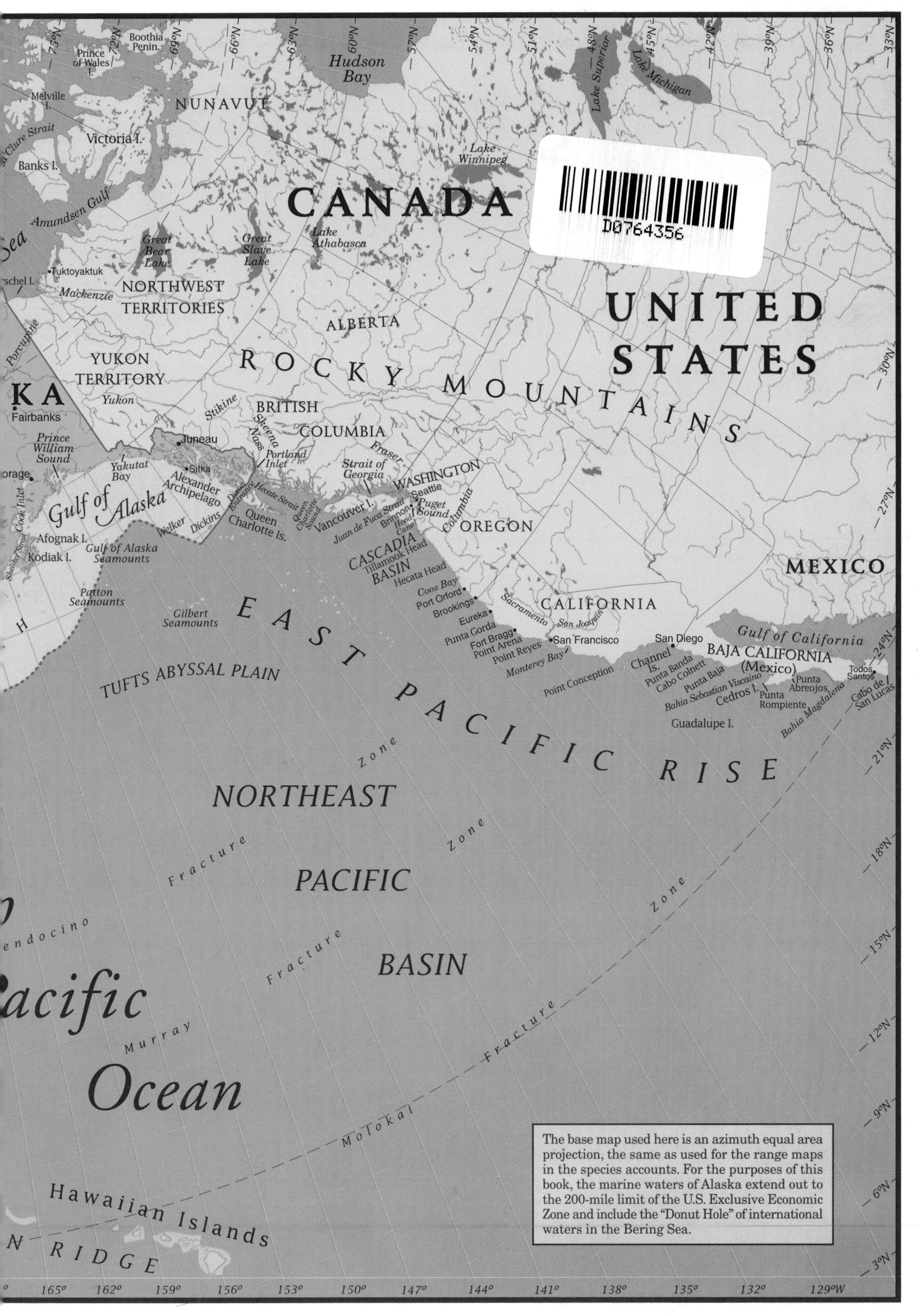

The base map used here is an azimuth equal area projection, the same as used for the range maps in the species accounts. For the purposes of this book, the marine waters of Alaska extend out to the 200-mile limit of the U.S. Exclusive Economic Zone and include the "Donut Hole" of international waters in the Bering Sea.

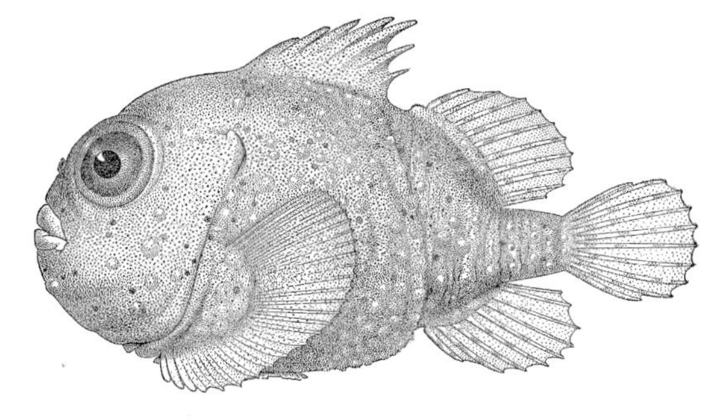

Fishes of Alaska

Funding for preparation and publication
of this book was provided primarily by

U.S. Geological Survey
Biological Resources Division

American Fisheries Society
Alaska Chapter

Fishes of Alaska

Catherine W. Mecklenburg
and
T. Anthony Mecklenburg

Point Stephens Research
Auke Bay, Alaska

Lyman K. Thorsteinson

U.S. Geological Survey
Western Fisheries Research Center
Seattle, Washington

American Fisheries Society
Bethesda, Maryland

2002

— In Memoriam —

Rae Baxter

Norman Joseph Wilimovsky

in recognition of their interest and contributions to our knowledge of the fishes of Alaska

To my parents,
Margaret Sampson Wimsatt
and
James McSherry Wimsatt,
sister, Tina, and brother, Sherry,
for their patience and understanding
— C.W.M.

Printed in the United States of America.
This book is printed on acid-free paper.

Library of Congress Catalog Card Number: 2001099776

ISBN 1-888569-07-7

American Fisheries Society
5410 Grosvenor Lane, Suite 110
Bethesda, Maryland 20814-2199
USA

FOREWORD

In November 1989, the membership of the Alaska Chapter of the American Fisheries Society unanimously approved an initiative to produce an identification guide to Alaska's fishes. A primary purpose was to bring needed scientific attention to some of Alaska's more poorly known fishes, particularly some of the marine and arctic species that are important in ecosystems but of little, or no, commercial significance. Past efforts to describe this fauna have been provisional in nature and focused on species perceived to be of direct value to humans. Prior to this book, there had been no singular, scientifically reliable documentation for this region. At one point, Dr. Norman J. Wilimovsky, an authority on Alaskan fishes, advised us that the chapter's representation of taxonomic contribution in its project description was potentially misleading and that broader objectives to organize inventory-level information about the Alaskan ichthyofauna in a current classification system would more adequately reflect its research purpose. This advice, about project clarity, was perhaps the singlemost important guidance we received to produce an authoritative account of this nation's northernmost ichthyofauna. The resultant book, *Fishes of Alaska,* is the seminal treatment of this region's aquatic biodiversity through synthesis and integration of inventory, descriptive, and taxonomic information. The publication's adherence to accepted standards of regional faunal monographs—species characteristics, geographic range, scientific nomenclature, identification keys, and illustrations—and high principles of scientific quality assure reference value over the Pacific Rim well into the twenty-first century.

Fishery resources hold a special place in Alaskan history. Archaeological records provide evidence of their prehistoric use by early human inhabitants of Beringia, now believed to be the ancestors of contemporary Alaska Natives. Today, fish contributions to the "seasonal round" of subsistence lifestyles are much better known. Alaskan fisheries are storied, holding recreational and commercial values worth billions of dollars annually. Historically, and beginning in the 1880s, regional salmon fisheries were an economic mainstay of a fledgling Territory of Alaska. More recently, with Alaska statehood (1959), federal enactment of the Magnuson Act (1976) and creation of an Exclusive Economic Zone (1983) and other governances, the management, magnitude, and ecosystem interactions of regional marine fisheries have changed dramatically. The North Pacific Ocean is a dynamic environment and its living resources respond to, or are influenced by, environmental change in ways and at scales that are not well understood. Understanding these processes and mechanisms is a long-term goal of adaptive management schemes, and because species are the basic units of ecosystems, their proper identification provides a basic, critical connection between oceanographic science and resource management.

Historically, obtaining institutional support for taxonomic investigations was difficult in Alaska in light of other research priorities. The Alaska Chapter's decision to sponsor this study was, in retrospect, extremely ambitious with respect to its objectives, availability of faunal expertise, and cooperative research and funding requirements. Without ready access to taxonomic data and information, and specialists by the Internet or other modern conveniences (e.g., interlibrary loan), and the technical and financial assistance of many, this project would not have been possible. Given this access, the study was visionary with respect to its timing, recognition of scientific need, and incorporation of novel methods for documenting fish diversity. Whereas conservation biologists had been advocating for faunal inventories and taxonomic undertakings since the early 1980s, and less frequently before, biodiversity issues only gained national prominence during the 1990s. The growing public awareness stemmed, in part, from mounting concerns about the legal and economic ramifications of the federal Endangered Species Act (1973). In addition, societal views toward the environment were changing and new ethics, with respect to ecosystem management and ecosystem services, were developing. Within this milieu of changing norms, the Alaska Chapter study also had a pragmatic origin. It reflected the combined knowledge and experience of its membership and their perceived need, as professionals, for reliable and valid species information to investigate and manage the sustainable fisheries and ecosystems in Alaska.

Unwittingly, by approving the preparation of a book on Alaskan fishes, the Alaska Chapter entered on a collision course with a national problem known as the taxonomic predicament. This concern addresses the nation's lack of taxonomic knowledge, infrastructure, and human resources. According to the Alaska Chapter's original planning, a manuscript by Alaskan biologist Rae Baxter entitled, *Annotated Keys to the Fishes of Alaska,* was believed to be nearing completion and the chapter's sponsorship would thus be limited to manuscript completion, orchestration of reviews, and book publication. Initial funding would be used for tasks associated with completing the draft including writing and conduct of a small number of specimen validation studies. A Fish Key Committee was formed to provide supervision and technical assistance for this work and the ensuing production phases of the book. During 1990, funds were provided to Mr. Baxter, and a review draft was expected by June 1991.

In a related step, a technical services contract was let to Catherine W. Mecklenburg and T. Anthony Mecklenburg for editorial support and eventual book production. Unfortunately, the author's death in March 1991 brought the effort to a premature conclusion. This was a crucial juncture in the project's history because we were faced with a difficult decision regarding continuation. Advice from several prominent West Coast ichthyologists was sought and, while the collective viewpoint was that the northern faunal work was needed, caution also was needed with respect to realism and timeliness in our project expectation. Much depended on the quality and completeness of Rae Baxter's unfinished work, and it seemed likely that our research and coordination requirements would be substantial considering that the specialized knowledge needed could not be found in a single individual or institution. Despite these cautions there was general support and the Fish Key Committee adopted a new approach that involved the Mecklenburgs using the unfinished manuscript, as much as possible, to prepare initial materials for scientific reviews. These reviews would indicate science quality, identify information gaps and research needs, and guide our future planning.

Although the scientific scope and approach was evolving, fund-raising remained a constant problem and a harrowing experience. Alaska, like the rest of the country, experienced an economic downturn in the early 1990s and, following the *Exxon Valdez* oil spill in 1989, there was continual turmoil in the science and management communities. On the project scene, the preparation of review materials was proving to be more complex than anticipated and it was clear that substantial new research would be required before, not after, an effective review process could be implemented. By 1994, the Alaska Chapter's financial investment was large and progress was stymied by funding and unsuspected scientific issues and problems. To complicate matters, the Fish Key Committee was losing its membership to nonvolunteer activities leaving its remaining members with the continual search for new funding. Despite these problems, there also were positive developments. The initial return of reviews for the first taxon accounts drafted were highly favorable and important in establishing the scientific credibility of the project.

The initial years were clouded by financial hardship and related uncertainty. It is a tribute to the Alaska Chapter, its executive committee, and the authors, that the work continued. In 1995, the National Biological Service (hereafter the U.S. Geological Survey) entered into cooperative research with the Alaska Chapter to complete the publication. The U.S. Geological Survey's primary mission is to assist land managers, particularly in the Department of the Interior, by providing them with the independent scientific information they need to make sound decisions about the use and conservation of natural resources. Major support already had been received from Interior's Minerals Management Service, U.S. Fish and Wildlife Service, and National Park Service, as well as other federal, state, and corporate organizations (National Marine Fisheries Service, North Pacific Fishery Management Council, Alaska Department of Fish and Game, Alaska Seafood Marketing Institute, British Petroleum Exploration (Alaska) Inc., and National Bank of Alaska). The Alaska Chapter's partnership approach typified the manner in which the U.S. Geological Survey addresses its science missions and the research was consistent with bureau goals for resource inventory and ecosystem understanding. In particular, it was consistent with science objectives for taxonomy, systematics, and museum studies. It was an important turn of events. The U.S. Geological Survey's participation created a stable research environment for the very first time in the project's seven year history to date.

By now, the authors and the Fish Key Committee were facing another important recognition. This was the growing realization that the evolved project, characterized by an expansion in research, analysis, and writing, could no longer be construed as a derivative of the unfinished *Annotated Keys to the Fishes of Alaska*. With the passage of time, *Annotated Keys* was no longer our template but an important information resource. The inclusion of this information in our species accounts was through incorporation by reference, where appropriate, following stylistic conventions consistent with scientific citation. In the end, this publication, representing joint research of the American Fisheries Society and the U.S. Geological Survey, reflects a more classical and detailed narrative than envisioned by Rae Baxter. We believe his vision of a "stripped-down" guide for field applications, perhaps in electronic format, represents a second-generation product whose eventual development will benefit from the testing of the keys and identification materials provided herein.

Fishes of Alaska is pioneering, not only for its documentation of Alaskan resources but also for its identification of scientific challenges to future investigators charged with understanding this part of Alaska's natural history. Sustainable fisheries and related management decisions will forever be dependent on accurate knowledge of the identity, distributions, and ecology of the species being used and those with which they interact. The Alaska Chapter hopes this guide helps those who continue to explore the richness of Alaska's fish resources.

William J. Wilson
Chairman, Fish Key Committee
Alaska Chapter, American Fisheries Society

PREFACE

What does it take to make a journey? A place to start from, something to leave behind.

— John Haines, *Moments and Journeys* (1981)

Alaska's first poet laureate writes eloquently about the importance of places and captures the spirit of journey we feel led to the preparation of this book. Our faunal monograph is about place — a northern region so vast and remote and so sparsely populated that few, if any one person, can truly appreciate the physical expanse, variety, and mosaic of environmental features that comprise its many fish habitats. Alaska stretches 2,700 miles from east to west and 1,700 miles north to south. Its surface area of 420 million acres, including 55 million acres of inland waters, is surrounded by 47,000 miles of coastline and two oceans overlying 1.5 billion acres of federal submerged lands. Like the theme portrayed in *Moments and Journeys,* this book is about life in Alaska's wilds. Our focus is on fishes and their geographic range across the gradient of physical habitats that compose Alaska and the surrounding federally managed waters. Our book, like the poet's introspection, has an identified time and spatial focus, addressing a brief period of geologic history and even shorter period of investigative research in Alaska. The description of this fauna began in the 1700s and continues today, but is an area of science that has left few scholarly landmarks behind. The self reflections of the trapper-poet in *Moments and Journeys* reflect a knowledge gained about faunal patterns that was greatly assisted by recorded history, animal collections, field observations, and the shared experience of others. This is also our history and within this largely recapitulative experience our journey ends, leaving behind a charted course that we hope marks a new era of systematic investigation in Alaska.

Our main purpose in writing this book was to provide an inventory of the fish species occurring in Alaska and a compilation of consistent information on the species in the framework of a modern classification. The inventory includes all the fish species known with certainty to exist in the marine and fresh waters of Alaska, species that have been reported from Alaska but because of some uncertainty in the record require additional documentation, and species that are likely to occur but have not yet been found in Alaska. The compilation of information focuses on classification, diagnostic morphological features, illustrations, geographic range and habitat, and documentation of the information presented. This catalog is the first to include such a compilation for the Alaskan ichthyofauna. Lists of Alaskan species have been published, but the most recent of those, by Quast and Hall (1972), was done as a preliminary effort, identified a small percentage of the relevant literature, and is 30 years old. The most recent compilation that attempted to include detailed information for the majority of Alaskan fish species, by Evermann and Goldsborough (1907), is nearly 100 years old. We hope this modern catalog of all Alaskan fish species with descriptive and source materials on each species under one cover will be a useful reference for fishery biologists, ichthyologists, environmental consultants, natural resource managers, editors, translators, students, naturalists, and others seeking authoritative information on the species.

Information on the classification, morphology, and distribution of Alaskan fish species is distributed throughout numerous publications, many of which are not readily available or are in languages other than English, and in various forms of unpublished data, so the necessity of reviewing and summarizing the information is quite evident. This book pulls together the relevant literature, including works obscure and difficult to assess, and critically reviews and extracts essential information. New observations are included from examination of specimens, museum collection databases, scientific survey databases, and communications with ichthyologists specializing in the various taxa. The compilation includes information on fish species in the Arctic Ocean off Alaska as well as the entire eastern Bering Sea, Gulf of Alaska, and Pacific Ocean south of the Aleutian Islands. Previous guides that include fish species of the Bering Sea and Gulf of Alaska did so only secondary to treatment of the more southern Pacific coast fish fauna from British Columbia through California. They do not cover the northern area of the Bering Sea, and address range in the Gulf of Alaska and Aleutian Islands only in the broadest of terms. Previous guides, in addition, only treat the species most commonly found and restrict coverage to shallow marine waters or to freshwaters. Hence, many of the species in this book are not included in other summaries, especially the Arctic species, deepsea species, and species which have Asian centers of distribution and are occasionally found in Alaskan waters. This book is the first to have researched the geographic ranges in Alaska of marine as well as freshwater fishes in detail and to depict them on individual maps for each species.

The species inventory and compilation of information, which together are our main focus, compose the major portion of the book, the Systematic Section. To maintain this focus we have kept the presentation of information in the preliminary pages to a minimum. A complete account of the history of ichthyological and fisheries research and exploration in Alaskan waters is not included. For Alaska, an account with enough detail to have value would make a volume by itself. A summary of previous lists and compilations of information on the Alaskan ichthyofauna is given in the Introduction, and the principal works and their authors are cited in the species accounts and in the introductions to the higher taxa. Likewise, a detailed description of the physical environmental setting, including oceanography and distribution of freshwater habitats, is outside the scope of this book. We provide a summary of major features with references to the literature so the reader may pursue the subject in more detail.

The Systematic Section includes introductions to the orders, families, and other selected higher taxa; an identification key to the families and keys to the species within the families; and one-page species accounts with documentation and commentary on the information presented. The main framework for presenting the information in the Systematic Section is the classification of families and higher taxa of fishes of the world by Nelson (1994). In the introductions to the families and higher taxa, comparing the inventory of Alaskan fish species to the world classification helps place the Alaskan ichthyofauna in perspective to all fishes. The introductions also summarize major morphological features that are diagnostic of the group, particularly as represented in the Alaskan fauna, identify characters useful in distinguishing among the species, highlight new information on species such as on known range, and point out differences from the previous published list of Alaskan fish species, that of Quast and Hall (1972). The term "recent" when used in this book in reference to the literature is meant in the context of occurring after Quast and Hall's inventory. Depending on the completeness of available information, the species accounts include summary statements on range and habitat, characters important for distinguishing the species, one or more illustrations of the species, and a map depicting range in Alaska. Sources of the data are cited and additional commentary is provided in the Notes & Sources section at the bottom of each species account. The notes document and comment on recent taxonomic changes and problems, recent extensions of known range, and records of occurrence in Alaska and closely adjacent marine waters.

Treatment is restricted primarily to adult fish. For a few families we include morphological characteristics and illustrations of early life history stages if those stages are sometimes the only evidence of occurrence or if they are apt to be confused with adults. The egg cases of skates (family Rajidae) frequently wash up on beaches or are brought up in nets and may be the only evidence of occurrence in an area, while the late juvenile stages of rockfishes (Scorpaenidae), eelpouts (Zoarcidae), and some other fishes are often mistaken for adults. In the past, juveniles of some species were mistakenly classified as different species from the adults. The accurate identification of juvenile salmons and trouts (subfamily Salmoninae) in the freshwaters of Alaska is important to fishery biologists in the region, so a key and drawings to help identify those juveniles are included.

To use the keys to identify a fish, one first determines what family it belongs to by using the Key to Fish Families in Alaska, then turns to the section on that family. There, the key to the Alaskan species in the family is used to carry the identification to species. Although identification keys are provided for all families represented in the accounts by two or more species, in many instances the species are identifiable without using the keys from the narration presented in the introductions to the families and the illustrations and morphological features given in the species accounts. Ideally, and for the greatest accuracy, both the key and the species accounts should be consulted. For large families, the introduction to the family describes the characters of each genus or subfamily represented in Alaskan waters, and each species account has selected characters that differentiate among the species. For the most abundant and well-documented Alaskan species, a glance at the range maps may help identify a specimen since a fish caught outside the range depicted for a species would probably not be that species.

Because users of this book will include fishery biologists, naturalists, students, and other nonichthyologists, some orientation and explanation of characters is provided. This includes definitions and diagrams of selected morphological features in the introductions to the families, and definitions of additional technical terms in the Glossary. For the most part, though, knowledge of fish morphology for persons wishing to study Alaska's fishes in more depth will be acquired from textbooks on ichthyology and comparative anatomy and from the specialized works cited for the various taxa.

The Gazetteer provides locations and geographical coordinates (latitudes and longitudes) for places mentioned in the text. Locality data are provided for place names in Russia, Canada, and other regions mentioned, not just for Alaska. Many of the place names are not the usual names included on maps or in the general atlases in most people's libraries. Maps showing major physiographic features and place names are provided inside the front and back covers of the book.

The Bibliography includes the works referred to in preparing this catalog. Pursuit of further information on some topics may require reference to additional literature, which is cited in the works listed.

For convenience in looking up species or other taxa, page numbers are given in the family keys and the List of Species in a Classification, as well as the Index. The species list may be more convenient for some readers, since it includes only the senior synonyms, not the junior synonyms and other names that are included in the detailed Index.

For the purposes of this book, Alaskan waters are the marine and fresh waters in the area encompassed by the heavy solid and dashed lines around Alaska on the map on the inside front cover of the book. The same outline is used for the range maps in the individual species accounts. The dashed lines north and south delimit the 200-mile Exclusive Economic Zone, also called the 200-mile limit or EEZ, which is coincident with the boundary of the Fishery Conservation Zone (U.S. Department of State 1977). The solid line in the west is the U.S.A.–Russia 1867 Convention Line, which coincides with the International Date Line. The solid line in the east is the U.S.–Canada border, between Alaska and Canada's Yukon Territory and Province of British Columbia. In the Bering Sea the line defining the EEZ for the most part runs coincidentally with the Date Line, but in the southern Bering Sea diverges eastward from that boundary and forms an area of international waters commonly called the "Donut Hole." Fish collected from the Donut Hole are counted as Alaskan.

For most of the species treated in this book there is adequate documentation that the species occurs within the geographic limits given above. For commercially important and regularly encountered species this is usually not an issue. For the less well-known species, this is not always so. Many similar-looking species have been confused in taxonomic works as well as in fishery survey and management reports. We cannot be assured of the validity of a record without adequate documentation. The best documentation of a species' existence is one or more voucher specimens, stored in museums and available for verification by examination. The best literature records cite voucher specimens by providing museum catalog numbers. Alternatively, if voucher specimens cannot be saved, written records can provide adequate documentation if critical diagnostic features observed in the specimens are included with other information in the catch record. For species that are unlikely to be confused with any others, catch records from fishery resource surveys may be adequate records of occurrence but must be used with caution. Photographs can be of considerable importance as part of the documentation, and the recent advent of digital cameras and their immediate popularity among museum workers and biologists in the field should result in significant improvements in documentation.

Reports of several species from Alaska cannot be confirmed for a number of reasons, yet the occurrence of some of those species in Alaska is not implausible from what we know of their life cycle requirements and their distribution outside the state. We retain the more plausible of those "unconfirmed" Alaskan species in this book, clearly label them as such, and discuss the available evidence in the appropriate family introductions and Range notes in the species accounts.

Like most other regional ichthyofaunal accounts, this book also includes species that have not been reported from Alaska but which are thought likely to occur in the region; again, judging from what we know of their behavior and distribution in other regions. Species known to inhabit closely adjacent waters are the most obvious choices to include. A few species in the category of potential Alaskan species are almost certain to exist in Alaska as they have been recorded, literally, within shouting distance of Alaska's borders. Some other species occur well outside Alaskan waters but within both the Bering Sea and the eastern Pacific Ocean, with records effectively bracketing the state, and those species likely occur in the intervening waters. On the other hand, some species with nearest records of occurrence hundreds of miles away are included as potential Alaskan species when they are known to have a wide distribution in the rest of the world and their life cycle and ecological requirements may be met in Alaska. Where choices had to be made to keep the book within manageable limits, benthic species, for example, which are in physical contact with the bottom and are not very mobile, may not be widespread and are less apt to be included. Pelagic deepsea species are more often included as likely Alaskan species than are intertidal species, because the former are more likely to be widespread. Generally speaking, continental shelf fishes appear to have relatively restricted distributions within large coastal ecosystems. In contrast, the distribution of continental slope species may extend across entire oceans in long ribbonlike bands along the rim of the deep ocean, and the species of the continental rise and the abyss are widespread across the deep basins. In a few cases we describe one member of a genus or family to enable identification of specimens found in Alaska to the appropriate group. A different species than we have selected as representative, or more than one species in the group, could eventually be discovered in Alaska.

Inadequate geographic sampling coverage partly explains the lack of Alaskan records for some species. As commercial fisheries exploit resources at greater depths and in new locations off the coasts of Alaska and scientific surveys respond to new information needs in underrepresented areas, the existence in Alaska of many of the species that we include here as potential Alaskan species may be verified. Some areas may never be adequately sampled. For example, the seafloor around the Aleutian Islands at slope depths is rough and impractical for bottom trawling. Although the use of submersibles is being explored, survey costs may prevent systematic surveys and the utility of submersibles for accurately identifying species is limited unless samples can be collected. Management interventions, such as the closure of fisheries or the creation of marine conservation zones, parks, and refuges could further prohibit or limit sampling opportunities in areas of incomplete inventory. New fishing technologies, including acoustic survey methods, continue to aid in locating, sampling, and documenting species occurrences in Alaska. Recent use of large, commercial-size nets in research surveys has produced greater knowledge of the life zones, abundance, and geographic ranges of large North Pacific mesopelagic fishes that previously were thought to be rare. This is a byproduct of greater sampling efficiency due to reduced net avoidance compared to sampling with the traditional research gear such as small midwater trawls and plankton nets. Environmental change may be accompanied by new species as conditions favor distributional shifts in response to global warming, oceanic regime shifts, El Niño events, or other large-scale changes in ecosystem conditions. Nonnative species may also be introduced into Alaska by humans, whether intentionally or not.

Only species that are currently recognized as valid are given a species account. This decision was not always easy, as the classification of certain genera and families represented in Alaska is in dire need of revision, and even some of the most well-studied families contain species that were originally described on the basis of specimens collected in Alaska but which may be synonymous with species known from other regions of the Pacific or Arctic oceans. The need for some nominal species to be reclassified as junior synonyms previously escaped attention primarily because there was no modern review of the Alaskan ichthyofauna. As a consequence of our review, we place several species in synonymy and suggest additional, potential synonymies that require further research. Merging additional species would decrease the total number of species in the inventory. Conversely, it is possible that some other species, as they are currently described, comprise more than one species and require redescription. There are several cases of forms once described as individual species that were later merged but are currently the subject of taxonomic studies that could reseparate them. This is the subject of ichthyology—the study of fish systematics—and pursuing it will undoubtedly lead to many changes to the inventory of Alaskan fish species presented here. We have tried to alert the reader to some of the changes in classification of species that may occur, which are the subjects of current research or should be studied. The identification of future research needs scattered throughout the narrative reflects significant results of our study.

Several species known to exist in Alaskan waters that have not yet been named will add to the inventory when they are formally described. However, for most of those forms research is ongoing and it would be premature to provide accounts of them in this book.

Many problems were encountered in determining which species occur in Alaska and delimiting their geographic ranges. One of the biggest problems was the large number of mistakes in the literature regarding records and ranges of Alaskan species or species that were erroneously reported to occur in Alaska. Even recent guides and ichthyological works perpetuate errors that were made many years ago. Previously this problem went largely unnoticed or without comment, probably because no in-depth study of the Alaskan fauna was attempted before now. We identify such errors in the species accounts in the Notes & Sources sections, to set the record straight for future researchers. The following are examples of the types of errors and problems found.

Several kinds of errors affected determination of range. Misconceptions regarding the geography of Alaska were evident and may have been partially due to the relatively late entry of Alaska as a United States territory, after the long period when it was a Russian possession. People were not knowledgeable about the geography of Alaska. As recently as the late 1920s, for instance, some American authors placed Simushir Island in Alaska, although it is one of the Kuril Islands off Russia. Common knowledge of the geography of the Russian Far East was also sketchy. Petropavlovsk and Avacha Bay were often given as Bering Sea localities, but they are on the southeastern coast of Kamchatka which is on the Pacific Ocean well south of the Aleutian Islands and Bering Sea. A huge portion of the Kamchatka Peninsula faces the western North Pacific, not the Bering Sea. Indeed, we had to closely examine most early works referring to fish records from Kamchatka, in English as well as in Russian, to determine whether the authors meant that portion of Kamchatka north or that south of the Aleutian chain. Records of occurrence often proved to be from the southern tip of Kamchatka and in the vicinity of the Kuril Islands. Faunistically, there is a difference, although it is least obvious with respect to pelagic species, with the southern, warmer water forms often showing up in the Bering Sea in warm years or, in the case of the large piscivores, during feeding excursions in any summer. As another example, Russian literature gives the Sea of Okhotsk as the collection locality for some fish specimens which were actually collected in Alaska at the time it was Russian America. Conversely, Alaskan localities with Russian-sounding place names have sometimes been referred to as being in Russia. Even in recent years the same mistakes have occasionally been made.

Other types of errors were made in reporting collection localities. For example, the location of U.S. Fish Commission steamer *Albatross* station 3213 was given in some faunal accounts as being north of Unalaska Island, in the Bering Sea, whereas the station actually was south of the Sanak Islands, in the Pacific Ocean. Authors have even given Alaska as the locality for *Albatross* stations that the ship's records show were in British Columbia, the Sea of Okhotsk, or elsewhere. We could correct those kinds of problems, but some problems with early collecting records may never be resolved. For example, the North Pacific Exploring Expedition of 1853–1856 collected at both Kamchatka and Bering Strait, and some specimens from that expedition cannot conclusively be determined to be from one or the other place. As well, the early naturalists had little conception of the laws of geographical distribution, and "America" or "the sea between Russia and America" was sometimes regarded as a sufficiently exact record of the origin of a specimen.

Errors in reporting an Alaskan distribution often occurred, evidently, from cursory or incautious use of works. Two works which were most often miscited are Gilbert's (1896) "The Ichthyological Collections of the Steamer Albatross during the Years 1890 and 1891," which included sections on Bering Sea, California, and Alaska and Washington but which authors have cited as pertaining only to Alaska;

and Evermann and Goldsborough's (1907) "Fishes of Alaska," which recorded collections from British Columbia and Washington as well as from Alaska. Bean (1881b) has been incorrectly attributed for Alaskan ranges of species which he only included in a supplementary list of species that he believed would eventually be found in Alaska, but still have not been found in the region.

Among the many pitfalls in the literature are discrepancies between the Russian originals and translations into English. An often-cited work on cyclopterids, for instance, gives Barents Sea in the Russian edition but this was translated to Bering Sea in the English edition. The problem is not always a matter of an incorrect translation. Sometimes the error is in the Russian. Taking an example in morphology, in the Russian edition of a work on northern fishes the drawings of the opercular lobe in eelpouts are incorrectly identified as to species, but this was corrected in the later translation into English.

Another problem frequently encountered in the ichthyological and fisheries biology literature is the perpetuation of errors by citing authors who did not themselves examine structures but relied on previous authors who may have made mistakes owing to scarcity of material and assumptions about what features a species should possess based on outdated classifications. By not noting that they did not themselves examine structures, authors not only carry along erroneous information, they give it the added credibility of having been independently supported. We hope to have avoided bestowing added credibility by citing our sources in each species account, and listing specimens we examined if they added significant new information. We are, of course, not the first to comment on this problem. Robins (1989), for instance, recounted an example wherein eel families were mistakenly assigned to a higher group with paired frontals when they in fact had united frontals.

In a related problem, in the early literature, especially, descriptions of new species rarely mentioned all of the characters used by other authors to describe closely related species, so unless specimens can be examined (and there may not be any in collections within reasonable study distance) one may be faced with making dangerous assumptions. This type of situation is one source of "missing" characters in the suite of characters we give for species within a genus or family; rather than assuming the state of a character, we omitted the character. The taxonomic histories of species also made accurate determination of their geographical ranges, as well as their features, difficult. For example, where authors gave a range for a species which later was recognized to include two species, it took some sleuthing to determine whether one or both species of the pair were recorded from Alaska, and where in Alaska.

Our range determinations were made, whenever possible, from original data sources. Numerous environmental syntheses and reviews, oil spill effects symposia, fishery survey reports, quarterly and annual contract reports, and technical memoranda give "range extensions" in and to Alaska or list poorly known, rare species without giving documentation. Such reports are problematical especially when they list species well outside the limits of range previously established from documented literature or voucher specimens. In some cases the catch localities were many hundreds of miles from the species' previously known limits of range, yet no comment on the unusual occurrence was made. Too often we found that adequate documentation did not exist. Usually, if voucher specimens were to have been saved they could not be found. In a few cases there were voucher specimens which proved to have been misidentified, but those did not constitute a problem.

An important source for range records was the National Marine Fisheries Service, Alaska Fisheries Science Center, Resource Assessment and Conservation Engineering Division (RACE) scientific survey database, when we could be assured the catches were accurately identified. Contributors to the database provided verification as necessary. The RACE database is largely based on trawl surveys, so intertidal and shallow subtidal species are generally not represented. The database is not without its problems but has been improving in recent years as knowledge on North Pacific fish species accumulates and the fishery biologists at RACE train survey workers, take photographs, and save specimens for vouchers which are deposited primarily in the University of Washington fish collection. Wherever we cite records from the RACE database in this book we indicate whether vouchers were saved (and if they were not, circles rather than dots are used to indicate the records on the range maps; see Range Maps in Structure of Accounts and Keys).

Permanent fish collections were the source of most previously unpublished records of occurrence and information on morphological features. No one museum contains examples of all the species occurring in Alaska, but the institutions in North America containing the most extensive collections from Alaska are the Smithsonian Institution, National Museum of Natural History; National Marine Fisheries Service, Auke Bay Laboratory; University of Washington, School of Aquatic and Fisheries Sciences; University of British Columbia, Cowan Vertebrate Museum; Royal British Columbia Museum; Scripps Institution of Oceanography; California Academy of Sciences; and University of Alaska Fairbanks. The Oregon State University, Museum of Natural History; Canadian Museum of Nature at Ottawa; and Museum of Comparative Zoology at Harvard University are among the several museums that contain less extensive Alaskan collections. There are also important Alaskan collections abroad. The largest is contained in the combined holdings of the branches of the Russian Academy of Sciences, with the main collection in St. Petersburg. The Hokkaido University, Laboratory of Marine Zoology collection has significant holdings from Alaska, particularly the Bering Sea.

It is only in recent years that museums have entered their catalog data (usually consisting of species name; catch locality, depth, and gear; number of specimens; and standard or total length) into computer databases. Computerization efforts are still ongoing so complete records for any museum are not yet online. It will be many years, for instance, before all the National Museum of Natural History fish holdings can be accessed online. Late in the project we were provided with printouts or data sheets containing the catalog data for fish specimens collected in Alaska and housed at the University of British Columbia, California Academy of Sciences, University of Washington, Canadian Museum of Nature, and Oregon State University. Most of those lists were incomplete, but were extremely helpful in identifying potentially important records of occurrence. The online databases used most frequently were those of the National Museum of Natural History, Scripps Institution of Oceanography, and University of Washington. The museum databases are not meant to provide accurate identifications of the specimens in the collections. Specimens accessioned into the collections are often identified only provisionally. Moreover, due to accumulating knowledge, identification of specimens is never fixed but can change. Accuracy of the identifications given in the catalogs or databases must be verified by examination of the specimens before they can be cited. When we could not examine specimens ourselves, either by traveling to the museum or having specimens sent to us, we relied on curators and collection managers to supply further information. Often, they confirmed or revised identifications upon examining the specimens. This effort was most important if a museum lot represented a possible extension of known range. Sometimes we were alerted to important museum records by ichthyologists who had collected the specimens or knew of them, and those experts provided additional information or reexamined specimens to provide verification, or we obtained details on catch records from the collection managers.

The Smithsonian Institution, National Museum of Natural History, Division of Fishes in Washington, D.C., houses the largest collection of preserved fishes in the world and was particularly useful to us because of the large number of type specimens it contains, as well as general holdings from Alaska. The National Museum is the main repository of the collections amassed by the U.S. Fish Commission steamer *Albatross* between 1882 and 1922. (The U.S. Fish Commission became the U.S. Bureau of Fisheries in 1903, and is succeeded by the National Marine Fisheries Service.) The *Albatross* was the first large ship designed especially for oceanographic research and included laboratories, storage space for specimens, and specialized bottom dredging and trawling equipment. She occupies an important place in the history of ichthyological research in Alaska, as she made several voyages to the Territory to collect specimens. Overall, she collected more marine specimens than any other ship, and most of the material collected was deposited at the Smithsonian Institution. One of the earliest catalogs of Alaskan fishes, by Evermann and Goldsborough (1907), was based largely on the *Albatross* collections. The collections are still being studied by scholars from all over the world and for this book were an important source for verifying published records of occurrence, discovering previously overlooked Alaskan records, and refining descriptions of morphological characters. The type collection has been enhanced over the years by exchanges of paratypes with other major museums. As well, authors often send paratypes to the National Museum, while depositing the holotypes in their own museums. Numerous other relevant collections have been deposited at the National Museum, and some have received little attention. A recent collection that provided several new records of eastern Bering Sea continental slope species was made by Daniel M. Cohen and Tomio Iwamoto in 1979 aboard the Japanese research vessel *Yakushi Maru*.

The National Marine Fisheries Service, Alaska Fisheries Science Center (AFSC), Auke Bay Laboratory near Juneau, Alaska, and the University of Alaska Fairbanks have the largest permanent fish collections in Alaska. The former contains voucher specimens accumulated from the early 1960s to the present in AFSC resource surveys, primarily of the Gulf of Alaska, Aleutian Islands, and southeastern Bering Sea using the NOAA RV *Miller Freeman,* NMFS RV *John N. Cobb,* and other research vessels as well as fishing vessels contracted for the surveys. The Auke Bay Laboratory collection was the basis for records of occurrence in Alaska reported by Quast and Hall (1972). The University of Alaska Fairbanks fish collection has received little professional attention in recent years. Its holdings include uncataloged voucher specimens from 1989–1991 surveys of the eastern Chukchi Sea using the chartered fishing vessel *Ocean Hope III* and the Japanese RV *Oshoro Maru,* which compose the majority of northeastern Chukchi Sea specimens available in museums, and a significant collection of Alaskan freshwater fishes from the years when the fish collection was curated by ichthyologist James E. Morrow.

Most deepwater Aleutian fish specimens in the University of British Columbia's (UBC) Cowan Vertebrate Museum were obtained by the International Pacific Halibut Commission surveys of 1961–1963, while shallow-water collections were made by biologists at the university, including Alex E. Peden and Norman J. Wilimovsky. Arctic collections were obtained largely by Norman J. Wilimovsky in 1954 aboard the RV *William E. Ripley* and N. J. Wilimovsky and Dayton L. Alverson in 1959 from the RV *John N. Cobb.* Significant freshwater collections from Alaska at UBC include those made by C. C. Lindsey and J. D. McPhail in the late 1950s. Specimens collected by S. J. Westrheim and others aboard the Fisheries Research Board of Canada's RV *G. B. Reed* in southeastern Alaska are at the UBC and other Canadian museums. Staff of the National Museums of Canada (now Canadian Museum of Nature) at Ottawa also collected in Alaska, and the collection also has material donated by Alaskan scientists. Recent collections include those made by Alaskans Kathy J. Frost and Lloyd F. Lowry during 1977–

1980 from the Chukchi and Beaufort seas. In 1983 Claude B. Renaud and colleagues from the Canadian Museum of Nature sampled fishes from the northern Bering Sea, the Arctic on either side of Point Barrow, and Resurrection Bay at Seward. Many collections originally cataloged at UBC were later transferred to the Canadian Museum of Nature, and that museum and the British Columbia Provincial Museum (Royal British Columbia Museum) often split collections. The latter museum contains Alaskan collections obtained aboard various vessels as well as scuba diving by Alex E. Peden during more than 25 years as curator of the collection.

Even with all those data sources, and we have only touched on them above, knowledge of many of the Alaskan fish species' ranges is rudimentary or practically nonexistent. Records in museums typically reflect the interests of the curators and contributors, not the true distribution of species. Some fish are so large they are rarely kept as voucher specimens and yet well enough known that, when caught, they are not reported as new records. For fish of any size, often no new records are published once a species has been described and named. Consequently, some species that appear to be rare in Alaska from the few dots included on our range maps, may not be as rare as the records suggest.

The effort to determine range of fish species in Alaska and to accurately describe their most basic morphological features reinforced the need for documentation by placement of voucher specimens in permanent collections. Representative samples need to be accumulated for future study, as well as to document occurrence in Alaska. Much emphasis is put on the reporting of rare species, but some of the most common fishes in Alaska are inadequately represented in permanent collections. This situation is not new in ichthyology, but repeats "the well-known fact that the commonest forms in nature are often the rarest as preserved specimens" (Evermann and Goldsborough 1907:271). As well, additional Alaskan specimens which have not been studied or reported still exist in museums. Museum collections such as the Smithsonian Institution's National Museum of Natural History fish holdings are enormous, and it will take many more research visits to comb the shelves and locate the majority of Alaskan specimens. Many specimens are identified only to order or family, and will never be identified to species unless this type of endeavor continues in the future. Moreover, the collections grow dramatically with new contributions every year. Our research also pointed out the need for continuing studies to more accurately describe the Alaskan species. As Jordan (1923:80) remarked, "we must not expect a degree of accuracy which the subject in question does not permit." With so much still unknown about the geographic range and morphological features of many Alaskan fish species, we cannot expect the material presented herein to be accurate in every respect. Many issues cannot be resolved from existing information. We hope this book will stimulate future research in the field and in the laboratory to address these issues, and will promote a greater recognition of the importance of reference museum collections for significant gains to be made. Viewing the book as a baseline to which new records can be added and hypotheses tested, we consider it to be, within the poet laureate's concept of journey, "a place to start from" and roadmap for a new journey.

ACKNOWLEDGMENTS

This book would not have been possible without the financial and administrative support of the American Fisheries Society (AFS) and the U.S. Geological Survey (USGS). Two individuals within these organizations deserve special recognition for their administrative contributions to the project. William J. Wilson of LGL Alaska Research Associates, Inc., donated longstanding service to the Alaska Chapter's Fish Key Committee, first as a member, and later as its chairman. In particular, for the past 8 years, Bill served as the Alaska Chapter's project manager providing technical liaison within that organization, to the USGS, with other agency sponsors, and to the authors. Bill's commitment was unwavering and he a singular source of organizational constancy throughout more than a decade of institutional and project changes. Bill's administrative oversight and coordination with various executive committee members allowed the Alaska Chapter to waive any overhead costs, representing a major financial contribution by the chapter and LGL to this project. We wish to recognize his personal contributions in drafting correspondence, developing and reviewing proposals, interviewing potential sponsors, developing contractual documents, monitoring contracts and budgets, reporting to AFS, negotiating printing details, and marketing of the book. The second individual we wish to extend our special gratitude to is David Bornholdt, USGS, for recognizing the scientific and management values of this research to the Department of the Interior bureaus. In 1995, upon learning about the Alaska Chapter's efforts to produce this book, Dave worked with the AFS to secure long-term funding by orchestrating the development of a funding proposal for the National Biological Survey's Systematics and Genetics science area. His assistance in project development activities and establishing a cooperative research agreement between the USGS and AFS was a critical turning point in this project's history. We also give special thanks to AFS executive directors Carl R. Sullivan, Paul Brouha, and Ghassan "Gus" N. Rassam, for additional AFS support and guidance. From the USGS national and regional leadership teams we thank Dennis Fenn (Associate Director, Biology), John D. Buffington (Director, Western Region), Allan Marmelstein (Associate Regional Biologist), and William Seitz (Associate Regional Director, Alaska), for many forms of organizational assistance and, perhaps most importantly, their continuing moral support.

The Alaska Chapter members unanimously approved this book's production as a formal AFS project during the 1989 annual meeting. As time would tell, this became the largest, most complex project ever undertaken by the chapter and we are grateful for its long-lasting support. This support was continuous through uncertain fiscal times and numerous changes in chapter presidents, executive committees, and the Fish Key Committee. The Alaska Chapter presidents who had direct responsibilities in administering this project were Alexander M. Milner, Gary Sanders, Alex C. Wertheimer, William Hauser, Joseph Webb, Kate Wedemeyer, Dana Schmidt, Peggy Merritt, Mason Bryant, Cindy Hartman, William Bechtol, Carol Ann Woody, and David Wiswar. The chapter treasurers were instrumental in the financial management of this project and included Jeff Koenings, Kate Wedemeyer, William Bechtol, Brenda Wright, Allen Bingham, Susan Walker, David Wiswar, and Bob Ourso. The Fish Key Committee was served by Randy Bailey, Robert M. Meyer, Alexander W. Milner, Melvin Monsen, William J. Wilson, L.K.T., and Martin D. Robards. Bill Wilson and Mel Monsen were the only continuous members of the Fish Key Committee providing institutional memory and liaison to the chapter's leadership. Alex C. Wertheimer provided technical assistance and fund raising support to the Fish Key Committee during early years of the project.

We dedicate this book to the memory of our friend and colleague Rae Baxter (1929–1991) of Red Mountain, Alaska. Rae's scientific curiosity about Alaska's fish and marine invertebrates and other native faunas was legendary. Following his retirement from the Alaska Department of Fish and Game, Rae was a common fixture aboard federally sponsored fishery surveys and research expeditions. His ichthyological knowledge and field expertise were invaluable and a marvel to those of us fortunate to have worked with him. Rae's special interest was collecting fish and invertebrate species from remote parts of Alaska where little, if any, previous sampling had been conducted. He loved the prospects of discovering extensions to known geographic ranges and new size records for Alaskan fishes. At the time of his death Rae was working for the Alaska Chapter to produce a set of annotated keys for publication. Unfortunately, his tragic death on 22 March 1991 prevented this work from being finished. We thank Rae's widow, Sera Baxter, for so graciously permitting us to borrow Rae's manuscript drafts, data, and volumes from his library, at the beginning of what turned out to be a completely different research requirement than the Alaska Chapter, and its authors, ever conceived.

The authors wish to specifically acknowledge the support of the late Norman J. Wilimovsky (1925-1997), University of British Columbia, for sharing his knowledge and experience with the senior author, especially during discussions of early drafts of the manuscript, and for his unsolicited contribution of previously unpublished illustrations of fishes, manuscripts, and data. He continued to help us shape this book even through the periods of illness that preceded his death on 31 December 1997. We co-dedicate the book to the memory of Dr. Wilimovsky in recognition of his many contributions through decades of research to our knowledge of the Alaskan fish fauna and his unstinted willingness to share with us the information he had so painstakingly gained.

Many other individuals and organizations provided information, advice, and encouragement during the course of preparing this book. Immediately following Rae Baxter's death, the Alaska Chapter solicited and received expert consultation about its research directions. We are thankful for the advice and recommendations and, in several instances, letters of support, from several well-respected West Coast and Alaska specialists. These individuals include William N. Eschmeyer, California Academy of Sciences; Richard H. Rosenblatt, Scripps Institution of Oceanography; Theodore W. Pietsch and James Wilder Orr, University of Washington; Lew Haldorson and James B. Reynolds, University of Alaska Fairbanks; Art Kendall, Gary Stauffer, and Bruce L. Wing, National Marine Fisheries Service (NMFS); and Waldo Wakefield, National Underwater Research Program. Their words of encouragement and caution, at such a critical juncture, were greatly appreciated, if not always followed.

We extend our gratitude to the museum curators and collection managers who so kindly helped us during visits to study their collections, lent specimens, supplied us with catalog data, examined and reported on specimens when we could not visit their museums, or assisted in other ways. We thank, in no particular order, Alex E. Peden and Kelly Sendall, Royal British Columbia Museum; Susan L. Jewett, Lisa Palmer, David G. Smith, and Jeffrey T. Williams, National Museum of Natural History (NMNH), Washington, D.C.; Boris A. Sheiko and colleagues at the Zoological Institute in St. Petersburg and other laboratories of the Russian Academy of Sciences; Bruce L. Wing, NMFS, Auke Bay Laboratory; Nora Foster, University of Alaska Fairbanks; William N. Eschmeyer, David Catania, and Jon Fong, California Academy of Sciences; Theodore W. Pietsch and Brian Urbain, University of Washington; J. Donald McPhail, University of British Columbia; Brian W. Coad, Canadian Museum of Nature, Ottawa; John R. Paxton, Australian Museum; Douglas F. Markle, Oregon State University; Richard H. Rosenblatt and H. J. Walker, Scripps Institution of Oceanography; and Jeffrey A. Seigel, Natural History Museum of Los Angeles County. We thank Karsten E. Hartel, Museum of Comparative Zoology, Harvard University, for hand carrying the unique holotype of *Eumicrotremus gyrinops* to C.W.M. at the NMNH, and Brian W. Coad for helping C.W.M. borrow the unique holotype of *Occella impi*. We thank James B. Reynolds, Stephen C. Jewett, and Max Holberg, University of Alaska Fairbanks, for locating and making available the uncataloged voucher specimens from surveys conducted during 1989–1991 in the eastern Chukchi Sea and Prince William Sound. Peter Frank, Canadian Museum of Nature, provided more than 800 fish collection data sheets for specimens collected in Alaska. To all others who contributed information from their collections and may not be mentioned in this Acknowledgments we also extend our thanks, and point out that they are cited in the main text and listed in the Personal Communications at the end of the book.

Several ichthyologists provided more or less continuous consultation to C.W.M. over a period of years, and we are deeply grateful to them. Boris A. Sheiko (at first with Kamchatka Institute of Ecology, now with the Zoological Institute in St. Petersburg) not only loaned specimens and examined specimens in Russian collections for us, he translated papers into English, discussed a myriad of topics, served as translator and liaison in discussions with his colleagues, and helped us coin vernaculars for continental slope and deepsea species. He critiqued, in detail, the chapters on Cottidae, Psychrolutidae, Liparidae, Cyclopteridae, Agonidae, and Pleuronectidae. Alex E. Peden (Royal British Columbia Museum) loaned specimens and examined specimens at British Columbia museums, contributed data and shared his views on numerous topics, mainly in Liparidae and Cottidae, and contributed a large number of illustrations based on Alaskan and British Columbia specimens. James Wilder Orr (NMFS, Alaska Fisheries Science Center, Seattle) reviewed the Elasmobranchii, Scorpaenidae, Cottidae, and Pleuronectiformes in greatest detail, and advised on many topics in those groups especially. He retrieved catch data on request from the Alaska Fisheries Science Center scientific survey database and provided evaluation of the accuracy of those data. Morgan S. Busby (NMFS, Alaska Fisheries Science Center) reviewed the Liparidae and Agonidae, and contributed valuable information on them from his research. In recent years M. Eric Anderson (J.L.B. Smith Institute of Ichthyology) provided discussions and information on the Zoarcoidei and reviewed, in greatest detail, the Zoarcidae, Stichaeidae, and Pholidae, as well as the list of species in a classification. Joseph S. Nelson (University of Alberta) spent a significant amount of time, even as he was intensively working on other projects, sharing his views on classification and fish names with us, reviewing the Psychrolutidae, and perusing a near-final draft of the entire manuscript. C.W.M. takes this opportunity to formally thank Joseph S. Nelson, Keith L. Jackson, and Boris A. Sheiko for their involvement, encouragement, and contribution of data to develop the presentation on *Malacocottus aleuticus* at the 2001 annual meeting of the American Society of Ichthyologists and Herpetologists; and Dr. Nelson for reviewing beforehand both that presentation and another on taxonomic discoveries that ensued from work on the *Fishes of Alaska*. We thank William N. Eschmeyer for encouragement in recent years, answering numerous questions on nomenclature, and sharing information and views on Oreosomatidae. Robert N. Lea (California Department of Fish and Game) provided discussion of nomenclatural problems, information on range records, and comments on a near-final draft of the book.

In addition to providing guidance and other assistance in the midyears of the project, Norman J. Wilimovsky reviewed drafts of the Scorpaeniformes, Perciformes, Pleuronectiformes, Tetraodontiformes, and key to families. Other reviewers were asked for help on specific families or other higher taxa, and we thank them for so kindly responding. They include Kenneth T. Alt (Salmonidae), Randy J. Brown (Esocidae and Umbridae), Alfred L. DeCicco (Salmonidae), Robert J. Behnke (Salmonidae), Bruce B. Collette (Scombridae), Kenneth J. Goldman (Elasmobranchii), Antony S. Harold (Sternoptychidae), Gerald R. Hoff (Macrouridae, Cottidae), Tomio Iwamoto (Macrouridae), Keith L. Jackson (Psychrolutidae), Milton Love (Scorpaenidae), Don E. McAllister (Zoarcidae), John D. McEachran (Rajidae), James E. Morrow (freshwater fishes), John R. Paxton (Gyrinomimidae), Theodore W. Pietsch (Lophiiformes), James D. Reist (Salmonidae), Martin D. Robards (Ammodytidae), David G. Smith (Albuliformes, Anguilliformes), and Duane E. Stevenson (Gobiidae). David C. Baker reviewed early drafts of the Scorpaenidae, Perciformes, and Pleuronectiformes. Akihiko Yatsu answered questions and provided papers on Pholidae; Claude B. Renaud on *Lampetra*, particularly the *L. alaskense* problem; Gento Shinohara on Cyclopteridae; Kaoru Kido on Liparidae; M. Yabe and Fumihito Muto on Cottidae; and Teodor T. Nalbant on Liparidae and Zoarcidae. Laurie E. Jarvela and William J. Wilson reviewed the introductory materials.

Arcady V. Balushkin answered questions on a variety of topics and facilitated communications with scientists of the Russian Academy of Sciences. Vladimir V. Fedorov, communicating through Boris A. Sheiko, supplied documentation for records on his unpublished master list of Russian Far East fish species, confirmed identifications of Bering Sea fishes in the fish collection of the Zoological Institute, and helped resolve a variety of problems. Kenneth D. Vogt was especially helpful in the early years, discussing Rae Baxter's taxonomic interpretations and loaning important papers; he read drafts and shared his views on the Myxinidae, Petromyzontidae, Cottidae, and Liparidae sections. Doyne W. Kessler provided records from the NMFS, Alaska Fisheries Science Center scientific survey database before retiring in 1994. The following persons also contributed information on range records and diagnostic characters, discussed taxonomic problems or other matters of content, or contributed literature or other information: Noel Alfonso, M. James Allen, Robert H. Armstrong, Andrey A. Balanov, James E. Blackburn, Edward L. Bousfield, Natalia V. Chernova, Joel Curtis, Jack L. Dean, Margaret F. Docker, Vladimir V. Dolganov, Denice Drass, David A. Ebert, Malcolm Francis, Kathy J. Frost, Douglas J. Frugé, Graham Gillespie, Richard Haight, Mysi Hoang, Philip N. Hooge, Keith L. Jackson, Mark R. Jennings, Robert Johnson, John F. Karinen, Jerrold Koerner, Ik-Soo Kim, Yoshihiko Machida, Scott Meyer, Ann C. Matarese, James H. McLean, Peter R. Møller, H. Geoffrey Moser, Kristen M. Munk, Victoria M. O'Connell, Glen T. Oliver, Wayne A. Palsson, Phillip Rigby, John E. Randall, James B. Reynolds, C. Richard Robins, Axayacatl Rocha-Olivares, David G. Roseneau, Michael F. Sigler, Elizabeth H. Sinclair, Elizabeth Sturm, Arnold Suzumoto, William Walker, Stanley H. Weitzman, and Jeffrey C. Williams.

The scientific review process was conducted by sending draft sections out to specialists over the years as the sections evolved. Personal communications cited are to C.W.M. and are on file at Point Stephens Research (P.O. Box 210307, Auke Bay, Alaska 99821). Decisions regarding taxonomy and other conclusions were the responsibility of C.W.M., and we acknowledge that they may not always be in accord with reviewers' opinions. Translations by B. A. Sheiko cited in the Bibliography are available from Point Stephens Research.

We thank David G. Roseneau, Don Dragoo, and Vernon Byrd for extending an invitation to the USGS to participate in the U.S. Fish and Wildlife Service's July 2001 Seabird, Marine Mammal, and Oceanography Coordinated Investigations (SMMOCI) research cruise to the Semidi Islands, western Gulf of Alaska. The cruise provided C.W.M. an additional opportunity to verify characters of several fish species from fresh specimens, and an excellent atmosphere in which to proof the entire manuscript.

We are fortunate to be able to include a large number of previously unpublished illustrations from the collection of Norman J. Wilimovsky, which were created by biological illustrators under his direction. Most of those illustrations are based on fish specimens collected in Alaskan waters. Alex E. Peden also loaned a large number of illustrations, some previously unpublished, which he commissioned. The Wilimovsky and Peden collections are the property of the Cowan Vertebrate Museum of the University of British Columbia and the Royal British Columbia Museum, respectively, and we gratefully extend our appreciation to the current curators at those institutions for the extended loan. Lisa Palmer provided several illustrations from the late 1800s and early 1900s in the NMNH, Division of Fishes archives. Several of those illustrations are published here for the first time, and include type specimens collected in Alaska. Olga Voskoboinikova and Igor Belousov, scientists of the Russian Academy of Sciences, prepared illustrations from specimens in the ichthyology collection of the Zoological Institute at St. Petersburg. We thank Arcady V. Balushkin, laboratory director, for overseeing production of those illustrations. Anatoly A. Andriashev provided copies of published illustrations from the Zoological Institute archives. Doris Alcorn drew specimens of *Bathyraja parmifera* on loan from the University of Washington. For previously unpublished illustrations, the artists are credited by name in the individual species accounts. Sandra Raredon, NMNH, Division of Fishes, took reference photographs and made radiographs of type and rare specimens. T.A.M. created the place names maps inside the front and back covers, the species range maps, and most of the diagrams in the family introductions (e.g., skate, hatchetfish, rockfish, sculpin features). C.W.M.

drew the sketches for the Key to Fish Families in Alaska and the teleost features on pages 109–112.

We thank the many publishers and authors who gave us permission to reproduce previously published illustrations. The works in which the illustrations first appeared are cited under the Figures subhead in the species accounts. Some publishers require separate acknowledgments, as follows. A few of the skate egg cases are extracted from an illustration in *A Field Guide to Pacific Coast Fishes of North America*; copyright © 1983 by William N. Eschmeyer, Olivia Walker Herald, Howard Hammann, and Jon Gnagy; and reprinted by permission of Houghton Mifflin Company, all rights reserved. Illustrations from the *Journal of the Fisheries Research Board of Canada* and the *Canadian Bulletin of Fisheries and Aquatic Sciences* published by Fisheries and Oceans Canada are reproduced with permission of the Minister of Public Works and Government Services Canada, 2001. Illustrations from the *Occasional Papers of the California Academy of Sciences* are used with permission of the California Academy of Sciences. Illustrations of eelpouts from Anderson (1989, 1994, 1995), Anderson and Peden (1988), and Gon and Heemstra (1990) are reproduced by permission of the J.L.B. Smith Institute of Ichthyology, Grahamstown, South Africa. Other persons and organizations who each gave permission for use of several illustrations include the American Society of Ichthyologists and Herpetologists, for illustrations in *Copeia*; Biogeographical Society of Japan, for *Fauna Japonica*; Robert J. Carveth for Carveth and Wilimovsky (1983ms); Jose I. Castro for Castro (1983); Food and Agriculture Organization of the United Nations for *FAO Species Catalogues*; Hokkaido University for *Memoirs of the Faculty of Fisheries*; Johannes Schmidt Foundation for *Dana-Reports*; Natural History Museum of Los Angeles County for *Contributions to Science* and *Natural History Museum of Los Angeles County Science Bulletin*; James E. Morrow for Morrow (1974, 1980); National Research Council of Canada for *Canadian Bulletin of Fisheries and Aquatic Sciences*; Natural History Museum and Institute, Chiba, Japan, for *Japanese Journal of Ichthyology*; Sears Foundation for Marine Research, Yale University, for *Fishes of the Western North Atlantic*; and University of California Press, *Bulletin of the Scripps Institution of Oceanography*. Others who gave permissions or provided illustrations were Noel Alfonso, Maureen A. Donnelly, Micheline Gilbert, Tomio Iwamoto, Moriya Keiko, Catherine Kempton, Ik-Soo Kim, David S. Lee, Katie Martin, Paul McClymont, J. Donald McPhail, J. G. Nielsen, Theodore W. Pietsch, C. Richard Robins, David G. Smith, Tomoki Sunobe, and Stanley H. Weitzman. In a few instances illustrations provided were not used in the book, but we appreciate the effort taken to provide them.

The color photographs were obtained and selected by L.K.T. and William J. Wilson. They reviewed hundreds of slides, photographs, and digital images. The photographs represent the work of many field biologists, often in adverse weather conditions, to document fish sampling efforts over a 40-year period dating back to surveys conducted in the early 1960s. Kristi Pullen developed a draft layout with scanned images received from L.K.T., then C.W.M. verified the species identifications, obtained additional photographs, and prepared the final layout. We especially thank Anthony J. Gharrett (curator of Jay Quast's photo collection), Donald E. Kramer, Milton Love, David G. Roseneau, Randy J. Brown, and Alfred L. DeCicco for use of their materials. We thank all the photographers for their generosity. Individual credits are given alongside each photograph. We thank James Wilder Orr and Gerald R. Hoff for reviewing the color section, as well as contributing several of the photographs.

The index is one of the most important parts of a book. Doris Alcorn prepared our index and proofed the final draft of the entire Systematic Section. She found inconsistencies in names and spelling, and other blunders, that might otherwise have gone unnoticed until too late.

Through the years, interlibrary loan services obtained several hundred items for us. We particularly thank Beth Bishop, Mendenhall Public Library, Juneau, and Beatrice Franklin, Egan Library, University of Alaska, Juneau, for providing rare and obscure works for reference, and many works in the original editions (some dating to the 1800s) so we could reproduce illustrations. Chip Thoma copied old and obscure publications and organized Rae Baxter's data sheets at the beginning of the project. Susan Thorsteinson obtained copies of several important reference works.

In these days of computer wonders, authors are sometimes called upon to do more than just research and writing. C.W.M. designed the book on a conventional typesetter in late 1990, wrote and revised drafts for several years on an Arche® PC-compatible in Corel®WordPerfect®, transferred sections to an Apple® Macintosh® G3 as they neared completion, and finished the book in Microsoft® Word® and Adobe® Pagemaker®. She thanks Olav J. Kvern for help with Pagemaker®. T.A.M. used a Macintosh® and Adobe® Freehand®, Photoshop®, and other applications to create the graphics, and provided high-resolution proofs throughout the years using an Agfa® imagesetter. We thank Charlie Jones, Printing Trade Co., Juneau, Alaska, for printing sample pages on various types of paper. Edwards Brothers Inc., Ann Arbor, Michigan, printed the book from disks prepared by C.W.M. and T.A.M. We thank Terri Salisbury and other technical staff at Edwards Brothers for advice on preparation of files for printing, coordination, and quality assurance. Janet Harry, Robert L. Kendall, Debbie Lehman, Robert Rand, Beth D. Staehle, Eric Wurzbacher, Carl Burger, and Aaron Lerner represented the AFS during production, printing, and distribution phases of the project. We thank Jim Wiener, Department of the Interior solicitor, for his provision of legal assistance in address of copyright, authorship, and intellectual freedom issues that surfaced in the conduct of this research.

Finally, we wish to formally acknowledge all of the other Alaska Chapter's sponsors who have not already been named. Our list includes individuals from various government agencies, the private sector, and in a special instance, one member of the Alaska Chapter. The funding identified herein primarily includes those sponsors that provided financial assistance during the performance period prior to 1995. Within the public agencies, several Department of the Interior bureaus provided the lion's share of financial help to publish Rae Baxter's annotated keys, and later, as the project evolved, to address new objectives to produce this book. On behalf of the Alaska Chapter, we wish to thank Cleveland J. Cowles, Robert M. Meyer, and Colleen Benner of the Minerals Management Service for their initial contribution and later supplemental funding in support of this effort. We thank Steve Rideout, Steve Klein, and Larry Petersen for U.S. Fish and Wildlife Service funding from the bureau's Global Climate Change Program in Alaska. We thank Al Lovaas and Ross Kavanaugh, formerly with the National Park Service, for their efforts to secure financial support through inventory objectives of the Alaska Region. From the Department of Commerce, special thanks to Steve Pennoyer and Alex C. Wertheimer are in order for National Marine Fisheries Service funding associated with two review sections of the book. Also, we thank the North Pacific Fishery Management Council for its response to a widely distributed funding solicitation to the North Pacific fishing community issued by the Fish Key Committee. The State of Alaska provided financial aid through the Alaska Seafood Marketing Institute (ASMI) and the Alaska Department of Fish and Game. We thank Kevin Sullivan of the ASMI and Jeff Koenings and Charles Meacham, Jr. of the ADFG for their agencys' support. From the private sector we thank Steve Taylor of British Petroleum Exploration (Alaska) Inc., William J. Wilson of LGL Alaska Research Associates, Inc., and the Rasmusson Foundation of the National Bank of Alaska for their financial contributions. Saving the best for last, we thank Tom Schroeder, formerly with the ADFG, of Homer, Alaska, who, as a private citizen, provided the very first gift, a check for $1,000, to assist the project following our initial proposal presentation at the Alaska Chapter's 1989 annual meeting. It was within this spirit of Alaskan partnership that this project was successfully completed.

CONTENTS

COLLECTION ABBREVIATIONS

Abbreviations used in the Systematic Section for permanent fish collections, as in specimen catalog numbers, are given below. Except for a few which have changed, the abbreviations are the same as given in the summaries by Leviton et al. (1985) and Leviton and Gibbs (1988). For some collections more than one abbreviation may currently be in use. If an abbreviation given in the family introductions or species accounts does not appear in the list, the reader is directed to the original literature source. In some cases the collection abbreviations are different from the abbreviations of the museums and academic institutions housing the collections (for those abbreviations, see opposite page).

AB	Auke Bay Laboratory, Alaska Fisheries Science Center, National Marine Fisheries Service, Auke Bay, Alaska, U.S.A.
AMNH	American Museum of Natural History, New York, U.S.A.
ANSP	Academy of Natural Sciences, Philadelphia, Pennsylvania, U.S.A.
BCPM	British Columbia Provincial Museum, Victoria, B.C., Canada. Now RBCM, Royal British Columbia Museum.
BMNH	Natural History Museum, London. Formerly British Museum of Natural History, London.
BPBM	Bernice P. Bishop Museum, Honolulu, Hawaii, U.S.A.
CAS	California Academy of Sciences, San Francisco, California, U.S.A.
CAS-IU	Currently at California Academy of Sciences, formerly at Indiana University.
CAS-SU	Currently at California Academy of Sciences, formerly at Stanford University.
CU	Cornell University Vertebrate Collections, Ithaca, New York, U.S.A.
HUMZ	Hokkaido University, Laboratory of Marine Zoology, Faculty of Fisheries, Hokkaido, Japan.
IOAN	Institute of Oceanology, Russian Academy of Sciences, Moscow, Russia.
KIE	Kamchatka Institute of Ecology, Russian Academy of Sciences, Far Eastern Branch, Petropavlovsk-Kamchatskiy, Russia.
LACM	Los Angeles County Museum of Natural History, Los Angeles, California, U.S.A.
MCZ	Museum of Comparative Zoology, Harvard University, Cambridge, Massachusetts, U.S.A.
NMC	National Museums of Canada, Ottawa, Canada. Now Canadian Museum of Nature.
OSU	Oregon State University, Museum of Natural History, Corvallis, Oregon, U.S.A. Also given as OS.
OSUO	Oregon State University, School of Oceanography, Corvallis, Oregon, U.S.A. Most specimens have been transferred to OSU main collection.
RBCM	Royal British Columbia Museum, Victoria, B.C., Canada. Formerly BCPM, British Columbia Provincial Museum.
SIO	Scripps Institution of Oceanography, La Jolla, California, U.S.A.
TINRO	Pacific Ocean Scientific Research Institute of Fisheries and Oceanography, Vladivostok, Russia.
UAM	University of Alaska, Fairbanks, Alaska, U.S.A.
UAMZ	University of Alberta Museum of Zoology, Alberta, Canada.
UBC	University of British Columbia, Cowan Vertebrate Museum, Vancouver, British Columbia, Canada. Also given as BC.
UMMZ	University of Michigan Museum of Zoology, Ann Arbor, Michigan, U.S.A.
USNM	Smithsonian Institution, National Museum of Natural History, Division of Fishes, Washington, D.C., U.S.A. Formerly U.S. National Museum.
UW	University of Washington, School of Aquatic and Fishery Sciences, Fish Collection, Seattle, Washington, U.S.A.
ZIN	Zoological Institute, Russian Academy of Sciences, St. Petersburg, Russia.
ZIAN	Zoological Institute, Russian Academy of Sciences, Leningrad. Same as ZIN.
ZISP	Zoological Institute, Russian Academy of Sciences, St. Petersburg. Used by some authors for ZIN.
ZIL	Now ZIN.
ZMMGU	Zoological Museum, Moscow State University, Moscow, Russia.

INSTITUTION ABBREVIATIONS

ABL — Auke Bay Laboratory, Alaska Fisheries Science Center, National Marine Fisheries Service, Auke Bay, Alaska.

ADFG — Alaska Department of Fish and Game.

AFS — American Fisheries Society.

AFSC — Alaska Fisheries Science Center, National Marine Fisheries Service, National Oceanic and Atmospheric Administration, U.S. Department of Commerce.

ASIH — American Society of Ichthyologists and Herpetologists.

BCF — Bureau of Commercial Fisheries. Now National Marine Fisheries Service.

CAS — California Academy of Sciences, San Francisco, California.

IFC — International Fisheries Commission. Now International North Pacific Fisheries Commission.

KIE — Kamchatka Institute of Ecology, Russian Academy of Sciences, Petropavlovsk-Kamchatsky, Russia.

NMFS — National Marine Fisheries Service, National Oceanic and Atmospheric Administration, U.S. Department of Commerce.

NMNH — National Museum of Natural History, Smithsonian Institution, Washington, D.C.

NOAA — National Oceanic and Atmospheric Administration, U.S. Department of Commerce.

OCSEAP — Outer Continental Shelf Environmental Assessment Program, U.S. Department of the Interior and U.S. Department of Commerce (existed 1975–1990).

RACE — Resource Assessment and Conservation Engineering Division, Alaska Fisheries Science Center, National Marine Fisheries Service, Seattle, Washington.

TINRO — Pacific Ocean Scientific Research Institute of Fisheries and Oceanography, Vladivostok, Russia.

USGS — U.S. Geological Survey, U.S. Department of the Interior.

USFWS — U.S. Fish and Wildlife Service, U.S. Department of the Interior.

UAF — University of Alaska, Fairbanks.

UBC — University of British Columbia, Vancouver, B.C.

UW — University of Washington, Seattle.

INTRODUCTION

More than a fourth of the species inhabiting the marine and freshwaters of Alaska were originally named and described from samples obtained in Alaska. Our summary table (see opposite page) shows a total of 143 species that were described on the basis of type material from Alaska and which are still recognized to be valid species. This is 27.4% of the 521 confirmed Alaskan species. There is also a large, uncounted number of nominal species that were described from Alaskan specimens but which were later found to be the same as other, previously described species. Just considering the large percentage of valid species named from specimens collected in Alaska and the authors' names and publication dates associated with them — from Pallas, 1787, to Orr and Busby, 2001 — gives an idea of the rich and complex history of expeditions of discovery and collecting in Alaska and research and writing on the region's ichthyofauna.

The first person associated with the study of the fishes of Alaska, as well as the Pacific coast of North America in general, was Georg Wilhelm Steller (1709–1745), a German naturalist sent by the Russian government on Vitus Bering's voyage of exploration in 1731 to study the animals of Alaska. Steller published descriptions under Russian names of five species of salmon from Alaska; these species still stand, and his conclusions about the trout have proved in general to be correct. As Jordan (1931) remarked, sorting out the complicated species of salmon and trout, before the time of Linnaeus, was a remarkable achievement. In 1811 another naturalist employed by the Russian government, Petrus Simon Pallas (1741–1811), completed an account of his explorations of the same area Steller had explored. He authenticated by repetition the work of Steller, and discovered many new species. In a work published in 1792, a compiler of natural history named Johann Julius Walbaum (1721–1800) gave scientific (binomial) names to the Pacific salmons and trouts; accordingly, his name is affixed as authority to the species which Steller discovered and described. Other material, including collections from the Bering Sea by the Russian navigator Krusenstern, was studied and published in transactions of the early scientific societies of Russia by Wilhelm Theophilus Tilesius (1775–1835). The histories of ichthyology by Jordan (1905), Hubbs (1964), and Myers (1964) provide a fairly complete review of Steller, Pallas, and others who left their mark in the development of knowledge of Alaska's fishes to the end of the nineteenth century. David Starr Jordan (1851–1931), who was the preeminent ichthyologist of North America during the late nineteenth and early twentieth centuries (Myers 1951), carried the outline of ichthyological history forward in his autobiography (Jordan 1922) and history of zoological explorations of the Pacific coast (Jordan 1931), which included much information that pertains to fishes of Alaska. Charles H. Gilbert (1859–1928), who ranks with Jordan as the foremost ichthyologist of the West Coast and was particularly significant in the development of knowledge of Alaskan fishes, is the subject of accounts by Dunn (1996a, 1996b, 1997). Jordan and Gilbert both collected fishes in Alaska. Hubbs (1964), highlighting the history of ichthyology in the United States after 1850, and Dymond (1964), of ichthyology in Canada including the Arctic, provided important references to knowledge of fishes of Alaska to the middle of the twentieth century.

Previous Inventories of the Fishes of Alaska

Few authors have listed the fish species occurring in Alaska as an object of their writing. Most lists were limited by expedition coverage or reflected the extent of a museum's holdings. The earliest list in English is the "List of the Fishes of Alaska" compiled by William H. Dall (1845–1927) and published in *Alaska and its Resources* (Dall 1870). The list includes only the most common species and several of them, owing to the primitive state of taxonomy at the time, are unidentifiable with names in use today. Dall's list gives 18 marine species as common in the seas off Alaska and 19 freshwater species in the Yukon River. *Alaska and its Resources* related Dall's observations as a naturalist in Alaska, including his tour as director of the Scientific Corps of the Western Union Telegraph Expedition which took the members to Norton Sound and the Yukon River. Unfortunately, fish collected by the expedition were not included, because they had not yet been studied and identified. It is an interesting historical point that Dall was in Alaska in 1867, leading the expedition, when the treaty of sale was agreed upon and the Russian holdings in America were transferred to the United States, making Alaska a U.S. territory.

Tarleton H. Bean (1846–1916), with the holdings of the Smithsonian Institution, United States National Museum (now National Museum of Natural History) at his disposal as curator of the fish collection, including Dall's and other early collectors' contributions, compiled "A Preliminary Catalogue of the Fishes of Alaskan and Adjacent Waters" for publication in the *Proceedings of the United States National Museum* (Bean 1881b). Bean's catalog is a list of families and species with the museum's holdings for each species identified by catalog number and name of collector. He listed 116 species in 33 families represented by museum records from the Territory of Alaska. The species listed are almost

Table of orders and the numbers of families, genera, and species treated in this book; numbers of species confirmed, reported but not confirmed, and possible but not reported in Alaska; numbers of confirmed Alaskan species by general habitat; and numbers of species originally described from specimens collected in Alaska. Alternate classifications of the higher taxa and questions concerning validity of species are addressed in the Taxon Accounts and Keys to Species.

	Numbers of taxa			Numbers of species			Species by habitat			Species with Alaskan type locality[2]
Order	Families	Genera	Species	Confirmed from Alaska	Reported but not confirmed	Probably in Alaska but not reported[1]	Salt water	Fresh water	Anadromous or euryhaline	
Myxiniformes	1	1	2	1	1	0	1	0	0	1
Petromyzontiformes	1	1	5	5	0	0	0	2	3	1
Chimaeriformes	1	1	1	1	0	0	1	0	0	0
Carcharhiniformes	3	4	4	2	1	1	2	0	0	0
Lamniformes	3	5	5	4	1	0	4	0	0	0
Hexanchiformes	1	2	2	1	1	0	1	0	0	0
Squaliformes	2	2	2	2	0	0	2	0	0	0
Squatiniformes	1	1	1	0	1	0	0	0	0	0
Rajiformes	3	4	14	12	1	1	12	0	0	4
Acipenseriformes	1	1	2	2	0	0	0	0	2	0
Albuliformes	1	2	2	1	0	1	1	0	0	0
Anguilliformes	3	5	6	4	0	2	4	0	0	0
Saccopharyngiformes	1	1	1	0	0	1	0	0	0	0
Clupeiformes	2	4	5	5	0	0	4	0	1	0
Cypriniformes	2	2	2	2	0	0	0	2	0	0
Esociformes	2	2	2	2	0	0	0	2	0	1
Osmeriformes	6	18	22	19	1	2	15	1	3	1
Salmoniformes	1	7	24	24	0	0	0	10	14	2
Stomiiformes	3	9	13	10	0	3	10	0	0	0
Aulopiformes	5	7	8	7	0	1	7	0	0	1
Myctophiformes	2	11	11	11	0	0	11	0	0	0
Lampridiformes	2	2	2	2	0	0	2	0	0	0
Percopsiformes	1	1	1	1	0	0	0	1	0	0
Ophidiiformes	2	3	3	2	0	1	2	0	0	0
Gadiformes	4	14	22	19	0	3	18	1	0	1
Batrachoidiformes	1	1	1	0	1	0	0	0	0	0
Lophiiformes	3	6	8	4	1	3	4	0	0	2
Beloniformes	1	1	1	1	0	0	1	0	0	0
Stephanoberyciformes	3	5	5	4	1	0	4	0	0	0
Beryciformes	1	1	1	0	0	1	0	0	0	0
Zeiformes	1	1	1	1	0	0	1	0	0	0
Gasterosteiformes	3	4	4	4	0	0	2	0	2	0
Scorpaeniformes	10	85	253	225	8	20	222	3	0	89
Perciformes	27	71	134	113	2	19	113	0	0	34
Pleuronectiformes	2	20	29	28	0	1	28	0	0	6
Tetraodontiformes	2	2	2	2	0	0	2	0	0	0
	108	307	601	521	20	60	474	22	25	143

[1] Most species in this category have been recorded just outside Alaska's borders in the Bering Sea or Pacific Ocean. Two or three species are included more for comparison with closely related species than for the likelihood of their occurrence in Alaska.
[2] Original description of the name-bearing taxon (senior synonym) was based wholly or partly on specimens collected in Alaska as all or part of the type series.

all shallow-water and intertidal species, because at that time the deepsea fishes of Alaska had not been sampled and remained to be discovered. In an appendix, Bean included the names of 99 species from adjacent waters which he believed would eventually be found within the limits of the Territory. Bean named several new species in his catalog but they were not described until later, largely in subsequent volumes of the *Proceedings*. The inventory of recorded Alaskan species was soon revised by Bean (in Nelson 1887) from 116 to 135. Three of the fishes described by Bean were named in honor of naturalists who collected in Alaska. He named the estuary eelpout, *Lycodes turneri* Bean, 1879, for Lucien M. Turner; and the Alaska whitefish, *Coregonus nelsonii* Bean, 1884, for Edward W. Nelson. Turner and Nelson were sent by the U.S. Army Signal Service to establish meteorological stations in Alaska. Turner (1886) collected specimens at Sanak Island, St. Michael (Yukon Delta, fresh and brackish waters), Saint Paul Island, and Unalaska, Atka, and Attu islands. Nelson (1887) collected specimens from various parts of the interior, from the Bering Sea to Fort Yukon and from the Kuskokwim River north to Point Barrow. Bean (1880) named the Alaska blackfish, *Dallia pectoralis,* in honor of William H. Dall for his contributions to the zoology of Alaska.

The next inventory for the entire Territory of Alaska was compiled by Barton W. Evermann (1853–1932) and Edmund L. Goldsborough (1868–1953). Working with the U.S. National Museum collection, Evermann and Goldsborough (1907) compiled "The Fishes of Alaska," published in the *Bulletin of the Bureau of Fisheries* for 1906. Their stated purpose was to record information concerning the habits, abundance, and distribution of salmon and other fishes obtained from investigations of the salmon fisheries of Alaska in 1903 and 1904, and to embody in the paper a complete review of the fishes of Alaska to date. They listed 265 species in 52 families, but a portion of this total was actually based on specimens obtained outside Alaska, in British Columbia and in Puget Sound, Washington. As with all such inventories, taxonomic changes make it difficult to compare the numbers given by different authors. Significant revisions had occurred by Evermann and Goldsborough's time and many more have occurred since then, with the net result being a lowering of the number of species that today would be recognized as valid. On the other hand, some species recorded from Alaska were overlooked. Evermann and Goldsborough (1907) described eight new species and commented on the taxonomy of others. For most species they did not give morphological features but listed museum records and catch localities; this accounting of records is an important research tool.

Evermann and Goldsborough's (1907) inventory benefited from the earliest collections made in deep water by scientists aboard the U.S. Fish Commission steamer *Albatross.* The *Albatross* was the first marine research vessel to be built by any nation. She was powered by two steam engines and rigged as a brigantine, and was the first government vessel to be provided with electric lights (Tanner 1885, 1897). Her work in Alaska began in 1888 and continued, primarily in the summers, through 1906. Available to Evermann and Goldsborough (1907) from the *Albatross* expeditions were samples collected by Bean (e.g., 1890b) from southeastern Alaska; Gilbert (1896) from north and south of the Aleutian Islands and in Bristol Bay; and Jordan and Gilbert (1899) from fur seal investigations in the Bering Sea, particularly around the Pribilof Islands and the vicinity of Unalaska and Bogoslof islands in the Aleutian Islands. The *Albatross* was the first research vessel to sample deep waters in Alaska and Evermann and Goldsborough's (1907) account included such rare deepwater species as *Histiobranchus bathybius,* obtained from the Bering Sea at a depth of 1,625 fathoms (2,972 m), which had been recorded by Gilbert (1896). Other than a single specimen collected off Mexico, that particular specimen is the only example of the species recorded from the eastern Pacific. Several other species obtained by the *Albatross* in Alaska are equally or nearly as rare in collections. Also available to Evermann and Goldsborough (1907) was Jordan and Evermann's (1896–1900) compendium on the fishes of North and Middle America, which contained descriptions of approximately 215 species recorded in Alaska.

Nearly 50 years after Evermann and Goldsborough's (1907) inventory, Norman J. Wilimovsky (1925–1997) listed 379 species in 74 families in his "List of the Fishes of Alaska" in the *Stanford Ichthyological Bulletin* (Wilimovsky 1954). In addition to the names of the species, he gave broad range statements, such as "Bering Sea – California." Unfortunately, documentation for the list and geographic ranges was not included but was intended to be published in later works which did not materialize. Samples forming the basis for Wilimovsky's list evidently included those he collected as a Stanford University graduate student accompanying James E. Böhlke on a 1951 collecting trip to Point Barrow. A few years after his list was published, and working as chief of marine fisheries investigations for the U.S. Fish and Wildlife Service in Alaska, Wilimovsky (1958) prepared his "Provisional Keys to the Fishes of Alaska," comprising keys to 388 Alaskan species. Distributed in a limited edition by the U.S. Fish and Wildlife Service, Fisheries Research Laboratory (now National Marine Fisheries Service, Auke Bay Laboratory), Juneau, Alaska, the supply was soon depleted. Wilimovsky's keys constituted the first single source aid to identification of the fishes of Alaska. Wilimovsky included vernacular names if they existed, as well as scientific names and broad range statements. Important footnotes on taxonomy were included, and the key couplets were fairly detailed. The keys, as well as the earlier list, have largely been superseded by subsequent taxonomic revisions and range records, but this was expected. As Wilimovsky pointed out, the inventory would be considerably enlarged before any definitive idea of the Territorial fish fauna would be attained. Wilimovsky's keys incorporated a few species that came to his attention while working in Alaska. Saving vouchers at the Auke Bay Laboratory, he started that agency's permanent

Puget Sound Maritime Historical Society

United States Fish Commission steamer *Albatross*.

fish collection and became its first curator but he soon moved to Canada and joined the faculty of the University of British Columbia. On 3 January 1959, shortly after Wilimovsky completed his keys, Alaska became the 49th state of the Union.

The Auke Bay Laboratory collection was curated next by Jay C. Quast, who with Elizabeth H. Hall surveyed the literature and the specimens housed in the collection and reported 431 confirmed Alaskan species in 81 families (Quast and Hall 1972). In addition, they listed 138 species from neighboring waters that they believed should be considered when identifying new collections. Quast and Hall (1972) described their report, "List of Fishes of Alaska and Adjacent Waters with a Guide to Some of Their Literature" (published in the *NOAA Technical Report* series), as a preliminary effort accomplished in a limited amount of time. Nevertheless, it was a significant synthesis of the literature on fish ranges in Alaska and, by listing the general catch localities for specimens accumulated in the laboratory collection since Wilimovsky's (1958) keys were prepared, provided much new information. The introduced literature included the report of Wilimovsky and Alex E. Peden's survey of the Aleutian Islands under the auspices of the Institute of Fisheries, University of British Columbia (Wilimovsky 1964), as well as much of the literature on geographic range that had been published in the time between Evermann and Goldsborough's (1907) account and Wilimovsky's (1954, 1958) list and keys. One of the most notable of those works, for the large number of Alaskan records it contains, is Gilbert and Burke's (1912a) "Fishes from Bering Sea and Kamchatka," which recorded collections obtained by the *Albatross* along the Aleutian chain in 1906 by shore collecting as well as bottom trawling and dredging. Alaskan localities sampled included Petrel Bank and Stalemate Bank. Thirty-five new species were described from this expedition. (For a detailed account of the expedition and Gilbert's involvement as chief naturalist, see Dunn [1996b].) Quast and Hall (1972) also had available the syntheses on freshwater fishes of Canada and Alaska by McPhail and Lindsey (1970); of the marine fishes of northeastern Siberia and the American Arctic by Walters (1955); and Clemens and Wilby's (1946, 1949, 1961) *Fishes of the Pacific Coast of Canada*. Another critical resource available to them was Jordan, Evermann, and Clark's (1930) checklist of fishes of North and Middle America with its listing of all junior synonyms. Major Russian and Japanese ichthyological works which included results from explorations of the Bering Sea and adjacent waters were also cited (e.g., Andriashev 1937, 1954; Schmidt 1950; Ishiyama 1967). As with the previous inventories, many of the species in Quast and Hall's (1972) inventory have been synonymized, so the number of valid species would now be recognized to be smaller.

The next significant syntheses of Alaskan fish species after Quast and Hall (1972) were not inventories of the entire state's ichthyofauna but addressed the freshwater and anadromous fishes. Building on years of research and collecting as biologist at the University of Alaska Fairbanks, James E. Morrow wrote *Illustrated Keys to the Freshwater Fishes of Alaska* (Morrow 1974) and *The Freshwater Fishes of Alaska* (Morrow 1980b). The latter publication included descriptions of the species, their habitats, and range in Alaska, and depicted the Alaskan ranges for each species on maps. It was preceded by McPhail and Lindsey's (1970) *Freshwater Fishes of Northwestern Canada and Alaska* and Scott and Crossman's (1973) *Freshwater Fishes of Canada,* and published at about the same time as Lee et al.'s (1980) *Atlas of North American Freshwater Fishes.*

Rae Baxter (1929–1991), treating the entire Alaskan ichthyofauna and starting from Wilimovsky's (1958) keys, included descriptive accounts of 581 Alaskan species and 50 from adjacent waters in a widely distributed but unfinished manuscript, "Annotated Keys to the Fishes of Alaska" (Baxter 1990ms). The number of Alaskan species is inflated compared to the present inventory, mostly by inclusion of nominal species which should have been classified as junior synonyms. On the other hand, several new species have been described in the intervening 12 years, and a few were overlooked. By 1990 an enormous body of literature that treated fishes of Alaska had been published but Baxter only had the opportunity, before his untimely death (22 March 1991), to accumulate and incorporate a relatively small portion. As a fishery biologist with the Alaska Department of Fish and Game and later as an independent investigator, Baxter participated in research on the Yukon River Delta and surveys in the Bering Sea and Gulf of Alaska. He also did some collecting near his home in Kachemak Bay and around the Kenai Peninsula off his skiff, which he had outfitted with a small trawl, and identified specimens sent to him by other investigators. Baxter adopted his own, personal view of the Alaskan ichthyofauna and how it should be classified and described. He reported extensions of known range and size but discarded most of the specimens he examined, so there are no voucher specimens confirming the extensions. His data sheets indicate that some specimens were saved, but we found few of those vouchers in museums. However, this does not mean they do not exist. They could be present in backlogged materials waiting to be accessioned into collections and not found when we asked curators about them. Most of the extensions have been superseded by more recent records.

Several major monographs and guides to the ichthyofaunas of other regions have been published since the works of Quast and Hall (1972) and Morrow (1980b) which include some of the species whose range extends into Alaskan waters or species which may yet be found in Alaska and which should be considered when identifying specimens collected in Alaska. The regional works most frequently consulted during preparation of this catalog are as follows. Works on marine species include Miller and Lea (1972), coastal fishes of California; Hart (1973), British Columbia, Canada; Eschmeyer and Herald (1983), eastern Pacific coast from Baja to Alaska (primarily to southeastern Alaska); Amaoka et al. (1983), northeastern Sea of Japan and Sea of Okhotsk off Hokkaido; Masuda et al. (1984), Japanese archipelago; Whitehead et al. (1984, 1986), northeastern Atlantic; Scott and Scott (1988), Atlantic coast of Canada, including much of the Arctic; and Gon and Heemstra (1990), the Southern Ocean. The Russian series of volumes on fishes of the Sea of Japan and adjacent areas of the Sea of Okhotsk and Yellow Sea (Lindberg and Legeza 1959, 1965; Lindberg and Krasyukova 1969, 1975, 1987; Lindberg and Fedorov 1993) were frequently consulted; all volumes except the two most recent have been translated into English. The major syntheses on freshwater species of North America are the atlas by Lee et al. (1980) and the field guide by Page and Burr (1991). The encyclopedia of Canadian fishes by Coad (1995) covers both freshwater and marine species. Regional treatments of individual orders or families, such as Kido (1988) and Kanayama (1991) on the Liparidae and Agonidae of Japan and adjacent waters, respectively, or worldwide treatment of individual taxa, such as Cohen et al. (1990) on Gadiformes of the world, are cited in the introductions to the higher taxa as well as in the species accounts.

The Current Inventory

The inventory presented in this book includes 521 species in 97 families with occurrence in Alaskan waters confirmed by adequate documentation. Another 20 species with reported but uncertain or unverifiable occurrence in Alaska and 60 from adjacent waters which should be considered when identifying new samples or problematical museum specimens are also included, for a total of 601 species in 108 families.

Comparing our inventory to the previous published inventory (Quast and Hall 1972) gives 90 more confirmed Alaskan species and 58 fewer species with uncertain occurrence in Alaska or believed to eventually be found in Alaska. Because of taxonomic changes it is difficult to assign any meaning to the differences. Some portion of the additional confirmed Alaskan species is accounted for by new records of occurrence which move some of Quast and Hall's potential Alaskan species to the confirmed side of the ledger. To that must be added the new species discovered and named since 1972 or that had been overlooked in obscure or foreign-language publications. Reducing Quast and Hall's list of confirmed Alaskan species because of the species that have since been synonymized would reduce that list significantly. The net number of species added by our inventory to the number of confirmed Alaskan species is, therefore, actually much larger than 90. Moreover, in selecting species which should be considered when identifying specimens from Alaska (what we sometimes call "potential" Alaskan species) we excluded several that were listed by Quast and Hall (1972).

Twenty-nine new species add names to the inventory of confirmed Alaskan species: *Lampetra alaskense* (Vladykov & Kott, 1978) (Alaskan brook lamprey); *Bathyraja lindbergi* Ishiyama & Ishihara, 1977 (Commander skate); *Bathyraja maculata* Ishiyama & Ishihara, 1977 (whiteblotched skate); *Bathyraja minispinosa* Ishiyama & Ishihara, 1977 (whitebrow skate); *Bathyraja taranetzi* (Dolganov, 1983) (mud skate); *Dolichopteryx parini* Kobyliansky & Fedorov, 2001 (winged spookfish); *Holtbyrnia latifrons* Sazonov, 1976 (teardrop tubeshoulder); *Maulisia argipalla* Matsui & Rosenblatt, 1979 (pitted tubeshoulder); *Anotopterus nikparini* Kukuev, 1998 (North Pacific daggertooth); *Bertella idiomorpha* Pietsch, 1973 (spikehead dreamer); *Adelosebastes latens* Eschmeyer, Abe, & Nakano, 1979 (Emperor rockfish); *Bolinia euryptera* Yabe, 1991 (broadfin sculpin); *Psychrolutes phrictus* Stein & Bond, 1978 (giant blobsculpin); *Careproctus canus* Kido, 1985 (gray snailfish); *Careproctus zachirus* Kido, 1985 (blacktip snailfish); *Liparis catharus* Vogt, 1973 (purity snailfish); *Paraliparis pectoralis* Stein, 1978 (pectoral snailfish); *Prognatholiparis ptychomandibularis* Orr & Busby, 2001 (wrinklejaw snailfish); *Pseudopentaceros wheeleri* Hardy, 1983 (North Pacific pelagic armorhead); *Lycenchelys alta* Toyoshima, 1985 (short eelpout); *Lycenchelys rosea* Toyoshima, 1985 (rosy eelpout); *Lycodapus endemoscotus* Peden & Anderson, 1978 (deepwater eelpout); *Lycodapus leptus* Peden & Anderson, 1981 (slender eelpout); *Lycodapus poecilus* Peden & Anderson, 1981 (variform eelpout); *Lycodapus psarostomatus* Peden & Anderson, 1981 (specklemouth eelpout); *Lycodes sagittarius* McAllister, 1976 (archer eelpout); *Opaeophacus acrogeneius* Bond & Stein, 1984 (bulldog eelpout); *Puzanovia rubra* Fedorov, 1975 (tough eelpout); and *Lepidopsetta polyxystra* Orr & Matarese, 2000 (northern rock sole). Two of those species represent North Pacific populations which have been separated from other species, and do not add numbers to the inventory: *Pseudopentaceros wheeleri* is a new name for the North Pacific armorhead and includes North Pacific records of *P. richardsoni,* which was on Quast and Hall's (1972) list; and *Anotopterus nikparini* is the North Pacific species of daggertooth which has been separated from *A. pharao.*

Among the many new species which have been described from adjacent waters in recent years are seven we include as potential Alaskan species: *Nemichthys larseni* Nielsen & Smith, 1978 (pale snipe eel); *Maulisia acuticeps* Sazonov, 1976 (dark tubeshoulder); *Coryphaenoides yaquinae* Iwamoto & Stein, 1974 (rough abyssal grenadier); *Paraliparis paucidens* Stein, 1978 (toothless snailfish); *Lycodapus pachysoma* Peden & Anderson, 1978 (stout eelpout); *Pachycara gymninium* Anderson & Peden, 1988 (nakednape eelpout); and *Pachycara lepinium* Anderson & Peden, 1988 (scalynape eelpout). One new species described from samples obtained in adjacent waters of British Columbia was reported in Alaska, but documentation for the Alaskan occurrence is lacking: *Hypsagonus mozinoi* (Wilimovsky & Wilson, 1978) (kelp poacher). Roughly 200 new species are being described worldwide each year (Eschmeyer 1998), and with increasing interest in Alaska's resources and biodiversity we may be assured that some of those new species will be named from discoveries in Alaska.

Further comparisons between this inventory and Quast and Hall's (1972) are made and the differences explained, by family, in the Systematic Section.

Composition of the Alaskan Ichthyofauna

Breaking the inventory down into various types of categories may help characterize the Alaskan ichthyofauna: taxonomic composition; numbers of endemic and nonindigenous species; composition by general habitat; and proportion of species utilized commercially.

Composition by Taxon

Jawless and cartilaginous fishes (Agnatha and Chondrichthyes) number 28 or 5.4% of the total of 521 species confirmed from Alaska. Numbers of ray-finned fishes (Actinopterygii) in Alaska total 493 or 94.6%.

The largest number of Alaskan species is in the order Scorpaeniformes, with 225 confirmed species (43% of the total of 521). Most of the Alaskan scorpaeniforms are members of the families Cottidae, Liparidae, Scorpaenidae, and Agonidae. The Perciformes is the second most speciose order in Alaska, represented by 113 species (21.7% of the total). Most of the Alaskan perciforms are in the families Zoarcidae and Stichaeidae. Following far behind the Scorpaeniformes and Perciformes in third and fourth place are the Pleuronectiformes (28 species, or 5.4%) and Salmoniformes (24 species, 4.6%), respectively. The greatest diversity in Alaska by number of families is in the Perciformes, with species in as many as 27 families, followed by the Scorpaeniformes, with representatives in 10 families (see table).

Eight families are represented in Alaska by more than 20 species each (counting confirmed Alaskan species from the List of Species in a Classification). These are the Cottidae (sculpins or cottids, 76 species); Liparidae (snailfishes, 56); Zoarcidae (eelpouts, 46); Scorpaenidae (rockfishes, 36); Pleuronectidae (righteye flounders, 26); Salmonidae (salmonids, 24); Stichaeidae (pricklebacks, 23); and Agonidae (poachers, 22). Altogether, the Alaskan species in those eight families comprise 309, or 59.3%, of the total of 521. Following them are 12 families represented by 5–12 species each. From most to least speciose in Alaska they are: Rajidae (skates, 12); Myctophidae (lanternfishes, 10) and Cyclopteridae (lumpsuckers, 10); Gadidae (cods, 9); Psychrolutidae (fathead sculpins, 8); Osmeridae (smelts, 7), Macrouridae (grenadiers, 7), Hexagrammidae (greenlings, 7), and Hemitripteridae (sailfin sculpins, 7); and Petromyzontidae (lampreys, 5), Pholidae (gunnels, 5), and Scombridae (mackerels, 5). The other 77 families are represented by four or fewer species.

Four families are included on the basis of uncertain or unverifiable Alaskan records: Squatinidae (angel sharks), Myliobatidae (eagle rays), Batrachoididae (toadfishes), and Gigantactinidae (whipnoses). Seven others are included as possibly being represented in Alaska: Triakidae (houndsharks), Torpedinidae (electric rays), Serrivomeridae (sawtooth eels), Cyematidae (bobtail eels), Sternoptychidae (marine hatchetfishes), Anoplogastridae (fangtooths), and Stromateidae (butterfishes). Dasyatidae (stingrays) and Trichiuridae (cutlassfishes), included by Quast and Hall (1972) as potential Alaskan families, are not included in the present inventory because northern records (Peden 1974, 1979c; Peden and Hughes 1986; Peden and Jamieson 1988) are rare and occur only into southern British Columbia waters, suggesting that species in these families are not likely to stray to Alaska.

Endemic Species

Twenty-one of the species treated in this book have been recorded only in Alaska. All are marine. Among the freshwater fishes, even the Alaska whitefish, *Coregonus nelsonii,* a species of questionable validity, has been recorded elsewhere (in Canada). The possible Alaskan endemics are members of the superfamilies Cottoidea and Cyclopteroidea. Six sculpins of the family Cottidae have been recorded only in Alaska: scaled sculpin, *Archistes biseriatus*; broadfin sculpin, *Bolinia euryptera*; spineless sculpin, *Phallocottus obtusus*; kelp sculpin, *Sigmistes caulias*; strangeline sculpin, *Stlegicottus xenogrammus*; and highbrow sculpin, *Triglops metopias.* Three lumpsuckers (Cyclopteridae) are known only from Alaska: Alaskan lumpsucker, *Eumicrotremus gyrinops*; toad lumpsucker, *E. phrynoides*; and docked snailfish, *Lethotremus muticus*. Twelve snailfishes (Liparidae) have been recorded only from Alaska. Most of them are represented by one or a few records: attenuate snailfish, *C. attenuatus*; Bowers Bank snailfish, *C. bowersianus*; gray snailfish, *C. canus*; shovelhead snailfish, *C. ectenes*; distalpore snailfish, *C. opisthotremus*; peachskin snailfish, *C. scottae*; stippled snailfish, *C. spectrum*; wrinklejaw snailfish, *Prognatholiparis ptychomandibularis*; elusive snailfish, *Crystallichthys cameliae*; minigill snailfish, *Gyrinichthys minytremus*; Bristol snailfish, *Liparis bristolensis*; and purity snailfish, *L. catharus.*

The apparent endemism of some of those marine species is probably an artifact of incomplete knowledge of the taxonomy of the species or limited sampling. There are several examples in this book of species that were believed to occur only in Alaska but which recent research has showed occur elsewhere. In 1992 we counted 40 or more species recorded only from Alaska (twice the number we ended up with). For example, the whitetail sculpin, *Malacocottus aleuticus,* was known for many years only from the description of one specimen obtained in the Bering Sea which subsequently was lost (Smith 1904), but has recently been found off the Kamchatka Peninsula, Russia, and Hokkaido Island, Japan, as well as in Prince William Sound, Alaska. The longfin Irish lord, *Hemilepidotus zapus,* was not known to occur outside Alaska from the time of its discovery in 1910 (Gilbert and Burke 1912a) until 1996, when it was obtained by Russian fishery biologists near the Kuril Islands. The bighead snailfish, *Liparis megacephalus,* was known only from the eastern Bering Sea and Aleutian Islands from records accumulated between 1912 and 1978, then Kim et al. (1993) recorded it from the Sea of Japan off South Korea. Several Alaskan species, even among those recently described, have proved to be the same as species described from specimens obtained elsewhere in the Pacific Ocean. For example, *Rhinoraja longi* Raschi & McEachran, 1991, described from specimens obtained near the Aleutian Islands, is a junior synonym of *Bathyraja taranetzi,* a species originally described from Russia. In the above list of possible endemics, *Eumicrotremus gyrinops* is likely to be a juvenile of some other species, *Liparis bristolensis* is probably a synonym of *L. tunicatus* and *Careproctus scottae* probably a synonym of *C. rastrinus,* and *Crystallichthys cameliae* may be a synonym of *C. mirabilis* or *C. cyclospilus.*

Nonindigenous Species

Three species have been introduced into Alaska or spread into Alaska from introductions elsewhere: American shad, *Alosa sapidissima*; brook trout, *Salvelinus fontinalis*; and Atlantic salmon, *Salmo salar.* The American shad, introduced to the Pacific coast of the United States from the Atlantic in the late 1800s, has become widespread although not abundant all the way to Alaska and to Siberia but does not reproduce in Alaska or Siberia. Brook trout, intentionally introduced into many lakes, rivers, and streams in southeastern Alaska starting in the early 1900s, have established populations in some of the lakes. Atlantic salmon in Alaska are escapees from Pacific Northwest fish farms, and have been found in marine waters from the Gulf of Alaska to the Bering Sea and in fresh water in southeastern Alaska. Naturally reproducing populations of Atlantic salmon have been reported in the wild in British Columbia, but not yet in Alaska. Yellow perch, *Perca flavescens,* were introduced to a private lake on the Kenai Peninsula but were eradicated in 2000 by the Alaska Department of Fish and Game. The introduction became known when the lake owner asked the agency to provide some northern pike, *Esox lucius,* as predators to reduce stunting of the perch from overcrowding.

General Habitat

Of the 521 species of fish well documented from Alaska, 474 (91%) almost exclusively inhabit salt water; 22 (4.2%) almost exclusively inhabit fresh water; and 25 (4.8%) spend parts of their life cycles, have adult populations, or appear to be equally at home in both salt and fresh water. The Alaskan marine species which have been recorded from fresh water include two sculpins (Cottidae), a surf perch (Embiotocidae), and two righteye flounders (Pleuronectidae). The Pacific staghorn sculpin, *Leptocottus armatus,* often enters the lower reaches of rivers and streams, and the fourhorn sculpin, *Myoxocephalus quadricornis,* is occasionally found high up rivers. The shiner perch, *Cymatogaster aggregata,* and Arctic flounder, *Pleuronectes glacialis,* sometimes enter fresh water. The starry flounder, *Platichthys stellatus,* enters fresh water to the limit of tidal influence, as well as coastal marshes and lakes. However, fresh water does not appear to be critical for the existence of those species and for a few others which occasionally enter brackish or fresh water. Similarly, in the freshwater category, the coastrange sculpin, *Cottus aleuticus,* can tolerate brackish water and is occasionally found in estuaries but the amount of time spent out of fresh water is relatively insignificant. The prickly sculpin, *C. asper,* tolerates salt water and is often found in brackish water, and some populations possibly move downstream to spawn in brackish water.

The species in the anadromous or euryhaline category show some degree of dependence on both environments, an ability to carry out major portions of their life cycles in both, or have populations in both. Among the Gasterosteidae, the threespine stickleback, *Gasterosteus aculeatus,* and the ninespine stickleback, *Pungitius pungitius,* have freshwater and marine or anadromous populations in Alaska. This category also includes the Salmonidae with, for example, the anadromous Pacific salmons (*Oncorhynchus*) which spend years at sea before entering their home streams to spawn in fresh water, and the amphidromous whitefishes (*Coregonus*) which as adults may make repeated feeding migrations to coastal waters before spawning in fresh water. Three anadromous species have not been reported from fresh water in Alaska: American shad, *Alosa sapidissima*; green sturgeon, *Acipenser medirostris*; and white sturgeon, *A. transmontanus.*

Commercial Fisheries

Commercial fisheries are an economic mainstay of Alaska even though only slightly more than 11% of its confirmed number of species are targeted by the fishing industry. Fifty-nine species in nine families are currently harvested in fisheries worth billions of dollars annually. Alaska currently produces 80% of all wild Pacific salmon harvested in the western United States and Canada and commercial harvests have, in recent years, exceeded 100 million fish annually. In order of abundance they are: pink salmon, *Oncorhynchus gorbuscha*; sockeye salmon, *O. nerka*; chum salmon, *O. keta*; coho salmon, *O. kisutch*; and Chinook salmon, *O. tshawytscha.* Two whitefish species (Arctic cisco, *Coregonus autumnalis*; least cisco, *C. sardinella*) are captured in a small (about 40,000 fish annually) commercial fishery on the Colville River.

Most of Alaska's commercial resources are harvested in the geographically extensive Gulf of Alaska and Bering Sea–Aleutian Island groundfish fisheries as targeted species or bycatch species. Alaska's groundfish resources include, in no particular order: Gadidae (walleye pollock, *Theragra chalcogramma*; Pacific cod, *Gadus macrocephalus*); Anoplopomatidae (sablefish, *Anoplopoma fimbria*); Pleuronectidae (arrowtooth flounder, *Atheresthes stomias*; deepsea sole, *Embassichthys bathybius*; rex sole, *Glyptocephalus zachirus*; flathead sole, *Hippoglossoides elassodon*; Pacific halibut, *Hippoglossus stenolepis*; butter sole, *Isopsetta isolepis*; northern rock sole, *Lepidopsetta polyxystra*; southern rock sole, *L. bilineata*; yellowfin sole, *Limanda aspera*; longhead dab, *L. proboscidea*; Dover sole, *Microstomus pacificus*; English sole, *Parophrys vetulus;* starry flounder, *Platichthys stellatus*; Alaska plaice, *Pleuronectes quadrituberculatus*; sand sole, *Psettichthys melanostictus*; Greenland halibut, *Reinhardtius hippoglossoides*); Hexagrammidae (lingcod, *Ophiodon elongatus;* Atka mackerel, *Pleurogrammus monopterygius*); Scorpaenidae (Pacific ocean perch, *Sebastes alutus*; rougheye rockfish, *S. aleutianus*; redbanded rockfish, *S. babcocki*; shortraker rockfish, *S. borealis*; copper rockfish, *S. caurinus*; dusky rockfish, *S. ciliatus*; darkblotched rockfish, *S. crameri*; widow rockfish, *S. entomelas*; yellowtail rockfish, *S. flavidus*; quillback rockfish, *S. maliger*; black rockfish, *S. melanops*; blue rockfish, *S. mystinus;* China rockfish, *S. nebulosus*; tiger rockfish, *S. nigrocinctus*; canary rockfish, *S. pinniger*; northern rockfish, *S. polyspinis*; redstripe rockfish, *S. proriger*; yellowmouth rockfish, *S. reedi*; yelloweye rockfish, *S. ruberrimus*; sharpchin rockfish, *S. zacentrus;* shortspine thornyhead, *Sebastolobus alascanus*; longspine thornyhead, *S. altivelis*; broadfin thornyhead, *S. macrochir*); Macrouridae (Pacific grenadier, *Coryphaenoides acrolepis*; smooth abyssal grenadier, *C. armatus*; popeye grenadier, *C. cinereus*; threadfin grenadier, *C. filifer*; ghostly grenadier, *C. leptolepis*; longfin grenadier, *C. longifilis*); and Rajidae (big skate, *Raja binoculata*; longnose skate, *R. rhina*). The biomass of groundfish in Alaska is very large compared to that in other parts of the world and the long-term potential yields (maximum sustainable yields) for the Gulf of Alaska and Bering Sea–Aleutian Islands regions are 450,000 metric tons (t) and 3 million t, respectively, excluding Pacific halibut (Low et al. 1998). The long-term potential for Pacific halibut in U.S. waters is 30,000 t.

Within the family Clupeidae, Pacific herring (*Clupea pallasii*) are the target of intense, short-term fisheries that occur each spring in southeastern Alaska, Prince William Sound, and Bristol Bay. Their abundance is highly variable from year to year.

Geologic Setting

The oldest known rocks in Alaska are from the Birch Creek schist of the Kantishna Hills and belong to the Precambrian era (Williams 1958, Thompson and Turk 1997). Between 520 and 185 million years ago (Ma), open ocean covered most of what is now Alaska (Williams 1958, Briggs 1995). Around 200 Ma, southern Alaska was beginning to form as a collage of distinct geologic fragments, or terranes, of suspected proto-Pacific Basin derivations (Winkler et al. 2000). Intervals of strong tectonism during the Jurassic period (208–144 Ma) buckled and fractured crustal foldbelts into Alaska's major mountain ranges that, with the exception of the Coast Range, occur in broad arcs with prevalent east–west trends. Raising of the Alaska Range, with North America's highest mountain, Mt. McKinley (6,194 m), created an arcuate wall that separated Pacific lowlands and tributary mountains from interior landforms draining into the Bering Sea. By the beginning of the Cretaceous period (140 Ma), the Brooks Range, Seward Peninsula, and most of southern and southeastern Alaska had been uplifted from the sea. Between 130 Ma and 100 Ma some parts of the present North Slope arctic plain had emerged from the sea, but other lowlands remained submerged for another 50–70 million years. The late Cretaceous was a time of widespread volcanism and transport of associated volcanic ash to Arctic marine sediments. Inland seas occupied much of the region represented by the present Chugach–Kenai–Kodiak mountain chain.

By the early Tertiary period (60 Ma), most of present day Alaska was above sea level. The Eocene epoch (60-40 Ma) was a time of intense volcanic activity, especially in south central Alaska, and ash from this period is found in the ancient sediments of many of the region's streams and lakes as well as in peat deposits north of the Alaska Range and around Cook Inlet. The climate was warm temperate, almost subtropical, and *Metasequoia* trees flourished as far north as the North Slope. The warming was accompanied by a sea level rise producing coastal seas and shelf areas around the deeper marine basins (Williams 1958; Briggs 1974, 1995). Throughout the succeeding Miocene and Pliocene epochs (24–2 Ma), the geography of Alaska was much like it is today; volcanoes were numerous and widespread, especially on the Seward Peninsula, around south-central Alaska, and along the Alaska Peninsula and Aleutian chain.

The climate continued to cool throughout most of the Tertiary and most volcanic activity became concentrated along the Alaska Peninsula and Aleutian chain. Toward the end of the Tertiary, during the early Pliocene epoch, global temperatures warmed and rising sea levels caused flooding of the Bering Strait (3.5 Ma). Fossil evidence suggests that this was probably the principal, but possibly not the first, opening of the strait (Hopkins 1994). Another cooling period began about 3 Ma and by the Quaternary period (2 Ma), a significant decline in global temperature resulted in the Ice Age, a relatively short interval of Pleistocene glaciation (Briggs 1995, Thompson and Turk 1997). Climatic conditions varied widely, resulting in alternating periods of ice advances and recessions. Glacial advances were geographically extensive and animal and plant extinction rates were high during such periods. Sedimentary records from the Gulf of Alaska indicate that grounded ice extended to the continental shelf break during the Pleistocene (Hampton et al. 1986). As the ice retreated, river, lake, and continental shelf environments were colonized by surviving species. The North American glacial maximum was reached during the Wisconsinan glacial period (Holocene epoch) between 18,000 and 17,000 years ago (Briggs 1995). During this period, all of Alaska from the Alaska Range south, including the Gulf of Alaska continental shelf, was covered with ice. By contrast, most of the northern region, known as Beringia, remained free of ice, connected, and habitable. Lindsey and McPhail (1970) identified Beringia as one of six North American refugia during the Wisconsinan.

Glacial, glacial-marine, and glacial-fluvial sediment was deposited in nearly all areas where ice advanced. During interglacials, as the climate warmed and the ice retreated, the region was inundated by the sea, giving rise to present geologic environments (Hampton et al. 1986). Today, additional sediment is delivered to Alaskan coasts by a few large rivers (Drake et al. 1980, Milliman and Meade 1983) and remnant glaciers (Hampton et al. 1986); for example, the Copper and Alsek rivers to the Gulf of Alaska, the Susitna River to Cook Inlet, the Yukon and Kuskokwim rivers to the Bering Sea, and the Mackenzie and Colville rivers to the southeastern Beaufort Sea. Examples of tidewater glaciers in the Gulf of Alaska include the Columbia and Malaspina glaciers. Glaciers continue to be a major topographic feature within the mountain ranges found along the northeastern Gulf of Alaska and throughout southeastern Alaska.

Contemporary Physical Setting

Alaska is an immense region encompassing a land area of nearly 1.5 million km^2 (365 million acres) with 223,000 km^2 (55.1 million acres) of inland waters, spanning 20 degrees of latitude and 62 degrees of longitude, and lying between the cold Arctic Ocean and warmer North Pacific Ocean. Alaska's geographic area is about half that of the contiguous 48 states and its coastlines account for more than 70% of the nation's total. It has an estimated 76,120 km (47,300 mi) of tidal shoreline, including islands and inlets to the head of tidewater, and more than 3,000 islands. Submerged federal lands off Alaska out to the 200-mile limit of the U.S. Exclusive Economic Zone comprise about 6 million km^2 (1.5 billion acres). The oceans have a tremendous influence on regional climate and Alaska is a land of harsh environmental extremes. Typical summer temperatures range from about 10°C (50°F) in southeastern Alaska to 35°C (95°F) in the interior, where in winter they drop below –44°C (–47°F). Annual rainfall averages about 390 cm (154 inches) in Ketchikan, but only 38 cm (15 inches) in Anchorage. Gale force winds often exceed 185 km per hour (100 knots) in the Bering Sea. Above the arctic circle (66°32'N), day lengths vary from 24 hours in summer to nil in winter.

With the exception of the Brooks Range and the Aleutian arc, Alaska's mountains are arranged concentrically around the Gulf of Alaska. From this arrangement of mountains Williams (1958) described four principal regions in Alaska where large-scale geologic and topographic features control climate and the distribution of all living resources: Pacific Mountain System, Interior and Western Alaska, Brooks

Range, and Arctic Slope. These are the basis of more recent classifications of biotic provinces by ecoregions (e.g., Bailey 1989, Bailey et al. 1994). The four regions are roughly equivalent to the arctic, continental, transitional, and maritime climatic zones recognized by Selkregg (1974–1976). The arctic zone extends from the central ridge of the Brooks Range north to the Arctic Ocean. Arctic environments are characterized by continuous permafrost, tundra, and low annual precipitation. Maritime influences are minor because of the nearly continuous frozen condition of the ocean surface. The continental zone includes Alaska's boreal forests extending south of the Brooks Range and inland from coastal maritime influences. Summer and winter temperatures are extreme and precipitation is light. The transitional zone extends as a near-coastal and coastal band of varying width from near Yakutat to Point Hope, where weather fluctuates between continental and maritime conditions and annual precipitation is highly variable. The maritime zone includes southeastern Alaska, north of Dixon Entrance, and a narrow coastal band extending around the Gulf of Alaska, along the southern side of the Alaska Peninsula, the Aleutian Islands, and islands in the Gulf of Alaska. Maritime conditions are temperate and include heavy rainfall, warm summers, cool winters, and persistently strong winds.

Freshwaters

Freshwater fish habitats are extensive in Alaska; they include bogs, muskegs, marshes, rivers and streams, mud flats, ponds, and lakes. The state has more than 3 million lakes larger than 8 hectares (20 acres) and 3,000 rivers. The three largest natural lakes in Alaska are Iliamna Lake (2,978 km^2), Becharof Lake (1,186 km^2), and Teshekpuk Lake (816 km^2). Alaska's largest rivers include the Colville and Sagavanirktok rivers draining into the Beaufort Sea; the Noatak River into the Chukchi Sea; the Yukon (including large tributaries such as the Koyukuk, Porcupine, and Tanana rivers) and Kuskokwim rivers into the Bering Sea; the Susitna River into Cook Inlet; the Copper and Alsek rivers into the Gulf of Alaska; and the Taku and Stikine rivers flowing into the marine waters of the Alexander Archipelago. Major deltas with significant fish and wildlife habitat values surround the mouths of the Yukon, Kuskokwim, Copper, and Stikine rivers. Flowing through Canada's Northwest Territories, the Mackenzie River delivers fresh water, sediments, and fishes to the Alaskan sector of the Beaufort Sea.

The geographic distribution of aquifers in Alaska and the physical extent of the various freshwater types were described by Madison et al. (1987) and Hall et al. (1994). Information about the physical and biological conditions of freshwater habitats and ecosystems has been summarized by region for rivers and streams (Craig 1989, Oswood 1989, Oswood et al. 1989, Thorsteinson et al. 1989, Reynolds 1997, Milner and York 2001), ponds and lakes (Hobbie 1984, Murray 1998), and coastal wetlands (Hall et al. 1994). Much information about Alaska's freshwater systems resides in unpublished reports. For example, during the 1980s, the Alaska Department of Fish and Game acquired several years of baseline information about the physical habitats and fishery resources of the Susitna River as part of its environmental assessment of the proposed Susitna River Hydroelectric Power Project. Oswood et al. (2000) described five tentative freshwater ichthyoregions related to the geographical similarities and differences in the fish assemblage and possible post-Pleistocene dispersals.

Two main categories of rivers occur in Alaska: those with headwaters in the arctic region and those with headwaters farther south. Flow in arctic rivers is mostly influenced by rain and melting snow and ice because of the barriers imposed by permafrost and consequently limited storage capacity of the active layer. Peak flows occur in spring and, in many arctic rivers, are elevated again in autumn, in response to snowmelt and summer warming. South of the Brooks Range, less dramatic autumnal peaks also occur in response to precipitation and glacial ice and snowmelt influences. Arctic rivers tend to remain cool throughout the short summer months due to cold meltwater additions. In summer, small shallow streams may be warmed to 10–20°C; however, those not fed by perennial mountain springs freeze solid in the winter months. Rivers with headwaters south of the arctic region are characterized by maximum flows in May and June, greatest flow variability in August and September, and relatively weak flows between December and April. Depending on region and river size, freezing may or may not occur. For rivers that freeze, flows are minimal prior to spring breakup. Summer temperatures tend to remain cool (6–8°C), especially in glacier-fed systems, but can have a wide annual range, typically 0–18°C.

Alaskan lakes are situated in topographic depressions or dammed river channels. Many Alaskan lakes are of glacial origin. Thermokarst lakes form in depressions that result from melting of permafrost. The time at which northern lakes, north of the arctic circle, become free of ice usually depends on temperature and wind speed in June. To the south, April and May temperatures, wind speeds, and whether or not rivers are part of the watershed, are important influences on this timing. Ice thaw begins when meltwater from surrounding watersheds flows onto the lake ice and enters cracks and holes on the surface. Shore leads then develop along the lake's perimeter and breakup ensues. The timing of ice-out ranges from early May in southern Alaska to mid-August in arctic settings. Thermal stratification may occur if water depth is sufficient; it is more common in the deeper lakes south of the arctic circle. In these lakes, wind produces mixing and a homogenous surface layer. Under calmer conditions, and no wind, stratification also can result from heating at the surface. Small arctic lakes can become quite warm (>10°C). Maximum surface water temperatures range from about 15°C in small lakes near the treeline, to 4-6°C farther north. Southern lakes, such as those on the Naknek system, attain maximum temperatures of about 12-15°C by mid-

August. Freeze-up occurs between September and October in high-latitude lakes and is much more variable farther south, where it usually occurs in November to January. Arctic lakes with depths less than 2.2 m often freeze to the bottom whereas water column temperatures of 0°C are not uncommon in larger, deeper lakes. Winter water temperatures in lakes in more temperate regions are generally warmer, but in some instances, under extreme weather conditions, thick ice can limit habitat available to resident fishes.

Marine Environment

The Pacific Ocean and the Arctic Ocean surround Alaska on the north, west, and south. The Pacific Ocean is the largest of the world's five oceans, followed by the Atlantic, Indian, Southern, and Arctic oceans. In the spring of 2000, the International Hydrographic Organization formally delimited a fifth ocean, the Southern Ocean, and thereby removed the portion of the Pacific Ocean south of 60°S. (There have been other definitions for the Southern Ocean.)

The Pacific Ocean is divided into the North Pacific and South Pacific at the equator. The Bering Sea, a major marginal sea of the North Pacific, bounds Alaska on the west, and the Gulf of Alaska, a major embayment, bounds the state on the south of the main land mass. The North Pacific Ocean proper washes the southern shores of the Aleutian Islands. For purposes of describing geographic ranges of fish species in this book's species accounts, the North Pacific south of the Aleutian Islands, the Gulf of Alaska, and the Bering Sea are treated as separate entities, but they are functionally part of the same system.

North Pacific Ocean

Most of the fish species inhabiting the marine waters of Alaska also occur in other regions of the North Pacific and Arctic oceans, so our descriptions of geographic ranges extend to those regions. The major marginal seas of the northwestern North Pacific off Asia that are most relevant in this book are the Sea of Okhotsk and Sea of Japan, as well as the Bering Sea. Major embayments include the Gulf of Anadyr and Karaginskiy Bay in the western Bering Sea. The Gulf of California is the nearest major embayment of the eastern North Pacific south of Alaska, and it is farther south than the Sea of Japan, at latitudes of the East China Sea and the Yellow Sea.

Major land features of the North Pacific include the Aleutian Islands, forming an arc bordering the Bering Sea to the north, and the islands of Honshu, Hokkaido, and Sakhalin in the western Pacific. The Kuril Islands extend from the southern tip of the Kamchatka Peninsula to Hokkaido. Honshu, Hokkaido, the Kurils, and the Aleutians are all part of the volcanic Ring of Fire circumscribing the Pacific Ocean. The Queen Charlotte Islands and Vancouver Island are the major islands of British Columbia.

The ocean floor in the eastern North Pacific Ocean is dominated by the Northeast Pacific Basin, separated from the Northwest Pacific Basin by the Emperor Seamounts and Hawaiian Ridge. The Japan Trench and Kuril–Kamchatka Trench, descending to depths as great as 9,750 m, border the Northwest Pacific Basin along Japan and southern Kamchatka to the Aleutian arc. The Aleutian Trench stretches across the Pacific south of the Aleutian chain from the northern end of the Emperor Seamounts to the central Gulf of Alaska and descends to depths over 8,000 m. (The lowest point of the Pacific Ocean is the Challenger Deep in the Mariana Trench, at 10,924 m.) The ocean off the west coast of North America does not descend to such great depths in trenches but rather is dominated by the East Pacific Rise broken by a series of east–west trending fracture zones. The Tufts Abyssal Plain south of Alaska and west of Oregon and Washington reaches about 4,000 m. The Cascadia Basin between the Tufts plain and the mainland descends to about 3,000 m. Seamounts rise from the floor of the East Pacific Rise in groups, such as the Patton and Gilbert seamount provinces, or as more or less isolated mounts, such as Welker and Dickins seamounts. Shallower regions are found along the continental shelves and the marginal seas. Sea ice forms in the Bering Sea and Sea of Okhotsk in winter.

The Pacific waters of Alaska, including the Bering Sea and Gulf of Alaska, are a portion of the region commonly known as the subarctic North Pacific. This region is bounded by the Bering Strait to the north and the Subarctic Boundary to the south. The Subarctic Boundary is the southern limit of the transitional zone in which the cold, low salinity upper water mass of the subarctic North Pacific and warm, high salinity subtropical water mass of the central North Pacific abut and mix. This feature persists across the ocean beyond coastal waters at approximately 40–42°N. The oceanography of the subarctic North Pacific is reasonably well known with respect to understanding of its physical (e.g., hydrography, currents, and circulation) and biological environments and major ecological processes (e.g., Dodimead et al. 1963; Tully 1964; Favorite et al. 1976, 1977; Hood and Calder 1981; Hood 1986; Molnia and Taylor 1994; National Research Council 1996; Loughlin and Ohtani 1999). It is a region of excess precipitation, seasonal heating and cooling, and strong winds and convective mixing. Investigators have attempted to relate fish distribution and abundance to the observed patterns of hydrographic structuring. Analysis by Willis (1984) of Isaacs-Kidd midwater trawl collections in the eastern North Pacific showed three faunal regions that appeared to be correlated with temperature and salinity fronts: subarctic, central, and southern. Focusing on the subarctic North Pacific and a larger database from midwater trawls, Willis et al. (1988) found distributional patterns of fishes to fall into two basic types: subarctic and transitional. Each of those types was subdivided based on physical structure of the subarctic North Pacific and the component ichthyofauna, resulting in five proposed faunal regions: eastern and western transition zones, Alaska Gyre, western subarctic, and Bering Sea. These faunal regions roughly coincided with the domains (areas of consistent

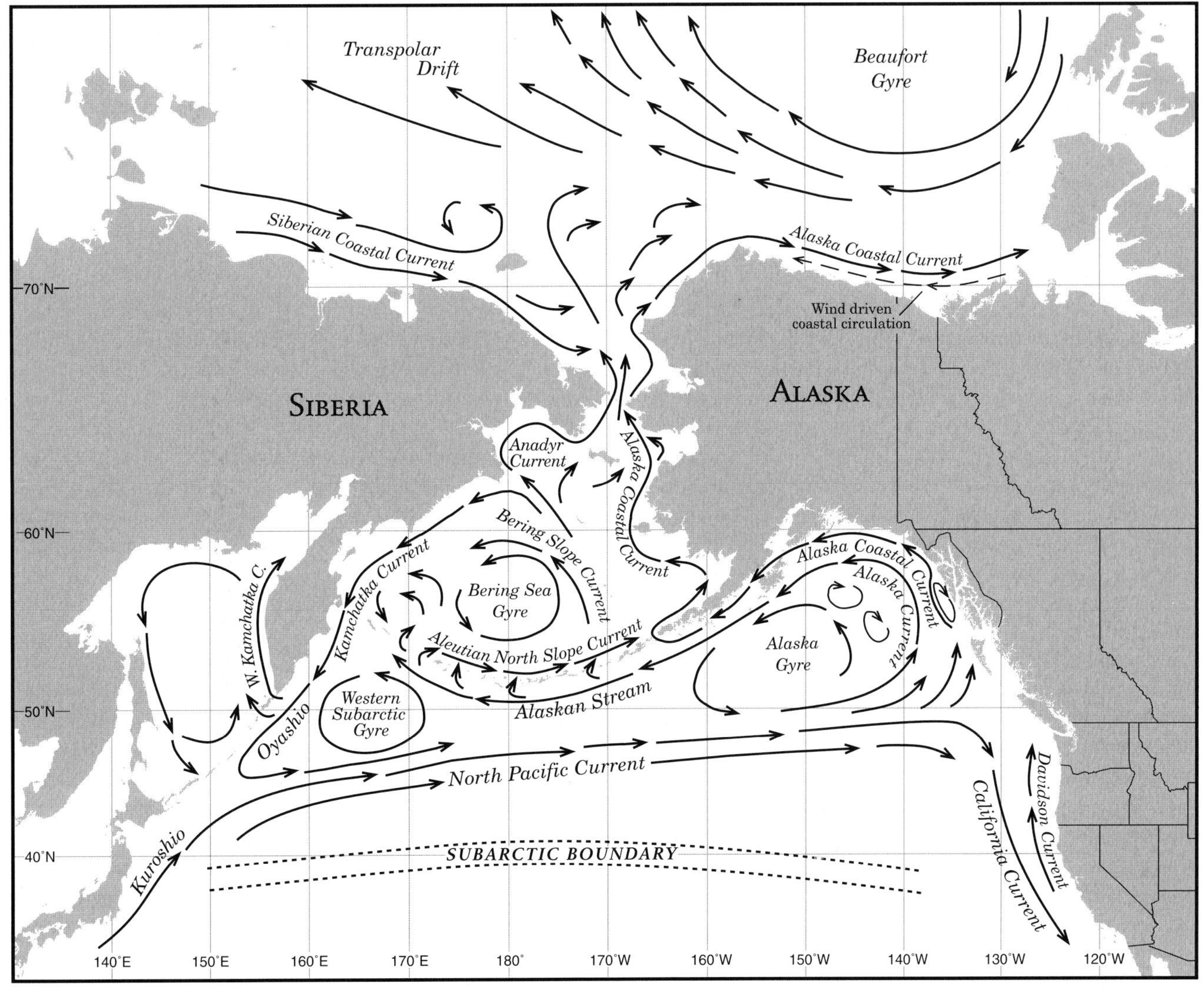

The main surface currents of the North Pacific and Arctic oceans off Alaska.
(After Favorite et al. 1976, Reed and Schumacher 1986, Johnson 1988, Niebauer and Schell 1993, Barrie et al. 1998, Reed and Stabeno 1999, Stabeno et al. 1999, Weingartner and George 2001.)

hydrographic structure and oceanographic behavior) of the subarctic lower zone defined by oceanographers (i.e., Dodimead et al. 1963). Willis et al. (1988) broadly compared mesopelagic species composition among the faunal regions. Sherman and Duda (1999) identified two large marine ecosystems in the subarctic North Pacific (Gulf of Alaska and Bering Sea) for management of Alaska's fisheries.

Surface currents in the North Pacific are dominated by a clockwise, warm-water gyre (broad circular system of currents). The Kuroshio is the Pacific's equivalent of the Atlantic's Gulf Stream, flowing north along Japan and joining the eastward flowing North Pacific Current to the coast of North America. The North Pacific Current feeds water into both the counterclockwise Alaska Gyre and the southward flowing California Current. The California Current is a wide, cold, sluggish current that follows the west coast of the United States as far as Baja California then flows west as the North Equatorial Current. The Davidson Current flows to the north inshore of the California Current over the continental shelf off northern California, Oregon, and Washington. The Alaska Current flows north into the Gulf of Alaska and then west, contributing to the Alaska Coastal Current and the Alaskan Stream. The origin of the Alaska Coastal Current, a feature common to most of the state's coast, is along the outer coast of southeastern Alaska. The Alaskan Stream flows west south of the Alaska Peninsula and Aleutian Islands, and enters the Bering Sea through island passes. The Kamchatka Current flows south along Kamchatka to the Northwest Pacific Basin, where the flow near the Kuril Islands, known as the Oyashio, moves south from the Bering Sea. Diverging into the Sea of Okhotsk and flowing north along Kamchatka is the West Kamchatka Current. The Western Subarctic Gyre is characterized by counterclockwise flows south of the western Aleutian Islands and the Commander Islands.

Gulf of Alaska

The Gulf of Alaska lies off the southern coast of Alaska and the western coast of Canada. To avoid confusion in the stated geographic ranges of fish species in the accounts we use a more restricted definition of the Gulf of Alaska to include waters from Dixon Entrance north, off Alaska only.

The bathymetry of the coastal Gulf of Alaska (in the broader sense) provides a contrast between a broad shelf region in the central and western gulf and a narrow, fjord-like region off southeastern Alaska and British Columbia. The shelf is punctuated by submarine canyons and by numerous embayments, including Cook Inlet, Prince William Sound, and Yakutat Bay. The continental shelf in the Gulf of Alaska is relatively broad (300 km) in the east, and comparatively narrow (100 km) south of the Aleutian Islands.

The largest islands in the Gulf of Alaska are Kodiak and Afognak islands in the Kodiak archipelago, separated from the mainland by Shelikof Strait; Montague and Hinchinbrook islands at the opening of Prince William Sound; and several islands in the Alexander Archipelago, including Baranof, Admiralty, Kupreanof, Kuiu, Prince of Wales, Etolin, Revillagigedo, and Dall islands. Groups of smaller islands are scattered along the coast, including the Sanak, Shumagin, and Semidi islands south of the Alaska Peninsula; the Trinity Islands off the south tip of Kodiak Island; and the Barren Islands between the Kodiak archipelago and the Kenai Peninsula. Several relatively isolated islands also dot the coastline, including Chirikof Island southeast of the Trinity Islands, St. Augustine in southwestern Cook Inlet, and Middleton Island well south of Prince William Sound. Dixon Entrance lies between the Alexander Archipelago of Alaska and the Queen Charlotte Islands of British Columbia. East of Dixon Entrance and north of Portland Inlet is Pearse Canal, continuing inland as Portland Canal and forming part of the Alaska–Canada border.

Southeastern Alaska's inside waters are diluted at the surface by runoff and precipitation and have salt added through exchanges with oceanic waters. Lower salinities and warmer surface temperatures characterize southeastern Alaskan waters and their net movement is generally seaward. In the offshore and coastal waters adjacent to southeastern Alaska's outer coastline Alaska Coastal Current flows are to the north and are dominated by a coastal jet approximately 20 km wide. The Alaska Coastal Current flows west along the inner shelf and enters the Bering Sea through Unimak Pass. Farther offshore, the Alaska Current is the dominant circulation feature extending approximately 75 km wide and to the shelf break.

The Gulf of Alaska's ocean circulation consists of the weak, eastward flowing North Pacific Current; the northward flowing Alaska Current; and the higher-speed, westward flowing alongshore current, the Alaskan Stream. The dominant circulation in the Gulf of Alaska is characterized by the large-scale, counterclockwise flow of the Alaska Gyre. The flow into the northeastern Gulf of Alaska often includes a large clockwise eddy off Baranof Island and similar and smaller-scale oceanographic features are common around the nearby seamounts. Farther offshore, the Alaskan Stream flows west off south central Alaska, south of the Alaska Peninsula and Aleutian Islands, and enters the Bering Sea through several major passes.

Bering Sea

The Bering Sea, named after the explorer Vitus Bering, covers over 2 million km^2 of the northernmost region of the Pacific Ocean. Its borders are defined to the north by western Alaska, the Bering Strait, and northeastern Siberia, and to the south by the arc of the Alaska Peninsula, Aleutian Islands, and Commander Islands. West of the Aleutian–Commander island chain the point delimiting the Bering Sea from the Pacific Ocean on the Kamchatka Peninsula is Cape Afrika. The Commander Islands of Russia, comprising Bering and Medny (or Copper) islands, are geologically part of the Aleutian Islands of Alaska. From west to east the major island groups of the Aleutian Islands are the Near Islands, named for their nearness to Russia; the Rat Islands, the Andreanof Islands, The Islands of Four Mountains, and the Fox Islands. The largest islands in the Bering Sea are St. Lawrence and Nunivak islands. The other major Bering Sea islands in Alaskan waters are St. Matthew Island and the Pribilof Islands, the latter called the Fur Seal Islands in early expedition accounts. Karaginskiy Island is the largest island in the western Bering Sea off Russia.

The major marginal bodies of water of the Bering Sea in Alaska are Norton Sound and Bristol Bay, the latter most famous for its salmon runs and fisheries. The major embayments off Russia include the Gulf of Anadyr and Karaginskiy Bay. The Bering Strait, which is only 85 km wide at its narrowest breadth, connects the Bering and Chukchi seas. From west to east the major (widest) passes, with their depths, from the North Pacific into the Bering Sea are Kamchatka Strait, 4,420 m; Near Strait between the Commander and Near islands, 2,000 m; Buldir Pass, 760 m; Kiska Pass, 120 m; Amchitka Pass, 1,082 m; Tanaga Pass, 377 m; Amukta Pass, 446 m; and Unimak Pass, only 80 m deep (Udintsev et al. 1959). The three largest rivers emptying into the Bering Sea are the Yukon and Kuskokwim rivers in Alaska and the Anadyr River in Russia.

The bathymetry of the Bering Sea can be divided into two primary regions: a continental shelf region less than 150–200 m deep to the northeast, and a deeper plain, 3,700–4,000 m deep, to the southwest. The boundary between the two regions is the steep scarp of the continental slope extending from near Cape Navarin, Russia, to Unimak Island at the eastern end of the Aleutian Islands. The continental slope drops sharply from the edge of the shelf to the floor of the Aleutian Basin. Bowers Ridge extends in a 460-km arc north and west from the Rat Islands and the Shirshov Ridge extends 670 km south from Cape Olyutorskiy. The Shirshov Ridge separates the Aleutian and Commander basins.

Northward flows of the Alaskan Stream through Near Strait, Amchitka Pass, and Amukta Pass are transported into the Bering Sea and produce the eastward-flowing Aleutian North Slope Current. This current is the major source of the Bering Slope Current which flows northwest of Unimak Pass and along the shelf edge and eventually joins the southward flowing Kamchatka Current to the west of the Aleutian Basin. Although there is some advection of Bering Sea water to the south through the Aleutian Island passes, the major outflow is associated with the Kamchatka Current. The Kamchatka Current flows south along the Kamchatka Peninsula to the Northwest Pacific Basin, where the flow near the Kuril Islands, the Oyashio, carries cold waters south from the Bering Sea. Diverging into the Okhotsk Sea and flowing north along the Kamchatka Peninsula is the West Kamchatka Current.

The Alaska Coastal Current flows along the coast north of the Alaska Peninsula, through Bristol Bay and Norton Sound, and through the Bering Strait into the Chukchi Sea. The Bering Sea has an expansive continental shelf (over 500 km wide in the east) and, in the southeastern region, the seasonal presence of frontal systems along the 50-, 100-, and 200-m isobaths results in three hydrographic domains: coastal, middle shelf, and outer shelf. The ecological significance of these fronts is great with respect to physical oceanography, ecosystem dynamics (primary production and efficiency of cropping by herbivores), and regional fisheries. The outer shelf domain is a pelagic ecosystem dominated by the walleye pollock, *Theragra chalcogramma*. The middle shelf domain, and to a lesser extent the coastal domain, is a benthic ecosystem dominated by flatfish and shellfish, including crabs. In the northern Bering Sea, upwelling of deep, nutrient-rich waters to surface layers west of St. Lawrence Island results in a northern shelf characterized by high biological productivity. Norton Sound is a depositional environment for Yukon and Kuskokwim river outflows entrained in the Alaska Coastal Current as it moves northward and into the Chukchi Sea. Sea ice coverage over the shelf can extend south of the Pribilof Islands in the Bering Sea during winter. In the west, the northward flowing Anadyr Current also transports Bering Sea water through the Bering Strait.

Arctic Ocean

The Arctic Ocean is located entirely within the arctic circle and is shallow relative to the Pacific and other oceans of the world. A large proportion of the Arctic is continental shelf. The average depth of the Arctic, including its marginal seas, is about 1,296 m, reaching a maximum of about 5,440 m. The marginal seas of the Arctic Ocean bordering Alaska are the Chukchi Sea and the Beaufort Sea, and Kotzebue Sound is the major arm of the Chukchi Sea in western Alaska. To the west, the Chukchi Sea borders northeastern Siberia and the Chukchi Peninsula, and west of the Chukchi Sea are the East Siberian and Laptev seas. The floor of the Arctic Ocean is crossed by several prominent ridges that restrict the circulation of the bottom water and divide the sea floor into several basins. The basin north of Alaska, with its southern portion forming the floor of the Beaufort Sea, is the Canada Basin, separated from the mainland by the continental slope and a narrow continental shelf. This basin reaches a depth of approximately 2,000 m and has deep water temperatures of –0.4°C.

The continental shelf west of Point Barrow, in the Chukchi Sea, is broad and continues to be so across Siberia in the East Siberian and Laptev seas. The continental shelf of Siberia is broken only by the New Siberian Islands and Wrangel Island. There are no similarly large islands in the Chukchi or Beaufort seas off Alaska. The largest island off Arctic Alaska is Barter Island at the east end of Camden Bay. Herschel Island is the nearest island to Alaska in the Canadian Arctic. Shifting barrier islands along the Arctic coast of Alaska form coastal lagoons. The largest lagoon in the Beaufort Sea is Simpson Lagoon enclosed by the Jones and Return islands west of Prudhoe Bay. Flaxman and other barrier islands form large lagoons west of Brownlow Point and Camden Bay. Approximately one half of the Chukchi coast is protected by spits, points of land, or barrier islands.

Regional environmental knowledge of the Arctic Ocean is less extensive than that for the North Pacific Ocean and reflects the comparative lack of commercial fisheries resources north of the Bering Strait. Existing oceanographic literature for the southern Chukchi Sea was reviewed and summarized by Hameedi and Naidu (1988). The results of physical oceanographic surveys of mesoscale processes in the Chukchi and Beaufort seas were reported by Johnson (1988), Aagaard et al. (1989), Niebauer and Schell (1993), Proshutninsky and Johnson (1997), and Weingartner (1997). Information describing arctic marine ecosystems was summarized by Barnes et al. (1984) and Lowry (1993). Regional ecosystems are characterized by relatively short trophic pathways between primary producers and apex predators, low primary productivity, and great seasonality in habitat use by migratory fish and wildlife. These qualities are consistent with limiting factors associated with the presence of sea ice.

The Chukchi Sea is fed by both Pacific and Arctic waters. The Pacific waters enter via Bering Strait and are modified on the Chukchi shelf. Arctic waters enter via Long Strait off Siberia and in up-shelf transport from the Arctic Ocean proper, for example, via Barrow Canyon. A weak current, the Siberian Coastal Current which is present in summer and fall, flows south from the Arctic Ocean through Bering Strait. The bulk of the exchange between the Arctic Ocean and more temperate regions is between the Arctic and Atlantic oceans, via the Greenland Sea. Water that does not exit gives rise to a circular current in the Arctic basin itself. This circular current causes relatively light ice over the Siberian seas. The Arctic Ocean is covered with ice throughout the year except along its fringes.

There is considerable temporal and spatial variability in the hydrographic structure of the Chukchi Sea and this relates to the nature of the transport and mixing of various water masses in the region. Three tongues of Pacific Ocean water are transported through the Bering Strait in association with the Alaska Coastal and Anadyr currents and the northward movement of Bering shelf water. In offshore waters of the southeastern Chukchi Sea, at depths between 20 and 30 m, Alaska coastal and Bering shelf waters are separated by an oceanic front that extends southward to Bering Strait from Cape Lisburne during the ice-free period. As the Alaska Coastal Current flows northward past Cape Lisburne and Icy Cape it diverges near Hannah Shoal, flowing as far as 100 km offshore and to the northwest, and closer inshore within 20–30 km of the coast. Offshore, Bering shelf waters are advected to the northwest and mix with Arctic waters east of Wrangel Island. Nearer the Alaska coast, a clockwise gyre is a regular feature near Point Franklin in summer months. The nearshore component of the Alaska Coastal Current diverges again in the Barrow Canyon area, flowing offshore and northwest, as well as in an easterly direction across the Beaufort Sea shelf and slope. In the western Chukchi Sea, the seasonally present Siberian Coastal Current, which merges with the Anadyr Current, fosters an east-to-west transport and mixing of Arctic and Bering shelf waters in central portions of the sea. The circulation and modification of Pacific and Arctic ocean water masses in the Chukchi Sea influences the properties of marine waters delivered to the Beaufort Sea and, on a broader geographic scale, the hydrography of currents associated with the Transpolar Drift and transport to the Atlantic Ocean.

The relatively narrow (50-100 km) Alaskan Beaufort Sea shelf extends about 600 km from Point Barrow to the Canadian border. It is covered with sea ice most of the year. In general, in early summer (late June) a brackish water mass resulting from river runoff and ice melt forms an essentially continuous, 1–10 km wide band along the coast. Cold, saline, marine water is present offshore and often underlies the brackish water. Astronomical tides have comparatively little influence on hydrography, their amplitudes being only about 0.3 m. The coastal brackish water band is progressively eroded during the summer by diminishing runoff and wind mixing. As suggested above, there are two substantially different circulation regimes on this shelf. Landward of about the 50-m isobath (inner shelf), the circulation has a large wind-driven component, particularly in summer. During the open-water season coastal winds are predominantly from the east, promoting regional upwelling. In winter the flow over the inner shelf is much less energetic, but still shows wind influence. Farther seaward, the dominant subsurface circulation feature is the Beaufort Undercurrent, which is directed eastward along the entire outer shelf and slope. It underlies a very large and very shallow flow regime in which the ice and uppermost ocean moves westward, representing the southern limb of the clockwise Beaufort Gyre. Hydrographic sampling has indicated the intrusion of Atlantic Ocean water over slope habitats to the west of the gyre along the Northwind Ridge and eastward along the slope and the clockwise circulation of the Beaufort Gyre.

Zoogeographic Setting

Information about the dispersal of fishes into Alaska or fishes that have possible centers of origin in the North Pacific is somewhat speculative as it is based on an incomplete fossil record and inferences on distributional analyses of contemporary data. The geologic framework emphasizes the importance of the opening and closing of the Bering Strait and refugia in Beringia in their significance to the evolution of the Alaskan fauna.

Freshwater Fishes

The zoogeography of Alaskan freshwater fishes was reviewed by McPhail and Lindsey (1970, 1986) and Lindsey and McPhail (1986). There is evidence of prehistoric dispersal of fishes from Asia to North America and from North America to Asia. The fall of global sea levels during the late Cretaceous created Beringia and established a migratory corridor between the two continents through the Cenozoic era.

The ice sheets of the Pleistocene had a profound effect on the distribution of freshwater fishes and other aquatic organisms. The glaciers eliminated aquatic life in all areas they occupied, changed the climate, and altered drainage basins. Their melting resulted in flooding, sea-level rise and associated flooding of coastal wetlands, and large lakes. These changes, occurring over millions of years, provided dispersal opportunities and mechanisms for migration and habitation of new freshwater environs (Lindsey and McPhail 1986). Oswood et al. (2000) analyzed Alaska's freshwater fauna with respect to identified biotic regions in order to study possible post-Pleistocene dispersal routes from refugia during the Wisconsinan glaciation. Their analysis suggests fish migrations from refugia in Beringia, Pacific Northwest, and Upper Mississippian regions were asymmetrical and that barriers such as those imposed by mountains, ice, and food limitations favored east to west dispersals into the Yukon River and interior Alaska and to Arctic and southern Alaska coastal areas. Zoogeographic patterns suggest a latitudinal effect on dispersals from south to north (i.e., from Pacific coast refugia) and that invading species from the Pacific Northwest were most successful in southeastern and south central Alaska. The existing data suggest that fewer freshwater species apparently were able to migrate into Alaska from other North American regions. For those that did, their relatively even distribution throughout Alaska suggests interregional movements within the major rivers of Alaska and the Mackenzie River of Canada. Terrestrial dispersal of fishes was greatly affected by tectonic, glacial, and volcanic events. The Tertiary landscapes of Alaska, the Yukon Territory, and western British Columbia were uplifted by tectonic events in the late Miocene and Pliocene (Lindsey and McPhail 1986). Changes in the erosion surface affected sources and rates and directions of freshwater flows (e.g., Yukon and Alsek rivers, other Gulf of Alaska drainages). Pleistocene glaciers further altered and blocked watersheds and the competition and movements of fishes therein. Volcanic effects on headwaters were equally dramatic as entire headwaters and their aquatic life could be moved or lost in response to widespread mudflows and flooding and effects of erosion and turbidity.

Contemporary distribution of Alaskan freshwater fishes has been reviewed by McPhail and Lindsey (1970), Lee et al. (1980), Morrow (1980), and Klein et al. (1998).

Marine Fishes

The major reviews of marine zoogeography are by Briggs (1974, 1995), who described a North Temperate Realm existing during the late Mesozoic era, and a North Pacific Province characterized by high endemism in Japanese–East Asian and North Pacific subprovinces during the early Cretaceous period (130 Ma). The late Cretaceous fall in sea level and resultant closing of the Bering Strait separated Pacific and Atlantic ocean marine fish populations that had been continuous in distribution for millions of years. Over time, this separation resulted in the evolution of a temperate, more diverse fauna in the Pacific than that found in the Arctic–Atlantic. The major sea level rise associated with global warming at the Cretaceous–Tertiary boundary, some 65 Ma, resulted in a massive extinction process. In the Pacific, the impacts to deepsea fishes of the central Pacific were less acute than those to the more northern fauna. However, the extinction losses were substantial and the estimated time spans associated with recovery of diversity range anywhere from 3 to 25 Ma (Briggs 1995). Eocene seas (37–58 Ma) were conducive to species dispersals because of the creation of inshore and continental shelf habitats associated with earth movements and global warming. Briggs (1995) suggested that most of the higher fish families were extant by the Eocene.

Biotic characteristics of fossil remains from the Arctic and Atlantic oceans and Antarctic seas suggest that the North Pacific functioned as a center of evolutionary radiation for marine species (Briggs 1974, 1984). The opening of the Bering Strait during the mid-Pliocene (3.5 Ma) connected long-isolated oceans and allowed a massive interchange of marine organisms of Pacific and Arctic–Atlantic origins. The Arctic Ocean was ice-free and its cold-temperate conditions allowed large numbers of North Pacific boreal fauna to invade the Arctic–North Atlantic (Vermeij 1991, Briggs 1995). A distributional analysis of the fossil records implies that the transarctic invasion was asymmetrical (Vermeij 1991) and that several fish families thought to have North Pacific origins (Salmonidae, Osmeridae, Hexagrammidae, Cottidae, Agonidae, Liparidae, Stichaeidae, and Pholidae) probably contributed at least one species each to the North Atlantic (Briggs 1995). Conversely, the family Gadidae, which developed primarily in the North Atlantic, is thought to have contributed two species to the North Pacific. The re-emergence of the Bering land bridge during the first Pliocene cooling episode (3 Ma) resulted in a transition to arctic conditions and caused severe declines in high-latitude temperatures. The colder temperatures led to the extirpation of many boreal species and to the evolution of the modern Arctic fauna.

Prior to this interval of global cooling, an Arctic biota extended southward into the central Bering Sea in the vicinity of Nunivak Island (east) and Cape Olyutorskiy (west). During the Pliocene glaciations and more recent glacial events, the fall in sea level and presence of the Bering land bridge acted to protect the Pacific species from the harsher conditions and higher extinction rates experienced by the North Atlantic fishes. The separation of oceans interrupted existing distributions and allowed distinct Pacific and Atlantic boreal faunal regions to evolve (Briggs 1995). The constant environmental change, over millions of years, corresponded to shifts in faunal distribution and, in many instances, promoted speciation through genetic drift and adaptations to variable ocean and climate conditions including barriers to preferred habitats and access to breeding populations (e.g., Williams 1958; Wilimovsky 1964; Alexander 1974; Briggs 1974, 1995; Gross 1987; Andriashev 1990; Vermeij 1991; Randall 1998). As an example, the family Scorpaenidae is believed to have radiated from somewhere in the western Pacific, perhaps near Japan, during the late Oligocene–early Miocene, about 30 Ma (Briggs 1974, 1984). The temperature swings associated with glacial and interglacial periods during the Pleistocene reduced the diversity of the northern fauna, especially in coastal and shallow-water areas where temperature conditions were negatively affected by more direct atmospheric interaction. Holocene warming and increased flooding reopened the Bering Strait 11,000 years ago.

Contemporary marine zoogeographic patterns have been reviewed for the Gulf of Alaska and Bering Sea (e.g., Andriashev 1939, Wilimovsky 1964, Hood and Calder 1981, Hood and Zimmerman 1986, Allen and Smith 1988, Wolotira et al. 1993, Mathisen and Coyle 1996, Loh et al. 1998, Robards et al. 1999) and to a much lesser extent, the Arctic Ocean (e.g., Andriashev 1937, Wilimovsky and Wolfe 1966, Hood and Burrell 1976, Frost and Lowry 1983, Craig 1984, Craig et al. 1985, Fechhelm et al. 1985, Barber et al. 1997, Reynolds 1997; Jarvela and Thorsteinson 1999). Marine ecological relationships have been described for the Gulf of Alaska (Hood and Zimmerman 1986); for the Bering Sea (Hood and Calder 1981, National Research Council 1996, Loughlin and Ohtani 1999); and the Arctic Ocean (e.g., Barnes et al. 1984, Murray et al. 1998, Molnia and Taylor 1994). Allen and Smith (1988) classified the most common fish species sampled by NMFS demersal trawls in the eastern North Pacific and Bering Sea by zoogeographic, life zone, and bathymetric patterns. Willis et al. (1988) analyzed distributional patterns of mesopelagic fishes from midwater trawls in the subarctic North Pacific.

SYSTEMATIC SECTION

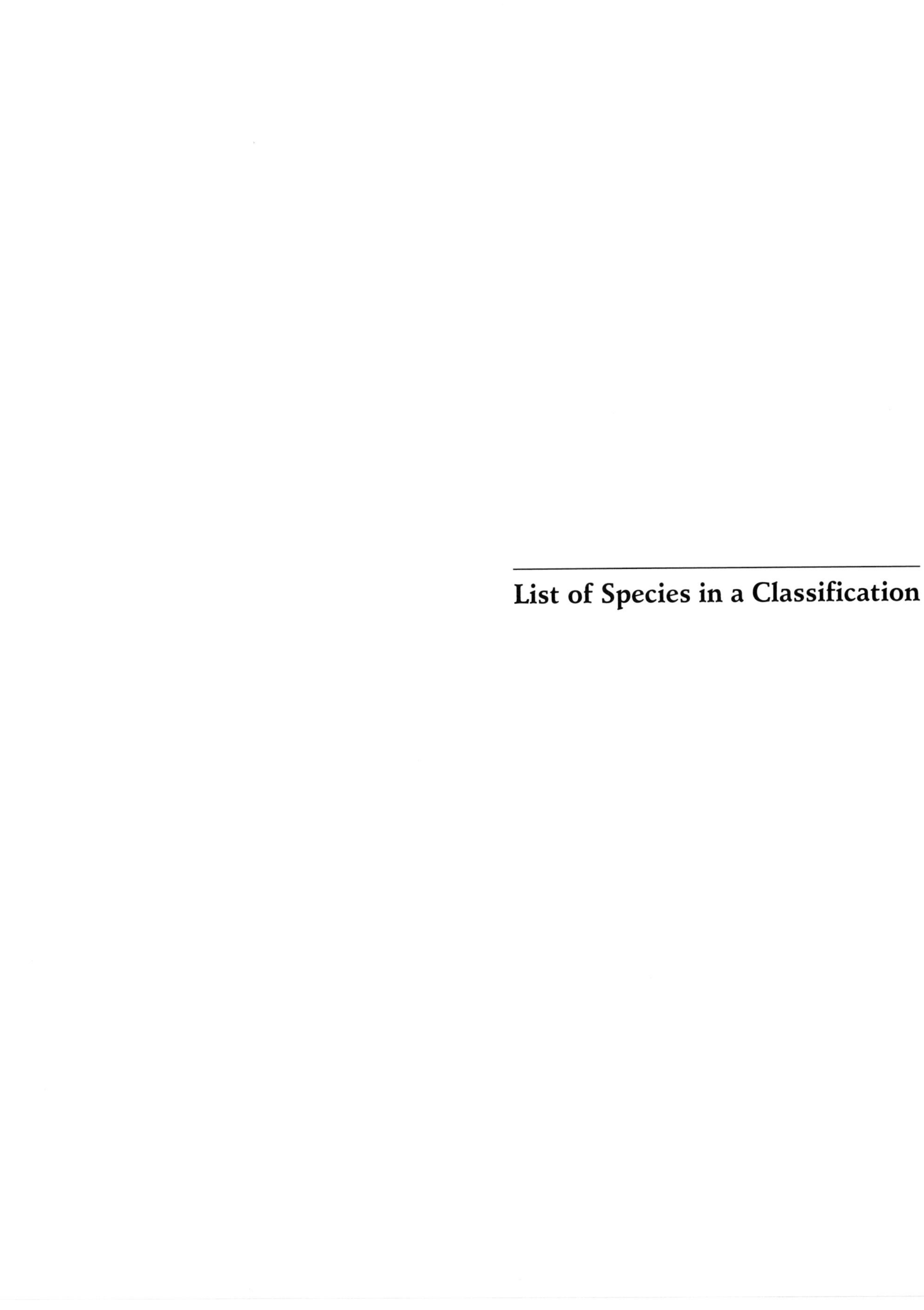

List of Species in a Classification

LIST OF SPECIES IN A CLASSIFICATION

There is no one, correct classification of fishes. Knowledge of fishes, no less than of any other organisms, constantly accumulates and relationships of the various groups must constantly be reexamined. The systematic framework for presenting the accounts in this book is the current edition of the widely used classification of higher fish taxa (subfamilies and above) by Nelson (1994). Changes will occur; see, for example, proposals in Stiassny (1996). However, we have refrained from anticipating changes and making adjustments which may or may not be accepted later.

The following classification includes the higher taxa known to contain Alaskan species, and the order of presentation of higher taxa in the accounts section follows this broadly phylogenetic sequence (after Nelson 1994). Genera and species are listed alphabetically, whereas in the accounts they are grouped by similarity of appearance. Sources for the classification of genera and species are cited in the introductions to the families and in the species accounts.

A plus sign (+) before a species name means the species has been reported from Alaska but the identification or capture locality is uncertain and not verifiable or not confirmed. An asterisk (*) means the species is likely to occur in Alaska but has not been reported from the region, or, rarely, is included in the accounts mainly for comparative purposes.

Page numbers are given for species accounts and introductions to families and other higher taxa. Family names are in bold capital letters for ease of reference.

STRUCTURE OF ACCOUNTS AND KEYS

The main portion of this book consists of a key to the families, introductions to the families and selected higher taxa, keys to the species in each family, and the one-page species accounts.

Keys

All keys in this book are structured the same. They consist of couplets of characters that, by process of elimination, guide the user to an identification. Identifying species by use of the keys begins with the key to the families. This key directs the user to the keys to the species in those families.

In any key, start with the first alternative in the first couplet. If the description fits the specimen, follow the direction given at the righthand margin: if a number in parentheses is given, go to the couplet with that number for the next character to consider; if a name is given, you have identified the specimen and the page number may be used to find the key to the species of that family (if you are working in the key to families) or the species itself (if working in a key to species of a family). If the first character in the couplet does not fit, go to the second character in the couplet, which will either give an identification or direct you to another couplet, and so on. Proceed down as many character couplets as necessary to identify the specimen. Do not skip characters. Whenever the key directs you to a new couplet, the new couplet has, in parentheses in the second column, the number from which you were referred; this facilitates backtracking through the key.

Introductions to Higher Taxa

The introductions to families and other higher taxa briefly give a group's physical appearance, habitat, geographical range, and numbers of genera and species; and summarize the major diagnostic characters of the group, characters that allow identification of species because they vary among the species, records of species new to the inventory of Alaskan fishes, and recent taxonomic revisions that affect the classification of Alaskan species. The summaries of characteristics are not meant to be full, detailed descriptions of any group, which may be found elsewhere, but to contain sufficient information to enable identification of fish specimens found in Alaska to the higher group and to place the group as represented in Alaska in context with the group as represented worldwide. Specialized morphological features used in the descriptions are defined, and often shown in diagrams. For families having several species in Alaska, the descriptive summaries extend to distinguishing features of subfamilies and genera.

Source materials are not cited in the taxon introductions if the information given is widely available, as in the major syntheses by Jordan and Evermann (1896–1900), McPhail and Lindsey (1970), Miller and Lea (1972), Hart (1973), Scott and Crossman (1973), Morrow (1980), and Eschmeyer and Herald (1983). Numbers of genera and species in families worldwide and some of the essential family characteristics are generally from Nelson (1984, 1994), as is the entire higher-taxon classification. Sources are cited for information on specialized characters or information that differs from that given in the major syntheses. For each family we cite the major taxonomic revisions which are our sources for classification of genera and species, and explain recent changes in classification or nomenclature, including any we make in this book. Comparing the present inventory to that of Quast and Hall (1972), we give our reasons for any differences. These generally include taxonomic reasons, such as synonymization of one species in another, and information on new records of occurrence.

Keys to the Species

Introductions to families which are represented in Alaska by two or more species include keys to the species. The title of each key specifies that the key is to the family as represented in Alaska, in order to emphasize the point that the keys are meant to apply only within the study area. In the jargon of taxonomy, the keys are "artificial," dealing with the species in a given region and not the full complement of species in the family worldwide.

Some species cannot be placed with certainty in the keys because they are not well studied and their published descriptions are incomplete with respect to characters currently used to distinguish species. Thus, some keys are provisional or experimental; for example, the keys to the Cyclopteridae and Liparidae. For some families the keys will not be easily used without special equipment or time spent in the laboratory. This is because observation of the diagnostic characters may require radiographs, dissection, staining, or other techniques. Some keys are, then, most useful in a laboratory situation, while others are usable in the field. Generally, however, we have tried to make them usable in both field and laboratory.

Mostly we have tried to give external characters but, for example, counts of vertebrae are necessary to categorize some species. This is where the main limitation of dichotomous keys makes itself evident. The need to sort the species into two groups at each successive character couplet may result in having to use characters that are difficult to assess. If a different sorting method is used it may be possible to identify the species without resorting to difficult characters. Computer software is available which should allow development of a database and method for identifying the fishes of Alaska that does not use dichotomous keys but identifies a specimen on the basis of an entire complex of characters which is examined in, essentially, one step.

Coloration is often important in determining species and it is used in some of the keys. In the keys, as well as in the species accounts, whenever we describe marks as pale versus dark rather than give specific colors it is because the contrast is more important than the actual color. In addition, colors fade in preservative and the pale–dark distinction is sometimes the only difference that remains in museum specimens.

In a few of the keys, some paths lead to groups of two or more closely similar species. From there, the user would examine the illustrations and descriptions in the species accounts to select a possible identification. However, in such groups the species may be synonymous or the level of knowledge about them is not sufficient to allow accurate discrimination. In either case, more study is required.

Format of Species Accounts

Within each family, the species are grouped by genus and according to overall similarity, following the order in which they key out.

Accounts are given only for full species, not for subspecies. Subspecies of Alaskan fish species are not well defined or universally recognized as valid entities. Those that have received the most attention and study, notably among the chars (Salmoninae), are mentioned in the Notes & Sources sections of the species accounts.

Each species account is limited to one page and includes scientific name, English vernacular (common) name, extralimital geographic range statement, and brief habitat statement; morphological characteristics distinguishing the species from other species in the family present in the study area; one or more illustrations of the fish; a map showing documented range or, in the case of the less well-studied species, depicting individual records of occurrence in Alaska; and a section of Notes & Sources.

Scientific Name

The scientific name of the species is given at the top left corner of the account. Following standard practice the genus (first word in the name) and species (second word) are italicized. The first letter of the genus is always capitalized, and the first letter of the species is always lower case. If the specific epithet is combined with a genus other than the genus in which the species was originally placed, the author(s) and date of the original name are enclosed in parentheses. For example, the parentheses in *Malacocottus aleuticus* (Smith, 1904) mean that Smith originally classified this species in a genus other than *Malacocottus*; in this example the original name was *Thecopterus aleuticus* Smith, 1904.

The original spelling of the species name is given unless it has been formally emended in the ichthyological literature. Consulting all the original descriptions to determine original spelling was not practical, since many are obscure and difficult to obtain. Fortunately, this is no longer a problem. Eschmeyer's (1998, 2001) recent catalog contains information on the original descriptions for all Recent fish species of the world. Readers familiar with the fifth edition of the American Fisheries Society list of North American continental shelf fish names (Robins et al. 1991a), which adopted an argument by Bailey and Robins (1988) for deleting the terminal *i* in some species names, will find the original spelling restored herein. An earlier edition of the International Code of Zoological Nomenclature (International Commission on Zoological Nomenclature 1984) was perceived by Bailey and Robins (1988) and some other authors as containing ambiguities regarding the correct spelling of names, but the latest edition of the Code (ICZN 1999) removed any ambiguity. The upcoming, sixth edition of the AFS list will also include the original spellings (J. S. Nelson, pers. comms., 2001).

The scientific name is followed by the name of the person who formally described and named the species in the ichthyological literature. This is the author name. Following usage in the Code, we use an ampersand (&) instead of the word "and" for dual authorship of scientific names, and interpose a comma between the name of the author and the date of publication. These two devices (ampersand and comma) distinguish the authors and publication dates of scientific names from citations of source materials. For example, we write Stein and Bond (1978) if citing that publication, but

Psychrolutes phrictus Stein & Bond, 1978, for the formal scientific name of the species they described.

Again following the Code, the actual date of publication is given and not the date on the title page of the work, if those dates are different. For example, the title page of the monograph on Arctic fishes by Goode and Bean (1896) bears the date 1895, but the work was not distributed (i.e., published) until 1896 (Cohen 1963a). For the many species that were first described in the volumes of the *Proceedings of the United States National Museum,* the date of publication can usually be determined because date of issuance of the individual articles was given in the table of contents or stamped on the signatures (groups of pages used in binding books), in addition to the volume date. The articles in each volume were commonly distributed as separates before the complete volume was published. For other works, several publications dealing with dates were consulted; e.g., Hays (1952) for the works of David Starr Jordan and United States National Museum (1947) for National Museum publications through 1946. The publication of Eschmeyer's (1998, 2001) catalog in the latter years of our effort rendered this exercise largely unnecessary.

Common Name

The common name is given at the upper right of each account. Following current convention, as reflected, for instance, in the AFS lists of fish names (Robins et al. 1991a,b), the common names are not italicized. Nor are they capitalized, except for elements that are proper names; for example, Arctic cod, named for its occurrence in the Arctic Ocean; or Pacific ocean perch (ocean in this example is not capitalized because it refers to the type of habitat, as opposed to a freshwater perch).

Common names may vary regionally and among authors. This book gives the names recommended by the American Fisheries Society Committee on Names of Fishes (Robins et al. 1991a,b) for fishes occurring in waters over the continental shelf (generally, shallower than 200 m). About one-third of the species treated in this book are deepsea and oceanic pelagic species or obscure, poorly known shelf species not on the AFS lists, and for them we generally give the oldest names found in the literature or, not finding any previous names, we coined names using the criteria of the AFS names committee (Robins et al. 1991a). Major sources of names included Hubbs et al. (1979) and Whitehead et al. (1984, 1986). In coining names, the main purpose was to attempt to establish and standardize common names for Alaskan fishes. (Since in this and some other instances the names are not in common use at all, some authors prefer to call them vernacular names, rather than common names.) For fish species occurring in waters of both Russia and Alaska, Boris A. Sheiko and C.W.M. worked to coin mutually acceptable names for use in upcoming publications (e.g., Sheiko and Fedorov 2000, Fedorov and Sheiko 2002, and this book). Some of those names are already in use in the literature, having been supplied by us in response to requests for names.

Following the criteria given by the AFS (Robins et al. 1991a), in coining names or choosing among available names we tried to pick names that are not intended to honor persons. The AFS recommends choosing vernacular names that refer to morphological features or geographic range. Hence we chose festive snailfish for *Liparis marmoratus,* for the bright, festive-looking coloration; veteran poacher for *Podothecus veternus* from the species name meaning old man or veteran in reference to a lack of teeth; slender eelpout for *Lycodapus leptus* because the species name means narrow or slender in reference to the emaciated look of most specimens; variform eelpout for *Lycodapus poecilus* from the species name meaning variform and referring to the variable forms of this fish; and so on. However, if only an honorific name was available and was in use, we chose this name in preference to coining a new vernacular; for example, Soldatov's lumpsucker for *Eumicrotremus soldatovi,* because the name has been used in many publications. Usually the choice of common name is obvious from the characteristics or range, but if not, an explanation is given in Notes & Sources. As well, widely used alternate names are sometimes given in Notes & Sources.

Range Statement

The statement below the scientific and common names includes the documented range of the species in Alaska and, in very general terms, the rest of the world. Usually the first part of the range statement gives the range in Alaska and the eastern Pacific Ocean, followed by the range in the western Pacific off Asian shores and progressing to other parts of the world. For some species the statement for Alaska comprises a few phrases giving a few known, disjunct records of the species. This is typically the case when species are represented in Alaska only by questionable or unverifiable reports of occurrence, or by one to a few confirmed records. Those uncertain and rare occurrences are usually listed separately in the range statement in lieu of a generalized statement which could give a false impression of the state of knowledge.

For the purpose of describing geographic range of species the southern limit of the Gulf of Alaska is taken to be a line running along the parallel at 54°30'N, from about the Alaska–British Columbia border at Dixon Entrance in the east to the southwest tip of Unimak Island. The imaginary line dips a few kilometers in the west to include the Sanak Islands. Thus the waters south of the Aleutians and west of Unimak Pass are considered to be in the North Pacific Ocean proper; and waters east of Unimak Pass and north of about 54°30'N, including the Sanak Islands and Shumagin Islands, are considered to be in the Gulf of Alaska. This differs from usage elsewhere and may not be correct hydrographically, but it causes less confusion when giving the ranges of species than if the Gulf of Alaska is taken to also include waters off British Columbia.

The Bering Sea is understood to be delimited in the south by the Aleutian chain, whereas in some early literature the coasts of Kamchatka and the Okhotsk Sea, as well as the Kuril Islands, were considered part of the Bering Sea. Such usage introduced much confusion regarding the ranges of Alaskan fishes.

Alaska is not divided into regions for the purposes of the range statements. References to western, northern, or eastern Gulf of Alaska, for example, are general and not delimited by specific landmarks. Southeastern Alaska is generally taken to include islands of the Alexander Archipelago and the mainland extending south from and including Yakutat.

References to northern, central, and southern British Columbia for marine fish ranges pertain to the coastal region of the province, not the interior which extends north adjacent to Alaska. Generally, northern British Columbia is the coastal and marine region north of Queen Charlotte Sound, the sound is central, and south of the sound is southern British Columbia.

Northern and southern Baja California, Mexico, are roughly equivalent to the political territories, Baja California and Baja California Sur.

Note that for Canada, the area encompassed by the Northwest Territories has changed. The eastern portion was split off in 1999 and given the name Nunavut.

Habitat Statement

Both the range statements and the habitat statements are based, as far as possible, on adults. For example, most literature accounts give 37 m as the minimum depth for *Sagamichthys abei,* but this is based on a record of four juveniles. The greater depths at which the adults live are given in the habitat statement while the 37-m juvenile record is mentioned, with citation of the literature source, in the Range section of the Notes & Sources. Some shallow depths given for species normally inhabiting greater depths could be due to catches of juveniles, but this type of detail is often not discernible from the available information.

Species are marine, inhabiting salt or brackish waters, if not stated to be freshwater or anadromous. Some authors prefer the term *amphidromous* for certain salmonids that do not undertake the oceanic migrations of the classically anadromous Pacific salmons but for simplicity we retain the general term. Gross (1987), McDowall (1987), and Craig (1989) address this subject.

Depth ranges are given for most species, but such statements are widely recognized as being estimates only. This is because most records are derived from tows made with open nets that capture fish as the net descends or ascends, and fish may be caught anywhere down to the maximum depth of the tow. Therefore, the maximum depth given is usually the maximum depth reached by a net. Most trawl-caught Alaskan records in the literature and museum collections are from nonclosing nets. Few surveys have used closing nets and depth-measuring devices. A few of the records cited are from the early years of oceanography when the only depth information given was the length of the cable used in the tow; for example, "1,200 m of wire out." Scuba diving has produced much new information on habitat of shallow, subtidal fishes. There is also some good depth information from research using manned and unmanned submersibles.

Depths are given in meters. When converting from fathoms we used several decimal places for accuracy.

Checklists of regional fish fauna typically characterize the living space of each species using tightly defined depth zones. However, the view of clearly defined communities zoned by depth appears to be too simplistic and somewhat out of date (Haedrich 1997). As well, the depth zone of many species is not well enough known to draw conclusions and apply a label. A universal terminology for this purpose is lacking and terms sometimes overlap in meaning. For the more well-known species we give living spaces in the most widely used, broad terms (e.g., epipelagic, mesopelagic, bathypelagic; or oceanic, neritic). Habitat terminology used in this guide is defined in the Glossary.

Selected Counts

For ray-finned fishes (actinopterygians) a line or two of meristic (countable) characters, such as numbers of fin rays, vertebrae, and gill rakers, is given below the habitat statement. The meristics provided are those most useful for identifying species within each family. They are tailored for the group. The Glossary gives the definitions and abbreviations used. More specialized counts which pertain within subfamilies or genera, but not to the entire family, are given in the two-column list of characters; for example, numbers of the oblique dermal folds in the various species of the genus *Triglops*, which are not present in most other cottids.

Counts were obtained from the ichthyological literature or from specimens examined during the course of research for this book. For any species, within the selected set of meristics, if counts are not given it is because they are not available. Accurate counts for some families, such as Liparidae in which rays are often buried in flesh, are difficult to obtain and the literature is sometimes difficult to assess. In the case of caudal fin rays, the counts are particularly difficult to assess because some investigators report only the principal rays whereas others report total rays without providing separate counts. It is only in recent years that radiographs have come to be commonly used as an aid for counting vertebrae and fin rays. Because radiographs allow greater accuracy, many of the older counts may not be comparable with the new.

Selected Characters (Bulleted Items)

The two columns of text marked by bullets give the characters which are most useful for identification. To facilitate comparison, the characters are always presented in the same order, progressing from coloration to maximum known size. As with the selected meristics, the characters listed vary according to the taxonomic group. For example, relative length of the second and third anal fin spines varies among species and is an important identifying character in rockfishes (Scorpaenidae), but not in pricklebacks (Stichaeidae).

If more than one species in a family is found in Alaska, characters that are most critical in distinguishing the most similar-looking species are indicated by bold type. Rarely, lack of bold type means species are not well enough known to enable us to point out any characters as being particularly significant.

As far as possible, the same set of characters is given for each species in a family or genus. Where characters are lacking in a set for one or more species, it is because the information is not available. For many taxa, characters were not reported in the older descriptions that today would be considered diagnostic or important supplementary characters. By the lack of complete character sets for some species, this book points out a research need.

Conversely, since the characters are selected for their use in distinguishing among species, many possible characters are not listed. Features which are common to all or most members of a family, for example, are generally not repeated in the species accounts (they are given in the family introductions). Emphasis is on consistency of characters within genera. It is not necessary, for example, to comment on the profile of the head in *Anarrhichthys ocellatus,* as other characters identify that species, but the profile is useful in distinguishing between *Anarhichas orientalis* and *A. denticulatus.* Additional description is available in the literature cited in Notes & Sources.

The characters are written, in traditional ichthyological style, in the singular number, to describe one side of the fish, even if the fish has two such structures; as in "pelvic fin absent." They are in the plural only when necessary to refer to a condition involving both sides, as in "gill membranes united." The plural is used elsewhere: in the keys, the Notes & Sources, and the introductions to the orders and families.

Rather than give a separate category for "similar species" as in some other regional guides, this guide presents similar species close to each other and indicates by bold type in the bulleted items the main characteristics which distinguish those species from each other. Occasionally we include a statement under Notes & Sources about differences between closely similar species; for example, if the distinction needs additional emphasis, there is some disagreement in the literature, or the taxonomy is unresolved.

Where qualifiers such as short or long, slender or robust are given they are meant relative to the condition in related species. There is no attempt to quantify all characters which differ by degree.

Measurements and proportions have been kept to a minimum. Any measurements given follow Hubbs and Lagler (1949) except for specialized measurements which are defined, with appropriate references cited, in the introductions to the families.

Maximum known length is always given as the last bulleted item. Total length (TL) is given if available, but often only standard length (SL) is available. We generally have not tried to estimate total length from standard length. Proportions vary by species and we only make conversions if both measurements are available for some specimens representing the species so that at least a rough proportion can be derived. Very occasionally we give fork length (FL), if that is all that is available in the literature.

Length is given in order to suggest the relative sizes of the species. Sample size is not given because it is rarely known. For well-known species, the size given is probably a rarely attained maximum size. In some of those cases, we have given a "usually" size in addition to the extreme, if available. For species known from only one or a few specimens the length given may not be at all representative of the adult population. Lengths are for mature individuals, as far as we know; some species are so poorly known that the only lengths available may be from immature individuals.

Lengths are given in millimeters or centimeters, depending on general fish size. For example, lengths of rockfishes (Scorpaenidae) are generally reported in centimeters, but most lumpsuckers (Cyclopteridae) are considerably smaller and their lengths are measured and reported in millimeters.

Weights are given for some commercial and game fishes, because often the weights of these fish are more well documented and there are few records of length. Weight is reported in kilograms.

Although lengths and weights are reported in metric units, often these are conversions from the U.S. standard. We used factors with three or four decimal places so that the fish would not "grow" by our conversions. Using only one or two decimal places makes inaccurate conversions and is a common cause of the discrepancies in reported fish lengths.

Illustrations of Fishes

Pictures of the fishes in this book were electronically scanned into digital format from a number of sources. If the illustration was published previously, the best possible reproduction was always sought. We used original editions, rather than later editions, reprints, or translations, if the original was the best reproduction; it was not always the best. If the same drawing was reproduced in several books, as in the monographs by Goode (1884), Goode and Bean (1896), Jordan and Evermann (1900), Evermann and Goldsborough (1907), and others which reused many of the same plates, the earliest use is cited but the best reproduction was used for this book.

Line drawings were used whenever possible because of the greater difficulty in reproducing continuous-tone illustrations. The latter were particularly problematical when scanning from publications, as electronic removal of printers' screens resulted in significant loss of detail and produced fuzziness.

Most previously published illustrations have been modified. Sometimes this was simply to enhance the reproduction but in many cases features were emphasized or added from examination of specimens. Significant changes are mentioned in Notes & Sources.

More than one illustration is included for some species. In some cases the additional illustrations show variation among the adults of a species, or differences due to age. They may emphasize important characters for identification. For example, the flatfish species accounts include a detailed illustration, as well as a diagram that emphasizes the lateral line configuration and fin and body shapes. For some other groups, young fish are shown if they have been confused with other species or occur in large enough sizes to have potential for being misidentified as adults of other species.

Whenever possible, we used illustrations based on specimens from Alaska or adjacent waters. Many of the illustrations that appear in this book for the first time, such as those prepared in the 1960s and 1970s under the direction of N. J. Wilimovsky (UBC collection), are based on Alaskan specimens. Those prepared in the 1970s and 1980s under A. E. Peden's supervision (RBCM collection) are mainly from Alaska and British Columbia. As well, most of the drawings in this book that were created in the late 1800s by artists of the Smithsonian Institution, National Museum of Natural History, Division of Fishes (USNM collection), were previously unpublished and were based on specimens from Alaska. The illustrations of *Bathyraja parmifera* are based on specimens in the UW collection which were collected from the Bering Sea.

Photographs of specimens were taken for the species accounts when no other illustration was available, and when we could locate specimens in good condition; for example, *Oneirodes thompsoni* and *Lethotremus muticus.* No depiction of the external appearance is available for a few poorly known species. Although we took photographs of some of the type specimens of those species, generally the condition of the types was poor and did not produce photographs that were useful for identifying the species.

Color photographs of about half of the Alaskan species are included in a special section of this book. Some do not show fish in Alaskan waters or specimens collected in Alaska, but many do. Additional color photographs of the most commonly encountered shallow-water fishes of the northeastern Pacific in their natural habitats may be found in guides by Lamb and Edgell (1986), Gotshall (1989), and Humann (1996). Kessler's (1985) guide provides photographs of dead but fresh specimens of Alaskan species arranged in standardized position, while Amaoka et al. (1984) and Masuda et al. (1984) include photographs of preserved specimens of many of the rarer species of the North Pacific Ocean as well. Kramer and O'Connell's (1988, 1995) guides to the rockfishes and flatfishes of the northeastern Pacific, and Orr et al.'s (2000) to the rockfishes, have color photographs of those fishes in standardized position. Color photographs of marine fishes of British Columbia are also available in Hart (1973), and freshwater fishes of Alaska in Morrow (1980). As well, the Worldwide Web is a good source of color photographs, at least of the more common, inshore species.

Range Maps

The maps showing known range in Alaska identify at a glance which species have been reported in Alaska and which have not, as well as the area in which each species has been found. The ranges depicted on the maps, as well as the range statements, are based on records of adults and late juveniles. Larvae and early juveniles often have a broader or different distribution than the late juveniles and adults of a species.

Depiction of range is by way of solid fill, dots, and circles. Dots and circles are used to indicate capture localities of specimens representing new, rare, or disjunct records, rather than losing visual tracking of new records or attempting to estimate a continuous range from insufficient or possibly anomalous data. Some dots and circles represent more than one collection. Through the course of several drafts many maps ended up with numerous dots, which suggests the species are more common in Alaska than previous literature indicated. However, in such cases the dots have been retained rather than changing to solid fills, in order to present and document the records.

Dots represent, as far as possible, verifiable records. These were gleaned from the ichthyological literature, examination of museum specimens, museum catalogs, and online museum collection databases. Curators and ichthyologists often confirmed identifications by examining specimens if C.W.M. or T.A.M. could not do this personally. The records are verifiable because the specimens are housed in permanent collections and can be examined. Rarely, the vouchers are photographs or videotapes. In some cases it is not clear from the literature if identifications are backed by vouchers. We accepted such a record as valid if it was judged likely to be correct from previously established knowledge of the species' range and the familiarity of the author who recorded the identification with the ichthyofauna.

Circles are for previously unpublished, unverifiable reports by knowledgeable persons. These include records from NMFS scientific surveys that are not backed by vouchers but are not likely to be misidentifications because the species are easily identified. In the best such cases, the records were retrieved from the database and their reliability evaluated by fishery biologists in charge of fish identification for the surveys. Other examples are extensions of known range Baxter (1990ms) claimed on the basis of specimens he examined which were not saved and deposited in museums, if his data records (Baxter, unpubl. data) were found and they demonstrated diagnostic features were observed, or the description of the species in the manuscript was correct in the diagnostic details. At least one Alaskan species may not be represented by specimens from Alaska in permanent collections (*Sebastes saxicola*), and for several species the limits of range in Alaska are not represented in collections. For those species, occurrence in Alaska is represented only or largely by circles. If specimens are caught in areas where circles are shown, examples should be saved and deposited in permanent collections.

Fills are used for ranges that are more well known. The species are generally commonly taken and include commercially important species and species commonly taken as bycatch, as well as commonly observed and collected inshore species. Fills may be based on a combination of verifiable records and other observations, such as NMFS scientific surveys or commercial catch records. While not every locality is represented by a museum specimen, the species are easily enough identified that the range depicted is probably accurate.

Gray fill is used for freshwater and anadromous species, and black for marine species. For benthic or demersal fishes the fill follows bathymetric contours of the typical range, not the known extremes of depth inhabited. To depict intertidal and shallow subtidal habitat the fill was extended out a little beyond the typical habitat range to make it show up on the small maps. For pelagic species the fill extends out to the approximate recorded distance offshore.

Notes & Sources

The Notes & Sources section at the bottom of each species account gives *selected* literature citations and other documentation. It identifies the most complete descriptions available in the literature, sources of the illustrations, information on known geographic range in Alaska, and, for some species, explanation of the maximum size reported in the last morphological characteristic marked by a bullet.

The currently valid scientific name of the species, from the top of the page, is repeated on the same line as the subheading "Notes & Sources," but with additional information. If the species has been classified in a subgenus and that usage has wide recognition among authors, the subgenus name is given in parentheses; for example, *Coryphaenoides (Bogoslovius) longifilis*. If an ichthyological work includes a description of a species that was contributed by someone other than the author(s) of the main work, this situation is clarified by giving the name of all authors involved; for example, *Sigmistes caulias* Rutter in Jordan & Evermann, 1898. This means that Rutter wrote the description of *Sigmistes caulias* which was published in the work by Jordan and Gilbert (1898).

Below the currently accepted scientific name we first list the original name of the species if the species has been moved to another genus, then synonyms and other names that have been used in literature giving Alaskan records of the species. These synonymic lists are not intended to provide a complete list of the junior synonyms or published references to each species. Enough synonymy has been given to connect this work with other descriptive works. Knowing the name under which the species was originally described enables one to search databases that use the original names, such as museum type catalogs, or to look up information on the type series and references to additional literature in Eschmeyer's (1998, 2001) catalog of fish types. Names of species which are recognized to be junior synonyms are given if the names have been applied to specimens collected in Alaska or their descriptions have been used as source material for the species account. Name combinations that differ from the valid name are listed if they are used in literature we cite.

Punctuation enables the reader to discriminate between original species descriptions and other name combinations. If the name is one associated with the original description of a species, the name, author, and date of publication of the description are given, with no terminal punctuation. If the name is a different combination applied to a previously described species, the name is followed by a colon and an example of a publication using the name, followed by a period. For example, in the synonymy of *Gymnelus viridis* there is an entry: "*Gymnelopsis stigma* (Lay & Bennett, 1839): Wilimovsky 1954." This means that Wilimovsky (1954) used the name *Gymnelopsis stigma* for the species originally described by Lay and Bennett (1839), which has since been placed in the synonymy of *Gymnelus viridis*. Such references are critical aids when consulting the older literature.

The first work to use a changed name in conjunction with records from Alaska is generally listed. For example, *Ophidium stigma* Lay & Bennett, 1839 was moved to *Gymnelis stigma* (Lay & Bennett, 1839) by Günther (1862), and the new combination was first used for specimens from Alaska by Bean (1881b). Therefore, we list Bean (1881b), but not necessarily Günther (1862). Sometimes we did not track names back to the earliest use pertaining to Alaskan specimens, but listed other early examples of use. The main purpose is to indicate to researchers using the older literature that there are records of occurrence, information on morphological features, or discussions of nomenclature under names other than those originally given to the species.

In the foregoing examples using *Gymnelus* the spelling *Gymnelis* is also given. This is because authors gave both spellings. *Gymnelus* is correct, as used in the original description of the genus by Reinhardt (1934). The nomenclatural history of Alaskan species contains several potentially confusing spelling pairs, which are included in the lists of selected synonyms in the species accounts.

Under the Notes & Sources heading we also comment on similarities among species, if we have not been able to determine significant differences by examining the literature and specimens. The similarities suggest synonymy but this could be a false impression gained from inadequate description in the literature, inadequate sampling of museum specimens, or misidentified museum specimens. The similarities noted could be topics for future taxonomic studies.

Sometimes, in this position, we give diagnostic characters of closely related species occurring outside Alaska which have in the past been confused with the Alaskan species, to prevent the mistake in future.

Any commentary we may have on common names is also given under the Notes & Sources heading.

Description

Selected descriptions of the species are cited under the Description subhead. The focus is on publications giving the most complete morphological descriptions and synonymies, to supplement as well as to document the information we give in the account. Several references may be cited. For many species more than one work is needed to make a complete description, or the published descriptions may not be clear and we list all pertinent works so that all may be taken in hand for further study. Occasionally, a newer work is cited if one or more of the older works might not be readily available. Reference is usually made to Jordan and Evermann's (1896–1900) compendium, *The Fishes of North and Middle America,* if their description has not been largely superseded by newer information.

Sometimes works are cited if they discuss classification or nomenclature of the species. All the works from which we drew morphological data for the account are cited. If the range and habitat information is not included in the works cited under Description, the additional works are cited separately under other subheads.

Much of the literature on North Pacific fishes is in the Russian language. To save space, page numbers are given only for the Russian editions, even though translations into English may be available (and usually have different page numbers). Available translations are listed in the Bibliography. In rare cases we did not have a Russian original so relied on, and give page numbers for, the translations.

If examination of specimens resulted in new data being added to the description, the specimens are listed under the Description heading. Specimens that were examined merely to verify characters or to clarify descriptions given in previous literature are not listed.

Collection abbreviations used in museum catalog numbers follow Leviton et al. (1985) and Leviton and Gibbs (1988), with a few exceptions. The abbreviations are listed toward the front of this book.

Regarding catalog numbers, the reader will avoid confusion by remembering that in museum collections, catalog numbers refer to all specimens in a lot. These may include several fishes that were captured together, in the same sample. Thus, a catalog number may apply to more than one specimen of a species or to specimens of more than one species.

Figures

Sources of the diagrams and illustrations of fishes and fish parts are given under the Figures subhead. The artist's name is given if the illustration has not previously been published. For full lateral views, and for some diagrams, we indicate if the specimen illustrated was a type specimen, give catalog number if the illustration has not been previously published or there is some other reason for giving it (e.g., a poorly studied group for which it is useful to retain detailed information while research is ongoing); total or standard length (whichever was reported), converted to metric; condition if this helps explain the figure, such as skinned or desiccated; and locality of capture. For many illustrations this information is not available.

Range

The Range section is primarily for documentation of geographic range in Alaska but may include notes on depth or other aspects of habitat, correct errors in the literature on any aspect of range (whether within or outside of Alaska), or provide information on range that is obscure or new enough that it has not yet entered the general literature. The emphasis is on known limits of range in Alaska, to identify the sources for the ranges depicted on our maps for each species (since we depict documented ranges, as far as possible). Question marks, dots, and circles on the maps are explained. For species not occurring in Alaska, we usually identify the nearest known locality of occurrence and cite the literature or other source. Problems with identification of species that affect our understanding of range are also mentioned here. Sources for the depth range are cited here if the information is not included in the references cited under the Description subhead. Under this and other subheads, citation of R. Baxter (unpubl. data) means data sheets or other Baxter records are on file (Point Stephens Research, P.O. Box 210307, Auke Bay, Alaska 99821) that provide documentation of the information to which the citation refers. Citation of Baxter (1990ms) refers to the technically unpublished but widely distributed manuscript, where the manuscript does not provide reference to data records or other source for the given information.

Museum catalog numbers and locality data are provided under Range if the records have not previously been published, or if there are only a few published records for a species. Otherwise, we generally just cite the sources of the data.

For most fish species there are far more museum specimens than are cited in the Range notes. There, emphasis is on documenting range limits, not listing all available records from between the limits.

Size

A note under Size is included if the maximum size (usually the last item in the righthand column of morphological features) needs some explanation, the source is not among the sources cited under Description, or there are so many citations under Description that it would be tedious to search through all of them to find the source for the size. A note is always given if the maximum size given in our account has not previously been reported. In addition to the source of the new size record, the previous record is cited. In a few instances we estimated total length from standard length. For example, if all but one or two species in a large family had total lengths reported for size, we estimated total length for those one or two species from their standard lengths using ratios derived from specimens for which both types of length are available.

Key to Fish Families in Alaska

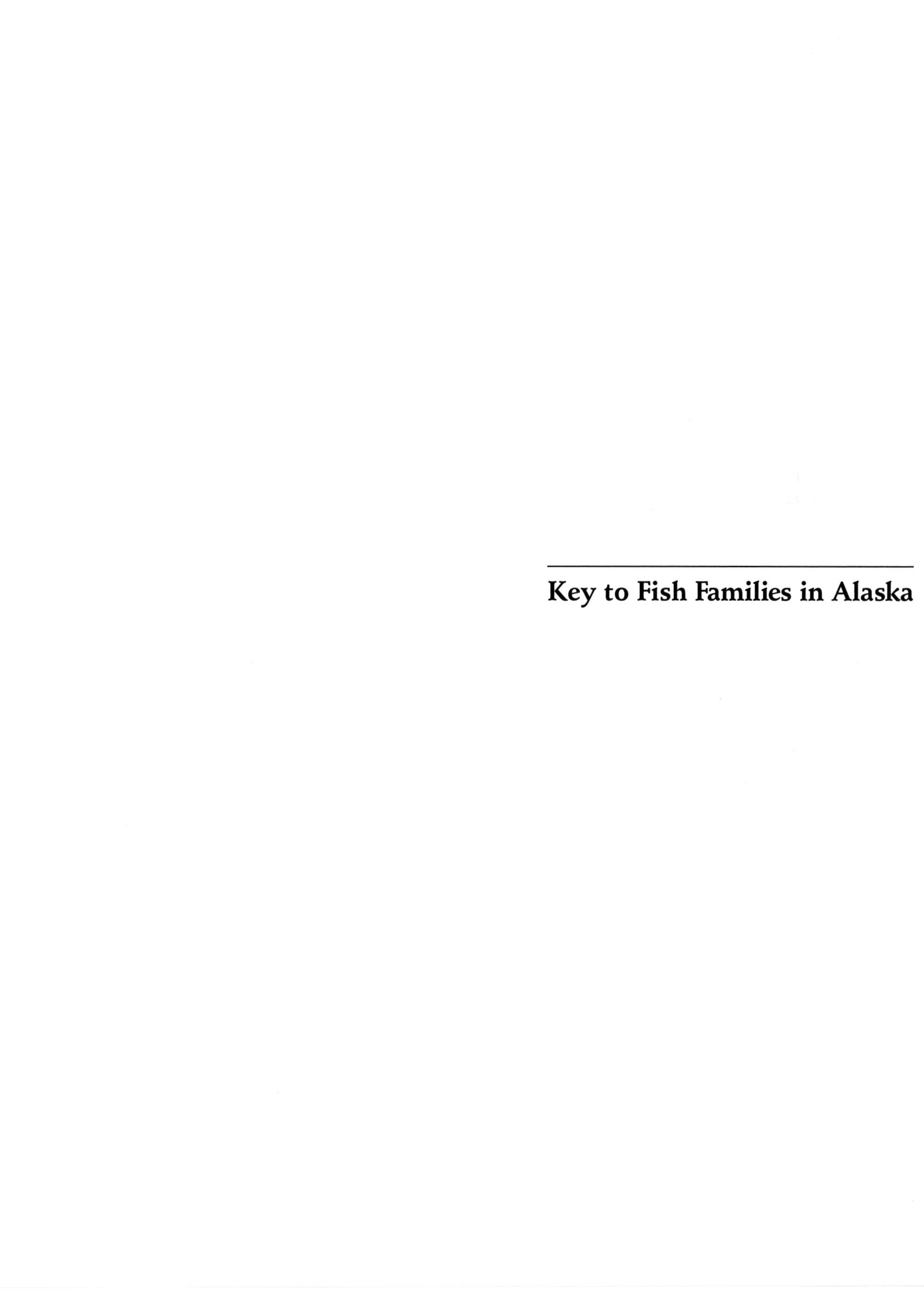

KEY TO FISH FAMILIES IN ALASKA

1 Mouth without jaws; one nostril (median); no paired fins or scales . . . . . (2)

1 Mouth with jaws; nostrils paired; paired fins and scales present or absent . . . . . (3)

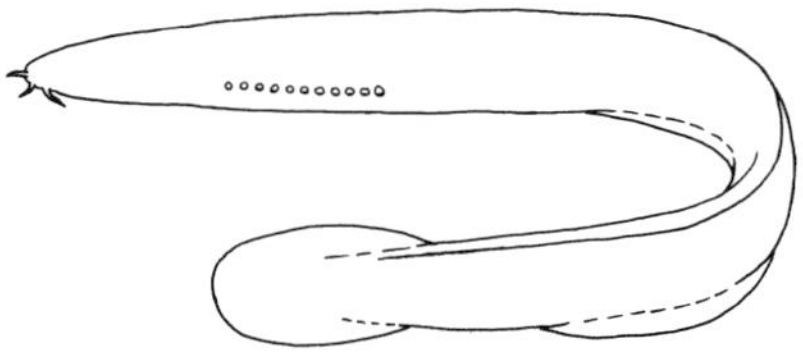

2 (1) Gill openings 10–15 on each side of body; barbels present around mouth; mouth a fleshy tunnel . . . . . **MYXINIDAE**, page 52

2 Gill openings 7 on each side of body; no barbels around mouth; mouth a toothed sucking disk . . . . . **PETROMYZONTIDAE**, page 56

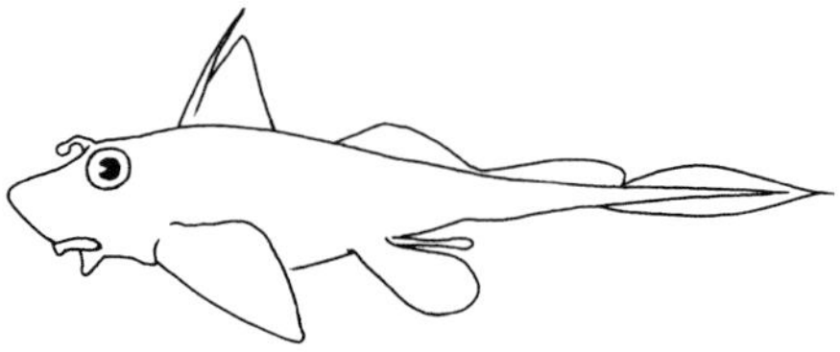

3 (1) First dorsal fin high and triangular, with stout serrate spine; second dorsal fin low, broadly notched; caudal fin pointed; scales absent . . . . . **CHIMAERIDAE**, page 67

3 First and second dorsal fins and caudal fin not as above; scales present or absent . . . . . (4)

4 (3) Gill openings 5–7 on each side . . . . . (5)

4 Gill openings 1 on each side. . . . . . (17)

5 (4) Gill openings 6 or 7 on each side . . . . . **HEXANCHIDAE**, page 82

5 Gill openings 5 on each side . . . . . (6)

6 (5) Gill openings mainly lateral; pectoral fin not continuous with head; body roundish in cross section or dorsoventrally flattened . . . . . (7)

6 Gill openings on ventral surface; pectoral fin continuous with head; body dorsoventrally flattened . . . . . (15)

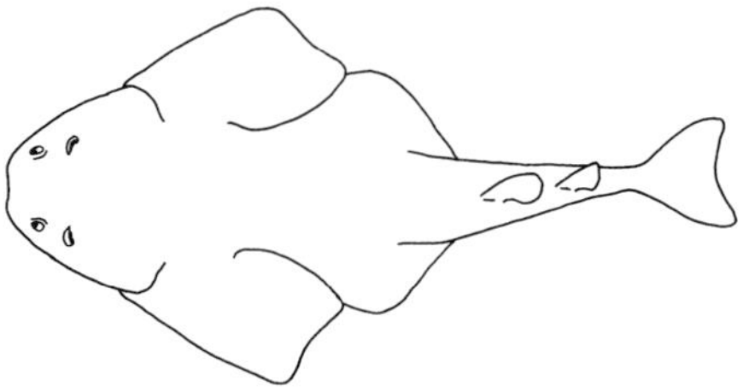

7 (6) Eyes dorsal; body dorsoventrally flattened . . . . . **SQUATINIDAE**, page 89

7 Eyes lateral; body not dorsoventrally flattened . . . . . (8)

8 (7) Anal fin absent . . . . . (9)

8 Anal fin present . . . . . (10)

9 (8) No spine at front of each dorsal fin . . . . . **DALATIIDAE**, page 85

9 Spine present at front of each dorsal fin . . . . . **SQUALIDAE**, page 87

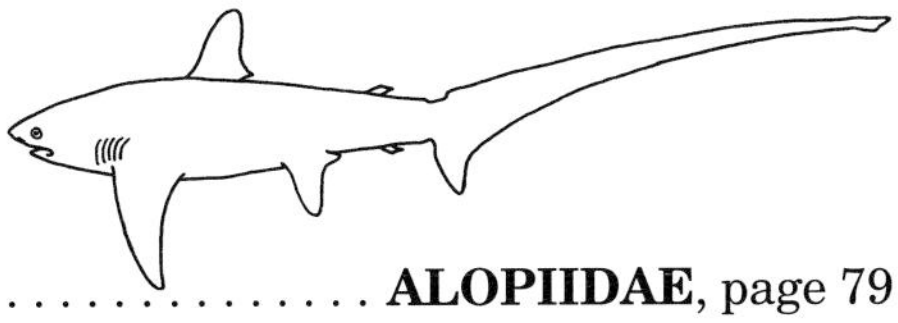

10 (8) Caudal fin greatly elongate, about equal to body length .... **ALOPIIDAE**, page 79

10 Caudal fin markedly shorter than body length ....(11)

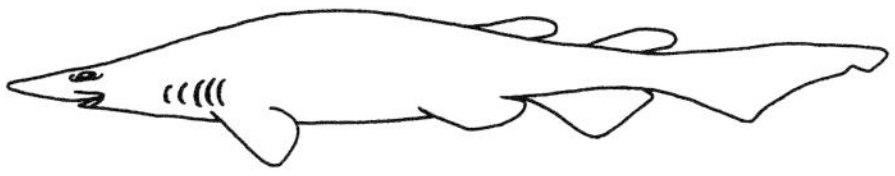

11 (10) Origin of first dorsal fin above or posterior to origin of pelvic fins .... **SCYLIORHINIDAE**, page 74

11 Origin of first dorsal fin well ahead of pelvic origin ......(12)

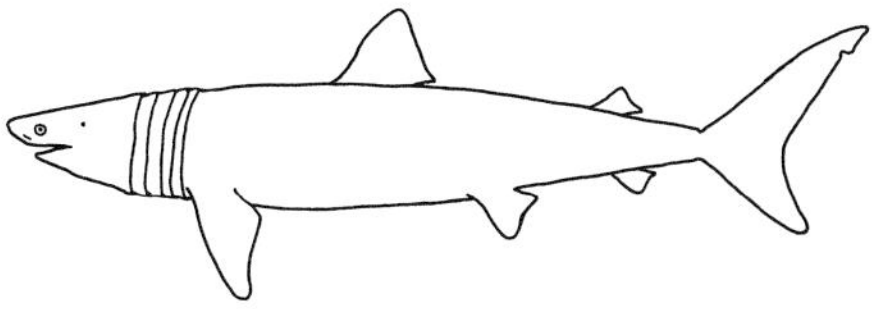

12 (11) Gill slits extremely large, extending from dorsal surface of body to ventral midline .... **CETORHINIDAE**, page 80

12 Gill slits mostly restricted to sides, not extending to dorsal surface or ventral midline ....(13)

13 (12) Gill slits large, extending well above middle of body and slightly onto ventral surface; all gill slits anterior to pectoral fin base .... **LAMNIDAE**, page 75

13 Gill slits not so large, not extending much above middle of body or onto ventral surface; last 2 gill slits above pectoral fin base ....(14)

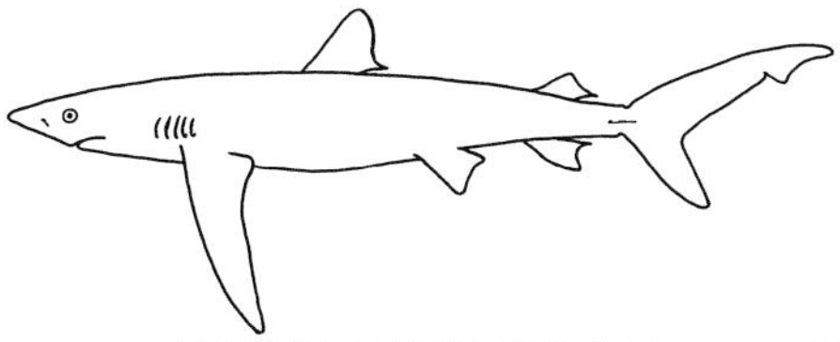

14 (13) Eyes round; low keel present on caudal peduncle; spiracles present or absent .... **CARCHARHINIDAE**, page 70

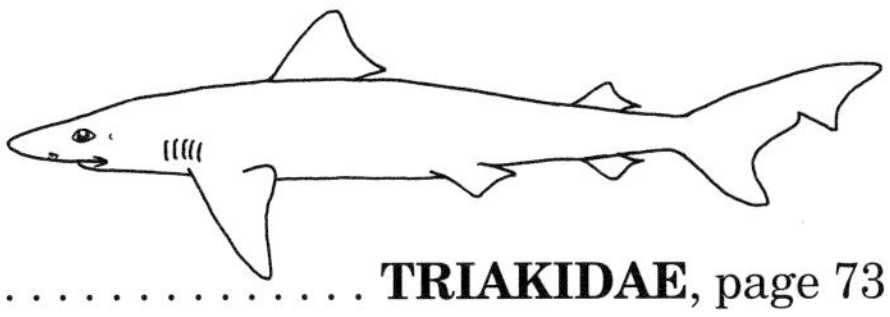

14 Eyes horizontally oval; no keel on caudal peduncle; spiracles present .... **TRIAKIDAE**, page 73

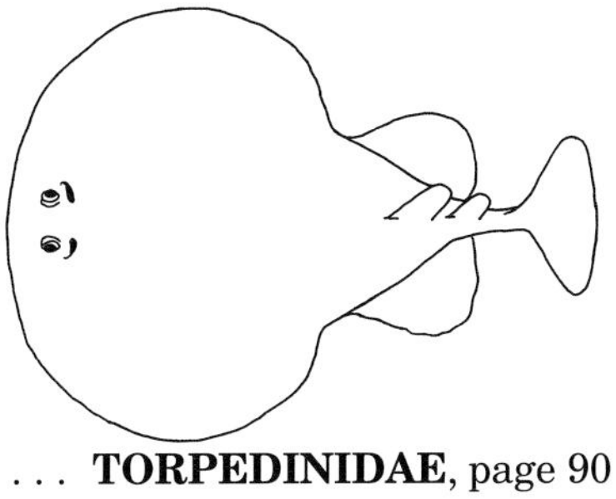

15 (6) Caudal fin well developed .... **TORPEDINIDAE**, page 90

15 Caudal fin absent or very small ....(16)

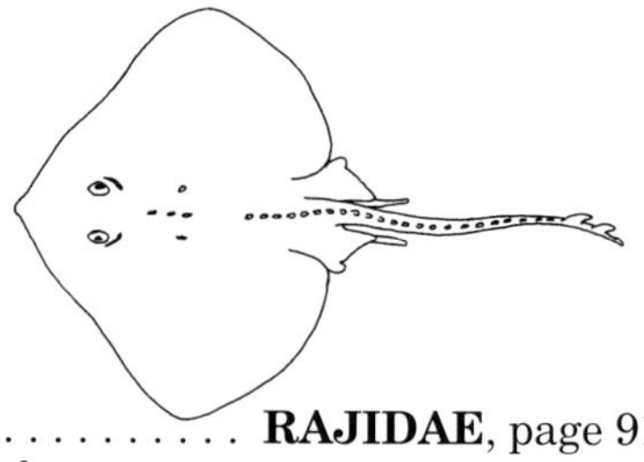

16 (15) Two dorsal fins, near tip of tail . . . . **RAJIDAE**, page 91

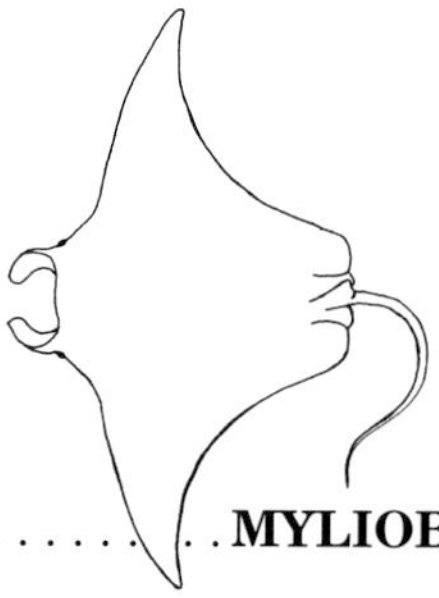

16 One dorsal fin, at base of tail . . . . **MYLIOBATIDAE**, page 108

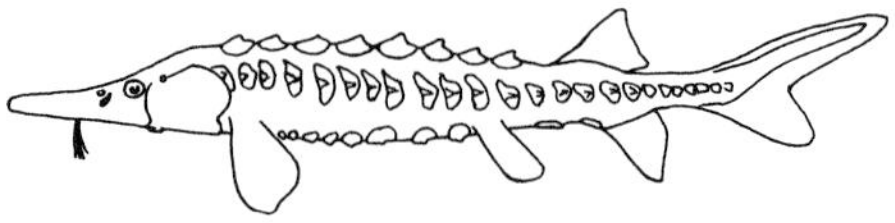

17 (4) Dorsal lobe of caudal fin distinctly larger than ventral lobe; 5 well-separated longitudinal rows of bony plates on body; mouth inferior, protrusible . . . . **ACIPENSERIDAE**, page 113

17 Dorsal lobe of caudal fin not obviously enlarged; without 5 well-separated longitudinal rows of bony plates on body; mouth not inferior and protrusible . . . . . . (18)

18 (17) Body shape variable but symmetrical, with one eye on each side and color similar on both sides . . . . (19)

18 Body compressed asymmetrically, with both eyes on same side and eyed side more strongly pigmented . . . . . . (115)

19 (18) Gill opening small, high on body, completely or mostly above pectoral fin; body short and deep; head and body laterally compressed . . . . (116)

19 Combination not as above . . . . (20)

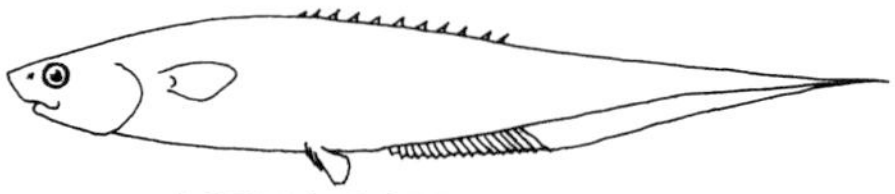

20 (19) Rayed dorsal fin represented by short, isolated spines . . . . **NOTACANTHIDAE**, page 116

20 Rayed dorsal fin not consisting only of isolated spines, or absent (adipose may be present) . . . . (21)

21 (20) Pelvic fins absent . . . . (22)

21 Pelvic fins present, may be modified as sucking disk . . . . . (45)

22 (21) Gill opening on side in front of pectoral base or on ventral surface below pectoral; no illicium on head . . . . . . (23)

22 Gill opening on side behind lower part of pectoral base; illicium on head in females . . . . (27)

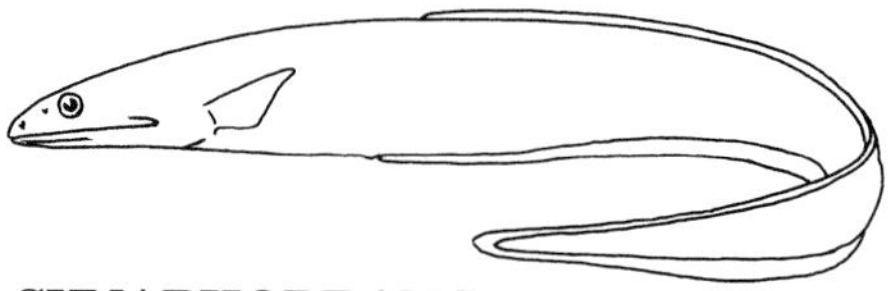

23 (22) Gill opening on ventral surface . . . . **SYNAPHOBRANCHIDAE**, page 120

23 Gill opening on side, may be high or low on body . . . . (24)

24 (23) Jaws long, slender, beaklike . . . . (25)

24 Jaws not long, slender, beaklike . . . . (29)

25 (24) Dorsal fin beginning on or just behind head . . . . **NEMICHTHYIDAE**, page 124

25 Dorsal fin beginning posterior to pectoral fins . . . . (26)

26 (25) Dorsal and anal fins decreasing in height posteriorly . . . . **SERRIVOMERIDAE**, page 128

26 Dorsal and anal fins increasing in height posteriorly . . . . **CYEMATIDAE**, page 130

27 (22) Cleft of mouth vertical to strongly oblique; 2 or 3 caruncles anterior to dorsal fin . . . . **CERATIIDAE**, page 300

27 Cleft of mouth horizontal or slightly oblique; no caruncles anterior to dorsal fin . . . . (28)

28 (27) Globose, with short caudal peduncle; illicium less than 60% of body length; illicium retractable . . . . **ONEIRODIDAE**, page 304

28 Elongate, with long caudal peduncle; illicium more than 60% of standard length; illicium not retractable . . . . **GIGANTACTINIDAE**, page 311

29 (24) Anal fin short-based, less than 25% of standard length, or absent . . . . (30)

29 Anal fin more than 25% of standard length . . . . (32)

30 (29) Dorsal fin extending from head to caudal fin; caudal fin asymmetrical, with dorsal lobe larger (adult only; juvenile has pelvic fins) . . . . **TRACHIPTERIDAE**, page 260

30 Dorsal fin short-based, located at about midbody or near caudal fin . . . . (31)

31 (30) Dorsal and anal fins opposite each other near caudal fin; skin loose and lacking scales, spinules, or other armor; mouth large, cleft extending way past eyes . . . . **CETOMIMIDAE**, page 323

31 Dorsal fin at about midbody, anal fin not easily discernible; dermal plates encircling body, giving armored look; mouth small, at end of elongate snout . . . . **SYNGNATHIDAE**, page 335

32 (29) Dorsal fin composed of spinous and soft-rayed portions, with shallow to deep notch between portions; large multifid cirrus over each eye (one species; others in family have pelvic fins) .... **COTTIDAE**, page 398

32 Dorsal fin composed of spines or soft rays, or both, but without notch if spinous and soft rays present; no multifid cirrus over each eye .... (33)

33 (32) Pectoral fins well developed; lower pectoral rays partly free (several species; others in family have pelvic disk) .... **LIPARIDAE**, page 571

33 Pectoral fins rudimentary to well developed; lower pectoral rays not partly free .... (34)

34 (33) Dorsal fin with soft rays only .... (35)

34 Dorsal fin with all spines or combination of stiff spines and soft rays .... (38)

35 (34) Dorsal and anal fins confluent with caudal fin .... (36)

35 Dorsal and anal fins not confluent with caudal fin .... (37)

36 (35) Body depth decreasing posteriorly; dorsal fin begins well anterior to midbody (several species; others in family have pelvic fins) .... **ZOARCIDAE**, page 671

36 Body depth greater posteriorly than anteriorly; dorsal fin begins at about midbody .... **SCYTALINIDAE**, page 787

37 (35) Numerous close-set diagonal creases on sides .... **AMMODYTIDAE**, page 795

37 No diagonal creases on sides (adult; juvenile has pelvic fins) .... **ICOSTEIDAE**, page 796

38 (34) Dorsal and anal fins confluent with caudal, tapering to point or filament .... (39)

38 Dorsal and anal fins separate from caudal, or confluent but distinct and not tapering to point or filament .... (40)

39 (38) Dorsal fin continuous from origin to caudal fin (one species; others in family have distinct caudal fins) .... **ANARHICHADIDAE**, page 781

39 Dorsal fin represented by isolated spines anteriorly .... **PTILICHTHYIDAE**, page 785

40 (38) Body depth at insertion of pectoral fin 11% of total length or less . . . . (41)

40 Body depth at insertion of pectoral fin 15% of total length or more . . . . (43)

41 (40) Mouth strongly oblique to vertical . . . . **CRYPTACANTHODIDAE**, page 770

41 Mouth horizontal . . . . (42)

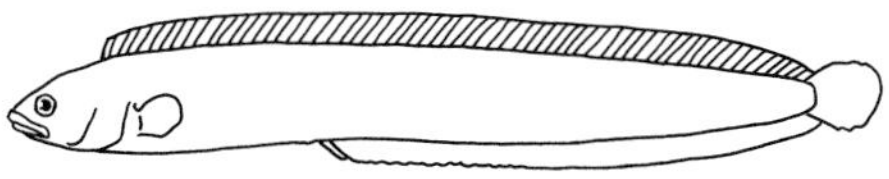

42 (41) Distance from tip of snout to anal fin origin less than distance from anal fin origin to base of caudal fin (part; others in family have pelvic fins) . . . . **STICHAEIDAE**, page 742

42 Distance from tip of snout to anal fin origin more than distance from anal fin origin to base of caudal fin; or if preanal distance about same or less, head has broad dark band through eye to lower cheek followed by broad pale band (part; others in family have pelvic fins) . . . . **PHOLIDAE**, page 773

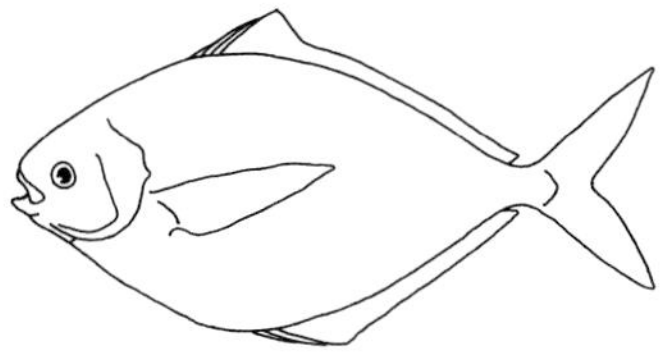

43 (40) Caudal fin forked; first few dorsal and anal fin spines higher than rest of fin . . . . **STROMATEIDAE**, page 814

43 Caudal fin truncate or rounded; first few dorsal and anal elements not higher than rest of fin . . . . (44)

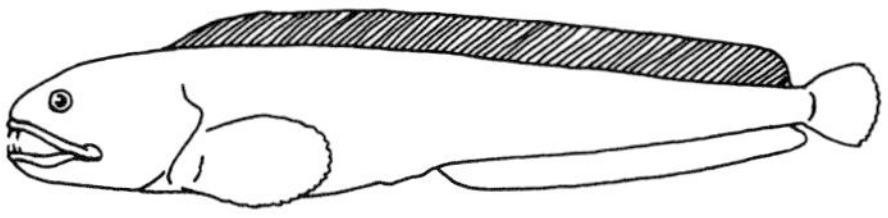

44 (43) Gill membranes attached to isthmus; caudal peduncle narrow (two species; other in family has tail tapering to point) . . . . **ANARHICHADIDAE**, page 781

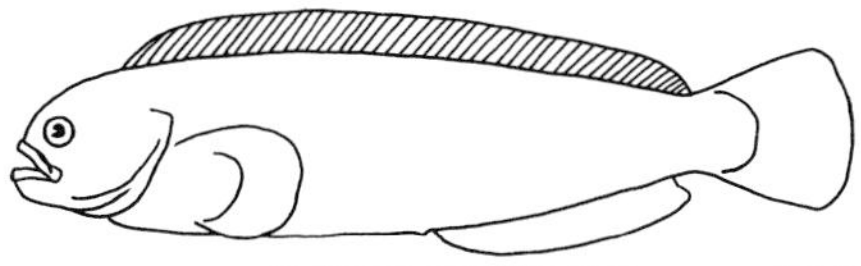

44 Gill membranes united, and free from isthmus; caudal peduncle deep . . . . **ZAPRORIDAE**, page 786

45 (21) Pelvic fins modified to form cone or sucking disk . . . . (46)

45 Pelvic fins not modified to form cone or sucking disk . . . . . (49)

46 (45) Pelvic fins modified to form cone . . . . **GOBIIDAE**, page 800

46 Pelvic fins modified to form sucking disk . . . . (47)

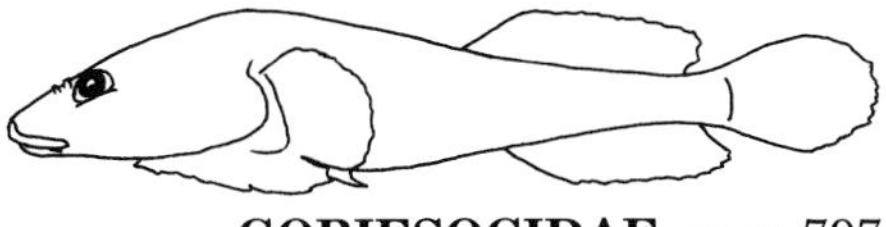

47 (46) Sucking disk formed of recognizable anterior and posterior parts . . . . **GOBIESOCIDAE**, page 797

47 Sucking disk similar anteriorly and posteriorly . . . . (48)

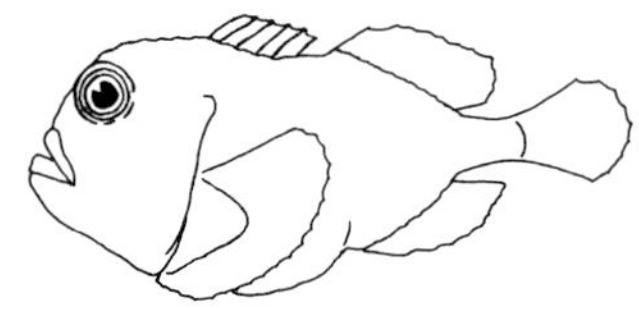

48 (47) Two dorsal fins, or one dorsal fin placed far back on body; mostly globose fishes, many with spiny tubercles .... **CYCLOPTERIDAE**, page 555

48 One dorsal fin, originating on or near head; mostly elongate fishes with no tubercles or prickles (most species in family; others without sucking disk) .... **LIPARIDAE**, page 571

49 (45) Pelvic fins abdominal (pelvic girdle without bony connection to pectoral girdle) ....(50)

49 Pelvic fins thoracic (pelvic girdle with bony connection to pectoral girdle) ....(78)

50 (49) One fin on back ....(51)

50 Two fins on back ....(64)

51 (50) Dorsal fin with rays absent, dorsal adipose fin present ....**ANOTOPTERIDAE**, page 240

51 Dorsal fin with rays present ....(52)

52 (51) Dorsal fin closer to caudal fin than to head ....(53)

52 Dorsal fin at about midbody ....(61)

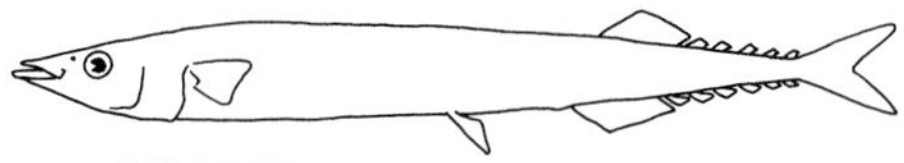

53 (52) Finlets present posterior to dorsal fin ....**SCOMBERESOCIDAE**, page 314

53 Finlets absent ....(54)

54 (53) Snout depressed; freshwater habitat ....(55)

54 Snout not depressed; marine habitat ....(56)

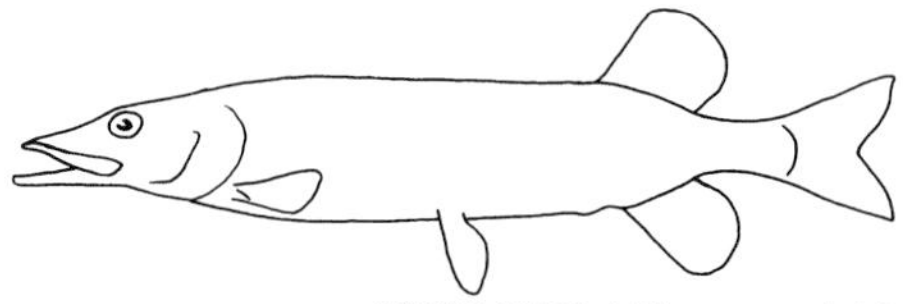

55 (54) Snout long, more than 2 times eye diameter; pectoral fin small and oblong, with 14–17 rays; caudal fin forked .... **ESOCIDAE**, page 143

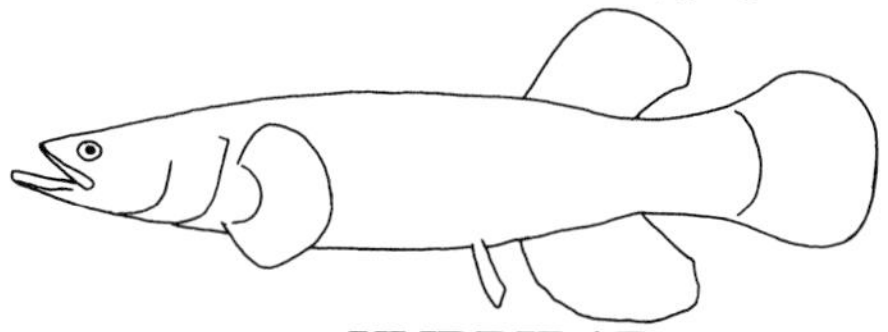

55 Snout short, less than 2 times eye diameter; pectoral fin large and round, with 29–38 rays; caudal fin round .... **UMBRIDAE**, page 145

56 (54) Maxillae form major portion of border of upper jaw in gape of mouth ....(57)

56 Premaxillae form major portion of border of upper jaw in gape of mouth ....(60)

57 (56) Shoulder apparatus (produces luminous fluid) present, with short tubular opening above pectoral fin base . . . . **PLATYTROCTIDAE**, page 157

57 Shoulder apparatus not present . . . . (58)

58 (57) Photophores absent . . . . **ALEPOCEPHALIDAE**, page 165

58 Photophores present . . . . (59)

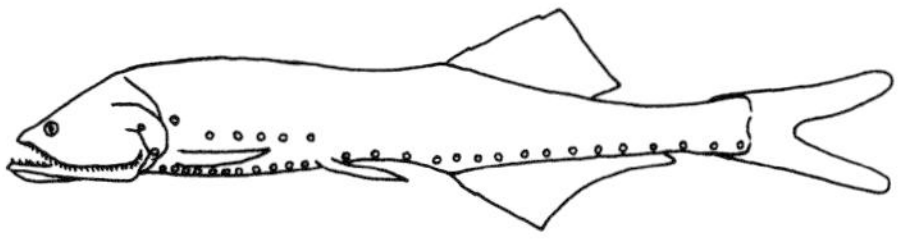

59 (58) Dorsal and anal fins posterior to midbody, with origins close to midbody; chin barbel absent . . . . **GONOSTOMATIDAE**, page 210

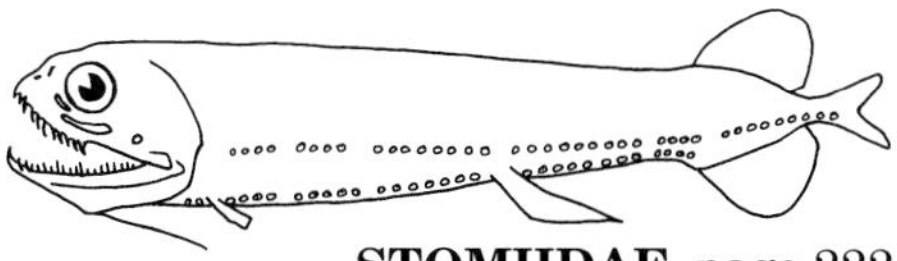

59 Dorsal and anal fins close to caudal fin, with origins far posterior to midbody; chin barbel present (may be very small, almost indiscernible) (all but one species in family; other has adipose fins, other differences) . . . . **STOMIIDAE**, page 222

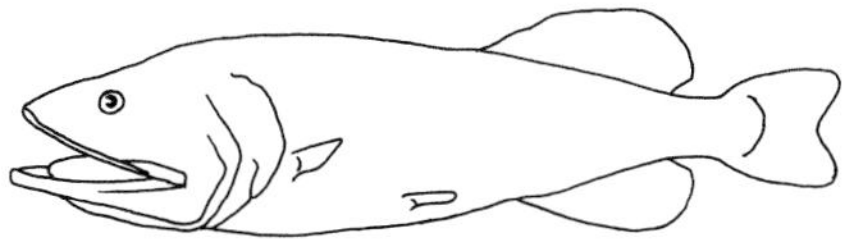

60 (56) Jaw teeth in broad villiform bands; body elongate, broad anteriorly; head depth not noticeably greater than length . . . . **BARBOURISIIDAE**, page 321

60 Jaw teeth long, fanglike, widely spaced; body short, strongly compressed, deep anteriorly; head depth noticeably greater than length . . . . **ANOPLOGASTRIDAE**, page 325

61 (52) Dorsal fin rays 14–21; branchiostegal rays 6 or more on each side; gill rakers long; marine habitat . . . . (62)

61 Dorsal fin rays 8–11; branchiostegal rays 3 on each side; gill rakers short; freshwater habitat . . . . (63)

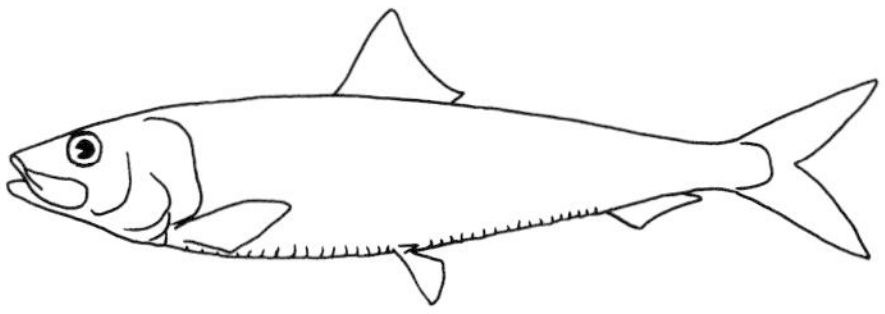

62 (61) Scutes present along belly; maxillae not extending posteriorly past eyes . . . . **CLUPEIDAE**, page 132

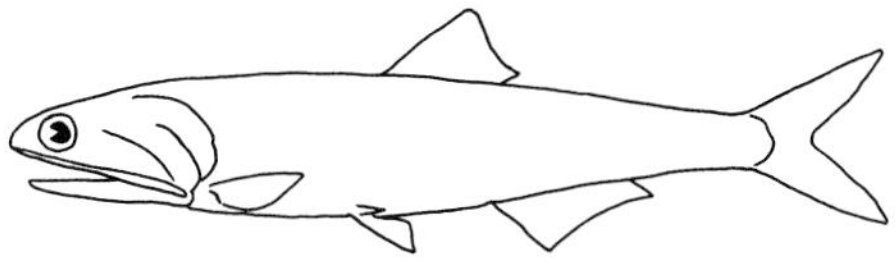

62 No scutes along belly; maxillae extending posteriorly far past eyes . . . . **ENGRAULIDAE**, page 137

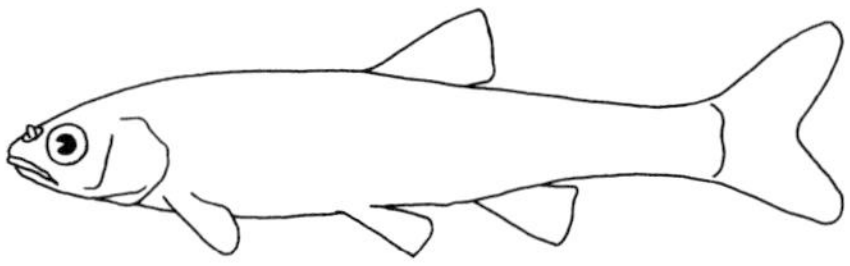

63 (61) Mouth subterminal; lips thin, without papillae . . . . **CYPRINIDAE**, page 140

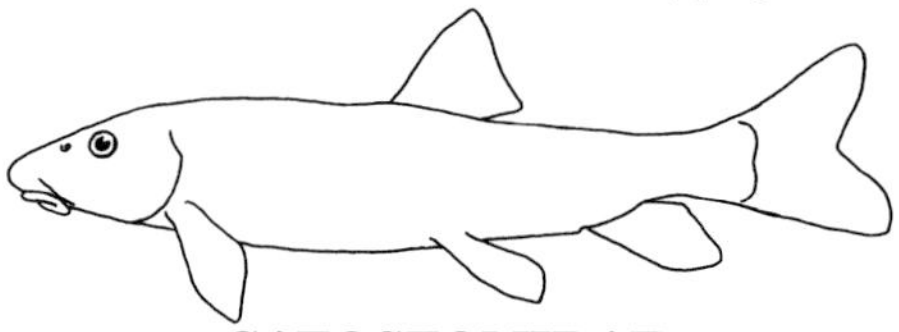

63 Mouth ventral; lips thick, covered with papillae . . . . **CATOSTOMIDAE**, page 142

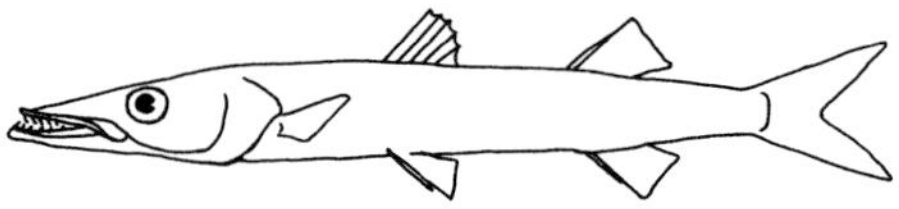

64 (50) Two fins on back, both with rays . . . . **SPHYRAENIDAE**, page 803

64 Two fins on back, one rayed and one adipose . . . . (65)

65 (64) Dorsal adipose fin with longer base than rayed dorsal fin base, and may be indistinct; photophores present, some arranged in parallel rows . . . . (66)

65 Dorsal adipose fin with shorter base than rayed dorsal fin base; photophores absent or present; if photophores present on body, not arranged in parallel rows . . . . (67)

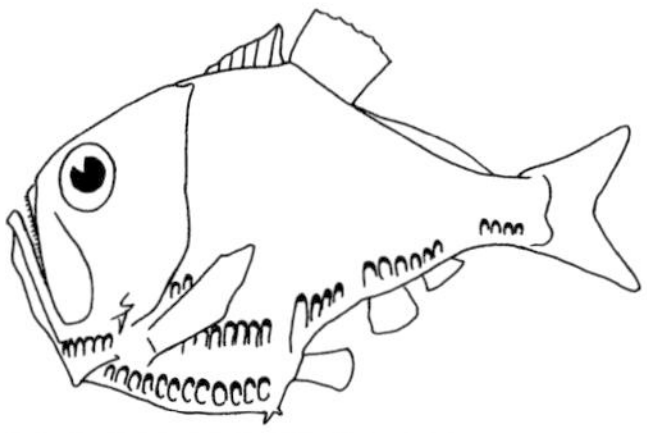

66 (65) Vertebral processes protrude and form dorsal "blade" that can resemble a spinous dorsal fin; body short, deep, strongly compressed; teeth needlelike and small . . . . **STERNOPTYCHIDAE**, page 219

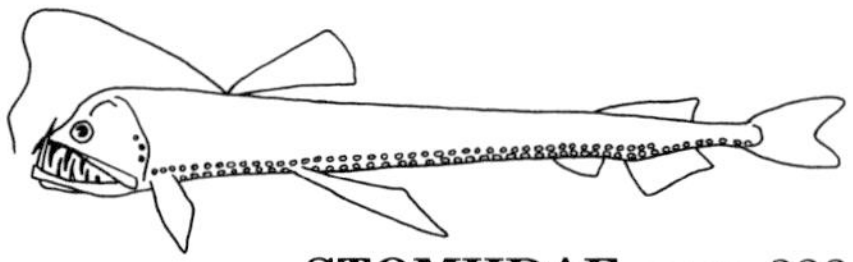

66 First dorsal fin ray long and whiplike; body elongate; teeth long and fanglike (one species; others in family lacking dorsal adipose fin) . . . . **STOMIIDAE**, page 222

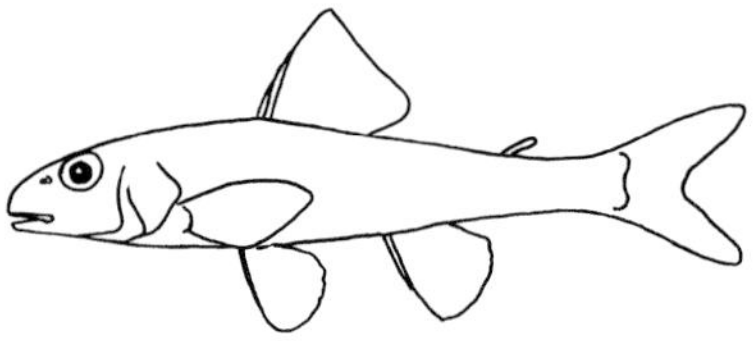

67 (65) Dorsal, anal, and pelvic fins with spines (although weak) anteriorly; freshwater habitat . . . . **PERCOPSIDAE**, page 262

67 No spines in fins; freshwater or marine habitat . . . . (68)

68 (67) Scales large and highly deciduous or absent; marine habitat . . . . (69)

68 Scales very small to large, not deciduous; freshwater or marine habitat . . . . (72)

69 (68) Mouth small, maxilla not extending below eye past front of pupil . . . . (70)

69 Mouth large, maxilla extending below eye to mideye or well past eye . . . . (73)

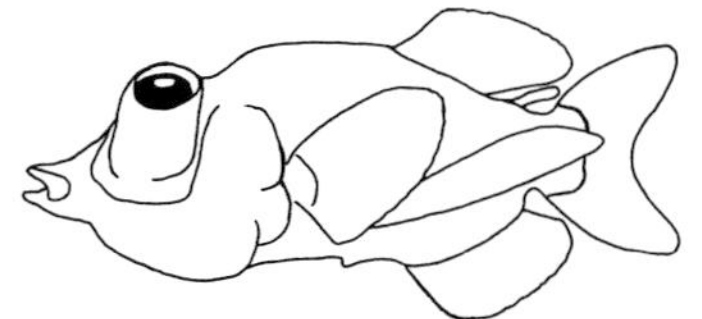

70 (69) Snout produced, with small mouth at end, maxilla not nearly reaching eye; eyes tubular, directed dorsally . . . . **OPISTHOPROCTIDAE**, page 154

70 Snout not produced, mouth reaching or nearly reaching front of eye; eyes not tubular, directed laterally . . . .(71)

71 (70) Branchiostegal rays 3; anal fin rays 8–11 . . . . **MICROSTOMATIDAE**, page 147

71 Branchiostegal rays 2; anal fin rays 10–28 . . . . **BATHYLAGIDAE**, page 149

72 (68) Pelvic axillary process absent . . . . **OSMERIDAE**, page 169

72 Pelvic axillary process present . . . . **SALMONIDAE**, page 178

73 (69) Body long and slender, depth less than 15% SL . . . .(74)

73 Body relatively short, depth more than 15% SL . . . .(77)

74 (73) Eyes directed upward, each with pearly area . . . . **SCOPELARCHIDAE**, page 229

74 Eyes directed laterally, without pearly area . . . .(75)

75 (74) Base of rayed dorsal fin longer than head length . . . . **ALEPISAURIDAE**, page 234

75 Base of rayed dorsal fin shorter than head length . . . .(76)

76 (75) Body almost round anteriorly, compressed posteriorly; eyes elliptical; rayed dorsal fin at about midbody . . . . **NOTOSUDIDAE**, page 232

76 Body compressed anteriorly, oval to round posteriorly; eyes round; rayed dorsal fin posterior to midbody . . . . **PARALEPIDIDAE**, page 236

77 (73) Photophores absent; eyes small, less than 15% of head length; anal fin origin far behind dorsal fin base . . . . **NEOSCOPELIDAE**, page 242

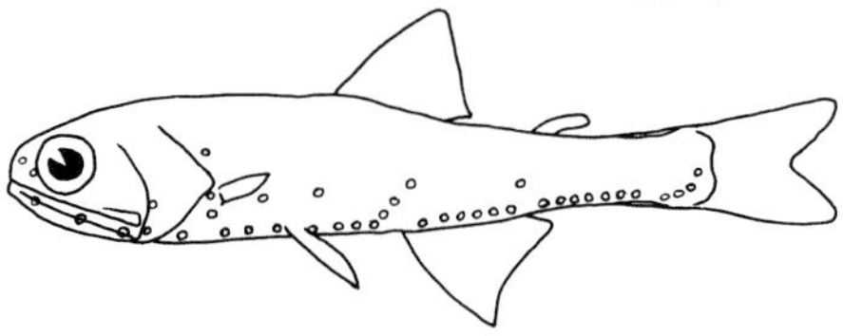

77 Photophores present; eyes large, more than 15% of head length; anal fin origin below base of dorsal fin or below or close behind dorsal fin insertion . . . . **MYCTOPHIDAE**, page 244

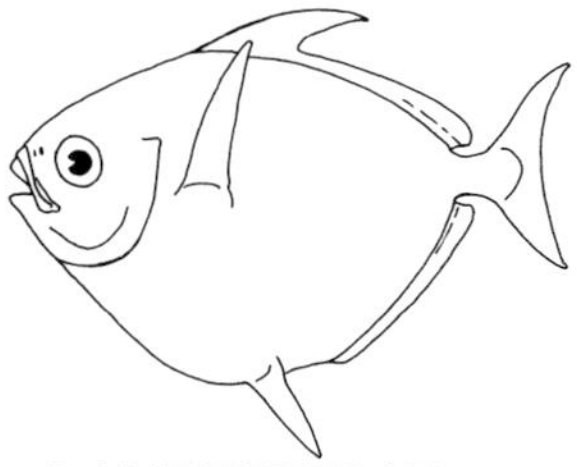

78 (49) Body short, deep, compressed; covered with silver spots; pectoral and pelvic fins long and falcate . . . . **LAMPRIDIDAE**, page 258

78 Combination not as above . . . . (79)

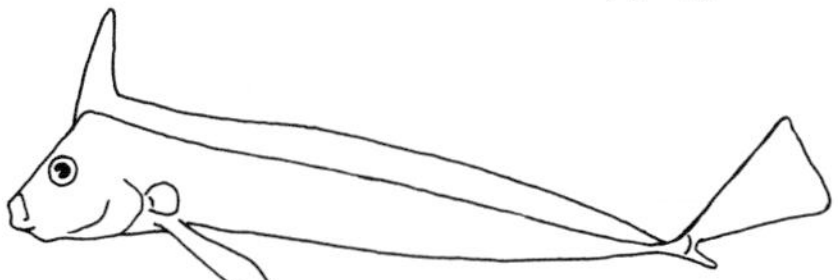

79 (78) Anal fin absent . . . . **TRACHIPTERIDAE**, page 260

79 Anal fin present . . . . (80)

80 (79) Pelvic fins with 1 spine and more than 5 soft rays . . . . (81)

80 Pelvic fins with all soft rays or 1 spine and 5 or fewer soft rays . . . . (82)

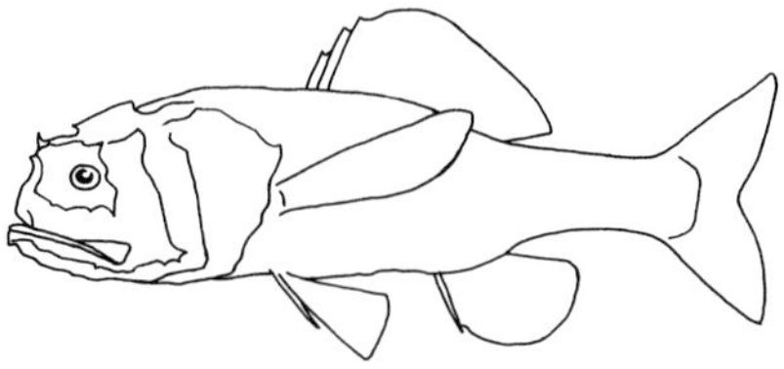

81 (80) Body elongate; eyes small, less than 25% HL . . . . **MELAMPHAIDAE**, page 316

81 Body short and deep; eyes large, more than 33% HL . . . . **OREOSOMATIDAE**, page 327

82 (80) Bony bridge (suborbital stay) connecting bones at lower part of eye to operculum, just under skin . . . . (97)

82 No suborbital stay . . . . (83)

83 (82) Pelvic fins with all soft rays or 1 spine and fewer than 5 soft rays . . . . (84)

83 Pelvic fins with 1 spine and 5 soft rays . . . . (103)

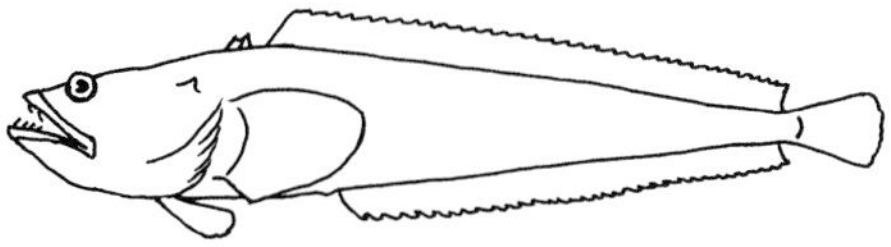

84 (83) Photophores present on sides and belly . . . . **BATRACHOIDIDAE**, page 298

84 No photophores on body . . . . (85)

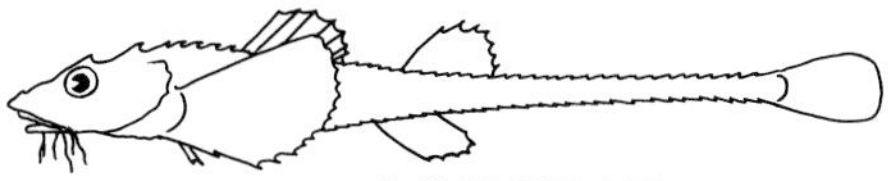

85 (84) Body encased in bony plates .... **AGONIDAE**, page 525

85 Body not encased in bony plates ....(86)

86 (85) Dorsal fin preceded by 2 or more isolated spines ....(87)

86 Dorsal fin not preceded by isolated spines ....(88)

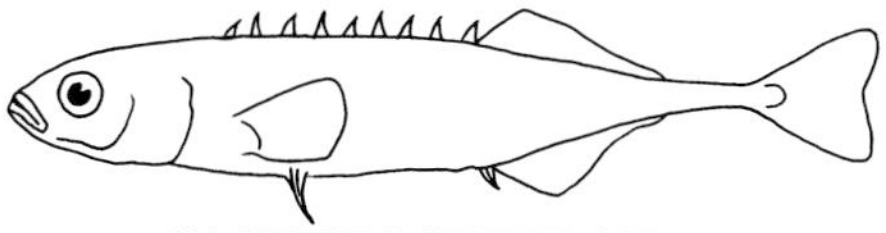

87 (86) Dorsal fin preceded by fewer than 15 isolated spines; snout not prolonged and tubular .... **GASTEROSTEIDAE**, page 332

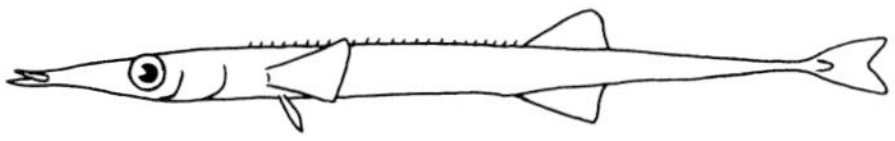

87 Dorsal fin preceded by more than 20 isolated spines; snout prolonged and tubular .... **AULORHYNCHIDAE**, page 330

88 (86) One dorsal fin ....(89)

88 More than one dorsal fin ....(94)

89 (88) No obvious spines in dorsal fin ....(90)

89 Dorsal fin wholly of spines ....(93)

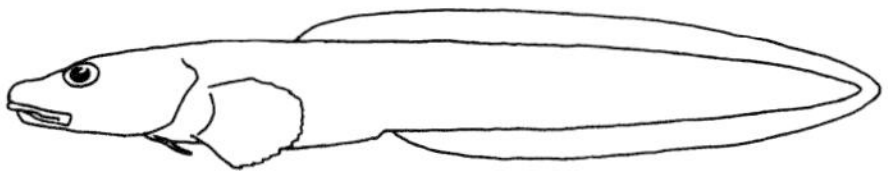

90 (89) Gill membranes joined to isthmus (several species; others in family lack pelvic fins) .... **ZOARCIDAE**, page 671

90 Gill membranes free or mostly free from isthmus ....(91)

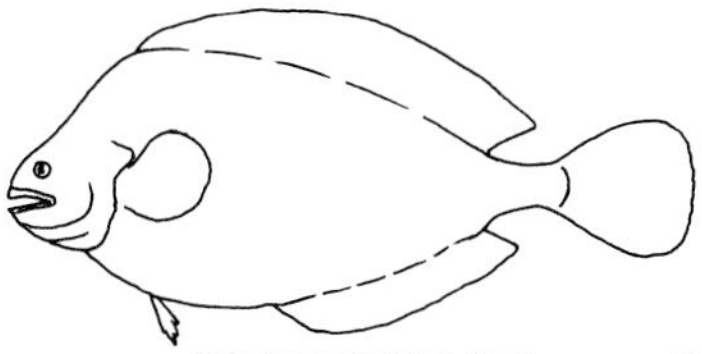

91 (90) Body deep; dorsal fin rays fewer than 60 (juvenile only; adults lack pelvic fins) .... **ICOSTEIDAE**, page 796

91 Body elongate; dorsal fin rays more than 70 ....(92)

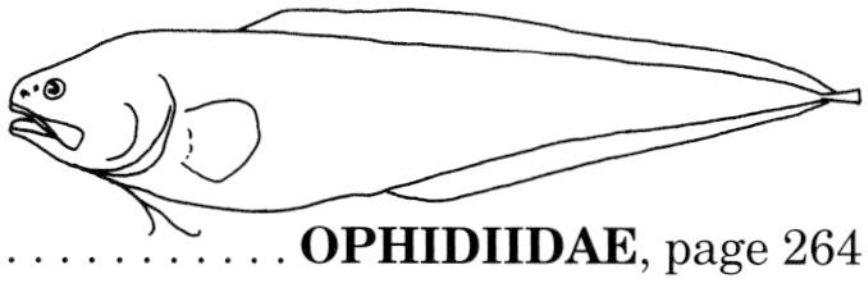

92 (91) Basibranchial teeth present; pores of sensory system on snout and lower jaw not prominent .... **OPHIDIIDAE**, page 264

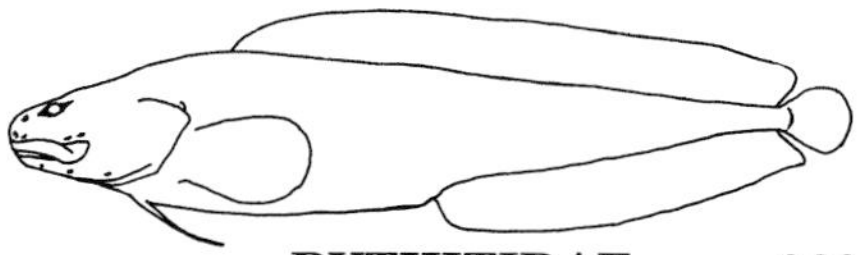

92 Basibranchial teeth absent; pores of sensory system on snout and lower jaw prominent .... **BYTHITIDAE**, page 266

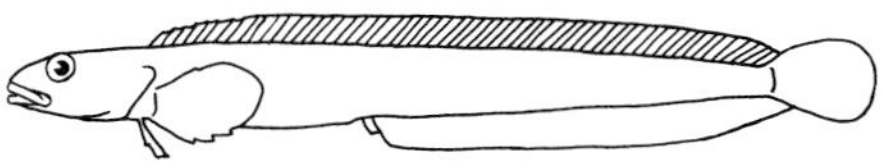

93 (89) Distance from snout to anal origin less than from anal origin to base of caudal fin; pelvic fins with 1 spine and 2–4 rays (others in family lack pelvic fins) .... **STICHAEIDAE**, page 742

93 Distance from snout to anal origin *usually* more than from anal origin to base of caudal fin; pelvic fins with 1 spine and 1 ray (others in family lack pelvic fins) .... **PHOLIDAE**, page 773

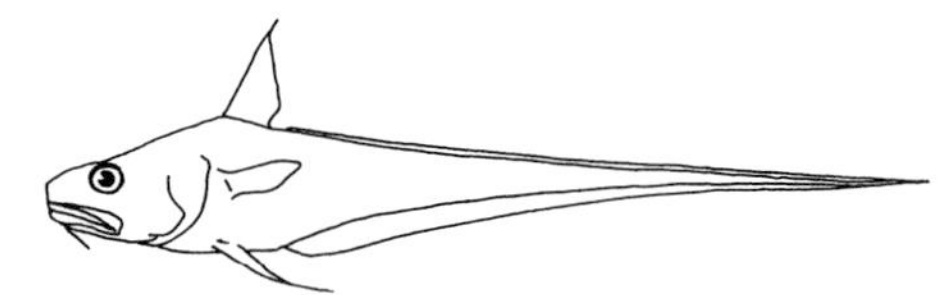

94 (88) No caudal fin; dorsal and anal fins tapering to point . . . . **MACROURIDAE**, page 269

94 Caudal fin present, and separate from dorsal and anal fins . . . . (95)

95 (94) Top of head with V-shaped crest, apex of V pointing posteriorly . . . . **MERLUCCIIDAE**, page 285

95 No V-shaped crest on top of head . . . . (96)

96 (95) Two dorsal fins, with first dorsal above pectoral fin; one anal fin, sometimes deeply notched and appearing to be two fins . . . .**MORIDAE**, page 280

96 Two dorsal fins, with first dorsal posterior to pectoral fin, and one anal fin (freshwater habitat); or three dorsal fins and two anal fins (marine habitat) . . . . **GADIDAE**, page 287

97 (82) Body uniformly covered with typical scales . . . . (98)

97 Body not uniformly covered with typical scales . . . . (100)

98 (97) Anal fin with 3 strong (stiff, robust) spines and 4–11 soft rays . . . . **SCORPAENIDAE**, page 337

98 Anal fin with 0–3 weak (flexible, thin) spines and 11–28 soft rays . . . . (99)

99 (98) Anterior nostril on each side well developed, posterior nostril reduced to small pore or absent . . . . **HEXAGRAMMIDAE**, page 387

99 Both nostrils on each side well developed . . . .**ANOPLOPOMATIDAE**, page 384

100 (97) Head large, about half of standard length; snout distinctly elongate; bilateral blunt bony ridges on top of head; lower pectoral fin rays free . . . . **RHAMPHOCOTTIDAE**, page 396

100 Combination not as above . . . . (101)

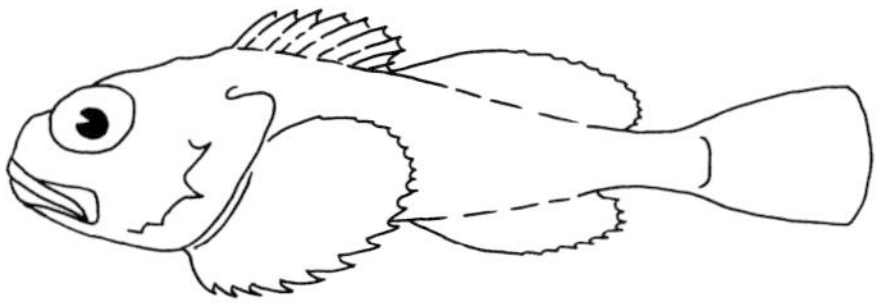

101 (100) Seven branchiostegal rays on each side; bases of dorsal and anal fins usually covered with skin and gelatinous tissue . . . . **PSYCHROLUTIDAE**, page 514

101 Six branchiostegal rays on each side; bases of dorsal and anal fins usually not covered with skin and gelatinous tissue . . . . (102)

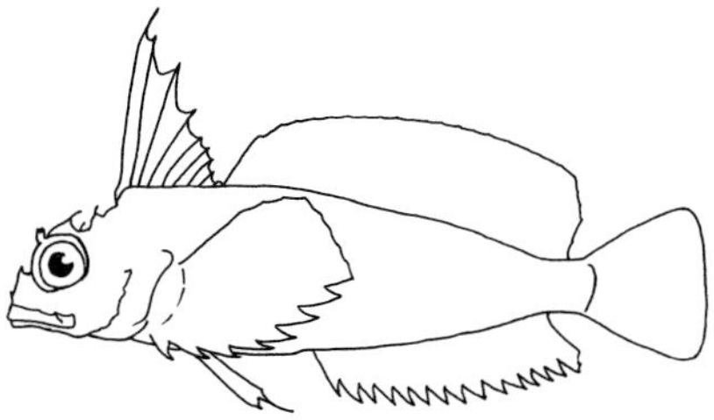

102 (101) Body densely covered with prickles (skin-covered spines, each on a buried platelike scale); no rows of typical scales or large, multispined platelike scales . . . . **HEMITRIPTERIDAE**, page 505

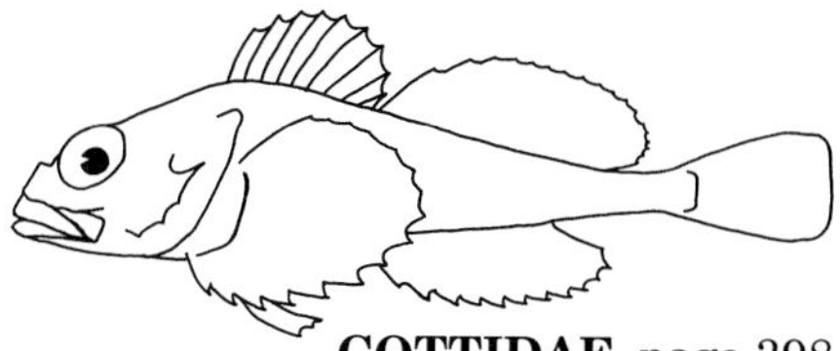

102 Body not densely covered with prickles, although widely scattered prickles or prickles in more or less definite arrangements, such as above or below lateral line, may be present; some species with rows of typical scales or multispined platelike scales . . . . **COTTIDAE**, page 398

103 (83) One fin on back, composed wholly of soft rays (first several rays may be unbranched) . . . . (104)

103 Two fins on back; or one fin with 4 or more stiff spines, usually set off from rest of fin by notch or other obvious differentiation . . . . (107)

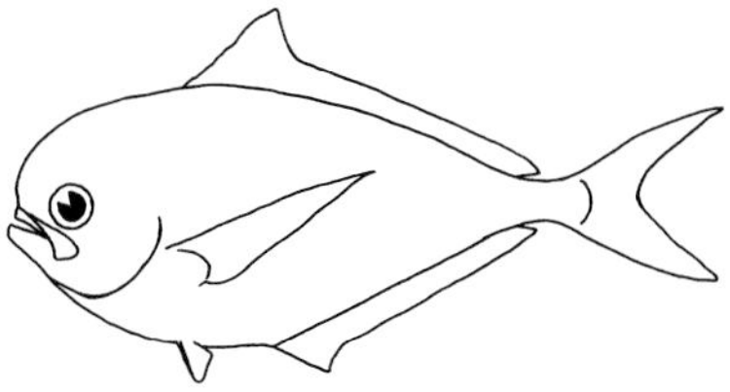

104 (103) Caudal fin forked . . . . **BRAMIDAE**, page 651

104 Caudal fin slightly emarginate to rounded . . . . (105)

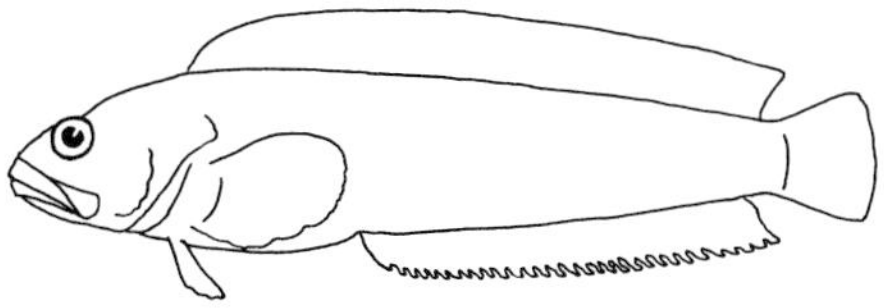

105 (104) Dorsal and anal fin bases not covered with flesh; dorsal and anal fins nearly even in height for their full length . . . . **BATHYMASTERIDAE**, page 665

105 Dorsal and anal fin bases covered with flesh; dorsal and anal fins not same height along full length . . . . (106)

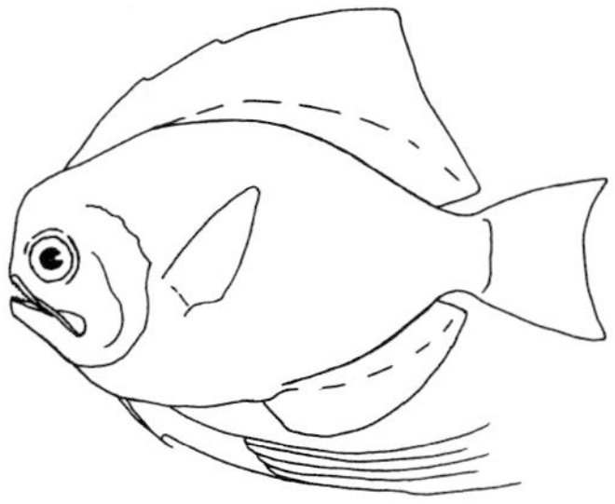

106 (105) Dorsal fin origin on head; pelvic fin rays drawn out as long filaments . . . . **CARISTIIDAE**, page 654

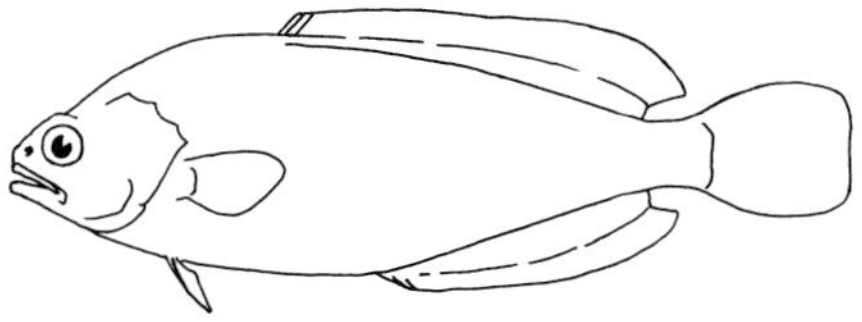

106 Dorsal fin origin posterior to head; pelvic fin rays not drawn out as long filaments . . . . **CENTROLOPHIDAE**, page 812

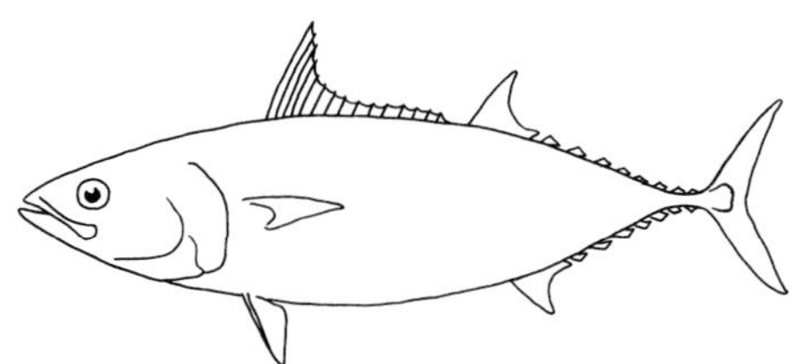

107 (103) Second dorsal fin followed by 4 or more finlets . . . . **SCOMBRIDAE**, page 804

107 Second dorsal fin not followed by 4 or more finlets . . . . . (108)

108 (107) Dorsal fins separated by distance about same as or greater than length of first dorsal base; anal fin with 3 spines and 7 or 8 rays . . . . **ACROPOMATIDAE**, page 646

108 Dorsal fins separate or spinous and rayed portions continuous; if separate, anal fin with more than 20 rays . . . . (109)

109 (108) Anal fin with more than 20 rays . . . . (110)

109 Anal fin with fewer than 20 rays . . . . (113)

110 (109) Lips fringed; mouth strongly oblique to vertical . . . . **TRICHODONTIDAE**, page 792

110 Lips not fringed; mouth horizontal . . . . (111)

111 (110) Mouth large, extending well past eyes . . . . **CHIASMODONTIDAE**, page 788

111 Mouth not large, not extending past front of eyes . . . . . . (112)

112 (111) Body elongate; two dorsal fins . . . . **CARANGIDAE**, page 648

112 Body deep; one dorsal fin . . . . **EMBIOTOCIDAE**, page 660

113 (109) Caudal fin forked; keels on each side of caudal peduncle . . . . **TETRAGONURIDAE**, page 813

113 Caudal fin slightly emarginate to slightly rounded; no keels on caudal peduncle . . . . (114)

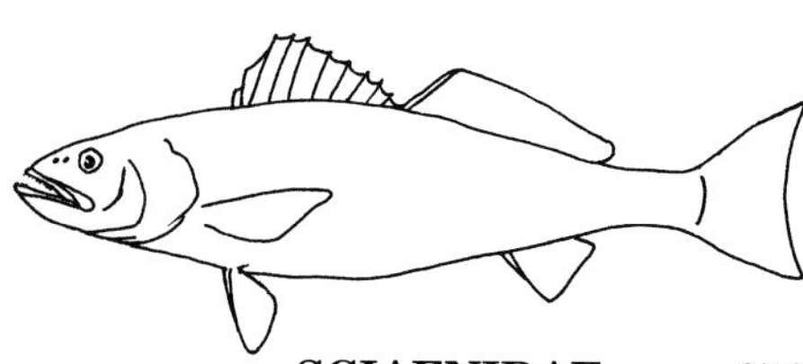

114 (113) Body elongate; head not encased in exposed, striated bone . . . . **SCIAENIDAE**, page 656

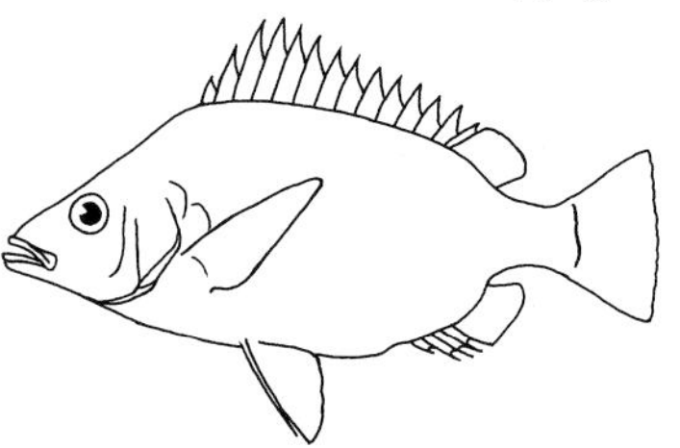

114 Body deep; head encased in exposed, striated bone . . . . **PENTACEROTIDAE**, page 658

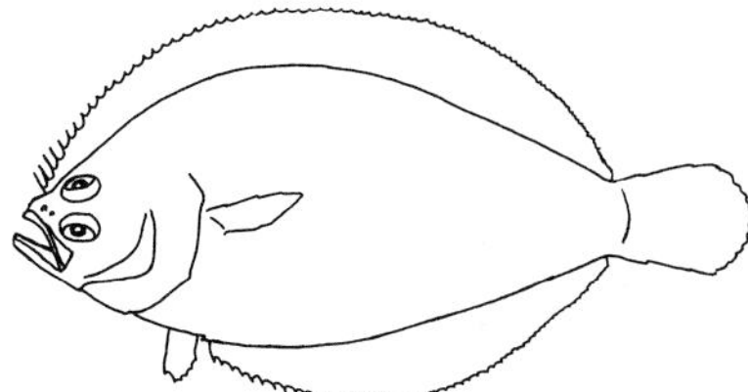

115 (18) Pelvic fins asymmetrically placed, with fin for eyed side on ridge of abdomen; eyes and color on left side of body . . . . **PARALICHTHYIDAE**, page 815

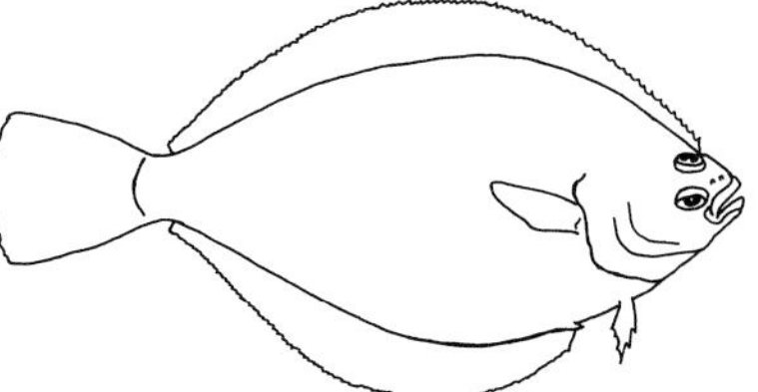

115 Pelvic fins symmetrically placed on sides of body; eyes and color usually on right side of body . . . . **PLEURONECTIDAE**, page 818

116 (19) Caudal peduncle with caudal fin present; 2 dorsal fins . . . . **BALISTIDAE**, page 850

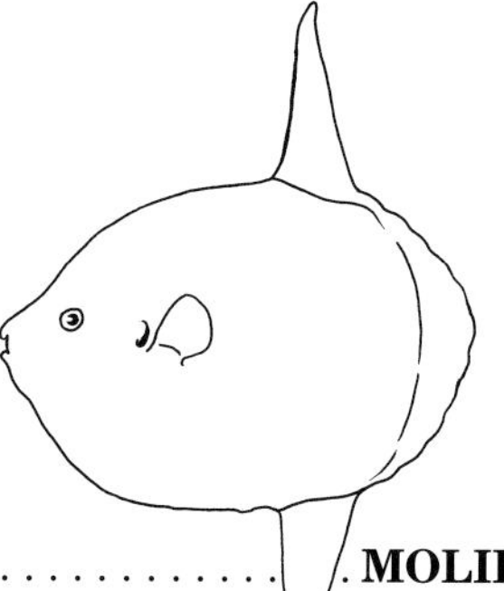

116 No caudal peduncle, no distinct caudal fin; 1 dorsal fin . . . . **MOLIDAE**, page 852

Milton Love

Pacific hagfish
Eptatretus stoutii

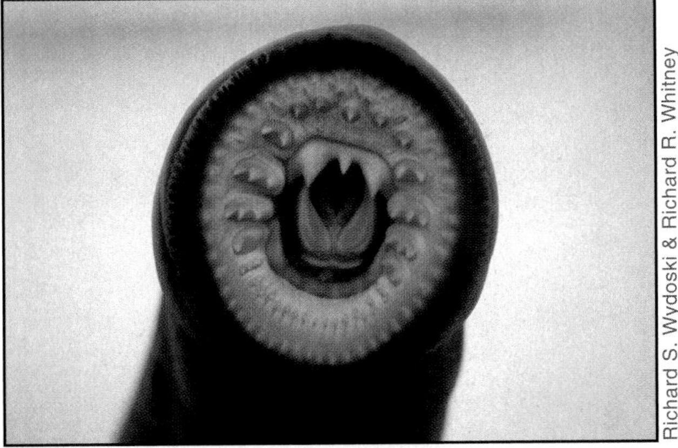
Richard S. Wydoski & Richard R. Whitney

Pacific lamprey
Lampetra tridentata

Marc C. Chamberlain

blue shark
Prionace glauca

Richard R. Straty

salmon shark
Lamna ditropis

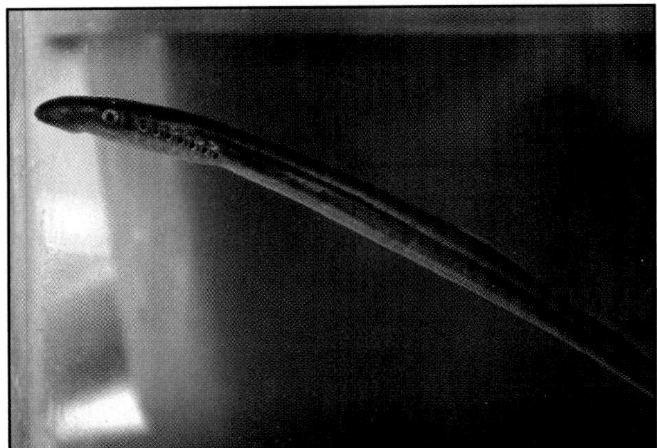
Jared Figurski

Pacific lamprey
Lampetra tridentata

Donald E. Kramer

spotted ratfish
Hydrolagus colliei

Donald E. Kramer

brown cat shark
Apristurus brunneus

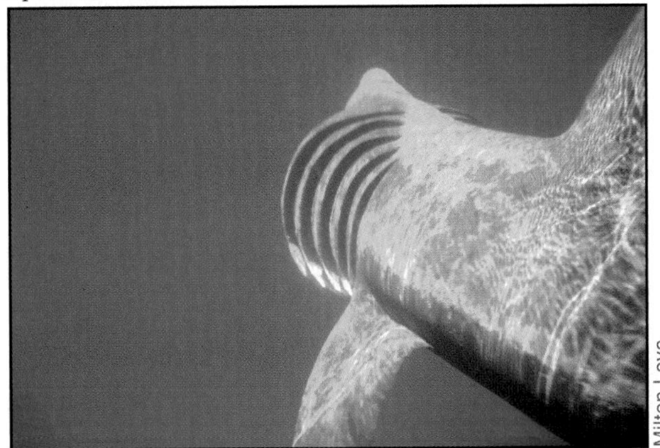
Milton Love

basking shark
Cetorhinus maximus

bluntnose sixgill shark
Hexanchus griseus

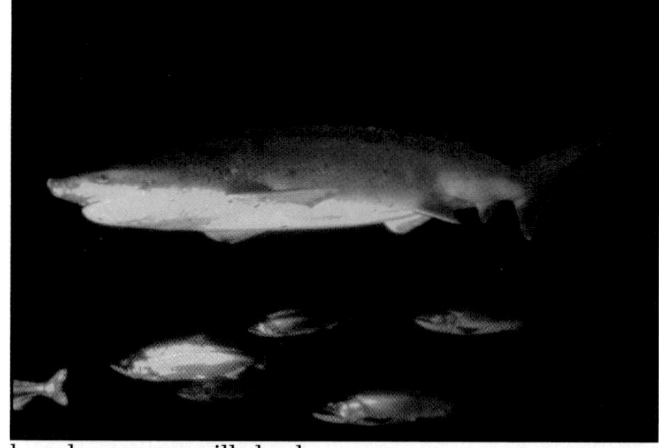

broadnose sevengill shark
Notorynchus cepedianus (not confirmed from Alaska)

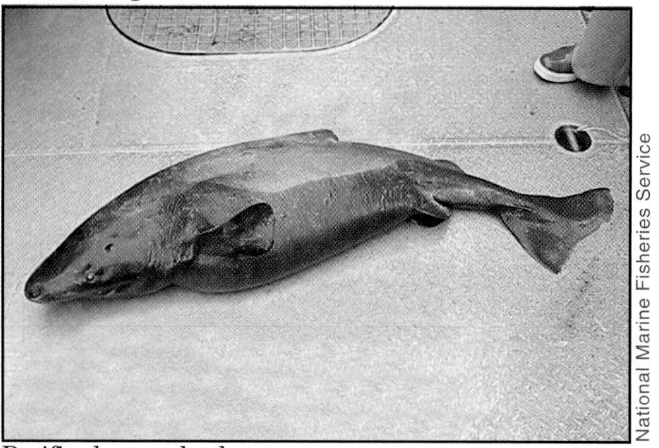

Pacific sleeper shark
Somniosus pacificus

spiny dogfish
Squalus acanthias

Pacific angel shark
Squatina californica (not confirmed from Alaska)

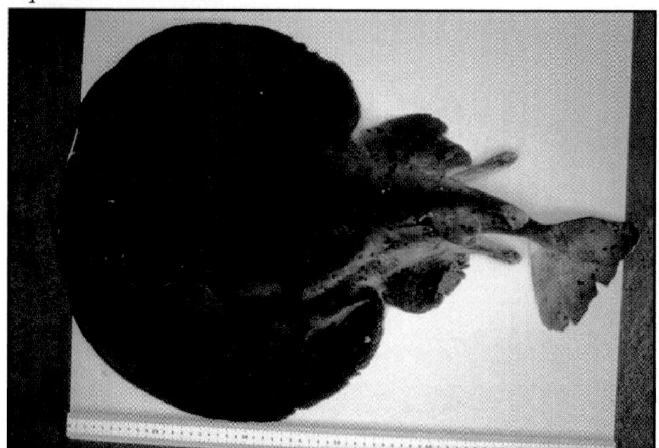

Pacific electric ray
Torpedo californica (not known from Alaska)

big skate (juvenile)
Raja binoculata

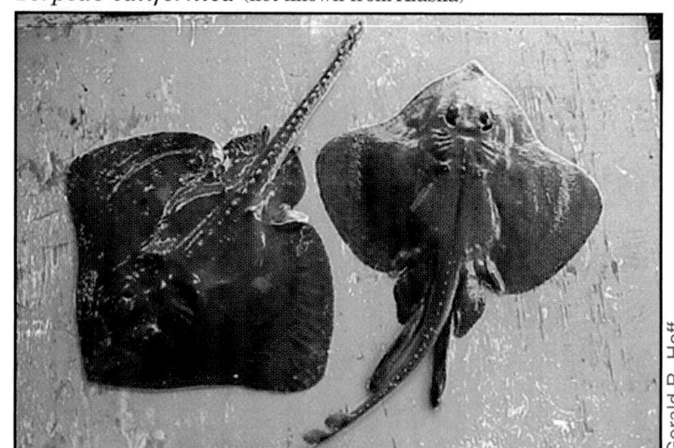

Alaska skate (left) and sandpaper skate (right)
Bathyraja parmifera and *B. interrupta*

Plate II

Gerald R. Hoff & James Wilder Orr

Okhotsk skate
Bathyraja violacea

Richard S. Wydoski & Richard R. Whitney

white sturgeon
Acipenser transmontanus

Donald E. Kramer

Pacific herring
Clupea pallasii

Milton Love

northern anchovy
Engraulis mordax

Richard S. Wydoski & Richard R. Whitney

green sturgeon
Acipenser medirostris

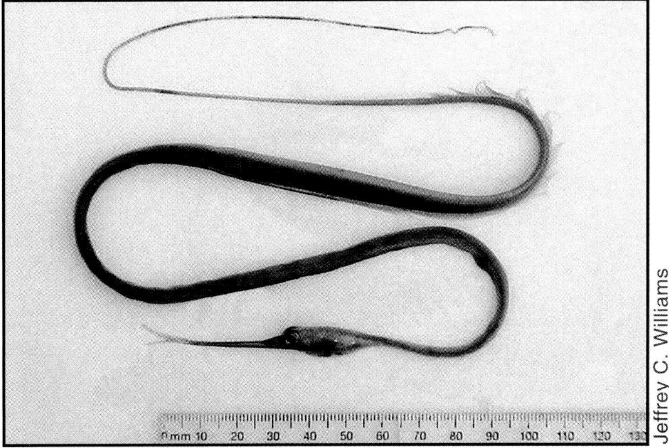

Jeffrey C. Williams

slender snipe eel
Nemichthys scolopaceus

Donald E. Kramer

American shad
Alosa sapidissima

John F. Scarola

lake chub
Couesius plumbeus

Randy J. Brown

longnose sucker
Catostomus catostomus

Randy J. Brown

northern pike
Esox lucius

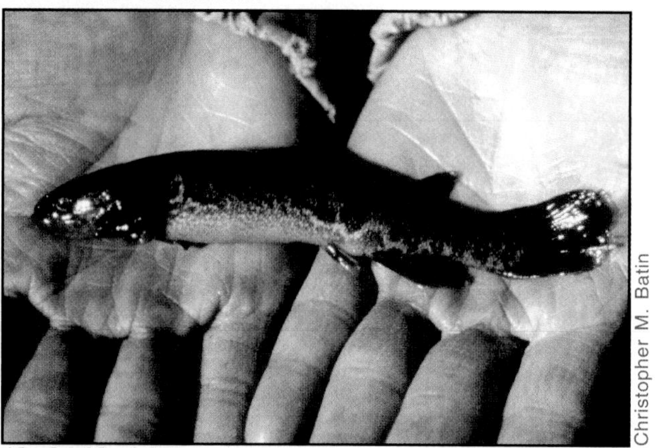
Christopher M. Batin

Alaska blackfish
Dallia pectoralis

Gerald R. Hoff

capelin
Mallotus villosus

National Marine Fisheries Service

surf smelt
Hypomesus pretiosus

Donald E. Kramer

rainbow smelt
Osmerus mordax

Richard S. Wydoski & Richard R. Whitney

eulachon
Thaleichthys pacificus

Richard S. Wydoski & Richard R. Whitney

longfin smelt
Spirinchus thaleichthys

Plate IV

Randy J. Brown

inconnu
Stenodus leucichthys

Kirk Waggoner

Arctic cisco
Coregonus autumnalis

Randy J. Brown

broad whitefish
Coregonus nasus

David G. Roseneau

Alaska whitefish
Coregonus nelsonii

Randy J. Brown

least cisco
Coregonus sardinella

Randy J. Brown

Bering cisco
Coregonus laurettae

John F. Scarola

lake whitefish
Coregonus clupeaformis

Randy J. Brown

humpback whitefish
Coregonus pidschian

round whitefish
Prosopium cylindraceum

Arctic grayling
Thymallus arcticus

brook trout
Salvelinus fontinalis

lake trout
Salvelinus namaycush

pygmy whitefish
Prosopium coulterii

Arctic grayling
Thymallus arcticus

lake trout
Salvelinus namaycush

Arctic char
Salvelinus alpinus

John H. Helle

Dolly Varden
Salvelinus malma

John F. Scarola

Atlantic salmon
Salmo salar

John F. Scarola

rainbow trout
Oncorhynchus mykiss

Richard S. Wydoski & Richard R. Whitney

pink salmon (breeding female)
Oncorhynchus gorbuscha

Christopher M. Batin

Dolly Varden
Salvelinus malma

Richard S. Wydoski & Richard R. Whitney

cutthroat trout
Oncorhynchus clarkii

Richard S. Wydoski & Richard R. Whitney

steelhead (breeding male)
Oncorhynchus mykiss

Richard S. Wydoski & Richard R. Whitney

pink salmon (breeding male)
Oncorhynchus gorbuscha

Christopher M. Batin

pink salmon (spawning migration)
Oncorhynchus gorbuscha

Donald E. Kramer

coho salmon (ocean fish)
Oncorhynchus kisutch

Richard S. Wydoski & Richard R. Whitney

coho salmon (breeding female)
Oncorhynchus kisutch

Richard S. Wydoski & Richard R. Whitney

coho salmon (breeding male)
Oncorhynchus kisutch

Richard S. Wydoski & Richard R. Whitney

Chinook salmon (breeding female)
Oncorhynchus tshawytscha

Richard S. Wydoski & Richard R. Whitney

Chinook salmon (breeding male)
Oncorhynchus tshawytscha

Christopher M. Batin

Chinook salmon (male on spawning ground)
Oncorhynchus tshawytscha

John H. Helle

chum salmon (spawning)
Oncorhynchus keta

Plate VIII

Richard S. Wydoski & Richard R. Whitney

chum salmon (breeding female)
Oncorhynchus keta

Richard S. Wydoski & Richard R. Whitney

sockeye salmon (breeding female)
Oncorhynchus nerka

Christopher M. Batin

sockeye salmon (spawning migration)
Oncorhynchus nerka

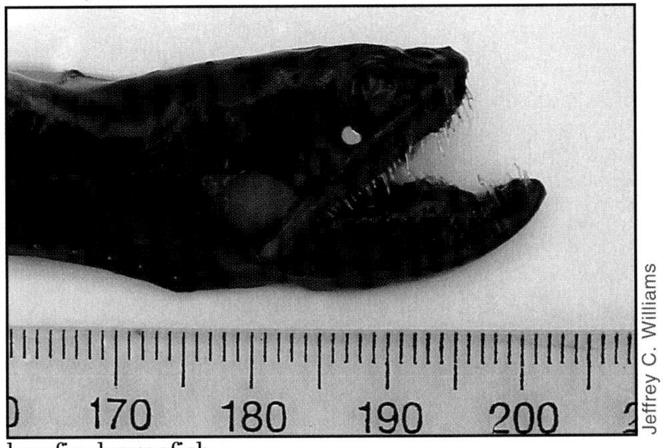

Jeffrey C. Williams

longfin dragonfish
Tactostoma macropus

Richard S. Wydoski & Richard R. Whitney

chum salmon (breeding male)
Oncorhynchus keta

Richard S. Wydoski & Richard R. Whitney

sockeye salmon (breeding male)
Oncorhynchus nerka

Jay C. Quast

Pacific viperfish
Chauliodus macouni

Steve Ebbert

longnose lancetfish
Alepisaurus ferox

Steve Ebbert

longnose lancetfish
Alepisaurus ferox

Donald E. Kramer

duckbill barracudina
Magnisudis atlantica

Doyne W. Kessler

brokenline lanternfish
Lampanyctus jordani

Daniel W. Gotshall

red brotula
Brosmophycis marginata

Donald E. Kramer

white barracudina
Arctozenus risso

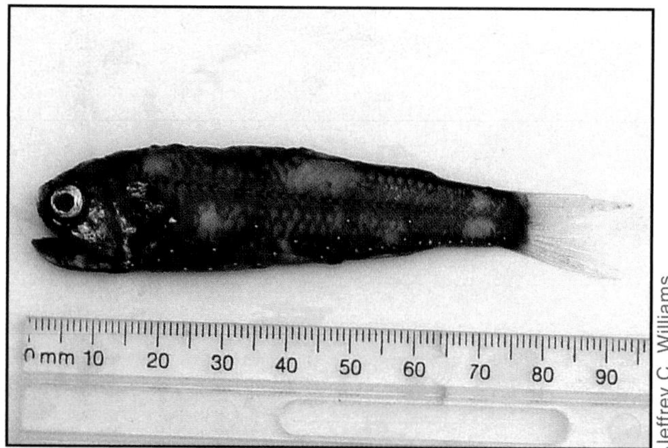

Jeffrey C. Williams

California headlightfish
Diaphus theta

Charles A. Purkett, Jr.

trout-perch
Percopsis omiscomaycus

Gerald R. Hoff

giant grenadier
Albatrossia pectoralis

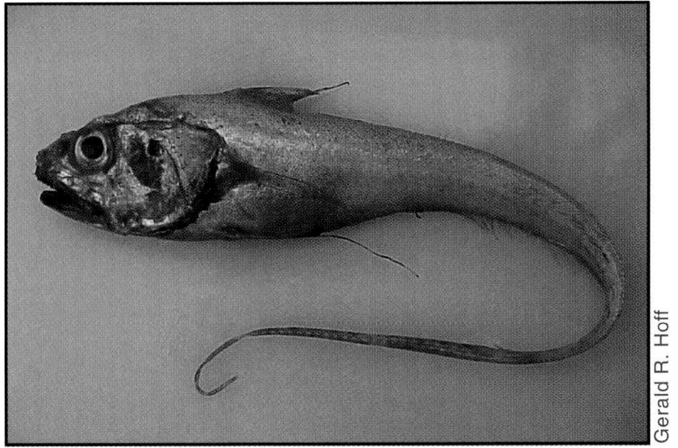
Gerald R. Hoff

longfin grenadier
Coryphaenoides longifilis

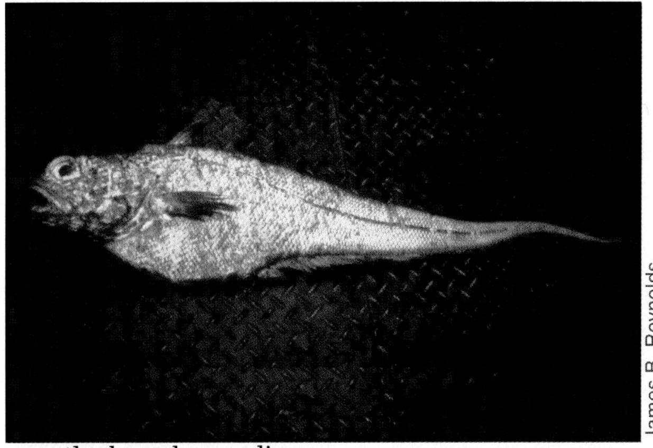
James B. Reynolds

smooth abyssal grenadier
Coryphaenoides armatus

Gerald R. Hoff

Pacific grenadier
Coryphaenoides acrolepis

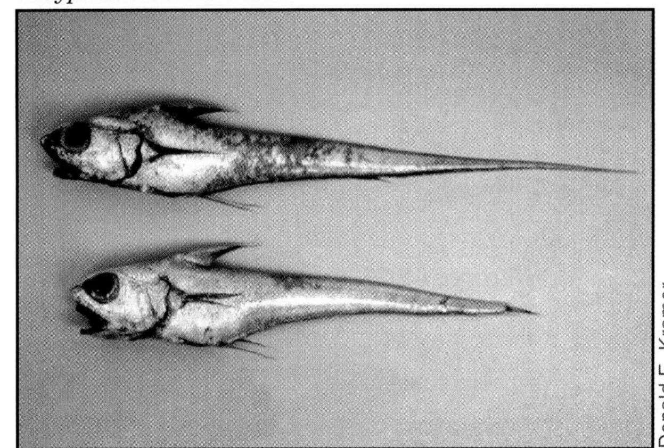
Donald E. Kramer

popeye grenadier
Coryphaenoides cinereus

Doyne W. Kessler

popeye grenadier
Coryphaenoides cinereus

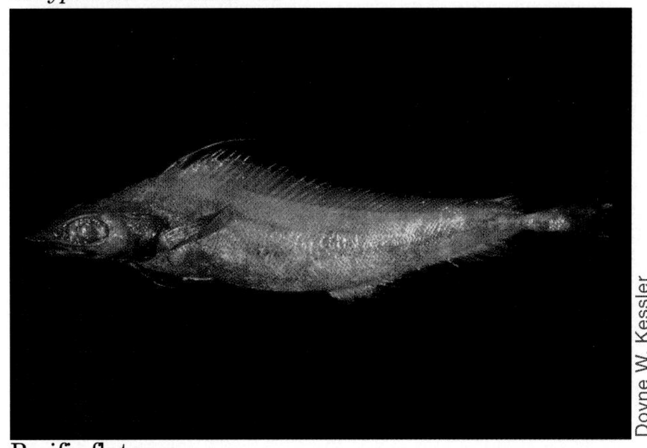
Doyne W. Kessler

Pacific flatnose
Antimora microlepis

Doyne W. Kessler

Pacific hake
Merluccius productus

John F. Scarola

burbot
Lota lota

David G. Roseneau

Arctic cod (upper) and saffron cod (lower)
Boreogadus saida and *Eleginus gracilis*

H. Richard Carlson

Pacific cod
Gadus macrocephalus

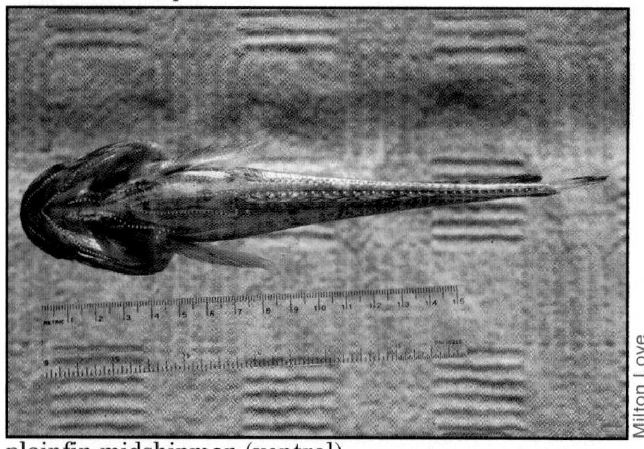
Milton Love

plainfin midshipman (ventral)
Porichthys notatus (not confirmed from Alaska)

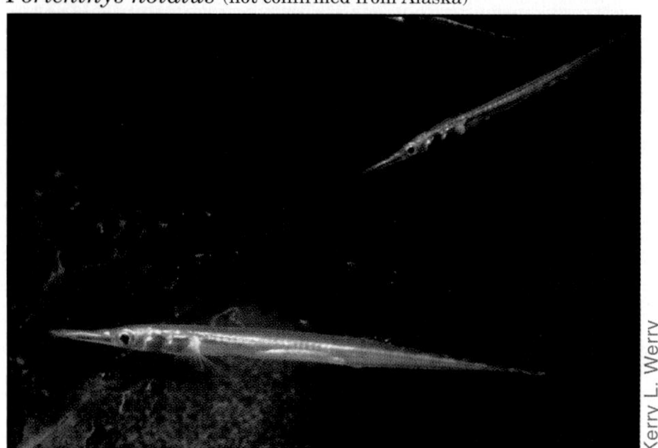
Kerry L. Werry

tubesnout
Aulorhynchus flavidus

Donald E. Kramer

walleye pollock
Theragra chalcogramma

Donald E. Kramer

plainfin midshipman
Porichthys notatus (not confirmed from Alaska)

Doyne W. Kessler

crested bigscale
Poromitra crassiceps

Brent Cooke

threespine stickleback
Gasterosteus aculeatus

David C. Heins & J. Michael Guill

ninespine stickleback
Pungitius pungitius

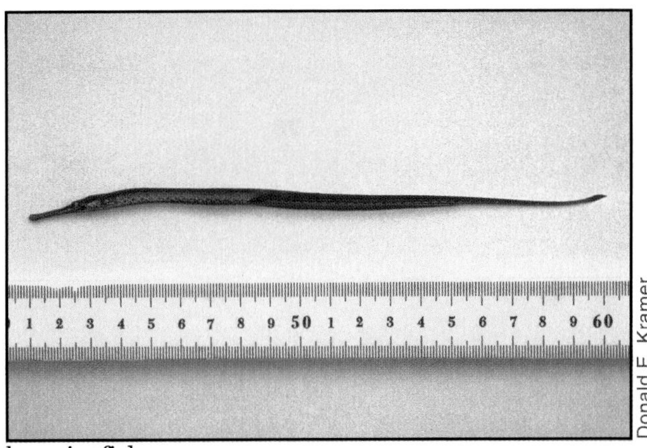

Donald E. Kramer

bay pipefish
Syngnathus leptorhynchus

Ann Cleveland

Emperor rockfish
Adelosebastes latens

Eric Lynn

longspine thornyhead
Sebastolobus altivelis

Donald E. Kramer

shortspine thornyhead
Sebastolobus alascanus

Milton Love

broadfin thornyhead
Sebastolobus macrochir

Donald E. Kramer

rosethorn rockfish
Sebastes helvomaculatus

Marc C. Chamberlain

tiger rockfish
Sebastes nigrocinctus

Donald E. Kramer

redbanded rockfish
Sebastes babcocki

Marc C. Chamberlain

China rockfish
Sebastes nebulosus

Frank S. Shipley

quillback rockfish
Sebastes maliger

Donald E. Kramer

brown rockfish
Sebastes auriculatus

Hitoshi Ida

gray rockfish
Sebastes glaucus

Donald E. Kramer

dusky rockfish (dark phase)
Sebastes ciliatus

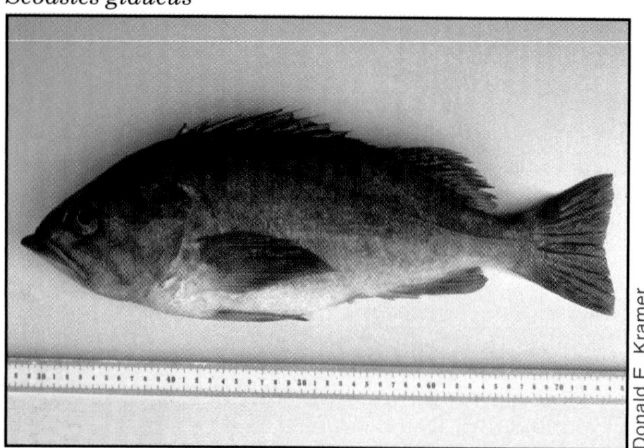
Donald E. Kramer

dusky rockfish (light phase)
Sebastes ciliatus

Donald E. Kramer

silvergray rockfish
Sebastes brevispinis

Donald E. Kramer

widow rockfish
Sebastes entomelas

Tim Herrlinger

blue rockfish
Sebastes mystinus (not confirmed from Alaska)

Milton Love

shortbelly rockfish
Sebastes jordani (not known from Alaska)

Donald E. Kramer

bocaccio
Sebastes paucispinis

Ken Wong

yellowtail rockfish
Sebastes flavidus

Mark D. Conlin

black rockfish
Sebastes melanops

Robert R. Lauth

northern rockfish
Sebastes polyspinis

Donald E. Kramer

copper rockfish
Sebastes caurinus

Donald E. Kramer

greenstriped rockfish
Sebastes elongatus

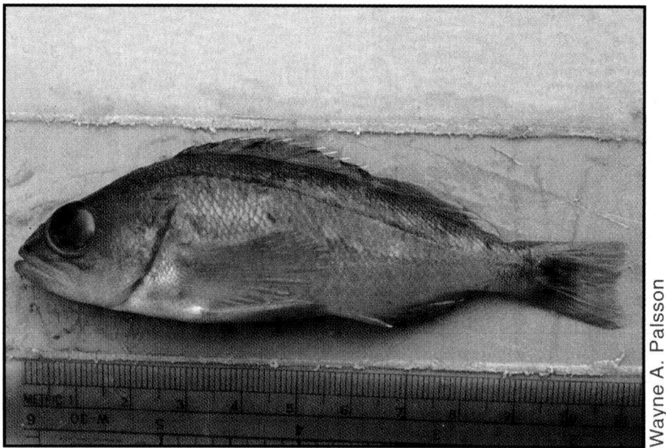
Wayne A. Palsson

Puget Sound rockfish
Sebastes emphaeus

Milton Love

canary rockfish
Sebastes pinniger

Donald E. Kramer

redstripe rockfish
Sebastes proriger

Donald E. Kramer

harlequin rockfish
Sebastes variegatus

Milton Love

pygmy rockfish
Sebastes wilsoni

Tim Herrlinger

vermilion rockfish
Sebastes miniatus

Donald E. Kramer

Pacific ocean perch
Sebastes alutus

Donald E. Kramer

yellowmouth rockfish
Sebastes reedi

Donald E. Kramer

splitnose rockfish
Sebastes diploproa

Donald E. Kramer

sharpchin rockfish
Sebastes zacentrus

Milton Love

yelloweye rockfish (juvenile)
Sebastes ruberrimus

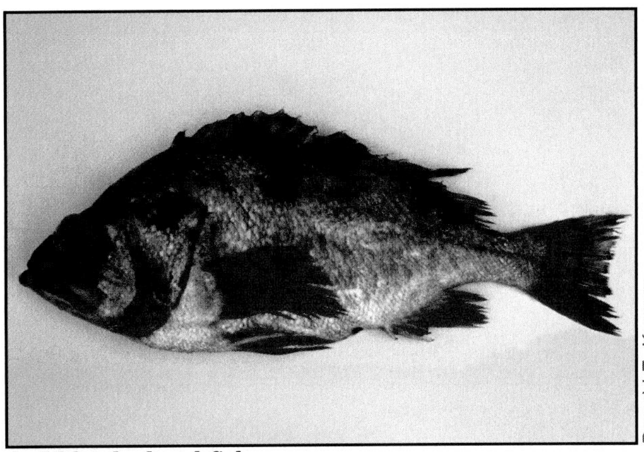
Donald E. Kramer

darkblotched rockfish
Sebastes crameri

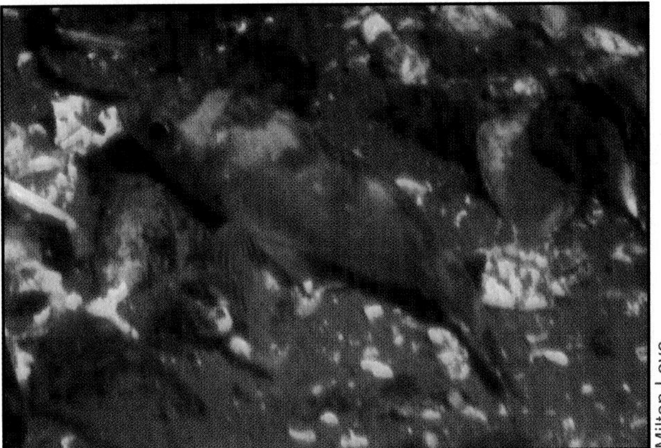
Milton Love

stripetail rockfish
Sebastes saxicola

Donald E. Kramer

yelloweye rockfish
Sebastes ruberrimus

Donald E. Kramer

rougheye rockfish
Sebastes aleutianus

shortraker rockfish
Sebastes borealis

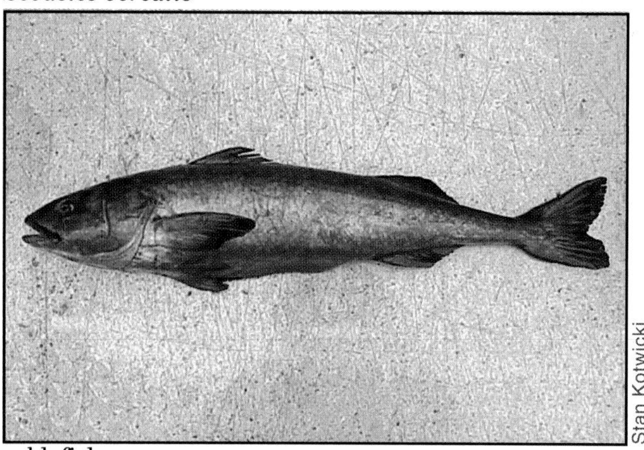

sablefish
Anoplopoma fimbria

skilfish (juvenile)
Erilepis zonifer

painted greenling
Oxylebius pictus

blackgill rockfish
Sebastes melanostomus (not confirmed from Alaska)

sablefish
Anoplopoma fimbria

painted greenling
Oxylebius pictus

lingcod
Ophiodon elongatus

Plate XVIII

Kerry L. Werry

lingcod
Ophiodon elongatus

Donald E. Kramer

Atka mackerel
Pleurogrammus monopterygius

Brent Cooke

whitespotted greenling
Hexagrammos stelleri

Mark D. Conlin

kelp greenling (female)
Hexagrammos decagrammus

Keith L. Jackson

kelp greenling (male)
Hexagrammos decagrammus

National Marine Fisheries Service

rock greenling
Hexagrammos lagocephalus

Donald E. Kramer

grunt sculpin
Rhamphocottus richardsonii

Donald E. Kramer

longfin sculpin
Jordania zonope

Catherine W. Mecklenburg

roughspine sculpin
Triglops macellus

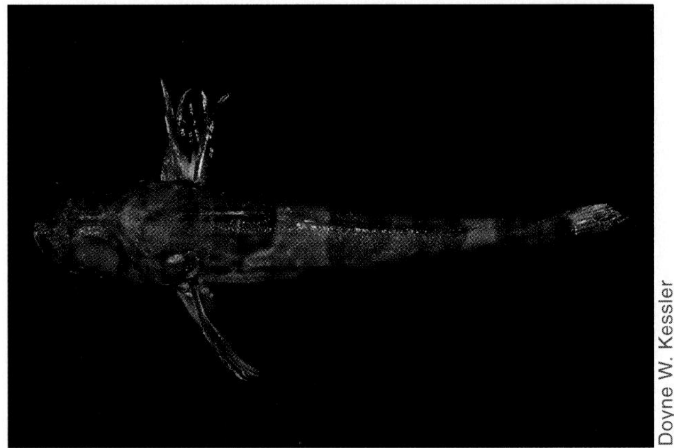

Doyne W. Kessler

spectacled sculpin
Triglops scepticus

Doyne W. Kessler

spectacled sculpin
Triglops scepticus

Gerald R. Hoff

ribbed sculpin
Triglops pingelii

Milton Love

cabezon
Scorpaenichthys marmoratus

Keith L. Jackson

cabezon
Scorpaenichthys marmoratus

Gerald R. Hoff

butterfly sculpin
Hemilepidotus papilio

Boris A. Sheiko

longfin Irish lord
Hemilepidotus zapus

Gerald R. Hoff

longfin Irish lord
Hemilepidotus zapus

Mark D. Conlin

red Irish lord
Hemilepidotus hemilepidotus

Marc C. Chamberlain

red Irish lord
Hemilepidotus hemilepidotus

Donald E. Kramer

yellow Irish lord
Hemilepidotus jordani

Gerald R. Hoff

threadfin sculpin
Icelinus filamentosus

Jared Figurski

slim sculpin
Radulinus asprellus

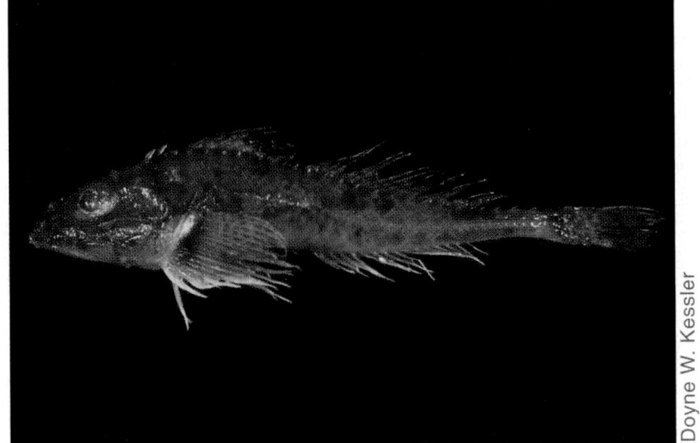
Doyne W. Kessler

thorny sculpin
Icelus spiniger

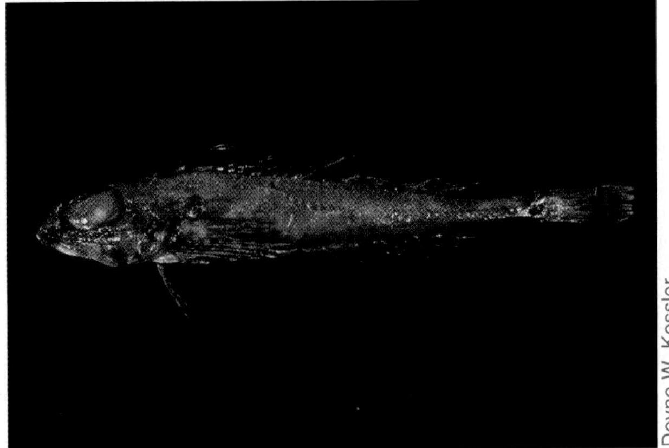
Doyne W. Kessler

wide-eye sculpin
Icelus euryops

Doyne W. Kessler

uncinate sculpin
Icelus uncinalis

Doyne W. Kessler

roughskin sculpin
Rastrinus scutiger

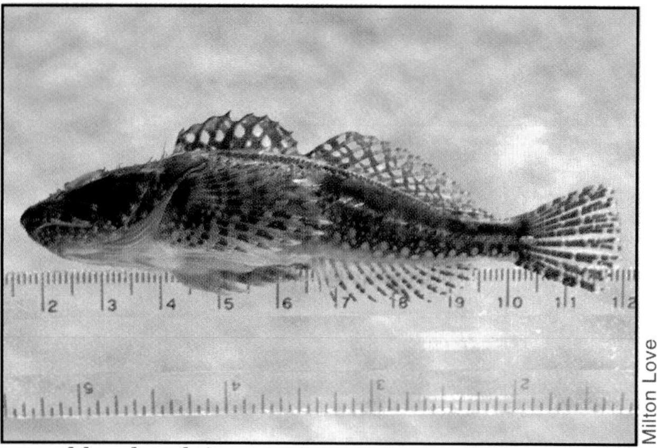
Milton Love

smoothhead sculpin
Artedius lateralis

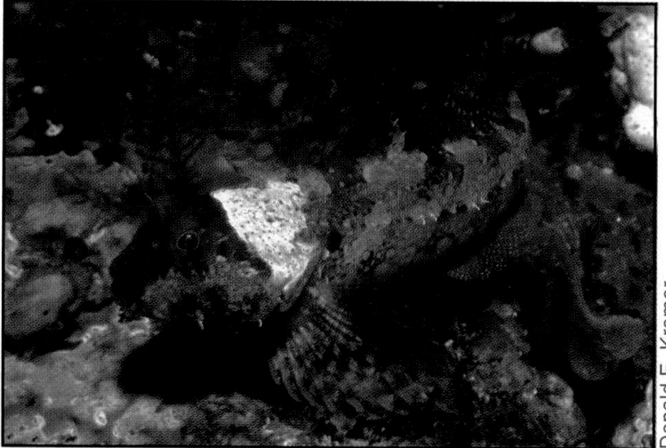
Donald E. Kramer

scalyhead sculpin
Artedius harringtoni

Gerald R. Hoff

threaded sculpin
Gymnocanthus pistilliger

Doyne W. Kessler

armorhead sculpin
Gymnocanthus galeatus

Keith L. Jackson

Pacific staghorn sculpin
Leptocottus armatus

Richard Herrmann

Pacific staghorn sculpin
Leptocottus armatus

John F. Scarola

slimy sculpin
Cottus cognatus

Richard S. Wydoski & Richard R. Whitney

coastrange sculpin
Cottus aleuticus

Mark D. Conlin

buffalo sculpin
Enophrys bison

H. Richard Carlson

leister sculpin
Enophrys lucasi

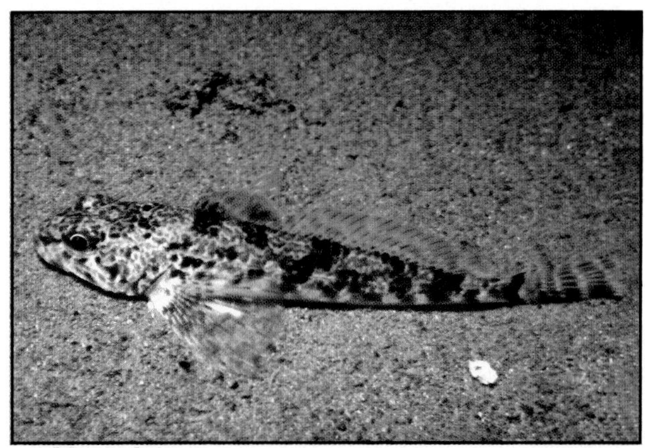
Donald E. Kramer

prickly sculpin
Cottus asper

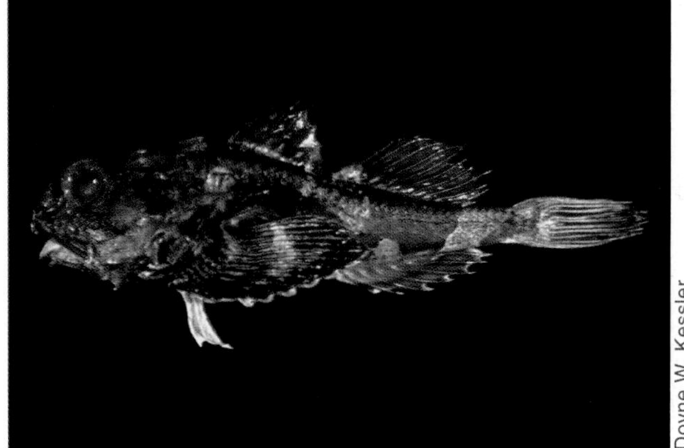
Doyne W. Kessler

buffalo sculpin
Enophrys bison

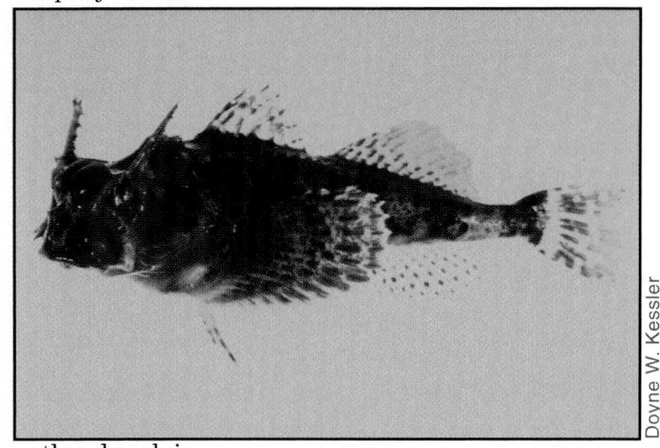
Doyne W. Kessler

antlered sculpin
Enophrys diceraus

Doyne W. Kessler

belligerent sculpin
Megalocottus platycephalus

Doyne W. Kessler

fourhorn sculpin
Myoxocephalus quadricornis

Jared Figurski

shorthorn sculpin (breeding male)
Myoxocephalus scorpius

Doyne W. Kessler

shorthorn sculpin (female)
Myoxocephalus scorpius

Richard Hockings

plain sculpin
Myoxocephalus jaok

Doyne W. Kessler

fourhorn sculpin
Myoxocephalus quadricornis

Jared Figurski

shorthorn sculpin (breeding male)
Myoxocephalus scorpius

Doyne W. Kessler

plain sculpin
Myoxocephalus jaok

Lou Barr

great sculpin
Myoxocephalus polyacanthocephalus

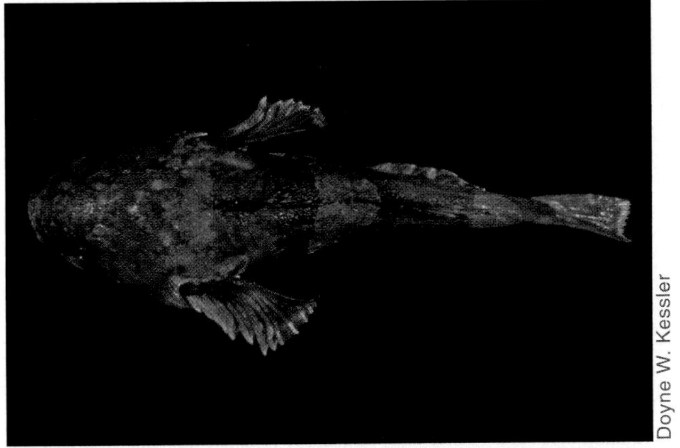
Doyne W. Kessler

great sculpin
Myoxocephalus polyacanthocephalus

Doyne W. Kessler

brightbelly sculpin (male)
Microcottus sellaris

Doyne W. Kessler

brightbelly sculpin (female)
Microcottus sellaris

Doyne W. Kessler

bigmouth sculpin
Hemitripterus bolini

Doyne W. Kessler

great sculpin
Myoxocephalus polyacanthocephalus

Doyne W. Kessler

brightbelly sculpin (male)
Microcottus sellaris

Rita M. O'Clair

tidepool sculpin
Oligocottus maculosus

Gerald R. Hoff

crested sculpin
Blepsias bilobus

Plate XXV

crested sculpin
Blepsias bilobus

sailfin sculpin
Nautichthys oculofasciatus

eyeshade sculpin
Nautichthys pribilovius

spinyhead sculpin
Dasycottus setiger

silverspotted sculpin
Blepsias cirrhosus

sailfin sculpin
Nautichthys oculofasciatus

spinyhead sculpin
Dasycottus setiger

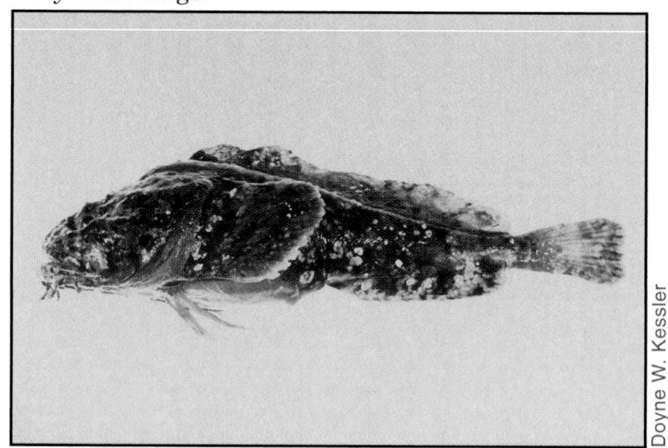

smoothcheek sculpin
Eurymen gyrinus

Plate XXVI

Erika I. Acuna

darkfin sculpin
Malacocottus zonurus

Gerald R. Hoff

dragon poacher
Percis japonica

Gerald R. Hoff

Bering poacher
Occella dodecaedron

Doyne W. Kessler

longnose poacher
Leptagonus leptorhynchus

Keith L. Jackson

darkfin sculpin
Malacocottus zonurus

Gerald R. Hoff

tubenose poacher
Pallasina barbata

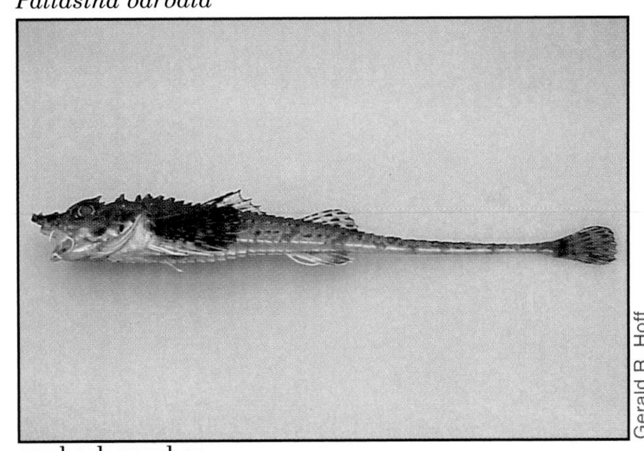
Gerald R. Hoff

sawback poacher
Leptagonus frenatus

Donald E. Kramer

northern spearnose poacher
Agonopsis vulsa

sturgeon poacher
Podothecus accipenserinus

sturgeon poacher
Podothecus accipenserinus

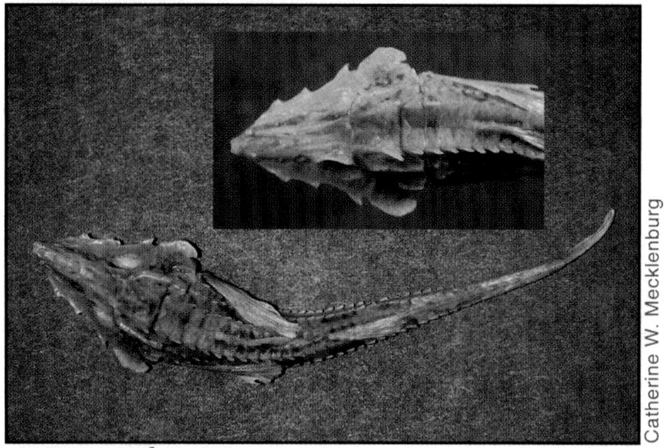

veteran poacher
Podothecus veternus

blackfin poacher (upper) and gray starsnout (lower)
Bathyagonus nigripinnis and *B. alascanus*

Arctic alligatorfish
Ulcina olrikii

alligatorfish
Aspidophoroides monopterygius

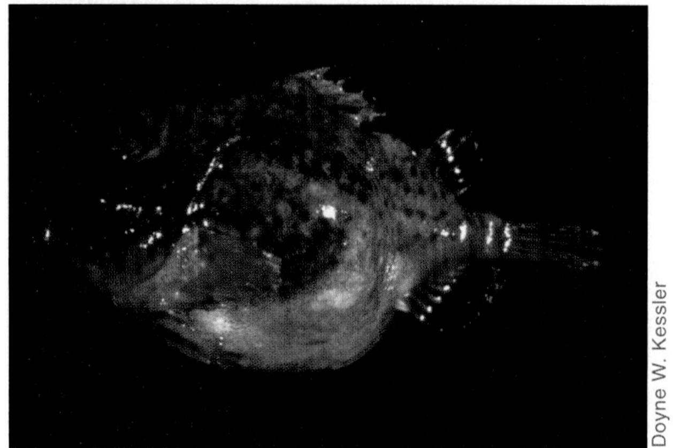

docked snailfish
Lethotremus muticus

Pacific spiny lumpsucker
Eumicrotremus orbis

showy snailfish
Liparis pulchellus

marbled snailfish
Liparis dennyi

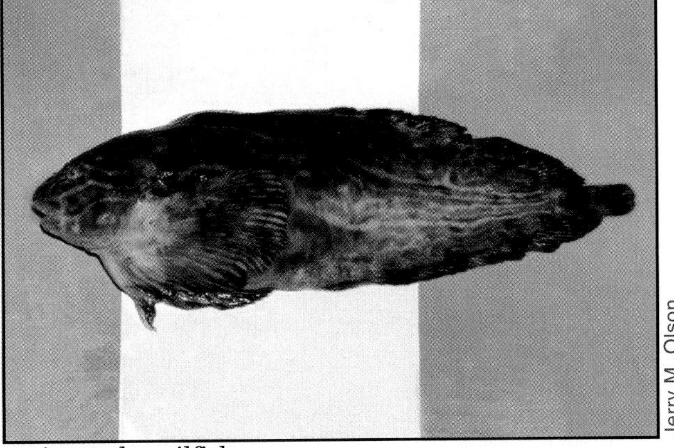

variegated snailfish
Liparis gibbus

variegated snailfish
Liparis gibbus

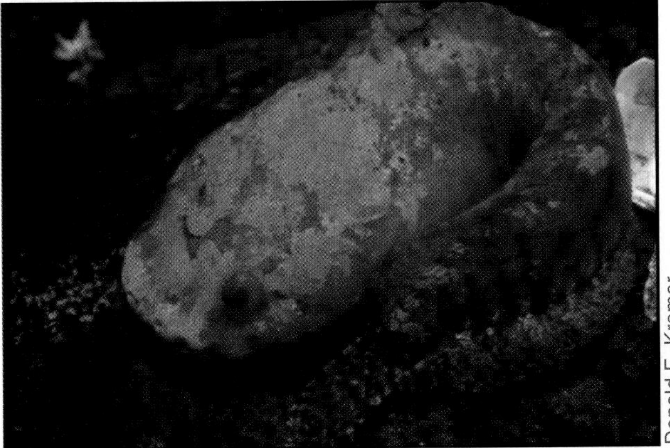

slipskin snailfish
Liparis fucensis

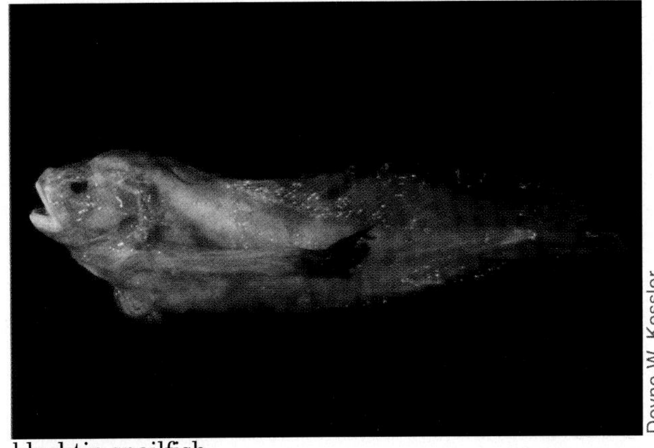

blacktip snailfish
Careproctus zachirus

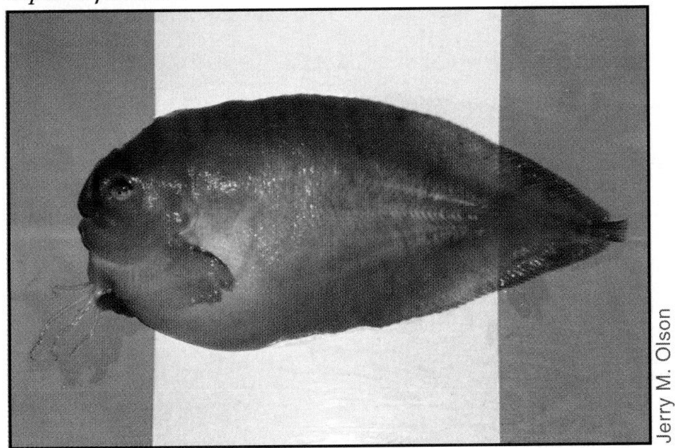

salmon snailfish
Careproctus rastrinus

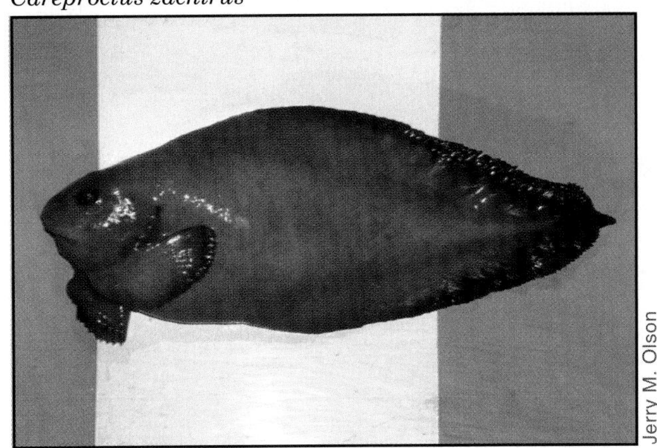

emarginate snailfish
Careproctus furcellus

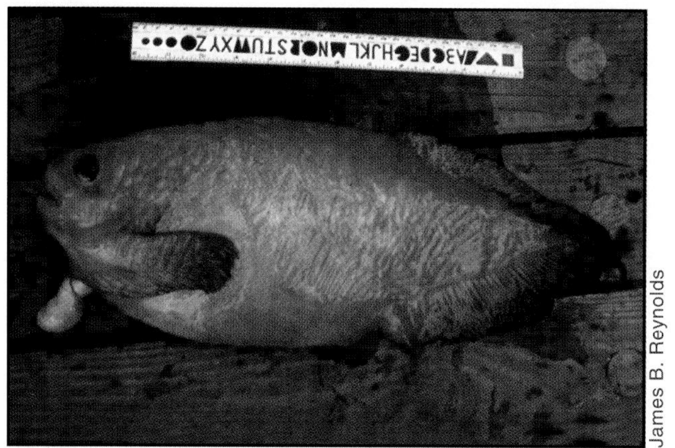
James B. Reynolds

blacktail snailfish
Careproctus melanurus

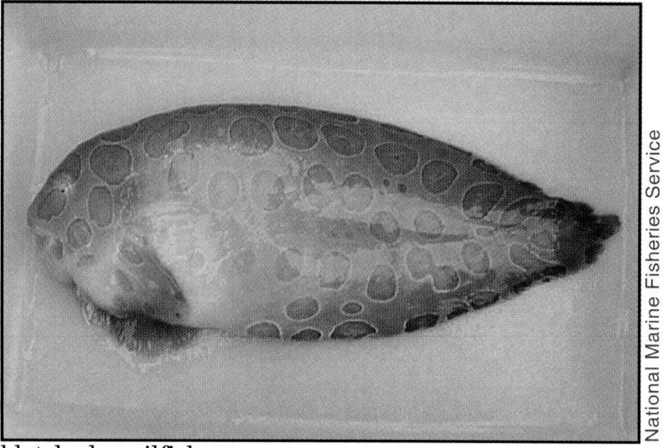
National Marine Fisheries Service

blotched snailfish
Crystallichthys cyclospilus

Milton Love

jack mackerel
Trachurus symmetricus

National Marine Fisheries Service

Pacific pomfret
Brama japonica

Alex E. Peden

smalldisk snailfish
Careproctus gilberti

Alex E. Peden

tadpole snailfish
Nectoliparis pelagicus

Marc C. Chamberlain

yellowtail jack
Seriola lalandi

Mark D. Conlin

white seabass
Atractoscion nobilis

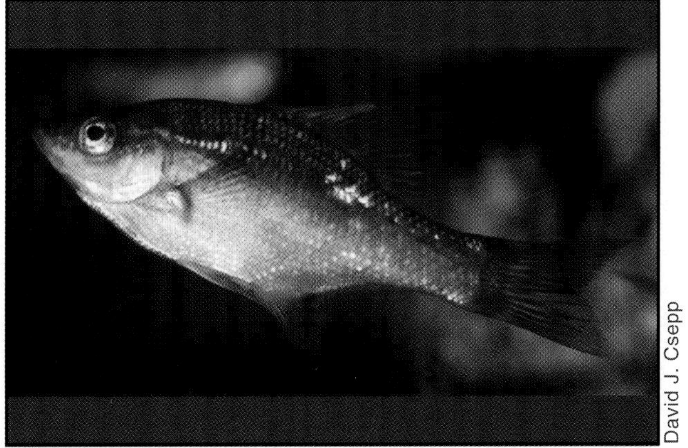

kelp perch
Brachyistius frenatus
David J. Csepp

striped seaperch
Embiotoca lateralis
Milton Love

northern ronquil
Ronquilus jordani
Jared Figurski

searcher
Bathymaster signatus
H. Richard Carlson

shiner perch
Cymatogaster aggregata
Donald E. Kramer

pile perch
Rhacochilus vacca (not confirmed from Alaska)
Daniel W. Gotshall

searcher
Bathymaster signatus
Jerry M. Olson

Alaskan ronquil
Bathymaster caeruleofasciatus
Brent Cooke

James B. Reynolds

marbled eelpout
Lycodes raridens

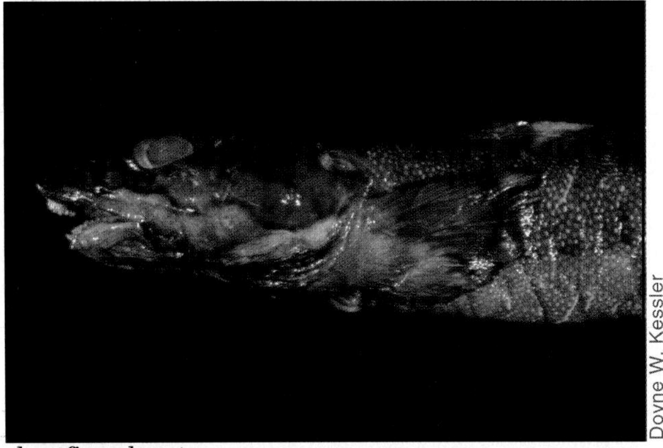
Doyne W. Kessler

shortfin eelpout
Lycodes brevipes

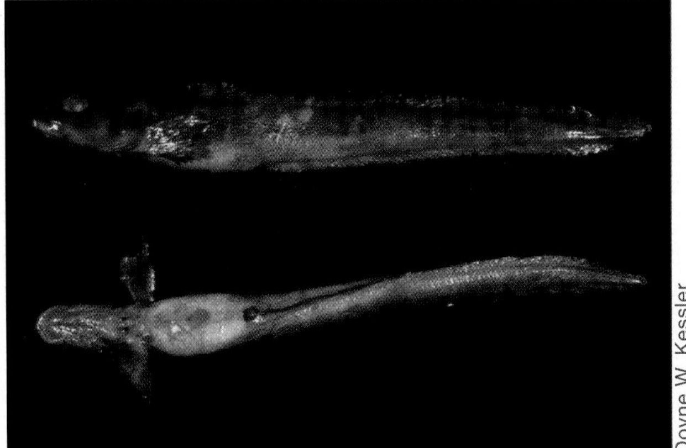
Doyne W. Kessler

black eelpout
Lycodes diapterus

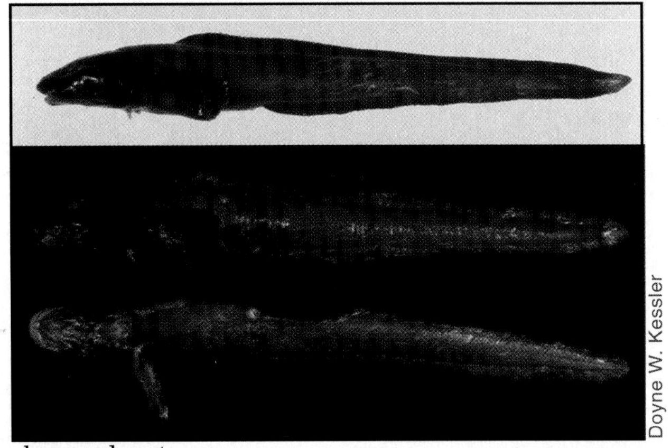
Doyne W. Kessler

ebony eelpout
Lycodes concolor

Jared Figurski

shortfin eelpout
Lycodes brevipes

Jerry M. Olson

wattled eelpout
Lycodes palearis

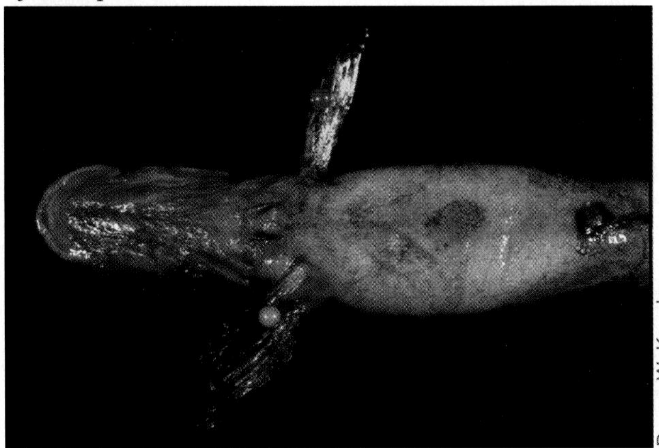
Doyne W. Kessler

black eelpout
Lycodes diapterus

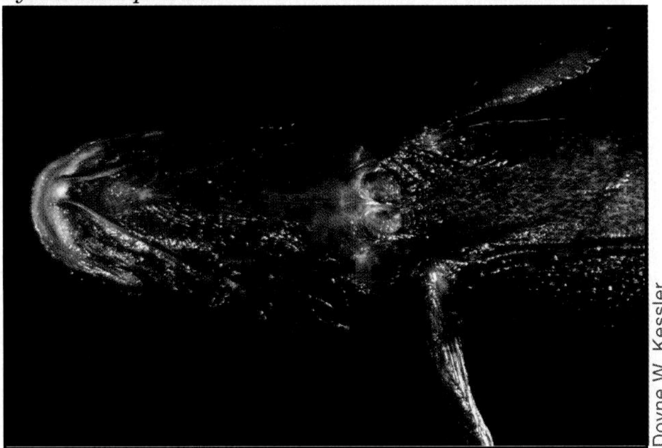
Doyne W. Kessler

ebony eelpout
Lycodes concolor

Gerald R. Hoff

twoline eelpout (young adult)
Bothrocara brunneum

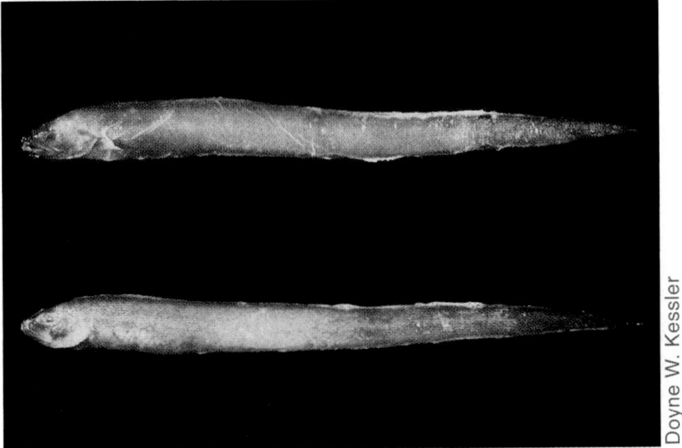

Doyne W. Kessler

lycodapine eelpouts
Lycodapus cf. *psarostomatus*

Donald E. Kramer

mosshead warbonnet
Chirolophis nugator

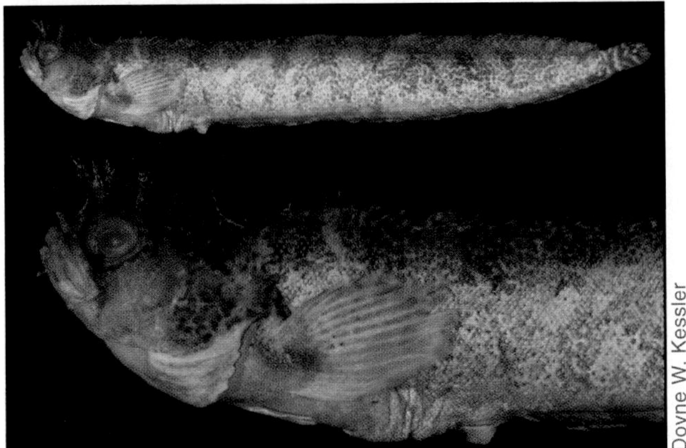

Doyne W. Kessler

nutcracker prickleback
Bryozoichthys lysimus

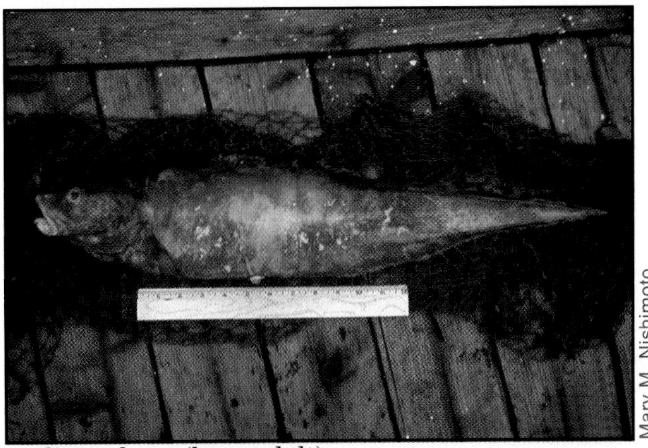

Mary M. Nishimoto

twoline eelpout (large adult)
Bothrocara brunneum

Charles E. O'Clair

Arctic shanny
Stichaeus punctatus

Lou Barr

decorated warbonnet
Chirolophis decoratus

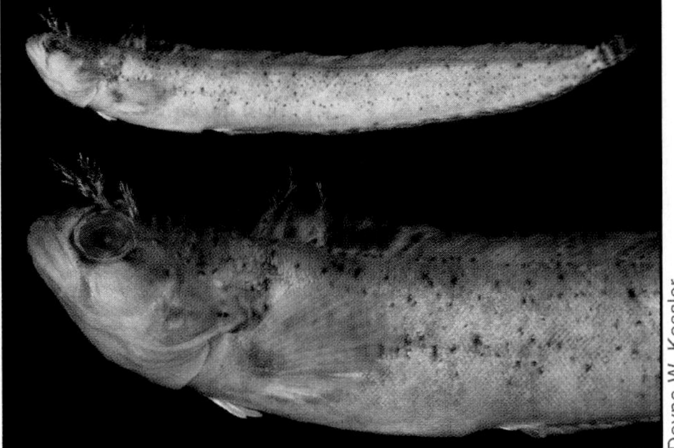

Doyne W. Kessler

pearly prickleback
Bryozoichthys marjorius

Donald D. Flescher

Jerry M. Olson

daubed shanny (upper) and blackline prickleback (lower)
Leptoclinus maculatus and *Acantholumpenus mackayi*

Kerry L. Werry

high cockscomb
Anoplarchus purpurescens

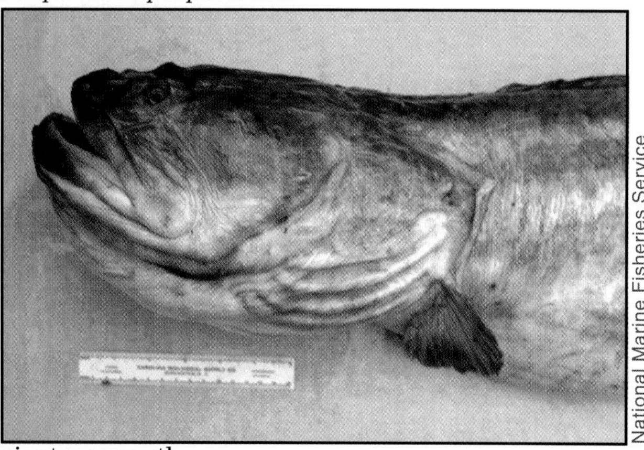

National Marine Fisheries Service

giant wrymouth
Cryptacanthodes giganteus

Kerry L. Werry

longfin gunnel
Pholis clemensi

Rita M. O'Clair

snake prickleback
Lumpenus sagitta

James B. Reynolds

giant wrymouth
Cryptacanthodes giganteus

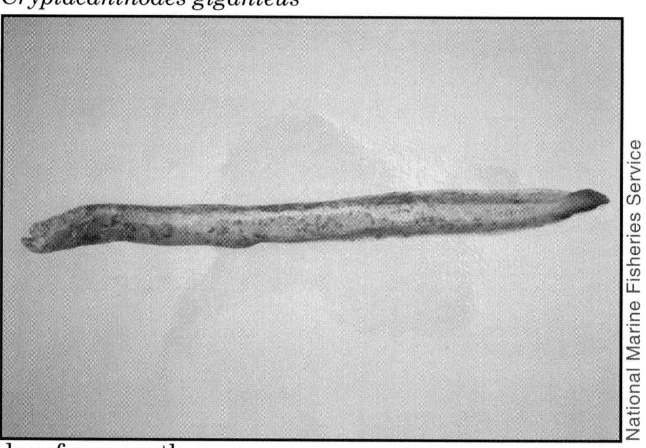

National Marine Fisheries Service

dwarf wrymouth
Cryptacanthodes aleutensis

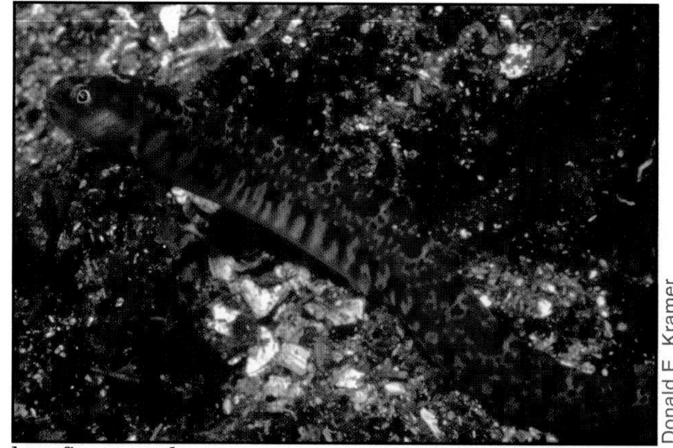

Donald E. Kramer

longfin gunnel
Pholis clemensi

crescent gunnel
Pholis laeta

wolf-eel (juvenile)
Anarrhichthys ocellatus

Bering wolffish (juvenile)
Anarhichas orientalis

prowfish (juvenile)
Zaprora silenus

prowfish
Zaprora silenus

Pacific sandfish (juvenile)
Trichodon trichodon

Pacific sandfish
Trichodon trichodon

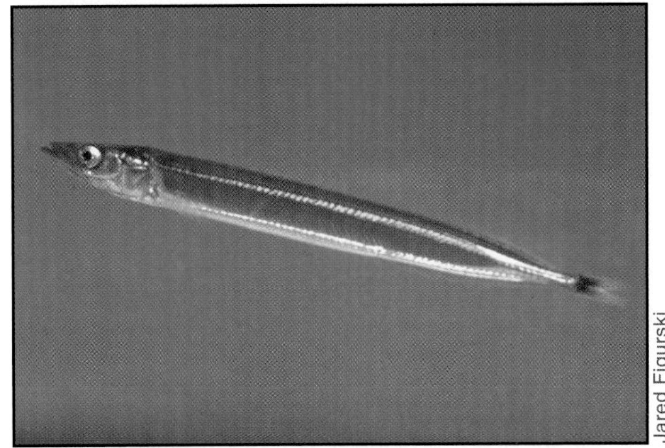

Pacific sand lance
Ammodytes hexapterus

Lou Barr

Pacific sand lance
Ammodytes hexapterus

Donald E. Kramer

northern clingfish
Gobiesox maeandricus

David J. Csepp

blackeye goby
Rhinogobiops nicholsii

Donald D. Flescher

chub mackerel
Scomber japonicus

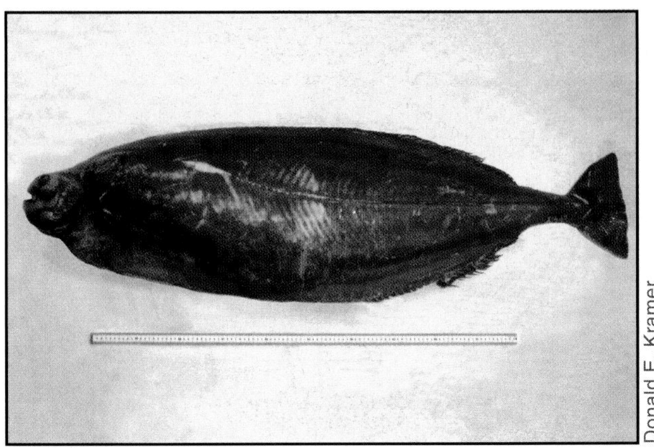
Donald E. Kramer

ragfish
Icosteus aenigmaticus

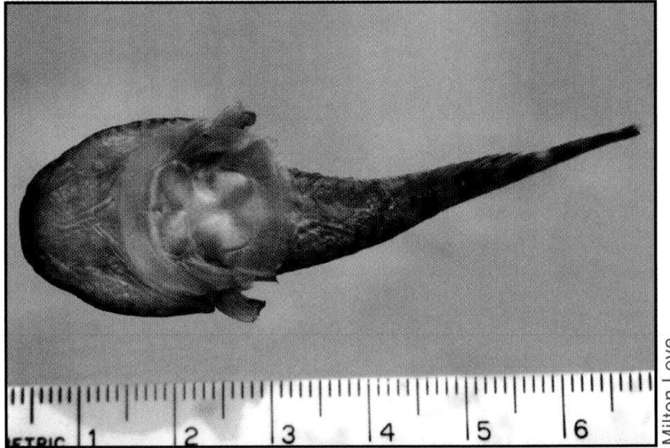
Milton Love

northern clingfish (ventral)
Gobiesox maeandricus

James Forte

Pacific barracuda
Sphyraena argentea

National Marine Fisheries Service

yellowfin tuna
Thunnus albacares (not confirmed from Alaska)

Daniel W. Gotshall

medusafish (juvenile)
Icichthys lockingtoni

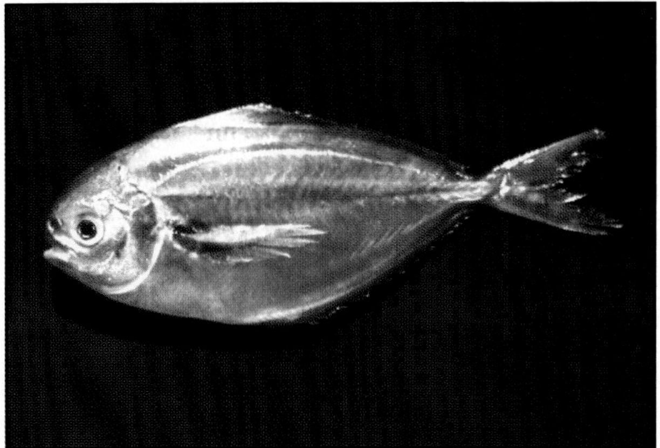
Milton Love

Pacific pompano
Peprilus simillimus (not known from Alaska)

Donald E. Kramer

Pacific sanddab
Citharichthys sordidus

Donald E. Kramer

Pacific sanddab
Citharichthys sordidus

Donald E. Kramer

Pacific halibut
Hippoglossus stenolepis

Donald E. Kramer

sand sole
Psettichthys melanostictus

Donald E. Kramer

slender sole
Lyopsetta exilis

Donald E. Kramer

petrale sole
Eopsetta jordani

Donald E. Kramer

flathead sole
Hippoglossoides elassodon

Gerald R. Hoff

Bering flounder
Hippoglossus robustus

Donald E. Kramer

Greenland halibut
Reinhardtius hippoglossoides

Donald E. Kramer

arrowtooth flounder
Atheresthes stomias

Jared Figurski

arrowtooth flounder
Atheresthes stomias

Donald E. Kramer

Kamchatka flounder
Atheresthes evermanni

Donald E. Kramer

starry flounder
Platichthys stellatus

Donald E. Kramer

roughscale sole
Clidoderma asperrimum

Plate XXXVIII

Donald E. Kramer

Alaska plaice
Pleuronectes quadrituberculatus

James B. Reynolds

Arctic flounder
Pleuronectes glacialis

Donald E. Kramer

southern rock sole
Lepidopsetta bilineata

James Wilder Orr

southern rock sole
Lepidopsetta bilineata

James Wilder Orr

northern rock sole
Lepidopsetta polyxystra

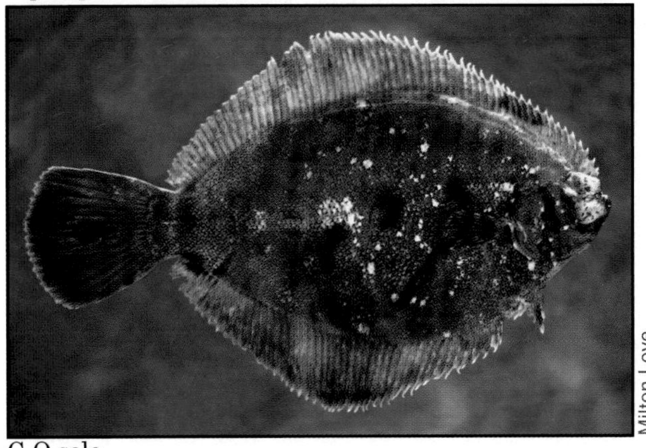
Milton Love

C-O sole
Pleuronichthys coenosus

Donald E. Kramer

curlfin sole
Pleuronichthys decurrens

Donald E. Kramer

English sole
Parophrys vetulus

Gerald R. Hoff

butter sole
Isopsetta isolepis

Gerald R. Hoff

yellowfin sole
Limanda aspera

Gerald R. Hoff

Sakhalin sole
Limanda sakhalinensis

Donald E. Kramer

deepsea sole
Embassichthys bathybius

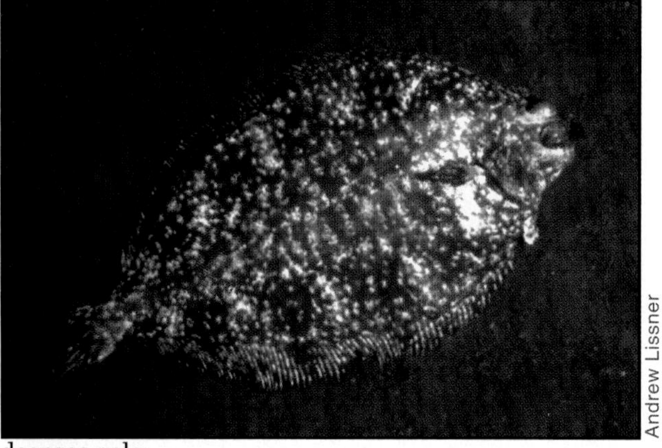
Andrew Lissner

deepsea sole
Embassichthys bathybius

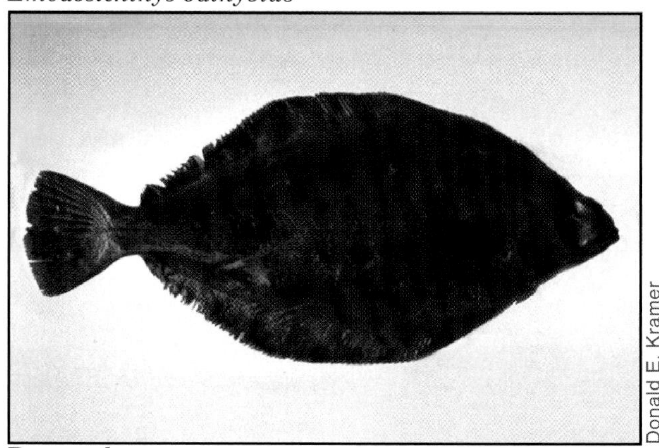
Donald E. Kramer

Dover sole
Microstomus pacificus

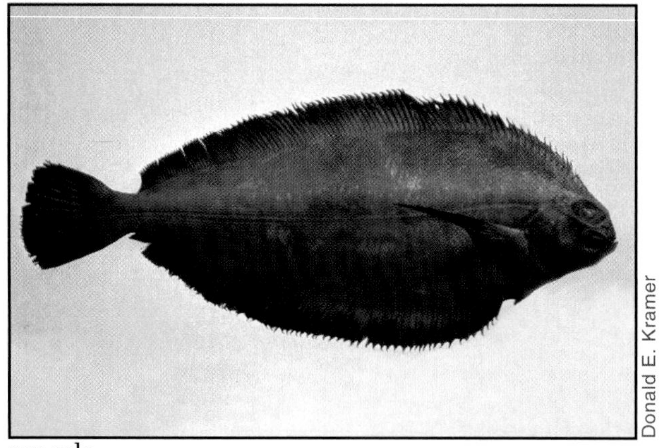
Donald E. Kramer

rex sole
Glyptocephalus zachirus

Marc C. Chamberlain

ocean sunfish
Mola mola

Superclass Agnatha
Jawless vertebrates

The three main groups of fishes of the world are well represented in the Alaskan fauna. These groups are the jawless fishes (Agnatha), including lampreys and hagfishes; the cartilaginous fishes (Chondrichthyes), including chimaeras, sharks, and skates; and the ray-finned fishes (Actinopterygii), including the sturgeons and all the bony fishes. Fishes of the superclass Agnatha, or jawless vertebrates, lack true jaws, although some forms have mouths structured for holding onto objects and noncalcified teeth for biting. They have a large, unrestricted notochord, and lack vertebrae. Although most authors classify agnathans as vertebrates, they are the most primitive members of the group. The fossil record indicates agnathans are the oldest of the fishlike animals. The only extant agnathans are the hagfishes (Myxinidae) and lampreys (Petromyzontidae).

Characters shared by hagfishes and lampreys include an elongate, cylindrical body; a single, median nostril; and no pelvic or pectoral fins or their girdles. The arrangement of the gills and branchial skeleton is entirely different from that of jaw-bearing vertebrates. The gills open to the surface through pores instead of slits and are pouches covered with endoderm and directed internally. The gill pouches, with their arteries and nerves, are inside of and supported by a cartilaginous basket, and the basket is fused to the neurocranium. The gill openings are located on the side of the fish in the Pacific agnathans; some other species have a single pore near the midventral line.

Most of the extinct jawless fishes had a bony exoskeleton. Fossil evidence suggests that the lampreys lost calcified tissue during their evolution, but there is less evidence for hagfish ancestors having had bone. The accumulating evidence from morphology of the extant forms and the fossil record suggests that hagfishes may be the most primitive agnathan group, and that the lampreys are more closely related to the gnathostomes (jawed vertebrates). The relationships of agnathans to each other and to jawed vertebrates are still subjects for study and debate. Existing knowledge of the evolutionary biology and systematics of agnathans has recently been reviewed by Foreman et al. (1985) and Forey and Janvier (1993, 1994).

In the classification used in this guide (Nelson 1994) the approximately 12 genera and 84 extant species of jawless fishes are grouped into two orders, each having only one family (Myxinidae and Petromyzontidae). The fishes of both groups are oviparous. They live primarily on the bottom and feed as scavengers, parasites, or predators on other fishes. At least one species of hagfish and five of lamprey represent these families in the Alaskan ichthyofauna.

Order Myxiniformes
Family Myxinidae
Hagfishes

Hagfishes are primitive or degenerate (opinions differ), bottom-dwelling, eel-like fishes with 5–16 pairs of gill pouches. They occur in temperate marine waters worldwide, typically on sandy or muddy substrates. The hagfish family contains five genera and about 60 species (Fernholm 1998) in two subfamilies. In the subfamily Eptatretinae, including the two species treated in this guide, the gill pouches have individual openings on the sides of the body. In the subfamily Myxininae the gill pouches have a single, common opening on each side.

All hagfishes have an evertible tongue equipped with teeth, and fleshy barbels around the nostril and mouth. Water enters through the single nostril above the mouth and through the nasopharyngeal duct, and exits via the gill openings and the pharyngocutaneous duct. In most species of *Eptatretus* the posteriormost gill opening on the left side is greatly expanded and confluent with the pharyngocutaneous duct. The dorsal and anal fins are absent, but the caudal fin can

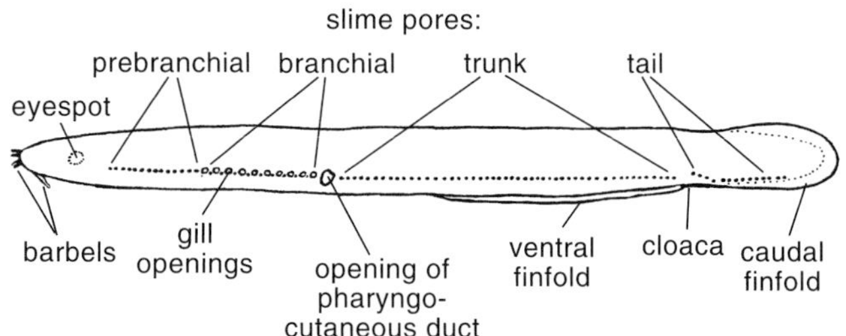

External features of hagfishes
(Adapted from Wisner and McMillan 1990.)

extend onto the dorsal surface of the body. The eyes are vestigial and covered by skin with, in some species, transparent (white in preserved specimens) eyespots, and are considered degenerate rather than primitive since the only known fossil hagfish had eyes (Bardack 1991). A row of about 70–200 slime- and thread-producing pores extends along each side.

Hagfishes feed on dead or moribund invertebrates and fish. They have been found in salmon, cods, flounders, and other fishes, which they enter by way of the mouth or anus. They are the only vertebrates in which the body fluids are isosmotic with seawater. Their slime is secreted in incredible amounts and is thought to be important in feeding and for defense. Hagfishes perform intricate knotting movements to free themselves of slime, escape capture, or tear off food (see illustrations in Hardisty 1979).

Female hagfishes produce large (up to 52 mm), elongate, yolky eggs in strings or clumps of up to 30 eggs held together by many hooked threads and a gelatinous substance. The young do not go through a larval stage.

The maximum length recorded for a hagfish is 1.1 m (36 inches), in *E. carlhubbsi* (not Alaskan). The two species reported to occur in Alaska and British Columbia probably do not reach more than 63.5 cm (25 inches), and specimens larger than about 51 cm (20 inches) are relatively rare.

The occurrence of hagfishes in Alaska is reliably documented for the southeastern part of the state, where they are represented by the black hagfish, *E. deani.* Although the Pacific hagfish, *E. stoutii,* has also been reported to occur in Alaska, its presence there has not been confirmed. It occurs in British Columbia and it may be that the fish has simply eluded capture in Alaska in recent years.

Wisner and McMillan (1990) provided much new information on the morphology and distribution of *E. deani* and *E. stoutii.* Fernholm (1998) reviewed hagfish characters and systematics.

Key to the Myxinidae of Alaska

1 Prebranchial slime pores usually 6–8 (range 4–10); body purplish black to dark brown, occasionally with pale spots and blotches; ventral finfold weakly developed, occasionally absent .... *Eptatretus deani,* page 54

1 Prebranchial slime pores usually 12–14 (range 10–16); body tan or light brown, commonly with pale spots and blotches; ventral finfold prominent... *Eptatretus stoutii,* page 55
(not confirmed from Alaska)

Eptatretus deani (Evermann & Goldsborough, 1907) **black hagfish**

Southeastern Alaska to central Baja California at Guadalupe Island.

On or near bottom at depths of 107–2,743 m.

- **Body purplish black to dark brown**, occasionally with pale spots and blotches; finfolds without pale margin except in spotted specimens; anterior part of head often pale.
- Eye not visible, marked by variably sized, prominent eyespot with irregular margin.
- **Ventral finfold weakly developed, occasionally absent**.
- **Prebranchial slime pores 4–10, usually 6–8**.
- Gill openings 10–12, usually 11.
- Length to about 63.5 cm TL.
- **Mature eggs large, up to 52 mm in length**, elongate, slightly curved, yellow.

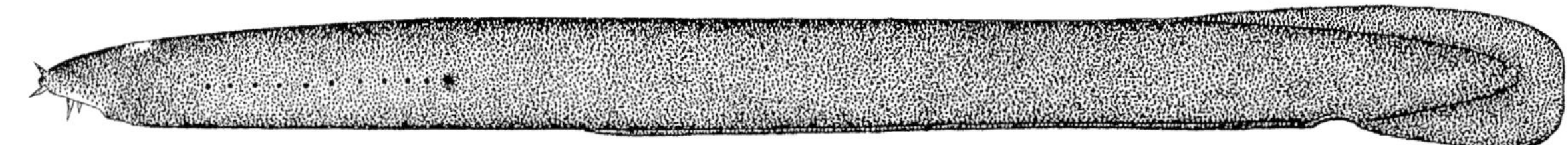

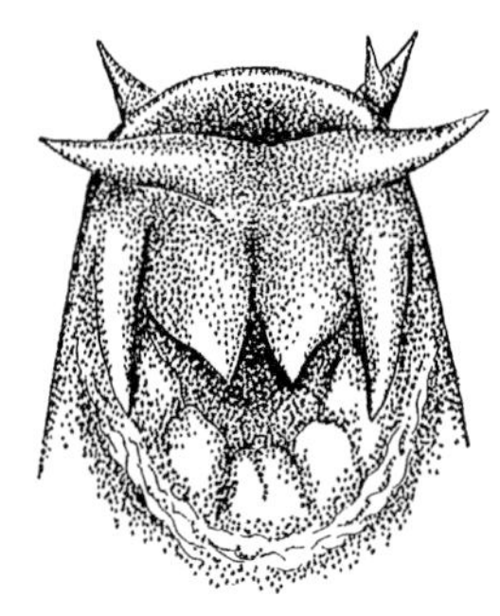

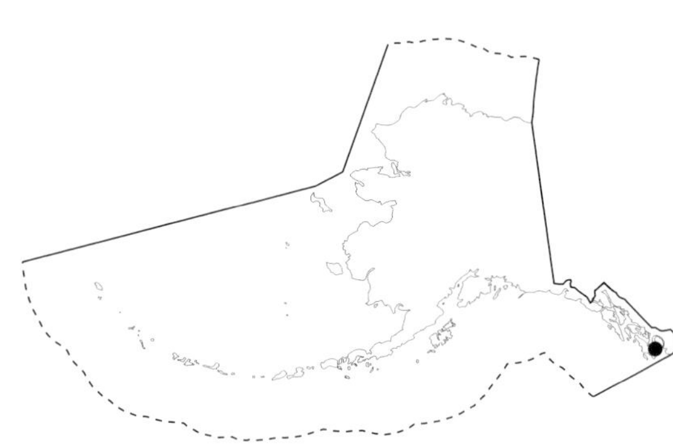

Notes & Sources — *Eptatretus deani* (Evermann & Goldsborough, 1907)
Polistotrema deani Evermann & Goldsborough, 1907
For detailed synonymy see Wisner and McMillan (1990).

Description: Evermann and Goldsborough 1907:225–226; Hart 1973:17–18; Wisner and McMillan 1990:793–795.

Figures: Bourne and McAllister 1969, fig. 1; 51 cm TL, south of Cape St. James, Queen Charlotte Islands.

Range: The holotype and 3 paratypes, described by Evermann and Goldsborough (1907), were collected from two localities on Behm Canal, southern southeastern Alaska: *Albatross* station 4235, off Square Island, Spacious Bay, Cleveland Peninsula, depth 238–353 m, bottom gray mud with black specks; and station 4238, off Nose Point, Revillagigedo Island, depth 419–422 m, bottom rocky mud. (Locality data are mixed up in Wisner and McMillan 1990.) Specimens in the ABL collection referred to by Quast and Hall (1972) are from the same vicinity. We did not find any other records of captures in Alaska. The northernmost British Columbia record is south of Cape St. James, the southern tip of the Queen Charlotte Islands, at 51°57'N, 130°58'W, where a 51-cm specimen (shown above) was caught on a longline hook baited with squid and set in 165-455 m (Bourne and McAllister 1969). *Eptatretus deani* generally occurs at much greater depths than *E. stoutii*. Wisner and McMillan (1990) reported capture depth of 2,743 m near Guadalupe Island (SIO 63-177).

Size: Hart (1973) reported length to "25 inches (63.5 cm)," possibly from rounding off 24.5 inches (about 62.2 cm) given by Evermann and Goldsborough (1907) for one of the paratypes. Largest of nearly 500 specimens examined by Wisner and McMillan (1990) was 554 mm TL.

Eptatretus stoutii (Lockington, 1878) **Pacific hagfish**

Southeastern Alaska records not confirmed; well documented from Vancouver Island, British Columbia, to central Baja California at Punta San Pablo.

On or near bottom at depths of 16–944 m.

- **Body tan or light brown**, usually with pale spots and blotches; ventral finfold with wide pale margin; gill openings with pale borders.
- Eye not visible, marked by small, prominent eyespot with well-defined margin.
- **Ventral finfold prominent**.
- **Prebranchial slime pores 10–16, usually 12–14**.
- Gill openings 10–14, usually 12.
- Length to 55 cm TL, possibly to 63.5 cm TL.
- **Mature eggs small, up to 29 mm in length**, elongate, slightly curved, yellow.

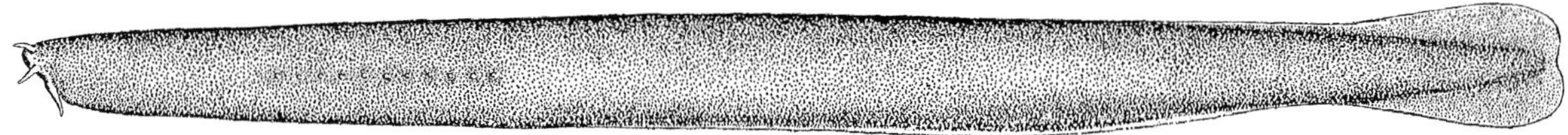

Notes & Sources — *Eptatretus stoutii* (Lockington, 1878)
Bdellostoma stoutii Lockington, 1878
Polistotrema stouti: Evermann and Goldsborough (1907:225–226), comparison with *P. deani*.
For detailed synonymy see Wisner and McMillan (1990).
Often spelled, incorrectly, with one *i*. Lockington (1878), in the original species description, spelled it *stoutii.*

Description: Hart 1973:18–19; Wisner and McMillan 1990: 795–798.

Figures: Hart 1973:18; 46 cm TL, Vancouver Island.

Range: Wisner and McMillan (1990:796) found no valid records of capture north of Nootka Bay (about 49°33'N, 126°38'W), Vancouver Island, British Columbia. They discounted UW 2738, a collection of four specimens labeled as *E. stoutii* from "S.E. Alaska," collected by the International Fish Commission in 1931, evidently because they believed the locality data to be incorrect; but they did not say why they thought this. Lot UW 6231, comprising three specimens cataloged as *Polistotrema stoutii* from Clarence Strait, southeastern Alaska, collected in 1950, is missing (UW online catalog), so the identification cannot be confirmed. Quast and Hall (1972, errata sheet) and Hart (1973) reported that Alaskan records had not been confirmed. The southernmost record is from Punta San Pablo, Baja California (Knaggs et al. 1975), but a range only to southern California is still given by some authors. Range of depths given in records for more than 1,500 specimens studied by Wisner and McMillan (1990) was 16–633 m. Grinols (1965) reported depth of 944 m off Washington.

Size: Hart (1973) reported length to "25 inches (63.5 cm)" in a general statement. Greatest total length reported by Wisner and McMillan (1990) for males was 550 mm, and for females, 515 mm.

Order Petromyzontiformes
Family Petromyzontidae
Lampreys

Lampreys, family Petromyzontidae, are eel-like fishes that lack jaws, bone, paired fins, and scales. They live in cool regions of the world, mostly in the Northern Hemisphere, and can be restricted to fresh water for their entire lives or anadromous, spending part of their lives in salt water but returning to fresh water to spawn. In either case, they die after spawning. There are about 40 extant species, with 5 occurring in Alaska.

Diagnostic characteristics of adult lampreys include 7 pairs of porelike external lateral gill openings; 1 or 2 dorsal fins, continuous with the caudal fin; a single, median nostril; a circular mouth forming a suction disk; and horny teeth on the oral disk and tongue.

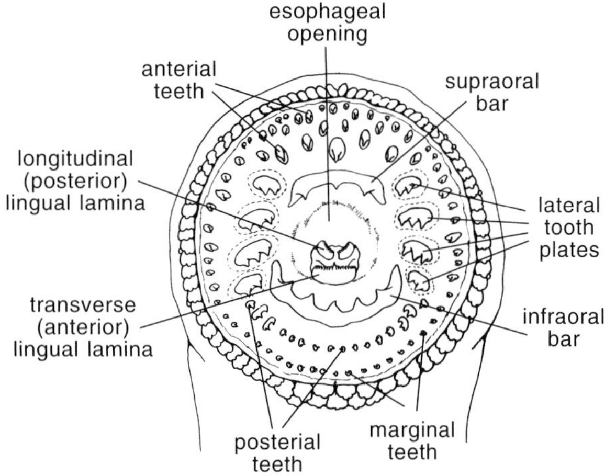

Dentition in *Lampetra tridentata*
(Adapted from Vladykov and Follett 1958.)

The number, arrangement, and size of the teeth are the most important criteria for identifying adult lampreys. Terminology is shown in the accompanying diagram of the disk and dentition in an Alaskan species, *Lampetra tridentata.* The terms *bar, lamina,* and *plate* are used interchangeably in the literature on lampreys. The supraoral tooth bar is immediately anterior to the front edge of the esophageal opening. The infraoral bar is immediately distal to the posterior edge of the esophageal opening. The tongue teeth are carried on a single transverse, anterior lamina and a pair of longitudinal, posterior lamina. Full descriptions of lamprey dentition can be found in Hubbs and Potter (1971) and Potter and Hilliard (1987).

In Nelson's (1994) classification, followed here, the subfamily Petromyzontinae comprises all of the Northern Hemisphere lampreys. Members of this group have a single supraoral tooth bar, rarely bearing more than 3 cusps (not more than 3 in Alaskan species). The Alaskan species are members of the tribe Lampetrini, in which the supraoral bar is broad, extending the width of the esophageal opening, and has an enlarged cusp at either end (the third cusp, usually present in Alaskan species only in *L. tridentata,* is at the middle of the bar). The Alaskan species are all in the genus *Lampetra.* Hubbs and Potter (1971), in a review of lamprey characters and revision of the taxonomy, included three subgenera in *Lampetra*: *Lampetra, Entosphenus,* and *Lethenteron.* Their allocation of species to subgenera, summarized in a helpful list by Potter (1980), is followed in this guide. Theirs is the prevailing usage among North American specialists, but some authors, including Vladykov and Follett (1967) and Vladykov and Kott (1976, 1978, 1979a, 1979b), preferred to treat the subgenera as distinct genera and others in their school, including Kottelat (1997), continue to do so. The main difference between *Entosphenus* and the other two subgenera is that *Entosphenus* has 4 pairs of lateral tooth plates and the others have 3 pairs. In subgenus *Lampetra* posterial teeth are lacking whereas they are present in *Lethenteron,* and the central laterals are typically tricuspid in *Lampetra* but bicuspid in *Lethenteron.* Other characters are given in the detailed key by Hubbs and Potter (1971). The question of subgenera is still being examined. An analysis of lamprey DNA by Docker et al. (1999) supports the view that *Entosphenus* is distinct from the others but showed considerable overlap between the other two subgenera.

The general development of the dentition, whether strong or weak, is closely tied to the two basic types of life cycle that occur in lampreys: parasitic and nonparasitic. The parasitic species include those that are anadromous and feed at sea before returning to fresh water to spawn, and others that do not leave fresh water. (A few anadromous species have given rise to landlocked lake forms, but not in Alaska.) Nonparasitic species stay in their natal streams and the adults are not only nonparasitic, they have a nonfunctional gut and do not feed at all. The adult phase is greatly abbreviated. As might be expected, the nonparasitic species generally have less well-developed dentitions with blunter teeth than the parasitic species. Although the teeth are stronger and sharper in the young adults of parasitic species, the teeth degenerate and become worn or lost as spawning time nears. Much of the tooth wear occurs as the fish progress during the spawning migration by holding onto rocks with their mouths.

Adult lampreys spawn in pits they excavate in stream riffles by removing stones with their mouths and fanning away fine particles with vibrations of the body. The sexes are separate. The eggs are small, not yolky, and number in the thousands. Eggs hatch into blind larvae called ammocoetes. The ammocoetes burrow into the sand or mud of quiet pools and backwaters and feed by filtering microorganisms and fine debris from the water. The following diagrams of the head and tail regions of a typical ammocoete show basic terminology.

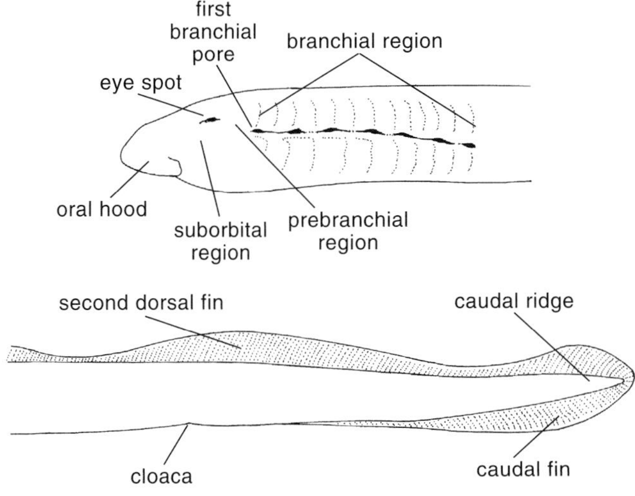

External features of lamprey ammocoetes
(Adapted from Richards et al. 1982.)

The ammocoetes metamorphose after 3–7 years, depending on species, into adults. Their transformation is radical, involving development of teeth and eyes, an isocercal caudal fin (hypocercal in the ammocoete), and other changes. (Only one other group of fishes has a distinctive, long-lived larval stage: the Elopomorpha, with a leptocephalus larva). The parasitic lampreys, after metamorphosis but before reproducing, feed on the flesh or the blood and other body fluids of other fish, sharks, and whales. The nonparasitic species live off their body reserves and reproduce and die the spring following their metamorphosis.

The maximum length of lamprey ammocoetes is about 10 cm and of parasitic adults is about 90 cm. Whereas parasitic lampreys rapidly increase in size after transformation, nonparasitic lampreys decrease in size and the ammocoetes are larger than the adults. Consequently, where sexually mature adults of closely related parasitic and nonparasitic species occur in the same streams, they can usually be separated on the basis of size. The ammocoetes, however, are difficult to identify to species with confidence. Ammocoetes of paired species (see below) are nearly identical and rarely can qualitative, morphometric, or meristic characters be used to distinguish them. Richards et al. (1982) raised ammocoetes in the laboratory to establish reliable criteria for distinguishing British Columbia species, and concluded that pigmentation patterns were the most reliable features.

Habitat and life history type are widely used to differentiate closely related lampreys. The prevailing hypothesis is that each of the nonparasitic lamprey species, with few exceptions, has evolved from an extant, probably anadromous, parasitic lamprey (e.g., Hardisty and Potter 1971, Vladykov and Kott 1979b, Potter 1980). The nonparasitic derivative of an ancestral parasitic species is called a *satellite species,* a term coined by Vladykov and Kott (1979b) to replace the older term *paired species* because there can be more than one derived species. Most authors also call any one of the satellite species in a group together with its ancestral form paired species. Although the satellite species show great morphological and genetic similarity to the ancestral species most specialists consider them distinct species because the different life history types appear to result in reproductive isolation. However, other authorities do not recognize life history type as a valid criterion of species differentiation and consider satellite species to be races or subspecies of the ancestral form.

It has been suggested that the evolution of freshwater nonparasitic lampreys may involve an intermediate freshwater feeding form, and there is evidence supporting this view (e.g., Beamish and Withler 1986, Youson and Beamish 1991). The occurrence of intermediate forms, although they may not be self-sustaining, may indicate reproductive isolation is not occurring in some populations, and the significance of intermediate forms along with the lack of genetic difference found in some paired species (e.g., Docker et al. 1999) requires further analysis with respect to the species question. Paired species in Alaska are the anadromous, parasitic *Lampetra ayresii* and its derivative the nonparasitic *L. richardsoni*; and *L. camtschatica* and its derivative *L. alaskense.*

Quast and Hall (1972) included four species of lamprey on their list of Alaskan fishes: Pacific lamprey, *Entosphenus tridentatus* (Gairdner); river lamprey, *Lampetra ayresii* (Günther); Arctic lamprey, *L. japonica* (Martens); and American brook lamprey, *L. lamottenii* (Lesueur). Following Hubbs and Potter (1971), we and most other authors, including Robins et al. (1991a), place *Entosphenus* in the synonymy of *Lampetra,* giving *L. tridentata* as the binomial for the Pacific lamprey. However, Kottelat (1997) and others in the school of Vladykov maintain the validity of *Entosphenus* as a genus (see commentary by Vladykov and Kott [1979b:6]). The Pacific lamprey occurs from southeastern Alaska to the Bering Sea and is one of the two most common lampreys in the state (the other is *L. camtschatica*).

The scientific name of the American river lamprey has not changed since the time of Quast and Hall's (1972) inventory, but it should be noted that, following provisions of the International Code of Zoological Nomenclature, the species name is correctly spelled *ayresii.* Many authors, including Quast and Hall (1972), Bailey and Robins (1988), and Robins et al. (1991a), dropped one *i*. This species occurs in southeastern Alaska.

The correct name for the Arctic lamprey is *L. camtschatica.* Kottelat (1997) found that this species name is available and, following the Code, has priority over *L. japonica,* the name previously in use. The Arctic lamprey is widespread in Alaska, except it is absent from the southeastern part of the state.

Alaskan specimens of a freshwater form identified by Quast and Hall (1972) and others as *L. lamottenii* were later referred to *Lethenteron alaskense* Vladykov & Kott, 1978, the Alaskan brook lamprey. Following Hubbs and Potter's (1971) classification of lamprey genera, the binomial is *Lampetra alaskense.* In Alaska this form occurs in some of the same streams as *L. camtschatica.* Outside Alaska, it has been recorded only from one locality in western Canada. To understand the nomenclatural history of *L. alaskense* it is important to know that *L. lamottenii* is an older name used for a time for American brook lamprey of eastern North America, now called *L. appendix* by some authorities (e.g., Robins et al. 1991a). The name *L. lamottenii,* along with the incorrect emendation *lamottei,* was suppressed in favor of a return to the name *L. appendix.* They are the same species. See Robins et al. (1980:68) for further explanation.

The taxonomic status of the Alaskan brook lamprey, *L. alaskense,* is unresolved, due largely to the differing viewpoints on significance of life history types in lamprey taxonomy and the consequent, presumed relationships of *L. alaskense* to both *L. camtschatica* and *L. appendix. Lampetra alaskense* has been variously treated as synonymous with *L. camtschatica* or *L. appendix,* as well as a distinct species. *Lampetra camtschatica* is widely viewed as being ancestral to both *L. appendix* and *L. alaskense* (as proposed by Vladykov and Kott 1979b); if life history is not a valid parameter for defining species, then on the basis of morphology and genetic similarity all three may be referred to *L. camtschatica* (the name having priority according to the Code).

Pending a different solution which may emerge from ongoing studies we choose to treat *L. alaskense* and *L. camtschatica* as species distinct from each other and from *L. appendix.* The following summary may help guide students of the Alaskan ichthyofauna through the literature on this complex subject. For clarity we use the binomials currently understood to be correct. Names actually used by authors can be found in the species account synonymies. Wilimovsky (1954, 1958) considered both *L. camtschatica* and the sympatric freshwater lamprey to be subspecies of *L. appendix,* and called the brook subspecies the Arctic brook lamprey. Heard (1966), who described the life history of this form in the Naknek river system, considered it to be a dwarfed form of *L. camtschatica* although he noted it was almost identical with *L. appendix.* McPhail and Lindsey (1970) regarded the Naknek population to be a nonparasitic phase of *L. camtschatica,* but also noted that *L. camtschatica* and *L. appendix* are closely similar and may not be specifically distinct. Quast and Hall (1972), following Wilimovsky (1954, 1958), identified the Alaskan freshwater form as American brook lamprey (*L. appendix*). Vladykov and Kott (1978, 1979b), who described *L. alaskense,* considered it to be closest to *L. appendix* but clearly distinct and standing with it as a satellite species of *L. camtschatica*; Potter (1980) also ascribed to this view. Bailey (1980) remarked that *L. alaskense* seems to differ from *L. appendix* chiefly in distribution, and Robins et al. (1980) judged it to be morphologically indistinguishable from *L. appendix* and excluded it as a distinct species from the American Fisheries Society list of North American fishes. Lindsey and McPhail (1986) treated *L. alaskense* as a distinct species by including it, along with *L. camtschatica,* on their list of fishes of the Yukon and Mackenzie river basins. Page and Burr (1991) treated *L. alaskense* as a possible subspecies of *L. appendix.* McAllister (1991), citing the interest of taxonomic stability until further data are published, retained *L. alaskense* as a distinct species on his list of Canadian fishes, as did Coad (1995) in his encyclopedia of Canadian fishes. Analysis of mitochrondrial DNA by Docker et al. (1999) indicated that *L. camtschatica* and *L. appendix* are closely related, although not identical as was the case with *L. ayresii* and *L. richardsoni* (see below). Relationship to *L. alaskense* was not examined, since the authors included it in the synonymy of *L. appendix.* Currently, a team of specialists are examining evolution of satellite species in lampreys of the world using mtDNA analysis, and will include recent material of *L. alaskense* collected from the lower Chena River near Fairbanks (C. B. Renaud, pers. comm., 29 Jul. 1998, 9 Jun. 2000).

The fifth Alaskan species is the western brook lamprey, *Lampetra richardsoni* Vladykov & Follett. Quast and Hall (1972) did not say why they excluded this species from their inventory, but ammocoetes from southeastern Alaska had been reported by Vladykov and Follett (1965) and it may be that Quast and Hall (1972) did not consider *L. richardsoni* a valid species but, rather, a life history variant of *L. ayresii*. Since then, in the 1980s, an ammocoete and three transformed individuals were collected from southeastern Alaska and identified as *L. richardsoni* by biologists of the National Marine Fisheries Service Auke Bay Laboratory (B. L. Wing, pers. comm., 13 Jun. 2000).

Like the taxonomic status of *L. alaskense* and *L. camtschatica,* the status of *L. richardsoni* depends on one's views regarding the significance of life history type and interpretation of recent findings in lamprey genetics. For example, populations of *L. richardsoni* have been discovered on Vancouver Island, British Columbia, that produce both the nonparasitic form and an intermediate, freshwater parasitic form, *L. richardsoni* var. *marifuga* (Beamish and Withler 1986, Youson and Beamish 1991). The forms are morphologically but not genetically distinguishable from each other and from *L. ayresii* (e.g., Docker et al. 1999). However, there is no evidence that the *marifuga* form successfully reproduces in nature, and apparent lack of genetic differentiation may be due to methodology. If speciation occurred within the last 10,000 years or so, in keeping with prevailing theory for speciation of freshwater fishes in areas that were recently glaciated, there would not necessarily be any differences yet detectable in the amount of mtDNA examined. A search for more variable nuclear markers may provide a higher degree of resolution (M. F. Docker, pers. comm., 25 Jul. 2000).

Several common names are currently in use for some lampreys. For example, *L. alaskense* is called the darktail lamprey, Alaskan lamprey, Alaskan brook lamprey, and Arctic brook lamprey. This guide uses lamprey names proposed by Vladykov and Kott (1979a), so *L. alaskense* is the Alaskan brook lamprey. Their rules for giving lampreys common names are: (1) parasitic species are named by their geographical area (e.g., Arctic lamprey, Pacific lamprey) or by their color (none of the Alaskan species is named for its color); and (2) nonparasitic species are distinguished by including the term *brook lamprey* (e.g., Alaskan brook lamprey, western brook lamprey).

The following key to adult lampreys of Alaska draws on information from several sources. Like keys to adult lampreys of other parts of the world, is it based on characters which have not become obscured or obliterated by the degenerative changes that accompany sexual maturation. In the nonparasitic species, particularly, degeneration may render structures difficult to discern and individuals are easiest to identify following transformation but before the spawning migration is well under way. For the key to ammocoetes, the key to British Columbia ammocoetes of Richards et al. (1982) was modified by adding the non-Canadian species *L. camtschatica*. Ammocoetes of *L. alaskense* have not been described, although Vladykov and Kott (1978) reported that some were collected in the Mackenzie River basin from the Martin River.

Key to Adults of Petromyzontidae of Alaska

1 Supraoral bar with 3 (rarely 2) cusps; 4 pairs of lateral tooth plates, the central 2 pairs each with 3 cusps; infraoral bar with 4–8 (usually 5 or 6) cusps . . . . *Lampetra tridentata,* page 61

1 Supraoral bar with 2 (rarely 3) cusps; 3 pairs of lateral tooth plates, each plate with 2 or 3 cusps; infraoral bar with 5–10 (usually 7 or 8) cusps . . . . (2)

2 (1) Posterial teeth present . . . . (3)

2 Posterial teeth absent . . . . (4)

3 (2) Supplementary marginal teeth absent from lateral areas of disk; cusps on tongue teeth well developed, pointed .... *Lampetra camtschatica,* page 62

3 A few supplementary marginal teeth present in lateral areas of disk; cusps on tongue teeth poorly developed, blunt .... *Lampetra alaskense,* page 63

4 (2) Anterial teeth prominent and sharp; large median tooth on tongue; teeth on lateral plates prominent; 3 (rarely 2) cusps on central lateral tooth plates .... *Lampetra ayresii,* page 64

4 Anterial teeth absent or inconspicuous and blunt; no median tooth on tongue, or median tooth present but blunt; teeth on lateral plates not prominent; 2 or 3 cusps on central lateral tooth plates .... *Lampetra richardsoni,* page 65

Key to Ammocoetes of Petromyzontidae of Alaska*

1 Tail heavily pigmented in caudal ridge area .... *Lampetra richardsoni,* page 65

1 Tail lightly pigmented in caudal ridge area .... (2)

2 (1) Body and head extensively pigmented, including lower half of oral hood .... *Lampetra tridentata,* page 61

2 Body and head lightly pigmented, or lower half of oral hood unpigmented .... (3)

3 (2) No prominent line of pigment behind eye spot................. *Lampetra camtschatica,* page 62

3 Prominent line of pigment behind eye spot .... *Lampetra ayresii,* page 64

*Ammocoetes of *L. alaskense* have not been described.

Lampetra tridentata (Richardson, 1836) **Pacific lamprey**

Eastern Chukchi Sea, one record off Cape Lisburne; other records are, at sea, from Bering Sea near Nome to northern Baja California at Punta Canoas; in fresh water, from Wood River and streams of Unalaska Island in western Alaska to northern Baja California at Rio Santo Domingo; rare to occasional marine records from Commander Islands, Pacific coast of Kamchatka, and Hokkaido.

Anadromous and parasitic, except for a few freshwater, nonparasitic populations in Oregon and California; at sea to depth of 1,463 m, usually less than 250 m; ammocoetes in silt, mud, and sand in shallow eddies and backwaters of streams for 4 or 5 years, then metamorphose; migrate to sea at age 5 or 6, feed at sea 12–14 months; migrate, taking 4 months, to headwater areas; spawn next spring.

- Blue-black to dark brown dorsally, pale or silver ventrally; dorsal and caudal fins dusky.
- **Supraoral bar with 3 cusps**, rarely 2.
- **Infraoral bar usually with 5 or 6 cusps**.
- **Lateral tooth plates 4, the central 2 pairs each with 3 sharp cusps**.
- Tongue with numerous (15–20) fine teeth, all about same size.
- Posterial teeth present.
- Length to 760 mm TL, typically 130–690 mm (much larger than other Alaskan lampreys).

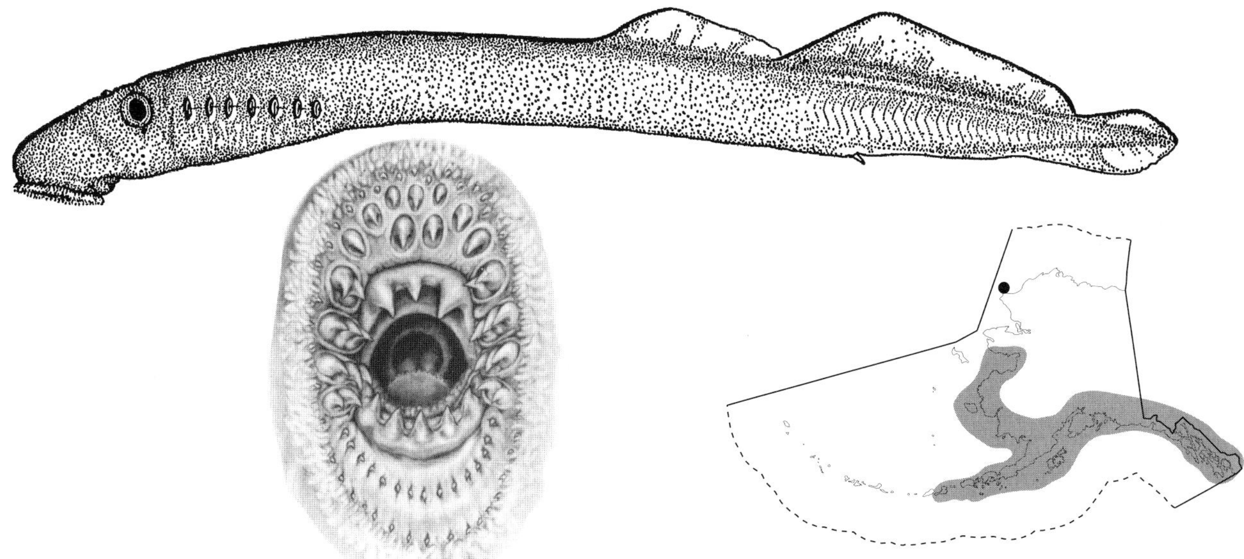

Notes & Sources — *Lampetra (Entosphenus) tridentata* (Richardson (ex Gairdner), 1836)
Petromyzon tridentatus Gairdner, 1836
Entosphenus tridentatus: Vladykov and Follett 1958, 1967; McPhail and Lindsey 1970; and others.
Hubbs and Potter (1971) classified *Entosphenus* as a subgenus of *Lampetra*; treatment not recognized by all authors.

Description: McPhail and Lindsey 1970:56–59; Scott and Crossman 1973:42–45; Morrow 1980:8–9; Coad 1995:506.

Figures: Lateral view: McPhail and Lindsey 1970:56. Disk: Morrow 1980, pl. 20A.

Range: Northernmost record is UBC 63-1190, a specimen from the Chukchi Sea off Cape Lisburne at 69°15'N, 165°55'W (N. J. Wilimovsky, pers. comm., 4 Apr. 1995); J. D. McPhail (pers. comm., 17 Jan. 2001) confirmed the identification. Nearest record to that is from Nome (Morrow 1980), a specimen collected in 1973 by Vogt (1988) 11 km southwest of Nome from an otter trawl sampling in 20 m of water. McPhail and Lindsey (1970) wrote that *L. tridentata* had been recorded from near St. Matthew Island, but that the only specimen they had seen from north of the Alaska Peninsula was a specimen from Wood River. Heard (1966) found none in the Naknek River system, despite extensive collecting there over several years. Gilbert (1896) reported a specimen was taken in one of the small streams of Unalaska Island, and Jordan and Gilbert (1899) reported five specimens in the stomach of a fur seal from Bering Sea. Fedorov and Sheiko (2002) reported it to be rare off the Commander Islands, Russia. Records from western Gulf of Alaska include UW 2678 from Uyak Bay, Kodiak Island; and UW 167 from 160 km southeast of Cape Chiniak at depth of 1,463 m (specimen collected in 1929 by the IFC). McPhail and Lindsey (1970) reported spawning in Copper River (drains to eastern Gulf of Alaska) in June. Lots UBC 63-211 and 63-212 (total of 5 specimens) are from Copper River, and UW 1674 (2), from Tazlina River, a Copper River tributary. Evermann and Goldsborough (1907) reported spawning populations in the Naha River near Loring and a stream flowing into Yes Bay. Quast and Hall (1972) also recorded it from southeastern Alaska; currently represented from seven localities in the ABL collection. Beamish and Levings (1991), reporting abundance and migrations in Nicola River, a tributary of Fraser River, British Columbia, estimated the average migration there of young adults to sea to be 100,000. Ruiz-Campos and Gonzalez-Guzman (1996) reported an ammocoete taken 600 m above the mouth of the Rio Santo Domingo, Baja California; this extended the known freshwater range south from Santa Ana River in southern California reported by Jordan and Evermann (1896b). Coad (1995) reported a maximum depth at sea of 250 m, and Fedorov and Sheiko (2002), 1,100 m.

Lampetra camtschatica (Tilesius, 1811) **Arctic lamprey**

Arctic coast to Kenai Peninsula; up Yukon River into Yukon Territory, also in Kuskokwim and Tanana river drainages; almost circumpolar, from Lapland south to Caspian Sea, eastward to Kamchatka and south to Korea, and eastward across North America to Northwest Territories and south to Great Slave Lake.

Anadromous, parasitic; at sea to depth of 50 m; ammocoetes in muddy margins and backwaters of rivers and lakes; transformed adults feed at sea or in lakes; spawn in gravel riffles and runs of clear streams.

- Blue-black to dark brown dorsally, yellow to light brown ventrally; dorsal fins light tan to gray; dark blotch on 2nd dorsal fin and on tail.
- Teeth on disk pointed, very sharp, well cornified (but becoming blunt in spawning individuals).
- Supraoral bar with 2 cusps (rarely 3).
- Infraoral bar with 5–10 cusps, usually 7 or 8.
- Lateral tooth plates 3, central pair with 2 cusps.
- **Tongue teeth well developed, pointed, sharp.**
- **Posterial teeth present.**
- **Supplementary marginal teeth absent** from lateral areas of disk.
- Length to 625 mm TL, typically 130–360 mm.

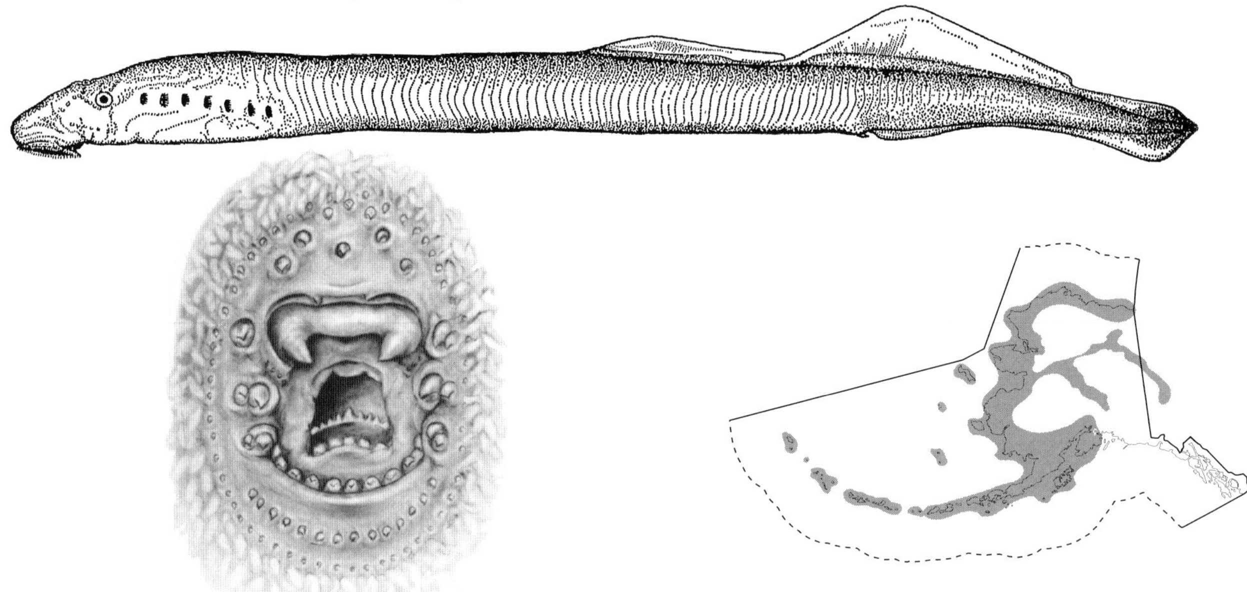

Notes & Sources — *Lampetra (Lethenteron) camtschatica* (Tilesius, 1811)
Petromyzon marinus camtschaticus Tilesius, 1811
Petromyzon borealis Girard, 1859
Petromyzon japonicus Martens, 1868
Ammocoetes aureus Bean, 1881
Lampetra aurea: Jordan and Evermann 1896b.
Lampetra japonica: Berg 1948.
Entosphenus lamottei japonicus: Wilimovsky 1954, 1958.
Lethenteron japonicum: Vladykov in Hureau and Monod 1973 and elsewhere.
Lethenteron camtschaticum: Kottelat 1997.

Kottelat (1997) determined that the name *Petromyzon marinus camtschaticus* Tilesius, 1811 has priority for the Arctic lamprey and classified the species in *Lethenteron,* giving the name *Lethenteron camtschaticum* (Tilesius). Classifying *Lethenteron* as a subgenus of *Lampetra* following Hubbs and Potter (1971) and changing the spelling of the specific epithet to match the gender of the genus, we use the name *Lampetra camtschatica.* Of interest is that this name was used by Pallas (1814:67, 1811) but Jordan and Evermann (1896b:13) did not use it on the ground that it was not intended as a binomial name, and listed it in the synonymy of *Lampetra aurea* (Bean).

The only parasitic member of subgenus *Lethenteron.* Probably ancestral to nonparasitic forms, including Alaskan brook lamprey, *L. alaskense,* and American brook lamprey, *L. appendix* (Vladykov and Kott 1979b, Potter 1980).

Freshwater form in Siberia and Japan currently is recognized as a distinct species, Siberian lamprey, *L. kessleri* (Poltorykhina 1974, Kottelat 1997, Reshetnikov et al. 1997).

Description: Heard 1966; McPhail and Lindsey 1970:50–55; Scott and Crossman 1973:58–61; Vladykov and Kott 1978; Morrow 1980:9–10; Page and Burr 1991:21–22.

Figures: Lateral view: McPhail and Lindsey 1970:50. Disk: Morrow 1980, pl. 20B.

Range: Most common lamprey in Alaska, well documented from the region by Bean (1881a), Turner (1886), Nelson (1887), Evermann and Goldsborough (1970), Walters (1953, 1955), Wilimovsky (1954, 1958), Heard (1966), McPhail and Lindsey (1970), Quast and Hall (1972), Morrow (1974, 1980), and many others. Fedorov and Sheiko (2002) reported it to be common in the vicinity of the Commander Islands, Russia, and gave a maximum depth of 50 m. In Alaska often found in the same streams as *L. alaskense.*

Lampetra alaskense (Vladykov & Kott, 1978) Alaskan brook lamprey

Alaska and Kenai peninsulas to Chatanika and Chena rivers near Fairbanks; Martin River, Mackenzie River basin, Northwest Territories; known only from those regions of northwestern North America.

Freshwater, nonparasitic; at about 4 years of age transforms from ammocoete in fall, moves downstream into lakes to overwinter; spawns the following spring and summer in shallows of lakes and rivers.

- Color of adults in preservative gray-brown dorsally, white ventrally; dark blotch on 2nd dorsal fin; tail dark.
- Teeth on disk blunt and weakly cornified.
- Supraoral bar with 2 cusps.
- Infraoral bar with 6–11 cusps.
- Lateral tooth plates 3, central pair with 2 cusps.
- **Tongue teeth poorly developed, blunt.**
- **Posterial teeth present.**
- **A few supplementary marginal teeth present** on lateral areas of disk.
- Length to 188 mm TL, typically 120–170 mm.

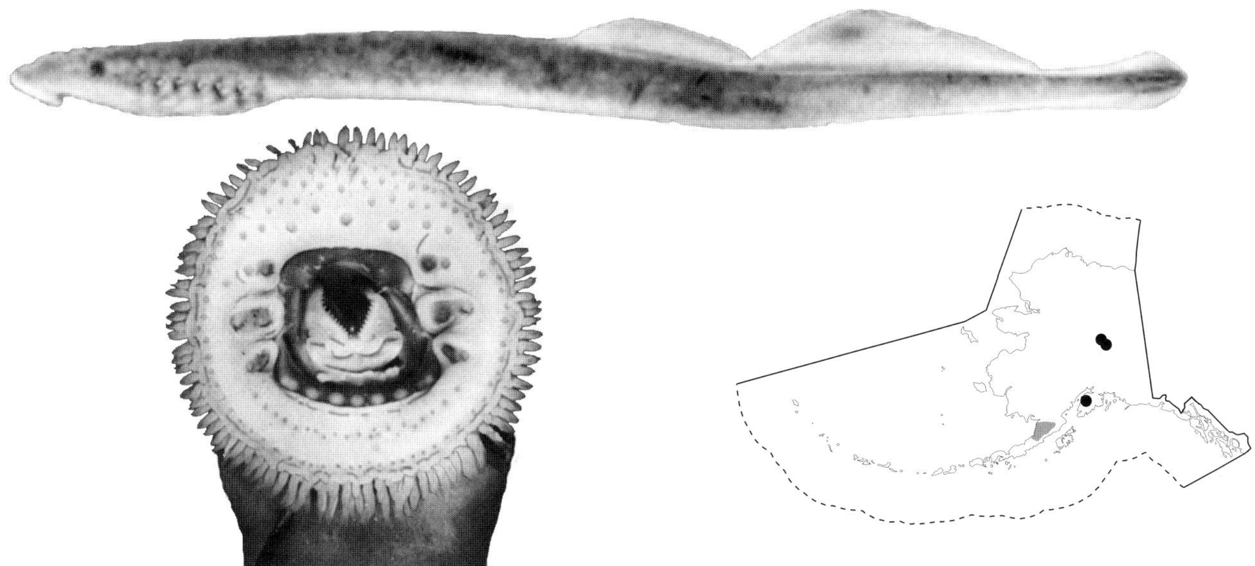

Notes & Sources — *Lampetra (Lethenteron) alaskense* (Vladykov & Kott, 1978)
Entosphenus lamottei lamottei (Lesueur): Wilimovsky 1954, 1958 (Alaskan part of range only).
Lampetra japonica: Heard 1966 ("dwarfed freshwater form").
Lampetra lamottenii (Lesueur): Hubbs and Lagler 1958, Quast and Hall 1972 (Alaskan references only).
Lethenteron alaskense Vladykov & Kott, 1978
Lampetra appendix alaskense: Page and Burr 1991.

Possibly a subspecies of American brook lamprey, *L. appendix* (DeKay, 1842). Hubbs and Lagler (1958) considered the Alaskan form to be the same or virtually indistinguishable and Wilimovsky (1954, 1958) considered both this form and *L. japonica* to be subspecies of American brook lamprey. Robins et al. (1980, 1991a) treated *L. alaskense* as junior synonym of *L. appendix*. There is no consensus. Currently, C. B. Renaud (pers. comm., 29 Jul. 1998, 9 Jun. 2000) and coworkers are working with mtDNA to examine relationships of these forms.

The species name *lamottenii* (originally *Petromyzon lamottenii* Lesueur, 1827), also spelled *lamottei*, was for a time used for American brook lamprey, then suppressed in favor of a return to *L. appendix*, but the status of the name *lamottenii* is uncertain. See Robins et al. (1980:68) and Eschmeyer (1998:866) for details and additional literature.

Thought to be a derivative of *L. camtschatica* (Vladykov and Kott 1979b, Potter 1980, Docker et al. 1999).

Similar form in eastern Russia is now recognized as Asiatic brook lamprey, *L. reissneri* (e.g., Reshetnikov et al. 1997).

Sometimes spelled, incorrectly, *L. alaskensis* (e.g., Potter 1980) or *L. alaskanse* (e.g., Vladykov et al. in Lee et al. 1980).

Description: Vladykov and Kott 1978; Coad 1995:24–25.

Figures: Vladykov and Kott 1978, figs. 1 and 3; holotype, male in spawning condition, 164 mm TL, West Creek, tributary of Brooks Lake, Alaska.

Range: Wilimovsky (1954, 1958) and Hubbs and Lagler (1958) identified this lamprey as *Entosphenus lamottei lamottei,* and gave a range in Alaska from central Alaska and the Yukon River system to the Gulf of Alaska. Specific localities in the Naknek system were reported by Heard (1966), who believed it to be the same as *L. japonica* (= *L. camtschatica*). Quast and Hall (1972) identified specimens from the Yukon River and Kenai Peninsula in the Auke Bay Laboratory collection as *L. lamottenii*. This form was described as *Lethenteron alaskense* by Vladykov and Kott (1978) from a sample of 67 metamorphosed lampreys collected from the Naknek River system, Alaska Peninsula, in 1962 and 1964 (by Heard); Chatanika River near Fairbanks, Alaska, in 1976; and Martin River, Mackenzie River basin, Northwest Territories, in winter 1972–1973. Four ammocoetes, also collected from the Martin River, were not described. Additional records from the Alaska Peninsula in the Kvichak, Egegik, and Ugashik river systems are shown on the map by Vladykov et al. (in Lee et al. 1980), who gave the Ugashik River as the westernmost known limit of range. Recently collected from the lower Chena River near Fairbanks (C. B. Renaud, pers. comm., 29 Jul. 1998).

Lampetra ayresii (Günther, 1870) American river lamprey

Southeastern Alaska north of Juneau at Tee Harbor to California at San Francisco Bay and the Sacramento-San Joaquin drainage; endemic to West Coast of North America.

Anadromous, parasitic; ammocoetes in sandy and muddy pools of streams; metamorphose to adult form in summer, migrate the next spring and early summer to feed in estuarine and coastal waters for 2–3 months; migrate upstream in fall to late winter, spawning the next spring in clear gravel riffles.

- Dark yellow or brown to silver-gray or blue-black dorsally, silver to white ventrally; fins yellow; tail with dark gray blotch.
- Teeth generally sharp (but becoming blunt in spawning individuals).
- Supraoral bar with 2 cusps.
- Infraoral bar with 7–10, usually 9, cusps; often bicuspid at each end of bar.
- **Lateral tooth plates 3, with 3 cusps on central pair** (rarely with 2 cusps).
- **Tongue with large triangular median tooth** and about 7 small teeth on each side.
- **Anterial teeth prominent, sharp.**
- **Posterial teeth absent.**
- Length to 311 mm TL, typically 120–290 mm.

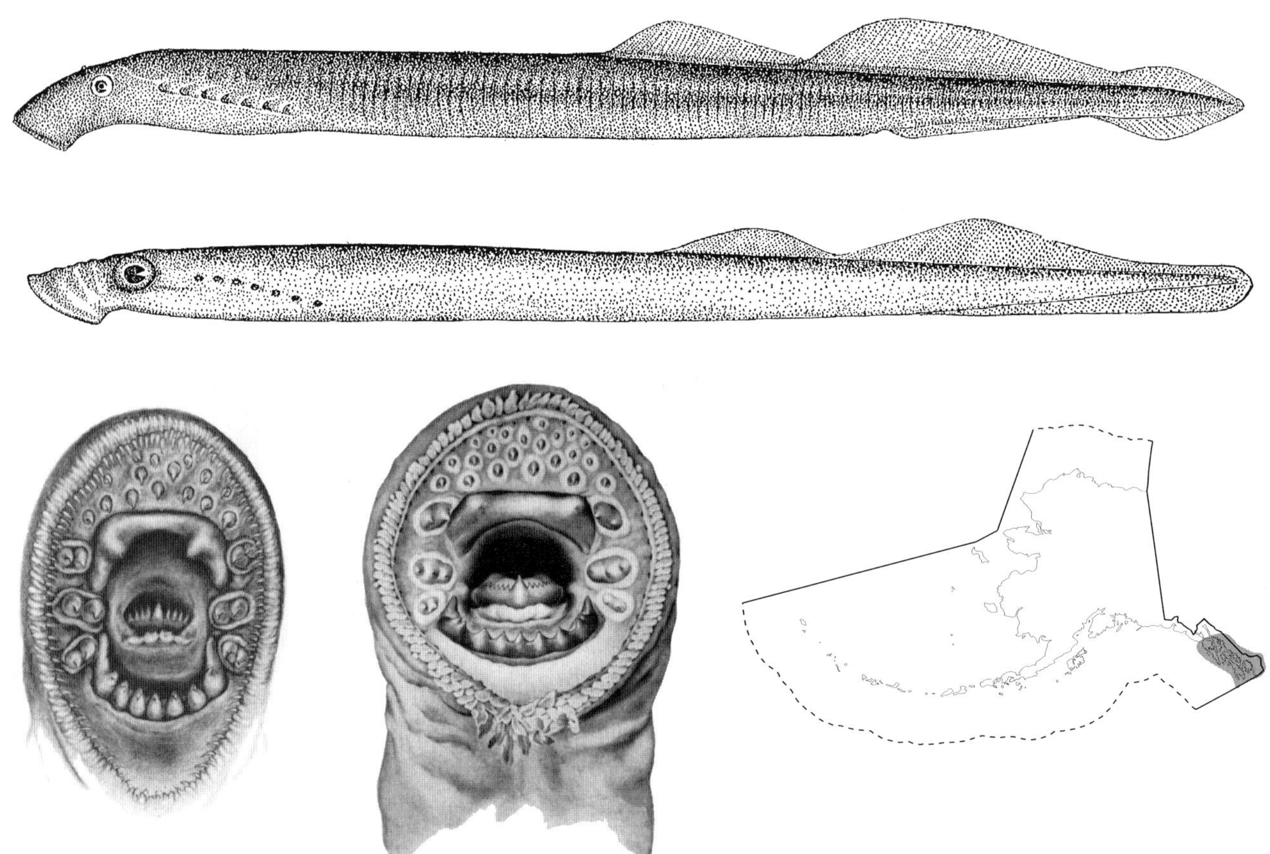

Notes & Sources — *Lampetra (Lampetra) ayresii* (Günther, 1870)
Petromyzon ayresii Günther, 1870

Description: Vladykov and Follett 1958; Scott and Crossman 1973:55–57; Morrow 1980:10–11; Page and Burr 1991:22–23; Coad 1995:594. Of 70 specimens of *L. ayresii* examined by Vladykov and Follett (1958), only 1 had a bicuspid central lateral tooth plate, and this was only on the right side of the disk.

Figures: Lateral views: Hart 1973:22; upper, 170 mm TL, Moresby Island, British Columbia; lower, 110 mm TL, off Fraser River, B.C. Disk at left: Morrow 1980, pl. 20C; presumably from Alaska; note bicuspid central lateral tooth plate. Disk at right: Vladykov and Follett 1958, fig. 2; neotype, female, 147 mm TL, San Francisco Bay.

Range: Previously recorded in Alaska from Stephens Passage (Quast and Hall 1972) and Tee Harbor (Scott and Crossman 1973). Recently B. L. Wing (pers. comm., 13 Jun. 2000) identified a transformed specimen taken in 1987 from Taku River as this species; the specimen is housed in ABL permanent collection. The UBC has collections from Tee Harbor–Lynn Canal area, Douglas Island, Taku River, and Portland Canal. In British Columbia, feeding adults are most common in Strait of Georgia and probably originated from the Fraser River since *L. ayresii* has not been found in any drainage flowing into the strait (Beamish and Withler 1986). In Strait of Georgia in 1975, an estimated 667,000 lampreys killed between 60 million and 600 million juvenile fish (Coad 1995). Not often found in Alaska.

Lampetra richardsoni Vladykov & Follett, 1965 **western brook lamprey**

Southeastern Alaska in Taku River to California in Sacramento–San Joaquin drainage; endemic to West Coast of North America.

Freshwater, nonparasitic; ammocoetes in silt or sand at margins of spawning streams, transform after about 6 years in summer through fall; overwinter without feeding, spawn in spring to early summer in coarse gravel and sand at head of riffle in quiet water, then die (live 4–6 months as adults).

- Brown, olive, or black dorsally; pale or silvery ventrally; fins olive-green and translucent; conspicuous dark area on caudal fin; in preservative, gray dorsally, whitish ventrally.
- Teeth generally blunt.
- Supraoral bar with 2 broad, blunt cusps.
- Infraoral bar with 7–9 cusps, rarely 6 or 10.
- **Lateral tooth plates 3, with 2 or 3 cusps on central pair.**
- **Median tongue tooth absent or, if present, blunt.**
- **Anterial teeth absent or peglike.**
- **Posterial teeth absent.**
- Length to 173 mm TL, typically 98–169 mm.

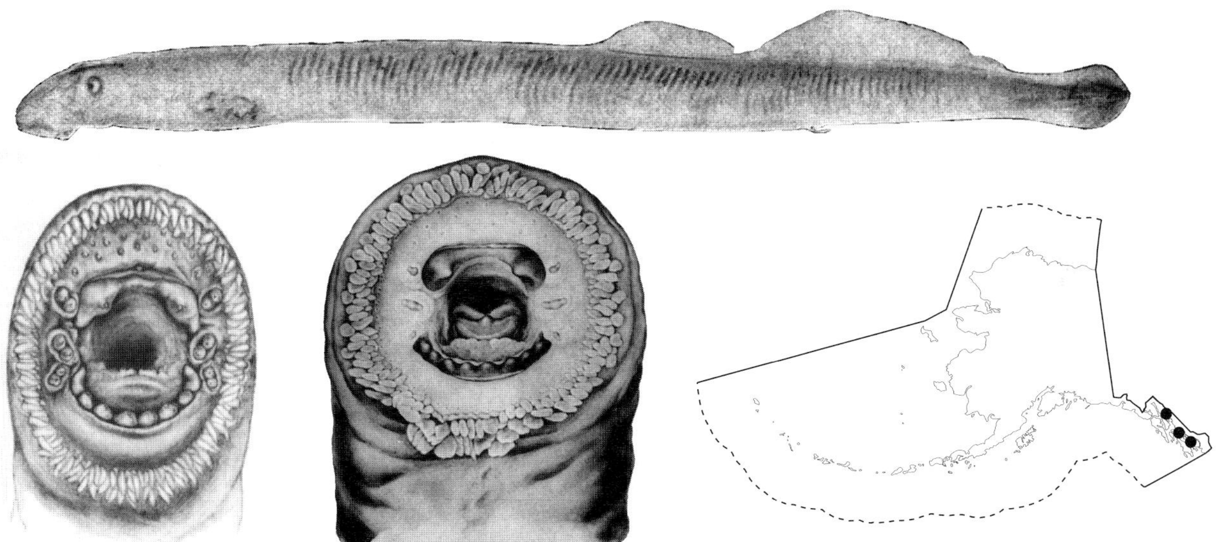

Notes & Sources — *Lampetra (Lampetra) richardsoni* Vladykov & Follett, 1965
Lampetra pacifica Vladykov, 1973

Considered to be a derivative of *L. ayresii* (Vladykov and Kott 1979b, Potter 1980). Mitochondrial DNA analysis showed *L. ayresii* and *L. richardsoni* to be genetically indistinguishable, but the methodology did not allow detection of differences that may have occurred in the past 10,000 years or so (Docker et al. 1999). A silvery, freshwater, parasitic intermediate form, *L. richardsoni* var. *marifuga,* is found on Vancouver Island, British Columbia (Beamish and Withler 1986, Youson and Beamish 1991).

The American Fisheries Society (Robins et al. 1991a), following a suggestion made by Bond and Kan (1986), placed the Pacific brook lamprey, *L. pacifica,* in the synonymy of the western brook lamprey, *L. richardsoni.* Described as a second nonparasitic derivative of *L. ayresii* by Vladykov (1973), *L. pacifica* inhabits streams of Oregon and California. It has been extirpated from southern California (Swift et al. 1993).

Description: Vladykov and Follett 1965; Scott and Crossman 1973:65–68; Morrow 1980:11–12; Page and Burr 1991:23; Coad 1995:833. Vladykov and Follett (1965) found that of 23 mostly spawning or close-to-spawning individuals, 21 (91%) had a bicuspid central lateral plate on both sides (19) or one side (2). Beamish and Withler (1986) found that in recently metamorphosed specimens (in which tooth or cusp counts are more reliable) the central lateral plate was *not* predominantly bicuspid.

Figures: Lateral view: Vladykov and Follett 1965, fig. 5; prespawning male, 154 mm TL, Smith Creek, Cultus Lake, B.C. Disk at left: Morrow 1980, pl. 20D. Disk at right: Vladykov and Follett 1965, fig. 4; paratype, prespawning male, 152 mm TL, Cultus Lake, British Columbia; note blunt median tooth on tongue and presence of tricuspid central lateral tooth plates.

Range: First record for Alaska comprised two ammocoetes (USNM 84411 and 84447; 106 and 175 mm TL) collected in 1907 from McDonald Lake, on the Cleveland Peninsula just north of Yes Bay (Vladykov and Follett 1965). B. L. Wing (pers. comm., 10 Oct. 1997) reported the only other Alaskan collections we know of: two specimens (AB 83-9; 98–121 mm SL) collected 20 Jun. 1982 by J. Heifitz from Bear Creek, Mitkof Island, the smaller transformed and the larger still with feathery feeding palps; and two transformed individuals (AB 87-31; 155–160 mm SL) collected 21 Jul. 1987 by M. Murphy and coworkers from Taku River. Not common in Alaska, but ammocoetes occur as densely as 170 per square meter elsewhere in the Pacific Northwest (Scott and Crossman 1973).

Size: Vladykov 1973; for *L. pacifica.* If *L. pacifica* is not treated as a junior synonym, maximum length recorded for *L. richardsoni* is 154 mm and typical range 101–149 mm (Vladykov and Follett 1965, Vladykov and Kott 1979b).

Superclass Gnathostomata
Jawed vertebrates

Gnathostomes, or jawed vertebrates, include amphibians, reptiles, birds, and mammals, as well as modern fishes. In addition to having jaws, gnathostomes have gill arches that are not fused to the neurocranium and are internal to the gill lamellae. The gills are covered with ectoderm and directed externally, and in fishes open to the surface through slits although the opercular opening, when present, in some species is small and porelike. Endochrondral bone is present, paired limbs and vertebral centra are usually present, there are three semicircular canals, and a bony exoskeleton is rarely developed. Worldwide about 48,100 species of extant jawed vertebrates have been identified. More than half, about 24,535 species, are fishes (Nelson 1994).

Grade Chondrichthiomorphi

Nelson (1994) classified the jawed vertebrates in three grades: Placodermiomorphi, Chondrichthiomorphi, and Teleostomi. The first is a group of extinct, armored fishes. The Chondrichthiomorphi comprises the elasmobranchs and other cartilaginous fishes, both fossil and living. The other jawed fishes amount to about half the species of the Teleostomi. This arrangement differs from Nelson's (1984) previous placement of all fishes in the grade Pisces and other jawed vertebrates in the grade Tetrapoda.

Class Chondrichthyes
Cartilaginous fishes

Living cartilaginous fishes are the holocephalans, represented in Alaskan waters by one species of chimaera, or ratfish, and the elasmobranchs, represented by several species of sharks and skates. The ratfish and most of the sharks that occur in Alaskan waters are warmer-water species and are relatively uncommon in Alaska or occur mostly off the southeastern coasts of the state. Most of the skates present in Alaska are relatively common in the region, especially in the Bering Sea.

In living cartilaginous fishes the skeleton is often calcified but seldom, if ever, ossified. The skull lacks sutures. The teeth in most species are not fused to the jaws and are replaced serially. Typically there is one nasal passage on each side, divided by a flap into incurrent and excurrent openings. The blood of most cartilaginous fishes has a high concentration of urea and trimethylene oxide, converted from toxic ammonia, which allows water to be drawn freely into the body. The swim bladder is absent, and an intestinal spiral valve is present. Fertilization is internal, accomplished via pelvic claspers of the male inserted in the female cloaca and oviducts.

Cartilaginous fishes produce embryos in leather-like cases, which are either permanent or temporary. Permanent egg cases are produced by the oviparous species, such as the skates (Rajidae) and cat sharks (Scyliorhinidae), in which the young undergo development completely within the shell and emerge similar to adult form. Each egg case contains one or more embryos, up to seven in *Raja binoculata.* Temporary egg cases are produced by ovoviviparous species, including soupfin shark, *Galeorhinus galeus,* and spiny dogfish, *Squalus acanthias.* The young, numbering one to four per shell, are encased only until their external gills begin to be absorbed. At this stage the shell ruptures and the young complete their development within the uterus. They are born more or less fully formed and the shell is resorbed or sloughed. In *S. acanthias* the discarded shell is a long, thin-walled tube, clear amber in color. Development to hatching takes a few months to a year or more—even to 2 years for *S. acanthias,* which may have the longest gestation of any vertebrate.

Empty egg cases of the permanent type from several species of skates are often found entangled in fishing nets or on beaches in Alaska. One species of shark that produces a permanent egg case, *Apristurus brunneus,* has been recorded from Alaska, but it does not reproduce in the region.

Subclass Holocephali
Holocephalans

The taxa representing the two main lines of evolution within the Chondrichthyes—the holocephalans and the elasmobranchs—are ranked as subclasses. The holocephalans are believed to be the more primitive lineage. Holocephalan characteristics include, among those listed by Nelson (1994): 4 gills covered by a flap, leaving a single external opening, on each side; no spiracles; slow tooth replacement; separate anal and urogenital openings (no cloaca); skin in adults naked; no stomach; and no ribs. Males have a clasping organ on the head, as well as the pelvic claspers common to elasmobranchs.

Extant holocephalans are classified in the superorder Holocephalimorpha, with teeth mainly consisting of a few large plates; the palatoquadrate fused to the cranium; and a dorsal fin spine usually present.

Order Chimaeriformes
Chimaeras

The order Chimaeriformes includes living and fossil chimaeras. The extant suborder is the Chimaeroidei, including chimaeras with two dorsal fins, the first erectile and short-based, the second nonerectile and long-based; and an inferior mouth. In Nelson's (1994) classification of fishes of the world, extant chimaeras are distributed among three families. One species exists in the marine waters off the southern coasts of Alaska.

Family Chimaeridae
Shortnose chimaeras

Shortnose chimaeras, also called ratfishes, inhabit marine waters of the Atlantic and Pacific oceans at shallow to moderate depths. The range of the spotted ratfish, *Hydrolagus colliei,* extends into Alaska, where it is occasionally captured in the eastern Gulf of Alaska as far north as Cape Spencer. A specimen taken off Kodiak Island in 1994 and recently reported by J. E. Blackburn (pers. comm., 23 Jul. 1998) is the only record from the western Gulf of Alaska.

Shortnose chimaeras have projecting, rounded snouts and are shortnosed only in comparison to species in other families of the order Chimaeriformes. They have large heads, gradually tapering bodies, and large, paddlelike pectoral fins. A poison gland associated with the dorsal spine produces venom that is painful to humans. The tail is diphycercal, and the anal fin is joined to or separate from the caudal fin. In species of the genus *Hydrolagus,* meaning "water hare," the head has a rabbitlike appearance partly owing to prominent, chisel-like tooth plates.

Shortnose chimaeras produce their young in two oval, bluntly pointed cases, with one embryo per case. The embryos take a year to develop. The maximum length recorded for chimaeras (all three families) is about 1.5 m (5 ft) (Nelson 1994). Spotted ratfish, *H. colliei,* reach almost 1 m (3.3 ft).

Hydrolagus colliei (Lay & Bennett, 1839) **spotted ratfish**

One record from western Gulf of Alaska east of Kodiak Island; more common from eastern Gulf of Alaska off Cape Spencer to Pacific Ocean off Baja California and to northern Gulf of California.

Taken from surface to depth of 913 m, usually near bottom at depths of 50–400 m.

- Silvery or brownish, with iridescent hues of gold, green, and blue; numerous white spots on body; dorsal and caudal fin margins dark; eyes green.
- Males with a club-shaped clasper on head; long, denticle-covered clasper (the copulatory organ) posterior to each pelvic fin; and shorter, hooked clasper lying in sheath anterior to each pelvic fin.
- First dorsal fin high and triangular, with stout, serrate spine; second dorsal long, low, and broadly notched; anal fin joined to caudal fin; caudal fin tapering to fine point.
- Scales absent, skin slippery.
- Lateral line canals prominent.
- Teeth prominent, projecting, directed forward.
- Length of adults to 97 cm TL.
- Egg case spindle-shaped, with one end drawn out into a filament and with longitudinal ridges, some elaborately fringed; length to 20 cm.

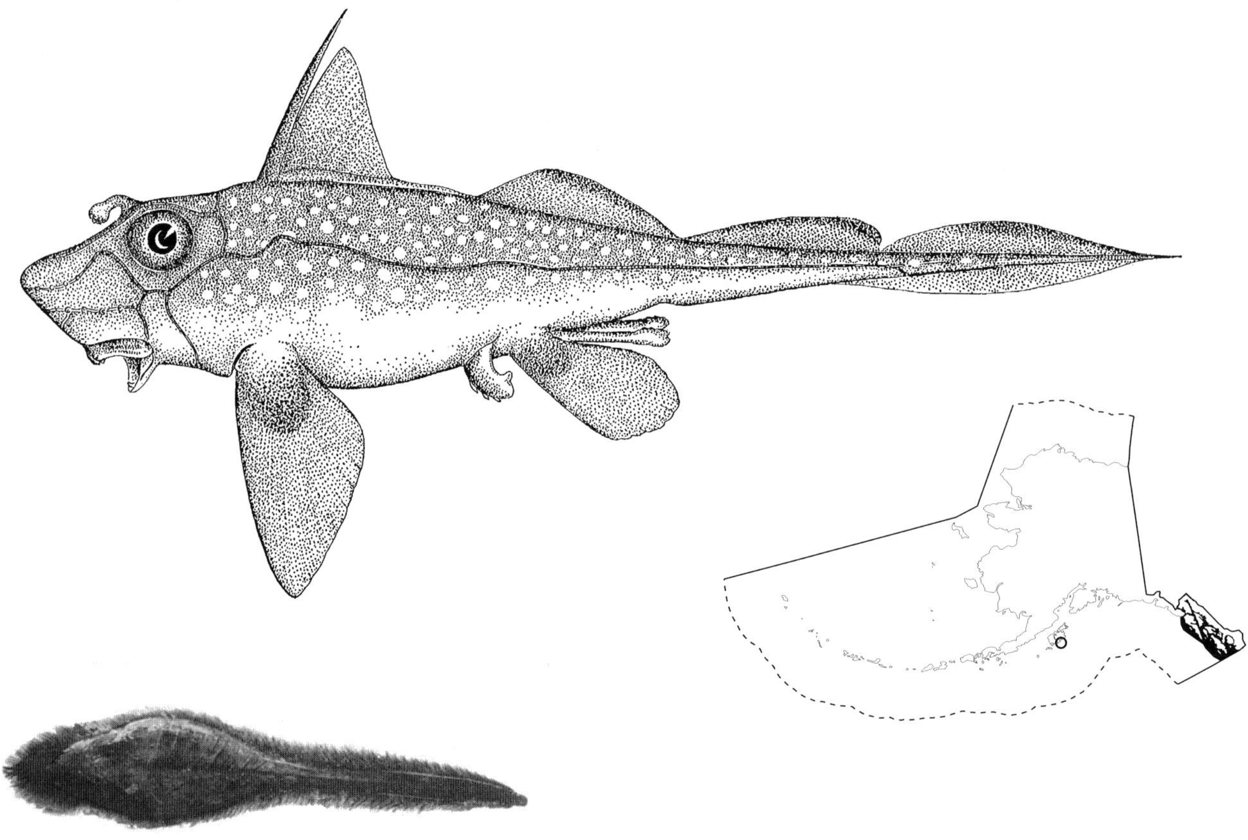

Notes & Sources — *Hydrolagus colliei* (Lay & Bennett, 1839)
Chimaera colliei Lay & Bennett, 1839

Description: Clemens and Wilby 1961:94–95; Hart 1973:66–67; Eschmeyer and Herald 1983:59.

Figures: Hart 1973:66; male. Egg case: Cox 1963, fig. 13.

Range: First recorded from Alaska by Bean (1881b), from specimens collected at unspecified localities in the Alexander Archipelago. Recorded from the Boca de Quadra and Kasaan Bay (*Albatross* dredging stations 4223 and 4246) and Port Alexander (taken by seine) by Evermann and Goldsborough (1907). A specimen taken by trawl net in 1994 off the east side of Kodiak Island (J. E. Blackburn, pers. comm., 23 Jul. 1998) is the only record from the western Gulf of Alaska. Allen and Smith (1988) reported *H. colliei* to be one of the most common fishes taken in 30 years (1953–1983) of NMFS demersal surveys of the eastern North Pacific, with 1,497 occurrences recorded. The northernmost occurrence was west of Cape Spencer, and the greatest frequency was on the outer shelf at depths of 100–150 m. Clemens and Wilby (1961) reported spotted ratfish to be abundant along the whole coast of British Columbia, and usually found there at depths below 73 m but occasionally in very shallow shore waters. They reported that egg capsules had been observed set upright in the mud in the intertidal zone (in Masset Inlet), that the young were commonly obtained in October and November in shrimp trawls, and that the adults were frequently taken in large numbers, particularly in October.

Subclass Elasmobranchii
Elasmobranchs

Elasmobranchs, including the extant sharks, skates, and rays, typically are predaceous fishes that rely more on smell and electroreception than sight for obtaining their food. They have large olfactory capsules and small eyes, and numerous teeth which are replaced rapidly. Other elasmobranch characteristics include 5–7 pairs of gill openings, rigid dorsal fins, and, usually, a pair of spiracles. Except for a relatively small number of species with intermediate shapes, sharks are more or less fusiform in shape while skates and rays are dorsoventrally flattened. In all sharks the gill openings are oriented laterally and the anterior edge of the pectoral fins is not attached to the sides of the head, whereas in skates and rays the gill openings are entirely ventral and the pectoral fins extend forward to attach to the sides of the head.

Elasmobranchs are primarily marine animals. Some species enter brackish estuaries, lagoons, and bays, and two species of sharks (not Alaskan) occur in rivers and in lakes with connections to the sea.

Living sharks, skates, and rays are classified in the superorder Euselachii (Nelson 1994). Classification of shark genera and species in this guide follows Compagno (1984). A recent checklist (Compagno 1999b) used a classification with minor differences. Some external features of sharks are shown in the diagram below, while features of skates are diagrammed in the introduction to the Rajidae.

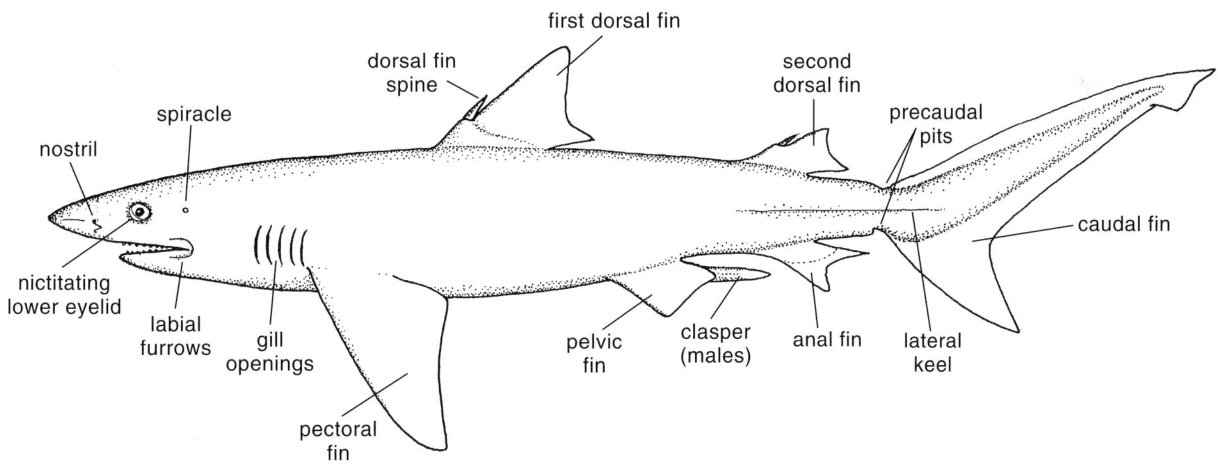

External features of sharks
(After Compagno 1984.)

Order Carcharhiniformes
Ground sharks

Ground sharks are the most diverse order of sharks. With more than 200 species, the group accounts for more than 60% of all shark species. Many of the sharks that are regularly implicated in attacks on people are included in this group. Four species distributed among three families—Carcharhinidae, Triakidae, and Scyliorhinidae—have been recorded from the marine waters of Alaska or waters nearby. Only one of those species, the blue shark, *Prionace glauca,* has been recorded more than once in Alaska.

External features that collectively distinguish the various ground sharks from other groups include the presence of 5 pairs of gill slits on the sides of the head, with the last 1–3 positioned over the bases of the pectoral fins; spiracles close behind the eyes in many species, or absent; eyes with true nictitating lower eyelids; a large mouth, extending behind the anterior ends of the eyes; labial furrows varying from large and on both jaws to absent; two dorsal fins; absence of spines associated with the dorsal fins; presence of an anal fin; a long dorsal caudal fin lobe; lack of a gap or small teeth between the anterior and lateral teeth; and absence of gill rakers. Ground sharks are variably oviparous, ovoviviparous, or viviparous.

Family Carcharhinidae
Requiem sharks

Requiem sharks are the dominant sharks in tropical waters but only a few range into temperate waters. One of those, the blue shark, *Prionace glauca,* has the widest geographic range of any elasmobranch. An epipelagic inhabitant of temperate and warm waters worldwide, it is especially characteristic for the subtropical regions. It migrates northward in summer, in the Pacific reaching the Gulf of Alaska in mid- to late summer. It is especially likely to be found there when the climate is influenced by El Niño. However, the blue shark prefers relatively cool water (7–15°C) and in northern regions is frequently reported close to the surface. To reach cool waters in the tropics it occupies greater depths. The blue shark is an offshore species but also frequents areas with a narrow continental shelf, like the eastern Gulf of Alaska. It has not been found in the Bering Sea or off the Aleutian Islands, but is frequently found in midocean south of the Aleutians as well as in the open waters of the Gulf of Alaska.

The tiger shark, *Galeocerdo cuvier,* also has a circumglobal distribution but is most typically found in a narrower range of warm waters. It is pelagic, and prefers coastal, turbid waters rather than the open ocean. Although tiger sharks prefer warm temperate and tropical coastal waters, they make long oceanic voyages and are often reported from cold waters; off Iceland, for example. Several authors (e.g., Bigelow and Schroeder 1948, Springer 1963, Seigel et al. 1995) have observed that excursions by tiger sharks into higher latitudes occur only during warm months. A sighting of tiger shark off Columbia Glacier in Prince William Sound, Alaska, was reported about the same time as reports of sightings of mantas (family Myliobatidae) in the area. The sightings occurred during the summer of 1983 when effects of an El Niño were strong and there were many confirmed records (Karinen et al. 1985, Schoener and Fluharty 1985, Pearcy and Schoener 1987) of southern species, and not only fishes, straying into northern regions. The wide-ranging behavior of the tiger shark and the sighting in Prince William Sound during an El Niño year both lend credence to the identification, although since the report was a sighting only, it cannot be confirmed.

Requiem sharks have round eyes and internal nictitating eyelids, and most have no spiracles (present in *G. cuvier*). The first dorsal fin is much larger than the second and is placed well ahead of the pelvic fins, precaudal pits are present, and the caudal fin has a strong ventral lobe. The teeth are bladelike, and often broader in the upper jaw.

All but one of the requiem sharks are viviparous. The exception is the tiger shark, which is ovoviviparous. Tiger sharks produce 10–82 large (51–76 cm TL) pups per litter (Randall 1992). Blue sharks produce 25–50 pups, and as many as 135, per litter; the young are smaller (35–51 cm TL) at birth than the young of tiger sharks (Castro 1983, Compagno 1984).

Most species of requiem sharks reach total lengths of 1–3 m (3.3–9.8 ft). *Galeocerdo cuvier* is exceptionally large, reaching 5.5 m (18 ft) or more, but the maximum size of 9.1 m (30 ft) which is sometimes reported for *G. cuvier* is not verifiable (Compagno 1984, Randall 1992).

Key to the Carcharhinidae of Alaska

1 Pectoral fins long and saberlike; snout long and pointed (viewed from below); labial furrows very short, at corners of mouth only; spiracles absent; back and upper sides dark blue, without stripes or spots . . . . *Prionace glauca,* page 71

1 Pectoral fins not long and saberlike; snout short and blunt (viewed from below); upper labial furrows long, reaching the eyes; spiracles present; back and upper sides gray, with dark stripes or spots (marks faded or obsolete in adults) . . . . *Galeocerdo cuvier,* page 72
(not confirmed from Alaska)

Prionace glauca (Linnaeus, 1758) **blue shark**

Eastern Pacific from Gulf of Alaska at Anton Larsen Bay, Kodiak Island, to Chile; circumglobal in temperate and tropical waters.

Pelagic, oceanic, typically where water depth is greater than 183 m (100 fathoms) and found from surface to depth of at least 152 m; often in areas with narrow continental shelf and off oceanic islands; often ventures inshore, to edges of kelp forests.

- **Dark blue dorsally, without stripes or spots**; white ventrally; pectoral and anal fins dusky; blue changes to slaty gray soon after death.
- **Snout pointed and long** (shorter than width of mouth); **spiracle absent**; **labial fold a slight groove at angle of mouth**.
- Low keel on caudal peduncle.
- **Pectoral fin long and saberlike**.
- Upper teeth with triangular, curved cusps with serrated edges and overlapping bases; lower teeth with triangular, erect cusps with smooth or finely serrated edges.
- Length to 383 cm TL or more.

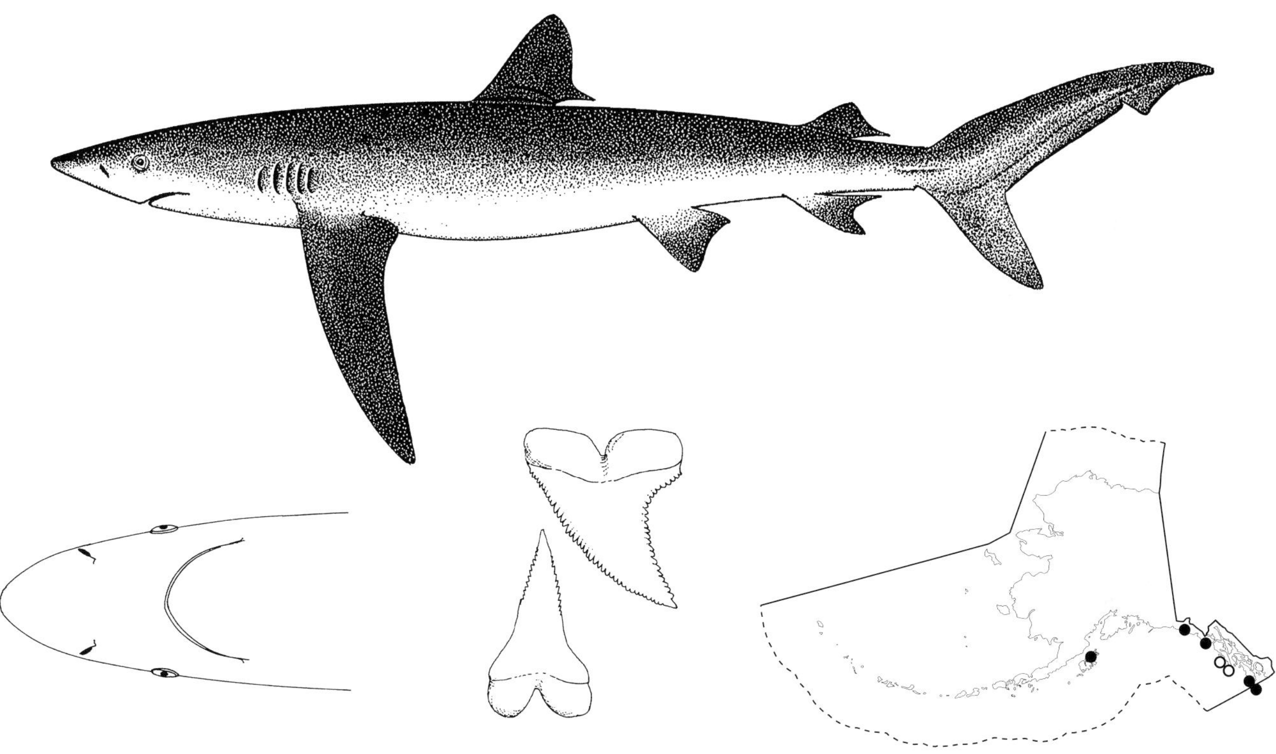

Notes & Sources — *Prionace glauca* (Linnaeus, 1758)
Squalus glaucus Linnaeus, 1758

Description: Bigelow and Schroeder 1948:282–292; Hart 1973:41–42; Castro 1983:147–148; Eschmeyer and Herald 1983:41; Compagno 1984:521–524, 1988:346–351.

Figures: Compagno 1984:522.

Range: Specimens caught in the Gulf of Alaska west of Cross Sound and Prince of Wales Island in July– September 1956 and 1957 during experimental epipelagic fishing indicated northward movement of the blue shark population in late spring and summer (Neave and Hanavan 1960). Analysis of bycatch data from North Pacific high seas salmon gillnet surveys in April through June from 1981 to 1991 indicated the same pattern, with blue sharks taken west of Dixon Entrance in July (Nakano and Nagasawa 1996). Karinen et al. (1985) confirmed identification of a specimen taken near Kodiak in October 1983, and reported unconfirmed sightings by reliable sources (ADFG biologists) off the outer coasts of southeastern Alaska in 1978 and in June-September 1983; B. L. Wing (pers. comm., 16 Apr. 1997) reported that the Kodiak Island specimen was caught at Anton Larsen Bay, and that he has seen specimens caught in southeastern Alaska during warm conditions. Most were less than 152 cm (5 ft) long, but he once had one that measured 183 cm (6 ft). Bob Johnson (ADFG, Yakutat, cited on U.S. Fish & Wildlife Service 1997–98 El Niño website) reported that blue sharks were caught in commercial nets in Yakutat Bay in September of 1997, a year with unusually strong El Niño effects. In British Columbia, blue sharks have been taken off the Queen Charlotte Islands and in some summers are common off the west coast of Vancouver Island (Clemens and Wilby 1946, 1961). Parin (1968) reviewed records of distribution worldwide.

Size: Compagno (1984) believed the 383-cm maximum size to be based on “reasonably good evidence,” while reports of lengths up to 4.8–6.5 m are unconfirmed.

Galeocerdo cuvier (Péron & Lesueur, 1822) **tiger shark**

Sighted at Prince William Sound, Alaska (not verifiable); well documented in eastern Pacific off southern California to Peru, including offshore islands; circumglobal in warm temperate and tropical seas.

Coastal pelagic, occurring from surface and intertidal area to depth of about 140 m; wide tolerance for different marine habitats but preferring turbid areas where runoff of fresh water may contribute to high density of prey organisms; sometimes strays far from typical range.

- **Gray dorsally, with vertical tiger-stripe marks**; marks faded or obsolete in adults; juveniles appearing mottled dorsolaterally, their spots fusing to form stripes with age.
- **Snout blunt and short** (shorter than width of mouth); **spiracle present**; **upper labial furrow long, reaching below eye**.
- Low keel on caudal peduncle.
- Pectoral fin not long and saberlike; upper caudal lobe sharply pointed.
- Upper and lower teeth cockscomb-shaped, curved, with heavy serrations and deep notch.
- Length to 550 cm TL, possibly to 740 cm or more.

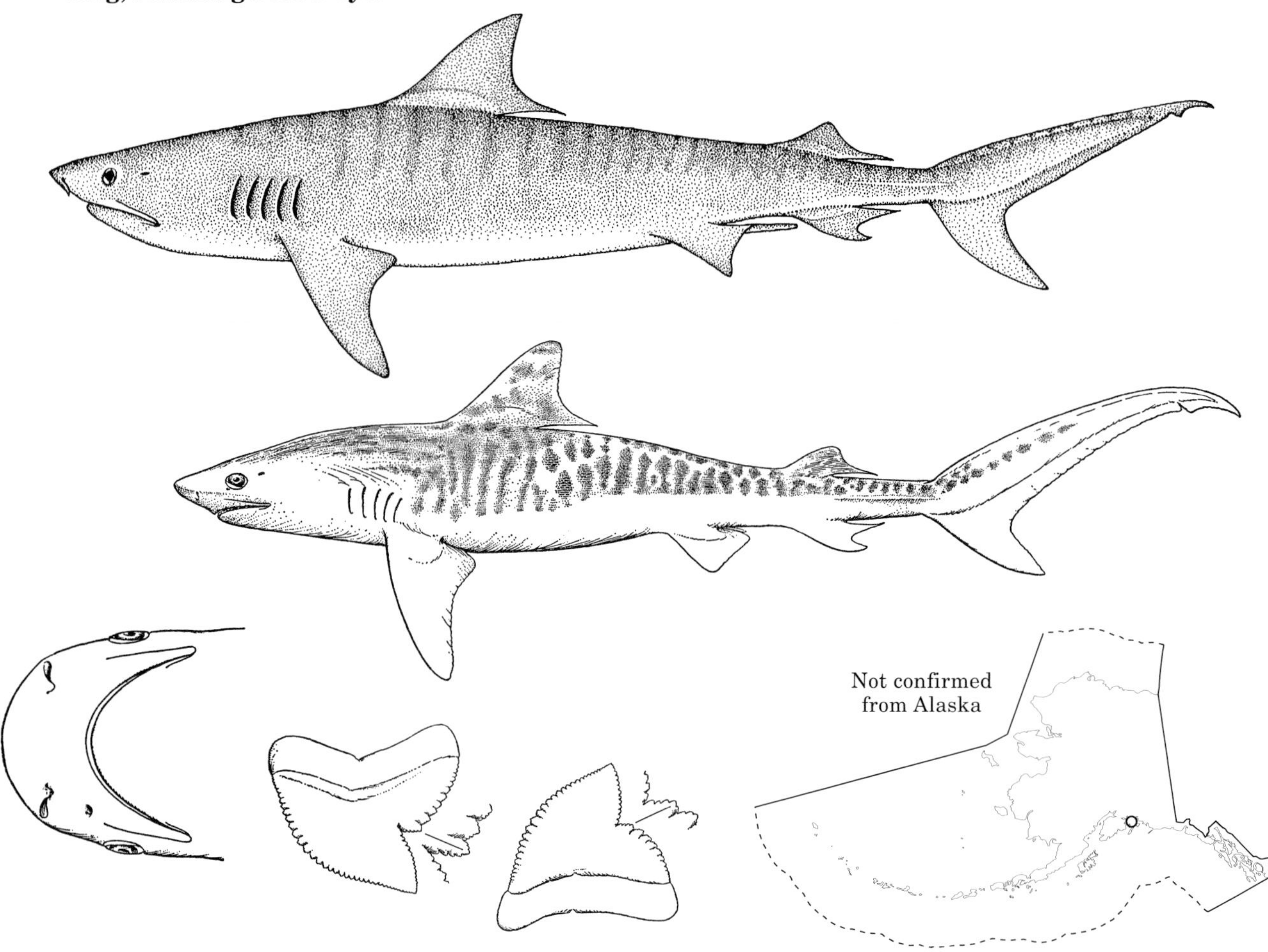

Notes & Sources — *Galeocerdo cuvier* (Péron & Lesueur in Lesueur, 1822)
Squalus cuvier Péron & Lesueur, 1822

Description: Bigelow and Schroeder 1948:266–275; Castro 1983:125–126; Eschmeyer and Herald 1983:40–41; Compagno 1984:503–506, 1988:278–346.

Figures: Upper full lateral view: Compagno 1984:504; adult male. Lower (a young male) and diagrams: Bigelow and Schroeder 1948, fig. 44.

Range: Karinen et al. (1985) reported a sighting by reliable sources (ADFG biologists) off Columbia Glacier, Prince William Sound, Alaska, in summer of 1983. Nearest reported areas of occurrence outside Alaska are southern Japan and southern California. Seigel et al. (1995) reported three juveniles taken off California near Los Angeles. One specimen was deposited in the LACM and is the only California record of *G. cuvier* based on museum material, as well as the first reported juvenile from California. The authors reviewed earlier, unconfirmed reports of specimens from California.

Size: One of the largest sharks. Adults 335–425 cm are common (Castro 1983), and a few large females reach over 550 cm (Compagno 1984). Compagno (1984, 1988) believed the reported length of 740 cm for a female caught off Indo-China to be possible. Authors agree that a reputed maximum length of about 910 cm cannot be confirmed. A length of 550 cm is the largest that seemed authentic to Randall (1992). Scofield (1941) reported a 270-cm female taken off California, but did not provide documentation.

Family Triakidae
Houndsharks

Houndsharks, also called topes or smoothhounds, are similar in appearance and closely related to requiem sharks (Carcharhinidae). *Galeorhinus galeus* and some other houndshark species have characteristics of both families and are considered transitional. The family is represented in temperate and warm seas, mostly along continental coasts near shore. No houndshark has been recorded from Alaska, but *G. galeus* has been known to occur nearby in northern British Columbia.

In houndsharks the eyes are horizontally oval; nictitating eyelids, small but conspicuous spiracles, and moderately to very long labial furrows are present; the first dorsal fin is well ahead of the pelvic fins; and precaudal pits are absent. In most houndsharks the teeth are blunt and molariform, or "pavementlike," the second dorsal is larger than the anal fin, and the caudal fin does not have a strong ventral lobe; in all these characters *G. galeus* is an exception. The Pacific population of *G. galeus* used to be classified as a separate species, *G. zyopterus,* called the soupfin shark.

Houndsharks are ovoviviparous or viviparous. *Galeorhinus galeus* is ovoviviparous, and produces 6–52 pups per litter. The largest houndsharks can reach 2.4 m (8 ft) at maturity, but most species are smaller.

Galeorhinus galeus (Linnaeus, 1758) **tope**

Eastern Pacific from northern British Columbia to Gulf of California; Peru and Chile; western South Pacific (not western North Pacific); eastern Atlantic and western South Atlantic (not western North Atlantic).

Coastal pelagic, often well offshore but not oceanic, found in surfline, shallow bays, and submarine canyons; feeds from surface to bottom, at depths of 2–471 m.

- Dark bluish gray to dusky dorsally, shading to white ventrally; in young under 61 cm, both dorsal fins and caudal fin black-tipped.
- Snout long and pointed.
- No keel on caudal peduncle.
- **Second dorsal fin and anal fin about same size**; **terminal lobe of caudal fin large**, about half length of upper lobe; **ventral caudal lobe well developed**.
- **Teeth bladelike**, compressed, and cuspidate, with oblique cusps and cusplets.
- Length to 195 cm TL.

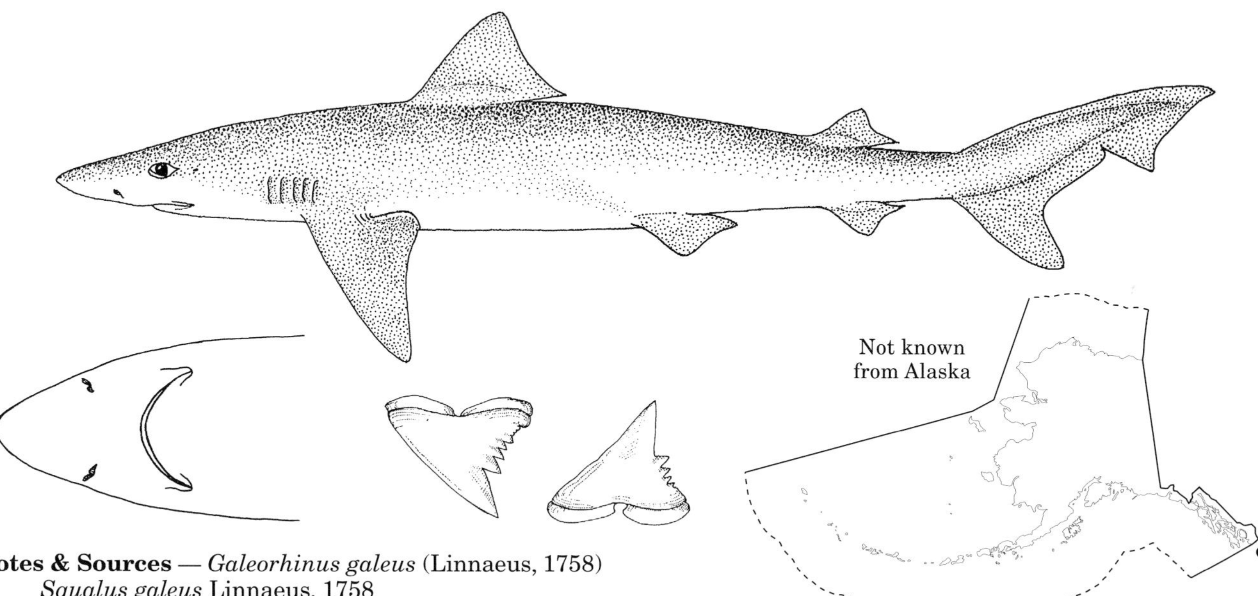

Notes & Sources — *Galeorhinus galeus* (Linnaeus, 1758)
Squalus galeus Linnaeus, 1758
Galeorhinus zyopterus Jordan & Gilbert, 1883

Description: Hart 1973:39–40; Eschmeyer and Herald 1983: 34; Compagno 1984:386–389, 1988:246–252.

Figures: Compagno 1984:386–387.

Range: When first recorded from British Columbia waters in 1891 *G. galeus* was "rather common" along the coast (Green 1891). Clemens and Wilby (1946) reported that a tope was captured off Banks Island, Queen Charlotte Islands, in 1914, and that "considerable numbers" had been captured by commercial fishermen from the west coast of Vancouver Island since 1939. The fishery for this species extended from California into British Columbia. Topes were caught "in about 25 fathoms with gill nets or with set lines baited with herring, suspended about 6 feet from the bottom." By 1946 demand for liver oils had dropped, the stock had been cut down, and the fishery declined to incidental captures (Hart 1973).

Family Scyliorhinidae
Cat sharks

Cat sharks typically have elongated eyes with nictitating eyelids and are inhabitants of warm southern seas. One species, the brown cat shark, *Apristurus brunneus,* occasionally enters British Columbia and southeastern Alaska waters, at the northern limit of its distribution. Evidence for its occurrence in Alaska consists of one specimen taken in an otter trawl in the eastern Gulf of Alaska off Icy Point in 1976 and reported on by Wilson and Hughes (1978).

In cat sharks spiracles are present, both dorsal fins are small and the first is above the pelvic fins, the anal fin is larger than either dorsal fin, precaudal pits are absent, and the teeth are small and cuspidate.

Most cat shark species are oviparous. Their smooth, amber egg cases, slightly constricted at one end, are easily recognized as products of this family. Most species at maturity are less than 80 cm (31.5 inches) in length; a few reach about 1.6 m (5.25 ft).

Apristurus brunneus (Gilbert, 1892) — **brown cat shark**

Eastern Pacific Ocean from southeastern Alaska off Icy Point to Panama.

On bottom to well off the bottom at depths of 33–1,306 m.

- Dark brown dorsally and ventrally with darker margins to fins and mouth.
- Body soft and flabby; snout and head long and laterally expanded.
- **First dorsal fin base over pelvic fin base; anal fin larger than either dorsal fin.**
- **Teeth small and cuspidate**, cusps elongate.
- Length to 68 cm TL.
- Egg case translucent, oblong, compressed, slightly constricted at one end, with a long, coiled tendril at each corner; body slightly over 50 mm long.

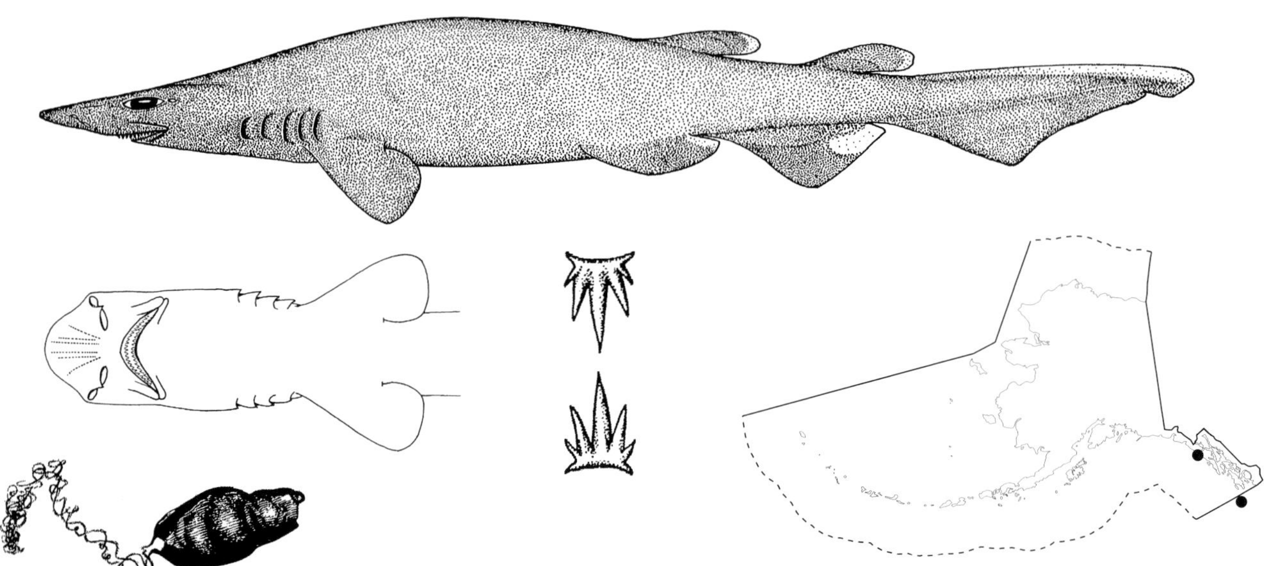

Notes & Sources — *Apristurus brunneus* (Gilbert, 1892)
Catulus brunneus Gilbert, 1892

Description: Cox 1963 (egg case); Hart 1973:38–39; Castro 1983:97–98; Compagno 1984:262–263.

Figures: Lateral and ventral: Compagno 1984:262. Teeth: Castro 1983:99. Egg case: Eschmeyer and Herald 1983:14.

Range: Wilson and Hughes (1978) recorded a 561-mm-TL specimen taken in a bottom trawl with 475 m maximum tow depth 6.5 km off Icy Point at about 58°N, 137°40'W, and reported that another had been taken south of the Alaska–British Columbia border off Langara Island at about 54°03'N, 133°W. The species is more common in southern British Columbia. Jones and Geen (1977) caught 65 during February and March 1974 in the Strait of Georgia. Brown cat sharks are generally benthic, but Jones and Geen found them at 201 m over a bottom depth of 373 m. They are taken at shallower depths in the northern part of their range (33–564 m in British Columbia and Alaska), but probably also occur there in deeper waters. Most (18) of the 23 records of catches deeper than 1,175 m in the NMFS survey database (provided by J. W. Orr, pers. comm., 12 May 2000) were from California north of Point Arena to northern Washington; all were from bottom trawls fishing on or close to the bottom. The deepest was 1,306 m, taken off northern California at 40°12'N, 125°08'W, in 1991. Reported to 1,189 m by Eschmeyer and Herald (1983).

Order Lamniformes
Lamniform sharks

With 16 species, the order Lamniformes is relatively small. Five species of lamniform shark occur in Alaska. They represent three families: Lamnidae, Alopiidae, and Cetorhinidae.

Like the Carcharhiniformes, most sharks of the order Lamniformes have an elongate snout and inferior mouth, no upper labial furrow, and no spines in front of the dorsal fins. In contrast to carcharhiniforms, lamniforms lack a lower nictitating membrane and the front teeth are usually the largest. The last 2 of the 5 gill slits in some species are above the pectoral fin. Spiracles are usually present behind the eyes.

In the uterus, developing lamniforms feed on unfertilized and fertilized eggs, and at least one species is a confirmed uterine cannibal, feeding on smaller siblings for a long time before birth.

Family Lamnidae
Mackerel sharks

Sharks in the family Lamnidae are fast, warm-blooded (endothermic), active pelagic and epibenthic swimmers. They often employ swift dashes and spectacular jumps when chasing prey. Their modified circulatory system enables them to retain a body temperature warmer than the surrounding water, permitting a higher level of activity and increasing the power of their muscles. Current research into their endothermy seeks to determine whether these sharks are homeothermic, like humans, or extremely good thermoregulators. Other questions surround the evolution of endothermy in lamnid and alopiid sharks (threshers are endotherms too), as it appears to have evolved independently in those two groups (see, e.g., Goldman 1997, Lowe and Goldman 2001). Lamnid sharks inhabit cold temperate as well as warm temperate to tropical waters.

Lamnid sharks have large gill openings; large, relatively few teeth; no gill rakers; and a nearly symmetrical caudal fin. The caudal peduncle has a strong lateral keel and precaudal pits.

The five species in this family are known to be dangerous to man or are considered dangerous because of their size and large teeth. Perhaps the most popularly well-known species is the white shark, *Carcharodon carcharias.* This shark is "perhaps the most formidable of fishlike vertebrates" (Compagno 1984). In some years during summer and fall white sharks are abundant in the Gulf of Alaska, and at times have been considered a plague to commercial fishermen (Royce 1963).

As its name suggests, the salmon shark, *Lamna ditropis,* feeds on salmon, but it also feeds on herring, sablefish, walleye pollock, rockfishes, and other fishes. This is the most common epipelagic shark in subarctic and cold-temperate North Pacific waters, and one of the three most common sharks in Alaska. In recent years, more sightings appear to be occurring in Prince William Sound, and research is under way to examine salmon shark abundance in the area.

The shortfin mako, *Isurus oxyrinchus,* has a bad reputation mainly for its numerous attacks on boats. It is called the shortfin mako in reference to its pectoral fins, but they are short only by contrast to the fins of its less well-known congener, the longfin mako, *Isurus paucus,* of warmer waters. Shortfin makos have been reported to occur south of the Aleutian Islands but it is not certain if catches or sightings were within the 200-mile limit or farther offshore.

Lamnid sharks are ovoviviparous. The largest lamnid is *C. carcharias,* with a maximum length of at least 6.0 m (19.5 ft).

Key to the Lamnidae of Alaska

1		Pectoral fin origin mostly below first dorsal fin; small secondary keel on base of caudal fin; teeth with lateral cusplets	*Lamna ditropis,* page 76
1		Pectoral fin origin mostly ahead of first dorsal fin; no secondary keel on base of caudal fin; teeth without lateral cusplets	(2)
2	(1)	Teeth broadly triangular, with serrated edges	*Carcharodon carcharias,* page 77
2		Teeth long and slender, with smooth edges	*Isurus oxyrinchus,* page 78 (not confirmed from Alaska)

Lamna ditropis Hubbs & Follett, 1947 **salmon shark**

Bering Sea, Gulf of Alaska, and North Pacific Ocean off Aleutian Islands to southern Baja California and to Japan and the Koreas, including Seas of Okhotsk and Japan; endemic to North Pacific.

Pelagic, coastal and oceanic; from surface to 650 m; most common offshore, also ranging inshore close to beaches.

- Dark bluish gray dorsally; white ventrally, with dusky spots and blotches.
- Body stout; snout short, conical.
- **First dorsal fin located above pectoral fin.**
- **Small secondary keel** on caudal base below strong caudal peduncle keel.
- **Teeth elongate and smooth**; lateral cusplets on most teeth, except in young sharks under 1 m long; intermediate teeth in upper jaw less than half height of anterior teeth.
- Length to 305 cm TL or more.

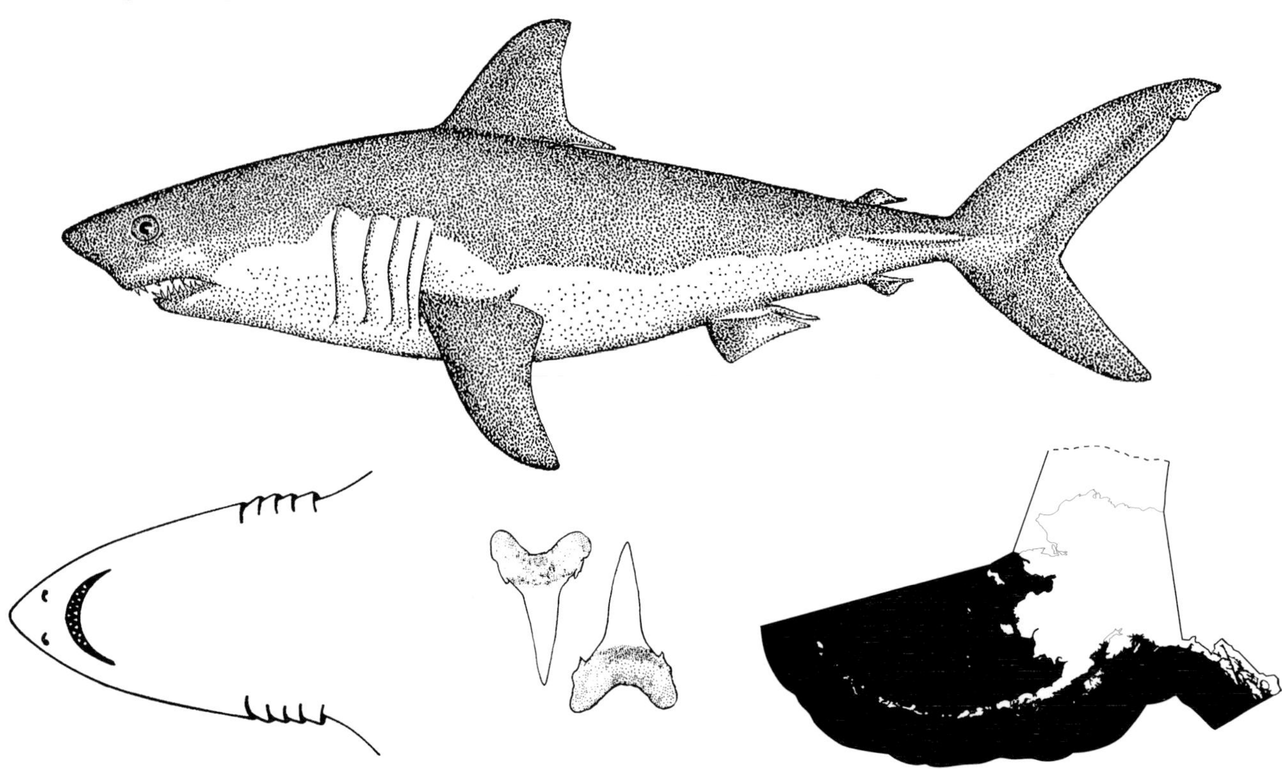

Notes & Sources — *Lamna ditropis* Hubbs & Follett, 1947
Isurus nasus (Bonnaterre, 1788): Clemens and Wilby 1946.
Lamna nasus (Bonnaterre, 1788): Bright 1960.

Description: Nakaya 1971:273–277; Hart 1973:36–37; Castro 1983:93–94; Compagno 1984:246–248.

Figures: Upper: Hart 1973:36, modified (secondary keel added). Ventral view: Castro 1983:93. Teeth: Miller and Lea 1972:39, modified.

Range: Neave and Hanavan (1960) found *L. ditropis* to be widespread in the Gulf of Alaska in mid- to late summer in 1956 and 1957, and reported it had been taken in the Bering Sea at 55°N in June. Nakano and Nagasawa (1996) reported occurrence during 1981–1991 in the Bering Sea north to about 60°N and all along the Aleutian chain in summer, mainly in June and July, but in the Gulf of Alaska only in July. At times *L. ditropis* is noted to be locally abundant, as along the Aleutian Islands, in Prince William Sound, in the southeastern Gulf of Alaska, in British Columbia, and off the northeast coast of Hokkaido. Increased abundance is often associated with the spring herring sac roe fishery, fall herring bait fishery, and summer returns of adult salmon for spawning. Since the mid-1990s there have been reports of increased salmon shark abundance in Prince William Sound. Interest in the sharks has increased and a small sport fishery has developed. Research is being conducted to examine salmon shark abundance in the area.

Fedorov and Sheiko (2002) reported *L. ditropis* to be common near the Commander Islands. They gave a maximum depth of 650 m. Compagno (1984) gave depth "to at least 152 m."

Occurrence in summer of small individuals (70–110 cm) in an area extending south of the Aleutian chain and Gulf of Alaska from about 45°N south of the Near Islands to 54°N west of the Queen Charlotte Islands and south to the subarctic boundary (40°N off Japan to 50°N off British Columbia) indicate that area to be a parturition and nursery ground (Nakano and Nagawasa 1996).

Size: Compagno (1984) and Compagno et al. (in Fischer et al. 1995) gave maximum of 305 cm, with maturation of males at 180–240 cm.

Carcharodon carcharias (Linnaeus, 1758) **white shark**

Eastern Pacific from Kenai Peninsula off Gulf of Alaska to Gulf of California and from Panama to Chile; worldwide, mostly amphitemperate.

Pelagic, coastal and offshore over continental and insular shelves; wanders into shallow water, even into the surf; found from surface to bottom, occasionally ranging down the continental slope, with a record depth of occurrence of 1,280 m.

- Slaty brown to blackish dorsally; white ventrally.
- Snout rather short, bluntly conical.
- **Dorsal fin origin largely behind pectoral fin.**
- Strong keel on caudal peduncle, **no secondary keel on caudal base.**
- **Teeth flat, triangular, broad, nearly straight, with serrated edges**; lateral cusplets in juveniles under 2 m long.
- Length to about 600 cm TL.

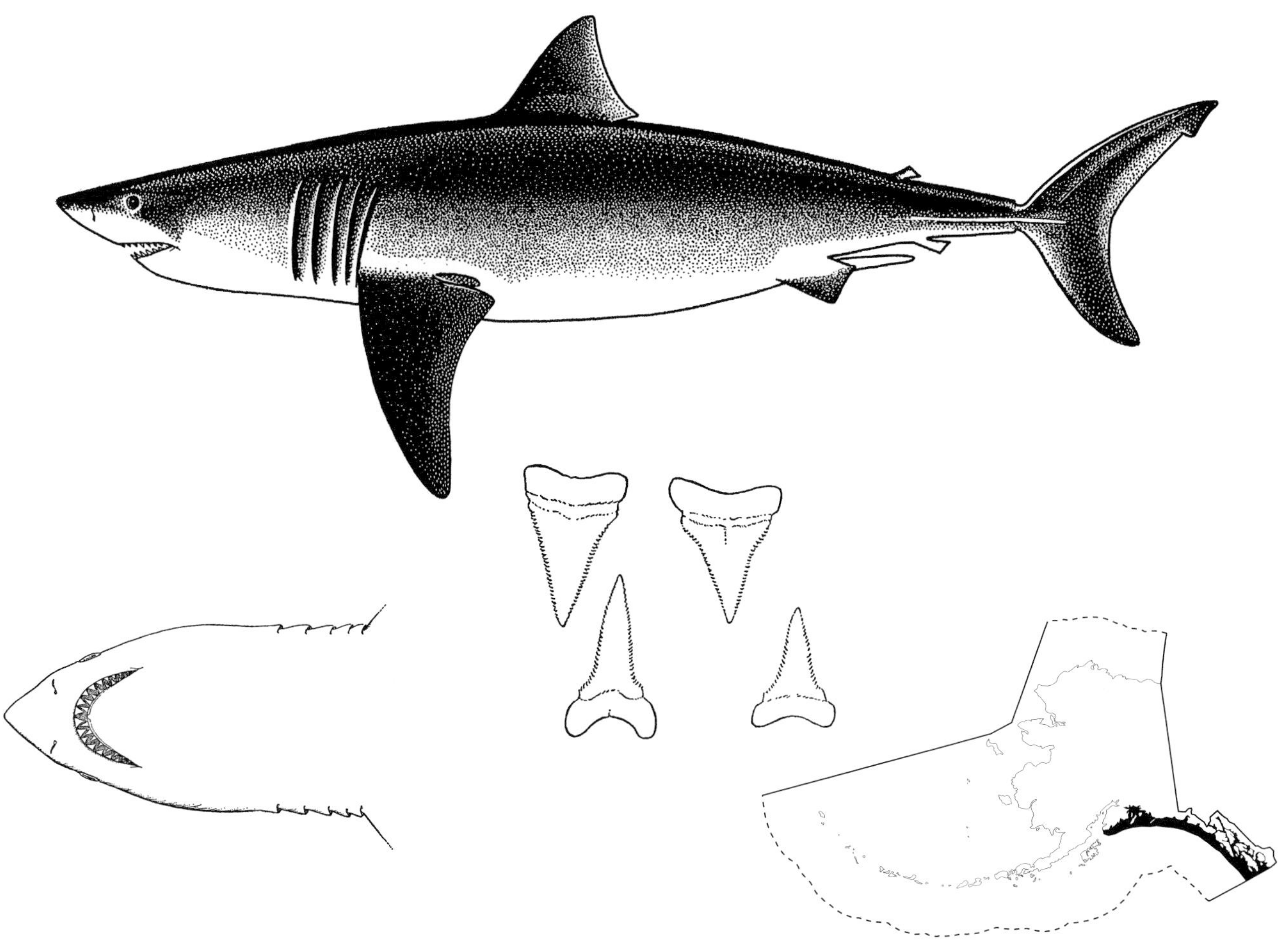

Notes & Sources — *Carcharodon carcharias* (Linnaeus, 1758)
Squalus carcharias Linnaeus, 1758

Description: Bigelow and Schroeder 1948:134–145; Castro 1983:88–90; Compagno 1984:238–241; Ellis and McCosker 1991.

Figures: Full lateral view: Compagno 1984:239. Ventral view and teeth (1st and 4th in each jaw): Bigelow and Schroeder 1948, figs. 20 and 21.

Range: Map by Compagno (1984) indicates range west in Gulf of Alaska to Kenai Peninsula. Royce (1963) reported numerous sightings in southeastern Alaska and a beached specimen at Craig (55°28'N, 133°08'W). Karinen et al. (1985) reported confirmed records from Cross Sound and unconfirmed sightings in Stephens Passage (Hobart Bay) and Lynn Canal in 1983 and 1984, when an increased incidence could have been associated with the effects of an El Niño event. White sharks were found in commercial nets in Yakutat Bay during the summer of 1997, during another strong El Niño (Bob Johnson, ADFG, cited on U.S. Fish & Wildlife Service 1997–98 El Niño website).

Size: Lengths of *C. carcharias* have been reported to reach as much as 12.2 m (40 feet). Randall (1987) investigated reports and reviewed available information on length and concluded that the largest *C. carcharias* reliably measured was a specimen from Australia, which was "19 feet 6 inches (6 m) long." He considered it probable that *C. carcharias* reaches more than 6.1 m (20 ft) but that irrefutable evidence of such a length has yet to be presented.

Isurus oxyrinchus Rafinesque, 1810 **shortfin mako**

Pacific Ocean south of Aleutian Islands and west of British Columbia to Chile, and to New Zealand; worldwide in temperate and tropical waters.

Pelagic, coastal and oceanic; occurs from surface down to at least 152 m; in extreme northern and southern parts of its range, tends to follow warm water masses poleward in summer.

- Deep blue to dark gray dorsally; white ventrally, without dark blotches.
- Snout long, acutely pointed.
- **Dorsal fin origin behind pectoral fin**; pectoral fin moderately long and broad, shorter than head.
- Strong keel on caudal peduncle, **no secondary keel on caudal base**.
- **Teeth flat, elongate, narrow, without serrations or cusplets**; anterior teeth narrower and more oblique than other teeth, and curved lingually at bases and labially at tips.
- Length to about 394 cm TL, possibly to 400 cm.

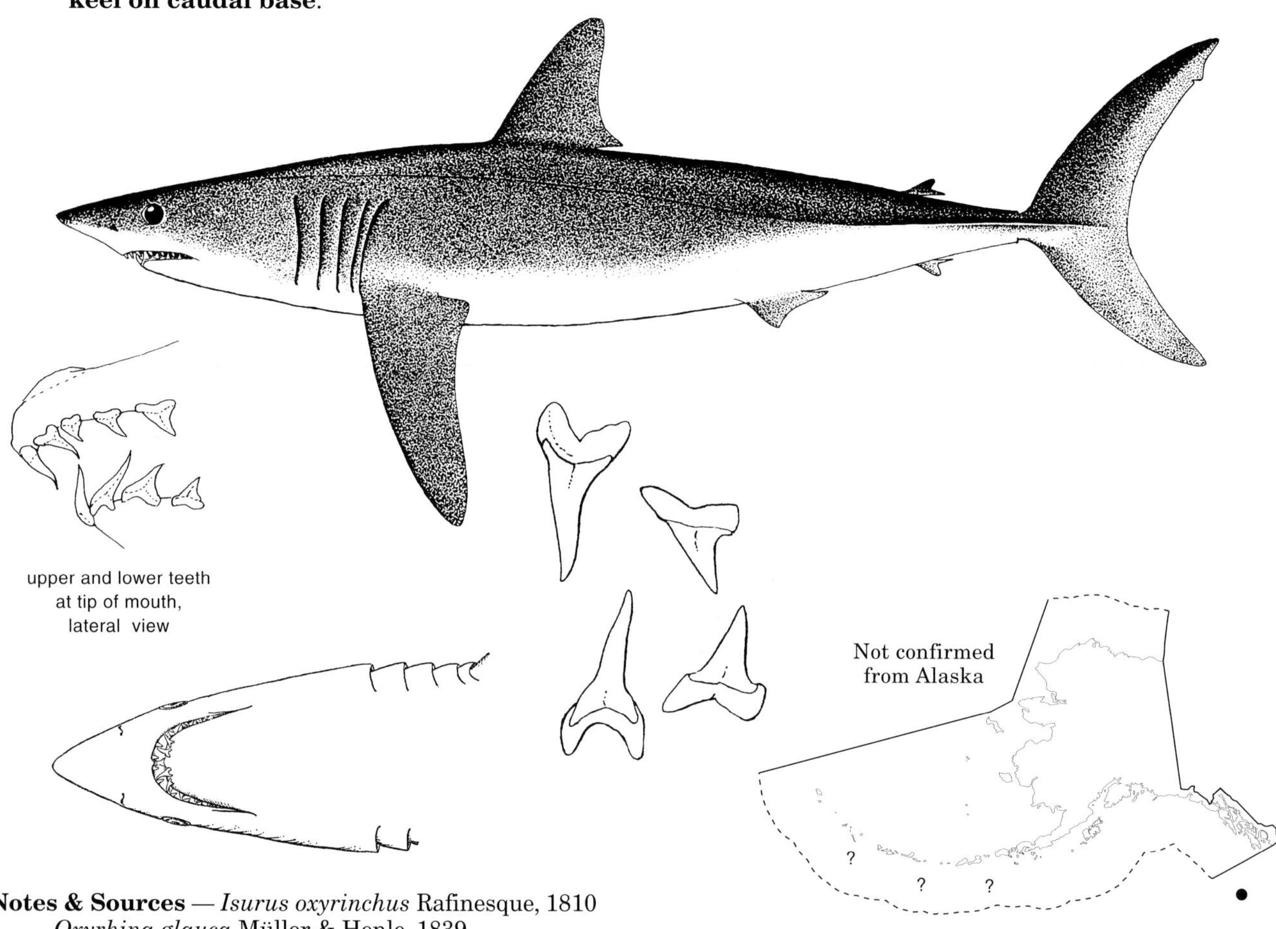

Notes & Sources — *Isurus oxyrinchus* Rafinesque, 1810
Oxyrhina glauca Müller & Henle, 1839
Isurus glaucus (Müller & Henle): Radovich 1961, McAllister 1990.
Heist et al. (1996) presented mitochondrial DNA evidence supporting the hypothesis that there is a single, worldwide population of shortfin mako, without subspecies.

Description: Bigelow and Schroeder 1948:124–133; Garrick 1967:674–677; Castro 1983:90–91; Compagno 1984:242–244.

Figures: Full lateral view: Compagno 1984:243. Ventral view and teeth (1st and 4th in each jaw): Bigelow and Schroeder 1948, figs. 18 and 19.

Range: Compagno (1981) gave range in central Pacific as extending from south of the Aleutian Islands to the Society Islands, with a map indicating occurrence all along and close to the Aleutians. However, reports of occurrence in Alaska that are documented with records of locality data and diagnostic features or voucher specimens are lacking in the literature and museum collections. The question marks on the above map indicate uncertainty as to actual localities, not whether the species occurs in the region. The first verifiable record from British Columbia waters was reported by Gillespie and Saunders (1994): a small (about 73 cm TL) specimen captured in August 1992 by a tuna boat trolling approximately 360 km due west of Cape St. James (51°53'N, 135°54'W), Queen Charlotte Islands. Previous reports of this species in Canadian waters existed (e.g., McAllister 1990), but were unconfirmed. A specimen caught in August 1959 off the Columbia River, Washington, represented a northward extension of known range at that time from central California (Radovich 1961). Not found farther north than 40°N in bycatch of North Pacific high seas salmon surveys from 1981 to 1991 (Nakano and Nagasawa 1996).

Family Alopiidae
Thresher sharks

Members of the family Alopiidae, or thresher sharks, have an enormous, curved caudal fin that is used to herd and stun their prey, primarily schooling fishes and squids. Other family characteristics include small gill slits; small, numerous teeth; gill rakers absent; precaudal pits present; and keels absent from the caudal peduncle. The family comprises three fairly well-known species. A study of phylogenetic relationships using allozymes provided evidence for the existence of a fourth species (Eitner 1995).

A specimen of *Alopias vulpinus,* a species occurring worldwide in warm and temperate seas along coasts as well as far from shore, was landed at Sitka, Alaska, in 1990. *Alopias vulpinus* is the largest of the threshers, with adult females reaching a total length of at least 5.5 m (18 ft).

Alopias vulpinus (Bonnaterre, 1788) **thresher shark**

Southeastern Gulf of Alaska, vicinity of Sitka; Goose Bay, Queen Charlotte Sound, British Columbia, to Baja California, Panama, and Chile, and to Japan; virtually circumglobal in warm seas.

Coastal over continental and insular shelves and epipelagic far from land; found from surface to 366 m.

- Slate blue, brown, or black dorsally; sometimes silvery, bluish, or golden on side; white with dark patches ventrally; white extending along lower side above pectoral fin base.
- No groove on side above gills; labial furrows present; eye small.
- **Dorsal caudal fin lobe curving, long, about 50% of total length**.
- Gill openings not extending onto dorsal surface of head, last 2 over pectoral base.
- Teeth small, curved, smooth, without cusplets; 3rd upper tooth and 1st lower tooth smaller than adjacent teeth.
- Length to 549 cm TL, possibly to 609 cm.

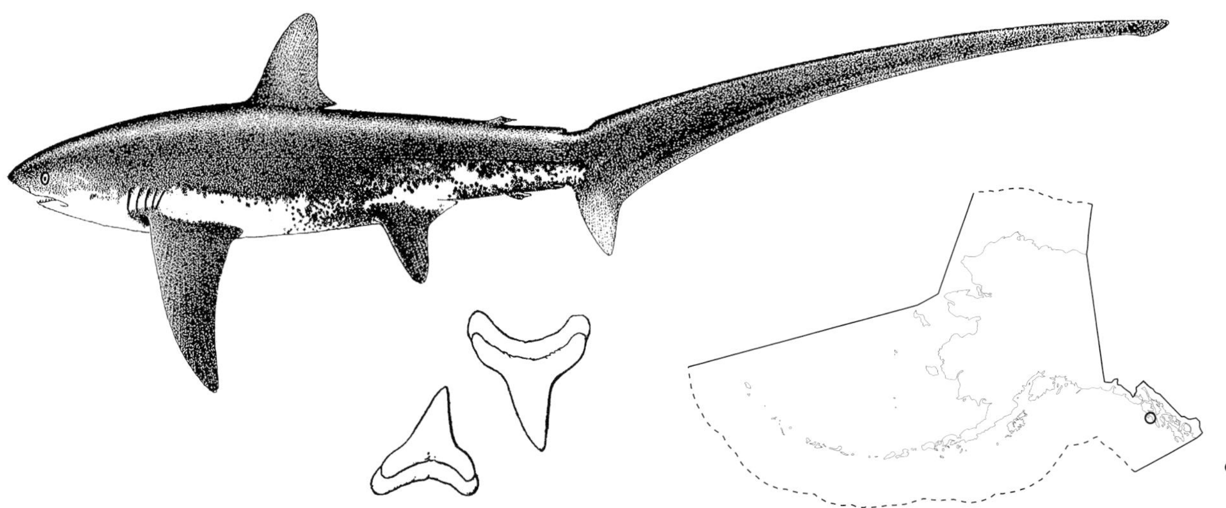

Notes & Sources — *Alopias vulpinus* (Bonnaterre, 1788)
Squalus vulpinus Bonnaterre, 1788
Alopias vulpes (Gmelin): Cowan 1938; specimen in fish trap in Juan de Fuca Strait near Sooke, British Columbia.
Also called common thresher. The American Fisheries Society (Robins et al. 1991a) uses the name thresher shark.

Description: Bigelow and Schroeder 1948:167–178; Hart 1973:30–31; Castro 1983:84–86; Eschmeyer and Herald 1983:27; Compagno 1984:232–233.

Figures: Compagno 1984:232. Teeth: Bigelow and Schroeder 1948, fig. 28.

Range: At the time of Quast and Hall's (1972) inventory of Alaskan fish species, thresher sharks had been reported in the eastern Pacific only as far north as British Columbia. Clemens and Wilby (1961) indicated a total of four British Columbia records, including one from "Goose Bay," and gave Johnstone Strait, Vancouver Island, as the northernmost record. Hart (1973) reported that the Goose Bay referred to is between Fitz Hugh and Smith sounds (in Queen Charlotte Sound), and indicated it to be the northernmost record. A specimen landed in 1990 at Sitka in a commercial catch is the first Alaskan record; B. L. Wing (pers. comm., 10 Oct. 1997) confirmed the identification. The catch locality was not recorded.

Size: Many authors give maximum length as 7.6 m (25 ft) or 6.1 m (20 ft). Compagno (1984) reported 6.1 m only as a possibility, with lengths of 319 cm to "at least" 420 cm for adult males and 376–549 cm for adult females.

Family Cetorhinidae
Basking sharks

The one extant member of the family Cetorhinidae, the basking shark, *Cetorhinus maximus,* has a wide distribution in boreal and temperate waters. The common name reflects the sharks' habit of lying with backs awash or on their sides, evidently sunning themselves, or swimming slowly at the surface with the dorsal fin and tip of the caudal fin exposed while feeding. One of three gigantic filter-feeding sharks (the others are megamouth, *Megachasma pelagios*; and whale shark, *Rhincodon typus*), the basking shark is unique in using only the passive flow of water through its pharynx generated by swimming to ingest food. It cruises with its mouth open and gills distended, occasionally closing the mouth to swallow. The other filter-feeding sharks assist food ingestion by pumping or gulping.

The bathymetric and migratory habits of basking sharks are poorly understood. One hypothesis is that they are epipelagic and oceanic, migrating toward the coast in certain seasons. In spring through summer they are most often seen in the eastern Pacific Ocean off the coasts of British Columbia to Washington, and off northern coasts of the western and eastern Atlantic. The few records from Alaska for which dates have been reported suggest a similar pattern to other northern locations. Basking sharks are most common in California bays in winter, when large schools, comprising several hundred individuals, are sometimes observed close to shore. At other times they may move into deeper water, settle to the bottom, and lose their food-gathering gill rakers until it is time to feed again. Spatial and seasonal population segregation may also occur, with pregnant females, for example, found deeper than individuals that are regularly seen basking at the surface. Compagno (1984), Lien and Fawcett (1986), Squire (1990), and Darling and Keogh (1994) reviewed and contributed to existing knowledge on basking shark distribution.

Evidently, basking sharks have been common at times in southeastern Alaska and may occur throughout the Gulf of Alaska and south of the Aleutian Islands, but specific Alaskan records are scarce. Occurrence in British Columbia waters is well documented and observations there suggest that basking sharks live in local, discrete, slow-breeding populations (Darling and Keogh 1994). They seem to be attracted to the propellers of slow-moving boats and often show injuries from encounters with them, and have a propensity for getting entangled in fishing gear, including prawn traps, salmon gill nets, and seine nets. Basking sharks in Barkley Sound, off Vancouver Island, were so numerous in the 1940s and 1950s they were sought and killed to reduce incidents of entanglement in fishing nets (Clemens and Wilby 1949, 1961). These days basking sharks are rarely seen in Barkley Sound, indicating that the majority of the population there was killed. A relatively small population (27 sharks have been identified) in Clayoquot Sound, Vancouver Island, may be the only aggregation remaining in British Columbia (Darling and Keogh 1994).

Morphological characteristics of basking sharks include enormous gill slits that practically encircle the head; a very large mouth, widely distensible at the corners; minute, numerous teeth; horny, bristlelike gill rakers; precaudal pits; and strong keels on the caudal peduncle. The skin of basking sharks, with islets separated by narrow channels, is different from that of all other sharks (Springer and Gilbert 1976). Young basking sharks have quite a different appearance, with snouts that are relatively longer than those of adults and obliquely truncate rather than rounded, and were once thought to represent a different species (Bigelow and Schroeder 1953).

The reproductive biology of basking sharks is poorly known. Gilmore (1993) reviewed existing information. Unlike any other shark, basking sharks produce millions of tiny eggs. A single ovary contained about 6 million eggs. Nevertheless, litter size may be small. The only published record of parturition is an account by Sund (1943), who reported that Norwegian fishermen observed a female giving birth to five live sharks and one stillborn as it was being towed to port. The pups were estimated to be between 1.5 and 2 m in length. Basking sharks are reported to reach 12.2–15.2 m (40–50 ft), but the largest adequately documented measurement is 9.8 m (32 ft). They are the second largest fish, surpassed only by the whale shark, *R. typus.*

Springer and Gilbert (1976) reviewed the many distinctive characters and taxonomic history of *Cetorhinus* and concluded that classification in Lamnidae, as some authors have done, is unjustified and recommended continued classification in Cetorhinidae, as done by Bigelow and Schroeder (1948, 1953). As well, there is disagreement over the makeup of the family Cetorhinidae, with some authors (e.g., Robins et al. 1991a) including *Megachasma.* However, *Megachasma* is so different, with its terminal mouth, shorter gill slits, unique, fingerlike gill rakers, and other distinguishing features, that Nelson (1994) and most other authors classify it separately from the Cetorhinidae.

Cetorhinus maximus (Gunnerus, 1765) **basking shark**

Gulf of Alaska and Pacific Ocean south of Aleutian Islands to Gulf of California and to Okhotsk, Japan, and Yellow seas; worldwide in cold waters.

Coastal pelagic, occurring well offshore and close to land, just off the surf zone; enters enclosed bays.

- Grayish brown or slaty gray to black dorsally; usually lighter, sometimes white, ventrally.
- Snout conical, rounded at tip; mouth large, arcuate, subterminal.
- Caudal peduncle with strong lateral keel.
- Caudal fin lunate, lower lobe often nearly as long as upper.
- Teeth minute (3–6 mm high), numerous (about 100 per row), with single cusp curved posteriorly; teeth similar in both jaws.
- **Gill slits enormous, extending from dorsal surface to ventral midline.**
- Gill rakers dark, long, bristlelike, periodically shed.
- Length to at least 980 cm TL.

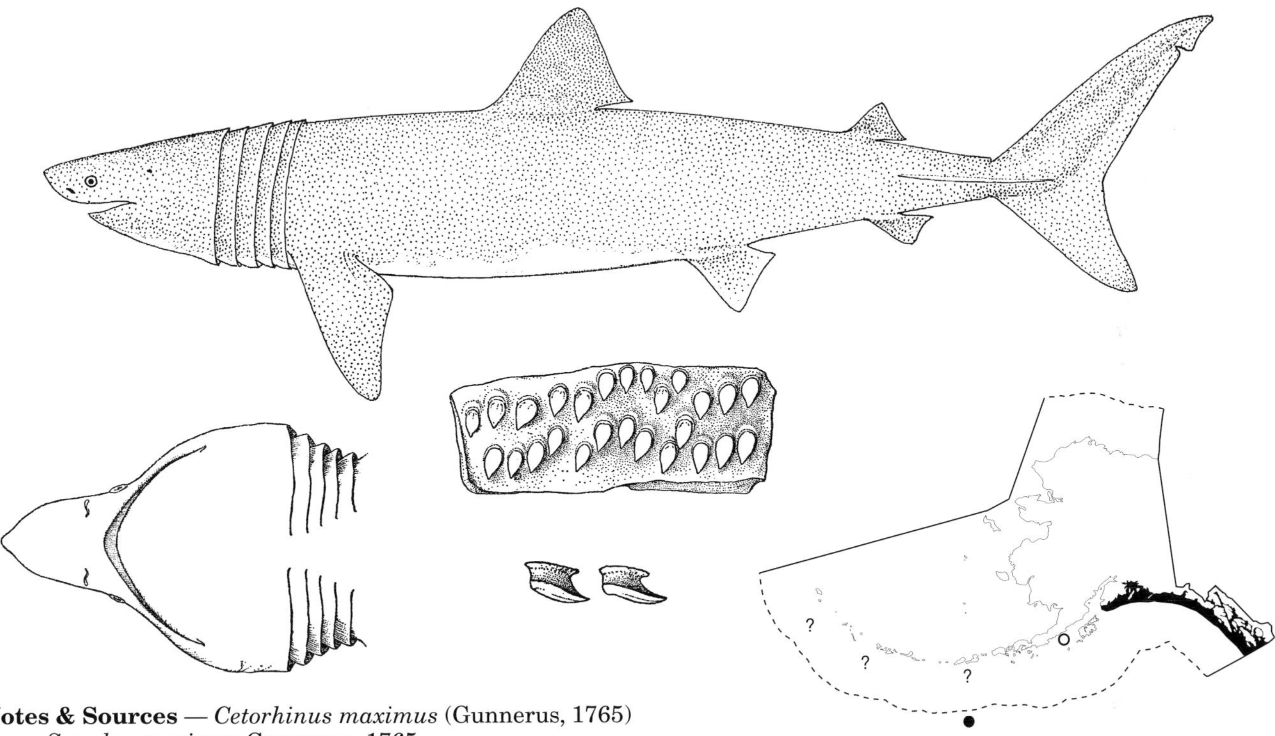

Notes & Sources — *Cetorhinus maximus* (Gunnerus, 1765)
Squalus maximus Gunnerus, 1765

The author's name is sometimes spelled Gunner (e.g., Jordan and Gilbert 1883:875; Jordan and Evermann 1896a,b; Clemens and Wilby 1946, 1949, 1961), but in his major work he used the Latinized spelling Gunnerus and this is, therefore, the more appropriate spelling for use with the species' name (W. N. Eschmeyer, pers. comm., 21 Aug. 2000).

Atlantic coast whalers used to call these sharks bone sharks, for the resemblance they saw in the long, dark gill rakers to the baleen, or "whalebone," of the baleen whales (Bigelow and Schroeder 1953).

Description: Bigelow and Schroeder 1948:146–160; Springer and Gilbert 1976; Castro 1983:86–88; Compagno 1984: 234–236.

Figures: Lateral view: Compagno 1984:234. Ventral view and teeth (section of upper jaw and lateral view of 2 teeth): Bigelow and Schroeder 1948, fig. 23.

Range: Indicated for Gulf of Alaska in general statements by Wilimovsky (1958), Clemens and Wilby (1961), and Quast and Hall (1972), without citing specific records. The map in Compagno (1984:235) has solid fill west to Kenai Peninsula, and question marks over western Gulf of Alaska and south of Aleutian Islands. Baxter (1990ms) gave range to Halibut Cove, Kachemak Bay, without citing documentation. The NMFS survey database has a record of one specimen taken off south side of Alaska Peninsula on 2 May 1981 at 56°49'N, 156°29'W (J. W. Orr, pers. comm., 4 Sep. 1997). Larkins (1964) reported that in high seas epipelagic fishing for salmon in the Bering Sea, North Pacific Ocean, and Gulf of Alaska over the period 1955–1961, one specimen was captured; this was in August 1958 at 50°00'N, 165°00'W. Basking sharks have been common at times in coastal waters of southeastern Alaska. Woodford (1996) showed photographs of basking sharks at least 5.7 m (12 ft) long taken in Clarence Strait in the 1940s. They were so common in Barkley Sound, British Columbia, in the 1940s and 1950s that entanglement in fishing nets caused a problem and a fisheries patrol boat was fitted with an underwater knife, with which several hundred basking sharks were killed (Clemens and Wilby 1961). Darling and Keogh (1994) reported that basking sharks are rarely sighted in Barkley Sound today, and that the only remaining aggregation in British Columbia may be a small group in Clayoquot Sound.

Size: Bigelow and Schroeder (1953), reviewing data from the Atlantic Ocean, considered that occasional reports of basking sharks reaching 15.2 m (50 ft) probably are not an exaggeration, but largest definite measurement they found was 980 cm (32 ft 2 inches). Castro (1983) gave average size of 700–900 cm (22–29 ft).

Order Hexanchiformes
Cow sharks and frill sharks

Sharks of the order Hexanchiformes, including cow sharks and frill sharks, have 6 or 7 pairs of gill slits; a single dorsal fin, without a spine; an anal fin; eyes without nictitating lower eyelids; and very small spiracles located well behind the eyes. All of the gill slits are anterior to the pectoral fins, labial furrows are reduced or absent, and there is no gap or small intermediate teeth between the anterior and lateral teeth.

The order contains two families, four genera, and five extant species. The Hexanchidae, with four species, is represented in Alaska by at least one species. The fifth species, in the other hexanchiform family, the Chlamydoselachidae, is the frill shark, *Chlamydoselachus anguineus.* In the Atlantic Ocean the frill shark occurs as far north as Norway, but in the Pacific Ocean it has not been recorded north of California.

Family Hexanchidae
Cow sharks

The family Hexanchidae, or cow sharks, comprises four species of deepwater sixgill and sevengill sharks. Cow sharks have a worldwide distribution in boreal and cold temperate to tropical seas. Most cow sharks are deepwater species, inhabiting outer continental shelves, continental slopes, insular shelves and slopes, and submarine canyons down to depths of at least 1,875 m, near the bottom or well above it; but occasionally are found near the surface or in shallow water. One species regularly inhabits shallow bays, often close to shore and near the surface.

Presence of the bluntnose sixgill shark, *Hexanchus griseus,* has been documented off the Aleutian Islands and southward, and the broadnose sevengill shark, *Notorynchus cepedianus,* off northern British Columbia and southward. Although the range of *N. cepedianus* has been stated to extend north to southeastern Alaska, records of diagnostic characters, locality data, or other information to support the claim are unknown.

Cow sharks have 6 or 7 gill slits (5 in most other sharks); 1 dorsal fin (2 in most other sharks); and a subterminal mouth with fanglike or long, narrow teeth in the upper jaw and large, comblike teeth with many cusplets in the lower jaw. The difference in the upper and lower teeth is most marked at the front of the mouth. The single dorsal fin is set far back on the body posterior to the pelvic fins. The caudal fin is elongate, and the caudal peduncle lacks keels and precaudal pits.

The only other sharks with 6 gill slits are the frill shark and one of the sawsharks. Those sharks do not occur in the eastern North Pacific north of California and, in any case, are easily identified. In the frill shark, family Chlamydoselachidae, the margin of the first gill is continuous across the throat, while in cow sharks it is not; the mouth is terminal rather than subterminal; and the teeth are alike in the upper and lower jaws, with three elongate cusps.

Cow sharks are ovoviviparous and the females of some species produce very large litters. *Hexanchus griseus,* for example, produces litters of 22–108 pups. Adult cow sharks range in maximum size from about 1.4 to 4.8 m (4.5 to 15.75 ft). The largest is *H. griseus.*

Key to the Hexanchidae of Alaska

1 Gill slits 6 on each side . . . . *Hexanchus griseus,* page 83

1 Gill slits 7 on each side . . . . *Notorynchus cepedianus,* page 84
not confirmed from Alaska)

Hexanchus griseus (Bonnaterre, 1788) **bluntnose sixgill shark**

North Pacific south of Aleutian Islands to California and to Japan; South Pacific; worldwide in deep temperate and tropical waters.

Benthic or pelagic, on continental and insular shelves and upper slopes, at depths from surface to at least 1,875 m.

- Dark brown or gray to black dorsally; slightly lighter ventrally; usually with lighter streak along side; unspotted; eye greenish.
- Head broad and depressed; snout rounded to bluntly pointed.
- One dorsal fin.
- **Gill slits 6.**
- **Upper and lower teeth strikingly different; lower lateral teeth sawlike, large, low, and long, with about 8–12 cusplets.**
- Length to at least 482 cm TL.

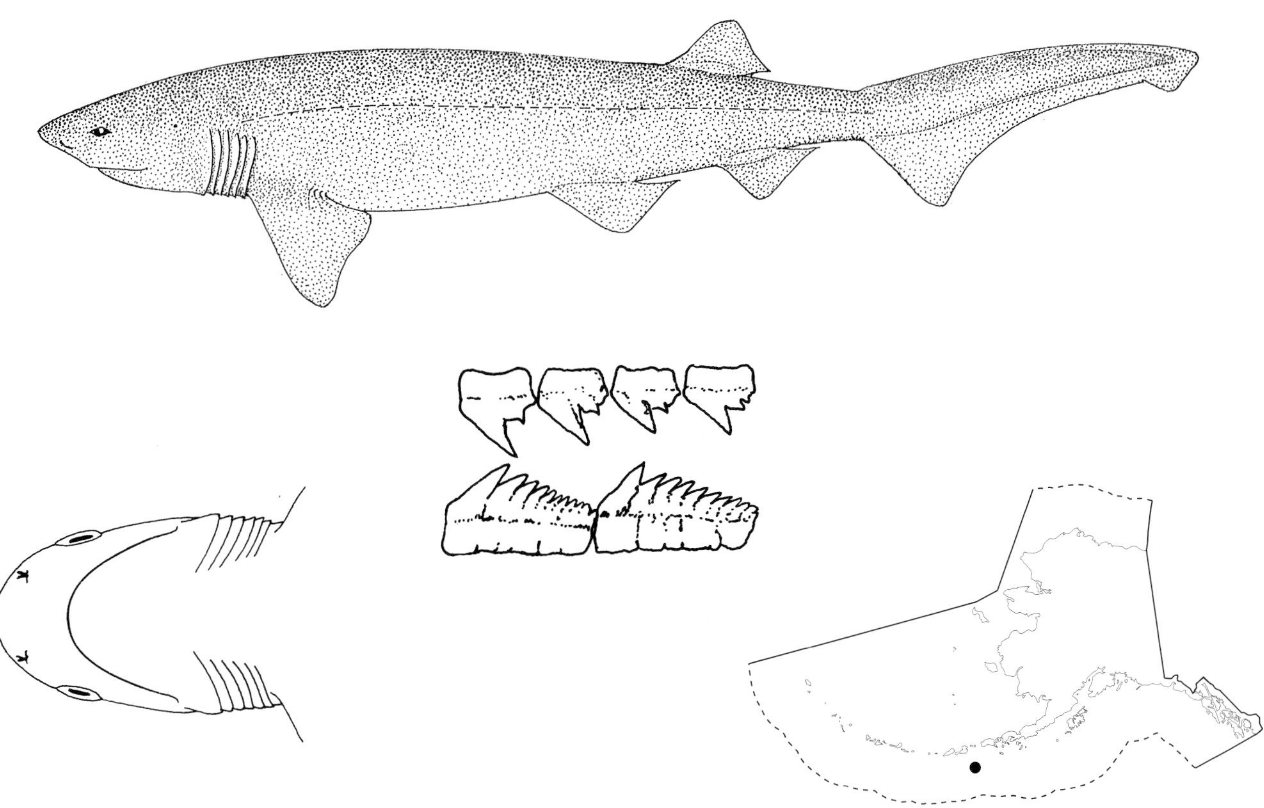

Notes & Sources — *Hexanchus griseus* (Bonnaterre, 1788)
Squalus griseus Bonnaterre, 1788
Hexanchus corinus Jordan & Gilbert, 1880
The bluntnose sixgill shark is sometimes called the mud shark, but this name is also used for the Pacific sleeper shark, *Somniosus pacificus,* a species which is much more common in Alaskan waters. Use of the name mud shark in newspapers and popular accounts without giving the scientific name has caused confusion regarding geographic range.

Description: Jordan and Gilbert 1880r; Bigelow and Schroeder 1948:78–87; Hart 1973:27–28; Castro 1983:37; Eschmeyer and Herald 1983:19; Compagno 1984:19–20.

Figures: Compagno 1984:19.

Range: Indicated for Gulf of Alaska in general statements by Wilimovsky (1958), Clemens and Wilby (1961), Quast and Hall (1972), and Hart (1973); no specific records were cited for Alaska. Larkins (1964) reported one specimen was taken in 7 years (1955–1961) of salmon fishing in the Bering Sea, North Pacific Ocean, and Gulf of Alaska, at 53°00'N, 165°00'W, in early September 1956. Clemens and Wilby (1946, 1949, 1961) reported it to be abundant in the Strait of Georgia, where it was caught in purse seines, especially during herring fishing season, on set-lines, and in sunken nets, trawls, and salmon traps.

Size: Clemens and Wilby (1946, 1949, 1961) and Hart (1973) reported a maximum length of "26 feet 5 inches" (8 m), but Castro (1983) stated that reports of such a large specimen are now known to be erroneous, and that the largest on record was a female 482 cm (15.8 ft) long.

Notorynchus cepedianus (Péron, 1807) **broadnose sevengill shark**

Southeastern Alaska, record not confirmed; well documented in North Pacific from northern British Columbia to Gulf of California and Japan to China; Peru to Chile; Australia and New Zealand; South Atlantic; mostly in temperate waters.

Benthic, neritic, on continental shelves; at depths to 46 m or more, often in shallow water less than 1 m deep and at the surface; moves into bays as the tide rises and out with its fall.

- Sandy gray to reddish brown; paler ventrally; numerous small black spots, sometimes also with white spots.
- Head broad and depressed; snout broadly rounded or bluntly pointed.
- One dorsal fin.
- **Gill slits 7.**
- **Upper and lower teeth strikingly different; lower teeth sawlike, large, high, and short, with 5 or 6 cusplets.**
- Length to 291 cm TL, possibly attaining lengths between 3 and 4 m.

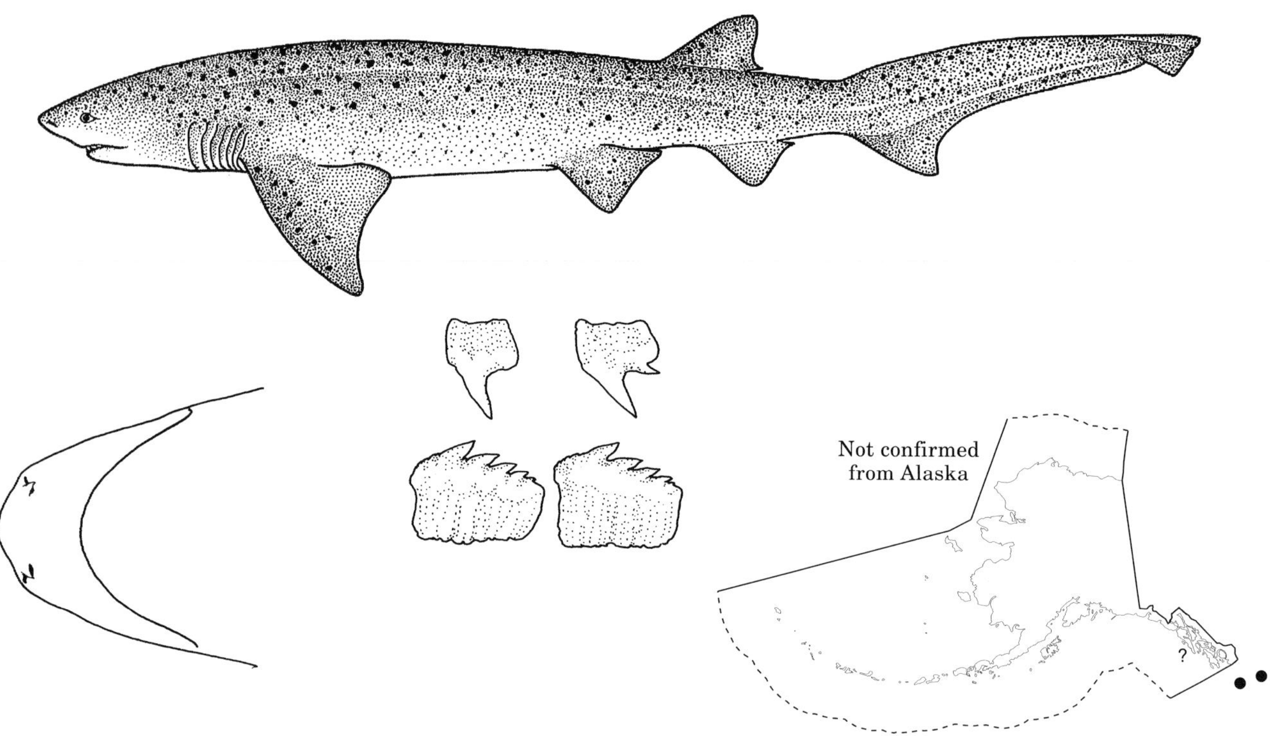

Notes & Sources — *Notorynchus cepedianus* (Péron, 1807)
Squalus cepedianus Péron, 1807
Notorynchus maculatus Ayres, 1855
Sevengill sharks from the eastern Pacific are classified by some researchers as *N. maculatus.*

Description: Hart 1973:28–29; Castro 1983:38–39; Eschmeyer and Herald 1983:19–20; Compagno 1984:22–23; Ebert 1989.

Figures: Compagno 1984:22.

Range: Compagno (1984) and previous authors, as well as Baxter (1990ms), gave British Columbia for the northern limit in the eastern Pacific. Quast and Hall (1972) listed this shark, as *N. maculatus,* as a species likely to occur in Alaska. Ebert (1986, 1989) gave a range to southeastern Alaska in general statements; specimens from Alaska could have been among the 32 specimens examined from California institutions, but Ebert did not give specimen data. Clemens and Wilby (1946) reported on occurrence in British Columbia. The northernmost catches were at Bonilla Island (53°30'N, 130°40'W) and Butedale (53°09'N, 128°41'W). They noted that sevengill sharks were obtained occasionally in otter trawls in the southern portion of the Strait of Georgia. No new records were reported for British Columbia by Clemens and Wilby (1949, 1961) or Hart (1973).

Size: Compagno (1984) reported that an old record at 4.6 m was based on *Hexanchus griseus*; and gave sizes at maturity for males of 150–180 cm, reaching at least 225 cm; and for females of 192–208 cm, reaching at least 288 cm. The 288-cm female was caught off New Zealand. Ebert (1989) gave a record length of 291 cm TL, from a female sevengill shark captured off California.

Order Squaliformes
Sleeper sharks and dogfish sharks

With 74 species, the Squaliformes is one of the largest orders of sharks. Many squaliforms inhabit deep water and are relatively sluggish and nonstreamlined, but the group is diverse and includes some highly mobile, fast-swimming species. Several are widespread in the world's oceans. Few, if any, have been implicated in attacks on humans. Two species of squaliform shark, one of them a sleeper shark and the other a dogfish shark, occur and are abundant in Alaskan waters. Recent evidence suggests their abundance has been increasing in parts of the Gulf of Alaska.

Squaliform sharks have 2 dorsal fins; no anal fin; 5 pairs of gill slits, all in front of the pectoral fin base; spiracles; and eyes without nictitating lower eyelids. The teeth are not well differentiated front to back, with none enlarged anteriorly or posteriorly and no gap or small intermediate teeth between the anterior and lateral teeth in the upper jaw.

The history of the order Squaliformes is long and complicated. In the simplest arrangement, followed fairly recently (e.g., Hart 1973), taxonomists included all "higher" sharks, meaning those with 5 gill slits and 2 dorsal fins, in the group. Currently the taxon is perceived as including relatively few species, with the makeup of the smaller group changing as understanding of their interrelationships grows. Eschmeyer and Herald (1983) and Compagno (1984), among other authors, classified the sleeper sharks and dogfish sharks in one family, the Squalidae. Following, in part, a cladistic analysis by Shirai (1992), Nelson (1994) and Eschmeyer (1998) classified them in separate families, the Dalatiidae and Squalidae.

Family Dalatiidae
Sleeper sharks

Sleeper sharks are sluggish, giving almost no resistance to capture. They live close to the bottom, where they scavenge for meals, but also swim toward the surface after prey. They consume a diverse array of both surface and bottom prey but fast-moving species, such as harbor seals and salmon, may be eaten as carrion rather than captured alive.

Most sleeper sharks lack spines in the dorsal fins, in contrast to dogfish sharks (Squalidae), which have a spine at the front of each dorsal fin; and luminous organs, appearing as black dots mainly on the ventral surface of the body, are present in all but the Pacific sleeper shark, *Somniosus pacificus.* This shark is a member of the subfamily Somniosinae, with representatives from the Arctic Ocean to the Southern Ocean. It inhabits the marine waters of Alaska from the Chukchi Sea to the Gulf of Alaska, and is one of the three most abundant sharks in the region (the others being spiny dogfish, *Squalus acanthias*; and salmon shark, *Lamna ditropis*). Once believed to be endemic to the North Pacific, *S. pacificus* was recently recorded from the southwest Atlantic (de Astarloa et al. 1999).

Starting in the early 1990s, increases in the numbers of Pacific sleeper sharks were observed in some areas of the Gulf of Alaska. In Prince William Sound catches of 20–30 sleeper sharks on one longline set of 100 hooks were common in 1997–1998, and 20–30% of the halibut catch was lost to the sharks. In Cook Inlet in 1998 they were eating the halibut as they were being brought to the surface, and fishermen often caught and killed the sharks so they could land the halibut. One longline set in the central Gulf of Alaska in 1998 came up with 67 sleeper sharks (L. B. Hulbert, pers. comm., 1 May 2000). Scientists are conducting research into the extent and possible causes of the apparent increase in abundance. It does not appear to be areawide. Available research data and incidental reports do not indicate an increase in Glacier Bay. Sleeper sharks are commonly found in Glacier Bay and there was high mortality from the longline fishery, but the fishery has been closed and numbers are expected to increase (P. N. Hooge, pers. comm., 22 May 2000).

The size of sleeper sharks in the Gulf of Alaska might also have been increasing. Sleeper sharks caught in Prince William Sound were reported to average about 1.2 m (4 ft) in the early 1990s and 2.4–3.0 m (8–10 ft) in 1998; and reports have recently come in of 6-m (20-ft) sleeper sharks in the Gulf of Alaska (L. B. Hulbert, pers. comm., 1 May 2000). However, documentation for sizes larger than 4.4 m (14.4 ft) in the Pacific Ocean is lacking.

Sleeper sharks are assumed to be ovoviviparous, although little is known about their reproduction or other aspects of their life history. Females can carry several hundred large yolky eggs, but embryos are unknown and the smallest sleeper shark on record measured 79 cm (31 inches) (Eschmeyer and Herald 1983).

Somniosus pacificus Bigelow & Schroeder, 1944 **Pacific sleeper shark**

Chukchi and Bering seas, and possibly East Siberian and Beaufort seas, to Pacific Ocean off southern Baja California and Japan, and Sea of Okhotsk; southwest Atlantic Ocean.

On or near bottom, sometimes at surface or intertidal, to depth of at least 2,000 m; typically at the greater depths in the southern part of its range.

- Uniformly blackish brown to slate green or gray, sometimes lightly streaked.
- Body robust and flaccid; snout long and rounded.
- No precaudal pits; lateral keel on caudal peduncle in some specimens.
- **Dorsal fins low, nearly equal in size, without spines at their origins**; first dorsal fin well ahead of pelvic fin; **anal fin absent**; caudal fin somewhat paddle-shaped, with large lower lobe.
- Upper teeth slender-cusped, narrow, thornlike; cusps of lower teeth short and low, strongly oblique, and roots very high.
- Length to 600 cm TL or more.

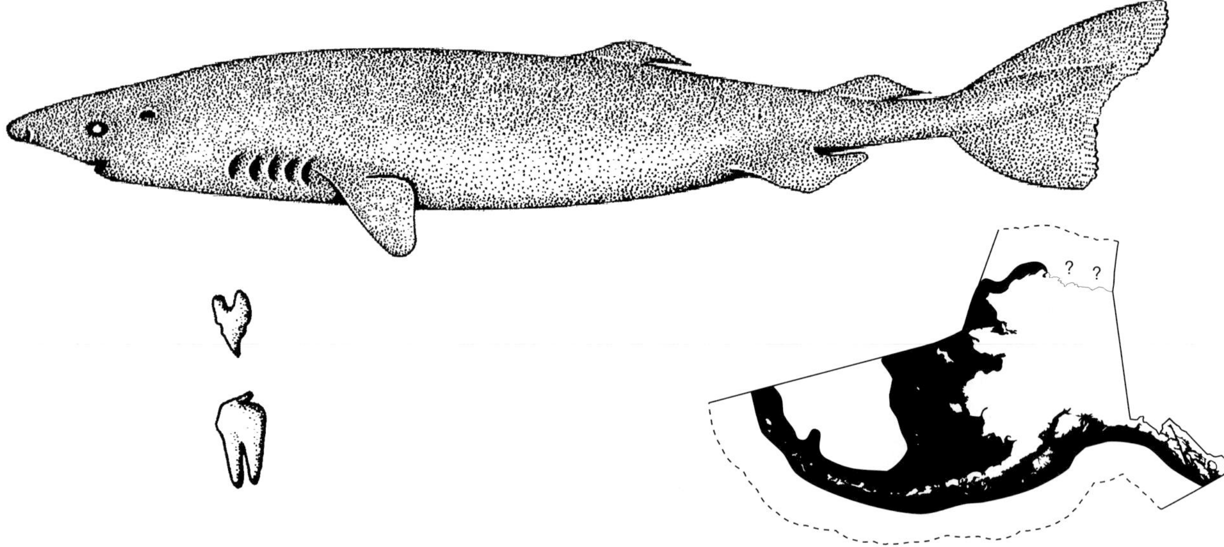

Notes & Sources — *Somniosus pacificus* Bigelow & Schroeder, 1944

In the late 1800s and early 1900s, specimens from Alaska were identified as Greenland shark, *Somniosus microcephalus* (Bloch & Schneider, 1801); e.g., Jordan and Gilbert 1881a, 1899. In *S. pacificus* the origin of the first dorsal fin is almost as near to the tip of the caudal fin as it is to the tip of the snout (pre-first dorsal length >43% of total length; Francis et al. 1988), while in *S. microcephalus* the origin of the first dorsal is much nearer to the tip of the snout than to the tip of the caudal fin.

Description: Bigelow and Schroeder 1944, 1948:514–516; Gotshall and Jow 1965; Hart 1973:43–44; Compagno 1984: 105–106; de Astarloa et al. 1999.

Figures: Castro 1983:64.

Range: Jordan and Gilbert (1899) reported it to be "not uncommon in the Bering Sea" and Andriashev (1939) listed it for the entire Bering Sea. Compagno's (1984) map indicated continuous range in the Chukchi Sea off Siberia and Alaska and included question marks for the East Siberian and Beaufort seas. Fedorov and Sheiko (2002) reported it to be common in the vicinity of the Commander Islands, and Sheiko (pers. comm., 23 Jan. 1999) reported that KIE biologists caught it frequently in 1994 on the Commander shelf northwest of Bering Island on longline hooks at depths below 300 m. J. W. Orr (pers. comm., 16 Apr. 1997) provided records from the central and western Aleutian Islands from the AFSC survey database. Yang and Page (1999) collected sleeper sharks from the western Gulf of Alaska in and south of Shelikof Strait at depths of 86–267 m. Orlov (1999) found that in the Bering Sea and in the Pacific Ocean near the Kuril Islands sleeper sharks occurred at 85–717 m, averaging around 450 m, with no evidence of a change-over to occupy deeper water in summer. Research- and commercial-caught sleeper sharks in Glacier Bay have been in soft-bottomed habitat at depths greater than 300 m (P. N. Hooge, pers. comm., 22 May 2000). Bright (1959) reported on a large (3.93 m) female sleeper shark stranded in a Kachemak Bay tidepool.

In the 1990s numbers of sleeper sharks may have increased in some areas of the Gulf of Alaska, including Prince William Sound, Cook Inlet, and the north-central Gulf of Alaska (L. B. Hulbert, pers. comm., 1 May 2000), while changes were not noticed in other areas, such as Glacier Bay (P. N. Hooge, pers. comm., 22 May 2000).

Size: Reported to reach more than 7 m, estimated from photographs taken in deep water (Compagno 1984). Documentation for 7.6 m TL given by Hart (1973) is lacking. A claim that specimens may reach 8 m TL (Issacs and Schwartzlose 1975) is unsubstantiated (D. A. Ebert, pers. comm., 15 Jul. 2001). Eschmeyer and Herald (1983) reported the largest sleeper shark captured in the Pacific Ocean was 4.4 m. Ebert et al. (1987) deposited parts of a 4.4-cm female in the CAS collection (CAS 33586). Orlov (1999), evidently not aware of that report, considered a 4.2-m female taken in 1988 in the Pacific off the Kuril Islands to be the largest adequately documented specimen. Females measuring 5 and 6 m were collected in 1997 in the southwest Atlantic (de Astarloa et al. 1999). The largest male sleeper sharks reported from the Pacific were 4.0 m TL (Phillips 1953) and from the Atlantic, 4.1 and 4.3 m (de Asterloa et al. 1999).

Family Squalidae
Dogfish sharks

Dogfish sharks inhabit boreal to tropical seas worldwide. They are sleek and fast-swimming, and travel in packs of hundreds to thousands of individuals. Distinguishing characters of dogfish sharks include: two dorsal fins, each with a spine at the front; teeth on the lower jaw not much larger than those of the upper jaw; an upper precaudal pit in most species; and a keel on each side of the caudal peduncle.

The spiny dogfish, *Squalus acanthias,* is possibly the most abundant and well-known living shark. Caught for human consumption, used in liver oil, pet food, fishmeal, fertilizer, and leather, and used in research and classroom dissection, it is the only shark that supports fisheries as large as those of the commercially important bony fishes. On the negative side, spiny dogfish are infamous for the damage they do to fishing gear and catches of other fishes.

Exhibiting wide salinity, temperature, and depth tolerances, spiny dogfish are the most widespread representative of the genus *Squalus* in the world's oceans, and were recently documented for the first time from subantarctic waters (Pshenichnov 1997). They mainly occur along coasts, both inshore and offshore. However, records of occurrence of immature and young adults in open ocean are not uncommon, and a few individuals tagged off the coasts of British Columbia and Washington have been recovered off Japan (Ketchen 1986, Nakano and Nagasawa 1996).

In Alaska, spiny dogfish are most abundant along the southern coasts. They are found there year round, but most commonly in spring through fall. Accounts from recreational and commercial fishers, longline surveys by the International Pacific Halibut Commission and the Alaska Department of Fish and Game, and other evidence indicate that spiny dogfish abundance may have increased in some areas of the Gulf of Alaska in recent years.

The spiny dogfish is ovoviviparous and produces up to 20 young per litter. Gestation ranges from 18 to 24 months, and at the higher end of this range is longer than gestation in any other vertebrate, even whales and elephants. Males mature at 59–72 cm, and females at 70–100 cm (Compagno 1984). Recently obtained data from the Strait of Georgia, British Columbia, indicate a median age at maturity for female spiny dogfish of 35.5 years and length of 94 cm (Saunders and McFarlane 1993). Spiny dogfish reach the maximum size reported for the species of 160 cm (5.25 ft) in the eastern North Pacific, but most individuals there are smaller, in the range of 61–122 cm (2–4 ft) (Eschmeyer and Herald 1983), and other populations reach smaller maximum sizes.

Squalus acanthias Linnaeus, 1758 **spiny dogfish**

Eastern Chukchi Sea, one record off Kotzebue; Bering Sea to Gulf of California and to southwestern Yellow Sea off China; South Pacific and Atlantic; not in tropical waters.

Coastal, inshore and offshore, from intertidal area and surface to depth of 1,244 m, usually taken near bottom at depths of 50–300 m; often in shallow bays; in schools segregated by size and sex, and as solitary individuals; individuals in open ocean are usually immature or recently matured adults.

- Slate gray or brown dorsally, lighter ventrally; one or two rows of small pale spots laterally on individuals up to 95 cm TL or more.
- Dorsal precaudal pit present; lateral keel present on caudal peduncle.
- First dorsal fin larger than second; **single spine at origin of each dorsal fin; anal fin absent.**
- Teeth in upper and lower jaws flattened, forming continuous cutting edge.
- Length to 160 cm TL.

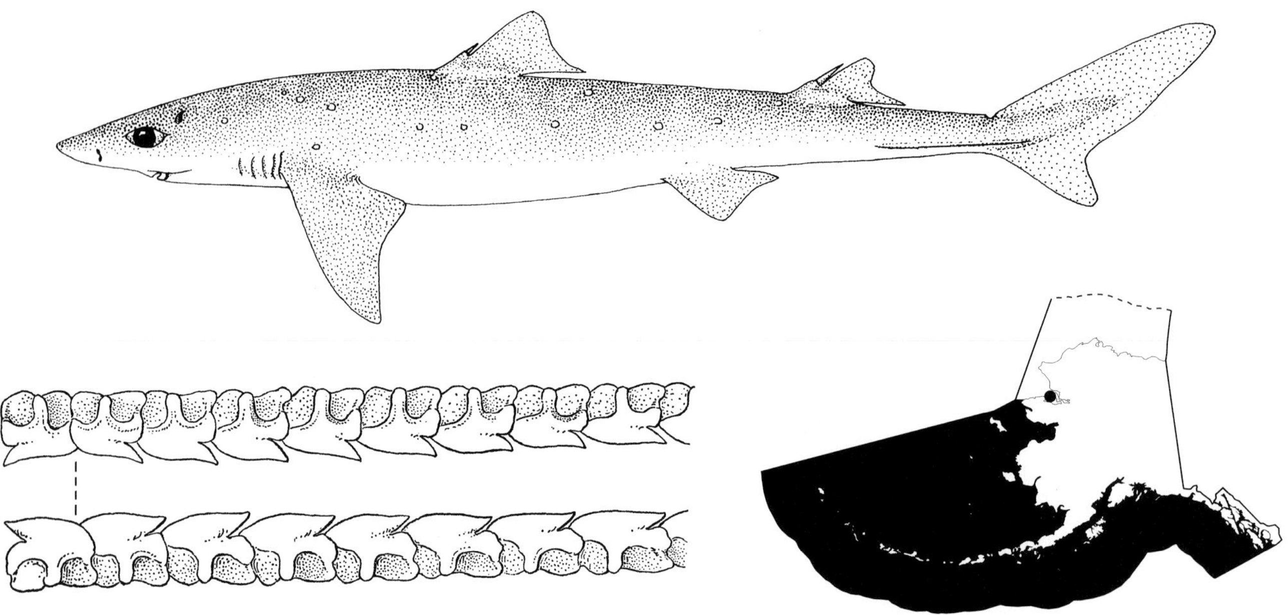

Notes & Sources — *Squalus acanthias* Linnaeus, 1758

Description: Bigelow and Schroeder 1948:455–473; Hart 1973:44–47; Castro 1983:55–57; Eschmeyer and Herald 1983:23; Compagno 1984:111–113.

Figures: Full lateral view: Compagno 1984:111. Teeth: Bigelow and Schroeder 1948, fig. 88.

Range: Compagno's (1984) map depicts range to Bering Strait, but specific records documenting distribution north of the southern portion of the Bering Sea are lacking from the literature. Andriashev (1939) reported spiny dogfish had not been found in the northern part of the Bering Sea, and were only questionably present in the western Bering Sea. Recorded west in Aleutian Islands to Attu Island by Okada and Kobayashi (1968). Reported to be rare in vicinity of Commander Islands, Russia, by Fedorov and Sheiko (2002). A specimen caught in a salmon gill net in the Chukchi Sea near Kotzebue in August 1986 may be the northernmost record. Identified by an ADFG biologist, it was 90 cm long and was mounted to hang in a bar at Kotzebue (B. L. Wing, pers. comm., 21 Feb. 1999). Specimens examined for taxonomic evaluation by Jones and Geen (1976) and records from surveys summarized by Allen and Smith (1988) and Nakano and Nagasawa (1996) provided more detailed information than previously available on occurrence in the southern portion of the Bering Sea. The northernmost record among 1,976 occurrences in NMFS surveys of 1953–1983 from California to Alaska was Zhemchug Canyon (Allen and Smith 1988). Immature and young adults were found in open ocean from north of 40°N to south of the Aleutian chain, as well as over the Aleutian Basin and eastern Bering Sea slope to about 60°N, along the Aleutian chain, and all across Gulf of Alaska offshore, as bycatch in North Pacific high seas salmon gillnet surveys in 1981–1991 (Nakano and Nagasawa 1996). Most authors give range as possibly to Gulf of California, but Compagno et al. (in Fischer et al. 1995) indicate this without question. First record for the subantarctic region was documented by Pshenichnov (1997), near Kerguelen Islands. Occasionally found deep; reported to 950 m by Fedorov and Sheiko (2002) and taken in NMFS AFSC surveys as deep as 1,244 m (J. W. Orr, pers. comm., 4 Sep. 1997).

Research surveys and anecdotal accounts indicate spiny dogfish have been increasing in some areas of the Gulf of Alaska, including Prince William Sound, and research is being undertaken to determine the extent and cause of the increase (L. B. Hulbert, pers. comm., 1 May 2000). T.A.M. caught two spiny dogfish, 56 and 62 cm TL, while sportfishing for halibut with herring-baited hook and line in Lynn Canal east of Shelter Island (southeastern Alaska) in the summer of 1998, which were the first we caught in more than 20 years of fishing the area.

Order Squatiniformes
Family Squatinidae
Angel sharks

The order Squatiniformes includes only the angel sharks, a family of bottom-dwelling inhabitants of shallow, mainly warm, coastal waters. Angel sharks are dorsoventrally flattened and greatly resemble skates, except their pectoral fins are not attached to the head, their five gill slits are ventrolateral instead of entirely ventral, and they have movable eyelids. They are ovoviviparous. The group is poorly known taxonomically and biologically, and a classification including 12 species is "provisional in the extreme" (Compagno 1984). One species, *Squatina californica,* occurs in the eastern Pacific Ocean. There is one record of its occurrence in southeastern Alaska, but it was problematic even when first published.

Squatina californica Ayres, 1859 — **Pacific angel shark**

Southeastern Alaska record not verifiable; well documented in eastern Pacific Ocean from Puget Sound, Washington, to Gulf of California and Ecuador to southern Chile.

On bottom at depths of 3–46 m in northern parts of range, to 183 m in Gulf of California; most common at depths of 15 m or less; buries itself in sand or mud, with eyes and upper parts showing.

- Grayish or reddish brown to blackish with dark speckles and spots dorsally; white ventrally.
- Body flattened, mouth terminal, eyes dorsal.
- Spiracles large; gill slits ventrolateral.
- Nostrils terminal; barbels on anterior margin.
- Pectoral fins greatly expanded; 2 spineless, small dorsal fins set far behind pelvic fins.
- Length to 152 cm TL, average about 100 cm.

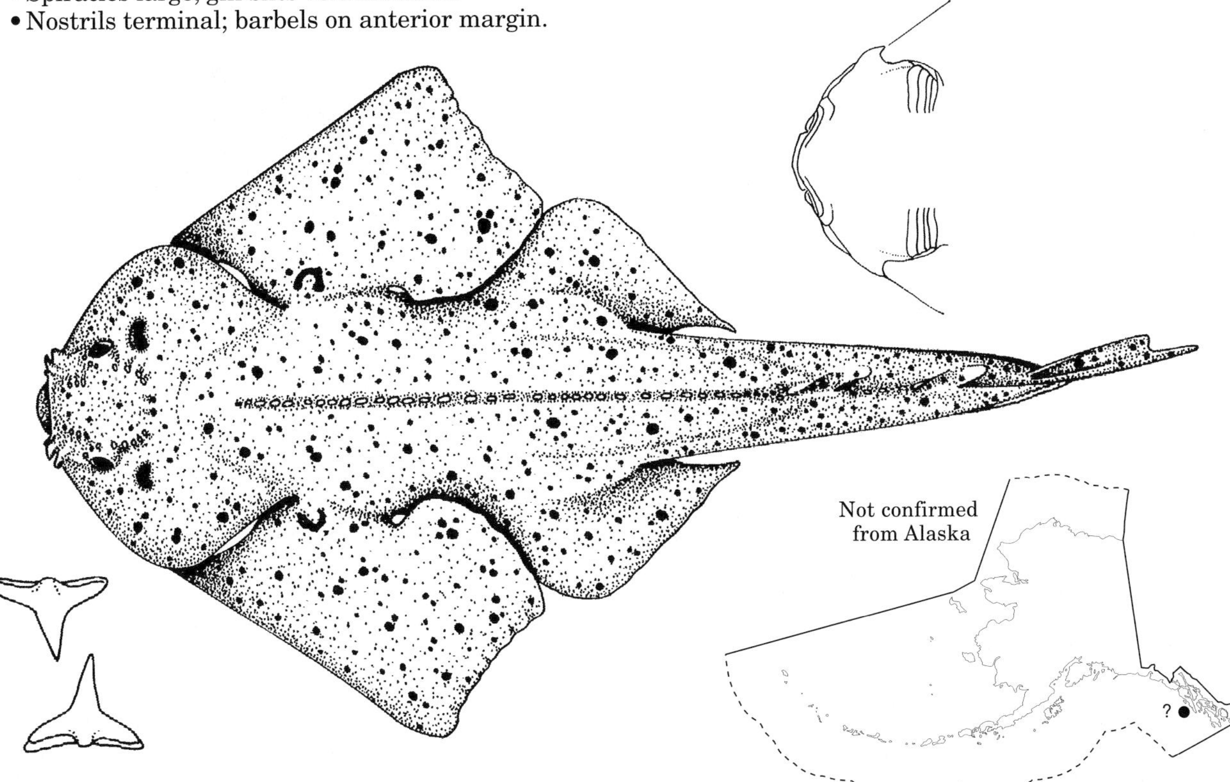

Notes & Sources — *Squatina californica* Ayres, 1859
Squatina squatina (Linnaeus): Evermann and Goldsborough 1907.
All angel sharks used to be classified as one species, *S. squatina* (Linnaeus, 1758).

Description: Castro 1983:71-72; Eschmeyer and Herald 1983:44; Compagno 1984:144–145.

Figures: Castro 1983:72, modified.

Range: Evermann and Goldsborough (1907:222, 228) reported that one specimen, "a female 14 inches long," from southeastern Alaska was in the USNM collection, but that the locality label had been lost. Theirs is the only record of occurrence in Alaska. Angel sharks have not been reported from British Columbia (Hart 1973, Peden 1998). The nearest well-documented locality is Puget Sound near Seattle, based on a specimen (UW 1508) recorded by Schultz et al. (1932). Rare north of California.

Order Rajiformes
Skates and rays

Skates and rays, or batoid fishes, are conspicuously flattened elasmobranchs with long-based pectoral fins attached to the sides of the head and continuous with the body, forming a disk. The gill slits are entirely ventral, and the teeth are pavementlike. All the batoid fishes are classified in the Rajiformes by Nelson (1994), but their interrelationships are not well understood. Recent phylogenetic analyses by Shirai (1996) and Carvalho (1996) support the one-order view, whereas McEachran et al. (1996) proposed several orders.

Family Torpedinidae
Electric rays

Electric rays have a relatively thick disk that is truncate or emarginate anteriorly and rounded on the sides, and a well-developed caudal fin. The electric organs, which are internal, at the base of each pectoral fin, produce a strong electric current for stunning prey and fending off enemies. Electric rays occur worldwide, primarily in warm seas, on sand and mud bottoms on continental and insular shelves and the upper slopes. They are ovoviviparous.

About 38 species of electric rays are known. None has been reported to venture into Alaskan waters, although the Pacific electric ray, *Torpedo californica,* has been found as far north in British Columbia as Dixon Entrance off Wiah Point, Graham Island.

Torpedo californica Ayres, 1855 **Pacific electric ray**

Northern British Columbia at Dixon Entrance to central Baja California at Sebastian Vizcaino Bay; Japan.

On or just above sandy bottom from depths of 3 m to about 425 m, usually shallower than 300 m.

- Dark blue to brownish gray with small dark spots, sometimes obsolete, dorsally; lighter ventrally.
- Caudal fin truncate, expanded.
- Skin entirely smooth.
- Length of females to 137 cm TL, males 91 cm TL.

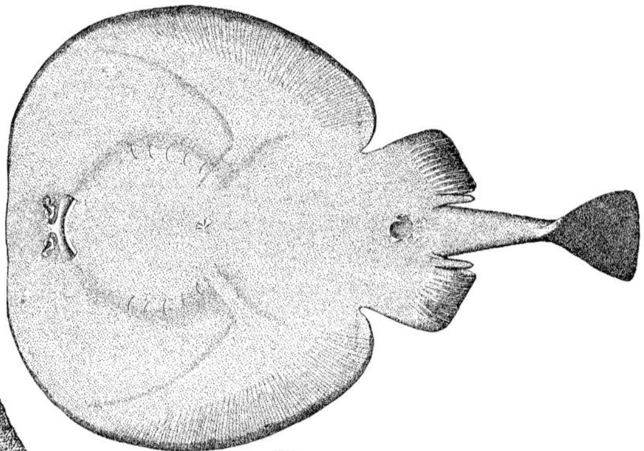

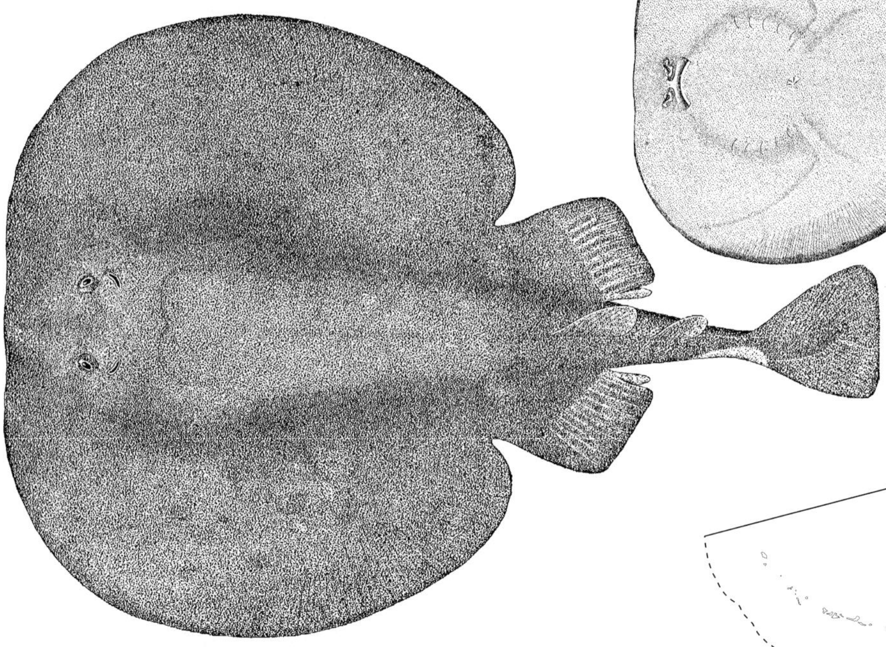

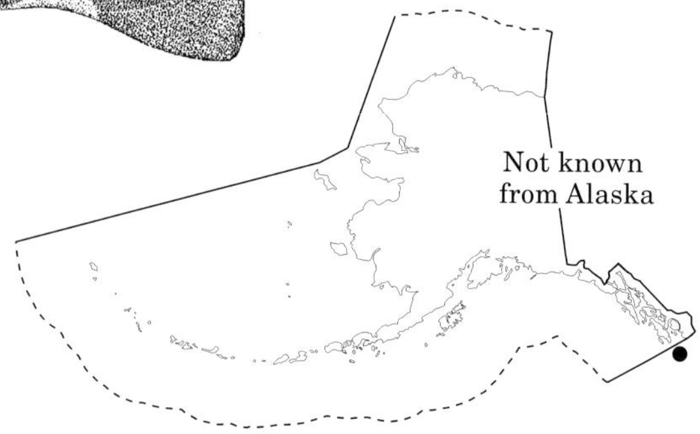

Not known from Alaska

Notes & Sources — *Torpedo californica* Ayres, 1855
Tetranarce californica: Clemens and Wilby 1946, 1949.

Description: Clemens and Wilby 1961:92–94; Hart 1973:50–51; Eschmeyer and Herald 1983:53–54.

Figures: Jordan and Evermann 1900, fig. 34.

Range: Clemens and Wilby (1961) reported specimen taken off Wiah Point in August 1960. Sporadically common in the past in British Columbia (Hart 1973). In NMFS bottom trawl surveys during 1953–1983, found no farther north than Cape Flattery, Washington (Allen and Smith 1988).

Family Rajidae
Skates

Skates inhabit marine waters nearly worldwide but are most common in cold temperate to tropical regions. They live on the bottom, both close to shore and in deep water to 3,000 m, and feed on benthic invertebrates and fishes. They prefer soft, muddy and sandy bottoms and often rest partly buried. Skates are readily identified to family by their triangular or kite-shaped (rhombic) disks, slender tails, and, in Alaskan species, presence of two small dorsal fins near the tip of the tail. Some species in other regions have one dorsal fin, or none. In most species the caudal fin is small or absent. In some species scattered denticles (also called prickles) cover much of the disk and tail, making the surface rough. A middorsal, or median, row of thorns (also called spines) on the tail is typical of many species, and in some extends to the nuchal or scapular region. Skates are oviparous, and produce eggs encased in a capsule with four drawn-out corners, or "horns." The skate family comprises about 228 valid species and 50 unnamed species worldwide (McEachran and Dunn 1998), with 12 valid species and an unknown number of undescribed species in Alaska.

Nearly 280 species is a large number, considering there are only about 800 species of cartilaginous fishes (Nelson 1994). However, skates are morphologically very similar, despite the high species diversity, and it has been difficult for systematists to define variation and infer phylogenetic relationships. Nelson (1994) chose not to recognize subfamilies of skates in his classification of fishes (followed in this guide). Recent progress and views on definition of skate clades may be understood from McEachran and Dunn (1998), who reviewed and summarized previous morphological studies and attempted to elucidate phylogenetic relationships by a cladistic analysis using 55 characters. Their analysis divided skates into two major clades, the Rajinae and

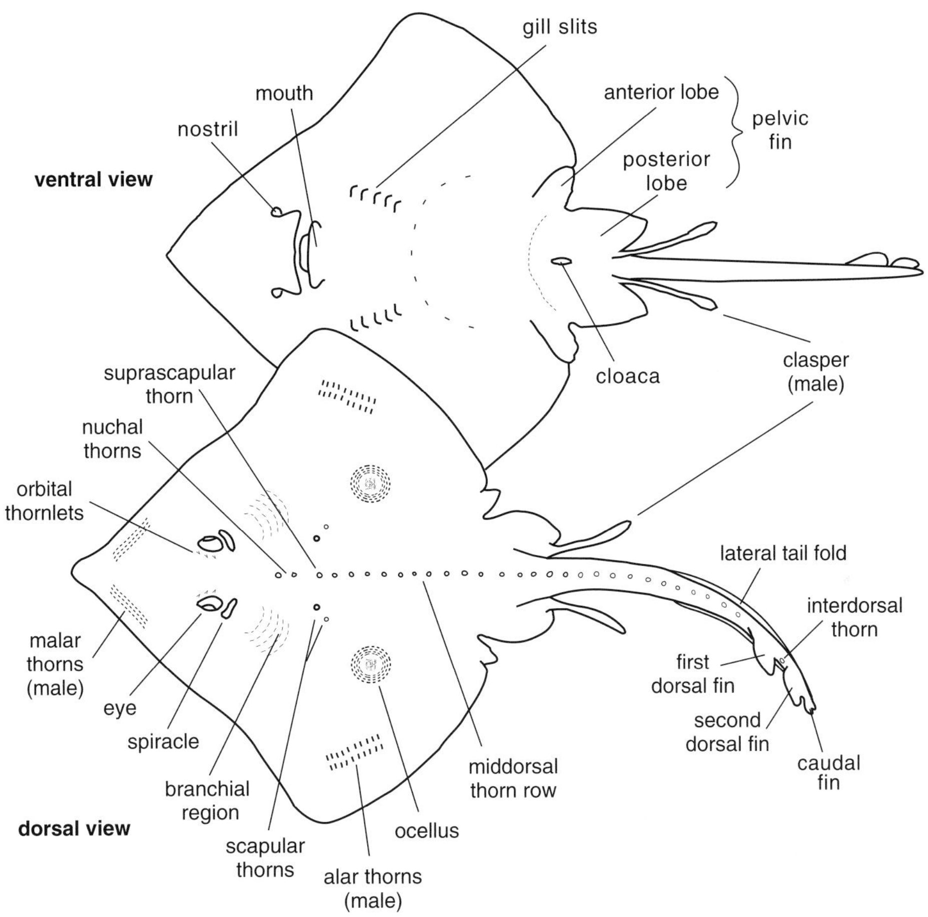

Some external features of skates

the Arhynchobatinae, defined by characters of the scapulocoracoids, basihyal cartilage, and clasper. The authors classified *Raja* and *Bathyraja,* the two genera of skates occurring in Alaskan waters, in Rajinae and Arhynchobatinae, respectively.

Because of the morphological conservatism of skates the limits of many genera and species, as well as the higher taxa, are not well defined, and the inventory and composition of Alaskan species given in this guide are less definite than for most other groups of fishes. Many of the old museum specimens, from Alaska and elsewhere, are in poor condition and no longer identifiable, many others are clearly misidentified, and yet others, not identified to family or genus, could represent unnamed species or species that have not been known previously to occur in Alaska. The early faunal accounts offer little help in determination of ranges of skates in Alaska. In "The Fishes of Alaska," Evermann and Goldsborough (1907) treated three eastern Pacific forms of *Raja* as synonymous which presently are considered to be valid species. Reviewing catch records from NMFS resource surveys in the eastern North Pacific from 1953 to 1983, Allen and Smith (1988) cautioned that most of the skate records represented misidentifications; J. W. Orr (pers. comm., 28 Jan. 1999) commented that the 1997 NMFS bottom trawl survey of the Aleutian Islands was the first Alaska survey for which he felt relatively confident about skate identifications.

Changes in nomenclature, as well as discoveries in Alaska of several species, have considerably changed the inventory of Alaskan fish species from that prepared by Quast and Hall (1972). In this guide many of the species formerly included in *Raja* are classified in *Bathyraja,* at least provisionally, following Ishiyama and Hubbs (1968) and Robins et al. (1991a). However, species currently classified in *Bathyraja* could belong in *Rhinoraja.* One of the main character states given by Ishiyama (1952) in the diagnosis of *Rhinoraja,* segmentation of the rostral cartilage (see below), has been found in some species of *Bathyraja,* as well as in other skate genera (e.g., McEachran and Compagno 1982, McEachran and Dunn 1998), and Ishihara and Ishiyama (1986), among others, have suggested that further study could show that *Rhinoraja* cannot be maintained as a separate genus. Russia's foremost skate expert, Dr. V. N. Dolganov, considers the genera to be synonymous but that the senior synonym is *Rhinoraja* (B. A. Sheiko, pers. comm., 7 Aug. 2000). *Rhinoraja* has priority by date of publication, but other factors could be involved. For this presentation we follow Ishihara and Ishiyama (1985, 1986), Stehmann (1986), J. D. McEachran (pers. comms., 1997, 1998), and others who retain the northeastern Pacific soft-nosed skates in *Bathyraja.*

Other recent changes affecting the inventory and names of Alaskan skates are the following. Ishiyama and Ishihara (1977) described three new species from specimens collected in the Bering Sea and western Pacific: Commander skate, *B. lindbergi*; whiteblotched skate, *B. maculata*; and whitebrow skate, *B. minispinosa.* Dolganov (1983b, 1985) described the mud skate, *B. taranetzi* (although he classified it in *Rhinoraja*), from specimens collected near the Kuril Islands, Russia, and *Bathyraja hubbsi,* described by Ishihara and Ishiyama (1985) from eastern Bering Sea (Alaska) to western Pacific specimens, was later recognized by Ishihara (1990) to be the same as *B. taranetzi.* Specimens from the Aleutian Islands described and named *Rhinoraja longi* by Raschi and McEachran (1991) are also indistinguishable from *B. taranetzi.*

As well, some skate species included on Quast and Hall's (1972) list have been synonymized with others on their list. Two have been referred to Alaska skate, *B. parmifera.* Dolganov (1983a, 1983b) referred the Asian skate *B. smirnovi* to *B. parmifera,* and Stehmann (1986) placed *Raja rosispinis,* described by Gill and Townsend (1897) from eastern Bering Sea specimens, in the same taxon. Ishihara and Ishiyama (1985) and Stehmann (1986) classified *B. kincaidii,* known from the Bering Sea to California, in *B. interrupta,* the sandpaper skate, previously known only from the Bering Sea.

The deepsea skate, *B. abyssicola,* was recorded from Alaska for the first time by Zorzi and Anderson (1990), off the Aleutian Islands. Another specimen (AB 95-19) was collected in 1995 in southeastern Alaska by NMFS Auke Bay Laboratory biologists. Quast and Hall (1972) had considered the deepsea skate to be a likely Alaskan species.

The poorly understood taxonomic relationships of some of the skates inhabiting Alaskan and adjacent waters affects conclusions regarding their geographic ranges. Dolganov (1983a, 1983b, 1999) believes *B. lindbergi* to be conspecific with *B. matsubarai,* a view followed in practice by Russian ichthyologists and fishery biologists (e.g., Orlov 1998a,b). However, North American workers, including J. D. McEachran (pers. comm., 4 Sep. 1997) and fishery biologists of the NMFS Alaska Fisheries Science Center (J.W. Orr, pers. comm., 28 Jan. 1999) classify *B. lindbergi* as a valid species.

The starry skate, *Raja stellulata* Jordan & Gilbert, 1880, was included in previous inventories of Alaskan fish species (e.g., Quast and Hall 1972) but it may not occur north of California. This species was recorded from Bristol Bay, the Aleutian Islands, and Kodiak Island by Gilbert (1896) and Jordan and Gilbert (1899), and in the next century from various localities in Alaska by other authors (e.g., Simenstad et al. 1971, Quast and Hall 1972, Allen and Smith 1988). However, Dolganov (1983a) referred Gilbert's (1896) Bering Sea specimens to *Bathyraja,* from Gilbert's description, and opined that *R. stellulata* is known with certainty only from California. Working with museum collections, one of us (C.W.M.) noticed that most specimens originally identified as *R. stellulata* had been referred to other species by various researchers, although the corrected identifications were not reported in the literature. Allen and Smith (1988) gave a map showing a broad range for *R. stellulata* in Alaska based on NMFS surveys during the period 1953–1983, but remarked that most Bering Sea specimens identified as this species were probably *Bathyraja parmifera.* All the Alaskan records of *R. stellulata* likely represent other species. No *R. stellulata* were taken in the NMFS 1997 bottom trawl survey of the Aleutian Islands, although both *R. rhina* and *R. binoculata* were caught (data provided by J. W. Orr, 28 Jan. 1999). Recently, J. D. McEachran (pers. comm., 8 Sep. 2000) reported that he has data sheets on eastern Pacific skates compiled by R. Ishiyama from research at U.S. museums, and the northernmost record in that set for *R. stellulata* is Eureka, California.

Some Alaskan records of *R. stellulata* may represent an unnamed species, but recognition of such specimens is confounded by weaknesses in the descriptions of *R. stellulata.* The early descriptions (Jordan and Gilbert 1880b, 1899; Gilbert 1896) do not mention all the features currently used to differentiate skate species, and, as well, may be based on specimens of more than one species. As a consequence, modern descriptions of *R. stellulata* vary. For example, the underside is described as being either smooth (Miller and Lea 1972, Hart 1973) or rough (Eschmeyer and Herald 1983), and this is an important diagnostic feature in skates. Although Hart (1973:61–62) gave an account under the name *R. stellulata,* C. L. Hubbs advised him that the description may represent a different and undescribed species; presumably, this applies to Hart's illustration of a specimen (UBC 65-728) from Bristol Bay, Alaska.

Quast and Hall (1972) listed California skate, *R. inornata* Jordan & Gilbert, 1881, as a species likely to be found in Alaska, but it has not been found north of the Strait of Juan de Fuca (Eschmeyer and Herald 1983) off Washington state. Gillespie (1993) and Peden (1998) did not list it for British Columbia. A specimen from Prince William Sound (UAM 761) identified as *R. inornata* is not that species, and does not fit descriptions of other *Raja* species (C.W.M., unpubl. data).

The broad skate, *Raja badia* Garman, 1899, has been found as far north in the eastern Pacific as southern British Columbia at 48°37'N, 126°57'W (Jean et al. 1981, Zorzi and Anderson 1988) and is considered extralimital for purposes of this guide. However, the relationship of this skate to the Arctic skate, *R. hyperborea* Collett, 1879, needs further study. Dolganov (1983a) opined that *R. badia* could be a junior synonym of *R. hyperborea.* Ishihara and Ishiyama (1986) noted that specimens from Japan fit the description of *R. hyperborea* given by Stehmann and Bürkel (in Whitehead et al. 1984), but Stehmann (pers. comm. in Zorzi and Anderson 1988) considered the taxonomic status of those specimens to be unresolved. Dolganov (1983a) recorded a specimen of *R. hyperborea* from the East Siberian Sea, indicating it could be a circumpolar species (previously recorded from the eastern Canadian Arctic to the Barents Sea). However, Dolganov's (1999) listing of *R. hyperborea* for the eastern Bering Sea is due, at least partly, to his practice (noted in Dolganov 1983a) of including *Raja rosispinis* Gill & Townsend, 1897, in *R. hyperborea.* Dolganov did not examine the type of *R. rosispinis* but both Stehmann (1986) and McEachran (pers. comm., 4 Sep. 1997) did, and they concluded it was synonymous with *Bathyraja parmifera.*

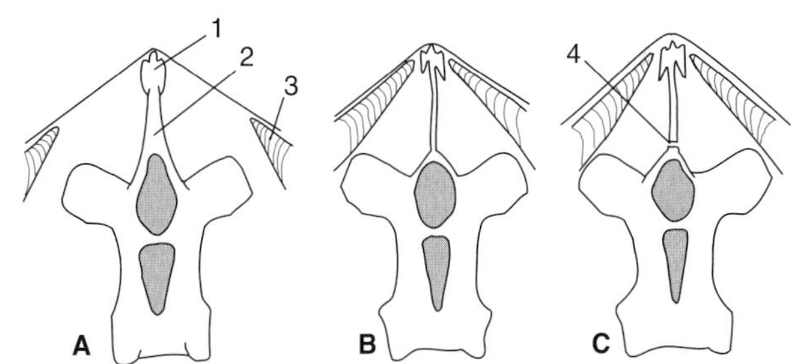

Structure of snout in skates

A, *Raja*; B and C, *Bathyraja*. 1, rostral appendix; 2, rostral cartilage; 3, pectoral radials (fin rays); 4, articulation between rostral cartilage and cranium.

It is possible to differentiate species of *Raja* from those of *Bathyraja* by the flexibility of their snouts. *Raja* species are sometimes called hard-nosed, because of their robust, stiff snouts, while *Bathyraja* species are soft-nosed, with flabby, pliable snouts. The differences in snout stiffness reflect the underlying structure (see diagram above). In *Raja* the rostral cartilage is stout but in *Bathyraja* it is slender and, in some species or populations, is separated at the base from the cranium. In *Raja* the anterior pectoral radials are far from the rostral appendix, whereas in *Bathyraja* they are close; this can be felt by manipulating the snout, or seen by holding the specimen up to a strong light.

The most useful features for differentiating the species in each genus are coloration; shape of the disk, particularly the anterior margin; distribution of thorns, thornlets (small thorns), and denticles; distribution of the sensory pores on the ventral surface; and notching, or indentation, of the pelvic fin (deep or shallow). In male skates the anterior margin of the disk is usually more concave than in females. Some morphometrics are useful. Tail length is measured from the center of the cloaca. Head length is measured from the snout tip to the junction of the cranium and vertebral column, the latter point discernible by pressing with a fingernail. Methodology for measurements follows Bigelow and Schroeder (1953) in measuring along the longitudinal and transverse body axes rather than from point to point as described by Hubbs and Ishiyama (1968); e.g., preorbital snout length is measured to an imaginary line connecting the anterior margins of the eyeballs, not to one eye or the other.

Maturing males of *Raja* and *Bathyraja* develop clawlike alar thorns near the wing tips that aid in holding the female during copulation. Males of some species of *Raja* have, as well, malar thorns on each side of the head. Although these specialized thorns are variable among species and may be phylogenetically informative (McEachran and Konstantinou 1996), the differences have not been defined for all species and are not used for identifying species.

Clasper characters are important in taxonomy but are not given in this guide because they are not needed to identify the Alaskan species, and they would only help to identify a small percentage of specimens (adult males). Definitions and discussion of skate clasper terminology are given in Ishiyama and Hubbs (1968) and Ishihara and Ishiyama (1985, 1986).

Skate egg cases are often brought to the surface in nets dragged over the bottom, or washed onto beaches. It would be useful to have a key to the egg cases but published descriptions of the cases of most species are not adequate for this purpose and the cases of some species have not been described. The egg cases of *Raja* are mostly smooth and have a short, tubelike horn at each of the four corners with a respiratory pore at the tip. Egg cases of *Bathyraja* are mostly rough and have a long horn at each of the corners with a respiratory pore near the middle of the horn; the apron at the anterior end is indented, while the margin of the apron at the posterior end is straight. The egg cases range in size, among the Alaskan species, from less than 50 mm (2 inches) long for sandpaper skate, *B. interrupta,* to more than 250 mm up to about 300 mm (12 inches) for big skate, *R. binoculata.* Egg cases are measured along the least length of the case. Cox (1963) and Ishiyama (1967) described egg cases of several North Pacific skate species. Studies of development in the laboratory (Berestovskii 1994) indicate that in northern seas embryonic development can take up to 5–6 years.

At maturity skates reach maximum sizes of at least 244 cm TL (8 ft), attained by *R. binoculata.* Most are smaller, ranging down to *B. taranetzi,* which may be the smallest Alaskan species with a recorded maximum length of 70 cm (27.5 inches).

The following key to adults of skate species in Alaska employs features described by Ishiyama (1967), Ishiyama and Ishihara (1977), Ishihara and Ishiyama (1985), Dolganov (1983b, 1985), Ishihara (1987), and Raschi and McEachran (1991), and contains refinements from a draft key provided by J. D. McEachran (pers. comm., 25 Aug. 1997).

Key to the Rajidae of Alaska

1 Snout stiff; pectoral fin radials (fin rays) not nearly reaching tip of snout; malar and alar thorns present on mature males .... Genus *Raja* (2)

1 Snout flexible; pectoral fin radials (fin rays) nearly reaching tip of snout; alar thorns present on mature males, malar thorns absent .... Genus *Bathyraja* (3)

2 (1) Ventral side light; pelvic fin shallowly notched .... *Raja binoculata,* page 96

2 Ventral side dark, especially anteriorly; pelvic fin deeply notched .... *Raja rhina,* page 97

3 (1) Scapular thorns present and strongly developed . . . . . (4)

3 Scapular thorns absent or only weakly developed . . . . . (6)

4 (3) Medial margins of orbits covered with thornlets; disk width 65% TL or greater . . . . . *Bathyraja parmifera,* page 98

4 Medial margins of orbits without thornlets; disk width less than 65% TL . . . . . (5)

5 (4) Snout long, preorbital snout length more than 70% HL; interdorsal space wide, more than half of length of first dorsal fin base; anterior area of ventral surface of disk with denticles . . . . . *Bathyraja aleutica,* page 99

5 Snout short, preorbital snout length less than 70% HL; interdorsal space narrow, less than half of length of first dorsal fin base; ventral surface of disk smooth, except for anteriormost area at tip of snout . . . . . *Bathyraja interrupta,* page 100

6 (3) Middorsal tail thorns strongly developed and about same size along length of tail . . . . . (7)

6 Middorsal tail thorns weakly developed and progressively decreasing in size posteriorly . . . . . (11)

7 (6) Middorsal thorns continuous from scapular region to origin of first dorsal fin . . . . . *Bathyraja lindbergi,* page 101

7 Middorsal thorns interrupted on disk, or no disk thorns present . . . . . (8)

8 (7) Ventral surface of disk and tail covered with denticles . . . . . *Bathyraja abyssicola,* page 102

8 Ventral surface of disk and tail almost entirely smooth . . . . . (9)

9 (8) Middorsal nuchal thorns always present, strongly developed, and more than 1; dorsal surface of disk with many white to yellow blotches . . . . . *Bathyraja maculata,* page 103

9 Middorsal nuchal thorns usually absent, if present weak and fewer than 3; dorsal surface of disk not scattered with many light blotches . . . . . (10)

10 (9) Interorbital region white, often distinctly bordering inner margins of eyes; interorbital space less than 20% HL . . . . . *Bathyraja minispinosa,* page 104

10 Interorbital region dark, same as ground color; interorbital space more than 20% HL . . . . . *Bathyraja trachura,* page 105

11 (6) Tail length (measured from center of cloaca) always more than pretail length; ventral surface of disk mostly white, tail mostly dark; dorsal surface of disk cinnamon, golden brown, or grayish brown with numerous small light and dark spots . . . . . *Bathyraja taranetzi,* page 106

11 Tail length usually less than pretail length; ventral surface of disk mostly white, tail also white except sometimes with narrow dark band along midline; dorsal surface of disk usually with dark (violet in fresh specimens) vermiculations or blotches, sometimes monotone, no white spots . . . . . *Bathyraja violacea,* page 107

Raja binoculata Girard, 1854 **big skate**

Eastern Bering Sea and Aleutian Islands, at least as far west as Unalaska Island, to Baja California in vicinity of Cedros Island; rare south of Point Conception, California.

On bottom at depths of 3–800 m; usually less than 200 m, on continental shelf.

- Dorsal surface dark gray, brown, or reddish brown, usually with large, dark-centered ocellus at base of each pectoral fin and white spots and scattered dark blotches; **ventral surface white to muddy white**, sometimes with dark blotches.
- **Snout stiff**, long, bluntly pointed, broadly triangular; margin of disk concave anterolaterally.
- **Pelvic fin shallowly notched**.
- One middorsal thorn in nuchal area, **continuous middorsal row starting near pelvic region**; scapular thorns absent; orbital thornlets present, but buried in skin in some large individuals.
- Length to 244 cm TL, rarely over 183 cm.
- Egg case with 2 curved ridges on upper surface, 2 keels on each side, and short horns; length over 25 cm (larger than any other skate's).

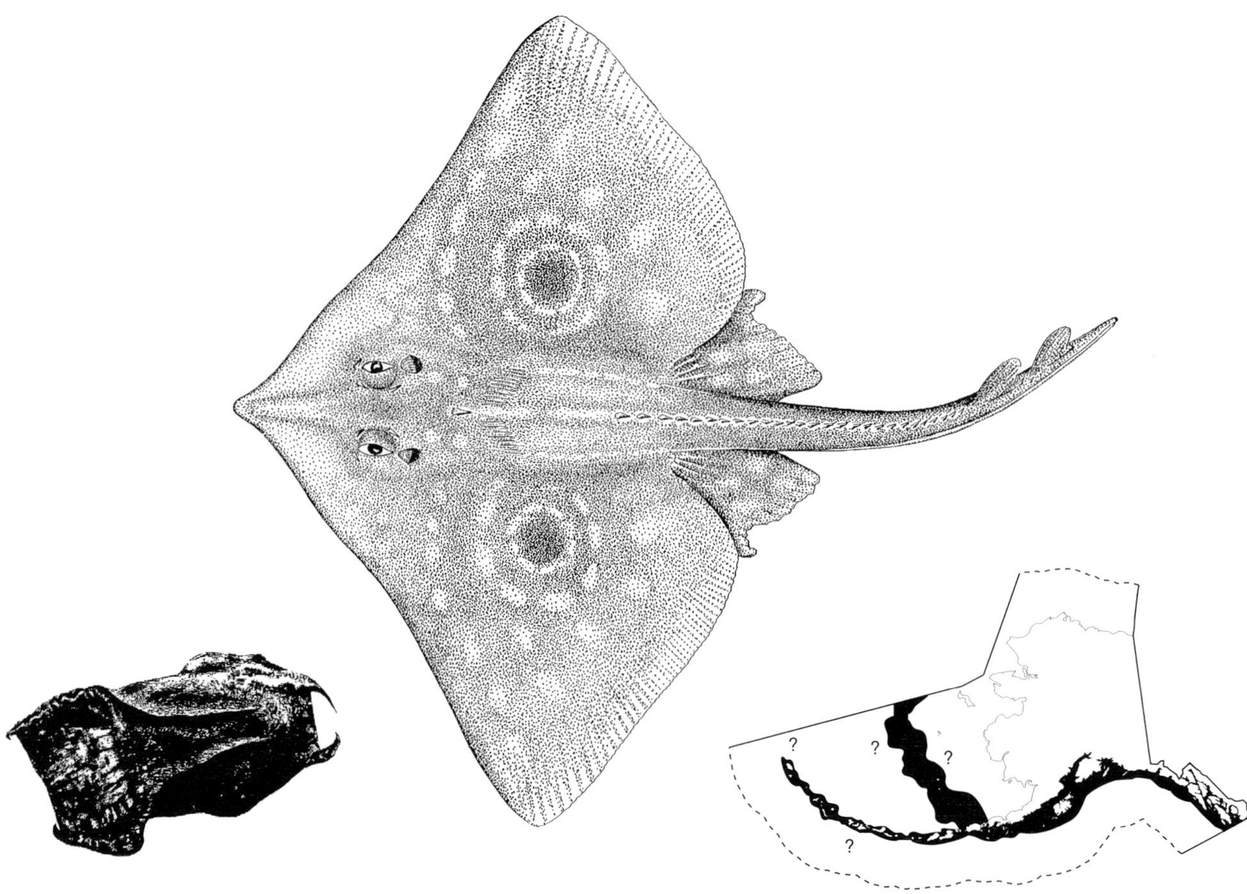

Notes & Sources — *Raja binoculata* Girard, 1854
Raia cooperi Girard, 1858

Description: Girard 1854:196; Miller and Lea 1972:48; Hart 1973:56–57; Eschmeyer and Herald 1983:51–52.

Figures: Dorsal view: Hart 1973:56; UBC 62-987, 44 cm TL, Resurrection Bay, Alaska. Egg case: Eschmeyer and Herald 1983:14.

Range: Bean (1881b, 1882) recorded *R. binoculata* from Sitka, Port Althorp, and Wrangell in southeastern Alaska; and from St. Paul (now city of Kodiak) in the western Gulf of Alaska. The account of Alaskan records by Evermann and Goldsborough (1907) is incorrect in today's terms, since they classified the Alaskan species of *Raja* as one species. Alaskan specimens at UBC are from Kasitsna Bay, Resurrection Bay, Frederick Sound, and Petersburg. Those in the ABL, NMNH, and UW collections are from the eastern Gulf of Alaska from Controller Bay near Katalla to Dixon Entrance. Northern and western limits of range in Bering Sea and Aleutian Islands are not known. Allen and Smith (1988) reported that specimens identified as *R. binoculata* taken in NMFS surveys during 1953–1983 west along the Aleutian chain to Stalemate Bank and along the Bering Sea outer shelf could have been misidentified *Bathyraja aleutica*. Simenstad et al. (1977) reported *R. binoculata* at Amchitka Island, but voucher specimens were not found. The 1997 NMFS survey of the Aleutian Islands netted six specimens among four tows, all of them around the eastern end of Unalaska Island at depths from 22 to 190 m (J. W. Orr, pers. comm., 28 Jan. 1999). Not listed for western Bering Sea and western Aleutian chain by Dolganov (1983a, 1999), Sheiko and Fedorov (2000), and Fedorov and Sheiko (2002).

Raja rhina Jordan & Gilbert, 1880 **longnose skate**

Southeastern Bering Sea to Pacific Ocean near Cedros Island, Baja California, and Gulf of California. On bottom at depths of 20 m to at least 622 m, usually at 55–350 m.

- Dorsal surface dark brown, with faint dark and light blotches; sometimes with pale-centered ocellus at base of each pectoral fin; **ventral surface bluish gray or mottled brown to black**.
- **Snout stiff, long, acutely pointed, tapering; anterior margin of disk strongly concave**.
- Pelvic fin deeply notched.
- **Middorsal row of thorns on tail only**, except for 1 or 2 nuchal thorns; scapular thorns absent; thorns dorsolaterally on tail in large specimens; orbital thornlets present.
- Length to about 137 cm TL.
- Egg case rough, with loose covering of fibers, and short horns; length to 13 cm.

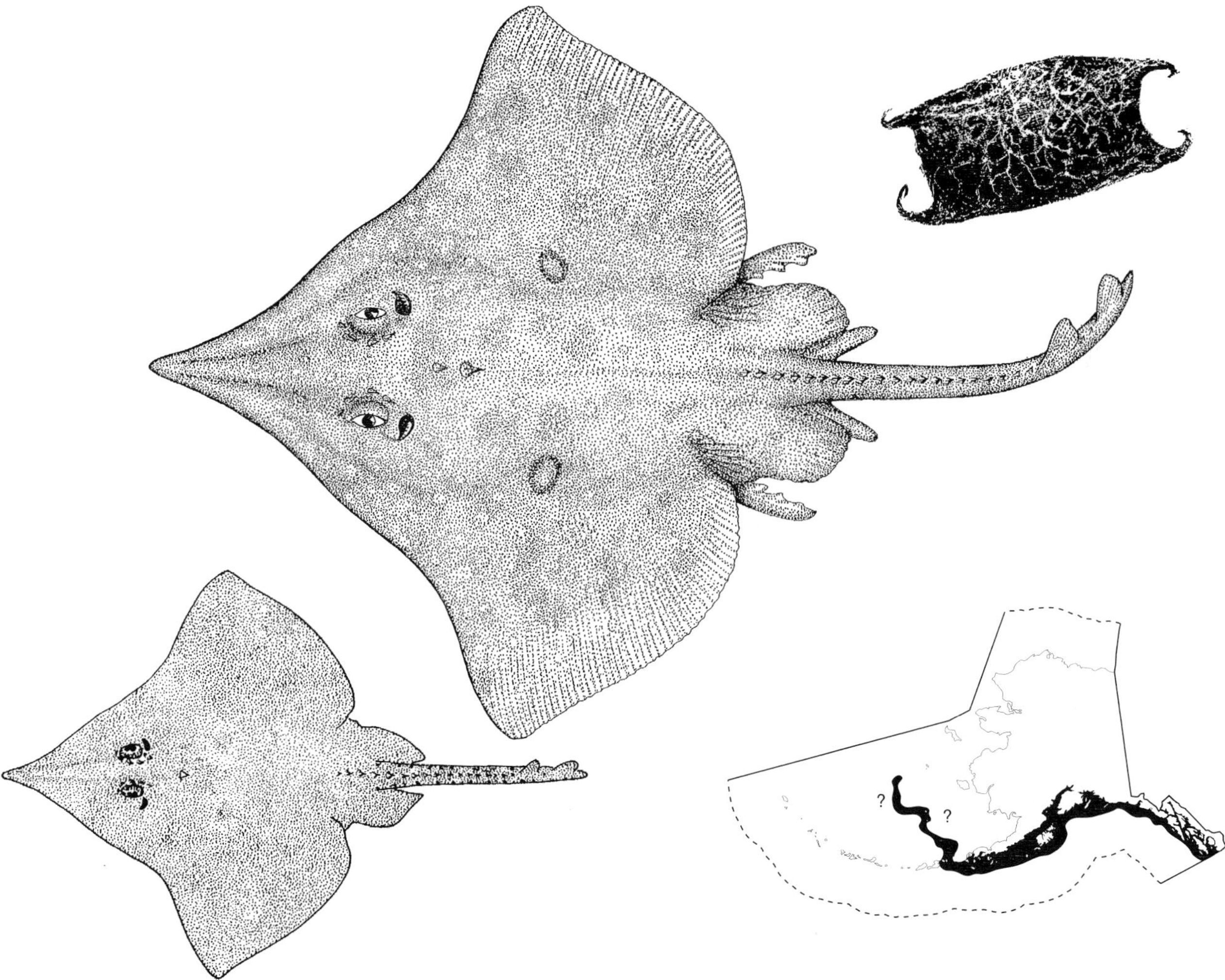

Notes & Sources — *Raja rhina* Jordan & Gilbert, 1880
Originally spelled *Raia*.

Description: Jordan and Gilbert 1880g:251–253; Miller and Lea 1972:47; Hart 1973:59–60; Eschmeyer and Herald 1983:52–53.

Figures: Larger dorsal view: Hart 1973:59; 22 cm TL, young male. Smaller dorsal view: Miller and Lea 1972:45. Miller and Lea's dorsal view shows dorsolateral tail thorns. A 101-cm adult male (photograph on file at Point Stephens Research) caught near Tee Harbor, Lynn Canal, in the summer of 1997 had strong dorsolateral tail thorns. Egg case: Eschmeyer and Herald 1983:14.

Range: Northern limit given as southeastern Alaska by Wilimovsky (1954, 1958), Quast and Hall (1972), and Eschmeyer and Herald (1983). Although NMFS survey data from 1953–1983 apparently extended known range into Bering Sea, *Bathyraja aleutica* could have been misidentified as *R. rhina* (Allen and Smith 1988). During the 1997 NMFS survey of the Aleutian Islands, two specimens identified as *R. rhina* were collected north of Akutan Island at 54°14'N, 165°54'W, depth 58 m, but not saved (J. W. Orr, pers. comm., 28 Jan. 1999). The westernmost records with vouchers may be Shelikof Strait (USNM 116319), Raspberry Strait off Afognak Island (USNM 103732), and Kiliuda Bay, Kodiak Island (CU 55942). Eschmeyer and Herald (1983) gave depth range of 55–622 m. Dolganov (1999) gave 20–340 m. Allen and Smith (1988) gave maximum of 650 m, with reservations.

Bathyraja parmifera (Bean, 1881) **Alaska skate**

Eastern Bering Sea and Aleutian Islands to eastern Gulf of Alaska; western Bering Sea and Commander Islands to Sea of Okhotsk, northern Sea of Japan, and Pacific off Hokkaido.

On bottom at depths of 20–1,425 m; usually at 90–250 m off Aleutian Islands, deeper in western Pacific.

- Dark grayish brown to olive brown dorsally with black spots, sometimes with variable, paired light spots; white ventrally, with dark blotches on tail.
- **Snout flexible**, blunt; **disk width 65% of total length or greater**.
- **Scapular thorns strong**, usually 2 on each side; middorsal row continuous from nuchal area to first dorsal fin or interrupted on back; usually 1 interdorsal thorn; anterior, medial, and posterior **orbital thornlets present**; coarse denticles on dorsal surface, ventral surface largely smooth.
- Length to 107 cm TL.
- Egg case striated; anterior horns short, posterior horns long, flat, tapered; length to 15 cm.

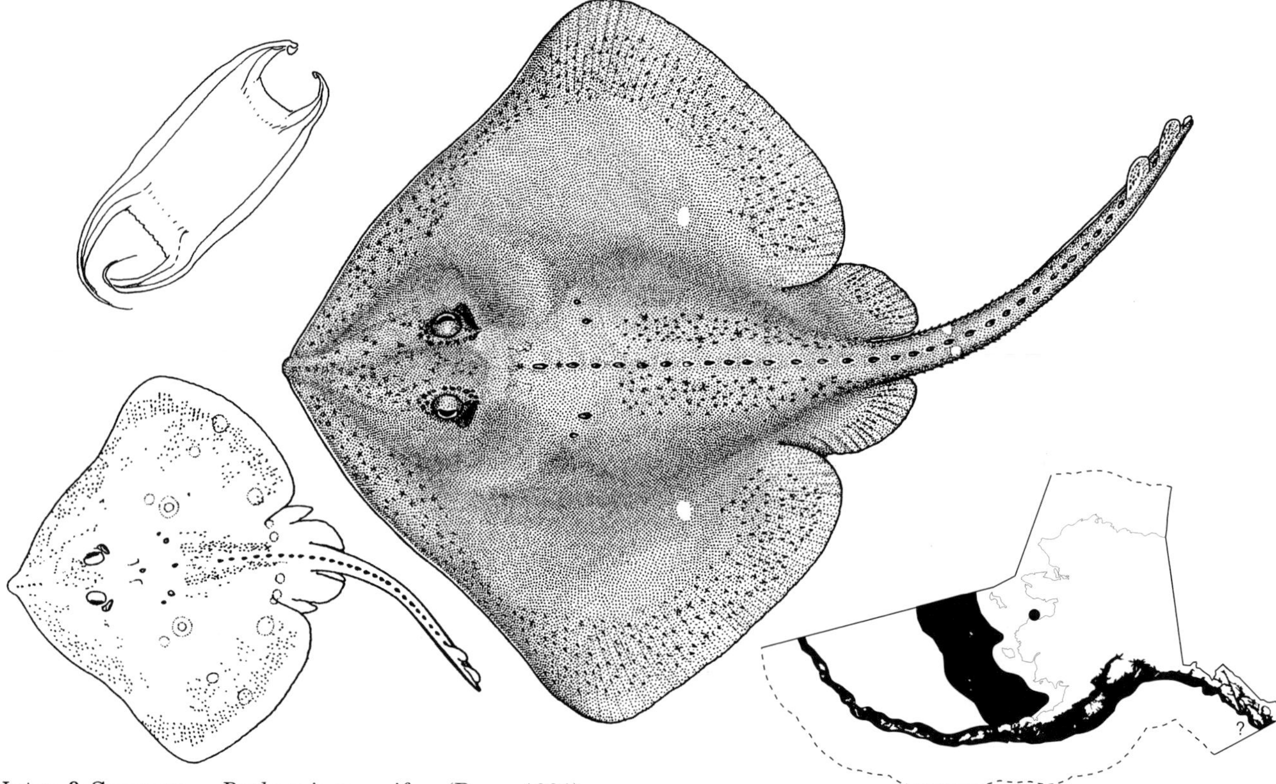

Notes & Sources — *Bathyraja parmifera* (Bean, 1881)

Raia parmifera Bean, 1881. Described from specimens taken off Unalaska Island, Alaska.

Raia rosispinis Gill & Townsend, 1897. Described from specimens taken in Bering Sea. Referred to *B. parmifera* by Stehmann (1986:263); J. D. McEachran (pers. comm., 4 Sep. 1997) recently examined the type, and concurs.

Raia obtusa Gill & Townsend, 1897. Described from Bering Sea specimens. Referred to *Raja rosispinis* by Jordan and Gilbert (1899) and to *B. parmifera* by Stehmann (1986:263).

Raja smirnovi Soldatov & Pavlenko, 1915. Reported from western Bering Sea to Sea of Japan, *R. smirnovi* was referred by Dolganov (1983a) to *B. parmifera*. Called *Breviraja smirnovi* by Ishiyama (1967).

Breviraja (Arctoraja) simoterus Ishiyama, 1967. Valid as *Bathyraja simoterus* according to Nakaya (in Masuda et al. 1984) and Stehmann (1986). Referred to *B. parmifera* by J. D. McEachran (pers. comm., 4 Sep. 1997).

Description: Bean 1881a:157–159; Gilbert 1896:395–396; Ishiyama 1967:62–68; Eschmeyer and Herald 1983:50; Nakaya in Amaoka et al. 1983:313.

Figures: Dorsal views: Point Stephens Research, artist Doris Alcorn, May 1999, eastern Bering Sea. Upper: UW 22338, young female, 656 mm TL. Lower: UW 22337, juvenile male, 541 mm TL. Egg case: Ishiyama 1967, fig. 19.

Range: Often taken in Bering Sea and western Gulf of Alaska but confused with other species. Allen and Smith (1988) declined to draw any conclusions regarding distribution from 1953–1983 NMFS surveys because of confusion with *Raja stellulata*. In 1997 NMFS demersal survey of Aleutian Islands, taken along entire chain west to Stalemate Bank, where survey ended; present in 85 net hauls, mostly less than 5 per haul but as many as 13; depth range 67–420 m, most at 90–250 m (data provided by J. W. Orr, 28 Jan. 1999). Northern and southern limits in Alaska are not well known. Turner collected a specimen at St. Michael, Norton Sound (listed by Bean 1881b). One from Frederick Sound identified by C. L. Hubbs and L. P. Schultz is in the University of Michigan collection (UMMZ 129014). Not listed for British Columbia by Peden (1998). Common in western Bering Sea (e.g., Sheiko and Fedorov 2000). Overall depth range is from Fedorov and Sheiko (2002). Taken at 300–1,100 m in Okhotsk Sea (Dudnik and Dolganov 1992).

Size: Orlov 1998b: 107 cm for adults from western Pacific.

Bathyraja aleutica (Gilbert, 1896) **Aleutian skate**

Bering Sea and Aleutian Islands to eastern Gulf of Alaska; southeastern limit in Alaska not known, range possibly extends to British Columbia; western Bering Sea to Sea of Okhotsk, northern Sea of Japan, and Pacific Ocean off Hokkaido.

On bottom at depths of 15–1,602 m; usually on outer shelf and upper slope at 100–800 m.

- Dorsal surface grayish brown to dusky olive with vaguely defined light areas; ventral surface white with grayish margins.
- Snout flexible, long, **preorbital snout length more than 70% of head length**; disk width less than 65% of total length.
- Interdorsal space wide, more than half the length first dorsal fin base.
- **Scapular thorns strong**, 1 or 2 on each side; mid-dorsal row continuous from nuchal area to first dorsal fin or interrupted over trunk; usually 2 interdorsal thorns; **orbital thornlets absent**; fine denticles covering dorsal surface, ventral surface of disk smooth except in head region.
- Length to 150 cm TL.
- Egg case rough, with long prickles, long horn at each corner; length to 14 cm.

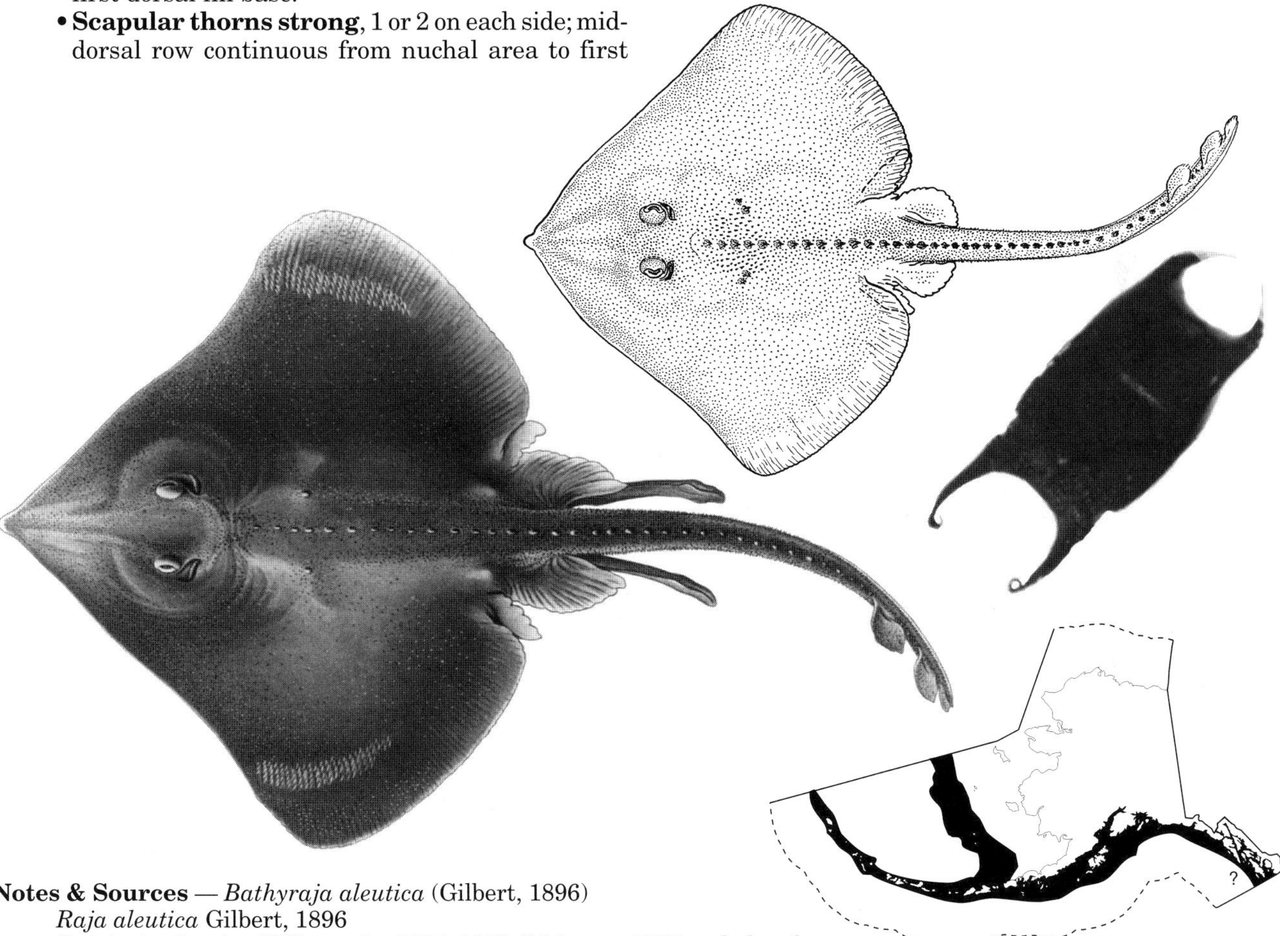

Notes & Sources — *Bathyraja aleutica* (Gilbert, 1896)
Raja aleutica Gilbert, 1896
Breviraja aleutica: Wilimovsky 1954, 1958; Ishiyama 1967 and elsewhere.
Because of the long snout of *B. aleutica,* especially in the males, this species is often confused with *Raja.*

Description: Gilbert 1896:397–398; Ishiyama 1967:58–61.

Figures: Ishiyama 1967, fig. 18A, pl. 25. Upper: young female, width 290 mm. Lower: adult male, 1,265 mm TL, width 870 mm. Egg case: Teshima and Tomonaga (1986, fig. 6).

Range: Allen and Smith (1988) concluded that in records from NMFS surveys during 1953–1983 many *B. aleutica* were misidentified as *B. interrupta, Raja binoculata,* and *R. rhina,* and did not provide a range map for *B. aleutica.* Teshima and Tomonaga (1986) reported distribution along upper slope and outer shelf in southeastern Bering Sea and western Gulf of Alaska at depths of 100–700 m from 1984 and 1985 Fisheries Agency of Japan–NMFS groundfish surveys. Taken along entire extent of Aleutian Islands from Unimak Pass to Stalemate Bank at depths of 87–474 m in 1997 NMFS survey of the islands (present in 39 net hauls; data provided by J. W. Orr, 28 Jan 1999). Wilimovsky (1954, 1958) gave a range of Bering Sea to southeastern Alaska, without citing documentation. The ABL collection has no specimens, and those at UBC are from western Gulf of Alaska and Bering Sea. Peden (1998) reported that the RBCM might have specimens from British Columbia, but that study of those specimens is incomplete. Dolganov (1999) and Sheiko and Fedorov (2000) reported occurrence off Asian coasts along the shelf and upper slope from Japan to Cape Navarin, and from there to the Pribilof Islands. Fedorov and Sheiko (2002) reported it to occur in the vicinity of the Commander Islands, and reported depth extremes given above. Dolganov (1999) reported 130–1,374 m.

Bathyraja interrupta (Gill & Townsend, 1897) **sandpaper skate**

Eastern Bering Sea and Aleutian Islands to Pacific Ocean off southern California at Cortes Bank.

On bottom at depths of 55–1,372 m, usually shallower than 500 m in Alaska.

- Dorsal surface dark brown to blackish, sometimes with white mottling; often with white spot on each side of tail; ventral surface of disk white, underside of tail mostly dark.
- Snout flexible, short, **preorbital snout length less than 75% of head length**; disk width less than 65% of total length.
- Interdorsal space narrow, less than half the length of first dorsal fin base.
- **Scapular thorns strong**, 1 or 2 each side; middorsal row from nape to first dorsal fin, continuous or interrupted; 0 or 1 interdorsal thorn; **orbital thornlets absent**; denticles densely covering dorsal surface, ventral surface smooth except at tip of snout.
- Length to 86 cm TL.
- Egg case rough, with coarse longitudinal fibers, side keels strong, horns long; small, length to 6 cm.

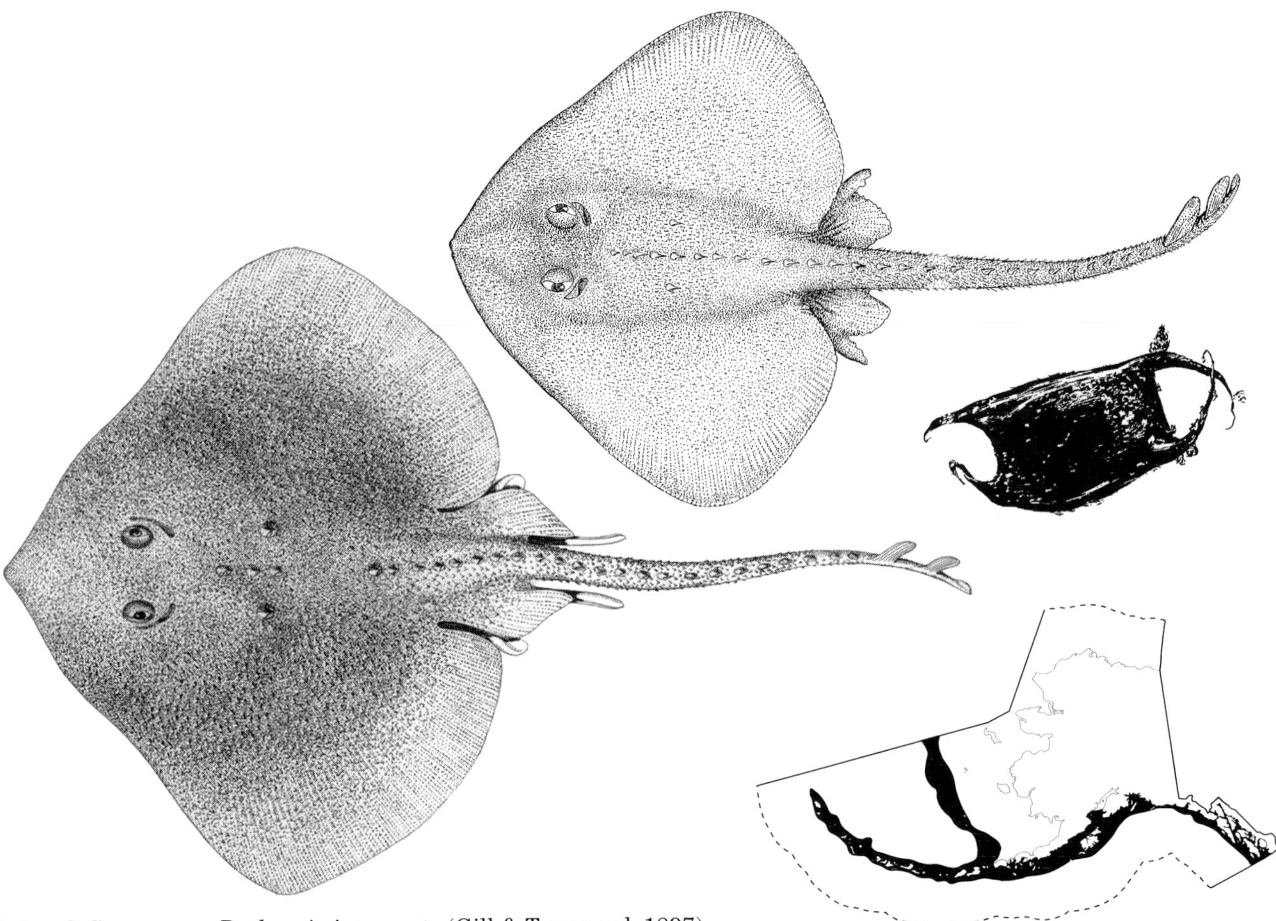

Notes & Sources — *Bathyraja interrupta* (Gill & Townsend, 1897)

Raia interrupta Gill & Townsend, 1897

Raia kincaidii Garman, 1908

Ishihara and Ishiyama (1985) classified *B. kincaidii* as a junior synonym of *B. interrupta.* Some authorities (e.g., Dolganov 1999) consider *Rhinoraja* to be the valid genus for the combined entity. The relationship between the *B. kincaidii* and *B. interrupta* forms and an additional, undescribed species in the northeastern Pacific generally included with *B. kincaidii* is not clear (J. D. McEachran, pers. comm., cited in Allen and Smith 1988:13).

Description: Gill and Townsend 1897:232; Eschmeyer and Herald 1983:50; Ishihara and Ishiyama 1985:152–160.

Figures: Upper: Hart 1973:58; young female, identified as *R. kincaidii,* 41 cm TL. Lower: Smithsonian Institution, NMNH, Division of Fishes, artist A. H. Baldwin; holotype of *R. interrupta,* USNM 48760, young male, 428 mm TL, Bering Sea. (Dorsal fins and interdorsal distance, which appear to be too small, may not be accurately depicted.) Egg case: Eschmeyer and Herald 1983:14.

Range: Type specimens are from the Bering Sea (Gill and Townsend 1897). Ishihara and Ishiyama (1985) summarized range from literature references and recorded additional specimens they examined from the Bering Sea and from the Pacific south of the Aleutian Islands. In 1997 NMFS survey of Aleutian Islands, taken from Unimak Pass to Stalemate Bank at depths of 93–457 m (present in 15 net hauls; data provided by J. W. Orr, 28 Jan. 1999). Thirteen specimens from Gulf of Alaska localities are in ABL collection, from off mouth of Taku River to Shumagin Islands. Depth range is from Miller and Lea (1972).

Bathyraja lindbergi Ishiyama & Ishihara, 1977 **Commander skate**

Eastern Bering Sea, Aleutian Islands, and unconfirmed report for western Gulf of Alaska; western Bering Sea and Commander Islands to Sea of Okhotsk off Hokkaido.

On bottom at depths of 120 m to at least 950 m, possibly to 2,000 m; usually deeper than 200 m.

- Both surfaces dark grayish brown, ventral surface sometimes whitish brown; dorsal surface rarely with white mottling; whitish around mouth and distally on anterior lobe of pelvic fin.
- Snout flexible, short, broad.
- **Scapular thorns absent; middorsal thorns more or less continuous from scapular region to first dorsal fin; thorns well developed along length of tail**; 0 or 1 interdorsal thorn; orbital thornlets absent; denticles on dorsal surface of disk, ventral surface smooth.
- Length to 93 cm TL.

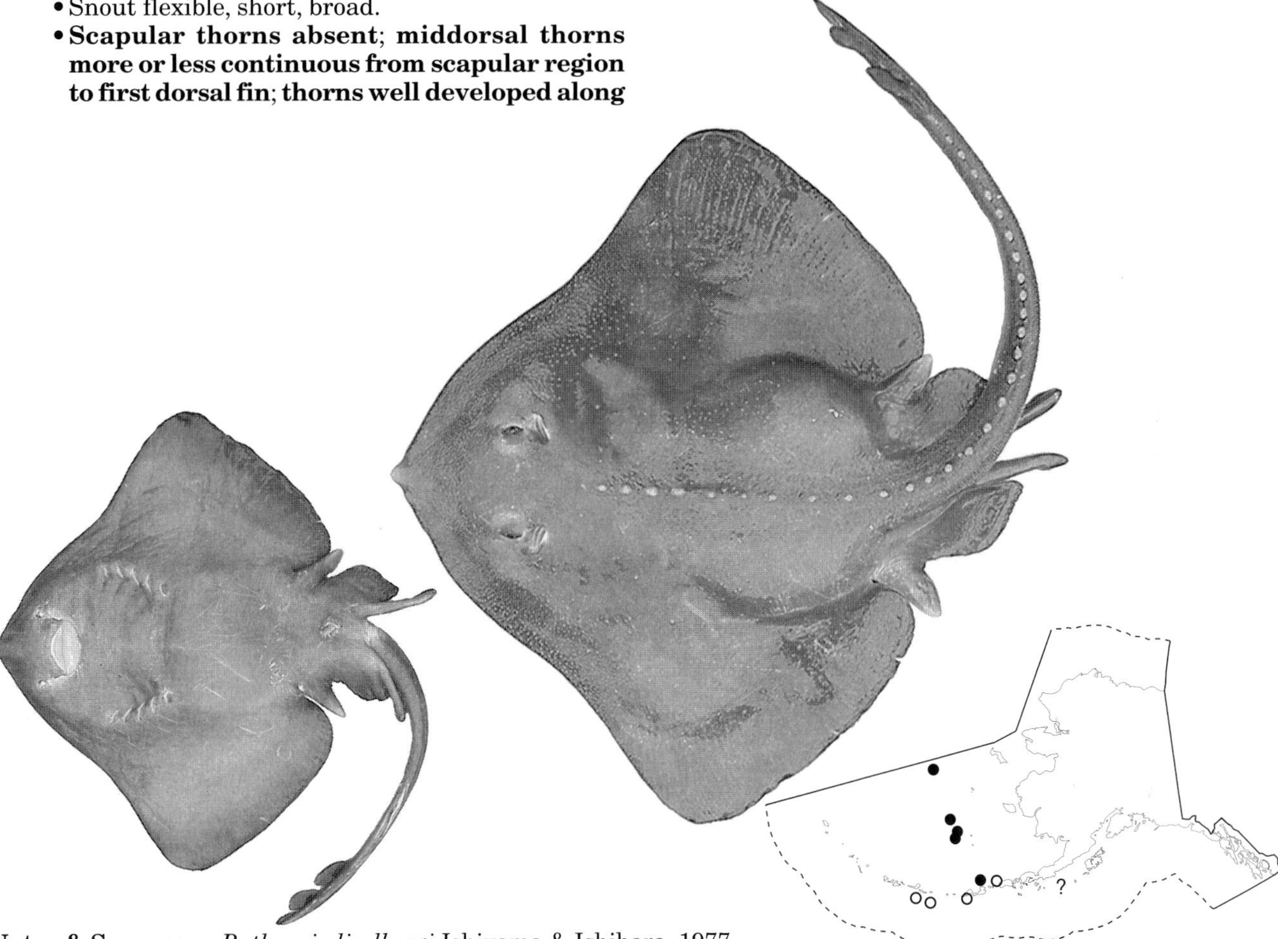

Notes & Sources — *Bathyraja lindbergi* Ishiyama & Ishihara, 1977

It is difficult to separate information on *B. lindbergi* from that published on closely related species. Russian ichthyologists classify *B. lindbergi, B. caeluronigricans,* and *B. notoroensis,* all described by Ishiyama and Ishihara (1977), as synonyms of *B. matsubarai* (Ishiyama, 1952). Ishiyama and Ishihara (1977) and Ishihara and Ishiyama (1985) considered coloration and middorsal thorn configuration to distinguish *B. lindbergi* from the others. *Bathyraja matsubarai,* for example, is dark purplish brown and has discontinuous middorsal thorns.

Description: Ishiyama and Ishihara 1977:82–83; Nakaya in Amaoka et al. 1983:312; Nakaya in Masuda et al. 1984, 1992:14. Egg case has not been described; probably similar to that of *B. maculata* (Ishiyama and Ishihara 1977).

Figures: Dorsal and ventral: NMFS, AFSC, Seattle; male, 93 cm TL, eastern Bering Sea slope.

Range: Dots on map represent localities for Alaskan specimens examined by Ishiyama and Ishihara (1977) and Ishihara and Ishiyama (1985), depth range 160–570 m; UW 26195, eastern Bering Sea at 60°29'N, 179°12'W; and specimen shown above, from 2000 NMFS bottom trawl survey (J. W. Orr, pers. comm., 30 Jan. 2001), 56°30'N, 172°03'W, depth 781 m. Circles represent localities from 1997 NMFS bottom trawl survey of the Aleutian Islands, not backed by voucher specimens; maximum depths for the four catches were 126–455 m (J. W. Orr, pers. comm., 28 Jan. 1999). Dolganov (1999) gave a range for *B. matsubarai,* which he does not consider distinguishable from *B. lindbergi,* to the western Gulf of Alaska but did not provide documentation. He gave an overall depth range of 180–1,773 m. Sheiko and Fedorov (2000) and Fedorov and Sheiko (2002) reported *B. matsubarai* to be common off the Commander Islands and Kamchatka and gave a depth range of 120–2,000 m. Recorded to 900–950 m for *B. lindbergi,* in the strict sense, from the Sea of Okhotsk off Hokkaido by Nakaya (in Amaoka et al. 1983).

Size: At 930 mm TL the specimen shown above is the largest on record. If *B. lindbergi* is a synonym of *B. matsubarai,* maximum is 98 cm TL, recorded by Orlov (1998b). Previously recorded to 87 cm TL by Ishihara and Ishiyama (1985).

Bathyraja abyssicola (Gilbert, 1896) **deepsea skate**

Pacific Ocean off Tanaga Island, Aleutian Islands; southeastern Alaska at Chatham Strait; northern British Columbia to southern California west of Coronado Islands; western Bering Sea to southern Japan off Honshu.

On bottom in deep water at depths of 362–2,904 m.

- Dorsal and ventral surfaces dark tan or gray to dark brown, ventral surface sometimes slightly darker; whitish around mouth, cloaca, gill slits, nostrils, and tips of anterior lobes of pelvic fin and claspers; white blotches sometimes present on abdomen.
- Snout flexible, long, narrow.
- **Scapular thorns absent**; **nuchal thorns 1–5, separated from more or less continuous row of strong thorns on trunk and tail**; 1 interdorsal thorn usually present; orbital thornlets absent; **disk densely covered with denticles on ventral surface, as well as dorsal**.
- Length to 157 cm TL.

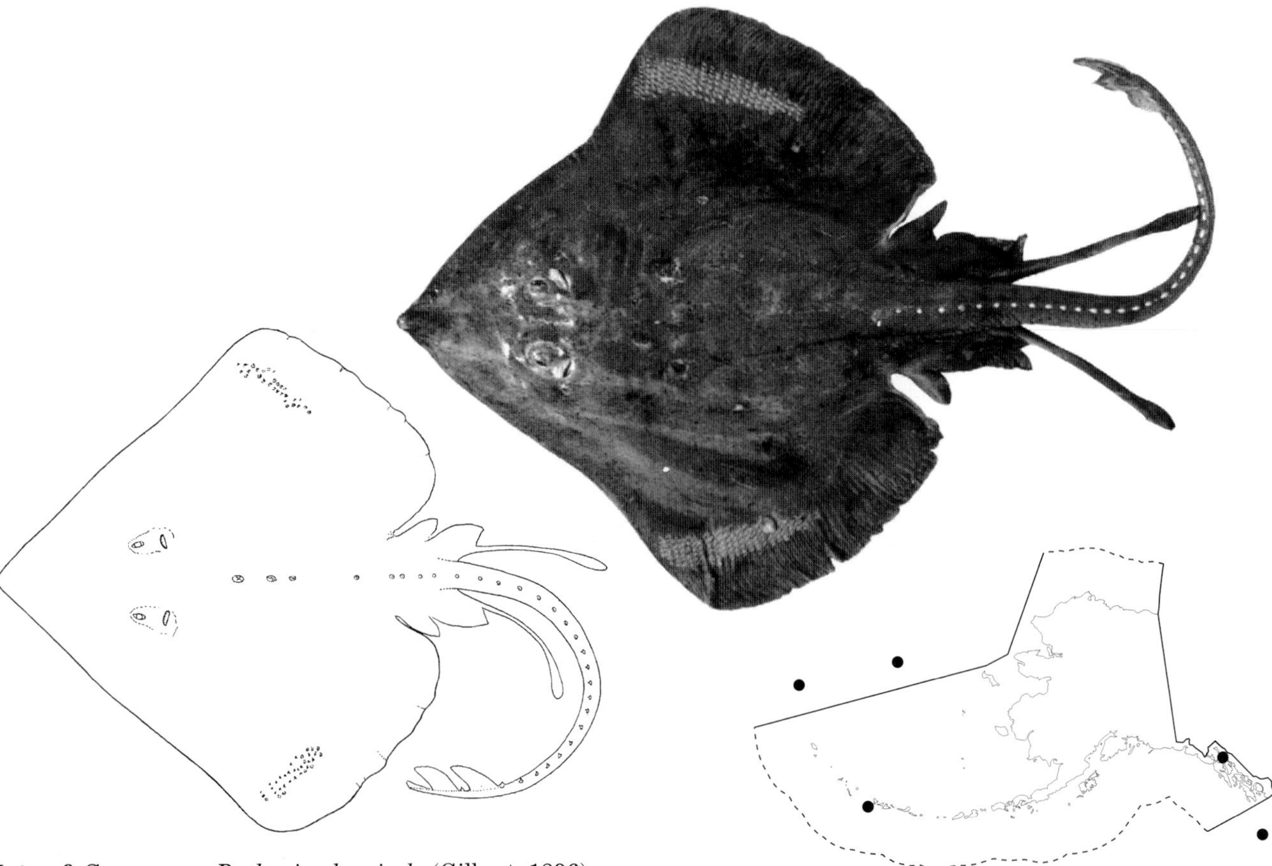

Notes & Sources — *Bathraja abyssicola* (Gilbert, 1896)
Raja abyssicola Gilbert, 1896

Description: Gilbert 1896:396; Ishihara and Ishiyama 1985:145–148; Zorzi and Anderson 1988:93, 95–101. The male specimen from Alaska lacked large white abdominal blotches (Zorzi and Anderson 1990).

Figures: Upper: Amaoka et al. 1983, pl. 9; 1,190 mm TL, Pacific off northern Honshu. Lower: Gilbert 1896, pl. 20; holotype, about 1,350 mm (Zorzi and Anderson 1988), off Queen Charlotte Islands, British Columbia.

Range: Zorzi and Anderson (1990) recorded a specimen taken south of Tanaga Island at 51°31'N, 178°07'W. The second specimen known from Alaska (AB 95-19) was collected in 1995 from northern Chatham Strait west of Point Retreat, depth 440 m, by J. F. Karinen aboard RV *John N. Cobb*. Nearest known locality in British Columbia waters is the type locality, *Albatross* station 3342, off the Queen Charlotte Islands at 52°39'N, 132°38'W, depth 2,904 m (Gilbert 1896). Hart (1973) incorrectly cited Wilimovsky (1954) for range to Bering Sea; there is no such statement in any of Wilimovsky's papers. Dolganov (1983a) examined a specimen from Bering Sea, but did not give catch locality. B. A. Sheiko (pers. comm., 15 Jan. 1999) collected two specimens in 1982 from northwestern Bering Sea at 61°23'N, 176°36'E, between Capes Olyutorskiy and Navarin, at depths of 1,325–1,370 m; also see Size, below. Zorzi and Anderson (1988) summarized available information on the 13 specimens previously reported in the literature, and redescribed the species using 9 new specimens from California. Southernmost record was LACM 38378, from West Cortes Basin, California, at 32°23'N, 119°25'W. Maximum recorded depth of 2,904 m (Gilbert 1896) is the greatest known for any skate.

Size: Sheiko and Tranbenkova 1998; from KIE 1257, including a female, 1,570 mm TL, and male, 1,325 mm TL, taken in 1994 northwest of Bering Island, 55°38'N, 164°52'E, depth range 500–600 m.

Bathyraja maculata Ishiyama & Ishihara, 1977 **whiteblotched skate**

Bering Sea and Aleutian Islands; western Bering Sea off Cape Navarin to Commander Islands, Pacific off Kamchatka and Kuril Islands, to Sea of Okhotsk and northern Sea of Japan.

On bottom at depths of 73–1,110 m, usually at 100–650 m.

- Dorsal surface gray, with **large, scattered white to yellow blotches**; ventral surface gray, with darker tail and disk margins.
- Snout flexible, short, broad; interorbital space wide and flat.
- Scapular thorns absent; **nuchal thorns present, strong, more than 1; no other middorsal thorns on disk**; middorsal tail thorns strongly developed; interdorsal thorns absent; orbital thornlets absent; denticles on dorsal surface, ventral surface mostly smooth.
- Length to 120 cm TL.
- Egg case rough, covered with fine prickles in longitudinal rows overlaid by dense covering of bands of silky fibers, lateral keels narrow, posterior apron wider than anterior apron; length to 10 cm.

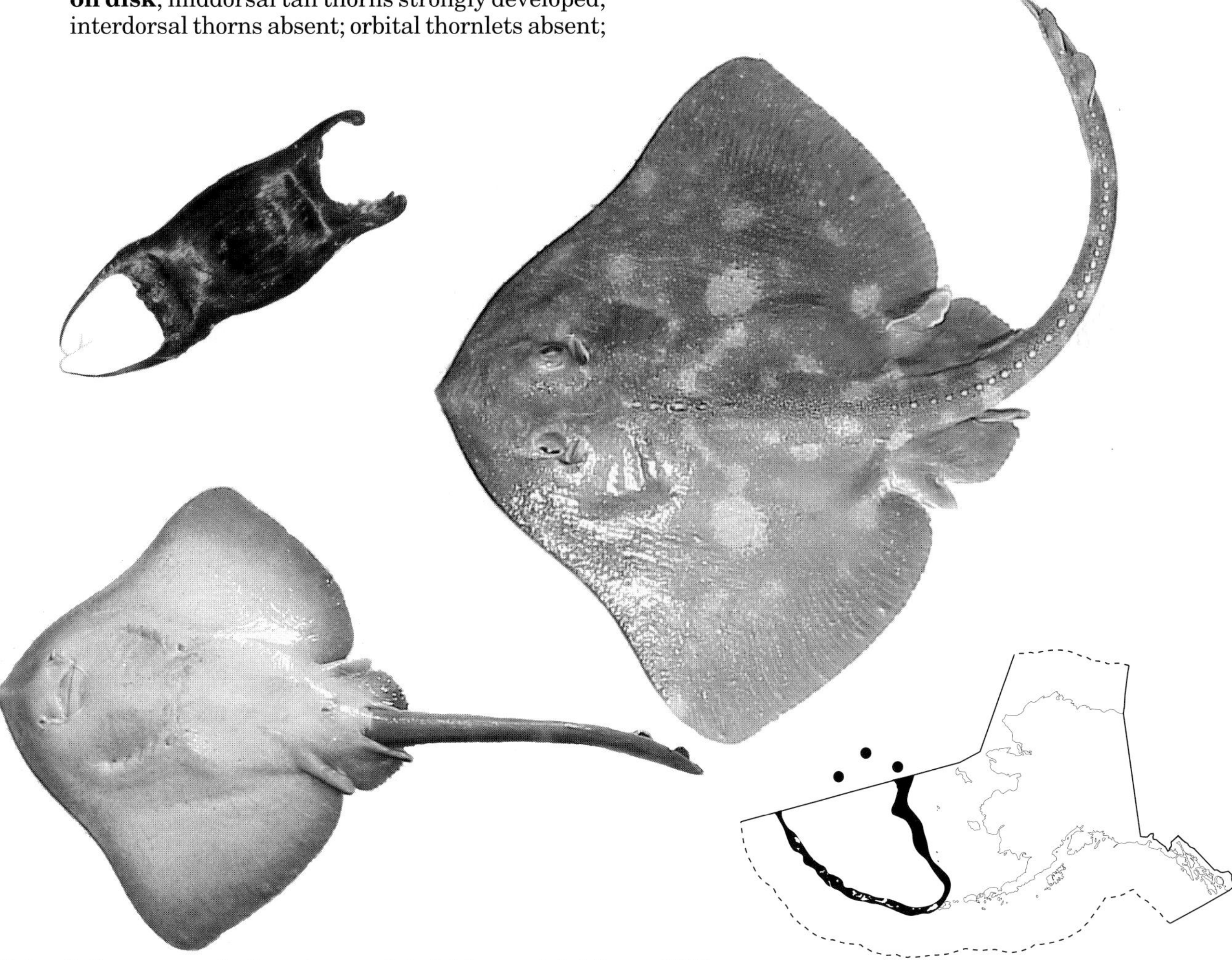

Notes & Sources — *Bathyraja maculata* Ishiyama & Ishihara, 1977
Also called spotted skate (e.g., Orlov 1998b).

Description: Ishiyama and Ishihara 1977:80–82.

Figures: Dorsal and ventral views: NMFS, AFSC, Seattle; male, 76 cm TL, eastern Bering Sea slope. Egg case: Ishiyama and Ishihara 1977, fig. 10B.

Range: Ishiyama and Ishihara (1977) and Ishihara and Ishiyama (1985) gave five eastern Bering Sea records and others from the western Bering Sea, at depths of 190–570 m. In the 1997 NMFS bottom trawl survey of the Aleutian Islands *B. maculata* was taken in 76 net tows, with as many as 75 individuals per catch, from 53°24'N, 168°41'W to 53°14'N, 170°49'E (Umnak Island to Stalemate Bank) at depths of 88–455 m; several specimens were deposited in the UW fish collection (J. W. Orr, pers. comm., 28 Jan. 1999). The specimen shown above was collected at 55°26'N, 168°19'W, depth 510 m, in the June 2000 NMFS survey of the eastern Bering Sea slope (J. W. Orr, pers. comm., 30 Jan. 2001). Others were captured, but all data from that survey were not available at the time of this writing (Feb. 2001). Dudnik and Dolganov (1992) gave depths of 327–672 m from the Sea of Okhotsk and Pacific off the northern Kuril Islands, and Orlov (1998a) gave 103–761 m from the Pacific off the northern Kuril Islands and southeastern Kamchatka. Dolganov (1999) summarized western Pacific records and gave an overall depth range of 150–1,110 m. Fedorov and Sheiko (2002) reported *B. maculata* to be common off the Commander Islands, and gave a minimum depth of 73 m.

Bathyraja minispinosa Ishiyama & Ishihara, 1977 **whitebrow skate**

Bering Sea and Aleutian Islands; western Bering Sea and Commander Islands to Pacific Ocean off Hokkaido and Sea of Okhotsk.

On bottom at depths of 150–1,420 m, usually at 200–800 m.

- Both surfaces dark brown to grayish brown, sometimes white or white with obscure gray mottles ventrally; ventral pores dark; lips white; **interorbital region generally white, often distinctly bordering inner margins of eyes.**
- Snout flexible, long, pointed; **interorbital space narrow, less than 20% of head length**, and slightly concave.
- Scapular thorns absent; **middorsal nuchal thorns often absent**, when present weak and fewer than 3; **no other middorsal thorns on disk**; middorsal tail thorns strongly developed; interdorsal thorns absent; orbital thornlets absent; fine denticles on dorsal surface, ventral surface smooth.
- Length to 83 cm TL.
- Egg case rough, densely covered with minute prickles in longitudinal rows, overlying silky fibers poorly developed, lateral keels narrow, posterior apron wider than anterior apron; length to 8 cm.

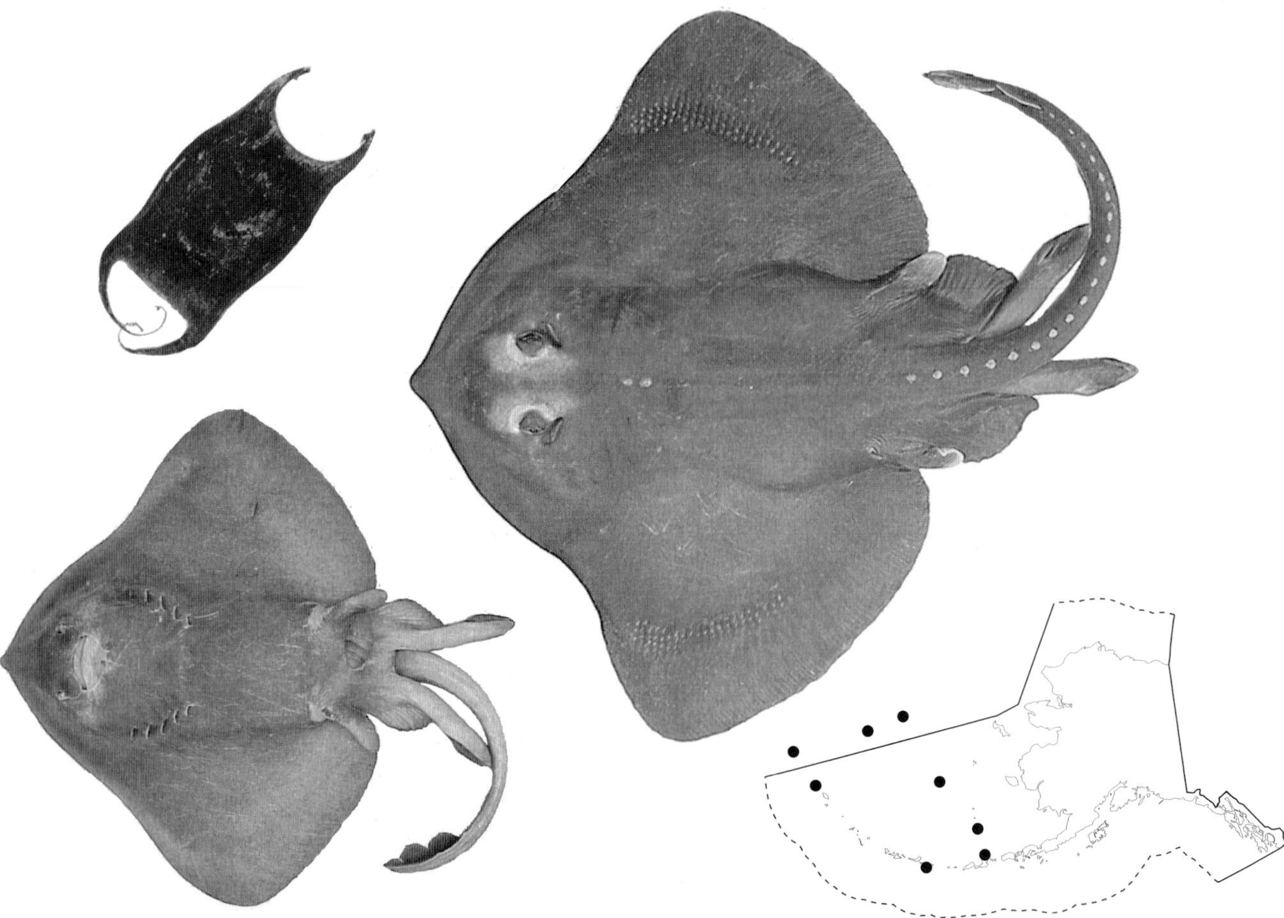

Notes & Sources — *Bathyraja minispinosa* Ishiyama & Ishihara, 1977
Also called bordered skate (e.g., Orlov 1998b) and smallthorn skate (Compagno 1999).

Description: Ishiyama and Ishihara 1977:83–86; Nakaya in Amaoka et al. 1983:312.

Figures: Dorsal and ventral views: NMFS, AFSC, Seattle; male, 78 cm TL, eastern Bering Sea slope. Egg case: Ishiyama and Ishihara 1977, fig. 10C.

Range: Ishiyama and Ishihara (1977) and Ishihara and Ishiyama (1985) gave two eastern Bering Sea records and others from western Bering Sea, at depths of 160–530 m. Taken in three net tows off Amlia and Attu islands during 1994 and 1997 NMFS surveys of the Aleutian Islands; a total of four specimens, with identification confirmed by J. W. Orr (pers. comm., 28 Jan. 1999). Localities were 53°06'N, 171°42'E, depth 461–465 m, in 1994 and1997; and 52°18'N, 173°06'W, depth 414 m, in 1997. Taken in NMFS survey along Bering Sea slope in June 2000; specimen shown above was taken at 56°05'N, 168°38'W, depth 623 m. Other data from that survey are not yet available (J. W. Orr, 30 Jan. 2001). Nakaya (in Amaoka et al. 1983) gave depths of 470–1,420 m for three specimens from the Sea of Okhotsk off Hokkaido. Dudnik and Dolganov (1992) found *B. minispinosa* at 492–1,020 m in the Sea of Okhotsk and Pacific Ocean off the northern Kuril Islands. Orlov (1998a) gave depths of 204–761 m for *B. minispinosa* in the Pacific off the northern Kuril Islands and southeastern Kamchatka. Fedorov and Sheiko (2002) reported it to be common near the Commander Islands, and gave minimum depth of 150 m.

Bathyraja trachura (Gilbert, 1892) **roughtail skate**

Eastern Bering Sea and Aleutian Islands to northern Baja California; western Bering Sea from Cape Navarin to Commander Islands, northern Kuril Islands, and Sea of Okhotsk.

On bottom in deep water at depths of 400–1,994 m.

- Both surfaces dark slate gray, black, or plum brown, but ventral surface sometimes slightly lighter; tip of anterior pelvic lobe, margin of cloaca, gill slits, mouth area whitish; rarely with white blotch over ventral branchial area; **interorbital region dark, same as ground color**.
- Snout flexible, short, broad, tip moderately produced; **interorbital space wide, more than 20% of head length**, and flat.
- Scapular thorns absent; **middorsal nuchal thorns usually absent**, when present weak and fewer than 3; **no other middorsal thorns on disk**; middorsal tail thorns strong and regularly arranged; interdorsal thorns absent; orbital thornlets absent; denticles on dorsal surface, ventral surface smooth.
- Length to 89 cm TL.
- Egg case smooth, horns long and slender; length of case to 12 cm.

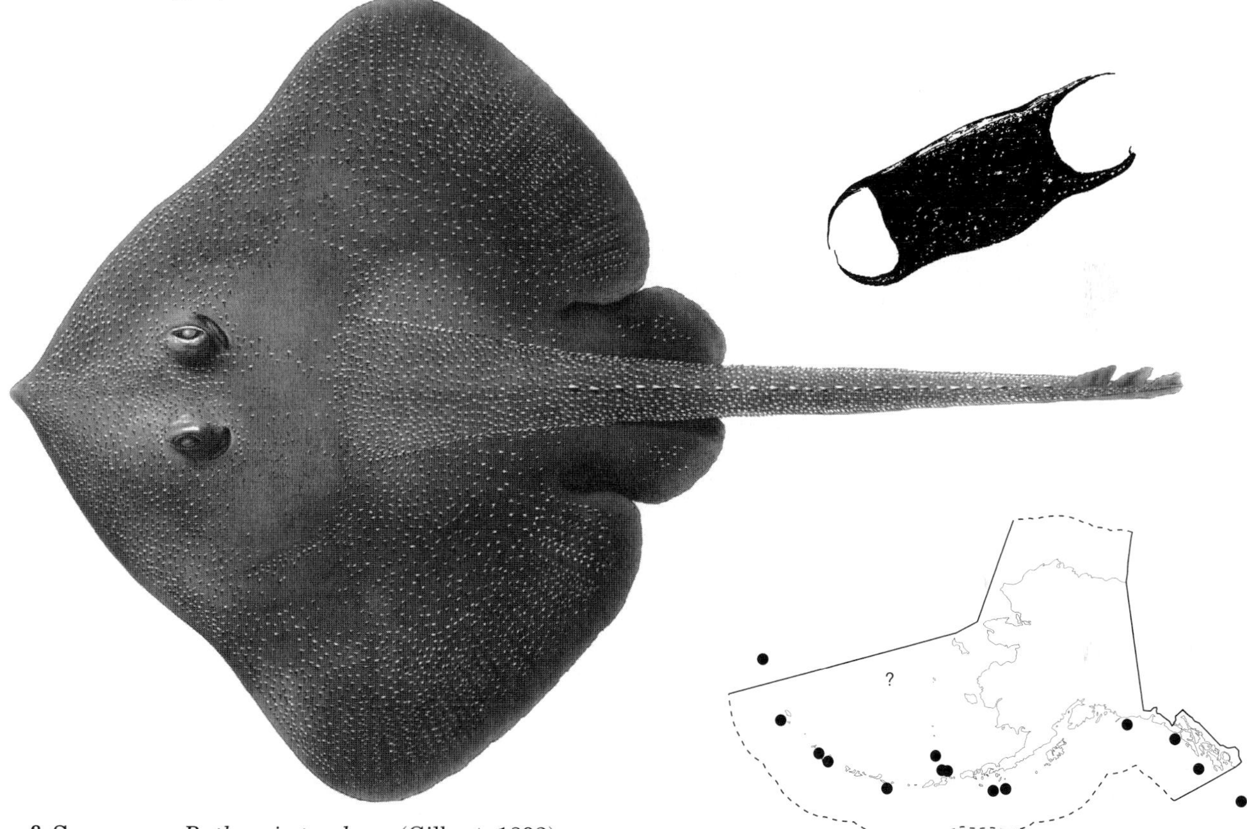

Notes & Sources — *Bathyraja trachura* (Gilbert, 1892)
Raia trachura Gilbert, 1892
Raja microtrachys Osburn & Nichols, 1916
Also called black skate. The whitish thorns and denticles stand out in sharp contrast to the dark background.

Description: Gilbert 1892:539–540; Townsend and Nichols 1925:6; Eschmeyer and Herald 1983:51; Ishiyama and Ishihara 1985:169–173.

Figures: Dorsal view: Royal British Columbia Museum, artist N. Eyolfson, Sep. 1982; BCPM 72-28, 492 mm TL, off southern Queen Charlotte Islands; specimen recorded by Peden (1974). Egg case: Eschmeyer and Herald 1983:14.

Range: First recorded from Alaska by Gilbert (1896), from *Albatross* station 3338, south of the Shumagin Islands at 54°19'N, 159°40'W, depth 1,143 m. Isakson et al. (1971) and Simenstad et al. (1977) reported it off Amchitka Island. Dolganov (1983a) examined 52 specimens from Bering Sea but did not report localities or catalog data. Ishihara and Ishiyama (1985:169) gave nine localities in eastern Bering Sea and Gulf of Alaska, at depths of 490–1,504 m, for specimens they examined. Two were from the eastern Gulf of Alaska: southeast of Cape Suckling at 59°34'N, 143°40'W, and west of Coronation Island at 55°37'N, 135°04'W. In 1998, one (AB 98-15) was taken west of Cross Sound by longline at 732–1,097 m; it matches literature descriptions and illustration (above). Two published records from British Columbia: off southern Queen Charlotte Islands, depth 1,134–1,262 m; and off Vancouver Island, 731–743 m (Peden 1974). Northern limit in Bering Sea is not well defined. Dolganov (1999) reported range, from surveys he participated in, to extend in Bering Sea along Koryak coast to Cape Navarin and southeast to Pribilof Islands, but did not give specific localities. Sheiko and Tranbenkova (1998) reported one specimen taken off Commander Islands, trawl depth range 400–500 m, and one in Karaginskiy Bay, depth range 440–480 m, which were the first published records with specific localities for Russia.

Bathyraja taranetzi (Dolganov, 1983) **mud skate**

Bering Sea and Aleutian Islands, and unconfirmed report from Gulf of Alaska; to Pacific coast of Kamchatka and northern Kuril Islands.

On bottom at depths of 81–1,000 m, usually at 150–550 m.

- Preserved specimens **cinnamon or grayish brown dorsally, with small light and dark spots and blotches; ventral surface white, with mostly brown tail,** margin of cloaca, and posterior margin of pectoral and pelvic fins.
- **Tail longer than pretail length** in adults.
- **No scapular thorns; middorsal nuchal thorns usually absent,** when present weak and fewer than 3; no other middorsal thorns on disk; **tail thorns unevenly distributed, usually fade to denticles distally;** dorsal surface, including branchial region, covered with denticles (sometimes sparse); ventral surface smooth.
- Length to 70 cm TL.

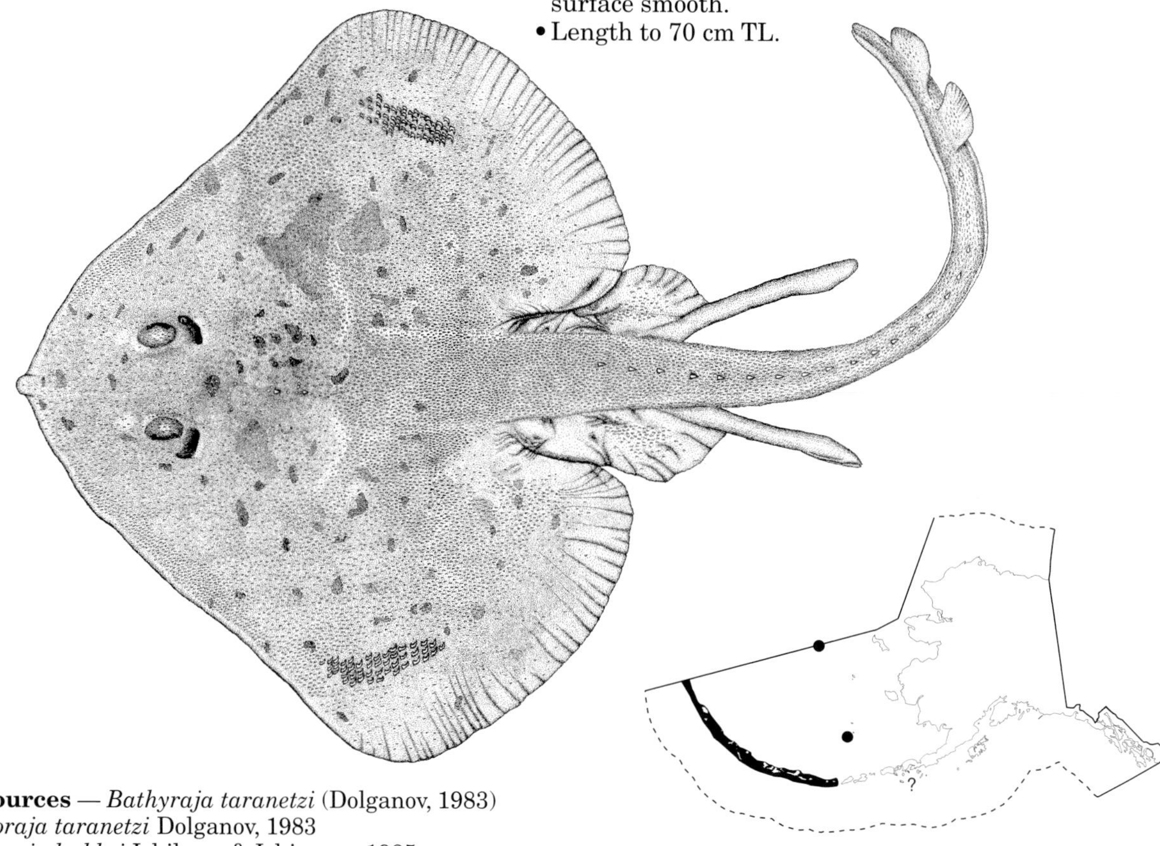

Notes & Sources — *Bathyraja taranetzi* (Dolganov, 1983)
Rhinoraja taranetzi Dolganov, 1983
Bathyraja hubbsi Ishihara & Ishiyama, 1985
Rhinoraja longi Raschi & McEachran, 1991

Ishihara (1990) classified *Bathyraja hubbsi,* described from Bering Sea and eastern Pacific specimens, as a junior synonym of *Rhinoraja taranetzi.* Eastern Pacific *Bathyraja* should be retained in *Bathyraja* pending further study of the relationships of *Bathyraja* and *Rhinoraja* and determination of priority should they be considered synonymous.

Authorities consulted (J. D. McEachran, 4 Sep. 1997; M. E. Anderson, 18 Nov. 1998) agree that *Rhinoraja longi,* described from the Aleutian Islands, is conspecific with *R. taranetzi,* described earlier from the Kuril Islands.

Description: Dolganov 1983b:65–78 and fig. 107 (in key), 1985: 128–130; Ishihara and Ishiyama 1985:148–152; Raschi and McEachran 1991. Egg case has not been described.

Figures: Raschi and McEachran 1991, fig. 1; holotype of *R. longi,* male, 529 mm TL, near Amchita Island, Alaska.

Range: Northernmost record is holotype of *B. hubbsi,* from Bering Sea at 61°11'N, 179°00'W, depth 400 m; other specimens examined by Ishihara and Ishiyama (1985) were from vicinity of Aleutian Islands, and Bering Sea and Pacific coasts of Kamchatka at depths of 190–590 m. Specimens described as *R. longi* by Raschi and McEachran (1991) were taken at several localities from Tanaga Island to Amchitka Island, at depths of 243–514 m. In 1997 NMFS survey of Aleutian Islands, *B. taranetzi* was taken in 57 net hauls, with as many as 20 per haul, extending from Samalga Pass at 52°57'N, 169°19'W to Stalemate Bank at 53°19'W, 170°36'E, depths 81–466 m; several are in the UW permanent collection (data from J. W. Orr, 28 Jan. 1999). The UW has a specimen (UW 42327) taken by NMFS in 1997 near St. George Island at head of Pribilof Canyon, 56°16'N, 169°26'W, depth 248 m. Fedorov and Sheiko (2002) listed it as common off the Commander Islands, and gave maximum depth of 1,000 m. Specimens from "Central Alaska" referred to *Raja trachura* by Walford (1935) and provisionally referred to *B. hubbsi* by Ishihara and Ishiyama (1985) are at least part of the basis for reports (e.g., Dolganov 1999) that *B. taranetzi* occurs in the Gulf of Alaska. As Ishihara and Ishiyama (1985) suggested, those specimens should be reexamined, if they can be found; details of catch locality, if available, should be reported.

Bathyraja violacea (Suvorov, 1935) **Okhotsk skate**

Northern and western Bering Sea, other Alaska reports not confirmed; Bering Sea and Pacific Ocean off Kamchatka and Commander and Kuril islands to Hokkaido and Sea of Okhotsk.

On bottom at depths of 20–1,100 m, usually at 100–800 m.

- **Dorsal surface with** lilac-violet hues and dark violet **vermiculations** (fresh specimens), or grayish brown with obscure dark blotches (preserved); can also be nearly monotone whether fresh or preserved; **ventral surface mostly white, including tail**, sometimes with dark blotches.
- **Tail length usually less than pretail length**.
- **No scapular or middorsal disk thorns**; **tail thorns unevenly distributed, fade to denticles distally**; denticles along medial side of eye enlarged; dorsal surface, except on branchial region, covered with denticles; ventral surface smooth.
- Length to 73 cm TL, possibly to 100 cm.

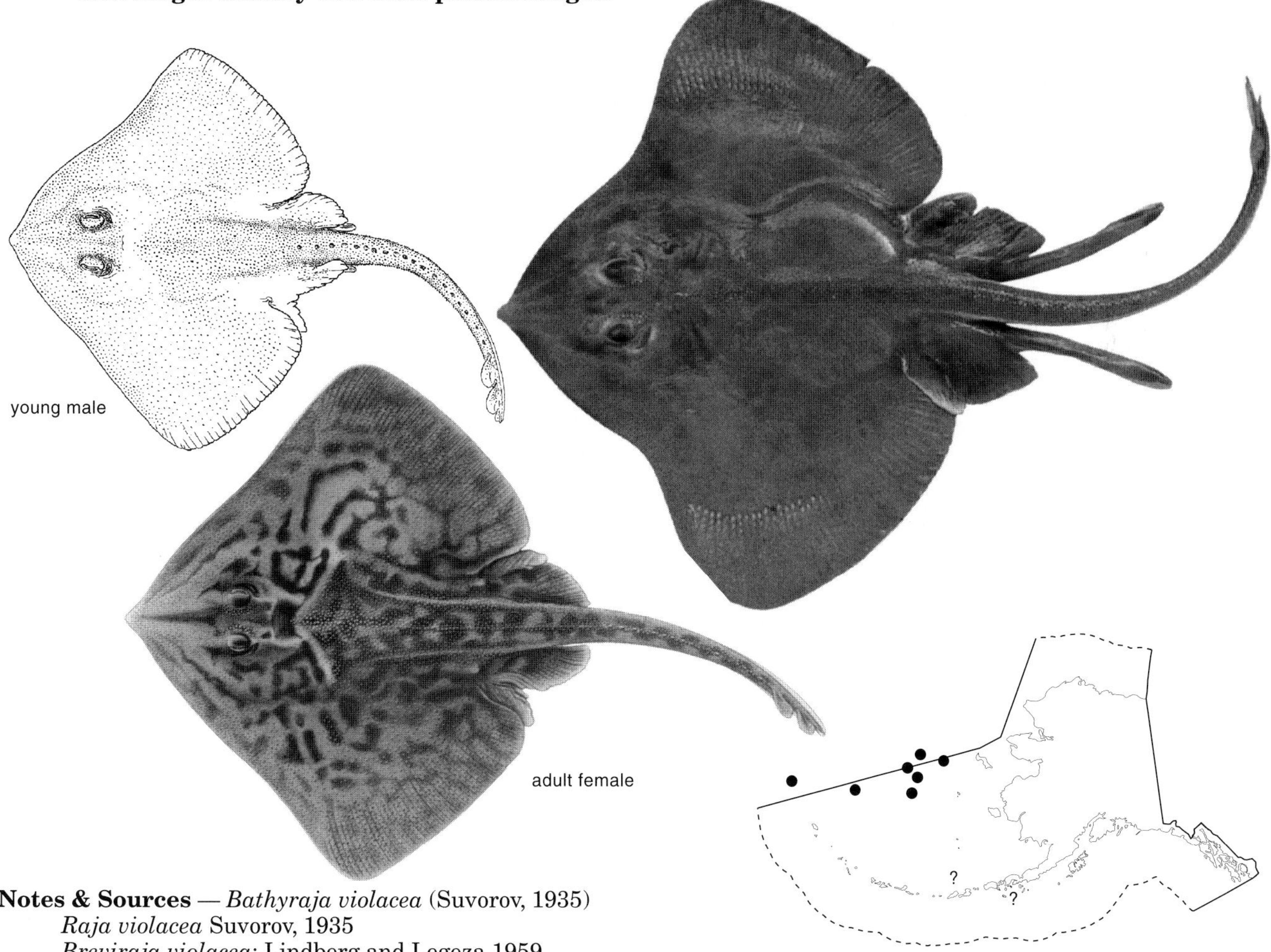

Notes & Sources — *Bathyraja violacea* (Suvorov, 1935)
Raja violacea Suvorov, 1935
Breviraja violacea: Lindberg and Legeza 1959.
Breviraja (*Bathyraja*) *violacea*: Ishiyama 1967.
Also called thornless skate (e.g., Orlov 1998b).

Description: Lindberg and Legeza 1959:133–135; Ishiyama 1967:51–53; Nakaya in Amaoka et al. 1983:310.

Figures: Adult male: Amaoka et al. 1983:220; 714 mm TL, off Hokkaido. Female: Ishiyama 1967, pl. 22; 710 mm TL, Sea of Okhotsk. Young male: Ishiyama 1967, fig. 15A; 273 mm disk width, off tip of Kamchatka.

Range: Andriashev (1937) described specimens under *Raja* sp. that he thought could be *B. violacea* from western Bering Sea north to Cape Navarin and the southern Gulf of Anadyr. Dolganov (1999) reported range to extend from Sea of Japan to Cape Navarin based on surveys he participated in, and to southeastern Bering Sea and western Gulf of Alaska based on literature reports, but latter part of range could reflect confusion in Russian practice, until recently, of *B. violacea* with other species. NMFS, AFSC records of *B. violacea* are from northern Bering Sea, with one to five specimens taken in each of five net hauls in 1990 (records supported by photographs; J. W. Orr, pers. comm., 30 Aug. 2000): 58°59'N, 177°35'W, depth 134 m; 60°19'N, 178°02'W, 152 m; 62°20'N, 176°00'W, 86 m; 61°00'N, 179°41'W, 187 m; 61°39'N, 179°55'W, 139 m. Dr. V. N. Dolganov (via A. A. Balanov, pers. comm., 5 Sep. 2000) provided data on western Bering Sea records, including one at 56°54'N, 174°37'E, depth 325 m. *Bathyraja violacea* is rare in the vicinity of the Commander Islands (Fedorov and Sheiko 2002).

Size: Orlov (1998b) recorded maximum of 73 cm TL from recent surveys in western Pacific. Lindberg and Legeza (1959) gave maximum of 1 m, but without documentation.

Family Myliobatidae

Eagle rays

In eagle rays the head is elevated above the disk and the eyes and spiracles are located on the sides of the head. These rays "fly" through the water using up and down movements of their "wings," in contrast to the undulating motion of skates (Rajidae) over the bottom. They inhabit warm temperate and tropical seas, yet in 1983, an El Niño year, a sighting of manta, *Manta birostris,* was reported from Prince William Sound. Otherwise, mantas are not known to occur farther north in the eastern Pacific than southern California.

The manta belongs to the Mobulinae, comprising mantas and devil rays, the only living vertebrates with three pairs of functional limbs. The cephalic pair direct food (small fishes and planktonic crustaceans) toward the mouth as the animal grazes, and are a subdivision of the pectorals. Mantas often swim at or near the surface, sometimes leaping or somersaulting out of the water and landing with a slap audible for miles. Occasionally they land on small boats, causing considerable damage, or tow them for miles when harpooned.

Manta birostris is 1.2 m (4 ft) across at birth and can grow to a width of 9.1 m (30 ft) and weight of more than 1,820 kg (4,000 lb), making it the largest member of the Rajiformes. The word *manta* is Spanish for blanket, and was used for this fish by pearl fishermen in South America who dreaded it for its reputation of devouring people after enveloping them in its vast wings. Actually, like filter-feeding sharks (basking shark, whale shark, megamouth), mantas strain their food out of the water and do not prey on humans.

Manta birostris (Walbaum, 1792) **manta**

Sighted at Prince William Sound, Alaska (record not verifiable); normally eastern Pacific from southern California to Peru, including Gulf of California and offshore islands; circumglobal in warm seas.

Pelagic, near surface; in eastern Pacific frequents coastal waters, elsewhere sometimes found far from land.

- Black to dark brown dorsally; white ventrally.
- **Head distinct from disk**; **long cephalic flaps**.
- Disk not quite twice as broad as long; tail about as long as disk.
- **Pectoral fins long and pointed**; **dorsal fin at base of tail**; no caudal fin.
- Body and tail covered with denticles, making surface very rough.
- Width to 9.1 m.

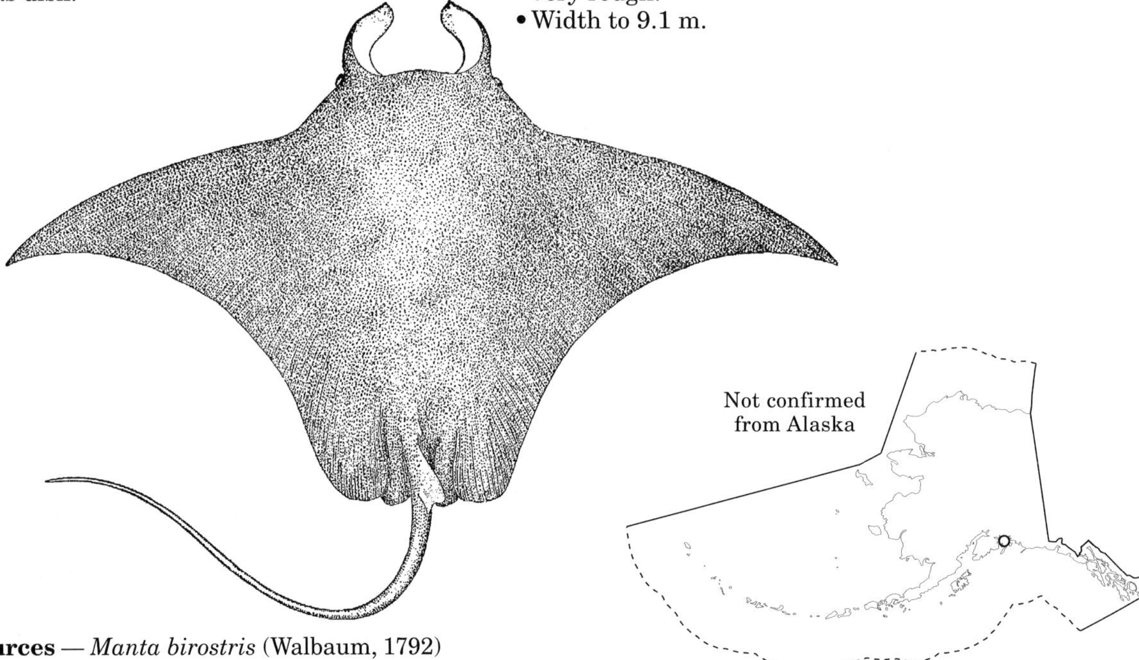

Notes & Sources — *Manta birostris* (Walbaum, 1792)
Raja birostris Walbaum, 1792
Manta hamiltoni (Newman, 1849)

Description: Jordan and Evermann 1896b:92–93; Eschmeyer and Herald 1983:57–58; Robins and Ray 1986:44–45.

Figure: Jordan and Evermann 1900, fig. 39.

Range: Karinen et al. (1985) reported that ADFG biologists sighted mantas (number not given) off Columbia Glacier in the summer of 1983, during an El Niño that brought several normally southern species to the Gulf of Alaska.

Size: McEachran and Capapé in Whitehead et al. 1984, McEachran and Notarbartolo-di-Sciara in Fischer et al. 1995. Size of eagle rays is usually reported as width.

Grade Teleostomi
Teleosts

In Nelson's (1994) classification of higher fish taxa the grade Teleostomi is a group within the superclass Gnathostomata that includes other jawed vertebrates as well as fishes. The grade comprises three classes, one of them (the Acanthodii) extinct. The other two classes, the Sarcopterygii and the Actinopterygii, form a group called the Euteleostomi by Nelson (1994). The group Euteleostomi includes all the bony fishes, plus the tetrapods. The formerly recognized class Osteichthyes (Nelson 1984), or bony fishes, is not a monophyletic group, and Nelson (1994) uses the name as a vernacular (osteichthyan) to denote those members of the class Sarcopterygii conventionally termed fishes (including coelacanths and lungfishes) together with the larger class Actinopterygii. Within this paraphyletic group (bony fishes) there are about 45 orders and 435 families, and more than 23,600 species. In the fresh and salt waters of Alaska, the teleosts are represented by about 27 orders, 92 families, and 496 or more species. All of the Alaskan teleost fishes are in the class Actinopterygii.

Class Actinopterygii
Ray-finned fishes

Like other osteichthyans, ray-finned fishes have jaws and a bony skeleton, and water exits the gills through a single opening on each side. They typically have branchiostegal rays and interopercles; nostrils placed relatively high up on the head; and ganoid, cycloid, or ctenoid scales, or the scales can be absent. Ray-finned fishes are grouped in two subclasses: Chondrostei and Neopterygii. In Alaska, two species of sturgeon represent the subclass Chondrostei while all the other ray-finned fishes are in the subclass Neopterygii.

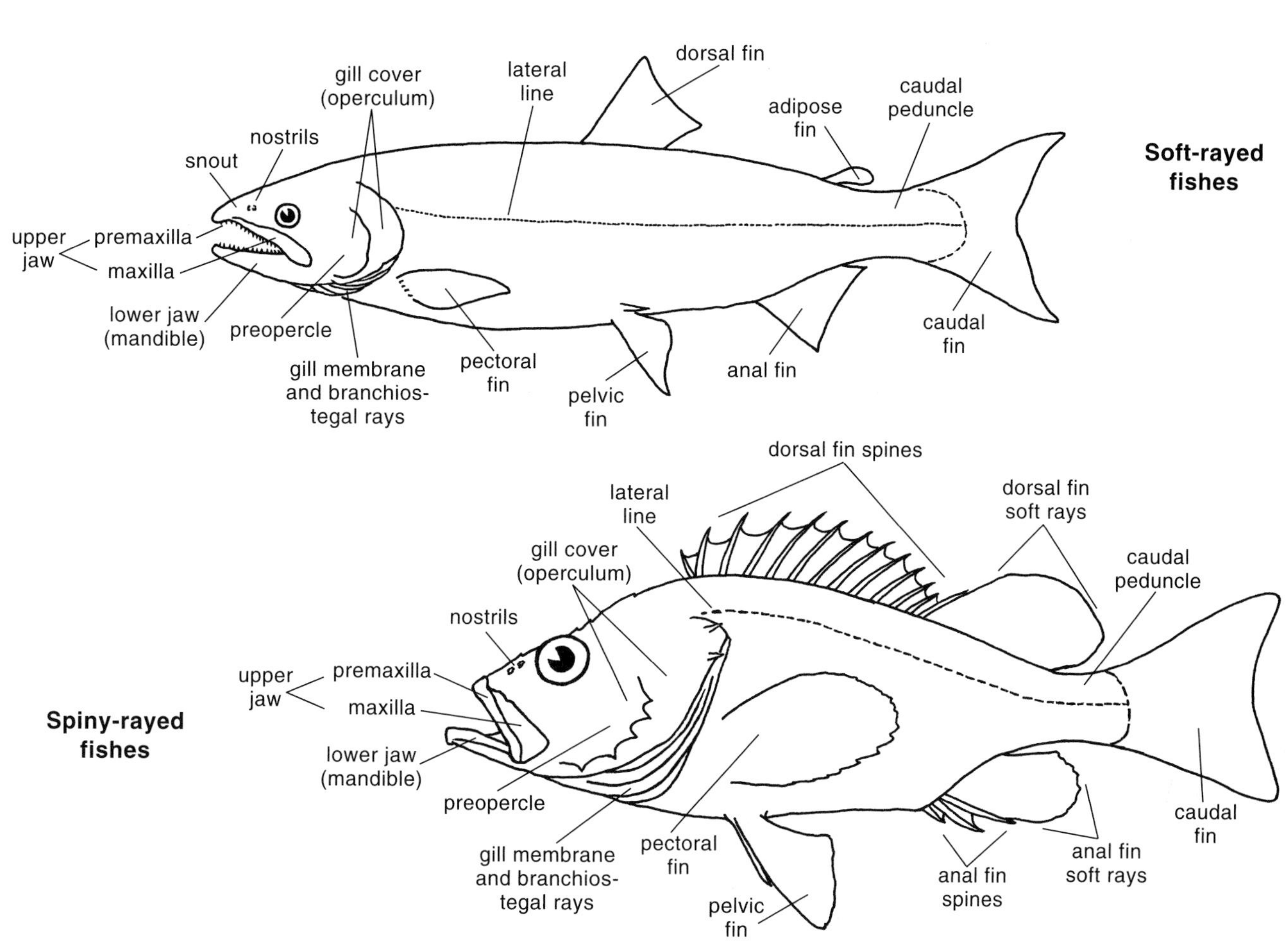

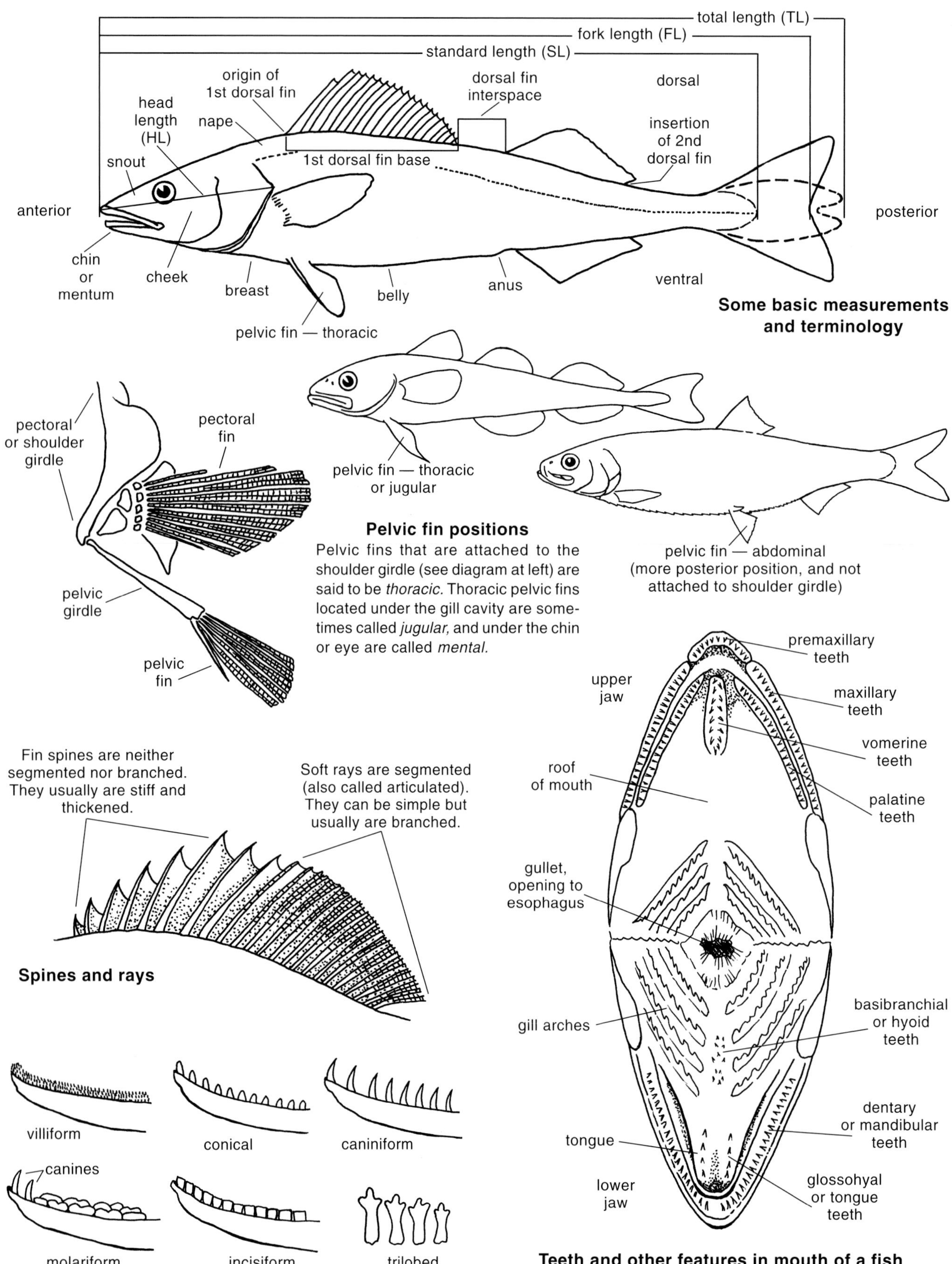

Some basic measurements and terminology

Pelvic fin positions

Pelvic fins that are attached to the shoulder girdle (see diagram at left) are said to be *thoracic.* Thoracic pelvic fins located under the gill cavity are sometimes called *jugular,* and under the chin or eye are called *mental.*

Spines and rays

Typical tooth types

Teeth and other features in mouth of a fish

Based on pink salmon, family Salmonidae. Fishes in other groups can have fewer or more types of teeth, in different arrangements.

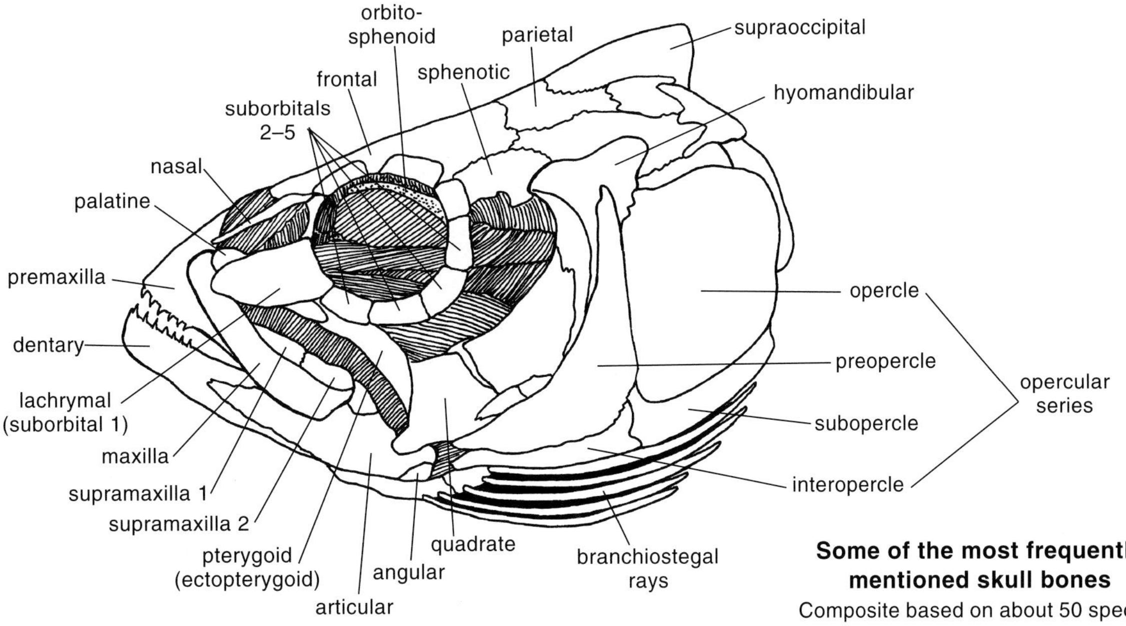

orbito-
sphenoid
parietal
supraoccipital
frontal
sphenotic
hyomandibular
suborbitals
2–5
nasal
palatine
premaxilla
opercle
dentary
preopercle
opercular
series
lachrymal
(suborbital 1)
subopercle
maxilla
interopercle
supramaxilla 1
supramaxilla 2
quadrate
pterygoid
(ectopterygoid)
angular
articular
branchiostegal
rays

Some of the most frequently mentioned skull bones

Composite based on about 50 species of teleosts. (Based on Gregory 1933.)

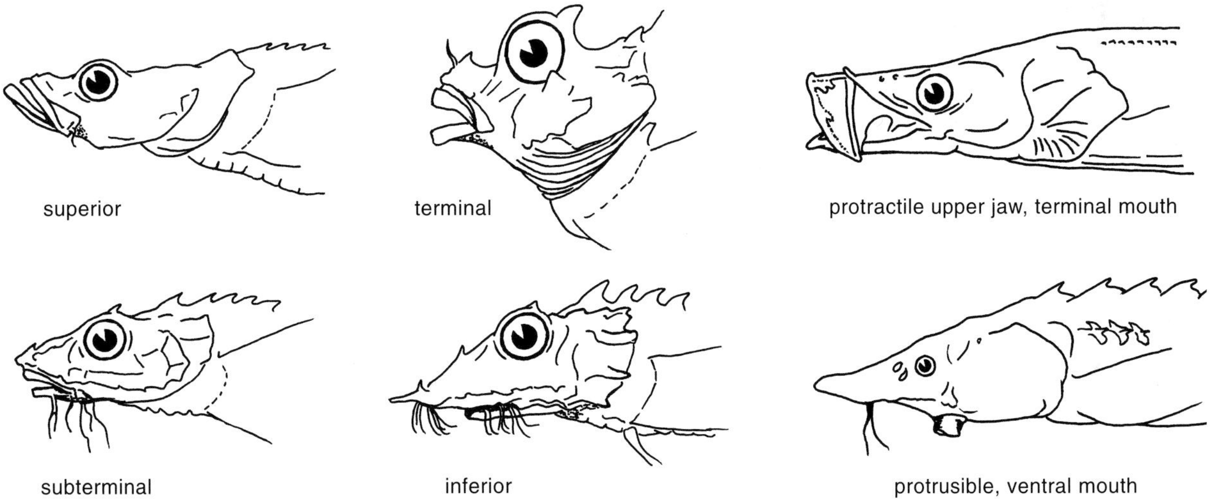

superior
terminal
protractile upper jaw, terminal mouth
subterminal
inferior
protrusible, ventral mouth

Examples of mouth shapes and types

Shown at left: four poachers, family Agonidae. Upper right: Pacific sand lance, family Ammodytidae. Lower right: white sturgeon, family Acipenseridae.

Caudal fin shapes

heterocercal
rounded
truncate
double truncate
pointed
slightly emarginate
or indented
moderately emarginate
or indented
double
emarginate
forked
or strongly indented
lunate

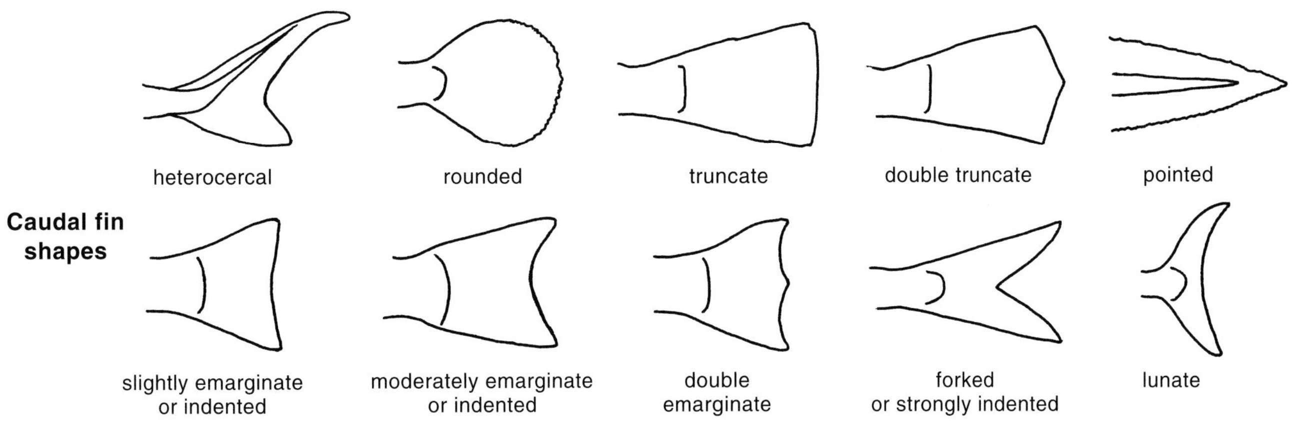

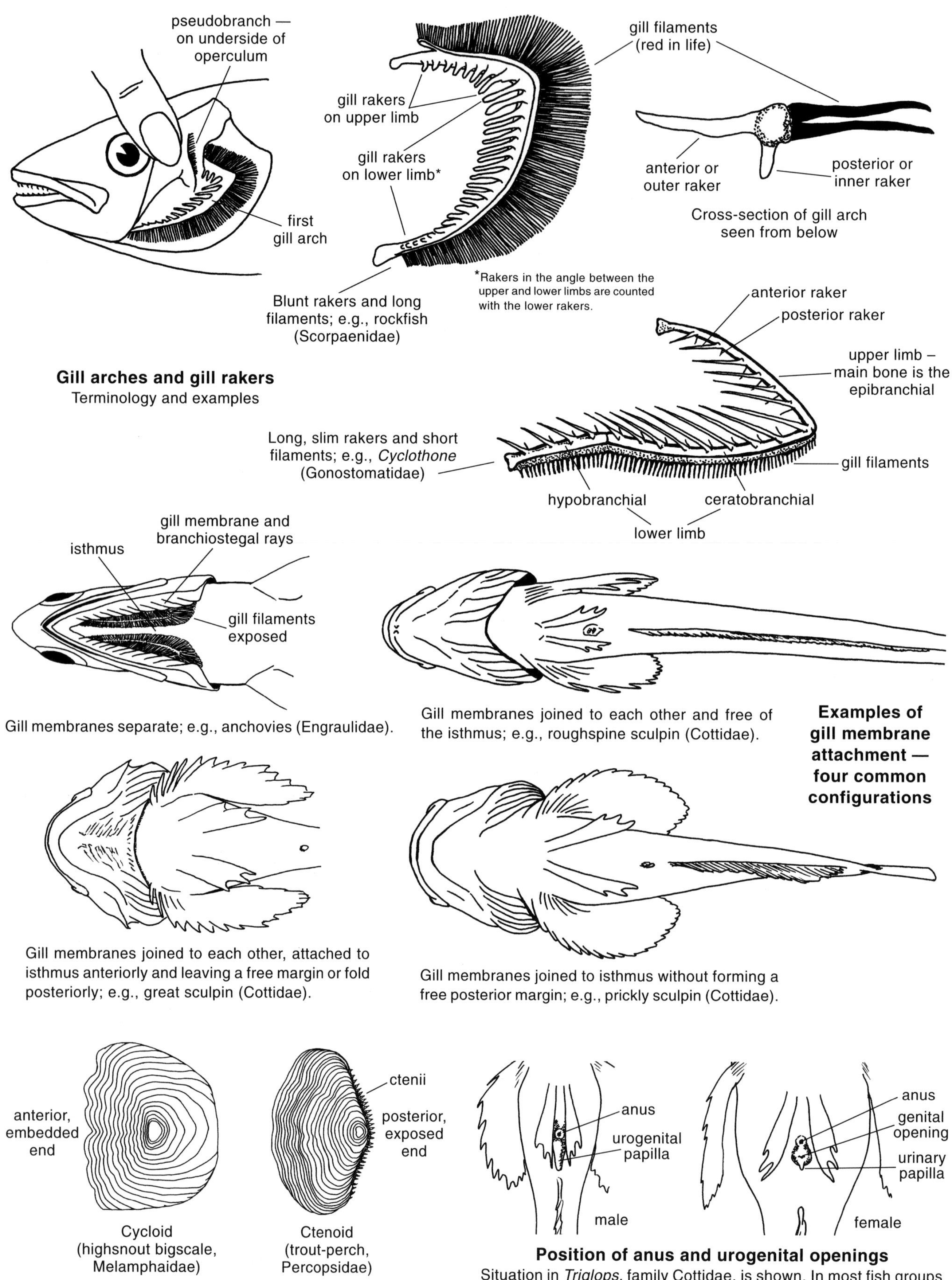

Gill arches and gill rakers
Terminology and examples

Gill membranes separate; e.g., anchovies (Engraulidae).

Gill membranes joined to each other and free of the isthmus; e.g., roughspine sculpin (Cottidae).

Examples of gill membrane attachment — four common configurations

Gill membranes joined to each other, attached to isthmus anteriorly and leaving a free margin or fold posteriorly; e.g., great sculpin (Cottidae).

Gill membranes joined to isthmus without forming a free posterior margin; e.g., prickly sculpin (Cottidae).

Cycloid (highsnout bigscale, Melamphaidae)

Ctenoid (trout-perch, Percopsidae)

Two common types of scales

Position of anus and urogenital openings
Situation in *Triglops,* family Cottidae, is shown. In most fish groups the sex organs are not so obviously differentiated externally.

Order Acipenseriformes
Sturgeons and paddlefishes

The Acipenseriformes is an ancient group of Northern Hemisphere fishes which presently contains 25 or 26 species in two families: sturgeons (Acipenseridae) and paddlefishes (Polyodontidae). Living representatives are descendants of ray-finned fishes, having secondarily developed a cartilaginous skeleton. They pursue freshwater or anadromous lifestyles, primarily on the bottom. Sturgeons and paddlefishes are characterized by, in addition to a largely cartilaginous skeleton, a flattened snout; heterocercal tail; sharklike fins with rays more numerous than the basals; one dorsal fin, placed far back on the body; reduced scales; and 1 branchiostegal ray. They have a spiral valve in the intestine, vertebrae without centra, a duct connecting the swim bladder to the gut, and one bone (the opercle) in the operculum. The order is represented in Alaska by two species of sturgeons. Bemis et al. (1997) reviewed the systematics of living and fossil members of the order.

Family Acipenseridae
Sturgeons

The Acipenseridae comprises four extant genera. With 16 or 17 species, *Acipenser* is the most speciose taxon in the family, as well as in the order. White sturgeon, *A. transmontanus,* and green sturgeon, *A. medirostris,* occur in southern Alaska. However, few adequately documented records exist of sturgeons in Alaska, and the majority of those are of individuals taken incidentally in salmon gill-net fisheries. Neither species spawns in Alaska. Both species are anadromous, more or less. Some populations of *A. transmontanus,* such as that in the Fraser River of British Columbia, do not move out to sea, and marine migration may not be an obligatory part of this species' life cycle.

Sturgeons have many distinctive features, including a depressed body; shovel-shaped snout; ventrally located, protrusible mouth; fleshy chemosensory barbels in front of the mouth; large bony scutes on the head and along the body; and a heterocercal caudal fin, with the upper lobe longer than the lower. The bony scutes are sharp in young fish but become blunt with age. The protrusible mouth vacuums up worms, mollusks, crustaceans, and other bottom-living organisms. Adult sturgeons lack teeth. In the Alaskan species spiracles are present (above and behind the eyes), the snout and caudal peduncle are subconical, the gill membranes are joined to the isthmus, and the mouth is transverse. The species are distinguishable from each other by numbers of fin rays and scutes.

Sturgeons are among the largest fishes, attaining lengths of 1–9 m (3–30 ft). The white sturgeon, reaching about 6 m (20 ft) and weighing up to 630 kg (1,387 lb) or more, is the largest freshwater fish in North America. Presently, however, due to a slow rate of growth, intensive fishing, and habitat loss, large fish are rarely taken. In British Columbia by about 1970, white sturgeon taken incidental to salmon fishing in the lower Fraser River measured 18–226 cm (7–89 inches) and weighed a maximum of 99 kg (218 lb). The green sturgeon, at least in the past, reached more than 2 m (about 7 ft) and 99 kg (218 lb), but has not been the focus of an organized fishery. As a food fish the green sturgeon is considered inferior, and was once thought to be poisonous.

Quast and Hall (1972) listed Siberian sturgeon, *A. baerii* Brandt, as a likely Alaskan species, following Walters' (1955) suggestion that it may occur in arctic Alaska. However, this species is believed to be restricted to rivers of the north coast of Russia. Ruban (1997) reviewed the contemporary distribution and taxonomic status of *A. baerii.*

Findeis (1997) reviewed acipenserid systematics and examined interrelationships among the genera using a cladistic analysis of osteological characters.

Key to the Acipenseridae of Alaska

1 Bony scutes in single row of 1–4 along midventral line
between anus and anal fin; scutes in lateral row 23–30 .... *Acipenser medirostris,* page 114

1 Bony scutes in two rows of 4–8 along midventral line
between anus and anal fin; scutes in lateral row 38–48 .... *Acipenser transmontanus,* page 115

Acipenser medirostris Ayres, 1854 **green sturgeon**

Rare records from Bering Sea; possible record from Copper River, northern Gulf of Alaska; southeastern Alaska to northern Baja California at Ensenada; and to Pacific coast of Kamchatka.

Anadromous; estuaries and mouths of large rivers; spawns close to coast, generally not ascending far up rivers (ascends far up Trinity and Klamath rivers, California, only); spawns south of Alaska.

D 29–42; A 18–30; GR 18–20.

- Olive to dark green above, greenish white below; sometimes with dark green stripes on belly and sides; viscera white.
- Barbels slightly closer to mouth than to tip of snout.
- Dorsal fin rays usually 33–35.
- Dorsal row of 7–12 scutes anterior to dorsal fin, 1 or 2 scutes posterior to dorsal fin; **scutes in lateral row 23–30**; scutes in ventrolateral row 7–11; **ventral scutes anterior to anal fin in 1 row** of 1–4 scutes.
- Length to more than 2 m TL, weight to 160 kg.

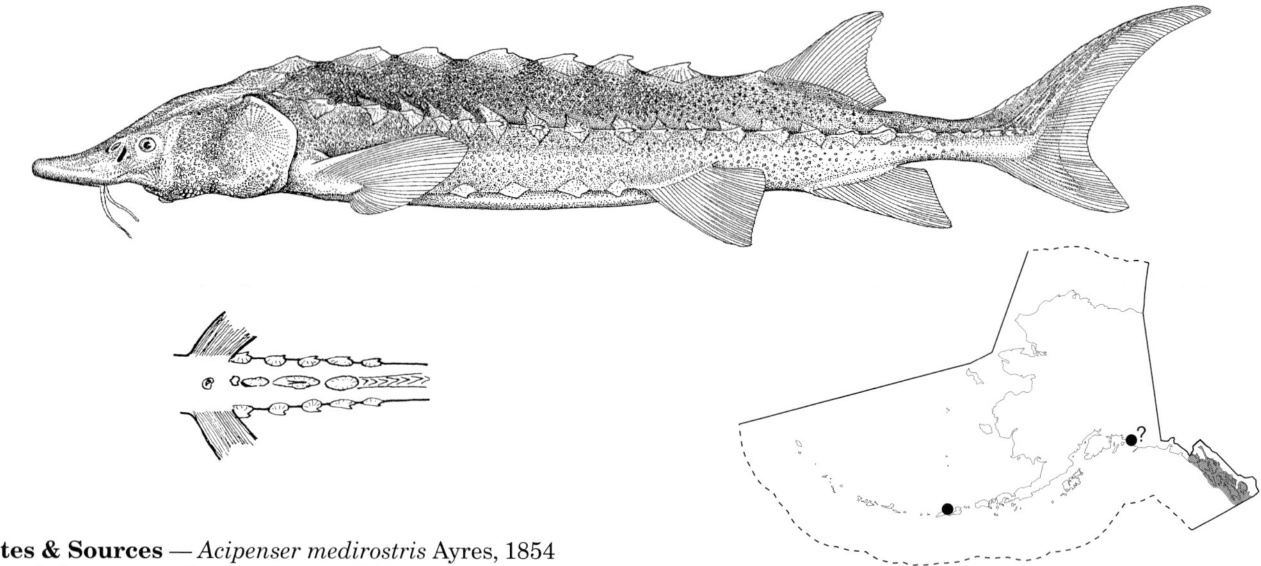

Notes & Sources — *Acipenser medirostris* Ayres, 1854
Acipenser acutirostris Ayres, 1854

The extralimital range statement (above) is affected by classification of *A. mikadoi* Hilgendorf, 1892, treated by most authors as a junior synonym or subspecies of *A. medirostris.* Lindberg and Legeza (1965) and Artyukhin and Andronov (1990) reviewed morphological characters and distributional records. Birstein et al. (1993, 1997) presented cytogenetic evidence, including differences in chromosome number, supporting the distinctiveness of the two species. *Acipenser mikadoi* ranges from the southern Okhotsk Sea and Japan to Korea.

Description: Hart 1973:82; Scott and Crossman 1973:90–92; Morrow 1980:13–14; Artyukhin and Andronov 1990.

Figures: University of British Columbia, artist R. Gowby, Aug. 1969; UBC 63-1064TO3, 107 mm TL, Flat Point, Taku Inlet, Alaska. Ventral scutes: Morrow 1974, fig. 7.

Range: Occurrence in eastern Bering Sea has been reported but is not well documented. Bean (1881b) doubted that a specimen (USNM 27697) reported to have been collected south of Bering Strait was "really Alaskan." Berg (1948:95) stated that the species is "probably present also in the Bering Sea." Andriashev and Panin (1953) reported a specimen from Olyutorskiy Bay as the first specimen known from the western Bering Sea. The statement by several authors that Magnin (1959), citing Russian sources, said it was fished commercially in the Bering Sea must have been due to mistranslation. Magnin (1959; in French), only cited Andriashev and Panin (1953) for the one Bering Sea record and did not say more. Lindberg and Legeza (1965) considered Andriashev and Panin's (1953) to be the only Bering Sea record. Wilimovsky (1964) reported *A. medirostris* from the northwest side of Unalaska Island on a list of Aleutian Islands fish species, without citing documentation. Evermann and Goldsborough (1907) wrote they were told of two specimens caught in the Copper River in 1897. Documentation is better for presence in southeastern Alaska. The only Alaskan record shown on maps by Scott and Crossman (1973) and Lee (in Lee et al. 1980) is at approximately the Taku River near Juneau. Quast and Hall (1972) reported specimens from southeastern Alaska in a general statement; documentation exists as specimens AB 63-245, AB 66-172, and AB-W 56-24 from the Taku River entrance. UBC 62-616TO3 is from the Taku River, and UBC 63-1064TO3 (shown above), from Taku Inlet. A specimen caught in 1988 in Stephens Passage is on display at the Juneau International Airport. Morrow (1980), reviewing Alaskan freshwater fishes, did not give specific Alaskan records of *A. medirostris.* Houston (1988) reported that a few are taken each year in northern British Columbia near the mouth of the Skeena River in the salmon gill-net fishery. They are most abundant in British Columbia in the southern part of the province. Hart (1973) reported that although *A. medirostris* were not common there, 75 fish weighing a total of 952 kg were taken in one day off Kyuquot Sound. They had been eating sand lance.

Acipenser transmontanus Richardson, 1836 **white sturgeon**

Northern Gulf of Alaska to northern Baja California at Ensenada.

Anadromous; estuaries and the sea as deep as 122 m, moving far inland in large rivers to spawn; spend much or all of their lives in fresh water in some areas; not known to spawn in Alaska.

D 44–48; A 28–31; GR 34–36.

- Gray, pale olive, or grayish brown dorsally; light gray to white ventrally; viscera black.
- Barbels slightly closer to tip of snout than to mouth.
- Dorsal fin rays usually 45.
- Dorsal row of 11–14 scutes anterior to dorsal fin, no scutes posterior to dorsal fin; **scutes in lateral row 38–48**; scutes in ventrolateral row 9–12; **ventral scutes anterior to anal fin in 2 rows** of 4–8 scutes.
- Length to 6 m TL, weight possibly to 817 kg.

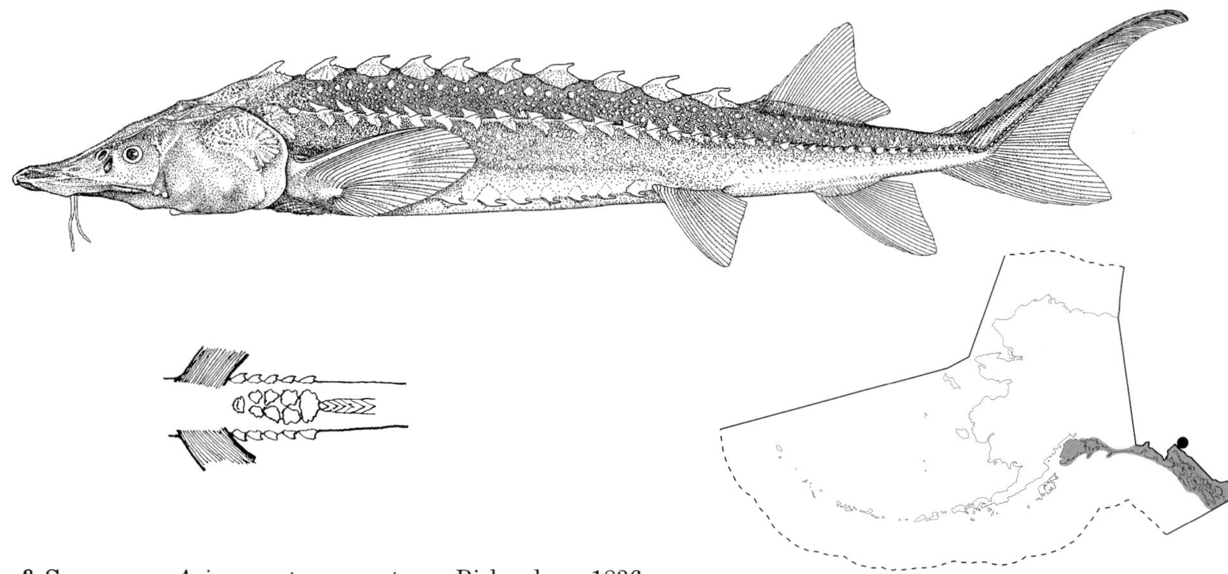

Notes & Sources — *Acipenser transmontanus* Richardson, 1836

Not *Acipenser aleutensis* Fitzinger in Fitzinger & Heckel, 1836. Described from a specimen reported to be from the Aleutian Islands, *A. aleutensis* was questionably included in the synonymy of *A. transmontanus* by Jordan and Evermann (1896b), and later without question by Jordan, Evermann, and Clark (1930) and others, most recently Scott and Crossmann (1973). However, Fitzinger's description does not fit *A. transmontanus*; e.g, 13–15 dorsal, 60–62 lateral, and 14–16 ventrolateral scutes. Indeed, Kottelat (1997) included *A. aleutensis* questionably in the synonymy of *A. ruthenus* Linnaeus, 1758, a species which is endemic to the rivers of east-central Europe. The specimen could not have been collected in Alaska.

Previously classified by some authors as a junior synonym of *A. transmontanus,* the Siberian sturgeon, *Acipenser baerii* Brandt, 1869, is currently recognized as a distinct species (Bemis et al. 1997, Ruban 1997).

Description: Hart 1973:83–84; Scott and Crossman 1973:96–100; Morrow 1980:14–16.

Figures: University of British Columbia, artist R. Gowby, Aug. 1969; UBC 59-599, 442 mm TL, British Columbia. Ventral scutes: Morrow 1974, fig. 6.

Range: Authors giving range to the Aleutian Islands for *A. transmontanus* (Scott and Crossman 1973, Lee et al. 1980) evidently did so on the basis of the erroneous locality data for the type of *A. aleutensis* (see above), since no other specimens from the Aleutians have been attributed to *A. transmontanus*. McPhail and Lindsey (1970) and Morrow (1974) gave Cook Inlet as the northern limit, the latter author stating it occurs "possibly also in Bristol Bay drainages." Morrow (1980) reported speculation that the "sea monster" of Lake Iliamna, Alaska, may be a white sturgeon, but this is only speculation; there are no confirmed records from the Bristol Bay drainage. Morrow's (1980) map depicts a range extending west as far as the Kenai Peninsula. None of the aforementioned authors cited specific Alaskan records. The northernmost record represented on the map by Lee (in Lee et al. 1980) is in British Columbia, inland near the Yukon Territory. A wall-mounted specimen (AB 76-68) from Lynn Canal on the north side of Berners Bay off Point Saint Mary is the only well-documented Alaskan record of white sturgeon that we found. The three known sizable populations are limited to the Fraser, Columbia, and Sacramento river systems. In British Columbia they occur in the upper Columbia River, as well as in the Fraser, and spawn in the Fraser. Hart (1973) reported that spawning eulachon are an important food for white sturgeon, and that some sturgeon migrations seem to be associated with eulachon availability.

Size: Clemens and Wilby (1946, 1949) cited a maximum reported weight of 817 kg, but later (Clemens and Wilby 1961) considered a record weight of 629 kg to be more reliable. Morrow (1980) wrote that it is reputed to attain a weight of over 860 kg. Authors concur on a maximum length of about 6 m.

Order Albuliformes
Bonefishes

Eels and eel-like fishes distributed among three orders in the subdivision Elopomorpha are represented in the Alaskan ichthyofauna: Albuliformes, Anguilliformes, and Saccopharyngiformes. Albuliform fishes differ from fishes in other orders by having the mandibular sensory canal lying in an open groove in the dentary and angular bones. In other elopomorphs the groove is roofed in at least the dentary. Although collectively called bonefishes, albuliforms vary in appearance and are grouped into eel-like and herringlike forms in two suborders. The suborder Notacanthoidei includes eel-like forms, and is represented in Alaska by the deepsea spiny eels of the family Notacanthidae. The suborder including herringlike forms, the Albuloidei, is not represented in Alaska.

Notacanthoids have pectoral fins located high on the sides, abdominal pelvic fins, and tails that taper to a point without a caudal fin or with a minute caudal fin. The tail tip regenerates if broken. Transparent skin, continuous with the skin of the head, covers the eyes. Other notacanthoid characteristics include: a prominent, posteriorly directed bony spine on the dorsal edge of the posterior end of the maxilla; upper jaw bordered by both premaxilla and maxilla; short dorsal fin base, or dorsal fin represented by isolated spines; long anal fin base; gill membranes separate or joined; 5–23 branchiostegal rays; and swim bladder present.

Like other elopomorph fishes, albuliforms possess a distinctive, long-lived larval stage known as a leptocephalus. The leptocephali are greatly compressed and transparent, and vary in shape from extremely elongate and ribbonlike to deep and leaflike. They exceed the adults in length and differ so much in appearance from them that few have been matched with adults. The leptocephali of notacanthoids can reach 2 m (6.5 ft) in length before metamorphosing, yet the largest adults are 122–152 cm (4–5 ft). Most leptocephali are found in temperate to tropical waters. None has been found off the coasts of Alaska, but at least one form occurs in closely adjacent waters (see order Anguilliformes). Notacanthoid leptocephali are differentiated from those of the orders Anguilliformes and Saccopharyngiformes

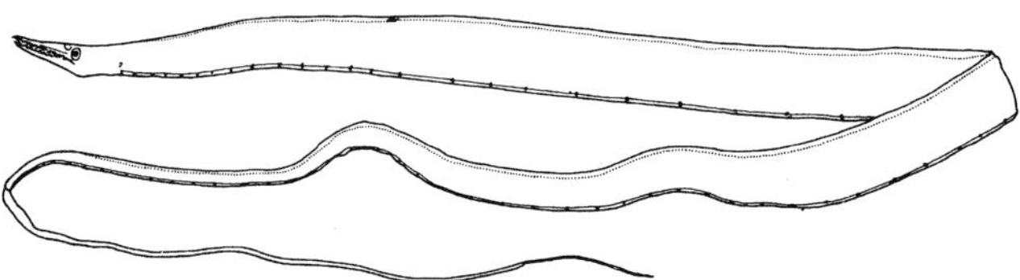

Notacanthoid leptocephalus
(After Matarese et al. 1989.)

by the absence of a caudal fin, instead having a single filament. Smith (1989b) provided an introduction to leptocephali, including the history of their study, biology, and identification, with a key to the orders. Hulet and Robins (1989) presented evidence that they believe indicates the leptocephalus is a primitive stage which has been eliminated in the higher ray-finned fishes, but there is no consensus on this point.

The varied morphology among adults within the elopomorph subdivision can be interpreted differently and several classifications have been proposed. Some taxonomists place the notacanthoids by themselves in an order, the Notacanthiformes, and the albuloids in their own order, the Elopiformes.

Family Notacanthidae
Deepsea spiny eels

The Notacanthidae have a worldwide distribution as benthic or benthopelagic inhabitants of outer continental shelf and slope waters. Known from depths of 125–4,900 m, they are called deepsea spiny eels to distinguish them from a family of freshwater, tropical spiny eels. Deepsea spiny eels have extremely elongate bodies but, unlike true eels (order Anguilliformes), have pelvic fins. Some authors prefer not to call them eels, instead using the term *tapirfish* in reference to the protruding snout of most species.

Morphological features of deepsea spiny eels also include a strongly compressed head and body; small, inferior mouth; dorsal fin composed of short, isolated spines; long-based anal fin, grading from spines anteriorly to soft rays posteriorly; minute, adherent cycloid scales; small teeth on the premaxillae, palatines, and dentaries but none on the maxillae; gill membranes united to each other and not connected to the isthmus by a frenum; well-developed gill rakers; and 6–13 branchiostegal rays. The pelvic fins are abdominal and their bases are connected ventrally.

Notacanthid fin spine and ray counts are highly variable, even among individuals captured in the same trawl, and some spines may be buried or difficult to distinguish from soft rays. The markedly different numbers of dorsal fin spines in the two eastern North Pacific species simplifies identification of those species.

Quast and Hall (1972) listed four notacanthids in their inventory of Alaskan fishes, but in revisions of the family and its genera McDowell (1973), Sulak et al. (1984), and Crabtree et al. (1985) classified them all in *Polyacanthonotus challengeri,* the longnose tapirfish. This species has not been reported from Alaska since Gilbert (1896) and Gill and Townsend (1897) described specimens collected in the southeastern Bering Sea more than a hundred years ago. The snubnosed spiny eel, *Notacanthus chemnitzii,* was not known to occur in the eastern North Pacific until Peden (1976) reported on four specimens taken off Oregon. That occurrence of *N. chemnitzii,* far from the previous records off Japan, suggests the species is widespread in the northern North Pacific and could be found in Alaskan waters.

Key to the Notacanthidae of Alaska

1 Dorsal spines more than 30 . . . . *Polyacanthonotus challengeri,* page 118

1 Dorsal spines fewer than 15 . . . . *Notacanthus chemnitzii,* page 119
(not known from Alaska)

Polyacanthonotus challengeri (Vaillant, 1888) **longnose tapirfish**

Southern Bering Sea; eastern North Pacific off southern British Columbia and Oregon; western North Pacific off Honshu; circumglobal, predominantly antitropical.

At depths of 1,260–3,753 m, most records below 2,000 m; benthopelagic.

D XXXII–XLVI; A XXVI–XXXV, about 130; Pec 10–15; Pel I,8–10; Br 8–10; GR 11–21; PC 3; Vert 254–284.

- **Creamy white to faintly pink**; posterior margins of anal and caudal fins and opercular flap black; mouth and gill membranes black.
- **Dorsal spines usually 32–38** (more than in *Notacanthus chemnitzii*).
- One row each of premaxillary, palatine, and mandibular teeth; all teeth clawlike, with tips smoothly recurved.
- Pyloric caeca very short, scarcely longer than broad, directed anteriorly.
- Length to 60 cm TL.

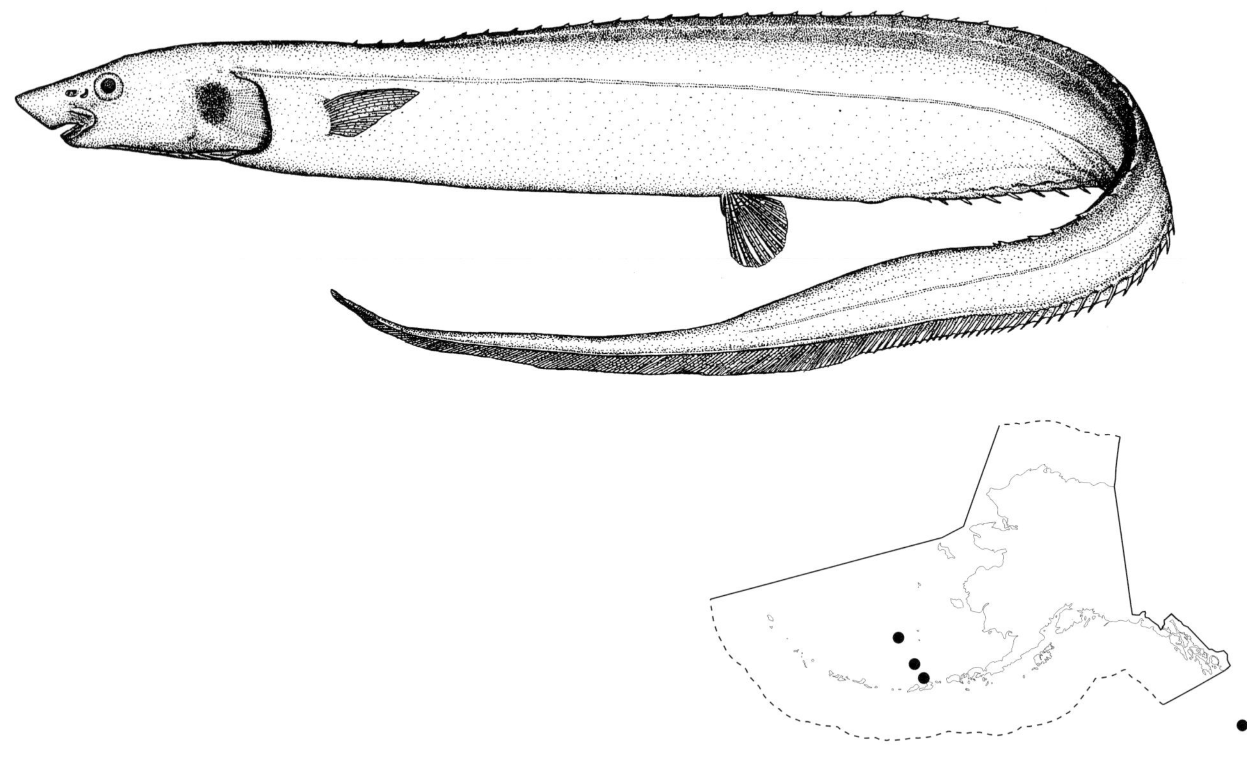

Notes & Sources — *Polyacanthonotus challengeri* (Vaillant, 1888)
Notacanthus challengeri Vaillant, 1888
Macdonaldia alta Gill & Townsend, 1897
Macdonaldia longa Gill & Townsend, 1897
Macdonaldia challengeri, Polyacanthonotus altus, P. longus: Quast and Hall 1972.
Complete synonymies were given by McDowell (1973) and Sulak et al. (1984).

Description: Stein and Butler 1971; McDowell 1973:161–173; Yabe in Amaoka et al. 1983:177; Sulak et al. 1984:65–66; Gon in Gon and Heemstra 1990:100–101.

Figure: Gon and Heemstra 1990:100; 46 cm TL, Kerguelen Islands, Indian Ocean.

Range: Recorded from three localities in the southeastern Bering Sea: by Gilbert (1896) west of Pribilof Islands at 56°12'N, 172°07'W, *Albatross* station 3308, depth 2,972 m; and by Gill and Townsend (1897) at 54°54'N, 168°59'W, *Albatross* station 3604, at depth of 2,562 m, and 54°11'N, 167°25'W, station 3607, at 1,805 m. Peden (1968) reported on the nearest record outside Alaska: from Pacific Ocean off Triangle Island, British Columbia, at 50°54'N, 130°06'W, two specimens taken in shrimp trawl at 2,103–2,196 m. Stein and Butler (1971) recorded specimens taken 120 km off Cape Falcon, Oregon. Minimum depth was recorded by Yabe (in Amaoka et al. 1983), and maximum depth by Sulak et al. (1984).

Notacanthus chemnitzii Bloch, 1788 — snubnosed spiny eel

Northeastern Pacific off Oregon and California; Japan; Greenland; probably distributed worldwide.

At depths of 128–3,285 m, usually captured at the greater depths; benthopelagic.

D V–XII; A XIII–XXI,110–130; Pec 12–17; Pel III–IV,6–11; Br 7–11; GR 12–17; PC 4; Vert 225–234.

- Head and body **uniformly dark brown**; margins of opercular flap and each fin blackish.
- **Dorsal spines usually 9 or 10** (fewer than in *Polyacanthonotus challengeri*).
- Teeth on premaxillae in 1 row, on palatines and dentaries in 2 or more rows; palatine and mandibular teeth more needlelike than clawlike.
- Pyloric caeca long, pointed, directed posteriorly.
- Length to more than 135 cm TL.

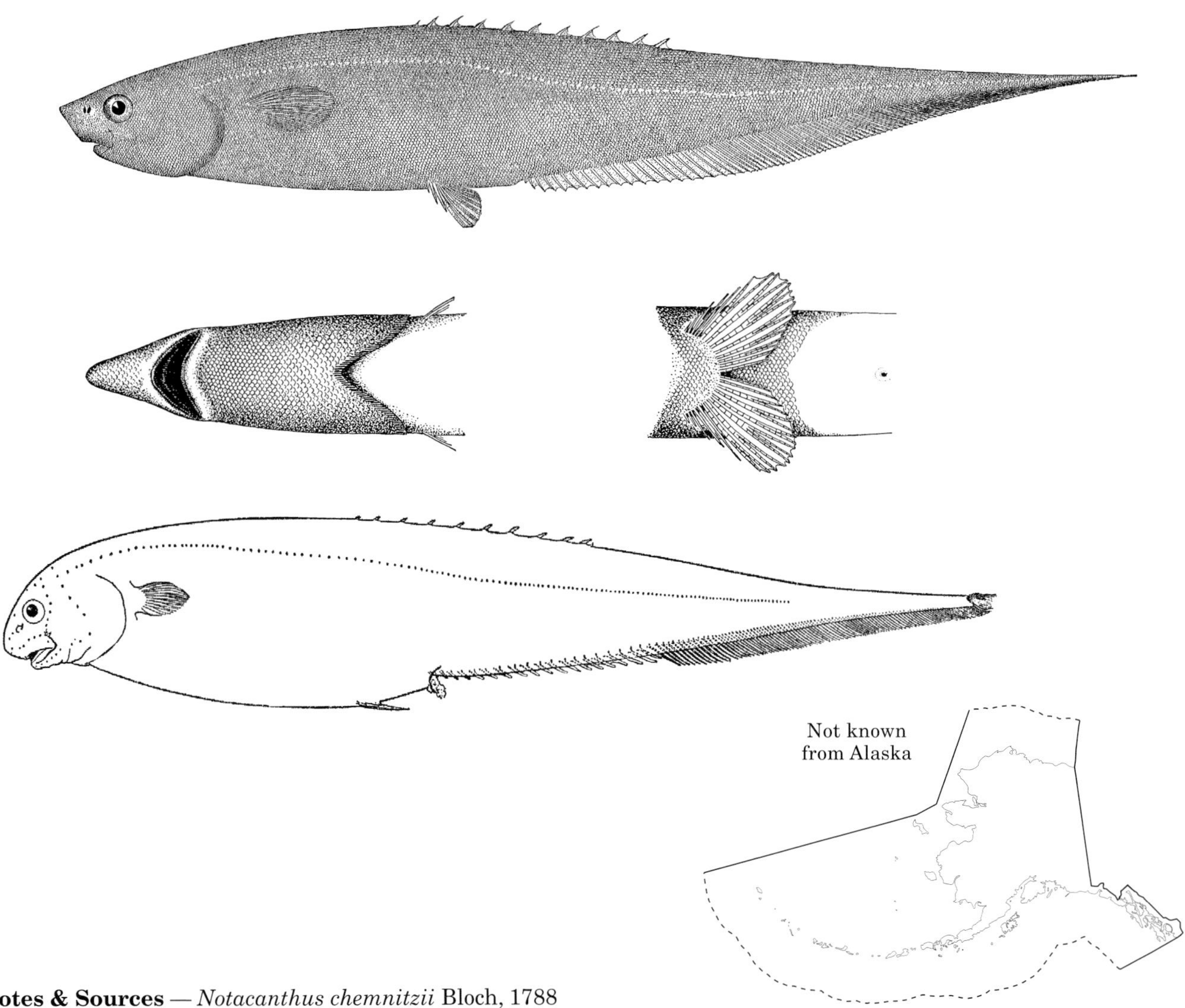

Notes & Sources — *Notacanthus chemnitzii* Bloch, 1788
Notacanthus phasganorus Goode, 1881
Notacanthus analis Gill, 1883
Coad (1995) called this species the largescale tapirfish.

Description: McDowell 1973:191–205; Peden 1976; Yabe in Amaoka et al. 1983:176; Lea and Rosenblatt 1987; Scott and Scott 1988:99–101; Coad 1995:397–398; Okamura and Takahashi in Okamura et al. 1995:61.

Figures: Upper: Goode and Bean 1896, figs. 184, 191A, 191B; 33 cm TL. Lower: Tucker and Jones 1951, pl. 7; 135 cm, tail broken. Both fish from western North Atlantic.

Range: Nearest record to Alaska comprises four specimens captured off Oregon in 1,536–1,554 m of water (Peden 1976). Lea and Rosenblatt (1987) recorded one specimen taken off Point Sur and one at the edge of Monterey Submarine Canyon, California. Minimum depth was recorded by McDowell (1973), and maximum by Yabe (in Amaoka et al. 1983).

Size: Estimated from centimeter scale shown with Tucker and Jones' (1951) figure of fish with tail tip broken off.

Order Anguilliformes
True eels

True eels, comprising 15 families with approximately 140 genera and 740 species, are widely distributed in the world's oceans but mainly inhabit tropical and subtropical regions. They occur in nearly every marine habitat, from coral reefs to the abyssal plain, and some species inhabit fresh water. One family is wholly catadromous. The specializations of true eels allow them to wedge through rocky crevices and other small openings, while some species are also adapted for burrowing in soft substrates or to exploit a pelagic lifestyle. Adults of four anguilliform species representing three families (Synaphobranchidae, Nemichthyidae, and Serrivomeridae) have been found in the marine waters of Alaska or nearby, off northern British Columbia.

Distinctive morphological characters of true eels include an elongate, compressed or rounded body with long-based, soft-rayed, dorsal and anal fins that are confluent with the caudal fin. All true eels lack pelvic fins, and many lack pectoral fins. In species having pectoral fins, the fins are high on the sides. The scales are cycloid, embedded, and mostly arranged in basketweave fashion if present, but in most eel species are absent. Gill rakers are absent. The gill membranes are united to the isthmus and the gill openings are small and slitlike or circular. The head and gill region are elongate, with the gills displaced posteriorly. There are 6–49 branchiostegal rays and 4 gill arches. The maxillae bear teeth and form most of the upper border of the mouth. Supramaxillae are absent. A swim bladder is present, and pyloric caeca and oviducts are absent.

Like the leptocephali of other elopomorphs, the various anguilliform leptocephali are restricted to relatively warm waters and are not likely to be found in Alaska. A possible exception is *Thalassenchelys coheni* Castle & Raju, a widespread North Pacific leptocephalus of uncertain family affinities. *Thalassenchelys* was referred to the Chlopsidae (formerly the Xenocongridae) by Castle and Raju (1975), but Smith (1979, 1994) and Lavenberg (1988) placed it in Anguilliformes incertae sedis. It keys out as an anguilliform leptocephalus from the small caudal fin, continuous with the dorsal and anal fins (Smith 1989b). *Thalassenchelys* is large, reaching at least 30 cm, and extremely deep-bodied. Some specimens contain developing eggs, indicating that *T. coheni* may be a neotenic species, in which transformation to an adult form does not occur, or the adult stage is short-lived. Eschmeyer and Herald (1983) called *T. coheni* the leaflike eel. It has been recorded from

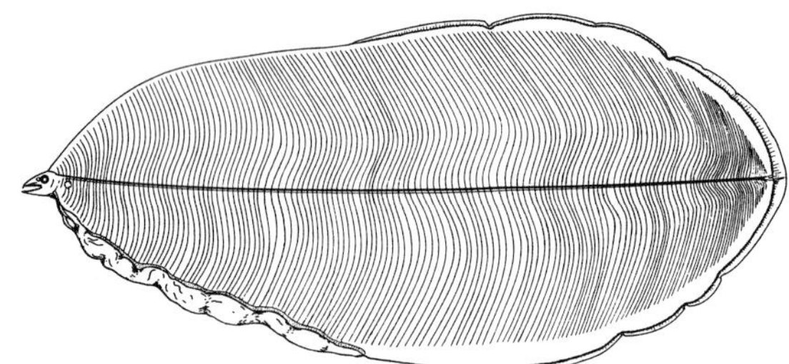

***Thalassenchelys coheni* leptocephalus**
(Adapted from Castle and Raju 1975; 246 mm TL.)

Baja California to British Columbia and across the Pacific Ocean nearly to Japan. A specimen of *T. coheni* (AB 95-32) caught west of northern Vancouver Island at 49°58'N, 130°32'W at a depth of 15 m or less in 1995 (B. L. Wing, pers. comm., 2 Jul. 1998) is the northernmost record. Peden (1998) reported that others are in the Royal British Columbia Museum; coordinates for one (RBCM 996-8-001) are 48°40'N, 126°43'W (K. Sendall, pers. comm., 22 Mar. 2000), placing it west of southern Vancouver Island. Detailed descriptions of *T. coheni* were given by Castle and Raju (1975), Smith (1979), and Shimokawa et al. (1995).

The Anguilliformes is a large and imperfectly known order, so classifications vary. Nelson's (1994) classification, following Robins (1989) and others, places the families represented in Alaska (by adults) in the suborder Congroidei, with fused frontal bones and with scales absent in most species. Robins (1989) gave a detailed list of anguilliform characteristics and discussed phylogenetic relationships within the order and with other elopomorphs.

Family Synaphobranchidae
Cutthroat eels

Gill slits low on the body and in many species meeting, or nearly meeting, on the ventral surface give the cutthroat eels their common name. Cutthroat eels are epibenthic predators and scavengers which primarily inhabit continental slopes and deeper bottoms in temperate to tropical waters. The geographic ranges of some synaphobranchid species are broad, extending nearly worldwide, and several exist in the North Pacific. As currently understood, the family comprises three subfamilies with 11 genera and 29 species (Sulak and

Shcherbachev 1997). Alaskan records include one well-documented example each of two of the most widespread species in the Synaphobranchinae: *Synaphobranchus affinis* and *Histiobranchus bathybius.*

In cutthroat eels the gill openings are located below the pectoral fins, or in that region. A few species lack pectoral fins, but not the two Alaskan species. Eels in the subfamily Synaphobranchinae, including the Alaskan species, have a long, lightly built lower jaw; a compressed, pointed head; and small, needle-like teeth. The body has scales, the gill openings are confluent ventrally or only slightly separated, and coloration is pale dorsally grading to darker ventrally. Vertebral numbers in the family range from 110 to 205. The leptocephali have telescopic eyes.

The valid record of *H. bathybius* in Alaska is an old one, and was included in the inventory by Quast and Hall (1972): a specimen taken west of the Pribilof Islands in 1890 by the U.S. Fish Commission research vessel *Albatross,* and described by Gilbert (1896). The mention of Bering Strait as an additional collection locality by Jordan and Evermann (1896a,b) is an error, perpetuating an incorrect statement made by Jordan and Davis (1891) regarding the collection locality for Gilbert's specimen. The record of *S. affinis* in the Bering Sea is relatively new: a single specimen collected southwest of the Pribilof Islands in 1962 by the Russian ichthyologist V. V. Fedorov during a survey using the research vessel *Adler* (B. A. Sheiko, pers. comm., 15 Feb. 2000), and later identified by Sulak and Shcherbachev (1997).

Histiobranchus has been classified from time to time as a junior synonym of *Synaphobranchus,* as in the systematic review of synaphobranchids emphasizing Atlantic species by Robins and Robins (1989). Sulak and Shcherbachev (1997) provided a worldwide synopsis of species in six genera of cutthroat eels and a detailed argument for reestablishing the distinctiveness of *Synaphobranchus* and *Histiobranchus.*

Key to the Synaphobranchidae of Alaska

1 Origin of dorsal fin far back, remote from head and directly above or slightly anterior or posterior to anus . . . . *Synaphobranchus affinis,* page 122

1 Origin of dorsal fin not far back, near head and anterior to anus and origin of anal fin . . . . *Histiobranchus bathybius,* page 123

Synaphobranchus affinis Günther, 1877 **slope cutthroat eel**

Bering Sea; circumglobal in temperate to tropical seas, including numerous records in southeastern Pacific, northwestern Pacific, and vicinity of Hawaiian Islands, but unknown in northeastern Pacific except for one Bering Sea record.

At depths of 290–2,334 m; primarily inhabiting middle to lower slope, mostly taken at 500–1,500 m.

Pec 14–18; Pel 0; Vert 125–150.

- Blackish to brownish or pinkish gray dorsally; darker ventrally; fins sometimes white-margined.
- Mouth long, maxilla extending well past eye; **anus located in anterior third of total length**.
- **Dorsal fin origin above anal fin origin or not far from this point**; pelvic fin absent; pectoral fin longer than half of gape length.
- Scales covering body; scales small, oval–elongate, in irregular groups at right angles to each other in loose basketweave pattern.
- Preoperculomandibular pores 11–14.
- Vomerine teeth very small, inconspicuous, essentially uniserial.
- **Gill openings ventrally placed and confluent along midline**.
- Length to 160 cm TL.

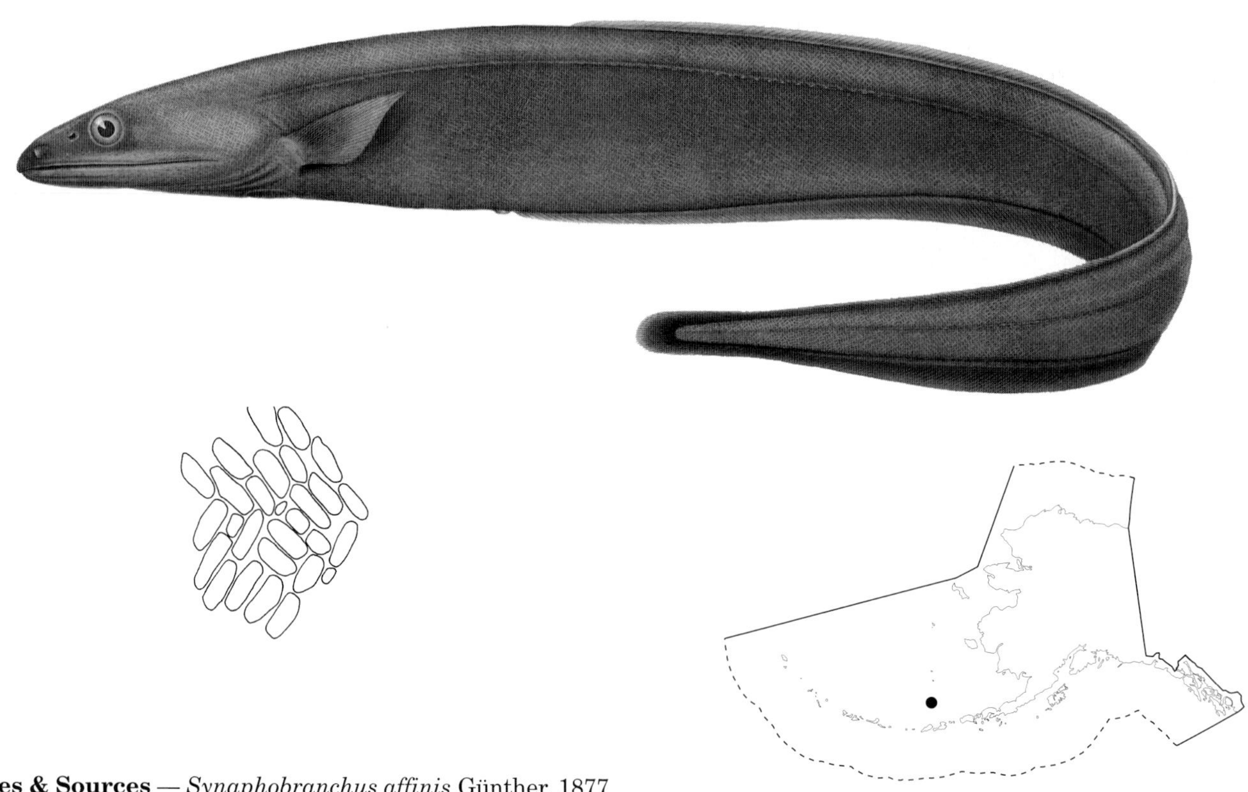

Notes & Sources — *Synaphobranchus affinis* Günther, 1877
Synaphobranchus brachysomus Gilbert, 1905
Usually distinguishable from other species of *Synaphobranchus* occurring in the North Pacific by position of the dorsal fin origin, which is well behind the anal fin origin in the other species.
Robins and Robins (1989) classified *S. brachysomus* in *S. affinis*.

Description: Gilbert 1905:583; Asano in Masuda et al. 1984:26; Robins and Robins 1989:223–225; Sulak and Shcherbachev 1997:1166–1171.

Figures: Full lateral view: Smithsonian Institution, NMNH, Division of Fishes, artist W. S. Atkinson; holotype of *S. brachysomus*, 71 cm TL, vicinity of Kauai, Hawaiian Islands. Scale pattern: after Sulak and Shcherbachev 1997, fig. 9A.

Range: Sulak and Shcherbachev (1997) determined that an eel (ZIN 37518) collected many years previously from the southeastern Bering Sea by Russian researchers is an example of *S. affinis*. They did not give the catch locality, but V. V. Fedorov (via B. A. Sheiko, pers. comm., 15 Feb. 2000) said he collected the specimen during a survey using the Russian research vessel *Adler* in 1962 at station 2, between the Pribilof Islands and Unalaska Island at great depths; this places it on the eastern slope of the Aleutian Basin. No records are known for the eastern Pacific south of Alaska, but several specimens have been collected from the western Pacific off the southern Kuril Islands and farther south. Shinohara and Matsuura (1997) recorded *S. affinis* from three stations in Suruga Bay in the central part of the Japanese archipelago; Suruga Bay reaches a depth of 2,500 m. Gilbert (1905) recorded specimens from several locations in the vicinity of the Hawaiian Islands.

Histiobranchus bathybius (Günther, 1877) deepwater cutthroat eel

Bering Sea; circumglobal in temperate to tropical seas, occasionally found in polar waters; known in eastern Pacific from one Bering Sea record and one off Mexico.

At depths of 644–4,700 m; primarily inhabiting continental rise, most specimens taken at depths of 2,000–3,500 m.

D 265–331; A 188–203; Pec 15; Pel 0; Br 15–19; Vert 122–146.

- Black to blackish brown; darker ventrally.
- Mouth long, eye over middle of its cleft; **anus located at middle of total length**.
- **Dorsal fin origin far forward, over pectoral fin**; pelvic fin absent; pectoral fin small, shorter than half of gape length.
- Scales covering body; scales small, elongate, in groups at right angles to each other in tight basketweave pattern.
- Preoperculomandibular pores 6–9.
- Vomerine teeth smaller than premaxillary teeth and becoming smaller posteriorly, irregularly biserial to multiserial.
- **Gill openings ventrally placed and distinctly separate**.
- Length to 90 cm TL.

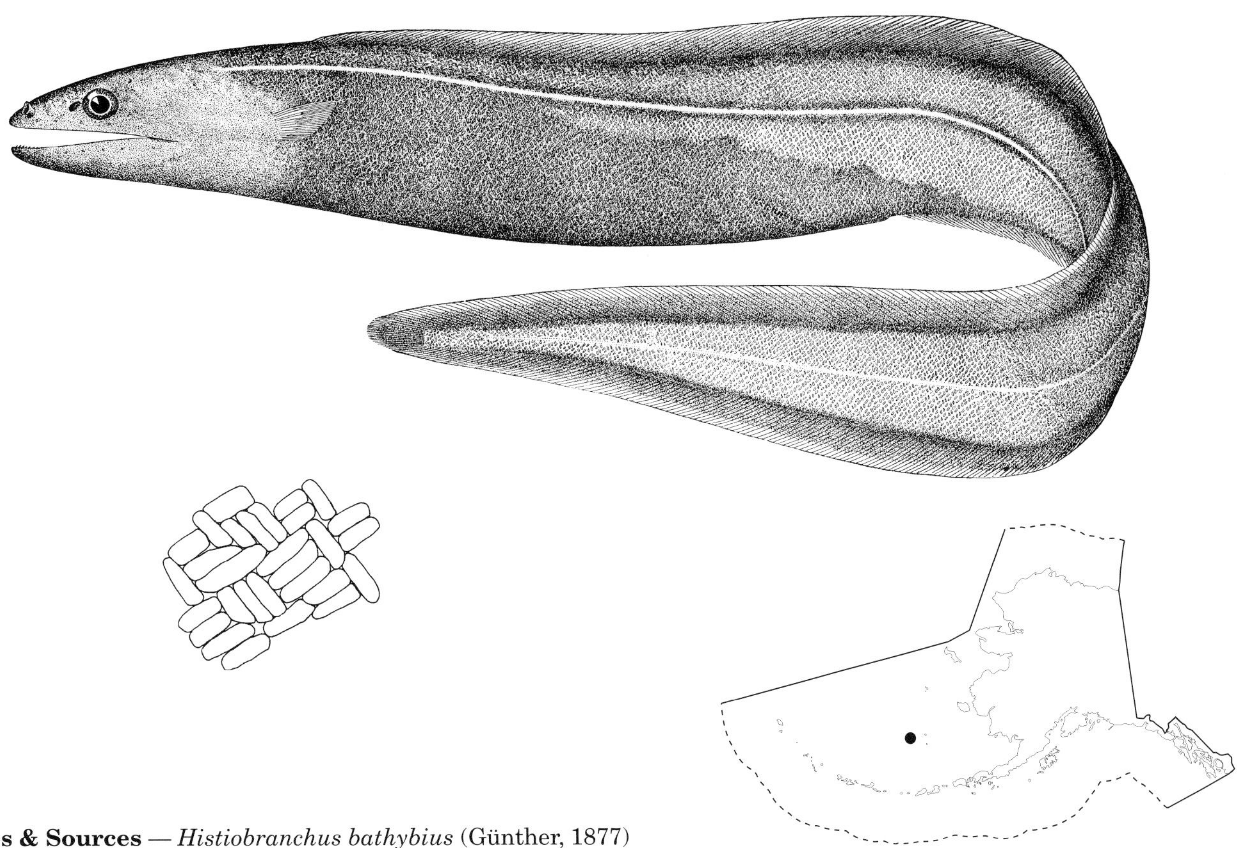

Notes & Sources — *Histiobranchus bathybius* (Günther, 1877)
Synaphobranchus bathybius Günther, 1877
Histiobranchus infernalis Gill, 1883

Description: Jordan and Evermann 1896b:352; Asano in Masuda et al. 1984:26; Okamura and Machida 1987:109; Robins and Robins 1989:230–232; Gon in Gon and Heemstra 1990:103–104; Sulak and Shcherbachev 1997:1166–1171.

Figures: Full lateral view: Goode and Bean 1896, fig. 165; western Atlantic. Scale pattern: after Sulak and Shcherbachev 1997, fig. 9F.

Range: Gilbert (1896) described a specimen (USNM 48693) taken in 1890 west of the Pribilof Islands at *Albatross* station 3308, 56°12'N, 172°07'W, with a deepsea trawl over a bottom of green ooze at 2,972 m of depth. Jordan and Evermann (1896a,b) incorrectly listed the Bering Strait as another collection locality, evidently following an incorrect statement by Jordan and Davis (1891:673) on the collection locality for Gilbert's specimen. (The paper on apodal eels by Jordan and Davis [1891] contains other errors that could have led to other misstatements on range of eels in Alaska. For example, in their summary list they give "A" to mean distribution in Alaska, but for most of the list the A obviously refers to the Atlantic.) The only eastern Pacific record outside the Bering Sea is a specimen taken in 1959 off the tip of Baja California in an otter trawl over a bottom depth of 3,000 m (SIO 59-269); evidently, the Mexican specimen mentioned by Sulak and Shcherbachev (1997). Known off Japan from numerous records, several of them recent (e.g., Shinohara and Matsuura 1997).

Family Nemichthyidae
Threadtail snipe eels

Threadtail snipe eels are slender, elongate midwater eels with jaws produced, except in ripe males, into a long, nonocclusible beak with many small posteriorly directed teeth. The beak is said to resemble that of a snipe, and several families of eels with similar jaws are commonly called snipe eels. Nemichthyid eels are called threadtail snipe eels because in some species the caudal fin is drawn out into a long, delicate filament. The Nemichthyidae is a small family comprising three genera with nine species. Two species have been recorded from Alaskan waters.

Other diagnostic characters of threadtail snipe eels include: dorsal and anal fins confluent with caudal fin; pectoral fins present; pelvic fins absent; dorsal fin origin near pectoral fin base; anus far in front of midbody; scales absent; lateral line complete, pores easily discernible; preopercle absent; gill openings limited to the sides, with gill membranes connected to the isthmus; and 170 to more than 750 vertebrae. Individuals of some species have been known to reach 145 cm (57 inches) or more in length. As the males reach sexual maturity the beak undergoes a drastic shortening and loss of teeth; these and other degenerative changes suggest that threadtail snipe eels spawn once and die.

Threadtail snipe eels are typically caught by research vessels using fine-mesh midwater trawls, but occasionally specimens are cast ashore by storms, caught in purse seines, or found in the stomachs of other fishes. Observers in submersibles have seen threadtail snipe eels hanging vertically in the water.

The two species of threadtail snipe eel known to occur in Alaska are blackline snipe eel, *Avocettina infans*, and slender snipe eel, *Nemichthys scolopaceus*. Records of each species from the region are rare. Their slender shape allows them to easily slip through collecting nets. Quast and Hall (1972) listed *A. gilli* as a confirmed Alaskan species, along with three others as likely Alaskan species: *A. infans, N. avocettta,* and *N. scolopaceus. Avocettina gilli* is now classified as a junior synonym of *A. infans*. Its presence in Alaska was recently documented by additional records. *Nemichthys avocetta* is a junior synonym of *N. scolopaceus*. A specimen of *N. scolopaceus* collected from the western Gulf of Alaska near Kodiak Island in 1998 is the first verifiable record from Alaska. In 2000, two more specimens were collected from the eastern Gulf of Alaska in Sitka Sound. The pale snipe eel, *N. larseni,* is included herein as a possible Alaskan species. Described in 1978 by Nielsen and Smith, this species is relatively new to science. A pale snipe eel collected in 1995 west of northern Washington represents a northward extension of the species' known range from Oregon.

Classification of threadtail snipe eels in this guide follows Nielsen and Smith (1978) and Smith and Nielsen (1989). Karmovskaya (1982, 1990) proposed a different classification but did not account for several eastern Pacific records or provide a detailed analysis. More study is needed, particularly of specimens from the north-central and northwestern Pacific, to resolve taxonomic problems in Nemichthyidae (Smith and Nielsen 1989).

Key to the Nemichthyidae of Alaska

1 Caudal filament absent; anus well behind pectoral fins; lateral line pores in 1 row; sensory ridges present on head behind eyes ...... *Avocettina infans,* page 125

1 Caudal filament present; anus below pectoral fins; lateral line pores in 3 rows; no sensory ridges on head behind eyes ...... (2)

2 (1) Rectangle outlining each quincunx of lateral-line pores longer than high; color dark; postorbital pores 3–20 (mean 10.7); preopercular pores 2–18 (mean 7.2) ...... *Nemichthys scolopaceus,* page 126

2 Rectangle outlining each quincunx of lateral-line pores shorter than high; color pale; postorbital pores 12–23 (mean 16.8); preopercular pores 8–17 (mean 11.5) ...... *Nemichthys larseni,* page 127
(not known from Alaska)

Avocettina infans (Günther, 1878) **blackline snipe eel**

Aleutian Islands to central Mexico, including Gulf of California; in all oceans, almost exclusively in Northern Hemisphere.

Surface to 4,571 m; primarily mesopelagic and upper bathypelagic; rarely, if ever, over continental shelf.

D 279–432; A 240–372; Pec 14–18; Pel 0; LLp 181–201; Vert 187–202.

- Dusky brown to black, with intensification of pigment along lateral line.
- Body moderately long; **elongate sensory ridges behind eye; jaw tips slightly expanded**.
- Dorsal fin origin near pectoral fin base, predorsal length 21–39% of preanal length; **no caudal filament**; pelvic fin absent.
- **Single row of large lateral line pores**, 1 per body segment.
- **Anus well behind pectoral fin**, a head length or more posterior to pectoral base.
- Length to 80 cm TL.

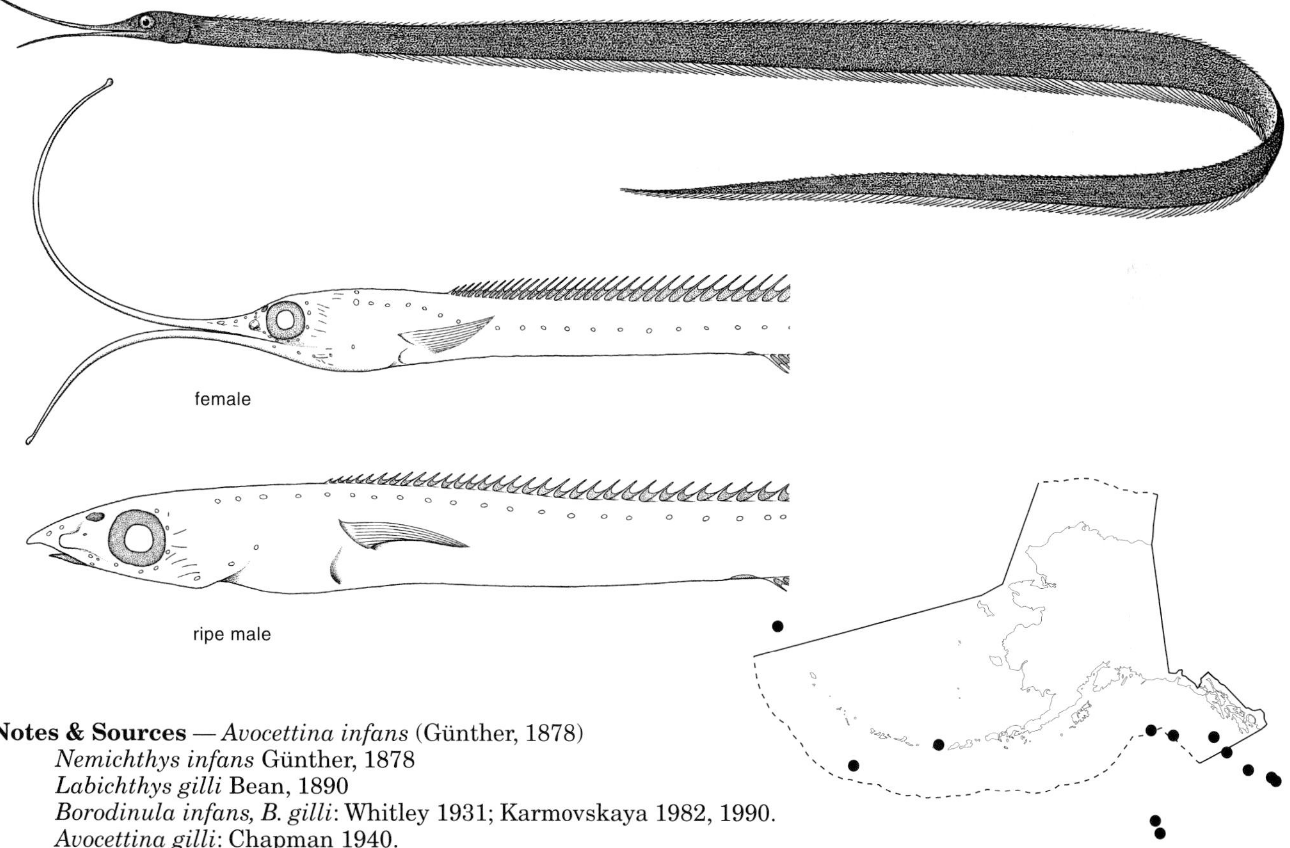

Notes & Sources — *Avocettina infans* (Günther, 1878)
Nemichthys infans Günther, 1878
Labichthys gilli Bean, 1890
Borodinula infans, B. gilli: Whitley 1931; Karmovskaya 1982, 1990.
Avocettina gilli: Chapman 1940.
Sympatric with smalleye snipe eel, *Avocettina bowersii* (Garman, 1899), in the southern part of its range but *A. bowersii* is not known to occur north of southern California.

Description: Bean 1890b:45; Nielsen and Smith 1978:24–29; Nielsen in Whitehead et al. 1986:552; Smith and Nielsen 1989:448–450. Preserved specimens range from nearly completely bleached and pale to uniformly black. The Chapman (1940) specimen with 157 pores has proven to be incomplete (Nielsen and Smith 1978).

Figures: Upper: Smithsonian Institution, NMNH, Division of Fishes, artist S. F. Denton, Apr. 1889; holotype of *L. gilli,* 462 mm TL, southeastern Alaska. Lower: Nielsen and Smith 1978: fig. 13.

Range: First recorded from Alaska by Bean (1890b), as holotype of *L. gilli* Bean from *Albatross* station 2859, west (*not* east as stated by Bean) of Prince of Wales Island at 55°20'N, 136°20'W, depth 2,870 m. Peden et al. (1985) recorded it from Alaska south of the Andreanof Islands at 49°14'N, 178°03'W (NMC 69-421); and near Yunaska Island at 53°03'N, 170°14'W (BCPM 980-568; found on deck, possibly regurgitated by predatory fish). Additional Alaskan specimens C.W.M. examined are: UW 26552 (2), 55°48'N, 141°55'W, Durgin Seamount, depth 704 m; and UW 26553 (1), 56°02'N, 144°23'W, Surveyor Seamount, depth 585 m. The former lot is the "*Aricotena bowersi*" listed, but misspelled and misidentified, by Hughes (1981). Shinohara et al. (1994) recorded two specimens south of the Alaska border at 53°57'N, 135°31'W, depth 1,300 m. Other nearby eastern Pacific records are those of Jordan (1896), Chapman (1940), Taylor (1967), Hart (1973), and Peden et al. (1985). Fedorov and Sheiko (2002) reported *A. infans* to occur, but rarely, near the Commander Islands, partly based on the Bering Sea record of Fedorov (1973a). *Avocettina infans* makes diurnal vertical migrations (Nielsen and Smith 1978).

Size: Smith and Nielsen 1989.

Nemichthys scolopaceus Richardson, 1848 **slender snipe eel**

Western Gulf of Alaska to South America; cosmopolitan in temperate and tropical seas to 42°S.

Surface to 3,656 m; attracted at night to surface by lights; primarily mesopelagic and upper bathypelagic, sometimes collected over continental shelf.

D and A more than 300 each; Pec 10–14; Pel 0; Vert 400 to 750 or more.

- **Brown**, darker ventrally (reversal of usual pattern in fishes).
- Body extremely long; **no sensory ridges behind eye; jaw tips pointed**.
- **Tail ending in long filament**, often broken off; pelvic fin absent.
- Postorbital pores 3–20 (mean 10.7); preopercular pores 2–18 (mean 7.2).
- **Lateral line pores in 3 rows**, forming units of 4 pores in rectangle with 5th pore in center (quincunx); **rectangles longer than high**.
- **Anus below pectoral fin**.
- Length to 145 cm TL.

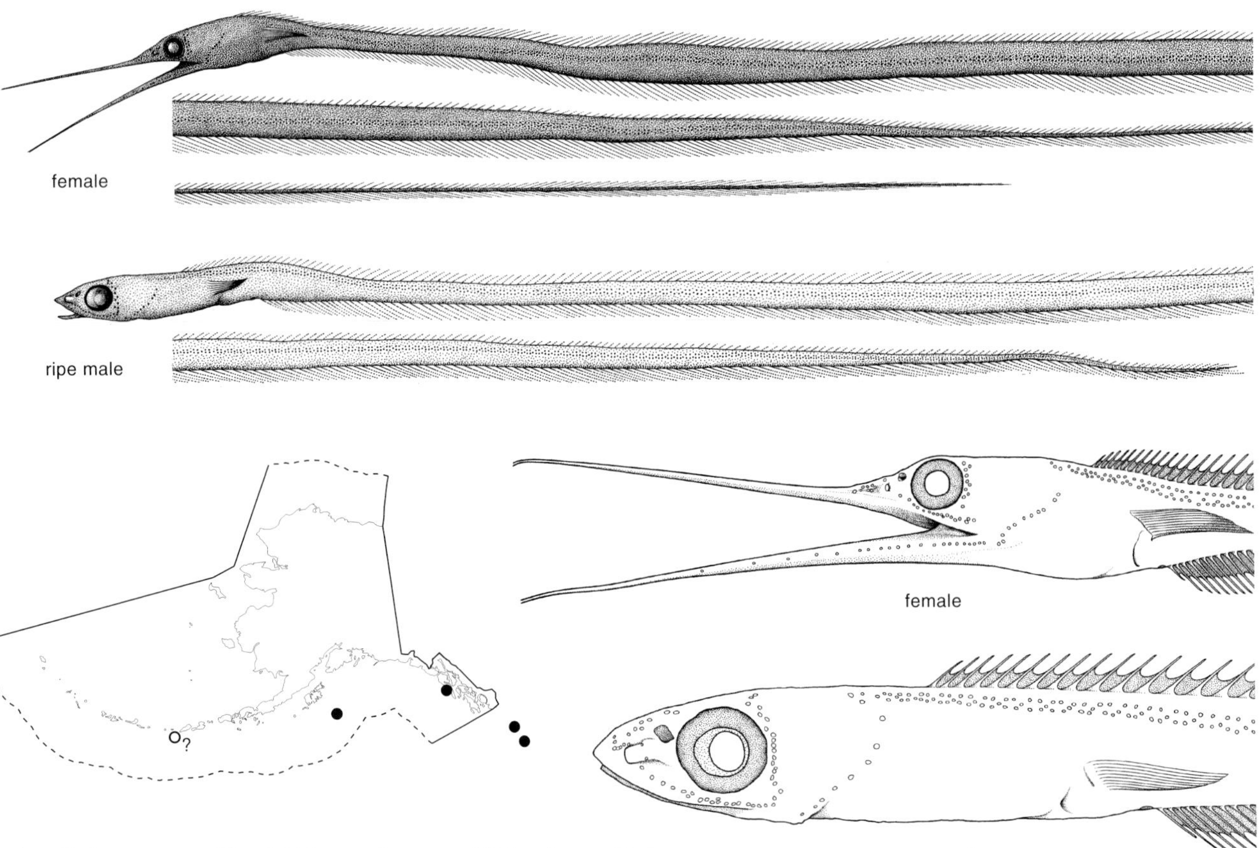

Notes & Sources — *Nemichthys scolopaceus* Richardson, 1848
Nemichthys avocetta Jordan & Gilbert, 1881
Also called brown snipe eel (e.g., Hubbs et al. 1979).

Description: Jordan and Gilbert 1881a:409–410; Nielsen and Smith 1978:38–47; Nielsen in Whitehead et al. 1986:553–554; Smith and Nielsen 1989:454–457.

Figures: Nielsen and Smith 1978, figs. 22 and 23; female, 680 mm TL; male, 460 mm TL; Atlantic Ocean.

Range: The first confirmed record from Alaska is a female (AB 98-19; over 60 cm TL) collected at 55°56'N, 150°47'W, off Cape Chiniak, Kodiak Island, at night on 29 Mar. 1998, depth 36–90 m; identified by D. G. Smith and C.W.M. Two specimens (610–645 mm TL) collected in Sitka Sound between St. Lazaria and Kruzof islands at 57°00'N, 135°43'W on 16 Jul. 2000 are the second Alaskan record (see color photograph in this book). They were captured in a modified herring trawl towed by the USFWS research vessel *Tiglax* at 15–25 m during 1406–1438 hours. Currently in the Point Stephens Research collection, the eels will be permanently housed at the UAF. British Columbia records include a specimen (UBC 53-326; Clemens and Wilby 1946) captured near Butedale (53°10'N, 128°40'W); one found on the beach at Beacon Hill, Victoria (Jordan 1896); one near Vancouver Island (BCPM 972-62); and one in the Strait of Georgia at 51°57'N, 128°25'W (UBC 53-207; Nielsen and Smith 1978). Fitch and Lavenberg (1968), Miller and Lea (1972), and Hart (1973) gave a range to Alaska, but documentation for those reports was not found. Quast and Hall (1972) and Nielsen and Smith (1978) gave British Columbia for known northern limit. Matarese et al. (1989) gave a range to the Aleutian Islands, but the NMFS survey database has no records of *N. scolopaceus* from Alaska; only one record, without a voucher specimen, of a *Nemichthys* not identified to species from 52°25'N, 169°30'W (J. W. Orr, pers. comm., 13 Nov. 1997).

Size: Miller and Lea 1972.

Nemichthys larseni Nielsen & Smith, 1978 **pale snipe eel**

Eastern North Pacific from west of Washington state to central Mexico, including Gulf of California, and west to Hawaii.

At depths of about 170–1,280 m; far from shore and mostly at mesopelagic depths.

D and A more than 300 each; Pec 10–12; Pel 0; Vert 400 or more.

- **Pale**; may turn dark gray as spawning condition is reached.
- Body extremely long; **no sensory ridges behind eye; jaw tips pointed**.
- **Tail ending in long filament**, often broken off; pelvic fin absent.
- Postorbital pores 12–23 (mean 16.8); preopercular pores 8–17 (mean 11.5).
- **Lateral line pores in 3 rows**, forming units of 4 pores in rectangle with 5th pore in center (quincunx); **rectangles higher than long or nearly square**.
- **Anus below pectoral fin**.
- Length to about 97 cm TL.

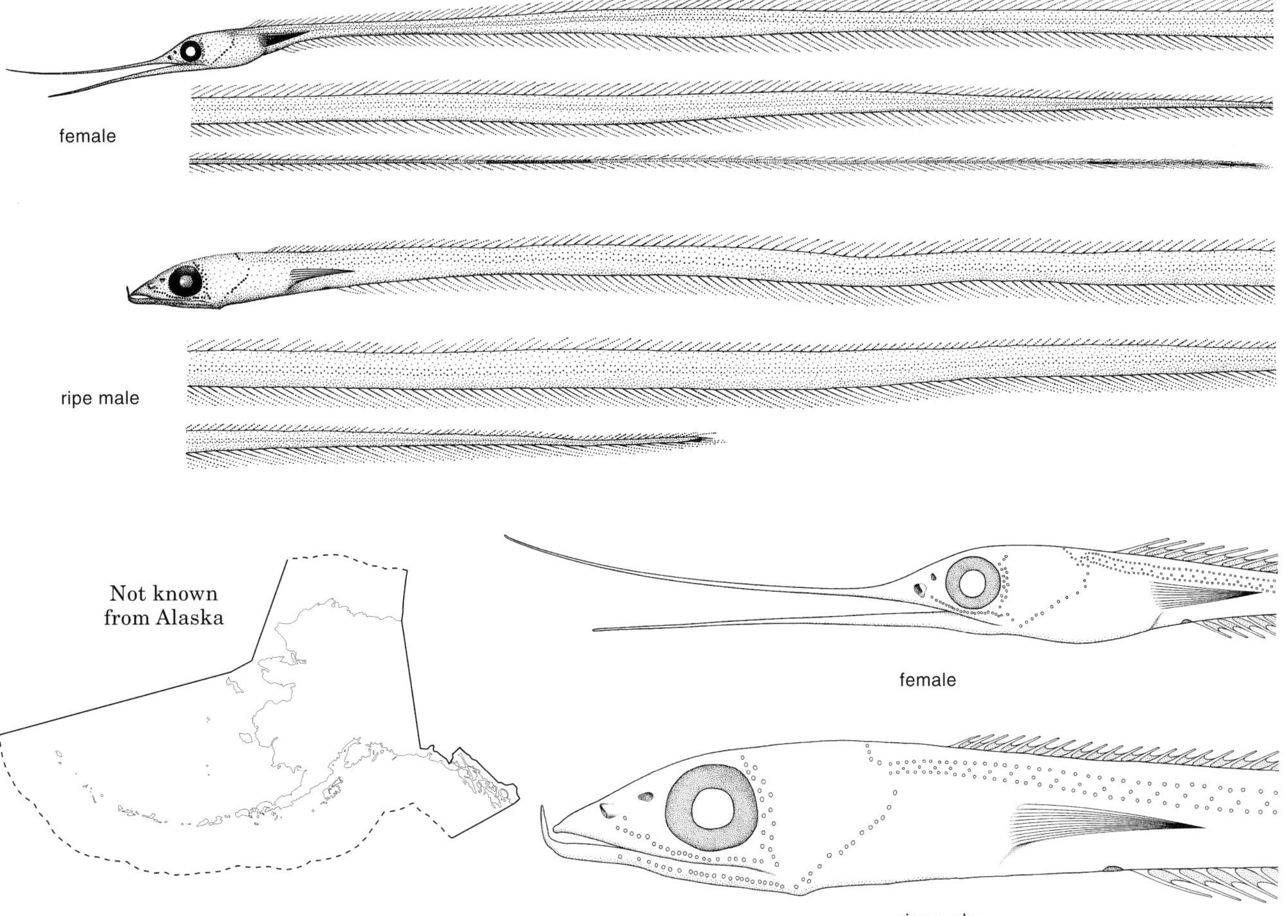

Notes & Sources — *Nemichthys larseni* Nielsen & Smith, 1978

Description: Nielsen and Smith 1978:38–47. Described from 23 specimens.

Figures: Nielsen and Smith 1978, figs. 34 and 35; holotype, female, 595 mm TL; paratype, male, 450 mm TL; eastern North Pacific Ocean.

Range: A specimen of *N. larseni* (AB 95-39) collected in 1995 west of Washington at 47°56'N, 131°26'W, trawl depth range 0–300 m, represents an extension northward of the recorded range from Oregon. Identified by D. G. Smith and C.W.M., 16 Nov. 1999, the specimen measures more than 60 cm TL and is whole but coiled (as is common for nemichthyid specimens), and accurate length could not be obtained without damaging it. Depths given above are from Nielsen and Smith (1978) for specimens they examined, and are maximum fishing depths of nonclosing nets. Northernmost specimen they examined was collected west of Oregon at 44°35'N, 125°44'W. There are no records of this species over the continental shelf.

Size: Most *Nemichthys* specimens are broken, with the tail filament and part of the beak missing, so Nielsen and Smith (1978) reported lengths as SL_{200}, which is defined as the distance from the posterior edge of the orbit to vertebra number 201. For holotype they gave SL_{200} 324 mm and TL 595 mm, giving SL_{200} = 54% of TL. The SL_{200} for the largest specimen examined was 522 mm, which would be *roughly* 967 mm TL.

Family Serrivomeridae
Sawtooth eels

Sawtooth eels pursue a pelagic lifestyle in temperate to tropical waters of the Pacific, Indian, and Atlantic oceans from near the surface to abyssal depths. The family as currently understood includes 10 species in three genera. With their long, slender jaws, sawtooth eels seem at first glance to resemble threadtail snipe eels (family Nemichthyidae), and are sometimes called snipe eels, but the groups are readily differentiated by several features. One of the most obvious is the more posterior placement of the dorsal fin in most sawtooth eels, well behind the head and behind the origin of the anal fin. The presence of sawlike teeth along the vomer, for which these eels are sometimes called sawpalates, is another critical diagnostic feature.

Other diagnostic morphological features of sawtooth eels include: dorsal and anal fins confluent with caudal fin; pectoral fins rudimentary or absent; pelvic fins absent; anus anterior to midbody; teeth on maxillae and dentaries small and acute, set in multiple rows; vomerine teeth enlarged, closely set in two or more rows; scales absent; lateral line pores minute; gill openings broad, starting high on the sides and connected ventrally, with gill membranes attached to the isthmus except at their posterior margins; branchiostegal rays 6 or 7; and vertebrae 137–170. Most species are black, with a silver coating. At maturity sawtooth eels attain maximum lengths of 20 cm (8 inches) in some species to 78 cm (31 inches) or more in others.

Three species of sawtooth eel occur in the eastern North Pacific Ocean as far north as Mexico or California, but only the crossthroat sawpalate, *Serrivomer jesperseni,* occurs north of California. This species has not been reported from Alaskan waters, but there are two British Columbia records. At the time Quast and Hall (1972) compiled their list of Alaskan fish species, one specimen of *S. jesperseni* had been recorded from Queen Charlotte Sound (Taylor 1967a,b). Since then, Peden and Hughes (1986) reported on a specimen collected off Vancouver Island.

The genus *Serrivomer* was revised most recently by Beebe and Crane (1936). Although the family Serrivomeridae contains some of the most common midwater eels of the world's oceans, they all require further study to definitively delineate the species (Castle in Smith and Heemstra 1986). Tighe (1989) reviewed family characteristics and western Atlantic species, but the taxonomy of *Serrivomer* on a worldwide basis has not been critically examined.

Serrivomer jesperseni Bauchot-Boutin, 1953 **crossthroat sawpalate**

Eastern Pacific from British Columbia to Gulf of Panama; south of about 25°N in central and western Pacific Ocean and in Indian Ocean.

At depths of 366–825 m over continental slope and rise; mesopelagic.

D 141–170; A 127–161; C 6; Pec 6–7; Pel 0; Vert 148–150.

- Dusky brown to blackish; mouth, gill cavities, and peritoneum black.
- Body greatly elongate and slender; snout beaklike, less than half of head length; lower jaw longer than upper; eye small, closer to snout tip than to gill opening.
- Dorsal fin origin well behind anus and anal fin origin; pectoral fin very small; pelvic fin absent.
- Multiple rows of small sharp teeth in upper and lower jaws; 2 rows of large bladelike teeth forming high serrated ridge along center of vomer, prominently entering profile of opened mouth.
- Lateral line pores not discernible.
- Length to 67 cm SL.

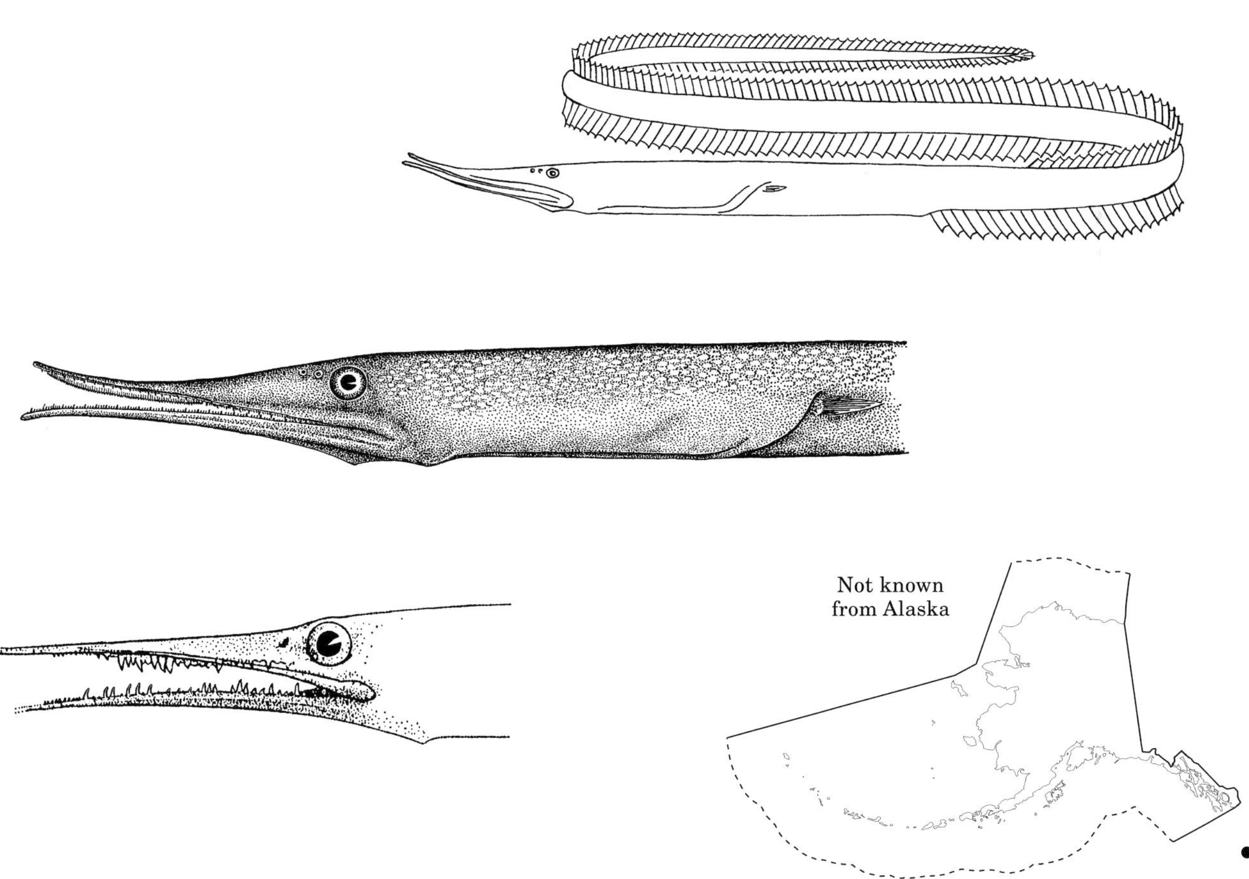

Notes & Sources — *Serrivomer jesperseni* Bauchot-Boutin, 1953

Description: Taylor 1967b:2108–2110; Hart 1973:86.

Figures: Whole fish and upper head: Hart 1973:86, after Garman 1899; from Gulf of Panama. Lower head: Taylor 1967b, fig. 2; off British Columbia.

Range: The nearest published record to Alaska is a specimen taken in Queen Charlotte Sound south of Cape St. James at 51°36'N, 131°09'W at 730–825 m in water 2,290–2,380 m deep, and described by Taylor (1967b). That record extended the known range north from the Gulf of Panama. Since then, specimens have been collected west of northern Baja California, including specimens housed in the Scripps Institution of Oceanography collection (e.g., SIO 72-374, 30°58'N, 155°20'W; SIO 76-81, 30°42'N, 147°23'W). The only other published record from British Columbia is based on a specimen taken in 1980 off Vancouver Island at 49°55'N, 126°35'W, at depth range of 366–512 m, reported on by Peden and Hughes (1986).

Size: SIO 64-21, 665 mm SL, collected in 1964 southwest of Bahia Magdalena at 24°11'N, 113°07'W. Previously recorded to 640 mm SL by Peden and Hughes (1986).

Order Saccopharyngiformes
Gulper eels

Fishes of the order Saccopharyngiformes are highly modified midwater eels. They are collectively called gulper eels after one of the order's two suborders, the Saccopharyngoidei, whose members have a highly distensible pharynx and can swallow extremely large prey. With their extreme skeletal reduction and other aberrant features, they are perhaps the most anatomically modified of all vertebrate species (Bertelsen et al. 1989). The Cyematoidei, which is the saccopharyngiform suborder most likely to be represented in Alaskan waters, shows less extreme modifications.

In Nelson's (1994) classification, followed here, the saccopharyngiforms are a separate order. However, there is disagreement over their precise relationships to the anguilliforms. Gulper eels were classified as a suborder in Anguilliformes by Greenwood (1977), Nelson (1984), and other authors partly because of having a leptocephalus stage and, as adults, an elongate, eel-like body form. However, Hulet and Robins (1989) believed the leptocephalus, a stage common to all elopomorph fishes, to be a shared primitive state and, as such, not usable for proving relationships between groups which have it. Gulper eel leptocephali are very deep-bodied and have V-shaped, rather than W-shaped, myomeres. Robins (1989) and Smith (1989a) reviewed the taxonomic history of the Saccopharyngiformes and summarized the reasons for separating saccopharyngiforms from the anguilliforms and from higher groups of bony fishes. One character unique to saccopharyngiforms, among all bony fishes, is the presence of connected efferent branchial arteries forming loops around and between the gill clefts. Small, pouched gills with plumelike gill filaments and projecting sensory papillae on the body lateral-line system are other shared derived features of fishes in this order. Their specializations also include absence of opercular bones and branchiostegal rays. Other structures absent in saccopharyngiforms are ribs, pelvic fins, scales, pyloric caeca, and swim bladder. The hyomandibular articulates with the neurocranium by a single condyle, the dorsal and anal fins are long, the fin rays are unsegmented, the caudal fin is absent or rudimentary, the gill openings are ventral or ventrolateral, and the jaws are greatly elongate.

Like anguilliforms, saccopharyngiforms probably die after spawning, and their leptocephali occur at shallower depths than the adults.

Family Cyematidae
Bobtail eels

The cyematids are sometimes called the bobtail snipe eels, but this is a holdover from their previous, long association with snipe eels in the order Anguilliformes. It is less confusing to call them bobtail eels; as in, for example, Hubbs et al. (1979). Two bobtail eel genera, each with one species, are recognized as valid by taxonomists. Both species are bathypelagic carnivores. They have a dartlike profile, from the long, pointed snout and slender body to the posteriorly positioned dorsal and anal fins with their rays increasing in length from front to back. *Cyema atrum* inhabits the Pacific, Indian, and Atlantic oceans at temperate to tropical latitudes, and appears to be the deepest-living of all the pelagic eels. This species has been reported from the eastern North Pacific Ocean as close to Alaska as Tillamook Head, Oregon. Following Quast and Hall (1972), *C. atrum* is included in this book as a possible future addition to the inventory of Alaskan species. The common name given by most authors for *C. atrum* is bobtail eel, but we call it the black bobtail eel to distinguish it from the other species, *Neocyema erythrosoma,* which is a translucent, bright red. *Neocyema* is less dartlike in shape. It is known from two specimens collected from the Atlantic Ocean off South Africa that appear to be either metamorphic leptocephali or neotenic adults. Bobtail eels are sometimes called arrow eels.

Bobtail eels have short bodies compared to other eels, and extremely small eyes. Like other saccopharyngiforms they lack branchiostegal rays and opercular bones, but they do not have some of the other striking features characteristic of saccopharyngiforms. The leptocephalus of *C. atrum* has the fewest myomeres (80 or less) of any known eel larva. Adult bobtail eels are small, not exceeding 16 cm (6.3 inches) in total length.

Robins (1989) summarized the evidence for removing the Cyematidae from the Anguilliformes and including them in the order Saccopharyngiformes. Smith (1989a) compared the Cyematidae to the Nemichthyidae and synthesized available information on the morphology and distribution of the Cyematidae and its two species. Cyematidae is the grammatically correct spelling, but Cyemidae is also in use.

Cyema atrum Günther, 1878 **black bobtail eel**

Pacific Ocean from Tillamook Head, Oregon, to Panama and to Japan; widespread in temperate to tropical regions of all oceans.

At depths of 330–5,100 m; mostly caught in lower mesopelagic to upper bathypelagic zones; leptocephali at shallower depths.

D 79–93; A 72–86; C 5–7; Pec 12–15; Pel 0; Vert 68–80.

- Opaque, dark brown to violet-black.
- Body delicate, relatively short, greatly compressed and bandlike, barely 3 mm thick; eye very small; snout and jaws prolonged into slender, nonocclusible beak; upper jaw slightly longer than lower; cleft of mouth extending posteriorly to end of head; opercular apparatus absent.
- Preanal length about two-thirds of total length.
- Dorsal fin origin above anus; dorsal and anal fins confluent with caudal; dorsal and anal fin rays becoming progressively longer posteriorly until just before tip of tail, then becoming abruptly shorter; caudal rays very short; pectoral fin well developed; pelvic fin absent.
- Lateral line on body without pores but with a series of small sensory papillae; additional series of papillae on head; head pores present.
- Teeth on mandible and maxilla minute, in multiple oblique rows forming rasplike surfaces; posterior end of maxilla with a ball-like patch of teeth; vomerine tooth patch elongate.
- Gill opening small, crescentic, on lower half of side, slightly anterior to pectoral fin.
- Length probably not more than 150 mm TL.

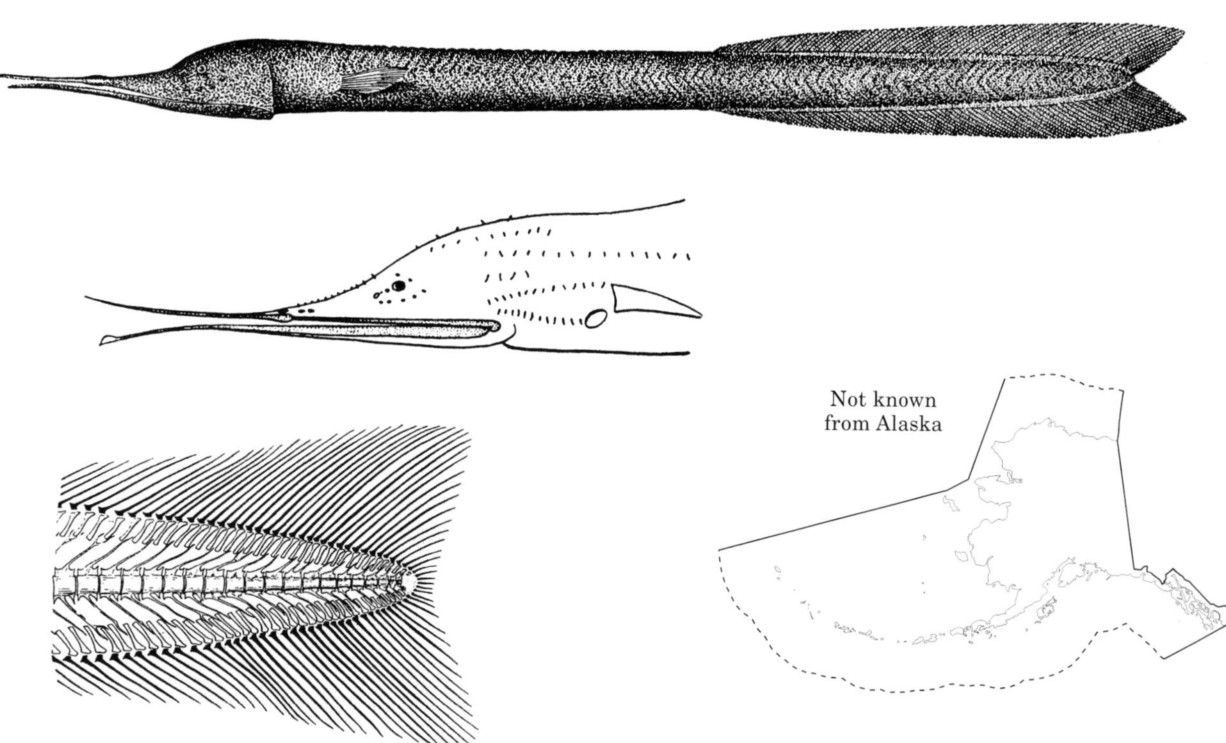

Notes & Sources — *Cyema atrum* Günther, 1878

Description: Günther 1887:265–266; Goode and Bean 1896: 154; Trewavas 1933:601–605; Castle in Smith and Heemstra 1986:192–193; Saldanha and Bauchot in Whitehead et al. 1986:557–558; Matarese et al. 1989:33; Smith 1989:633–635; Aizawa and Sakamoto 1993. Some authors count the sensory papillae along the body lateral line as pores. The dorsal fin origin is sometimes slightly ahead of the anal fin, above the anus, not directly above the anal fin origin.

Figures: Upper: Goode and Bean 1896: fig. 176, after Günther 1878; South Pacific. Diagram of head, showing cirri, pores, location of gill opening: modified from Bertin 1937, fig. 9. Skeleton of tail: Trewavas 1933, fig. 3.

Range: Nearest record is that of an adult specimen taken with bottom sampling gear off Tillamook Head, Oregon, at 45°45'N, 125°09'W, depth 1,646 m (Grinols 1966b). Aizawa and Sakamoto (1993) described the first adult specimen known from Japan, taken in 1991 off Kyushu by midwater trawl with 5,062 m of wire out. Minimum depth: Bertin 1937. Maximum depth: Grey 1956.

Size: Smith 1989a. Maximum length reported from study material is 134 mm TL, recorded by Bertin (1934). Most specimens are broken at one or both ends. Length of 60 cm given by Castle (in Smith and Heemstra 1986) is obviously a mistake.

Order Clupeiformes
Herrings and anchovies

Herrings, anchovies, and other clupeiforms are pelagic, schooling fishes of major importance in the world's commercial fisheries. The order contains two suborders with five families, about 100 genera, and more than 350 species. All but one of the species are classified in the suborder Clupeoidei, which is the largest suborder of nondomesticated vertebrates harvested by man. About 60 species in various groups make up half the world catch of fishes, and a third of those prime species are clupeoids (Whitehead 1985). In Alaska, clupeoids are represented by species in two families: Clupeidae and Engraulidae. The Clupeidae contains herringlike clupeoids, easily recognized by their keel of scutes along the belly, and the Engraulidae contains anchovylike clupeoids, distinguished by their projecting, "piglike" snout and large mouth. The Pacific herring, *Clupea pallasii,* is abundant and widespread in Alaska and is important there as a regional economic resource as well as food for marine mammals, while four other species are found occasionally or rarely in the region.

Fishery workers have little difficulty in picking clupeoids out of the net, but there are so many exceptions in features used by taxonomists in the past to define the clupeoids that modern diagnoses rely mainly on internal features, such as a characteristic coupling of the swim bladder, inner ear, and head canal system. This involves the *recessus lateralis,* a special cranial chamber where sensory canals meet around the inner ear. The system is unique to clupeiforms. It probably monitors information necessary for schooling and detection of predators and other hazards (Whitehead 1985).

Body shape varies greatly among clupeoids, from round to greatly compressed. Most are silvery fishes. Other features include: no spines in the fins; single, short dorsal fin usually located near the midpoint of the body; anal fin usually short; caudal fin forked, with 19 principal caudal fin rays; pectoral fins low on the body; and pelvic fins below the dorsal fin. There is no lateral line canal with pored scales along the sides, except occasionally for 1 or 2 pores behind the gill opening. The scales are cycloid, completely cover the body, and frequently deciduous. Almost all clupeoids have a pelvic scute immediately in front of the pelvic fins, some have additional scutes in front of and behind the pelvic scute, and a few species, not including those in Alaska, have scutes in front of the dorsal fin. One to several axillary scales lie above the bases of the first pectoral and pelvic fin rays. Some species have enlarged scales on the base of the caudal fin. The maxillae usually have 2 supramaxillae along the upper edge. The jaws, palatines, and vomer usually bear small conical teeth. Most clupeoids are plankton feeders, with long and sometimes very numerous gill rakers. Authors usually report numbers of gill rakers on the lower half of the first gill arch (on the ceratobranchial), not the total number. The gill membranes are separate. Most clupeoids have 6 or 7 branchiostegal rays. Clupeoids have a swim bladder which is joined by a duct to the esophagus or stomach (physostomous).

The clupeoids were once classified with certain other primitive bony fishes in an order called the Isospondyli, but it is now universally recognized that those groups have no common ancestry. The life history of some, for example, includes a leptocephalus stage which allies them with the eels, whereas the clupeoids lack a leptocephalus larva. Keys and summaries of morphological features, geographic distribution, habitat, and economic importance of clupeoids of the world are contained in catalogs by Whitehead (1985) and Whitehead et al. (1988).

Family Clupeidae
Herrings

The family Clupeidae includes herrings, shads, sardines, sprats, and other herringlike fishes. Calling them clupeids avoids confusion. There are several freshwater and anadromous clupeids, but most are marine. They typically aggregate in schools and feed on plankton near the surface, usually in shallow coastal waters. American shad, *Alosa sapidissima,* can reach 76 cm (30 inches) in length, but most clupeids attain maximum lengths of less than 25 cm (10 inches). The family contains about 56 genera and 180 species in five subfamilies. Three clupeid species occur in Alaska. A catalog of the clupeids of the world by Whitehead (1985) has keys to the genera and descriptions of the species.

Clupeids are easily distinguished from their close relatives the anchovies (Engraulidae) by their short, deep lower jaw; terminal or slightly superior mouth; and the presence of ventral scutes. Other family characteristics include such externally visible features as, usually, the lack of scales on the head, and small teeth or absence of teeth. The anal fin is fairly short, with 12–29 rays, and placed well behind the last dorsal fin ray. The pelvic fins have 7–10 rays, with 8 or 9 in the Alaskan species. The scales are fairly large, with 35–65 in the midlateral series. Clupeids have numerous gill rakers, increasing in number with age; 5–10 branchiostegal rays; and 37–59 vertebrae. The Alaskan species are in two subfamilies: the Clupeinae, with upper jaw rounded and not notched when viewed from the front, and the Alosinae, with the upper jaw not evenly rounded in front but with a distinct notch into which the symphysis of the lower jaw fits. The scales are firmly attached in the Alosinae.

In clupeids scutes continue forward from the pelvic scute to the gill opening, forming the prepelvic series; and behind the pelvic scute is a small scute between the pelvic fins which is the first of the postpelvic series. Scute shape and numbers are useful for distinguishing among the three Alaskan species. The two numbers in the notation giving numbers of abdominal scutes (e.g., 28 + 13 in *Clupea pallasii*) are for the prepelvic scutes, including the pelvic scute, and postpelvic scutes (see diagram).

Three clupeid species occur in Alaskan waters. The Pacific herring, *Clupea pallasii,* is distributed off all the coasts of Alaska and is seasonally and locally abundant. The Pacific sardine, *Sardinops sagax,* occurs, although rarely, in the southeastern part of the state during years of high abundance of the eastern North Pacific population, and may be expected off western Alaska when the western North Pacific population is in high abundance. There used to be an important commercial fishery for sardines in British Columbia before it collapsed in the mid-1940s, and no sardines were reported from the region after the 1950s until 1992 and 1993, when they started to show up again. Adult Pacific sardines captured by surface trawl and gill net in southeastern Alaska in 1998 were the first known captures of adult sardines in Alaska since 1931 (Wing et al. 2000). American shad, *Alosa sapidissima,* were introduced to the Pacific in the late 1800s from the Atlantic, and now can be found from the Gulf of California to Alaska and Russia. Fishers pick up a few shad each year in salmon nets in Alaska but there are no known breeding populations in the state. They are mostly taken in southeastern Alaska, but there have been occasional records from Cook Inlet, off Kodiak Island, and Bristol Bay.

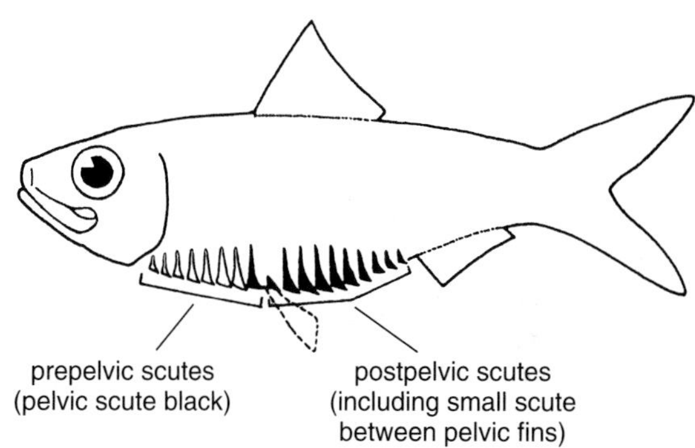

Ventral scutes in clupeids
(After Whitehead 1985.)

Classification of the Alaskan clupeids in this guide follows the classification used in the worldwide review by Whitehead (1985), except that the Pacific sardine is treated as one widely distributed species, *S. sagax,* following Svetovidov (1952) and Parrish et al. (1989), not separated into several species.

Key to the Clupeidae of Alaska

1		No enlarged scales on base of caudal fin; no radial striations on operculum; no black spots on sides of body	*Clupea pallasii,* page 134
1		Enlarged scales present on base of caudal fin; radial striations present on operculum; black spots on sides of body	(2)
2	(1)	Body terete; keels on abdominal scutes weak; radial striations on operculum fine; lateral black spots usually not in single row, irregularly arranged	*Sardinops sagax,* page 135
2		Body deep, compressed; abdominal scutes strongly keeled; radial striations on operculum coarse; lateral black spots usually in single row	*Alosa sapidissima,* page 136

Clupea pallasii Valenciennes, 1847 — Pacific herring

Coppermine River, Canada, and White Sea, Russia, in Arctic Ocean to northern Baja California and Japan and Korea in Pacific Ocean.

Coastal and offshore, pelagic, schooling, from surface to depth of 250 m; almost always caught at depths less than 150 m; usually found inshore in harbors and large estuaries during spawning in spring (in winter farther south); spawn in inter- and subtidal zones.

D 15–21; A 13–20; Pec 17–19; Pel 8–9; Ls 38–54; GR 63–73; Vert 51–57.

- Metallic blue-green to olive green dorsally; silvery ventrally; **no black spots laterally**; peritoneum black.
- Body moderately compressed.
- Lower jaw slightly projecting beyond upper; upper jaw without median notch; maxilla not extending beyond eye.
- Dorsal fin centered at about midpoint of body or slightly posterior to midpoint; **no enlarged scales on base of caudal fin**.
- **No striations on operculum**.
- Ventral scutes 28 + 13; keels moderately developed, not strong.
- Fine teeth present on vomer; no teeth on jaws.
- Length to 46 cm TL.

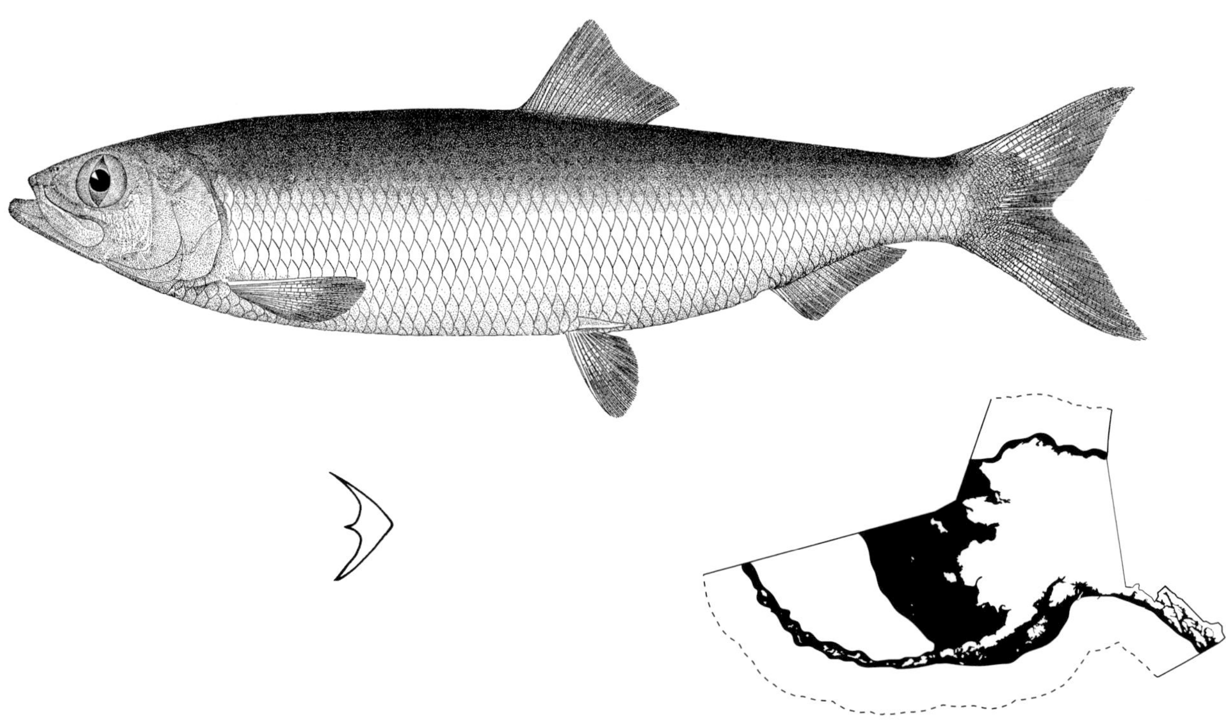

Notes & Sources — *Clupea pallasii* Valenciennes in Cuvier & Valenciennes, 1847
Clupea mirabilis Girard, 1854
Clupea harengus pallasi Svetovidov, 1952
Considered by some researchers to be a subspecies of Atlantic herring, *C. harengus,* but by others (e.g., Uyeno and Sato in Masuda et al. 1984, Whitehead 1985, Grant 1986, Rass and Wheeler 1991, Swift et al. 1993), from biochemical and life history information, to be a distinct species.

Description: Hart 1973:96–100; Morrow 1980:17–20; Whitehead 1985:115–118; Coad 1995:504–506.

Figures: Turner 1886, pl. 14; about 307 mm TL, from St. Michael. Abdominal scute (ventral view): Miller and Lea 1972:55.

Range: One of the most abundant fishes along the coasts of Alaska, although abundance is seasonal and varies from year to year. Region of greatest abundance in North America is along the coasts of western and southern Alaska and British Columbia. Herring are not particularly abundant along northern Chukchi and Beaufort coasts. Range was most recently depicted on maps by Morrow (1980), Whitehead (1985), and Allen and Smith (1988). An extreme depth of 475 m and other unusually deep catches reported by Allen and Smith (1988) were probably from fish entering the net above the maximum depth of the tow. Pacific herring in Alaska move offshore in winter and onshore in spring for spawning.

Size: Miller and Lea 1972, Eschmeyer et al. 1983, Coad 1995. Hart (1973) reported length in British Columbia to reach 33 cm but seldom to exceed 25 cm. Morrow (1980) considered average adult size in Alaska to be around 25 cm.

Sardinops sagax (Jenyns, 1842) **Pacific sardine**

Eastern North Pacific from southeastern Alaska to southern Baja California and Gulf of California; western North Pacific off eastern Kamchatka at about 54°N to south of Japan; other populations in eastern South Pacific, western South Pacific, and off southern Africa.

Coastal, pelagic, in large schools, from surface to depth of 150 m; migratory, with northward movement of eastern North Pacific population between California and British Columbia waters in summer.

D 17–20; A 17–20; Pec 17; Pel 8–9; Ls 52–60; GR 21–23 + 44–110; Vert 48–54.

- Metallic blue-green dorsally, silvery ventrally; **usually with several dark spots variably arranged laterally**; peritoneum black.
- Body elongate and rounded.
- Jaws about equal; no median notch in upper jaw; maxilla not extending beyond eye.
- Dorsal fin centered at midpoint of body or slightly anterior to midpoint; enlarged scales present on upper and lower lobes of caudal fin.
- **Fine striations present on operculum.**
- **Ventral scutes weakly keeled, points barely protruding beyond scales**, 18 + 14.
- Teeth absent.
- Length to 41 cm TL, usually less than 30 cm.

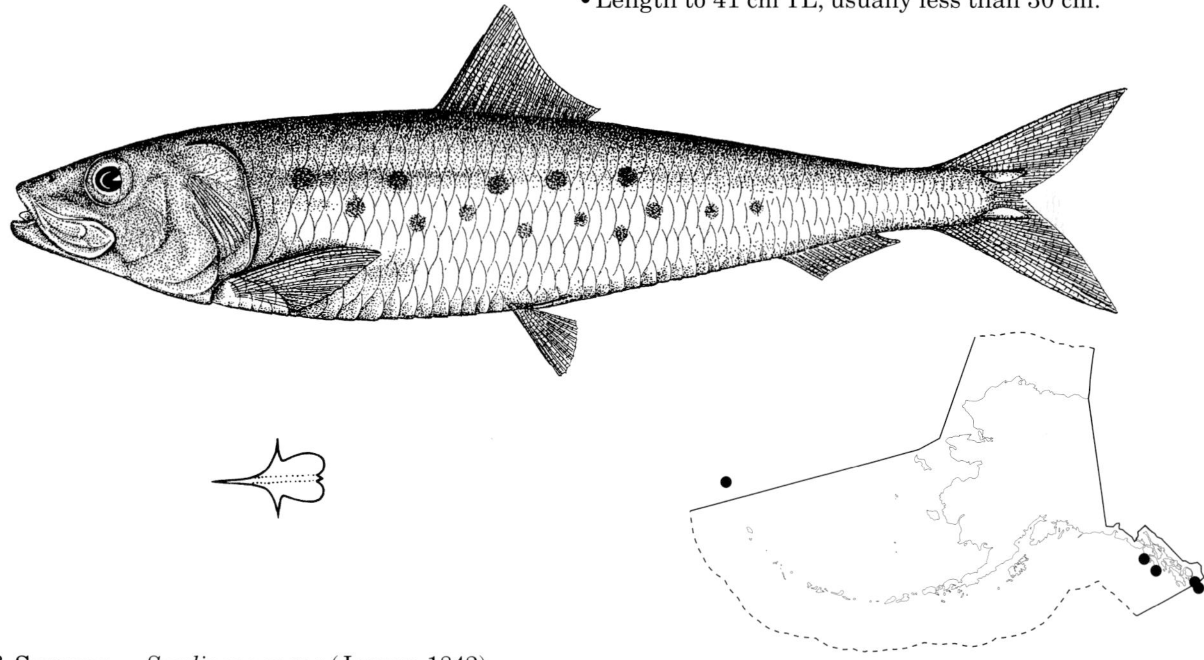

Notes & Sources — *Sardinops sagax* (Jenyns, 1842)

Sardinops caeruleus (Girard, 1854): Whitehead 1985, and others; eastern North Pacific.

Sardinops melanostictus (Temminck & Schlegel, 1946): Whitehead 1985, and others; western North Pacific.

Detailed history of this species and its nomenclature was given by Parrish et al. (1989).

Also called pilchard or California pilchard.

Description: Miller and Lea 1972:54; Hart 1973:100–103; McGowan and Berry 1984; Whitehead 1985:57–59; Coad 1995:509–510.

Figures: Hart 1973:100; UBC 53-228, Goose Island, British Columbia. Abdominal scute (ventral view): Miller and Lea 1972:55.

Range: Schultz et al. (1932) reported that more than 20 sardines were taken in 1931 in several loads of herring near Cape Ommaney, in southeastern Alaska, and that sardines were unusually abundant that year on British Columbia fishing grounds. Wing et al. (2000) reported the first known captures in southeastern Alaska since then: two adult sardines taken off Garnet Point near Nakat Bay, Kanagunut Island (54°45'N, 130°42'W), and eight others taken west of Khaz Point, Chichagof Island, at 57°31'N, 136°34'W; both catches were in summer of 1998, a year of unusually strong El Niño warming of the Pacific. Fishers reported that sardines were common but not numerous in eastern Dixon Entrance that year (Wing et al. 2000). Parrish et al. (1989) gave 57°N as the northern limit off Alaska, that limit reached only in times of high abundance, with the northern limit about 35°N, off southern California, in times of low abundance. Since sardines occur in the Kuroshio Current system as well, catches could be expected off western Alaska. Andriashev (1939) and Fedorov and Sheiko (2002) reported occurrence of sardines in the western Bering Sea. Kenya (1982) reported that schools of 2-year-old western Pacific sardines were encountered east of 171°E in 1980. M. S. Busby (pers. comm., 29 Dec. 1999) has two larvae collected near the Shumagin Islands in 1992, and suggested they are products of sardines from the eastern Pacific population. Schweigert (1988) reviewed historical catches of sardines in British Columbia. Hargreaves et al. (1994) reported on sardines caught in 1992 and 1993 in British Columbia waters, as the first confirmed catches there since the 1950s. They captured 0.5 tonne of sardines in one tow during a midwater trawl survey off Barkley Sound.

Size: Clemens and Wilby 1961.

Alosa sapidissima (Wilson, 1811) **American shad**

Eastern Bering Sea to Pacific coast of Baja California at Todos Santos Bay; Atlantic coasts from Labrador to Florida. Introduced to Pacific coasts via Sacramento River, California, in 1871–1881, and spread north to Kamchatka and Bering Sea and south to Baja California.

Epipelagic and anadromous, in schools, traveling more than 600 km up some East Coast rivers.

D 15–20; A 17–25; Pec 14–18; Pel 9; Ls 50–64; GR 56–76; Vert 53–59.

- Metallic blue or green dorsally, silvery white ventrally; **dark spots dorsolaterally, usually in 1 row**, occasionally 2 rows, rarely 3; peritoneum pale gray to silvery.
- Body deep and compressed.
- Lower jaw pointed, fitting into **median notch in upper jaw**; notch absent in fish less than about 15 cm long; maxilla not extending beyond eye.
- **Radiating striations on operculum coarse**.
- Dorsal fin centered anterior to midpoint of body; enlarged scales present above and below middle of caudal fin at base.
- **Ventral scutes strongly keeled**, 18-24 + 12-19.
- Teeth absent in adults.
- Length to 76 cm TL, weight to 6.8 kg.

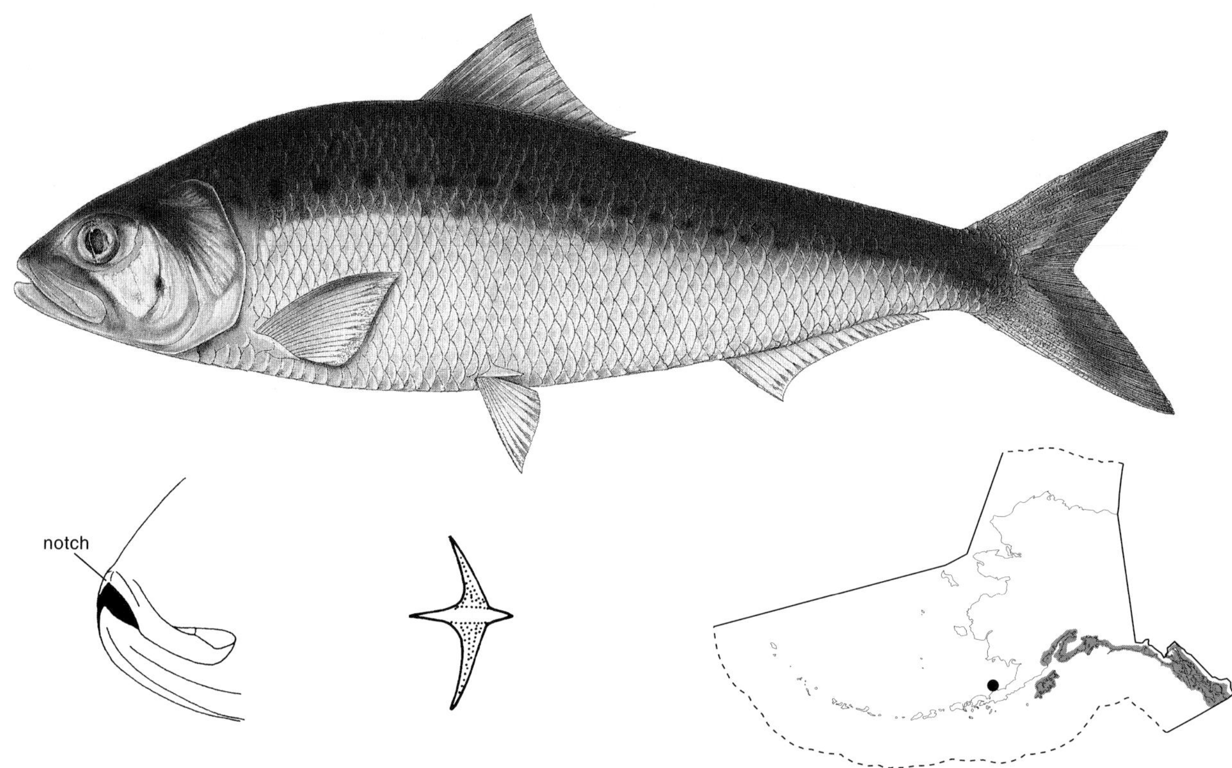

Notes & Sources — *Alosa sapidissima* (Wilson, 1811)

Description: Hart 1973:95–96; Morrow 1980:20–22; Whitehead 1985:206–207; Coad 1995:29–30.

Figures: University of British Columbia, artist P. Drukker-Brammall; UBC 63-946, 400 mm SL, British Columbia. Abdominal scute (ventral view): Miller and Lea 1972:55. Diagram of mouth: Whitehead 1985:42

Range: Baxter (1990ms) reported a specimen (UAM uncataloged) captured in Bristol Bay northeast of Port Moller at about 56°15'N, 160°22'W; this represents an extension of the recorded range westward in Alaska from Kodiak Island. Morrow (1980) reviewed Alaskan records and concluded that shad have never been more than strays in the region. The earliest Alaskan records are from the Stikine River near Wrangell in 1891 (Smith 1896), Cook Inlet in 1904 (Evermann and Goldsborough 1907), and Kodiak Island in 1926 and 1937 (Welander 1940). Quast and Hall (1972) noted that specimens from southeastern Alaska were in the ABL permanent collection; the collection presently has specimens from five localities. Thirty years of NMFS bottom trawl surveys in the northeastern Pacific yielded 192 occurrences distributed from southwestern Vancouver Island, British Columbia, to Monterey Bay, California (Allen and Smith 1988). None was from Alaska. Hart (1973) reported that in British Columbia shad occurred in moderate numbers in the Fraser River, less commonly in Rivers Inlet, and in catches of schooling fishes away from river mouths. Chereshnev and Zharnikov (1989) reported the first find of shad in the Anadyr River, Russia: a single, 48-cm-TL, prespawning female found in a catch of chum salmon in August 1987. One of the salmon had been tagged at Unimak Island, Alaska. The authors concluded that the occurrence of shad in the Anadyr River was accidental, like previous Asian records (from Kamchatka), but that the climate and other ecological conditions would allow naturalization as far north as Anadyr Bay. Shad had not been reported off the Asian coast since the 1950s.

Family Engraulidae
Anchovies

Anchovies are primarily marine coastal and schooling fishes, inhabiting subarctic to subantarctic waters of all the oceans. Some species enter brackish or fresh water to feed or spawn and a few, although not any of the North American species, live permanently in fresh water. Most anchovies are small plankton-feeders reaching maximum lengths of 10–25 cm (4–10 inches). The family Engraulidae contains 16 genera with 139 species in two subfamilies. Whitehead et al. (1988) provided a worldwide review of the family with keys to the genera and descriptions of the species.

The most obvious external feature differentiating anchovies from herrings (Clupeidae) is their head, with its prominent, projecting snout, and long jaws extending well behind the eyes. In most genera, including *Engraulis,* the genus represented in Alaska, the anal fin is short-based, with 15–25 rays, and the pelvic fins have 6 rays. All engraulids have a pelvic scute with lateral arms. Most Indo-Pacific species have pre- and postpelvic scutes and a few have a spinelike scute just before the dorsal fin, but *Engraulis* lacks such scutes. The scales are moderately large, about 30–60 along midside, and easily shed. Most anchovy species have small or minute teeth in the jaws. The gill rakers are usually short and not very numerous, but in *Engraulis* they are long, slender, and numerous; the number of rakers increases with size of the fish. The branchiostegal rays number 7–19, and vertebrae 38–49.

Two species of anchovy have been reported from Alaska as rare finds: the northern anchovy, *Engraulis mordax,* and the Japanese anchovy, *E. japonicus.* Quast and Hall (1972) listed the northern anchovy as a species likely to occur off Alaska, but it was not reported from Alaska until 1997, when anchovies were found in the stomachs of coho salmon (*Oncorhynchus kisutch*) caught west of Yakutat; 1997 was a year marked by unusually strong El Niño warming. Northern anchovies are most abundant from San Francisco, California, to Bahia Magdalena, Mexico. Anchovy populations fluctuate widely, and northern anchovies were abundant enough in the 1940s in British Columbia to be fished commercially, but today are not available abundantly or consistently enough there for commercial use. The northern anchovy is not known to overlap in its distribution with any other anchovy. The other eastern Pacific species of *Engraulis,* the Peruvian anchoveta, *E. ringens,* is found only off South America.

A report of Japanese anchovy, *E. japonicus,* in Alaskan waters south of the western Aleutian Islands (Birman 1958) evidently was overlooked during compilation of the previous regional inventory (Quast and Hall 1972). The Japanese anchovy is most abundant along the coasts of Japan. Parin (1968) explained the catches south of Alaska as a chance find, the fish having been carried from coastal waters of Japan to the open ocean by currents in the zone of activity of the Kuroshio.

Key to the Engraulidae of Alaska

1 Tip of maxilla pointed, extending beyond tip of 2nd supramaxilla; no gill rakers present on hind face of 3rd epibranchial; pseudobranch shorter than eye or just equal to it . . . . *Engraulis mordax,* page 138

1 Tip of maxilla blunt, not extending beyond tip of 2nd supramaxilla; a few small rakers present on hind face of 3rd epibranchial; pseudobranch longer than eye . . . . *Engraulis japonicus,* page 139

Engraulis mordax Girard, 1854 **northern anchovy**

Eastern Gulf of Alaska, one record off Yakutat; Queen Charlotte Islands, British Columbia, to Cape San Lucas, Baja California, and Gulf of California; most abundant from San Francisco to Bahia Magdalena.

Near surface to depth of 310 m; epi- and mesopelagic; usually coastal and within about 30 km of shore, but occurring to 480 km offshore, in large tightly packed schools; entering bays and inlets in summer.

D 14–19; A 19–26; Pec 13–20; Pel 6; Ls 41–50; GR 28–41 + 37–45; Vert 43–47.

- Metallic bluish or greenish dorsally; silvery ventrally; silver stripe along side in young individuals, disappearing with age.
- Body slender, elongate, round in cross-section, depth 5 or 6 times in standard length.
- Snout short, sharply pointed, protruding beyond lower jaw; mouth extremely large; **maxilla tip sharply pointed, reaching well onto preopercle and projecting well beyond tip of 2nd supramaxilla**.
- **Anal fin origin below base of last dorsal fin ray or slightly posterior to it**; anal fin relatively long, with more rays than in *E. japonicus*.
- Gill rakers long, slender; lower rakers 37–45; **no gill rakers on hind face of 3rd epibranchial**.
- **Pseudobranch shorter than eye or just equal to it**.
- Length to about 25 cm TL, 21 cm SL; about 12 and 14 cm SL at 2 and 3 years.

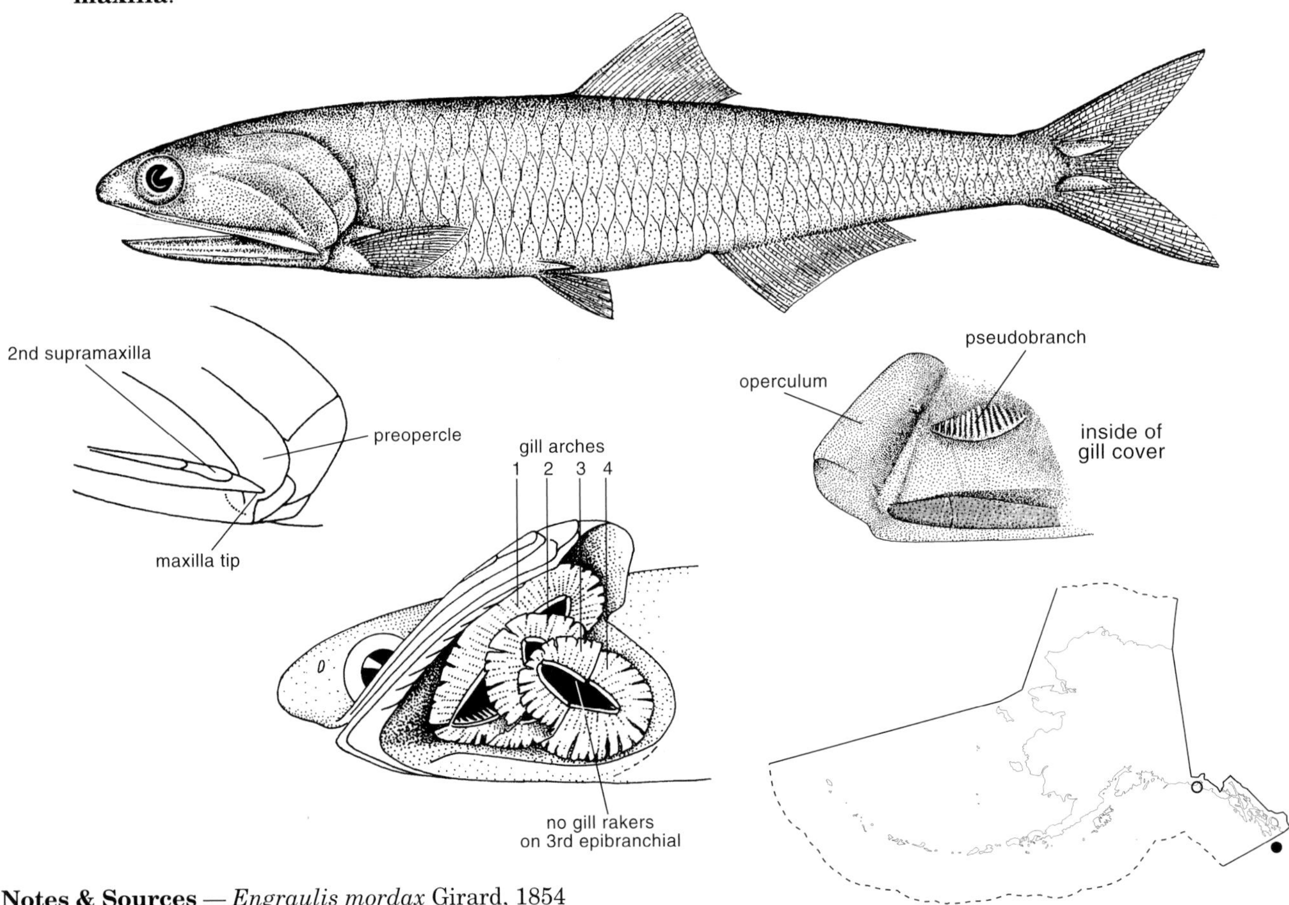

Notes & Sources — *Engraulis mordax* Girard, 1854
Also called California anchovy.

Description: Miller and Lea 1972:56; Hart 1973:104–106; Whitehead et al. 1988:320–321.

Figures: Full lateral view: Hart 1973:104; 16 cm TL, Departure Bay, British Columbia. Diagrams: Whitehead et al. 1988:308, 311, 320.

Range: Anchovies were found in the stomachs of salmon caught off Yakutat in August of 1997, an unusually strong El Niño year. The fisher, a National Weather Service forecaster, recorded a surface temperature of 63°F at the time, whereas the normal range for the Gulf of Alaska is in the mid-50s (Associated Press, *Juneau Empire,* 3 Sep. 1997). C.W.M. contacted Joel Curtis, the fisher, in January 2000, and his description of the anchovies confirmed the identification. He reported that 10 or more coho salmon (*Oncorhynchus kisutch*) he caught by hand trolling about 20 miles from shore in pockets of cold water below 59°F had anchovies in their guts. Previously recorded as close to Alaska as the Queen Charlotte Islands, anchovies currently occur sporadically in British Columbia but have been abundant there at times, as in the early 1940s when a small commercial fishery was based in the Strait of Georgia (Hart 1973). Hammann and Cisneros-Mata (1989) recorded extension of the known range of northern anchovy to the Gulf of California.

Engraulis japonicus Temminck & Schlegel, 1846 — **Japanese anchovy**

Pacific Ocean south of western Aleutian Islands, one record; western Pacific, from southern Sea of Okhotsk, Sea of Japan, and Pacific coasts of Japan to Taiwan, with rare records south to Philippines and north to southeastern Kamchatka.

Near surface, epipelagic and coastal, but also occurring to over 1,000 km from shore and depth of 150 m, forming large schools; tending to move northward and inshore, to bays and inlets, in summer, but without well-defined migrations.

D 14–16; A 14–18; Pel 6; Ls 42–44; GR lower 27–43; Vert 44–47.

- Metallic bluish or greenish dorsally; silvery ventrally; silver stripe along side, disappearing with age.
- Body slender, elongate, oval in cross-section, depth about 6 times in standard length.
- Snout short, sharply pointed, protruding beyond lower jaw; mouth extremely large; **maxilla tip rounded, reaching almost to anterior border of preopercle, not projecting beyond tip of 2nd supramaxilla**.
- **Anal fin origin well behind base of last dorsal fin ray**; anal fin relatively short, with fewer rays than in *E. mordax*.
- Gill rakers long, slender; lower rakers 27–43; **gill rakers present on hind face of 3rd epibranchial**.
- **Pseudobranch longer than eye, reaching onto inner face of operculum**.
- Length to about 16 cm SL; usually 12–14 cm.

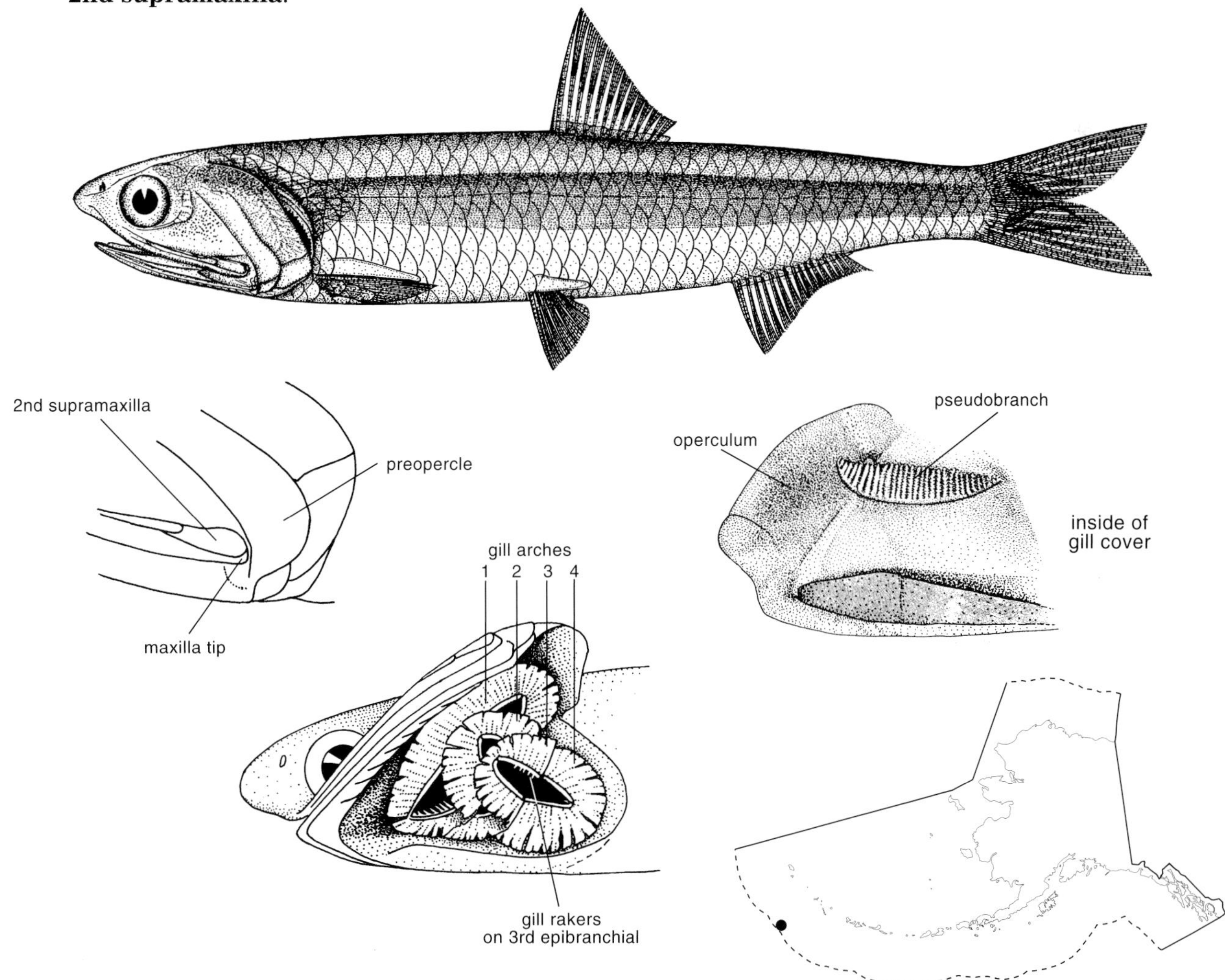

Notes & Sources — *Engraulis japonicus* Temminck & Schlegel, 1846

Description: Lindberg and Legeza 1965:70–71; Uyeno in Masuda et al. 1984:20; Whitehead et al. 1988:316–317, 318–319 (characters same as those of European anchovy, *E. encrasicolus*).

Figures: Whitehead et al. 1988:307, 311, 319.

Range: Birman (1958) reported catches of *E. japonicus* in August and September 1956 south of the western Aleutian Islands within the area 47–49°N, 172–176°E, and between there and the Kuril Islands. Recorded, but rarely, off southeastern Kamchatka (Lindberg 1935, Panin 1936, Lindberg and Legeza 1965). Most abundant along coasts of Japan.

Order Cypriniformes
Minnows and suckers

The order Cypriniformes, containing minnows, carps, loaches, suckers, and allied forms, is a large order of freshwater fishes with about 2,660 species in 280 genera and five families. Many of the small species are popular aquarium fishes, while in Asia the large species of carp are used for food. Members of the group are native to North America, Eurasia, and Africa, but are present in greatest diversity in southeast Asia. Two families, Cyprinidae and Catostomidae, are represented by one species each in Alaska.

A unique feature of cypriniforms and other members of the series Ostariophysi is the Weberian apparatus, which aids in detection of sound and involves modifications of the ossicles, ligaments, and vertebrae between the swim bladder and the ears. In addition, cypriniforms lack teeth in the jaws and palate but have lower pharyngeal teeth that press upward against a cartilaginous pad covering a process of the basioccipital bone. The pad is tough and horny in the Cyprinidae and soft in the Catostomidae. Other diagnostic morphological features of most or all cypriniforms include: upper jaw protractile; adipose fins absent; dorsal fin present; caudal fin homocercal; scales cycloid, covering body but absent from head; branchiostegal rays 3; swim bladder connected to gut by a duct; and intermuscular bones present. Enlarged and stiffened spinelike rays are present at the front of the dorsal and anal fins in some cypriniforms.

Family Cyprinidae
Minnows

Minnows, carps, shiners, chubs, and other fishes in the family Cyprinidae occur in diverse freshwater habitats from swift-running, cold streams to warm bogs in North America, Africa, and Eurasia. This is the largest family of freshwater fishes, with more than 2,100 species or almost 10% of the world's total. With the possible exception of the Gobiidae, the Cyprinidae is also the most speciose family of vertebrates. The greatest number of species is native to China and southeast Asia. About 270 are native to North America. The only minnow in Alaska is the lake chub, *Couesius plumbeus,* which occurs in the Yukon River drainage.

Characters defining the family Cyprinidae include pharyngeal teeth in 1–3 rows with never more than 8 teeth in any row; thin lips, without plicae or papillae; barbels present or absent; upper jaw usually bordered by premaxilla, entirely or almost entirely exluding the maxilla from the gape; upper jaw protrusible; and spinelike rays present in the dorsal fin of some species.

Maximum lengths attained by cyprinids range from 12 mm (0.5 inch) to nearly 3 m (10 ft), and weights can reach 130 kg (285 lb) or more. Both extremes are found in southeast Asian species. The Alaskan species, *C. plumbeus,* reaches about 23 cm (9 inches).

Sexual dimorphism is often conspicuous in minnows as they undergo changes during the spawning season. Some species, which are usually silvery, develop bright red and yellow coloration, and breeding males have nuptial tubercles on the head, body, and fin rays. The tubercles and swollen fin rays aid in clasping the female and are also used to fight other males and to clean nests.

Mayden (1991) reviewed systematics and biology of New World Cyprinidae. Nelson (1994) and Bond (1996) summarized the morphological characteristics and worldwide distribution of the family.

Couesius plumbeus (Agassiz, 1850) **lake chub**

Yukon River and its tributaries, from Nulato upstream; south to Columbia River drainage in Washington, Platte system in Colorado, southern Lake Michigan, and New York; endemic to North America.

Any body of fresh water, large or small, running or standing, clear or very muddy; even found in outlets of hot streams; in Alaska, much more common in heavily silted main rivers than in clear tributaries; most common in fairly shallow water but moving into deeper parts of lakes during hot weather.

D 8; A 7–9; Pec 13–18; Pel 7–9; LLp 53–79; GR 4–9; Vert 39–44.

- Brown to green dorsally; silvery ventrally; dark stripe along side, darkest on young fish and large males; sometimes with black specks on sides and belly; orange patches on side of head and at base of pectoral fin in breeding males variably present, not known to occur in Alaskan populations.
- Body elongate, slender, moderately compressed; mouth fairly small, slightly oblique; upper jaw extending slightly beyond lower jaw; eye large, 20–33% of head length; head flattened above and below.
- Small but well-developed barbel near posterior end of maxilla.
- No spinelike rays in dorsal fin or anal fin; dorsal fin origin over or slightly behind pelvic fin origin; caudal fin moderately forked, with rounded lobes.
- Fine tubercles on head, just behind head to dorsal fin, and on upper rays of pectoral fin in breeding adults, better developed in males than in females.
- Lateral line complete.
- Gill rakers short.
- Length to 227 mm TL; most adults 50–100 mm.

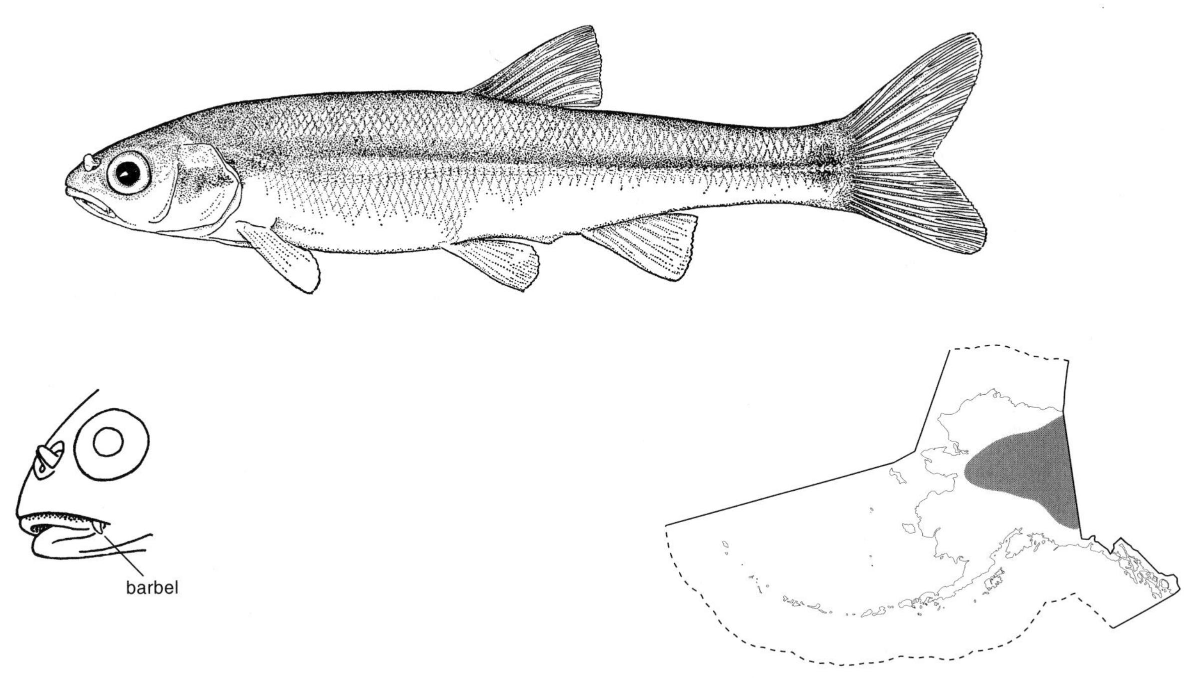

Notes & Sources — *Couesius plumbeus* (Agassiz, 1850)
Gobio plumbeus Agassiz, 1850
Hybopsis plumbea (Agassiz): Wilimovsky 1954, 1958.

Description: McPhail and Lindsey 1970:242–245; Scott and Crossman 1973:401–406; Morrow 1980:171–172; Page and Burr 1991:89–90.

Figures: McPhail and Lindsey 1970:218, 242.

Range: Most northern-occurring minnow in North America. In Alaska confined to the Yukon-Koyukuk-Tanana-Porcupine drainage from about Nulato on upstream, and usually abundant where found (Morrow 1980). Abundant in headwaters of all the major Yukon River tributaries, but only as far downstream as Fairbanks, and absent from Bristol Bay, Kuskokwim River, and North Slope. Evidently, entered the Yukon system from the Mackenzie. *Couesius plumbeus* is absent where *Dallia pectoralis* is abundant (Lindsey and McPhail 1986). McPhail and Lindsey (1970) reported that lake chub frequent the outlets of hot springs, including the lower pools of Liard Hot Springs on the Alaska Highway and springs near Atlin Lake, British Columbia.

Family Catostomidae
Suckers

Suckers are freshwater fishes that primarily inhabit North America. The family includes 65 species, with only 2 occurring in other countries. One of those two species is endemic to southern China. The other is the longnose sucker, *Catostomus catostomus,* which inhabits rivers and lakes of eastern Siberia and North America and is the only species of sucker living in Alaska.

A ventral mouth with thick papillose lips, creating suction to ingest invertebrates from stream and lake beds, gives the family its common name. In addition, suckers have a single row of 16 or more pharyngeal teeth, and the upper jaw is usually bordered by the premaxilla and maxilla. Suckers are tetraploids.

The maximum total length reached by suckers is about 1 m (39 inches), attained in an endangered species (*C. luxatus*) endemic to Oregon and California, but most species reach less than 60 cm (23.5 inches). Although *C. catostomus* has been known to reach at least 65 cm (25.5 inches) in Canada, reported lengths for Alaskan populations have been much smaller.

Catostomus catostomus (Forster, 1773) **longnose sucker**

Throughout mainland Alaska, absent from islands of Alaska; western Canada south to British Columbia and Washington; Arctic coasts from Siberia to New York, except absent from Chukchi Peninsula.

Clear, cold freshwaters, on the bottom; recorded at depths to 183 m.

D 9–11; A 7; Pec 16–18; Pel 10–11; LLp 90–120; GR 23–30; Vert 45–47.

- Reddish brown, dark brassy green, or gray to black dorsally; white ventrally; brownish black lateral stripe turning red in breeding fish.
- Body elongate and rounded; mouth ventral, protrusible, lips thick and covered with papillae; eye small, 22–31% of snout length.
- No spinelike rays in dorsal or anal fin; caudal fin forked.
- Tubercles on breeding males on anal fin, lower lobe of caudal fin, and head.
- Gill rakers short.
- Length to 64 cm FL.

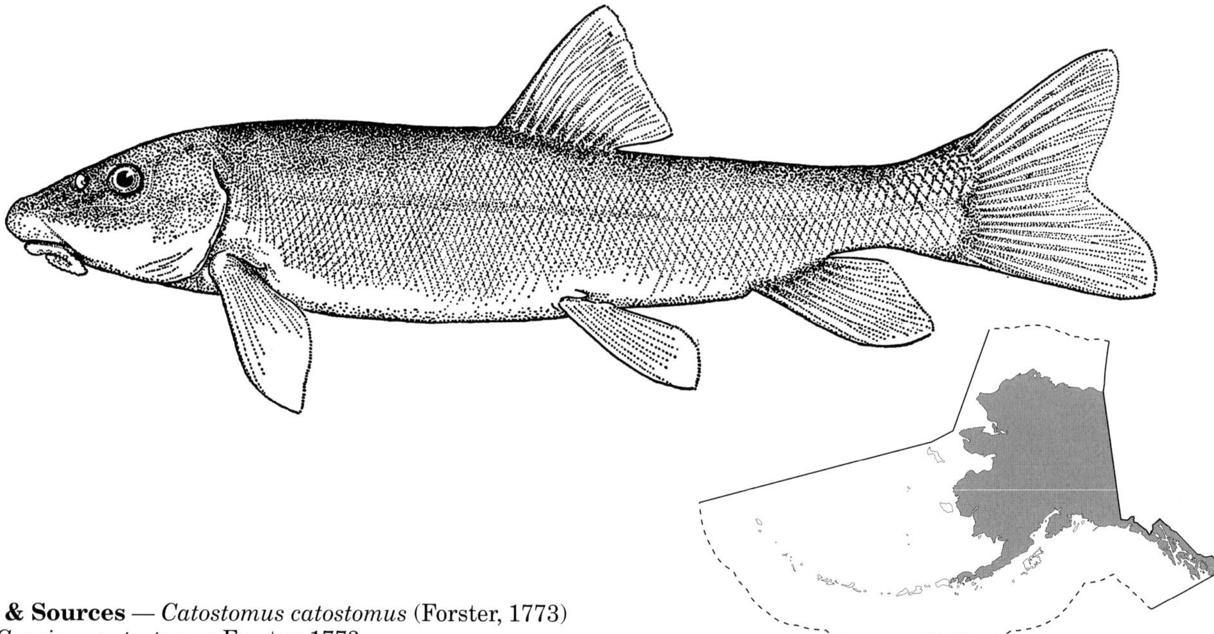

Notes & Sources — *Catostomus catostomus* (Forster, 1773)
Cyprinus catostomus Forster, 1773

Description: McPhail and Lindsey 1970:284–187; Scott and Crossman 1973:531–535; Morrow 1980:173–175.

Figure: McPhail and Lindsey 1970:284.

Range: Morrow (1980) mapped range of the longnose sucker in Alaska. This species has the widest geographic distribution of any catostomid. Its present distribution in relation to glacial history was described and discussed by Lindsey and McPhail (1986) and McPhail and Taylor (1999). Longnose suckers are absent from the Chukchi Peninsula and rivers that once drained the Bering land bridge, consistent with a theory of pre-Illinoian dispersal from North America into Asia. They are absent from the Anadyr and Amguema rivers but present farther west in the Kolyma River. This gap suggests they were extirpated beween Bering Strait and the Kolyma by the heavy glaciation of eastern Siberia.

Size: Keleher 1961: specimens from Quebec.

Order Esociformes
Pikes and mudminnows

The order Esociformes includes about 10 extant species in four genera distributed among two families: pikes, family Esocidae; and mudminnows, family Umbridae. Pikes and mudminnows are found only in freshwaters of the Northern Hemisphere. One species in each of the two families occurs in Alaska.

Pikes and mudminnows have flattened snouts, elongate bodies with posteriorly located dorsal and anal fins, no spines in the fins, no adipose fin, no breeding tubercles, no pyloric caeca, and no teeth in the maxillae. The maxillae are included in the gape but form a relatively small part of the mouth border. The dorsal and anal fins are short-based, and opposite each other. The pelvic fins are abdominal. The mesocoracoid is lacking from the pectoral girdle and the orbitosphenoid from the skull (advanced characteristics), while preethmoids are present (primitive characteristic).

The relationships of the pikes and mudminnows to other teleosts are a matter for study and debate. Johnson and Patterson (1996) reviewed the relationships of lower teleostean fishes using molecular and morphological data and the fossil record, and proposed major changes in the classification of the groups involved. They also corrected seriously flawed data published in the early 1990s on the subject. With respect to pikes and mudminnows, the evidence presented by Johnson and Patterson (1996), among other authors (e.g., Jamieson 1991), supports classification of these fishes in a separate order (Esociformes) as done by Greenwood et al. (1966), Nelson (1994), and Eschmeyer (1998). Previously some authors (e.g., Gosline 1971) included them in Salmoniformes, and a few still do (e.g., López et al. 2000).

Opinions also differ on interrelationships within the order Esociformes and, therefore, there is no widely accepted classification of esociform families. In Nelson's (1994) classification (followed in this guide), the Esocidae contains one genus: *Esox*; and the Umbridae contains three: *Dallia, Umbra,* and *Novumbra.* Nelson (1994) reviewed various possibilities that have been advanced. Recently, López et al. (2000) suggested that a natural classification of pikes and mudminnows requires reassigning *Dallia* and *Novumbra* to the Esocidae, leaving only *Umbra* in the Umbridae. If one decided to adopt that classification the two Alaskan genera (*Esox* and *Dallia*) would be included in the family Esocidae, and the Umbridae would not be represented in Alaska.

Family Esocidae
Pikes

Pikes have elongate, moderately compressed bodies; elongate, flattened snouts; and many large, sharp teeth. Family characteristics also include well-developed pelvic fins with 10 or more rays; a forked caudal fin; a complete lateral line; 10–20 branchiostegal rays; and 43–67 vertebrae. The family comprises five species in one genus.

The northern pike, *Esox lucius,* has a circumpolar distribution. In Alaska this species is widespread in Arctic Ocean and Bering Sea drainages. Northern pike do not occur naturally in northeastern Pacific drainages except in the Ahrnklin River drainage in Alaska and the headwaters of the Alsek and Taku rivers in the Yukon Territory and British Columbia. In some Alaskan localities northern pike are not a native species but were introduced by transplants. As Morrow (1980) pointed out in his review of freshwater fishes of Alaska, introductions of pike are either a nuisance or a blessing, according to one's point of view. Adult pike are voracious predators, feeding on fish and occasionally other animals, even birds, and are believed to be a serious predator of young waterfowl. In Alaska coregonids (Salmonidae) appear to be the major food item.

In some regions of the world the northern pike is highly regarded as a food fish, but in others has a reputation for muddy flavor and bonyness. Morrow (1980) considered the poor reputation as a food fish unjust, since the muddy taste can be eliminated by skinning and the excess bones removed by proper filleting.

Because they reach large sizes and put up a good fight, pikes are usually favorite game fishes in regions where they occur. The angling record for a northern pike, *E. lucius,* is a fish 133 cm (52.4 inches) long and weighing 21 kg (46 lb), caught in New York. One weighing about 20.5 kg (45 lb) was taken near Circle, Alaska, in the early 1960s. Most northern pike caught by anglers in Alaska weigh 1–3 kg (2.2–6.6 lb), and one weighing more than 11 kg (24 lb) would be considered remarkable (Morrow 1980). The largest pike is the muskellunge, *E. masquinongy,* of eastern North America, with a maximum length of 183 cm (72 inches; Page and Burr 1991).

Esox lucius Linnaeus, 1758 **northern pike**

Arctic coasts and interior of Alaska to Alaska Peninsula streams draining into Bristol Bay; isolated populations in Ahrnklin River and ponds near Yakutat; introduced to Susitna River and lakes and streams on Kenai Peninsula and around Anchorage; North America and Eurasia from arctic to temperate environments, south in North America to Nebraska and in Europe to northern Italy.

Clear vegetated lakes, quiet pools and backwaters of creeks, and small to large rivers; in spring moving inshore or upstream to marsh areas to spawn.

D 17–25; A 14–22; Pec 14–17; Pel 10–11; LLp 55–65; Ls 105–148; Br 13–16; PC 0; Vert 57–65.

- Dark grayish green to green or dark brown dorsally; creamy white ventrally; irregular longitudinal rows of yellow spots on side; median fins green, yellow, orange, or red, marked with dark blotches; pectoral and pelvic fins dusky; inconspicuous dark vertical line below eye.
- Body elongate, slender, moderately compressed; snout long, dorsoventrally flattened; mouth large, maxilla reaching to eye; lower jaw often projecting beyond upper.
- Dorsal and anal fins positioned posteriorly on body; caudal fin forked.
- Cheek fully scaled; preopercle partly scaled.
- Mandibular pores 5 or 6 (usually 5).
- Large canine teeth on inner edge of palatines, head of vomer, and lower jaw; smaller sharp, curved teeth on premaxillae, palatines, vomer, tongue, basibranchials, and pharyngobranchials.
- Gill rakers present as patches of sharp teeth.
- Length to 133 cm TL in North America.

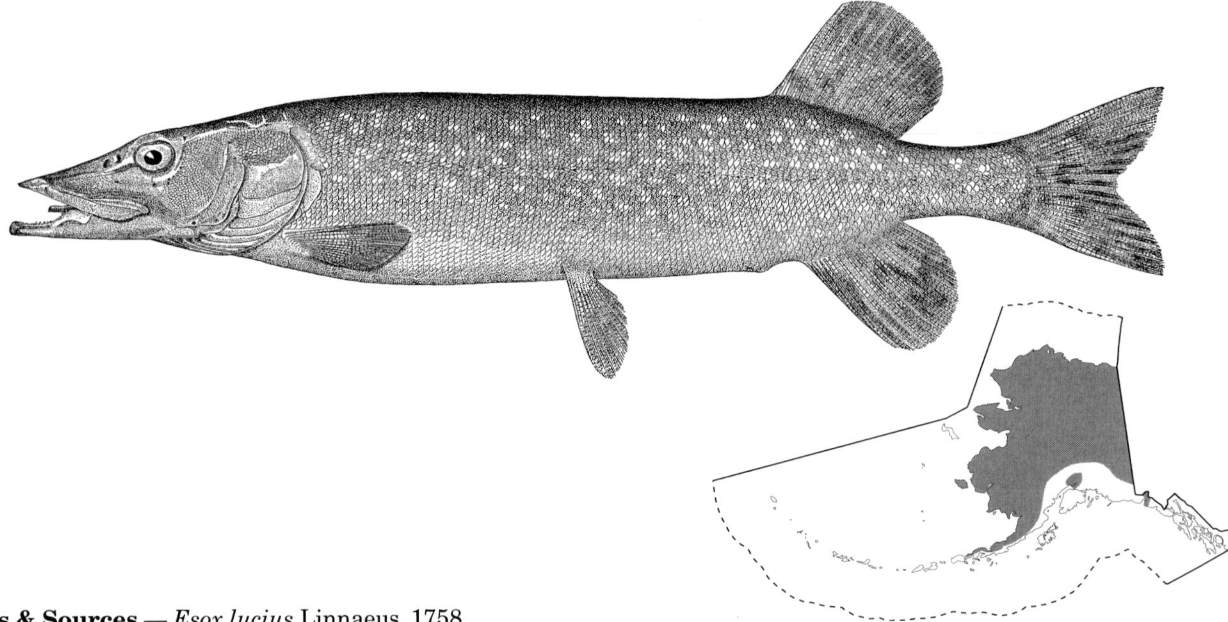

Notes & Sources — *Esox lucius* Linnaeus, 1758

Lucius lucius: Jordan and Evermann 1896, 1900; Evermann and Goldsborough 1907.

In Alaska *E. lucius* are easily recognized from their duckbill snout, posteriorly positioned dorsal and anal fins, and large mouth with many sharp teeth because they are the only pike in the state. Some of the other differences listed above, including coloration, numbers of mandibular pores and branchiostegal rays, and coverage of scales on the cheek, distinguish *E. lucius* from species in other regions.

Description: McPhail and Lindsey 1970:206–210; Scott and Crossman 1973:356–363; Crossman in Lee et al. 1980:133; Morrow 1974:59, 1980:165–169; Page and Burr 1991:61.

Figure: Goode 1884, pl. 183; Michigan.

Range: Mapped by Crossman (in Lee et al. 1980) and Morrow (1980). Early Alaskan records include those of Bean (1881a) and Nelson (18887) from the Yukon River and Townsend (1887) from the Kobuk River. McPhail and Lindsey (1986) and Lindsey and McPhail (1986), reviewing the freshwater fishes of Cascadia (Columbia River system and rivers north to the Stikine) and the Yukon and Mackenzie basins, reported *E. lucius* to be absent from the Stikine, Copper, and Susitna drainages of the Gulf of Alaska. In Pleistocene times it broke through from the Yukon River and entered Gulf of Alaska drainages in only a few places. Most populations of *E. lucius* in Alaska, including those of the Alaska Peninsula, entered from Beringia (Lindsey and McPhail 1986). Northern pike do not occur naturally in eastern North Pacific drainages except in Alaska in the Ahrnklin River drainage and in the Yukon Territory and British Columbia in the headwaters of the Alsek and Taku rivers (Morrow 1980). Illegal transplants in the 1970s by private individuals placed northern pike in the Susitna River drainage (Morrow 1980). Northern pike illegally stocked in the 1990s on the Kenai Peninsula and in the Anchorage area have jeopardized local sport fisheries by preying on rainbow trout and other stocked species to the extent the ADFG stocking programs for many lakes have had to be curtailed, to avoid using public dollars to feed the illegally introduced pike (B. Stratton in ADFG *Currents,* Winter 2000–2001).

Family Umbridae
Mudminnows

The family Umbridae, or mudminnows, contains three genera with at least five species (see discussion on this page). Like other esociforms, mudminnows occur only in freshwaters of the Northern Hemisphere. One species exists in Alaska: the Alaska blackfish, *Dallia pectoralis.* This species is locally abundant in Alaska in drainages of the Bering, Chukchi, and western Beaufort seas, and also occurs in eastern Siberia.

In mudminnows the snout is short compared to that of the Esocidae (pikes), and their bodies are cylindrical anteriorly and compressed posteriorly. They have a rounded caudal fin (compared to forked in Esocidae); smaller pelvic fins (2–7 rays), placed close to the anal fin; fewer pores in the infraorbital canal (not more than 3); fewer (5–9) branchiostegal rays; and more (32–42) vertebrae. In Alaska blackfish the pelvic fins are particularly small and may, although rarely, be absent or represented by only 1 ray.

Mudminnows are relatively small fishes, with the largest, which is the Alaska blackfish, possibly reaching 35 cm (almost 14 inches) in total length. Blackfish that large were reported by villagers of the eastern Chukchi Peninsula (Gudkov 1998). Alaska blackfish up to 25.4 cm (10 inches) are "not uncommon" in the Yukon-Kuskokwim Delta, and have been recorded up to 30.4 cm (12 inches) and 366 g (0.82 lb) in the area around Anchorage. At least one specimen caught in Alaska measured 33 cm (13 inches) (Morrow 1980).

Mudminnows can breathe atmospheric oxygen and survive in poorly oxygenated water unsuitable for other fishes. Turner (1886), during an expedition to the Yukon-Kuskokwim Delta, found them at times in sphagnum-covered areas which seemed "to contain but sufficient water to more than moisten the skin of the fish." Modern research (summarized by Morrow 1980) shows that Alaska blackfish can withstand complete absence of oxygen for up to 24 hours if the temperature is 0°C. Blackfish also have a legendary tolerance to cold. Turner (1886) said they could remain in baskets for weeks, and when thawed out the fish would be "as lively as ever." He saw blackfish thrown up alive by dogs after their stomachs thawed them out. Scientists who investigated this claim concluded that Alaska blackfish can survive after freezing parts of the body, even the head, but cannot withstand complete freezing (Scholander et al. 1953).

Alaska blackfish are not native to some of the localities in Alaska they now inhabit. Populations on St. Paul Island and around Anchorage were artificially introduced, the former intentionally. Blackfish accidentally introduced into lakes at Anchorage in the early 1950s thrived and the species spread via interconnecting waterways, as well as additional, illicit transplants, to other lakes in the area and became a serious problem in managing the rainbow trout sport fishery (Morrow 1980).

Classification of *Dallia* species is currently a matter of debate. In this guide *D. delicatissima* Smitt, 1881, and *D. admirabilis* Chereshnev & Balushkin, 1980, of northeastern Siberia are included in the synonymy of *D. pectoralis.* However, some taxonomists consider them to be valid species. Type localities for *D. delicatissima* include Port Clarence in Alaska, as well as the Chukchi Peninsula of Russia. Jordan and Evermann (1896b), Berg (1948), and McPhail and Lindsey (1970) classified *D. delicatissima* as a junior synonym of *D. pectoralis,* and for a while this view was generally accepted. However, Balushkin and Chereshnev (1982) and Chereshnev (1990, 1996) resurrected *D. delicatissima,* believing it to be a valid species. Andreev and Reshetnikov (1981) considered separation of *D. admirabilis* from *D. pectoralis* to be questionable, and Reshetnikov et al. (1997) questioned recognition of both *D. admirabilis* and *D. delicatissima.*

As well, the relationship of *Dallia* to other esociforms is not settled. Most classifications (e.g., Nelson 1994, Eschmeyer 1998) place *Dallia* in the Umbridae, but it has at times been classified in a separate family, the Dalliidae (e.g., Jordan and Evermann 1896), and some authors continue to do so (e.g., Bond 1996). Other possibilities have been explored. A study of external morphometry (Reist 1987) suggested that *Dallia* is more similar to pikes, genus *Esox,* than are the other umbrids. Evidence from a phylogenetic analysis using DNA sequencing (López et al. 2000) suggested *Dallia* should be classified in the family Esocidae.

Dallia pectoralis Bean, 1880 — Alaska blackfish

St. Lawrence, St. Matthew, and Nunivak islands, and in mainland Alaska west from Colville River along Arctic coast and south in Bering Sea drainages to Alaska Peninsula at Grass Creek (flows to Herendeen Bay); in Yukon-Tanana drainage as far upstream as Big Eldorado Creek, near Fairbanks; introduced to St. Paul Island and to lakes at Anchorage; northeastern Russia on Chukchi Peninsula.

Tundra freshwaters, usually in heavily vegetated swamps and ponds, occasionally in medium to large rivers and lakes with abundant vegetation.

D 10–16; A 11–16; Pec 29–38; Pel 0–4; Ls 76–100; GR 9–12; Br 7–8; PC 0; Vert 40–42.

- Dark green or brown dorsally; pale ventrally; irregular bars or blotches on side; body and fins with dark brownish speckling; median fins with pale margins, becoming pink to red in spawning males.
- Body elongate, cylindrical anteriorly and compressed posteriorly; snout short and depressed; mouth large, maxilla extending beyond mideye; lower jaw protruding beyond upper.
- Dorsal and anal fins positioned posteriorly on body; caudal fin broad and rounded; pectoral fin large and rounded; pelvic fin small, usually 3 rays in Alaskan specimens, and close to anus.
- Scales tiny and embedded; scale coverage on head strongly developed, extending anteriorly beyond posterior nostrils and onto lower jaw.
- Lateral line complete but pores minute and inconspicuous.
- Small, sharp teeth on premaxillae, palatines, vomer, and lower jaw (no teeth on maxillae, tongue, or basibranchials).
- Gill rakers short.
- Length to about 35 cm TL, in most areas rarely exceeding 20 cm.

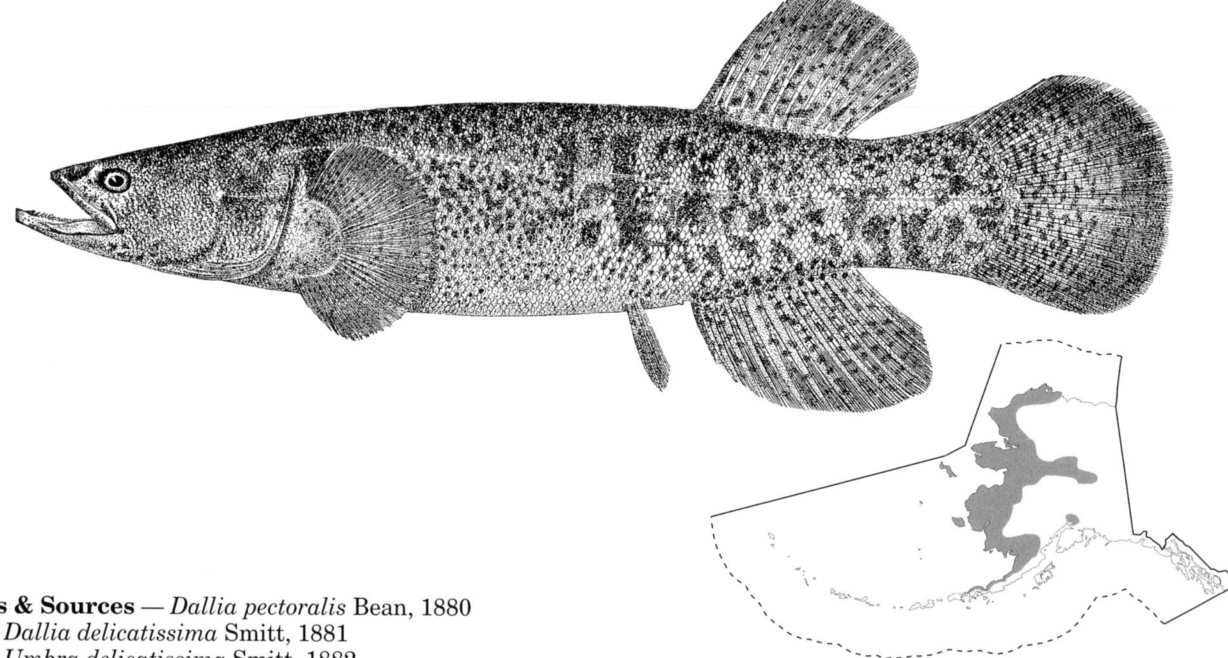

Notes & Sources — *Dallia pectoralis* Bean, 1880
Dallia delicatissima Smitt, 1881
Umbra delicatissima Smitt, 1882
Dallia admirabilis Chereshnev & Balushkin, 1980, was described as having fewer (22–30) pectoral fin rays, more limited scale coverage on the head, reduction of the seismosensory system of the head, and other differences from *D. pectoralis.* Andreev and Reshetnikov (1981) considered it to be a junior synonym of *D. pectoralis.*

Description: McPhail and Lindsey 1970:212–215; Scott and Crossman 1973:338–341; Morrow 1980:161–163; Chereshnev and Balushkin 1980; Balushkin and Chereshnev 1982:53–54. Pelvic fin rays are absent in some Siberian fish (*D. delicatissima* form), but absence is unknown in Alaskan populations.

Figure: Goode 1884, pl. 185; 208 mm TL, St. Michael, Alaska.

Range: Recorded range in North America was depicted on maps by McPhail and Lindsey (1970), Scott and Crossman (1973), Rohde (in Lee et al. 1980), and Morrow (1980). The known range was extended to Grass Creek, a small stream flowing to Herendeen Bay on the north side of the Alaska Peninsula, where Wagner (1988) found small specimens (50–62 mm) during a stream survey. The species is endemic to Beringia. Where present in Alaska it is usually abundant. However, it has a curiously circumscribed natural range. There is no evident barrier to its further dispersal, but there may be exclusion between *Dallia* and the cyprinid *Couesius plumbeus.* The ranges of the two species in Alaska are almost exactly complementary and may possibly be explained, at least in part, by predation on the young of *Dallia* by *Couesius,* which entered Alaska from the east (Lindsey and McPhail 1986). The description of range of *D. pectoralis* in Siberia by Scott and Crossman (1973) was updated by Chereshnev and Balushkin (1980), Balushkin and Chereshnev (1982), and Gudkov (1998).

Size: Gudkov 1998: unconfirmed report by Chukchi Peninsula residents of *Dallia* reaching 35 cm in tundra lakes.

Order Osmeriformes
Argentines and smelts

The order Osmeriformes includes argentines, slickheads, tubeshoulders, smelts, and other fishes which are similar in overall appearance to trouts, salmons, and whitefishes and are classified by some taxonomists with those fishes in the order Salmoniformes. Osmeriforms are small (typically under 30 cm), mostly silvery fishes. Fresh specimens of some smelts and argentines have a cucumber-like odor. The order contains two suborders and 13 families with about 74 genera and 235 species. The suborder Argentinoidei contains deepsea forage fishes and is represented in Alaska by 12–15 species in five families: Microstomatidae, Bathylagidae, Opisthoproctidae, Alepocephalidae, and Platytroctidae. The suborder Osmeroidei contains diadromous or freshwater fishes, represented in Alaska by seven species in the family Osmeridae. Morphological characteristics of the order include: maxilla in the gape of the mouth; no spines in the fins; dorsal adipose fin present or absent; nuptial tubercles usually absent; scales cycloid; and orbitosphenoid and basisphenoid absent. The first basibranchial has a ventral, cartilaginous vane. Most species have numerous long gill rakers.

Views on the relationships of osmeriform fishes vary considerably and alternative classifications to that followed here (Nelson 1994) have been proposed. From a cladistic analysis using 200 characters, Johnson and Patterson (1996) suggested a substantially different treatment. Their classification represents a return, in part, to earlier views that the osmeriforms belong with the salmoniforms. They proposed raising the suborder Argentinoidei to a new order, the Argentiniformes, and moving the suborder Osmeroidei to the order Salmoniformes as the sister-group to the suborder Salmonoidei. There would be no order Osmeriformes. The proposal is well supported by the evidence, and in future works J. S. Nelson (pers. comm., 29 Aug. 2000) intends to recognize Argentiniformes and classify Osmeridae with Salmonidae in Salmoniformes.

Family Microstomatidae
Pencilsmelts

The small-mouthed, long-bodied pencilsmelts are pelagic inhabitants of the subpolar to tropical regions of all oceans. The family contains three genera and 16 or 17 species. One species, *Nansenia candida,* occurs in offshore Alaskan waters. Its presence over Gulf of Alaska seamounts was reported by Hughes (1981), and in the central Bering Sea by Balanov and Il'insky (1992) and Balanov and Fedorov (1996). At the time Quast and Hall (1972) compiled their inventory of Alaskan fish species *N. candida* had been reported as close to Alaska as the Pacific Ocean off northern British Columbia. They called it the white pencilsmelt from the species name *candida,* which is Latin for "shining white" and refers to the bright, silvery appearance of the fish. Recent usage (e.g., Hubbs et al. 1979, Coad 1995, Peden 1998) favors the name bluethroat argentine.

In pencilsmelts the body is long and slender, and rounded to slightly compressed; the mouth is small, not reaching past the front of the eyes; the dorsal fin is at about midbody, above or behind the pelvic fins, and the anal fin is farther back; a dorsal adipose fin is present or absent; the anal fin base is about equal to or shorter than the caudal peduncle length; and the pectoral fins are on the side, usually at midside or above. Other pencilsmelt characteristics include: parietals usually meeting along midline; postcleithra present; mesocoracoids absent; swim bladder physoclistous and well developed; teeth present on vomer, palatines, and dentaries, absent from premaxilla, maxilla, and tongue; scales deciduous, and absent from the head; and lateral line scales extending onto the caudal fin. Basic counts for the family are: dorsal fin rays 9–12, anal rays 7–10, pectoral rays 7–14, pelvic rays 8–12, gill rakers on the first arch 21–46; branchiostegal rays 3 or 4, and vertebrae 35–50. Their nearest relatives, the Bathylagidae, have more anal fin rays and fewer branchiostegal rays.

In future works J. S. Nelson (pers. comm., 29 Aug. 2000) intends to recognize the close relationship of microstomatids and bathylagids by combining them in the Microstomatidae. Kobyliansky (1990) argued in detail that the Microstomatidae and Bathylagidae are sister-groups and classified them as subfamilies of Microstomatidae, an assessment that coincides with observations of Greenwood and Rosen (1971) and, most recently, Johnson and Patterson (1996).

Kawaguchi and Butler (1984) revised the classification of the genus *Nansenia.* Species of *Nansenia* were formerly placed in the family Argentinidae.

Nansenia candida Cohen, 1958 **bluethroat argentine**

Southern Bering Sea and Gulf of Alaska to Pacific Ocean off Baja California, and to Pacific off southern Kuril Islands and northern Japan.

Near surface to depth of about 1,500 m; epipelagic to mesopelagic.

D 9–12; A 8–11; Pec 9–12; Pel 9–11; GR 25–32; Br 3; PC 7–9; Vert 44–50.

- Bright and silvery in life; brown in preservative; bluish on nape, preopercle, and throat; fins clear.
- Body slender, moderately compressed.
- Transparent bones arching around dorsal and posterior margin of eye.
- Dorsal fin located at midbody or slightly posterior to midbody; dorsal adipose fin present, above anal fin; pectoral fin inserted low on side, upper end of pectoral base at midpoint between lateral line and ventral margin of body or slightly lower; pelvic fin base below posterior part of dorsal fin; anal fin origin slightly in advance of adipose fin; fewer anal fin rays than in Bathylagidae.
- Teeth on head of vomer and lower jaw conical, closely spaced in picket-fence arrangement.
- Length to 239 mm SL.

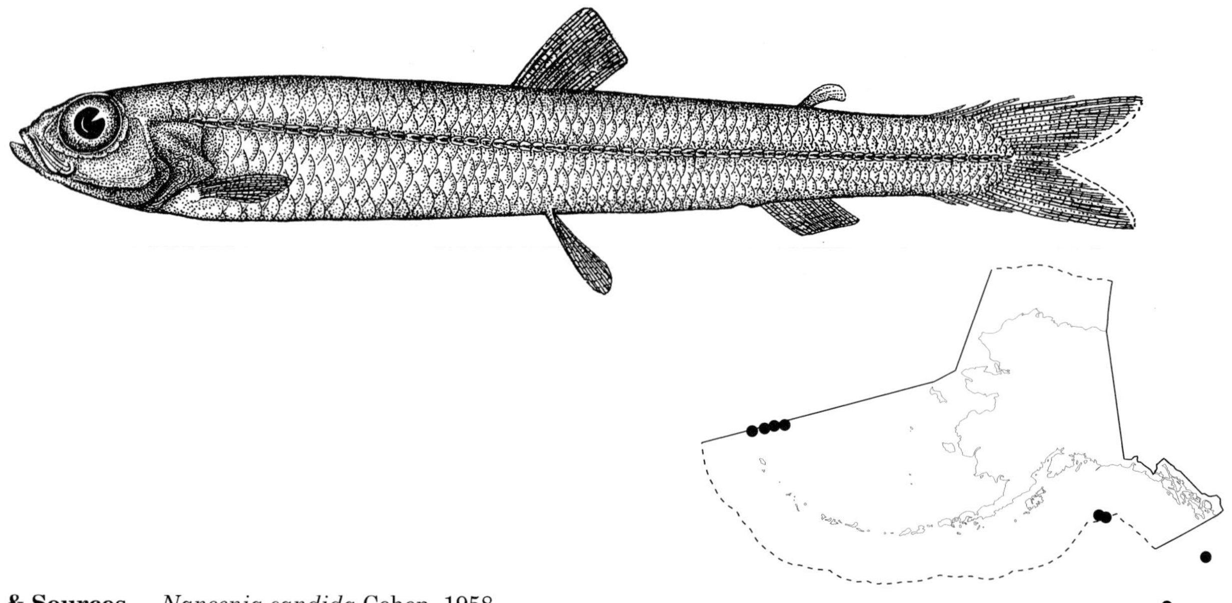

Notes & Sources — *Nansenia candida* Cohen, 1958
Nansenia sanrikuensis Kanayama & Amaoka, 1983

Kawaguchi and Butler (1984) considered the status of *N. sanrikuensis* as a distinct species questionable, pointing out that only vertebral counts separated *N. candida,* with 44–47 vertebrae, and *N. sanrikuensis,* with 48–49. Vertebral counts of 47–50 for seven specimens of *N. sanrikuensis* taken east of the southern Kuril Islands (Parin et al. 1995) bridge the difference and provide further evidence of an east–west geographical cline in *N. candida*.

Species of *Nansenia* are difficult to distinguish from each other; presence of only 3 branchiostegal rays narrows the choice to four species, and only one of those (*N. candida*) occurs in the Pacific Ocean as far north as Alaska.

Description: Cohen 1958a:53–54; Hart 1973:151–152; Kanayama and Amaoka in Amaoka et al. 1983:77–79; Kawaguchi and Butler 1984:4–7; Parin et al. 1995:195.

Figure: Hart 1973:151; 18 cm TL, off British Columbia.

Range: Possibly more common than indicated by the few dots on our map but Alaskan records are rare, perhaps because this narrow fish could easily pass through most nets and most surveys do not sample its preferred depths. Balanov and Il'insky (1992) reported they captured large, sexually mature specimens in the Bering Sea but did not give localities. Analyzing a sample of 490 hauls conducted in 1989 and 1990 in the Bering Sea, Sinclair et al. (1999) reported *N. candida* in 6% of hauls at 500–1,000 m and 2% of hauls at 200–500 m, without giving localities. Balanov and Fedorov (1996) recorded seven specimens (145–197 mm SL) taken at four localities in the Bering Sea at depths of 500–1,000 m: ZIN 49572, at 54°08'N, 170°13'E; ZIN 49573, at 54°59'N, 170°59'E; ZIN 49574, at 55°26'N, 171°59'E; and ZIN 49575, at 55°58'N, 172°53'E. Hughes (1981) reported that *N. candida* were obtained in 1979 by midwater trawls at depths of 549–622 m over Quinn and Surveyor seamounts, centered at 56°18'N, 145°13'W, and 56°03'N, 144°19'W, respectively. The northernmost record given by Kawaguchi and Butler (1984) in their revision of the family was at 52°13'N, 133°12'W (UBC 65-524), from one of the specimens recorded by Taylor (1967b). Taylor (1967b) recorded it from as far north off British Columbia as 52°17'N, 133°10'W; it was taken at depths of 730–825 m in the daytime and in early evening at 100–330 m in water depths of 2,220–2,750 m. Peden et al. (1985) reported that none was taken at Canadian Ocean Station Papa but that one specimen was captured at 49°34'N, 138°56'W. Kanayama and Amaoka (in Amaoka et al. 1983) recorded *N. candida* from the Pacific off northern Honshu, and Parin et al. (1995) and Ivanov (1997) off the southern Kuril Islands.

Family Bathylagidae
Deepsea smelts

Deepsea smelts inhabit meso- to bathypelagic zones of the world's oceans. The most recent revision of the family (Kobyliansky 1986) recognizes eight genera and 19 species, which have been divided for convenience into two groups (Cohen 1964, Peden 1981c, Kobyliansky 1985). Species in one group are dark (chocolate brown or bluish black), have a short gill slit not reaching up to the middle of the side, and are typically taken in relatively deep water. Species in the other group are light-colored (mostly silvery), have longer gill slits reaching to or above midside, and usually occur higher up in the water column. Other differences exist, such as, in the light group, a more slender and compressed body and a flatter dorsal profile of the head. Four bathylagid species inhabit the Bering Sea and Gulf of Alaska. *Leuroglossus schmidti* and *Lipolagus ochotensis* belong to the light group, and *Pseudobathylagus milleri* and *Bathylagus pacificus* to the dark group. The distinction by color is most evident in life. In preservative the light-colored species turn dark but still can be distinguished as they take on a characteristic (of the light group) coloration of yellowish brown belly and sides and dark brown back (Kobyliansky 1985).

Deepsea smelts are some of the most common mesopelagic fishes of the Bering Sea and Gulf of Alaska. In the Bering Sea, for example, the four Alaskan bathylagids are among the top eight most frequently occurring mesopelagic species (the others are in Myctophidae and Stomiidae). In some years *L. schmidti* has the second highest biomass, after the myctophid *Stenobrachius leucopsarus* (Sobolevsky et al. 1996, Sinclair et al. 1999).

Diagnostic features of bathylagids include: body elongate, in some species relatively deep anteriorly and tapering to a narrow caudal peduncle; eyes large, located near tip of short, blunt snout; mouth small, not extending beyond front of eye; dorsal fin at about midbody; anal fin near caudal fin, and usually longer than caudal peduncle; dorsal adipose fin present; pelvic fins inserted below or slightly behind dorsal fin; pectoral fins inserted low, near ventral surface of body; parietals not meeting along midline; teeth present on vomer, palatines, and dentaries, absent from premaxilla, maxilla, and tongue; scales large and highly deciduous; lateral line complete, but not always easily discernible; postcleithra and mesocoracoids absent; and swim bladder absent. Basic counts are: dorsal fin rays 6–13; anal fin rays 10–28; pectoral fin rays 7–16; pelvic fin rays 6–11; branchiostegal rays 2; and vertebrae 38–55.

Quast and Hall (1972) listed six deepsea smelt species from Alaska. Revisions to the family account for the lower number (four) in the present inventory. Gilbert (1915) synonymized *Bathylagus borealis* Gilbert in *B. pacificus* Gilbert, a revision followed by most authors (e.g., Norman 1930, Chapman 1940) but overlooked by Quast and Hall (1972). *Bathylagus callorhini* (Lucas), from its description (the types no longer exist), appears to be a junior synonym of *Leuroglossus schmidti* Rass (Dunn 1983). After some confusion, Alaskan specimens of *B. stilbius* (Gilbert) are classified in *L. schmidti*. Cohen (1956) synonymized *L. schmidti* in *L. stilbius*, which he later (Cohen 1964) placed in *Bathylagus*. Peden (1981c) retained the name *Leuroglossus* and presented evidence favoring recognition of both *L. stilbius* and *L. schmidti* in the North Pacific, with *L. schmidti* occurring north of the Strait of Juan de Fuca and *L. stilbius* to the south. This view was confirmed by Dunn (1983).

The names of two other Alaskan bathylagids changed when Kobyliansky (1986) revised the family, placing *Bathylagus ochotensis* Schmidt in *Lipolagus* and *B. milleri* Jordan & Gilbert in *Pseudobathylagus*.

Key to the Bathylagidae of Alaska

1 Gill slit long, reaching up to or above midside of body; anal fin base not much longer than dorsal fin base, or about same length . . . . (2)

1 Gill slit short, not reaching up to midside of body; anal fin base about twice length, or more, of dorsal fin base . . . . (3)

2 (1) Snout slightly longer than diameter of eye; anal fin rays usually 11–13 . . . . *Leuroglossus schmidti,* page 150

2 Snout much shorter than diameter of eye; anal fin rays usually 14 or 15 . . . . *Lipolagus ochotensis,* page 151

3 (2) Pelvic fin base below anterior portion of dorsal fin base; anal fin rays usually 22–26; pectoral rays 11–16; scales along midside 23–27 . . . . *Pseudobathylagus milleri,* page 152

3 Pelvic fin base below posterior portion of dorsal fin base; anal fin rays usually 18–20; pectoral rays 7–11; scales along midside 37–44 . . . . *Bathylagus pacificus,* page 153

Leuroglossus schmidti Rass, 1955 — northern smoothtongue

Bering Sea and North Pacific Ocean to southern British Columbia and to Sea of Okhotsk and northern Honshu, Japan.

Near surface to depth of 1,800 m, usually taken at 150–500 m; adults at upper mesopelagic depths in daytime and migrating to epipelagic depths, as shallow as 0–50 m, at night.

D 9–11; A 10–14; Pec 7–9; Pel 8–9; GR 25–29; Br 2; Vert 47–52.

- Silver; darker dorsally.
- Body slender and compressed; snout pointed; **eye relatively small, diameter slightly shorter than snout length**; median, knob-like process in posterior area of interorbital space; lower jaw projecting beyond upper jaw.
- Posterodorsal margin of opercle convex, in continuous curve with rest of opercular margin; **radial striations on operculum**.
- **Anal fin base short, almost equal to dorsal fin base**; pelvic fin base below anterior portion of dorsal fin base; anal rays usually 13 or fewer.
- Dorsal end of gill slit reaching above middle of side of body.
- Length to 200 mm SL or more in open ocean, typically less than 100 mm SL in coastal waters.

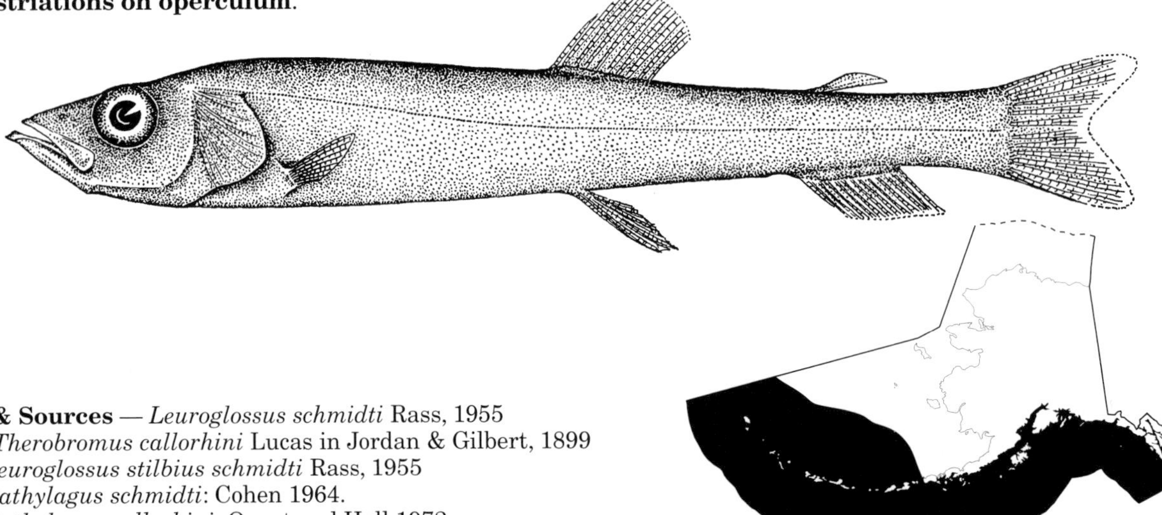

Notes & Sources — *Leuroglossus schmidti* Rass, 1955
?*Therobromus callorhini* Lucas in Jordan & Gilbert, 1899
Leuroglossus stilbius schmidti Rass, 1955
Bathylagus schmidti: Cohen 1964.
Bathylagus callorhini: Quast and Hall 1972.
Bathylagus stilbius: Quast and Hall 1972, specimens from Alaska.

Therobromus callorhini was described by Lucas (in Jordan and Gilbert 1899) from bones found in the stomachs of fur seals collected in the eastern Bering Sea. If, as has been suggested, this form is synonymous with *L. schmidti,* then technically the name should be *Leuroglossus callorhini.* However, the name *Therobromus callorhini* fell into disuse and, following provisions of the International Code of Zoological Nomenclature, Dunn (1983) considered the valid name of the northern smoothtongue to be *L. schmidti.* The type material of *T. callorhini* no longer exists.

Description: Rass 1955:329; Hart 1973:156–157; Peden 1981c; Dunn 1983; Kanayama in Amaoka et al. 1983:315; Uyeno in Masuda et al. 1984:41.

Figure: Hart 1973:156; 10 cm TL, from Alaska.

Range: Allen and Smith (1988:19) and Willis et al. (1988, fig. 28) plotted records from surveys of Bering Sea and North Pacific. The species is scattered throughout the mesopelagic zone. Allen and Smith (1988) remarked that the apparent concentration along the slope on their map is an artifact, reflecting the distribution of demersal trawl tows rather than distribution of the species. Sobolevsky et al. (1996) and Sinclair et al. (1999) reported distribution in recent surveys in the Bering Sea. A. A. Balanov (pers. comm., 23 Aug. 2000) reported that adults there were found as shallow as 0–50 m at night. However, in the Bering Sea in spring and summer, when daylight hours are increased, vertical migrations are not as distinct as in winter (Sobolevsky et al. 1996). In the Strait of Georgia, British Columbia, two 24-hour sampling series in April 1982 indicated that juveniles and adults did not migrate vertically, and that adults remained below 240 m (Mason and Phillips (1985). Earlier, Barraclough (1967) reported 16 individuals 45–90 mm in length were taken there at depths of 5–10 m at night.

Size: Mason and Phillips (1985) .

Lipolagus ochotensis (Schmidt, 1938) **popeye blacksmelt**

Bering Sea and North Pacific to Baja California and to Sea of Okhotsk and southern Honshu, Japan.

Near surface to depth of 6,100 m, usually taken at 200–1,000 m; adults generally remaining at and migrating within mesopelagic depths but sometimes found in lower epipelagic zone at night.

D 9–12; A 12–17; Pec 8–11; Pel 9–10; Ls 45–48; GR 24–29; Br 2; Vert 47–49.

- Silver; faint dark blotches along back.
- Body slender and compressed; snout somewhat pointed; **eye large, diameter much greater than snout length**; median, knob-like process in posterior area of interorbital space; jaws about equal in length or lower jaw slightly protruding.
- Posterodorsal margin of opercle notched or concave; **radial striations on operculum**, sometimes extending slightly beyond operculum as spines.
- **Anal fin base about same length as or slightly shorter than dorsal fin base**; pelvic fin base below posterior portion of dorsal fin base; anal rays usually 14 or 15.
- Dorsal end of gill slit reaching to or above middle of side of body.
- Length to 180 mm TL.

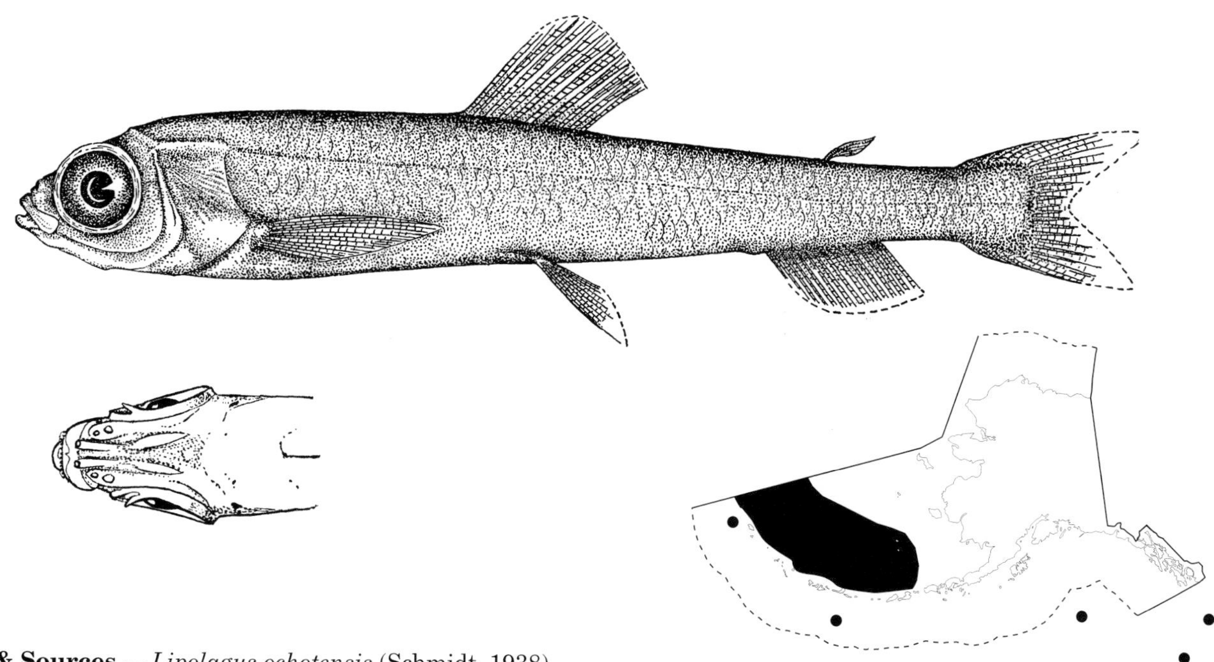

Notes & Sources — *Lipolagus ochotensis* (Schmidt, 1938)
Bathylagus ochotensis Schmidt, 1938

Description: Schmidt 1950:51–52; McAllister 1959:39; Kanayama in Amaoka et al. 1983:180, 316; Uyeno in Masuda et al. 1984:41; Kobyliansky 1985:9–11.

Figures: Hart 1973:154; 12 cm TL, off Cape St. James, British Columbia. Dorsal view of head: Schmidt 1950, pl. 1; 95 mm TL, Sea of Okhotsk. The longitudinal, vertical lamellae in the interorbital space occur in other bathylagids, including *Pseudobathylagus milleri* (Jordan and Evermann 1898, Cohen 1966), and may not differentiate the species.

Range: Records with locality data for Alaska outside the Bering Sea are scarce. Rather than estimate limits south of the Aleutian Islands and in the Gulf of Alaska on the above map, we give dots for the few available records. Taylor (1967b) reported specimens taken west of the Queen Charlotte Islands, British Columbia, and summarized previous records, including specimens collected by Aron (1960) south of the Aleutians at 50°47'N, 174°31'W. McAllister (1959) recorded *L. ochotensis* from 50°N, 135°W (*not* 55°N, as reported by Hart [1973]). Willis et al.'s (1988, fig. 20) map, based on a review of data from numerous surveys, shows one record in the eastern Bering Sea and one south of the Aleutian Islands, with others in the southern Gulf of Alaska and across the Pacific to the Commander Islands and southern Kamchatka to the southern Kuril Islands. Most records in the eastern Pacific are offshore at latitudes of British Columbia and farther south. Kobyliansky (1985) reported occurrence in the western Bering Sea as far north as 58°N, south of Cape Olyutorskiy. Sobolevsky et al. (1996) and Sinclair et al. (1999) reported it to be one of the most common mesopelagic fish species of the Bering Sea in surveys extending north to Cape Navarin. The latter authors reported *L. ochotensis* in 98% of about 500 tows at 500–1,000 m, and in 69% of the tows at 200–500 m. Like other bathylagids, it undergoes vertical migrations and does not form concentrations. From surveys extending from the Kuril Islands to the northern Bering Sea, A. A. Balanov (pers. comm., 23 Aug. 2000) reported that *L. ochotensis* generally does not migrate as far as the epipelagic zone but is sometimes found there at night. Miya (1995) found that in Sagami Bay, central Japan, larvae did not occur above 200 m but remained in the upper mesopelagic zone at about 300–600 m during both day and night.

Size: Miller and Lea 1972. Males and females attain maturity at about 70 mm and 100 mm SL, respectively (Miya 1995).

Pseudobathylagus milleri (Jordan & Gilbert, 1898) **stout blacksmelt**

Bering Sea and North Pacific Ocean to southern California and to southern Sea of Okhotsk and southern Honshu, Japan.

At depths of 60–6,600 m; adults generally remaining at and migrating within lower mesopelagic and bathypelagic depths, and not ascending to epipelagic zone.

D 6–9; A 20–28; Pec 11–16; Pel 6–8; Ls 23–27; GR 25–27; Br 2; Vert 51–55.

- Metallic blackish brown to black; gill membranes bluish black.
- Body slender and compressed, moderately robust anteriorly; snout short; eye large, diameter about twice snout length or larger; no knob-like process in interorbital space posteriorly; lower jaw and lips slightly protruding.
- Posterodorsal margin of opercle straight; no radial striations on operculum.
- **Anal fin base long, twice length of dorsal fin base or longer**; anal fin rays usually 22–26; **pelvic fin base below anterior portion of dorsal fin base**.
- Dorsal end of gill slit not reaching middle of side of body.
- Length to 216 mm TL.

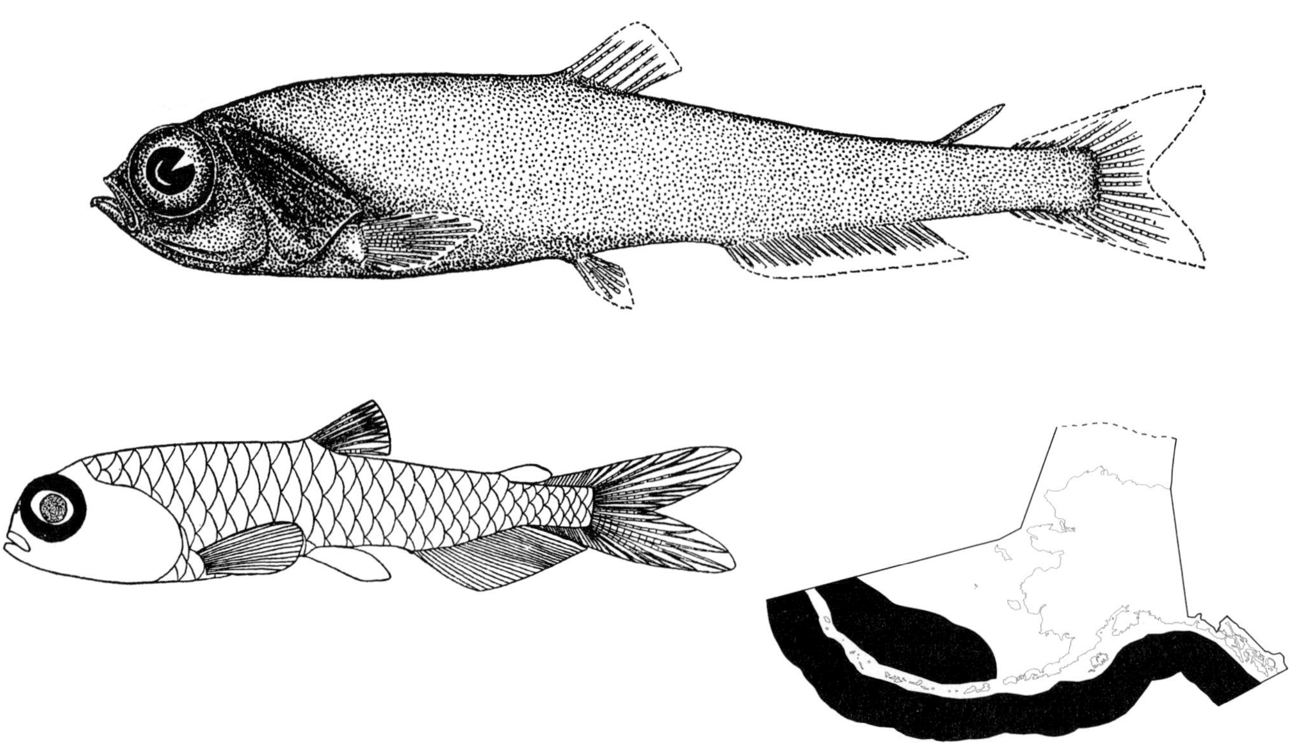

Notes & Sources — *Pseudobathylagus milleri* (Jordan & Gilbert in Jordan & Evermann, 1898)
Bathylagus milleri Jordan & Gilbert in Jordan & Evermann, 1898
Bathylagus alascanus Chapman, 1939

Description: Jordan and Evermann 1898:2825; Chapman 1939:505–507; Cohen 1966; Hart 1973:153; Kanayama in Amaoka et al. 1983:179, 317; Uyeno in Masuda et al. 1984:41.

Figures: Upper: Hart 1973:153; 7.8 cm TL, off Queen Charlotte Sound, British Columbia. Lower: Chapman 1939:fig. 58; 83 mm without caudal fin, from northern Gulf of Alaska.

Range: Chapman (1939) recorded *P. milleri* at numerous stations extending from southern tip of Queen Charlotte Islands off Cape St. James through the Gulf of Alaska to south of the Shumagin Islands. Willis et al. (1988, fig. 27) plotted records from the southcentral and southeastern Bering Sea, the Aleutian Islands, and other North Pacific localities. Shinohara et al. (1994) recorded additional specimens from the Gulf of Alaska and south of the Aleutian Islands. Fedorov and Sheiko (2002) reported *P. milleri* to be abundant in the vicinity of the Commander Islands. Sinclair et al. (1999) reported occurrence in the Bering Sea in 98% of about 500 tows at 500–1,000 m, and in 42% of the tows at 200–500 m. Sobolevsky et al. (1996) and A.A. Balanov (pers. comm., 23 Aug. 2000) reported that it does not rise to the epipelagic zone. Pearcy et al. (1982) found that off Oregon *B. milleri* migrated from about 650 m during the day to 500 m or above at night. Peden et al. (1985), reporting on daylight hauls at Canada's Ocean Station Papa, said young *P. milleri* (less than 60 mm SL) were most abundant at depths of 500–600 m, whereas individuals larger than 100 mm SL were more common in nets reaching 800 m or deeper.

Size: Miller and Lea 1972.

Bathylagus pacificus Gilbert, 1890 — **slender blacksmelt**

Southern Bering Sea and North Pacific to Gulf of California and to Sea of Okhotsk and Honshu, Japan.

At depths of 150–7,700 m; adults generally remaining at lower mesopelagic and bathypelagic depths, and not ascending to epipelagic zone.

D 8–13; A 15–22; Pec 7–11; Pel 7–10; Ls 37–44; GR 27–33; Br 2; Vert 45–49.

- Metallic blackish brown to black; head blue-black.
- Body slender and compressed; snout short; eye diameter about twice snout length; no knob-like process in interorbital space posteriorly; lower jaw projecting.
- Posterodorsal margin of opercle projecting posteriorly or straight, not indented; no radial striations on operculum.
- **Anal fin base long, twice length of dorsal fin base or longer**; anal fin rays usually 18–20; **pelvic fin base below posterior portion of dorsal fin base**.
- Dorsal end of gill slit not reaching middle of side of body.
- Length to about 254 mm TL.

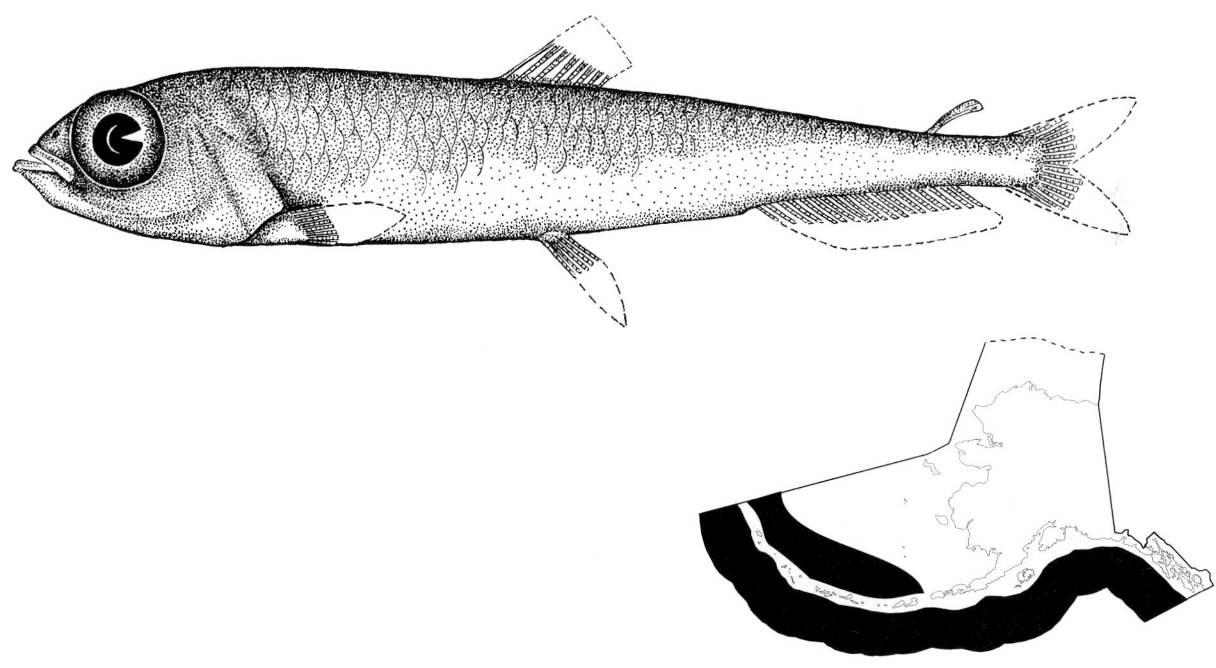

Notes & Sources — *Bathylagus pacificus* Gilbert, 1890
Bathylagus borealis Gilbert, 1896

Description: Gilbert 1890:55, 1896:402; Chapman 1940:3–5; Hart 1973:155; Kanayama in Amaoka et al. 1983:180, 316; Uyeno in Masuda et al. 1984:41.

Figure: Hart 1973:155; 14 cm TL, off Triangle Island, British Columbia.

Range: Gilbert (1896) described specimens taken north of Unalaska Island. Chapman (1940) reported records from south of the Semidi Islands and throughout the Gulf of Alaska offshore to west of the Queen Charlotte Islands. Midwater trawl catches of *B. pacificus* mapped by Willis et al. (1988, fig. 23) were distributed widely in the southern Bering Sea and throughout the Gulf of Alaska and northern North Pacific offshore. Fedorov and Sheiko (2002) reported *B. pacificus* to be abundant in the vicinity of the Commander Islands. Sinclair et al. (1999) reported occurrence in the Bering Sea in 100% of about 500 tows at 500–1,000 m, and in 33% of the tows at 200–500 m. *Bathylagus pacificus* does not migrate to the epipelagic zone (e.g., A. A. Balanov, pers. comm., 23 Aug. 2000), and studies by Pearcy et al. (1982) off Oregon indicate it does not undergo significant diel vertical migration within the mesopelagic zone. Peden et al. (1985), analyzing daylight catches at Canada's Ocean Station Papa, found that individuals under 70 mm SL were most abundant in hauls reaching 600–800 m, whereas fish larger than 100 mm SL were usually taken in hauls reaching 800 m or deeper. Reports from epipelagic and upper mesopelagic depths probably represent larvae and juveniles, or fishing range of nets rather than actual depth of capture (true also of *Pseudobathylagus milleri*, and to a lesser extent of *Lipolagus ochotensis*).

Size: Fitch and Lavenberg 1968. Maximum length given by Miller and Lea (1972) was 190.5 mm TL. Most specimens reported are much smaller. Largest of 25 specimens examined by Chapman (1940) was 155 mm SL.

Family Opisthoproctidae
Spookfishes

Spookfishes, also called barreleyes, are mesopelagic to bathypelagic fishes with many shapes, from short and compressed to elongate and cylindrical; unusually long paired fins; and tubular eyes. The eyes are directed anteriorly, dorsally, or dorsolaterally in the various species and provide binocular vision and increased efficiency in light perception. The family contains six genera with 11 described species distributed primarily in temperate to tropical regions of the Pacific, Indian, and Atlantic oceans. At least two spookfish species occur within the 200-mile limit off Alaska: barreleye, *Macropinna microstoma,* and winged spookfish, *Dolichopteryx parini.* Several species of *Dolichopteryx* have been described, but *M. microstoma* is the only species known in *Macropinna.*

Other distinguishing morphological features of spookfishes include: snout more or less produced; mouth very small, not reaching eye; premaxillae rudimentary or absent; maxillae thin, scalelike, easily lost; dorsal and anal fins far back on body; dorsal adipose fin usually present; pelvic fins abdominal, well developed, base position variable; pectoral fin base lateral, usually high on side of body; vomerine, palatine, and dentary teeth present or absent; scales large, cycloid, deciduous; lateral line running straight along lateral midline, not continuing onto caudal fin; frontal bones fused; parietal bones not meeting on midline; postcleithra and mesocoracoids absent; swim bladder usually absent; photophores present in some species, often associated with the eyes; branchiostegal rays 2–4; and vertebrae about 34–84. Spookfishes are soft and delicate, and usually are badly damaged during capture. Although most species lack a swim bladder they are not particularly efficient swimmers; Cohen (1964) suggested that the elongation of the paired fins and, in some species, the high, forward placement of the pelvic fins provide partial solution to this problem. Winged spookfish, *D. parini,* grow to more than 22 cm (8.7 inches) in total length but most spookfish species are under 7.6 cm (3 inches).

The barreleye, *M. microstoma,* is widespread in the North Pacific. Several records document its occurrence in Alaska. The winged spookfish, *Dolichopteryx parini,* may also be widely distributed in the North Pacific but records of it are scarce and include few from Alaska. Describing *D. parini,* Kobyliansky and Fedorov (2001) gave a range extending from California to the Bering Sea and to Japan and the Sea of Okhotsk. Owing to discrepancies in the published descriptions, the inclusion of a spookfish recorded by Hart (1973) as *Dolichopteryx* sp. from Ocean Station Papa in the synonymy of *D. parini* is not entirely convincing. Kobyliansky and Fedorov (2001) also included specimens recorded as *Dolichopteryx* sp. from Japan and California by Fujii (in Masuda et al. 1984) and Moser (in Moser et al. 1996), respectively, in the synonymy, but expressed reservation later in their text. They noted that the diagnostic characters reported by Fujii and Moser included lower numbers of dorsal and anal fin rays, outside the range of the *D. parini* type material, and suggested those records may represent another species. Hart (1973) did not report fin ray counts for the Station Papa specimen and details of coloration and fin lengths differ from those given for *D. parini,* so it is possible that Hart's record should also have been included only provisionally in the synonymy. Specimens of *Dolichopteryx* collected in the future from Alaska and other regions in the eastern North Pacific may help to resolve this problem.

Quast and Hall (1972) included *M. microstoma* on their list of Alaskan fish species, but *Dolichopteryx* had not yet been reported from the region.

The most recent description and classification of the Opisthoproctidae (Cohen 1964) primarily treats the western North Atlantic species. There is no detailed synopsis of species inhabiting the Pacific Ocean.

Key to the Opisthoproctidae of Alaska

1 Body deep and compressed . . . . *Macropinna microstoma,* page 155

1 Body elongate and subcylindrical . . . . *Dolichopteryx parini,* page 156

Macropinna microstoma Chapman, 1939 **barreleye**

Bering Sea to eastern South Pacific west of Islas Juan Fernández, Chile, and to western North Pacific off Kuril Islands and northern Japan.

Midwater at depths of 16–1,015 m; primarily mesopelagic.

D 11–12; A 14; Pec 17–19; Pel 9–10; LLs 23–26; Br 3–4; Vert 34–37.

- Dark brown.
- **Body deep** and compressed.
- Snout shovel-like; mouth tiny.
- Eye large, tubular, directed dorsally.
- Dorsal and anal fins far back on body; **dorsal adipose fin present**; anal fin origin below middle of dorsal fin base; pelvic fin closer to pectoral fin than to anal fin; pectoral and pelvic fins long, pectoral fin almost reaching anal fin origin and pelvic fin reaching caudal peduncle.
- Gill membranes broadly united to each other and attached to isthmus leaving broad free margin.
- Length to 160 mm TL.

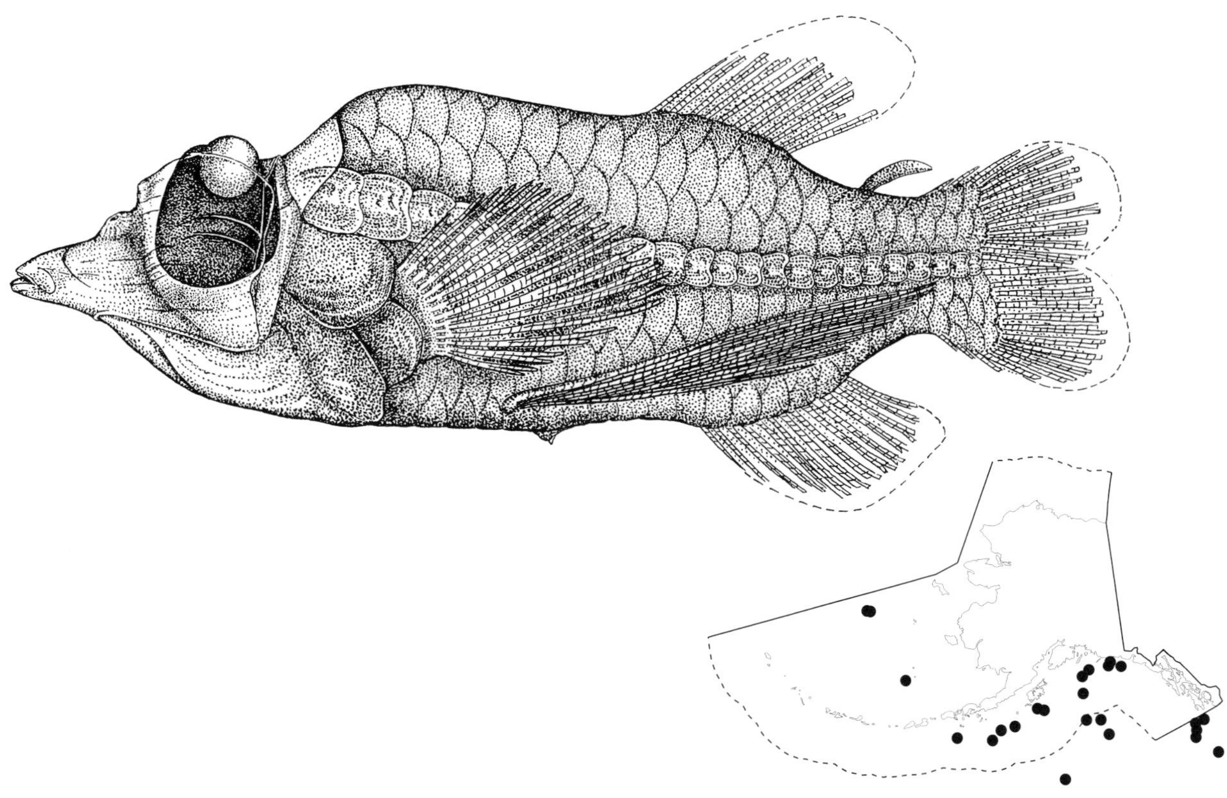

Notes & Sources — *Macropinna microstoma* Chapman, 1939

Description: Chapman 1939:509–515; Hart 1973:159–160.

Figure: Hart 1973:159; 9 cm TL, off British Columbia.

Range: Chapman (1939) recorded numerous larval to adult specimens taken by the International Fisheries Commission in the Gulf of Alaska incidental to halibut investigations. Localities ranged from southwest of Kodiak Island at 53°52'N, 158°29'W, to south of Cape St. Elias at 59°21'N, 143°51'W, off Alaska, and south to 51°46'N, 131°37'W off the Queen Charlotte Islands, British Columbia. Fedorov (1973a) reported *M. microstoma* from the Bering Sea but without providing locality or other data. Yabe et al. (1981) provided the first confirmed records from the Bering Sea, including one specimen taken at 59°48'N, 178°47'W, and one at 59°53'N, 178°54'W. The coordinates they gave for the third specimen (USNM 220876) are incorrect; NMNH records give 56°00'N, 170°21'W, bottom depth 708–780 m. Records plotted by Willis et al. (1988, fig. 36) from a compilation of midwater trawl surveys in the North Pacific included one in southeastern Bering Sea at about the same locality as Yabe et al.'s (1981) southernmost record, and one south of the eastern Aleutian Islands. *Macropinna* is a characteristic member of the mesopelagic fauna of the temperate North Pacific (Yabe et al. 1981). It does not form concentrations but is scattered, like most other mesopelagic fishes. Fedorov and Sheiko (2001) reported it to be abundant off the Commander Islands and gave new depth extremes (16–1,015 m). Previously reported at depths of 99–891 m, after Grinols (1965).

Size: Miller and Lea (1972), in a general statement. A specimen of similar large size from California is in lot SIO 63-379; catalog gives size of 133 mm SL which, from SL = 83% TL (R. Baxter, unpubl. data), would be about 160 mm TL. Most specimens on record are under 100 mm SL, but larger specimens are not particularly unusual. Some specimens from California in the SIO collection are 119–120 mm SL, Peden et al. (1985) reported that specimens west of British Columbia at Ocean Station Papa reached at least 120 mm SL, and Hughes (1981) reported that 16 barreleye measuring 60–140 mm FL were obtained in 1979 in the Gulf of Alaska over Quinn and Surveyor seamounts.

Dolichopteryx parini Kobyliansky & Fedorov, 2001 **winged spookfish**

Southern Bering Sea and North Pacific Ocean to southern British Columbia and to Honshu, Japan, and Sea of Okhotsk; possibly throughout the North Pacific.

Midwater at depths of about 200–1,000 m, possibly shallower; mesopelagic.

D 9–13; A 8–11; Pec 14–15; Pel 9–11; GR 26-28; Br 2; Vert 46–47.

- Whitish, with dark scale pockets; paired fins black, median fins lightly pigmented or dark; dark peritoneum visible through body wall.
- **Body elongate** and subcylindrical.
- Mouth terminal, very small.
- Eye large, tubular, directed dorsally.
- Dorsal and anal fins far back on body; **dorsal adipose fin present**; anal fin origin below middle of dorsal fin; pectoral and pelvic fins long, pectoral fin reaching nearly to or beyond anal fin origin and pelvic fin nearly to or beyond caudal fin base.
- Gill membranes broadly united to each other and attached to isthmus leaving broad free margin.
- Length to 217 mm SL.

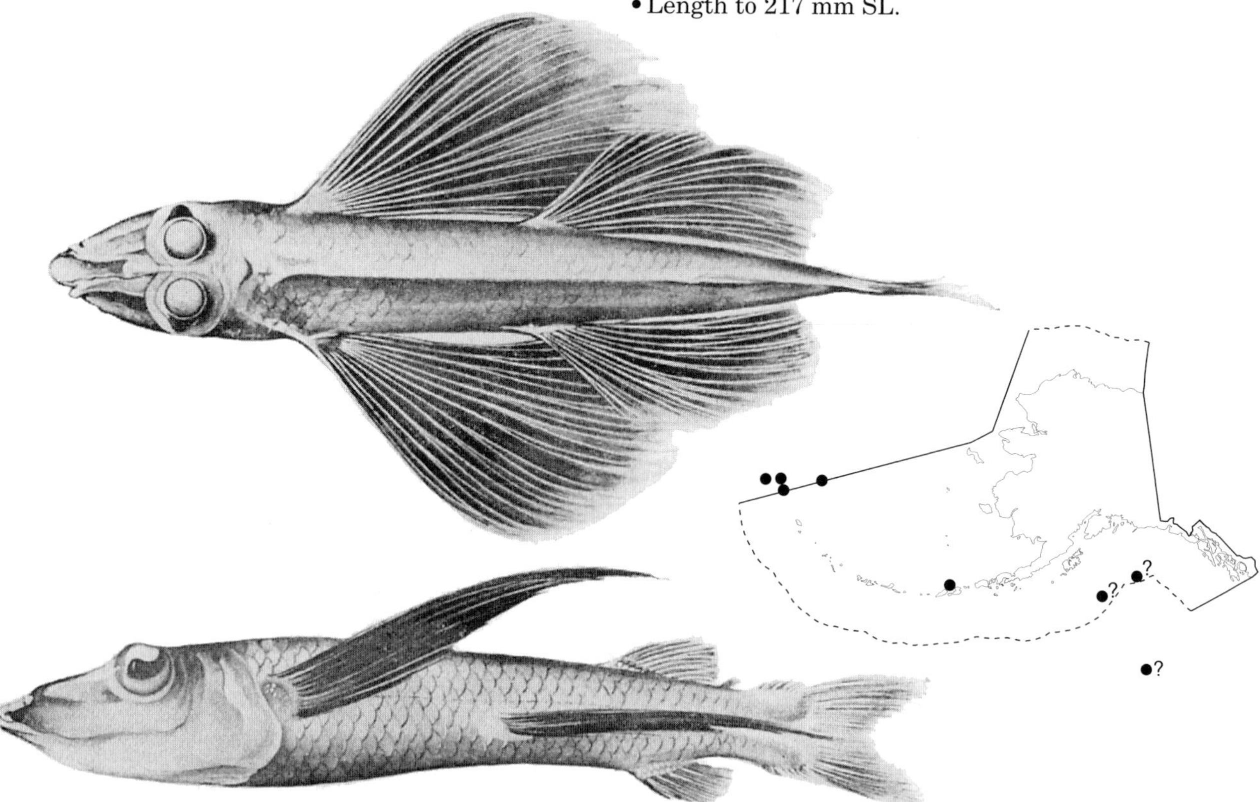

Notes & Sources — *Dolichopteryx parini* Kobyliansky & Fedorov, 2001

Dolichopteryx sp. recorded by Hart (1973) from the eastern North Pacific west of British Columbia, Fujii (in Masuda et al. 1984) from "warm waters" of the western North Pacific, and Moser (in Moser et al. 1996) from the California Current are provisionally included in the synonymy following Kobyliansky and Fedorov (2001). The determination of those records and some others from the North Pacific is still a matter for study. Counts given by Fujii (in Masuda et al. 1984) are: D 9, A 8, Pec 15, Pel 9; and by Moser (in Moser et al. 1996) are: D 9, A 8, Pec 14–15, Pel 11, Vert 45. For *D. parini,* Kobyliansky and Fedorov (2001) gave D 11–13, A 10–11, Pec 15, Pel 10–11.

Description: Hart 1973:158–159; Fujii in Masuda et al. 1984: 42; Kobyliansky and Fedorov 2001.

Figures: Hart 1973:158; Ocean Station Papa.

Range: Balanov and Il'insky (1992) reported two large, mature specimens from the Bering Sea. Localities for those and other Bering Sea specimens were given by Fedorov and Parin (1998) and Kobyliansky and Fedorov (2001): ZIN 40872 (1 specimen), 53°41'N, 167°30'W, depth 560–700 m; ZIN uncataloged (3), 54°55'N, 169°14'E, 200–500 m; ZIN 49599 (2 paratypes, 161–170 mm SL), 55°58'N, 172°53'E, 500–1,000 m; and ZIN 49970 (2 paratypes, 125–152 mm SL), 53°01'N, 170°01'E, 0–200 m. They also listed records from west of Vancouver Island (ZIN 40871), the Sea of Okhotsk (ZIN 48800, holotype), and off the southern Kuril Islands. Recently, A. A. Balanov (pers. comm., 3 Feb. 1999) collected specimens (4 juveniles, 2 adults) from the Pacific off northern Honshu which he identified as *D. parini.* Hart (1973) recorded one specimen as *Dolichopteryx* sp. from Ocean Station Papa. Hughes (1981) reported specimens of *Dolichopteryx* sp. measuring 200 mm FL obtained by midwater tows over Patton and Quinn seamounts in 1979. Vouchers were to be sent to the University of Washington (Hughes 1981), but the UW collection does not have any records of *Dolichopteryx* (B. W. Urbain, pers. comm., 1 Feb. 1999).

Size: The holotype, from the Sea of Okhotsk, is 217 mm SL (Kobyliansky and Fedorov 2001).

Family Platytroctidae
Tubeshoulders

Tubeshoulders, family Platytroctidae, and slickheads, family Alepocephalidae, are closely related, dark-colored deepsea fishes of the superfamily Alepocephaloidea. Tubeshoulders are mesopelagic and bathypelagic midwater fishes, generally occupying the 200–2,000-m depth range, while most slickheads (as adults) are associated with the bottom, usually at greater depths. The presence of a tube, often supported by a modified scale, below the lateral line and above the pectoral fin distinguishes the tubeshoulders. This tube is the external opening of a shoulder organ that secretes a blue-green luminous fluid. The shoulder apparatus is unique to the tubeshoulder family. Some tubeshoulders also have light organs, mostly on the ventral surface, which is somewhat flattened. The tubeshoulder family contains about 13 genera and 35 species, and is represented in all oceans. The presence of four species within the 200-mile limit off Alaska in the Bering Sea or Gulf of Alaska is known from one to a few records each: shining tubeshoulder, *Sagamichthys abei*; pitted tubeshoulder, *Maulisia argipalla*; teardrop tubeshoulder, *Holtbyrnia latifrons*; and lanternjaw tubeshoulder, *H. innesi*. The dark tubeshoulder, *M. acuticeps,* has been found in the Bering Sea over the Shirshov Ridge and is included in this book as another possible Alaskan species.

Although the adults of many deepsea fishes occur at the greater depths of record whereas the young inhabit shallower depths, this may not be true for tubeshoulders. Matsui (1991) found that young stages of *S. abei* and *H. latifrons* occurred over the entire depth range of the species. Diel vertical migration, a behavior of many deepsea pelagic fishes, evidently does not occur among tubeshoulders. Matsui and Rosenblatt (1987) discounted earlier claims that some tubeshoulder species migrate toward the surface at night. These authors also noted that records of tubeshoulders from depths 200 m and shallower are extremely rare and that the single record from the Pacific Ocean, which involved *S. abei,* is probably an error. Existing records of tubeshoulders from depths greater than 2,000 m are probably based on fish entering the nets at depths shallower than the maximum depth of the tow. Tubeshoulders tend to occur near continents, islands, submarine ridges, and seamounts.

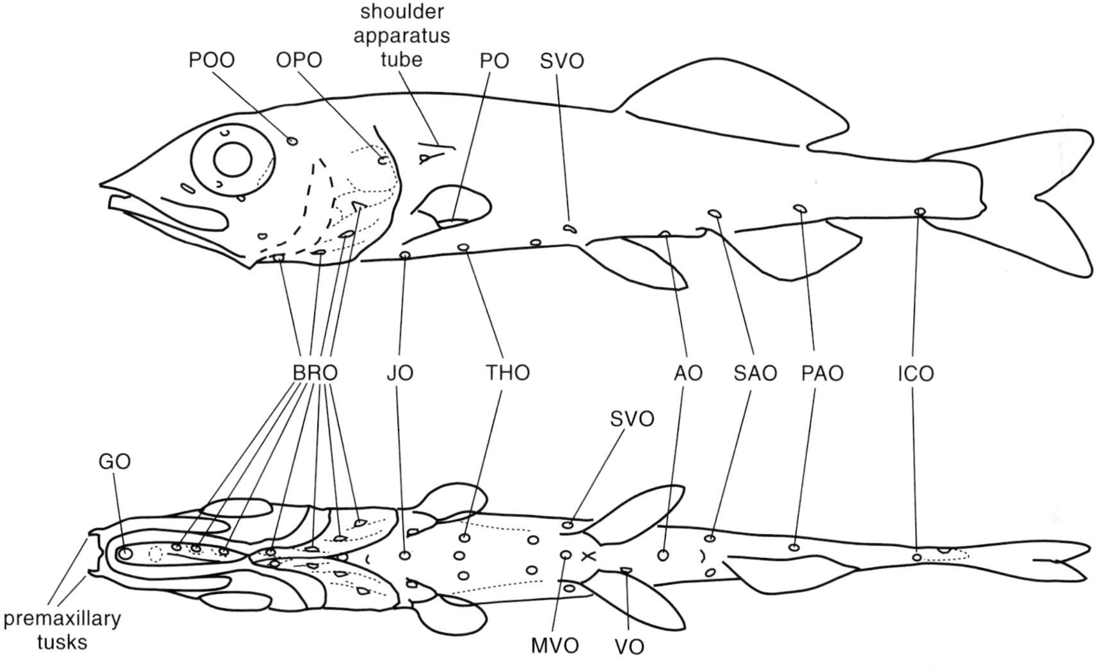

Major features and photophores in tubeshoulders

GO, gular organ; POO, postorbital organ; OPO, opercular organ; BRO, branchiostegal organs; JO, jugular organ; PO, pectoral organ; THO, thoracic organ; MVO, midventral organ; SVO, supraventral organ; VO, ventral organ; AO, anal organ; SAO, supra-anal organ; PAO, postanal organ; ICO, infracaudal organ. (Adapted from Parr 1960.)

Locations of the shoulder apparatus and major photophores in tubeshoulders are shown in the diagram on the preceding page. Photophores which disappear in adults, are rudimentary, or are not found in the three genera in our area are not labeled. Sometimes the photophores are covered by dark tissue so that the middle is blacked out (see illustration with the account for *S. abei*). In damaged specimens it may be difficult to find any photophores, but the supra-anal organ (SAO) is usually discernible even in poor specimens and is a reliable indicator of the presence of a photophore system (Parr 1960). In all the Alaskan species, except *S. abei,* the anterior premaxillary teeth are enlarged into "tusks" and project horizontally, and scales are absent from the head. In *S. abei* scales are not only present on the head, they are arranged opposite the usual fashion with each scale overlapping the scale before it so that the anterior end of each scale is exposed, not the posterior end. Other diagnostic characters of tubeshoulders include: body slightly to strongly compressed, elongate to moderately deep; head and eyes moderate to large; mouth usually large; dorsal and anal fins far back on body, the dorsal fin usually with a few more rays than the anal fin; pectoral fins small but with numerous rays (14–28); pelvic fins at about midpoint of body (absent in a non-Alaskan species); scales cycloid and thin; lateral line marked by enlarged scales or papillae, or absent; teeth small, except for the tusks; branchiostegal rays 4–8; and vertebrae 40–52. Like other alepocephaloids, in tubeshoulders the parietal bones are separated by the supraoccipital, the dorsal part of the opercle is reduced, mesocoracoids are present, and adipose fin and swim bladder are absent.

Tubeshoulders range in maximum recorded size from about 13 cm (5.1 inches) to 30 cm (11.8 inches) in standard length (few total lengths are available). *Sagamichthys abei* and *M. acuticeps,* at about 25 cm SL, are the largest species treated in this guide.

Only *S. abei* was listed in the inventory of Alaskan fish species by Quast and Hall (1972), and there only as a species likely to occur in the area. It has since been recorded from Alaska in the Bering Sea and Gulf of Alaska, and there are additional records from nearby waters off British Columbia. The present inventory also reflects revisions of the family by Sazonov (1976), Matsui and Rosenblatt (1987), and Sazonov et al. (1993), as well as recently published extensions of known range of some species into the region. The first record of *M. acuticeps* from the Bering Sea off Russia (Balanov 1992) demonstrates this species is widely distributed—Peru, Japan, and now east of Karaginskiy Island—and could also exist in U.S. waters. Specimens formerly identified as *M. mauli* Parr from the Bering Sea and North Pacific have been placed in the synonymy of *M. argipalla* Matsui & Rosenblatt; these include a specimen from the eastern Bering Sea identified as *M. mauli* by Fedorov (1973a). Records of *M. mauli* from the North Atlantic are the only certain records of that species. Specimens formerly identified as *H. macrops* Maul from the eastern Pacific are now in the synonymy of *H. latifrons* Sazonov, and distribution of *H. macrops* is now considered to be restricted to the Atlantic Ocean. Therefore, the current inventory includes *M. argipalla* but not *M. mauli,* and *H. latifrons* but not *H. macrops.*

Following other classifications in use at the time, Quast and Hall (1972) included *S. abei* in the Alepocephalidae. The relationships of these groups are still a matter of debate. Begle (1992), from a cladistic analysis of the superfamily Alepocephaloidea, placed all the families in a single, monophyletic family Alepocephalidae without any subfamilies. From further analysis using additional characters, Johnson and Patterson (1996) argued that some characters which had been interpreted as derived are primitive and, with other evidence they presented, support separation of the families. Johnson and Patterson's (1996) cladograms place Platytroctidae as the sister-group of other alepocephaloids, whereas Begle's (1992) cladogram places platytroctids in the terminal position. Some authors still use the name Searsidae or Searsiidae for the tubeshoulders, but Sazonov (1980) replaced it with the name Platytroctidae.

The following key to the tubeshoulders of Alaska and nearby waters is drawn mainly from the key constructed by Matsui and Rosenblatt (1987).

Key to the Platytroctidae of Alaska

1 Head mostly covered with scales; photophores present;
JO a transverse bar (may be blacked out by dark tissue);
premaxillary tusks absent or rudimentary . . . . *Sagamichthys abei,* page 160

1 No scales on head; photophores present or absent; if photophores present, JO absent or longitudinal; premaxillary tusks present . . . . . (2)

2 (1) Widest part of head above eyes; supraorbitals slanting down over anterodorsal part of eyes; 2nd premaxillary tusk directed more laterally than 1st, not parallel to it; cleithral symphysis produced as a blunt spine; if photophores present, JO absent, THO round . . . . . genus *Maulisia* (3)

2 Widest part of head behind eyes; supraorbitals cupped over most of eyes; 2nd premaxillary tusk parallel to 1st; cleithral symphysis normal, not produced as a spine; JO a longitudinal bar, THO a transverse bar . . . . . genus *Holtbyrnia* (4)

3 (2) Large pit several scale rows wide behind supracleithrum (shoulder pit); photophores present; JO absent, THO round; snout relatively short, 21–26% HL; premaxilla with 4–8 teeth behind tusks . . . . . *Maulisia argipalla,* page 161

3 No shoulder pit; photophores absent; snout relatively long, 26–31% HL; premaxilla with 7–10 teeth behind tusks . . . . . *Maulisia acuticeps,* page 162 (not known from Alaska)

4 (2) GO less than its diameter behind symphysis (essentially at symphysis); gill filaments long, about 3–6% SL at junction of ceratobranchial and epibranchial, bases of filaments not united; gill rakers on first arch 25–31 . . . . . *Holtbyrnia latifrons,* page 163

4 GO at least 1.5 organ-diameters behind symphysis; gill filaments short, 0.6–0.8% SL at junction of ceratobranchial and epibranchial, bases of filaments united; gill rakers on first arch 18–25 (rarely 24 or 25) . . . . . *Holtbyrnia innesi,* page 164

Sagamichthys abei Parr, 1953 **shining tubeshoulder**

Bering Sea and eastern Pacific Ocean to southern South America, across North Pacific to Kamchatka and south to Sea of Okhotsk and to southern Japan.

At depths of 200–1,240 m, usually taken at 300–1,000 m; mesopelagic.

D 15–18; A 13–16; Pec 14–18; Pel 8–10; Ls 110–125; GR 7–9 + 16–19 (24–29); Br 8; Vert 50–52.

- Adults black, juveniles gray-blue.
- Photophores present: GO, POO, OPO, BRO, JO, PO, THO, MVO, SVO, VO, PAO, ICO; **photophores barlike across ventral surface; JO a transverse bar**.
- **Scales covering most of head**, with reverse arrangement (reverse imbricate).
- Lateral line canal with slight dorsal jog before joining cephalic lateralis canal.
- **Premaxillary tusks rudimentary or absent.**
- Length to 252 mm SL.

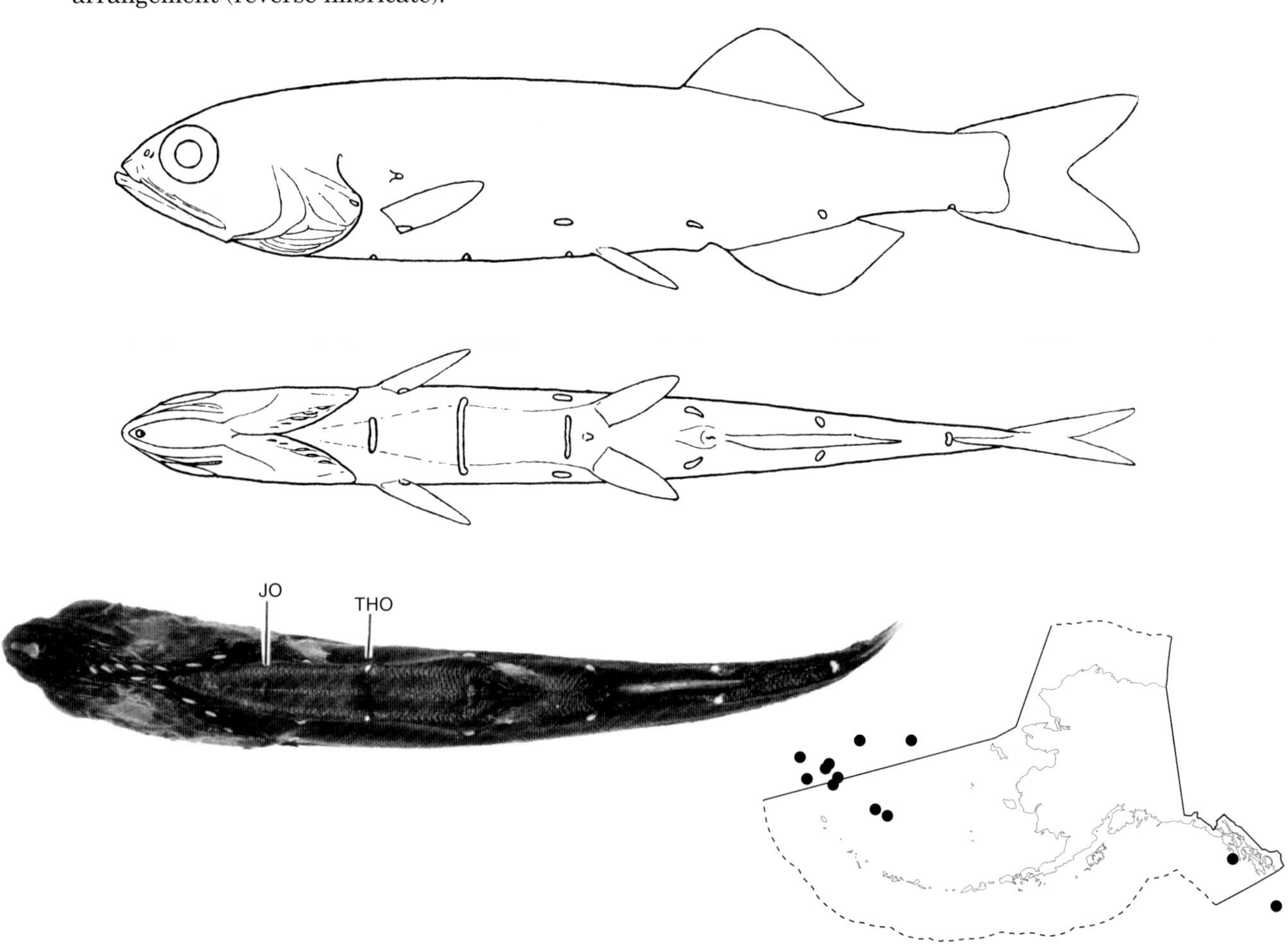

Notes & Sources — *Sagamichthys abei* Parr, 1953

Description: Parr 1960:42–45; Matsui and Rosenblatt 1987: 68–69; Sazonov et al. 1993:44–45.

Figures: Upper: Parr 1960, fig. 29. Lower: Matsui and Rosenblatt 1987, fig. 2, showing ventral photophores; THO is blacked out at the middle with only the ends exposed, and JO is covered by dark tissue.

Range: NMC 65-406 contains a specimen collected by S. J. Westrheim and J. W. Scoggan on 3 Sep. 1965 southwest of Baranof Island, southeastern Alaska, at 56°14'N, 135°32'W, depth 260–451 m; confirmed by B. W. Coad (pers. comm., 26 Apr. 1999). Nearest records outside Alaska in eastern Pacific are specimens from British Columbia at 52°18'N, 133°11' and 133°13'W at trawl depths of 510–595 m over a bottom depth of 2,650 m (Taylor 1967a,b); and at 48°N, 126'W at three stations at trawl depths of 439–530 m over bottom depths of 2,012–2,377 m (Peden 1974). Sazonov et al. (1993) recorded several specimens from Bering Sea, including the following localities in Alaska: 55°26'N, 172°E, 500–1,000 m; 55°30'N, 177°27'E, 200–500 m; and 55°37'N, 178°59'E, 320 m. Ivanov (1997) reported *S. abei* composed 10.7–13.0% by frequency of occurrence of fishes and cephalopods caught in surveys during 1991–1992 at 200–500-m depths in the Pacific off southern Kamchatka and the Kuril Islands. Record of four juveniles taken at an estimated depth of 37 m over water 130 m deep (Berry and Perkins 1966), which is much shallower than reported for any other platytroctid, is probably a mistake; no tubeshoulders were taken in over 30,000 open 1-m plankton net tows in a program sampling to depths of 150-200 m (Matsui and Rosenblatt 1987).

Maulisia argipalla Matsui & Rosenblatt, 1979 **pitted tubeshoulder**

Eastern Bering Sea north of Semisopochnoi Island; western Bering Sea near Karaginskiy Trench; eastern Pacific off southern British Columbia to Chile; Sea of Okhotsk; Indian and Atlantic oceans.

At depths of 475-1,340 m, most records from nets sampling at 500–1,000 m; mesopelagic.

D 17–23; A 15–19; Pec 17–20; Pel 7–9; Ls 77–100; GR 7–8 + 16–18 (23–27); Br 8–9; Vert 43–47.

- White tissue around posterior border of orbit, extending forward ventrally to about mideye.
- **Photophores present**: GO, BRO, PO, THO, MVO, SVO, SAO, PAO, ICO; **THO round**; **JO absent**.
- **Pit several scale rows wide in shoulder behind supracleithrum**.
- **Supraorbital forming hood over antero-dorsal part of eye**; **snout relatively short**, 21–26% of head length.
- Lateral line marked by papillae or neuromasts, without modified scales.
- Tusks present, 1st pointing forward, 2nd pointing more laterally; premaxilla with about 4–8 teeth behind tusks.
- Fewer gill rakers than in *M. acuticeps.*
- Length to 195 mm SL.

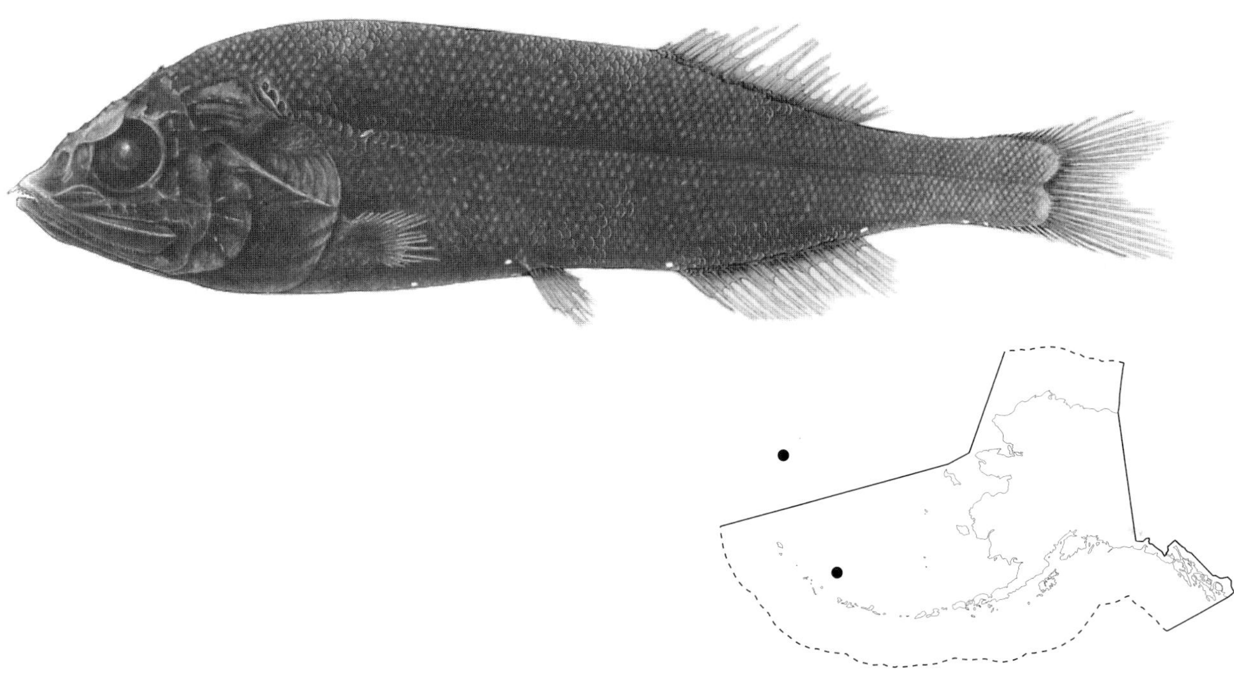

Notes & Sources — *Maulisia (Maulisia) argipalla* Matsui & Rosenblatt, 1979

Maulisia mauli: Fedorov 1973:48 (listed, Bering Sea); Peden 1974:49–50, fig. 2 (specimen taken off Cape Flattery, Washington, in southern British Columbia waters); Sazonov 1976b, fig. 20 (distribution).

Description: Matsui and Rosenblatt 1979:65–68, 1987:92–93; Balanov 1992:136; Sazonov et al. 1993:55–57.

Figure: Royal British Columbia Museum, artist P. Drukker-Brammall; 151 mm SL, west of Cape Flattery in British Columbia, 48°09'W, 126°43'W.

Range: Sazonov (1976b) reported a specimen of *M. mauli* taken off the Aleutian Islands at 53°25'N, 179°59'W, depth 810–825 m, which had been listed by Fedorov (1973) without locality data; this record represents *M. argipalla* (Matsui and Rosenblatt 1987, Balanov 1992, Sazonov et al. 1993). Matsui and Rosenblatt (1987) placed other records of North Pacific *M. mauli* in *M. argipalla* as well, including a specimen (see illustration above) taken west of southern British Columbia and recorded by Peden (1974); Peden (1998) listed *M. argipalla* in the British Columbia fauna, not *M. mauli*. Balanov (1992) recorded an adult female (136 mm SL) and a juvenile (68 mm SL) caught near the Karaginskiy Trench at 59°02'N, 166°55'E, by trawl towed at 500–1,000 m over a bottom depth of 3,300 m. The British Columbia specimen (Peden 1974) was taken in a trawl net sampling at 475–530 m over bottom depths of 2,195–2,377 m. Species is widespread but known from a small number of scattered records.

Maulisia acuticeps Sazonov, 1976 **dark tubeshoulder**

Western Bering Sea east of Karaginskiy Island; Pacific Ocean off Peru, Japan, and Australia; South Atlantic; possible records off Galápagos Islands and in North Atlantic.

At depths of about 200–1,500 m, possible records to 2,000–2,600 m; mesopelagic to bathypelagic.

D 18–22; A 15–18; Pec 12–16; Pel 7–8; Ls 95–100; GR 8–9 + 20–22 (28–31); Vert 43.

- White tissue around posterior border of orbit, extending forward ventrally to about mideye.
- **Photophores absent**.
- **No pit in shoulder behind supracleithrum**.
- **Supraorbital forming hood over antero-dorsal part of eye; snout relatively long**, 26–31% of head length.
- Lateral line marked by papillae or neuromasts, without modified scales.
- Tusks present, 1st pointing forward, 2nd pointing more laterally; premaxilla with about 7–10 teeth behind tusks.
- More gill rakers than in *M. argipalla.*
- Length to 255 mm SL.

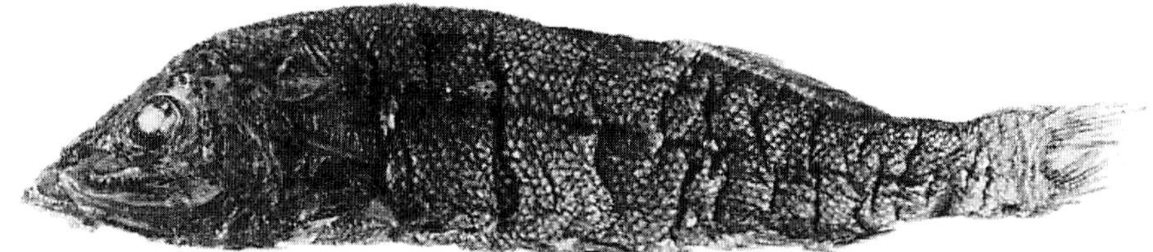

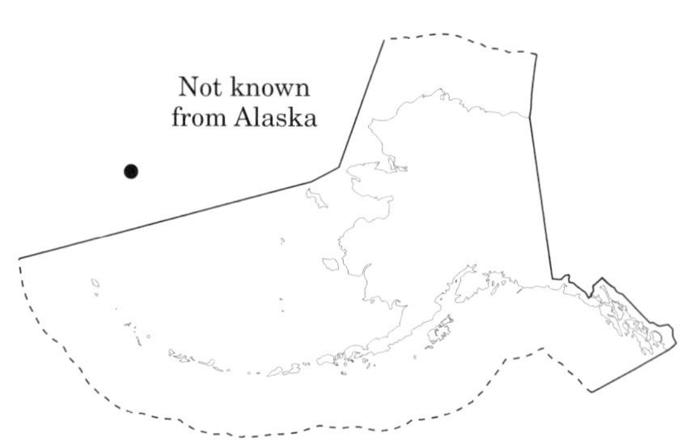

Notes & Sources — *Maulisia (Aphanichthys) acuticeps* Sazonov, 1976

Maulisia isaacsi (Galápagos Islands) and *M. microlepis* (North and South Atlantic) may be junior synonyms of *M. acuticeps* (Sazonov et al. 1993).

Description: Sazonov 1976a:23–24; Matsui and Rosenblatt 1987:95; Balanov 1992:134–135; Sazonov et al. 1993:53–55.

Figure: Matsui and Rosenblatt 1987, fig. 26D; 173 mm SL, Kuroshio region.

Range: Nearest published record to Alaska is that of Balanov (1992): one specimen, 196 mm SL, taken east of Karaginskiy Island at 59°46'N, 169°46'E, at the northern part of the Shirshov Ridge. Balanov (1992) gave a trawl depth range of 200–500 m over a bottom depth of 3,300 m for the specimen (ZMMGU 18693), but Sazonov et al. (1993) gave 500–1,000 m. Other records are widespread but rare, and include the holotype and paratype taken off the coast of Peru (Sazonov 1976a), one specimen taken off the east coast of Japan (Matsui and Rosenblatt 1987), and one specimen off the east coast of Australia and one in the South Atlantic off Africa (Sazonov et al. 1993). Including *M. microlepis* in the synonymy would increase the depth range to 2,000–2,600 m.

Holtbyrnia latifrons Sazonov, 1976 **teardrop tubeshoulder**

Gulf of Alaska to northern Chile; western Bering Sea; most records are from California to Chile.

At depths of about 300–1,400 m, usually taken in nets sampling from below 300 m to less than 1,000 m; mesopelagic.

D 17–21; A 14–20; Pec 16–20; Pel 8–9; Ls 95–115; GR 7–9 + 18–21 (25–31); Br 8–9; Vert 46–50.

- Two patches of white tissue behind eye separated by less than length of ventral body.
- Photophores present: GO, POO, OPO, BRO, JO, PO, THO, MVO, SVO, VO, SAO, PAO, ICO; **GO less than its diameter from mandibular symphysis** (0.4–1.5% of standard length); **JO longitudinal**, teardrop-shaped, with pointed end forward; THO a transverse bar.
- **Supraorbital cupped over most of eye**.
- Lateral line with enlarged, modified scales that continue onto caudal rays.
- Premaxillary tusks present, pointing forward.
- **More gill rakers than in *H. innesi*; gill filaments long**, about 3–6% of standard length at junction of ceratobranchial and epibranchial, bases of filaments not united.
- Length to 200 mm TL.

Notes & Sources — *Holtbyrnia latifrons* Sazonov, 1976

Holtbyrnia macrops: Peden 1974:49, table 1. For complete synonymy see Matsui and Rosenblatt (1987).

Matsui (1991) suggested that *H. latifrons* may be a junior synonym of *H. baucoti* Mayer & Nalbant, 1972, but that *H. baucoti* was inadequately described and he had no additional information on the holotype.

Called teardrop tubeshoulder by Peden (1974, 1998), for the teardrop-shaped JO photophore. Called streaklight tubeshoulder by Hubbs et al. (1979).

Description: Sazonov 1976a:20–23; Matsui and Rosenblatt 1987:60; Sazonov et al. 1993:49–50.

Figure: Royal British Columbia Museum, artist K. Uldall-Ekman, Dec. 1984; BCPM 979-11245, 106 mm SL, Ocean Station Papa (50°N, 145°W).

Range: Peden et al. (1985) identified a specimen (107 mm SL) taken near Surveyor Seamount at approximately 57°N, 144°30'W, and one (106 mm SL; see illustration on this page) from Ocean Station Papa as *H. macrops*. Peden (1974) had earlier recorded the occurrence of *H. macrops* west of Cape Flattery, Washington. Matsui and Rosenblatt (1987) referred records of *H. macrops* from the Pacific Ocean to the synonymy of *H. latifrons*, which would make the Surveyor Seamount specimen the first record from Alaska. The Cape Flattery specimen was collected at trawling depths of 439–484 m over a bottom of 2,012 m, and the Ocean Station Papa specimen at a depth less than 650 m. Sazonov et al. (1993) recorded a specimen from the western Bering Sea at 59°N, 171°04'E, depth range 500–1,000 m; as well as an additional specimen from the Gulf of Alaska at 57°42'N, 137°01'W, depth range 610–780 m.

Holtbyrnia innesi (Fowler, 1934) **lanternjaw tubeshoulder**

Bering Sea, central North Pacific, eastern Pacific off Peru, and western Pacific off southern Kamchatka and Kuril Islands to South China Sea and Celebes Sea; Indian and Atlantic oceans.

At depths of 200–1,300 m, usually taken at 500–1,000 m; mesopelagic.

D 18–22; A 14–19; Pec 16–20; Pel 7–9; Ls 94–110; GR 5–8 + 15–16 (18–25); Br 8; Vert 46–48.

- Two patches of white tissue behind eye separated by more than length of ventral body.
- Photophores present: GO, POO, OPO, BRO, JO, PO, THO, MVO, SVO, VO, SAO, PAO, ICO; **GO more than its diameter from mandibular symphysis** (about 3.5% of standard length); **JO longitudinal**; THO a transverse bar.
- **Supraorbital cupped over most of eye.**
- Lateral line with enlarged, modified scales that continue onto caudal rays.
- Premaxillary tusks present, pointing forward.
- **Fewer gill rakers than in *H. latifrons***; gill filaments short, 0.6–0.8% of standard length at junction of ceratobranchial and epibranchial, bases of filaments united.
- Length to 215 mm SL.

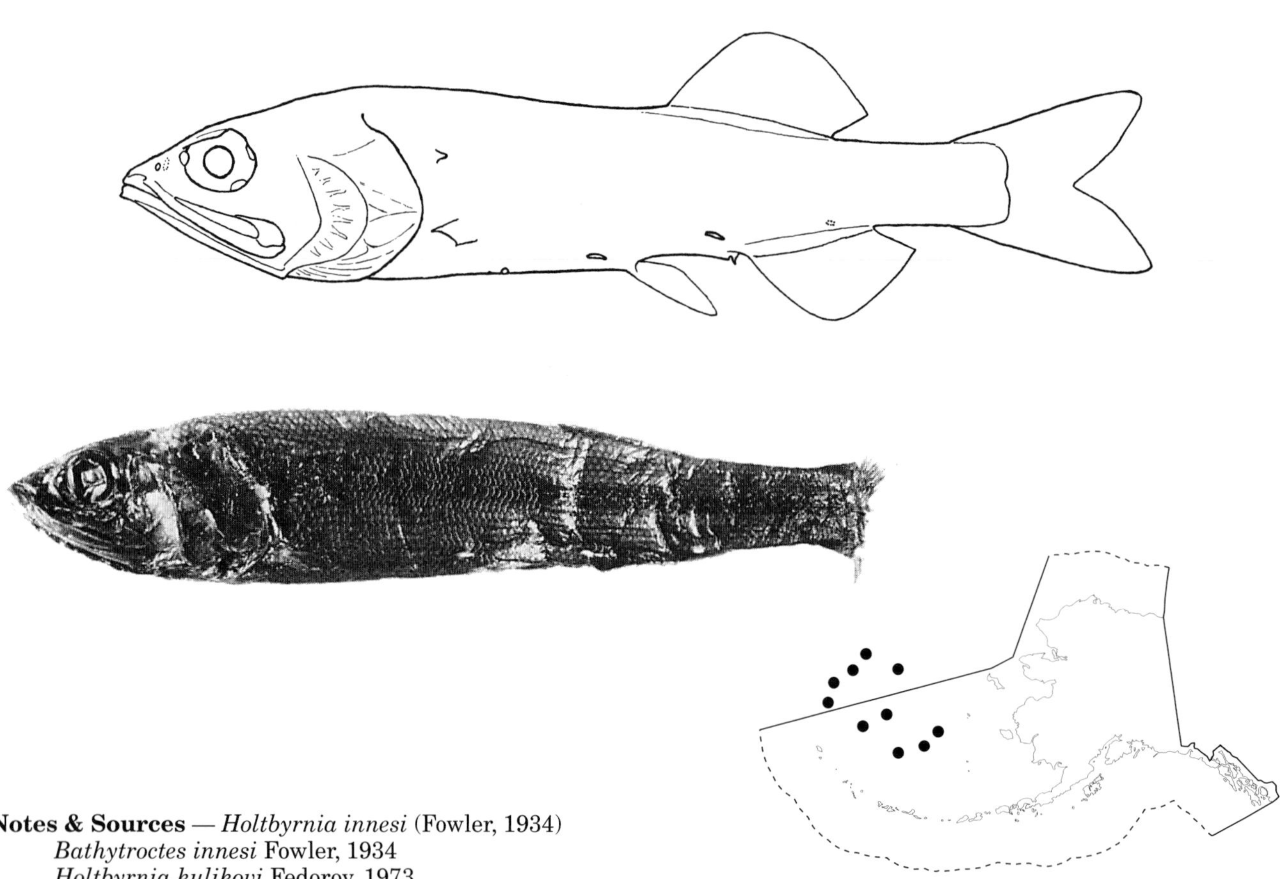

Notes & Sources — *Holtbyrnia innesi* (Fowler, 1934)
Bathytroctes innesi Fowler, 1934
Holtbyrnia kulikovi Fedorov, 1973
Holtbyrnia conocephala Sazonov, 1976

Matsui and Rosenblatt (1987) placed records of *H. kulikovi* in the synonymy of *H. innesi*. This was confirmed by Sazonov et al. (1993), who also placed *H. conocephala* in *H. innesi*.

Called lanternjaw tubeshoulder in allusion to the more posteriorly placed gular organ (GO), which is closer to the chin in *H. latifrons*.

Description: Matsui and Rosenblatt 1987:58–59; Sazonov et al. 1993:45–49.

Figures: Upper: Parr 1960, fig. 45. Lower: Matsui and Rosenblatt 1987, fig. 23B; 152 mm SL, North Atlantic.

Range: Fedorov (1973a:48) listed *H. kulikovi* from the Bering Sea and called it a new species, but without giving a description (making the name a nomen nudum) or locality. Sazonov (1976a) described a specimen taken at 58°15'N, 175°20'W, depth less than 570 m, as the holotype of *H. kulikovi*. Sazonov et al. (1993) recorded several specimens of *H. innesi* from the Bering Sea, including the following localities in Alaska: 56°02'N, 175°58'E, 500–1,000 m; 57°58'N, 177°54'E, 500–1,000 m; 55°52'N, 178°24'W, 500–1,000 m; and 57°00'N, 176°00'W, 200–500 m. Ivanov (1997) reported *H. innesi* made up 17.9–30.4% by frequency of occurrence of the fishes and cephalopods taken at upper mesopelagic depths (200–500 m) in their sampling regions off southern Kamchatka and the Kuril Islands in 1991–1992. Two specimens from Peru (Sazonov 1976b) are the only published record of *H. innesi* from the eastern Pacific.

Family Alepocephalidae
Slickheads

In slickheads the skin on the head is smooth, thin, and without scales. They are deepsea fishes, with most species occurring below 1,000 m. Half-grown and juvenile individuals live at midwater depths well above the bottom but larger adults live in close association with the bottom. Slickheads are adapted to process jellyfish and other gelatinous prey and closely match them in basic composition, consisting of about 90% water (Gartner et al. 1997). The family includes about 20 genera and more than 90 species (Sazonov and Markle in Gon and Heemstra 1990), with representatives in all oceans. Occurrence of one slickhead species in Alaska is substantiated by one record, while two other species possibly exist in the region.

Slickhead characters include: body slightly compressed, elongate to moderately deep; head and eyes often large; skin slippery, flesh soft and mushy; pectoral fin often reduced; pelvic fins at midpoint of body or farther back, often small; scales cycloid, and usually present; teeth usually small; gill covers large in some species; gill rakers long and numerous; and branchiostegal rays 5–13. Slickheads lack the luminous-fluid-filled shoulder sac of the platytroctids, but photophores are present in some species. Like other alepocephaloids, slickheads have the dorsal and anal fins located far back on the body and lack an adipose fin and swim bladder. They range in maximum size at maturity from about 10 cm (4 inches) to more than a meter. The largest may be an Atlantic species, *Alepocephalus bairdii*, with a maximum recorded standard length of 100 cm (39 inches). The three species treated in this guide are in about the midrange for the family, with maximum standard lengths of 38–73 cm (15–29 inches), and lack photophores.

The salmon slickhead, *Conocara salmoneum*, was originally described from a specimen collected in 1895 from the Bering Sea off Alaska (Gill and Townsend 1897), and has not been recorded again north of California. Quast and Hall (1972) included it on their list of Alaskan fishes under its original name, *Ericara salmonea*. Two additional slickheads are included in the present inventory as possible Alaskan species. The California slickhead, *A. tenebrosus*, has been reported but not confirmed from the eastern Bering Sea. The softskin slickhead, *Rouleina attrita*, has recently been collected in the western Bering Sea over the Shirshov Ridge (Sazonov et al. 1993). Available evidence indicates it is a circumglobal species, and although well documented from the western Pacific Ocean it is not yet known from the eastern Pacific.

Recent reviews of the Alepocephalidae are available for the Indian Ocean (Sazonov and Ivanov 1980), northeastern Atlantic (Markle and Quéro in Whitehead et al. 1984), southeastern Atlantic and southwestern Indian oceans off southern Africa (Markle in Smith and Heemstra 1986), eastern tropical Atlantic (Markle and Sazonov in Quéro et al. 1990), Southern Ocean (Sazonov and Markle in Gon and Heemstra 1990), and western Pacific (Sazonov et al. 1993), but not for the eastern Pacific.

Key to the Alepocephalidae of Alaska

1		Body completely naked (except for ringlike scales standing on edge inside and supporting body lateral line canal)	*Rouleina attrita*, page 166 (not known from Alaska)
1		Body covered with deciduous scales (at least scale pockets remain)	(2)
2	(1)	Dorsal fin origin above or slightly anterior to anal fin origin; scales of lateral line enlarged, forming raised ridge; maxilla extending to anterior portion of eye	*Alepocephalus tenebrosus*, page 167 (not confirmed from Alaska)
2		Dorsal fin origin posterior to anal fin origin; scales of lateral line not greatly enlarged; maxilla extending to posterior margin of eye	*Conocara salmoneum*, page 168

Rouleina attrita (Vaillant, 1888) **softskin slickhead**

Western Bering Sea over Shirshov Ridge; Greenland; Southern Ocean; circumglobal in temperate and tropical waters.

Near bottom on continental slopes and submarine ridges, recorded from depths of 800–2,102 m; at 800–1,540 m in Pacific Ocean; benthopelagic.

D 16–21; A 17–21; Pec 4–8; Pel 6–8; LL 43–48; GR 5–8 + 17–21; Br 5–6; PC 7–11; Vert 43–48.

- Uniformly black, except sometimes bluish on gill membranes, around eyes, and on bases of fins.
- Body moderately elongate; head large, 30% of standard length or more; orbit diameter shorter than snout; **maxilla extending past eye and greatly expanded posteriorly**; 1 supramaxilla.
- Photophores absent.
- Dorsal and anal fins opposite each other; pectoral fin small, usually with 6 or 7 rays.
- **Scales absent** except in lateral line canal.
- Lateral line extending onto caudal fin; narrow ringlike scales standing on edge inside canal.
- Sensory papillae on body, head, and fin rays numerous, especially along lateral line; papillae more noticeable in specimens under 155 mm SL.
- Teeth in 1 row on premaxilla, maxilla, and dentary; vomerine and palatine teeth absent.
- Gill rakers united at bases, free parts very short.
- Testes ribbonlike, in convoluted folds but never in discrete lobes.
- Length to 38 cm SL.

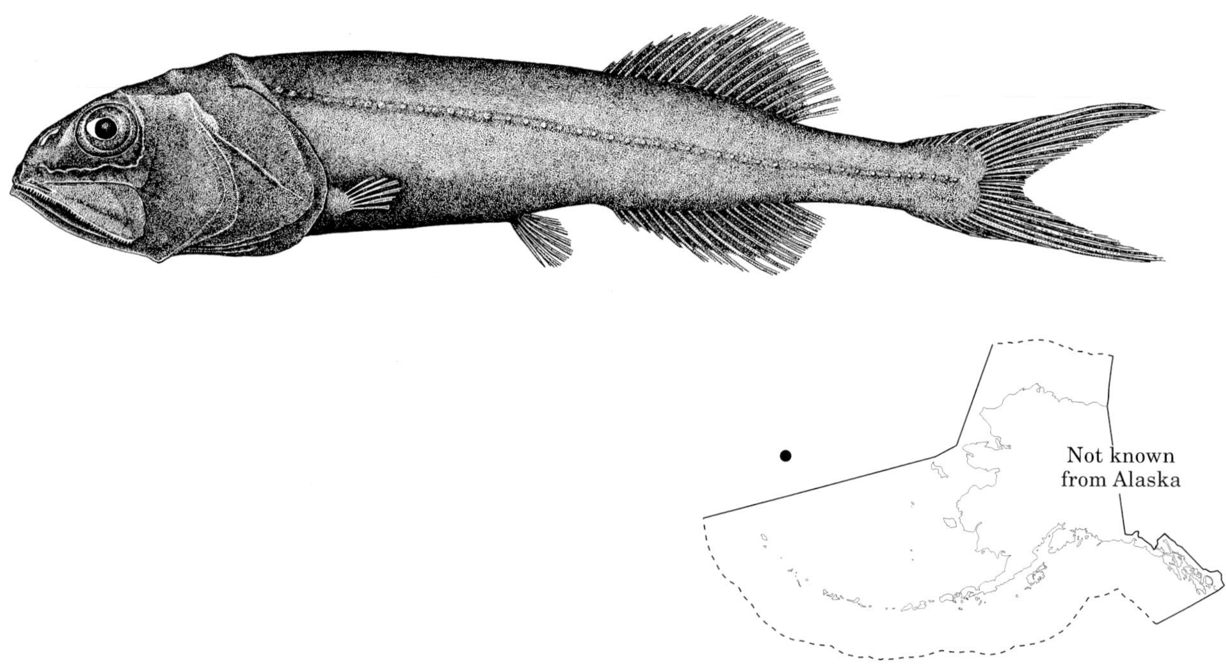

Notes & Sources — *Rouleina attrita* (Vaillant, 1888)

Bathytroctes attritus Vaillant, 1888

Distinguishable from *R. maderensis* by the lack of photophores, lower number of lateral line scales, and convoluted testes. *Rouleina maderensis* occurs at shallower depths (mainly 600–1,200 m); it has not been recorded from the North Pacific but is present in the southeastern Pacific.

Description: Markle 1978:81–84; Markle and Quéro in Whitehead et al. 1986:249; Sazonov and Markle in Gon and Heemstra 1990:114; Sazonov et al. 1993:59–60; Nakamura and Okamura in Okamura et al. 1995:77.

Figure: Gon and Heemstra 1990:114; 37.5 cm SL, Atlantic Ocean.

Range: Nearest known occurrence is western Bering Sea over the Shirshov Ridge, a 203-mm-SL specimen (ZIN 42302) recorded by Sazonov et al. (1993). Other specimens they recorded (26 in all) were from the Sea of Okhotsk and the western Pacific Ocean, with localities in the Pacific extending from well south of the Near Islands at 46°15'N, 169°36'E to and along the coast of Honshu and east of Taiwan at 24°07'N, 150°E. Usually taken in bottom trawls.

Alepocephalus tenebrosus Gilbert, 1892 — **California slickhead**

Eastern Bering Sea reports not verifiable; well documented from eastern North Pacific west of Barkley Sound, southern British Columbia, to central Baja California off Guadalupe Island; also reported from Chile.

Near bottom at 294–1,646 m, with greater extremes reported but not confirmed; most often taken at about 600–1,200 m; benthopelagic.

D 17; A 17–18; Pec 10; Pel 6–7; Ls about 90–105; GR 7–8 + 17–18; Br 6–7; PC 14–16; Vert 53–55.

- Uniformly blue-black.
- Body compressed, moderately elongate; head large, 30% of standard length or more; **maxilla extending to anterior portion of eye**, not greatly expanded posteriorly; 2 supramaxillae.
- Photophores absent.
- **Dorsal fin origin above or slightly anterior to anal fin origin**; pectoral fin well developed, with 10 rays.
- **Body covered with thin, deciduous scales**; scales extending onto dorsal and anal fins for one-third their height; no scales on head.
- **Scales of lateral line enlarged, forming raised ridge**.
- Teeth in 1 irregular row on premaxilla, dentary, and palatine; maxillary and vomerine teeth absent.
- Gill membranes not united to each other, and free from isthmus; gill rakers longer than wide, not united at bases.
- Testes in discrete lobes.
- Length to 61 cm TL; usually less than 40 cm SL.

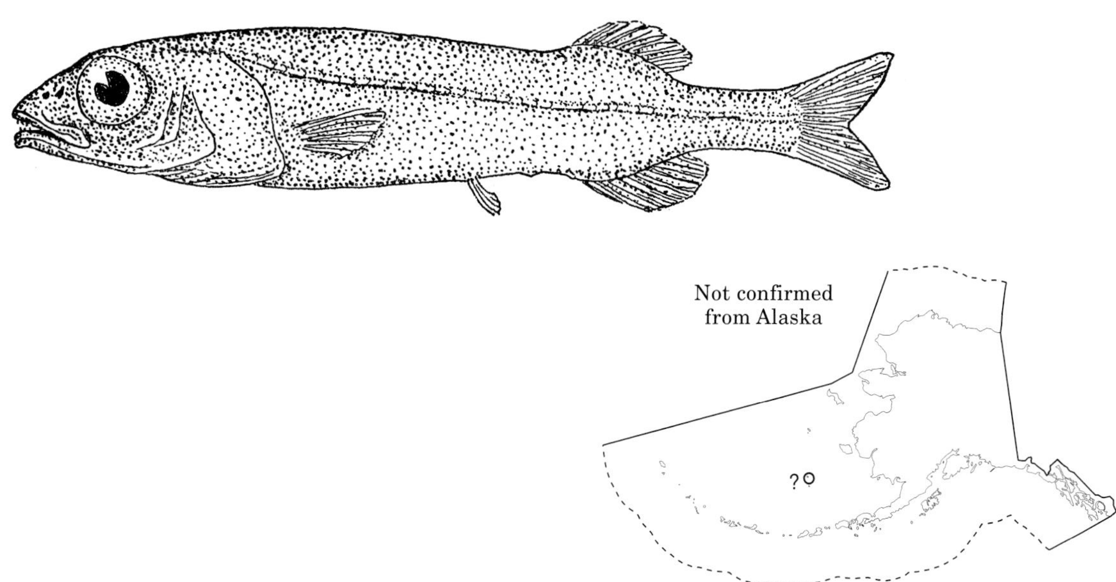

Notes & Sources — *Alepocephalus tenebrosus* Gilbert, 1892

Description: Gilbert 1892:545–546; Grinols and Heyamoto 1965:1157–1163.

Figure: Barnhart 1936, fig. 52.

Range: Voucher specimens from Alaska are lacking. The NMFS resource survey database has one record from the Bering Sea at 56°58'N, 170°16'W, but it is not associated with a voucher specimen (J. W. Orr, pers. comm., 13 Nov. 1997). A range north to the Bering Sea was given by Miller and Lea (1972) and Eschmeyer and Herald (1983). Not listed for Alaska by Wilimovsky (1954, 1958) or Quast and Hall (1972). Grinols and Heyamoto (1965), in a review of the distribution and taxonomic status of the species, gave range as extending north to Oregon. The first adequately documented record from British Columbia was provided by Peden (1997b): eight specimens from Barkley Canyon west of southern Vancouver Island.

The depth range of 46–5,486 m (150–18,000 feet) given by Fitch and Lavenberg (1968:17) may apply to the family as a whole, not necessarily to *A. tenebrosus*. The given extremes are not documented by specific records in the literature. Grinols and Heyamoto (1965) gave a range of 294–1,503 m for records available at that time. Alton (1972:620) recorded a maximum depth of 1,646 m for specimens taken off Oregon. The specimens recorded by Peden (1997b) from west of Vancouver Island were taken between 562 and 959 m. Usually taken in bottom trawls.

Size: Fitch and Lavenberg 1968. The largest specimen in 64 SIO collections, some containing several specimens, is 550 mm SL, a specimen from Monterey Bay (SIO 91-118); a few are 400–448 mm, but the rest are smaller.

Conocara salmoneum (Gill & Townsend, 1897) **salmon slickhead**

One record from southwest of Pribilof Islands, Bering Sea, and one off Santa Catalina Island, southern California; Atlantic off southwestern Ireland, Cape Verde Islands, and Antilles.

At depths of about 2,400–4,200 m, usually below 3,000 m; benthopelagic.

D 17–21; A 24–28; Pec 10–12; Pel 6–7; Ls 130–140; GR 1–3 + 12–13; Br 6; PC 2; Vert 51–53.

- Body and fins dark brown, head nearly black.
- Body moderately elongate, rounded, but compressed posteriorly; head large, 30% of standard length or more; **maxilla extending to mideye to posterior edge of eye**; premaxillae forming sharp platelike "visor."
- Photophores absent.
- **Dorsal fin origin slightly posterior to anal fin origin; anal fin noticeably longer-based than dorsal fin**; pectoral fin well developed, 10 or more rays.
- **Body covered with small, barely imbricate scales**; scales absent from fins and head.
- Lateral line scales not greatly enlarged.
- Premaxillary and mandibular teeth in narrow band anteriorly, in 1 row laterally; palatine teeth in 1 row; maxillary and vomerine teeth absent.
- Upper gill rakers 3 or fewer.
- Length to at least 73 cm SL.

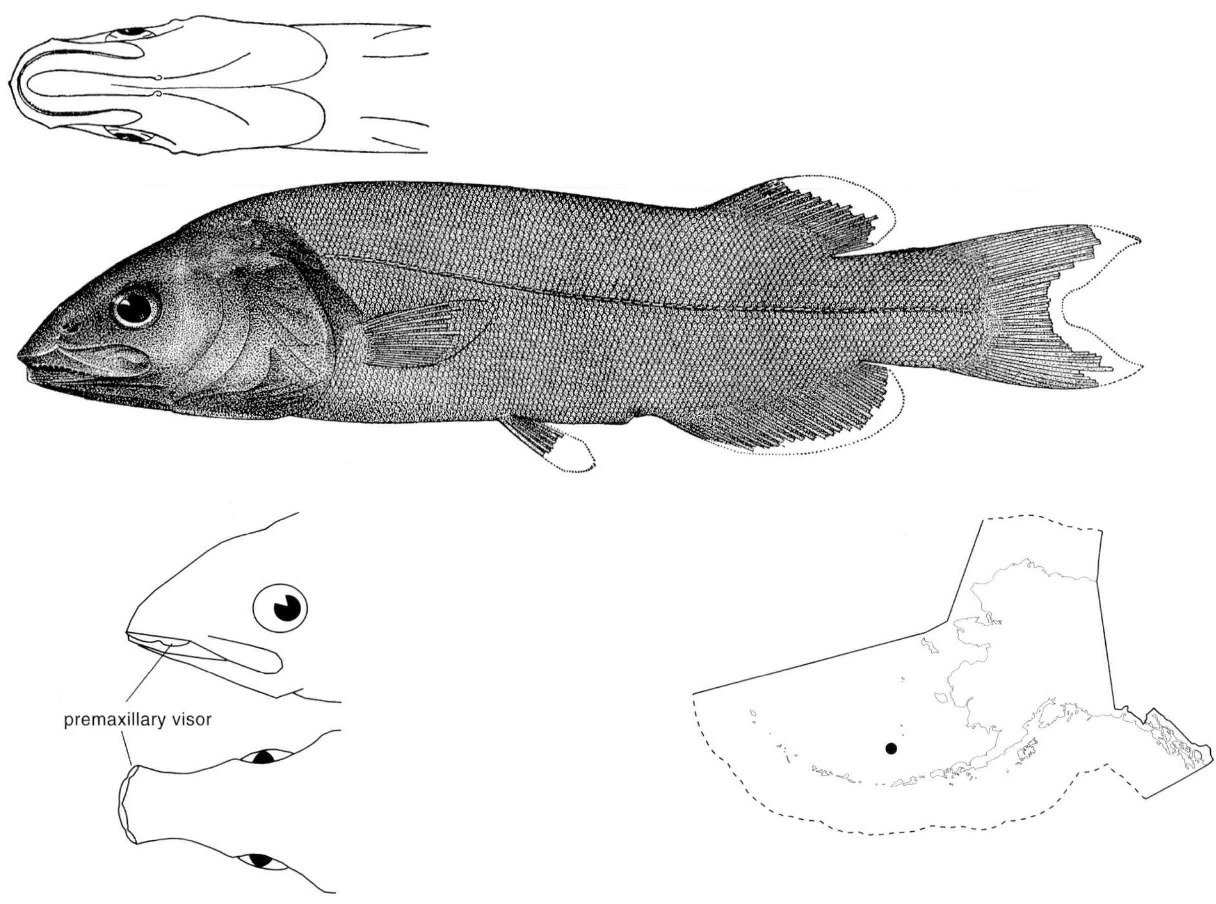

Notes & Sources — *Conocara salmoneum* (Gill & Townsend, 1897)
Ericara salmonea Gill & Townsend, 1897
Xenognathus profundorum Gilbert, 1915

Description: Gill and Townsend 1897:232; Gilbert 1915: 311–312; Markle and Quéro in Whitehead et al. 1984: 241; Sazonov et al. 1993:65–66.

Figures: Upper, with ventral view of head: Gilbert 1915, pl. 14, fig. 2; type of *Xenognathus profundorum*, off Santa Catalina Island, California. Premaxillary visor: redrawn from Markle and Quéro in Whitehead et al. 1984:238.

Range: Few records of this species are known. The only record from Alaska is that of Gill and Townsend (1897), from *Albatross* station 3603, Bering Sea at 55°23'N, 170°31'W, at depth of 3,239 m. The only other record from the Pacific is the holotype (unique) of *X. profundorum*, described by Gilbert (1915), which was obtained by dredging off California by the *Albatross* at depths of 2,469–3,991 m.

Family Osmeridae
Smelts

Smelts are slender, silvery, shallow-water fishes found only in temperate and cold regions of the Northern Hemisphere. They occur in both fresh and salt water, usually in schools, and are important food and forage fishes. Some species congregate in huge numbers prior to spawning. Most species spawn on sand or gravel. Species which are entirely marine spawn on ocean beaches at high tide, and in Alaska these include capelin, *Mallotus villosus*; surf smelt, *Hypomesus pretiosus*; and night smelt, *Spirinchus starksi*. Several species are anadromous or have anadromous populations and ascend freshwater streams to spawn, including three Alaskan species: rainbow smelt, *Osmerus mordax*; eulachon, *Thaleichthys pacificus*; and longfin smelt, *S. thaleichthys*. A few inhabit only fresh water, such as the pond smelt, *H. olidus*. With a revision of the genus *Hypomesus* and a new species described recently from the Kuril Islands (Saruwatari et al 1997), the family has seven recognized genera and 15 or 16 species, with the exact number of species depending on classification within the other genera. Alaska is home to four genera and seven species. However, *S. starksi* is known in Alaska from only one record.

Smelts are distinguishable from similar-looking fishes by the combination of absence of a pelvic axillary process, presence of a dorsal adipose fin, and a lower jaw that protrudes beyond the upper. Several species have a cucumber-like odor, although it is not detectable by all observers or they remark on the likeness of the odor to other things. Swan (1880b), for example, likened the odor of eulachon, *T. pacificus*, to bruised leaves of wild syringa, *Philadelphus*, a shrub of the Pacific Northwest coast. Most smelts are extremely oily and have excellent flavor.

Other morphological features in the complex distinguishing smelts from other fishes include: pelvic fins well developed, mainly horizontal, with 8 rays (except 9 in *Mallotus*); caudal fin forked, with 19 principal rays; lateral line usually incomplete; teeth present on premaxillae, maxillae, dentaries, vomer, palatines, and tongue; mesocoracoids present; branchiostegal rays 5–10 (6–8 in Alaskan species); pyloric caeca 0–12; and vertebrae 51–78 (51–73 in Alaskan species). Nelson (1994) listed additional characters. Differences in the vomerine, palatine, and tongue teeth are helpful in differentiating the Alaskan species.

Sexual dimorphism is strong in some smelt species. Males often have longer fins and different coloration than females, and, as breeding season approaches, can develop nuptial tubercles, a swollen area or "shelf" at the base of the anal fin, and swollen ridges along midside.

Adults of some smelt species reach 40 cm (almost 16 inches) in total length, but they rarely exceed about 30 cm (almost 12 inches). Maximum lengths are not well documented, especially for populations in Alaska, possibly because some species can be so abundant it may not seem worthwhile or important to report size.

In this guide, following Nelson (1994), the suborder Osmeroidei is classified in the order Osmeriformes. However, Johnson and Patterson (1996) recently addressed the question of osmeroid relationships using a cladistic analysis that indicated osmeroids are the sister-group of the Salmonoidei, and classified both groups in the order Salmoniformes. This alternative may be followed in future works.

Relationships within Osmeridae are a more difficult problem. As Johnson and Patterson (1996) remarked, osmerids are unique in the disparity of opinion on their interrelationships. Johnson and Patterson's analysis of morphological characters strongly suggests that *Hypomesus* is the basal genus and *Thaleichthys* and *Spirinchus* are derived osmerids. *Osmerus* and *Mallotus* are somewhere in between.

The current inventory of Alaskan smelt species differs from Quast and Hall's (1972) mainly by not including whitebait smelt, *Allosmerus elongatus*. The nearest record of whitebait smelt is from the Strait of Juan de Fuca off Vancouver Island, which is the only British Columbia record (Hart 1973). Whitebait smelt are most abundant off northern California. The rainbow smelt was called *O. eperlanus* (Linnaeus) on Quast and Hall's (1972) list, but that name is now in use only for European rainbow smelt. North American rainbow smelt have been called *O. mordax* (Mitchill) since Kljukanov (1969) found both species to be sympatric in the White Sea. Kljukanov (1969) called the North Pacific–Arctic form *O. mordax dentex*, the name later used by Hart (1973), but most authors no longer consider the subspecies distinction valid.

The following key to the smelts of Alaska relies heavily on characters from McAllister (1963). To distinguish between *S. thaleichthys* and *S. starksi* it is helpful to hold the head over a protractor, with the mouth closed (see couplet number 6). Since the pelvic fins are attached practically horizontally on the body, the leading edge of the fin base may appropriately be called the origin, in the same way the term is traditionally used in ichthyology for the dorsal and anal fins.

Key to the Osmeridae of Alaska

1 Teeth on tongue minute, villiform; maxilla not reaching past middle of eye . . . . . (2)

1 Teeth on tongue medium conical or large caniniform; maxilla reaching almost to posterior margin of eye or past eye . . . . . (4)

2 (1) Scales tiny, lateral line with 170–220 scales; pectoral fin rays 16–22 . . . . . *Mallotus villosus,* page 171

2 Scales moderate to large, midlateral scales fewer than 80; pectoral fin rays 10–17 . . . . . (3)

3 (2) Adipose fin base more than 20% HL; adipose eyelid absent; anal fin rays long, 43–56% HL; pectoral fins long, 50–80% of distance between pectoral and pelvic fin bases; midlateral scales usually 51–60 (range 51–62) . . . . . *Hypomesus olidus,* page 172

3 Adipose fin base less than 20% HL; adipose eyelid present; anal fin rays short, 29–38% HL; pectoral fins short, extending 41–48% of distance between pectoral and pelvic fin bases; midlateral scales usually 66–73 (range 66–76) . . . . . *Hypomesus pretiosus,* page 173

4 (1) Canine teeth present on vomer; gill rakers on lower limb of 1st arch 13–24 . . . . . (5)

4 No canine teeth on vomer; gill rakers on lower limb of 1st arch 24–34 . . . . . (6)

5 (4) Operculum lacking obvious concentric striae; anal fin rays usually 12–16 (range 11–18); pelvic fin origin opposite or posterior to dorsal fin origin; gill rakers on upper limb of first arch 8–14 . . . . . *Osmerus mordax,* page 174

5 Operculum with obvious concentric striae; anal fin rays usually 18–22 (range 17–23); pelvic fin origin anterior to dorsal fin origin; gill rakers on upper limb of first arch 4–6 . . . . . *Thaleichthys pacificus,* page 175

6 (4) Anal fin high, longest ray 45–71% HL; pectoral fin long, extending 84% or more of distance to pelvic fin origin, sometimes past pelvic origin; midlateral scales large, usually 55–62 (range 54–63); snout blunt, with steep premaxilla forming angle of 68–90 degrees to forehead . . . . . *Spirinchus thaleichthys,* page 176

6 Anal fin low, longest ray 32–45% HL; pectoral fin short, extending 84% or less of distance to pelvic fin origin; midlateral scales moderate, usually 62–65 (range 60–66); snout pointed, with premaxilla forming angle of 54–65 degrees to forehead . . . . . *Spirinchus starksi,* page 177

Mallotus villosus (Müller, 1776) **capelin**

Beaufort Sea to Strait of Juan de Fuca, across southern Arctic Canada, and south in western Atlantic Ocean to Cape Cod; in western Pacific to Japan and Korea; Sea of Okhotsk; circumboreal–Arctic.

Marine, pelagic; from surface to depth of 200 m in coastal areas and on offshore banks; migrates inshore to spawn on beaches.

D 10–18; A 16–26; Pec 16–22; Pel 9; LLs 170–220; GR 8–14 + 24–35 (33–48); Br 7–8; PC 3–9; Vert 62–73.

- Blue or olive green to yellow-green dorsally; silvery white laterally and ventrally.
- Mouth moderate, maxilla extending to or almost to mideye.
- **Adipose fin long-based**, more than 1.5 times eye diameter; **pectoral rays numerous** (usually 17–20); pelvic fin origin anterior to or below dorsal fin origin; **pelvic fin ray 9 small**, much shorter than other rays.
- **Scales very small** (170–220 along lateral line).
- Lateral line complete.
- Vomerine teeth small, in arch across vomer; palatine teeth all small; tongue teeth minute, villiform.
- Breeding males develop raised ridge of 4 rows of overlapping, elongated scales along lateral line, ends of the scales giving a hairy appearance to the ridge; tubercles on head and pectoral, pelvic, and caudal fins; and enlarged ridge along base of anal fin.
- Length to 252 mm TL.

Notes & Sources — *Mallotus villosus* (Müller, 1776)
Clupea villosa Müller, 1776
Salmo catervarius Pennant, 1784
Mallotus catervarius: Schultz 1937.
Sudis squamosa Chapman, 1939

Description: McAllister 1963:38–41; Hart 1973:141–143; Coad 1995:183–185.

Figure: University of British Columbia, artist P. Drukker-Brammall, 1967; UBC 63-642, male, 136 mm SL, Alaska.

Range: Although pelagic, *M. villosus* was one of the most common species taken in NMFS demersal trawl surveys (as the nets were being raised from the bottom), with 30 years of data from the North Pacific and Bering Sea plotted by Allen and Smith (1988). Their surveys found *M. villosus* only as far west as Great Sitkin Island, but Wilimovsky (1964) recorded the species at Attu Island. Barber et al. (1997) found it in bottom trawl surveys of tye northeastern Chukchi Sea in 1990 and 1991; UAM uncataloged materials from the surveys include examples of this species from 70°00'N, 163°28'W, at depth of 27 m. Murdoch (1885) was the first to record *M. villosus* from Point Barrow, and there are numerous specimens collected by N. J. Wilimovsky at Point Barrow in the UBC fish collection. Walters (1955), reviewing fishes of Arctic America and Siberia, reported that there were no previous records of *M. villosus* from Point Barrow to Herschel Island, Yukon Territory, but that N. J. Wilimovsky found the species in between those localities. The latter portion of the range is documented by, e.g., UBC 63-600, 70°27'N, 149°02'W, Beechey Point; UBC 63-599, 70°34'N, 150°17'W, Thetis Island; and UBC 63-593, 70°55'N, 153°05'W, Pitt Point. Hunter et al. (1984) plotted Canadian Arctic records, including several in the vicinity of Herschel Island and the Mackenzie Delta. Chapman (1939) described a specimen from the Gulf of Alaska as the holotype of a new species, *Sudis squamosus*; Hubbs and Chapman (1951) corrected the error. Fedorov and Sheiko (2002) reported *M. villosus* to be abundant in the vicinity of the Commander Islands. Occasional reports of capelin caught deeper than 200 m, including an extreme record of 725 m (Allen and Smith 1988), are probably due to fish entering the nets above the maximum depth of the tow.

Size: Attained by a female, 10 years old and about to spawn, in Newfoundland. Greatest length cited for North Pacific is 21.8 cm (Hart 1973).

Hypomesus olidus (Pallas, 1814) **pond smelt**

Beaufort Sea drainages and south along Bering Sea coastal regions to Copper River, northern Gulf of Alaska, and east across Arctic Canada to lower Mackenzie River system and Coronation Gulf; Chukchi Peninsula to Wonsan, North Korea, and northern Siberia west to Alazaya River.

Freshwater species occurring in ponds, lakes, and streams; only occasionally entering brackish water.

D 7–11; A 12–18; Pec 9–13; Pel 8–9; Ls 51–62; GR 8–12 + 17–22 (26–34); Br 6–8; PC 1–5; Vert 51–62.

- Yellow-brown to olive green dorsally; silvery white ventrally; poorly defined silver stripe along middle of side, turning dark in preservative; snout and operculum speckled.
- **Adipose eyelid absent**.
- **Mouth small, maxilla not reaching or barely reaching mideye**.
- **Adipose fin base equal to or longer than eye diameter, or more than 20% of head length; anal fin rays long**, longest anal ray 43–56% of head length; **pectoral fin long**, reaching 50–80% of distance between pectoral and pelvic fin bases; pelvic fin origin below or anterior to dorsal fin origin; pelvic fin in males almost reaching anal fin, shorter in females.
- **Midlateral scales fewer (usually 51–60) than in *H. pretiosus*.**
- Lateral line incomplete, extending less than a head's length along body.
- None of teeth enlarged; arch of small teeth across vomer; palatine teeth small; tongue teeth minute, villiform.
- Fewer pyloric caeca (usually 2) than in *H. pretiosus*.
- Pneumatic duct attached behind anterior end of swim bladder.
- Males develop breeding tubercles on head, scales, and fin rays.
- Length to 200 mm TL; usually under 150 mm.

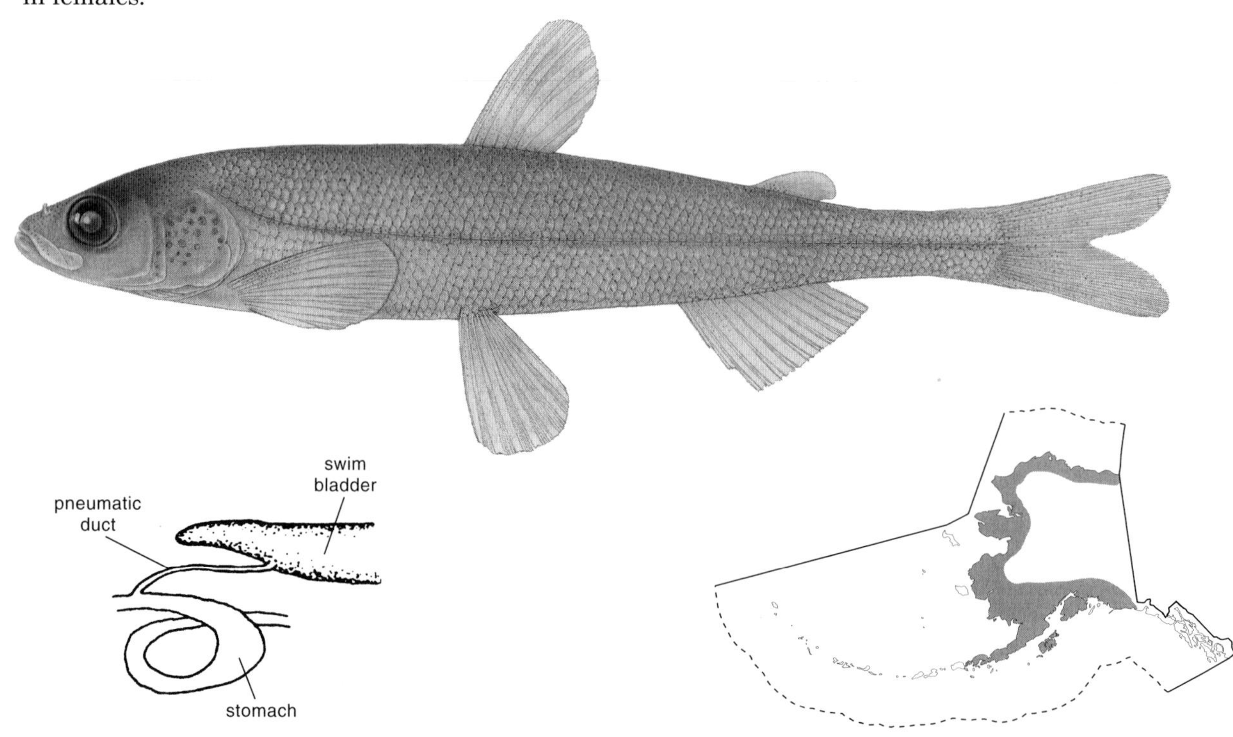

Notes & Sources — *Hypomesus olidus* (Pallas, 1814)
Salmo (Osmerus) olidus Pallas, 1814

Description: McAllister 1963:31–34; McPhail and Lindsey 1970:200–203; Morrow 1980:151–154; Saruwatari et al. 1997:73–76.

Figures: University of British Columbia, artist P. Drucker-Brammall, Nov. 1966; UBC 63-740, 101 mm SL, Kuskokwim River, Alaska. Diagram: after McAllister 1963:27.

Range: Jordan and Evermann (1896b) noted pond smelt were "excessively abundant" around St. Michael, on Norton Sound. McAllister (1963) and Saruwatari et al. (1997) gave collection data for numerous Alaskan records. Range in Alaska was mapped most recently by McAllister et al. (in Lee et al. 1980), Morrow (1980), and Page and Burr (1991). McAllister (1963) found this species in brackish water along the Mackenzie Delta at Inuvik, and Coad (1995) reported it enters brackish water along the Tuktoyaktuk Peninsula. *Hypomesus olidus* has been confused with other species of *Hypomesus,* so care should be taken in using the earlier literature (McAllister 1963).

Hypomesus pretiosus (Girard, 1855) **surf smelt**

North side of Alaska Peninsula at Izembek Bay and Gulf of Alaska to Long Beach, California.

Marine; sometimes found in brackish water, rarely in fresh water; spawns in surf of ocean beaches in coarse sand and fine gravel.

D 8–11; A 12–17; Pec 13–17; Pel 8–9; Ls 65–76; GR 9–13 + 20–25 (30–36); Br 7–8; PC 4–8; Vert 62–70.

- Light green to yellow-brown dorsally; silvery yellow or white ventrally; bright silver stripe along side, turning dark in preservative.
- **Adipose eyelid well developed**.
- **Mouth small, maxilla not reaching mideye**.
- **Adipose fin base less than eye diameter, or less than 20% of head length; anal fin rays short**, longest anal ray 29–38% of head length; **pectoral fin short**, extending 41–48% of distance between pectoral and pelvic fin bases; pelvic fin origin below or posterior to dorsal fin origin; pelvic fin not extending near anal fin in either sex.
- **Midlateral scales more (usually 66–73) than in *H. olidus***.
- Lateral line incomplete, extending less than a head's length along body.
- None of teeth enlarged; arch of small teeth across vomer; palatine teeth small; tongue teeth minute, villiform.
- More pyloric caeca (usually 6) than in *H. olidus*.
- Pneumatic duct attached to anterior end of swim bladder.
- Males develop breeding tubercles on scales and fin rays.
- Length to 305 mm TL; usually under 200 mm.

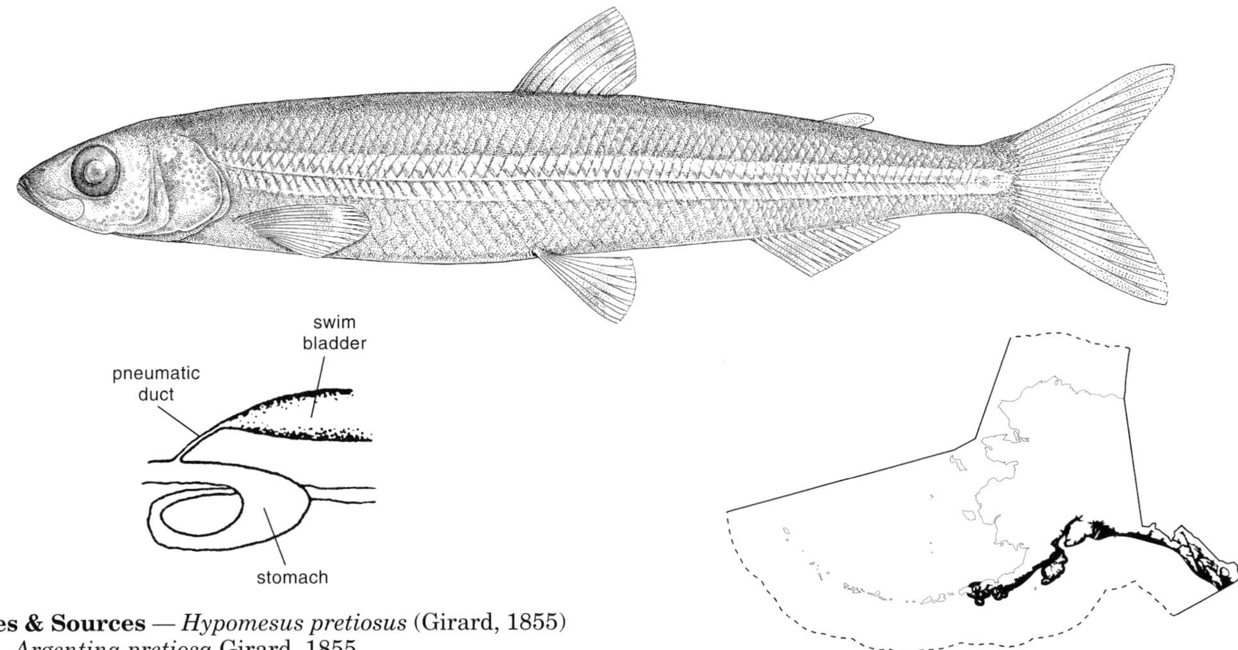

Notes & Sources — *Hypomesus pretiosus* (Girard, 1855)
Argentina pretiosa Girard, 1855
Hypomesus pretiosus pretiosus: McAllister 1963.

A closely related western Pacific form with a range from southern Kamchatka to Korea was treated as a subspecies of *H. pretiosus, H. p. japonicus,* by McAllister (1963), McAllister (in Lee et al. 1980), Morrow (1980), Eschmeyer and Herald (1983), and Uyeno (in Masuda et al. 1984). Its meristics are somewhat different (e.g., lower fin ray and higher midlateral scale counts) from those of *H. p. pretiosus,* so we were careful to include only meristics based on eastern Pacific records above. It is not correct, as some authors have stated, that the range of *H. p. japonicus* extends to Alaska. After we prepared this species account, Saruwatari et al. (1997) revised the genus *Hypomesus* and recognized both *H. pretiosus* and *H. japonicus* as valid species.

Description: McAllister 1963:28–30; Morrow 1980:152–154; Coad 1995:778–779; Saruwatari et al. 1997:78–79.

Figures: University of British Columbia, artist P. Drukker-Brammall; UBC 63-272, 84 mm SL, Toledo Harbor, Baranof Island, Alaska. Diagram: after McAllister 1963:27.

Range: Morrow (1980) recorded range to Herendeen Bay, approximately 55°50'N, 160°50'W, on the north side of the Alaska Peninsula. McAllister (in Lee et al. 1980) recorded a new westernmost record, at Izembek Bay, about 55°20'N, 162°48'W, and a northern record at Olsen Bay, about 60°43'N, 146°12'W, Prince William Sound. The latter two records are documented by UBC 63-1439 and UBC 63-394, respectively. The UBC also has examples from Port Gravina and Orca Inlet, Prince William Sound. Phinney and Dahlberg (1968) recorded *H. pretiosus* from Chignik Lagoon, on the south side of the Alaska Peninsula.

Size: Maximum length of 305 mm TL given by Hart (1973) for California fish, without documentation, was repeated by McAllister (in Lee et al. 1980) and Coad (1995). Morrow (1980) gave maximum of 254 mm for California fish, citing Roedel (1953), and reported that the maximum size of northern fish is about 200–230 mm.

Osmerus mordax (Mitchill, 1814) **rainbow smelt**

Beaufort Sea to Barkley Sound, British Columbia, possibly to Heceta Head, Oregon; across Arctic Canada to Bathurst Inlet, and Labrador to Pennsylvania; western Pacific to Sea of Okhotsk and to Wonsan, North Korea; across Arctic Russia to White Sea.

Anadromous; from surface to depth of 150 m, occasionally deeper, near coast; ascends freshwater streams to spawn, usually only a few hundred meters to a few kilometers upstream.

D 8–11; A 11–18; Pec 9–14; Pel 8; Ls 62–72; GR 8–14 + 15–24 (26–37); Br 6–8; PC 4–9; Vert 58–70.

- Olive green speckled with black dorsally; silvery band laterally; white ventrally.
- Mouth large, **maxilla extending to posterior part of eye or past eye**; **operculum lacking striae**.
- Adipose fin base less than eye diameter; relatively few anal fin rays (usually 12–16); pelvic fin origin below or slightly posterior to dorsal fin origin.
- Lateral line incomplete, ceasing anterior to pelvic fin insertion.
- **One large canine on each side of vomer**, sometimes accompanied by smaller canines; palatine teeth enlarged anteriorly; **prominent conical to caniniform teeth on tongue**.
- Breeding males develop numerous tubercles on head, body, and fins; lateral ridge may develop.
- Length to 356 mm TL.

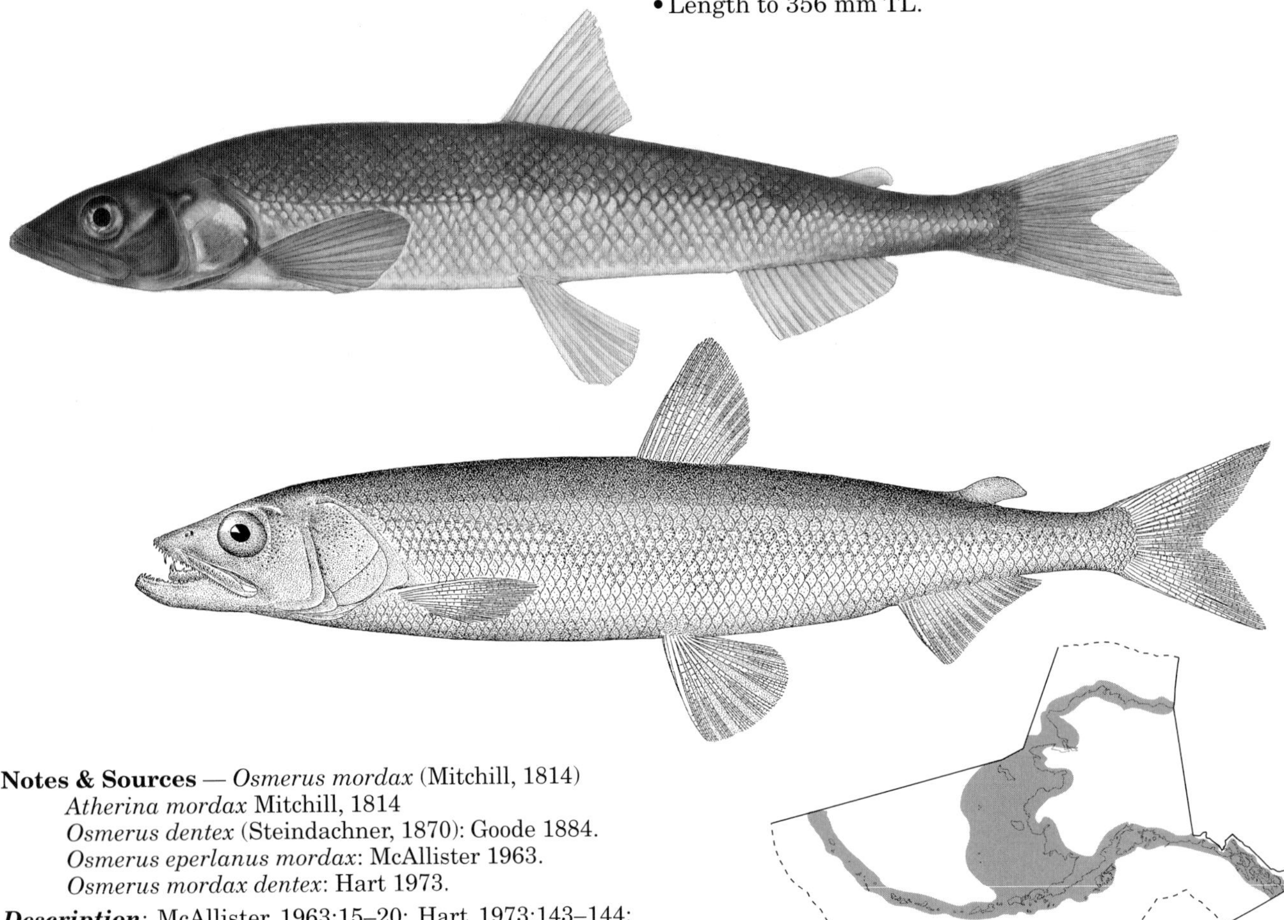

Notes & Sources — *Osmerus mordax* (Mitchill, 1814)
Atherina mordax Mitchill, 1814
Osmerus dentex (Steindachner, 1870): Goode 1884.
Osmerus eperlanus mordax: McAllister 1963.
Osmerus mordax dentex: Hart 1973.

Description: McAllister 1963:15–20; Hart 1973:143–144; Morrow 1980:155–159; Coad 1995:567–568.

Figures: Upper: University of British Columbia, artist P. Drukker-Brammall, Oct. 1966; UBC 63-1128, 197 mm SL, inlet at Wainwright, Alaska. Lower: Goode 1884, pl. 199; 305 mm TL, Port Clarence, Alaska.

Range: Most recently mapped by McAllister et al. (in Lee et al. 1980), Morrow (1980), and Allen and Smith (1988). The latter authors reported catches in demersal tows reaching to deeper than 150 m, including an occurrence at 425 m, but noted that the fish, being pelagic, were probably captured nearer to the surface. Haldorson and Craig (1984) found *O. mordax* to be abundant in winter in Harrison Bay near the mouth of the Colville River. Hunter et al. (1984) plotted Canadian Arctic records, including several near Herschel Island and the Mackenzie Delta. Fedorov and Sheiko (2002) reported *O. mordax* to be abundant near the Commander Islands. It is least common in Alaska in the Gulf of Alaska. A record in the NMFS survey database (data provided by J. W. Orr, 13 Nov. 1997) from Heceta Head, Oregon (44°08'N), represents an extension of the known range southward from Barkley Sound, British Columbia, recorded by Hart (1973). Upstream migrations of more than 1,000 km occur in Siberia (Berg 1948).

Size: Scott and Scott 1988.

Thaleichthys pacificus (Richardson, 1836) **eulachon**

Bering Sea west of St. Matthew Island, off Kuskokwim Bay and Nushagak River, and Bowers Bank and central Aleutian Islands through coastal Gulf of Alaska to central California at Point Conception.

Anadromous; from surface to depth of 300 m, occasionally deeper, near coast; ascends freshwater streams to spawn, up to 160 km upstream; most die after spawning, but some survive to spawn once more.

D 10–13; A 17–23; Pec 10–12; Pel 8; LLs 70–78; GR 4–6 + 13–18 (17–23); Br 6–8; PC 8–12; Vert 65–72.

- Bluish to bluish black or brown, with fine black speckling dorsally; silvery white laterally and ventrally.
- Mouth large, maxilla reaching to or beyond posterior margin of eye; **obvious concentric striae on operculum**.
- Adipose fin base less than eye diameter; pelvic fin of males sometimes reaching anus, always shorter in females; **pelvic fin base anterior to dorsal fin origin**.
- Lateral line complete.
- Vomer with 1 pair large canines; palatine teeth larger anteriorly; tongue teeth medium conical to large caniniform; all teeth tend to be lost in spawners, particularly males.
- **Few gill rakers (4–6) on upper limb of first arch**.
- Breeding males develop midlateral ridge formed by swollen muscles, and fine tubercles on head, body, and fins.
- Length to 254 mm TL.

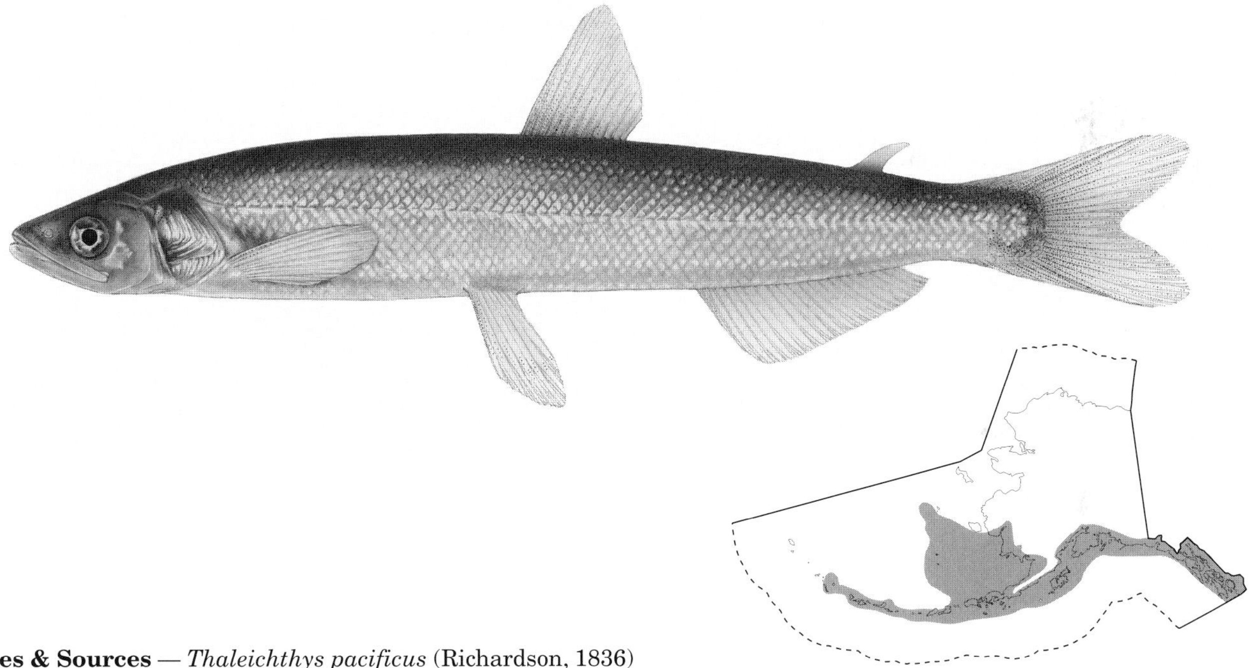

Notes & Sources — *Thaleichthys pacificus* (Richardson, 1836)
Salmo (Mallotus?) pacificus Richardson (ex Gairdner), 1836
Osmerus albatrossis Jordan & Gilbert in Jordan & Evermann, 1898 (also in Jordan & Gilbert, 1899)
Lestidium (Bathysudis) parri Chapman, 1939
Sometimes called candlefish because it is so oily that when dried it can be used as a candle (Swan 1880b).

Description: McAllister 1963:23–24; Hart 1973:148–150; Morrow 1980: 154–155; Coad 1995:269–270.

Figure: University of British Columbia, artist P. Drukker-Brammall, Nov. 1966; UBC 65-94, 161 mm SL, Nagai Island, Alaska.

Range: One of the most commonly found fishes in Alaska. In the late nineteenth century, Swan (1880b) reported they were present "in countless myriads in the waters of Alaska Territory." Range was mapped most recently by McAllister and Parker (in Lee et al. 1980), Morrow (1980), and Allen and Smith (1988). The latter authors reported that eulachon were taken in nets towed as deep as 625 m, but that the fish could have been captured near the surface; more than 96% of the occurrences in their database were from depths of 300 m or less. Juveniles of *T. pacificus* from the northern Gulf of Alaska were described as a new species by Chapman (1939); the error was corrected by Hubbs and Chapman (1951). Anderson (1977) recorded two specimens from Monterey Bay, extending the known range southward from Bodega Head. The NMFS survey database has records of occurrence as far south as Point Conception (J. W. Orr, pers. comm., 13 Nov. 1997).

Size: Morrow (1980) gave a maximum known length of 22.5 cm FL, from Bering Strait specimens examined by Taranetz (1933). Hart (1973) believed that records of larger sizes should be viewed with suspicion. Miller and Lea (1972) gave a length of 30.5 cm TL ("about 12 inches"), but later (in 1976 addendum) reported it had not been verified and gave a length of 25.4 cm TL (10.0 inches) for a specimen from the Bering Sea. Some authors continue to give the improbable 30.5-cm length.

Spirinchus thaleichthys (Ayres, 1860) **longfin smelt**

Shelikof Strait, southwestern Gulf of Alaska, to Monterey Bay, central California.

Anadromous; a few landlocked populations occur south of Alaska; along coast, from surface to depth of about 137 m.

D 8–10; A 15–22; Pec 10–12; Pel 8; Ls 54–63; GR 10–13 + 26–34 (38–47); Br 7–8; PC 4–6; Vert 54–61.

- Brown to olive brown dorsally; silvery laterally; white ventrally; ripe males darker laterally with profuse stippling dorsally and on scale margins.
- **Snout blunt, with premaxilla steep, forming angle of 68–90 degrees to forehead**; maxilla extending to or almost to posterior margin of eye.
- Adipose fin base length two-thirds of to equal to eye diameter; **longest anal fin ray 45–71% of head length**; **pectoral fin long**, extending 84–128% of distance to pelvic fin base; pelvic fin origin below or slightly anterior to dorsal fin origin.
- **Midlateral scales fewer (usually 55–62) than in *S. starksi*.**
- Lateral line incomplete, extending about a head's length along body.
- **Series of small teeth in arc across vomer**; palatine teeth small; **tongue teeth caniniform**.
- Gill rakers long.
- Breeding males develop anal shelf, protruding lateral line, and tubercles on scales and fins.
- Length to 200 mm TL.

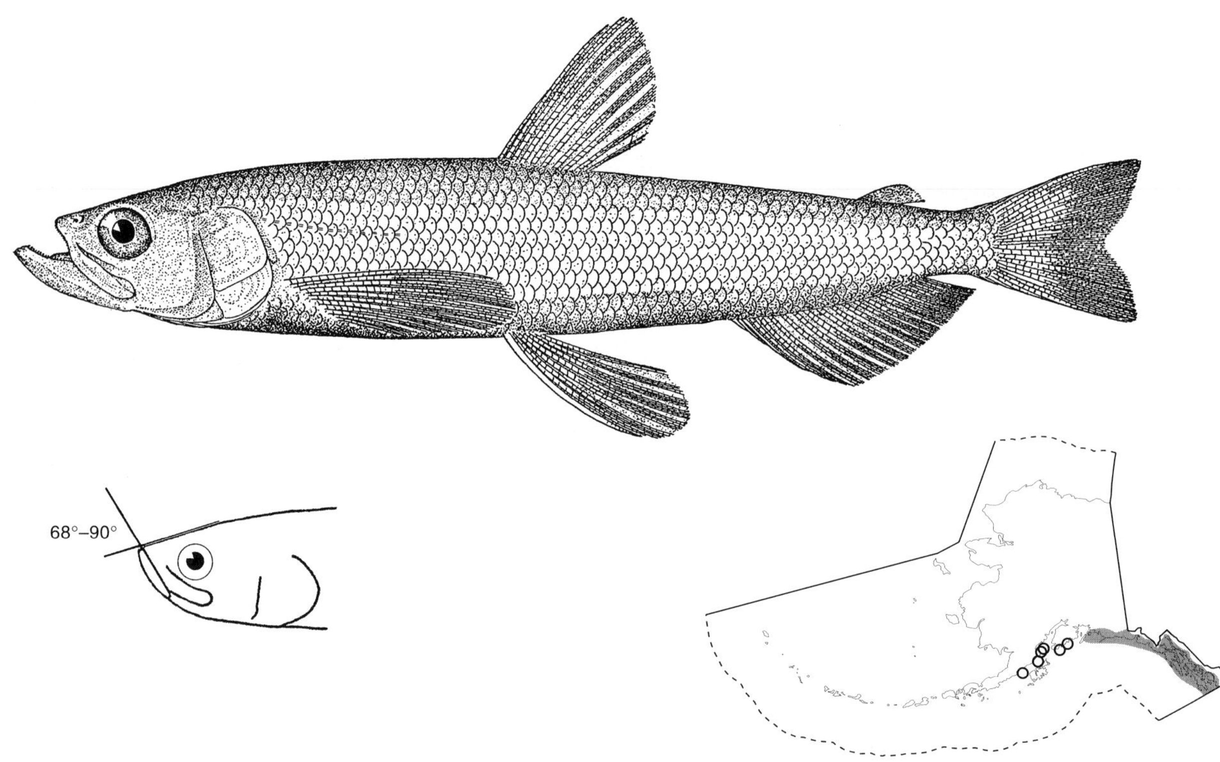

Notes & Sources — *Spirinchus thaleichthys* (Ayres, 1860)
Osmerus thaleichthys Ayres, 1860
Spirinchus dilatus Schultz & Chapman, 1934

Description: McAllister 1963:10–14; Hart 1973:146–147; Morrow 1980:150–151.

Figures: Jordan and Evermann 1900, fig. 227, modified; San Francisco. Diagram: adapted from McAllister 1963:8.

Range: Statements of range to Bering Sea for this species are unsubstantiated. Hubbs (1925) long ago pointed out that the record reported by Gilbert (1896) from the Nushagak River in the Bristol Bay area is an error, that the specimens were pond smelt, *Hypomesus olidus.* The westernmost, adequately documented, published record is that of Dryfoos (1961), for specimens taken in the vicinity of Hinchinbrook Island, off Prince William Sound, at 60°12'N, 146°15'W; identification of the specimens (12, in UW 15548) was verified by McAllister (1963). Circles on the above map represent nine records of occurrence west of Prince William Sound from the NMFS survey database, provided by J. W. Orr (pers. comm., 13 Nov. 1997): 57°20'N, 156°26'W; 58°00'N, 154°39'W; 58°18'N, 154°16'W; 59°30'N, 153°14'W; 59°38'N, 152°58'W; 59°36'N, 151°22'W; 59°36'N, 151°20'W; 59°38'N, 151°13'W; 59°43'N, 151°09'W; surveys were during 1963–1989. This species is anadromous in Alaska but landlocked populations exist elsewhere, as in Harrison Lake, British Columbia, and Lakes Union and Washington in Seattle, Washington.

Size: Morrow (1980) and Coad (1995); neither author cited documentation. Other authors (e.g., Hart 1973, Eschmeyer and Herald 1983) report smaller maximum sizes, up to 15.2 cm TL.

Spirinchus starksi (Fisk, 1913) — night smelt

Southeastern Gulf of Alaska at Shelikof Bay to southern California off Point Arguello.

Marine; surface to depth of 128 m; spawns in surf at night; caught while spawning, or occasionally on hook and line.

D 8–11; A 15–21; Pec 10–11; Pel 8; Ls 60–66; GR 8–13 + 24–31 (32–45); Br 7–8; PC 4–8; Vert 60–64.

- Brownish green dorsally; silvery laterally and ventrally.
- **Snout pointed, with premaxilla relatively horizontal, forming angle of 54–65 degrees to forehead**; maxilla extending to just short of to beyond posterior margin of eye.
- Adipose fin base length two-thirds of to equal to eye diameter; **longest anal fin ray 32–45% of head length**; **pectoral fin short**, extending 84% or less of distance to pelvic fin base; pelvic fin origin slightly anterior to dorsal fin origin.
- **Midlateral scales more (usually 62–65) than in *S. thaleichthys*.**
- Lateral line incomplete, extending less than a head's length along body.
- **Series of small teeth in arc across vomer**; palatine teeth small; **tongue teeth caniniform**.
- Gill rakers short.
- Breeding males with anal shelf and lateral ridge absent or only slightly developed; tubercles on head, scales, and lower fins.
- Length to 230 mm TL.

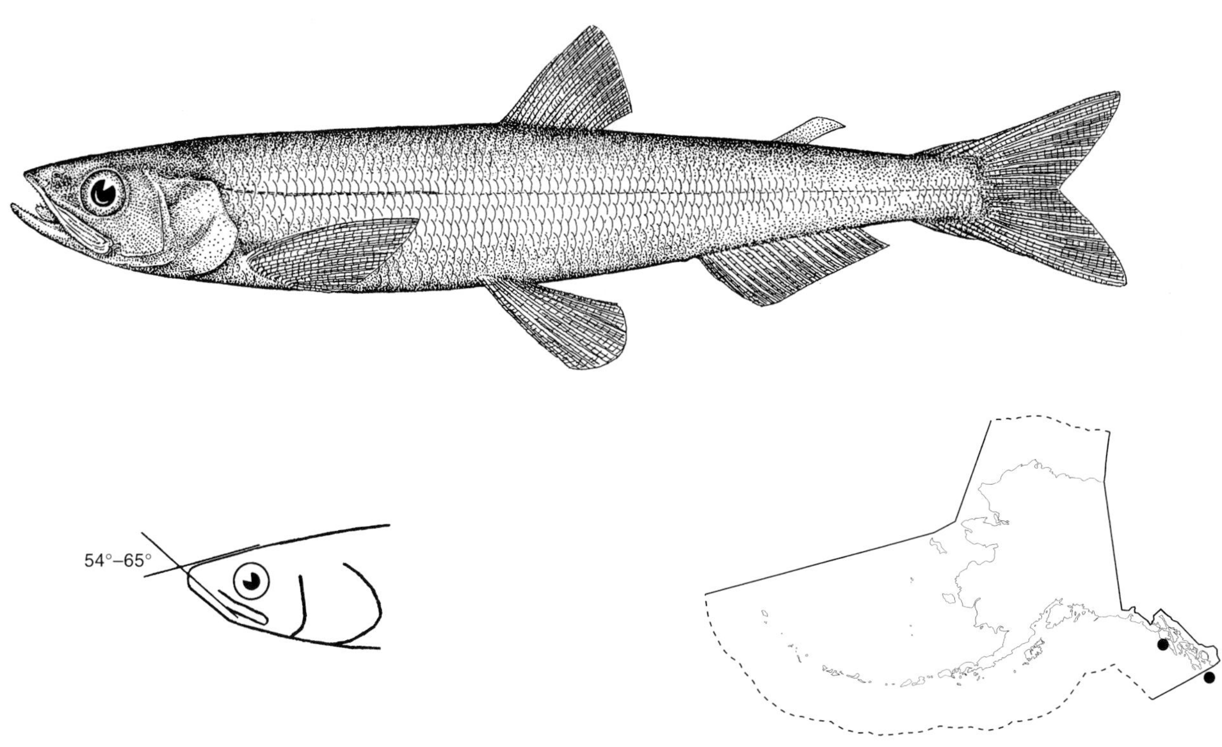

Notes & Sources — *Spirinchus starksi* (Fisk, 1913)
Osmerus starksi Fisk, 1913

Description: McAllister 1963:14–15; Hart 1973:145–146; Coad 1995:468.

Figures: Hart 1973:145; 11 cm TL, Hecate Strait, British Columbia. Diagram: after McAllister 1963:8.

Range: The only published record from Alaska comprises 12 specimens (UW 15547) from Shelikof Bay, in the southeastern Gulf of Alaska near Sitka at about 57°08'N, 135°48'W (Dryfoos 1961); identity of those specimens was verified by McAllister (1963). Recorded from Hecate Strait at 54°30'N, 131°50'W, off Graham Island, Queen Charlotte Islands, by Hart (1973).

Size: Eschmeyer and Herald (1983) and Coad (1995). Previously reported to 140 mm TL (Miller and Lea 1972) or 121 mm TL (Hart 1973). Largest examined by McAllister (1963) was 112 mm SL.

Order Salmoniformes
Salmoniforms

Salmoniforms include about 70 species of whitefishes, graylings, salmons, trouts, and chars, all classified in the Salmonidae, which is the only family in the order Salmoniformes. The characters of the order, then, are those of the family. For consistency this guide follows the classification by Nelson (1994) but, as with other taxa, views on the relationships of the salmoniforms vary and different classifications exist. Most recently, Johnson and Patterson (1996) proposed that smelts (Osmeridae) are the sister-group of salmonids (Salmonidae), and that to express this relationship they should be classified together in the Salmoniformes. This is not a totally new idea, but Johnson and Patterson provided new evidence supporting it. Among the 11 characters they listed that are common to osmerids and salmonids are a single supramaxilla, absence of radii on the scales, absence of epipleural bones, and presence of nuptial tubercles and diadromy in some species. They proposed classifying the Salmoniformes in two suborders, Osmeroidei and Salmonoidei, allowing room to express relationships in either group as they are resolved. Following the work of Sanford (1990), Stearley and Smith (1993), and others, they proposed including two families in the Salmonoidei: Salmonidae, with the subfamilies Thymallinae (graylings) and Salmoninae (trouts, salmons, and chars); and Coregonidae (whitefishes). In a future revision to his classification, J. S. Nelson (pers. comm., Aug. 2000) may combine Osmeridae and Salmonidae in Salmoniformes, but probably would not split the Salmonidae into smaller groups.

Family Salmonidae
Salmonids

Fishery workers commonly use the name salmonid to refer to the various species in the family Salmonidae as a group. Using any of the less encompassing names, including whitefish, trout, salmon, or char, when the whole group is meant could be confusing. By any name, however, they are some of the best known of the world's fishes. All salmonids spawn in fresh water and many are anadromous, spending part of their life at sea. They are fished for subsistence, commercial gain, and recreation both at sea and in fresh water, and farming of some species is hugely successful. Salmonids are native to cool waters of the Northern Hemisphere, but several species have been transplanted outside their native ranges and a few now occur virtually worldwide.

Diagnostic features of salmonids include a rounded or moderately compressed body; no spines in the fins; a dorsal adipose fin, with the anal fin below it; 1 dorsal fin, located at about the middle of the body; pectoral fins positioned low on the body; abdominal pelvic fins; a distinct pelvic axillary process; cycloid scales, which are confined to the body and often very small; a distinct lateral line; and gill membranes extending far forward, free from the isthmus. The mouth can be large and well toothed to small and toothless. The pectoral girdle has a mesocoracoid, the last 3 vertebrae are turned up, the eye muscles pass through a deep posterior myodome and attach to the trunk muscles, and the swim bladder is connected to the esophagus. Salmonids have 7–20 branchiostegal rays, 11–210 pyloric caeca, and 50–75 vertebrae. They have tetraploid karyotypes. At maturity the largest salmonids can reach about 1.5 m (5 feet) in length.

Subfamily Coregoninae
Whitefishes

Various, unrelated fishes around the world are called whitefishes for their white or silvery color without spots or other marks. In North America the name applies to species in the subfamily Coregoninae. Whitefishes are found in Alaska in all river systems north of the Alaska Range, and the Copper, Susitna, and Alsek systems south of the Alaska Range. Eight to ten or more species are present in the region, with the number depending on how some forms are classified.

The main features distinguishing whitefishes from other salmonids are large scales, usually not numbering more than 110 along the lateral line; small, weak teeth or absence of teeth; and the absence of parr marks in the young, except in genus *Prosopium.* In *Prosopium* the marks are round or longitudinally ovoid and can persist beyond the juvenile stage, but in Thymallinae and Salmoninae the marks are typically vertically ovoid and disappear at smoltification. Other whitefish characteristics include: fewer than 16 dorsal fin rays; no teeth on the maxillae; vomer usually small and without teeth; orbitosphenoid present; and suprapreopercular absent.

Whitefishes develop nuptial tubercles and in most species in which they are prominent in the males, the females also have them but they are only feebly developed. Like Pacific salmons, genus *Oncorhynchus,* some anadromous whitefishes show fidelity to their natal streams for spawning. Unlike Pacific salmons, whitefishes generally do not die after spawning and anadromous species do not spend most of their lives at sea. When at sea, anadromous whitefishes stay in estuarine coastal waters and do not make oceanic migrations.

Identifying whitefishes can be difficult. Checking nonoverlapping characters will first narrow the choices to groups of closely related species. Round whitefishes, genus *Prosopium,* have a single flap between each pair of nostrils and the young have parr marks. Inconnu, ciscoes, and lake whitefishes (*Stenodus* and *Coregonus*) have two flaps between the nostrils and the young do

nostril with singe flap—*Prosopium*

nostril with double flap—*Stenodus* and *Coregonus*

not bear parr marks. (A magnifying glass is needed to see the nostril flaps.) Inconnu (*Stenodus*) and ciscoes (*Coregonus autumnalis, C. laurettae, C. sardinella*) have terminal or superior mouths. Broad whitefish (*C. nasus*) and lake whitefishes (*C. clupeaformis, C. nelsonii, C. pidschian*), as well as *Prosopium,* have inferior mouths. *Stenodus* is easily distinguished from *Coregonus* by its large mouth and lower number of gill rakers.

Some of the most closely related species are fairly easily separated, and some are not. The round whitefish, *P. cylindraceum,* has more lateral line scales and a smaller eye, and is much larger at maturity than the pygmy whitefish, *P. coulterii.* Adults of least cisco, *C. sardinella,* are easily distinguished from adults of *C. autumnalis* and *C. laurettae* by a superior mouth, with slightly projecting lower jaw, and dusky or black pelvic fins. Identification of young least cisco can be difficult because the dusky fin coloration does not appear until the fish are about 15 cm long. Arctic cisco, *C. autumnalis,* and Bering cisco, *C. laurettae,* are not easily separated except by counting gill rakers, and some authors do not recognize them as separate species. Recent genetic tests and gill raker counts in samples from the Colville River confirm their distinctiveness (Bickham et al. 1989, 1997).

Broad whitefish, *C. nasus,* have short gill rakers, a wide head, and rounded to flat head profile compared to the humpback whitefishes, *C. pidschian, C. clupeaformis,* and *C. nelsonii.* The only way to tell the humpback whitefishes apart is by modal gill raker counts. McPhail and Lindsey (1970) treated the humpback whitefishes collectively as a "*Coregonus clupeaformis* complex." Alt (1979), from data on humpback whitefishes in several Alaskan localities, concluded that there is considerable overlap in life history parameters and no clear pattern of distribution of gill raker counts and that it may be appropriate to consider the humpback whitefish in Alaska a single species for management purposes. Other authors, including Morrow (1980), follow Starks' (1926) admonition that "a question would better remain in the form of a question than in the form of an incorrect answer," and treat the three Alaskan forms as possibly distinct. Following Morrow (1980), we take the conservative approach. If the forms are shown to be the same, the correct name would be *C. pidschian* (Gmelin, 1789), as that name has priority by date over *C. clupeaformis* (Mitchill, 1818). The third species in the complex, the Alaska whitefish, *C. nelsonii* Bean, 1884, was described later.

Hybridization among whitefishes is common and there are several hybrid studies for almost all pairs of whitefish crosses (e.g., Alt 1971, Reist et al. 1992). Hybridization is believed not to result from intergeneric pairing but to occur when species spawn at the same time and in the same place, simultaneously broadcasting their reproductive products. Presence of hybrids can pose a challenge when attempting to identify species.

The following key to the Alaskan whitefishes is modified from keys by McPhail and Lindsey (1970) and Morrow (1980).

Key to the Coregoninae of Alaska

1 Mouth terminal or superior, lower jaw equal to or projecting beyond upper jaw; profile of upper lip not overhanging lower jaw . . . . (2)

1 Mouth inferior, upper jaw projecting beyond lower jaw; profile of upper lip vertical or overhanging lower jaw . . . . (5)

2 (1) Mouth large, maxilla reaching to below posterior edge of pupil; gill rakers on lower limb of first arch fewer than 18 .... *Stenodus leucichthys,* page 181

2 Mouth moderate, maxilla not reaching to below posterior edge of pupil; gill rakers on lower limb of first arch 20 or more .... (3)

3 (2) Mouth superior, lower jaw projecting slightly beyond upper jaw; pelvic fins dusky or black in adults .... *Coregonus sardinella,* page 182

3 Mouth terminal, lower jaw not projecting beyond upper jaw; pelvic fins always pale .... (4)

4 (3) Gill rakers usually 26–31 on lower limb of first arch, total on first arch 41–48.................... *Coregonus autumnalis,* page 183

4 Gill rakers usually 18–25 on lower limb of first arch, total on first arch 35–39.................... *Coregonus laurettae,* page 184

5 (1) Adipose eyelid without distinct notch below posterior edge of pupil; nostrils on each side separated by double flap.................... (6)

5 Adipose eyelid with distinct notch below posterior edge of pupil; nostrils on each side separated by single flap .... (9)

6 (5) Gill rakers short, longest less than 20% of interorbital width; profile of head smoothly convex, except barely concave in large fish; hump behind head absent, or not prominent; maxilla depth more than 50% of its length .... *Coregonus nasus,* page 185

6 Gill rakers long, longest more than 20% of interorbital width; profile of head distinctly concave between snout and nape; hump behind head prominent in adults; maxilla depth less than 50% of its length .... (7)

7 (6) Total gill rakers on first arch 24–33, modal counts 26 or more.................... *Coregonus clupeaformis,* page 186

7 Total gill rakers on first arch 19–27, modal counts 25 or fewer .... (8)

8 (7) Total gill rakers on first arch 23–27, modal counts 24 or 25 .... *Coregonus nelsonii,* page 187

8 Total gill rakers on first arch 19–24, modal counts 21 or 22 .... *Coregonus pidschian,* page 188

9 (5) Lateral line scales 74 or more; snout pointed when seen from above; eye small, 14–20% HL; pyloric caeca 50 or more; adults to 56 cm TL .... *Prosopium cylindraceum,* page 189

9 Lateral line scales 70 or less; snout blunt when seen from above; eye moderate, 25–30% HL; pyloric caeca fewer than 40; adults 28 cm TL or less .... *Prosopium coulterii,* page 190

Stenodus leucichthys (Güldenstadt, 1772) **inconnu**

Arctic Alaska to northern Bering Sea drainages, in Colville, Meade, Kobuk, Selawik, Yukon, and Kuskokwim systems; Siberia to White Sea and south to Kamchatka; Caspian Sea drainages; Mackenzie River and east to Anderson River in Canada.

Freshwater; rivers and streams, some populations in brackish lakes and delta waters; migrate upstream to spawn.

D 11–19; A 14–19; Pec 14–17; Pel 11–12; LLs 90–115; GR 17–24; Br 9–12; PC 144–211; Vert 63–69.

- Silvery; green, blue, or pale brown dorsally; silvery white ventrally; margins of dorsal and caudal fins dusky; other fins pale.
- Body not much compressed; head long, 24–28% of total length; eye diameter about 15% of head length; snout prominent, about 23% of head length; nostrils with double flap between openings; **maxilla reaching to below posterior margin of pupil or beyond; lower jaw protruding** beyond upper jaw.
- Dorsal fin high and pointed; adipose fin present; pelvic axillary process well developed.
- Teeth very small, in velvetlike bands on both jaws and on vomer, palatines, and tongue.
- **Fewer than 18 gill rakers on lower limb of first arch.**
- Length to 140 cm TL.

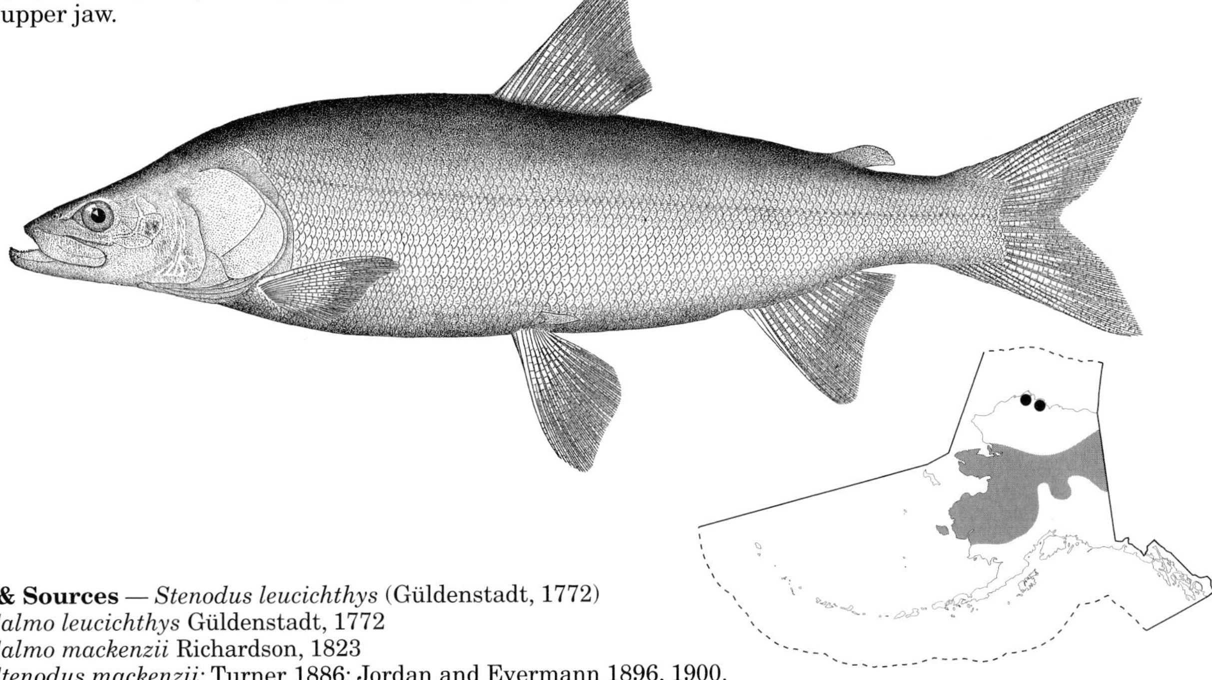

Notes & Sources — *Stenodus leucichthys* (Güldenstadt, 1772)
Salmo leucichthys Güldenstadt, 1772
Salmo mackenzii Richardson, 1823
Stenodus mackenzii: Turner 1886; Jordan and Evermann 1896, 1900.
In Alaska often called sheefish from the Yupik and Innuit Eskimo name for this fish.

Description: Berg 1948:308–312; Alt 1969; McPhail and Lindsey 1970:74–77; Scott and Crossman 1973:295–298; Morrow 1980:25–27; Page and Burr 1991:44.

Figure: Turner 1886, pl. 12; 580 mm TL, Nulato, Alaska.

Range: Mapped most recently by McAllister and Platania (in Lee et al. 1980), Morrow (1980), and Page and Burr (1991). Range in Alaska was summarized by Morrow (1980) as follows. Present in Yukon River and its tributaries from the mouth to Teslin Lake, Yukon Territory, but does not ascend Tanana River much beyond Fairbanks. Migrates up Koyukuk River at least as far as Alatna. Not found north or east of Kobuk River, except for a few fish reported from Meade and Colville rivers. Inconnu in Alaska, Morrow (1980) reported, constitute five distinct populations that mix little with each other: Minto Flats and upper Yukon River groups, which are year-round residents, wintering in the large rivers and moving relatively short distances to clear streams to spawn; Kuskokwim and lower Yukon River groups, which winter in the delta areas of these streams, the fish of the lower Yukon traveling 1,600 km to spawn in the Alatna River and the spawning area of the Kuskokwim group not definitely known; and the Kobuk–Selawik population, which winters in the brackish waters of Selawik Lake and Hotham Inlet and moves as far as 670 km up Kobuk River to spawn. From more recent work, K. T. Alt (pers. comm., 26 May 2000) reported that distinct populations are found in the upper Nowitna River, the upper Porcupine River, and the Salmon Fork of the Black River. He reported that fish of the lower Yukon River population also spawn in the main Yukon River between Beaver and Circle, and the Kuskokwim River group spawns in Highpower Creek and Big River. Alt also reported that inconnu have been stocked in interior Alaska lakes, with reproductive success noted at Four Mile Lake near Tok. The species has not been found in North Slope rivers in recent years (K. T. Alt and A. L. DeCicco, pers. comms., 26 May 2000).

Size: Total length of a specimen captured in population assessment work by ADFG in 1996 was 140 cm (A. L. DeCicco, pers. comm., 26 May 2000). Reported by Page and Burr (1991) to reach 125 cm TL.

Coregonus sardinella Valenciennes, 1848 **least cisco**

Arctic coast to Bristol Bay and in most streams and lakes north of Alaska Range and throughout Yukon and Kuskokwim drainages; south in Mackenzie River to Fort Simpson and east across Arctic coast of Canada to Bathurst Inlet and Cambridge Bay; Bering Strait and Siberia to White Sea.

Anadromous and landlocked, freshwater forms; coastal waters, estuaries, large lakes, and rivers; landlocked forms in upper Yukon and lakes near Bristol Bay.

D 12–14; A 11–13; Pec 14–17; Pel 8–12; LLs 78–98; GR 41–53; Br 8–9; PC 74–111; Vert 58–64.

- Brownish to dark green dorsally; silvery white ventrally; back and dorsal fin sometimes with dark spots; **pelvic fins dusky to black**, but not until fish are about 15 cm long.
- Body slightly to moderately compressed; head length less than 25% of total length; eye large, 26–32% of head length; snout about 25% of head length; nostrils with double flap between openings; maxilla not extending past mideye; **lower jaw protruding slightly** beyond upper.
- Dorsal fin high and falcate; adipose fin present; pectoral fin narrow; pelvic axillary process distinct.
- Teeth absent, or reduced to slight asperities on tongue.
- Gill rakers long and slender.
- Length to 47 cm TL.

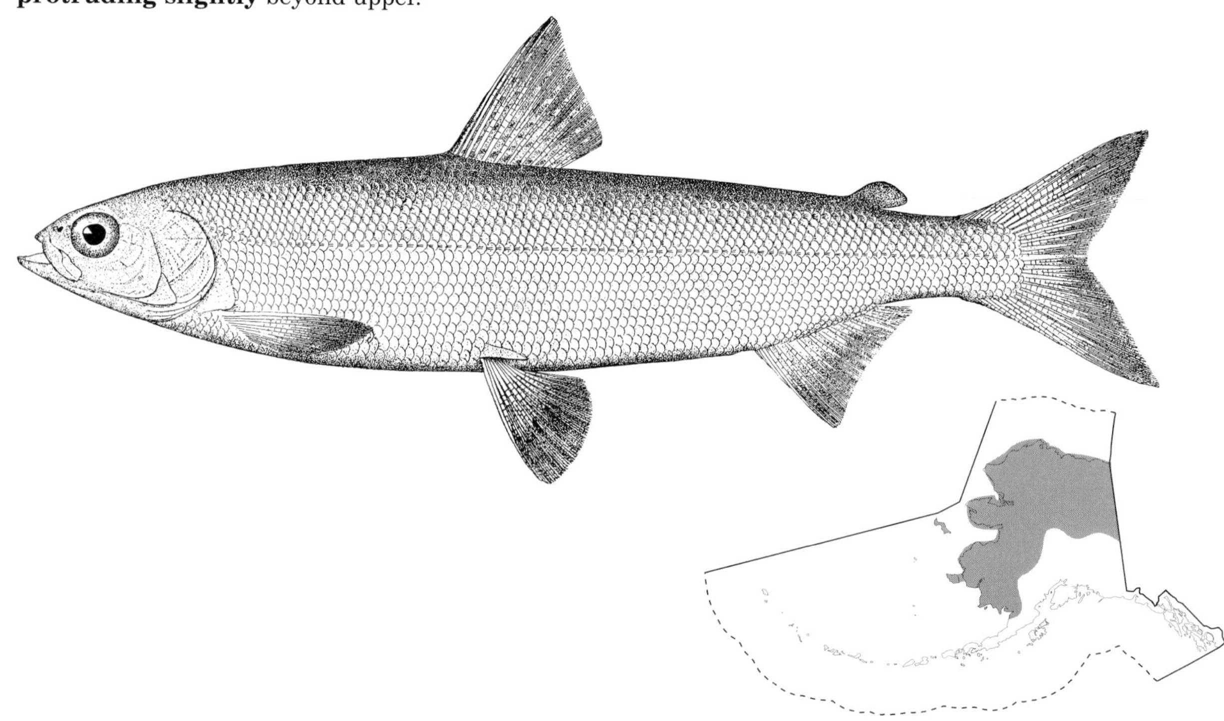

Notes & Sources — *Coregonus sardinella* Valenciennes in Cuvier & Valenciennes, 1848
Coregonus merkii Günther, 1866
Coregonus pusillus Bean, 1889
Argyrosomus pusillus: Evermann and Smith 1896.
Four forms: (1) anadromous form occurring in Arctic drainages and lower Yukon River has spotted back and dorsal fin, 48–53 gill rakers on first arch, reaches 47 cm TL; (2) dwarf, nonanadromous form in Naknek and Iliamna lakes lacks spots, has 49–53 rakers, reaches 18 cm TL; (3) nonanadromous form in upper Yukon lakes has extensively spotted back and dorsal fin, 48–52 gill rakers, reaches 47 cm TL; and (4) nonanadromous form occurring elsewhere lacks spots, has 41–47 rakers, reaches 22 cm TL (Page and Burr 1991).

Description: Bean 1889; Evermann and Smith 1896:312–313; Berg 1948:328–333; McPhail and Lindsey 1970:96–101; Scott and Crossman 1973:262–265; Morrow 1980:27–29; Page and Burr 1991:42. Morrow (1980) stated that in Alaska spawning tubercles are not developed in *C. sardinella* by either sex, contrary to earlier statements by other authors.

Figure: Evermann and Smith 1896, pl. 23, modified from Goode 1884, pl. 198A; 254 mm TL, northern Alaska.

Range: Mapped by Clarke (in Lee et al. 1980), Morrow (1980), and Page and Burr (1991). The *C. pusillus* types were obtained in the Kuwuk River (now Kobuk River), Alaska, by C. H. Townsend (Bean 1889). (Kowak River, the type locality given in the NMNH online catalog, and Putnam River, also sometimes given for the type locality (e.g., Eschmeyer 1998), are other old names for the Kobuk River.) The holotype (unique) of *C. merkii* is from Siberia. Although lake-dwelling populations are nonmigratory, *C. sardinella* living in streams or reaching brackish water undergo upstream spawning migrations.

Size: Page and Burr 1991.

Coregonus autumnalis (Pallas, 1776) **Arctic cisco**

Point Barrow, Alaska, to Murchison River, Northwest Territories, ascending Mackenzie River to Fort Simpson; Arctic Siberia to White Sea; landlocked populations in Lake Baikal and some Irish lakes.

Anadromous and landlocked, freshwater populations; estuaries, rivers, and lakes.

D 10–12; A 12–14; Pec 14–17; Pel 11–12; LLs 82–110; GR 41–48; Br 8; PC 113–183; Vert 64–67.

- Brown to dark green dorsally; silvery ventrally; no black dots on body or white spots on fins; dorsal and caudal fins dusky; **anal, pectoral, and pelvic fins pale**, almost colorless.
- Body slightly compressed; head less than 25% of total length; eye diameter 20–24% of head length; snout about 25% of head length, a little longer than eye diameter; nostrils with double flap between openings; maxilla extending to about mideye; mouth terminal, lower jaw not protruding beyond upper.
- Adipose fin and pelvic axillary process present.
- Teeth absent from jaws in adults; patch of teeth on tongue.
- **Gill rakers on lower limb of first arch more (26–31) than in *C. laurettae***; rakers long and slender.
- Length to 64 cm TL.

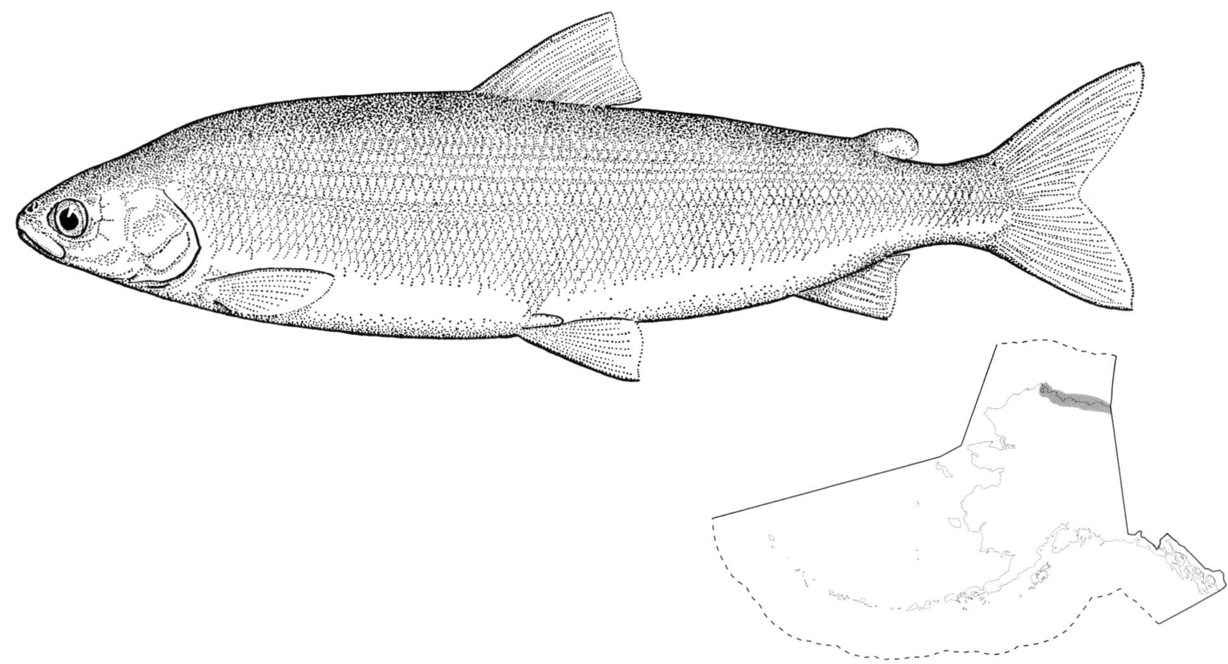

Notes & Sources — *Coregonus autumnalis* (Pallas, 1776)
Salmo autumnalis Pallas, 1776

Dymond (1943) and Berg (1948) included *C. laurettae* of Alaska and Canada as a junior synonym of *C. autumnalis.* McPhail (1966) and Chereshnev (1984) presented morphological evidence supporting the distinctiveness of both species. Most authors have treated them as distinct (e.g., Clarke in Lee et al. 1980, Morrow 1980, Lindsey and McPhail 1986, Robins et al. 1991a). Dillinger (1989) again questioned their specific status and Page and Burr (1991) treated them as subspecies of *C. autumnalis,* pointing to the occurrence of intergrades in the Mackenzie River. Bickham et al. (1997) assessed the degree of differentiation using gill raker counts and mitochondrial DNA haplotypes of samples from the Colville River delta and concluded the forms are valid species.

Description: Berg 1948:336–346; McPhail 1966; McPhail and Lindsey 1970:102–105; Scott and Crossman 1973:244–246; Morrow 1980:30–31; Page and Burr 1991:42. Bickham et al. (1997:225) found absence of dots and spots to be a distinguishing character of *C. autumnalis* (N = 49) in the Colville River delta; this character may not be present in other regions. The authors did not indicate if rakers at the angle of the arch were counted as lower or upper; regardless of exact number, however, the distinction of higher counts in *C. autumnalis* held true. Overlap occurred in only 3 specimens out of a total of 69.

Figure: McPhail and Lindsey 1970:102.

Range: Records were mapped most recently by Clarke (in Lee et al. 1980), Morrow (1980), and Page and Burr (1991). *Coregonus autumnalis* is much more tolerant of salt water than other coregonids (Nikolskii 1961). Migrates as much as 1,000 km upstream to spawn (Roguski and Komarek 1971). Natal stream fidelity was demonstrated for Arctic cisco by Bickham et al. (1989). Sympatric with *C. laurettae* from Colville River to Point Barrow.

Size: Berg 1948; specimens from Siberia. Morrow (1980) noted that North American fish average 35–40 cm.

Coregonus laurettae Bean, 1881 — Bering cisco

Alaska from Beaufort Sea coast at Oliktok Point to Kenai Peninsula on Cook Inlet, northern Gulf of Alaska; Yukon River upstream to Fort Yukon, also Porcupine River; Chegitun River, eastern Siberia.

Primarily freshwater and coastal marine, but anadromous populations are known; most fish apparently winter in salt or brackish water near river mouths, but some possibly winter in fresh water far upstream; undertake extensive spawning migrations.

D 11–13; A 12–14; Pec 14–17; Pel 10–12; LLs 76–95; GR 35–39; Br 8–9; PC 71–123; Vert 62–65.

- Brownish to dark green dorsally; silvery ventrally; black dots with faint halos on body, or white spots on fins, or both; dorsal and caudal fins dusky; **anal, pectoral, and pelvic fins pale**, almost colorless.
- Body slightly compressed; head length 22–25% of total length; eye diameter about equal to snout; snout 20–25% of head length; nostrils with double flap between openings; maxilla extending to mideye; mouth terminal, lower jaw not protruding or only slightly protruding beyond upper.
- Adipose fin and pelvic axillary process present.
- Teeth usually absent from jaws in adults, rarely a few small teeth present on lower jaw; small patch of teeth on tongue.
- **Gill rakers on lower limb of first arch fewer (18–25) than in *C. autumnalis***; rakers long and slender.
- Length to 48 cm FL.

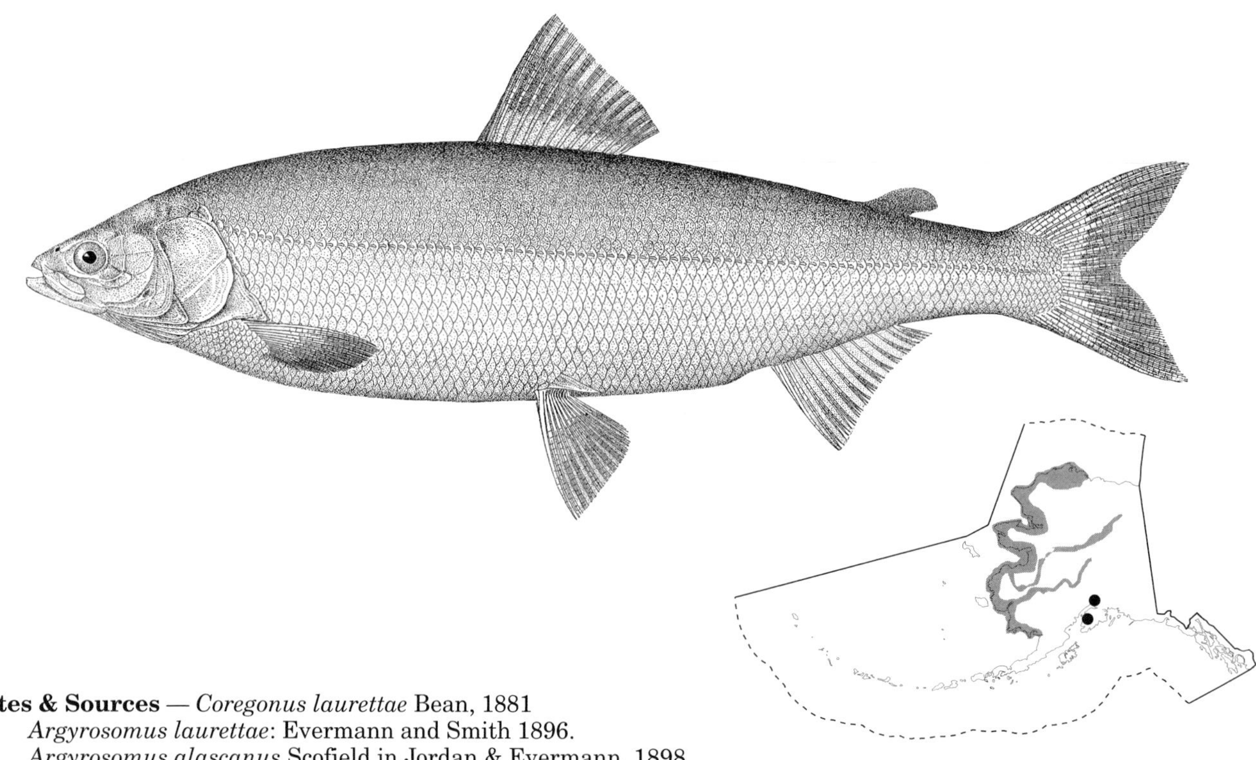

Notes & Sources — *Coregonus laurettae* Bean, 1881
Argyrosomus laurettae: Evermann and Smith 1896.
Argyrosomus alascanus Scofield in Jordan & Evermann, 1898
Often confused with *C. autumnalis*. See Notes & Sources for *C. autumnalis*.

Description: McPhail 1966; McPhail and Lindsey 1970:106–109; Alt 1973; Scott and Crossman 1973:255–256; Morrow 1980:29–30. Bickham et al. (1997:225) found black dots on body and white spots on fins in *C. laurettae* (N = 20) in Colville River delta; this character may not hold true for other regions. The distinction of lower gill raker counts in *C. laurettae* was confirmed, but their method of counting was not defined and their counts cannot be added to totals given above.

Figure: Goode 1884, pl. 198B; 381 mm TL, Point Barrow, Alaska.

Range: Alaskan records were mapped by Clarke (in Lee et al. 1980) and Morrow (1980). *Coregonus laurettae* was described by Bean (1881a) from specimens taken at Point Barrow and at Port Clarence on Yukon River, Alaska, and named for his wife, Lauretta. *Argyrosomus alascanus* was described by Scofield in Jordan and Evermann (1898) and in Scofield (1899) from Point Hope, Alaska. Records from the mouth of Ship Creek, Knik Arm, at Anchorage and the Kenai River on the Kenai Peninsula (McPhail 1966, Morrow 1980) remain the easternmost known occurrences in Gulf of Alaska drainages. An anadromous population inhabits the Kukokwim River (K. T. Alt, pers. comm., 26 May 2000). Chereshnev (1984) described the first specimens known from Russia: 2 males, 335 and 352 mm SL, taken in mouth of Chegitun River, Chukchi Peninsula.

Size: Largest known (48 cm FL) was recorded by Alt (1973): a female from Hess Creek, Alaska. Morrow (1980) noted that average size of adults is about 30 cm TL.

Coregonus nasus (Pallas, 1776) **broad whitefish**

Alaskan Beaufort, Chukchi, and Bering drainages to Kuskokwim Bay; in Canada, east to Perry River, Nunavut; westward across Siberia to Pechora River, south to Korfa Bay, and to Penzhina River on Sea of Okhotsk.

Fresh water, usually in streams; less often found in lakes and estuaries; anadromous, but not venturing far seaward from brackish water.

D 10–13; A 11–14; Pec 16–17; Pel 11–12; LLs 84–102; GR 18–25; Br 8–9; PC about 140 to more than 150; Vert 60–65.

- Olive brown to nearly black dorsally; silvery laterally; white to yellowish ventrally; fins dusky to black, except pale in young fish.
- Body strongly compressed; head short, 15–20% of fork length; **dorsal profile of head rounded to flat**, except slightly concave in large fish; eye small, 12–16% of head length; snout blunt, short, equal to or less than diameter of eye; nostrils with double flap between openings; mouth small, maxilla reaching to below anterior edge of eye; **maxilla broad, length less than twice its width**; upper jaw slightly overhanging lower.
- Adipose fin relatively large; pelvic axillary process present.
- Males develop prominent nuptial tubercles on lateral scales.
- Teeth absent except for small patch on tongue.
- **Gill rakers short and blunt**, length less than 20% of interorbital width.
- Length to 71 cm TL.

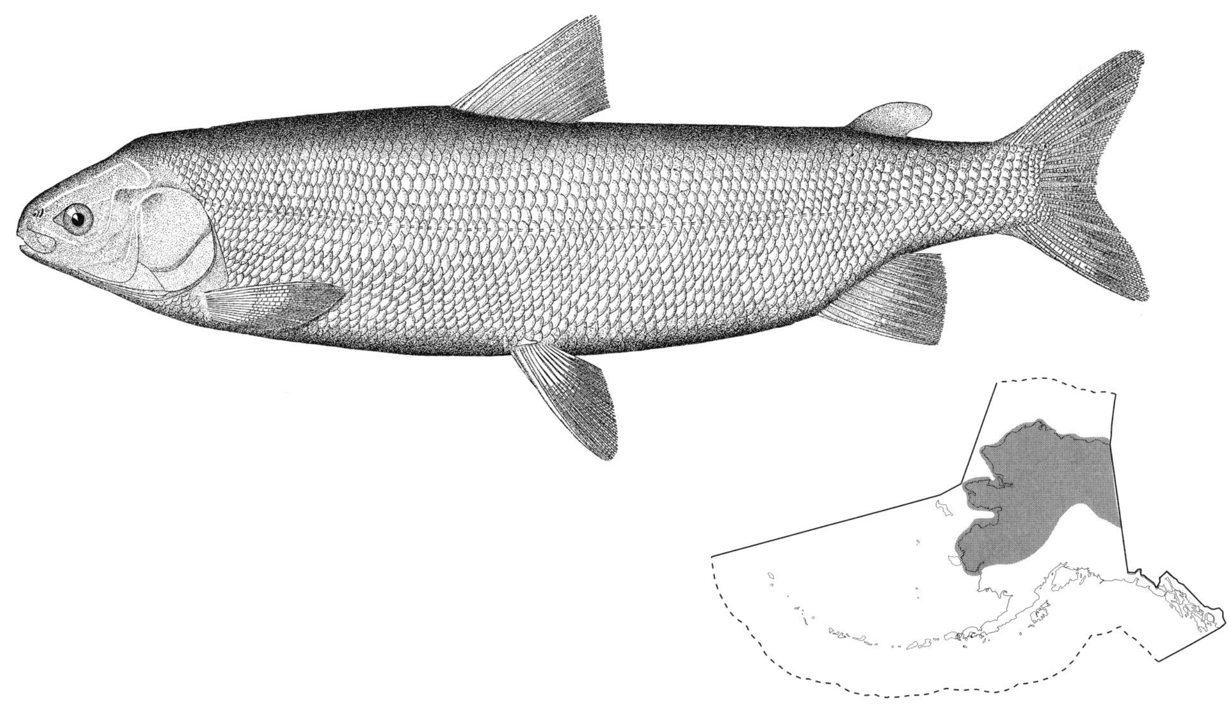

Notes & Sources — *Coregonus nasus* (Pallas, 1776)
Salmo nasus Pallas, 1776
Coregonus kennicotti Milner in Jordan & Gilbert, 1883
Lindsey (1962) placed *C. kennicotti* in synonymy of *C. nasus,* and described distinctions between *C. nasus* and other North American whitefishes, particularly those in the *C. clupeaformis* complex.

Description: Berg 1948:353–357; Lindsey 1962; McPhail and Lindsey 1970:86–89; Scott and Crossman 1973:278–280; Morrow 1980:34–35; Page and Burr 1991:39.

Figure: Turner 1886, pl. 11; identified as *C. kennicottii* drawn from specimens taken from Yukon River at Nulato, Alaska, by W. H. Dall. Evermann and Smith (1896, pl. 15) gave Meade River, Alaska, for collection locality, and size of 20 inches (508 mm).

Range: Lindsey (1962) reviewed Alaskan records. Range was mapped most recently by Lee and McAllister (in Lee et al. 1980), Morrow (1980), and Page and Burr (1991). Broad whitefish occur broadly in Alaska from the Kuskokwim River to the Arctic coast, present in the Yukon River from mouth to headwaters; in the Tanana River drainage from Minto Flats and the Tolovana, Chatanika, and Chena rivers, and probably farther upstream as well; and in most, if not all, of the rivers draining into the Beaufort Sea, Chukchi Sea, and northern Bering Sea (Morrow 1980).

Size: Page and Burr 1991. The largest Alaskan specimen recorded was 67 cm FL, from the Colville River at Umiat (Alt and Kogl 1973).

Coregonus clupeaformis (Mitchill, 1818) **lake whitefish**

In Alaska, recorded with reasonable certainty from Paxson and Crosswind lakes in Copper River drainage and Lake Louise and Tyone Lake in the Susitna drainage; widely distributed across Canada and northern United States, south into New England, Great Lakes basin, and Minnesota; introduced into Montana, Idaho, and Washington.

Primarily fresh water, in large lakes and rivers; less often, outside Alaska, found in streams or brackish water; relatively sedentary, majority of fish staying within 16 km of spawning ground.

D 11–13; A 10–14; Pec 15–17; Pel 11–12; LLs 77–95; GR 24–33; Br 8–10; PC 140–222; Vert 55–64.

- Dark brown to midnight blue dorsally; silver laterally; white ventrally.
- Body moderately compressed; head short, less than 25% of fork length; dorsal profile of head concave due to **prominent nuchal hump** in adults; eye small, diameter 20–25% of head length; snout 27–35% of head length; nostrils with double flap between openings; mouth small, maxilla extending to below anterior third of eye; **maxilla length twice width or more**; upper jaw overhanging lower.
- Adipose fin and pelvic axillary process present.
- Males develop prominent nuptial tubercles on lateral scales.
- Teeth absent except for small patch on tongue.
- **Gill rakers on first arch usually 26 or more; gill rakers longer than 20% of interorbital width**.
- Length to 80 cm TL.

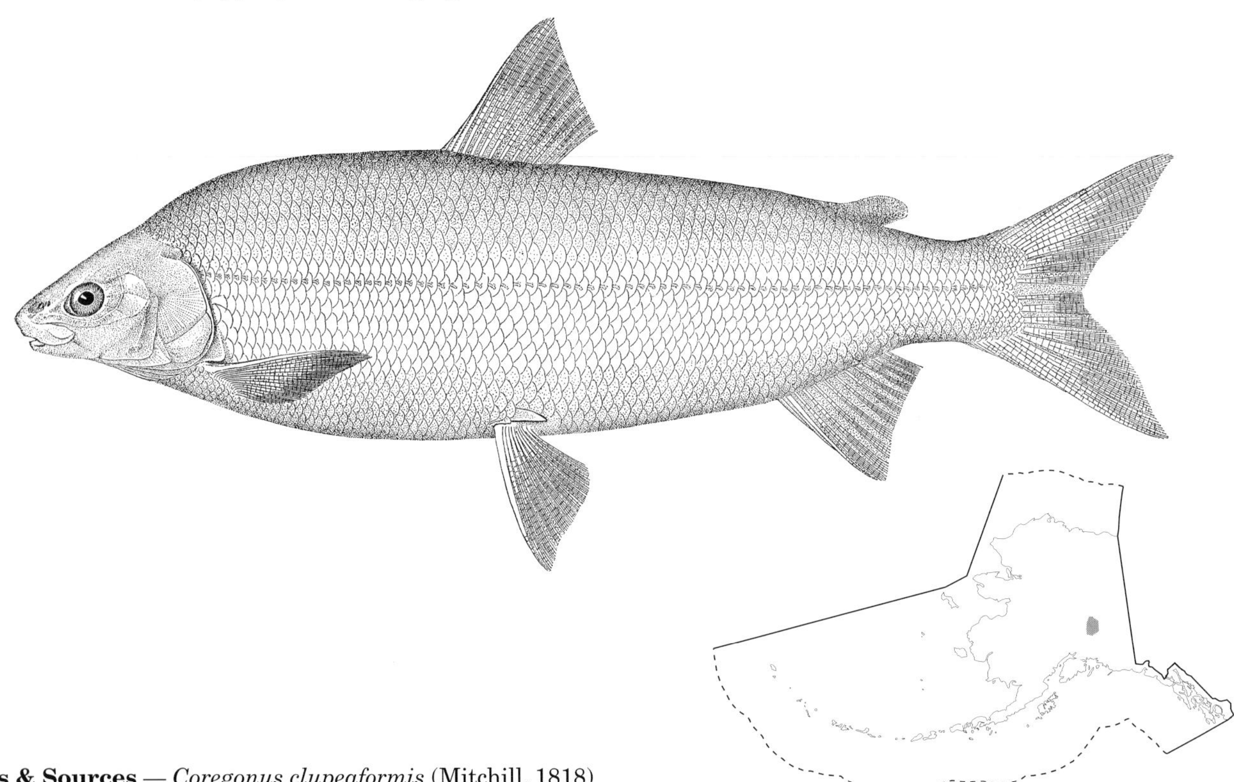

Notes & Sources — *Coregonus clupeaformis* (Mitchill, 1818)
Salmo clupeaformis Mitchill, 1818
Coregonus clupeiformis: Goode 1884, Evermann and Smith 1896, other early authors.
One of three Alaskan species of humpback whitefishes in the "*Coregonus clupeaformis* complex" (McPhail and Lindsey 1970); not recognized by all authors as distinct species, distinguishable from each other only by modal gill raker counts. McPhail and Lindsey (1970) summarized possible relationships among *C. pidschian, C. nelsonii,* and *C. clupeaformis.*

Description: McPhail and Lindsey 1970:78–85; Morrow 1980:38–39; Page and Burr 1991:40.

Figure: Goode 1884, pl. 196; 483 mm TL, from Detroit River, Michigan.

Range: Maps by Parker et al. (in Lee et al. 1980) and Page and Burr (1991) indicate wide distribution in Alaska, but Morrow (1980) stated that records of distribution in Alaska are not completely reliable due to confusion with other species in the *C. clupeaformis* complex, as well as other whitefishes. Possibly ecologically distinct from others in the complex, with this species, *C. clupeaformis,* not anadromous and found mostly in large lakes (Morrow 1980).

Size: Page and Burr (1991) gave length of 80 cm TL, evidently following Parker et al. (in Lee et al. 1980), who gave maximum length of 798 mm TL. Morrow (1980), applying length-weight relationship given by Dryer (1963) to largest weight on record, from a 19-kg lake whitefish taken in Lake Superior, gave possible total length of 125 cm.

Coregonus nelsonii Bean, 1884 **Alaska whitefish**

Alaska in Yukon River and its tributaries from Nulato to Canada border, Tanana and Koyokuk river systems, Paxson Lake, Copper River system; Lake Minchumina; Mackenzie River delta and lakes in western Canada.

Fresh water; primarily in streams and rivers, rarely found in lakes; some evidence exists of anadromous populations in Yukon River that reach salt water.

D 11–13; A 10–14; Pec 15–17; Pel 11–12; LLs 77–95; GR 22–27; Br 8–10; Vert 60–63.

- Dark brown to midnight blue dorsally; silver laterally; white ventrally.
- Body moderately compressed; head short, less than 25% of fork length; dorsal profile of head concave due to **prominent nuchal hump** in adults; eye small, diameter 20–25% of head length; snout 27–35% of head length; nostrils with double flap between openings; mouth small, maxilla extending to below anterior third of eye; **maxilla length twice width or more**; upper jaw overhanging lower.
- Adipose fin and pelvic axillary process present.
- Males develop prominent nuptial tubercles on lateral scales.
- Teeth absent except for small patch on tongue.
- **Gill rakers on first arch usually 24 or 25**; **gill rakers longer than 20% of interorbital width**.
- Length to about 56 cm TL.

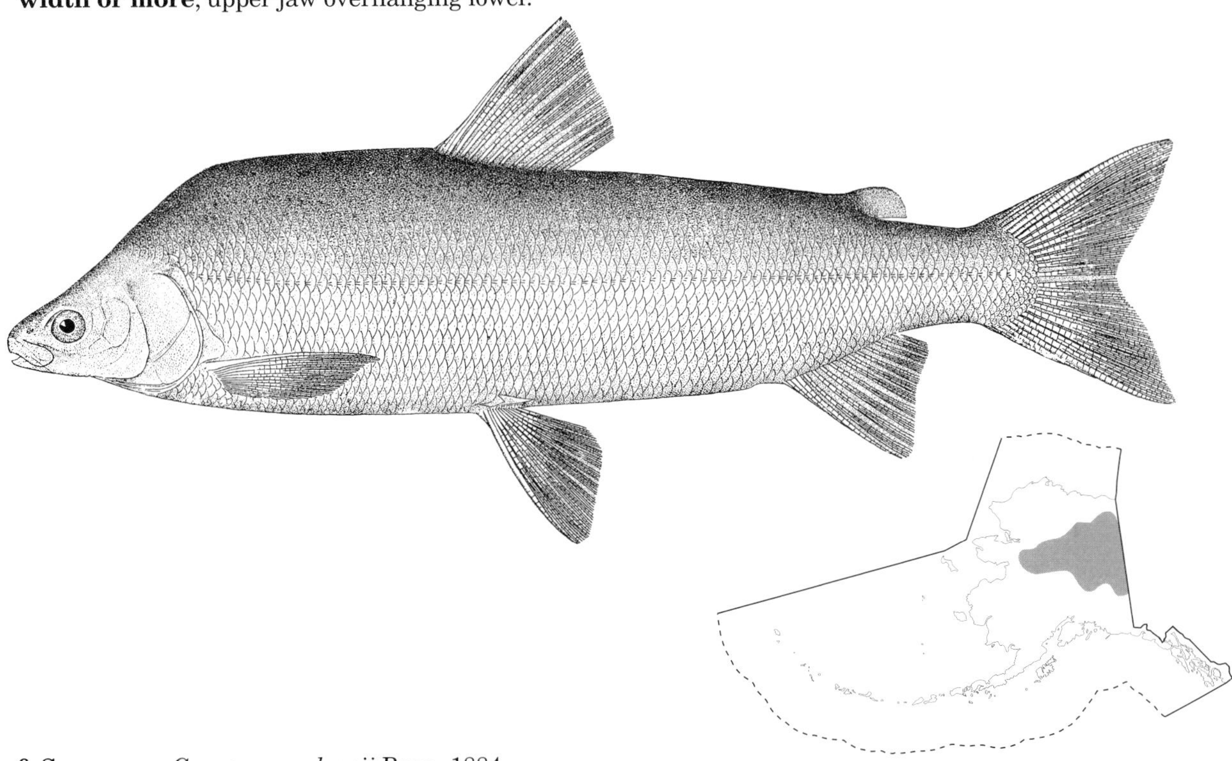

Notes & Sources — *Coregonus nelsonii* Bean, 1884

Spelling of species name with two *i*'s is correct, as in Bean's (1884) original description, although spelling with one *i* is commonly seen.

One of three Alaskan species in the humpback whitefish complex; not recognized by all authors as distinct species, distinguishable from each other only by modal gill raker counts. *Coregonus nelsonii* could be a distinct species with intermediate gill raker numbers between *C. pidschian* and *C. clupeaformis* or a hybrid of those two (McPhail and Lindsey 1970:82).

Description: Bean 1884c; Morrow 1980:35–37; Page and Burr 1991:40.

Figure: Evermann and Smith 1896, pl. 18; 457 mm TL, Nulato, Alaska.

Range: Above map is based on those of Morrow (1980) and Page and Burr (1991). When Bean (1884c) first described *C. nelsonii,* naming as the type a specimen from Nulato, Alaska, it was known to occur in the territory from Bristol Bay to the "extremity of the territory," and had already been confused with *C. clupeaformis* and other whitefish species. As with other species in the humpback whitefish complex, the range of *C. nelsonii* is not known with any confidence due to difficulty of identifying them. Morrow (1980) pointed to possible ecological distinction from other species in humpback whitefish complex, with *C. nelsonii* mostly a stream dweller, rarely encountered in lakes and apparently not tolerating salt water. However, K. T. Alt (pers. comm., 26 May 2000) reported that populations traveling past Rampart in September and spawning farther up the Yukon River do reach salt water.

Size: Alt 1971a: Chatanika River, Alaska.

Coregonus pidschian (Gmelin, 1789) **humpback whitefish**

Most Alaskan rivers emptying into western Beaufort Sea, Chukchi Sea, and Bering Sea; throughout Kuskokwim River drainage and well above Umiat in Colville River; eastward at least to Sagavanirktok River, Alaska; westward across Siberia to Kara Sea; upper Atlin Lake, Yukon Territory.

Anadromous; coastal waters near shore; overwinters near river mouths; some populations possibly never going to sea.

D 11–13; A 10–14; Pec 15–17; Pel 11–12; LLs 77–95; GR 17–25; Br 8–10; Vert 58–63.

- Dark brown to midnight blue dorsally; silver laterally; white ventrally.
- Body moderately compressed; head short, less than 25% of fork length; dorsal profile of head concave due to **prominent nuchal hump** in adults; eye small, diameter 20–25% of head length; snout 27–35% of head length; nostrils with double flap between openings; mouth small, maxilla extending to below anterior third of eye; **maxilla length twice width or more**; upper jaw overhanging lower.
- Adipose fin and pelvic axillary process present.
- Males develop prominent nuptial tubercles on lateral scales.
- Teeth absent except for small patch on tongue.
- **Gill rakers on first arch usually 21–23; gill rakers longer than 20% of interorbital width**.
- Pearl organs possibly far fewer in number and less well developed than in *C. nelsonii.*
- Length to 46 cm TL.

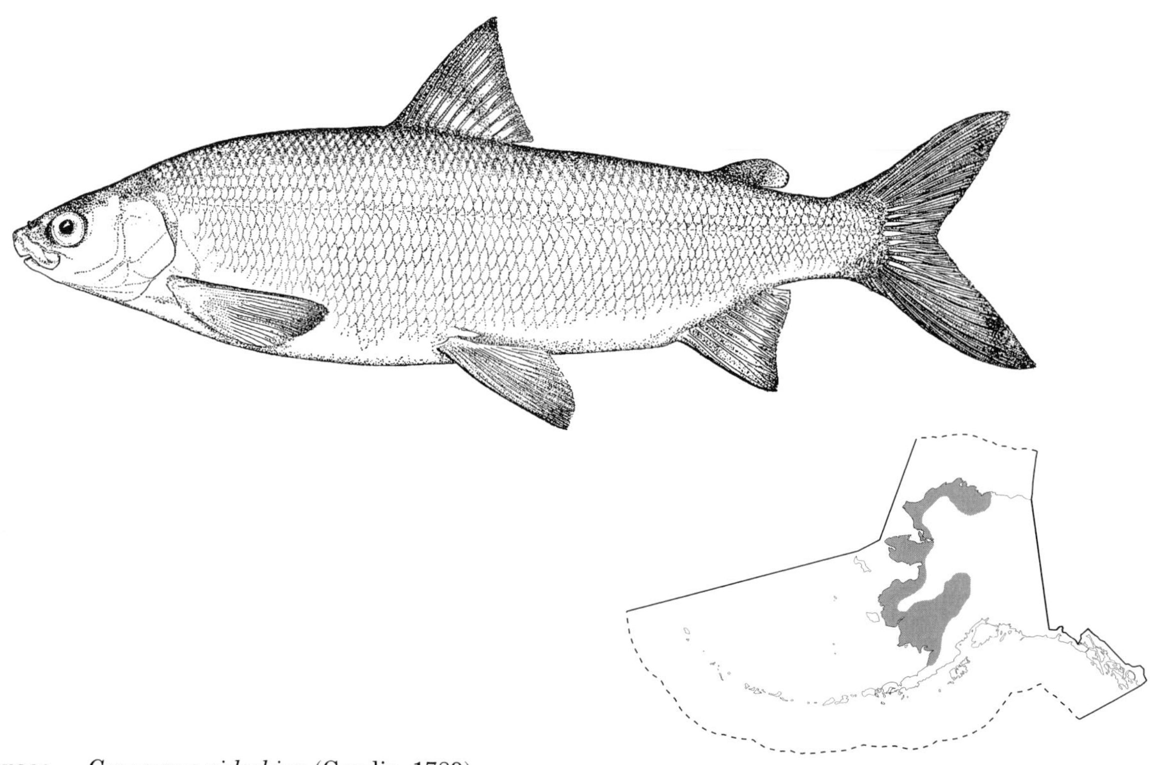

Notes & Sources — *Coregonus pidschian* (Gmelin, 1789)
Salmo pidschian Gmelin, 1789
Coregonus lavaretus pidschian (Gmelin): Berg 1948.
One of three Alaskan species in the humpback whitefish complex; not recognized by all authors as distinct species, distinguishable from each other only by modal gill raker counts.

Description: Berg 1948:393, 401–402; McPhail and Lindsey 1970:78–85; Morrow 1980:37–38. See also Alt 1979; Lee et al. 1980:88; Page and Burr 1991:41.

Figure: None available of a specimen originally identified as *C. pidschian* in the strict sense. This illustration, from McPhail and Lindsey (1970:78), depicts an unspecified member of the humpback whitefish complex; lack of nuchal hump indicates it is a young fish.

Range: Above map is based on those of Morrow (1980) and Page and Burr (1991). As with other forms in the humpback whitefish complex, distributional records of *C. pidschian* in Alaska must be viewed with caution because fishery biologists often have applied the various species names to humpback whitefish without collecting adequate samples for accurate identification (Morrow 1980). A possible ecological distinction is that *C. pidschian* is truly anadromous, at least in some areas, and may winter at sea near river mouths (Morrow 1980). Migrates at least 1,600 km inland, to vicinity of Fort Yukon (K. T. Alt, pers. comm., 26 May 2000).

Size: Page and Burr 1991.

Prosopium cylindraceum (Pallas, 1784) **round whitefish**

Mainland Alaska from North Slope to Taku River near Juneau; northern interior British Columbia; arctic Canada, Great Lakes (except Lake Erie), Labrador to Connecticut; in Asia west to Yenisei River and south to Kamchatka.

Fresh water; shallow areas of lakes and clear rivers and streams; rarely in brackish water.

D 11–15; A 10–13; Pec 14–17; Pel 9–11; LLs 74–108; GR 14–21; Br 6–9; PC 50–130; Vert 58–65.

- Bronze to greenish bronze dorsally; silvery white ventrally; fins usually more or less colorless or slightly dusky; anal and pelvic fins sometimes amber, becoming orange at spawning time; juveniles with black spots in 2 or 3 longitudinal rows, the dorsal row often coalescing across the back.
- Body cylindrical; head short, about 20% of fork length; dorsal profile behind head not much elevated; snout short, about 22% of head length; **snout pointed when seen from above**; eye diameter equal to or less than snout length, 14–20% of head length; **notch present in adipose eyelid** posteroventrally; **single flap between nostril openings**; maxilla reaching nearly to anterior edge of eye in large specimens, as far as pupil in smaller specimens; mouth subterminal, upper jaw protruding beyond lower jaw.
- Adipose fin and pelvic axillary process present.
- Males develop prominent nuptial tubercles on lateral scales.
- **Lateral line scales 74 or more**; usually 22–24 scales around caudal peduncle.
- Teeth absent from jaws, vomer, palatines; small patch of embedded teeth on tongue.
- Gill rakers short and stout.
- Pyloric caeca 50 or more.
- Length to 56 cm TL.

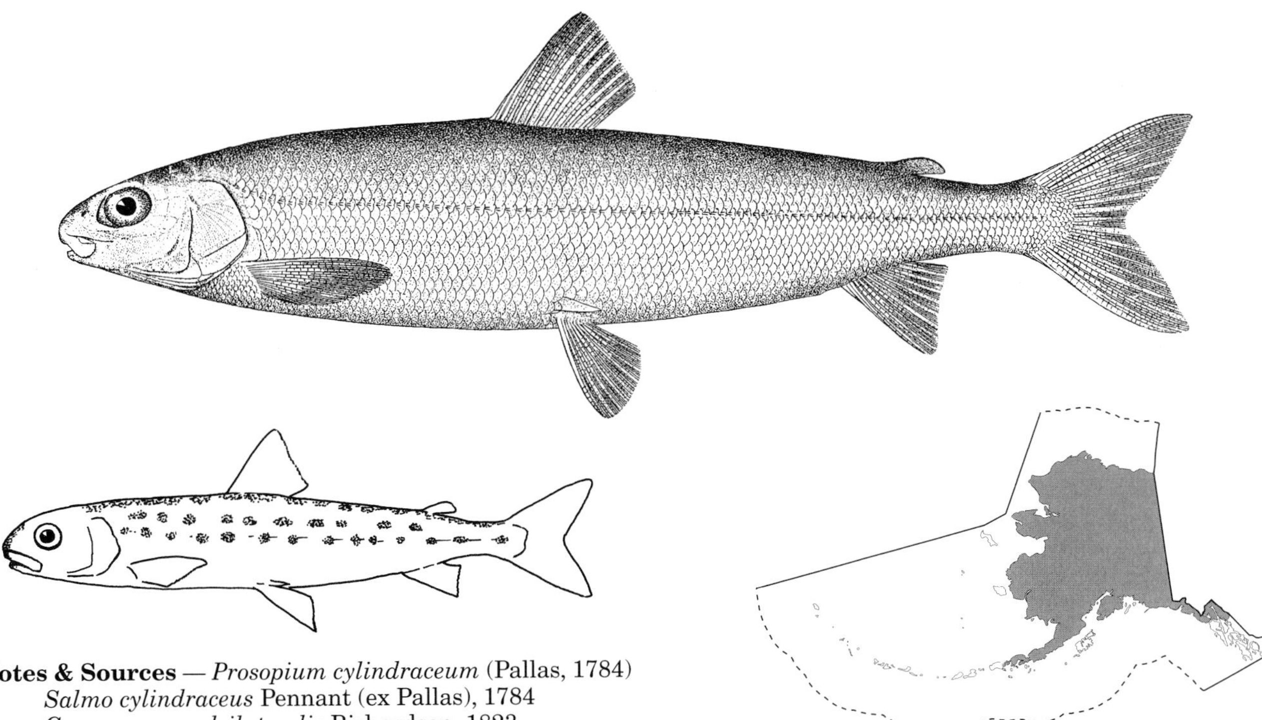

Notes & Sources — *Prosopium cylindraceum* (Pallas, 1784)
Salmo cylindraceus Pennant (ex Pallas), 1784
Coregonus quadrilateralis Richardson, 1823
Coregonus cylindraceus: Berg 1948.

Description: Evermann and Smith 1896:296–297; Berg 1948:417–421; McPhail and Lindsey 1970:110–113; Scott and Crossman 1973:286–291; Morrow 1980:32–34; Page and Burr 1991:47.

Figures: Upper: Evermann and Smith 1896, pl. 16; 279 mm TL, New Hampshire. Lower (juvenile): composite by C.W.M. based on specimens and Scott and Crossman 1973:286. Black spots are most intense at lengths of 50–75 mm but may be visible on dead specimens up to 265 mm long. The marks are round or at most longitudinally ovoid, and not ventrally ovoid as in Salmoninae.

Range: Alaskan and North American ranges were mapped most recently by Morrow (1980), Rohde (in Lee et al. 1980), and Page and Burr (1991). Distribution in eastern Russia is patchy, and not known east of the Amguema River except for a relict population in the extreme southeastern part of the Chukchi Peninsula reported by Gudkov (1999). Gudkov compared that population and specimens collected from the Seward Peninsula, Alaska. He gave competition with grayling (*Thymallus arcticus*) for food in the small rivers of the Chukchi Peninsula and lack of spawning habitat (swift-running rivers) as likely causes for the general extinction of round whitefish from the Chukchi Peninsula. Gudkov pointed out that although round whitefish coexist with grayling in small rivers of the Seward Peninsula, there the populations of Pacific salmon are larger and their eggs and carcasses are available for consumption by both grayling and round whitefish.

Prosopium coulterii (Eigenmann & Eigenmann, 1892) **pygmy whitefish**

Chignik, Naknek, and Wood river systems in southwestern Alaska and Copper River system in southcentral Alaska; Washington, Montana, British Columbia, and Yukon Territory in Columbia, Fraser, Skeena, Alsek, Peace, Liard, and upper Yukon systems; Lake Superior.

Fresh water; deep lakes and swift, cold streams.

D 10–13; A 10–14; Pec 13–18; Pel 9–11; LLs 50–70; GR 12–21; Br 6–9; PC 13–33; Vert 49–55.

- Brownish, often with green tints, dorsally; silvery white ventrally; juveniles with 7–14 large round black marks along side, persisting in all but the largest adults.
- Body cylindrical; head moderate, about 22% of fork length; dorsal profile behind head not much elevated; snout short; **snout broadly rounded when seen from above**; eye large, diameter usually greater than snout length, 25–30% of head length; **notch present in adipose eyelid** posteroventrally; **single flap between nostril openings**; maxilla reaching anterior edge of eye in large specimens, farther in smaller ones; mouth subterminal, upper jaw protruding beyond lower jaw.
- Adipose fin present; **pelvic axillary process small**, often rudimentary.
- **Lateral line scales 70 or fewer**; usually 16–20 scales around caudal peduncle.
- Gill rakers short and stout.
- Pyloric caeca fewer than 40.
- Length to 28 cm TL.

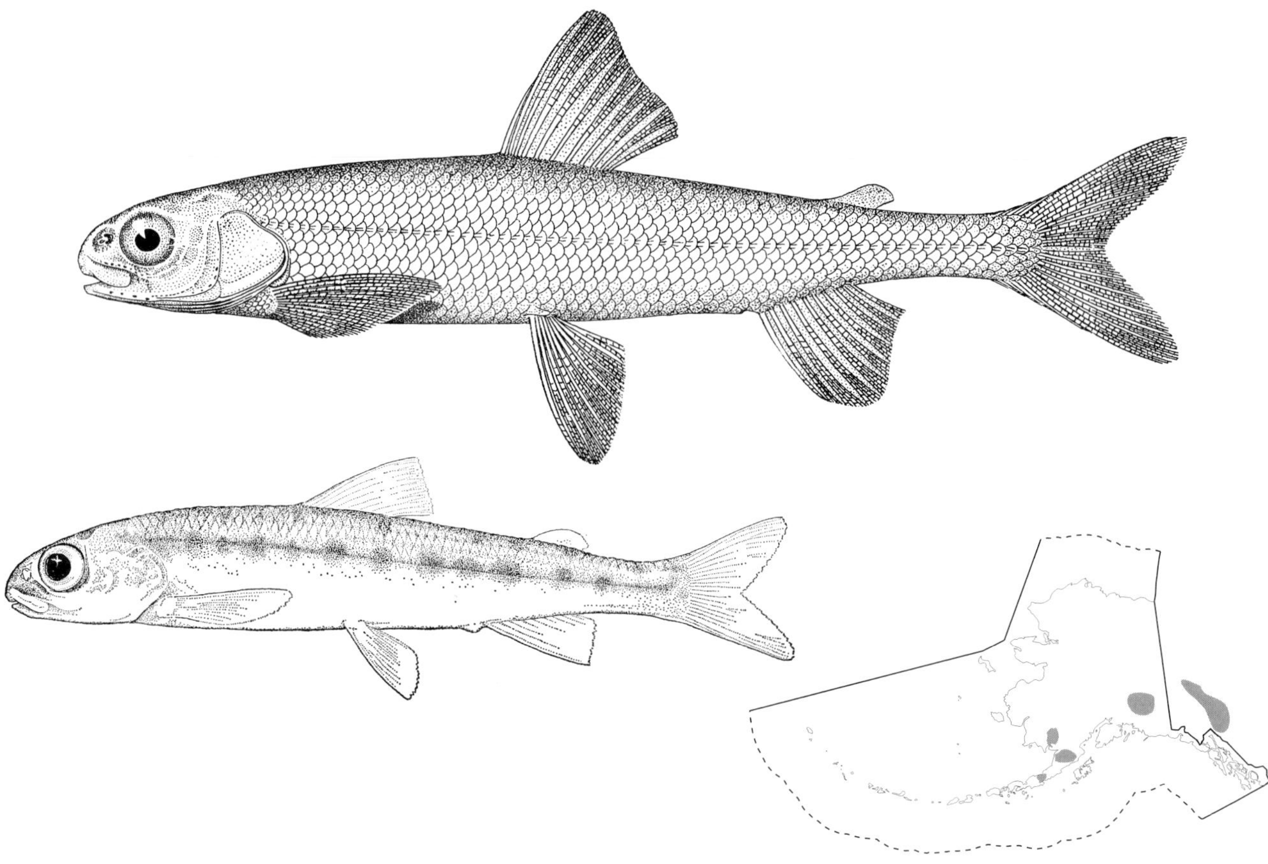

Notes & Sources — *Prosopium coulterii* (Eigenmann & Eigenmann, 1892)

Coregonus coulterii Eigenmann & Eigenmann, 1892

Species name was spelled with two *i*'s by Eigenmann and Eigenmann (1892) in the original description of the species. The International Code of Zoological Nomenclature specifies that the original spelling is the correct spelling.

Description: Evermann and Smith 1896:290–291; McPhail and Lindsey 1970:118–121; Scott and Crossman 1973:282–285; Morrow 1980:31–32; Page and Burr 1991:45.

Figures: Upper: Evermann and Smith 1896, pl. 12; lectotype, 109 mm TL, Kicking Horse River at Field, British Columbia. Lower: McPhail and Lindsey 1970:118.

Range: Mapped by Rohde and Platania (in Lee et al. 1980), Morrow (1980), and Page and Burr (1991), but without collections from Tazlina, Klutina, and Tonsina lakes in the Copper River drainage recorded by Bird and Roberson (1979). The species is probably more widespread but must be specifically looked for. It was not known from Lake Superior until 1955 (R. J. Behnke, pers. comm., 29 Aug. 2000). Heard and Hartman (1965) provided detailed information on distribution and life history of this species in the Naknek River system, Alaska.

Subfamily Thymallinae
Graylings

Graylings externally resemble whitefishes of the genus *Coregonus* except that they are more colorful; the dorsal fin of the adults, particularly the males, is greatly enlarged; and parr marks are present on the young. The brilliant, iridescent coloration of the male in spawning dress has been likened to that of a peacock. The grayling subfamily contains one genus with four or five species. They are strictly freshwater inhabitants, and popular sport fishes. The species occurring in Alaska, *Thymallus arcticus,* is widespread across northern Asia and North America. Graylings were given the name *Thymallus* because, when fresh, they were said to have the scent of water-thyme (Jordan 1905).

In contrast to the subfamilies Coregoninae and Salmoninae, graylings have a long-based dorsal fin (usually more than 17 rays) and lack orbitosphenoids and suprapreopercles. Unlike the Coregoninae, but like the Salmoninae, graylings have maxillary teeth.

Thymallus arcticus (Pallas, 1776) — **Arctic grayling**

Alaskan mainland, St. Lawrence and Nunivak islands, and northern Canada to west side of Hudson Bay; headwaters of Missouri River in Montana; Asian mainland west to Kara and Ob rivers of Siberia and Eroo (Yoroo) River in northern Mongolia, and south to Yalu River on North Korea–China border.

Clear waters of large rivers, rocky streams, and lakes; spawn in small, gravelly streams.

D 17–25; A 10–15; Pec 14–16; Pel 10–11; LLs 75–103; GR 14–23; Br 8–9; PC 13–21; Vert 58–62.

- Iridescent blue, blue-gray, or purple dorsally; silver-gray to blue laterally, often with pink or lavender wash; small blue-black spots on sides, more numerous anteriorly; juveniles with 10–20 parr marks below 2 or 3 rows of black spots.
- Mouth terminal; maxilla reaching to mideye.
- **Dorsal fin large**, in adult males reaching adipose fin when depressed; pelvic axillary process present.
- Teeth small, present on jaws, vomer, palatines, and tongue, except absent from tongue in large adults.
- Nuptial tubercles develop on caudal region.
- Length to 76 cm TL, weight to 2.7 kg.

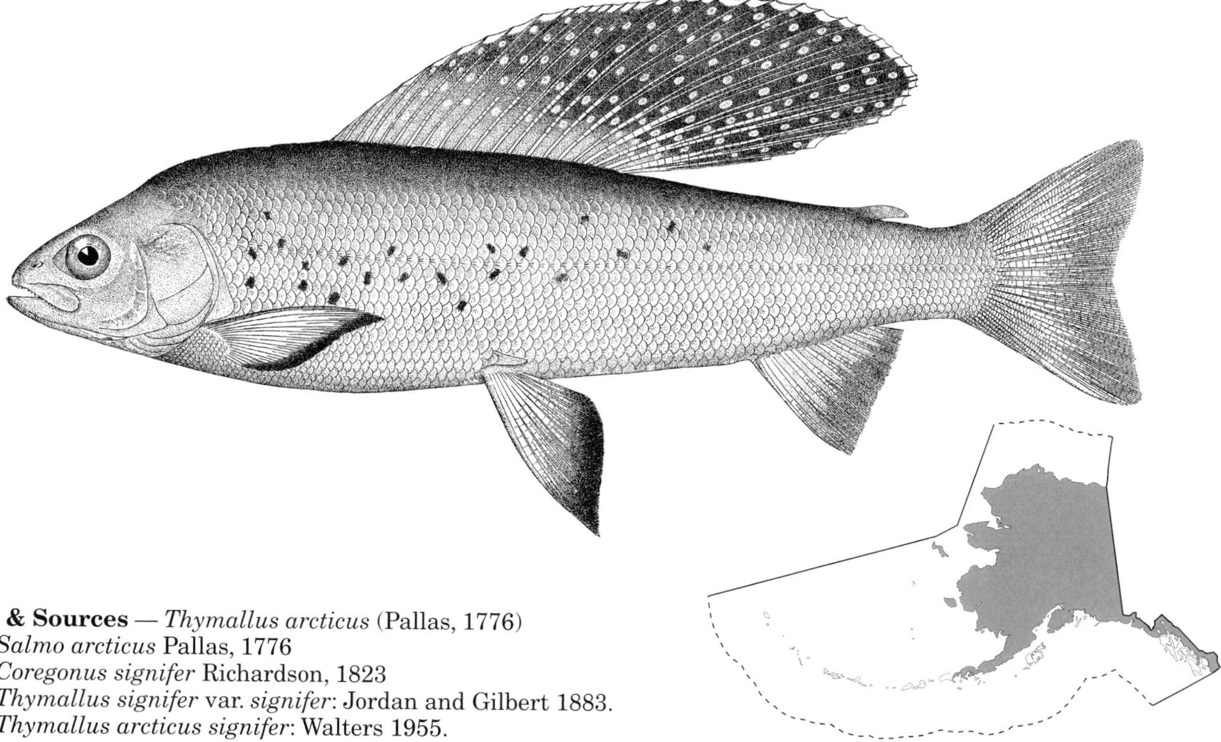

Notes & Sources — *Thymallus arcticus* (Pallas, 1776)
Salmo arcticus Pallas, 1776
Coregonus signifer Richardson, 1823
Thymallus signifer var. *signifer*: Jordan and Gilbert 1883.
Thymallus arcticus signifer: Walters 1955.

Description: McPhail and Lindsey 1970:124–128; Scott and Crossman 1973:300–305; Morrow 1980:145–147; Coad 1995:39–41.

Figure: Turner 1886, pl. 13; 34 cm TL, St. Michael, Alaska (south shore of Norton Sound).

Range: Mapped most recently by Morrow (1980), Rohde (in Lee et al. 1980), and Page and Burr (1991).

Size: World, all-tackle angling record, from Katseyedie River, Northwest Territories; average angler-caught fish would be about 30–35 cm long and weigh 450–700 g (Morrow 1980).

Subfamily Salmoninae
Trouts, salmons, and chars

The subfamily Salmoninae comprises seven extant genera and at least 30 species of trouts, salmons, and chars. A conservative classification of the forms found in Alaska, followed in this guide, recognizes 13 species in three genera. Further study may reveal existence of additional species within some of the currently named species, as ichthyologists are still trying to determine species limits and provide an optimal classification for the group. Salmonines exhibit remarkable variation in sexual dimorphism, coloration, life history, and adaptability to local conditions. There is an enormous body of literature on their phylogeny and classification. Reviews and analyses by Behnke (1989), Smith and Stearley (1989), Grewe et al. (1990), Sanford (1990), Phillips and Pleyte (1991), Stearley and Smith (1993), Osinov and Pavlov (1998), and Osinov (1999, 2001) are a few of the recent studies which could be consulted for discussion and references to previous work.

Salmonines typically have very small scales, with more than 100 along the lateral line; well-developed teeth; a truncate to shallowly forked caudal fin (deeply forked only in lake trout, *Salvelinus namaycush*); and prominent parr marks on the young (lacking only in pink salmon, *Oncorhynchus gorbuscha*). Teeth are carried on the premaxillae, maxillae, dentaries, vomer, palatines, tongue, and, in some species (*Salvelinus* species and cutthroat trout, *O. clarkii*), on the basibranchials; the main differences among species are in the vomerine dentition. Salmonines have fewer than 16 dorsal fin rays, and orbitosphenoids and suprapreoperculars are present.

Like other salmonids, trouts and salmons inhabit fresh water or spend variable amounts of time at sea and migrate to fresh water to spawn. Pacific salmon, genus *Oncorhynchus,* spend most of their lives at sea and return to fresh water only to spawn. They migrate back to the same streams in which they hatched. During their ocean stay they undertake extensive migrations and are epipelagic, although some stocks can be found deep, to 200 m or more. Some populations of anadromous chars, genus *Salvelinus,* move between the sea and fresh water for other than reproductive purposes, and at sea generally stay close to shore and avoid high-salinity water.

Breeding tubercles are generally absent in salmonines. They develop on some males of lake trout, *S. namaycush,* but disappear rapidly after spawning season. Colors and body shapes change, often dramatically, in some species before breeding. The jaws, particularly in males of the Pacific salmons, genus *Oncorhynchus,* become elongate and hooked, forming a kype.

Salmonines of the genus *Salvelinus* are collectively or individually called chars or charrs. The spelling with one *r* is used more frequently by North American authors than in Europe. Morton (1980) gave a history of the name and it spelling. Chars have cylindrical, troutlike bodies, light spots (pink, red, yellow, cream) on the body, a white leading edge on the pelvic and anal fins, scales along the lateral line that are smaller than the surrounding scales and do not overlap each other, and teeth on the head of the vomer but not the shaft. They have slightly emarginate to forked caudal fins.

Trouts and salmons are cylindrical (*O. mykiss, O. clarkii*) or moderately compressed (other *Oncorhynchus* and *Salmo salar*) and usually have black spots or specks on the body or caudal fin. They do not have a white leading edge on the lower fins (except in some *O. mykiss,* especially juveniles), the scales along the lateral line are as large as or larger than the adjacent scales and overlap each other, and teeth are present on the head and shaft of the vomer. Trouts in genus *Oncorhynchus* have 8–12 principal anal fin rays while Pacific salmon have 13–19, and rarely 12. Adults of species in *Oncorhynchus* and *Salmo* have truncate to slightly emarginate caudal fins, never deeply forked (except in juveniles). Atlantic salmon, *Salmo salar,* which occurs as an invasive species in Alaska, has 8–11 anal fin rays and is further distinguishable from both Pacific salmons and trouts (*Oncorhynchus*) by the presence of large black spots on the operculum.

Placement of the species of *Salvelinus* in the subgenera *Salvelinus, Cristivomer,* and *Baione* in this guide follows Behnke (1989) and Grewe et al. (1990). The composition of subgenus *Salvelinus,* including the so-called *S. alpinus–S. malma* (Arctic char–Dolly Varden) complex, was for a long time in taxonomic disarray but has to some extent been resolved, with North American authors, at least, recognizing each as a distinct species (see discussions by Behnke 1980, 1984, 1989). Confusion still exists regarding recognition of forms within those two species. Following Behnke (1980, 1984, 1989; pers. comm., 13 Oct. 1998), classification in this guide recognizes two forms of *S. alpinus* and two of *S. malma* in Alaska as subspecies (see the Notes & Sources in the species accounts). One of those forms, the Taranetz char of western Alaska and the Chukchi Peninsula, is sympatric with Dolly Varden, *S. malma,* and is considered by some authors (e.g., Chereshnev 1996) to be a distinct species, *S. taranetzi*; following Behnke, we recognize it as a well-marked subspecies, *S. alpinus taranetzi*.

For many years the bull trout, *S. confluentus,* was considered to be conspecific with *S. malma* (e.g., McPhail 1961) but studies by Cavender (1978) and Haas and McPhail (1991) conclusively demonstrated the bull trout is a distinct species. There are recent records of bull trout from the Taku River in Alaska and the species is included herein as a new addition to the inventory of Alaskan fish species.

The angayukaksurak char, *S. anaktuvukensis,* inhabiting headwaters of the Brooks Range, Alaska, was described as a new species by Morrow (1973). The validity of this species is not recognized by all authors. McCart (1980) and Lindsey and McPhail (1986) considered it to be a form of *S. alpinus,* and R. J. Behnke (pers. comm., 13 Oct. 1998) believes it to be a landlocked form of *S. malma.* Robins et al. (1984, 1991a) excluded the Angayukaksurak char from the American Fisheries Society list of North American fishes pending better understanding of its status. It would key out from the second choice in couplet 5 (relatively low numbers of gill rakers and pyloric caeca) of our key, as a velvety black or dark brown char with fiery red spots. Walters (1955) was the first to mention the presence of this form of char in Alaska. The complete taxonomic history was given by Morrow (in Lee et al. 1980:112).

The kundscha or East Siberian char, *Salvelinus leucomaenis,* was included on Quast and Hall's (1972) list of fishes of Alaska as a species likely to be found in Alaska, but it appears to be restricted to Asian coasts from Japan and the Sea of Okhotsk to eastern Kamchatka as far north as Korfa Bay (Chereshnev 1996, Reshetnikov et al. 1997). Specimens previously identified as *S. leucomaenis* from the Commander Islands (e.g., Andriashev 1939) have been reidentified as *S. malma* (B. A. Sheiko, pers. comm., 22 Feb. 2000).

Alaskan trouts formerly classified in *Salmo* are currently classified in *Oncorhynchus* by North American taxonomists, and fewer species are recognized as valid in the North Pacific than at the time of Quast and Hall's (1972) writing. From morphological, cytological, and biochemical genetic evidence provided by Behnke (1966), Okazaki (1984), and others, Smith and Stearley (1989) recognized the conspecificity of North American and Kamchatkan rainbow trout and steelhead and classified the North American form (then called *Salmo gairdneri)* in the synonymy of the Asian species (*S. mykiss*); and showed that they and other Pacific trouts then classified in genus *Salmo* are more closely related to Pacific salmons in genus *Oncorhynchus* than they are to Atlantic salmon and brown trout in genus *Salmo.* Stearley and Smith (1993) provided a complete taxonomic history and additional evidence relating to this problem.

Russian researchers classify the Pacific trouts in *Parasalmo* (e.g., Mednikov et al. 1999) or maintain that further study is needed before combining them with *Oncorhynchus* (e.g., Osinov 1999). Stearley and Smith (1993) considered that the subgenera *Oncorhynchus,* for Pacific salmons, and *Rhabdofario,* for Pacific trouts, need further analysis but they are convenient categories and we use them, following Nelson (1994). The name *Rhabdofario* has priority over *Parasalmo,* as shown by Smith and Stearley (1989).

Salmo penshinensis Pallas, a form known from Kamchatka, Russia, and listed by Quast and Hall (1972) as a potential addition to the Alaskan ichthyofauna, is now recognized by most Russian authors as the anadromous (Kamchatka steelhead) form of *O. mykiss,* although they (e.g., Reshetnikov et al. 1997) call it *Parasalmo mykiss.*

The cherry or masu salmon, *O. masou,* also listed by Quast and Hall (1972) as a species likely to be found in Alaska, evidently is restricted to Asian coasts from western and southeastern Kamchatka to Japan (Kato 1991, Chereshnev 1996, Reshetnikov et al. 1997).

The following key to adults of the Salmoninae of Alaska uses characters from keys by McPhail and Lindsey (1970) and Morrow (1980), with others added to accommodate addition of *Salmo salar* and *Salvelinus confluentus* and deletion of *S. anaktuvukensis.* Salmon species caught at sea look a lot alike and it can be difficult, even for experienced observers, to identify them. Once identified using the key, specimens should be carefully checked against the characters given in the species accounts.

Key to Adults of the Salmoninae of Alaska

1 Principal anal fin rays 8–12 . . . . (2)

1 Principal anal fin rays 13–19 (in rare cases 12) . . . . (9)

2 (1) Teeth present on head of vomer, absent from shaft; spots on body pale or red, never brown or black .... (3)

2 Teeth present on both head and shaft of vomer; spots on body dark brown or black, if present .... (7)

3 (2) Obvious green or cream vermiculations on back, dorsal fin, and caudal fin; black line behind white leading edge on pectoral, pelvic, and anal fins; caudal fin truncate to only slightly indented .... *Salvelinus fontinalis,* page 197

3 Sometimes with subtle, gray vermiculations on back; no black line behind white leading edge on pectoral, pelvic, and anal fins, although dusky area may be present; caudal fin forked .... (4)

4 (3) Caudal fin sharply forked; body color dark green to grayish, with numerous oval or irregular whitish to yellow spots on sides and back; no bright orange or red on body; pyloric caeca 90–200 .... *Salvelinus namaycush,* page 198

4 Caudal fin shallowly forked; spots on body round, in live specimens red, pink, or yellow; pyloric caeca 13–75 .... (5)

5 (4) Usually 21–30 gill rakers on first arch; pyloric caeca usually 35 or more (range 30–75) .... *Salvelinus alpinus,* page 199

5 Usually 14–21 gill rakers on first arch; pyloric caeca usually less than 35 (range 17–36) .... (6)

6 (5) Head length usually less than 25% SL; top of head convex, with eye not near dorsal profile; maxilla straight; usually 11–12 branchiostegal rays; mandibular pores 6 .... *Salvelinus malma,* page 200

6 Head length usually more than 25% SL; top of head flat, with eye near or intersecting dorsal profile; maxilla curved downward; usually 13–15 branchiostegal rays; mandibular pores 7–9 .... *Salvelinus confluentus,* page 201

7 (2) Maxilla barely reaching or almost reaching below posterior margin of eye; spots, if present, usually not on dorsal fin or caudal fin .... *Salmo salar,* page 202

7 Maxilla reaching below posterior margin of eye to well past eye; spots, if present, usually on dorsal and caudal fins .... (8)

8 (7) Small teeth present on floor of mouth behind tongue (basibranchial teeth); red or orange streak along underside of each side of jaw (often pale or absent in ocean fish or recent migrants to fresh water); no red stripe on sides .... *Oncorhynchus clarkii,* page 203

8 No teeth on floor of mouth behind tongue (basibranchial teeth); no red or orange streak along underside of each side of jaw (except present in some fish in Kuskokwim system); well-developed red stripe along sides in spawning adults .... *Oncorhynchus mykiss,* page 204

9 (1) Distinct black spots present on back and caudal fin .... (10)

9 No distinct black spots on back or caudal fin, fine black speckling usually present .... (12)

10 (9) Spots on back and caudal fin large, more or less oval, longest as long as diameter of eye; scales small, 170 or more in first row above lateral line . . . . *Oncorhynchus gorbuscha,* page 205

10 Spots on back and caudal fin small, largest much smaller than eye diameter; scales moderate in size, 155 or fewer in first row above lateral line . . . . (11)

11 (10) Gums white or pale; black spots on caudal fin on upper lobe only or absent; pyloric caeca fewer than 100 . . . . *Oncorhynchus kisutch,* page 206

11 Gums black; black spots on both lobes of caudal fin; pyloric caeca 120 or more . . . . *Oncorhynchus tshawytscha,* page 207

12 (9) Gill rakers on first arch short, stout, smooth, widely spaced, 28 or fewer; irregular dark vertical bands in fish migrating to fresh water . . . . *Oncorhynchus keta,* page 208

12 Gill rakers on first arch long, slender, rough, closely spaced, 30–39; no dark vertical bands . . . . *Oncorhynchus nerka,* page 209

The following key to juveniles of the Salmoninae of Alaska is drawn primarily from the key by McPhail and Lindsey (1970). Morrow's (1974) drawings of juveniles are included in the species accounts. Other keys to juvenile salmonids, using additional or different characters, are available. The key by McConnell and Snyder (1972) uses external features only, and is most useful in the field. Trautman's (1973) key to presmolt Pacific salmon in Alaska contains instructions for identifying salmon at different presmolt sizes, relying heavily on gill raker and pyloric caeca counts, and is an essential tool for laboratory work.

Key to Juveniles (5–13 cm TL) of the Salmoninae of Alaska

1 Principal anal rays 8–12 . . . . (2)

1 Principal anal rays 13 or more (in rare cases 12) . . . . (6)

2 (1) No dark spots on dorsal fin and first dorsal ray not black (lake trout, *S. namaycush,* may have faint dark bars on dorsal fin) . . . . (3)

2 Distinct dark spots present on dorsal fin or first dorsal ray black . . . . (4)

3 (2) Parr marks along lateral line in form of vertical bars; width of dark areas usually equal to or less than width of light areas; predorsal distance about one-half of standard length . . . . *Salvelinus namaycush,* page 198

3 Parr marks along lateral line in form of irregular, often rectangular, blotches; width of dark areas along lateral line greater than width of light areas; predorsal distance less than one-half of standard length . . . . *Salvelinus alpinus,* page 199
. . . . *Salvelinus malma,* page 200
. . . . *Salvelinus confluentus,* page 201

4 (2) Red or yellow spots on lateral line between or on parr marks (may be missing in hatchery-reared fish and in preserved specimens); combined width of dark areas along lateral line about equal to or greater than width of light areas . . . . . (5)

4 No red or yellow spots along lateral line; combined width of dark areas along lateral line less than width of light areas . . . . . (6)

5 (4) Pectoral fins short, not as long as depressed dorsal fin; caudal fin not deeply forked, the center rays definitely more than half the length of the longest; no dark spots on operculum . . . . . *Salvelinus fontinalis,* page 197

5 Pectoral fins long, as long as depressed dorsal fin; caudal fin deeply forked, the center rays about half the length of the longest; dark spots on operculum . . . . . *Salmo salar,* page 202

6 (4) Usually 4 or fewer (rarely 5) dark marks along dorsal midline in front of dorsal fin; black border of adipose fin usually with more than 1 break; maxilla may reach to or past rear margin of eye (not in very small fish) . . . . . *Oncorhynchus clarkii,* page 203

6 Usually 5–10 dark marks along dorsal midline in front of dorsal fin; black border of adipose fin unbroken or with 1 break; maxilla not reaching rear margin of eye . . . . . *Oncorhynchus mykiss,* page 204

7 (1) No parr marks; maximum length in fresh water about 5 cm . . . . . *Oncorhynchus gorbuscha,* page 205

7 Parr marks present; maximum length in fresh water 12.5 cm or even more . . . . . (8)

8 (7) Parr marks in form of tall vertical bars almost bisected by lateral line, the tallest marks much longer than vertical diameter of eye . . . . . (9)

8 Parr marks oval or elliptical and short, most reaching barely if at all below lateral line, none much longer than vertical diameter of eye . . . . . (10)

9 (8) First anal fin ray elongate, producing concave outer margin on anal fin; anal fin usually with dark pigment behind white leading edge; adipose fin uniformly dark . . . . . *Oncorhynchus kisutch,* page 206

9 First anal fin ray not elongate, outer margin of anal fin not strongly concave; anal fin usually without dark pigment behind leading edge; adipose fin pigmented only around margin . . . . . *Oncorhynchus tshawytscha,* page 207

10 (8) Black spots on back irregular in position, if present; maximum size in fresh water about 6.5 cm; gill rakers on lower limb of first arch about 14 . . . . . *Oncorhynchus keta,* page 208

10 Row of definite black spots on bask; maximum size in fresh water about 46 cm in landlocked populations, about 20 cm in anadromous populations; gill rakers on lower limb of first arch about 18 . . . . . *Oncorhynchus nerka,* page 209

Salvelinus fontinalis (Mitchill, 1814) **brook trout**

Introduced to southeastern Alaska; native to eastern North America, introduced to higher elevations in western North America, including western Canadian provinces, and temperate regions of South America, Europe, Asia, and Australasia.

Fresh water; clear, cold, well-oxygenated creeks, small to medium rivers, lakes; some populations anadromous in Hudson Bay and Atlantic Canada, staying at sea a few months and never venturing more than a few kilometers from river mouths.

D 9–14; A 8–13; Pec 10–15; Pel 7–10; LLs 109–132; GR 13–22; Br 8–13; PC 20–55; Vert 57–62.

- Greenish to brown dorsally; prominent green or cream **vermiculations on head, back, and dorsal and caudal fins**; lighter ventrally; **numerous pale spots and some red spots**, the latter with blue halos, on side; **pectoral, pelvic, and anal fins with white leading edge followed by black line**, rest of fin yellow to dusky red; spawning male brilliant orange or red ventrolaterally, bordered below by black on each side delimiting white belly.
- Body only slightly compressed; caudal peduncle deep; maxilla extending well beyond eye; breeding males develop kype.
- **Caudal fin truncate or slightly emarginate**; adipose fin and pelvic axillary process present.
- Scales minute, 195–243 in midlateral series.
- Teeth on head of vomer but not on shaft.
- Teeth present along mesial margin of gill rakers.
- Usually 1 less branchiostegal ray on right side.
- Length to 70 cm TL.

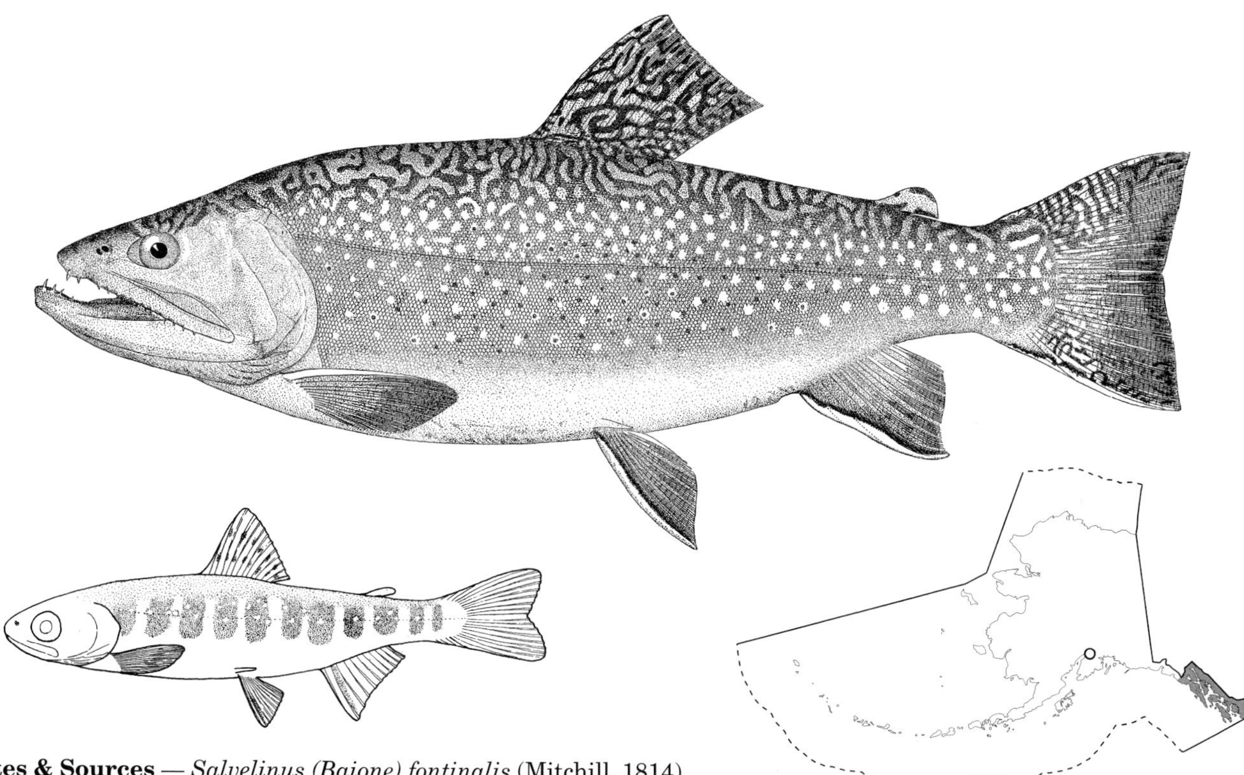

Notes & Sources — *Salvelinus (Baione) fontinalis* (Mitchill, 1814)
Salmo fontinalis Mitchill, 1814
In Alaska, hybridizes readily with native Dolly Varden, *S. malma,* and the hybrid is inferior to both parent species (Morrow 1980).

Description: Scott and Crossman 1973:208–213; Morrow 1980:53–55; Power 1980; Page and Burr 1991:48; Coad 1995:161–163. Like the stripes on a zebra, whether the vermiculations are dark or light may depend on one's viewpoint. Blue haloes are also present in some populations of Dolly Varden, *S. malma.*

Figures: Adult: Goode 1884, pl. 192; 40 cm TL, New York. Juvenile: Morrow 1974, fig. 29; 9 cm TL.

Range: Introduced, starting in 1918, in southeastern Alaska (MacCrimmon and Campbell 1969, MacCrimmon et al. 1971), where into the 1950s many rivers, streams, and lakes were stocked. Brook trout survived in some of the lakes as far north as Haines and Skagway and provide good sport fishing. Sources outside of Alaska included Colorado, but the source for most of the systems that now support brook trout populations in southeastern Alaska was the federal Yes Bay Hatchery at McDonald Lake, which was shut down in 1933. Baxter (1990ms) gave the "Cook Inlet Basin" as a transplant location and commented that the introduction there was probably not successful. Power (1980) gave a detailed account of the life history of the brook trout.

Size: Reported to reach 86 cm, but Morrow (1980) remarked that reports of brook trout over 70 cm invariably turned out to be attributable to Arctic char, *S. alpinus.*

Salvelinus namaycush (Walbaum, 1792) **lake trout**

Arctic Alaska and Alaska Peninsula to Yukon Territory and British Columbia, continuing east across mainland northern North America; southern limits of native range associated with extent of Pleistocene glaciation; widely introduced outside original range in United States, a few introductions into Europe, South America, and New Zealand.

Fresh water; deep, cold lakes; generally absent from lowland regions such as Yukon–Kuskokwim valleys; does not tolerate salt water.

D 8–10; A 8–10; Pec 12–17; Pel 8–11; LLs 116–138; GR 16–26; Br 10–14; PC 81–210; Vert 61–69.

- Light green, brown, gray, dark green, or nearly black; usually **dark green back and sides with profuse, irregularly shaped white to yellow spots; no pink or red spots on body**; sometimes with light gray vermiculations on head and back; sometimes so silvery that spots are hard to see; belly white; roof of mouth and tip of jaws white; pectoral, pelvic, and anal fins sometimes with white leading edge, dusky area (but not a distinct black line) behind white, then orange tinge; spawning male paler on back, develops dark stripe on side.
- Body more or less terete; caudal peduncle slender; maxilla reaching well past eye in adults; breeding males do not develop kype.
- Dorsal fin set slightly farther back on body than in other *Salvelinus*; **caudal fin deeply forked**; adipose fin and pelvic axillary process present.
- Scales minute, 175–228 in oblique rows; breeding tubercles develop on some scales but disappear rapidly after spawning.
- Teeth on head of vomer but not on shaft.
- Teeth present along mesial margin of gill rakers.
- Pyloric caeca numerous, usually 120–180.
- Length to 126 cm TL, weight to 46.3 kg (largest of all *Salvelinus*).

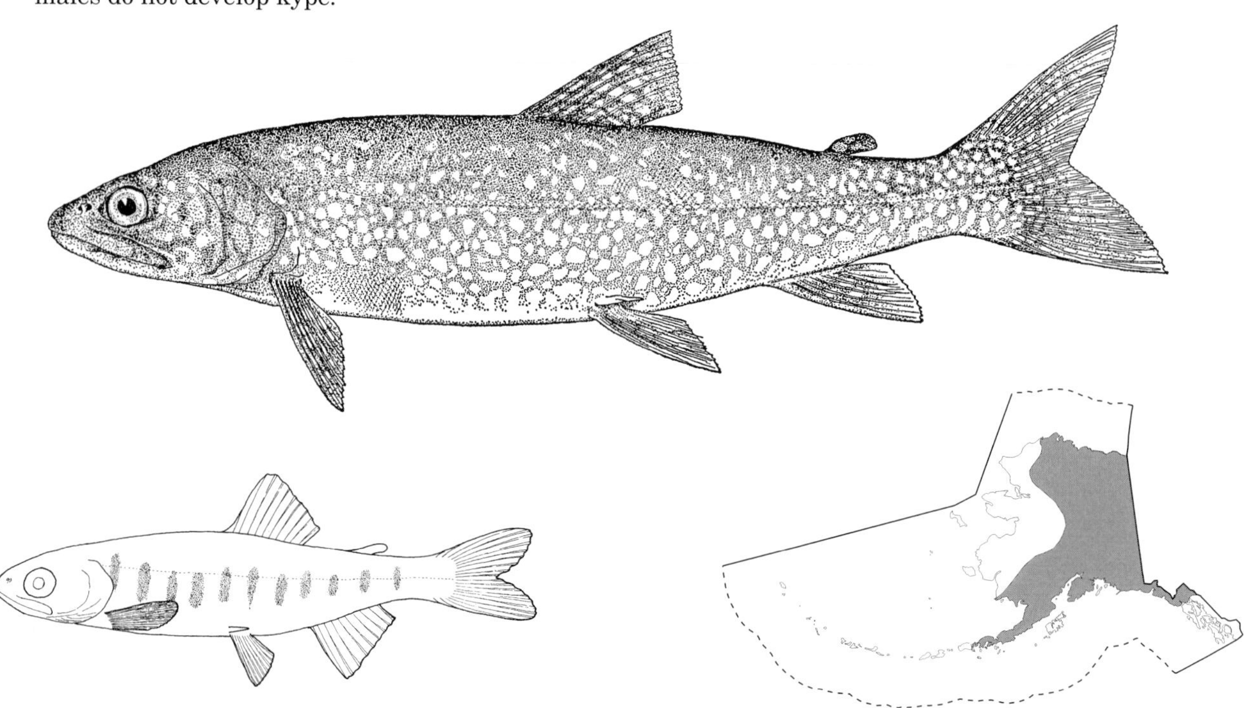

Notes & Sources — *Salvelinus (Cristivomer) namaycush* (Walbaum, 1792)

Salmo namaycush Walbaum, 1792

Cristivomer namaycush: Gill and Jordan (in Jordan 1878:356). Placed in *Salvelinus* by Jordan and Gilbert (1883:317). *Cristivomer* refers to raised crest behind chevron of vomer, free from the shaft and armed with teeth.

Behnke (1980) and Cavender (1980) placed *Salvelinus namaycush* in subgenus *Cristivomer* to emphasize its morphological and ecological distinctions. Nelson (1994) placed it in *Baione,* following the work of Cavender and Kimura (1989) and Phillips and Pleyte (1991), but acknowledged that other studies, such as that of Grewe et al. (1990), support placement in subgenus *Cristivomer.*

Description: Scott and Crossman 1973:220–227; Martin and Olver 1980; Morrow 1980:55–58; Page and Burr 1991:48; Coad 1995:384–386. Vermiculations on head and back are never as pronounced as in *S. fontinalis.*

Figures: Adult: McPhail and Lindsey 1970:136. Juvenile: Morrow 1974, fig. 32; 12.5 cm TL

Range: The distribution map for *S. namaycush* by Martin et al. (in Lee et al. 1980) includes several records from Alaska not included in previous accounts (e.g., Scott and Crossman 1973) or on Morrow's (1980) map.

Salvelinus alpinus (Linnaeus, 1758) **Arctic char**

Arctic Alaska to Bering Sea and Gulf of Alaska drainages to Kenai Peninsula and Kodiak Island; Siberia to Japan; across Canada to Newfoundland and south to New England; Greenland; circumpolar.

Anadromous and resident freshwater lacustrine populations; spawn in lakes; lacustrine, no direct evidence of anadromy, in Alaska; commonly anadromous on Chukchi Peninsula.

D 10–12; A 11–15; Pec 14–16; Pel 9–11; LLs 123–152; GR 22–35; Br 10–13, total 20–24; PC 35–75; Vert 61–70.

- Brown to greenish brown dorsally; lighter ventrally; pink to red spots on back and sides, **largest spots usually larger than pupil**; spots sparse, typically 15–20 below lateral line; leading edges of pectoral, pelvic, and pectoral fins, and sometimes caudal fin, white; spawning adults, especially males, orange to red ventrally, including pectoral, pelvic, and anal fins.
- **Maxilla extending only to posterior edge of eye or slightly beyond; kype absent or only feebly developed in spawning males.**
- Median number of anal fin rays 11; caudal fin forked; adipose fin and pelvic axillary process present.
- Teeth on head of vomer but not on shaft.
- Gill rakers variable in form (see Notes, below); teeth absent from mesial margin; usually more gill rakers than in *S. malma* and *S. confluentus*.
- Total branchiostegal rays usually 22 or 23.
- **Pyloric caeca usually 35 or more** (more than in *S. malma* and *S. confluentus*).
- Length to 96 cm TL.

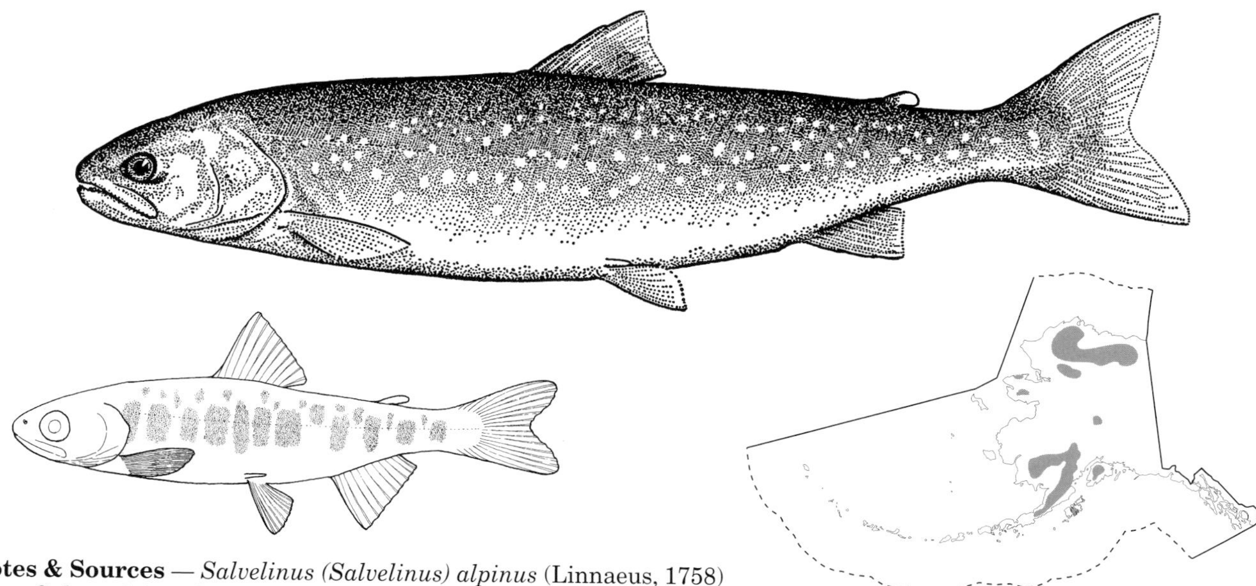

Notes & Sources — *Salvelinus (Salvelinus) alpinus* (Linnaeus, 1758)
Salmo alpinus Linnaeus, 1758

The form most commonly found in Alaska is *Salvelinus alpinus taranetzi,* the form also occurring in lakes and rivers of the Chukchi Peninsula and Kamchatka. This form was called the Bristol Bay–Gulf of Alaska form of *S. alpinus* by McPhail (1961). In Chukotka it runs to the sea, but generally does not in Alaska. Scanlon (2000) found marine-derived strontium in otoliths of this form of Arctic char from Becharof Lake, Alaska, but the origin of the strontium is unknown, and possibly from sockeye salmon eggs consumed by the char. Thus there is no direct documentation of anadromy, although the presence of the strontium is highly suggestive (R. J. Behnke, pers. comm., 29 Aug. 2000). Gill rakers usually number 20–27, and typically are short and stout. Gill rakers of Taranetz char from three Kenai Peninsula lakes sent to R. J. Behnke (pers. comm., 13 Oct. 1998) by J. L. Dean are longer and thinner than usual, hence intermediate between this form and the northern form (see next note).

A northern form, which is the same as the "eastern Arctic charr" of McPhail and Lindsey (1970), occurs as resident lacustrine populations in some lakes west of the Mackenzie River where they are sympatric with anadromous *S. malma*. Behnke (1984) suggested that the northern form, which also occurs in eastern Siberia lakes, the Taymyr region, and in Lake Coomarsharn, Ireland, be called *S. alpinus erythrinus.* Gill rakers usually number 25–30, and typically are long and thin.

Description: Scott and Crossman 1973:201–207; Johnson 1980; Morrow 1980:58–60; Chereshnev 1982.

Figures: Adult: McPhail and Lindsey 1970:142. Juvenile: Morrow 1974, fig. 33; 10 cm TL (same as Dolly Varden; characters differentiating juveniles of *S. alpinus, S. malma,* and *S. confluentus* are not well known).

Range: Distribution in Alaska was recently mapped by DeCicco (1997). Populations of both subspecies are sympatric with populations of *S. malma* in Alaska.

Size: Page and Burr 1991. Various lengths have been reported as maximum sizes for *S. alpinus,* but because of taxonomic confusion with other *Salvelinus* species it is difficult to determine which reports actually pertain to any given species. Morrow (1980) reported that the largest Arctic char known is one from the Northwest Territories weighing 13.5 kg. Alaskan records he mentioned were 5 kg or less.

Salvelinus malma (Walbaum, 1792) **Dolly Varden**

Arctic Alaska to northern Washington and to Mackenzie River in Canada; Chukchi Peninsula and Kamchatka to Japan and Korea; including most islands with suitable, fast-moving streams.

Anadromous, overwintering in lakes and spawning in tributaries to the lake, or resident in tributaries; a few landlocked, lacustrine populations on North Slope of Brooks Range in Alaska.

D 10–12; A 9–13; Pec 14–16; Pel 8–11; LLs 105–142; GR 11–26; Br 10–15, total 19–25; PC 17–36; Vert 60–71.

- Olive green to dark blue or brown dorsally; yellow, orange, or red spots on side; **largest spots usually smaller than pupil of eye**; spots profuse, typically 60–80 below lateral line; pectoral, pelvic, and anal fins with white leading edge and black or red line behind; spawning males orange to red ventrally.
- Head slightly compressed, frontals usually peaking at midline; snout deeper than in *S. confluentus*; maxilla extending beyond eye, but not as far past eye as in *S. confluentus*; spawning males **develop distinct kype**.
- **Median number of anal fin rays 11**; caudal fin usually indented but not sharply forked; adipose fin and pelvic axillary process present.
- Mandibular pores usually 6.
- Teeth on head of vomer but not on shaft.
- Gill rakers strongly compressed, finely tapered; teeth absent from mesial margin.
- **Total number of branchiostegal rays usually 21–23**.
- Length to 100 cm TL.

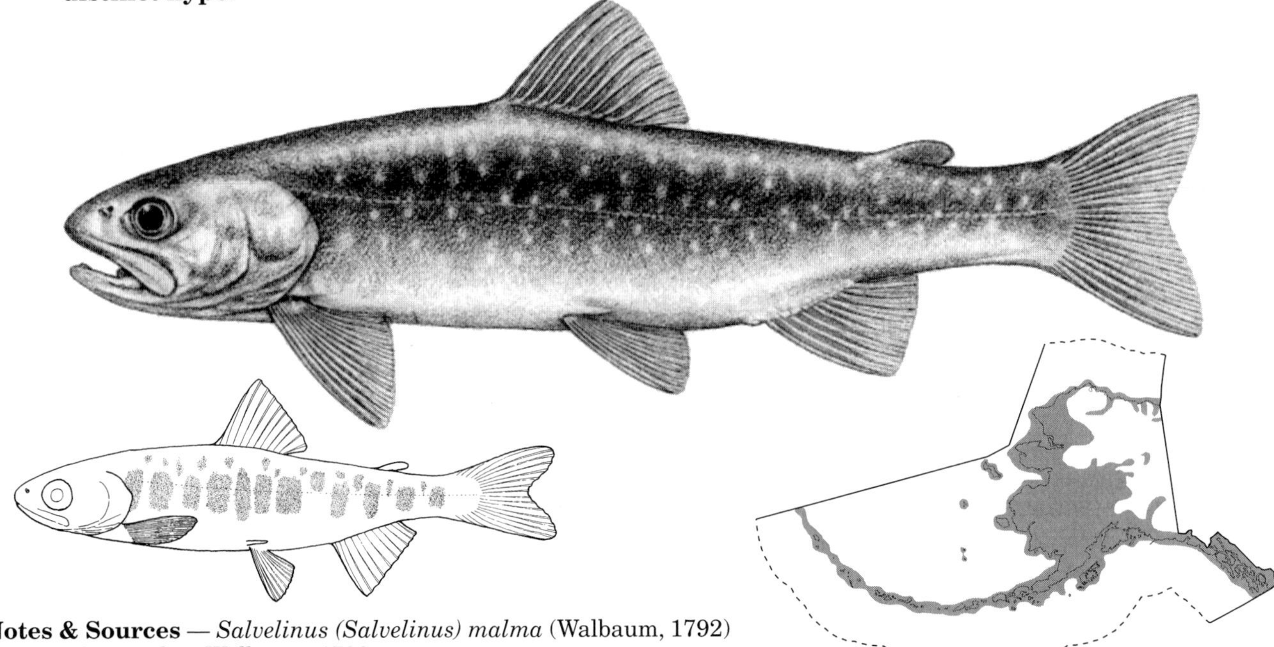

Notes & Sources — *Salvelinus (Salvelinus) malma* (Walbaum, 1792)
Salmo malma Walbaum, 1792

Dolly Varden was the name of a colorfully dressed character in Charles Dickens' story *Barnaby Rudge.*

Haas and McPhail (1991) found that the best individual characters for differentiating *S. malma* and *S. confluentus* were total number of branchiostegal rays, anal fin ray number, and ratio of upper jaw length to body length; in that order.

Of the several subspecies that have been proposed (see Morton 1970), two in Alaska have gained general recognition. Behnke (1980, 1984) distinguished the southern form, tentatively called *S. malma lordi,* occurring south of the Alaska Peninsula to Washington, with fewer gill rakers (usually 18 or 19) and vertebrae (usually 62–64), from the northern form, *S. malma malma,* occurring in northern Asia and in North America from the north side of the Alaska Peninsula to the Mackenzie River, with more gill rakers (usually 21 or 22) and vertebrae (usually 66–68).

A golden-fin, mostly dwarf form mentioned by some authors as *S. malma tudes* (Morton 1970) is common above high falls in tributaries of Karluk Lake and in several Kenai Peninsula watersheds (J. L. Dean, pers. comm., 2 Oct. 2001).

Cavender (1978) found that on average the head is shorter in *S. malma* (23% SL) than in *S. confluentus* (26% SL), but that *S. confluentus* has shorter heads than average in the Taku River basin.

Description: Scott and Crossman 1973:214–219; Cavender 1978, 1980; Morrow 1980:60–63; Chereshnev 1982; Haas and McPhail 1991; Coad 1995:252–254.

Figures: Adult: Haas and McPhail 1991, fig. 6. Juvenile: Morrow 1974, fig. 33; 10 cm TL (same as Arctic char).

Range: Recorded from Attu Island to the Sanak Islands by Wilimovsky (1964). Distribution in the rest of Alaska was mapped by Haas and McPhail (1991) and DeCicco (1997). The most widely distributed and most marine-adapted Alaskan char. Migrations between freshwaters of Alaska and northeastern Asia were documented by DeCicco (1992).

Size: Various sizes have been reported as maximal for *S. malma,* but *S. malma, S. alpinus,* and *S. confluentus* were confused for so long it is difficult to determine which reports actually pertain to *S. malma.* A. L. DeCicco (pers. comm., 26 May 2000) reported *S. malma* reaches 100 cm or more and 8.6 kg in Wulik River, northwestern Alaska. Elsewhere in Alaska, adults rarely exceed 3 kg (Morrow 1980).

Salvelinus confluentus (Suckley, 1859) **bull trout**

Rocky Mountain and Cascade ranges of northwestern North America on both sides of Continental Divide from about 61°N to 41°N, including Skeena and Taku rivers of British Columbia and Alaska, and Bering Sea drainage at headwaters of Yukon River near British Columbia–Yukon Territory boundary.

Fresh water; well inland and generally nonanadromous; can tolerate salinity, but have not been collected from any offshore islands or far out to sea.

A 9–15; GR 14–20; Br 12–16, total 24–31; PC 21–36; Vert 62–67.

- Olive green to blue-gray dorsally; gray to greenish laterally with white to yellow, pink, or red spots; lower fins with white leading edge but without contrasting black band behind; spawning males orange to red on belly.
- **Head flat on top**, frontals sloping only slightly away from midline; eye near dorsal profile; **maxilla curved downward**, extending well beyond eye, farther past eye than in *S. malma*; some spawning males develop **barely evident kype**.
- **Median number of anal fin rays 12**; caudal fin distinctly indented but not sharply forked; adipose fin and pelvic axillary process present.
- Mandibular pores usually 7–9 (per side).
- Teeth on head of vomer but not on shaft.
- Gill rakers stout and oval; strong teeth present on mesial margin.
- **Total number of branchiostegal rays usually 26–29**; tendency for 1 more on left side.
- Length to 103 cm TL or more, weight to 18.3 kg.

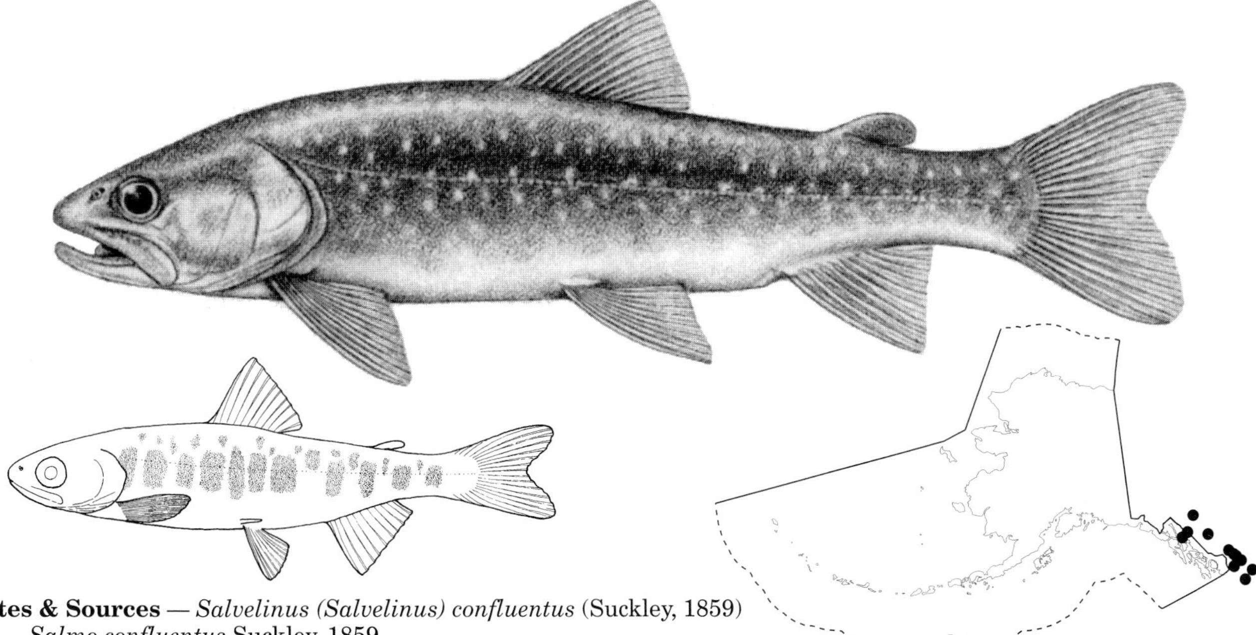

Notes & Sources — *Salvelinus (Salvelinus) confluentus* (Suckley, 1859)
Salmo confluentus Suckley, 1859

Long confused with *Salvelinus malma*. Jordan and Gilbert (1883) placed *S. confluentus* in synonymy with *S. malma*. Cavender (1978) provided evidence favoring specific distinction of *S. confluentus*. Haas and McPhail (1991) found that the best individual characters for differentiating the two species were total number of branchiostegal rays, anal fin ray number, and ratio of upper jaw length to body length. In most cases the number of branchiostegal rays differentiates the two species. Where this is not the case, the following LDF (linear discriminant function) formula should be used: 0.629 × branchiostegal ray number + 0.178 × anal fin ray number + 37.210 × total upper jaw length/standard length – 21.8. The interpretation is that char > 0 are bull trout and < 0 are Dolly Varden.

Description: Cavender 1978; Haas and McPhail 1991; Page and Burr 1991:50; Coad 1995:171–172.

Figures: Adult: Haas and McPhail 1991, fig. 6. Juvenile: Morrow 1974, fig. 33; 10 cm TL (same as Dolly Varden; characters differentiating juveniles of *S. alpinus, S. malma,* and *S. confluentus* have not been published).

Range: Cavender (1978) recorded 5 specimens (NMC 68-896; 150–246 mm SL) from Flannigan Slough, Taku River, at the Alaska–British Columbia boundary. The ABL has specimens taken farther downriver on Canyon Island and across the Taku from the mouth of the Wright River (B. L. Wing, pers. comm., 8 Jan. 2001). Cavender (1978) found that *S. confluentus* and *S. malma* are sympatric in the Taku Basin of southeastern Alaska and northern British Columbia, the Skeena Basin of British Columbia, and the Puget Sound region of Washington. Haas and McPhail (1991) recorded bull trout well up the Stikine, Nass, Skeena, and other British Columbia rivers near southern southeastern Alaska, and headwaters of the Yukon River just south of the British Columbia–Yukon boundary. Bull trout probably entered the Taku River from the east, from the Liard River via Yukon headwaters or directly from the Liard, as the continental ice sheet was retreating; i.e., not by coastal route (Haas and McPhail 1991).

Size: A 103-cm-TL specimen weighed 14.5 kg, another of unspecified length weighed 18.3 kg; originally reported as records for *S. malma* but the specimens probably were misidentified *S. confluentus* (Morrow 1980).

Salmo salar Linnaeus, 1758 — Atlantic salmon

Eastern Bering Sea and Gulf of Alaska, mostly as escapees from aquaculture pens in British Columbia and Washington; introduced in Pacific Ocean; natural reproduction in British Columbia recently documented; native to both sides of North Atlantic, with range in western Atlantic south to Connecticut River.

Anadromous; reside in fresh water 2–4 years, spend 1–6 years at sea, then spawn in natal streams; many die after spawning, some survive and spawn once or twice more; many landlocked populations in eastern Canada and New England.

D 10–12; A 8–11; Pec 14–15; Pel 9–10; LLs 109–124; GR 15–20; Br 10–13; PC 40–74; Vert 58–61.

- Brown, green, or blue dorsally; silver laterally; white ventrally; **black spots, some x- or y-shaped, on body** dorsolaterally and sometimes on caudal fin; **black spots on operculum**; spawning fish of both sexes bronze-purple overall, with or without reddish spots.
- Head small, pointed; maxilla extending below mid-eye, beyond eye only in large adult males; spawning males develop kype.
- Caudal fin slightly indented; adipose fin and pelvic axillary process present.
- Vomer with teeth on head and shaft, those on shaft weak or deciduous.
- Length to 150 cm TL, weight to 35.9 kg.

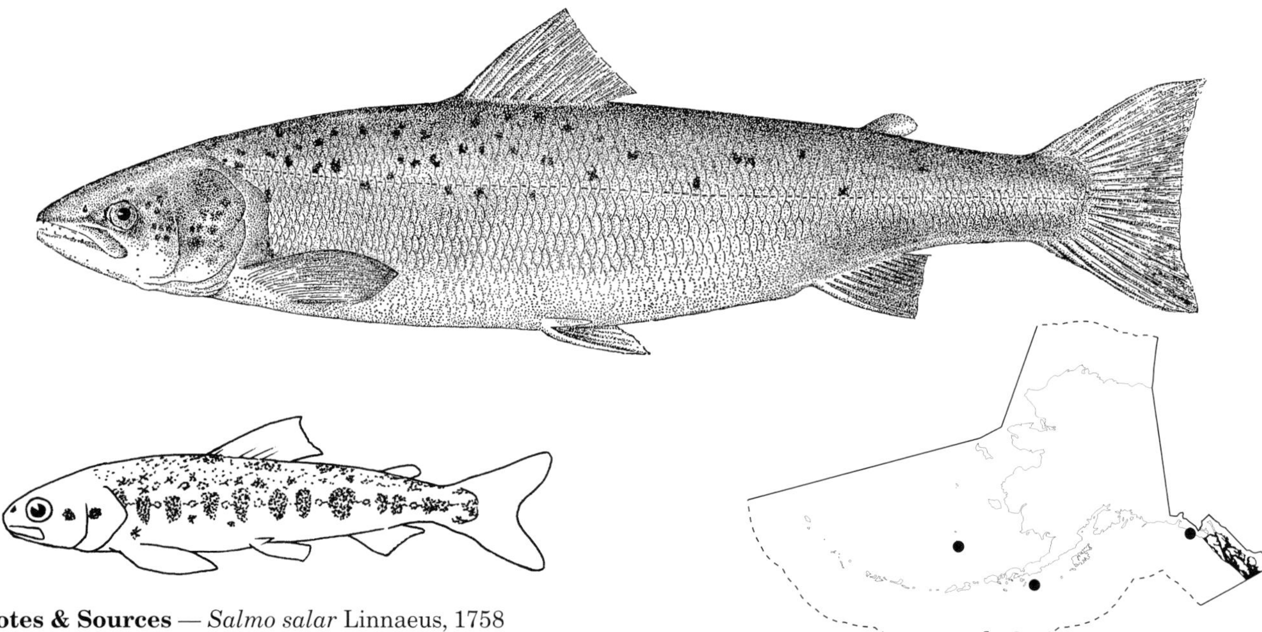

Notes & Sources — *Salmo salar* Linnaeus, 1758

Description: Scott and Scott 1988:129–134; Page and Burr 1991:50–51; Coad 1995:62–64.

Figures: Adult: Scott and Scott 1988:129. Juvenile: redrawn from McPhail and Lindsey 1970:133.

Range: Farming of Atlantic salmon started in Washington and British Columbia in the 1980s, and escapees have been found to be widely distributed in marine waters from Washington to Alaska. Wing et al. (1992) published the first record of Atlantic salmon in Alaska, citing several occurrences in southeastern Alaska near Wrangell and describing an immature female (48.5 cm SL) taken near Cape Cross by a commercial salmon troller. McKinnell et al. (1997) gave an update on occurrence in the North Pacific, including the capture of a single fish in 1994 near Nagai Island of the Shumagin Island group. McKinnell and Thomson (1997) gave additional information on Atlantic salmon in the North Pacific, noting that the ocean catch of 135 fish in Alaska in 1996 exceeded the sum of catches in all previous years, that the number caught in fresh water in British Columbia has been increasing, and that Atlantic salmon caught on Vancouver Island were feeding in fresh water. Brodeur and Busby (1998) recorded the first Bering Sea occurrence: an immature male (58 cm SL) caught during NMFS research at 56°16'N, 169°26'W, in 1997. Adult Atlantic salmon were caught in fresh water in Alaska in 1998 near Ketchikan (by angler in Ward Creek) and near Yakutat in 2000 (angled at least 6.4 km [4 miles] up the Doame River) and 2001 (lower Situk River, in commercial catch); one fish was caught in each case. The Situk River fish had been feeding, and there are other, undocumented reports from Alaska rivers (ADFG information reported in *Anchorage Daily Times,* 15 October 2001). Volpe et al. (2000) documented natural reproduction of *S. salar* in the Tsitika River on the northeast coast of Vancouver Island, and suggested that Atlantic salmon may constitute an invasive species in British Columbia. From 1988 to 1995 at least 97,800 Atlantic salmon escaped from net pens in British Columbia (McKinnell et al. 1997), and 35,000 escaped at once in Aug. 2000 from a net pen in Johnstone Strait off the northern tip of Vancouver Island (radio announcement). Atlantic salmon escaping in such huge numbers, the discovery of self-sustaining populations in British Columbia, and the recent finding of adults in fresh water in Alaska constitute a matter of great concern with respect to the potential for competition with local Pacific salmon stocks.

Oncorhynchus clarkii (Richardson, 1836) **cutthroat trout**

Kenai Peninsula at Gore Point to Eel River, California, including islands with suitable habitat in Gulf of Alaska and penetrating as far inland in British Columbia as Skeena River headwaters.

Anadromous and nonmigratory freshwater stocks; prefers smaller streams or those with long, slow stretches before entering sea; sea-run cutthroat in Alaska migrate to sea 2 or 3 years after hatching, remain at sea 12–150 days, most staying close to home stream; most spawn 2 or 3 times.

D 8–11; A 8–12; Pec 12–15; Pel 9–10; LLs 116–230; GR 14–22; Br 10–12; PC 24–57; Vert 59–64.

- Silvery to brassy with yellowish tints; **small, densely packed, irregularly shaped dark brown or black spots on body, head, and fins**; **red or orange streak on underside of lower jaw** on each side; spots fewer and cutthroat marks absent or inconspicuous in fish at sea or fresh from sea; no red stripe along side.
- Maxilla extending well beyond eye; spawning males develop slight kype.
- Caudal fin slightly indented; adipose fin and pelvic axillary process present.
- Vomer with teeth on head and shaft, those on shaft well developed; **patch of small basibranchial teeth** (behind tongue between gills) usually present.
- Gill rakers short and blunt.
- Length to 99 cm TL, weight to 18.6 kg.

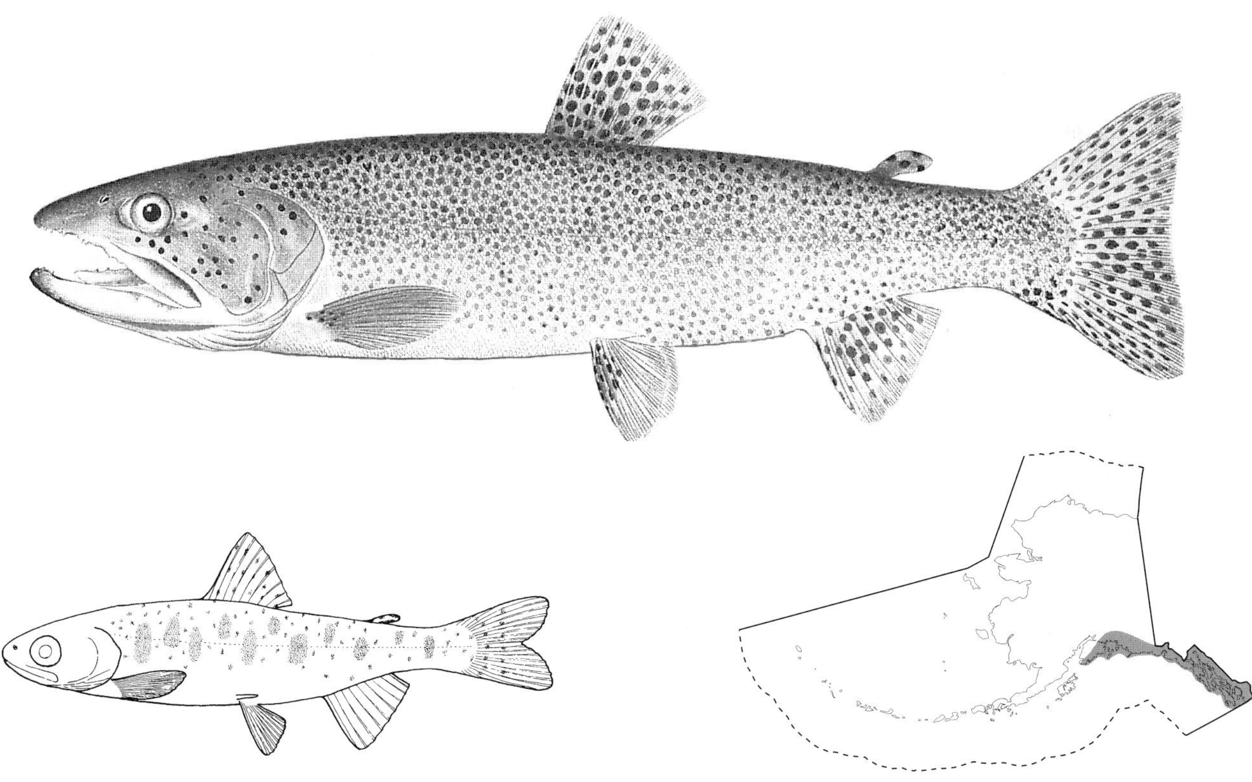

Notes & Sources — *Oncorhynchus (Rhabdofario) clarkii* (Richardson, 1836)
Salmo clarkii Richardson, 1836
Some authors spell the species name with one *i,* but the International Code of Zoological Nomenclature (1999) specifies the spelling used in the original species description as the correct spelling.
The form present in Alaska is the coastal cutthroat trout, *Oncorhynchus clarkii clarkii*. Behnke (1992) described distinguishing morphological characters and geographic distribution of the subspecies.

Description: Morrow 1980:48–50; Behnke 1992:53, 61–72; Coad 1995:211.

Figures: Adult: Evermann and Goldsborough 1907, pl. 37. Juvenile: Morrow 1974, fig. 31; 9 cm TL.

Range: Behnke (1992) gave the Prince William Sound area, bounded by Gore Point on the Kenai Peninsula, for the northwestern extent of distribution of *O. clarkii clarkii.* This species is very difficult to separate from *O. mykiss* at the northwestern end of its range based on color patterns and basibranchial teeth. It is widely stocked in lakes within and outside its original range. Normally occurs less than 150 km from the coast.

Oncorhynchus mykiss (Walbaum, 1792) **rainbow trout**

Coastal waters and drainages from Kuskokwim River and Port Moller to Mexico and to Kamchatka; Peace and Athabasca rivers in Canada; introduced in interior Alaska, and widely introduced elsewhere.

Freshwater and anadromous populations, called rainbow trout and steelhead; stream-dwelling rainbows stay in short sections of stream, lake-dwellers migrate to spawning streams; steelhead run to sea after 1–4 years, stay there 1–4 years, spawn in natal stream; usually survive spawning but repeat spawning is rare.

D 10–12; A 8–12; Pec 11–17; Pel 9–10; LLs 100–161; GR 15–24; Br 8–13; PC 27–80; Vert 60–66.

- Dark blue to greenish or brownish dorsally; silvery white or pale yellow ventrally; **reddish stripe along side**, except in steelhead fresh from sea; **small dark brown or black spots on back, sides, and dorsal and caudal fins**.
- Maxilla extending to posterior margin of eye to well beyond eye; breeding males develop kype.
- Caudal fin nearly truncate in large fish; adipose fin and pelvic axillary process present.
- Vomer with teeth on head and shaft; **basibranchial teeth generally absent**.
- Length to 122 cm TL, weight to 23.6 kg.

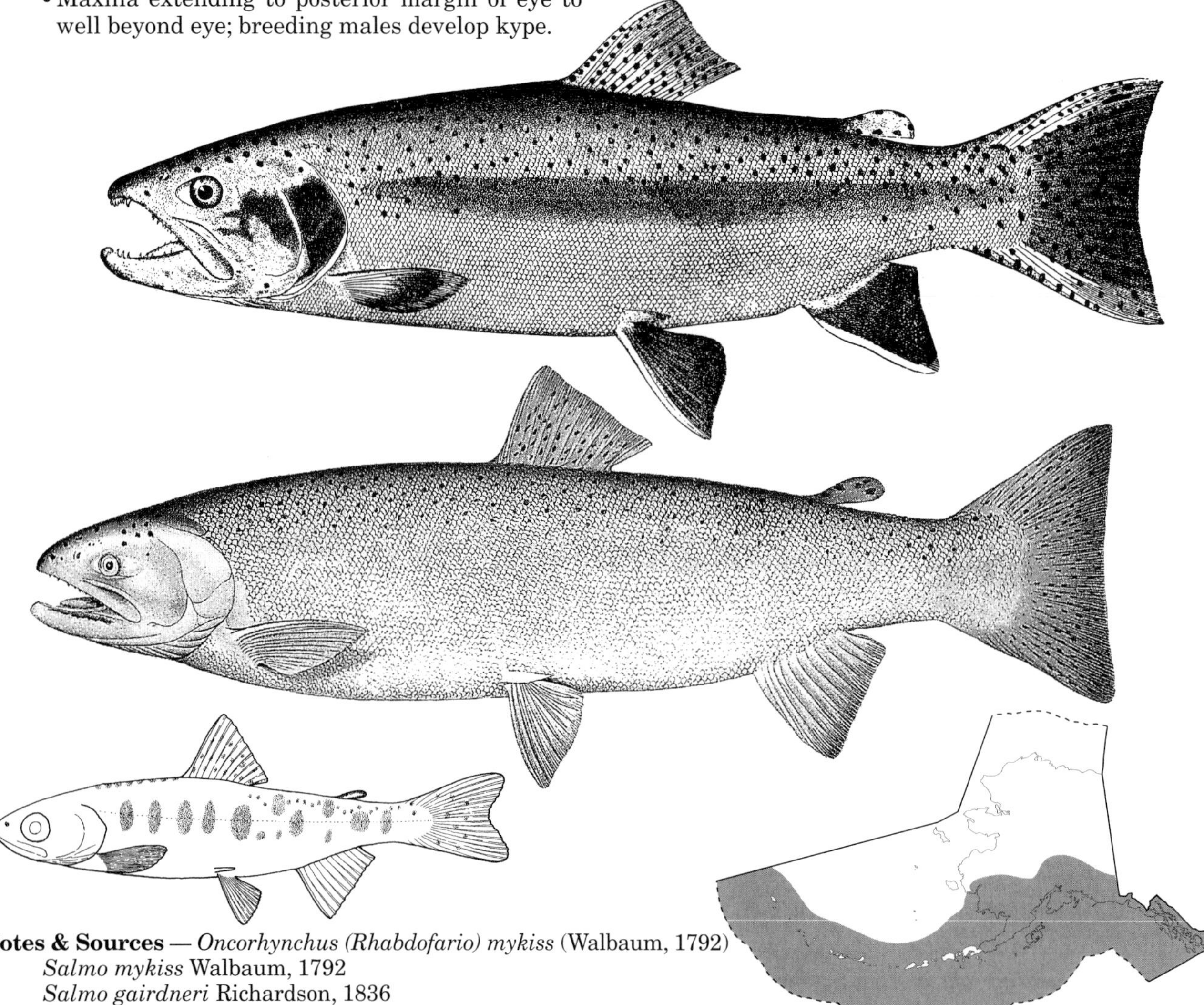

Notes & Sources — *Oncorhynchus (Rhabdofario) mykiss* (Walbaum, 1792)
Salmo mykiss Walbaum, 1792
Salmo gairdneri Richardson, 1836
Salmo irideus Gibbons, 1855
For taxonomic history see Smith and Stearley (1989) and Behnke (1992).
The form present in Alaska is the coastal rainbow trout, *Oncorhynchus mykiss irideus.* Complete descriptions of the morphology and distributions of the subspecies were given by Behnke (1992).
Steelhead (anadromous) could be confused with coho salmon, *O. kisutch,* but steelhead has a completely white mouth cavity, whereas coho salmon has white gums but the rest of the mouth cavity is dark (Hagerman 1951).

Description: Morrow 1980:50–53; Page and Burr 1991:54–55; Behnke 1992:193–201; Coad 1995:568–569.

Figures: Upper: Jordan and Evermann 1900, fig. 216; rainbow trout, Missouri. Lower: Evermann and Goldsborough 1907, pl. 38; steelhead. Juvenile: Morrow 1974, fig. 30; 9 cm TL.

Range: Morrow (1980) and Behnke (1992) summarized freshwater range. Northwestern limits of freshwater range are southern tributaries of the Kuskokwim River and the Port Moller region of the Alaska Peninsula. Hart (1973) and Brodeur (1988) mapped ocean distribution.

Oncorhynchus gorbuscha (Walbaum, 1792) **pink salmon**

Beaufort Sea coast of Alaska to Sacramento River in central California, and to Japan and North Korea; in Canada to Mackenzie River delta; northern Siberia to Yana and Lena rivers; during ocean phase, found throughout North Pacific and Bering Sea north of about 40°N.

Anadromous; run to sea right after emerging from gravel; in sea, stay close to shore until 6–8 cm long, then move offshore; after 18 months in sea, return to spawn in natal streams but often wander; die soon after spawning; due to 2-year life cycle, runs in odd- and even-numbered years are genetically separated, with observable, though minor, morphological differences; generally do not reach far upstream, often spawn in lower tidal areas.

D 10–15; A 13–19; Pec 14–17; Pel 9–11; LLs 147–205; GR 24–35; Br 9–15; PC 95–224; Vert 63–72.

- At sea, metallic blue to blue-green dorsally, silver laterally, white ventrally; large **oval black spots on body dorsolaterally and on both lobes of caudal fin**; breeding males dark on back, red with brownish green blotches on side, breeding females similar but less distinctly colored.
- Males develop pronounced hump and elongate, hooked snout and lower jaw during spawning.
- Adipose fin and pelvic axillary process present.
- Scales very small, usually more than 170 lateral scales.
- Vomer with teeth on head and shaft.
- Gill rakers moderately long, closely spaced.
- Length to 76 cm TL, weight to 6.4 kg (smallest of the Pacific salmons).

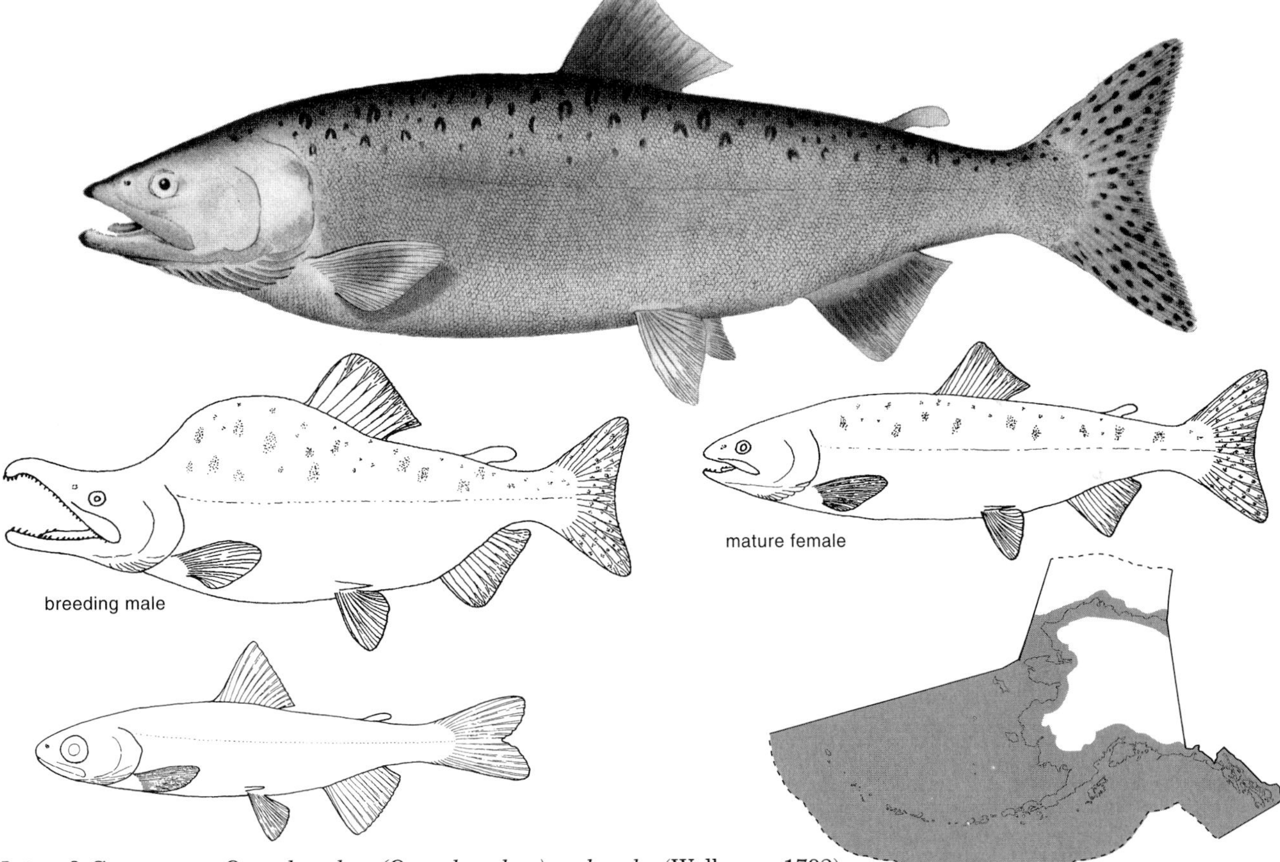

Notes & Sources — *Oncorhynchus (Oncorhynchus) gorbuscha* (Walbaum, 1792)
Salmo gorbuscha Walbaum, 1792
Also called humpback salmon.

Description: Hart 1973:108–111; Scott and Crossman 1973: 148–152; Morrow 1980:64–67; Page and Burr 1991:53; Coad 1995:531–533.

Figures: Upper: Evermann and Goldsborough 1907, pl. 23; adult male. Below: Morrow 1974, figs. 24, 34; juvenile 5 cm TL.

Range: Heard (1991) reviewed distribution and life history in detail. Spawning runs in North America are most substantial from Bering Strait to Washington. Pink salmon, and to a lesser degree chum salmon, are the only salmon species to occur with any regularity and to maintain small populations in Beaufort coast drainages (Craig and Haldorson 1986). State and private artificial propagation in Alaska of billions of pink salmon and chum salmon has made them the dominant commercially caught salmon in Alaska in biomass, but with less value per pound than other species. Most reports from streams of central California, and those occasionally heard of as far south as La Jolla, represent strays and not self-perpetuating runs.

Oncorhynchus kisutch (Walbaum, 1792) **coho salmon**

Point Hope, Alaska, except for rare strays farther north along Chukchi and Beaufort coasts, to Monterey Bay, California, with strays to Chamalu Bay, Baja California; in Asia, Anadyr River and its estuary, and Kamchatka to northern Japan and North Korea.

Anadromous; run to sea usually after 1 year, up to 4 years, in freshwater pools, avoiding riffles; in sea, gradually move offshore and travel major current systems; return to spawn after 2 or 3 years at sea, with about 85% of those returning entering the natal stream; die soon after spawning; typically in short coastal streams, but spawn in Yukon system at least as far upriver as the Tanana.

D 9–13; A 12–17; Pec 12–16; Pel 9–11; LLs 112–148; GR 18–25; Br 11–15; PC 45–114; Vert 61–69.

- At sea, metallic blue dorsally, silver laterally, white ventrally; **small black spots on body dorsolaterally and on upper lobe of caudal fin; gums at base of teeth in lower jaw white**; breeding male with dusky green back and head, bright red side, black belly; breeding female with bronze to pinkish red side.
- Males develop elongate, hooked upper and lower jaws and slight hump during spawning run.
- Adipose fin and pelvic axillary process present.
- Scales relatively large.
- Vomer with teeth on head and shaft.
- Gill rakers rough, short, widely spaced.
- Length to 108 cm TL, weight to 17.7 kg.

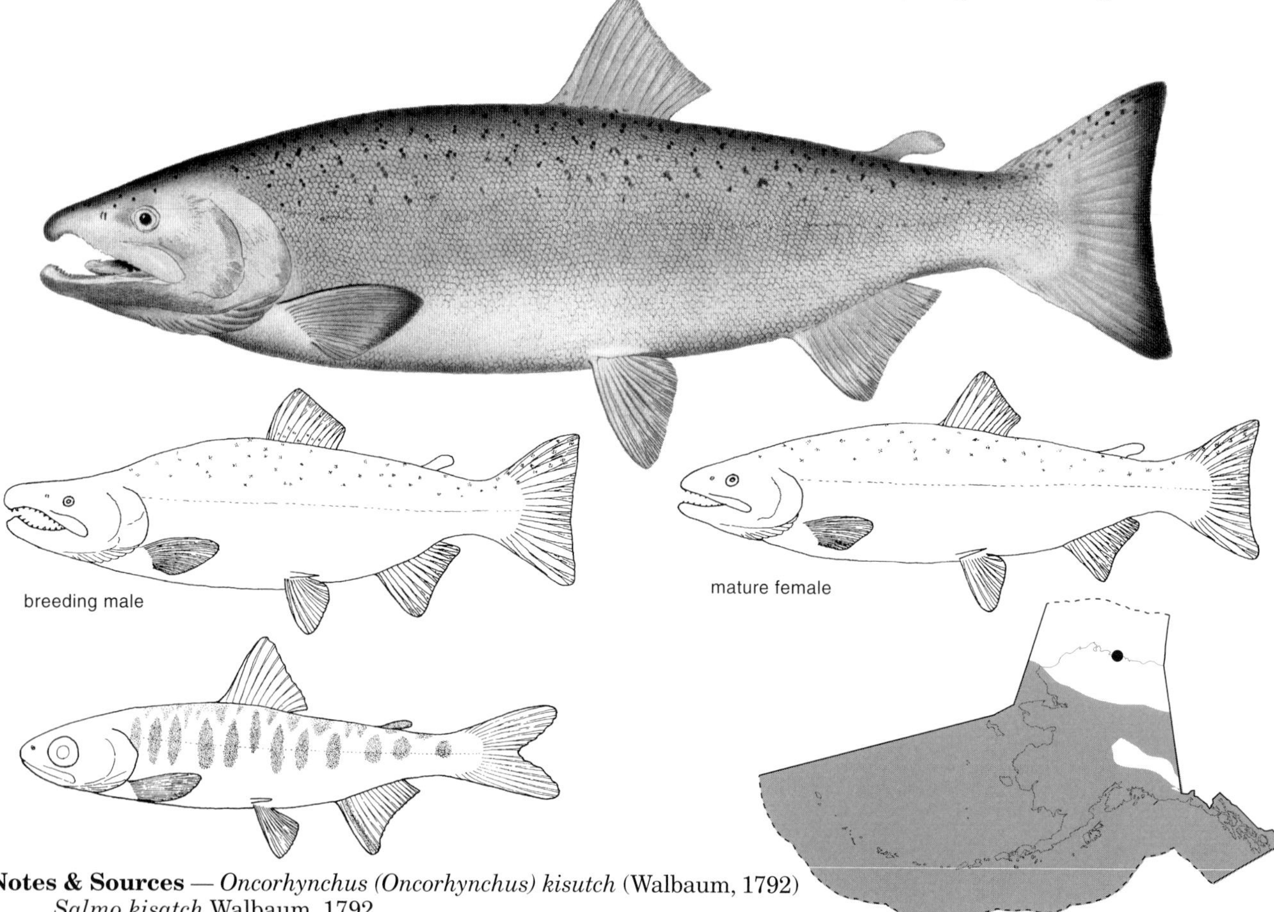

Notes & Sources — *Oncorhynchus (Oncorhynchus) kisutch* (Walbaum, 1792)
Salmo kisatch Walbaum, 1792
The spelling *kisutch* is in general use, probably after Pennant's name *kysutch,* and, following provisions of the International Code of Zoological Nomenclature effective 1 Jan. 2000, should be retained (Eschmeyer 2001).
Also called silver salmon.

Description: Hart 1973:115–118; Scott and Crossman 1973: 158–164; Morrow 1980:72–75; Page and Burr 1991:53; Coad 1995:215–217.

Figures: Upper: Evermann and Goldsborough 1907, pl. 31; adult male. Others: Morrow 1974, figs. 26, 37; juvenile 10 cm TL.

Range: Sandercock (1991) reviewed distribution and life history. The northernmost coho salmon population is found in the Kukpuk River (Wahle and Pearson 1987), near Point Hope. Craig and Haldorson (1986), reviewing occurrence north of Point Hope, found one or two records of single specimens in salt water at Prudhoe Bay. Well documented as far up the Yukon system as the Tanana, but since both coho salmon and chum salon are known as silver salmon in interior Alaska, reports of coho salmon in the Chandalar and tributaries of the Porcupine should be viewed with skepticism until they can be verified (Morrow 1980). Nowhere as numerous as chum, pink, or sockeye salmon.

Oncorhynchus tshawytscha (Walbaum, 1792) **Chinook salmon**

Point Hope, Alaska, except for rare strays farther north along Chukchi and Beaufort coasts as far east as Coppermine River in Canada, south to Ventura River, California, with strays to Baja California; in Asia, Anadyr River to northern Japan; transplanted to Great Lakes, New Zealand, Chile, other areas.

Anadromous; run to sea after 3 months to 2 years in fresh water; in sea, some remain near shore but others migrate extensively, traveling 1,600 km or more out to sea and descending to 200 m or more; return to spawn in natal rivers after 1–5 years at sea; die soon after spawning; spawn in large rivers from near tidewater to over 3,200 km upstream in headwaters of the Yukon River.

D 10–14; A 13–19; Pec 14–17; Pel 10–11; LLs 130–165; GR 16–30; Br 13–19; PC 90–240; Vert 67–75.

- At sea, metallic dark green to blue-black dorsally, silver laterally, white ventrally; **small black spots on both lobes of caudal fin and on back**; **gums at base of teeth in lower jaw black**; breeding fish change to olive brown, red, or purplish, with change more marked in males.
- Males develop elongate, hooked jaws and enlarged anterior jaw teeth during spawning run.
- Adipose fin and pelvic axillary process present.
- Scales relatively large.
- Vomer with teeth on head and shaft.
- Gill rakers rough, short, widely spaced.
- Length to 160 cm TL, weight to 61.2 kg; rarely over 23 kg (largest of the Pacific salmons).

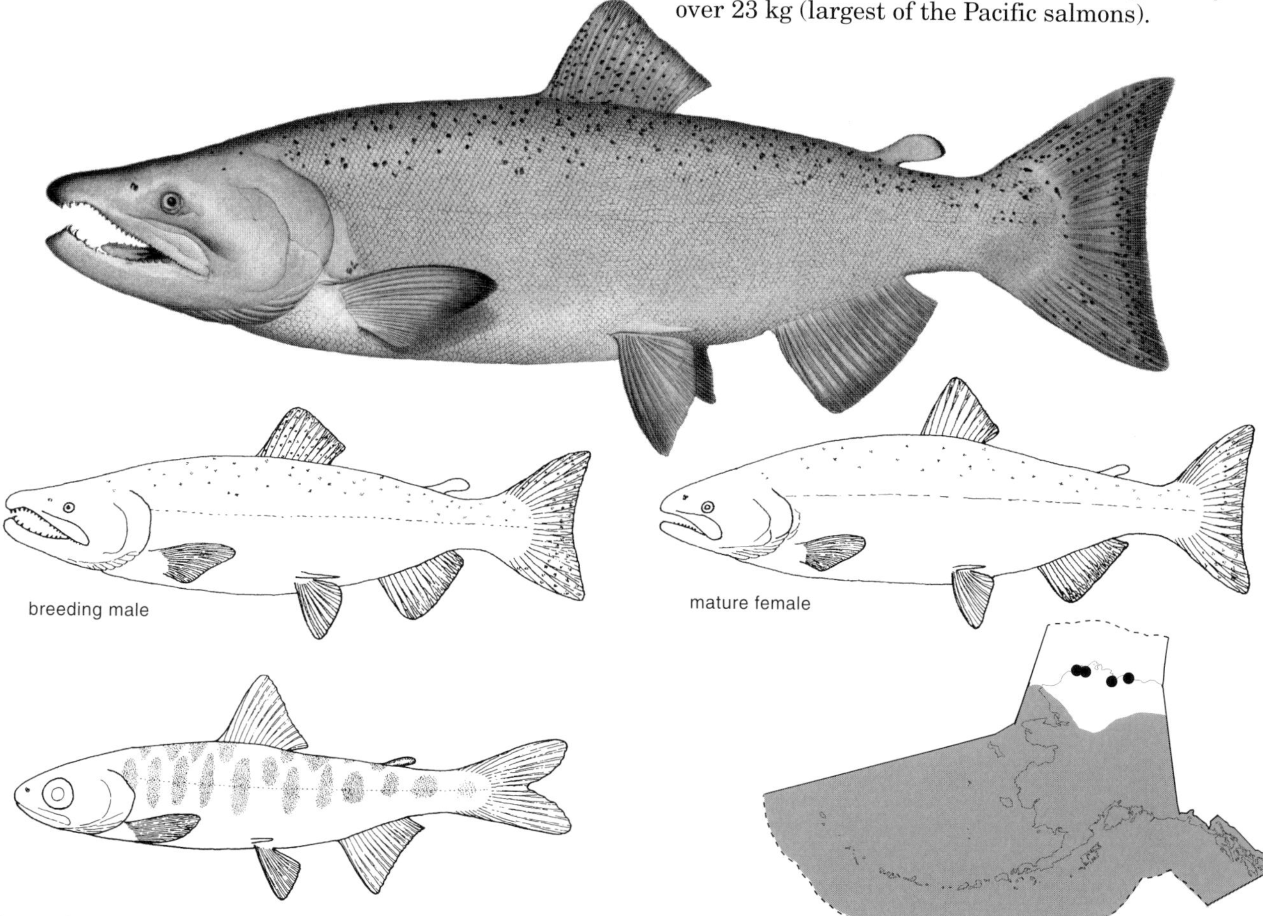

Notes & Sources — *Oncorhynchus (Oncorhynchus) tshawytscha* (Walbaum, 1792)
Salmo tshawytscha Walbaum, 1792
Salmo tschawytscha Bloch & Schneider, 1801
Oncorhynchus chouicha: Jordan and Gilbert 1883:307; they called *tshawytscha* "a barbarous spelling of the word *chouicha*."
Also known as king salmon. Species name *tshawytscha* is pronounced "choweecha" (Goode 1884).

Description: Hart 1973:124–126; Scott and Crossman 1973: 172–177; Morrow 1980:67–69; Page and Burr 1991:52; Coad 1995:202–204.

Figures: Upper: Evermann and Goldsborough 1907, pl. 29; adult male. Others: Morrow 1974, figs. 25, 38; juvenile 12.5 cm TL.

Range: Healey (1991) reviewed distribution and life history in detail. Spawning runs in North America are most substantial from Kotzebue Sound to central California. Craig and Haldorson (1986), reviewing occurrence north of Point Hope, found records of strays in the Kuk and Colville rivers, off Wainwright, and in Prudhoe Bay. Cruz-Agüero (1999) documented the first record from Baja California: a mature female caught by an angler at 27°54'N, 114°17'W.

Oncorhynchus keta (Walbaum, 1792) **chum salmon**

Beaufort Sea coast of Alaska to Sacramento River in central California, with strays to Del Mar, near Mexico border, and to Kyushu Island of southern Japan and Naktong River in Korea; in Canada to Mackenzie and Anderson rivers; arctic coast of Siberia to Lena River (Laptev Sea).

Anadromous; run to sea right after emerging from gravel; in sea, after spending several months close to shore, disperse to open ocean and are found as deep as 61 m; after 3–5 years in sea, return to spawn in natal streams; die a few days after spawning; some stocks have short runs, to 160 km upstream, or spawn in tidal areas, others travel farther, to 3,200 km in headwaters of Yukon River.

D 10–14; A 13–17; Pec 14–16; Pel 10–11; LLs 124–153; GR 18–28; Br 12–16; PC 163–249; Vert 59–71.

- At sea, metallic dark blue dorsally, silvery laterally and ventrally; **no distinct black spots**, but fine speckling may be present; breeding fish become dirty red on side and dusky below and develop irregular purplish green bands on side, with changes more marked in males.
- Males develop elongate, hooked jaws and enlarged anterior teeth during spawning run.
- Adipose fin and pelvic axillary process present.
- Scales relatively large.
- Vomer with teeth on head and shaft.
- **Gill rakers smooth, fairly short, stout, widely spaced, fewer than 30**.
- Length to 109 cm TL, weight to 20.8 kg.

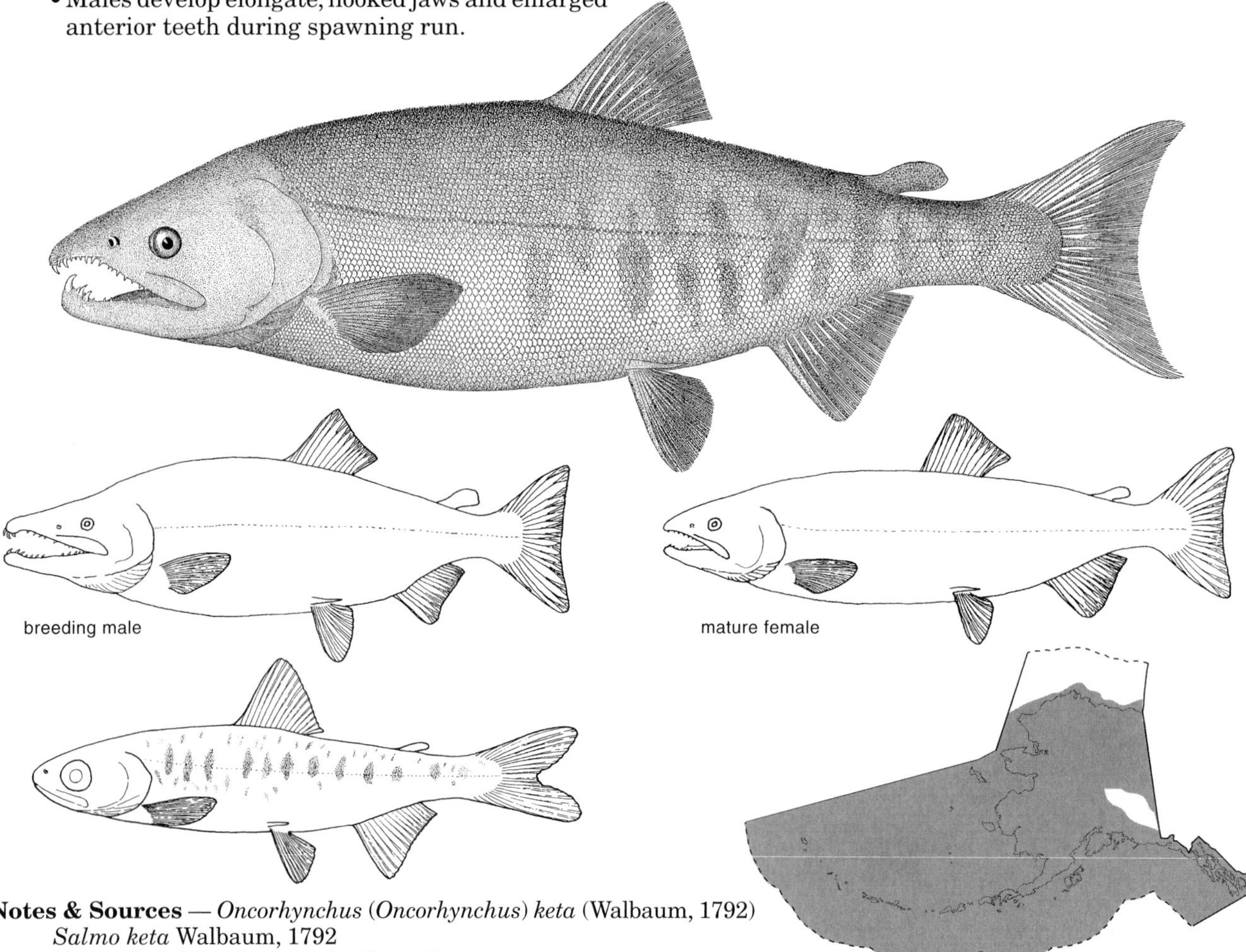

Notes & Sources — *Oncorhynchus (Oncorhynchus) keta* (Walbaum, 1792)
Salmo keta Walbaum, 1792
Also called dog salmon and calico salmon.

Description: Hart 1973:112–114; Scott and Crossman 1973:153–158; Morrow 1980:69–72; Page and Burr 1991:52; Coad 1995:206–208.

Figures: Upper: Goode 1884, pl. 188B; breeding male, near Anchorage, Cook Inlet, Alaska. Others: Morrow 1974, figs. 27, 36; juvenile 10 cm TL.

Range: Burgner (1991) reviewed distribution and life history in detail. Most abundant from Kotzebue Sound to Columbia River. Seasonal stocks occur as summer and autumn chums. Autumn stocks have larger fish, older age composition, and higher fecundity. The only true summer chum salmon in North America may be in the Yukon River. Others called summer chum salmon are probably early autumn runs. Chum salmon and pink salmon are the only salmon species to have self-sustaining populations, although small, in Beaufort coast rivers. Chum salmon runs in southeastern Alaska have recently been enhanced by releases of large numbers of juveniles from private and public aquaculture facilities. No freshwater residents or landlocked forms have been reported.

Oncorhynchus nerka (Walbaum, 1792) **sockeye salmon**

Sockeye spawn from Point Hope, Alaska, to Klamath River in California; strays to Bathurst Inlet in Canadian Arctic; in Asia, Anadyr River to Hokkaido, Japan; kokanee from Kenai Peninsula to Deschutes River in Oregon, and Japan and Siberia, and introduced widely elsewhere.

Anadromous and freshwater populations, called sockeye and kokanee, respectively; sockeye run to sea after 1 or 2 years in lakes; in sea, grow awhile close to shore then head into ocean, spreading across North Pacific north of 40°N; return to natal streams to spawn after 1–4 years at sea; die after spawning; make more use of lake rearing habitat that other salmon species.

D 11–16; A 13–18; Pec 11–21; Pel 9–11; LLs 120–150; GR 28–40; Gr 11–16; PC 45–115; Vert 56–67.

- At sea, metallic dark blue to greenish blue on head and back, silver laterally, white to silver ventrally; **typically no distinct black spots on back or fins; if black spots present, they are smaller than pupil and limited to lobes of caudal fin or irregular marks on dorsal fin**; at spawning, male changes to bright to olive green on head, brilliant red body, grayish to green paired fins and tail; some populations turning dull green to yellowish with little red; females less brilliantly colored.
- Males develop elongate, hooked jaws, enlarged anterior teeth, slight hump during spawning run.
- Adipose fin and pelvic axillary process present.
- Vomer with teeth on head and shaft.
- **Gill rakers long, slender, serrated, closely set, usually 30 or more.**
- Length to 84 cm TL, weight to 7 kg as sockeye; length to 53.3 cm as kokanee.

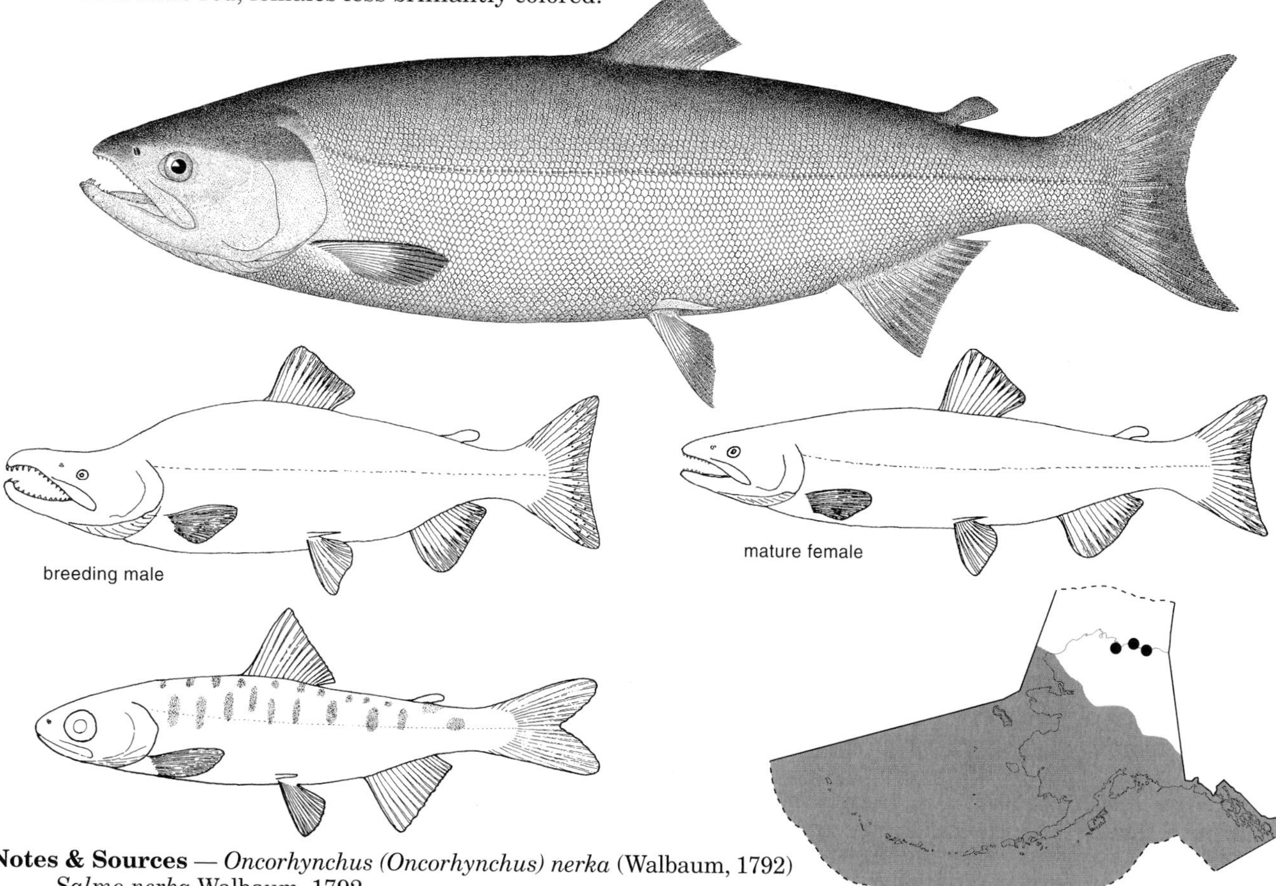

Notes & Sources — *Oncorhynchus (Oncorhynchus) nerka* (Walbaum, 1792)
Salmo nerka Walbaum, 1792
Sockeye salmon are also known as red salmon, and kokanee as blueback salmon.

Description: Hart 1973:118–123; Scott and Crossman 1973: 165–171 (emphasizes kokanee); Morrow 1980:75–78; Page and Burr 1991:52; Coad 1995:722–725.

Figures: Upper: Goode 1884, pl. 191A; blueback salmon, Columbia River. Others: Morrow 1974, figs. 328, 35; juvenile 9.5 cm TL.

Range: Burgner (1991) reviewed distribution and life history in detail. Sockeye salmon are most abundant in the Fraser River system of British Columbia and Bristol Bay system of Alaska. Bristol Bay runs, including those of the Kvichak, Naknek, Ugashik, Egegik, and Nushagak rivers, are famed worldwide as prime producers, with runs of tens of millions of fish in good years. Taken in the Yukon River as far upstream as Rampart. Rare south of the Columbia River. Craig and Haldorson (1986) listed rare records of stray sockeye salmon north of Point Hope, including the Colville River, Simpson Lagoon, and Canning River in Alaska, as well as the Mackenzie River and Bathurst Inlet in Canada.

Order Stomiiformes
Stomiiforms

The stomiiforms are a morphologically diverse group of four families of deepwater oceanic fishes. They vary in form from the elongate, almost eel-like dragonfishes (Stomiidae) to the compressed, deep-bodied hatchetfishes (Sternoptychidae). One obvious, commonly held feature of stomiiforms is an extremely large mouth, extending way past the eye, for which some authors (e.g., Coad 1995) call the group the widemouth order.

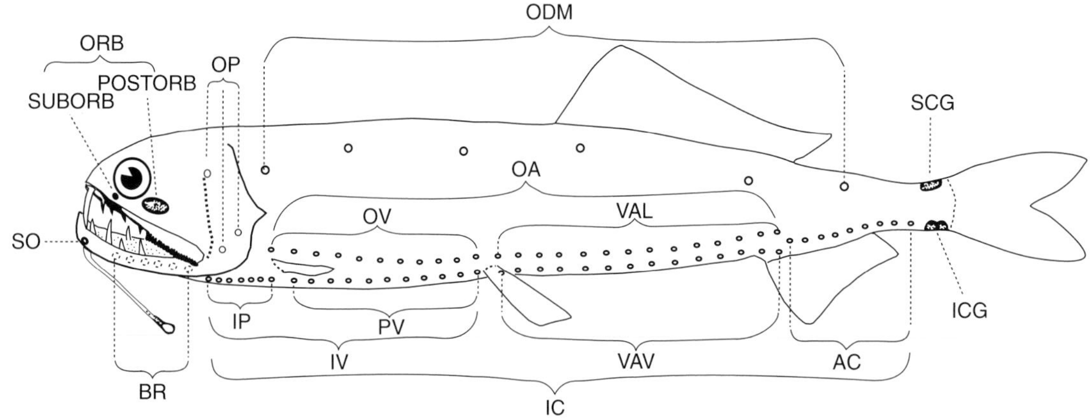

Major photophores and luminous glands in stomiiforms (except Sternoptychidae)
ORB, orbital; SUBORB, suborbital; POSTORB, postorbital; SO, symphyseal; BR, branchiostegal; OP, opercular; ODM, photophores along dorsal margin of body; OV, lateral series behind operculum to above pelvic insertion; VAL, lateral series from above pelvic insertion to end of row above caudal fin; OA, all photophores in lateral series; IP, ventral series, isthmus to pectoral insertion; PV, ventral series, pectoral to pelvic insertion; IV, ventral series, prepelvic; VAV, ventral series, pelvic insertion to anal origin if row is continuous with AC, or to end if AC row is separate; AC, above anal fin to end of row if distinct from VAV, or anal origin to end of row if continuous with VAV; IC, all photophores in ventral series; SCG, supracaudal luminous gland; ICG, infracaudal luminous gland.

Another distinctive feature is the presence of luminescent organs, which serve various functions in the near-dark to dark mesopelagic to bathypelagic levels at which these fishes live.

Other diagnostic stomiiform characters include the presence of complex chin barbels in some species; premaxilla and maxilla both included in gape of mouth, and both bearing teeth; teeth bristlelike or fanglike and hinged anteriorly; scales, if present, cycloid and easily lost; no spines in the fins; pectoral and dorsal fins, and dorsal and ventral adipose fins variably present or absent; pelvic fin rays 4–9; and branchiostegal rays 5–24. Coloration in stomiiforms is dark brown or black, or silvery with metallic tints. The light organs are white to yellow, blue, green, purple, and red.

The structure of stomiiform photophores, type of tooth attachment, arrangement of jaw muscles and ligaments, and features of the branchial arches are among the characters used by Fink and Weitzman (1982) to diagnose the order. Weitzman (1974) revised the family classification, and Harold and Weitzman (1996) examined interrelationships of the families.

Photophore numbers and arrangement are important characters for identifying stomiiform families and species. The accompanying diagram shows photophore terminology applicable to all stomiiforms, except terminology for the Sternoptychidae is different and is shown in the introduction to that family.

Family Gonostomatidae
Bristlemouths

Bristlemouths have numerous, fine teeth, with those on the maxilla showing as a long bristly fringe when the mouth is closed. Some bristlemouth species are highly abundant, and none is believed to be rare. Even the bathypelagic species often number more than 10 individuals in a single tow of a net (Miya and Nishida 1996). In some seas, species of *Cyclothone* are the most numerous deepsea fishes. Bristlemouths are most abundant in temperate to tropical waters, and also found at subarctic and antarctic latitudes. Five species of *Cyclothone* and one of *Sigmops* occur within the U.S. 200-mile fishery zone off Alaska.

Other diagnostic morphological features of bristlemouths include: body elongate, not extremely compressed; chin barbel absent; adipose fin present or absent; anal fin rays 16–68; branchiostegal rays 12–16, with 4–6 on the epihyal (posterior ceratohyal); branchiostegal photophores 7–16; isthmus photophores present or absent; and serial photophores separate, not grouped in common glands. Nelson (1994) recognized two subfamilies. Species treated in this guide are in Gonostomatinae, in which the adipose fin may be present or absent, the anal fin rays number 16–31 and vertebrae 29–40, and isthmus photophores are lacking. Bristlemouths are black, brown, or white, with transparent and translucent sections.

Most bristlemouths stay at meso- to bathypelagic depths day and night, in contrast to other midwater deep-sea fishes that undertake extensive vertical migrations, such as lanternfishes (Myctophidae). Species of *Sigmops* migrate vertically, but *Cyclothone* do not undertake well-defined diurnal migrations. Some evidence of minor, irregular migration exists, such as off the coast of Oregon where some individuals of *C. signata* rise to less than 100 m at night, some *C. pseudopallida* to 500 m, and some *C. atraria* to 800 m (Willis and Pearcy 1982). Larvae and juveniles of both genera are most often found at the shallower depths. Kashkin (1995) summarized regional depth records for species of *Cyclothone.*

Classification of the Alaskan species of bristlemouths follows revisions by Mukhacheva (1964, 1969, 1972, 1974) and Miya and Nishida (2000). Quast and Hall (1972) listed both *C. pacifica* Mukhacheva and *C. atraria* Gilbert, but Mukhacheva (1969, 1974) synonymized the two nominal species in *C. atraria.* This guide adds two species to the inventory of Alaskan species: *C. alba* and *C. pseudopallida,* both recorded from Alaska by Mukhacheva (1964). Additional Alaskan records of *C. pseudopallida* have been published (Shinohara et al. 1994) or are in museum collections (e.g., SIO 53-330), but no further specimens of *C. alba* have been reported. However, some records probably represent misidentifications. *Cyclothone alba* is closely similar to *C. signata,* and *C. pseudopallida* to *C. pallida.*

Bristlemouths are delicate, mostly small fishes. Maximum sizes in the family reach 36 cm (14 inches), but most species are under 7.6 cm (3 inches). *Sigmops* are larger than *Cyclothone.* The largest Alaskan bristlemouth is *S. gracilis,* reaching 13.3 cm SL (5.24 inches), while the smallest is *C. alba,* at 3.4 cm SL (1.3 inches). The small sizes given for *Cyclothone* species are not artifacts of small sample size, as they are for species in some less well-known families, because samples used in taxonomic studies of most bristlemouth species comprise several thousand fish (e.g., Mukhacheva 1964, 1974). Miya and Nishida (1996) used gene sequencing methodology to examine the phylogeny of the 13 recognized species of *Cyclothone,* and related their evolutionary history, including trends to miniaturization and larval-like body plan, to their surroundings.

Sigmops and *Cyclothone* are closely related but are distinguishable from each other by photophore configuration, dentition, and numbers of anal fin rays, as specified in the key and species accounts. The most obvious difference in the dentition is the presence of well-spaced, long, slender teeth with markedly shorter teeth between them in the maxilla of *Sigmops,* compared to close-set, short maxillary teeth, none of them markedly enlarged, in *Cyclothone.* In some species of *Cyclothone* some of the teeth are moderately enlarged,

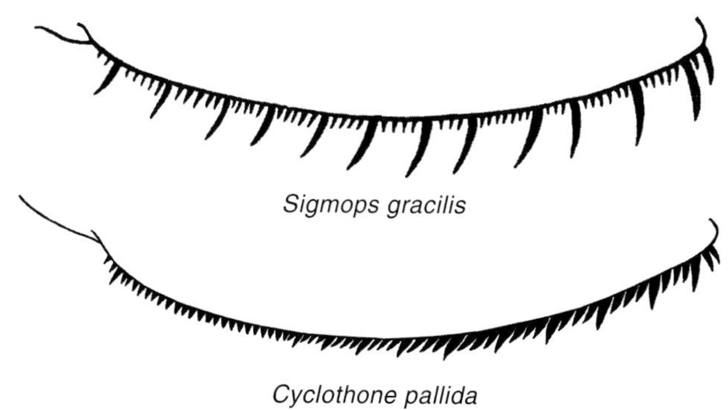

Maxillary teeth (left side) of *Sigmops* and *Cyclothone*
(After Grey 1964, Kawaguchi 1971.)

but they are never as long as in *Sigmops.* As well, species of *Sigmops* have more vertebrae (37–42) than *Cyclothone* (29–33). Most *Sigmops* have a dorsal adipose fin, but this fin is absent in the Alaskan species *S. gracilis,* as it is in *Cyclothone.*

Bristlemouths have 1 orbital photophore (ORB), always below the front of the eye. The anterior and posterior photophores (OV and VAL) in the lateral series can be difficult to differentiate in *Cyclothone,* as they may be continuous, and emphasis should be on counting the total number in the lateral series (OA). In Alaskan species the first OA is elevated. A dissecting microscope must be used to determine the full extent of the precaudal luminous glands, and damage to the skin, fading in preservative, and individual variation prevent their general use in identification. Alaskan bristlemouths have 2 opercular photophores (OP). Some species of *Cyclothone* have luminescent stripes between the OP, but the stripes are not always discernible.

The following key was constructed from characters used by Grey (1964), Mukhacheva (1964, 1974), and Kawaguchi (1971) in their keys.

Key to the Gonostomatidae of Alaska

1 SO present; ODM present; OA 11–21; anal fin rays 21–31; maxilla with a row of well spaced, long, slender teeth, and markedly shorter teeth in the interspaces .... *Sigmops gracilis,* page 213

1 SO absent; ODM absent; OA 6–10; anal fin rays 16–21; maxilla with a row of close-set, short teeth increasing in size posteriorly, some of them moderately enlarged .... genus *Cyclothone* (2)

2 (1) One gill raker in angle of first arch; gill rakers 12–15; body color white .... (3)

2 Two gill rakers in angle of first arch; gill rakers 18–24; body more or less colored .... (4)

3 (2) Gill filaments short, fused into wide convex band on hypobranchial; BR photophores 8; OA 6; VAV usually 3 (rarely 4); AC 11–12 .... *Cyclothone alba,* page 214

3 Gill filaments long, usually free along their entire length but sometimes fused into narrow band along hypobranchial, especially in fish caught in western part of range; BR photophores 9–10; OA 7; VAV usually 4 (rarely 3); AC 13–14 .... *Cyclothone signata,* page 215

4 (2) Skin densely pigmented dark brown or black ventrally as well as dorsally, anal fin pterygiophores and black peritoneum generally not visible externally .... *Cyclothone atraria,* page 216

4 Skin transparent, not pigmented or only lightly pigmented vemtrally, anal fin pterygiophores and black peritoneum visible externally .... (5)

5 (4) Gill rakers on first arch 18–20; gill filaments fused at base into obvious transparent band along ceratobranchial and into broad convex band along hypobranchial; first and second VAV photophores close together; dorsal fin base and dorsal half to three-fourths of body pigmented .... *Cyclothone pseudopallida,* page 217

5 Gill rakers on first arch 21–24; gill filaments mostly free, fused only at base into narrow band along ceratobranchial and hypobranchial; VAV photophores evenly spaced; dorsal fin base not pigmented or only lightly pigmented .... *Cyclothone pallida,* page 218

Sigmops gracilis (Günther, 1878) **slender fangjaw**

Bering Sea and Pacific Ocean, widespread in subarctic to subtropical waters mainly west of 143°W and north of 15°N; most abundant in western North Pacific at latitudes of southern Kuril Islands to Taiwan.

Near surface to depth of 4,389 m; primarily mesopelagic, usually taken at depths of 800 m or less; migrates toward surface at night; larvae and juveniles in upper 200 m.

D 10–14; A 26–30; Pec 9–10; Pel 7–8; GR 20–22; Vert 40–42.
SO 1; ORB 1; OP 2; BR 9; ODM 6; OA 11–14; IV 15; VAV 4–5; AC 17–19; IC 35–39.

- Dark brown or black, with metallic sheen; in life OA silvery blue, ICG reddish.
- Infracaudal luminous gland (ICG) present, consisting of 2 or 3 spots on short rays of caudal fin.
- **SO present**; **row of 6 widely separated ODM present**; OA 11 or more, irregularly arranged.
- Adipose fin absent; anal fin considerably longer-based than dorsal fin; **more anal rays than in *Cyclothone***; dorsal fin origin behind anal origin, above 4th or 5th anal ray.
- Scales absent, no trace of scale pouches.
- **Upper jaw teeth a series of widely spaced, slender fangs with short teeth in interspaces.**
- Anus posterior to midpoint of distance between pelvic fin base and anal fin origin.
- Length to 133 mm SL.

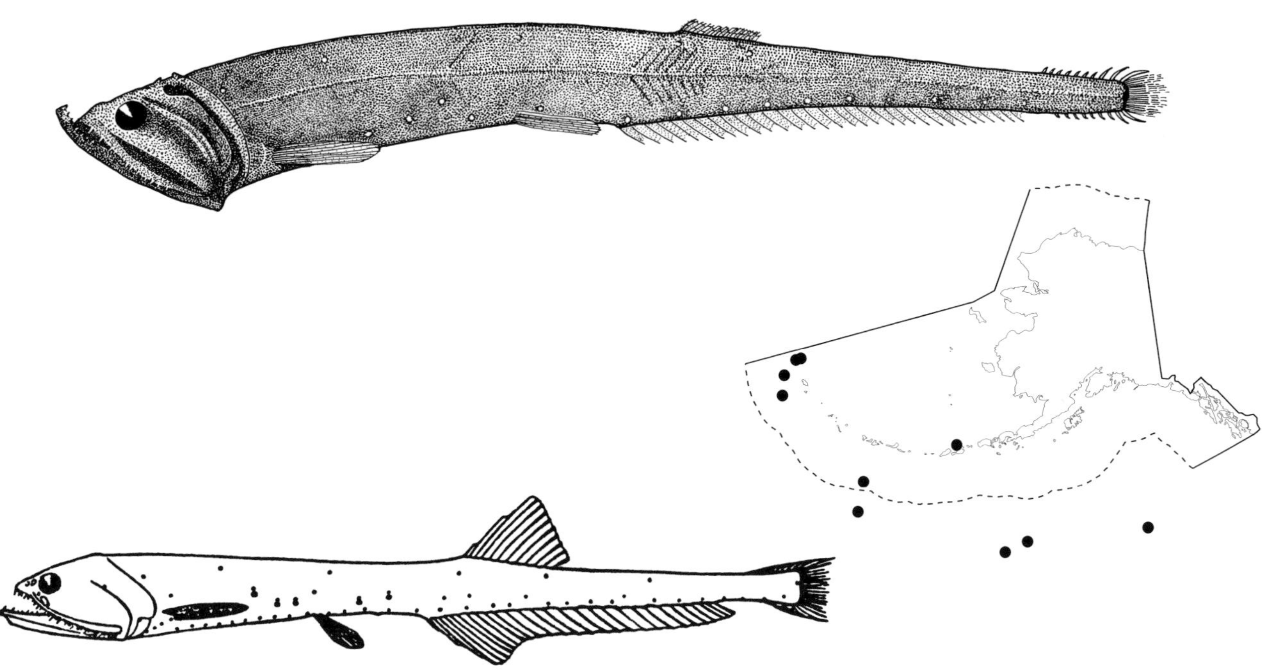

Notes & Sources — *Sigmops gracilis* (Günther, 1878)
Gonostoma gracile Günther, 1878
Miya and Nishida (2000) revised the classification of *Gonostoma*. They resurrected the genus *Sigmops* Gill, 1883 for the clade comprising five dark-colored species, leaving two light-colored species in *Gonostoma* Rafinesque, 1810.

Description: Kawaguchi 1971:418–419; Mukhacheva 1972: 225–229 (42–50 of transl.); Fujii in Masuda et al. 1984:45–46; Coad 1995:693–694.

Figure: Upper: Russian Academy of Sciences, Zoological Institute, St. Petersburg, artist O. S. Voskoboinikova, Dec. 2000; modified; ZIN 37577, 147 mm SL (specimen in poor condition, some photophores not discernible). Lower: Mukhacheva 1972, fig. 7; female, 102 mm SL, western Pacific Ocean (idealized diagram showing position of most photophores).

Range: Catch localities reported by Mukhacheva (1972) were mostly in the western Pacific and included three off the western Aleutian Islands: 54°30'N, 171°09'E; 52°23'N, 170°49'E; and 51°21'N, 172°14'E. A specimen in SIO 53-330 is from 53°55'N, 171°11'E; and SIO 51-371 is from south of Alaska at 48°48'N, 157°39'W. More-recent collections reported by Peden et al. (1985), although including a specimen from the eastern Pacific at 50°N, 145°W, substantiated greater abundance in the western Pacific, west of 177°W at latitudes of the southern Kuril Islands and Japan. Records plotted on a map summarizing available records by Willis et al. (1988, fig. 37) included localities north of Unalaska Island and south of the Aleutian Islands. Fedorov and Sheiko (2002) reported *S. gracilis* to be common in the vicinity of the Commander Islands.

Size: Largest of 677 adults measured by Mukhacheva (1972) was 133.2 mm SL.

Cyclothone alba Brauer, 1906 **white bristlemouth**

Bering Sea and western Pacific to Tasman Sea, east to about 140°W in tropical and subtropical North Pacific and to South America in South Pacific; widespread in Atlantic and Indian oceans.

Near surface to depth of about 4,000 m; primarily mesopelagic, mostly taken at 300–1,000 m.

D 12–14; A 17–20; Pec 9–10; Pel 6–7; GR 14; PC 4.
ORB 1; OP 2; BR 8; OV 6; VAL 0; OA 6; IV 13; VAV 3–4; AC 11–12; IC 28–29.

- **White, with dark pigment visible through transparent skin before vertical fins and between pterygiophores**; black pigment along branchiostegal rays and on base and margin of gill membranes; fewer large stellate melanophores on cheeks and body than in *C. signata.*
- Precaudal and cheek luminescent glands absent.
- Photophores larger than in most other species of *Cyclothone*; **BR photophores 8; VAV usually 3**; if VAV 4, last frequently at base of first anal fin ray; rarely 2 AC between anal fin and caudal fin; if AC 2, second at base of first caudal ray.
- Scales absent, no trace of scale pouches.
- Anus almost at pelvic fin base, much closer than midpoint between pelvic base and anal fin origin.
- **One gill raker in angle of first arch; gill filaments fused into wide convex band along edge of hypobranchial**.
- Length to 34 mm SL.

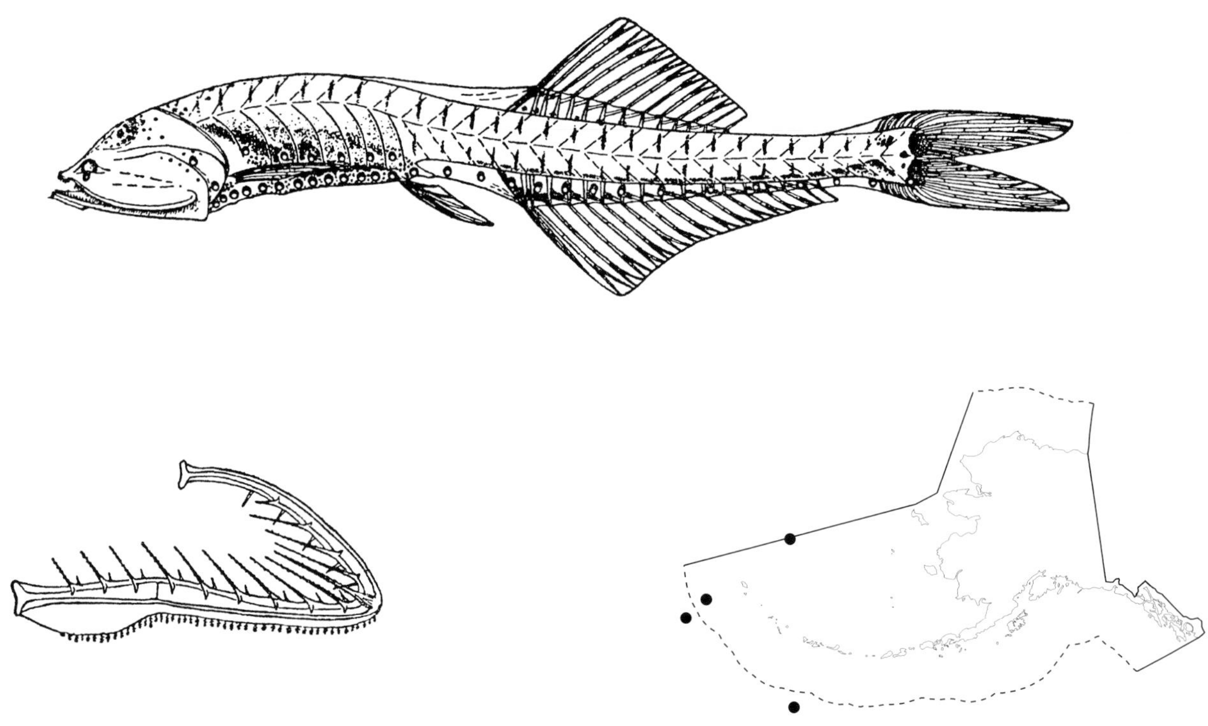

Notes & Sources — *Cyclothone alba* Brauer, 1906
Cyclothone signata var. *alba* Brauer, 1906

Description: Mukhacheva 1964:96–98 (101–104 of transl.), 1974:192–195; Kawaguchi 1971; Fujii in Masuda et al. 1984:46.

Figures: Mukhacheva 1964, fig. 2, modified; 22 mm SL, western Pacific; typical first gill arch.

Range: Mukhacheva (1964) recorded two specimens taken by the RV *Vitiaz* within the 200-mile limit off Alaska: one in Bering Sea at 57°49'N, 175°01'E (station 1557, in 1952), and one south of the Near Islands at 50°28'N, 171°00'E (station 3360, in 1954); as well as two just outside the limit at 48°48'N, 170°35'E (station 3363, in 1954), and 47°19'N, 175°57'W (station 4066, in 1958). *Cyclothone alba* primarily inhabits tropical and subtropical waters, but the nearly complete lack of northern North Pacific records could be due to confusion with the closely related *C. signata.*

Cyclothone signata Garman, 1899 — showy bristlemouth

Bering Sea and eastern North Pacific to South America at about 35°S, and west at tropical latitudes to 175°W; endemic to Pacific Ocean.

Near surface to depth of 1,000 m; primarily upper mesopelagic, mostly taken at 300–500 m.

D 12–14; A 17–20; Pec 9–10; Pel 6–7; GR 12–15; PC 3–4.
ORB 1; OP 2; BR 9–10; OV 7; VAL 0; OA 7; IV 13; VAV 3–4; AC 13–14; IC 30–31.

- **White, with dark pigment visible through transparent skin anterior to vertical fins and between pterygiophores**; black pigment along branchiostegal rays and on base and margin of gill membranes; large stellate melanophores on cheeks, back, and lateral midline in some fish.
- Precaudal and cheek luminescent glands absent.
- Photophores larger than in most other species of *Cyclothone*; **BR photophores usually 9**; **VAV usually 4, all evenly spaced**; 2 AC between anal fin and caudal fin, the second of these often at base of first caudal ray.
- Scales absent.
- Anus almost at pelvic fin base, much closer than midpoint between pelvic base and anal fin origin.
- **One gill raker in angle of first arch**; **gill filaments mostly free**; filaments sometimes fused, especially in individuals from western part of range, into narrow band along edge of hypobranchial.
- Length to 44 mm SL.

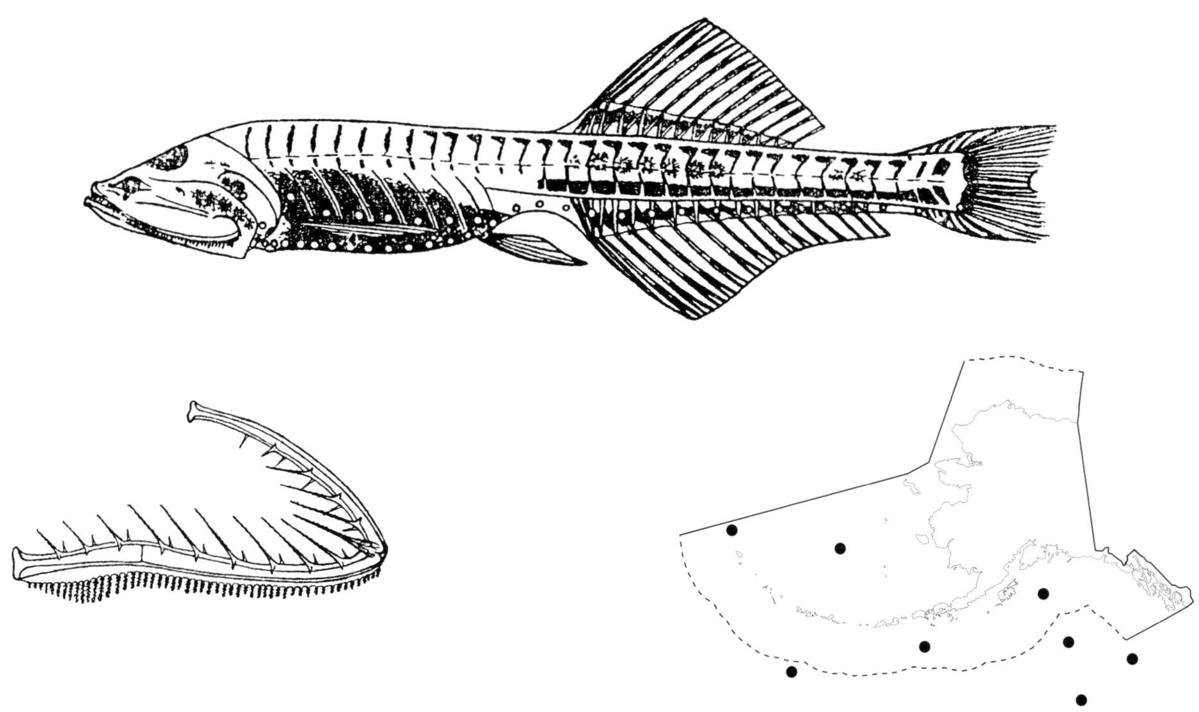

Notes & Sources — *Cyclothone signata* Garman, 1899

Description: Mukhacheva 1964:98–102 (104–105 of transl.), 1974:196; Kawaguchi 1971; Peden 1974:53–55; Peden and Hughes 1986:1–2.

Figure: Mukhacheva 1964, fig. 4, modified; 31.5 mm SL, tropical eastern North Pacific; typical first gill arch.

Range: Willis et al. (1988, fig. 11) reported occurrence of *C. signata* in 20 of 761 midwater tows in the North Pacific, including several broadly distributed off Alaska in the Bering Sea, Gulf of Alaska, and south of the Aleutian Islands. It is possible that some of these records represent *C. alba*. A specimen of *C. signata* from Canada's Ocean Station Papa (50°N, 145°W) reported by Peden et al. (1985) represented an extension northward of the range known at that time, from Cape Flattery, Washington (Peden 1974). Peden and Hughes (1986) reviewed British Columbia records; all were from the southern region of the province. Willis and Pearcy (1982) found that, off the coast of Oregon, *C. signata* was most abundant at 500 m both day and night but there was some evidence, agreeing with previous studies, that some individuals migrate from 500–600 m in the daytime into the upper 100 m at night.

Size: Largest of 281 specimens in SIO 93-261, taken in 1991 at 32°25'N, 127°44'W. Other large specimens are in SIO 87-22 (41 mm SL) and SIO 87-30 (40 mm SL), taken in 1986 at 32°50'N, 124°07'W. Previously recorded to 37.7 mm SL by Peden and Hughes (1986).

Cyclothone atraria Gilbert, 1905 **black bristlemouth**

Bering Sea and North Pacific, mostly north of Tropic of Cancer; Sea of Okhotsk; endemic to North Pacific.

Near surface to depth of 3,400 m; primarily lower mesopelagic and bathypelagic, mostly taken at 600–2,000 m.

D 12–14; A 17–20; Pec 9–10; Pel 6; GR 21–23; PC 3–4.
ORB 1; OP 2; BR 8–10; OV 7; VAL 2–3; OA 9–10; IV 13–14; VAV 5; AC 14–16; IC 32–34.

- **Dark brown or black**; densely pigmented, pterygiophores not visible externally; **area immediately anterior to anal origin densely pigmented externally and not transparent**; black peritoneum ending above area between 3rd and 4th VAV, usually not visible externally; specimens under 20 mm SL lighter, frequently with transparent but pigmented areas in front of dorsal and anal fins.
- SCG and ING present but weakly developed; luminescent strip between OP photophores.
- Photophores very small; OA rarely 10; **VAV 5**; last 3 AC between anal fin and caudal fin.
- Scales covering body, with **scale pockets usually detectable**.
- Anus at middle of distance between pelvic fin base and anal origin, or slightly posterior to middle, just before or beside 3rd VAV.
- **Two gill rakers in angle of first arch**; **gill filaments long and almost entirely free**.
- Pyloric caeca usually 3.
- Length to 62 mm SL.

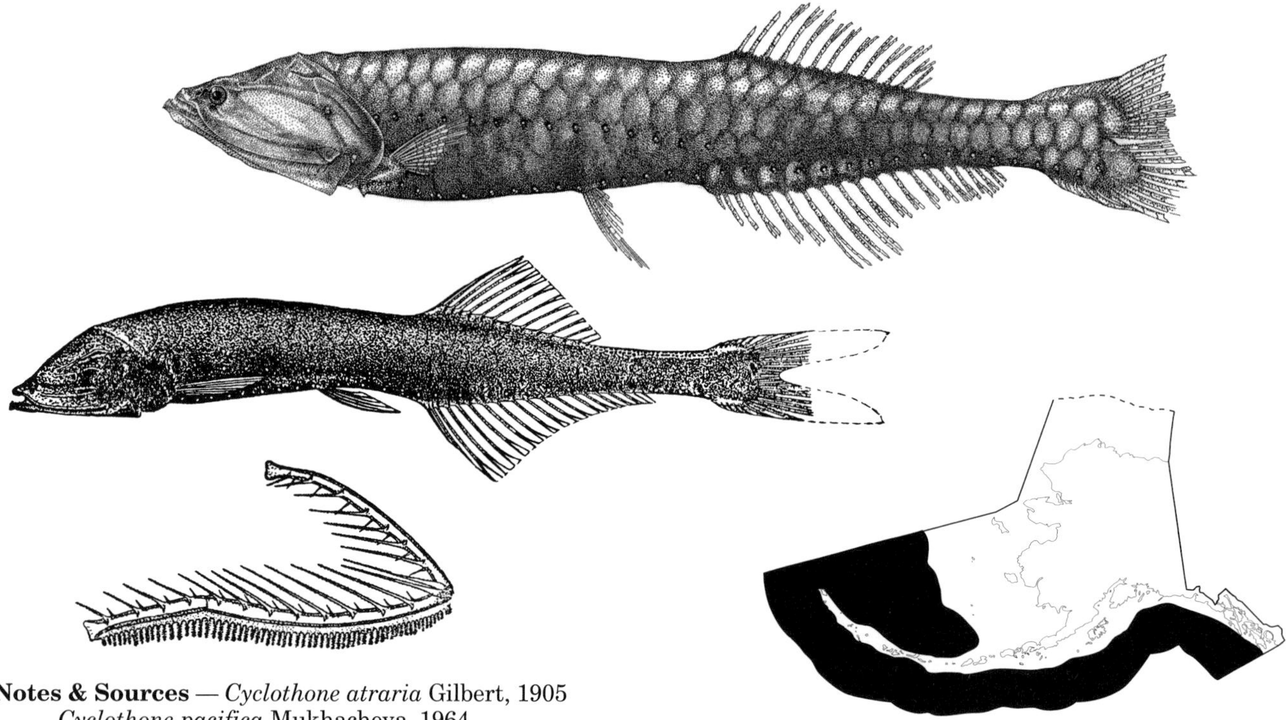

Notes & Sources — *Cyclothone atraria* Gilbert, 1905
Cyclothone pacifica Mukhacheva, 1964
Cyclothone microdon: North Pacific specimens only.
Mukhacheva (1964) included North Pacific records of *C. microdon* in *C. pacifica*, and later (Mukhacheva 1969, 1974) classified *C. pacifica* as a synonym of *C. atraria* after a study by Berry and Perkins (1966) and further work. The closely related *C. microdon* (Günther) has fused gill filaments and occurs in the South Pacific and Atlantic oceans.

Description: Gilbert 1905:605; Mukhacheva 1964:114–117 (121–124 of transl.), 1974:214; Kawaguchi 1971; Fuji in Masuda et al. 1984:46.

Figures: Upper: Smithsonian Institution, NMNH, Division of Fishes, artist M. Dalen; USNM 149537, 54 mm SL. Lower: Mukhacheva 1964, fig. 13, modified; 46.2 mm SL, Pacific Ocean north of Hawaii; typical first gill arch.

Range: Most abundant species of *Cyclothone* in the northern North Pacific. Chapman (1940) reported specimens large enough to be identified by adult characters were taken from the Shumagin Islands to the coast of Washington in 1926–1934 by International Pacific Fisheries Commission plankton hauls incidental to collecting halibut eggs and larvae. Mukhacheva (1964) recorded numerous catches in the Bering Sea and Pacific Ocean off southern Alaska, taken in midwater trawls by the RV *Vitiaz* in the 1950s. The northernmost catch was at 59°52'N, 168°17'W. Willis et al. (1988, fig. 25), summarizing data from other midwater trawls, reported *C. atraria* in 83 out of 761 tows, many in the Gulf of Alaska and southern Bering Sea. Stated by some authors to be absent off the coast of California, but numerous specimens taken off the California coast are currently in collections; e.g., at SIO. Museum specimens cataloged as *C. atraria* from near the Equator and in the South Pacific could be misidentified *C. microdon*. Fedorov and Sheiko (2002) gave maximum depth of 3,400 m.

Cyclothone pseudopallida Mukhacheva, 1964 — phantom bristlemouth

Bering Sea and North Pacific Ocean to South America and Australia; widespread in Pacific, Indian, and Atlantic oceans from about 60°N to 63°S, except absent from Seas of Okhotsk and Japan.

Near surface to depth of about 3,000 m; primarily mesopelagic, mostly taken at 200–1,000 m.

D 12–14; A 17–21; Pec 9–10; Pel 6–7; GR 18–20; PC 4; Vert 31–33.
ORB 1; OP 2; BR 9–11; OV 7; VAL 1; OA 8; IV 12–13; VAV 4–5; AC 14–15; IC 31–33.

- Body gray or grayish brown; skin over anal fin base transparent and not pigmented, pterygiophores visible externally, and patches of internal pigment visible between pterygiophores; **area immediately anterior to anal fin origin transparent**, lacking pigment externally; **border between dorsal, pigmented portion and ventral, unpigmented portion of body distinct**; black peritoneum ending above or just behind 2nd VAV, clearly visible through skin.
- SCG and ICG present but weakly developed.
- Photophores on body small, but larger than in *C. pallida* or *C. atraria*; **VAV usually 5, with first 2 closer together than others**; last 2 AC between anal fin and caudal fin.
- Scales present, but **scale pockets usually not detectable**.
- Anus much closer to pelvic fin base than to anal fin origin, usually between 2nd and 3rd VAV, rarely just before 2nd VAV.
- **Two gill rakers in angle of first arch**; gill rakers fewer (18–20) than in *C. pallida*; **gill filaments fused at base into noticeable transparent strip along ceratobranchial and broad convex band along hypobranchial**.
- Length to 58 mm SL.

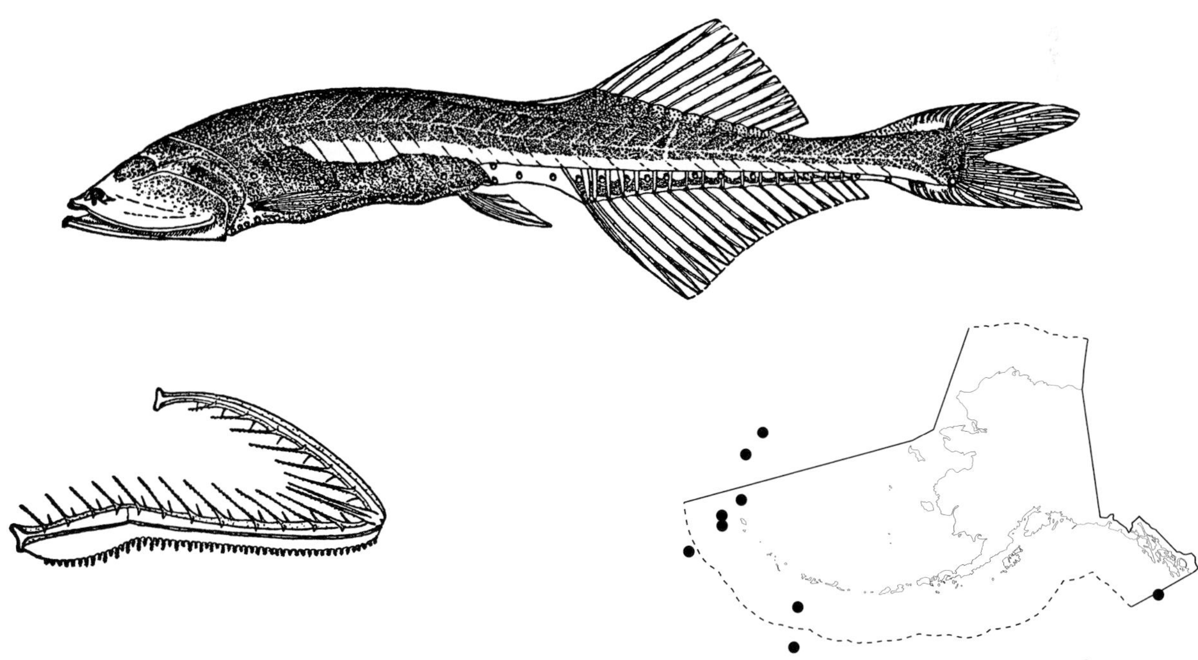

Notes & Sources — *Cyclothone pseudopallida* Mukhacheva, 1964

Description: Mukhacheva 1964:104–107 (110–113 of transl.), 1974:203–205; Kawaguchi 1971; Fujii in Masuda et al. 1984:46; Miya 1994.

Figures: Mukhacheva 1964, fig. 7, modified; 42.0 mm SL, western North Pacific; typical first gill arch.

Range: Mukhacheva (1964: Supplement) recorded several specimens taken in 1954–1958 in Alaskan waters and just outside the 200-mile limit by RV *Vitiaz*: 52°23'N, 170°49'E (station 3357); 51°52'N, 172°03'E (station 3358); 48°48'N, 170°35'E (station 3362); and 47°19'N, 175°57'W (station 4066). The northernmost catch reported by Mukhacheva (1964) was in the western Bering Sea at 59°03'N, 167°57'E (station 1599). Pearcy et al. (1979) reported a specimen from the western Bering Sea at 57°11'N, 169°05'E. SIO 53-330 is an Alaskan record, with three specimens taken in 1953 in the Bering Sea at 53°55'N, 171°11'E. Shinohara et al. (1994) recorded specimens taken in a beam trawl survey in 1988 in Alaskan waters south of the Aleutian Islands at 49°58'N, 176°57'W (HUMZ 114313), and just south of the Alaska border west of Dixon Entrance at 53°58'N, 135°31'W (HUMZ 114311). The latter record, published with diagnostic characters, substantiates occurrence in the Gulf of Alaska. Miya (1994), Kashkin (1995), and Miya and Nishida (1996) indicated it to be absent from the Gulf of Alaska. Additional northern records are those of Peden et al. (1985) from Ocean Station Papa; and Peden and Hughes (1986) from southern British Columbia. Not reported by Willis et al. (1988) in their summary of data from North Pacific midwater surveys (761 hauls). SIO 61-43, from 63°05'S, 178°44'E, may be the southernmost record.

Cyclothone pallida Brauer, 1902 — **tan bristlemouth**

Southern Bering Sea and North Pacific Ocean south of Aleutian Islands to South America and to Kuril Islands; widespread in warm waters of Pacific, Indian, and Atlantic oceans from 40°N to 40°S.

Near surface to depth of about 3,000 m; primarily mesopelagic and upper bathypelagic, mostly taken at 200–2,000 m.

D 12–14; A 17–19; Pec 9–11; Pel 6; GR 21–24; PC 4.
ORB 1; OP 2; BR 9–11; OV 7; VAL 1–2; OA 8–9; IV 13; VAV 4–5; AC 15–16; IC 32–34.

- Light brown or brown; skin over anal base transparent but sparsely pigmented, pterygiophores visible through skin, and spaces between pterygiophores not pigmented internally; **area immediately anterior to anal fin origin transparent**, sometimes sparsely pigmented externally; black peritoneum ending above area between 2nd and 3rd VAV, clearly observed through skin.
- SCG and ICG well developed; luminescent strip between OP photophores.
- Body photophores small, but larger than in *C. atraria*; **VAV usually 5, evenly spaced**; last 3 AC between anal fin and caudal fin.
- Scales present, but **scale pockets usually not detectable**.
- Anus much closer to pelvic fin base than to anal fin origin, usually between 2nd and 3rd VAV, rarely just before 2nd VAV.
- **Two gill rakers in angle of first arch**; more gill rakers (21–24) than in *C. pseudopallida*; **gill filaments free**.
- Length to 75 mm SL.

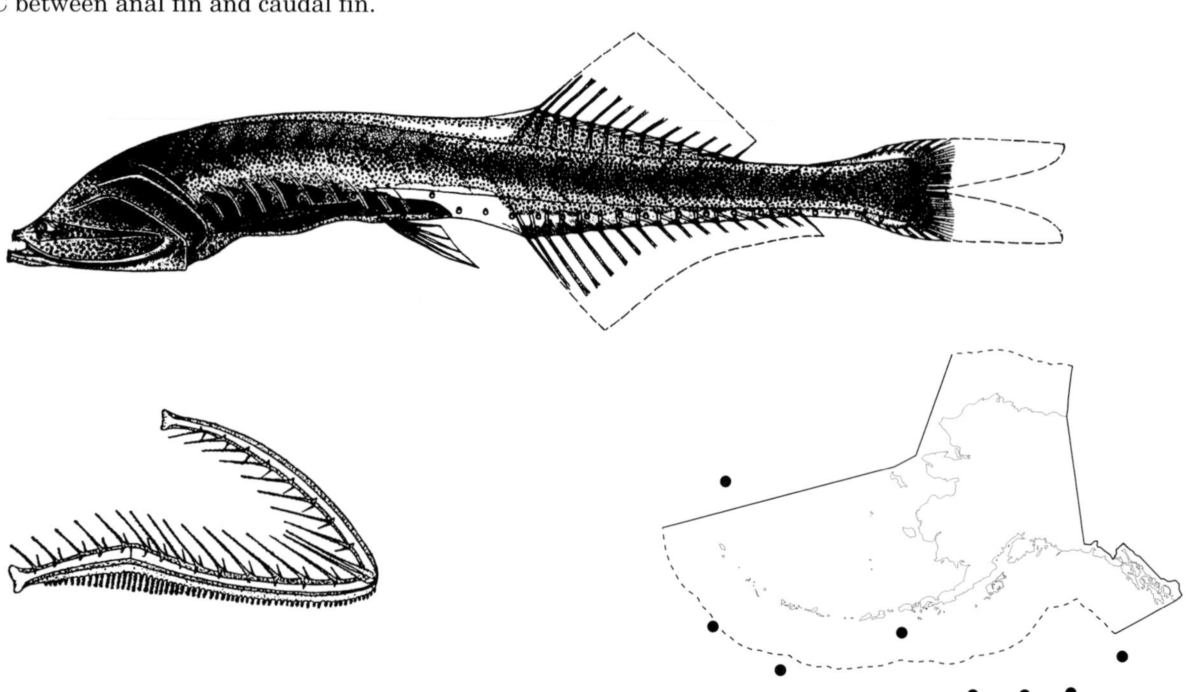

Notes & Sources — *Cyclothone pallida* Brauer, 1902

Description: Mukhacheva 1964:107–111 (113–117 of transl.), 1974:206–210; Kawaguchi 1971; Fujii in Masuda et al. 1984:46.

Figures: Mukhacheva 1964, fig. 9, modified; 38.0 mm SL, western North Pacific; typical first gill arch.

Range: Mukhacheva's (1964) Pacific Ocean data suggest that *C. pallida* is a more southern species than *C. pseudopallida,* but northern records of *C. pallida* have been accumulating. Records cited in her treatise on *Cyclothone* of the world (Mukhacheva 1974) extend in the Atlantic north to 62°N, and in the Pacific include a record from approximately 50°N, 155°W. Pearcy et al. (1979) reported a specimen caught in Russian waters at 57°11'N, 169°05'E, depth 520 m, to be the first Bering Sea record. Willis et al. (1988, fig. 26) reported *C. pallida* were found in 12 of 761 tows, with their map depicting 1 occurrence in Alaskan waters south of Unimak Island, 1 in the western Bering Sea which may be the same as Pearcy et al.'s (1979) record, and 4 in the Pacific south of the 200-mile limit. Peden et al. (1985) recorded *C. pallida* from Ocean Station Papa (50°N, 145°W) and noted that both *C. pallida* and *C. pseudopallida* occurred there. Peden and Jamieson (1988) recorded *C. pallida* from the Pacific off southern British Columbia at 48°08'N, 126°37'W. Kashkin (1995) and Miya and Nishida (1996) gave a range for *C. pallida* extending no farther north than 40°N, evidently overlooking the aforementioned records. *Cyclothone pallida* and *C. pseudopallida* can be difficult to differentiate and some records, especially older ones, are from misidentified material.

Size: Kobayashi 1973.

Family Sternoptychidae
Marine hatchetfishes

The Sternoptychidae, or marine hatchetfishes, are silvery, elongate- to deep-bodied, bioluminescent, meso- and bathypelagic fishes. They occur in all major oceans. The group includes 10 genera with a total of 57 species. The lowcrest hatchetfish, *Argyropelecus sladeni,* has been found in Russian waters of the western Bering Sea and off British Columbia in the eastern Pacific, and probably occurs within the 200-mile Exclusive Economic Zone off Alaska as well.

Hatchetfishes are distinguished from their close relatives the bristlemouths, family Gonostomatidae, by the presence of 6–10 branchiostegal rays (vs. 12–16), 6 branchiostegal photophores (vs. 7–16), and at least some of the serial photophores grouped together into compound light organs, appearing as black or silvery bands. Isthmus photophores are present. Hatchetfishes have well-developed pseudobranchs compared to other stomiiforms, in which they are reduced or absent. Nelson's (1994) classification divides the group into two subfamilies: the Sternoptychinae and the Maurolicinae. With their extremely deep, strongly compressed silvery bodies and nearly vertical mouths, the Sternoptychinae, for which some authors reserve the common name, hatchetfishes, are easily distinguished from other fishes. The Maurolicinae, sometimes called, simply, maurolicines, are elongate and never extremely compressed. The family takes its name from the Greek *sternon* (chest) and *ptyx* (plate), in reference to the bony abdominal keel present in some genera.

Argyropelecus sladeni belongs to the subfamily Sternoptychinae, which contains three phylogenetically divergent genera with a total of 43 species (Harold 1994). Species in the genus *Argyropelecus* have a "dorsal blade," which is the bony structure resembling a fin with spines immediately in front of the dorsal fin. The dorsal blade is actually composed of externally projecting supraneurals, or first-dorsal pterygiophores. *Argyropelecus* species have "telescopic" eyes, on tubes that fit into grooves in the frontal bone; an abdominal keel of bony scalelike plates below the abdominal photophores; and spines on the preopercle. In some species the anal fin is divided.

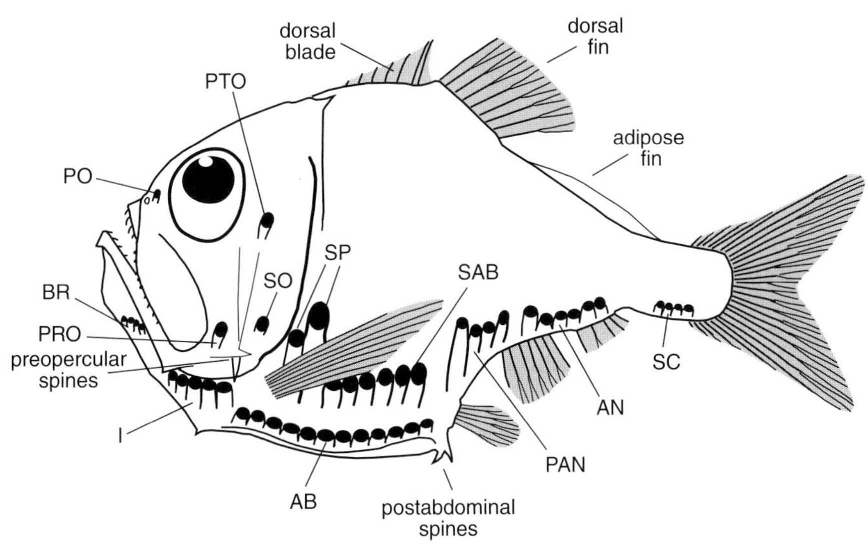

Photophores and spines of Sternoptychidae, particularly *Argyropelecus*
PO, preorbital; PTO, postorbital; PRO, preopercular; SO, subopercular; I, isthmus; BR, branchiostegal; SP, suprapectoral; SAB, supra-abdominal; AB, abdominal; PAN, preanal; AN, anal; SC, subcaudal.

Terminology used in this guide for photophores of Sternoptychidae is from Baird (1971). (Other systems are available; e.g., Harold 1994). The photophore configuration shown in the diagram above is typical for *Argyropelecus.* The characters in bold type in the species account distinguish *A. sladeni* from other species of *Argyropelecus,* particularly those in the *A. lychnus* complex (discussed on the next page). Preopercular spine characteristics in the *A. lychnus* complex are sometimes variable, and borderline cases occasionally occur. As well, due to the damage that many specimens in midwater collections sustain, all diagnostic characters are not always discernible.

Quast and Hall (1972) included *Argyropelecus lychnus* in their inventory as a potential addition to the Alaskan ichthyofauna on the basis of records that had been reported from British Columbia. Currently, *A. sladeni* is recognized as the species occurring in the region (e.g., Gillespie 1993, Peden 1998). It is worth recounting the history of local records and taxonomy of this species to prevent further misidentifications or misunderstanding the available literature. The local history begins with the first and revised first editions of *Fishes of the Pacific Coast of Canada,* in which Clemens and Wilby (1946, 1949) identified the first record of a hatchetfish from British Columbia, obtained by shrimp trawl in the Strait of Georgia in English Bay, as *A. olfersii.* Barraclough (1956) recorded the second British Columbia specimen, taken in a shrimp trawl off the mouth of the Fraser River, as *A. sladeni* and examined and referred the earlier specimen recorded as *A. olfersii* to *A. sladeni.* Consequently, in their later edition Clemens and Wilby (1961) referred British Columbia specimens to *A. sladeni,* including a third individual found on the beach at Pedder Bay, Sooke Harbour. In that same year, Schultz (1961b) revised the hatchetfish family. He classified *A. sladeni* as a subspecies in an *A. lychnus* complex including *A. l. lychnus, A. l. sladeni,* and *A. l. hawaiensis,* and considered *A. l. lychnus* to be an eastern Pacific form and *A. l. sladeni* to be a western Pacific form. However, Schultz (1961b) included Clemens and Wilby's (1946) record of *A. olfersii* in *A. lychnus lychnus,* evidently overlooking Barraclough's (1956) reexamination and referral of the specimen to *A. sladeni,* and second British Columbia record. No specimens from British Columbia or north of California were included in the lists of specimens examined by Schultz (1961b), and Clemens and Wilby's (1961) new edition was not yet available. Quast and Hall (1972) and Hart (1973) followed Schultz (1961b) and a later review by Schultz (1964), and referred northeastern Pacific specimens to *A. lychnus.* Unfortunately, a newer revision of the hatchetfishes, by Baird (1971), was not yet available. Baird (1971) recognized both *A. sladeni* and *A. lychnus* at the species level and classified *A. l. hawaiensis* in the synonymy of *A. sladeni.* He included *A. lychnus, A. sladeni,* and *A. olfersii,* as well as another very deep-bodied species, *A. aculeatus,* in the *A. lychnus* species complex. Harold (1993), in an analysis of the phylogenetic relationships of the species of *Argyropelecus,* agreed with Baird's assessment of this complex but added a fourth species, *A. hemigymnus.*

A problem with Baird's (1971) review, with respect to northern records of hatchetfishes, was perpetuation of Schultz's (1961b) mistake of including Clemens and Wilby's (1946, 1949) British Columbia record in the synonymy of *A. lychnus.* That this was unintentional is evident from Baird's (1971) text and map, giving a range for *A. lychnus* extending no farther north than California.

The similarity of appearance and complicated nomenclatural history of species in the *A. lychnus* complex have resulted in much confusion in identifying examples from the North Pacific, not just those from British Columbia. *Argyropelecus sladeni* occurs in both the eastern and the western North and South Pacific. *Argyropelecus lychnus* co-occurs with *A. sladeni* off the coast of California but is not known to occur farther north. *Argyropelecus olfersii* occurs in the northeastern North Atlantic to 65°N, but in the Pacific seems to be restricted to the South Pacific south of 30°S. *Argyropelecus aculeatus* and *A. hemigymnus* are widespread in the world's oceans but have not been found north of about 37°N and 45°N, respectively, in the Pacific.

Other hatchetfish species are found, albeit rarely, in the northeastern Pacific at latitudes of southern British Columbia, at the extremes of their subtropical–tropical ranges. These include the bottlelight, *Danaphos oculatus* (Maurolicinae), recorded by Peden and Hughes (1986) from 50°N, 128°W; this is the only known record north of Oregon. Peden (1974) recorded highlight hatchetfish, *Sternoptyx pseudobscura* (Sternoptychinae), off southern British Columbia; the species had previously not been known north of California. Those two species are not likely to be found in Alaska, but if they are it should be possible to identify them to genus by the following features. *Danaphos* is readily differentiated from *Argyropelecus* and *Sternoptyx* by its elongate body, greater number of anal fin rays (24–25), fewer dorsal fin rays (6), and different photophore pattern. *Sternoptyx* has the deep, compressed body of the Sternoptychinae but is distinguished from *Argyropelecus* by having normal eyes (not telescopic); a large, triangular, transparent membrane above the anal fin rays through which greatly enlarged pterygiophores are visible; 10 (vs. 12) abdominal photophores; and 3 (vs. 6) anal photophores (among other differences).

Argyropelecus sladeni Regan, 1908 **lowcrest hatchetfish**

Western Bering Sea; eastern Pacific off British Columbia to southern South America; western Pacific to New Zealand; widely found in temperate to tropical waters of Pacific, Indian, and Atlantic oceans.

At depths of 55–600 m; 100–375 m at night, 350–600 m during day; primarily mesopelagic.

D 9; A 12; Pec 10–11; GR 17–21; Vert 35–37.
PO 1; PTO 1; PRO1; SO 1; I 6; BR 6; SP 2; SAB 6; AB 12; PAN 4; AN 6; SC 4.

- **Distinct pigment spots along lateral midline**, especially evident in smaller specimens.
- SAB, PAN, AN, and SC photophores not in a continuous straight line; 1st PAN raised well above 2nd, which is even with or above 3rd; SC photophores closely spaced.
- Body and head strongly compressed; **body depth about 50% or less of standard length**.
- Eyes telescopic, lens dorsally oriented.
- Two separate postabdominal spines; **postabdominal spines small, about equal in length, with anterior spine squared off or blunt** (except in very small individuals).
- **Upper preopercular spine long, extending beyond posterior border of preopercle, and directed posteriorly and, usually, dorsally; lower preopercular spine directed ventrally and often slightly posteriorly**.
- **Dorsal blade low, height about 33% or less of its length**; anal fin gap with 3 haemal spines lacking pterygiophores.
- Scales below SC smooth, without spinules.
- Teeth small, recurved, no large canines present.
- Gill rakers medium to long, slightly dentate.
- Length to 67 mm SL.

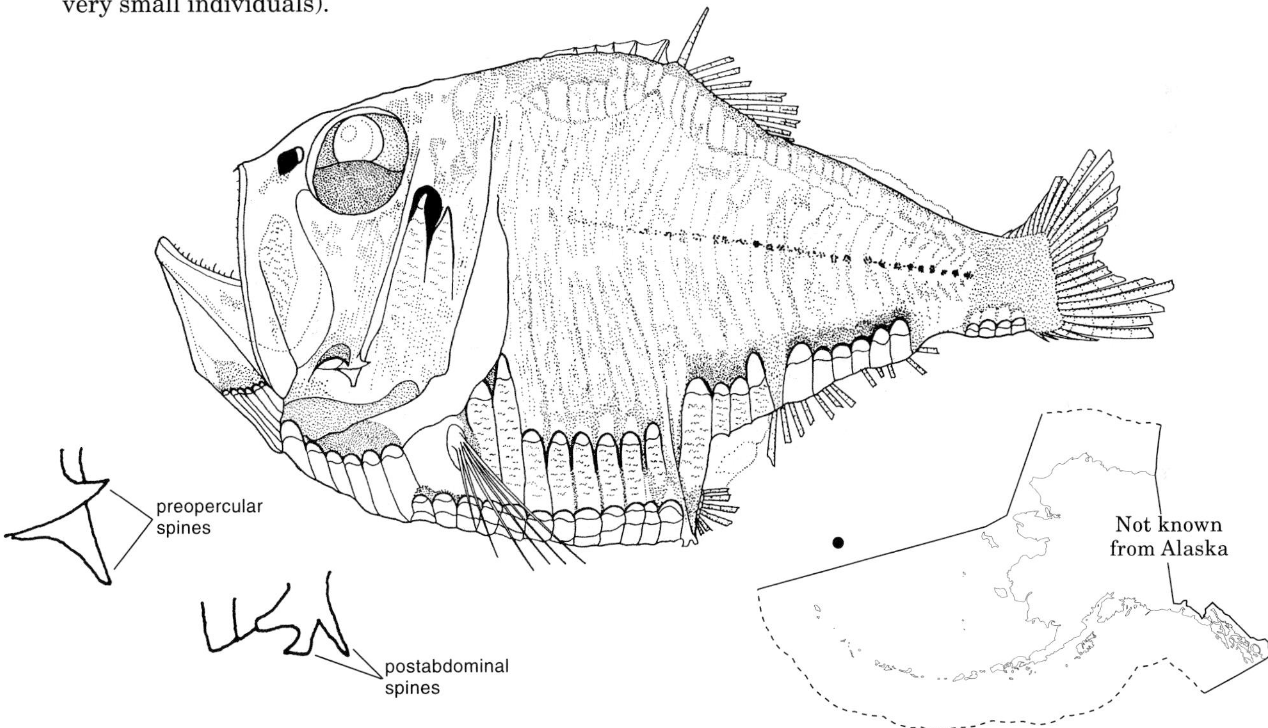

Notes & Sources — *Argyropelecus sladeni* Regan, 1908
Argyropelecus olfersii: British Columbia record of Clemens and Wilby (1946, 1949) (not of Cuvier, 1829).
Argyropelecus lychnus hawaiensis Schultz, 1961
Argyropelecus lychnus sladeni Schultz, 1961
Argyropelecus lychnus lychnus Schultz, 1961: in part; including British Columbia records cited by Hart (1973).

Baird (1971) revised *Argyropelecus*, recognizing *A. sladeni* and *A. lychnus* as distinct species. Harold (1993) concurred, and stated that *A. lychnus* co-occurs with *A. sladeni* off the coast of California with no evidence of interbreeding. As currently understood, *A. lychnus* does not occur much farther north in the Pacific than 35°N.

Description: Baird 1971:31–34, 56–63; Fujii in Masuda et al. 1984:48; Weitzman in Smith and Heemstra 1986:257; Balanov 1992:133.

Figures: Baird 1971, fig. 43; 43 mm SL. For a good photograph, see Shinohara et al. (1994:60). Illustrations in Clemens and Wilby (1946, 1961) and Hart (1973) show a combination of characters suggesting they were drawn from specimens or illustrations of more than one species.

Range: Nearest known occurrence is a 49-mm-SL specimen recorded by Balanov (1992) from 57°12'N, 171°02'E, over the Commander Basin, taken by trawl at 200–500 m. Next nearest records are from south of 50°N, including specimens taken off southern British Columbia (Clemens and Wilby 1946, 1961; Barraclough 1956); and beyond the 200-mile limit south of the western Gulf of Alaska (Shinohara et al. 1994). Minimum depth: Clemens and Wilby (1946, 1949), specimen from Strait of Georgia, British Columbia, taken in a shrimp trawl.

Family Stomiidae
Barbeled dragonfishes

The Stomiidae are photophore- and barbel-bearing, mainly deepsea, pelagic, predatory fishes. Formerly scattered in six families, the barbeled dragonfishes were combined into one family (Fink 1985) with about 230 species in 26 genera (Weitzman 1997). This guide treats six species, each in a different genus distributed among three subfamilies.

Features distinguishing the Stomiidae from other stomiiforms include the presence of only 1 suborbital bone, compared to 2–6; one or no supramaxilla; and photophores without ducts. Most species have a barbel on the underside of the head associated with the hyoid apparatus, and in some species the barbel has light organs. All stomiids have large mouths, with the gape extending well past the eye, and well developed teeth. In most species some of the premaxillary, maxillary, and mandibular teeth are long and fanglike, with some depressible. Stomiids lack vomerine teeth. The adults have no true gill rakers. Stomiid coloration is dark brown to black, providing strong contrast to the photophores. Most stomiids are under 30 cm (12 inches) in total length but at least one, *Tactostoma macropus,* reaches more than 41 cm (16 inches).

The Stomiinae, with scales or hexagonal scalelike markings, are represented in Alaska by *Chauliodus macouni,* a member of the tribe Chauliodontini, or viperfishes, in which the dorsal fin is far forward on the body, the first dorsal ray is greatly elongate, and dorsal and ventral adipose fins are present. Three other Alaskan species are in *Tactostoma, Bathophilus,* and *Pachystomias* of the Melanostomiinae, or scaleless black dragonfishes, which have the dorsal fin far back on the body and one or both adipose fins lacking. The Malacosteinae, or loosejaws, are represented in this guide by *Aristostomias* and *Malacosteus.* Members of this subfamily also lack scales, have the dorsal fin far back on the body, and lack adipose fins, but their most distinguishing feature is their mouth, with extremely long jaws and no floor. They can thrust their lower jaw far forward to impale prey on their fangs. Although included in Melanostomiinae in Nelson's (1994) classification, *Pachystomias,* with its near absence of a floor in the mouth, may be more closely related to the Malacosteinae.

Quast and Hall (1972) included four dragonfish species in their inventory: two confirmed and two likely to occur in Alaska. The two most well-known species in the region are Pacific viperfish, *C. macouni,* and longfin dragonfish, *T. macropus.* Shining loosejaw, *Aristostomias scintillans,* is still not known with certainty from the region, but there is one record of highfin dragonfish, *Bathophilus flemingi,* from the central Gulf of Alaska near the 200-mile limit. The present inventory includes two additional dragonfish species. Balanov and Fedorov (1996) recorded large-eye dragonfish, *Pachystomias microdon,* in Alaska over Bowers Ridge in the Bering Sea; and shortnose loosejaw, *Malacosteus niger,* near Alaska in Russian waters over the Commander Basin.

Key to the Stomiidae of Alaska

1		Dorsal fin toward front of body, first dorsal ray greatly elongated; dorsal and ventral adipose fins present	*Chauliodus macouni,* page 223
1		Dorsal fin far back on body, first dorsal ray not greatly elongated; no adipose fins	(2)
2	(1)	Pectoral fin absent	*Tactostoma macropus,* page 224
2		Pectoral fin present	(3)
3	(2)	Pelvic fins positioned high on side of body	*Bathophilus flemingi,* page 225
3		Pelvic fins positioned ventrally	(4)
4	(3)	Large photophore below eye, and smaller photophores anterior and posterior to eye; teeth not particularly large	*Pachystomias microdon,* page 226
4		Large photophore below eye, and photophore posterior to eye but no photophore anterior to eye; some teeth long and fanglike	(5)

5 (4) Hyoid barbel present; serial photophores well developed, conspicuous; 2 pairs of nostrils; largest orbital photophore anteroventral . . . . *Aristostomias scintillans,* page 227 (not known from Alaska)

5 Hyoid barbel absent; serial photophores poorly developed, inconspicuous; 1 pair of nostrils; largest orbital photophore posteroventral . . . . *Malacosteus niger,* page 228 (not known from Alaska)

Chauliodus macouni Bean, 1890 — **Pacific viperfish**

Bering Sea to Gulf of California and across North Pacific Ocean to Kuril Islands and Japan.

Primarily meso- to bathypelagic; reported at depths of 25–4,390 m, usually collected at 250–950 m.

D 6–7; A 10–13; Pec 10–13; Pel 7.
OV 17–20; VAL 24–28; OA 43–46; IP 9–11; PV 17–20; VAV 24–28; AC 9–14; IC 65–69.

- POSTORB elongate, triangular, located behind a vertical through posterior margin of orbit.
- Minute chin barbel sometimes present.
- **Dorsal fin well anterior to base of pelvic fin; dorsal ray 1 greatly elongated; dorsal adipose fin present**, above anal fin; **ventral adipose fin present**, in front of anal fin.
- Fanglike teeth on premaxilla and lower jaw; 3rd tooth on premaxilla longer than 4th.
- Length to 27 cm SL.

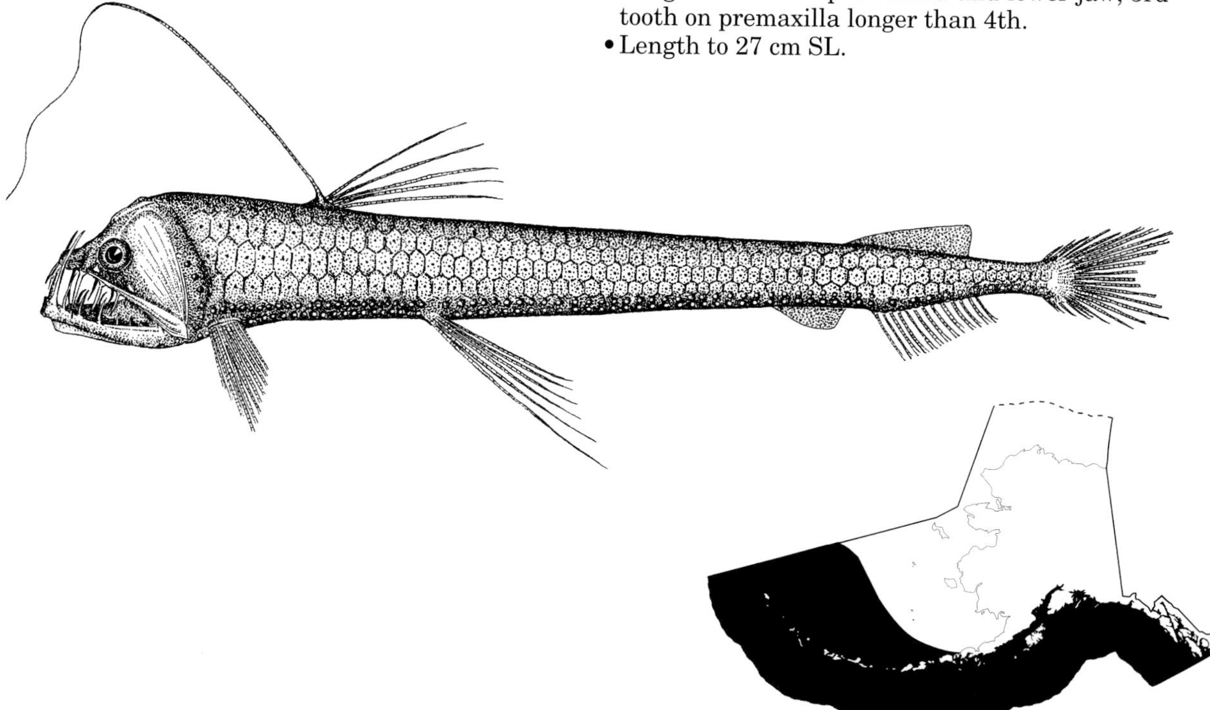

Notes & Sources — *Chauliodus macouni* Bean, 1890

Shape and position of the postorbital photophore and relative size of 3rd and 4th premaxillary teeth distinguish *C. macouni* from *C. sloani* Bloch & Schneider, 1801, known from warmer waters south of Alaska. In *C. sloani* POSTORB is round and located below or in front of a vertical through the posterior margin of the orbit, and the 3rd premaxillary tooth is shorter than the 4th.

Parin and Novikova (1974) revised the genus *Chauliodus.*

Description: Bean 1890b:44; Gilbert 1896:402; Chapman 1940:5–11; Barraclough 1950; Hart 1973:171–172; Parin and Novikova 1974:268–275; Fujii in Masuda et al. 1984:48.

Figure: Hart 1973:171; 22 cm TL, off British Columbia.

Range: Well documented from numerous records in Alaska. For example, Willis et al. 1988, fig. 24: taken in 258 out of 761 mesopelagic midwater tows in the North Pacific and Bering Sea. NMFS survey records plotted by Allen and Smith (1988) extended the known distribution farther north, over the continental slope to west of St. Matthew Island. Northern limit is not clear from the literature. Records in western Bering Sea extend as least as far north as 60°N (Parin and Novikova 1974). Maximum depth of 4,390 m was reported by Fedorov and Sheiko (2002).

Tactostoma macropus Bolin, 1939 **longfin dragonfish**

Bering Sea to southern California and across North Pacific Ocean to Japan and Sea of Okhotsk; more common in eastern North Pacific.

Primarily meso- and bathypelagic; recorded from depths of 25 m or less to 2,000 m, usually at 200–500 m.

D 12–18; A 15–20; Pec 0; Pel 9–10.
OV 43–44; VAL 18–20; IV 54–55; VAV 19–20; AC 11–12.

- **Body extremely elongate, almost cylindrical**; **lower jaw longer than upper and strongly curved upward**.
- Serial photophores small, numerous, arranged in parallel lateral and ventral lines; body and fins studded with small luminous flecks and patches.
- Chin barbel short, less than diameter of eye.
- Dorsal and anal fins far back on body; **pectoral fin absent**; pelvic fin low on body, long (but often partially torn off during collection); adipose fins absent.
- Numerous large teeth in multiple groups; fang-like teeth along each side of tongue.
- Length to 41 cm SL.

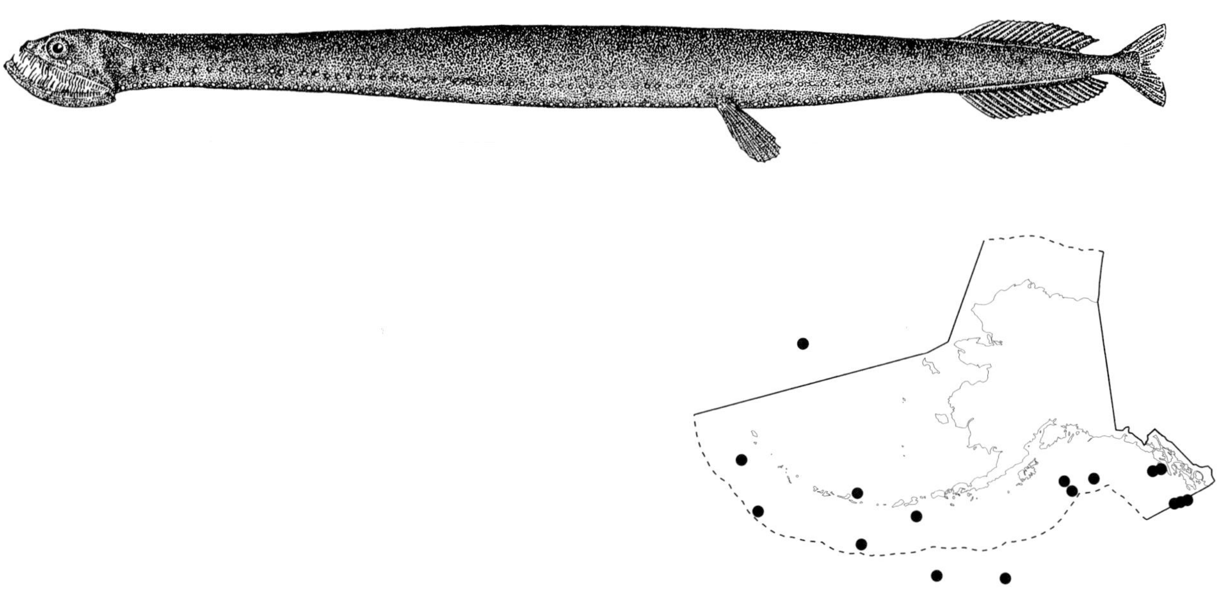

Notes & Sources — *Tactostoma macropus* Bolin, 1939

Description: Bolin 1939a; Hart 1973:167–168; Amaoka et al. 1983:182; Fujii in Masuda et al. 1984:52; Balanov et al. 1995:93–94.

Figure: Hart 1973:167; about 17 cm, composite.

Range: Willis et al. 1988, fig. 19: taken in 156 midwater tows out of 761, distributed widely in Gulf of Alaska and North Pacific; Alaskan localities were one just north of the eastern Aleutian Islands and others south of the chain and west to the west-central Aleutians. Shinohara et al. (1994) reported additional North Pacific records, including some south of the Aleutian Islands at 48°50'N, 178°17'E and 47°26'N, 174°56'W. Il'insky et al. (1995) recorded *T. macropus* relatively far north in the Bering Sea, at 60°37'N, 172°26'E, and noted that its occasional presence in the Bering Sea may be due to transport from Pacific waters through Aleutian Island passes (supported by low abundance in the Bering Sea and localized distribution in the vicinity of major currents). Quast and Hall (1972) recorded *T. macropus* from southeastern Alaska (two specimens in Auke Bay Laboratory museum), and Hart (1973) recorded it off Cape Spencer, Alaska. On 16 Jul. 2000 between 1406 and 1438 hours the USFWS research vessel *Tiglax* captured a 240-mm-TL specimen in a modified herring trawl towed at depths of 15–25 m in Sitka Sound between St. Lazaria and Kruzof islands at 57°00'N, 135°43'W. This catch represents a new minimum depth record for the species. Hart (1973) reported a minimum depth of 31 m. The *Tiglax* specimen, currently in C.W.M. and T.A.M.'s reference collection, will be deposited in the UAF permanent collection.

Size: Il'insky et al. 1995.

Bathophilus flemingi Aron & McCrery, 1958 **highfin dragonfish**

Gulf of Alaska and eastern North Pacific Ocean to Baja California.

Primarily meso- and bathypelagic, recorded from depths less than 60 m to 1,372 m.

D 15–16; A 16–17; Pec 4–7; Pel 15–19; Vert 44–48.
OV 13–17; VAL 12–14; IP 4–5; PV 6–17; VAV 6–13; AC 4–7.

- Folds along ventral surface of body.
- Serial photophores difficult to count due to damage, epidermis readily flaking off; **OV photophores arching to a level above pelvic fin base, VAL resuming below pelvic base**.
- Barbel long, up to 4 times body length; barbel without enlarged, bulbous tip.
- **Pelvic fin placed high on side of body**; pectoral and pelvic fin rays long and fragile; adipose fins absent.
- Teeth large, sharp, widely spaced.
- Length to 16.5 cm TL.

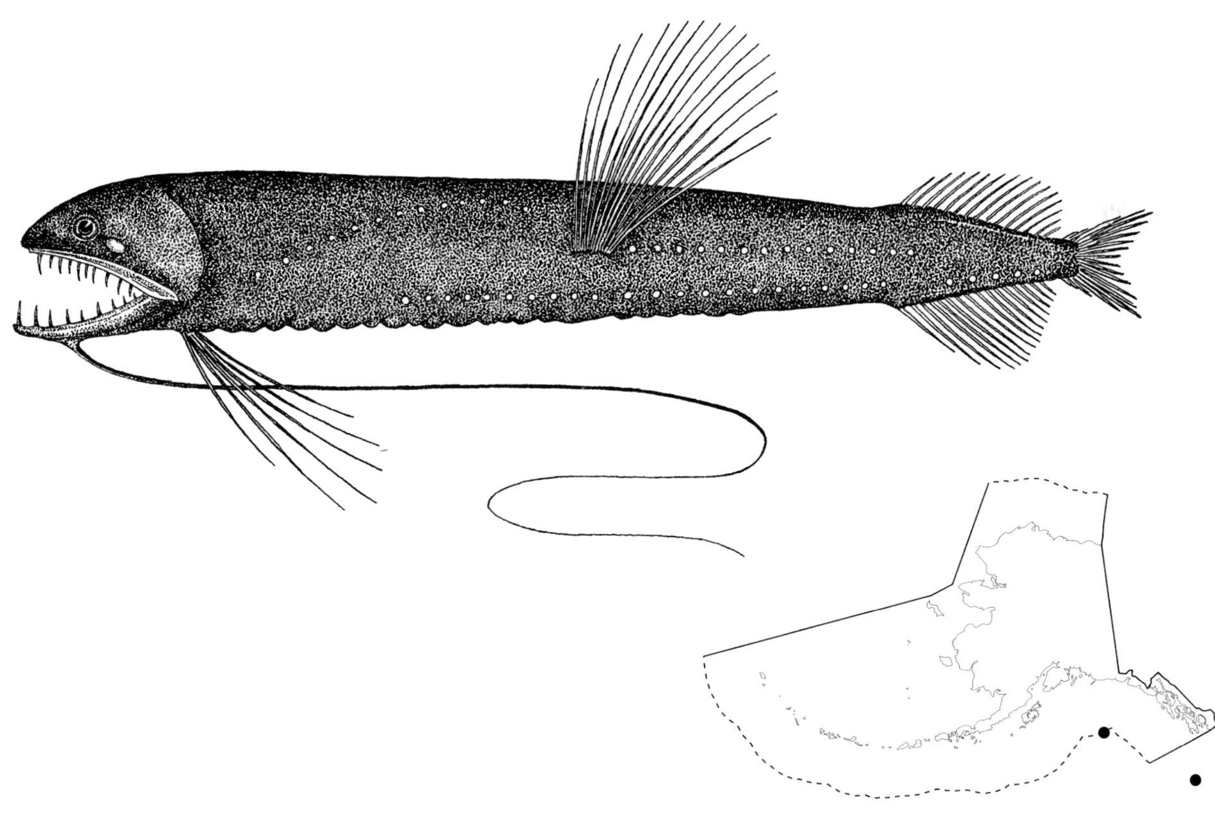

Notes & Sources — *Bathophilus flemingi* Aron & McCrery, 1958

Description: Aron and McCrery 1958; Barnett and Gibbs 1968; Hart 1973:165–166.

Figure: Hart 1973:165; 13 cm TL, Bowie Seamount.

Range: Willis et al. 1988, fig. 4: taken in 25 of 761 midwater tows in the North Pacific, including one record from approximately 56°N, 144°W, just outside or on the imaginary line delimiting the 200-mile Exclusive Economic Zone off Alaska; the rest were in the northeastern Pacific at northern British Columbia latitudes and southward. Taylor (1967a) recorded *B. flemingi* from about 50 miles southwest of Tasu Sound and from Bowie Seamount, about 52°30'N, 136°20'W. Recorded from Canada's Ocean Station Papa (50°N, 145°W) at depths less than 60 m during night tows by Peden et al. (1985).

Pachystomias microdon (Günther, 1878) **large-eye dragonfish**

One record from southern Bering Sea over Bowers Ridge; widespread in Pacific and Atlantic oceans.

Meso- to bathypelagic; recorded to depth of 4,463 m, possibly migrating toward surface at night.

D 21–24; A 23–29; Pec 4–6; Pel 7–9; Vert 48–53.
OV 17–19; VAL 12–16; OA 30–33; IP 8–9; PV 14–18; VAV 12–16; AC 8–11; IC 42–49.

- Eye large, snout equal to or shorter than eye; nostrils paired.
- Fold of skin connecting branches of lower jaw anteriorly; behind this, a thin transparent membrane connecting right and left rami and forming floor of mouth.
- **SUBORB large and sausage-shaped**, rose or greenish yellow; **small patch anterior to eye**, of same color, apparently part of SUBORB; small red **POSTORB well behind eye**, just above upper jaw.
- Serial photophores violet to red, in ventral and lateral series divided by spaces into groups; skin with minute scattered organs, especially on head.
- Barbel tapering to filament, 3–50% of standard length, generally decreasing with growth.
- Pelvic fin low on body; adipose fins absent.
- **Teeth not particularly large**; jaw teeth uniserial, slender, curved.
- Length to more than 22 cm SL.

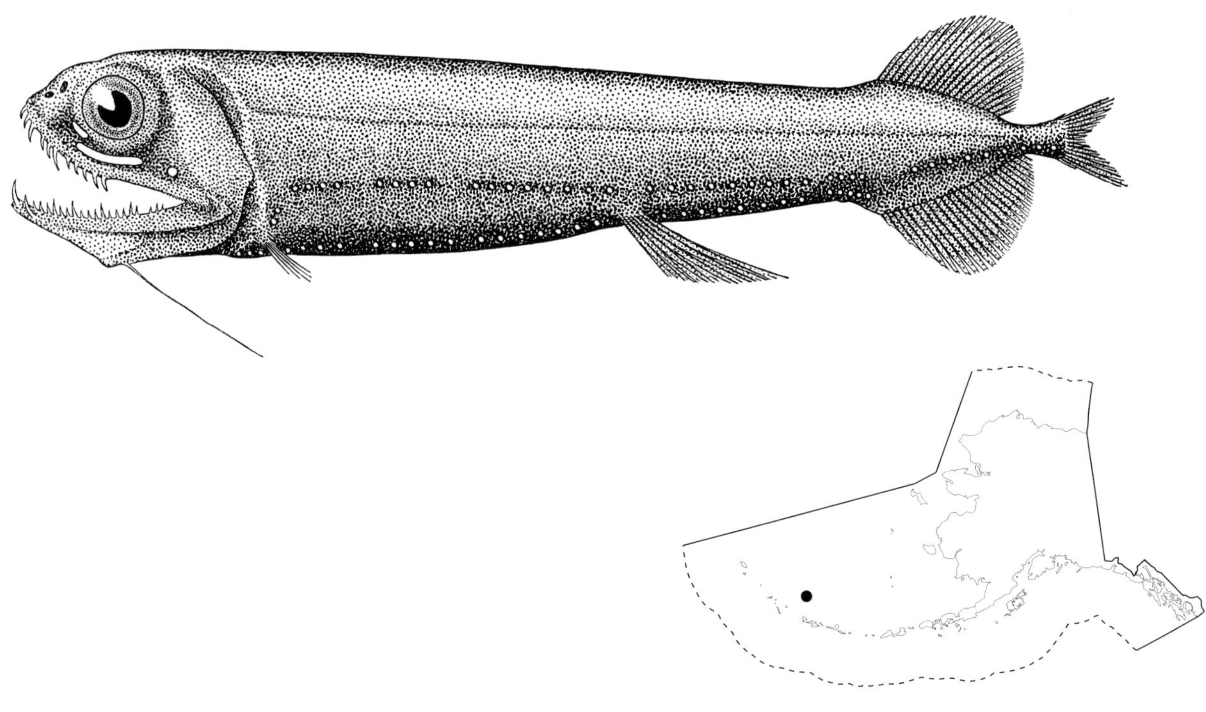

Notes & Sources — *Pachystomias microdon* (Günther, 1878)
Echiostoma microdon Günther, 1878
Pachystomias atlanticus Regan & Trewavas, 1930
Called "largeye" by Coad (1995). The French vernacular is *drague grands-yeux.*

Description: Regan and Trewavas 1930:70–71; Morrow and Gibbs 1964:374–377; Fujii in Masuda et al. 1984:51–52; Gibbs in Whitehead et al. 1986:361.

Figure: Regan and Trewavas 1930, pl. 6, fig. 1; holotype of *Pachystomias atlanticus,* 165 mm SL.

Range: Balanov and Fedorov (1996) recorded the first specimen collected in Alaska: a male measuring 169 mm SL, taken at 53°32'N, 179°19'W, in a net towed from depth of 1,000 m up to 500 m. There are no records from adjacent waters. Nearest record in the eastern Pacific may be SIO 71-296 from the North Central Gyre at 27°27'N, 155°27'W, a specimen measuring 183.5 mm SL. Nearest records in the western Pacific are from Japan and Australia. Known mainly from tropical and subtropical regions.

Aristostomias scintillans (Gilbert, 1915) **shining loosejaw**

Northeastern North Pacific Ocean west of southern British Columbia to latitudes of central Baja California. Primarily meso- to bathypelagic, recorded at depths of 29–1,008 m.

D 21–23; A 25–29; Pec 4–5; Pel 4–7.

- Eye relatively small, **snout longer than eye**; **nostrils paired**.
- Hyoids and mandibular symphysis connected only by a single muscular cord; no floor in mouth.
- Large, red **SUBORB anteroventral in position**; small, green POSTORB with anterior edge under posterior edge of eye.
- Serial photophores forming lateral and ventral series low on body, lateral series not elevated anteriorly; serial counts uncertain due to damage to specimens; numerous minute luminous bodies on head, body, and fins.
- **Barbel long**, extending more than half of body length, with enlarged, luminous pink tip.
- Pectoral and pelvic fin rays free of membranes; pelvic fin low on body; adipose fins absent.
- Teeth long and sharp, some fanglike.
- Length to 23 cm TL.

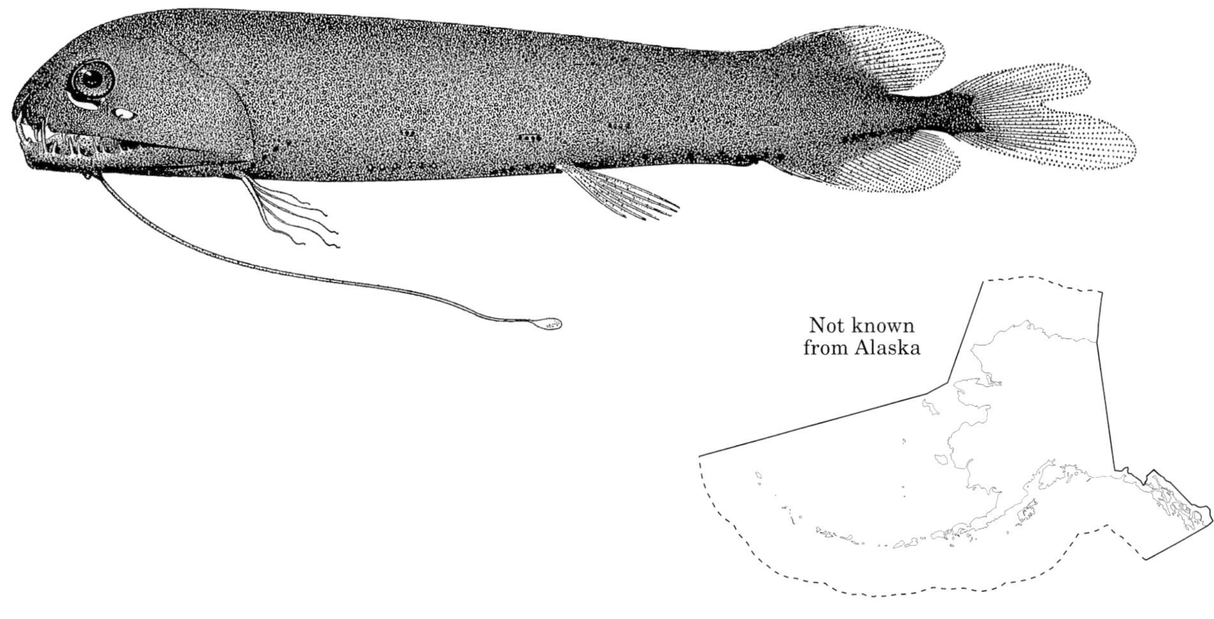

Notes & Sources — *Aristostomias scintillans* (Gilbert, 1915)
Zastomias scintillans Gilbert, 1915

Description: Gilbert 1915:322–323; Regan and Trewavas 1930:138–139; Hart 1973:169–170.

Figure: Gilbert 1915, pl. 15, fig. 4; holotype, 72 mm SL, Monterey Bay, California.

Range: Matarese et al. (1989) gave a range to Bering Sea for *A. scintillans,* but this may have been an estimate. We found no records of this species from the Bering Sea. The northernmost adequately documented occurrence in the Pacific Ocean may be a specimen reported by Aron (1960), from west of southern British Columbia at 50°13'N, 138°26'W. It was collected at a depth of 29 m, the minimum depth known for the species. The maximum depth reported is 711–1,008 m, for the holotype, captured off California (Gilbert 1915). Daylight tows at Ocean Station Papa that descended to depths of 600 or 800 m captured *A. scintillans*; night tows at depths less than 60 m captured smaller specimens (Peden et al. 1985).

Malacosteus niger Ayres, 1848 **shortnose loosejaw**

Western Bering Sea; eastern North Pacific Ocean at 50°N, 145°W; worldwide from subarctic to tropical waters, recorded from 66°N to 20°S in Atlantic Ocean.

Meso- and bathypelagic, recorded at depths of 200–3,886 m.

D 14–21; A 17–23; Pec 2–5; Pel 6–7; Vert 47–49.
OA 7–15; IC 12–22.

- **Snout very short, less than half of eye**; **one pair of nostrils**.
- Hyoids and mandibular symphysis connected only by a single muscular cord; lower jaw not connected by membrane to isthmus, leaving floor of mouth open.
- Large, dark red, comma-shaped **SUBORB below and slightly behind eye**; green POSTORB well behind eye; POSTORB more than 25% diameter of eye in specimens of 100 mm or over.
- Photophores on body and branchiostegal membranes small, inconspicuous, single or in small groups.
- **Barbel absent**.
- Pelvic fin low on body; adipose fins absent.
- Teeth long and sharp, some fanglike; fangs in lower jaw much longer than those in upper jaw.
- Length to almost 24 cm SL.

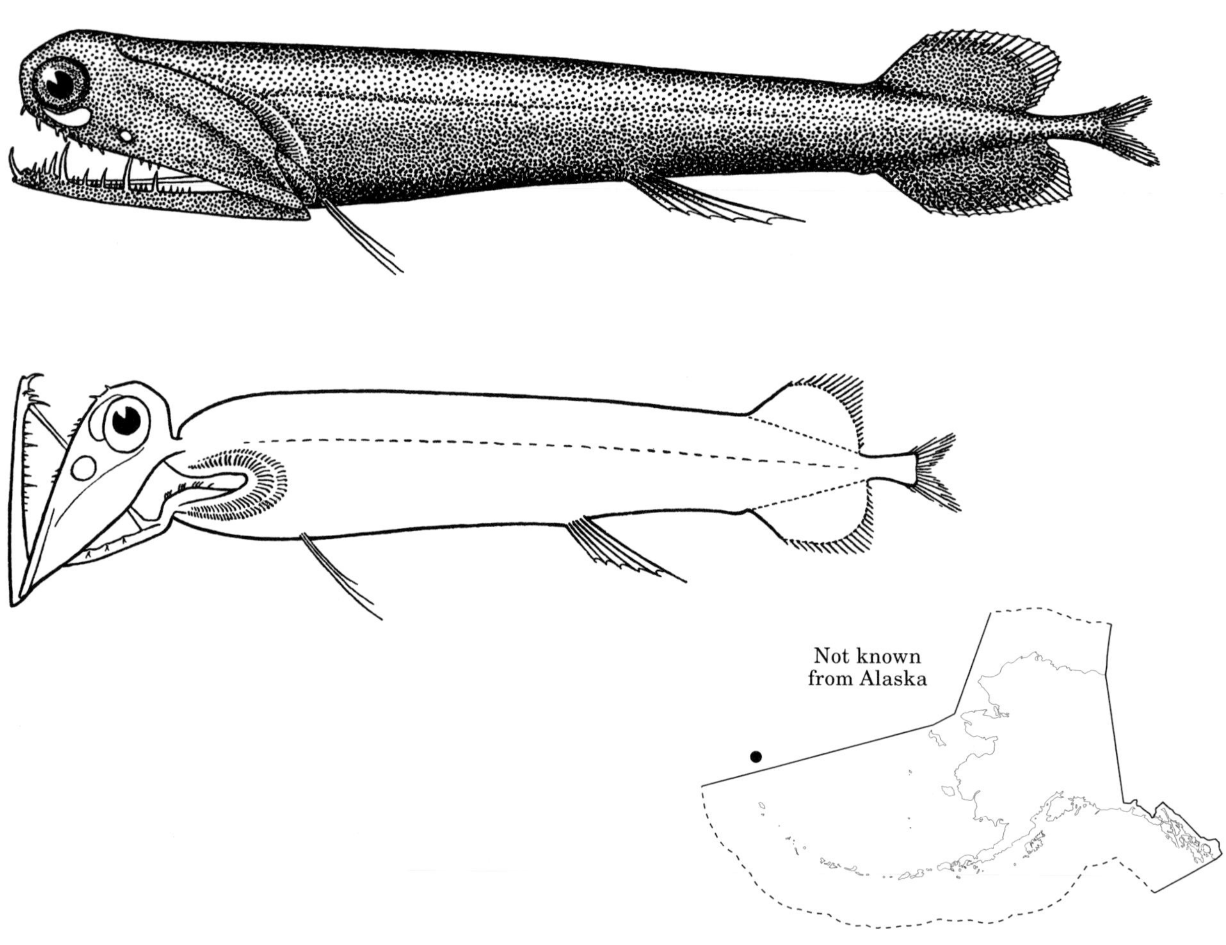

Notes & Sources — *Malacosteus niger* Ayres, 1848
Malacosteus danae Regan & Trewavas, 1930

Description: Regan and Trewavas 1930:142–143; Morrow 1964:545–548; Fujii in Masuda et al. 1984:53; Gibbs in Whitehead et al. 1986:369; Nielsen and Schwägermann in Okamura et al. 1995:94.

Figures: Upper: Regan and Trewavas 1930, pl. 14, fig. 1; Gulf of Panama. Lower: Ibid, fig. 138.

Range: Balanov and Fedorov (1996) recorded a 176-mm-SL specimen from western Bering Sea at 55°58'N, 169°02'E, in tow from 500 m to 200 m. Recorded from Canada's Ocean Station Papa by Peden et al. (1985); nearest previous record was California. Maximum depth: Machida in Okamura and Kitajima 1984.

ORDER AULOPIFORMES
Aulopiforms

Aulopiforms are benthic and pelagic predatory fishes that until recently were classified in the order Myctophiformes (Neoscopelidae and Myctophidae). Most of the aulopiforms lack photophores, and the group exhibits a wide range of shapes and sizes. The Alaskan aulopiforms are moderately to markedly elongate and range in recorded maximum length from about 24 cm (9.5 inches), found in slender barracudina, *Lestidiops ringens,* to 230 cm (91 inches) in longnose lancetfish, *Alepisaurus ferox.* Although the adults of most aulopiform species are benthic some species have reentered the pelagic realm. All 8 of the aulopiform species occurring in Alaska are pelagic, but this number represents only a small portion of the order, which has about 220 species in 42 genera.

Taxonomically the Aulopiformes is defined by internal features, including certain specializations of the gill arches, absence of a swim bladder, and fusion of the medial processes of the pelvic girdle. Like other lower teleosts, aulopiforms have only soft rays in the fins (no spines). The pectoral fins are set low on the body compared to high on the side in myctophiforms. The dentition is highly variable, with upper jaw teeth in 1 row, generally small, and numerous; lower jaw teeth absent in some species and in 2–4 rows in others, with the innermost teeth depressible when present; and palatine teeth in 1 or 2 rows. Normal gill rakers are lacking, replaced by teeth on bony plates. Several of the aulopiform families are synchronous hermaphrodites, with functional ovotestes.

Relationships within the order were examined through a cladistic analysis of 118 morphological characters by Baldwin and Johnson (1996) which suggested a somewhat different classification of suborders and families than used in this guide following Nelson (1994). Reverting, in part, to previous classifications (e.g., Rosen 1973), they moved the family Scopelarchidae from the suborder Chlorophthalmoidei to the suborder Alepisauroidei, and reassigned *Anotopterus* to the family Paralepididae (included by Nelson in Anotopteridae).

FAMILY SCOPELARCHIDAE
Pearleyes

Pearleyes have more or less tubular, upward-directed eyes with a glistening, pearly area on the eyeball. The systematics and distribution of pearleyes were studied by Johnson (1974, 1982), who recognized 17 species in four genera. Two cold-water species endemic to the North Pacific occur off southern Alaska. *Benthalbella linguidens* may be restricted to oceanic waters and is known in Alaska from only one record, while *B. dentata* inhabits both coastal and oceanic waters and is caught fairly frequently in Alaska.

Pearleyes have compressed bodies, cycloid scales, dorsal adipose fins, strong teeth on the tongue, and well-developed pseudobranchs. Pelvic fin rays are invariably 9, and branchiostegal rays 8. The most important meristic characters used to distinguish the species are counts of the dorsal, anal, and pectoral fin rays; lateral line scales; and vertebrae. Positions of the anal and adipose fins and relative length of the pectoral fins are also helpful in differentiating the two Alaskan species.

Longfin pearleye, *Benthalbella linguidens,* is new to the inventory since Quast and Hall (1972) tallied the Alaskan species. Peden et al. (1985) recorded a specimen collected over Surveyor Seamount, in the eastern Gulf of Alaska west of Baranof Island.

Key to the Scopelarchidae of Alaska

1 Adipose fin posterior to a vertical line drawn through base of last anal fin ray; dorsal fin rays usually 6 or 7; anal fin rays 17–21; lateral line scales 54–58 . . . . *Benthalbella dentata,* page 230

1 Adipose fin anterior to a vertical line drawn through base of last anal fin ray; dorsal fin rays usually 8 or 9; anal fin rays 26–30; lateral line scales 65–67 . . . . *Benthalbella linguidens,* page 231

Benthalbella dentata (Chapman, 1939) **northern pearleye**

Southern Bering Sea and Gulf of Alaska to Pacific Ocean off Baja California and Japan, including midocean and Seas of Okhotsk and Japan.

Mesopelagic; recorded from depths of 90–1,340 m, adults usually taken deeper than 500 m.

D 6–8; A 17–21; Pec 20–25; LLs 54–58; Vert 54–55.

- **Adipose fin posterior to a vertical through insertion of anal fin.**
- Dorsal fin rays usually 6 or 7; anal fin base short (compared to *B. linguidens*); pectoral fin reduced in size, rays short and slender.
- **Lateral line scales fewer than in *B. linguidens*.**
- Length to 28 cm TL or more.

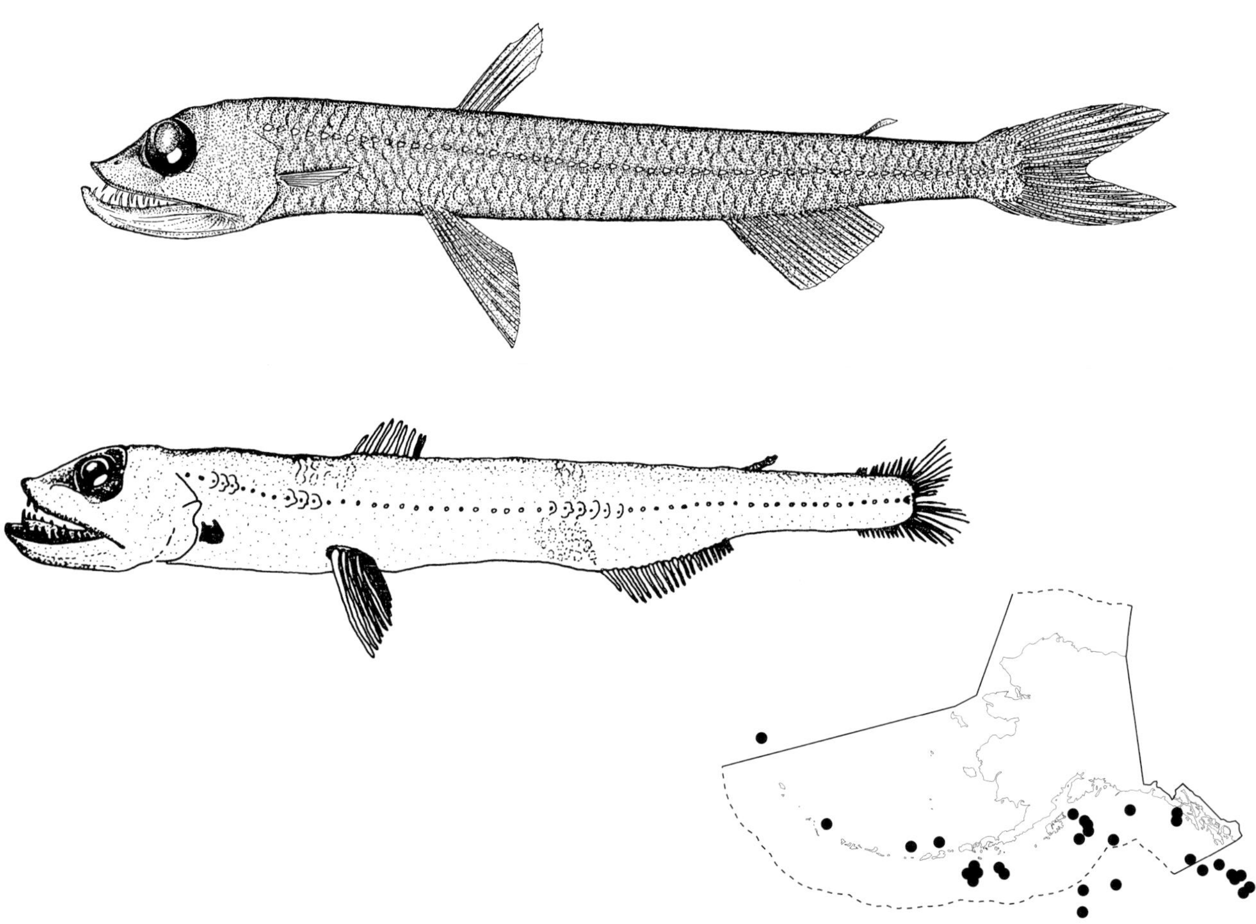

Notes & Sources — *Benthalbella dentata* (Chapman, 1939)
Neoscopelarchoides dentatus Chapman, 1939

Description: Chapman 1939:530–532; Johnson 1974:64–71; Hart 1973:179–180; Yamamoto in Amaoka et al. 1983:187, 320; Fujii in Masuda et al. 1984:63.

Figures: Upper: Hart 1973:179; 24 cm TL, British Columbia. Lower: Johnson 1974, fig. 16A; 148 mm SL.

Range: Chapman (1939) recorded catches from several Gulf of Alaska localities, including that of the holotype at 56°22'N, 145°54'W; station data are given in Thompson and Van Cleve (1936). Willis et al. (1988, fig. 35) plotted 32 additional occurrences of *B. dentata* in the North Pacific, including several from the Gulf of Alaska and one in the Bering Sea north of Unalaska Island. Lot UW 22477 is a 241-mm-SL specimen taken in 1992 north of the Islands of Four Mountains at 53°43'N, 170°13'W, depth 90 m; and SIO 94-243 includes a 220-mm-SL specimen taken north of Semisopochnoi Island at 52°10'N, 179°30'E, depth 246 m. The ABL museum has specimens from Icy Strait in the Gulf of Alaska. Hughes (1981) reported *B. dentata* were obtained in 1979 in midwater tows at depths of 549–622 m over Patton, Surveyor, and Quinn seamounts. Peden et al. (1985) reported *B. dentata* were taken in nets towed at depths of 500–1,200 m at Ocean Station Papa (50°N, 145°W). Probably more widely distributed in the Bering Sea and south of the Aleutian Islands than indicated by the few records we found. Fedorov and Sheiko (2002) reported it to be common in the vicinity of the Commander Islands.

Size: Using SL = 85% from Baxter (1990ms) gives an estimated TL of 283 mm for the 241-mm-SL UW 22477 and another of the same standard length recorded by Shinohara et al. (1996) from the Pacific coast of northern Honshu.

Benthalbella linguidens (Mead & Böhlke, 1953) **longfin pearleye**

Gulf of Alaska and North Pacific Ocean to Oregon and northern Japan.

Meso- to bathypelagic; recorded from depths of 13–3,660 m, usually taken at depths less than 1,000 m.

D 7–10; A 26–30; Pec 23–27; LLs 65–67; Vert 63–64.

- **Adipose fin base anterior to a vertical through last anal fin ray.**
- Dorsal fin rays usually 8 or 9; anal fin base long (compared to *B. dentata*); pectoral fin well developed, relatively long, although not reaching pelvic fin base.
- **Lateral line scales more than in *B. dentata*.**
- Length to about 36 cm TL.

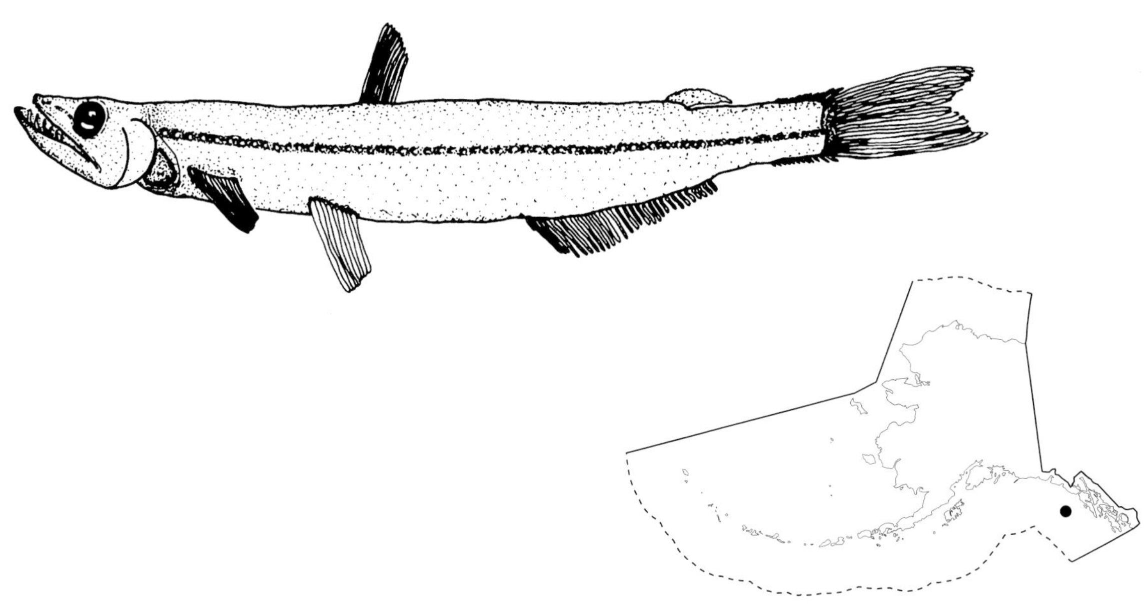

Notes & Sources — *Benthalbella linguidens* (Mead & Böhlke, 1953)
Scopelarchus linguidens Mead & Böhlke, 1953

Description: Mead and Böhlke 1953:241–245; Johnson 1974:84–88; Yamamoto in Amaoka et al. 1983:186; Fujii in Masuda et al. 1984:63; Parin et al. 1995:197.

Figure: Johnson 1974, fig. 25; 221 mm SL.

Range: Peden et al. (1985) examined an uncataloged specimen in the UW collection taken over Surveyor Seamount at about 57°N, 138°56'W, evidently the only confirmed record from Alaska; and two specimens from Canada's Ocean Station Papa in depths less than 650 m. Table 2 in Willis et al. (1988) indicates 4 captures of *B. linguidens* in 761 midwater tows in the North Pacific. Those four were scattered in the western subarctic and transitional zones and the Alaska Gyre; the locations were not given but it is doubtful that any were from within the 200-mile limit off Alaska. The species is known from rare catches in the eastern Pacific but appears to be more abundant in the western Pacific off the southern Kuril Islands and northern Japan. Recent records from southern Kuril Islands include those of Parin et al. (1995) and Ivanov (1997).

Size: Using 320 mm TL and 273 mm SL measured by Baxter (1990ms) from one of the Ocean Station Papa specimens in BCPM 979-11245 gives SL = 85% TL. Applying this proportion to a 306.5-mm-SL specimen recorded by Yamamoto (in Amaoka et al. 1983) gives 361 mm TL.

Family Notosudidae
Waryfishes

Waryfishes are elongate, slender, aulopiform fishes with large, egg-shaped eyes and spatulate snouts. They are also called paperbones, for their fragile, thin skeletons. This character, however, is shared with many other deepsea fishes. Waryfishes primarily inhabit the mesopelagic realm or are mesobenthopelagic. Part of the population, mostly the younger fish, migrates to the epipelagic zone at night. Waryfishes are highly active and can easily dodge trawls, especially the smaller nets typically used for scientific surveys.

Bertelsen et al. (1976), in the most recent comprehensive review and revision of the family, recognized 19 waryfish species in 3 genera as being valid. Scaly waryfish, *Scopelosaurus harryi,* occur in Alaska in the Bering Sea over the Aleutian Basin. They likely occur in the Gulf of Alaska as well, but occurrence there is not adequately documented. Some authors recognize a second species in the North Pacific Ocean, the longfin waryfish, *S. adleri.* Bertelsen et al. (1976) classified *S. adleri* as a junior synonym of *S. harryi.* Although there is fairly good evidence for the presence of two species in the North Pacific (Balanov and Savinykh 1999, Savinykh and Balanov 2000, Balanov 2001), there is not enough information at this time on records of *Scopelosaurus* from Alaska and other areas of the eastern North Pacific to differentiate them with confidence.

Waryfishes are almost round anteriorly, becoming more and more compressed from the anus to the caudal fin. Their eyes have an elliptical pupil in a round lens with a prominent lenseless space (aphakic aperture). They have a small dorsal fin located about halfway along the body, a posteriorly located anal fin with an adipose fin above it, and pectoral fins placed well up on the sides. Waryfishes are similar in shape to barracudinas (Paralepididae), but in waryfishes the dorsal and pelvic fins are farther forward on the body, closer to the pelvic fins. The last rays of the dorsal and anal fins are divided completely to the base, and most investigators count them as one ray. The scales are large, cycloid, and highly deciduous. The jaws have numerous small, pointed teeth, with 1 or 2 rows in the upper jaw and 3 or 4 rows in the lower. Like most other aulopiforms, waryfishes lack photophores and a swim bladder. Coloration of the adults is light brown to dark brown, with the darkest pigmentation on the head. The most important characters used for distinguishing the species of *Scopelosaurus* are meristics, particularly counts of the gill rakers, pyloric caeca, and vertebrae.

The largest waryfish on record is the type specimen of *Scopelosaurus hamiltoni* (not Alaskan), which measures 50.5 cm (20 inches) to the end of the longest unbroken caudal ray. Other species range in maximum size at maturity down to about 21 cm (8.25 inches).

In a revision of the family, Marshall (1966) replaced the name Notosudidae with the name Scopelosauridae, but Paxton (1972) pointed out that according to the rules of nomenclature Notosudidae Parr, 1928 has priority.

Quast and Hall (1972) listed *S. harryi* as a potential Alaskan species. However, it had already been recorded from Alaska in the Bering Sea, albeit under the name *Notosudis adleri* (Fedorov 1967) which was later classified as a synonym of *S. harryi* (Bertelsen et al. 1976).

For years *S. harryi* was believed to be rare in the Bering Sea and northwestern Pacific, but recent surveys (e.g., Balanov et al. 1995, Il'insky et al. 1995) found *S. harryi* to be abundant in the western region of the Aleutian Basin, as well as in other areas of the western Bering Sea and northwestern Pacific Ocean off Russia, in some years. Il'insky et al. (1995) reported catching as many as 25 specimens per 1-hour tow in large commercial nets fishing in mesopelagic waters of the western Bering Sea, including the Aleutian Basin, in 1989–1992. Savinykh (1993) attributed a greater concentration in the western Pacific, as opposed to open ocean waters, to a benthic mode of reproduction and restriction of juveniles and adults to continental margins and underwater rises. Il'insky et al. (1995) noted that only large individuals (18–24 cm) were found in the Bering Sea, Sea of Okhotsk, and the Pacific off the Kuril Islands, Kamchatka, and British Columbia, and suggested that medium-size fish (13–18 cm) inhabit the central waters of the subarctic Pacific and, as they grow, move to the peripheral regions and undergo further dispersal into subarctic waters only after attaining lengths in excess of 17 cm. Spawning grounds are in temperate and subtropical waters off Japan and California. The broad geographical range of *S. harryi* as adults suggests they actively migrate, using the subarctic Pacific as a foraging ground. Major concentrations of *S. harryi* are not found near the continental slopes and are rare in the Sea of Okhotsk, which is somewhat isolated from major oceanic circulation patterns.

Scopelosaurus harryi (Mead, 1953) **scaly waryfish**

Bering Sea to North Pacific off southern California and Japan and to Sea of Okhotsk; widespread in Pacific between 60°N and 20°N.

Mesopelagic; recorded from depths of 20–1,310 m, usually taken at 200–800 m; a portion of the population, mainly juveniles, makes nocturnal vertical migrations to the epipelagic zone.

D 10–12; A 17–19; Pec 10–14; Pel 9; GR 0–2 + 1 + 17–19; PC 16–21; Vert 58–61.

- Dark overall, including fins; mouth black; pores of mandibular canal not outlined in black; no silvery scales along ventral surface of body; black patch on pectoral fin; no distinct black spot surrounding anus.
- Dorsal fin at about midbody, posterior to vertical through pelvic fin base but closer to pelvic fin than to anal fin; pectoral fin short for genus, not quite reaching pelvic fin, but reaching much closer to pelvic fin than in family Paralepididae.
- Length to 32 cm SL.

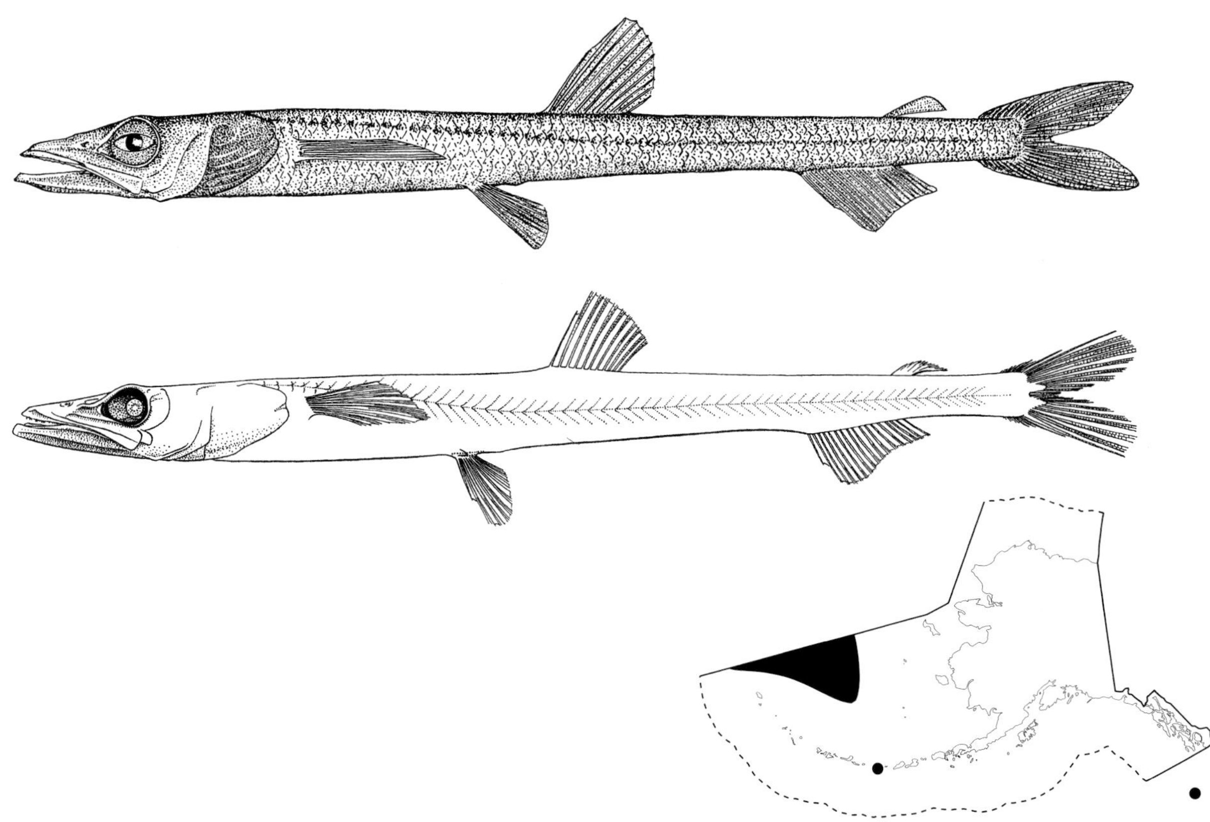

Notes & Sources — *Scopelosaurus harryi* (Mead in Mead & Taylor, 1953)
Notosudis adleri Fedorov, 1967

Bertelsen et al. (1976) classified *N. adleri* in *S. harryi.* Balanov and Savinykh (1999) and Saviniykh and Balanov (2000) presented evidence suggesting both forms are valid species of *Scopelosaurus.* However, the information is difficult to interpret. Examining museum specimens from the Bering Sea and northeastern Pacific and using the key presented by Balanov and Savinikh (1999), C.W.M. and museum curators were unable to differentiate the species. Fishery scientists working with material from Alaska were either unable to differentiate the species or elected to retain *S. harryi* for specimens they collected. Most museum specimens of *Scopelosaurus* are in poor condition, partly owing to damage sustained by these delicate fish during collection, and there are not many in museums. New material must be accumulated and studied to address the validity of the species and determination of their distribution in the eastern Pacific Ocean.

Description: Mead and Taylor 1953:578–580; Bertelsen et al. 1976:80–87; Yamamoto in Amaoka et al. 1983:320; Fujii in Masuda et al. 1984:64.

Figures: Upper: Hart 1973:184; 19 cm TL, off Tasu Sound. Lower: Bertelsen et al. 1976, fig. 54; 175 mm SL, off central British Columbia.

Range: Fedorov 1967: Bering Sea, 58°16'N, 175°13'E, in 620–650 m. Il'insky et al. 1995: numerous specimens taken in mesopelagic surveys using large commercial trawl nets over the Commander and Aleutian basins, and off the coasts of Russia from about Cape Navarin to the Kuril Islands. NMC 81-500: an adult specimen collected by A. E. Peden from southeast of Yunaska Island among the Islands of Four Mountains at 52°43'N, 170°47'W. Taylor 1967b: nearest British Columbia records, at 51°26'N, 131°09'W, and 52°11'N, 133°11'W.

Family Alepisauridae
Lancetfishes

Lancetfishes are large, carnivorous, aulopiform fishes that primarily inhabit warm waters of the world's oceans at mesopelagic depths. Reaching a length of 2.3 m (7.6 feet), they are the largest of the predacious alepisauroids. For their voracious appetites, lancetfishes have been called wolves of the sea, and many species of fishes were first discovered in the stomachs of lancetfishes. With a long, slender body, dorsal adipose fin, and small anal fin, lancetfishes are easily recognized as alepisauroids. A long, sail-like dorsal fin, reaching from near the back of the head to a point above the anal fin and with rays as much as half the length of the fish, readily identifies them as alepisaurids. As currently classified following Gibbs and Wilimovsky (1966), the family comprises one genus with two species. The longnose lancetfish, *Alepisaurus ferox,* occurs off southern Alaska.

Other diagnostic morphological characteristics of lancetfishes include a weak skeleton, a flaccid body covered with pores, and a prominent, fleshy keel along each side. The whole fish has a translucent quality, enhanced by loose outer epidermal layers, and a drawing published in 1707 of the first record of a lancetfish was labeled as a "jelly fish." The first ray of the dorsal, anal, and pectoral fins is thickened and armed with minute serrations on the outer margin. The pectoral fins are larger than in other alepisauroids, and attached horizontally. Some of the lower jaw and palatine teeth are strikingly elongate and sharp. The gill rakers have tufts of depressible filaments. Scales and photophores, as well as the swim bladder, are absent.

The flesh, though flaccid, is said to have a sweet and excellent taste (Gibbs and Wilimovsky 1966), but even the largest fish would not produce much meat. The largest weight on record is 6.8 kg (15 pounds) (Eschmeyer and Herald 1983), not much for a fish reaching more than 2 m (more than 7 feet).

Lancetfishes are primarily oceanic but commonly approach shore, presumably to feed. They are voracious feeders, ingesting squids, fishes, salps, and other prey, and their stomachs are a source of biological specimens as ingested food organisms seem to be little damaged by their teeth (Hart 1973). Lancetfishes are often found floundering in the surf or stranded on beaches. Either washed ashore or fished in shallow to deep waters, many lancetfishes have been found to be heavily infested with nematode and tapeworm parasites. Although lancetfishes occur in surface waters they are believed to be primarily inhabitants of the bathypelagic realm (Hubbs and Wilimovsky 1966).

For awhile lancetfishes were thought to be rare, but the accumulation of numerous records and accounts indicates these fish can be quite common. Alaska Maritime National Wildlife Refuge (USFWS) biologists find two or three or more longnose lancetfish on the beach each year in the western Aleutian Islands. The biologists often see the fish floundering and rolling around near shore, apparently disoriented. They are often reported to the biologists as "giant barracudas" (J. C. Williams, pers. comm., 12 Mar. 2001). Russian biologists find several lancetfish every year washed up on the beaches of the Commander Islands (B. A. Sheiko, pers. comm., 23 Jan. 1999). Peden et al. (1985) reported *A. ferox* were frequently caught by Canadian weathership crews at Ocean Station Papa (50°N, 145°W), where the fish was considered a nuisance because of its habit of wrapping itself around the fishing line. LeBrasseur (1967) reported 72 lancetfish were caught at the station during 1958–1966 by line fishing using a 183-m wire with lures.

The longnose lancetfish was included on previous lists of the fishes of Alaska, but under different names than *Alepisaurus ferox,* the name presently in use. Bean (1881b), believing two species were present, used the names *Alepidosaurus ferox* and *A. borealis.* Evermann and Goldsborough (1907) called them *Plagyodus aesculapius* and *A. borealis.* Wilimovsky (1954, 1958) listed one species from Alaska and used the name *A. borealis,* but later (Wilimovsky 1964) referred it to *A. richardsonii,* the name used by Quast and Hall (1972).

Although the shortnose lancetfish, *A. brevirostris,* is known to inhabit all major oceans, including the South Pacific, it has not been recorded from the North Pacific. For their review of the Alepisauridae, Gibbs and Wilimovsky (1966) could not reexamine all of the many early Alaskan records of alepisaurids and listed most of those records under *Alepisaurus* as nominal references not identifiable to species. Subsequently, authors have assumed that all of the early Alaskan records represent *A. ferox.* Characters differentiating *A. ferox* and *A. brevirostris* are given in the Notes & Sources section of the following account of *A. ferox.*

Alepisaurus ferox Lowe, 1833 **longnose lancetfish**

Southern Bering Sea and Aleutian Islands to Chile and to Japan and Sea of Okhotsk; Atlantic Ocean. Near surface to depth of 1,830 m, primarily oceanic but often found close to shore; epi- to bathypelagic.

D 30–43; A 15–18; Pec 13–15; Pel 8–10; GR 2–6 + 16–24 (20–30); Vert 48–52.

- Iridescent and generally rather pale; brown or bluish black dorsally, lighter ventrally; fins dark brown to black; lateral keel black; no horizontal row of white spots on dorsal fin; abdomen may appear striped, from black peritoneum showing between muscle strips.
- Body elongate, slender; prominent, low keel along posterior half of each side; head length more than 17% of standard length; snout length 33–50% of head length.
- Dorsal fin high, sail-like, and long, originating above posterior margin of opercle and extending almost to adipose fin; a few anterior dorsal fin rays usually exserted and free; caudal fin deeply forked, lobes pointed, upper lobe often longer and terminating in filament.
- Lateral line of lipped, small pores; tiny, closely spaced pores covering entire surface of body.
- Small teeth in both jaws; large, daggerlike teeth on palatines and a few in lower jaw.
- Length to about 231 cm TL.

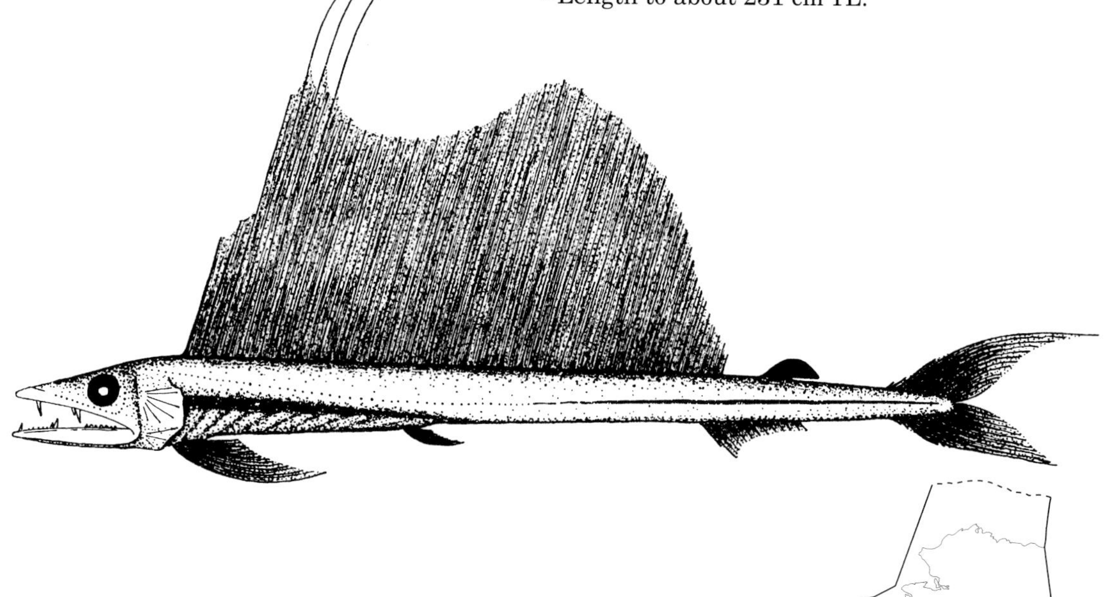

Notes & Sources — *Alepisaurus ferox* Lowe, 1833
Alepisaurus richardsonii Bleeker, 1855
Alepidosaurus borealis Gill, 1862
Alepidosaurus aesculapius Bean in Jordan & Gilbert, 1883
Plagyodus aesculapius: Jordan and Gilbert 1899, Evermann and Goldsborough 1907.
Plagyodus borealis: Evermann and Goldsborough 1907.

In *A. brevirostris* Gibbs, 1960 the coloration is generally darker; the dorsal fin is low in front, has no exserted, free rays, and its origin is over the middle of the opercle; head length is equal to or less than 15% SL; snout length is less than 33% HL; and the dorsal fin has a horizontal row of white spots. The number of dorsal fin rays is usually greater (typically 42–46) than in *A. ferox* (typically 32–42).

Description: Gibbs 1960:5–9; Gibbs and Wilimovsky 1966; Miller and Lea 1972:61; Hart 1973:175–176; Fujii in Masuda et al. 1984:77.

Figure: Gibbs 1960, fig. 1.

Range: Alaskan records include: Bean (in Jordan and Gilbert 1883), Iliuliuk, Unalaska Island; Jordan and Gilbert (1899), Unalaska Island, said to be common there; Scheffer (1959), beached on Amchitka Island; Larkins (1964), southern Bering Sea and Aleutian Islands, localities not given; Wilimovsky (1964), Semichi, Adak, Amchitka, and Unalaska islands; Isakson et al. (1971), Amchitka Island; D. G. Roseneau (pers. comm., 9 Mar. 2001), Kanaga and Aiktak islands. One was found freshly dead on a beach at Little Sitkin Island in June 2000 (S. Ebbert, pers. comm., 13 Feb. 2001). The Kanaga and Little Sitkin lancetfish had been eating squid and other fish (D. G. Roseneau, pers. comm., 9 Mar. 2001). Specimen AB 94-16 was found on the beach south of Ketchikan; and AB 98-72, south of Unalaska Island at 53°40'N, 166°51'W. The question mark on the above map indicates uncertainty about the northern limit of range. Most dots represent fish found washed ashore or floundering in the surf. The paucity of records from the Gulf of Alaska is curious, since lancetfish are commonly found in adjacent waters (e.g., LeBrasseur 1967, Peden et al. 1985).

Size: Gibbs and Wilimovsky (1966) gave a standard length of 208 cm for an *A. ferox* that washed ashore at Monterey Bay, California. Using SL = 89–91% TL from measurements in Kobayashi and Ueno (1956) yields a total length of 231 cm.

Family Paralepididae
Barracudinas

Barracudinas are elongate, slender, swift-swimming oceanic fishes with compressed, pointed heads, and bodies that are compressed anteriorly and oval to cylindrical posteriorly. Like waryfishes (Notosudidae) they have fragile, thin skeletons, but their eyes are round, with round pupils, not elliptical, and their shapes are opposite those of waryfishes, which are round anteriorly and compressed posteriorly. Barracudinas occur in all oceans, from arctic to antarctic waters but most abundantly in the tropics, at midwater depths to the surface. The family contains 12 genera and about 56 species, with 3 species known to occur in Alaska or nearby waters.

Morphological features of barracudinas include a small dorsal fin (9–16 rays) located slightly posterior to midbody; a long (20–50 rays) anal fin placed well behind the dorsal fin; a dorsal adipose fin; and, in some genera, a ventral adipose fin. The paired fins are small and the pelvic fins are far back on the body, closer to the dorsal fin than to the pectoral fin. The scales, in species having them, are deciduous and usually are missing from museum specimens, except for embedded scales along the lateral line. The lateral line is conspicuous. The mouth is large, and has alternately fixed and depressible fanglike teeth on the lower jaw and palatines, and fangs on the premaxilla followed by sawlike caniniform teeth. Old individuals often lack teeth. Barracudinas have 8 branchiostegal rays on each side and 53–121 vertebrae (63–91 in the three species treated in this guide). Two genera, not among those treated here, have light organs.

Barracudinas attain total lengths of about 15 cm (6 inches) to 50 cm (20 inches) or more. Specimens of *Magnisudis atlantica* caught in recent surveys in the northwestern Pacific measured 40–47 cm SL and were immature (Il'insky et al. 1995).

Following the most recent revision of the family (Rofen 1966a), Nelson (1994) classified the Paralepididae in two subfamilies. The species treated in this guide belong to the subfamily Paralepidinae, with two tribes. Members of the tribe Paralepidini have the body and much of the head covered with scales, and include the two Alaskan species: white barracudina, *Arctozenus risso,* and duckbill barracudina, *Magnisudis atlantica.* Post (1987) recently revised the Paralepidini. Species in the tribe Lestidiini lack scales except along the lateral line, and include slender barracudina, *Lestidiops ringens,* a probable Alaskan species.

One of the most interesting things about barracudinas is their swimming behavior. Some swim vertically, like "silvery javelins," darting up and down in spurts or drifting slowly, "stiffly erect like asparagus," and make abrupt turns from head-up to head-down positions (Rofen 1966a). Janssen et al. (1992) related the head-up swimming attitude of *A. risso* to features of the trunk lateral line and the aphakic space of the eyes as adaptations to minimize self-induced oscillations which would affect visual and lateral-line function.

At the time of Quast and Hall's (1972) inventory of Alaskan fish species no paralepidids had been found in Alaskan waters but they considered two were likely to be found in the region. *Lestidium ringens,* now classified in *Lestidiops,* still has not been collected in Alaska although it has been found just outside the 200-mile limit in the Bering Sea (Balanov 2000), south of the Gulf of Alaska (Peden et al. 1985), and off British Columbia (Hart 1973). *Notolepis rissoi,* now called *Arctozenus risso,* has been collected within the 200-mile limit over Gulf of Alaska seamounts (Hughes 1981) and in the western Bering Sea (Il'insky et al. 1995). *Magnisudis atlantica* is new to the roster of Alaskan species, with one specimen found close to the international boundary in the Bering Sea (Il'insky et al. 1995) and one in the eastern Gulf of Alaska (J. W. Orr, pers. comm., 13 Nov. 1997).

Barracudinas caught in Alaska and nearby waters are probably on foraging migrations. Recent surveys suggest that, like *Scopelosaurus* (family Notosudidae) and many epipelagic fish species, barracudinas spawn in the subtropical zone and forage in subarctic waters. The barracudinas move into the deep basins of the northern North Pacific and western Bering Sea in fall and winter (Balanov et al. 1995, Il'insky et al. 1995).

Key to the Paralepididae of Alaska

1 Pelvic fins well in front of a vertical line extending down from dorsal fin origin; scales absent except along lateral line . . . . *Lestidiops ringens,* page 237
(not known from Alaska)

1 Pelvic fins below or behind a vertical line from dorsal fin origin; body covered with scales . . . . (2)

2 (1) Pelvic fins mostly behind a vertical from dorsal fin insertion; anal fin rays 28 or more . . . . *Arctozenus risso,* page 238

2 Pelvic fins mostly below dorsal fin; anal fin rays 25 or less . . . . *Magnisudis atlantica,* page 239

Lestidiops ringens (Jordan & Gilbert, 1880) **slender barracudina**

Western Bering Sea, eastern Pacific midocean and offshore of British Columbia to central Baja California; Gulf of California; western Pacific off southern Kamchatka to southern Kuril Islands.

At depths of 29–3,920 m; primarily mesopelagic.

D 9–12; A 26–33; Pec 10–12; Pel 8–9; LLs 115–120; Vert 84–91.

- Light greenish brown dorsally, silvery ventrally; no dark spot anterior to eye.
- Extremely slender body and head; ridges between pelvic fins and anus, joined anterior to anus; no ventral luminous organ from head to pelvic fins.
- **Pelvic fin well in front of dorsal fin**; ventral adipose fin present, extending from anus to anal fin but barely evident in some specimens.
- **Scales absent except along lateral line.**
- Anus posterior to pelvic fin and anterior to dorsal fin origin.
- Each gill raker a bony base bearing a few small teeth.
- Length to 240 mm SL.

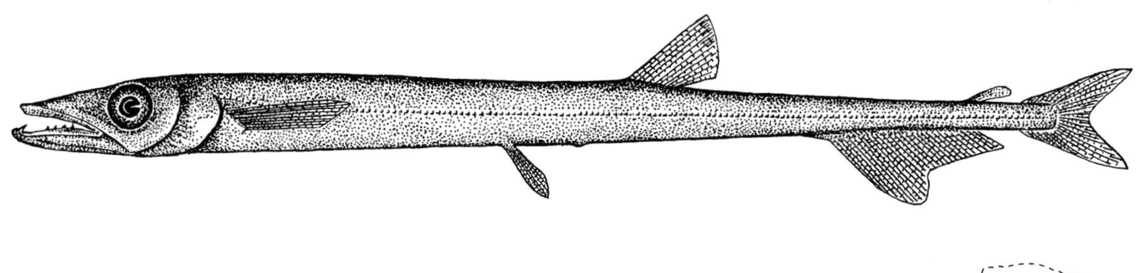

Notes & Sources — *Lestidiops ringens* (Jordan & Gilbert, 1880)
Sudis ringens Jordan & Gilbert, 1880
Lestidium elongatum Ege, 1953
Lestidiops ringens: Rofen 1966a.
Lestidium ringens: Quast and Hall 1972, Hart 1973.
The lack of a ventral, longitudinal luminous duct distinguishes *Lestidiops* from *Lestidium.*

Description: Jordan & Gilbert 1880i; Ege 1953:61–62; Hart 1973:181–182; Peden et al. 1985:6, table 2; Coad 1995: 691–692; Balanov 2000:806.

Figure: Hart 1973:181; 22 cm TL, off Tasu Sound, B.C.

Range: Called the most abundant barracudina of the eastern North Pacific by Rofen (1966a), *L. ringens* has not been recorded from Alaskan waters although it undoubtedly occurs there. Balanov (2000) recorded seven specimens (173–192 mm SL) collected from the western Bering Sea at 55°03'N, 170°58'E at a trawl depth range of 200–500 m over bottom depths of 3,300–3,880 m in two hauls in September and November 1990. The northernmost catch locality published for the eastern North Pacific is 52°17'N, 147°24'W, at less than 50 m of depth, reported by Peden et al. (1985). The map constructed by Willis et al. (1988, fig. 10) from records of 671 midwater tows indicates 36 occurrences in the eastern North Pacific with several at British Columbia latitudes, including one at about 52°N, 149°W. British Columbia records given by Hart (1973) were from south of Tasu Sound at about 52°15'N, 132°W; at 51°26'N, 131°06'W; and localities farther south. Parin et al. (1995) reported the first records from the northwestern Pacific, comprising five individuals (205–240 mm SL) collected in 1992 south of the southern Kuril Islands. Balanov (1997) reported occurrence of *L. ringens* in surveys in 1991 and 1992 off the Kuril Islands and southeastern Kamchatka at depths of 200–500 m. Castro-Aguirre (1991) reported *L. ringens* from the Gulf of California, as the southernmost record in the eastern Pacific.

Size: Parin et al. 1995.

Arctozenus risso (Bonaparte, 1840) **white barracudina**

Western Bering Sea and North Pacific Ocean south of Aleutian Islands and off British Columbia to Baja California and Japan, and Sea of Okhotsk; worldwide in cold (adults), temperate, and tropical waters.

At depths of 50–2,200 m, singly or in small schools; primarily mesopelagic, rarely found in upper 200 m, some pseudoceanic; portion of population, primarily juveniles, migrates at night to epipelagic zone; in Pacific in fall and winter migrates north through Kamchatka and Near straits into western Bering Sea.

D 9–11; A 28–33; Pec 10–13; Pel 9–10; GR 8 + 26 (34); LLs 59–68; Vert 75–85.

- Bright silvery, with dark pigment along back; brown when dead or preserved; **black area at base of anterior rays of anal fin**.
- **Pelvic fin mostly behind dorsal fin base**; anal fin longer-based than in *Magnisudis atlantica*; no ventral adipose fin.
- Head length less than one-fourth of standard length.
- **Body covered with scales**, but deciduous and likely to be represented mostly by empty scale pockets.
- Pores present in lateral line scales.
- Anus between pelvic fins.
- Each gill raker an elongate bony base bearing numerous needlelike teeth.
- Length to 310 mm SL.

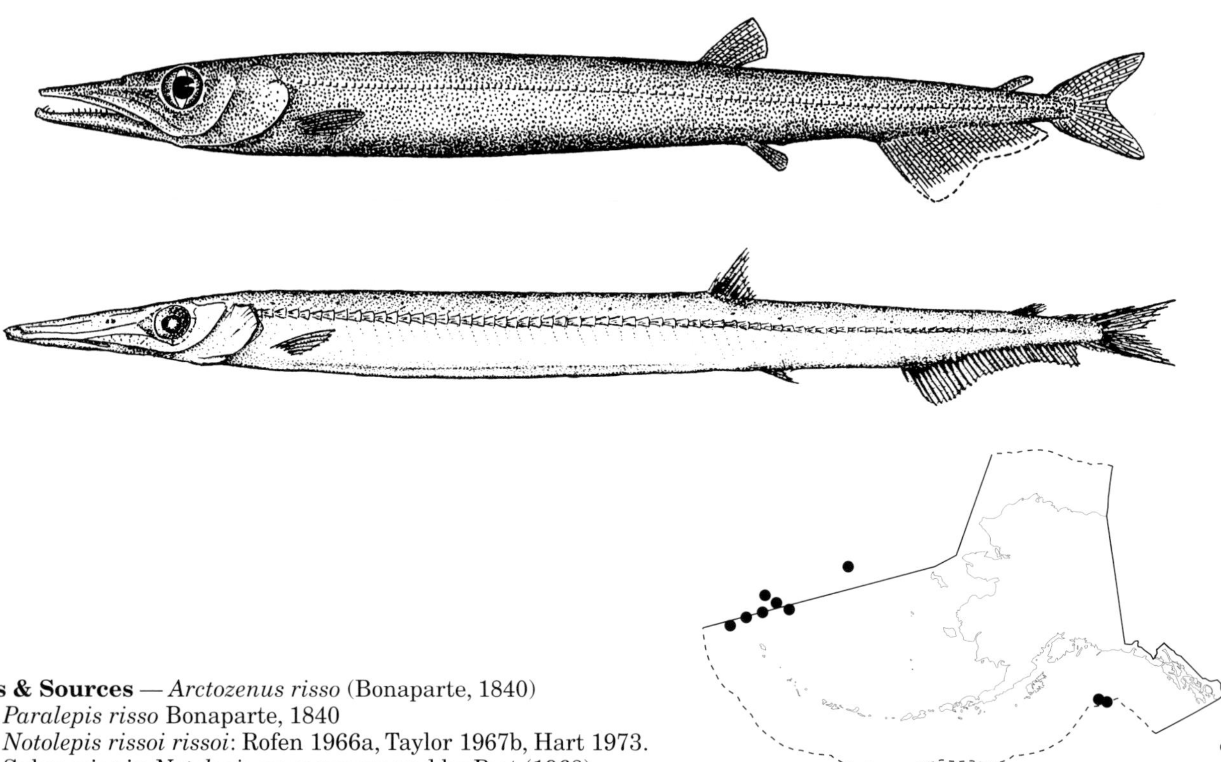

Notes & Sources — *Arctozenus risso* (Bonaparte, 1840)
Paralepis risso Bonaparte, 1840
Notolepis rissoi rissoi: Rofen 1966a, Taylor 1967b, Hart 1973.
Subspecies in *Notolepis* were suppressed by Post (1968).
Arctozenus rissoi: Post 1987.
Spelling of species name is correct as *risso,* as it appeared in the original description (Eschmeyer 1998).
The common name white barracudina is from Robins et al. (1991a). Ribbon barracudina is another frequently seen vernacular (e.g., Hubbs et al. 1979, Peden 1998).

Description: Rofen 1966a:280–295; Hart 1973:182–183; Post in Whitehead et al. 1984:503; Post 1987:79–88; Post in Okamura et al. 1995:96.

Figures: Upper: Hart 1973:182; 23 cm TL, Pacific Ocean off Cape St. James, British Columbia. Lower: Post 1987, fig. 1A; 22 cm SL, North Atlantic.

Range: Balanov et al. (1995) collected 10 specimens (231–256 mm SL) in November 1990 in the western Bering Sea at 55°58'N, 170°01'E, not far from the U.S.–Russia boundary, at trawl depths of 200–500 m over a bottom depth of 3,000 m. Il'insky et al. (1995) reported large *A. risso* (18–29 cm SL) to be common during October–December in 1989–1992, with as many as 6–10 specimens per hour of trawling, off eastern Kamchatka and in the vicinity of the Near and Commander islands. The northernmost occurrence was at 61°41'N, 176°22'E. Hughes (1981) reported *A. risso* was obtained in midwater trawls fishing at 549–623 m over Surveyor and Quinn seamounts. The nearest British Columbia record was reported by Taylor (1967b), from 51°30'N, 131°34'W, southwest of Cape St. James, Queen Charlotte Islands. Il'insky et al. (1995) reported that the vertical range of *A. risso* includes the entire mesopelagic and epilepagic zones, although this species is "much rarer" in the upper 200 m than is *Scopelosaurus harryi,* and is "extremely rare" in the upper 50 m.

Size: Fujii in Masuda et al. 1984.

Magnisudis atlantica (Krøyer, 1868) **duckbill barracudina**

Bering Sea to Pacific Ocean off Baja California and Japan, and Sea of Okhotsk; widespread primarily in temperate to tropical waters of North Pacific and North Atlantic oceans.

Epi- to bathypelagic, from near surface to depth of 2,000 m; some large individuals found near the coast and specimens sometimes found washed ashore.

D 9–11; A 20–25; Pec 15–18; Pel 9–10; GR 6–8 + 27–30 (34–40); LLs 55–61; Vert 63–67.

- Brownish; lighter ventrally; fins and their bases darker; no black area at base of anterior rays of anal fin.
- Head length about one-fourth of standard length.
- **Pelvic fin below dorsal fin**; anal fin shorter-based than in *Arctozenus risso*; no ventral adipose fin.
- **Body covered with scales**, although deciduous and easily shed.
- Pores absent from lateral line scales.
- Anus at level of pelvic fin tips.
- Each gill raker an elongate bony base bearing numerous needlelike teeth.
- Length to about 500 mm SL.

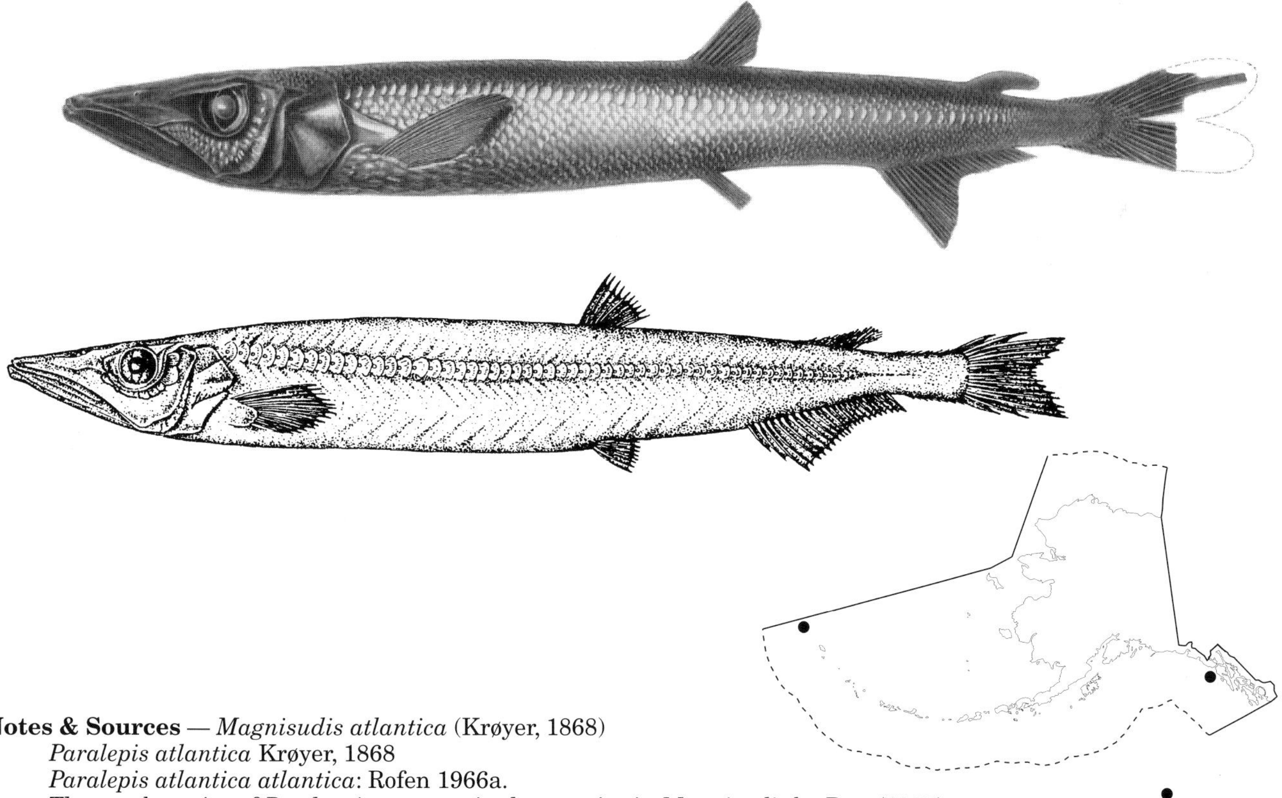

Notes & Sources — *Magnisudis atlantica* (Krøyer, 1868)
Paralepis atlantica Krøyer, 1868
Paralepis atlantica atlantica: Rofen 1966a.
Three subspecies of *P. atlantica* were raised to species in *Magnisudis* by Post (1987).

Description: Rofen 1966a:222–243; Peden 1979c; Post in Whitehead et al. 1984:504; Post 1987:88–94 and table 5; Balanov et al. 1995:92–93 and table; Post in Okamura et al. 1995:97.

Figures: Upper: Royal British Columbia Museum, artist N. Eyolfson, Aug. 1982; NMC 76-442, 286 mm SL, eastern North Pacific, Ocean Station Papa; this fish was described by Peden (1979c). Lower: Post 1987, fig. 3A; 410 mm SL. What appear to be pores in the lateral line scales in Post's illustration of a skinned specimen are openings in an irregular system of canals between the scales formed by fusion of the lateral and medial surfaces of each scale; they would not be visible in fresh or well-preserved specimens, as shown in Peden's illustration.

Range: Il'insky et al. (1995) reported seven specimens (405–470 mm SL) were taken as isolated individuals in survey samples from Pacific waters of the Kuril Islands to the southern Bering Sea during 1990–1992. One was from the Bering Sea at 53°52'N, 170°06'E, on or close enough to the international boundary to be considered an Alaskan record. James W. Orr (pers. comm., 13 Nov. 1997) identified a specimen (UW uncataloged) collected from the eastern Gulf of Alaska at 57°55'N, 137°07'W as this species; he commented that other northern records are in the NMFS survey database but cannot be verified. Previously, the northernmost record for the eastern Pacific Ocean was a specimen from Ocean Station Papa (50°N, 145°W), reported by Peden (1979c). Peden and Jamieson (1988) recorded a specimen (410 mm SL) from 48°N, 126°W, north of Cape Flattery. Two of Il'insky et al.'s (1995) specimens were taken at less than 6 m of depth, one from less than 50 m, and three in the upper and one in the lower mesopelagic zone.

Size: Il'insky et al. (1995) gave a length of 470 mm SL for an immature individual. Post (in Okamura et al. 1995) estimated the maximum length for the species to be about 500 mm SL.

Family Anotopteridae
Daggertooths

Large, daggerlike palatine teeth give the anotopterids their common English name, while a flexible chin projection, said to resemble the false beards of the Egyptian pharaohs, gives them the French common name, *pharaons.* The name *Anotopterus pharao* was bestowed by Zugmayer (1911), who gave the first scientific description of anotopterids. Daggertooths are widely distributed throughout the world's oceans in subarctic to subtropical waters at midwater depths to the surface. They are present in surface waters (to 10 m) at night, when they feed on salmon and other epipelagic fishes, and have adaptations for swallowing large prey. The stomach and body wall are distensible and the pectoral girdle is free from the cranium, allowing the bones to expand laterally.

Other morphological features of daggertooths include a strongly rodlike appearance enhanced by the lack of a dorsal fin and presence of only a small dorsal adipose fin and small anal fin placed far back on the body near the caudal fin. The paired fins are also small, and the pectoral fins are inserted vertically. The head is large and compressed, with long, pointed jaws. The skeleton is poorly ossified. Adults have a single lateral line with various accessory pores, but juveniles have the skin of the entire body evenly penetrated by closely spaced minute pores; the latter condition persists in lancetfishes (Alepisauridae) into adulthood. The jaw teeth include both fixed and depressible series and are much smaller than the palatine teeth. Adults tend to lose their teeth. There are 7 branchiostegal rays on each side, and the membranes are separate from each other and not joined to the isthmus. Scales, gill rakers, and photophores are absent.

Revisers of the family have offered different classifications of the Anotopteridae, including one to several species in one genus. Although Hubbs et al. (1953) combined all species of *Anotopterus* described at that time into one species, *A. pharao,* Marshall (1955) suggested that separate species, at least in the Atlantic, would be warranted once a larger amount of material was collected. Rofen (1966b) concurred with Hubbs et al. (1953), in considering that the observed diversity, such as in numbers of palatine teeth and vertebrae, was the variability of form to be expected from a single wide-ranging species. Only 35 specimens were known at that time and only 12 were available for detailed study. Kukuev (1998) examined 116 specimens and and reviewed other available data, and recognized three geographically isolated species: one each in the North Atlantic (*A. pharao*) and North Pacific (*A. nikparini*) oceans, and one circumglobal species in the Southern Ocean (*A. vorax*). He named the North Pacific species after the Russian ichthyologist Nikolai V. Parin.

Numerous specimens of *A. nikparini* have been recorded from Alaska and the species is, undoubtedly, even more abundant in the region than indicated by the records. As with barracudinas, the streamlined form of daggertooths suggests they are swift swimmers that can readily avoid collecting nets (Rofen 1966b). Salmon often bear slash marks attributable to attacks by daggertooths (Welch et al. 1991, Balanov and Radchenko 1998). Up to 12% of adult sockeye salmon (*Oncorhynchus nerka*) returning to British Columbia waters each year bear such marks (Gilhausen 1989).

Immature daggertooths feed in cold subarctic and subantarctic waters, and spawning takes place on the perimetry of subtropical waters. In adulthood reaching as much as 146 cm (57.5 inches) in total length, the North Pacific daggertooth could be the largest daggertooth species. Measurements on record for specimens from Alaska range up to about 100 cm (39.4 inches).

Daggertooths are characterized by most authors as bathypelagic, and have been captured as deep as 2,750 m off Japan (Fujii in Masuda et al. 1984). However, they are most often taken near the surface and in the mesopelagic zone, where they feed on herring (Engraulidae), salmon (Salmonidae), Atka mackerel (Hexagrammidae), sauries (Scomberesocidae), and other pelagic fishes. Balanov and Radchenko (1998) analyzed the diet of daggertooths in relation to their dentitions and the resulting types of wounds. The pattern of wounds inflicted by *Anotopterus* on salmon and other prey suggests daggertooths wait with their heads up in anticipation of prey and attack from below, as is typical of many mesopelagic predators.

The inclusion of *Anotopterus* in its own family, separate from the Paralepididae, follows the classification by Nelson (1994), after Rofen (1966b) and others. A close relationship of daggertooths to the Paralepididae has long been recognized. Johnson (1982) proposed that daggertooths are the sister group to the Paralepididae, forming a monophyletic lineage. Baldwin and Johnson (1996) assigned *Anotopterus* to Paralepididae in their classification of the Aulopiformes.

Anotopterus nikparini Kukuev, 1998 — North Pacific daggertooth

Bering Sea and Gulf of Alaska south in Pacific waters to about 25°N, south of Baja California and Japan.

Near surface to depth of 2,750 m, usually taken above 700 m; primarily epipelagic to mesopelagic; near surface at night.

D 0; A 14–17; Pec 13–16; Pel 9–10; Vert 78–80.

- Dark brownish; silvery ventrally; caudal fin dark; pectoral and pelvic fins black.
- Extremely elongate body; on large adults, a pair of dermal keels midlaterally on each side; small, flexible projection at tip of lower jaw.
- **No rayed dorsal fin**; dorsal adipose fin present.
- Scales absent.
- **Palatine teeth daggerlike**, usually 9–10 (range 5–11); premaxillary and dentary teeth more numerous and much smaller; vomerine teeth absent; teeth sometimes lost in adults.
- Gill membranes joined forward, below anterior edge of eye, and free from isthmus.
- Length to 146 cm TL, weight to 1.6 kg.

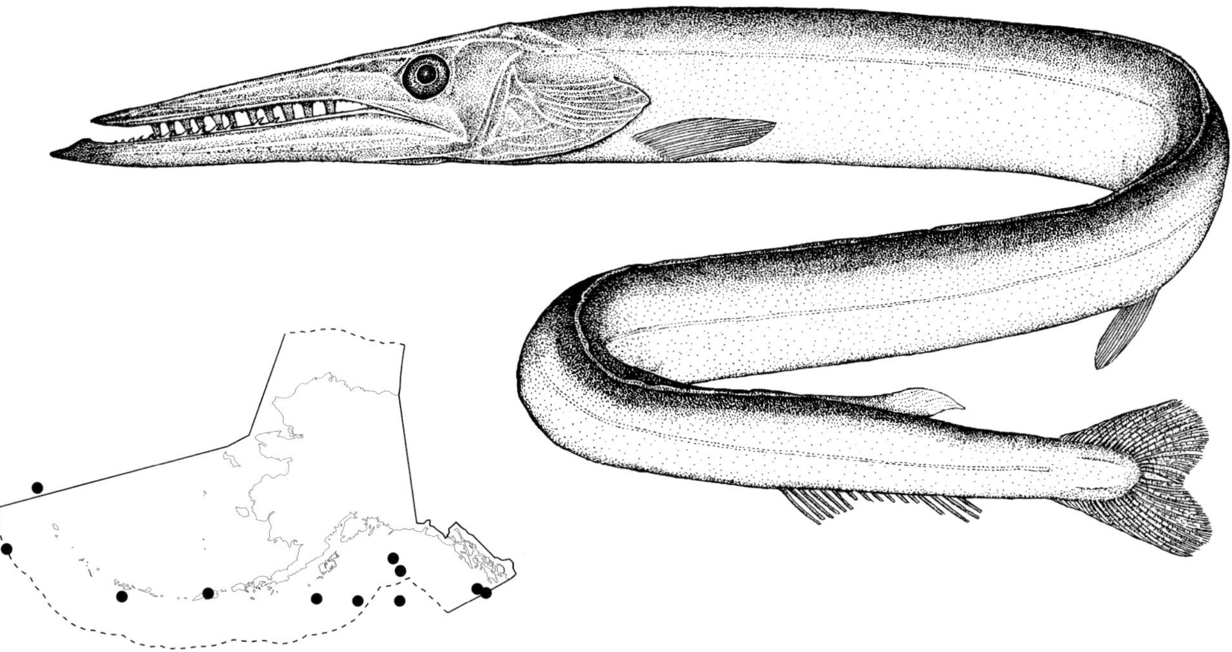

Notes & Sources — *Anotopterus nikparini* Kukuev, 1998

Anotopterus pharao Zugmayer, 1911 (North Pacific specimens only)

Anotopterus nikparini differs from the other two anotopterid species by having a larger number of vertebrae; larger head with a greater depth (head depth in adults 29–33% of lower jaw length); stronger, straighter, more regularly arranged palatine teeth; slightly posterior pectoral fin base; slightly higher number of anal fin rays; uniformly black paired fins; and other differences in morphometrics (Kukuev 1998).

Description: Hubbs et al. 1953; Rofen 1966b:498–510; Fujii in Masuda et al. 1984:77–78; Kukuev 1998. Shelekhov and Baginskii (2000) provided additional references and observations on loss of teeth in daggertooths during maturation and approach of reproductive season. Daggertooths may spawn once and then die.

Figure: Gon and Heemstra 1990:142; 98 cm SL, off Cape Mendocino, Humboldt, California.

Range: Alaskan records include: Kobayashi and Ueno (1956), southwest of Attu Island; Welander et al. (1957), south of Kiska Island; Neave (1959), Taylor (1959), and Larkins (1964), Gulf of Alaska; Wilimovsky (1964), northwest Unalaska Island; Polutov (1966), between the Commander and Aleutian islands, south of the Aleutians, and in Gulf of Alaska; Quast and Hall (1972), southeastern Alaska (AB 61-40, 960 mm SL, from about 57°N, 144°W). Kukuev (1998) reported on several large specimens (up to 928 mm SL) taken in the Bering Sea; localities were not specified. Fedorov and Sheiko (2002) reported this species to be common in the vicinity of the Commander Islands. Polutov (1966) reported it from as far north in the Bering Sea as Olyutorskiy Bay, but without giving specific localities. KIE 2007, taken in January 1998, is from Olyutorskiy Bay at 60°02'N, 168°03'E, depth 150–200 m (B. A. Sheiko, pers. comm., 23 Jan. 1999). Species is also commonly taken in the eastern Pacific at latitudes of British Columbia; e.g., Peden et al. (1985) reported that daggertooths were inadvertently angled by Canadian weathership crews while they fished for salmon (50°N, 145°W). Nagasawa (1993) and Kukuev (1998) reported other North Pacific records. Daggertooths are often caught in gill nets and found in stomachs of other fishes, including lancetfish (*Alepisaurus*), halibut, albacore, and salmon shark.

Size: Miller and Lea 1972, Eschmeyer and Herald 1983.

Order Myctophiformes
Myctophiforms

Members of the order Myctophiformes are deepsea pelagic and benthopelagic fishes. Most of them have numerous photophores on the body and head, for which Coad (1995) called the order the lanternfish order. These small fishes, most not exceeding 20 cm (8 inches), occur in large numbers and are important "forage fishes," serving as fodder for squids, other fishes, and marine mammals. Many myctophiform fishes undergo a diurnal vertical migration of several hundred meters so that during the daytime most species are in greatest numbers between 300 and 1,200 m, whereas at night peak abundance is between 10 and 100 m. They occur in large schools and form a major component of the deep scattering layer of the oceans.

As currently understood, the order comprises two families, Neoscopelidae and Myctophidae, with 35 genera and about 240 species. Both families have representatives in the marine waters off the coasts of Alaska.

In addition to the presence of photophores in most species, distinguishing characters of myctophiform fishes include: compressed head and body; lateral eyes; large, terminal mouth, with maxillae extending beyond the eyes and excluded from the gape by the premaxillae; an adipose fin; no spines in the fins; abdominal pelvic fins, usually with 8 rays; forked caudal fin; cycloid scales in most species; swim bladder usually present, and physoclistous; 7–11 branchiostegal rays; well-developed gill rakers; and 28–45 vertebrae.The presence of upper pharyngobranchials and retractor muscles like those of generalized paracanthopterygians is the main character cited by Rosen (1973) to distinguish the Myctophiformes from the Aulopiformes.

An investigation of the relationships of Myctophiformes by Stiassny (1996) provided evidence corroborating the monophyly of the Neoscopelidae and of the Myctophidae. However, she concluded, the resolution of myctophid intrarelationships remains an outstanding problem in teleostean systematics, at least partly due to concentration on the disposition of photophores and the exclusion of studies on variation in other features.

Family Neoscopelidae
Blackchins

Comprising three genera and six species, the family Neoscopelidae is the smaller of the two extant families of myctophiforms. Two genera, including *Scopelengys,* the genus represented in Alaska, lack photophores. Members of this family primarily inhabit tropical and subtropical regions and none was known to occur in the Bering Sea or in Alaskan waters until Balanov and Il'inskiy (1992) and Balanov and Fedorov (1996) reported specimens of Pacific blackchin, *S. tristis,* from the continental slope near Cape Olyutorskiy and southeastern portions of the Commander and Aleutian basins. *Scopelengys tristis* is a commonly occurring blackchin species in the northeastern Pacific Ocean at relatively low latitudes.

Characteristics of the family Neoscopelidae include an anal fin origin far behind the dorsal fin base; presence of a long, slender supramaxilla along the dorsal margin of the maxilla; a maxilla with a greatly expanded, truncate posterior portion; and lack of a suborbital shelf. Bands of small teeth are present on the jaws, palatines, vomer, and basibranchials. The lateral line is weakly developed. Only *Scopelengys* lacks a swim bladder. Two of the three blackchin genera, including *Scopelengys,* have small eyes.

Butler and Ahlstrom (1976) reviewed the genus *Scopelengys* and described the mid-Pacific species *S. clarkei,* comparing it to its only congener, *S. tristis.* Nafpaktitus (1977) reviewed the family.

Scopelengys tristis Alcock, 1890 **Pacific blackchin**

Southern Bering Sea; most common in eastern mid-Pacific and off Santa Barbara, California, to mid-Chile; across Pacific to Japan to Indonesia; tropical and subtropical Atlantic and Indian oceans.

Oceanic, meso- to bathypelagic, possibly also benthopelagic; adults tend to occur deeper than 1,000 m, to 3,350 m or more, and young (less than 100 mm) at 500–800 m; no evidence of vertical migration.

D 11–13; A 12–14; Pec 14–17; GR 7–15; PC 8; Vert 29–32.

- Color uniform black.
- Weakly ossified skeleton and flaccid musculature.
- Head large, 26–30% of standard length; dorsal profile of head concave; lower jaw projecting; eye small, 10–13% of head length; maxilla extending well past eye; width of maxilla at posterior end greater than diameter of eye.
- Anal fin origin well behind vertical through dorsal fin insertion.
- Photophores absent.
- Scales large, cycloid, highly deciduous (rarely present in freshly caught or preserved specimens).
- Jaws and palatines with bands of villiform teeth; vomer with small patch of teeth on each side.
- Length to 194 mm SL.

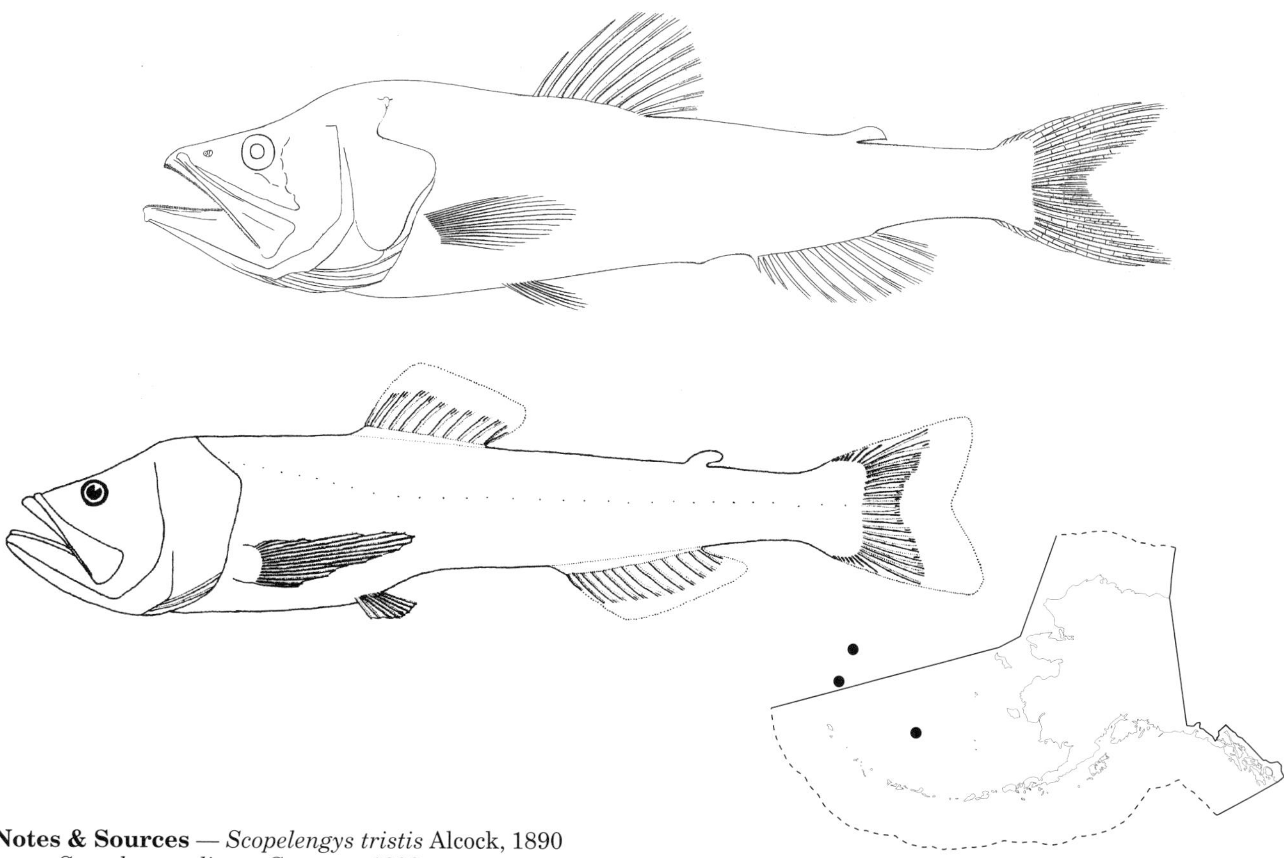

Notes & Sources — *Scopelengys tristis* Alcock, 1890
Scopelengys dispar Garman, 1899
Scopelengys clarkei Butler & Ahlstrom, 1976, a species inhabiting the mid-Pacific, has a lower number of pectoral fin rays (12–13) and more vertebrae (34–35), among other differences from *S. tristis*. The status of *S. clarkei* as a distinct species was questioned by Bekker and Shcherbachev (1990), but upheld by Balanov and Fedorov (1996).

Description: Alcock 1890:302–303; Garman 1899:254–256; Bolin 1939a:94–95; Butler and Ahlstrom 1976:143–148; Nafpaktitus 1977:4–6.

Figures: Upper: Garman 1899, pl. 54, fig. 2; off Pacific coast of Panama. Lower: Butler and Ahlstrom 1976, fig. 2A; 126 mm SL, Pacific Ocean.

Range: Aleutian Basin at 55°52'N, 177°30'W, one specimen taken by midwater trawl towed from 1,000 m to 500 m (Balanov and Fedorov 1996). The same authors recorded specimens taken at 56°03'N, 171°03'E in the Commander Basin, and off Cape Olyutorskiy. They did not report sizes. Uyeno and Kishida (1976) described a 178-mm-SL specimen collected in the East China Sea by midwater trawl at 660 m, the first record off Japan. Bekker and Shcherbachev (1990) recorded specimens taken by bottom trawls from submarine ridges and the continental slope in the Indian Ocean, South China Sea, and western Pacific Ocean, and considered those catches to demonstrate a benthopelagic lifestyle for the species. However, the specimens could have been captured in midwater as the trawl was raised. Nafpaktitus (1977) noted that capture data indicate young *S. tristis* inhabit shallower depths than the adults. Most specimens, adults as well as young, have been taken in midwater trawls.

Family Myctophidae
Lanternfishes

Lanternfishes, also called lampfishes or myctophids, have relatively large eyes and numerous discrete, round photophores which produce gold, orange, blue, green, red, and other colors of light. The photophores, each having a light gland, reflecting layer, and lens, are arranged in distinct groups. Many species also have other luminous tissue, including glands on the caudal peduncle, organs around the eyes, patches on various parts of the body, and minute secondary photophores associated with each scale. Myctophids are found in all oceans from near the surface to moderately great depths and occur in such tremendous schools their extent is measured in miles. Most species occur shallower than 1,000 m, and most migrate toward the surface at night to feed on plankton. They are the most speciose family of mesopelagic fishes, with about 235 valid species. In many regions of the world, including the basin waters of the Bering Sea and the Gulf of Alaska, the number of myctophids in each midwater trawl catch far outnumbers species of other mesopelagic families. They are potentially an important commercial resource but, because of processing difficulties and low market price related to their small size, short duration of storage, presence of photophores, and a black film in the abdominal cavity, currently are not heavily exploited. Myctophids are important food for squids, larger fishes, and marine mammals, and constitute a critical part of the ocean ecosystem as they convert plankton to food for the next higher trophic level.

Accounts for 10 lanternfish species are included in this guide. The occurrence of eight species in Alaskan waters, primarily in the southern Bering Sea, Pacific Ocean south of the Aleutian Islands, and Gulf of Alaska, is well known from occasional to numerous catches. The glacier lanternfish, *Benthosema glaciale,* is the only Arctic lanternfish species in Alaska. Its presence in the region is substantiated by only one or two records. The taillight lanternfish, *Tarletonbeania taylori,* is known in Alaska from a single Bristol Bay record, but other specimens have been caught not far outside the 200-mile limit off southern Alaska. Some of the more common species are abundant in the region. For example, Nagasawa et al. (1997) reported that in midwater trawl surveys conducted in the Bering Sea in 1991–1994, northern lampfish, *Stenobrachius leucopsarus,* were found to be widespread and abundant over the Aleutian Basin and were the most numerous species caught, followed by northern smoothtongue, *Leuroglossus schmidti* (family Bathylagidae).

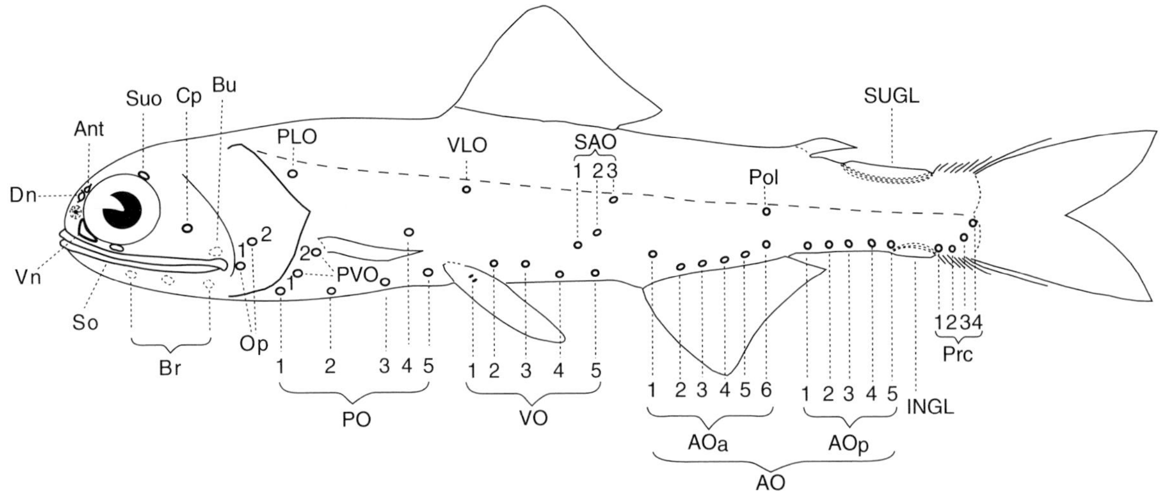

Major photophores and luminous tissue in lanternfishes
Ant, antorbital; Dn, Dorsonasal; Vn, ventronasal; Suo, supraorbital, So, suborbital; Br, branchiostegal; Cp, cheek; Bu, buccal; Op, opercular; PLO, suprapectoral organ; PVO, subpectoral organ; PO, pectoral or thoracic organs; VLO, supraventral organ; VO, ventral organs; SAO, supra-anal organs; AO, anal organs; AOa, anterior anal; AOp, posterior anal; Pol, posterolateral; Prc, precaudal; SUGL, supracaudal luminous gland; INGL, infracaudal luminous gland.

By far the most characteristic feature of lanternfishes is the presence of photophores, and since each species has its own photophore pattern the location and number of photophores are critical for identifying the species. The diagram above (drawn from several sources) shows standard terminology for the commonly occurring photophores and patches of luminous tissue. Some species have additional luminous organs but they are not always evident, due to damage. Luminous scales, in particular, are often missing, since myctophid scales in general are highly deciduous.

To some extent the photophore patterns are sexually dimorphic within species. In fact, some species are so similar in appearance to each other that only the males can be distinguished as belonging to a different species by the shape of their caudal luminous glands. For those species identification of the females has to be assumed by their presence in the same net as the males.

An obvious difference between the lanternfish species in this guide and the closely related *Scopelengys* (Neoscopelidae), is that the anal fin origin in the lanternfishes is below the dorsal fin or not far behind it, whereas the anal fin is far behind the dorsal fin in *Scopelengys.* Other characteristics of lanternfishes include large eyes, a compressed snout, and a rudimentary supramaxilla or no supramaxilla. The wide range given for gill raker numbers of some species may be due to the practice of some authors of counting only the lathelike rakers, and not the rudimentary rakers. Counts for branchiostegal rays are not given in the species accounts because they are difficult to count accurately without staining or dissection and few numbers are available for the species.

Current classifications of lanternfishes (e.g., Paxton 1972, Wisner 1974, Paxton et al. 1984) include two subfamilies: Myctophinae and Lampanyctinae. Diagnostic characters of Myctophinae include relatively short jaws; unsculptured circumorbital bones with an extensive orbital shelf; a ventral position for most photophores, including the precaudal series with only two; lack of secondary photophores and cheek photophores; restriction of luminous tissue to the caudal glands; and sexual dimorphism of the caudal glands. Those characters are found in none or few of the Lampanyctinae. Within the Lampanyctinae are found extremely long jaws; sculptured circumorbital bones with a moderate orbital shelf; a number of photophores near or above the lateral line, including the last of the precaudal series which usually numbers from 3 to 9; presence of secondary photophores and luminous tissue over the body; presence of cheek photophores; and lack of sexual dimorphism in the caudal luminous glands. Representatives of both subfamilies occur in Alaska.

Quast and Hall (1972) included 13 species of lanternfish on their list of Alaskan fish species, along with 3 others they thought were likely to occur, although not yet reported, in the region. Results of systematic and distributional studies since then, primarily those of Paxton (1972), Wisner (1974), and Peden et al. (1985), allow refinement of the Alaskan inventory through better understanding of the family's taxonomy and accumulation of records. As well, there are syntheses of older mesopelagic surveys (e.g., Willis et al. 1988) and several reports on more recent surveys (e.g., Shinohara et al. 1994) in the Pacific Ocean.The following nine species reported from Alaska by various authors are not likely to occur in Alaska or have been shown to be the same as other species.

Broadhead lanternfish, *Hygophum reinhardtii* (Lütken, 1892), are widespread in the Pacific and Atlantic oceans from about 40°N to 40°S, with few individuals known from outside that range. Wilimovsky (1954, 1958) gave a range to the Gulf of Alaska, and Quast and Hall (1972), citing Wilimovsky, included the species in their inventory; however, documentation for this range has not been found. Wisner (1974) and Bekker (1983) did not acknowledge records of *H. reinhardtii* north of 30° and 40°N, respectively. Willis et al. (1988) reported occurrence of this lanternfish in only 1 of 761 midwater tows in the subarctic Pacific Ocean; this tow was at an unspecified location south of 50°N, and could represent a different species.

Protomyctophum crockeri (Bolin, 1939), California flashlightfish, occurs in the eastern Pacific off southern British Columbia to Baja California. It was listed by Quast and Hall (1972) under *Hierops crockeri,* as a species likely to occur in Alaska. All of the 60 catches with *P. crockeri* in 761 midwater tows in the subarctic North Pacific were south of about 50°N in the east and 45°N in the west (Willis et al. 1988). The species was taken no closer to Alaska than 45°N, 170°W in recent larval net and beam trawl collections (Shinohara et al. 1994).

Symbolophorus californiense (Eigenmann & Eigenmann, 1889), bigfin lanternfish, occurs in the eastern Pacific from southern British Columbia latitudes to Mexico. Clemens and Wilby (1961) gave a range north to the Gulf of Alaska, probably referring, by a broader definition of the Gulf than most authors use, to waters off British Columbia. Subsequently, Grinols (1965), Quast and Hall (1972), and Hart (1973) gave a range to Alaska, without citing further documentation. Maps for *S. californiense* by Bekker (1983) and Willis et al. (1988) indicated no records farther north than 50°N. The nearest to Alaska reported by Peden et al. (1985) were from 49° and 50°N, 145°W. Shinohara et al. (1994) reported none taken closer to Alaska than 45°N, 170°W.

Electrona risso (Cocco, 1829), chubby lanternfish, has a circumglobal distribution, and has been recorded in the eastern Pacific from Oregon to Baja California. It was not included in inventories by Wilimovsky (1954, 1958) or Quast and Hall (1972), but Baxter (1990ms) believed it might occur in Alaska. However, only 2 out of a total of 761 midwater tows in the North Pacific were reported to have captured *E. risso;* those 2 were in the eastern Pacific somewhere south of 50°N (Willis et al. 1988), and it is not certain if vouchers exist.

Notoscopelus japonicus (Tanaka, 1908), fluorescent lampfish or spiny lanternfish, was also included in Baxter's (1990ms) manuscript. This species is widespread in the western North Pacific south of 45°N, but has not been confirmed in the eastern Pacific. Peden et al. (1985) and Peden and Hughes (1986) recounted the confused nomenclature of *Notoscopelus* in the northeastern North Pacific and referred records of Aron (1960) and Clemens and Wilby (1961) concerning *Notoscopelus* at British Columbia latitudes to *N. japonicus,* and suggested that Hart's (1973) record and illustration from Canadian waters may be a misidentified *Lampanyctus.*

Notoscopelus resplendens (Richardson, 1845), the patchwork lampfish, was considered likely to occur in Alaska by Quast and Hall (1972). This species is widely distributed in warm waters, and in the North Pacific occurs off southern California to Chile and to Japan. British Columbia records were referred to *N. japonicus* by Peden et al. (1985) and Peden and Hughes (1986), who concluded that *N. resplendens* resides well south of British Columbia.

Ceratoscopelus townsendi (Eigenmann & Eigenmann, 1889), dogtooth lampfish, was listed by Quast and Hall (1972) as a likely Alaskan species on the basis of British Columbia records of Aron (1962). Hart (1973) reported that the species occurs, but rarely, off British Columbia. The Canadian records probably refer to a different species. Wisner's (1974) range map indicates *C. townsendi* south of 45°N. It may be confined to the eastern North Pacific from northern California to Mexico.

Idiolychnus urolampus (Gilbert & Cramer, 1897) is known from scattered records in the tropical regions of the Pacific and Indian oceans (Wisner 1974). The map for this species by Bekker (1983) has a dot off Yakutat, Alaska, but this undoubtedly is a printer or artist's error; no such record is mentioned in Bekker's text, or by Bekker (1993) in his more recent review of *I. urolampus.* This species was valid as *Lobiancha urolampa* in Wisner (1974).

Lampanyctus beringensis Schmidt, 1933, described from Bering Island specimens, was listed for Alaska by Wilimovsky (1954) and Quast and Hall (1972) but curently is classified in *Stenobrachius leucopsarus* (an Alaskan species).

The following key first separates the two subfamilies, so that the Myctophinae appear first in the species accounts, followed by the Lampanyctinae.

Key to the Myctophidae of Alaska

1 Prc 1 or 2; no secondary photophores . . . . (2)

1 Prc 3–5; secondary photophores present or absent . . . . (5)

2 (1) PLO ventral to or distinctly dorsal to pectoral base; jaws short, extending less than one-half eye diameter behind orbit; mouth terminal, snout not projecting; procurrent caudal rays not fused . . . . (3)

2 PLO opposite pectoral base; jaws moderate, extending one-half eye diameter behind orbit; mouth subterminal, snout projecting; procurrent caudal rays weakly fused at tips . . . . (4)

3 (2) PLO and PVO1 juxtaposed, nearly on same level and below level of PVO2; AO continuous, not distinctly divided into two groups; Pol absent; Prc2 not elevated . . . . . *Protomyctophum thompsoni,* page 248

3 PLO dorsal to level of pectoral base, above level of PO1 and PO2; AO discontinuous, divided into AOa and AOp groups; 1 distinct Pol; Prc2 elevated, near lateral line . . . . *Benthosema glaciale,* page 249

4 (2) Males with short, bulky SUGL and INGL . . . . *Tarletonbeania taylori,* page 250

4 SUGL of males long and slender, usually filling supracaudal space; INGL of male, if present, short and weakly developed, hidden under body scales . . . . *Tarletonbeania crenularis,* page 251

5 (1) Dn present; PLO much closer to pectoral fin base than to lateral line . . . . *Diaphus theta,* page 252

5 Dn absent; PLO closer to lateral line than to pectoral fin base . . . . (6)

6 (5) One Pol . . . . genus *Stenobrachius* (7)

6 Two Pol . . . . (8)

7 (6) Usually 4 VO (range 3–5), the VO1–2 interspace larger than the rest; usually 4 Prc (range 3–5), in even curve; SUGL with 5–8 luminous scales; INGL with 7–9 scales, filling entire infracaudal space; body moderately robust. . . . . . *Stenobrachius leucopsarus,* page 253

7 Usually 5 VO (range 4–6); usually 3 Prc, rarely 4; SUGL with 2–4 luminous scales; INGL with 5–6 scales, filling about three-fourths of infracaudal space; body slender . . . . *Stenobrachius nannochir,* page 254

8 (6) Pectoral fins long, extending well past base of pelvic fins, to or almost to anal fin origin; abruptly elevated AOa2, AOa3, and often AOa4; extra PLO near pectoral origin. . . . . *Lampanyctus jordani,* page 255

8 Pectoral fins short, not reaching base of pelvic fins or not reaching much past base of pelvic fins; no AOa photophores abruptly elevated; no extra PLO near pectoral origin . . . . (9)

9 (8) Photophores notably small; SAO3 about over anal fin origin; VLO much closer to lateral line than to pelvic fin base . . . . *Nannobrachium regale,* page 256

9 Photophores not notably small; SAO3 behind vertical through anal fin origin; VLO a little below midway between lateral line and pelvic fin base . . . . *Nannobrachium ritteri,* page 257

Protomyctophum thompsoni (Chapman, 1944) **bigeye lanternfish**

Southern Bering Sea to Pacific Ocean off central California and across Pacific to Hokkaido; widespread in subarctic North Pacific; usually found north of 40°N.

Mesopelagic, to depth of 1,370 m; usually taken at 200–500 m, day and night.

D 11–13; A 21–25; Pec 14–17; GR 16–20; Vert 37–39.
VO4; SAO 3; AO 14–17; Pol 0; Prc 2.

- Metallic blue dorsally, bright silvery ventrally.
- Mouth terminal, **snout not projecting**; maxilla greatly expanded posteriorly.
- Single SUGL or INGL present, depending on sex.
- Dn absent; Vn small; **PLO ventral to pectoral base**, nearly hidden by subopercle, anterior to PVO1; SAO slightly angled; **SAO2 nearer to SAO3 than to SAO1**; SAO1 directly above or above and slightly in advance of VO3; **AO continuous, not distinctly divided into AOa and AOp; no Pol**; Prc1–2 interspace less than a photophore diameter; Prc2 not elevated.
- Lateral line pores not distinct.
- Length to 70 mm TL.

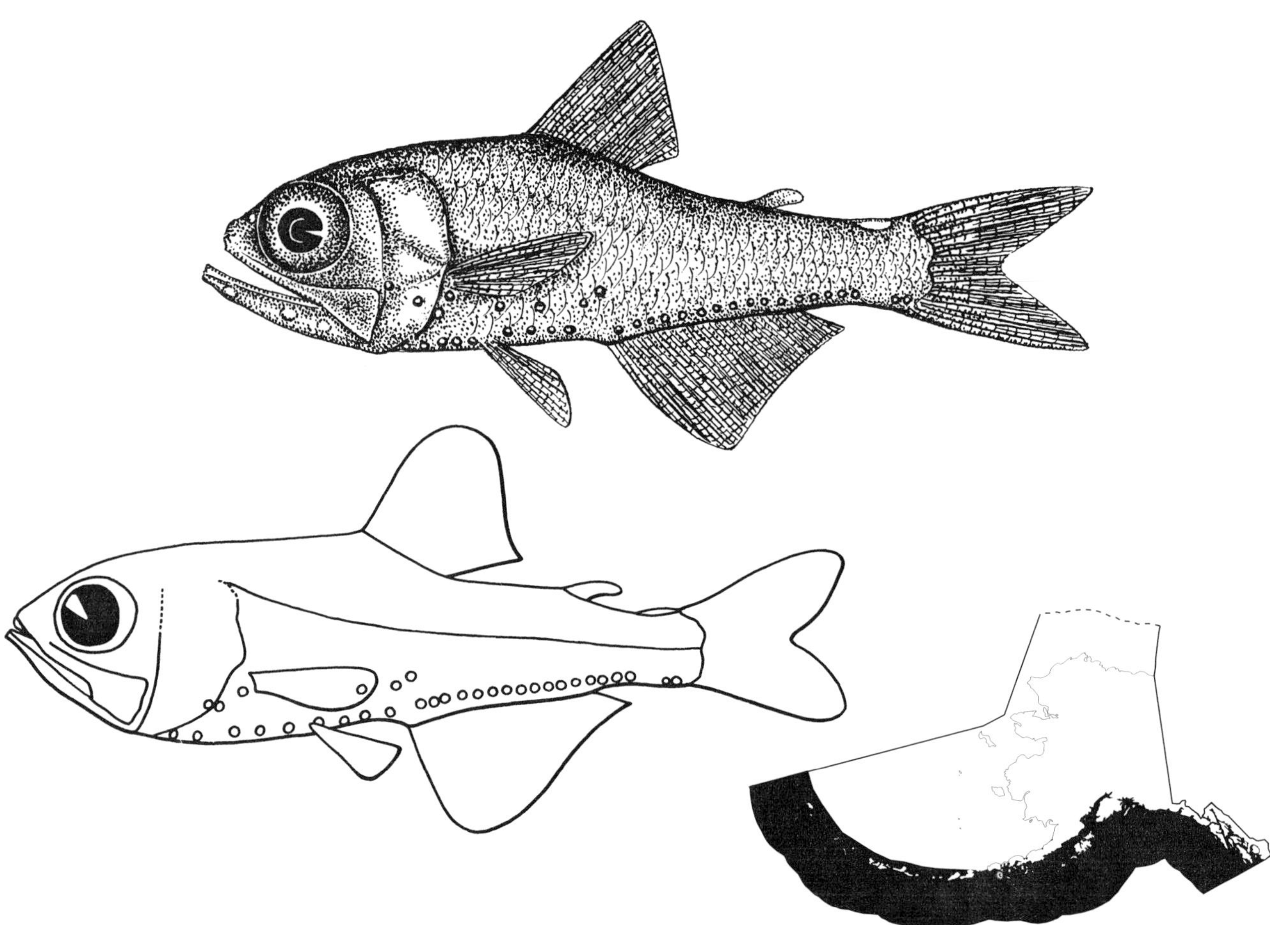

Notes & Sources — *Protomyctophum thompsoni* (Chapman, 1944)
Electrona thompsoni Chapman, 1944 (replacement name for *Myctophum oculeum* Chapman, 1939)
Hierops thompsoni: Quast and Hall 1972.
Classified by Paxton (1972, 1979) and Wisner (1974) in subgenus *Hierops,* but Peden et al. (1985) presented evidence suggesting that growth of the eyes, used as a distinguishing character for the subgenus, is allometric, with the eyes shifting from a telescopic condition in juveniles to a more normal condition in adults. The interorbital region is very narrow in juveniles and becomes wider with growth.

Description: Chapman 1939:524–527; Hart 1973:196–197; Wisner 1974:25; Fujii in Masuda et al. 1984:65; Peden et al. 1985: 6–7, table 7.

Figures: Upper: Hart 1973:196. Lower: Bekker 1983, fig. 6C.

Range: Occurs but is not abundant in Bering Sea near the Aleutian Islands, and is probably carried there by currents through the interisland passes. Mapped by Bekker (1983, fig. 58) and Willis et al. (1988, fig. 29). The latter plotted locations of 269 tows which captured *P. thompsoni* out of total of 761: Alaska records were heavily distributed in Gulf of Alaska and south of the Aleutian Islands but very few north of the Aleutians. Shinohara et al. (1994) reported similar distribution from more recent surveys. Maximum depth: Sheiko and Fedorov 2000.

Benthosema glaciale (Reinhardt, 1837) **glacier lanternfish**

Chukchi Sea off Point Barrow, Alaska; eastern Canadian Arctic and North Atlantic Ocean to Cape Hatteras; Mediterranean Sea.

Epi- to mesopelagic; near surface to depth of 225 m at night, and 275–1,250 m during the day.

D 12–15; A 17–19; Pec 10–13; GR 15–20; Vert 35–37.
PO 5; VO 5; AO 11–14; Pol 1; Prc 2.

- Mouth terminal, **snout not projecting**; maxilla notably expanded posteriorly.
- SUGL and INGL heavily bordered with dark pigment; SUGL small, elongate, beginning just before first procurrent caudal ray; INGL smaller, composed of 2 coalesced parts.
- Dn and Vn small, Vn sometimes absent; **PLO anterodorsal to pectoral base**, well above PVO1 and PVO2; VLO about midway between lateral line and pelvic fin base, about on level of SAO1–2; VO2 elevated; SAO1–3 in nearly straight horizontal or angled line; **AOa and AOp discontinuous**; **1 Pol**; **Prc2 elevated**, one diameter below lateral line.
- Lateral line pores fairly distinct.
- Length to 103 mm TL, usually less than 70 mm.

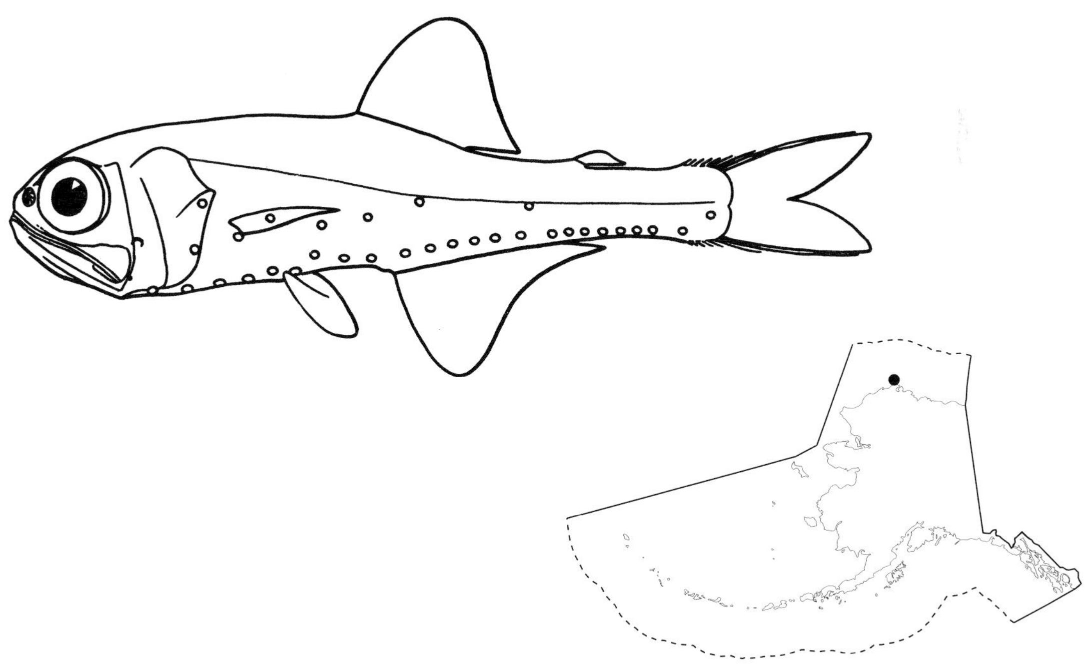

Notes & Sources — *Benthosema glaciale* (Reinhardt, 1837)
Scopelus glacialis Reinhardt, 1837

Description: Wisner 1974:40–41; Coad 1995:313; Hulley in Okamura et al. 1995:100. Wisner (1974) noted that of 14 specimens, the smallest male with caudal luminous glands was 59 mm SL, and the smallest female, 36 mm SL.

Figure: Bekker 1983, fig. 9C.

Range: The most abundant Atlantic myctophid, but very few records are known from the Canadian Arctic and only one or two from Alaska. Listed for Arctic Alaska by Wilimovsky (1954) and Quast and Hall (1972). Wisner (1974) included it as a "remotely possible item" in the Pacific ichthyofauna on the basis of one specimen reported from the Arctic Ocean off Point Barrow by Walters (1955). The latter author noted that the Alaskan specimen had been collected by N. J. Wilimovsky. Lot UBC 63-601 is a specimen from the Chukchi Sea off Point Barrow at 71°23'N, 156°28'W, identified as *B. glaciale,* which may be the same specimen referred to by Walters (1955). Nearest records outside Alaska are from southern Baffin Bay (Coad 1995).

Tarletonbeania taylori Mead, 1953 **taillight lanternfish**

Southeastern Bering Sea and Pacific Ocean, most common from 50°N to 30°N, to latitudes of California and northern Japan; records of occurrence north of 45°N are unreliable unless based on males.

Epi- to mesopelagic, migrating to near surface at night.

D 12–14; A 17–20; Pec 11–15; GR 14–18; Vert 40–42.
PO 6–7; VO 5–7; SAO 3; AO 14–18; Pol 1; Prc 1.

- **Snout slightly projecting**; caudal peduncle narrow and long, depth less than eye diameter.
- **SUGL and INGL short and bulky in males; SUGL and INGL absent in females**.
- Suo present; **PLO opposite pectoral base**, above level of dorsal PVO, hidden by edge of subopercle; SAO series angled; 1 Prc.
- Lateral line undeveloped externally, only the first 2 or 3 scales perforated.
- Gill rakers well developed.
- Length to 70 mm TL.

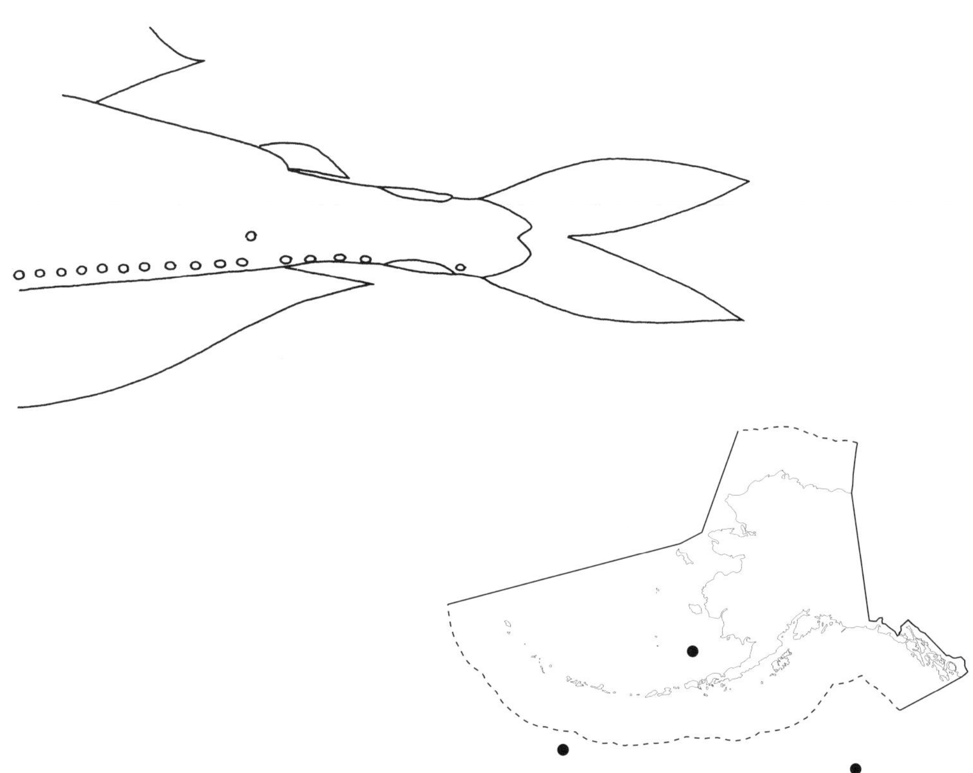

Notes & Sources — *Tarletonbeania taylori* Mead, 1953

Females cannot be distinguished from females of *T. crenularis*; only males can, by the presence of short, bulky supracaudal and infracaudal photophores.

Description: Wisner 1959, 1974:82–83; Fujii in Masuda et al. 1984:67; Peden et al. 1985:9.

Figures: Wisner 1974, fig. 70; male.

Range: Shinohara et al. (1994) recorded adult specimens, including males, from just outside the 200-mile limit south of the Aleutian Islands at 47°26'N, 174°56'W, and farther south; as well as larvae in Bristol Bay at 56°59'N, 165°00'W. Previous reports of occurrence in Alaska (e.g., Matarese et al. 1989) were based on personal communications without supporting documentation. Previously recorded, with documentation, as close to Alaska as 50°N, 145°W (Ocean Station Papa) by Peden et al. (1985).

Tarletonbeania crenularis (Jordan & Gilbert, 1880) **blue lanternfish**

Bering Sea range uncertain; Pacific Ocean south of Aleutian Islands and Gulf of Alaska to Mexico and across Pacific to Japan; distributed mainly in subarctic eastern North Pacific.

Epi- to mesopelagic, from surface to depth of 832 m.

D 11–14; A 17–20; Pec 11–15; GR 14–18; Vert 40–41.
PO 6–7; VO 5–7; SAO 3; AO 13–16; Pol 1; Prc 1.

- **Snout slightly projecting**; caudal peduncle narrow and long, depth less than eye diameter.
- **SUGL long and slender in males**, SUGL absent in females; INGL short and bulky in males, **INGL absent or long and slender in females**.
- Suo present; **PLO opposite pectoral base**, above level of dorsal PVO, hidden by edge of subopercle; SAO series angled; 1 Prc.
- Lateral line undeveloped externally, only the first 2 or 3 scales perforated.
- Gill rakers well developed.
- Length to 70 mm TL.

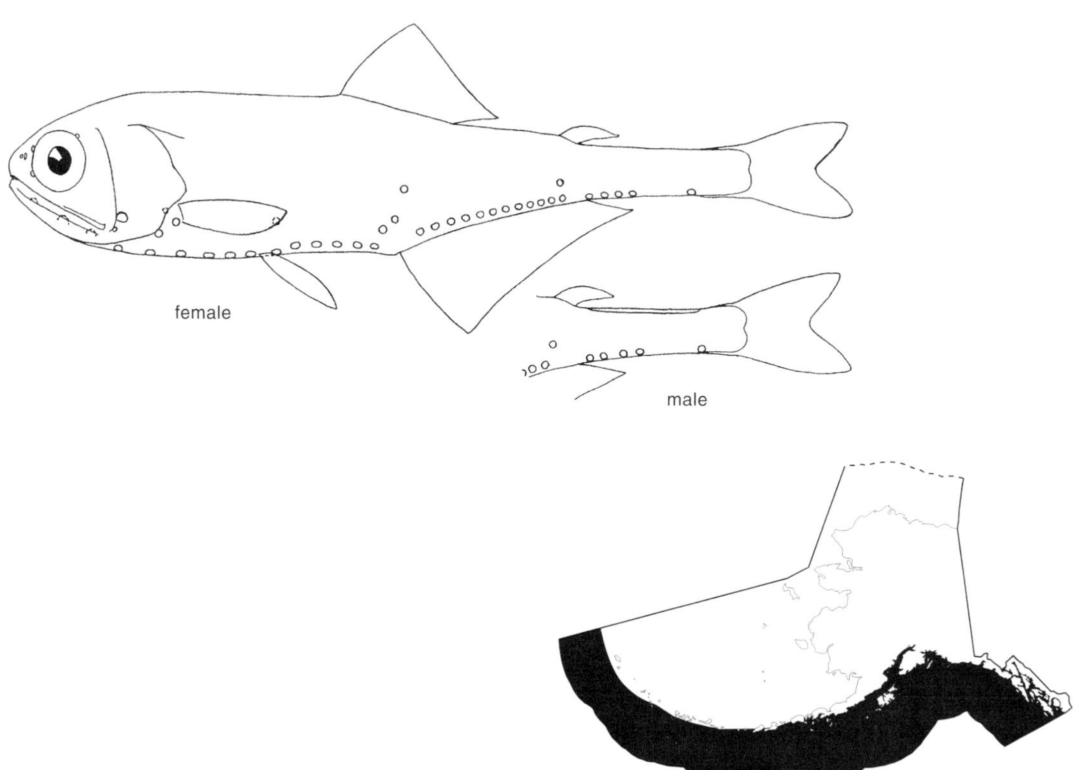

Notes & Sources — *Tarletonbeania crenularis* (Jordan & Gilbert, 1880)
Myctophum crenulare Jordan & Gilbert, 1880

Similar to *T. taylori,* except for the differences in SUGL and INGL, and treated by some authors as a junior synonym of *T. taylori.* Peden et al. (1985) provided data on sympatry supporting separation of *T. taylori* and *T. crenularis* as distinct species. They recorded apparent hybrids of the two forms from Ocean Station Papa.

Females cannot be distinguished from females of *T. taylori*; only the males can, by presence of a long, thin supracaudal gland and absence of the infracaudal gland or, occasionally, presence of a long, thin infracaudal gland.

Description: Chapman 1940:14–16; Wisner 1959, 1974:82; Peden et al. 1985:8–9.

Figures: Bolin 1939b, fig. 5.

Range: Mapped from Bekker (1983, fig. 69) and Willis et al. (1988, fig. 34). The latter reported that *T. crenularis* was captured in 194 of 761 midwater tows; several were in the northern Gulf of Alaska and just south of the Aleutian Islands. Peden et al. (1985) reported that most of their *Tarletonbeania* from Ocean Station Papa were *T. taylori,* but that one was *T. crenularis* and two appeared to be hybrids. Matarese et al. (1989) gave a range to the Bering Sea, but without citing documentation. Fedorov and Sheiko (2002) characterized abundance as common in the vicinity of the Commander Islands. Probably occurs in Alaskan waters in the southern Bering Sea over the Aleutian Basin, but voucher specimens are lacking.

Diaphus theta Eigenmann & Eigenmann, 1890 **California headlightfish**

Southern Bering Sea just north of Aleutian Islands, throughout Gulf of Alaska and North Pacific to Baja California and Japan; widespread in subarctic North Pacific.

Epi- to mesopelagic; at 400–800 m in daytime, migrating at night to depths of 10–60 m.

D 12–14; A 12–14; Pec 10–12; GR 19–23; Vert 34–36.
PO5; VO 5; AO 10–12; Pol 1; Prc 4.

- **Large suprapectoral luminous scale present**; SUGL and INGL absent.
- **Dn, Vn, and So present**; PVO1 and PVO2 in straight line with PO1 or nearly so; **PLO and VLO much nearer to pectoral and pelvic bases than to lateral line**; SAO3, Pol, and Prc4, two to three diameters below lateral line; SAO series usually equally spaced and in line with VO5; SAO2 often a little behind a line through SAO1–3; SAO2–3 interspace infrequently slightly greater than that of SAO1–2; AOa1 usually on level of adjacent AOa photophores but occasionally slightly elevated, though seldom by a full diameter; **last 1 or 2 AOa elevated to form curve with Pol**; Pol and last AOa interspace usually larger than spaces between other AOa photophores.
- Length to 90 mm SL, usually less than 75 mm.

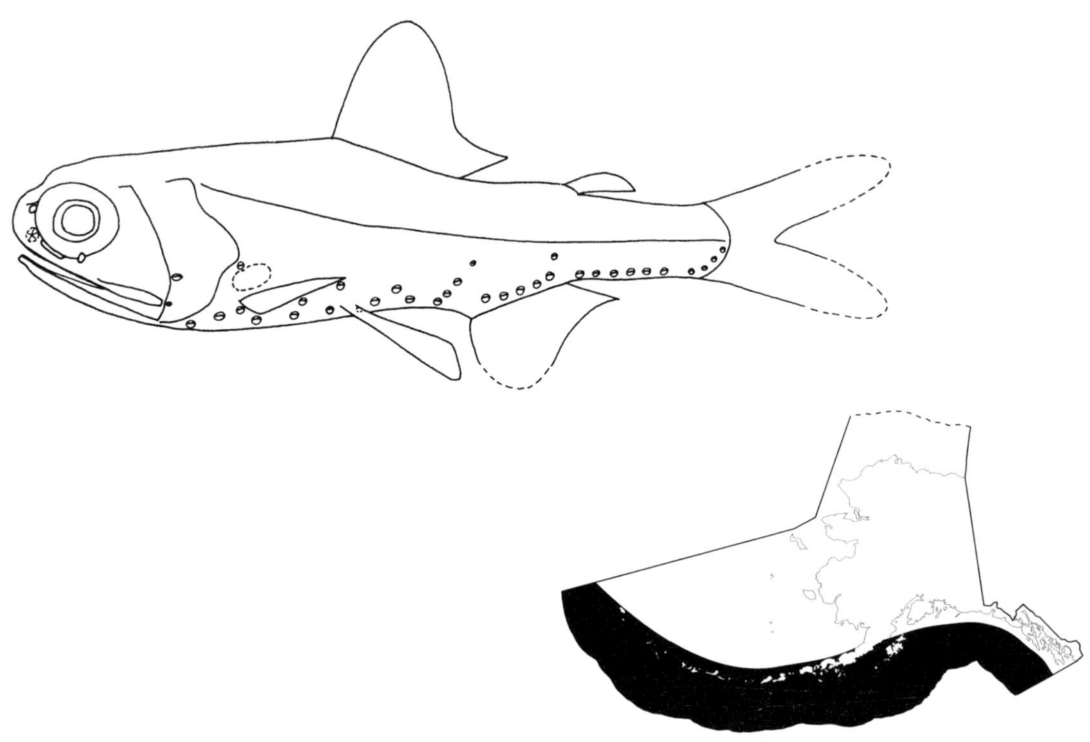

Notes & Sources — *Diaphus theta* Eigenmann & Eigenmann, 1890
Diaphus protoculus Gilbert, 1891

Description: Wisner 1974:140–141; Fujii in Masuda et al. 1984:72; Peden et al. 1985:6.
Figure: Wisner 1974, fig. 125.
Range: Occurs but is not abundant in the Bering Sea north of the Aleutian Islands. Mapped from Bekker (1983, fig. 76) and Willis et al. (1988, fig. 30). The latter plotted 335 tows which captured *D. theta* out of a total of 761 tows. Alaskan records were distributed throughout the Gulf of Alaska and North Pacific with a few records among and just north of the Aleutian Islands. Shinohara et al. (1994) reported similar distribution in their surveys.

Stenobrachius leucopsarus (Eigenmann & Eigenmann, 1890) **northern lampfish**

Southern Bering Sea, Gulf of Alaska, and North Pacific to latitudes of Baja California (about 29°N, 115°W) and across Pacific to southern Japan off Honshu; widespread in subarctic North Pacific.

Epi- to mesopelagic; at depths of 200–1,000 m in daytime, migrating abruptly after sunset to depths of 30 m or less.

D 13–15; A 14–16; Pec 8–11; GR 17–22; Vert 35–37.
PO 5; VO 3–5; AO 12–14; Pol 1; Prc 3–5.

- **Body silvery; fins light gray, unpigmented distally; photophores blue-green.**
- Body moderately robust; caudal peduncle deeper than in *S. nannochir*.
- **SUGL and INGL long; SUGL with 5–8 luminous scales, origin below tip of adipose fin; INGL with 7–9 scales, occupying entire ventral surface of caudal peduncle**; SUGL and INGL present in both sexes.
- Dn absent; Vn present; PO4 much elevated; **usually 4 VO,** with VO1–2 interspace larger than the rest; SAO in relatively straight line, in line, or nearly so, with last VO; SAO usually 3, but 2 or 4 not uncommon; **1 Pol**; usually 4 Prc, in even curve.
- Length to 112 mm SL.

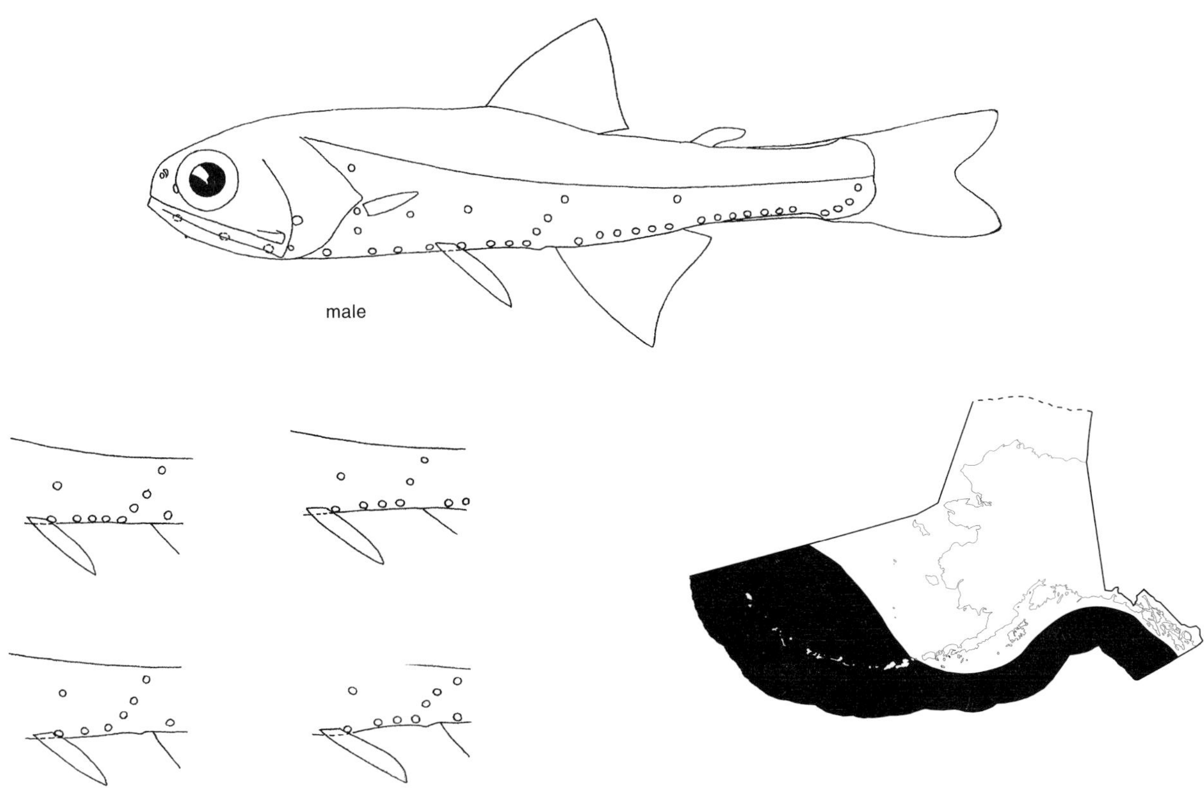

Variations in VO and SAO photophores

Notes & Sources — *Stenobrachius leucopsarus* (Eigenmann & Eigenmann, 1890)
Myctophum (Stenobrachius) leucopsarum Eigenmann & Eigenmann, 1890
Nannobrachium leucopsarum: Gilbert 1896.
Lampanyctus beringensis Schmidt, 1933
Lampanyctus leucopsarus: Chapman 1940.

Description: Gilbert 1896:399; Chapman 1940:16–33; Wisner 1974:159–160; Peden 1974:56–57; Fujii in Masuda et al. 1984:69; Peden et al. 1985:8, tables 9–12.

Figure: Bolin 1939b, fig. 19.

Range: Mapped from Chapman (1940), Bekker (1983, fig. 87), Willis et al. (1988, fig. 21), and Shinohara et al. (1994). Abundant in Bering Sea as well as south of the Aleutian Islands. Willis et al. (1988) plotted 578 tows that captured *S. leucopsarus* out of a total of 761 tows in North Pacific midwaters, with numerous records off Alaska. Brodeur et al. (1999) and Sinclair et al. (1999) reported this species to be the most abundant lanternfish in the Bering Sea in surveys conducted in the 1980s and early 1990s.

Stenobrachius nannochir (Gilbert, 1890) **garnet lampfish**

Southern Bering Sea, Gulf of Alaska, and North Pacific to latitudes of California and Japan; widespread in subarctic North Pacific.

Mesopelagic, to depth of 1,000 m; few found above 500 m; usually taken deeper than *S. leucopsarus.*

D 13–14; A 14–16; Pec 8–10; GR 17–25; Vert 36–39.
PO 5; VO 4–6; AO 13–15; Pol 1; Prc 3–4.

- **Body very dark, fins black; photophores red.**
- Body slender; caudal peduncle not as deep as in *S. leucopsarus*.
- **SUGL and INGL relatively short; SUGL with 2–4 luminous scales, origin well behind adipose fin; INGL with 5–6 scales, occupying about half to three-fourths of ventral aspect of caudal peduncle**; SUGL and INGL present in both sexes.
- Dn absent; Vn present; PO4 much elevated; **usually 5 VO**; SAO in relatively straight line, in line, or nearly so, with last VO; **1 Pol**; usually 3 Prc.
- Length to 110 mm SL.

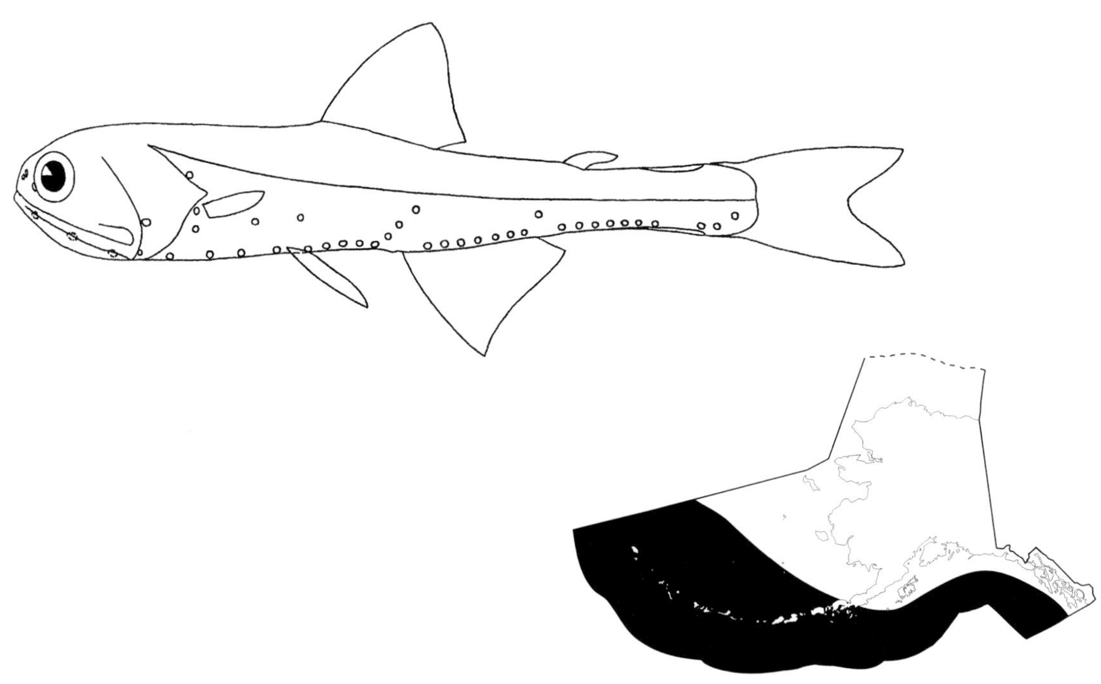

Notes & Sources — *Stenobrachius nannochir* (Gilbert, 1890)
Myctophum nannochir Gilbert, 1890
Nannobrachium nannochir: Gilbert 1896.

Description: Gilbert 1896:399–400; Chapman 1940:28–29, 30–32; Wisner 1974:161–162; Peden 1974:56–57; Peden et al. 1985:8, tables 9–12. Peden et al. (1985) noted that they readily differentiated *S. nannochir* and *S. leucopsarus* even though specimens were badly abraded in net tows.

Figure: Bolin 1939b, fig. 20.

Range: Mapped from Bekker (1983, fig. 87), Willis et al. (1988, fig. 22), and Shinohara et al. (1994). Willis et al. (1988) reported *S. nannochir* taken in 167 of 761 midwater tows, with many records off Alaska. Peden et al. (1985) reported that hauls in northeastern North Pacific from below 500 m captured proportionally many more *S. nannochir* than *S. leucopsarus.* Specimens measuring less than 50 mm SL were most abundant near 600-m depths while the largest fish (up to 124 mm SL) were common in 800-m depths. None were taken shallower than 500 m.

Lampanyctus jordani Gilbert, 1913 — brokenline lanternfish

Bering Sea and Gulf of Alaska to southern California and across Pacific to Japan and Sea of Okhotsk; widespread in subarctic North Pacific, most common in western North Pacific.

Epi- to mesopelagic; to depth of about 1,400 m in daytime, from 200 m to near surface at night.

D 10–14; A 16–20; Pec 13–17; GR 20–25; Vert 38–40.
PO 5; VO 4; AO 14–18; Pol 2; Prc 4.

- **Pectoral fin long**, about 80–110% of head length; pectoral base broad.
- Luminous scales at base of adipose fin; INGL short; SUGL and INGL present in both sexes.
- Dn absent; Vn small; body photophores not notably small; **extra PLO close above pectoral fin origin**; PVO1 well below PVO2; PO4 elevated; VO2 slightly elevated; **VLO close to lateral line**; SAO3 above anal fin origin; **AOa2, AOa3, and often AOa4 abruptly elevated**.
- Length to 140 mm SL.

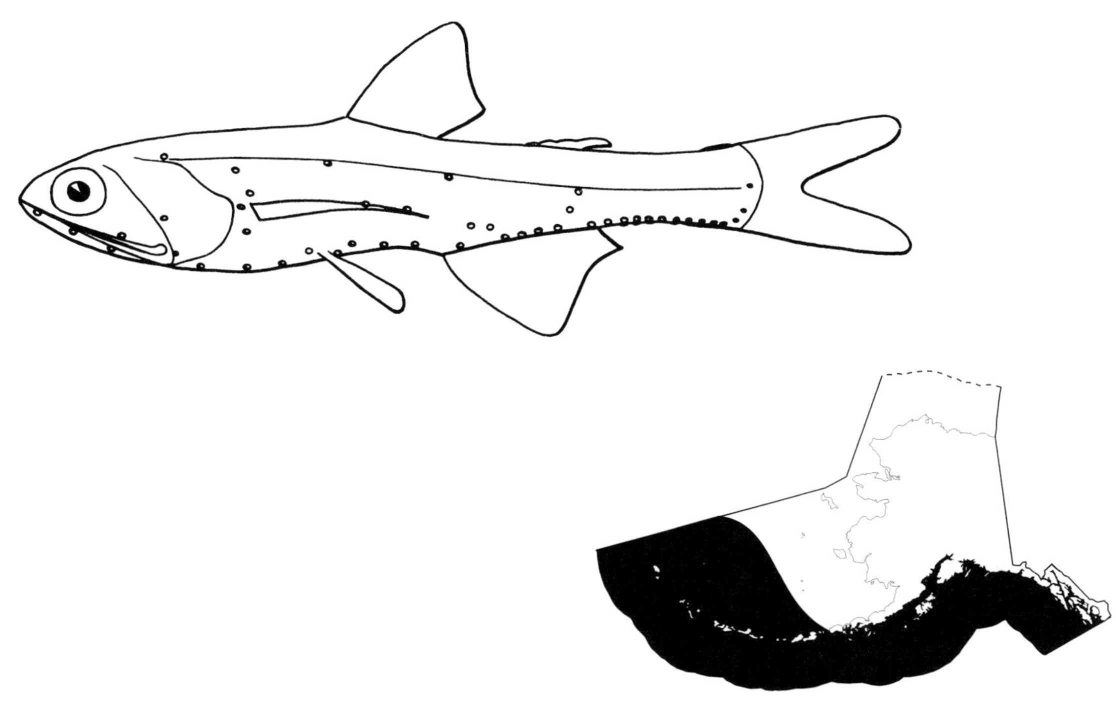

Notes & Sources — *Lampanyctus jordani* Gilbert, 1913

Description: Wisner 1970, 1974:190–191; Fujii in Masuda et al. 1984:70; Peden et al. 1985:6, table 3; Shinohara et al. 1994:76.

Figure: Bekker 1983, fig. 38B.

Range: Mapped from Wisner (1970; 1974, fig. 180), Bekker (1983, fig. 88), Willis et al. (1988, fig. 38), and Shinohara et al. (1988). In North Pacific survey catches summarized by Willis et al. (1988) it was taken in 57 of 761 tows, a few of them in Alaska in the Gulf of Alaska and south of the Alaska Peninsula and the Aleutian Islands, but none in the Bering Sea except in the southwest, off Russia. Few records are from the Bering Sea and the solid fill on our map, after Bekker (1983), may misrepresent range in the Bering Sea.

Nannobrachium regale (Gilbert, 1892) **pinpoint lampfish**

Bering Sea, Gulf of Alaska, and North Pacific to south of Bahia Magdalena, Baja California, and to northern Japan; widespread in subarctic North Pacific.

Epi- to mesopelagic, to depth of 1,500 m; rises to near surface at night, least depth of capture 50 m.

D 14–17; A 16–19; Pec 11–14; GR 12–19; Vert 36–39.
PO 5; VO 4; AO 13–15; Pol 2; Prc 4.

- Pectoral fin short, not reaching past base of pelvic fin; pectoral base narrow.
- No luminous gland at base of adipose fin; INGL long, originating below AOp2–3; SUGL and INGL present in both sexes.
- Dn absent; Vn small; **body photophores notably small**; PVO1 well below PVO2; PO4 elevated; VO2 not elevated; **SAO3 above or anterior to anal fin origin**; **VLO much closer to lateral line than to pelvic base**; line through VLO and SAO1 passes far below SAO3; AOa series often slightly curved.
- Length to 183 mm SL.

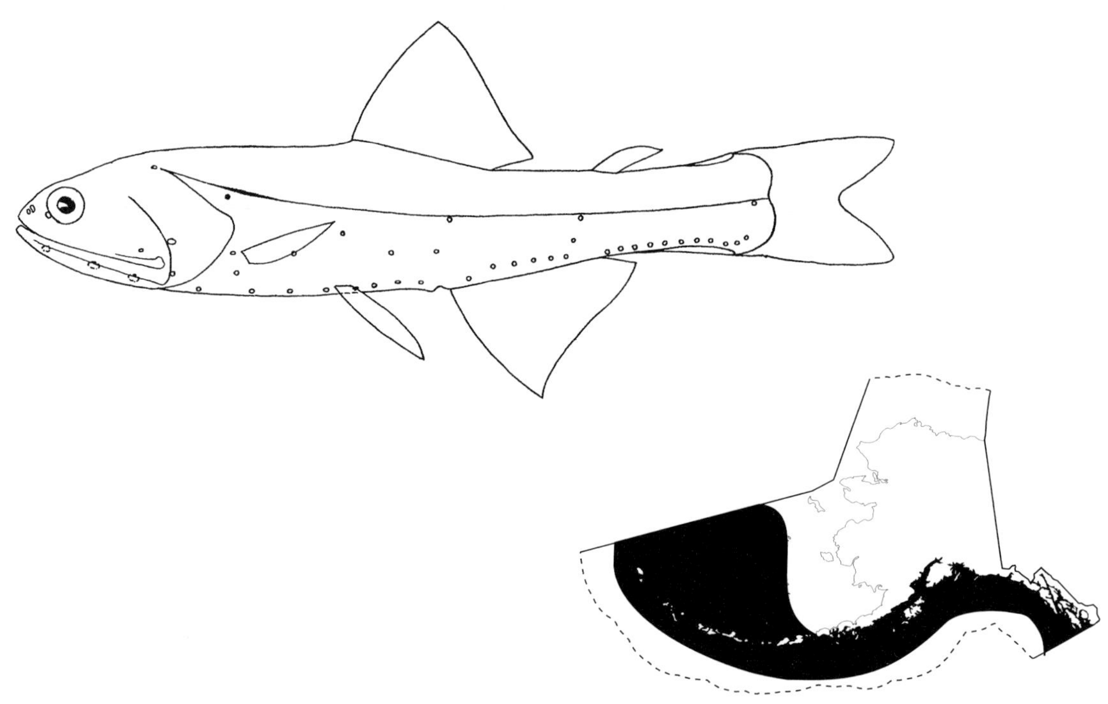

Notes & Sources — *Nannobrachium regale* (Gilbert, 1892)
Myctophum regale Gilbert, 1892
Lampanyctus micropunctatus Chapman, 1939
Lampanyctus regalis: Paxton 1979, Robins et al. 1991, and others.
Classified in *Nannobrachium* by Zahuranec (2000). The genus name refers to the relatively short pectoral fin (compare to pectoral fin of *Lampanyctus jordani*).

Description: Chapman 1939:527–530; Wisner 1974:173; Fujii in Masuda et al. 1984:69; Peden et al. 1985:6–7, table 4; Shinohara et al. 1994:76; Zahuranec 2000:23–26 and appendix tables.

Figure: Bolin 1939b, fig. 25.

Range: Mapped from Wisner (1974, fig. 158), Bekker (1983, fig. 92), Willis et al. (1988, fig. 33), and Shinohara et al. (1994). Willis et al. (1988) reported *N. regale* in 58 of 761 tows, many of them in Alaska in the Gulf of Alaska and south of the Alaska Peninsula and Unimak Pass, and at least one in the vicinity of Attu Island; several catches were in the southwestern Bering Sea off Russia. Few records are from the south-central Bering Sea and solid fill on the above map in that region, after the distribution pattern shown in Bekker's (1983) monograph, may misrepresent the northern limit of the species' range.

Size: This is a large myctophid, and the largest occurring in Alaska. The largest *N. regale* on record is a 183-mm-SL specimen from Japan. The maximum size reported for the eastern Pacific is 170 mm SL (Zahuranec 2000).

Nannobrachium ritteri (Gilbert, 1915) **broadfin lanternfish**

Northeastern Pacific Ocean south of Aleutian Islands and Gulf of Alaska to Mexico.

Epi- to mesopelagic; at depths to 1,100 m in daytime, rising at night to least depth of 20 m.

D 13–16; A 17–19; Pec 11–13; GR 13–18; Vert 36–38.
PO 5; VO 4; AO 14–17; Pol 2; Prc 4.

- Pelvic fin short, not reaching past base of pelvic fin; pectoral base narrow.
- INGL covering three-fourths or less of ventral surface of caudal peduncle; SUGL and INGL present in both sexes.
- Dn absent; Vn small; body photophores not notably small; PVO1 well below PVO2; PO4 elevated; VO2 not elevated; **VLO on line through SAO1 and SAO2 and a little below midway between lateral line and pelvic base; SAO3 well behind vertical from anal origin**; Prc4 slightly behind vertical from Prc3.
- Length to 120 mm SL.

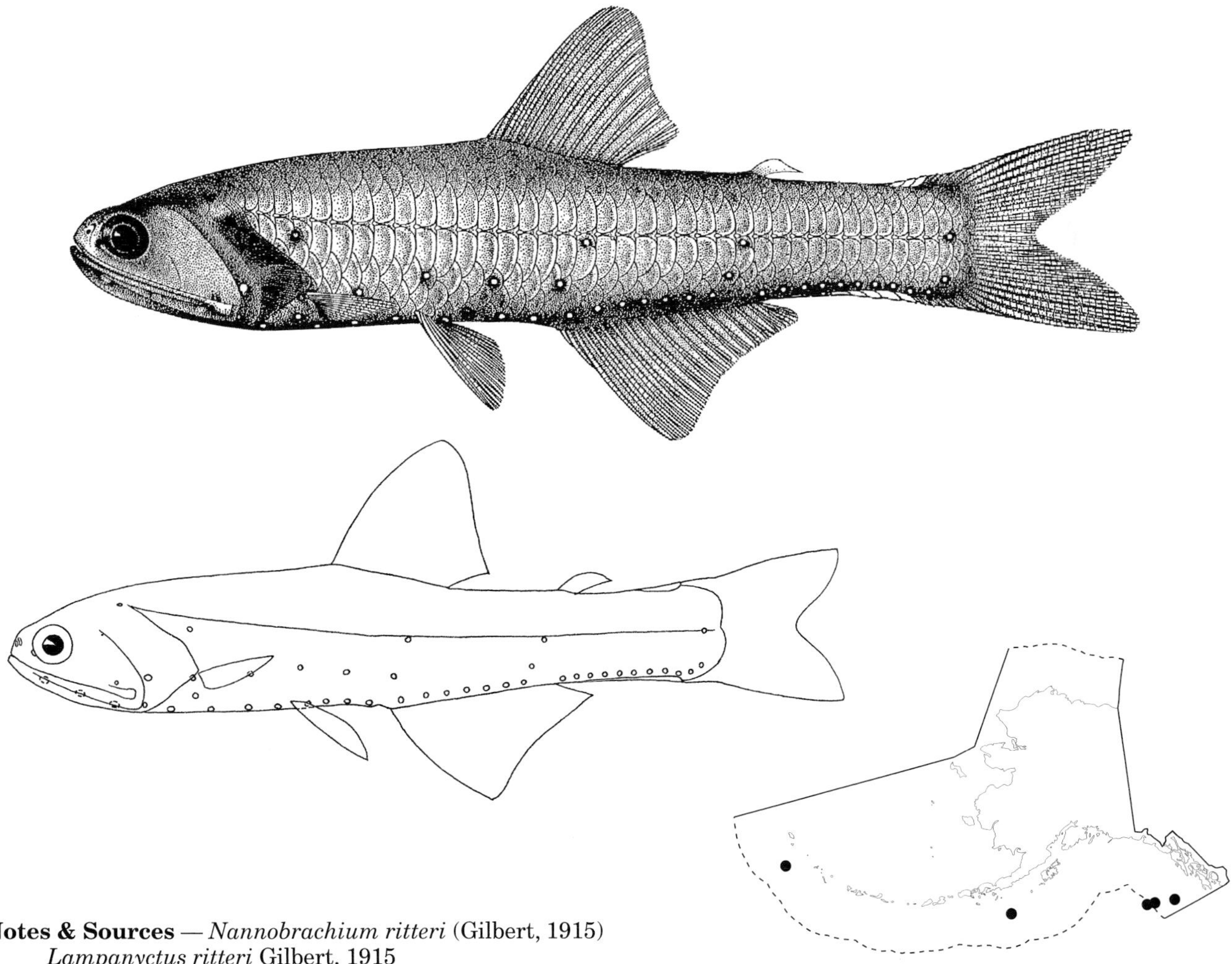

Notes & Sources — *Nannobrachium ritteri* (Gilbert, 1915)
Lampanyctus ritteri Gilbert, 1915
Classified in *Nannobrachium* by Zahuranec (2000).

Description: Gilbert 1915:318–321; Wisner 1974:170–172; Peden et al. 1985:7, table 5; Shinohara et al. 1994:73–74; Zahuranec 2000:26–28 and appendix tables.

Figures: Upper: Gilbert 1915, pl. 15, fig. 3. Lower: Bolin 1939b, fig. 24. The labels for *N. ritteri* and *Notoscopelus resplendens* in Clemens and Wilby (1961, figs. 70 and 72) are switched. The figure on page 195 of Hart (1973) is labeled *N. resplendens* but looks like *Nannobrachium ritteri.*

Range: Willis et al. 1988, fig. 3: taken in 109 of 761 midwater tows; a few were off Alaska but the vast majority were in the eastern North Pacific at latitudes of southern British Columbia to northern California (where the study terminated). Shinohara et al. 1994: collected by beam trawl in the Gulf of Alaska at 54°59'N, 141°59'W. Matarese et al. (1989) gave a range to the Bering Sea, evidently based on records that are no longer considered to be accurate. J. W. Orr (pers. comm., 13 Nov. 1997) reported that the NMFS survey database has records from the Bering Sea but that all myctophid identifications to species level in the database were suspect and he knows of no specimens retained to verify those records. None of the 929 specimens examined by Zahuranec (2000) was from the Bering Sea.

Order Lampridiformes
Lampridiforms

Lampridiforms are a diverse group of oceanic fishes with representatives in all the seas of the world. Their diversity is reflected in the large number of families (seven) containing a relatively small number of genera (12) and species (19). Their body forms place them in two main groups: species with deep bodies, symmetrical caudal fins, and well-developed skeletons, referred to as the bathysomes; and species with long, ribbonlike bodies, asymmetrical caudal fins, and weak skeletons, referred to as the taeniosomes. One of each type occurs in the marine waters of Alaska.

As well as having striking shapes, lampridiforms are highly colored. Many species are silvery, with red fins, as are the two species occurring in Alaska. Other diagnostic lampridiform characters include lack of true spines in the fins; a long dorsal fin, usually with the anterior portion much higher than the rest of the fin; a long to much reduced anal fin; and pelvic fins which are usually thoracic, or they can be absent. Lampridiforms have a unique type of protrusible upper jaw; a posteriorly placed mesethmoid and lack of a ligamentous attachment between the palatines and maxillae allows the maxillae to carry the premaxillae forward in the feeding posture. The premaxillae exclude the maxillae from the gape. Many lampridiform fishes have no scales, and when present they are usually small and cycloid. When present, the swim bladder is physoclistous.

Most lampridiforms are large fishes. The oarfish, *Regalecus glesne* (which does not occur in Alaska), reaches 11 m (35 ft) and probably is the source of many sea-serpent tales. The Alaskan species can reach at least 1.8 m (6 ft).

The composition of the order Lampridiformes has changed markedly over the years. Olney et al. (1993) surveyed characters and used a cladistic analysis to establish a monophyletic grouping of families.

Family Lamprididae
Opahs

The opah family exemplifies the bathysomic form of lampridiforms and comprises two species in one genus, *Lampris,* with a circumglobal distribution in tropical and temperate seas. These predatory fishes of the open ocean occur near the surface to depths of about 500 m. The more cosmopolitan of the two species, the spotted opah, *L. guttatus,* occurs in the northeastern Pacific as far north as the Gulf of Alaska off Icy Bay, near Yakutat, but records from Alaska are rare and the fish probably ventures there only in El Niño years.

Opahs are easily identified by their oval, strongly compressed shape (they are known as moonfish in some regions of the world), silvery blue and red body scattered with silver spots, and brilliant vermilion fins. Their dorsal and anal fins are long but low, except for a high portion at the front of the dorsal fin, and the anal fin is shorter-based than the dorsal fin. The pectoral fins are long and attached horizontally on the upper third of the body. Cruising speed is probably maintained by pectoral swimming (Rosenblatt and Johnson 1976). The pelvic fins, also long, are attached to the pectoral girdle. Other family characteristics include: body covered with small, cycloid, deciduous scales; lateral line highly arched anteriorly; teeth absent in adults, present in juveniles; large swim bladder; 6 branchiostegal rays; and 43–46 vertebrae. Radical morphological changes occur in *L. guttatus* during development, including an increase in body depth and decreases in length of the anterior dorsal fin rays and the pelvic fins. The fully adult shape is not reached until 50 cm SL or so.

Lampris guttatus is the larger of the two opah species, reaching a total length of about 183 cm (6 ft) and weight of about 273 kg (600 lb).

Lampris guttatus was included on Quast and Hall's (1972) list of fishes of Alaska and in Hart's (1973) guide to Pacific fishes of Canada as *L. regius,* with opah for the vernacular. Since then, Palmer (in Hureau and Monod 1973) brought the name *L. guttatus* back into use and Palmer and Oelschläger (1976) demonstrated its validity according to the International Code of Zoological Nomenclature. In addition, Parin and Kukuyev (1983) showed that there are two valid species of opah, not just one, and Gon (in Gon and Heemstra 1990) coined the name spotted opah to distinguish the opah that occasionally occurs off Alaska from the other species, *L. immaculatus,* which he called the southern opah.

Another recent change is reversion of the spelling of the family name from Lampridae back to Lamprididae, the spelling preferred by Gill (1872, 1903), who established the family. Patterson (1993) reviewed the history of the family name and concluded that the proper stem is *lamprid-*, which also applies to the order Lampridiformes, established by Goodrich (1909).

Lampris guttatus (Brünnich, 1788) **spotted opah**

North Pacific from Gulf of Alaska at Icy Bay and south of Aleutian Islands to Baja California off Cape San Lucas and to Japan; worldwide in temperate and tropical seas.

Oceanic, pelagic, at depths near surface to 512 m; usually found in lower epipelagic zone.

D 48–55; A 33–42; Pec 20–25; Pel 13–17; GR 15–16; Vert 46.

- Iridescent blue and red dorsally shading to silver flushed with light red ventrally; body covered with silver spots; fins bright red.
- Body compressed and deep; ventral body contour much steeper than dorsal contour; caudal peduncle slender.
- Anterior part of dorsal fin, pectoral, and pelvic fins long and falcate; caudal fin sharply but shallowly forked or lunate; pelvic fin inserted below or slightly behind posterior edge of pectoral base.
- Scales minute, cycloid.
- Length to 183 cm TL, weight to 273 kg.

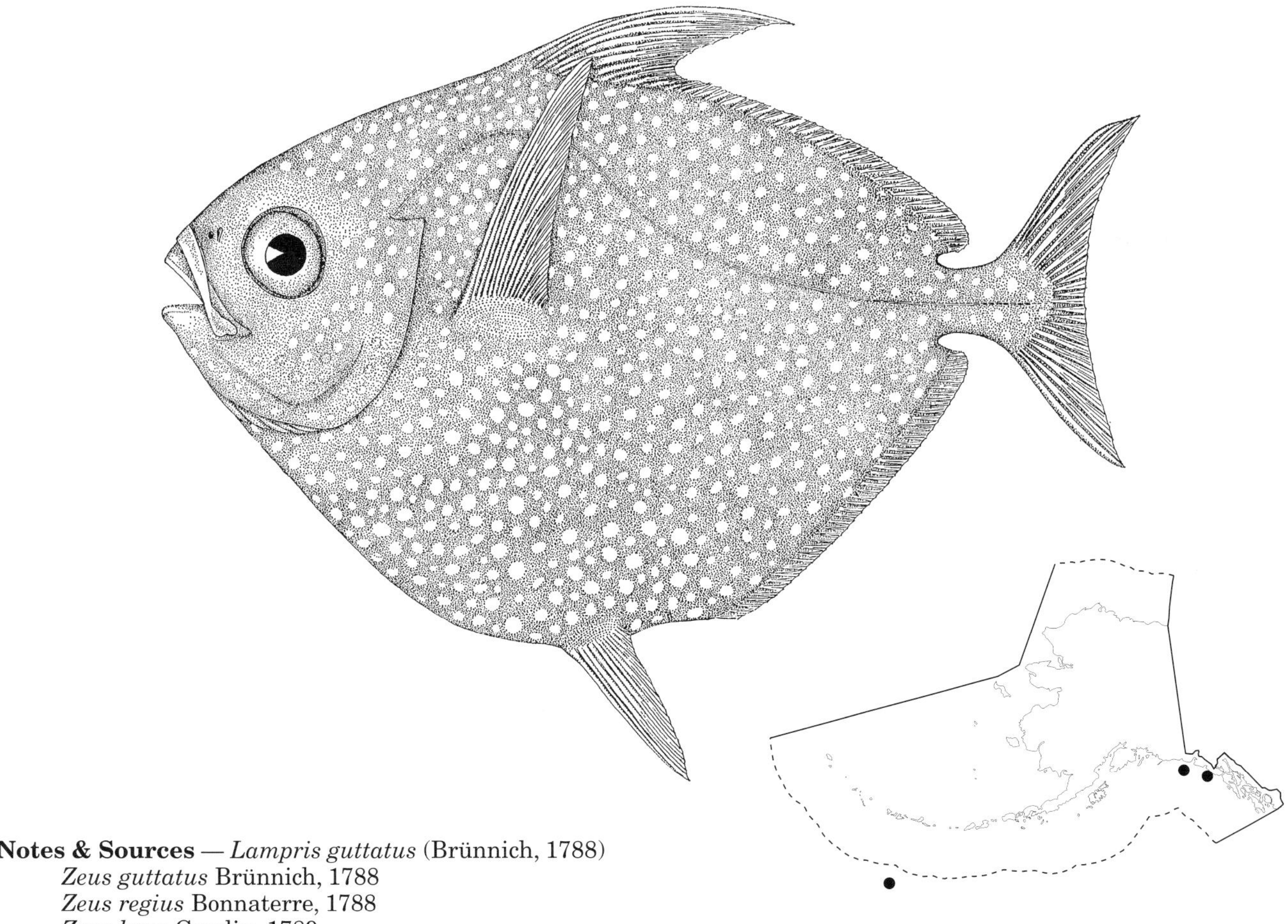

Notes & Sources — *Lampris guttatus* (Brünnich, 1788)
Zeus guttatus Brünnich, 1788
Zeus regius Bonnaterre, 1788
Zeus luna Gmelin, 1789

The name *Lampris regius* (Bonnaterre) is still used by some authors, although the name *L. guttatus* (Brünnich) has priority. The two names are considered as synonyms simultaneously published. The first reviser (Müller 1806) chose to use the name *L. guttatus* and in so doing, determined priority (Palmer and Oelschläger 1976).

Description: Hart 1973:269–270; Eschmeyer and Herald 1983:119; Gon in Gon and Heemstra 1990:215–216.

Figure: Leim and Scott 1966:227.

Range: Recorded from Icy Bay, near Yakutat, at 59°12'N, 141°42'W by Bell and Kask (1936); one specimen (USNM 104524), 51.3 cm TL, taken on longline halibut gear at or above 91 m. A story by K. Diakanoff and color photograph in the *Alaskan Southeaster* (March 1998, Vol. 7, No. 1) document the catch of a small specimen (8 kg dressed weight) 3.7 km offshore from La Perouse Glacier on the Fairweather Grounds on 9 Aug. 1992, on trolling gear at 7–11 m. Larkins (1964) reported one opah taken in 1955 south of the Aleutian Islands at 48°00'N, 175°00'W, just outside the 200-mile Exclusive Economic Zone, during salmon gillnetting research. The catch locality for USNM 84407 (a skin), collected in 1913, is uncertain; one catalog entry states it to be from Alaska but another specifies Carpenter Bay, which is on the coast of Moresby Island, northern British Columbia. No records have been published for British Columbia since Clemens and Wilby (1949) reported catches off the coast of Vancouver Island.

Family Trachipteridae
Ribbonfishes

Ribbonfishes, family Trachipteridae, exemplify the taeniosomic form of lampridiform fishes. They are widely distributed in all seas except the Southern Ocean, and are frequently taken as bycatch of one to a few individuals in nets fishing near the surface to depths of about 640 m, as well as found in the stomachs of deep-feeding predatory fishes such as albacore and lancetfish. Although occasionally they are found in the surf or washed up on beaches, these fish probably occur near shore only accidentally. Little is known about their habits but they have been observed from submersibles to orient themselves at a 45° angle with the head up and move by undulating the dorsal fin. Four species of ribbonfish inhabit the eastern Pacific Ocean. One is known to occur in Alaska. King-of-the-salmon, *Trachipterus altivelis,* are occasionally caught in the Gulf of Alaska and southeastern Bering Sea.

Ribbonfishes are elongate and compressed, as suggested by the name, and extremely delicate owing to weak skeletons. Completely whole specimens are rare due to breakage from entanglement in collecting gear and weight of other fishes in the catch. Ribbonfish fin characteristics include a long dorsal fin beginning on the head; lack of an anal fin; a caudal fin mainly consisting of an upper lobe; small pectoral fins, inserted horizontally; and rudimentary or no pelvic fins. In ribbonfishes scales are absent or, when present, deciduous and cycloid or modified ctenoid; teeth are present; the swim bladder is rudimentary or absent; ribs are absent; and 6 branchiostegal rays support the gill membrane of each side. Vertebral counts range from 62 to 111, with 90 or more in the Alaskan species. Like most other lampridiforms, ribbonfishes have silver bodies and red fins.

Allometric growth in ribbonfishes results in some radical changes in body shape, fin length, and other characters. In *T. altivelis* changes include reduction of the pelvic fins to rudiments, reduction of the lower lobe of the caudal fin to a few short spines and development of a long upward lobe, development of rasplike tubercles (modified ctenoid scales) along the ventral midline, and loss of dark blotches on the body.

The maximum confirmed length for a ribbonfish is 186 cm (6.1 ft), recorded by Hart (1973) for *T. altivelis,* although specimens up to 244 cm (8 ft) have been reported. Being so slim, ribbonfishes do not weigh much. Fitch (1964) noted that a ripe female about 167 cm (5.5 ft) in length weighed only 4.04 kg (8.9 lb).

Trachipterus altivelis was named king-of-the-salmon by the Makah Indians of the Pacific Northwest who believed this fish led the salmon into the rivers to spawn each year (Fitch 1964), and that killing it would cause the salmon runs to cease (Jordan and Evermann 1898). Accumulated knowledge suggests this fish probably occurs near shore only accidentally.

Trachipterus altivelis Kner, 1859 **king-of-the-salmon**

Southeastern Bering Sea and Gulf of Alaska to Chile and offshore halfway to the Hawaiian Islands. Offshore from surface to about 640 m, in inside waters as well as open ocean; mesopelagic.

D 163–191; A 0; Pec 9–11; Pel 6–7; LLp 262–306; LLs 106–122; GR 12–16; Vert 90–94.

- Body dusky silver with red fins; juveniles and young adults with evenly spaced dark spots, 4–5 above and 1–2 below the lateral line.
- Head deep, compressed, mouth small; body elongate, compressed, tapering to fine caudal peduncle; ventral body contour straight for entire length; dorsal contour descending in straight line from nuchal crest to caudal fin origin.
- First 3–6 dorsal fin rays elongate; anal fin absent; eccentric caudal fin with dorsally directed, fan-shaped upper lobe and rays of lower lobe reduced to stumps; pectoral fin small; pelvic fin reduced to base in adults.
- Modified ctenoid scales present as sharp-tipped tubercles covering body, enlarged along ventral surface; small prickles along fin rays; and inconspicuous prickles along lateral line.
- Jaws with several canine teeth as well as numerous minute, weak teeth.
- Length to 186 cm TL.

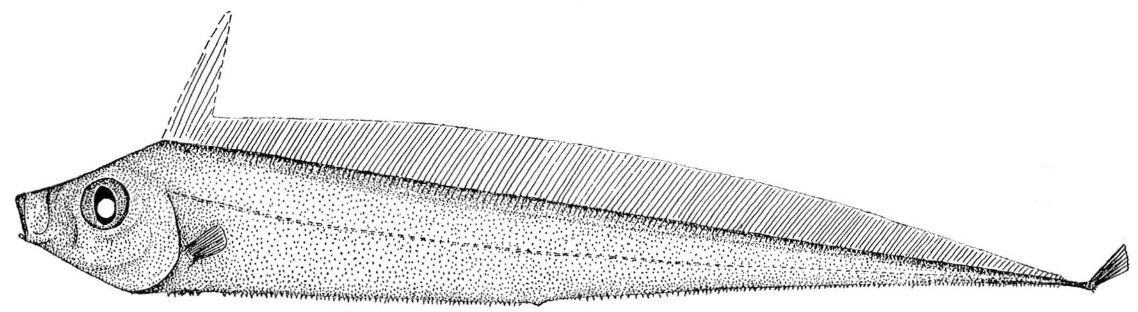

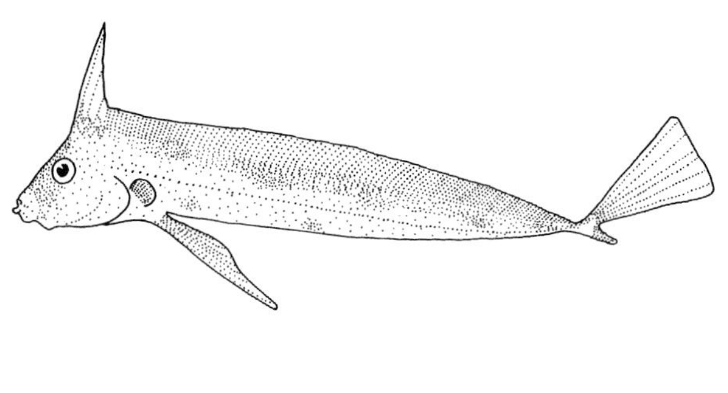

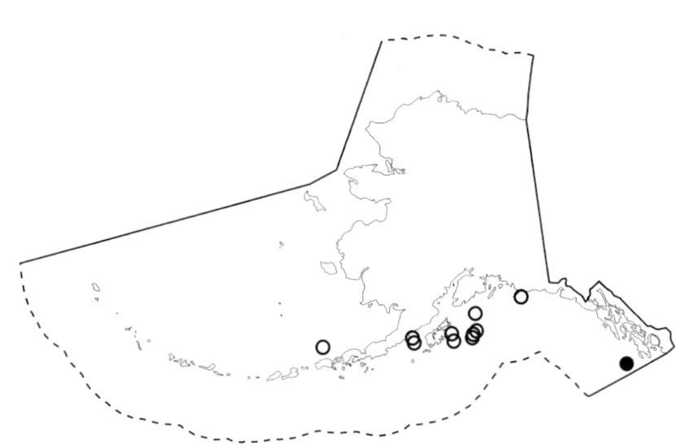

Notes & Sources — *Trachipterus altivelis* Kner, 1859
Trachypterus rexsalmonorum Jordan & Gilbert, 1894
Trachypterus seleniris Snyder, 1908

Description: Fitch 1964:233–236; Hart 1973:271–272; Eschmeyer and Herald 1983:121.

Figures: Upper: Hart 1973:271; BC 65-590, 186 cm TL, Sooke, British Columbia (greatest confirmed length in the literature). Lower: Miller and Lea 1972:86; juvenile.

Range: Fitch (1964) seems to have been the first to give Alaska as the northern limit, but he and subsequent authors did not cite voucher specimens or give specific localities in Alaska waters. Lot AB 99-3 comprises five specimens taken west of Cape Augustine at 54°58'N, 134°21'W, depth 0–20 m, by the FV *Great Pacific* on 24 Jul. 1998. Open circles on the above map represent catch localities in the NMFS survey database reported by D. W. Kessler (pers. comm., 20 Jun. 1994); these records are not backed by voucher specimens, but the species is easy to identify and not likely to have been confused with others.

Order Percopsiformes
Percopsiforms

The Percopsiformes is an order of freshwater fishes that combine some of the characters exhibited by the more primitive troutlike fishes (e.g., small adipose fin, pelvic fins placed well behind the pectorals) and the more advanced spiny rayed fishes (spines in fins, ctenoid scales, perchlike mouth). For the combination of troutlike and perchlike features, some members of the order are called trout-perches. This is a small order, with two suborders represented by living species and comprising three families, six genera, and nine species. Pecopsiforms occur only in North America, and include the cavefishes of the southern and eastern United States. One species, *Percopsis omiscomaycus,* occurs in Alaska.

In percopsiforms the premaxilla borders the entire upper jaw (maxilla is not in the gape), and is not protractile; the ectopterygoids and palatines bear teeth; and the orbitosphenoid, basisphenoid, and suborbital shelf are absent. Spines are usually present in the dorsal and anal fins but are soft and weak; the pelvic fins, when present, are positioned behind the pectoral fins; and some species have an adipose fin. Scales are ctenoid in some species, cycloid in others. Percopsiforms have 6 branchiostegal rays and 28–36 vertebrae.

Percopsiforms are small fishes, attaining maximum sizes of about 6.2 cm (2.5 inches) to 20 cm (7.75 inches). *Percopsis omiscomaycus* is the largest species.

Family Percopsidae
Trout-perches

The family Percopsidae comprises two species: the trout-perch, *Percopsis omiscomaycus,* and the sand roller, *P. transmontana.* Sand rollers, occurring in the Columbia River Basin in Idaho, Washington, and Oregon, have a much more restricted distribution than trout-perch, which occur across northern North America to Alaska. Trout-perch inhabit fairly deep water in lakes or deep pools in streams, but move into shallow water for spawning and to feed at night.In Alaska they have been found in the Porcupine and Yukon drainages, out to the edge of the Yukon Delta. They are not common in Alaska but are abundant in other areas.

Percopsids have a large, naked head; a subterminal mouth; ctenoid body scales; no teeth on the vomer; an adipose fin; a dorsal fin with 1–3 weak spines and 9–12 soft rays; an anal fin with 1 or 2 weak spines and 5–8 soft rays; pectoral fins reaching well posterior to the bases of the pelvic fins; and subthoracic pelvic fins with 1 weak spine and 7–9 rays. The combination of ctenoid scales, weak spines in the dorsal and anal fins, long pectoral fins, and presence of an adipose fin distinguishes *P. omiscomaycus* from all other Alaskan freshwater fishes. In addition, the arrangement of the pyloric caeca is unique among Alaskan freshwater fishes and provides a good character for identifying remains in stomach contents since the caeca are resistant to digestion and can be recognized after most other ingested tissues are in an advanced state of digestion.

Although *P. omiscomaycus* are reported to reach 20 cm (7.75 inches) in length, in most areas they are half this size or less. In Alaska they reach a maximum of about 8 cm (3.15 inches).

Percopsis omiscomaycus (Walbaum, 1792) **trout-perch**

Porcupine River and mainstem Yukon River to outer edge of Yukon Delta; boreal North America; relatively rare in Alaska.

Fairly deep water (10–61 m) in lakes, deep pools in streams, or under cut banks, roots, or debris; in shallower water for feeding at night or for spawning, usually over sand.

D I–III,9–11 + adipose; A I,5–8; Pec 12–15; Pel I,8–9; LLp 41–60; GR 8–13; PC 7–14; Vert 33–36.

- Silver, with purplish or yellow tinge dorsally; body partly transparent; rows of small dark spots along dorsal midline, above lateral line, and along lateral line; fins transparent.
- Body elongate, terete, noticeably heavier toward head.
- Mouth small, subterminal; maxilla not reaching level of eye.
- Spines present in dorsal, anal, and pelvic fins; pectoral fin reaching posterior to base of pelvic fin; pelvic fin abdominal; adipose fin present.
- Large, rough (ctenoid) scales on body; head naked.
- Lateral line complete, nearly straight.
- Pyloric caeca arrangement unique, see figure.
- Length to 200 mm TL, usually 75–100 mm.

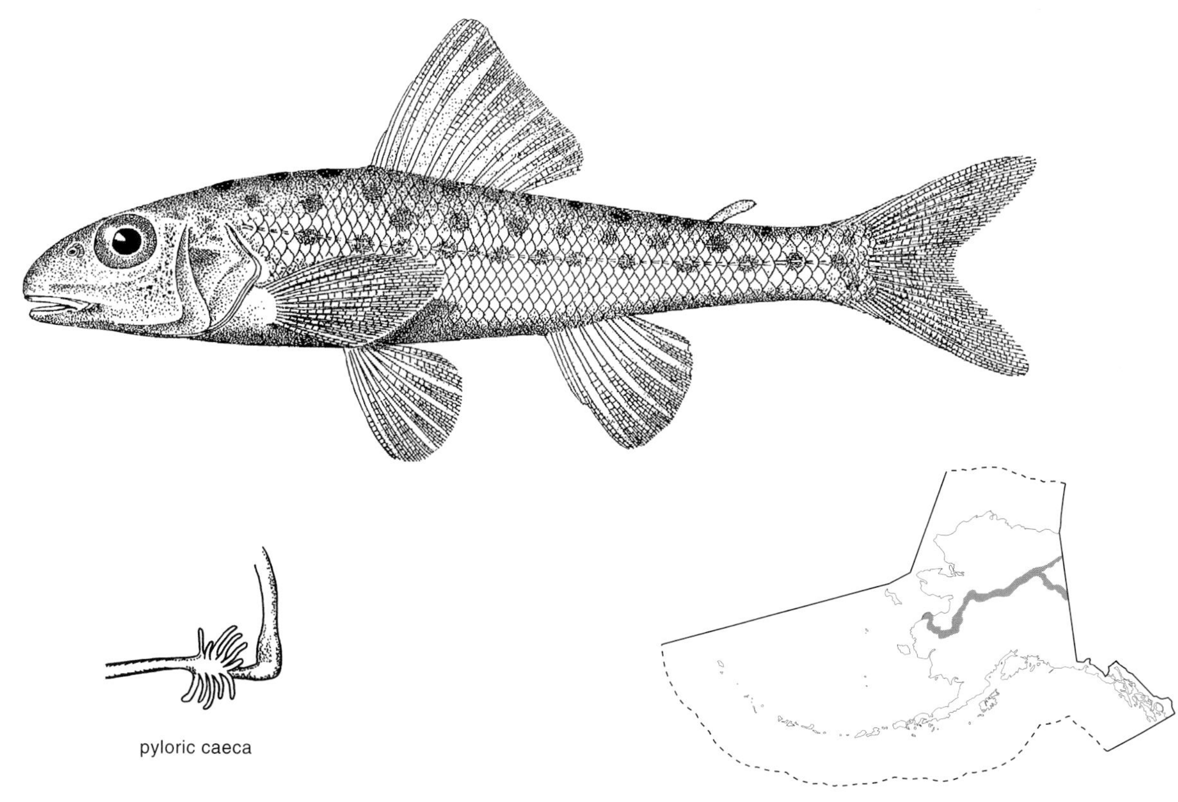

Notes & Sources — *Percopsis omiscomaycus* (Walbaum, 1792)
Salmo omiscomaycus Walbaum, 1792
Percopsis guttatus Agassiz, 1850

Description: McPhail and Lindsey 1970:290–293; Scott and Crossman 1973:678–682; Morrow 1980:177–179.

Figures: Jordan and Evermann 1900, fig. 329; Iowa. Pyloric caeca: based on Scott and Crossman 1973:679 and specimen.

Range: North American range was mapped most recently by Gilbert and Lee (in Lee et al. 1980) and Page and Burr (1991), and range in Alaska by McPhail and Lindsey (1970) and Morrow (1980). The ABL has samples from the Yukon River. Baxter (1990ms) collected numerous specimens in June 1985 from the outer edge of the Yukon Delta at the mouths of Apoon Pass, Elongozhik Pass, and Bugomowik Pass, extending the known range more than 150 km down the Yukon from the mouth of the Andreafsky River.

Size: Gilbert and Lee in Lee et al. 1980.

Order Ophidiiformes
Ophidiiforms

Ophidiiforms are thought to be related to gadiforms and, like some cod relatives, are elongate, tapering fishes with long-based dorsal and anal fins. Many species occupy benthic, deepsea habitats. A few live in brackish or freshwater caves in tropical climates and are blind or have reduced eyes. Poorly developed eyes are also common among the deepsea species.

Containing about 367 species, 93 genera, and four families (Nielsen et al. 1999), the order is a relatively large one. It contains two suborders, which are defined by the presence or absence of viviparity. The Bythitoidei are live-bearing fishes, represented in Alaskan waters by the family Bythitidae. The Ophidioidei are oviparous, and are represented in Alaska by the Ophidiidae.

In ophidiiforms the dorsal and anal fins extend to and are usually joined with the caudal fin, which is absent in some species; and dorsal and anal fin pterygiophores are more numerous than the adjacent vertebrae. The pelvic fins have 1 or 2 soft rays each or are absent, and when present are inserted at about the level of the preopercle or farther anteriorly and are relatively close together. The fin rays are soft; although a short pelvic fin spine is present in some species it is hidden, and not included in meristic counts by most authors. The nostrils are paired on each side. Most genera have one or more patches of teeth on the basibranchials. The branchiostegal rays number 7–9 and the count can be a useful character, but achieving an accurate count can require stripping away darkly pigmented or thick skin. Nearly all ophidiiform species have short tubercles as well as "long" or "developed" gill rakers on the first arch and some authors report only the long rakers; comparable counts are not available for all species.

Ophidiiforms range in maximum size from about 13 cm (5 inches) to 2 m (6.6 ft). The largest sizes are attained in the cusk-eel family, Ophidiidae.

Because of similarities of the ophidiiforms to gadiform fishes, particularly to the Macrouridae, some researchers classify them in the Gadiformes. In the past, some researchers placed them in the Perciformes. Cohen and Nielsen (1978) summarized the characters of the group, accorded it ordinal rank, and provided a new classification of the order. Nielsen et al. (1999) provided an updating and enlargement of Cohen and Nielsen (1978), and summarized conclusions of recent studies addressing the relationships of the various taxa. The order Ophidiiformes is paraphyletic as currently organized but serves for purposes of convenience.

Family Ophidiidae
Cusk-eels

Cusk-eels occur in all oceans in a wide range of habitats, from tidepools to abyssal plains. Many of the species are benthopelagic at great depths. A member of this group, *Abyssobrotula galatheae* (not Alaskan), holds the deepsea record for all fishes, with one taken at 8,370 m in the Puerto Rico Trench. None of the 218 known species (Nielsen et al. 1999) is particularly common.

The one ophidiid species known to exist in Alaskan waters is the giant cusk-eel, *Spectrunculus grandis.* Its presence in the region was confirmed by Quast and Hall (1972), who reported a specimen from Cook Inlet. Changes with growth in *Spectrunculus* include repositioning of the mouth from vertical to horizontal and development of tissue covering the eyes, and until fairly recently the postlarval and adult stages of *S. grandis* were classified as two different species. The Alaskan specimen is a postlarva and Quast and Hall (1972) recorded it as *S. radcliffei,* the name in use at that time for postlarvae of the giant cusk-eel.

As with other families in the suborder Ophidioidei, in most members of the Ophidiidae the anterior nostril is placed well above the upper lip, not immediately above it. All species are oviparous, and males lack an external intromittent organ. The dorsal and anal fins often connect with the caudal fin, appearing as one continuous fin that tapers to a point.

Characters distinguishing the Ophidiidae from other ophidioids include: supramaxilla present; dorsal fin rays usually equal to or longer than the opposing anal rays; anus and anal fin origin posterior to tip of pectoral fin; pelvic fins rarely absent; one or more spines on the opercle in some species; scales present; and median basibranchial tooth patches present or absent.

Pacific Ocean cusk-eels attain a wide range of sizes, from about 18 cm (7 inches) to 200 cm (6.6 ft). The largest *S. grandis* recorded from the eastern Pacific is an individual measuring 135 cm (4.4 ft) in total length caught off California (Hubbs and Follett 1978).

Spectrunculus grandis (Günther, 1877) **giant cusk-eel**

Gulf of Alaska at Kasitsna Bay, Cook Inlet; northern British Columbia at Tasu Sound, Queen Charlotte Islands, to California and to Japan; South Pacific off New Zealand; Atlantic Ocean.

Benthopelagic at depths of 800–4,300 m, most often taken at 2,000–3,000 m; postlarval stage pelagic, found between surface and 1,700 m but mostly epipelagic.

D 113–148; A 73–113; Pec 21–33; Pel 2; Br 8; GR 7–13; Vert precaudal 18–25, total 70–84.

- In preservative males dusky cream, females light gray-brown; in life pinkish orange.
- Head small, less than half preanal length; snout fleshy, rounded, longer than eye; mouth large, maxilla extending past eye; anterior nostril with thick, fleshy raised rim.
- Eyes large, protruding, with clear corneas in small specimens, to small, recessed, covered with translucent or opaque tissue in large specimens.
- Opercular spine strong.
- Pectoral fins short, not reaching anus; pelvic fins close together on isthmus below preopercle.
- Head and body covered with small, thin cycloid scales; dorsal, anal, and pectoral fins scaled.
- Lateral line short, reaching to or slightly beyond origin of dorsal fin.
- Small villiform teeth on jaws, basibranchials, vomer, and palatines; vomerine tooth patch diamond-shaped; 2 median basibranchial tooth patches (anterior long, posterior short).
- Length to 138 cm TL.

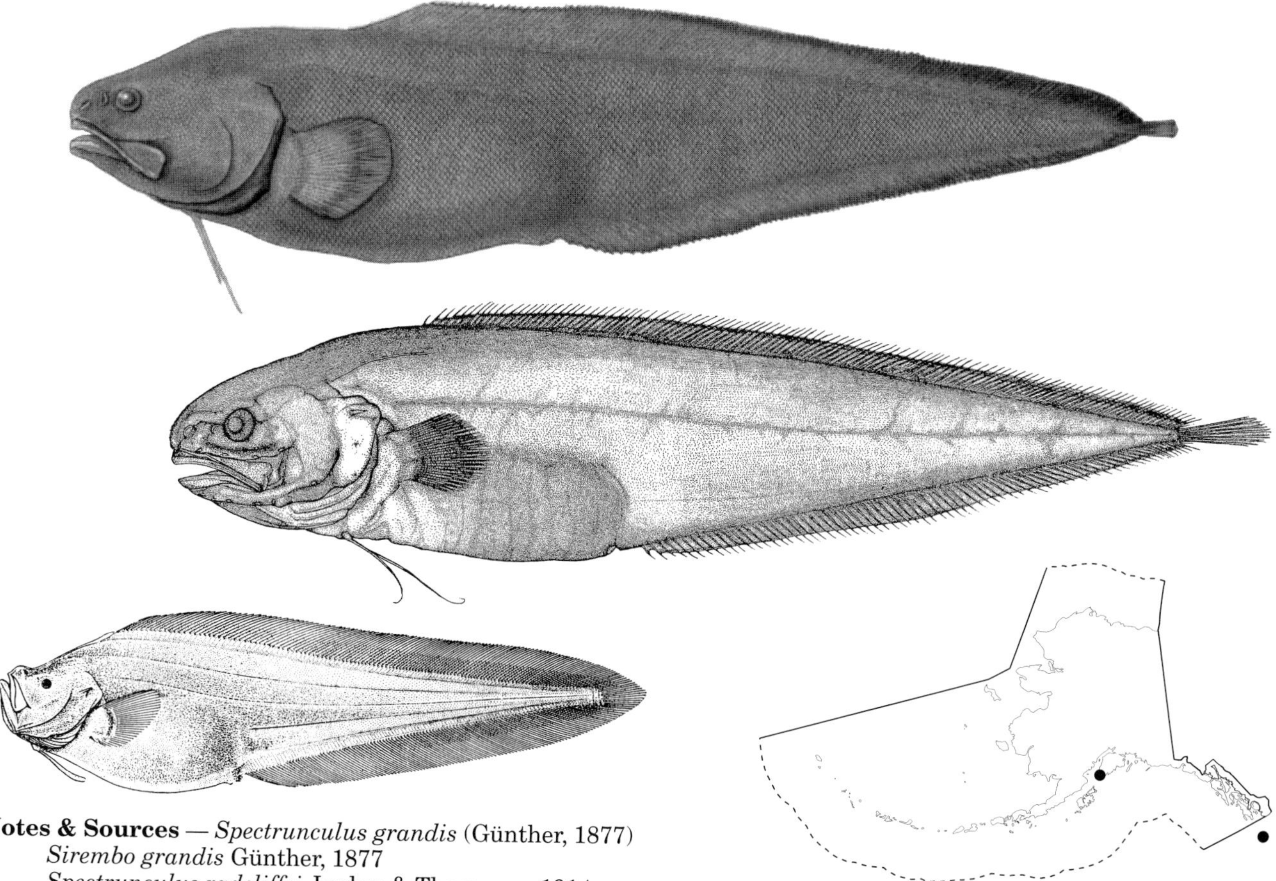

Notes & Sources — *Spectrunculus grandis* (Günther, 1877)
Sirembo grandis Günther, 1877
Spectrunculus radcliffei Jordan & Thompson, 1914
Parabassogigas grandis: Hubbs and Follett 1978 (and others).
Nielsen and Hureau (1980) considered *Spectrunculus* to represent the postlarval and *Parabassogigas* the juvenile and adult stages of the same genus.

Description: Eagle 1969; Cohen and Nielsen 1978:36–37, 39–40; Hubbs and Follett 1978; Nielsen and Hureau 1980; Machida et al. 1987. Account in Nielsen et al. (1999:90) is based on Nielsen and Hureau (1980).

Figures: Top: Royal British Columbia Museum, artist K. Uldall-Ekman, Oct. 1983; RBCM 980-121, adult, west of Queen Charlotte Islands, B.C. Middle: Eagle 1969, fig. 1; adult, 351 mm SL. Bottom: Jordan and Thompson 1914, pl. 37, fig. 3; holotype of *S. radcliffei,* postlarva, 56 mm SL.

Range: Kasitsna Bay (Quast and Hall 1972), a 52-mm postlarva taken pelagically on 23 Oct. 1963, originally in ABL collection, now USNM 202103; Nielsen and Hureau (1980) confirmed the identification as *S. grandis.* Peden and Hughes (1986) confirmed records of six specimens from British Columbia; two from Tasu Sound are the closest to Alaska.

Size: Abe and Hiramoto 1984; specimen taken off Japan.

FAMILY BYTHITIDAE
Viviparous brotulas

Viviparous brotulas resemble cusk-eels (Ophidiidae) except that fertilization is internal and the males have an external intromittent organ. Most of the 32 genera and 96 species (Nielsen et al. 1999) are shallow-water fishes, but some are benthopelagic and occur at depths to at least 2,600 m. A few species inhabit fresh water.

At least three species of viviparous brotula occur off the Pacific coast of North America. The red brotula, *Brosmophycis marginata,* is a cryptic, shallow-water fish known in Alaska from one specimen collected in the Alexander Archipelago near Petersburg (Schultz and DeLacy 1936). *Thalassobathia pelagica* is a pelagic deepsea brotula which was recently found in the western Bering Sea in the southern area of the Commander Basin (Balanov and Fedorov 1996) close to the Russia–United States boundary. This brotula is included in this book as a likely Alaskan species.

In addition to their viviparity and in common with other members of the suborder Bythitoidei, most bythitids have the anterior nostril positioned immediately above the upper lip. Other bythitoid characters include: caudal fin separate from or connected with the dorsal and anal fins; pelvic fins present or absent, and if present attached to the body at about the level of the preopercles; median basibranchial tooth patches absent; swim bladder present or absent; and 9–48 precaudal vertebrae.

Characters distinguishing the Bythitidae from other viviparous bythitoids include: scales present in all but a few species; swim bladder present; opercular spine usually present and strong; pyloric caeca present; and 9–22 precaudal vertebrae. The subfamily to which *B. marginata* belongs, the Brosmophycinae, has the caudal fin free from the dorsal and anal fins and contains mostly small, shallow-water, reef-dwelling fishes. Some of them, previous to the classification by Cohen and Nielsen (1978), were placed in the Brotulidae (e.g., Quast and Hall 1972). *Thalassobathia pelagica* is a member of the Bythitinae, with a caudal fin joined to the dorsal and anal fins. The Bythitinae are a more diverse group, found from shallow to abyssal depths, but most species live at moderate depths. Meso- and bathypelagic species, like *T. pelagica,* exhibit modifications for such life in their poorly ossified skeleton and small, tissue-filled swim bladder. In *B. marginata* the long, delicate pelvic fins, similar to those serving as tactile organs in many other benthic species, stand in sharp contrast to the short, skin-covered pelvic rays of *T. pelagica.* Similarly, *Thalassobathia* is one of the few bythitoids with an elevated anterior nostril; a low-positioned nostril probably would not have functional significance for a pelagic fish.

The key below will serve to distinguish the genera *Brosmophycis* and *Thalassobathia* but will not separate *T. pelagica* from its only congener, *T. nelsoni.* In describing *T. nelsoni* from two specimens taken off the coast of Chile, Lee (1974) gave shorter gill filaments, larger eyes, and a more slender body as the important distinguishing characters. For many nominal taxa, morphometric characters based on small samples have proved to be inadequate as diagnostic characters when the supposed distinctions disappear with acquisition of additional specimens. Although a few differences between *T. pelagica* and *T. nelsoni* in meristics are apparent, the combined counts for the two species do not exceed ranges found in many other species, and most other counts for the two nominal forms overlap. Balanov and Fedorov (1996) found the Bering Sea specimen to be more similar, but not exactly identical, to the Atlantic species *T. pelagica* and referred it to that species rather than suggesting the possibility of a third species. Eye diameter in the Bering Sea specimen, for example, is intermediate. Following Balanov and Fedorov (1996), in this guide we provisionally recognize *T. pelagica* as the likely Bering Sea species pending accumulation and study of additional specimens.

Most species of viviparous brotula, including *T. pelagica,* attain maximum lengths of about 15–30 cm (6–12 inches). *Brosmophycis marginata,* reaching about 46 cm (18 inches), is exceptionally large.

Key to the Bythitidae of Alaska

1 Caudal fin separate from dorsal and anal fins; pelvic fins reaching well past pectoral fin base . . . . *Brosmophycis marginata,* page 267

1 Caudal fin confluent with dorsal and anal fins and tapering to point; pelvic fins short, barely reaching pectoral base . . . . *Thalassobathia pelagica,* page 268 (not known from Alaska)

Brosmophycis marginata (Ayres, 1854) **red brotula**

Southeastern Alaska off Petersburg to northern Baja California off Ensenada.

Rocky areas in caves and crevices at depths of 3–256 m; occasionally found in crab traps and in stomachs of other benthic fishes, such as *Spectrunculus grandis*.

D 98–110; A 72–81; Pec 20–26; Pel 2; Br 7; LLp 64; Ls about 170; Vert precaudal 16–17, total 63–65.

- Bright red to brown dorsally, paler ventrally; fins red; mucus covering body reddish.
- Body covered with thick mucus; loose, thick skin on head, body, and bases of fins.
- Head compressed, small, 20–25% of standard length; body elongate, moderately compressed; mouth large, maxilla extending well past eye; eye diameter less than snout length; maxilla reduced to a dorsal plate above end of premaxilla; **anterior nostril immediately above upper lip**, without tube.
- Opercular spine weak.
- Numerous papillae on head, larger on snout and lower jaw.
- **Caudal fin free from dorsal and anal fins**; **anal fin origin at about midlength of fish**; **pelvic fins long, extending posterior to pectoral base**, inserted close together near base of isthmus, each with 2 rays forming a slender filament, outer ray twice length of inner ray.
- Pores of cephalic sensory system on snout and lower jaw pronounced.
- Lateral line in 2 parts: upper ending at about midbody; lower extending from above anus to caudal fin along midline.
- Body covered with minute, embedded, cycloid scales.
- Small, sharp, villiform teeth on jaws, vomer, and palatines; suprabranchial teeth present, basibranchial teeth absent.
- Gill rakers reduced, few developed on first arch.
- Length to 46 cm TL.

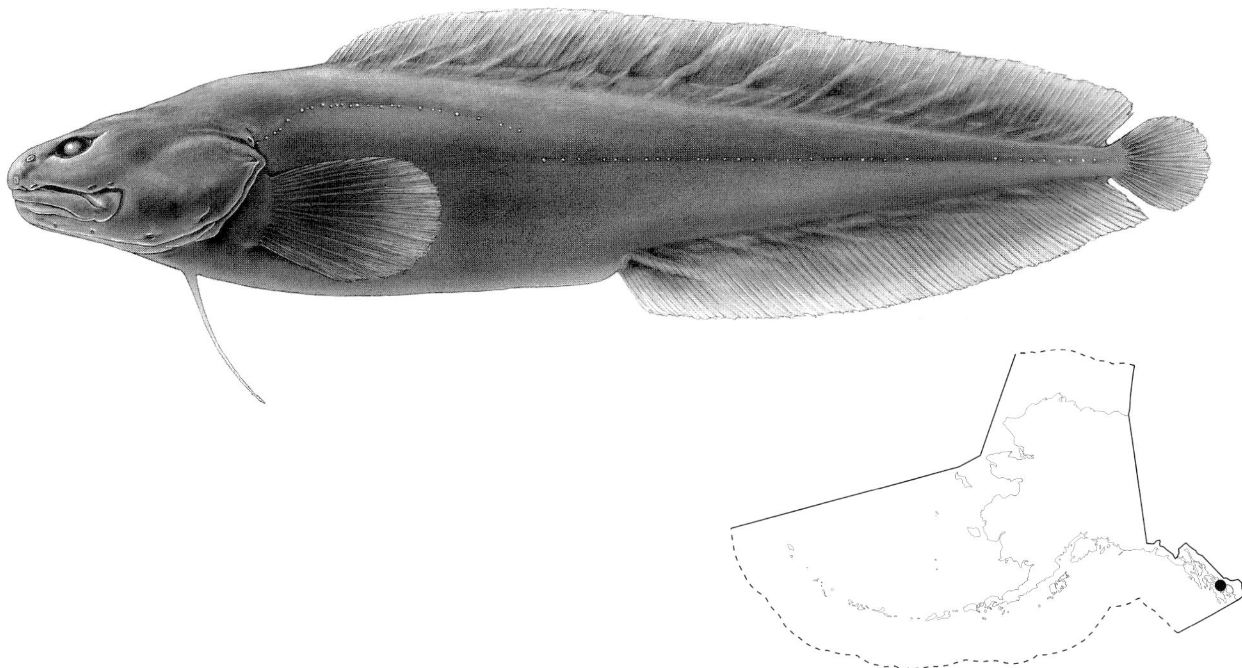

Notes & Sources — *Brosmophycis marginata* (Ayres, 1854)
Brosmius marginatus Ayres, 1854

Description: Jordan and Evermann 1898:2502; Follett 1970:480–481; Miller and Lea 1976:239 (dorsal ray counts); Cohen and Nielsen 1978:53–54; Eschmeyer and Herald 1983:103. The species account in Nielsen et al. (1999:121–122) is based on the same information.

Figure: University of British Columbia, artist P. Drukker-Brammall, Apr. 1974; UBC 61-89, 244 mm SL, Freeman Passage, British Columbia.

Range: An asterisk by the Petersburg locality listed for this species in Schultz and DeLacy's (1936) catalog of Washington and Oregon fishes indicates they saw one or more specimens from Petersburg, but they did not cite voucher collections. UW 2589, a specimen collected in 1920 from the Petersburg area, could be a specimen they saw. This is a common, but secretive, fish south of Alaska, including inside waters of British Columbia.

Size: Miller and Lea (1976) stated it had been reported to reach 51 cm but that the largest recorded recently in California was 41 cm. Other authors (e.g., Eschmeyer and Herald 1983) give a maximum length of 46 cm.

Thalassobathia pelagica Cohen, 1963 **pelagic brotula**

Commander Basin, western Bering Sea; Atlantic Ocean, tropical to temperate, to 60°N.
Mesopelagic and bathypelagic at depths of 500–1,000 m.

D 72–79; A 58–65; Pec 22–29; Pel 2; Br 7; GR 7–10; LLp 30 + 35; Vert precaudal 12, total 46–51.

- In alcohol light brown, head and fins darker.
- Bones poorly ossified, making body lax; skin thick, covering fins as well as body.
- Head compressed, small, about 20% of standard length; body compressed, relatively short and stubby; anterior profile of head blunt; mouth large, maxilla extending well beyond eye; maxilla narrow posteriorly; eye diameter greater than snout length; **anterior nostril placed high on snout**, without tube.
- **Dorsal and anal fins confluent with caudal, tapering to point; anal fin origin anterior to midlength of fish; pelvic fins short, reaching only to or slightly beyond pectoral base**, each with 2 fleshy rays, inner ray longer than outer.
- Scales absent, or widely scattered, embedded cycloid scales present on posterior third of body.
- Pores of cephalic sensory system prominent.
- Lateral lines 2, indistinct: upper extending from above gill opening for about 2/3 of body length; lower from above anus to caudal fin along midline; each lateral line marked with small, dark papillae.
- Short, needlelike teeth on jaws, vomer, and palatines; suprabranchial teeth present, basibranchial teeth absent.
- Gill rakers reduced, better developed on medial surface of first arch than on lateral surface.
- Length to 260 mm SL.

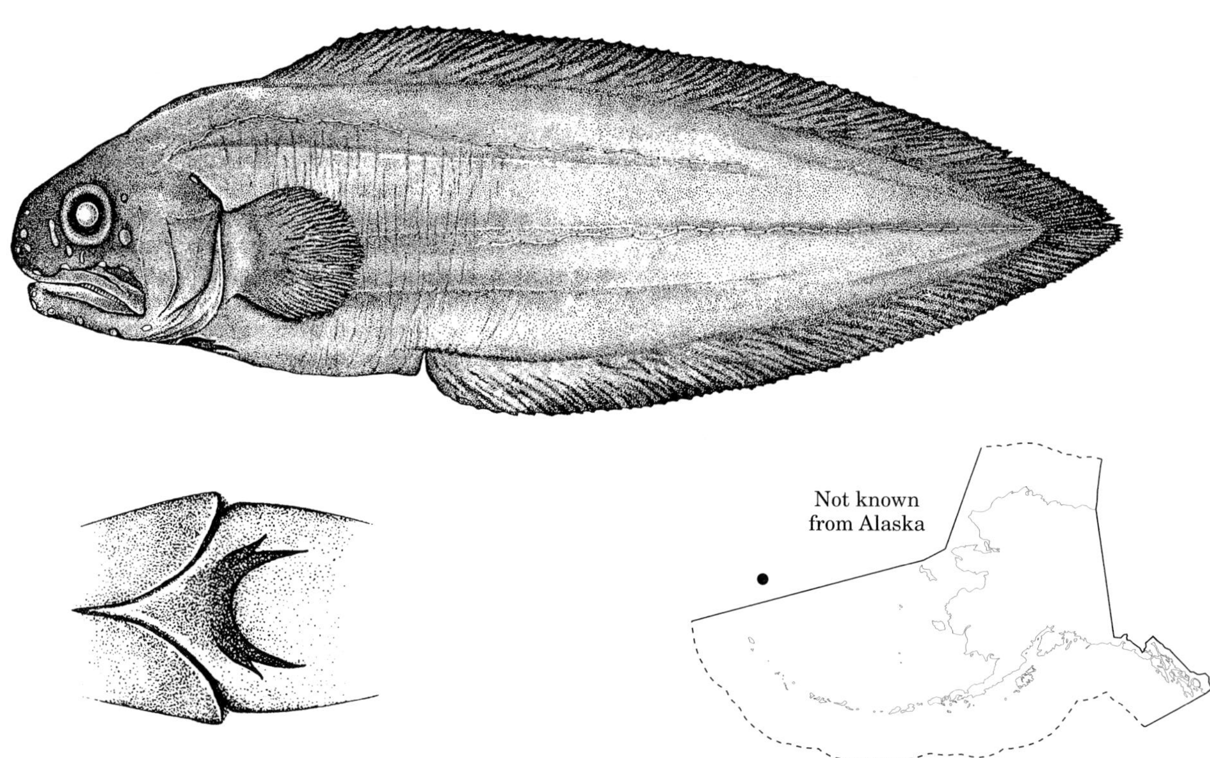

Notes & Sources — *Thalassobathia pelagica* Cohen, 1963

Closely similar to *T. nelsoni* Lee, 1974, known from the Pacific Ocean off Chile at depths above 2,000 m in water 3,620–6,990 m deep. Counts for *T. nelsoni*: D 78–81, A 62–65, Pec 19–20, Pel 2, Br 7, Vert 51–52. Balanov and Fedorov (1996) remarked that their specimen from the Commander Basin differs from both species and, while it is closer to *T. pelagica,* the identification is disputable.

Description: Cohen 1963b; Lee 1974; Cohen and Nielsen 1978: 51–52; Balanov and Fedorov 1996. The account in Nielsen et al. (1999:111–112) is based on the same information.

Figures: Cohen 1963b, figs. 1 and 2C; holotype, 221 mm SL, northwest Atlantic. Ventral view shows pelvic fins and separate gill membranes.

Range: Balanov and Fedorov (1996) reported on the first discovery from the Pacific Ocean: a female, 157 mm SL, taken in the southern area of the Commander Basin at 56°31'N, 170°00'E, by midwater trawl net towed obliquely from 1,000 m to 500 m. Other records are from the Atlantic Ocean.

Order Gadiformes
Gadiforms

The order Gadiformes includes cods and their close relatives. Many of them are commercially important, the combined catch composing more than one-fourth of the world's marine fish catch. This is a complex, highly polymorphic taxon with a large number of poorly known species and a wealth of information, particularly on habitat and fisheries, on others. The higher systematics of the order is in a confused state. Nelson's (1994) classification includes 12 families with 85 genera and about 482 species. Cohen (1989) reviewed developments in gadiform systematics, and Cohen et al. (1990) compiled information primarily on commercially valuable species and provided keys for their identification.

Gadiforms occur in all oceans, predominantly as benthopelagic fishes of cool waters, whether shallow in high and mid-latitudes or deep in the tropics. One species (*Lota lota*) is confined to fresh water. Four gadiform families are represented in Alaska: Macrouridae, Moridae, Merlucciidae, and Gadidae.

Although no external or internal characters uniquely define the order Gadiformes, many species share features that serve to generally portray the group. Their fins lack true spines (some rays are spine-like and counted as spines by most authors). The dorsal and anal fins are long-based and often separated into two or three fins. The pelvic fins are thoracic and in some species reduced to filaments, but rarely absent; they are not close together like they are in Ophidiiformes. The scales are usually cycloid, rarely ctenoid. Many species have a chin barbel. The premaxilla forms the entire margin of the upper jaw and in some species is protractile. Gadiforms have 6–8 branchiostegal rays.

Family Macrouridae
Grenadiers

Grenadiers, also called rattails, have a short trunk and a compressed, greatly elongate tail tapering to a slender point. Primarily predators and scavengers of the sea floor, grenadiers follow a benthopelagic mode of life typically at depths of 200–2,000 m. They occur throughout the world but mostly at tropical and subtropical latitudes. The Macrouridae is a large family, with four subfamilies and about 285 species currently recognized. The 8 species treated in this guide are in the subfamily Macrourinae, by far the largest subfamily, with at least 255 species and representatives all over the world except in the high Arctic.

Most of the Alaskan grenadiers are distributed among four subgenera of *Coryphaenoides* (*Bogoslovius, Nematonurus, Chalinura,* and *Coryphaenoides*) recognized by Iwamoto (in Cohen et al. 1990). Some workers classify the subgenera as valid genera. Species of subgenus *Coryphaenoides* are more or less confined to continental slope habitats, whereas species of *Chalinura* and *Nematonurus* also occur in ocean basins at depths below 4,000 m and are considered abyssal (Wilson 1994). The one known species of subgenus *Bogoslovius* (*Coryphaenoides longifilis*) occurs over the slope.

Grenadiers typically have large eyes with a ridge below each which is produced into a rostrum over an inferior mouth, and many have a chin barbel. The anus is located just before the anal fin in *Albatrossia* and *Coryphaenoides* but farther anteriorly in some other genera. Some grenadier species, although not those in Alaska, have a ventral light organ. All but two species have two dorsal fins. They all have one anal fin, and no caudal fin. The second dorsal fin and anal fin are long, and joined at the tip of the tail. The anterior rays of the second dorsal fin may be difficult to discern and the tail is often broken off, and few authors give counts for the second dorsal or anal fin. The first dorsal fin is high, and in most species the two anteriormost rays are spinous. The first spinous ray is minute and closely appressed to the base of the second ray, which is often prolonged beyond the rest of the fin and, in the Alaskan species, has a serrated leading edge.

Grenadier scales are cycloid but with the exposed area of each scale often covered with sharp spinules in ridgelike rows. Scale architecture differs among the species and is useful in identification, but the spinules become reduced with age in large species (over 60 cm). Scale row counts can also be helpful in identification; the following accounts give scale counts between the midbase of the first dorsal fin and the lateral line (Ds). Some species have stout, scutelike scales at the snout tip, and some have rows of coarse scutes on the head.

In grenadiers teeth are present only on the jaws, not on the vomer or palatines, and arranged in sparse single series of enlarged canines to broad villiform bands. In most species the gill rakers are tubercular. Species in some non-Alaskan genera lack gill rakers on the outer side of the first gill arch. Some authors give counts only for the inner series and others for the outer series, rarely both, so comparable counts are often lacking. The grenadier species treated in this guide have 6 branchiostegal rays, and gill membranes that are united to each other and variably joined to the isthmus. The swim bladder is well developed except in the bathypelagic species. Few authors report counts of vertebrae for grenadiers, and those that do, usually report counts only for the precaudal vertebrae. Grenadiers have 10–16 precaudal vertebrae and numerous, often more than 100, total vertebrae. Coloration of Alaskan grenadiers is whitish to brown, without distinguishing marks such as spots or bars.

The subfamily Macrourinae, including the Alaskan and other northeastern Pacific macrourids, has rays of the second dorsal fin much shorter than those of the anal fin, the first and second dorsal fins separated by a distinct gap, gill rakers all tubercular, and the outer gill slit restricted by folds of skin. This subfamily includes the smallest and largest species in the family, from 12 cm (4.7 inches) in some species to more than 150 cm (5 ft) in *Albatrossia pectoralis.*

Among the body proportions most useful for identifying grenadiers are the length of the abdomen, expressed as distance from the isthmus (at anterior end of scaled area of chest) to the anal fin or anus as a percentage of head length. Methods of measurement for grenadiers have most recently been given by Iwamoto and Sazonov (1988).

Discrepancies between the present inventory and earlier lists of Alaskan grenadiers are due mostly to suppression of nominal species. Three of the species in this guide incorporate seven of the species listed by Quast and Hall (1972): *Coryphaenoides armatus* now includes *C. cyclolepis* and *C. suborbitalis*; *C. acrolepis* includes *C. firmisquamis*; and *C. filifer* includes *C. lepturus. Coryphaenoides clarki* is a junior synonym of *C. longifilis,* and *C. serrula* is a junior synonym of *C. leptolepis.* Iwamoto (in Cohen et al. 1990) resurrected Jordan and Evermann's (1898) old name *Albatrossia pectoralis* for the giant rattail (in *Coryphaenoides, Chalinura,* or *Nematonurus* on previous lists).

The taxonomic status of an additional nominal species, *Coryphaenoides (Chalinura) liocephalus,* is problematical. We include it questionably in the synonymy of *C. leptolepis.* Günther (1877) described the species *C. leptolepis* on the basis of a few specimens from the Pacific off Yokohama (one specimen), the mid-Pacific (two), and the Atlantic off Brazil (one); and later (Günther 1887) referred the Pacific specimens to a new species, *C. liocephalus*. However, Günther's descriptions do not adequately distinguish the species and taxonomists have been unable to distinguish them. Most specimens collected since the time of Günther that could be referred to one of these forms (and there have been many) have been identified as *C. leptolepis,* whether from the Pacific or the Atlantic (e.g., Wilson 1994), probably since that name has priority if the forms are synonymous. Only one specimen from the eastern Pacific has been recorded in the literature as *C. liocephalus* (Hart 1973; off British Columbia), the name that would be valid for the Pacific form if it is distinct from Atlantic *C. leptolepis.* Specimens taken off Japan have been recognized as *C. liocephalus* (e.g., Okamura in Masuda et al. 1984). Dr. T. Iwamoto (pers. comm., 31 Aug. 1999) suggested that tissue samples collected near the type localities of the two nominal species could help determine if significant differences exist, and that if the two species are different, specimens called *C. leptolepis* from the North Pacific (including Bean's [1890b] *Chalinura serrula* from Alaska) are really *Coryphaenoides liocephalus* and *C. leptolepis* would be the name for the Atlantic species.

In all, the occurrence of seven grenadier species in waters off Alaska is adequately documented. *Albatrossia pectoralis* and *C. cinereus* are fairly common in the region, while *C. longifilis, C. armatus, C. filifer,* and *C. leptolepis* are rare or their habitat (deep) is inadequately sampled. *Coryphaenoides acrolepis* is probably fairly common off Alaska but documented captures are scanty, especially for the Gulf of Alaska.

Coryphaenoides spinulosus (Gilbert & Burke, 1912), listed by Wilimovsky (1954, 1958) and Quast and Hall (1972) as an Alaskan species with a Bering Sea distribution, is not included in this guide. The only record is the unique holotype, from the western Pacific off Avacha Bay, southern Kamchatka (*not* from Bering Sea).

Coryphaenoides (Nematonurus) yaquinae Iwamoto & Stein, 1974 is similar to but replaces *C. armatus* at depths greater than 4,300 m in the North Pacific (Wilson and Waples 1983), and is included herein as a potential addition to the Alaskan fauna. Recorded to depths of about 5,825 m, *C. yaquinae* may be the deepest-living grenadier. Although the northernmost known occurrence of *C. yaquinae* is about 45°N, 154°W, off Oregon, the species could replace *C. armatus* at great depths off the Aleutian Islands and in the Gulf of Alaska.

Nezumia stelgidolepis (Gilbert, 1890) is another widespread macrourine grenadier of the eastern Pacific, known from southern Peru to British Columbia off Vancouver Island. However, it occurs in much shallower waters, in 277–909 m, which have been more completely explored than the great depths at which *C. yaquinae* occurs. With 7 branchiostegal rays, anus closer to the pelvic fins than to the anal fin, and a light organ anterior to the anus, *N. stelgidolepis* would immediately be distinguishable from other grenadiers in the region. A complete description of *N. stelgidolepis* was given by Iwamoto (1979).

Key to the Macrouridae of Alaska

1 Pelvic fin rays 6–8, usually 7; 10–15 rows of scales between midbase of first dorsal fin and lateral line; maxilla extending past orbit; first pelvic ray not extending much beyond others ..... *Albatrossia pectoralis,* page 272

1 Pelvic fin rays 7–13, rarely 7; scales small to large, usually fewer than 10 rows between midbase of first dorsal fin and lateral line; maxilla extending from front of pupil to beyond orbit; first pelvic ray usually extending well beyond others .... (2)

2 (1) Outer pelvic fin rays greatly prolonged, longer than head (136–232% HL); chin barbel very small, 1–4% HL; first dorsal fin with 2 spinous and 12–14 segmented rays; premaxillary teeth in 2 rows, mandibular teeth in 1 row.................. *Coryphaenoides longifilis,* page 273

2 Outer pelvic fin rays less than 150% HL; barbel rudimentary to well developed, 0–37% HL; first dorsal fin with 2 spinous and 7–13 (rarely 14) segmented rays; premaxillary teeth in 1 row to a broad band, mandibular teeth in 1 row to a narrow band .... (3)

3 (2) No enlarged scutes on tip of snout .... (4)

3 Enlarged scutes present on tip of snout .... (6)

4 (3) Isthmus to anus distance 65–88% HL; color whitish with deciduous scale covering removed .... *Coryphaenoides leptolepis,* page 274

4 Isthmus to anus distance 89–135% HL; color dark gray or dark brown to blackish .... (5)

5 (4) Premaxillary teeth usually in 2 distinct rows with outer series enlarged, smaller inner row sometimes lost in large specimens; mandibular teeth in 1 distinct row............... *Coryphaenoides armatus,* page 275

5 Premaxillary teeth in 2 or more irregular rows with outer series enlarged; mandibular teeth in patch or 2 irregular rows near symphysis and1 distinct row posteriorly........... *Coryphaenoides yaquinae,* page 276 (not known from Alaska)

6 (3) Entire orbital rim black; entire leading edge of snout with enlarged tubercular scales.............................. *Coryphaenoides acrolepis,* page 277

6 Orbital rim black only anteroventrally; leading edge of snout with enlarged tubercular scales only at tip and lateral angles .... (7)

7 (6) Color very pale, whitish in life; interorbital space broad, 24–30% HL; relatively narrow suborbital shelf with anteroventral process; scales on suborbital shelf thin and deciduous except anteriorly .... *Coryphaenoides cinereus,* page 278

7 Color medium to dark brown; interorbital space narrow, 19–23% HL; relatively broad suborbital shelf without anteroventral process; scales on suborbital shelf stout and embedded.. *Coryphaenoides filifer,* page 279

Albatrossia pectoralis (Gilbert, 1892) **giant grenadier**

Bering Sea from Navarin Canyon and Pacific Ocean off Aleutian Islands to northern Baja California; and to Sea of Okhotsk and Pacific off northern Honshu, Japan.

On or near sandy mud bottom at depths of 140–2,189 m, usually 300–900 m; young fish bathypelagic, settling to bottom at about 50–60 cm in length.

D II,7–9; Pec 16–21; Pel 6–8; Ds 10–12; GR outer 5–7, inner 12–14; PC 12–16; Vert precaudal 13–15.

- Olive gray-brown; fins, lateral line, lips, lower surface of snout blackish; denuded specimens whitish.
- Isthmus to anal origin 88–123% of head length; head broad, width more than 50% of length; snout slightly protruding beyond mouth; maxilla extending beyond eye; orbit diameter 19–23% of head length.
- **Barbel short and fine**.
- Dorsal fin interspace 10–21% of head length; anal fin origin posterior to origin of second dorsal fin; **first pelvic ray usually not extending much beyond others; pelvic rays usually 7**.
- **Scales very small**, elongate, deciduous, with 3–6 spinous ridges in small specimens to fewer ridges and no spinules in larger specimens.
- Head pores small and inconspicuous.
- Lateral line large and strongly marked.
- Teeth spaced, not crowded; premaxillary teeth in 2 irregular rows, outer slightly enlarged; mandibular teeth in 1–3 (usually 1) irregular rows.
- Gill membranes joined to isthmus, no free fold.
- Length to 150 cm TL or more.

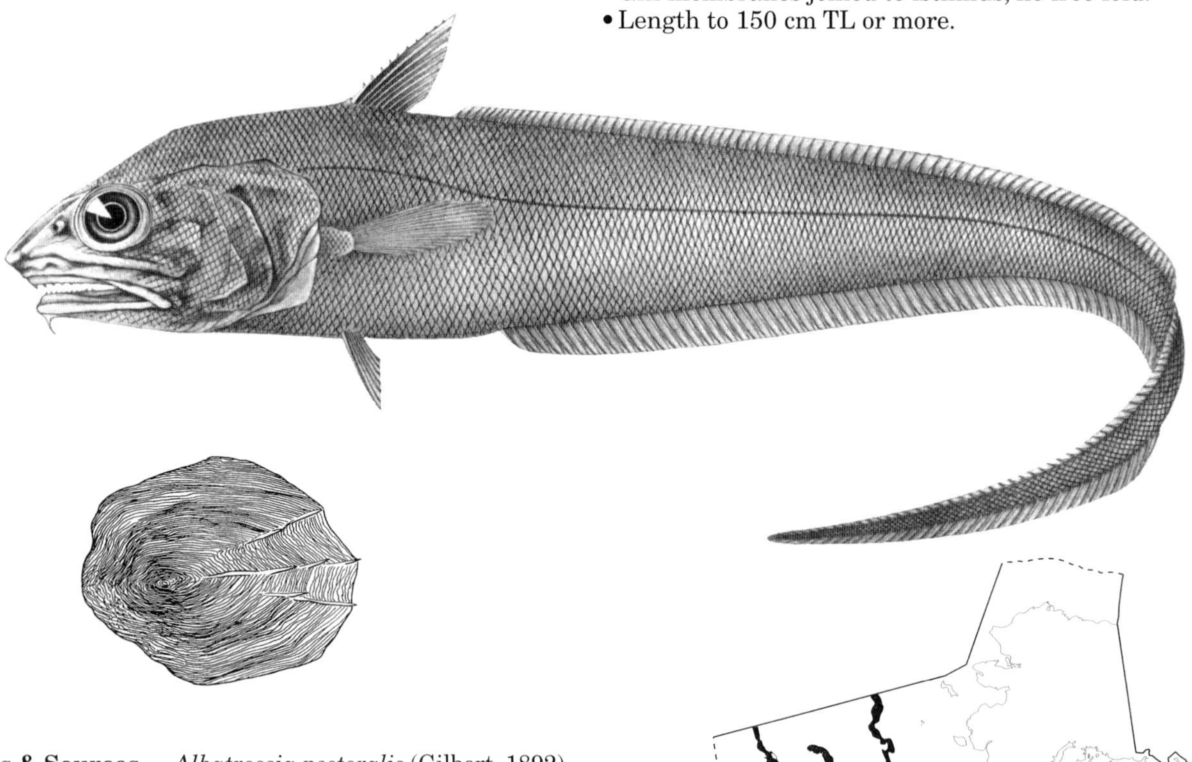

Notes & Sources — *Albatrossia pectoralis* (Gilbert, 1892)
Macrurus (Malacocephalus) pectoralis Gilbert, 1892
Macrurus (Nematonurus) magnus Gill & Townsend, 1897
Albatrossia pectoralis: Jordan and Evermann 1898:2573 (new genus).
Ateleobrachium pterotum Gilbert & Burke, 1912
Nematonurus pectoralis: Gilbert and Hubbs 1916, Andriashev 1937.
Coryphaenoides pectoralis: Iwamoto and Stein 1974.

A small swim bladder and elongate, comb-shaped sagitta otolith are two of the most consistent characters distinguishing the genus *Albatrossia* from *Coryphaenoides* (Iwamoto in Cohen et al. 1990).

The synonymy of *Ateleobrachium pterotum,* which was based on a larval specimen taken off Kamchatka, in *A. pectoralis* was established by Endo et al. (1993).

Description: Gilbert and Hubbs 1916:161–162; Andriashev 1937:75–77; Okamura 1970:118–121; Iwamoto and Stein 1974:37–41; Iwamoto in Cohen et al. 1990:110–111.

Figures: Okamura 1970, pl. 25. Scale: Cohen et al. 1990, fig. 236.

Range: Numerous records backed by voucher specimens document the Alaskan portion of the range as mapped from NMFS bottom trawl surveys by Allen and Smith (1988). Early records include those of Gill and Townsend (1897) from southwest of Pribilof Islands and Jordan and Gilbert (1899) off Bogoslof Island. Andriashev (1937) recorded it from Bering Island, Russia. Snytko (1987) reported it from seamounts in the Gulf of Alaska, including Welker, Surveyor, Jakomini, Pratt, and Durgin.

Coryphaenoides longifilis Günther, 1877 **longfin grenadier**

Bering Sea to Sea of Okhotsk off Kuril Islands and Pacific off southern Japan.
Benthopelagic, at depths of 700–2,025 m.

D II,12–14; Pec 15–18; Pel 9–10; Ds 11–13; GR outer 6–7, inner 14–16; PC 10–12; Vert precaudal 14–15.

- Light brown or gray; fins dusky; lips, gill membranes, mouth and gill cavities dark brown; denuded specimens whitish.
- Isthmus to anal origin 74–87% of head length; head compressed; snout barely protruding beyond mouth; maxilla extending to rear portion of eye to beyond eye; orbit diameter 20–25% of head length; interopercle broadly exposed beyond preopercle.
- **Barbel rudimentary**.
- Dorsal fin interspace narrow, less than length of base of first dorsal fin, 11–15% of head length; anal fin origin slightly posterior to origin of second dorsal fin; **pectoral fin reaching well beyond anal fin origin; first pelvic ray greatly prolonged, to 200% of head length**.
- **Scales small**, deciduous, with 3–6 spinous ridges in small specimens, the spinules obscure in larger specimens.
- Sensory pores on head well developed.
- Lateral line distinct.
- Premaxillary teeth in 2 distinct, widely separated rows, outer series enlarged and widely spaced, inner teeth nearly horizontal and close together; mandibular teeth in 1 row.
- Gill membranes joined to isthmus leaving narrow free edge.
- Length to 86 cm TL.

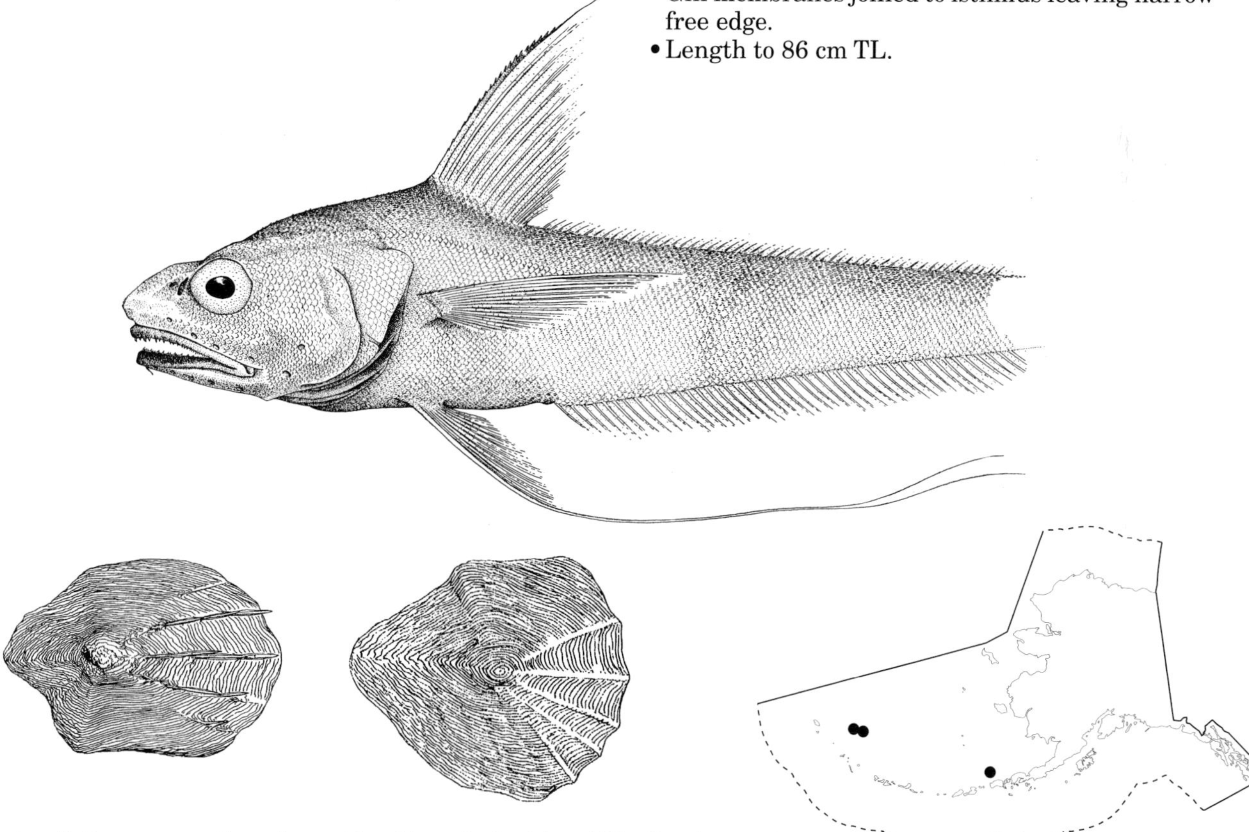

Notes & Sources — *Coryphaenoides (Bogoslovius) longifilis* Günther, 1877
Macrurus (Nematonurus) longifilis Günther, 1887
Bogoslovius clarki Jordan & Gilbert in Jordan & Evermann, 1898
Dolloa longifilis Jordan, 1900
Nematonurus clarki: Gilbert and Burke 1912a.
Coryphaenoides (Nematonurus) longifilis: Gilbert and Hubbs 1916, Iwamoto and Stein 1974.

Description: Jordan and Evermann 1898:2575; Jordan and Gilbert 1899:487–488; Iwamoto and Stein 1974:24–25; Okamura 1970:121–124; Okamura in Masuda et al. 1984:96; Iwamoto in Cohen et al. 1990: 211–212.

Figures: Jordan and Gilbert 1899, pl. 83, type of *Bogoslovius clarki,* off Bogoslof Island. Scale at left: Cohen et al. 1990, fig. 488; at right: Günther 1887, pl. 35.

Range: Known in Alaska from four specimens taken in Bering Sea off Bogoslof Island at *Albatross* station 3634, 54°51'N, 167°27'W, depth 1,214 m (Jordan and Evermann 1898), and several on Bowers Bank at stations 4768, 4774, and 4775, depths 1,019–1,397 m (Gilbert and Burke 1912a). A specimen taken in 1982 by the Russian RV *Darwin* at 60°27'N, 173°31'E, depth 1,090–1,200 m (B. A. Sheiko, pers. comm., 15 Jan. 1999), is the northernmost Bering Sea record. Dudnik and Dolganov (1992) recorded *C. longifilis* from the Sea of Okhotsk and the Pacific off the northern Kuril Islands at 915–2,025 m. Most other records are from southern Japan.

Coryphaenoides leptolepis Günther, 1877 **ghostly grenadier**

Gulf of Alaska west of Prince of Wales Island; northeastern Pacific from latitudes of central British Columbia to Baja California southwest of Cabo de San Lucas and to Pacific off Japan; North Atlantic.

Soft bottom at depths of 640–4,100 m.

D II,7–10; Pec 18–22; Pel 9–11; Ds 6–8; GR outer 8–13; Vert precaudal 12.

- Brown; fins dusky; lips and mouth, gill membranes, peritoneum black; **denuded specimens whitish**.
- Flesh and bones relatively soft.
- **Isthmus to anus 65–88% of head length**; snout broadly rounded in life (can look pointed in preserved specimens), not strongly protruding; maxilla extending to posterior edge of eye to beyond eye; orbit diameter 15–20% of head length; **posterior end of interopercle exposed as slender, naked sliver**.
- Barbel long, length 25% HL.
- Dorsal fin interspace 27–50% of head length; anal fin origin anterior to second dorsal fin origin; outer pelvic ray thicker than others and elongate, reaching well past anal fin origin.
- **Scales thin, deciduous, smooth or with weak spinules** on 5–7 low divergent ridges; broad naked area dorsally behind leading edge of snout on either side of median ridge.
- Sensory pores on head large and conspicuous.
- Lateral line distinct.
- **Premaxillary dentition a broad villiform band of minute teeth with distinctly enlarged, spaced outer series**; mandibular teeth in 1 row, except in bands in young individuals.
- Gill membranes narrowly connected to isthmus, forming broad posterior free fold.
- Length to more than 46 cm TL.

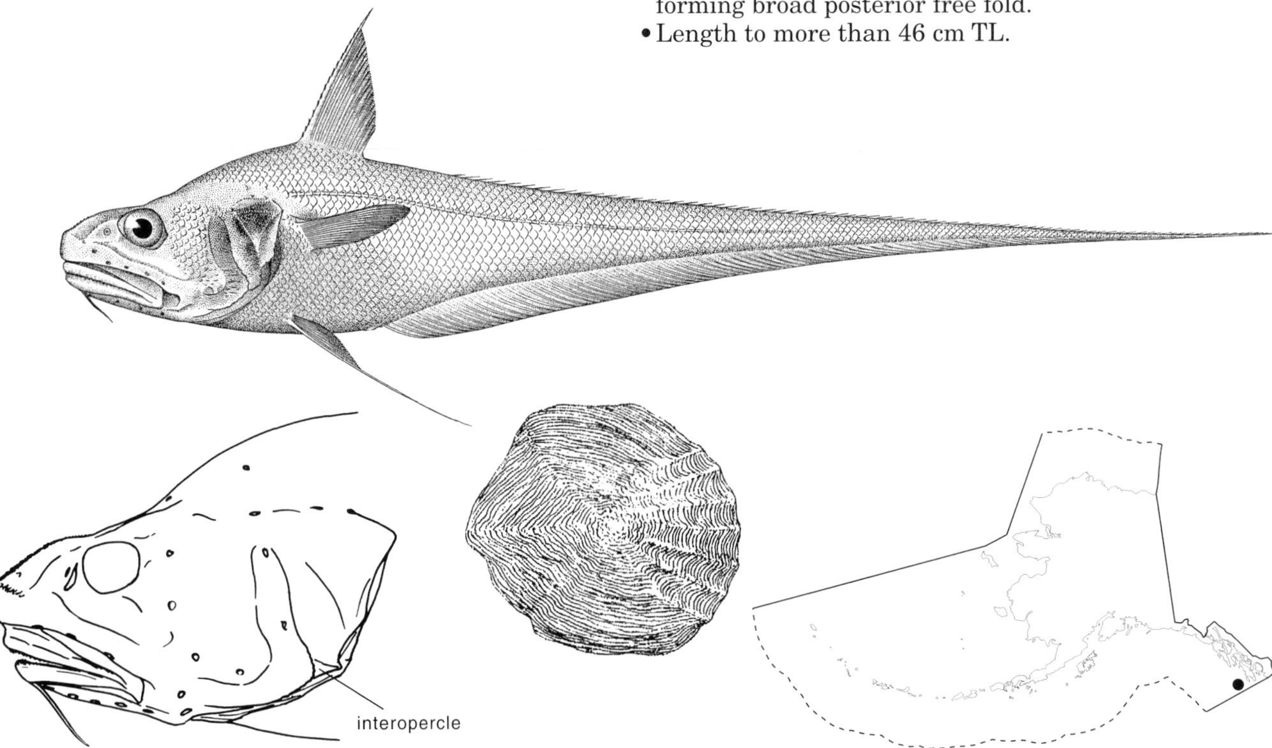

Notes & Sources — *Coryphaenoides (Chalinura) leptolepis* Günther, 1877
Chalinura serrula Bean, 1890
?*Macrurus liocephalus* Günther, 1887
Chalinura simula Goode & Bean, 1883
The possible synonymy of *Coryphaenoides liocephalus* in *C. leptolepis* is discussed in the introduction to this family.

Description: Günther 1877:441, 1887:144; Bean 1890b:37; Iwamoto and Stein 1974:42–46.

Figures: Upper: Smithsonian Institution, NMNH, Division of Fishes, artist S. F. Denton, 1890; holotype of *Chalinura serrula,* USNM 45358, 32 cm TL, west of Prince of Wales Island, Alaska. Scale: Günther 1887, pl. 31. Diagram of head: Iwamoto and Stein 1974, fig. 24.

Range: The only Alaskan record comprises the three type specimens of *Chalinura serrula* Bean, 1890 taken west (*not* east as stated by Bean [1890b]) of Prince of Wales Island at *Albatross* station 3634, 55°20'N, 136°20'W, depth 2,870 m. Nearest recorded British Columbia specimens were taken off Triangle Island, Queen Charlotte Sound (UBC 64-444; Iwamoto and Stein 1974). SIO 65-240 may be southernmost record in Pacific, at 22°34'N, 110°09'W, southwest of Cabo de San Lucas. Minimum depth: Günther (1877), for holotype, 46 cm TL, off Pernambuco, Brazil, *Challenger* station 122. Maximum depth: SIO 91-152, 94 mm (SL), 34°44'N, 123°08'W, Jun. 1990; and SIO 91-154, 240 mm, 34°44'N, 123°11'W, Feb. 1990.

Coryphaenoides armatus (Hector, 1875) — smooth abyssal grenadier

Southeastern Bering Sea and Pacific south of Aleutian Islands; Pacific off northern British Columbia to South America, Japan, and Southern Ocean; Atlantic Ocean; all oceans except Arctic.

In North Pacific limited to depths of 2,000–4,300 m on deeper portion of continental slope and upper rise and co-occurring with *C. yaquinae* at depths of 3,400–4,300 m; to 4,700 m in Atlantic.

D II,8–10; Pec 17–22; Pel 10–12; Ds 6–8; GR outer 7–9, inner 11–14; Vert precaudal 13–15.

- **Dark brown to blackish**; fins, lower part of head, gill cavities, and peritoneum blackish.
- **Isthmus to anus 89–135% of head length**; snout strongly protruding in small specimens, less prominent in larger fish; maxilla extending to posterior portion of eye; orbit diameter 18–27% of head length; lips thick, papillose.
- Barbel well developed, 11–19% of head length.
- Dorsal fin interspace longer than base of first dorsal fin, 39–77% of head length; anal fin origin anterior to second dorsal fin origin; first pelvic ray usually not reaching anus.
- **Scales deciduous, with 3–10 rows of small spinules, the spinules diminishing with age**; **4 or 5 rows of small scales on suborbital shelf**; scales present on mandibular rami.
- Sensory pores on head prominent.
- Lateral line conspicuous.
- **Premaxillary teeth usually in 2 distinct rows with teeth in outer row enlarged, inner row sometimes lost in large specimens**; **mandibular teeth in 1 distinct row**.
- Gill membranes joined to isthmus leaving, at most, a narrow free edge.
- Length to 102 cm TL.

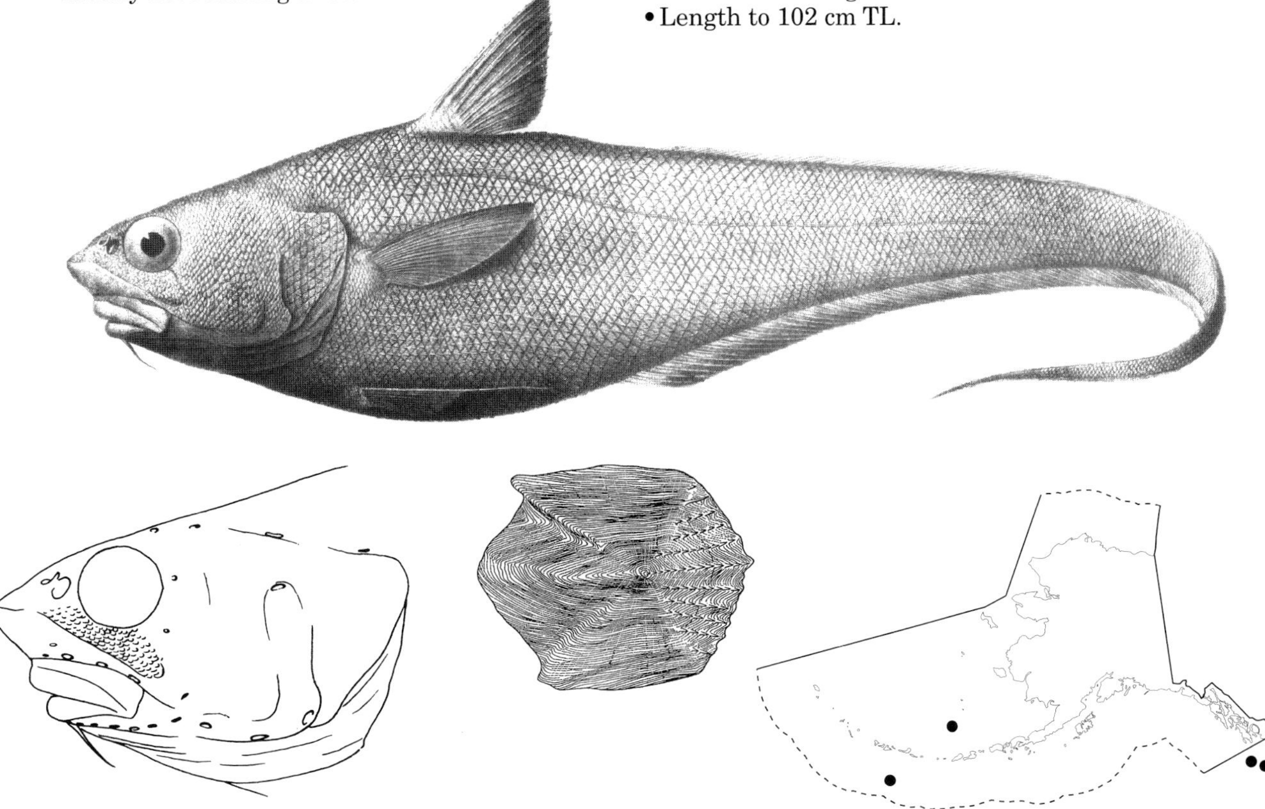

Notes & Sources — *Coryphaenoides (Nematonurus) armatus* (Hector, 1875)
Macrurus armatus Hector, 1875
Macrurus cyclolepis Gilbert, 1896
Macrurus (Nematonurus) suborbitalis Gill & Townsend, 1897
Wilson and Waples (1984) recognized two subspecies: *C. a. variabilis* (Günther, 1878) in the North Pacific and *C. a. armatus* (Hector, 1875) in the South Pacific and the Atlantic.

Description: Gilbert 1896:458; Hart 1973:252–253; Iwamoto and Stein 1974:27–34; Wilson and Waples 1983, 1984; Iwamoto in Cohen et al. 1990:205; Endo and Okamura 1992.

Figures: Günther 1887, pl. 40. Scale: Cohen et al. 1990, fig. 478. Head: Iwamoto and Stein 1974, fig. 15B.

Range: Two records from Alaska: Bering Sea southwest of Pribilof Islands at *Albatross* station 3603, 55°23'N, 170°31'W, 3,239 m (Gill and Townsend 1897), and just north of Kanaga Island of the Aleutian Islands, 52°18'N, 177°00'W, 3,300 m (Wilson and Waples 1984). Nearest known localities outside Alaska: off Graham Island, British Columbia, at 53°33'N, 133°38'W, about 1,830 m (Hart 1973); and off Moresby Island, B.C., *Albatross* station 3342, 52°39'N, 132°38'W, 2,904 m (Gilbert 1896). Endo and Okamura (1992) reported the first record from western North Pacific: 15 specimens taken in fish trap in Japan Trench at 4,100 m.

Coryphaenoides yaquinae Iwamoto & Stein, 1974 **rough abyssal grenadier**

Eastern, western, and mid-North Pacific Ocean at latitudes of Oregon to Equator.

At depths of about 3,400–6,450 m on ocean floor and lower continental rise, co-occurring with *C. armatus* at depths of 3,400–4,300 m.

D II,8–10; Pec 16–22; Pel 8–11; Ds 5–8; GR outer 7–9, inner 11–13; PC 10–11; Vert precaudal 13–14.

- **Dark gray to bluish gray**; fins dusky; lips, orbit, barbel, opercle, posterior margins of gill membranes blackish; peritoneum black.
- **Isthmus to anus 100–122% of head length; snout pointed, strongly protruding**; maxilla extending to posterior edge of eye to beyond eye; orbit diameter 16–22% of head length; lips fleshy and papillose.
- Barbel well developed, 16–18% of head length.
- Dorsal fin interspace longer than first dorsal fin base, 44–51% of head length; anal fin origin anterior to second dorsal fin origin; first pelvic ray extending slightly posterior to anal fin origin.
- **Scales relatively adherent, with 3–7 strong, sharp ridges of close-set spinules; usually only 2 rows of scales on suborbital shelf**; broad naked area dorsally on snout on either side of median ridge; scales absent from mandibular rami.
- Sensory head pores and lateral line not as prominent as in *C. armatus*.
- **Premaxillary teeth usually in 2 or more irregular rows, teeth in outer row much enlarged; mandibular teeth in small patch or 2 irregular rows near symphysis, and 1 distinct row posteriorly**.
- Gill membranes joined to isthmus leaving moderately broad to narrow free margin.
- Length to 77 cm TL.

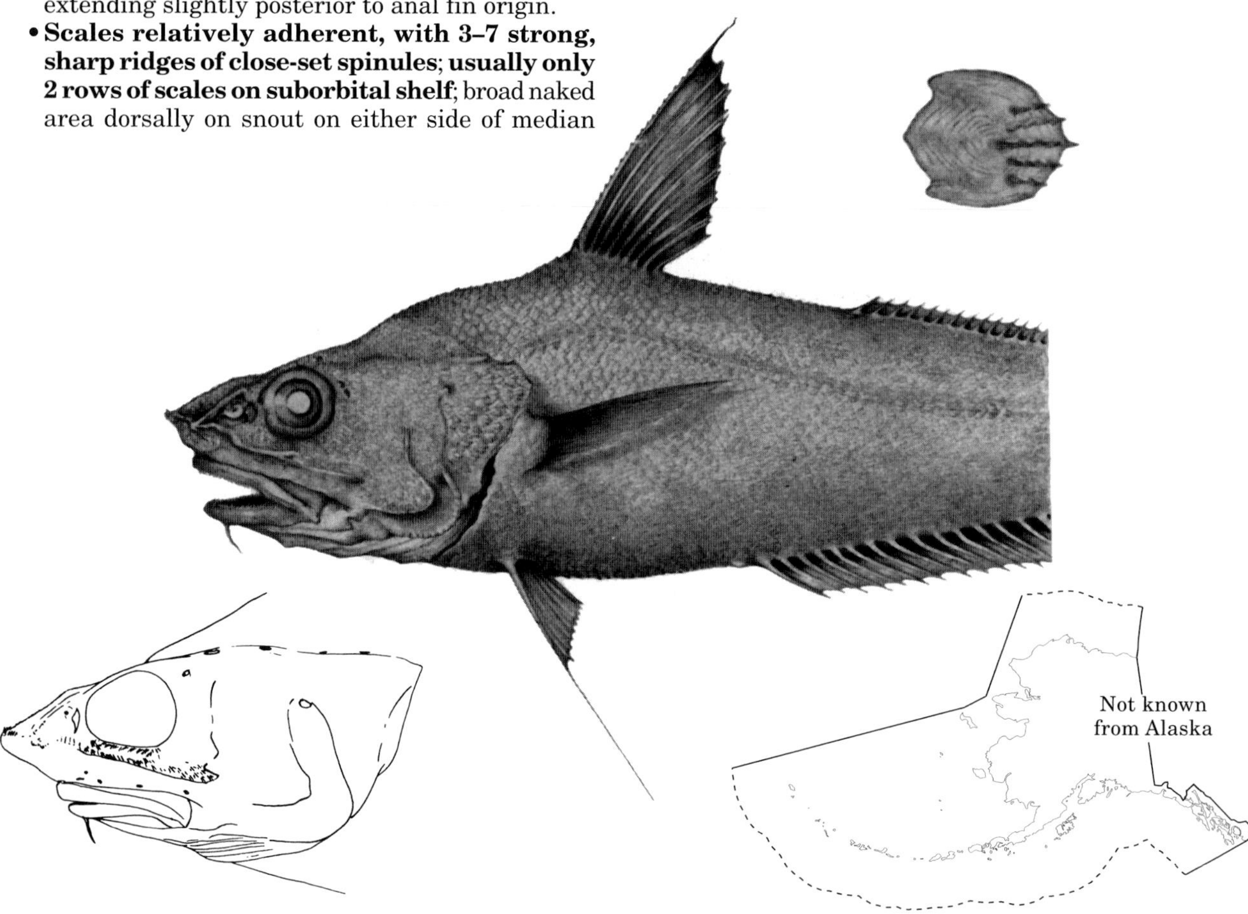

Notes & Sources — *Coryphaenoides (Nematonurus) yaquinae* Iwamoto & Stein, 1974

The species name is from the research vessel *Yaquina,* which collected the types.

In *C. yaquinae* the scales are generally coarser and less deciduous than those of *C. armatus,* but the premaxillary dentition provides the most reliable, least variable distinguishing character (Wilson and Waples 1983).

Wilson and Waples (1983) recounted the complex nomenclatural history of *C. yaquinae* and identified records previously referred to *C. armatus.*

Description: Iwamoto and Stein 1974:34–37; Wilson and Waples 1983; Endo and Okamura 1992.

Figures: Iwamoto and Stein 1974, figs. 15A, 20. Holotype, 376 mm TL, Tufts Abyssal Plain, off Oregon.

Range: Nearest collection localities to Alaska are those of the type series, taken off Oregon at 44°40'N, 133°37'W, depth 3,724 m, and specimens taken in mid-Pacific at 45°01'N, 153°50'W, depth 5,180 m. Endo and Okamura (1992) described specimens (28) taken by beam trawl and fish trap at depths of 4,100–6,450 m around the Japan Trench, constituting a new depth record and the first confirmed occurrence in the western Pacific.

Coryphaenoides acrolepis (Bean, 1884) **Pacific grenadier**

Bering Sea and Aleutian Islands to Baja California and to Sea of Okhotsk and Pacific off Japan.

Over continental slope, usually at depths of 600–2,500 m, reported as shallow as 35 m and 155 m; primarily benthopelagic but also captured thousands of meters above bottom.

D II,8–11; Pec 17–22; Pel 8–9; Ds 7–10; GR outer 5–7; PC 12–14; Vert precaudal 13–16.

- Medium brown to dark brown or blackish; fins dark; gill and mouth cavities and peritoneum black; **entire orbital rim black**.
- Isthmus to anal fin 82–100% of head length; snout prominent; maxilla extending to posterior portion of eye; orbit diameter 24–31% of head length.
- Barbel length 11–19% of head length.
- Dorsal fin interspace shorter than length of first dorsal fin base, 8–15% of head length; anal fin origin below second dorsal fin; pelvic fin relatively short, 50–70% of head length.
- Scales adherent, with 3–5 diverging rows of coarse spinules; **entire leading edge of snout covered with stout ridged scutes**.
- Teeth in 2 irregular rows or in a narrow band in both jaws, the lower teeth somewhat smaller.
- Gill membranes attached to isthmus leaving only a narrow free edge, if any.
- Length to more than 87 cm TL.

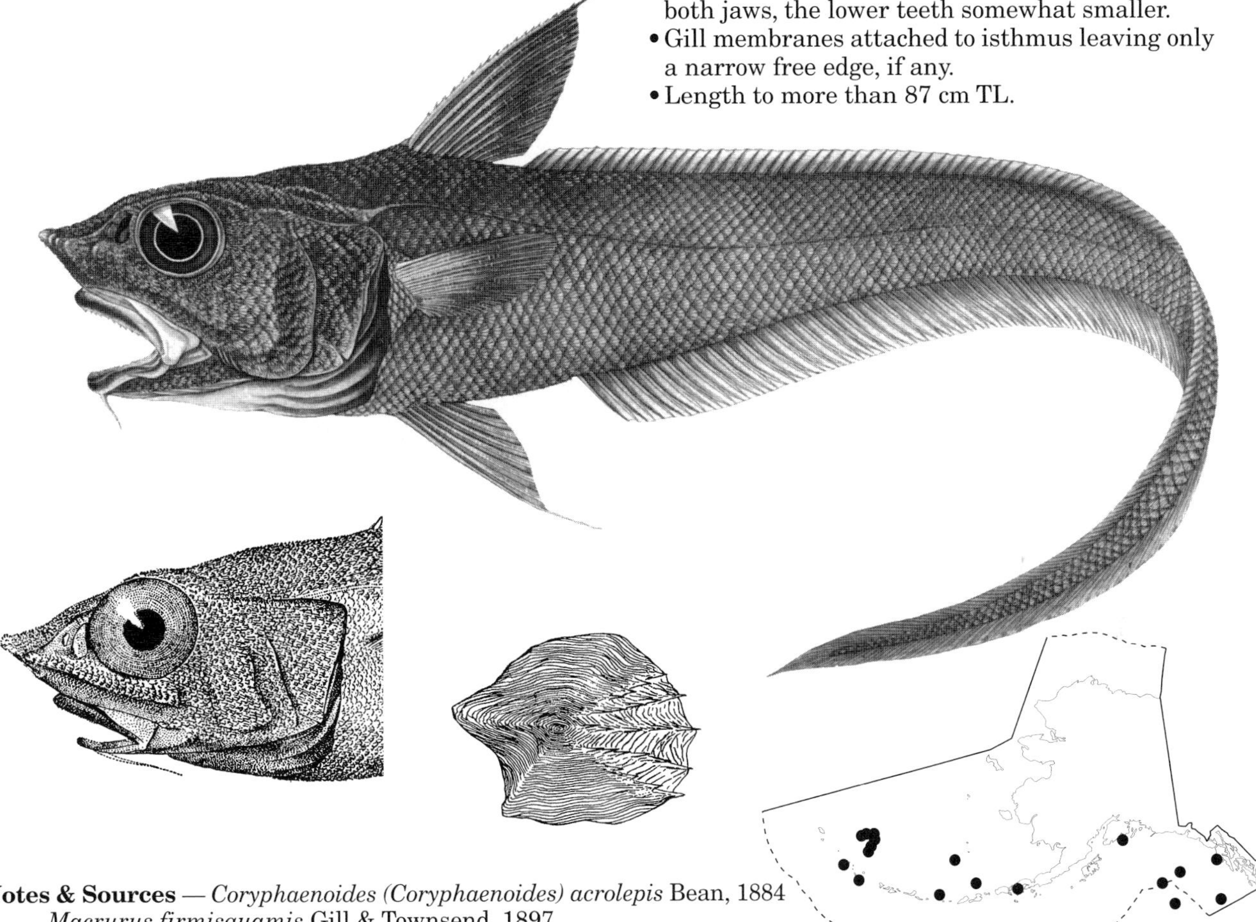

Notes & Sources — *Coryphaenoides (Coryphaenoides) acrolepis* Bean, 1884
Macrurus firmisquamis Gill & Townsend, 1897
Macrourus acrolepis: Jordan and Gilbert 1899.
Bogoslovius firmisquamis: Evermann and Goldsborough 1907.
Coryphaenoides bonanox Jordan & Thompson, 1914
Distinguished from *C. filifer* by its fewer pelvic fin rays (usually 8 vs. 9 or 10 in *C. filifer*) and segmented rays in first dorsal fin (usually 9–11 vs. 12 or 13 in *C. filifer*), the less elongate fin rays, the more adherent scales with stouter spinules, and an entirely black orbital rim (Iwamoto in Cohen et al. 1990).

Description: Bean 1884:262; Hart 1973:251–252; Iwamoto and Stein 1974:12–13; Okamura in Masuda et al. 1984:96; Iwamoto in Cohen et al. 1990:202.

Figures: Full lateral: Okamura 1970, pl. 27. Head: Jordan and Gilbert 1899, pl. 82; juvenile, Bering Sea off Bogoslof Island. Scale: Cohen et al. 1990, fig. 472.

Range: The best-known rattail in the entire North Pacific, broadly distributed and abundant in boreal slope waters of the North Pacific basin (Iwamoto and Stein 1974). Bering Sea records are those of Gill and Townsend (1897), Jordan and Gilbert (1899), Gilbert and Burke (1912a), and Simenstad et al. (1977). Gulf of Alaska records include specimens at ABL taken off Seward and Chichagof Island (B. L. Wing, pers. comm., 11 Apr. 1996), and catches reported by Snytko (1987) from Surveyor, Dickins, Pratt, and Durgin seamounts. Minimum recorded depths: 35 m at *Albatross* station 3274, south of Aleutian Islands, and 155 m at station 3784, in Bering Sea (Evermann and Goldsborough 1907).

Coryphaenoides cinereus (Gilbert, 1896) **popeye grenadier**

Bering Sea and Aleutian Islands to Oregon and to Sea of Okhotsk and Pacific off Japan.

Benthopelagic at depths of 225–2,832 m, most common at 400–950 m in Bering Sea and Gulf of Alaska, deeper off Japan.

D II,10–14; Pec 17–23; Pel 8–10; Ds 8; GR 8–14; PC 5–7; Vert precaudal 13–14.

- Light grayish brown; fins blackish to dusky; mouth and gill cavities black; orbital rim black only anteroventrally; denuded specimens whitish.
- Head broad; maxilla extending to rear portion of eye; **interorbital space broad, width 24–30% of head length; relatively narrow suborbital shelf with anteroventral process**; orbit diameter 26–34% of head length; posterior end of interopercle naked and broadly rounded.
- Barbel very short, 2–8% of head length.
- Dorsal fin interspace 15–22% of head length; **anal fin origin slightly anterior to second dorsal fin origin**; fins moderately large, height of first dorsal 85–105% of head length, pelvic fin 67–141% of head length (longer in males).
- Scales rather deciduous, bearing 3–10 subparallel ridges with short, sharp spines; **scales on suborbital shelf thin and deciduous** except for a few at anteriormost end; **snout tipped with broad spinous scute**; leading edge of snout with enlarged scutes only at tip and at lateral angles.
- Grooved scales of lateral line discontinuous.
- Teeth small, fine, in narrow bands on both jaws.
- Gill membranes narrowly attached to isthmus anteriorly leaving free fold posteriorly.
- Length to 56 cm TL, usually less than 45 cm.

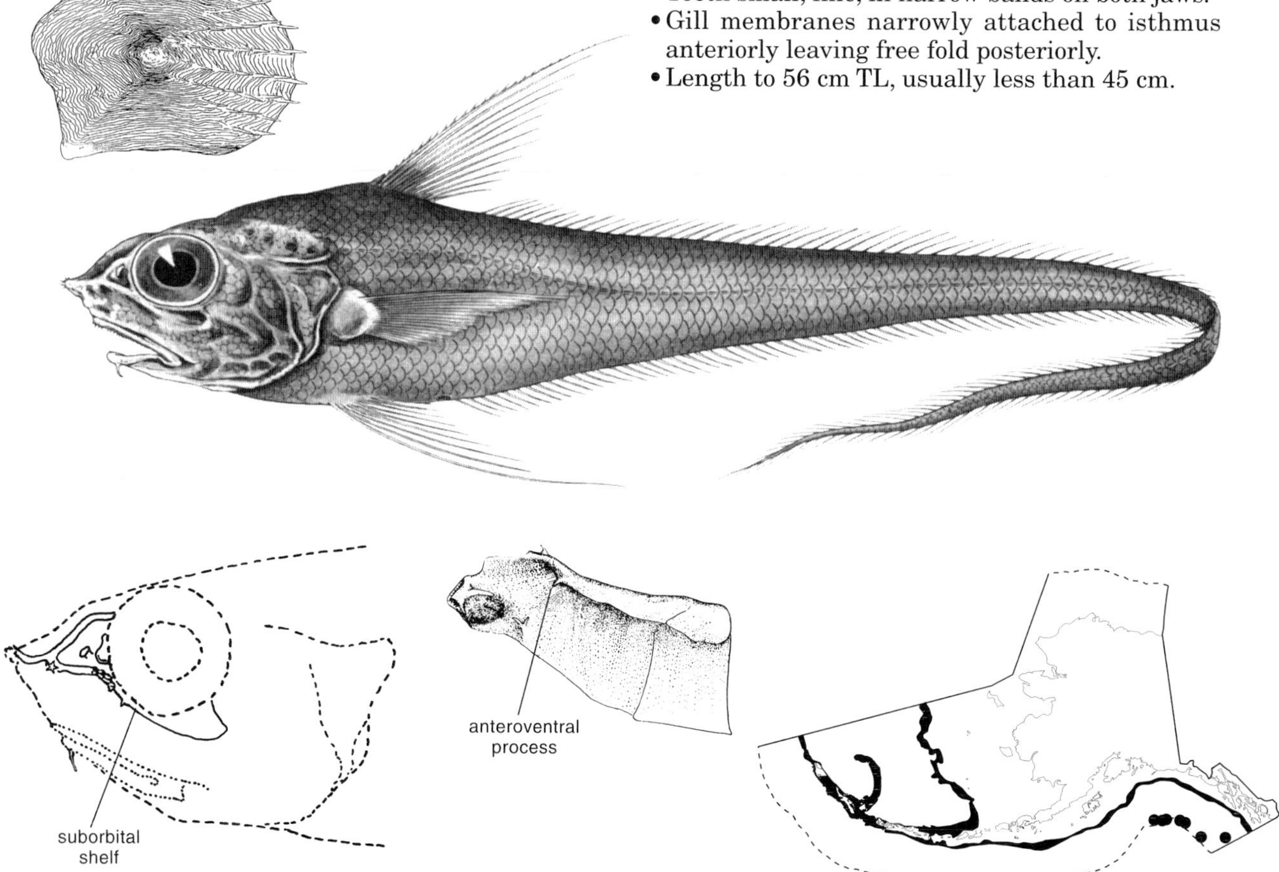

Notes & Sources — *Coryphaenoides (Coryphaenoides) cinereus* (Gilbert, 1896)
Macrurus cinereus Gilbert, 1896
Often difficult to distinguish from *C. filifer.*

Description: Gilbert 1896:457; Iwamoto and Stein 1974:20; Okamura in Masuda et al. 1984:96; Iwamoto in Cohen et al. 1990:207.

Figures: Full lateral: Okamura 1970, pl. 28. Scale: Cohen et al. 1990, fig. 482. Head and suborbital bone: Iwamoto and Stein 1974, figs. 4B and 5B.

Range: Allen and Smith (1988) mapped range in Bering Sea and Aleutian Islands from NMFS surveys. Type localities: north of Unalaska Island, *Albatross* stations 3307 and 3329, 730-1,889 m; south of Ookamok Island, station 3340, 1,271 m. The numerous Alaskan records include those of Gilbert (1896), Jordan and Evermann (1896), Evermann and Goldsborough (1907), Gilbert and Burke (1912a), and Iwamoto and Stein (1974). Snytko (1987) reported *C. cinereus* from Gulf of Alaska seamounts Welker, Dickins, Surveyor, Jakomini, Pratt, Durgin, and Horton.

Coryphaenoides filifer (Gilbert, 1896) **threadfin grenadier**

Southeastern Bering Sea and Aleutian Islands; northern British Columbia off Moresby Island, Queen Charlotte Islands, to southern California; Sea of Okhotsk.

Soft bottom at depths of 2,067–2,904 m.

D II–III,11–14; Pec 17–23; Pel 8–10; Ds 8–11; GR 5–11; PC 10.

- Dark brown; black on fins, nostrils, ventral surfaces of snout, lips, and gill membranes; orbital rim black only anteroventrally.
- Isthmus to anus 68–108% of head length; head broad; maxilla extending to rear portion of eye; **interorbital space narrow, width 19–23% of head length; relatively broad suborbital shelf with no anteroventral process**; orbit diameter 22–30% of head length; interopercle broad and slightly exposed posteriorly, with small, loose scales.
- Barbel length 6–13% HL.
- Dorsal fin interspace shorter than first dorsal fin base, 9–29% of head length; **anal fin origin below second dorsal fin**; pelvic fin long, 74–135% of head length.
- Scales rather deciduous, with 3–7 parallel to slightly diverging spinous ridges; **scales on suborbital shelf stout and embedded; snout tipped with broad spinous scute**, generally larger than in *C. cinereus*; leading edge of snout with enlarged scutes only at tip and at lateral angles.
- Lateral line more distinct and not as interrupted as in *C. cinereus*.
- Teeth small, fine, in narrow bands on both jaws; sometimes with enlarged outer teeth on premaxilla.
- Gill membranes closely joined to isthmus with no free fold present.
- Length to 66 cm TL.

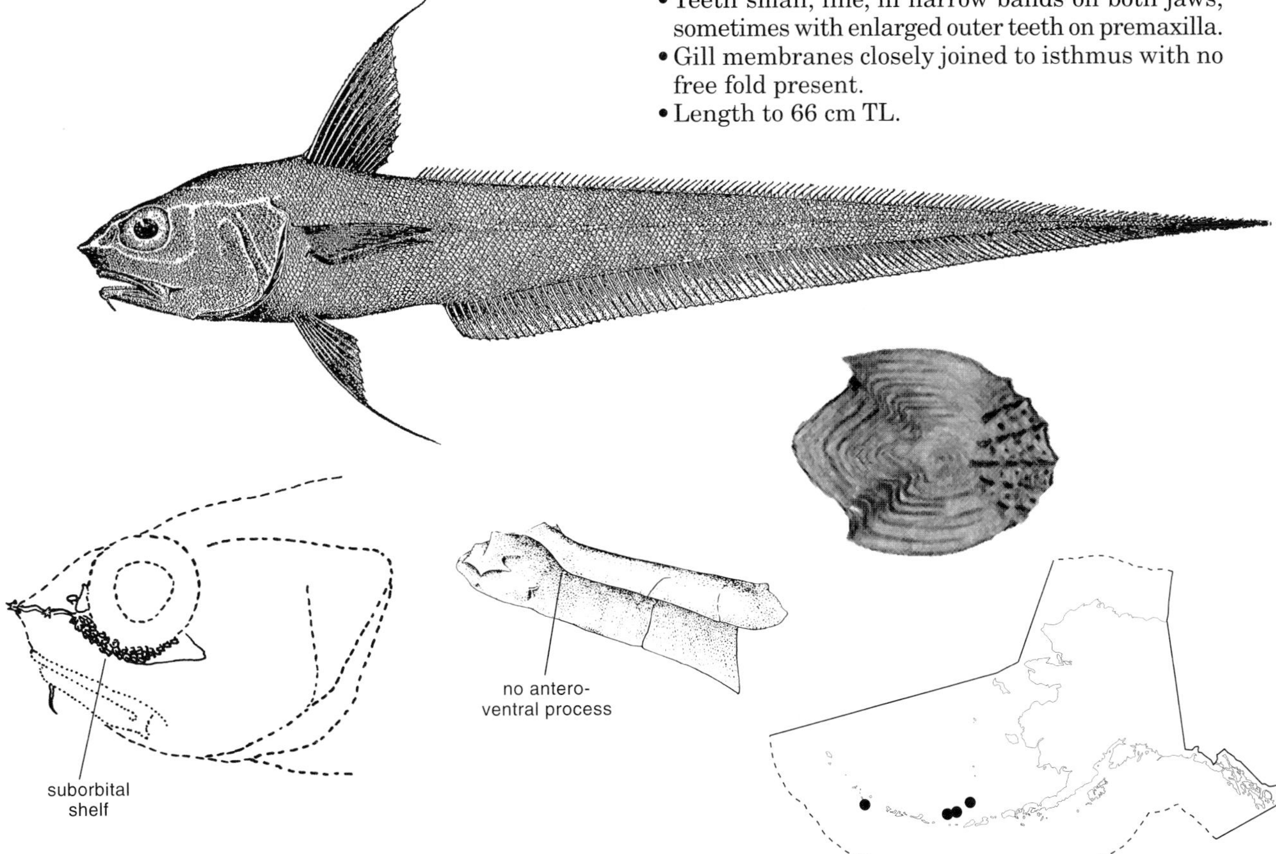

Notes & Sources — *Coryphaenoides (Coryphaenoides) filifer* (Gilbert, 1896)
Chalinura filifera Gilbert, 1896
Macrurus dorsalis Gill & Townsend, 1897
Macrurus lepturus Gill & Townsend, 1897

Description: Gilbert 1896:458; Gilbert and Burke 1912a:91–92; Iwamoto and Stein 1974:17.

Figures: Full lateral: Gilbert and Burke 1912a:91; type of *Macrurus lepturus,* south of Pribilof Islands. Head, suborbital bone, scale: Iwamoto and Stein 1974, figs. 4A, 5A, 8.

Range: Alaskan records are from southwest of Pribilof Islands at *Albatross* station 3604, 54°54'N, 168°59'W, depth 2,562 m (Gill and Townsend 1897); off Yunaska Island at station 4764, 53°20'N, 171°00'W, depth 2,067 m, and station 4765, 53°12'N, 171°37'W, depth 2,226 m (Gilbert and Burke 1912a); and Amchitka Island (Isakson et al. 1971, confirmed in Simenstad et al. 1977). Vouchers from Gulf of Alaska are needed. Specimens from Gulf of Alaska identified as *C. filifer* by Quast and Hall (1972) are referable to *C. cinereus.* Documented range was extended to Sea of Okhotsk by Endo et al. (1994). Nearest record outside Alaska is that of Gilbert (1896), from west of Moresby Island, British Columbia, at *Albatross* station 3342, 52°39'W, 132°38'W, depth 2,904 m.

Family Moridae
Codlings

Among the many common names for the Moridae are deepsea cods, morid cods, moras, hakelings, and codlings. Most species inhabit deep water, to depths beyond 2,500 m, but some inhabit shallow coastal areas. The family is represented in all seas and comprises about 100 recognized species, many of them known from only one specimen. Paulin (1989) provided an overview of the family, but there is no up-to-date classification for the entire group and no consensus on how many genera should be recognized.

The occurrence of two morid species off the coasts of Alaska is well documented, while at least two others probably occur in the region although their presence has not yet been confirmed. Pacific flatnose, *Antimora microlepis,* are commonly taken over the continental slope in the Bering Sea and Gulf of Alaska. Longfin codling, *Laemonema longipes,* are occasionally caught over the slope in the Bering Sea. Slender codling, also called dainty mora, *Halargyreus johnsonii,* have been caught close to Alaska in the Bering Sea southwest of Cape Navarin (B. A. Sheiko, pers. comm., 15 Jan. 1999) and the northeast Pacific Ocean at Canadian weathership Ocean Station Papa (50°N, 145°W; Peden et al. 1985). Northern gray hakeling, *Lepidion schmidti,* occur as close to Alaska as the vicinity of the Commander Islands, Russia (Sheiko and Tranbenkova 1998).

Taxonomically the family Moridae is defined by four features: a swim bladder–auditory capsule (otophysic) connection, a caudal fin with several hypurals, the neural spine of the first vertebra firmly connected to the skull, and distinctive otoliths (Cohen 1984). Other diagnostic characters, some useful for distinguishing the genera and species, include: body tapering to very narrow caudal peduncle; caudal fin separate from dorsal and anal fins; fins lacking spines; two or three (usually two) dorsal fins; and one anal fin, which in some species is deeply notched, or, rarely, two anal fins. Some species have a chin barbel. Vomerine teeth are present or absent, and palatine teeth always absent. The scales are small and cycloid. The gill rakers are usually small. The vertebral count range for the family is 41–72, and for species in this guide, 50–58. Some morids, although not the species in or near Alaska, have a light organ between the pelvic fins.

Most codlings are moderate-sized fish in the 50- to 70-cm (20- to 27-inch) range, but for the whole family sizes range from 13 cm (5 inches) to 90 cm (35.4 inches) in total length.

Quast and Hall (1972) included one species of codling in their inventory of Alaskan fish species, using the name *Antimora rostrata.* Since then, Small (1981) reviewed the genus *Antimora* and recognized two valid species. The one in Alaska is *A. microlepis*; this species is restricted to the Bering Sea and North Pacific Ocean. *Antimora rostrata* occurs in all oceans except the North Pacific. Nakaya et al. (1980) reviewed *Lepidion* from the western North Pacific, and Meléndez and Markle (1997) examined the systematics of *Laemonema.*

Key to the Moridae of Alaska

1 Anal fin not notched . . . . (2)

1 Anal fin notched . . . . (3)

2 (1) Anal fin origin opposite origin of second dorsal fin; lower jaw slightly projecting beyond upper jaw; chin barbel absent; first dorsal fin ray not filamentous . . . . *Laemonema longipes,* page 281

2 Anal fin origin posterior to level of origin of second dorsal fin; upper jaw projecting beyond lower jaw; chin barbel present; first dorsal fin ray filamentous . . . . *Lepidion schmidti,* page 282 (not known from Alaska)

3 (1) Snout strongly projecting, depressed, and keeled; chin barbel present; first ray of first dorsal fin greatly elongate . . . . *Antimora microlepis,* page 283

3 Lower jaw strongly projecting; snout not depressed and keeled; chin barbel absent; first dorsal ray not particularly elongate . . . . . *Halargyreus johnsonii,* page 284 (not known from Alaska)

Laemonema longipes Schmidt, 1938 — **longfin codling**

Bering Sea and Pacific Ocean south of Aleutian Islands to Sea of Okhotsk and Pacific off southern Japan. Near bottom on continental slope at depths of 200–2,025 m; benthopelagic.

D 5–6 + 49–53; A 45–51; Pec 15–18; Pel 2; Ds 10–11; GR 25–30; Vert 49–53.

- Brown dorsally; silvery ventrally, breast sometimes dark blue; fins, oral and gill cavities, and peritoneum black.
- Head relatively small, 21–23% of standard length; body low, compressed, and elongate, body depth 15–17% of standard length; eye diameter less than snout length; **lower jaw slightly protruding**; maxilla extending to mideye to posterior edge of pupil.
- **Chin barbel absent**.
- **No elongated filament in first dorsal fin**; **anal fin not notched**; **anal fin origin below origin of second dorsal fin**; pectoral and pelvic fins extending beyond origin of anal fin; pelvic fin filamentous.
- Mandibular teeth uniserial; premaxillary teeth uniserial anteriorly, villiform posteriorly; vomerine teeth caniniform, in V-shaped patch.
- Length to 60 cm TL.

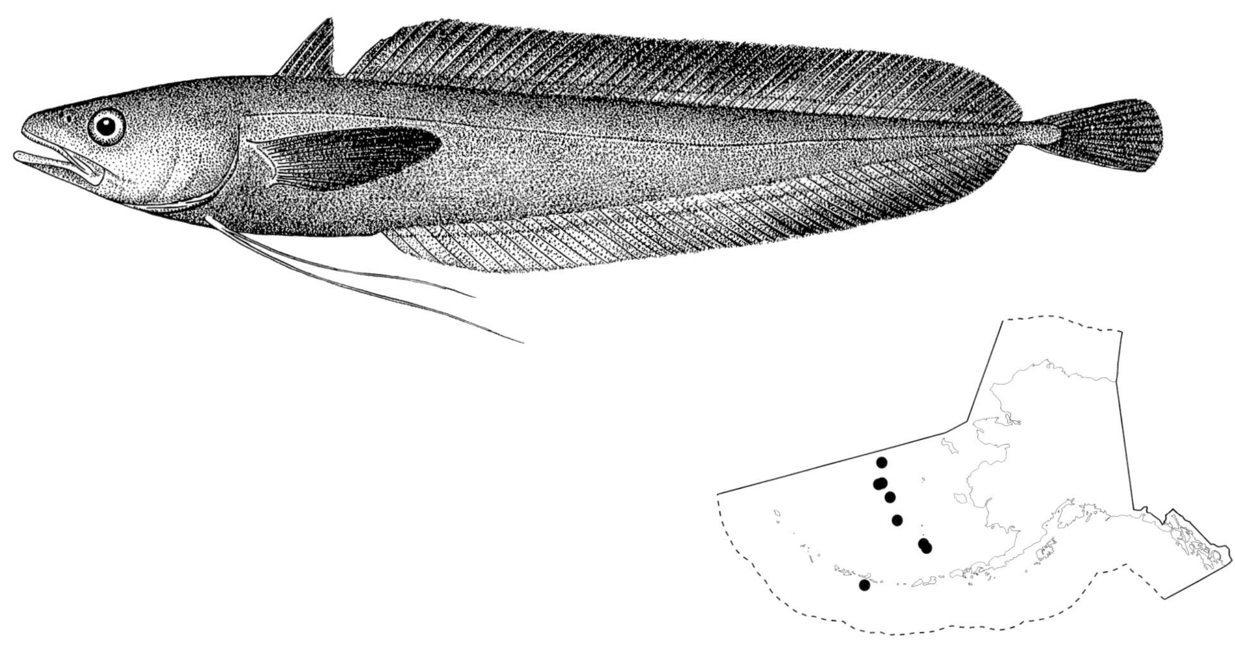

Notes & Sources — *Laemonema longipes* Schmidt, 1938

Description: Svetovidov 1948:68–69; Lindberg and Legeza 1965:243–244; Yabe et al. 1981:354; Sawada in Amaoka et al. 1983:190, 322; Okamura in Masuda et al. 1984:91; Cohen in Cohen et al. 1990:363; Meléndez and Markle 1997:645–646.

Figure: Cohen et al. 1990, fig. 785.

Range: Previously published records of occurrence in North American waters comprise two specimens from 56°00'N, 169°16'W (HUMZ 82892, USNM 220877) and one from an unspecified area of the eastern Bering Sea (UW 20772) reported by Yabe et al. (1981). Additional examples from the Bering Sea, taken in the early 1980s by various research vessels and including one or two specimens in each lot, are: UW 21536, 58°18'N, 175°25'W, depth 500 m; UW 29004, 56°06'N, 168°40'W, 850 m; UW 29006, 58°46'N, 177°34'W, 390 m; UW 29007, 60°03'N, 179°07'W, 550 m; UW 29008, 58°46'N, 178°03'W, 550 m; UW 29009, 57°05'N, 173°33'W, 500 m; and UW 29010, 52°14'N, 173°55'W, 470 m. Savin (1993) gave depth range of 200–2,000 m. Dudnik and Dolganov (1992) gave maximum depth of 2,025 m. One of the few commercially sought morids, longfin codling are most abundant in the western Pacific off Japan and the Kuril Islands. Savin (1993) suggested that living in bathyal waters under relatively constant environmental conditions allows the fish to penetrate as far north as the Bering Sea and Gulf of Alaska on feeding migrations, but did not give specific records from those regions. Records documenting presence in the Gulf of Alaska appear to be lacking.

Lepidion schmidti Svetovidov, 1936 **northern gray hakeling**

Western Bering Sea off Bering Island to Sea of Okhotsk and to Pacific Ocean off southern Japan and at Emperor Seamounts; eastern Atlantic Ocean.

Near bottom at depths of 315–1,520 m; benthopelagic.

D 4–6 + 47–50; A 39–42; Pec 21–23; Pel 7; Ds 23–27; GR 14–18; Vert 17–18 + 37–40.

- Body uniformly grayish brown to blackish brown; lateral line and paired fins blackish brown; outer portions of median fins blackish brown.
- Head depressed, large, depth 27–31% of standard length; body elongate, depth 18–23% of standard length; snout long, more than 1.5 times eye diameter; **upper jaw protruding**; maxilla extending to posterior edge of eye or beyond.
- **Chin barbel present**.
- **First ray of first dorsal fin minute, second ray (or first, if minute ray absent) greatly elongate**; **anal fin margin straight or slightly concave, *not* distinctly notched**; **anal fin origin posterior to second dorsal fin origin**, at about midpoint of body; caudal fin truncate; pectoral and pelvic fins short, not reaching level of anal fin; outermost pelvic fin rays filamentous.
- Teeth villiform, in broad bands on both jaws; vomerine teeth villiform, in broad V-shaped patch.
- Length to 101 cm TL.

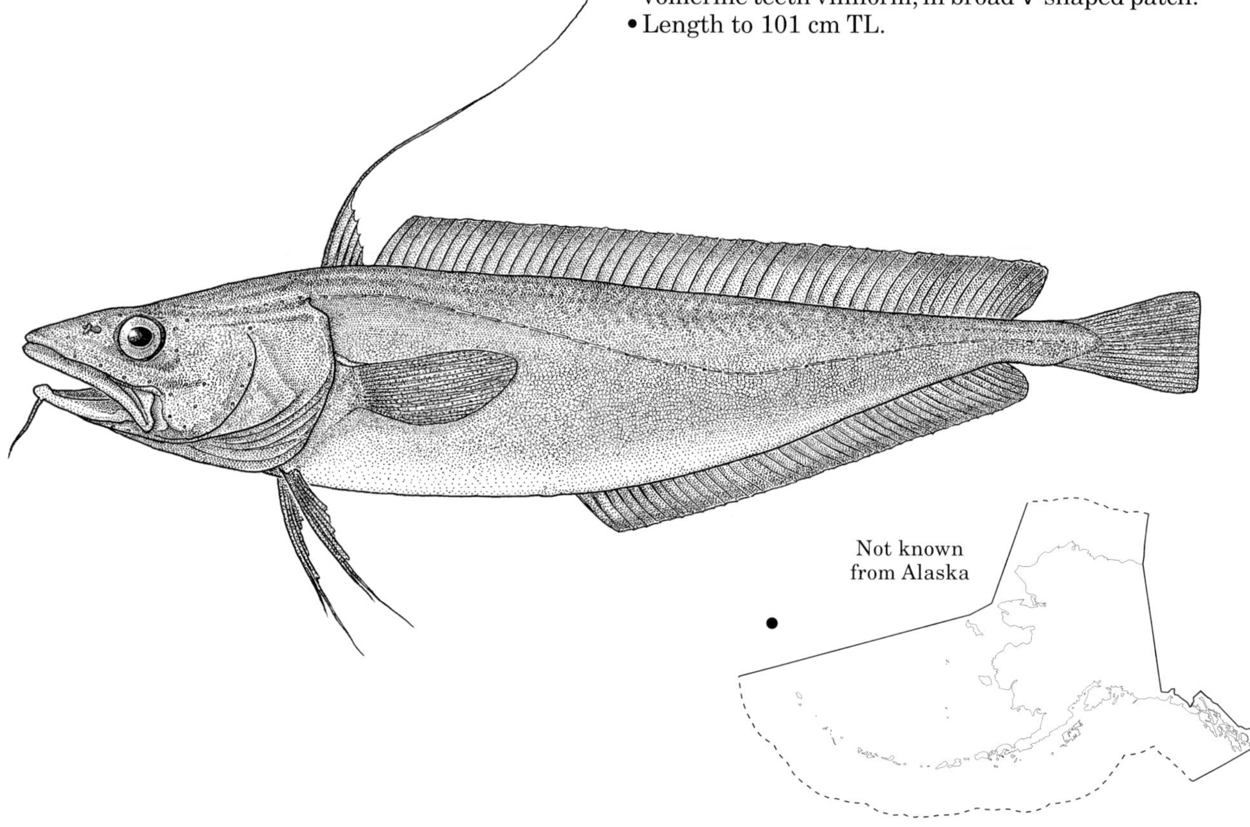

Notes & Sources — *Lepidion schmidti* Svetovidov, 1936

Description: Svetovidov 1936; Nakaya et al. 1980; Sawada in Amaoka et al. 1983:189; Okamura in Masuda et al. 1984:90. (Not treated by Cohen in Cohen et al. 1990.)

Figure: Russian Academy of Sciences, Zoological Institute, St. Petersburg, artist I. Belousov, 30 Jun. 1999; holotype, ZIN 22883, 497 mm SL. For photograph see Amaoka et al. (1983:98) or Masuda et al. (1984, pl. 78-A), which both have the same photograph.

Range: One specimen (KIE 1264, male, 595 mm SL) taken by longline northwest of Bering Island at 55°38'N, 164°52'E, depth 500–600 m, in 1994 (Sheiko and Tranbenkova 1998) represents the nearest documented record to Alaska. Minimum depth of 315 m was reported by Dudnik and Dolganov (1992).

Antimora microlepis Bean, 1890 — Pacific flatnose

Bering Sea and Pacific Ocean south of Aleutian Islands to Gulf of California and to Sea of Okhotsk and Pacific off southern Japan; tropical mid-North Pacific.

Near bottom at depths of 175–3,048 m, usually at 500–950 m over continental slope; benthopelagic.

D 4–5 + 50–55; A 36–42; Pec 18–20; Pel 6–7; Ds 11; GR 15–20; Vert 57–58.

- Gray, bluish, pale brown, or nearly black; pectoral, pelvic, and caudal fins blackish.
- Body compressed, robust to elongate depending on condition; **snout protruding, strikingly depressed and forming shelf over mouth**, the shelf extending posteriorly as keel below eye; eye diameter about same as or less than snout length; maxilla extending to posterior part of eye.
- **Chin barbel present**.
- **First dorsal ray elongate**; **anal fin originating well past midpoint of body and deeply indented at middle of fin**; pectoral and pelvic fins falling well short of anal fin origin; second pelvic fin ray elongated into filament.
- Jaw teeth villiform; vomer with small round patch of minute teeth.
- Length to 66 cm TL.

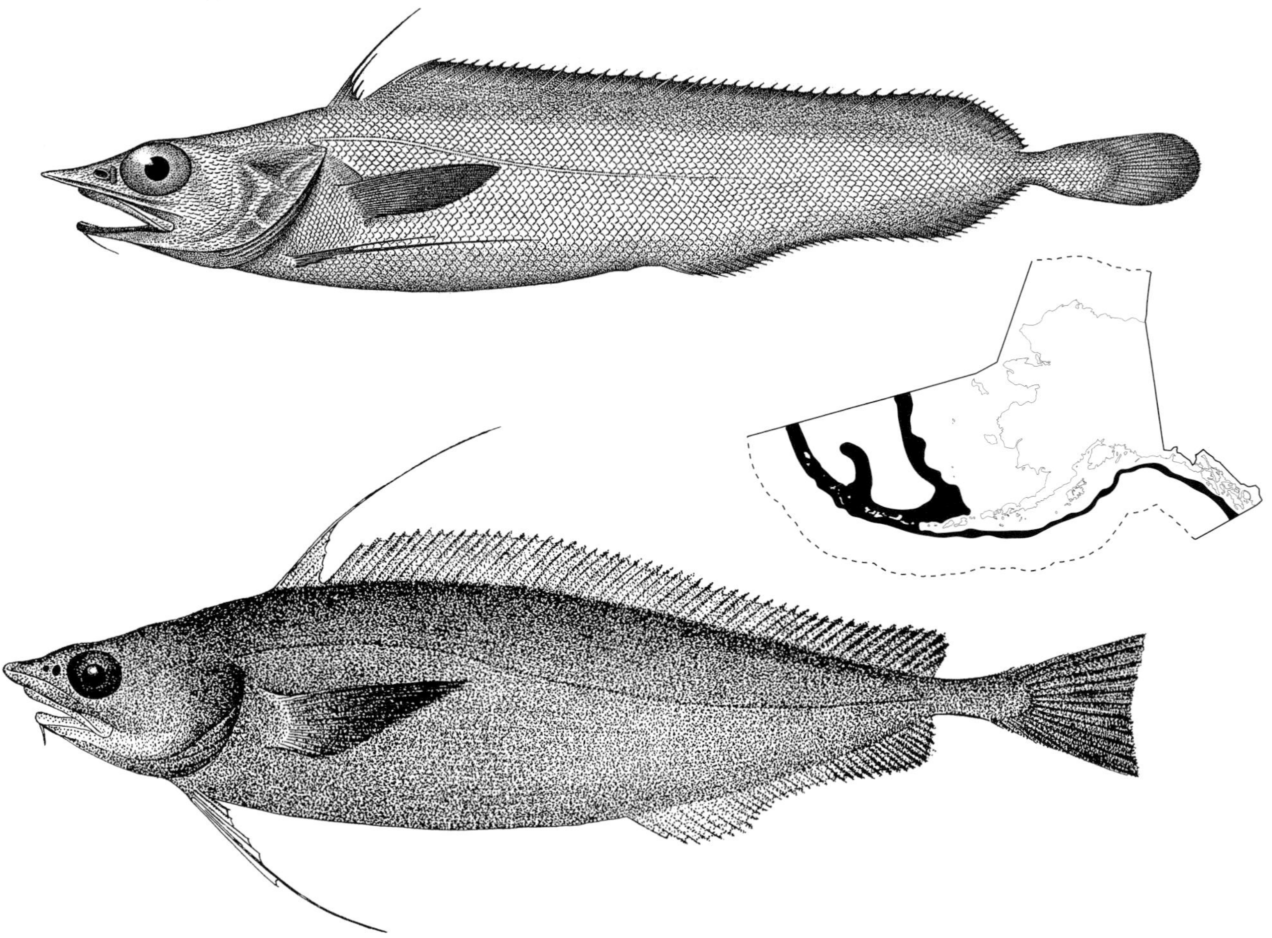

Notes & Sources — *Antimora microlepis* Bean, 1890

Distinguishable from *A. rostrata* (Günther, 1878), inhabiting all oceans except the North Pacific, by length and number of gill filaments on first arch: relatively long and numbering 93–103 in *A. microlepis*; and relatively short and numbering 76–90 in *A. rostrata*.

Description: Bean 1890b:38; Lindberg and Legeza 1965:239–240; Hart 1973:220–221; Sawada in Amaoka et al. 1983: 323; Okamura in Masuda et al. 1984:90; Cohen in Cohen et al. 1990:353.

Figures: Upper: Smithsonian Insitution, NMNH, Division of Fishes, artist S. F. Denton, 10 Apr. 1889; syntype, USNM 45361, 263 mm TL, *Albatross* station 2860, off Cape St. James, Queen Charlotte Islands, British Columbia, depth 1,602 m. Lower: Cohen et al. 1990, fig. 767.

Range: One of the most common species taken in NMFS bottom trawl surveys of the Bering Sea and North Pacific, and found in those surveys as far north as Navarin Canyon and west in the Aleutians to Attu Island (Allen and Smith 1988). Commonly taken as bycatch by trawlers fishing for deepwater species of flatfish and rockfish. Early Alaskan records include those of Gilbert and Burke (1912a) from Agattu Island and Bowers Bank. Hughes (1981) recorded it from Surveyor and Welker seamounts.

Halargyreus johnsonii Günther, 1862 **slender codling**

Northwestern Bering Sea; Pacific Ocean south of Gulf of Alaska to California and to Japan and Sea of Okhotsk; subarctic and subantarctic to temperate waters in the Atlantic Ocean, as well as the Pacific.

Over continental slope at depths of 508–1,500 m; benthopelagic to pelagic.

D 6–9 + 47–59; A 41–52; Pec 14–19; Pel 5–6; Ds 7–8; GR 20–28; Vert 52–57.

- Fresh specimens reddish brown on silvery background; in alcohol light brown to whitish gray; mouth and gill cavities black.
- Body elongate, compressed; eye diameter about equal to or less than snout length; **lower jaw protruding**; maxilla extending to mideye.
- **Chin barbel absent.**
- **No elongate filament in first dorsal fin; anal fin origin posterior to origin of second dorsal fin, near midpoint of body; anal fin deeply indented, sometimes appearing as two fins**; caudal fin emarginate; pectoral and pelvic fins not reaching anal fin origin; outer 2 pelvic rays elongate.
- Jaw teeth villiform; vomerine teeth absent.
- Anterior gill rakers of 1st arch longer than gill filaments.
- Length to 56 cm TL.

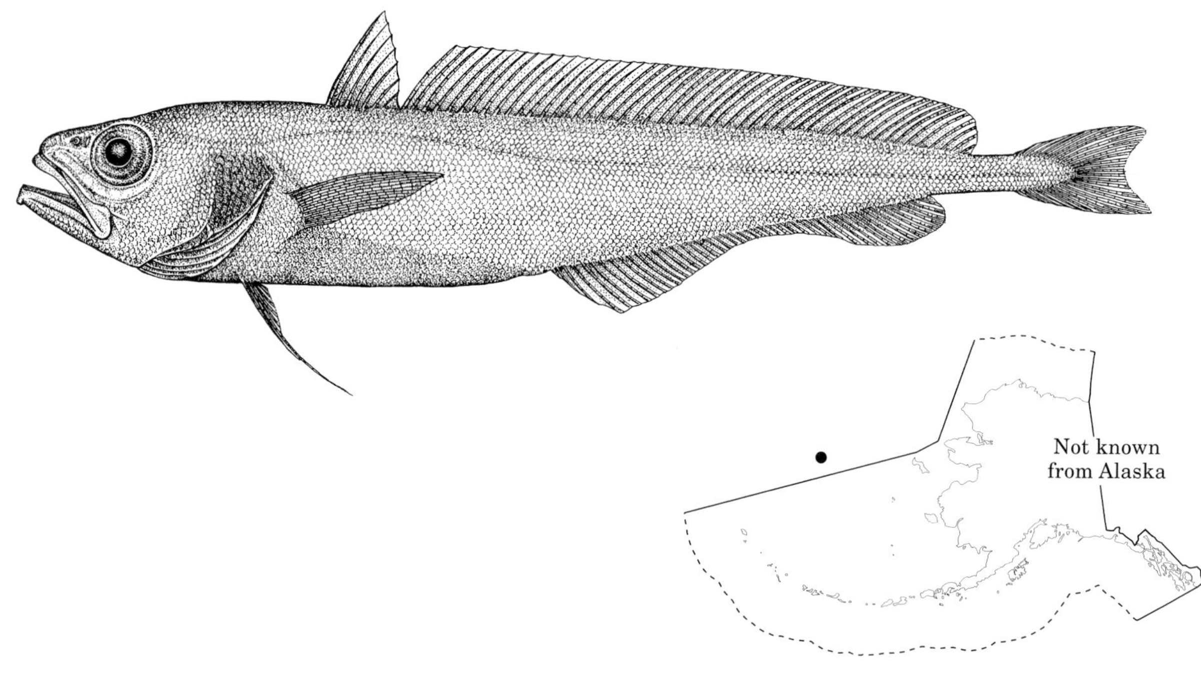

Notes & Sources — *Halargyreus johnsonii* Günther, 1862
Also called dainty mora.

Description: Templeman 1968; Sawada in Amaoka et al. 1983:190, 322; Okamura in Masuda et al. 1984:90; Cohen in Cohen et al. 1990:360; Chiu et al. in Gon and Heemstra 1990:184–185; Okamura in Okamura et al. 1995:107.

Figure: Gon and Heemstra 1990, fig. 3; 28 cm SL, eastern South Pacific (52°20'S, 158°29'E).

Range: Peden et al. (1985) recorded a specimen (NMC 76-31) taken from midocean west of southern British Columbia at Ocean Station Papa at a depth of 1,500 m; they included a photograph. The only other published records for the eastern North Pacific are one from off northern Washington, one off southern Washingon, and one off California, reported by Logan et al. (1993). The nearest record to Alaska was recently reported by B. A. Sheiko (pers. comm., 15 Jan. 1999): one specimen (KIE uncataloged) collected from the northwestern Bering Sea at 61°24'N, 176°24'E, depth range 1,090–1,120 m, on 31 Jul. 1982 by the Russian research vessel *Darwin*.

Family Merlucciidae
Merluccid hakes

Members of the family Merlucciidae are called merlucciids or merluccid hakes to distinguish them from hakes in other families. In some parts of the world they are called whiting, but that name is also used for some other gadiforms. The group was previously classified as a subfamily of Gadidae. As presently understood (Howes 1991a), the Merlucciidae has one genus, *Merluccius,* with 13 species. The species are distributed in the Atlantic and Pacific oceans mainly over the continental shelf and upper slope, but some enter estuaries and others inhabit waters deeper than 1,000 m.

The Pacific hake, *Merluccius productus,* is the only merlucciid inhabiting the northeastern Pacific. In Alaska this species is occasionally found in the inside waters of the Alexander Archipelago as well as off the outer coasts of the Gulf of Alaska and the Pacific side of the Aleutian Islands. Pacific hake are most likely to occur off Alaska during their summer and fall northward migration, which is accompanied by movement toward shore and into shallower water.

Important taxonomic characteristics of merluccid hakes include a V-shaped ridge on the roof of the skull (see diagram), a "pseudospine" at the anterior end of the dorsal fin (also in some macrourids), two hypural bones in the caudal fin, and first vertebra firmly fused with the cranium (attachment is looser in morids; Inada 1989). The pseudospine is the first principal dorsal fin ray, which is spinelike but is considered to be in a developmental stage from the soft ray to the spine (Okamura 1970). Some investigators count the pseudospine with the rays, as in this guide, while others count it separately, as a spine. In merlucciids the swim bladder and auditory capsule are not connected (as they are in morids).

Other distinguishing features of merluccid hakes include presence of two dorsal fins and one anal fin, and a separate, distinct caudal fin. The second dorsal fin and the anal fin are deeply notched toward their

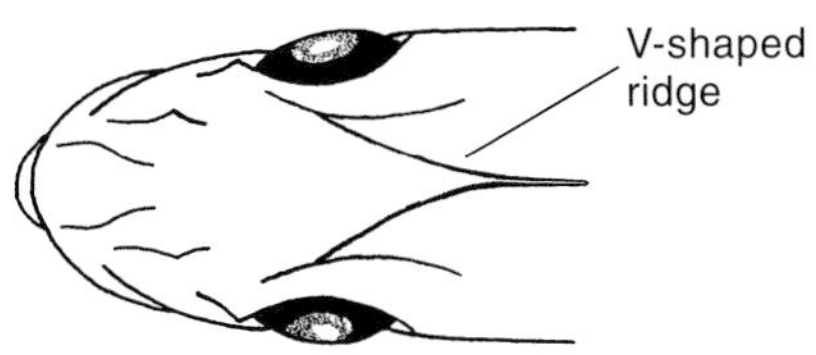

posterior ends. The mouth is terminal, large, and has long teeth, and the lower jaw projects slightly and lacks a chin barbel. Teeth are present on the vomer but lacking on the palatines. The scales are tiny, cycloid, and easily rubbed off. The gill rakers are well developed and vary in shape and number by species, providing characters helpful for identification. Except in occasional individuals, merluccid hakes have 7 branchiostegal rays.

Merluccid hakes range in maximum total length from about 40 cm (1.3 ft) to 140 cm (4.5 ft). Pacific hake reach about 91 cm (4 ft) but in commercial catches sizes under 60 cm (2 ft) are most common.

Merluccius productus (Ayres, 1855) **Pacific hake**

Casco Cove, Attu Island; Gulf of Alaska to southern Baja California at Bahia Magdalena.

Oceanic and coastal near surface to depth of 914 m, usually at 50–450 m; largely pelagic, in schools.

D 10–13 + 39–44; A 37–44; Pec 14–16; Pel 6–8; LLs 125–144; Ds 13; GR 18–23; Vert 53–54.

- Body silvery gray dorsally, white ventrally; mouth and gill cavity black.
- **V-shaped ridge on top of head**; eye diameter less than snout length; **lower jaw protruding**; maxilla extending to mideye.
- **Chin barbel absent**.
- **Second dorsal fin and anal fin both deeply notched**; pectoral fin usually reaching or extending beyond origin of anal fin; caudal fin margin basically truncate, becoming slightly emarginate or forked with age.
- Teeth strong, pointed, in bands on jaws and vomer.
- Gill rakers long and slender with pointed tips.
- Length to 91 cm TL.

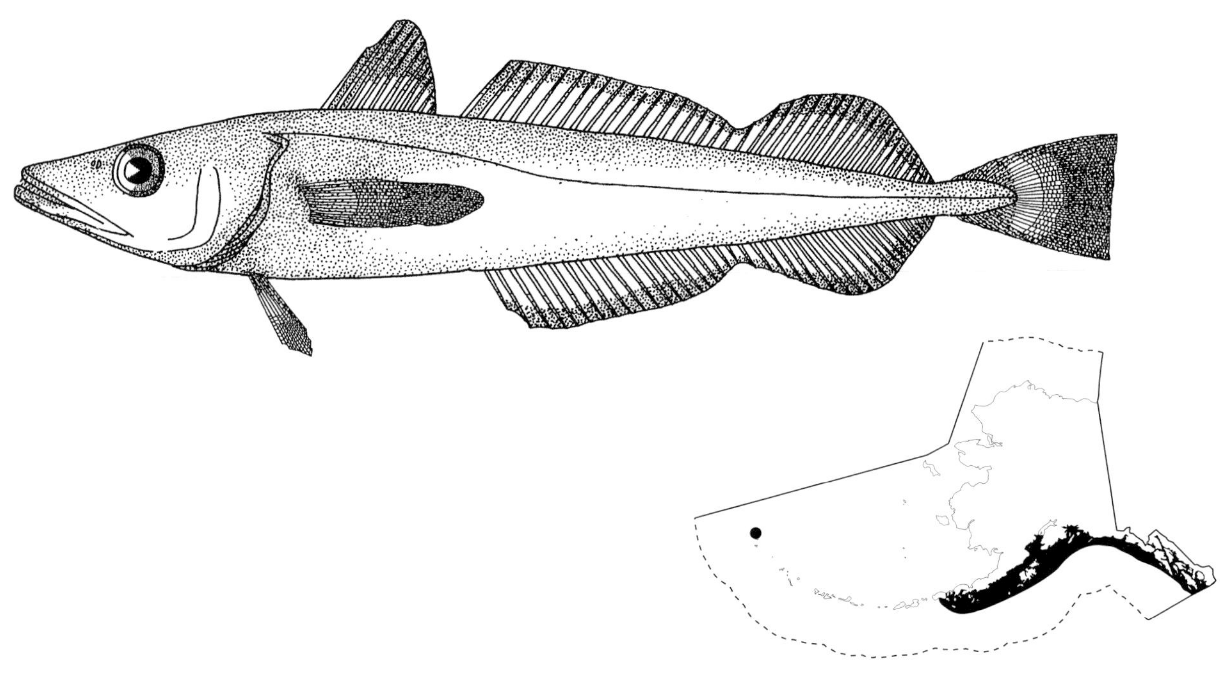

Notes & Sources — *Merluccius productus* (Ayres, 1855)
Merlangus productus Ayres, 1855

Description: Hart 1973:225–226; Inada in Cohen et al. 1990: 342–343.

Figure: Cohen et al. 1990, fig. 743.

Range: Wilimovsky (1954, 1958) gave the Gulf of Alaska for the northern limit in general statements. Inada (in Cohen et al. 1990) reported the range to extend north to Vancouver Island, British Columbia, and discounted "a record from the Gulf of Alaska." However, Quast and Hall (1972) reported presence of specimens from southeastern Alaska in the NMFS Auke Bay Laboratory collection, and more specimens (e.g., from Katlian Bay and Lisianski Inlet) have since been added to the collection. Hake are not rare in the Gulf of Alaska. Carlson et al. (1982) reported hake off Point Arden, Stephens Passage; and R. Haight collected one from a trawl net in Fritz Cove (B. L. Wing, pers. comm., 11 Apr. 1996). Allen and Smith (1988) reported this species was taken in NMFS resource surveys at several Gulf of Alaska localities, including the vicinity of Sanak Island, southwest of Prince William Sound, and at Dixon Entrance, as well as off coasts of northern British Columbia. The UBC collection contains a specimen (UBC 65-5) from Casco Cove, on the southeastern coast of Attu Island. Listed as a component of the sublittoral ichthyofauna on the continental slope of the Bering Sea by Fedorov (1973a). However, there have been no other reports of occurrence in the Bering Sea. Voucher specimens are needed to confirm continued existence in the Bering Sea. Hart (1973) reported that the species was common along the entire British Columbia coast. A report for the Gulf of California (Roedel 1953) was discounted by J. Arvizu (pers. comm. cited by Allen and Smith 1988). A report from Asia at Tatar Strait was discounted by Svetovidov (1948).

Family Gadidae
Cods

Cods, family Gadidae, are marine fishes except for the burbot, *Lota lota,* which exclusively inhabits fresh water. Most cod species inhabit continental shelves at coldwater latitudes in the North Atlantic Ocean. Relatively few are distributed in the Arctic and Pacific oceans. The family includes about 30 species with 9 occurring in Alaska. Walleye pollock, *Theragra chalcogramma,* and Pacific cod, *Gadus macrocephalus,* are the most abundant marine species in Alaska and are commercially important while saffron cod, *Eleginus gracilis,* Pacific tomcod, *Microgadus proximus,* and Arctic cod, *Boreogadus saida,* are next abundant and sought by subsistence fishers. Burbot, *L. lota,* are sought by subsistence fishers but are not the target of a commercial fishery in Alaska, as they are in Russia. The presence of three Arctic marine cod species in Alaska is known from only one or a few records each: polar cod, *Arctogadus glacialis,* collected by K. J. Frost and L. F. Lowry northeast of Point Barrow in 1977 and preserved in the fish collection of the Canadian Museum of Nature at Ottawa; and toothed cod, *A. borisovi,* and ogac, *G. ogac,* recorded from the Alaskan sector of the Beaufort Sea in previous publications (e.g., Walters 1955).

Morphological features distinguishing the Gadidae include: caudal fin separate from the dorsal and anal fins and not tapering to a point; fins lacking spines; teeth small, in bands on the jaws and head of the vomer but usually absent from the palatines; small, cycloid scales; swim bladder not connected with the auditory capsules (no otophysic connection); and one hypural bone in the caudal fin.

In Nelson's (1994) classification the Gadidae comprise two subfamilies. The subfamily Lotinae, including *L. lota,* is characterized by the presence of one or two dorsal fins and one anal fin; presence of a chin barbel; a rounded caudal fin; and eggs with an oil globule. Members of the subfamily Gadinae have three dorsal fins and two anal fins; usually a chin barbel; a truncate or emarginate caudal fin; and eggs without an oil globule. The subfamily Gadinae is the most advanced taxon in the order Gadiformes.

The numbers of dorsal and anal fins, caudal fin shape, chin barbel development, presence or absence of pores of the cephalic sensory canals, configuration of the lateral line on the body, and other external characters are usually sufficient for identifying gadids obtained in Alaskan waters. The numbers of fin rays are roughly similar in the Alaskan species and not helpful for identification. The counts show the usual increases in number in specimens from higher- to lower-temperature waters. Vertebral counts range from 48 to 67 for the Alaskan species and overlap greatly among species. As with vertebral counts for most other fish families, counts for gadids are not often reported in the literature and sample sizes are small for some species. The number of branchiostegal rays ranges from 6 to 8 and varies among individuals in most species.

The Atlantic cod, *Gadus morhua,* is the largest of the world's gadids, with a recorded maximum total length of 183 cm (6 ft). The nine Alaskan species range from about 37 cm (14.6 inches) in *Microgadus proximus* to 152 cm (5 ft) in *L. lota.*

Although *G. ogac* was reported from Arctic Alaska by Walters (1955) on the basis of specimens collected by N. J. Wilimovsky, it was not included on lists of Alaskan fish species by Wilimovsky (1954, 1958) or Quast and Hall (1972). The discrepancy likely reflects the changing taxonomic status of the ogac. At times, both ogac and Pacific cod, *G. macrocephalus,* have been classified as junior synonyms of Atlantic cod, *G. morhua.* Although differences of opinion still exist, presently the prevailing opinion is that the three species are valid (e.g., Cohen et al. 1990). Studies have not found molecular differences between *G. ogac* and *G. macrocephalus*; for example, examination of 896 base pairs found identical gene sequences (Carr et al. 1999). However, although such demonstrations in these and in other species may indicate continued gene flow and argue for synonymy, they may not be a reason for rejecting species status (Nelson 2000). Commenting on the findings of Carr et al. (1999), C. R. Renaud (pers. comm., 22 Jan. 2001) remarked that the lack of difference in base pairs examined does not discount the differences in morphology between *G. ogac* and *G. macrocephalus*; specifically, in testicular lobe shape and breeding tubercle shape (Renaud 1989). Several recent accounts give a range for *G. ogac* extending to Alaska. Presence of ogac near Alaska in western Arctic Canada is well documented (e.g., Hunter et al. 1984), but vouchers are needed from Alaska.

The following key is adapted from the key to gadid genera by Cohen (in Cohen et al. 1990), with characters added for the species. Our key does not use a pale lateral line to distinguish *Gadus* from other genera, as some keys do, because published accounts disagree as to whether *G. ogac* has a pale or dark lateral line, and Schultz and Welander (1935) found that specimens of *G. macrocephalus* from Japan have a dark lateral line.

Key to the Gadidae of Alaska

1		Dorsal fins 2, anal fin 1; caudal fin rounded; freshwater habitat	*Lota lota,* page 289
1		Dorsal fins 3, anal fins 2; caudal fin truncate to lunate; marine habitat	(2)
2	(1)	Lateral line pores on head absent, although small papillae or pits may be present	(3)
2		Lateral line pores present on head	(7)
3	(2)	Body lateral line interrupted along its entire length	(4)
3		Body lateral line continuous along all or part of its length	(6)
4	(3)	Scales nonoverlapping; scales with tubercles giving skin coarse sandpaper texture; palatine teeth never present	*Boreogadus saida,* page 290
4		Scales overlapping; scales without tubercles, skin feeling rough only from overlapping scales; palatine teeth usually present	(5)
5	(4)	Chin barbel absent, except sometimes for barely discernible rudiment	*Arctogadus glacialis,* page 291
5		Chin barbel well developed	*Arctogadus borisovi,* page 292
6	(3)	Lateral line continuous to origin of second dorsal fin; parapophyses expanded at their tips	*Eleginus gracilis,* page 293
6		Lateral line continuous to end of third dorsal fin; parapophyses not expanded at their tips	*Microgadus proximus,* page 294
7	(2)	Lower jaw longer than upper jaw; chin barbel minute or absent; lateral line interrupted at origin of second dorsal fin	*Theragra chalcogramma,* page 295
7		Lower jaw shorter than upper jaw; chin barbel longer than pupil; lateral line continuous to caudal peduncle	(8)
8	(7)	Predorsal distance more than about 33% SL; dorsally light grayish brown with brown and yellowish spots and blotches; median fin margins white	*Gadus macrocephalus,* page 296
8		Predorsal distance less than about 33% SL; dorsally dark brown to blackish without distinct spots or blotches; dorsal and caudal fin margins black	*Gadus ogac,* page 297

Lota lota (Linnaeus, 1758) **burbot**

Throughout Alaska except for offshore islands and most of southeastern Alaska; circumarctic, generally as far south as 40°N, in North America south to Tennessee.

Fresh water; deep in rivers and lakes to 213 m; as shallow as 0.3 m during spawning under the ice or to feed at night in summer.

D 8–16 + 60–80; A 58–79; Pec 17–21; Pel 5–8; GR 7–12; Vert 50–67.

- Yellow, light tan, to brown with darker brown or black mottling; dark line along anal fin margin.
- Head depressed, broad; body elongate, robust, nearly round anteriorly, compressed behind anus; eye small, diameter about 30% of snout length; anterior nostril in prominent barbel-like tube; mouth terminal.
- Chin barbel well developed.
- **Two dorsal fins, one anal fin**; dorsal and anal fins sometimes slightly connected to caudal base; caudal fin distinct, rounded; second ray of pelvic fin elongate and filamentous, falling short of tip of pectoral fin.
- Lateral line continuous to about end of dorsal and anal fin bases, then interrupted.
- Palatine teeth absent.
- Length to 152 cm TL, weight to 34 kg, historically; today usually much smaller, with angler-caught burbot averaging 0.5–1.0 kg.

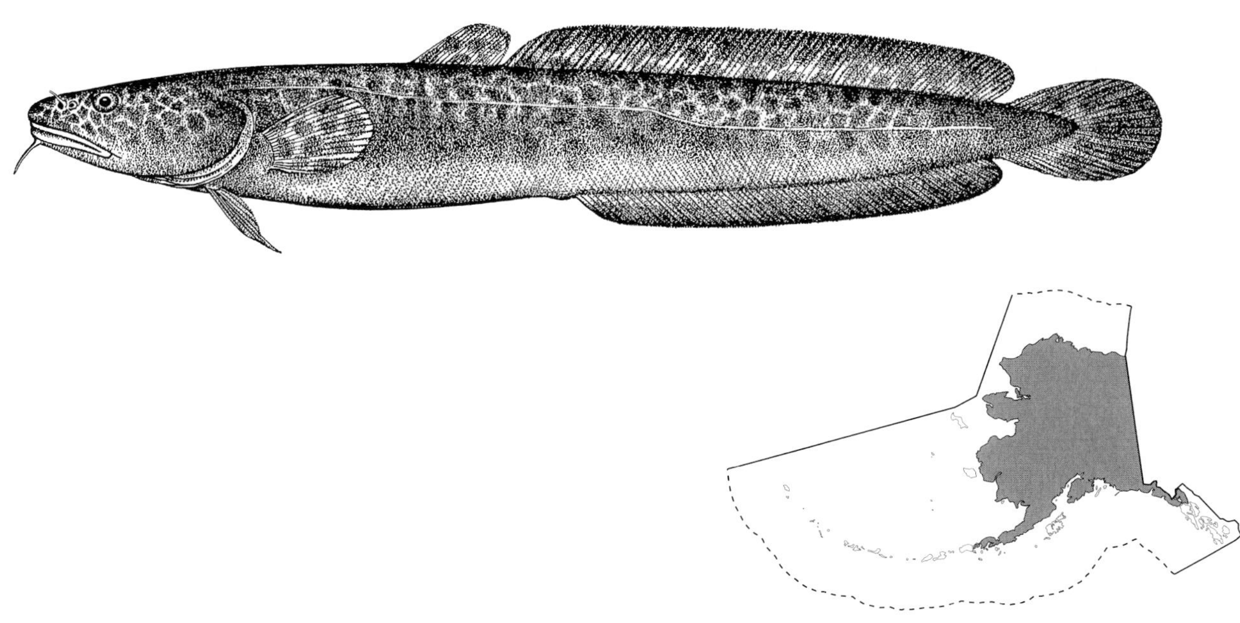

Notes & Sources — *Lota lota* (Linnaeus, 1758)
Lota maculosa Lesueur: Dall 1870, Bean 1881b, Turner 1886.

Description: McPhail and Lindsey 1970:296–300; Morrow 1980:181–184; Cohen in Cohen et al. 1990:53.

Figure: Cohen et al. 1990, fig. 99.

Range: The text and map by Page and Burr (1991) indicate distribution throughout Alaska, but presence of burbot in south-central and southeastern Alaska is not adequately documented. Maps by McPhail and Lindsey (1970), Scott and Crossmann (1973), and Lee and Gilbert (in Lee et al. 1980) show no records in those areas. Quast and Hall (1972) reported existence of a specimen from the Copper River Basin in the Auke Bay Laboratory collection. This was in lot AB 66-132 (146 mm SL), caught in a minnow trap in Mendeltna Creek near the Glenn Highway bridge; specimen now in collection of Northeastern Louisiana State College, Monroe, LA (B. L. Wing, pers. comm., 21 Nov. 2000). The map by Morrow (1980) indicates range south to northern southeastern Alaska, but specific records were not cited in the text. Absent from coastal British Columbia and Washington, as well, on Scott and Crossman's (1973) map. Range extends south to 40°N east of the Coast Mountains.

Size: Dall (1870) and Turner (1886) reported the largest known sizes (to 152.4 cm TL and 34 kg), from their expeditions to Alaska, but in recent years the fish have run smaller. Morrow (1980) gave a weight of 10.2 kg for the angling record for the state.

Boreogadus saida (Lepechin, 1774) **Arctic cod**

Beaufort Sea to Bristol Bay and Pribilof Islands in eastern Bering Sea, and to Cape Olyutorskiy in western Bering Sea; circumpolar, to White Sea, Iceland, Greenland, Gulf of St. Lawrence, Hudson Bay.

Brackish lagoons, river mouths, and ocean to depths of 731 m, usually near shore at less than 100 m, also occurring to 175 km offshore; often associated with presence of ice but also present in ice-free nearshore waters and found in coastal habitats in both summer and winter.

D 10–17 + 11–18 + 16–24; A 13–21 + 17–23; Pec 18–19; Pel 6; GR 37–47; Vert 49–58.

- Brownish dorsally, with fine black dots and violet or yellowish sheen; silvery white ventrally; fins dusky yellow or gray, darker toward margins; dorsal and caudal fins with white margins, anal fins with black margins.
- Body slender, strongly tapering from large head; **jaws about equal or lower jaw protruding**; eye large, diameter 25–32% of head length.
- Chin barbel minute, length much less than pupil diameter.
- Three dorsal fins, two anal fins; origin of first anal fin below first dorsal fin interspace or origin of second dorsal; base of third dorsal fin longer than base of second dorsal; **caudal fin deeply emarginate**, lobes rounded.
- **Scales nonoverlapping**, circular, embedded, with bony tubercles giving the skin the texture of coarse sandpaper.
- Head lacking lateral line pores (small pits may be present); **body lateral line interrupted for entire length, with strong wavy curves below second dorsal fin**.
- **Palatine teeth absent**.
- Length to 40 cm TL, usually less than 25 cm.

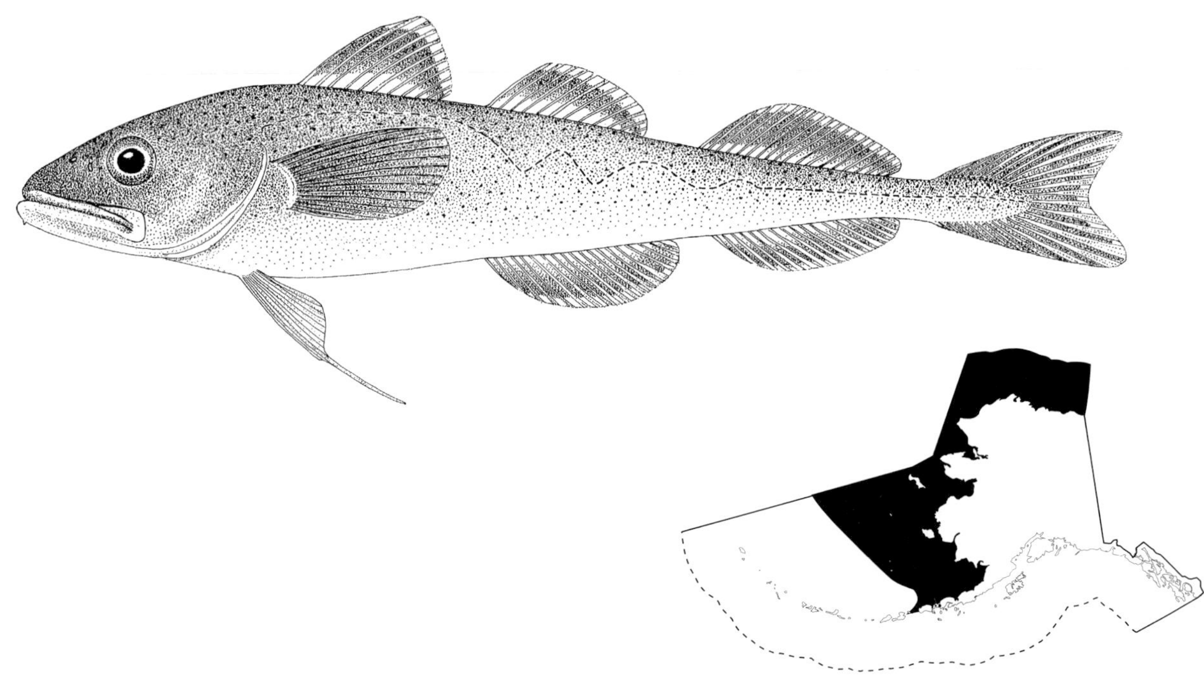

Notes & Sources — *Boreogadus saida* (Lepechin, 1774)
Gadus saida Lepechin, 1774
Frequently called polar cod, which can be confusing when the scientific name is not given. The American Fisheries Society (Robins et al. 1991) uses polar cod for *Arctogadus glacialis*. Conversely, the name Arctic cod is often used, as in European literature, for Atlantic cod, *Gadus morhua*.

Description: Svetovidov 1948:199–203; Andriashev 1954: 184–187; Morrow 1980:184–185; Robins and Ray 1986:92; Scott and Scott 1988:260–262; Cohen in Cohen et al. 1990:27; Endo in Okamura et al. 1995:110.

Figure: Cohen et al. 1990, fig. 62.

Range: Andriashev (1954) listed early records, including those from Alaska starting with Murdoch (1885) from Point Barrow, and Turner (1886) and Nelson (1887) from Norton Sound. Lowry and Frost (1981) reviewed distribution in the Bering, Chukchi, and Beaufort seas, and Craig et al. (1982) provided details of ecology in Beaufort Sea coastal waters. Allen and Smith (1988) reported *B. saida* in NMFS survey catches south to Bristol Bay. Barber et al. (1997) found it to be the most abundant fish in demersal surveys of the northeastern Chukchi Sea in 1990 and 1991. Cohen (in Cohen et al. 1990) mapped worldwide distribution.

Arctogadus glacialis (Peters, 1872) **polar cod**

Beaufort Sea northeast of Barrow; Arctic Canada from Beaufort Sea to Ellesmere Island and northern Baffin Island; western and eastern Greenland; Barents Sea; East Siberian Sea and western Chukchi Sea over continental slope.

Pelagic, in schools; mainly far from shore at or beyond edge of continental shelf near surface to depth of about 1,000 m; usually caught under drifting ice at 0–25 m over great depths, and in ice cracks.

D 9–16 + 15–24 + 18–25; A 16–24 + 15–26; Pec 18–22; Pel 6; GR 27–35; Vert 54–60.

- Brownish gray dorsally; bluish gray ventrally; anal fins gray, other fins black; juveniles light gray with chocolate-brown head and fins.
- Head large, 25–31% of standard length; jaws about equal or lower jaw slightly protruding; eye large, diameter 17–25% of head length.
- **Chin barbel rudimentary or absent**.
- Three dorsal fins, two anal fins; **caudal fin deeply emarginate** or forked; pectoral fin nearly reaching origin of first anal fin.
- **Scales overlapping**, elliptical, deciduous, not bearing tubercles.
- Head lacking lateral line pores; body lateral line interrupted along entire length, dipping below lateral midline above origin of first anal fin then ascending and continuing posteriorly along midline.
- **Palatine teeth small, usually present**.
- Length to 41 cm SL (about 45 cm TL).

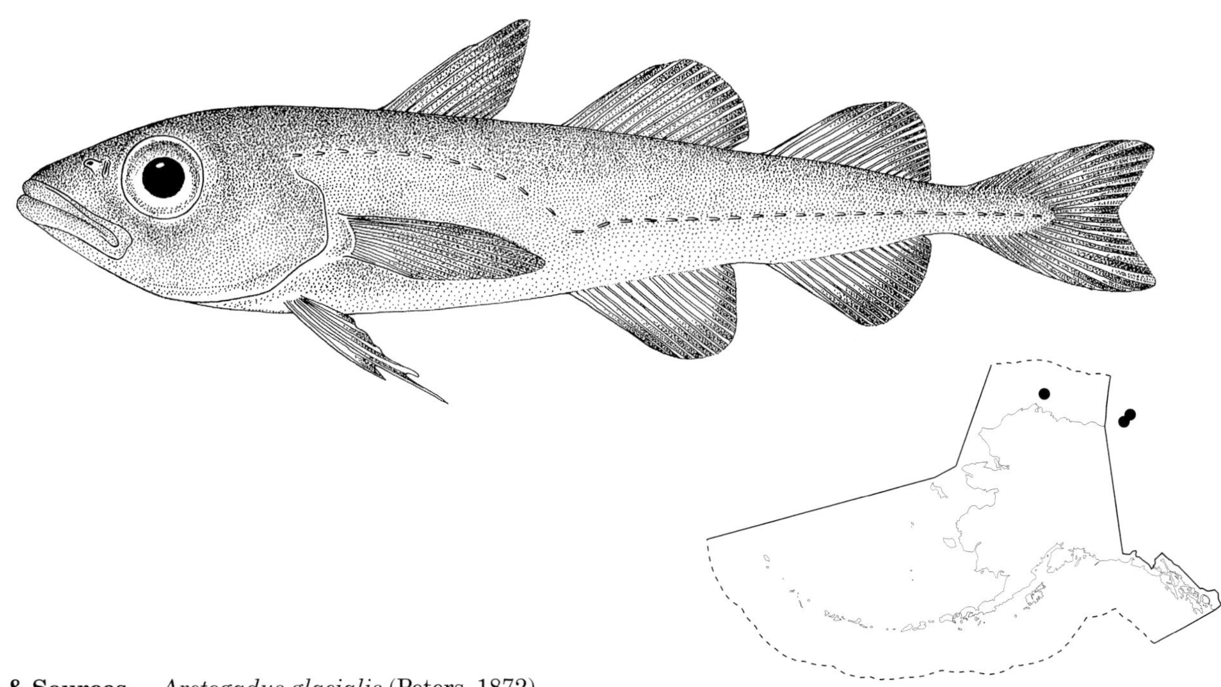

Notes & Sources — *Arctogadus glacialis* (Peters, 1872)

Gadus glacialis Peters, 1872

Nielsen and Jensen (1967) and Boulva (1972) reported morphometrics differing between *A. glacialis* and *A. borisovi,* such as larger eye and narrower interorbital space, on average, in *A. glacialis.* However, only the absence of the chin barbel unambiguously differentiates *A. glacialis* from *A. borisovi*; when "rudimentary" in *A. glacialis* it is a barely detectible nubbin, essentially absent.

Also called Arctic cod (e.g., Okamura et al. 1995), but the American Fisheries Society (Robins et al. 1991) uses the name Arctic cod for *Boreogadus saida.*

Description: Andriashev 1957; Nielsen and Jensen 1967:6–13; Boulva 1972; Robins and Ray 1986:92; Cohen in Cohen et al. 1990:26; Coad 1995:539–540; Endo in Okamura et al. 1995:109.

Figure: Cohen et al. 1990, fig. 60.

Range: Usually found far north of the 200-mile Exclusive Economic Zone, but in Sep. 1977 K. J. Frost and L. F. Lowry collected a specimen (NMC 82-0027) 100 km northeast of Barrow, at 71°59'N, 155°42'W, depth 150 m. (Although taken by bottom trawl, this pelagic fish could have been captured not at the bottom but closer to the surface, when the net was hauled in.) Polar cod are more or less closely associated with permanent ice or drifting ice of various kinds, but the presence of ice is not essential (Borkin and Mel'yantsev 1984). Escaping from seals, these fish have been observed to throw themselves out onto the ice through seal holes (Jensen 1948). Hunter et al. (1984) confirmed records from Canada as close to Alaska as Liverpool Bay, Tuktoyaktuk Peninsula.

Size: Applying TL = 110.9% SL from Boulva (1972) to maximum of 41 cm SL from Coad (1995) gives 45.5 cm TL.

Arctogadus borisovi Dryagin, 1932 **toothed cod**

Beaufort Sea off Point Barrow; coasts of Canadian Beaufort Sea and Arctic archipelago to northern Baffin Island and Ellef Ringnes Island; northern and southern coasts of Greenland; coasts of Arctic Siberia.

Near bottom in small, dense schools in littoral and brackish waters, usually at depths of 17–40 m, but also far from shore under pack ice or drifting ice.

D 9–14 + 16–23 + 19–25; A 16–25 + 16–25; Pec 16–23; Pel 6; GR 30–38; Vert 58–59.

- Dark olive dorsally; light gray with dark spots ventrally.
- Head large, 26–33% of standard length; jaws about equal or lower jaw slightly protruding; eye large, diameter 18–22% of head length.
- **Chin barbel well developed**.
- Three dorsal fins, two anal fins; **caudal fin deeply emarginate** or forked; pectoral fin not reaching origin of first anal fin.
- **Scales overlapping**, elliptical, not bearing tubercles.
- Head lacking lateral line pores, or with few, very small pores; body lateral line interrupted along entire length, strongly dipping above origin of first anal fin but not dipping below midline.
- **Palatine teeth well developed**.
- Length to 60 cm TL.

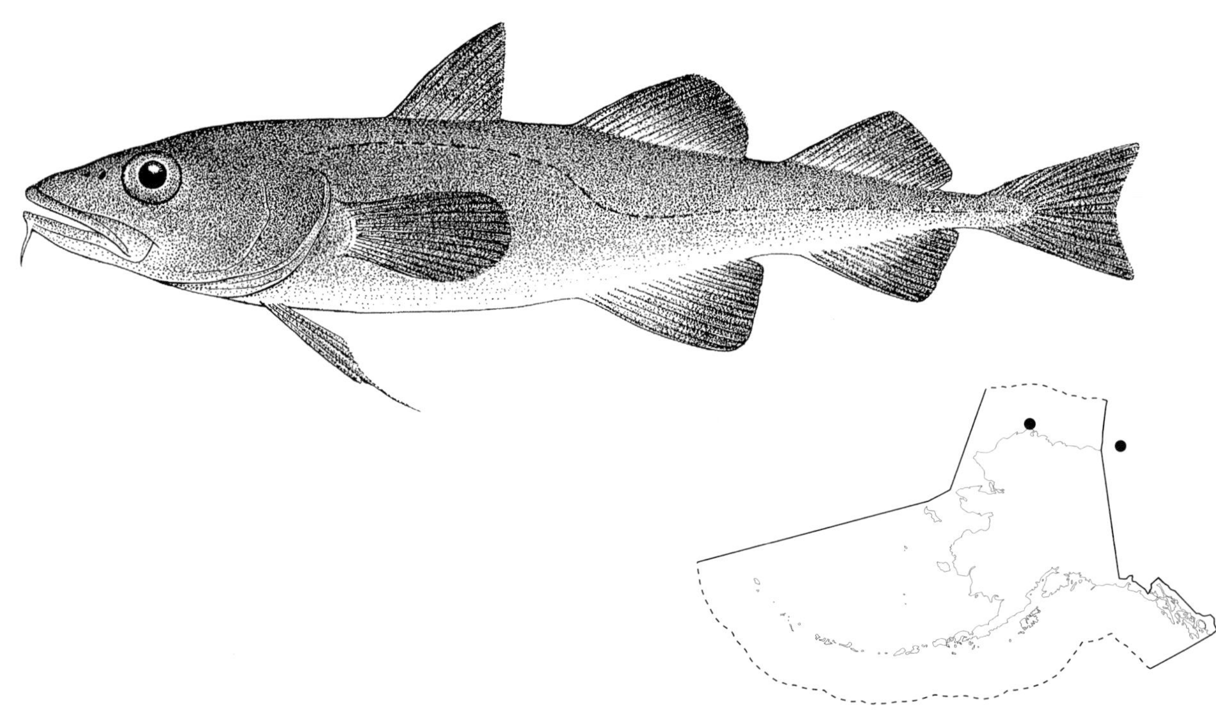

Notes & Sources — *Arctogadus borisovi* Dryagin, 1932
Boreogadus pearyi Nichols & Maxwell, 1933
Nielsen and Jensen (1967) and Boulva (1972) reported morphometrics differing between *A. borisovi* and *A. glacialis*, such as smaller eye and wider interorbital space, on average, in *A. borisovi.* However, only the presence of a well-developed chin barbel unambiguously differentiates *A. borisovi* from *A. glacialis.*

Description: Andriashev 1954:188–190; Nielsen and Jensen 1967:6, 14–24; Boulva 1972; Robins and Ray 1986:92; Cohen in Cohen et al. 1990:25; Coad 1995:807–808.
Figure: Cohen et al. 1990, fig. 58.
Range: Walters (1955) recorded this species from Alaska on the basis of a specimen collected by N. J. Wilimovsky off Point Barrow; the same record was cited by Nielsen and Jensen (1967) and Quast and Hall (1972). Although *A. borisovi* is usually taken close to shore near the bottom, one was found at a drifting ice station far north of Alaska, at 77°12'N, 168°12'W, with 34 specimens of *A. glacialis* (Nielsen and Jensen 1967). Hunter et al. (1984) confirmed records from western Canada as close to Alaska as Liverpool Bay, Tuktoyaktuk Peninsula, with fewer records from that area than for *A. glacialis.*

Eleginus gracilis (Tilesius, 1810) **saffron cod**

Beaufort Sea and Chukchi Sea through eastern Bering Sea to southeastern Gulf of Alaska off Sitka, and east in Arctic to Dease Strait in western Canada; East Siberian Sea to Yellow Sea.

Demersal, usually taken in coastal Alaska waters at less than 60 m, but as deep as 200 m off Japan; also enters brackish waters, and rivers up to limit of tidal influence.

D 11–16 + 15–23 + 18–22; A 20–27 + 19–23; Pec 18–21; Pel 6; GR 14–25; Vert 57–64.

- Body washed with yellow; brown to gray-green with mottling dorsally; yellow to white ventrally; dorsal and caudal fin margins white; pectoral fin yellow.
- Body slender, trunk slightly robust; snout bulbous; **upper jaw slightly protruding**.
- Chin barbel not longer than pupil diameter.
- Three dorsal fins, two anal fins; origin of first anal fin opposite or slightly anterior to origin of second dorsal fin; caudal fin truncate; pectoral fin falling well short of anal fin.
- Head lacking lateral line pores; **body lateral line continuous to about origin of second dorsal fin**, then interrupted to caudal fin.
- Palatine teeth absent.
- **Anus below insertion of first dorsal fin or first interspace**.
- Tips of parapophyses beginning on about vertebral centrum 9 or 10 swollen and hollow, containing outpouchings of swim bladder.
- Length to 55 cm TL.

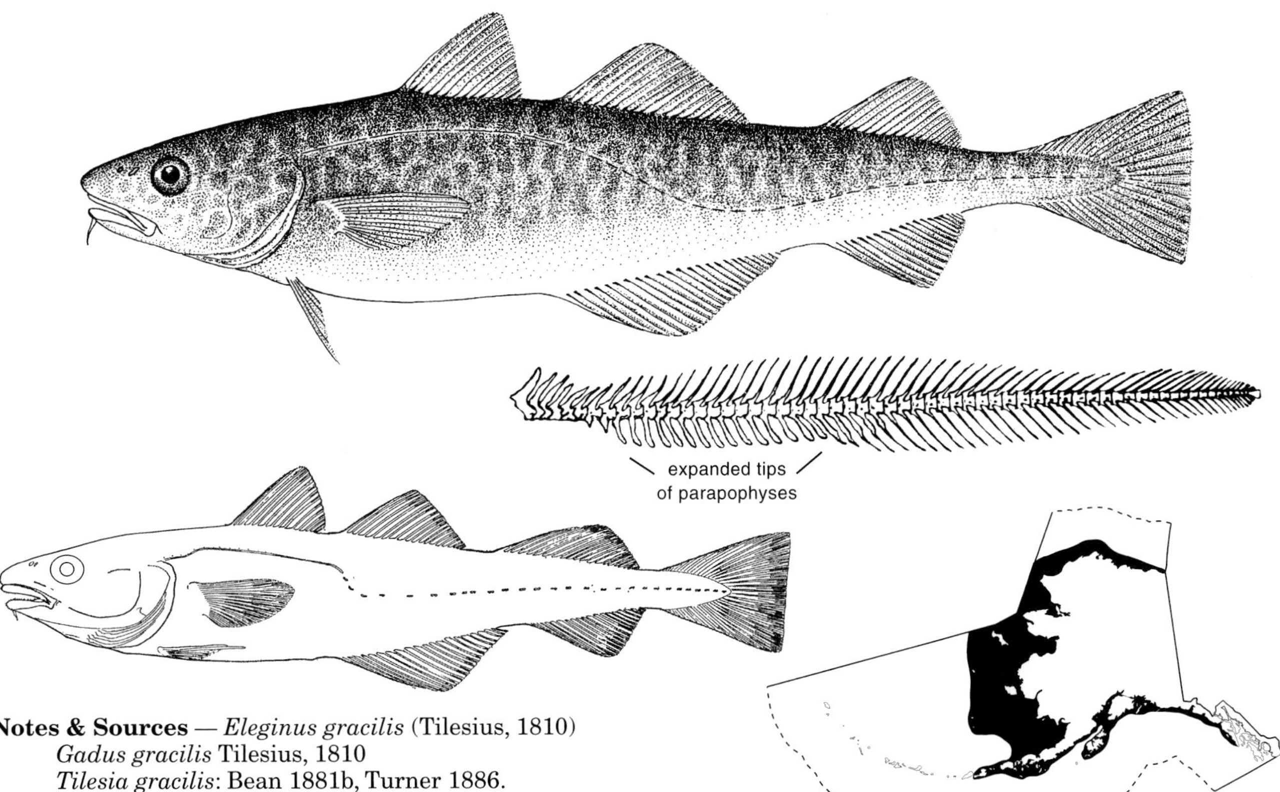

Notes & Sources — *Eleginus gracilis* (Tilesius, 1810)
Gadus gracilis Tilesius, 1810
Tilesia gracilis: Bean 1881b, Turner 1886.
Pleurogadus navaga: Nelson 1887.
Eleginus navaga: Evermann and Goldsborough 1907 (in part).
Early records confused *E. navaga* of Arctic eastern Europe with *E. gracilis* (as well as other genera). Walters (1955) considered Arctic American specimens of *Eleginus* to be intermediate in form and considered them a subspecies of *E. navaga*. Although current opinion classifies Arctic American specimens with the North Pacific form, *E. gracilis*, additional taxonomic study is needed to precisely delimit ranges.

Description: Schultz and Welander 1935:133–137; Svetovidov 1948:191–198, 1965; Walters 1955:299–300; Morrow 1980:187–188; Okamura in Masuda et al. 1984:92; Cohen in Cohen et al. 1990:34; Vasil'eva 1997.

Figures: Upper: Cohen et al. 1990, fig. 73. Lower: Schultz and Welander 1935, fig. 8; 215 mm SL, Sitkalidak Strait, Alaska. Vertebral column: Svetovidov 1948:304, fig. 1.

Range: Recorded by Walters (1955) from Point Barrow and Baxter (1990ms and unpubl. data) from Prudhoe Bay. The southeasternmost record is from Sitka (Svetovidov 1948), but the species is rarely taken in the Gulf of Alaska. Schultz and Welander (1935) referred most of the Alaskan specimens recorded by Evermann and Goldsborough (1907) under *E. navaga* to other genera. Reported from northwest Unalaska Island and the Krenitzin Islands by Wilimovsky (1964). Allen and Smith (1988) mapped occurrences in the Chukchi and Bering seas from NMFS resource surveys. Barber et al. (1997) found *E. gracilis* to be the second most abundant fish after *Boreogadus saida* in surveys of the northeastern Chukchi Sea in 1990 and 1991. Hunter et al. (1984) confirmed records from western Arctic Canada near the Alaska border.

Microgadus proximus (Girard, 1854) **Pacific tomcod**

Southeastern Bering Sea and Aleutian Islands to central California off Point Sal.

Demersal, at depths of 25–260 m over sand bottom, usually shallower than 120 m; sometimes enters brackish water.

D 9–15 + 16–21 + 17–24; A 20–29 + 18–24; Pec 19; Pel 6–7; GR 22–28; Vert 53–60.

- Grayish yellow or tan to olive green dorsally, without spots or mottling; white ventrally; fins gray to brown, tips dusky; peritoneum speckled black, denser dorsally.
- Body fairly robust; **upper jaw slightly protruding**.
- Chin barbel shorter or only slightly longer than pupil diameter.
- Three dorsal fins, two anal fins; origin of first anal fin slightly anterior to origin of first dorsal fin; caudal fin truncate; pectoral fin nearly reaching origin of anal fin.
- Head lacking lateral line pores (small pits sometimes present); **body lateral line continuous to insertion of third dorsal fin**, then interrupted to caudal fin.
- Palatine teeth absent.
- Gill rakers on first arch usually more than 25.
- **Anus below posterior fourth of first dorsal fin**.
- Tips of parapophyses of precaudal vertebrae not expanded, without processes of swim bladder entering into them.
- Length to 37 cm TL.

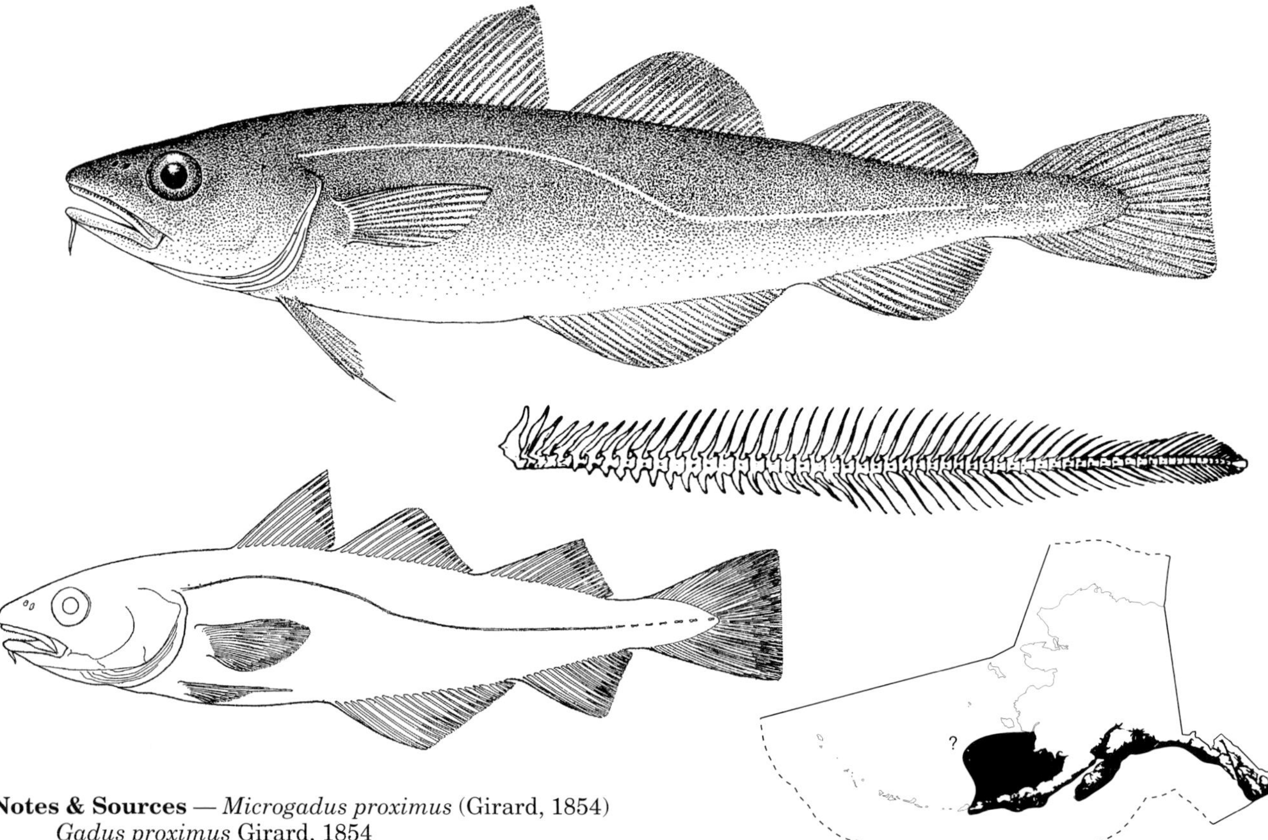

Notes & Sources — *Microgadus proximus* (Girard, 1854)
Gadus proximus Girard, 1854
Often confused with *Eleginus gracilis* in earlier accounts.

Description: Schultz and Welander 1935:134–137; Svetovidov 1948:188–190; Miller and Lea 1972:76; Hart 1973:226–227; Eschmeyer and Herald 1983:98; Matarese et al. 1989:196; Cohen in Cohen et al. 1990:58.

Figures: Upper: Cohen et al. 1990, fig. 106. Lower: Schultz and Welander 1935, fig. 9; 193 mm SL, Yaquina Bay, Oregon. Vertebral column: Svetovidov 1948:303, fig. 5.

Range: Northern limit of occurrence in Bering Sea is uncertain. Allen and Smith (1988) remarked that specimens identified in NMFS surveys as *M. proximus* from Kuskokwim Bay, Bristol Bay, and the Pribilof Islands may represent *Eleginus gracilis*. However, Tanner (1894:5) earlier reported *M. proximus* off St. Paul Island. Recorded by Jordan and Evermann (1898), Evermann and Goldsborough (1907), and Wilimovsky (1964) from Unalaska. Lot UBC 63-911S comprises five specimens caught at Kiska Harbor and identified as *M. proximus*.

Size: Baxter 1990ms; specimen measuring 345 mm SL and 371 mm TL taken in the northern Gulf of Alaska by a NMFS bottom trawl survey in 1986; specimen was not saved, but data recorded by Baxter support the identification. Baxter (unpubl. data) also took notes on a specimen measuring 323 mm TL taken during an ADFG survey in 1987 off Barabara Point in Kachemak Bay. Previously reported to reach only 30.5 cm TL by other authors, but few specific records are given in the literature.

Theragra chalcogramma (Pallas, 1814) **walleye pollock**

Chukchi Sea through Bering Sea and Aleutian Islands to central California off Carmel; and to Commander Islands and Okhotsk and Japan seas.

Generally demersal at depths of 30–300 m, recorded to 950 m; also taken pelagically, near surface and in midwater across Aleutian Basin; performs diurnal vertical migrations.

D 10–13 + 12–18 + 14–20; A 15–24 + 15–23; Pec 17–22; Pel 5–7; GR 33–42; Vert 48–54.

- Olive green to brown dorsally; silvery, with dark mottling and blotches dorsally and interrupted stripes of dark brassy olive laterally; white ventrally; fins brown or dusky gray to black; peritoneum dark gray to black.
- Body elongate and compressed; head about 27% of standard length; **lower jaw protruding**; eye large, diameter 21–30% of head length.
- **Chin barbel minute or absent**.
- Three dorsal fins, two anal fins; origin of first anal fin opposite origin of second dorsal fin; caudal fin moderately emarginate to truncate.
- Lateral line pores present on head; body lateral line continuous to origin of second dorsal fin, then interrupted.
- Palatine teeth absent.
- **Anus below first dorsal fin interspace**.
- Parapophyses not expanded at their tips.
- Length to 91 cm TL.

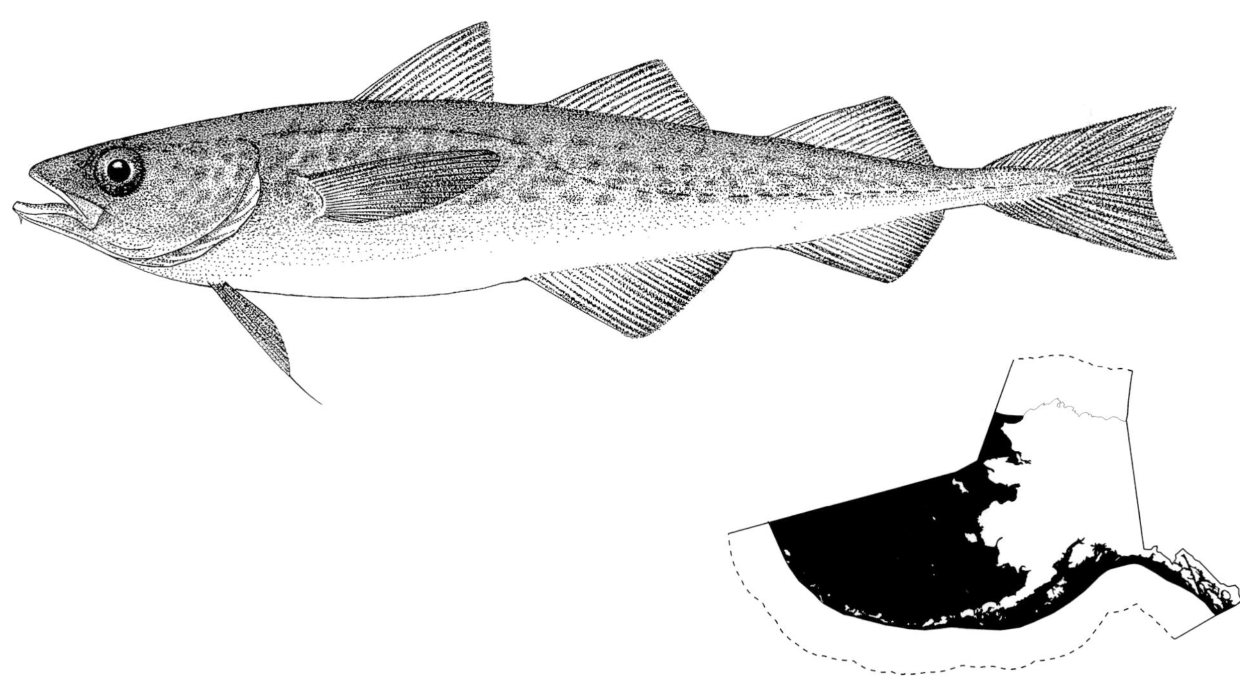

Notes & Sources — *Theragra chalcogramma* (Pallas (ex Steller), 1814)
Gadus chalcogrammus Pallas (ex Steller), 1814
Pollachius chalcogrammus fucensis Jordan & Gilbert, 1893

Description: Schultz and Welander 1935:137–138; Wilimovsky 1967:3–20; Hart 1973:228–229; Eschmeyer and Herald 1983:98; Okamura in Masuda et al. 1984:92; Cohen in Cohen et al. 1990:75.

Figures: Cohen et al. 1990, fig. 139.

Range: In NMFS bottom trawl surveys during 1953–1983, found as far north in the Chukchi Sea as Kivalina, throughout the Aleutian Islands, and over the Aleutian Basin in the Bering Sea (Allen and Smith 1988). This was the eighth most abundant species in the 1990 UAF bottom trawl survey of the northeastern Chukchi Sea, with an estimated abundance of 138 fish/km^2, but was not found in the 1991 survey of the same area. The unpublished haul-catch listing for the 1990 survey (*Ocean Hope III,* cruise 90-2) indicates the northernmost catch was in haul 95, west of Point Lay at 69°26'N, 166°04'W, at a depth of 42 m, although the survey extended northwest of Point Barrow; and that the fish were juveniles weighing 45 g or less. Walleye pollock are an important commercial species, contributing the largest of all demersal fish resources to the Nation's fisheries. The largest catches are from the outer shelf and slope of the eastern Bering Sea.

Gadus macrocephalus Tilesius, 1810 **Pacific cod**

Eastern Chukchi Sea, not confirmed; Bering Strait to southern California off Santa Monica, and to Yellow Sea off Manchuria, China.

Benthic, also pelagic over deep water; near surface to 875 m, usually less than 350 m; deep in winter, shallow in spring and summer; migratory species.

D 10–16 + 13–20 + 14–21; A 16–25 + 14–22; Pec 19–22; Pel 6–7; GR 18–24; Vert 50–55.

- **Light gray-brown** dorsally, whitish ventrally; **brown to yellowish spots and blotches dorsolaterally**; lateral line pale; **median fin margins white**; peritoneum black.
- Body robust; head large, length 25–33% of standard length, and broad, interorbital space 18–25% of head length; **snout slightly protruding**; eye moderate, diameter 13–20% of head length.
- Chin barbel long, almost equal to or longer than eye diameter.
- Three dorsal fins and two anal fins; **predorsal distance more than about 33% (33–36%) of standard length**; origin of first anal fin slightly posterior to origin of second dorsal fin; caudal fin truncate to slightly emarginate.
- Lateral line pores present on head; body lateral line distinct, arched over pectoral fin, continuous nearly to caudal peduncle.
- Palatine teeth absent.
- Anus under origin of second dorsal fin.
- Testicular lobes smooth (unindented) in males in spawning condition; breeding tubercles very short and hillock-shaped in spawning males and females.
- Length to 120 cm TL, average trawl-caught fish 70–75 cm and weighing about 4.5 kg.

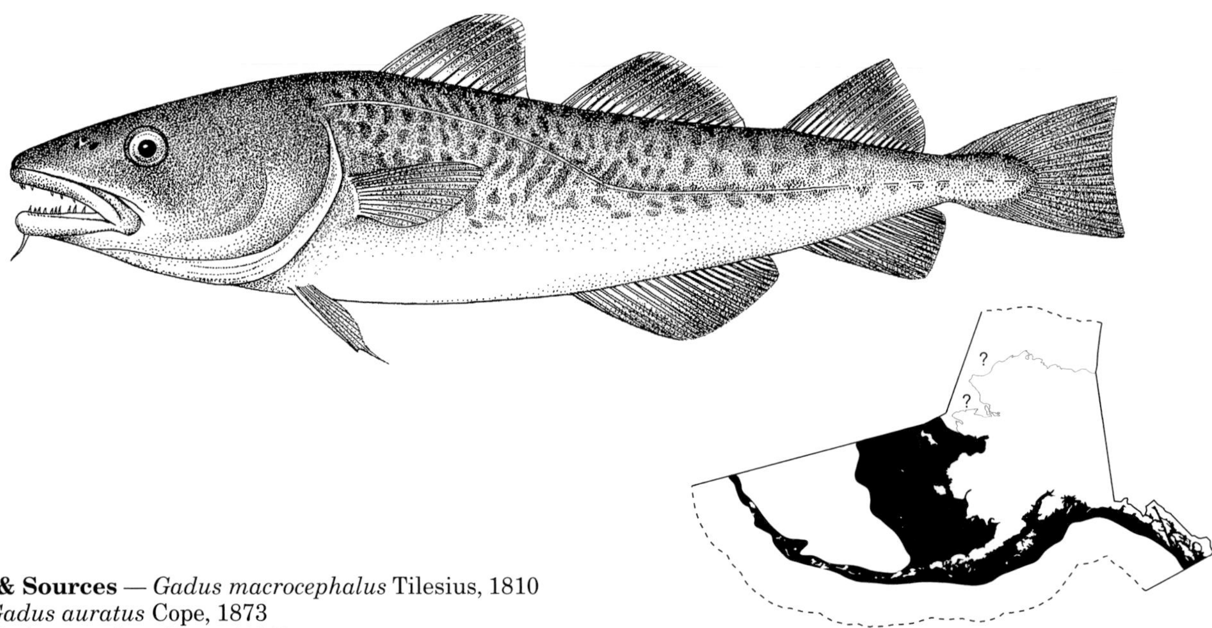

Notes & Sources — *Gadus macrocephalus* Tilesius, 1810
Gadus auratus Cope, 1873
Gadus morrhua: Bean 1881b.
Gadus morhua macrocephalus: Berg 1933, Svetovidov 1948, Andriashev 1954, Quast and Hall 1972.
Classification in same species with Atlantic cod, *G. morhua,* has been abandoned by most researchers; exceptions include Svetovidov (in Whitehead et al. 1986). Renaud (1989) gave differences in testicular lobe and breeding tubercle morphologies as evidence for distinctiveness of *G. macrocephalus* and *G. ogac.*

Description: Schultz and Welander 1935:129–133; Andriashev 1954:175–177; Wilimovsky et al. 1967:21–37; Hart 1973:222–224; Morrow 1980:185–186; Eschmeyer and Herald 1983:97; Okamura in Masuda et al. 1984:92; Renaud 1989:239; Cohen in Cohen et al. 1990:42.

Figure: Cohen et al. 1990, fig. 84.

Range: Reported but not confirmed from the eastern Chukchi Sea. Relatively well documented in the Bering Sea as far north as St. Lawrence Island (e.g., Andriashev 1954); Cape Rodney, Norton Sound (Allen and Smith 1988); and Lavrentiya Bay (Svetovidov 1948). Barber et al. (1997) reported *G. macrocephalus* in the 1990 UAF survey of the northeastern Chukchi Sea, with an estimated abundance of 44 fish/km^2; it was not found in the 1991 survey of the same area. The unpublished haul-catch listing for the 1990 survey (*Ocean Hope III,* cruise 90-2) indicates the northernmost occurrence was haul 46, 70°22'N, 162°43'W, depth 31 m, west of Icy Cape (survey extended northwest of Point Barrow); and that the fish were juveniles weighing 45 g or less. R. Baxter (unpubl. data) recorded data from a 13-cm-TL specimen from haul 46 but did not include characters differentiating *G. macrocephalus* from *G. ogac.* No *G. macrocephalus* were found among survey vouchers at the UAF (C.W.M.). The species was not found in previous eastern Chukchi Sea surveys (Alverson and Wilimovsky 1966, Quast 1972, Frost and Lowry 1983, Fechhelm et al. 1985).

Gadus ogac Richardson, 1836 **ogac**

Alaskan Beaufort Sea to west coast of Greenland and Atlantic coast of Canada south to Gulf of St. Lawrence and Cape Breton Island; disjunct population in White Sea.

Close to coast, from surface to depth of 200 m; occasionally found offshore to depth of 400 m in southern parts of range; nonmigratory species.

D 12–17 + 14–22 + 15–21; A 17–25 + 15–21; Pec 19; Pel 6; GR 19–43; Vert 51–57.

- **Blackish**, frequently almost olive black and uniformly monotone, sometimes shading to yellow or white ventrally; **no distinct spots on body**; chin barbel black, lateral line dark; **dorsal and caudal fin margins black**; pectoral and pelvic fins reddish brown to black; peritoneum black.
- Body robust; head large, length 25–28% of standard length, and broad, interorbital space 18–25% of head length; **snout slightly protruding**; eye large, diameter 21–23% of head length.
- Chin barbel long, almost equal to or longer than eye diameter.
- Three dorsal fins and two anal fins; **predorsal distance less than about 33% (30–33%) of standard length**; origin of first anal fin slightly posterior to origin of second dorsal fin; caudal fin truncate to slightly emarginate.
- Lateral line pores present on head; body lateral line distinct, arched over pectoral fin, continuous nearly to caudal peduncle.
- Palatine teeth absent.
- Anus under origin of second dorsal fin.
- Testicular lobes crenate in males in spawning condition; breeding tubercles long and club-shaped in spawning males and females.
- Length to 71 cm TL, weight to 7 kg.

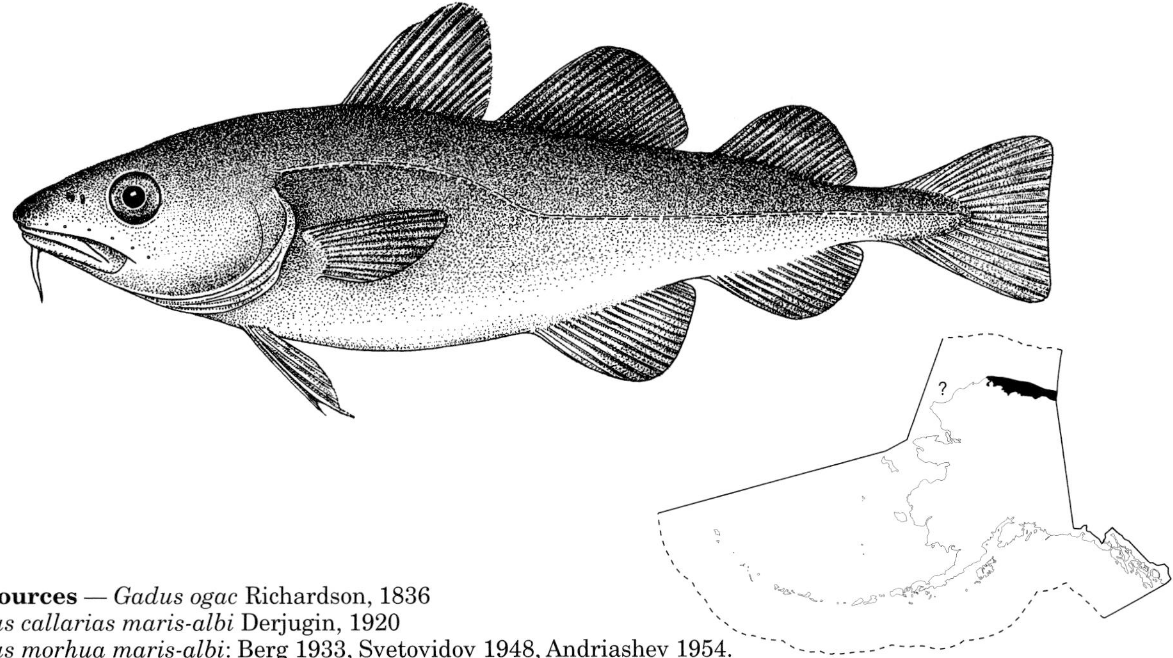

Notes & Sources — *Gadus ogac* Richardson, 1836
Gadus callarias maris-albi Derjugin, 1920
Gadus morhua maris-albi: Berg 1933, Svetovidov 1948, Andriashev 1954.
Gadus morhua ogac: Svetovidov 1948.
Also called Greenland cod.

Classification of *G. ogac* and *G. macrocephalus* as junior synonyms of Atlantic cod, *G. morhua,* has been abandoned by most researchers; exceptions include Svetovidov (in Whitehead et al. 1986). Renaud (1989), considering karyological, electrophoretic, and morphological data, argued for separation of the three species. Differences in testicular lobes and breeding tubercles were the strongest evidence supporting separation of *G. ogac* and *G. macrocephalus.*

Description: Schultz and Welander 1935:130–133; Svetovidov 1948:178–179; Andriashev 1954:173–174; Walters 1955:298–299; Scott and Scott 1988:270–271; Cohen in Cohen et al. 1990:47–48; Coad 1995:492–493; Endo in Okamura et al. 1995:113.

Figure: Cohen et al. 1990, fig. 89.

Range: Recorded from Alaskan Beaufort Sea between Point Barrow and Smith Bay by Walters (1955) from specimens collected by N. J. Wilimovsky, but the current whereabouts of those specimens are unknown. The map by Cohen (in Cohen et al. 1990) depicts range of *G. ogac* in a solid band from Point Barrow into Canada. Hunter et al. (1984) confirmed records of *G. ogac* in western Canada as close to Alaska as Mackenzie Bay. The citation of Carey (1978) for a report of *G. morhua ogac* (= *G. ogac*) from the northeastern Chukchi Sea and Beaufort Sea in table 3 of Frost and Lowry (1983) is, evidently, an error. However, it is possible that reports of *G. macrocephalus* in the region are from misidentified *G. ogac.* Specimens from Arctic Alaska believed to represent either species should be preserved for accurate identification and further study.

Order Batrachoidiformes
Batrachoidiforms

The order Batrachoidiformes contains mostly dull-colored fishes with large, depressed heads on bodies that are stout anteriorly. Some species can produce sounds with the swim bladder and can live out of the water for several hours. Some older classifications placed batrachoidiform fishes in the same order as the anglerfishes (order Lophiiformes). Nelson (1994), following Patterson and Rosen (1989), retained the separate orders. The latter authors applied the term Pediculati to include both orders.

Diagnostic characters of the order Batrachoidiformes include: eyes more dorsal than lateral and tending to protrude; mouth large and bordered by both premaxilla and maxilla; photophores present or absent; a pore, or foramen, in the axis of the pectoral fin in some species; pelvic fins jugular in position and having 1 spine and 2 or 3 rays; scales usually absent, small cycloid scales present in some; 3 pairs of gills; small gill openings; separate gill membranes broadly joined to isthmus; 6 branchiostegal rays; swim bladder present; and pyloric caeca absent.

The order contains one family, the Batrachoididae. One species has been reported to occur in coastal waters of southeastern Alaska.

Family Batrachoididae
Toadfishes

The toadfish family, Batrachoididae, has 19 genera and 69 species distributed among three subfamilies. They are primarily bottom-dwelling coastal fishes that rarely enter brackish water; a few species are confined to fresh water. The family is represented in the Pacific, Indian, and Atlantic oceans. The genus *Porichthys* is endemic to the New World. One species, the plainfin midshipman, *P. notatus,* occurs in the Pacific Northwest. This species is commonly reported to occur as far north as Sitka, Alaska, but adequate documentation for occurrence in Alaska is lacking. Walker and Rosenblatt (1988), in reviewing records of Pacific species of *Porichthys,* found no authenticated records from Alaska and gave Smith Sound, in southern British Columbia, as the northernmost record that could be substantiated.

Members of the Batrachoididae have a small spinous dorsal fin with 2–4 spines, long-based rayed dorsal and anal fins that almost reach the caudal fin, and a prominent opercular spine. Some species have hollow dorsal spines and opercular spines that connect with venom glands and can inflict painful wounds; subopercular spines; and a foramen opening from a gland in the base of each pectoral fin. The number of lateral lines and presence or absence of photophores, scales, and canine teeth vary with subfamily and species.

Species in the subfamily Porichthyinae have 2 solid dorsal fin spines and a solid opercular spine (no venom glands); no subopercular spine; no scales; several lateral lines; and canine teeth. This is the only toadfish subfamily with species having photophores, and they are present only in the 14 species of *Porichthys.* The presence of photophores is unusual in shallow-water fishes, and *Porichthys* are the only coastal fishes of the Americas with photophores.

The total known range of the plainfin midshipman is from British Columbia to southern Baja California, but despite numerous collections no specimens have been recorded from between northern Washington and southern Oregon. Walker and Rosenblatt (1988) reported that electrophoretic analysis did not reveal substantial differences between specimens from either side of the apparent gap.

The name midshipman comes from the arrangement of the numerous photophores in lines, which suggests the appearance of rows of buttons. The Pacific Northwest species is called the plainfin midshipman because it lacks the small spots that are present on the specklefin midshipman, *P. myriaster,* of California and Mexico. Some of the common names that have been used for the plainfin midshipman reflect the ecology of the species, such as mud-fish and cat-fish, while others reflect its ability to make sounds, such as singing fish and drummer. Midshipmen spend much of their time buried in the silt, but also rise off the bottom to swim about. The sounds they achieve by vibrating the otoliths against the swim bladder include a repertoire of grunts, squeaks, whistles, hums, and croaks.

Adults of most toadfish species reach about 30.5 cm (12 inches) in total length. *Porichthys notatus* is larger than average, reaching about 38 cm (15 inches).

Taxonomic revisions including Pacific species of *Porichthys* are those of Hubbs and Schultz (1939) and Walker and Rosenblatt (1988).

Porichthys notatus Girard, 1854 **plainfin midshipman**

Alaskan records erroneous or uncertain; southern British Columbia at Smith Sound to Magdalena Bay, southern Baja California.

On sand or mud bottoms from intertidal to depth of 366 m, usually less than 250 m; often found partially buried.

D II + 33–38; A 30–35; Pec 15–20; Pel I,2; GR 9–17; Vert 41–45.

- Dark gray to olive green dorsally, yellowish ventrally; 5–9 dark saddles in small specimens; dorsal and pectoral fins without small spots; dorsal fin usually with large spot anteriorly, and occasionally with 1 or 2 oblique bars anteriorly; margin of caudal fin with distinct, dark band.
- Rows of photophores on underside of head and body and lower side.
- Eyes protruding and positioned dorsally; mouth large, maxilla extending past eye.
- Single, solid opercular spine; no subopercular spines.
- Spinous dorsal fin very small; rayed dorsal fin and anal fin long, emarginate, of even height.
- Scales absent.
- Four lateral lines on side of head and body, with cirri.
- Vomer with 2 large canine teeth.
- Gill membranes separate, attached to isthmus.
- Length to 38 cm TL.

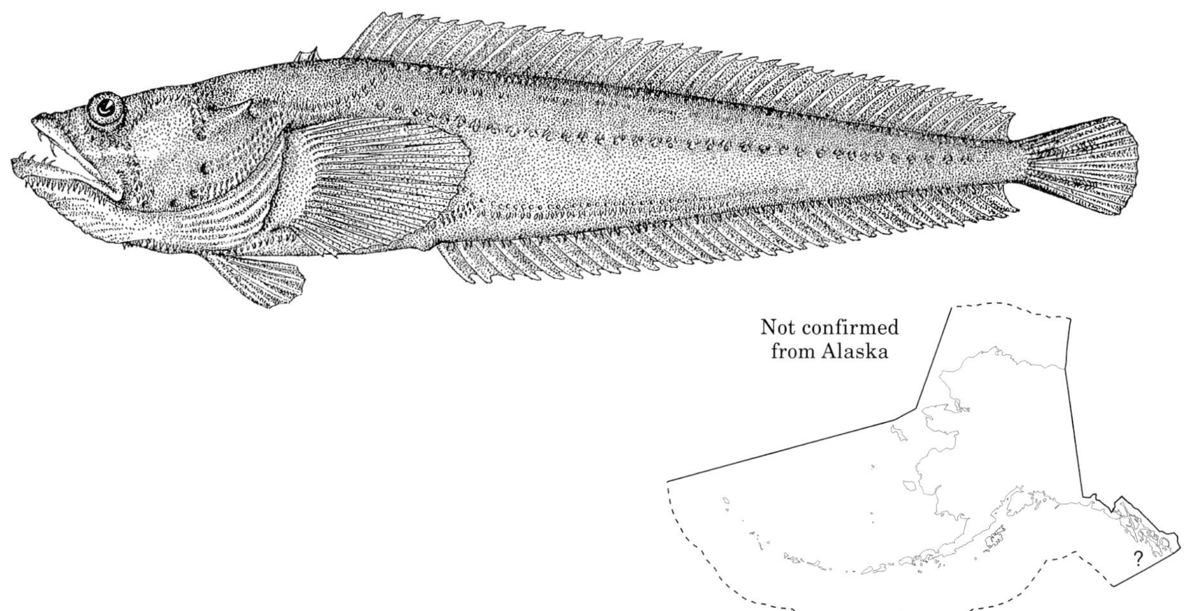

Notes & Sources — *Porichthys notatus* Girard, 1854

Since *Porichthys notatus* is the only species of midshipman occurring north of southern California, the subfamily and generic characters given above are sufficient to identify specimens from the Pacific Northwest to Alaska. The only specific characters given above are meristics, details of coloration, and maximum length.

Description: Hubbs and Schultz 1939; Arora 1948; Hart 1973:207–209; Walker and Rosenblatt 1988:893–895 and tables.

Figures: Hart 1973:207; 24 cm TL, British Columbia.

Range: Most authors give Sitka or southeastern Alaska as the northern limit of range for *P. notatus,* but no one has been able to confirm an Alaskan record. Walker and Rosenblatt (1988) attributed the original record to Evermann and Goldsborough (1907), but the latter authors listed specimens from southern British Columbia only, not from Alaska. Hubbs and Schultz (1939) suggested that the locality data were erroneous for three specimens said to be from Alaska and referred by Greene (1889) to *P. notatus,* and stated they had seen no specimens from Alaska themselves. The photophore numbers given by Greene (1889) indicate a different species, and *P. notatus* is the only species known to exist in the eastern North Pacific. The only other "record" Hubbs and Schultz (1939) said they knew of from Alaska was a statement by Starks and Morris (1907:230) giving Sitka as the northern limit. However, Starks and Morris (1907) actually gave Puget Sound as the northern limit. Wilimovsky (1954, 1958) and Quast and Hall (1972) gave southeastern Alaska as the northern limit but specified "Alaska record not verified." The label on a jar with one specimen (149 mm TL) of *P. notatus* in the University of Alaska Fairbanks collection (UAM 51) reads "Presume taken in Alaska." Walker and Rosenblatt (1988) reported they could not find any authenticated records for Alaska, and gave the northernmost documented record to be Smith Sound, British Columbia (51°20'N, 127°32'W). Hart (1973) reported that *P. notatus* is common in the Strait of Georgia and along the west coast of Vancouver Island at least as far north as Nootka Sound (about 49°45'N). Replaced by *P. mimeticus* Walker & Rosenblatt, 1988, in Gulf of California; named for its close resemblance to *P. notatus.*

Order Lophiiformes
Anglerfishes

Anglerfishes have a rod, line, and lure on the head for attracting prey. They inhabit marine waters, and fall into two ecological groups: species living on the bottom or attached to drifting seaweed, usually in shallow water; and those occupying the water column at great depths. The deepsea anglerfishes compose the superfamily Ceratioidea, and include the anglerfishes treated in this guide. Like many midwater fishes, ceratioids pass their entire larval life in the food-rich, sunlit water of the upper 200 m. At metamorphosis they descend to live at greater depths, usually between 500 and 2,500 m.

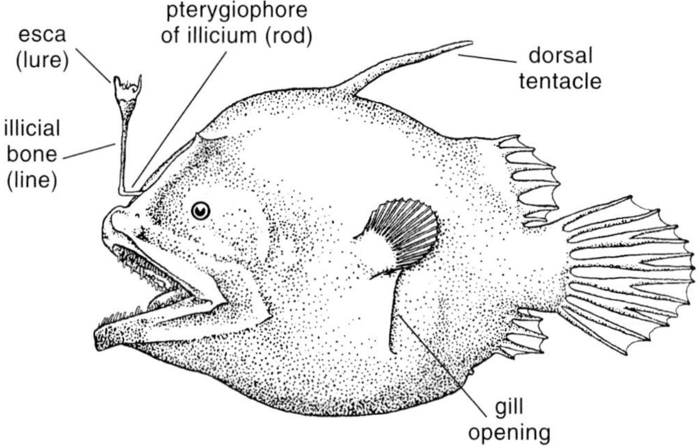

Some external features of anglerfishes

The angling apparatus is called the illicium, and is composed of modified dorsal fin spines. The base, or rod, is a modified pterygiophore which in some families is long and moves forward and backward, within the head, to attract prey and entice it into the mouth. When the pterygiophore is retracted in the larger individuals of some species the structure actually protrudes out the dorsal surface of the body, where it is encased in an evagination of the skin which has been referred to as a tentacle, papilla, or spine. The fishing line is the illicial bone, and the lure or bait is called an esca.

Diagnostic lophiiform characters also include: a tubelike gill opening below or behind the pectoral fin base; pelvic fins usually absent; pectoral fins fanlike, on a long peduncle (radials elongate); scales absent but skin often prickly; 5 or 6 branchiostegal rays; no ribs; and swim bladder, when present, physoclistous.

Diagnostic features of ceratioid anglerfishes include: 12–30 pectoral fin rays; 8 or 9 caudal rays; pelvic fins absent; long, slender, depressible teeth; pseudobranchs absent; and 19–24 vertebrae. They exhibit extreme sexual dimorphism. The males are dwarfed, lack an external illicium, have denticular teeth on the tips of the jaws, and, in most families, have well-developed eyes. Males in some families are parasitic on the females. In most ceratioid species the female has a large photophore in the esca, and light organs are often present elsewhere on the body. The escal light attracts appropriate males, because the esca is different for each species, as well as prey. The taxonomy of the suborder is based mainly on the females.

Ceratioid anglerfishes are soft-bodied and easily damaged, and shrink during preservation. Many measurements are difficult to take with accuracy and are highly variable intraspecifically. Thus, distinguishing the species based on females relies heavily on differences in the illicium, particularly the esca.

Family Ceratiidae
Seadevils

Seadevils, family Ceratiidae, are a small but relatively well-known group of anglerfishes of the meso- and bathypelagic suborder Ceratioidei. The family as currently understood includes two genera: *Ceratias,* with three species, and *Cryptopsaras,* with one species. Two species, both of them widely distributed in the Pacific, Indian, and Atlantic oceans, are treated in this guide. The northern seadevil, *Ceratias holboelli,* has occasionally been taken in the eastern Bering Sea and the Gulf of Alaska. Although the triplewart seadevil, *Cryptopsaras couesii,* has not been recorded from Alaska, its cosmopolitan distribution, including a capture at 63°N off Iceland, suggests it could occur in the region. Seadevils are usually taken at depths of 400–2,000 m, but several large female *Ceratias holboelli* have been taken in relatively shallow water, as shallow as 120 m, in the Bering Sea and high latitudes of the North Atlantic.

The females of the Ceratiidae differ from those of other ceratioid families by having the cleft of the mouth vertical to strongly oblique, the posterior end of the pterygiophore of the illicium emerging from the dorsal midline of the trunk, and two or three caruncles just anterior to the dorsal fin. The caruncles are modified dorsal fin rays, each bearing an area of bioluminescent tissue. They decrease in size after sexual maturity, and are minute in large individuals. The eyes in females degenerate with age and in large specimens are barely discernible beneath a layer of tissue. Seadevils have 3–5, nearly always 4, dorsal fin rays; 4 anal fin rays; 8 or 9 caudal fin rays; and 6 branchiostegal rays. The bilateral, sphenotic spines, which are prominent in some ceratioid families, such as the Oneirodidae, are absent. The skin is covered with close-set dermal spines. Several of the family characteristics can be seen in this diagram of a female *Cryptopsaras couesii* (after Bertelsen 1951):

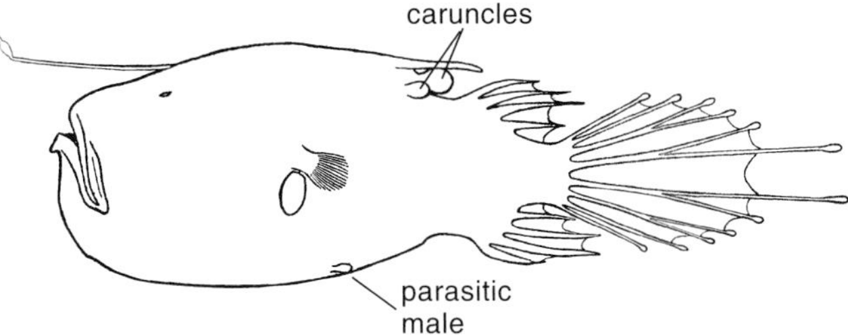

The photophores shown on the caudal fin are often missing due to damage, and in this genus the illicial bone is greatly reduced and covered by escal tissue, so that the angling apparatus is composed primarily of the pterygiophore of the illicium and the esca.

Mature male seadevils are parasitic on females. They are dwarfed, lack an external illicium, and are equipped with denticular teeth for attaching themselves to the females. They have a pair of large denticular teeth on the snout, which are fused at the base and articulate with the pterygiophore of the illicium, and two pairs on the tip of the lower jaw; no jaw teeth; large eyes; minute olfactory organs; and no caruncles. Dorsal, anal, and caudal fin ray counts are the same in the males as in the females.

Before they become attached to a female, male seadevils are similar to this specimen of *Himantolophus* (from Parr 1930), which, although it belongs to a different anglerfish family, has the same general features as a ceratiid male:

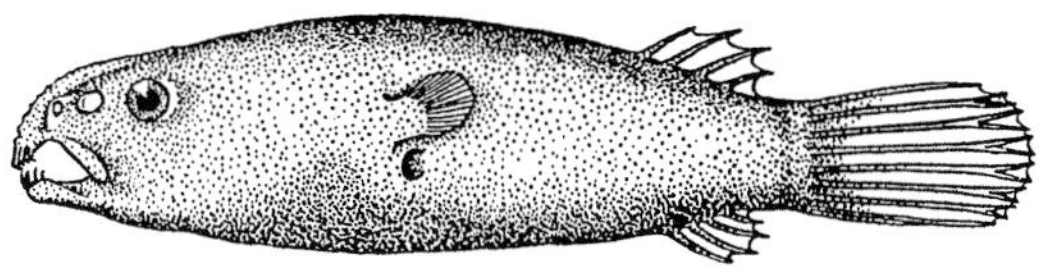

Soon after attachment, which can be anywhere on the body but is often ventrolaterally on the trunk, the mouth parts fuse to the female as in this specimen of *Ceratias holboelli* (from Bertelsen 1943):

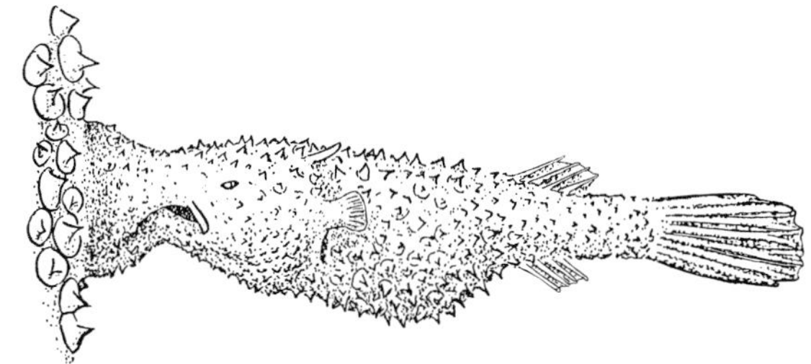

After awhile the male is barely identifiable as a fish, as in this specimen of *Cryptopsaras couesii* (from Bertelsen 1951):

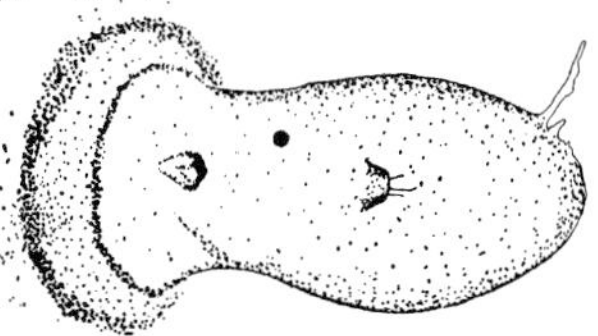

Cryptopsaras and *Ceratias* are easily distinguished from each other by the presence of three dorsal caruncles in the former and two in the latter. The most useful characters for identifying species of *Ceratias* are morphology of the esca, illicial bone length, and presence or absence of vomerine teeth. Color is not a useful distinguishing character, as ceratiids, at least in preservative, are uniformly dark red-brown to black. Morphometrics are of little use because, as in other soft fishes, measurements of ceratiids can be greatly affected by shrinkage during preservation.

Characters that allow identification of *Ceratias* males to species have not been found; larvae, males, and unmetamorphosed females have been described by Bertelsen (1951) and Pietsch (1986).

Seadevils are recent additions to the inventory of Alaskan fish species. None was known to exist in or near Alaskan waters at the time of Quast and Hall's (1972) inventory. Matarese et al. (1989), citing Pietsch (1986), listed one more species of seadevil from the Bering Sea than we do: "*Ceratias* sp." However, the Bering Sea *Ceratias* sp. referred to by Pietsch (1986:487 and fig. 6) comprised two adult females which could not be identified because the escae were missing and the specimens lacked vomerine teeth; they do not necessarily represent an additional or undescribed species.

The largest seadevil is *Ceratias holboelli,* with a maximum length of 145 cm (57 inches) or more. Male seadevils do not exceed 16 cm (6.3 inches) in length.

Key to the Ceratiidae of Alaska
(adolescent and adult females)

1 Three caruncles on dorsal midline of trunk just anterior to dorsal fin; subopercle with conspicuous spine on anterodorsal margin; caudal fin rays 8 . . . . *Cryptopsaras couesii,* this page (not known from Alaska)

1 Two caruncles on dorsal midline of trunk just anterior to dorsal fin; subopercle without spine on anterodorsal margin; caudal fin rays 9, the lowermost only a small remnant . . . . *Ceratias holboelli,* page 303

Cryptopsaras couesii Gill, 1883 **triplewart seadevil**

Monterey Bay, California, to Peru, and Japan to New Zealand; Hawaiian Islands; Greenland; all major oceans, with overall latitudinal range of 63°N to 43°S.

At depths of 75–4,000 m, majority taken at depths of 500–1,250 m; mesopelagic to bathypelagic.

D 4, rarely 5; A 4; C 8; Pec 14–18; Pel 0.

- **Three dorsal caruncles**.
- Esca with single filament at tip, and one or more pairs of filaments arising from base.
- Illicial bone reduced to a small remnant.
- Skin covered with fine, close-set dermal spinules.
- Vomerine teeth 2–10.
- Length to about 44 cm TL.

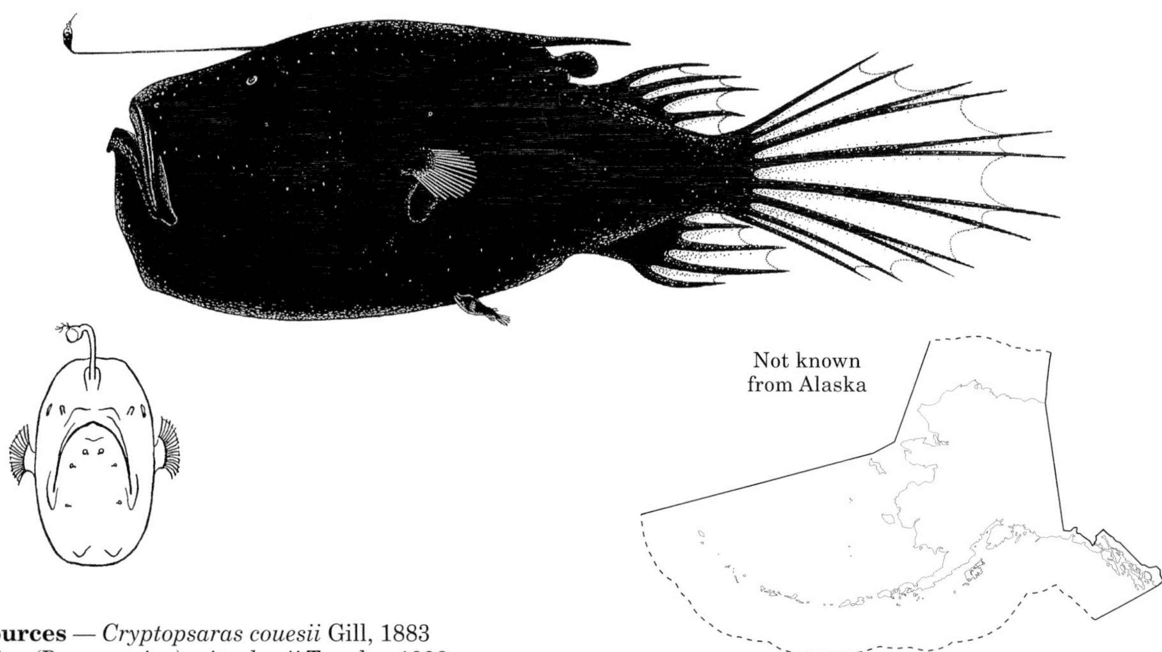

Notes & Sources — *Cryptopsaras couesii* Gill, 1883
Ceratias (Paraceratias) mitsukurii Tanaka, 1908

Description: Bertelsen 1951:138–145; Amaoka in Masuda et al. 1984:108; Pietsch 1986:488–490.

Figures: Full lateral: Pietsch 1986, fig. 7. Anterior: Norman 1930, fig. 44

Range: Nearest records to Alaska are from off Hokkaido, Japan, and Monterey Bay, California (Pietsch 1986). The northernmost record is a single specimen from Iceland, at 63°N (Saemundsson 1922).

Size: Largest known is a specimen from Sagami Bay, Japan (holotype of *Ceratias mitsukurii*), with a length of 44 cm to the tip of the longest caudal rays, which were broken and lacked their tips (Tanaka 1911).

Ceratias holboelli Krøyer, 1845 — northern seadevil

Bering Sea and Gulf of Alaska; Pacific Ocean off British Columbia, central California, Japan, and Hawaiian Islands; nearly cosmopolitan in world oceans, excluding Southern Ocean.

At depths of 120–3,400 m, most commonly 400–2,000 m; mesopelagic to bathypelagic.

D 4, rarely 3; A 4; C 9; Pec 15–19; Pel 0.

- **Two dorsal caruncles**, minute in specimens over 40 cm SL.
- Single slender escal appendage with as many as three short filaments on each side.
- Ninth or lowermost caudal ray reduced to a remnant, totally embedded in skin.
- Skin covered with close-set dermal spinules.
- Vomerine teeth 0–6, present in nearly all specimens less than 80 mm SL and in about 25% of larger specimens.
- Length to about 145 cm TL.

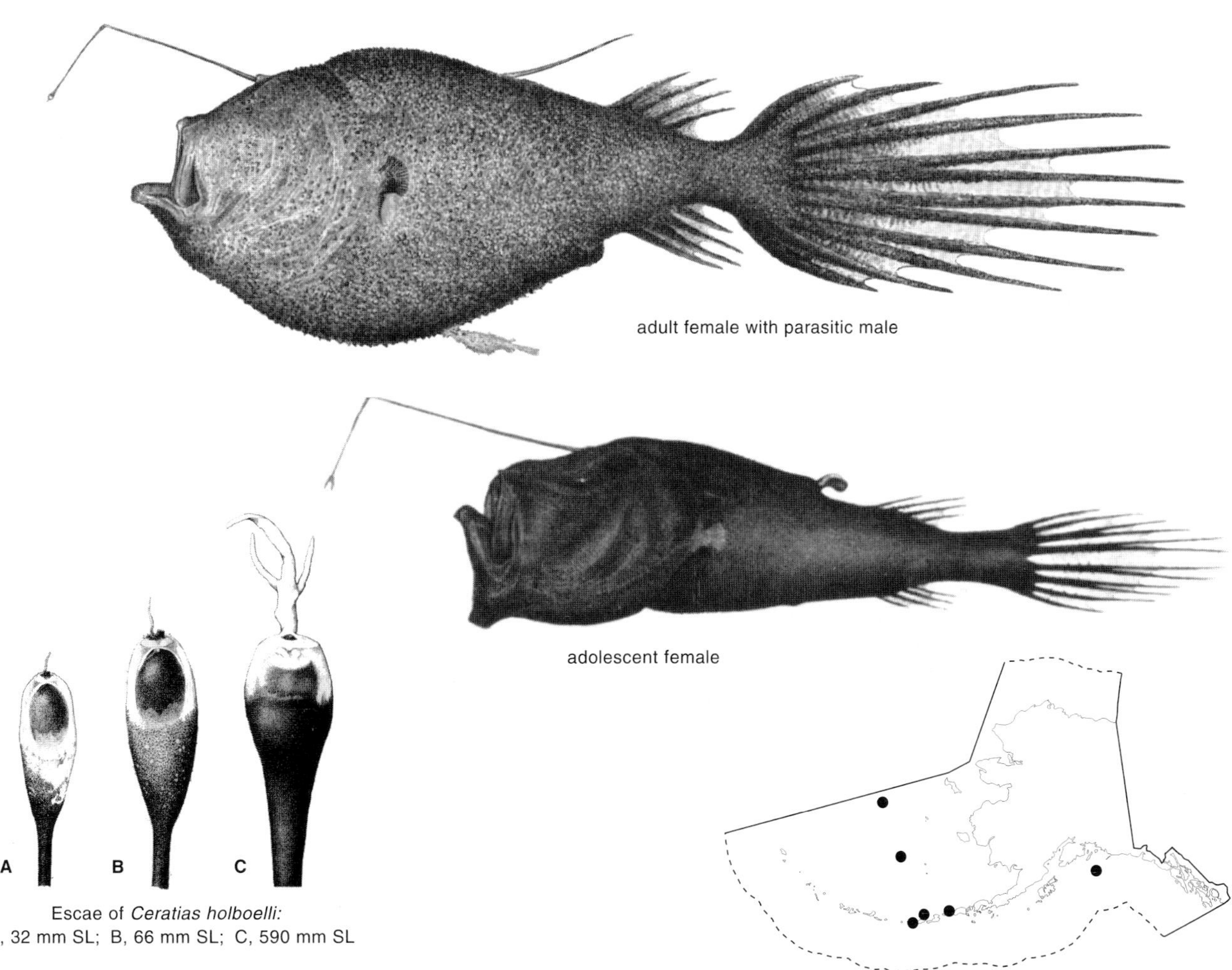

adult female with parasitic male

adolescent female

Escae of *Ceratias holboelli:* A, 32 mm SL; B, 66 mm SL; C, 590 mm SL

Notes & Sources — *Ceratias holboelli* Krøyer, 1845

Specimens of *C. uranoscopus* Murray, 1877, were once thought to be the young of *C. holboelli.* Differences include a complete lack of distal appendages on the esca of *C. uranoscopus,* as well as smaller size (not known to reach more than 32 cm TL) and different geographic range (not recorded closer to Alaska than the Hawaiian Islands).

Description: Bertelsen 1943, 1951:132–138; Clarke 1950; Amaoka in Masuda et al. 1984:108; Pietsch 1986:484–485.

Figures: Full lateral views: Bertelsen 1951, frontispiece. Escae: Pietsch 1986, fig. 2.

Range: Recorded by Pietsch (1986) from 60°02'N, 179°00'W (UW 20952) and 56°57'N, 173°42'W (UW 20951). Other Alaskan specimens, collected in 1990 and 1991 at depths of 315–503 m and identified by T. W. Pietsch, are from 54°32'N, 165°36'W (UW 21615); 53°51'N, 168°43'W (UW 21616); and 53°10'N, 169°28'W (UW 21617). An adult female was collected from the Gulf of Alaska, Middleton Island area, at about 59°N, 147°W and depth of about 768 m on 10 Jun. 1989; it has been deposited in the ABL permanent collection (B. L. Wing, pers. comm., 11 Apr. 1996). The first records from British Columbia were a specimen caught in 1993 and another in 1995 by commercial fishing vessels (Peden 1997a). Catch localities for the British Columbia records were not reported.

Size: Pietsch in Smith and Heemstra 1986.

Family Oneirodidae
Dreamers

The family name Oneirodidae is derived from the Greek word meaning "dreamlike" in allusion to the bizarre, almost unbelievable shapes of these fishes, like something out of a dream, but it could as well refer to their seemingly dreamlike state as they are passively carried along by water movements in the deep sea. The family includes about 16 genera with about 60 species (Nelson 1994), and has representatives in all the oceans. This guide includes accounts for three dreamer species that are known to occur in Alaska and two from adjacent waters that might yet be found in Alaska. Several examples of Alaska dreamer, *Oneirodes thompsoni,* and bulbous dreamer, *O. bulbosus,* have been documented from the Bering Sea and Gulf of Alaska. Spikehead dreamer, *Bertella idiomorpha,* is known in Alaska from one Bering Sea record and one from the southwestern Gulf of Alaska. Cosmopolitan dreamer, *O. eschrichtii,* has been found almost everywhere but in Alaska, while smooth dreamer, *Chaenophryne melanorhabdus,* occurs off British Columbia.

Female dreamers tend to be globose and soft. They have an angling apparatus with a rodlike pterygiophore which, when retracted, extends out the dorsal midline, as in Ceratiidae; a well-developed spine on each cone-shaped sphenotic; greatly concave foreheads due to enlarged frontal bones, in contrast to the convex foreheads of ceratiids; and jaws that are usually equal anteriorly or with the lower slightly projecting, and often with a well-developed symphyseal spine. Family characteristics also include 4–8 dorsal fin rays; 4–7 anal fin rays; bifurcate opercle; hyomandibular with double head (except single in *Bertella*); 6 branchiostegal rays; and 18–21 vertebrae. (See Pietsch [1974] for osteology of dreamers.) Skin spines are lacking, except for microscopic dermal spines in *Oneirodes.* Dreamers are dark brown to black except for the escal bulb and appendages; the oral cavity and viscera, except for the outer surface of the stomach wall, are unpigmented.

In dreamers the skin sheath ("tentacle" of some authors) that receives the posterior end of the pterygiophore of the illicium when it is retracted is about halfway between the sphenotic spines and dorsal fin. In seadevils (Ceratiidae) it is closer to the dorsal fin.

Dreamers typically reproduce through nonparasitic attachment of the male onto the body of the female. Parasitic males have been observed in one genus (Pietsch 1976). In male dreamers the posterior end of the upper denticular teeth is remote from the anterior end of the pterygiophore of the illicium; the eyes and posterior nostrils are lateral, while the anterior nostrils are close together and directed anteriorly; and the olfactory organs are large. Fin ray counts are the same as those of the females.

The list of Alaskan fish species by Quast and Hall (1972) had a somewhat different roster of dreamers, but was compiled before Pietsch (1973, 1974, 1975) described *Bertella* and reviewed the systematics and distribution of *Oneirodes* and *Chaenophryne.* One of the most important considerations pertaining to the Alaskan species is that, owing largely to great similarities in their escal morphology, *O. thompsoni* had been sunk in the synonymy of *O. acanthias,* while *O. bulbosus* had been classified in *O. eschrichtii.* Therefore, *O. acanthias* and *O. eschrichtii* became known as the species to recognize off Alaska. Pietsch (1974) demonstrated that all four species are distinct, which means that *O. thompsoni* and *O. bulbosus* are the forms typically occurring in Alaskan waters. The others have more southerly distributions. Escal morphology and main latitudinal ranges in the eastern North Pacific for the four species are summarized in the diagram above. Although the range of *O. eschrichtii* is not presently known to extend to Alaska, the species' nearly cosmopolitan distribution and a record from the Kuril–Kamchatka Trench at 49°N suggest it may yet be found in Alaska.

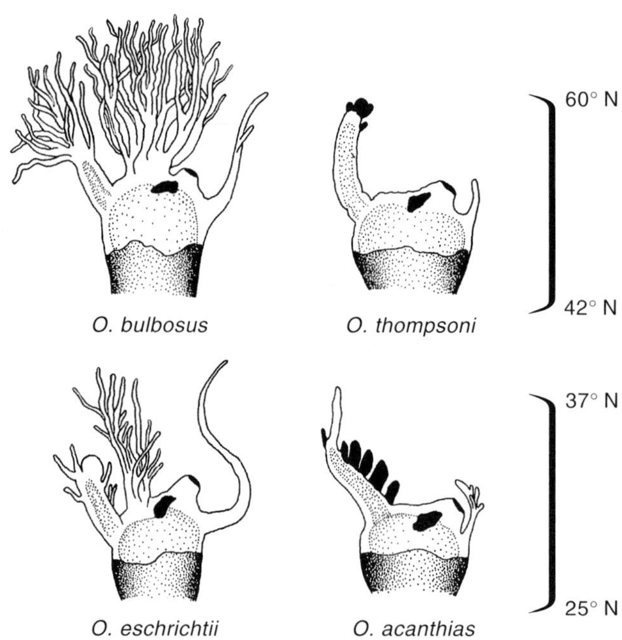

Escae and main latitudinal ranges in eastern North Pacific Ocean of four *Oneirodes* species
(After Pietsch 1974.)

Chaenophryne parviconus was listed as a potential addition to the Alaskan ichthyofauna by Quast and Hall (1972) on the basis of a record from British Columbia provisionally identified as that species by Taylor (1967b). However, Pietsch (1975) synonymized *C. parviconus* in *C. draco,* a form that does not occur in the northeastern Pacific, and provided updated, more detailed descriptions of all the *Chaenophryne* species he considered valid. Peden et al. (1985) concluded that the species to recognize off British Columbia is *C. melanorhabdus,* while noting the presence of another species, *C. longiceps,* as far north as Oregon.

Key to the Oneirodidae of Alaska

(adolescent and adult females)

1 Skin covering caudal fin to some distance from fin base; anal fin rays 5, rarely 4 or 6; sphenotic spines present or absent; dorsal margin of frontal bones straight or curved; lower jaw with or without symphyseal spine . . . . . . (2)

1 Skin not extending onto caudal fin past fin base; anal fin rays 4, very rarely 5; sphenotic spines well developed; frontal bones convex along entire dorsolateral margin; lower jaw with well-developed symphyseal spine . . . . . . (3)

2 (1) Body fusiform; dorsal profile of frontal bones straight; sphenotic spines strong; symphyseal spine strong; spines at mandibular angles strong; esca with one short appendage . . . . *Bertella idiomorpha,* page 306

2 Body globular; dorsal profile of frontal bones convex; sphenotic spines absent; symphyseal spine rudimentary; spines at mandibular angles rudimentary or absent; esca with more than one appendage . . . . . . *Chaenophryne melanorhabdus,* page 307
(not known from Alaska)

3 (1) Esca without filamentous medial appendages . . . . . . *Oneirodes thompsoni,* page 308

3 Esca with filamentous medial appendages almost half as long as escal bulb to longer than escal bulb . . . . . . (4)

4 (3) Anterior escal appendage bearing papillae and short filaments at distal tip, posterior appendage unbranched; posterior margin of upper part of subopercle not indented . . . . *Oneirodes eschrichtii,* page 309
(not known from Alaska)

4 Anterior escal appendage divided distally into many long filaments, posterior appendage usually with 1 or 2 short branches; posterior margin of upper part of subopercle usually indented to deeply notched . . . . . . *Oneirodes bulbosus,* page 310

Bertella idiomorpha Pietsch, 1973 — spikehead dreamer

Bering Sea and Gulf of Alaska to Gulf of California and to western North Pacific off southern Japan.
Taken in nets fishing to depths of 500–2,900 m; mesopelagic and bathypelagic to bathybenthic.

D 5–6; A 5, rarely 4; C 9, rarely 8; Pec 17–21; Pel 0; Vert 20.

- **Body moderately fusiform**; **dorsal profile of frontal bone straight**.
- **Sphenotic spine strong**; lower jaw with **strong symphyseal spine** and 3 spines (quadrate, mandibular, and angular) on posterior angle; **quadrate and angular spines large**.
- **Esca with one short posterior appendage**.
- Usually more anal fin rays than in *Oneirodes.*
- **Skin extending past base of caudal fin**.
- Length to 101 mm SL.

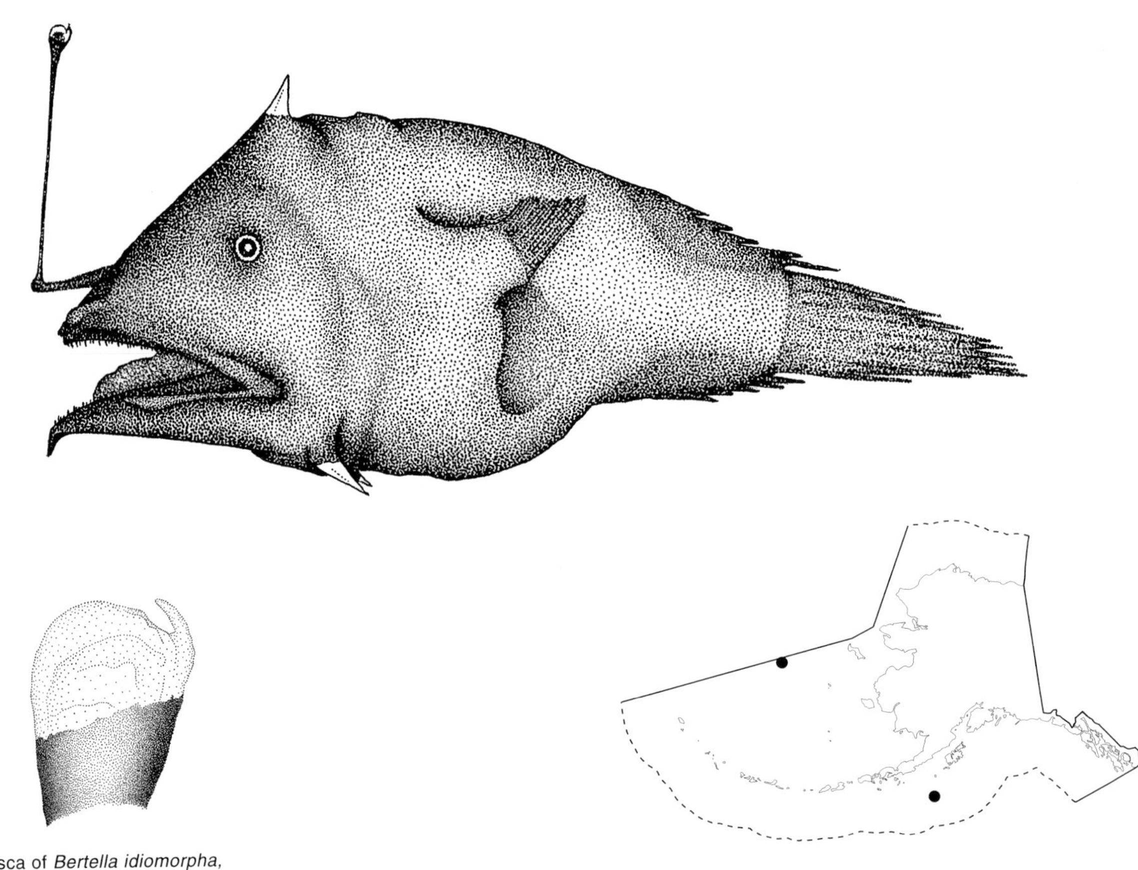

Esca of *Bertella idiomorpha*, left side, 84 mm SL

Notes & Sources — *Bertella idiomorpha* Pietsch, 1973
The genus *Bertella* is monotypic, as currently known.

Description: Pietsch 1973; Amaoka in Masuda et al. 1984: 106.

Figures: Pietsch 1973, figs. 3 and 5.

Range: One of the paratypes described by Pietsch (1973) was a specimen (OSUO 1045, 84 mm SL) from the Gulf of Alaska at 54°37'N, 155°33'W. Balanov and Fedorov (1996) recorded a specimen (ZIN 49598, 101 mm SL) taken over the continental slope southeast of Cape Navarin, on the U.S. side of the international border at 60°28'N, 180°00', in a midwater trawl pulled obliquely from 1,000 m to 500 m. Other recent Pacific records are those of Parin et al. (1995) off the southern Kuril Islands, and Shinohara et al. (1996) off Honshu. Nearest published record outside Alaska is a paratype (SIO 60-51) from 44°06'N, 161°39'W (Pietsch 1973). Vertical distribution is not well known. *Bertella* has been caught in plankton nets and open midwater and bottom trawl nets towed as deep as 2,900 m over bottom depths of 805–5,920 m. It has not been reported from net tows with maximum depths of less than 500 m. Usually caught well above bottom; e.g., holotype was caught in a net towed through 0–940 m over bottom depth of 2,377–3,475 m. However, caught often enough near bottom (suggested by frequency of catches in bottom trawls) that Balanov and Fedorov (1996) characterized life zone as mesopelagic to bathybenthic.

Size: Balanov and Fedorov 1996.

Chaenophryne melanorhabdus Regan & Trewavas, 1932 **smooth dreamer**

Eastern Pacific over continental slope from southern British Columbia to Gulf of Panama.

Between approximately 200 m and an unknown lower limit; most specimens have been collected below 450 m; evidently, concentrated between 300 and 1,000 m; mesopelagic.

D 6–8; A 5, rarely 6; C 9; Pec 16–18; Pel 0; Vert 19.

- Body globular; **dorsal profile of frontal bone strongly convex**.
- **Sphenotic spine absent; symphyseal and articular spines of lower jaw rudimentary; angular spine absent**.
- Esca with 1 filamentous anterolateral appendage on each side; single, elongate, anterior appendage; no medial appendage; posterior appendage with swollen basal portion and a compressed distal portion bearing filaments.
- Usually more anal fin rays than in *Oneirodes*.
- **Skin extending past base of caudal fin**.
- Length to 97 mm SL.

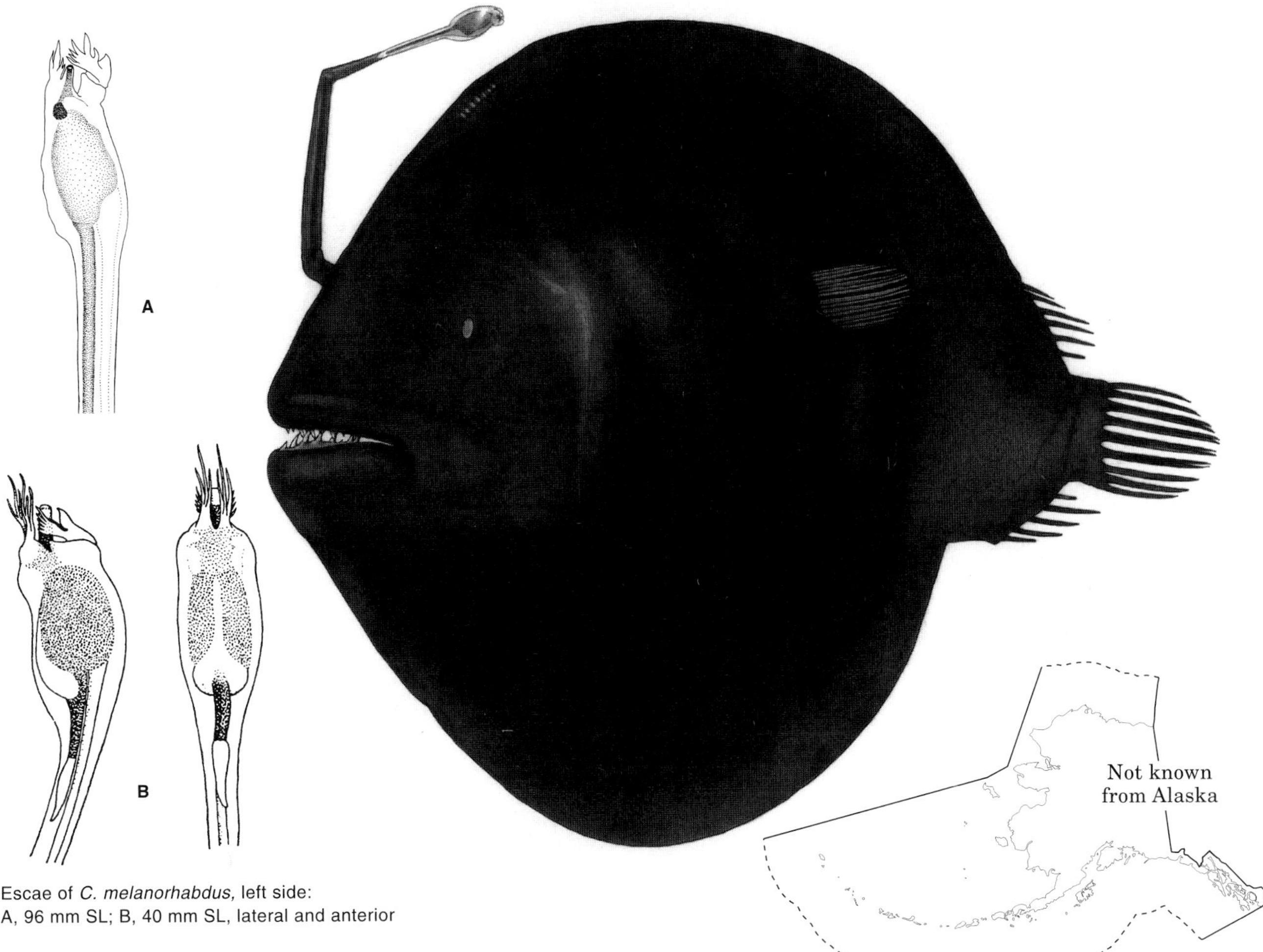

Escae of *C. melanorhabdus*, left side:
A, 96 mm SL; B, 40 mm SL, lateral and anterior

Notes & Sources — *Chaenophryne melanorhabdus* Regan & Trewavas, 1932

The escal characters easily separate *C. melanorhabdus* from other species of *Chaenophryne*. In addition, it has fewer pectoral fin rays (16 or 17, rarely 18) than the partly sympatric species *C. longiceps* (17–22, rarely less than 18).

Description: Pietsch 1975:81 (key), 90–92.

Figures: Full lateral: Royal British Columbia Museum, artist K. Shuster, Mar. 1982; BCPM 972-64, 65 mm SL, off Cape Flattery. Escae: 40 mm SL from Regan and Trewavas 1932, 96 mm SL from Pietsch 1975. Illustration of *Chaenophryne* by Hart (1973) inadvertently mixed esca of one species and body of another (Peden et al. 1985).

Range: Nearest record to Alaska is a specimen taken off Cape Flattery (see illustration above); it was originally identified as *Oneirodes* sp. by Peden (1975) and later referred to *C. melanorhabdus* by Peden et al. (1985). The only other published record of *Chaenophryne* from nearby waters is a damaged specimen unidentifiable as to species taken southwest of Cape St. James at 51°26'N, 131°98'W. Taylor (1967b) assigned the specimen to *C.* cf. *parviconus* on the basis of existing information on distribution of *Chaenophryne* species; Hart (1973) attributed the record to *C. parviconus,* without question. Pietsch (1975) later placed *C. parviconus* in the synonymy of *C. draco,* which is not known to occur in the northeastern Pacific; and provided new descriptions of *C. melanorhabdus* and another northeastern Pacific form, *C. longiceps*.

Oneirodes thompsoni (Schultz, 1934) **Alaska dreamer**

Bering Sea and Gulf of Alaska to northern California and across Pacific to Honshu and Sea of Okhotsk. At depths of 500–1,500 m or more, with most occurring at 600–1,250 m; mesopelagic and bathypelagic.

D 5–6; A 4; C 9; Pec 14–17; Pel 0; Vert 18–20.

- Body globular; frontal bone convex along entire dorsolateral margin.
- Sphenotic spine well developed; symphyseal spine well developed; articular spines present, quadrate spine larger than mandibular spine; angular spine absent.
- **Medial escal appendages absent.**
- Fewer anal fin rays than in either *Chaenophryne* or *Bertella*.
- **Skin not extending past caudal fin base.**
- Length to 150 mm SL, 194 mm TL.

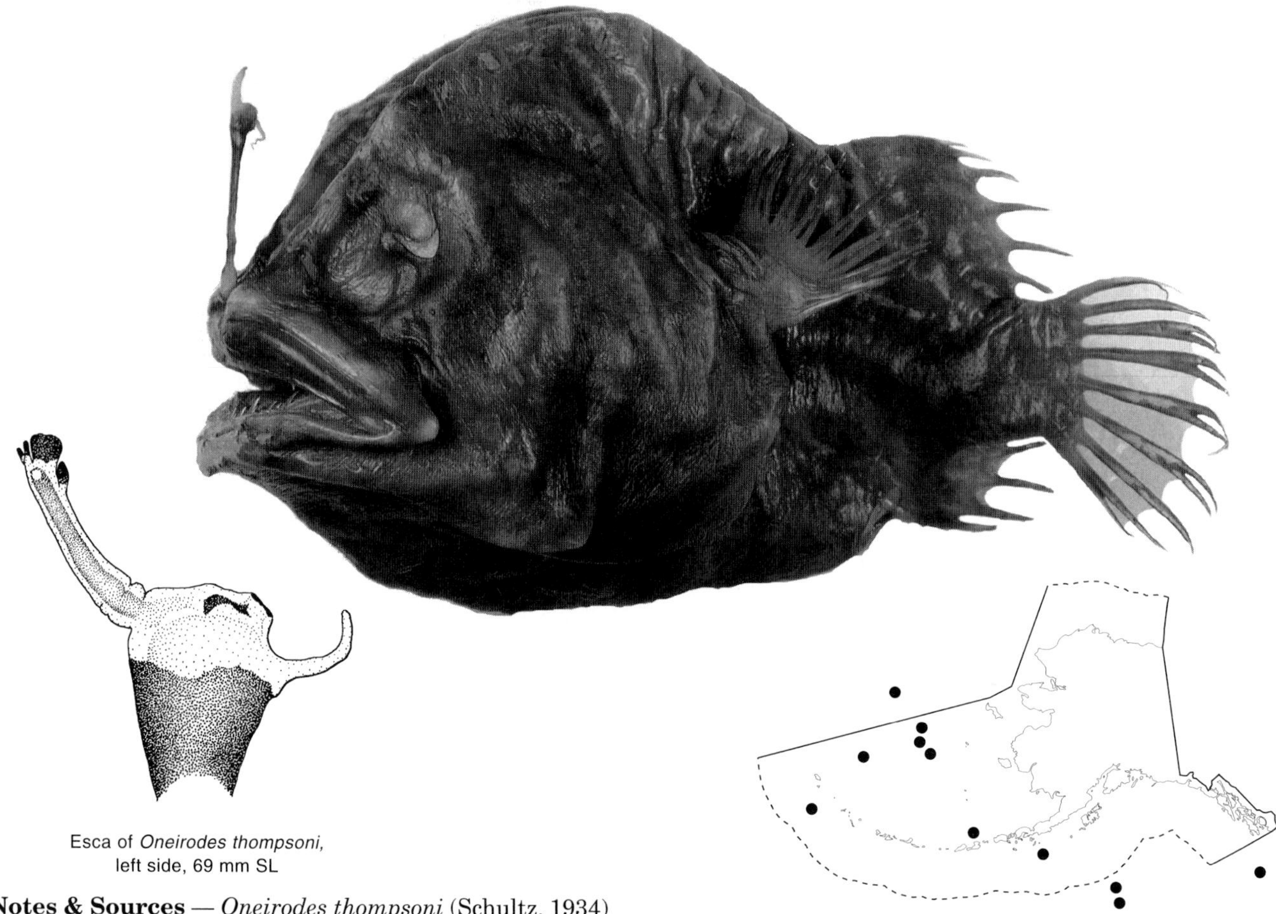

Esca of *Oneirodes thompsoni*, left side, 69 mm SL

Notes & Sources — *Oneirodes thompsoni* (Schultz, 1934)
Dolopichthys thompsoni Schultz, 1934

Bertelsen (1951) placed *D. thompsoni* in the synonymy of *O. acanthias* (Gilbert, 1915), and populations off British Columbia and Alaska became known under that name (e.g., Hart 1973). On the basis of additional material Pietsch (1974) resurrected the species *thompsoni. Oneirodes acanthias,* as currently known, while evidently endemic to the eastern Pacific has not been found farther north than approximately 38°N.

Description: Pietsch 1974:68–70; Amaoka in Masuda et al. 1984:106.

Figures: Full lateral: UAM 3492, 103 mm SL, 127 mm TL, central Bering Sea; photograph by T.A.M. Esca: Pietsch 1974, fig. 87.

Range: The holotype is from the Gulf of Alaska at 54°13'N, 159°06'W, depth range 0–900 m (Schultz 1934a). Pietsch (1974) gave locality data for several Alaskan specimens, taken in midwater and bottom trawls: 61°21'N, 176°18'E, 0–1,020 m; 60°01'N, 179°08'W, 0–680 m; 58°52'N, 178°18'W, 0–720 m; 58°36'N, 176°02'W, 0–700 m; 54°34'N, 167°36'W, 0–720 m; as well as several from nearby in the western Bering Sea and across the Pacific Ocean from Kamchatka to British Columbia. Pietsch's (1974:92) map shows an additional Alaskan record at about 51°N, 175°E. See below, under Size, for another. UAM 3492, shown above, has no locality data other than central Bering Sea. Southernmost record given by Pietsch (1974) was 41°20'N, 144°10'W. Recorded by Shinohara et al. (1996) off Pacific coast of Honshu as far south as 36°31'N, in trawl nets towed along bottom as deep as 930–2,056 m. Amaoka (in Masuda et al. 1984) reported *O. thompsoni* in Sea of Okhotsk as well.

Size: R. Baxter, unpubl. data; lengths of an uncataloged OSUO specimen from 56°02'N, 176°25'E, depth 622–724 m. Previously recorded to 14 cm SL by Amaoka (in Masuda et al. 1984).

Oneirodes eschrichtii Lütken, 1871 **cosmopolitan dreamer**

Pacific, Indian, Atlantic, and Southern oceans; north in Pacific to about 33°N except for one specimen from Kuril–Kamchatka Trench; in Atlantic north to Greenland at about 61°N; nearly cosmopolitan.

Taken in gear fishing to maximum depths of 150–6,200 m; mesopelagic and bathypelagic.

D 5–7; A 4; C 9; Pec 15–19; Pel 0.

- Body globular; frontal bone convex along entire dorsolateral margin.
- Sphenotic spine well developed; symphyseal spine well developed; articular spines present, quadrate spine larger than mandibular spine; angular spine absent.
- **Anterior escal appendage without numerous, tapering distal filaments**; medial escal appendages more than twice length of escal bulb in medium-size specimens (A in figure), to less than half length of escal bulb in largest specimens (C); **medial escal appendages not as highly branched as in *O. bulbosus***.
- Fewer anal fin rays than in either *Chaenophryne* or *Bertella*.
- **Skin not extending past caudal fin base**.
- Length to 213 mm SL.

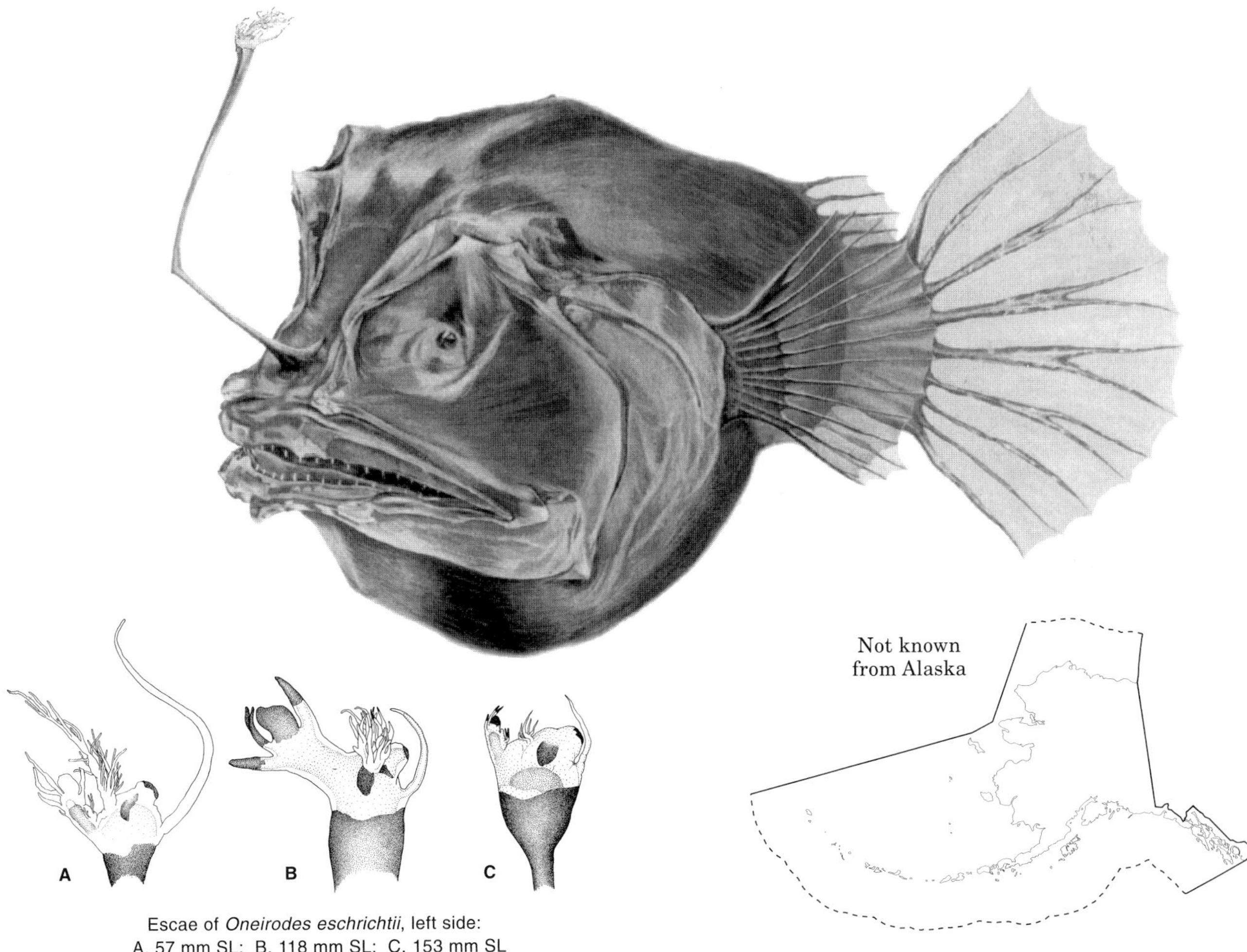

Escae of *Oneirodes eschrichtii*, left side: A, 57 mm SL; B, 118 mm SL; C, 153 mm SL

Notes & Sources — *Oneirodes eschrichtii* Lütken, 1871

Bertelsen (1951) classified *O. bulbosus,* including records from Alaska, as synonymous with *O. eschrichtii.* Pietsch (1974) resurrected *O. bulbosus* as a distinct species. None of the remaining records of *O. eschrichtii* is from Alaska.

Description: Pietsch 1974:44–52; Amaoka in Masuda et al. 1984:106.

Figures: Pietsch 1974, frontispiece and fig. 65.

Range: The nearest published record is a specimen from the Kuril–Kamchatka Trench at 49°29'N, 158°41'E identified by Rass (1955) as a different species and assigned by Pietsch (1974) to *O. eschrichtii.* Other Pacific Ocean records are from south of 33°N. The type specimen was taken off the southwest coast of Greenland. That record and other specimens from northern latitudes in the Atlantic, such as those taken off Ireland, and the nearly cosmopolitan distribution already recorded, suggest the species could occur at far-northern latitudes in the Pacific as well.

Oneirodes bulbosus Chapman, 1939 **bulbous dreamer**

Bering Sea and Gulf of Alaska to southern British Columbia and across Pacific to southern Kuril Islands; one record in midocean eastern Pacific west of Oregon.

At depths of 500–1,500 m, most occurring at 600–1,000 m; mesopelagic.

D 6–7; A 4; C 9; Pec 15–18; Pel 0; Vert 19–20.

- Body globular; frontal bone convex along entire dorsolateral margin.
- Sphenotic and symphyseal spines well developed; articular spines present, quadrate spine larger than mandibular spine; angular spine absent.
- **Anterior escal appendage with numerous, tapering distal filaments**; pair of **medial escal appendages highly branched**, 2–5 times length of escal bulb in large specimens.
- Fewer anal fin rays than in either *Chaenophryne* or *Bertella*.
- **Skin not extending past caudal fin base.**
- Length to 117 mm SL.

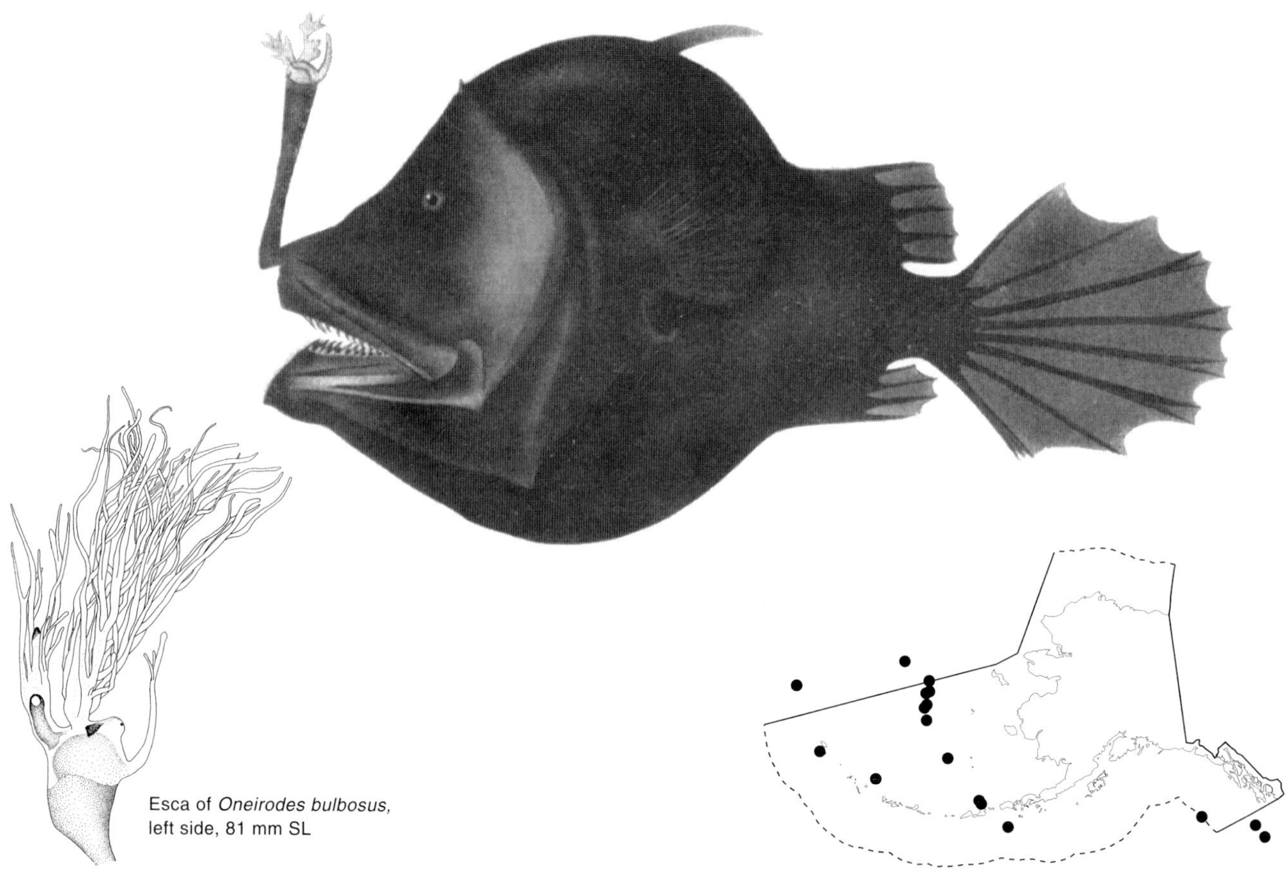

Esca of *Oneirodes bulbosus*, left side, 81 mm SL

Notes & Sources — *Oneirodes bulbosus* Chapman, 1939

Following Bertelsen (1951), some authors synonymized records of *O. bulbosus* in the *O. eschrichtii* group. Pietsch (1974) resurrected *O. bulbosus* as a distinct species. Peden et al. (1985) confirmed that specimens taken more recently west of British Columbia at Ocean Station Papa are readily identifiable with Pietsch's (1974) description of *O. bulbosus* and that *O. bulbosus* is the form to recognize off British Columbia.

Description: Pietsch 1974:52–54; Amaoka in Masuda et al. 1984:106.

Figures: Full lateral: Clemens and Wilby 1961, fig. 281. Esca: Pietsch 1974, fig. 71. (Hart's [1973] illustration of *O. eschrichtii* is based on Chapman's [1939] drawing of *O. bulbosus*.)

Range: Holotype, described by Chapman (1939), was taken west of the northern end of Graham Island, British Columbia. Since then, numerous examples have been collected from Alaska and nearby waters. Pietsch (1974) gave locality data for many of them, from 61°21'N, 176°18'E in the Bering Sea to the Gulf of Alaska. Specimens collected more recently (1979–1983) and identified by T. W. Pietsch, J. W. Orr, and K. M. Howe include: UW 21471, 59°12'N, 178°26'W, 640 m; UW 21472, 58°58'N, 178°20'W, 650 m; UW 21474, 52°14'N, 173°55'E, 470 m; UW 25506, 60°25'N, 179°00'W, no depth; UW 25508, 56°28'N, 172°45'W, 732 m; UW 25509, 60°11'N, 179°00'W, 600 m; and UW 25510, from 55°08'N, 140°20'W, 787 m (depths are maximum depth of tow). The southernmost record given by Pietsch (1974) was 43°48'N, 149°55'W.

Size: UW 21472 (online database).

FAMILY GIGANTACTINIDAE
Whipnoses

Females of the family Gigantactinidae, with their elongate bodies and long caudal peduncles, are streamlined compared to females of the Ceratiidae and Oneirodidae, and immediately recognizable by their extremely long illicium. The family comprises two genera: *Gigantactis,* with 20 species, and the monotypic *Rhynchactis.* They are widely distributed in all the major oceans of the world in a broad belt limited by the Arctic and Antarctic polar fronts, with northern- and southernmost records at about 63°N and 63°S. They are probably the most hydrodynamically efficient and most capable of prolonged horizontal movement of all ceratioids and tend to inhabit deeper strata where physicochemical differences between water masses are minimized, so they have broad horizontal ranges compared to other ceratioids (Bertelsen et al. 1981).

The family Gigantactinidae was not included on the list of fishes of Alaska by Quast and Hall (1972), but a note written in the margin of Baxter's (1990ms) draft keys to the fishes of Alaska indicates he knew of a report or specimen of *Gigantactis vanhoeffeni* found "off south side of Kodiak Island, May 1989." Our search for further information on this possible record was unsuccessful. However, most whipnoses have wide distributions and it is reasonable to expect that at least one species will be found in Alaskan waters, even if not *G. vanhoeffeni.* Some possibilities are mentioned after the following summary of family characteristics.

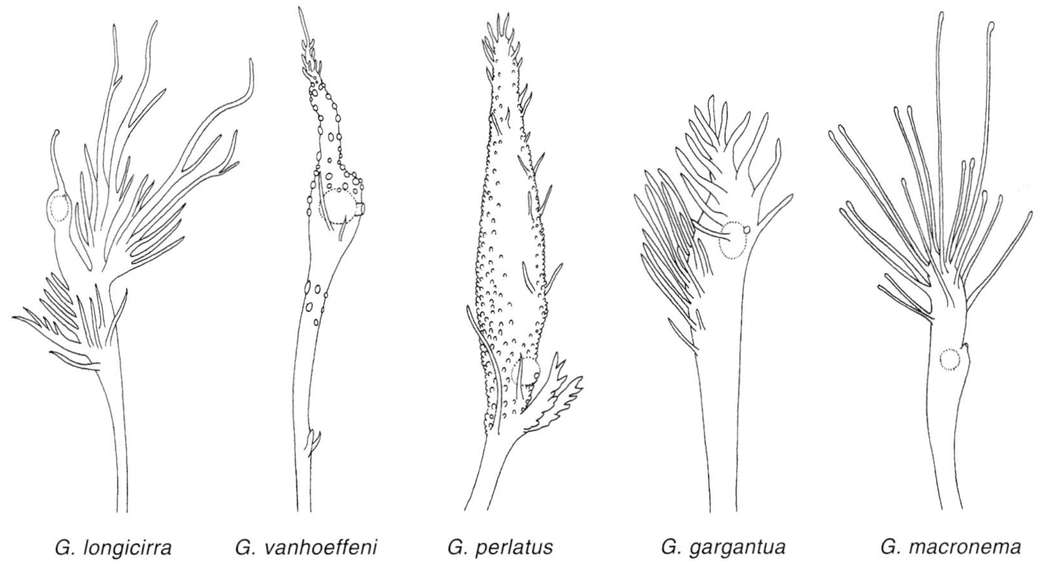

Examples of *Gigantactis* escae
(After Bertelsen et al. 1981.)

The morphology, systematics, and distribution of the family Gigantactinidae were the subject of a detailed study by Bertelsen et al. (1981). Since then, Kharin (1984) described a new species, *G. balushkini,* from the North Pacific off northern Japan, and there have been several records extending the known range of other whipnoses in the North Pacific.

Female whipnoses can be distinguished from other ceratioids by their elongate bodies; long caudal peduncle, more than 20% SL; and long illicium, greater than 60% SL to more than 350% SL. The posterior end of the pterygiophore of the illicium butts against the supraoccipital, and the angling apparatus is not retractable like it is in Ceratiidae and Oneirodidae. In *Gigantactis* the anterior end of the pterygiophore of the illicium extends slightly beyond the tip of the upper jaw, making the snout unusually pointed and protruded forward beyond the lower jaw. Sphenotic spines are absent, and the vomer is absent. The maxilla of *Gigantactis* females is represented by a threadlike remnant; and the dentaries are not ankylosed, so that the rami of the lower jaw can rotate relative to each other. The dentaries bear several rows of strong, recurved teeth. The eyes of adult female gigantactinids are very small, and sunk beneath a transparent layer of skin. Fin characteristics include a dorsal fin with 3–10 rays and anal fin with 3–8 rays; pectoral fins usually with 17–19 rays, ranging to 14–22 rays; and 9 caudal rays. The pelvic fins are absent, as in other ceratioids. All of the caudal fin rays in adult female *Gigantactis* are unbranched, in contrast to the branched caudal rays of other ceratioids. The ninth caudal ray is very small and covered by skin. Gigantactinids have 6 (rarely 7) branchiostegal rays, and spinulose skin.

Rhynchactis leptonema, the only species in its genus, is a highly derived species which differs from *Gigantactis* in several characters. Females lack a photophore-bearing escal bulb, frontal and parietal bones, and maxillae, and have a truncated snout, ankylosed dentaries, and branched caudal rays.

As with the Ceratiidae and Oneirodidae, in the Gigantactinidae the identification of species based on females relies primarily on morphology of the illicium and esca. In *Gigantactis* the bulb of the esca is more or less club-shaped and more slender than in most other ceratioids. An assortment of *Gigantactis* escae is shown in the illustration on the preceding page.

Males of gigantactinid species for which the males are known, are nonparasitic. They have minute eyes and large olfactory organs. The anterior nostrils are close together and open anteriorly. They typically have 3–6 upper denticular and 4–7 lower denticular teeth; all or nearly all of them are mutually free. The upper denticular teeth are not connected to the pterygiophore of the illicium. The hyomandibular has a single head. Although the males of many gigantactinid species are fairly well known, males of *G. vanhoeffeni* have not yet been identified.

The largest of 165 female whipnoses examined by Bertelsen et al. (1981) was 40.8 cm SL (16 inches); the largest of 50 males was 2.2 cm SL (0.87 inch). The largest female *G. vanhoeffeni* measured 34.0 cm SL (13.4 inches). Standard length of whipnoses is measured from the tip of the pterygiophore of the illicium to the posteriormost point on the margin of the hypural plate (Bertelsen et al. 1981).

At the time Bertelsen et al. (1981) prepared their review, the northernmost record of *G. vanhoeffeni* in the Pacific Ocean was from about 40°N off northern California, although a specimen had been collected in the Atlantic off Greenland at 63°N. This is the most commonly found whipnose in the North Pacific and, indeed, elsewhere in the world. A specimen (OS 13915) recently collected off Oregon extends the known range north in the eastern Pacific to about 44°N (D. F. Markle, pers. comm., 5 Nov. 1999). However, other species of *Gigantactis* are also proving to be distributed farther north as they become better known. A specimen (OS 17560; 317 mm SL) collected off northern Oregon at 45°28'N, 124°51'W in a bottom trawl at about 969 m of depth most likely is *G. gargantua* Bertelsen, Pietsch, and Lavenberg, 1981 (D. F. Markle, pers. comm., 5 Nov. 1999). Previously, *G. gargantua* was known only from the southern Indian Ocean, the eastern North Pacific off the Hawaiian Islands and southern California, and the western Pacific off northern Honshu (Bertelsen et al. 1981, Amaoka in Amaoka et al. 1983). Fedorov (1994) recorded *G. elsmani* Bertelsen, Pietsch, & Lavenberg, 1981, from the Okhotsk Sea between 43°N and 48°N. It had been known only from four specimens scattered in the Atlantic and eastern South Pacific until Amaoka (in Amaoka et al. 1983) recorded a specimen from the North Pacific off northern Honshu. Other forms which should be considered when identifying future whipnose specimens from Alaska are *G. kreffti, G. longicirra, G. macronema, G. perlatus,* and *Rhynchactis leptonema,* which are all widespread forms; *G. savagei,* which is known only from the North Pacific; and *G. balushkini,* from the Pacific off Japan.

Since the record of *G. vanhoeffeni* from Alaska suggested by Baxter (1990ms) has not been verified and so many other species could possibly be in the region, *G. vanhoeffeni* is included in this guide only to represent the family and serve as an example whereby a specimen could at least be identified to family. *Gigantactis vanhoeffini* is the type of a group of species characterized by having a darkly pigmented, spinulose, distal prolongation of the escal bulb. The *G. vanhoeffeni* group includes *G. paxtoni* and, although this particular species is not likely to be found off Alaska, an illustration of it is included in the account on the next page because it shows the family characters exceedingly well and the species is closely related to *G. vanhoeffeni.* Available drawings of *G. vanhoeffini* (Chen 1903, Gill 1904) lack detail and are inaccurate. (Photographs have been published; see, for example, a specimen from Greenland in Okamura et al. [1995:133].) *Gigantactis paxtoni* has a longer illicium (170–200% SL) than other members of the species group, including *G. vanhoeffeni* (less than 120% SL); and its caudal fin rays are more extensively covered with skin than in *G. vanhoeffeni.* It is most similar to *G. balushkini* from Japan.

Gigantactis vanhoeffeni Brauer, 1902 **cosmopolitan whipnose**

Gulf of Alaska in vicinity of Kodiak Island, report unconfirmed; Pacific Ocean off Oregon, California, Japan, and in midocean; Indian and Atlantic oceans; overall known latitudinal range 63°N to 15°S.

At depths of 300–5,300 m, most commonly 700–1,300 m; mesopelagic to bathypelagic.

D 5–7; A 5–6, rarely 7; Pec 17–18, rarely 19; Pel 0; C 9; Br 6; Vert 22.

- Black; paired papillae and tips of distal filaments of esca bright red.
- Illicial length less than 120% SL (71–112% in specimens greater than 25 mm SL).
- Escal bulb with elongate, distal prolongation; bulb and prolongation bearing distally flattened papillae; distal and proximal escal filaments present.
- Illicium with a posterior pair of papillae below the escal bulb.
- Caudal fin rays less than 45% SL; ninth or lowermost caudal ray reduced and embedded in skin; caudal skin coverage weakly developed.
- Length to at least 34 cm SL.

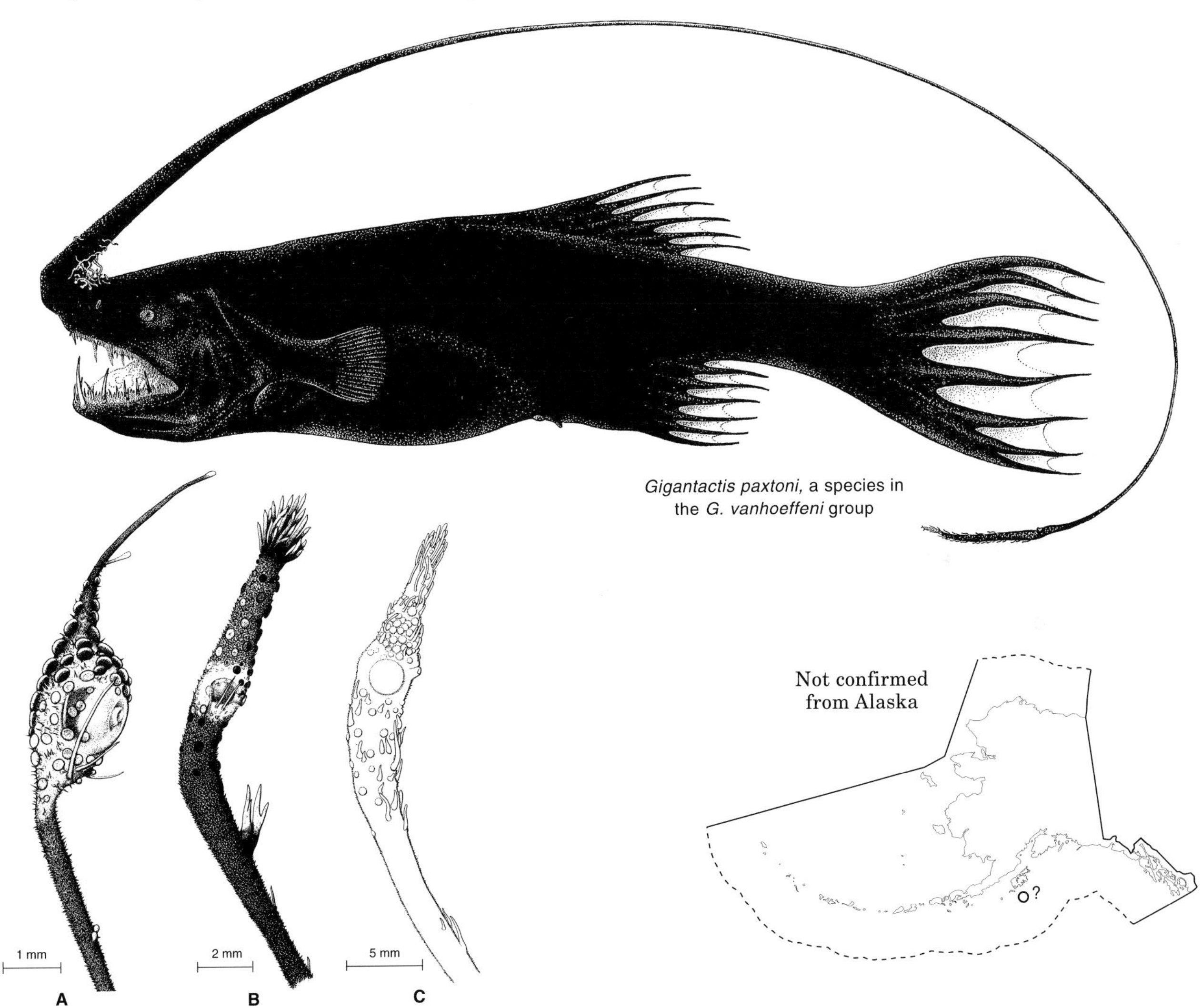

Gigantactis paxtoni, a species in the *G. vanhoeffeni* group

Escae of *Gigantactis vanhoeffeni,* left side: A, 38 mm SL; B, 152 mm SL; C, 270 mm SL

Notes & Sources — *Gigantactis vanhoeffeni* Brauer, 1902

Description: Bertelsen et al. 1981:31; Amaoka in Amaoka et al. 1983:198; Amaoka in Masuda et al. 1984:106.

Figures: Bertelsen et al. 1981. Full lateral view: *G. paxtoni* Bertelsen, Pietsch, & Lavenberg, 1981, a member of the *G. vanhoeffeni* group; holotype, 237 mm SL.

Range: A cryptic marginal note by Baxter (1990ms) indicated he knew of a specimen of *G. vanhoeffeni* taken off the south side of Kodiak Island in May 1989, but we have not found a voucher specimen or further information on this possible record. The northernmost adequately documented record for the eastern North Pacific is a specimen (OS 13915) collected off Brookings, Oregon (about 44°N), in a bottom trawl at a depth of 915 m; identified and reported by D. F. Markle (pers. comm., 5 Nov. 1999).

Order Beloniformes
Flyingfishes

The order Beloniformes primarily comprises active, epipelagic fishes of warm seas. Relatively few species inhabit fresh water or weak brackish water, or occur in temperate seas. Marine flyingfishes, halfbeaks, and needlefishes are some of the more familiar members of the order. Five families with nearly 200 species are included in the group. One species in the family Scomberesocidae occurs in Alaska.

The complex of characters defining beloniforms taxonomically includes a slender, elongate body; fixed, nonprotrusible upper jaw; soft rays (no spines) in all fins; dorsal and anal fins placed far back on the body; caudal fin with 13 principal rays, and more of them in the lower lobe than the upper lobe; pectoral fins placed high on the sides; abdominal pelvic fins with 6 rays; and a physoclistic swim bladder. The maxillae are excluded from the gape, the lower pharyngeal bones are fused to each other, and orbitosphenoid and mesocoracoid are lacking. The Scomberesocidae are in the suborder Belonoidei, called the Exocoetoidei by some authors, which have the lateral line low on the body (except absent in some species), a single nasal opening on each side, elongate lower jaw at some stage of the life history, and 6–15 branchiostegal rays; and the superfamily Scomberesocoidea, with small scales, usually a relatively large mouth, and both jaws usually elongate.

Family Scomberesocidae
Sauries

The saury family, or Scomberesocidae, includes four monotypic genera. All four species are marine and epipelagic in tropical and temperate seas. The Pacific saury, *Cololabis saira,* is restricted to the North Pacific Ocean, where it ranges, usually in schools well offshore, south to Mexico and to the Kuril Islands and Japan, and north to the Gulf of Alaska and Bering Sea. Occurrence of sauries over the continental shelf in the Gulf of Alaska and Bering Sea is typically noted in late summer when they move north on feeding migrations and may be most evident during unusually warm conditions, including El Niños. Pacific sauries can be attracted at night to lights and caught in nets, and are one of the most popular food fishes in Japan.

In sauries the posterior portions of the dorsal and anal fins are modified into several finlets, as commonly found in scombroid fishes (tunas and mackerels). Other saury characteristics include slender, pikelike bodies; jaws ranging from long slender beaks with both jaws produced to relatively short beaks with only the lower jaw produced; small mouth opening, not extending below the eyes; small scales; relatively small teeth; and 54–70 vertebrae.

Two of the four saury species are dwarfed, as adults not exceeding about 13 cm (5 inches) in total length, while the largest reaches 50 cm (20 inches) or more. *Cololabis saira* is the second largest saury, reaching about 44 cm (17 inches).

Cololabis saira (Brevoort, 1856) **Pacific saury**

Southeastern Bering Sea, Pacific Ocean south of Aleutian chain, and Gulf of Alaska to Mexico off Revillagigedo Islands; western Bering Sea from Olyutorskiy Bay to Pacific Ocean and Sea of Okhotsk off Kuril Islands and Japan.

Epipelagic, in schools offshore; to depth of 229 m, but usually near surface.

D 9–12 + 5–6 finlets; A 12–14 + 5–7 finlets; Pec 12–15; Pel 6; Br 12–15; Ls (midlateral) 128–148; GR 32–43; Vert 62–69.

- Dark green to blue dorsally, silver ventrally.
- Body slender and elongate; head pointed, jaws moderately (but not extremely) produced into blunt beaks, lower beak projecting beyond upper; mouth small, maxilla not nearly reaching eye.
- Dorsal and anal finlets present.
- Lateral line very low on body near ventral surface, and extending along body over anal fin base.
- Gill rakers numerous, very closely spaced.
- Length to about 44 cm TL.

Notes & Sources — *Cololabis saira* (Brevoort, 1856)
Scomberesox saira Brevoort, 1856

Description: Hart 1973:257–260; Hubbs and Wisner 1980: 522; Eschmeyer and Herald 1983:116; Yoshino in Masuda et al. 1984:79.

Figure: University of British Columbia, artist P. Drukker-Brammall; UBC 65-392, 207 mm SL, south of Adak Island, Alaska.

Range: Hubbs and Wisner (1980) and Brodeur (1988) depicted distribution of *C. saira*. Hubbs and Wisner (1980) found no records from the central or eastern Bering Sea, only from the western Bering Sea along the coast of Kamchatka north to Olyutorskiy Bay at about 60°N. Brodeur (1988), after Kobayashi et al. (1968) and Macy et al. (1978), depicted the ranges of three subpopulations, with that of the central subpopulation extending into the southeastern Bering Sea. We did not find voucher specimens or other documentation substantiating occurrence in the Bering Sea off Alaska; the above map reproduces the Bering Sea range depicted by Brodeur (1988). Specific Alaskan records extend from south of the Near Islands, recorded by Birman (1958) and Larkins (1964); to the northern Gulf of Alaska at 58°32'N, 148°13'W (UAM 3271, two specimens over 25 cm TL collected in 1979); and to the eastern Gulf of Alaska at 54°06'N, 139°23'W (LeBrasseur 1964).

Size: Hubbs and Wisner (1980) give a maximum size of 40 cm SL in two places (pages 522 and 529), but 35 cm SL in another place (page 523). Taking the more frequently given measurement and estimating standard length at about 90% of total length from illustrations and UAM 3271 gives a total length of roughly 44 cm.

Order Stephanoberyciformes
Stephanoberyciforms

All the remaining orders of fishes in this guide are classified in the series Percomorpha. Most fishes in this taxon have thoracic or jugular pelvic fins, with the pelvic girdle directly or ligamentously attached to the cleithrum or coracoid of the pectoral girdle; a ventrally displaced anterior pelvic process; pectoral fins inserted high on the sides of the body; and pelvic fins with 1 spine in addition to the soft rays.

The order Stephanoberyciformes contains marine fishes in nine families with 86 species. Three families are represented in Alaska, in deep water: Melamphaidae, Barbourisiidae, and Cetomimidae. Stephanoberyciforms typically have a roundish body, single dorsal fin placed well back on the body, toothless palate, and exceptionally thin skull bones. They have a uniquely modified extrascapular and lack an orbitosphenoid. Weak dorsal spines are present in some species, and a few lack pelvic fins.

Many problems concerning interrelationships of percomorphs remain to be resolved, so opinions on their classification differ. Nelson (1994) took a conservative approach and classified the Stephanoberyciformes, Beryciformes, and Zeiformes in the series Percomorpha, while acknowledging that Johnson and Patterson (1993) challenged the monophyly of the resulting taxon. Johnson (1993) reviewed progress in studies of percomorph phylogeny, and Parenti and Song (1996) reviewed relationships within the superorder Acanthopterygii (including the series Percomorpha and Atherinomorpha) and implications of new information from comparative neuroanatomy. As well, different theories exist on the relationships of the Stephanoberyciformes and Beryciformes. Nelson (1994) summarized recent arguments.

Family Melamphaidae
Bigscales

Fishes of the family Melamphaidae, commonly called bigscales or ridgeheads, are small, dark brown or black deepsea fishes with large, cycloid, deciduous scales and ridged, cavernous heads. Bigscales are found in all oceans except the Arctic and the Mediterranean Sea. The family includes five genera with 33 species. Three species, each in a different genus, have been reported off the coast of Alaska, although the presence of one of them in the region has not been confirmed.

Adult bigscales are mesopelagic and bathypelagic while the juveniles are found at shallower depths. As well, bigscales tend to occur at lesser depths in the northern than in the southern portions of their distribution. For example, in the subarctic region the upper limit for *Melamphaes lugubris* adults and young adults is 200–250 m, and for juveniles is 50–75 m; while in the south they are deeper, below 400–500 m and 200–300 m, respectively (Ebeling 1962).

Bigscales have moderately compressed, oblong to fusiform bodies and abruptly angular or rounded anterodorsal profiles; heads highly sculptured with ridges and crests; blunt snouts; and large mouths. The sensory canals of the head are massive, making caverns in the superficial bones, and are not covered by bone, as in typical percomorphs, but only by epidermis stretched between paper-thin bony partitions. The frontal ridges (one on each of the paired frontals), a spine between the nostrils in front of the eyes, and condition (with or without serrations and spines) of the preopercular margin, particularly around the angle, provide some of the most important characters for differentiating bigscale species. The accompanying diagram of the head region in front of the opercle shows these features, using *Poromitra* sp. as an example. Bigscales have a single dorsal fin with 1–3 weak spines

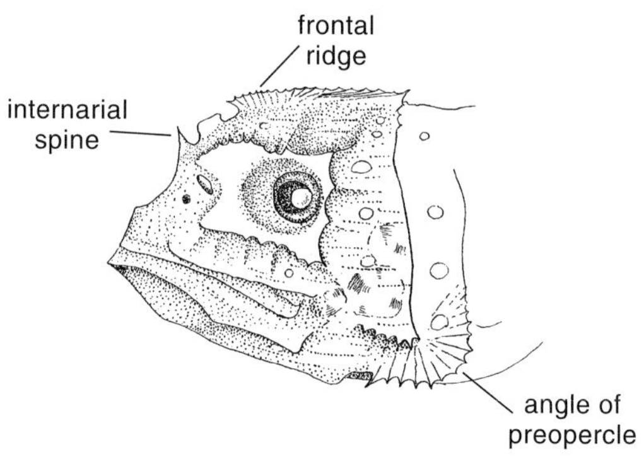

Some features that differ among bigscales
(After Ebeling 1962.)

and about 9–18 soft rays; a shorter anal fin with 1 or 2 spines and about 7–11 soft rays, positioned posterior to a vertical through mid-base of the dorsal fin or slightly behind the dorsal fin; pelvic fins below or slightly posterior to the pectoral fins, with 1 spine and 6–8 soft rays; and caudal fin with 3 or 4 small dorsal and ventral procurrent spines. Bigscales frequently and naturally lose some of their scales and replace them, but most are rubbed off during capture and scale counts must be done from the scale pockets. Numerous parallel embossed lines decorate most of the head epidermis and are supplied with nerve endings from branches from the superficial nerves of the head. Cephalic sensory canal pores occur singly or in groups of 2–4. The lateral line is rudimentary, reduced to 1 or 2 pored scales behind the dorsal edge of the operculum. The jaw teeth are tiny and pointed, arranged in single rows or bands. The branchiostegal rays number 7 or 8, and the vertebrae 23–31. Adults of most bigscale species reach maximum lengths of 10–15 cm (4–6 inches).

The presence of highsnout bigscale, *Melamphaes lugubris,* and crested bigscale, *Poromitra crassiceps,* in Alaska is well documented, with numerous records of each from throughout the Gulf of Alaska, around the Aleutian Islands, and into the Bering Sea to 55–56°N. Occurrence of longjaw bigscale, *Scopeloberyx robustus,* in Alaska, reported by Wilimovsky (1954, 1958) and Quast and Hall (1972) under the name *S. nycterinus,* has not been verified.

The family Melamphaidae was most recently revised, with emphasis on northwestern Atlantic species, by Ebeling and Weed (1973). Earlier, Ebeling (1962) revised the genus *Melamphaes* worldwide.

Key to the Melamphaidae of Alaska

1		Frontal ridges crestlike, with serrated margins; conspicuous spine between nostrils; ventral margin, angle, and most of posterior margin of preopercle serrate	*Poromitra crassiceps,* page 318
1		Frontal ridges not crestlike, or crestlike but with margins more or less smooth (damage may cause edges to be ragged); spine between nostrils absent or inconspicuous; margin of preopercle smooth, no spines around angle	(2)
2	(1)	Total dorsal fin spines and rays 17 or more	*Melamphaes lugubris,* page 319
2		Total dorsal fin spines and rays 15 or fewer	*Scopeloberyx robustus,* page 320 (not confirmed from Alaska)

Poromitra crassiceps (Günther, 1878) **crested bigscale**

Southern Bering Sea and Gulf of Alaska to Chile and to Japan; nearly cosmopolitan, definitely excluded only from Arctic Ocean and Mediterranean Sea.

Adults at depths of 600–3,400 m, juveniles found more shallowly; mesopelagic and bathpelagic.

D III,11–15; A I,8–12; Pec 13–15; Pel I,7–8; Br 8; Ls 29–37; GR 8–12 + 18–24 (27–36); Vert 26–29.

- Snout moderately blunt, mouth oblique.
- **Frontal ridges crestlike, margins serrate**; **internarial spine conspicuous**; maxilla extending to below posterior edge of eye or past eye; **numerous small spines around angle of preopercle**.
- Anal fin origin below 5th to 8th ray from posterior end of dorsal fin.
- Head pores large or moderate in size, usually single (seldom in groups).
- Teeth in upper and lower jaws in 1 row.
- Length to 180 mm SL.

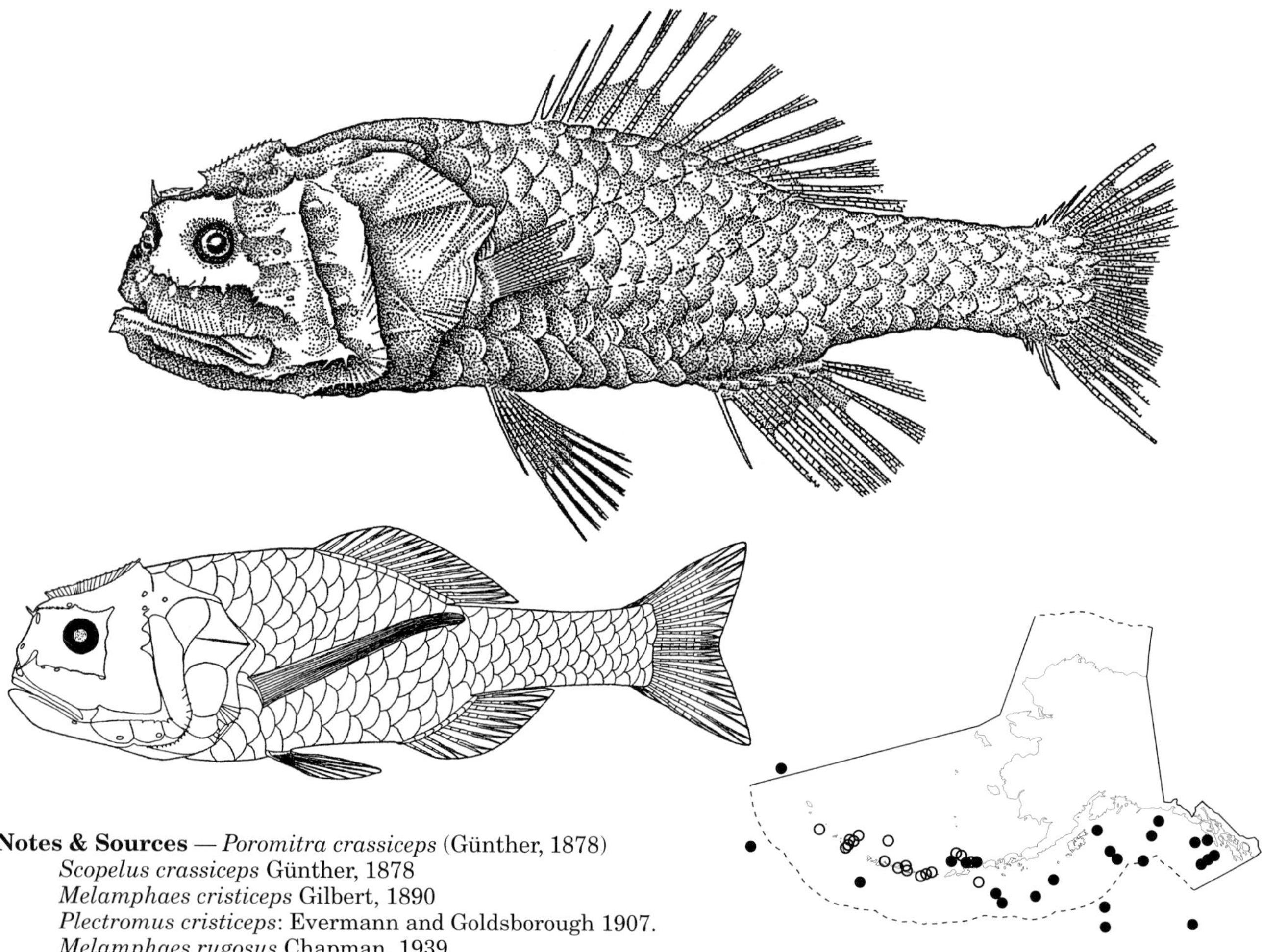

Notes & Sources — *Poromitra crassiceps* (Günther, 1878)
Scopelus crassiceps Günther, 1878
Melamphaes cristiceps Gilbert, 1890
Plectromus cristiceps: Evermann and Goldsborough 1907.
Melamphaes rugosus Chapman, 1939
Poromitra cristiceps: Fujii (in Masuda et al. 1984) considered *P. cristiceps* to be a species distinct from *P. crassiceps*.

Description: Chapman 1939:535–537; Ebeling and Weed 1973:440–444; Ebeling 1975:314 (key); Parin and Ebeling 1980:tables 1–3; Fujii in Masuda et al. 1984:110.

Figures: Upper: Ebeling and Weed 1973, fig. 21; 116 mm SL. Lower: Chapman 1939, fig. 69; holotype of *Melamphaes rugosus*, 94 mm SL, eastern Gulf of Alaska.

Range: Recorded from eastern Gulf of Alaska off Cape Edgecumbe by Evermann and Goldsborough (1907), and at 55°32'N, 136°25'W by Chapman (1939). Indicated for the Bering Sea by Wilimovsky (1954, 1958) and eastern Aleutian Islands by Quast and Hall (1972) in general statements. Willis et al. (1988, fig. 31) found 40 records of *P. crassiceps* in 761 North Pacific midwater tows, with some in the Gulf of Alaska and Pacific Ocean south of the Aleutian Islands, as well as one record in the southern Bering Sea. The NMFS survey database contains records (circles on above map) from the southern Bering Sea and Aleutian Islands west nearly to Attu Island (D. W. Kessler, pers. comm., 20 Jun. 1994). Specimens from the Bering Sea in permanent collections include RBCM 980-596, 54°22'N, 165°57'W, a specimen taken from the stomach of a cod (A. E. Peden, pers. comm., 11 Jan. 1995); and UW 25599, 54°31'N, 167°04'W, two specimens collected in 1979 (UW online catalog). Reported to be common in vicinity of the Commander Islands (Fedorov and Sheiko 2001).

Size: Parin and Ebeling 1980: table 3.

Melamphaes lugubris Gilbert, 1890 **highsnout bigscale**

Subarctic North Pacific including Bering Sea from about 56°N to northern Baja California and to Japan. Adults at depths of 150–1,500 m, juveniles found more shallowly; mesopelagic and bathypelagic.

D III,14–16; A I,7–9; Pec 15–17; Pel I,6–7; Br 8; Ls 26–35; GR 5–6 + 15–17 (19–23); Vert 28–31.

- Snout extremely blunt, mouth strongly oblique.
- **Frontal ridges low, not serrate; internarial spine not conspicuous**; maxilla barely reaching below rear edge of eye; **no spines on margin of preopercle**, angle sometimes slightly produced.
- **Total dorsal fin spines and rays 17 or more**; anal fin origin below last to 3rd from last dorsal fin ray or slightly behind last dorsal ray.
- Eight scales (usually missing) covering opercle, interopercle, and subopercle.
- Head pores small to moderate in size, some in groups of 2 or 3.
- Teeth in jaws in bands of 2–6 irregular rows.
- Length to 89 mm SL.

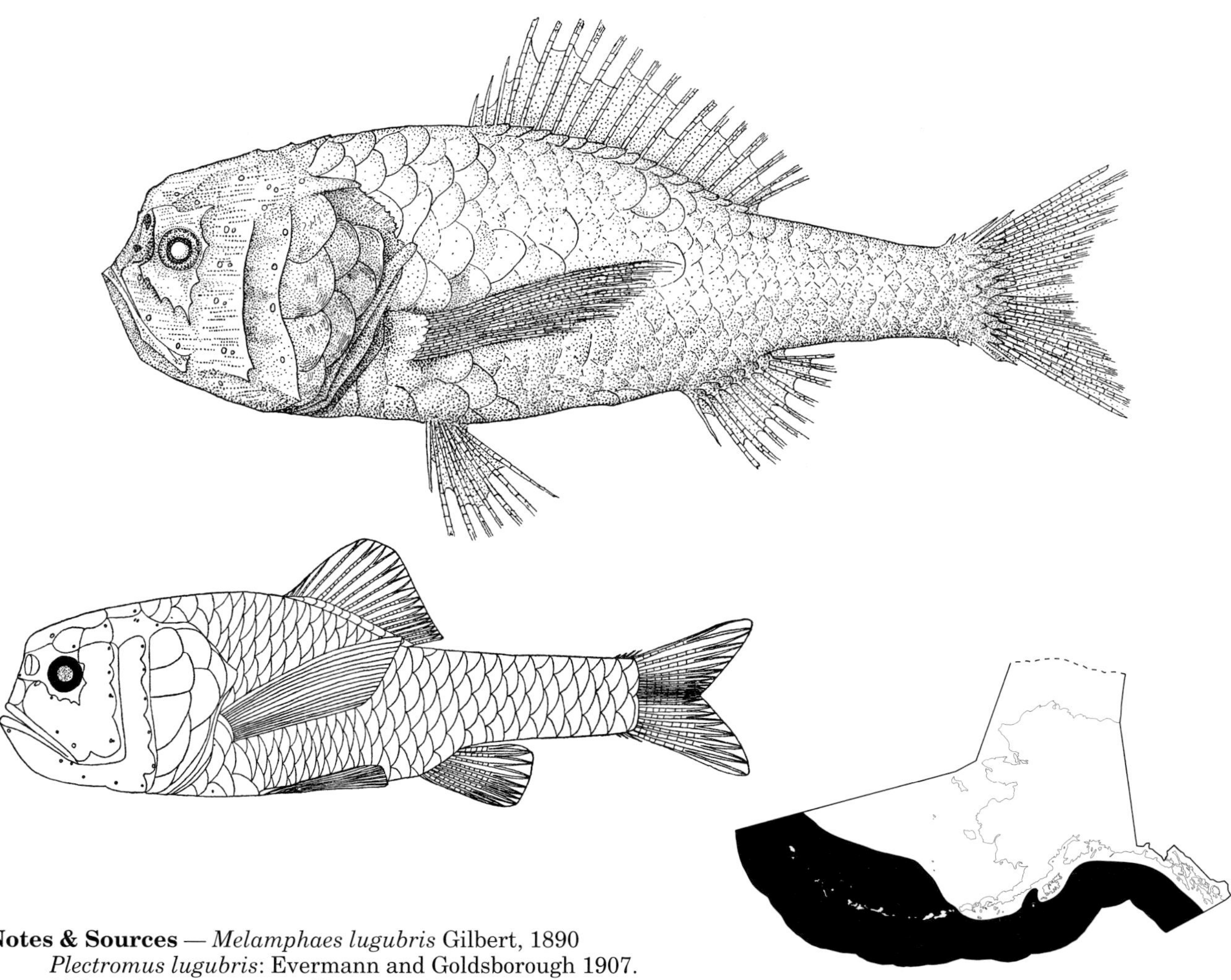

Notes & Sources — *Melamphaes lugubris* Gilbert, 1890
Plectromus lugubris: Evermann and Goldsborough 1907.
Melamphaes cavernosus Chapman, 1939

Description: Chapman 1939:533–534; Ebeling 1962:36–43; Fujii in Masuda et al. 1984:111. Although Gilbert (1890) reported 14 pectoral rays for the holotype, Ebeling (1962) counted 16. A high number (usually 16, rarely 15 or 17) distinguishes *M. lugubris* from its congeners.

Figures: Upper: Ebeling 1962, fig. 18; 87.5 mm SL, Pacific Ocean west of Washington. Lower: Chapman 1939, fig. 68; holotype of *M. lugubris,* 70 mm SL, western Gulf of Alaska.

Range: Early Alaskan records include those of Gilbert (1896) from north of Unalaska Island and Chapman (1939) from eastern and western Gulf of Alaska. Ebeling (1962) provided locality data for several records from the Pacific south of the Aleutian Islands, including Attu Island, throughout the Gulf of Alaska, and southern Bering Sea. Willis et al. (1988, fig. 32) found records of 69 occurrences in 761 midwater tows in the North Pacific; many were from Alaska. Parin and Kotlyar (1998) reported that records of *M. nycterinus* from the Pacific off eastern Kamchatka and the Kuril Islands reported by Rass (1954) and included by Ebeling and Weed (1973) in the synonymy of *S. robustus* actually refer to *M. lugubris.* Reported by Fedorov and Sheiko (2001) to be common in the vicinity of the Commander Islands .

Size: Largest of 24 adults measured by Ebeling (1962).

Scopeloberyx robustus (Günther, 1887) **longjaw bigscale**

Gulf of Alaska reports doubtful; subarctic North Pacific to California and Japan; Sea of Okhotsk; nearly cosmopolitan, definitely excluded only from Arctic Ocean and Mediterranean Sea.

Adults at depths of 500–3,384 m. juveniles found more shallowly; mesopelagic and bathypelagic.

D II–III,9–13; A I,7–9; Pec 11–14; Pel I,6–8; Br 8; Ls 28–33; GR 4–7 + 14–19 (19–24); Vert 23–28.

- Snout moderately elongate, mouth oblique.
- **Frontal ridges present, but margins smooth**; **internarial spine not conspicuous**; maxilla extending well beyond eye; **no spines on margin of preopercle**.
- **Total dorsal fin spines and rays 15 or fewer**; anal fin origin below last to 3rd from last dorsal fin ray.
- Head pores large or moderate in size, usually single.
- Teeth in upper and lower jaws in 2–4 rows at widest parts.
- Length to 100 mm SL.

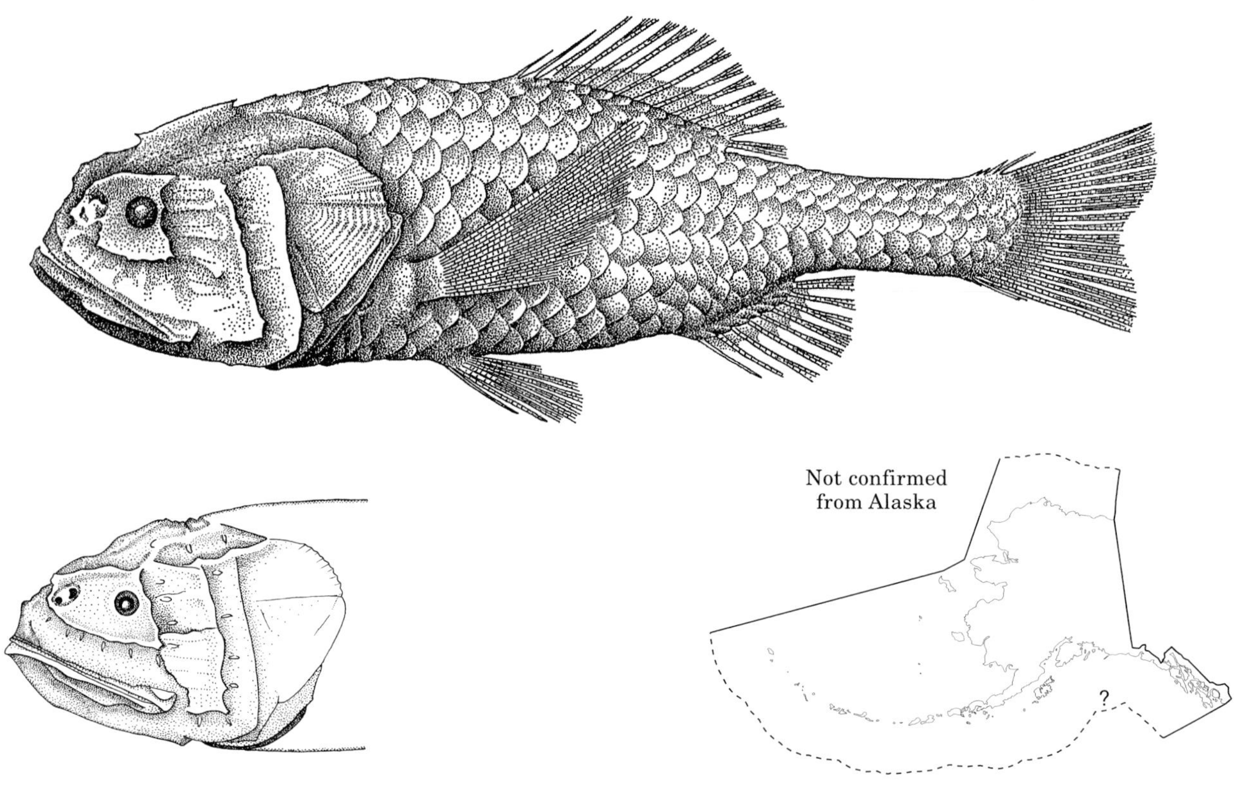

Notes & Sources — *Scopeloberyx robustus* (Günther, 1887)
Melamphaes robustus Günther, 1887
Plectromus robustus: Goode and Bean 1896.
Melamphaes nycterinus Gilbert, 1915
Scopeloberyx nycterinus: Ebeling 1962.
Maul (in Whitehead et al. 1986:763) placed *M. nycterinus* Gilbert in the synonymy of *S. robustus* (Günther).

Description: Goode and Bean 1896:180; Ebeling and Weed 1973:446–449; Fujii in Masuda et al. 1984:110; Parin and Kotlyar 1998.

Figures: Full lateral view: Ebeling and Weed 1973, fig. 22; holotype, 85 mm SL, mid-Atlantic. Head: Ebeling 1962, fig. 8A; *Scopeloberyx* sp. (most of skin removed).

Range: Range was reported, as *S. nycterinus,* to the Gulf of Alaska by Wilimovsky (1954, 1958) and Quast and Hall (1972) in general statements, without specific localities or other data. Willis et al. (1988) reported *S. robustus* to occur rarely in the North Pacific, representing less than 0.1% of individuals taken in midwater tows in subarctic waters (their Alaska Gyre and Western Subarctic zoogeographical regions); *S. robustus* records were not depicted on a map, and they could all be from south of the 200-mile limit. We did not find specimens from Alaska in museum collections. Not recorded from British Columbia. Parin and Kotlyar (1998) described the first records for the Sea of Okhotsk. They stated that the indication of occurrence of *M. nycterinus* in the Bering Sea by Rass (1954) actually pertains to *M. lugubris,* and should not have been included by Ebeling and Weed (1973) in the synonymy of *S. robustus.*

Size: Largest of 163 young adults examined by Ebeling and Weed (1973).

Family Barbourisiidae
Velvet whalefishes

Three families of whalefishes are included in the superfamily Cetomimoidea of the order Stephanoberyciformes: Barbourisiidae, Cetomimidae, and Rondeletiidae. The whalefishes all have the same basic shape, with huge mouths, large heads, and tapering bodies. The three families contain about 11 genera and 38 species, with most of them in the Cetomimidae. The whalefish families used to be classified by themselves in their own taxon, as a suborder (Cetomimoidei) in Beryciformes or as an order (Cetomimiformes). Recent classifications (e.g., Nelson 1994) include two other, nonwhalefish families in the superfamily Cetomimoidea, making a total of five families with 18 genera and about 47 species. They are mostly rare, deepsea fishes. A unifying feature of the five-family taxon is complete absence of fin spines. Nelson (1984, 1994) and Moore (1993) recounted the taxonomic history and reviewed the families in this group.

Whalefishes, in addition to their large mouths, whale-shaped bodies, and lack of fin spines, have loose skin and highly distensible stomachs. Other features include: dorsal and anal fins far back on the body and opposite one another; pelvic fins abdominal or absent; cephalic sensory canals covered by skin and opening through large pores; body lateral line composed of enormous hollow tubes; no swim bladder; no orbitosphenoid; and supramaxilla absent or reduced. Most whalefishes are black or dark brown suffused with orange or red. Whalefishes, despite their name, are fairly small fishes, attaining sizes to about 39 cm TL (15.3 inches).

Whalefishes generally occur worldwide in tropical and temperate seas. Neither of the two species of Rondeletiidae, the redmouth whalefishes, has been found off the coast of Alaska (although one occurs farther south in the Pacific, from California to Japan), but one species each of the Barbourisiidae, or velvet whalefishes, and the Cetomimidae, or flabby whalefishes, have been collected off the Aleutian Islands. The Barbourisiidae is sometimes called the red whalefish family (e.g., Nelson 1984, 1994), for the color of the one known species, *Barbourisia rufa.* Calling the family the velvet whalefish family (e.g., Eschmeyer and Herald 1983) calls attention to a diagnostic character of the skin. A different color than red might be more likely in a newly discovered species than a major difference in the character of the skin.

The red whalefish, currently the sole known member of the family Barbourisiidae, has tough skin densely covered with fine spinules which give it a furry feeling. The skin is uniformly bright orange-red, not brownish black suffused with red like some other whalefishes, and lacks the melanophores that make other whalefishes appear black or dark brown (Herring 1976). The pectoral fins are high on the body, and pelvic fins are present (and abdominal). The red whalefish has 4 gill arches, large gill slits, and slender, fairly long gill rakers. Pleural ribs and pyloric caeca are present.

The presence of pelvic fins, furry character of the skin, and well-developed, slender gill rakers readily distinguish the Barbourisiidae from the closely related Cetomimidae, despite the similarity in general form.

Velvet whalefishes are rare but widely distributed in the world's oceans. Most records are from low latitudes. In the Atlantic Ocean, one specimen was caught in the Labrador Sea off the Newfoundland shelf (at 56°20'N; Karrer 1976). Another individual was caught somewhere off Greenland (Amaoka in Okamura et al. 1995). (The precise locality for the Greenland specimen was not reported.) This guide reports the first records of *B. rufa* from Alaska, comprising one specimen taken north and one south of the central Aleutian Islands in 1979 and 1982; both specimens are in the University of Washington College of Fisheries collection. The velvet whalefish family was not included on Quast and Hall's (1972) list of Alaskan fishes, because at that time *B. rufa* was not known to occur farther north in the Pacific Ocean than Japan or California.

Barbourisia rufa Parr, 1945 **red whalefish**

Southeastern Bering Sea north of Amlia Island and Pacific Ocean south of Amukta Pass, Aleutian Islands; North Pacific off Washington, California, Hawaiian Islands, and Japan, and on Emperor Seamounts; worldwide at low latitudes, recorded as far north as Greenland.

Near bottom or in midwater over continental slopes and seamounts at depths of 120–2,000 m; benthopelagic and pelagic.

D 20–23; A 14–18; Pec 12–14; Pel 6; Br 7–8; LLp 25–32; GR 4–6 + 13–16 (19–21); PC 9–14; Vert 40–44.

- Body and fins uniformly bright red.
- Mouth large, maxilla extending way past eye; lower jaw projecting beyond upper.
- Pectoral and pelvic fins small but well developed.
- Skin tough, loose, densely covered with minute spinules, making surface velvety to the touch.
- Lateral line opening through continuous row of large pored scales.
- Teeth on jaws in broad villiform bands extending the whole length of each jaw; vomerine teeth present as round patch of villiform teeth, or absent; palatine teeth absent.
- Length to 390 mm TL.

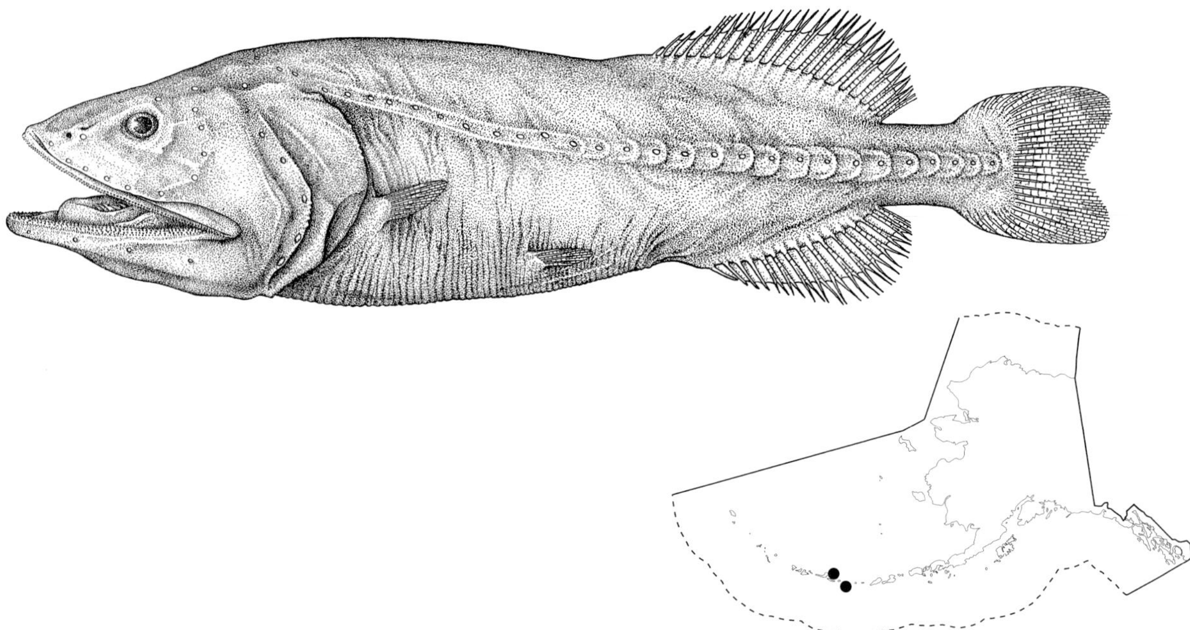

Notes & Sources — *Barbourisia rufa* Parr, 1945

Description: Parr 1945, 1946b; Rofen 1959:259; Karrer 1976: 376; Amaoka in Masuda et al. 1984:115; Okamura in Okamura et al. 1985:440, 654; Amaoka in Okamura et al. 1995:148; Kotlyar 1995.

Figure: Parr 1945, pl. 1; holotype, 180 mm SL, Gulf of Mexico.

Range: Two specimens from the vicinity of the central Aleutian Islands are the first records from Alaska: UW 21483 (250 mm SL), taken north of Amlia Island at 52°31'N, 173°11'W, depth 555 m, on 18 Apr. 1979; and UW 21010 (312 mm SL, 363 mm TL), taken just south of Amukta Pass at 52°06'N, 171°52'W, depth 176 m, on 10 Dec. 1982. UW 29669 contains a specimen (320 mm SL) taken off the Washington coast, 47°40'N, 125°30'W, depth 1,006–1,097 m, by otter trawl on 5 Mar. 1995; identified by B. K. Urbain and J. A. Lopez. Previously published records of *Barbourisia rufa* in the Pacific Ocean extended only as far north as about 45°N (Paxton and Bray in Smith and Heemstra 1986, Kotlyar 1995). Fitch (1979) reported the first specimen taken off California, which was found on a freezer room floor, and Lea (1987) recorded the second California specimen, caught by a trawler fishing at a depth of 988 m. The net haul in which the second California specimen was taken also included Dover sole, *Microstomus pacificus*; sablefish, *Anoplopoma fimbria*; and shortspine thornyhead, *Sebastolobus alascanus*. Often taken high in the water column; e.g., the holotype was taken in the Gulf of Mexico at depths of 750–1,000 m over a bottom depth of 1,637 m, and the second known specimen was taken off Madagascar at an estimated fishing depth of 450–700 m over bottom depths of 1,070–1,360 m. Kotlyar (1995) gave a list of records and depths, and suggested that lifestyle is basically benthopelagic with feeding migrations into midwater. The statement of range in Matarese et al. (1989:256) giving the Arctic Ocean as the northern limit for *B. rufa* lacks documentation. The northernmost record at that time, which was reported by Karrer (1976), was a 310-mm specimen taken in 1976 off the continental shelf in the Labrador Sea at 56°20'N, 57°30'W, depth 800–850 m. Recently, Amaoka (in Okamura et al. 1995) described a 341-mm-SL specimen taken at a depth of 1,139 m off Greenland, but coordinates or other catch locality data were not reported.

Size: Scott and Scott (1988): specimen caught east of Newfoundland in 1982 at 50°49'N, 49°40'W, depth 1,250 m.

Family Cetomimidae
Flabby whalefishes

With about nine genera and 35 species the family Cetomimidae, or flabby whalefishes, is the largest family of whalefishes. It was also the most poorly known, until Paxton (1989) studied available specimens (more than 500), summarized knowledge of the family at the genus level, and described new genera and species. Many of the 35 or so species indicated by Paxton's analysis to be distinct remain to be described in future papers.

Cetomimid whalefishes are second only to the dreamers (Oneirodidae) in being the most species-rich family in the bathypelagic zone, and may be the most abundant family below 1,800 m. They are distributed in all oceans, except they are absent from the Mediterranean Sea. Like the whipnoses (Gigantactinidae), several of the cetomimids have cosmopolitan distributions. Paxton (1989) reported their overall known latitudinal distribution to be between 52°N and 72°S.

A specimen of *Gyrinomimus* collected in 1990 from the Bering Sea north of Dutch Harbor provides the second record of the genus from Alaska. Paxton (pers. comm., 3 Sep. 1999) examined the specimen and identified it as *Gyrinomimus* sp. nov. B2, one of the several new species he plans to describe. He reported that he has more than 20 specimens of this species from the northeastern and northwestern Pacific, making it the most common cetomimid in the North Pacific. Two specimens from the Bering Sea previously identified as *Cetomimus* sp. by Fedorov (1973a) also represent Paxton's undescribed common North Pacific species of *Gyrinomimus* (Fedorov and Parin 1998). One of those specimens was caught in Alaska in 1971 very near the collection locality of the 1990 specimen, and is the first record from Alaska; the other was collected in 1955 from Russian waters of the western Bering Sea.

No other cetomimid genera are known to occur in the Bering Sea. Authors who listed *Cetomimus* from the region evidently did so on the basis of the specimens (Fedorov 1973a) which have recently been referred to *Gyrinomimus.* On the other hand, more than one species of *Gyrinomimus* inhabits the subarctic and temperate North Pacific (Paxton 1989), so it is possible that more than one species occurs in Alaskan waters.

Because the new species have not been formally described, this guide can include only a generic account for *Gyrinomimus.* The illustrations of *G. bruuni* and Paxton's (1989) *Gyrinomimus* sp. nov. C are included as examples of the genus. No illustrations of *Gyrinomimus* sp. nov. B2 are available at this time. The list of morphological features and the comparisons under Notes & Sources on the next page should allow differentiation of *Gyrinomimus* specimens from other cetomimids, including the one other relatively common genus in the North Pacific, *Cetomimus.*

Most captures of cetomimids are from depths below 1,000 m. Parin and Fedorov (1998) reported depths of 2,500–3,400 m for *Gyrinomimus* taken in the Sea of Okhotsk. A few species are mesopelagic as juveniles and small adults, and some species are probably benthopelagic part of the time. Although the vast majority of individuals have been taken in midwater trawls fishing well off the bottom, a few have been taken in trawls fishing within 100 m of the bottom at 1,200–2,400 m and in a bottom trap at 2,400 m (Paxton 1989). The depth of 240 m or less for the recent Alaskan record (an adult measuring 297 mm SL) is unusually shallow.

Cetomimid whalefishes have soft, flabby, smooth skin. Their color is brownish black mixed with reddish orange. Other cetomimid features include: eyes tiny or rudimentary; dorsal and anal fin rays 11–37; pelvic fins absent; gill arches usually 3, in some species 4; gill rakers club-shaped or as toothed knobs, tooth plates, or individual teeth; pleural ribs absent; pyloric caeca absent; and vertebrae 38–59. The body lateral line is set deeply in the skin and pierced by large pores. The lateral line scales are in the bottom of the canal, with a neuromast on top of each scale and the pores located over the spaces between scales.

Cavernous tissue is present around the anus and sometimes the fin bases and other areas in cetomimids, and some species have flaps of skin hanging over the base of the anal fin. The functions of the cavernous tissue and anal lappets are unknown. Harry (1952) believed the cavernous tissue to be luminous, but no cetomimid has been captured alive to confirm this idea, and histological studies have not provided an answer. The anal lappets differ among species and are sometimes associated with other mysterious features, like networks of vessels or curtainlike folds of the anal fin membrane. They are fragile and easily torn off during capture.

Gyrinomimus, with a maximum known length of 39 cm (15 inches), is the largest of the flabby whalefishes. Other genera reach 13–25 cm (5–10 inches). Males were recently found for the first time, and are only 30–50 mm (1–2 inches) long (Paxton 1990).

Gyrinomimus sp.

Southern Bering Sea; Sea of Okhotsk; Pacific, Atlantic, and Indian oceans; worldwide at low latitudes.
At depths of 240–3,400 m; center of vertical distribution below 1,000 m; bathypelagic.

D 14–21; A 14–20; Pec 18–23; Pel 0; Br 6; LLp 12–23; GR 0 (bony plates); PC 0; Vert 47–59.

- Brownish black mixed with reddish orange.
- Mouth large, maxilla extending well beyond eye, nearly to opercular margin; eye tiny.
- Cavernous tissue around anus and often along dorsal and anal fin bases and above pectoral fins.
- Skin loose and smooth, lacking scales or spinules.
- Lateral line scales narrowly rectangular or strap-like and curved.
- **Jaw and palatine teeth elongate, and closely set in distinct longitudinal rows; vomerine tooth patch rectangular or laterally elongate and flat.**
- Free gill arches 3; gill rakers as solid, flat tooth plates covering most of lateral face of each arch.
- Length to 390 mm TL.

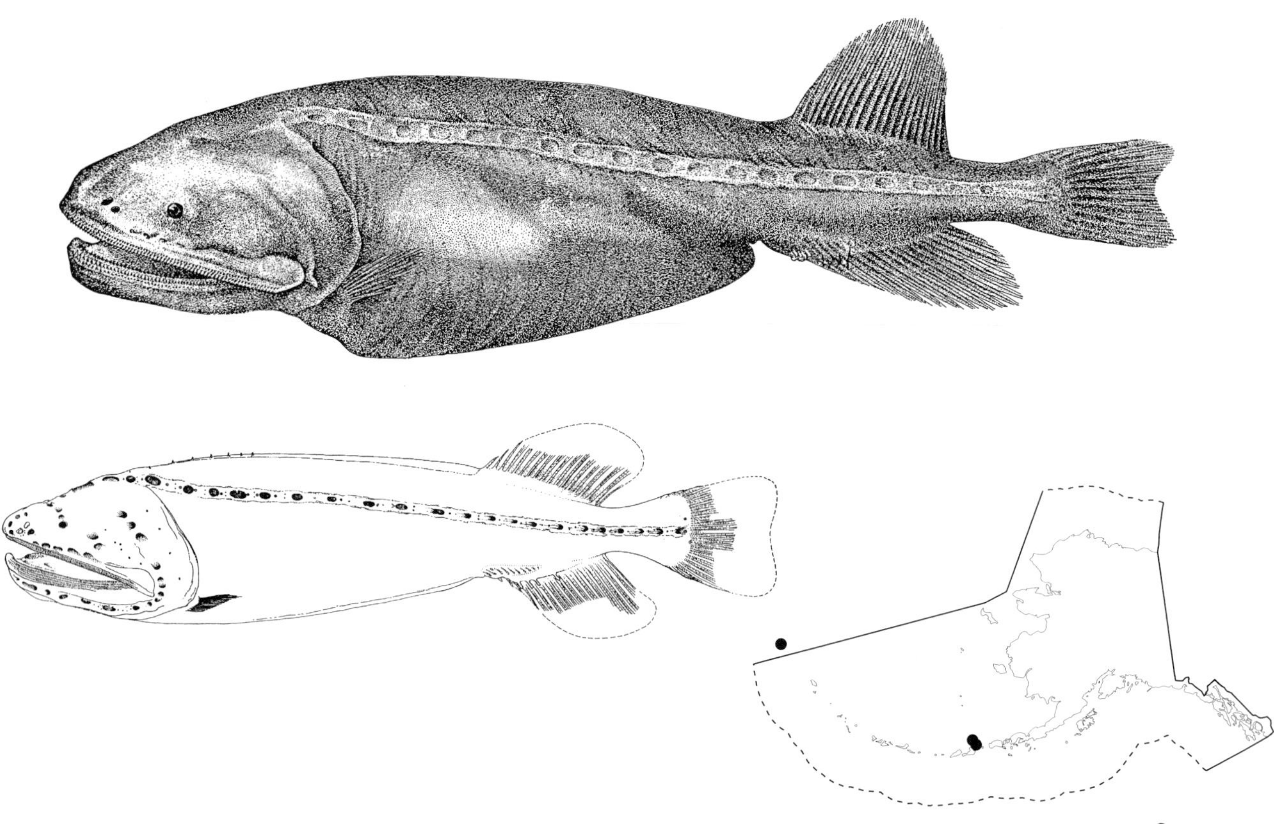

Notes & Sources — *Gyrinomimus* sp.

The characters in bold type (above) distinguish *Gyrinomimus* from the most similar genus, *Cetomimus*. In *Cetomimus* the jaw and palatine teeth are short, and set in indistinct diagonal rows, and the vomerine tooth patch is round or elliptical and dome-shaped. *Cetostoma* differs from all other cetomimid genera in having higher numbers of dorsal (29–37) and anal (26–34) fin rays, longitudinal skin ridges on the belly, and posterior portion of the anal fin membrane in curtainlike folds.

Description: Paxton 1989:175–177.

Figures: Upper: Rofen 1959, pl. 1, fig. 2; *G. bruuni,* stomach distended with food. Lower: Paxton 1989, fig. 26; *Gyrinomimus* sp. C, schematic showing head pores.

Range: A specimen collected from the Bering Sea north of Dutch Harbor is the second record of *Gyrinomimus* from Alaska: UW 21484 (297 mm SL), caught by bottom trawl at 54°09'N, 166°20'W, depth 240 m, on 23 Mar. 1990, and recently identified by Paxton (pers. comm., 3 Sep. 1999) as an undescribed species, *Gyrinomimus* sp. nov. B2. Other specimens, evidently of the same species, are known from the Bering Sea: ZIN 40548, collected in 1971 at 54°35'N, 166°51'W, not far from where the UW specimen was collected in 1990; and ZIN 47892, collected in 1955 in Russian waters of the Bering Sea at 53°48'N, 166°54'E. They originally were identified by Fedorov (1973a) as *Cetomimus* sp., but recently were referred by Paxton to *Gyrinomimus* (Balanov and Il'insky 1992; Fedorov and Parin 1998; B. A. Sheiko, pers. comm., 15 Mar. 2000). A specimen of *Gyrinomimus* taken at 50°N, 145°W could belong to the same species (Peden et al. 1985). Paxton (pers. comm., 3 Sep. 1999) also identified a juvenile (UW 21463, 90.5 mm SL) caught off Oregon at 44°48'N, 130°19'W in a sediment trap set at 100 m above bottom in water 2,125 m deep, in July 1990, as *Gyrinomimus* sp. nov. B2. He reported that this species has been collected as far south in the North Pacific Ocean as 39°N, and is the most common cetomimid in the North Pacific.

ORDER BERYCIFORMES
Beryciforms

The order Beryciformes follows the order Stephanoberyciformes as one of two successive sister-groups of higher acanthopterygians. That is, both groups are close to representing the ancestral stock from which more advanced fishes evolved, but have morphological features reflecting independent evolution away from the ancestral line. Johnson and Patterson (1993) described characters allying the beryciforms with higher acanthopterygians and separating them from the stephanoberyciforms. Accordingly, Nelson (1994) classified seven families comprising 28 genera and 123 species in the order Beryciformes.

The beryciforms are marine species. Some of them inhabit shallow tropical waters and some are deepsea fishes with more cosmopolitan distributions. None of the species has been discovered in Alaska, but one, a member of the Anoplogastridae, has been collected from the North Pacific Ocean west of British Columbia.

Beryciform fishes have short, deep, compressed bodies and, typically, spines in one or more fins. Other diagnostic features include: orbitosphenoid present; mesocoracoid absent; pelvic fins thoracic or subthoracic, usually with more than 5 pelvic fin rays; caudal fin with 18 or 19 principal rays and a few procurrent rays dorsally and ventrally; maxillae more or less protrusible and usually partially included in the gape of the mouth; and cycloid or ctenoid scales. All known beryciforms have a distinctive feature of the supraorbital sensory canal called Jakubowski's organ, involving modifications of the nasal and lachrymal bones and innervation of neuromasts by the buccal nerve rather than by the supraorbital nerve. Beryciforms lack a fourth pharyngobranchial cartilage, a structure which is present in most stephanoberyciforms.

FAMILY ANOPLOGASTRIDAE
Fangtooths

Fangtooths, also called ogrefishes, are deepsea fishes with large heads and mouths, and huge fangs. The family comprises two species, both in the same genus. The longhorn fangtooth, *Anoplogaster cornuta,* has a worldwide distribution from temperate to tropical latitudes and is the species most likely to be found off the coast of Alaska. At the time of Quast and Hall's (1972) inventory of Alaskan fish species the nearest confirmed record of *A. cornuta* was a specimen taken off Tillamook Head, Oregon (Grinols 1966b). Since then, *A. cornuta* has been recorded farther north, to about 50°N in the Pacific off the coast of Vancouver Island, British Columbia (A. E. Peden in Anonymous 1997), and in the Sea of Okhotsk (Kotlyar 1986). It has been taken as far north as 64°26'N in the Atlantic Ocean (Karrer 1976).

Diagnostic morphological features of fangtooths include: body short, deep, compressed; head large, sculptured-looking, with crests and spines; mouth large and diagonal; teeth long and fanglike; eyes small, less than snout length; anal fin much shorter-based than dorsal fin; scales ctenoid and very small; lateral line an open groove only partly covered by scales; gill arches 4; pseudobranchs present; branchiostegal rays 8–9; swim bladder present; and vertebrae 25–28. Unlike most other beryciforms, fangtooths lack spines in the fins. The anteriormost rays of the dorsal, anal, and pelvic fins are not branched and are counted by some authors as spines, but they are not stiff or thickened. *Anoplogaster cornuta* individuals are known to reach a maximum size of about 16 cm (6.3 inches). Adults of the other species, *A. brachycera,* are unknown.

Early growth of fangtooths takes place in the epipelagic zone. They undergo a marked metamorphosis from juvenile to adult, which for a while resulted in classification of the juveniles and adults as different species. Among other changes that occur, the jaw teeth are depressible in juveniles but fixed in adults, and juveniles are silvery but adults are dark brown or black. One of the most obvious changes in *A. cornuta* is reduction in size of the temporal and preopercular spines. In *A. cornuta* juveniles these spines are very long, and the temporal spines give the species its common name, longhorn fangtooth. Juveniles of *A. brachycera* have short temporal and preopercular spines and are called shorthorn fangtooths.

Woods and Sonoda (1973) synthesized information available at the time of their study on *A. cornuta.* Kotlyar (1986) described the new species *A. brachycera,* and provided additional information on *A. cornuta* and characterization of the family. This guide follows Nelson (1984, 1994) and Eschmeyer (1998) in using the spelling Anoplogastridae, instead of the variant Anoplogasteridae.

Anoplogaster cornuta (Valenciennes, 1833) **longhorn fangtooth**

Eastern Pacific Ocean from southern British Columbia to northern Chile and Gulf of Panama; mid-Pacific; Sea of Okhotsk and western Pacific Ocean from Hokkaido almost to New Zealand; nearly worldwide.

Adults at depths of 75–4,992 m, juveniles as shallow as 2 m; mesopelagic to bathypelagic.

D 17–19; A 7–9; Pec 13–16; Pel 7; GR 16–23; PC 5–10; Vert 25–28.

- Adults dark brown to black.
- Body short and compressed, deep anteriorly; head large, depth noticeably greater than length; head strongly sculptured, with ridges, grooves, and spines; no suborbital shelf; opercular bones small.
- Mouth large, upper jaw almost as long as head.
- Scales small, ctenoid, not overlapping; each scale elevated on short, stout pedicel.
- Jaw teeth long, fanglike, widely spaced, in 3 pairs on upper jaw and 4 pairs on lower jaw.
- Length to 160 mm SL.

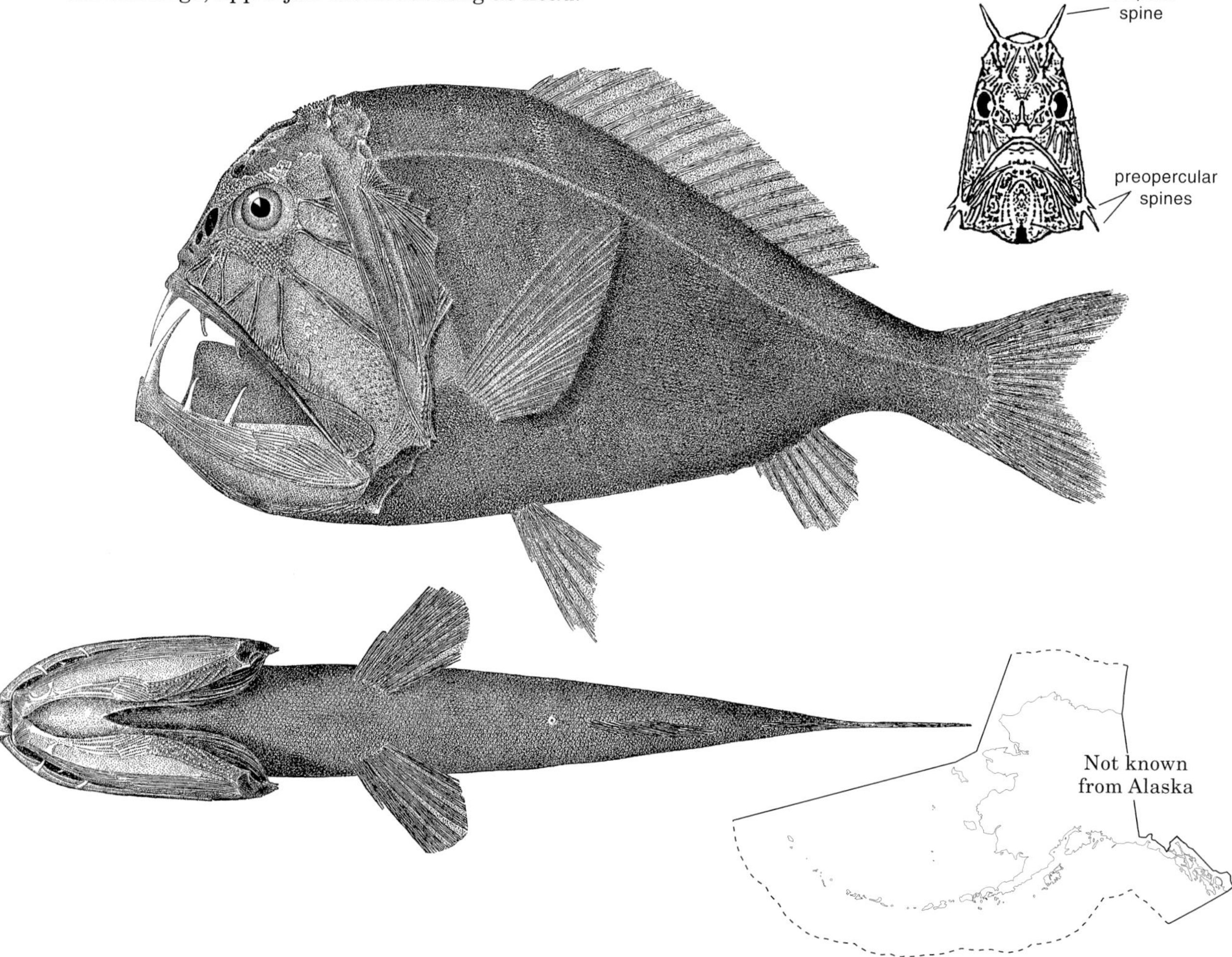

Notes & Sources — *Anoplogaster cornuta* (Valenciennes in Cuvier & Valenciennes, 1833)
Hoplostethus cornutus Valenciennes in Cuvier & Valenciennes, 1833
Caulolepis longidens Gill, 1883

Description: Woods and Sonoda 1973:386–394; Shimizu in Masuda et al. 1984:109; Kotlyar 1986.

Figures: Lateral and ventral: Goode and Bean 1896, pl. 55, fig. 204; 119 mm TL, Atlantic Ocean. Anterior: redrawn from Kotlyar 1986, fig. 2E; juvenile, 57 mm SL; shows temporal and preopercular spines, which in this size fish are already considerably reduced.

Range: Fitch and Lavenberg (1968) reported the range of *A. cornuta* to extend north to British Columbia, but did not cite documentation or specific localities. The first solid record from British Columbia is a specimen taken off the west coast of Vancouver Island and identified by A. E. Peden (Anonymous 1997). The specimen, about 13 cm long, was caught in a trawl net fishing for *Sebastolobus altivelis* at a depth range of 950–975 m. Previously the northernmost record in the eastern North Pacific was a specimen (UW 16745) collected at 45°55'N, 124°48'W, off Tillamook Head, Oregon, and reported on by Grinols (1966b). Kotlyar (1986) reported *A. cornuta* from the Sea of Okhotsk; the northernmost was from 50°02'N, 153°54'E. Shimizu (1978) reported on a specimen taken off Cape Erimo, Hokkaido, which was the first adult *A. cornuta* recorded from the western North Pacific. Northernmost record in Atlantic Ocean is 64°26'N, 57°18'W, a 126-mm-SL specimen reported by Karrer (1976).

Order Zeiformes
Zeiforms

Zeiforms are marine, primarily deepsea, fishes with representatives in the tropical and temperate areas of all the oceans. Young zeiforms are pelagic, while adults are typically taken near bottom. The order includes dories, boarfishes, oreos, and their allies, making a total of six families with about 20 genera and 39 species. The oreos, family Oreosomatidae, are represented off the coast of Alaska by one species.

Zeiforms generally have deep, compressed bodies, large eyes, and oblique mouths with protrusible jaws. Their fins have spines as well as rays, the spinous part of the dorsal fin is separated from the rayed portion by a notch, and the rays of the dorsal, anal, and pectoral fins are not branched. Other zeiform characters include: dorsal fin spines 5–10; anal fin spines 0–4; pelvic fins with 1 spine and 5–9 rays; orbitosphenoid absent; simple posttemporal fused to the skull; branchiostegal rays 5–8; swim bladder present; and vertebrae 21–46. Most zeiforms attain adult lengths of about 15–30 cm (6–12 inches).

The affinities of the zeiforms are not well understood. The classical view, retained by Nelson (1994), places them in a position as a preperciform percomorph. Among the possibilities presented by Johnson and Patterson (1993) is placement between their orders Stephanoberyciformes and Beryciformes. As currently defined, the order might not be a natural unit, with some families belonging in other taxa.

Family Oreosomatidae
Oreos

Oreos have an extra life history stage that is so unlike the juvenile and adults that a metamorphosis occurs between it and the juvenile stage. This stage is clearly postlarval in development, and is called the prejuvenile stage. Adult oreos are deepwater demersal fishes inhabiting the continental slope and seamounts, while prejuveniles and juveniles usually occur in offshore surface and midwaters. Oreos are found nearly worldwide, but most live in the Southern Hemisphere.

Oreos were classified with dories in the family Zeidae until Myers (1960) removed them to their own family. Myers named the new family after the genus *Oreosoma,* which was the first oreo genus described. The genus was named in 1829 by the French zoologist Georges Cuvier (1769–1832) from the Greek *oreos* ("mountain") and *soma* ("body"), after the "hills" (modified scales) he observed on a juvenile specimen. As currently understood, the family contains five genera and nine species. The oxeye oreo, *Allocyttus folletti,* is widespread in the North Pacific from California to Japan, and several specimens have been collected off Alaska from the Bering Sea and the Pacific Ocean south of the Aleutian Islands and Gulf of Alaska.

Adult oreos have deep, compressed bodies; upturned, protrusible mouths; large eyes; small, cycloid or ctenoid scales; both spines and rays in the dorsal, anal, and pelvic fins; moderately long-based dorsal and anal fins, with about 30 or more elements; fan-shaped pectoral fins with 17 or more rays; and 34–43 vertebrae. The fin spines range from very weak to strong and differ in length relative to one another, depending on species. The pelagic prejuveniles have expanded abdomens, leathery skin covered by minute tubercles, and two rows of large tubercles on the lower region of the sides between the pectoral and pelvic fins. The enlarged tubercles have been called cones, scutes, platelike scales, or plates. When prejuveniles undergo transformation, which in some species does not occur until the fish reach 10–15 cm (4–6 inches), the abdomen shrinks, the abdominal scutes are reduced or lost, cycloid body scales develop, and the eyes become extremely large. The coloration of most species changes from dark spots on a light background to uniformly dark. Due to the great difference in appearance of the young and the adults, some oreo prejuveniles were once described as distinct species. Oreos attain a maximum size of 61 cm (24 inches; Eschmeyer and Herald 1983), but most species are smaller.

The first oreo record from the North Pacific was a 10.5-cm-SL prejuvenile identified by Welander et al. (1957) as a warty dory (also called coster dory), *A. verrucosus* Gilchrist. Taken south of Alaska at 50°N, 150°W, the specimen was believed to represent an extension of the known range north from Australia. Shortly thereafter Myers (1960) described a new species, *A. folletti,* from specimens collected off California. After that, identification of specimens from the North Pacific became confused, with some authors maintaining that *A. folletti* was a junior synonym of *A. verrucosus* or that other species were involved. Eschmeyer and Herald

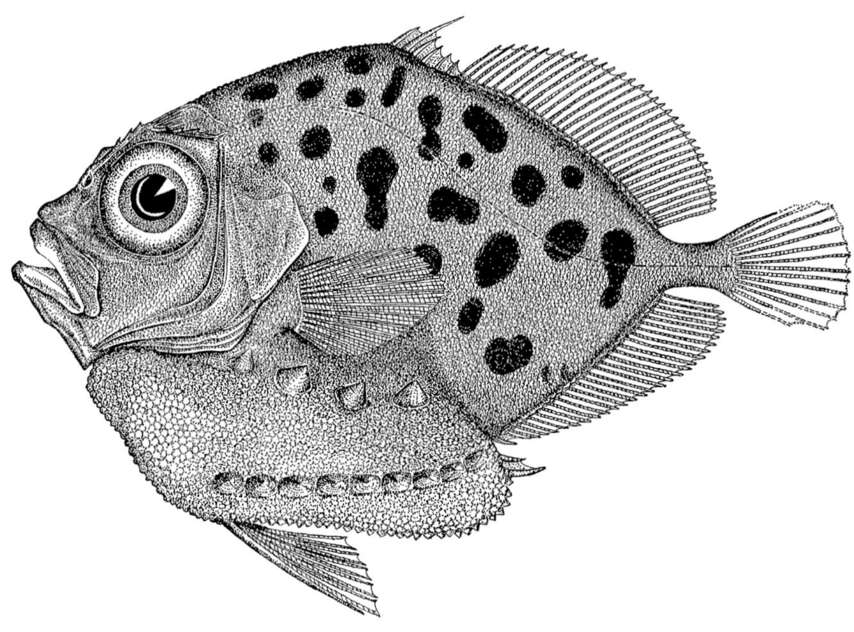

Prejuvenile of oxeye oreo, *Allocyttus folletti* Myers, 1960
UW 40273 (formerly UBC 64-11), 13 cm TL, mid-Pacific west of British Columbia
(After Hart 1973.)

(1983) considered that *A. folletti* is the form in the North Pacific. James et al. (1988) revised the taxonomy of southern ocean oreos, confirming that *A. verrucosus* is endemic to the South Pacific and that North Pacific oreos are different. A revised description of *A. folletti,* including transformation to the adult stage and review of existing records, is being prepared (W. N. Eschmeyer, C.W.M., and others). Morphological features essential for identification and records from Alaska and adjacent waters are given in the following account. Hart's (1973) illustration of the prejuvenile described by Welander et al. (1957) is reproduced above.

Quast and Hall (1972) included *A. verrucosus* on their list of Alaskan fishes on the basis of specimens collected south of the Aleutian Islands and identified as *A. verrucosus* by Kobayashi et al. (1968), but the specimens were actually collected well south of the 200-mile Exclusive Economic Zone. (Those specimens are referred herein to *A. folletti* on the basis of the published description.) Hughes (1981) reported that one or more oreos which he identified as *A. verrucosus* were taken over Surveyor Seamount just within or outside the 200-mile limit in the Gulf of Alaska; voucher specimens were to have been saved, but currently cannot be found. Cook and Long (1985) provided the first verifiable record of *A. folletti* in Alaskan waters, comprising specimens captured over the Bering Sea slope and later identified as *A. folletti* by W. N. Eschmeyer. Those specimens and several others from Alaska, both prejuvenile and adult, are housed in the permanent collections of the University of Washington, Royal British Columbia Museum, and other institutions.

Allocyttus folletti Myers, 1960 **oxeye oreo**

Bering Sea and Pacific Ocean to central California off Point Sur and to Honshu, Japan.

Most adults caught near bottom at 360–860 m, one record from 47–292 m, in bottom trawls; prejuveniles taken near surface offshore and in midocean by midwater trawls, gill nets, and purse seines.

D V–VII,30–36; A III,30–32; Pec 19–21; Pel I,6–7; LLp 85–97+3–7 C; GR 3–7+15–25 (24–32); Vert 39–41.

- Adults uniformly dark brown; juveniles spotted.
- Body deep and compressed; caudal peduncle slender; mouth upturned, protractile; eye very large.
- Fin spines stout; spines in dorsal and anal fins decreasing in height posteriorly.
- Prejuveniles with 2 rows of large scutes between pectoral and pelvic fins; scutes in upper row larger, less numerous (3–5), more conelike than scutes in lower row (9 or more); scutes of both rows reduced or lost, leaving flat areas, in adults.
- Adults with rough, spiny scales on belly, between eyes, on nape, and in rows at base of dorsal and anal fins, and cycloid scales on cheek, side, lateral line, and caudal peduncle.
- Length to 42 cm TL or more.

Notes & Sources — *Allocyttus folletti* Myers, 1960

Pending results of ongoing study, the synonymy provisionally includes records of *A. verrucosus* listed below under Range. *Allocyttus verrucosus* of the South Pacific has fewer fin elements and vertebrae (D V–VII,27–32; A II–III,25–30; Pec 17–20; Vert 34–37); more cones (7 or more) in the upper abdominal row; and larger spots in the prejuvenile.

Description: Welander et al. 1957; Myers 1960; Kobayashi et al. 1968; Anderson et al. 1979:262; Eschmeyer and Herald 1983:126; Kido in Amaoka et al. 1983:203; Nagtegaal 1983; Gillespie and Saunders 1994:348.

Figure: Royal British Columbia Museum, artist N. Eyolfson, Sep. 1982; BCPM 979-11396, 310 mm SL.

Range: Records from Alaska include: Cook and Long (1985): 3 specimens (OS 7895, UW 20831, UW 20832; 185–302 mm SL), Bering Sea slope, depths 500–600 m. A. E. Peden (pers. comm., 11 Jan. 1995): 2 specimens (BCPM 986-118), 7 miles south of Kaga Point, Kagalaska Island. Hughes (1981): Surveyor Seamount, 165–430 m, midwater trawl. UW collection has: 1 juvenile (UW 22692, 97 mm SL), south of Chirikof Island, 52°32'N, 155°35'W, taken by purse seine; 1 adult (UW 22694, 223 mm SL), west of Pribilof Islands, 56°33'N, 172°31'W, depth 360 m; and 5 adults (UW 22695–22699, 255–325 mm SL) taken at 5 stations north of Akutan Pass and Krenitzin Islands at 366–640 m. Open circles: NMFS survey database (D. W. Kessler, pers. comm., 20 Jun. 1994). Records from adjacent waters include: Welander et al. (1957), as *A. verrucosus*: juvenile, at 50°N, 150°W, gill net. Hart (1973), as *Allocyttus* sp.: juvenile, from stomach of a lancetfish, *Alepisaurus ferox,* at 50°N, 145°W. Gillespie and Saunders (1994): 1 specimen (262 mm SL) off Englefield Bay, Queen Charlotte Islands (about 53°N, 132°35'W), 388–540 m. BCPM 994-00120-001 (330 mm SL) is from Rennel Sound, 53°16'N, 133°05'W, 530 m. Nagtegaal (1983): 1 adult, Hecate Strait, 47–292 m. Northernmost record: KIE uncataloged, female, 358 mm TL, 60°38'N, 172°40'E, 550–560 m (reported as *A. verrucosus*; B. A. Sheiko, pers. comm., 15 Jan. 1999). Kobayashi et al. (1968): 2 juveniles, outside U.S. waters south of Aleutian Islands, 45°58'N, 170°58'W, gill net; 1 immature female (222 mm SL), western Bering Sea, 59°07'N, 166°12'E, 485 m. Abe and Hotta (1962; 181 mm SL, 600–700 m) and Kido (in Amaoka et al. 1983; 292 mm SL, 815–860 m) reported on specimens, as *A. verrucosus,* from Japan.

Size: Holotype, SU 15377, 347 mm SL = at least 42 cm TL.

Order Gasterosteiformes
Gasterosteiforms

The order Gasterosteiformes contains nearshore marine, brackish, and freshwater fishes in two suborders with 11 families and nearly 260 species. Seahorses (which do not occur in Alaska) are probably the most familiar members of the group to nonscientists. Many gasterosteiform species have dermal plates, small mouths, and long snouts, and most have elongate bodies. Diagnostic features also include: supramaxilla, orbitosphenoid, and basisphenoid absent; pelvic girdle never attached directly to the cleithra; postcleithrum a single bone or absent; and branchiostegal rays 1–5. Gasterosteiforms typically are small fishes, with few species reaching lengths of more than 18 cm (7 inches). The tropical trumpetfishes and cornetfishes reach lengths of 80–180 cm (31–71 inches).

Males of the suborder Gasteroidei construct nests of plant material using glue produced by their kidneys. Species in this suborder occur only in the Northern Hemisphere. The group is represented in Alaska by the families Aulorhynchidae and Gasterosteidae. Shared features include: protractile upper jaws, lack of a postcleithrum, circumorbital bones present in addition to the lachrymal, pelvic fins placed below the pectoral fins, and presence of isolated dorsal spines followed by a soft-rayed dorsal fin. Species in the suborder Syngnathoidei have nonprotractile upper jaws, no circumorbital bones other than the lachrymal, pelvic fins located on the abdomen or absent, and no ribs. The Syngnathoidei are represented in Alaska by the family Syngnathidae. The gasterosteiform suborders are classified by some taxonomists in separate orders.

Like the relationships of so many other fish groups, those of the gasterosteiforms, both within the order and between it and other taxa, are subject to different interpretations. Johnson and Patterson (1993) examined possible gasterosteiform relationships. Nelson (1994) summarized recent views and provided references to pertinent literature.

Family Aulorhynchidae
Tubesnouts

Species of the tubesnout family occur only in salt water along coasts of the North Pacific Ocean. There are two species: *Aulorhynchus flavidus* from the Gulf of Alaska south to Baja California, and *Aulichthys japonicus* from northern Japan to Korea. Tubesnouts are schooling fishes of inshore areas, with schools sometimes numbering millions of fish. *Aulorhynchus flavidus* males guard egg clumps spawned on stems of seaweed, and dispersal of eggs may occur when clumps rip off during storms (Marliave 1976). *Aulichthys japonicus* spawns in the peribranchial cavity of the tunicate *Halocynthia* (Ida in Masuda et al. 1984). Tubesnouts are also commonly called needlefishes.

Diagnostic tubesnout features include: elongate, cylindrical body; bony scutes on sides; 23–27 small, free dorsal spines followed by a dorsal fin with 9–11 rays; anal fin opposite rayed dorsal fin and with about the same number of rays; 13 caudal fin rays; pelvic fins with 1 spine and 4 rays; 4 branchiostegal rays; circumorbital ring complete posteriorly; and 52–56 vertebrae.

Some classifications, including that followed by the American Fisheries Society (Robins et al. 1991a), combine the Aulorhynchidae and Gasterosteidae in one family. Nelson (1994) chose to retain them as separate families until relationships within the suborder Gasteroidei are better understood. The Aulorhynchidae could be paraphyletic, as molecular data suggest that the western Pacific tubesnout is more closely related to sticklebacks (Gasterosteidae) than to the eastern Pacific tubesnout (Nelson 1994).

Aulorhynchus flavidus Gill, 1861 — **tubesnout**

Captains Bay, Unalaska Island, record uncertain; southwest Alaska Peninsula at Pavlof Bay; Kodiak Island to central Baja California at Punta Rocosa.

Near surface to depth of 30 m, usually in schools; eelgrass beds, kelp forests, rocky areas, and over sand, often near pilings and under docks; sometimes well offshore; nests built of kelp stems above bottom, usually deeper than 10 m.

D XXIII–XXVII + 9–11; A I,9–10; Pec I,9–10; Pel I,4; Br 4; LLp 52; GR 25–31; Vert 52–56.

- Silvery brown to olive green with darker bars; dark stripe on head, often extending onto body; silvery patch between operculum and pectoral fin; pelvic fin bright red and snout phosphorescent in breeding males.
- Body spindle-shaped and rigid; snout long and tubular, with small mouth at tip; eye large; caudal peduncle strongly keeled, making it broader than deep.
- Numerous short, isolated spines preceding triangular, soft-rayed dorsal fin; anal fin opposite and about same size as dorsal fin; caudal fin small and forked; pectoral fin broad; pelvic fin below pectoral fin.
- Thin, embedded bony plates along side.
- Length to 188 mm TL.

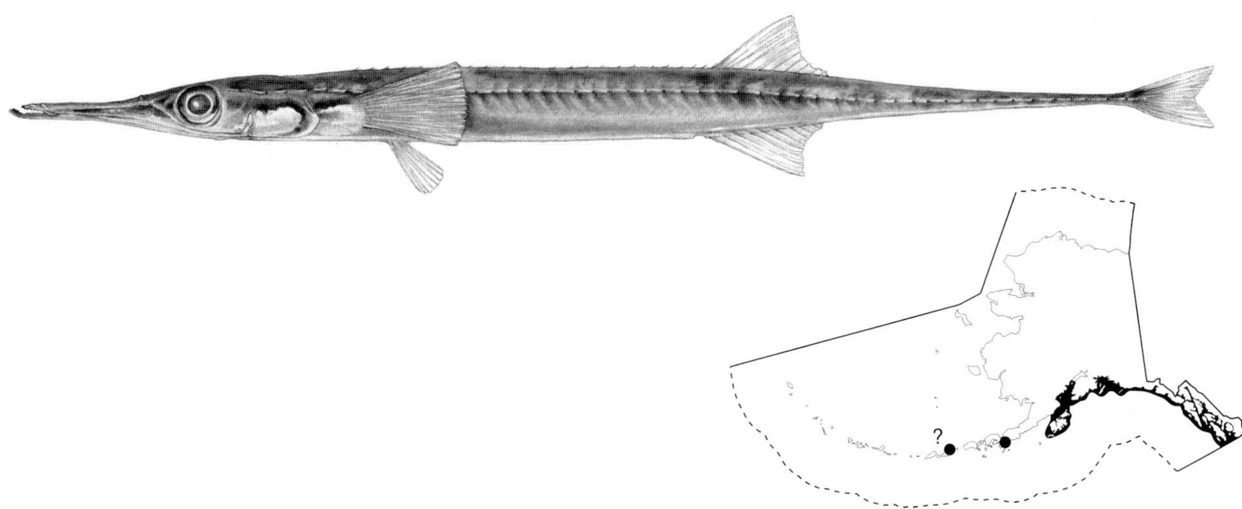

Notes & Sources — *Aulorhynchus flavidus* Gill, 1861

Description: Miller and Lea 1972:88; Hart 1973:273–275; Eschmeyer and Herald 1983:128; Coad 1995:816–817.

Figures: University of British Columbia, artist P. Drukker-Brammall; UBC 63-235, 121 mm SL, Silver Bay, Alaska.

Range: Range given as extending north to Sitka or southeastern Alaska by Wilimovsky (1954, 1958), Miller and Lea (1972), Quast and Hall (1972), Hart (1973), Eschmeyer and Herald (1983), and Lamb and Edgell (1986). Examples from southeastern Alaska in ABL collection are from Samsing Cove near Sitka, Traitors Cove near Ketchikan, Paul Bight in Skowl Arm, Steamer Bay, and Clarence Strait. Sometimes found in abundance in eastern Gulf of Alaska localities; NMC 61-163 includes 56 specimens from San Juan Batista Island, taken in beach seine in 0–1 m of water. We usually notice tubesnouts in the summer at Tee Harbor, north of Juneau, and B. L. Wing (pers. comm., 9 Mar. 2000) reports there is usually a school under the ABL float in the summer. Records exist that document extension of the known range farther north and west. Found in OCSEAP studies west to Kodiak Island (Blackburn and Jackson 1982) and north to Danger Island, Zaikof Bay, and Schooner Rock, Prince William Sound (Rosenthal 1980), and Kachemak Bay, Cook Inlet (Dames and Moore 1979). Indication of occurrence at Kodiak, Cook Inlet, and Prince William Sound in table by Rogers et al. (1986) is based on those reports. Previously unreported examples from northern Gulf of Alaska, all collected by the International Fisheries Commission in 1928–1932, are: UW 155, Yakutat Bay; UW 3825, Hanning Bay, Prince William Sound; and UW 4268, Zaikof Bay, Prince William Sound. Collection UBC 62-489 includes a specimen from Pavlof Bay, on the southwest end of the Alaska Peninsula at 55°36'N, 161°28'W. A specimen (UW 3090) collected by beach seine in 1932 by L. Townsend of the IFC at Captains Bay, Unalaska Island, 53°52'N, 166°34'W, may be the westernmost record, but the UW database indicates the exact locality could be incorrect. Reported to be very uncommon to rare around Kodiak Island by J. E. Blackburn (pers. comm., 9 Mar. 2000). Southernmost record may be SIO 52-164, from 28°45'N, 114°24'W, at Punta Rocosa, Baja California. Previously reported south to northern Baja California at Punta Rompiente by Miller and Lea (1972).

Size: Coad 1995. Length of 7 inches was given by previous authors, variously converted to 17.7, 17.9, or 18 cm. R. Baxter (unpubl. data) found a specimen measuring 180.2 mm TL among OSUO uncataloged material, providing further confirmation (in addition to Coad 1995) of sizes 18 cm and over.

Family Gasterosteidae
Sticklebacks

Sticklebacks inhabit coastal marine and fresh waters of the Northern Hemisphere, primarily in temperate to subarctic regions. There are marine, anadromous, and freshwater forms, and some species have both anadromous and strictly freshwater populations. Their common name comes from the isolated spines preceding the soft dorsal fin. Although more than 60 species of sticklebacks have been described, less than a dozen, with some of them in "species complexes," are now considered valid. Their interesting behavior, including nest building and guarding of eggs and fry by the males, wide range of salinity tolerance, phenotypic responsiveness to environmental factors, and recently evolved genetic diversity have made them famous among scientists, who have made sticklebacks the subject of several books and thousands of research papers. Sticklebacks are also popular aquarium fishes. Two species occur in Alaska: threespine stickleback, *Gasterosteus aculeatus,* and ninespine stickleback, *Pungitius pungitius.* Both species are widely distributed in the state, except that *G. aculeatus* is rarely found north of the Bristol Bay region or far inland and *P. pungitius* has not been recorded from southern Alaska east of the Kenai Peninsula.

Sticklebacks typically have a moderately elongate body; bony scutes instead of scales on the sides; 3 or more well-developed, free spines in front of a dorsal fin with 6–14 rays; pelvic fins with 1 strong spine and 0–3 rays; 12 caudal fin rays; 3 branchiostegal rays; and 28–42 vertebrae. The circumorbital ring is incomplete posteriorly. In relatively rare cases the free dorsal spines are reduced to 0–2, or bony scutes are absent. The numbers of fin rays, body plates, gill rakers, and vertebrae are highly variable in sticklebacks.

Interpretation of the genetic diversity of sticklebacks is one of the most challenging problems in ichthyology. The taxonomy of both of the species resident in Alaska is problematical. The *G. aculeatus* complex shows such diversity in body plates and other characters worldwide that at least 45 species have been described. A period of synonymizing the nominal species followed realization that the variation was probably not the result of genetic divergence but of phenotypic variation. Among the studies reporting on phenotypic variation in Alaskan *G. aculeatus* are those of Narver (1969) on sticklebacks from Chignik River system lakes; Kynard and Curry (1976), from Auke Lake; and Francis et al. (1985), from Knik Lake. Recent studies indicate reproductive isolation may be established in some sympatric forms, and species-level differences are being suggested for some of them.

From analysis of allozyme variation in the *G. aculeatus* complex, Haglund et al. (1992a) concluded there is a recognizable unit that should be considered *G. aculeatus,* but that it can only be recognized on the basis of allozyme characters. The authors were not able to describe the unit using morphological features. The work suggested other divergent forms, such as an evolutionary unit in Japan, but, again, the variation cannot at this time be extended to taxonomic recognition.

Haglund et al.'s (1992b) study of allozyme variation in the *P. pungitius* complex indicated the presence of three clades in that complex, and they recommended naming the North American unit *P. occidentalis* (Cuvier, 1829), after the first ninespine stickleback species described from the New World. Keivany and Nelson (2000) classified North American forms in *P. pungitius.* They analyzed osteology and meristic features of the nominal taxa in *Pungitius* and recognized five subspecies, with *P. p. occidentalis* the form occurring in Alaska from Cook Inlet to the Arctic, and *P. p. pungitius* implied to be the form to expect along the Aleutian Islands. However, the recent analyses did not include samples from the Bering Sea and North Pacific off western Alaska and eastern Siberia, so distribution of subspecies in this region is not clearly defined. Generally speaking, more information on geographic variation in molecular characters as well as morphological characters of Alaskan populations is needed to delimit subspecies in the region.

Key to the Gasterosteidae of Alaska

1 Free spines anterior to soft dorsal fin 2–4; gill membranes united to isthmus . . . . *Gasterosteus aculeatus,* page 333

1 Free spines anterior to soft dorsal fin 7–13; gill membranes free from isthmus . . . . *Pungitius pungitius,* page 334

Gasterosteus aculeatus Linnaeus, 1758 **threespine stickleback**

Simpson Lagoon, Beaufort Sea; Point Lay and Cape Thompson, Chukchi Sea; Bering Sea and Pacific Ocean to Monterey Bay, central California, and to Korea; in fresh water south to Rio Rosario, Baja California; Seas of Okhotsk and Japan; disjunct in North America, absent from western arctic Canada; Hudson Bay and Atlantic coast to Chesapeake Bay; arctic Europe and Asia south to Syria.

Marine, brackish, and fresh waters; anadromous and resident freshwater forms; shallow vegetated areas of lakes, ponds, rivers, streams; marshes; usually over mud or sand, to depth of 27 m; often near surface far from land, recorded to about 800 km offshore; benthic and pelagic; nests built on sandy bottom.

D II–IV,7–14; A I,6–11; Pec 8–11; Pel I,1; Br 3–4; GR 17–27; PC 1–2; Vert 30–34.

- Freshwater fish usually mottled brown or greenish; anadromous fish silvery green to bluish black; yellow, white, or silvery ventrally; breeding males turn brilliant bluish or green, with bright blue eyes and red or orange belly and throat.
- Body moderately elongate; snout short; maxilla not reaching anterior margin of eye; bony lateral keel on caudal peduncle in anadromous fish.
- **Isolated dorsal spines usually 3, last very short**; anal fin shorter-based than soft dorsal fin, origin several rays posterior to origin of dorsal; pectoral fin margin nearly truncate; pelvic fin spine long, strong, serrated.
- Well-developed, vertically elongate, lateral bony plates usually present; up to 37 plates all along side in marine and anadromous fish, reduced to 0–9 anteriorly in some freshwater fish.
- **Gill membranes broadly united to isthmus**.
- Length to 102 mm TL, usually under 75 mm TL.

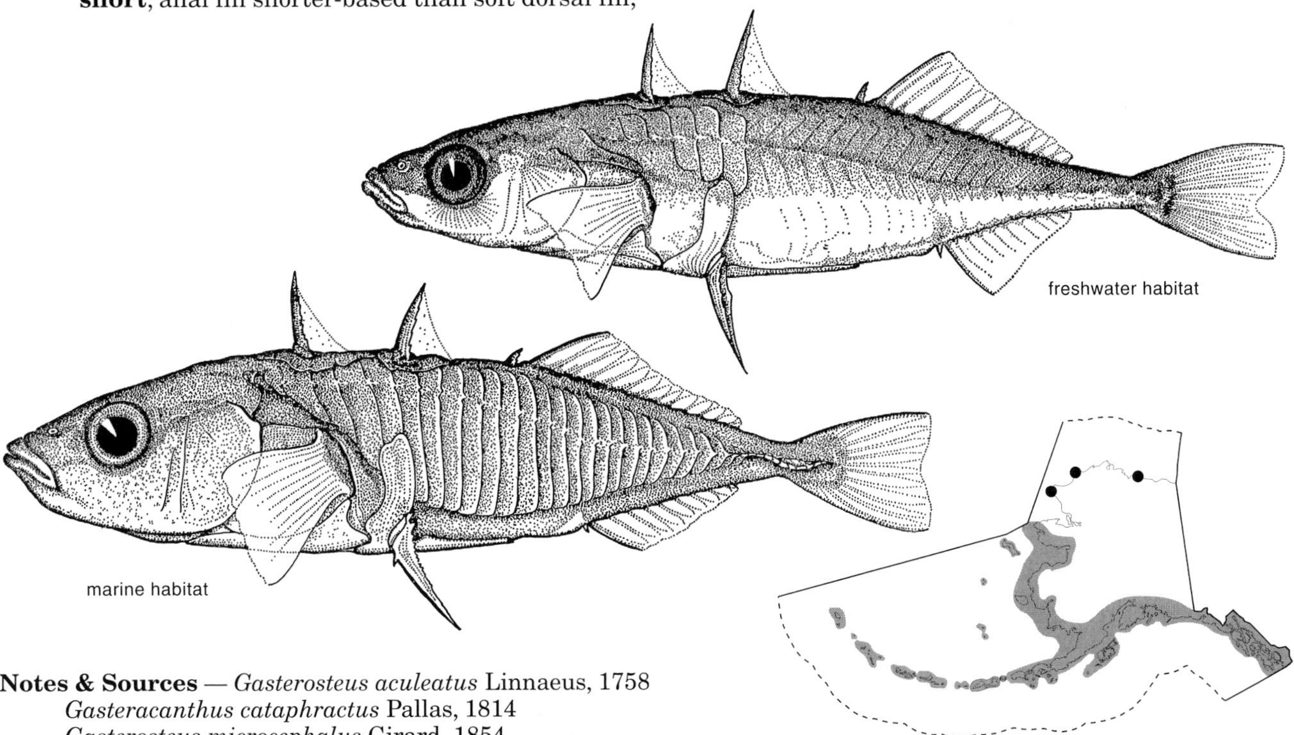

Notes & Sources — *Gasterosteus aculeatus* Linnaeus, 1758
Gasteracanthus cataphractus Pallas, 1814
Gasterosteus microcephalus Girard, 1854
Gasterosteus cataphractus: Bean 1881b, Elliott 1882, Jordan and Evermann 1896.

A search of Eschmeyer's (1998) catalog of types yielded 45 synonyms. An analysis by Haglund et al. (1992a) of allozyme variation in Asian, North American, and European populations supported recognition of a cohesive taxonomic unit, including most samples, as *G. aculeatus.* Further work could show that recognition of some subspecies is justified.

Description: McPhail and Lindsey 1970:310–315; Morrow 1980:189–192; Eschmeyer and Herald 1983:128; Page and Burr 1991:243; Coad 1995:797–799.

Figures: McPhail and Lindsey 1970:310.

Range: Evermann and Goldsborough (1907) listed Alaskan records from Bering Strait to southeastern Alaska, including the Pribilof Islands and Aleutian chain west to Kiska. Wilimovsky (1964) recorded it west to Attu Island. Records north of Bristol Bay are relatively rare: Martin et al. (1986), Yukon Delta; McPhail and Lindsey (1970), St. Lawrence Island; Scofield (1899), Bering Strait at Grantley Harbor; Fechhelm et al. (1984), Point Lay; and Craig and Haldorson (1979), Simpson Lagoon. Collection UBC 64-10 is from Ogotoruk Creek, Cape Thompson; UBC 63-1295, from St. Matthew Island; and UBC 65-639, 65-743, and 65-824, from Nunivak Island. Sometimes found far from shore. LeBrasseur (1964) reported several catches numbering 1–5,000 fish up to 55 mm SL south of Kodiak Island at 55°03'N, 153°30'W. Clemens and Wilby (1961) reported that over 4,000 specimens were obtained in a 10-minute surface tow with a 3-foot trawl offshore in the Gulf of Alaska, and McPhail and Lindsey (1970) that "a number" had been captured 500 miles (805 km) from land in the Gulf of Alaska, but the authors did not give localities.

Pungitius pungitius (Linnaeus, 1758) **ninespine stickleback**

Arctic, Bering Sea, and Gulf of Alaska coasts and interior to Kenai Peninsula; Siberia south to Korea; Seas of Okhotsk and Japan; northeastern British Columbia, Alberta, Mackenzie Valley to Great Lakes, all eastern Canada, and Atlantic coast south to New Jersey; northern Europe and Asia; circumboreal.

Marine, brackish, and fresh waters; anadromous and resident freshwater forms; shallow vegetated areas of lakes, ponds, and pools in slow streams, sometimes in open water to depth of 110 m; marine populations most common in marshes and estuaries near shore; benthic and pelagic; nests built off bottom in vegetation or on bottom.

D VI–XII,7–13; A I,8–11; Pec 10–11; Pel I,1; Br 3; GR 10–15; PC 0; Vert 30–35.

- Dull olive to light brown dorsally; darker mottling or blotches laterally; yellowish to silvery white ventrally; breeding colors variable, males turning black on belly and under chin.
- Body elongate, slender; snout short; maxilla not reaching or barely reaching anterior margin of eye; caudal peduncle long and slender; bony lateral keel on caudal peduncle, sometimes extending anteriorly to below origin of soft dorsal fin.
- **Isolated dorsal fin spines usually 9**, angled alternately to left and right; anal fin base about same length as soft dorsal, anal fin spine opposite 1st soft-dorsal ray; pectoral fin margin rounded; pelvic fin spine strong.
- No large bony plates on side in Alaskan fish; 0–15 small bony plates along lateral line anteriorly.
- **Gill membranes united to each other and free from isthmus**.
- Length to 90 mm TL, usually under 65 mm TL.

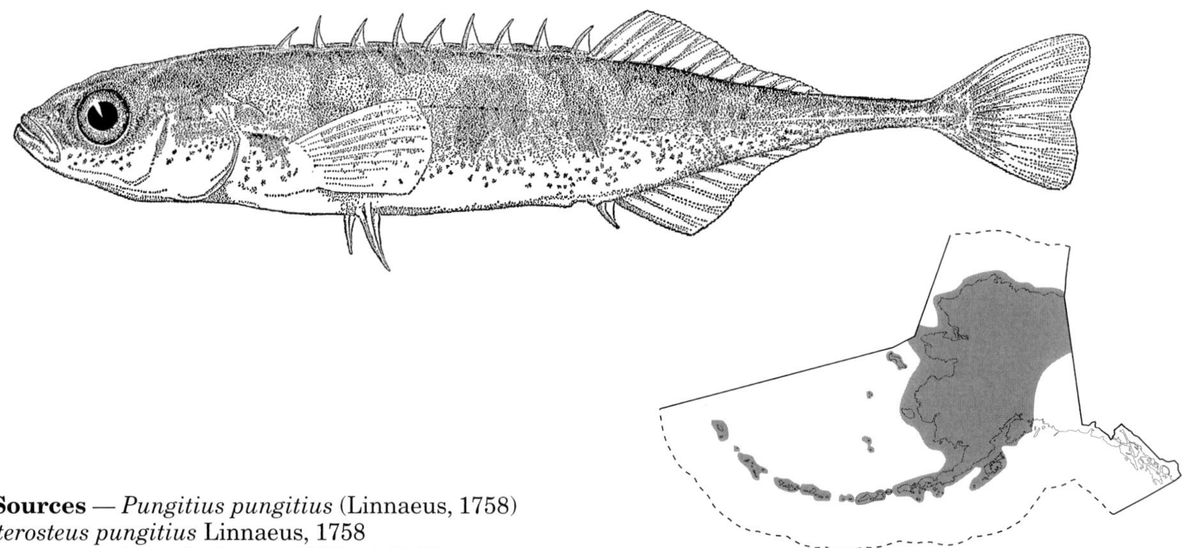

Notes & Sources — *Pungitius pungitius* (Linnaeus, 1758)
Gasterosteus pungitius Linnaeus, 1758
Pygosteus pungitius: Jordan and Gilbert 1877.

One of the conclusions Haglund (1992b) reached from a study of allozyme variation in *Pungitius* was that the form in North America should be recognized as *P. occidentalis.* Nelson believed (1994 and pers. comm., 15 Mar. 2000) that more work is necessary to produce a stable taxonomy. Keivany and Nelson (2000), from study of osteological features and meristics, argued for keeping the North American form as *P. pungitius.* They recognized five subspecies in *P. pungitius.* The major diagnostic feature differentiating the Alaskan subspecies *P. p. pungitius* and *P. p. occidentalis* is presence of long and oblique haemal and neural spines on preural 4 in the former, versus short and horizontal spines in the latter. More studies are needed to determine subspecies limits in Alaska and eastern Russia.

Description: Morrow 1980:192–194; Page and Burr 1991: 242; Coad 1995:469–470.

Figure: McPhail and Lindsey 1970:306.

Range: Bean (1881b) and Evermann and Goldsborough (1907) listed early Alaskan records from Point Barrow to Kodiak Island. Wilimovsky (1964) reported occurrence along the Aleutian Islands from Attu Island to the Sanak Islands. McPhail and Lindsey (1970) indicated several Chukchi and Beaufort Sea coastal records on their map; examples are in the NMC and UBC collections. Taken at numerous stations in Norton and Kotzebue sounds in NMFS resource surveys (D. W. Kessler, pers. comm., 20 Jun. 1994). UBC 63-744, 65-642, and 65-824 include examples from Nunivak Island. Not indicated on Morrow's (1980) map for the Kodiak archipelago, but Bean (1882) recorded it from St. Paul (now Kodiak), Rutter (1899) from a brook near the mouth of Alitak Bay, and Evermann and Goldsborough (1907) from Karluk River near its source. Scott and Crossman (1973) stated that the known range extends to the Kenai Peninsula side of Cook Inlet but their map depicts range only around the head of Cook Inlet. UBC 58-199 includes specimens from a pond on Bird Point, Turnagain Arm (head of Cook Inlet). Not indicated for the Kenai Peninsula on maps by Morrow (1980) and McAllister and Parker (in Lee et al. 1980), but Page and Burr's (1991) map depicts range throughout the Kenai Peninsula.

Family Syngnathidae
Pipefishes

Species in the family Syngnathidae typically occur in shallow marine and brackish waters at tropical and subtropical latitudes. A few inhabit fresh water or relatively cool waters. The family contains 52 genera and about 215 species, with representatives in the Pacific, Indian, and Atlantic oceans. It includes seahorses and seadragons, as well as pipefishes, but only the latter are represented in Alaska. The range of one eastern Pacific species, the bay pipefish, *Syngnathus leptorhynchus,* reaches Alaska, where the species has been found as far north and west as Prince William Sound. It is the only syngnathid occurring north of California.

The most obvious distinguishing morphological feature of syngnathids is the series of dermal plates encircling the body and giving it a segmented look. Syngnathid reproductive adaptations are curious, as females place their fertilized eggs in a special area on the underside of the trunk or tail of the male, where they are carried and hatched. In some genera the brood area is developed into a pouch, which splits to release the young. Other diagnostic characters of syngnathids include: no spines in the fins; 1 dorsal fin, with 15–60 rays, sometimes absent; anal fin very small, with 2–6 rays, or absent; caudal fin sometimes absent; pectoral fins small but moderately well developed, with 10–23 rays; pelvic fins always absent; gill openings very small, with gill membranes broadly fused to the isthmus and anterior part of the body; 4 complete gill arches; pseudobranchs present; ribs absent; teeth absent from the jaws; and 1–3 branchiostegal rays. In some species the caudal peduncle is prehensile and used for holding onto objects. Fritzsche (1980) provided a complete list of features in a revision of the eastern Pacific Syngnathidae.

With poorly developed fins, syngnathids do not swim well but protect themselves by mimicking their surroundings. The seadragons of Australia have leaf-like appendages and float with the current, and are difficult to distinguish from fronds of algae. The bay pipefish is variously colored to match eelgrass and other local vegetation and glides slowly along, often with its body held stiffly upright.

Most syngnathids are small, with some attaining only 2.5 cm (1 inch) in length, but the species range in size up to about 65 cm (25.6 inches).

Syngnathus leptorhynchus Girard, 1854 **bay pipefish**

Northcentral Gulf of Alaska at Prince William Sound to southern Baja California at Bahia Santa Maria.

Close to shore, from surface to depth of 3 m; typically in eelgrass in bays, occasionally near shore outside of bays; sometimes in vicinity of docks and pilings.

D 28–44; A 2–3; Pec 11–13; Pel 0; Br 3; Vert 56–64.

- Various shades of brown, purple, or green, irregularly mottled, spotted, or striped.
- Body flexible, extremely elongate, hexagonal in cross section anteriorly, quadrilateral posteriorly; body covered with encircling dermal plates; mouth very small, at tip of elongate snout.
- Spinous dorsal fin absent; soft dorsal fin located at about middle of body and of even height throughout; anal fin present in both sexes but minute; caudal fin small, fanlike; pectoral fin extending posteriorly over about 1.3 rings; pelvic fin absent.
- Dermal rings: trunk, 16–21; tail, 36–46; total, 53–63.
- Gill slit a small opening at posterodorsal margin of opercle.
- Brood pouch with protective plates on underside of caudal peduncle in males.
- Length to 385 mm TL.

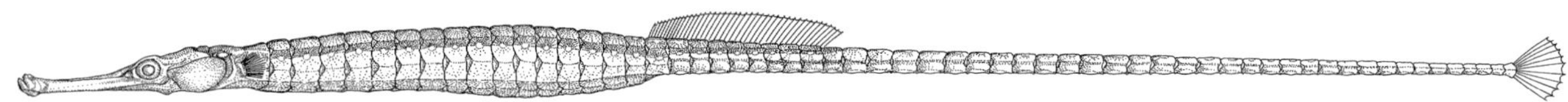

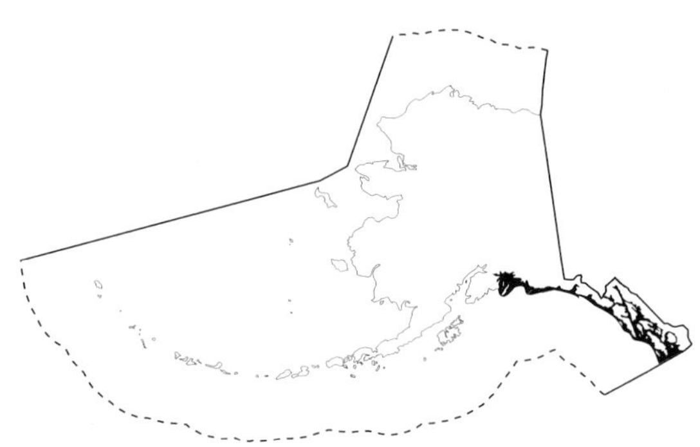

Notes & Sources — *Syngnathus leptorhynchus* Girard, 1854

Syngnathus griseolineatus Ayres, 1854

Siphostoma griseolineatum: Evermann and Goldsborough 1907.

Detailed synonymy given by Fritzsche (1980) seems complete to that time except for exclusion of range records given by Evermann and Goldsborough (1907) and Hart (1973).

Since *S. leptorhynchus* is the only species of pipefish likely to be found in Alaska, the family and generic characters are sufficient to identify it. Counting the fin rays and dermal rings is not necessary.

Description: Hart 1973:278–279; Fritzsche 1980:184, 198–199, 210–215; Eschmeyer and Herald 1983:131.

Figure: University of British Columbia, artist R. Wood, Feb. 1969; UBC 60-526, 224 mm SL, Port San Antonio, Alaska.

Range: In spring of 1989 Orsi et al. (1991) collected 257 specimens from eight widely distributed sites in Prince William Sound. The northwesternmost samples were from Wells Passage and Long Bay, at the entrance to Port Wells. Orsi et al. (1991) cited unpublished NMFS Auke Bay Laboratory and Canadian Museum of Nature (NMC collection) records which, with previously published records, indicate continuous distribution from Prince William Sound to Baja California. Additional records from southeastern Alaska are: UAM 128, from Tongass Narrows; UAM 3038, the Boca de Quadra; UBC 60-526, Port San Antonio, Baker Island; UBC 61-508, Polk Inlet, Prince of Wales Island; UBC 63-1255, Little Port Walter, Baranof Island; UW 14054, Ward Cove, Revillagigedo Island; UW 14074, Meyers Chuck, north of Ketchikan; and UW 14075, Tongass Narrows near Ketchikan. Given its abundance and wide distribution in Prince William Sound, *S. leptorhynchus* probably occurs even farther west in the Gulf of Alaska.

Size: Bayer 1980. Sizes of 130 specimens collected in June 1989 in Prince William Sound ranged from 104 to 337 mm (Orsi et al. 1991).

Order Scorpaeniformes
Mailcheeked fishes

The order Scorpaeniformes takes its common name, the mailcheeked fishes, from presence of a suborbital stay. The stay is a prolongation of the third suborbital bone, which extends across the cheek to the preopercle. This is the only diagnostic feature common to all members of the order. However, the suborbital stay may have evolved independently in more than one family, so the order may not be a monophyletic unit and its makeup is a matter of much debate. In many species the head has spines, and some are covered with bony plates. Most species have large, broad-based pectoral fins, often with the lower rays partly free and fingerlike.

Worldwide the order has more than 1,275 species in 25 families. All are marine, except for about 52 species of cottoids confined to fresh water. This guide includes accounts for 253 scorpaeniform species in 10 families, with only 3 species typically occurring in fresh water. Most of the Alaskan mailcheeked fishes are in the suborders Cottoidei and Scorpaenoidei. Counting only the species confirmed from Alaska by adequate documentation, the greatest numbers of cottoids are in Cottidae (sculpins) with 76 species, Liparidae (snailfishes) with 56, and Agonidae (poachers) with 22. The family Scorpaenidae (rockfishes) of the suborder Scorpaenoidei is represented in Alaska by at least 36 species.

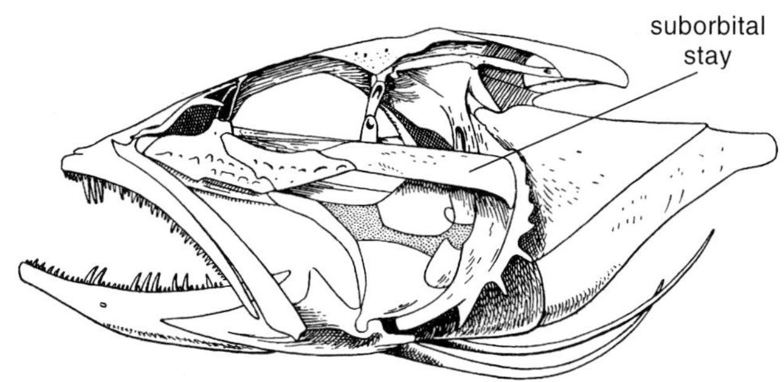

Location of suborbital stay in mailcheeked fishes
Skull of lingcod, *Ophiodon elongatus.* (After Boulenger 1904.)

Family Scorpaenidae
Rockfishes

The family Scorpaenidae, commonly called rockfishes or scorpionfishes, is a commercially important group of about 115 species of basslike, typically spiny-headed fishes. Most species inhabit rocky areas in shallow to moderately deep waters, while some are found farther offshore on silty and sandy, soft bottoms. As with most marine fishes, the young often occupy shallower water depths than the adults. The family is represented in Alaska by 32 species in the genus *Sebastes,* 3 species in the genus *Sebastolobus,* and 1 species of *Adelosebastes.* Accounts for three additional species of *Sebastes* inhabiting nearby waters or which have been reported but not confirmed in Alaska are also included in this guide.

Rockfishes belong to the suborder Scorpaenoidei, which includes the world's most venomous fishes. They carry the venom in the fin spines. Although the venom of the Scorpaenidae is not as potent to humans as that of some families from the western Pacific, a jab from a rockfish spine can cause severe pain, swelling, and fever. Characters distinguishing the Scorpaenidae from other families in the suborder include the presence of more than 24 vertebrae and a projecting mouth.

Other diagnostic characters of the Scorpaenidae include: ridges and spines on top of the head; 5 spines on the preopercle; 2 spines on the upper angle of the opercle; dorsal fin with (in the Alaskan species) 12–18 spines and 6–17 soft rays, with the spinous and soft-rayed portions continuous but distinctly notched before the last spine; anal fin with 3 spines and 4–11 soft rays; slightly rounded to strongly emarginate caudal fin; rounded or wedge-shaped pectoral fins with 14–20 rays, sometimes notched between upper and lower portions; pelvic fins with 1 spine and 5 rays; a uniformly scaly body; a single body lateral line canal, opening through numerous pored scales; teeth in patches in both jaws, the vomer, and the palatines; large gill openings, with gill membranes free from the isthmus; long, well-developed gill rakers; 7 branchiostegal rays; and 25–31 vertebrae. *Sebastes* species have swim bladders, whereas *Sebastolobus* and *Adelosebastes* do not. *Sebastes* give birth to live young, whereas *Sebastolobus* and *Adelosebastes* lay eggs in a gelatinous mass. Coloration in rockfishes ranges from red and orange to brown and black, and can be mottled, blotched, banded, striped, spotted, or relatively uniform.

Many rockfishes are large enough to be sought for their value as food for humans, and the smallest species are commonly found in the stomachs of other rockfishes as well as marine mammals. Alaskan rockfish species range in total length from about 18 cm (7.2 inches), attained by some Puget Sound rockfish, *S. emphaeus*, to 105 cm (41.5 inches), attained by shortraker rockfish, *S. borealis*. Rockfishes can live for many years. An unusually large, 45-cm (17.8-inch) China rockfish, *S. nebulosus*, was estimated to be 70 years old (Ueber 1989), and there are reports of shortraker rockfish and rougheye rockfish, *S. aleutianus,* aged at more than 120 years (Chilton and Beamish 1982). Biologists at the Alaska Department of Fish and Game Age Determination Laboratory recently aged a rougheye rockfish captured in southeastern Alaska at 205 years. Even in the worst-case error scenario, the fish would be 170 years old, which is still the oldest known fish of any species (K. M. Munk, pers. comm., 27 Dec. 2000).

The most useful characters for identifying rockfishes are coloration, the various head and cheek spines, fin spine and ray counts and relative size, and fin shape. Appearance of the symphyseal knob, size of the mouth (expressed by posterior extension of the maxilla), shape of the head between the eyes (concave to convex), scale coverage, and gill raker numbers can also be helpful.

With few exceptions, which are noted in the species accounts, and compared to fishes in some other families the coloration of each species of rockfish is remarkably constant. The colors given in the accounts pertain to live or freshly caught specimens, as the colors change or fade shortly after death and, especially, in preservative. While it is possible to identify rockfishes using the key, the characters given in the species accounts, and the black and white illustrations, color photographs make the job much easier. As well, several rockfish species have markedly different juvenile and adult coloration. Examples among the Alaskan species are vermilion rockfish, *S. miniatus*; bocaccio, *S. paucispinis*; and yelloweye rockfish, *S. ruberrimus*.

Rockfish head and cheek spines and ridges are shown in the diagram below (no one species has all of the structures shown). The paired series of spines on top of the head numbered 1–8 are collectively called *head spines* in the species accounts, where they are listed in the lefthand column of diagnostic characters. Prominence of the head spines is expressed as absent or weak to very strong. They are considered strong, or prominent, if the spines over the eye are easily visible when the fish is held at about normal reading distance. A head spine number in parentheses indicates that the spine can be present or absent. Other spines which vary in their presence or prominence and shape and can be useful in identification are those on the suborbital stay, along the lower rim of the eye, on the lachrymal bone, on the subopercle or interopercle (loosely referred to as subopercular spines), and above the operculum (supracleithral and cleithral spines). The lachrymal processes (usually two) can be barely evident, low and rounded, triangular, or produced into spines and can bear more than one spine each.

In rockfishes the last ray in the dorsal and anal fins usually is doubled but originates from a common

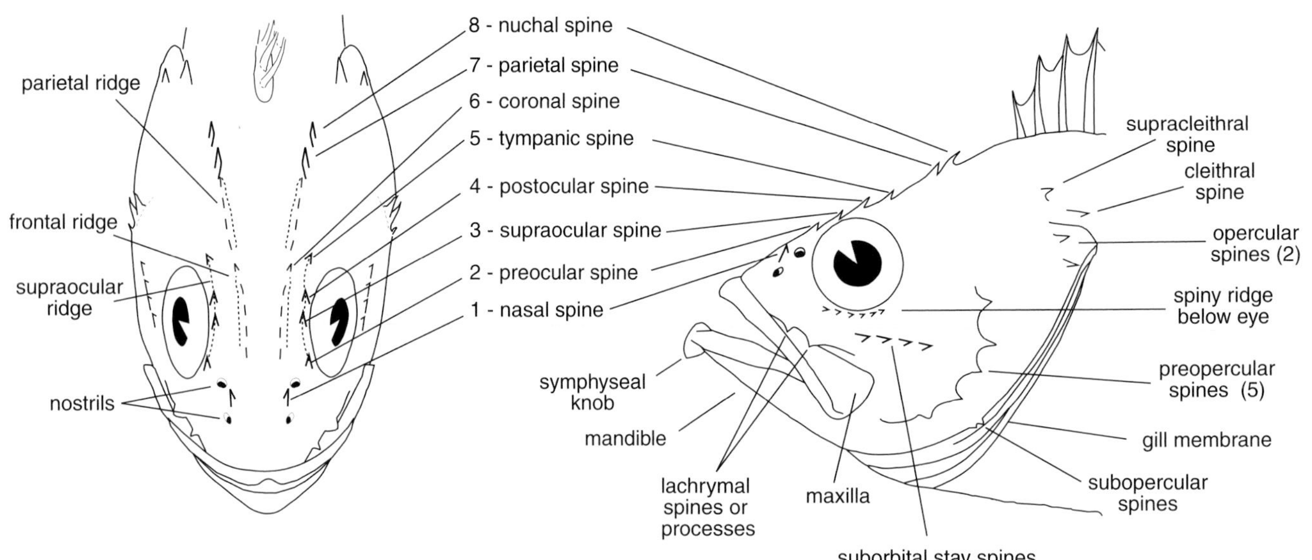

Rockfish head spines and structures

base and is counted by most workers as 1 ray. The total number of pores in the lateral line (LLp) includes all pores, without separate reference to pores following the structural base of the fin.

Anal fin spine lengths are expressed as the condition of the second spine relative to the third when the spines are depressed against the body.

For subfamilies we follow Nelson (1994) and place *Sebastes* in Sebastinae and *Adelosebastes* and *Sebastolobus* in Sebastolobinae. No nomenclatural changes for Alaskan rockfishes have occurred at the genus or species level since the inventory by Quast and Hall (1972). Use of the name *Sebastodes* for many North Pacific rockfishes had already been discarded in favor of using the same name as the Atlantic genus *Sebastes.* Proposed subgenera of *Sebastes* are subjects of current research (e.g., Gharrett et al. 2001). Kendall (1991, 2001) reviewed subgenera which have been proposed over the years.

An addition to the inventory of Alaskan fishes is the Emperor rockfish, *Adelosebastes latens,* a new species described by Eschmeyer et al. (1979) from a specimen caught at the Emperor Seamounts of the Hawaiian submarine ridge and recently collected south of the western Aleutian Islands by Orr and Baker (1996).

Rockfish species confirmed in Alaska after Quast and Hall (1972) suggested they probably occur in the region are broadfin thornyhead, *Sebastolobus macrochir*; gray rockfish, *Sebastes glaucus*; chilipepper, *S. goodei*; and vermilion rockfish, *S. miniatus. Sebastolobus macrochir* had actually been recorded from U.S. waters south of Cape Navarin by Barsukov (1964), but this record was overlooked; additional specimens have since been caught off the western Aleutian Islands. A record of *Sebastes glaucus* from south of the Aleutian Islands (Orr and Baker 1996) extended the known range for that species to Alaska from the western Bering Sea. The capture of *S. goodei* over Gulf of Alaska seamounts (Snytko 1986) and *S. miniatus* in Prince William Sound (O'Connell et al. 1992) extended their known ranges north to Alaska from British Columbia.

Accounts for three rockfish species that have been reported but not confirmed in Alaska are included in this guide. The shortbelly rockfish, *S. jordani,* has been recorded as far north as British Columbia; reports from demersal trawl catches in Alaska at Granite Island off the Kenai Peninsula were regarded as misidentifications by Allen and Smith (1988). Reports of blackgill rockfish, *S. melanostomus,* in the Bering Sea and Gulf of Alaska are not supported by voucher specimens and probably represent confusion with shortraker rockfish, *S. borealis*, or rougheye rockfish, *S. aleutianus* (e.g., Barsukov 1970; Tsyuki and Westrheim 1970; J. W. Orr, pers. comm., 29 Jan. 2001). Blackgill rockfish have, however, recently been taken close to Alaska off northern British Columbia (Workman et al. 1998). Quast and Hall (1972) considered all reports of blue rockfish, *S. mystinus,* in Alaska doubtful and probably referable to dusky rockfish, *S. ciliatus,* or black rockfish, *S. melanops,* and there are still no confirmed records of *S. mystinus* north of British Columbia.

Wilimovsky (1954) listed *S. ruber* Ayres from the Gulf of Alaska but later dropped it from his keys to the fishes of Alaska (Wilimovsky 1958), saying it was synonymous with *S. ruberrimus,* which is not entirely correct. Quast and Hall (1972) continued to list *S. ruber* from Alaska. The confusion is understandable. Jordan et al. (1930) listed *Sebastes ruber* Ayres in the synonymy of *S. auriculatus* and "*Sebastes ruber* of early writers, not of Ayres" in the synonymy of *S. ruberrimus.* This nomenclatural problem as it relates to Alaskan records is moot, however, because R. N. Lea (pers. comm., 3 Jun. 1998) recently examined the only specimen from Alaska recorded as *S. ruber* (USNM 29129) and concluded that it represents *S. alutus.* Bean (1882) collected the specimen from southeastern Alaska in 1881 and identified it as *Sebastichthys ruber.* It was not until 1890 that Gilbert (1890) described *Sebastes alutus.*

Sebastes aurora and *S. rosaceus,* listed as possible Alaskan species by Quast and Hall (1972), are not included in the present inventory because they have not been reported to occur north of Vancouver Island (and there only rarely) or Puget Sound, respectively.

The number of rockfishes on the list of Alaskan species could increase by one if dusky rockfish, *S. ciliatus,* is shown to comprise two species: a light dusky form and a dark dusky form. Morphological and genetic studies attempting to elucidate the systematic status of *S. ciliatus* are under way. Since the early 1900s, fisheries workers have been identifying *S. ciliatus* as the light form, whereas the original description and illustration appear to describe the dark form. Presence of the dark form in Alaska, especially where the two forms occur in the Aleutian Islands, has led to much confusion because species such as *S. melanops* and *S. mystinus* have been confused with *S. ciliatus* (Orr et al. 1997). The problem may be further complicated by, for instance, presence in Alaska of more than one morph of the light form (J. W. Orr, pers. comm., 19 Nov. 1997).

The following key will be less useful for work on faded specimens in museum collections than on freshly caught fish because it relies heavily on color. However, use of color in identifying rockfishes is unavoidable.

Key to the Scorpaenidae of Alaska

1		Pectoral fin slightly bilobed, lower rays thickened and partly free; pectoral fin rays 20–24; head spines very strong	(2)
1		Pectoral fin not bilobed, lower rays not thickened and not partly free; pectoral fin rays 14–20; head spines absent or weak to very strong	genus *Sebastes* (5)
2	(1)	Dorsal fin spines 12 or 13; dorsal fin soft rays 12 or 13; spines absent from suborbital stay or 1 or 2 weak spines present	*Adelosebastes latens,* page 345
2		Dorsal fin spines 13–16 (rarely 13); dorsal fin soft rays 6–10; several strong spines on suborbital stay	genus *Sebastolobus* (3)
3	(2)	Dorsal fin spine 3 obviously longest, spine 4 rarely slightly longer, with following spines markedly shorter; gill cavity mostly dusky	*Sebastolobus altivelis,* page 346
3		Dorsal fin spines 3–5 usually longest, with following spines not markedly, but gradually, shorter; gill cavity red to pale in life, pale in preservative	(4)
4	(3)	Body relatively elongate, caudal peduncle depth more than 43% of body depth at base of anal fin; lower pectoral fin rays not highly branched	*Sebastolobus alascanus,* page 347
4		Body relatively deep, caudal peduncle depth less than 43% of body depth at base of anal fin; lower pectoral fin rays highly branched	*Sebastolobus macrochir,* page 348
5	(1)	Four or five white blotches above lateral line	*Sebastes helvomaculatus,* page 349
5		No white blotches above lateral line	(6)
6	(5)	Four or five red or black vertical bands on sides and extending onto dorsal fins and below lateral line	(7)
6		No red or black vertical bands on sides and extending onto dorsal fins and below lateral line (dark blotches can be present, but not distinct bands)	(8)
7	(6)	Color pink or orange with 4 or 5 dark red or black bands; no distinct band on caudal peduncle (some dark pigment can be present); all 8 head spines present, strong, some much divided	*Sebastes nigrocinctus,* page 350
7		Color pink and white with 4 red bands; 4th band on caudal peduncle; head spines 1, 2, 4, 7 present, moderate to strong	*Sebastes babcocki,* page 351
8	(6)	Background color predominantly yellowish brown, brown, greenish gray, dark gray, black, or blue-black; any pink occurs mainly ventrally	(9)
8		Background color dark red, red, pink, orange, yellow, or some combination that makes selecting either predominantly red to yellow or brown to black difficult	(18)

9 (8) Head spines strong . . . . . . (10)

9 Head spines weak . . . . . . (12)

10 (9) Broad yellow stripe along lateral line to caudal fin . . . . . . *Sebastes nebulosus,* page 352

10 No yellow stripe reaching to caudal fin . . . . . . (11)

11 (10) Large yellowish area on spinous dorsal fin; body brown mottled with yellow and orange; spinous dorsal fin deeply incised, higher than soft dorsal fin . . . . . . *Sebastes maliger,* page 353

11 No large yellow area on spinous dorsal fin; body brown to blackish brown tinged with brownish red and pink; spinous dorsal fin not particularly deeply incised, not much higher than soft dorsal fin . . . . . . *Sebastes auriculatus,* page 354

12 (9) Dorsal fin spines 14; scales absent from maxilla; supracleithral and cleithral spines absent . . . . . . *Sebastes glaucus,* page 355

12 Dorsal fin spines 13, rarely 12 or 14; scales present on maxilla; supracleithral and cleithral spines weak to strong, supracleithral spine usually present . . . . . . (13)

13 (12) Head spines all typically absent; only spines 1 and 7 occasionally present and if present weak to very weak; vertebrae 28 . . . . . . *Sebastes ciliatus,* page 356

13 Head spine 1 (at least) present, weak to very weak; some combination of spines 2, 3, 4, 5, and 7 also can be present, and if present weak to very weak; vertebrae 26 or 27 . . . . . . (14)

14 (13) Supracleithral and cleithral spines both moderately strong to strong . . . . . . (15)

14 Supracleithral spine weak or absent, cleithral spine weak to moderately strong . . . . . . (16)

15 (14) Symphyseal knob large; maxilla extending to below rear edge of pupil to rear edge of eye; distal margin of anal fin nearly vertical or slightly slanted anteriorly; greenish to silvery gray dorsally, pink to white ventrally . . . . . . *Sebastes brevispinis,* page 357

15 Symphyseal knob absent; maxillary extending to below mideye; distal margin of anal fin strongly slanted posteriorly; golden brown to dusky brown with traces of yellow and red, lighter ventrally . . . . . . *Sebastes entomelas,* page 358

16 (14) Color olive green to grayish brown, with strong yellow cast . . . . . . *Sebastes flavidus,* page 359

16 Color mainly gray to black, without green or yellow . . . . . . (17)

17 (16) Dorsal fin soft rays usually 16 (range 15–17); anal fin soft rays usually 9 (range 8–10); mouth relatively small, maxilla extending to below mideye to rear edge of pupil; distal margin of anal fin straight and vertical or slightly slanted posteriorly . . . . . . *Sebastes mystinus,* page 360
(not confirmed from Alaska)

17 Dorsal fin soft rays usually 14 or 15 (range 13–16); anal fin soft rays usually 8 (range 7–9); mouth relatively large, maxilla extending to below rear edge of pupil to rear edge of eye; distal margin of anal fin rounded below and slanting anteriorly above . . . . *Sebastes melanops,* page 361

18 (8) Anus about midway between pelvic and anal fins . . . . *Sebastes jordani,* page 362 (not known from Alaska)

18 Anus close to anal fin . . . . (19)

19 (18) Dorsal fin spines 14; symphyseal knob strong; dark greenish gray on red background; lower pectoral fin rays white on distal portion . . . . *Sebastes polyspinis,* page 363

19 Dorsal fin spines 13 (rarely 14 or 15); symphyseal knob weak to strong; color not greenish gray on red background; lower pectoral fin rays not white on distal portion . . . . (20)

20 (19) Anal fin spines small; head spines weak or obsolete; lateral line scales 60–90 . . . . (21)

20 Anal fin spines not small; head spines weak to strong; lateral line scales 32–67 . . . . (22)

21 (20) Mouth large, maxilla extending to below rear edge of eye to beyond eye; symphyseal knob absent, lower jaw massive and strongly projecting; pectoral fin rays usually 15 (range 14–16); gill rakers on first arch 27–32 . . . . *Sebastes paucispinis,* page 364

21 Mouth moderate, maxilla extending to mideye; symphyseal knob strong, directed forward; pectoral fin rays usually 17 (range 16–18); gill rakers on first arch 34–39 . . . . *Sebastes goodei,* page 365

22 (20) Brown to copper with pink and yellow blotches; white on lower sides and belly; posterior two-thirds of lateral line in light area; no olive green; head spines strong . . . . *Sebastes caurinus,* page 366

22 Body color with more red, pink, or orange than brown to copper; not usually white on lower sides and belly; can have some olive green; head spines weak to strong . . . . (23)

23 (22) Body relatively slender and elongate; head spines moderate to strong; symphyseal knob absent to weak; adults not larger than 37 or 38 cm TL . . . . (24)

23 Body relatively deep; head spines weak to strong; symphyseal knob absent to strong; adults attaining 39–108 cm TL (only two species smaller than 46 cm TL) . . . . (27)

24 (23) Gill rakers on first arch 28–33; broken olive green stripes dorsolaterally on pink background; lateral line in distinct pink area . . . . *Sebastes elongatus,* page 367

24 Gill rakers on first arch 36–43; coloration different from above . . . . (25)

25 (24) Pectoral fin rays usually 18 (rarely 17 or 19); reddish pink to deep red with olive or brown blotches; posterior two-thirds of lateral line in well-defined clear area; red band on margin of caudal fin; adults not larger than 37 cm TL . . . . *Sebastes variegatus,* page 368

25 Pectoral fin rays usually 17 (rarely 16 or 18); copper red to light brown with or without olive or brown blotches; lateral line not in well-defined clear area; no red band on margin of caudal fin; adults not larger than 23 cm TL . . . . . (26)

26 (25) Anal fin rays usually 7 (range 6–7); distal margin of anal fin rounded; caudal fin emarginate; copper red with dark olive blotches; green bands radiating from eye . . . . . *Sebastes emphaeus,* page 369

26 Anal fin rays usually 6 (range 5–7); distal margin of anal fin almost straight; caudal fin truncate; light brown flushed with red, often with dark blotches dorsally; no green bands radiating from eye . . . . . *Sebastes wilsoni,* page 370

27 (23) Distal margin of anal fin strongly slanted anteriorly; body yellow-orange or red, generally with gray mottling . . . . . (28)

27 Distal margin of anal fin not strongly slanted anteriorly; body orange to red, generally without gray mottling . . . . . (29)

28 (27) Underside of lower jaw smooth (scales embedded); lateral line in pale gray area, strongly contrasting with yellow-orange body; low lachrymal process anteriorly, sharply triangular spine posteriorly . . . . . *Sebastes pinniger,* page 371

28 Underside of lower jaw rough (scales not embedded); lateral line not in clear gray area, not strongly contrasting with background (red); both lachrymal spines sharply triangular . . . . . *Sebastes miniatus,* page 372

29 (27) Head spines weak; subopercular spines present; lachrymal spines absent to moderate . . . . . (30)

29 Head spines moderate to very strong; subopercular spines present or absent; lachrymal spines usually moderate to strong . . . . . (32)

30 (29) Lateral line in light red stripe bordered by olive green mottling above and below; white areas at base of anal fin spines, between pelvic fin rays 4 and 5, and on proximal part of pectoral fin; symphyseal knob long and conspicuous; head spine 3 absent . . . . . *Sebastes proriger,* page 373

30 Lateral line not bordered by olive green mottling above and below; discrete white areas at fin bases and on fins absent; symphyseal knob weak to long and conspicuous; head spine 3 present or absent . . . . . (31)

31 (30) Symphyseal knob long and conspicuous; lateral line scales 43–55; pectoral fin rays usually 18 (less commonly 17; rarely 15, 16, or 19); dark blotch if present on opercle diffuse, not distinct; inside of mouth mainly pink, with some duskiness . . . . . *Sebastes alutus,* page 374

31 Symphyseal knob weak to moderate; lateral line scales 57–67; pectoral fin rays usually 19 (less commonly 18; rarely 20); discrete dark olive green blotch on upper area of opercle; inside of mouth with yellow and black blotches . . . . . *Sebastes reedi,* page 375

32 (29) Body deep, depth at insertion of pelvic fins greater than head length; head spine 3 present; 3 black blotches below spinous dorsal fin, 1 below soft dorsal, and 1 on caudal peduncle; black spot on opercle . . . . . *Sebastes crameri,* page 376

32 Body not so deep, depth at insertion of pelvic fins same as or less than head length; head spine 3 present or absent; black blotches, if present, vague . . . . (33)

33 (32) Head spine 3 (supraocular) absent . . . . (34)

33 Head spine 3 (supraocular) present . . . . (36)

34 (33) Rose red, no yellow; prominent knobs bordering notch at front of upper jaw . . . . *Sebastes diploproa,* page 377

34 Yellow-pink or red with yellow ventrally; no prominent knobs bordering notch in upper jaw . . . . (35)

35 (34) Yellow-pink with light green and with vague dusky blotches dorsally; silvery pink ventrally; caudal fin with green streaks, at least on upper portion; no dark forked bar from eye to operculum; subopercular spines present; dorsal soft rays usually 12 (range 11–13) . . . . *Sebastes saxicola,* page 378

35 Light red with vague dusky blotches dorsally; reddish yellow ventrally; dark forked bar from eye to operculum; subopercular spines usually absent; dorsal soft rays usually 14 (range 13–15) . . . . *Sebastes zacentrus,* page 379

36 (33) Bright yellow-orange; belly white to yellow; young fish, under about 30 cm TL, darker, redder, including belly, and with white stripe along lateral line and shorter white stripe below; ocular and parietal ridges high and rough in larger fish, making spines difficult to count . . . . *Sebastes ruberrimus,* page 380

36 Bright red, dusky red, dark pink, or orange-pink, with little or no yellow; belly pink or reddish; juveniles sometimes with white belly, but no white stripes on sides even in juveniles and young adults; ocular and parietal ridges not particularly high and rough . . . . (37)

37 (36) Ridge below lower rim of eye with 2–10 spines; lateral line scales 47–55 . . . . *Sebastes aleutianus,* page 381

37 No ridge and no spine below lower rim of eye or slight ridge with 1 or 2 spines; lateral line scales 32–46 . . . . (38)

38 (37) Body reddish pink to orange-pink; mouth, gill cavity, and gill membranes red to red-black; no black in fold above upper jaw; gill rakers on first arch usually 27–30 (range 27–31); large pores on lower jaw . . . . *Sebastes borealis,* page 382

38 Body dark red; mouth, gill cavity, and upper portion of gill membranes black; black area in fold above upper jaw; gill rakers on first arch usually 31–33 (range 27–34); pores on lower jaw not particularly large . . . . *Sebastes melanostomus,* page 383 (not confirmed from Alaska)

Adelosebastes latens Eschmeyer, Abe, & Nakano, 1979 **Emperor rockfish**

Pacific Ocean south of Delarof Islands, Alaska; and at Emperor Seamounts.

Seamounts and continental slope at depths of 687–1,200 m.

D XII–XIII,12–13; A III,5; Pec 20–23; LLp 28–29; LLs 74–100; GR 23–27; Vert 26.

- Bright crimson-red; dusky mottling dorsally, forming 3 vague saddles; margins of operculum and membranes of spinous dorsal fin dusky; ventral pectoral fin rays pink; dusky area on upper pectoral rays; gill cavity black; peritoneum dark.
- **Body relatively deep**.
- Head spines: 1, 2, 3, 4, 5, 7, 8; very strong.
- Interorbital space concave; **suborbital stay spines absent or 1–2 weak spines present**.
- **Dorsal fin spines fewer and dorsal soft rays more than in *Sebastolobus***; anal fin spine 2 longer than 3; **pectoral fin with slight notch, lower rays thickened and tips free**.
- Smaller scales (more than 70 in lateral line) than in *Sebastolobus* and most *Sebastes*.
- Length to 41 cm TL.

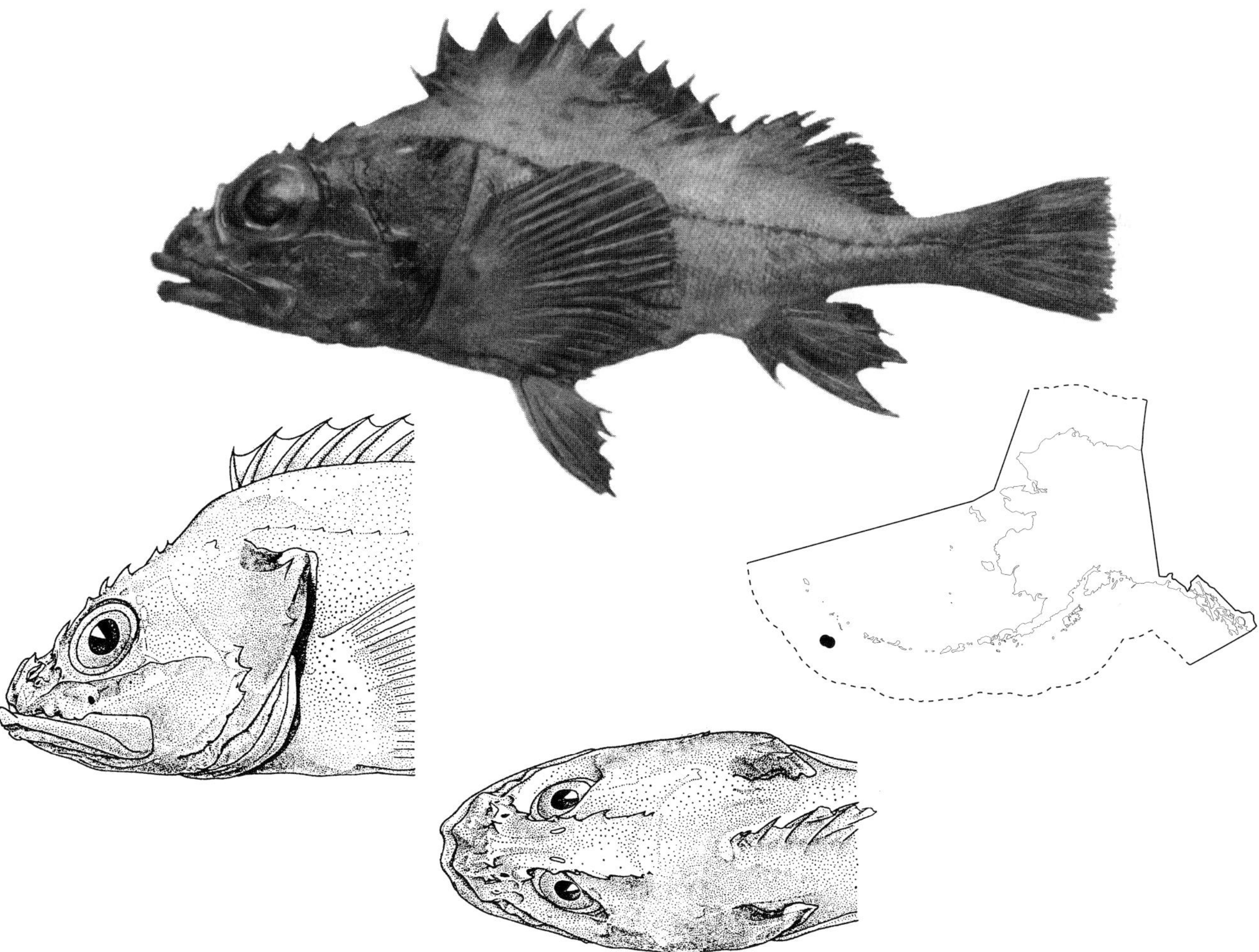

Notes & Sources — *Adelosebastes latens* Eschmeyer, Abe, & Nakano, 1979

Smaller individuals, less than 288 mm SL, are nearly uniform red in life, and adults 325–335 mm SL have more black and dusky markings, including the broad, diffuse bands dorsally. Any spines present on the suborbital ridge are more strongly developed in adults, although still weaker than in *Sebastolobus*.

Description: Eschmeyer et al. 1979; Barsukov et al. 1983; Amaoka in Masuda et al. 1984:315; Orr and Baker 1996a; Orr et al. 2000:21. Orr and Baker (1996a) reported 18 pectoral fin rays on the left side of one Alaskan specimen, but considered it to be anomalous.

Figures: Masuda et al. 1984, pl. 281-G; 19 cm SL. Head, lateral and ventral: Eschmeyer et al. 1979, fig. 1; holotype, 28 cm SL (scales not shown).

Range: Recorded in Alaska from the Aleutian Islands south of Ilak Island in the Delarof Islands by Orr and Baker (1996a); one specimen from 51°22'N, 178°10'W, depth 732 m, and one from 51°21'N, 178°48'W, depth 687 m, caught in commercial longline operations targeting sablefish. Previous records are from the Emperor Seamounts, from 34° to 41°N and 170° to 172°E; specimens were caught in bottom trawls and shrimp pots.

Sebastolobus altivelis Gilbert, 1896 **longspine thornyhead**

Western Gulf of Alaska to southern Baja California off Cape San Lucas.
Bottom, on continental slope at depths of 201–1,756 m.

D XV–XVII,8–10; A III,4–6; Pec 22–24; LLp 28–32; LLs 32–38; GR 21–26; Vert 29.

- Bright red; black areas on fins; underside of head purplish red; **gill cavity mostly dusky**; peritoneum white with black dots, uniformly blackish in juveniles.
- **Body relatively elongate**, caudal peduncle depth more than 43% of body depth at base of anal fin.
- Head spines: 1, 2, 3, 4, 5, 7, 8; very strong.
- Maxilla extending to rear edge of pupil; **interorbital space concave; several strong spines on suborbital stay**.
- **Dorsal fin spine 3 obviously longest**; spine 4 rarely slightly longer, this occurring more frequently in juveniles; anal fin spine 2 longer than 3; **pectoral fin notched, lower rays not highly branched**, lowest rays thickened and tips free.
- Length to 38 cm TL.

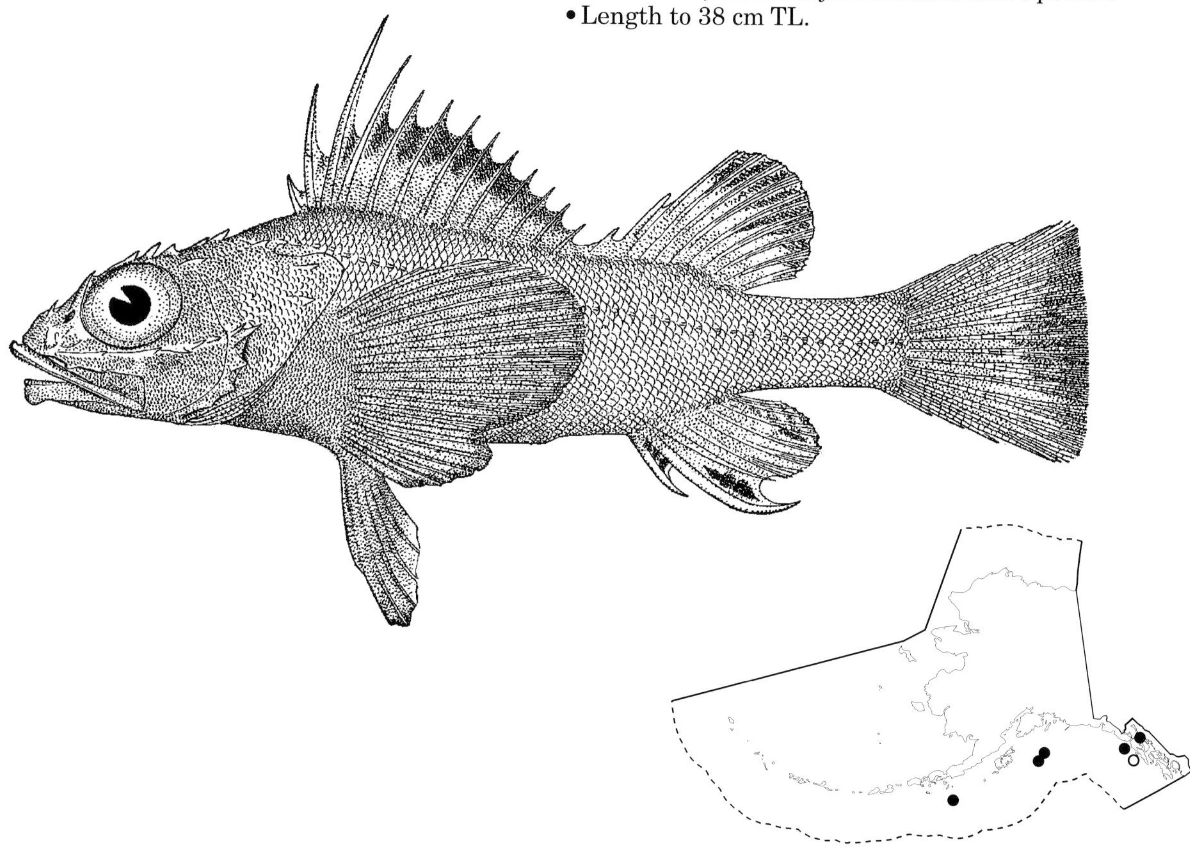

Notes & Sources — *Sebastolobus altivelis* Gilbert, 1896

Description: Phillips 1957:34–35; Barsukov 1964:235–236 of transl.; Hart 1973:453–454; Eschmeyer and Herald 1983: 153; Kramer and O'Connell 1995:73; Orr et al. 2000:20.

Figure: Jordan and Evermann 1900, fig. 654; holotype, 32.5 cm TL, from south of Alaska Peninsula.

Range: Previously given in general statements as north to the Bering Sea (Phillips 1957) or the Aleutian Islands (Schultz 1936, Barsukov 1964, Miller and Lea 1972, Quast and Hall 1972, Hart 1973, Kramer and O'Connell 1995), but only to the Gulf of Alaska by Orr et al. (2000). Although the NMFS survey database contains a few Bering Sea records for this species, J. W. Orr (pers. comm., 2 Apr. 1999) doubts their validity, and they are not associated with voucher specimens. The nearest adequately documented record to the Bering Sea may be the holotype, taken south of the Shumagin Islands at *Albatross* station 3338 in 1,143 m of water (Gilbert 1896). Position of this station was 54°19'N, 159°40'W (Tanner 1893). Quast and Hall (1972) reported *S. altivelis* from southeastern Alaska, based on AB 62-488 from Favorite Channel at 58°35'N, 135°04'W, depth 494 m. Recent records include AB 86-1, off Cape Cross, 57°51'N, 137°24'W, 823 m; AB 94-8, northern Gulf of Alaska, 57°50'N, 149°13'W, 880–910 m; and AB 94-9S, northern Gulf of Alaska, 58°10'N, 148°39'W, 800–860 m. Meristic and other characters (R. Baxter, unpubl. data; specimens not saved) of two specimens collected off Sitka by the 1987 NMFS triennial bottom trawl survey are appropriate for this species. Probably more common in the Gulf of Alaska than suggested by the few voucher specimens. The NMFS bottom trawl surveys, and even the sablefish longline surveys, are generally too shallow to catch this fish (B. L. Wing, pers. comm., 30 Mar. 1999).

Sebastolobus alascanus Bean, 1890 **shortspine thornyhead**

Bering Sea and Aleutian Islands to central Baja California off Cedros Island; less common in western Bering Sea south to Commander Islands, common from Cape Afrika southward along Pacific side of Kuril Islands, relatively rare in Seas of Okhotsk and Japan.

Bottom at depths of 17–1,524 m, usually at 100–800 m.

D XV–XVIII,8–9; A III,4–5; Pec 21–23; LLp 29–33; LLs 35–46; GR 18–23; Vert 29–31.

- Bright red to pink; usually with dusky to black areas on fins; dark blotch between dorsal spines 1–4 and another between posterior spines; **underside of head white**; **gill cavity mostly pale**, dusky blotch inside operculum; peritoneum white, or white with black dots.
- **Body relatively elongate**, caudal peduncle depth more than 43% of body depth at base of anal fin.
- Head spines: 1, 2, 3, 4, 5, 7, 8; very strong.
- Maxilla extending to rear edge of eye or beyond; **interorbital space concave**; **several strong spines on suborbital stay**.
- **Dorsal fin spine 4 or 5 longest, rarely spine 3, none of them greatly differing in length from adjacent spines**; anal fin spine 2 longer than 3; **pectoral fin notched, lower rays not highly branched**, lowest rays thickened and tips free.
- Length to 80 cm SL.

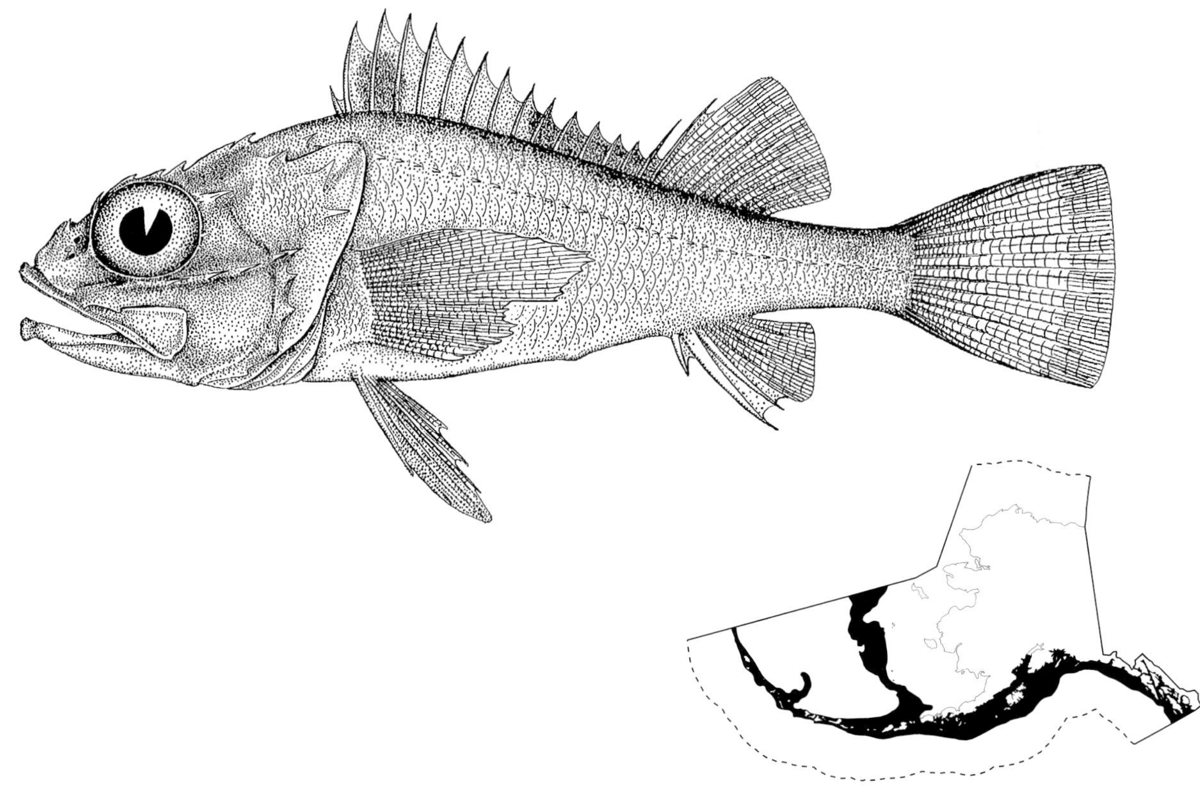

Notes & Sources — *Sebastolobus alascanus* Bean, 1890

Description: Phillips 1957:36–37; Barsukov 1964:234–235 of transl.; Hart 1973:451–452; Amaoka in Masuda et al. 1984:316; Kramer and O'Connell 1995:71; Orr et al. 2000:20.

Figure: Hart 1973:451, modified; 28 cm TL.

Range: Range given by Barsukov (1964) as San Diego north to the Bering Sea, along the continental slope and off the Commander Islands; distribution along Asian coasts was unknown. Range in the eastern Bering Sea and North Pacific was more precisely defined by Allen and Smith (1988), primarily from NMFS demersal trawl survey data, with distribution north to Navarin Canyon and west in the Aleutian Islands to Stalemate Bank. Recent reports document presence from western Bering Sea to Sea of Okhotsk (e.g., Dudnik and Dolganov 1992, Orlov 1998a). Fedorov and Sheiko (2002) reported *S. alascanus* to be abundant in the vicinity of the Commander Islands, and gave depth range of 17–1,524 m.

Size: Amaoka in Masuda et al. 1984. Recorded to 76 cm TL in eastern Pacific (Kramer and O'Connell 1995).

Sebastolobus macrochir (Günther, 1877) **broadfin thornyhead**

Eastern Bering Sea slope and Pacific off central and western Aleutian Islands; rare in western Bering Sea south of Cape Navarin to Commander Islands and Pacific off southeastern Kamchatka, common in Pacific off Kuril Islands, and Okhotsk and Japan seas.

Bottom at depths of 110–1,504 m.

D XIII–XVI,6–10; A III,4–6; Pec 21–23; LLp 31–32; LLs 35–38; GR 18–22; Vert 27–30.

- Bright red; large black blotch posteriorly on spinous dorsal fin, dusky area between anal fin spines; **gill cavity red, in preservative pale**; peritoneum pale.
- **Body relatively deep**, caudal peduncle depth less than 43% of body depth at base of anal fin.
- Head spines: 1, 2, 3, 4, 5, 7, 8; very strong.
- Maxilla extending beyond mideye; **interorbital space flattish**; **several strong spines on suborbital stay**.
- **Dorsal fin spine 3 longest, but usually not markedly longer than following spines**, rarely spine 2, 4, 5, or 6 longest; anal fin spine 2 same length or slightly longer than 3; **pectoral fin notched, lower rays highly branched, lowest rays thickened, elongate, and with tips free**; pelvic fin long, reaching to or near anal fin origin, outer rays thickened in some specimens.
- Length to 35 cm TL.

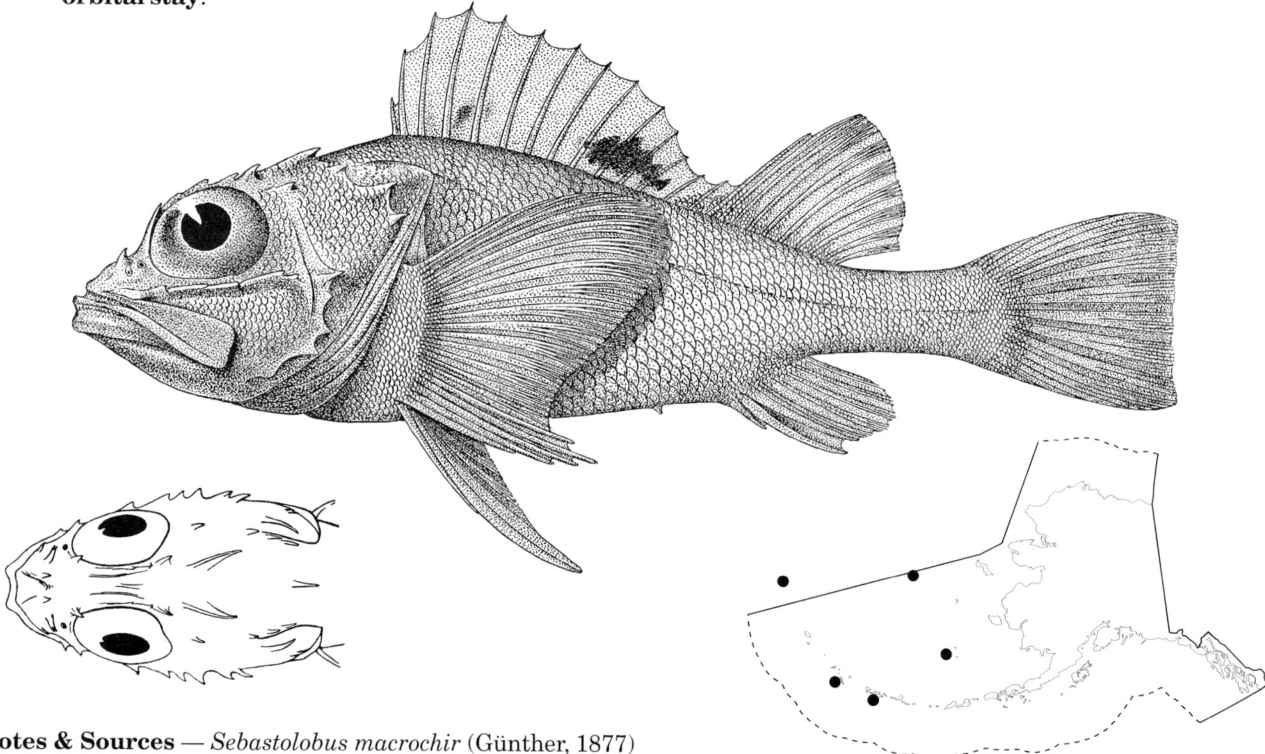

Notes & Sources — *Sebastolobus macrochir* (Günther, 1877)
Sebastes macrochir Günther, 1877
Appeared again as new species in Günther (1880), but 1877 date has priority (Eschmeyer 1998).
The common name "broadbanded thornyhead," given by Robins et al. (1991a), was an error. The species name means *broad hand,* a reference to the pectoral fins. We use the name broadfin thornyhead, recommended by the American Fisheries Society Committee on Names of Fishes (J. S. Nelson, pers. comm., 31 Apr. 2001).

Description: Günther 1877:434–435; Jordan and Starks 1904a:94–95; Barsukov 1964:233–234 of transl.; Kanayama in Amaoka et al. 1983:336; Amaoka in Masuda et al. 1984: 315–316; Lindberg and Krasyukova 1987:89–91; Shinohara and Amaoka 1993; Orr et al. 2000:21.

Figures: Lindberg and Krasyukova 1987, fig. 44; 241 mm TL, Japan.

Range: Recorded by Barsukov (1964) from Bering Sea south of Cape Navarin at 60°44'N, 179°45'W, depth 360–400 m; on the U.S. side of the international boundary. Reported from the Aleutian Islands by Robins et al. (1991a) in a general statement. Specific localities south of the Aleutians were provided by J. W. Orr (pers. comm., 2 Apr. 1999) from NMFS surveys in 1997: 51°27'N, 178°35'E, depth 368 m; and 51°54'N, 176°38'W, depth 376 m. In June 2000 the NMFS caught a specimen west of the Pribilof Islands at 56°30'N, 172°03'W, at depth of about 788 m (average depth of tow; J. W. Orr, pers. comm., 5 Sep. 2000). Although the NMFS survey database contains numerous earlier eastern Bering Sea records for this species, Orr believes they probably all represent *S. alascanus,* the common species of the eastern Pacific having been misidentified as the common species of the western Pacific. Reported to be present but rare in the Commander Islands vicinity by Fedorov and Sheiko (2002); they gave a depth range of 110–1,504 m. Previously reported as deep as 1,280 m (e.g., Lindberg and Krasyukova 1987). *Sebastolobus macrochir* is an important commercial fish in Japan.

Sebastes helvomaculatus Ayres, 1859 **rosethorn rockfish**

Western Gulf of Alaska east of Sitkinak Island to Baja California north of San Benito Islands.
Around rocky reefs and seamounts at depths to 549 m, usually offshore at depths of 125–350 m.

D XII–XIV,12–14; A III,6–7; Pec 15–18; LLp 34–45; LLs 42–48; GR 28–33; Vert 26.

- Yellow-orange, with light olivaceous mottling dorsally; **4 or 5 white blotches bordered or tinged with pink or orange dorsally**; lighter ventrally; dusky area on opercle; fins pink, with yellow-green areas; mouth and gill cavity pink and white, often with some yellow; peritoneum gray with black dots or black.
- Head spines: 1, 2, 3, 4, 5, 7, (8); strong to very strong.
- Symphyseal knob moderately strong; maxilla extending to mideye to rear edge of pupil; interorbital space concave; small subopercular spines present or absent; lachrymal with small process anteriorly and triangular spine posteriorly, occasionally with two triangular spines.
- **Anal fin spine 2 longer than 3**; distal margin of anal fin vertical or slightly slanted anteriorly; caudal fin slightly to moderately emarginate; **pectoral rays typically 16**.
- Length to 41 cm TL.

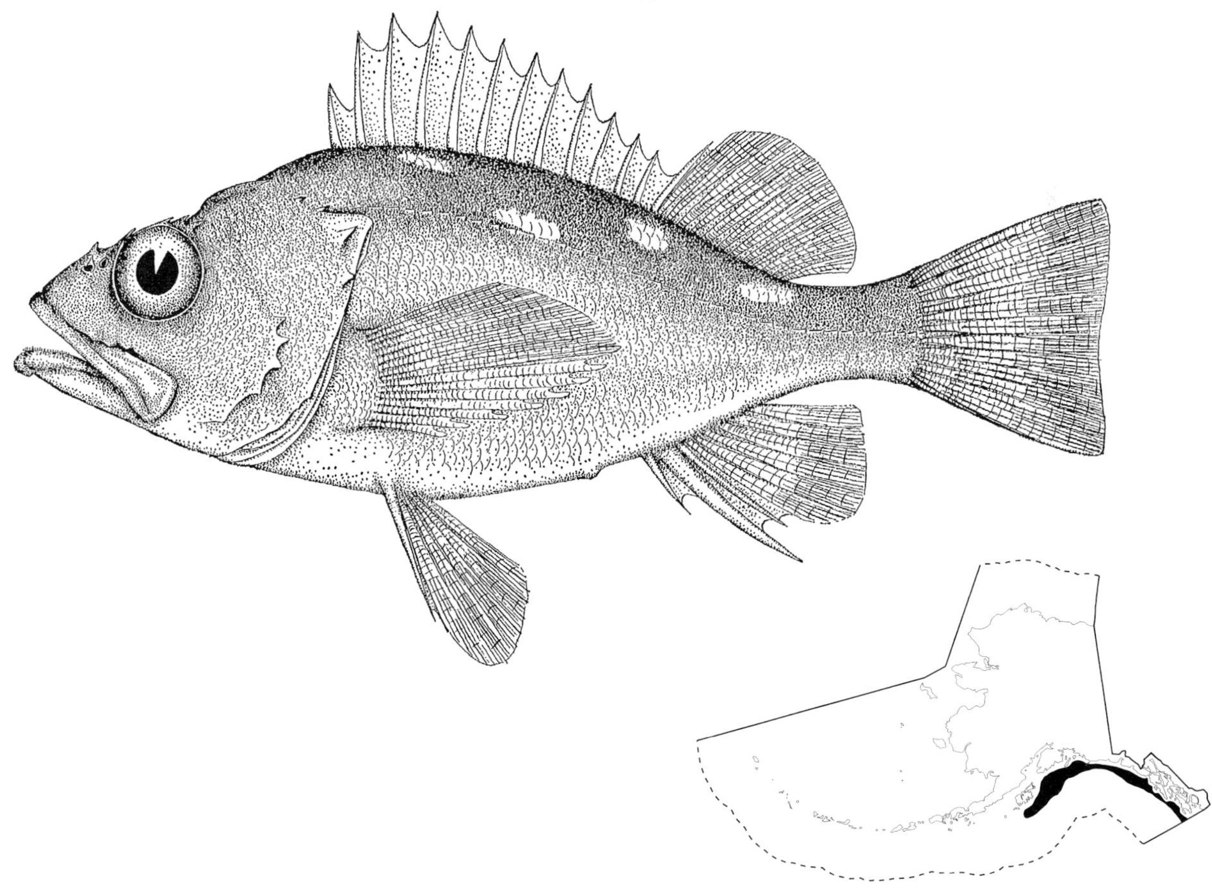

Notes & Sources — *Sebastes helvomaculatus* Ayres, 1859

Description: Phillips 1957:118–119; Hart 1973:421–422; Eschmeyer and Herald 1983:141; Kramer and O'Connell 1995:33; Orr et al. 2000:37. Description is not in Jordan and Evermann (1898) because they mistakenly synonymized *S. helvomaculatus* Ayres with *S. rosaceus* Girard (not Alaskan). Chen (1986) reported that in a sample of 73 fish, only 1 had 12 and 1 had 14 dorsal fin spines.

Figure: Hart 1973:421; 28 cm TL, British Columbia.

Range: Recorded from east of Sitkinak Island at 56°22'N, 152°21'W (AB 67-63), by Nishimoto (1970). Distribution of the 469 occurrences mapped by Allen and Smith (1988) and catch localities of voucher specimens in museums indicate the species is relatively rare west of Icy Bay (about 141°30'W, in the eastern Gulf of Alaska). Westrheim (1965) described three specimens taken 65 miles east of Cape Saint Elias, at 59°33'N, 142°34'W. The ABL has six lots from localities farther southeast, including Yakutat and Cape Fairweather, recorded by Quast and Hall (1972), as well as one from south of Kodiak Island (AB 69-25). Krieger (1993) observed *S. helvomaculatus* from a submersible over the outer continental shelf off southeastern Alaska. Snytko (1986) reported extension of the known range south (from Guadalupe Island) to 28°33'N, 115°25'W, a few kilometers north of San Benito Islands off Ranger Bank.

Sebastes nigrocinctus Ayres, 1859 **tiger rockfish**

Northwestern Gulf of Alaska at Marmot Bay off The Triplets to southern California at Tanner and Cortes banks.

Around rocky reefs and boulder fields, at depths of 18–274 m; usually deeper than 55 m; solitary, often hidden in crevices, and not often taken in trawl nets.

D XII–XIII,12–15; A III,6–7; Pec 18–20; LLp 36–50; LLs 44–53; GR 27–32; Vert 26.

- **Pink to orange, with 4 or 5 dark red or black bands**; 4th and 5th bands extending down from second dorsal fin; **no distinct band on caudal peduncle**; 2 bars radiating down and back from eye; anal and pelvic fin tips dark in juveniles; mouth and gill cavity pink; peritoneum white.
- Body very deep.
- Head spines: 1, 2, 3, 4, 5, 6, 7, 8; strong; some spines much divided.
- Symphyseal knob obsolete or absent; maxilla extending to mideye to beyond eye; **interorbital space strongly concave, parietal ridges thick and coarse**; subopercular spines absent; lachrymal with low process anteriorly, triangular spine posteriorly.
- Anal fin spine 2 slightly longer or shorter than 3 or about same length; distal margin of anal fin rounded; caudal fin slightly rounded.
- Length to 61 cm TL.

Notes & Sources — *Sebastes nigrocinctus* Ayres, 1859

Description: Jordan and Evermann 1898:1827–1828; Phillips 1957:134–135; Hart 1973:433–434; Eschmeyer and Herald 1983:145;Kramer and O'Connell 1995:49; Orr et al. 2000:36. One fish in a sample of nine had 12 dorsal fin spines (Chen 1986).

Figure: University of British Columbia, artist P. Drukker-Brammall; UBC 63-938, 248 mm SL, Malaspina Strait, south side of Pearson Island, British Columbia.

Range: A photograph by Kessler (1985:41) shows a 40-cm *S. nigrocinctus* captured 27 Aug. 1981 northeast of Kodiak Island in Marmot Bay at The Triplets, off the first rock closest to Ouzinkie (D. W. Kessler, pers. comm., 20 Jun. 1994); this is the westernmost adequately documented record. Quast and Hall (1972) earlier recorded a range extension to Cape Resurrection on the Kenai Peninsula (AB 70-66; 302 mm SL). Rosenthal (1980) found it off Schooner Rock, Prince William Sound. UBC 62-996 is from Kachemak Bay off Nubble Point, McDonald Spit. Voucher specimens from southeastern Alaska include NMC 68-1849 (2 specimens) from 23 km southwest of Sitka; AB 84-69 (13 small specimens, 37–43 mm SL) from off Cape Ommaney; and UBC 63-188 (1) from east of Rose Island. Lissner and Dorsey (1986) reported extension of known range south (from Point Buchon) to Tanner and Cortes banks.

Sebastes babcocki (Thompson, 1915) **redbanded rockfish**

Bering Sea at Zhemchug Canyon and Aleutian Islands off Amchitka Island to southern California off San Diego.

Offshore reefs, seamounts, and smoother bottoms at depths of 49–625 m; most commonly in deep water at 150–400 m.

D XIII,13–15; A III,6–8; Pec 17–20; LLp 41–51; LLs 56–64; GR 29–33; Vert 26.

- **Pink and white with 4 broad red bands** that fade in large specimens (and in alcohol); 1st band extending from front of spinous dorsal fin and top of head over and behind operculum to pectoral fin; 2nd band usually curving anteriorly above lateral line, ending on lower side; 3rd band extending from second dorsal onto anal fin; **4th band on caudal peduncle**; 1 or 2 red bands radiating from eye; usually some black on median fins; peritoneum gray or mottled with black.
- Head spines: 1, 2, 4, (5), 7; moderate to strong.
- Symphyseal knob small; maxilla extending to mideye to rear edge of eye; **interorbital space flat to slightly concave**; subopercular spines usually absent; lachrymal spines prominent, posterior spine usually multifid.
- Anal fin spine 2 longer and much thicker than 3; distal margin of anal fin rounded or slightly slanted posteriorly; caudal fin emarginate.
- Length to 65 cm TL.

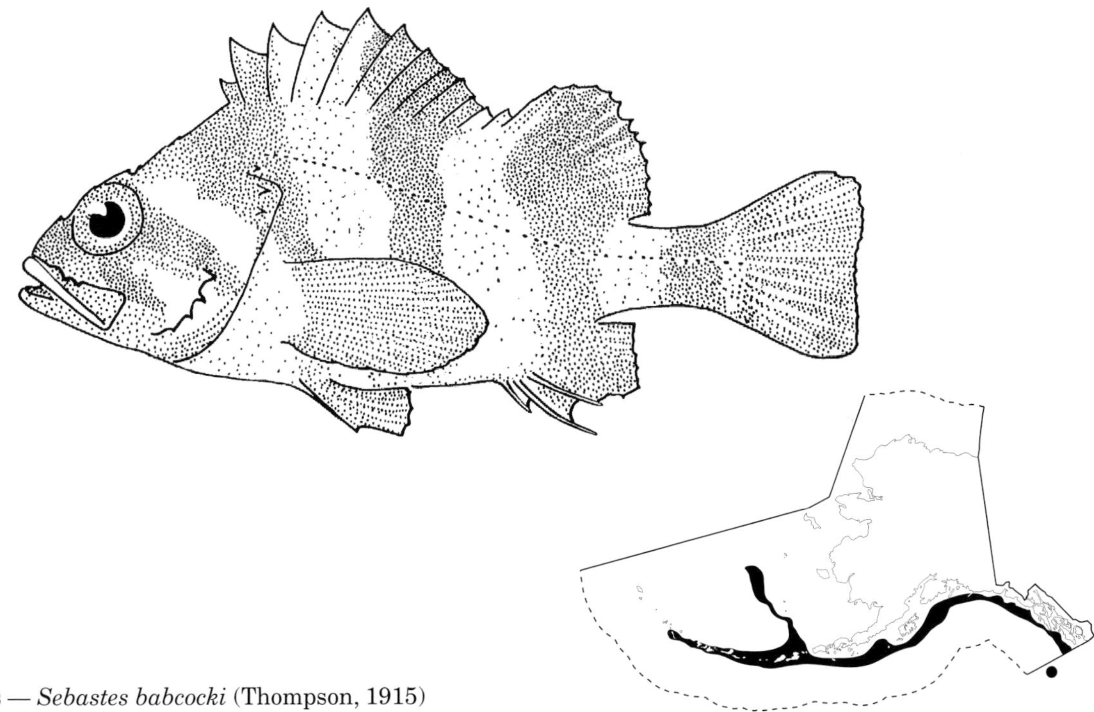

Notes & Sources — *Sebastes babcocki* (Thompson, 1915)
Sebastodes babcocki Thompson, 1915
A similar species, *S. rubrivinctus* Jordan & Gilbert, 1880, has been confused with *S. babcocki* in Alaska. However, *S. rubrivinctus* is rarely found north of San Francisco. Snytko and Fedorov (1975) reported *S. rubrivinctus* from off Washington at 46°42'N, 124°47'W, and Snytko (1986) reported both species west of Washington at Cobb Seamount. Allen and Smith (1988:56) discussed identification of these species in the NMFS survey database.

Description: Thompson 1915; Rosenblatt and Chen 1972; Hart 1973:401–402; Eschmeyer and Herald 1983:135; Kramer and O'Connell 1995:9; Orr et al. 2000:35.

Figure: Miller and Lea 1972:103.

Range: The type specimen was taken off Middleton Island, Alaska (Thompson 1915). Notices of extensions of known range of *S. rubrivinctus* to Gulf of Alaska and Aleutian Islands (e.g., Heyamoto and Hitz 1962, Barsukov 1964, Best and Eldridge 1969) were shown by Rosenblatt and Chen (1972) to represent *S. babcocki.* Recorded from Amchitka Island by Best and Eldridge (1969), as *S. rubrivinctus,* and by Simenstad et al. (1977). NMFS survey data (706 occurrences in more than 30 years of surveys) extended known range north to Bering Sea at Zhemchug Canyon (Allen and Smith 1988); that locality was far distant from the nearest other catch locality, south of Tigalda Island near Unimak Pass. The available information, including unpublished museum records, indicates *S. babcocki* is relatively rare west and north of Unimak Pass. Snytko (1986) reported one specimen (58 cm FL) was taken at Hodgkins Seamount, 53°15'N, 135°45'W, depth 240-250 m.

Size: R. N. Lea (pers. comm., 6 Mar. 2001) reported maximum verifiable record of 65.5 cm TL, from specimen taken off Davenport, Santa Cruz County, California, in gill net set at 311–393 m on 5 Apr. 1995. Previous record was 64 cm TL (Miller and Lea 1972).

Sebastes nebulosus Ayres, 1854 **China rockfish**

Western Gulf of Alaska at Kodiak Island to southern California off Redondo Beach and San Nicholas Island.

Over reefs and in crevices at depths of 3–128 m, most commonly shallower than 91 m; found more often on open coasts than inside waters.

D XIII,12–14; A III,6–8; Pec 17–19; LLp 37–48; ; LLs 43–48; GR 26–31; Vert 26.

- **Blue-black**, mottled and splotched with yellow, white, and bluish white; more white ventrally; **broad yellow stripe starting at dorsal fin spines 3 and 4 and continuing along lateral line to caudal fin**; fins blue-black, finely speckled; mouth and gill cavity mainly white; peritoneum silvery white.
- Head spines: 1, 2, 4, 5, 7; strong and high, encased in thick skin.
- Symphyseal knob small or absent; maxilla extending to posterior part of eye to beyond eye; **interorbital space deeply concave**; subopercular spines usually present; lachrymal processes present and rounded or somewhat triangular.
- Anal fin spine 2 as long or longer than 3; distal margin of anal fin rounded; caudal fin slightly rounded.
- Length to 45 cm TL.

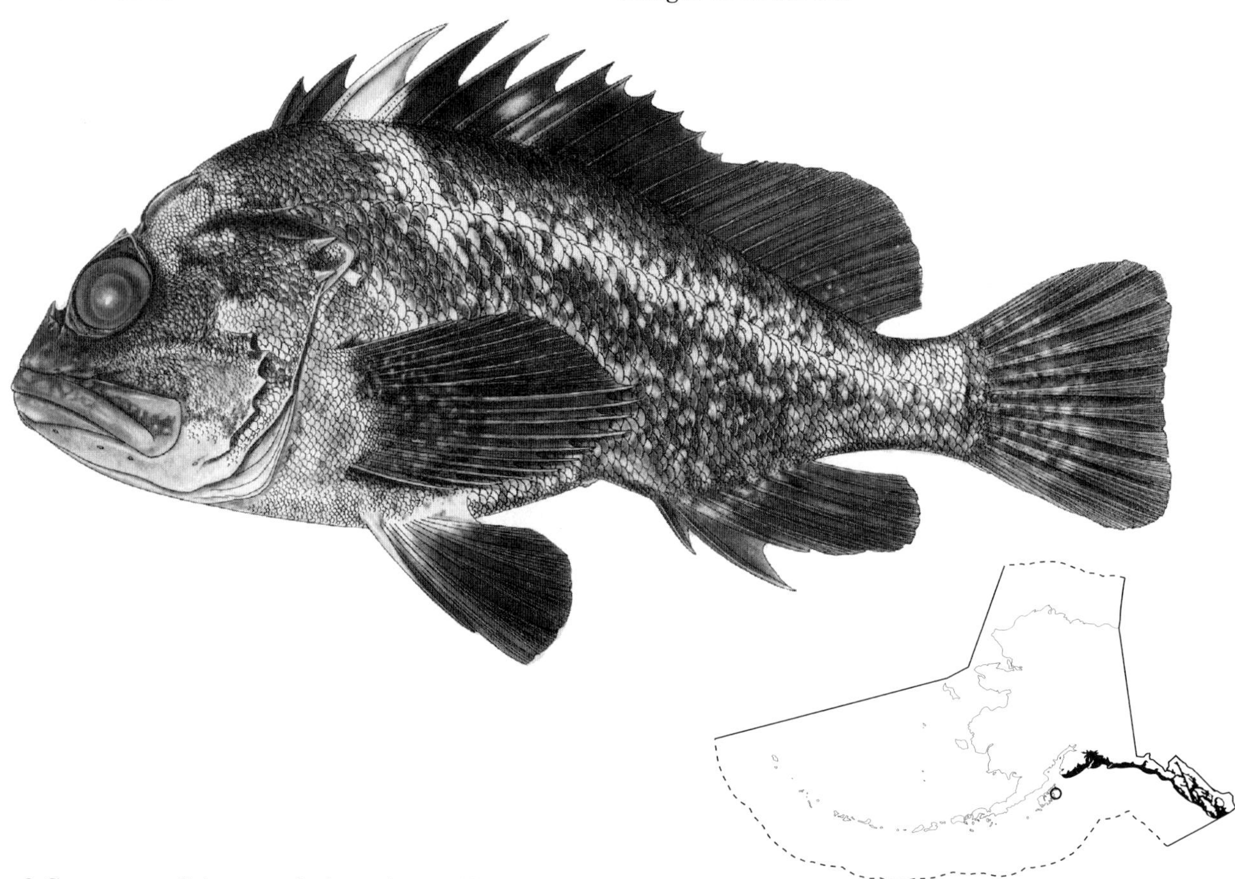

Notes & Sources — *Sebastes nebulosus* Ayres, 1854

Walford (1931) remarked that this fish was highly prized by the Chinese in San Francisco; hence the common name.

Description: Jordan and Evermann 1898:1826–1827; Phillips 1957:126–127; Hart 1973:431–432; Eschmeyer and Herald 1983:145; Kramer and O'Connell 1995:47; Orr et al. 2000:32.

Figure: University of British Columbia, artist P. Drukker-Brammall; UBC 65-576, 240 mm SL, Klokachef Island.

Range: Wilimovsky (1954) gave southeastern Alaska for northern limit. Rosenthal (1980) claimed extension of known range north to Danger Island, Zaikof Point, and Schooner Rock in Prince William Sound. Kramer and O'Connell (1988, 1995) gave Kachemak Bay, Cook Inlet, without specific documentation. J. E. Blackburn (pers. comm., 23 Jul. 1998) reported catches off Kodiak Island at Williams Reef in Chiniak Bay in 1996, and Afognak Island at Izhut Bay in 1984; records are on file at ADFG, Kodiak. Specimens from Alaska are not common in museum collections. Those we know of are from southeastern Alaska. AB 62-338 and AB 70-139 are from Skowl Arm, and AB 67-242 is from Katlian Bay (one specimen each). UBC 65-373 has three specimens from Biorka Island at 56°51'N, 135°32'W; and UBC 65-576, three specimens from Klokachef Island off south point at 57°24'N, 135°53'W. More abundant off British Columbia and farther south. Known range was extended south from previous records to Redondo Beach (about 33°51'N, 118°23'W) off southern shore of Monterey Bay by Fitch and Schultz (1978), and to San Nicholas Island (about 33°14'N, 119°31'W) by M. S. Love (pers. comm., 30 Jul. 1999).

Size: Ueber 1989.

Sebastes maliger (Jordan & Gilbert, 1880) **quillback rockfish**

Western Gulf of Alaska at Kodiak Island to southern California off San Miguel Island.

Close to or on rocky bottom and reefs inshore to depth of 274 m, usually found shallower than 145 m.

D XIII,12–14; A III,6–8; Pec 16–18; LLp 34–48; LLs 39–45; GR 29–34; Vert 26.

- **Grayish brown mottled with yellow anteriorly, and orange-brown spots on lower, anterior part of body**; fins dark brown or blackish except for **large white to yellow area on spinous dorsal fin**; mouth and gill cavity white, with some yellow; peritoneum silvery white.
- Head spines: 1, 2, 4, 5, 7; strong.
- Symphyseal knob obsolete or absent; maxilla extending to rear edge of eye; **interorbital space slightly convex to slightly concave**; subopercular spines present; lachrymal spines weak or absent.
- **Spinous dorsal fin deeply incised and high**; anal fin spine 2 shorter than 3 or about equal; distal margin of anal fin rounded; caudal fin slightly rounded.
- Length to 61 cm TL.

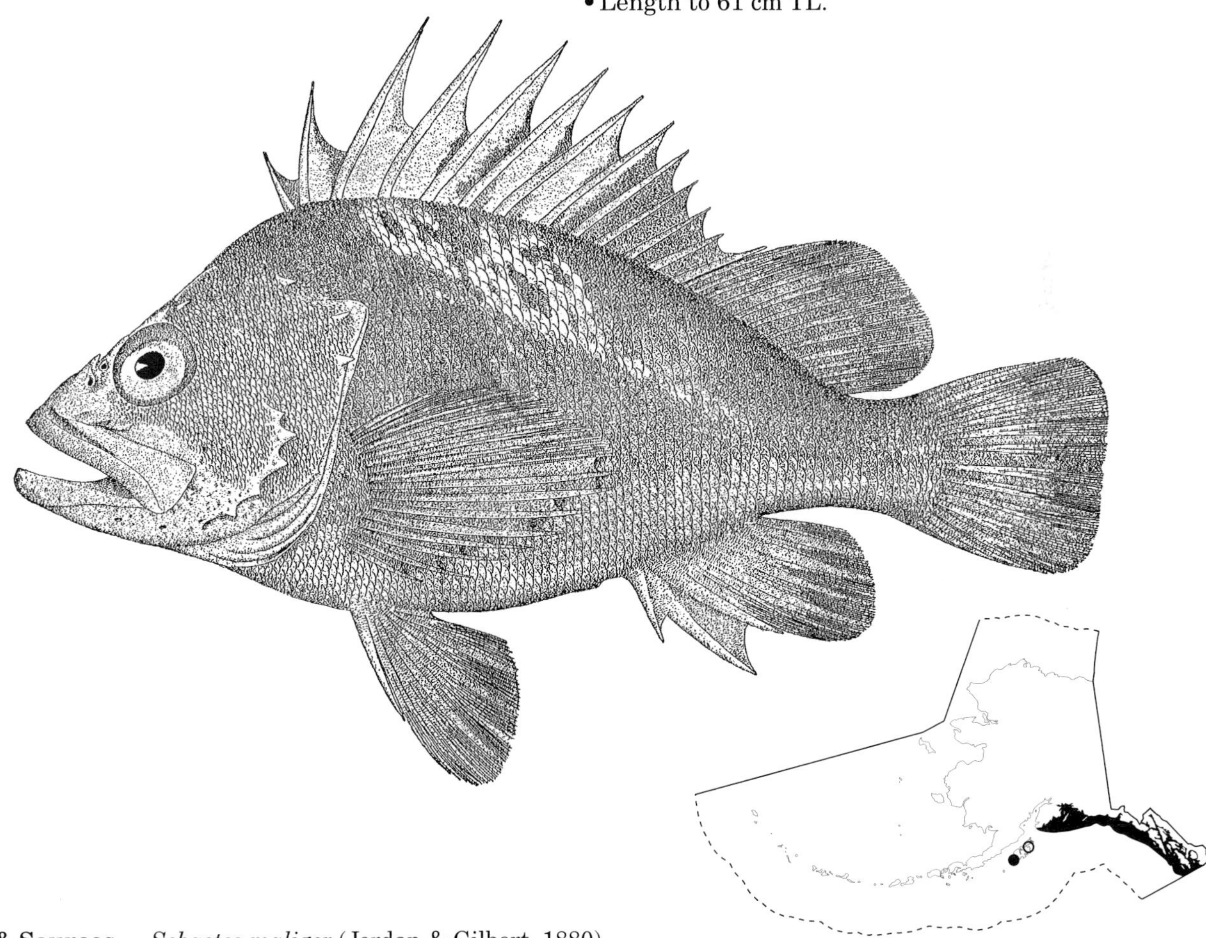

Notes & Sources — *Sebastes maliger* (Jordan & Gilbert, 1880)
Sebastichthys maliger Jordan & Gilbert, 1880

Description: Jordan and Evermann 1898:1822–1823; Phillips 1957:94–95; Hart 1973:424–425; Eschmeyer and Herald 1983:142; Kramer and O'Connell 1995:37; Love and Lea 1997; Orr et al. 2000:32.

Figures: Jordan and Evermann 1900, fig. 665; 32 cm TL, Sitka, Alaska.

Range: J. E. Blackburn (pers. comm., 23 Jul. 1998) reported catches at Kodiak Island off The Triplets in Marmot Bay and Afognak Island in Izhut Bay, both in 1984; records are on file at ADFG, Kodiak. The identification of UW 3070 from Alitak Bay, Kodiak Island, cannot be verified because the specimen is missing (UW online catalog). However, Blackburn's records from the Kodiak archipelago indicate it was probably valid. Recorded as far west as the Kenai Peninsula by Quast and Hall (1972). Rosenthal (1980) reported *S. maliger* from Danger Island, Zaikof Point, and Schooner Rock in Prince William Sound. The UBC collection has specimens from as far north as Evans Island, 60°04'N, 147°59'W (UBC 62-984) and Middleton Island (UBC 58-333), and south nearly to the British Columbia border. Specimens from southeastern Alaska are fairly common in museum collections. Love and Lea (1997) reported specimens representing extension of the recorded range to southern California off San Miguel Island; the southernmost was taken at 34°00'N, 119°30'W.

Size: Kramer and O'Connell (1995) reported average length of 36 cm for *S. maliger* in the southeastern Alaska commercial fishery.

Sebastes auriculatus Girard, 1854 **brown rockfish**

Northern Gulf of Alaska at Prince William Sound to central Baja California at Hipolito Bay.

Shallow water, to depth of 128 m but usually less than 55 m, most commonly in areas of abundant kelp and around low profile reefs in sandy or silty areas.

D XIII,12–15; A III,5–8; Pec 15–19; LLp 40–50; LLs 45–52; GR 25–30; Vert 26–27.

- Light brown to blackish brown with darker brown mottling and vague bands and streaks; tinged with brownish red; **dark brown blotch on upper portion of opercle**; **underside of lower jaw and throat pinkish**; **fins dusky and pink**; mouth and gill cavity mainly white; peritoneum silvery white.
- Head spines: 1, 2, 4, 5, (6), 7, (8); strong.
- Symphyseal knob small or absent; maxilla extending to rear edge of pupil to beyond eye; **interorbital space slightly convex to flat**; subopercular spines present; lachrymal usually with small low process followed by larger spine.
- Anal fin spine 2 shorter or longer than 3; distal margin of anal fin rounded; caudal fin slightly rounded.
- Length to 56 cm TL.

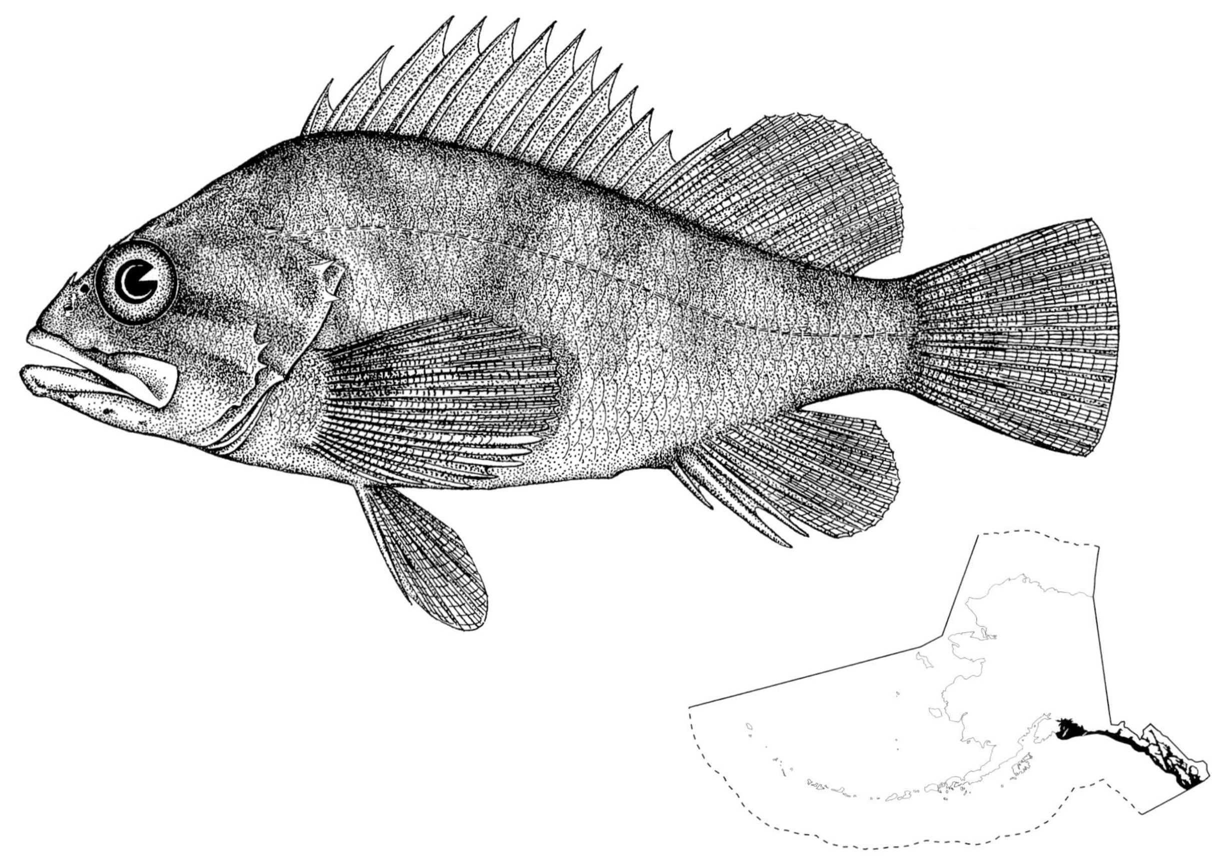

Notes & Sources — *Sebastes auriculatus* Girard, 1854

Description: Jordan and Evermann 1898:1817–1819; Phillips 1957:74–75; Hart 1973:398–399; Eschmeyer and Herald 1983:134; Kramer and O'Connell 1995:5; Orr et al. 2000:31.

Figure: Hart 1973:398; 16 cm TL, Hecate Strait, British Columbia.

Range: Northern limit was given as southeastern Alaska by Wilimovsky (1954), without documentation. Quast and Hall (1972) reported presence of specimens from southeastern Alaska in ABL collection; AB 63-164 and AB 63-172 are from Prince of Wales Island. More recent ABL collections include AB 88-22 (2 specimens), from Coronation Island, 55°53'N, 134°14'W. Rosenthal (1980) reported *S. auriculatus* from Prince William Sound, without giving a specific locality in the sound, as an extension of the known range northward from southeastern Alaska; reported from Prince William Sound by Rogers et al. (1986), on the basis of OCSEAP studies that included Rosenthal's (1980) report. Kramer and O'Connell (1995) reported *S. auriculatus* to be uncommon north of Prince of Wales Island. Hart (1973) reported that it is not commonly observed in British Columbia but probably is widely, if sparsely, distributed there in shallow waters.

Sebastes glaucus Hilgendorf, 1880 **gray rockfish**

Aleutian Islands south of Atka Island; western Bering Sea from Olyutorskiy Bay to Commander Islands and Pacific Ocean off Kamchatka to northern parts of Okhotsk and Japan seas.

Above and on bottom at depths of 2–550 m, usually shallower than 200 m; move inshore to release larvae.

D XIV,14–17; A III,7–9; Pec 18–20; LLp 37–52; LLs 48–78; GR 34–41; Vert 29–30.

- **Dark gray with yellow tinge**, yellow especially prominent in fins; darker bars radiating from eye; in preservative, dark brown with darker mottling; peritoneum dark.
- **Head spines: 1, others obsolete**.
- Symphyseal knob small or absent; maxilla extending to rear edge of pupil to rear edge of eye; interorbital space strongly convex; **supracleithral and cleithral spines absent**; both lachrymal processes present, each long and low.
- **Dorsal fin spines 14**; anal fin spine 2 shorter than 3; distal margin of anal fin rounded, slightly slanted posteriorly; caudal fin margin slightly emarginate.
- Scales absent from maxilla.
- Length to 59 cm TL.

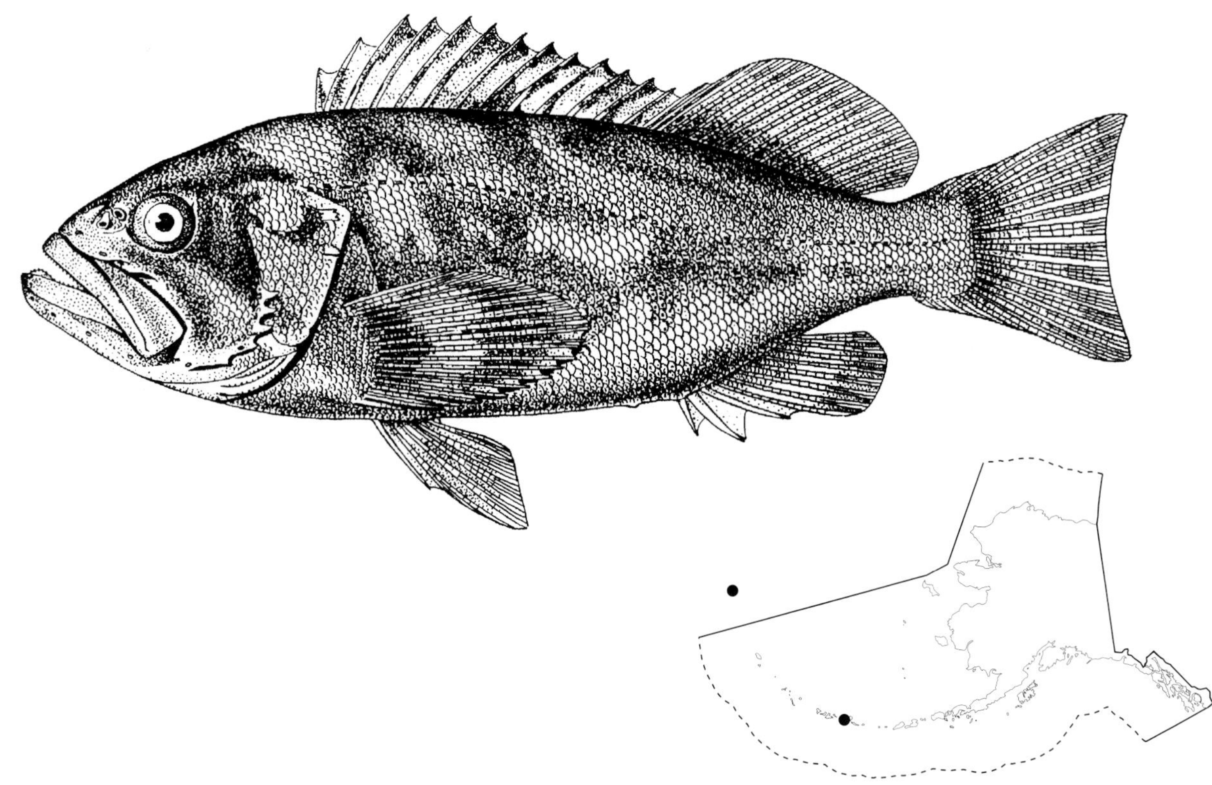

Notes & Sources — *Sebastes glaucus* Hilgendorf, 1880
Called blue rockfish by Russian authors.

Description: Jordan and Starks 1904a:97–98; Barsukov 1964:258 of transl.; Amaoka in Masuda et al. 1984:310; Lindberg and Krasyukova 1987:38–40; Orr and Baker 1996a; Orr et al. 2000:28.

Figure: Lindberg and Krasyukova 1987, fig. 11; 466 mm TL, Commander Islands.

Range: Orr and Baker (1996a) reported first record for Alaska: two specimens taken south of Atka Island at 52°19'N, 174°40'W, depth 122 m; and 52°20'N, 174°38'W, depth 123 m. Fedorov and Sheiko (2002) reported it to be abundant at the Commander Islands and gave a depth range of 10–320 m. Lindberg and Krasyukova (1987) recorded depths of 25 m for ZIN 43918 and 27 m for ZIN 43919, both from the Sea of Okhotsk; and depths of 125–276 m from previous literature. Orr et al. (2000) gave a maximum depth of 550 m, which is unusually deep; the catch was reported by the NMFS observer program, but without a voucher specimen (J. W. Orr, pers. comm., 23 Jun. 1999). Kondrat'ev (1996) and Panchenko (1996) reported on biology of this species in the Sea of Okhotsk. In Tauyskaya Bay adults are common at depths less than 30 m for most of the year, and move to 2–5 m to release larvae in early summer.

Size: Amaoka (in Masuda et al. 1984) gave a maximum size of about 50 cm SL, whereas other authors, even those writing more recently, give 50 cm TL. Panchenko (1996) reported a range for *S. glaucus* collected in the southern Sea of Okhotsk in 1994 of 33–50 cm SL. Using a rough estimate of SL = 85% TL gives a maximum of 59 cm TL.

Sebastes ciliatus (Tilesius, 1813) **dusky rockfish**

Bering Sea and Aleutian Islands to southern British Columbia at Johnstone Strait; western Bering Sea from Cape Olyutorskiy to Commander Islands and Pacific off south tip of Kamchatka.

In schools around rocky reefs; light form to depth of 525 m, most commonly at 100–300 m; dark form shallower, recorded to 153 m, usually taken shallower than 100 m.

D XIII,13–16; A III,7–9; Pec 17–19; LLp 41–54; LLs 46–58; GR 32–36; Vert 28.

- Light form greenish to yellowish brown dorsally, pink or lighter ventrally, olive or brown bands radiating from eye, fins gray tinged pink or orange, peritoneum light to dark; dark form uniformly dark gray to bluish black, fins dark gray to black, peritoneum dark.
- **Head spines**: (1), (7); weak to very weak; **all typically absent**.
- Symphyseal knob moderate in light form, small or obsolete in dark form; maxilla extending to mideye to beyond eye; interorbital space convex; supracleithral and cleithral spines both moderately strong; subopercular spines present or absent; lachrymal processes barely evident or strong, rounded lobes.
- Anal fin spine 2 shorter than 3 or about equal; distal margin of anal fin rounded to almost straight and vertical or slightly slanted posteriorly; caudal fin emarginate to practically truncate.
- Scales present on maxilla.
- Length to 53 cm TL.

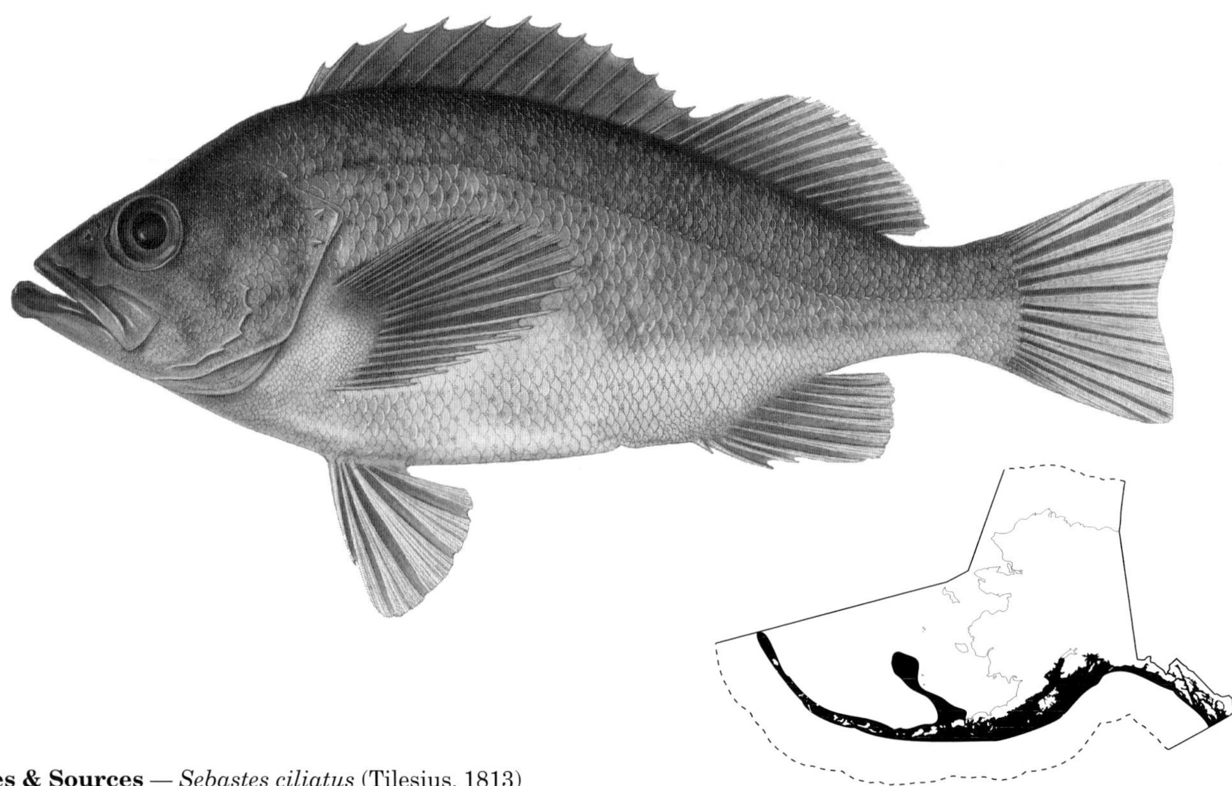

Notes & Sources — *Sebastes ciliatus* (Tilesius, 1813)
Epinephelus ciliatus Tilesius, 1813

Light and dark dusky rockfishes are sometimes taken in the same catch but the light form typically occurs in deeper water, is a target of the trawl fishery, and is most common at the northern end of the range. Seeb (1986) suggested that the two forms are distinct species. Orr et al. (2000) treated them separately, with the dark form labeled *Sebastes* sp. cf. *ciliatus*. Since the forms have not been described and named as valid species (they might not be distinct; study is ongoing), in this guide they are treated as a single entity.

Description: Barsukov 1964:256–257 of transl.; Hart 1973: 409–410; Westrheim 1973; Eschmeyer and Herald 1983: 136; Shinohara, Yabe, and Honma 1994; Kramer and O'Connell 1995:17; Orr et al. 2000:26.

Figure: University of British Columbia, artist P. Drukker-Brammall; UBC 62-42, light form, 297 mm SL, off Saturna Island, British Columbia.

Range: Allen and Smith (1988) reported range to Zhemchug Canyon in the Bering Sea and Agattu Island from NMFS surveys. Richards and Westrheim (1988) documented range south to Johnstone Strait, British Columbia. Shinohara, Yabe, and Honma (1994) reported the first record from Japan, off eastern Hokkaido. Sheiko and Tranbenkova (1998) recorded specimens from the Commander Islands, off Cape Olyutorskiy, and off the south tip of Kamchatka near Cape Lopatka. Western Pacific and Bering Sea records are of the light form; both forms are present from the Aleutian Islands to British Columbia.

Sebastes brevispinis (Bean, 1884) **silvergray rockfish**

Southeastern Bering Sea to Pacific Ocean off central Baja California at Bahia Sebastian Vizcaino.

Around reefs and over soft bottoms, from surface to 375 m, most commonly at 100–300 m.

D XIII,13–17; A III,7–8; Pec 16–18; LLp 44–53; LLs 58–70; GR 33–36; Vert 26.

- **Dark greenish to silvery gray dorsally and laterally, pink to white ventrally**; lateral line in narrow pinkish stripe; **lower portions of anal, pectoral, and pelvic fins tinged orange or pink**; lips blackish; peritoneum white, with or without black dots.
- Head spines: 1, 2, 7; weak.
- **Lower jaw strongly projecting**; **symphyseal knob large**; maxilla extending to rear edge of pupil to rear edge of eye; interorbital space convex; supracleithral and cleithral spines strong; subopercular spines present or absent; lachrymal with small rounded process followed by single or multifid spine.
- Anal fin spine 2 slightly shorter than 3 or about same length; distal margin of anal fin nearly vertical or slanted slightly anteriorly; caudal fin emarginate.
- Scales present on maxilla.
- Length to 71 cm TL.

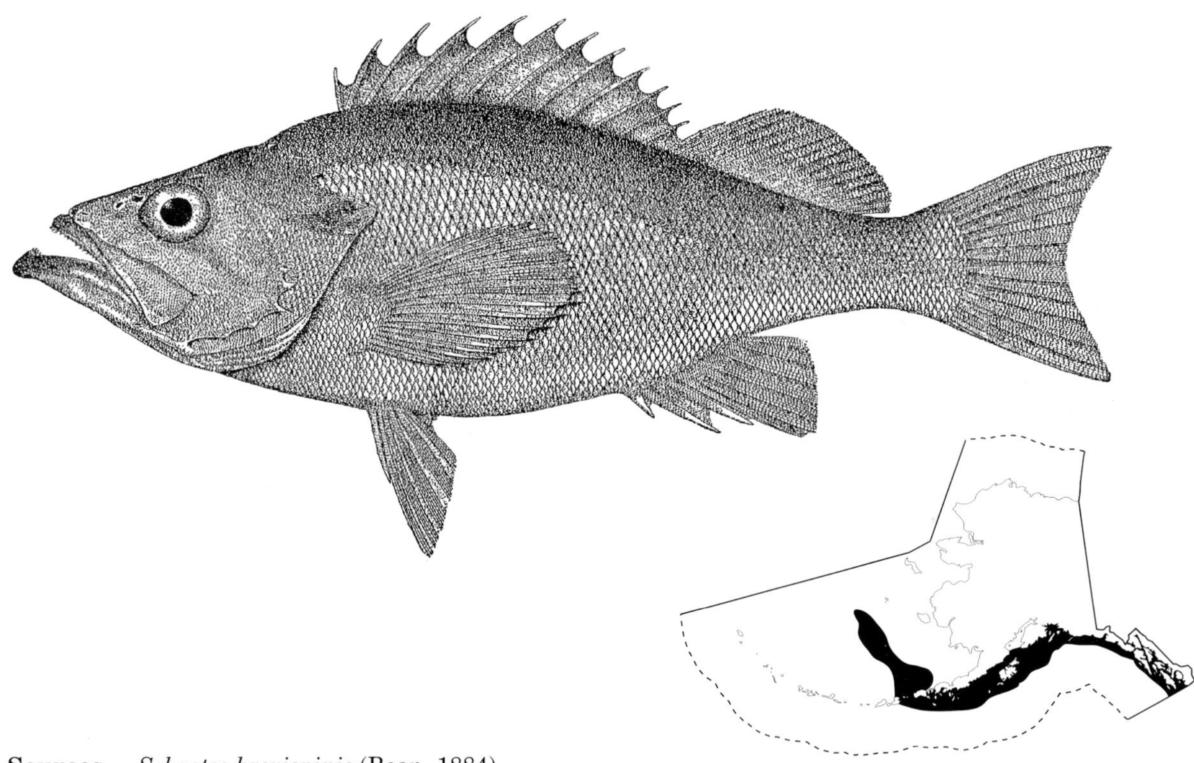

Notes & Sources — *Sebastes brevispinis* (Bean, 1884)

Sebastes proriger: Jordan and Gilbert 1883:950; Alaskan specimens.

Sebastichthys proriger brevispinis Bean, 1884

Sebastichthys brevispinis Bean, 1895

Closely similar to *S. paucispinis*, but differentiated by pectoral fin rays (usually 17 or 18 in *S. brevispinis* versus 14–16 in *S. paucispinis*), anal fin rays (7 or rarely 8 versus 8–10), gill rakers on first arch (33–36 versus 27–32), and symphyseal knob (prominent versus absent).

Description: Bean 1895; Jordan and Evermann 1898:1787–1788; Phillips 1957:42–43; Hart 1973:405–406; Eschmeyer and Herald 1983:135; Kramer and O'Connell 1995:13; Orr et al. 2000:28.

Figure: Jordan and Evermann 1900, fig. 658; holotype, 36 cm TL, Hassler Harbor, Annette Island, Alaska. This species is easier to identify from a photograph showing color than from this illustration.

Range: Taken in NMFS surveys west to Sanak Island, in the extreme southwestern part of the Gulf of Alaska near Unimak Pass (Allen and Smith 1988). Many authors have given the Bering Sea as the northern limit (e.g., Wilimovsky 1954, 1958; Phillips 1957; Quast and Hall 1972; Miller and Lea 1972; Fedorov 1973a; Hart 1973), but without giving localities or other data. Snytko (1986) reported catches at three eastern Bering Sea localities: 57°55'N, 173°43'W, depth 130 m; 57°51'N, 173°50'W, depth 135–136 m; and 57°41'N, 174°12'W, depth 145 m; lengths were 20–61 cm FL. There are no records from the Bering Sea in the NMFS AFSC scientific survey database, but there are some from along the Bering Sea slope in the observer program database; J. W. Orr (pers. comm., 23 Jun. 1999) considers the observer program records to be reliable, as observers correctly identified the species in tests. Snytko and Fedorov (1974) reported extension of the known range south (from Santa Barbara) to Bahia Sebastian Vizcaino.

Sebastes entomelas (Jordan & Gilbert, 1880) **widow rockfish**

Western Gulf of Alaska at Albatross Bank to Baja California at Todos Santos Bay.

In schools around offshore reefs, seamounts, and in midwater from near surface to depths of 600–800 m; usually taken shallower than 350 m.

D XIII,14–16; A III,7–10; Pec 17–19; LLp 52–60; LLs 58–66; GR 34–38; Vert 26–27.

- Golden brown to dusky brown, with traces of yellow and red; vague blotches dorsolaterally; lighter ventrally; fins brown to black; **fin membranes black except spinous dorsal lighter** and caudal fin sometimes with blotchy white bar; young fish with streaks of orange; mouth and gill cavity white, with dusky areas; peritoneum dark gray with black dots, or black.
- Head spines: 1, 2, (3), (4), (5), (7); weak.
- **Symphyseal knob absent**; maxilla extending to mideye; interorbital space convex; supracleithral and cleithral spines both moderately strong; small subopercular spines present or absent; lachrymal spines or processes absent.
- Anal fin spine 2 shorter than 3, except spine 2 can be slightly longer in fish under about 20 cm; **distal margin of anal fin strongly slanted posteriorly**; caudal fin strongly emarginate.
- Scales present on maxilla.
- Length to 59 cm TL.

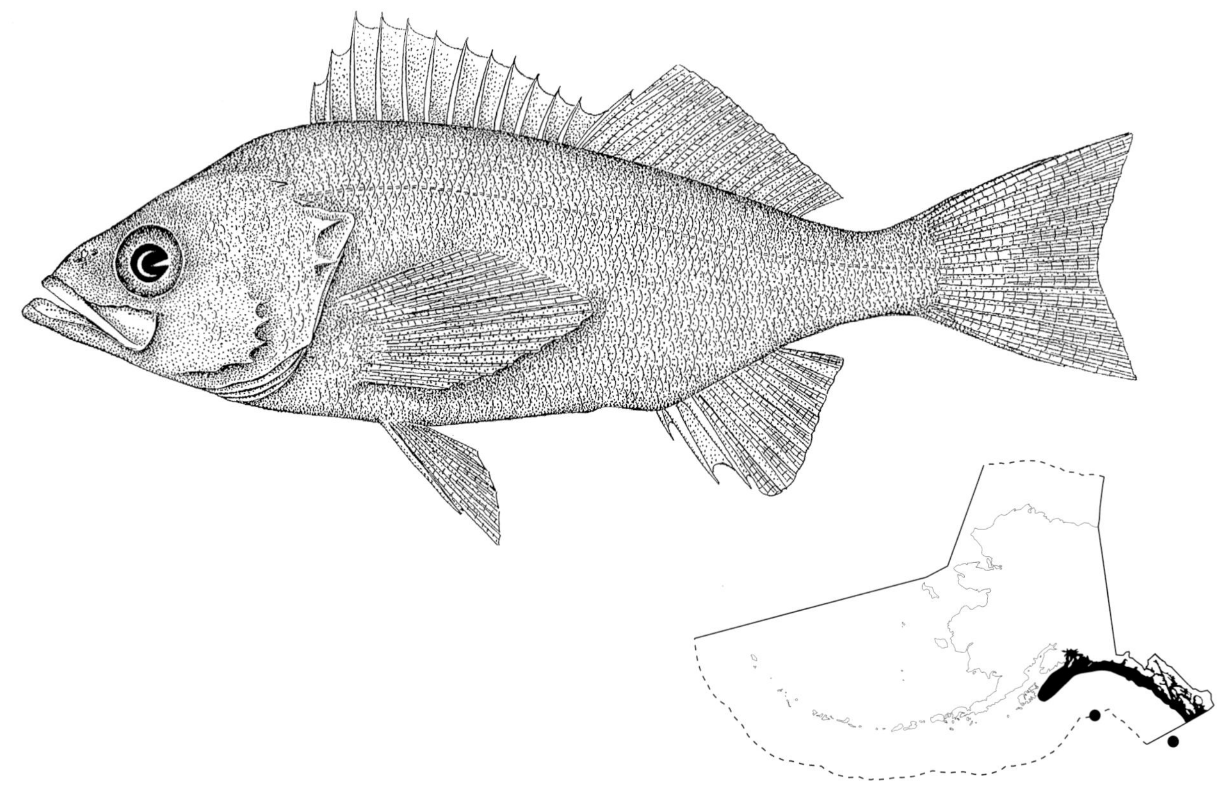

Notes & Sources — *Sebastes entomelas* (Jordan & Gilbert, 1880)
Sebastichthys entomelas Jordan & Gilbert, 1880

Description: Jordan and Evermann 1898:1785; Phillips 1957:46–47; Barsukov 1964:253 of transl.; McAllister and Westrheim 1965; Hart 1973:417–418; Eschmeyer and Herald 1983:139; Kramer and O'Connell 1995:27; Orr et al. 2000:30.

Figure: Hart 1973:417; 44 cm TL, British Columbia.

Range: Taken as far west in Gulf of Alaska as Albatross Bank, east of Kodiak Island, by NMFS surveys (Allen and Smith 1988). The species is well represented in museum collections from Alaskan localities within the range indicated by solid black on the above map. Snytko (1986) reported catches by benthic and demersal trawls from offshore seamounts, some of them within the 200-mile limit off Alaska and nearby: at Surveyor Seamount, 56°03'N, 144°21'W, depth 600–800 m; and at Hodgkins Seamount, 53°15'N, 135°45'W, depth 240–250 m; sizes were 27–46 cm FL. The Surveyor Seamount record at 600–800 m is unusually deep; previous records are from less than 550 m.

Sebastes flavidus (Ayres, 1862) **yellowtail rockfish**

Eastern Aleutian Islands south of Unalaska Island to southern California off La Jolla.

In schools around offshore reefs from near surface to depth of 549 m, most commonly at 50–250 m.

D XII–XIII,14–16; A III,7–9; Pec 17–19; LLp 49–55; LLs 55–60; GR 34–39; Vert 26.

- Olive green to grayish brown with yellow wash and vague blotches dorsally; fine brown speckles on side; white ventrally; **fins dusky green with strong yellow cast**; lower rays of pectoral fin tinged with pink; mouth and gill cavity light gray, sometimes tinged with yellow; peritoneum silvery white, with black speckling in young fish.
- Head spines: 1, (2), (7); weak.
- Symphyseal knob small to moderate; maxilla extending to rear edge of pupil to rear edge of eye; interorbital space convex; supracleithral and cleithral spines weak, supracleithral spine sometimes absent; subopercular spine usually absent; lachrymal spines or processes absent.
- Anal fin spine 2 shorter than 3; **distal margin of anal fin mainly vertical**; caudal fin moderately emarginate.
- Scales present on maxilla.
- Length to 66 cm TL.

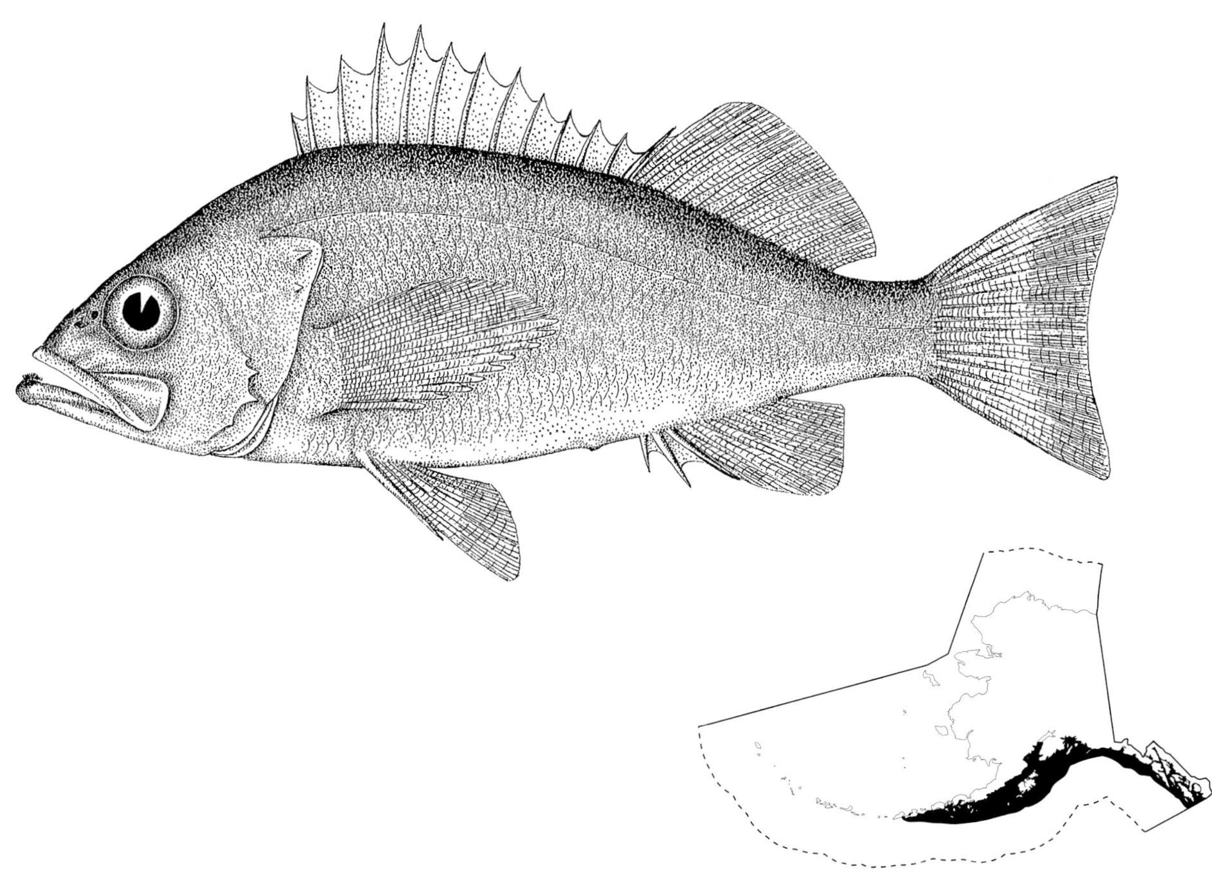

Notes & Sources — *Sebastes flavidus* (Ayres, 1862)
Sebastodes flavidus Ayres, 1862

Description: Jordan and Evermann 1898:1781–1782; Phillips 1957:56–57; Hart 1973:418–419; Eschmeyer and Herald 1983:140; Kramer and O'Connell 1995:29; Orr et al. 2000: 29. The presence of 12 dorsal fin spines is not common in *S. flavidus*; Chen (1986) reported an occurrence of 1 in a sample of 17 fish.

Figure: Hart 1973:418; 31 cm TL, British Columbia.

Range: Westrheim (1966b) recorded range to western Gulf of Alaska off Kodiak Island. Snytko (1986) reported it from farther west at localities off the Shumagin Islands, with depths of 105–230 m; westernmost was 54°25'N, 161°16'W. Reported off coasts of Gulf of Alaska and west to the Aleutian Islands just south of Unalaska Island in NMFS surveys (Allen and Smith 1988). *Sebastes flavidus* is well represented from throughout the Alaskan portion of its range in institutional collections.

Sebastes mystinus (Jordan & Gilbert, 1881) **blue rockfish**

Eastern Gulf of Alaska off Sitka, records uncertain; British Columbia to northern Baja California off Punta Banda.

In schools off bottom over reefs and pinnacles from near surface to depth of 549 m; most commonly found at depths of 60–300 m.

D XIII,15–17; A III,8–10; Pec 16–19; LLp 47–53; LLs 50–56; GR 32–38; Vert 26–27.

- **Blue-black or black dorsally, lighter ventrally**; **vague bands over top of head and radiating back from eye**; fine black flecks on body; fins dark, tipped with blue; juveniles gray, with irregular reddish streaks; mouth and gill cavity dusky white; peritoneum light gray to black, fading to white with a few black flecks or dusky patches in largest fish.
- Head smooth and rounded; body deep, with evenly curved dorsal and ventral outlines.
- Head spines: 1, 2, (3), (4), (5); **nasal and preocular spines weak, others usually absent**.
- Symphyseal knob small or absent; **maxilla extending to mideye to rear edge of pupil**; interorbital space convex; supracleithral spine weak or absent, cleithral moderately strong; small subopercular spines present; 1 low lachrymal process or spine occasionally present.
- Anal fin spine 2 shorter than 3; **distal margin of anal fin straight and vertical or slightly slanted posteriorly**; caudal fin emarginate.
- Scales present on maxilla.
- Length to 53 cm TL.

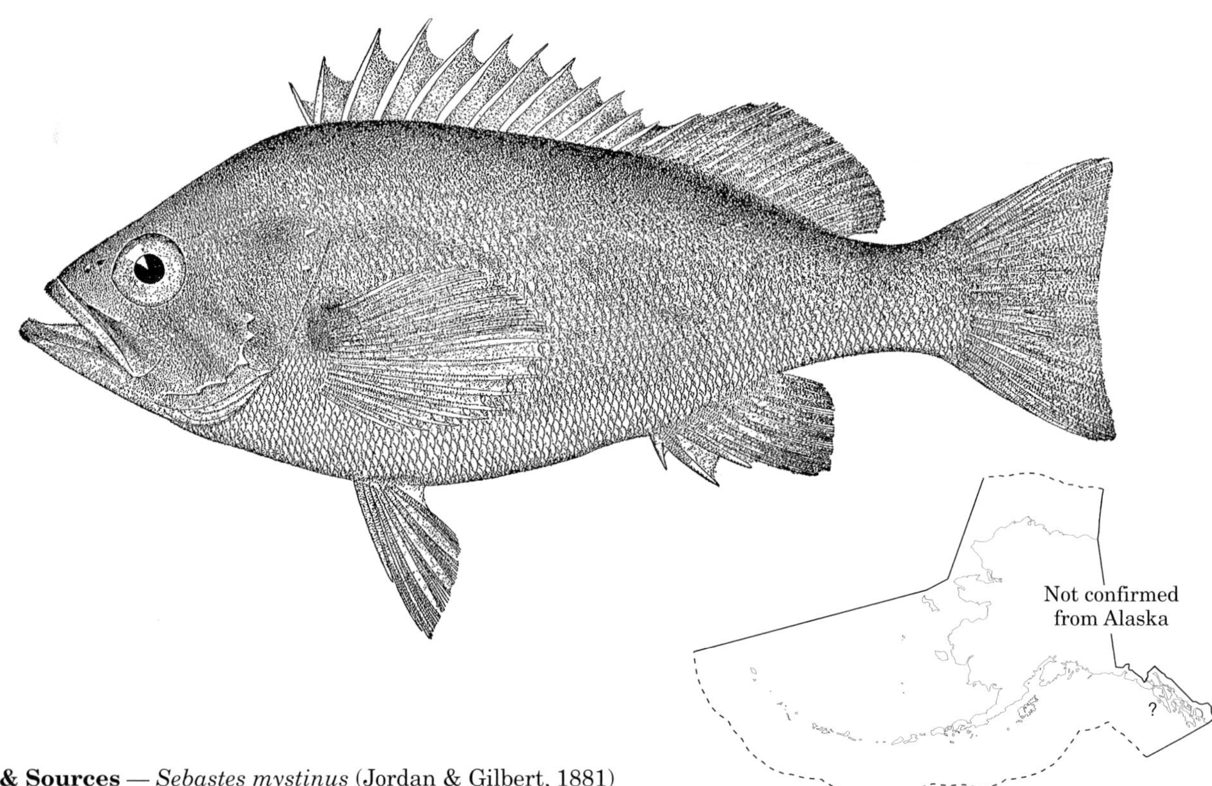

Notes & Sources — *Sebastes mystinus* (Jordan & Gilbert, 1881)
Sebastichthys mystinus Jordan & Gilbert, 1881
This species has been confused with others, primarily *Sebastes melanops* and *S. ciliatus*, since before it was named and described by Jordan and Gilbert (1881c).

Description: Jordan and Evermann 1898:1784–1785; Phillips 1957:52–53; Hart 1973:429–430; Eschmeyer and Herald 1983:144; Kramer and O'Connell 1995:45; Orr et al. 2000:27.

Figure: Jordan and Evermann 1900, fig. 657; 30 cm TL, Monterey, California.

Range: Reported from time to time from the eastern Bering Sea and western Gulf of Alaska, but such reports are believed to be incorrect. All specimens identified as *S. mystinus* from the Bering Sea in the NMFS observer program are probably the dark form of the dusky rockfish, *S. ciliatus* (J. E. Blackburn, pers. comm., 23 Jul. 1998). Quast and Hall (1972) considered all reports of occurrence of *S. mystinus* in Alaska doubtful. Kramer and O'Connell (1988) reported that fish from Kodiak Island once thought to be *S. mystinus* are now identified as *S. ciliatus* and, more recently (Kramer and O'Connell 1995), that the occurrence of *S. mystinus* in Alaskan waters is still under debate. They mentioned that fish tentatively identified as *S. mystinus* were collected near Sitka, and included a photograph of one of them (which in coloration, at least, does not look like *S. mystinus*). Hart (1973) remarked that *S. mystinus* is not frequently encountered in British Columbia; the fish illustrated in Hart (1973:429) has too large a mouth to be this species.

Sebastes melanops Girard, 1856 **black rockfish**

Aleutian Islands off Amchitka Island to southern California off Huntington Beach.

In schools from surface to depth of 366 m around rocky reefs, usually found shallower than 150 m; have been seen feeding on Pacific sand lance, *Ammodytes hexapterus,* at the surface.

D XIII–XIV,13–16; A III,7–9; Pec 18–20; LLp 46–55; LLs 50–55; GR 32–39; Vert 26.

- Dark gray to black dorsally, lighter ventrally; some light gray mottling on back; fins blackish except pelvic fins lighter; mouth and gill cavity light gray; peritoneum silvery white.
- **Head spines: 1, 2, (4); weak to very weak.**
- Symphyseal knob obsolete or absent; maxilla extending to rear edge of pupil to rear edge of eye; interorbital space convex; supracleithral spine usually absent, cleithral weak; subopercular spines usually absent; lachrymal processes or spines absent.
- Anal fin spine 2 shorter than 3; **distal margin of anal fin slightly rounded below and slanting anteriorly above**; caudal fin emarginate.
- Scales present on maxilla.
- Length to 65 cm TL.

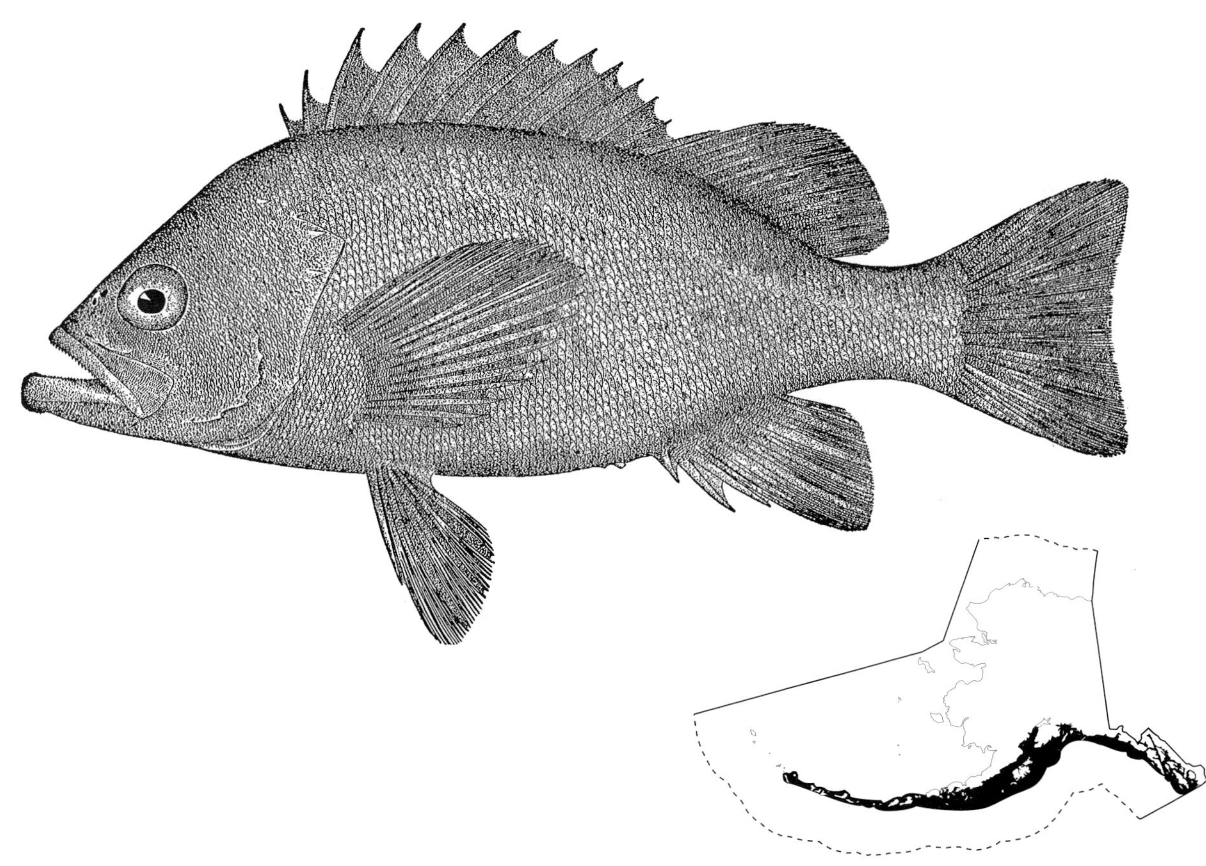

Notes & Sources — *Sebastes melanops* Girard, 1856

Description: Jordan and Evermann 1898:1782–1783; Phillips 1957:54–55; Barsukov 1964:255–256 of transl.; Hart 1973: 426–427; Eschmeyer and Herald 1983:143; Kramer and O'Connell 1995:39; Orr et al. 2000:27.

Figure: Jordan and Evermann 1900, fig. 655; 39 cm TL, Sitka, Alaska.

Range: Recorded west in the Aleutian Islands to Amchitka Island by Wilimovsky (1964). R. Baxter (unpubl. data) examined a specimen in the OSUO collection which was taken just south of Atka Island in 1983, at 21–27 m of depth. Early records include Kodiak Island and Sitka (e.g., Jordan and Evermann 1898). Blackburn and Jackson (1982) reported it from the east side of Kodiak Island, Rosenthal (1980) from Prince William Sound, and Rogers et al. (1986) from Cook Inlet. Most Alaskan specimens in museums are from southeastern Alaska, but the entire range in Alaska is represented. Commonly caught on sport gear and troll gear.

Size: Lea et al. 1999: 64.8 cm, central California. Previously reported to 63 cm TL (e.g., Kramer and O'Connell 1995).

Sebastes jordani (Gilbert, 1896) **shortbelly rockfish**

Eastern Pacific Ocean off southern British Columbia at La Perouse Bank to southern Baja California west of Todos Santos.

In schools, offshore and off bottom; adults at depths of 91–350 m, usually at 50–250 m; juveniles taken at the shallower depths and near surface.

D XIII,13–16; A III,8–11; Pec 19–22; LLp 52–64; LLs 65; GR 40–47; Vert 26.

- **Olive pink dorsally, becoming light pink on sides; silvery white ventrally**; fins reddish pink; mouth and gill cavity white and pink; peritoneum gray with black dots or black.
- **Body slender and elongate**.
- Head spines: 1, 2, 4, 5, 7; weak.
- Symphyseal knob small; maxilla extending barely to front of pupil or to mideye; interorbital space flat to convex; subopercular spines absent; small lachrymal spines usually present, posterior spine directed backward.
- Anal fin spine 2 shorter than 3 or about same length; distal margin of anal fin slanted posteriorly; caudal fin strongly emarginate, almost forked.
- **Anus about midway between pelvic and anal fins**.
- Length to 35 cm TL or more.

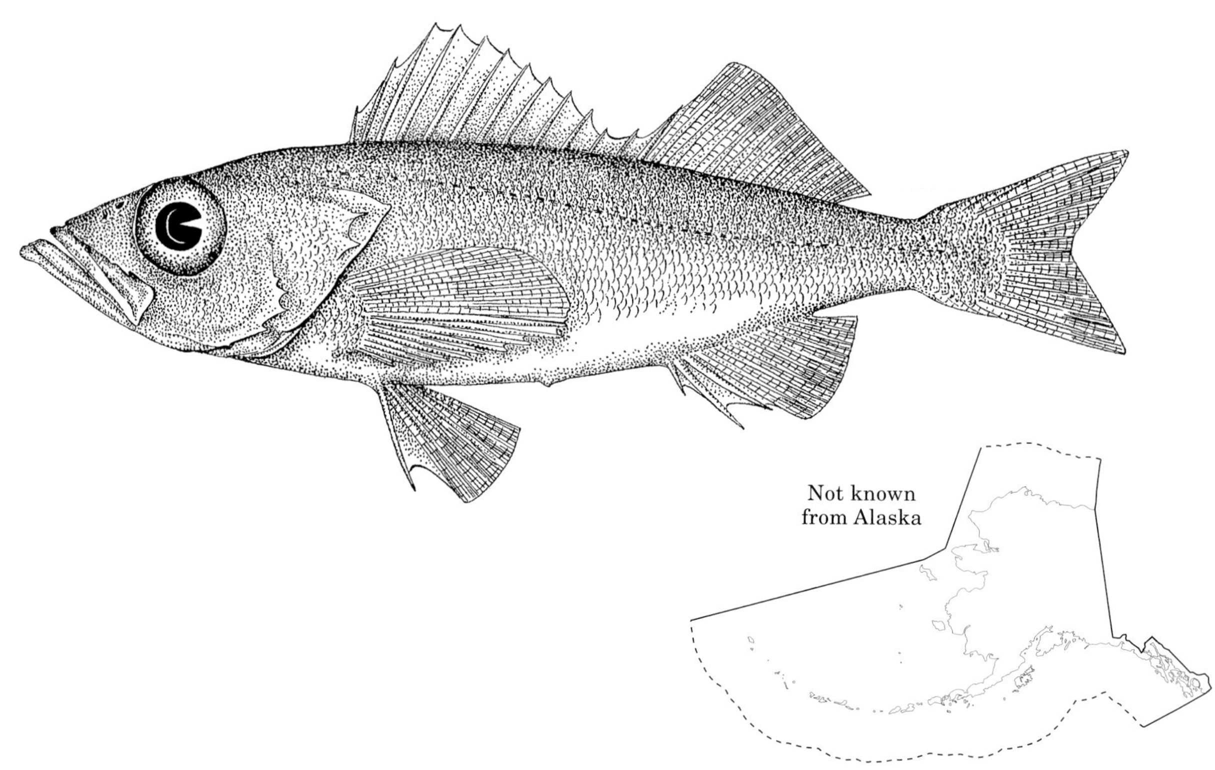

Notes & Sources — *Sebastes jordani* (Gilbert, 1896)
Sebastodes jordani Gilbert, 1896

Description: Jordan and Evermann 1898:1778–1779; Phillips 1957:38–39; Hart 1973:423–424; Eschmeyer and Herald 1983:141; Kramer and O'Connell 1995:35; Orr et al. 2000:10.

Figure: Hart 1973:423; 21 cm TL, off Vancouver Island.

Range: Catches off Granite Island, Kenai Peninsula, reported to represent this species were considered by Allen and Smith (1988) to be questionable. Quast and Hall (1972) included *S. jordani* on their list of fishes as a species to be considered when identifying unusual specimens from the southeastern Gulf of Alaska. Kramer and O'Connell (1995) and Orr et al. (2000) believed it to be absent from Alaskan waters. Northernmost adequately documented records are those of Westrheim and Pletcher (1966), from La Perouse Bank off Vancouver Island; and Snytko (1986), from slightly farther north at 48°58'N, 126°43'W, depth 180 m. Snytko (1986) extended the known range south (from San Benito Island) to southern Baja California at 23°28'N, 110°43'W, depth 230 m.

Size: Pearson et al. 1993: "in excess of 34 cm fork length" at Cobb Seamount. Previously reported to reach 32 cm TL (eg., Eschmeyer and Herald 1983).

Sebastes polyspinis (Taranetz & Moiseev, 1933) **northern rockfish**

Bering Sea at Pervenets Canyon and Aleutian Islands at Stalemate Bank to northern British Columbia off Graham Island; western Bering Sea off northeastern Kamchatka and Commander Islands, present but rare in Pacific Ocean from Cape Afrika to Kuril Islands.

Mostly offshore at depths of 73–740 m, usually at 100–300 m.

D XIV,13–16; A III,7–9; Pec 17–19; LLp 43–53; LLs 69–70; GR 35–39; Vert 28.

- **Dark greenish gray on red background** with red-orange or brown specks and fine green spots; red-orange to white ventrally; dark bands radiate from eye; top of head dark; fins reddish to dusky red; **lower pectoral fin rays white on distal portion**; gill cavity silvery; peritoneum dark.
- Head spines: 1, (2), (4), (7); very weak.
- **Symphyseal knob strong**; maxilla extending to mideye to rear edge of eye; interorbital space convex; subopercular spines present or absent; lachrymal processes, if present, long and low.
- **Dorsal fin spines 14**; anal fin spines 2 and 3 about same length or 3 slightly longer; distal margin of anal fin straight and slanted posteriorly; caudal fin strongly emarginate.
- Length to 41 cm TL.

Notes & Sources — *Sebastes polyspinis* (Taranetz & Moiseev in Taranetz, 1933)
Sebastodes polyspinis Taranetz & Moiseev in Taranetz, 1933

Description: Taranetz 1933:69; Barsukov 1964:257–258 of transl.; Westrheim and Tsuyuki 1971; Eschmeyer and Herald 1983:146–147; Kramer and O'Connell 1995:55; Orr et al. 2000:22.

Figure: University of British Columbia, artist P. Drukker-Brammall; UBC 62-443, 234 mm SL, off Fox Islands, Alaska.

Range: Distribution of 856 occurrences in NMFS resource surveys during 1953–1983 was north to Pervenets Canyon, west to Stalemate Bank, and east to southeastern Alaska and continuing south to Graham Island, British Columbia (Allen and Smith 1988). Most of the catches were west of Prince William Sound. Range in Alaska is well documented in museum collections. The type series was collected from the Pribilof Islands, Alaska, as well as the east coast of the Kamchatka Peninsula, Russia. Fedorov and Sheiko (2002) reported *S. polyspinis* to be abundant off the Commander Islands and gave a new maximum depth of 740 m. Previously reported to 625 m by Allen and Smith (1988).

Sebastes paucispinis Ayres, 1854 **bocaccio**

Western Gulf of Alaska south of Shumagin Islands and Alaska Peninsula to central Baja California off Punta Blanca.

Around reefs and seamounts and over soft bottoms; adults at depths of 20–475 m, usually at 50–300 m; juveniles near surface and in inshore waters.

D XIII–XV,13–15; A III,8–10; Pec 14–16; LLp 51–70; LLs 72–90; GR 27–32; Vert 26.

- Light olive brown dorsally grading to reddish brown laterally and to red or pink ventrally; occasionally bright red or golden orange; small brown spots on sides in specimens under 25 cm; lateral line creamy or pinkish brown; mouth and gill cavity white, with some pink and dusky; peritoneum silvery white with a few black dots, with numerous black dots in fish under about 25 cm.
- Body deep, especially in larger fish.
- Head spines: 1, 7; weak.
- **Symphyseal knob absent, but lower jaw massive, strongly projecting, tip thickened**; head profile concave over eye; maxilla extending to rear edge of eye to beyond eye; interorbital space convex; subopercular spines absent; lachrymal processes obsolete in adults, 2 small spines present in fish under 25 cm.
- **Anal fin spines small**; anal spine 2 shorter than 3; distal margin of anal fin slightly rounded, nearly vertical or slanted posteriorly; caudal fin emarginate.
- Length to 91 cm TL.

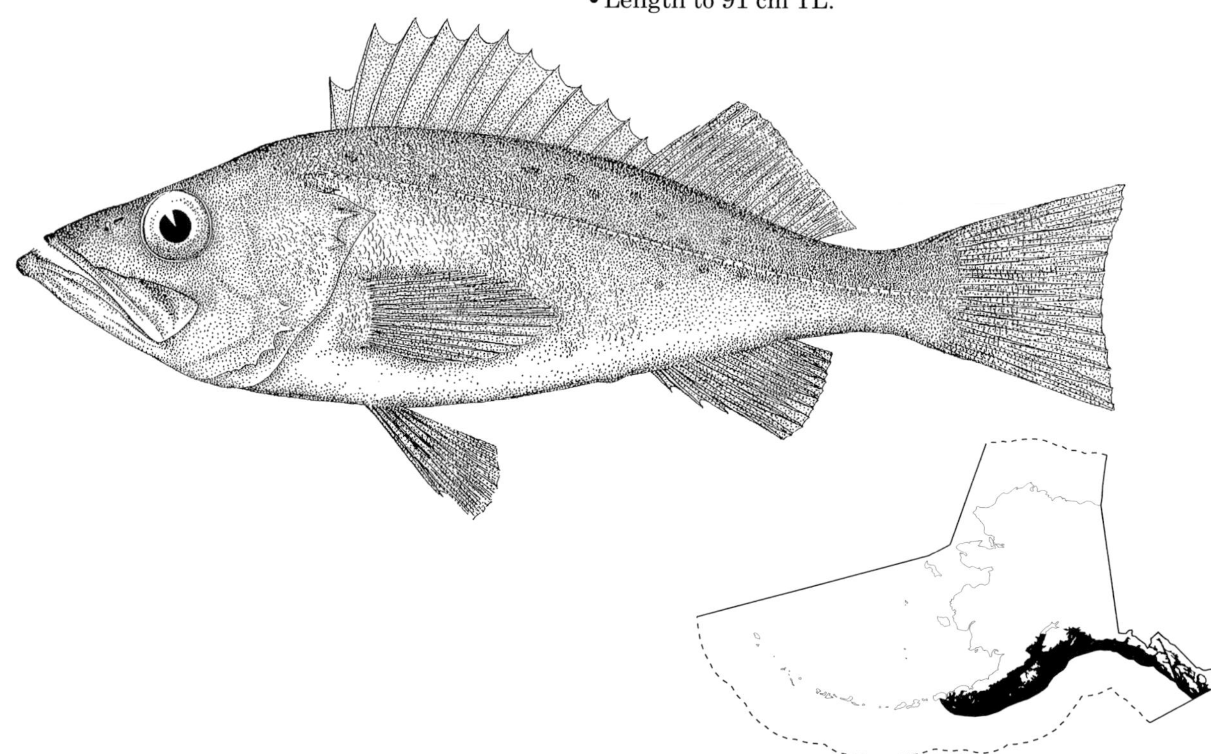

Notes & Sources — *Sebastes paucispinis* Ayres, 1854

Closely similar to *S. brevispinis,* but differentiated by pectoral fin rays (14–16 in *S. paucispinis* versus 17 or 18 in *S. brevispinis*), anal fin rays (8–10 versus 7, rarely 8), gill rakers on first arch (27–32 versus 33–36), and symphyseal knob (absent versus strong).

Description: Jordan and Evermann 1898:1780–1781; Phillips 1957:40–41; Hart 1973:435–436; Eschmeyer and Herald 1983:145; Kramer and O'Connell 1995:51; Orr et al. 2000:10. Of 43 specimens examined by Chen (1986), 1 had 15 dorsal fin spines, 1 had 14, and the rest had 13.

Figure: Hart 1973:435; 17 cm TL, British Columbia.

Range: Snytko (1986) reported the westernmost record, from south of the Shumagin Islands at 54°17'N, 161°25'W, depth 160–175 m. Reported from the south coast of the Alaska Peninsula in the vicinity of Stepovak Bay, from southeast of Kodiak Island, and from a few eastern Gulf of Alaska localities by Allen and Smith (1988). Previous reports of occurrence as far west as Kodiak Island evidently were based on Alverson et al.'s (1964) report of catches in the general Gulf of Alaska area, which did not give localities. Few Alaskan records are backed by voucher specimens. Those that are, are from southeastern Alaska. Westrheim (1966b) recorded it from near Kruzof Island at 57°14'N, 136°13'W. The UBC has specimens from Washington Bay (UBC 63-1343); Port Armstrong (UBC 63-157) and Port Conclusion (UBC 65-525), Baranof Island; and west of Noyes Island (UBC 63-157). Quast and Hall (1972) noted presence of specimens from southeastern Alaska in the ABL permanent collection. The map by Allen and Smith (1988) indicates that few of the 651 occurrences in 30 years of NMFS trawl surveys were from Alaska. Snytko (1986) reported *S. paucispinis* at Cobb and other seamounts south of Alaska.

Sebastes goodei (Eigenmann & Eigenmann, 1890) **chilipepper**

Eastern Gulf of Alaska at Pratt and Durgin seamounts to Pacific Ocean off southern Baja California at Bahia Magdalena.

Around reefs and seamounts as well as over soft bottoms from near surface to depth of 425 m and possibly to 900 m, usually at depths of 50–350 m.

D XIII,13–14; A III,8–9; Pec 16–18; LLp 50–57; LLs 60–77; GR 34–39; Vert 26.

- Pinkish red; white ventrally; **lateral line in red area**; fins pinkish red, median fins with dusky areas; light olive on back in fish under 25 cm; mouth and gill cavity pinkish white, sometimes with one or two patches of light dusky; peritoneum silvery white, with black dots in small fish.
- Body slender, not particularly deep.
- Head spines: (1), (3), (7); weak, all usually obsolete in adults.
- **Symphyseal knob moderately strong, sharp, directed forward**; maxilla extending to mideye; interorbital space convex; supracleithral spine weak, almost obsolete, cleithral spine moderately strong; subopercular spines absent; weak lachrymal spines present or absent in adults, usually small, sharp spines present in fish under 25 cm.
- **Anal fin spines small**; anal spine 2 same length or slightly shorter than 3 (with fin depressed); distal margin of anal fin slanted posteriorly and rounded.
- Length to 59 cm TL.

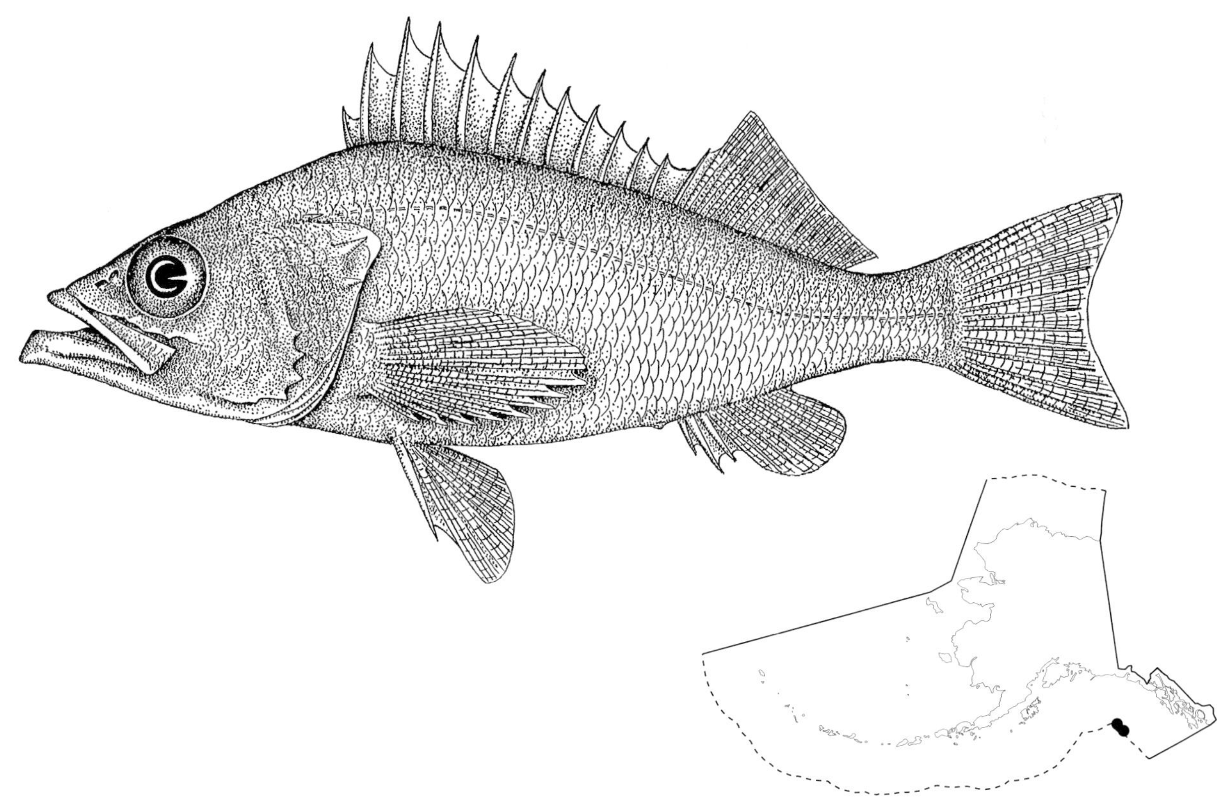

Notes & Sources — *Sebastes goodei* (Eigenmann & Eigenmann, 1890)
Sebastodes goodei Eigenmann & Eigenmann, 1890

Description: Jordan and Evermann 1898:1779–1780; Phillips 1957:44–45; Hart 1973:420–421; Eschmeyer and Herald 1983:140; Kramer and O'Connell 1995:31; Orr et al. 2000:9.

Figure: Hart 1973:420; 35 cm TL, off Vancouver Island.

Range: Known in Alaska from two specimens taken at seamounts, reported by Snytko (1986): one measuring 54 cm FL from Pratt Seamount, at 56°10'N, 142°32'W, depth 840–900 m; and one 45 cm FL from Durgin Seamount, at 55°50'N, 141°56'W, depth 720–730 m. Nearest locality along coast reported from NMFS surveys is southern Queen Charlotte Sound, British Columbia (Allen and Smith 1988). Recorded from slightly farther south, off northwest coast of Vancouver Island at 50°39'N, 128°39'W by Westrheim (1965). Other records are from southernmost British Columbia and farther south. Most common off California to northern Baja California. With a maximum trawling depth range of 720–900 m, Snytko's (1986) seamount records are exceptionally deep, indicating the fish may have entered the net as it was being raised, not at the maximum depth of the tows. Other records are from depths less than 425 m.

Size: M. S. Love (pers. comm., 26 Dec. 2000) reported a total length of 59 cm for a chilipepper from Monterey, California. Previously reported to reach 56 cm TL (e.g., Hart 1973).

Sebastes caurinus Richardson, 1845 **copper rockfish**

Western Gulf of Alaska east of Kodiak Island to central Baja California off San Benito Islands.
Close to bottom in rocky, shallow-water areas to depth of 183 m, usually shallower than 120 m.

D XIII,11–14; A III,5–7; Pec 16–18; LLp 37–47; LLs 39–45; GR 26–32; Vert 25–26.

- Dark brown to olive brown washed with **copper pink** and yellow; **white on lower sides and belly**, turning copper pink during exposure to air; **posterior two-thirds of lateral line in light area**; 2 yellow or copper bands radiate posteriorly from eye; spinous dorsal and anal fins with some white, soft dorsal and caudal fins mostly blackish brown; pectoral and pelvic fins coppery; peritoneum silvery white.
- Head spines: 1, 2, 4, 5, 7; strong.
- Symphyseal knob small or absent; maxilla extending to posterior part of eye to beyond eye; interorbital space moderately convex to flat; subopercular spines present; lachrymal usually with low process followed by triangular spine.
- Anal fin spine 2 slightly longer or shorter than 3, or about equal; distal margin of anal fin rounded below, with upper portion slanted anteriorly; caudal fin truncate or slightly rounded.
- Length to 66 cm TL.

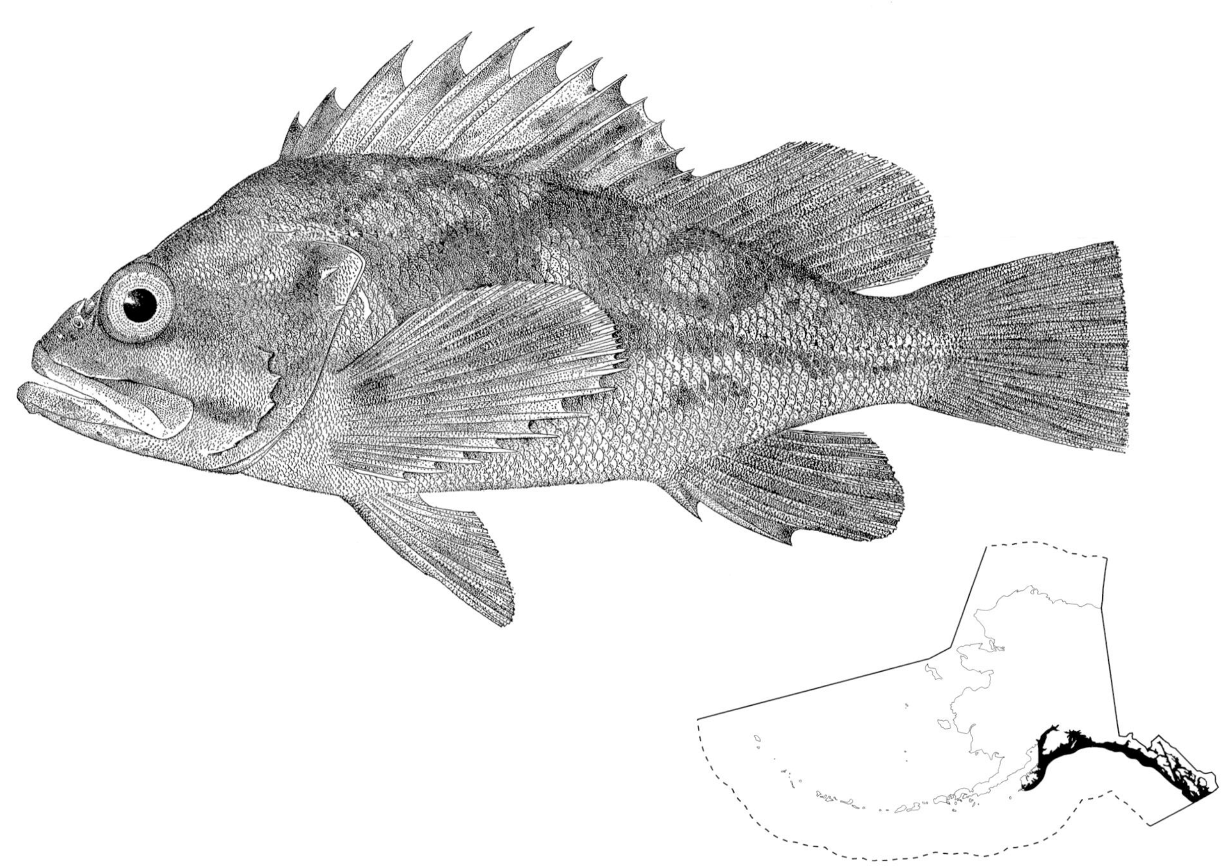

Notes & Sources — *Sebastes caurinus* Richardson, 1845

Description: Jordan and Evermann 1898:1820–1821; Phillips 1957:96–97; Barsukov 1964:246 of transl.; Hart 1973: 407–408; Eschmeyer and Herald 1983:136; Kramer and O'Connell 1995:15; Orr et al. 2000:23.

Figure: Jordan and Gilbert 1899, pl. 49; 29 cm TL, Sitka.

Range: Southwesternmost record in the Gulf of Alaska was reported by Snytko (1986), from specimens taken east of Kodiak Island at 56°22'N, 152°25'W, at depths of 90–120 m; specimens were 26–28 cm TL. Records from the northern Gulf of Alaska are from Jakalof Bay, an embayment of Kachemak Bay, lower Cook Inlet (Dames and Moore 1979); Port Dick, on the outer coast of the Kenai Peninsula (Westrheim 1966a); and Zaikof Bay, Prince William Sound (Rosenthal 1980). There are fairly numerous specimens from within the range depicted on the above map at ABL, NMNH, UBC, and UW.

Size: W. A. Palsson (pers. comm., 3 Jan. 2001) reported that data from Washington Department of Fish and Wildlife recreational creel census surveys include several *S. caurinus* 60 cm or larger, including a 66-cm fish taken in 1978 from south Puget Sound; he personally observed a 60-cm fish in 1997 near Seattle at Edmonds Underwater Park, which is a long-term harvest refuge. Previously reported to reach 58 cm TL (e.g., Kramer and O'Connell 1995).

Sebastes elongatus Ayres, 1859 **greenstriped rockfish**

Western Gulf of Alaska off Chirikof Island to central Baja California off Cedros Island.

Over sandy or silty bottoms inshore and offshore at depths of 12–495 m, most common at 100–250 m.

D XIII,12–14; A III,5–7; Pec 16–18; LLp 37–47; LLs 42–55; GR 28–33; Vert 26.

- **Irregular, broken olive green stripes dorsally and laterally on pink background**; pale red to white ventrally; **lateral line in distinct pink area**; fins with dusky and greenish areas, most evident on median fins; pectoral and pelvic fins mostly pale red; mouth and gill cavity white, with some pink; peritoneum light gray or dusky, with black dots.
- Body slender and elongate.
- Head spines: 1, 2, 4, 5, 7; strong.
- Symphyseal knob obsolete or absent; maxilla extending to mideye to rear of pupil; interorbital space concave; strong subopercular spines present; lachrymal processes barely evident.
- **Anal fin spine 2 obviously longer than 3**; distal margin of anal fin straight and vertical or slightly slanted anteriorly; caudal fin emarginate.
- Length to 43 cm TL.

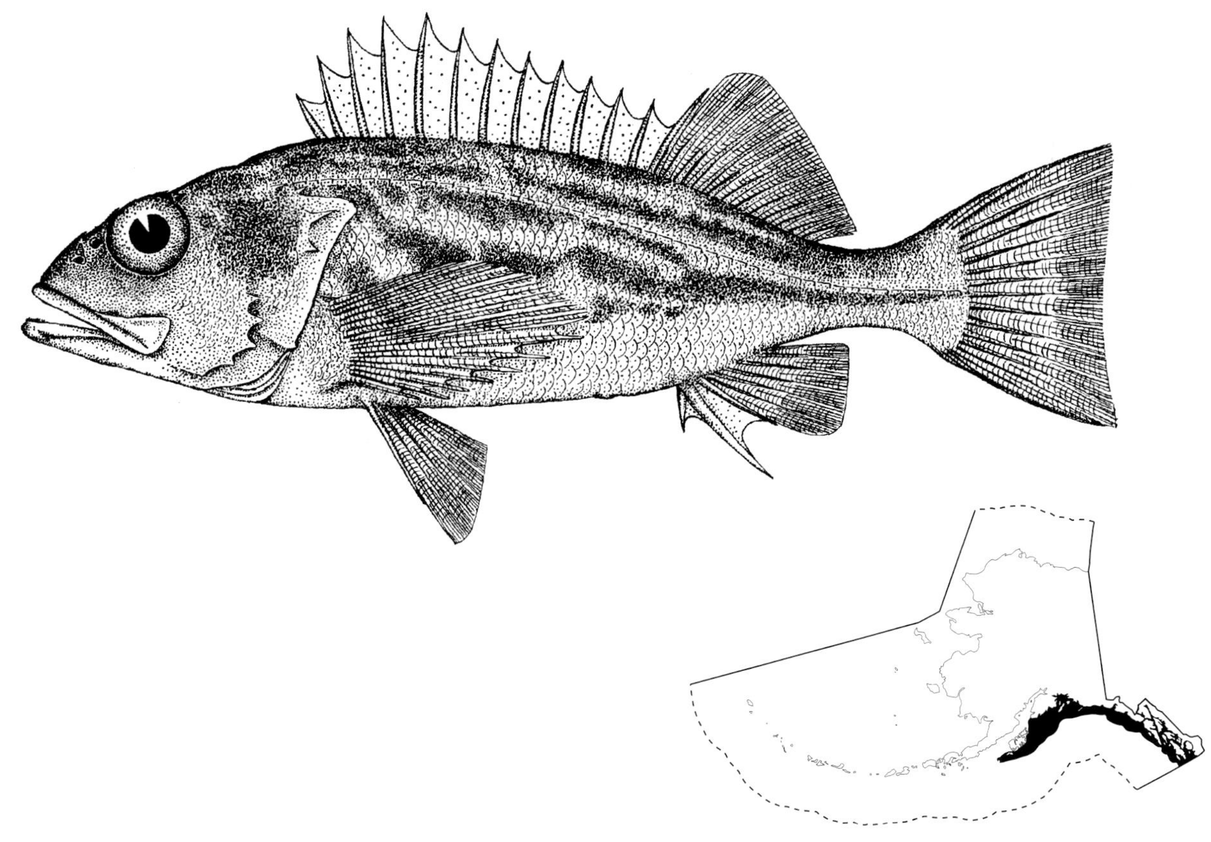

Notes & Sources — *Sebastes elongatus* Ayres, 1859

Description: Jordan and Evermann 1898:1815–1816; Phillips 1957:108–109; Hart 1973:414–415; Eschmeyer and Herald 1983:138; Kramer and O'Connell 1995:23; Orr et al. 2000:23.

Figure: Hart 1973:414; 27 cm TL, British Columbia.

Range: Recorded west in Gulf of Alaska to just north of Chirikof Island by Allen and Smith (1988). Westrheim (1966a) recorded it from Prince William Sound near Montague Island, 2 miles southeast of Green Island; and off Forrester Island in the southeastern Gulf of Alaska. Quast and Hall (1972) recorded it from Katlian Bay and Baranof Island. Taken in trawl surveys (Allen and Smith 1988) at a few localities in the Gulf of Alaska, but most of the 759 occurrences reported were from south of Alaska. Krieger (1993) observed *S. elongatus* from a submersible over the outer continental shelf off southeastern Alaska. Hart (1973) reported it to be fairly common in the Strait of Georgia, British Columbia. One of the few rockfishes consistently found on sandy or silty bottoms. Shaw (1999) gave depth range of 12–495 m, extended from range of 25–425 m reported by Allen and Smith (1988).

Size: Shaw 1999. Previously reported to reach 38 cm TL (e.g., Hart 1973).

Sebastes variegatus Quast, 1971 **harlequin rockfish**

Southeastern Bering Sea and Aleutian Islands at Bowers Bank to Pacific Ocean off Oregon.

Deep water, inshore and offshore; adults at depths of 49–558 m, usually at 100–300 m; juveniles shallower.

D XIII,13–15; A III,6–7; Pec 17–19; LLp 42–52; LLs 46–58; GR 36–41; Vert 27.

- Reddish pink to deep red with olive or brown blotches; **posterior two-thirds of lateral line in well-defined clear area**; tip of mandible blackish; dorsal fin membranes black, **second dorsal, anal, and caudal fins black with red margins**; **clear red terminal band on caudal fin**; peritoneum dark brown to black.
- Slender and elongate compared to *S. zacentrus*.
- Head spines: 1, 2, 4, 5, 7, (8); moderate to strong.
- **Symphyseal knob weak or absent**; maxilla extending to mideye to rear edge of pupil; interorbital space flat to convex.
- **Anal fin spine 2 longer and stronger than 3**; distal margin of anal fin slanted posteriorly; caudal fin emarginate.
- Length to 37 cm TL.

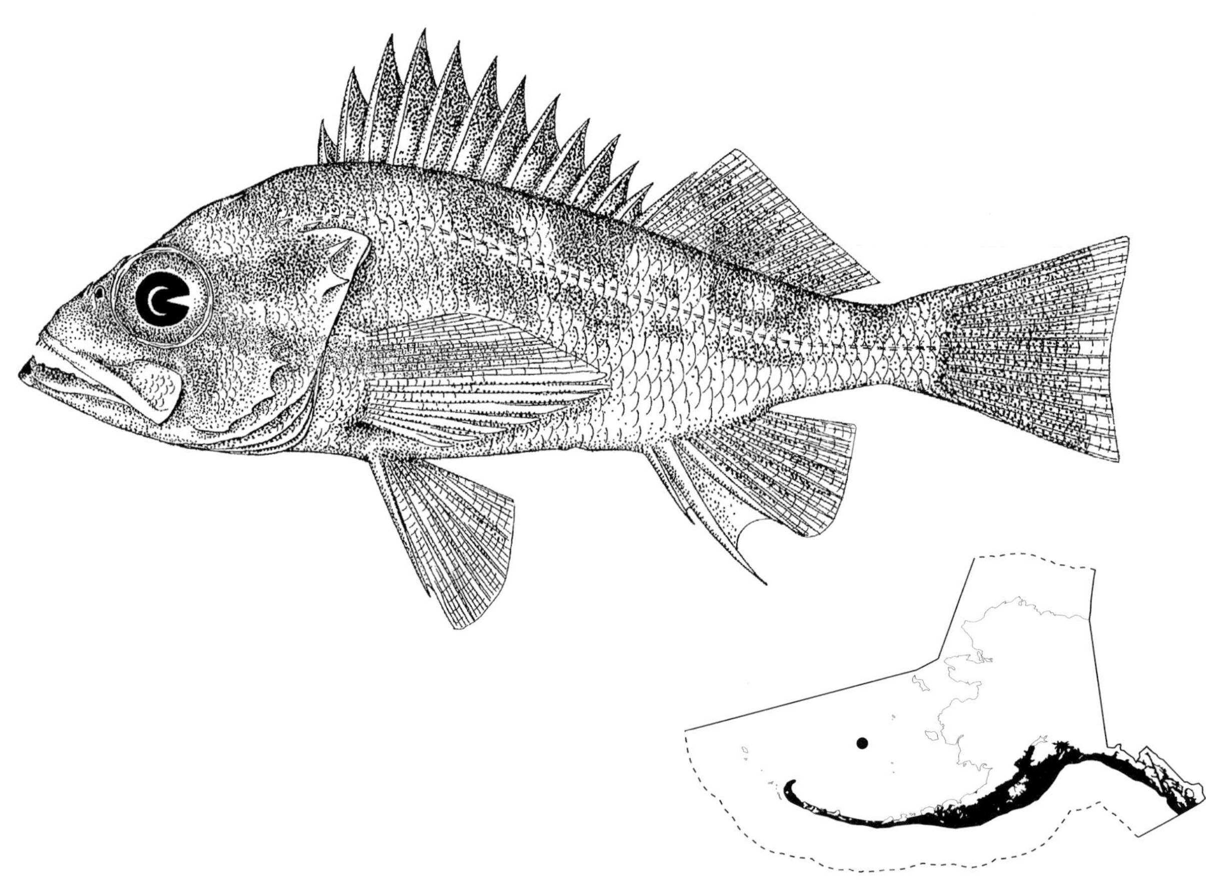

Notes & Sources — *Sebastes variegatus* Quast, 1971

Most similar to *S. zacentrus*, but distinguishable from it by at least the characters in bold type.

Description: Quast 1971; Hart 1973:446–447; Eschmeyer and Herald 1983:152; Kramer and O'Connell 1995:65; Orr et al. 2000:13.

Figure: Hart 1973:446; 27 cm TL, Icy Bay, Alaska.

Range: One record from Bering Sea, reported by Snytko and Fedorov (1974): 57°27'N, 173°54'W. Snytko (1986) reported catches at three localities off south side of Aleutian Islands; westernmost was at 51°36'N, 176°32'W; depth range was 160–225 m; fish measured 21–32 cm FL. Reported as far west as Bowers Bank in the Aleutian Islands from NMFS survey data by Allen and Smith (1988); most catches were in Gulf of Alaska. Well represented from Kodiak Island to southeastern Alaska in museum collections. Gillespie and Saunders (1994) reported specimens from the west coast of Vancouver Island, representing the southernmost confirmed record for the species at that time (1994) and the first inshore collection. Orr and Baker (1996b) reported extension of known range south to Washington and Oregon.

Sebastes emphaeus (Starks, 1911) **Puget Sound rockfish**

Northern Gulf of Alaska off Kenai Peninsula to northern California off Punta Gorda.

In schools off bottom and around rocky reefs near surface to depth of 366 m, usually less than 91 m.

D XIII,13–15; A III,6–7; Pec 16–18; LLp 40–46; LLs 41–46; GR 37–41; Vert 27–28.

- **Copper red with dark olive blotches**; **green bands radiating from eye**; spinous dorsal fin dark green with bright red tips; outer portion of soft dorsal fin bright red, base of fin dark; paired fins and anal fin clear, bright red; mouth red; peritoneum dark.
- Body slender and elongate.
- Head spines: 1, 2, 4, 5, 7; moderate to strong.
- Symphyseal knob weak or absent; maxilla extending to mideye; interorbital space slightly convex to flat; 1 subopercular spine present; 2 low lachrymal processes.
- Anal fin spine 2 longer than 3; **anal fin rays usually 7**; **distal margin of anal fin rounded**, slightly slanted posteriorly; caudal fin emarginate.
- Length to 18 cm TL (a very small *Sebastes*).

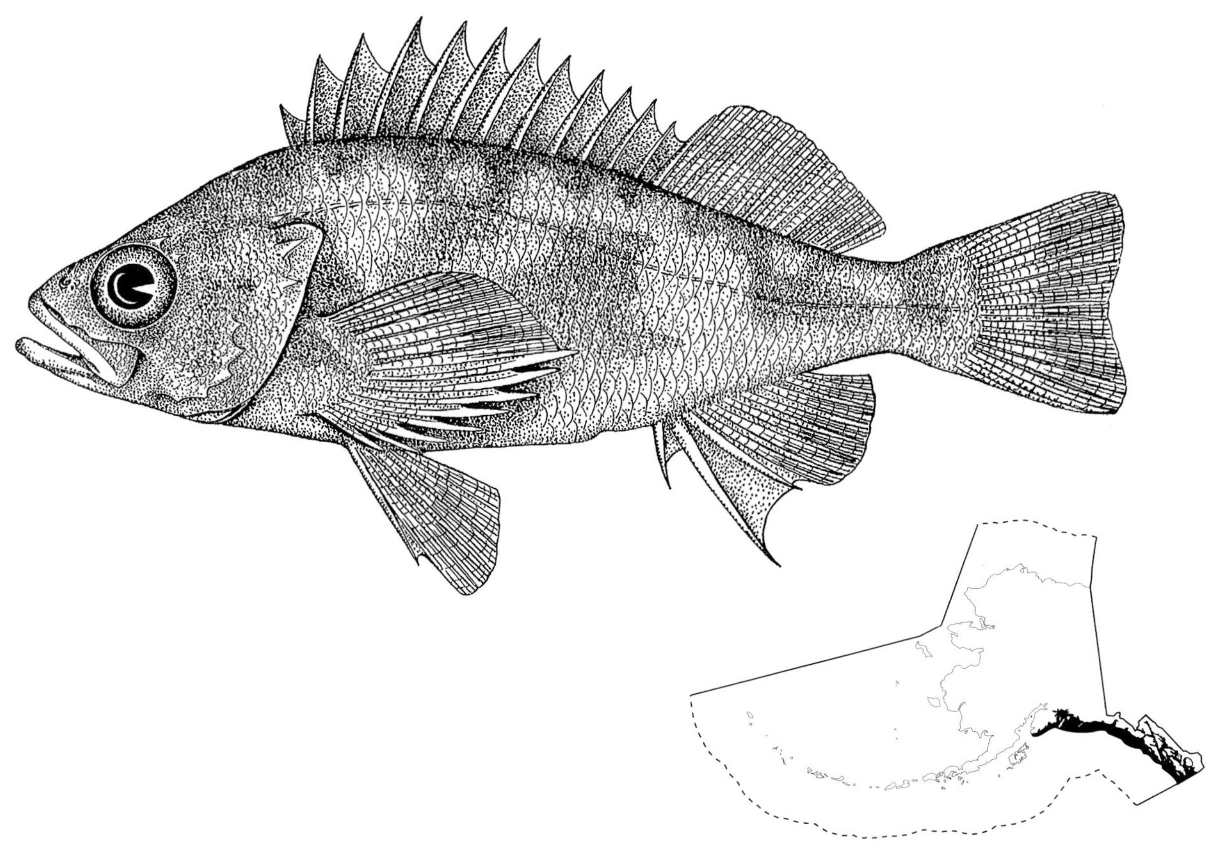

Notes & Sources — *Sebastes emphaeus* (Starks, 1911)
Sebastodes emphaeus Starks, 1911

Description: Starks 1911; Hart 1973:415–416; Eschmeyer and Herald 1983:138; Kramer and O'Connell 1995:25; Orr et al. 2000:24.

Figure: Hart 1973:415; from a drawing of a type specimen.

Range: Recorded as far north and west in the Gulf of Alaska as the Kenai Peninsula (Quast and Hall 1972) (AB 64-699 and AB 70-259, south tip of the peninsula); and Danger Island, Prince William Sound (Rosenthal 1980). Specimens in UW 21708 and SIO 91-58 were collected more recently from Prince William Sound, on 5 Sep. 1990 at 59°60'N, 146°14'W, in an otter trawl on mud and gravel bottom at a depth of 60 m. Quast and Hall (1972) also recorded it from southeastern Alaska (ABL southeastern Alaska records for this species include Port Conclusion, Big Port Walter, Port Althorp, and Funter Bay). Their Alaskan records were northern extensions of the range as known at that time, from Puget Sound. The species was not confirmed from Canada until later, by Peden and Wilson (1976); Hart (1973) had mentioned the existence of a tentative British Columbia record. Specimens were collected by automatic jigging machine and with spears while scuba diving off the southwest coast of Baranof Island by Rosenthal et al. (1988), who characterized the species as pelagic, occurring in schools off the bottom during the day. Statements giving range to Punta Gorda, Baja California (e.g., Gotshall 1989), result from a geographic mixup; the Punta Gorda referred to is in northern California.

Sebastes wilsoni (Gilbert, 1915) **pygmy rockfish**

Northern Gulf of Alaska off Kenai Peninsula to southern California at Cortes Bank.
At depths of 29–274 m, usually offshore.

D XIII–XIV,13–15; A III,5–7; Pec 16–18; LLp 37–46; LLs 45–50; GR 37–43; Vert 27–28.

- **Light brown flushed with red**; distinctly lighter ventrally; 4 or 5 dark blotches along base of dorsal fin, usually not extending to lateral line; operculum sometimes with vague dark blotching; irregular, brownish red or orange stripe along and below lateral line; mouth and gill cavity whitish; peritoneum black.
- Body slender and elongate.
- Head spines: 1, 2, 4, 5, 7; strong.
- Symphyseal knob weak or absent; maxilla extending to mideye; interorbital space flat to barely concave; subopercular spines usually absent; 2 low lachrymal processes.
- Anal fin spine 2 longer than 3; **anal fin rays usually 6**; **distal margin of anal fin almost straight** and nearly vertical or slanted posteriorly; caudal fin truncate.
- Length to 23 cm TL (a very small *Sebastes*).

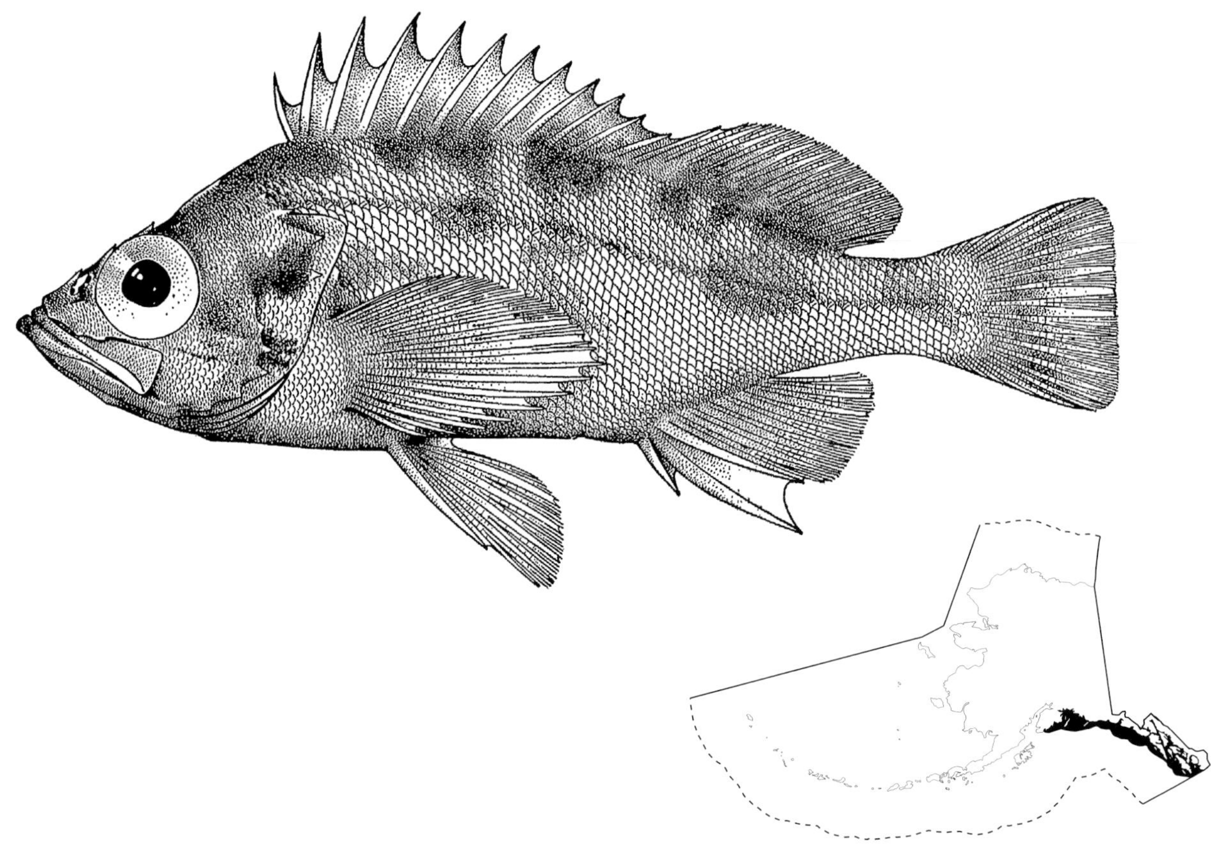

Notes & Sources — *Sebastes wilsoni* (Gilbert, 1915)
Sebastodes wilsoni Gilbert, 1915

Description: Gilbert 1915:333–335; Phillips 1957:100–101; Hart 1973:448–449; Eschmeyer and Herald 1983:152; Kramer and O'Connell 1995:67; Orr et al. 2000:24. Chen (1986) found 14 dorsal fin spines in 1 fish in a sample of 26.

Figure: Gilbert 1915, pl. 16, fig. 8; holotype, 145 mm TL, Monterey Bay, California.

Range: Recorded from Kenai Peninsula and southeastern Alaska by Quast and Hall (1972); on basis of AB 70-257 from 59°12'N, 150°52'W (1 specimen, 126 mm SL); and AB 71-24, 71-25, and 72-33 (7 specimens, 70–124 mm SL) from the mouth of Lisianski Inlet off Cross Sound. Baxter (1990ms, unpubl. data) examined three specimens (132–155 mm SL, 161–191 mm TL) caught in one trawl net haul south of the Kenai Peninsula near Prince William Sound at 59°34'N, 148°38'W, depth 90 m, during NMFS surveys in 1987 (specimens not saved).

Sebastes pinniger (Gill, 1864) **canary rockfish**

Western Gulf of Alaska south of Shelikof Strait to northern Baja California off Cape Colnett.

In schools around reefs and over hard bottoms; adults at depths of 18–425 m, usually at 50–250 m.

D XIII,13–16; A III,7; Pec 16–18; LLp 39–47; LLs 43–50; GR 40–45; Vert 26.

- **Gray mottled with yellow to orange, appearing orange overall; fins bright orange**; 3 orange stripes across head; black blotch on posterior portion of spinous dorsal fin in fish under 30 cm; **lateral line in light gray area**, contrasting with yellow-orange; mouth and gill cavity white, mottled with yellow, pink, and dusky; peritoneum white, with black dots in young fish.
- Head spines: 1, 2, 3, 4, 5, 7; moderate to strong.
- Symphyseal knob weak; maxilla extending to rear edge of pupil to rear edge of eye; interorbital space convex; weak subopercular spines present or absent; **low lachrymal process anteriorly, sharply triangular spine posteriorly**.
- Anal fin spine 2 shorter than 3; **distal margin of anal fin strongly slanted anteriorly**; pelvic fin distinctly pointed, usually reaching to anus; caudal fin moderately to strongly emarginate.
- **Underside of lower jaw smooth**, with scales embedded.
- Length to 76 cm TL.

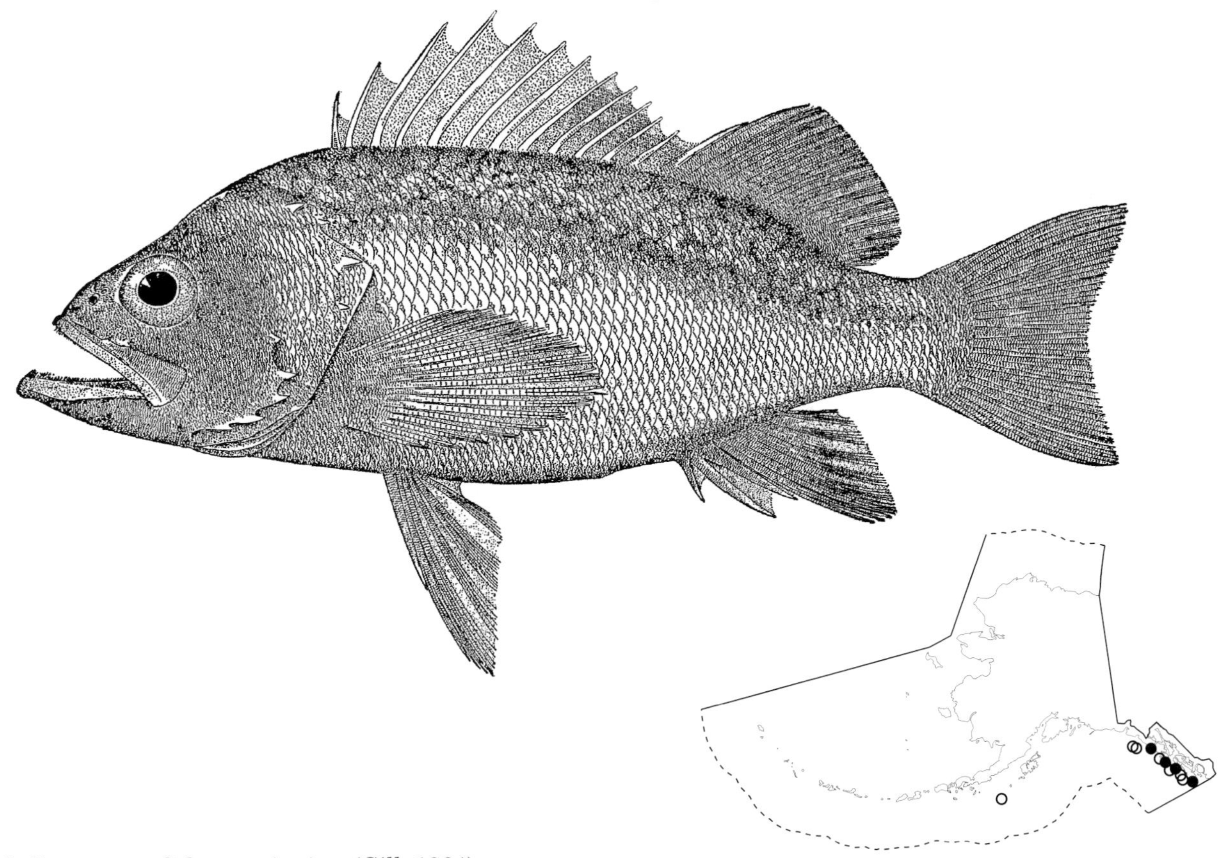

Notes & Sources — *Sebastes pinniger* (Gill, 1864)
Sebastosomus pinniger Gill, 1864

Description: Jordan and Evermann 1898:1793–1794; Phillips 1957:60–61; Westrheim 1966b; Hart 1973:437–438; Eschmeyer and Herald 1983:146; Kramer and O'Connell 1995:53; Orr et al. 2000:18.

Figure: Jordan and Evermann 1900, fig. 662; Neah Bay, Washington.

Range: Reported by Alverson et al. (1964) from Shelikof Strait area, without giving specific localities; and from south of Shelikof Strait by Allen and Smith (1988), who also reported catches from the eastern Gulf of Alaska off Yakutat Foreland and outer coasts of the Alexander Archipelago. The northernmost catch locality recorded in the literature and backed by a voucher specimen is that of Westrheim (1966b) from west of Cape Bartolome (UBC 65-791), about 55°16'N, 134°07'W. Quast and Hall (1972) reported the presence of additional specimens in the ABL collection; those are in lots AB 67-122 and 68-172 from Katlian Bay, AB 71-5 and 72-31 from Port Conclusion, and AB 72-40 from Lisianski Inlet. At about 58°07'N, 137°27'W, Lisianski Inlet is the northernmost documented limit of range for the species. Documented by many more records from southern British Columbia and southward than from Alaska, although it may be more common in Alaska than suggested by trawl surveys since much of its habitat is untrawlable. Examples from northern and western Gulf of Alaska should be placed in permanent collections.

Sebastes miniatus (Jordan & Gilbert, 1880) **vermilion rockfish**

Prince William Sound at Zaikof Bay, Montague Island; southeastern Alaska off Cape Bartolome and northern British Columbia at Gillen Harbour to central Baja California off San Benito Islands.

Rocky reefs and seamounts at depths of 12–400 m, usually deeper than 183 m.

D XIII,13–15; A III,6–8; Pec 16–18; LLp 40–48; LLs 45–48; GR 35–43; Vert 26–27.

- **Deep dark red, mottled with gray dorsally and laterally**; **fins red**; fins often edged with black, and black blotch in posterior portion of soft dorsal fin posteriorly, especially in fish under 35 cm; 3 obscure orange stripes radiating from eye; **lateral line not in clear gray area**; peritoneum silvery white in large specimens.
- Head spines: 1, 2, 3, 4, 5, 7, (8); weak to moderate.
- Symphyseal knob low, projecting downward; maxilla extending to mideye to slightly beyond eye; interorbital space convex; subopercular spines present or absent; **both lachrymal spines sharply triangular**.
- Anal fin spine 2 about same length or slightly shorter than 3; **distal margin of anal fin slanted strongly anteriorly**; pelvic fin extending to anus; caudal fin slightly to moderately emarginate.
- **Underside of lower jaw with rough scales**.
- Length to 76 cm TL.

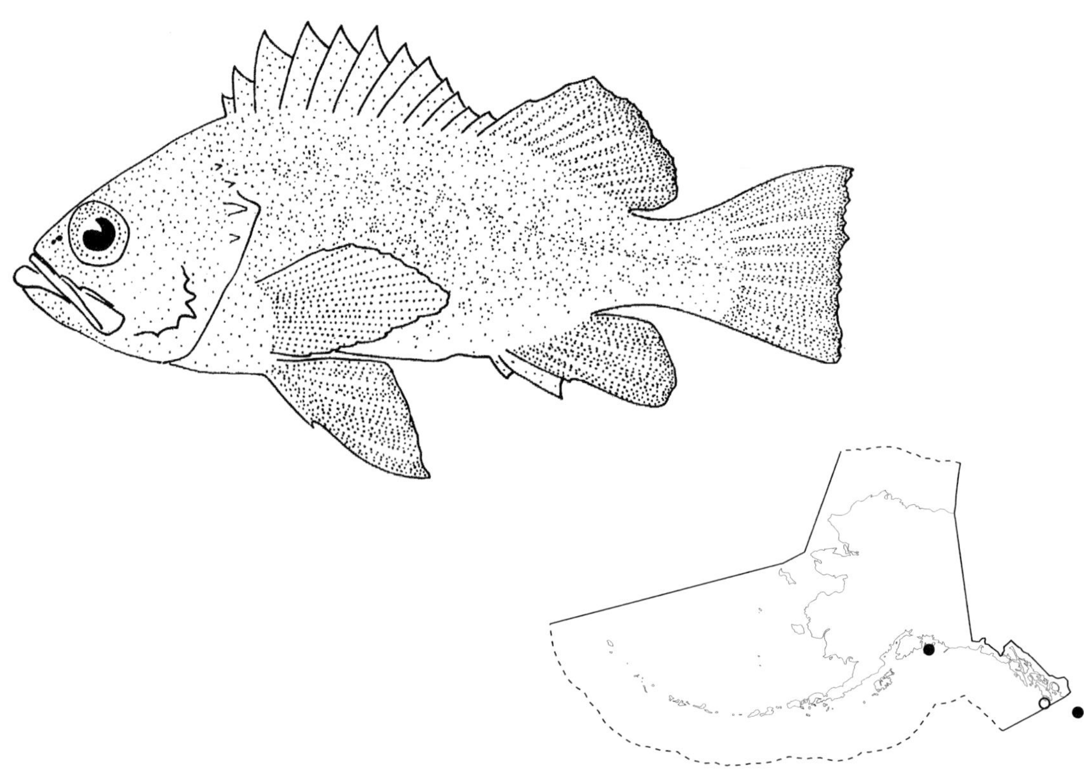

Notes & Sources — *Sebastes miniatus* (Jordan & Gilbert, 1880)
Sebastichthys miniatus Jordan & Gilbert, 1880

Description: Jordan and Evermann 1898:1794–1795; Phillips 1957:62–63; Westrheim 1966b; Hart 1973:428–429; Eschmeyer and Herald 1983:144; Kramer and O'Connell 1995:43; Orr et al. 2000:18.

Figure: Miller and Lea 1972:111.

Range: Recorded from Zaikof Bay, Prince William Sound, at 60°14'N, 146°58'W (O'Connell et al. 1992); the specimen (AB 90-21) is missing from the ABL collection. It was collected in 12 m of water by a diver and was determined to be *S. miniatus* from having rough scales on the mandible and fin ray counts within the range given above. Reported from southeastern Alaska off Cape Bartolome (Kramer and O'Connell 1988, 1995) in a general statement without specific documentation; voucher specimens or catch records were not found. The nearest adequately documented occurrence outside Alaska is from Gillen Harbour, British Columbia, at 52°59'N, 129°35'W, recorded by Peden and Wilson (1976); this record extended the geographic range known at that time north by 400 km. Snytko (1986) reported the first records from seamounts, at Eickelberg and unnamed seamounts west of southern British Columbia and Washington.

Sebastes proriger (Jordan & Gilbert, 1880) **redstripe rockfish**

Southeastern Bering Sea at Pribilof Canyon and Aleutian Islands off Amchitka Island to Pacific Ocean off southern Baja California.

In schools over rocky bottom at depths of 12–425 m, usually at 100–300 m.

D XIII,14–15; A III,6–7; Pec 16–18; LLp 47–55; LLs 55–60; GR 36–43; Vert 27.

- Light red mottled with olive dorsally and flushed with yellow ventrolaterally; **lateral line in distinct continuous light red stripe bordered by olive green mottling**; vague olive streaks radiating from eye; dusky blotch on operculum; lips and tip of lower jaw blackish; fins reddish; portions of spinous dorsal fin and caudal fin blackish or dark olive; pectoral and pelvic fins with yellow cast; **whitish areas at base of anal fin spines, on membranes between pelvic fin rays 4 and 5 and between body and pelvic fin ray 5, and proximal part of pectoral fin**; peritoneum brownish black or black.
- **Head spines**: 1, 2, 4, 5, 7; **weak**.
- **Symphyseal knob long, conspicuous**, directed forward; maxilla extending to rear edge of pupil; interorbital space slightly convex; subopercular spines present; lachrymal processes rounded, rarely produced into spines.
- Anal fin spine 2 thicker and about same length or slightly shorter or longer than 3; distal margin of anal fin straight and nearly vertical or slanted posteriorly; caudal fin moderately to strongly emarginate.
- Length to 52 cm TL.

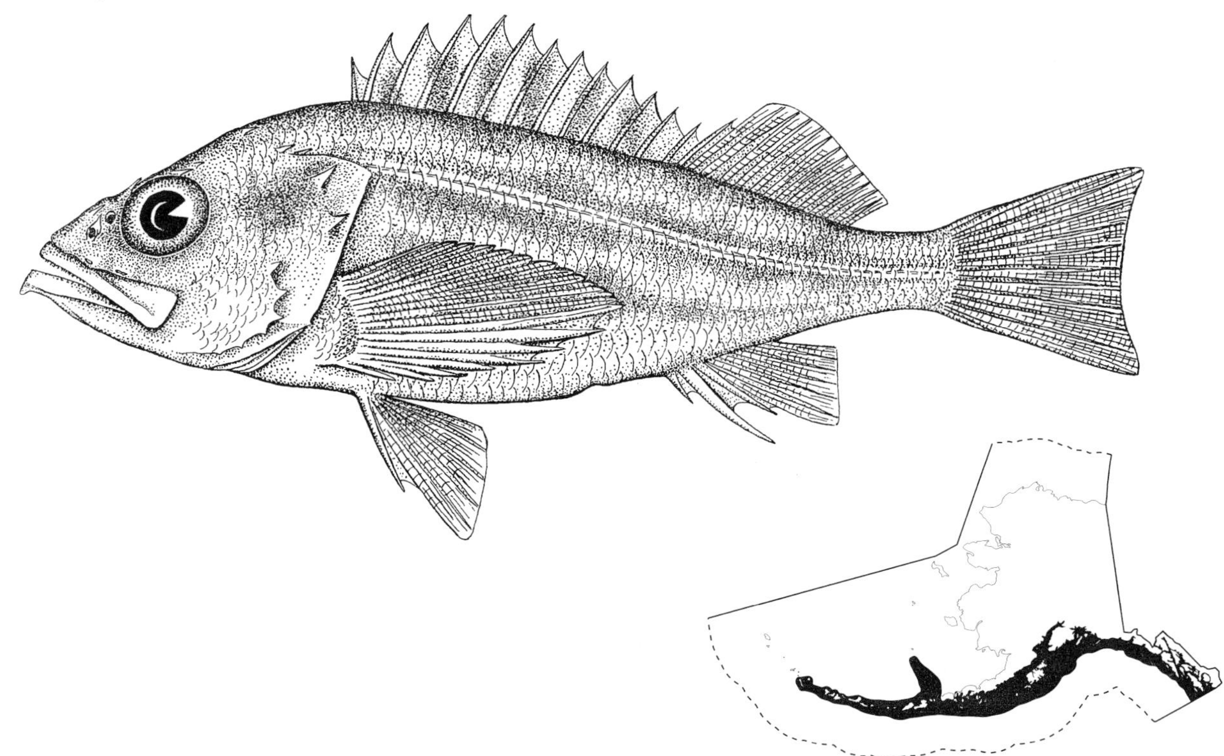

Notes & Sources — *Sebastes proriger* (Jordan & Gilbert, 1880)
Sebastichthys proriger Jordan & Gilbert, 1880

Description: Jordan and Evermann 1898:1792–1793; Phillips 1957:68–69; Barsukov 1964:252–253; Hart 1973:439–440; Eschmeyer and Herald 1983:147; Kramer and O'Connell 1995:57; Orr et al. 2000:8. Length of second anal fin spine relative to third varies, often with age. It can be distinctly longer than the third (Jordan and Gilbert 1880p), slightly shorter than the third (Phillips 1957), or about the same length or slightly longer than the third (Barsukov 1964).

Figure: Hart 1973:439, modified by enlarging symphyseal knob; 33 cm TL, British Columbia.

Range: Reported in NMFS surveys as far north in Bering Sea as Pribilof Canyon by Allen and Smith (1988), and from Amchitka Island by Isakson et al. (1971) and Simenstad et al. (1977). Only 427 occurrences were reported in more than 30 years of trawl surveys of the eastern Bering Sea and North Pacific Ocean (Allen and Smith 1988), but *S. proriger* inhabits generally nontrawlable, rocky areas, so the surveys could not adequately sample *S. proriger* habitat. The ABL has many examples, mostly longlined, from the Gulf of Alaska off Kodiak Island and Cook Inlet through the Alexander Archipelago. Most abundant from Gulf of Alaska to Oregon. Known range was extended south from San Diego (e.g., Phillips 1957) to southern Baja Californa at 26°46'N, 114°07'W by Snytko and Fedorov (1975).

Sebastes alutus (Gilbert, 1890) **Pacific ocean perch**

Bering Sea at Navarin Canyon and Aleutian Islands to central Baja California off Punta Blanca; and to southern Japan and Sea of Okhotsk.

Adults in schools over flat, pebble bottom and juveniles in more rugged habitat including cobble, boulders, and seamounts; near surface to depth of 825 m, usually at 100–450 m.

D XIII–XIV,13–17; A III,6–9; Pec 15–19; LLp 44–55; LLs 43–55; GR 30–39; Vert 27.

- Bright to light red; olive brown blotches dorsally and on caudal peduncle, base of pectoral fin, and operculum, the **dark blotches most discrete at base of soft dorsal fin**; **fins red, without white areas**; **lateral line in red area but not bordered by dark mottling**; mouth mainly pink, with some duskiness; gill cavity dusky; peritoneum gray with black dots or black.
- **Head spines**: 1, 2, (**3**), 4, 5, 7; **weak**; **spine 3 more often present than absent**.
- **Symphyseal knob long, conspicuous**, directed forward; maxilla extending to mideye to rear edge of eye; interorbital space flat to slightly convex; subopercular spines present; small lachrymal spines or rounded processes present.
- Anal fin spine 2 slightly shorter than 3 in adults, equal to or longer than 3 in juveniles; distal margin of anal fin nearly vertical or slightly slanted posteriorly; caudal fin strongly emarginate.
- Length to 55 cm TL.

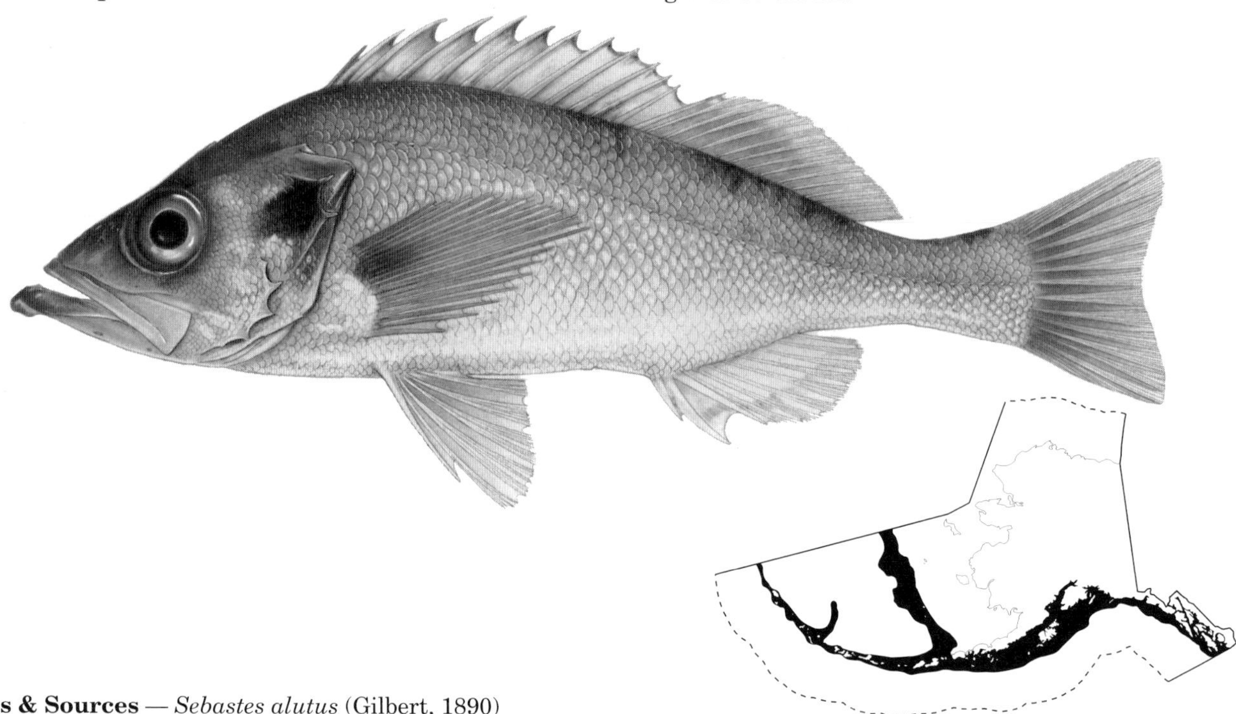

Notes & Sources — *Sebastes alutus* (Gilbert, 1890)

Sebastichthys ruber: Bean 1882:472; USNM 29129, from Kygani Strait (Dixon Entrance), examined and determined to represent *Sebastes alutus* by R. N. Lea (pers. comm., 3 Jun. 1998).

Sebastichthys alutus Gilbert, 1890

The presence of the supraocular spine (number 3) can be a useful character in distinguishing *S. alutus* from *S. proriger*. Although the lateral line scale counts differ, they are notoriously difficult to count accurately (J. W. Orr, pers. comm., 23 Jun. 1999).

Description: Jordan and Evermann 1898:1790–1792; Phillips 1957:78–79; Barsukov 1964:250–252 of transl.; Hart 1973: 396–397; Eschmeyer and Herald 1983:133; Amaoka in Masuda et al. 1984:311; Kramer and O'Connell 1995:3; Orr et al. 2000:8. Only 1 of 15 specimens examined by Chen (1986) had 14 dorsal fin spines. Quast (1987) analyzed morphometric characters by geographic area, sex, and age; symphyseal knob becomes relatively larger and third anal fin spine relatively shorter with age.

Figure: University of British Columbia, artist P. Drukker-Brammall; UBC 62-464, 292 mm SL, south of Fox Islands, Alaska.

Range: Early Alaskan records include those of Gilbert (1896) from Bristol Bay and the Aleutian Islands, and Gilbert and Burke (1912a) from Attu Island (and the Commander Islands, Russia). Allen and Smith (1988) mapped range in Alaska and the eastern Pacific from 4,378 occurrences in NMFS bottom trawl surveys. The NMFS surveys confirmed range west in the Aleutian Islands to Stalemate Bank, and Fedorov and Sheiko (2002) reported *S. alutus* to be abundant off the Commander Islands, Russia. Larvae and juveniles may drift into the Chukchi Sea, as suggested, for example, by the provisional identification by Quast (1972) of early juveniles taken off Cape Lisburne. Snytko (1986) reported adult *S. alutus* well south of the previous record (La Jolla; e.g., Phillips 1957) off Punta Blanca at 29°08'N, 115°26'W, trawl depth range 300–350 m; as well as at seamounts west of Washington and off western Kamchatka.

Sebastes reedi (Westrheim & Tsuyuki, 1967) **yellowmouth rockfish**

Western and northern Gulf of Alaska, reports unconfirmed; southeastern Alaska off Sitka to northern California between Point Arena and Bodega Bay.

Offshore over very rough bottom at depths of 141–366 m.

D XIII,13–15; A III,7–8; Pec 18–20; LLp 47–55; LLs 57–67; GR 30–36; Vert 26.

- **Red mixed with yellow-orange**; **mixed with black in fish under 40 cm**; **diffuse olivaceous mottling dorsally**, not extending below lateral line; **dark olive blotch on opercle**; fins red; **inside of mouth whitish, with yellow, red, and black blotches**; peritoneum silvery gray with black dots to black.
- Head spines: 1, 2, 3, 4, 5, (6), 7; weak (supraocular absent in *S. proriger*, nuchal present in *S. crameri*).
- **Symphyseal knob weak to moderate**, projecting forward; maxilla extending to mideye to rear edge of pupil; interorbital space flat to convex; subopercular spines present; lachrymal spines weak to moderate.
- Anal fin spine 2 thicker and usually shorter than spine 3; distal margin of anal fin slanted posteriorly; caudal fin strongly emarginate.
- Lateral line scales more than in *S. alutus* (57–67 versus 49–55).
- Gill rakers on first arch fewer than in *S. proriger* (30–36 versus 38–43).
- Length to 58 cm TL.

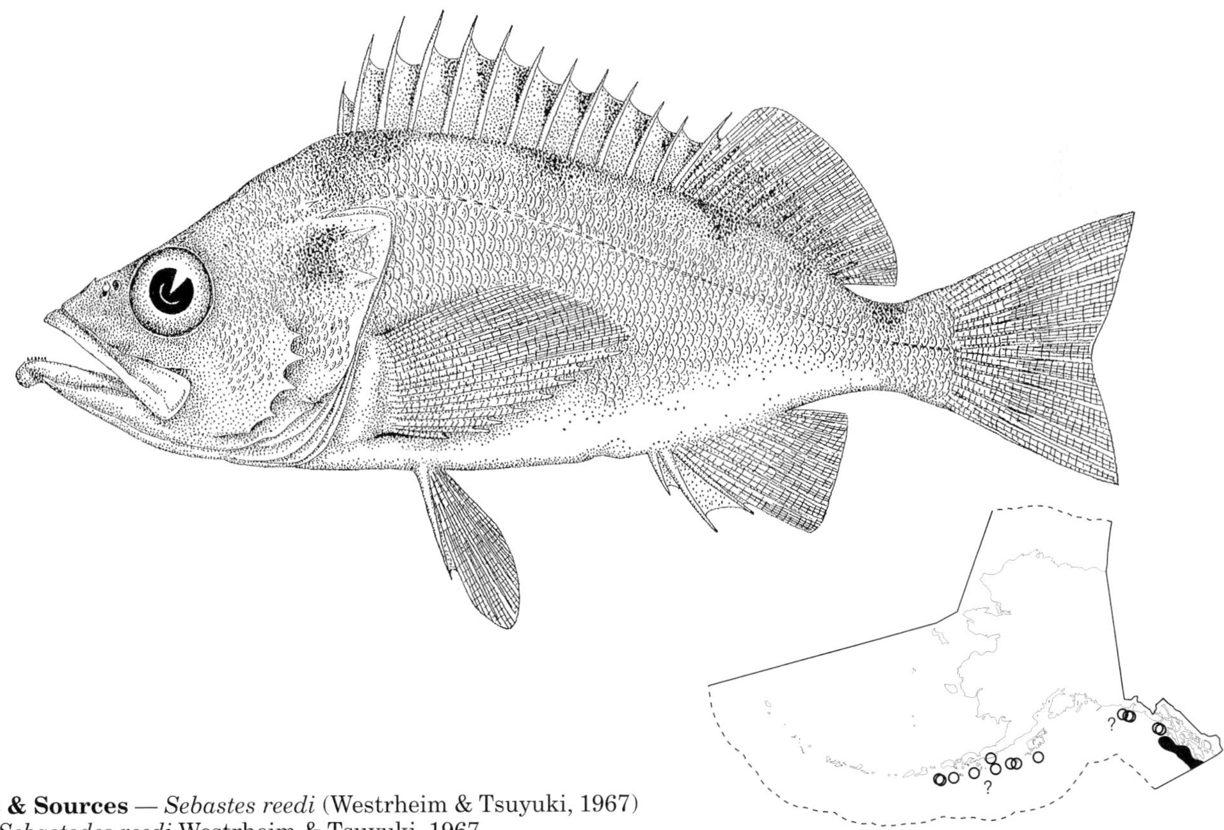

Notes & Sources — *Sebastes reedi* (Westrheim & Tsuyuki, 1967)
Sebastodes reedi Westrheim & Tsuyuki, 1967
Closely resembles *S. alutus, S. crameri,* and *S. proriger.* The main distinguishing characters are given above.

Description: Westrheim and Tsuyuki 1967; Hart 1973:440–441; Eschmeyer and Herald 1983:147; Kramer and O'Connell 1995:59; Orr et al. 2000:9.

Figure: Hart 1973:440; 42 cm TL.

Range: Documented as far north as Sitka by Westrheim and Tsuyuki (1967) from RV *G. B. Reed* trawl catches. Voucher specimens include NMC 66-269 and 66-273 from west of Forrester Island and UBC 65-791 from west of Cape Bartolome. Reported from farther north and west in the Gulf of Alaska (e.g., Baxter 1990ms), but without voucher specimens. Circles on our map represent localities from the NMFS survey database retrieved by D. W. Kessler (pers. comm., 20 Jun. 1994). From more recent observations, J. W. Orr (pers. comm., 13 Nov. 1997) believes the earlier records could represent other species; he went to extraordinary lengths to try to verify a possible Bering Sea record for us and concluded that it probably represented a different species. Most Alaskan records are from offshore localities; we found none from inside waters of the Alexander Archipelago. The NMFS survey database gives depths of 100–431 m for *S. reedi* (greater than range reported in the literature), but there are no voucher specimens. Orr et al. (2000) gave maximum depth of 366 m for *S. reedi.* Snytko (1986) reported extension of the known range south from vicinity of Crescent City (Eschmeyer and Herald 1983) at about 41°N, to 38°18'N, 123°45'W, depth range 260–270 m; specimens measured 50–52 cm FL.

Sebastes crameri (Jordan, 1897) **darkblotched rockfish**

Southeast of Zhemchug Canyon in eastern Bering Sea and Aleutian Islands off Tanaga Island to southern California off Santa Catalina Island.

Over soft bottom at depths of 29–600 m, usually at 100–400 m.

D XII–XIII,13–15; A III,6–8; Pec 18–20; LLp 40–51; LLs 48–62; GR 29–34; Vert 26.

- **Pinkish red**; **young fish often washed with light yellow-green**; **5 black patches dorsally, some extending below lateral line** (3 under spinous dorsal fin, 1 under soft dorsal fin, 1 on caudal peduncle); **black blotch on opercle**; fins red, with some black; **mouth mostly black in large fish**, mostly pink in small fish; peritoneum brown with black dots to all black.
- **Body deep**, depth at pelvic fin insertion greater than head length.
- Head spines: 1, 2, 3, 4, 5, 7, 8; moderate to strong; nuchal and parietal spines occasionally coalesced.
- Symphyseal knob moderate to strong, directed downward; maxilla extending to mideye to rear edge of pupil; interorbital space slightly to moderately convex; subopercular spines present; both lachrymal spines present, posterior sometimes doubled.
- Anal fin spine 2 thicker and about same length or slightly shorter than 3; distal margin of anal fin slightly rounded, nearly vertical or slanted posteriorly; caudal fin strongly emarginate.
- Length to 58 cm TL.

Notes & Sources — *Sebastes crameri* (Jordan in Gilbert, 1897)
Sebastodes crameri Jordan in Gilbert, 1897

Description: Jordan and Evermann 1898:1799–1800; Phillips 1957:66–67; Hart 1973:410–411; Eschmeyer and Herald 1983:137; Kramer and O'Connell 1995:19; Orr et al. 2000: 12. In a sample of 21 specimens, only 1 had 12 dorsal fin spines (Chen 1986).

Figure: Hart 1973:410; 40 cm TL.

Range: Survey data reported by Allen and Smith (1988) included 1,013 occurrences of this species in the southeastern Bering Sea and eastern Pacific Ocean to California, providing, they stated, a more precise description of range than previous records allowed. We did not find voucher specimens from the Bering Sea in museum collections. Most specimens in permanent collections are from southeastern Alaska. UBC 62-659 is from south of the Alaska Peninsula at 55°49'N, 157°34'W. Snytko (1986) doubted existence of *S. crameri* in the Bering Sea; westernmost record he reported was at 55°31'N, 158°34'W, depth 160–167 m. However, Orr et al. (2000) gave a range to the Bering Sea. Specimens from the Bering Sea should be saved and added to permanent collections.

Sebastes diploproa (Gilbert, 1890) **splitnose rockfish**

Western Gulf of Alaska off Sanak Islands to central Baja California off Cedros Island.

Deep water offshore over soft, level bottoms; adults at depths of 80–800 m, usually shallower than 450 m.

D XIII,11–14; A III,5–8; Pec 17–18; LLp 32–43; LLs 53–57; GR 32–37; Vert 26.

- **Rose red**; **silvery white ventrally**; lateral line red; fins red, with variable amounts of black; mouth and gill cavity pink and white; peritoneum black.
- Head spines: 1, 2, 4, 5, 7; strong.
- Symphyseal knob small; **premaxillae produced anteriorly, forming prominent dentigerous knobs on either side of a groove** into which fits the tip of the mandible; interorbital space concave; upper opercular spine strong, extending past opercular flap in some specimens; supracleithral spine usually weak, cleithral moderately strong; subopercular spines usually present; **lachrymal spines strong**.
- Anal fin spine 2 longer than 3 or about the same; distal margin of anal fin rounded below, upper portion nearly vertical or slanted posteriorly; caudal fin moderately emarginate.
- Length to 46 cm TL.

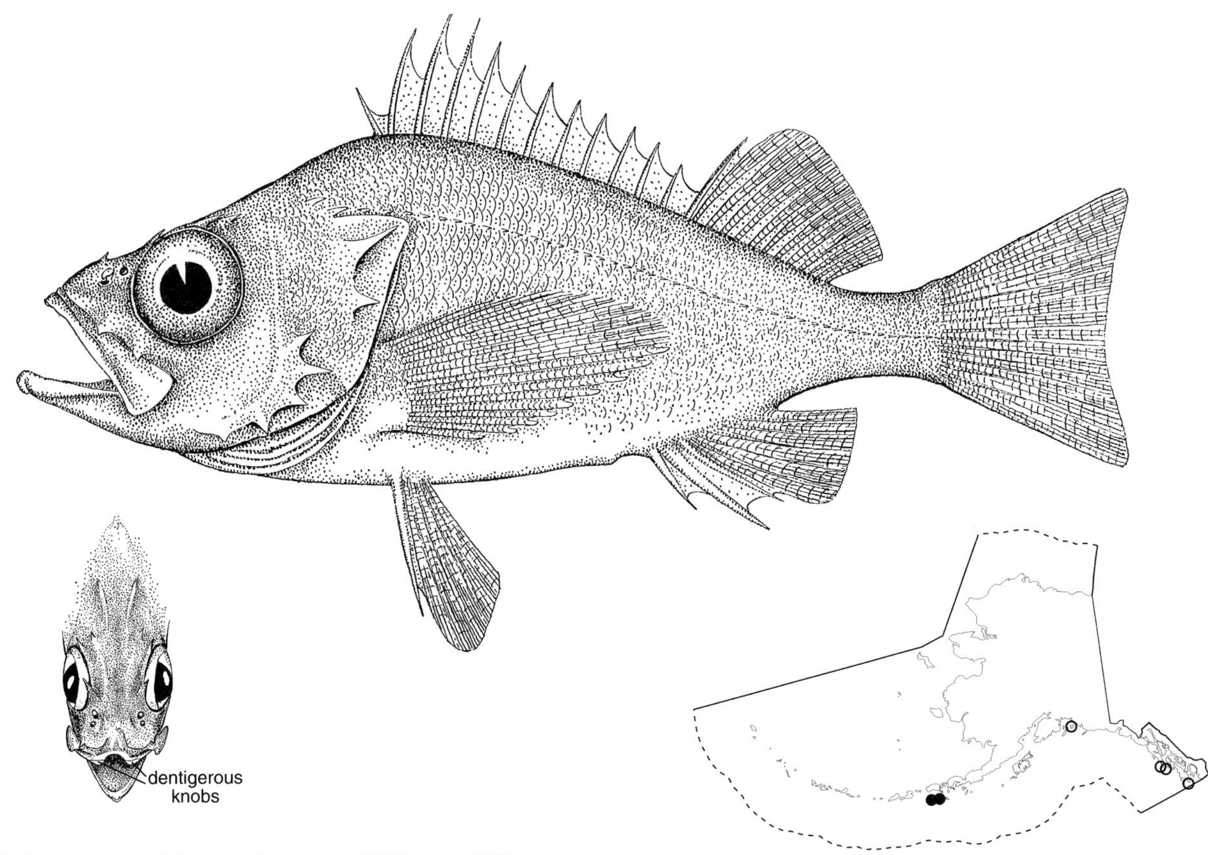

Notes & Sources — *Sebastes diploproa* (Gilbert, 1890)
Sebastichthys diploproa Gilbert, 1890

Description: Jordan and Evermann 1898:1801–1802; Phillips 1957:86–87; Hart 1973:412–413; Eschmeyer and Herald 1983:138; Kramer and O'Connell 1995:21; Orr et al. 2000:14.

Figures: Hart 1973:412; 17 cm TL, British Columbia.

Range: Not included in inventories of Alaskan fish species by Wilimovsky (1954, 1958). Reported from southeastern Alaska and from Alaska Peninsula by Alverson et al. (1964) from records of groundfish explorations, without giving specific localities; and from Prince William Sound by Miller and Lea (1972). Hart's (1973) report of range to Alaska Peninsula probably was based on that of Alverson et al. (1964). Phillips (1957) gave Vancouver, British Columbia, and Grinols (1965), Quast and Hall (1972), and Eschmeyer and Herald (1983) gave southeastern Alaska for northern limit. Snytko (1986) reported catches from two localities off the Sanak Islands in the western Gulf of Alaska: 53°52'N, 163°31'W, depth 95 m; and 54°05'N, 163°08'W, depth 80–85 m; fish measured 26–37 cm FL. NMFS resource assessment surveys reviewed by Allen and Smith (1988) indicated range to Prince William Sound, but few of the 724 occurrences in 30 years of surveys were from Alaska (circles on the above map; each could represent more than one occurrence). R. Baxter (unpubl. data) examined a specimen obtained in southeastern Alaska at 56°15'N, 135°33'W, depth 263 m, during a NMFS survey in 1987, but the specimen was not saved. We found no voucher specimens from Alaska in museum collections. This species is most common off southern California.

Sebastes saxicola (Gilbert, 1890) **stripetail rockfish**

Eastern Gulf of Alaska at Yakutat Bay to central Baja California at Bahia Sebastian Vizcaino.

Offshore, on soft bottoms and around reefs at depths of 25–547 m, usually at 100–350 m.

D XIII,11–13; A III,5–8; Pec 15–18; LLp 35–43; LLs 43–53; GR 30–35; Vert 26.

- **Yellow-pink** with some light green; several vague dusky blotches dorsally, these darker in young fish; silvery pink ventrally; fins pink, with some yellow; **caudal fin with green streaks**; mouth and gill cavity white; peritoneum black.
- Eye large, 31–34% of head length.
- Head spines: 1, 2, 4, 5, 7, (8); moderate to strong.
- Symphyseal knob strong, directed forward; maxilla extending to mideye to rear edge of pupil; interorbital space flat to slightly concave; subopercular spines present; **lachrymal spines strong**, either one occasionally double.
- **Anal fin spine 2 slightly longer than 3**; distal margin of anal fin nearly straight, and almost vertical or slightly slanted posteriorly; caudal fin moderately emarginate.
- Length to 41 cm TL.

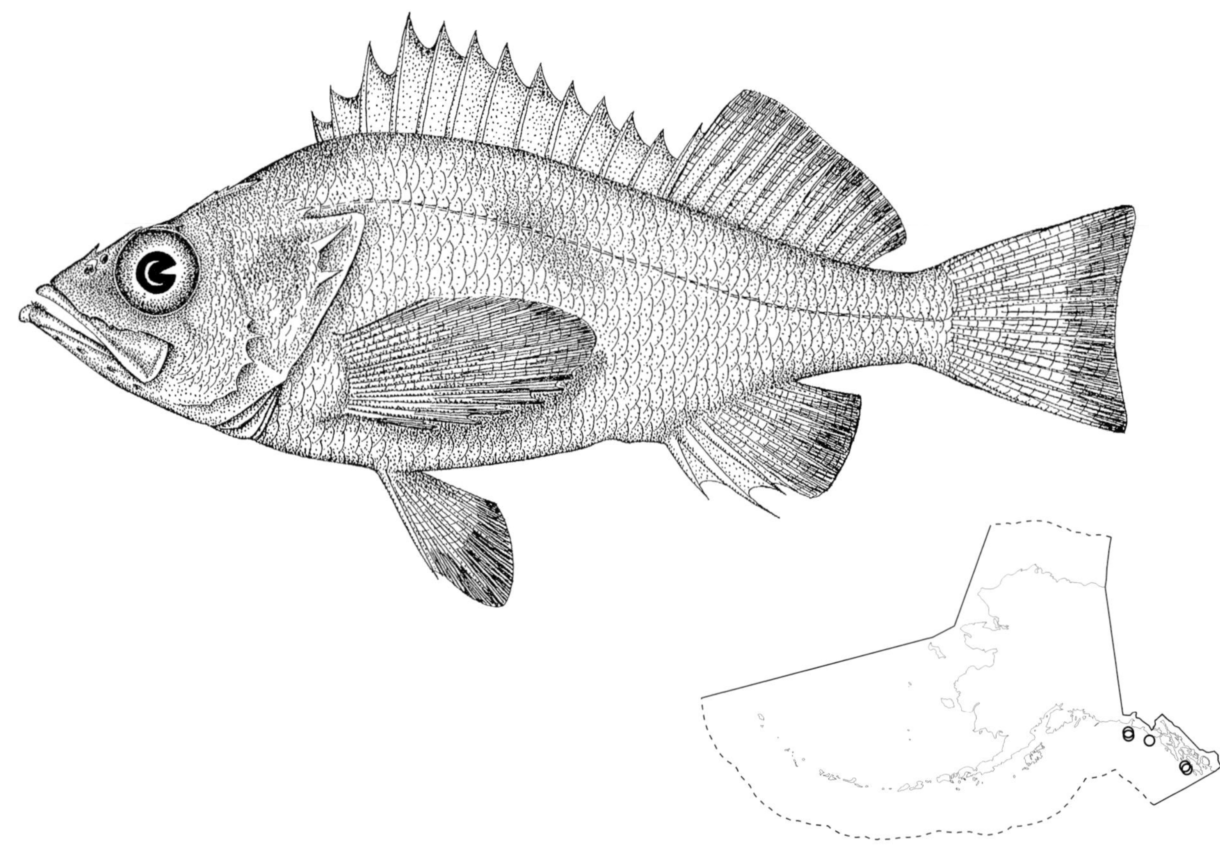

Notes & Sources — *Sebastes saxicola* (Gilbert, 1890)
Sebastichthys saxicola Gilbert, 1890

Description: Jordan and Evermann 1898:1798–1799; Phillips 1957:80–81; Hart 1973:444–445; Eschmeyer and Herald 1983:150; Kramer and O'Connell 1995:63; Orr et al. 2000:13.

Figure: Hart 1973:444; 31 cm TL.

Range: Allen and Smith (1988) mapped 432 occurrences of *S. saxicola* from 30 years of NMFS resource surveys in the eastern North Pacific. A few catches were off the outer coasts of southeastern Alaska, with the northernmost off Yakutat Bay (circles on the above map; each could represent more than one occurrence). The rest were from Washington and farther south, although Hart (1973) reported that the species occurs in British Columbia waters off the outer coasts and in the Strait of Georgia. We found no voucher specimens from Alaska in museum collections.

Sebastes zacentrus (Gilbert, 1890) **sharpchin rockfish**

Attu Island, Aleutian Islands, to southern California off San Diego.

Soft bottom and on seamounts at depths of 25–660 m, usually at 100–350 m.

D XIII,13–15; A III,7–8; Pec 16–18; LLp 39–47; LLs 43–59; GR 31–41; Vert 27.

- **Light red** with vague dark brown blotches extending onto dorsal fin and below lateral line; reddish yellow ventrally; **dark forked bar from eye to operculum**; **lateral line in area same color as background or only slightly darker**; mouth and gill cavity pink and white with yellow mottling; peritoneum black.
- Head spines: 1, 2, 4, 5, 7; strong.
- Symphyseal knob strong, directed forward; maxilla extending to mideye to rear edge of pupil; interorbital space slightly convex to slightly concave; **subopercular spines usually absent**; lachrymal spines bluntly triangular, the posterior sometimes bifid; **short ridge on lachrymal forming shelf under nostrils**.
- **Anal fin spine 2 slightly longer than 3**; distal margin of anal fin nearly straight, nearly vertical; caudal fin slightly to moderately emarginate.
- Length to 45 cm TL.

Notes & Sources — *Sebastes zacentrus* (Gilbert, 1890)
Sebastichthys zacentrus Gilbert, 1890

Description: Jordan and Evermann 1898:1814–1815; Gilbert 1915:331–333; Phillips 1957:102–103; Barsukov 1964:249–250 of transl.; Hart 1973:450–451; Eschmeyer and Herald 1983:152; Kramer and O'Connell 1995:69; Orr et al. 2000:12.

Figure: University of British Columbia, artist P. Drukker-Brammall; UBC 65-5, 207 mm SL, Attu Island, Alaska.

Range: Recorded range is extended west to Attu Island by UBC 65-5 (see illustration above); caught on east side of Casco Cove. Previously recorded to Semisopochnoi Island by Allen and Smith (1988) from NMFS surveys. Records from the Aleutian Islands are relatively rare. Most of the 694 occurrences mapped by Allen and Smith (1988) from NMFS surveys were from the Gulf of Alaska to California. Well represented, although not common, in museum collections from Sanak and Shumagin islands to southeastern Alaska. Snytko (1986) reported catches from seamounts, including Surveyor Seamount at 56°03'N, 144°03'W, depth 610–660 m; and Hodgkins Seamount at 53°15'N, 135°45'W, 200–250 m; fish were 11–37 cm FL. Depth range of 610–660 m (Snytko 1986) is the maximum recorded. Previously reported to 475 m by Allen and Smith (1988).

Sebastes ruberrimus (Cramer, 1895) **yelloweye rockfish**

Aleutian Islands south of Umnak Island to northern Baja California off Ensenada.
Around rocky reefs and boulder fields at depths of 15–549 m, usually at 50–400 m.

D XIII,13–16; A III,5–8; Pec 18–20; LLp 39–46; LLs 45–50; GR 25–30; Vert 26.

- **Red dorsally, yellow-orange laterally**, white to yellow ventrally; fins usually with black tips; **juveniles and young adults darker, redder, with more black, and with white stripe along lateral line and shorter stripe below**; eye bright yellow; mouth and gill cavity white, with some light pink or yellow; peritoneum silvery white, with a few scattered black dots.
- Head spines: 1, 2, 3, 4, 5, (6), 7, (8); strong to very strong.
- Symphyseal knob broad, low, rounded; maxilla extending to rear edge of pupil to just beyond eye; interorbital space slightly concave; **ocular and parietal ridges high and rugose in larger fish**; subopercular spines present; lachrymal processes present, usually a small lobe followed by a larger, triangular projection.
- Anal fin spine 2 about same length as 3 or slightly longer, but much thicker; distal margin of anal fin rounded; caudal fin slightly emarginate or nearly truncate but with slightly rounded tips.
- Length to 91 cm TL (one of the largest *Sebastes*).

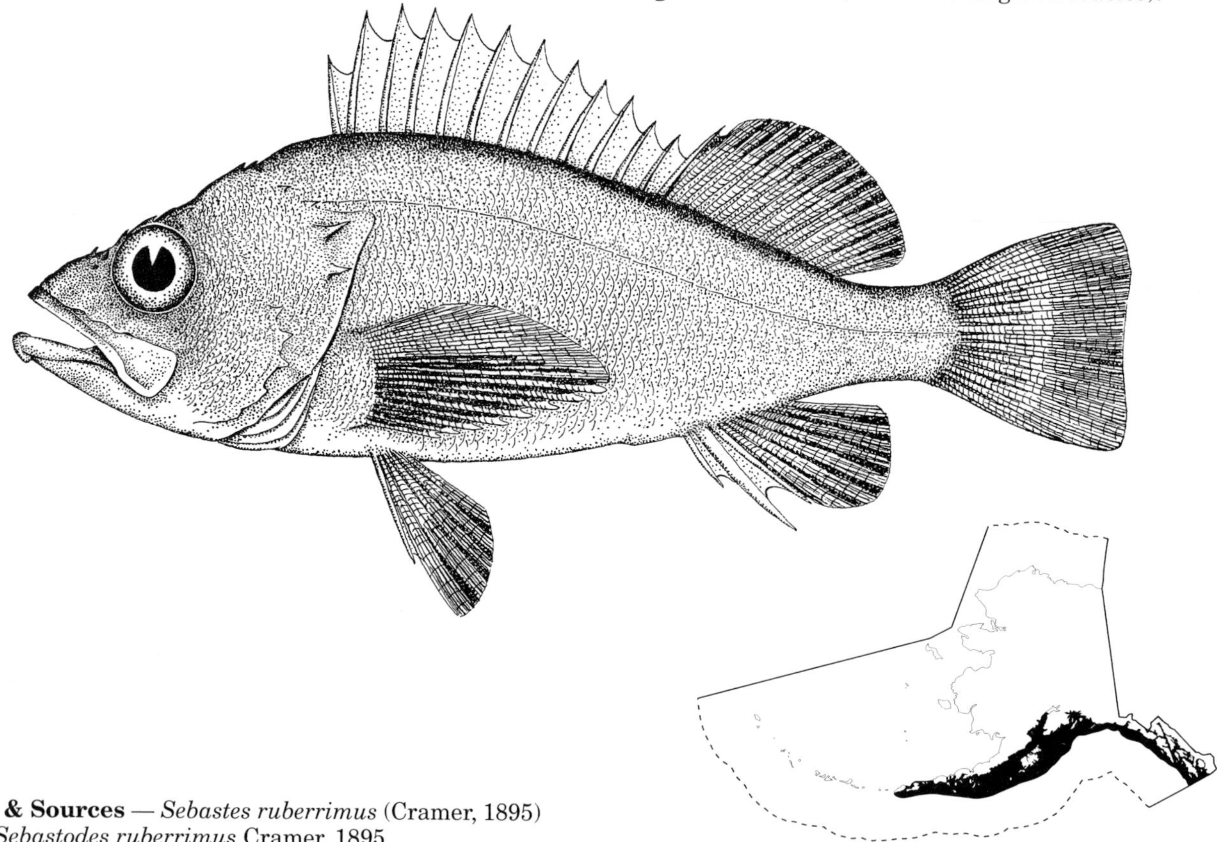

Notes & Sources — *Sebastes ruberrimus* (Cramer, 1895)
Sebastodes ruberrimus Cramer, 1895
Sebastodes bilineatus Welander & Alverson, 1954
Young are so differently colored they were described as a new species by Welander and Alverson (1954); the error was corrected by Hubbs (1959).
The vernacular can be misleading, as some other rockfishes have yellow eyes.

Description: Jordan and Evermann 1898:1805–1806; Phillips 1957:104–105; Barsukov 1964:245–246 of transl.; Hart 1973:442–443; Eschmeyer and Herald 1985:148; Kramer and O'Connell 1995:61; Orr et al. 2000:16.

Figure: Hart 1973:442; 21 cm TL, British Columbia.

Range: Taken in NMFS bottom trawl surveys as far west off the south side of the Aleutian Islands as Umnak Island and Unimak Pass (Allen and Smith 1988). The western-most-caught voucher specimen we found is NMC 81-494, from about 50 km south of Unimak Island at 52°48'N, 168°46'W, collected by A. E. Peden in 1980. Reported off the north side of Unalaska Island by the NMFS marine observer program and documented by photographs (D. C. Baker, pers. comm., 29 Oct. 1991). Quast and Hall (1972) reported presence of specimens from the Gulf of Alaska, including southeastern Alaska, in ABL permanent collection. Five lots from Alaska are in UBC collection, with catch localities from south of the Shumagin Islands (UBC 62-693) to Suemez Island, Ulloa Channel (UBC 61-546). *Sebastes ruberrimus* is a target species in the longline fishery in southeastern Alaska, but less common off Alaskan coasts than in British Columbia and farther south.

Sebastes aleutianus (Jordan & Evermann, 1898) **rougheye rockfish**

Bering Sea at Navarin Basin and Aleutian Islands at Stalemate Bank to southern California off San Diego; western Bering Sea to Pacific Ocean off Kuril Islands and northern Hokkaido; not in Sea of Okhotsk.

Near and on bottom at depths of 25–900 m, usually at 100–500 m; large fish prefer soft, gently sloping substrates with boulders; also found on seamounts.

D XII–XIV,12–15; A III,6–8; Pec 17–19; LLp 29–37; LLs 47–55; GR 29–35; Vert 27.

- **Red**, often with vague dusky bands and blotches, especially dorsally; posterior part of lateral line usually pink, standing out slightly from darker body; **occasionally predominantly dusky red with dark bands radiating from eye**; usually with black margins on all fins except pectoral; dusky blotch on opercle, both inside and out; mouth and gill cavities red and black, white in juveniles; peritoneum pale, with large black dots.
- Head spines: 1, 2, 3, 4, 5, 6, 7, 8; strong.
- Symphyseal knob broad, low, projecting downward; maxilla extending to rear edge of pupil to rear edge of eye; interorbital space convex to flat; **2–10 spines on ridge below eye**, rarely 0 or 1 spine; 1–6 subopercular spines; lachrymal spines well developed, occasionally multifid.
- Anal fin spine 2 usually shorter than 3 in large adults, may reach tip of spine 3 in smaller specimens; distal margin of anal fin rounded or almost straight and slanted posteriorly; caudal fin slightly to moderately emarginate.
- Length to 97 cm TL (a large *Sebastes*).

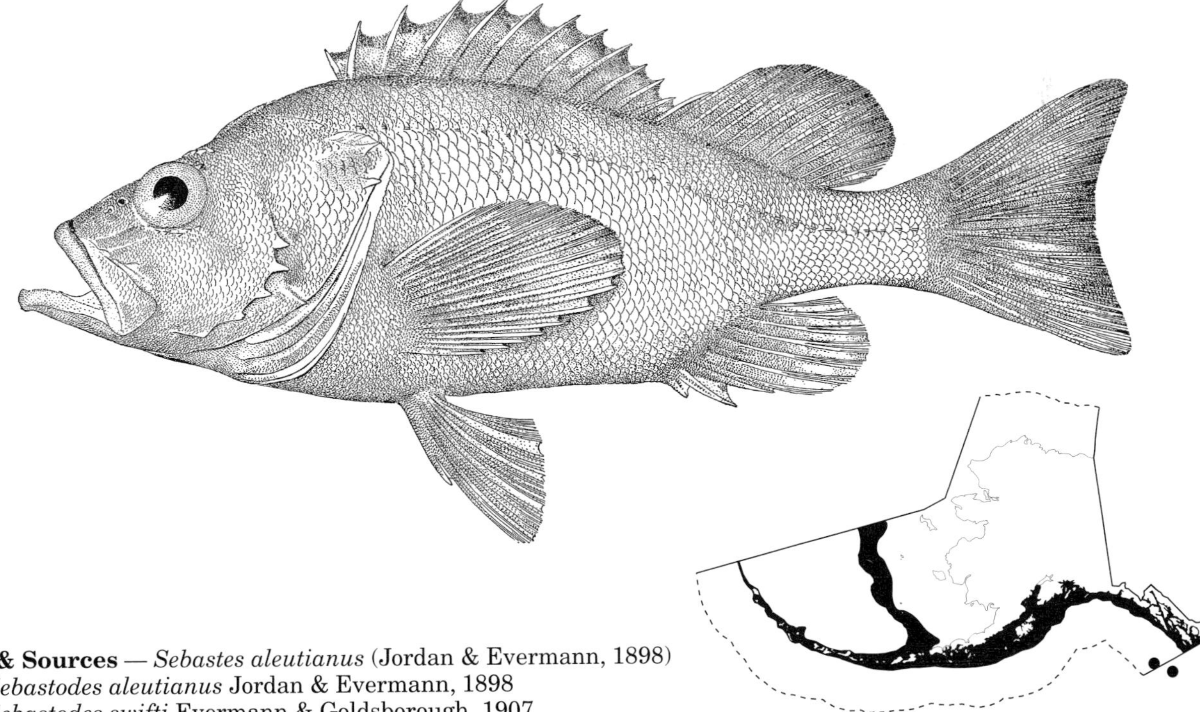

Notes & Sources — *Sebastes aleutianus* (Jordan & Evermann, 1898)
Sebastodes aleutianus Jordan & Evermann, 1898
Sebastodes swifti Evermann & Goldsborough, 1907
Sebastodes melanostictus Matsubara, 1934

Wilimovsky (1958:49) placed *S. swifti,* which had been described by Evermann and Goldsborough (1907:285–286) from two small fish collected at Yes Bay and Kasaan Bay, Alaska, in the synonymy of *S. aleutianus.* The correctness of the synonymy is clear from the description of *S. swifti.*

Description: Jordan and Evermann 1898:1795–1796; Phillips 1957:82–83; Barsukov 1964:239–242 of transl.; Hart 1973:394–395; Eschmeyer and Herald 1983:133; Amaoka in Masuda et al. 1984:311; Kramer and O'Connell 1995:1; Orr et al. 2000:16. Rarely with other than 13 dorsal fin spines. Chen (1986) found 1 specimen with 14 spines in a sample of 22.

Figure: Jordan and Gilbert 1899, pl. 48 modified to repair damaged fins; type, 46 cm TL or more (types ranged from 46 to 68 cm), off Karluk, Kodiak Island.

Range: NMFS survey data summarized by Allen and Smith (1988) confirmed earlier Alaskan records and provided a more precise description of range. Their map depicting the distribution of 2,151 occurrences in 30 years of surveys of eastern North Pacific and Bering Sea shows that *S. aleutianus* is more common in the north-central and eastern Gulf of Alaska than is *S. borealis.* This is reflected in museum holdings as well. Fedorov and Sheiko (2002) reported *S. aleutianus* to be common in the vicinity of the Commander Islands and gave a new maximum depth of 900 m. Krieger and Ito (1999) described seafloor habitat from observations using a manned submersible in the eastern Gulf of Alaska. Snytko (1986) reported *S. aleutianus* in catches at seamounts, including Dickens Seamount at 54°30'N, 137°00'W, and Hodgkins Seamount at 53°15'N, 135°45'W; fish lengths were 44–61 cm FL.

Sebastes borealis Barsukov, 1970 **shortraker rockfish**

Bering Sea at Navarin Canyon and Aleutian Islands at Stalemate Bank to southern California off Point Conception; western Bering Sea from Cape Olyutorskiy to Sea of Okhotsk and Pacific off northern Hokkaido.

Near or on bottom in deep water offshore to depth of about 1,200 m, most commonly at 100–600 m; rugged, steep-sloped habitat to moderately sloped, smooth, silty bottom with boulders.

D XIII,12–15; A III,6–8; Pec 17–20; LLp 28–32; LLs 36–46; GR 27–31; Vert 27–28.

- **Pink to orange-pink** with vague dusky bands which are most prominent in young fish; belly just as dark or only a little lighter than sides; fins reddish, edged with black; eye yellow; mouth, gill cavity, and gill membranes red to red-black; peritoneum light gray with black dots.
- **Large pores on lower jaw** which are much larger than in other species of *Sebastes*.
- Head spines: 1, 2, 3, 4, 5, (6), 7, 8; moderate to strong.
- Symphyseal knob obsolete to moderate; maxilla extending to rear area of pupil to rear edge of eye; interorbital space convex to flat; **0 or rarely 1 weak spine below eye** on orbital rim; subopercular spines present or absent; lachrymal spines variously developed.
- Anal fin spine 2 shorter than 3; distal margin of anal fin rounded, upper portion usually slanted anteriorly in large fish; caudal fin slightly emarginate.
- Length to 120 cm TL (largest *Sebastes* in Alaska).

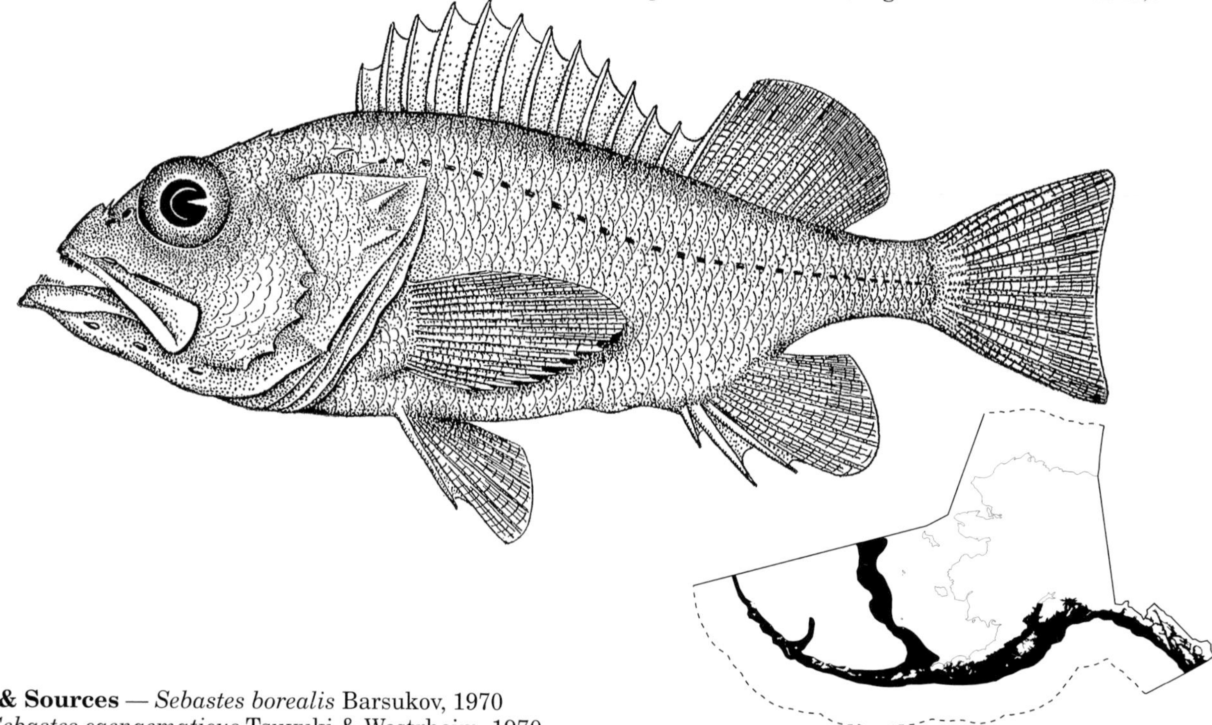

Notes & Sources — *Sebastes borealis* Barsukov, 1970
Sebastes caenaematicus Tsuyuki & Westrheim, 1970
This species was described in 1970 by Russian and American researchers working independently. Barsukov's (1970) description was published earlier in the year than Tsuyuki and Westrheim's (1970), so *S. borealis,* the name given by Barsukov, has priority.

Description: Barsukov 1970; Hart 1973:403–404; Amaoka in Masuda et al. 1984:311; Eschmeyer and Herald 1983: 135; Kramer and O'Connell 1995:11; Orr et al. 2000:17.

Figure: Hart 1973:403; 54 cm TL, off Vancouver Island.

Range: Data from NMFS surveys summarized by Allen and Smith (1988) provided a more precise description of range in Alaska than previously available. Most of their records (670 occurrences in 30 years of trawl surveys) were from the western Gulf of Alaska, Aleutian Islands, and Bering Sea slope. Relatively few were from the eastern Gulf of Alaska, and specimens from the eastern Gulf are rare in museum collections. Krieger (1992) observed *S. borealis* at several sites in southeastern Alaska. Rutecki et al. (1997) reported that the eastern Gulf of Alaska produces high catch rates of both *S. borealis* and *S. aleutianus.* Krieger and Ito (1999) observed both species in the same region from a submersible, and noted that it was not always possible to distinguish between them from the submersible. Some specimens identified as *S. borealis* from the Gulf of Alaska and British Columbia in museum collections are *S. aleutianus.* Tokranov and Davydov (1997) gave detailed data on distribution in western Bering Sea and Pacific off Kamchatka. Sheiko and Fedorov (2000) reported a new maximum depth of 1,200 m.

Size: Novikov (1974, cited in Tokranov and Davydov 1998) gave a maximum size of 120 cm TL. Tokranov and Davydov (1998) reported a maximum of 116 cm TL in catches off eastern Kamchatka in 1992–1995. Reported to reach 108 cm TL in the eastern Pacific (e.g., Kramer and O'Connell 1995).

Sebastes melanostomus (Eigenmann & Eigenmann, 1890) **blackgill rockfish**

Southeastern Alaska, reports unconfirmed; northern British Columbia to central Baja California near Cedros Island.

Deep water over soft bottom and on seamounts at depths of 125–768 m, usually at 250–600 m.

D XIII,12–15; A III,6–8; Pec 17–20; LLp 28–34; LLs 32–34; GR 27–34; Vert 26.

- **Dark red**; vague dusky bands dorsally, most prominent in young fish; fins red, most with black tips; **black area in fold above upper jaw; mouth, gill cavity, and upper portion of gill membrane black; peritoneum black**.
- Head spines: 1, 2, 3, 4, 5, 7, 8; strong.
- Symphyseal knob large, projecting downward; maxilla extending to mideye to rear edge of eye; interorbital space flat to slightly concave; **0–2 spines below eye** on orbital rim, posterior spine sometimes double; subopercular spines absent; 2 lachrymal spines present, posterior sometimes double.
- Anal fin spine 2 usually shorter than 3; distal margin of anal fin slightly rounded or almost straight and nearly vertical; caudal fin truncate to moderately emarginate.
- Gill rakers usually 31–33, compared to 27–30 in *S. borealis*.
- Length to 61 cm TL.

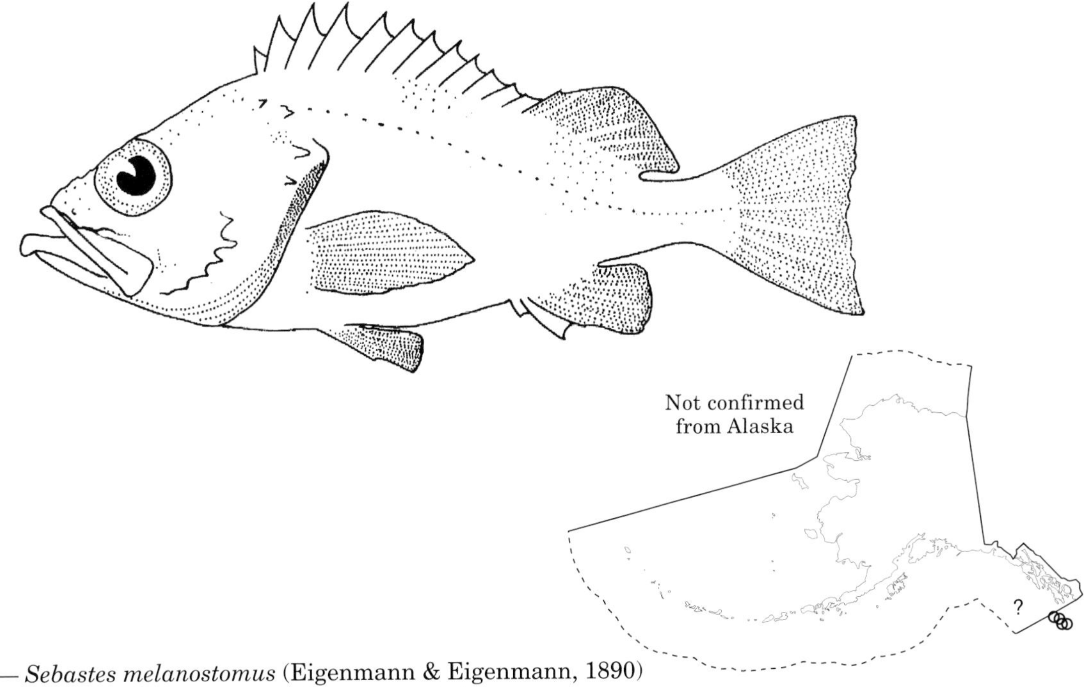

Notes & Sources — *Sebastes melanostomus* (Eigenmann & Eigenmann, 1890)
Sebastodes melanostomus Eigenmann & Eigenmann, 1890
Sebastichthys introniger Gilbert, 1890
Caution: Not all records identified as *S. introniger* are *Sebastes melanostomus.* Specimens reported from the Aleutian Islands by Gilbert (1896) are *S. aleutianus* (Barsukov 1970).
Most easily confused with *S. borealis* but distinguishable by coloration and, usually, number of gill rakers.

Description: Jordan and Evermann 1898:1803; Phillips 1957:84–85; Eschmeyer and Herald 1983:143; Kramer and O'Connell 1995:41; Orr et al. 2000:17.

Figure: Miller and Lea 1972:107.

Range: Reports for the Bering Sea and Aleutian Islands, such as Quast and Hall (1972) after Phillips (1957) and Barsukov (1964), and a recent report by Mito et al. (1999), probably represent *S. borealis,* which was not recognized and described as a species until 1970, or *S. aleutianus.* This point was made by Barsukov (1970) and Tsyuki and Westrheim (1970), but the problem continues to present itself. Many "vouchers" of field-identified *S. melanostomus* have been brought back from the Bering Sea by NMFS observers, but J. W. Orr (pers. comm., 29 Jan. 2001) reidentified all of them he has seen as either *S. borealis* or, less commonly, *S. aleutianus.* Apparently, Orr reported, any black on the gill membranes is taken to be diagnostic for *S. melanostomus,* despite training to the contrary. In southeastern Alaska, *S. melanostomus* has been reported twice in commercial catches landed at Ketchikan but the identification is unconfirmed (Kramer and O'Connell 1988, 1995). Allen and Smith (1988) and Orr et al. (2000) gave Washington for the northern confirmed limit. Workman et al. (1998) caught *S. melanostomus* in 1997 from the *Ocean Selector* off the west coast of the Queen Charlotte Islands; several were caught near the Alaskan border, with the northernmost at 54°17'N, 133°09'W. Unfortunately, the voucher specimen was lost in a freezer mishap (G. Gillespie, pers. comm., 3 Jan. 2001). In 1999, Gillespie caught *S. melanostomus* from the *W. E. Ricker* as far north as 49°09'N, 127°01'W, off central Vancouver Island, which are the northernmost records supported by voucher specimens (RBCM uncataloged).

Family Anoplopomatidae
Sablefishes

Members of the family Anoplopomatidae are collectively called sablefishes or coalfishes for their coloration. There are two species: the sablefish, *Anoplopoma fimbria,* and the skilfish, *Erilepis zonifer.* They occur only in marine waters of the North Pacific, where their ranges extend from Alaska to California and to Japan.

Anoplopoma fimbria is an important commercial species. In the fishing industry it is more often called blackcod than sablefish, the name assigned by the American Fisheries Society (Robins et al. 1991a). The skilfish, *E. zonifer,* is less common, not a specific target of the fisheries, and its range does not extend as far south or north as that of *A. fimbria.* Sablefish (*A. fimbria*) are commonly caught from the Bering Sea to the Gulf of Alaska. Skilfish, however, have not been confirmed in the Bering Sea. They are rarely reported from within the 200-mile limit south of the Aleutian Islands or in the Gulf of Alaska, and those records mostly represent immature fish. Reports of skilfish in the Bering Sea lack documentation. After reviewing available records Phillips (1966) concluded skilfish were absent from the Bering Sea, and we found no recent or verifiable records that would negate that conclusion. The capture of a juvenile skilfish just south of Unimak Island in 1998 (UW 42329) suggests juveniles might occasionally travel north of the Aleutians.

Adults of both sablefish species inhabit fairly deep water. Adult sablefish (*A. fimbria*) are most abundant in commercial quantities at depths of about 365–915 m and have been caught as deep as 2,740 m. Skilfish have been caught as deep as 439 m. Sablefish live near the bottom and are found in nearshore as well as offshore waters whereas skilfish are usually taken far offshore. As with many other marine fish species, the younger individuals inhabit the surface and upper waters of the ocean before descending into deeper waters.

Like other scorpaeniforms, sablefishes have a suborbital stay. Quast (1965), however, considered that the family has little affinity to other scorpaeniforms and speculated that the suborbital stay may have originated independently in the sablefish lineage.

Features common to the two sablefish species that, taken together, distinguish them from other scorpaeniforms include lack of spines, ridges, or cirri on the head; presence of two dorsal fins, the first spinous and the second mainly of soft rays; an anal fin mainly of soft rays; thoracic pelvic fins with 1 spine and 5 rays; two well-developed nostrils on each side; gill membranes attached to the isthmus; 6 branchiostegal rays; a single lateral line; and a swim bladder. The anal fin spines are not strong, like they are in the rockfishes (Scorpaenidae), and can be difficult to discern. The two sablefish species are easily distinguished from each other by the configuration of the dorsal and anal fins, as indicated in the key and in the species accounts.

Sablefish, *A. fimbria,* reach a maximum length of about 114 cm (3 ft 9 inches) while skilfish, *E. zonifer,* can reach 183 cm (6 ft). Neither species has been known to attain such a great size in recent years. Most skilfish taken in Alaskan waters are juveniles.

Key to the Anoplopomatidae of Alaska

1 Dorsal fins well separated, by more than twice diameter of eye; second dorsal fin and anal fin bases about equal in length, with their origins opposite each other . . . . *Anoplopoma fimbria,* page 385

1 Dorsal fins close together, almost touching; second dorsal fin base longer than anal fin base, with origin of anal fin posterior to origin of second dorsal fin . . . . *Erilepis zonifer,* page 386

Anoplopoma fimbria (Pallas, 1814) **sablefish**

Bering Sea south of St. Lawrence Island and Aleutian Islands to central Baja California off Cedros Island; western Bering Sea and Commander Islands to Japan.

Near bottom over soft substrate at water depths to 2,740 m, usually less than 700 m; young often near shore and shallower.

D XVII–XXX + I,16–21; A II–III,15–20; Pec 14–16; Pel I,5; LLs 190–195; GR 18–25; Vert 61–66.

- Blackish, dark gray, or dark greenish gray dorsally, gray to white ventrally.
- Body elongate.
- First dorsal fin not set in shallow groove.
- **First and second dorsal fins set well apart**, interspace more than twice width of eye; **bases of dorsal fins about same length or second dorsal fin base shorter**; **anal fin origin below origin of second dorsal fin**; spines in second dorsal fin and anal fin typically embedded and difficult to discern.
- Small, weakly ctenoid scales on head and body; scales absent from fins.
- One body lateral line, following dorsal contour.
- Teeth fine and in patches, on both jaws, vomer, and palatines.
- Gill membranes broadly attached to isthmus.
- Length to 114 cm TL, weight to 25 kg.

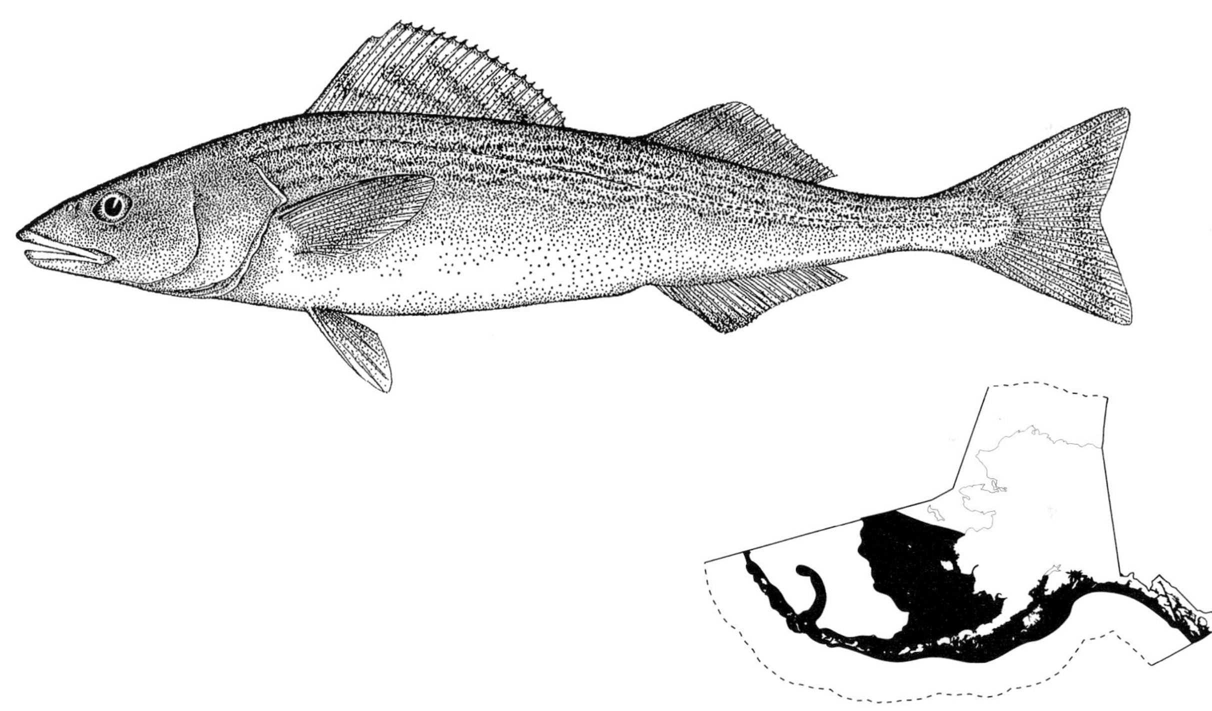

Notes & Sources — *Anoplopoma fimbria* (Pallas, 1814)
Gadus fimbria Pallas, 1814

Description: Jordan and Evermann 1898:1862; Miller and Lea 1972:113; Hart 1973:455–457; Amaoka in Masuda et al. 1984:320.

Figure: Hart 1973:455; 25 cm TL, off Nagai Island, Alaska.

Range: The type specimens were probably collected in Alaska at the Aleutian Islands (Eschmeyer 1998). NMFS survey catches reported by Allen and Smith (1988) outlined the known range of *A. fimbria* in Alaska, extending from the Bering Sea southeast of St. Lawrence Island to Stalemate Bank and Ulm Plateau in the Aleutian Islands, and along Bowers Ridge.

Size: Baxter (1990ms), citing data provided by Norman Parks, NOAA, NMFS, Seattle, Washington, for a 114-cm-TL fish weighing 15.3 kg. The maximum weight of 57 kg given by Roedel (1948) and Hart (1973) is mythical. Bell and Gharrett (1945) reported that the captain of a halibut vessel operating off southeastern Alaska in 1916 had caught a blackcod (sablefish) weighing 126 pounds (57 kg) with the head and viscera removed. However, as Phillips (1966) pointed out, that dressed weight would represent a whole fish weighing about 189 pounds (86 kg), which is appropriate for a skilfish but much too large for a sablefish. He gave a weight of 56 pounds (25.4 kg) for the largest authenticated sablefish, taken off California in 1930. Sablefish usually weigh less than 25 pounds (11.3 kg). Clemens and Wilby (1961) considered sablefish 36 inches (91 cm) in length and 40 pounds (18.1 kg) large and gave a maximum length of 40 inches (102 cm).

Erilepis zonifer (Lockington, 1880) skilfish

Pacific Ocean south of Aleutian Islands and southern Gulf of Alaska to central California at Monterey Bay, and to western Pacific off southeastern Kamchatka and Kuril Islands to northern Japan.

Adults offshore, close to bottom at depths of 200–439 m; juveniles and young adults to about 110 cm TL taken at and near surface, sometimes close to shore.

D XII–XIV + I–II,15–17; A II–III,11–14; Pec 16–19; Pel I,5; LLp 133; LLs 120–130; GR 21–22; Vert 45–46.

- Large adults more or less uniformly black dorsally, lighter ventrally; young fish dark blue-gray, green, or black with large white and gray blotches, these blotches fading with growth but retained until at least 90 cm TL.
- Body stout.
- First dorsal fin set in shallow groove.
- **Two dorsal fins set close together**, interspace less than width of eye; **base of second dorsal fin longer than first dorsal fin**; **origin of anal fin posterior to origin of second dorsal fin**; anal fin base shorter than base of second dorsal; spines in second dorsal fin and anal fin often buried and difficult to discern.
- Ctenoid scales on soft-rayed fins, as well as head and body.
- One body lateral line, nearly straight.
- Teeth conical, in 2 rows in lower jaw and in a band in upper jaw.
- Gill membranes attached to isthmus except at posterior margin.
- Length to 183 cm TL, weight to 91 kg.

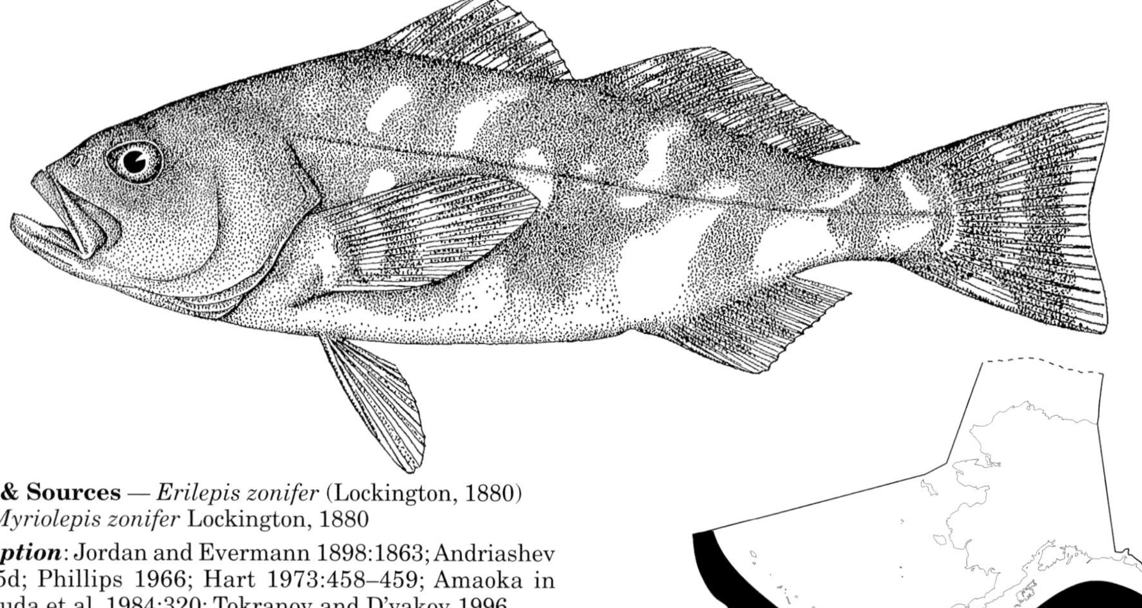

Notes & Sources — *Erilepis zonifer* (Lockington, 1880)
Myriolepis zonifer Lockington, 1880

Description: Jordan and Evermann 1898:1863; Andriashev 1955d; Phillips 1966; Hart 1973:458–459; Amaoka in Masuda et al. 1984:320; Tokranov and D'yakov 1996.

Figure: Hart 1973:458; 29 cm TL, British Columbia.

Range: Depicted on map from rare reports of juveniles. Reported from southeastern Alaska in 1916, but locality was later corrected (Thompson 1917) to British Columbia. A fish caught off southeastern Alaska that weighed 57 kg dressed out and was reported to be a sablefish, *Anoplopoma fimbria,* was probably a skilfish (Phillips 1966), but details are unknown. Neave (1959) reported two small specimens taken in surface gill nets in the Gulf of Alaska at 55°N, 145°W, outside the 200-mile limit, in the summer of 1958. Larkins (1964) reported skilfish caught near the surface south of the Aleutian Islands ("between Aleutian Islands and 50°N") and in the Gulf of Alaska ("north of 54°N and east of 160°W") between 1955 and 1961 during salmon gill-net fishing. Skilfish were present as rare individuals in 4% of the sets in those two areas. LeBrasseur (1967) reported that from 1958 to 1966, 33 skilfish, all weighing less than 0.9 kg (2 lb), were caught by crews line fishing at Canada's Ocean Station Papa (50°N, 145°W); gear was a hand gurdy with 183 m of sounding wire, a 14-kg weight at the end, and lures on 1.8-m leaders at 5–9-m intervals. The only voucher specimen from Alaska in a museum may be UW 42329, a 53-cm-SL juvenile caught 10 Jun. 1998 south of Unimak Island at 54°40'N, 163°50'W, and identified by D. Adams and B. K. Urbain. The only Gulf of Alaska specimen at the ABL (AB 61-39) is a 35-cm-SL juvenile from about 54°N, 141°W, just outside the 200-mile limit, and is the record cited by Quast and Hall (1972). B. L. Wing (pers. comm., 12 Apr. 1999) recalled a 20-pound (9-kg) fish being taken off the Fairweather Ground in the late 1970s by a salmon troller, and seeing photographs of a 30-pound (14-kg) fish taken by sablefish longliner off southeastern Alaska in about 1995. Tokranov and D'yakov (1996) recorded two adult skilfish (126–130 cm TL) taken east of Shiashkotan Island at depths of 220-400 m, and Mukhametov and Volodin (1999) recorded another (120 cm TL) from the same area at 361–415 m; previously known off Russia from juveniles caught near the surface east of Iturup Island and Cape Lopatka. The maximum recorded depth of 439 m (Clemens and Wilby 1961) is for two adults (112–178 cm TL) taken west of Queen Charlotte Islands.

Family Hexagrammidae
Greenlings

The family Hexagrammidae is a small group of marine scorpaeniform bottom fishes that is endemic to the North Pacific. Comprising four or five genera with 9–11 species, depending on classifiation employed, the family is the most speciose of the families occurring only in the North Pacific. Seven species of greenling occur in Alaska. Atka mackerel, *Pleurogrammus monopterygius,* and lingcod, *Ophiodon elongatus,* inhabit shallow inshore waters to moderate depths, reaching 475–575 m. Painted greenling, *Oxylebius pictus,* and the four species of *Hexagrammos* in Alaska inhabit much shallower inshore waters and are rarely found deeper than 100 m. *Pleurogrammus monopterygius* is the only greenling that is pelagic as an adult. The others are primarily demersal. All seven species occur in the Gulf of Alaska. Four species are also found in the Bering Sea and one, the whitespotted greenling, *H. stelleri,* has been found in the Chukchi and Beaufort seas.

Greenlings lack head spines and ridges. Most species have a pair of cirri above the eyes, and some have two pairs. Several greenling species have five lateral lines. All have a single, long-based dorsal fin, usually with a notch between the spines and soft rays. The anal fin is roughly half the length of the dorsal and has 0–3 flexible spines followed by soft rays; the spines are usually weak and difficult to distinguish as spines. The pelvic fins are thoracic and have 1 spine and 5 rays. The anterior nostril on each side is well developed but the posterior nostril is reduced to a small pore or absent. The gill membranes are broadly joined and free of the isthmus except in *Ophiodon,* in which they are joined to each other only anteriorly. (Fusion of the gill membranes to the isthmus was reported, incorrectly, by some authors; in hexagrammids the gill membranes are free of the isthmus.) Six branchiostegal rays support each gill membrane. The teeth are usually small and the scales ctenoid, and a swim bladder is absent. In the Alaskan species the vertebrae range in number from 36 to 63.

Coloration in greenlings can vary with local habitat, sex, size, and geographic region. Sexual dimorphism in coloration is particularly marked in kelp greenling, *H. decagrammus.*

Adults of most greenling species attain lengths of 61 cm (2 ft) or less. The largest is *Ophiodon elongatus,* which reaches 152 cm (5 ft). All of the greenlings are reported to have good flavor, but only *O. elongatus* and *P. monopterygius* are commercially important species.

The only change in the list of Alaskan greenling species since Quast and Hall (1972) inventoried the regional ichthyofauna is the addition of *Oxylebius pictus,* discovered in Prince William Sound and the Alexander Archipelago by Orsi et al. (1991). The nomenclature for the greenlings is the same, including synonymy of *P. azonus* in *P. monopterygius* and *H. superciliosus* in *H. lagocephalus,* and follows Quast (1964a, 1965), Kendall and Vinter (1984), Nelson (1994), and Shinohara (1994).

In Nelson's (1994) classification, *Pleurogrammus monopterygius, Ophiodon elongatus,* and *Oxylebius pictus* are each in their own, monotypic subfamilies, while the species of *Hexagrammos* are in another subfamily. Some classifications (e.g., Eschmeyer 1998) place *Oxylebius pictus* with the combfishes in a separate family, the Zaniolepididae. Nelson (1994) classified combfishes in Hexagrammidae as a subfamily that does not include *O. pictus.* Combfishes differ from other greenlings in having comblike scales and unperforated lateral line scales, and in other ways. One of the two known species of combfishes occurs as far north as Vancouver Island, British Columbia.

The key to Alaskan greenlings first separates the monotypic subfamilies, and ends with Hexagramminae. The key is essentially that of A. E. Peden from the 1975 revised print of Hart's (1973) *Pacific Fishes of Canada,* except for the addition of characters to distinguish *P. monopterygius,* which at that time was not known to occur off British Columbia. For the three monotypic subfamilies the characters separating the species are the same as those distinguishing the subfamilies. Within Hexagramminae, distinguishing characters include body and caudal peduncle depth, caudal fin shape, eye color, lateral line configuration, and number and size of head cirri. The second, third, and fifth lateral lines are complete in all *Hexagrammos* species, while the first and fourth are variously developed and offer important specific characters.

Key to the Hexagrammidae of Alaska

1		One lateral line canal on each side of body	(2)
1		More than one lateral line canal on each side of body	(3)
2	(1)	Maxilla not reaching or barely reaching anterior margin of eye; vertical dark bands on sides of body and caudal fin	*Oxylebius pictus,* page 389
2		Maxilla reaching posterior margin of eye or extending past eye; no distinct bands on sides of body	*Ophiodon elongatus,* page 390
3	(1)	Dorsal fin not notched between spines and soft rays	*Pleurogrammus monopterygius,* page 391
3		Dorsal fin with notch between spines and soft rays	(4)
4	(3)	Fourth lateral line short, not extending past tip of depressed pelvic fin	(5)
4		Fourth lateral line long, reaching to posterior area of anal fin	(6)
5	(4)	Dorsal fin spines usually more than 20; first (uppermost) lateral line canal reaching to midpoint of spinous dorsal fin; caudal peduncle slender, depth less than snout length	*Hexagrammos stelleri,* page 392
5		Dorsal fin spines usually fewer than 20; first (uppermost) lateral line canal reaching to posterior area of soft-rayed dorsal fin; caudal peduncle stout, depth greater than snout length	*Hexagrammos octogrammus,* page 393
6	(4)	Multifid cirrus above each eye and a pair of minute cirri in slight depression midway between middle of eye and origin of dorsal fin	*Hexagrammos decagrammus,* page 394
6		Large, densely fringed, multifid cirrus above eye but no other cirri between eye and origin of dorsal fin	*Hexagrammos lagocephalus,* page 395

Oxylebius pictus Gill, 1862 **painted greenling**

Prince William Sound at Snug Harbor to central Baja California at San Benito Islands.

Rocky reefs from the intertidal area to depth of about 49 m; often observed clinging to steep rock faces.

D XIV–XVII,13–17; A III–IV,12–15; Pec 14–17; Pel I,5; GR 9–14; Vert 36–39.

- Creamy white to grayish brown background with **5–7 distinct red bands** on body and median fins; 3 dark bars radiate from eye, 1 anteriorly, 2 posteriorly; male turns nearly black and bars of female turn brown during breeding season.
- **Head elongate and pointed**; **maxilla barely reaching front of eye**.
- **Two pairs of cirri on head**: one pair above eyes and one between eyes and dorsal fin.
- Dorsal fin divided past middle by shallow notch between spines and rays; anal fin usually with 3 spines, of which the second is longest; caudal fin rounded.
- One lateral line.
- Length to 25 cm TL.

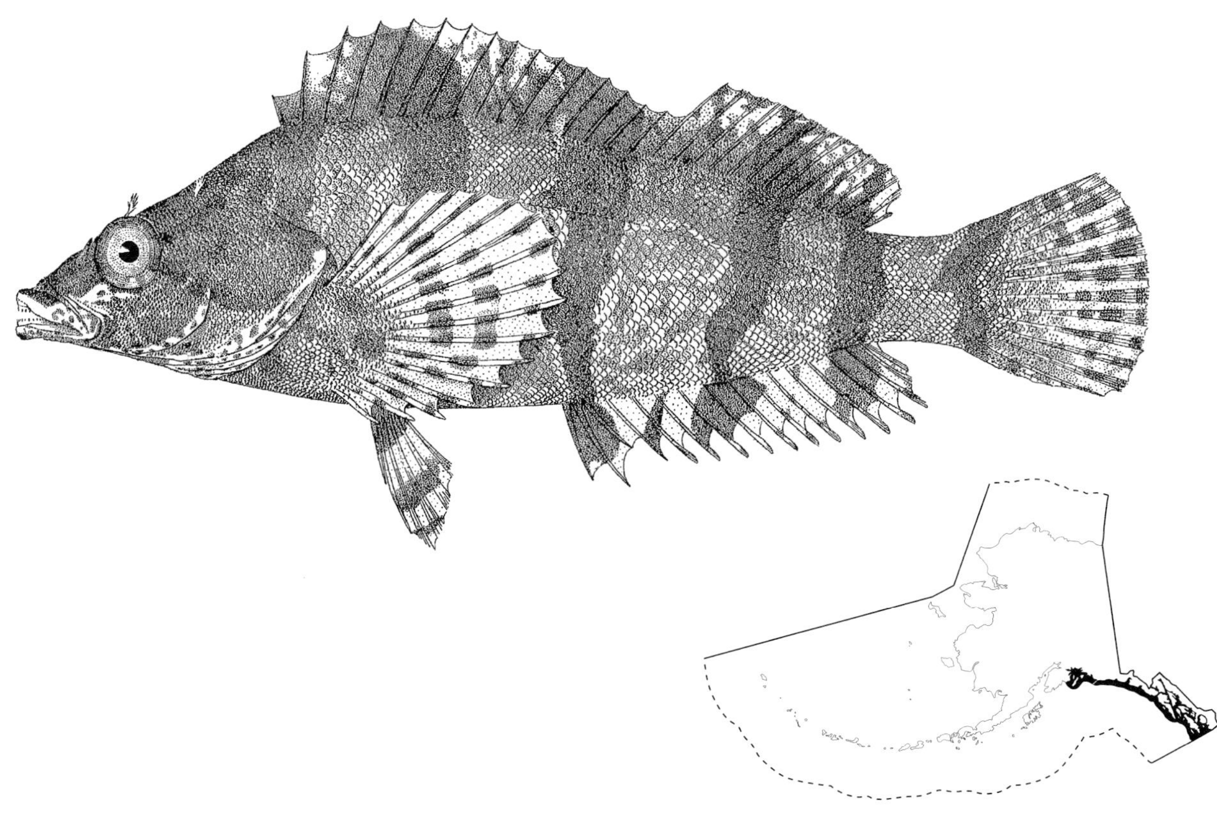

Notes & Sources — *Oxylebius pictus* Gill, 1862

Description: Jordan and Evermann 1898:1878–1879; Miller and Lea 1972:114; Hart 1973:470–471; Eschmeyer and Herald 1983:157.

Figure: Jordan and Starks 1895, pl. 78; Monterey, California. Humann's (1996:104–105) guide has photographs of brown and red variations.

Range: Recorded range was extended by Orsi et al. (1991) from British Columbia north to Prince William Sound, where they found it adjacent to a steep rock face in Snug Harbor. They noted that a previous report of range west to Kodiak Island was incorrect. At the time of Orsi et al.'s (1991) report the only other known capture localities in Alaska were Steamer Bay (AB 78-59, AB 82-3) and Aleutkina Bay (voucher specimen not indicated). The ABL fish collection currently contains examples from Kasaan Bay (AB 93-8) and Clarence Strait (AB 93-12). While scuba diving, Peden and Wilson (1976) collected specimens and observed others hiding among bryozoans and hydroids on rock faces in British Columbia near the Alaska border; the northernmost locality was Brundige Inlet at 54°37'N, 130°51'W. The statement by Humann (1996) giving range to the Bering Sea for *O. pictus* evidently is based on older reports that have been discounted.

Ophiodon elongatus Girard, 1854 **lingcod**

Southwestern Gulf of Alaska off Shumagin Islands to northern Baja California off Punta San Carlos.

Near and on bottom around rocky areas, reefs, and kelp beds, especially in areas of strong tidal movement; inshore and to depth of 475 m, usually shallower than 300 m.

D XXII–XXVIII,18–24; A III,23–25; Pec 16–18; Pel I,5; GR 21–26; Vert 57–59.

- Black, gray, or brown with shades of blue or green; darker mottling and eye-sized yellow or orange spots dorsally and laterally; amount of mottling variable, from little or none to dense; meat often blue or green.
- **Mouth large**, maxilla extending to rear edge of eye or beyond.
- Large, multifid or paddle-shaped cirrus over each eye.
- **Dorsal fin divided past middle by deep notch** between spines and rays; anal fin with 3 spines; caudal fin truncate or slightly emarginate
- **One lateral line**.
- **Small, smooth (cycloid) scales on body**.
- **Jaws with large canine teeth** interspersed with small teeth.
- Length to 152 cm TL.

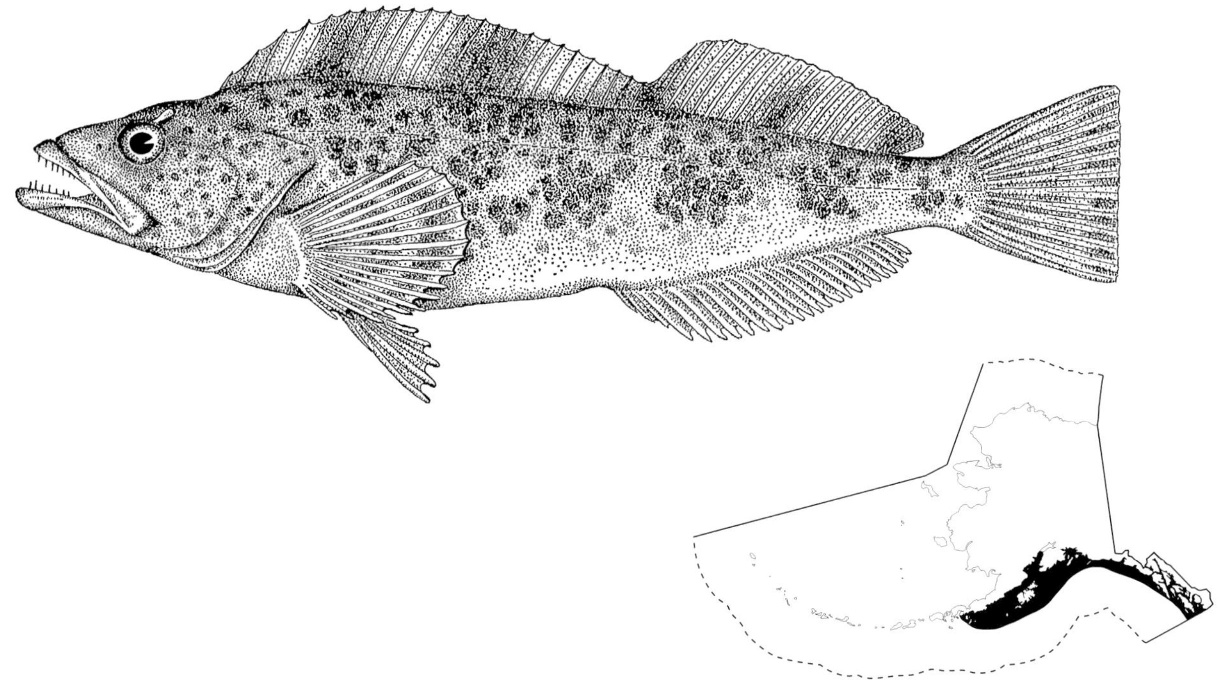

Notes & Sources — *Ophiodon elongatus* Girard, 1854

The vernacular reflects a superficial resemblance to the European ling (*Molva*), noted by early settlers in the Pacific Northwest and differentiated by them by adding the word "cod."

Description: Jordan and Evermann 1898:1875–1876; Phillips 1959; Hart 1973:467–469; Eschmeyer and Herald 1983: 156–157. From a submersible, O'Connell (1993) observed lingcod behavior in southeastern Alaska off Sitka. Coloration of the fish, which were about 30–115 cm in length, ranged from dark gray with little mottling to tan with much mottling. It was not clear whether this dimorphism was sexual or related to stage of maturity. All nest-guarding individuals, which presumably were male, were dark, with little or no mottling. See Humann (1996:108–109) for photographs of three striking color variations.

Figure: Hart 1973:467; 23 cm TL, Queen Charlotte Islands, British Columbia.

Range: West in Alaska to Shumagin Islands (Hart 1973). Some authors give a Bering Sea range for lingcod, but Quast and Hall (1972) and Hart (1973) considered it doubtful and our searches of museum records, which failed to find any lingcod from the Bering Sea, support that conclusion. The westernmost of 1,021 occurrences reported by Allen and Smith (1988) from 30 years of NMFS surveys was southwest of Chirikof Island (south of Shelikof Strait).

Size: Wilby 1937.

Pleurogrammus monopterygius (Pallas, 1810) **Atka mackerel**

Bering Sea and Aleutian Islands to southern California off Redondo Beach, rarely found south of Alaska; western Bering Sea and Commander Islands to Sea of Japan and Yellow Sea.

Lower intertidal to depth of 575 m, usually shallower than 300 m; primarily pelagic as adults; travel in schools and enter inshore waters to spawn.

D XXI–XXIV,24–30; A 23–28; Pec 22–28; Pel I,5; GR 22–28; Vert 58–63.

- Yellowish gray to olive green or dark blue-green dorsally; paler ventrally; almost always 6 or 7 dark bands on body; dorsal fin yellow or orange, anal and pelvic fins largely black, lower part of pectoral black, upper part of pectoral fin and caudal fin amber to reddish.
- Maxilla extending to below front edge of eye to pupil.
- **No cirri on head**.
- **Dorsal fin not notched**; anal fin usually without a spine; **caudal fin deeply forked**.
- Five separate lateral lines on body: 1st, 2nd, and 5th lines extending to or past caudal peduncle, 3rd terminating above middle of anal fin, 4th terminating above tip of depressed pelvic fin rays; 2nd line running high but ending along middle of caudal peduncle, considered primary lateral line.
- Length to 60 cm SL.

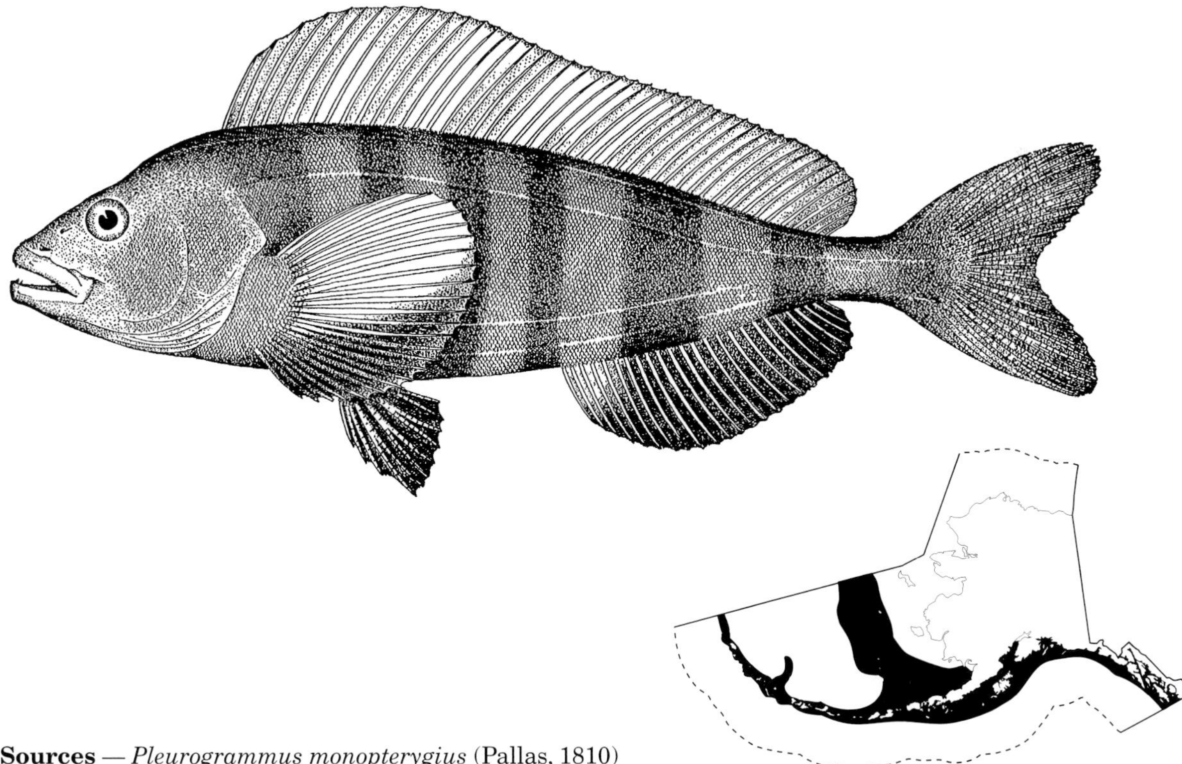

Notes & Sources — *Pleurogrammus monopterygius* (Pallas, 1810)
Labrax monopterygius Pallas, 1810
Pleurogrammus azonus Jordan & Metz, 1913

Quast (1964a, 1965), Kendall and Vinter (1984), and Nelson (1994) included the western Pacific form *P. azonus* in the synonymy of *P. monopterygius*. Researchers in Russia and Japan (e.g., Amaoka in Masuda et al. 1984, Lindberg and Krasyukova 1987, Shinohara 1994, Shinohara and Amaoka 1994) maintain it is a distinct species.

Description: Jordan and Evermann 1898:1864–1866; Eschmeyer and Herald 1983:157; Amaoka in Masuda et al. 1984:321.

Figure: Jordan and Evermann 1900, fig. 676; Atka Island, Alaska.

Range: Described in 1810 from specimens collected in the vicinity of Unalaska Island. Allen and Smith (1988) mapped distribution from NMFS resource surveys spanning a period of 30 years (1953–1983), with a range in Alaska north to about 63°N in the Bering Sea (northeast of Cape Navarin), west to Stalemate Bank and Bowers Bank off the Aleutian Islands, and east to Icy Cape in the eastern Gulf of Alaska. Although abundant in parts of its range there are relatively few specimens in museums, this status not having changed much since Quast (1964) noted there were not enough specimens available for meristic studies. Not recorded from British Columbia until the late 1970s, when a small specimen (126 mm SL) was captured at Hunger Harbour, Tasu Sound, Queen Charlotte Islands (Peden 1977).

Size: Reported to reach 50 cm TL in the eastern Pacific (e.g., Miller and Lea 1972, Eschmeyer and Herald 1983). A specimen caught in the Bering Sea at 60°33'N, 171°52'E, at a depth of 102 m by Russian research vessel *Novokotovsk* in Jul. 1990 was 51 cm TL (R. Baxter, unpubl. data; specimen not saved). Amaoka (in Masuda et al. 1984) gave a maximum length of 60 cm SL for *P. azonus* (= *P. monopterygius*).

Hexagrammos stelleri Tilesius, 1810 **whitespotted greenling**

Beaufort Sea at Simpson Cove; Chukchi Sea to Puget Sound and to Sea of Japan.

Around reefs and kelp beds from intertidal area to depth of 175 m, usually shallower than 100 m.

D XX–XXV,18–22; A 22–25; Pec 18–20; Pel I,5; GR 16–20; Vert 51–56.

- Brown to green, tinged orange and yellow; white ventrally; often with large black spot on dorsal fin anteriorly; body and head usually with small white spots; anal fin yellow, often with brown bars, other fins with dark streaks or dots; eye golden yellow.
- **Caudal peduncle slender**, depth less than snout length.
- Maxilla extending to front of eye.
- Moderately large cirrus above each eye.
- Dorsal fin divided past middle by notch; **dorsal fin spines usually more than 20**.
- Five lateral lines; **1st lateral line short, extending to midpoint of spinous dorsal fin**; **4th lateral line short, extending past base of pelvic fin** but not beyond depressed tip, occasionally forked in front of pelvic fin base.
- Length to 48 cm TL.

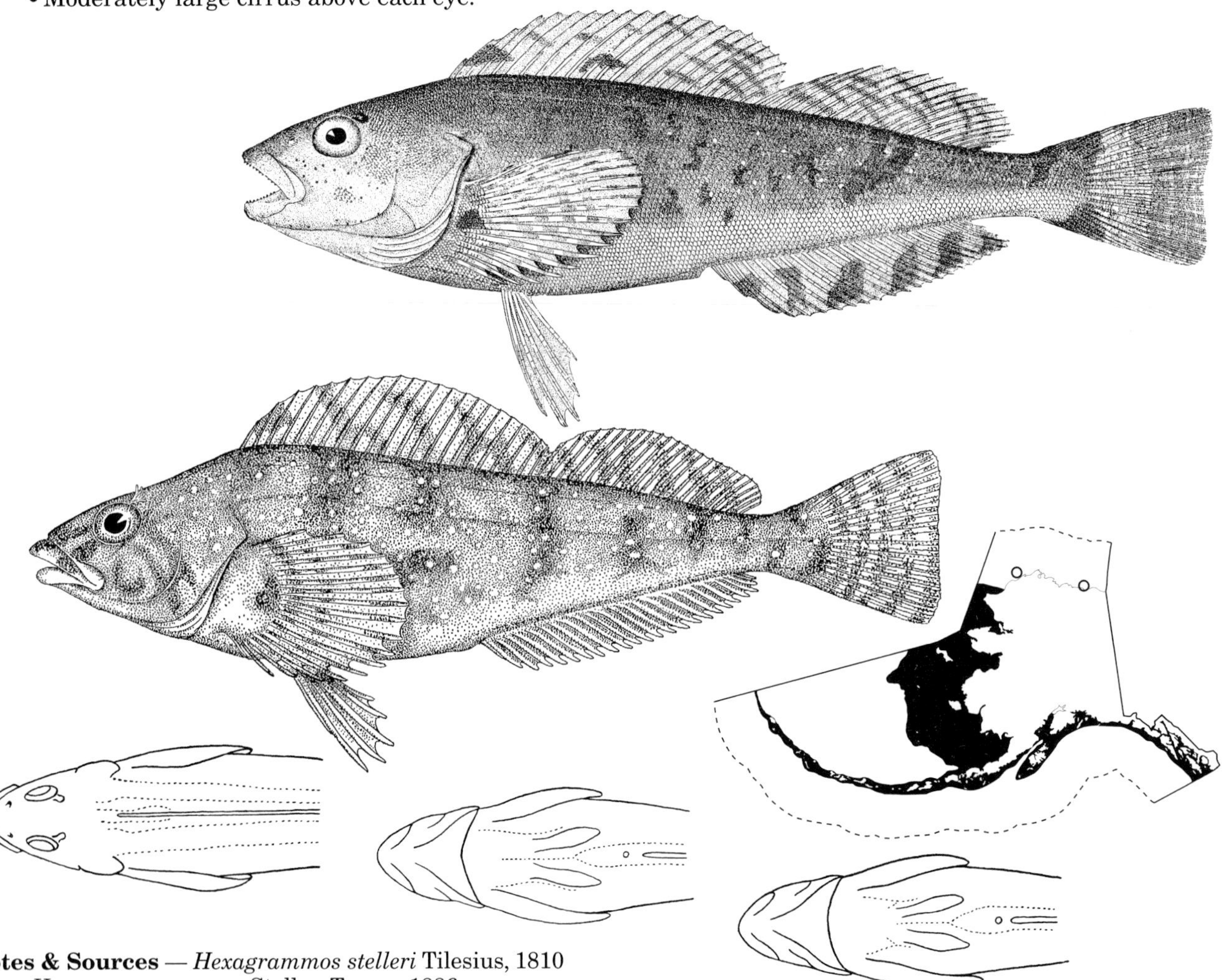

Notes & Sources — *Hexagrammos stelleri* Tilesius, 1810
Hexagrammus asper Steller: Turner 1886.

Description: Jordan and Evermann 1898:1871–1872; Andriashev 1954:343–345; Hart 1973:466–467; Eschmeyer and Herald 1983:156.

Figures: Upper: Turner 1886, pl. 8; 24 cm TL, western Alaska. Lower: Hart 1973:466; female, 20 cm TL, Halibut Cove, Kachemak Bay, Alaska. Diagrams: Lindberg and Krasyukova 1987, fig. 68; dorsal view shows lateral lines 1–3; ventral views, lines 4 and 5 with two variations of line 4.

Range: Numerous records from Alaska. Among the most recent are: Attu Island to Cold Bay (Wilimovsky 1964); Bristol Bay, Kodiak Island, Cook Inlet, southeastern Alaska (Quast and Hall 1972); Prince William Sound (Rosenthal 1980); Kodiak Island, east side (Blackburn and Jackson 1982); Point Hope (Fechhelm et al. 1985); Norton Sound (Sample and Wolotira 1985); north side of Alaska Peninsula (Isakson et al. 1986); Yukon Delta (Martin et al. 1986). Taken in NMFS surveys from northeast of Cape Lisburne to Unimak Island and east to Cordova (Allen and Smith 1988). R. Baxter (unpubl. data) identified a juvenile (79 mm TL) collected in 1989 at Simpson Cove, Beaufort Sea, and remarked in a letter to the collector (M. Osborne, USFWS, Fairbanks) that a juvenile had also been caught in the Chukchi Sea northwest of Wainwright. Reports from Oregon and northern California (e.g., Roedel 1953, Andriashev 1954) lack documentation.

Hexagrammos octogrammus (Pallas, 1814) **masked greenling**

Bering Sea from St. Lawrence Island and Aleutian Islands to northern British Columbia off Banks Island; western Bering Sea at Karaginskiy Bay and Commander Islands to Okhotsk and Japan seas.

Nearshore rocky areas at depths of 6–31 m.

D XVII–XX,22–25; A 23–26; Pec 18–19; Pel I,5; GR 14–17; Vert 50–54.

- Green to brown; dark mottling and spots; supraorbital cirrus black; eye red.
- **Caudal peduncle stout**, depth greater than snout length.
- Maxilla extending to front of pupil.
- One moderately large cirrus above each eye.
- Dorsal fin divided at about the middle by a notch; **dorsal fin spines usually fewer than 20**, with short cirri at tips.
- Five lateral lines; **1st lateral line long, extending to posterior part of soft dorsal** (about ray 13); **4th lateral line short, not extending past pelvic fin**, forked in front of pelvic fin base.
- Length to 28 cm TL.

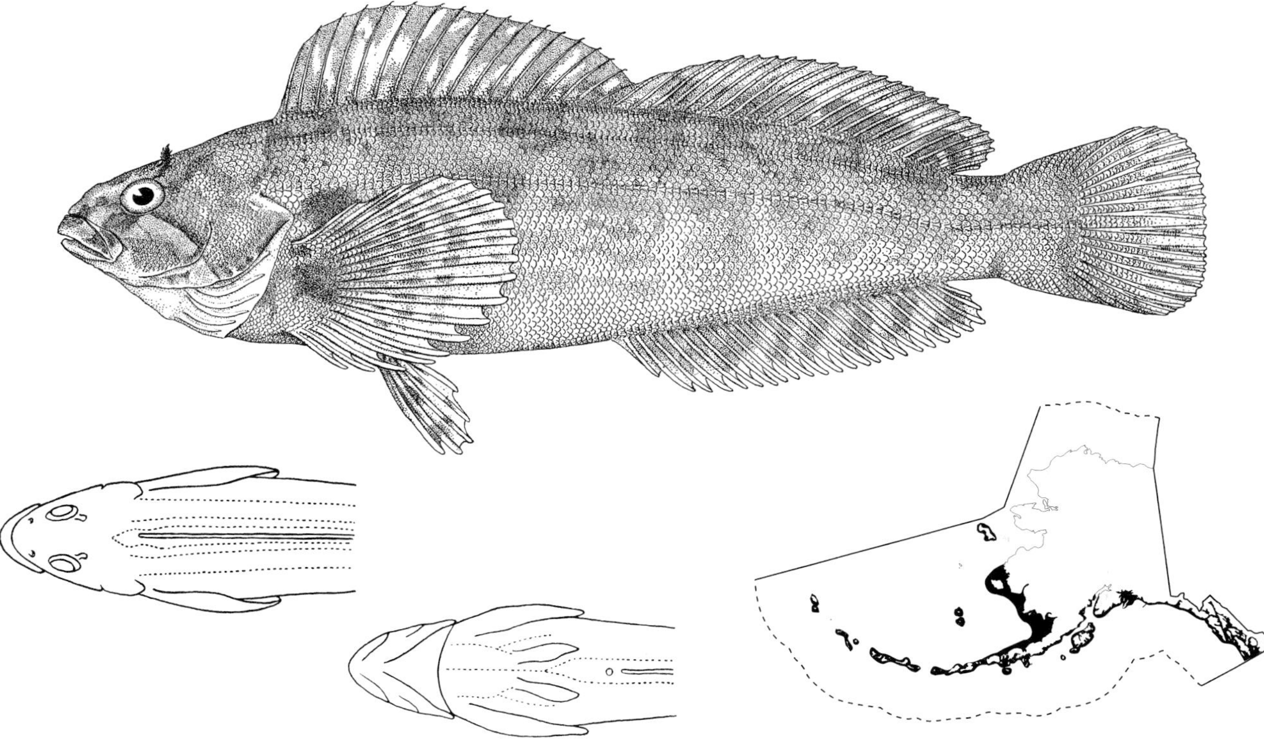

Notes & Sources — *Hexagrammos octogrammus* (Pallas, 1814)
Labrax octogrammus Pallas, 1814
Chirus ordinatus Cope, 1873
Hexagrammos ordinatus: Jordan and Gilbert 1883.

Description: Jordan and Evermann 1898:1869–1871; Jordan and Starks 1903a:1009–1011; Hart 1973:464–465; Eschmeyer and Herald 1983:156; Amaoka in Masuda et al. 1984:320.

Figures: Full lateral: Jordan and Gilbert 1899, pl. 50; Unalaska Island. Lateral line diagrams: Lindberg and Krasyukova 1987, fig. 67; dorsal shows lines 1–3; ventral shows lines 4 and 5.

Range: Said to be most common greenling in Bering Sea (Jordan and Gilbert 1899, Kendall and Vinter 1984), but published records do not document range north of the Aleutian Islands. Early records documenting range from the Sea of Okhotsk through the Aleutian Islands to Sitka were summarized by Evermann and Goldsborough (1907) and Schmidt (1950). More recent records include: Attu to Krenitzin islands (Wilimovsky 1964); Samsing Cove near Sitka (Quast 1968); lower Cook Inlet (Blackburn et al. 1980); Prince William Sound (Rosenthal 1980); and Kodiak Island (Blackburn and Jackson 1982). The most northerly-caught museum specimens may be three in UBC 60-380, from St. Lawrence Island at Tomname Lagoon, 63°18'N, 169°26'W; A. E. Peden (pers. comm., 26 Apr. 1999) examined them and confirmed the identification. Other examples from the island, in UBC 60-384, are probably also this species. The UBC also has several examples from St. Paul Island and Izembek Bay. Lot NMC 79-793 from north of Nunivak Island at 61°37'N, 168°11'W includes a specimen; identified by D. E. McAllister, its depth of capture at 31 m represents a new maximum depth, extended from 26 m recorded by Schmidt (1950). The species was first recorded south of Alaska near Prince Rupert by Peden (1971), and later from Banks Island by Peden and Wilson (1976).

Hexagrammos decagrammus (Pallas, 1810) **kelp greenling**

Aleutian Islands from Attu Island to Gulf of Alaska coasts and to southern California off La Jolla.

Rocky reefs and kelp beds to depth of about 46 m.

D XX–XXIII,22–26; A 0–I,21–25; Pec 18–20; Pel I,5; GR 15–20; Vert 52–57.

- Male olive brown to bluish gray, with irregular blue spots mostly anteriorly; female background color lighter, speckled all over with reddish brown to gold spots, face and fins with various shades of golden yellow; eye yellow.
- Maxilla extending from almost to front edge of eye to front edge of pupil.
- **Two pairs of cirri on head**, one above eyes and one smaller pair on occiput in slight depression.
- Dorsal fin divided at about middle by deep notch; usually 1 small spine at anterior end of anal fin.
- Five lateral lines; 1st lateral line extending to middle of soft dorsal fin; **4th lateral line long, extending nearly to or past end of anal fin**.
- Length to 53 cm TL.

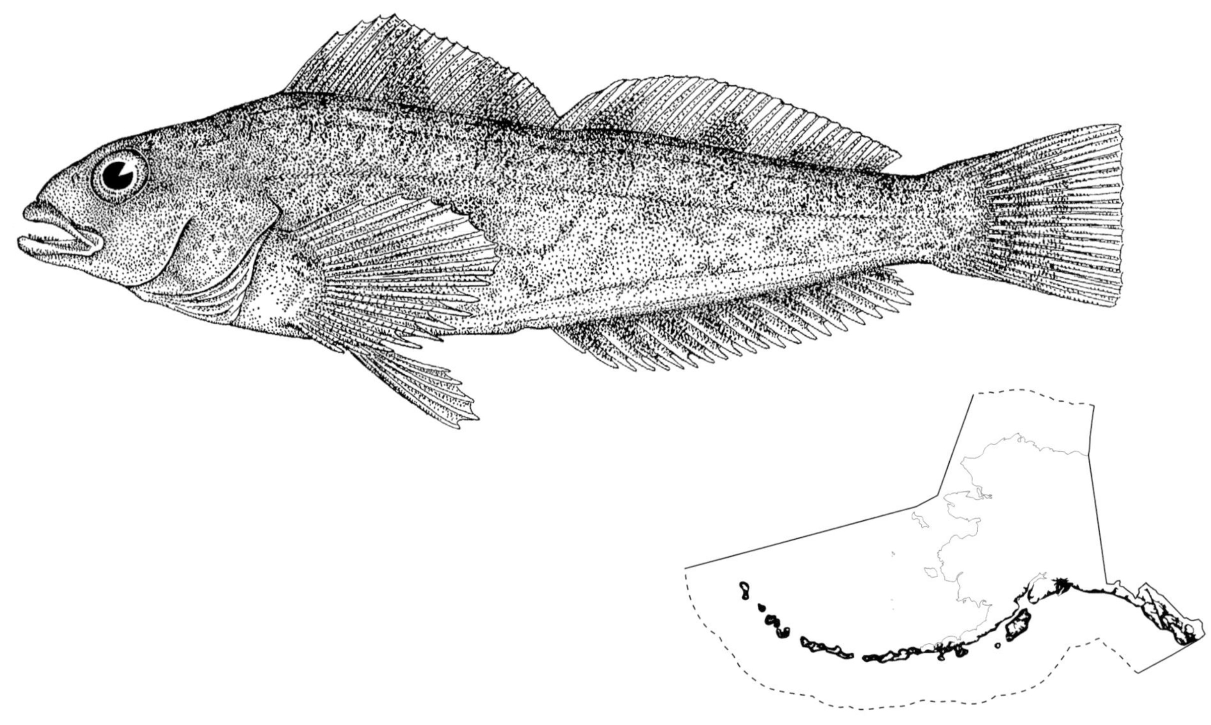

Notes & Sources — *Hexagrammos decagrammus* (Pallas, 1810)
Labrax decagrammus Pallas, 1810

Description: Jordan and Evermann 1898:1867–1869; Hart 1973:461–462; Eschmeyer and Herald 1983:155.

Figure: Hart 1973:461; 14 cm TL, Washington. The occipital cirri are small and difficult to see; not shown in illustration. Photographs in Humann (1996:106–107) show color variations.

Range: Holotype was taken off Cape St. Elias, Alaska. Early records from Point Conception to Kodiak and Unalaska islands were summarized by Evermann and Goldsborough (1907). Other Alaskan records include: Attu to Unimak islands (Wilimovsky 1964); Shumagin Islands, Kodiak Island, Yakutat Bay, Lituya Bay, southeastern Alaska (Quast and Hall 1972); Amchitka Island (Simenstad et al. 1977); Prince William Sound (Rosenthal 1980); and Kodiak Island (Blackburn and Jackson 1982). Peden and Wilson (1976) found many specimens north and south of the Alaska–British Columbia border. There are numerous specimens from throughout the species' range in Alaska in museum collections, but because of its preference for shallow rocky habitat it is not often taken in trawl surveys. Probably also occurs north of the Aleutian Islands. Juveniles were collected with a larval net near the Pribilof Islands in 1995–1997 (A. C. Matarese, unpubl. data provided by J. W. Orr, Nov. 1997).

Hexagrammos lagocephalus (Pallas, 1810) **rock greenling**

Eastern Bering Sea and Aleutian Islands from Attu Island to south-central California off Point Conception; and western Bering Sea and Commander Islands to Okhotsk, Japan, and Yellow seas.

Shallow rocky areas, especially along exposed coasts, to depth of 80 m, usually shallower than 21 m.

D XIX–XXIII,20–25; A 0–I,21–25; Pec 18–21; Pel I,5; GR 14–18; Vert 52–57.

- Green to brown with dark (red or orange in male) mottling; lighter ventrally; often with dark spot above pectoral fin base; mouth cavity typically blue, flesh and bones sometimes blue; female with oblong, blue or other light-color spots on body; eye red.
- Maxilla extending to mideye.
- **Large cirrus above each eye**, length usually greater than pupil diameter; **no other cirri on top of head**.
- Dorsal fin divided at about middle by deep notch; dorsal fin spines with short cirrus at tip; occasionally 1 spine at anterior end of anal fin.
- Five lateral lines; 1st lateral line extending beyond middle of soft dorsal fin; **4th lateral line long, extending above posterior half of anal fin for a variable distance**.
- Length to 61 cm TL.

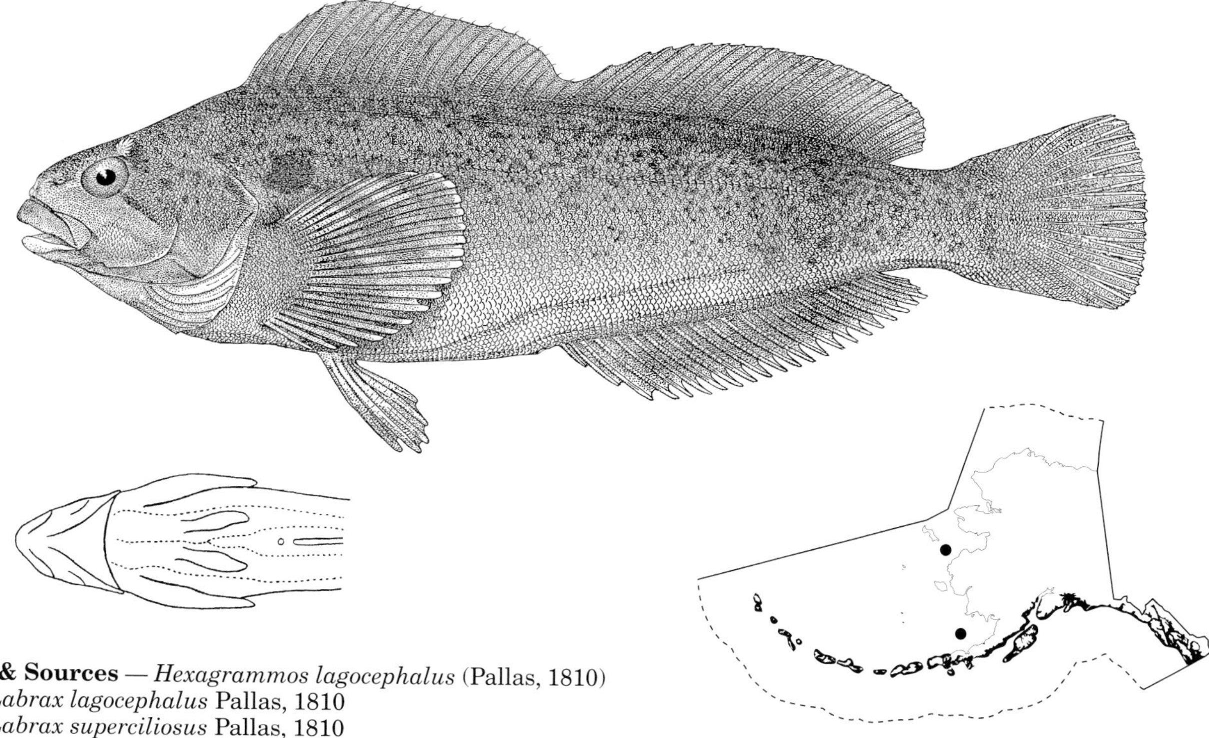

Notes & Sources — *Hexagrammos lagocephalus* (Pallas, 1810)
Labrax lagocephalus Pallas, 1810
Labrax superciliosus Pallas, 1810
Hexagrammus scaber Bean, 1881

Classification of *Hexagrammos superciliosus* in *H. lagocephalus* follows Quast (1964a, 1965), Kendall and Vinter (1984), Nelson (1994), and Shinohara (1994). Some researchers maintain the two nominal species are distinct on the basis of a shorter supraorbital cirrus (shorter than pupil diameter), no dark spot above the pectoral fin, and fewer precaudal vertebrae in *H. lagocephalus.* Recently, B. A. Sheiko (pers. comm., 15 Jan. 1999) reported that among numerous specimens taken along eastern Kamchatka and the Commander Islands he never saw one with supraorbital cirri larger than the pupil but that he has seen specimens with a dark spot above the pectoral fin. Meristic data are needed to determine if a cline in numbers of precaudal vertebrae occurs (Quast 1964a).

Description: Jordan and Evermann 1898:1872–1875; Jordan and Starks 1903a:1011–1012; Hart 1973:463–464; Eschmeyer and Herald 1983:154–155; Amaoka in Masuda et al. 1984:320; Lindberg and Krasyukova 1987:125, 130–132.

Figures: Full lateral: Jordan and Gilbert 1899, pl. 51 modified by adding cirri to dorsal fin spines; Robben Island, Sea of Okhotsk. Diagram of lateral lines 4 and 5: Lindberg and Krasyukova 1987, fig. 69.

Range: The range of *H. superciliosus* was given by Jordan and Gilbert (1899) as Bering Island to Monterey, and of *H. lagocephalus* as the Kuril Islands to Bering Island. Most researchers in the United States and Canada in recent years have not differentiated the forms. Recorded limits in Alaska are from the north side of the Alaska Peninsula east to Izembek Bay (Gilbert 1896, Wilimovsky 1964), and west in the Aleutians to Attu Island (Jordan and Gilbert 1899). Lot NMC 79-802 includes two specimens collected from the northeastern Bering Sea at 63°03'N, 166°38'W, depth 28 m, in 1979 by K. J. Frost and L. F. Lowry; identification was confirmed by D. E. McAllister. The UBC has many Alaskan specimens, collected from Bristol Bay at about 57°N, 162°W (UBC 63-361) and throughout the Aleutian Islands to Cape Bartolome in southeastern Alaska (UBC 60-526, UBC 65-582).

Family Rhamphocottidae
Grunt sculpins

The grunt sculpin, *Rhamphocottus richardsonii,* is a distinctive-looking marine cottoid fish with a large head and long snout, for which Starks (1921) called the family the horsehead sculpins. Nelson (1994) called the family the grunt sculpins. When removed from the water they grunt and hiss.

The one known species has a broad range in the eastern Pacific from the Gulf of Alaska south at least as far as Santa Monica Bay, California. Grunt sculpins also occur in the western Pacific, but not as commonly. Their lower pectoral fin rays are long and free of each other, and used to crawl along the bottom and over rocks. One of their most frequently seen postures is a curled position which may be related to their habit, often observed by scuba divers, of taking shelter in empty shells, especially those of the giant barnacle, *Balanus nubilis.* Grunt sculpins are found in tidepools and shallow waters, especially off Alaska and in the Pacific Northwest. Farther south they tend to occupy the deeper parts of their depth range, to about 165 m, where the water is cooler.

This little fish, not known to attain a size greater than 8.9 cm (3.5 inches), is the sole representative of its family and is easily identified by its large head, elongate snout, bilateral blunt bony ridges on top of the head, and free pectoral fin rays. Like most sculpins it has two completely separate dorsal fins, the first spinous and the second composed of soft rays. The gill opening is small, not extending below the lower edge of the pectoral fin as it does in other sculpins. The body is covered with small, multifid spines. Palatine teeth are absent, there are 6 branchiostegal rays, and all fin rays are unbranched.

Some taxonomists classify grunt sculpins in the Cottidae. Washington et al. (1984) and Yabe (1985) believed them to be the primitive sister group to the other members of the superfamily Cottoidea and recognized the relationship by classifying them in a separate family.

Rhamphocottus richardsonii Günther, 1874 — grunt sculpin

Bering Sea, record not confirmed; well documented from Gulf of Alaska to southern California at Santa Monica Bay; Japan.

Rocky bottoms and areas of sand mixed with rubble from the intertidal zone to depth of 165 m; not often found in tidepools.

D VII–IX + 12–14; A 6–8; Pec 14–18; Pel I,3–4; Vert 24–28.

- Creamy yellow with irregular dark brown streaks running obliquely across body and radiating from eye; caudal peduncle bright red; fins bright red; not always with red, sometimes more orange.
- **Head large**, about half of standard length; **snout elongate**; **dorsal profile high**.
- **Head with 2 heavy blunt ridges** ending in blunt spines at occiput; interorbital space deeply concave; preopercular spine single, sharp, long.
- **Lower pectoral fin rays free**.
- **Head and body covered with multipointed spinous plates**, each buried beneath a papilla with the points piercing the end.
- Jaws and vomer with teeth in villiform bands; palatine teeth absent.
- Gill membranes attached to isthmus, leaving small gill opening mainly above pectoral fin base.
- Length to 89 mm TL.

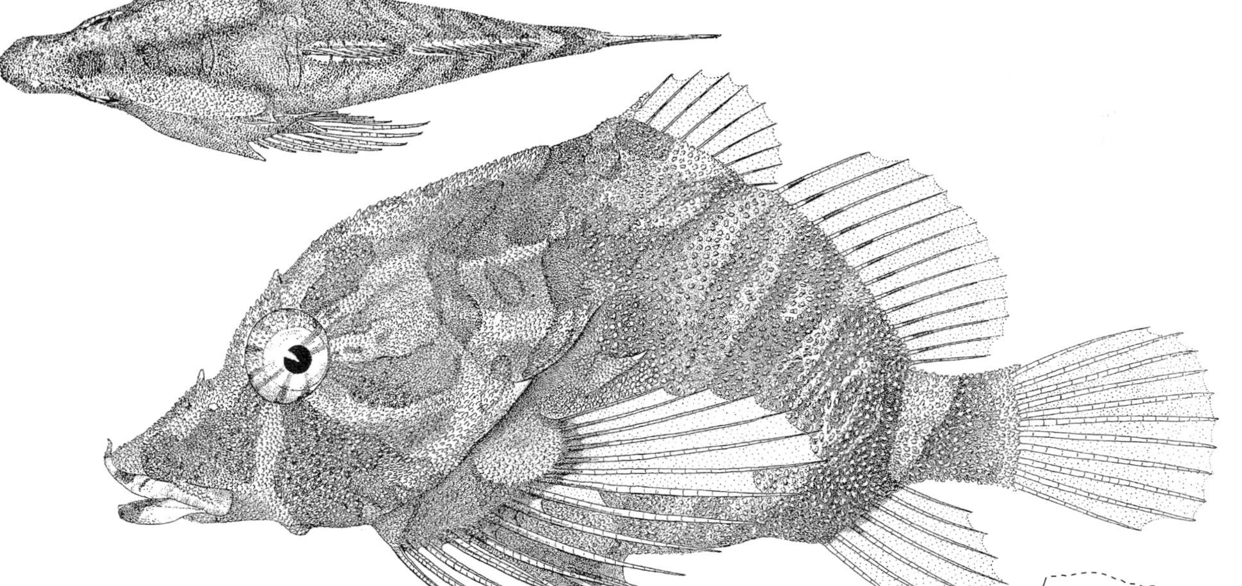

Notes & Sources — *Rhamphocottus richardsonii* Günther, 1874
Spelling is correct with two *i*'s, the spelling used by Günther (1874).

Description: Günther 1874:369–370; Jordan and Starks 1895:813–815; Jordan and Evermann 1898:2029–2031; Johnson 1918; Abe 1963.

Figures: Lateral view: Jordan and Starks 1895, pl. 87; 76 mm TL, Port Orchard, Washington. Dorsal, ventral: Jordan and Evermann 1900, fig. 742; California.

Range: First recorded from Alaska from St. Paul, Kodiak Island, by Bean (1881b:252). Northern limit of range given as Bering Sea by Wilimovsky (1954) and subsequent authors, without specific documentation. St. Paul is an old name, used in the 1800s, for the city of Kodiak, and it is possible that the locality was incorrectly interpreted to be St. Paul Island. Generally distributed through coastal British Columbia (Hart 1973) and the Pacific Northwest (Lamb and Edgell 1986). Museum collections include numerous specimens from the Gulf of Alaska; e.g., UBC has specimens from Kodiak Island, UW from Kodiak Island and Wrangell Island, and ABL from Alexander Archipelago localities. Baxter (1990ms; unpubl. data) collected one at Port Dick, Kenai Peninsula, in a shrimp pot. Often collected by divers and displayed in aquaria (e.g., at ABL). This species is rare in Japan (Yabe in Masuda et al. 1984) but common along eastern North Pacific coasts.

Size: Humann 1996.

Family Cottidae
Sculpins

The Cottidae are the largest family of sculpins, with, worldwide, about 70 genera and 300 species. They are primarily demersal inhabitants of cold, northern, marine coastal waters, with relatively few representatives in fresh water or, as adults, in offshore deep water. Whereas the juveniles and adults are benthic, the larvae are planktonic and sometimes are found farther offshore. All but four cottid species occur in the Northern Hemisphere, where the most speciose region comprises the Bering Sea and North Pacific Ocean. A few species are edible and good eating such as the Irish lords, genus *Hemilepidotus,* and cabezon, *Scorpaenichthys marmoratus,* but they are not commercially important. For general discussion these sculpins are called cottids to avoid confusion with other sculpins of the superfamily Cottoidea. This guide includes accounts of 87 cottid species in 35 genera.

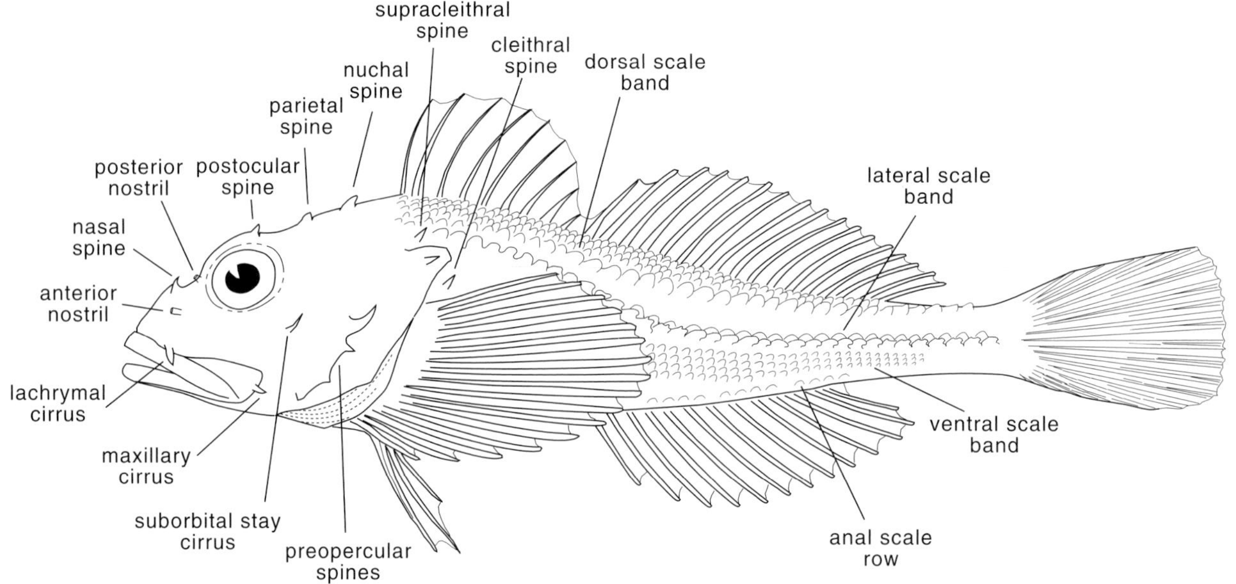

Some external features of cottids

Like other scorpaeniform fishes, cottids have a suborbital stay. Except for that they are an extremely variable group that may best be characterized by what features they lack compared to other scorpaeniforms. Most cottid species occurring in Alaska are distinguishable from rockfishes (Scorpaenidae), greenlings (Hexagrammidae), and sablefishes (Anoplopomatidae) by not being completely covered with typical scales (as opposed to prickly papillae or bony plates); in the few Alaskan cottids that have fuller scale coverage the scales below the lateral line are arranged in oblique, fold-like rows, unlike scales in any other scorpaeniform group. Cottids differ from sailfin sculpins (Hemitripteridae) and grunt sculpins (Rhamphocottidae) by not being densely covered with prickles, and from most fathead sculpins (Psychrolutidae) by not being extremely tadpole-shaped and not having loose skin over a gelatinous layer. They differ from poachers (Agonidae) by not being completely covered with bony plates. Unlike lumpsuckers (Cyclopteridae) and most snailfishes (Liparidae), cottids lack an adhesive disk formed from specialized pelvic fins.

The relationships of the Cottidae to other groups in the superfamily Cottoidea were studied by Yabe (1985), who defined cottids as a monophyletic group having one autapomorphy (presence of the lateral process of the hyomandibular) and a unique combination of nine synapomorphies (e.g., absence of tooth plate on third epibranchial, presence of 6 branchiostegal rays, presence of two supratemporals, and absence of stay behind last pterygiophore).

Characters readily observed without dissection that in combination distinguish the Cottidae, and which in those cases having varying expressions can be used to identify genera and species, are as follows. In cottids the body is never entirely covered by organized rows of scales; it can have bands of scales with intervening naked areas, be entirely naked, or have only scattered prickles protruding through fleshy papillae, but is never encased in heavy armor. The enlarged, plate-like scales of some groups are armed with spines. The lateral line system is well developed, and in some genera numerous branches, called secondary canals or canalicules, are present and open by way of secondary pores, also called accessory or supplementary pores. Cottids have one body lateral line, which is usually complete, with 1 or 2 pores extending onto the caudal base. Counts of lateral line pores (LLp) and scales (LLs) include the pores or scales extending beyond the posterior margin of the hypural plate. Pore counts are given for forms with reduced or deeply embedded scales, in lieu of scale counts.

Most cottids have well-separated spinous and soft-rayed dorsal fins, but in a few genera the portions are continuous or only slightly attached at the base. The spinous portion in most species is shorter-based than the soft portion, and has fewer than 20 spines. The anal fin lacks spines. The pectoral fins are large and fan-shaped, with lower rays often thickened and partly free although they are never completely free and specialized as tactile organs. In males of some species the pectoral or pelvic rays, or both, are pectinate, bearing bony ctenii; called setae or combs by some authors. Pelvic fins are present in all but one of the Alaskan species and have 1 spine and 2–5 rays. The pelvic fin spine is usually short and closely adnate to the rays, thus difficult to discern without dissection.

The gill membranes are never free but are fused to the isthmus, or united to each other and variously attached to the isthmus leaving part or all of the joined membrane free from the isthmus; the connection may be determined by running a dissecting needle from side to side under the membrane.

All cottids have villiform or cardiform bands of teeth on the jaws, while vomerine and palatine teeth are variably present. Frequently the vomerine teeth are in a patch on each side of the vomer and could be mistaken for palatine teeth.

Nasal spines are usually well developed but can be covered with skin or, in old individuals, truncated. Head spines are variously developed, and the term includes postocular spines as well as parietal and nuchal spines, the latter collectively called occipital spines. In many species instead of sharp head spines there are definite bumps, called protuberances or tubercles. The usual number of preopercular spines is 4, although all but one are obscure or weak in many cottid species. In counting, preopercular spine 1 is the most dorsal, and 4 is most ventral. Spine 1 is usually the longest and strongest, and can be simple or multifid. The dorsal surface of the major preopercular spine can bear sharp protuberances called spinules (or barbs, thorns, or cusps by some authors). Fleshy cirri can be present or absent, and when present are most developed on the head and along the lateral line. Cirri immediately above and behind the eye are called postocular cirri, those above the middle of the eye are supraocular, and those above the front of the eye are preocular.

The usual position of the anus in cottids is an orbit diameter or less in front of the anal fin. The genital papilla of males in some species is enlarged to form an intromittent organ. Females of some species have a small urogenital papilla.

Authors rarely report vertebral numbers for cottids, so counts are not available for all species and the few numbers reported for others may not be representative. Vertebral counts in the Alaskan species range from 25 in *Zesticelus profundorum* to 54 in *Triglops forficatus* (counts include the hypural). Cottids typically have 6 branchiostegal rays; some species occasionally have 5 or 7. Gill rakers are usually poorly developed in cottids as low spiny knobs or obsolete, and most researchers do not report counts. In cottids pseudobranchs are present, the swim bladder is absent, and there are few pyloric caeca (4–8).

Cottids exhibit wide variation in color, and in distribution of pigment from nearly uniform to heavily mottled, spotted, and banded. In some genera there is much variability within species, individually, with growth, and between the sexes.

Size can be helpful for identifying cottids. The largest is *Scorpaenichthys marmoratus,* with a maximum recorded length of about 99 cm (39 inches) and weight of about 13.6 kg (30 lb). Among species occurring in Alaska, sizes range down to about 6 cm (2.4 inches), in *Ruscarius meanyi.* When collecting sculpins in the intertidal zone it may be helpful to know that small and intermediate-size individuals of species that can reach large sizes, such as *S. marmoratus*, are often found in tidepools and could be confused with adults of smaller-sized species.

Relationships within the Cottidae are incompletely understood and most genera have not been classified into well-defined subfamilies. The following summary includes a few of the most distinctive characters of each genus, and defines terminology. For genera represented by more than one species, reference is made to the most recent systematic study of the genus. The few more-or-less well-defined subfamilies are identified. The order in which the genera are summarized follows the key and species accounts.

Synchirus is the only cottid genus with pectoral fins united across the breast, and ***Ascelichthys*** is the only genus without pelvic fins.

Jordania is superficially most similar, although not necessarily closely related, to ***Triglops***. In both genera the scales below the lateral line are closely set in oblique rows. Pietsch (1994) recently revised the classification of *Triglops* species, and the indices included in our species accounts are from the hundreds of specimens he examined. To count the oblique scale rows, Pietsch (1994) cautioned, count only those that cut across a straight-line transect beginning beneath the pectoral fin and continuing along close to and strictly parallel with the base of the anal fin to the extremity of the caudal peduncle. The folds across the breast are called transverse or cross folds as distinguished from the oblique rows on the sides below the lateral line. In life *Triglops* are olive brown to chocolate brown or dusky dorsally and silvery white ventrally.

Paricelinus superficially resembles *Triglops* but lacks the oblique folds of scales, is covered with prickles below as well as above the lateral line, and has a single row of enlarged scales each bearing a prominent, recurved spine, along the base of the dorsal fins.

Scorpaenichthys has a median, flaplike cirrus on the snout and smooth skin, without obvious scales or prickles. Although it has deeply embedded scales along the lateral line they are usually not discernible.

Hemilepidotus species always have three bands of scales: a dorsal band close to the dorsal fin, a lateral band which includes the lateral line scales and a row dorsal and close to the lateral line, and a ventral band between the lateral row and the anal fin. Some species also have an anal row running close to the anal fin. The numbers of rows in each band are important in identifying species. The dorsal rows are counted below the middle of the spinous dorsal fin and the ventral rows above the middle of the anal fin. Peden (1978) revised this genus.

Chitonotus is most similar to *Icelinus* but has a deep notch in the dorsal fin between the third and fourth spines, strongly ctenoid scales covering the upper part of the head and body, and 3 rays in each pelvic fin. ***Icelinus*** species have 2 rows of platelike ctenoid scales just below the dorsal fins, with the number of rows not increasing anteriorly and not extending onto and across the nape; platelike lateral line scales; and 2 rays in each pelvic fin. Spines and bony protuberances are absent from the top of the head in most species. Peden's (1984) key to the species of *Icelinus* includes all the Alaskan species.

Archistes is similar to *Icelinus* but has a more robust body, with an elevated dorsal profile anteriorly; 1 or 2 rows of platelike ctenoid scales close to the dorsal fins, with the number of rows increasing anteriorly and with the scales in one species extending onto and across the nape but not in the other species; anus positioned closer to the pelvic fin base than to the anal fin; more rays in the soft dorsal and anal fins than in *Icelinus*; and 3 pelvic fin rays. Taranetz (1941) included *Archaulus,* described by Gilbert and Burke (1912a) from Alaskan specimens, in the synonymy of *Archistes* but this has generally been overlooked.

Radulinus species are relatively elongate and have a flat dorsal profile, practically straight from the top of the head to the caudal fin; 1–4 rows of ctenoid scales immediately above the lateral line, at least anteriorly, and separated by a naked area from the dorsal fins; lateral line placed high on the body; and no spines on top of the head. Bolin (1944) reviewed the two species occurring in California as well as Alaska, *R. boleoides* and *R. asprellus,* and Hart (1973) summarized information on all three species.

Stelgistrum is similar to *Icelinus* and *Archistes* in having 1 or more rows of platelike ctenoid scales immediately below the dorsal fins and separated by a naked area from the platelike lateral line scales. Unlike *Archistes,* the anus in *Stelgistrum* is close to the anal fin. Unlike *Icelinus,* in *Stelgistrum* the number of rows in the dorsal band increases anteriorly and the scales extend onto and across the nape, the pelvic fins each have 3 rays, and bony protuberances and spines are completely lacking from the top of the head. Palatine teeth are absent in *Stelgistrum* and present in *Icelinus* and in *Archistes.* The most recent revision of *Stegistrum* is that of Andriashev (1935).

Thyriscus is more compressed (side to side) than most cottids and has an elevated dorsal profile anteriorly. The pectoral fins with the lower rays elongate and thickened and membranes deeply incised, coupled with the lack of scales except along the lateral line and in the pectoral axil, distinguish this genus from all other cottid genera.

Icelus has one row of large, spiny platelike scales below the dorsal fins, in some species with smaller scales between the platelike scales; spiny, tubular rather than platelike, lateral line scales; and in some species additional, small scales above or below the lateral line; scales on pectoral axil ("axillary scales") and on upper portion of eye; a definite nuchal spine or protuberance, and in some species a parietal spine (both loosely called occipital spines or spines on top of the head in other groups). ***Rastrinus*** is so closely related to *Icelus* that some researchers classify it in that genus. *Rastrinus* differs in lacking parietal and nuchal spines, and in having the body above and below the lateral line completely covered with small spiny scales and lacking the dorsal row of enlarged platelike scales. The genera *Icelus* and *Rastrinus* were revised by D. W. Nelson (1984).

Stlegicottus is similar to *Rastrinus* but the lateral line does not extend beyond the anal fin; the lateral lines scales, although tubular, are broken by a longitudinal slit; and the pectoral fins are small, measuring less than the diameter of the eye.

In Alaskan species of ***Artedius*** the lateral line scales are embedded and smooth or embedded and with exposed ctenoid margins; a dorsal scale band of several scale rows is present below the dorsal fins, does not contain the greatly enlarged, platelike scales of some other genera, and in some species extends to the lateral line; the posterior nostril tube is markedly longer than the anterior tube (the reverse is true of most other genera); and cirri are present along the lateral line as well as on the head. ***Ruscarius*** in some ways is similar to *Artedius* but has spiny scales nearly completely covering the body above the lateral line; enlarged, ctenoid lateral line scales; and posterior nostril tubes that are not tubular, having only slightly elevated margins. Begle (1989) provided a taxonomic revision of *Artedius* and *Ruscarius.*

Gymnocanthus is the only Alaskan cottid genus which lacks teeth on the vomer in adults (weak but present in *Zesticelus profundorum*). Other distinctive characters include flat bony plates on the nape and top of the head, no other scales except for a few plates in the pectoral axil, lateral line scales as embedded tubules, few or no cirri on the head and body, and a long uppermost preopercular spine with 1 or more recurved spinules on the dorsal surface. Wilson (1973) reviewed six species in this genus but we found the descriptions of *G. galeatus* and *G. detrisus* by Bean (1881b) and Gilbert and Burke (1912a), respectively, and the review by Andriashev (1954) of *G. tricuspis, G. pistilliger,* and *G. galeatus* to be generally sufficient for distinguishing the four Alaskan species.

In ***Leptocottus*** the gill membranes are broadly joined to the isthmus, without leaving a free margin posteriorly. In all the genera summarized above, the gill membranes are free from the isthmus posteriorly (except for *Hemilepidotus spinosus,* in which there is no free margin posteriorly but which has other distinguishing characters, including the presence of scales). *Leptocottus* lacks scales, bony plates on the head, cirri, and nasal spines; and has a robust upper preopercular spine with 2 or more spinules and a very large mouth, with maxillae usually extending beyond the eyes. *Leptocottus* is primarily marine but often enters lower reaches of rivers and streams.

Cottus is a genus of freshwater fishes, but two of the three Alaskan species are also found in estuarine waters. These sculpins can have small prickles in the pectoral axil or scattered on the back and sides, but no bony plates or other scales, and no nasal spines; and a relatively short, simple upper preopercular spine. Morrow (1980) reviewed Alaskan *Cottus* species.

Enophrys species also have gill membranes that are attached to the isthmus without leaving a free margin, but they are marine fishes with plates along the lateral line; prickly scales below the lateral line anteriorly in some species; very long, sharp upper preopercular spine; sharp nasal spines; and a high nuchal ridge. Sandercock and Wilimovsky (1968) revised the genus *Enophrys.*

In the remaining genera the gill membranes are free from the isthmus at least posteriorly. Neyelov (1979) classified *Trichocottus, Megalocottus, Myoxocephalus, Microcottus,* and *Porocottus,* along with *Enophrys,* in one subfamily, the Myoxocephalinae. In members of this subfamily the interorbital space is equal to or wider than the vertical eye diameter; the lateral line canal has branches (or canalicules) which open through secondary (or accessory) pores dorsal and ventral to the usual pores, giving the appearance of 3 lateral lines; there is no large caudal pore at the end of the lateral line canal; and the rays of the second dorsal fin, anal fin, and pectoral fins are not branched (as well as other, less obvious differences). In *Trichocottus, Megalocottus,* and *Myoxocephalus* the uppermost preopercular spine is long and usually straight, and a slit or pore is present behind the fourth gill arch.

Trichocottus, in addition, has numerous fleshy cirri on the sides of the head, snout, jaws, and lateral line; and prickly bony plates on the sides behind the posterior half of the pectoral fins, but no other scales.

Megalocottus, in addition to the long, nearly straight upper preopercular spine and an opening behind the fourth gill arch, has a projecting lower jaw, spiny plates in uneven rows above and below the lateral line, and few or no cirri.

In ***Myoxocephalus*** the long, straight upper preopercular spine and opening behind the last gill arch are accompanied by a lower jaw that does not extend past the upper, and absence of cirri from the cheeks, jaws, and lateral line. Neyelov (1979) reviewed the species of *Myoxocephalus.* His work, Walters' (1955) review of Arctic species, and the key to *Myoxocephalus* by Carveth and Wilimovsky (1983ms) were important references for the *Myoxocephalus* accounts in this guide.

In ***Microcottus*** and ***Porocottus*** species the upper preopercular spine is abruptly curved upward and is shorter than in most *Myoxocephalus* species. There is no slit or pore behind the fourth gill arch. ***Microcottus*** differs by having each pelvic fin attached to the body by a wide membrane, and if cirri are present behind the eye (postocular) and on the top of the head (occipital) they are simple. ***Porocottus*** has the usual attachment of the pelvic fins to the body and the postocular and occipital cirri are usually multifid. *Microcottus* and *Porocottus* were classified by Neyelov (1976, 1979) in the tribe Microcottini. A revision of the Microcottini is the subject of ongoing research by M. Yabe (pers. comm., 25 Dec. 2000).

Neyelov (1979) classified *Zesticelus, Artediellichthys,* and *Artediellus* in the subfamily Artediellinae. These sculpins have broad pectoral fins with high numbers of rays, usually more than 18 and up to 26; a relatively narrow interorbital space, less than the vertical eye diameter; branched second dorsal, anal, and pectoral fins; 1 or 2 rows of body lateral line pores; and a large caudal pore at the end of the lateral line.

In ***Zesticelus*** the preopercular and mandibular pores of the cephalic lateral line system are distinctly enlarged, there are fewer than 20 pores in the main row of body lateral line pores, and the upper preopercular spine is long and gently curved upward.

In ***Artediellichthys*** and ***Artediellus*** the upper preopercular spine is sharply hooked upward and the body lateral line opens through one row of pores along the lower edge of the canal. Diagnostic characters of ***Artediellichthys*** include a broad, platelike suborbital stay; doubled nasal spines; and absence of cirri from the posterior ends of the maxillae. In contrast, species of ***Artediellus*** have a narrow, rodlike suborbital stay; simple or no nasal spines; and a cirrus at the posterior end of each maxilla. Taxonomic works on these genera by Schmidt (1927, 1937b), Andriashev (1961), Neyelov (1979), and D. W. Nelson (1986) are significant sources of information on the Alaskan species.

Bolinia, a genus described fairly recently (Yabe 1991), has characters appropriate to the Artediellinae but is distinguished by its two complete rows of lateral line pores and extremely high number of pectoral rays (27–31). In most other characters it is similar to *Artediellichthys* and *Artediellus,* the hookear sculpins.

The remaining cottid genera have relatively few pectoral fin rays, never more than 16; never any bony plates or scales, and only prickly papillae in one species; no postocular or occipital spines; and only the uppermost preopercular spine well developed. In ***Phallocottus,*** in addition, the nasal spines are barely evident, weak and covered with skin; the uppermost preopercular spine is blunt and rounded; the anus is close to the pelvic fins; the lateral line is strongly arched anteriorly; and palatine teeth are absent. Schultz (1938) considered *Phallocottus* to be most similar to the subfamily Oligocottinae, in which Hubbs (1926) included *Sigmistes, Oligocottus,* and *Clinocottus.*

Sigmistes has its anus close to the pelvic fins; strong nasal spines; a short, slender, sharp upper preopercular spine; a strongly arched lateral line; and teeth on the palatines, although they are weak or obscure.

Oligocottus has its anus close to the anal fin; well developed nasal spines; a short, simple or multifid upper preopercular spine; a lateral line that descends anteriorly but is not strongly arched; and relatively strong palatine teeth. In males one or more of the anterior anal fin rays is markedly enlarged. The most recent revision of *Oligocottus* is that of Bolin (1944). Bolin (1947) later discussed the characters of both *Oligocottus* and *Clinocottus* in detail.

Clinocottus has its anus in the middle third of the distance between the pelvic fin base and anal fin origin; well developed nasal spines; a short, simple, blunt or sharp upper preopercular spine; a lateral line that descends anteriorly but is not strongly arched; and relatively strong palatine teeth. In males the genital papilla is exceptionally large and stout.

The plan for the cottid key and species accounts in this guide was to keep closely related genera together but this was not always possible due to the limitations of a traditional dichotomous key and the lack of consensus regarding relationships of some of the genera. For example, *Artedius* keyed out well in advance of *Oligocottus* and *Clinocottus,* but some researchers believe the three genera are closely related. Washington (1986), from larval characters, considered *Artedius* to be most closely related to *Oligocottus* and *Clinocottus,* whereas Begle (1989), in a cladistic analysis, found slight evidence (only one character: ossification of the opercle) supporting the clade consisting of these three genera. Using parsimony analyses, Strauss (1993) reexamined the data presented by Washington (1986) and Begle (1989) and concluded that evidence for a close relationship of *Clinocottus* and *Oligocottus* as sister groups is weak.

Six cottid species are new to the inventory of Alaskan fish species since that of Quast and Hall (1972). *Bolinia euryptera,* described by Yabe (1991) from specimens taken around the central Aleutian Islands, is a new addition to the list of named cottid species as well as to the list of Alaskan species. *Artediellichthys nigripinnis* was recorded by Neyelov (1979) from the Bering Sea and Gulf of Alaska, extending the known range east from Cape Navarin. *Radulinus taylori* was collected just north of the Alaska–British Columbia border by Peden and Wilson (1976). This guide records extensions of known range to Alaska for *Radulinus boleoides,* taken east of Kodiak Island and extending the recorded range from British Columbia; *Trichocottus brashnikovi,* taken near St. Lawrence Island and extending the known range from the western Bering Sea off Cape Navarin; and *Artediellus ochotensis,* collected in the eastern Chukchi Sea and extending the known range from the Commander Islands and Cape Navarin.

Six species included on Quast and Hall's (1972) list as potential additions to the inventory of Alaskan fishes are now known to occur in the region. Peden and Wilson (1976) collected *Artedius meanyi* (= *Ruscarius meanyi*) and *Oligocottus rimensis* near the Canadian border in southeastern Alaska. Records published for the first time in this guide extend the range of *Artediellus gomojunovi* to St. Matthew and St. Lawrence islands from Bering Strait off the Chukchi Peninsula; *Icelinus tenuis* to southeastern Alaska at Revillagigedo Channel and near Noyes Island, from British Columbia; and *Stelgistrum concinnum* to the Pribilof and Aleutian islands, from the western Bering Sea off Cape Olyutorskiy. Specimens of *Icelinus filamentosus* were taken south of Kodiak Island and the Kenai Peninsula in NMFS bottom trawl surveys (Allen and Smith 1988), and specimens collected near Petersburg in 1920 were recently determined to be this species.

Three species listed as probable Alaskan fishes by Quast and Hall (1972) are still not known from Alaska, but the known range of two has been extended closer to Alaska. *Archistes plumarius,* previously known only from the Kuril Islands, has been found at Medny Island, Russia (Fedorov and Sheiko 2002). *Artediellus camchaticus,* also previously recorded only as close to Alaska as the Kuril Islands, has been discovered at the Commander Islands (Fedorov and Sheiko 2002) and Cape Navarin (Sheiko and Fedorov 2000). *Triglops jordani* has not been confirmed from Alaska despite earlier reports of its presence in the region.

Species newly added as potential additions to the regional fauna are *Chitonotus pugetensis,* found in northern British Columbia close to the Alaskan border (Peden and Wilson 1976); *Triglops nybelini,* which is known from numerous records in the Canadian Arctic as close to Alaska as the Mackenzie Delta (Hunter et al. 1984); and *Porocottus camtschaticus,* occurring along the coast of eastern Kamchatka. *Stelgistrum stejnegeri,* a species inhabiting the Sea of Okhotsk and Pacific Ocean off the Kuril Islands, is included in this guide because it has been confused with Alaskan species of *Stelgistrum* and it is helpful to compare all the species in this relatively poorly known genus when identifying specimens.

The presence in Alaska of three species listed by Quast and Hall (1972) as Alaskan species is not adequately documented: *Hemilepidotus gilberti, Artediellus miacanthus,* and *A. uncinatus.* The first two are included in this guide as potential additions to the Alaskan fauna, while the third has been dropped from the inventory. *Hemilepidotus gilberti,* an inhabitant of the western Pacific, has been recorded close to Alaska near Bering Island (Peden 1978). Specimens of *Artediellus miacanthus* collected off St. Lawrence Island, Alaska, and nearby in the Gulf of Anadyr, Russia (Andriashev 1937), were lost (Andriashev 1961). The species is common at the Commander Islands (Fedorov and Sheiko 2002) and occurs along Russian shores north at least to Cape Navarin (Sheiko and Fedorov 2000). Its existence in Alaskan waters is likely but its presence cannot be confirmed from available information.

A cottid from Point Barrow was identified by Walters (1955) as *Artediellus uncinatus* (Reinhardt, 1835), but with the caveat that it might be *A. dydymovi* Soldatov, 1915. Later studies on the taxonomy of *Artediellus* (e.g., Andriashev 1961) suggested that specimens identified by Walters as *A. dydymovi* belong in the synonymy of *A. gomojunovi* Taranetz, 1933. The nearest confirmed records to Alaska among all records of *A. uncinatus* known from Arctic Canada (Hunter et al. 1984; Van Guelpen 1986; Coad 1995; N. Alfonso, pers. comm., 5 Apr. 2001) are from Davis Strait between Greenland and Baffin Island, and Hudson Strait. A record (Holeton 1974) from the Canadian high Arctic at Resolute Bay (95°W longitude) is probably a misidentification; it has been disregarded by subsequent authors (e.g., Scott and Scott 1988) and, in any case, is too far from Alaska to provide justification for considering *A. uncinatus* a probable Alaskan species. If *A. uncinatus* is found in Alaska it should be recognizable from its white spots, for which it is called the snowflake hookear sculpin. The white spots are most pronounced on the dorsal fins of the males. Additional diagnostic characters of *A. uncinatus* were reviewed by Nelson (1986) and Van Guelpen (1986). Scott and Scott (1988) summarized information on the species. The American Fisheries Society (Robins et al. 1991a) calls this fish the Arctic hookear sculpin.

Four other species previously reported from Alaska are no longer considered likely to occur in the region and are not included in this guide: *Cottus gulosus* (Girard, 1854); *Artediellus ingens* Nelson, 1986; *Artedius notospilotus* Girard, 1856; and *Myoxocephalus brandtii* (Steindachner, 1867). Specimens recorded as *C. gulosus* from southeastern Alaska at Loring and the Boca de Quadra by Evermann and Goldsborough (1907) were found in the mid-1970s to have been misidentified (Morrow 1980). Existence of *C. gulosus* in Alaska was considered doubtful by Wilimovsky (1954b) and Quast and Hall (1972). The species is adequately documented only from Washington to California.

Artediellus ingens, a cottid described by Nelson (1986), has been recorded only from the Kuril Islands. Baxter (1990ms) included *A. ingens* on his list of Alaskan species, but the specimens he identified as *A. ingens* in the University of Washington collection were later reidentified as *Bolinia euryptera,* an Alaskan species that was described (Yabe 1991) after Baxter's death.

Artedius notospilotus was reported from Prince William Sound by Rosenthal (1980) and from Cook Inlet by Rogers et al. (1986) but those authors' identifications were made before Begle (1989) revised *Artedius.* Although *A. notospilotus* has been reported from time to time from British Columbia as well, further examination of voucher specimens has always revealed an alternate species (A. E. Peden, pers. comm., 5 Sep. 1996). The confirmed northern record for *A. notospilotus* is Puget Sound (Eschmeyer and Herald 1983).

Myoxocephalus brandtii was included on Baxter's (1990ms) list of Alaskan species. However, *M. brandtii* is known mainly from the Kuril Islands and Seas of Okhotsk and Japan, and has been recorded only as close to Alaska as the western Bering Sea off Karaginskiy Island, Russia (Schmidt 1929, 1950). It inhabits shallow water close to shore so can be expected to have a relatively limited distribution.

Some species listed by Quast and Hall (1972) are now classified as junior synonyms of other Alaskan species. These are *Cottus protrusus* Schultz & Spoor, classified in *C. aleuticus* Gilbert by Morrow (1980); *Icelus vicinalis* Gilbert, classified in *I. euryops* Bean by Nelson (1984); *Megalocottus laticeps* (Gilbert), classified in *M. platycephalus* (Pallas) by Neyelov (1979) and others; *Oncocottus hexacornis* (Richardson), classified in *M. quadricornis* (Linnaeus) by Neyelov (1979) and others; and *Porocottus quadratus* Bean, classified in *Microcottus sellaris* (Gilbert) by Neyelov (1976).

Quast and Hall (1972) also listed *Myoxocephalus mednius* Bean, known from the Aleutian Islands as well as from Medny Island in the Commander group; *Porocottus bradfordi* Rutter, from the Aleutian Islands and Kodiak Island; and *Crossias albomaculatus* Schmidt, recorded from St. Paul Island in the Bering Sea and from Frederick Sound in southeastern Alaska. In this guide *Myoxocephalus mednius* is classified in *Porocottus,* giving the name *P. mednius* (Bean), and includes *P. bradfordi* and *C. albomaculatus.* This treatment differs from that of Neyelov (1976, 1979), who classified *C. albomaculatus* in *P. bradfordi* as a subspecies, *P. b. albomaculatus,* occurring from the western Aleutian Islands to the Kuril Islands; distinguished that form from *P. b. bradfordi,* occurring in the eastern Bering Sea and Gulf of Alaska; and provisionally listed *M. mednius* as a junior synonym of *P. b. albomaculatus.* However, the species name *mednius* has priority by date of publication (earlier in 1898 than *P. bradfordi*) and neither of the other names has been in widespread use, especially outside the ichthyological literature, so *mednius* is available and appropriate. From examination of specimens (C.W.M.), including the holotype of *M. mednius* (USNM 33863), which was not available to Neyelov (1976, 1979), and from descriptions in the ichthyological literature, it is clear that the synonymy of *P. bradfordi* in *P. mednius* is warranted. The holotype of *M. mednius* was also examined by F. Muto (pers. comm., 15 Dec. 2000) and M. Yabe (pers. comm., 25 Dec. 2000), whose preliminary conclusion is that they too believe *M. mednius* Bean is a synonym of *Porocottus.* North American ichthyologists have not distinguished subspecies of *P. bradfordi* (= *P. mednius*) in museum collections. If there are two distinguishable forms they are sympatric in the western Aleutian Islands, and possibly throughout the chain.

All records of *P. mednius* have not yet been reexamined to determine their proper allocation. Some Asian records attributed to this species may represent other species. Conversely, most specimens of *P. mednius* in North American museum collections are misidentified and cataloged under other species names, including *Crossias allisii* (= *Porocottus allisii*), which is known from the Kuril Islands to the Sea of Japan but which does not occur in Alaska; and some *P. mednius* from Russia are misidentified as *P. quadrifilis* (see below).

Records attributed to *Porocottus quadrifilis* Gill have been problematical with regard to both identity and geographic locality. Like other authors, Quast and Hall (1972) listed the Bering Sea and Bering Strait, Alaska, as collection localities for *P. quadrifilis*. However, all but one of the early Alaskan records are attributable to *Microcottus sellaris*. The only one that is *P. quadrifilis* is the unique holotype described by Gill (1859), and it is not at all certain that it is an Alaskan specimen, or even that it was collected at Bering Strait. Although Gill (1959) stated that it was caught at Bering Strait, he did not say it was caught on the Alaskan side of the strait; it was assumed to be Alaskan by subsequent authors. Neyelov (1976, 1979), evidently from records of specimens that were misidentified as *P. quadrifilis*, gave Norton Sound for the type locality. The NMNH Division of Fishes collection ledger, the jar label, and Bean (1881b) give "Awatska Bay" or "Avatcha Bay" (= Avacha Bay), Kamchatka, for the locality. The North Pacific Exploring Expedition of 1853–1856, which collected the specimen, visited both Kamchatka and Bering Strait. We may never know the true collection locality. However, Gill (1859) reported that the holotype of *Boreocottus axillaris* (= *Myoxocephalus scorpioides*) was caught with *P. quadrifilis*. Since *M. scorpioides* is primarily an Arctic species, not found off southern Kamchatka (where Avacha Bay is located), this lends support for a Bering Strait locality. Although the ledger and Bean (1881b) give Avacha Bay for the *B. axillaris* type locality, Andriashev (1954) stated that this was an error and gave Bering Strait for the locality, following Gill (1859).

Sculpins collected from several localities in Alaska and Russia have been identified as *P. quadrifilis* since Gill (1859) described the species. However, examination of those specimens indicates they were misidentified and that *P. quadrifilis* is known only from Gill's holotype. Specimens from Alaska, including those recorded by Nelson (1887) from Norton Sound and Gilbert (1896) from Bristol Bay, are mostly misidentified *Microcottus sellaris* (examined by C.W.M.) and are readily determined to be that species from the wide membrane that connects each pelvic fin to the body, the presence of postocular and occipital spines, and other characters. The problem of mistaken identity and specimens from Russia was not as obvious, because those specimens represent a more closely related species, *P. mednius*. Comparison of the *P. quadrifilis* holotype (USNM 6227; C.W.M., Jan. 1998, Nov. 1999) and an illustration of it from the NMNH Division of Fishes archives (see species account) with descriptions of specimens identified by Taranetz (1935b) and Matyushin (1990) as *P. quadrifilis* from the Chukchi Peninsula revealed major discrepancies. In identifying a specimen of *Porocottus* that washed up on the beach at Lavrentiya Bay as *P. quadrifilis*, Taranetz (1935b) assumed that certain characters reported by Gill (1859) were mistakes. For example, Taranetz's sculpin had 18 dorsal fin soft rays and Gill (1859) had reported 13 rays, so Taranetz assumed the 13 was a typographical error for 18; and his specimen had three pairs of head cirri whereas Gill (1859) reported two pairs, so Taranetz assumed Gill had simply missed one pair. Taranetz's redescription and specimen became the model for *P. quadrifilis* for subsequent authors. However, Gill was not mistaken in the number of dorsal fin rays. Unfortunately, the holotype is in poor condition and we cannot know the true number of cirri. The description of Taranetz's (1935b) Lavrentiya Bay specimen, which was expanded by Andriashev (1954) and Neyelov (1976, 1979), and Matyushin's (1990) description of specimens collected later at Provideniya Bay seemed to C.W.M. to fit descriptions of *P. mednius*. Consequently, B. A. Sheiko (pers. comm., 8 Aug. 2001) reexamined Taranetz's (1935b) and Matyushin's (1990) specimens, as well as others identified as *P. quadrifilis* in the Russian Academy of Sciences Zoological Institute and Kamchatka Institute of Ecology. He found no differences between them and specimens of *P. mednius*.

Myoxocephalus scorpius, which does commonly occur in Alaska, also has a confused taxonomic history. Walters (1955) synonymized *M. verrucosus*, which Bean (1881a) had described from Alaska, in *M. scorpius groenlandicus*, but Neyelov (1979) maintained them as distinct forms. Both Walters (1955) and Neyelov (1979) recognized the Atlantic subspecies *M. scorpius scorpius* to be valid. Some authors have treated the three forms as full species. In this guide they are all considered to represent one species, *M. scorpius*. The so-called stellate sculpin, *Myoxocephalus* sp., thought by Cowan and Wilimovsky (1976ms) to be an additional, closely related species ranging from the Gulf of Alaska to British Columbia, is also referable to *M. scorpius*. These conclusions are based on study of an unpublished key to *Myoxocephalus* by Carveth and Wilimovsky (1983ms) and detailed illustrations of specimens from Alaska and British Columbia (in archives of Royal British Columbia Museum and University of British Columbia), examination of museum specimens, and consultation with Wilimovsky in 1996. Peden (1998) listed one form, *M. scorpius,* from British Columbia and later (pers. comm., 3 May 1999) confirmed that the specimens recorded as *Myoxocephalus* sp. by Peden and Wilson (1976) are *M. scorpius.* Records of *M. verrucosus* from NMFS surveys off Alaska reported by Allen and Smith (1988) also should be attributed to *M. scorpius.*

Quast and Hall (1972) questioned the validity of *Enophrys lucasi* (Jordan & Gilbert) as a species distinct from *E. diceraus* (Pallas) and referred possible *E. lucasi* specimens in the NMFS Auke Bay Laboratory collection to *E. diceraus.* Neyelov (1979) synonymized *E. lucasi* in *E. diceraus,* but without examining specimens from the eastern Pacific. Peden and Wilson (1976) and Peden (1998) referred British Columbia specimens to *E. lucasi.* Further research on the interrelationships of *E. diceraus* and *E. lucasi* should include molecular data as a level of information in addition to the morphological differences, and examination of a series in sympatry.

A few sculpin species on Quast and Hall's (1972) list have undergone name changes due to shifts at the generic level (and not for the first time): *Myoxocephalus platycephalus* (Pallas), now *Megalocottus platycephalus* (Pallas); *Oxycottus acuticeps* (Gilbert), now *Clinocottus acuticeps* (Gilbert); and *Porocottus sellaris* (Gilbert), now *Microcottus sellaris* (Gilbert). *Sternias xenostethus* (Gilbert) is now *Triglops xenostethus* Gilbert, having been returned to its original genus by Wilimovsky (1979ms) and Pietsch (1994). *Archaulus biseriatus* Gilbert & Burke is classified in *Archistes*; Taranetz (1941) suggested the synonymy, and features of specimens recently examined (C.W.M., unpubl. data), including type specimens, confirm the synonymy.

Of the 87 cottid species treated in this guide, only 17 were included among the 124 species of fishes that Allen and Smith (1988) found to be most common in the eastern North Pacific from more than 30 years of NMFS demersal surveys; and one of those species (threadfin sculpin, *Icelinus filamentosus*), although common south of Alaska, is known in Alaska from only a few records. Our search indicates 43 marine cottid species and 3 freshwater species are common in Alaska, at least to the extent they are well enough documented that we indicate their known range in Alaska by solid shading on the maps. Thirty other species, with records represented only by dots on the maps, are relatively rare in Alaska or their presence is inadequately documented in museums or the literature. Three other species have been reported but not confirmed in Alaska, and eight species in this guide have not been reported from Alaska but occur nearby.

Classification of cottid species is addressed above. At the family level, Rhamphocottidae, Hemitripteridae, and Psychrolutidae were recognized by Yabe (1985) and others as lineages distinct from Cottidae, whereas they were all classified in one family at the time of Quast and Hall's (1972) inventory. Most researchers consider it premature to define subfamilies. Taranetz (1941) showed no such hesitation and his cottid subfamilies, while largely no longer workable due to the body of accumulated knowledge which points to too many exceptions, are helpful if viewed as phenetic groupings, like those of Washington (1981). The current situation is not much different from when Jordan and Starks (1904:232) wrote of cottids that "almost every species has an individuality of its own, and among the marine forms it is necessary to recognize almost as many genera as species. It is impossible to throw these small genera together into large groups." The most recent study of the relationships of the cottid genera (Yabe 1985) supports Jordan and Starks' (1904) conclusion that, of the various forms, the genus *Jordania* is nearest to the primitive scaly stock, *Cottus* exemplifies freshwater specialization, and *Zesticelus* deepwater specialization.

Key to the Cottidae of Alaska

1 Pectoral fins joined on the breast . . . . *Synchirus gilli,* page 418

1 Pectoral fins not meeting each other . . . . (2)

2 (1) Pelvic fins absent . . . . *Ascelichthys rhodorus,* page 419

2 Pelvic fins present . . . . (3)

3 (2) Gill membranes united to each other and free from isthmus or attached to isthmus for part of the distance anteriorly, forming

a wide to narrow (referring to distance front to back, not side to side) free portion (or "fold") across isthmus posteriorly; or (*Hemilepidotus spinosus* only) gill membranes completely attached to isthmus without leaving free portion posteriorly and spinous dorsal fin notched between 3rd and 4th spines . . . . (4)

3 Gill membranes broadly attached to isthmus, leaving at most a crease across isthmus posteriorly; spinous dorsal fin not notched anteriorly . . . . (51)

4 (3) Scales below lateral line arranged in separate, oblique rows or folds of serrated scales . . . . (5)

4 Scales, if present, below lateral line not in separate, oblique rows . . . . (13)

5 (4) Dorsal fin spines 17 or 18, soft rays 15–17; pelvic fin with 4–5 rays; long cirri above eyes, shorter cirri on top of head; palatine teeth present . . . . *Jordania zonope,* page 420

5 Dorsal fin spines 9–13, soft rays 21–32; pelvic fin with 3 rays; no cirri above eyes or on top of head; palatine teeth absent . . . . genus *Triglops* (6)

6 (5) Breast covered with irregular clusters of small, close-set scales; transverse folds absent from breast . . . . *Triglops xenostethus,* page 421

6 Breast naked or with small scales embedded within widely spaced, transverse dermal folds . . . . (7)

7 (6) Dorsolateral scale row (approximately midway between lateral line and base of dorsal fin) absent or containing fewer than 24 minute scales, barely distinguishable from surrounding scales . . . . (8)

7 Dorsolateral scale row well developed (especially at anterior and beneath insertion of spinous dorsal fin), containing 18 or more enlarged scales . . . . (9)

8 (7) Breast with 4–11 transverse dermal folds; pectoral fin rays 18–21; caudal fin forked . . . . *Triglops jordani,* page 422 (not confirmed from Alaska)

8 Breast nearly always naked, without transverse dermal folds; pectoral fin rays 15–17; caudal fin emarginate to nearly truncate . . . . *Triglops macellus,* page 423

9 (7) Caudal fin truncate or deeply forked; oblique dermal folds on trunk below lateral line 108 or more . . . . (10)

9 Caudal fin rounded, truncate, or emarginate, but never forked; oblique dermal folds on trunk below lateral line 105 or fewer . . . . (11)

10 (9) Caudal fin deeply forked; skin of exposed portion of maxilla naked; dermal folds of breast 5–10; interorbital space broad, width 16–21% HL . . . . *Triglops forficatus,* page 424

10 Caudal fin more or less truncate; skin of exposed portion of maxilla covered with rough, close-set granular scales (may be lost in poorly preserved specimens); dermal folds of breast 14–23; interorbital space narrow, width 5–10% HL . . . . *Triglops scepticus,* page 425

11 (9) Lower jaw projecting beyond upper jaw; body darkly pigmented, saddles beneath dorsal fins and on caudal peduncle absent or only faintly present; breast, sides of belly, and especially peritoneum densely peppered with small melanophores . . . . *Triglops nybelini,* page 426 (not known from Alaska)

11 Jaws equal or upper jaw projecting beyond lower; body lightly pigmented, with 4 or 5 dark saddles, 1 beneath spinous dorsal fin, 2 or 3 beneath soft dorsal fin, and 1 on caudal peduncle; breast and sides of belly unpigmented, peritoneum unpigmented or at most lightly covered with small, widely spaced melanophores . . . . (12)

12 (11) Caudal fin emarginate; pectoral fin rays usually 20 or 21 (range 19–22); oblique dermal folds 66–105; interorbital width 11–18% HL . . . . *Triglops metopias,* page 427

12 Caudal fin truncate to slightly rounded; pectoral fin rays usually 17–19 (range 17–21); oblique dermal folds 49–69; interorbital width 6–10% HL . . . . *Triglops pingelii,* page 428

13 (4) Pelvic fins with 4 or 5 rays . . . . (14)

13 Pelvic fins with 2 or 3 rays . . . . (21)

14 (13) Single row of hooked scutes below dorsal fins . . . . *Paricelinus hopliticus,* page 429 (not known from Alaska)

14 No row of scutes along base of dorsal fins . . . . (15)

15 (14) Scales deeply embedded, may not be apparent, skin smooth; median, flaplike cirrus on snout . . . . *Scorpaenichthys marmoratus,* page 430

15 Scales not deeply embedded, skin rough in places; no median, flaplike cirrus on snout . . . . genus *Hemilepidotus* (16)

16 (15) Dorsal scale band of 3 rows of scales; dorsal fin spines 1–3 gradually increasing in height, spinous dorsal fin membrane not notched between spines 3 and 4; first few dorsal fin spines greatly exserted in males (subgenus *Melletes*) . . . . *Hemilepidotus papilio,* page 431

16 Dorsal scale band of 4–8 rows of scales; dorsal fin spine 3 about same height as spine 2 or lower, spinous dorsal fin membrane notched between spines 3 and 4 first few dorsal spines not greatly exserted in males . . . . (17)

17 (16) Dorsal scale band of 6–8 rows; ventral scale band of 4 or 5 rows of scales; gill membranes attached to isthmus posteriorly without leaving free fold across isthmus (subgenus *Calycilepidotus*) . . . . *Hemilepidotus spinosus,* page 432

17 Dorsal scale band of 4 or 5 rows; ventral scale band of 6–9 rows of scales; gill membranes united to each other, forming broad free fold across isthmus in most species, and joined to isthmus anteriorly leaving a narrow fold posteriorly in one species (subgenus *Hemilepidotus*) . . . . (18)

18 (17) First dorsal fin spine longer than second; frontal cirrus (medial to postocular cirrus) reduced or absent . . . . *Hemilepidotus gilberti,* page 433 (not known from Alaska)

18 First dorsal spine usually shorter than second; frontal cirrus (medial to postocular cirrus) well developed, usually multifid in larger specimens . . . . . (19)

19 (18) Lateral line pores 58 or fewer; scales present on caudal peduncle between levels of dorsal scale band and lateral line; anal scale row present in adults; pelvic fins of ripe males longer than head . . . . . *Hemilepidotus zapus,* page 434

19 Lateral line pores 59 or more; scales usually absent from caudal peduncle between levels of dorsal scale band and lateral line; anal scale row usually absent in adults; pelvic fins of ripe males shorter than head . . . . . (20)

20 (19) Pectoral fin rays 16 or fewer, or if 17, total number of rays in dorsal, anal, and both pectoral fins fewer than 70 (63–68); width of maxillary cirrus more than half its length; nasal cirrus multifid; posterior dorsal and anal fin rays branched . . . . . *Hemilepidotus hemilepidotus,* page 435

20 Pectoral fin rays 18 or more, or if 17, total number of rays in dorsal, anal, and both pectoral fins more than 70 (71–78); width of maxillary cirrus less than half its length; nasal cirrus simple; dorsal and anal fin rays unbranched . . . . . *Hemilepidotus jordani,* page 436

21 (13) Body with scales in organized rows extending posteriorly past pectoral fin tip; scale rows may be above and along lateral line, or only along lateral line . . . . . (22)

21 Body without organized rows of scales extending posteriorly past pectoral fin tip; may have scattered bony or spiny plates, warts, or papillae, or be entirely naked . . . . . (42)

22 (21) Upper preopercular spine with 2 or more dorsally directed spinules . . . . . (23)

22 Upper preopercular spine simple, bifid, or bifid with single dorsal spinule . . . . . (27)

23 (22) Pelvic fins with 3 rays; spinous dorsal fin deeply notched between spines 3 and 4 . . . . . *Chitonotus pugetensis,* page 437 (not known from Alaska)

23 Pelvic fins with 2 rays, may be hard to count; spinous dorsal fin not notched between spines 3 and 4 . . . . . genus *Icelinus* (24)

24 (23) Dorsal fin with first 1 or 2 spines greatly elongate . . . . . (25)

24 Dorsal fin with first 2 dorsal spines about same length as 3rd . . . . . (26)

25 (24) Two distinct pairs of postocular spines; no cirri on nasal spine; dorsal scale band extending to about 5th to 11th soft dorsal ray . . . . . *Icelinus tenuis,* page 438

25 Postocular spines absent; long cirrus at base of nasal spine; dorsal scale band extending to below base of last 2 soft dorsal rays . . . . . *Icelinus filamentosus,* page 439

26 (24) Dorsal scale band not extending beyond insertion of soft dorsal fin . . . . *Icelinus burchami,* page 440

26 Dorsal scale band extending beyond insertion of soft dorsal fin onto caudal peduncle . . . . *Icelinus borealis,* page 441

27 (22) Anus close to pelvic fin origin (in adults) . . . . (28)

27 Anus not close to pelvic fin origin . . . . (29)

28 (27) One row of platelike scales below soft dorsal fin; scales of one side not extending across nape to other side . . . . *Archistes plumarius,* page 442 (not known from Alaska)

28 Two rows of platelike scales below soft dorsal fin; scales of each side connecting across nape . . . . *Archistes biseriatus,* page 443

29 (27) Palatine teeth absent . . . . (30)

29 Palatine teeth present . . . . (35)

30 (29) Dorsal profile not arched, nearly straight from eye to caudal peduncle; lateral line descending little anteriorly, running high on body to end of line; 1–4 rows of scales above and closely adjacent to lateral line scales; males with elongate, conical genital papilla . . . . genus *Radulinus* (31)

30 Dorsal profile arched at nape and anterior part of body; lateral line strongly descending anteriorly, running relatively low on body to end of line; rows of scales above lateral line separated from lateral line scales by wide space without obvious scales; males without elongate genital papilla . . . . genus *Stelgistrum* (33)

31 (30) Anal fin rays 13–17; dorsal scales usually in more than 1 row above lateral line scales; dorsal scales extending to below posterior portion of second dorsal fin . . . . *Radulinus taylori,* page 444

31 Anal fin rays 20–23; dorsal scales as 1 row of small scales above lateral line scales; dorsal scales not extending beyond middle of second dorsal fin . . . . (32)

32 (31) Snout longer than eye; nasal spines short, triangular; pelvic fins short, length about equal to or less than width of pectoral fin base . . . . *Radulinus boleoides,* page 445

32 Snout equal to or shorter than eye; nasal spines long, needlelike; pelvic fins long, length about equal to or greater than width of pectoral fin base . . . . *Radulinus asprellus,* page 446

33 (30) Rough scales present on dorsal fin spines and rays, nape, sides of head, and snout; platelike scales of dorsal scale band extending almost to base of caudal fin; maxilla extending to mideye to posterior edge of eye . . . . *Stelgistrum stejnegeri,* page 447 (not known from Alaska)

33 Scales absent from dorsal fin spines and rays, sides of head, and snout (may be present on nape); dorsal scale band reaching almost to base of last rays of soft dorsal fin or extending to base of caudal fin; maxilla extending to anterior edge of eye or nearly to posterior edge of eye . . . . (34)

34 (33) Dorsal scale band extending to base of caudal fin; scales in dorsal band (counted below posterior portion of spinous dorsal fin) in no more than 2 rows; scales of lower row in dorsal band large and platelike; maxilla extending to anterior edge of eye to mideye; 4 pairs of fleshy cirri on top of head, including multifid postocular cirrus .... *Stelgistrum concinnum,* page 448

34 Dorsal scale band not extending past insertion of soft dorsal fin; scales in dorsal band (counted below posterior portion of spinous dorsal fin) in more than 2 rows; scales in dorsal band not particularly large; maxilla extending to mideye or nearly to posterior edge of eye; up to 3 pairs of cirri on top of head, including bifid postorbital cirrus .... *Stelgistrum beringianum,* page 449

35 (29) Scales in row between lateral line and dorsal fins enlarged and platelike, or absent .... (36)

35 Scales between lateral line and dorsal fins not enlarged and platelike .... (44)

36 (35) No scales above lateral line; lower pectoral fin rays thickened and with membanes deeply incised, the uppermost of these rays exserted well beyond rest of fin .... *Thyriscus anoplus,* page 450

36 Distinct band of scales dorsally, including row of enlarged platelike scales; lower portion of pectoral fin not as above .... genus *Icelus* (37)

37 (36) Each scale of dorsal row of platelike scales bearing a single, strong spine .... *Icelus spiniger,* page 451

37 Each scale of dorsal row of platelike scales bearing a ridge of several small spinules .... (38)

38 (37) Pectoral axil with well-developed rows of scales; short ventral scale row usually present; nasal tubes black .... *Icelus canaliculatus,* page 452

38 Scales below lateral line absent or reduced to patch on pectoral axil; nasal tubes pale .... (39)

39 (38) Spine present on suborbital stay .... *Icelus euryops,* page 453

39 Spine absent from suborbital stay .... (40)

40 (39) Lateral line scales extending past posterior edge of hypural plate, 1 lateral line scale on caudal rays; dorsal and ventral caudal peduncle scales absent; postocular cirrus narrow at base, broad and multifid distally, not darkly pigmented .... *Icelus uncinalis,* page 454

40 Lateral line scales not extending past posterior edge of hypural plate; no lateral line scales on caudal rays; dorsal and ventral caudal peduncle scales present or absent; postocular cirrus usually simple, slender, gently tapering distally, if broad and multifid, then darkly pigmented .... (41)

41 (40) Lateral line scales extending to posterior edge of hypural plate; caudal peduncle scales absent, or present only above lateral line; axillary scales 1–14; rows of scales between dorsal scale row and lateral line absent; row of scales just above anal fin absent; male genital papilla flattened or

spatulate, with a short, curved or hooklike terminal appendage . . . . *Icelus spatula,* page 455

41 Lateral line scales incomplete posteriorly, terminating on or before anterior portion of caudal peduncle (rarely extending to posterior edge of hypural plate); caudal peduncle scales generally present above and below midline; axillary scales 9–30; row of small scales often present between dorsal scale row and lateral line; row of small scales often present just above anal fin; genital papilla of male cylindrical, with elongate, tapering terminal appendage . . . . *Icelus bicornis,* page 456

42 (21) Vomerine and palatine teeth present; 4 preopercular spines, upper not much larger than rest; body covered with small prickly scales . . . . (43)

42 Vomerine or palatine teeth absent; upper preopercular spine usually distinctly longer than rest; body naked or covered with small prickly scales . . . . (47)

43 (42) Lateral line complete, extending to or nearly to caudal fin base; pelvic fins not short . . . . *Rastrinus scutiger,* page 457

43 Lateral line incomplete, not extending beyond second dorsal fin; pelvic fins short, less than eye length . . . . *Stlegicottus xenogrammus,* page 458

44 (35) Scales absent from top of head; lateral line scales embedded, making lateral line smooth to touch . . . . *Artedius lateralis,* page 459

44 Scales on top of head, may be scattered; lateral line scales embedded or not . . . . (45)

45 (44) Cirrus absent from upper anterior edge of orbit; dorsal body scales in band originating under base of 2nd or 3rd dorsal fin spine, separated from head scales by naked area or preceded by scales so minute and scattered that they do not obscure the definite origin of the band; lateral line scales embedded and smooth . . . . *Artedius fenestralis,* page 460

45 Cirrus present on upper anterior edge of orbit; dorsal body scales merging with head scales; lateral line scales not embedded, feeling rough . . . . (46)

46 (45) Dorsolateral scales in distinct band of several rows with naked area below dorsal fins, especially below first dorsal, and above lateral line; no scales on eye; upper preopercular spine stout and flattened; posterior nostril tube markedly longer than anterior tube; total length up to 100 mm or more . . . . . *Artedius harringtoni,* page 461

46 Scales nearly completely covering body above lateral line; scales on upper part of eye; upper preopercular spine long and narrow; posterior nostril not tubular, its margins only slightly elevated; total length up to 60 mm . . . . *Ruscarius meanyi,* page 462

47 (42) Vomer without teeth. . . . . genus *Gymnocanthus* (48)

47 Vomer with teeth . . . . (57)

48 (47) Interorbital space broad, width 14–19% HL. . . . . *Gymnocanthus detrisus,* page 463

48 Interorbital space narrow, width less than 10% HL. . . . . (49)

49 (48) No occipital tubercles . . . . . . *Gymnocanthus tricuspis,* page 464

49 One to three pairs of occipital tubercles . . . . . . (50)

50 (49) Two or three pairs of prominent occipital tubercles; total count for both dorsal fins, both pectoral fins, and anal fin 80 or less; bony plates of interorbital space not extending onto rim of orbit; long cirri with expanded ends behind pectoral fin in males . . . . . . *Gymnocanthus pistilliger,* page 465

50 One or two pairs of low occipital tubercles; total count for both dorsal fins, both pectoral fins, and anal fin 81 or more; bony plates of interorbital space extending onto rim of orbit; no long cirri behind pectoral fin in males . . . . . . *Gymnocanthus galeatus,* page 466

51 (3) Lateral line without bony plates . . . . . . (52)

51 Lateral line with bony plates . . . . . . genus *Enophrys* (55)

52 (51) Upper preopercular spine long, robust, and antlerlike, with 2–6 spinules . . . . . . *Leptocottus armatus,* page 467

52 Upper preopercular spine short and simple, without spinules . . . . . . genus *Cottus* (53)

53 (52) Lateral line ending under middle of second dorsal fin, although there may be isolated pores farther behind; 2 mandibular pores on tip of chin at midline . . . . . . *Cottus cognatus,* page 468

53 Lateral line extending posterior to anal fin; 1 mandibular pore on tip of chin at midline . . . . . . (54)

54 (53) Palatine teeth present, well developed; posterior nostril not tubular; prickles usually present on back and sides, sometimes only in pectoral axil . . . . . . *Cottus asper,* page 469

54 Palatine teeth absent or only poorly developed; posterior nostril tubular; prickles usually absent, except sometimes present in pectoral axil . . . . . . *Cottus aleuticus,* page 470

55 (51) Uppermost preopercular spine simple, without spinules; combined total of second dorsal and anal fin rays 22 or less; lateral line plates without keels; edge of lachrymal bone straight, not extending over maxilla . . . . . . *Enophrys bison,* page 471

55 Uppermost preopercular spine with 1–8 recurved spinules; combined total of second dorsal and anal fin rays 23 or more; lateral line plates with 1 or 2 keels; lachrymal bone expanded as flange extending over maxilla . . . . . . (56)

56 (55) Uppermost preopercular spine long, equal to or greater than distance from posterior rim of orbit to posterior edge of nuchal ridge (rarely shorter); second dorsal rays usually 14 (range 13–15); anal fin rays usually 12 (range 11–13) . . . . . . *Enophrys diceraus,* page 472

56 Uppermost preopercular spine relatively short, generally much less than distance from posterior rim of orbit to posterior edge of nuchal ridge; second dorsal rays usually 13 (range 10–14); anal fin rays usually 10 or 11 (range 9–11) . . . . . . *Enophrys lucasi,* page 473

57 (47) Pectoral fin rays 12–19 (rarely 19); dorsal, anal, and pectoral fin rays unbranched; uppermost preopercular spine simple or multifid, straight or gently curved upward; lateral line canal with or without bend downward on caudal peduncle . . . . . (58)

57 Pectoral fin rays 18–31 (rarely 18); dorsal, anal, and pectoral fin rays branched; uppermost preopercular spine simple, strongly hooked upward, or if not strongly hooked but long and curved, preopercular and mandibular pores obviously enlarged; lateral line canal without downward bend on caudal peduncle . . . . . (71)

58 (57) Lateral line with accessory canals and pores giving appearance of many pores along lateral line; palatines without teeth; lateral line often with bend downward on caudal peduncle . . . . . (59)

58 Lateral line without accessory canals and pores; palatines with teeth, or if without teeth lateral line strongly arched anteriorly; lateral line without bend on caudal peduncle . . . . . (79)

59 (58) Uppermost preopercular spine usually straight; slit or pore present behind fourth gill arch; ascending process of premaxilla always shorter than length of premaxilla; pectoral fin rays 14–19; pelvic fins usually not reaching anus, occasionally reaching anus in males . . . . . (60)

59 Uppermost preopercular spine usually curved upward; no slit or pore behind fourth gill arch; ascending process of premaxilla longer or equal to length of premaxilla; pectoral fin rays 12–17; pelvic fins usually reaching anus in females and extending beyond anus in males . . . . . (68)

60 (59) Cirri present on cheeks, lower jaw, and lateral line . . . . . *Trichocottus brashnikovi,* page 474

60 Cirri absent from cheeks, lower jaw, and lateral line . . . . . (61)

61 (60) Lower jaw distinctly extending past upper jaw; supracleithral spine fork-shaped or double, upper spine not visible in all specimens . . . . . *Megalocottus platycephalus,* page 475

61 Lower jaw not extending past upper jaw; supracleithral spine straight and single . . . . . genus *Myoxocephalus* (62)

62 (61) Bony projections absent from top of head; numerous small cirri on top of head . . . . . *Myoxocephalus niger,* page 476

62 Bony projections variously developed on top of head, with conspicuous spines, protuberances, or digitating ridges present; without numerous small cirri on top of head . . . . . (63)

63 (62) Digitating ridges absent from head; protuberances or spines present on head . . . . . (64)

63 Digitating ridges present on head . . . . . (66)

64 (63) Spinous and soft dorsal fins well separated, interspace 1 eye diameter or more; postocular and occipital protuberances present, variously developed, in some specimens well developed and with rough, wartlike surface . . . . . *Myoxocephalus quadricornis,* page 477

64 Dorsal fins confluent or nearly so . . . . . (65)

65 (64) Pectoral fin rays typically 16–18 (range 14–19); usually 2 postocular and 2 occipital protuberances or spines on each side, cirri present on protuberances in some specimens; warts present on top of head or absent; platelike scales above lateral line with depressed center and spines around margin . . . . *Myoxocephalus scorpius,* page 478

65 Pectoral fin rays typically 15 (range 14–16); 1 weak postocular and 1 weak occipital spine or protuberance on each side, each with stout cirrus; numerous hard, sharp-tipped warts on top of head; platelike scales above lateral line anteriorly with raised centers and entirely covered with spines . . . . *Myoxocephalus scorpioides,* page 479

66 (63) Postocular and occipital protuberances absent; postocular cirrus present; occipital cirrus present in some specimens; cirrus often present on posterior end of maxilla; digitate ridges behind eyes covered with thick skin . . . . *Myoxocephalus stelleri,* page 480

66 Postocular and occipital protuberances present; cirri absent; digitate ridges behind eyes not covered with thick skin . . . . (67)

67 (66) Dentary lip present (on each side of lower jaw); anal fin rays 13–15. . . . . *Myoxocephalus jaok,* page 481

67 Dentary lip absent (loose skin fold may be present but when teased with probe, fold will not be elaborated as a distinct structure); anal fin rays 11–13 . . . . *Myoxocephalus polyacanthocephalus,* page 482

68 (59) Pelvic fins connected to belly by wide membrane for a fourth to half their length; postocular and occipital spines or bony protuberances present . . . . *Microcottus sellaris,* page 483

68 Pelvic fins connected to belly by membrane only at their base; top of head without bony spines or protuberances . . . . genus *Porocottus* (69)

69 (68) Dorsal fin soft rays 13 or 14; two pairs of head cirri (postocular and occipital), cirri simple . . . . *Porocottus quadrifilis,* page 484 (not confirmed from Alaska)

69 Dorsal fin soft rays 14–19 (rarely 14); two or three pairs of head cirri, with or without additional cirri between; postocular cirri multifid, other head cirri usually multifid . . . . (70)

70 (69) Two pairs of head cirri; postocular cirri with 8–20 branches . . . . *Porocottus camtschaticus,* page 485 (not known from Alaska)

70 Three pairs of head cirri; postocular cirri with 2–9 branches . . . . *Porocottus mednius,* page 486

71 (57) Upper preopercular spine long and gently curved upward; preopercular and mandibular pores obviously enlarged; lateral line pores fewer than 20 . . . . *Zesticelus profundorum,* page 487

71 Upper preopercular spine sharply hooked upward; preopercular and mandibular pores not enlarged; lateral line pores more than 20 . . . . (72)

72 (71) Pectoral fin rays usually 29–30 (range 27–31); palatine teeth absent (with rare exception); body lateral line canal opening through 2 rows of pores . . . . *Bolinia euryptera,* page 488

72 Pectoral fin rays 18–28; palatine teeth present; body lateral line canal opening through 1 row of pores along lower edge of canal . . . . (73)

73 (72) Suborbital stay platelike (broad and spatulate); nasal spine of each side doubled; cirrus absent from posterior end of maxilla . . . . *Artediellichthys nigripinnis,* page 489

73 Suborbital stay sticklike (narrow and round); nasal spines single or absent; cirrus present on posterior end of maxilla . . . . genus *Artediellus* (74)

74 (73) Small spinule on inner surface of upper preopercular spine; occipital protuberances strong; interorbital space convex . . . . *Artediellus gomojunovi,* page 490

74 Spinule absent from inner surface of upper preopercular spine; occipital protuberances low or absent; interorbital space flat to concave . . . . (75)

75 (74) Occipital protuberances low; nasal spines absent; numerous fleshy cirri present on head and anterior part of lateral line; anterior mandibular pore single . . . . *Artediellus scaber,* page 491

75 Occipital protuberances absent; nasal spines absent or present but small; cirri few or numerous; anterior mandibular pore single or paired . . . . (76)

76 (75) Anterior mandibular pore single; numerous cirri on head; cirrus at posterior end of maxilla often branched; in males, membrane at tips of spines of first dorsal fin expanded and paddlelike . . . . *Artediellus pacificus,* page 492

76 Anterior mandibular pore paired; few or numerous cirri on head; cirrus at posterior end of maxilla simple; in males, membrane at tips of spines of first dorsal fin not expanded and paddlelike . . . . (77)

77 (76) Cirri absent except for long, slender cirrus on posterior end of maxilla; caudal peduncle long and slender, depth usually less than 35% of its length; pectoral fin rays 23–26; several dark spots on first dorsal fin but no large black spot posteriorly on first dorsal . . . . *Artediellus camchaticus,* page 493 (not known from Alaska)

77 Postocular and occipital cirri present, as well as maxillary cirrus; caudal peduncle short and stout, depth greater than 35% of its length; pectoral fin rays 20–24; large round black spot posteriorly on first dorsal fin in males, often present but not as well developed in females . . . . (78)

78 (77) Lateral line pores 24–33; numerous large fleshy cirri, usually including lachrymal, preopercular, cleithral, and anterior lateral line cirri . . . . *Artediellus ochotensis,* page 494

78 Lateral line pores 14–24; lachrymal, preopercular, cleithral, and anterior lateral line cirri absent . . . . *Artediellus miacanthus*, page 495 (not confirmed from Alaska)

79 (58) Anus close to base of pelvic fins; lateral line strongly arched anteriorly . . . . (80)

79 Anus in middle third of distance between pelvic fins and anal fin origin or close to anal fin; lateral line strongly arched or not . . . . (82)

80 (79) Nasal spines obscure; anal fin rays 22–25; palatine teeth absent . . . . *Phallocottus obtusus*, page 496

80 Nasal spines well developed; anal fin rays 14–21; palatine teeth present, may be difficult to discern . . . . (81)

81 (80) Rays in second dorsal fin 24–27; anal fin rays 17–20 . . . . *Sigmistes smithi*, page 497

81 Rays in second dorsal fin 19–21; anal fin rays 14–17 . . . . *Sigmistes caulias*, page 498

82 (79) Anus close to anal fin origin . . . . genus *Oligocottus* (83)

82 Anus in middle third of area between pelvic fin base and anal fin origin . . . . genus *Clinocottus* (85)

83 (82) Body covered with small slender spines . . . . *Oligocottus rimensis*, page 499

83 Body without scales or spines . . . . (84)

84 (83) No cirri on nasal spine base; cirri on body single or paired, those on lateral line confined mostly to anterior portion . . . . *Oligocottus maculosus*, page 500

84 Cirrus at base of nasal spine on posterior side; cirri on body in groups of 3–6 along lateral line and in 2 rows above it . . . . *Oligocottus snyderi*, page 501

85 (82) One or two cirri at end of maxilla; inner pelvic ray widely attached to belly by membrane . . . . *Clinocottus acuticeps*, page 502

85 No cirri on maxilla; inner pelvic ray not widely attached to belly by membrane . . . . (86)

86 (85) Upper lip strictly terminal; small fleshy tubercle in median line of groove that limits the upper lip dorsally; no cirri behind opercular flap between upper pectoral fin base and lateral line; head in dorsal view moderately pointed and angular, definitely not hemispherical . . . . *Clinocottus embyrum*, page 503

86 Upper lip inferior, except in young; no fleshy tubercle in groove that limits the upper lip dorsally; a patch of cirri behind opercular flap between pectoral base and lateral line; head in dorsal view very bluntly rounded, hemispherical . . . . *Clinocottus globiceps*, page 504

Synchirus gilli Bean, 1890 **manacled sculpin**

Unalaska Island; western Gulf of Alaska at Kodiak Island to southern California at San Miguel Island. Tidepools and shallow water, often in kelp; mainly intertidal; clings to pilings, rocks, other objects.

D VIII–X + 19–21; A 18–21; Pec 21–24; Pel I,3; LLp 39–42; Vert 38–39.

- Translucent olive green to brown; male with silvery lateral stripe.
- Head pointed and slender; body elongate and slender.
- Nasal spine present; no spines on top of head.
- One preopercular spine, short and bifid.
- Nasal, postocular, and preopercular cirri present or absent.
- **Pectoral fins united ventrally**, forming cuplike structure (used for clinging to objects); pelvic fins posteriorly positioned (owing to unusually long pubic bones).
- Ctenoid scales along lateral line and sometimes along base of dorsal fins.
- Vomerine teeth present; palatine teeth present or absent.
- Genital papilla of males elongate, retractable into deep pit.
- Gill membranes united, free from isthmus.
- Length to 69 mm TL, possibly larger.

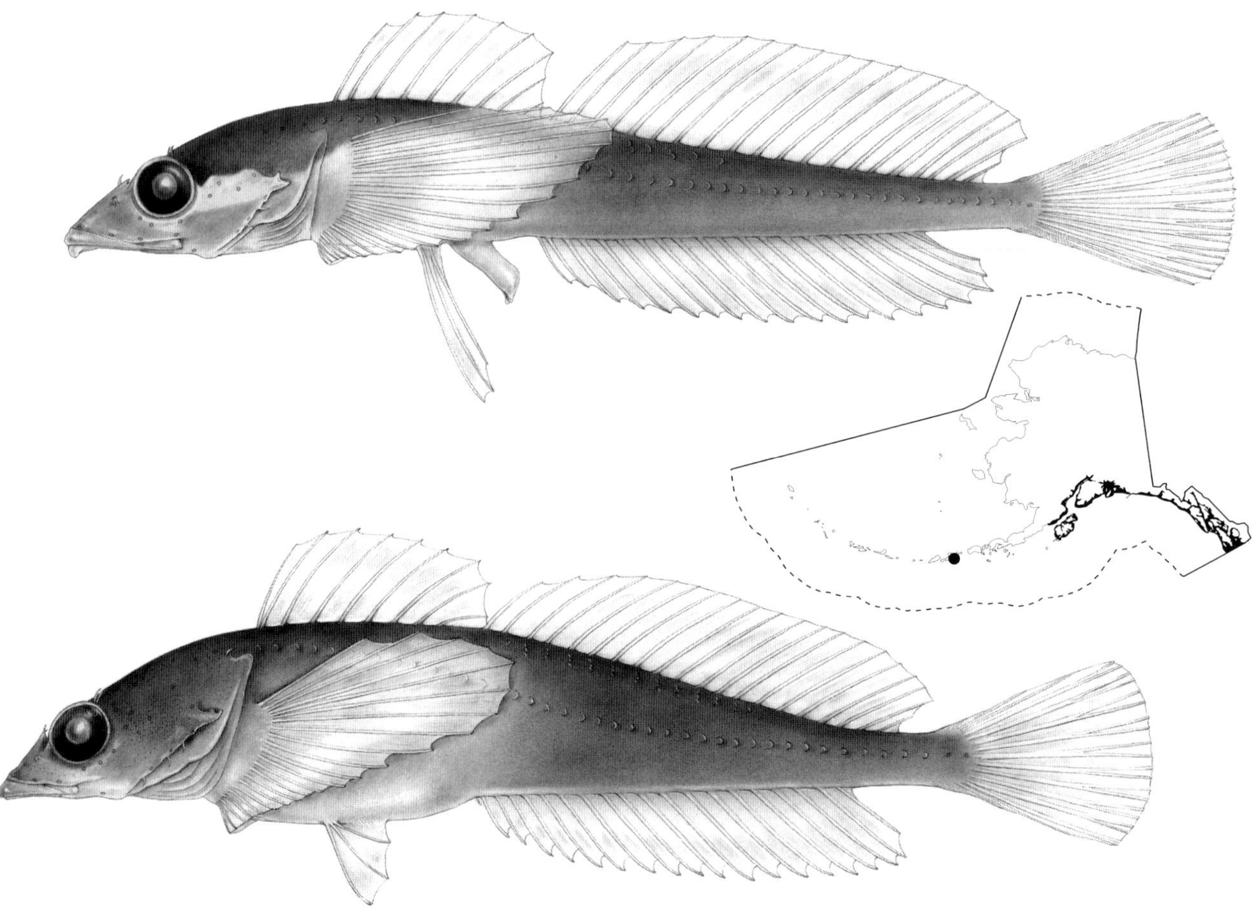

Notes & Sources — *Synchirus gilli* Bean, 1890

Convergent in appearance to *Rimicola muscarum* (Perciformes, Gobiesocidae) in coloration; fin specialization to form adhesive disk; low, elongate, lateral profile; small size; and preference for kelp zone (Krejsa 1964).

Description: Bean 1890a; Jordan and Evermann 1898:2023–2024; Miller and Erdman 1948; Bolin 1950:200; Krejsa 1964; Hart 1973:542.

Figures: University of British Columbia, artist P. Drukker-Brammall, May 1966. Upper: male, UBC 62–884, 38 mm SL. Lower: female, UBC 62-867, 47 mm SL. Sooke, B.C.

Range: Known range is extended west to Unalaska Island, near head of Usof Bay, 53°30'N, 166°45'W, by specimen in UBC 65-104. Recorded from four sites in Prince William Sound by Orsi et al. (1991). Other Alaskan records include Kodiak Island (Harris and Hartt 1977), Funter Bay (Orsi and Landingham 1985), and other Gulf of Alaska sites (Orsi et al. 1991). Baxter (1990ms) observed numerous specimens and collected five (not saved) in 1983 on the north side of Hesketh Island, Kachemak Bay.

Size: Miller and Lea (1972) gave maximum of 69 mm TL. Baxter (1990ms) reported 80 mm TL, but without citing documentation. Largest of 224 specimens measured by Krejsa (1964) was 54.5 mm SL, or about 65 mm TL using SL = 83–86% TL from Baxter (1990ms).

Ascelichthys rhodorus Jordan & Gilbert, 1880

rosylip sculpin

Prince William Sound at head of Olsen Bay; southeastern Alaska at Sitka to northern California at Moss Beach.

Tidepools, rocky shoreline, and gravel beaches along exposed coasts, and in eel grass in bays; subtidal to depths of 15 m, often found at low tide under rocks.

D VII–X,17–20; A 13–16; Pec 16–18; Pel 0; LLp 35–39; Vert 35–36.

- Dark olive brown shading to dusky ventrally; lips edged with dark red or cinnamon; fins dusky, spinous dorsal fin edged with bright crimson.
- Nasal tubes long.
- Nasal spine absent; no spines on top of head.
- One preopercular spine, stout and skin-covered.
- Multifid cirrus above posterior part of eye; several cirri above opercular flap.
- Dorsal fin continuous, with shallow to deep notch between spinous and soft-rayed portions; soft dorsal higher than spinous; **pelvic fin absent**.
- Skin smooth, without scales, prickles, or papillae.
- Vomerine and palatine teeth present.
- Genital papilla of males small and conical.
- Gill membranes united, free from isthmus.
- Length to 150 mm TL.

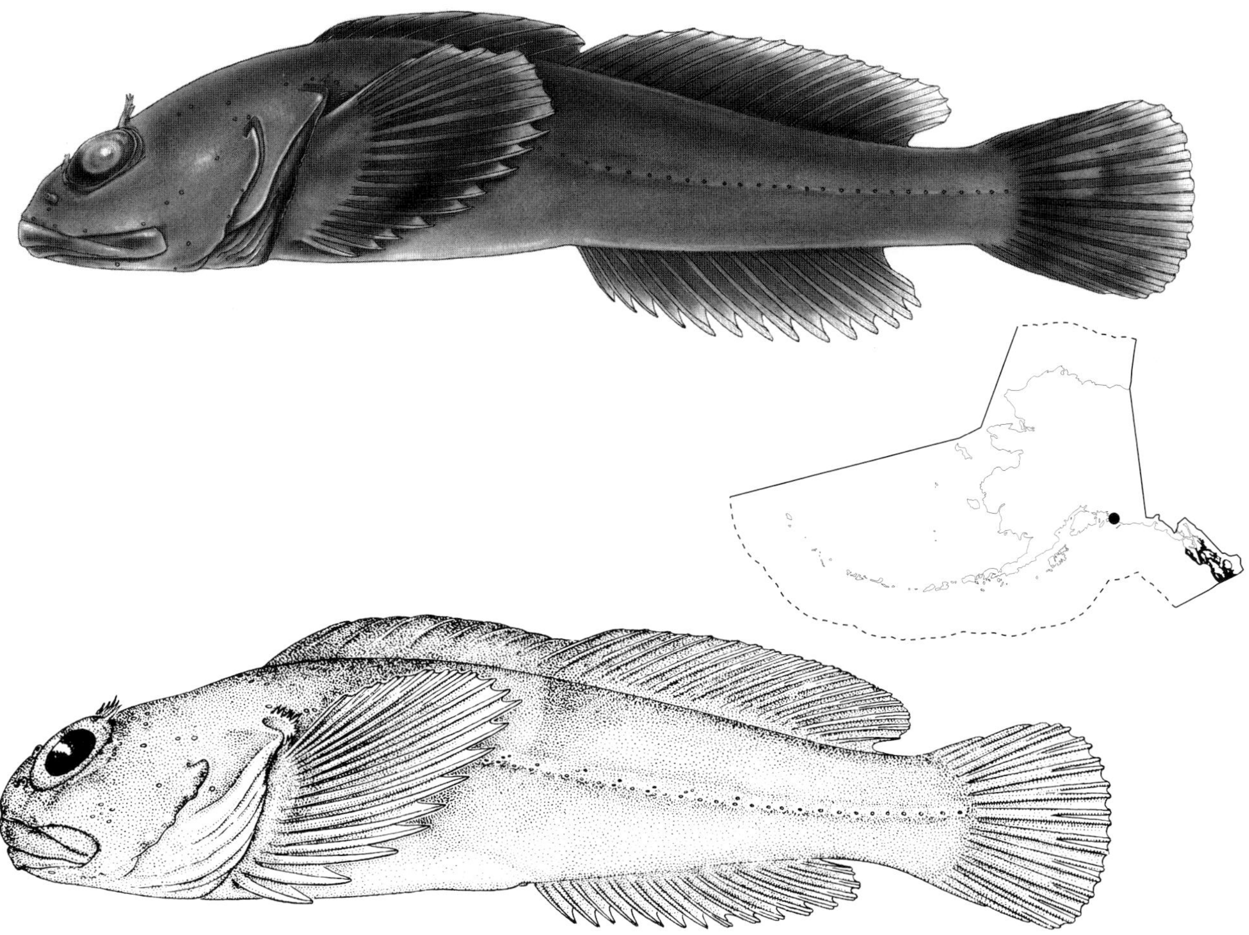

Notes & Sources — *Ascelichthys rhodorus* Jordan & Gilbert, 1880

Description: Jordan and Gilbert 1880h; Jordan and Evermann 1898:2024–2025; Bolin 1944:88–90; Miller and Lea 1972:118; Hart 1973:484–485.

Figures: Upper: University of British Columbia, artist P. Drukker-Brammall, Mar. 1966; UBC 65-574, 62 mm SL, Klokachef Island, Alaska. Lower: Bolin 1944, fig. 34.

Range: Known range is extended from southeastern Alaska to Prince William Sound at head of Olsen Bay, 60°43'N, 146°12'W, by UBC 63-499; identification was confirmed by N. J. Wilimovsky (pers. comm., 29 Feb. 1996). Reported north to Sitka by Jordan et al. (1930). Species is common in tidepools from British Columbia (Hart 1973) to California (Eschmeyer and Herald 1983), but we found few examples from Alaska. The UBC has 26 specimens from Klokachef Island, north of Sitka (one is shown in illustration above), as well as specimens from farther south in the Alexander Archipelago at Coronation Island (UBC 65-524) and Dall Island (UBC 65-517). The UW has a specimen from Noyes Island (UW 5204), and NMC from southwestern Prince of Wales Island (NMC 61-8).

Jordania zonope Starks, 1895 **longfin sculpin**

Prince William Sound at Danger Island; southeastern Alaska at Baranof Island to central California at Diablo Canyon.

Intertidal zone to depth of 38 m in rocky areas and kelp, usually subtidal; clings to vertical rock faces.

D XVII–XVIII + 15–17; A 22–24; Pec 13–14; Pel I,5 (rarely 4); LLp 48–51; Vert 46–48.

- Greenish to reddish or yellowish brown, sometimes marked with red, orange, and blue; **wide dark and narrow light bars on cheek**; 6–8 dark saddles dorsally, large dark blotches along midside; caudal fin often bright orange or yellow; pelvic fin black.
- Body elongate and slender.
- Nasal spine present; no spines on top of head.
- Two preopercular spines; upper very small, lower well developed and curved upward.
- **Cirri on either side of each nasal spine, above eye, and on top of head**.
- **Dorsal fins similar in size and shape**; **dorsal and anal fins all long-based**; **anal fin origin below posterior third of spinous dorsal**.
- Body above lateral line covered with closely set, irregularly positioned ctenoid scales; scales below lateral line forming long, oblique, serrated rows.
- Vomerine and palatine teeth present.
- Anus not advanced in position.
- Genital papilla of males small and conical.
- Gill membranes broadly united, free of isthmus.
- Length to 150 mm TL.

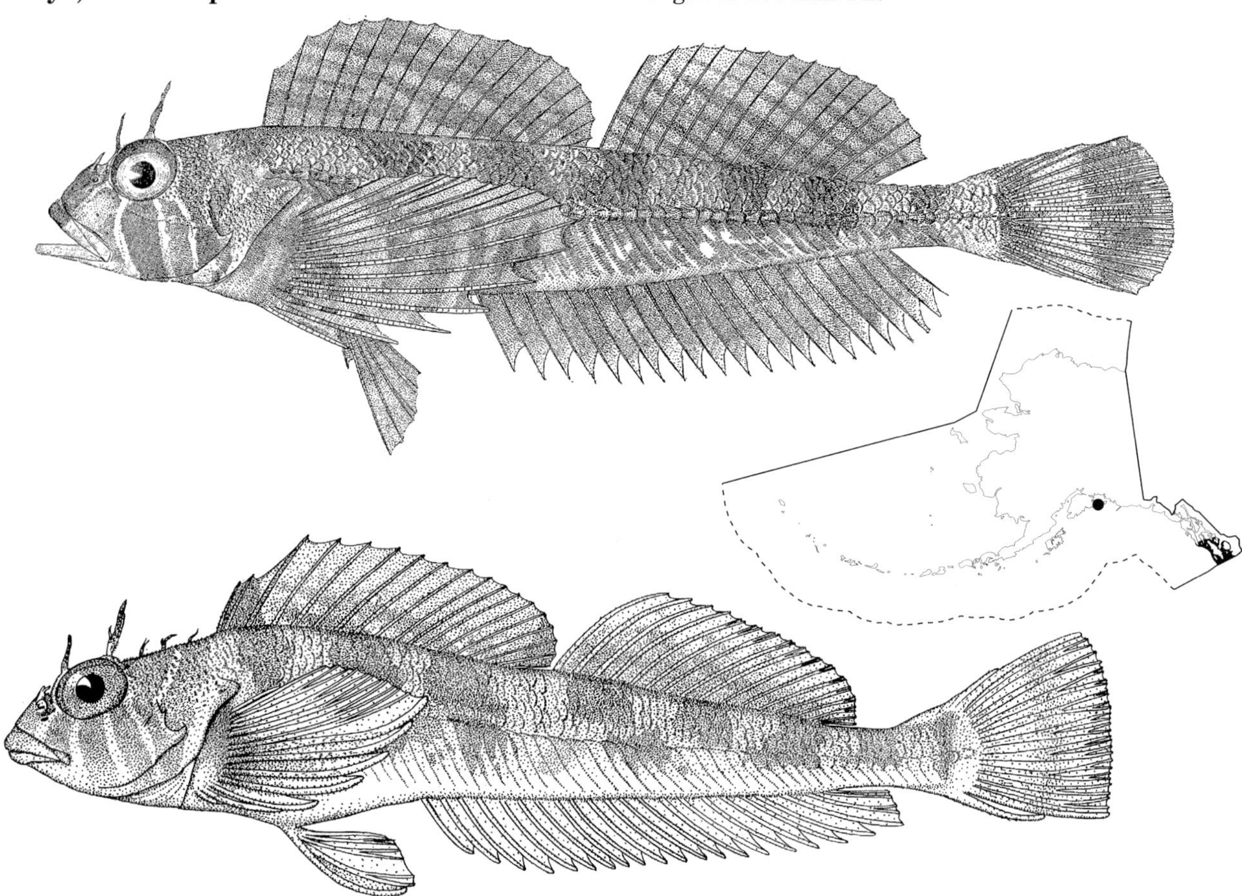

Notes & Sources — *Jordania zonope* Starks, 1895

Because of its superficial appearance *Jordania* is placed near species of the genus *Triglops* in this guide, but its relationships are obscure and further study may indicate *Jordania* has a closer affinity to other genera. The close-set, oblique dermal folds shared with *Triglops* are thought to have been independently derived (Yabe 1985).

Description: Jordan and Evermann 1898:1884–1885; Bolin 1944:9–11; Hart 1973:516–517. Vertebral counts from Howe and Richardson (1978).

Figures: Upper: Jordan and Starks 1895, pl. 79; type, CAS-SU 3124, 102 mm TL, Port Orchard, Puget Sound, Washington. Lower: Bolin 1944, fig. 2. The guide by Humann (1996) includes photographs of three color variations.

Range: Collected from Danger Island at western entrance to Prince William Sound at depth of 22 m by Rosenthal (1980); two of those specimens are in UW 22030. Previously recorded from Port Walter, Baranof Island, approximately 56°23'N, 134°48'W (AB 72-71, AB 72-72) by J. C. Quast (pers. comm. in Peden and Wilson 1976). Numerous collections by Peden and Wilson (1976) north of the British Columbia border suggest the species is common in the southern portion of the Alexander Archipelago. *Jordania zonope* is most commonly collected by scuba divers.

Triglops xenostethus Gilbert, 1896 **scalybreasted sculpin**

Southern Bering Sea and Aleutian Islands; Commander Islands; Kuril Islands.

Rock, gravel, broken shell, and fine gravel bottoms at depths of 62–178 m.

D X–XI + 22–24, A 22–24; Pec 15–18; Pel I,3; LLs 45–47; Vert 43–46.

- Grayish brown dorsally, creamy white ventrally; broad dark saddles across back; peritoneum pale.
- Body slightly compressed.
- Interorbital width 5.8–7.9% HL; orbit length 30.2–37.9% HL; snout length 22.4–28.8% HL.
- Nasal spine present; no spines on top of head.
- Four preopercular spines, all small.
- No cirri on head.
- Caudal fin truncate to slightly rounded.
- Body above lateral line covered with prickles; row of 35–47 enlarged scales dorsolaterally; lateral line with platelike scales; scales below lateral line on 70–98 oblique dermal folds; **cluster of closely set scales on breast**; **folds absent from breast**.
- Vomerine teeth present; palatine teeth absent.
- Anus about halfway between pelvic and anal fins.
- Males with unusually large, anteriorly directed genital papilla, length 13–19% SL.
- Gill membranes united, free from isthmus.
- Length to 97 mm SL (about 114 mm TL).

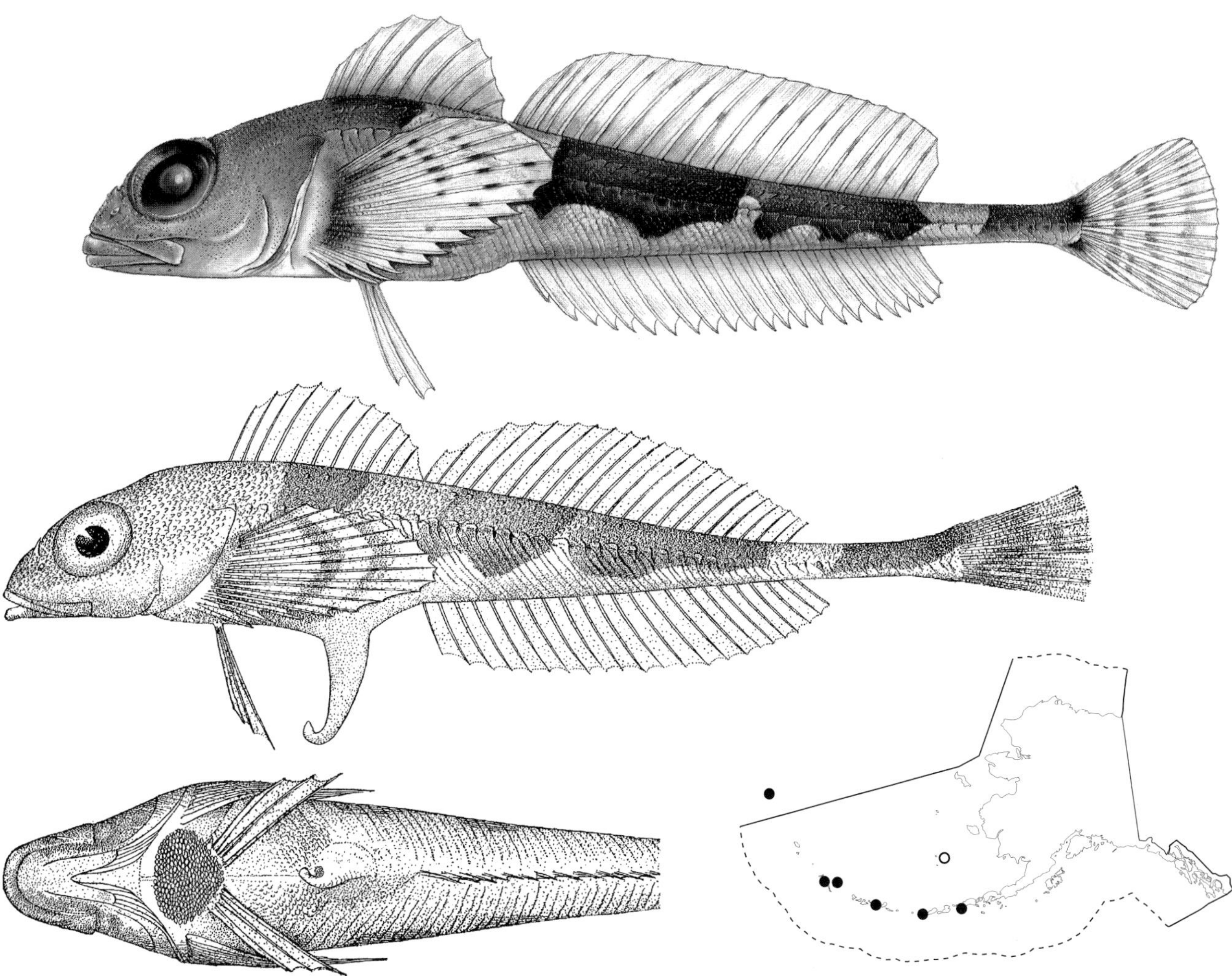

Notes & Sources — *Triglops xenostethus* Gilbert, 1896

Sternias xenostethus: Jordan and Evermann 1898. Replaced in *Triglops* by Wilimovsky (1979ms) and Pietsch (1994).

Description: Gilbert 1896:429; Jordan and Evermann 1898: 1926–1927; Pietsch 1994:344–347.

Figures: Upper: University of British Columbia, artist P. Drukker-Brammall, Oct. 1965; CAS-SU 22346, 73 mm SL, *Albatross* station 4777, Petrel Bank, Bering Sea, Alaska. Lower: Gilbert 1896, pl. 29; holotype (unique), 66 mm TL, *Albatross* station 3220, Unimak Pass, Alaska.

Range: Dots in Alaska on map: specimens Pietsch (1994) examined, and type locality. Gilbert and Burke 1912a: Petrel Bank–Semisopochnoi Island. Baxter 1990ms: Pribilof Islands; specimen not saved. Taken near Commander Islands in early 1950s (ZIN 33664 and 33665; B. A. Sheiko, pers. comm., 30 Jun. 1999). Recorded from northern Kuril Islands at depth of 178 m by Sheiko and Tranbenkova (1998).

Triglops jordani (Jordan & Starks, 1904) **Sakhalin sculpin**

Eastern Bering Sea, records doubtful or not verifiable; western North Pacific Ocean from southern Kamchatka at Avacha Bay to Sea of Okhotsk and Sea of Japan to northern South Korea.

Mud, sand, and pebble bottoms at depths of 22–348 m, usually at depths of 38–256 m.

D IX–XI + 25–29; A 26–29; Pec 18–21; Pel I,3; LLs 49–52; Vert 47–49.

- Grayish brown dorsally, white ventrally; broad, dark saddles across back; peritoneum pale.
- Head and body compressed; snout pointed.
- Interorbital width 9.9–11.6% HL; orbit length 26.7–30.3% HL; snout length 30.0–34.8% HL.
- Nasal spine present; no spines on top of head.
- Four preopercular spines, all small.
- No cirri on head.
- **Caudal fin forked**.
- Body above lateral line densely covered with fine prickly scales; **dorsolateral scale row absent or with 24 or fewer minute scales**; lateral line with large, platelike scales; scales below lateral line on 79–131 oblique dermal folds; 4–11 scale rows on breast; 8–15 close-set rows of tiny scales on eyeball dorsally.
- Vomerine teeth present; palatine teeth absent.
- Anus about halfway between pelvic and anal fins.
- Males with anteriorly directed genital papilla, length 7–10% SL.
- Gill membranes united, free from isthmus.
- Length to 168 mm SL (roughly 198 mm TL).

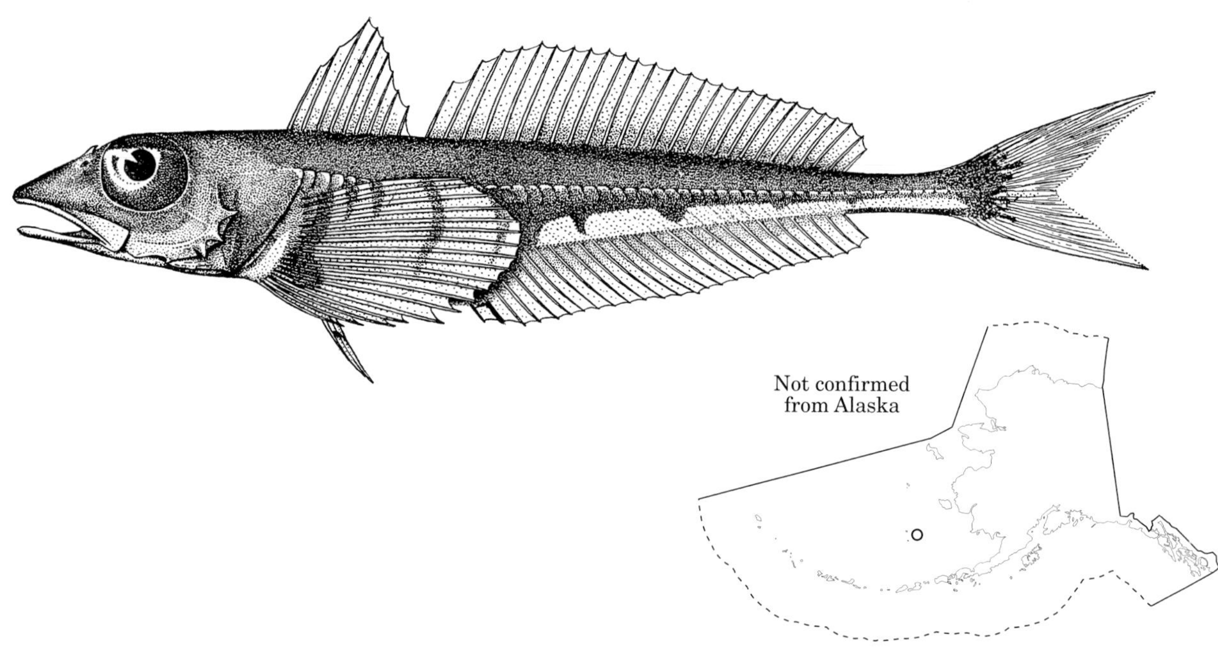

Not confirmed from Alaska

Notes & Sources — *Triglops jordani* (Jordan & Starks (ex Schmidt), 1904)

Elanura jordani Schmidt, 1903. Not available, appeared with name and localities but no description; valid with Jordan and Starks, as above, as authors (Eschmeyer 1998:818).

Prionistius jordani Jordan & Starks, 1904

Triglops jordani: Gilbert and Burke 1912a:50, 51 (new combination).

Description: Jordan and Starks 1904b:252–254; Schmidt 1950:144–145; Lindberg and Krasyukova 1987:177–179; Pietsch 1994:351–354.

Figure: Lindberg and Krasyukova 1987, fig. 107, after Jordan and Starks 1904b; lectotype, female, 74 mm SL, Peter the Great Bay. Pietsch (1994:352) noted that forking of caudal fin is exaggerated in this illustration.

Range: Baxter (1990ms) identified two specimens caught near the Pribilof Islands at about 56°45'N, 169°22'W (NMFS survey, *Miller Freeman,* 19 Apr. 1984, depth 78–86 m) as this species; the data recorded by Baxter are appropriate, but the identification cannot be confirmed because no specimens were saved. Schmidt (1929, 1950) referred to one specimen from Nikolai Inlet in the Bering Sea, but the location is uncertain; there is a Nikolai Cove near Chignik, Alaska, but that is on the Gulf of Alaska, and the St. Nicholas Bay in the northern Anadyr Estuary referred to by Andriashev (1954:395) surely is too far north for *T. jordani*. B. A. Sheiko (pers. comm., 6 Jun. 1999) could not determine the locality from Russian maps, and considers the northernmost record for *T. jordani* to be Avacha Bay. Schmidt (1950) commented that the collection of a specimen from Avacha Bay showed the species occurs in the western Bering Sea, but Avacha Bay is far south of the Bering Sea on the Pacific coast of southeastern Kamchatka. Kim and Youn (1992) recorded the first find from Korea.

Triglops macellus (Bean, 1884) **roughspine sculpin**

Eastern Bering Sea from north of St. Matthew and Nunivak islands, and Aleutian Islands from Rat Islands to eastern Pacific off Washington.

Flat or sloping bottom at depths of 18–275 m, usually at 30–166 m, rarely deeper than 200 m.

D X–XII + 25–29; A 27–31; Pec 15–17; Pel I,3; LLs 49–55; Vert 49–51.

- Dark brown to olive green dorsally, cream ventrally; dark saddles across back; **dark, narrow bars on rays of dorsal and caudal fins and upper part of pectoral fin**; fin membranes clear.
- Head and body depressed; body very narrow and elongate; snout pointed.
- Interorbital width 4.5–7.7% HL; orbit length 27.2–33.0% HL; snout length 26.3–32.4% HL.
- Nasal spine present; no spines on top of head.
- Four preopercular spines; all very short, lowermost obscure.
- No cirri on head.
- Lower pectoral fin rays exserted and produced; **caudal fin emarginate to nearly truncate**.
- Body above lateral line densely covered with fine prickly scales; **dorsolateral scale row absent**; lateral line with large, platelike scales; scales below lateral line on 122–162 oblique dermal folds; **dermal folds absent from breast**; 1–3 close-set rows of tiny scales on eyeball dorsally.
- Vomerine teeth present; palatine teeth absent.
- Anus about halfway between pelvic and anal fins.
- Males with anteriorly directed genital papilla, length 8.5–12.0% SL.
- Gill membranes united, free from isthmus.
- Length to 264 mm SL (about 300 mm TL) or more.

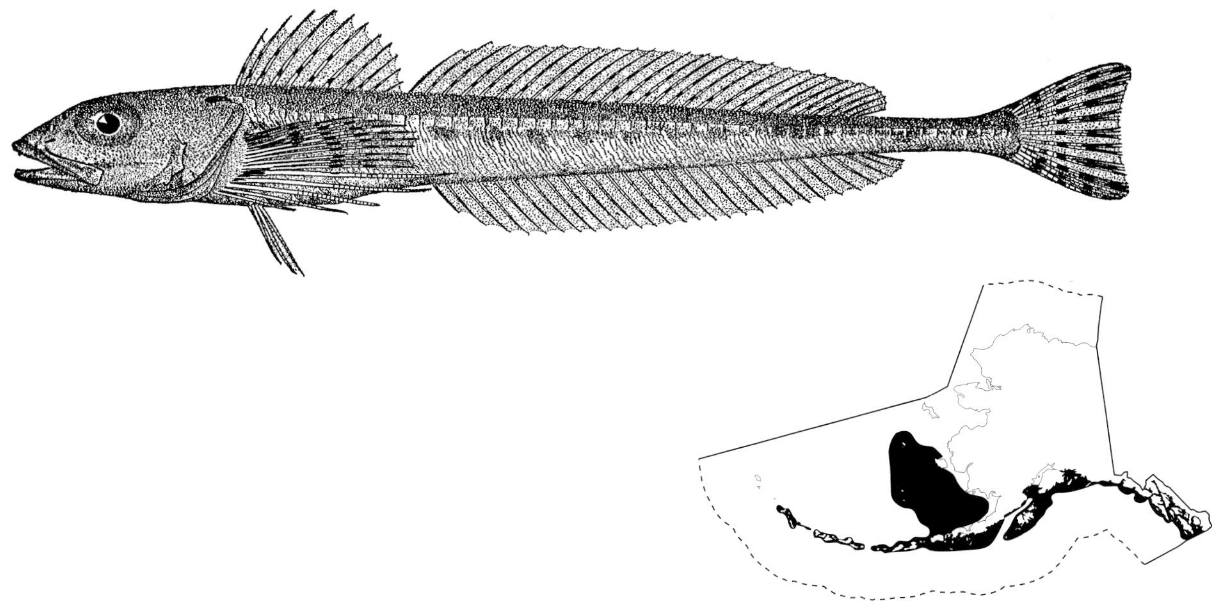

Notes & Sources — *Triglops macellus* (Bean, 1884)
Prionistius macellus Bean, 1884
Triglops macellus: Schmidt 1929:514 (new combination).

Description: Bean 1884a:355–359; Jordan and Evermann 1898:1927–1930; Pietsch 1994:347–350.

Figure: Jordan and Evermann 1900, fig. 701; holotype, USNM 31958, female, 154 mm SL, Carter Bay, British Columbia.

Range: Baxter (1990ms, unpubl. data) examined two specimens (not saved) taken near Kiska Island at 51°46'N, 177°21'E by *Miller Freeman* during NMFS survey, 20 Aug. 1986, depth 148 m. Previously reported as far west in the Aleutians as Amchitka Island (Isakson et al. 1971). Allen and Smith (1988), from 30 years of NMFS bottom trawl surveys, reported the range of the species to extend northwest of St. Matthew and Nunivak islands. Pietsch (1994) listed locality data for numerous museum specimens, many of them from Alaska. Another is UAM 3396, a 252-mm-TL specimen collected off Kodiak Island at 57°33'N, 152°02'W in 1978 by K. J. Frost.

Size: One of Baxter's (1990ms) Kiska Island specimens measured 275.5 mm SL and 312 mm TL. Since the specimen was not saved, the documented maximum size is 264 mm SL (Pietsch 1994; CAS 76537), which, using SL = 88% TL from Baxter's measurements, is about 300 mm TL.

Triglops forficatus (Gilbert, 1896) **scissortail sculpin**

Bering Sea and throughout Aleutian Islands to Cook Inlet; eastern Gulf of Alaska at False Point Retreat; western Bering Sea off Cape Navarin to Commander Islands and Pacific to northern Kuril Islands.

Sand, pebble, gravel, and broken shell bottoms at depths of 20–425 m, usually at 75–200 m.

D X–XI + 28–30; A 29–32; Pec 20–22; Pel I,3; LLs 53–56; Vert 52–54.

- Dark brown dorsally, cream ventrally; usually with dark saddles; **caudal fin tips with black band**; peritoneum with widely spaced dark dots.
- Body slender, elongate, distinctly compressed; snout pointed; lower jaw very slightly projecting.
- Interorbital width 16.2–21.4% HL; orbit length 30.4–34.7% HL; snout length 25.4–29.8% HL.
- Nasal spine present; no spines on top of head.
- Four preopercular spines, all small to obscure.
- No cirri on head.
- Lower pectoral fin rays exserted; **caudal fin deeply forked**.
- Body above lateral line densely covered with fine prickly scales; **dorsolateral scale row well developed**, with 22–32 enlarged scales; lateral line with large, platelike scales; scales below lateral line on 108–138 oblique dermal folds; 5–10 scale rows on breast; 12–22 close-set rows of tiny scales on eyeball dorsally.
- Vomerine teeth present; palatine teeth absent.
- Anus about halfway between pelvic and anal fins.
- Males with anteriorly directed genital papilla, length 7–10% SL.
- Gill membranes united, free from isthmus.
- Length to 275 mm SL (about 323 mm TL).

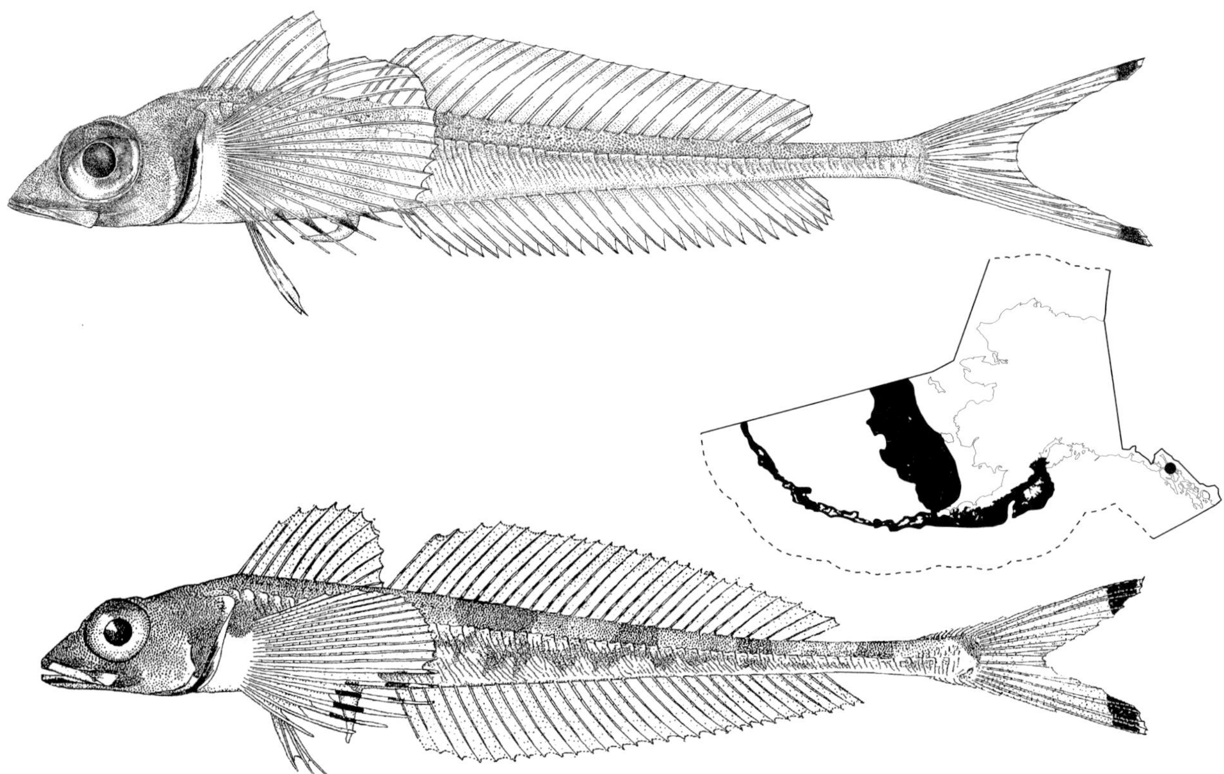

Notes & Sources — *Triglops forficatus* (Gilbert, 1896)
Elanura forficata Gilbert, 1896

Description: Gilbert 1896:430–431; Jordan and Evermann 1898:1930–1932; Pietsch 1994:354–357.

Figures: Upper: University of British Columbia, artist P. Drukker-Brammall, Aug. 1965; UBC 62-526, male, 143 mm SL, off Kodiak Island east of Cape Alitak. Lower: Gilbert 1896, pl. 30; lectotype, MCZ 28266, male, 169 mm SL, *Albatross* station 3214, south of Sanak Islands, Alaska.

Range: Allen and Smith (1988) reported catches north to Cape Navarin in the Bering Sea and east to Albatross Bank northeast of Kodiak Island from 30 years of NMFS bottom trawl surveys. Pietsch (1994) gave locality data for more than 200 specimens, most of them from Alaska and ranging from the Bering Sea and west of Attu Island (UW 21362, 52°48'N, 172°37'E) to northeast of Kodiak Island; one specimen (OSU 8734) was taken far east of the others off False Point Retreat in southeastern Alaska. (Two disjunct sites in southern Gulf of Alaska on Pietsch's [1994:356] map are errors from incorrect cataloging data.) Baxter (1990ms) collected specimens (not saved) from Kachemak Bay, Cook Inlet. Fedorov and Sheiko (2002) listed *T. forficatus* among the Commander Islands ichthyofauna.

Size: Using SL = 85% TL for *T. forficatus* from Baxter (1990ms), the documented maximum size of 275 mm SL (HUMZ 117596; Pietsch 1994) is about 323 mm TL.

Triglops scepticus Gilbert, 1896 — **spectacled sculpin**

Bering Sea and throughout Aleutian Islands to southeastern Alaska at Cape Ommaney; western Bering Sea from Capes Navarin and Olyutorskiy to Commander Islands and to southern Sea of Okhotsk, Tatar Strait, Pacific Ocean off northern Honshu, and Sea of Japan to North Korea at Wonsan.

Mud, sand, pebble, gravel, and broken shell bottoms at depths of 25–925 m, usually at 100–380 m.

D X–XII + 21–24; A 22–25; Pec 18–20; Pel I,3; LLs 32–48; Vert 45–46.

- Brown dorsally, cream ventrally; dark saddles usually present, sometimes very faint; irregular dark blotches on sides and fins; **caudal fin with broad, dark bands**; peritoneum densely covered with black dots.
- Body relatively short and stout, distinctly compressed; snout blunt; **lower jaw slightly protruding**.
- Interorbital width 4.9–9.8% HL; orbit length 33.3–46.6% HL; snout length 20.9–28.1% HL.
- Nasal spine present; no spines on top of head.
- Four preopercular spines, all small.
- No cirri on head.
- **Caudal fin more or less truncate**.
- **Exposed portion of maxilla covered with rough scales**; body above lateral line densely covered with fine prickly scales; row of 30–60 enlarged scales dorsolaterally, may be indistinct; lateral line with large, platelike scales; scales below lateral line on 145–198 oblique dermal folds; 14–23 scale rows on breast; **scales on eyeball anteriorly, dorsally, and ventrally**, surrounding pupil in some specimens.
- Vomerine teeth present; palatine teeth absent.
- Anus about halfway between pelvic and anal fins.
- Males with anteriorly directed genital papilla, length 11–24% SL.
- Gill membranes united, free from isthmus.
- Length to 308 mm SL (about 354 mm TL).

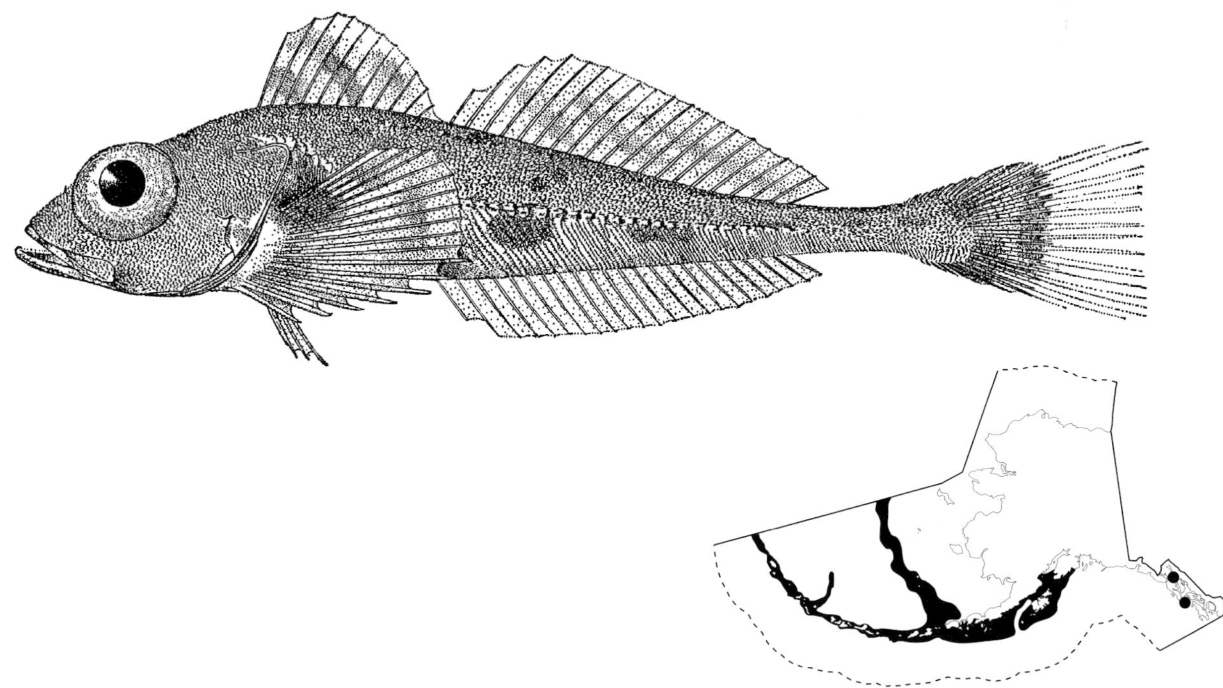

Notes & Sources — *Triglops scepticus* Gilbert, 1896

Description: Gilbert 1896:428–429; Jordan and Evermann 1898:1925–1926; Pietsch 1994:358–361.

Figure: Gilbert 1896, pl. 28; lectotype, CAS-SU 2426, female, 138 mm SL, *Albatross* station 3339, south of Alaska Peninsula, 54°46'N, 157°43'W.

Range: Taken in NMFS bottom trawl surveys west to Stalemate Bank and north to Navarin Canyon (Allen and Smith 1988). Capture localities for nearly 700 specimens examined by Pietsch (1994) extended in the Bering Sea to near Cape Navarin, throughout the Aleutian chain and over Bowers Ridge, south to southern Honshu, Japan, and east to the tip of the Kenai Peninsula and Gulf of Alaska east of Kodiak Island. Slightly farther east, USNM 208312 is from Port Bainbridge, east coast of Kenai Peninsula, 59°56'N, 148°24'W. A few of Pietsch's (1994) specimens were from southeastern Alaska off False Point Retreat (OSU 8717) and off Cape Ommaney (AB 90-14 and 90-15). Shinohara et al. (1996) recorded *T. scepticus* from the Pacific coast of northern Honshu. Kim and Youn (1992), citing Mori (1952), reported it from Wonsan, North Korea.

Size: Using SL = 87% TL for this species from Baxter's (1990ms) measurements gives 354 mm TL for the largest specimen examined by Pietsch (1994).

Triglops nybelini Jensen, 1944 — bigeye sculpin

Arctic Ocean from western Canada off Mackenzie Bay and in Amundsen Gulf, east to Baffin Island, Greenland, Jan Mayen Island, and Spitsbergen, to Barents Sea, Kara Sea, and Laptev Sea.

Silty or muddy bottoms at depths of 9–930 m; usually taken deeper than 200 m, only occasionally in inshore waters.

D X–XII + 24–29; A 24–28; Pec 20–23; Pel I,3; LLp 48–52; Vert 46–49.

- Dark brown dorsally, cream ventrally; broken or complete dark lines along side, some below lateral line; **rarely any trace of dark saddles**; **base of caudal fin with small dark spot ventrally and usually dorsally**; dark spots on rays of lower portion of pectoral fin; peritoneum densely covered with small dark dots.
- Body relatively short and stout, distinctly compressed; head compressed; snout pointed; **lower jaw slightly protruding**.
- Interorbital width 10.8–14.6% HL; orbit length 32.9–40.0% HL; snout length 24.8–29.5% HL.
- Nasal spine present; no spines on top of head.
- Four preopercular spines, all small.
- No cirri on head.
- **Caudal fin truncate to slightly rounded**.
- Body above lateral line densely covered with fine prickly scales; row of 29–47 enlarged scales dorsolaterally, in large specimens weakly differentiated; lateral line with large, platelike scales; scales below lateral line on 63–95 oblique dermal folds; 10–15 scale rows on breast; 12–16 close-set rows of tiny scales on eyeball dorsally.
- Vomerine teeth present; palatine teeth absent.
- Anus about halfway between pelvic and anal fins.
- Males with anteriorly directed genital papilla, length 13–16% SL.
- Gill membranes united, free from isthmus.
- Length to 170 mm TL.

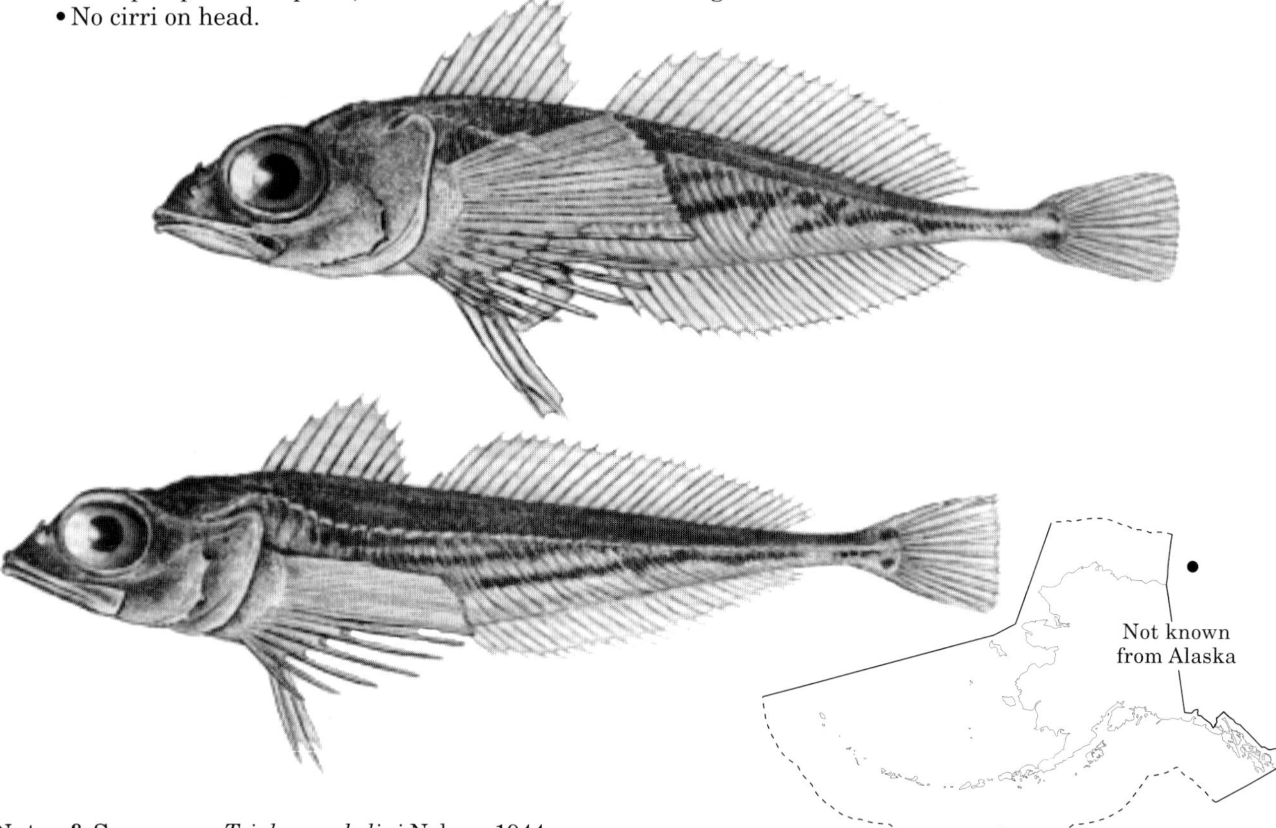

Notes & Sources — *Triglops nybelini* Nelsen, 1944

Until Jensen (1944) described *T. nybelini,* this species and *T. pingelii* were often confused. Characters distinguishing *T. nybelini* from *T. pingelii* include the protruding lower jaw; short snout and long orbit; high number of pectoral fin rays; heavily pigmented peritoneum; overall dark coloration, nearly always lacking dark saddles; and middle pelvic fin ray longest in both sexes (3rd ray longest in both sexes in *T. pingelii*).

Description: Jensen 1944:24–29; Andriashev 1949:12–15; Scott and Scott 1988:510–511; Pietsch 1994:361–365.

Figures: Jensen 1944, pl. 3; type series, western Greenland. Upper: male, 123 mm TL. Lower: female, 120 mm TL.

Range: Nearest records are from east of the Alaska–Yukon boundary in the Beaufort Sea north of the Mackenzie River Delta. Hunter et al. (1984:pl. 16) indicated a record from that area on their map, and Pietsch (1994) examined a specimen (ROM 51605) collected later (in 1986) from the same area, at 70°40'N, 135°51'W, depth 232–240 m. Hunter et al.'s (1984) map also indicates several records from Amundsen Gulf, so the species does not seem to be particularly rare in western Canada and probably occurs in the Beaufort Sea off Alaska as well.

Triglops metopias Gilbert & Burke, 1912 — **highbrow sculpin**

Aleutian Islands off Amchitka and Semisopochnoi islands to southeastern Alaska at Auke Bay.

Sand, silty sand, fine gravel, pebble, and broken shell bottoms at depths of 15–132 m.

D X–XI + 24–28; A 24–28; Pec 19–22; Pel I,3; LLs 48–52; Vert 47–49.

- Brownish gray dorsally, white ventrally; vague dark saddles across back; distinct dark blotches below lateral line; male with dark spot near tips of dorsal and ventral caudal fin rays; **peritoneum pale or with a few widely spaced dark dots**.
- Head and body compressed; body relatively short and stout; snout pointed; jaws equal or upper slightly protruding.
- **Interorbital width 11.2–17.7% HL**; orbit length 26.9–32.5% HL; snout length 27.7–36.0% HL.
- Nasal spine present; no spines on top of head.
- Four preopercular spines; all small, uppermost sharp, lower three blunt.
- No cirri on head.
- **Caudal fin emarginate**.
- Body above lateral line densely covered with fine prickly scales; **dorsolateral scale row well developed**, with 18–39 enlarged scales; lateral line with large, platelike scales; **scales below lateral line on 66–105 oblique dermal folds**; 0–9 scale rows on breast; 10–12 close-set rows of tiny scales on eyeball dorsally.
- Vomerine teeth present; palatine teeth absent.
- Anus about halfway between pelvic and anal fins.
- Males with anteriorly directed genital papilla, 7–10% SL in males over 100 mm SL, 1–4% SL in smaller males.
- Gill membranes united, free from isthmus.
- Length to 167 mm SL.

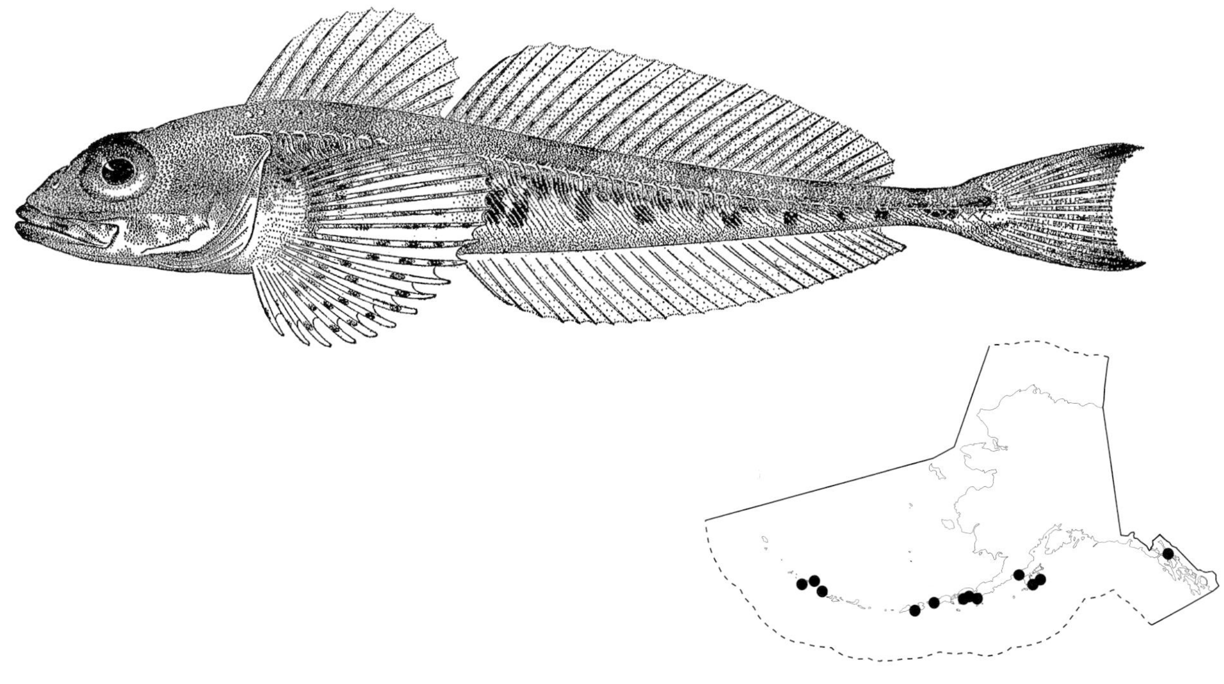

Notes & Sources — *Triglops metopias* Gilbert & Burke, 1912

Description: Gilbert and Burke 1912a:50–51; Pietsch 1994: 365–368.

Figure: Gilbert and Burke 1912a, fig. 8; holotype, male, 123 mm SL, 144 mm TL, *Albatross* station 4777, Petrel Bank, Bering Sea, Alaska.

Range: Not well represented in permanent collections. Sixteen lots, including 53 specimens, were listed by Pietsch (1994). Those, with an additional specimen from Kachemak Bay east of Homer Spit (UBC 62-995), for a total of 17 lots, are the only known specimens. Quast (1968) recorded the minimum depth of 15.5 m, for a specimen taken in a shrimp try net on silty sand bottom in Auke Bay (AB 63-182). Maximum known depth is for specimens recorded by Gilbert and Burke (1912a) from *Albatross* station 4779, taken by beam trawl on bottom of sand, pebbles, and broken shell at 99–102 m.

Triglops pingelii Reinhardt, 1837 **ribbed sculpin**

Beaufort and Chukchi seas to Aleutian Islands at Stalemate Bank to Puget Sound, Washington; and western Bering Sea to Commander Islands and Sea of Japan to North Korea at Wonsan; circumpolar.

Sand, pebble, gravel, and rocky bottoms at depths of 4.6–482 m, most often at 20–150 m.

D X–XIII + 23–26; A 21–27; Pec 17–21; Pel I,3; LLs 47–51; Vert 45–51.

- Olive brown dorsally, whitish ventrally; vague black saddles across back; **black spots or streaks below lateral line, connected in males to form broken or continuous stripe**; caudal fin with dark spots dorsally and ventrally near its tips; peritoneum pale or with few, widely spaced dark dots.
- Head and body compressed; body relatively short and stout; snout pointed; upper jaw slightly protruding.
- **Interorbital width 6.5–10.0% HL**; orbit length 25.6–31.6% HL; snout length 26.5–33.3% HL.
- Nasal spine present; no spines on top of head.
- Four preopercular spines; all small, upper three directed posteriorly, lowest directed ventrally.
- No cirri on head.
- **Caudal fin truncate to slightly rounded**.
- Body above lateral line densely covered with fine prickly scales; **dorsolateral scale row well developed**, with 26–36 enlarged scales; lateral line with large, platelike scales; **scales below lateral line on 49–69 oblique dermal folds**; 2–10 scale rows on breast; 10–12 close-set rows of tiny scales on eyeball dorsally.
- Vomerine teeth present; palatine teeth absent.
- Anus about halfway between pelvic and anal fins.
- Males with anteriorly directed genital papilla, length 5.8–11.7% SL.
- Gill membranes united, free from isthmus.
- Length to 202 mm SL (about 232 mm TL) or more.

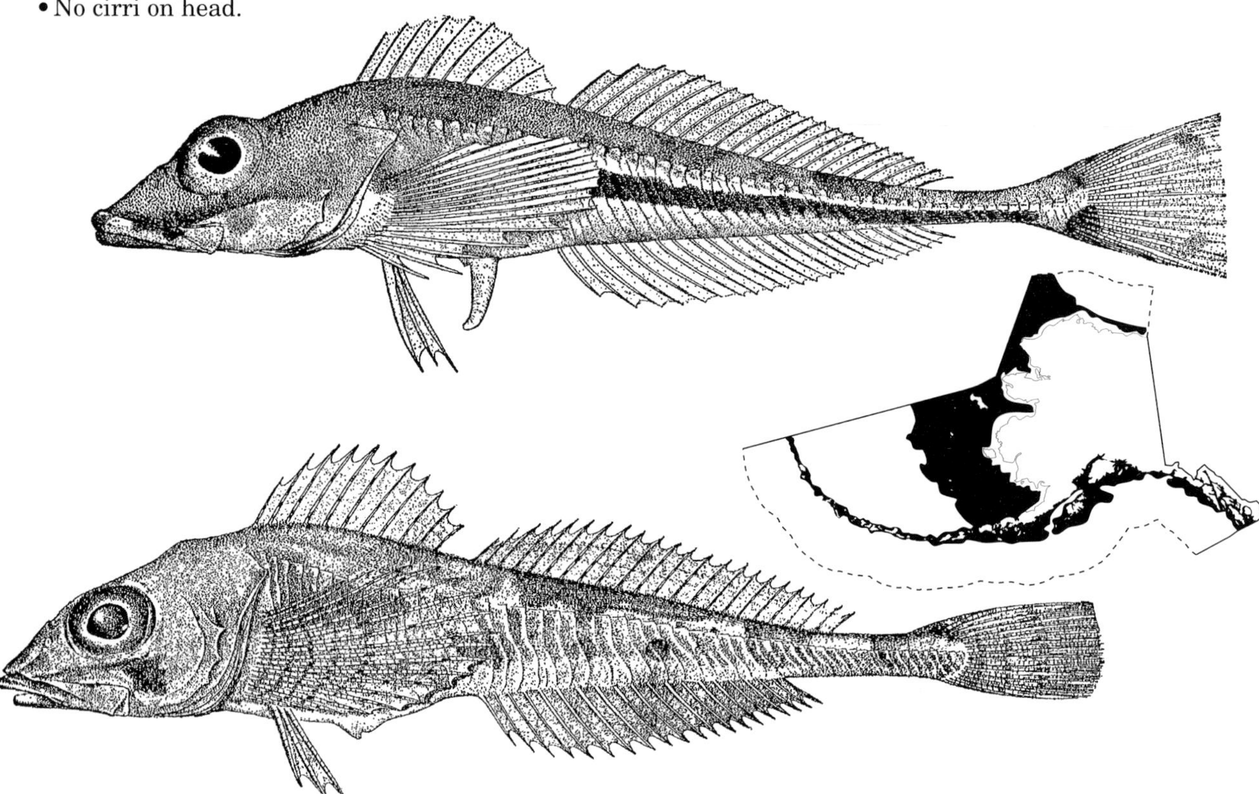

Notes & Sources — *Triglops pingelii* Reinhardt, 1837
Triglops beani Gilbert, 1896

Description: Gilbert 1896:426–427; Jordan and Starks 1904b:250–252; Andriashev 1949:6–9 of transl., 1954:350–353; Schmidt 1950:142–143; Pietsch 1994:374–379.

Figures: Upper: Gilbert 1896, pl. 28; syntype of *T. beani*, male, 123 mm SL, *Albatross* station 3296, Bristol Bay, Alaska. Lower: Goode and Bean 1896, fig. 256; female, off Halifax, Nova Scotia.

Range: The most widely distributed species of the genus and one of the most abundant sculpins in Alaska. Range in the eastern Bering Sea and Pacific Ocean was mapped by Allen and Smith (1988) from 617 occurrences in NMFS bottom trawl surveys. Pietsch (1994) gave locality data for 819 museum specimens, including hundreds of locations in Alaska. Hunter et al. (1984) mapped additional records from eastern Beaufort Sea near Alaska. Least common in Alaska in eastern Gulf of Alaska. Reported by Kim and Youn (1992), citing Mori (1952), from Wonsan, North Korea.

Size: A specimen obtained near Amchitka Island measured 211 mm SL, 242 mm TL (Baxter 1990ms). It was not saved, so verifiable maximum size is 202 mm SL (HUMZ 76742), largest of 819 specimens examined by Pietsch (1994); using SL = 87% TL from Baxter (1990ms) gives 232 mm TL.

Paricelinus hopliticus Eigenmann & Eigenmann, 1889 — **thornback sculpin**

Northern British Columbia near Banks Island, Hecate Strait, to southern California at Cortes Bank off San Diego.

Nearshore rocky bottom at depths to 183 m, usually deeper than 20 m.

D XII–XIII + 19–20; A 23–24; Pec 14–15; Pel I,5; LLs 44–45; Vert 42.

- Olive green dorsally, grayish ventrally; indistinct brownish bars on back; dusky purplish blotches on side; yellow-brown flecks along lateral line, with blue spots below.
- Nasal spine strong; **spines present on occiput and behind and below eye**.
- Three preopercular spines; sharp and slightly curved, middle spine longest.
- Large, fringed postocular cirrus; cirri posterior to maxilla and on cheek.
- **Anal fin longer-based than soft-rayed dorsal fin**, origin below insertion of spinous dorsal fin; lower pectoral rays exserted and produced.
- Prickly scales covering most of body and head; lateral line scales enlarged; **single row of enlarged scales along base of dorsal fin, each with prominent, recurved spine**.
- Vomerine and palatine teeth present.
- Anus close to origin of anal fin.
- Gill membranes united, free from isthmus.
- Length to 194 mm TL.

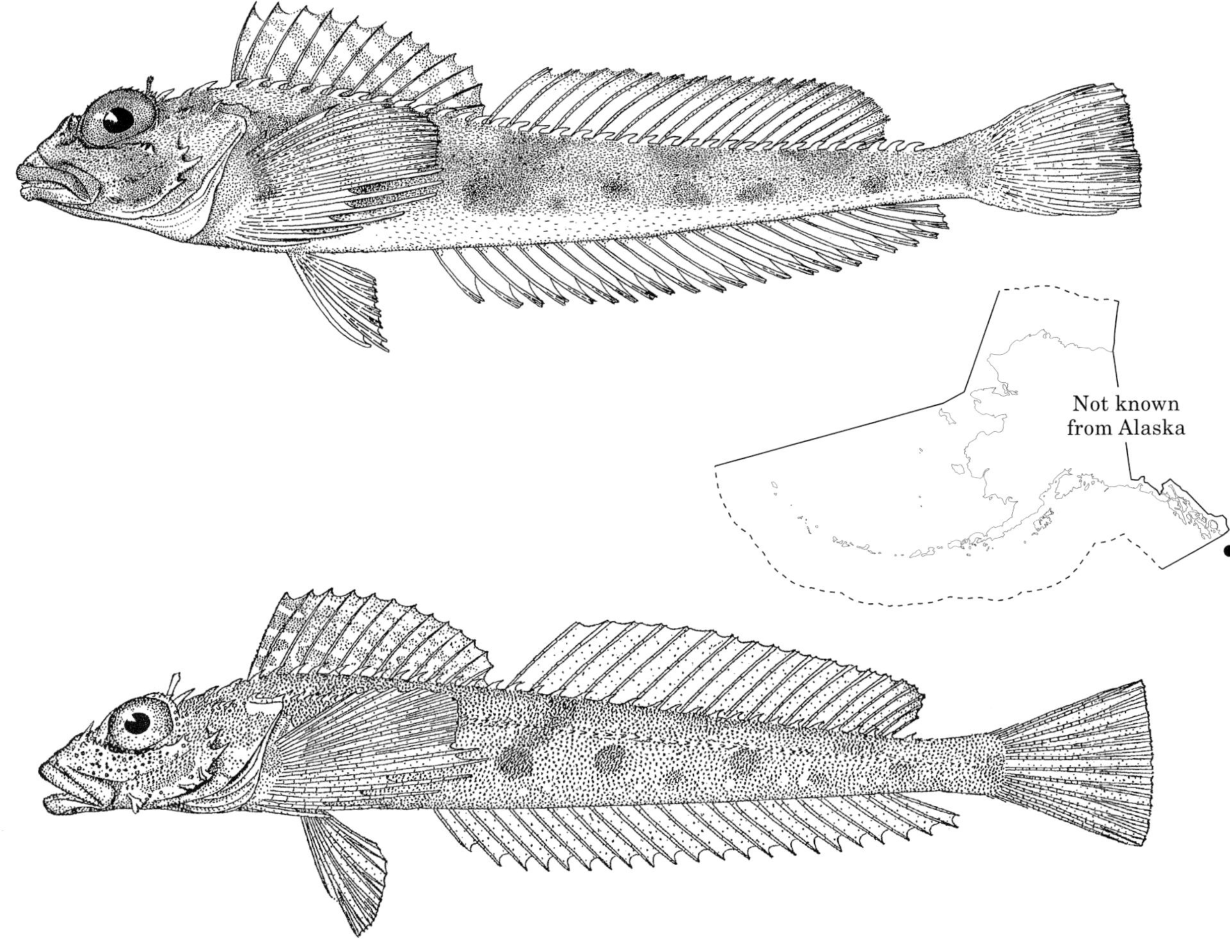

Notes & Sources — *Paricelinus hopliticus* Eigenmann & Eigenmann, 1889
Paricelinus thoburni Gilbert, 1896
Alcidea thoburni: Jordan and Evermann 1898, 1900 (new genus).

Description: Jordan and Evermann 1898:1885–1888; Bolin 1944:11–13; Hart 1973:532–533; Howe and Richardson 1978 (some meristics); Eschmeyer and Herald 1983:179.

Figures: Upper: Bolin 1944, fig. 3. Lower: Gilbert 1896, pl. 30, middle figure; holotype (unique) of *Paricelinus thoburni,* USNM 64324, off Oregon.

Range: Nearest record to Alaska is from approximately 53°12'N, 130°16'W, near Banks Island, Hecate Strait, British Columbia (Barraclough and Ketchen 1963). Lamb and Edgell (1986) reported that scuba divers see this species below 20 m in the Pacific Northwest and that, contrary to previous reports, it is not rare.

Size: Miller and Lea 1972.

Scorpaenichthys marmoratus (Ayres, 1854) **cabezon**

Southeastern Alaska in vicinity of Sitka to central Baja California at Point Abreojos.

Intertidal area and to water depth of 76 m on hard bottoms; small and intermediate sized individuals often found in tidepools, larger fish found in deeper water; adults move inshore to feed at high tide.

D VIII–XII + 15–19; A 11–14; Pec 14–16; Pel I,5 (rarely 4); LLp 71–88 + 4–8; Vert 35–36.

- Cherry red to green or brown, blotched and reticulated with various shades of yellow and brown to green and blue; flesh bluish, but variable.
- Head large; body robust, skin thick.
- Nasal spines strong; no spines on top of head.
- Three preopercular spines; all small and simple, upper two longest, third sometimes obscure.
- **Median, flaplike cirrus on snout**; large, fringed postocular cirrus; fleshy cirrus at posterior end of maxilla.
- Spinous and soft portions of dorsal fin nearly or completely separate; profile of spinous portion depressed near middle; pelvic fin in males not greatly lengthened or with conspicuous ctenii.
- **Skin smooth, without scales or prickles** (scales are present along lateral line, but deeply embedded and not always readily discernible).
- Vomerine and palatine teeth present.
- Gill membranes united, free from isthmus.
- Length to 990 mm TL; weight to 13.6 kg.

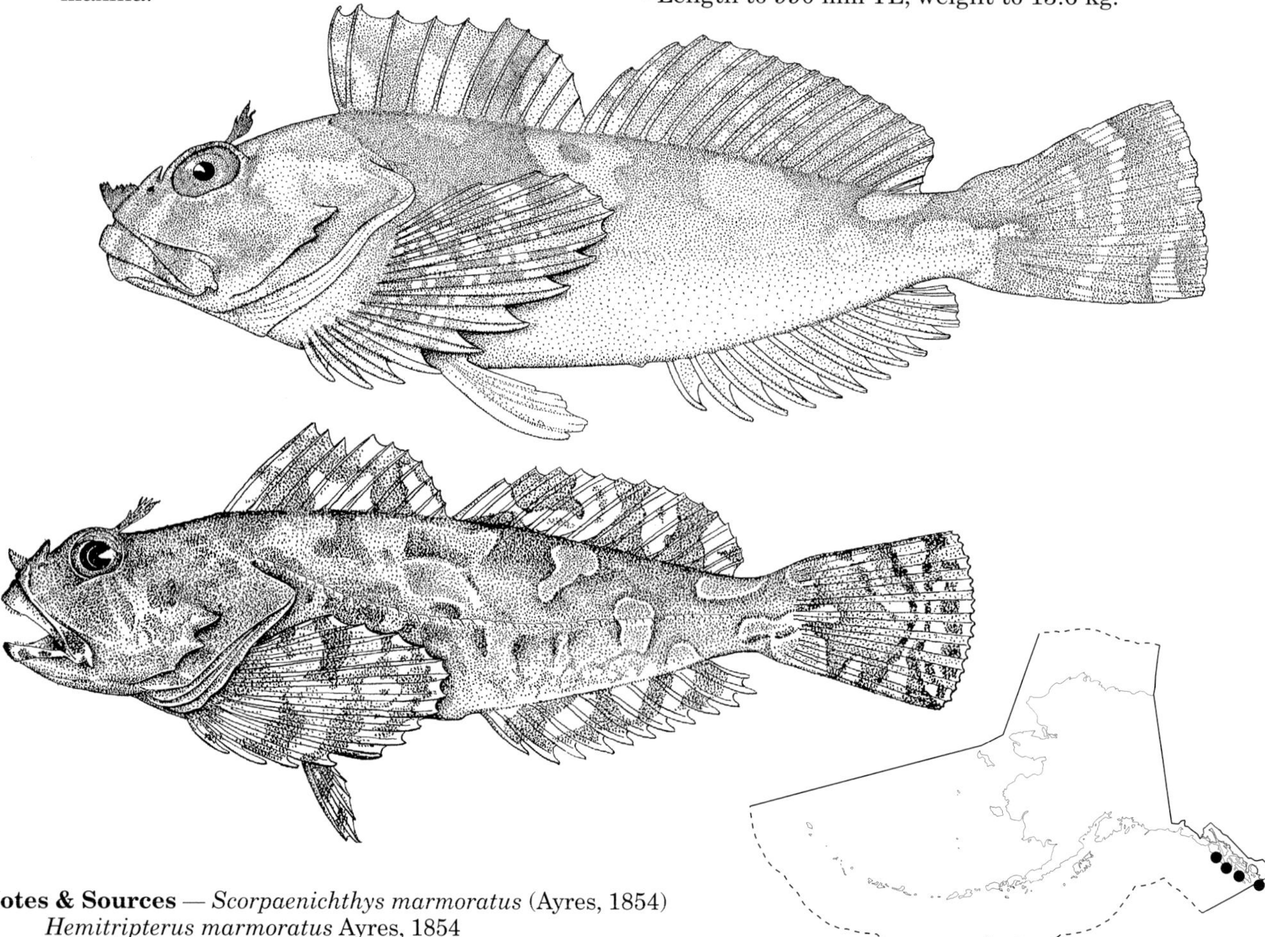

Notes & Sources — *Scorpaenichthys marmoratus* (Ayres, 1854)
Hemitripterus marmoratus Ayres, 1854
Caution: Cabezon are good to eat, but the roe is poisonous.

Description: Jordan and Evermann 1898:1889; Bolin 1944:6–8; O'Connell 1953; Hart 1973:540–541; Howe and Richardson 1978 (dorsal fin ray and vertebral counts).

Figures: Upper: Bolin 1944, fig. 1. Lower: Hart 1973:540; 180 mm TL, Saturna Island, British Columbia.

Range: Quast (1968) recorded extension of known range into Alaska based on a small specimen (93 mm SL; AB 64-954) from Samsing Cove, near Sitka. Rogers et al. (1986) reported cabezon were found in southeastern Alaska in OCSEAP studies during 1976–1982, but did not give specific documentation. There are anecdotal reports of adult cabezon being caught by recreational fishers and observed from a manned submersible and by scuba divers in the Sitka and Craig–Klawock areas, and larvae have been collected off Cape Muzon. The ABL has recently collected juveniles from Sandy Cove (near Sitka), Klawock, and Little Port Walter (B. L. Wing, pers. comm., 21 Jun. 2001). Scuba diving in northernmost British Columbia, Peden and Wilson (1976) collected three small specimens (79–87 mm SL) at one site. Dots on the above map represent the records of juveniles. Evidently, the species is well distributed off southern southeastern Alaska coasts, although not commonly caught. Clemens and Wilby (1961) reported cabezon to be common in British Columbia south of the Queen Charlotte Islands.

Hemilepidotus papilio (Bean, 1880) **butterfly sculpin**

Southeastern Chukchi Sea to Aleutian Islands west to Buldir Island; western Bering Sea to Commander Islands and Pacific off Kamchatka to Sea of Okhotsk and northern Sea of Japan off Hokkaido.

Intertidal area, sometimes in tidepools, and to depth of 320 m; usually at depths shallower than 150 m.

D XI–XIII,19–22; A 16–18; Pec 16–18; Pel I,4; LLp 49–65; PC 4–7; Vert 40.

- Males yellowish or gray and black; females brownish to reddish; usually with 4 darker bars on back and extending onto dorsal fin.
- Nasal spine moderate; postocular and occipital spines prominent and rounded.
- Four preopercular spines; second spine longest.
- Maxillary and other cirri short or absent.
- Dorsal fin continuous; **first 3 dorsal fin spines increasing in height, no conspicuous notch in fin profile between 3rd and 4th spines**; pelvic fin of males very long and with conspicuous ctenii.
- Three bands of scales, plus anal scale row above anal fin; **scales of ventral band much smaller than those of other bands**; **rows of ventral scale band and anal row evenly spaced between lateral line and anal fin**; usually 3 (2–4) rows in dorsal band; 15–26 scales in row above lateral line; about 4 rows in ventral band.
- Vomerine and palatine teeth present.
- Gill membranes united, attached anteriorly to isthmus leaving wide free portion posteriorly.
- Length to 300 mm SL (about 370 mm TL).

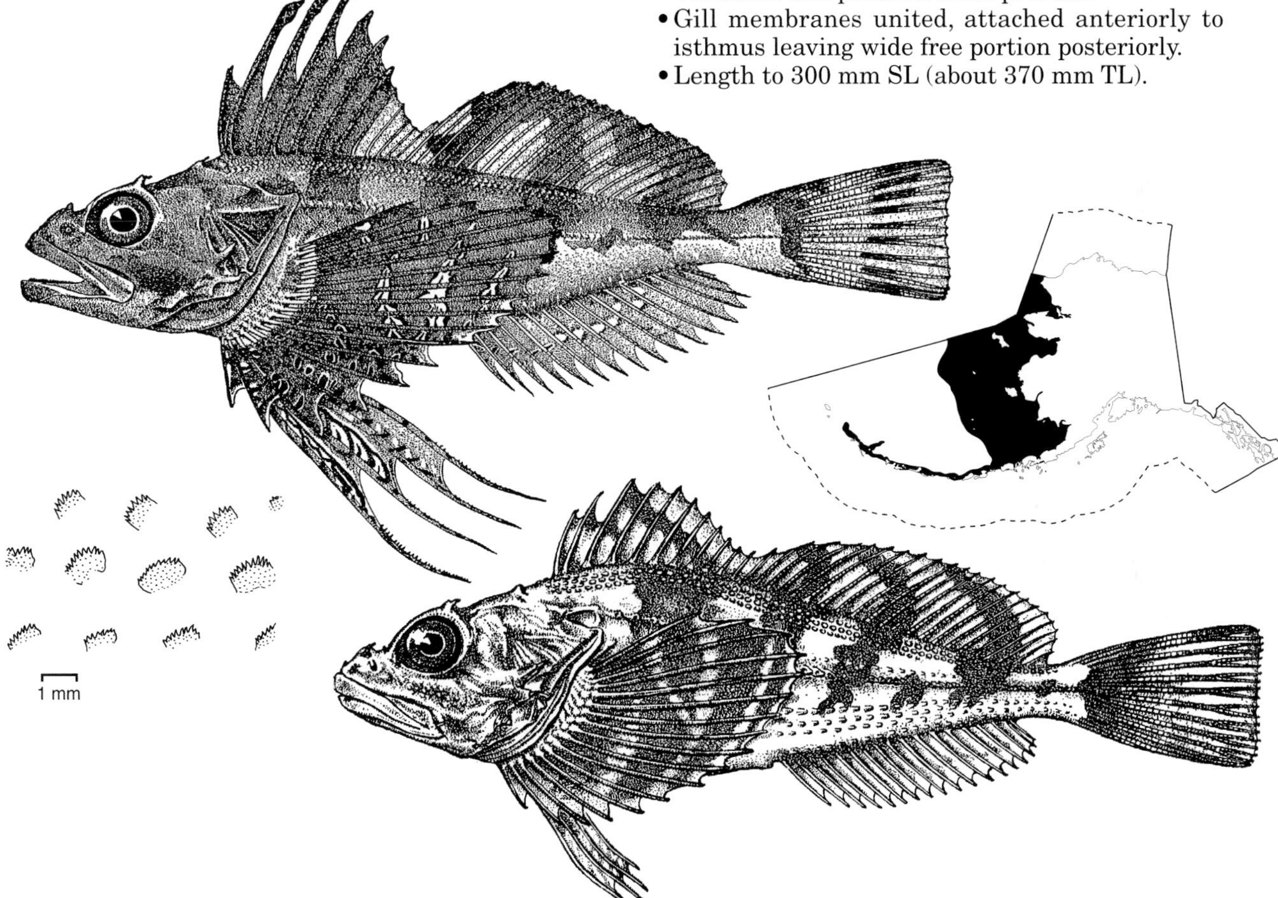

Notes & Sources — *Hemilepidotus (Melletes) papilio* (Bean, 1880)
Melletes papilio Bean, 1880
The name *Melletes* means "a loiterer, from its habit of remaining in shallow pools when the tide recedes, where it is taken by hand in great quantities by the natives" (Bean 1880).

Description: Bean 1880:354–357; Jordan and Evermann 1898:1932–1934; Peden 1978:41–43.

Figures: Upper: Jordan and Evermann 1900, fig. 703; holotype (unique), male, 185 mm SL, St. Paul Island. Lower: Lindberg and Krasyukova 1987, fig. 111, after Andriashev 1954; female, 162 mm TL, Bering Sea off Cape Navarin. Scales in dorsal scale band: Peden 1978, fig. 8.

Range: Reported from Bering Strait by Andriashev (1937). AB 63-215 (38 mm SL) is from eastern Chukchi Sea at 67°30'N, 166°47'W. Reported from northeastern Chukchi Sea by Barber et al. (1997), without specific localities. UAM uncataloged specimens with appropriate diagnostic characters include one (59 mm TL) taken at 66°51'N, 168°03'W, depth 30 m, in 1989; and one (141 mm TL) from 68°25'N, 166°40'W, 17 m, in 1991. Found west in Aleutian Islands to Buldir Island in NMFS surveys (Allen and Smith 1988). Easternmost voucher may be UBC 65-1285, from 56°30'N, 165°30'W. Probably occurs throughout the Aleutian chain. Fedorov and Sheiko (2002) reported it to be common at the Commander Islands and gave a maximum depth of 320 m.

Hemilepidotus spinosus Ayres, 1854 **brown Irish lord**

Northern Gulf of Alaska at Kachemak Bay, Cook Inlet, to southern California at Santa Barbara Islands.

Intertidal and to depth of 97 m along rocky, wave-swept coasts; often among weed-covered rocks of outer coast tidepools.

D XI,18–20; A 14–16; Pec 14–16; Pel I,4; LLp 57–67; PC 4; Vert 36.

- Shades of brown with dark mottling; top of head often with brick red; whitish ventrally; dark saddles; fins mottled with blackish and reddish.
- Nasal spine large, blunt, skin-covered; ridges on head, becoming rugose in large specimens.
- Four preopercular spines; upper two or three longest and stout, fourth small and sharp.
- Cirri on head numerous, some broad and large; small cirri along lateral line, with a few white flap-like cirri posteriorly.
- Dorsal fin continuous; 3rd dorsal spine shorter than 2nd and 4th, forming obvious notch in fin profile.
- Three bands of scales; anal row absent; all scales of bands similar in size; **6–8 rows in dorsal scale band** below spinous dorsal fin; 18–37 scales in row above lateral line; **4 or 5 rows in ventral band**.
- Vomerine and palatine teeth present.
- **Gill membranes united, joined to isthmus without leaving a free margin posteriorly**.
- Length to 290 mm TL.

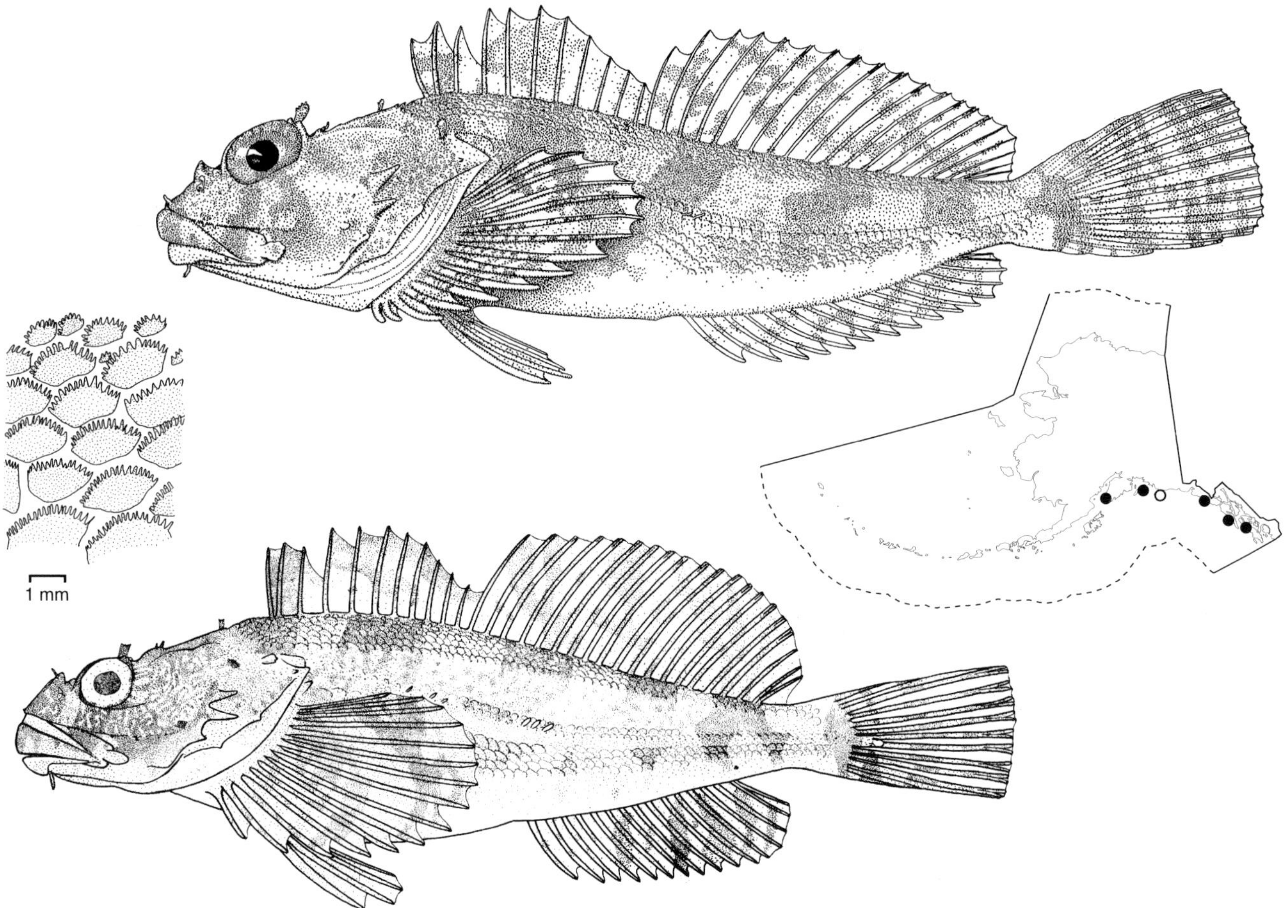

Notes & Sources — *Hemilepidotus (Calycilepidotus) spinosus* Ayres, 1854
Calycilepidotus spinosus Ayres, 1855

Description: Jordan and Evermann 1898:1936–1937; Bolin 1944:15–17; Hart 1973:504–505; Peden 1978:18–23.

Figures: Upper: Bolin 1944, fig. 4. Lower: Peden 1978, fig. 6; female, about 203 mm TL. Scales in dorsal scale band: Peden 1978, fig. 8.

Range: Record from Puffin Bay, 50 miles south of Sitka by Peden (1966b) was a northern extension of known range from British Columbia and the first known occurrence in Alaskan waters. Additional southeastern Alaska record was referred to in a general statement by Quast and Hall (1972); this was based on AB 70-146, a specimen from Eliza Harbor, Frederick Sound. Dames and Moore (1979) found *H. spinosus* at Kachemak Bay and Rosenthal (1980) claimed an extension of the known range north to Prince William Sound off Zaikof Point; these evidently were the basis of Rogers et al.'s (1986) listings from Cook Inlet and Prince William Sound. A UBC specimen (UBC 72-4) taken near Cape Fairweather at 58°58'N, 138°00'W is identified as *H. spinosus*. R. Baxter (unpubl. data) examined a specimen (145 mm SL, 179 mm TL; not saved) taken off Kayak Island during a NMFS bottom trawl survey in 1987.

Size: Eschmeyer and Herald 1983.

Hemilepidotus gilberti Jordan & Starks, 1904 **banded Irish lord**

Western Bering Sea off Commander Islands and northwest Pacific Ocean off Kamchatka to Honshu, Sea of Okhotsk, and Sea of Japan to North Korea.

Bottom in shallow water to depth of 604 m, usually over outer continental shelf at depths of 50–200 m.

D XI–XII,20–23; A 14–19; Pec 15–17; Pel I,4; LLp 56–66; PC 4–5; Vert 36–39.

- Olive green dorsally; pinkish white ventrally; dark bands dusky olive dorsally, dusky red ventrally; males with violet tinge and some yellow, golden green, and orange spots and mottlings.
- Nasal spine strong and sharp; ridges present on head, becoming rugose in large specimens.
- Four preopercular spines; upper three sharp, second longest; **fourth preopercular spine directed ventrally, broad and flat**.
- Most cirri small, some reduced or absent; cirrus at posterior end of maxilla large, thin, broad.
- Dorsal fin continuous; **1st dorsal spine longer than 2nd**; 3rd dorsal spine shorter than 2nd and 4th, forming obvious notch in fin profile; pelvic fin of males very long and with conspicuous ctenii.
- Three bands of scales, plus **anal scale row** above anal fin to abdomen; all scales of bands similar in size; 4 (rarely 5) rows in dorsal scale band below spinous dorsal fin; 14–35 scales in row above lateral line; **8 or 9 rows in ventral band**.
- Vomerine and palatine teeth present.
- Gill membranes united, attached anteriorly to isthmus leaving wide free portion posteriorly.
- Length to 360 mm SL (about 430 mm TL).

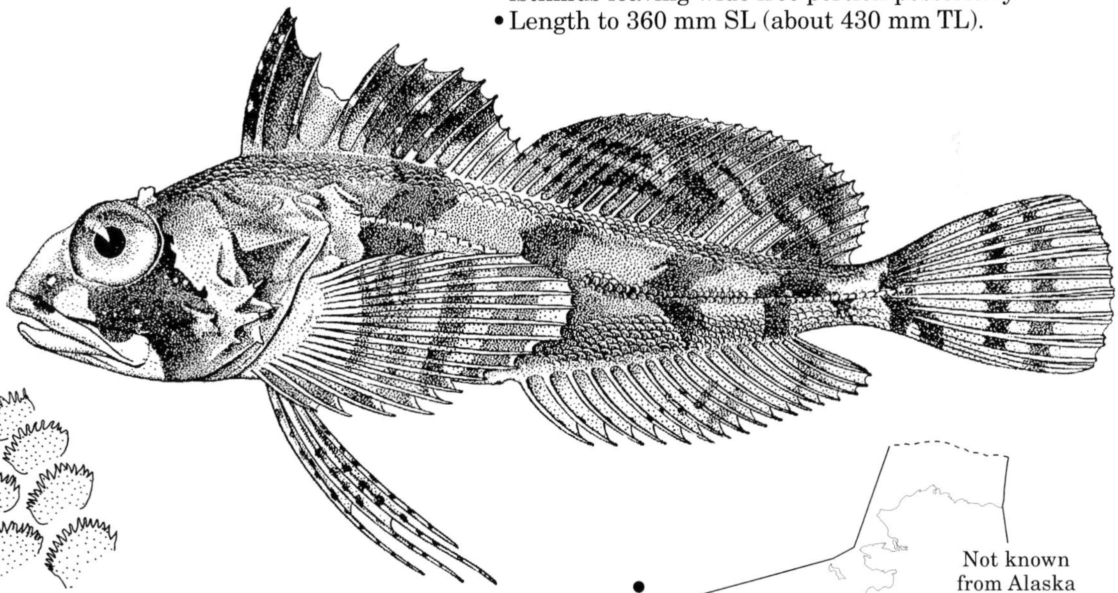

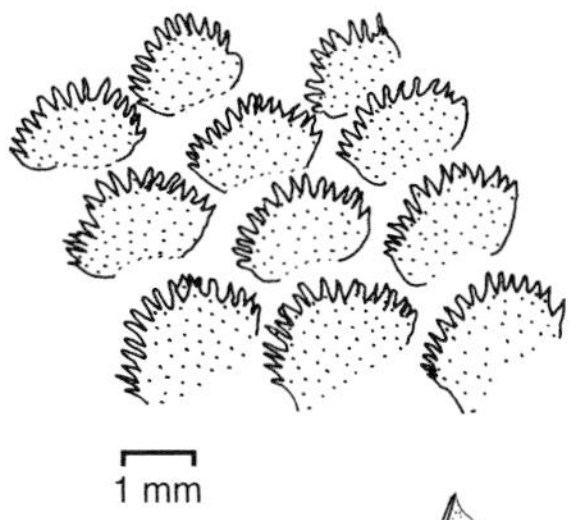

1 mm

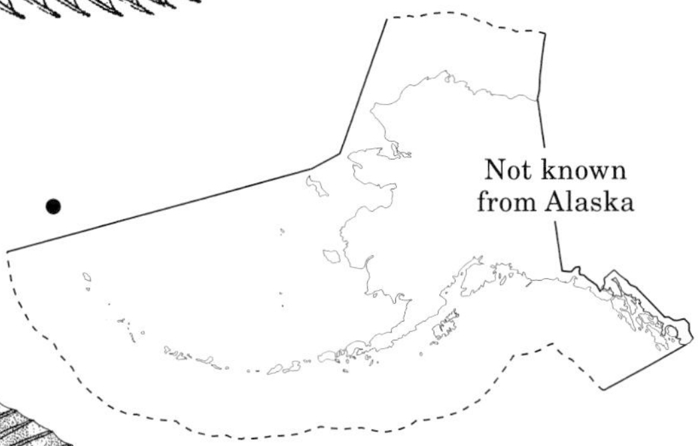

Not known from Alaska

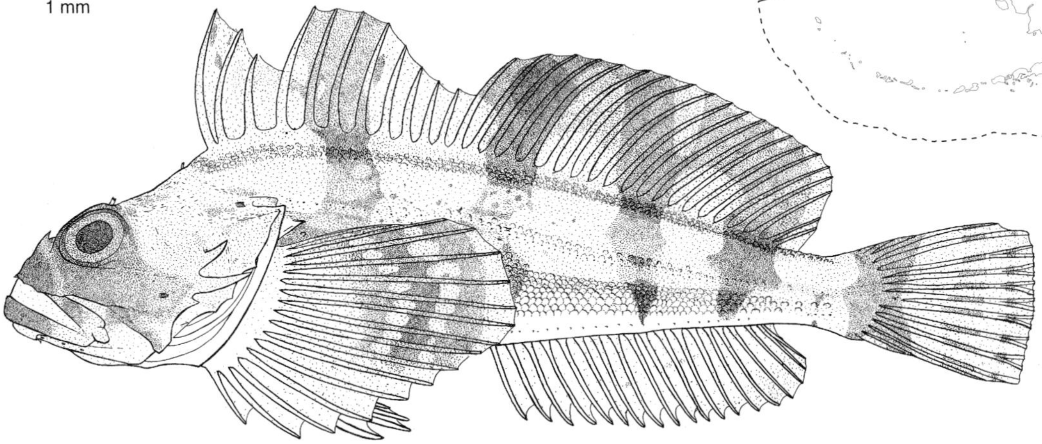

Notes & Sources — *Hemilepidotus (Hemilepidotus) gilberti* Jordan & Starks, 1904

Description: Jordan and Starks 1904b:254–256; Peden 1978:36–39; Lindberg and Krasyukova 1987:181–182.

Figures: Upper: Lindberg and Krasyukova 1987, fig. 109, after Jordan and Starks 1904b, fig. 10; male, 225 mm TL, Hakodate, Japan. Lower: Peden 1978, fig. 19; female, about 320 mm TL, Sea of Okhotsk. Scales in dorsal scale band: Peden 1978, fig. 8.

Range: Nearest known occurrence is Bering Island (Peden 1978). Shinohara et al. 1996: Pacific coast of northern Honshu. Depths: Fedorov and Sheiko (2002).

Hemilepidotus zapus Gilbert & Burke, 1912 **longfin Irish lord**

Aleutian Islands from Attu Island to Chagulak Island; southwestern Gulf of Alaska off Chernabura Island; northern Kuril Islands.

Bottom at depths of 61–128 m; juveniles and adults appear to be strictly subtidal.

D XI–XII,20–22; A 16–17; Pec 15–17; Pel I,4; LLp 47–58; PC 4; Vert 37–38.

- Pink to red with dark red to reddish black bands; white ventrally; in alcohol yellow and brown.
- Nasal spine strong and sharp; ridges present on head, becoming rugose in large specimens.
- Four preopercular spines; upper two longest and sharp, third smaller but evident under skin, **fourth spine sharp** and pointed ventrally.
- Most cirri broad, but thin and weak; postocular and occipital cirri multifid; **small frontal cirrus present** posteromedial to postocular cirrus; cirrus at posterior end of maxilla large, thin, broad.
- Dorsal fin continuous; **1st dorsal spine shorter than 2nd**; 3rd dorsal spine shorter than 2nd and 4th, forming obvious notch in fin profile; pelvic fin of males very long and with conspicuous ctenii.
- Three bands of scales, plus **anal scale row** above anal fin to abdomen; all scales of bands similar in size; 4 or 5 rows in dorsal band below spinous dorsal fin; 16–27 scales in row above lateral line; 8 or 9 rows in ventral band; **at least 1, usually 2–8, scales on caudal peduncle between levels of dorsal and lateral scale bands**.
- Vomerine and palatine teeth present.
- Gill membranes united, attached anteriorly to isthmus leaving wide free portion posteriorly.
- Length to 237 mm SL, 287 mm TL.

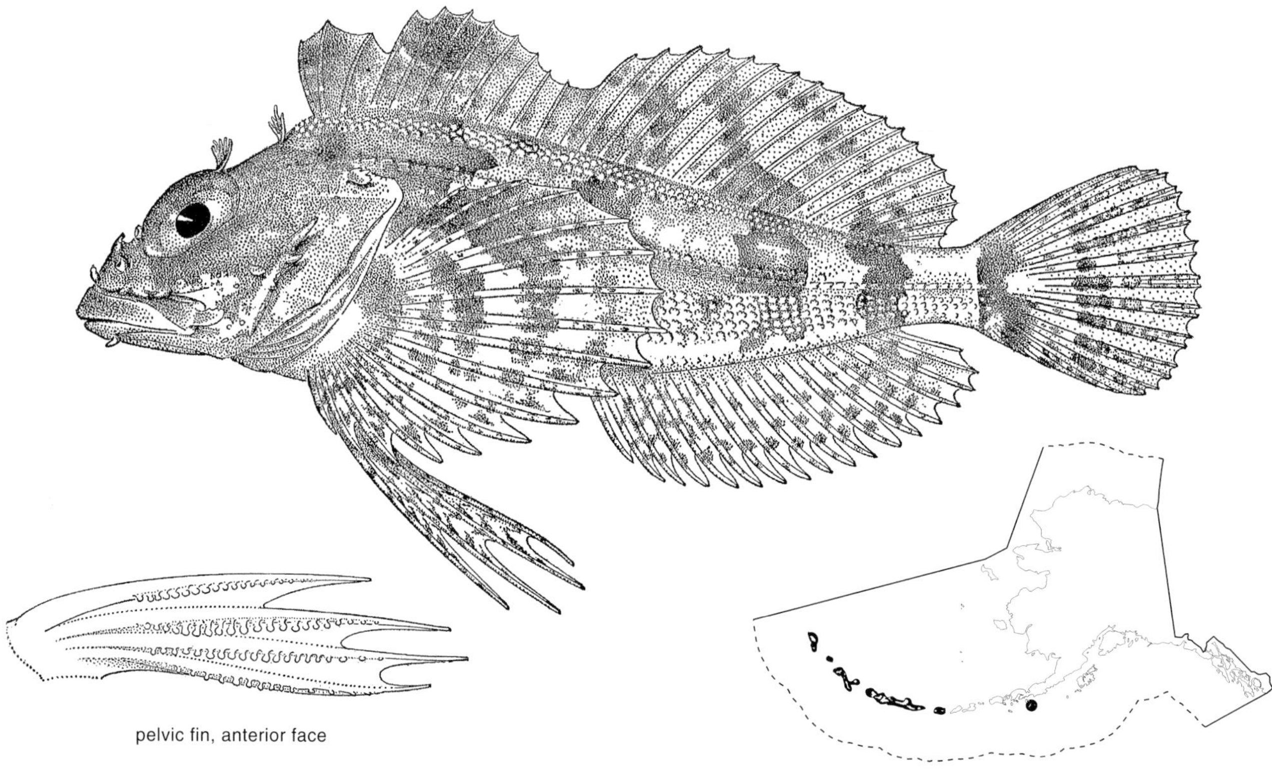

pelvic fin, anterior face

Notes & Sources — *Hemilepidotus (Hemilepidotus) zapus* Gilbert & Burke, 1912

Description: Gilbert and Burke 1912a:54–56; Peden 1978: 28–31.

Figures: Gilbert and Burke 1912a, figs. 10, 10a; type, male, 127 mm TL, near Attu Island, Alaska, *Albatross* station 4782.

Range: Previously recorded from Attu Island (Gilbert and Burke 1912a) to Chagulak Island (Peden 1978). UBC 63-333 (1 specimen) is from Chernabura Island, which is farther east. A specimen (AB 63-215) recorded by Quast and Hall (1972) as an extension of known range to the Chukchi Sea has diagnostic characters of *H. papilio.* Not listed in Commander Islands inventory by Fedorov and Sheiko (2002). Specimens collected by A. M. Orlov during bottom trawl surveys by the *Toru Maru 58* in 1996 (1 specimen) and 1999 (33 specimens) southeast of Onekotan Island (northern Kuril Islands), mostly near the top of a seamount, represent a significant extension of the known range to the west (B. A. Sheiko, pers. comms. and photograph, 22 Apr.–3 Sep. 1999). The specimen taken in 1996 (KIE 2287; 158 mm SL, 196 mm TL) at 48°26'N, 154°41'E, with depth range 122–128 m represents a new maximum depth (coordinates and depths not yet available for 1999 survey). Previously recorded to 108 m by Gilbert and Burke (1912a).

Size: A female from the 1999 Onekotan Island survey, which will be housed in the ZIN collection.

Hemilepidotus hemilepidotus (Tilesius, 1811) **red Irish lord**

Southeastern Bering Sea and throughout Aleutian Islands to California at Mussel Point, Monterey Bay; western Bering Sea and Commander Islands to Pacific Ocean off southeastern Kamchatka.

Tidepools and to depth of 48 m on protected and exposed coasts; prefer rocky habitats, especially where bottom is clean and coralline algae predominate.

D XI,17–20; A 13–16; Pec 15–17; Pel I,4; LLp 59–68; PC 6–7; Vert 35–37.

- Red to orange, pink, or brown; white, brown, and black mottling; dark saddles; whitish ventrally.
- Nasal spine strong, prominent; ridges on head, becoming rugose in large specimens.
- Four preopercular spines; upper two long, sharp, first often longer; lower two small and blunt.
- Postocular, frontal, occipital cirri well developed; **nasal cirri present, fringed**; **maxillary cirrus broad**, width more than half its length.
- Dorsal fin continuous; first 3 dorsal spines shorter than 4th, and membrane between 3rd and 4th incised; 1st spine seldom longer than 2nd; **posterior dorsal fin rays branched**.
- Three bands of scales; anal row rarely present; all scales of bands similar in size; **4 or 5 rows in dorsal scale band** below spinous dorsal fin; 7–27 scales in row above lateral line; **6 or 7 rows in ventral band**.
- Vomerine and palatine teeth present.
- **Gill membranes united, attached along isthmus leaving only a narrow free margin posteriorly**, about a pupil diameter in width.
- Length to 510 mm TL, rarely over 375 mm TL.

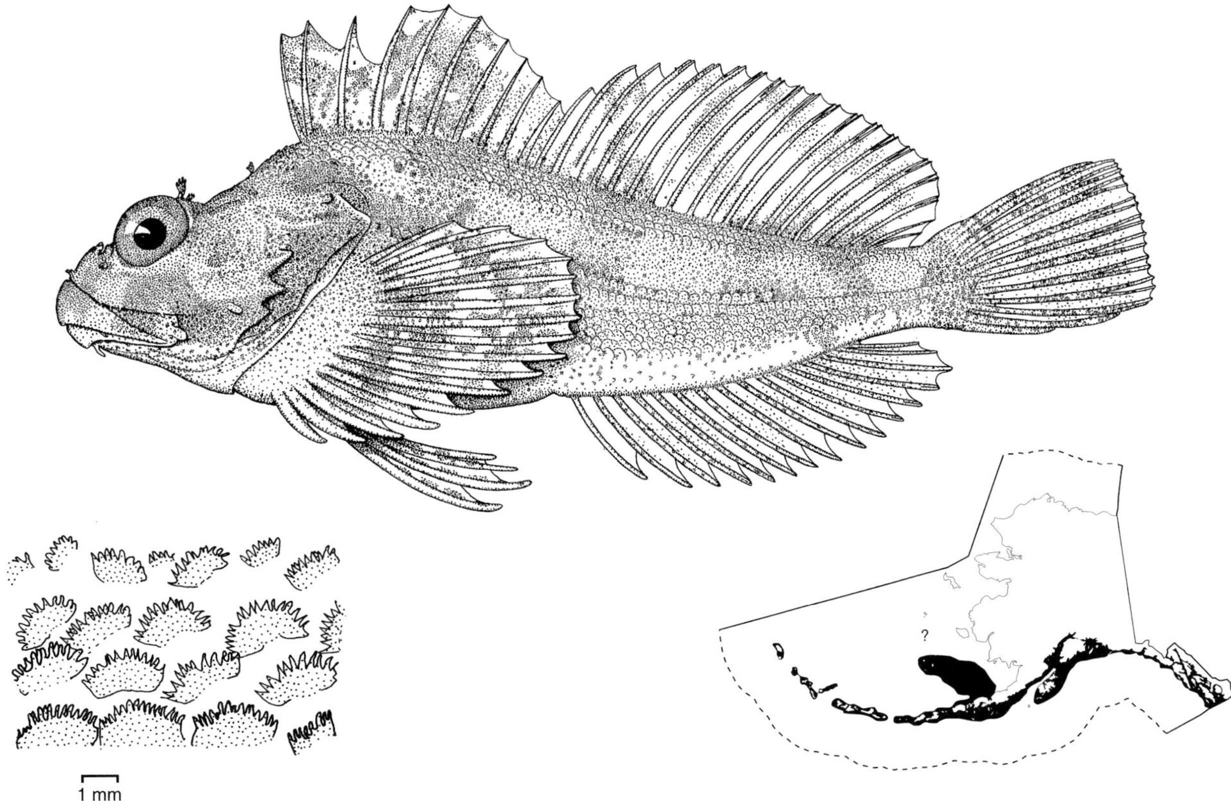

Notes & Sources — *Hemilepidotus (Hemilepidotus) hemilepidotus* (Tilesius, 1811)
Cottus hemilepidotus Tilesius, 1811

Description: Jordan and Evermann 1898:1935–1936; Bolin 1944:17–19; Hart 1973:502–503; Peden 1978:24–28; Eschmeyer and Herald 1983:170.

Figures: Bolin 1944, fig. 5. Scales in dorsal scale band: Peden 1978, fig. 8.

Range: Northernmost limit in Bering Sea documented by adult voucher specimens is St. Paul Island, where it was found in tidepools (Peden 1978). Gilbert (1896) recorded numerous specimens less than an inch long taken at the surface off St. Paul Island. Commonly taken in NMFS bottom trawl surveys in the eastern North Pacific, but range in Bering Sea is uncertain because of confusion with female *H. papilio* (Allen and Smith 1988). Quast and Hall (1972) reported *H. hemilepidotus* from Bristol Bay. The type series includes specimens from the Bering Sea but with no definite localities recorded (Eschmeyer 1998). Lots NMC 84-163 and 84-165 include specimens collected in 1983 from Resurrection Bay off the Seward Marine Center dock. Other Alaskan records were mapped by Peden (1978).

Hemilepidotus jordani Bean, 1881 **yellow Irish lord**

Southeastern Chukchi Sea and Bering Sea to Aleutian Islands and southeastern Alaska at Port Conclusion; Gulf of Anadyr to Commander Islands, eastern Kamchatka, northern Kuril Islands, and Sea of Okhotsk.

Soft bottoms, usually at subtidal depths to 110 m; rarely found deeper than 250 m, reported to 579 m; juveniles occasionally found in rocky tidepools.

D XI–XII,18–23; A 16–18; Pec 17–19; Pel I,4; LLp 59–68; PC 4–5; Vert 37–39.

- Yellowish tan to dark brown; vague dark saddles; white to yellow ventrally; **gill membranes yellow**.
- Nasal spine strong and sharp; ridges present on head, becoming rugose in large specimens.
- Four preopercular spines, second usually longest.
- Cirri weak; postocular, frontal, occipital present; **nasal cirrus simple**, very small; **maxillary cirrus narrow**, width less than half its length.
- Dorsal fin continuous; 3rd spine shorter than 4th, forming notch in fin profile, and membrane between them incised; 1st spine usually shorter than 2nd; **posterior dorsal fin rays unbranched**.
- Three bands of scales; anal row usually absent; all scales of bands similar in size; 4 or 5 rows in dorsal band below spinous dorsal fin; 18–34 scales in row above lateral line; about 8 rows in ventral band.
- Vomerine and palatine teeth present.
- Gill membranes united, attached anteriorly to isthmus leaving wide free portion posteriorly.
- Length to about 500 mm TL.

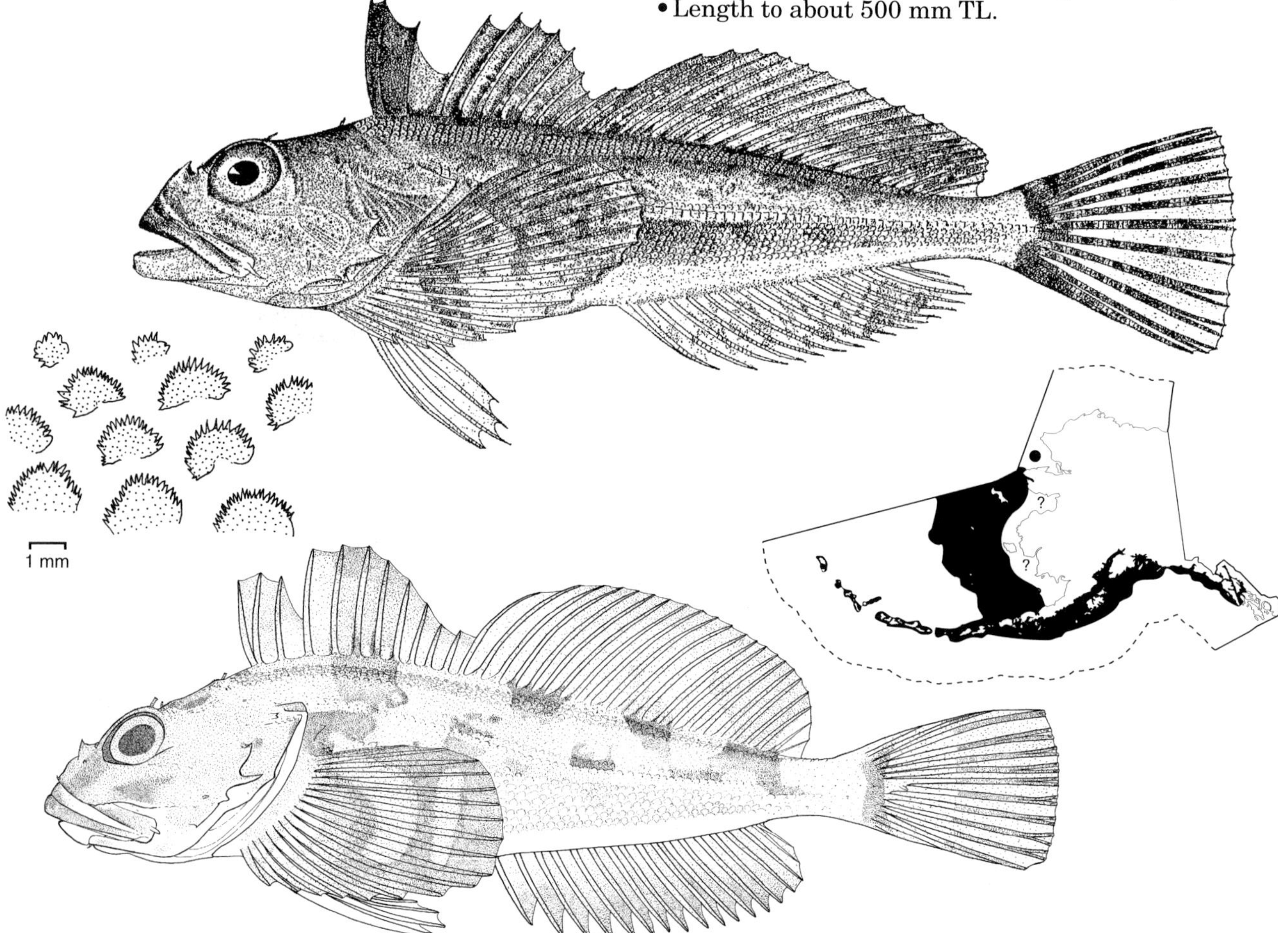

Notes & Sources — *Hemilepidotus (Hemilepidotus) jordani* Bean, 1881

Description: Peden 1978:32–36.

Figures: Upper: Jordan and Evermann 1900, fig. 703; lectotype, about 335 mm TL, Unalaska, Alaska. Lower: Peden 1978, fig. 17; female, about 314 mm TL, Sea of Okhotsk. Scales in dorsal band: Peden 1978, fig. 8.

Range: Found, in 4,000 occurrences in 30 years of NMFS bottom trawl surveys, from southeastern Chukchi Sea to Aleutian Islands and along Gulf of Alaska coasts to Icy Strait (Allen and Smith 1988). Recorded from Sitka by Evermann and Goldsborough (1907), and from southeastern Alaska in a general statement by Quast and Hall (1972); ABL museum contains several examples from the Alexander Archipelago, as far south as Port Conclusion (AB 71-5). Maximum depth: Fedorov and Sheiko 2002.

Size: Baxter (1990ms) reported 365 mm SL, 468.5 mm TL for a specimen taken in a 1986 NMFS survey near Unalaska Island at 54°14'N, 166°02'W, depth 49 m. Yabe (in Masuda et al. 1984) gave a maximum length of 41 cm SL, which works out to 500 mm TL using SL = 80% TL from Baxter's Unalaska Island specimen.

Chitonotus pugetensis (Steindachner, 1876) **roughback sculpin**

Northern British Columbia at Brundige Inlet to southern Baja California.

Sand, silt, and mud bottoms, from intertidal to depth of 142 m; most common at depths of 8–73 m.

D X–XI + 14–17, A 14–17; Pec 16–18; Pel I,3; LLs 37–40; Vert 35–36.

- Pale grayish green to brown dorsally, white ventrally; dark brown saddles; margin of spinous dorsal fin black; pectoral fin yellow; males in breeding season often have red blotches below lateral line and below spinous dorsal, and red to orange, lavender, or white patch above eyes; color and markings can change with substrate.
- Postocular and parietal spines present.
- Four preopercular spines; first longest, with bifid tip and spinules along dorsal surface.
- Nasal, eyeball, postocular, and maxillary cirri present.
- **Spinous dorsal fin membrane deeply incised between 3rd and 4th spines**; 1st through 3rd spines decreasing in height, 1st spine often greatly elongate but length highly variable.
- **Strongly ctenoid scales covering upper part of head and body**; lateral line scales enlarged.
- Vomerine and palatine teeth present.
- Gill membranes united, free from isthmus.
- Length to 230 mm TL.

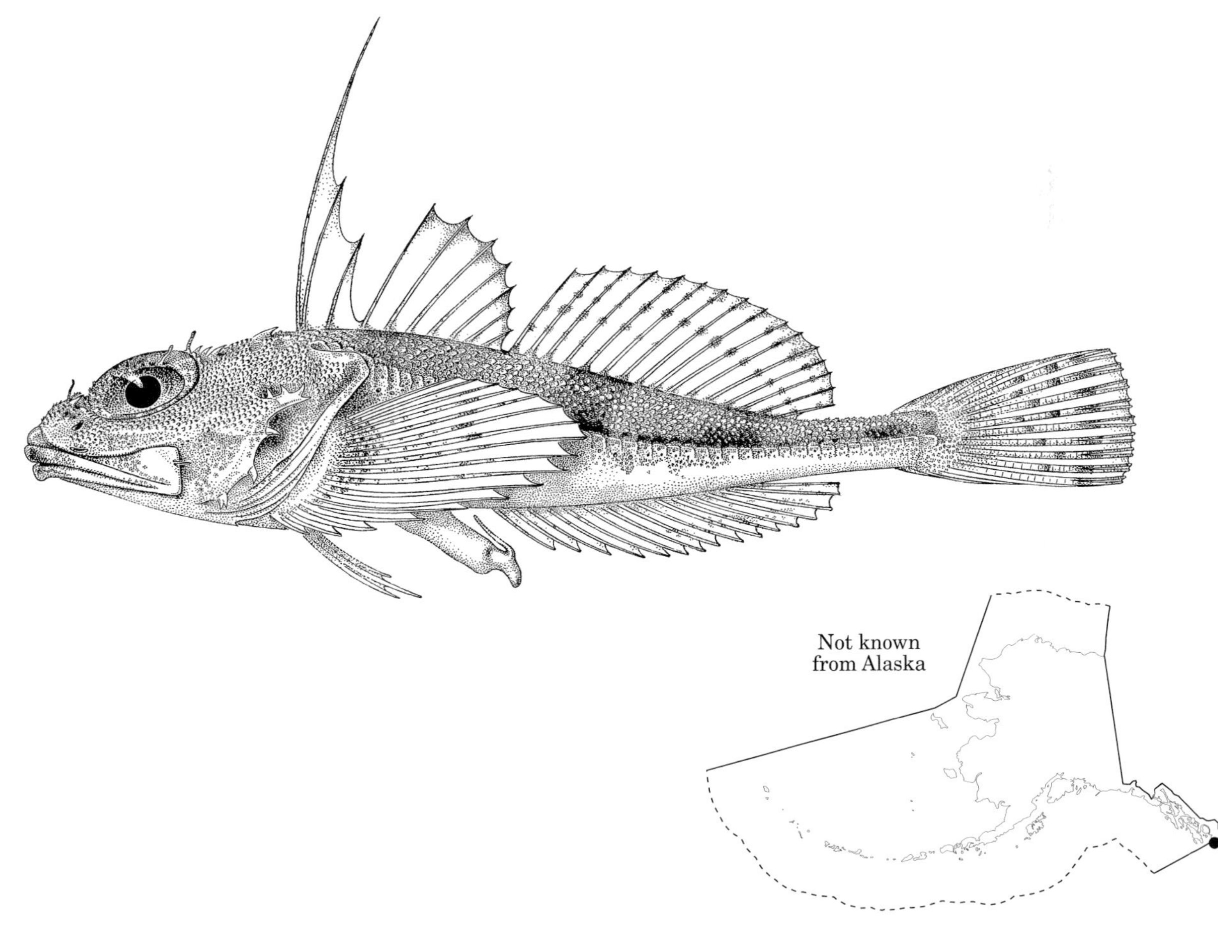

Notes & Sources — *Chitonotus pugetensis* (Steindachner, 1876)
Artedius pugetensis Steindachner, 1876

Description: Jordan and Evermann 1898:1890–1891; Bolin 1944:19–22; Hart 1973:491–492; Eschmeyer and Herald 1983:164; Humann 1996:66, 67.

Figure: Bolin 1944, fig. 6; male. The guide by Humann (1996) includes photographs of three color variations.

Range: Known to occur just south of the Alaska–British Columbia border. Peden and Wilson (1976) collected specimens and observed others while scuba diving at several nearby sites; the northernmost occurrence was at Brundige Inlet at 54°36'N, 130°51'W.

Icelinus tenuis Gilbert, 1890 **spotfin sculpin**

Southeastern Alaska to central Baja California off San Benito Islands.

Sandy and silty bottoms at depths of 12–373 m, occasionally found on rocky reefs.

D IX–XI + 16–19; A 13–17; Pec 15–17; Pel I,2; LLs 39–43; Vert 37–39.

- Light brown and gray with darker mottling, often with patches of brilliant red, rose, or lavender; several dark saddles; male with dusky spot on first dorsal fin.
- Body very slender and elongate.
- **Top of head concave behind eyes.**
- **Two distinct spines behind eye on each side.**
- Four preopercular spines; first longest, with spinules on dorsal surface.
- **No nasal cirri**; large, flat postocular cirrus; long cirrus on middle of fronto-parietal ridge; maxillary cirrus small.
- **First 2 dorsal fin spines greatly elongate**, first spine usually longer than second and sometimes ornamented at tip.
- **Two rows of scales below dorsal fins, extending to 5th to 11th soft ray**; lateral line scales platelike; 5–19 scales in pectoral axil.
- Anterior pair of mandibular pores opening into common pit on symphysis.
- Vomerine and palatine teeth present.
- Gill membranes united, free from isthmus.
- Length to 159 mm TL.

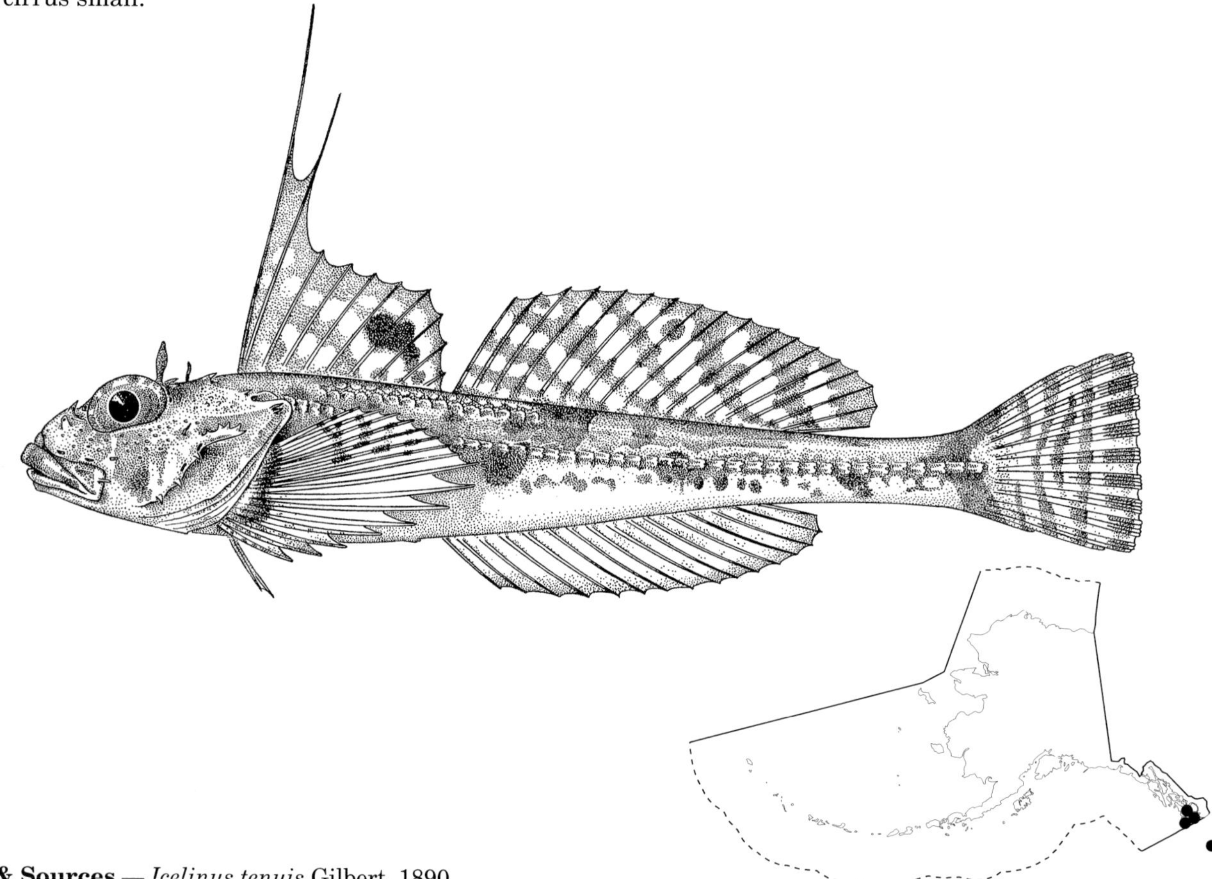

Notes & Sources — *Icelinus tenuis* Gilbert, 1890
Tarandichthys tenuis: Jordan and Evermann 1898.

Description: Bolin 1936a:155, 1944:26–28; Hart 1973:513–514; Peden 1984.

Figure: Bolin 1944, fig. 8. The guide by Humann (1996) includes photographs showing several color variations.

Range: Bolin (1936a) stated that the record given by Jordan et al. (1930) of an Alaskan distribution was an error resulting from too literal an acceptance of the title of Evermann and Goldsborough's report *The Fishes of Alaska.* However, examples of the species have since been found in waters of the Alexander Archipelago, and documented by voucher specimens. The northernmost record comprises two specimens (USNM 131264; 102 and 159 mm TL) taken from Behm Canal near Ketchikan in Nov. 1944 in "trawl catch of the *Charles T.*" by Lyle Anderson; the specimens are in excellent condition. B. W. Coad (pers. comm., 26 Apr. 1999) confirmed the identification of a specimen (NMC 65-412) taken west of Noyes Island at 55°25'N, 134°48'W, depth 214–218 m, as *I. tenuis*. Another example is a specimen (AB 77-34) collected in a shrimp pot in 1977 in Revillagigedo Channel near the Boca de Quadra at a depth 46 m; identified by E. L. Hall. Nearest reported locality of occurrence outside Alaska is Tasu Sound, Queen Charlotte Islands (Hart 1973). Scuba divers have reported *I. tenuis* south of Alaska at depths as shallow as 12 m (Humann 1996).

Size: USNM 131264. Previously reported to reach 140 mm TL (e.g., Hart 1973).

Icelinus filamentosus Gilbert, 1890 **threadfin sculpin**

Gulf of Alaska near Chirikof Island, south of Kenai Peninsula, and near Petersburg; southern British Columbia to southern California at Point Loma and Cortes Bank.

Sandy and muddy bottoms at depths of 18–373 m.

D IX–XII + 15–18; A 13–16; Pec 16–18; Pel I,2; LLs 37–41; Vert 34–37.

- Light gray to brown, mottled and blotched with darker and lighter shades; usually with dark saddles; whitish ventrally.
- **Head behind eyes not concave.**
- **No distinct postocular spines.**
- **Long cirrus at base of nasal spine**; large, flat postocular cirrus; 2 well-developed cirri on frontoparietal ridge; long maxillary cirrus.
- Four preopercular spines; first longest, with spinules on dorsal surface; second sometimes difficult to discern; short spine on subopercle.
- **First 2 dorsal fin spines extremely elongate**, often of nearly equal length, 2nd sometimes longer, both sometimes plumose.
- **Two rows of scales below dorsal fins, extending to below last 2 soft rays**; lateral line scales platelike; 2–6 scales in pectoral axil.
- Anterior pair of mandibular pores opening into common pit on symphysis.
- Vomerine and palatine teeth present.
- Gill membranes united, free from isthmus.
- Length to 270 mm TL.

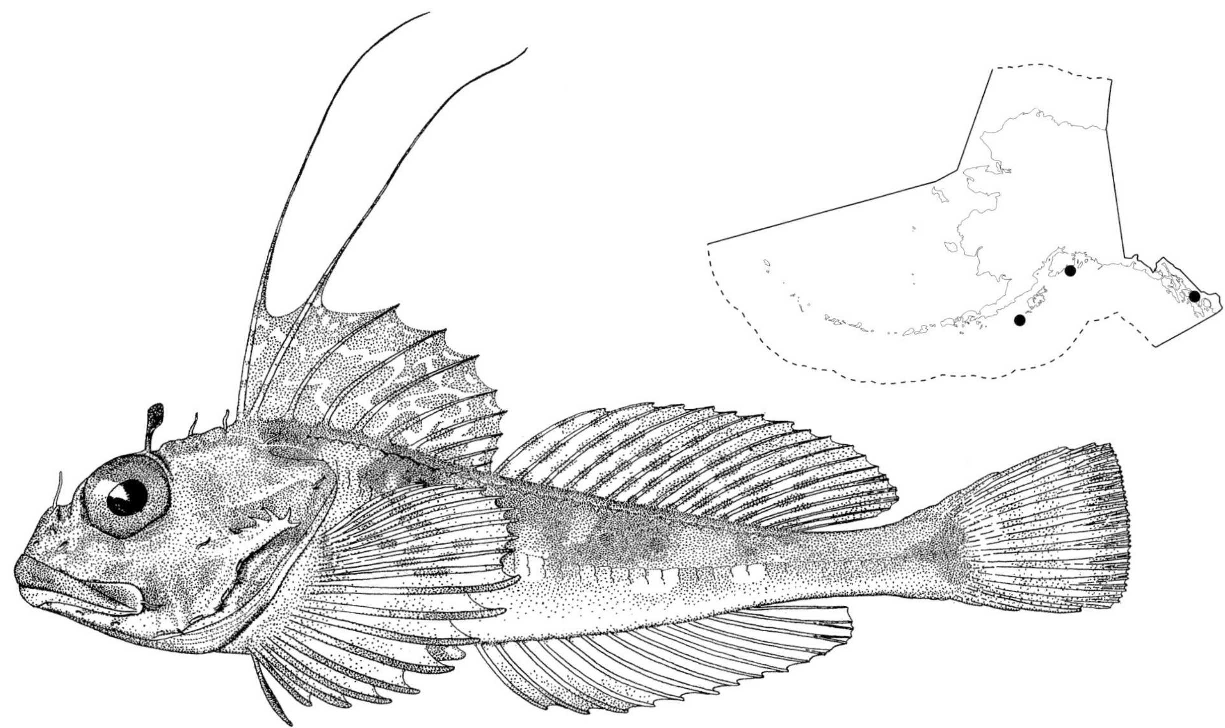

Notes & Sources — *Icelinus filamentosus* Gilbert, 1890
Tarandichthys filamentosus: Jordan 1896, Jordan and Evermann 1898.

Description: Bolin 1936a:154–155; 1944:24–26; Hart 1973: 510–511; Peden 1984. First two dorsal spines are often broken off by collecting gear.

Figure: Bolin 1944, fig. 7.

Range: Bolin (1936a) noted that attribution of an Alaskan record by Jordan et al. (1930) was an error, based on too literal an interpretation of the title of Evermann and Goldsborough's (1907) work, *The Fishes of Alaska*. The St. Mary's Mission, *Albatross* station 4193, referred to by the latter authors was in southern British Columbia off the Strait of Georgia at the mouth of the Fraser River, at the present-day New Westminster. Hart (1973) listed British Columbia records. Allen and Smith (1988) reported *I. filamentosus* was taken in Alaska east of Chirikof Island and south of the Kenai Peninsula in NMFS bottom trawl surveys. The rest of the 130 occurrences they reported were off Vancouver Island and farther south. The identification of two specimens (UW 2588) collected in 1920 from the Petersburg area as *I. filamentosus* was confirmed by J. W. Orr (pers. comm., 4 Aug. 1999). Humann (1996) reported that, south of Alaska, *I. filamentosus* is rarely found above safe scuba diving limits. However, the 800-m lower limit given in an unpublished summary cited by Allen and Smith (1988) is probably a mistake, or is the maximum depth of a trawl and not the depth at which the fish entered the net.

Icelinus burchami Evermann & Goldsborough, 1907 **dusky sculpin**

Southeastern Alaska at Behm Canal off Loring to southern California off La Jolla.

Various bottoms, including gravel and rock, at depths of 61–567 m, most often taken near dropoffs; sometimes captured in prawn traps.

D IX–X + 16–18; A 12–14; Pec 16–19; Pel I,2; LLs 36–40; Vert 36–37.

- Color in preservative yellowish brown with small whitish spots and dark irregular blotches.
- Top of head flat or slightly concave.
- **No distinct postocular spines**.
- Four preopercular spines; first longest, with spinules on dorsal surface; no spine on subopercle.
- **No nasal cirrus**; large, flat postocular cirrus; parietal cirri present; maxillary cirrus small.
- **First or second dorsal fin spines not longer than third or fourth**; cirri on tips of dorsal fin spines; pelvic fin very small, not extending more than one-third of distance to anal fin origin.
- **Two rows of scales below dorsal fins, extending to next to last dorsal ray or not beyond insertion of second dorsal fin**; lateral line scales platelike; no scales on pectoral axil.
- **Pores of head large**; anterior mandibular pores opening separately on either side of symphysis.
- Vomerine and palatine teeth present.
- Gill membranes united, free from isthmus.
- Length to 129 mm TL.

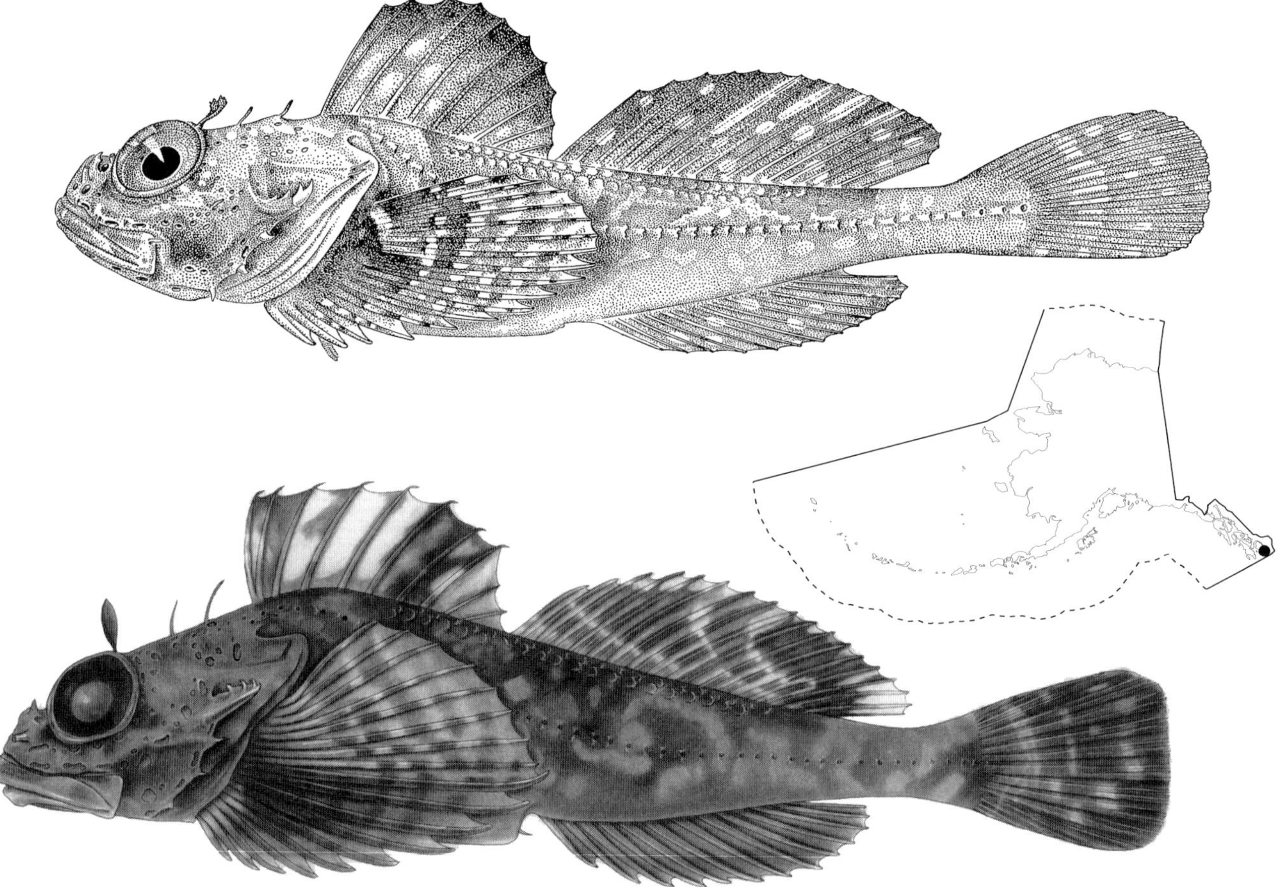

Notes & Sources — *Icelinus burchami* Evermann & Goldsborough, 1907
Icelinus fuscescens Gilbert, 1915
Lower meristic counts for specimens south of Point Conception, California, led Peden (1981b) to provisionally assign the northern and southern populations to subspecies: *I. b. burchami* and *I. b. fuscescens,* respectively.

Description: Bolin 1936a:156; 1944:30–31; Barraclough and Butler 1965; Hart 1973:508–509; Eschmeyer and Herald 1983:172; Peden 1984. Meristic character counts given above are for *I. b. burchami,* from Peden (1981b).

Figures: Upper: Bolin 1944, fig. 10. Lower: Royal British Columbia Museum, artist P. Drukker-Brammall, spring 1981; BCPM 977-19, Howe Sound, British Columbia.

Range: Described by Evermann and Goldsborough (1907) from specimens collected in Behm Canal off Loring, Alaska, *Albatross* dredging station 4228, at depths of 75–245 m on bottom of gravel with sponges at beginning of haul and rocky bottom at end of haul (station data from Fassett 1905). No additional Alaskan examples have been reported. British Columbia records are from the southern Strait of Georgia (Hart 1973, Peden 1981b).

Icelinus borealis Gilbert, 1896 — northern sculpin

Bristol Bay and Aleutian Islands off Attu Island to southern Puget Sound, Washington.

Mud, silt, sand, gravel, pebble, and shell bottoms at depths of 4.6–247 m.

D IX–XI + 14–17; A 11–14; Pec 14–17; Pel I,2; LLs 37–40; Vert 35–36.

- Mottled and blotched shades of brown, gray, and white; often with dark saddles; males with dark patches anteriorly and posteriorly on first dorsal.
- Top of head gently concave.
- **No distinct postocular spines**.
- Four preopercular spines; first longest, with spinules on dorsal surface; second (close to base of first) often absent or difficult to discern; small spine at lower angle of subopercle.
- **Long cirrus at base of nasal spine**; long postocular cirrus; parietal cirri present; maxillary cirrus small.
- **First or second dorsal fin spines not longer than third or fourth spines**; cirri on tips of dorsal spines; pelvic fin extending more than one-third of distance to anal origin.
- **Two rows of scales below dorsal fins, extending onto caudal peduncle**; lateral line scales platelike; no scales on pectoral axil.
- Anterior pair of mandibular pores opening into common pit on symphysis.
- Vomerine and palatine teeth present.
- Gill membranes united, free from isthmus.
- Length to 101 mm TL.

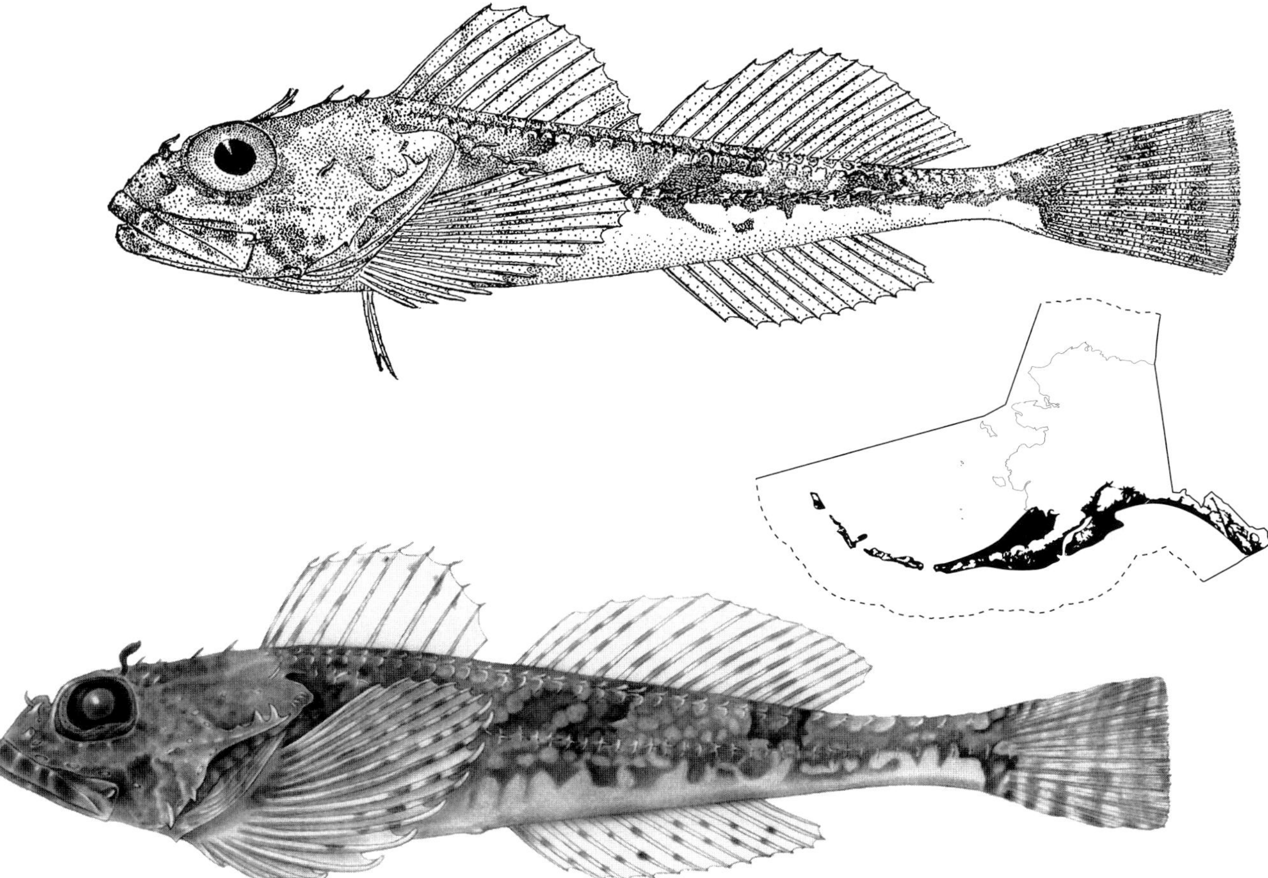

Notes & Sources — *Icelinus borealis* Gilbert, 1896

Description: Gilbert 1896:415–416; Bolin 1936a:159.

Figures: Upper: Gilbert 1896, pl. 25; type, 75 mm TL, Unimak Pass, Aleutian Islands, *Albatross* station 3223. (All four preopercular spines are shown.) Lower: Royal British Columbia Museum, artist P. Drukker-Brammall, summer 1980; BCPM 974-488, 78 mm SL, Wales Harbour, British Columbia. See Humann (1996:67) for color photograph.

Range: Recorded by Gilbert (1896) from specimens taken at 14 *Albatross* stations north and south of the Aleutian Islands and in Bristol Bay, at depths of 20 m (station 3235) to 234 m (station 3226). (The maximum depth of 221 m reported by Gilbert [1896] for those stations is incorrect.) Gilbert and Burke (1912a) recorded it from Attu Island and Petrel Bank at depths to 247 m. Quast and Hall (1972) reported specimens from Unimak, Krenitzin, Shumagin, Trinity, and Kodiak islands, Cook Inlet, and southeastern Alaska in the ABL collection. Peden and Wilson (1976) found numerous specimens at sites north and south of the Alaska–British Columbia border, at depths as shallow as 4.6 m. Other museums (e.g., UBC, UW) also have samples from Alaska. *Icelinus borealis* is the most common species of *Icelinus* in Alaska.

Archistes plumarius Jordan & Gilbert, 1898 **plumed sculpin**

Medny Island, Commander Islands; Ushishir Island, Kuril Islands.

On bottom at depth of 40 m at Medny Island; depth of capture at Ushishir Island not recorded.

D X,23; A 18; Pec 15; Pel I,3; LLs 44.

- Color in preservative light grayish olive, with dark saddles, irregular blotches, and marbling; dusky marking of sides enclosing round spots of pale ground color; pectoral with large black blotch; **dorsal fin with irregular markings**; anal, caudal and pectoral indistinctly barred; pelvic fin plain.
- Head and body compressed.
- No spines above eye or on top of head.
- Four preopercular spines; first moderately long and sharp, lower three obsolete, concealed beneath skin.
- Long nasal cirrus; long, fringed postocular cirrus; 2 bifid or multifid occipital cirri; short maxillary cirrus; as well as others.
- **Dorsal fin continuous, notched between spinous and soft portions**; dorsal fin spines with flat, multifid cirri.
- **One row of platelike scales below dorsal fin**, number of rows increasing anteriorly to fill space between dorsal fin and lateral line, but **scales not extending across nape to other side**; lateral line scales platelike.
- Vomerine and palatine teeth present.
- Anus immediately posterior to pelvic fin base.
- Gill membranes united, free from isthmus.
- Length to 72 mm TL.

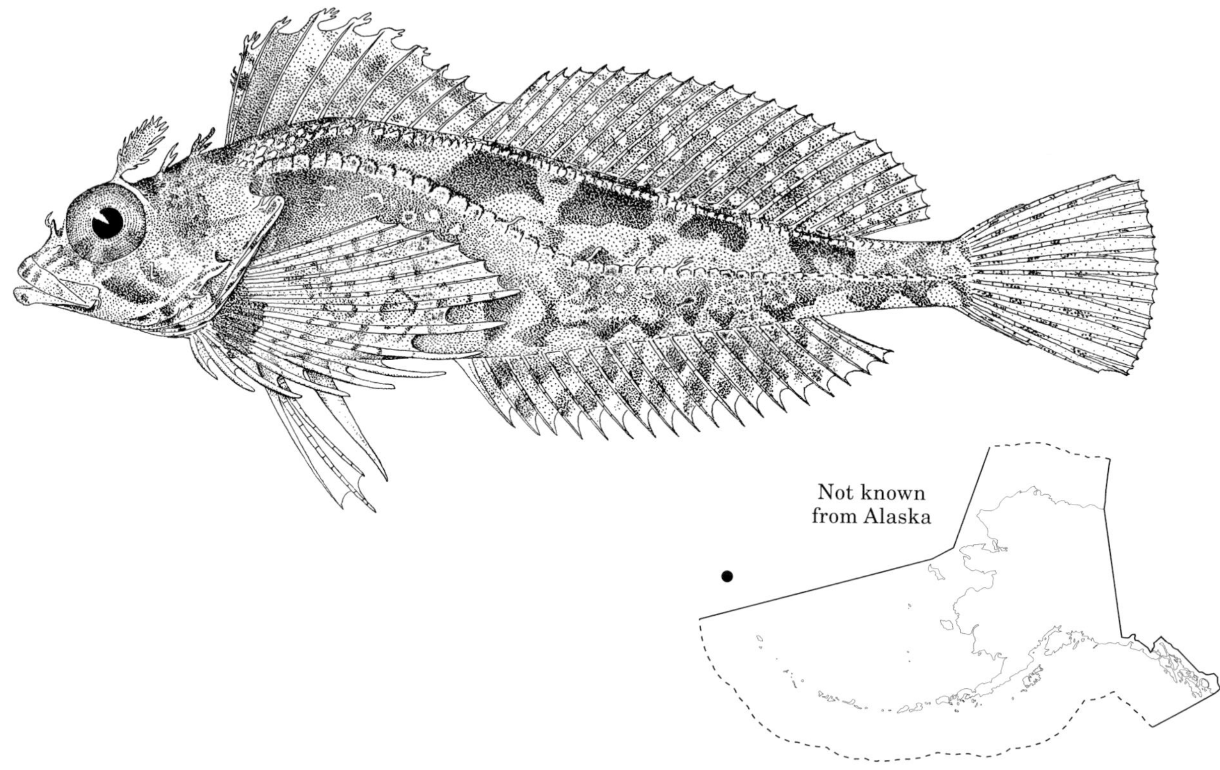

Notes & Sources — *Archistes plumarius* Jordan & Gilbert in Jordan & Evermann, 1898

Similar to *A. biseriatus* but, judging from one specimen (the unique holotype), *A. plumarius* is distinguishable by the lower dorsal and anal fin ray counts, as well as the characters indicated in bold type above.

Description: Jordan and Evermann 1898:1900–1901; Jordan and Gilbert 1899:454–455; Jordan and Starks 1904b:239–240 (all same description). For pectoral fin rays previous descriptions give 15 or 16, the illustration shows 15, and C.W.M. counted 15 on each side when examining the holotype (USNM 48233) on 15 Nov. 1999.

Figure: Jordan and Gilbert 1899, pl. 53: holotype (unique), USNM 48233, male, 72 mm TL, Ushishir Island, Kuril Islands.

Range: Listed by Quast and Hall (1972) as a potential addition to the inventory of Alaskan fish species; at that time, known only from the one holotype specimen from the Kuril Islands. Fedorov and Sheiko (2002) listed the species for the Commander Islands on the basis of ZIN 45555, one specimen taken off Medny Island at a depth of 40 m by bottom trawl in 1973 and recently identified by V. M. Matyushin (B. A. Sheiko, pers. comm., 15 Jan. 1999). A. A. Balanov (pers. comm., 23 Aug. 2000) also examined the Medny Island specimen and believes it to be an example of *A. plumarius*; he plans to describe it in a future publication.

Archistes biseriatus (Gilbert & Burke, 1912) **scaled sculpin**

Petrel Bank, Bering Sea, northeast of Semisopochnoi Island.

At depths of 79–102 m.

D IX–X + 28–29; A 22–23; Pec 16–17; Pel I,3; LLs 47.

- Color in life light olive dorsally, tinged with salmon or pinkish; marked with dark saddles, bars, marbling, and spots in blue, yellowish brown, carmine, orange, and pink; whitish on breast and belly; **soft dorsal fin with broad bars** of brownish yellow or green with light blue intervals; pelvic fin whitish in females, blue-black in males.
- Head and body compressed.
- No spines above eye or on top of head.
- Four preopercular spines; first longest, lower two or three concealed beneath skin.
- Nasal cirrus small and delicate, not always discernible; long, fringed postocular cirrus; 2 simple or bifid occipital cirri; short maxillary cirrus; other cirri present, including some on lateral line scales.
- **Spinous and soft-rayed portions of dorsal fin almost completely separate**, connected by membrane near base; dorsal fin spines with flat, multifid cirri.
- **Two rows of platelike scales below dorsal fins**, number of rows increasing anteriorly to fill space between dorsal fin and lateral line, with **scales extending across nape to connect with scales on other side**; lateral line scales platelike.
- Vomerine and palatine teeth present.
- Anus immediately posterior to pelvic fin base.
- Gill membranes united, free from isthmus.
- Length to 160 mm TL.

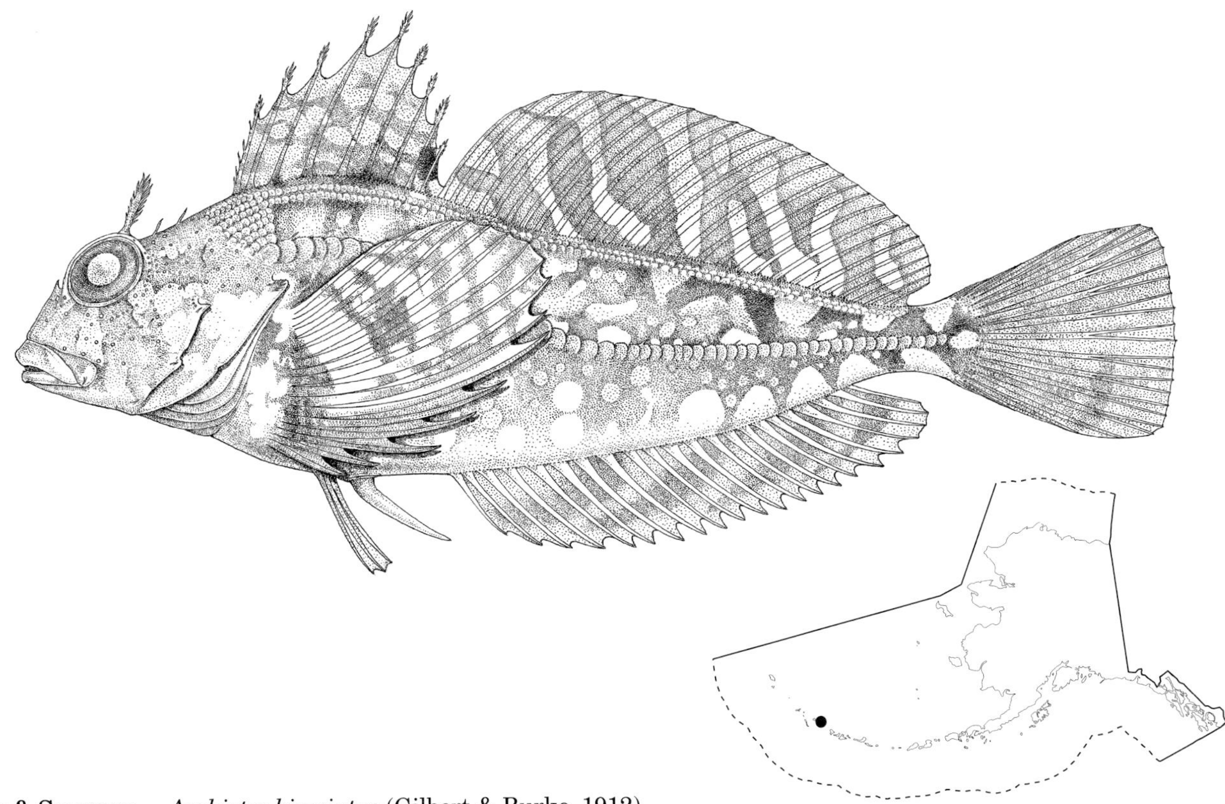

Notes & Sources — *Archistes biseriatus* (Gilbert & Burke, 1912)
Archaulus biseriatus Gilbert & Burke, 1912
Taranetz (1941) included *Archaulus* in the synonymy of *Archistes* Jordan & Gilbert, 1898.

Description: Gilbert and Burke 1912a:36–38; they reported that 9 of the 10 specimens had D IX, and 1 had D X. They gave a count of 16 for pectoral fin rays in all specimens. Examining four syntypes (USNM 74504, 3 specimens; USNM 70879, 1 specimen) on 17 Nov. 1999, C.W.M. also counted 16, except for 17 on the left side in one specimen.

Figure: University of British Columbia, artist P. Drukker-Brammall; composite of paratype, USNM 74503, male, 83 mm SL, and illustration in Gilbert and Burke (1912a, fig. 1) of holotype, USNM 74365, male, 154 mm TL; Petrel Bank, Bering Sea.

Range: No specimens have been reported since Gilbert and Burke (1912a) described the 10 type specimens collected from Petrel Bank at *Albatross* stations 4777 (52°11'N, 179°49'E), 4778 (52°12'N, 179°52'E), and 4779 (52°11'N, 179°57'W), at depths of 79–102 m. (Although their text gives a maximum depth of 99 m, the station data tables give a maximum depth at station 4779 of 102 m.)

Radulinus taylori (Gilbert, 1912) **spinynose sculpin**

Southeastern Alaska off Fillmore Island and other sites near Alaska–British Columbia border to northern Washington at San Juan Islands.

Sand and shell bottom near rocky outcroppings at subtidal depths, usually 5–18 m, reported to 50 m.

D X–XI + 14–17; A 13–17; Pec 16–18; Pel I,3; LLs 34–37; Vert 33–35.

- Olive brown dorsally, lighter ventrally; 4 dark saddles; brown bars on pectoral and caudal fins.
- Body elongate, subcircular; **body deeper than in other *Radulinus***; dorsal profile not much arched, nearly straight from eye to caudal peduncle; **snout length equal to or less than eye diameter**.
- Nasal spine strong; no spines on top of head.
- Three preopercular spines; lowermost obscure.
- Nasal cirri absent; short postocular and parietal cirri present; no cirri on maxilla or sides of head; a few cirri along midside below lateral line.
- **Rays of second dorsal fin and anal fin each fewer than 17**.
- **Ctenoid scales immediately above lateral line** in 1–4 irregular rows **extending to about third to last soft dorsal ray; naked area between scales and dorsal fins**; lateral line scales enlarged; a few scales on occiput, interorbital space, and below orbit; snout naked.
- Lateral line slightly sloping anteriorly then running high on body and straight to caudal fin.
- Vomerine teeth present; palatine teeth absent.
- Anus close to anal fin origin.
- Genital papilla of males elongate and conical.
- Gill membranes united, free from isthmus.
- Length to 74 mm TL.

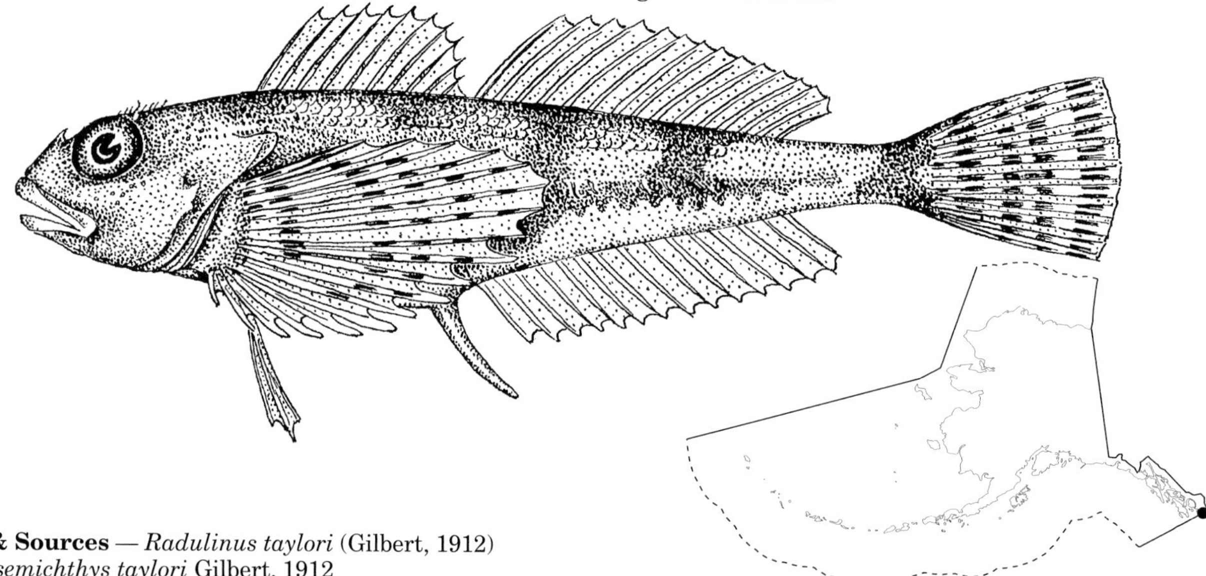

Notes & Sources — *Radulinus taylori* (Gilbert, 1912)

Asemichthys taylori Gilbert, 1912

Classified in *Radulinus* by Clemens and Wilby (1961), Peden and Wilson (1976), Wilimovsky (1979ms), Eschmeyer and Herald (1983), and some other authors; but not universally accepted. The differences Gilbert (1912) gave to differentiate *Asemichthys* from *Radulinus* are not sufficient to erect a new genus: shorter body, fewer vertebrae, shorter dorsal and anal fins, and absence or reduction of spines or ridges on the opercle and preopercle. The differences are well within the range of variation seen in many cottid genera. Specimens collected since Gilbert (1912) described this species have almost closed the meristic gaps, and they indicate more similarities, such as in the shape of the male genital papilla (holotype [unique] is a female) and the presence of a row of minute spinous projections on the eyeball between the upper edge of the orbit and the pupil. Howe and Richardson (1978), reviewing meristic variation in marine sculpins, also concluded that *Asemichthys* should be classified in *Radulinus*. They commented that it appears to occupy an intermediate relationship between subgenus *Radulinellus* and subgenus *Radulinus* (subgenera following Bolin 1950). Yabe (1985) found no difference in the *Radulinus* group of sculpins (including both *Radulinus* and *Asemichthys*) in characters he examined; the *Radulinus* group was characterized by absence of the entopterygoid (a synapomorphy). Although *R. taylori* has a deeper body than other *Radulinus* species, a similar range of body shapes exists in other genera; e.g., in *Triglops*, from relatively short, robust forms to elongate, slim forms.

Description: Gilbert 1912:215–216; Wilby 1936; Hart 1973: 485–486; Peden and Wilson 1976:238–239.

Figures: Hart 1973:485; BCPM 63-732, 68 mm TL, Keats Island, British Columbia.

Range: Fifty-five specimens collected at Male Point, Fillmore Island, and three closely adjacent sites in southeastern Alaska near the British Columbia border in 1974 by Peden and Wilson (1976) are the only published Alaskan records; northernmost site is 54°51'N, 130°27'W. Those specimens are housed in the RBCM collection. Coffie (1998), reviewing the status of the species in Canada, concluded it has not been collected since 1963, the most recent collection date for specimens in the UBC museum. However, Peden and Wilson (1976) found *R. taylori* to be common in northern British Columbia in 1974.

Size: Largest of the 55 specimens recorded from Alaska by Peden and Wilson (1976) was 74 mm TL. Previous size record was 57 mm, reported by Hart (1973).

Radulinus boleoides Gilbert, 1898 **darter sculpin**

Gulf of Alaska east of Kodiak Island; northern British Columbia off Langara Island to southern California off Santa Catalina Island.

Sand and gravel bottom at depths of 15–146 m.

D X + 20–21; A 21–23; Pec 18–20; Pel I,3; LLs 39–40; Vert 39–40.

- Olive gray dorsally, silvery and white ventrally; 3 or 4 dark saddles; dark blotches along midside; brown bars on dorsal, caudal, and pectoral fins.
- Body very elongate; subcircular; dorsal profile straight to caudal peduncle; **snout length greater than (120–150%) eye diameter**.
- **Nasal spine short**; no spines on top of head.
- Two preopercular spines, at most, developed as evident points.
- Small cirrus on posterior part of eyeball; head cirri small and obscure if present; no cirri below lateral line.
- **Rays of second dorsal fin and anal fin each more than 19; pelvic fin short, little more (100–120%) than width of pectoral base**.
- **Ctenoid scales immediately above lateral line in 1 row extending to about middle of second dorsal fin; naked area between scales and dorsal fins**; lateral line scales enlarged; scales on occiput, opercular flap, snout, interorbital space, below and behind eye.
- Lateral line running high on body and straight to caudal fin.
- Vomerine teeth present; palatine teeth absent.
- Anus close to anal fin origin.
- Genital papilla of males elongate and conical.
- Gill membranes united, free from isthmus.
- Length to 127 mm SL (about 149 mm TL).

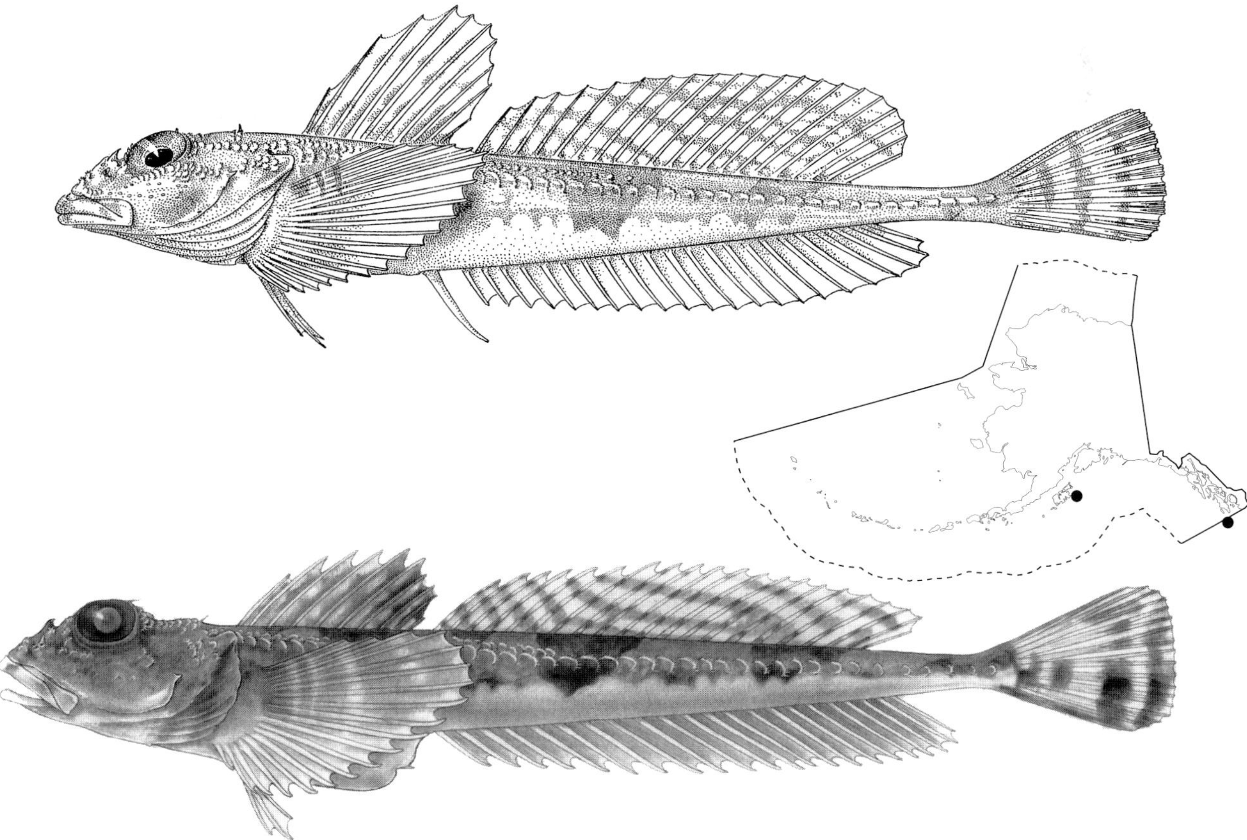

Notes & Sources — *Radulinus boleoides* Gilbert in Jordan & Evermann, 1898

Description: Jordan and Evermann 1898:1919–1920; Bolin 1944:38–39; Hart 1973:536–537; Peden 1972:168–169.

Figures: Upper: Bolin 1944, fig. 14; male. Lower: Royal British Columbia Museum, artist P. Drukker-Brammall, Dec. 1978; female, BCPM 978-145, British Columbia at 48°42'N, 123°22'W (size not available, specimen was lost).

Range: UW 22027, a 127-mm-SL specimen taken by the *Pacific Harvester* at 57°53'N, 151°01'W, depth 77 m, on 14 Jul. 1981 and identified by K. M. Howe, represents an extension of the known range. Nearest record outside Alaska is from 54°12'N, 133°01'W, depth 73 m, off Langara Island, B.C. (Peden 1972). McPhail (1969) reported a sand and gravel bottom for the first British Columbia record, off the north end of Vancouver Island. Minimum depth: Eschmeyer and Herald (1983). Rare in museum collections.

Size: Using SL = 85% TL from a male specimen in BCPM 978-145 measuring 122 mm SL, 143 mm TL, gives 149 mm TL for the 127-mm-SL specimen in UW 22027. Previously given as 14 cm TL in a general statement, converted from 5.5 inches (Hart 1973).

Radulinus asprellus Gilbert, 1890 **slim sculpin**

Aleutian Islands off Amchitka Island; western Gulf of Alaska off Kodiak Island to northern Baja California off Coronado Islands.

Soft bottom at depths of 18–283 m.

D VIII–XI + 20–23; A 22–25; Pec 17–20; Pel I,3; LLs 38–41; Vert 38–39.

- Light olive green mottled with orange-brown dorsally, creamy white ventrally; vague dark saddles; diffuse dark blotches along lateral line; brown bars on dorsal, caudal, and pectoral fins; males with dark spot posteriorly on first dorsal.
- Body very elongate; subcircular; dorsal profile straight to caudal peduncle; **snout length less than or equal (70–100%) to eye diameter**.
- **Nasal spine long and slender**; no spines on top of head.
- Four preopercular spines; first long and sharp, second triangulate and sharp, others blunt in adults.
- No cirrus on eyeball; head cirri small and obscure if present; no cirri below lateral line.
- **Rays of second dorsal fin and anal fin each more than 19; pelvic fin long, more than 1.5 times (170–260%) width of pectoral base.**
- **Ctenoid scales immediately above lateral line in 1 row extending to about middle of second dorsal fin; naked area between scales and dorsal fins**; lateral line scales enlarged; very few scales on head, absent from snout, interorbital space almost entirely naked.
- Lateral line running high on body and straight to caudal fin.
- Vomerine teeth present; palatine teeth absent.
- Anus close to anal fin origin.
- Genital papilla of males elongate and conical.
- Gill membranes united, free from isthmus.
- Length to 152 mm TL.

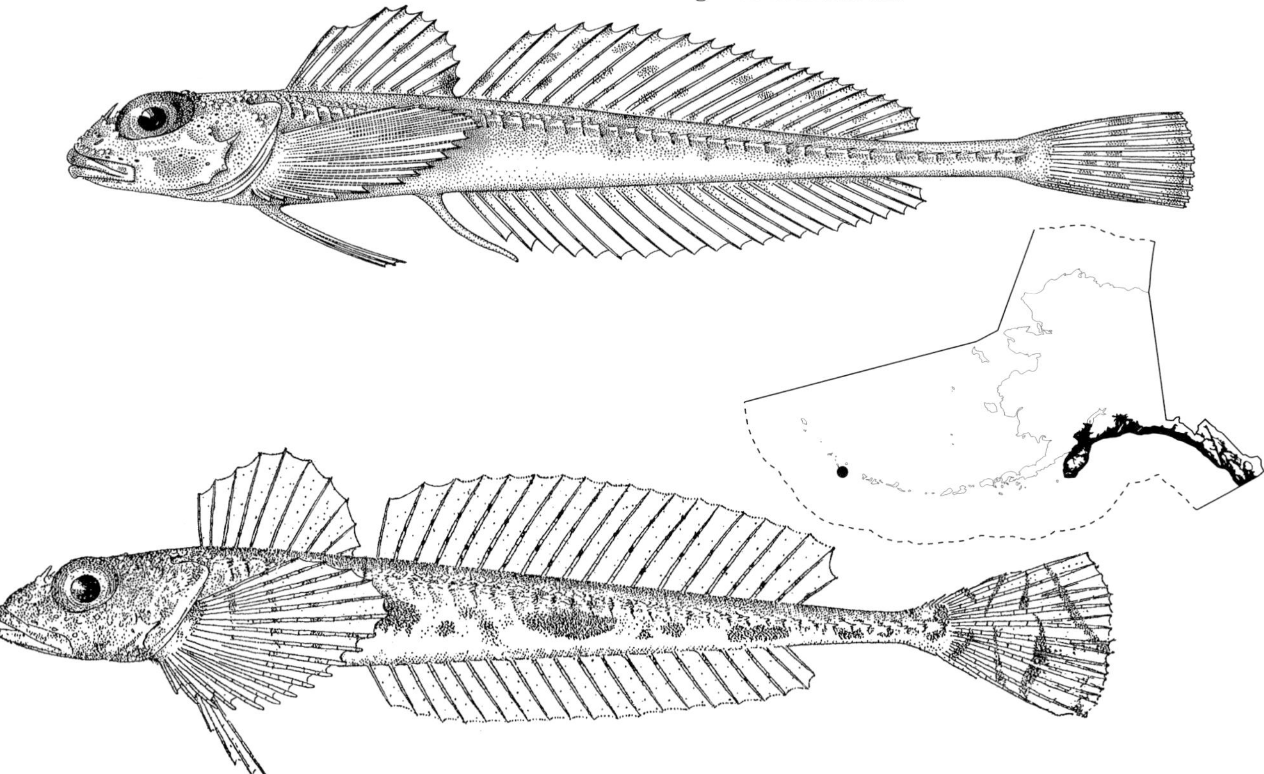

Notes & Sources — *Radulinus asprellus* Gilbert, 1890

Description: Jordan and Evermann 1898:1920–1921; Bolin 1944:40–41; Hart 1973:535–536.

Figures: Upper: Bolin 1944, fig. 15; male. Lower: Jordan and Starks, 1895, pl. 81; female, about 97 mm TL, Puget Sound, near Seattle.

Range: Previously published Alaskan records: Hubbs and Schultz (1941), specimens from south of Kodiak Island, Kasaan Bay, and Petersburg; Isakson et al. (1971; confirmed in Simenstad et al. 1977), from Amchitka Island; and Blackburn and Jackson (1982), from east side of Kodiak Island. The ABL specimens referred to by Quast and Hall (1972) are from the Kodiak Island vicinity; Gulf of Alaska; Chichagof Island at Lisianski Inlet, Ogden Passage, and Khaz Bay; and Baranof Island at Katlian Bay and Port Conclusion. Others are in UW 15710, from Tenakee Inlet; UAM 1808, Fairweather Ground; UAM 1588, from Port Valdez, Prince William Sound; UW 22029 and UBC 65-145, east side of Kodiak Island; UBC 62-676, off Cape Karluk; SIO 76-299, Kodiak shelf at 56°43'N, 153°22'; and SIO 93-169, off Cormorant Rock, Uyak Bay, Kodiak Island. Baxter (1990ms, unpubl. data) examined specimens from Kachemak Bay (specimens not saved).

Stelgistrum stejnegeri Jordan & Gilbert, 1898 — furseal sculpin

Northwestern Pacific Ocean at Avacha Bay to Kuril Islands, southern Sea of Okhotsk, and Sea of Japan off Hokkaido.

Sandy bottom at depths of 18–100 m.

D VIII–X + 16–18; A 11–14; Pec 15–18; Pel I,3; LLs 37–40.

- Light grayish olive dorsally, creamy white ventrally; **4 broad dusky bands**, 1 from spinous dorsal to axil, **1 below anterior and 1 below posterior portion of soft dorsal**, 1 at base of caudal fin; bands broken and mingling with mottling below lateral line.
- Dorsal profile high at nape and anterior part of body; snout profile not abrupt; **maxilla extending to mideye to posterior edge of eye**.
- Nasal spines short and strong; deep transverse groove behind nasal spines; no spines or ridges on top of head.
- Four preopercular spines; upper longest, simple, curved upward; lower three short and sharp.
- Three pairs of simple cirri on top of head, including postocular; cirri on end of maxilla, suborbital stay, lateral line plates; cirri absent from nasal spine and preopercle.
- Spinous and soft-rayed portions of dorsal fin nearly or completely separate.
- **More than 2 scale rows close to dorsal fins**, separated from lateral line by wide space without scales; **lowest row of dorsal scales enlarged, platelike, and extending onto caudal peduncle**; **scales on dorsal fin spines and rays, top and sides of head, and snout**; lateral line scales large, platelike; all scales spiny.
- Lateral line strongly sloping anteriorly then running low on body to caudal fin.
- Vomerine teeth present; palatine teeth absent.
- Anus close to anal fin origin.
- Males without elongate genital papilla.
- Gill membranes united, free from isthmus.
- Length to 90 mm TL.

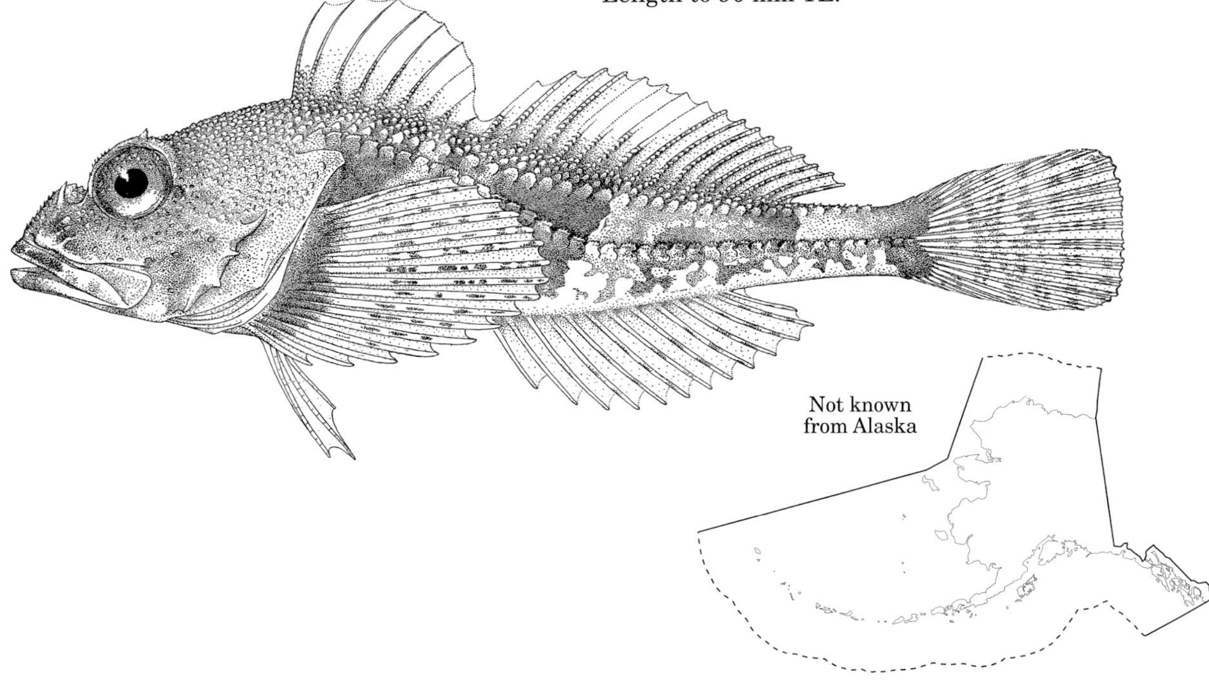

Notes & Sources — *Stelgistrum stejnegeri* Jordan & Gilbert in Jordan & Evermann, 1898

Species name is sometimes spelled *steinegeri,* but *stejnegeri* was the spelling published first.

The vernacular refers to the fur-seal investigations under which the holotype specimen was collected.

Description: Jordan and Evermann 1898:1921–1922; Jordan and Gilbert 1899:456–457; Jordan and Starks 1904b:248–250; Andriashev 1935:294–297; Lindberg and Krasyukova 1987:195–196. KIE uncataloged, 3 specimens (72–85 mm TL) from Sea of Okhotsk.

Figure: Jordan and Gilbert 1899, pl. 54; holotype (unique), 52 mm TL, *Albatross* station 3645, off Robben Island.

Range: *Not* known to occur in the Bering Sea. Jordan and Evermann (1898:1922) gave the type locality as "Bering Sea, off Robben Island." However, Robben Island (Ostrov Tyuleniy) is in the Sea of Okhotsk off Sakhalin, where the *Albatross* made collections in 1896 after it left the Bering Sea. Evidently the error was noticed by Jordan and Starks (1904b:250), who gave the locality simply as: "Sea, off Robben Island." They reported the second known specimen, from Aniva Bay, Sakhalin, and the species is now recognized to be one of the abundant sculpins of that region. Jordan and Gilbert (1899) gave the type locality only as Robben Island; apparently the title of their work, *The Fishes of Bering Sea,* is taken too literally by some authors.

Stelgistrum concinnum Andriashev, 1935 **largeplate sculpin**

Aleutian Islands and eastern Bering Sea at Pribilof Islands; western Bering Sea off Cape Olyutorskiy.

Rocky bottom to depth of 32 m; among rocks covered with calcareous algae, kelp and other brown algae, and sea urchins.

D IX + 17–19; A 14–15; Pec 14–15; Pel I,3; LLs 42.

- Pink in life, in alcohol light tan, marked with brown and dusky; **broad dusky bands** extending to lateral line, 1 below spinous dorsal, **3 below soft dorsal**, 1 on caudal peduncle, all with narrow bars extending ventrally from and between them.
- Dorsal profile high at nape and anterior part of body; snout abrupt in larger specimens; **maxilla extending to anterior edge of eye to mideye**.
- Nasal spines long, strong; deep transverse groove behind nasal spines; no spines on top of head.
- Four preopercular spines; upper long, simple, curved upward; second short, triangular; lower two obsolete.
- Usually 4 pairs of cirri on top of head, including multifid postocular pair; maxillary cirrus short to long, always present; cirri on nasal spine, suborbital stay, and preopercle in some specimens.
- Spinous and soft-rayed portions of dorsal fin nearly or completely separate; pectoral fin very long, extending to about 7th to 9th soft dorsal ray; pelvic fin reaching anal fin origin.
- **One or two scale rows close to dorsal fins**, separated from lateral line by wide naked space; **lower row of dorsal scales greatly enlarged, platelike, extending almost to caudal base**; **scales mostly absent from fin rays and snout**, few on cheek, numerous on top of head; lateral line scales large, platelike; scales spiny.
- Lateral line strongly sloping anteriorly then running low on body to caudal fin.
- Vomerine teeth present; palatine teeth absent.
- Anus close to anal fin origin.
- Males without elongate genital papilla.
- Gill membranes united, free from isthmus.
- Length to 51 mm SL (about 62 mm TL).

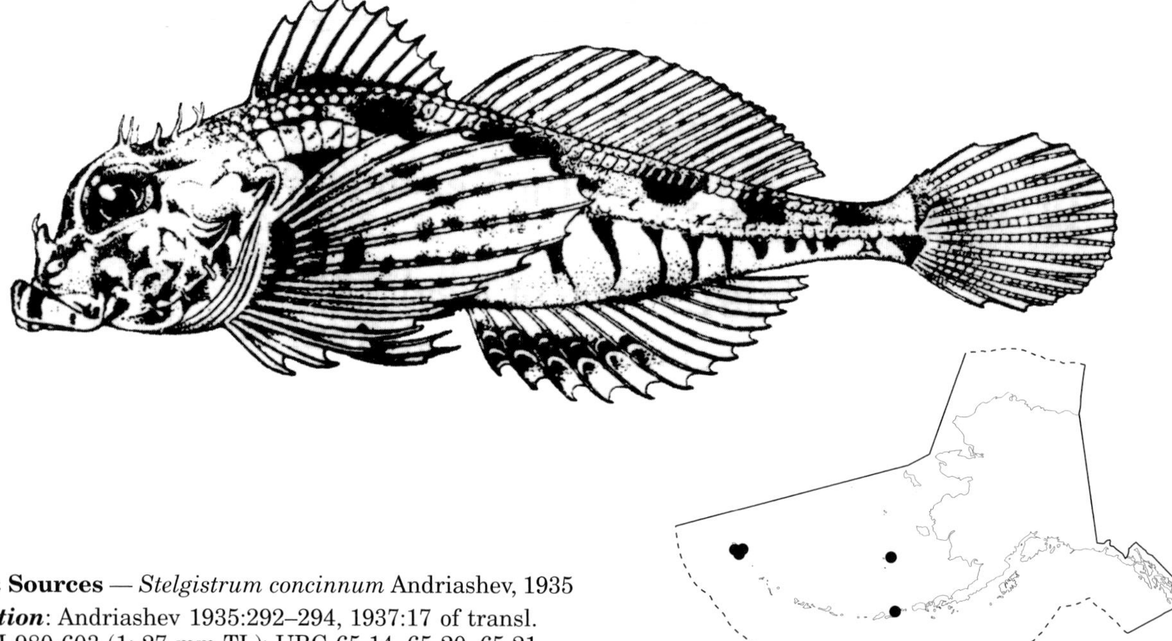

Notes & Sources — *Stelgistrum concinnum* Andriashev, 1935

Description: Andriashev 1935:292–294, 1937:17 of transl. BCPM 980-603 (1; 27 mm TL); UBC 65-14, 65-20, 65-21 (40; 16–24 mm TL); AB 80-49 (1; 56 mm TL). Fin ray counts for 14 of the Alaskan specimens are included above.

Figure: Andriashev 1935, fig. 1; holotype, 51 mm SL, Cape Olyutorskiy. Caudal fin not as rounded in Alaskan specimens; more like *S. beringianum*. Ten dorsal-fin spines could be artist's error; Andriashev (1935, 1937) reported nine, as C.W.M. found in Alaskan specimens.

Range: The ABL, BCPM, and UBC specimens listed above are the first records from Alaska. The ABL specimen was collected in 1975 by N. Calvin and R. J. Ellis from Otter Island in the Pribilof group at depths of 6–9 m; later identified by C.W.M. as *S. concinnum.* The BCPM and UBC specimens were collected by A. E. Peden in clear, shallow water (0–6 m) with nil to slight wave surge while snorkeling and using fish toxicant along rocky shores in 1964 at Binnacle and Armeria bays, Agattu Island (UBC specimens); and in 1980 at Captains Bay, Unalaska Island (BCPM 980-603). Peden also collected *Stelgistrum* at Nizki Island (UBC 65-29) in 1964. At the Agattu and Nizki sites the bottom was large pebbles and rocks covered with red and pink calcareous algae, with growth of *Fucus, Ulva,* and other brown algae according to depth, and many sea urchins. Andriashev (1935) described specimens taken off Cape Olyutorskiy at 31–32 m on rocky bottom.

Size: Using SL = 82% TL from Alaskan specimens gives 62 mm TL for the holotype. Most specimens examined (by C.W.M.) are small but those over 21 mm TL have well-developed scalation and cirri, and fin ray counts are appropriate.

Stelgistrum beringianum Gilbert & Burke, 1912 **smallplate sculpin**

Western Aleutian Islands at Attu Island and Petrel Bank; Commander Islands; western Bering Sea off Cape Olyutorskiy.

Bottom at depths of 32–95 m.

D IX + 18–19; A 12–13; Pec 16–17; Pel I,3; LLs 38–41; Vert 36.

- Body with **4 conspicuous black bands**; 1 under spinous dorsal, **2 under soft dorsal**, 1 on caudal peduncle; last 2 bands divided below lateral line into diverging branches; bands below soft dorsal continuing onto fin as oblique bars.
- Dorsal profile high at nape and anterior part of body; snout not abrupt; **maxilla extending to mid-eye or to posterior edge of eye**.
- Nasal spines short and strong; deep transverse groove behind nasal spines; no spines or ridges on top of head.
- Four preopercular spines; upper longest, simple, curved upward; lower three short, strong, sharp.
- Up to 3 pairs of cirri on top of head, including bifid postocular cirrus, all may be absent; cirri on nasal spine, posterior end of maxilla, and along lateral line in some specimens.
- Spinous and soft-rayed portions of dorsal fin nearly or completely separate.
- **More than 2 scale rows close to dorsal fins**, separated from lateral line by wide space without scales below second dorsal fin; **lowest row of scales distinctly, but not greatly, enlarged; dorsal scales not extending beyond insertion of soft dorsal fin; scales absent or very few on fin rays, top and sides of head, and snout**, except for scales behind eye; numerous scales on nape as continuation of bands anteriorly and meeting on nape; lateral line scales platelike; all scales spiny.
- Lateral line strongly sloping anteriorly then running low on body to caudal fin.
- Vomerine teeth present; palatine teeth absent.
- Anus immediately anterior to anal fin origin.
- Males without elongate genital papilla.
- Gill membranes united, free from isthmus.
- Length to 77 mm SL (about 94 mm TL).

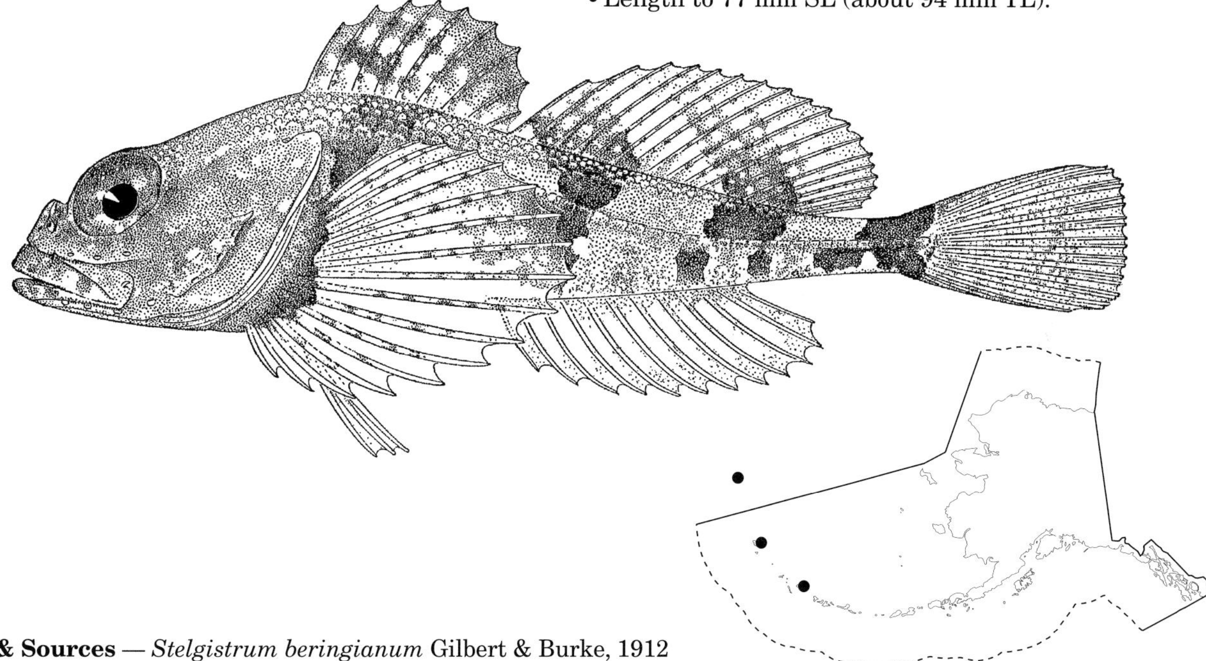

Notes & Sources — *Stelgistrum beringianum* Gilbert & Burke, 1912

Stelgistrops beringiana: Hubbs 1926a.

Hubbs (1926a) considered *Stelgistrum beringianum* to be so different from *S. stejnegeri* that he erected a new genus, *Stelgistrops,* for it, whereas Soldatov and Lindberg (1930) classified it in the synonymy of *S. stejnegeri*. Andriashev (1935) classified them as separate species in the same genus and described them in greater detail.

Description: Gilbert and Burke 1912a:52–53; Andriashev 1935:290–292, 1937:16–17 of transl.; Howe and Richardson 1978 (vertebral count). USNM 38985 (1; 36 mm SL).

Figure: Gilbert and Burke 1912a, fig. 9; holotype, 44 mm TL, *Albatross* station 4777, Petrel Bank, Aleutian Islands.

Range: Species was described by Gilbert and Burke (1912a) from specimens collected at Petrel Bank at depths of 79–95 m. Listed for Attu Island by Wilimovsky (1964), without citing documentation. Bean and Bean (1896:242) recorded a sculpin from the stomach of a cod collected at Bering Island as *Artedius lateralis* (USNM 38985), but Hubbs (1926a) reexamined it and referred it to *S. beringianum*; examining it on 12 Nov. 1999, C.W.M. found it to be a clear example of this species. Andriashev (1935) recorded *S. beringianum* off Cape Olyutorskiy at depths of 32–34 m, where *S. concinnum* was taken in one of the same net hauls.

Size: Largest reported by Andriashev (1935) was 77 mm SL; using SL = 82% TL from measurements of the holotype (36 mm SL, 44 mm TL) gives 94 mm TL. (Caudal fin is missing from USNM 38985.)

Thyriscus anoplus Gilbert & Burke, 1912 **sponge sculpin**

Aleutian Islands from Attu Island to Islands of Four Mountains, and Commander Islands to northern Kuril Islands.

Rocky bottoms with complicated relief and covered with sponges; at depths of 104–800 m, usually at depths of 300–400 m.

D IX–XI + 19–21; A 17–18; Pec 15; Pel I,3; LLs 42–43; Vert 38–39.

- Color in alcohol light olive brown dorsally, pale ventrally; 1 dusky band below spinous dorsal, 3 below soft-rayed dorsal (with first of these 3 doubled), 1 on caudal peduncle joining additional dark band at base of caudal fin; fins barred; cirri on top of head blackish.
- Body compressed, especially along base of spinous dorsal fin; head deeper than wide; occiput slightly concave; maxilla extending to posterior edge of eye or beyond.
- Nasal spines short and strong; deep transverse groove behind nasal spines; no spines or ridges on top of head.
- Four preopercular spines; all simple and short, uppermost scarcely longer than other three.
- Three pairs of long cirri on top of head, including broad, fringed postocular cirrus; minute cirrus on end of maxilla and one at base of opercular flap.
- Dorsal fins completely separate or slightly joined by membrane at base; wide membranous tags at tips of dorsal fin spines; **lower pectoral rays thickened, with membranes deeply incised and 2 or 3 uppermost rays in this group exserted**, longest reaching base of 7th anal ray.
- **Skin smooth except for large, platelike, spiny lateral line scales and spiny scales in pectoral axil**.
- Vomerine and palatine teeth present.
- Anus close to anal fin (74–85% of distance between pelvic and anal fin bases).
- Genital papilla of males over about 85 mm TL well developed, bulbous at base, tapering to point.
- Gill membranes united, free from isthmus.
- Length to 145 mm TL.

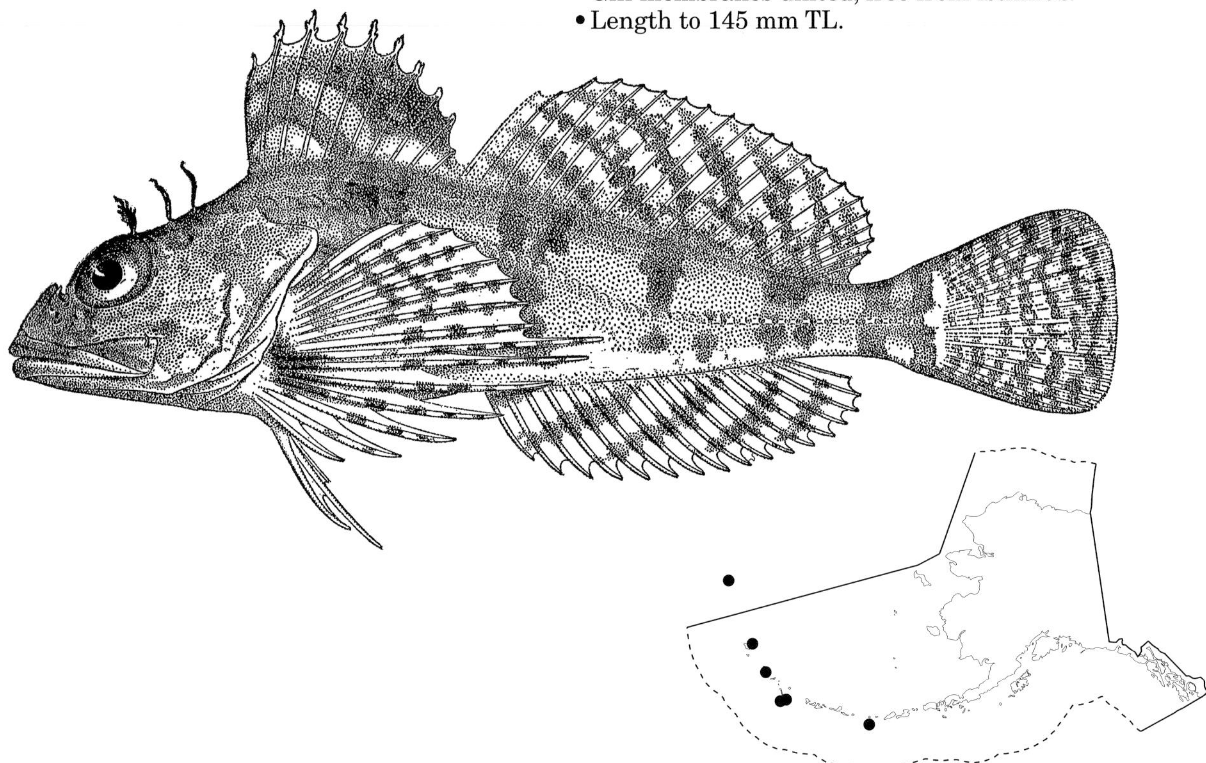

Notes & Sources — *Thyriscus anoplus* Gilbert & Burke, 1912

Description: Gilbert and Burke 1912a:43–44; Tokranov 1998b. CAS 47752 (4 specimens, 91–115 mm TL).

Figure: Gilbert and Burke 1912a, fig. 4; holotype (unique), USNM 74368, female, 109 mm TL, *Albatross* station 4782, Bering Sea off Attu Island, Alaska.

Range: The type locality is north of Attu Island at a depth of 104 m. No other Alaskan records have been published, although several specimens are in museum collections. Specimens at CAS are: CAS 47688, from south of Amchitka Island at 51°31'N, 179°45'E, depth 351–488 m; CAS 47752, south of Amchita at 51°19'N, 178°59'E, depth 230–256 m; and CAS 48211, near Buldir Island at 52°16'N, 175°52'E, depth 244–264 m. The UW has an uncataloged specimen from south of the Islands of Four Mountains and OSU has one from an unspecified locality in the Aleutian Islands (R. Baxter, unpubl. data). Tokranov (1998b) provided details on distribution, habitat, and aspects of life history from trawl surveys in the Pacific off the northern Kuril Islands, where it is fairly common. Fedorov and Sheiko (2002) reported it to be common near the Commander Islands.

Icelus spiniger Gilbert, 1896 — **thorny sculpin**

Bering Sea from Cape Navarin and Aleutian Islands to southern British Columbia at La Perouse Bank, and to Sea of Okhotsk.

Bottom at depths of 30–770 m, usually at 150–350 m.

D VIII–X + 19–23; A 15–19; Pec 17–20; Pel I,3; LLs 42–45; Vert 40–42.

- Body tan, underside whitish; 4 narrow brown bars dorsally; vague splotches laterally; first dorsal fin often with black blotches; second dorsal, caudal, and pectoral fins vaguely barred.
- Body elongate, slender; head wider than deep; eye large, about 1.5 times snout length.
- Parietal spine absent; nuchal spine long, sharp; 1 or 2 suborbital stay spines; lachrymal spines absent.
- Four preopercular spines, uppermost bifid.
- Postocular cirrus present; parietal cirrus present or absent; other cirri absent.
- **Each scale of dorsal row of platelike scales bearing a single, strong spine**; axillary scales 2–17; scale rows between dorsal row and lateral line and between lateral line and anal fin absent; dorsal and ventral caudal peduncle scales present; lateral line scales extending onto caudal fin.
- Vomerine and palatine teeth present.
- Genital papilla of males with spatulate basal portion; terminal appendage curved or hooklike.
- Gill membranes united, free from isthmus.
- Length to 280 mm TL.

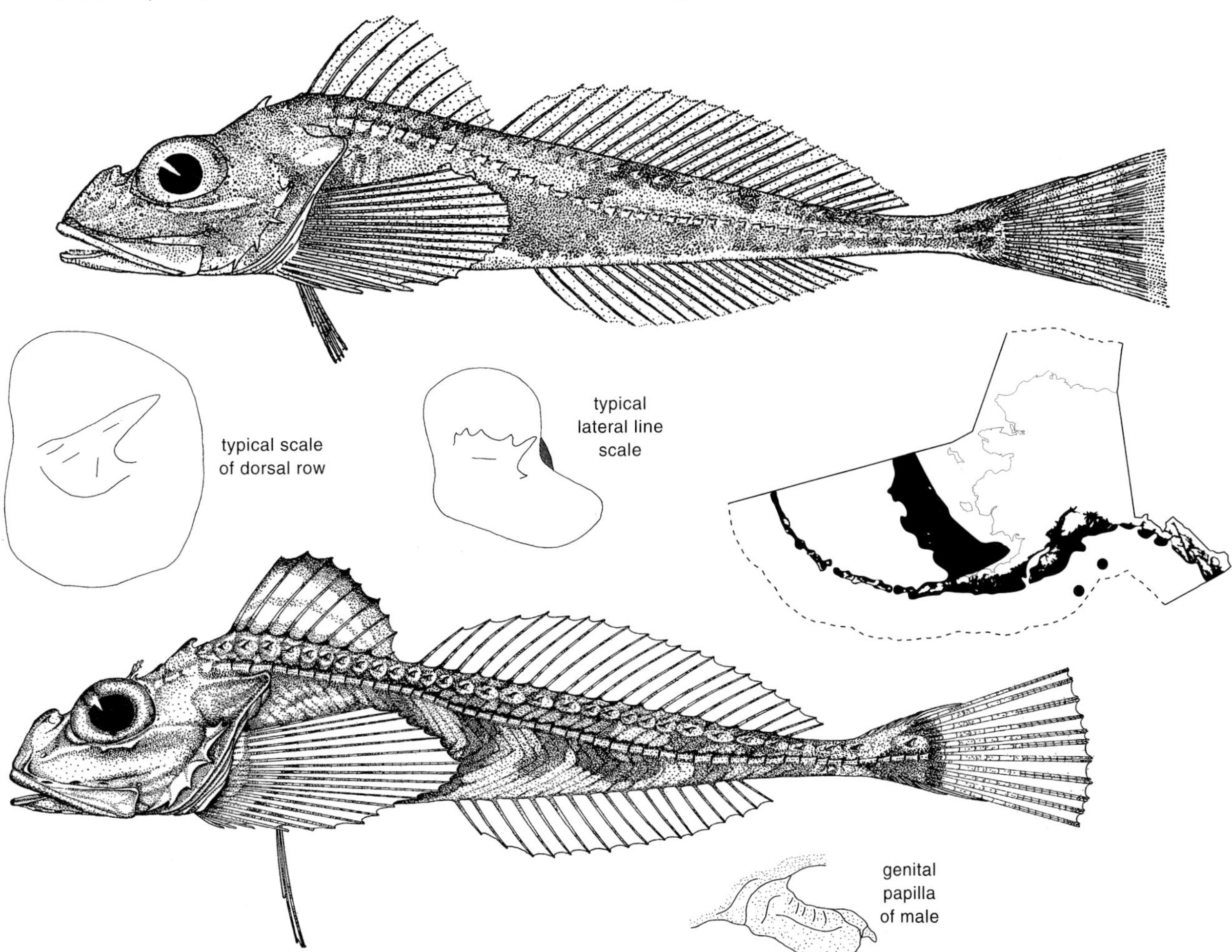

Notes & Sources — *Icelus spiniger* Gilbert, 1896

Description: Gilbert 1896:412; D. W. Nelson 1984:24–25.

Figures: Upper: Gilbert 1896, pl. 24; lectotype, female, about 118 mm SL, 140 mm TL, *Albatross* station 3278, Bristol Bay, Alaska. Lower: Barraclough 1971, fig. 1; desiccated or skinned, but shows more diagnostic details. Scales, genital papilla: Nelson 1984, figs. 18D, 19C, 23I.

Range: Nelson (1984) and Peden and Hughes (1986) listed locality data for many Alaskan records. Allen and Smith (1988) mapped range in eastern Bering Sea and Pacific Ocean from 30 years of NMFS demersal trawl surveys. Westernmost locality in Aleutian Islands reported by Nelson (1984) and Allen and Smith (1988) was Agattu Island. Fedorov and Sheiko (2002) reported it to be common off the Commander Islands. Barber et al. (1997) reported it was taken at one station in 1990 northeastern Chukchi Sea survey, but did not comment on the unusual record or give specific documentation; C.W.M. did not find this species represented in the voucher collection (at UAF) for the cruise.

Icelus canaliculatus Gilbert, 1896 **blacknose sculpin**

Bering Sea from Navarin Canyon to Bristol Bay, usually along continental slope, and off Aleutian Islands east to Akutan Island, possibly to Gulf of Alaska; and to southern Sea of Okhotsk off Hokkaido.

Bottom at depths of 20–1,005 m, most commonly collected at 250–900 m; often taken with *I. euryops*.

D VII–VIII + 22–25; A 18–20; Pec 15–19; Pel I,3; LLs 43–46; Vert 37–39.

- Color in life blackish, in preservative yellowish brown; vague darker saddles; **nasal tubes black**; genital papilla of males dark proximally, whitish distally.
- Body elongate, slender; head wider than deep; eye large, about 1.5 times snout length.
- Parietal spine absent; nuchal spines short, sharp; 1 suborbital stay spine; lachrymal spine absent.
- Four preopercular spines; uppermost simple, bifid, or trifid.
- Postocular, parietal, opercular, and maxillary cirri present; other cirri absent.
- Dorsal row of enlarged, platelike scales bearing spinules, and with smaller scales interspersed; **axillary scales 14–39**; scale rows between dorsal row and lateral line usually absent; **row of small scales usually present just above anal fin base**; dorsal and ventral caudal peduncle scales present; lateral line scales extending onto caudal fin.
- Suborbital pores of cephalic sensory system large, with smaller pores clustered around them.
- Vomerine and palatine teeth present.
- Genital papilla of males with cylindrical basal portion and large, curved terminal appendage.
- Gill membranes united, free from isthmus.
- Length to 232 mm TL.

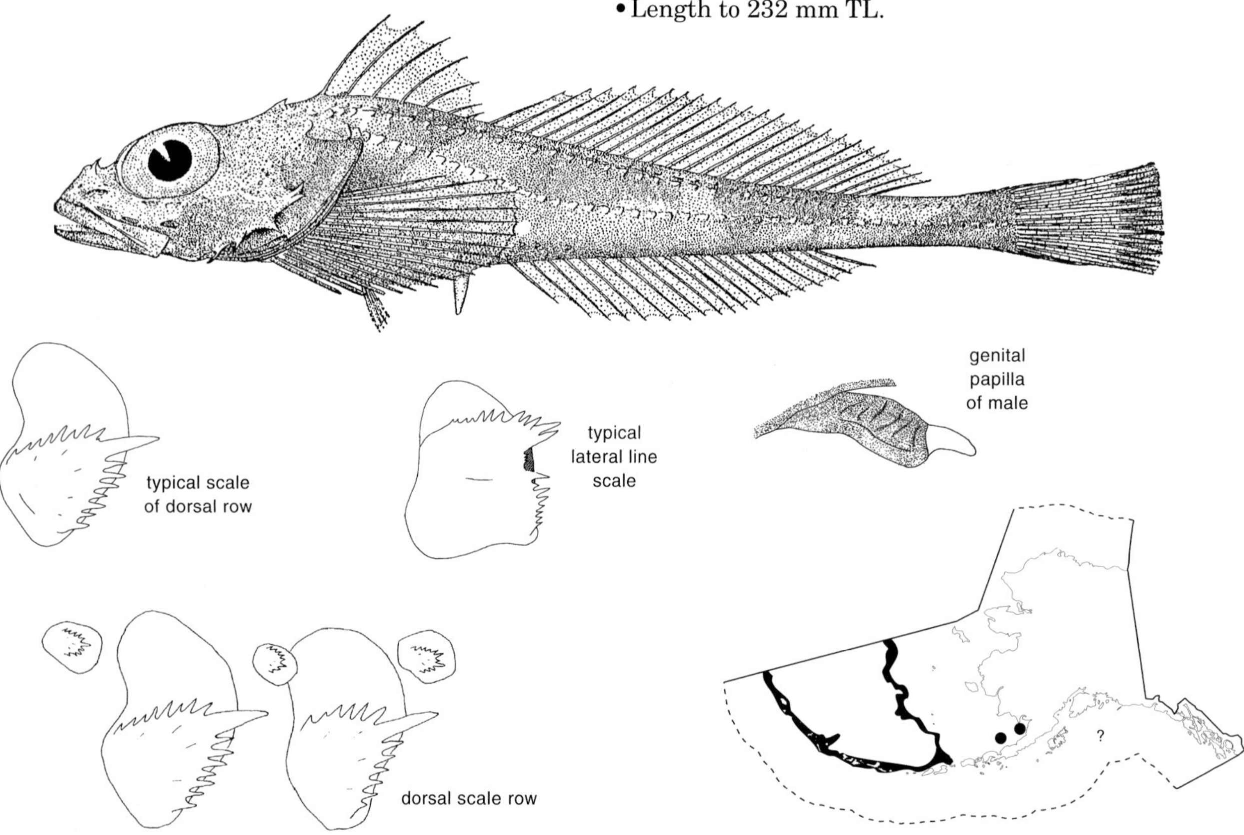

Notes & Sources — *Icelus canaliculatus* Gilbert, 1896

The specific name, *canaliculatus*, refers to the numerous small canals associated with the larger canals of the cephalic lateral line sensory system.

Description: Gilbert 1896:412–413; D. W. Nelson 1984:32–33.

Figures: Gilbert 1896, pl. 24; lectotype, male, about 94 mm SL, 105 mm TL, *Albatross* station 3329, north of Unalaska Island, Bering Sea, Alaska. Scales, genital papilla: Nelson 1984, figs. 18C, 19B, 23D, 31B.

Range: Taken from Agattu Island to Akutan Island in NMFS demersal trawl surveys (Allen and Smith 1988). Locality data for voucher specimens from inner Bristol Bay and other Alaskan localities were given by Nelson (1984). UBC 63-362 includes two other examples from Bristol Bay, at about 57°N, 162°W. We could not identify the literature source of a Gulf of Alaska occurrence referred to by Allen and Smith (1988), and we did not find any specimens from the Gulf of Alaska in museum collections. Yabe et al. (1983) reported collection of a male *I. canaliculatus* at a depth of 1,005 m in the Sea of Okhotsk. Fedorov and Sheiko (2002) reported *I. canaliculatus* to be common in the vicinity of the Commander Islands.

Icelus euryops Bean, 1890 **wide-eye sculpin**

Bering Sea from Navarin Canyon along continental slope to Unimak Pass; western Gulf of Alaska near Trinity Islands.

Bottom at depths of 200–740 m; often taken with *I. canaliculatus*.

D VIII–X + 20–23; A 15–19; Pec 16–18; Pel I,3; LLs 43–45.

- Light brown to gray, sometimes with 4 dark bands dorsally; fin rays black except lower portion of pectoral base light; belly dark gray except anal papilla white; **nasal tubes pale**, similar to snout; **head cirri black**.
- Body elongate, slender; head wider than deep; eye large, about twice snout length.
- Parietal spine absent; nuchal spine short, sharp; 1 suborbital stay spine; lachrymal spine absent.
- Four preopercular spines, first bifid.
- Postocular, parietal, nuchal, and opercular cirri present; other cirri absent.
- Dorsal row of enlarged, platelike scales bearing spinules, and with smaller scales scattered among them; **1–3 rows of scales between dorsal scale row and lateral line**; axillary scales 10–27; scale rows between lateral line and anal fin absent; dorsal and ventral caudal peduncle scales present; lateral line scales extending onto caudal fin.
- Suborbital pores of cephalic lateral line large, but without smaller pores clustered around them.
- Vomerine and palatine teeth present.
- Genital papilla of male cylindrical, dorsoventrally flattened, with large, curved terminal appendage.
- Gill membranes united, free from isthmus.
- Length to 164 mm TL.

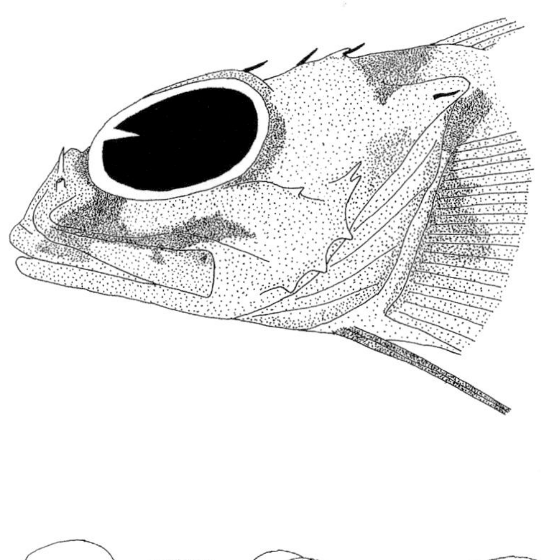

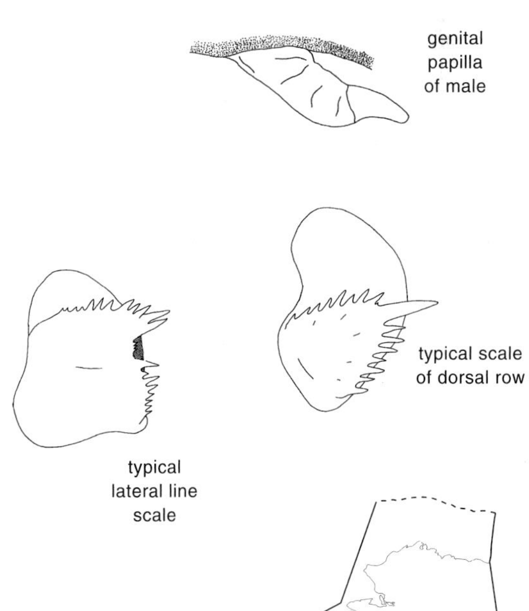

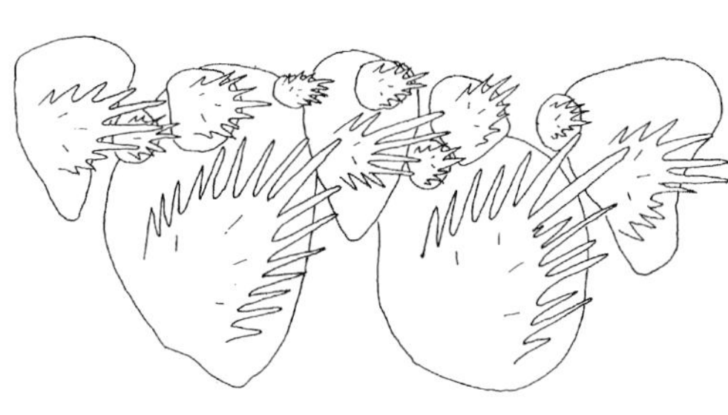

dorsal scale row

Notes & Sources — *Icelus euryops* Bean, 1890
Icelus vicinalis Gilbert, 1896
The specific name, *euryops,* means "wide eye" and refers to the characteristically large eye of the species.

Description: Bean 1890b:41; Gilbert 1896:413–415; Jordan and Evermann 1898:1915–1917; D. W. Nelson 1984:30–32.

Figures: Nelson 1984, figs. 18C, 19B, 23C, 30, 31A.

Range: Type locality of *I. euryops* is near the Trinity Islands at 56°00'N, 154°20'W; depth 290 m, *Albatross* station 2853. Nelson (1984) stated that the type is the only Gulf of Alaska record, and gave locality data for known Bering Sea specimens. The type locality of *I. vicinalis* (= *I. euryops*) is usually given as Bristol Bay. However, all of the types were taken west of Bristol Bay, at localities north of Unimak Pass, Unalaska Island, and Umnak Pass. *Icelus euryops* commonly occurs with *I. canaliculatus.*

Size: Baxter 1990ms: BCPM 980-18, a specimen measuring 139.7 mm SL and 164.4 mm TL taken from the southern Bering Sea at 60°58'N, 179°03'W. Probably similar in total length to the largest specimen examined by Nelson (1984), which was 141 mm SL.

Icelus uncinalis Gilbert & Burke, 1912 **uncinate sculpin**

Western Bering Sea north of Attu Island and Semisopochnoi Island, and Commander Islands.
Bottom in relatively shallow water at depths of 70–247 m.

D IX + 19–20; A 14–16; Pec 17–18; Pel I,3; LLs 41–42.

- Light brown dorsally, creamy white ventrally; 4 darker saddles, including 1 posteriorly on caudal peduncle; nasal tubes and head cirri pale, similar to surrounding coloration.
- Body elongate, compressed; eye large, about 1.5 to 2 times snout length.
- Parietal and nuchal spines present, short, sharp; lachrymal and suborbital stay spines absent.
- Four preopercular spines, first simple or bifid.
- **Postocular cirrus present, narrow at base and widening distally, usually branched or multifid at tip**; parietal, opercular, suborbital stay cirri present or absent; other cirri absent.
- Dorsal row of enlarged, platelike scales bearing spinules; axillary scales 12–20; scales between dorsal row and lateral line and between lateral line and anal fin absent; **dorsal and ventral caudal peduncle scales absent**; **lateral line scales extending onto caudal fin (1 scale on caudal rays)**.
- Vomerine and palatine teeth present.
- Genital papilla of males cylindrical and slightly dorsoventrally flattened, with short, curved terminal appendage.
- Gill membranes united, free from isthmus.
- Length to 97 mm TL.

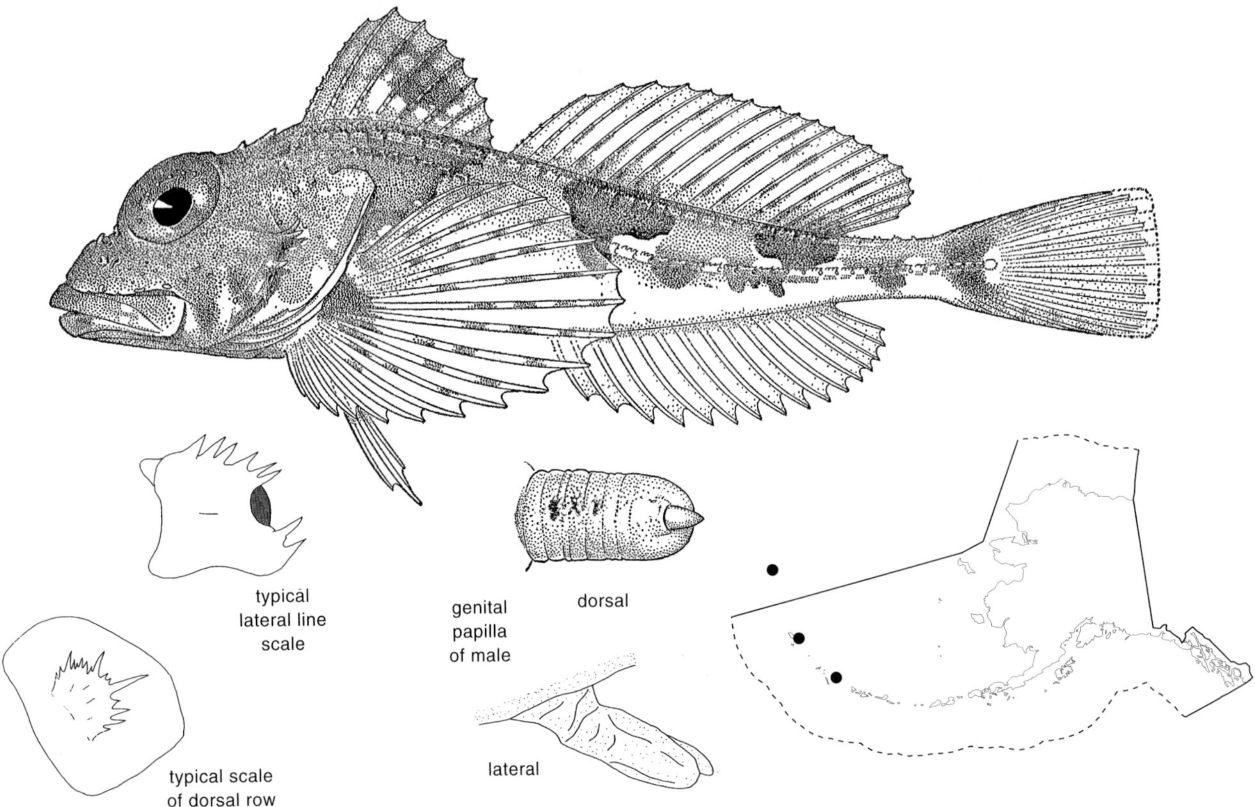

Notes & Sources — *Icelus uncinalis* Gilbert & Burke, 1912
The name *uncinalis* means "small hook," and refers to the male genital papilla.

Description: Gilbert and Burke 1912a:39–41; D. W. Nelson 1984:52–53.

Figures: Gilbert and Burke 1912a, figs. 2, 2a (dorsal view of genital papilla); holotype, 97 mm TL, *Albatross* station 4784, off Attu Island, Bering Sea, Alaska. Scales, genital papilla (lateral view): Nelson 1984, figs. 18B, 19A, 23E.

Range: Nelson (1984) concluded, from analysis of the systematics and distribution of *Icelus,* that *I. uncinalis* has been collected only in the western Bering Sea. Voucher specimens include Gilbert and Burke's (1912a) 12 specimens collected off Bering Island, off Attu Island, and near Semisopochnoi Island on Petrel Bank by the *Albatross* in 1906, and specimens taken off Bering Island in 1950 by the Soviet research vessel *Vitiaz* and examined by Nelson (1984). Accounts of the species in the eastern Bering Sea, Sea of Okhotsk, and Sea of Japan are attributable to *I. spatula* and other *Icelus* species (Nelson 1984). Eastern Bering Sea specimens in the NMC collection identified as *I. uncinalis* were examined by B. W. Coad (pers. comm., 28 Apr. 1999), who concluded they too were attributable to *I. spatula*. ABL specimens listed by Quast and Hall (1972) from the Gulf of Alaska are also referable to *I. spatula* using Nelson's (1984) key. Minimum depth: Fedorov and Sheiko 2002.

Icelus spatula Gilbert & Burke, 1912 — **spatulate sculpin**

Beaufort, Chukchi, and eastern Bering seas to eastern Gulf of Alaska at Glacier Bay; western Chukchi Sea to Pacific Ocean off Kamchatka and Sea of Okhotsk; Arctic seas of Canada to west Greenland and Labrador; and in Arctic seas of Russia.

Bottom in relatively shallow water at depths of 12–365 m.

D VII–XI + 18–22; A 13–18; Pec 16–20; Pel I,3; LLs 33–43; Vert 39–41.

- Light brown dorsally, creamy white ventrally; 4 or 5 dark saddles; coloration varying geographically (lighter or darker, freckles present or absent, saddles distinct or vague); nasal tubes pale, similar to snout; head cirri pale or black.
- Body elongate, compressed; head about as deep as wide; eye large, about 1.5 to 2 times snout length.
- Parietal and nuchal spines present, shape variable; lachrymal and suborbital stay spines absent.
- Four preopercular spines, first simple or bifid.
- Postocular cirrus present, shape (and pigmentation) variable; parietal, opercular, suborbital stay cirri present or absent; other cirri absent.
- Dorsal row of enlarged, platelike scales bearing spinules; axillary scales 1–14; scales between dorsal row and lateral line and between lateral line and anal fin absent; **caudal peduncle scales absent, or present only above lateral line**; **lateral line scales extending to posterior edge of hypural plate**.
- Vomerine and palatine teeth present.
- Genital papilla of males spatulate or dorsoventrally flattened, with curved or hooklike terminal appendage (terminal appendage shape variable).
- Gill membranes united, free from isthmus.
- Length to 116 mm SL (about 140 mm TL).

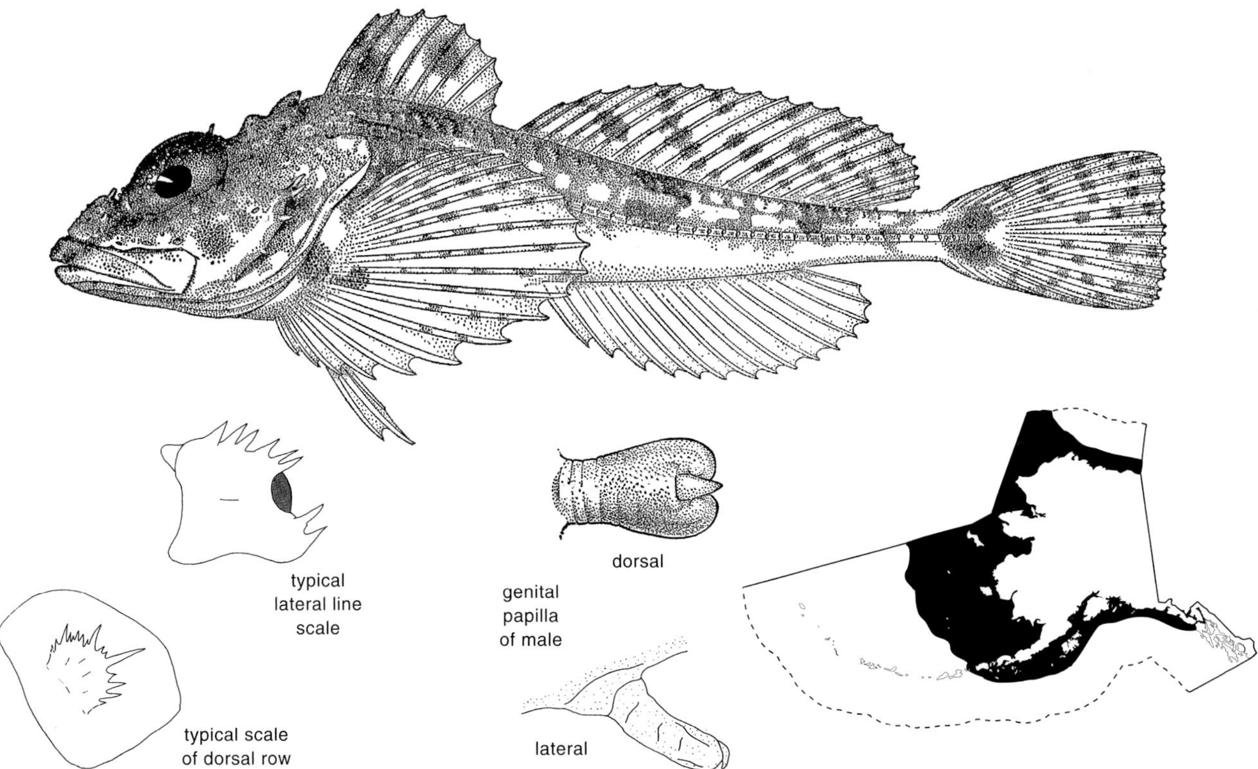

Notes & Sources — *Icelus spatula* Gilbert & Burke, 1912

The name *spatula* refers to the spatulate shape of the male genital papilla.

D. W. Nelson (1984) gave a complete synonymy, including many records previously referred to *I. bicornis* and *I. uncinalis.*

Description: Gilbert and Burke 1912a:41–43; D. W. Nelson 1984:41–50.

Figures: Gilbert and Burke 1912, figs. 3, 3a (dorsal view of genital papilla); holotype, male, 69 mm TL, *Albatross* station 4794, Avacha Bay, southeast Kamchatka. Scales, genital papilla (lateral view): Nelson 1984, figs. 18B, 19A, 23G.

Range: Nelson (1984) gave locality data for numerous specimens from Alaska. Quast and Hall (1972) recorded *I. spatula* from Glacier Bay. Specimens at ABL originally identified as *I. uncinalis* from Unimak Pass, the Shumagin Islands, Kodiak Island, and Cook Inlet are referable to *I. spatula* using Nelson's (1984) key. UBC 61-516 and 62-994 are single specimens from Kachemak Bay, Cook Inlet. Fedorov and Sheiko (2002) reported it to be common in vicinity of the Commander Islands. We did not find records of occurrence from the Aleutian Islands west of Unimak Pass.

Size: Nelson 1984: largest of 510 specimens examined.

Icelus bicornis (Reinhardt, 1840) **twohorn sculpin**

Beaufort Sea; nearly circumpolar, not found in Chukchi Sea or East Siberian Sea.

Bottom at depths of 17–560 m; Alaskan records from depths of 50–159 m.

D VIII–X + 18–21; A 12–16; Pec 16–18; Pel I,3; LLs 33–43; Vert 40–43.

- Yellowish brown dorsally, whitish ventrally; many brown spots; nasal tubes pale, similar to snout; cirri pale, similar to dorsal surface of head.
- Body elongate, compressed; head profile steeper than in *I. spatula*; eye large, about 1.5 to 2 times snout length; supraocular ridge usually much more prominent than in *I. spatula*.
- Parietal spine short, blunt; nuchal spine blunt or pointed; lachrymal and suborbital stay spines absent.
- Four preopercular spines, first bifid or trifid.
- Postocular cirrus present; parietal, opercular, suborbital stay cirri present or absent.
- Dorsal row of enlarged, platelike scales bearing spinules; axillary scales 9–30; **1 or more rows of small scales often present between dorsal scale row and lateral line and between lateral line and anal fin**; **dorsal and ventral caudal peduncle scales present** (occasionally absent); **lateral line scales not extending onto caudal peduncle**.
- Vomerine and palatine teeth present.
- Genital papilla of males with cylindrical basal portion and long, tapering terminal appendage.
- Gill membranes united, free from isthmus.
- Length to 116 mm TL.

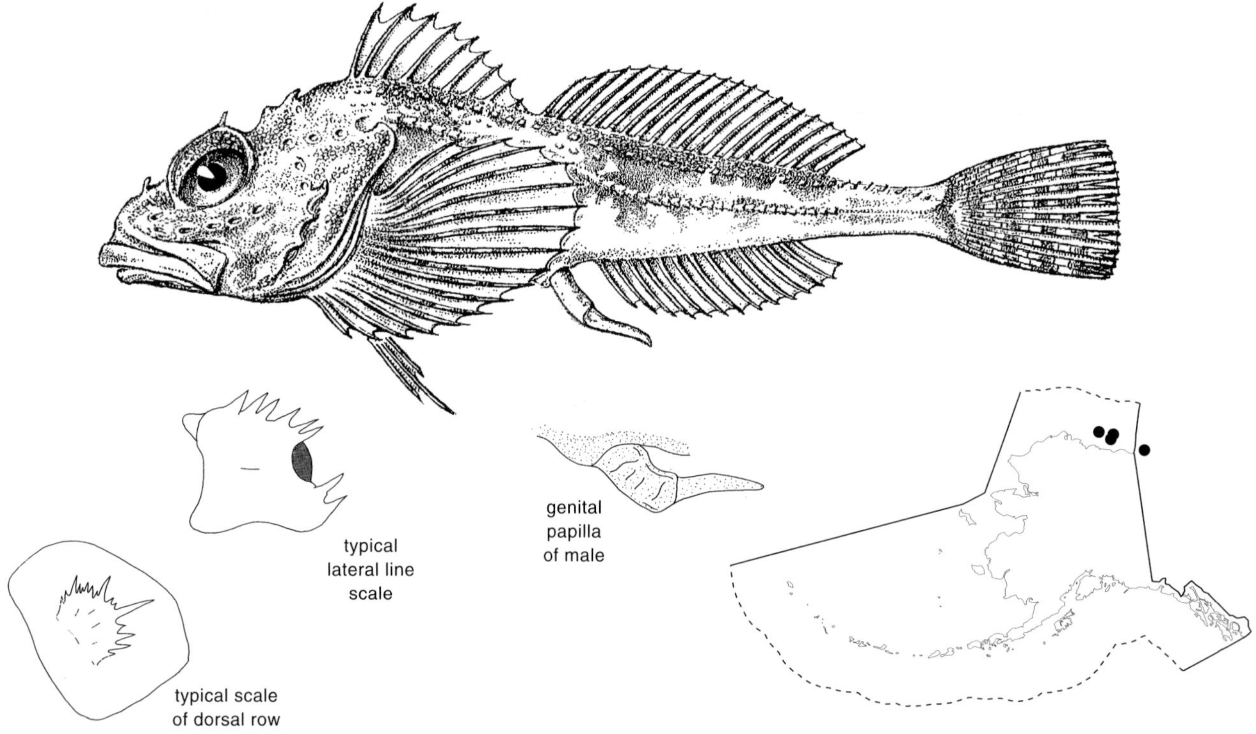

Notes & Sources — *Icelus bicornis* (Reinhardt, 1840)
Cottus bicornis Reinhardt, 1840
D. W. Nelson's (1984) synonymy identified many Alaskan records that had been incorrectly attributed to *I. bicornis.* The name *bicornis,* meaning "two-horned," refers to the two pairs of spines, parietal and nuchal, on the occiput.

Description: Andriashev 1954:361–392; McAllister 1963b: 53–55; D. W. Nelson 1984:35–41; Scott and Scott 1988:498–499.

Figures: Andriashev 1954, fig. 202; male, 61 mm TL, Barents Sea. Scales, genital papilla: Nelson 1984, figs. 18B, 19A, 23H.

Range: In early literature *I. bicornis* was not distinguished from *I. spatula.* Several Alaskan records originally attributed to *I. bicornis* represent *I. spatula.* From reexamining hundreds of specimens Nelson (1984) concluded that *I. bicornis* has been documented in Alaska only in the eastern Beaufort Sea, although it probably coexists with *I. spatula* from about Point Barrow eastward. Alaskan records given by Nelson (1984) are NMC 74-281 (7 specimens), 70°33'N, 145°45'W; and NMC 79-509 (7), 70°50'N, 145°31'W. NMC records indicate they were taken at depths of 50 m and 110 m, respectively. Others are NMC 74-283 (28), 70°41'N, 145°23'W, depth 79 m; and NMC 74-289 (5), 71°11'N, 148°32'W, depth 159 m. All four NMC lots were taken by otter trawl, and were identified by D. E. McAllister. Hunter et al. (1984) confirmed records from Canadian Arctic as close to Alaska as Herschel Island.

Rastrinus scutiger (Bean, 1890) **roughskin sculpin**

Aleutian Islands from Attu Island to western Gulf of Alaska at Trinity Islands; Commander Islands. Muddy and sandy bottoms at depths of 120–512 m; reported to 740 m.

D IX–X + 18–21; A 17–19; Pec 17–19; Pel I,3; LLs 43–44; Vert 39–41.

- Color in preservative light brown dorsally, whitish ventrally; irregular dark blotches on back and sides, some extending onto dorsal and anal fins; dark streak running forward from eye and across premaxilla, leaving tip of snout pale; head cirri dark.
- Body elongate, compressed; head depth about equal to head width; eye large, about 1.5 to 2 times snout length.
- Parietal, nuchal, and suborbital stay spines absent.
- Four preopercular spines; all small, uppermost simple or bifid.
- Postocular, parietal, nuchal, suborbital stay, and opercular cirri present.
- First dorsal fin longer than second, especially in males.
- **Body above and below lateral line completely covered with small, spiny scales; dorsal rows of enlarged, platelike scales absent**; axillary scales present; scales present on eye.
- **Lateral line extending to or nearly to caudal fin base.**
- Vomerine and palatine teeth present.
- Anus well in front of anal fin origin.
- Genital papilla of males cylindrical, dorsoventrally flattened, with hooklike terminal appendage.
- Gill membranes united, free from isthmus.
- Length to 86 mm SL (about 100 mm TL).

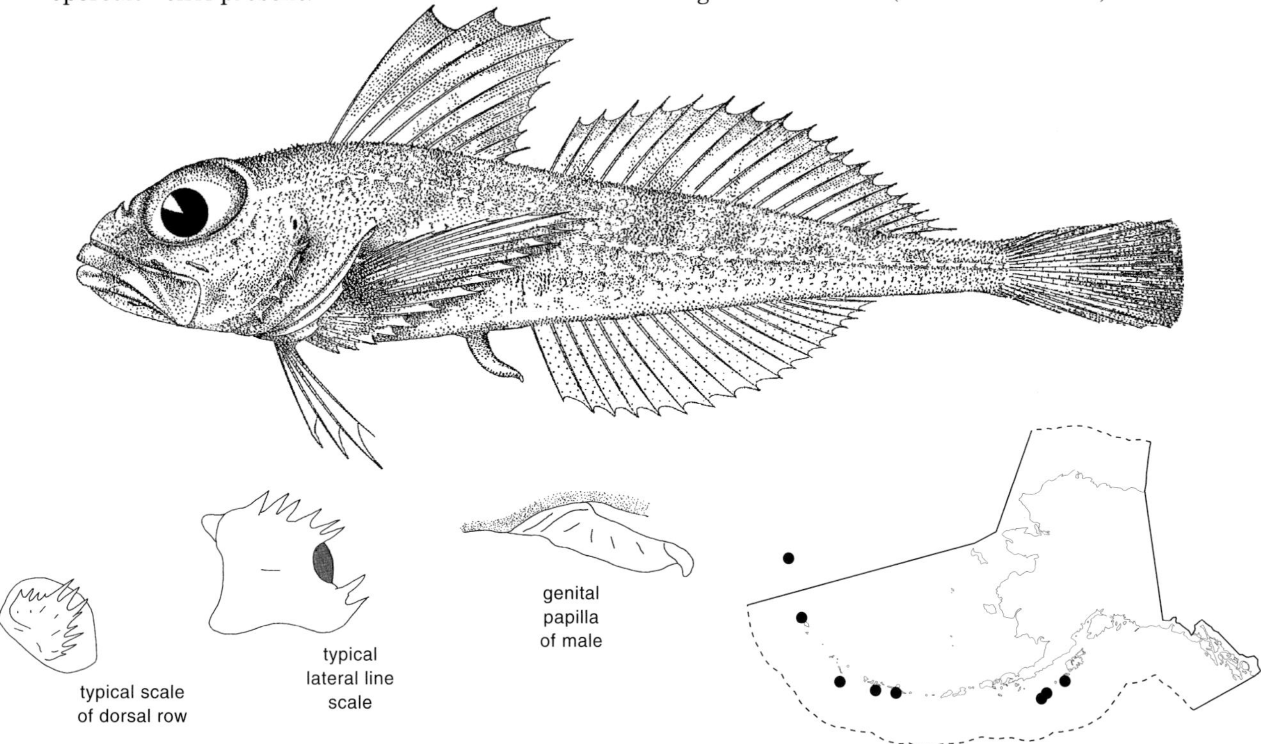

Notes & Sources — *Rastrinus scutiger* (Bean, 1890)
Icelus scutiger Bean, 1890
Jordan and Evermann (1896a, 1898) erected the genus *Rastrinus* to accommodate *Rastrinus scutiger*. Taranetz (1935a) later returned it to *Icelus*. Because incorporating the character states of *Rastrinus,* such as absence of parietal and nuchal spines (the latter present in all *Icelus*), broadens the diagnosis of *Icelus* so much that some other cottid genera would have to be included, Nelson (1984) resurrected the genus *Rastrinus*.

Description: Bean 1890b:41; Gilbert 1896:415; D. W. Nelson 1984:17–18.

Figures: Jordan and Evermann 1900, fig. 692, male, about 73 mm TL. Scales, genital papilla: Nelson 1984, figs. 18A, 19A, 23A.

Range: Type locality is near Trinity Islands, Alaska, *Albatross* station 2853, at 56°00'N, 154°20'W, depth 291 m (Bean 1890b). Recorded from south of the Alaska Peninsula, *Albatross* station 3339, depth 252 m, by Gilbert (1896); and off Attu Island, Alaska, station 4784, depth 247 m, and Bering Island, Russia, station 4790, depth 117 m, by Gilbert and Burke (1912a). The capture locality for the "Bering Sea" specimen referred to by Quast and Hall (1972) is uncertain; the specimen could have been caught off the Shumagin Islands, western Gulf of Alaska, instead (ABL records). Nelson (1984) recorded five OSU lots taken near Amchitka, Adak, and Atka islands. UBC 65-67 (1 specimen) is from southwest of the Semidi Islands at 55°08'N, 156°57'W.

Size: Nelson 1984: largest of 45 specimens examined.

Stlegicottus xenogrammus Bolin, 1936

strangeline sculpin

Bering Sea north of Rat Islands, Aleutian Islands.
Sand and broken shell bottom at depth of 494 m.

D IX + 19; A 17; Pec 18; Pel I,3; LLs about 30.

- Color in preservative brownish yellow; vague, reddish brown blotches extending below lateral line; reddish brown bars extending from eye over tip of lower jaw, maxilla, and toward opercle.
- Head and anterior part of body subovate, set off from rest of body at level of anal fin origin ventrally by broad transverse groove; body slightly compressed; eye large, about 1.5 times snout length; anterior nostril in well developed tube.
- Nasal spine strong; no spines on top of head.
- Four preopercular spines; first longest, all simple.
- Postocular, parietal, and nuchal cirri present; cirrus near angle of opercle; no cirri on body.
- First dorsal fin higher than second; pelvic fin small, less than eye length.
- **Scales irregular, present on head, interorbital space, dorsal surface of body, above and below lateral line**; scales bearing slender, slightly curved spines; about 3 rows of same type of spines on dorsal surface of eyeball; lateral line scales short and tubular, broken by a longitudinal slit and having a single spine at upper posterior angle and another at lower posterior angle.
- Pores of head well developed; suborbital series very large.
- **Lateral line not extending beyond anal fin.**
- Vomerine and palatine teeth present.
- Anus about one-fourth of distance to pelvic base from anal fin.
- Genital papilla short, bluntly conical.
- Gill membranes united, free from isthmus.
- Length of holotype (unique) 29.1 mm SL.

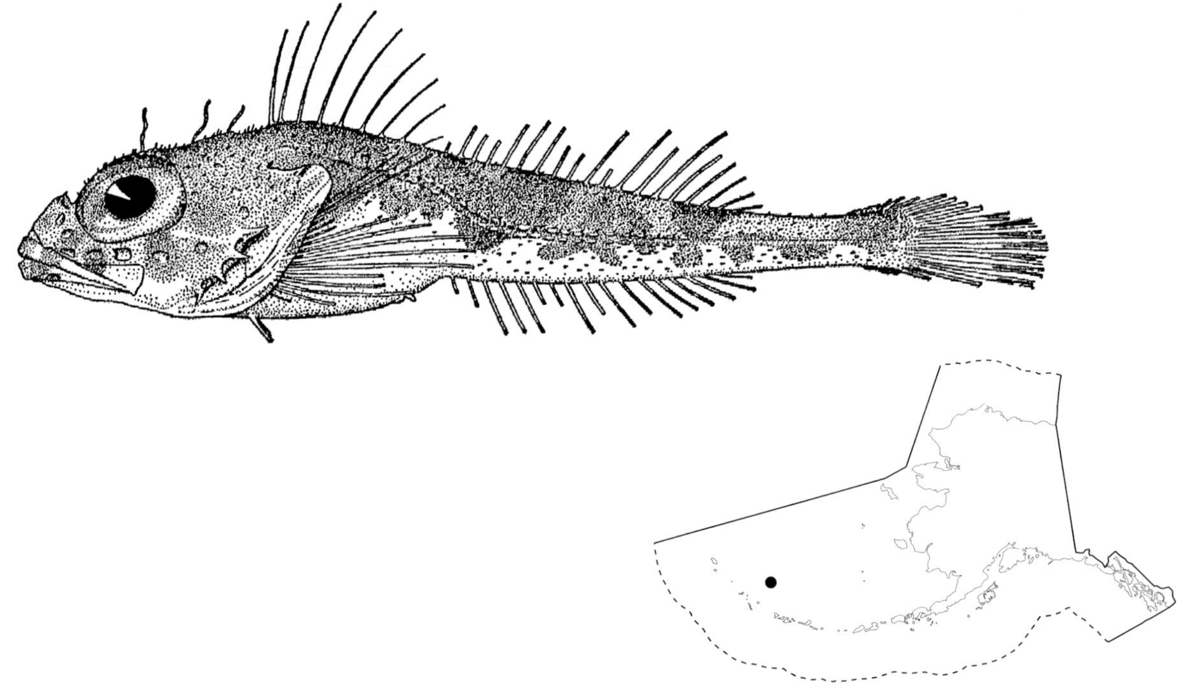

Notes & Sources — *Stlegicottus xenogrammus* Bolin, 1936

The specific epithet *xenogrammus,* from Greek, means "strange line" and refers to the broad transverse groove which forms "a line of demarcation" ventrally between the anterior and posterior portions of the body.

Bolin (1936b) speculated that the isolated genus *Stlegicottus* represents an early offshoot from the line of descent that later gave rise to *Artedius* and *Stelgistrum.*

Description: Bolin 1936b:36–38.

Figure: Bolin 1936b, fig. 8 (damaged specimen); holotype (unique), USNM 102108, male, 29.1 mm SL, Bering Sea north of Rat Islands, Alaska.

Range: Known from one specimen (USNM 102108) collected in 1900 in an "8-foot Tanner beam trawl" (Townsend 1901) at *Albatross* station 3785, in the Bering Sea 150 miles north of the Rat Islands at a depth of 494 m on a bottom of gray sand and broken shells. Curiously, this specimen was taken in the same net haul as the unique holotype of *Thecopterus (= Malacocottus) aleuticus* (Psychrolutidae), a species which was not known again to science for nearly 100 years, then rediscovered in Alaskan and Russian waters. Maybe *S. xenogrammus* will also turn up again.

Artedius lateralis (Girard, 1854) **smoothhead sculpin**

Western Gulf of Alaska at Sanak Island to northern Baja California at Bahia San Quintin.

Tidepools and intertidal zone to depth of 14 m; along rocky coasts and in sandy areas with eel grass.

D XII–X + 15–17; A 12–14; Pec 14–16; Pel I,3; LLp 36–38; Vert 32–34.

- Greenish to brown dorsally, with red highlights; red or blue-green to creamy white and yellow ventrally, with or without spots; body with 2 or more dark bars; bones and flesh sometimes blue.
- Body heavy and robust, particularly anteriorly; head broad and depressed.
- Maxilla extending to rear edge of pupil to rear edge of eye; posterior nostril tube markedly longer than anterior.
- Spines generally absent from top of head, bony protuberances sometimes present in large adults.
- Four preopercular spines; first usually bifid, others usually obsolete.
- No preocular cirrus; various other cirri on head; single to triple cirri along lateral line.
- **No scales on head**; **dorsal band of ctenoid scales** 6–11 rows deep anteriorly, separated by scaleless areas from base of dorsal fin and from lateral line, **extending as far as level of next to last or last dorsal ray**; **lateral line scales embedded and smooth**.
- Vomerine and palatine teeth present.
- Genital papilla of males small and conical.
- Gill membranes united, free from isthmus.
- Length to 140 mm TL.

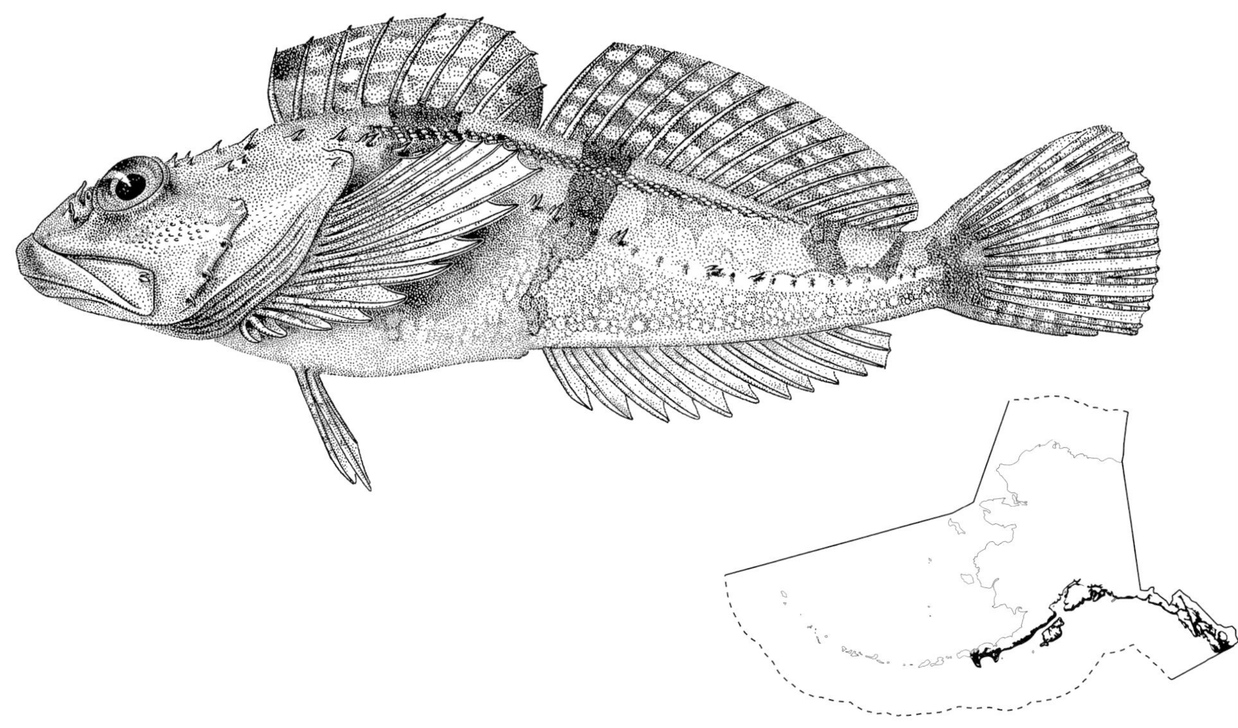

Notes & Sources — *Artedius lateralis* (Girard, 1854)
Scorpaenichthys lateralis Girard, 1854
Artedius delacyi Hubbs & Schultz, 1941
Hubbard and Reeder (1965) presented evidence supporting the synonymy of *A. delacyi* with *A. lateralis* using specimens from Kodiak Island, and Quast (1968) provided further evidence using specimens from Sitka.

Description: Hubbs and Schultz 1941:4–8; Bolin 1944:55–57; Hart 1973:481–482; Begle 1989:648.

Figure: Bolin 1944, fig. 21.

Range: Not known from Bering Sea or Aleutian Islands. An early record from Bering Island in the Commander group as *A. lateralis* (Bean and Bean 1896) was noted by Hubbs (1926b) to be attributable to *Stelgistrum beringianum,* and a record from Unalaska (Jordan and Gilbert 1899) was referred to *A. fenestralis* by Hubbs and Schultz (1941). The latter authors described *A. delacyi* (= *A. lateralis*) from specimens collected in a tidepool at Uyak Bay, Kodiak Island. Hubbard and Reeder (1965) collected specimens at 13 localities on Kodiak Island. Rogers et al. (1986) listed *A. lateralis* from Cook Inlet and Prince William Sound from Dames and Moore (1980) and other OCSEAP studies, and Barber et al. (1996) also from Prince William Sound. Quast (1968) recorded specimens from Baranof Island, Sitka, Barlow Cove, and Skowl Arm in southeastern Alaska. Museum collections have additional Alaskan specimens. UBC 63-333, from Sanak Island tidepools, 54°37'N, 162°21'W, is the westernmost record found.

Size: Peden and Wilson 1976.

Artedius fenestralis Jordan & Gilbert, 1883 **padded sculpin**

Aleutian Islands at Unalaska Island to southern California at Diablo Cove, San Luis Obispo County.

Intertidal and to depth of 55 m, usually less than 20 m, along rocky coastlines and in sandy areas with eelgrass; also found in tidepools, although not as commonly as *A. lateralis.*

D VIII–X + 16–18; A 12–14; Pec 14–16; Pel I,3; LLp 37–39; Vert 32–35.

- Olive green, orange or yellowish dorsally; pale orange to bluish gray ventrally; dark saddles and bars on body; ocelli on anterior and posterior margins of spinous dorsal fin.
- Body heavy and robust, particularly anteriorly; head broad and depressed.
- Maxilla extending to rear edge of pupil; posterior nostril tube markedly longer than anterior.
- Spines generally absent from top of head; low, blunt, postocular spines present in large adults.
- Four preopercular spines; first largest, multifid; others usually obsolete.
- No preocular cirrus; various other cirri on head; single to triple cirri along lateral line.
- **Ctenoid scales on top of head and under eye**; scales of head separated from dorsal scale band or are so small they do not obscure origin of dorsal band; **dorsal scale band** 9–11 rows deep anteriorly, **extending beyond insertion of dorsal fin** to meet scales of other side and form dense patch on caudal peduncle; **dorsal scale band usually not distinctly separated from dorsal fin or from lateral line, with irregular scales intervening**; **lateral line scales embedded and smooth**.
- Vomerine and palatine teeth present.
- Genital papilla of males small and conical.
- Gill membranes united, free from isthmus.
- Length to 140 mm TL.

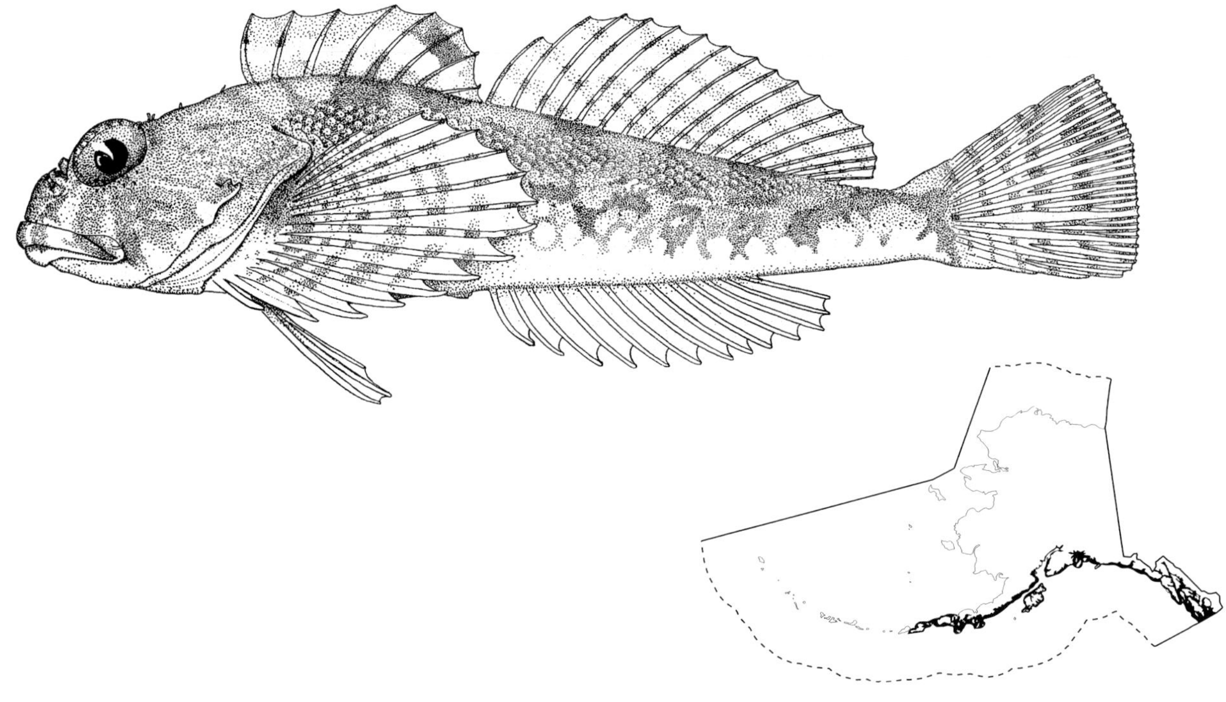

Notes & Sources — *Artedius fenestralis* Jordan & Gilbert, 1883
Astrolytes fenestralis: Jordan and Starks 1895.

Description: Bolin 1944:48–50; Hart 1973:478–479.

Figure: Bolin 1944, fig. 18.

Range: Recorded from Unalaska and from Sanborn Harbor, Nagai Island, in the Shumagin group by Bean (1881b) as *A. notospilotus* and referred to *A. fenestralis* by Jordan and Gilbert (1899). Evermann and Goldsborough (1907) recorded it from Karluk, Metlakatla, and Loring; Gilbert and Burke (1912a) from a tidepool at Unalaska Island; Wilimovsky (1964) from Cold Bay and Izembek Bay; Quast and Hall (1972) from Cook Inlet; and Peden and Wilson (1976) from sites just north of British Columbia. Rogers et al. (1986) reported it for Cook Inlet and Prince William Sound from OCSEAP research. Lots NMC 61-91 and 61-107 are from Prince William Sound. Museum collections include examples from numerous other localities in Alaska. Often taken in beach seines.

Artedius harringtoni (Starks, 1896) **scalyhead sculpin**

Aleutian Islands at Unalaska Island; western Gulf of Alaska at Kodiak Island to southern California at San Miguel Island.

Tidepools and rocky intertidal and subtidal areas to depth of 21 m.

D IX + 15–18; A 10–14; Pec 13–15; Pel I,3; LLs 36–40; Vert 32–34.

- Brown and orange to olive, often with red and pink; pale spots and mottling ventrolaterally blending with white or tan belly; dark red or brownish black saddles; bars radiating from eye; often with red blotch near margin of first dorsal fin anteriorly; anal fin of male with hexagonal latticework lacking darker pigmentation.
- Maxilla extending to pupil; posterior nostril tube markedly longer than anterior.
- No spines or protuberances on top of head.
- Four preopercular spines; first flattened, short, bifid or trifid; second minute; others obsolete.
- **Large, fringed preocular cirrus**; various other cirri on head; cirri along lateral line.
- Incised membrane of anal fin convex in males, concave in females.
- **Ctenoid scales on head, not below front of eye**; scales of head tending to merge with dorsal band; **dorsal scale band** 9–16 deep anteriorly, usually separated by scaleless areas from spinous dorsal fin and from lateral line, **extending beyond insertion of dorsal fin** to meet scales of other side and form dense patch on caudal peduncle; **lateral line scales slightly enlarged, embedded, with ctenoid margins exposed**.
- Vomerine and palatine teeth present.
- Genital papilla of mature males enlarged, conical, terminating in slender projection.
- Gill membranes united, free from isthmus.
- Branchiostegal rays 7.
- Length to 102 mm TL.

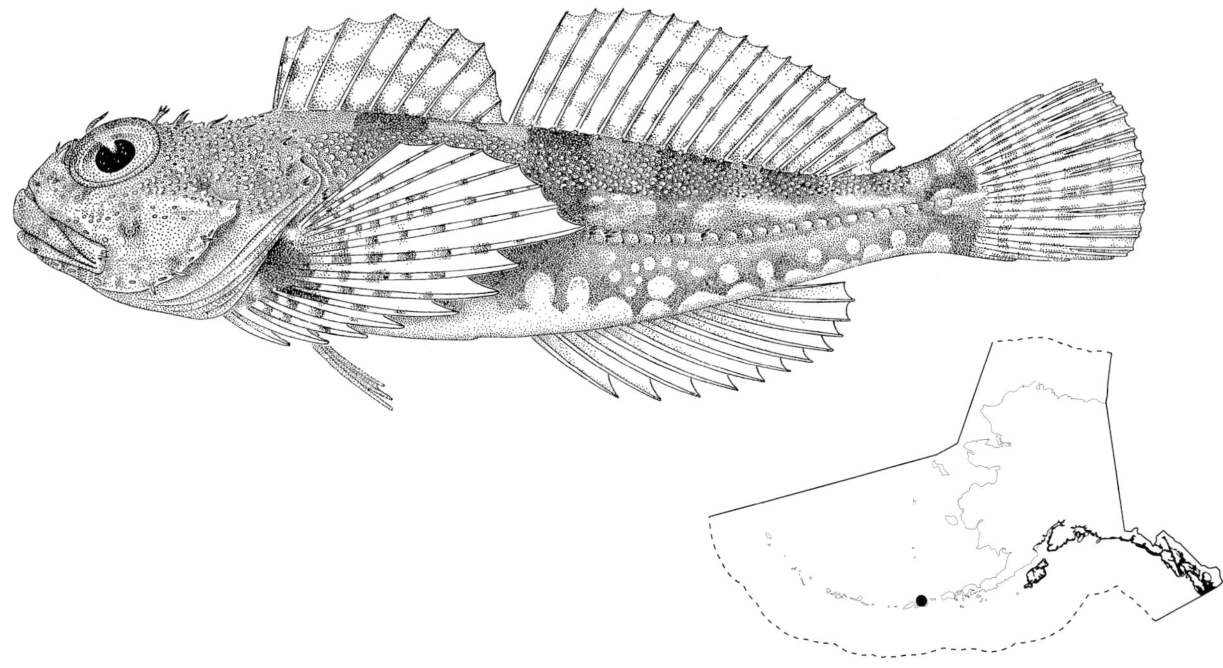

Notes & Sources — *Artedius harringtoni* (Starks, 1896)
Axyrias harringtoni Starks, 1896

Description: Bolin 1944:45–47; Hart 1973:479–480; Begle 1989:648.

Figure: Bolin 1944, fig. 17.

Range: Recorded by Hubbard and Reeder (1965) from four Kodiak Island rocky tidepool localities; by Quast (1968) from Skowl Arm, Prince of Wales Island, taken subtidally in shrimp traps, and Samsing Cove, near Sitka, taken intertidally by a diver; and Peden and Wilson (1976), from diving at several sites north and south of the Alaska–British Columbia border. OCSEAP investigators found *A. harringtoni* at Kachemak Bay and Prince William Sound (Rogers et al. 1986); voucher specimens include UW 25318, 25322, and 25325. Well represented in museum collections from localities throughout coastal Gulf of Alaska to Kodiak Island. As well, A. E. Peden (pers. comm., 5 Sep. 1996) collected specimens from Captains Bay, Unalaska Island, in 1980 by scuba diving; those specimens are in BCPM 980-603, 980-605, and 980-606.

Ruscarius meanyi Jordan & Starks, 1895 — Puget Sound sculpin

Southeastern Alaska at Fillmore Island to northern California at Arena Cove.

Intertidal and subtidal areas on large rocks or vertical rock faces to depths of 82 m; usually found at shallow subtidal depths, about 1.5–20 m below low-tide levels.

D IX–XI + 14–17; A 10–13; Pec 14–16; Pel I,2–3; LLp 36–39; Vert 33–35.

- Green to cream with vague, dark saddles dorsally and narrow dark bars below lateral line.
- Body round or slightly depressed anteriorly, slightly compressed posteriorly; head depressed.
- Maxilla extending to posterior part of pupil; posterior nostril not tubular, its margins only slightly elevated; anterior tube long, slightly fringed.
- No spines or tubercles on top of head.
- Four preopercular spines; first elongate, bifid.
- **Long, simple preocular cirrus**; **long, triple postocular cirrus**; no nasal cirrus; various other, shorter cirri on head; single and double cirri along lateral line.
- Cirrus at tip of each dorsal fin spine; first two anal fin rays thickened and curved in males.
- **Ctenoid scales on top of head, cheek, around and under eye**; scales on side continuous with scales on head; **scales nearly completely covering body above lateral line**, with at most a gap 1 or 2 scales wide above lateral line; lateral line scales enlarged, ctenoid; no scales below lateral line; **scales covering upper fifth of eye**.
- Vomerine and palatine teeth present.
- Genital papilla of males not enlarged.
- Gill membranes united, free from isthmus.
- Length to 59 mm TL.

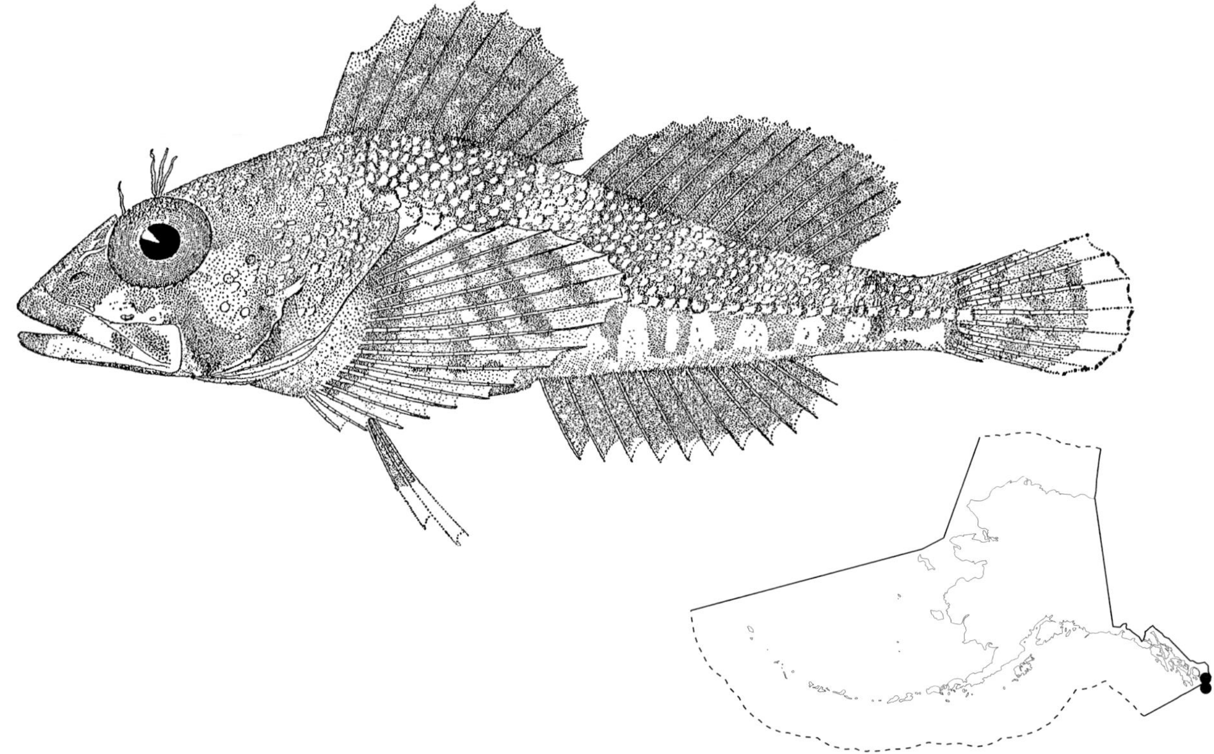

Notes & Sources — *Ruscarius meanyi* Jordan & Starks, 1895

Classified in genus *Artedius* by Rosenblatt and Wilkie (1963), and reassigned to *Ruscarius* by Begle (1989).

Description: Jordan and Starks 1895:805–807; Rosenblatt and Wilkie 1963:1505–1507; Hart 1973:483–484; Begle 1989:648–649. Rosenblatt and Wilkie (1963) gave counts of 15 and 16 for the soft-dorsal rays in specimens they examined and provided a recount of 16 rays for the syntypes, which Jordan and Starks (1895) had reported and illustrated as 14. Counts from additional specimens by Peden and Wilson (1976) and Howe and Richardson (1978) confirm that counts as low as 14 can occur. Researchers (Lea 1974, Howe and Richardson 1978, Begle 1989) examining the same specimens disagree on whether they have 2 or 3 pelvic fin rays.

Figure: Jordan and Starks 1895, pl. 80; lectotype, CAS-SU 3127, about 33 mm TL, near Port Orchard, Puget Sound, Washington. (Some features listed above are not shown in this illustration of a damaged specimen.)

Range: The known range was extended northward into Alaska by a specimen collected off Male Point, Fillmore Island, 54°48'N, 130°38'W, and recorded by Peden and Wilson (1976); they collected additional specimens from several sites a few kilometers south of the Alaska–Canada border. Recorded from Graham Island, British Columbia, at a depth of 82 m by Peden (1972).

Size: Eschmeyer and Herald 1983.

Gymnocanthus detrisus Gilbert & Burke, 1912 **purplegray sculpin**

Bering Sea to Seas of Okhotsk and Japan.

Bottom at depths of 15–450 m.

D IX–XI + 14–18; A 15–20; Pec 18–21; Pel I,3; LLp 39–49; Vert 38–40.

- Body purplish gray in preservative, reticulated with lighter gray dorsally; head reddish, with black marks at end of snout and on cheek; black bars on dorsal, caudal, and pectoral fins.
- Body elongate, stout, depressed; head depressed; **interorbital space broad, width 14–19% of head length**, relatively flat and smooth.
- Strong postocular tubercle present; occipital ridges well developed, with low tubercles.
- Four preopercular spines; first elongate, with 3–5 spinules on dorsal surface.
- No cirri on head or body.
- Pelvic fins longer in males than females.
- Scales absent except for a few bony plates in pectoral axil and scattered plates on interorbital space, occiput, cheek, and upper part of opercle; interorbital plates smaller and more numerous than in *G. galeatus*; lateral line scales as embedded tubules.
- Vomerine and palatine teeth absent.
- Genital papilla of males elongate and conical.
- Gill membranes united, attached to isthmus anteriorly leaving wide free portion posteriorly.
- Length to 360 mm TL.

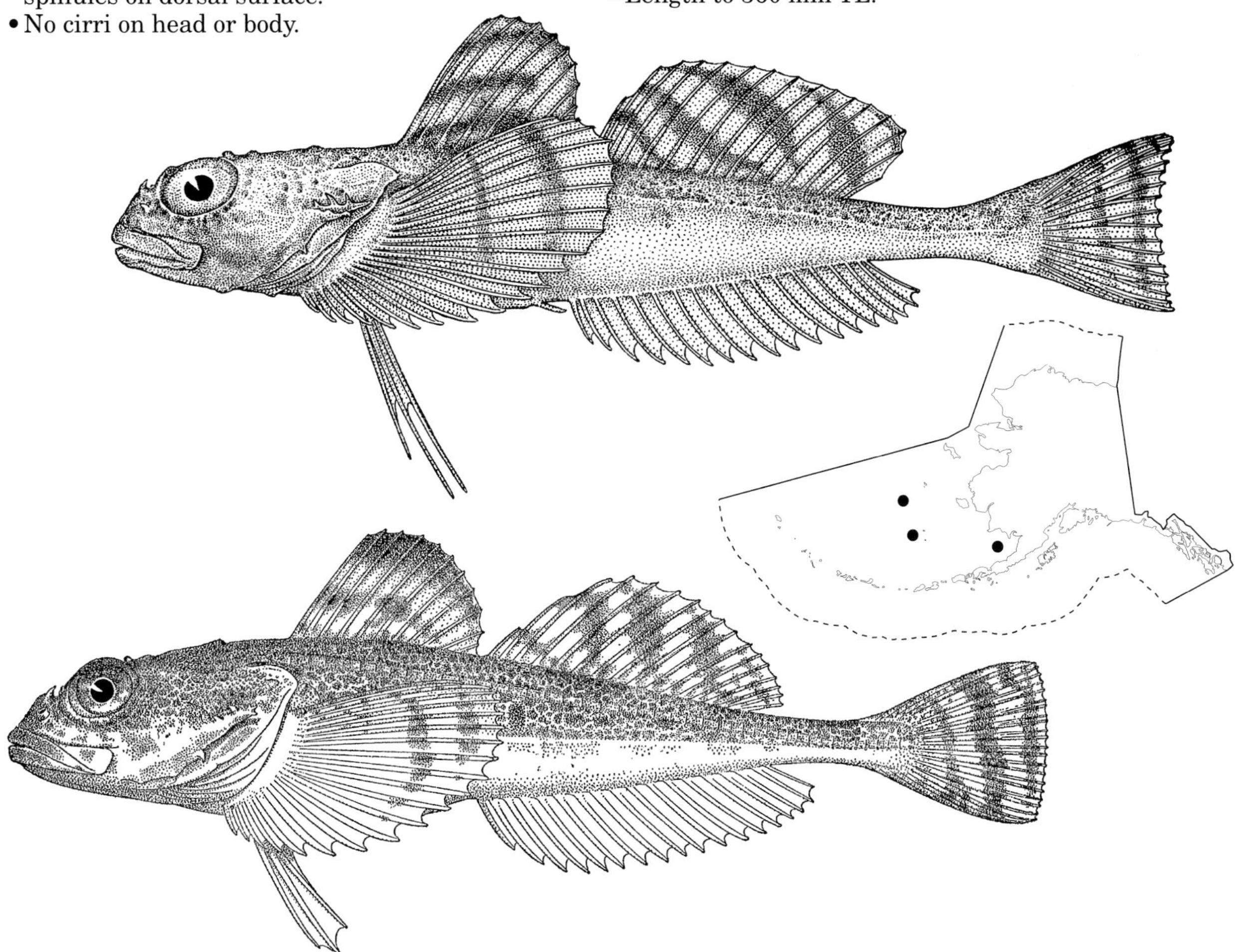

Notes & Sources — *Gymnocanthus detrisus* Gilbert & Burke, 1912

Description: Gilbert and Burke 1912a:61–63; Watanabe 1960:61–64.

Figures: Upper: Watanabe 1960, pl. 23, fig. 2; male. Lower: Gilbert and Burke 1912a, fig. 13; type, female, 175 mm TL, west coast of Kamchatka, Sea of Okhotsk.

Range: Recorded from Bristol Bay by Quast and Hall (1972; AB 70-124, male, 230 mm SL). A specimen (UW uncataloged) was collected in 1997 southwest of Saint Matthew Island at 59°20'N, 173°47'W, depth 44 m; a male, 265 mm SL, 315 mm TL, with counts of D X + 17, A 18, and Pec 20, interorbital width 16.4% HL, and smoother head scalation than in *G. galeatus* (J. Hoff, pers. comm., 14 Jan. 1998). Another (UW uncataloged) was collected in 1998 west of the Pribilof Islands at 57°20'N, 171°29'W, depth 99 m; a male, 258 mm SL (J. W. Orr, pers. comm., 31 Oct. 2000). Minimum depth of 15 m was given by Fedorov and Sheiko (2002).

Size: Baxter (1990ms, unpubl. data) reported lengths of 355 and 360 mm TL for two females taken off Cape Olyutorskiy by Russian research vessel *Novokotovsk* in 1990. Counts were D X + 16–17, A 18, Pec 20, LLp 39–41, Vert 39–40 (specimens were not saved). Largest specimen examined by Watanabe (1960) was 320 mm TL.

Gymnocanthus tricuspis (Reinhardt, 1830) **Arctic staghorn sculpin**

Beaufort and Chukchi seas to northern Bering Sea; circumpolar.

Bottom from close to shore to depth of 240 m.

D X–XII + 14–17; A 15–19; Pec 16–21; Pel I,3; LLp 39–45; Vert 36–40.

- **Dark brown dorsally, without reticulated pattern**; dark blotches extending below lateral line and more or less strongly demarcated from pale yellowish background; first dorsal fin of males blackish, with scattered white spots; dark bars on dorsal and pectoral fins.
- Body elongate, stout, depressed; head depressed, width usually more than 80% of head length; interorbital space narrow, width less than 10% of head length, concave.
- Postocular and **occipital protuberances weak or obscure**.
- Four preopercular spines; first elongate, bearing spinules (usually 3) on dorsal surface.
- No cirri on head or body.
- Pelvic fin rays very long and exserted in males; inner surface of pectoral and pelvic fins pectinate in large males.
- Scales absent except for a few in pectoral axil and rough, scattered to continuous bony plates on occiput and interorbital space; rough plates not always present on interorbital space, and when present, **plates not extending onto upper edge of orbit**; interorbital plates smaller and more numerous than in *G. galeatus*; lateral line scales as embedded tubules.
- Vomerine and palatine teeth absent.
- Genital papilla of males elongate and conical.
- Gill membranes united, attached to isthmus anteriorly leaving wide free portion posteriorly.
- Length to 299 mm TL, usually under 150 mm TL.

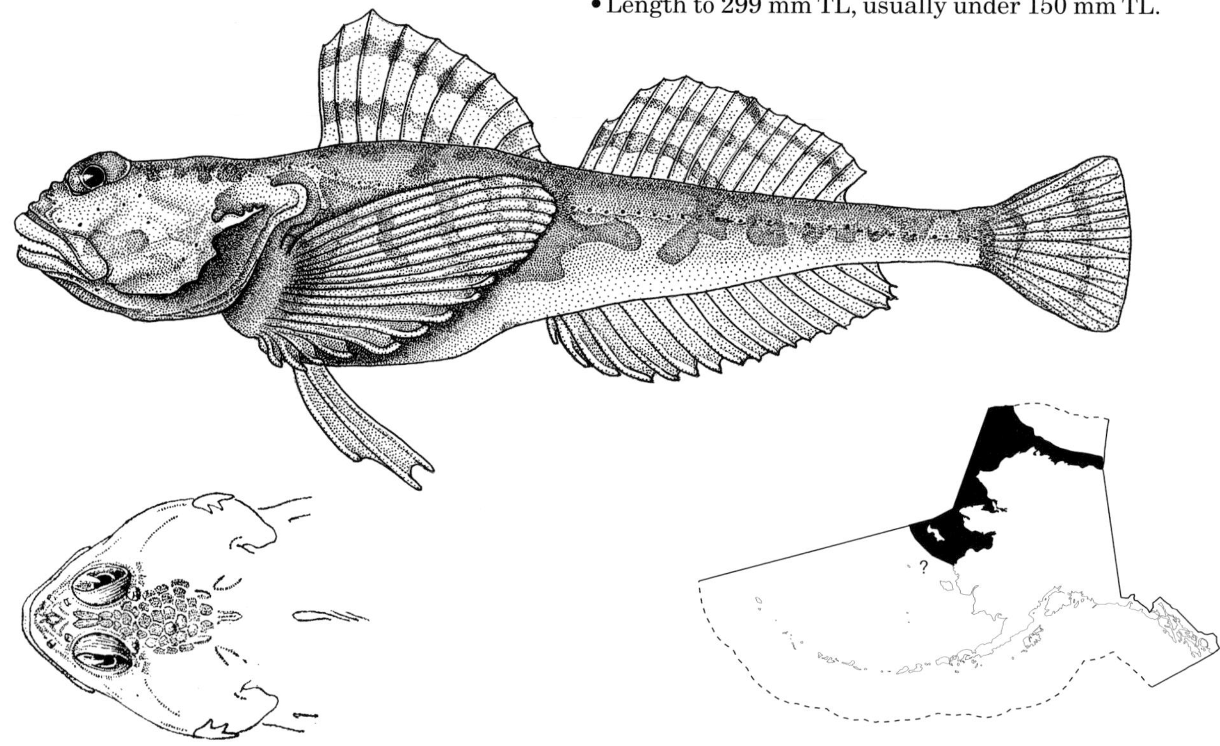

Notes & Sources — *Gymnocanthus tricuspis* (Reinhardt, 1830)
Cottus tricuspis Reinhardt, 1830

Description: Andriashev 1954:368–372; Walters 1955:313–314; Leim and Scott 1966:348–350.

Figures: Lateral view: Russian Academy of Sciences, Zoological Institute, St. Petersburg, artist I. Belousov, May 2001; ZIN 33520, female, 130 mm SL, 151 mm TL, Anadyr Gulf. Dorsal view of head: Andriashev 1954, fig. 208-1; female, 177 mm TL, Murman coast.

Range: This circumpolar species was reported in NMFS surveys at the Aleutian Islands and in the southeastern Bering Sea (Allen and Smith 1988), but G. R. Hoff (pers. comm., 14 Jan. 1998), who has been conducting a study of *Gymnocanthus,* considers those reports to be doubtful and that the species probably does not occur south of Nunivak and St. Matthew islands. The southernmost Bering Sea museum specimen listed among hundreds examined by Wilson (1973) is UW 7314, taken south of St. Lawrence Island at 62°16'N, 168°06'W. Distribution north of St. Lawrence Island is well documented by published records and specimens in permanent collections. Walters (1955) noted that the specimens recorded as *G. galeatus* by Bean (1881b, 1883) from Cape Sabine and by Scofield (1899) from Point Barrow represent *G. tricuspis.* Additional specimens recorded by Walters (1955) from Point Barrow were taken in water as shallow as 7.6 m.

Gymnocanthus pistilliger (Pallas, 1814) **threaded sculpin**

Bering Sea from Port Clarence to Aleutian Islands and to southeastern Alaska at Oliver Inlet, Stephens Passage; to Commander Islands, Sea of Okhotsk, and Sea of Japan to South Korea at Pusan.

Soft bottoms in shallow water; rarely found deeper than 100 m, although reported to 325 m.

D IX–XI + 13–16; A 14–18; Pec 15–20; Pel I,3; LLp 34–37; Vert 35–38.

- Brown dorsally, reticulated with light brown; white ventrally; 4 vague, dusky saddles; first dorsal fin of males with white spots; dorsal, caudal, pectoral, sometimes pelvic, fins barred; tips of pistil-like cirri of males bright white.
- Body elongate, stout, depressed; head depressed; interorbital space less than 10% of head length.
- Postocular and **2 or 3 pairs of occipital protuberances usually well developed**.
- Four preopercular spines; first elongate, bearing 1–4 spinules on dorsal surface.
- Postocular cirrus usually absent in adults; **long, pistil-like cirri under pectoral fin in males**.
- Dorsal fin spines usually 9–10, dorsal rays 14–15, anal rays 16, pectoral 18–19; **total count for both dorsals, both pectorals, and anal fin 80 or less**; in males, pelvic fin longer, rays partly free; pectoral rays of males pectinate on inner surface.
- Scales absent except for weak plates on occipital and nuchal regions; **interorbital space usually smooth, plates never extending onto rim of orbit**; lateral line scales as embedded tubules.
- Vomerine and palatine teeth absent.
- Gill membranes united, attached to isthmus anteriorly leaving wide free portion posteriorly.
- Genital papilla of males elongate and conical.
- Length to 292 mm TL.

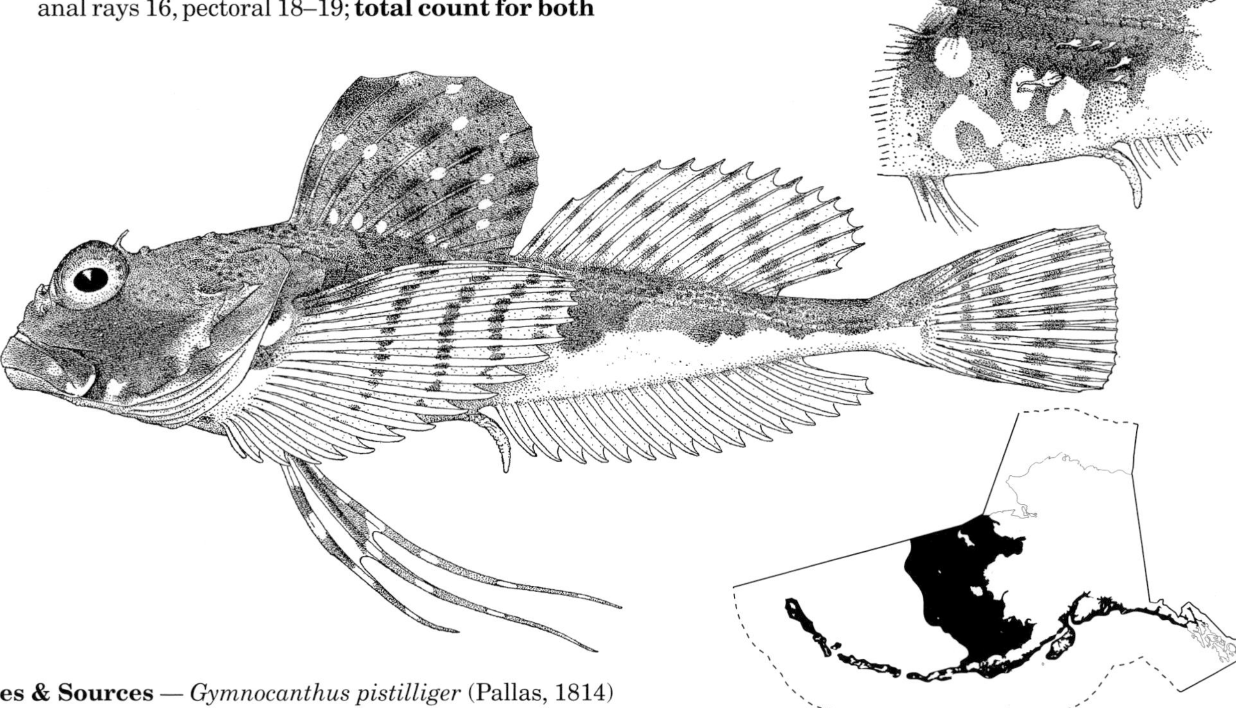

Notes & Sources — *Gymnocanthus pistilliger* (Pallas, 1814)
Cottus pistilliger Pallas, 1814

Description: Jordan and Starks 1904b:290–292; Andriashev 1954:372–373. Total fin ray count from Wilson (1973: fig. 24), minus 1 to compensate for method.

Figures: Jordan and Gilbert 1899, pl. 58; male, about 125 mm TL, Avacha Bay, Kamchatka.

Range: Westernmost Aleutian Islands record is a specimen from Kiska Island (Bean 1881b), but the species is abundant at the Commander Islands (Fedorov and Sheiko 2002) and likely occurs throughout the chain. Northernmost record is that of Scofield (1899), who described specimens from Port Clarence; appropriate characters include the meristics and, in the males, the "mushroom-like filaments" behind the pectoral fins. Andriashev (1954) doubted Scofield's record, but it may be valid. Lot NMC 58-93 includes an 85-mm-SL female collected adjacent to Port Clarence at Grantley Harbor at 4–6 m of depth in 1913. Found in NMFS surveys as far north as Norton Sound and west of St. Lawrence Island (Allen and Smith 1988). Probably not in the Arctic Ocean, or there only rarely. Specimens recorded from Point Belcher by Bean (1881b) are too small (about 25 mm long) to be reliably identified (Walters 1955). Quast and Hall (1972) extended known range to Kodiak Island and southeastern Alaska. UBC 62-792 contains two specimens from Oliver Inlet, Stephens Passage. Much more common in Bering Sea than in Gulf of Alaska. The type series includes material from Unalaska Island (Eschmeyer 1998). Hoff (2000) reported on the biology and ecology of this species in Bristol Bay. Reported from Pusan, South Korea, by Kim and Youn (1992), citing Chyung and Kim (1959). Reported as deep as 325 m (Allen and Smith 1988) but fish could have entered the net at a shallower depth than maximum tow depth.

Size: Wilson 1973.

Gymnocanthus galeatus Bean, 1881 **armorhead sculpin**

Bering Sea and Aleutian Islands to central British Columbia at Wales Island; western Bering Sea and Commander Islands to northern Sea of Japan off Hokkaido.

Soft bottom near shore and to depth of 579 m, most common between 50 and 165 m.

D X–XII + 14–17; A 17–20; Pec 19–21; Pel I,3; LLp 41–65; Vert 37–40.

- Brown to olivaceous or gray, lightly reticulated, dorsally; white ventrally; 4 or 5 blackish saddles, extending below lateral line; dorsal, caudal, and pectoral fins barred.
- Body more elongate than in *G. pistilliger*; **head slightly compressed, width usually less than 75% of head length**; interorbital space narrow, less than 10% of head length, concave.
- Postocular tubercle moderately prominent; 1 or 2 pairs of low occipital tubercles.
- Four preopercular spines; first elongate, bearing 1–3 spinules on dorsal surface.
- No cirri on head or body.
- Dorsal fin spines usually 10 or 11, dorsal rays 15–17, anal 18 or 19, pectoral 20; **total fin ray count of dorsal, both pectoral, and anal fins of 81 or more**; pelvic fin longer in males.
- Scales absent except for a few bony plates in pectoral axil and **rough plates covering top of head and interorbital space, plates extending onto rim of orbit**; lateral line scales as embedded tubules.
- Vomerine and palatine teeth absent.
- Genital papilla of males elongate and conical.
- Gill membranes united, attached to isthmus anteriorly leaving wide free portion posteriorly.
- Length to 360 mm TL.

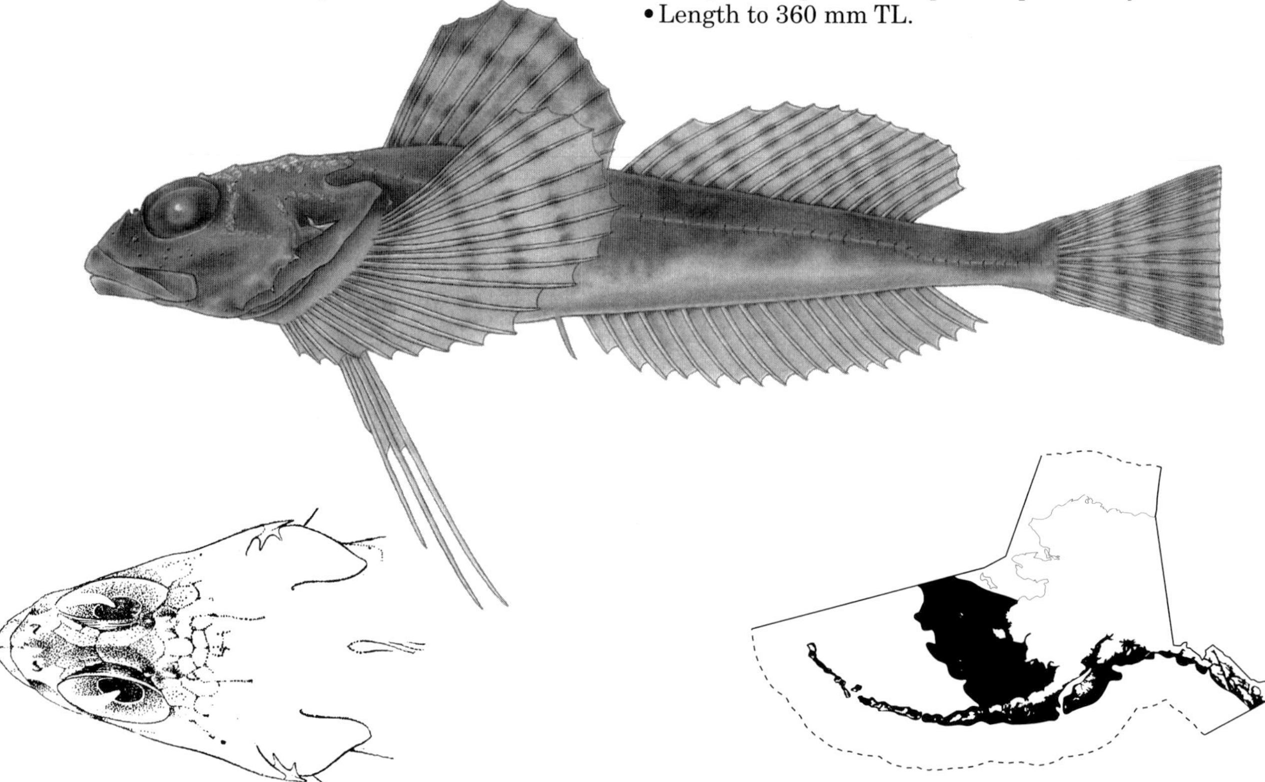

Notes & Sources — *Gymnocanthus galeatus* Bean, 1881
Gymnacanthus galeatus Bean, 1881
The original genus should have been spelled *Gymnocanthus,* after *Gymnocanthus* Swainson, 1839 (Eschmeyer 1998).

Description: Bean 1881a:153; Andriashev 1954:373–374; Watanabe 1960:59–61. Total fin ray count from Wilson (1973: fig. 24), minus 1 to compensate for method of counting last anal ray when doubled.

Figures: Royal British Columbia Museum, artist K. Uldall-Ekman, Jan. 1976; UBC 62-645, male, near Sitkalidak Island, Alaska. Dorsal view of head: Andriashev 1937, fig. 5.

Range: Bean (1881a) based the description of this species on specimens collected from Iliuliuk (= Unalaska). Quast and Hall (1972) listed other early records and reported the presence of specimens in the ABL collection from the Bering Sea to southeastern Alaska. Allen and Smith (1988) reported *G. galeatus* was taken in NMFS resource surveys from Agattu Island north nearly to St. Lawrence Island and east to Afognak Island. Fedorov and Sheiko (2002) reported it to be abundant at the Commander Islands and gave a new maximum depth (579 m). Recorded as far south of Alaska as Wales Island, British Columbia, at 54°47'N, 130°36'W (Peden and Wilson 1976). Vladykov's (1933) record of this species from Hudson Bay represents another species; *G. galeatus* is not known from the Atlantic.

Size: Eschmeyer and Herald 1983.

Leptocottus armatus Girard, 1854 — Pacific staghorn sculpin

Southeastern Bering Sea at Port Moller to north-central Baja California at San Quintin Bay.

Tidepools and intertidal to subtidal silt, sand, and broken shell bottoms and eelgrass beds; found as deep as 91 m; tolerates fresh water and often found in lower reaches of rivers and streams; sometimes buried in sand with only the eyes protruding.

D V–IX + 15–21; A 14–20; Pec 19; Pel I,4; LLp 37–42; Vert 37–39.

- Greenish brown to gray with some yellow dorsally; white to orange-yellow ventrally; **black spot near posterior margin of spinous dorsal fin**; dorsal, caudal, and pectoral fins creamy or golden yellow with green or dusky bars; caudal fin tinged deep red and anal fin margin light red in mature females.
- Body elongate, subcylindrical anteriorly and somewhat compressed posteriorly; head large, depressed, and broad; mouth large, maxilla extending to posterior edge of eye or beyond.
- Nasal spine absent, low median bump present.
- **Three preopercular spines, first elongate, robust, bearing 2–6 spinules** on dorsal surface; lower two spines simple, less prominent.
- Cirri absent from head and body.
- **Scales absent from head and body**.
- Lateral line distinct, nearly straight, extending to caudal fin.
- Vomerine and palatine teeth present.
- Gill membranes joined to isthmus without leaving free posterior margin.
- Length to 480 mm TL.

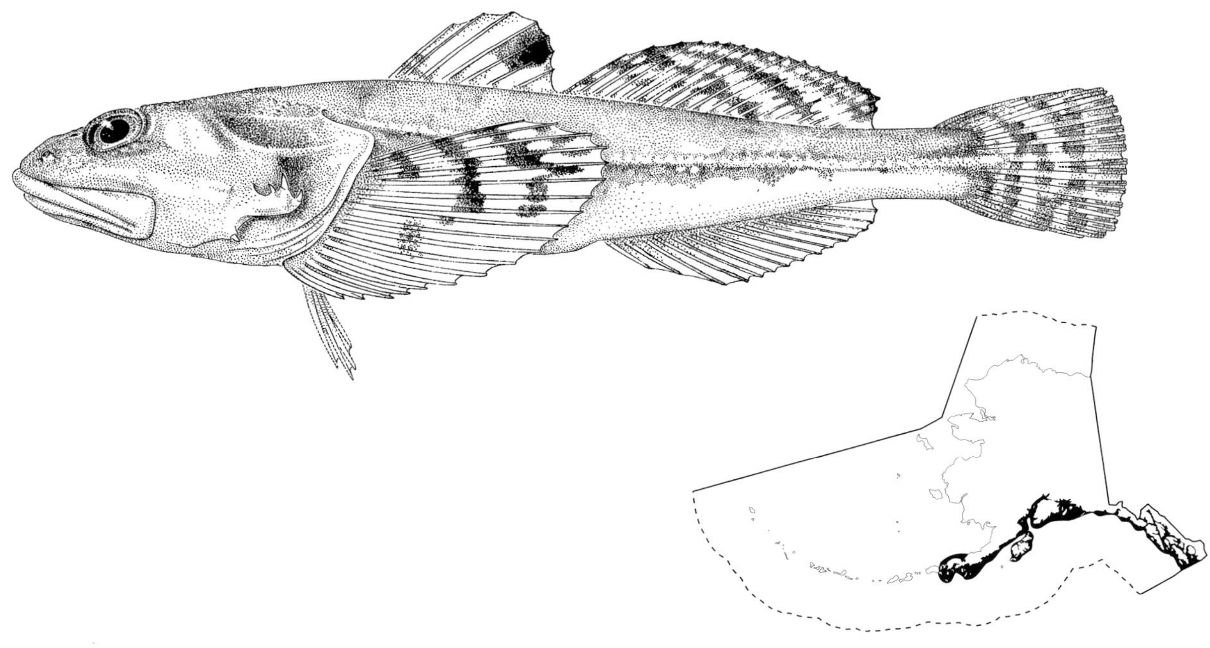

Notes & Sources — *Leptocottus armatus* Girard, 1854

Description: Bolin 1944:97–99; Jones 1962; Hart 1973:518–519; Morrow 1980:205–206; Coad 1995:512–513.

Figure: Bolin 1944, fig. 38.

Range: Phinney (1972) recorded a northwestward extension of known range to Chignik Bay. Soon afterward, Paulson and Smith (1974) extended the known range to the Bering Sea at Izembek Lagoon, where they found *L. armatus* to be a common resident in all habitats examined, including shallow and deep eelgrass beds, channels, and intertidal sand flats. They observed foxes catching them in the surf. In 1989 R. Baxter (unpubl. data) collected specimens from about 140 km farther east, at the low intertidal area under a cannery at Port Moller (specimens not saved). This is a commonly occurring species throughout its reported range in Alaska, and well represented from the region in published records (e.g., Bean 1881b, Rutter 1899, Evermann and Goldsborough 1907, Bolin 1944, Quast and Hall 1972) and in museum collections. Gunter (1942) recorded it from fresh water on Admiralty Island, and Heard et al. (1969) from 3.2 km above the mouth of the Katmai River. This fish can be a nuisance because it often takes baited hooks intended for other fishes and gets caught in gill nets.

Cottus cognatus Richardson, 1836 **slimy sculpin**

Arctic Alaska mainland, St. Lawrence and Nunivak islands, and eastern Aleutian Islands to southeastern Alaska at Stikine River; east across North America through the Great Lakes and along the East Coast to Virginia; eastern Chukchi Peninsula to Anadyr River.

Fresh water; lakes from near shore to depth of 210 m, most common at 37–108 m; and bottom of streams, particularly those with fast current and rocky bottoms.

D VI–X + 14–19; A 10–14; Pec 12–16; Pel I,3–4; LLp 12–27; Vert 31–35.

- Dark brown, green, or gray dorsally; whitish ventrally, often with orange tint; sometimes with vague dark bands on body and caudal peduncle; first dorsal fin dark at base, clear at margin; other fins barred; breeding males darker, with red or orange margin on first dorsal fin.
- Body nearly round anteriorly, strongly compressed posteriorly; head depressed, broad; eye more or less on top of head; maxilla extending to front of eye to mideye.
- Nasal spine absent, low median bump present.
- Three preopercular spines; first broad, curved upward; lower two obscure.
- Cirri absent from head and body.
- Dorsal fins touching or joined at base; **first 2 dorsal spines far apart**; caudal fin rounded.
- Scales absent, except small prickles sometimes present in pectoral axil.
- Two median occipital pores; **anterior pair of mandibular pores separate**.
- **Lateral line short, main portion ending below second dorsal fin**, usually with a few isolated pores beyond main portion.
- Vomerine teeth present; palatine teeth almost always absent.
- Genital papilla of males twice the length of that in females and more triangular.
- Gill membranes joined to isthmus without leaving free posterior margin.
- Length to 128 mm TL, most less than 75 mm TL.

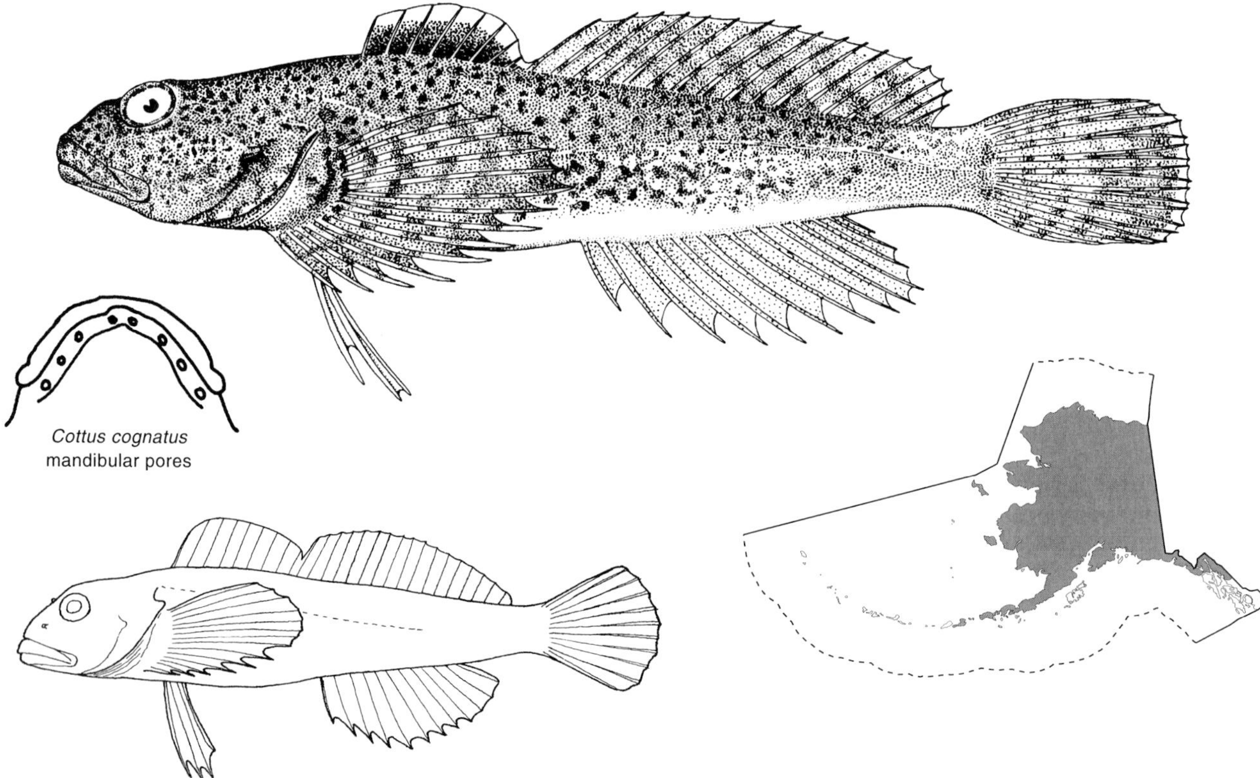

Notes & Sources — *Cottus cognatus* Richardson, 1836
Cottus chamberlaini Evermann & Goldsborough, 1907

Description: McAllister and Lindsey 1961:75–76; Morrow 1980:200–202; Coad 1995:698–699.

Figures: Upper: National Museums of Canada, Ottawa; specimen data not available. Lower: Morrow 1974, fig. 58. Diagram of mandibular pores: Morrow 1980, fig. 57.

Range: Morrow (1980) summarized and mapped range in Alaska. Wallace et al. (in Lee et al. 1980) mapped North American records. Extent of range in the Aleutian Islands is not clear from the literature. The westernmost record from the Aleutians may be USNM 91842, a specimen from Unalaska Island collected in 1930 by L. P. Schultz.

Cottus asper Richardson, 1836 **prickly sculpin**

Seward, Alaska, to Ventura River, southern California.

Fresh water, in coastal and inland rivers and lakes, as well as estuaries and nearshore marine waters; prefers quiet waters, like pools; some populations migrate downstream and spawn in brackish waters.

D VII–XI + 18–23; A 12–19; Pec 14–18; Pel I,4 (rarely 3 or 5); LLp 28–43; Vert 34–36.

- Dark brown, greenish, or gray dorsally; white to yellow ventrally; dark bands on body; breeding males darker than females; blackish blotches on first dorsal fin; fins barred; first dorsal fin with narrow, orange edge in both sexes.
- Body nearly round anteriorly, strongly compressed posteriorly; head depressed, broad; eye more or less on top of head; maxilla extending from mideye to posterior edge of pupil; **posterior nostril not tubular**.
- Nasal spine absent, low median bump present.
- Two or three preopercular spines; upper small, sharp; others obscure.
- Cirri absent from head and body.
- Dorsal fins touching; first 2 dorsal fin spines relatively close together; pectoral rays usually more than 15; caudal fin truncate or slightly rounded.
- **Prickles on body**, usually on back and sides but occasionally only a patch in pectoral axil.
- **Anterior pair of mandibular pores opening into same pit, appearing as one pore**.
- **Lateral line complete, extending to caudal fin**.
- Vomerine and **palatine teeth present**.
- Genital papilla of males long and triangular, that of females short and round.
- Gill membranes joined to isthmus without leaving free posterior margin.
- Length to 192 mm SL, most not over 150 mm TL.

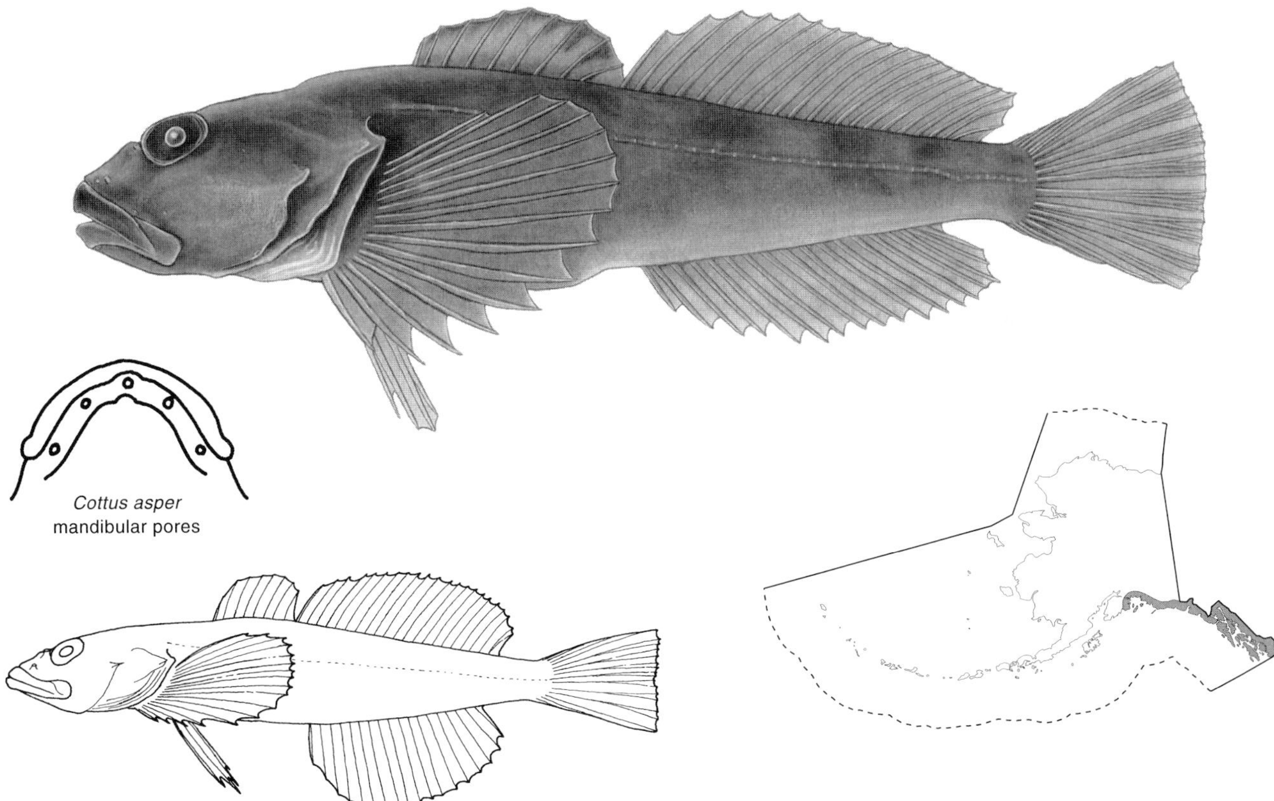

Cottus asper
mandibular pores

Notes & Sources — *Cottus asper* Richardson, 1836

Description: McAllister and Lindsey 1961:70–73; Morrow 1980:202–204; Coad 1995:548–549. Prickles most often cover the body in inland populations, while restriction of prickles to the pectoral axil is more common in coastal populations (Coad 1995).

Figures: Upper: Royal British Columbia Museum, artist K. Uldall-Ekman, 1983; BCPM 981-76, Brooks Peninsula, British Columbia. Lower: Morrow 1974, fig. 59. Mandibular pore diagram: Morrow, fig. 58.

Range: Morrow (1980) summarized range records from Alaska, and Wallace (in Lee et al. 1980) from the entire range of the species. Recorded west as far as Seward by Morrow (1980).

Size: Coad (1995) considered the previously reported maximum length of 300–305 mm TL (12 inches; e.g., McPhail and Lindsey 1970) to be questionable and gave a recorded maximum size of 192 mm SL.

Cottus aleuticus Gilbert, 1896 **coastrange sculpin**

Kobuk River isolated population; Bristol Bay, Alaska Peninsula, and Aleutian Island drainages from Attu Island to southern California at Oso Flaco Creek, Santa Barbara County.

Fresh and brackish waters; usually found in fast, gravel-bed streams but also occurs in sand- and mud-bottomed lakes and in estuaries and nearshore coastal waters.

D VIII–X + 16–20; A 12–16; Pec 13–16; Pel I,4; LLp 32–44; Vert 34–38.

- Dark brown, green, or gray dorsally; white ventrally; darker blotches on sides and vague bands below second dorsal and on caudal peduncle; chin heavily speckled; fins thinly barred; spawning males with orange-edged first dorsal fin.
- Body nearly round anteriorly, strongly compressed posteriorly; head depressed, broad; eye more or less on top of head; maxilla extending to anterior edge of eye to mideye; **posterior nostril tubular**.
- Nasal spine absent, low median bump present.
- Two or three preopercular spines; upper short, distinct; others obscure.
- Cirri absent from head and body.
- Dorsal fins touching; first 2 dorsal fin spines close together; pectoral rays usually 14; caudal fin truncate.
- Scales absent, except small prickles sometimes present in pectoral axil.
- **Anterior pair of mandibular pores opening into same pit, appearing as one pore**.
- **Lateral line complete, extending to caudal fin**, usually with marked flexion on caudal peduncle.
- Vomerine teeth present; **palatine teeth absent**.
- Genital papilla of males long.
- Gill membranes joined to isthmus without leaving free posterior margin.
- Length to 170 mm TL, most under 115 mm TL.

Notes & Sources — *Cottus aleuticus* Gilbert, 1896
Uranidea microstoma Lockington, 1880
Cottus protrusus Schultz & Spoor, 1933

Description: McAllister and Lindsey 1961:74–75; Morrow 1980:204–205; Coad 1995:212–213.

Figures: Upper: Royal British Columbia Museum, artist K. Uldall-Ekman, Jul. 1984; BCPM 971-86, 81 mm SL, Graham Island, Queen Charlotte Islands, British Columbia. Lower: Morrow 1974, fig. 60.

Range: Gilbert (1896) described *C. aleuticus* from specimens collected in a small stream passing through the village of Iliuliuk (= Unalaska). The fish were abundant in the upper, strictly freshwater portion as well as the lower, brackish portion of the stream. Specimens collected from a small lake on Unalaska Island were described under the name *C. protrusus* by Schultz and Spoor (1933). The type locality of *Uranidea microstoma* (= *C. aleuticus*) is St. Paul, an old name for the town of Kodiak. Morrow (1980) and Wallace (in Lee et al. 1980) summarized and mapped range records from Alaska, giving a range in the Aleutian Islands west to Kiska. Lot USNM 126974 comprises two specimens collected from a stream on Attu Island by a U.S. Bureau of Fisheries survey in 1921. Morrow (1980) noted the presence of an isolated population in the Kobuk River north of Bering Strait some 800 km away from the nearest Bristol Bay record. Swift et al. (1993) extended the known range in California south to Oso Flaco Creek (LACM 35163-1).

Enophrys bison (Girard, 1854) **buffalo sculpin**

Western Gulf of Alaska at Uyak Bay, Kodiak Island, to central California at Monterey Bay.

Inshore rocky and sandy areas to depths of 20 m; only occasionally found in tidepools.

D VII–IX + 9–13; A 8–10; Pec 15–18; Pel I,3; LLs 30–35; Vert 29–31.

- Dark brown, green-black, or white with black mottling; ivory or white ventrally; 3 or 4 dark bands; often with purplish plates on head; dorsal, caudal, and pectoral fins heavily spotted and barred with black; anal, pectoral, and pelvic fin margins orange.
- Body robust anteriorly, subcircular in cross section; somewhat compressed posterior to anus; head massive; maxilla extending beyond pupil.
- Orbit protruding above profile of head; frontoparietal ridge strong, ending in elevated nuchal ridge; exposed head bones covered with minute osseous tubercles.
- **Lachrymal bone not expanded as flange extending over maxilla**.
- **First preopercular spine long (27–48% of head length), with serrated base but without spinules**, other three strong and sharp; opercle with 2 spines.
- One or more cirri on posterior end of maxilla.
- Cirri on tips of dorsal fin spines; **second dorsal and anal fin rays total 22 or less**.
- Scales absent except for lateral line scales.
- **Lateral line** high on body, comprising greatly enlarged, raised **plates without keels**.
- Vomerine teeth present; palatine teeth absent.
- Genital papilla of males not enlarged.
- Gill membranes joined to isthmus without leaving free posterior margin.
- Length to 371 mm TL.

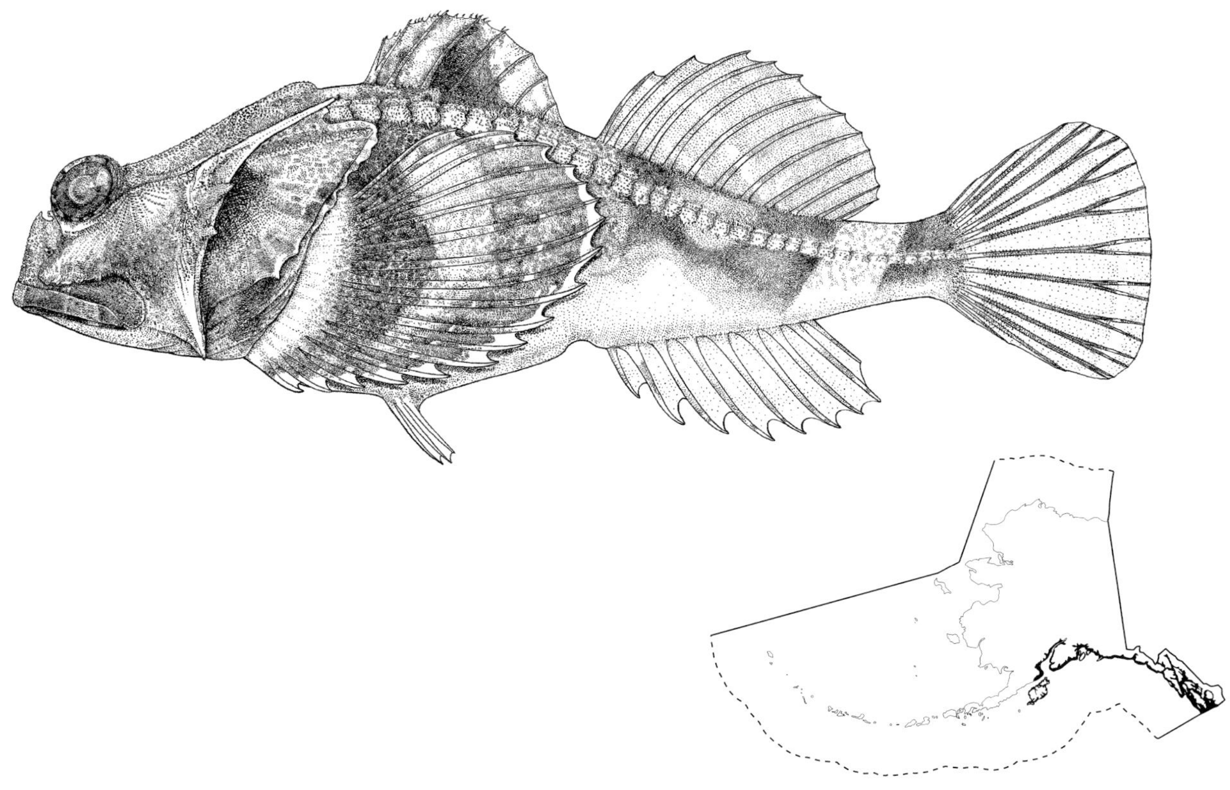

Notes & Sources — *Enophrys bison* (Girard, 1854)
Aspicottus bison Girard, 1854
Aspidocottus bison: Bean 1881b.

Description: Bolin 1944:91–93; Sandercock and Wilimovsky 1968:844–846; Hart 1973:499–500; Coad 1995:169.

Figure: University of British Columbia, artist P. Drukker-Brammall, Mar. 1966; UBC 62-558, male, 138 mm SL, Chatham Strait, Alaska.

Range: Well represented from Alaska in museum collections, with localities for all examples, even those most recently collected, falling within the range recorded by Sandercock and Wilimovsky (1968): north to Ocean Cape in the northeastern Gulf of Alaska (UBC 65-568) and west to Uyak Bay on the west coast of Kodiak Island (UBC 64-42).

Size: Miller and Lea 1972.

Enophrys diceraus (Pallas, 1788) **antlered sculpin**

Chukchi Sea off Point Barrow to Aleutian Islands and to southeastern Alaska at Fort Tongass; western Chukchi and Bering seas to Commander Islands, Sea of Okhotsk, and Sea of Japan to South Korea.

Stony bottom at depths of 13–350 m; rarely deeper than 100 m.

D VII–VIII + 13–15; A 11–13; Pec 16–19; Pel I,3; LLs 34–38; Vert 31–34.

- Greenish and reddish, marbled and spotted; often with 3 or 4 dark bands; some cirri centered in pale spots on side; pale yellow ventrally; fins with irregular bars.
- Body robust anteriorly, ovate in cross section; only slightly compressed posterior to anus; head massive; maxilla extending beyond pupil.
- Orbit protruding above profile of head; frontoparietal ridge strong, ending in much-elevated nuchal ridge; exposed head bones covered with minute osseous tubercles.
- **Lachrymal bone expanded as forked flange with sharp points** extending over maxilla.
- **First preopercular spine long (34–59% of head length), with 2–8 spinules**, other three strong and sharp; opercle with 2 sharp spines.
- Cirri on chin, posterior end of maxilla, preopercular margin, and below lateral line.
- **Total of second dorsal and anal fin rays 23 or more**.
- Prickly scales below lateral line anteriorly.
- **Lateral line plates with 1 or 2 keels**.
- Vomerine teeth present; palatine teeth absent.
- Genital papilla of males elongate and conical.
- Gill membranes joined to isthmus without leaving free margin posteriorly.
- Length to 280 mm TL.

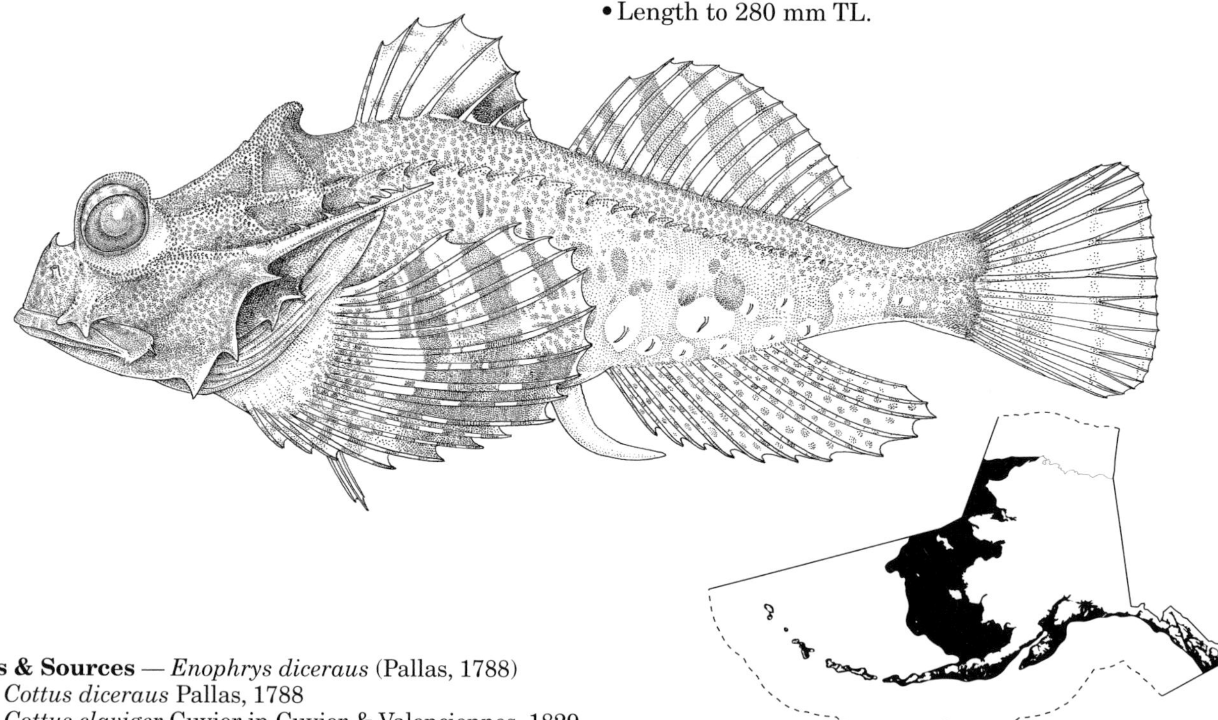

Notes & Sources — *Enophrys diceraus* (Pallas, 1788)
Cottus diceraus Pallas, 1788
Cottus claviger Cuvier in Cuvier & Valenciennes, 1829

Quast and Hall (1972) did not distinguish between *E. diceraus* and *E. lucasi,* because they were not convinced the differences described by Sandercock and Wilimovsky (1968) in their revision of the genus were not size-specific. This has been a controversial point ever since Jordan and Gilbert (1899:459) stated that it seemed possible *E. lucasi* was based on juvenile *E. diceraus.* Evermann and Goldsborough (1907) claimed the species were not distinguishable but Gilbert and Burke (1912a) maintained they were. Peden and Wilson (1976) believed them to be distinguishable by the larger preopercular spine and tendency for more anal fin rays in *E. diceraus.* Neyelov (1979) commented that at best the two represent subspecies of *E. diceraus*; however, he did not study examples from the eastern Pacific.

Description: Jordan and Gilbert 1883:711; Jordan and Evermann 1898:1938–1941; Gilbert and Burke 1912a:56–57; Sandercock and Wilimovsky 1968:835–837.

Figure: University of British Columbia, artist P. Drukker-Brammall, Mar. 1966; UBC 61-65, male, 126 mm SL, Chukchi Sea, Alaska.

Range: In Alaska, north to Point Barrow (Neyelov 1979); west to Amchitka Pass (Gilbert and Burke 1912a) and Amchitka Island (Simenstad et al. 1977); and south to Fort Tongass (54°44'N, 130°42'W; Bean 1884a). Neyelov (1979) did not give documentation for range to Point Barrow. Sandercock and Wilimovksy (1968) recorded *E. diceraus* northeast of Cape Lisburne at 69°16'N, 164°22'W (UBC 61-105). Allen and Smith (1988) reported it in survey catches from Point Hope to Bristol Bay and off Tanaga Island. Occurrence off Commander Islands (Andriashev 1954) indicates continuous distribution along Aleutian chain. Kim and Youn 1992: northern South Korea. Habitat: Gilbert 1896, Andriashev 1954, Allen and Smith 1988, Fedorov and Sheiko 2002.

Size: Neyelov 1979.

Enophrys lucasi (Jordan & Gilbert, 1898) **leister sculpin**

Bering Strait off Little Diomede Island to British Columbia near Port McNeill; Commander Islands.

Shallow water near shore to depth of about 17 m, in rocky areas with minimal amounts of sediment among bryozoans and hydroids.

D VII–VIII + 10–14; A 9–11; Pec 17–19; Pel I,3; LLs 34–37; Vert 32.

- Background color light olive, thickly covered with dusky spots; 3 or 4 dark bands; some cirri centered in pale spots on side; pale yellow ventrally; fins with pale yellow bars and spots; anal and pelvic fins with dark spots along rays.
- Body robust anteriorly, ovate in cross section, slightly compressed; head massive; maxilla extending beyond pupil.
- Orbit protruding above profile of head; frontoparietal ridge strong, ending in much-elevated nuchal ridge; exposed head bones covered with minute osseous tubercles.
- **Lachrymal bone expanded as rounded lobe bearing 2 low projections** extending over maxilla.
- **First preopercular spine long (24–48% of head length), with 1–4 spinules**, other three strong and sharp; opercle with 2 sharp spines.
- Cirri on posterior end of maxilla, preopercular margin, and below lateral line.
- Cirri on tips of dorsal fin spines; **total of second dorsal and anal fin rays 23 or more**.
- Prickly scales below lateral line anteriorly.
- **Lateral line plates with 1 or 2 keels**.
- Vomerine teeth present; palatine teeth absent.
- Genital papilla of males elongate and conical.
- Gill membranes joined to isthmus without leaving free margin posteriorly.
- Length to 204 mm SL (about 250 mm TL).

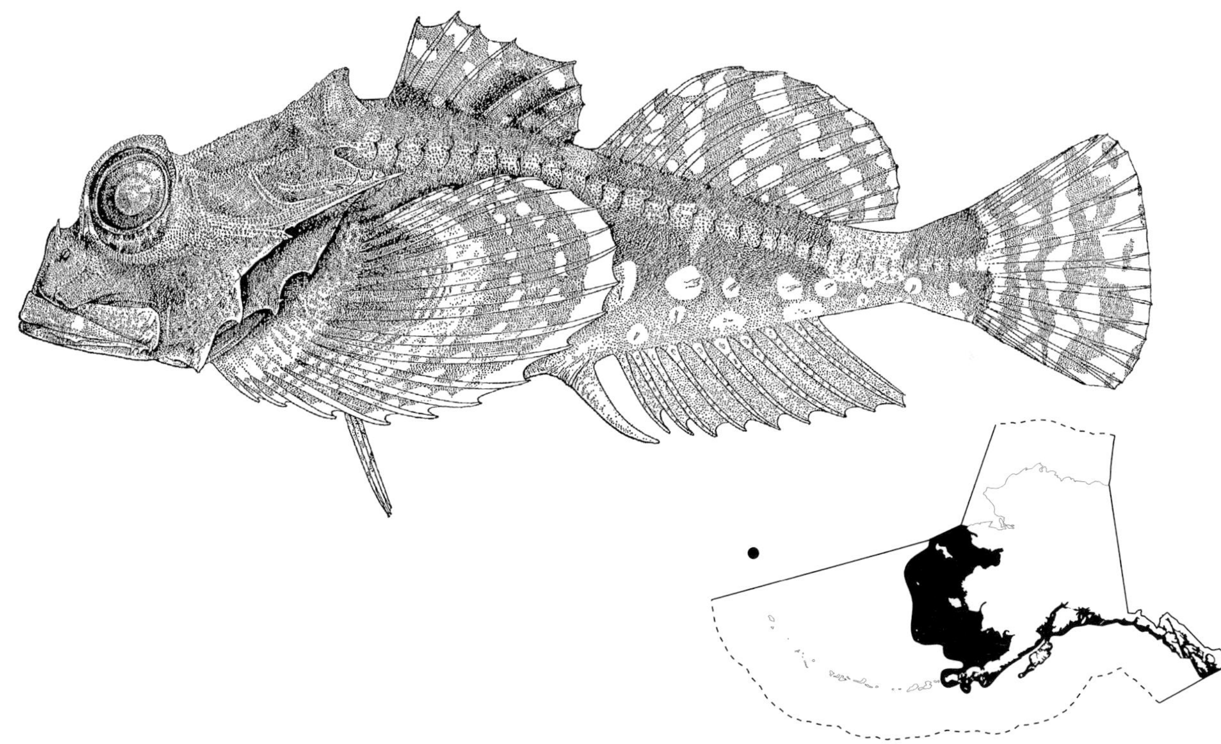

Notes & Sources — *Enophrys lucasi* (Jordan & Gilbert in Jordan & Evermann, 1898)
Cottus clavigero: Smitt 1893; Bering Island specimen, placed in synonymy by Sandercock and Wilimovsky (1968).
Ceratocottus lucasi Jordan & Gilbert in Jordan & Evermann, 1898
Included by some taxonomists in the synonymy of *E. diceraus* (see Notes & Sources on preceding page).

Description: Jordan and Evermann 1898:1940; Jordan and Gilbert 1899:459–460; Sandercock and Wilimovsky 1968: 838–839; Peden and Wilson 1976:236–237.

Figure: University of British Columbia, artist P. Drukker-Brammall; UBC 62-548, male, 162 mm SL, Sanak I., Alaska.

Range: The type specimens include one from the stomach of a cod and one from a halibut, both captured near St. Paul Island (Jordan and Gilbert 1899). Sandercock and Wilimovsky (1968) recorded specimens from Little Diomede Island in Bering Strait (UBC 63-142) to Craig in the Alexander Archipelago (UBC 63-171). Peden and Wilson (1976) extended known range to sites farther south in Alaska and in northern British Columbia. The westernmost collection locality in the Aleutian Islands recorded by Sandercock and Wilimovsky (1968) is south of Unimak Island at 53°54'N, 163°58'W (UBC 62-471). They placed the Avacha Bay, Kamchatka, record of Jordan and Gilbert (1899) in *E. diceraus,* but assumed distribution of *C. lucasi* to be continuous along the Aleutian chain from the Bering Island record of Smitt (1893). Habitat: Peden and Wilson 1976.

Trichocottus brashnikovi Soldatov & Pavlenko, 1915 **hairhead sculpin**

Northeastern Bering Sea between St. Lawrence Island and Seward Peninsula; western Bering Sea off Cape Navarin; Sea of Okhotsk and northern Sea of Japan off Tatar Strait.

Sandy bottom at depths of 7–87 m.

D IX–XI + 15–16; A 12–14; Pec 18–19; Pel I,3; LLs 36–38.

- Color in alcohol dark gray dorsally, light ventrally; vague dark bands below dorsal fins and on caudal peduncle; 1 or 2 bright white spots above anal fin.
- Head large, slightly depressed; body almost fusiform; body covered with thin skin.
- Nasal spine strong, embedded in skin; no spines or bony protuberances on top of head.
- Three strong preopercular spines, first longest.
- Top and sides of head, snout, jaws, lateral line with **numerous cirri**, some large, flat, fringed; nasal and supraocular cirri sometimes absent; strong, simple cirrus in center of each white spot above anal fin.
- Scales absent except for 3 short rows (1–4 scales in each row) of partially embedded **prickly bony plates on side above and partly hidden behind distal half of pectoral fin** and extending slightly posterior to tip of fin.
- Numerous small pores on head, giving granular appearance.
- Lateral line straight, with 3 rows of pores.
- Vomerine teeth present; palatine teeth absent.
- Gill membranes united to each other and free from isthmus or attached to isthmus anteriorly.
- Length to 225 mm TL.

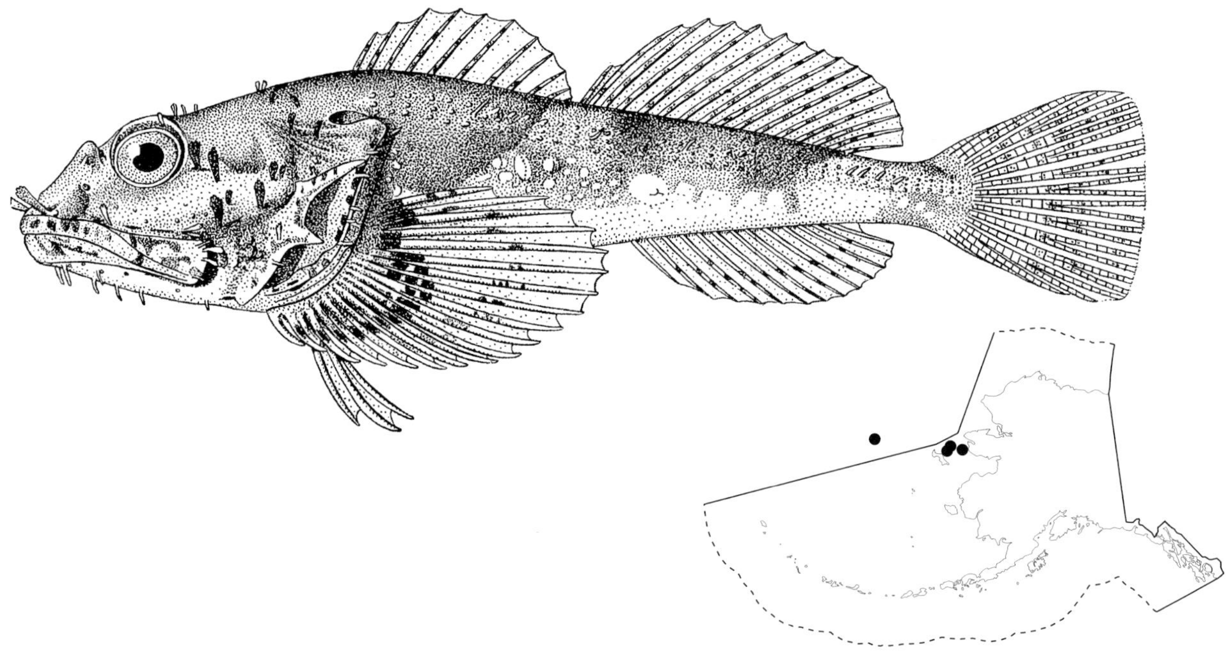

Notes & Sources — *Trichocottus brashnikovi* Soldatov & Pavlenko, 1915

Trichocottus brashnicovi: Neyelov 1979, Yabe 1985, Lindberg and Krasyukova 1987. Spelled *brashnikovi* by Soldatov and Pavlenko (1915).

Taranetz (1935a, 1937, 1941) placed *Trichocottus* in the synonymy of *Taurocottus,* believing that teeth are sometimes absent from the palatines also in *Taurocottus.* Neyelov (1979), however, determined that the fish without palatine teeth attributed to *Taurocottus bergii* by Taranetz were typical *Trichocottus brashnikovi.* Yabe (1985) treated both genera as valid taxa in his classification of the Cottoidea.

Description: Soldatov and Lindberg 1930:210–212; Neyelov 1979:69, 115, 143; Lindberg and Krasyukova 1987:227–229. KIE 1156(2), from Sea of Okhotsk, data provided by B. A. Sheiko (pers. comm., 25 Jul. 1999).

Figure: Lindberg and Krasyukova 1987, fig. 142, after Soldatov and Pavlenko 1915; 198 mm TL, Tatar Strait.

Range: First records for Alaska are as follows: UW 15756 (male, 133 mm SL) and UW 16397 (female, 190 mm SL), taken on 27 Jun. 1949 in otter trawl at depth of 38–40 m by the RV *Deep Sea* near St. Lawrence Island at 63°58'N, 169°05'W; UW 25675 (male, 131 mm SL), taken 29 Sep. 1976 by RV *Miller Freeman* at 63°43', 169°26'W, depth 70 m; and OS 11994 (male, 135 mm SL), taken in 1982 by RV *Miller Freeman* at 64°15'N, 167°06'W, depth 26 m (reported by J. W. Orr, pers. comm., 24 Mar. 1998, 31 Oct. 2000). The only record from the western Bering Sea is a specimen (ZIN 40075) identified by V. V. Fedorov, taken northeast of Cape Navarin at 62°38'N, 179°47'E (Lindberg and Krasyukova 1987). The correct capture locality for two specimens (ZIN 21848) reported to be from Bering Sea near Karaginskiy Island (Lindberg and Krasyukova 1987) is the Sea of Okhotsk; the error was caused by a typographical error in the longitude given on the jar label (B. A. Sheiko, pers. comm., 24 Dec. 1998).

Megalocottus platycephalus (Pallas, 1814) **belligerent sculpin**

Eastern Chukchi Sea off Point Barrow to eastern Bering Sea at Herendeen Bay; and western Chukchi Sea off Chukchi Peninsula to Sea of Okhotsk, and Sea of Japan to Peter the Great Bay.

Coastal brackish waters at depths to 30 m; regularly enters lower reaches of rivers.

D VIII–X + 12–15; A 11–13; Pec 15–18; Pel I,3; LLp 36–43.

- Olive brown with white marks to gray-brown with yellow marks; light spots ventrolaterally; belly white along midline, underside of head dark; all fins spotted and barred.
- Head wide, strongly depressed, depth much greater than width; **lower jaw projecting**.
- Top and sides of head verrucose.
- Postocular and occipital protuberances or spines present, sometimes with short cirri.
- Four preopercular spines; first longest, third and fourth weak or obsolete; **supracleithral spine double**, upper not always visible.
- Spiny plates in uneven rows above and below lateral line.
- Lateral line with 3 rows of pores.
- Vomerine teeth present; palatine teeth absent.
- Gill membrane free from isthmus posteriorly.
- Length to 350 mm TL or more.

Notes & Sources — *Megalocottus platycephalus* (Pallas, 1814)
Cottus platycephalus Pallas, 1814
Cottus taeniopterus Kner, 1868
Acanthocottus laticeps Gilbert, 1896
Myoxocephalus platycephalus (Pallas): Walters 1955, Quast and Hall 1972.
Megalocottus laticeps (Gilbert): Quast and Hall 1972.

Description: Turner 1886:94; Gilbert 1896:422–423; Jordan and Evermann 1898:1987–1989; Andriashev 1954:391–393; Walters 1955:315; Neyelov 1979:129–131.

Figures: Andriashev 1954, figs. 219, 220; male, 250 mm TL, Provideniya Bay, Chukchi Peninsula, Russia.

Range: Description by Pallas (1814, cited by Eschmeyer 1998) was based on material from Russian America (Alaska), as well as Kamchatka and the Sea of Okhotsk. Later, range in Alaska was recorded south to Herendeen Bay (Gilbert 1896) and north to Point Barrow (Scofield 1899). Walters (1955) examined specimens from Point Belcher, Eschscholtz Bay, and Point Barrow. The UBC collection contains many specimens from Alaska: Point Barrow (UBC 63-611); Wainwright (UBC 63-1117, 63-1128); Point Hope (UBC 63-1468); St. Lawrence Island (UBC 60-380, 60-384); Nunivak Island (UBC 63-743, 65-643, 65-644, 65-645); Hooper Bay (UBC 63-311, 63-315, 63-319); and other localities.

Size: Andriashev 1954: specimens from Provideniya Bay. Maximum length of 42 cm was reported for specimens captured off western Kamchatka (Tokranov 1994), but specimens collected in Alaska have measured 350 mm TL and under.

Myoxocephalus niger (Bean, 1881) **warthead sculpin**

Pribilof Islands, Aleutian Islands to Amak Island in Bering Sea, to western Gulf of Alaska at Sanak and Shumagin islands; Commander Islands to coasts of Sea of Okhotsk and northern Sea of Japan.

Intertidal, usually in rocky pools and crevices.

D IX–X + 15–17; A 10–13; Pec 15–18; Pel I,3; LLp 36–40; Vert 36–39.

- Typically almost black, in black lava rock habitat; sides mottled with lighter brown; white blotches and spots ventrolaterally and on fins; specimens from granitic rocks sand-colored.
- **Greatly thickened skin, partially concealing nasal and opercular spines and bases of fins.**
- No bony ridges or protuberances on top of head.
- Uppermost preopercular spine about same size as eye, second shorter and often concealed by skin.
- **Numerous warts with cirri on top of head**, which often obscure postocular and occipital cirri.
- Dorsal spine tips with fine, short cirri.
- Scales absent.
- Lateral line with 3 rows of pores.
- Vomerine teeth present; palatine teeth absent.
- Gill membrane free from isthmus posteriorly.
- Length to 270 mm TL.

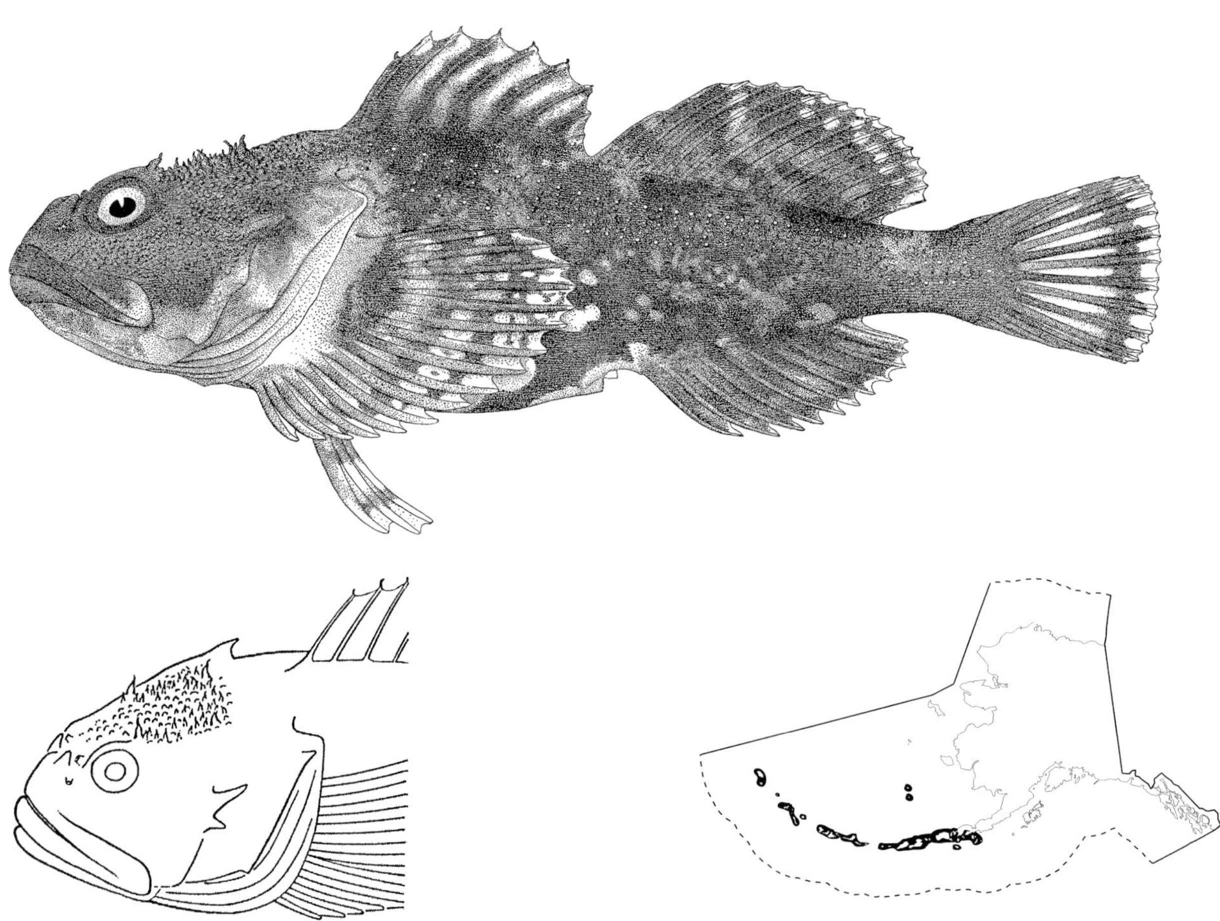

Notes & Sources — *Myoxocephalus niger* (Bean, 1881)
Cottus niger Bean, 1881

Description: Bean 1881a:151–152; Jordan and Evermann 1898:1985–1986; Jordan and Gilbert 1899:465–466; Schmidt 1950:149–150; Watanabe 1960:78–80; Neyelov 1979:123.

Figures: Jordan and Gilbert 1899, pl. 65; 230 mm TL, St. Paul Island. Diagram of head: Carveth and Wilimovsky 1983ms.

Range: The type specimens (Bean 1881a) were collected at St. Paul Island, Bering Sea, where it was reported by Elliott (1882) to be a common beach cottoid in 1872. Bean (1881b) soon recorded it also from Sanborn Harbor, Shumagin Islands. Wilimovsky (1964) recorded it from the Aleutian Islands at Attu, Agattu, Semichi, Buldir, Amchitka, Adak, Great Sitkin, and Atka islands, and the Islands of Four Mountains. The UBC collection contains numerous voucher specimens from those localities as well as Nizki, Shemya, and Umnak islands, and the Sanak Islands at Caton Island. Easternmost record in Bering Sea is lot UBC 65-142, from Amak Island off Cold Bay. Pinchuk (1976) found 46 specimens on Bering Island in the Commander group.

Myoxocephalus quadricornis (Linnaeus, 1758) **fourhorn sculpin**

Beaufort Sea coast to St. Lawrence Island and Norton Sound; off Russia to Gulf of Anadyr; circumpolar.

Salt and brackish waters to fresh water, to depth of about 20 m; ascends rivers for considerable distances, often more than 100 km.

D VI–X + 11–16; A 12–17; Pec 15–18; Pel I,3; LLp about 45; Vert 37–43.

- Dark gray dorsally, paler ventrally; dark saddles below dorsal fins; soft dorsal, anal, caudal, and pectoral fins barred.
- Head depressed, width greater than depth.
- No sharp spines on top of head; **postocular and occipital protuberances present, with rough, wart-like surface in some specimens**.
- Four preopercular spines, first straight or slightly curved, lower two short and pointing ventrally.
- Cirri absent from head and body.
- **Dorsal fins separated by space about equal to eye diameter or more**.
- Scales absent except for irregular rows of spiny plates above and below lateral line, poorly developed or absent in females and young.
- Lateral line a single row of pores fading behind anal insertion or extending to caudal fin.
- Vomerine teeth present; palatine teeth absent.
- Gill membrane free from isthmus posteriorly.
- Length to 365 mm TL, usually not over 280 mm.

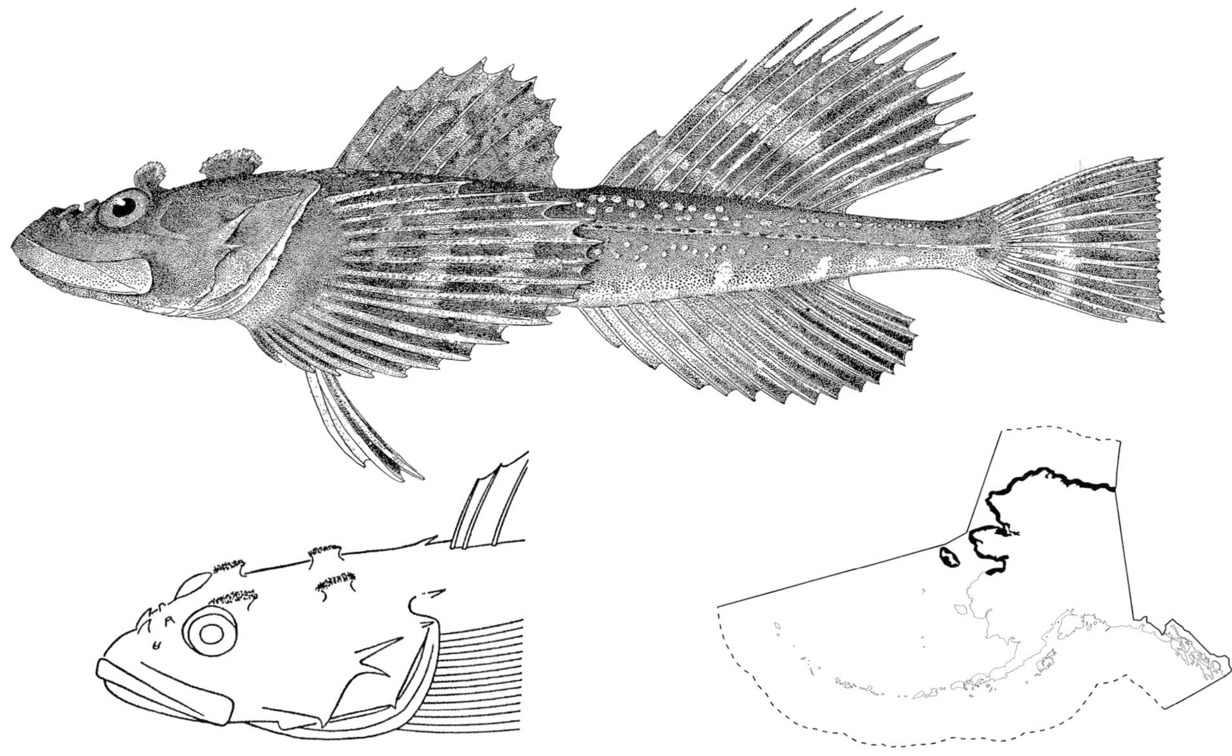

Notes & Sources — *Myoxocephalus quadricornis* (Linnaeus, 1758)
Cottus quadricornis Linnaeus, 1758
Cottus hexacornis Richardson, 1823
Oncocottus quadricornis: Jordan and Evermann 1898, 1900.
Oncocottus hexacornis: Jordan and Gilbert 1899.
Called *Triglopsis quadricornis* by some authors, including Neyelov (1979) and Fedorov (in Whitehead et al. 1986:1259). See those works and Kottelat (1997) for detailed synonymies.

Description: Jordan and Evermann 1898:2001–2004; Andriashev 1954:387–391; Walters 1955:315–318; Scott and Crossman 1973:842–847; Morrow 1980:207–209.

Figures: Jordan and Gilbert 1899, pl. 68; 197 mm TL, Herschel Island, Beaufort Sea, Canada. Diagram of head: Carveth and Wilimovsky 1983ms.

Range: No reliable records of *M. quadricornis* south of Norton Sound or the Gulf of Anadyr are known. Walters (1955) attributed the Kodiak Island record of *Oncocottus hexacornis* by Evermann and Goldsborough (1907) to *M. jaok,* and Andriashev (1954) noted that the record of Bean and Bean (1896) from Bering Island was based on incorrect identification of fry. A dwarf, strictly lacustrine form that occurs in the Great Lakes and other deep lakes of arctic Canada is often considered a separate species, or at least a subspecies, *M. quadricornis thompsoni.* It has not been found in Alaska. Morrow (1980) opined that it could be present in some of the unexplored lakes of Alaska. It is possible, though, as pointed out by B. L. Wing (pers. comm., 5 Aug. 1997), that it is not present in Alaska, due to lack of suitable habitat. Alaska does not have such large, deep lakes as are found in arctic Canada.

Myoxocephalus scorpius (Linnaeus, 1758) **shorthorn sculpin**

Beaufort Sea to northern British Columbia; Laptev Sea to Kamchatka Bay and Commander Islands; Canadian Arctic to Greenland and northwest Atlantic; northeast Atlantic and seas of northern Europe.

Shallow water near shore to depth of 550 m, most common at depths less than 70 m.

D VII–XII + 13–19; A 9–15; Pec 14–19; Pel I,3; LLp 39–45; Vert 34–39.

- Greenish brown to blackish, with yellow and orange tinges and dark mottling; belly white to orange, red, or brown with large white spots; fins brown, green, or yellow, with paler spots and bars.
- Head depressed; caudal peduncle shorter and stouter than in *M. scorpioides.*
- **Top of head strongly verrucose or not**.
- **Usually 2 postocular and 2 occipital protuberances or spines** on each side; one or both of either pair often lacking; with or without cirri.
- Usually 3 preopercular spines, uppermost longest.
- **Platelike scales above lateral line round, with depressed center and numerous short spines around margin**; fewer, scattered plates below lateral line with spines on posterior edge.
- Lateral line with 3 rows of pores.
- Vomerine teeth present; palatine teeth absent.
- Gill membrane free from isthmus posteriorly.
- Length to 600 mm TL, usually under 350 mm.

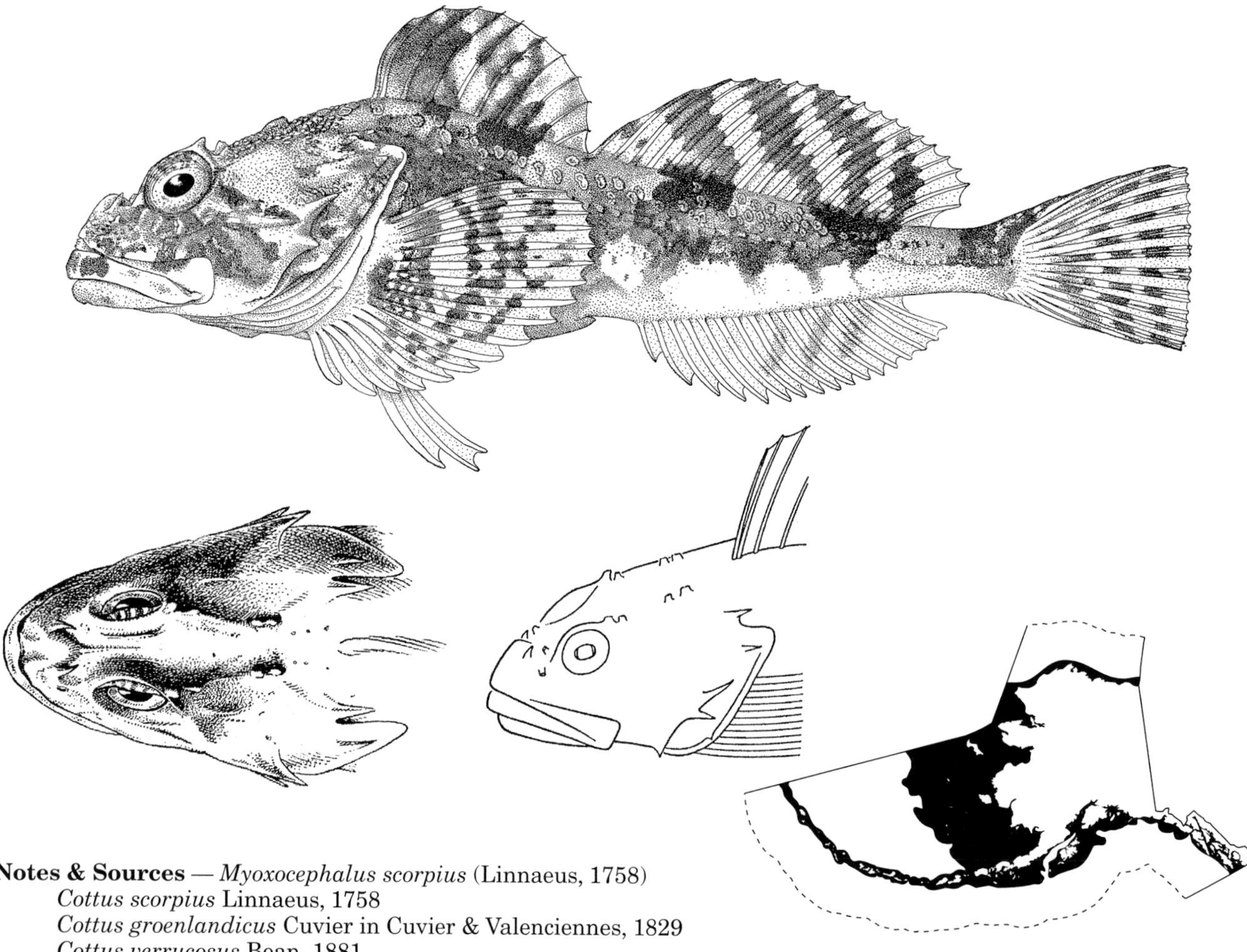

Notes & Sources — *Myoxocephalus scorpius* (Linnaeus, 1758)
Cottus scorpius Linnaeus, 1758
Cottus groenlandicus Cuvier in Cuvier & Valenciennes, 1829
Cottus verrucosus Bean, 1881
Walters (1955), reviewing Arctic species of *Myoxocephalus,* concluded that *M. scorpius* is a highly variable species represented by two subspecies, *M. s. groenlandicus* and *M. s. scorpius,* and that *M. verrucosus* is identical to *M. s. groenlandicus.* Some authors, following Neyelov (1979), maintain that all three forms are distinct.

Description: Bean 1881a:152–153; Jordan and Evermann 1898:1974–1975, 1979–1980; Andriashev 1954:377–380; 383–387; Walters 1955:318–320; Neyelov 1979:127–129.

Figures: Jordan and Gilbert 1899, pl. 66; 230 mm TL, Bristol Bay, Alaska, *Albatross* station 3232, 58°31'N, 157°34'W. Heads: dorsal: Andriashev 1954, fig. 215(1); dorsolateral: Carveth and Wilimovsky 1983ms.

Range: The UBC collection contains specimens from throughout the species' range in Alaska; e.g., UBC 63-846, Flaxman Island; UBC 63-1009, Attu Island; and UBC 63-81, Gastineau Channel. Specimens recorded by Peden and Wilson (1976) as *Myoxocephalus* sp. from Welcome Harbour, B.C., are referable to *M. scorpius* (A. E. Peden, pers. comm., 3 May 1999) and are the southernmost record.

Myoxocephalus scorpioides (Fabricius, 1780) **Arctic sculpin**

East Siberian Sea through Alaskan and Canadian Arctic to Greenland and south to Gulf of St. Lawrence in Atlantic; south to Norton Sound and Gulf of Anadyr in Bering Sea.

Shallow coastal waters from shore to depth of 25 m.

D VIII–X + 14–17; A 11–13; Pec 14–16; Pel I,3; LLp 36–42; Vert 35–38.

- Purplish blue or blackish with white mottling and spots and darker bands; cream to orange tinges; in males, belly orange-red with wide white stripe along midline, and sides below pectoral fin and above anal fin with dark-outlined silvery or white spots; fins spotted and barred.
- Head depressed; caudal peduncle longer and more slender than in *M. scorpius*.
- **Top of head covered with numerous hard, sharp-tipped warty protuberances**.
- **Postocular and occipital spines weak, in adults skin-covered, each spine with stout cirrus**.
- Four preopercular spines, uppermost longest, lower two mere tubercles.
- **Scattered plates with numerous small spines above lateral line**, anterior plates entirely covered with spines in adult males; fewer, scattered plates below lateral line.
- Lateral line with 3 rows of pores.
- Vomerine teeth present; palatine teeth absent.
- Gill membrane free from isthmus posteriorly.
- Length to 238 mm TL.

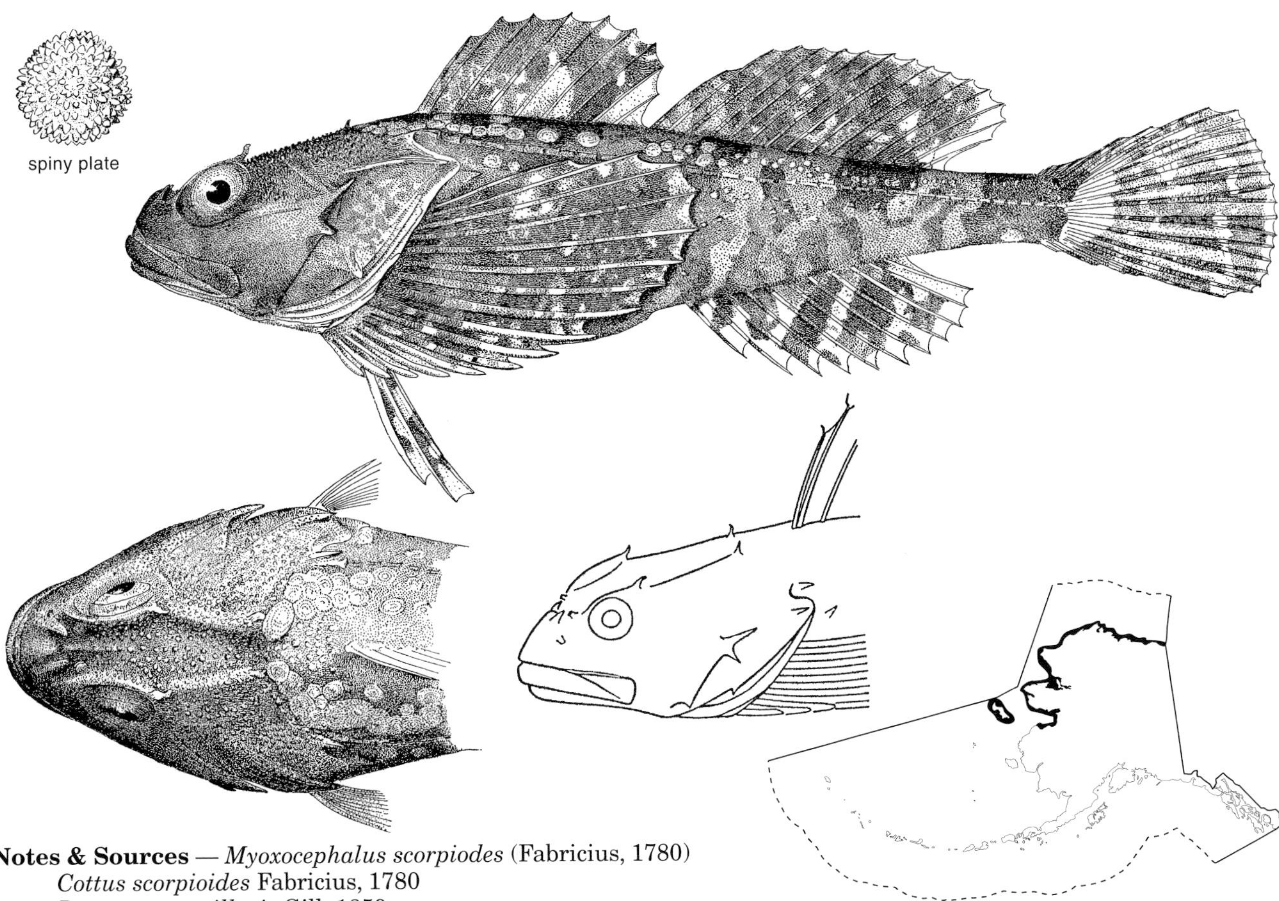

Notes & Sources — *Myoxocephalus scorpiodes* (Fabricius, 1780)
Cottus scorpioides Fabricius, 1780
Boreocottus axillaris Gill, 1859
Walters (1955) reviewed diagnostic characters and concluded that *M. axillaris* is identical to *M. scorpioides*.

Description: Gill 1859:166; Scofield 1899:500; Andriashev 1954:380–383; Walters 1955:318–319; Neyelov 1979:124.

Figures: Jordan and Gilbert 1899, pl. 67a and page 466; Alaska (reported to be from Herendeen Bay but NMNH records indicate locality uncertain, probably Port Clarence). Diagram of head: Carveth and Wilimovsky 1983ms.

Range: Recorded from Bering Strait by Gill (1859); St. Michael by Nelson (1887); Port Clarence by Scofield (1899); and St. Lawrence Island by Rendahl (1931). The record from Bering Island, Russia, of Bean and Bean (1896; USNM 39428) is referable to *Porocottus* (e.g., pelvic fins reach beyond origin of anal fin as in *Porocottus* males). Soldatov and Lindberg (1930) and Taranetz (1937) reported that *M. scorpioides* was not found at Atka Island, contrary to earlier reports. Most museum specimens from Alaska are from Barrow (e.g., UBC 63-639, 63-1136, 63-1175, 63-1438) to Norton Sound (e.g., UBC 60-377). Specimens identified as *M. scorpioides* from farther south, including records of Scofield (1899) from Chignik Bay and Herendeen Bay, are misidentified or have questionable locality data. B.A. Sheiko (pers. comm., 25 Jul. 1999), from Russian records, concluded that southern limit in western Bering Sea is Gulf of Anadyr.

Myoxocephalus stelleri Tilesius, 1811 **frog sculpin**

Unalaska Island, Aleutian Islands, to southeastern Alaska at Port Conclusion; Commander Islands and east coast of Kamchatka to Sea of Okhotsk and to Sea of Japan to South Korea.

Coastal waters near shore to depth of 55 m; sometimes in lower reaches of streams and in river mouths.

D VIII–X + 14–17; A 11–14; Pec 15–18; Pel I,3; LLp 34–41; Vert 37.

- Brown dorsally; dusky blotches and mottling; 3 light gray bands, 1 around caudal peduncle; ventral side of head mottled in young, nearly uniform whitish in adults; fins barred and spotted; males with round white spots on side.
- Head large, wide, depressed; **lips greatly thickened**; top of head verrucose.
- **Postocular and occipital spines absent; usually a cluster of short digitate ridges behind eye,** covered with thick skin.
- Three preopercular spines, uppermost longest.
- **Postocular cirrus present**; **occipital cirrus often present**; often a cirrus on end of maxilla.
- Skin naked, or with a few small, spiny plates in adult males mostly below lateral line.
- Lateral line with 3 rows of pores.
- Vomerine teeth present; palatine teeth absent.
- Gill membrane free from isthmus posteriorly.
- Length to 580 mm TL, usually under 300 mm.

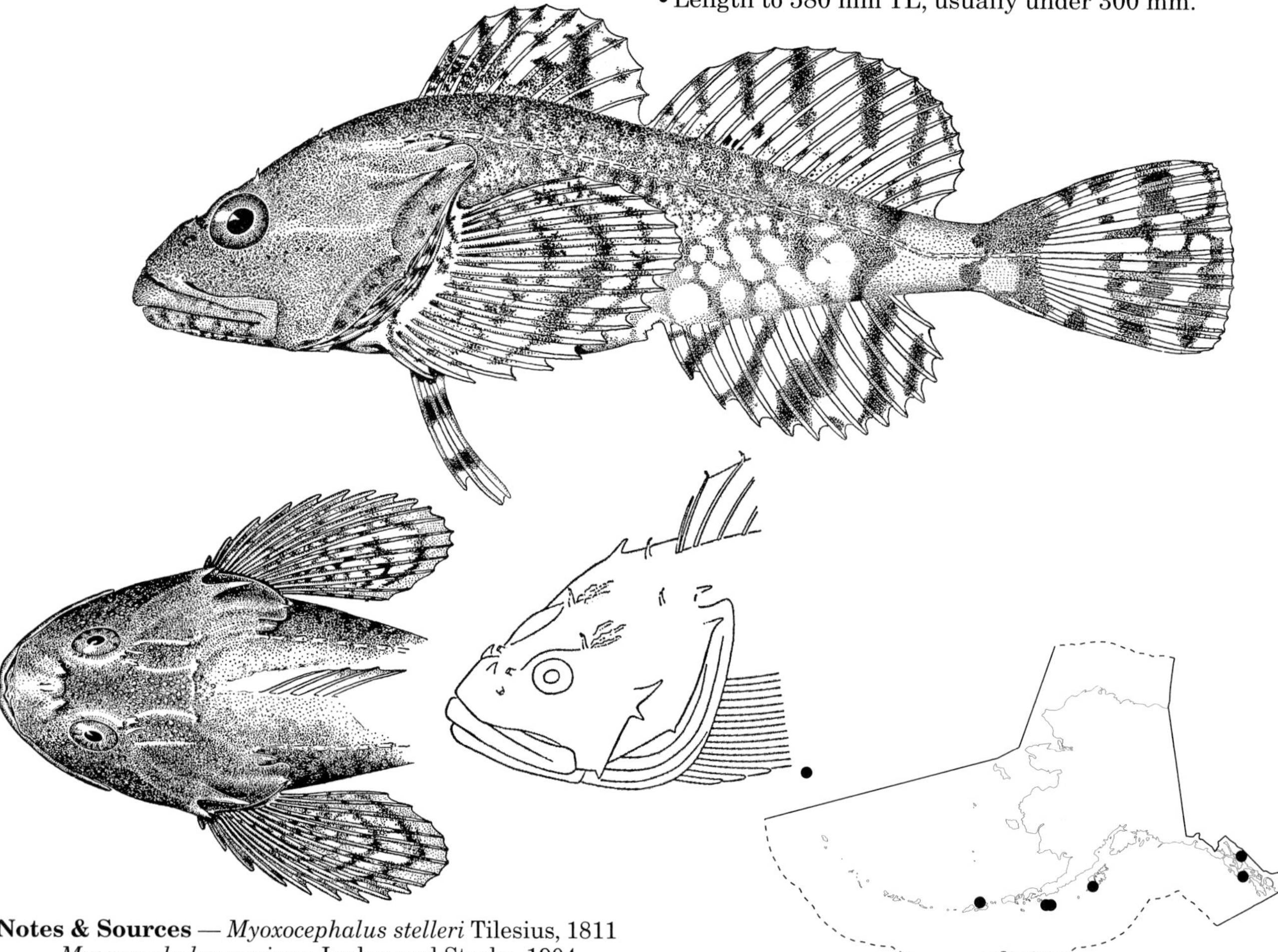

Notes & Sources — *Myoxocephalus stelleri* Tilesius, 1811
Myoxocephalus raninus Jordan and Starks, 1904
Confused with *M. verrucosus* (= *M. scorpius*) in early accounts (e.g., Evermann and Goldsborough 1907).
Called frog sculpin because the speckled throat and belly reminded G. W. Steller of the coloration of a frog.

Description: Jordan and Gilbert 1899:463–465; Jordan and Starks 1904b:277–281; Andriashev 1954:375–377; Watanabe 1960:82–84; Neyelov 1979:124.

Figures: Jordan and Gilbert 1899, pl. 64a and page 464; about 178 mm TL, Petropavlovsk, Kamchatka. Dorsolateral view of head: Carveth and Wilimovsky 1983ms. Walters (1955: 319) wrote that the illustration for *M. stelleri* in Jordan and Evermann (1900) and Evermann and Goldsborough (1907) is not of *M. stelleri* and probably represents *M. scorpius*.

Range: Previously recorded from northwest Unalaska Island (Wilimovsky 1964). Museums contain few examples from Alaska. At UBC: Lazy Bay, southern Kodiak Island (UBC 62-713); and Simeonof Island, Shumagin Islands (UBC 63-1302). At ABL: Big Koniuji Island, Shumagin Islands (AB 66-954); Point Louisa, Stephens Passage (AB 72-74); and Big Port Walter (AB 71-12) and Port Conclusion (AB 71-5, 71-6), southeast coast of Baranof Island. Specimens from Bering Strait (e.g., Rendahl 1931) and Chukchi Sea (e.g., NMC 79-505) identified as *M. stelleri* are referable to *M. scorpius* or are too small to be reliably identified.

Myoxocephalus jaok (Cuvier, 1829) **plain sculpin**

Chukchi Sea to Bering Sea, eastern Aleutian Islands, and Gulf of Alaska to Kachemak Bay, Cook Inlet; southeastern Alaska at Limestone Inlet; to Okhotsk and Japan seas as far as northern North Korea.

Sand and mud bottoms from intertidal zone to depths usually not greater than 80 m; rarely taken deeper than 150 m, reported to 550 m.

D VIII–X + 14–17; A 13–15; Pec 16–18; Pel I,3; LLp 35–42; Vert 35–38.

- Gray, with many small black spots; white ventrally; no saddles or bands on body; large white spots ventrolaterally; fins barred and spotted.
- Head narrow and depressed; body slender; mouth U-shaped; **dentary lip on each side of lower jaw**; top and sides of head covered with warts.
- **Postocular and occipital spines present; cluster of short digitate ridges behind eye**, not covered with skin.
- Usually 3 preopercular spines, uppermost longest.
- Cirri absent from head and body.
- Soft dorsal fin rays usually 15–17, anal rays 13–15 (more than *M. polyacanthocephalus*).
- Numerous spiny bony plates above lateral line; fewer, smaller prickly plates below lateral line.
- Lateral line with 3 rows of pores.
- Vomerine teeth present; palatine teeth absent.
- Gill membrane free from isthmus posteriorly.
- Length to 600 mm TL.

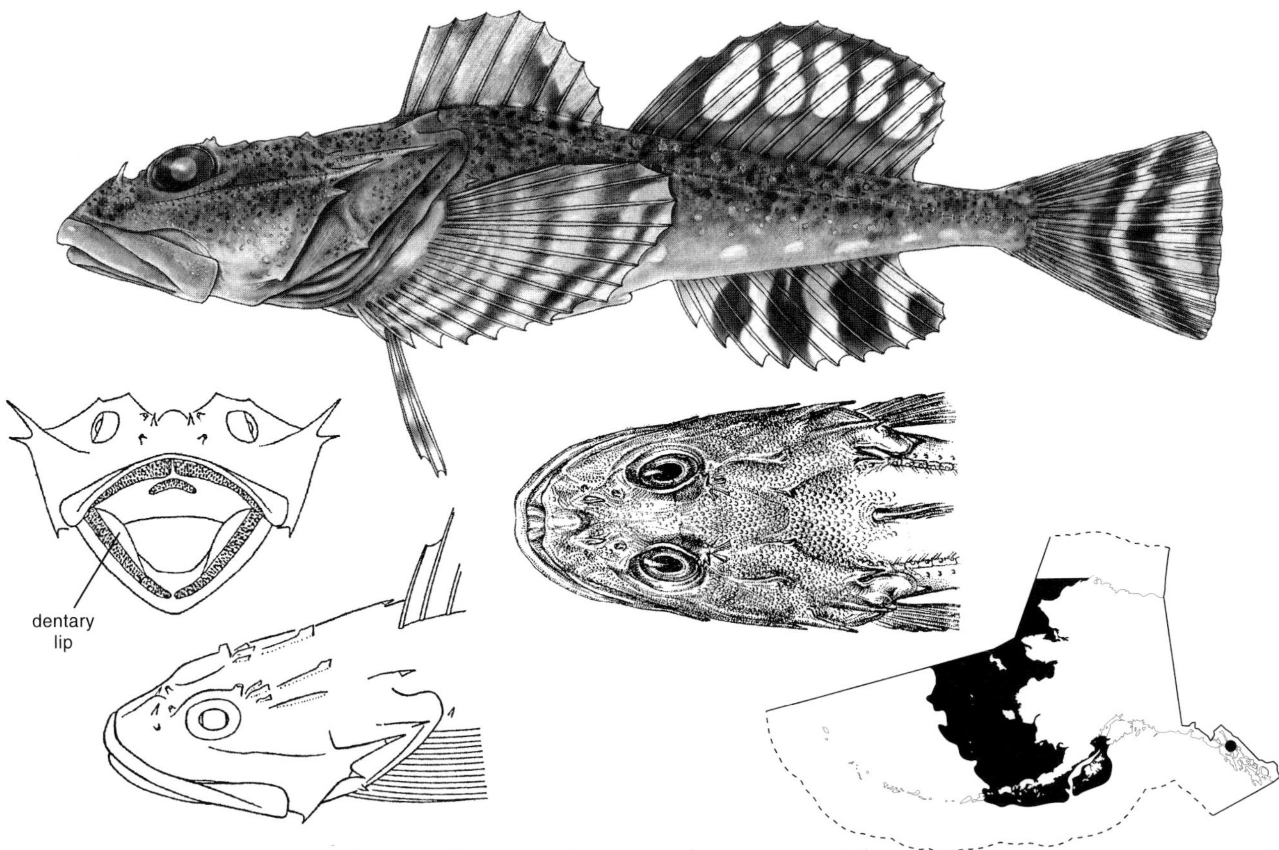

Notes & Sources — *Myoxocephalus jaok* (Cuvier in Cuvier & Valenciennes, 1829)
Cottus jaok Cuvier in Cuvier & Valenciennes, 1829
Cottus humilis Bean, 1881
Acanthocottus humilis: Gilbert 1896.

Description: Bean 1881a:149–151; Gilbert 1896:421; Jordan and Gilbert 1899:462–463; Andriashev 1954:386–387; Watanabe 1960:75–77; Neyelov 1979:126; Howe and Richardson 1978 (vertebral counts); Carveth and Wilimovsky 1983ms.

Figures: University of British Columbia, artist P. Drukker-Brammall, May 1966; UBC 65-83T17, west of Unga Island, Alaska. Diagrams: Carveth and Wilimovsky 1983ms. Dorsal view of head: Andriashev 1954, fig. 209(2).

Range: North at least as far as Point Belcher, northeast of Wainwright (Bean 1883, Walters 1955); and west in the Aleutians to Unalaska Island (Evermann and Goldsborough 1907). Recorded by Quast and Hall (1972) from Cold Bay, on south side of Alaska Peninsula. The UBC has examples from Bering Sea to Kodiak archipelago and Cook Inlet; easternmost is from Aurora Lagoon, Kachemak Bay (UBC 62-998). Eschmeyer and Herald (1983) reported range to southeastern Alaska; AB 67-155, comprising two specimens identified in 1977 by E. L. Hall, is from Limestone Inlet. Allen and Smith (1988) reported that *M. jaok* was taken as far north as Kotzebue Sound and east to Kodiak Island in NMFS bottom trawl surveys.

Myoxocephalus polyacanthocephalus (Pallas, 1814) **great sculpin**

Bering Sea and Aleutian Islands to southern Puget Sound, Washington; Gulf of Anadyr to Sea of Okhotsk and eastern Sea of Japan.

Sand and mud bottoms and around rocks, usually found from intertidal zone to depths less than 200 m, but not rare at 200–300 m; reported to 775 m.

D VIII–X + 13–16; A 11–13; Pec 16–18; Pel I,3; LLp 36–40; Vert 36–39.

- Olive brown or gray dorsally, mottled with yellow to orange-red; usually with 3 or 4 dark, irregular saddles; belly white; small white spots ventrolaterally; fins barred and spotted.
- Head wide; body robust; mouth rounded; **lateral dentary lip absent**; top and sides of head covered with warts.
- **Postocular and occipital spines present; cluster of short digitate ridges behind eye**, not covered with skin.
- Usually 3 preopercular spines, uppermost longest.
- Cirri absent from head and body.
- Soft dorsal fin rays 13–16, anal rays usually 11–12 (fewer than *M. jaok*).
- Scales absent, except for prickles embedded in papillae on head and sometimes above lateral line in very large males.
- Lateral line with 3 rows of pores.
- Vomerine teeth present; palatine teeth absent.
- Gill membrane free from isthmus posteriorly.
- Length to at least 760 mm TL.

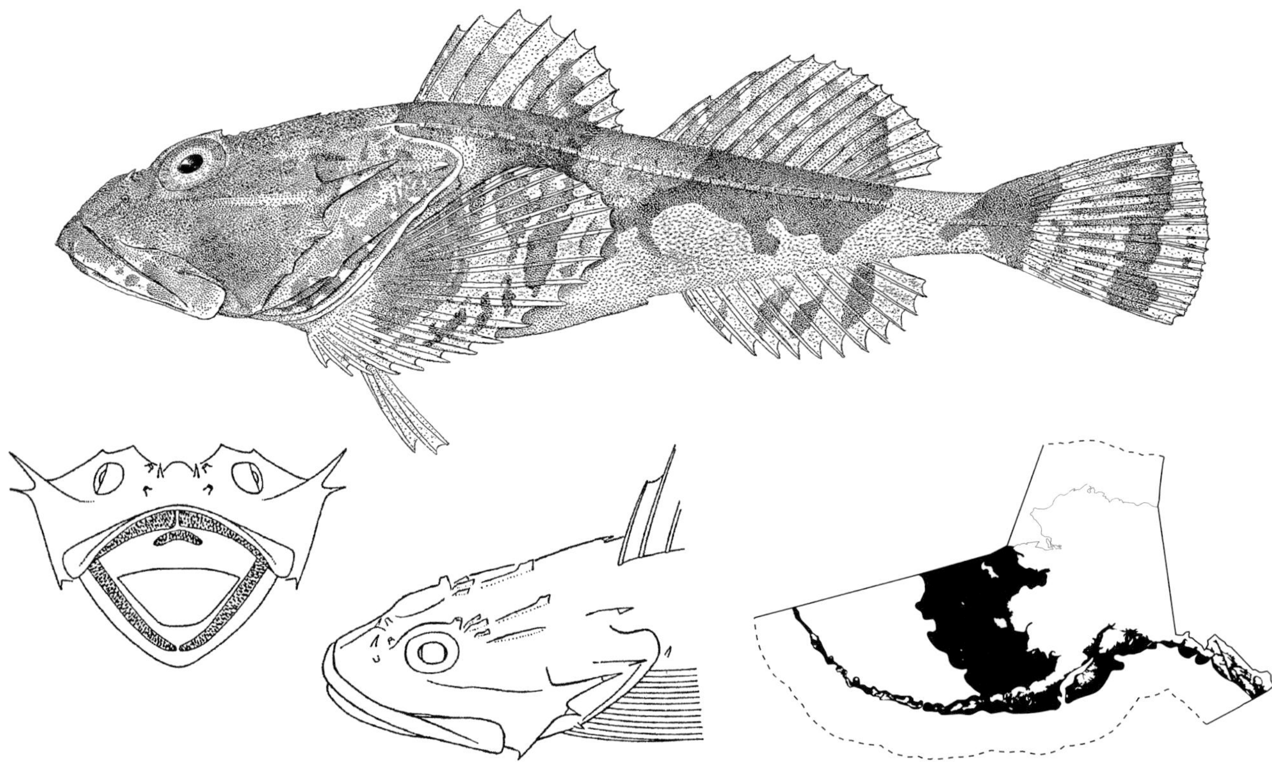

Notes & Sources — *Myoxocephalus polyacanthocephalus* (Pallas, 1814)
Cottus polyacanthocephalus Pallas, 1814

Description: Jordan and Starks 1904b:272–273; Hart 1973: 521–522; Howe and Richardson 1978 (vertebral counts); Neyelov 1979:125–126; Eschmeyer and Herald 1983:176; Carveth and Wilimovsky 1983ms.

Figures: Jordan and Gilbert 1899, pl. 63; 186 mm TL, Unalaska. Diagrams: Carveth and Wilimovsky 1983ms (dorsolateral view intentionally the same as for *M. jaok*; young fish, especially, can be similar in appearance).

Range: A common sculpin in Alaskan waters, well represented from the southern Bering Sea and throughout the Aleutian Islands and Gulf of Alaska in published records (e.g., Evermann and Goldsborough 1907, Wilimovsky 1964, Quast and Hall 1972) and museum collections. The holotype (unique) is from Alaska, but with no definite locality (Kodiak, Aleutian Islands; Eschmeyer 2001). The northern limit in the Bering Sea off Alaska is not clear. Allen and Smith (1988) reported survey catches north to about 62°N, but they noted that some records could be misidentified *M. verrucosus* (= *M. scorpius*) or *M. jaok*. The northernmost Bering Sea locality represented among more than 280 lots of *M. polyacanthocephalus* from Alaska at UBC is Bristol Bay near Walrus Island at 58°48'N, 160°00'W (UBC 62-657). Probably occurs along Alaskan coasts north to Bering Strait. Neyelov (1979) reported its range north along Asian coasts to reach Lavrentiya Bay. Incorrectly reported by some authors to be absent from Sea of Okhotsk. Tokranov (1984) reported dense aggregations off west Kamchatka, with catches of 1 to 1.5 tonnes per hour of trawling.

Microcottus sellaris (Gilbert, 1896) **brightbelly sculpin**

Chukchi Sea to southern Bering Sea and Aleutian Islands; Gulf of Anadyr to Commander Islands, to southern Sea of Okhotsk, Kuril Islands, and northern Sea of Japan.

Coastal areas to depth of about 50 m, often in brackish water.

D VII–IX + 12–14; A 10–12; Pec 15–18; Pel I,3; LLp 32–34.

- Body purplish, spotted and mottled in black and white, or red and black, with 2 or more white bars and bright yellow belly; pelvic fin with black or red spots along rays; female not as brightly colored.
- Head deep, profile abrupt.
- **Postocular and occipital spines or protuberances present, usually bearing simple cirri**.
- **First preopercular spine round**, curved upward, **second spine at least half length of first**; **spines on opercle, subopercle, interopercle variously developed, often strong**.
- Single cirrus on tip of each dorsal fin spine; **pelvic fin united to belly by wide membrane**.
- Scales absent except for weak, slightly prickly papillae below lateral line.
- Numerous secondary pores on head.
- Lateral line with 3 rows of pores.
- Vomerine teeth present; palatine teeth absent.
- Gill membrane free from isthmus posteriorly.
- Length to 125 mm TL.

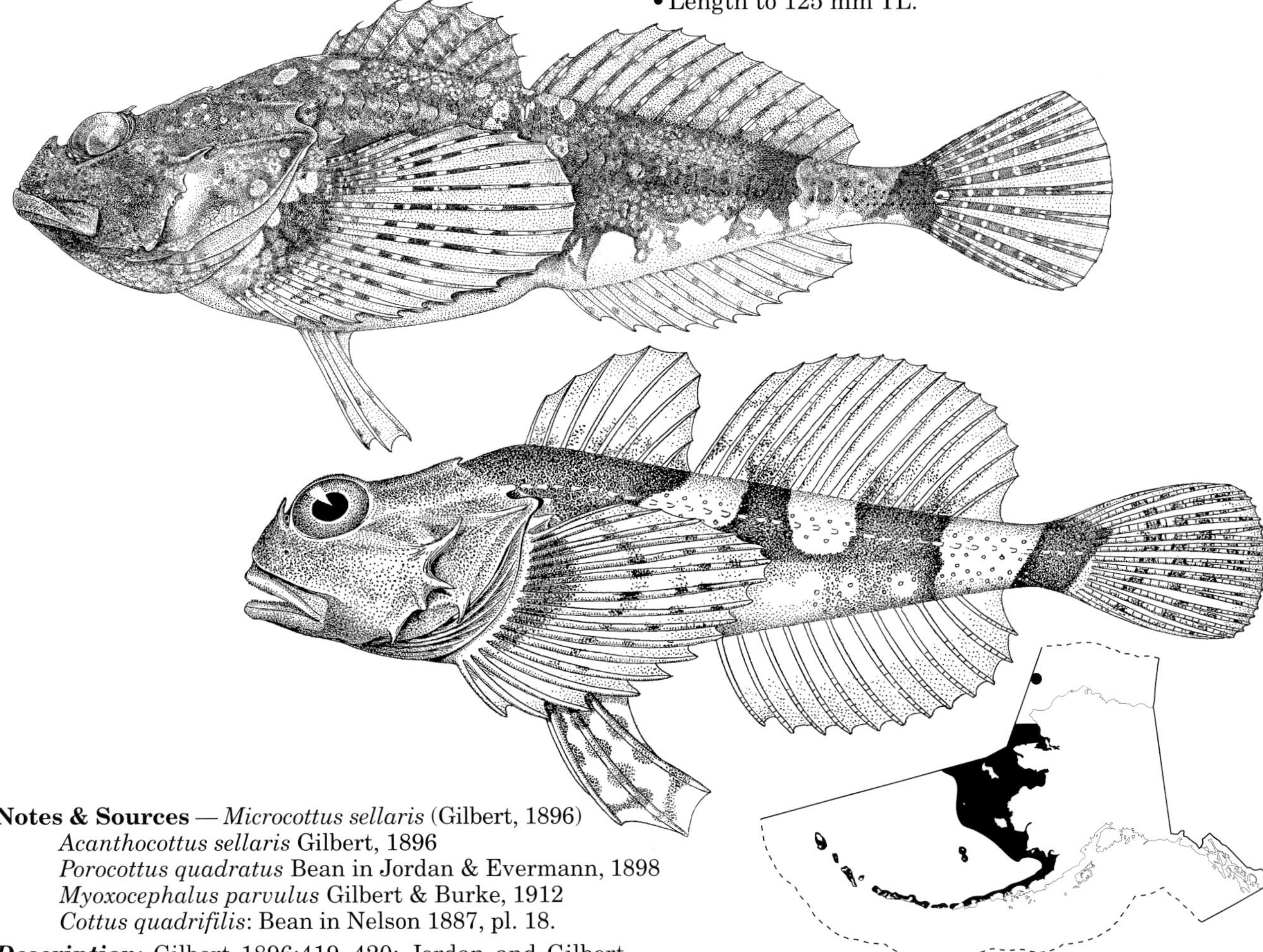

Notes & Sources — *Microcottus sellaris* (Gilbert, 1896)
Acanthocottus sellaris Gilbert, 1896
Porocottus quadratus Bean in Jordan & Evermann, 1898
Myoxocephalus parvulus Gilbert & Burke, 1912
Cottus quadrifilis: Bean in Nelson 1887, pl. 18.

Description: Gilbert 1896:419–420; Jordan and Gilbert 1899:466–467; Gilbert and Burke 1912a:59–60; Taranetz 1935b:179; Hubbs and Schultz 1941:9–11; Andriashev 1954:394–395; Neyelov 1976:86–89, 1979:134–135.

Figures: Upper: University of British Columbia, artist P. Drukker-Brammall; UBC 63-1443, St. Paul Island, Alaska. Lower: Jordan and Gilbert 1899, pl. 67b; Bering I., Russia.

Range: Previous records: St. Michael (Nelson 1887), Bristol Bay (Gilbert 1896), and St. Paul Island (Hubbs and Schultz 1941). The UBC has specimens taken off Kivalina (UBC 63-1470); and St. Lawrence, St. Paul, and Attu islands (several lots each). AB 82-1, 82-27, and 82-28 are from Bristol Bay. Cataloged as *P. quadrifilis* but correctly *M. sellaris*: USNM 32943 (1; 102 mm TL), Kegiktowik (= Kegiktowruk or Klikitarik); 32961 and 32963 (2; about 51–72 mm SL), St. Michael; 34046 (12; 69–96 mm TL), Bristol Bay. Northern record (confirmed by C.W.M.) is a UAM uncataloged specimen (69 mm TL) from 71°30'N, 167°06'W, depth 48 m, taken in UAF survey of eastern Chukchi Sea in 1990. The species was reported on the list of fishes from the survey (Barber et al. 1997), without locality data or commentary on this unique northern record; the haul-catch listing (unpublished) indicates only the one specimen was caught.

Porocottus quadrifilis Gill, 1859 **Gill's fringed sculpin**

One record, with locality uncertain: probably Bering Strait on Russian or Alaskan coast.

Habitat not known.

D VIII + 13; A 11; Pec about 21; Pel I,3.

- Purple, irregularly spotted with black; dark spot under eye, and another on maxilla (not shown); dorsal, caudal, and pectoral fins irregularly variegated with black; large dark spots on pectoral fin.
- Head large, depressed, subrhomboidal; body anteriorly subcylindrical, rapidly declining to caudal.
- Nasal spines small; top of head without bony spines and ridges.
- **First preopercular spine long, sharply curved upward, second and third spines obsolete, fourth small, directed anteroventrally**; no longitudinal rib or spine on opercle.
- **One pair of simple postocular cirri and one pair of simple occipital cirri** (not shown).
- Membrane of first dorsal fin bearing small cirri along margin; **fewer dorsal fin elements than in most *P. mednius* and *P. camtschaticus***; pectoral fin reaching anal fin origin.
- Scales absent.
- Large pores on head and lower jaw.
- Lateral line opening by pores in raised papillae, under a cutaneous keel.
- Vomerine teeth present; palatine teeth absent.
- Gill membrane continuous over isthmus and attached to isthmus along midline almost as far posteriorly as margin of membrane.
- Branchiostegal rays 5?
- Length of holotype about 51 mm TL.

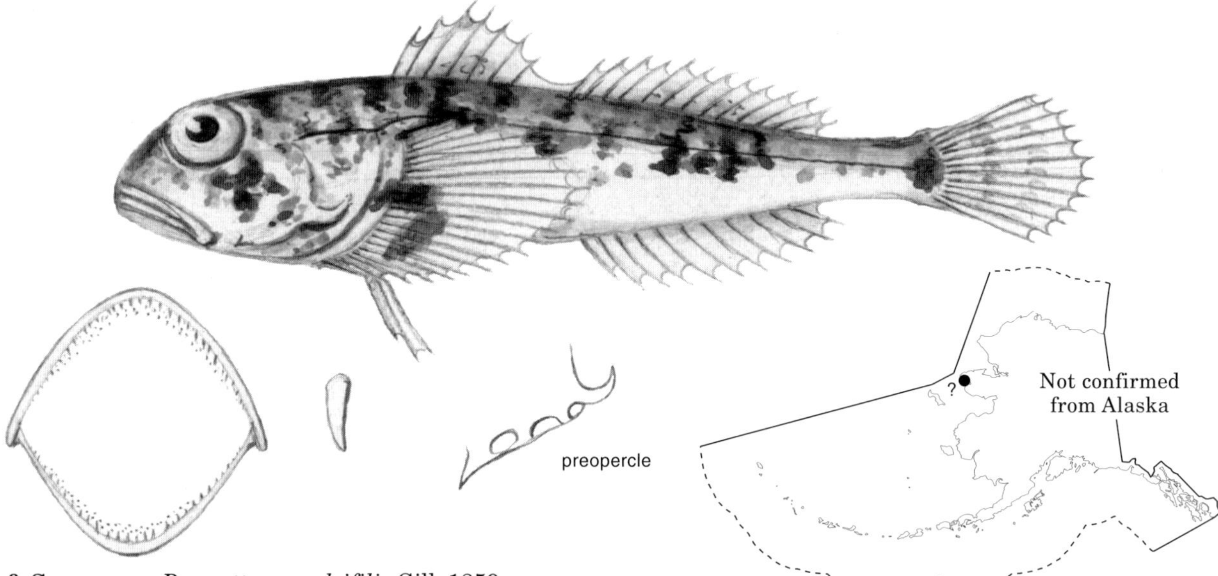

Notes & Sources — *Porocottus quadrifilis* Gill, 1859

Named *quadrifilis* by Gill (1859) for having two pairs of cirri on the top of the head. The only specimen known with certainty is the holotype. Authors from Bean (1881b) to Matyushin (1990) identified specimens as *P. quadrifilis* but those specimens actually represent *P. mednius, Microcottus sellaris,* and other species.

Gill's fringed sculpin was chosen for the vernacular in order to emphasize identity with Gill's holotype.

Description: Gill 1859:166. The holotype (USNM 6227) has deteriorated, with the skin gone, much of the head missing, and the tail broken off, but the dorsal and anal fin rays are countable from the exposed pterygiophores. As well, there is an illustration (see above), done near the time of collection. (A radiograph exists, but the specimen was placed ventral side down on the plate and the dorsal and anal fin rays are not visible; D.G. Smith, pers. comm., 20 Dec. 2000). Counts from the specimen are 8 dorsal fin spines, 14 dorsal rays, and 12 anal rays. The illustration shows 7 dorsal spines, 13 dorsal rays, and 11 anal rays, indicating the element from the last pterygiophore in each series was not externally visible. Gill (1859) reported 8 dorsal fin spines and 13 dorsal rays (no other counts). He reported 5 branchiostegal rays, although cottids typically have 6. Damage to the holotype prevents determination of actual branchiostegal ray count.

For additional discussion, see introduction to the Cottidae.

Figures: Smithsonian Institution, NMNH, Division of Fishes; USNM 6227, holotype (unique), 51 mm TL as measured from the illustration (bears notation 1:1).

Range: Described by Gill (1859:166) from one specimen collected at Bering Strait. He did not report which side of the strait. Other authors assumed the type locality was in Alaska, possibly from other early records attributed to *P. quadrifilis.* Wilimovsky (1954, 1958) and Quast and Hall (1972) included *P. quadrifilis* on lists of fishes of Alaska based on earlier reports. However, records from Alaska attributed to *P. quadrifilis,* including specimens at NMNH from Norton Sound, Kegiktowik (Nelson 1887), and Bristol Bay (Gilbert 1896), are *Microcottus sellaris* (specimens examined by C.W.M.). Neyelov (1976) gave Norton Sound for the type locality, possibly connecting it with those early, incorrect records. Specimens from Russia recorded as *P. quadrifilis* by Taranetz (1935b) and Matyushin (1990) were reexamined by B. A. Sheiko (pers. comm., 8 Aug. 2001), who found them not to differ from *P. mednius.*

Porocottus camtschaticus (Schmidt, 1916) **Kamchatka fringed sculpin**

Southeastern and southwestern Kamchatka Peninsula and northern Kuril Islands.

Tidepools, and intertidal and subtidal zones among pebbles, rocks, and thickets of algae to depth of 40 m.

D VIII–IX + 18–19; A 13–15; Pec 15; Pel I,3; LLp 39–40.

- Tan, with dark brown mottling and widely scattered black dots dorsally and laterally; vague dark saddles; large, pale spots behind pectoral fin ventrolaterally; broad dark streaks at pectoral base; first dorsal fin dusky brown; second dorsal dusky, with irregular white bars and margin; other fins pale, with dusky brown and gray bars, little pigment on pelvic fins; head cirri dusky, darkest at base.
- Nasal spines well developed, covered with skin; top of head without bony spines and ridges.
- **First preopercular spine broad, almost flat, sharply curved upward, second spine short and blunt, third and fourth spines obscure**.
- **Two pairs of cirri on top of head; postocular cirri cockscomb-like and with 8–20 branches**; occipital cirri simple or with 2–4 branches; occasionally with simple cirri between the larger cirri.
- Membrane of first dorsal fin bearing small cirri along margin at and adjacent to spine tips; pectoral fin in males extending beyond anal fin origin, in females reaching or nearly reaching anal fin origin; pelvic fin in males reaching anal fin origin, in females reaching anus; pelvic fin with ctenii in large males.
- Scales absent.
- Numerous pores on head; body lateral line with 3 rows of pores, central row in ridge and difficult to discern.
- Vomerine teeth present; palatine teeth absent.
- Gill membrane free from isthmus posteriorly.
- Length to 98 mm TL.

Notes & Sources — *Porocottus camtschaticus* (Schmidt, 1916)
Crossias camtschaticus Schmidt, 1916
Taranetz (1935b) classified this species in *Porocottus.*

Description: Soldatov and Lindberg 1930:232–233; Schmidt 1950:158; Neyelov 1976:94–96. KIE uncataloged, 2 specimens, 68 and 75 mm TL, tidepools at Staritschkof Island, southeastern Kamchatka. The head cirri in juvenile *P. camtschaticus* may in general be less well developed than in the adults; B.A. Sheiko (pers. comm., 24 Aug. 2001) reported that 25–30-mm-SL juveniles from western Kamchatka had postocular cirri with 2–4 branches.

Figures: KIE uncataloged, male, 75 mm TL, southeastern Kamchatka; photographs by C.W.M.

Range: This species is abundant along the southeastern Kamchatka coast but has not been recorded from the Commander Islands or Aleutian Islands. Ongoing studies of *Porocottus* from Kamchatka and Alaska by B.A. Sheiko and C.W.M. have shown that at least one other species, *P. mednius,* has a wider distribution than previously recognized, from the Kuril Islands and eastern Kamchatka to southeastern Alaska. It is possible that *P. camtschaticus,* which is the only other species of *Porocottus* known to inhabit eastern Kamchatka, could also have a wider distribution than is currently recorded.

Size: Soldatov and Lindberg 1930.

Porocottus mednius (Bean, 1898) **Aleutian fringed sculpin**

Pribilof and Aleutian islands to Gulf of Alaska at Kodiak Island; southeastern Alaska at Frederick Sound; Chukchi Peninsula at Bering Strait to Commander Islands, southeastern Kamchatka, and Kuril Islands.

Tidepools and intertidal zone.

D VII–X + 14–19; A 11–15; Pec 13–15; Pel I,3; LLp 35–42; Vert 34–37.

- Olive brown mottled with lavender-pink, brick red, and brown; ventrolaterally, males reddish pink with bright white or silvery spots, females and young watery green; white ventrally.
- Head slightly depressed; body round anteriorly, compressed posterior to anus.
- Top of head without bony spines and ridges.
- **First preopercular spine wide at base, curved upward, almost flat, second spine small and knoblike**, lower two spines weak or obscure.
- **Three pairs of multifid cirri and several simple cirri on top of head.**
- First dorsal fin membrane bearing cirri along margin; pectoral fin reaching beyond anal fin origin in males, reaching anal origin in females; pelvic fin with ctenii in males.
- A few prickles present in males below lateral line.
- Body lateral line opening through 3 rows of pores.
- Vomerine teeth present; palatine teeth absent.
- Gill membrane free from isthmus posteriorly.
- Length to 82 mm TL.

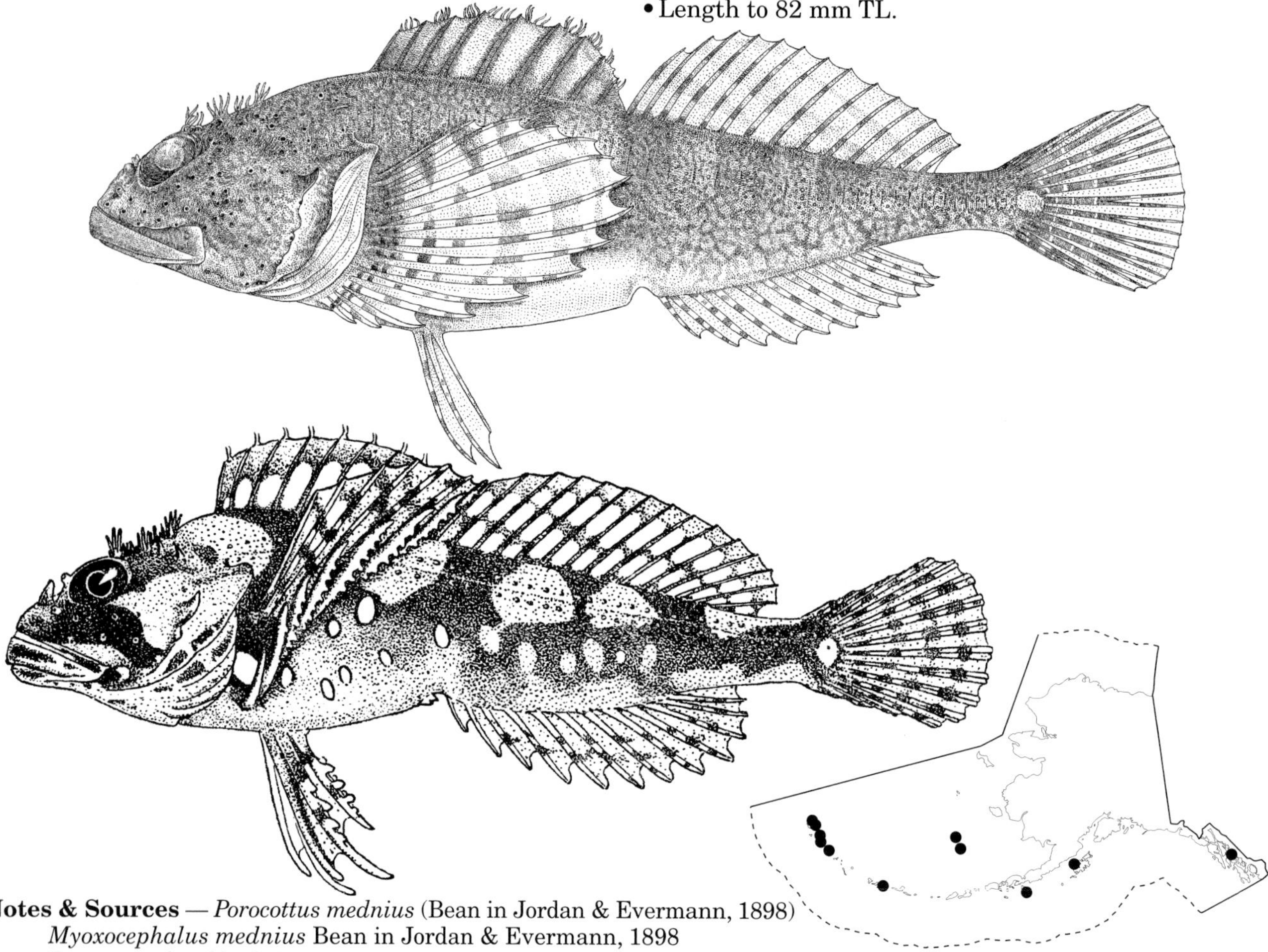

Notes & Sources — *Porocottus mednius* (Bean in Jordan & Evermann, 1898)
Myoxocephalus mednius Bean in Jordan & Evermann, 1898
Porocottus bradfordi Rutter in Jordan & Evermann, 1898
Crossias albomaculatus Schmidt, 1916
Porocottus quadrifilis: non-Gill specimens: Taranetz 1935b, description of ZIN 25472, misidentified; Andriashev 1954:396, description; Neyelov 1976:105–106, additional data from ZIN 25472; Neyelov 1979:137–138, keys, based on ZIN 25472; Matyushin 1990, description of 14 specimens in ZIN 45116, 48150, and 48151, misidentified.

Description: Jordan and Evermann 1898:1983–1984, 2862–2863; Hubbs and Schultz 1941:14–16; Neyelov 1976:101–105; Howe and Richardson 1978 (low-end vertebral count).

Figures: Upper: University of British Columbia, artist P. Drukker-Brammall; UBC 63-1412, 75 mm SL, Buldir Island, Alaska. Lower: Soldatov and Lindberg 1930, fig. 41, dorsal fin cirri corrected (error noted by Hubbs and Schultz 1941).

Range: Karluk, Kodiak Island (Rutter 1899; "most common fish in the rock pools"); Attu and Agattu islands (Gilbert and Burke 1912a); St. Paul I. and Frederick Sound (Hubbs and Schultz 1941). The UBC has 45 lots from tidepools at St. Paul, St. George, Attu, Agattu, Nizki, Shemya, Buldir, Adak, and Chernabura islands, identified as *Crossias allisii*.

Size: USNM 1608, collected in 1903 from Karluk.

Zesticelus profundorum (Gilbert, 1896) **flabby sculpin**

Bering Sea and Aleutian Islands to northern Baja California and to southeastern Kamchatka at Avacha Bay. Deep water, recorded from depths of 730–2,580 m.

D V–VII + 10–13; A 8–11; Pec 19–21; Pel I,2–3; LLp 14–18; Vert 25–26.

- Light brown dorsally; dark brown below lateral line; fins blackish, mouth and gill cavity dusky.
- Nasal spine absent; occipital spine sharp, short, recumbent, and simple or bifid; smaller, erect spine lateral to occipital spine on posttemporal.
- **First preopercular spine long, gently curved upward**, and sharp; others sharply pointed.
- Cirri absent.
- Scales absent, not even prickles or papillae.
- **Pores of infraorbital, preopercular, and mandibular series very large**.
- Body **lateral line opening through a row of fewer than 20 large, widely spaced pores**, with a smaller pore above each large pore anteriorly; no lateral line plates or scales.
- Vomerine teeth weak; palatine teeth absent.
- Gill membrane joined to isthmus leaving free margin posteriorly.
- Length to 64 mm TL.

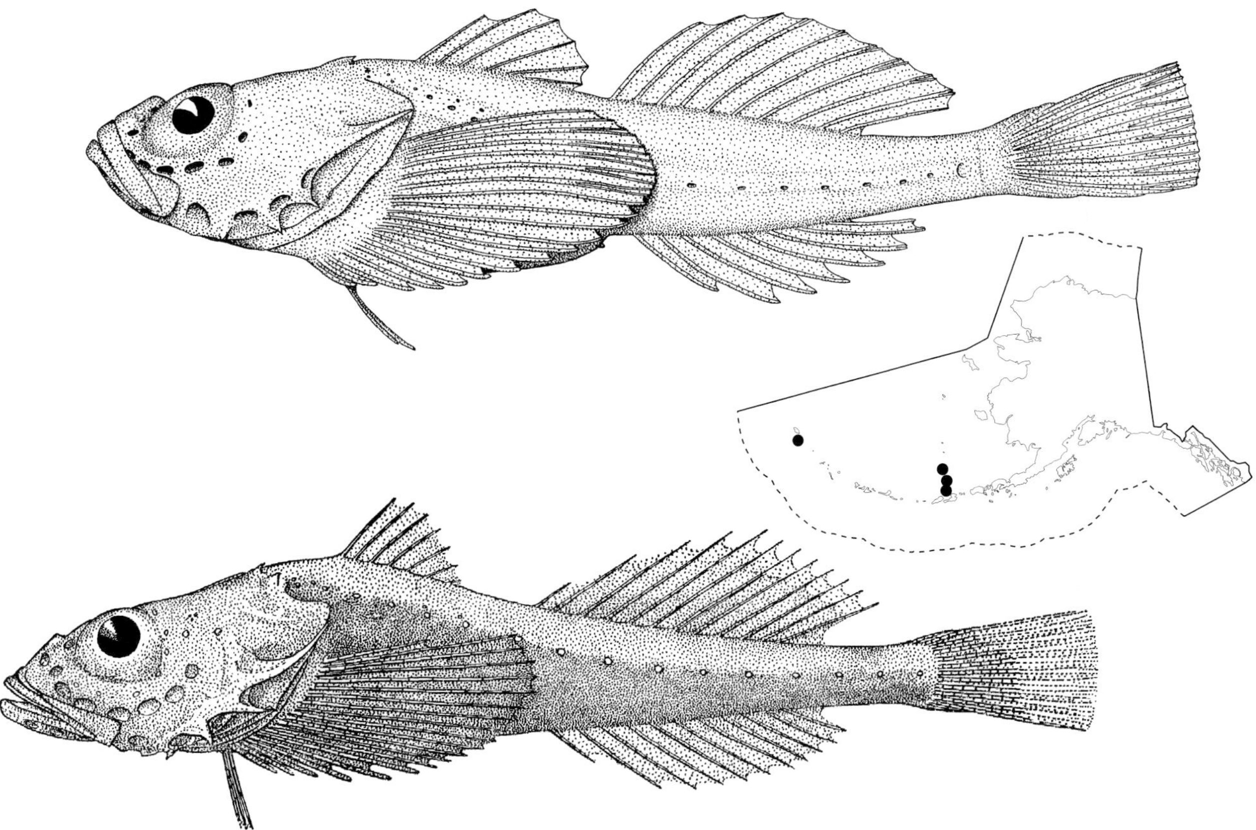

Notes & Sources — *Zesticelus profundorum* (Gilbert, 1896)
Acanthocottus profundorum Gilbert, 1896

Description: Gilbert 1896:423–424; Jordan and Evermann 1898:1990–1991; Gilbert and Burke 1912a:61; Gilbert 1915:342; Bolin 1944:95–96; Howe and Richardson 1978 (vertebral counts); Neyelov 1979:92–93, 160–161; Eschmeyer and Herald 1983:184.

Figures: Upper: Bolin 1944, fig. 37. Lower: Gilbert 1896, pl. 27, modified by removing row of small pores above large lateral line pores posteriorly; about 55 mm TL, *Albatross* station 3329, north of Unalaska Island.

Range: Few specimens have been reported. Alaskan records are: Gilbert (1896), three specimens (types) from north of Unalaska Island, *Albatross* station 3329, 53°56'N, 167°08'W, depth 730 m; Jordan and Evermann (1898), one specimen from north of Bogoslof Island, station 3634, 54°51'N, 167°27'W, depth 1,214 m; Gilbert and Burke (1912a), one specimen taken between Petrel Bank and Agattu Island, station 4781, 52°14'N, 174°13'E, depth 882 m; and Bolin (1944), south of the Pribilof Islands, 55°51'N, 169°18'N, number of specimens and depth not given (but coordinates place this record over the continental slope). Although recorded in the eastern Bering Sea only in the southern portion, the species occurs in the northern portion of the western Bering Sea. In 1974 V. V. Fedorov collected a specimen (ZIN 42440) at 61°02'N, 175°35'E, at a depth of 1,010 m (B.A. Sheiko, pers. comm., 18 Sep. 2001). Reports of *Z. profundorum* at a depth of 88 m may stem from a printer's error. The species otherwise is known only from deep water, 730 m (Gilbert 1896) or more, and is not on the American Fisheries Society list (Robins et al. 1991a) of species occurring over the North American continental shelf.

Bolinia euryptera Yabe, 1991 — broadfin sculpin

Bering Sea off Aleutian Islands in vicinity of Amukta, Carlisle, and Semisopochnoi islands.
Deep water at depths of 201–410 m.

D VIII–IX + 15–18; A 14–16; Pec 27–31; Pel I,3; LLp 34–37; Vert 32–35.

- Color in alcohol brown dorsally; dusky white ventrally; dark saddles; white spots below lateral line; numerous small pale spots on head; maxillary cirrus pale, cirri on top of head dark; 2 distinct broad stripes on first dorsal fin; large pale spot near base of pectoral fin.
- Head and body depressed.
- Interorbital space narrow, less than height of eye.
- Nasal spine sharp; no spines or protuberances on top of head.
- **Two primary preopercular spines: upper strongly hooked, lower sharp and directed anteroventrally**; accessory, descending spine on lateral surface of preopercle above base of upper primary spine, usually covered with thick skin.
- Small postocular cirrus; 1 or 2 small cirri on frontal region, 2 cirri on parietal region; robust cirrus on posterior end of maxilla.
- **Large number of pectoral fin rays**, usually 29 or 30.
- Scales absent except for subcutaneous lateral-line scales.
- Cephalic sensory system well developed, with secondary canals and pores; separate pores on either side of mandibular symphysis.
- **Body lateral line pores in 2 rows** to base of caudal fin, forming almost straight line.
- Vomerine teeth present; palatine teeth usually absent.
- Gill membranes broadly united, free of isthmus.
- Length to 189 mm SL.

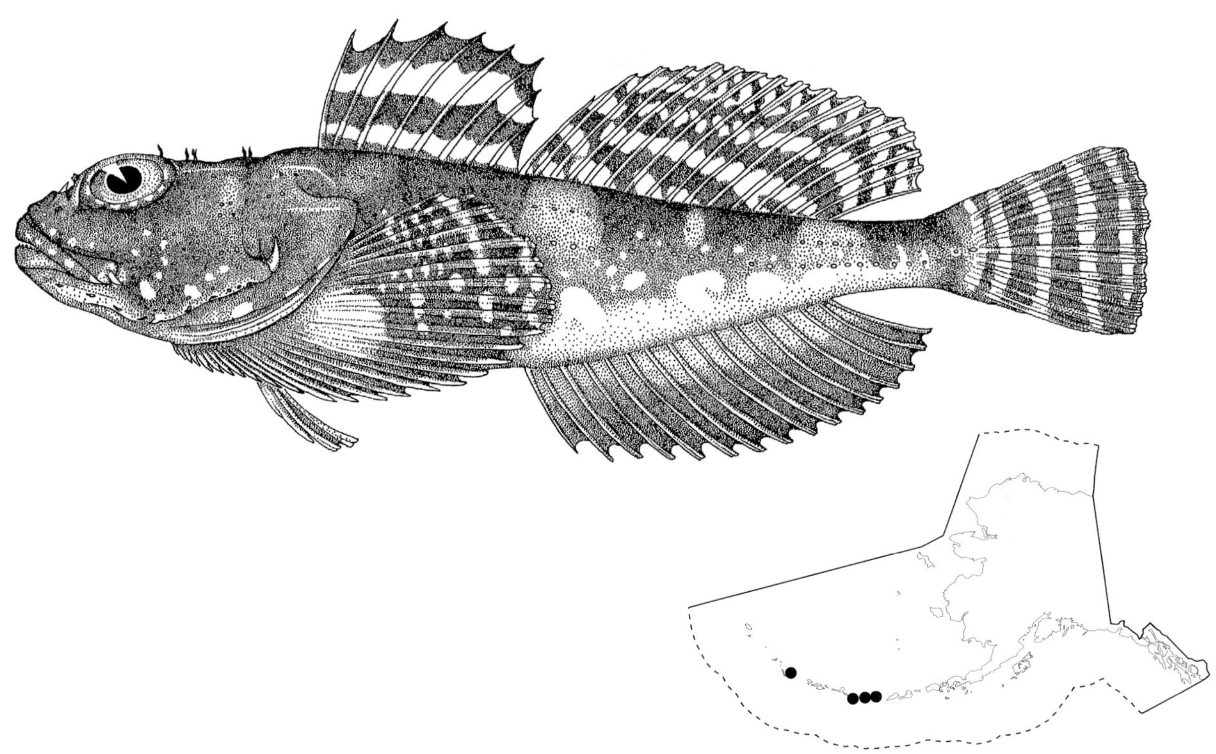

Notes & Sources — *Bolinia euryptera* Yabe, 1991

The word *primary* is used above to distinguish the preopercular spines on the posterior margin of the preopercle from the *accessory* spine on the lateral surface above the base of the uppermost primary spine.

Description: Yabe 1991.

Figure: Yabe 1991, fig. 1; holotype, male, 176 mm SL, near Amukta Pass, Aleutian Islands (52°52'N, 171°13'W).

Range: Described by Yabe (1991) from 60 specimens collected over a period of 10 years from the central Aleutian Islands, mostly off the Bering Sea side of the islands. No information on habitat other than depth was reported.

Artediellichthys nigripinnis (Schmidt, 1937) **blackfin hookear sculpin**

South-central Bering Sea; eastern Gulf of Alaska; western Bering Sea off Cape Navarin to Pacific Ocean off Kuril Islands and to Sea of Okhotsk.

Deep water at depths of 200–592 m, on bottom and in water column over bottom depths to 3,730 m.

D VII–IX + 12–13; A 9–11; Pec 21–23; Pel I,3; LLp 23–31.

- Yellowish gray, darker on head and tail; **dorsal, anal, pectoral, and pelvic fins completely black**; caudal fin dusky.
- Head and anterior part of body depressed; body compressed posteriorly; body elongate.
- Interorbital space very narrow, much less than height of eye; suborbital stay broad, spatulate.
- **Two large nasal spines with coalesced bases on each side**; small postocular protuberance but no spine; occipital spine present.
- Four preopercular spines, first strongly hooked dorsally, second shorter and directed posteroventrally, third concealed in skin, fourth a triangular prominence directed ventrally.
- **Cirrus on dorsal part of eye present or absent, few or no other cirri on head**; maxillary cirrus absent.
- First dorsal fin low, membrane incised.
- Scales and prickles absent except for a few scales below lateral line anteriorly.
- Numerous secondary head pores; separate pores on either side of mandibular symphysis.
- Lateral line pores in one row along lower edge of canal.
- Vomerine and palatine teeth present.
- Gill membranes broadly united, free of isthmus.
- Genital papilla of males small and cylindrical.
- Length to 137 mm TL.

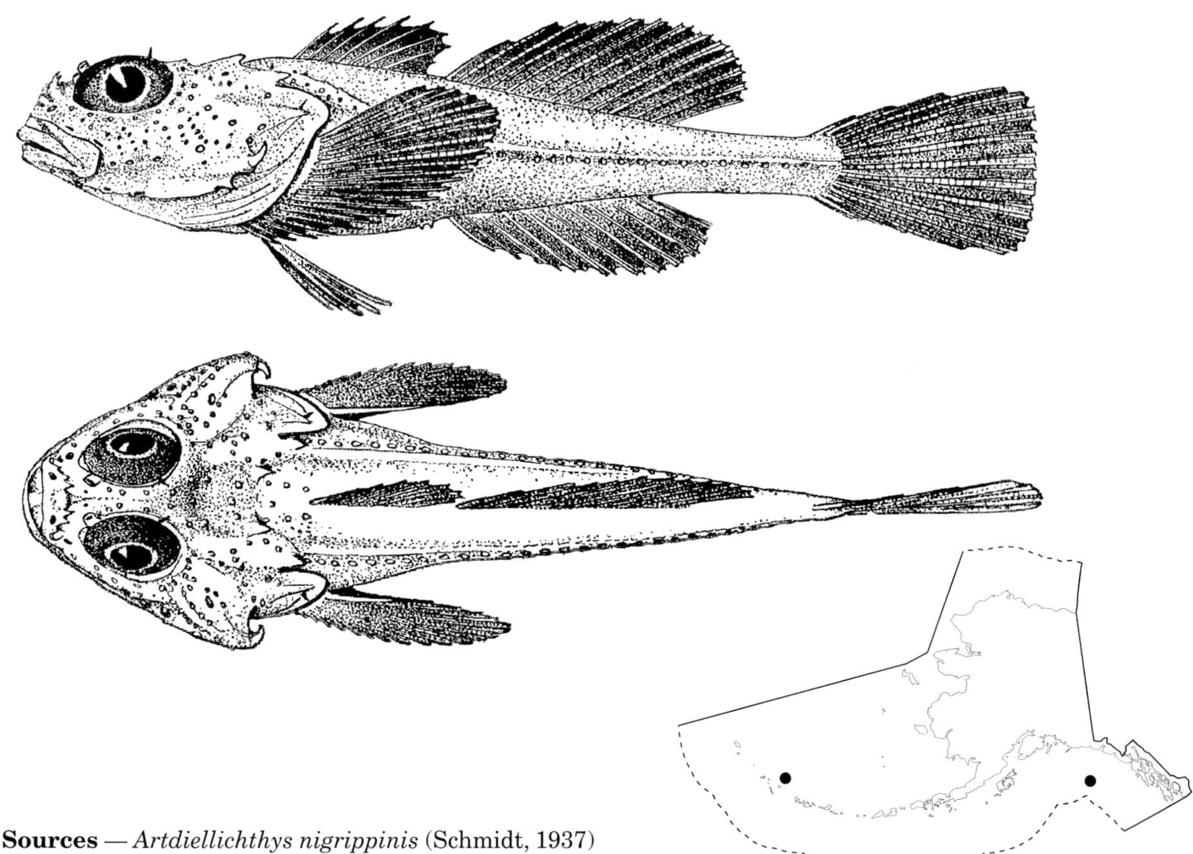

Notes & Sources — *Artdiellichthys nigrippinis* (Schmidt, 1937)
Artediellus nigrippinis Schmidt, 1937
Taranetz (1941) classified *A. nigripinnis* Schmidt, 1937 in a new subgenus, *Artediellichthys* Taranetz. Neyelov (1979) raised *Artediellichthys* to full generic status. Yabe (1985) classified *Artediellichthys* and *Artediellus* as genera distinct from each other in his revision of the Cottoidea.

Description: Schmidt 1937b:571–572, 1950:167–168; Neyelov 1979:159–160.

Figures: Schmidt 1950, pl. 13; Sea of Okhotsk.

Range: Recorded from two localities in Alaska by Neyelov (1979): southern Bering Sea at 53°53'N, 179°57'E, depth 300 m (ZIN 40580); and eastern Gulf of Alaska at 57°34'N, 142°30'W, taken at depth of about 200 m over bottom depth of 2,730 m (ZIN 42064). Collected by V. V. Fedorov during 1963–1967 along the eastern Kamchatka coast north to Cape Navarin (B. A. Sheiko, pers. comm., 15 Jan. 1999). Schmidt (1950) recorded it from the central Sea of Okhotsk, as well as off the west coast of Kamchatka. Tokranov (2001) reported on the biology of this species in Pacific waters of the northern Kuril Islands and southeastern Kamchatka.

Artediellus gomojunovi Taranetz, 1933 — spinyhook sculpin

Point Barrow, Alaska, record not confirmed; Bering Sea to Kuril Islands.

Rock-and-pebble bottom, often mixed with sand, at depths of 37–380 m; rare on clay and mud bottoms.

D VII–VIII + 13–14; A 11–12; Pec 20–22; Pel I,3; LLp 20–29; Vert 31–32.

- Light brown; 3 dark bands on body, including 1 on caudal peduncle; black blotch on posterior part of first dorsal fin, larger in males than in females; dorsal, caudal, and pectoral fins barred.
- Caudal peduncle slender, least depth about third of length.
- Interorbital space narrow, less than height of eye, and convex; suborbital stay slender, rod-shaped.
- Nasal spine present; postocular protuberance absent; **occipital protuberance prominent**.
- **Upper preopercular spine with small spinule on inner surface** and strongly hooked dorsally, lower spine pointing ventrally.
- No cirri except for small maxillary cirrus; short cirrus on upper portion of eye or occipital bump sometimes present.
- First dorsal fin low in both sexes, membrane not deeply incised.
- Scales absent; skin smooth, not granular.
- Few secondary pores on head; anterior mandibular pore single.
- Lateral line pores in one row along lower edge.
- Vomerine and palatine teeth present.
- Gill membrane free of isthmus posteriorly.
- Length to 76 mm TL.

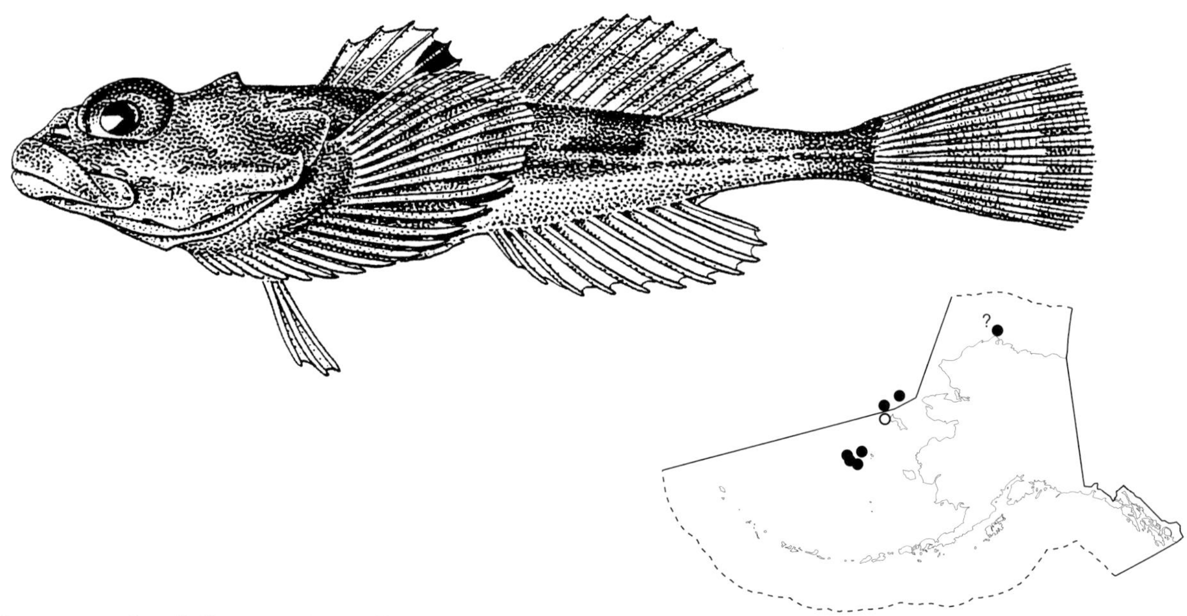

Notes & Sources — *Artediellus gomojunovi* Taranetz, 1933
Artediellus dydymovi gomojunovi Taranetz, 1933
Called spinyhook sculpin in reference to the spinule on the inner surface of the upper preopercular spine.

Description: Taranetz 1933:71; Andriashev 1937:26 of transl., 1954:405–406, 1961:233–235; Neyelov 1979:155, 156; D. W. Nelson 1986:43.

Figure: Andriashev 1961, fig. 2; male, 71 mm TL, western Bering Sea near Koryak coast (61°40'N).

Range: Described by Taranetz (1933) from specimens collected in the Gulf of Anadyr near Cape Chukotskiy and in Olyutorskiy Bay. He commented that *A. gomojunovi* is widely distributed in the western Bering Sea and is not rare in the Gulf of Anadyr. Quast and Hall (1972) listed it as a probable Alaskan species. Specimens have since been discovered in Alaska. Some were identified by D. W. Nelson in the course of research for a revision of *Artediellus*: UAM 2748 (3 specimens, 64–74 mm TL), 60°47'N, 173°41'W, depth 76 m, collected by K. J. Frost, 27 May 1978; UAM 2749 (3 specimens, 49–52 mm TL), 60°59'N, 172°50'W, depth 60 m, same collector and date; and UW 20981 (11 specimens, 59–70 mm SL), 60°20'N, 173°26'W. The UAM specimens are excellent, well preserved examples of *A. gomojunovi* (C.W.M.). Another Alaskan record was reported by J. W. Orr (pers. comm., 31 Oct. 2000): UW uncataloged (41 mm SL), 60°11'N, 173°02'W, depth 58 m, collected 21 Jul. 1998. All of the UAM and UW specimens were taken west of St. Matthew Island. Walters (1955) tentatively listed a 35-mm-SL specimen from Point Barrow (USNM 152901) under *A. uncinatus* and remarked that it was probably closer to *A. dydymovi*. Andriashev (1961) suggested it was an example of the closely related *A. gomojunovi*. The specimen was not found in recent searches, and may have been lost. R. Baxter (unpubl. data) identified a specimen captured in 1990 just west of St. Lawrence Island at 63°18'N, 172°00'W, depth 56 m, as *A. gomojunovi* (specimen was not saved). In a survey of the Kuril Islands in 1982, *A. gomojunovi* was found to be abundant near Simushir Island at depths of 320–380 m (B. A. Sheiko, pers. comm., 5 Feb. 1999).

Artediellus scaber Knipowitsch, 1907 **hamecon**

Beaufort and Chukchi seas to south of St. Lawrence Island in eastern Bering Sea; Cook Inlet; western Bering Sea south to Cape Navarin; east to Somerset Island, Canada; west to Barents and Kara seas.

Mud and clay bottoms in coastal salt and brackish waters at depths of 10–55 m, reported to 93 m.

D VII–IX + 12–14; A 10–13; Pec 18–23; Pel I,3; LLp 21–31.

- Grayish brown, with large blotches or bars; **males with black blotch on posterior part of first dorsal fin**; orange bars on fins.
- Interorbital space narrow, less than height of eye; suborbital stay slender, rod-shaped.
- **Nasal spine absent**; low occipital protuberance present; top of head and nape with fine tubercles.
- Two preopercular spines, upper hooked dorsally, lower directed ventrally.
- **Numerous fleshy cirri**: lachrymal, maxillary, eye, postocular, occipital, nape, preopercular, opercular, cleithral, anterior part of lateral line.
- First dorsal fin low in females, high in males, membrane incised.
- Scales absent.
- Head pores large; **anterior mandibular pore single**, not paired.
- Lateral line pores in one row along lower edge.
- Vomerine and palatine teeth present.
- Gill membrane free of isthmus psoteriorly.
- Length to 89 mm TL.

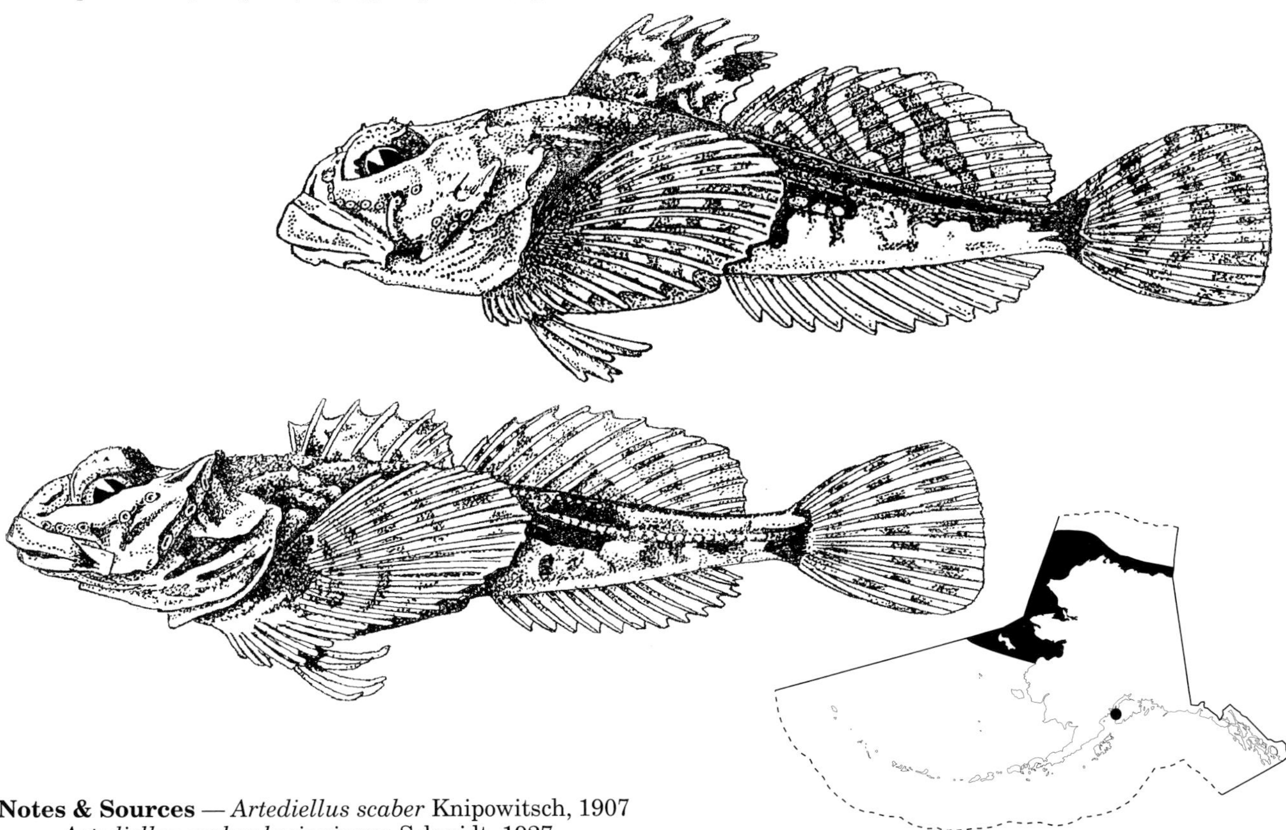

Notes & Sources — *Artediellus scaber* Knipowitsch, 1907
Artediellus scaber beringianus Schmidt, 1927

Also called rough hookear for the granular skin on the top of the head and anterior portion of the back, but the skin is often smoother in Alaskan specimens. The unpaired anterior mandibular pore, absence of nasal spines, and black spot on the first dorsal fin of males are characteristic of all populations, including those in Alaska.

Description: Knipowitsch 1907:18–29; Schmidt 1927:7–8; Andriashev 1937:25–26 of transl., 1954:409–410, 1961: 240–241; McAllister 1963b:51–52; Neyelov 1979:155.

Figures: Knipowitsch 1907. Upper: male, 73 mm TL, Laptev Sea. Lower: female, 72 mm TL, Kara Sea.

Range: Museums have many examples from Alaska but few records have been published: Walters (1953a, 1955), Alverson and Wilimovsky (1966), and Quast and Hall (1972); from Bering Strait to Barrow. Barber et al. (1997) found it to be the 7th most abundant species in demersal surveys of the northeastern Chukchi Sea in 1990 and 1991; voucher specimens are in UAM collection. Easternmost Alaskan Beaufort Sea examples are NMC 81-128, near Demarcation Bay at 69°40'N, 141°05'W, and NMC 81-132, east of Humphrey Point at 69°58'N, 142°12'W; both collected by K. J. Frost and L. F. Lowry and identified by D. E. McAllister. Southernmost Alaskan records are from St. Lawrence Island (UBC 63-1201, 63°06'N, 171°42'W) and Ninilchik, Cook Inlet (UBC 63-1029, 60°03'N, 151°40'W); A. E. Peden (pers. comm., 28 Apr. 1999) examined them and reported that identification as *A. scaber* is correct. McAllister (1963b) recorded *A. scaber* from sites around Herschel Island, east of the U.S.–Canada border. Recorded east to Somerset Island in the Canadian Arctic by Hunter et al. (1984).

Artediellus pacificus Gilbert, 1896 — **hookhorn sculpin**

Eastern Chukchi Sea, record uncertain; Bering Sea and Aleutian Islands to southeastern Alaska at Limestone Inlet; and to Sea of Okhotsk and northern Sea of Japan.

Mud and sand bottom at 15–250 m.

D VI–VIII + 11–13; A 11–13; Pec 21–25; Pel I,3; LLp 19–26.

- Small light brown spots dorsally; pale ventrally; vague dark bands on body; expanded tips of first dorsal fin of males black; first dorsal fin without black spot; dorsal, caudal, pectoral fins barred.
- Caudal peduncle short and stout, depth 40–50% of its length.
- Interorbital space narrow, less than height of eye; suborbital stay slender, rod-shaped.
- Nasal spines small, often buried in skin; postocular and occipital protuberances absent.
- Two preopercular spines, upper strongly hooked dorsally, lower pointed ventrally.
- **Cirri numerous**: eye, postocular, occipital, lachrymal, preopercular, opercular, cleithral, anterior lateral line, some rarely absent; **maxillary cirrus long, sometimes branched**.
- **First dorsal fin in males high, incised membranes expanded and paddlelike at tips**.
- Scales absent; skin smooth, not granular.
- Secondary head pores absent; **anterior mandibular pore single**.
- Lateral line pores in one row along lower edge.
- Vomerine and palatine teeth present.
- Genital papilla of males small and conical.
- Gill membrane free of isthmus posteriorly.
- Length to 87 mm SL (about 105 mm TL).

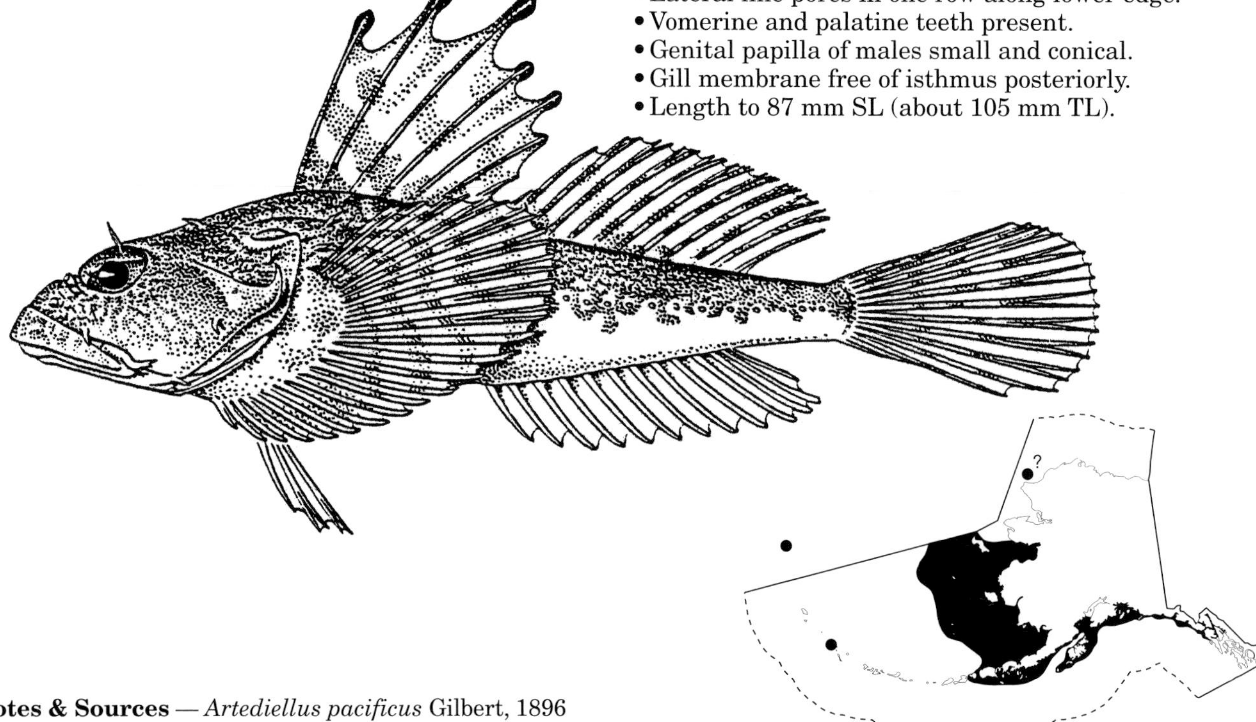

Notes & Sources — *Artediellus pacificus* Gilbert, 1896
Blennicottus clarki Evermann & Goldsborough, 1907

Hubbs (1926a) noted that *B. clarki,* taken near Kiska Island, belongs in *Artediellus.* Andriashev (1961) considered it likely to be identical with *A. pacificus,* but was uncertain because of the inexact illustration and description in Evermann and Goldsborough (1907). Neyelov (1979) formally included it in the synonymy of *A. pacificus.*

Also called Pacific hookear sculpin (Eschmeyer and Herald 1983) or paddled sculpin (Sheiko and Fedorov 2000).

Description: Gilbert 1896:416–417; Jordan and Starks 1904b:244–245; Evermann and Goldsborough 1907:323–324; Andriashev 1961:236–238; Neyelov 1979:154, 157.

Figure: Andriashev 1961, fig. 3; Olyutorskiy Bay.

Range: Included on list of northeastern Chukchi Sea fishes from 1990 and 1991 surveys by Barber et al. (1997), but specimens were not found among the vouchers for those surveys at UAM. Northernmost locality in eastern Bering Sea supported by voucher specimen is 63°40'N, 167°28'W, northeast of St. Lawrence Island (UW 11740). Reported north to southern Gulf of Anadyr in western Bering Sea (Andriashev 1937, Neyelov 1979). Previous Alaskan records include: north of Unalaska Island, Bristol Bay, and south of Sanak Islands (type series; Gilbert 1896); St. Paul Island and Karluk (Jordan and Evermann 1898); Kiska Island (Evermann and Goldsborough 1907); Barren Islands and Auke Bay (Quast 1968); south of Krenitzin and Unimak islands (Quast and Hall 1972; ABL records). Additional Bering Sea vouchers are AB 72-57, NMC 79-511 and 79-515; and UAM 2446, 2453, and 3338. AB 67-79, 67-141, 67-288, and 68-252 are from Limestone Inlet, south of Juneau, southeastern Alaska. Common at Commander Islands (Fedorov and Sheiko 2002). Maximum depth of 250 m is from UAM 2453 (2 specimens), taken by Tucker trawl, 27 May 1975, at 57°01'N, 168°59'W. Voucher specimens are needed from the Aleutian Islands and Chukchi Sea.

Size: UW 20988, eastern Bering Sea at 58°51'N, 175°13'W. Previously recorded to 82 mm TL by Andriashev (1961).

Artediellus camchaticus Gilbert & Burke, 1912 **clownfin sculpin**

Western Bering Sea from Cape Navarin to Commander Islands, and Pacific Ocean off southeastern Kamchatka and Kuril Islands to Okhotsk Sea coast of Hokkaido.

At depths of 35–520 m, usually 80–130 m.

D VII–IX + 10–15; A 10–14; Pec 23–26; Pel I,3; LLp 29–34.

- Color in alcohol brown, with lighter reticulating lines and small light spots; first dorsal fin of males usually with large roundish brown spots, but **no black spot on posterior portion of first dorsal**; dark bars on second dorsal, caudal, and pectoral fins, least distinct on pectoral.
- **Caudal peduncle long and slender, depth usually less than 35% of its length**.
- Interorbital space narrow, less than height of eye; suborbital stay slender, rod-shaped.
- Nasal spine small, covered with skin; postocular and occipital protuberances absent.
- Two preopercular spines, upper strongly hooked dorsally, lower pointing ventrally.
- **No cirri on head except for long, slender cirrus on maxilla**.
- First dorsal fin high in male, deeply incised; usually **more pectoral fin rays than in _A. ochotensis_**.
- Scales absent.
- Pores on top of head large; secondary head pores absent; **anterior mandibular pore paired**.
- Lateral line pores in one row along lower edge.
- Vomerine and palatine teeth present.
- Genital papilla of males short and conical.
- Gill membrane free of isthmus posteriorly.
- Length to 132 mm TL.

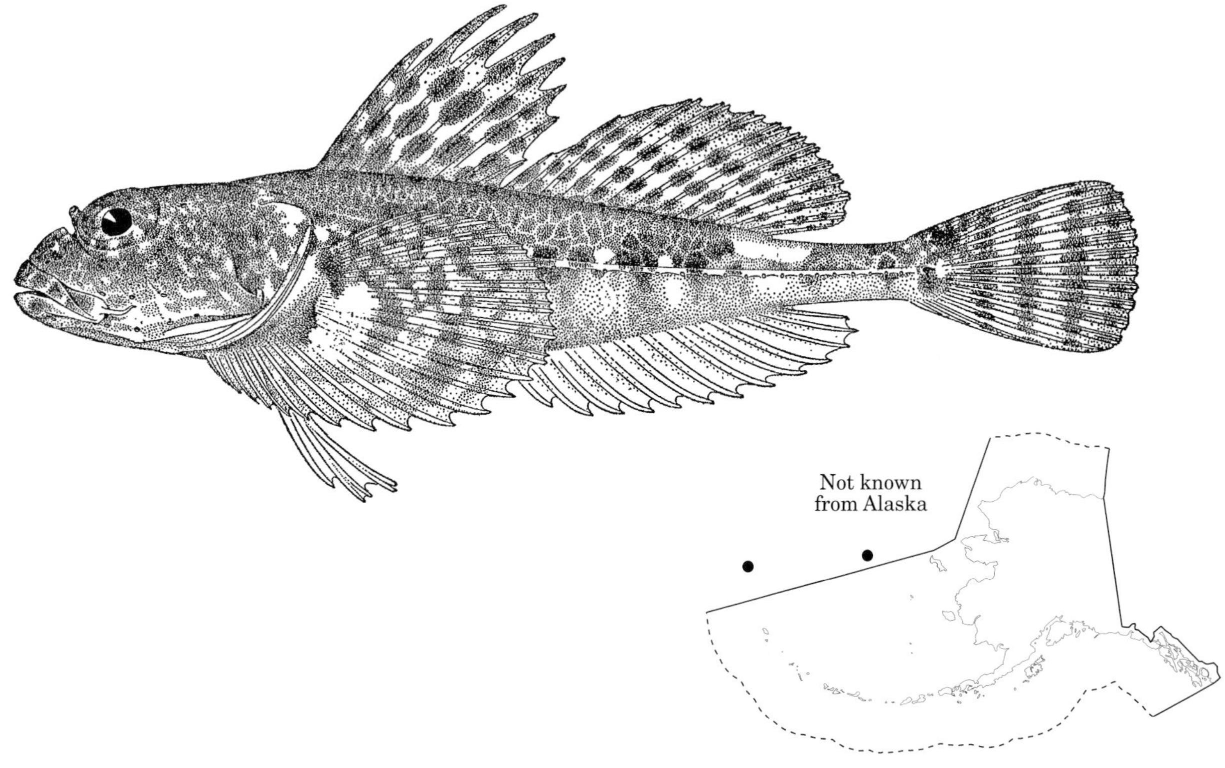

Notes & Sources — _Artediellus camchaticus_ Gilbert & Burke, 1912
Artediellus ochotensis morpha _camchaticus_: Schmidt 1927.

Description: Gilbert and Burke 1912a:46–47; Schmidt 1927:4, 1950:164–165; Andriashev 1961:235–236; Neyelov 1979:157.

Figure: Gilbert and Burke 1912a, fig. 6; type, male, 117 mm TL, _Albatross_ station 4795, off Avacha Bay, southeast coast of Kamchatka, 52°47'N, 158°44'E.

Range: Nearest known areas of occurrence are the vicinity of the Commander Islands, where specimens were collected by V. V. Fedorov during surveys in 1963–1967 (B. A. Sheiko, pers. comm., 15 Jan. 1999), and Cape Navarin, the northern limit of range reported by Sheiko and Fedorov (2000). Recorded from Okhotsk coast of Hokkaido by Yabe (in Masuda et al. 1984). Depths: Fedorov and Sheiko 2002.

Artediellus ochotensis Gilbert & Burke, 1912 **Okhotsk hookear sculpin**

Northeastern Chukchi Sea; western Bering Sea from Gulf of Anadyr south along Kamchatka coast and off Commander Islands, and Pacific Ocean to Kuril Islands, Sea of Okhotsk, and Sea of Japan to Peter the Great Bay.

At depths of 4–100 m, usually shallower than 50 m.

D VII–VIII + 12–15; A 11–14; Pec 20–23; Pel I,3; LLp 24–33.

- Head and dorsal region of body finely vermiculated with light reddish brown; light reddish spots on body; first dorsal fin with small reddish brown blotches; **males with round black spot on posterior part of first dorsal fin** and bright chrome yellow anal fin; dark reddish brown bars on second dorsal, caudal, and pectoral fins.
- **Caudal peduncle short and stout, depth more than 35% of its length**.
- Interorbital space narrow, less than height of eye; suborbital stay slender, rod-shaped.
- Nasal spine present, but minute; postocular and occipital protuberances absent.
- Two preopercular spines, upper strongly hooked dorsally, lower pointing ventrally.
- **Numerous large, thick cirri**: lachrymal, maxillary, eye, postocular, occipital, nuchal, preopercular, opercular, suborbital stay (occasionally absent), anterior part of lateral line; maxillary cirrus simple.
- First dorsal fin of males high, with deeply incised membrane; usually **fewer pectoral fin rays than in *A. camchaticus***.
- Scales absent.
- Pores on top of head large; secondary head pores absent; **anterior mandibular pore paired**.
- **Lateral line pores** in one row along lower edge; **almost always more than in *A. miacanthus***.
- Vomerine and palatine teeth present.
- Genital papilla of males small and conical.
- Gill membrane free of isthmus posteriorly, sometimes with only a narrow free margin.
- Length to 102 mm TL.

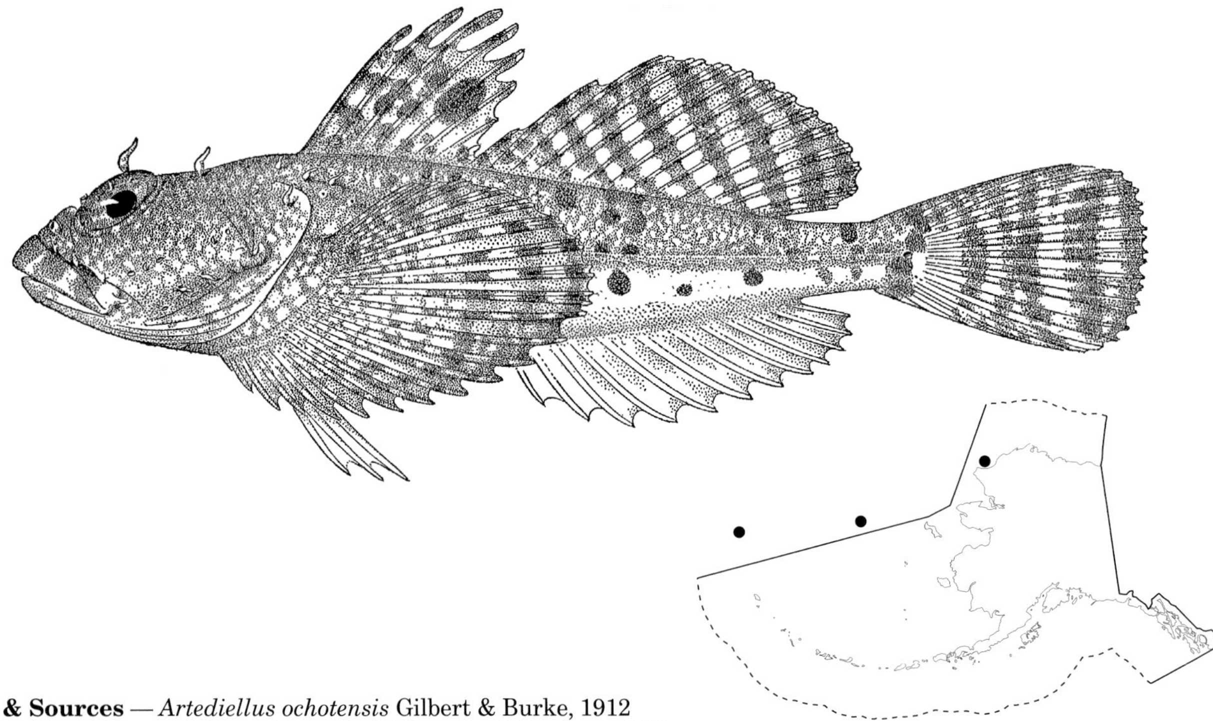

Notes & Sources — *Artediellus ochotensis* Gilbert & Burke, 1912
Artediellus pacificus ochotensis: Soldatov and Lindberg 1930.

Description: Gilbert and Burke 1912a:44–46; Schmidt 1927:3–4; Andriashev 1961:238–239; Neyelov 1979:157; Lindberg and Krasyukova 1987:233–235.

Figure: Gilbert and Burke 1912a, fig. 5; holotype, male, 94 mm TL, *Albatross* station 4798, off western Kamchatka.

Range: The first record for Alaska is USNM 313488, comprising four specimens (32–51 mm TL) from the Chukchi Sea at 69°16'N, 164°22'W, depth 22 m, collected during RV *John N. Cobb* Project Chariot cruise on 25 Aug. 1959. A note in the jar indicates the specimens were identified as *A. ochotensis* by M. Yabe in Oct. 1998; C.W.M., examining them on 13 Nov. 1999, found them to have the appropriate diagnostic characters, including large, fleshy cirri exactly as in Jordan and Gilbert's (1912a) illustration, 21 pectoral fin rays, caudal peduncle short and stout, anterior mandibular pore paired, and 28 or more lateral line pores. Nearest records outside Alaska are from the western Bering Sea off Cape Navarin (Sheiko and Fedorov 2000), and in the vicinity of the Commander Islands (Fedorov and Sheiko 2002). The latter record is based on collections by V. V. Fedorov during surveys in 1963–1967 (B. A. Sheiko, pers. comm., 15 Jan. 1999).

Artediellus miacanthus Gilbert & Burke, 1912 **smallhook sculpin**

Record from Bering Sea southeast of St. Lawrence Island not verifiable; western Bering Sea from Cape Navarin, and possibly Gulf of Anadyr, along eastern Kamchatka to Pacific Ocean off Cape Lopatka and Paramushir Island.

Sandy bottom at 33–293 m, usually shallower than 160 m.

D VI–VIII + 12–15; A 10–13; Pec 21–24; Pel I,3; LLp 14–24.

- Color in alcohol grayish, coarsely mottled and blotched dorsolaterally with brown; **round black spot on posterior part of first dorsal fin in males**, present but poorly expressed in females; second dorsal, caudal, and pectoral fins barred; 1 or 2 rows of dark spots also on anal fin of males.
- **Caudal peduncle short and stout, depth more than 35% of its length.**
- Interorbital space narrow, less than height of eye; suborbital stay slender, rod-shaped.
- Nasal spine absent; postocular and occipital protuberances absent.
- Two preopercular spines, upper strongly hooked dorsally, lower directed ventrally; upper usually not as large as in other *Artediellus*.
- **Lachrymal, preopercular, cleithral, anterior lateral line cirri always absent**; small, simple maxillary cirrus; eye, postocular, occipital, and opercular cirri usually present.
- First dorsal fin of males high, with incised membrane; usually fewer pectoral fin rays than in *A. camchaticus*.
- Scales absent; skin smooth, not granular.
- Secondary head pores absent; **anterior mandibular pore paired**.
- **Lateral line pores** in one row along lower edge; **almost always fewer than in *A. ochotensis***.
- Vomerine and palatine teeth present.
- Genital papilla of males small and conical.
- Gill membrane free of isthmus posteriorly.
- Length to 72 mm TL.

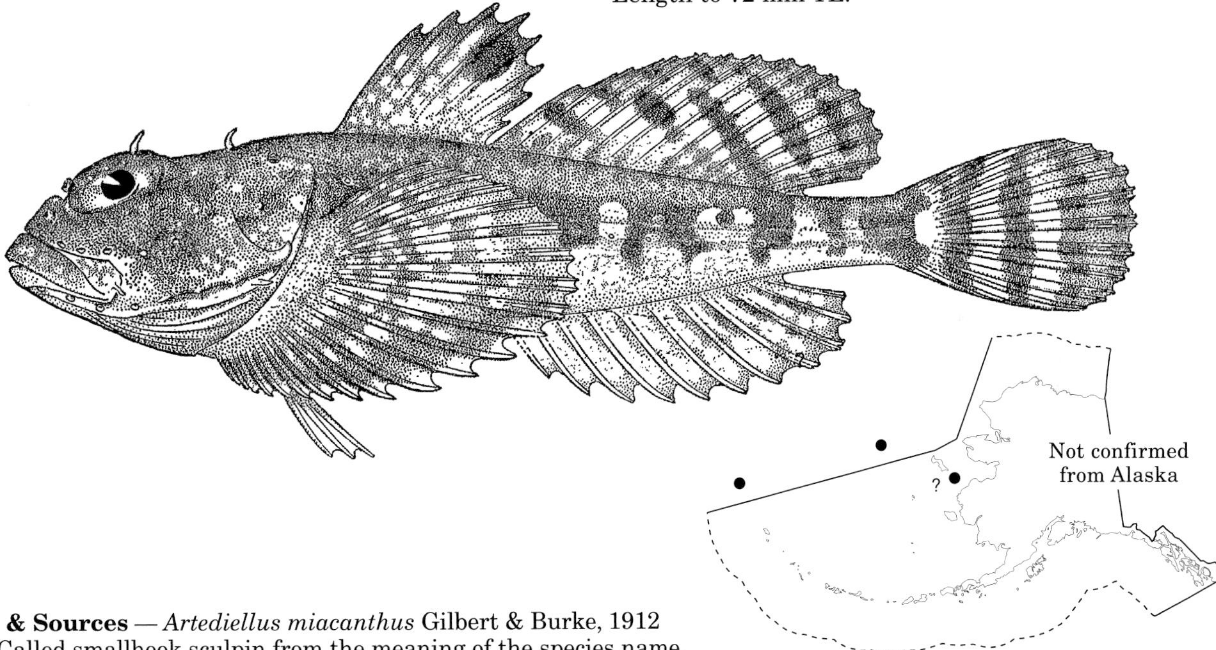

Notes & Sources — *Artediellus miacanthus* Gilbert & Burke, 1912
Called smallhook sculpin from the meaning of the species name.

Description: Gilbert and Burke 1912a:47–49; Schmidt 1927:5, 1950:162–163; Andriashev 1961:239–240; Neyelov 1979:154, 156.

Figure: Gilbert and Burke 1912a, fig. 7; holotype, male, 66 mm TL, *Albatross* station 4795, off eastern Kamchatka, 52°47'N, 158°44'E.

Range: D. W. Nelson (1986) indicated its range to be restricted to the western Bering Sea, but the type specimens were from the Pacific Ocean off southeastern Kamchatka and Neyelov (1979) gave a range for *A. miacanthus* south to Cape Lopatka and Paramushir Island. Specimens recorded by Andriashev (1937) from southeast of St. Lawrence Island and the Gulf of Anadyr were later lost, and Andriashev (1961) stated that the species was absent from Russian collections from areas north of Kamchatka Bay (west of the Commander Islands). From more recent data Fedorov and Sheiko (2002) reported it to be common at the Commander Islands, and Sheiko and Fedorov (2000) reported it north to Cape Navarin. UBC 62-802 from the vicinity of Gambell (St. Lawrence Island), cataloged as *A. miacanthus,* was examined by A. E. Peden (pers. comm., 28 Apr. 1999), who found it to be deteriorated but with enough diagnostic characters preserved to indicate it does *not* belong (e.g., median chin pore) to this species. Another specimen from Bering Sea cataloged as *A. miacanthus,* UAM 3388, is an example of *A. pacificus* (examined by C.W.M., 25 Oct. 2000). Occurrence of *A. miacanthus* in Alaskan waters remains unconfirmed. Not confirmed from Seas of Okhotsk and Japan; those records (Gilbert and Burke 1912a, specimens from *Albatross* station 5025, Sakhalin Island; Schmidt 1927, 1950) were placed in the synonymy of *A. aporosus* Soldatov, 1921 (not an Alaskan species) by Neyelov (1979).

Phallocottus obtusus Schultz, 1938 — **spineless sculpin**

Aleutian Islands at Amchitka and Igitkin islands.

Close to shore.

D X–XII + 22–24; A 22–25; Pec 14–16; Pel I,3; LLp 48–49; Vert 47.

- Color in alcohol light brown dorsally; pale yellow ventrally; body finely speckled with tiny black dots; ocelli and black spots on head and body; fins with faint, irregular bars.
- Snout blunt; body deep and compressed.
- **Nasal spine obscure**; no spines on top of head.
- Four preopercular spines; first short, blunt or rounded, lower three obscure.
- Simple cirri over each concealed nasal spine, on occiput, on each pore of anterior portion of lateral line; large multibranched cirrus over eye.
- **One long cirrus at tip of each dorsal fin spine except the first**; spinous dorsal of mature males much higher than in females.
- Skin smooth, scales absent.
- Lateral line strongly arched anteriorly.
- Vomerine teeth present; **palatine teeth absent**.
- **Anus near pelvic fin base**.
- Genital papilla of males long and conical.
- Gill membranes broadly united, free of isthmus.
- Length to 69 mm TL.

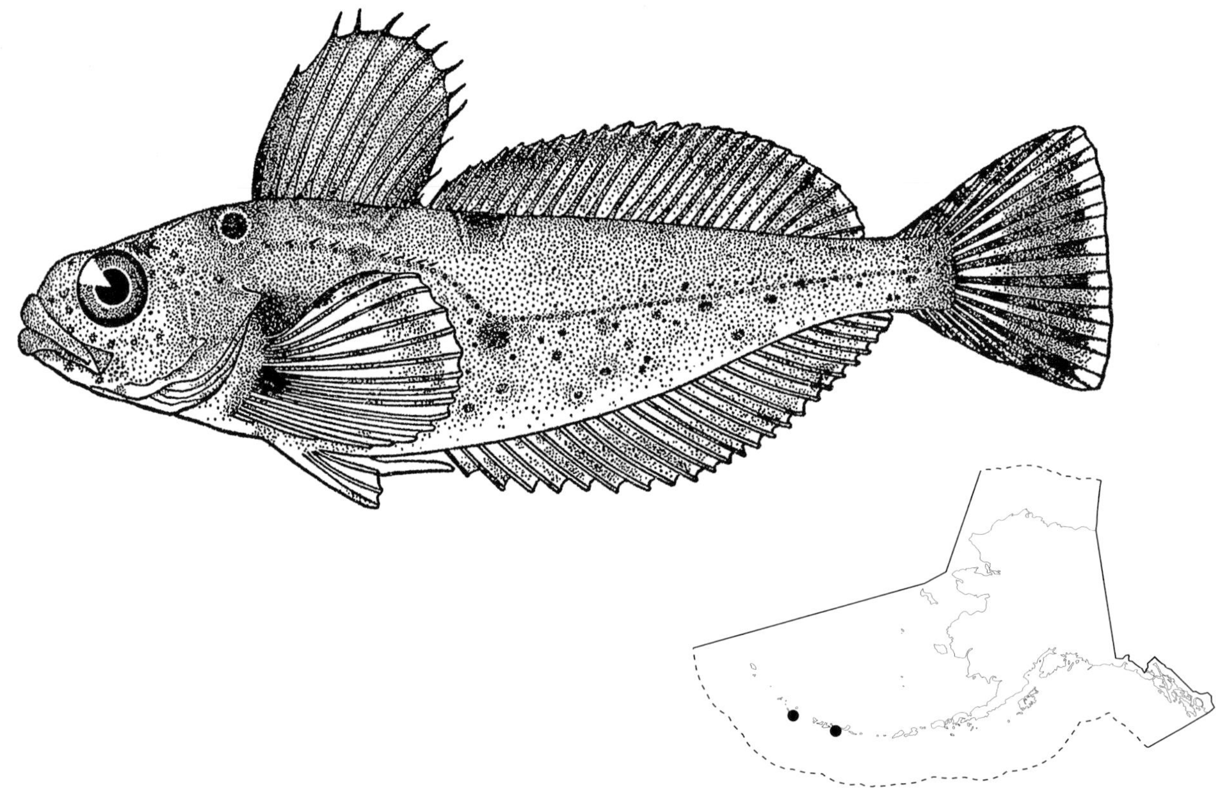

Notes & Sources — *Phallocottus obtusus* Schultz, 1938

The scientific name refers to the large conical genital papilla and the bluntly rounded upper opercular spine.

Description: Schultz 1938a:188–190; Howe and Richardson 1978 (fin ray counts); R. Baxter, unpubl. data on USNM 105280 (holotype, total length) and USNM 105281 (one paratype, vertebral count).

Figure: Schultz 1938a, fig. 70; holotype, USNM 105280, male, 69 mm TL, Igitkin Island, Aleutian Islands.

Range: Described from six specimens collected in a beach seine at Igitkin Island (Schultz 1938a). Later recorded from Amchitka Island by Wilimovsky (1964); UBC 63-919 is one specimen collected off the south side of Igitkin Island, and UBC 63-1010 includes 22 specimens collected at Kirilof wharf, Constantine Harbor, Amchitka Island.

Sigmistes smithi Schultz, 1938 **arched sculpin**

Aleutian Islands from Attu to Chagulak; southern Kuril Islands.

Intertidal area and tidepools.

D VIII–X + 24–27; A 17–20; Pec 13–15; Pel I,3; LLp 45–46.

- Color in alcohol pale yellowish, body and head speckled with tiny black dots, denser dorsally, paler ventrally; faint blackish band from eye to tip of snout, with light streak through middle of band and including anterior nostril; small pale gray spots along base of dorsal fin.
- Body deep and compressed.
- Nasal spine strong; no spines on top of head.
- Four preopercular spines, first short, thin, curved dorsally, lower three weak or obsolete.
- Pair of cirri on each nasal spine; multifid postocular cirrus; simple cirri on top of head; simple cirrus at each pore of lateral line anteriorly.
- Cirrus at tip of each dorsal fin spine; **soft dorsal fin origin at level anterior to anal fin origin**; dorsal fins sometimes continuous at base; **caudal rays not branched**.
- Scales, including prickles or papillae, absent.
- Lateral line strongly arched anteriorly.
- Vomerine teeth present; palatine teeth present but weak or obscure.
- Anus closer to pelvic fin base than to anal fin.
- Genital papilla of males long and conical.
- Gill membranes broadly united, free of isthmus.
- Length to 45 mm SL (about 55 mm TL) or more.

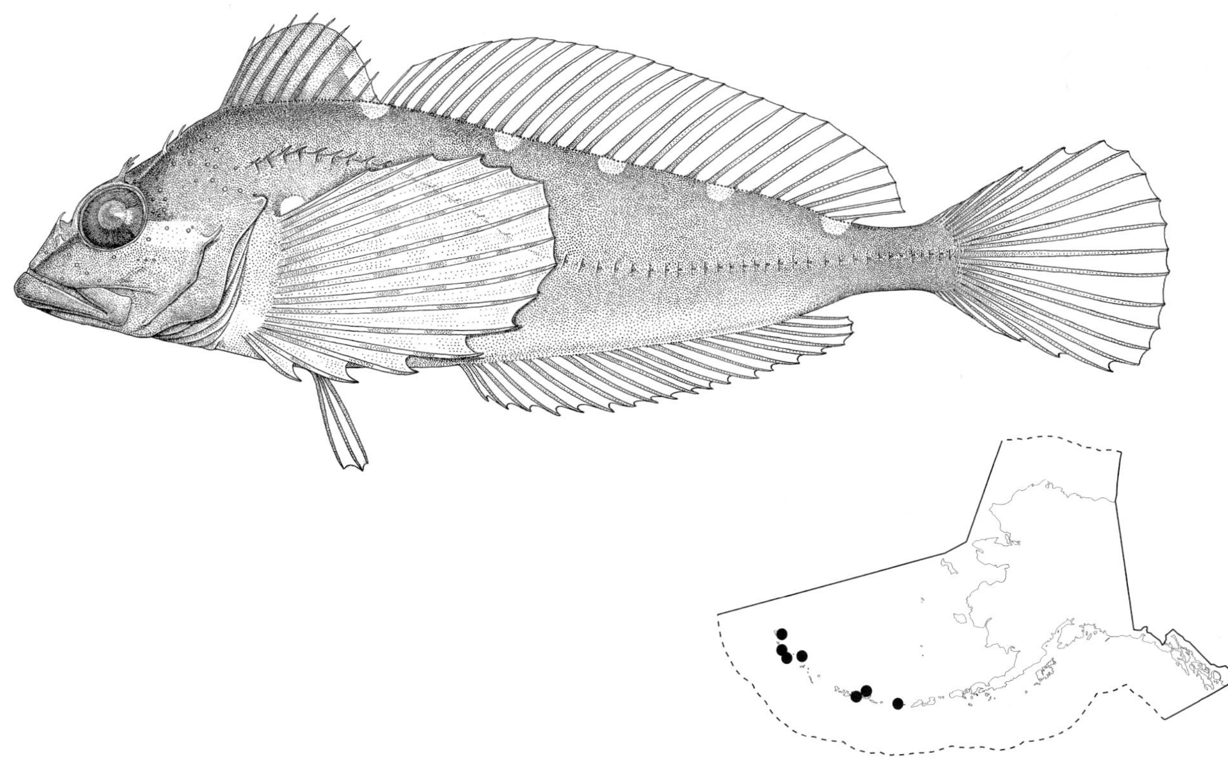

Notes & Sources — *Sigmistes smithi* Schultz, 1938

Description: Schultz 1938a:190–191 (3 specimens); Howe and Richardson 1978 (meristics from 11 specimens); R. Baxter, unpubl. data on USNM 105282 (holotype, lengths).

Figure: University of British Columbia, artist P. Drukker-Brammall; UBC 65-29, 45 mm SL, Nizki Island, Aleutian Islands.

Range: Described from three specimens collected at Igitkin Island (Schultz 1938a). Recorded from several localities from Attu Island to Chagulak Island by Wilimovsky (1964); voucher specimens at UBC are from Attu, Agattu, Nizki, Buldir, Adak, and Chagulak islands. Yabe et al. (2001) reported the first record of *S. smithi* from the southern Kuril Islands, which is also the first record outside of Alaska.

Size: Holotype is 37 mm SL and 45 mm TL, giving ratio of SL = 82.2% TL (R. Baxter, unpubl. data). From that, the 45-mm-SL specimen in UBC 65-29 illustrated above is about 55 mm TL. The source of Baxter's (1990ms) maximum length of 80 mm TL has not been determined.

Sigmistes caulias Rutter, 1898 **kelp sculpin**

Pribilof Islands, Aleutian Islands from Attu to Tigalda, and western Gulf of Alaska at Kodiak Island. Intertidal area and tidepools.

D VIII–X + 19–21; A 14–17; Pec 13–14; Pel I,3; Vert 37–38.

- Color in life pale pinkish; usually with 3–5 pale blotches with black margins along base of dorsal fins, sometimes other pale spots and blotches laterally; dark line from snout through eye to preopercular spine, bordered by pale line along midline of snout; spinous dorsal dusky, nearly black along margin, sometimes with pale blotch; soft dorsal fin and anal fin with dusky bars.
- Body deep and compressed.
- Nasal spine strong; no spines on top of head.
- Four preopercular spines, first short, thin, curved dorsally, lower three weak or obsolete.
- Small cirrus near tip of snout; one or two cirri on each nasal spine; multifid postocular cirrus; simple or multifid cirri on top of head; preopercular and opercular cirri present; a few cirri at anterior end of lateral line, present or absent.
- Simple or multifid cirrus at tip of each dorsal fin spine; dorsal fin spines widely spaced; **soft dorsal and anal fin origins opposite each other**; dorsal fins sometimes continuous at base; **caudal fin rays branched**.
- Scales, including prickles or papillae, absent.
- Lateral line strongly arched anteriorly.
- Vomerine teeth present; palatine teeth present but weak or obscure.
- Anus close to pelvic fin base.
- Genital papilla of males long, conical, pointed.
- Gill membranes broadly united, free of isthmus.
- Length to 76 mm TL.

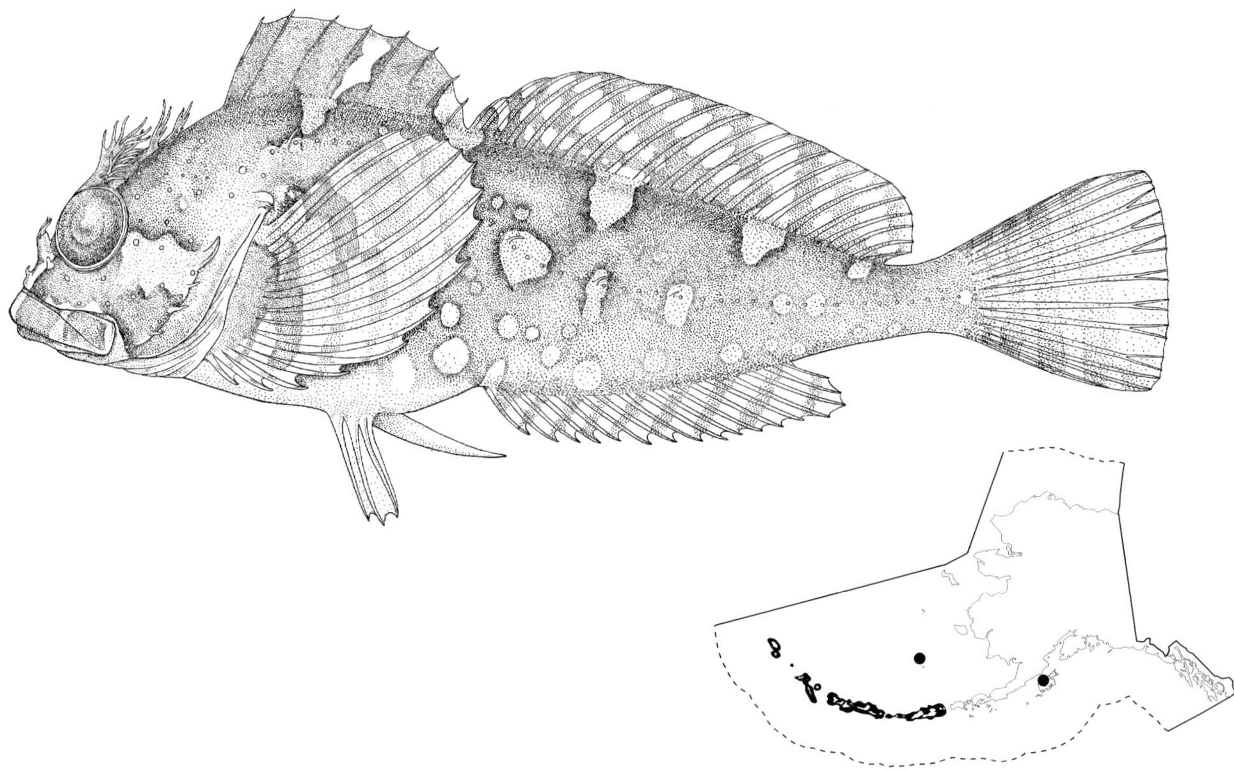

Notes & Sources — *Sigmistes caulias* Rutter in Jordan & Evermann, 1898

Description: Jordan and Evermann 1898:2863–2864; Rutter 1899:190–191; Howe and Richardson 1978 (meristics from 4–100 specimens); UAM 1967 (2; 39–52 mm TL).

Figure: University of British Columbia, artist P. Drukker-Brammall; UBC 63-898, 51 mm SL, tidepool at east end of Shemya Island, Aleutian Islands.

Range: Described by Rutter from specimens collected from tidepools at Karluk, Kodiak Island. Gilbert and Burke (1912a) recorded three specimens from tidepools on Agattu Island. Wilimovsky (1964) recorded it from Attu Island to Krenitzin Islands; the latter is represented by voucher specimens from Tigalda Island (UBC 63-1311). Collected by A. E. Peden from Nateekin Bay, north coast of Unalaska Island, in 1980 (NMC 81-496). Specimens in UBC 63-1446 and 63-1458, from tidepools at St. Paul Island, extend the published range north in the Bering Sea. UAM 1967 comprises two additional specimens from Agattu Island, collected in 1974 and identified by J. E. Morrow. Reported range to Baja California (e.g., Quast and Hall 1972) is incorrect. *Sigmistes caulias* is much more numerous than *S. smithi* in museum collections.

Size: Rutter 1899; largest of the Karluk type specimens.

Oligocottus rimensis (Greeley, 1899) **saddleback sculpin**

Southeastern Alaska at Kakul Narrows to northern Baja California.

Tidepools and shallow rocky and gravelly areas near shoreline, often in kelp; usually in lower tidepools.

D VIII–X + 16–19; A 13–15; Pec 13–15; Pel I,3; LLp 35–41; Vert 34–37.

- Light olive green or red tinged with lavender and blue; 4 or 5 brown saddles with pale blue borders; dark mottling along lateral line; brownish green ventrolaterally; pale yellow ventrally; some specimens almost uniformly greenish brown; soft dorsal, anal, and caudal fins barred with red.
- Head small, snout blunt; body slender and elongate, not greatly compressed.
- Nasal spine small; no spines on top of head.
- **Uppermost preopercular spine simple**; others weak or obsolete; all skin-covered.
- Cirri at base of nasal spine, on end of maxilla, on preopercle; postocular (1 pair) and occipital (3 pairs) cirri usually longer; cirri along anterior half of lateral line; cirri usually simple.
- First two anal rays in males elongate, membrane deeply incised.
- **Scales present as scattered prickly papillae** on body, absent from head.
- Lateral line not strongly arched.
- Vomerine and palatine teeth present.
- Anus close to anal fin origin.
- Genital papilla of males slender and conical, as long as eye diameter; sheathed in deep depression and not visible when not protruded.
- Gill membranes broadly united, free of isthmus.
- Length to 65 mm TL.

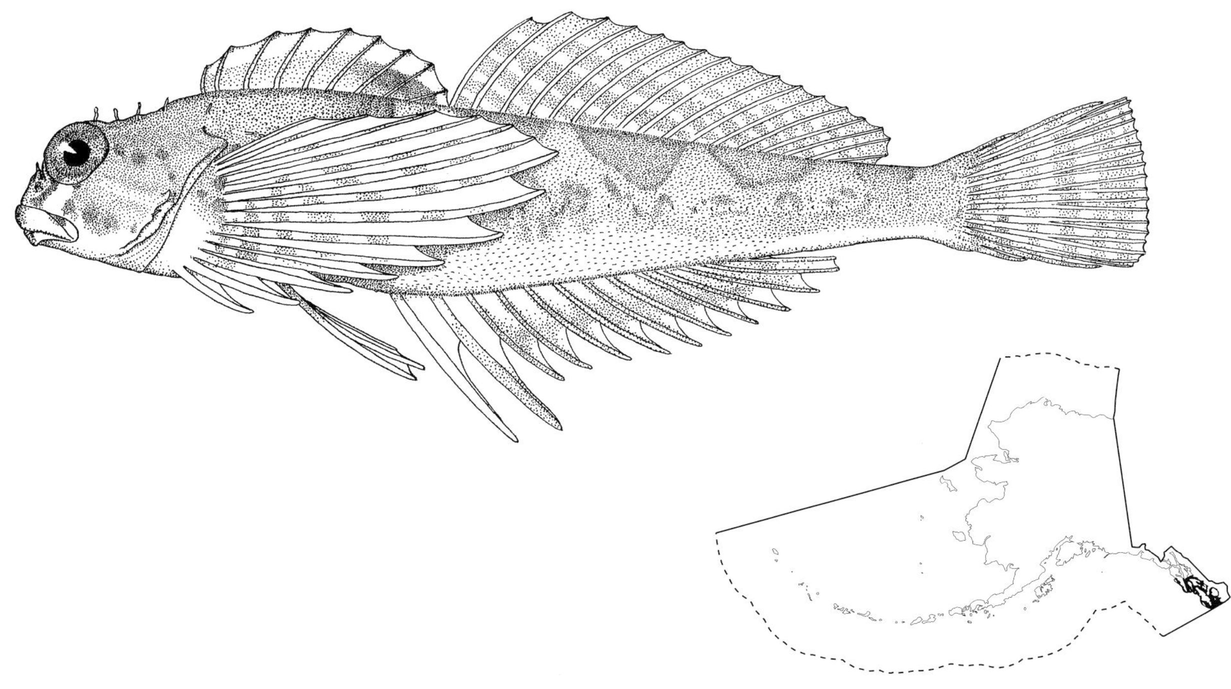

Notes & Sources — *Oligocottus rimensis* (Greeley, 1899)
Rusciculus rimensis Greely, 1899
Stelgidonotus latifrons Gilbert & Thompson, 1905

Description: Jordan and Evermann 1900:3179–3180; Evermann and Goldsborough 1907:298–299; Bolin 1944:63–64; Hart 1973:529–530.

Figure: Bolin 1944, fig. 24; male.

Range: Peden and Wilson (1976) recorded specimens representing extension of the known range north from the southern Strait of Georgia (Hart 1973) to northern British Columbia and southeastern Alaska. The Alaskan specimens they recorded are, from north to south: NMC 61-32, Kakul Narrows, 57°22'N, 135°41'W; UBC 65-527, Port Conclusion; UBC 65-581, Barrier Island; and UBC 65-519, Dall Island, Cape Muzon.

Size: Miller and Lea 1972.

Oligocottus maculosus Girard, 1856 **tidepool sculpin**

Southeastern Bering Sea at Pribilof Islands to southern California at Los Angeles County.

Tidepools and along shoreline; in areas with rough surf inhabits the higher, more sheltered places.

D VIII–IX + 15–18; A 11–14; Pec 13–15; Pel I,3; LLp 35–41; Vert 33–34.

- Greenish gray to reddish, variously spotted and mottled; dark saddles; whitish ventrally; some specimens nearly uniform in color; spinous dorsal fin often dusky, with orange anterior margin and large clear spots; bars rusty brown on caudal fin, dusky on pectoral fin.
- Head large, snout blunt; body somewhat compressed; caudal peduncle short and stout.
- Nasal spine strong; no spines on top of head.
- **Uppermost preopercular spine bifid to quadrifid**; others obsolete; all skin-covered.
- **Cirri absent from base of nasal spine**; 1–3 at end of maxilla, 1–7 along upper margin of orbit, cirri on top of head variable; cirri on preopercle, anterior half of lateral line, but **absent above lateral line**; most cirri simple.
- Cirri at tips of dorsal fin spines; first 3 anal fin rays on mature males enlarged.
- **Scales, including prickles, absent**.
- Lateral line not strongly arched.
- Vomerine and palatine teeth present.
- Anus close to anal fin origin.
- Genital papilla of males long and slender, permanently external.
- Gill membranes broadly united, free of isthmus.
- Length to 90 mm TL.

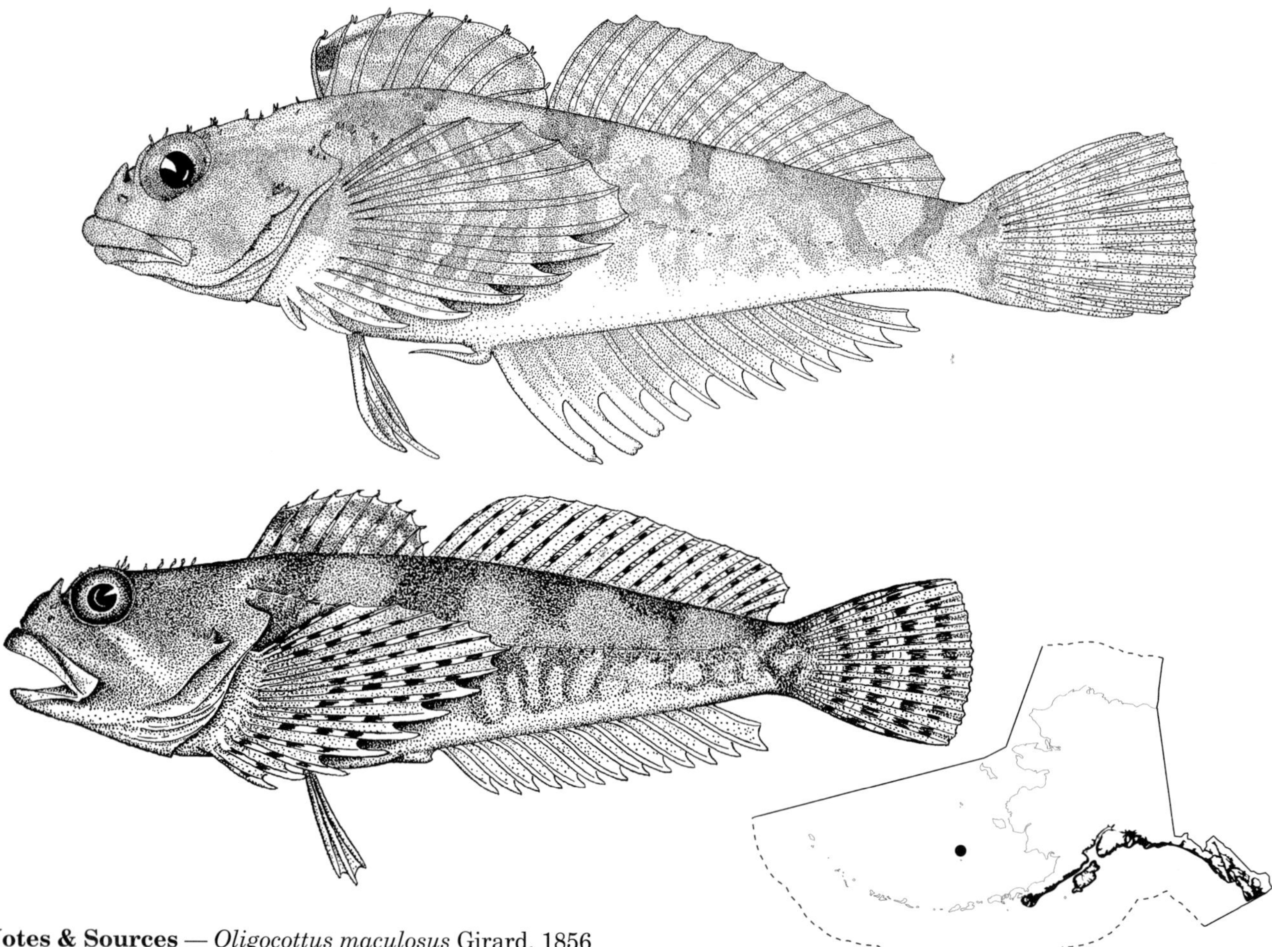

Notes & Sources — *Oligocottus maculosus* Girard, 1856
Oligocottus borealis Jordan & Snyder in Jordan, 1896

Description: Bolin 1944:65–67; Hart 1973:527–528.

Figures: Upper: Bolin 1944, fig. 25; male. Lower: Hart 1973: 527; female, 9 cm TL, Departure Bay, British Columbia.

Range: Well documented from Gulf of Alaska localities by published records (e.g., Evermann and Goldsborough 1907) and additional specimens in museum collections. Howe and Richardson (1978) considered occurrence west of Gulf of Alaska doubtful. UBC 63-1296 is from St. Paul Island at Lincoln Bight. Westernmost Gulf of Alaska collections at UBC are from the Shumagin Islands (UBC 63-1304, 65-87), and northernmost is from Prince William Sound at Galena Bay (UBC 63-484). Reported to occur along Russian shores on basis of specimens collected by Il'ya Vosnesenskiy in the mid-1800s; however, those specimens are incorrectly labeled and are from Sitka and other former Russian American possessions (B.A. Sheiko, pers. comm., 26 Aug. 1999).

Oligocottus snyderi Greeley, 1898 **fluffy sculpin**

Western Gulf of Alaska at Chernabura Island; southeastern Alaska at Samsing Cove, near Sitka, to northern Baja California; common north of San Francisco.

Tidepools and shallow rocky areas, often in algae.

D VII–IX + 17–20; A 12–15; Pec 13–15; Pel I,3; LLp 37–41; Vert 34–37.

- Bright green to reddish brown, spotted and mottled pink and lavender, highly variable; some specimens nearly uniform in color; chin usually spotted or marbled with white; fins barred.
- Head small; body robust.
- Nasal spine strong; no spines of top of head.
- **Uppermost preopercular spine usually bifid**, rarely trifid; others obsolete; all skin-covered.
- **Cirri present at base of nasal spine**, above eye, on top of head, preopercle, anterior two-thirds of lateral line, **along base of dorsal fin**; most cirri clustered; **maxillary cirrus absent**.
- Cirri at tips of dorsal fin spines; first anal fin ray enlarged and first 2 rays separate from rest of fin in males.
- **Scales, including prickles, absent**.
- Lateral line not strongly arched.
- Vomerine and palatine teeth present.
- Anus close to anal fin origin.
- Genital papilla of males long and slender, permanently external.
- Gill membranes broadly united, free of isthmus.
- Length to 90 mm TL.

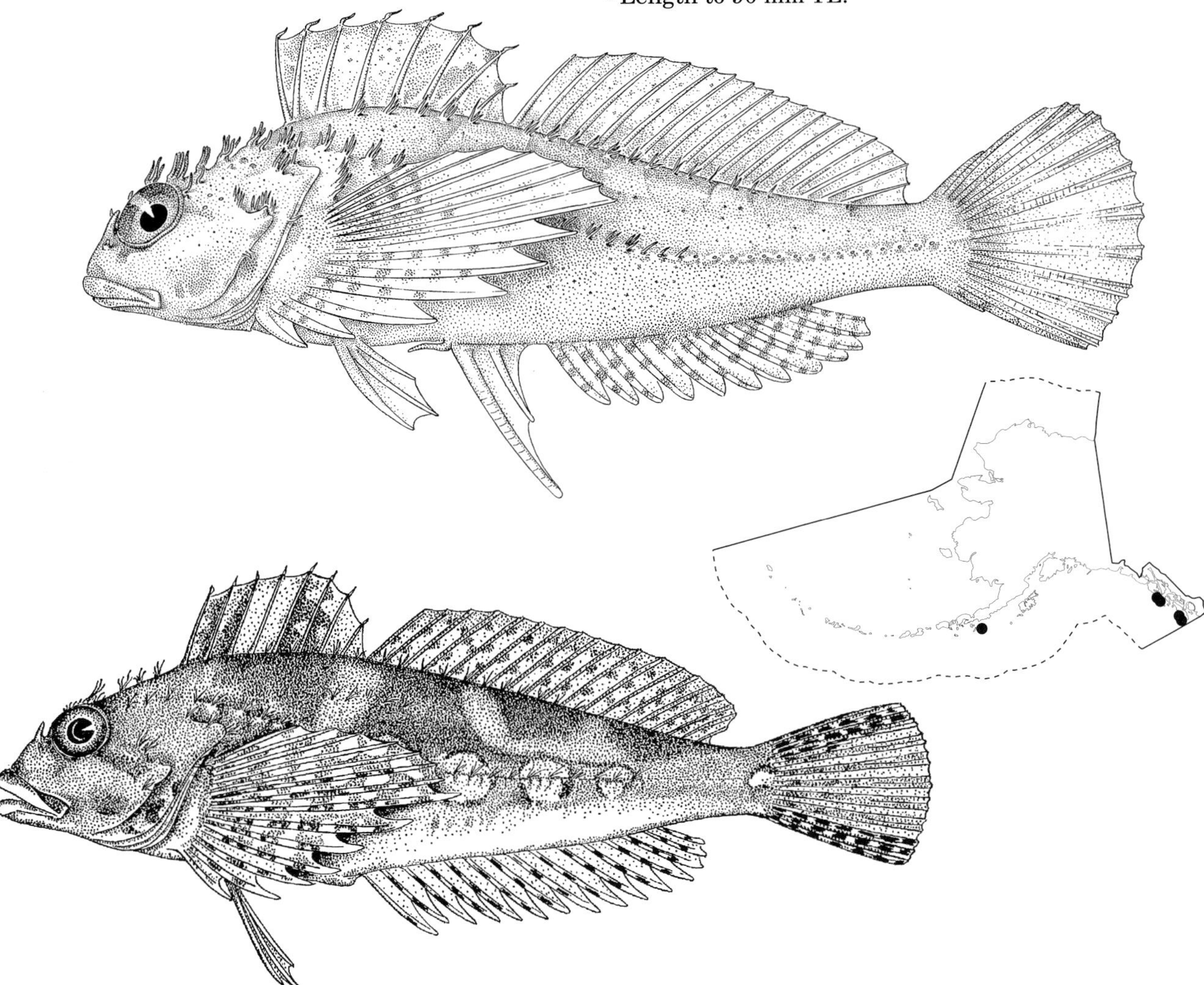

Notes & Sources — *Oligocottus snyderi* Greeley in Jordan & Evermann, 1898

Description: Bolin 1944:67–70; Hart 1973:530–531.

Figures: Upper: Bolin 1944, fig. 26; male. Lower: Hart 1973: 530; female, 9 cm TL, British Columbia.

Range: Recorded by Quast (1968) from Samsing Cove, near Sitka (ABL specimens), as an extension of known range into Alaska from British Columbia. Other voucher specimens from southeastern Alaska in permanent collections are from Volga Island, near Sitka (UBC 65-536, 65-537); Klokachef Island (UBC 65-573); Tava Island (NMC 61-25); San Juan Batista Island (NMC 61-163); and Cape Muzon, Dall Island (UBC 65-518, 65-519). Westernmost example is from Chernabura Island (UBC 63-333).

Clinocottus acuticeps (Gilbert, 1896) **sharpnose sculpin**

Aleutian Islands to central California at Big Sur River.

Intertidal area and to depth of about 20 m, sometimes in sheltered tidepools in upper intertidal; rocky or sandy bottoms, often in eelgrass and seaweed; often in brackish water, occasionally in fresh water.

D VII–IX + 13–17; A 9–13; Pec 13–15; Pel I,3; LLp 34–38; Vert 31–33.

- Slate gray, pinkish, brownish green, or emerald green; several saddles; white, pale green, to tan ventrally; dark area at anterior end of dorsal fin; dorsal, anal, caudal, pectoral fins barred.
- Snout sharp or steep in profile; body slender.
- Nasal spine strong; no spines on top of head.
- Uppermost preopercular spine simple, small, blunt or sharp; lower three obsolete.
- Nasal, eye, postocular, occipital, preopercular, anterior lateral line, 1 or 2 **maxillary cirri present**; no cirri below dorsal fins.
- Cirri on tips of first dorsal fin spines; **inner pelvic fin ray attached to belly by membrane**.
- Scales, including prickles, absent.
- Lateral line not strongly arched.
- Vomerine and palatine teeth present.
- Anus in middle third of area between pelvic fin base and anal fin origin, closer to pelvic base.
- Genital papilla of males unusually large and stout, and trilobed at tip.
- Gill membranes broadly united, free of isthmus.
- Length to 63 mm TL.

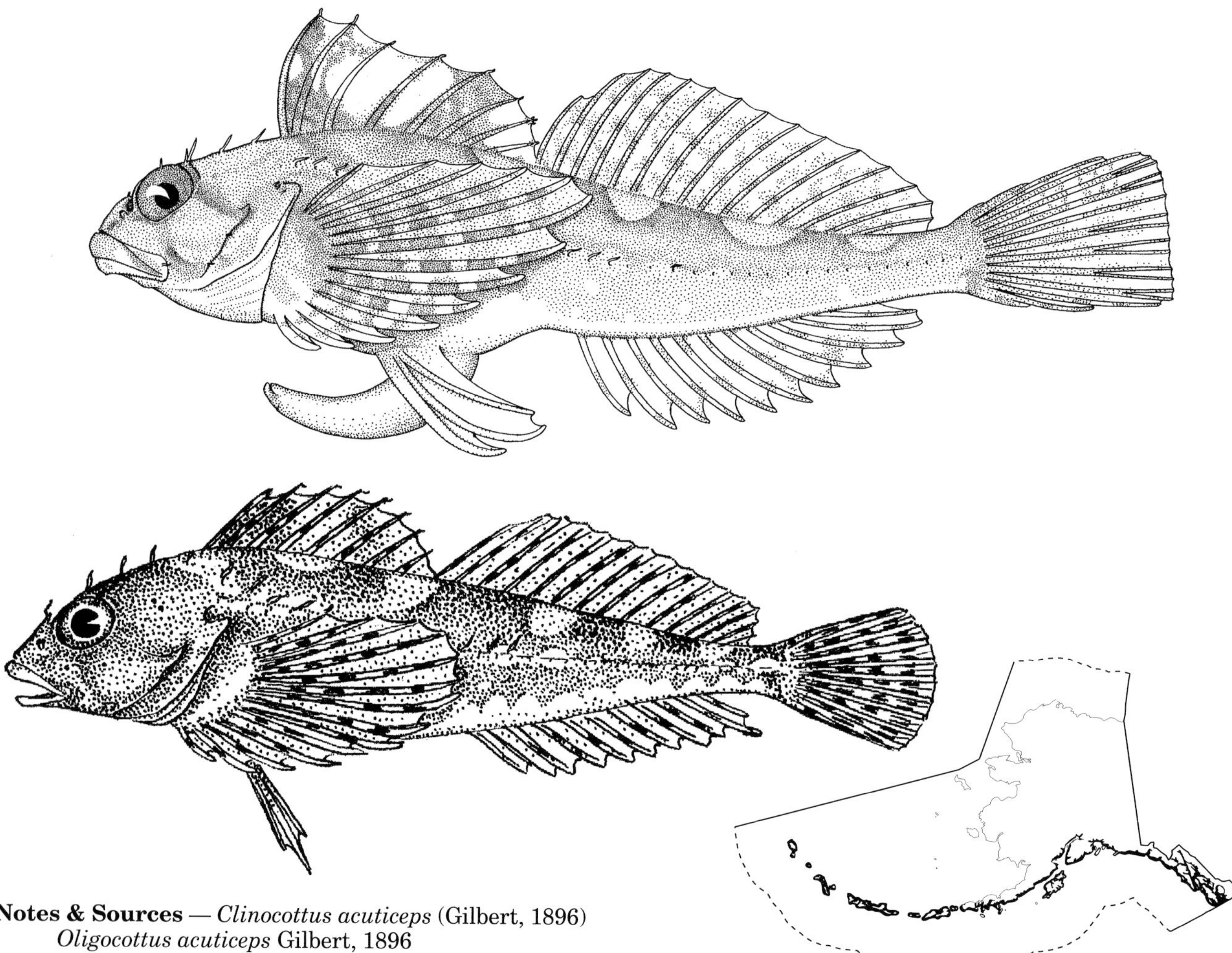

Notes & Sources — *Clinocottus acuticeps* (Gilbert, 1896)
Oligocottus acuticeps Gilbert, 1896
Oxycottus acuticeps: Jordan and Evermann 1898.

Description: Gilbert 1896:432; Bean and Bean 1899; Bolin 1944:84–86; Hart 1973:493–494; Morrow 1980:209.

Figures: Upper: Bolin 1944, fig. 32; male. Lower: Hart 1973:493; female, 53 mm TL, British Columbia.

Range: Morrow 1980:210, map. Type locality is Unalaska harbor, Unalaska. Well documented from Alaska; e.g., Sitka and Kodiak by Bean and Bean (1899); Prince William Sound by Jordan and Gilbert (1899); Karluk by Rutter (1899); Attu, Agattu, and Atka islands by Gilbert and Burke (1912a); and other Aleutian islands by Wilimovsky (1964). Bean (1881b) recorded specimens as *Oligocottus globiceps* from Adak and Amchitka islands, but the specimens were reexamined and referred to *C. acuticeps* by Hubbs (1926a). UW 3617 is from a freshwater lake in the vicinity of Makushin Bay, Unalaska Island. There are no specific records from north of the Aleutian Islands.

Clinocottus embryum (Jordan & Starks, 1895) **calico sculpin**

Aleutian Islands to northern Baja California at Punta Banda; most common from Puget Sound northward. Rocky and sandy intertidal areas, most often in tidepools in middle intertidal zone.

D VIII–X + 14–17; A 9–12; Pec 12–15; Pel I,3; LLp 35–40; Vert 33–34.

- Green to maroon or pink; mottled in darker shades; several saddles; white to greenish ventrally; dorsal fins sometimes with dark margin.
- **Snout pointed in dorsal view**, steep in lateral profile; body robust.
- **Small fleshy tubercle on median line in groove behind upper lip**.
- Nasal spine moderate; no spines on top of head.
- Upper preopercular spine simple, small, blunt; others obsolete.
- Nasal, postocular, occipital, opercular, anterior lateral line cirri present; **no cirri on maxilla or behind opercular flap**, or below dorsal fins.
- Inner pelvic ray not joined to belly by membrane.
- Scales, including prickles, absent.
- Lateral line not strongly arched.
- Vomerine and palatine teeth present.
- Anus about halfway between pelvic base and anal fin origin, or slightly nearer anal origin.
- Genital papilla of males wide at base.
- Gill membranes broadly united, free of isthmus.
- Length to 70 mm TL.

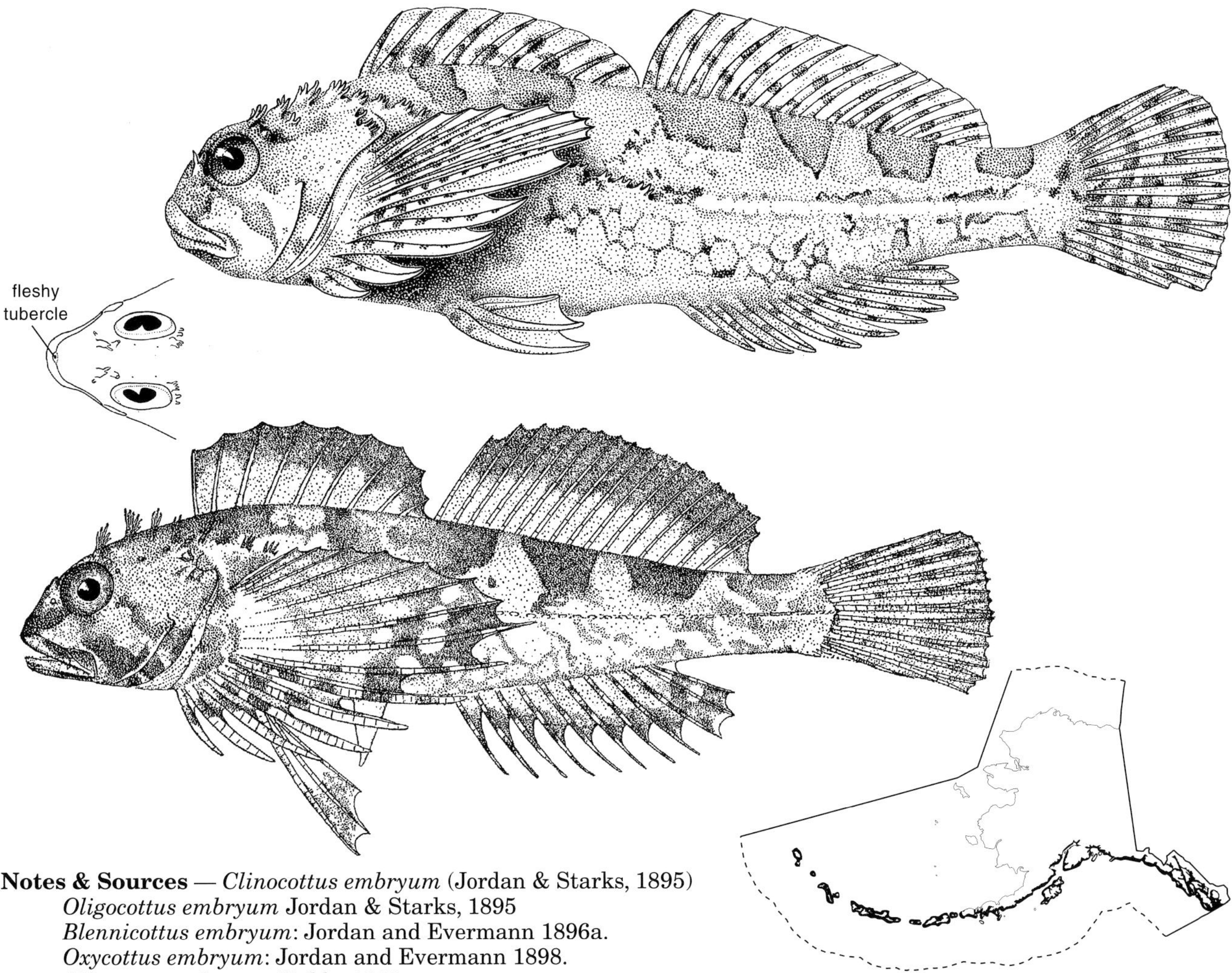

Notes & Sources — *Clinocottus embryum* (Jordan & Starks, 1895)
Oligocottus embryum Jordan & Starks, 1895
Blennicottus embryum: Jordan and Evermann 1896a.
Oxycottus embryum: Jordan and Evermann 1898.
Allocottus embryum: Hubbs 1926a.

Description: Jordan and Starks 1895:808–810; Bolin 1944: 78–79; Hart 1973:494–495.

Figures: Upper: Bolin 1944, fig. 29; female. Lower: Jordan and Starks 1895, pl. 82; type, male, Neah Bay, Washington. Diagram: Miller and Lea 1972:132.

Range: Recorded from Karluk by Evermann and Goldsborough (1907); Attu and Unalaska by Gilbert and Burke (1912a); Attu, Semichi, Buldir, Kiska, Amchitka, Adak, Great Sitkin, Atka, Amlia, Umnak, Unalaska, Krenitzin, and Unimak islands by Wilimovsky (1964). The UBC collection includes many examples from the Aleutians and from southeastern Alaska (e.g., Cape Spencer, UBC 65-543; Yakobi Island, UBC 65-546, 65-547; Port Conclusion, UBC 65-526, 65-527; Baker Island, UBC 65-582; Duke Island, UBC 65-510; Forrester Island, UBC 65-584). We did not find specific records from north of the Aleutian Islands.

Clinocottus globiceps (Girard, 1858) **mosshead sculpin**

Western Gulf of Alaska at Chernabura and Kodiak islands to southern California at Gaviota.

Rocky and sandy intertidal areas; in tidepools, or rocky areas in strong surf, under rocks or among seaweed; sometimes rests out of the water on rocks.

D IX–X + 15–17; A 10–12; Pec 13–14; Pel I,3; LLp 35–38; Vert 32–34.

- Reddish brown to olive green; usually spotted and vermiculated with white; dark bars on body; yellow to brown ventrally; fins barred.
- **Snout rounded in dorsal view**, steep in lateral profile; body robust.
- Nasal spine moderate; no spines on top of head.
- Upper preopercular spine simple, blunt; others obsolete.
- **Many cirri on head, including interorbital space, behind opercular flap**, lateral line anteriorly; **no cirri on maxilla** or below dorsal fins.
- Inner pelvic ray not joined to belly by membrane.
- Scales, including prickles, absent.
- Lateral line curved, not strongly arched.
- Vomerine and palatine teeth present.
- Anus in middle third of area between pelvic fin base and anal fin origin, closer to anal origin.
- Genital papilla of males lobed and slightly expanded distally.
- Gill membranes broadly united, free of isthmus.
- Length to 190 mm TL.

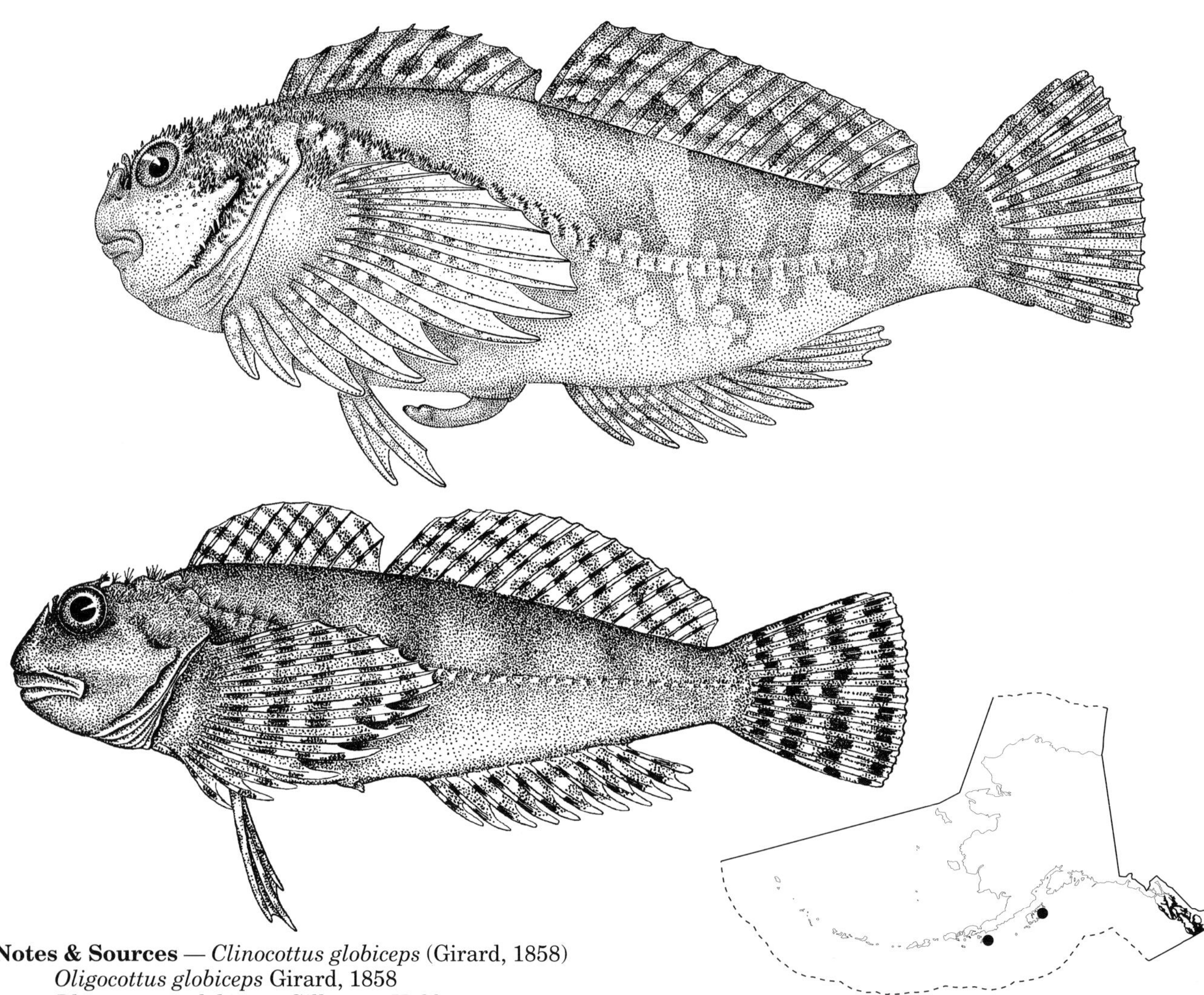

Notes & Sources — *Clinocottus globiceps* (Girard, 1858)
Oligocottus globiceps Girard, 1858
Blennicottus globiceps: Gill 1862, Hubbs 1926a.

Description: Bolin 1944:81–83; Hart 1973:496–497.

Figures: Upper: Bolin 1944, fig. 31; male. Lower: Hart 1973: 496; female, 12 cm TL, Vargas Island, British Columbia.

Range: Bean 1881b: Chagafka (= Shahafka) Cove, Kodiak Island, and Sitka. Specimens listed by Bean (1881b) from Adak and Amchitka islands were referred by Hubbs (1926a) to *C. acuticeps.* Additional records: Chernabura Island (UBC 63-333); Yakobi Island (UBC 65-547); Klokachef Island (UBC 65-578); Port Armstrong (UBC 63-158, 63-164, 63-165); Puffin Bay (NMC 61-160); southern Prince of Wales Island (NMC 61-10, UBC 65-514); Dall Island (UBC 65-518); Duke Island (UBC 65-510).

Family Hemitripteridae
Sailfin sculpins

The family Hemitripteridae comprises eight species of demersal marine fishes which are closely related to and classified with the Cottidae in the superfamily Cottoidea. Seven hemitripterid species occur in Alaska and other regions of the North Pacific.

Tall fins are a special mark of hemitripterids, from which the group takes the vernacular, sailfin sculpins. In some sailfin sculpins the first dorsal fin is exceptionally long. Characters defining sailfin sculpins as a taxon different from other cottoid families, including the Cottidae, are the presence of numerous prickles on the head and body; a knobby fronto-parietal ridge; broad, platelike epurals; and absence of the basihyal bone. The prickles, called papillae by some authors, are modified platelike scales bearing a single skin-covered spine.

Like most cottids, sailfin sculpins have two dorsal fins, low spinous plates or knobs for gill rakers, 6 branchiostegal rays, a well-developed lateral line which in most species opens through more than 20 pores, no swim bladder, and, in the males of some species, an external genital papilla. The preopercle bears 3 or 4 spines, which are mostly blunt and skin-covered. The gill membranes are broadly attached to the isthmus or form a free fold across the isthmus. Vomerine and palatine teeth are present. Except in *Hemitripterus* species, which have very large mouths extending back beyond the eyes, sailfin sculpins have moderate-sized mouths with the maxillae reaching mideye. Bands and other pigmentation, such as the diagonal bars through the eyes in *Nautichthys* species, are helpful in identification but the colors themselves can vary with habitat, particularly in the species of *Hemitripterus.*

Maximum sizes attained by sailfin sculpins range from about 8 cm (3.2 inches) for shortmast sculpin, *Nautichthys robustus,* to about 73 cm (28.7 inches) for bigmouth sculpin, *Hemitripterus bolini.*

The shaggy sea raven, *H. villosus,* primarily inhabits shallow waters off Russia and Japan; reports of its occurrence in Alaska in recent years have not been adequately documented or confirmed. The taxonomic history of *H. villosus* and evidence for existence of this species in Alaska are confusing. Soon after Lockington (1880g) named a new species, *H. cavifrons,* from a specimen collected at Kodiak Island, Bean (1881b) compared it to the sea raven, *H. americanus* (Gmelin, 1789), of eastern Canada and New England, and concluded they were the same species. Jordan and Starks (1904b), however, believed Lockington's *H. cavifrons* to be identical with *Cottus villosus* Pallas, 1811 (which is now classified in *Hemitripterus*). *Hemitripterus villosus* is so close to the Atlantic species, Schmidt (1904, 1927, 1950) and Andriashev (1937, 1939) continued to equate the two or to classify *H. villosus* as a subspecies of *H. americanus,* but in recent years the status of the sea ravens of the western Pacific (*H. villosus*) and Atlantic (*H. americanus*) as distinct species has been universally accepted.

In Alaska the greater confusion is between the species *H. villosus* and *H. bolini,* which also are very similar. *Hemitripterus bolini* is found at moderate water depths primarily from Alaska to California. All reports of *H. villosus* in Alaska, except that of Lockington (1880g), have proved to represent *H. bolini* or are not verifiable for lack of voucher specimens. A conspicuous difference between the species is that in *H. villosus* the first few dorsal fin spines are distinctly higher than the remaining spines and are separated from them by a deep notch. In some specimens the notch extends all the way to the back, separating the spinous dorsal into two fins. Chapman (1940), however, described a juvenile of *H. bolini* (39 mm SL) caught south of the Shumagin Islands that had the first three spines of the dorsal fin decidedly higher than the rest. He concluded that the height of the first few dorsal rays is variable in the young of *H. bolini,* and that the young of the two species are more similar in appearance than the adults. The only other major difference is the greater number of dorsal fin spines in *H. villosus,* and this character carries more weight than configuration of the fin in differentiating *H. villosus* from *H. bolini* (e.g., Chapman's specimen). Lockington's (1880g) Kodiak Island specimen had the requisite number of dorsal fin spines for *H. villosus,* as well as configuration, so its identification is not in question. The species prefers shallow, rocky, untrawlable habitats, so the absence of additional discoveries in Alaska could be due to lack of sampling coverage. From Cape Lopatka at the southern tip of Kamchatka to Cape Olyutorskiy on the Bering Sea, divers find *H. villosus* "almost behind every fifth stone" (B. A. Sheiko, pers. comm., 15 Jan. 1999), and Andriashev (1937, 1939) reported it to be abundant at the Commander Islands and along Russian Bering Sea coasts in general. Therefore, occasional reports of this species from the western Aleutian Islands and Bering Sea off Alaska would not be surprising. Lockington's Kodiak Island, Gulf of Alaska, record is extraordinary, but there is no particular evidence placing it in question.

Presence of both species of *Blepsias* and *Nautichthys pribilovius* in the Gulf of Alaska and Bering Sea is well documented; *N. oculofasciatus* is confirmed in Alaska only in the Gulf of Alaska. *Nautichthys robustus* occurs in the Bering Sea as well, but is known in Alaska from relatively few records.

Previous inventories of Alaskan fishes included the hemitripterids in the Cottidae. However, Washington et al. (1984) and Yabe (1985) provided evidence that the lineage comprising *Hemitripterus, Nautichthys,* and *Blepsias* is the sister group to the Agonidae. Classifying the Hemitripteridae as a separate family expresses that relationship.

No new hemitripterid species have been described in recent years, nor any species added to the inventory of Alaskan species from new records extending known range into the region. The only change is in nomenclature and reflects recognition that the differences between *H. bolini* and *H. villosus* do not merit separation at the genus level. This also has a confusing history, starting with *Hemitripterus marmoratus,* which was described by Bean (1890b) from specimens collected at Sitkalidak Island, Alaska. *Hemitripterus marmoratus* was placed in a new genus by Jordan and Evermann (in Jordan 1896), giving the binomial *Ulca marmorata.* Later, however, Myers (1934) observed that the species name was already in use for another sculpin (cabezon, *Scorpaenichthys marmoratus*), and replaced the name *U. marmorata* with *U. bolini.* The first use as *Hemitripterus bolini* may have been by Clemens and Wilby (1961), and this has been the principal usage by North American authors ever since (Lea and Quirollo 1986). *Ulca bolini* is the name used in recent Russian works reporting this fish at southeastern Kamchatka and the Kuril Islands (e.g., Orlov 1998a, Poltev and Muhkametov 1999, Sheiko and Fedorov 2000).

Key to the Hemitripteridae of Alaska

1 Caudal fin rays unbranched; conspicuous cirri on lower jaw .... (2)

1 Caudal fin rays branched; no cirri on lower jaw .... (5)

2 (1) Base of first dorsal fin longer than base of second dorsal; 11 or more dorsal fin spines; head depressed .... (3)

2 Base of first dorsal fin shorter than base of second dorsal; 9 or fewer dorsal fin spines; head compressed .... (4)

3 (2) First dorsal fin with 15 or fewer spines; sometimes with notch behind 3rd or 4th dorsal fin spine; pectoral fin reaching to below last spine of first dorsal fin or beyond .... *Hemitripterus bolini,* page 507

3 First dorsal fin with 16 or more spines; notch behind 3rd or 4th dorsal fin spine; pectoral fin usually not reaching to below last spine of first dorsal fin .... *Hemitripterus villosus,* page 508

4 (2) First dorsal fin not notched; no smooth areas on body .... *Blepsias bilobus,* page 509

4 First dorsal fin deeply notched; smooth, silvery areas on sides .... *Blepsias cirrhosus,* page 510

5 (1) First dorsal fin height more than twice length of base of first dorsal; second dorsal fin rays 27 or more; pectoral fin rays 13 or 14 .... *Nautichthys oculofasciatus,* page 511

5 First dorsal fin height less than twice length of base of first dorsal; second dorsal fin rays 26 or fewer; pectoral fin rays 14–17 .... (6)

6 (5) Spines on occiput rounded; second dorsal fin rays 22–26; anal fin rays 15–20 (usually 16 or 17) .... *Nautichthys pribilovius,* page 512

6 Spines on occiput pointed; second dorsal fin rays 19–21; anal fin rays 14–16 (usually 14 or 15) .... *Nautichthys robustus,* page 513

Hemitripterus bolini (Myers, 1934) **bigmouth sculpin**

Bering Sea from Cape Navarin to north side of Alaska Peninsula, and Aleutian Islands to Pacific Ocean off northern California at Eureka; to western Pacific off Kamchatka and northern Kuril islands.

Bottom at depths of 25–925 m, most common offshore at depths of 100–300 m.

D XIII–XV + 11–12; A 11–14; Pec 20–23; Pel I,3; LLp 40–42; Vert 38–40.

- Mottled gray to brown dorsally, lighter ventrally; 4 or 5 vague darker saddles across back; reddish, yellow-brown, and orange patches and highlights.
- **Head large and depressed; mouth extremely large, maxilla extending well beyond eye.**
- **Numerous blunt spines on head**; nasal spines small and sharp, with rounded knob between.
- Four preopercular spines: upper 2 longest and pointed, lower 2 blunt, lowest a low triangle.
- **Numerous cirri, many complex, mainly on head.**
- **Spinous dorsal fin base longer than soft dorsal**; dorsal fin spines greatly exserted, with long, flat filaments at tips; first few dorsal spines usually not markedly higher or set off from rest by deep notch; **dorsal spines 15 or fewer**; pectoral fin reaching nearly to or beyond an imaginary line extending down from insertion of spinous dorsal fin.
- Prickles covering body and extending onto fins.
- Gill membranes united, forming wide free fold across isthmus.
- Length to 734 mm TL.

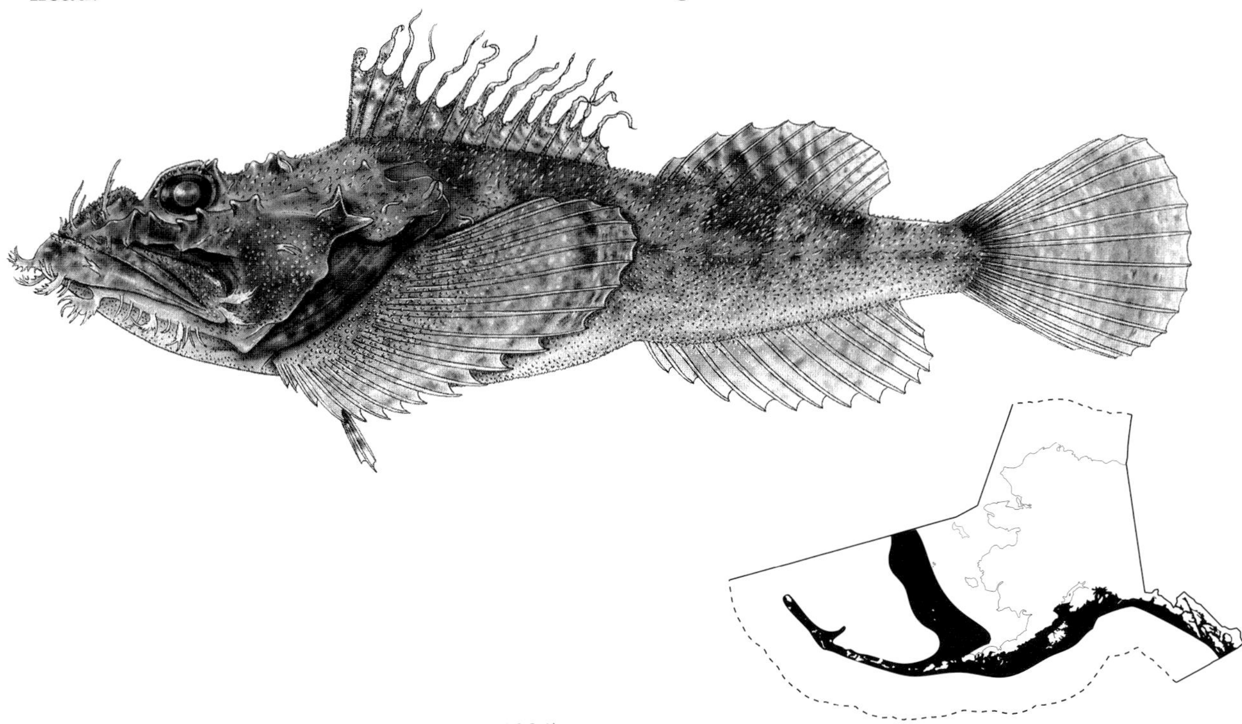

Notes & Sources — *Hemitripterus bolini* (Myers, 1934)

Ulca bolini Myers, 1934. Replacement name for *Hemitripterus marmoratus* Bean, 1890, preoccupied by *Hemitripterus marmoratus* Ayres, 1854.

Hemitripterus villosus: Wilimovsky 1954, 1958, 1964 (Bering Sea and Aleutian Islands range limits evidently based on Unalaska Island record of *H. marmoratus* Bean); Isakson et al. 1971; Quast and Hall 1972 (Bering Sea listing).

Lea and Quirollo (1986) gave a synonymy with additional details.

Description: Gilbert 1896:474; Jordan and Evermann 1898:2021–2022; Andriashev 1937:30 of transl.; Chapman 1940:36–39; Hart 1973:505–506; Matarese et al. 1989 (vertebral counts).

Figure: University of British Columbia, artist P. Drukker-Brammall, May 1966; UBC 62-516, 225 mm SL, east of Sanak Island off Davidson Bank, Alaska.

Range: The type locality is *Albatross* station 2855, in the western Gulf of Alaska off Sitkalidak Island at a depth of 126 m. Records in the literature and additional specimens in museum collections are numerous and document the eastern North Pacific and Bering Sea range depicted from NMFS survey data by Allen and Smith (1988). In the western Bering Sea, recorded as far north as Cape Navarin by Taranetz (1933, 1935a). Orlov (1998a) documented range south to the northern Kuril Islands. In research trawling for shelf species off southeastern Kamchatka and the northern Kuril Islands, Poltev and Mukhametov (1999) found that adult bigmouth sculpins occurred predominantly at depths of 200–300 m, and juveniles at 100–200 m.

Size: Lea and Quirollo (1986) reported a gravid female, the first record of the species from California, with a length of 73 cm TL and weight of 8.5 kg. R. Baxter (unpubl. data) examined a specimen of similar length (734 mm TL) but weighing 10.6 kg, caught just north of Unalaska Island (specimen not saved, sex not recorded). Poltev and Mukhametov (1999) reported another 73-cm specimen, this one caught in 1998 near the northern Kuril Islands.

Hemitripterus villosus (Pallas, 1814) **shaggy sea raven**

Kodiak Island; western Bering Sea from Cape Olyutorskiy to Commander Islands and Pacific Ocean from Cape Afrika to Japan, Sea of Okhotsk, and Sea of Japan to South Korea.

Rocky and sandy bottoms at depths of 16–112 m; prefers shallow, rocky habitat near the coast.

D XVI–XVIX + 11–13; A 12–16; Pec 18–20; Pel I,3; LLp 40–46; Vert 39–41.

- Reddish brown or olive to dark gray dorsally with large, irregular dark spots; dorsal and caudal fins dull crimson; fins mottled with dark brown or dark gray; lighter ventrally.
- **Head large and depressed; mouth extremely large, maxilla extending well beyond eye.**
- **Numerous blunt spines on head**; nasal spines small and sharp, with rounded knob between.
- Four preopercular spines: upper 2 longest and pointed, lower 2 blunt, lowest a low triangle.
- **Numerous cirri, many complex, mainly on head.**

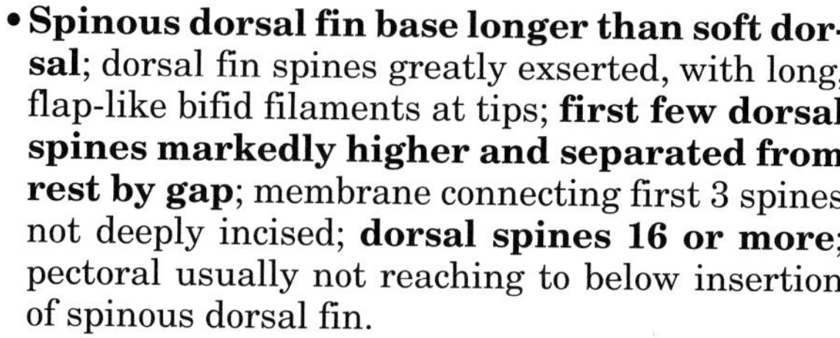

- **Spinous dorsal fin base longer than soft dorsal**; dorsal fin spines greatly exserted, with long, flap-like bifid filaments at tips; **first few dorsal spines markedly higher and separated from rest by gap**; membrane connecting first 3 spines not deeply incised; **dorsal spines 16 or more**; pectoral usually not reaching to below insertion of spinous dorsal fin.
- Prickles covering body, smaller and more dense below lateral line.
- Gill membranes united, forming wide free fold across isthmus.
- Length to 500 mm TL.

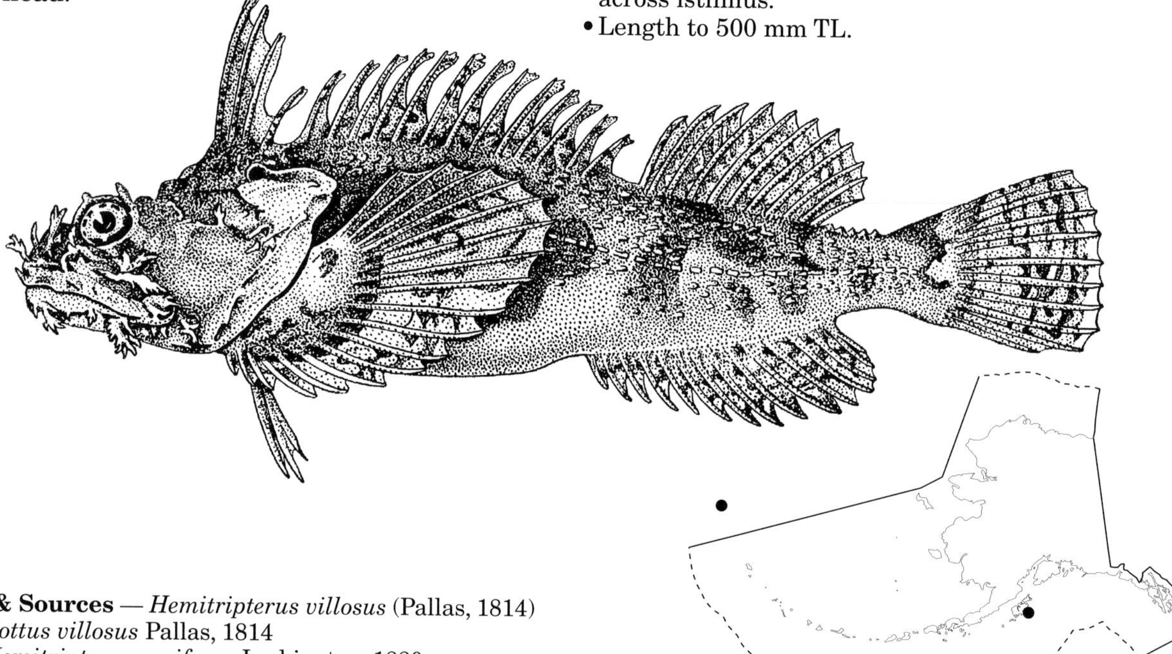

Notes & Sources — *Hemitripterus villosus* (Pallas, 1814)
Cottus villosus Pallas, 1814
Hemitripterus cavifrons Lockington, 1880
Hemitripterus americanus (Gmelin): Bean 1881b (Lockington's type).
Hemitripterus americanus villosus (Pallas): Andriashev 1937, 1939; Schmidt 1950.

Description: Lockington 1880g; Jordan and Starks 1904b: 326–328; Andriashev 1937:30–32 of transl.; Schmidt 1950: 180–181; Yabe in Masuda et al. 1984:323; Lindberg and Krasyukova 1987:256–257.

Figure: Lindberg and Krasyukova 1987, fig. 165, after Watanabe 1960; 422 mm TL, Sea of Japan.

Range: One specimen reported to be from Kodiak Island was the basis of *H. cavifrons* Lockington, 1880. Unfortunately, the holotype (unique) cannot be found (Eschmeyer 1998); once housed at the CAS, it may have been destroyed in the San Francisco fire of 1906. Reports of *H. villosus* from the Bering Sea off Alaska by Wilimovsky (1954, 1958, 1964) and Quast and Hall (1972) were partly based on Gilbert's (1896) specimens of *H. marmoratus* from north of Unalaska Island, but Lea and Quirollo (1986) later synonymized those in *H. bolini*. Isakson et al. (1971) included *H. villosus* on their list of Amchitka Island fishes, but in a later report that used the same data Simenstad et al. (1977) listed *H. bolini* instead, indicating they revised the identification to species. The NMFS scientific survey database has three records attributed to *H. villosus* from the western Aleutian Islands; they lack voucher specimens but there is a photograph of one fish, and it looks like *H. bolini* (J. W. Orr, pers. comm., 6 Aug. 1998). They were taken in bottom trawls fishing to depths of 155–270 m, which is deep for *H. villosus*. Specimens from Prince William Sound (UAM 416, UAM 1145) identified as *H. villosus* have the wrong number of dorsal fin spines (13 and 14, respectively) and are obvious examples of *H. bolini* (C.W.M.). Andriashev (1937, 1939) reported *H. villosus* to be common at the Commander Islands. Kim and Youn (1992) recorded catches of *H. villosus* from five stations off the east coast of South Korea. Few depths have been reported; deepest was given by Jordan and Snyder (1904b), off Honshu at 75–112 m (*Albatross* stations 3770 and 3771). Scuba divers report it to be an abundant solitary predator in shallow rocky habitats between Capes Olyutorskiy and Lopatka (B. A. Sheiko, pers. comm., 15 Jan. 1999).

Blepsias bilobus Cuvier, 1829 **crested sculpin**

Chukchi and Bering seas and Aleutian Islands from Amchitka Island to northern British Columbia; western Chukchi Sea to Commander Islands and Okhotsk and Japan seas.

Near bottom to depth of 190 m, usually near shore or over continental slope at depths less than 120 m.

D VII–IX + 20–22; A 18–20; Pec 15–17; Pel I,3; LLs 52–53; Vert 37–38.

- Orange-brown to olive green with darker blotches dorsally, or white with olive to black mottling.
- Body compressed.
- Top of head with bony ridges, no strong spines; nasal spines low, recurved.
- Four preopercular spines: blunt, second longest.
- **Prominent, simple cirri on snout and lower jaw.**
- Spinous dorsal fin base shorter than soft dorsal; **spinous dorsal without deep notch**; **pectoral fin rays 15 or more.**
- **Prickles densely cover body, without naked areas, and bases of fins.**
- Gill membranes united, forming free fold across isthmus.
- Length to 270 mm TL.

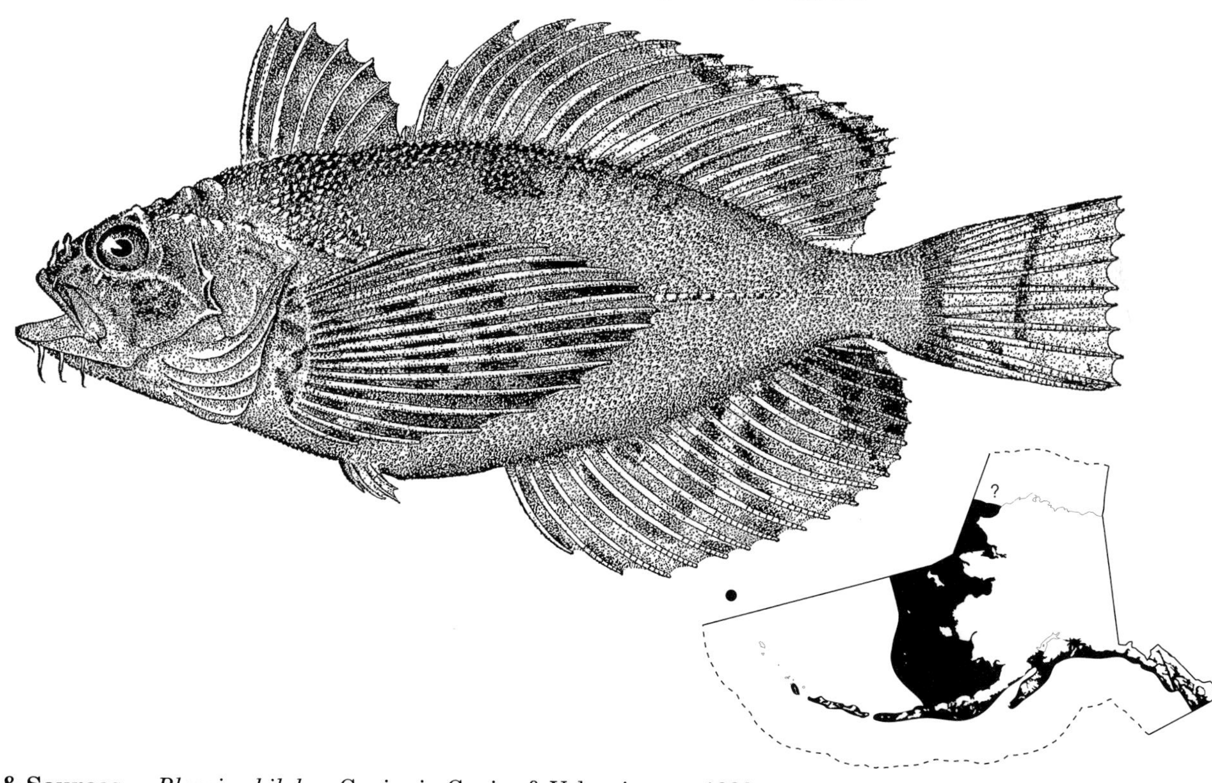

Notes & Sources — *Blepsias bilobus* Cuvier in Cuvier & Valenciennes, 1829

Histiocottus bilobus (Cuvier, 1829): Jordan and Evermann 1898, 1900. However, Schmidt (1950) united the two genera because the only essential difference between them is the presence of a notch in the first dorsal fin of *B. cirrhosus*.

Description: Jordan and Evermann 1898:2018; Schmidt 1950:174–175; Hart 1973:487–488; Eschmeyer and Herald 1983:164; Yabe in Masuda et al. 1984:323; Lindberg and Krasyukova 1987:258–259; Matarese et al. 1989:448 (vertebral counts); Coad 1995:230.

Figure: Jordan and Evermann 1900, fig. 736; 154 mm TL, St. Paul (now city of Kodiak), Alaska.

Range: Well documented from numerous localities in Bering Sea and Gulf of Alaska and continuing to British Columbia, but northern limit of range is not well defined. R. Baxter (unpubl. data) examined samples from Chukchi Sea at 68°53'N, 166°26'W, depth 35 m, and 69°49'N, 164°09'W, depth 29 m, from a 1990 UAF survey (Barber et al. [1997] listed species but did not give localities); and a specimen from Norton Sound, depth 13 m, from a 1985 NMFS survey. No specimens were saved, however, and future samples from the Arctic should be kept as vouchers. *Blepsias bilobus* was observed from remote-operated vehicle near St. Paul Island in 1995; vouchers are in UW collection (J. W. Orr, pers. comm., 13 Nov. 1997). Samples taken near St. Lawrence Island to southeastern Alaska are in ABL, UBC, and UW collections. Brodeur et al. (1999) reported *B. bilobus* in survey catches along western Bering Sea coasts north to Bering Strait, as well as in eastern Bering Sea. Wilimovsky (1964) recorded it at the Krenitzin Islands, and the UW has a specimen from Amchitka Island (UW 25355) collected in 1971 by C. S. Simenstad. Probably occurs west to Attu Island, but voucher specimens are lacking. Collected by Stejneger from Bering Island (Jordan and Gilbert 1899). Maximum depth of 190 m is from UW 25335, a 22-cm-SL specimen taken north of Akun Island and Unimak Pass in 1980 in a "modified eastern trawl." Other records are from less than 120 m.

Size: R. Baxter, unpubl. data: a specimen taken north of Alaska Peninsula, depth 90 m, measured 270 mm TL and weighed 407 g; specimen was not saved, but data are appropriate. Maximum size generally given is 25 cm TL (e.g., Hart 1973).

Blepsias cirrhosus (Pallas, 1811) **silverspotted sculpin**

Southeastern Bering Sea and Aleutian Islands from Attu Island to central California off San Simeon; and Commander Islands to Okhotsk and Japan seas.

Near shore to depth of about 47 m among seaweed and rocks.

D VI–X + 20–25; A 18–22; Pec 11–14; Pel I,3; LLp 43–57; Vert 37–39.

- Golden brown to olive green dorsally, copper red to yellow ventrally; dark patches often present dorsolaterally; bright silvery white patches below lateral line behind pectoral fin, and often on fins and cheeks.
- Body compressed.
- Top of head with bony ridges, no strong spines; nasal spines low, recurved.
- Four preopercular spines: blunt, second longest.
- **Prominent, simple cirri on snout and lower jaw**.
- Spinous dorsal fin base shorter than soft dorsal; **spinous dorsal deeply notched, nearly forming 2 fins; pectoral fin rays 14 or fewer**.
- **Prickles closely packed on body but absent from pectoral axil, around posterior part of lateral line, and silvery patches**.
- Gill membranes united, forming free fold across isthmus.
- Length to 200 mm SL.

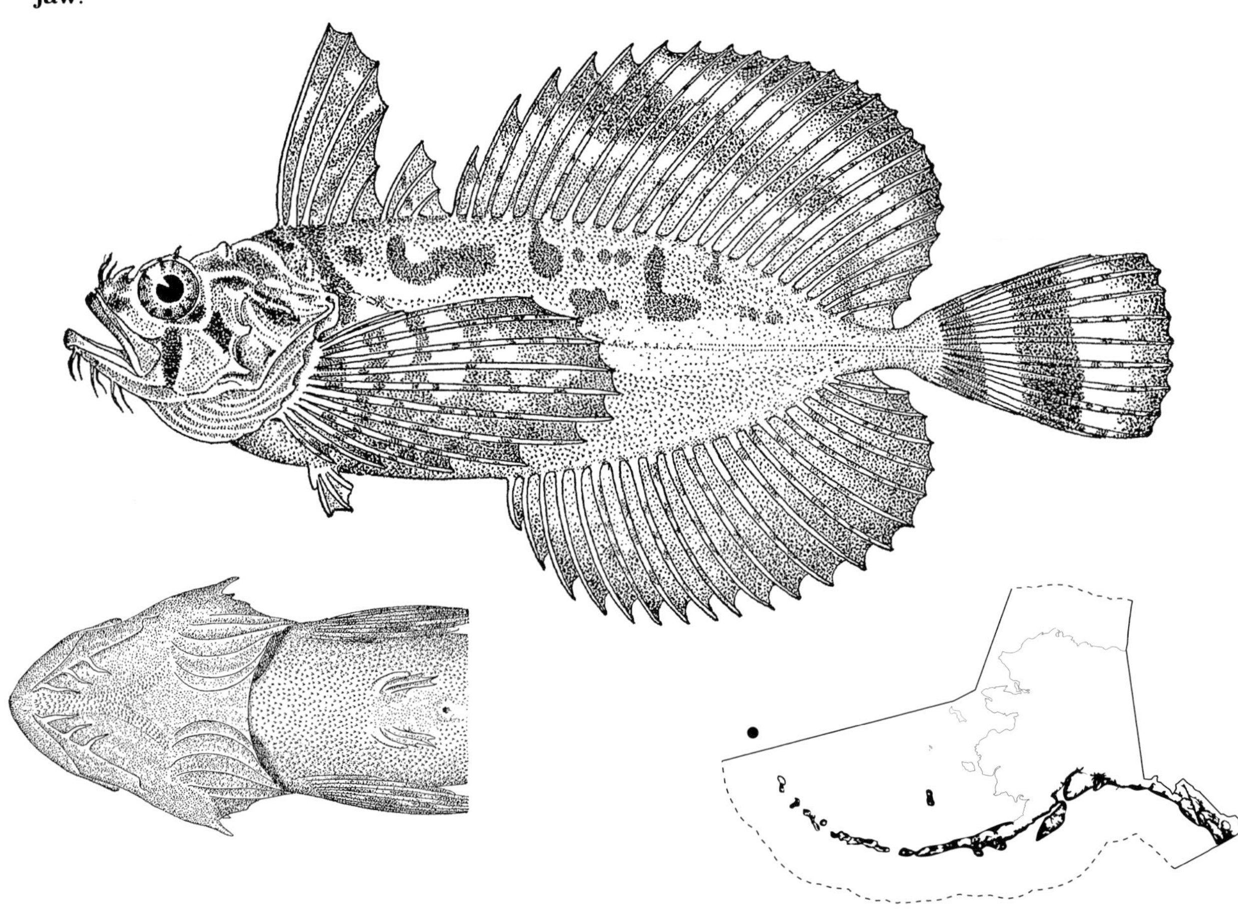

Notes & Sources — *Blepsias cirrhosus* (Pallas, 1811)
Trachinus cirrhosus Pallas, 1811
Blepsias draciscus Jordan and Starks, 1904

Description: Jordan and Evermann 1898:2018–2019; Jordan and Starks 1904b:322–324; Bolin 1944:99–102; Hart 1973:489–490; Eschmeyer and Herald 1983:164; Yabe in Masuda et al. 1984:323; Lindberg and Krasyukova 1987: 259–261; Matarese et al. 1989:450 (vertebral counts); Coad 1995:685.

Figures: Jordan and Evermann 1900, fig. 737; Strait of Juan de Fuca, Washington; and St. Paul (now city of Kodiak), Kodiak Island, Alaska (ventral view).

Range: Recorded by Bean (1881b) from several localities from St. Paul Island to Sitka. Wilimovsky (1964) recorded it from Attu Island, and Isakson et al. (1986) collected it along the north shore of the Alaska Peninsula. Numerous specimens exist in permanent collections, including some from southernmost southeastern Alaska and continuing into British Columbia, and from the Aleutian Islands to the Commander Islands, Russia, to the Kamchatka coast. *Blepsias cirrhosus* is often displayed in marine aquaria.

Size: Coad 1995.

Nautichthys oculofasciatus (Girard, 1858) **sailfin sculpin**

Western Gulf of Alaska to southern California at San Miguel Island.

Intertidal zone, sometimes in tidepools, and to depth of 110 m, mostly on rocky bottom and often in areas with algae.

D VIII–IX + 27–30; A 16–21; Pec 13–14; Pel I,3; LLp 41–46; Vert 40–41.

- Orange-brown to pale gray with blackish blotches; **black bar through eye and across cheek**; first dorsal fin blackish.
- Nape short; base of first dorsal fin enlarged and elevated.
- Head spines strong, rounded; nasal spines well developed, sharp.
- Three preopercular spines: blunt, first longest.
- Large cirrus on eye; smaller cirri on head spines and posterior end of maxilla.
- Spinous dorsal fin base shorter than soft dorsal; **first 3–5 dorsal fin spines very long, more than twice as long as base of fin**; **soft dorsal rays more than 26**.
- Prickles dense, except some areas such as pectoral axilla and along base of anal fin naked.
- Gill membranes broadly attached to isthmus, with no free fold.
- Length to 203 mm TL.

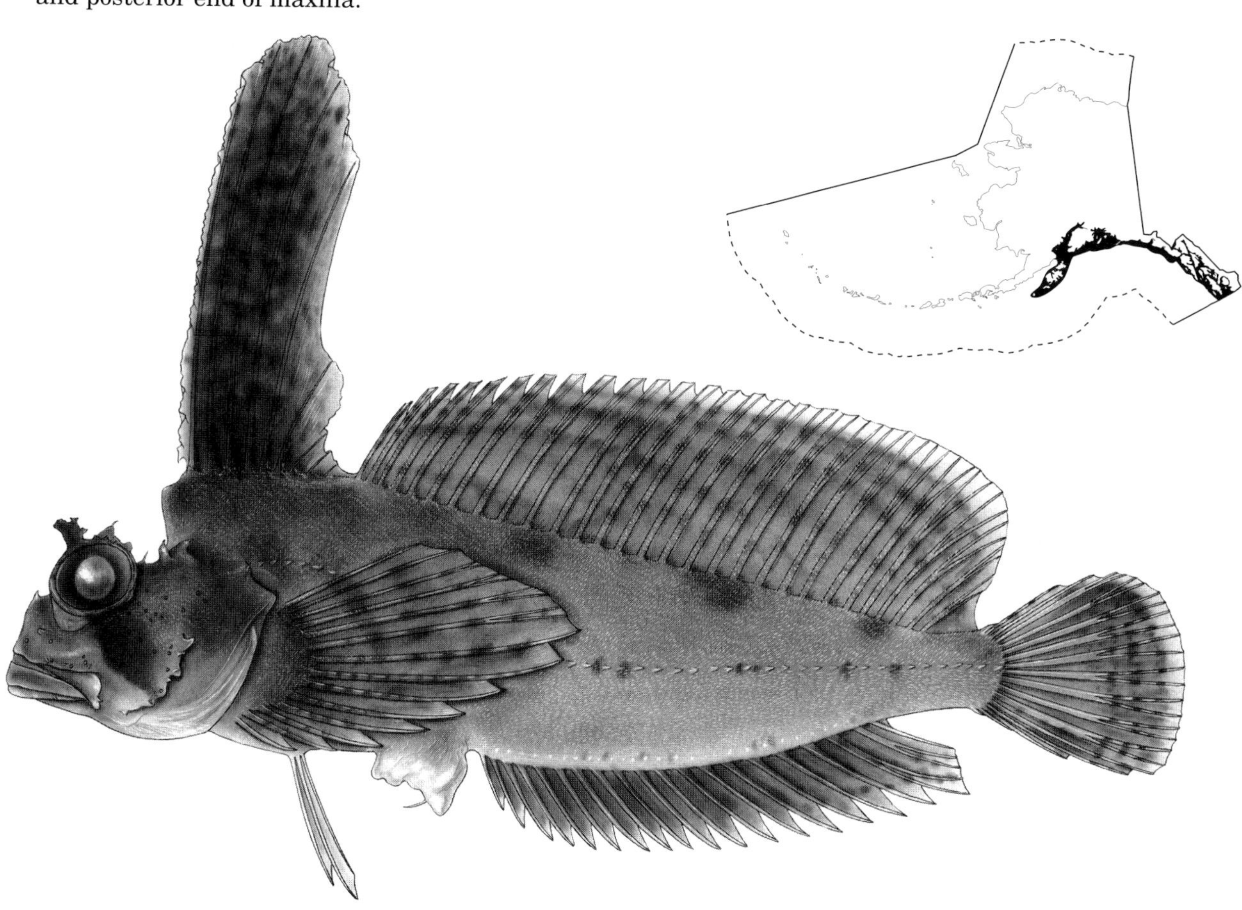

Notes & Sources — *Nautichthys oculofasciatus* (Girard, 1858)
Blepsias oculofasciatus Girard, 1858

Description: Bolin 1944:102–104; Peden 1970:4; Hart 1973: 522–524; Matarese et al. 1989:454.

Figure: University of British Columbia, artist P. Drukker-Brammall, Nov. 1965; UBC 65-44, male, 146 mm SL, Uyak Bay, Kodiak Island, Alaska.

Range: Hubbard and Reeder (1965) recorded extension of the known range west to Kodiak Island, and Rosenthal (1980) north to Prince William Sound. The UBC has specimens from Kodiak Island (see illustration on this page) and Kachemak Bay, as well as southeastern Alaska. ABL specimens are from southeastern Alaska. Peden and Wilson (1976) collected it by scuba diving at several sites north and south of the Alaska–British Columbia border. The species is not rare in the Gulf of Alaska. Bolin (1944) noted that the northern limit of its range was not known with certainty due to confusion with *N. pribilovius,* and Schmidt (1950) and Andriashev (1954) included Bering Sea records of *N. oculofasciatus* in the synonymy of *N. pribilovius.* Hart (1973) also concluded *N. oculofasciatus* was absent from the Bering Sea. The species currently is believed to be endemic to the eastern Pacific (e.g., Yabe et al. 1983). Recently, B. A. Sheiko (pers. comm., 28 May 1999) confirmed the lack of adequately documented records of *N. oculofasciatus* from Russian waters.

Nautichthys pribilovius (Jordan & Gilbert, 1898) **eyeshade sculpin**

Chukchi Sea off Wainwright to Bering Sea and Aleutian Islands from Attu Island to southeastern Alaska at Steamer Bay; Gulf of Anadyr to Commander Islands and to Okhotsk and Japan seas.

Bottom from near shore to depth of 422 m; usually shallower than 135 m in eastern Bering Sea and Gulf of Alaska; typically found deeper than *N. oculofasciatus* and *N. robustus*.

D VII–X + 22–26; A 15–20; Pec 14–17; Pel I,3; LLp 37–42; Vert 36–38.

- Brown to gray with vague darker blotches; **black bar through eye and across cheek**; first dorsal fin dusky.
- Nape short; base of first dorsal fin enlarged and elevated.
- **Head spines rounded**; nasal spines prominent.
- Four preopercular spines: blunt, first longest.
- Large cirrus on eye; smaller cirri on head spines, posterior end of maxilla, and suborbital stay.
- Spinous dorsal fin base shorter than soft dorsal; spinous dorsal fin height less than twice length of base of fin; **soft dorsal rays 22 or more**.
- Prickles extend onto dorsal fins and pectoral fin.
- Gill membranes broadly attached to isthmus, with no free fold.
- Length to 109 mm TL.

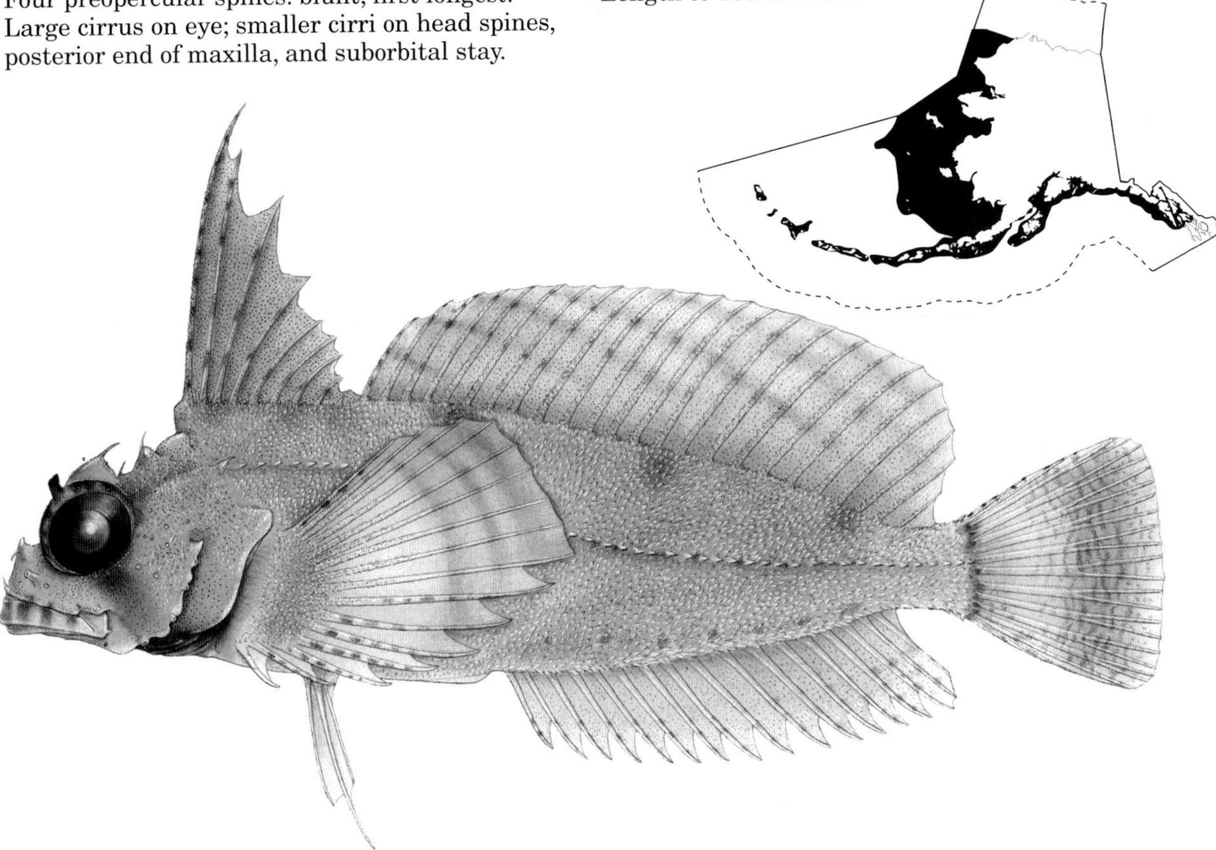

Notes & Sources — *Nautichthys pribilovius* (Jordan & Gilbert in Jordan & Evermann, 1898)
Nautiscus pribilovius Jordan & Gilbert in Jordan & Evermann, 1898
Nautichthys oculofasciatus: Gilbert (1896) and other Bering Sea reports (misidentifications).

Description: Jordan and Evermann 1898:2019–2020 (same as in Jordan and Gilbert 1899); Schmidt 1950:173–174; Andriashev 1954:411–412; Yabe et al. 1983:461–462.

Figure: University of British Columbia, artist P. Drukker-Brammall, Nov. 1965; UBC 61-88, male, 71 mm SL, Chukchi Sea, Alaska.

Range: The type locality is *Albatross station* 3635, in the Bering Sea off St. George Island, Pribilof Islands. Recorded by Gilbert (1896) as *N. oculofasciatus* from Bristol Bay and south of the Alaska Peninsula. Numerous Alaskan records have been published since then, from Wainwright on the Chukchi Sea (Peden 1970) and Attu Island in the Aleutian Islands (Wilimovsky 1964) to Stephens Passage in southeastern Alaska (Quast and Hall 1972). Found to be present but uncommon in the northeastern Chukchi Sea by UAF surveys in 1990 and 1991 (Barber et al. 1997). Specimens with appropriate diagnostic characters obtained in 1991 near Wainwright are among UAM uncataloged materials examined by C.W.M. from the UAF surveys. A specimen from Steamer Bay (AB 84-44) extends the known southern limit of range a few kilometers to the south beyond Quast and Hall's (1972) Stephens Passage record. Sheiko and Fedorov (2000) reported a maximum depth of 422 m off the coast of Russia, but eastern Pacific records are from shallower depths.

Size: R. Baxter, unpubl. data: specimen collected during NMFS survey off Pribilof Islands in Sep. 1985; specimen was not saved, but meristics and other characters recorded indicate the identification is correct. Previously recorded to 88 mm TL by Andriashev (1954).

Nautichthys robustus Peden, 1970 **shortmast sculpin**

Bering Sea and Aleutian Islands to northern Washington.

Near shore to depth of 97 m on sand, pebble, and rock bottoms and in shallow exposed areas.

D VII–IX + 19–21; A 14–16; Pec 14–16; Pel I,3; LLp 35–39; Vert 35.

- Brown to gray with vague darker blotches; **black bar through eye and across cheek**; first dorsal fin dusky.
- Nape short; base of first dorsal fin enlarged and elevated.
- **Head spines sharply pointed**; nasal spines strong and sharp.
- Four preopercular spines: upper 2 short and broad, lower 2 reduced.
- Large cirrus on eye; smaller cirri on head spines, posterior end of maxilla, and suborbital margin.
- Spinous dorsal fin base shorter than soft dorsal; spinous dorsal fin height less than to slightly greater than length of base of fin; **soft dorsal rays 21 or fewer**.
- Prickles dense on body, scattered on dorsal fins, caudal fin, and upper portion of pectoral fin.
- Gill membranes broadly attached to isthmus, with no free fold.
- Length to 80 mm TL.

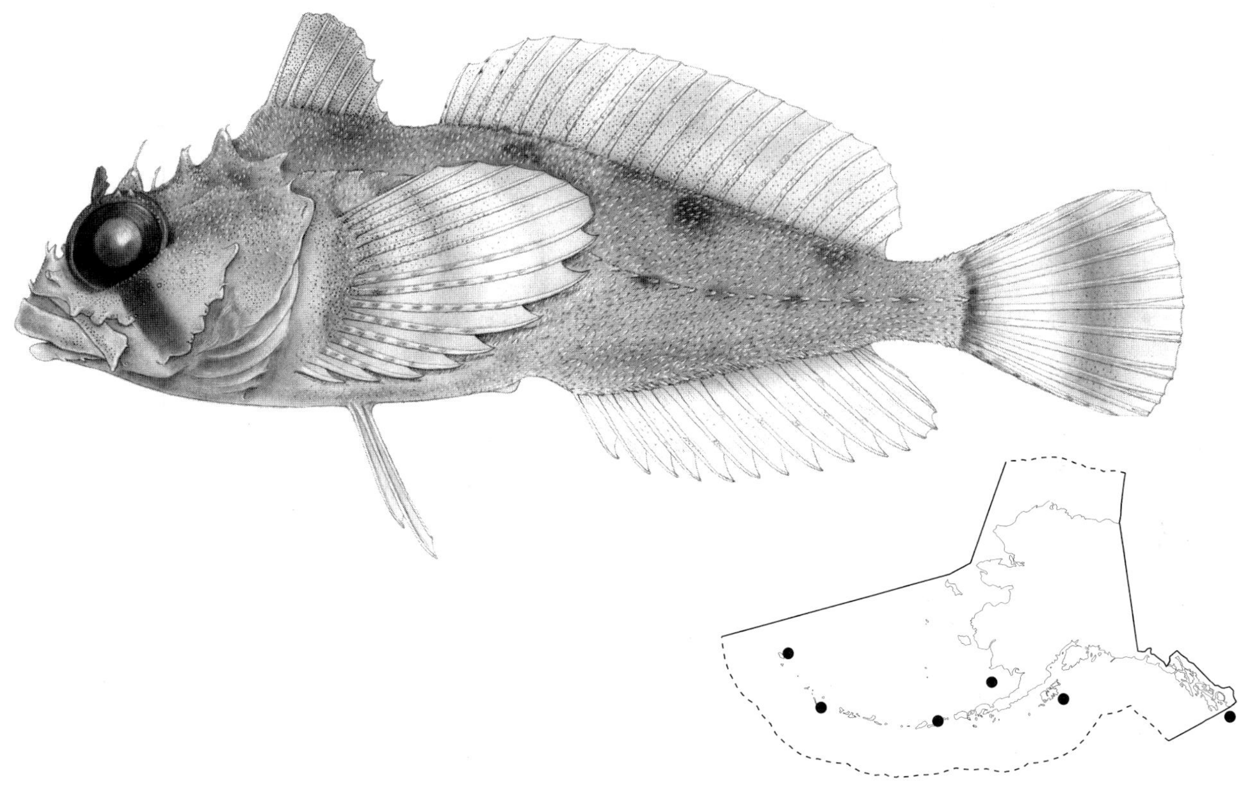

Notes & Sources — *Nautichthys robustus* Peden, 1970

Description: Peden 1970:2–4, tables 1 and 2; Peden 1972; Matarese et al. 1989:454 (vertebral count).

Figure: University of British Columbia, artist P. Drukker-Brammall, Nov. 1965; paratype, UBC 63-886, 39.5 mm SL, Murder Point, Attu Island, Alaska.

Range: Previously recorded from Attu Island (the type locality), Amchitka Island, and Bristol Bay by Peden (1970, 1972). Peden collected additional examples during scuba diving at Captains Bay, Unalaska Island, in August 1980 (e.g., BCPM 980-606 and NMC 81-495). Five specimens in UW 27795 compose the only record from farther north, collected at Norton Sound at 64°20'N, 164°13'W, during a survey using the RV *Miller Freeman* in 1976. The only record from the Gulf of Alaska may be a specimen in SIO 76-300, collected in 1976 off Kodiak at 57°40'N, 150°37'W, depth 97 m. The latter specimen represents a new maximum depth record; previous maximum was 73 m, recorded by Peden (1972) for specimens (USNM 127026) obtained by the *Albatross* off the northern coast of Washington in 1888. This species is not nearly as common in Alaska as *N. pribilovius.* The closest record outside Alaska is from British Columbia at Dixon Entrance off the Queen Charlotte Islands, 54°01'N, 132°35'W (Peden 1970). Sheiko and Fedorov (2000) listed *N. robustus* for the Bering Sea coast of Russia north of Cape Olyutorskiy (general statement, localities not given).

Size: UW 27795 includes a specimen measuring 66 mm SL. Using SL = 82% TL derived from measurements given by Peden (1970) gives 80 mm TL for the UW specimen. Previously recorded to maximum of 64 mm TL by Peden (1970).

Family Psychrolutidae
Fathead sculpins

The family Psychrolutidae includes about 30 species of loose-skinned, demersal marine cottoid fishes called fathead, soft, or blob sculpins. Their tadpole shape and movable skin over a clear, gelatinous layer gives them the general appearance of snailfishes (family Liparidae), except for lacking a pelvic disk. They are widely distributed in temperate to arctic regions from inshore shallow waters to depths as great as 2,800 m. Eight or nine species, possibly more, occur in Alaskan waters. Two of the described species may be synonymous, and there may be additional, undescribed species.

Connection of the operculomandibular sensory canal to the infraorbital canal and absence of pores between actinosts distinguish psychrolutids from other members of the suborder Cottoidei (Yabe 1985), while the presence of well-developed bony arches, which may bear spines, over the lateral line system of the head distinguishes psychrolutids from all other members of the superfamily Cottoidea (Nelson 1982).

Characters which as a complex distinguish the family from other cottoids include: interorbital space usually wider than diameter of eye; cranial arch spines present or absent; preopercular spines usually absent; spinous and soft-rayed portions of dorsal fin usually continuous, and their bases, especially that of the spinous dorsal, covered by skin and gelatinous tissue; pelvic fins with 1 spine and 3 soft rays each, their bases buried in skin; body scaleless or with plates bearing prickles; cirri present or absent; lateral line opening through 20 or fewer widely spaced pores in a single row; palatine teeth absent, vomerine teeth present or absent; 7 branchiostegal rays; gill membranes completely attached to the isthmus or forming a free fold posteriorly; 28–39 vertebrae; swim bladder absent; and genital papilla present in males of some species.

The largest fathead sculpin is the giant blobsculpin, *Psychrolutes phrictus,* with a maximum recorded length of about 70 cm (27.6 inches). Adult tadpole sculpins, *P. paradoxus,* attain 7 cm (2.75 inches) total length.

The Sadko sculpin, *Cottunculus sadko,* is a new addition to the inventory of Alaskan fish species. Specimens from the Beaufort Sea off Alaska examined by Nelson (1982) represent an extension of the known range from the Kara Sea. *Psychrolutes phrictus,* described in the late 1970s (Stein and Bond 1978) from specimens taken off Oregon, is another new addition to the inventory. It has been collected from deep waters of the southern Bering Sea off the Aleutian Islands.

The darkfin sculpin, *Malacocottus zonurus,* is relatively common in the Bering Sea and Gulf of Alaska. The blackfin sculpin, *M. kincaidi,* is absent from Alaska, and may be synonymous with *M. zonurus.* Described from the Trinity Islands, Alaska, *Malacocottus zonurus* Bean, 1890, was diagnosed as having an accessory preopercular spine. This spine was lacking in an otherwise similar species, *M. kincaidi* Gilbert & Thompson, 1905, from Puget Sound, Washington. Through time, presence of the accessory spine became associated in the literature with the wrong species (e.g., Clemens and Wilby 1949, 1961; Hart 1973; Coad 1995). The mixup stems, in part, from Watanabe (1960), who described *M. zonurus* under the name *M. kincaidi* with Bean, incorrectly, as author. The two species names appear to have been used interchangeably by some museum workers. Quast and Hall (1972) reported only *M. kincaidi* from Alaska. However, all Alaskan specimens identified as *M. kincaidi* that we and Vogt (1987b) examined are referable to *M. zonurus.* The name *M. zonurus* Bean, 1890 has priority over *M. kincaidi* Gilbert & Thompson, 1905.

Shinohara et al. (1992) found presence of the accessory spine to be variable in the Asian species *M. gibber,* and concluded that this character has no taxonomic significance. Observing variability in this character in the type specimens of *M. zonurus,* and finding no apparent differences in other characters between type specimens of *M. zonurus* and *M. kincaidi,* we considered classifying *M. kincaidi* in the synonymy of *M. zonurus.* However, we did not examine many specimens identified as *M. kincaidi* from Puget Sound. *Malacocottus kincaidi* may represent populations of *M. zonurus* that more often than not lack an accessory preopercular spine, or it could be a species distinct from *M. zonurus* but inadequately described. Shinohara et al. (1992) believed one of the best characters distinguishing *M. gibber* from *M. zonurus* to be the condition of the cranial bony arches (narrow versus broad). This and other characters should be compared in specimens of *Malacocottus* from Puget Sound and British Columbia.

The classification of Psychrolutidae used herein follows Jackson and Nelson (1998), except for addition of the whitetail sculpin, *Malacocottus aleuticus.* This species was described by Smith (1904) on the basis of one specimen collected from the Bering Sea north of the Rat Islands. The unique holotype was lost before the species description was published (Smith 1904). Smith erected a new genus, *Thecopterus,* for this species. However, specimens collected in recent years from such widely separated areas as Prince William Sound, Alaska, and the Sea of Okhotsk off Russia and Japan likely represent Smith's species, and they do not differ in any significant way from *Malacocottus*. A team of investigators are developing a redescription of *M. aleuticus* and intend to designate a neotype from this material (Mecklenburg et al. 2001). Richardson and Bond (1978), from a collection of larvae and juveniles, suggested that a second species (in addition to *M. zonurus*) with an accessory preopercular spine may exist in the eastern North Pacific. *Malacocottus aleuticus* may be that species. Its relation to *M. gibber* and other *Malacocottus* species is not clear.

Key to the Psychrolutidae of Alaska

1 Spines present on head or preopercle, or conspicuous cirri present on lower jaw; interorbital width (between exposed portion of eyes) less than 2 times diameter of exposed eye . . . . . (2)

1 Spines absent from head and preopercle and conspicuous cirri absent from lower jaw; interorbital width more than 2 times diameter of exposed eye . . . . . (7)

2 (1) Gill membranes attached to each other and free from isthmus posteriorly . . . . . (3)

2 Gill membranes attached to isthmus without free posterior fold . . . . . (4)

3 (2) Head and preopercular spines present; dorsal fins separate or only slightly connected . . . . . *Dasycottus setiger,* page 516

3 Head and preopercular spines absent; dorsal fins continuous or slightly notched . . . . . *Eurymen gyrinus,* page 517

4 (2) Head spines strong; preopercular spines blunt and crestlike; body covered with numerous spiny tubercles . . . . . *Cottunculus sadko,* page 518

4 Head spines inconspicuous; preopercular spines sharp and long; body not covered with spinous tubercles (fine prickles present in some specimens) . . . . . (5)

5 (4) Caudal peduncle and caudal fin pale, without dark bands . . . . . *Malacocottus aleuticus,* page 519

5 Caudal peduncle and caudal fin with dark bands . . . . . (6)

6 (5) Laterally directed accessory preopercular spine usually present at base of second major preopercular spine . . . . . *Malacocottus zonurus,* page 520

6 Laterally directed accessory preopercular spine absent . . . . . *Malacocottus kincaidi,* page 521

7 (1) Spinous portion of dorsal fin not distinctly lower than soft-rayed portion; dorsal and anal fins extending onto caudal fin base; pectoral fin rays 14–18 . . . . . *Psychrolutes sigalutes,* page 522

7 Spinous portion of dorsal fin distinctly lower than soft-rayed portion; dorsal and anal fins free of caudal fin base; pectoral fin rays 19–26 . . . . . (8)

8 (7) Head large, more than 40% SL; skin relatively tough and thick; no distinct bands or other patterns; maximum TL about 70 cm . . . . . *Psychrolutes phrictus,* page 523

8 Head length less than 40% SL; skin loose and thin; distinct bands, bars, and patches; maximum TL about 6.5 cm . . . . . *Psychrolutes paradoxus,* page 524

Dasycottus setiger Bean, 1890 **spinyhead sculpin**

Bering Sea from Navarin Canyon and Aleutian Islands to Pacific Ocean off Washington; western Bering Sea to Commander Islands and to Pacific coast of northern Honshu, Sea of Okhotsk, and Sea of Japan.

Soft bottom at depths of 15–850 m, usually on middle shelf to upper slope at 50–300 m.

D VIII–XI,13–16; A 12–16; Pec 22–26; Pel I,3; LLp 13–16; GR 9–15; Vert 33–35.

- Pinkish gray with gray to dark brown blotches and bars on head, body, and fins.
- Head large; lower jaw protruding; snout broad and humped.
- Maxilla extending to posterior edge of eye; interorbital space about same as or not much wider than eye, concave.
- **Four spines, variously directed, above eye; occipital spine large, single or double.**
- **Four preopercular spines.**
- **Numerous cirri scattered on head and body.**
- **Dorsal fins separate or slightly connected;** bases of fins covered with loose skin.
- Spiny scales at base of spinous dorsal fin in 1 or 2 irregular rows; scattered spiny plates below lateral line.
- Vomerine teeth present; palatine teeth absent.
- Gill membranes united to each other, forming broad fold across isthmus.
- Length to 450 mm TL.

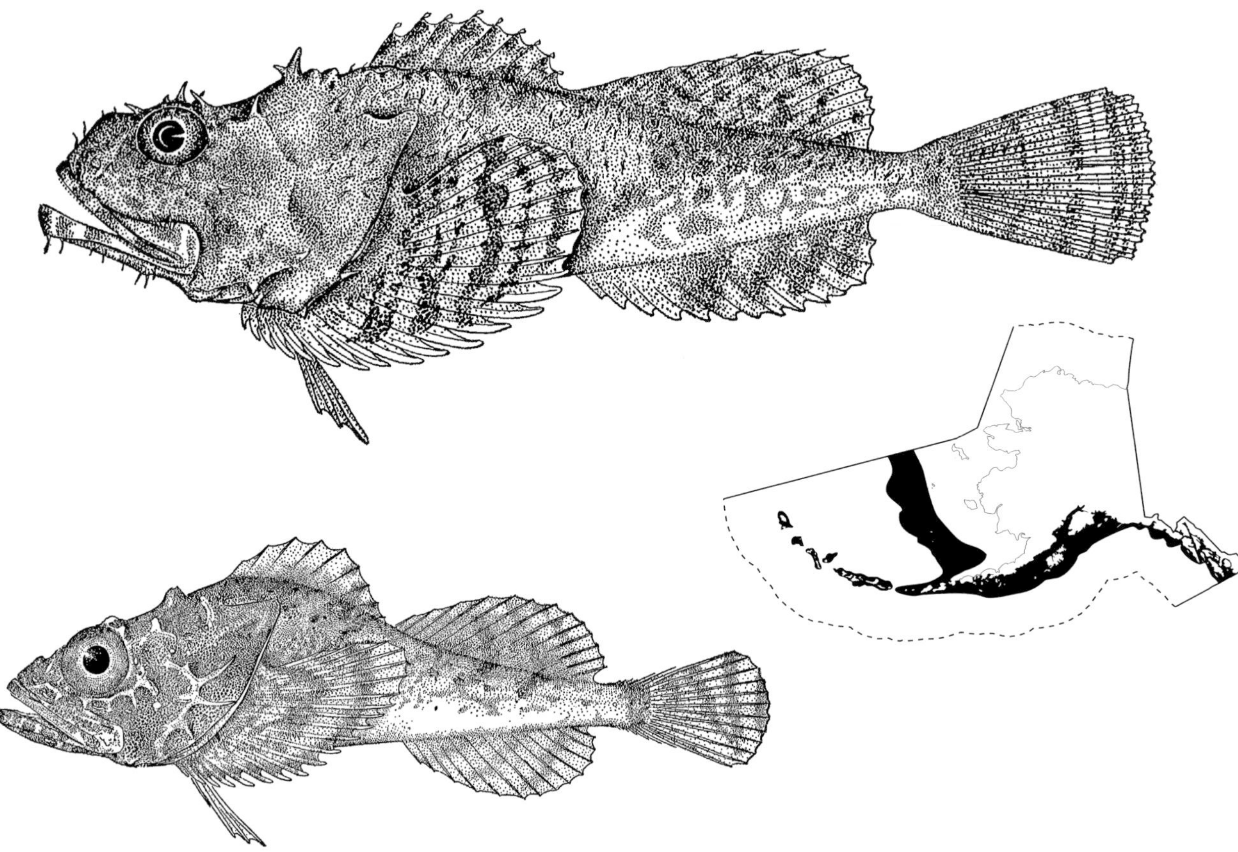

Notes & Sources — *Dasycottus setiger* Bean, 1890

Description: Gilbert 1896:411; Watanabe 1960:175–177; Hart 1973:497–498; Nelson 1982:1473; Yabe in Amaoka et al. 1983:214; Yabe in Masuda et al. 1984:330; Lindberg and Krasyukova 1987:268.

Figures: Upper: Hart 1973:497; 20 cm TL, Alaska. Lower: Jordan and Starks 1895, pl. 83; 48 mm TL, Unalaska.

Range: This species was named and described from specimens collected off Sitkalidak Island, Alaska, *Albatross* station 2855, at a depth of 126 m (Bean 1890). Allen and Smith (1988) mapped 2,802 records of occurrence in the northeastern Pacific and Bering Sea from 30 years of resource surveys. Well represented in museum collections from within the depicted range. Depth range: Fedorov and Sheiko 2002. Tokranov and Orlov (2001a) reported spatial and bathymetric distribution of *D. setiger* in the Pacific waters off southeastern Kamchatka and the northern Kuril islands. There, most catches were in the range of 100–300 m. In the eastern Bering Sea, Aleutian Islands, and Gulf of Alaska, Allen and Smith (1988) found that most catches were from 50 to 200 m.

Size: Tokranov and Orlov 2001b: individuals caught in the western Bering Sea in 1997 attained lengths to 45 cm TL. The largest record from the eastern Bering Sea may be a specimen collected in 1983 that measured 305 mm SL and 378 mm TL (R. Baxter, unpubl. data); the specimen was not saved, but data recorded support the identification.

Eurymen gyrinus Gilbert & Burke, 1912 **smoothcheek sculpin**

Chukchi and Bering seas to Aleutian Islands and to western Gulf of Alaska at Kodiak Island; to Commander Islands, Sea of Okhotsk, Sea of Japan to South Korea, and Pacific Ocean to Honshu Island.

Bottom at depths of 14–494 m.

D VIII–IX,19–25 = 27–33; A 15–18; Pec 22–27; Pel I,3; LLp 15–20; GR 8–11; Vert 35–39.

- Coloration highly variable according to habitat; broad dark band at base of caudal fin usually present even in smallest specimens.
- Maxilla extending to rear edge of pupil to beyond eye; interorbital space about same diameter as eye, flat.
- **Head and preopercular spines absent**.
- Many short cirri on top of head, cheeks, and operculum; wide, flat, **forked and doubled cirri at posterior end of maxilla and on lower jaw.**
- **Spinous and soft dorsal fins continuous, with notch between portions and some or all spines free in juveniles and young adults**.
- Many small, raised, white-rimmed pores on head.
- Vomerine teeth present; palatine teeth absent.
- Gill membranes united to each other, attached to isthmus anteriorly and forming narrow to broad fold across isthmus posteriorly.
- Length to 388 mm TL.

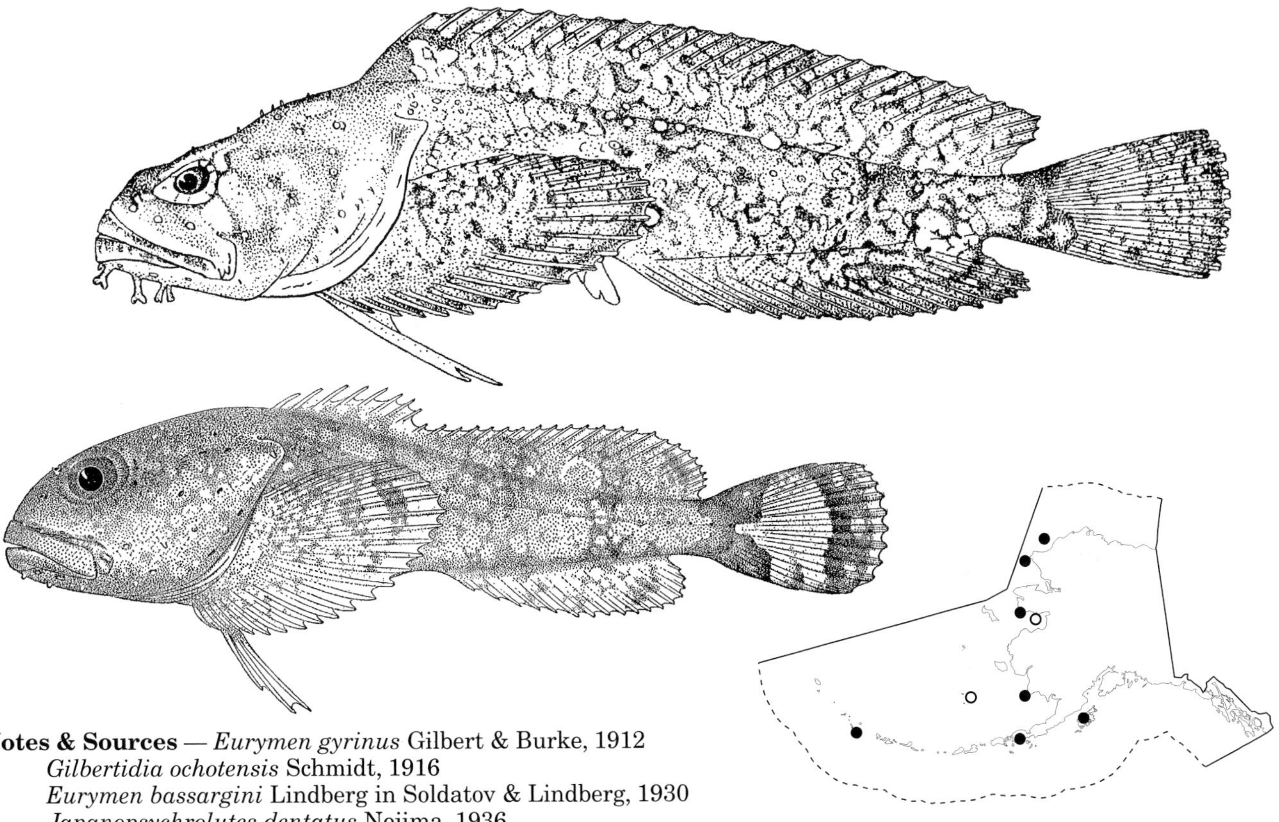

Notes & Sources — *Eurymen gyrinus* Gilbert & Burke, 1912
Gilbertidia ochotensis Schmidt, 1916
Eurymen bassargini Lindberg in Soldatov & Lindberg, 1930
Japanopsychrolutes dentatus Nojima, 1936

Description: Gilbert and Burke 1912a:64–65; Soldatov and Lindberg 1930:282–287; Schmidt 1937b; Watanabe 1960:188–193; Nelson 1982:1478–1480; Lindberg and Krasyukova 1987:265–267. Dorsal fin spines and soft rays are not easily distinguishable because of skin covering and are usually included in one count.

Figures: Upper: Lindberg and Krasyukova 1987, fig. 171, after Soldatov and Lindberg 1930; 320 mm TL, Peter the Great Bay, Sea of Japan. Lower: Gilbert and Burke 1912a, fig. 14; holotype (unique), 50 mm TL, *Albatross* station 4795, off Avachinskaya Bay, east Kamchatka.

Range: Northernmost records are from UAF surveys of eastern Chukchi Sea in 1990 and 1991. Barber et al. (1997) reported this species was caught during the surveys, but that paper did not give catch data. Among UAM uncataloged specimens examined by C.W.M. are: one (124 mm TL) from 70°00'N, 164°56'W, depth 38 m, 22 Sep. 1991; and two (105–114 mm TL) from 68°25'N, 166°40'W, depth 17 m, 3 Sep. 1991. Alaskan records also include: Aleutian Islands at Constantine Harbor, Amchitka Island (Wilimovsky 1964; UBC 63-300); Bering Sea at Cape Newenham and Gulf of Alaska at Larsen Bay, Kodiak Island (Quast and Hall 1972; AB 66-1139, 71-368); Bering Strait about 70 km southeast of Sinuk, Seward Peninsula, at 64°20'N, 165°20'W (Nelson 1982; NMC 79-633). Another specimen (UW 25685) was collected off Cape Newenham in 1981. USNM 119387 comprises two specimens collected in 1940 from Canoe Bay, Alaska Peninsula. Specimens identified as *E. gyrinus* by R. Baxter (unpubl. data) were taken by NMFS surveys at Norton Sound and the Pribilof Islands (no voucher specimens, but meristics and other recorded data are appropriate for this species). Kim et al. (1993) reported the first collections from Korea.

Cottunculus sadko Essipov, 1937 — Sadko sculpin

Beaufort Sea off Alaska; rare records from other areas of Arctic Ocean, including Kara Sea and vicinity of Faroe Islands.

Muddy bottom at depths of 300–839 m; deep troughs and upper part of continental slope.

D VIII–IX,13–15; A 11; Pec 18; Pel I,3; LLp about 11; Vert 28–29.

- Dark band across head; body with 3 vague dark gray bands against grayish background; pectoral fin dark gray with light margin.
- Head large, wide, deep; interorbital space wider than eye diameter, flat.
- **Head spines strong**.
- **Four crestlike preopercular spines separating enormous grooves** for openings of cephalic lateral line system.
- Cirri absent from head and body.
- **Spinous and soft-rayed portions of dorsal fin continuous, spinous portion low**, buried.
- Body covered with numerous prickles arranged in groups forming spinous tubercles not touching each other.
- Vomerine teeth present; palatine teeth absent.
- Gill membranes broadly attached to isthmus, without posterior fold.
- Length to 166 mm TL.

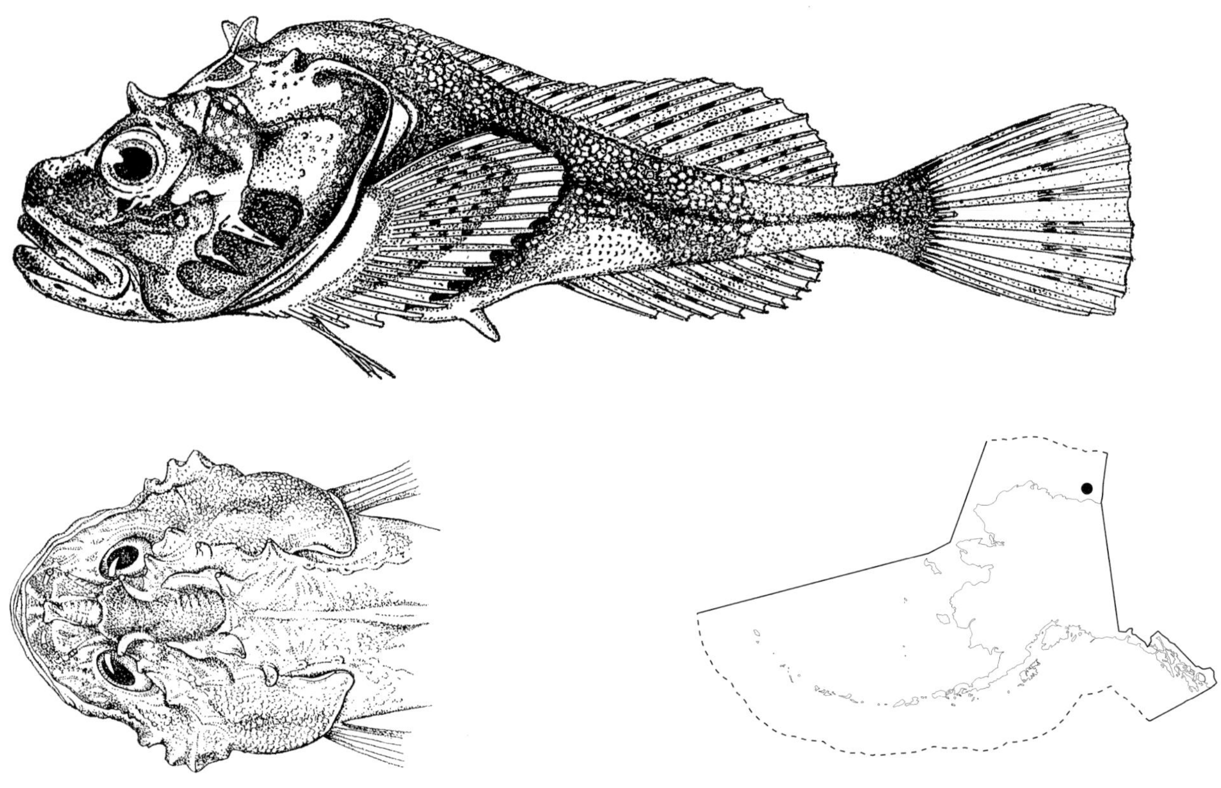

Notes & Sources — *Cottunculus sadko* Essipov, 1937

Another Arctic Ocean fathead sculpin species, *Cottunculus microps* Collett, 1875, is distinguishable from *C. sadko* by having more than 12 lateral line pores, rather than fewer; head in dorsal view roundish, not markedly compressed anteriorly as in *C. sadko*; and blunt occipital spines, not pointed as in *C. sadko* (Nelson 1989).

Some of the first specimens of this species known to science were collected by a Russian expedition exploring the depths of the central Polar Basin using the vessel *Sadko*.

Description: Essipov 1937:95–96; Andriashev 1954:419–421; Nelson 1982:1474–1475, 1478; Fedorov and Nelson in Whitehead et al. 1986:1271–1272.

Figures: Essipov 1937, fig. 2; type, male, 166 mm TL, Voronin Trough in the Kara Sea. Dorsal view of head: Andriashev 1954, fig. 237; same specimen.

Range: One record from Alaska: Beaufort Sea at 70°43'N, 143°43'W (Nelson 1982; NMC 74-275). Nearest records outside of Alaska are the specimens described by Essipov (1937) and Andriashev (1954) from the northern part of the Kara Sea. Very rare.

Malacocottus aleuticus (Smith, 1904) **whitetail sculpin**

Prince William Sound; Bering Sea north of Rat Islands; Pacific Ocean off southeastern Kamchatka and Sea of Okhotsk off southwest coast of Kamchatka, eastern Sakhalin Island, and Hokkaido Island.

Holotype dredged from sand and broken shell bottom at depth of 494 m; others taken by bottom trawls to 560 m, and pelagically in nets towed as deep as 500–1,000 m over bottom depths to 3,500 m.

D VIII–X,13–15; A 10–13; Pec 19–22; Pel I,2 or 3; GR 6–11; Vert 31–32.

- Body minutely speckled with black; broad black bands from soft dorsal fin to anal fin and behind pectoral axil; **caudal peduncle and fin white**.
- Head large, broad; body short, compressed, deep, tapering abruptly from origin of first dorsal.
- Maxilla extending to anterior edge of pupil; interorbital space much less than eye diameter.
- No head spines; protuberances weak to moderate.
- **Four preopercular spines, almost always with an accessory (fifth) spine in front of the second and directed laterally**; first two primary spines and accessory spine the longest, and enclosing a triangular space; third and fourth spines smaller, fourth usually obsolete.
- Cirri absent, except sometimes over eye.
- Dorsal fins continuous at base or indistinctly separate; bases of dorsal, anal, pectoral, and pelvic fins covered with loose skin; pelvic fin very small, less than pupil diameter, sometimes difficult to discern buried in loose layer.
- Skin smooth, without spiny tubercles or papillae.
- Vomerine and palatine teeth absent.
- Gill membranes broadly attached to isthmus, without free posterior fold.
- Length to 98 mm TL.

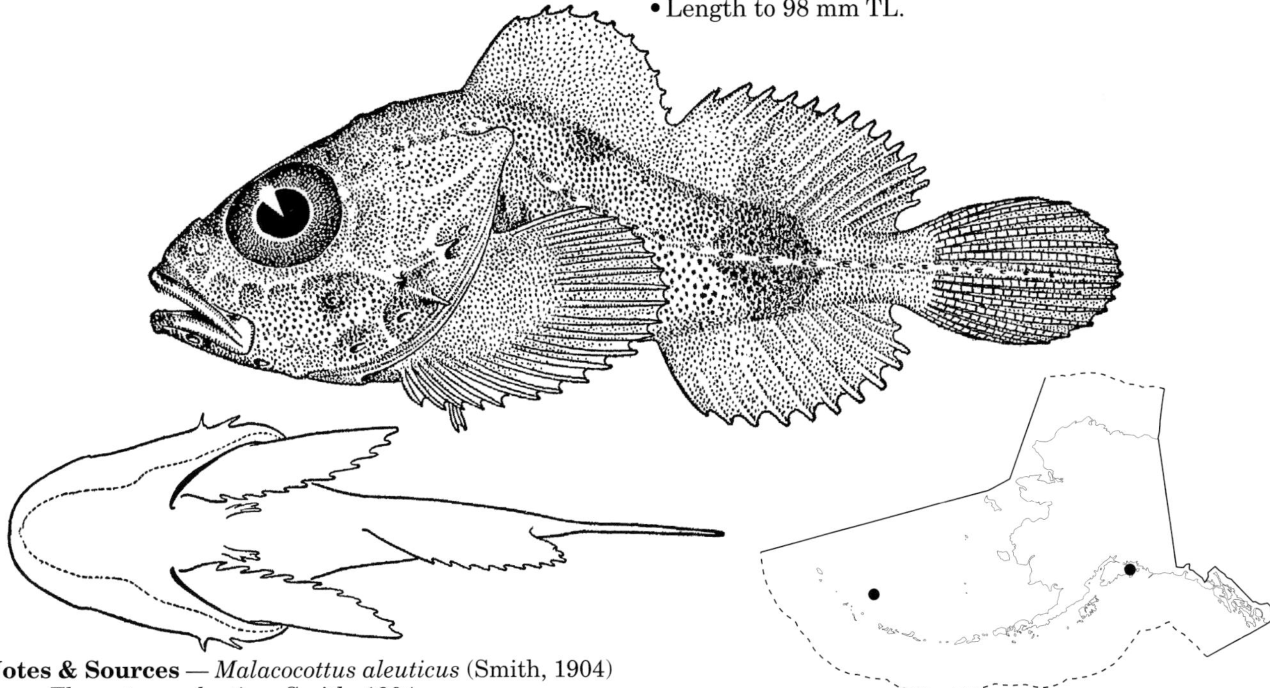

Notes & Sources — *Malacocottus aleuticus* (Smith, 1904)
Thecopterus aleuticus Smith, 1904

Smith (1904) observed a resemblance to *Malacocottus* but considered the presence of vomerine teeth, lack of cirri, and connected dorsal fins to be significant differences. From new material it appears that Smith mistook papillae in the roof of the mouth for vomerine teeth and that the other differences are variable within the species. The genus name, *Thecopterus,* is from the Greek for "sheath" and "fin," evidently in allusion to the loose skin covering the body and fins. The loose layer is marked in most specimens but this feature, too, is variable in species of *Malacocottus.*

Description: Smith 1904; B. A. Sheiko, K. L. Jackson, J. S. Nelson, and C.W.M., data from UAM 2812, UAMZ 7685 and 7686, and KIE uncataloged (see Range). Smith (1904) reported I,2 for the pelvic fins, but stated that the unusual formula could not be verified because the specimen was mislaid. The new specimens invariably have I,3, the usual formula for psychrolutids.

Figures: Smith 1904, fig. 1; holotype (unique), 40 mm TL, Bering Sea north of Rat Islands, Aleutian Islands.

Range: Described from one specimen dredged from the bottom at *Albatross* station 3785, 150 miles north of Rat Islands (Smith 1904). Two specimens (UAM 2812; 46 and 48 mm TL) collected in 1983 by vertical tow from 200 m to the surface at Eshamy Bay, Prince William Sound, 60°29'N, 146°51'W, are the only other Alaskan record (R. Baxter, unpubl. data; confirmed by our team). Fedorov and Parin (1998) identified a specimen from southeastern Kamchatka as *Thecopterus aleuticus.* UAMZ 7685 and UAMZ 7686 (54 and 63 mm TL) were collected from the Okhotsk Sea off Hokkaido. B. A. Sheiko provided 9 specimens (KIE uncataloged; 63–80 mm TL) collected in 2000 from the Sea of Okhotsk off southern Kamchatka, and reported the existence of several other lots from the central and southern Okhotsk Sea in ZIN and other Russian Academy of Sciences collections; the specimens were taken in both bottom and midwater trawls.

Size: B. A. Sheiko, pers. comm., 8 Aug. 2001: ZIN 49077.

Malacocottus zonurus Bean, 1890 — darkfin sculpin

Bering Sea and Aleutian Islands to Pacific Ocean off Washington; to Commander Islands and to Kuril Islands, Sea of Okhotsk, Sea of Japan to South Korea, and Pacific Ocean to Honshu Island, Japan.

Bottom at depths of 95–1,980 m, usually on outer continental shelf and upper slope at 100–500 m.

D VIII–X + 12–15; A 9–12; Pec 19–23; Pel I,3; LLp 12–20; GR 4–9; Vert 30–33.

- Light grayish brown, with vague dark brown to blackish bands; fins with dark and light bands and white margins; **caudal fin with black bands**.
- Maxilla extending to mideye; interorbital space narrower than eye diameter, shallowly concave.
- Nasal and head spines obsolete; occiput with pair of blunt protuberances.
- **Four preopercular spines, almost always with an accessory (fifth) spine in front of the second and directed laterally**; first three spines typically long and strong; fourth spine shortest but strong, in some specimens partially concealed.
- One long cirrus on opercular angle and several shorter cirri on upper portion of eyeball, nape, opercle, and jaws.
- Dorsal fins separate but touching or nearly touching; bases of fins covered with loose skin.
- Head and upper anterior part of body with sparsely distributed fine prickles.
- Vomerine and palatine teeth absent.
- Gill membranes broadly attached to isthmus, without free posterior fold.
- Length to 350 mm TL.

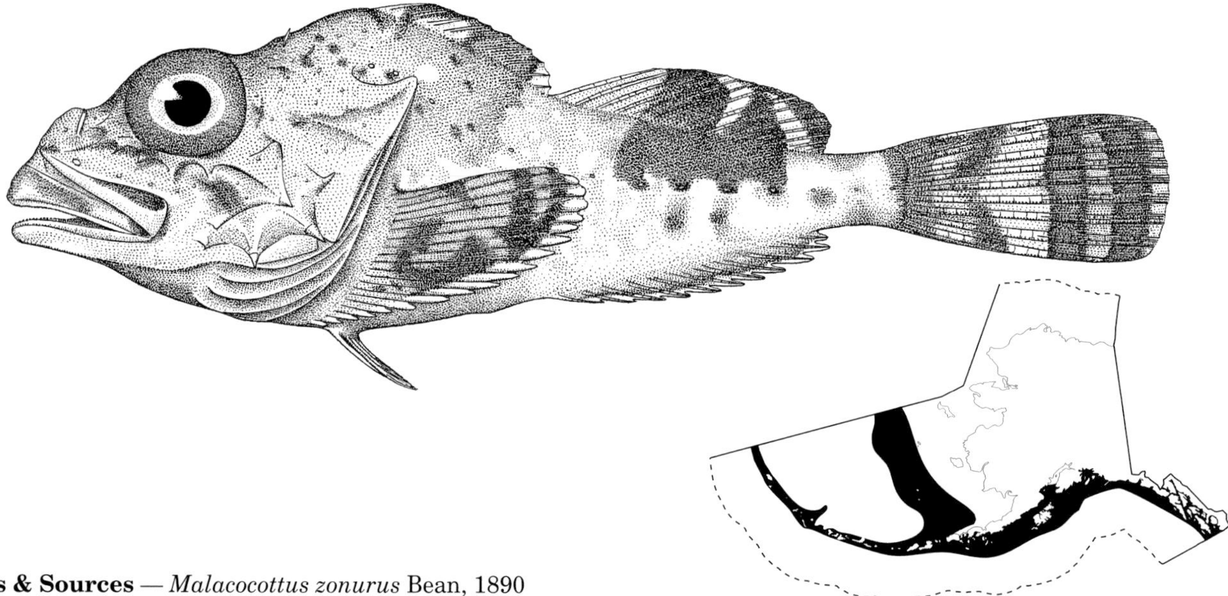

Notes & Sources — *Malacocottus zonurus* Bean, 1890

"*Malacocottus kincaidi* Bean, 1890": Watanabe 1960 (incorrect combination).

Some authors, evidently seeing no difference between the two nominal species *M. zonurus* and *M. kincaidi,* have used the names interchangeably. However, the name *M. zonurus* Bean, 1890 has priority over *M. kincaidi* Gilbert & Thompson, 1905. While noting that recognition of both species is questionable, Peden (1998) flagged the reputed distinction by coining a new vernacular, spinycheek blobsculpin, for *M. zonurus.*

Description: Bean 1890b:42–43 and Gilbert 1896:411 (both repeated in Jordan and Evermann 1898:1994–1995); Nelson 1982:1473; Yabe in Amaoka et al. 1983:215; Lindberg and Krasyukova 1987:271–273; Shinohara et al. 1992. Sometimes, but rarely, the accessory spine is obsolete (noted in ABL, SIO, and UAM specimens), and in the two "cotypes" examined (in USNM 44643; 55 and 57 mm TL) 1 of 4 sides lacked the accessory spine. The *accessory spine* referred to here and by other authors on *Malacocottus* is the same as a *secondary spine* as defined by Jackson and Nelson (1998).

Figure: Smithsonian Institution, NMNH, Division of Fishes, artist S. F. Denton, 4 May 1889; type, 121 mm TL, *Albatross* station 2853, off Trinity Islands, Alaska. Modified to correct the dorsal fin rays. Original illustration has branched dorsal rays, but bears the handwritten notation: "Dorsal rays should be simple." The beaklike mouth is inaccurate. This shape is not evident in specimens, including the type series.

Range: Bean (1890b) described specimens from the Trinity Islands, Alaska, and Gilbert (1896) from Unimak Pass. Specimens from Alaska in museum collections identified as *M. kincaidi* are *M. zonurus.* The ranges depicted by Allen and Smith (1988) from NMFS resource surveys indicate catches were misidentified; the range and number of occurrences given for *M. kincaidi* are more likely for *M. zonurus.* Evermann and Goldsborough (1907) were correct to attribute Alaskan records to *M. zonurus,* not in error as asserted by Clemens and Wilby (1949, 1961). The latter authors and Hart (1973) gave incorrect descriptions of *M. kincaidi,* which would have resulted in identification errors. Depth range: Yabe (in Amaoka et al. 1983), Shinohara et al. (1992).

Size: Tokranov and Orlov 2001a,b: specimens from Pacific waters off the northern Kuril Islands and southeastern Kamchatka reached 35 cm TL. Largest record from Alaska may be 31 cm TL for a specimen from the Aleutian Islands, collected in 1986 (R. Baxter, unpubl. data); specimen was not saved, but data recorded confirm the identification.

Malacocottus kincaidi Gilbert & Thompson, 1905 **blackfin sculpin**

Not confirmed from Alaska; British Columbia to Puget Sound, Washington.

Bottom in shallow water.

D VIII–X + 13–15; A 11–12; Pec 19–22; Pel I,3; LLp 14–17; GR 8–12; Vert 31–34.

- Light grayish brown, with vague dark brown to blackish bands; fins with dark and light bands and white margins; **caudal fin with black bands**.
- Body less robust than in *M. zonurus.*
- Maxilla extending to mideye; interorbital space narrower than eye diameter, shallowly concave.
- Nasal and head spines obsolete; occipital protuberances weak to moderate.
- Two slender diverging spines on upper angle of preopercle, with a third below and anterior to them directed ventrally and anteriorly; fourth spine small or obscure; **usually no trace of accessory spine at base of second preopercular spine**.
- Cirri absent from head and eyeball or fewer than in *M. zonurus.*
- Dorsal fins separate but touching or nearly touching; bases of fins covered with loose skin.
- Fine prickles present on head and body.
- Vomerine and palatine teeth absent.
- Gill membranes broadly attached to isthmus, without free posterior fold.
- Length to 106 mm TL.

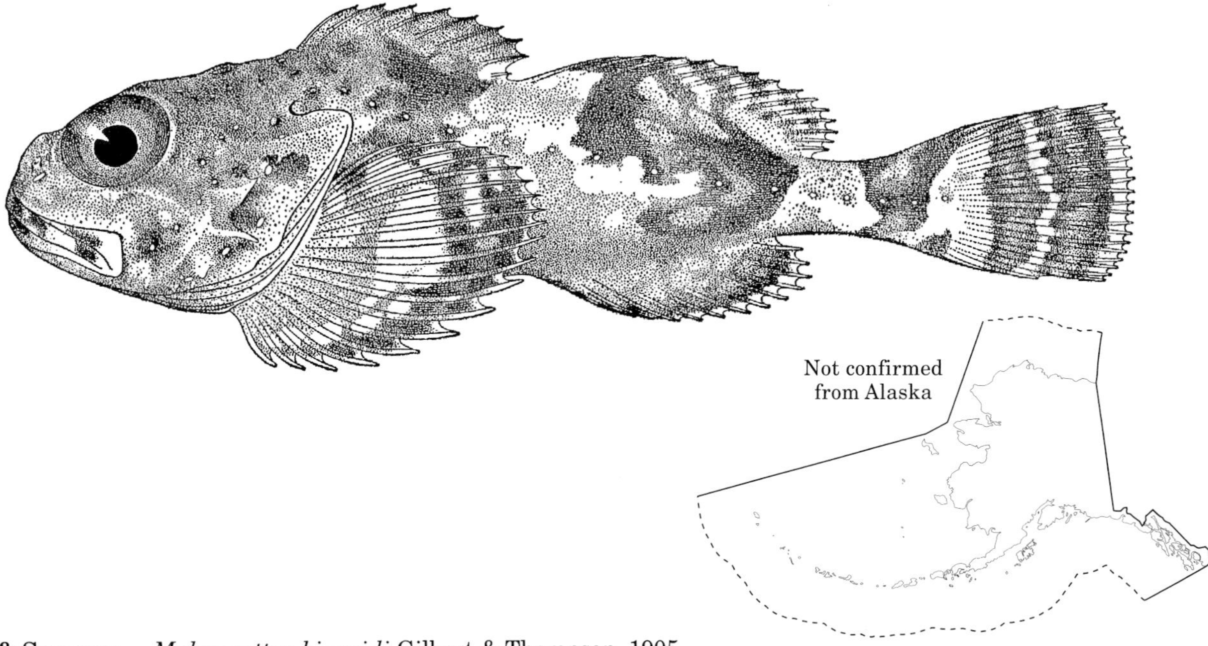

Notes & Sources — *Malacocottus kincaidi* Gilbert & Thompson, 1905

Often confused with *M. zonurus* Bean, 1890, and possibly a junior synonym of that species (e.g., Nelson 1982). Because of the confusion, most published accounts under the name *M. kincaidi* include characters of *M. zonurus.* Therefore, our account for *M. kincaidi* is based only on the original description and on museum lots in which specimens lack the accessory preopercular spine (the only possibly significant difference given in the original species descriptions).

Description: Gilbert and Thompson 1905:979–981; Nelson 1982:1473 (UAMZ specimens only). Rae Baxter, unpubl. data: OSU 7072 (3 specimens; 104–106 mm TL). Keith L. Jackson, unpubl. data: UAMZ 3186.7 (3; 41–46 mm SL), UAMZ 4497(9; 42–52 mm SL). One specimen in UAMZ 4497 has an accessory preopercular spine on the left side. All others cited here lack the accessory spine.

Figure: Gilbert and Thompson 1905, fig. 2; 65 mm TL, from Brinnon, Hood Canal, Washington. The illustrations in Clemens and Wilby (1949, 1961), Hart (1973), and Coad (1995) look like *M. zonurus* with the accessory preopercular spine visible.

Range: The type series (11 specimens) was collected from Hood Canal, Puget Sound, Washington. Specimens examined by R. Baxter (unpubl. data) were also from Hood Canal (OSU 7072); and by Nelson (1982) and K. L. Jackson (unpubl. data) were from British Columbia at Trevor Channel, Vancouver Island (UAMZ 3186.7) and Malaspina Strait, Strait of Georgia (UAMZ 4497). Occurrence in Alaska has not been confirmed. Vogt (1987) examined all specimens from Alaska in the UAM collection identified as *M. kincaidi* and concluded they are specimens of *M. zonurus*; examining them in 2000, C.W.M. concurred. The numerous Alaskan specimens at ABL originally identified as *M. kincaidi* are *M. zonurus* (checked by C.W.M.). Other museums, such as RBCM, SIO, UBC, and UW, have Alaskan specimens once identified as *M. kincaidi* but later referred to *M. zonurus* by other researchers. In more than 30 years of fieldwork in Alaska, Baxter (1990ms, unpubl. data) collected many specimens he identified as *M. zonurus* but found none referable to *M. kincaidi.* Depth range is not clear from the literature because of confusion with *M. zonurus.* Gilbert and Thompson (1905) noted that *M. kincaidi* was "easily dredged in shallow water" in Puget Sound.

Size: R. Baxter, unpubl. data: OSU 7072. Greater lengths have been reported, but they may not represent *M. kincaidi.*

Psychrolutes sigalutes (Jordan & Starks, 1895) **soft sculpin**

Aleutian Islands off Adak Island to southern Puget Sound, Washington; Commander Islands.

Rocky areas, among sponges, and silty bottom, from near shore to depth of 225 m.

D VII–IX,14–19; A 12–15; Pec 14–18; Pel I,3; LLp 11–14; GR 8–13; Vert 33–35.

- Pinkish gray to dark brownish gray, with darker marbling; eye orange.
- Especially liparid-like in appearance, except for lack of pelvic disk.
- Maxilla extending to rear edge of eye, posterior portion buried in skin; interorbital area flexible, broad, convex to nearly flat.
- Head and preopercular spines absent.
- **Spinous and soft-rayed portions of dorsal fin continuous and same height**; dorsal and anal fins and bases of pectoral and pelvic fins buried in skin; **dorsal and anal fins extending onto base of caudal fin**; fewer pectoral fin rays than in *P. phrictus* and *P. paradoxus*.
- Skin covered with small papillae.
- Vomerine and palatine teeth absent.
- Gill membranes broadly attached to isthmus, without free posterior fold.
- Length to 83 mm TL.

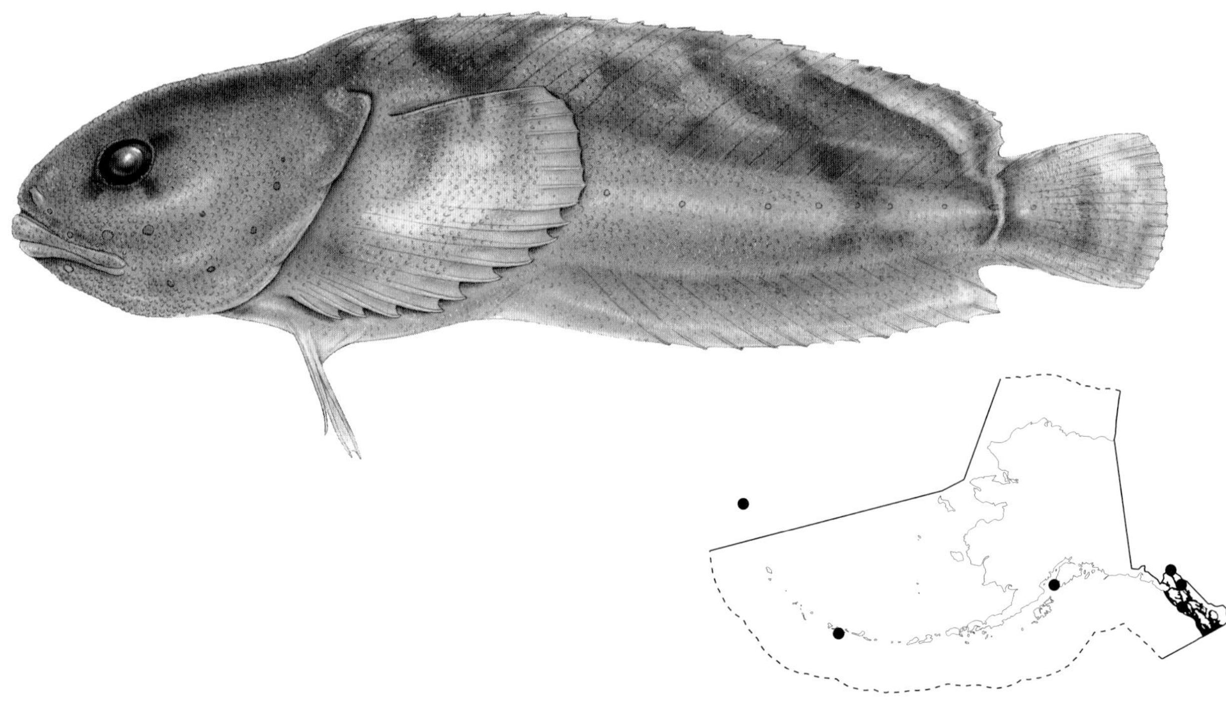

Notes & Sources — *Psychrolutes sigalutes* (Jordan & Starks, 1895)
Gilbertina sigalutes Jordan & Starks, 1895
Gilbertina, preoccupied in Mollusca, was replaced by *Gilbertidia.* Nelson (1982) placed *G. sigalutes* in *Psychrolutes,* but some researchers retain genus *Gilbertidia.*

Description: Jordan and Starks 1895:811–813; Welander and Alverson 1954:40–41; Hart 1973:501–502 (except erroneous dorsal ray count); Nelson 1982:1489; Eschmeyer and Herald 1983:169.

Figure: University of British Columbia, artist P. Drukker-Brammall, Feb. 1966; UBC 63-1422, 61 mm SL, Finger Bay, Adak Island, Alaska.

Range: Occurrence in southeastern Alaska well documented; e.g., at Chilkoot Inlet, Funter Bay, and Loring by Evermann and Goldsborough (1907), and several sites near the British Columbia border by Peden and Wilson (1976). Also known from Adak Island (Wilimovsky 1964) and from Kasitsna Bay, an embayment of Kachemak Bay (UBC 63-118). Listed as rare at Commander Islands by Fedorov and Sheiko (2002). Peden and Wilson (1976) found the species on rocky as well as silty bottoms while scuba diving in southeastern Alaska and northern British Columbia, but cited evidence suggesting that when the juveniles settle, those settling in rocky areas are more likely to survive than those on muddy bottoms.

Psychrolutes phrictus Stein & Bond, 1978 **giant blobsculpin**

Eastern Bering Sea to Pacific Ocean off southern California at San Diego; western Bering Sea from Cape Navarin to Commander Islands and to Seas of Okhotsk and Japan, and Pacific off northern Honshu.

Bottom on middle and lower continental slope at depths of 480–2,800 m.

D VII–IX,19–20; A 12–14; Pec 22–26; Pel I,3; LLp 12–14; GR 9–13; Vert 33–36.

- Grayish or blackish, sometimes mottled with white; **no distinct bands or other patterns**.
- **Head large (41–61% SL)**; **body enormously globular**; **skin relatively tough and thick**.
- Maxilla extending to mideye or beyond; interorbital area flexible, broad, slightly convex.
- Head and preopercular spines absent.
- **Head and body scattered with small cirri**.
- Spinous and soft-rayed portions of dorsal fin continuous, **spinous portion low**, buried.
- Prickles on head and body in specimens less than 50 mm SL.
- Vomerine and palatine teeth absent.
- Gill membranes broadly attached to isthmus, without posterior fold.
- Length to 700 mm TL (**much larger than *P. sigalutes* and *P. paradoxus***).

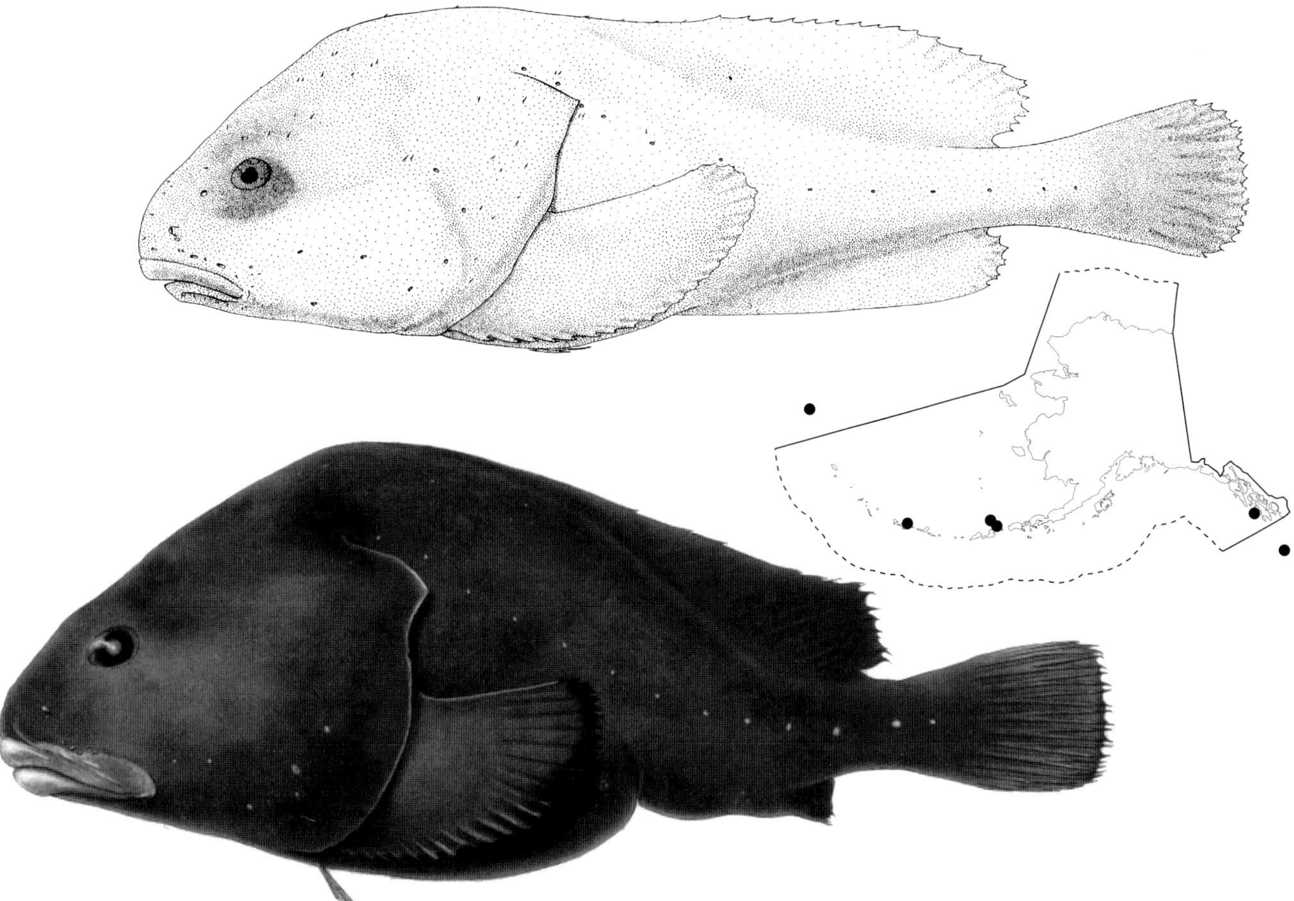

Notes & Sources — *Psychrolutes phrictus* Stein & Bond, 1978

Description: Stein and Bond 1978; Matarese and Stein 1980.

Figures: Upper: Stein and Bond 1978, fig. 1; holotype, female, 38 cm SL, off Oregon at 2,800 m. Lower: Royal British Columbia Museum, artist N. Eyolfson, Dec. 1983; BCPM 979-11148, 41 cm SL, off Vancouver Island, British Columbia.

Range: Matarese and Stein (1980) recorded 18 specimens taken from the Bering Sea north of Unalaska Island at depths of 685–1,320 m. The NMFS Auke Bay Laboratory has specimens taken from the Alexander Archipelago west of Craig by sablefish longline (AB 93-20, depth 1,280 m; AB 95-1, depth not recorded). In the late 1970s a specimen about 60 cm long ("about 2 feet") washed up on Adak Island and was still alive when found (D. Roseneau, pers. comm., Feb. 2001; see photograph in this book). The nearest known locality of occurrence outside Alaska in the eastern Pacific is Tasu Sound, Queen Charlotte Islands, recorded by Peden and Ostermann (1980). The species has proved to be widespread since it was first described by Stein and Bond (1978) from specimens taken off Oregon and California. Yabe et al. (1983) and Shinohara et al. (1996) recorded *P. phrictus* from Japan, and Sheiko and Tranbenkova (1998) from Russia off the Commander Islands (KIE 1265, 55°38'N, 164°52'E, depth 500–600 m). V. V. Fedorov has records off Russia from Cape Navarin to the Kuril Islands (B. A. Sheiko, pers. comm., 15 Jan. 1999) .

Psychrolutes paradoxus Günther, 1861 **tadpole sculpin**

Bering Sea from Norton Sound and Aleutian Islands to Puget Sound, Washington; Cape Olyutorskiy to Commander Islands and to Okhotsk and Japan seas.

Soft and rocky bottoms on continental shelf, recorded from depths of 9–240 m.

D IX–XII,12–17; A 12–14; Pec 19–23; Pel I,3; Vert 34–35.

- Creamy white to light brown with **distinct dark brown bars and patches on body and fins**.
- **Head not so large (usually 33% SL or less); tadpole shaped**, broad anteriorly, compressed posteriorly; **skin loose, thin, jellylike**.
- Maxilla extending to mideye; interorbital area flexible, broad, flat to convex.
- Head and preopercular spines absent.
- No scattered cirri on head and body.
- Spinous and soft-rayed portions of dorsal fin continuous, **spinous portion low**, mostly buried.
- Numerous small, blunt papillae on body and fins.
- Vomerine and palatine teeth absent.
- Gill membranes broadly attached to isthmus, without posterior fold.
- Length to 65 mm TL (**much smaller than *P. phrictus***).

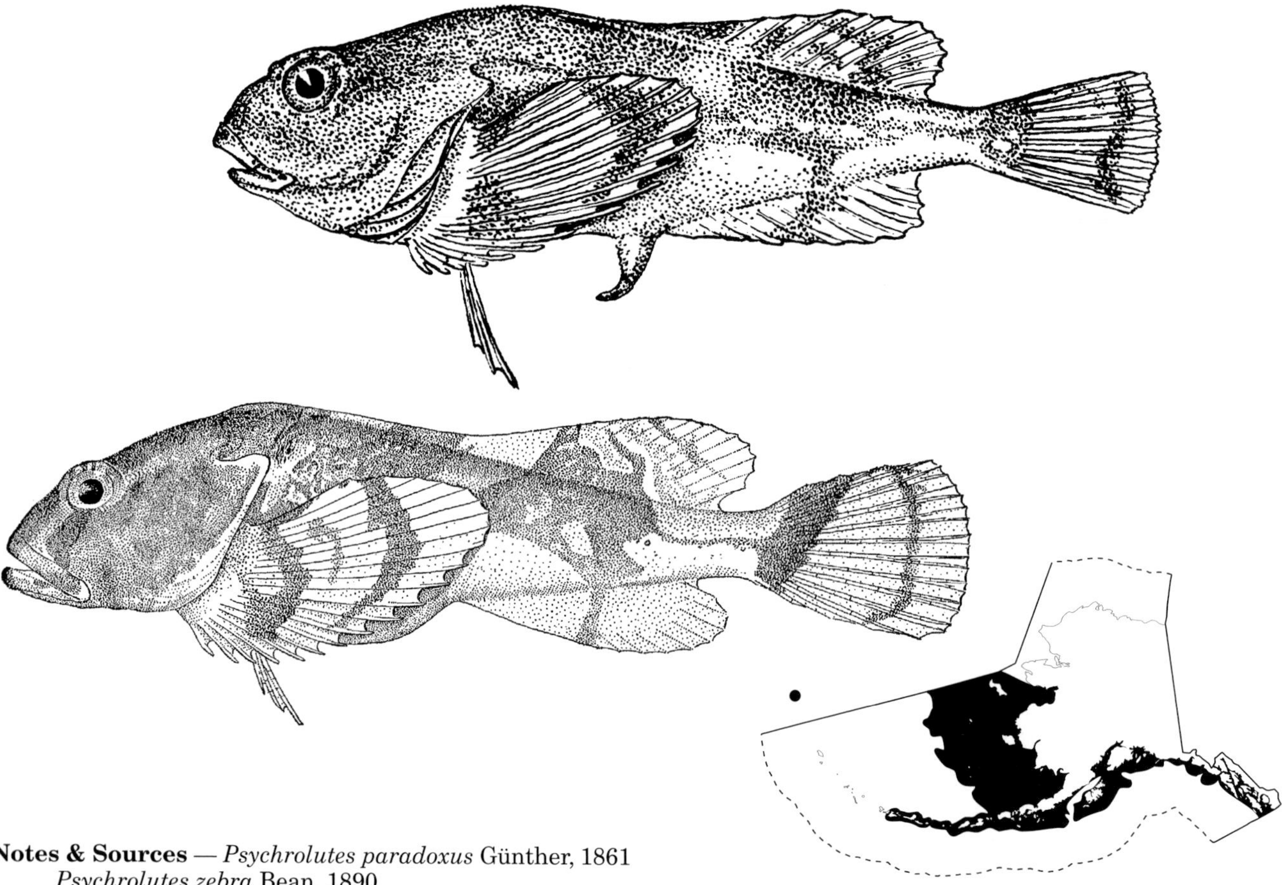

Notes & Sources — *Psychrolutes paradoxus* Günther, 1861
Psychrolutes zebra Bean, 1890

Description: Bean 1890b:43–44; Jordan and Evermann 1898:2026–2027; Andriashev 1937:23 of transl.; Hart 1973:533–534; Nelson 1982:1488–1489; Lindberg and Krasyukova 1987:263.

Figures: Upper: Hart 1973:533; male, 4.6 cm TL, Rennell Sound, British Columbia. Lower: Jordan and Starks 1895, pl. 65; female, about 53 mm TL, Puget Sound near Port Orchard, Washington.

Range: Among the numerous published records are: Bean (1881b, 1890b) from Kodiak Island and from Aleutian Islands between Unga and Nagai islands; Gilbert (1896) from south of Alaska Peninsula through Unimak Pass to north of Unalaska Island and in Bristol Bay; Jordan and Gilbert (1899) from St. Paul Island and Karluk; Evermann and Goldsborough (1907) from Boca de Quadra, Behm Canal, Lynn Canal, Afognak Island, Alitak Bay, Chignik Bay, Uyak Bay, Shelikof Strait; Wilimovsky (1964) from Adak Island; Quast and Hall (1972) from Cook Inlet and other localities; Sample and Wolotira (1985) from Norton Sound. Occurrence at many other Alaskan localities is documented by specimens in museum collections. Although recorded west only as far as Adak Island, distribution is probably continuous throughout the Aleutian chain. Recorded by Fedorov and Sheiko (2002) from Commander Islands, Russia. Compared to *P. phrictus* and *P. sigalutes, P. paradoxus* is common in Alaska.

Family Agonidae
Poachers

Poachers are bottom-dwelling cottoid fishes with bodies completely covered by bony plates. The plates give poachers the appearance of being covered in alligator skin, for which some species are called alligatorfishes. The family occurs primarily in the North Pacific Ocean north of Japan and northern Mexico, the Bering Sea, and the Arctic Ocean. Poachers are usually found at moderate depths but occupy a wide range of habitats from tidepools to the continental slope at depths to nearly 1,300 m. In the most recent revision of poacher taxonomy, by Kanayama (1991), the family comprises four subfamilies with 20 genera and 45 species. Twenty-two species occur and are well documented in Alaska, and one other has been reported but not confirmed in Alaska. Accounts for two species from nearby waters of British Columbia are also included in this guide.

Diagnostic characters of poachers include the body covering of bony plates, an elongate shape (usually), two dorsal fins (usually), unbranched fin rays, and no swim bladder. When present, the first dorsal fin has 2–21 spines. The second dorsal fin has 4–14 rays, and the anal fin has 4–28 rays. In the Alaskan species the counts are all at the low end of those ranges. The caudal fin ray count throughout the family varies little, with 10–12 principal rays. The pectoral fins in Alaskan species have 10–19 rays. The lower pectoral rays in some species are thickened and exserted, and used for climbing rocks and other surfaces. The pelvic fins are thoracic and invariably have 1 spine and 2 rays; they are longer in adult males than in females. The Alaskan species have 6 branchiostegal rays, except for some individuals of *Pallasina barbata* which have 5. In all poachers the gill membranes are united, but can be free from or variously joined to the isthmus. The vertebral count for the family ranges from 29, expressed in the Alaskan species *Bothragonus swanii,* to 54, in the Alaskan species *Aspidophoroides monopterygius.* Sexual dimorphism is often evident in brighter coloration of the males, as well as in differences in fin lengths.

Members of the four poacher subfamilies can be distinguished from each other by the position of the mouth, relative length of the jaws, and fusion or nonfusion of the gill membranes to the isthmus. In the subfamily Percidinae the mouth is terminal, the jaws are about equal, and the gill membranes are free from the isthmus. In the Agoninae the mouth is subterminal or inferior, the upper jaw projects beyond the lower, and the gill membranes are joined to the isthmus. In the Anoplagoninae the mouth is terminal, rarely superior, and the gill membranes are joined to the isthmus; except that in *Ulcina olrikii, Aspidophoroides monopterygius,* and *Anoplagonus inermis* the gill membranes are largely free. In the Brachyopsinae the mouth is superior, the lower jaw projects beyond the upper jaw, and the gill membranes are free from the isthmus. The Alaskan species are distributed among all four subfamilies.

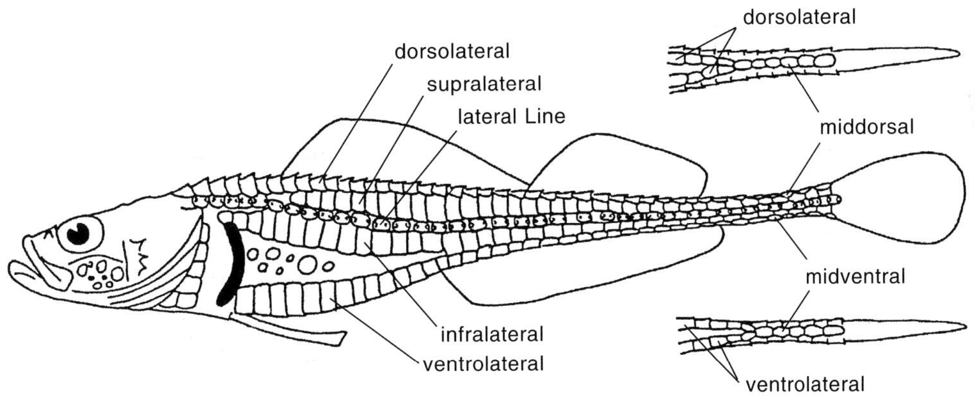

Rows of bony plates on poachers
(After Kanayama in Masuda et al. 1984.)

Among the characters most useful for identifying poacher species are the numbers and configurations of bony plates. The rows on the trunk and caudal peduncle are shown in the accompanying diagram. The terminology used is that of Gruchy (1969). On the trunk the plates form a pair of *dorsolateral* rows, one on either side of the dorsal midline. These rows usually disappear posterior to the second dorsal fin, on the peduncle, where they are replaced by a single *middorsal* row. Below each dorsolateral row is the *supralateral* row, then the *lateral line,* and below that the *infralateral* row; and, finally, the *ventrolateral* row on either side of the ventral midline, which is replaced with a single row of *midventral* plates on the caudal peduncle.

One or more rows can be absent, and the dorsolateral–middorsal and ventrolateral–midventral transitions can occur at different places on the peduncle. Gruchy (1969) found the supralateral and infralateral rows to be the only uniform rows and the easiest to enumerate in species he examined. Subsequently, most investigators have reported counts for those rows. Among the species included in this guide, the supralateral row is absent in *Ulcina olrikii, Aspidophoroides monopterygius,* and *Anoplagonus inermis* and helps to identify those species, while the infralateral row is present in all. The number of lateral line plates compared to supralateral and infralateral plates is also helpful, because it describes how far the plates extend along the lateral line before they disappear and the supra- and infralateral rows abut on the lateral line. To take an extreme example, *Hypsagonus quadricornis* has only 6–11 lateral line plates, posterior to which the supra- and infralateral rows, up to 32 plates each, meet on the lateral line; compared to *Agonopsis vulsa* in which the lateral line plates (up to 42) number about the same as the supra- and infralateral plates and form a complete row to the caudal fin.

In the following pages, counts of the supralateral (SLP), lateral line (LLP), and infralateral (ILP) plates are given in addition to counts of the dorsal, anal, and pectoral fin rays, and vertebrae. The plate counts are mainly from Kanayama (1991), since he provided counts for all species in Alaska and, since they were counted by the same person, one may be assured the counts are comparable. Coloration, number and arrangement of head spines and barbels, and position of the dorsal and anal fins also vary among poacher species and are useful for identification.

Adults of most poacher species reach total lengths of 15 cm (6 inches) or less. The dragon poacher, *Percis japonica,* is a giant compared to the other species in this guide, with a recorded maximum length of 42 cm (16.5 inches). The smallest of the Alaskan poachers is the Arctic alligatorfish, *Ulcina olrikii,* which reaches 8.6 cm (3.4 inches).

Twelve of the twenty-five species in this guide are relatively abundant (with known range represented by solid black fill on our maps) off the coasts of Alaska while ten are less common or rare (records represented by dots) in the region. The kelp poacher, *Hypsagonus mozinoi,* occurs just south of the Alaska–Canada border and undoubtedly also occurs in Alaska but its presence has not been confirmed. It was reported once near Sitka but the whereabouts of the specimen, if it was kept, are not known. The remaining two species have not been reported from Alaska but occur nearby in northern British Columbia. The blacktip and bluespotted poachers, *Xeneretmus latifrons* and *X. triacanthus,* should be considered when identifying specimens from the eastern Gulf of Alaska.

Three poacher species are new additions to Quast and Hall's (1972) inventory of Alaskan fishes.The kelp poacher, *H. mozinoi,* was described by Wilimovsky and Wilson (1978); known to occur from California to British Columbia, it has been reported once but not confirmed from southeastern Alaska. The smootheye poacher, *X. leiops,* also known from California to British Columbia, was recorded from southeastern Alaska off Forrester Island by Peden and Jamieson (1988); this is the only record of the species from Alaska. As a result of corrected identifications of specimens the veteran poacher, *Podothecus veternus,* is now known to be a member of the Alaskan ichthyofauna. One example of *P. veternus* was collected in 1975 by V. V. Barsukov from nearby Provideniya Bay on the coast of the Chukchi Peninsula (Lindberg and Krasyukova 1987), but the species was not known to occur in Alaska until B. A. Sheiko (pers. comms., May–Dec. 1998), examining poachers in museum collections in 1997, discovered that *P. veternus* had been confused with sturgeon poacher, *P. accipenserinus.* The veteran poacher seems to be as abundant in the northern Bering Sea and Chukchi Sea off Alaska as the sturgeon poacher is in the southern Bering Sea and along Aleutian Islands and Gulf of Alaska coasts.

The dragon poacher, *Percis japonica,* and Atlantic poacher, *Leptagonus decagonus,* listed by Quast and Hall (1972) as potentially occurring in Alaska, are now known from several Alaskan localities. The bluespotted poacher, *Xeneretmus triacanthus,* is added to the list as a potential Alaskan species because it was recorded from nearby northern British Columbia at Kwatna Inlet by Peden and Gruchy (1971).

Other differences from Quast and Hall's (1972) inventory result from changes in taxonomy. *Agonopsis emmelane* is now classified as a synonym of *A. vulsa* following Hubbs et al. (1979) and Lea and Dempster (1982). *Asterotheca alascana, A. infraspinata,* and *A. pentacantha* are classified in *Bathyagonus* following Fitch (1973). Kanayama (1991) revised the classification of several other species. *Aspidophoroides bartoni,* the Aleutian alligatorfish described by Gilbert (1896), was synonymized in *A. monopterygius*. The warty poacher, *Occella verrucosa*, was moved to the genus *Chesnonia*, but *C. verrucosa* is so similar to the Bering poacher, *O. dodecaedron*, the two are often confused and it is helpful to know that separation into different genera depends on a character that is not externally visible (presence of an ectopterygoid in *Chesnonia*). Other changes made by Kanayama (1991) affecting the taxonomy of Alaskan species include moving the kelp poacher, *Agonomalus mozinoi*, to genus *Hypsagonus*; and sawback and longnose poachers, *Sarritor frenatus* and *S. leptorhynchus*, to *Leptagonus*. Jordan et al. (1930) classified the Arctic alligatorfish, *Aspidophoroides olrikii*, in *Ulcina*. *Aspidophoroides güntherii*, an alligatorfish species described by Bean (1885) from Alaskan specimens, is synonymous with *Ulcina olrikii*, as suggested long ago by Jordan and Evermann (1896a, 1898) and recently confirmed by Kanayama (1991).

We classify pixie poacher, *Occella impi* Gruchy, as a junior synonym of *Stellerina xyosterna* (Jordan & Gilbert). The holotype and only known specimen, collected in northern British Columbia and described by Gruchy (1970), is a juvenile (21 mm TL) of *S. xyosterna*. The holotype was examined and compared with juveniles of *S. xyosterna* and other species by B. A. Sheiko (pers. comm., 21 Oct. 1999), who made the following observations. The main differences of *O. impi* from *S. xyosterna* given by Gruchy (1970) were presence of vomerine and palatine teeth, and a large number of infralateral plates. Sheiko found no such teeth in the holotype, only granular skin. The seemingly large number of infralateral plates is due to the young age of the holotype, since in such small specimens all the infralateral plates are equally developed; during growth of the individual the plates enlarge, except for the anterior plates (under the pectoral fins) which remain small and without spines and, in older individuals, do not get counted as infralateral plates. *Stellerina* differs from other poacher genera by the absence of pores in nearly all the canals on top of the head, and in the holotype of *O. impi* such pores are absent even though infraorbital and other pores are present. The mandible is sharply angled downward, as in *Stellerina*; the illustration of the holotype incorrectly depicts this character. Although the anus is nearer to the origin of the anal fin than to the bases of the pelvic fins, this is related to the young age of the specimen. In agonids, with growth the anus becomes closer to the pelvic fins. As in *S. xyosterna*, the *O. impi* holotype has spinous plates on the breast and gular region. Finally, nearly all counts coincide with those of *S. xyosterna*. Slightly greater numbers in some counts may be explained by the habitation of the *O. impi* holotype near the northern boundary of *S. xyosterna's* range.

The following key draws on sources cited in the species accounts, with refinements from personal observations (C.W.M.). Sheiko (pers. comm., 21 Dec. 1998) provided the snout length distinction for couplet 12, and improvements to couplet 5. A few of the fin ray and vertebral counts in the species accounts are from Busby (1998), although not cited individually in the accounts.

Key to the Agonidae of Alaska

1 Two dorsal fins present; distinct supralateral plate row present . . . . . (2)

1 One dorsal fin (spinous dorsal absent); distinct supralateral plate row absent . . . . . (23)

2 (1) Gill membranes united, free from isthmus . . . . . (3)

2 Gill membranes united, narrowly or broadly attached to isthmus, with or without free margin or fold posteriorly . . . . . (9)

3 (2) Body compressed or rounded in cross section; lower jaw not projecting; body plates spinous; first dorsal fin at nape . . . . . (4)

3 Body more or less depressed; lower jaw projecting; body plates spinous or not; first dorsal fin well behind nape . . . . . (6)

4 (3) Body elongate; no barbel on snout; dorsal fins well separated . . . . . *Percis japonica*, page 530

4 Body short and deep; barbel on snout; dorsal fins moderately close together . . . . . (5)

5 (4) Lateral line plates less than 16; two anteriormost lateral line plates enlarged; ventrolateral plates anterior to anal fin indistinct . . . . *Hypsagonus quadricornis,* page 531

5 Lateral line plates more than 15; all lateral line plates equal in size; ventrolateral plates anterior to anal fin forming distinct ridge. . . . . *Hypsagonus mozinoi,* page 532
(not confirmed from Alaska)

6 (3) Snout long, tubelike; barbel at tip of lower jaw . . . . *Pallasina barbata,* page 533

6 Snout not tubelike; no chin barbel . . . . (7)

7 (6) Breast with numerous prickles, no plates; anal fin rays 7–9; pectoral fin rays 16–19 . . . . *Stellerina xyosterna,* page 534

7 Breast with plates; anal fin rays 10–16, rarely 7–9; pectoral fin rays 13–16. . . . . (8)

8 (7) Anal fin rays 7–13, usually 10–12 . . . . *Chesnonia verrucosa,* page 535

8 Anal fin rays 13–16, usually 14–16 . . . . *Occella dodecaedron,* page 536

9 (2) Tip of snout without freely movable plate . . . . (10)

9 Tip of snout with freely movable plate . . . . (15)

10 (9) No spines at tip of snout . . . . (11)

10 Two anteriorly directed spines at tip of snout . . . . (13)

11 (10) Barbel on ventral surface of snout rudimentary or absent . . . . *Leptagonus decagonus,* page 537

11 Pair of barbels on ventral surface of snout . . . . (12)

12 (11) Snout length (tip of snout to anterior margin of orbit) less than postorbital distance (orbit to posterior margin of operculum); free nasal margin serrated, with small spines; second infraorbital spine with supplementary knob . . . . *Leptagonus frenatus,* page 538

12 Snout length greater than postorbital distance; free nasal margin usually smooth; second infraorbital spine usually without supplementary knob . . . . *Leptagonus leptorhynchus,* page 539

13 (10) Gill membranes with cirri or barbels, 1 or more on each branchiostegal ray; barbels on cheeks, snout, around mouth, but not always under snout; occipital pit present . . . . *Agonopsis vulsa,* page 540

13 Gill membranes without cirri or barbels; bunches of barbels under tip of snout and on corners of mouth; mouth has gap when closed . . . . (14)

14 (13) Barbels in patch on snout numbering 13–19; uppermost preopercular spine not expanded laterally . . . . *Podothecus accipenserinus,* page 541

14 Barbels in patch on snout numbering 6–11; uppermost preopercular spine expanded laterally . . . . *Podothecus veternus,* page 542

15 (9) Occiput with distinct, deep pit or pair of pits . . . . (16)

15 Occiput without distinct pit . . . . (17)

16 (15) Occiput with distinct, deep pit; rostral plate without spine; body short and broad, especially anteriorly . . . . *Bothragonus swanii,* page 543

16 Occiput with distinct pair of pits or heart-shaped pit; rostral plate with vertical spine at tip; body elongate and slender . . . . *Odontopyxis trispinosa,* page 544

17 (15) Spines on rostral plate in starlike arrangement with 5 or more points, 3 of them dorsally directed . . . . genus *Bathyagonus* (18)

17 One dorsally directed spine on rostral plate . . . . genus *Xeneretmus* (21)

18 (17) Fins uniformly black; lower jaw projecting beyond upper jaw . . . . *Bathyagonus nigripinnis,* page 545

18 Fins not uniformly black; lower jaw not projecting beyond upper jaw . . . . (19)

19 (18) Two median pairs of plates immediately in front of pelvic fins; supralateral plates 40 or more; infralateral plates 39 or more . . . . *Bathyagonus pentacanthus,* page 546

19 One median pair of plates or single plate immediately in front of pelvic fins; supralateral plates less than 40; infralateral plates less than 39 . . . . (20)

20 (19) Free lachrymal margin smooth; 2 spines on infraorbital ridge; anal fin origin below dorsal fin interspace . . . . *Bathyagonus alascanus,* page 547

20 Free lachrymal margin serrated; 3 spines on infraorbital ridge; anal fin origin below insertion of first dorsal fin . . . . *Bathyagonus infraspinatus,* page 548

21 (17) Eyeball without spinous processes . . . . *Xeneretmus leiops,* page 549

21 Row of 2–6 spinous processes on dorsal area of eyeball . . . . (22)

22 (21) One major barbel at posterior end of maxilla, occasionally with 2 or 3 minor barbels . . . . *Xeneretmus latifrons,* page 550 (not known from Alaska)

22 Two major barbels at posterior end of maxilla . . . . *Xeneretmus triacanthus,* page 551 (not known from Alaska)

23 (1) Barbel present on end of maxilla; predorsal plates 17 or less . . . . *Ulcina olrikii,* page 552

23 No barbel on end of maxilla; predorsal plates 18 or more . . . . (24)

24 (23) Nasal spines present; no median dorsal row of plates behind occiput . . . . *Aspidophoroides monopterygius,* page 553

24 Nasal spines absent; median row of small plates extending from occiput halfway to dorsal fin origin . . . . *Anoplagonus inermis,* page 554

Percis japonica (Pallas, 1769) **dragon poacher**

Bering Sea from southern part of Gulf of Anadyr to Gulf of Alaska and to Okhotsk and Japan seas. Rocky gravel and muddy sand bottoms at depths of 87–450 m, most abundant off Japan at 150–250 m.

D V–VII + 6–8; A 7–9; Pec 11–13; SLP 34–43; LLP 30–40; ILP 33–38; Vert 40–42.

- Light brown, with 4 or 5 dark brown bands; belly whitish; saddle-like dark brown blotch on nape.
- Elongate; **dorsal profile high at nape**.
- **No snout barbel**.
- **Long nasal tube, reaching upper jaw**.
- **Dorsal fins far apart**, anal fin origin well behind a vertical line through insertion of first dorsal; first dorsal fin at nape.
- **Sharp, hooked spines on body plates**; tiny prickles on head, body, and fins.
- Gill membranes united, free from isthmus.
- Length to 420 mm TL.

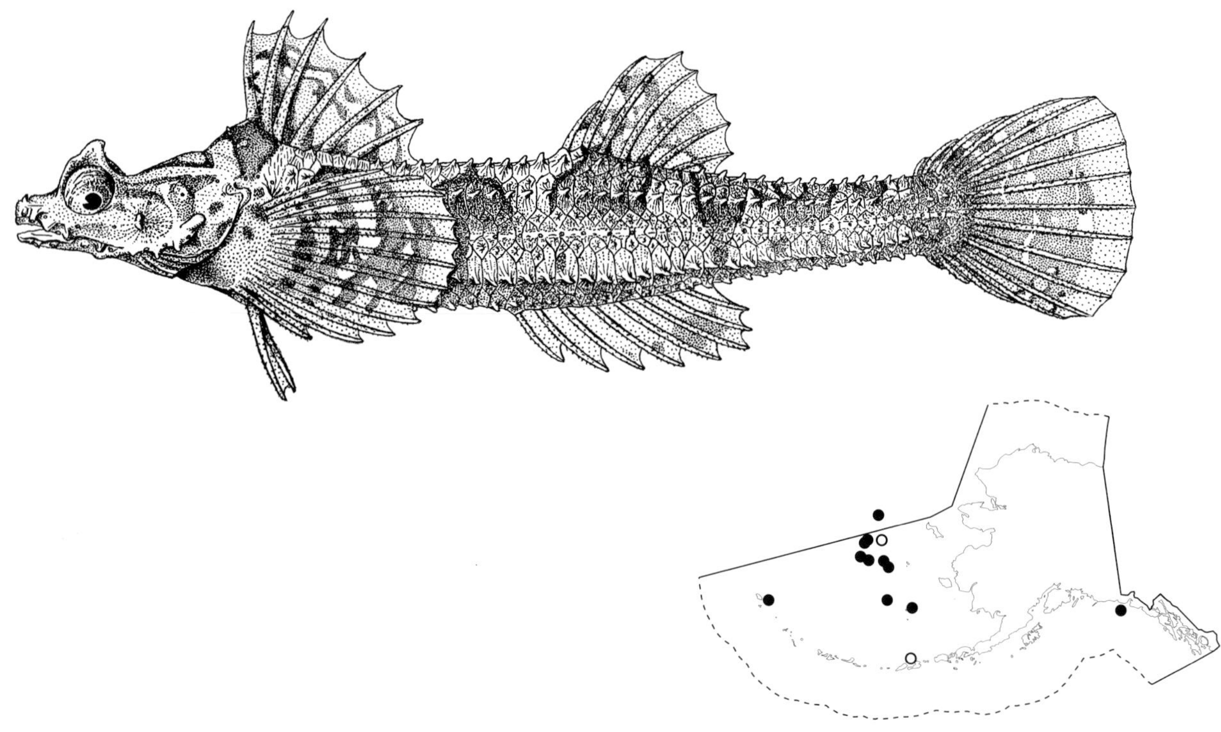

Notes & Sources — *Percis japonica* (Pallas, 1769)
Cottus japonicus Pallas, 1769
The specific epithet is spelled *japonica* to agree with the feminine gender of *Percis* (Sheiko 1993).

Description: Jordan and Evermann 1898:2034–2036; Lindberg and Krasyukova 1987:281; Kanayama 1991:27–29. SLP and ILP counts from B. A. Sheiko (pers. comm., 21 Dec. 1998) based on KIE and UW specimens.

Figure: Lindberg and Krasyukova 1987, fig. 181; ZIN 17452, 275 mm TL, Tatar Strait.

Range: Primarily an Asian species but known from several localities off Alaska. First reported from Bering Sea by T. T. Nalbant (in Schultz 1967), who mentioned it was taken there by the Romanian trawler *Galatzi* and later (Nalbant 1994) reported the locality was over the shelf of the Near Islands. Yabe et al. 1981: HUMZ 84945, 59°28'N, 178°12'W, depth 280 m; NMFS Kodiak laboratory, 57°16'N, 172°56'W; J. Long and D. W. Kessler, pers. comm., northwest of Unalaska Island. Kanayama 1991: HUMZ 84945, 59°28'N, 178°09'W, 28 m; HUMZ 85345, 59°25'N, 177°39'W, 321 m; HUMZ 86090, 60°00'N, 175°29'W, 123 m; HUMZ 86117, 60°38'N, 179°00'W, 295 m; Far Sea Fisheries Research Laboratory, 62°45'N, 179°30'W, 87 m; HUMZ 33813, 59°28'N, 141°29'W (the only Gulf of Alaska record). SIO 91-82 comprises one specimen from 60°47'N, 179°28'W. UW 28562 is from 57°20'N, 168°58'W, 68 m. Baxter (1990ms) examined OSU 8403, from 59°40'N, 174°28'W; and a specimen (not saved) taken by the Russian RV *Novokotovsk*, haul 312, on 28 Jun. 1990 at 61°21'N, 176°58'W, depth 116 m.

Size: Lindberg and Krasyukova 1987.

Hypsagonus quadricornis (Valenciennes, 1829) **fourhorn poacher**

Bering Sea and Aleutian Islands to Puget Sound, Washington; and to Commander Islands and Okhotsk and northern Japan seas.

Rocky sand, gravel, or pebble bottoms at depths of 15–452 m, usually shallower than 126 m.

D VIII–XI + 5–7; A 8–11; Pec 12–14; SLP 25–32; LLP 6–11; ILP 28–32; Vert 35–37.

- Reddish brown, with yellow, red, and brown bands and blotches; dark band along caudal fin margin; sometimes with hydroids and seaweeds on skin.
- **Dorsal profile high at nape**.
- Postocular spine absent.
- **Barbel at tip of snout**.
- **Dorsal fins close together**, anal fin origin below first dorsal fin; first dorsal fin at nape.
- **Lateral line plates less than 15**, first 2 with an enlarged spine; supralateral and infralateral plates meet on lateral line posteriorly; large spines on body plates.
- Gill membranes united, free from isthmus.
- Length to 105 mm TL.

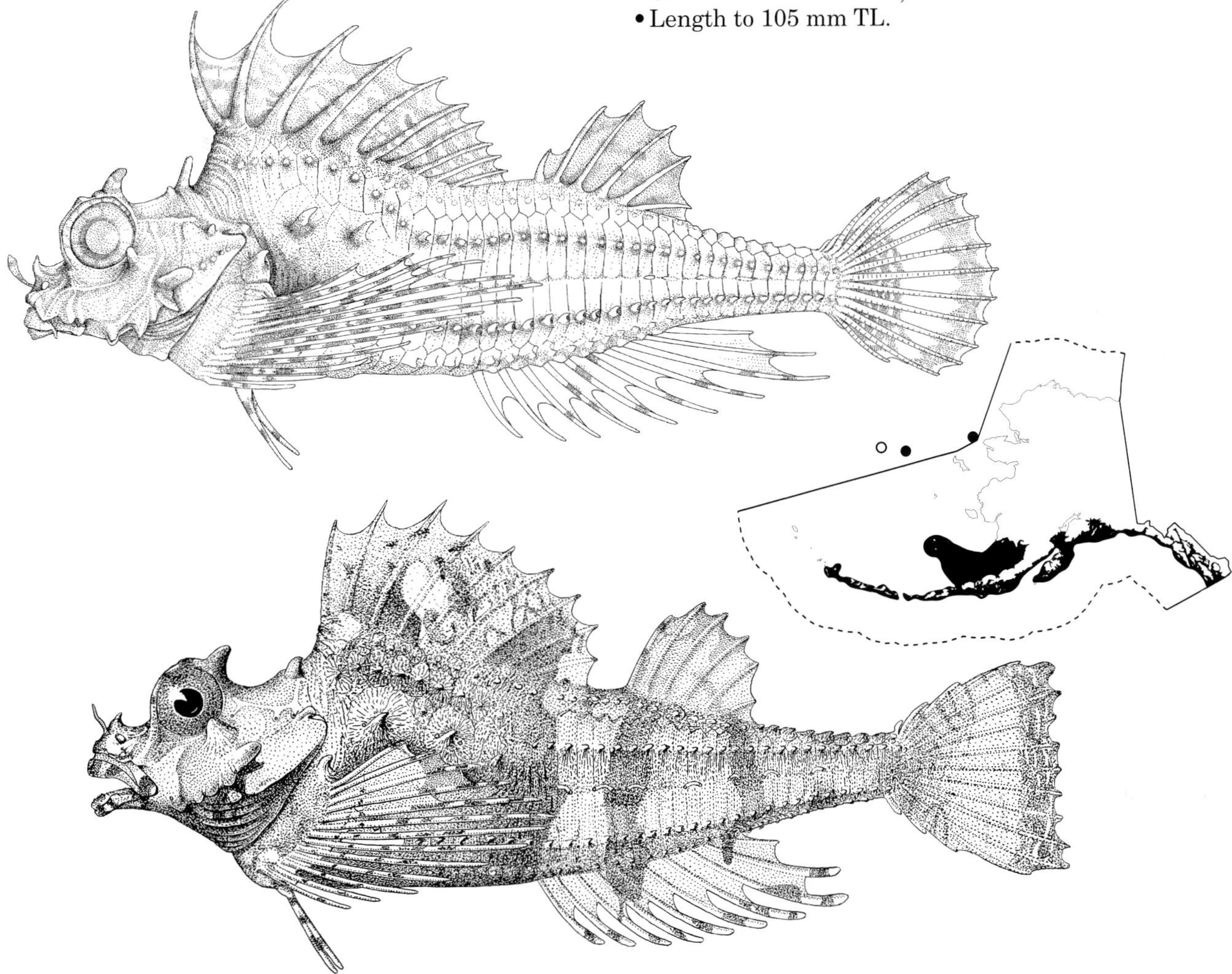

Notes & Sources — *Hypsagonus quadricornis* (Valenciennes in Cuvier & Valenciennes, 1829)
Aspidophorus quadricornis Valenciennes in Cuvier & Valenciennes, 1829
Sheiko (1993:75) corrected the authorship, previously attributed to Cuvier. Valenciennes provided both the description and the species name.

Description: Jordan and Evermann 1898:2038–2041; Lindberg and Krasyukova 1987:295; Kanayama 1991:17–19.

Figures: Upper: University of British Columbia, artist R. Wood, Dec. 1968; UBC 63-929, 69 mm SL, desiccated, south of Alaska Peninsula. Lower: Lindberg and Krasyukova 1987, fig. 186; ZIN 43471, 76 mm TL, Sea of Okhotsk.

Range: There are numerous records of this species for the Gulf of Alaska and for the Bering Sea north to Bristol Bay (58°23'N, 160°00'W; Kanayama 1991) and the Pribilof Islands (BCPM 985-227, 56°40'N, 169°30'W) and west to Amchitka Island (Isakson et al. 1971) and Semisopochnoi Island (Gilbert and Burke 1912a). From nearby waters: west of Little Diomede Island (Andriashev 1937, 1954); 62°45'N, 179°30'W (Kanayama 1991); 61°59'N, 177°04'E (R. Baxter, unpubl. data; *Novokotovsk,* 8 Jul. 1990, specimen not saved). Maximum depth (452 m) was reported by Sheiko and Fedorov (2000).

Size: Taranetz 1933.

Hypsagonus mozinoi (Wilimovsky & Wilson, 1978) **kelp poacher**

Sitka, report unverifiable; well documented from northern British Columbia at Dixon Entrance to central California at San Simeon Point.

Open coast tidepools and shallow rocky areas to depth of about 11 m.

D VII–IX + 6–8; A 10–12; Pec 11–12; SLP 27–29; LLP 18–21; ILP 28–29; Vert 34.

- Scarlet red, brown, and white; body covered with small sponges and seaweed.
- **Dorsal profile high at nape.**
- Postocular spine present.
- **Barbel at tip of snout.**
- **Dorsal fins close together**, anal fin origin below first dorsal fin; first dorsal fin at nape.
- **Lateral line plates more than 15**, without an enlarged spine; supralateral and infralateral plates not meeting on lateral line; large spines on body plates; body covered with prickles.
- Gill membranes united, free from isthmus.
- Length to 89 mm TL.

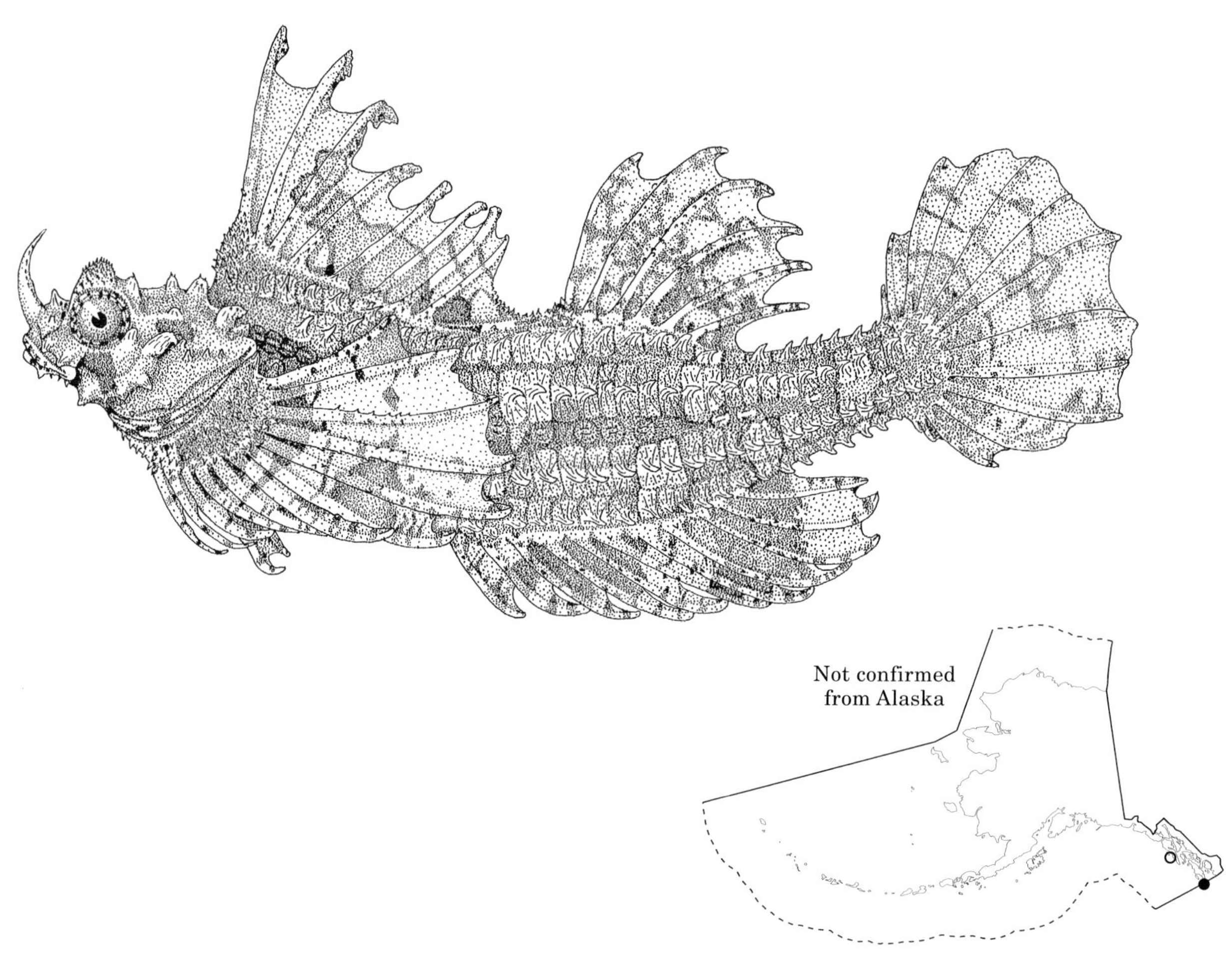

Notes & Sources — *Hypsagonus mozinoi* (Wilimovsky & Wilson, 1978)
Agonomalus sp.: Miller and Lea 1972, Barraclough and Peden 1976, Peden and Wilson 1976.
Agonomalus mozinoi Wilimovsky & Wilson, 1978
Classified in *Hypsagonus* by Kanayama (1991). Sheiko (1993) maintained *Agonomalus* as a distinct genus.

Description: Wilimovsky and Wilson 1978; Kanayama 1991:15–17. LLP count increased by B. A. Sheiko (pers. comm., 21 Dec. 1998) from KIE specimens.

Figure: Kanayama 1991, fig. 3; UCLA 63-256, 55 mm SL, California.

Range: For occurrence in Alaska, there is only an unverifiable report of a specimen collected off Sitka by a scuba diver in 1988 (B. L. Wing, pers. comm., 10 Mar. 1999). The nearest confirmed record is from just south of the Alaska-Canada boundary at Langara Island, Dixon Entrance, at 54°13'N, 132°58'W (BCPM 976-1303; Peden and Wilson 1976).

Size: Eschmeyer and Herald 1983.

Pallasina barbata (Steindachner, 1876) **tubenose poacher**

Eastern Chukchi and Bering seas, St. Lawrence Island, and Aleutian Islands to northern California at Bodega Bay; Commander Islands and southern Kamchatka through Kuril Islands, Okhotsk and Japan seas to Wonsan, Korea.

Intertidal and subtidal to depth of 27 m among eelgrass and algae over sand and gravel bottoms; greater depths reported but not documented. Unlike most poachers, swims well off bottom.

D IV–IX + 6–9; A 8–14; Pec 10–13; SLP 33–52; LLP 44–54; ILP 39–48; Vert 42–52.

- Gray to brownish, paler ventrally; belly golden in large adults; dorsal and pectoral fins spotted; fins pale, except caudal fin dark.
- **Snout long, tubelike**; lower jaw projecting beyond upper jaw; mouth slightly upturned.
- **Barbel at tip of lower jaw**, inconspicuous to more than 150% of head length; **no barbel on snout tip or at posterior end of maxilla**.
- Distance between dorsal fins varies from touching to width of one or two plates.
- Body plates smooth, main rows with blunt spines or knobs.
- Gill membranes united, free from isthmus.
- Length to 208 mm TL.

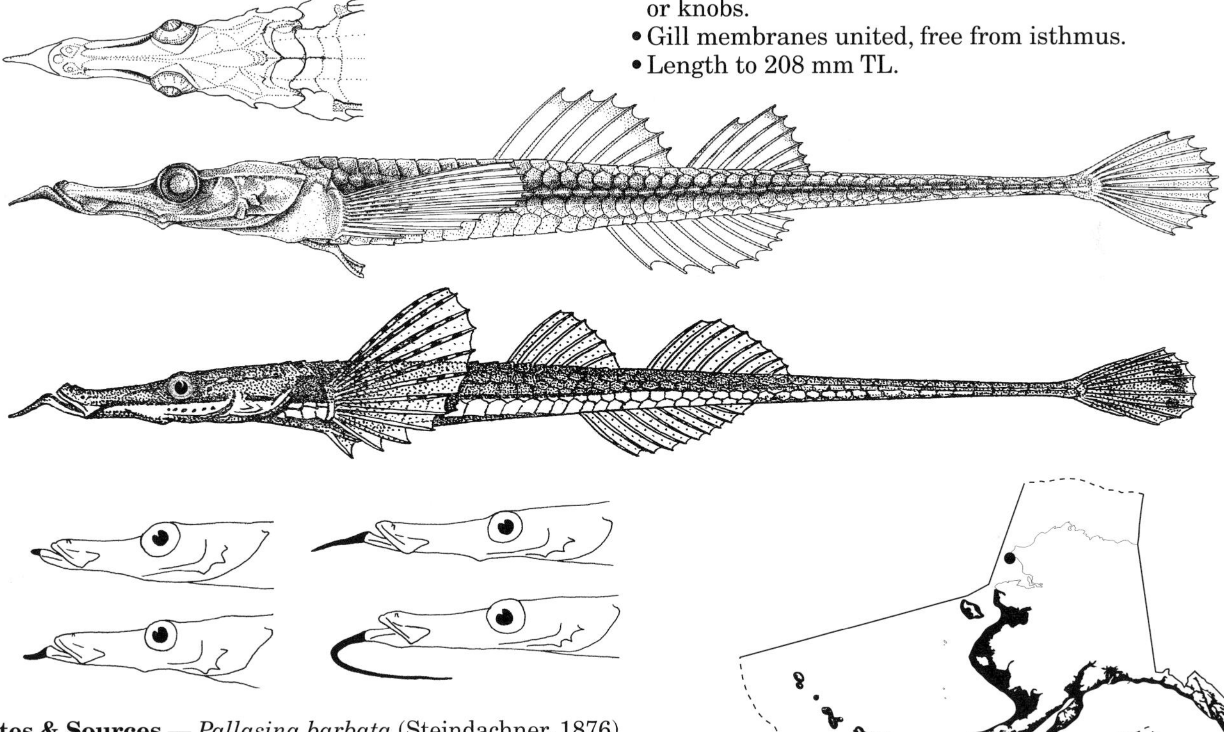

Notes & Sources — *Pallasina barbata* (Steindachner, 1876)
Siphagonus barbatus Steindachner, 1876
Pallasina aix Starks, 1896
Pallasina eryngia Jordan & Richardson, 1907

Classified as a subspecies or synonym of *P. barbata* by some authors (e.g., Gilbert and Burke 1912a, Barraclough 1952, Hemphill and Follett 1958, Kanayama 1991), the eastern Pacific *P. aix* is classified as a species by others (e.g., Lindberg and Krasyukova 1987, Sheiko 1993). A similar situation pertains for western Pacific *P. eryngia.* Chin barbel length and numbers of pectoral rays and prepelvic plates (2 or 3) are some differentiating features cited, but they are highly variable, with different combinations in local populations and overlap of individual characters among populations.

Description: Jordan and Evermann 1898:2049–2051; Gilbert and Burke 1912a:65–67; Barraclough 1952; Hemphill and Follett 1958; Lindberg and Krasyukova 1987:321; Kanayama 1991:114–117.

Figures: Upper: University of British Columbia, artist R. Wood, Dec. 1968; UBC 65-39, 127 mm SL, desiccated, Izembek Bay, Alaska. Lower: Lindberg and Krasyukova 1987, fig. 197; ZIN 18864, 167 mm SL, Sea of Japan. Barbel length variations: Kanayama 1991, fig. 52. In specimens collected in 1991 from Chukchi Sea off Alaska (see Range) the barbel is as long as the longest shown in Kanayama's diagrams. It is shorter in specimens from Bering Sea and Gulf of Alaska.

Range: The type came from Port Clarence, Alaska, just south of Bering Strait. Frequently taken as far north as Port Clarence (e.g., Steindachner 1876, Bean 1881b) and St. Lawrence Island (Rendahl 1931) and west to Attu Island (UBC 63-1005, 65-1, 65-4, 65-23, 65-24); no records from vicinity of St. Matthew Island and the Pribilof Islands, although the species probably occurs there. Walters (1955) believed Arctic records were erroneous. However, uncataloged vouchers at UAF from Chukchi Sea surveys include two (124 and 125 mm TL) with obvious diagnostic characters of *P. barbata* (C.W.M.) taken at 68°25'N, 166°40'W, depth 17 m, on 23 Sep. 1991; species was included on the survey catch list by Barber et al. (1997). Specimens in NMC 79-800 (two, identified by B. W. Coad) were taken southwest of Nunivak Island at 59°26'N, 166°20'W, depth 27 m.

Size: Kanayama 1991.

Stellerina xyosterna (Jordan & Gilbert, 1880) **pricklebreast poacher**

Northern Gulf of Alaska at Icy Bay to northern Baja California at San Carlos Bay.

Nearshore mud or sand bottoms at depths of 2–91 m, usually shallower than 75 m.

D VI–VIII + 5–7; A 7–9; Pec 16–19; SLP 28–31; LLP 34–38; ILP 28–31; Vert 34–37.

- Light olive brown, paler ventrally; spotted dorsally; pectoral fin with dark band on distal half and clear tip; dorsal fins black along margins, anal fin black posteriorly; caudal fin black.
- Long, depressed head; body and tail depressed to caudal fin; lower jaw projecting beyond upper; mouth upturned.
- Sharp, posteriorly directed nasal spine.
- **Long barbel at posterior end of maxilla**.
- Dorsal fins close together, separated by length of one or two plates.
- **Breast with numerous prickles, no plates**; body plates with sharp, slightly curved spines.
- Vomerine and palatine teeth absent in adults.
- Gill membranes united, free from isthmus.
- Length to 165 mm TL.

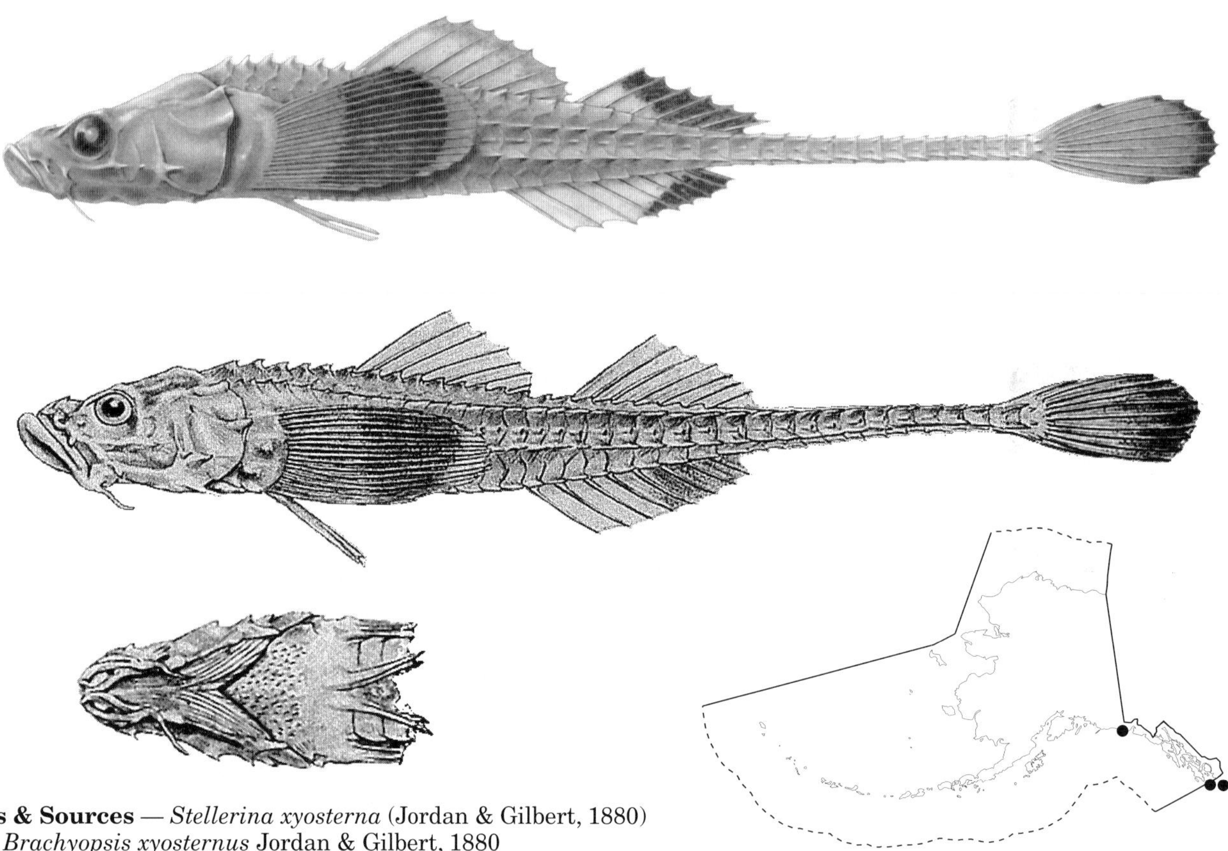

Notes & Sources — *Stellerina xyosterna* (Jordan & Gilbert, 1880)
Brachyopsis xyosternus Jordan & Gilbert, 1880
Occella impi Gruchy, 1970

No specimens have been referred to *O. impi* since the species was described by Gruchy (1970), from one small (20.6 mm TL) specimen collected in northern British Columbia. To A. E. Peden (pers. comm., 1987, in Matarese et al. 1989), the features of *O. impi* suggested it might be a juvenile of *S. xyosterna*. Recently, B. A. Sheiko (pers. comm., 21 Oct. 1999) examined the holotype (NMC 60-283), as well as juveniles of *S. xyosterna,* and confirmed the synonymy. See the introduction to the Agonidae (page 527 herein) for details.

Description: Jordan and Gilbert 1880e; Jordan and Evermann 1898:2042–2043; Gruchy 1970; Kanayama 1991:95–96.

Figures: Upper: Royal British Columbia Museum, artist N. Eyolfson, Dec. 1983; BCPM 965-2, size not recorded but not same specimen as lower illustration, Strait of Juan de Fuca, British Columbia. Lower: Barraclough and Peden 1976, fig. 1; also from BCPM 965-2, 83 mm SL, modified.

Range: One previous Alaskan record: a 79-mm-SL specimen taken in an otter trawl by the RV *Miller Freeman* at Icy Bay at 59°53'N, 141°51'W, depth 27–29 m (CAS 47039; Peden and Jamieson 1988). UAM uncataloged material includes two specimens (133 and 153 mm TL) that were taken in the same net haul as Peden and Jamieson's (1988) specimen; characters include A 9, Pec 18, one long simple cirrus at end of maxilla, prickles on breast, strongly upturned mouth, and appropriate coloration (dorsal fins scrunched down too tightly to count elements without damaging specimens). Nearest British Columbia records are from McIntyre Bay and inside the bar off Fife Point, Graham Island (Barraclough and Peden 1976). The unique holotype of *O. impi* (= *S. xyosterna*) was also collected at McIntyre Bay, from the mouth of the Skonun River (Gruchy 1970).

Size: Jordan and Evermann 1898.

Chesnonia verrucosa (Lockington, 1880) **warty poacher**

Southeastern Bering Sea at Bristol Bay; eastern Gulf of Alaska at Shelikof Bay; southern British Columbia off Vancouver Island to central California off Point Montara.

Soft bottoms at depths of 20–274 m.

D VII–X + 6–9; A 7–13; Pec 13–15; SLP 33–35; LLP 36–40; ILP 35–37; Vert 34–38.

- Grayish or brownish, lighter ventrally; dark bands on body and dorsal fins variable; pelvic fin orange and black in males, pale in females.
- Long, depressed head; body and tail depressed throughout; upturned mouth.
- Nasal spine absent or blunt.
- Short barbel at posterior end of maxilla.
- Dorsal fins touching or nearly so; **anal fin base long, usually 10–12 rays**; pelvic fin in males long, extending to anal fin, and expanded.
- **Plates of belly bluntly spinous**.
- Anus close to base of pelvic fins, as usual in agonids.
- Gill membranes united, free from isthmus.
- Length to 200 mm TL.

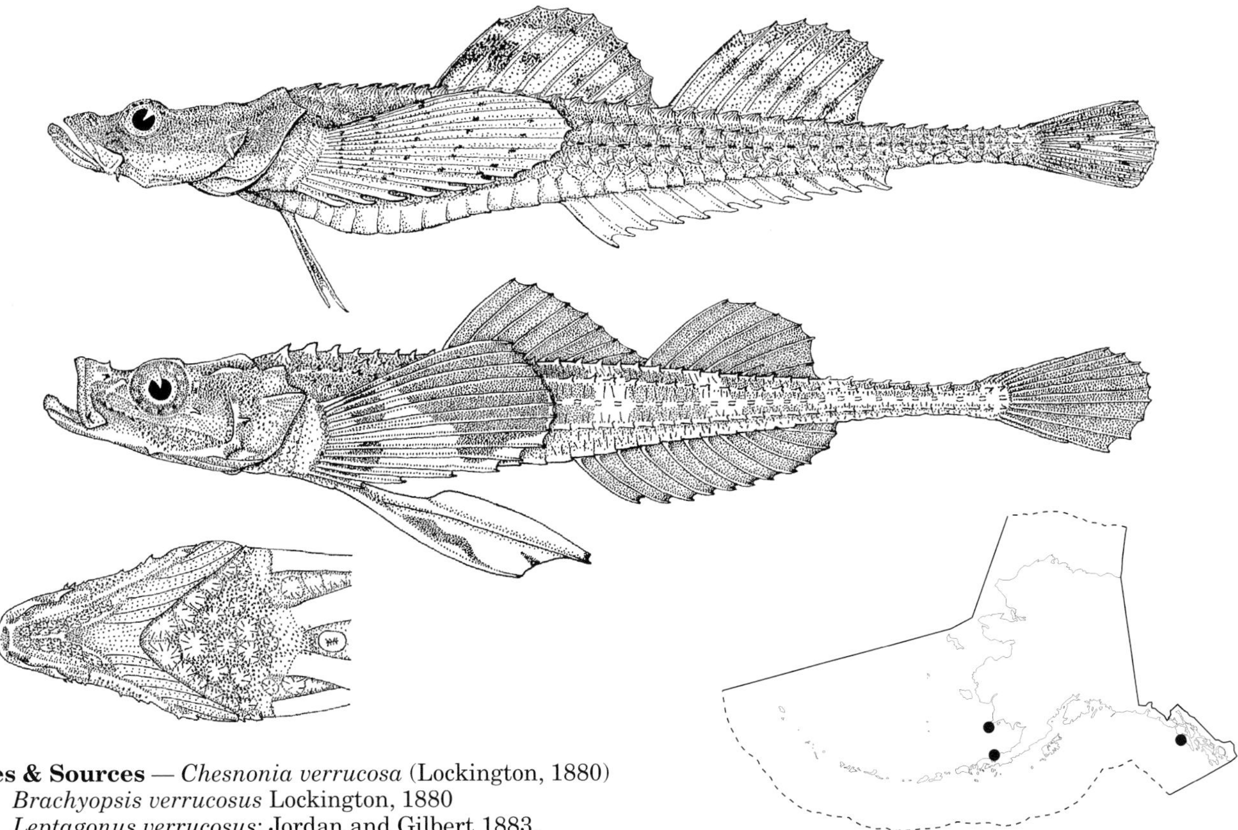

Notes & Sources — *Chesnonia verrucosa* (Lockington, 1880)
Brachyopsis verrucosus Lockington, 1880
Leptagonus verrucosus: Jordan and Gilbert 1883.
Occa verrucosa: Jordan and Evermann 1898.
Chesnonia verrucosa: Iredale and Whitley (1969) proposed *Chesnonia* as a substitute name for *Occa,* which was preoccupied as a genus of bird.
Occella verrucosa: Bailey and Gruchy 1970.
Kanayama (1991) maintained *Chesnonia* as a distinct genus based on presence of a large ectopterygoid.
Easily confused with *Occella dodecaedron,* but anal fin ray counts are different.

Description: Lockington 1880c; Jordan and Evermann 1898: 2043–2044; Gruchy 1969; Kanayama 1991:97–99.

Figures: Upper: Hart 1973:562; UBC 65-711, female, 160 mm TL, Bristol Bay, Alaska. Lower: Kanayama 1991, fig. 43; HUMZ 51923, male, 99 mm SL, Pacific off Oregon.

Range: Occurrence in Alaska not well documented due to confusion with *Occella dodecaedron* and other agonids. Dryfoos (1961) reported two specimens from Shelikof Bay, southeastern Alaska, with diagnostic fin ray counts. Quast and Hall (1972) reported extension of known range to Bering Sea based on AB 67-175, a specimen from Herendeen Bay, Port Moller. Hart's (1973) illustration of *C. verrucosa* (see above) is based on one of five specimens in UBC 65-711, from Bristol Bay at 58°15'N, 162°15'W. Reports of range to "Shelikof" and "Shelikof Str." (Miller and Lea 1972, Eschmeyer and Herald 1983) probably refer to Shelikof Bay in the eastern Gulf of Alaska from the report by Dryfoos (1961), not to Shelikof Strait in the western Gulf of Alaska. CAS 47039, from Gulf of Alaska near Icy Bay, originally identified as this species was referred to *Stellerina xyosterna* by Peden and Jamieson (1988). Other Alaskan specimens C.W.M. found identified as *C. verrucosa* in museum collections are *O. dodecaedron* or *S. xyosterna.* Allen and Smith (1988) gave a range map for *C. verrucosa* based on NMFS surveys, but warned of likely confusion with *O. dodecaedron.*

Size: Jordan and Evermann 1898.

Occella dodecaedron (Tilesius, 1813) **Bering poacher**

Eastern Chukchi Sea at Kotzebue Sound; eastern Bering Sea at Norton Sound to western Gulf of Alaska; western Bering Sea at Gulf of Anadyr to Pacific Ocean off Kamchatka and Kuril Islands, and Okhotsk and northern Japan seas to Peter the Great Bay.

On or over sandy and muddy bottoms, sometimes in *Laminaria* thickets; at 5–47 m, rarely deeper.

D VIII–XI + 6–9; A 13–16; Pec 14–16; SLP 33–40; LLP 37–44; ILP 36–39; Vert 37–40.

- Brownish olive, lighter ventrally; pectoral fin orange with 4 or 5 rows of blackish dots; pelvic fin in males with dark membranes, white in females.
- Head depressed; body as far as middle of first dorsal fin depressed, becoming gradually compressed behind.
- Short barbel at posterior end of maxilla.
- Dorsal fins close together or connecting; **anal fin base long, usually 14–16 rays**; pelvic fin in males not extending to anal fin.
- **Plates of belly nearly smooth**.
- Anus a little farther removed from base of pelvic fins than usual in agonids.
- Gill membranes united, free from isthmus.
- Length to 216 mm TL.

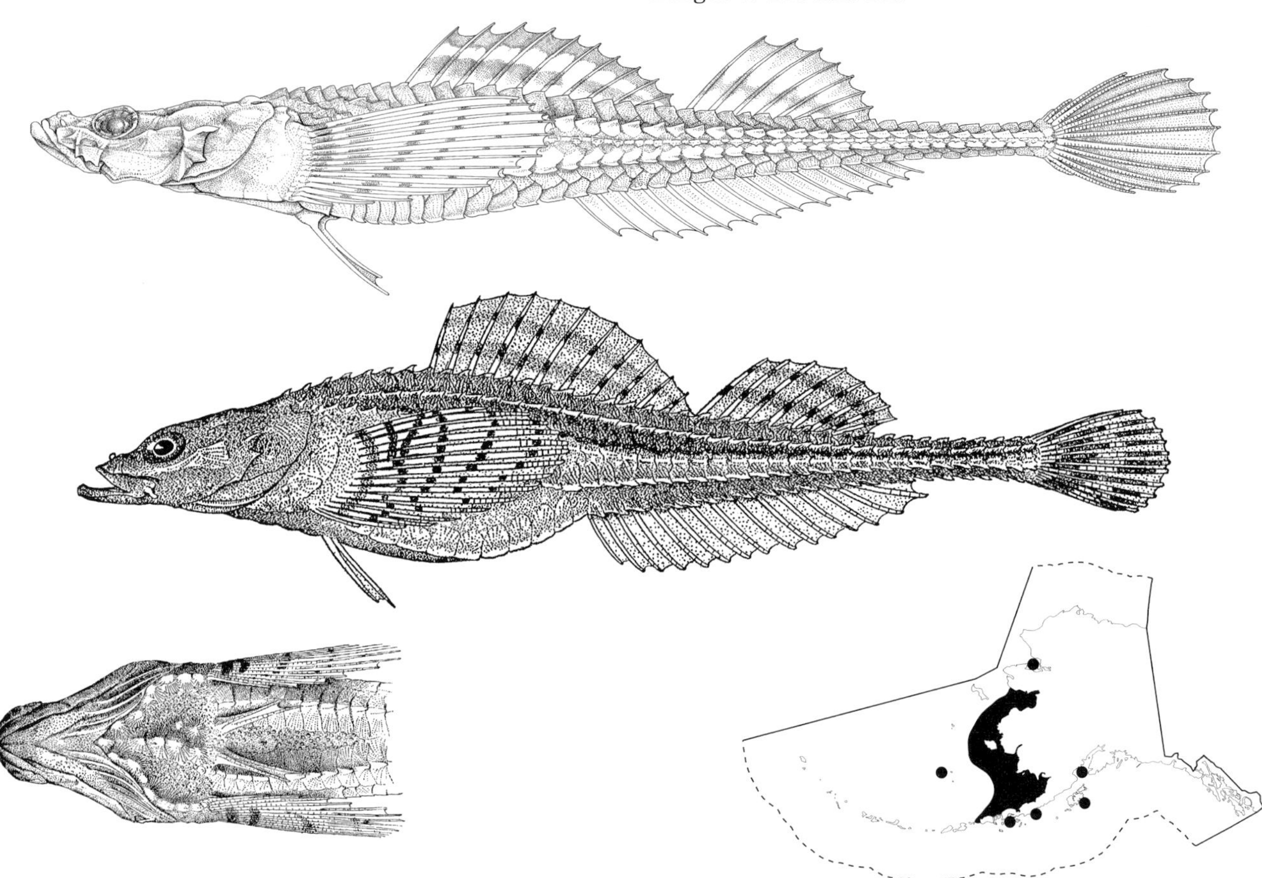

Notes & Sources — *Occella dodecaedron* (Tilesius, 1813)
Agonus dodecaedron Tilesius, 1813
Occa dodecaedron: Jordan and Evermann 1898. *Occa dodecaedra*: Wilimovsky 1954.

Description: Jordan and Evermann 1898:2044–2046; Kanayama 1991:100–102.

Figures: Upper: University of British Columbia, artist R. Wood, Jan. 1969; UBC 60-377, 120 mm SL, desiccated, Bering Sea between Nome and Safety Sound, Alaska. Lower: Jordan and Evermann 1900, fig. 743. Ventral view: Jordan and Gilbert 1899:470.

Range: Distribution in the eastern Bering Sea from Norton Sound to Alaska Peninsula is well documented by Nelson (1887), Gilbert (1896), Quast and Hall (1972), and others, as well as additional museum holdings (e.g., UBC 60-377, Norton Sound between Nome and Safety Sound; USNM 266649–266652, Izembek Lagoon and vicinity). Records outside this range are relatively rare. Allen and Smith (1988): NMFS trawl records from Kotzebue Sound and west of St. Paul Island. Records south of Alaska Peninsula: Phinney (1972), Chignik Bay off Cape Kumliun and near Pavlof Bay; Harris and Hartt (1977), Rogers and Wangerin (1980), and Blackburn and Jackson (1982), east side of Kodiak Island; and Blackburn et al. (1980), lower Cook Inlet. ZIN 44627 from Gulf of Anadyr is northernmost record in western Bering Sea (B. A. Sheiko, pers. comm., 21 Dec. 1998).

Size: R. Baxter, unpubl. data; *Chapman,* Bristol Bay, 10 Jun. 1984, specimen not saved. Reported to reach 190 mm TL (ZIN 42868) by Lindberg and Krasyukova (1987).

Leptagonus decagonus (Bloch & Schneider, 1801) **Atlantic poacher**

Bering and Chukchi seas, east through Arctic Ocean to northern North Atlantic Ocean and eastern Canada; western Bering Sea at Gulf of Anadyr to northern Sea of Okhotsk and to Tatar Strait.

Mud and sand bottoms at depths of 24–930 m; usually shallower than 200 m in Chukchi and Bering seas.

D V–VIII + 5–8; A 5–8; Pec 13–17; SLP 36–41; LLP 21–32; ILP 38–43; Vert 44–49.

- Yellowish gray, with indefinite grayish brown bands and patches; pectoral and caudal fins brownish black toward tips.
- Mouth subterminal; snout projecting slightly beyond mouth.
- **No spines directed forward at tip of snout; free nasal margin serrated; spine on second infraorbital with a supplementary spine or knob.**
- **Barbels (paired): 4 around posterior end of maxilla and angle of mouth, and 1 (bifurcate) on side of lower jaw; infrequently with paired or single small barbel on underside of snout.**
- Keels of body plates strongly developed, with sharp recurved spines.
- Gill membranes united, joined to isthmus without leaving a fold or with only a narrow, rudimentary fold.
- Length to 226 mm TL.

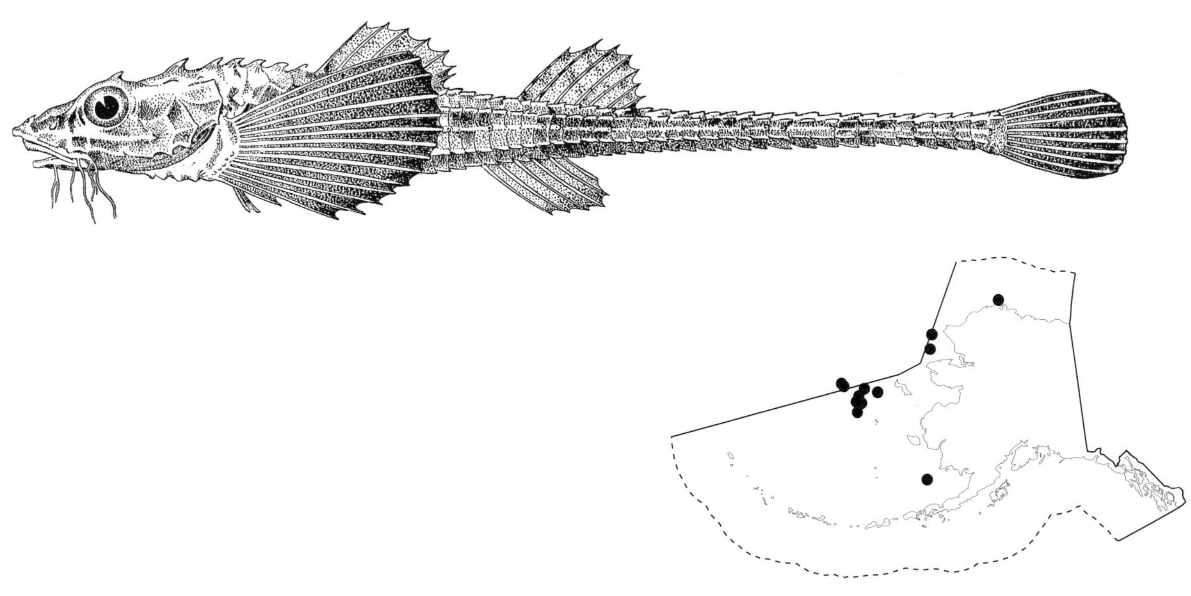

Notes & Sources — *Leptagonus decagonus* (Bloch & Schneider, 1801)
Agonus decagonus Bloch & Schneider, 1801
Podothecus decagonus: Goode and Bean 1896.

Description: Jordan and Evermann 1898:2052–2054; Andriashev 1954:427–429; Scott and Scott 1988:513–514; Kanayama 1991:37–39.

Figure: Goode and Bean 1896, fig. 259; Arctic Ocean.

Range: Andriashev (1937, 1954) suggested that the juvenile specimen of *Podothecus acipenserinus* listed from Cape Lisburne by Bean (1881b) was *L. decagonus.* Quast and Hall (1972) reported occurrence of *L. decagonus* in Alaska to be uncertain. Specimens examined by Kanayama (1991) included at least 11 from the northern Bering Sea, many of them from U.S. waters. The northernmost record from Alaska is UBC 63-1224, a specimen taken in the Arctic off Point Barrow at 71°19'N, 156°44'W, and identified by N. J. Wilimovsky. Southernmost may be UW 28587, from Bristol Bay at 57°40'N, 163°23'W, depth 44 m. UW 15284 is from Chukchi Sea at 68°18'N, 168°15'W, confirmed by B. A. Sheiko (pers. comm., 21 Dec. 1998). Other UW specimens are from localities in the northern Bering Sea close to those recorded by Kanayama (1991). NMC 79-809 comprises four specimens taken southwest of St. Lawrence Island at 62°42'N, 174°58'W, depth 80 m, and identified by B. W. Coad. UAM 1173 is a specimen from the eastern Chukchi Sea at 67°10'N, 168°35'W, with identification confirmed by R. Baxter (unpubl. data). Minimum depth: Sheiko and Fedorov (2000), from ZIN specimens.

Size: Scott and Scott 1988.

Leptagonus frenatus (Gilbert, 1896) **sawback poacher**

Norton Sound, Bering Sea, to Stalemate Bank and Bowers Bank and to northern British Columbia at Observatory Inlet; western Bering Sea at Glubokaya Bay to Pacific coast of Hokkaido, Japan.

On bottom at depths of 18–975 m, usually on outer shelf in water depths of 50–450 m.

D VI–IX + 6–8; A 6–8; Pec 14–17; SLP 41–45; LLP 28–46; ILP 41–45; Vert 45–48.

- Brown dorsally, whitish ventrally; dark blotches and bands; dorsal fins brown, with white spots; anal fin mostly white; caudal fin brown; pectoral fin brown, with or without white blotch on upper portion near base; pelvic fin white or brown.
- Mouth subterminal; snout projects beyond mouth.
- **No spines directed forward at snout tip; free nasal margin serrated, with small spines; spine on second infraorbital with a supplementary spine or knob.**
- **Barbels (paired): 3 at posterior end of maxilla, 1 a little anterior to them, 1 (bifurcate) on side of lower jaw, and 1 on underside of snout.**
- Keels of body plates strongly developed, with sharp recurved spines.
- Gill membranes united, joined to isthmus without a fold or with only a narrow, rudimentary fold.
- Length to 242 mm SL.

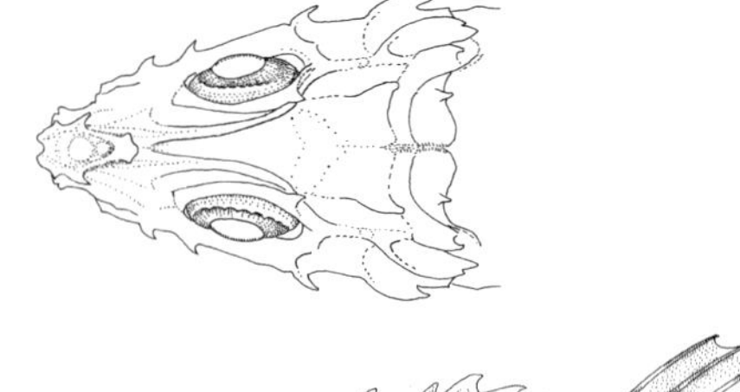

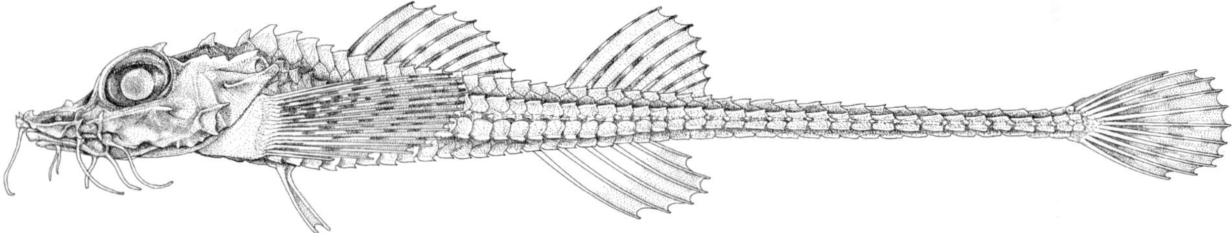

Notes & Sources — *Leptagonus frenatus* (Gilbert, 1896)
Odontopyxis frenatus Gilbert, 1896
Sarritor frenatus: Jordan and Evermann 1898.
Sarritor frenatus occidentalis Lindberg & Andriashev in Andriashev, 1937
Kanayama (1991) classified *Sarritor* in *Leptagonus,* but not all authors (e.g., Sheiko 1993) concur.

Description: Gilbert 1896:435–437; Jordan and Evermann 1898:2073–2075; Kanayama 1980, 1991:39–42. Ranges for anal and pectoral fin ray counts were increased by counts from 93 specimens collected in the vicinity of Cape Navarin (B. A. Sheiko, pers. comm., 21 Dec. 1998).

Figures: Upper: University of British Columbia, artist R. Wood, Dec. 1968; UBC 61-542, 152 mm SL, dessicated specimen, near Douglas Island, southeastern Alaska. Lower: Royal British Columbia Museum, artist K. Shuster, Mar. 1983; BCPM 983-335, 197 mm SL, British Columbia.

Range: The type series was obtained by the *Albatross* from numerous stations (16) north and south of the Aleutian Chain and Alaska Peninsula at depths of 29–642 m (Gilbert 1896). Distribution off Alaska is well documented by additional records, including Evermann and Goldsborough (1907), Wilimovsky (1964), and Quast and Hall (1972). Documented limits in Alaska are Norton Sound in the north, west along the Aleutian Islands to Stalemate Bank and Bowers Bank (Allen and Smith 1988), and south to Petersburg (Freeman 1951), continuing to northern British Columbia at Alice Arm, off Observatory Inlet (Hughes and Kashino 1984).

Size: Kanayama 1980.

Leptagonus leptorhynchus (Gilbert, 1896) **longnose poacher**

Southeastern Bering Sea and Aleutian Islands to northern Gulf of Alaska at Prince William Sound; western Bering Sea to Commander Islands, Pacific coast of northern Japan, and Okhotsk and Japan seas.

Sand, gravel, muddy sand, sand-pebble-shell, and other soft bottoms at depths of 14.6–345 m; reported to reach 974 m.

D VI–IX + 5–8; A 5–8; Pec 13–15; SLP 35–42; LLP 20–33; ILP 39–43; Vert 42–45.

- Dark brown dorsally, white ventrally; indistinct dark bands and blotches; dorsal, anal, and pelvic fins white; first dorsal with dark brown bands, second dorsal with a few dark spots; upper portion of pectoral fin brown, lower portion white; caudal fin dark brown.
- Mouth subterminal; **snout elongate, slender, projecting well beyond mouth**.
- **No spines directed forward at snout tip; free nasal margin smooth; spine on second infraorbital without a supplementary spine**.
- **Barbels (paired): 3 at posterior end of maxilla, 1 a little anterior to them, 1 (sometimes bifurcate) on lower jaw, and 1 under snout**.
- **Spines on body plates not as well developed as in other *Leptagonus***.
- Gill membranes united, joined to isthmus without a fold or with only a narrow, rudimentary fold.
- Length to 200 mm SL.

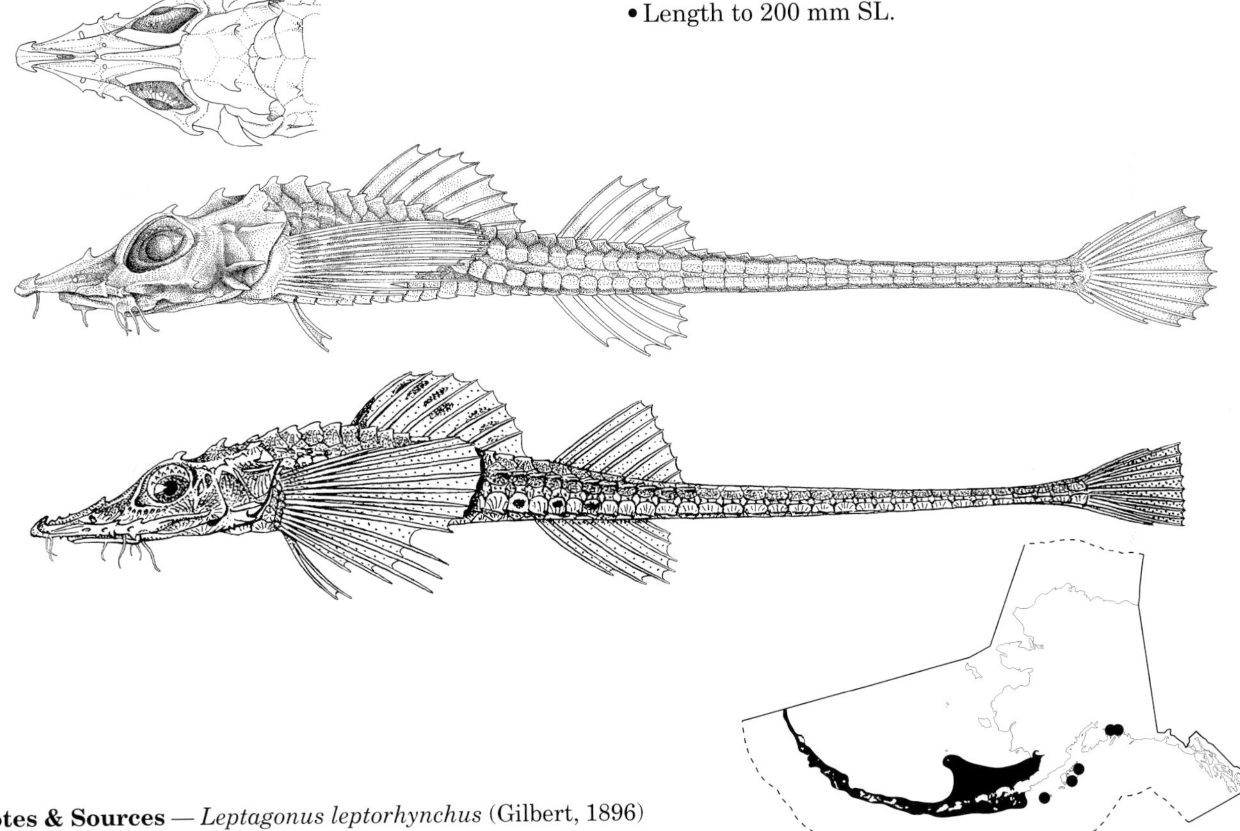

Notes & Sources — *Leptagonus leptorhynchus* (Gilbert, 1896)
Odontopyxis leptorhynchus Gilbert, 1896
Sarritor leptorhynchus: Jordan and Evermann 1898.
Kanayama (1991) classified *Sarritor* in *Leptagonus,* but not all authors (e.g., Sheiko 1993) concur.

Description: Gilbert 1896:437; Jordan and Evermann 1898:2075–2076; Kanayama 1991:42–45.

Figures: Upper: University of British Columbia, artist R. Wood, Dec. 1968; UBC 65-146, 138 mm SL, desiccated, off Kodiak Island, Alaska. Lower: Lindberg and Krasyukova 1987, fig. 202; ZIN 12314, 157 mm SL, Sea of Japan.

Range: The type series was collected from inner Bristol Bay by Gilbert (1896) aboard the *Albatross.* R. Baxter (unpubl. data) examined specimens near the Pribilof Islands at 56°30'N, 169°45'W and 56°45'N, 169°20'W during a NMFS survey in April 1984. The species probably occurs farther north off Alaska, as it does off Russia; Kanayama (1991) examined specimens from 61°27'N, 174°30'E. Specimens described by Gilbert (1896) were collected around Unimak Island and Unimak Pass, as well as inner Bristol Bay. Recorded west in Aleutian Islands as far as Amchitka Island (Simenstad et al. 1977), but probably occurs throughout the chain; Gilbert and Burke (1912a) found this species at the Commander Islands. Recorded from Shumagin Islands by Quast and Hall (1972). Gulf of Alaska records include: UBC 62-442 and 62-659, southwest of Chirikof Island; UBC 65-146, off southeast coast Kodiak Island at 57°20'N, 153°22'W; UW 28583, north of Kodiak Island at 57°53'N, 152°43'W; UW 27345 and 27376, Prince William Sound. UW records were confirmed by B. A. Sheiko (pers. comm., 21 Dec. 1998).

Size: Kanayama 1991.

Agonopsis vulsa (Jordan & Gilbert, 1880) **northern spearnose poacher**

Northern Gulf of Alaska at Kachemak Bay to southern California off Point Loma.

Soft level bottom at depths of 5–180 m, and sometimes in tidepools.

D VIII–X + 7–9; A 10–12; Pec 13–15; SLP 37–41; LLP 40–42; ILP 36–38; Vert 38–42.

- Dark brown dorsally, white ventrally; irregular white bars laterally; snout black; pelvic fin dark brown, with white tip; semitransparent light spot on caudal fin.
- Mouth inferior; snout projecting.
- **Shallow pit on occipital region**.
- Tip of snout with 2 pairs of spines: 1 directed forward, with tips skin-covered; and 1 curving upward, outward, and slightly backward.
- Two irregular rows of spines on eyeball.
- **Barbels and cirri on opercle, interopercle, maxilla, chin, mandible, and gill membranes; not always present on underside of snout; fine cirri on lips**.
- Vomerine and palatine teeth present.
- Gill membranes united, joined to isthmus.
- Length to 200 mm TL.

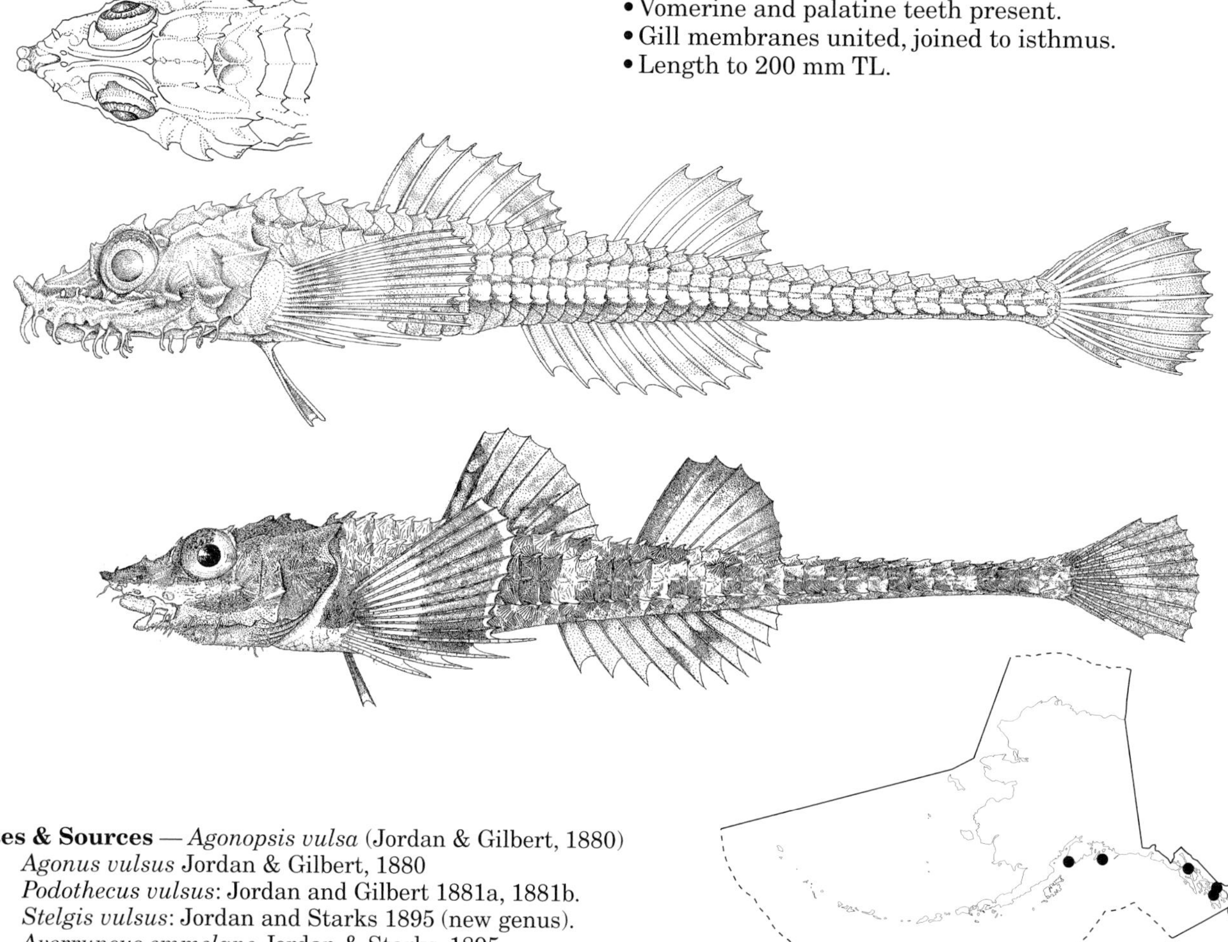

Notes & Sources — *Agonopsis vulsa* (Jordan & Gilbert, 1880)
Agonus vulsus Jordan & Gilbert, 1880
Podothecus vulsus: Jordan and Gilbert 1881a, 1881b.
Stelgis vulsus: Jordan and Starks 1895 (new genus).
Averruncus emmelane Jordan & Starks, 1895
Xystes axinophrys Jordan & Starks, 1895
Agonopsis emmelane: Wilimovsky 1954, 1958. Hubbs, Follett, and Dempster (1979) and Lea and Dempster (1982) classified *A. emmelane* as a junior synonym of *Agonus vulsus* with the binomen *Agonopsis vulsa*.

Description: Jordan and Gilbert 1880q; Jordan and Starks 1895:821–827; Jordan and Evermann 1898:2067–2071; Gilbert 1915:343; Kanayama 1991:63–65.

Figures: Upper: University of British Columbia, artist R. Wood, Dec. 1968; UBC 53-66, 133 mm SL, desiccated, British Columbia. Lower: Jordan and Starks 1895, pl. 91; type of *Averruncus emmelane*, 180 mm TL, Port Orchard, Washington.

Range: Listed from southeastern Alaska by Wilimovsky (1954, 1958). Quast and Hall (1972) reported extension of known range to the northern Gulf of Alaska; based on AB 64-627 from east of Montague Island at 59°52'N, 147°13'W. Other northern records are a specimen in SIO 67-162, from a Kasitsna Bay tidepool; and one in UBC 65-154, collected a few kilometers away in Kachemak Bay. UW 22382, from the Bering Sea at 55°11'N, 165°11'W, was originally identified as *A. vulsa,* but B. A. Sheiko determined it to be an example of *Leptagonus frenatus* (UW online catalog). There are no confirmed records of *A. vulsa* from the Bering Sea. Records for southeastern Alaska include AB 77-92, Steamer Bay, Etolin Island; AB 89-29, Yakobi Rock; and UW 1619 and 1656, Wrangell Island. Peden and Wilson (1976) recorded British Columbia specimens taken from Brundige Inlet at 54°36'N, 130°51'W, and slightly farther south.

Size: Miller and Lea 1972.

Podothecus accipenserinus (Tilesius, 1813) **sturgeon poacher**

Bering Sea and Aleutian Islands from Attu Island to northern California at Point Reyes; western Bering Sea south of Cape Navarin to Commander Islands, and Pacific Ocean to Sea of Okhotsk off southwestern Kamchatka and northern Kuril Islands.

Soft bottoms at depths of 2–300 m.

D VIII–X + 7–8; A 7–9; Pec 17–19; SLP 28–31; LLP 38–40; ILP 36–38; Vert 39–42.

- Yellowish brown to gray-brown with dark bands dorsally, white to orange ventrally; cirri under snout yellow, around mouth white; dorsal and caudal fin margins black; anal fin with dark blotch posteriorly; pectoral fin pale, with indistinct bands and dark lower portion; pelvic fin pale or dark.
- **Mouth inferior, with gap when closed**; snout greatly projecting.
- Tip of snout with 2 pairs of spines: 1 pointed forward and 1 curving backward and outward.
- **Uppermost preopercular spine not expanded laterally**.
- No spines on eyeball.
- **Dense clusters of barbels under snout and at corner of mouth on each side; 13–19 barbels in each patch on snout**; no barbels or cirri on gill membranes.
- Teeth present on upper and lower jaws; vomerine and palatine teeth absent.
- Gill membranes united, joined to isthmus without free fold.
- Length to 305 mm TL.

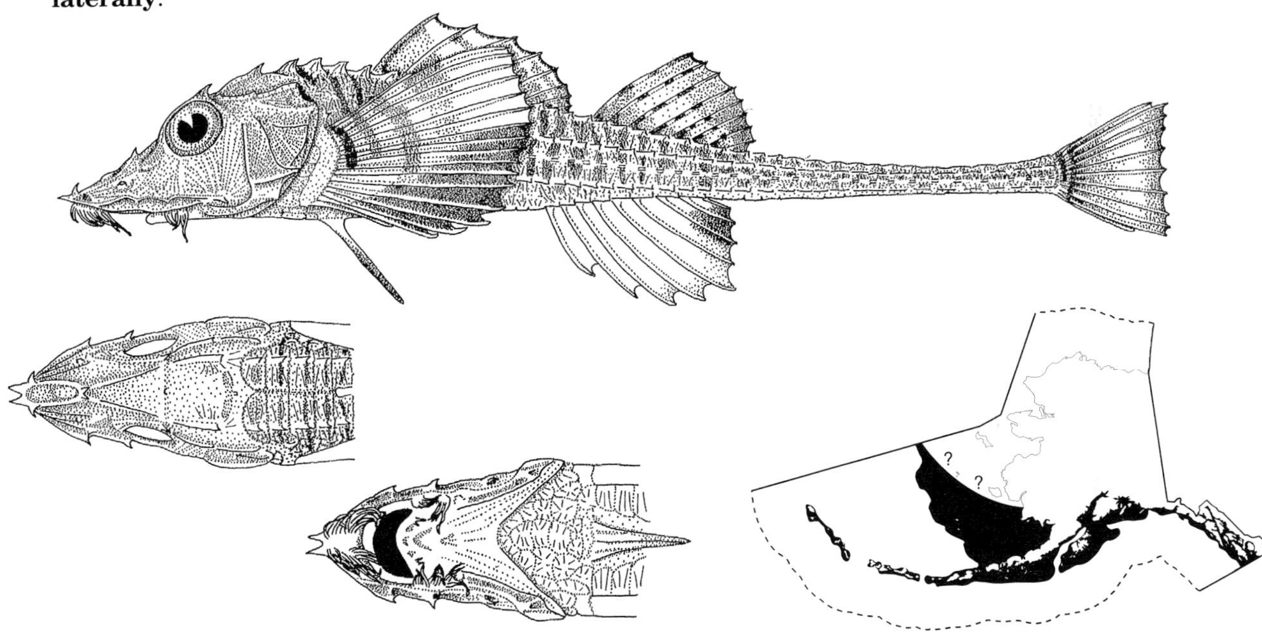

Notes & Sources — *Podothecus accipenserinus* (Tilesius, 1813)
Agonus accipenserinus Tilesius, 1813
Phalangistes acipenserinus Pallas, 1814
Although for many years authors followed Pallas (1814) and spelled the specific epithet with one *c*, this is incorrect. Sheiko (1993), writing in Russian in his taxonomic catalog of agonids, reported the error; for details in English, see Eschmeyer (2001).

Description: Jordan and Evermann 1898:2061–2062; Andriashev 1954:431–432; Hart 1973:550; Kanayama 1991:46–48.

Figures: Kanayama 1991, fig. 16; HUMZ 76796, 193 mm SL, Bristol Bay, Alaska.

Range: Specimens in UW, ABL, ZIN, and KIE collections examined by B. A. Sheiko (pers. comms., May–Dec. 1998) indicate range of this species in the eastern Bering Sea may extend north only to the vicinity of St. Matthew Island, whereas previously it was believed to extend north into the Alaskan Beaufort Sea. *Podothecus accipenserinus* is sympatric with *P. veternus* in the western portion of its range from Cape Navarin to the northern Kuril Islands, and, evidently, is replaced by *P. veternus* in the Chukchi and Beaufort seas. UAM uncataloged vouchers from the Chukchi Sea recorded as *P. accipenserinus* (Barber et al. 1997) were determined by C.W.M. to be examples of *P. veternus*. Walters (1955) noted that a small specimen (2.8 cm) from Cape Lisburne, Chukchi Sea, recorded as *P. accipenserinus* by Bean (1881b, 1883) had been destroyed, so the identification could not be verified; it lacked snout barbels and probably was a different species. A specimen from Point Barrow collected and identified as *P. accipenserinus* by N. J. Wilimovsky and cited by Walters (1955) is missing, but presence of others in the UBC collection (which holds most of Wilimovsky's specimens) referable to *P. veternus* suggests this record also represents *P. veternus*. Survey catches of *P. accipenserinus* north of St. Matthew Island reported by Allen and Smith (1988) probably represent, at least in part, *P. veternus*.

Size: Jordan and Evermann 1898.

Podothecus veternus Jordan & Starks, 1895 **veteran poacher**

Beaufort and Chukchi seas to eastern Bering Sea near St. Matthew Island, and to Okhotsk and Japan seas. Soft bottoms at depths of 18–240 m.

D VIII–IX + 7–8; A 7–9; Pec 15–17; SLP 28–31; LLP 37–42; ILP 34–38; Vert 41.

- In preservative, brown dorsally with dark bands, lighter ventrally; cirri under snout and around mouth pale; dorsal fins with dark margins and dark streaks at bases; caudal fin fin dark; pectoral fin pale, with dark margin and indistinct dark bands; anal and pelvic fins colorless.
- **Mouth inferior, with gap when closed**; snout greatly projecting.
- Tip of snout with 2 pairs of spines: 1 pointed forward and 1 curving backward and outward.
- **Uppermost preopercular spine expanded laterally**.
- No spines on eyeball.
- **Dense clusters of barbels under snout and at corner of mouth on each side; 6–11 barbels in each patch on snout**; no barbels or cirri on gill membranes.
- Teeth absent from upper jaw, present on lower jaw; vomerine and palatine teeth absent.
- Gill membranes united, joined to isthmus without free fold.
- Length to 285 mm TL.

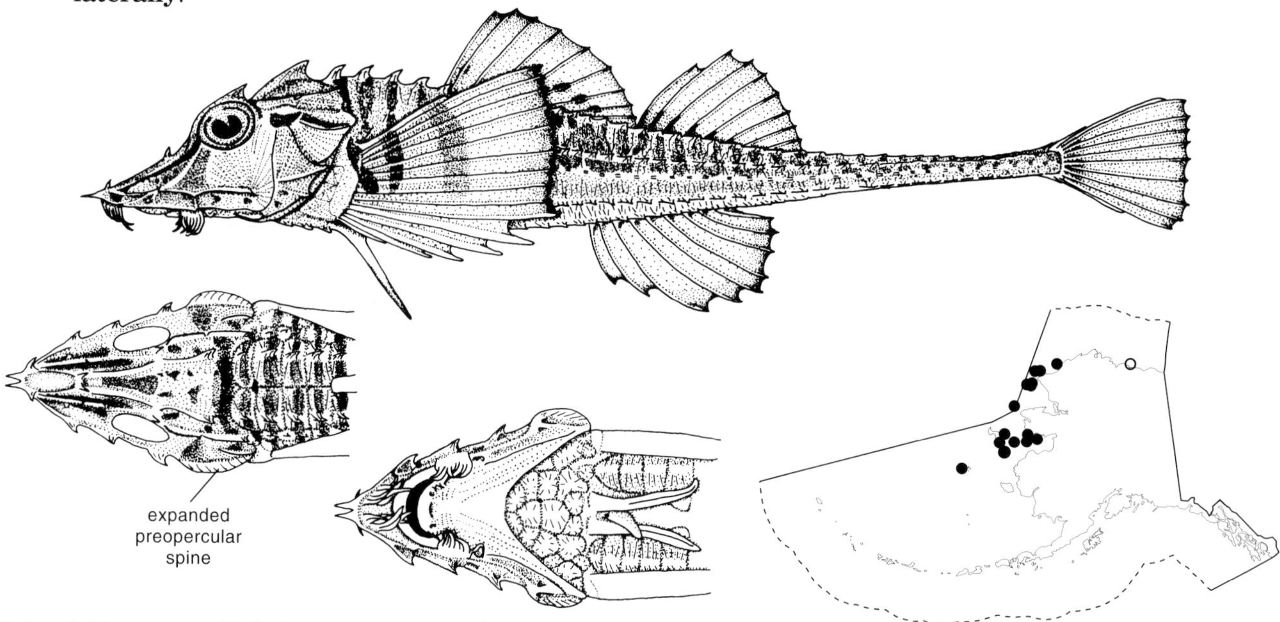

Notes & Sources — *Podothecus veternus* Jordan & Starks, 1895
Podothecus hamlini Jordan & Gilbert in Jordan & Evermenn, 1898
Sheiko (1993) classified *P. hamlini* in the synonymy of *P. veternus.*
The species name *veternus* means "old man" or "veteran," in allusion to the lack of teeth (Jordan and Evermann 1898:2064); hence the suggested vernacular, veteran poacher.

Description: Jordan and Starks 1895:819–821; Jordan and Evermann 1898:2056–2058, 2063–2064; Lindberg and Krasyukova 1987:337–339; Kanayama 1991:49–51.

Figures: Kanayama 1991, fig. 17; HUMZ 58950, 138 mm SL, Sea of Okhotsk.

Range: Most dots on our map represent ABL and UW lots previously identified as *P. accipenserinus* but examined and referred to *P. veternus* by B. A. Sheiko (pers. comms., May–Dec. 1998). The dot in Russian waters of Bering Strait represents KIE 2098 (B. A. Sheiko, pers. comm., 8 Sep. 1998); previously recorded in western Bering Sea as far north as Provideniya Bay (Lindberg and Krasyukova 1987). The northernmost Alaskan record identified by Sheiko is AB 70-167, taken off Point Lay at 69°43'N, 163°34'W, and the southernmost is UW 28156, near St. Matthew Island at 60°40'N, 172°49'W. C.W.M. examined UAM uncataloged vouchers from the eastern Chukchi Sea identified by Barber et al. (1997) as P. *accipenserinus*, and they also are *P. veternus.* Five specimens (91–123 mm TL) from three localities were examined: 70°22'N, 162°53'W, 30 m; 70°00'N, 163°28'W, 38 m; and 70°00'N, 164°56'W, 33 m. They have 8–10 barbels in each snout-tip patch, and the uppermost preopercular spine is strongly expanded. Additional museum specimens should be examined to more precisely describe the range of each species. The UBC has several lots from the Chukchi Sea identified as *P. accipenserinus* that probably represent *P. veternus*; an illustration of UBC 61-88 clearly depicts this species. Some, or all, of the records mapped by Allen and Smith (1988) for *P. accipenserinus* north of Saint Matthew Island likely represent *P. veternus.* Jarvela and Thorsteinson (1999) reported catching one *P. accipenserinus* in the Beaufort Sea, which, given the information presented here, was likely a *P. veternus* (voucher specimen was lost); catch locality (L.K.T., unpubl. data) was near the Endicott Causeway at 70°13'N, 147°35'W. The holotype (unique) is from the Gulf of Patience, Sea of Okhotsk, not from Puget Sound (as the title of Jordan and Starks' [1895] work might suggest).

Size: Lindberg and Krasyukova 1987.

Bothragonus swanii (Steindachner, 1876) **rockhead**

Western Gulf of Alaska at Kodiak Island to central California at Lion Rock, San Luis Obispo County.

Along exposed coasts in the intertidal area and to depth of about 18 m, often found in rocky or pebble-bottomed tidepools among sponges and various other flora and fauna.

D II–V + 4–6; A 4–5; Pec 10–12; SLP 26–28; LLP 31–32; ILP 28–30; Vert 29–32.

- Brown mottled with red and brown, to red or orange with black bars; most fins spotted; pectoral fin with wide light band near base.
- **Head and front of body broad, strongly compressed behind; large, deep occipital pit with club-shaped processes inside**.
- **Dorsal and anal fins small, especially first dorsal**.
- **Body plates large, rounded, smooth**.
- Gill membranes united, broadly joined to isthmus leaving only a thin crease across isthmus.
- Length to 89 mm TL.

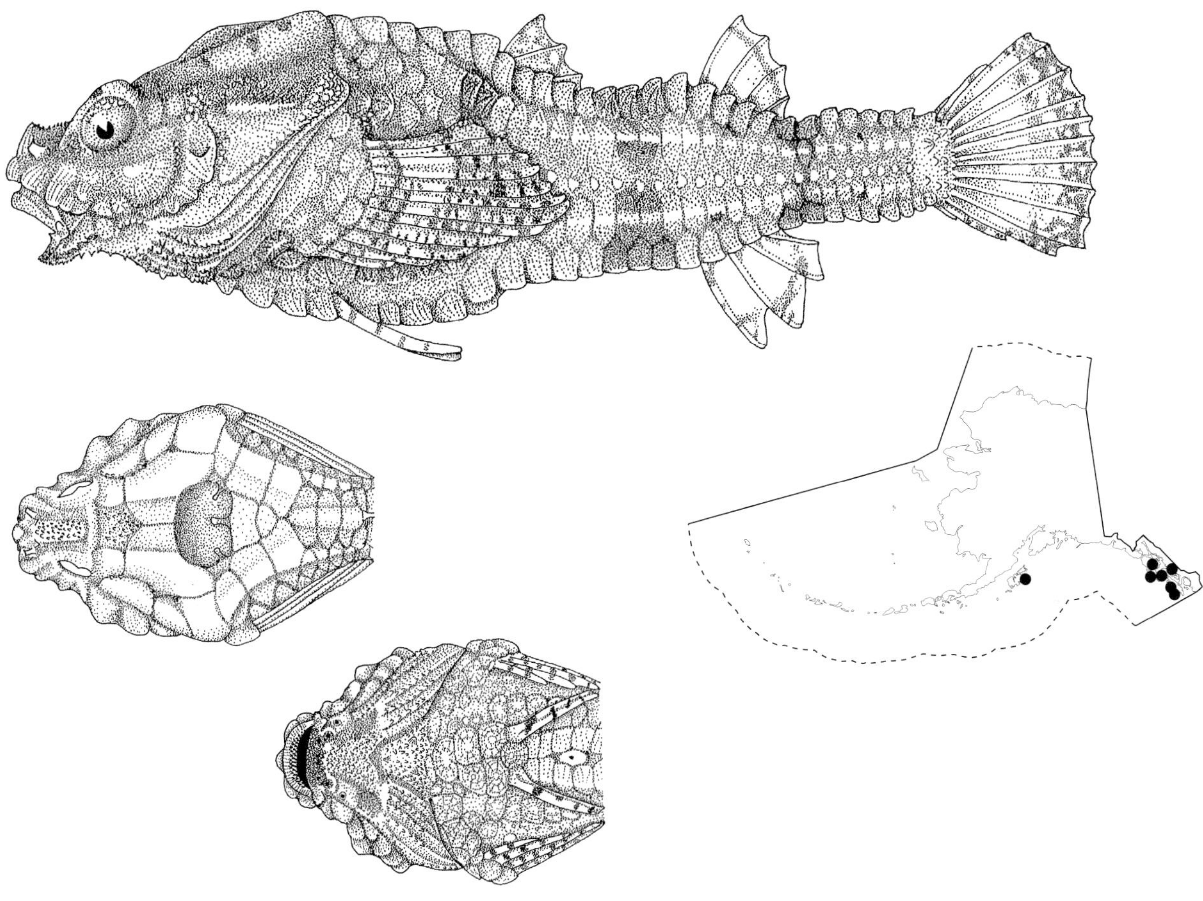

Notes & Sources — *Bothragonus swanii* (Steindachner, 1876)
Hypsagonus swanii Steindachner, 1876

Description: Jordan and Evermann 1898:2086–2088; Hart 1973:558–559; Leipertz 1988; Kanayama 1991:69–70. Leipertz (1988) proposed that the deep occipital pit mimics sponge and sea squirt openings and, in conjunction with coloration, enhances the rockhead's ability to hide from predators. The pit may also serve sensory functions as part of the lateralis system (M. Busby, pers. comm., 18 May 1998).

Figures: Kanayama 1991, fig. 25; HUMZ 51922, 49.5 mm SL, California.

Range: Previous Alaskan records are those of Hubbard and Reeder (1965) from Shearwater Bay, Kodiak Island; and Quast (1968) from Samsing Cove, Baranof Island (AB 64-954). Additional examples from southeastern Alaska include AB 77-111 from Steamer Bay, Etolin Island; UBC 65-574, southeast point of Klokachef Island; UBC 65-527, Port Conclusion, Baranof Island; and UBC 65-582, Baker Island. NMC 61-163 contains two specimens from a tidepool on San Juan Batista Island, one tomato red with black bars and the other yellow-brown with black bars (NMC records).

Size: Hart 1973.

Odontopyxis trispinosa Lockington, 1880 **pygmy poacher**

Southeastern Bering Sea, record not verifiable; Gulf of Alaska at Prince William Sound to Baja California off Cedros Island.

Sand or mud bottoms at depths of 5–373 m; at the greater depths in the southern part of the range.

D III–VI + 5–7; A 5–7; Pec 13–15; SLP 34–38; LLP 35–39; ILP 35–36; Vert 37–42.

- Gray to olive brown, paler ventrally; 6 or 7 dark blotches or bands.
- **Heart-shaped or double occipital pit**.
- **Vertical spine at tip of snout**, as well as pair of nasal spines farther back on snout.
- **Single barbel at posterior end of maxilla**.
- Body plates with moderately developed spines.
- Gill membranes united, broadly joined to isthmus without fold across isthmus or with only a very slight fold.
- Length to 95 mm TL.

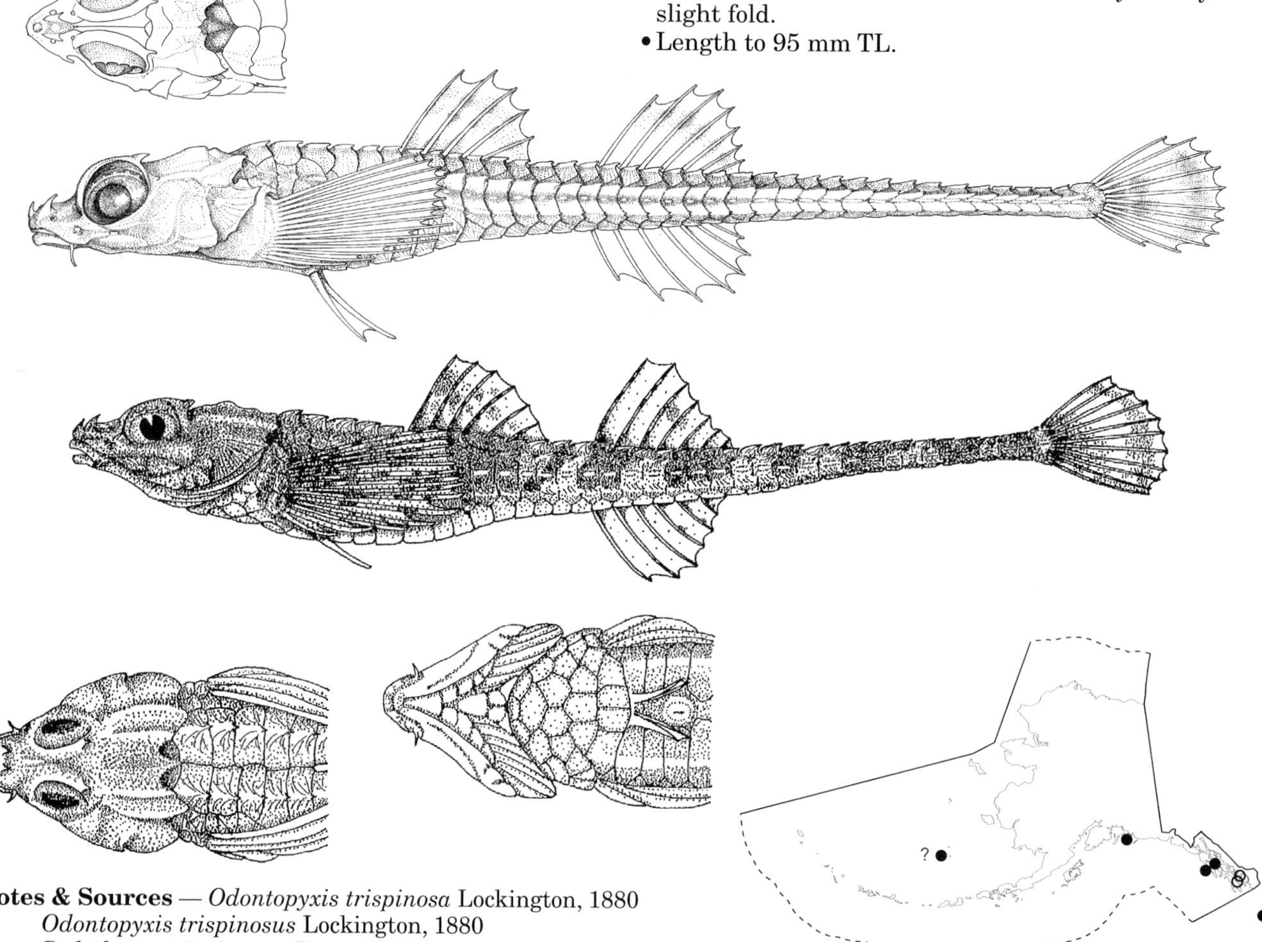

Notes & Sources — *Odontopyxis trispinosa* Lockington, 1880
Odontopyxis trispinosus Lockington, 1880
Podothecus trispinosus: Bean 1881b.
The specific epithet should be spelled *trispinosa* to agree with the gender (feminine) of the genus (e.g., Eschmeyer and Herald 1983, Sheiko 1993, Eschmeyer 1998).

Description: Lockington 1880a:328–330; Jordan and Evermann 1898:2085; Hubbs 1942; Kanayama 1991:84–85.

Figures: Upper: University of British Columbia, artist R. Wood, Jan. 1969; UBC 53-73, 70 mm SL, desiccated, British Columbia. Lower: Kanayama 1991, fig. 35; BCPM 978-144, 63 mm SL, off Vancouver Island, British Columbia.

Range: Bean (1881b) reported *O. trispinosa* from Sitka, and Evermann and Goldborough (1907) stated it had been "seen" at Behm Canal and Kasaan Bay (open circles on the above map). Quast and Hall's (1972) southeastern Alaska record is based on AB 67-40, from Katlian Bay, Baranof Island. The only Prince William Sound record is UW 40951, confirmed by B. A. Sheiko (pers. comm., 21 Dec. 1998), from Northwest Bay, Eleanor Island, depth 40 m. UAM 1066, obtained from Prince William Sound and identified as this species, is *Bathyagonus infraspinatus* (examined by C.W.M., 16 Nov. 2000). The CAS catalog lists one lot from the Bering Sea near St. Paul Island (CAS 104057, 57°06'N, 170°35'W), but it cannot be found (J. Fong, pers. comm., 10 Mar. 1999) and identification has not been confirmed. Peden and Wilson (1976) found the species at Griffith Harbour and other northern British Columbia sites at shallow subtidal depths. Clemens and Wilby (1949) noted it was taken in shrimp trawls at 18–72 m off British Columbia. Gilbert (1896) recorded it from depths of 20–86 m off California, except at 373 m south of Monterey Bay; and later (Gilbert 1915) at depths of 18–143 m off southern California.

Size: Eschmeyer and Herald 1983.

Bathyagonus nigripinnis Gilbert, 1890 — **blackfin poacher**

Eastern Bering Sea and Aleutian Islands to northern California off Eureka; western Bering Sea from Navarin Canyon to Commander Islands, southeastern Kamchatka, and northern Kuril Islands.

Fine sand or mud bottoms at depths of 18–1,247 m, most often taken on outer shelf and upper slope at depths of 90–800 m; one of the few deepwater poachers.

D IV–VIII + 5–8; A 6–10; Pec 14–17; SLP 39–44; LLP 40–46; ILP 38–43; Vert 43–46.

- Brown; bluish black gill membrane; **fins uniformly black or bluish black**.
- **Lower jaw projecting beyond upper jaw**.
- Free lachrymal margin finely serrated; infraorbital ridge serrated, ending as sharp spine directed posterolaterally; 2–4 spinous plates below ridge; 0–5 spinous processes on eyeball.
- Rostral plate with 3 spines directed dorsally and 2 laterally.
- Two small barbels at posterior end of maxilla; no barbels on mandible.
- Anal fin origin below dorsal fin interspace.
- More plates in supralateral and infralateral rows than in *B. alascanus* or *B. infraspinatus*.
- Gill membranes united, broadly joined to isthmus without free fold across isthmus.
- Length to 242 mm TL.

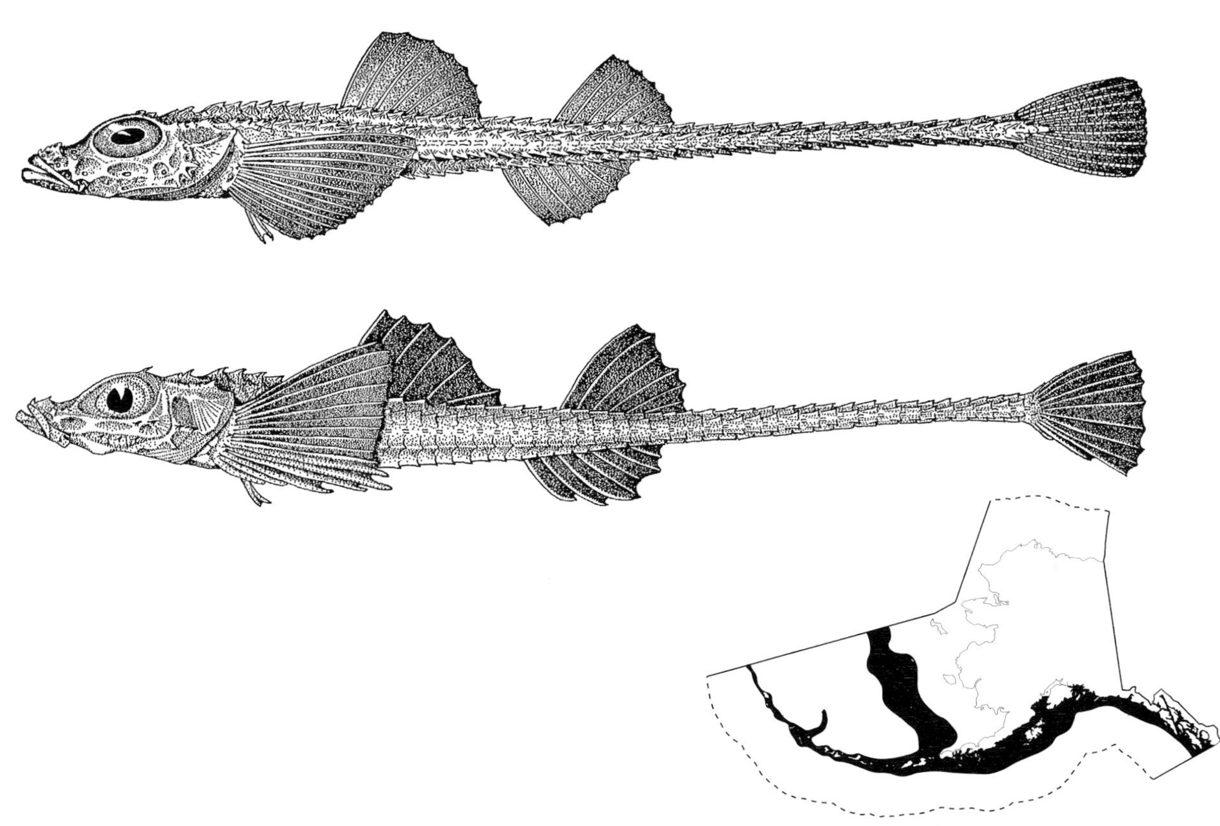

Notes & Sources — *Bathyagonus nigripinnis* Gilbert, 1890

Called blackfin starsnout by Hubbs et al. (1979) and McAllister (1990) to be consistent with the common names of other species in the genus *Bathyagonus,* but the name blackfin poacher is given by the American Society of Ichthyologists and Herpetologists and American Fisheries Society on their list of common names of North American continental shelf fishes (e.g., Robins et al. 1991a).

Description: Gilbert 1890:89–90; Jordan and Evermann 1898:2078–2079; Fitch 1973; Kanayama 1991:73–74. Dorsal and anal fin spine and ray counts were extended by B. A. Sheiko (pers. comm., 21 Dec. 1998) from a sample of 213 specimens collected in the northwestern Bering Sea.

Figures: Upper: Jordan and Evermann 1900, fig. 753; USNM 46614, Aleutian Islands. Lower: Kanayama 1991, fig. 27; HUMZ 84261, central Bering Sea, Alaska.

Range: The most abundant and widely distributed of the four species of *Bathyagonus* occurring in Alaska. Distribution off Alaska well documented by, for example, Jordan and Gilbert (1899), Evermann and Goldsborough (1907), Quast and Hall (1972), and Kanayama (1991). NMFS survey data reported by Allen and Smith (1988) extended the known range north to St. Matthew Island and Navarin Canyon. Maximum depth: Sheiko and Fedorov 2000.

Size: Tokranov (2000d) reported a maximum size of 242 mm TL in females and 239 mm TL in males in trawl catches off southeastern Kamchatka and the northern Kuril Islands. Previously recorded to 210 mm TL in the eastern Pacific by Eschmeyer and Herald (1983).

Bathyagonus pentacanthus (Gilbert, 1890) **bigeye poacher**

Western Gulf of Alaska near Chirikof Island to Cortes Bank near San Diego, California.
Mud or sand bottoms in deep waters, usually at about 100–375 m, reported to depth of 910 m.

D V–VIII + 5–8; A 6–9; Pec 14–16; SLP 40–45; LLP 39–46; ILP 39–43; Vert 40–46.

- Olive brown dorsally, same or paler ventrally; 4–6 indistinct dark bands on body; **dusky areas on dorsal and pectoral fins; anal and pelvic fins mostly pale; caudal fin dusky to black.**
- **Lower jaw not projecting beyond upper jaw.**
- Free lachrymal margin smooth; infraorbital ridge weakly serrated, with 3 spines (1 on lachrymal, 2 on 2nd infraorbital); 3 spinous plates below ridge; 4 or 5 spinous processes on eyeball.
- Rostral plate with 3 spines directed dorsally and 2 laterally.
- One or two barbels at posterior end of maxilla; barbels on mandible small, not always present.
- Anal fin origin below dorsal fin interspace.
- More plates in supralateral and infralateral rows than in *B. alascanus* or *B. infraspinatus*; **two pairs of plates immediately in front of pelvic fins.**
- Gill membranes united, broadly joined to isthmus anteriorly but narrowly attached to isthmus along sides posteriorly, leaving narrow median portion free over isthmus.
- Length to 262 mm TL.

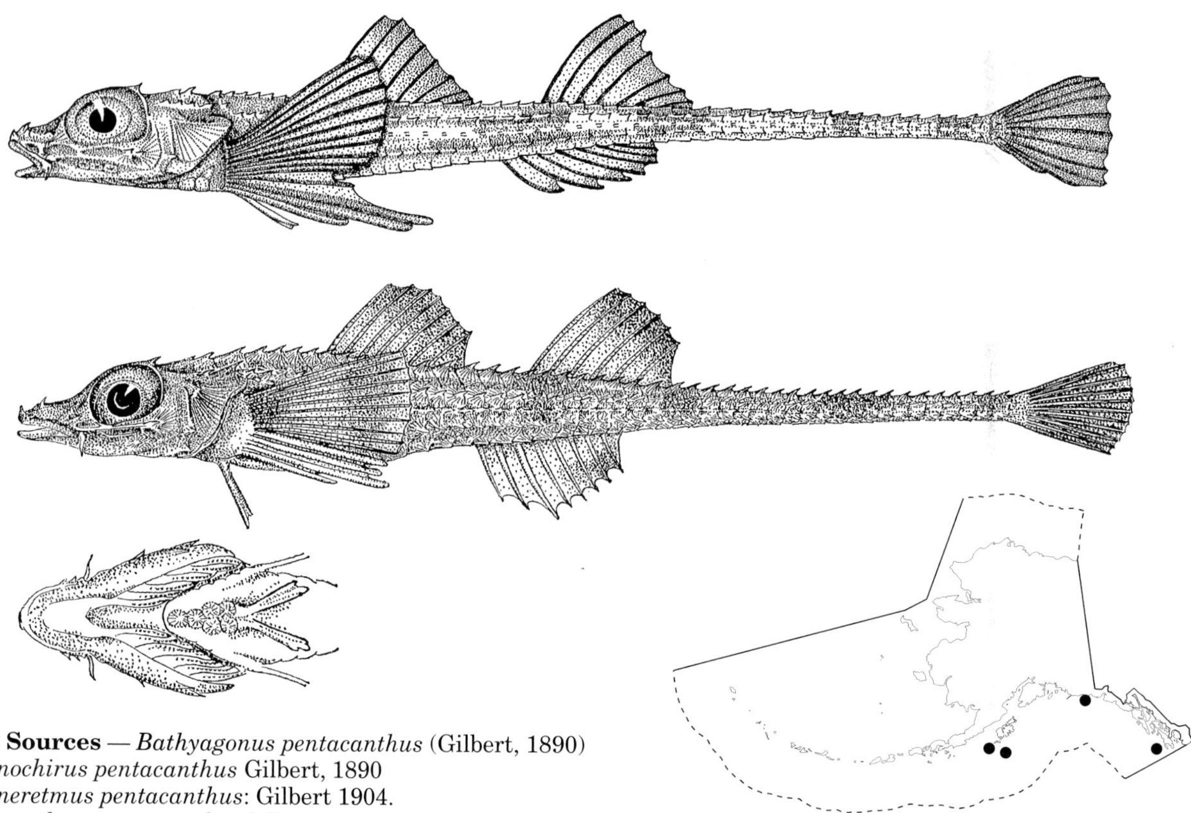

Notes & Sources — *Bathyagonus pentacanthus* (Gilbert, 1890)
Xenochirus pentacanthus Gilbert, 1890
Xeneretmus pentacanthus: Gilbert 1904.
Asterotheca pentacantha: Gilbert 1915.
Fitch (1973) classified *Asterotheca* in *Bathyagonus*.
Called bigeye starsnout by Hubbs et al. (1979) and McAllister (1990), but the American Fisheries Society and the American Society of Ichthyologists and Herpetologists (e.g., Robins et al. 1991a) prefer the name bigeye poacher.

Description: Gilbert 1890:91–92; 1915:344; Jordan and Evermann 1898:2080–1081; Fitch 1973; Kanayama 1991: 74–76.

Figures: Upper: Kanayama 1991, fig. 28; HUMZ 62264, eastern Gulf of Alaska. Lower: Hart 1973:556, modified; UBC 65-59, 240 mm TL, western Gulf of Alaska.

Range: Fitch (1973) determined that all previous records from the Bering Sea and Alaska attributed to *B. pentacanthus* were based on incorrect identifications by Evermann and Goldsborough (1907). The only Alaskan record he considered valid was a specimen from the western Gulf of Alaska near Chirikof Island (UBC 65-59, 55°49'N, 154°58'W; see illustration above). Kanayama (1991) recorded a specimen from the eastern Gulf of Alaska west of Dall Island (HUMZ 62264, 55°23'N, 134°52'W; also shown above). B. A. Sheiko (pers. comm., 21 Dec. 1998) confirmed identification of a specimen from southeast of Kodiak Island (ZIN 47243, 55°58'N, 153°54'W, depth 260–270 m), and R. Baxter (unpubl. data) examined two from practically the same locality (55°58'N, 154°00'W, depth 304 m, *Miller Freeman,* 20 Apr. 1986, specimens not saved). Another is UAM 2420 (198 mm TL), from the northeastern Gulf of Alaska at 59°46'N, 142°23'W, depth 149–161 m (confirmed by C.W.M.).

Size: R. Baxter, unpubl. data: one of the specimens collected 20 Apr. 1986 southeast of Kodiak Island (see above). Reported by Hart (1973) to reach 240 mm TL.

Bathyagonus alascanus (Gilbert, 1896) — **gray starsnout**

Southeastern Bering Sea west of Pribilof Islands to Pacific Ocean off northern California.

Sand or mud bottoms at depths of 18–252 m.

D V–VIII + 5–8; A 6–8; Pec 14–16; SLP 36–37; LLP 39–41; ILP 34–36; Vert 39–42.

- Brown to greenish gray dorsally, lighter ventrally; dark blotches or bands on body; **fins pale**; **bars on dorsal, caudal, and pectoral fins**.
- Lower jaw not projecting beyond upper jaw.
- **Free lachrymal margin smooth**; **2 spines on infraorbital ridge** (1 on lachrymal, 1 on 2nd infraorbital); **2 or 3 tightly joined nonspinous plates below ridge**; 5–10 spinous processes on eyeball.
- Rostral plate with 3 vertical and 2 lateral spines; or with additional spines.
- Two barbels at posterior end of maxilla; 1 or 2 short barbels on each side of mandible.
- Anal fin origin below dorsal fin interspace.
- **Single pair of plates or single plate immediately in front of pelvic fins in median row of plates**.
- Gill membranes united, broadly joined to isthmus anteriorly, leaving a free fold posteriorly.
- Length to 141 mm TL.

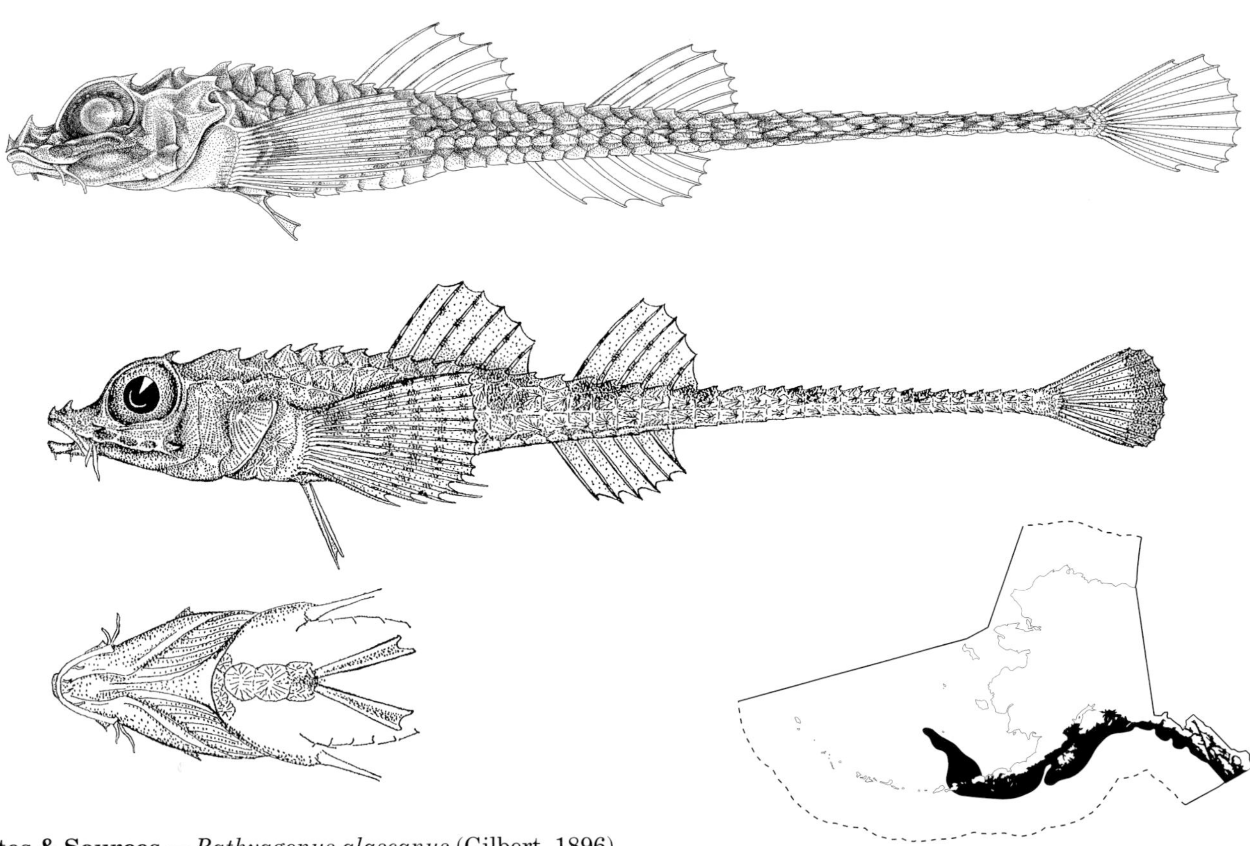

Notes & Sources — *Bathyagonus alascanus* (Gilbert, 1896)
Xenochirus alascanus Gilbert, 1896
Xeneretmus alascanus: Gilbert 1904.
Asterotheca alascana: Gilbert 1915.

Description: Gilbert 1896:438; Jordan and Evermann 1898: 2081–2082; Kanayama 1991:76–77.

Figures: Upper: University of British Columbia, artist R. Wood; UBC 61-542, 114 mm SL, desiccated, off Douglas Island, Alaska. Lower: Hart 1973:553, modified; UBC 55-240, 100 mm TL, Burrard Inlet, British Columbia.

Range: The northernmost record is from one of the syntypes (Gilbert 1896), collected at 56°56'N, 172°55'W, *Albatross* station 3309; the same expedition collected samples around Unimak Island to north of Unalaska Island at 53°56'N, 166°29'W (station 3334). Depths for the type series were 64–252 m. There are numerous published records (e.g., Jordan and Gilbert 1899, Quast and Hall 1972), as well as unpublished records, from within the range indicated on the above map. For example, from specimens examined by C.W.M.: UAM 419 (129 mm TL), off Shumagin Islands, depth 97–102 m; and UAM 482 (two specimens, 98–102 mm TL), near Pribilof Islands, depth 229–249 m. Kulikov (1964) reported this species from the Commander Islands on the basis of a 291-mm-TL specimen, but no description was given and B. A. Sheiko (pers. comm., 21 Dec. 1998) discounted the record from the specimen's size, which is much too large for *B. alascanus*.

Size: R. Baxter, unpubl. data: specimen collected by ADFG survey, Kachemak Bay, 13 Oct. 1987, not saved. Reported by Hart (1973) to reach 130 mm TL.

Bathyagonus infraspinatus (Gilbert, 1904) **spinycheek starsnout**

Southeastern Bering Sea from vicinity of Pribilof Islands and Islands of Four Mountains to Pacific Ocean off northern California near Eureka.

Sand and mud bottoms at depths of 6–183 m.

D V–VIII + 5–8; A 5–8; Pec 14–16; SLP 35–36; LLP 37–39; ILP 34–35; Vert 38–39.

- Olive green to brown dorsally, whitish ventrally; 5 or 6 dark blotches or bands on body; **fins pale; bars on dorsal, caudal and pectoral fins.**
- Lower jaw not projecting beyond upper jaw.
- **Free lachrymal margin serrated; 3 spines on infraorbital ridge** (1 on lachrymal, 1 each on 1st and 2nd infraorbital); **3 spinous plates below ridge**; 6–10 spinous processes on eyeball.
- Rostral plate with 3 vertical and 2 lateral spines; or with additional spines.
- Two barbels at posterior end of maxilla; 2 small barbels on each side of mandible near tip, posterior barbel sometimes double.
- Anal fin origin below insertion of first dorsal fin.
- **Single pair of plates or single plate immediately in front of pelvic fins in median row of plates.**
- Gill membranes united, attached to isthmus along sides leaving a narrow free median portion.
- Length to 143 mm TL.

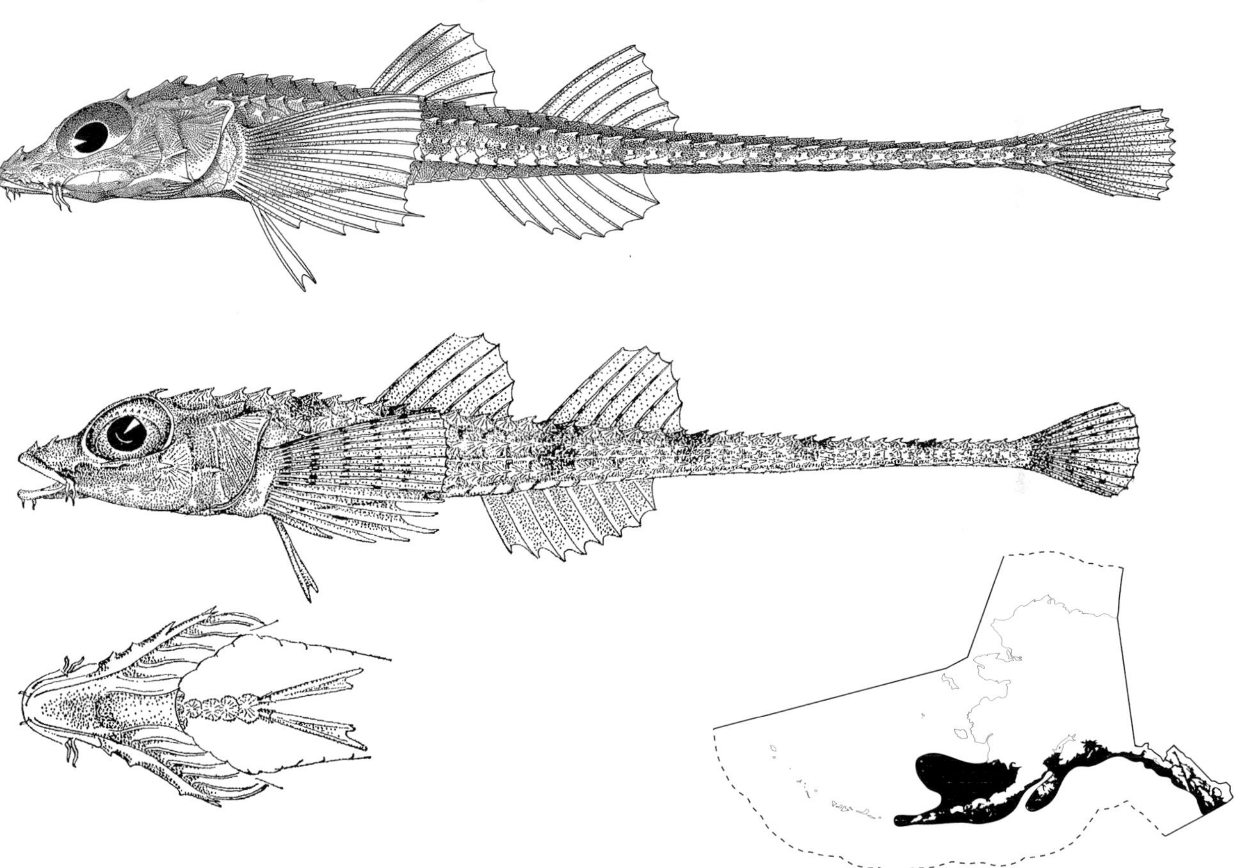

Notes & Sources — *Bathyagonus infraspinatus* (Gilbert, 1904)
Xeneretmus infraspinatus Gilbert, 1904
Asterotheca infraspinata: Gilbert 1915.

Description: Gilbert 1904:262–263, 1915:344; Fitch 1966b; Kanayama 1991:77–78.

Figures: Upper: Gilbert 1904, pl. 27; holotype, 99 mm TL, off Cape Flattery, Washington. Lower: Hart 1973:554, modified; UBC 54-95, 95 mm TL, Burrard Inlet, British Columbia.

Range: Reported from Unimak Pass (*Albatross* station 3259, 54°41'N, 165°05'W) by Gilbert and Thompson (1905). Fitch (1973) referred a specimen identified as *B. pentacanthus* by Evermann and Goldsborough (1907) from nearby station 3547 (54°16'N, 165°45'W) to *B. infraspinatus.* USNM 207979 is from just north of Unalaska Island at 53°56'N, 166°37'W; formerly in the ABL collection, this is the Aleutian Islands record reported by Quast and Hall (1972). UBC 62-912 from the Islands of Four Mountains at about 53°20'N, 170°W, appears to be the westernmost record. Specimens taken near St. George Island (about 56°45'N, 169°30'W) during surveys in 1984 were identified as this species by R. Baxter (unpubl. data; specimens not saved). Vouchers or reports of this species north of the Pribilof Islands are unknown. Holdings at ABL, CAS, SIO, and NMNH confirm wide distribution along Gulf of Alaska coasts within the range depicted by black fill on the above map.

Size: OSU 85544 (R. Baxter, unpubl. data). Reported by Hart (1973) to reach 121 mm TL

Xeneretmus leiops Gilbert, 1915 **smootheye poacher**

Eastern Pacific Ocean off southeastern Alaska west of Forrester Island to southern California off Santa Catalina Island.

Bottom at depths of 37–399 m.

D VI–VII + 6–8; A 5–8; Pec 13–15; SLP 41–45; LLP 42–45; ILP 38–42; Vert 39–42.

- Dusky olive dorsally, whitish ventrally; dark blotches on sides; snout tip black; fins pale; **black on first dorsal and dusky on second dorsal fin along margins, extending toward body anteriorly especially on first dorsal fin**.
- **No plates below infraorbital ridge; no spinous processes on eyeball**.
- Rostral plate with 1 dorsally directed spine, and often 1 tiny laterally directed spine on each side.
- **One barbel at posterior end of maxilla**; 1–4 small barbels on mandible near tip on margins of first and second mandibular pores.
- Anal fin origin below second dorsal fin origin.
- Plates on breast oval, the anterior plates not touching each other.
- Gill membranes united, broadly joined to isthmus leaving a narrow free fold.
- Length to 225 mm SL, 270 mm TL.

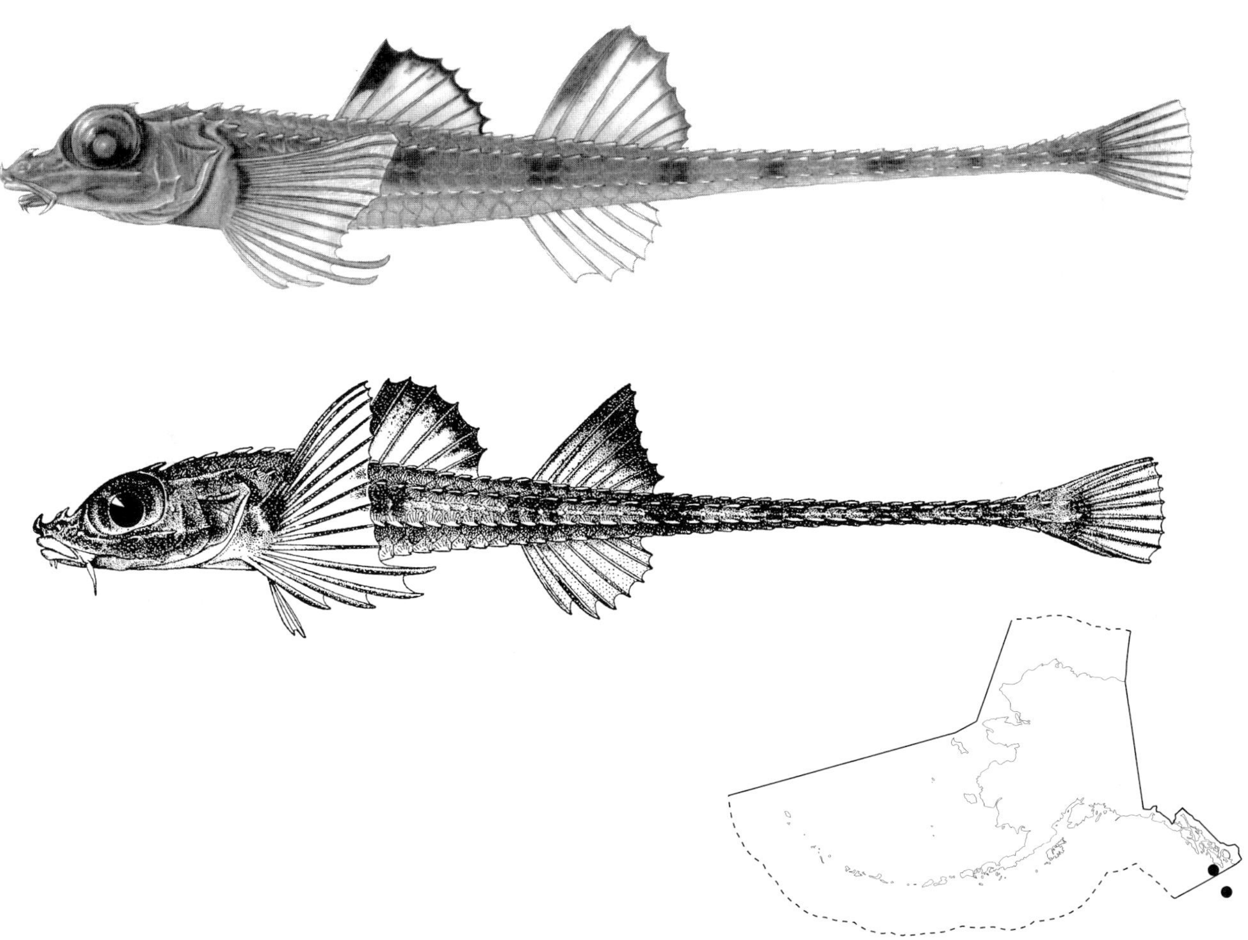

Notes & Sources — *Xeneretmus leiops* Gilbert, 1915
Xenopyxis leiops: Jordan, Evermann, and Clark 1930.
Kanayama (1991) classified *Xenopyxis* as a synonym of *Xeneretmus,* whereas Leipertz (1985) and Sheiko (1993) considered it to be valid as a subgenus of *Xeneretmus.*
The spelling *Xenertmus* (e.g., Kanayama 1991) is incorrect.

Description: Gilbert 1915:345, 348–350; Barraclough and Peden 1976:table 1; Leipertz 1985; Kanayama 1991:82–83.
Figures: Upper: Royal British Columbia Museum, artist N. Eyolfson, Feb. 1982; BCPM 972-6, west of Vancouver Island, British Columbia. Lower: Gilbert 1915, fig. 11 (not 10; figures were transposed); holotype, USNM 75813, 176 mm TL, off Santa Catalina Island, California.
Range: One record from Alaska: off Forrester Island at 54°42'N, 134°W (NMC 66-268; Peden and Jamieson 1988). Northernmost British Columbia record is Rennell Sound at 53°21'N, 133°04'W (NMC 67-348; Leipertz 1985). Barraclough and Peden (1976) reported the first records for British Columbia, as far north as 48°48'N.
Size: Barraclough and Peden 1976.

Xeneretmus latifrons (Gilbert, 1890) **blacktip poacher**

Rennell Sound and Skidegate Channel, British Columbia, to northern Baja California off Cape Colnett. Sand and mud bottoms at depths of 18–399 m; at the greater depths in southern regions.

D VI–VIII + 6–8; A 6–9; Pec 13–15; SLP 36–42; LLP 39–42; ILP 35–40; Vert 39–43.

- Brown or tan; sometimes with 5–8 dark bars on body; **black margin of uniform width on first dorsal fin**; margin unevenly dark on second dorsal fin.
- **No plates (rarely 1) below infraorbital ridge; 3–6 spinous processes on eyeball.**
- Rostral plate with 1 dorsally directed spine, and usually 1 laterally directed spine on each side.
- **One barbel at posterior end of maxilla**; 2 small barbels on mandible, 1 at each posterior margin of first and second mandibular pores.
- Anal fin origin below dorsal fin interspace.
- Plates on breast usually in contact, completely covering the area.
- Gill membranes united, broadly joined to isthmus leaving a narrow to moderate free fold.
- Length to 190 mm TL.

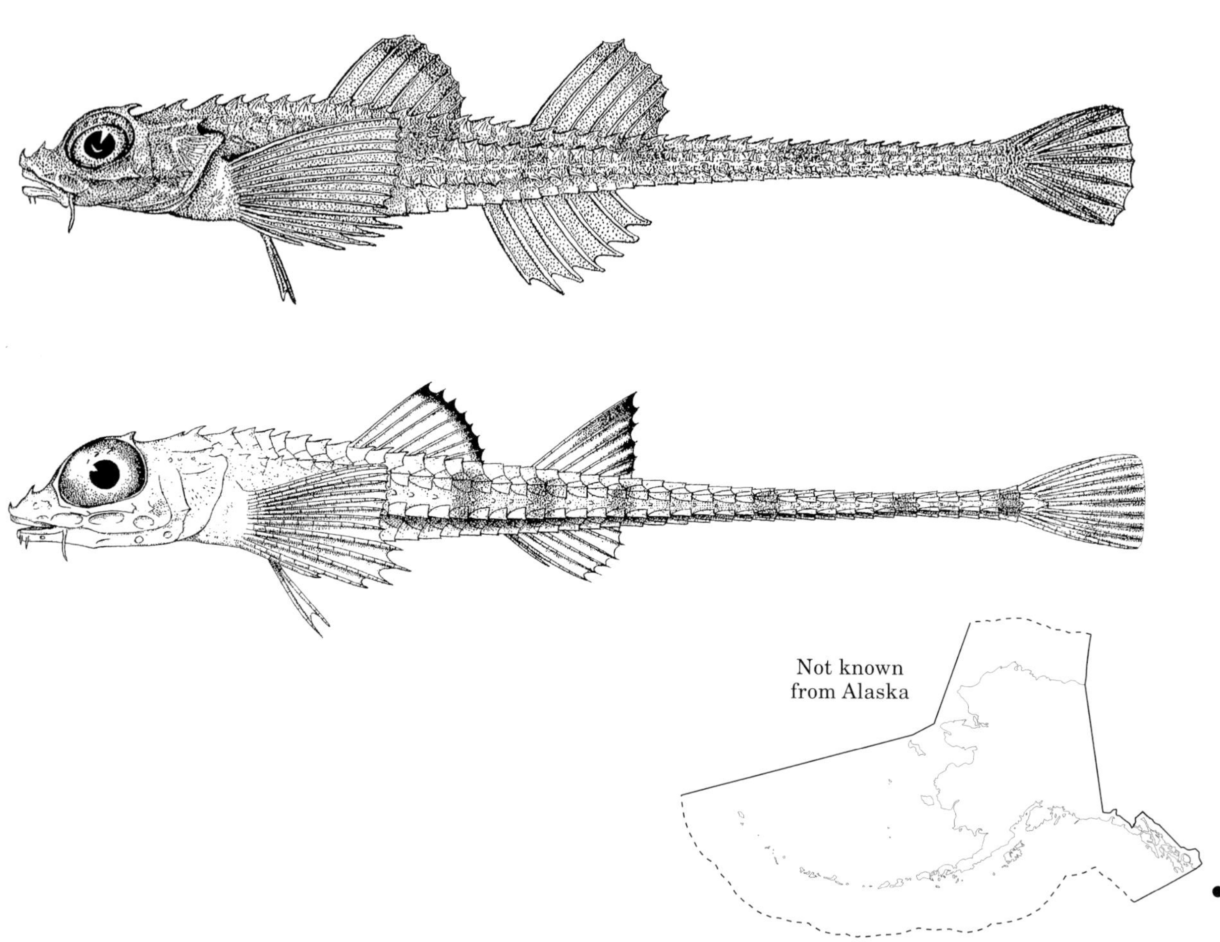

Notes & Sources — *Xeneretmus latifrons* (Gilbert, 1890)
Xenochirus latifrons Gilbert, 1890
Xenopyxis latifrons: Jordan, Evermann, and Clark 1930.
Kanayama (1991) classified *Xenopyxis* as a synonym of *Xeneretmus,* whereas Leipertz (1985) and Sheiko (1993) considered it to be valid as a subgenus of *Xeneretmus.*
The spelling *Xenertmus* (e.g., Kanayama 1991) is incorrect.

Description: Gilbert 1890:92–93, 1915:345–347; Jordan and Evermann 1898:2082–2083; Barraclough and Peden 1976: table 1; Leipertz 1985; Kanayama 1991:80–82.

Figures: Upper: Hart 1973:566, modified; UBC 65-469, 130 mm TL, Pendrell Sound, British Columbia. Lower: Leipertz 1985, fig. 15; 142 mm SL.

Range: Specimens at RBCM from Rennell Sound (BCPM 990-110-1, 53°25'N, 132°43'W) and Skidegate Inlet (BCPM 991-340-1, 53°12'N, 132°05'W) are northernmost British Columbia records (A. E. Peden, pers. comm., 11 Jan. 1995). Previously recorded from British Columbia at Kwatna Inlet, at 52°07'N, 127°38'W (NMC 65-259; Leipertz 1985).

Size: Eschmeyer and Herald 1983.

Xeneretmus triacanthus (Gilbert, 1890) **bluespotted poacher**

Pacific Ocean from northern British Columbia at Kwatna Inlet to northern Baja California at Punta Baja. Sand and mud bottoms at depths of 73–373 m.

D V–VII + 6–7; A 5–7; Pec 12–14; SLP 38–43; LLP 39–42; ILP 38–40; Vert 41–42.

- Olive brown dorsally, paler ventrally; usually with bright **blue spots on and behind head**; about 6 dark blotches on body; **fin rays and spines dusky**; **no black margin on dorsal fins**.
- **Plates below infraorbital ridge 1–4; row of 2–6 spinous processes on eyeball**.
- Rostral plate with 1 dorsally directed spine, and 1 small laterally directed spine on each side.
- **Two, rarely three, barbels at posterior end of maxilla**; 3 small barbels on mandible, 1 at each posterior margin of first 3 mandibular pores.
- Anal fin origin below second dorsal fin origin.
- Gill membranes united, broadly joined to isthmus without a free fold or with a very narrow fold.
- Length to 178 mm TL.

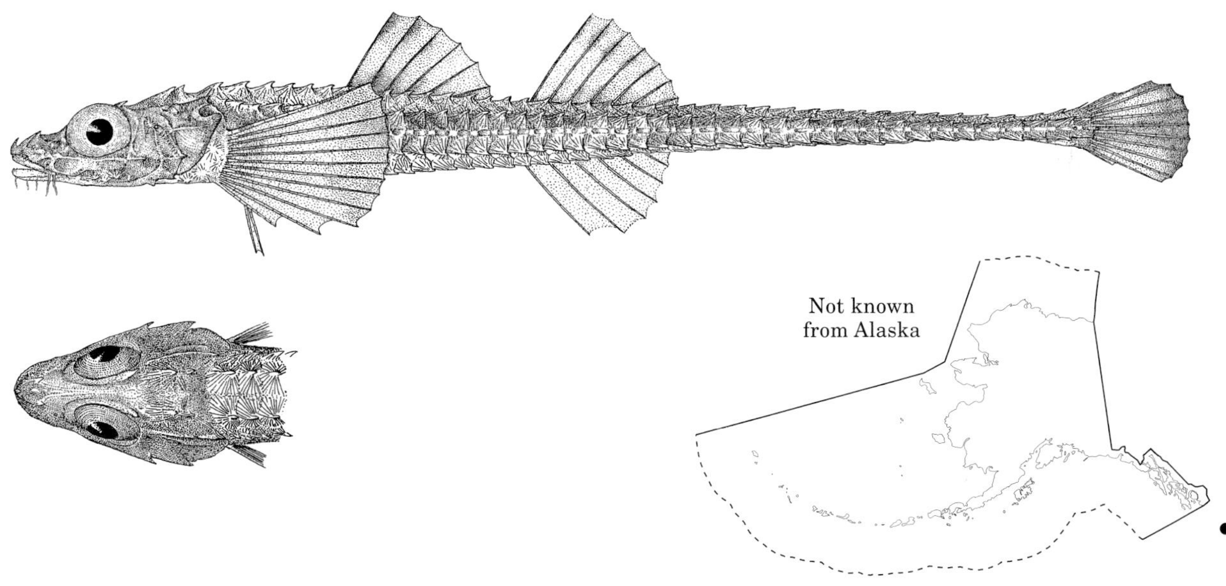

Notes & Sources — *Xeneretmus triacanthus* (Gilbert, 1890)
Xenochirus triacanthus Gilbert, 1890
Leipertz (1985) and Sheiko (1993) classified *Xeneretmus triacanthus* in subgenus *Xeneretmus*. Kanayama (1991) did not recognize subgenera of *Xeneretmus*.
The spelling *Xenertmus* (e.g., Kanayama 1991) is incorrect.

Description: Gilbert 1890:91, 1915:346, 352–353; Jordan and Evermann 1898:2084; Peden and Gruchy 1971; Barraclough and Peden 1976:table 1; Leipertz 1985; Kanayama 1991: 79–80.

Figures: Jordan and Starks 1895, pl. 93; 89 mm TL, Port Orchard, Puget Sound (lower three or four pectoral fin rays are thickened and exserted in larger specimens).

Range: Northernmost record is from Kwatna Inlet, British Columbia, at 52°03'N, 127°35'W (NMC 65-258; Peden and Gruchy 1971). The Kwatna Inlet record was the first for Canada, and an extension of known range north from Puget Sound. Maximum depth: Coad 1995.

Size: Jordan and Evermann 1898.

Ulcina olrikii (Lütken, 1876) **Arctic alligatorfish**

Arctic Ocean to northern Bering Sea south of St. Lawrence Island and in Gulf of Anadyr; across Canadian Arctic to Greenland and south to Newfoundland in Atlantic Ocean; circumpolar.

Sand, mud, and rocky bottoms at depths of 7–520 m; at shallower end of range, less than 100 m, off Alaska.

D 5–7; A 5–7; Pec 12–16; SLP 0; LLP 26–32; ILP 34–37; Vert 37–40.

- Brownish to olive green dorsally, whitish ventrally; dark bands on body; dorsal fin white, with two dark greenish bands; pectoral fin pale, with dark spots; anal and pelvic fins white; caudal fin white at margin and center.
- Body robust, depth more than 12% of standard length.
- Head large, more than 20% of standard length; mouth small, terminal.
- **Nasal spine (paired) small to well developed**.
- **Short barbel on posterior end of maxilla**.
- **First dorsal fin absent**.
- **Supralateral plates absent**; low lateral line plate count, less than 35.
- Gill membranes united, narrowly joined to isthmus anteriorly, free posteriorly.
- To 86 mm TL, usually less than 75 mm TL.

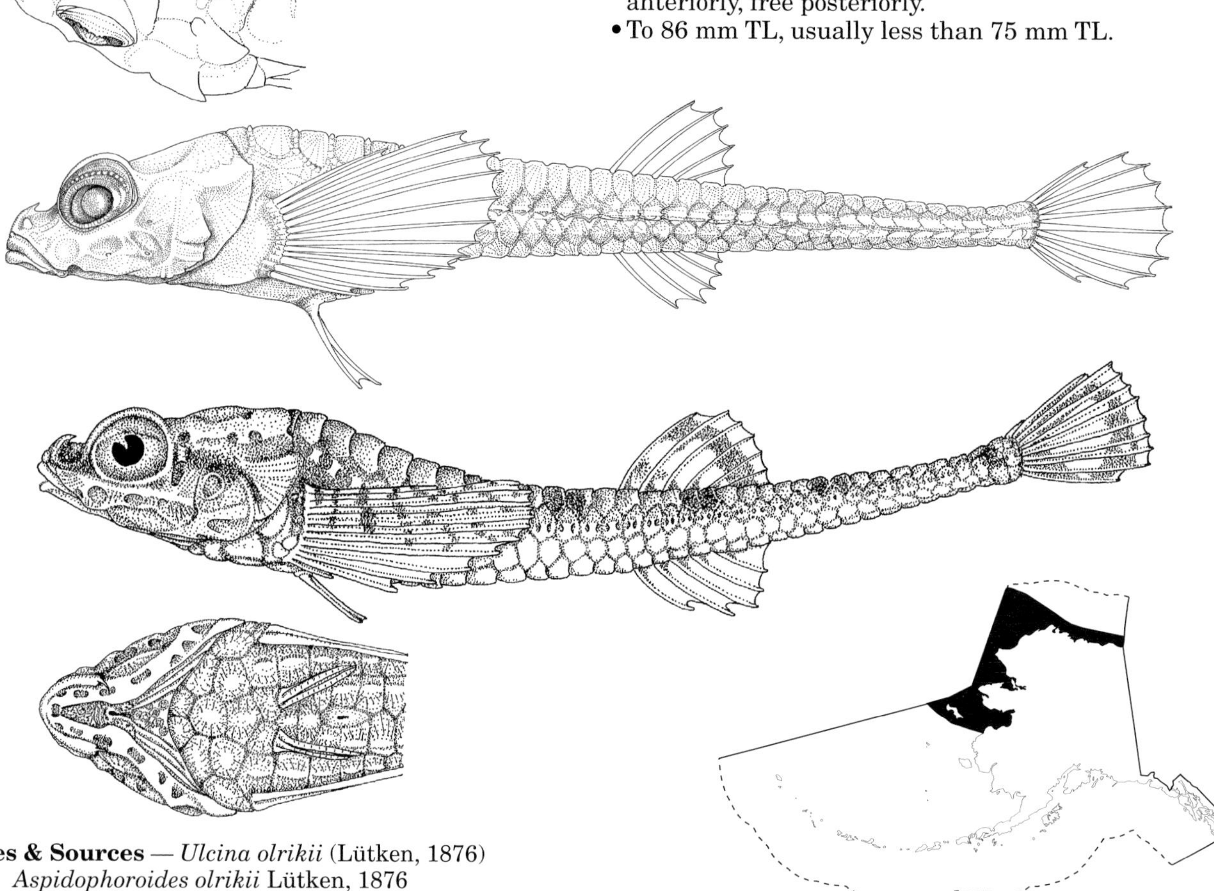

Notes & Sources — *Ulcina olrikii* (Lütken, 1876)
Aspidophoroides olrikii Lütken, 1876
Aspidophoroides güntherii Bean, 1885
Ulcina Cramer in Jordan & Evermann, 1896a
Ulcina olriki, U. güntheri: Jordan et al. 1930:397. Rendahl (1931) synonymized the two forms.

Description: Bean 1885; Jordan and Evermann 1898:2088–2091; Kanayama 1991:86–87. Nasal spines were small in Alaskan specimens described by Bean (1885).

Figures: Upper: University of British Columbia, artist R. Wood, Jan. 1969; UBC 63-1208, 51 mm SL, desiccated, Bering Strait, Alaska. Lower: Kanayama 1991, fig. 36; HUMZ 69035, 49 mm SL, northwestern Bering Sea.

Range: Walters (1955) recorded this species from Point Barrow and Kotzebue Sound to northern Bering Sea. First reported from the Beaufort Sea by McAllister (1962), near Herschel Island, Yukon Territory. Alaskan Beaufort Sea localities represented in collections include vicinity of Prudhoe Bay (CAS 45450 and 45451; 147–149°W), Smith Bay (UBC 63-851; 154°W), and near Point Barrow (UBC 63-615, 63-635, 63-636, 63-654; 156°W). Southernmost records from eastern Bering Sea are NMC 79-805 (5 specimens), taken at 62°08'N, 171°52'W, depth 51 m; and NMC 79-809 (1), from 62°42'N, 174°58'W, depth 80 m, collected by L. F. Lowry and K. J. Frost and identified by B. W. Coad. Lot UW 41437 was collected south of St. Lawrence Island at 63°00'N, 171°19'W, 51 m. Maximum depth: Sheiko and Fedorov 2000.

Size: Jensen 1942.

Aspidophoroides monopterygius (Bloch, 1786) **alligatorfish**

Eastern Chukchi Sea, Bering Sea, and Aleutian Islands west to Amchitka Island, and to Gulf of Alaska at Prince William Sound; Gulf of Anadyr to Japan and Okhotsk seas; western Atlantic from west Greenland to New Jersey.

Sand and mud bottoms at depths of 8–500 m, almost always shallower than 200 m.

D 4–6; A 4–6; Pec 9–11; SLP 0; LLP 47–53; ILP 47–53; Vert 48–54.

- Brownish to olive green dorsally, whitish ventrally; faint dark bands on body; pectoral fin with whitish lower lobe; caudal fin margin pale; pelvic fin white.
- Body slender, depth less than 12% of standard length.
- Head small, length less than 20% of standard length; mouth small, terminal.
- **Nasal spine (paired) present.**
- **No barbel on maxilla.**
- **First dorsal fin absent.**
- **Supralateral plates absent**; high lateral line plate count, more than 45; no median dorsal row of plates behind occiput.
- Gill membranes united, narrowly joined to isthmus anteriorly, free posteriorly.
- Length to 178 mm TL.

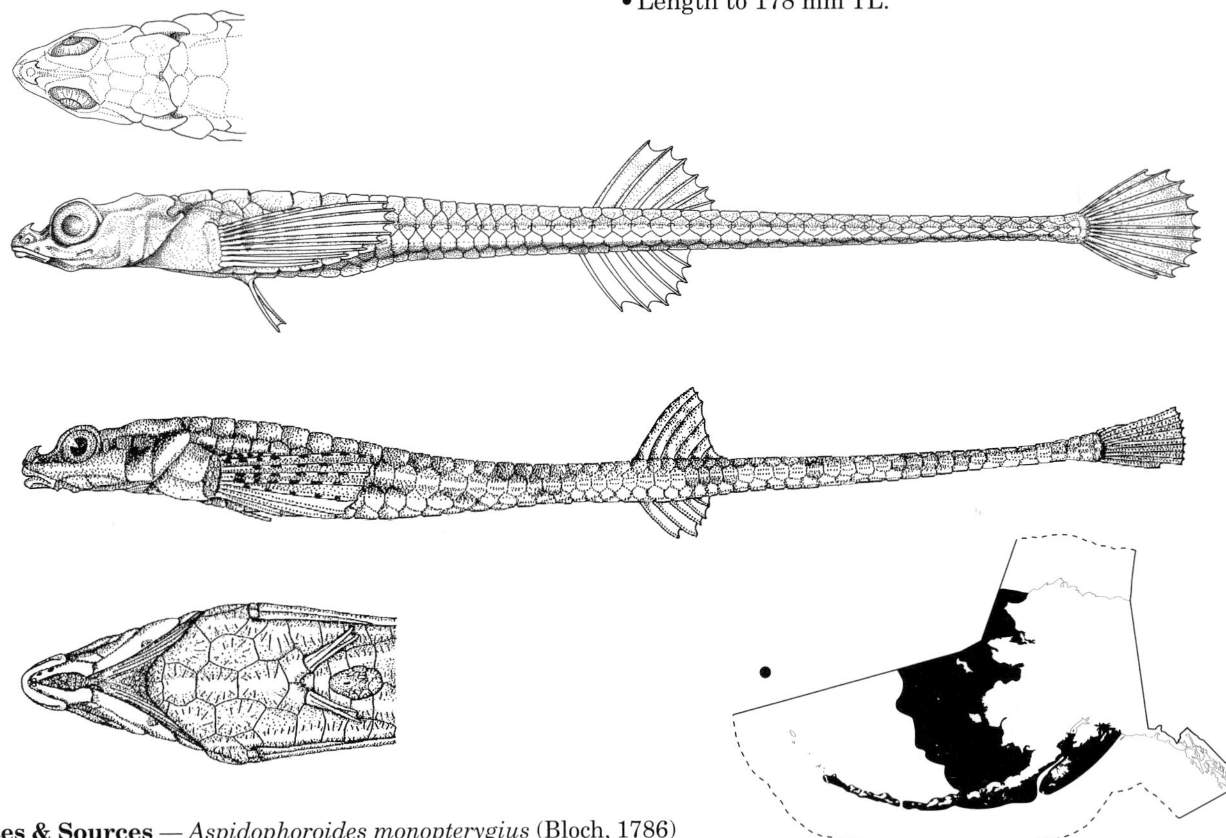

Notes & Sources — *Aspidophoroides monopterygius* (Bloch, 1786)
Cottus monopterygius Bloch, 1786
Aspidophoroides bartoni Gilbert, 1896
Kanayama (1991) synonymized *A. bartoni* in *A. monopterygius*; not universally accepted (e.g., Sheiko 1993).

Description: Gilbert 1896:434; Jordan and Evermann 1898: 2091–2093; Scott and Scott 1988:514–515; Kanayama 1991:88–91.

Figures: Upper: University of British Columbia, artist R. Wood, Jan. 1969; UBC 63-360, 122.5 mm SL, desiccated, Bristol Bay, Alaska. Lower: Kanayama 1991, fig. 37; HUMZ 76642, 136.5 mm SL, eastern Bering Sea, Alaska.

Range: Gilbert (1896) described *A. bartoni* (= *A. monopterygius*) from specimens taken at several *Albatross* stations: off St. Paul Island, in Bristol Bay, and south of the eastern Aleutian Islands. Limits of range in Alaska from previous records: Chukchi Sea (Quast 1972); Amchitka Island (Isakson et al. 1971; and UBC 63-1010); Cook Inlet (Rogers et al. 1986). Taken in NMFS surveys mapped by Allen and Smith (1988) from the Bering Sea at Pervenets Canyon and Nunivak Island to the Gulf of Alaska off Kodiak Island at Albatross Bank. A specimen from Kachemak Bay examined by R. Baxter (unpubl. data) had diagnostic characters of this species (specimen not saved). UW 29703(1) and UW 29732(1) from Prince William Sound were determined by B. A. Sheiko (pers. comm., 21 Dec. 1999) to be examples of *A. bartoni* (= *A. monopterygius*). Probably occurs throughout the Aleutian chain. Fedorov and Sheiko (2002), for example, reported it from the Commander Islands. They gave new range-wide depth extremes of 8–500 m. Only 2 of 184 occurrences off Alaska reported by Allen and Smith (1988) were from depths greater than 200 m.

Size: Lindberg and Krasyukova 1987.

Anoplagonus inermis (Günther, 1860) **smooth alligatorfish**

Aleutian Islands at Petrel Bank to northern California off Point Arena.

Sand, gravel, or rocky bottoms at depths of 5–108 m; often near rock outcroppings.

D 4–6; A 4–5; Pec 8–11; SLP 0; LLP 38–42; ILP 38–42; Vert 41–45.

- Dark brown or gray; several vague darker bands on body; pale band or patches on caudal fin.
- Body slender, depth less than 12% of standard length; **dorsal surface of body broadly concave**.
- Head small, length less than 20% of standard length; mouth small, terminal.
- **No nasal spines or head barbels**.
- **First dorsal fin absent**.
- **Supralateral plates absent**; high lateral line plate count, 38 or more; median row of plates extending from occiput halfway to dorsal fin origin.
- Gill membranes united, narrowly joined to isthmus anteriorly, free posteriorly.
- Length to 150 mm TL.

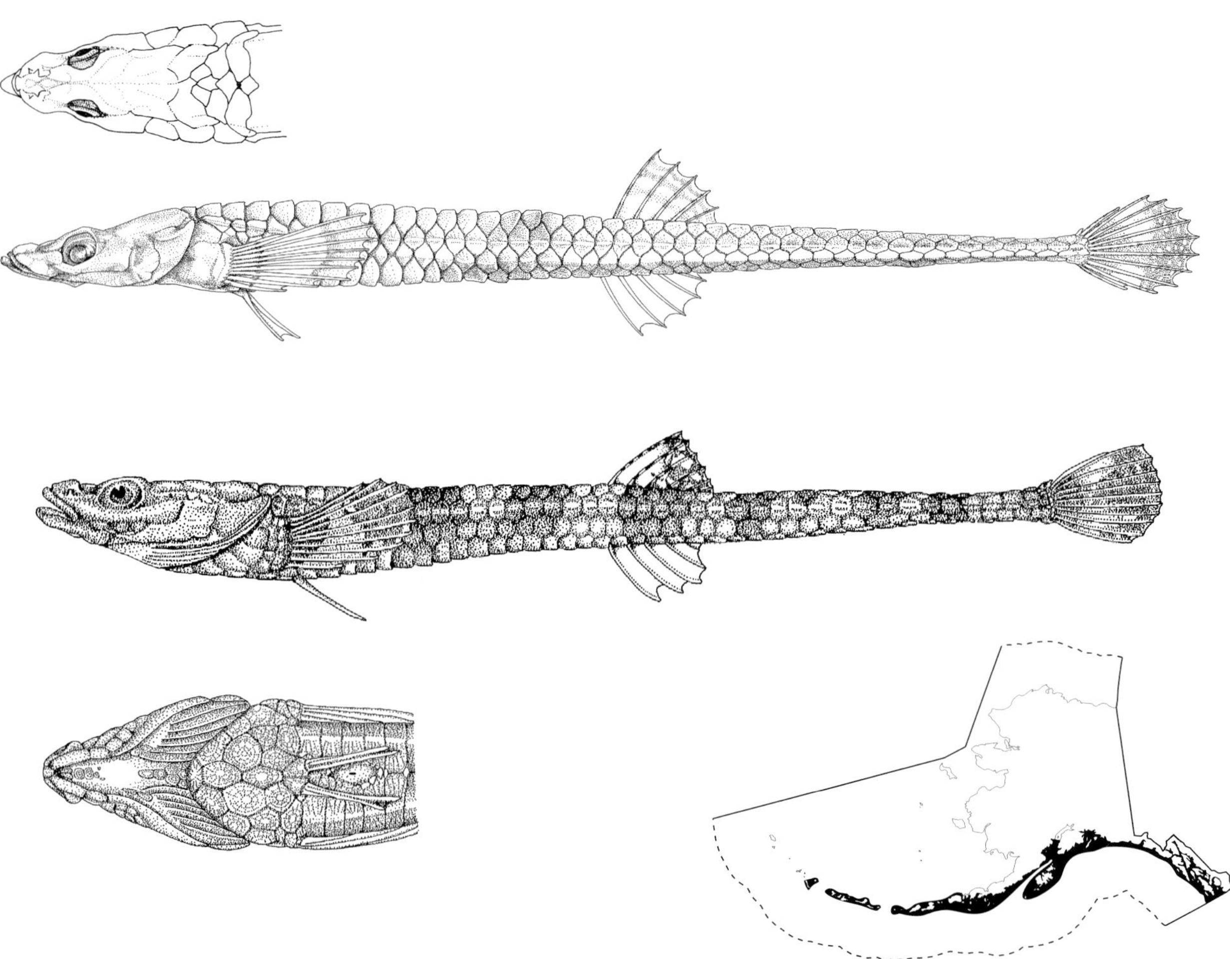

Notes & Sources — *Anoplagonus inermis* (Günther, 1860)
Aspidophoroides inermis Günther, 1860

Description: Jordan and Evermann 1898:2093–2094; Hart 1973:552; Kanayama 1991:92–93; Busby 1998:65–67. Sheiko (pers. comm., 21 Dec. 1988) reported LLP count of 38 for UW 14185, lower than range of 41–42 reported by Kanayama (1991).

Figures: Upper: University of British Columbia, artist R. Wood; UBC 65-146, 143.5 mm SL, desiccated, off Kodiak Island. Lower: Kanayama 1991, fig. 39; BCPM 978-102, 83 mm SL, near Vancouver Island, British Columbia.

Range: Wide distribution in Gulf of Alaska documented by Quast and Hall (1972), Rosenthal (1980), Blackburn and Jackson (1982), and additional specimens in museum holdings. Known from the Bering Sea only off the Aleutian Islands. Collected by Gilbert (1896) north and south of Unimak and Unalaska islands (*not* in Bristol Bay), and Gilbert and Burke (1912a) at Petrel Bank near Semisopochnoi Island. Records from Korea were referred to a different species by Lindberg (1950). Minimum depth: Lamb and Edgell 1986. Maximum depth: Gilbert 1896.

Size: Hart 1973.

Family Cyclopteridae
Lumpsuckers

Lumpsuckers inhabit cold marine waters of the Northern Hemisphere. Most species live on the bottom on the continental shelf, while a few occur pelagically in deeper waters. Like the closely related snailfishes (Liparidae), lumpsuckers have a disk on the underside of the body, formed by modified pelvic fins, for clinging to rocks and other objects; and a short gill opening high on the body. Unlike snailfishes, lumpsuckers have globose bodies with short tails. Most have two dorsal fins. The dorsal and anal fins are short-based, and are not confluent with the caudal fin; there is a distinct caudal peduncle. All but a few lumpsuckers have spiny tubercles on the head and body. The most recent revision of the family, by Ueno (1970), included 7 genera and 27 species. This guide includes accounts for 13 species. The occurrence of 10 species in Alaska has been confirmed; 3 others, known to be present in adjacent waters, probably also occur in Alaska.

Because of their similarities, lumpsuckers and snailfishes are classified by some authors in the same family (Cyclopteridae). Nelson (1994) accommodated the monophyly of the combined groups by classifying them in the superfamily Cyclopteroidea. An old name for the combined entity is the Discoboli. Within the order Scorpaeniformes, the lumpsuckers and snailfishes are most closely related to the sculpins and poachers, superfamily Cottoidea, and are classified with them in the suborder Cottoidei. Thus the term *cottoid* refers to all those forms.

Pelagic lumpsuckers, like the smooth lumpsucker, *Aptocyclus ventricosus,* and Soldatov's lumpsucker, *Eumicrotremus soldatovi,* undergo extensive migrations to reach their coastal spawning grounds (Il'inskii and Radchenko 1992, Orlov 1994). Female lumpsuckers lay their eggs in a sticky, spongy mass on rocks and seaweed or in mollusk shells, and in some species the male guards the eggs. The largest species at maturity is the lumpfish, *Cyclopterus lumpus,* the common species of the Atlantic Ocean, which can reach 61 cm (2 feet) in length. The largest species in Alaska is *A. ventricosus,* with a maximum length of 42 cm (16.5 inches). Most are smaller. Some Alaskan species, including *Lethotremus muticus,* may not attain lengths greater than about 6.5 cm (about 2.6 inches). *Lethotremus awae,* a dwarf species inhabiting the northwestern Pacific Ocean, matures at about 2 cm (less than 1 inch).

The most important characteristics for differentiating the lumpsuckers are presence or absence of the first dorsal fin, and the presence or absence and distribution of armor or appendages on the skin. The absence of the first dorsal fin and complete lack of tubercles, warts, or other bony or dermal appendages define the subfamily Aptocyclinae with its one species, the smooth lumpsucker, *Aptocyclus ventricosus.* In the subfamily Cyclopterinae the first dorsal fin projects above the profile of the back, although in some species in the adults it is very low and mostly buried. It can be heavily overgrown with skin, obscuring the spines, or not heavily overgrown and with the spines clearly visible. The bases of the second dorsal fin and the anal fin are embedded in skin. The skin has conical bony tubercles, papillae, or warts, or may be completely smooth. The length of the nostril tubes was once thought to have taxonomic value, but it varies widely within species; generally the anterior nostril tube is short and wide and the posterior tube long and narrow.

Lumpsuckers exhibit considerable variation within species. For example, taking changes with age, in some *E. birulai* juveniles the first dorsal fin is high but gradually becomes buried in the skin and is barely discernible in large adults. Some species, such as *E. lindbergi,* do not develop spiny tubercles until they reach 40 mm SL or more; whereas in others, such as *E. orbis,* the tubercles are obvious even at 16 mm SL or less. The sexes can be greatly different; for example, in some species the males may develop armor but not the females, and coloration can be different. There may also be great variability among individuals of a given age, with, for example, some juvenile *E. birulai* having high first dorsal fins but others of the same size already having them buried. Finally, lumpsuckers can inflate themselves and this greatly changes their appearance. In inflated specimens the tubercles are relatively far apart and body shape more spherical, making them almost unidentifiable with uninflated individuals. The naked species (e.g., *L. muticus, A. ventricosus*), as well as the armored (e.g., *E. phrynoides, E. orbis*), have this ability. The Diodontidae (Tetraodontiformes), a family of tropical fishes, combine inflation and body spines as a defense mechanism and accomplish inflation by pumping water into the stomach, which has many pleats and expands dramatically. The mechanism of inflation and related behavior in lumpsuckers has not been studied.

The variability in appearance, coupled with a paucity of specimens of several species in study collections, has resulted in much taxonomic confusion. Knowledge of age- and sex-related changes and the extent of individual variation is still rudimentary.

Consequently, interrelationships and species limits in Cyclopteridae are not well understood. Lindberg and Legeza (1955) and Ueno (1970) conducted taxonomic reviews of the family, but few specimens of several species, and none of three Alaskan species (*Lethotremus muticus, E. phrynoides, E. gyrinops*), were available to those researchers. Since their work, a few significant contributions to knowledge of cyclopterids at the species level have been made. For example, taking an Alaskan species, Kido and Shinohara (1996) demonstrated that specimens identified as *Pelagocyclus vitiazi* are the young of *Aptocyclus ventricosus*. Departures from Ueno (1970) in classification of species in this guide also include removal of *Cyclopteropsis phrynoides* and *C. lindbergi* to *Eumicrotremus* and resurrection of *C. inarmatus*. The Notes sections in the species accounts give brief explanations of the changes. However, studies on cyclopterid taxonomy are ongoing and many problems remain. *Cyclopteropsis inarmatus, E. birulai, E. gyrinops, E. phrynoides,* and *L. muticus* are particularly problematical. *Eumicrotremus gyrinops* and *C. inarmatus* may not be valid species. The other three seem to be good species but have been confused with each other in the literature and in museum collections.

Differences in our list of Alaskan cyclopterids from that compiled by Quast and Hall (1972) are as follows. *Cyclopterichthys glaber* Steindachner is now recognized to be conspecific with *Aptocyclus ventricosus* (e.g., Ueno 1970), as is *Pelagocyclus vitiazi* (Kido and Shinohara 1996). *Cyclopteropsis bergi* Popov, *C. brashnikovi* (Schmidt), *C. popovi* Soldatov, and *Cyclopsis tentacularis* Popov, which were listed by Quast and Hall (1972) as potential additions to the list of Alaskan fishes, are not treated in this guide because they have not been found outside the Sea of Okhotsk and appear to be restricted to that area.

Eumicrotremus soldatovi, which was included on previous lists of Alaskan fishes as a possible member of the regional ichthyofauna, was collected in Alaska near Bowers Ridge, Bering Sea (Ueno 1970). New additions to the inventory as species likely to be found in Alaska are *E. lindbergi* (Soldatov & Lindberg) and, if it is, indeed, a valid species, *Cyclopteropsis inarmatus* Mednikov & Prokhorov; both are known to be present in nearby waters of the western Bering Sea.

Eumicrotremus spinosus (Müller) is retained on the list as a likely Alaskan species. This species mainly inhabits the Arctic Ocean from Greenland to western Russia but has been reported from Canada as close to Alaska as the Beaufort Sea off the Mackenzie Delta, and some museum specimens identified as other species may upon further examination prove to be *E. spinosus.*

Most of the Alaskan species have rarely been recorded in Alaska. There is one Alaskan record each of *E. soldatovi* and *E. barbatus.* The most widespread species in Alaska are *A. ventricosus* and *E. orbis,* found from the Bering Sea and Aleutian Islands to southeastern Alaska; and *E. phrynoides,* from the southern Bering Sea to the north central Gulf of Alaska. Lumpsuckers occur from the Arctic Ocean to Puget Sound in the eastern Pacific and to the Koreas in the western Pacific.

Key to the Cyclopteridae of Alaska

1 First dorsal fin absent; skin without bony or dermal appendages . . . . *Aptocyclus ventricosus,* page 558

1 First dorsal fin present, projecting above profile of back; skin with or without bony or dermal appendages . . . . (2)

2 (1) Skin naked except for a few microscopic, slightly raised spicule clusters ("rosettes") or single spicules on first dorsal fin and dorsal rim of orbit in some specimens over 35 mm TL . . . . . *Lethotremus muticus,* page 559

2 Skin with spiny or nonspiny raised bony plates or conical tubercles, dermal bumps ("warts"), or papillae . . . . (3)

3 (2) Body covered with nonbony warts; no spiny or nonspiny bony plates, tubercles, or papillae with bony bases . . . . *Cyclopteropsis inarmatus,* page 560 (not known from Alaska)

3 Body with warts with a bony base, spiny rosettes, spiny conical tubercles, or papillae with raised bony bases . . . . (4)

4 (3) Body with warts, many larger than eye, with subcutaneous bony bases; spiny conical tubercles on some specimens over 35 mm TL (tubercles can be hidden in heavy mucus); no dermal papillae projecting from subcutaneous round bases .... *Eumicrotremus lindbergi,* page 561 (not known from Alaska)

4 Body without numerous large warts; with few or many spiny rosettes or conical tubercles; with or without dermal papillae projecting from round bases .... (5)

5 (4) Body with numerous, close-set, low spiny tubercles smaller than pupil; first dorsal fin covered with heavy skin......... *Eumicrotremus phrynoides,* page 562

5 Body with scattered tubercles or large conical tubercles; first dorsal fin covered with heavy skin or not .... (6)

6 (5) Dermal papillae projecting from subcutaneous round bases on head, cheeks, chin, throat, and sometimes other areas...... *Eumicrotremus barbatus,* page 563

6 Dermal papillae not present .... (7)

7 (6) Head and body naked except for distantly spaced low spiny tubercles smaller than eye.......... *Eumicrotremus gyrinops,* page 564

7 Head and body with numerous conical spiny tubercles .... (8)

8 (7) First dorsal fin covered with thick skin, fin rays not visible from outside except at tips, or buried in the skin .... (9)

8 First dorsal fin not heavily covered with skin, fin rays easily distinguishable from outside........ (11)

9 (8) First dorsal fin buried in adults; head and chin with numerous small tubercles .... *Eumicrotremus birulai,* page 565

9 First dorsal fin high in adults, not buried; head and chin with or without small tubercles .... (10)

10 (9) First dorsal fin entirely enveloped by thick skin, with small tubercles on top and larger ones on sides; body spherical; dorsal fin interspace not longer than base of first dorsal fin .... *Eumicrotremus derjugini,* page 566

10 First dorsal fin enveloped by thick skin, without obvious tubercles; body elongate; dorsal fin interspace longer than base of first dorsal fin .... *Eumicrotremus soldatovi,* page 567

11 (8) Small tubercles in 6–8 irregular rows on interorbital region .... *Eumicrotremus andriashevi,* page 568

11 Large tubercles in 4 regular rows on interorbital region........ (12)

12 (11) Inner row of large interorbital tubercles diverging and decreasing in size posteriorly, extending between dorsal row and continuation of outer interorbital (or postorbital) row .... *Eumicrotremus orbis,* page 569

12 Inner row of large interorbital tubercles not diverging and decreasing in size posteriorly (no row between dorsal row and postorbital row) .... *Eumicrotremus spinosus,* page 570 (not known from Alaska)

Aptocyclus ventricosus (Pallas, 1769) **smooth lumpsucker**

Bering Sea to Pacific Ocean south of Aleutian Islands and Gulf of Alaska to Mathieson Channel, British Columbia; from Providence Bay, Gulf of Anadyr, to Sea of Japan off Pusan, South Korea.

Pelagic, usually found in deep waters, taken from surface to depths greater than 500 m; migrate to spawn in littoral waters of Bering Sea in December–June.

D IV–VI + 8–12; A 6–9; C 9-12; Pec 19–22.

- Dark gray, lighter ventrally; fins darker; small black spots dorsally in some specimens.
- Body globular, especially when inflated, or subelongate; skin wrinkled on deflated specimens.
- Skin naked, no tubercles or scales.
- **First dorsal fin completely embedded under skin.**
- Disk rudimentary in young, well developed in adults.
- Length to 420 mm TL.

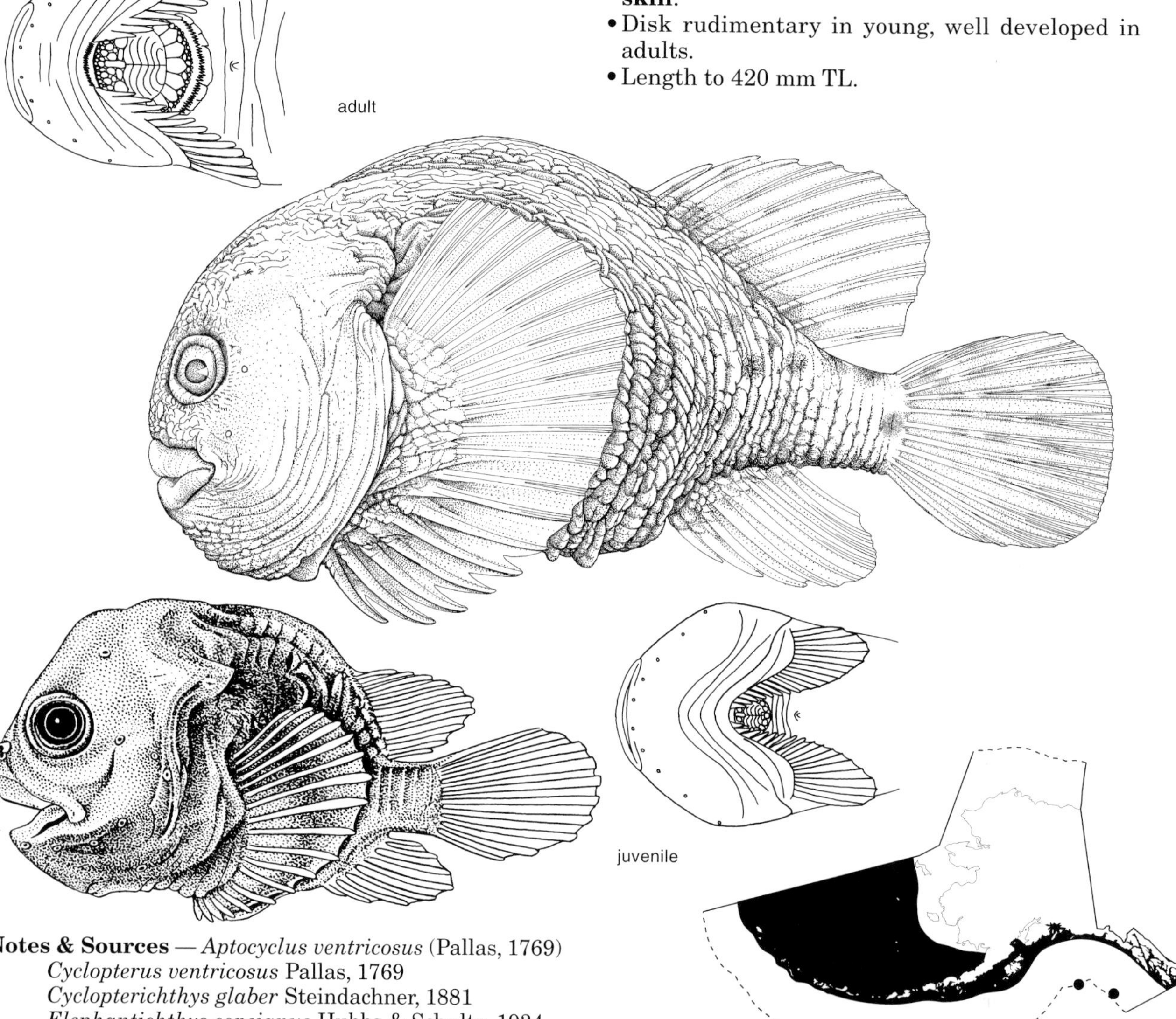

Notes & Sources — *Aptocyclus ventricosus* (Pallas, 1769)
Cyclopterus ventricosus Pallas, 1769
Cyclopterichthys glaber Steindachner, 1881
Elephantichthys copeianus Hubbs & Schultz, 1934
Pelagocyclus vitiazi Lindberg & Legeza, 1955

Description: Ueno 1970:132–148; Kido in Masuda et al. 1984:337; Kido and Shinohara 1996.

Figures: Adult, lateral: University of British Columbia, artist R. Wood, Mar. 1969; UBC 60-457, 160 mm SL, Nushagak Bay, Alaska; ventral: Ueno 1970, fig. 57C, same lot. Juvenile, lateral: Lindberg and Krasyukova 1987 after Lindberg and Legeza 1955; 24.6 mm SL, Pacific off Kuril Islands; ventral: Ueno 1970, fig. 62C; a type specimen.

Range: Pelagic lifestyle is well documented. Yoshida and Yamaguchi (1985) and Il'inskii and Radchenko (1992) described distribution, diet, and migrations in Bering Sea. Midwater trawl surveys capture *A. ventricosus* primarily over the outer shelf and slope and across the Aleutian Basin. Allen and Smith (1988) mapped Bering Sea and Gulf of Alaska records from demersal trawl surveys, which likely captured *A. ventricosus* nearer the surface than at maximum depth of the tows. Snytko (1987) recorded *A. ventricosus* from Welker and Surveyor seamounts.

Size: D. Baker (pers. comm., 29 Oct. 1991). Previously recorded to 405 mm TL (Lindberg and Krasyukova 1987).

Lethotremus muticus Gilbert, 1896 — docked snailfish

Eastern Bering Sea and Aleutian Islands from Unimak Pass to Amchitka Island.

Sand, gravel, and pebble bottoms at depths of 99–329 m.

D VII + 10–11; A 9–11; C 10–11; Pec 23–28.

- Head and body naked, **without spiny tubercles, warts, or long papillae; a few fine (microscopic), isolated spicules and spicule clusters on some individuals larger than 35 mm SL,** mainly along rim of orbit dorsally and on anterior margin of first dorsal fin.
- Anterior nostril tube wide, posterior narrow; both equally long, or posterior with barely raised rim.
- **First dorsal fin covered with thick skin**; even in smallest specimens examined, spines not visible; tentacle-like extensions of skin from spine tips or skin tags elsewhere on fin in some specimens.
- Operculomandibular pores, when evident, 5 each side, with or without raised rims; anterior mandibular pores occasionally opening through short tubes, but not long and barbel-like.
- Single pore in tube at origin of lateral line, not always evident in larger specimens.
- Length to 62 mm TL.

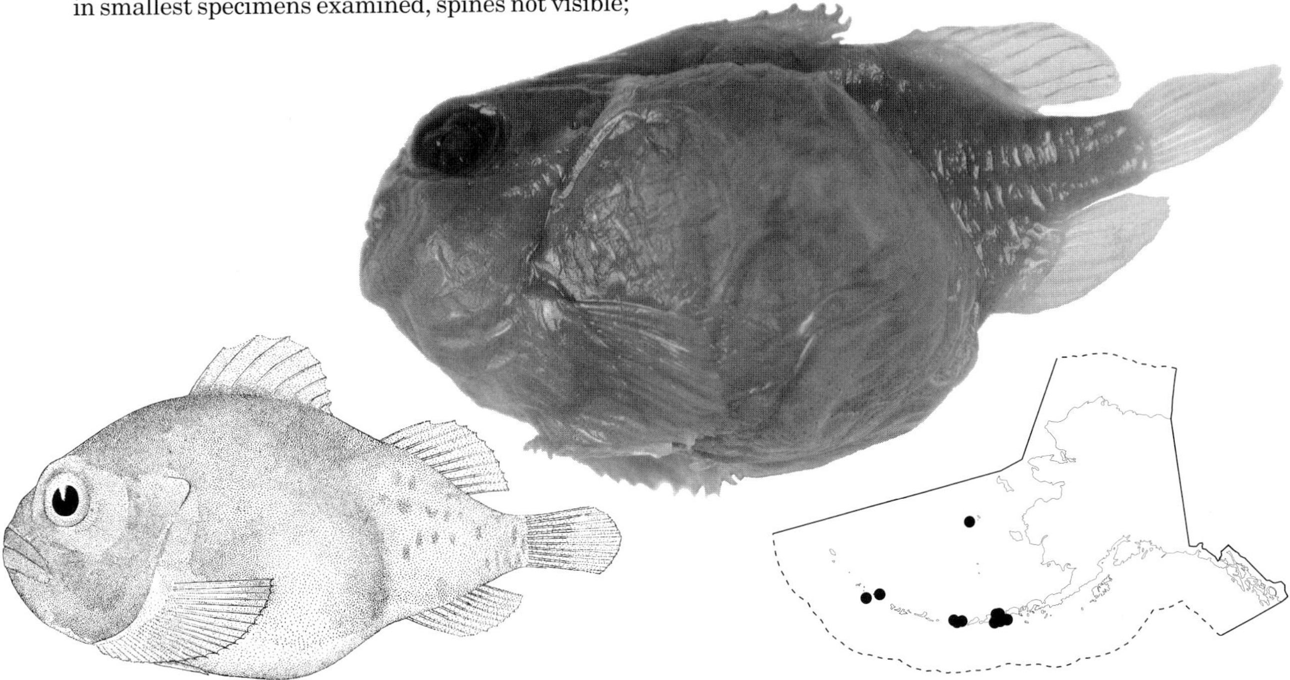

Notes & Sources — *Lethotremus muticus* Gilbert, 1896

Gilbert (1896) did not designate a type specimen in the original description, but he provided an illustration. In 1998, searching shelves at NMNH, C.W.M. found a specimen (USNM 53806) of *L. muticus* collected in 1888 that was labeled "Drawn." The length of the specimen (31 mm SL) and damaged condition of the fins match the illustration. Gilbert's (1896) paper was based on 1890 and 1891 *Albatross* collections and listed only the three specimens that were collected then. The subject of the illustration was referred to by Jordan and Evermann (1900) as the type, but they connected it with the wrong specimen by giving the wrong station number. Establishing USNM 53806 as the lectotype makes it clear that there are four specimens in the type series, not just the three listed by Gilbert, and identifies this particular specimen as the name-bearing type of the taxon.

Description: Gilbert 1896:449; Gilbert and Burke 1912a:70. Those descriptions are based on individuals 37 mm TL or smaller. Characters given above are from specimens up to 50.5 mm SL (BCPM 980-565). A female of 49 mm SL in BCPM 980-565 had about 120 well-developed eggs.

Figures: Upper: BCPM 980-565, 50.5 mm SL, 62 mm TL, north of Yunaska Island; by C.W.M. Lower: Gilbert 1896, pl. 31; lectotype, USNM 53806, 31 mm SL, Unimak Pass. The lectotype and two paralectotypes (USNM 48614 and 59376) have 7 dorsal spines and thick skin covering the spinous dorsal fin. Depiction of 8 spines in the drawing evidently an error; and the drawing does not depict a fin lacking thick skin cover, as interpreted by some authors, but a damaged fin.

Range: Lectotype (USNM 53806): *Albatross* station 2844, 53°56'N, 165°40'W, depth 99 m. Paralectotypes: station 3223, 54°26'N, 165°32'W, depth 102 m (USNM 48614 [21 mm SL], SU 103093); and sta. 3258, 54°48'N, 165°13'W, depth 128 m (USNM 59376; 29 mm SL). Gilbert and Burke (1912a): two (USNM 70877; 18–26 mm SL) from Petrel Bank, sta. 4779, 52°11'N, 179°57'W, depth 99 m. Others examined include BCPM 980-565 (4; 46–62 mm TL), 52°46'N, 170°39'W; BCPM 990-223 (1; 42 mm TL), Alaska; BCPM 980-588 (1; 43 mm TL), 54°15'N, 165°57'W; AB 66-1039 (2; 41.5–45 mm TL), 54°26'N, 165°38'W, 113–124 m; AB 66-1051 (1; 37 mm TL), 53°35'N, 166°05'W, 99–102 m; AB 66-1056 (2; 38–46.5 mm TL), 54°03'N, 164°47'W, 104–106 m. Isakson et al. (1971): offshore Amchitka Island. Others in collections include: NMC 78-320 (2 adults), near St. Matthew Island, 60°05'N, 172°50'W; SIO 94-182 (1; 32 mm SL), 53°03'N, 169°56'W, 138 m; SIO 94-190 (1; 32 mm SL), 52°51'N, 170°32'W, 329 m.

Cyclopteropsis inarmatus Mednikov & Prokhorov, 1956 **bumpy lumpsucker**

Western Bering Sea between Capes Navarin and Olyutorskiy; possible new records from Sea of Okhotsk and Bering Sea south of Cape Olyutorskiy presently being studied.

Stony bottom at depths of 100–150 m; possible new records would extend range to pebbly bottom and depths of 49–150 m .

D VI + 12; A 10; C 9; Pec 27.

- Profile steep from top of head to mouth; lower jaw strongly protruding.
- **No bony conical tubercles or spiny plates; skin with low bumps and leathery tubercles lacking subdermal bony plates** on head and body, including top of head, chin, throat, pectoral fin base.
- Anterior nostril tube short, posterior longer and narrow.
- **First dorsal fin overgrown with skin**, rays barely visible and of about equal length.
- Pores present on head and cheeks.
- Length to 64 mm TL.

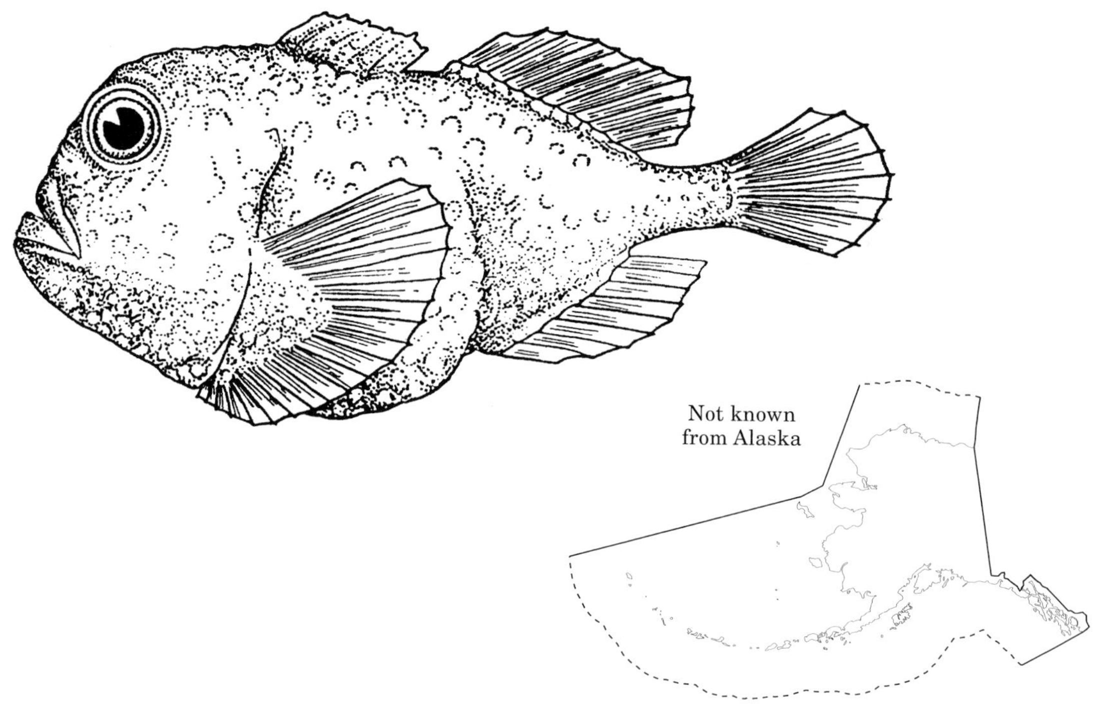

Notes & Sources — *Cyclopteropsis inarmatus* Mednikov & Prokhorov, 1956

Ueno (1970) placed *Cyclopteropsis inarmatus* in the synonymy of *C. phrynoides* (= *Eumicrotremus phrynoides*), without examining type specimens of either nominal species. He believed the type of *E. phrynoides* to be a juvenile and *C. inarmatus* an adult of the same species. However, *E. phrynoides* has many low spiny tubercles and these were lacking in the types of *C. inarmatus.* Mednikov and Prokhorov (1956) considered *C. inarmatus* to be more similar to *C. lindbergi* (= *Eumicrotremus lindbergi*) and *Lethotremus muticus.* Sheiko and Fedorov (2000) listed *C. inarmatus* as a distinct species based on examination of recently collected specimens (B. A. Sheiko, pers. comms., Jun.–Oct. 2000). However, a sample of those specimens (KIE 1458, KIE 2307) examined by C.W.M. exhibits diagnostic characters of *E. lindbergi. Lethotremus muticus* does not have the bumps described and portrayed by Mednikov and Prokhorov (1956) for *C. inarmatus.* Unfortunately, the type specimens of *C. inarmatus* were not found in the Russian Academy of Sciences fish collections, and may have been lost (B.A. Sheiko, pers. comm., 9 Aug. 2000), so they cannot be examined in an attempt to resolve the issue. *Cyclopteropsis inarmatus* could be a junior synonym of *E. lindbergi* or *E. phrynoides,* but it could with equal reason be considered a distinct species.

Description: Mednikov and Prokhorov 1956.

Figure: Mednikov and Prokhorov 1956, fig. 1; a type specimen, 62 mm TL, western Bering Sea.

Range: Described from two specimens caught in the western Bering Sea between Capes Olyutorskiy and Navarin by bottom trawl on stony substrate at depths of 100–150 m, and known with certainty only from those two specimens. Recently collected specimens from the western Bering Sea off northeastern Kamchatka and the Sea of Okhotsk off northwestern Kamchatka which may represent *C. inarmatus* are currently being studied (by B. A. Sheiko and C.W.M.).

Eumicrotremus lindbergi (Soldatov, 1930) **Lindberg's lumpsucker**

Western Bering Sea northeast of Dezhneva Bay to Pacific Ocean off southeastern Kamchatka, Sea of Okhotsk, Tatar Strait, and Sea of Japan to Korea.

Pebble and sand bottoms at depths of 49–118 m.

D VI–VII + 10–11; A 9–11; C 9–11; Pec 25–28.

- Light grayish brown dorsally, whitish ventrally; large and small dark brown spots on head and on body dorsolaterally; tiny, widely scattered, low, black protuberances; skin covering first dorsal fin colored like back; other fins mostly white.
- **Body covered with large dermal elevations** ("warts") with subdermal bony plates; head with smaller warts; **high, spiny conical tubercles on some specimens 40 mm SL and over**, becoming more numerous and covering most of body in largest individuals; heavy covering of mucus hides most tubercles; tubercles cone-shaped, taller, and with stronger spines than in *E. phrynoides.*
- First dorsal fin enveloped in thick skin.
- Head, operculomandibular canal, anterior lateral line pores well developed; no barbel-like tubes.
- Imperforate papillae along lateral line.
- Length to 74 mm TL.

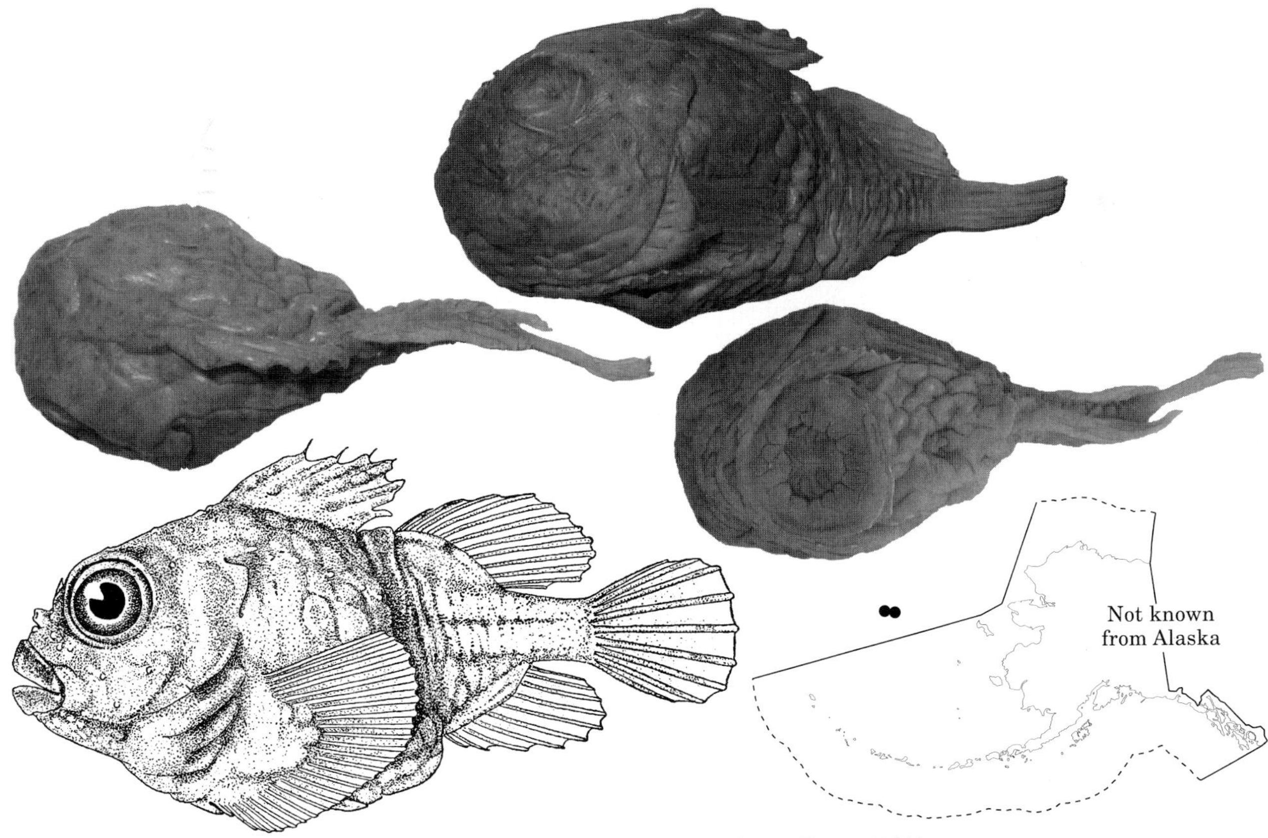

Notes & Sources — *Eumicrotremus lindbergi* (Soldatov in Soldatov & Lindberg, 1930)
Cyclopteropsis lindbergi Soldatov in Soldatov & Lindberg, 1930
Lethotremus fuscopunctatus Oshima, 1957
Ueno (1970) examined type specimens (from Sea of Japan) and placed *L. fuscopunctatus* in synonymy of *C. lindbergi.*
Classified herein in *Eumicrotremus* because in some specimens (e.g., USNM 149360, KIE 2306) body has conical spiny tubercles posteriorly as well as anteriorly. In *Cyclopteropsis* Soldatov & Popov, amended by Lindberg and Legeza (1955) and Ueno (1970), conical bony tubercles, if present, are located only on the anterior part of the body.

Description: Soldatov and Lindberg 1930:318–321; Lindberg and Legeza 1955:452–453; Ueno 1970:119, 122; Kido in Masuda et al. 1984:337. KIE 1458 (2; 40–42 mm SL), Koryak coast; KIE 2306 (1; 52 mm SL) and KIE 2307 (1; 47 mm SL), northwest Kamchatka; and USNM 149360 (2; 49–59 mm SL), Korea.

Figures: Drawing: Soldatov and Lindberg 1930, fig. 51; holotype (unique), 38 mm SL, 50 mm TL, Tatar Strait. Photographs: USNM 149360, 59 mm SL, 74 mm TL, Korea. See color photograph in Masuda et al. 1984 (pl. 303-H).

Range: Records nearest to Alaska are KIE 1458, off Koryak coast near Dezhneva Bay at 61°38'N, 174°59'E, depth 49 m; and UBC 60-549 (1; 44 mm SL), farther east at 61°55'N, 176°20'E (not Cape Olyutorskiy as given by Ueno 1970). The latter specimen, listed by Ueno (1970) under *E. phrynoides,* is missing, but an illustration of it dated 30 Mar. 1969 (UBC collection, copy on file at Point Stephens Research) exhibits characters of *E. lindbergi* and UBC records indicate G. S. Arita examined the specimen on 9 Nov. 1967 and identified it as *C.* cf. *lindbergi.*

Eumicrotremus phrynoides Gilbert & Burke, 1912 **toad lumpsucker**

Aleutian Islands and western Gulf of Alaska.

Sand, broken shell, and gravel bottoms at depths of 69–172 m.

D VI–VII + 10–11; A 9–10; C 10; Pec 25–27.

- Skin densely covered with dark specks, and sparsely with widely scattered, small dark spots.
- Head and body covered with **tubercles smaller than pupil, some with rosettes of short spines protruding and others concealed, forming bumps** or "warts"; in specimens not swollen with air or water, overall appearance bumpy and corrugated; when swollen, skin, except for spiny tubercles, appears smooth; **few or no spiny tubercles on throat**.
- Anterior nostril tube wide, posterior narrow; both equally long or posterior shorter or barely raised.
- **First dorsal fin covered with thick skin**, spines not visible through skin; tentacle-like extensions of skin from spine tips and skin tags on sides of fin in some specimens.
- Operculomandibular pores, up to 4, sometimes evident, lacking barbel-like tubes.
- Single pore in tube or with barely raised rim at origin of lateral line, not evident in all specimens.
- Length to 74 mm TL.

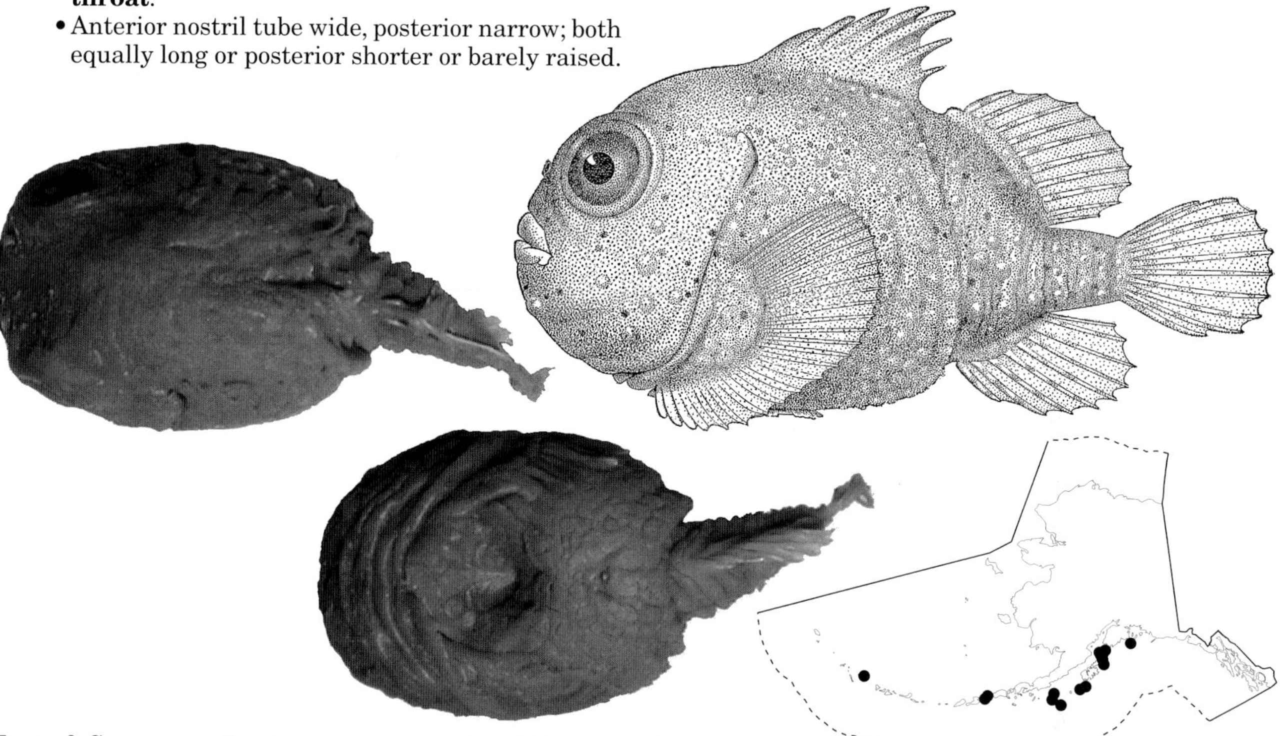

Notes & Sources — *Eumicrotremus phrynoides* Gilbert & Burke, 1912
Cyclopteropsis phrynoides: Soldatov and Lindberg 1930. *Cyclopterocottus phrynoides*: Popov 1930.
Reinstated in genus *Eumicrotremus* by Lindberg and Legeza (1955) because of widely distributed spiny tubercles.
Replaced in *Cyclopteropsis* by Ueno (1970), without examining the holotype. The description by Ueno (1970:114–116) does not include features of the holotype of *E. phrynoides* (e.g., presence of spiny tubercles posteriorly) and may be based on specimens of more than one species. *Cyclopteropsis inarmatus* Mednikov & Prokhorov, 1956, placed in the synonymy of *E. phrynoides* by Ueno, may not belong in the synonymy. A specimen from UBC 60-549 listed under *C. phrynoides* by Ueno has features of *C.* (= *Eumicrotremus*) *lindbergi*.

Description: Gilbert and Burke 1912a:69–70. Holotype and additional specimens examined are listed under Range.

Figures: Holotype (unique), USNM 74378, 30 mm SL, 38 mm TL, Petrel Bank, Alaska. Lateral view: Gilbert and Burke 1912a, fig. 15. Dorsal and ventral: Smithsonian Institution, NMNH, Division of Fishes.

Range: Gilbert and Burke (1912a): one specimen from *Albatross* station 4779, Petrel Bank near Semisopochnoi Island, 52°11'N, 179°57'W, 99–102 m. Specimens identified at time of collection in 1960s by M. Yesaki, and recently confirmed by C.W.M.: AB 64-717 (4; 34–41 mm SL), 59°05'N, 152°23'W; AB 64-725 (3; 40–48 mm SL), 59°09'N, 152°34'W; AB 64-753 (2; 34–45 mm SL), 58°45'N, 152°02'W; AB 64-756 (1; 42 mm SL), 58°24'N, 151°48'W; AB 64-831 (48–50 mm SL), 56°16'N, 153°55'W; and AB 64-834 (1; 54 mm SL), 56°06'N, 154°28'W. Some of the ABL lots from the 1960s are now in other collections; e.g., SIO 69-109, 59°54'N, 148°02'W, 69–71 m; SIO 72-234, 59°01'N, 152°29'W, 143–150 m; USNM 207981, 58°26'N, 151°51'W, 104–106 m; and UAM 637, 56°21'N, 153°55'W. Specimens previously identified as *L. muticus, E. derjugini,* and *E. gyrinops* having characters of *E. phrynoides* are: AB 66-1038 (13; 37–46 mm SL), 54°24'N, 165°21'W, 143–159 m; AB 66-1040 (2; 29–37 mm SL), 54°37'N, 165°28'W, 165–172 m; AB 66-1042 (6; 30–40 mm SL), 54°33'N, 165°29'W, 90–91 m; AB 66-1043 (1; 41 mm SL), 54°22'N, 165°46'W, 110–115 m; UBC 62-659 (1; 53 mm SL), 55°49'N, 157°34'W; UBC 62-669 (1; 58 mm SL), 55°18'N, 158°00'W; and UBC 62-672 (1; 63 mm SL, 74 mm TL), 55°55'N, 156°45'W.

Eumicrotremus barbatus (Lindberg & Legeza, 1955) **papillose lumpsucker**

Pacific Ocean off Igitkin Island in the Aleutian Islands; Paramushir Island, Kuril Islands; Sea of Okhotsk off northern Hokkaido.

Igitkin Island specimen collected "at the shore." Depth of 74 m reported for Kuril Islands specimen and 210 m for Sea of Okhotsk specimen.

D VII + 9–11; A 10; C 11; Pec 23–25.

- **Tubercles on head and body low, with large bases and weak spinules**; some tubercles as large as eye; no tubercles on interorbital region.
- First dorsal fin high, covered with thin skin except tips of some spines free.
- Many dermal **papillae projecting from subcutaneous round bases** on upper part of head and cheeks, chin, throat, first dorsal fin, bases of second dorsal, pectoral, and anal fins, and caudal region; not always present on all of those areas.
- Mandibular pores with long, barbel-like tubes; nostril tubes unusually long.
- Length to 65 mm TL.

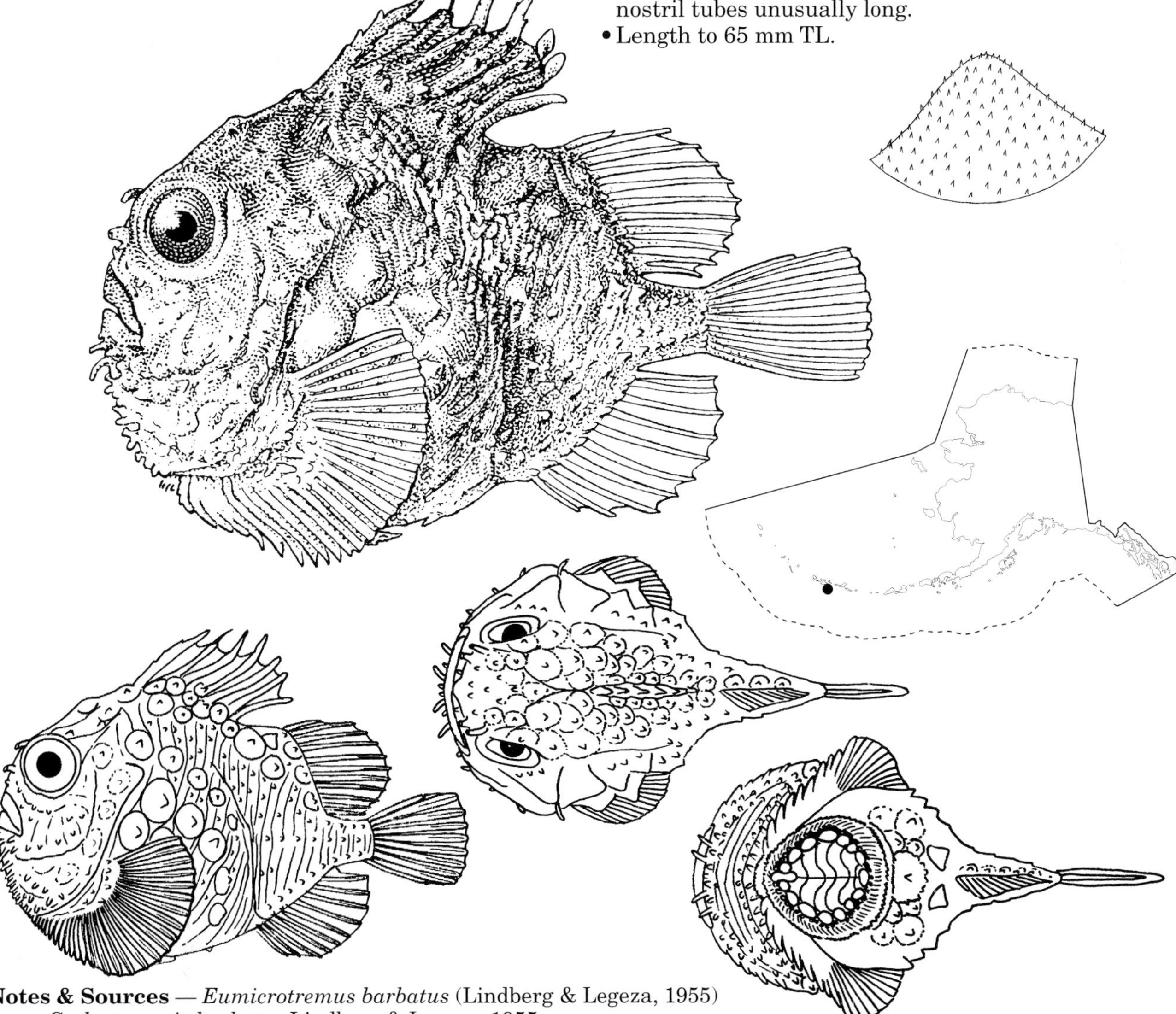

Notes & Sources — *Eumicrotremus barbatus* (Lindberg & Legeza, 1955)

Cyclopteropsis barbatus Lindberg & Legeza, 1955

Classified in *Eumicrotremus* by Ueno (1970), partly because the subcutaneous round bases of the dermal papillae on the posterior part of the body can be considered to be modified bony tubercles, and in the diagnosis of *Cyclopteropsis* Soldatov & Popov, 1929, bony tubercles are absent from the posterior part of the body.

Description: Lindberg and Legeza 1955:449–452; Ueno 1970: 102–105; Kido 1984a.

Figures: Full lateral: Lindberg and Legeza 1955; 65 mm TL, Pacific Ocean off Paramushir Island, Russia. Diagrams: Ueno 1970, fig. 46A-D; UBC 63-919, 46 mm SL, south side of Igitkin Island, Aleutian Islands, Alaska.

Range: Known from three records comprising one specimen each: Igitkin Island, Aleutian Islands, 51°59'N, 175°52'W (Wilimovsky 1964, Ueno 1970); Pacific Ocean off Paramushir Island, Kuril Islands (Lindberg and Legeza 1955); and Sea of Okhotsk off Abashiri, Hokkaido (Kido 1984a).

Eumicrotremus gyrinops (Garman, 1892) **Alaskan lumpsucker**

Southeastern Bering Sea off St. Paul Island; records from St. George Island, Unalaska Island, and Gulf of Alaska south of Alaska Peninsula uncertain or unconfirmed.

Holotype collected in shallow water, depth not reported.

D VIII + 9; A 9; C 10; Pec 24.

- Body relatively elongate, subtriangular in cross section.
- **Body and head smooth and naked except for small, distantly spaced spiny conical tubercles** on interorbital space, top of head, below dorsal fins, on side above and posterior to pectoral fin and between second dorsal and anal fin origins.
- First dorsal fin covered with thick skin at least at base (entire fin may be covered).
- Long, barbel-like mandibular pore tubes.
- Length of holotype 37.5 mm SL.

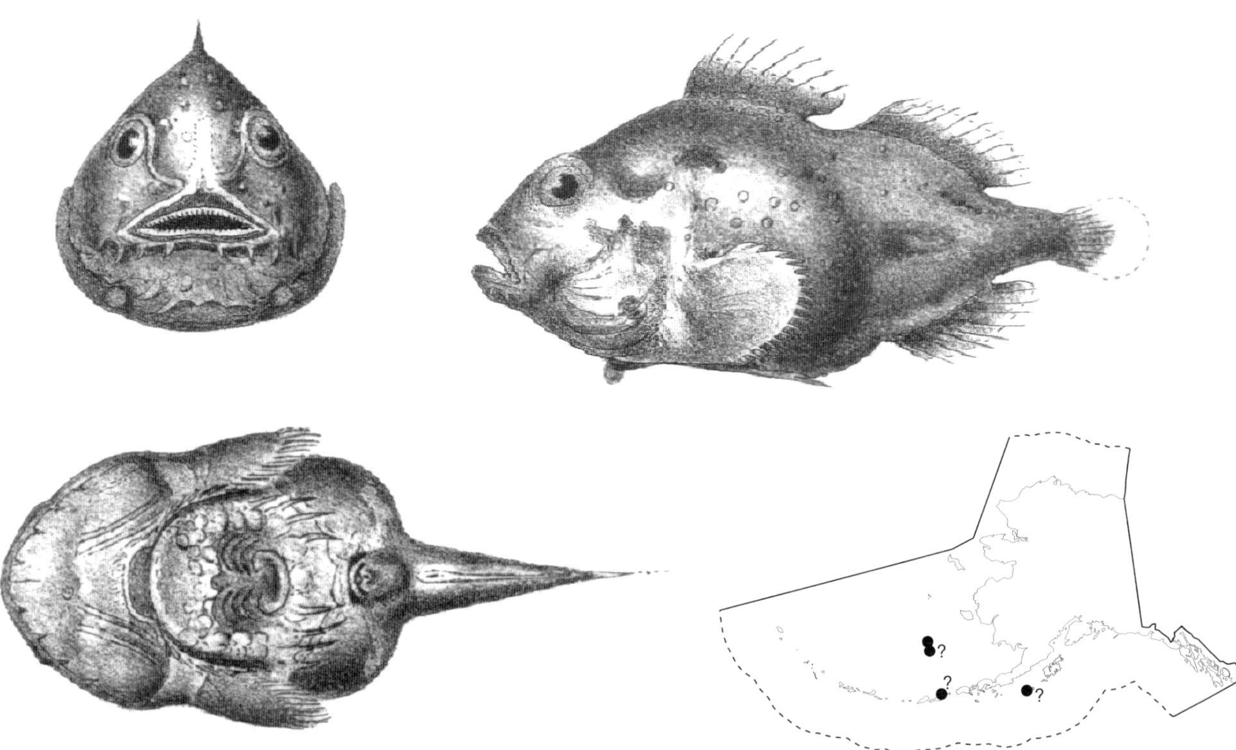

Notes & Sources — *Eumicrotremus gyrinops* (Garman, 1892)
Cyclopteroides gyrinops Garman, 1892

Lindberg and Legeza (1955) classified *Cyclopteroides* as a junior synonym of *Eumicrotremus* because of the presence of small spiny tubercles in regular rows. The authors considered the small size of the tubercles to be a diagnostic feature, differentiating this species from all others of the genus *Eumicrotremus.* However, in *E. phrynoides,* even in individuals larger than the holotype of *E. gyrinops,* the tubercles are about the same size or smaller.

The holotype (MCZ 16026) has more spiny tubercles than indicated in Garman's (1892) illustrations, but fewer than most other armored lumpsuckers. It is possible that the holotype is an immature individual of some other species.

Description: Garman 1892:37–39. Descriptions of this species by Ueno (1970) and others repeat Garman's description, since authors did not examine the holotype. Examination of the holotype (by C.W.M. and B. A. Sheiko) confirms suggestion made by other authors that free tips of dorsal, anal, and pectoral fins; appearance of pelvic disk; exaggerated, sculptured-looking features of the head; and dark blotches described and illustrated by Garman are due to the condition of the specimen, which seems to have been partly deteriorated and dried out before preservation.

Figures: Garman 1892, pl. 11, figs. 4–6; holotype (unique), MCZ 16026, 37.5 mm SL, 43 mm to end of broken caudal fin tips, St. Paul Island, Alaska.

Range: The only record other than the holotype comprises "a few young specimens" from Golinski Harbor (now Dutch Harbor), Unalaska Island, reported by Jordan and Gilbert (1899). Those specimens may no longer be in existence; C.W.M. did not find them in searches of the NMNH collection in 1998 and 2000. A University of British Columbia specimen (UBC 62-672) from south of the Alaska Peninsula identified as this species has the characteristics of *E. phrynoides.* An Auke Bay Laboratory specimen (AB 76-99; 26 mm SL) from the vicinity of St. George Island identified as *E. gyrinops* is slightly deteriorated and possibly too small, with undeveloped characters, for accurate identification; but has fairly dense spiny tubercles, unlike *E. gyrinops.*

Eumicrotremus birulai Popov, 1928 **Siberian lumpsucker**

Western Gulf of Alaska; western Bering Sea to Okhotsk and Japan seas and Pacific Ocean off Hokkaido. Mud, sand, and rocky gravel bottoms at depths of 30–900 m; juveniles usually shallower than 100 m.

D VI–VII + 9–12; A 9–11; C 9–12; Pec 25–29.

- Head and body with **numerous spiny tubercles, all smaller to about same size as eye**; cheeks, chin, throat, and pectoral fin base densely covered with tubercles in adults, but possibly not in all juveniles; 3 rows on caudal peduncle.
- **In adults first dorsal fin low, skin-covered; spine tips visible or fin evident by row of small tubercles**; in some juveniles first dorsal fin high.
- Length to 108 mm SL, 135 mm TL; mature at about 60 mm TL.

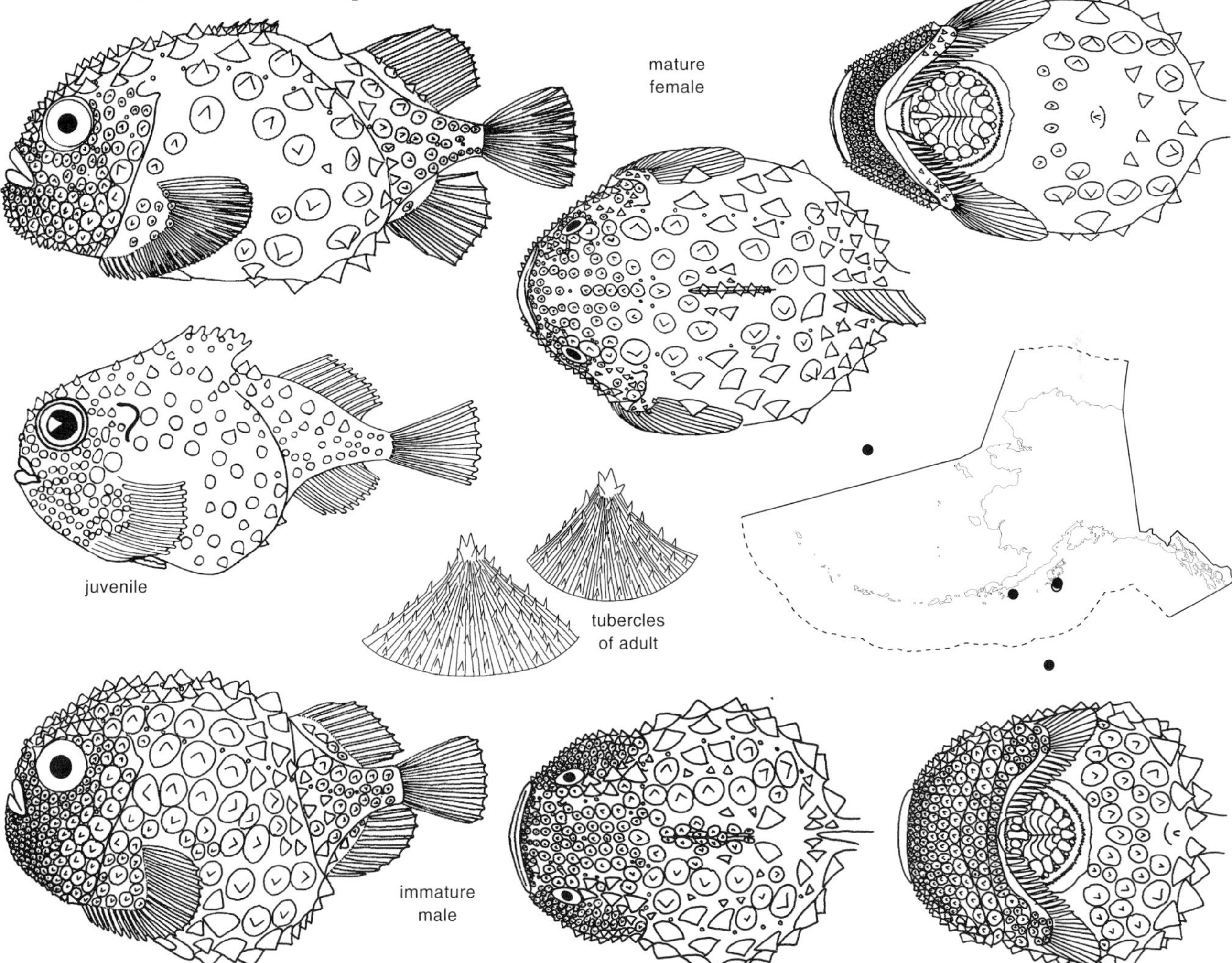

Notes & Sources — *Eumicrotremus birulai* Popov, 1928
Possibly confused in Alaska with *E. phrynoides*. All spiny tubercles are smaller than the pupil in *E. phrynoides*.

Description: Popov 1928:48–51; Lindberg and Legeza 1955: 416–420; Ueno 1970:83–91; Kido in Amaoka et al. 1983:341. It is possible that Gulf of Alaska specimens recorded by Ueno (1970) as *E. birulai* (see below) were *E. phrynoides,* and account for some confusion in Ueno's decription of *E. birulai.*

Figures: Most from Ueno 1970. Adult female: fig. 38; UBC 62-523, 109 mm TL, Sea of Okhotsk. Young male: fig. 39; UBC 60-296, 57 mm TL, off Shikotan Island. Juvenile at center left: Lindberg and Legeza 1955, fig. 17; 53 mm TL, Gulf of Tatary; note high first dorsal fin.

Range: Ueno (1970) identified HFRS 63-19, south of Gulf of Alaska at 50°43'N, 153°15'W; and HFRS 63-20, southeast of Kodiak Island at 56°42'N, 153°15'W, as *E. birulai.* Hamada (1982) identified two specimens (40 and 43 mm SL) from south of Kodiak (55°34'N, 153°16'W) as *E. birulai,* but Hamada's description and drawings suggest the fish may have been *E. phrynoides* (the specimens were not saved). USNM 333400 (65 mm TL), collected in August 1987 and identified as *E. derjugini* from 55°22'N, 158°58'W, is *E. birulai.* This species was recorded from the western Bering Sea as far north as Natalii Bay, 61°10'N, by Lindberg and Legeza (1955). Three juveniles (30–44 mm TL) in KIE uncataloged material examined by C.W.M. are from 61°38'N, 175°01'E, depth 49 m. Not recorded from eastern Bering Sea but probably occurs there.

Size: Ueno's (1970: fig. 41) sample included specimens up to 108 mm SL; standard length is about 80% of total length for this species, giving 135 mm TL.

Eumicrotremus derjugini Popov, 1926 **leatherfin lumpsucker**

Beaufort Sea; uncertain records from Chukchi Sea; Canadian Arctic to Greenland and Labrador, and Norwegian, Barents, Kara, and Laptev seas; isolated population in northern Sea of Okhotsk.

Mud, gravel, and stony bottoms at depths of 50–930 m; most records shallower than 275 m.

D VI–VII + 11–13; A 10–13; C 9–11; Pec 25–27.

- **Largest tubercles on body distinctly larger than pupil diameter; chin, throat, and pectoral fin base naked**; tubercles on caudal peduncle in 2 rows; no tubercles between disk and anus; 5 or 6 irregular rows of small tubercles on interorbital space; tubercles well developed even in juveniles 25 mm in total length, although not as numerous as in adults.
- **First dorsal fin keel-like, covered with thick skin and tubercles**, spines not discernible.
- Length to 127 mm TL.

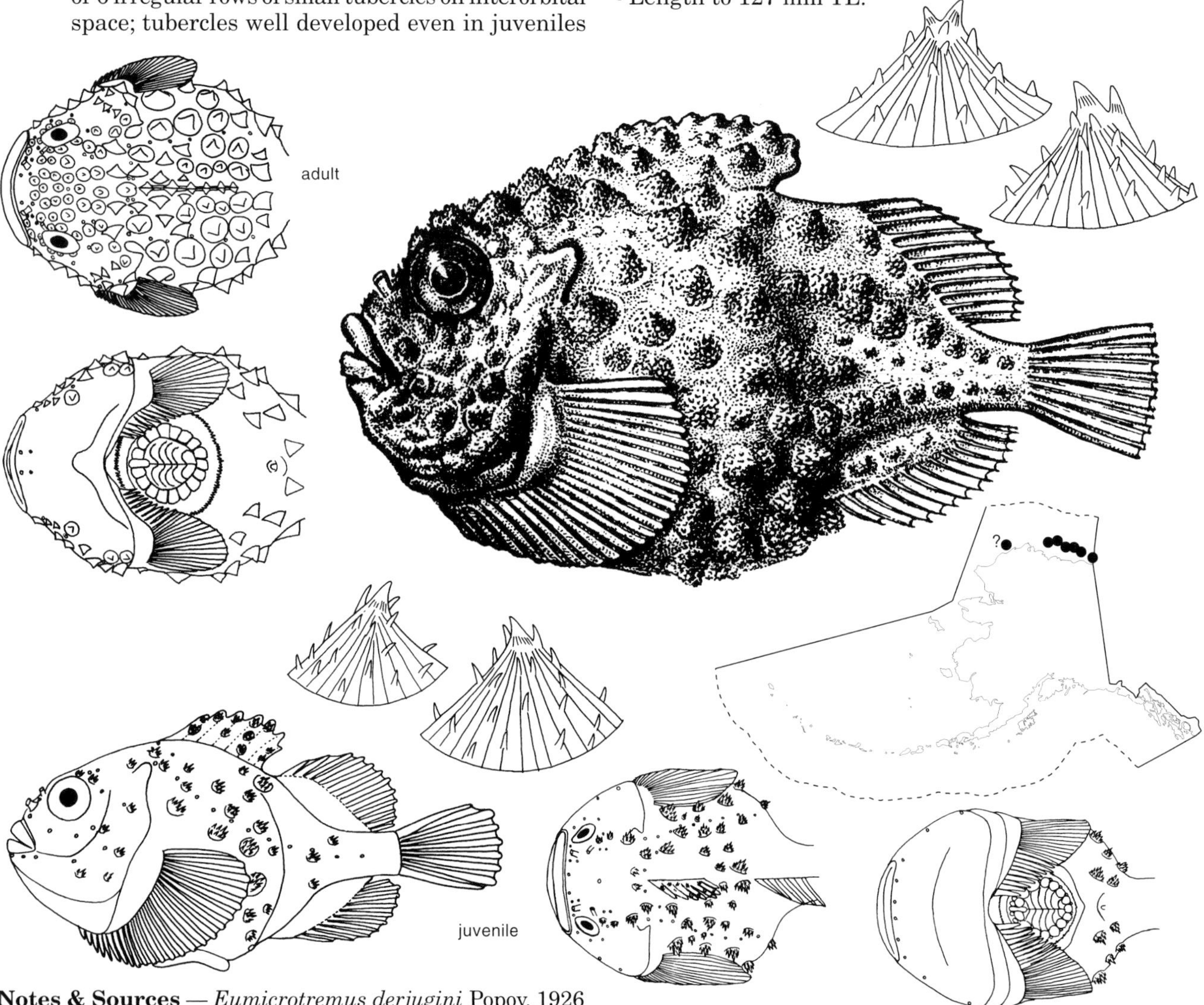

Notes & Sources — *Eumicrotremus derjugini* Popov, 1926

Description: Jensen 1944:53–54; Andriashev 1954:447–449; Lindberg and Legeza 1955:420–423; Ueno 1970:165–172; Scott and Scott 1988:520-521.

Figures: Adult, lateral: Andriashev 1954, fig. 256; 95 mm TL; dorsal, ventral: Ueno 1970, fig. 70B,C; 61 mm TL. Juvenile: fig. 71A–C; 37 mm TL. Tubercles: fig. 73C–F. All from Barents Sea.

Range: Listed by Wilimovsky (1954) from Arctic Alaska. Frost and Lowry (1983) caught 3 specimens west and 26 east of Prudhoe Bay in water 50–110 m deep (some are at UAF, including UAM 2679). Other Alaska records are NMC 74-283, 70°41'N, 145°23'W, 79 m; NMC 74-289, 71°11'N, 148°32'W, 158 m; and NMC 79-510, 70°47'N, 146°33'W, 56 m. UBC specimens from Chukchi Sea identified as *E. derjugini* are missing (UBC 63-1123, off Wainwright) or too small for accurate identification (UBC 63-1119; 16.5 mm SL). Not found in Bering Sea (Andriashev 1954). References to Bering Sea for this species in English translation of Lindberg and Legeza (1955) are incorrect; Russian edition gives Barents Sea. Documentation is lacking for occurrence in Chukchi and Siberian seas reported by Ueno (1970). Hunter et al. (1984) confirmed Canadian Arctic records as close to Alaska as Franklin Bay. Rogers et al. (1986) listed it from Cook Inlet, but we disregard this report since specific documentation was not given and other information indicates *E. derjugini* is absent from Gulf of Alaska.

Eumicrotremus soldatovi Popov, 1930 — Soldatov's lumpsucker

Recorded once from Bering Sea, near northwest end of Bowers Ridge; common in Sea of Okhotsk.

Pelagic; observed from submersible at 80 m over bottom of 230 m, taken in midwater trawls to 350 m; makes diurnal vertical migrations with primary prey, hyperiids; migrates to coastal areas for spawning.

D VI–VII + 11–12; A 10; C 9–11; Pec 24–26.

- **Body relatively elongate**.
- **Interorbital space naked or with a few small scattered tubercles; 3 pairs of tubercles between dorsal fins**.
- Tubercles with distinct radial ridges from top of cone to base on body and head.
- First dorsal fin high, triangular, covered with thick skin, spines not visible except for tips; **dorsal fin interspace same as or greater than length of first dorsal fin base**.
- Operculomandibular pores without long tubes.
- Length to about 260 mm TL.

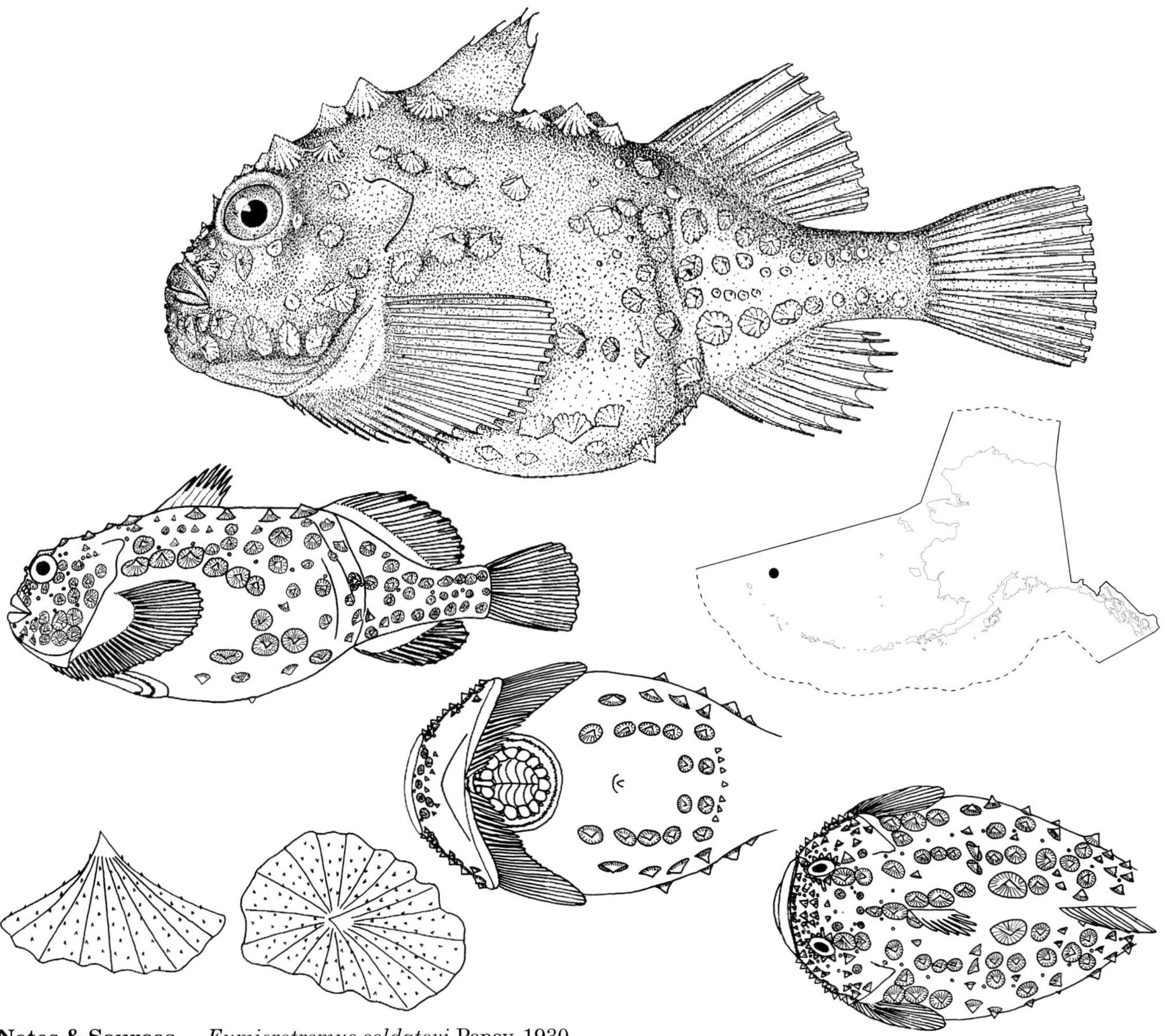

Notes & Sources — *Eumicrotremus soldatovi* Popov, 1930

Description: Soldatov and Lindberg 1930:310–314, 321; Lindberg and Legeza 1955:413–416; Ueno 1970:99–102. Descriptions, which are based on few specimens, say 6 dorsal fin spines; Ueno's (1970) pl. 3 and fig. 45 show 7.

Figures: Upper: Soldatov and Lindberg 1930, fig. 50; 150 mm TL, Sea of Okhotsk. Lower: Ueno 1970, fig. 45A–E; UBC 60-298, 191 mm SL, Bering Sea.

Range: Ueno (1970) recorded a specimen (UBC 60-298) from Bering Sea at 55°23'N, 175°38'E. Orlov (1994) described life history and distribution in Sea of Okhotsk, where the species is abundant.

Size: Ueno (1970:102) gave length of 191 mm SL for the Bering Sea and largest Sea of Okhotsk specimens; scale provided for fig. 45A indicates 260 mm TL for the Bering Sea specimen. Orlov (1994) reported a maximum length of 250 mm in a sample of 292 specimens from the Sea of Okhotsk.

Eumicrotremus andriashevi Perminov, 1936 **pimpled lumpsucker**

Chukchi Sea to Bering Sea south of St. Lawrence Island, and to northern Kuril Islands near Paramushir Island and Sea of Okhotsk.

Mud, sand, and pebble bottoms at depths of 20–83 m.

D VI–VII + 10–12; A 10–12; C 10–11; Pec 23–27.

- **Interorbital space with 6–8 irregular rows of small tubercles**; well-developed midoccipital row of tubercles; tubercles on posterior part of body irregularly arranged.
- **First dorsal fin covered with thin, smooth skin** and small, scattered spinules; dorsal fin spines all visible, tips free.
- Mandibular pores with long tubes.
- Length to 97 mm TL.

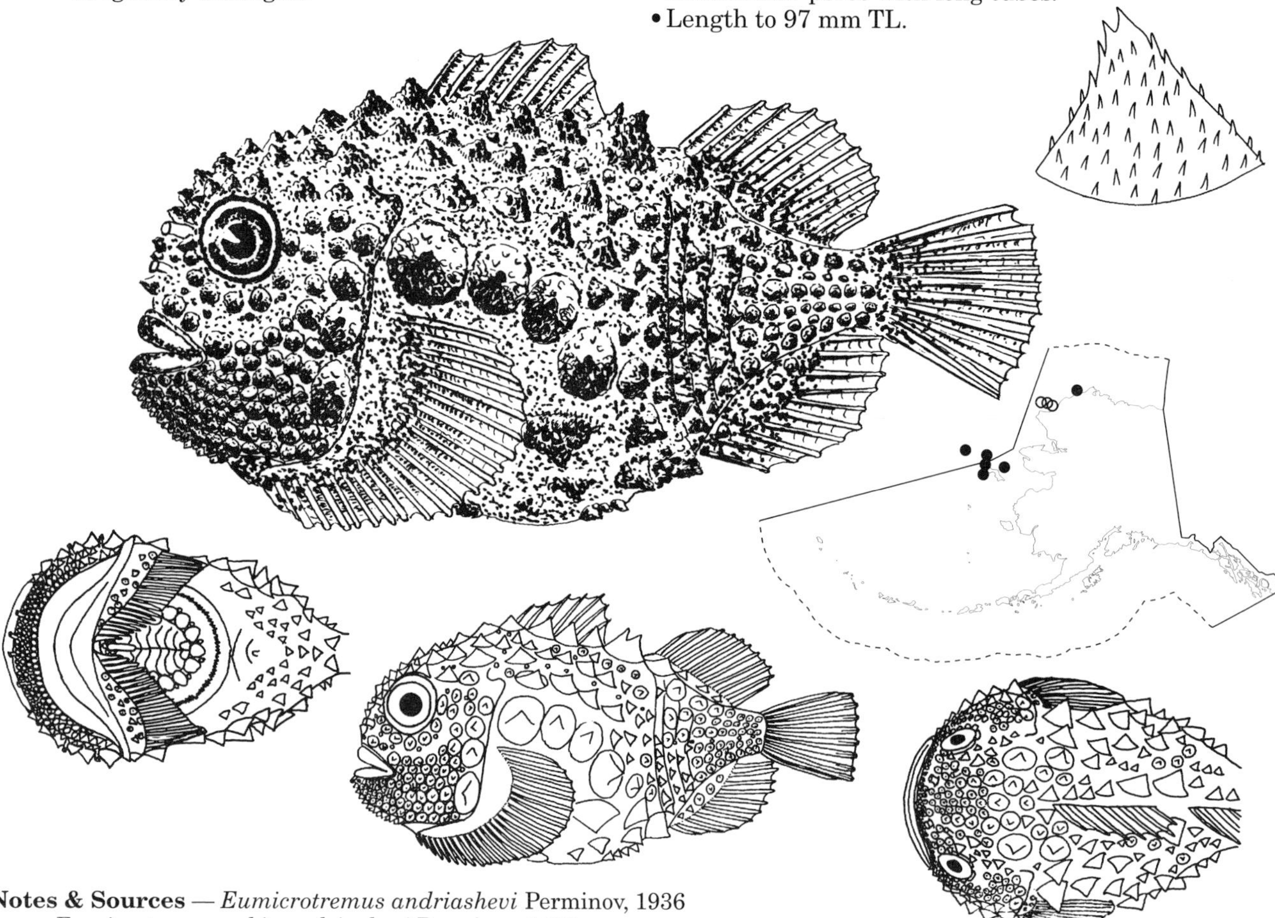

Notes & Sources — *Eumicrotremus andriashevi* Perminov, 1936
Eumicrotremus orbis andriashevi Perminov, 1936
Ueno (1970:80) provided detailed synonymy, but Chukchi Sea location given for specimen of Andriashev (1937, fig. 7) is incorrect (see Range, below). Records almost inextricably mixed up with those of *E. orbis* and *E. spinosus* in the literature. Lindberg and Legeza (1955) included *E. terraenovae* Myers & Böhlke, 1950, from Newfoundland in *E. andriashevi*, thereby extending the range of the latter to the Atlantic; however, Ueno (1970) removed it from the synonymy. *Eumicrotremis andriashevi* is not known to occur outside the Pacific.
Removed by mistake from American Fisheries Society list of North American fishes by Robins et al. (1991a).

Description: Perminov 1936:118–120; Lindberg and Legeza 1955:408–410, figs. 10 and 11; Ueno 1970:80–83.

Figures: Ueno 1970, pl. 10(1), figs. 36B, 37A–C; ZIAS 33762, 49 mm SL, 55 mm TL, near Anadyr Bay.

Range: Ueno (1970:83) gave range to Chukchi Sea, but at that time no records had been published from north of Bering Strait. Several specimens were recorded off the Chukchi Peninsula but none farther north than Lavrentiya Bay (Bering Sea). The juvenile specimen reported by Andriashev (1937, fig. 7) was caught in the Bering Sea between Cape Chaplina and St. Lawrence Island. Ueno (1970) examined four from vicinity of St. Lawrence Island: UW 14738(3), 63°56'N, 169°05'W; and UW 14739(1), 63°50'N, 172°05'W. Perminov's (1936) specimens included 70 from south of the Chukchi Peninsula at 64°07'N, 175°57'W; and 2 from south of St. Lawrence Island at 63°05'N, 171°47'W. Included on list of fish species from northeastern Chukchi Sea by Barber et al. (1997), without locality data. Voucher specimens among UAM uncataloged material include four (49–79 mm TL) from 71°00'N, 159°21'W, depth 27 m, collected 21 Sep. 1991. Others, from the unpublished cruise report for the UAF 1990 survey of the northeastern Chukchi Sea, are indicated by circles. Sheiko and Fedorov (2000) gave minimum depth of 20 m. KIE uncataloged specimens (on loan to C.W.M.) from Litke Strait and Gulf of Anadyr were collected on mud, sand, and shingle bottoms.

Eumicrotremus orbis (Günther, 1861) **Pacific spiny lumpsucker**

Bering Sea to Puget Sound, Washington, and to Sea of Okhotsk and Pacific Ocean off Hokkaido, Japan. Sand, pebble, and stony bottoms, usually found at shallow depths to 200 m although reported to 575 m.

D V–VII + 9–12; A 9–11; C 9–12; Pec 19–27.

- Males orange to reddish brown, females pale green.
- Tubercles well developed, with numerous strong, sharp spinules; **4 rows of large tubercles on interorbital region, inner 2 rows each diverging posteriorly to form row of small tubercles between dorsal row and postorbital row.**
- Chin, throat, and pectoral fin base densely covered with small tubercles; tubercles in females larger and more numerous than those in males.
- **First dorsal fin high, not thickly covered with skin**, spines covered with small tubercles.
- Operculomandibular pores with barbel-like tubes.
- Length to 127 mm TL.

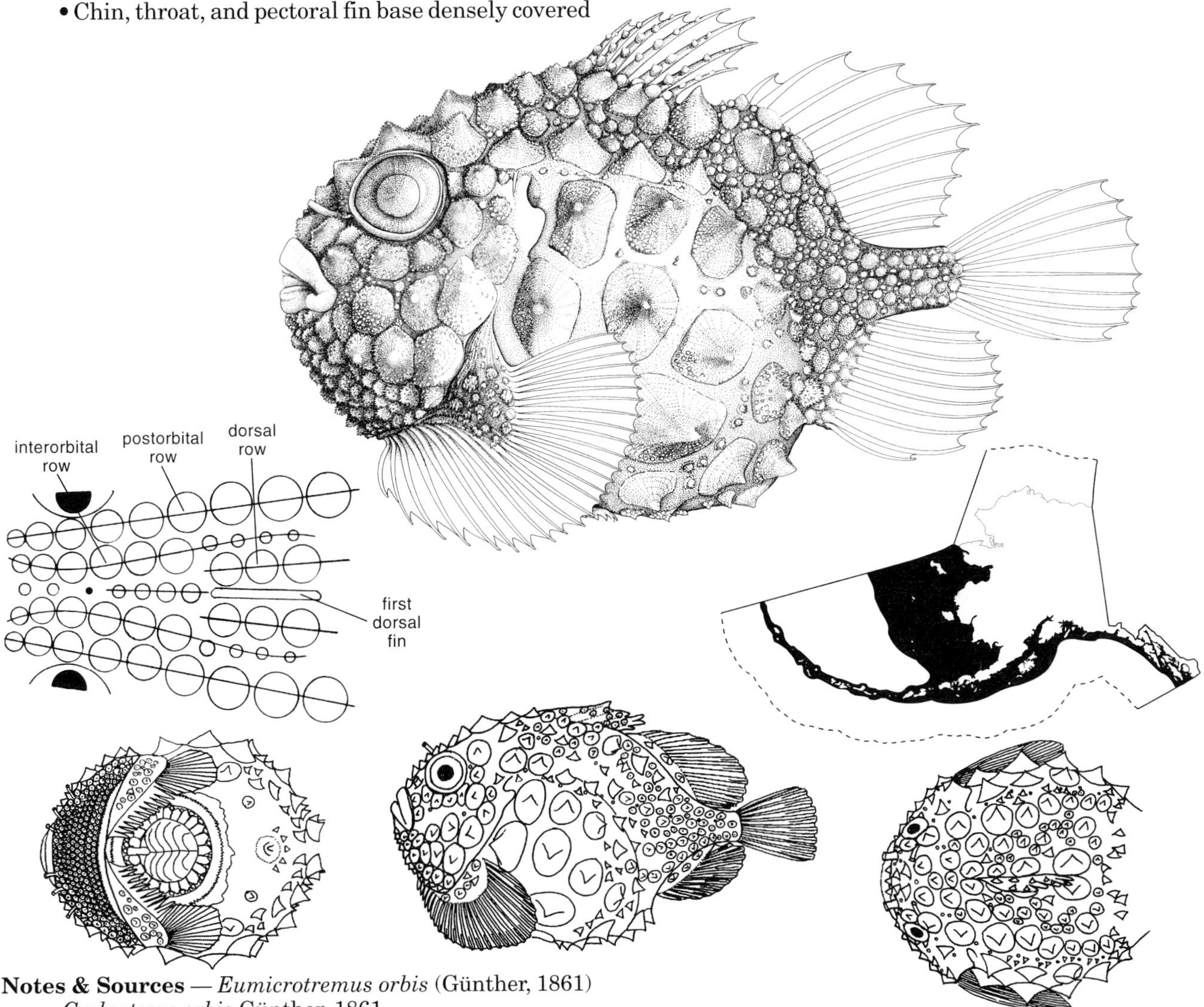

Notes & Sources — *Eumicrotremus orbis* (Günther, 1861)
Cyclopterus orbis Günther, 1861
Many museum specimens from Alaska cataloged as *E. spinosus* are misidentified *E. orbis.* Ueno (1970) corrected several such records.

Description: Andriashev 1937:37–38; Arita 1969; Ueno 1970:64–70. Examination of specimens from Alaska, Russia, and Canada confirms tubercle pattern on top of head as described by Ueno (1970) to be excellent method for differentiating *E. orbis* and *E. spinosus.*

Figures: Upper: University of British Columbia, artist R. Wood, Feb. 1969; UBC 62-663, 55 mm SL, Unimak Pass, Alaska. Lower: Ueno 1970, fig. 30A–C; UBC 62-245, Vancouver, British Columbia; tubercle pattern on top of head, fig. 67A.

Range: Recorded between St. Lawrence Island and Chukchi Peninsula by Andriashev (1937). Allen and Smith (1988) reported it in surveys as far north as Bering Strait and south to Baranof Island. Recorded from Amchitka Island by Isakson et al. (1971). USNM 333401 is from Kiska Island. Grebnitzki collected it near Bering Island in 1886 (USNM 54246). Barber et al. (1997) listed it from Chukchi Sea, but voucher specimens (UAM uncataloged) are *E. andriashevi.* A juvenile (UBC 63-1119; 16.5 mm SL) collected off Point Marsh, 70°38'N, 160°19'W, and identified as *E. derjugini* has features of *E. orbis,* including very large tubercles.

Eumicrotremus spinosus (Fabricius, 1776) **Atlantic spiny lumpsucker**

Eastern Beaufort Sea and Canadian high Arctic to Greenland, western Atlantic Ocean south to Cape Cod, and eastern Atlantic and Arctic oceans to Kara and Barents seas and Novaya Zemlya.

Stony bottom or soft bottom mixed with stones, mostly in shallow water; usually at 5–200 m, rarely deeper, with records to 400 m and one at 930 m.

D VI–VII + 10–13; A 10–13; C 9–11; Pec 21–27.

- Olivaceous to brown, sometimes with darker bands posteriorly; whitish ventrally.
- Throat and ventral surface between disk and anus with dermal folds but no tubercles.
- Tubercles well developed, with numerous strong, sharp spinules; **4 rows of large tubercles on interorbital region, no extension of inner 2 rows between dorsal and postorbital rows**.
- Chin and pectoral fin base covered with small tubercles; throat mostly lacking tubercles.
- **First dorsal fin high, not thickly covered with skin**, a few small tubercles on spines.
- Operculomandibular pores with barbel-like tubes.
- Length to 137 mm TL.

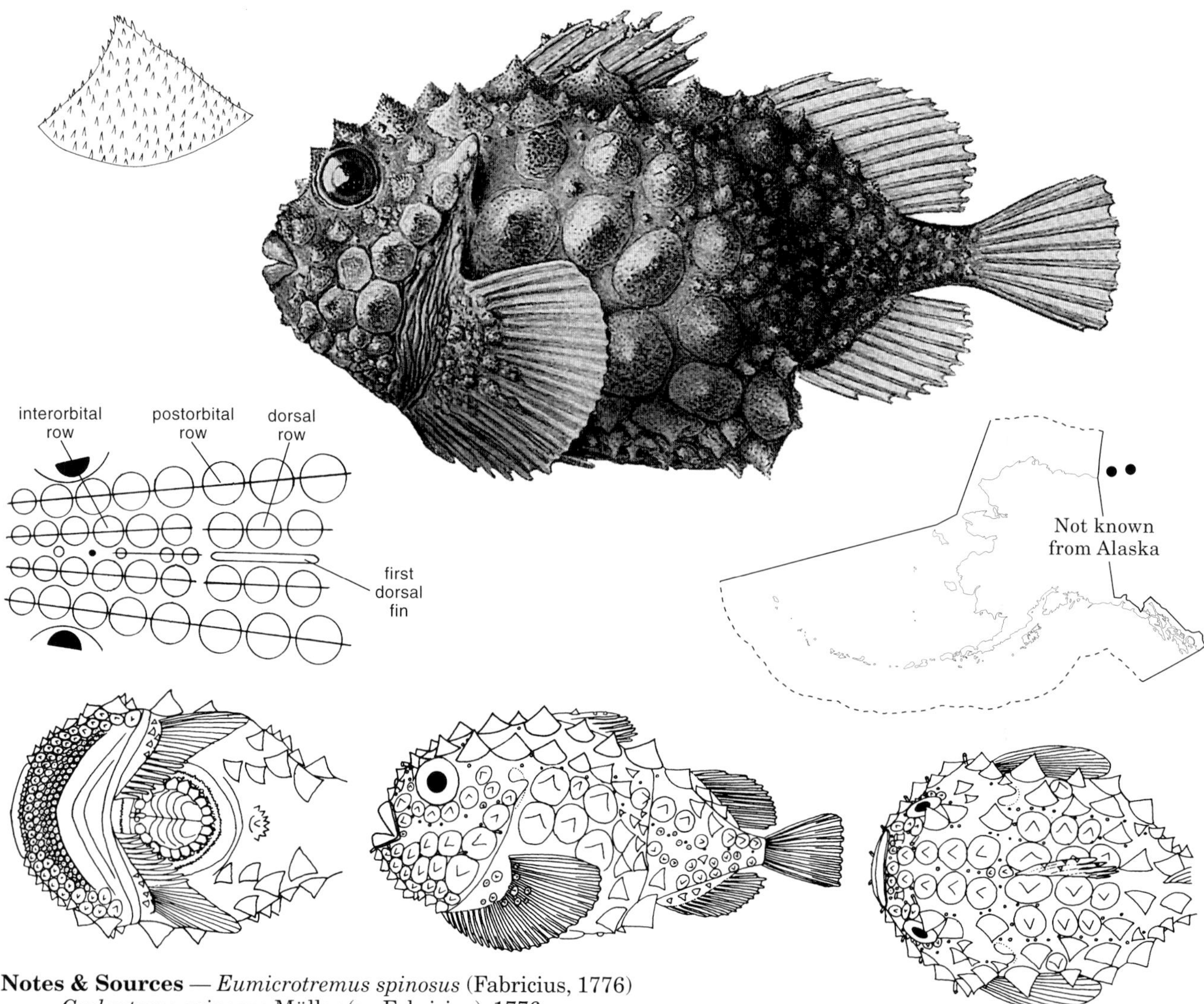

Notes & Sources — *Eumicrotremus spinosus* (Fabricius, 1776)
Cyclopterus spinosus Müller (ex Fabricius), 1776

Description: Jensen 1944:48–53; Andriashev 1954:442–446; Ueno 1970:156–162; Scott and Scott 1988:521–522.

Figures: Upper: Jensen 1944, pl. 7; 100 mm TL, Davis Strait between Greenland and Baffin Island. Lower and tubercle: Ueno 1970, fig. 66A–D; UBC 61-29, Jens Munk Island, west coast Baffin Island; tubercle pattern on top of head, fig. 67B.

Range: For a time *E. orbis* was considered by some authors to be conspecific with *E. spinosus,* and numerous old specimens of *E. orbis* from Alaska and other regions of the North Pacific in museum collections are still cataloged as *E. spinosus.* On the other hand, some specimens from Alaska identified as *E. orbis, E. andriashevi,* and *E. derjugini* may be referable to *E. spinosus*; study is under way. Map of Canadian Arctic records by Hunter et al. (1984) shows several *E. spinosus* near Alaska off the Mackenzie Delta and in Franklin Bay.

Family Liparidae
Snailfishes

Snailfishes (family Liparidae) are marine cottoid fishes that typically are tadpole-shaped, soft, and covered with gelatinous tissue. They are closely related to the lumpsuckers (Cyclopteridae) and, like them, many snailfishes have a ventral sucking disk derived from the pelvic fins with which they attach themselves to rocks, algae, and other objects. Unlike lumpsuckers, snailfishes are elongate in the tail region and lack bony tubercles.

Snailfishes are distributed through a wide range of cold and temperate marine habitats from tidepools to depths of almost 8 km. Most species pursue benthic lifestyles while relatively few are pelagic or benthopelagic. They have a bipolar distribution pattern, with more than half of the family's roughly 200 currently recognized species occurring in the Northern Hemisphere and the rest, 89 species in the most recent count (Andriashev and Stein 1998), in the Southern Hemisphere. The Liparidae are the richest and taxonomically most complex fauna in the North Pacific, which is generally considered to be the region of origin for this family. Fifty-six liparid species are known to occur in Alaska and seven more have been reported from Alaska but with some uncertainty or are included from adjacent waters, making a total of sixty-three species—nearly a third of the world's total—treated in this guide.

In snailfishes (Liparidae) the body cavity is shorter than the caudal region, compared to a body cavity about as long as the caudal region in lumpsuckers (Cyclopteridae). Snailfishes usually have one dorsal fin, not two as in lumpsuckers, and the dorsal and anal fins are long-based compared to the fins of lumpsuckers. The anal fin, for example, in Alaskan snailfishes has 21–73 rays, whereas the range in Alaskan lumpsuckers is 6–13. Snailfishes have 36–86 vertebrae, and lumpsuckers have 23–29. In most species of snailfish the pelvic disk is present, but in others it has been reduced to a rudiment or is completely absent. The operculum is usually produced posteriorly to form a flap or lobe, partly covering the gill opening.

Snailfishes range in size at maturity from a few centimeters (a couple of inches) to at least 50 cm (around 20 inches). The largest species in all the genera except *Paraliparis* are found in the North Pacific Ocean, where they attain the greatest size around Japan. Species with geographic ranges extending from American to Asian coasts attain the greatest size in the latter region (Burke 1930). Since the sizes reported in the literature for many species are based on very small samples they may not reflect size at full maturity.

Most of the Alaskan snailfish species are in three genera: *Liparis* (17), *Careproctus* (23), and *Paraliparis* (6). Three are in *Crystallichthys,* two each in *Elassodiscus* and *Rhinoliparis,* and one each in *Acantholiparis, Gyrinichthys, Lipariscus, Nectoliparis,* and *Prognatholiparis.* The number of *Paraliparis* species currently known to occur in Alaska could be artificially low, as members of this genus inhabit mainly deep waters which have been insufficiently sampled, and many are of a size and shape (small and narrow) that allows them to pass through the large-mesh nets of commercial trawlers. It is difficult to say, though, as other factors tend to limit their distribution. Deepwater snailfishes, as well as eelpouts (Perciformes: Zoarcidae), are different from most fishes because their eggs and larvae are more likely to develop at the same depths as inhabited by the adults. The eggs and larvae of most other fishes are produced in the surface waters, and maturing adults of deepwater species descend as they grow to maturity. This suggests that deep basins, submarine canyons, and other physiographic features could restrict distribution of deepwater snailfishes (and eelpouts); for example, the Kuril Basin in the Sea of Okhotsk or the fjords of southeastern Alaska (N. J. Wilimovsky, pers. comm., 1996). Opportunities for dispersion of deepwater *Careproctus* and *Paraliparis* are limited when compared to species of *Liparis* having planktonic larvae (Andriashev 1990). Females of some species of *Careproctus* deposit their eggs in the gill chambers of crabs by way of an ovipositor, and at least one species of *Liparis* lays its eggs in scallops (see, for example, Peden and Corbett 1973, Able and Musick 1976, Somerton and Donaldson 1998).

The following summary of the major diagnostic features of the snailfish genera represented in Alaska is offered as an aid to identification, supplementing the key provided later in this section. Taxonomists have not grouped the genera into subfamilies.

Liparis species have two nostrils on each side; pseudobranchs, comprising about 5 filaments; pelvic disk; 6 branchiostegal rays; trilobed teeth; pectoral fin rays about the same in number or more than the anal fin rays; anus usually about midway between the disk and the anal fin or closer to the anal fin than to the disk; and body coloration variegated within species. Most species of the genus inhabit coastal regions. *Liparis* is typically a tidepool genus, but is represented down to depths of about 450 m.

Careproctus species have a single nostril on each side; no pseudobranchs; a pelvic disk; snout without barbels; 6 branchiostegal rays; trilobed or simple teeth; pectoral fin rays typically fewer than anal fin rays; anus closer to the disk than to the anal fin; and body without spots, stripes, or mottling, and any significant pigmentation usually restricted to the fins. Most *Careproctus* species inhabit the dimly lighted regions, with an extreme range of occurrence of about 100–3,335 m.

Prognatholiparis, comprising the single species *P. ptychomandibularis,* has several of the diagnostic features of *Careproctus* but has a strongly protruding lower jaw and heavily wrinkled snout and jaws, features not seen in any other snailfish.

Gyrinichthys, also comprising a single species, *G. minytremus,* is similar to species of *Careproctus* but has a gill opening that is high above the pectoral fin and is so small it will not admit a dissecting needle.

Crystallichthys is also most similar to *Careproctus* but differs in having spots or bars on the body and a unique, horizontally divided pupil.

Elassodiscus species are distinguished by a markedly reduced ventral disk in which the rays are absent. The nearest approach to this condition in another genus is *Careproctus ostentum,* in which the disk is minute but perfect in structure.

In ***Paraliparis*** there is a single nostril, pseudobranchs are absent, the ventral disk is entirely absent, and there are 6 branchiostegal rays. Most species of *Paraliparis* and *Elassodiscus* inhabit waters deeper than 500 m. While occurring at about the same depth range as *Careproctus* and *Crystallichthys,* their greatest abundance is about 350 m deeper, at about 900 m.

Species of ***Rhinoliparis*** have barbels on the snout, and ***Acantholiparis*** species have opercular spines. Otherwise they are most similar to *Paraliparis.*

Lipariscus and ***Nectoliparis*** are pelagic species that are similar to *Paraliparis* in lacking a pelvic disk but have 5 branchiostegal rays. *Nectoliparis pelagicus* is easily identified by a gill slit that is entirely in front of the pectoral fin.

It is difficult to differentiate some of the species in the three most speciose snailfish genera. The most generalized species of *Liparis, Careproctus,* and *Paraliparis* exist in the North Pacific, making it particularly difficult to identify species in this region. Characters most helpful for identifying species of *Liparis, Careproctus*, and *Paraliparis* in Alaska, drawn mainly from Burke (1930), Stein (1978), and Able and McAllister (1980), are as follows. Species diverging the most from the characterizations are the easiest to identify. *Liparis* is sometimes doubly difficult to identify to the species level because it is the most generalized of the large liparid genera, and, as with the other large genera, the primitive forms of *Liparis* are in the North Pacific. The tidepool species typically have a short, stout body which is wide and depressed anteriorly. The body is typically firm. The size of the eye varies with age, as in other fishes, but comparing eye size in specimens of similar length helps distinguish some species. The size and position of the gill slit is highly useful for distinguishing among species. Unfortunately, damage to the tissues during collection often prevents accurate determination of the extent of the gill slit. The number of dorsal fin rays, presence or absence of a notch in the anterior portion of the dorsal fin, and extent of the fin's connection with the caudal fin are good diagnostic characters for *Liparis.* The dorsal fin notch is more characteristic of the shallow-water than the deepwater species. Important characteristics of the anal fin are the number of rays and the extent of connection with the caudal fin. The connection of the anal fin with the caudal typically is slightly greater than the connection of the dorsal with the caudal. The caudal fin is always strong and broad in *Liparis* species and offers no distinguishing characters. However, features of the pectoral fin are useful for identification. In nearly all species of *Liparis* the number of pectoral rays is greater than or similar to the number of anal rays. In most species the pectoral is notched, in that the rays near the middle of the fin are shorter than some of those below. The rays of the lower lobe are thickened and partly free. The size of the pelvic disk, usually given as a percentage of head length, is important for distinguishing a few species. The disk is round or slightly oval, but never triangular as in some *Careproctus*. The pyloric caeca are always on the right side in *Liparis.* They usually are present, but overlap greatly in number among the species. Only *Liparis greeni* has such a high number, more than 200 and all matted together, that they can be used without counting them to distinguish this species from the rest. "Thumbtack" prickles, named for their shape, are present on some specimens of some species. The extent of variability within species is not well understood; sometimes presence of prickles seems to be sexually dimorphic. *Liparis* species, while generally dull colored, can be highly variable in coloration with some individuals uniformly colored and others with bars, lines, blotches, and mottlings.

In typical *Careproctus* the body is elongate, compressed and deepened, and enveloped in gelatinous tissue. The head is compressed, with its depth greater than its width. The profile of the snout rises gradually or abruptly from the upper lip. The posterior nostril is absent. The position of the nostril opening varies in its relation to the eye, depending somewhat on the shape of the head. The eye is typically larger and more prominent than in *Liparis*. The pupil ranges in size from almost a point to comprising the major part of the eye. Position of the pores varies. In some species the maxillary and mandibular pores are sunken in pits, and in some the anterior mandibular pores have a common opening. However, the condition of the skin in preserved specimens can make it difficult to discern the pores. In most species the gill slit is wholly above the pectoral fin base. The dorsal fin notch is absent or only faintly indicated. The number of pectoral fin rays, the extent of the pectoral notch, and length of the lower lobe are helpful in distinguishing the species. (See Sakurai and Kido [1992] for description and photographs of *C. rastrinus* using the lower lobe to find food; the rays have taste buds.) The pectoral typically has a smaller number of rays than the anal fin (compared to the opposite tendency in *Liparis*). Differences in size and shape of the pelvic disk are also useful. The anus is usually close behind the disk and the distance varies little. Most species have fewer than 20 pyloric caeca. The caeca are on the left side of the body due to the shorter alimentary tract, and usually are long and pointed. Some species have thumbtack- or cactuslike prickles, but the presence of prickles can be a sexually dimorphic or age-dependent character. *Careproctus* species are never distinctly variegated, mottled, barred, or striped. Most are uniformly colored, and in species that are not the pigmentation pattern is usually constant.

In *Paraliparis* the body is compressed, but does not attain the depth of some species of *Careproctus*. Body shape of *Paraliparis* varies from moderately stout and elongate, to very heavy anteriorly and attenuate posteriorly, to very slender overall. *Paraliparis* species are typically frail and soft. The head is usually compressed, the width seldom if ever equal to the depth. The snout is deep and abrupt, in only a few species projecting slightly. The profile of the head is typically rather low and rises gradually to the nape. The single nostril presents no characters of specific value, nor does the eye. The head pores are usually small and difficult to distinguish. Because the pores, in general, are difficult to discern and easily damaged in snailfishes, pore configurations are not given for each species in this guide. For critical work the reader may wish to consult the scheme of head pore location given by Andriashev (1986: fig. 3), who corrected earlier inaccuracies by Burke (1930), Stein (1978), and Able and McAllister (1980). In a few species the anterior pair of mandibular pores are united and have a common opening. In most *Paraliparis* the gill slit is entirely above the base of the pectoral fin but in a few species it extends down in front of the pectoral fin base. In some species the size of the gill slit is unknown due to the torn condition of the skin. The teeth display a wider range of modification than in other genera of Liparidae, ranging from trilobed in *P. dactylosus* to simple or arrow-shaped as in *P. pectoralis*. Other differences in the dentition are not easy to use as diagnostic characters because they vary with age (in all genera). The number of caudal fin rays is useful but the caudal area is often badly damaged. The pectoral fin has some of the most important distinguishing characters, including the number of rays, extent of the pectoral notch and development of the middle pectoral rays, length of the lower pectoral lobe, and the level at which the upper edge of the pectoral is attached to the body. The number of pyloric caeca is greatly reduced in *Paraliparis*, to 5–18. As in *Careproctus* the caeca are on the left side. *Paraliparis* species are generally without prickles. Color varies from white or pinkish to black and is generally uniform. Color of the peritoneum, stomach, gill cavity, and mouth help distinguish some species.

Five new species have been described and recorded from Alaska since Quast and Hall (1972) prepared their inventory of the region's fish species. *Liparis catharus* was described by Vogt (1973) from a single specimen collected in southeastern Alaska. *Careproctus canus* and *C. zachirus* were described by Kido (1985) from Bering Sea material. *Paraliparis pectoralis* was described by Stein (1978) on the basis of specimens taken off Oregon, and later recorded from the central Bering Sea by Kido (1984b). *Prognatholiparis ptychomandibularis,* a new genus as well as a new species, was described by Orr and Busby (2001) from one specimen caught in Seguam Pass in the central Aleutian Islands.

Two species were collected in Alaska after Quast and Hall (1972) listed them as likely to be found in Alaskan waters. *Careproctus pycnosoma,* previously known only from off Cape Rollin, Simushir Island of the Kuril Islands, was recorded by Kido (1985) from the Bering Sea northwest of Umnak Island. Kido (1992) also recorded several examples of *Elassodiscus tremebundus* from the eastern Bering Sea; the species was previously known from the Pacific Ocean off the southeastern coast of Kamchatka.

Gilbert and Burke's (1912a) record of *Acantholiparis opercularis* from the North Pacific Ocean near the Shumagin Islands is an Alaskan record which apparently was overlooked in previous inventories.

A specimen taken from the Bering Sea near St. Lawrence Island was identified by Busby and Chernova (2001) as *Liparis marmoratus*. The only other records of *L. marmoratus* are a few specimens from the Sea of Okhotsk. Quast and Hall (1972) listed *L. marmoratus* as a potential addition to the Alaskan ichthyofauna.

Paraliparis melanobranchus, a species that was known only from the unique, holotype specimen taken in the Sea of Okhotsk and two unverified records from the Pacific off Oregon, was recently caught off the west coast of Vancouver Island, British Columbia (Peden 1997ms). This indication of broad distribution in the North Pacific and the species' possible pelagic lifestyle reinforce the proposal (Quast and Hall 1972) that it is likely to occur in Alaskan waters.

Liparis mednius, Paraliparis paucidens, and *P. rosaceus* are new additions to the inventory as potentially occurring in Alaska. *Liparis mednius* is known only from the Commander Islands and might be a junior synonym of *L. micraspidophorus,* which occurs in Alaska. *Paraliparis paucidens* was recorded off Graham Island close to the Alaska–British Columbia border (Stein and Peden 1979), and *P. rosaceus* from slightly farther south, off Tasu Sound (Peden and Ostermann 1980). Andriashev (1990) estimated the range of *P. rosaceus* to extend throughout the Gulf of Alaska and across the Pacific south of the Aleutian Islands to Asia.

Several snailfish species of the western Pacific Ocean and Okhotsk and Japan seas listed by Quast and Hall (1972) as potential additions to the Alaskan fauna are not included in this guide. They still have not been recorded from Alaskan waters, several are known from only one or a few specimens, and due to their habitat preferences most species are relatively restricted in distribution: *Liparis curilensis* Gilbert & Burke, *L. dulkeiti* Soldatov, *L. latifrons* Schmidt, *L. punctatus* Schmidt, *L. rhodosoma* Gilbert & Burke, *L. schantarensis* (Lindberg & Dulkeit), *Careproctus amblystomopsis* Andriashev, *C. cypseluroides* Schmidt, *C. mederi* Schmidt, *C. melanuroides* Schmidt, *C. nigricans* Schmidt, *C. rastrinoides* Schmidt, *C. roseofuscus* Gilbert & Burke, *C. seraphinnae* Schmidt, and *C. trachysoma* Gilbert & Burke. Discovery of species in the eastern Pacific that were previously known only from the Sea of Okhotsk and other Asian seas is more apt to occur with pelagic species of *Paraliparis* than with benthic *Liparis* and *Careproctus,* especially species which may be restricted to deep cold spots such as the Kuril Basin. In addition, as pointed out by Gilbert and Burke (1912b), the liparid fauna of the Bering Sea is generally distinct from that of the Sea of Okhotsk and seas to the south. *Liparis liparis* (Linnaeus), a European Arctic species, also has not been found any closer to Alaska.

Sources for the classification of liparid genera and species occurring in Alaska include the revision of the entire family, as it was known at the time, by Burke (1930), and more recent, regional treatments, particularly those by Stein (1978) on deepwater liparids off Oregon, Able and McAllister (1980) on *Liparis* species of Arctic Canada, and Kido (1988) on the Liparidae of Japan and adjacent waters. Many of the Alaskan species have not been included in a recent taxonomic review.

Synonymies followed in this guide that differ from past inventories of Alaskan fish species (e.g., Quast and Hall 1972) include *Careproctus acanthodes* and *C. pellucidus* in *C. rastrinus*; *Liparis cyclostigma* in *L. gibbus*; *L. herschelinus* in *L. tunicatus*; *L. koefoedi* in *L. fabricii*; *Polypera* in *Liparis*; and *Temnocora* in *Careproctus.* Kido (1988, 1993) classified all liparids without pelvic disks in *Paraliparis*, including *Rhinoliparis, Acantholiparis,* and *Lipariscus,* but most workers retain the older genera. *Paraliparis* as defined by Kido (1988) is probably polyphyletic, as indicated, for example, by a cladogram of liparid genera by Balushkin (1996). Kido (1988, 1992) also classified *Elassodiscus* in *Paraliparis,* but the presence of a rudimentary disk in *Elassodiscus* supports continued recognition of that genus (Pitruk and Fedorov 1993b).

From examination of specimens and review of the literature we classify *Liparis beringianus* (Gilbert & Burke) as a junior synonym of *L. greeni* (Jordan & Starks). Both N. J. Wilimovsky and A. E. Peden (pers. comms., 1995–1997), specialists in the Alaskan and eastern North Pacific fish fauna, agreed, stating they could not see enough difference among specimens to distinguish *L. beringianus.* Museum collections have numerous lots identified as *L. greeni* but none or very few as *L. beringianus.* Burke (1930) noted that *L. beringianus,* known from relatively small individuals, could represent the young of *L. greeni.*

A few other possible synonymies are mentioned in the Notes & Sources for the individual species. For example, *Liparis bristolensis* (Burke) is likely a junior synonym of *L. tunicatus* Reinhardt. Data presented by Able and McAllister (1980) indicate the synonymy but it was not pursued because *L. bristolensis* was extralimital to their study of Arctic Canadian *Liparis* and Burke's 1912 date of publication did not bring into question the nomenclature for *L. tunicatus* (D. A. McAllister, pers. comm., 23 Jul. 1998). Burke (1930) recognized that *Liparis grebnitzkii,* known from only one specimen from the Commander Islands, could be conspecific with *L. callyodon*. While some questions of synonymy might be resolved by study of existing specimens, others will remain unanswered without additional samples from field collections. Other potential synonymies may become evident with further study. For example, several species of *Careproctus* that are known from one or a few very small individuals could represent juveniles or young adults of other species.

At least one previously proposed synonymy of *Liparis* species was studied in detail, and the results support retention of both species. Able and McAllister (1980) suggested that *L. gibbus* and *L. dennyi* are conspecific, but Peden (1997ms) showed the two species to be distinctly different in habitat preference in the area of sympatry (from the Aleutian Islands to Portland Inlet in British Columbia), as well as showing very little overlap in meristics despite clines such that northern *L. dennyi* having fewer median fin rays and vertebrae could overlap southern *L. gibbus.*

Undescribed snailfish species known to exist in the marine waters off Alaska will affect future inventories. For example, A. E. Peden and K. Sendall (pers. comms., 2000) are studying a species of *Careproctus* from southern Alaska and British Columbia that is closely related to *C. melanurus* but occurs in deeper water. Somerton and Donaldson (1998) reported that an unnamed, red *Careproctus* in the Bering Sea deposits its eggs in the branchial chambers of lithodid crabs.

The horizontal distribution of many of the deepwater benthic species in Alaskan waters is unknown. Some appear to be widely distributed but restricted to narrow bands along the continental slope, like *Careproctus gilberti, Elassodiscus caudatus, Paraliparis cephalus, P. deani,* and *P. dactylosus.* Abyssal plain species, such as *P. rosaceus,* are probably more widespread than suggested by current information, as samples from offshore deep waters, including the Gulf of Alaska and the Aleutian Basin, are scarce. Benthic snailfishes inhabiting shallow water, less than 200 m, generally are widespread in their geographic area of inhabitance, to the extent of limitations imposed by temperature or wide stretches of deep water. Pelagic species, such as *Nectoliparis pelagicus* and *Lipariscus nanus,* are very widespread. However, many snailfishes are found in midwater and because of small size usually are taken accidentally. Special nets with small mesh size are needed to catch them, not commercial trawls except for the larger species.

For liparids, perhaps more so than for any other fish family in Alaska, the numerous published records based on misidentifications and the presence of misidentified specimens in museum collections make it additionally difficult to determine geographic range as well as to list comparable morphological features. Several liparids have not been illustrated in the literature and lack adequate descriptions. Consequently, museum collections have, for example, specimens catalogued as *C. spectrum* that could be *C. melanurus* or *C. cypselurus,* and vice versa.

Allen and Smith (1988), in their review of the geographic ranges of common demersal species of the Bering Sea and eastern North Pacific, reported that good field characters are lacking to distinguish several species, including *C. colletti* and *C. furcellus,* as well as *C. cypselurus* and *C. melanurus.* Since they were unable to determine the distribution of individual species they gave a range for the group, which they called the "blacktail snailfish complex," and opined that the dominant species in the Bering Sea is *C. cypselurus.* Our studies suggest it is probably *C. furcellus.* Similarly, Allen and Smith (1988) grouped *C. osborni* (not Alaskan), *C. phasma, C. rastrinus,* and *C. scottae* in a "pink snailfish complex." However, *Careproctus phasma* is not similar to the others, and *C. rastrinus* and *C. scottae* are probably the same species. *Careproctus osborni* (Townsend & Nichols) is a synonym of *C. gilberti* (M. E. Anderson, pers. comm., 15 Apr. 1999). More research is needed to identify existing museum specimens and provide accurate diagnostic descriptions in order to more precisely determine geographic ranges.

Another problem regarding snailfish taxonomy and identification is that many species are small, jellylike, and delicate, hence easily damaged during collection and preservation. This is especially true of the deepwater species, and is one reason they are relatively uncommon in museum collections.

The following key and species accounts reflect the limitations of the existing information. Authors have not always described the same characters for each species or have taken measurements differently, so comparable data are not available for all species. For species that are known from only one or a few, often damaged, specimens, some character states may never be known. Some of the character states given in the kay are based on only one specimen, and to separate some species we resorted to differences in habitat and geographic range. Trying to separate species that may be synonymous (e.g., *L. tunicatus* and *L. bristolensis, L. micraspidophorus* and *L. mednius, L. callyodon* and *L. grebnitzkii, Careproctus rastrinus* and *C. scottae*) led to some particularly labored distinctions. The key and species accounts have *Liparis* at the beginning as the most generalized or primitive of the forms and end with *Nectoliparis* as the most specialized or advanced, which is the phylogeny suggested by Burke (1930) and, most recently, Balushkin (1996).

The family name is correctly spelled Liparidae, not, as often seen in the taxonomic literature, Liparididae (Vogt 1988a). The gender of *Liparis* is masculine, not feminine (International Commission on Zoological Nomenclature 1992, 1993), so, to be consistent, species names in *Liparis* are spelled with a masculine ending.

Key to the Liparidae of Alaska

1		Nostrils double on each side; pelvic disk present and well developed; pseudobranchs present	genus *Liparis* (2)
1		Nostrils single on each side; pelvic disk present and well developed to rudimentary or absent; pseudobranchs absent	(21)
2	(1)	Dorsal fin extending onto caudal fin for more than one-fifth of caudal fin length	(3)
2		Dorsal fin not extending onto caudal fin or barely extending past caudal fin base	(12)
3	(2)	Dorsal and anal fins extending onto caudal fin for nearly its entire length; pectoral fin rays less numerous than anal fin rays	*Liparis pulchellus,* page 583
3		Dorsal and anal fins not extending onto caudal fin for nearly its entire length; pectoral fin rays either more or less numerous than anal fin rays	(4)
4	(3)	Gill opening long, extending down in front of 8 or more pectoral fin rays; adults reaching 450 mm TL or more; usually taken in waters less than 100 m deep	(5)
4		Gill opening extending down in front of fewer than 6 pectoral fin rays; or if extending in front of more than 6 pectoral rays, adults reaching less than 167 mm TL; habitat shallow, usually less than 75 m	(8)
5	(4)	Dorsal fin rays usually 37–40; anal fin rays usually 30–33; adults not over 305 mm TL	*Liparis dennyi,* page 584
5		Dorsal fin rays usually more than 40; anal fin rays usually 33 or more; adults reaching more than 450 mm TL	(6)
6	(5)	Dorsal fin rays usually 41–44; anal fin rays usually 33–36; vertebrae 44–50	*Liparis gibbus,* page 585
6		Dorsal fin rays usually 44–47; anal fin rays usually 36–38; vertebrae 48–52	(7)
7	(6)	Prickles present on head and body; basic color gray to pinkish	*Liparis ochotensis,* page 586
7		Prickles absent; basic color pale violet	*Liparis catharus,* page 587

8 (4) Mouth small, maxilla not reaching vertical with eye; color rosy orange, with large brownish bands and blotches . . . . *Liparis marmoratus,* page 588

8 Mouth moderate in size, maxilla reaching to below front of eye to mideye; coloration variable, can be similar to above . . . . (9)

9 (8) Dorsal fin not notched; peritoneum pale; prickles usually absent; Beaufort Sea to Bering Sea south of St. Lawrence Island . . . . *Liparis tunicatus,* page 589

9 Dorsal fin notched or not notched; peritoneum pale or black; prickles present or absent; Beaufort Sea to Gulf of Alaska . . . . (10)

10 (9) Anterior dorsal fin rays usually set off by shallow notch; prickles present; peritoneum pale; gill opening extending down in front of 2–5 pectoral fin rays . . . . *Liparis bristolensis,* page 590

10 Dorsal fin not notched; prickles present or absent; peritoneum pale or black; gill opening extending down in front of 3–14 pectoral fin rays . . . . (11)

11 (10) Peritoneum pale; habitat mainly subarctic, Bering Sea from about St. Matthew Island and farther south, in water usually shallower than 75 m . . . . *Liparis megacephalus,* page 591

11 Peritoneum black; habitat arctic, Beaufort and possibly Chukchi seas, in water usually deeper than 75 m . . . . *Liparis fabricii,* page 592

12 (2) Tips of dorsal and anal fin rays free or fin margins crenulate . . . . (13)

12 Tips of dorsal and anal fin rays not free, fin margins not unusually crenulate . . . . (14)

13 (12) Anus far back, nearer to anal fin than to disk; more pectoral fin rays (38–43) than dorsal fin rays (33–35); disk length less than 50% HL . . . . *Liparis fucensis,* page 593

13 Anus slightly closer to disk than to anal fin; about same number of pectoral and dorsal fin rays (30–33); disk length more than 50% HL . . . . *Liparis rutteri,* page 594

14 (12) Dorsal fin not notched, notch faintly indicated, or dorsal fin lobe present but low and broadly rounded . . . . (15)

14 Dorsal fin notch deep, forming distinct anterior lobe . . . . (16)

15 (14) Dorsal fin not notched or notch faintly indicated; dorsal fin rays 34–37, anal fin rays 29–31 . . . . *Liparis cyclopus,* page 595

15 Dorsal fin lobe low, broadly rounded, hardly evident in some specimens; dorsal fin rays 30–32; anal fin rays 24–26 . . . . *Liparis mucosus,* page 596

16 (14) Dorsal fin rays 31–33, anal fin rays 21–25; gill opening extending down in front of 1–5 pectoral fin rays . . . . (17)

16 Dorsal fin rays 32–40, anal fin rays 25–32; gill opening entirely above pectoral fin base or extending down in front of 1 ray . . . . (18)

17 (16) Disk length less than 50% HL; prickles absent; anus slightly closer to disk than to anal fin or equidistant .... *Liparis florae,* page 597

17 Disk length more than 50% HL; prickles present; anus noticeably closer to disk than to anal fin .... *Liparis micraspidophorus,* page 598

18 (16) Prickles present .... *Liparis mednius,* page 599 (not known from Alaska)

18 Prickles absent .... (19)

19 (18) Dorsal fin rays 37–40, anal fin rays 29–32, pectoral fin rays 33–37; pyloric caeca more than 200 .... *Liparis greeni,* page 600

19 Dorsal fin rays 32–35, anal fin rays 25–27, pectoral fin rays 25–29; pyloric caeca fewer than 100 .... (20)

20 (19) Solid olive brown to purplish, often with fine black specks on sides and back and bars on the fins; body and fins dark .... *Liparis callyodon,* page 601

20 Brown, with darker head and back; fins grayish, except pectoral fin yellowish; without spots or bars on body or fins......... *Liparis grebnitzkii,* page 602 (not known from Alaska)

21 (1) Disk present, can be rudimentary and difficult to discern .... (22)

21 Disk absent.. (50)

22 (21) Disk well developed .... (23)

22 Disk rudimentary.. genus *Elassodiscus* (49)

23 (22) Lower jaw strongly protruding; prominent folds and flaps of skin on jaws and snout .... *Prognatholiparis ptychomandibularis,* page 603

23 Lower jaw not strongly protruding; no prominent folds and flaps of skin on jaws and snout .... (24)

24 (23) Gill opening a minute pore .... *Gyrinichthys minytremus,* page 604

24 Gill opening well developed .... (25)

25 (24) Dorsal fin distinctly but shallowly notched anteriorly; pupil a horizontal slit.................................. *Careproctus candidus,* page 605

25 Dorsal fin not notched; pupil round, oval, or a horizontal slit .... (26)

26 (25) Body with light or dark spots or blotches; pupil probably a horizontal slit in all species (not recorded for all specimens) .... genus *Crystallichthys* (47)

26 Body without colored spots or blotches; pupil round or oval .... (27)

27 (26) Upper pectoral fin lobe greatly elongate, posterior part black ..... *Careproctus zachirus,* page 606

27 Upper pectoral fin lobe not as above .... (28)

28 (27) Body uniformly gray; median fin margins dark; opercular flap projection absent .... *Careproctus canus,* page 607

28 Body color other than above; opercular flap projection present .... (29)

29 (28) Small flap of tissue in front of some of the head pores . . . . *Careproctus pycnosoma,* page 608

29 No flaps in front of head pores . . . . (30)

30 (29) Mouth very large; pyloric caeca on right side of body; lower rays of pectoral fin forming a distinct lobe . . . . *Careproctus ovigerum,* page 609 (not known from Alaska)

30 Mouth not so large; pyloric caeca on left side of body; lower rays of pectoral fin not forming a distinct lobe . . . . (31)

31 (30) Low fin ray counts: dorsal less than 45, anal less than 35, pectoral less than 25 . . . . *Careproctus abbreviatus,* page 610

31 High fin rays counts: dorsal 45 or more, anal 36 or more, pectoral 25 or more . . . . (32)

32 (31) Disk triangular; dorsal and anal fins connected to caudal but ending abruptly, forming notches, not confluent with caudal; if snout projecting, peritoneum black and adults relatively large (maximum lengths 397–461 mm TL) . . . . (33)

32 Disk round or oval; dorsal and anal fins set off by notches or confluent with caudal fin; if snout projecting, peritoneum pale and adults relatively small (maximum length to 186 mm TL) . . . . (37)

33 (32) Snout blunt; profile rising steeply from mouth; lower pectoral fin rays longer than upper; peritoneum pale . . . . (34)

33 Snout blunt or projecting; profile rising gradually from mouth; lower pectoral fin rays longer or not longer than upper rays; peritoneum black . . . . (35)

34 (33) Gill opening extending down in front of 1–6 pectoral fin rays, rarely entirely above pectoral fin . . . . *Careproctus rastrinus,* page 611

34 Gill opening entirely above pectoral fin or extending down in front of 1–3 rays . . . . *Careproctus scottae,* page 612

35 (33) Pectoral fin base not strongly horizontal, extending down from level above angle of mouth; lower pectoral fin rays longer than upper and mostly free; teeth long, recurved, lanceolate; pectoral fin rays 25–31 . . . . *Careproctus colletti,* page 613

35 Pectoral fin base mainly horizontal, extending down and forward from level with angle of mouth; anterior pectoral fin rays not longer than posterior and free or not free; teeth not recurved, most with slight shoulders; pectoral fin rays 32–40 . . . . (36)

36 (35) Caudal fin slightly emarginate, nearly truncate when spread, rarely almost falcate; snout distinctly projecting; pectoral fin not notched, anterior rays free only at tips; body relatively deep anteriorly, tapering gradually to caudal but not strongly attenuate . . . . *Careproctus furcellus,* page 614

36 Caudal fin falcate; snout not projecting or only slightly projecting; pectoral fin not notched or slightly notched, anterior rays partly free; body relatively attenuate, not heavy anteriorly . . . . *Careproctus cypselurus,* page 615

37 (32) Dorsal and anal fins confluent with caudal, forming bluntly pointed tail; snout blunt, not projecting . . . . . (38)

37 Dorsal and anal fins extending onto caudal but not confluent, not forming bluntly pointed tail; snout blunt or not, and projecting or not . . . . . (40)

38 (37) Disk oval, longer than wide; pectoral fin base horizontal; caudal fin and posterior parts of dorsal and anal fins black; peritoneum black . . . . . *Careproctus melanurus,* page 616

38 Disk round or wider than long; little or no dark pigment on body or fins; peritoneum pale . . . . . (39)

39 (38) Disk wider than long; disk smaller than eye, disk length about 25% HL; skin transparent, loose . . . . . *Careproctus spectrum,* page 617

39 Disk probably round; disk larger than eye, disk length 30–38% HL; skin opaque, relatively thick . . . . . *Careproctus phasma,* page 618

40 (37) Snout thick, rounded, elongate, distinctly projecting . . . . . *Careproctus simus,* page 619

40 Snout not elongate or distinctly projecting . . . . . (41)

41 (40) Eye large, 24–27% HL, pupil large, round; body stout . . . . . *Careproctus bowersianus,* page 620

41 Eye not particularly large, or if eye large, body extremely attentuate . . . . . (42)

42 (41) Occiput swollen; body slightly humped at nape; pupil small; gill opening extending down in front of 1–4 pectoral fin rays . . . . . *Careproctus mollis,* page 621

42 Head depressed, occiput not swollen; body not humped at nape; pupil small to moderate; gill opening above pectoral fin or extending down in front of 5–14 pectoral rays . . . . . (43)

43 (42) Anus far back, closer to anal fin than to disk . . . . . *Careproctus opisthotremus,* page 622

43 Anus closer to disk or equidistant . . . . . (44)

44 (43) Gill opening entirely above pectoral fin; body extremely attentuate; disk length 21–27% HL . . . . . (45)

44 Gill opening extending down in front of 8–17 pectoral fin rays; body elongate but not particularly attenuate; disk length 14% HL or less . . . . . (46)

45 (44) Snout deep, not projecting; peritoneum black . . . . . *Careproctus attenuatus,* page 623

45 Snout not deep, snout distinctly projecting; peritoneum pale . . . . . *Careproctus ectenes,* page 624

46 (44) Disk small, length 6–14% HL; lower lobe of pectoral fin relatively long, 72–78% HL, in some specimens . . . . . *Careproctus gilberti,* page 625

46 Disk minute, length 5% HL or less; lower lobe of pectoral fin relatively short, 22–42% HL, in some specimens . . . . . *Careproctus ostentum,* page 626

47 (26) Head and anterior part of body not strongly compressed; pectoral fin rays 28 . . . . *Crystallichthys cameliae,* page 627

47 Head and body strongly compressed, the sides nearly vertical; pectoral fin rays 30–35 . . . . (48)

48 (47) Snout conical, distinctly projecting beyond premaxillae; blotches present or absent dorsally on head and body; if present, blotches not distinctly outlined by darker border . . . . *Crystallichthys mirabilis,* page 628 (not confirmed from Alaska)

48 Snout broadly rounded, slightly to moderately projecting; dark and light blotches all over; dark blotches outlined by darker border . . . . *Crystallichthys cyclospilus,* page 629

49 (22) Lower pectoral fin rays not as long as upper rays; profile not strongly arched at occiput and nape; dorsal and anal fin profiles not decreasing in height until relatively far posteriorly, making elongate elliptical shape . . . . *Elassodiscus tremebundus,* page 630

49 Lower pectoral fin rays longer than upper and almost completely free; dorsal profile strongly arched at occiput and nape; profile decreasing gradually to caudal fin . . . . *Elassodiscus caudatus,* page 631

50 (21) Barbels present on snout . . . . (51)

50 No barbels on snout . . . . (52)

51 (50) Barbels on tip of snout 2; teeth strongly lobed . . . . *Rhinoliparis barbulifer,* page 632

51 Barbels on tip of snout 9 (some may be missing due to damage); teeth simple . . . . *Rhinoliparis attentuatus,* page 633

52 (50) Operculum with 2 distinct dorsally and laterally directed spines . . . . *Acantholiparis opercularis,* page 634

52 No spines on operculum . . . . (53)

53 (52) Pectoral fin rays 28–32 . . . . (54)

53 Pectoral fin rays 12–25 . . . . (55)

54 (53) Teeth lobed . . . . *Paraliparis dactylosus,* page 635

54 Teeth simple . . . . *Paraliparis pectoralis,* page 636

55 (53) Movable cartilaginous rod on each side of mandible . . . . *Paraliparis paucidens,* page 637 (not known from Alaska)

55 No movable cartilaginous rod on each side of mandible . . . . (56)

56 (55) Gill slit large, extending from above pectoral fin base down in front of 10–13 pectoral fin rays . . . . (57)

56 Gill slit not so large, either entirely above or entirely in front of pectoral fin base . . . . (58)

57 (56) Entirely black, except for pyloric caeca; pectoral fins with two wholly distinct lobes, with 2 or 3 rudimentary, buried rays between lobes; profile of head not concave over eye; prickles absent; dorsal fin rays 58–61, anal fin rays 54, pectoral fin rays 23 . . . . *Paraliparis holomelas,* page 638

57 Translucent pale brown, lips and fins pinkish; pectoral fins notched without really being divided into two; profile of head over eye concave; prickles present on base of lower lobe of pectoral fin; dorsal fin rays 56–57, anal fin rays 44–48, pectoral fin rays 18–22 . . . . *Paraliparis deani,* page 639

58 (56) Branchiostegal rays 6 . . . . (59)

58 Branchiostegal rays 5 . . . . (62)

59 (58) Pectoral fin high, upper edge level with upper part of pupil . . . . *Paraliparis ulochir,* page 640

59 Pectoral fin relatively low, upper edge below level of lower part of eye . . . . (60)

60 (59) Mouth oblique; knob on mandibular symphysis present, fits into wide notch at juncture of premaxillae; head and anterior part of body greatly enlarged relative to rest of body; pectoral fin rays 14–16 . . . . *Paraliparis cephalus,* page 641

60 Mouth horizontal; no knob on mandibular symphysis; head and anterior part of body enlarged or not relative to rest of body; pectoral fin rays 17–22 . . . . (61)

61 (60) Profile not arched over occiput, body deepest posterior to pectoral fin and not strongly attentuate; body stout, gelatinous tissue thick and adherent to body; body rose red, pinkish, or bluish with pink tint; adults relatively large, to 400 mm TL . . . . *Paraliparis rosaceus,* page 642
(not known from Alaska)

61 Profile arched over occiput, body deepest anteriorly, just behind head, rest of body strongly attenuate; body slender, skin held away from body by liquid; body bright orange-red or brick red; adults relatively small, probably less than 100 mm TL . . . . *Paraliparis melanobranchus,* page 643
(not known from Alaska)

62 (58) Gill opening entirely above pectoral fin; pectoral fin rays 12–16; intermediate pectoral fin rays widely spaced but well developed, not rudimentary . . . . *Lipariscus nanus,* page 644

62 Gill opening entirely in front of pectoral fin; pectoral fin rays 19–25; intermediate pectoral fin rays widely spaced and rudimentary . . . . *Nectoliparis pelagicus,* page 645

Liparis pulchellus Ayres, 1855 **showy snailfish**

Southeastern Bering Sea and Aleutian Islands to central California at Monterey Bay.

Soft bottoms at depths of about 9–183 m, most records from less than 90 m.

D 47–53; A 39–42; Pec 36–37; PC 32; Vert 51–53.

- Coloration variable: light to dark brown, lighter ventrally; plain or with dots and wavy lines.
- Dorsal fin smoothly contoured, no anterior notch; **dorsal and anal fins extend onto caudal for nearly its whole length**, connection with caudal fin gradual; dorsal fin rays more than 45; **pectoral fin rays fewer than anal fin rays.**
- Gill opening extending to just above pectoral fin or in front of 1–7 rays, usually only to 4th ray.
- Length to 254 mm TL; mature at 70–90 mm TL.

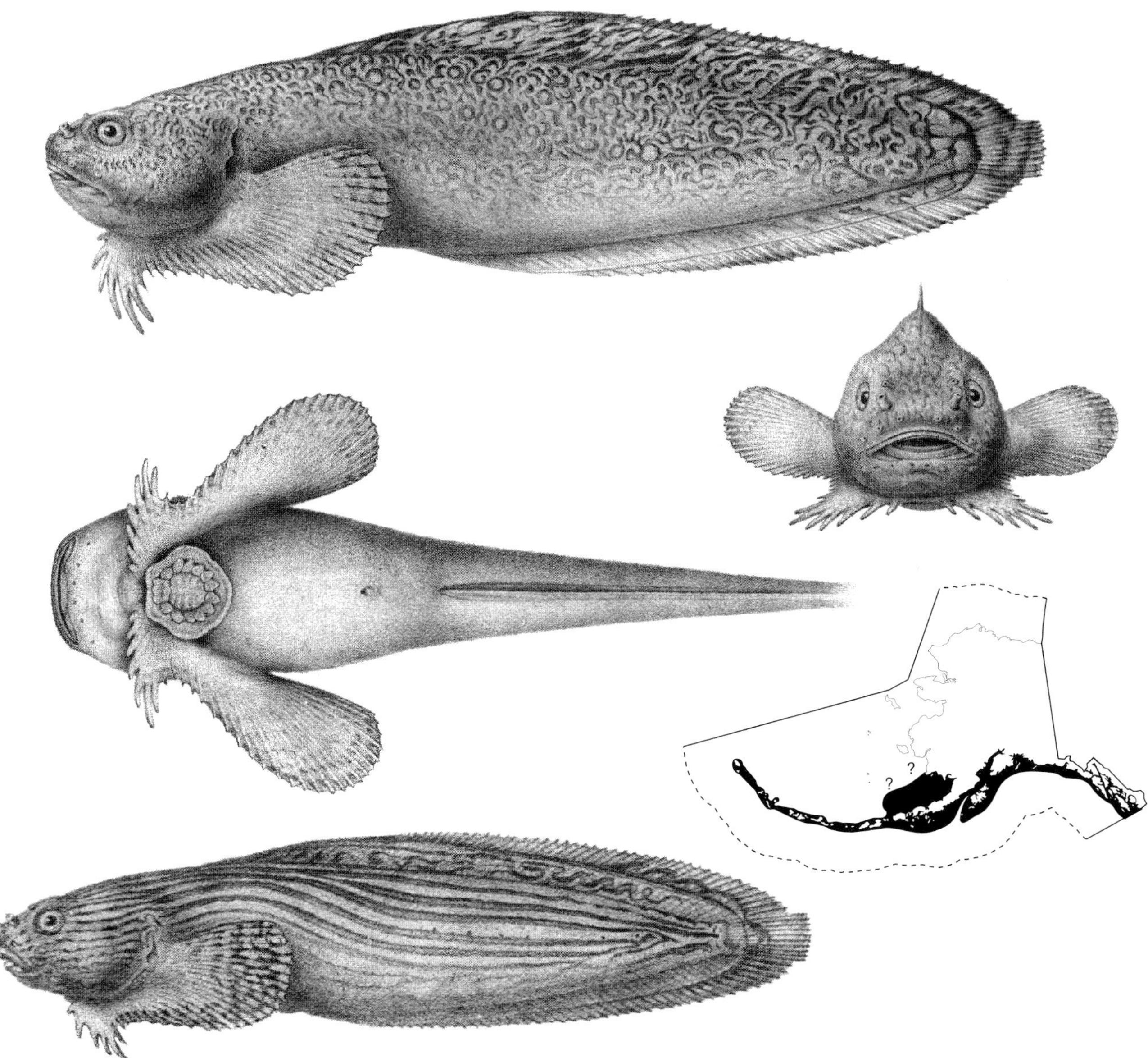

Notes & Sources — *Liparis pulchellus* Ayres, 1855

Description: Burke 1930:88–89; Hart 1973:588–589; Miller and Lea 1972:138–139; Johnson 1969.

Figures: Garman 1892, pl. 4, figs. 1, 3, 4; pl. 5, fig. 6.

Range: Earliest Alaskan records are from Unalaska and Kodiak islands (Bean 1881b) and Bristol Bay (Gilbert 1896). Well represented in museum collections; e.g., UBC 65-4, Attu Island; UBC 62-843, Kachemak Bay. Least common in Bering Sea, and range there is not clear from available records. Specimens once identified as *L. pulchellus* from Peter the Great Bay (Sea of Japan) were determined by Schmidt (1950) to be *L. ochotensis* and no other possible Asian specimens have been reported.

Size: Miller and Lea 1972. Largest of 220 taken off Humboldt Bay, California, was 205 mm TL (Johnson 1969).

Liparis dennyi Jordan & Starks, 1895 **marbled snailfish**

Eastern Aleutian Islands to Puget Sound, Washington; Bering Sea and western Aleutian records not confirmed. Shallow waters to depth of about 225 m, usually shallower; rarely, if ever, found in tidepools.

D 36–41; A 29–34; C 12; Pec 36–39; PC 19–31; Vert 41–45.

- Coloration variable: pink with black fin tips, mottled, striped, or brown with fine white spots.
- Jaws equal or nearly so; usually a few of the upper teeth show when the mouth is closed.
- Dorsal fin slightly notched anteriorly or not; dorsal and anal fins extend well onto caudal fin, anal fin usually slightly farther than dorsal; **dorsal fin rays usually 37–40, anal usually 30–33**.
- **Vertebrae usually 42–45**; **dorsal and anal fin rays and vertebrae total 108–119, usually 109–118**.
- Posterior nostril with rim raised anteriorly into a fingerlike projection.
- Gill opening extending down in front of 9–20 pectoral fin rays.
- Length to 305 mm TL (smaller than *L. gibbus*).

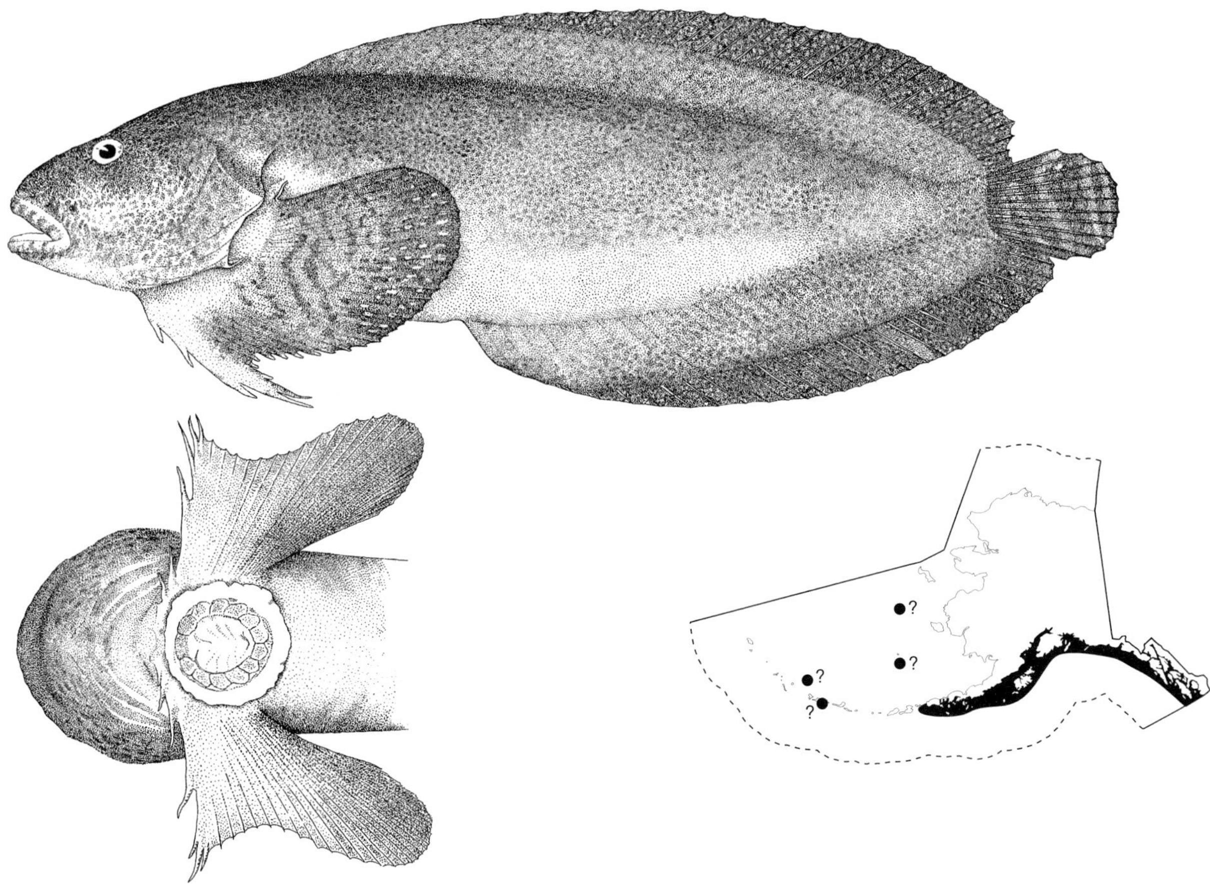

Notes & Sources — *Liparis dennyi* Jordan & Starks, 1895

Difficult to distinguish from *L. gibbus* and additional research is needed to determine differences between these forms, although distributional and size differences suggest each species is biologically distinct (Peden 1997ms).

Description: Jordan and Starks 1895:835–837; Burke 1930:77–79; Peden 1997ms.

Figures: Jordan and Starks 1895, pl. 98; holotype (unique), about 203 mm TL, from Admiralty Inlet, near Seattle.

Range: Numerous published records (e.g., Burke 1930, Quast and Hall 1972) and specimens in ABL, NMNH, RBCM, UAM, UBC, and UW fish collections indicate distribution in the area filled with solid black on the above map. Identification of specimens represented by dots should, perhaps, be verified because of possible confusion with *L. gibbus*: UBC 62-848 (3), north of Rat Islands, about 52°59'N, 179°W; UBC 63-342 and 63-343 (1 each), Sweeper Cove, Adak Island, 51°51'N, 176°37'W; UW 7349 (1), vicinity of St. Matthew Island; and UW 14782 (1), St. George Island.

Burke (1930) concluded that the Alaska Peninsula separated *L. dennyi* and the arctic species *L. gibbus,* but they appear to be sympatric at least from the eastern Aleutian Islands to British Columbia. In samples from southeastern Alaska and Portland Inlet, British Columbia, *L. dennyi* tended to be smaller and from shallower water (caught with toxicants and scuba gear), or trawl-caught near the entrances of inlets rather than in deep water; while *L. gibbus* was most commonly taken well within inlets and in deeper waters where colder temperatures would be expected (at least in summer) (Peden 1997ms).

Size: Hart 1973.

Liparis gibbus Bean, 1881 **variegated snailfish**

Arctic Alaska to Bering Sea and Aleutian Islands, and Gulf of Alaska to northern British Columbia; to Commander Islands, southeastern Kamchatka, and northern Kuril Islands; circumpolar.

Benthic, taken over rock, sand, and mud bottoms on the continental shelf and upper slope, usually at depths less than 200 m but reported to 647 m; most common in offshore waters, like *L. fabricii.*

D 37–46; A 31–37; Pec 35–45; PC 16–42; Vert 44–50.

- Coloration highly variable: pink, brown with tan stripes, tan with fin margins black, or brownish with large blackish spots; peritoneum pale.
- Thumbtack prickles present on mature males on head, body, and dorsal fin.
- Dorsal fin not notched; dorsal and anal fins usually extend well onto caudal fin, anal fin slightly farther than dorsal; **dorsal fin rays usually 41–44, anal fin rays usually 33–36**.
- **Vertebrae usually 46–49; dorsal and anal rays and vertebrae total 119–128, usually 121–128**.
- Gill opening extending ventrally in front of 8–16 pectoral rays, usually about 14.
- Length to 524 mm TL.

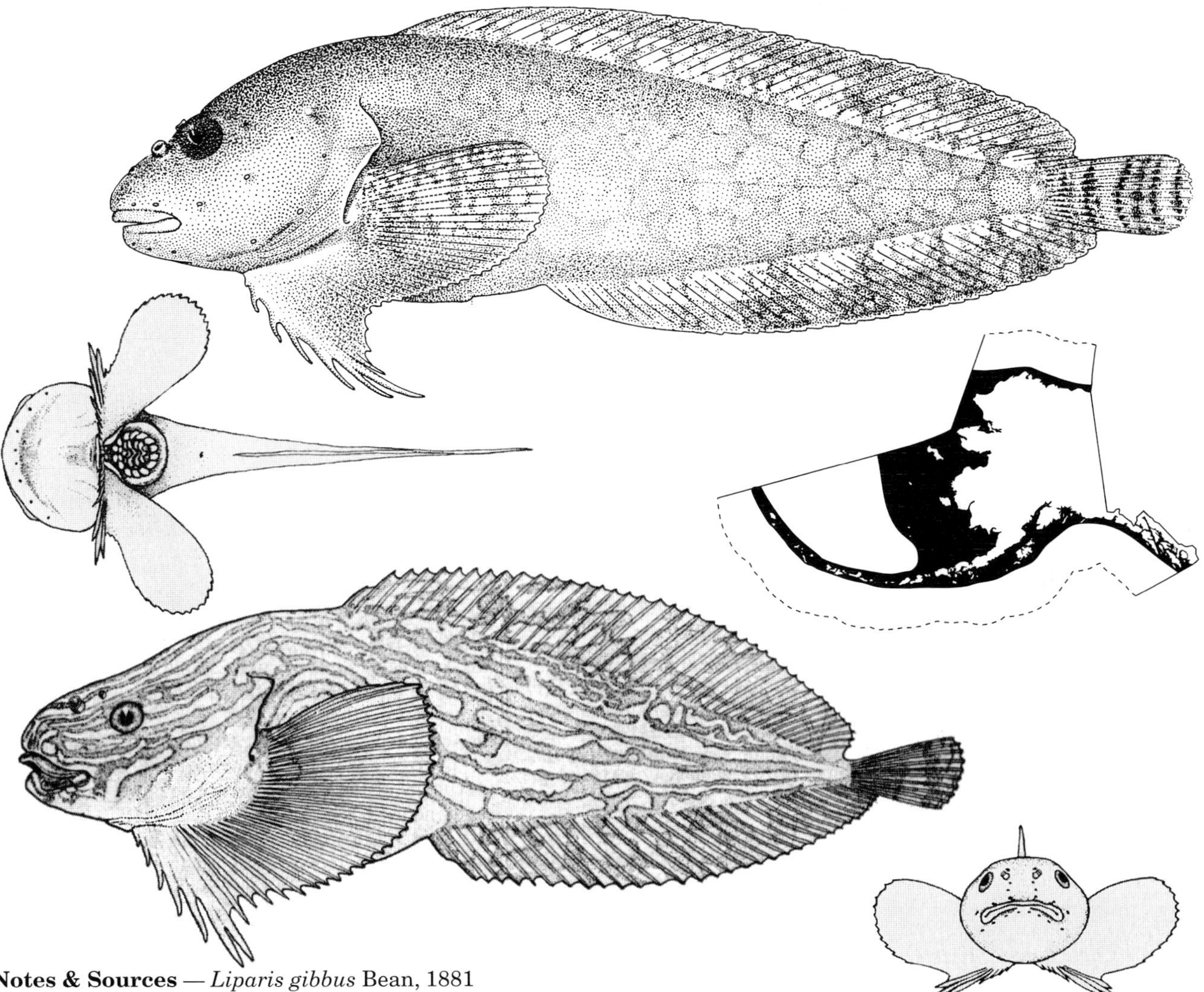

Notes & Sources — *Liparis gibbus* Bean, 1881
Liparis cyclostigma Gilbert, 1896
Cyclogaster cyclostigma: Gilbert and Burke 1912a.
Gilbert and Burke (1912a:73–74) considered this species to be distinguished from *L. dennyi* by the broad, depressed snout; larger, more prominent eye; longer nostril tube; and more projecting snout.

Description: Able and McAllister 1980:25–32, tables 1–7; Able 1990:487–488, tables 1–5; Chernova 1991:39–46.
Figures: Upper: Gilbert and Burke 1912a, fig. 18; about 147 mm TL, Petrel Bank, Bering Sea. Lower: Able and McAllister 1980: fig. 7B, 132 mm SL, Hudson Bay.
Range: Able and McAllister 1980, fig. 7D; Able 1990, fig. 4. Type specimens (Bean 1881a) were obtained near Unalaska and St. Paul islands. Recorded range was extended to Eurasian Arctic by Chernova (1991) and to British Columbia at Alice Arm near Portland Inlet by Peden (1997ms). Maximum depth: V. V. Fedorov (pers. comm. via B. A. Sheiko, 12 May 1998); specimens collected off northern Kuril Islands.

Liparis ochotensis Schmidt, 1904 — Okhotsk snailfish

Gulf of Alaska records uncertain; Bering Sea; Pacific Ocean off southeastern Kamchatka to Kuril Islands and Hokkaido, and Okhotsk and Japan seas.

Shallow waters to extreme depth record of 761 m, usually taken at 50–300 m.

D 43–48; A 35–39; C 10–11; Pec 39–45; PC 16–38; Vert 48–52.

- Coloration variable: gray or brown to pinkish; white-spotted, black-spotted, speckled, dusted, striped, mottled, reticulated, or plain; dorsal and anal fin margins often black; peritoneum pale.
- **Thumbtack prickles present on head and body in mature males and females**.
- Dorsal fin not notched; dorsal fin extending onto caudal fin for one-fourth to one-half of its length, anal fin slightly farther; usually **more dorsal and anal rays and vertebrae than *L. gibbus*.**
- Gill opening extending ventrally in front of 11–18 pectoral fin rays.
- Length to 740 mm SL.

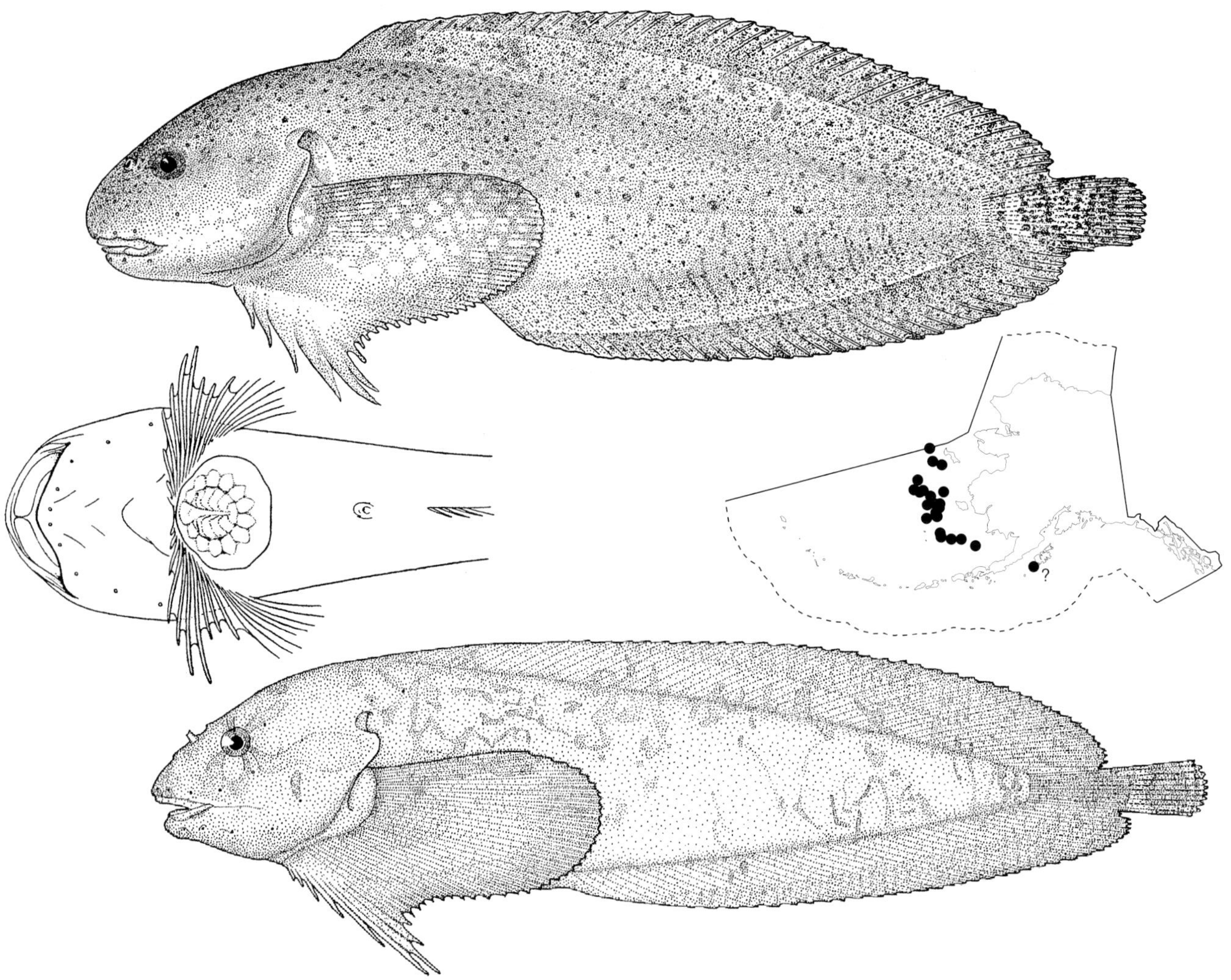

Notes & Sources — *Liparis ochotensis* Schmidt, 1904
Cyclogaster ochotensis (Schmidt): Gilbert and Burke 1912b.
Burke (1930:79) believed *L. ochotensis* and *L. gibbus* to be closely related, but distinguishable by a larger number of dorsal and anal rays and the presence of prickles in *L. ochotensis*.

Description: Gilbert and Burke 1912b:359; Burke 1930:80–81; Kido 1988:178–181.

Figures: Upper: Gilbert and Burke 1912b, pl. 42, fig. 3; 465 mm TL. Ventral view: Lindberg and Krasyukova 1987, fig. 249, after Schmidt 1904b. Lower: Kido 1988, fig. 27; 185 mm SL. All from southern Sea of Okhotsk.

Range: Bering Sea: dots represent HUMZ collections (data provided by M. S. Busby, 28 Jan. 1998). Specimens at ABL from Kodiak Island (Quast and Hall 1972) look the same as recently collected *L. gibbus* and need further study. Maximum depth: V. V. Fedorov, unpubl. data (B. A. Sheiko, pers. comm., 12 May 1998); southeastern Kamchatka. Tokranov (2000a): 100–338 m off southeastern Kamchatka and northern Kuril Islands in the 1990s.

Size: Tokranov (2000b) reported a size range of 27–74 cm SL in a sample of 275 specimens.

Liparis catharus Vogt, 1973 — purity snailfish

Southeastern Alaska at Bradfield Canal.

Taken in beam trawl at depth of about 137 m.

D 46; A 36; C 12; Pec 37; PC 27; Vert 50.

- **Body and head pale purplish violet, with small blue rings on head**; fins black; peritoneum cream colored.
- Snout projecting, upper teeth showing when mouth is closed.
- Prickles absent.
- Dorsal fin not notched; dorsal fin extending onto about one-half of caudal fin, anal fin about three-fourths.
- Disk length 43% of head length.
- Gill opening extending down in front of 18 pectoral fin rays.
- Holotype (unique) 469 mm SL, 559 mm TL.

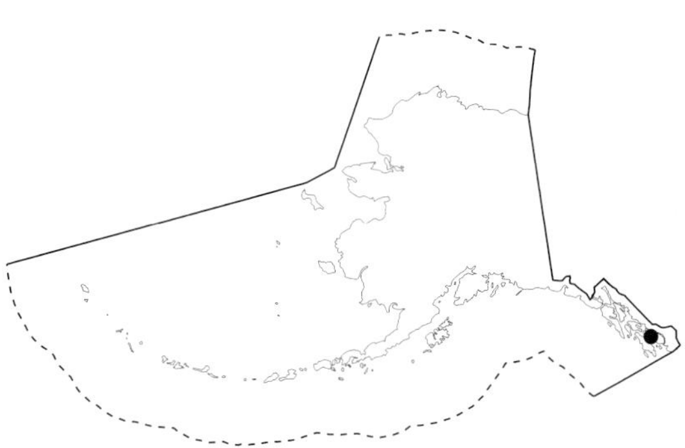

Notes & Sources — *Liparis catharus* Vogt, 1973

Some researchers, remarking on the close similarity of *L. catharus, L. gibbus,* and *L. ochotensis,* believe more examples need to be examined to determine if the three nominal species are distinct from each other. However, no specimens attributed to *L. catharus* have been recorded since the original description (Vogt 1973) was published. A snailfish (AB uncataloged) captured in the Juneau area in 1974 and tentatively identified as *L. catharus* (R. Baxter, unpubl. data) is more likely an example of *L. gibbus* (M. S. Busby, pers. comm., 16 Aug. 1996). Briefly examining the holotype of *L. catharus* (UAM 704) in November 2000, C.W.M. found the colors to be faded and could not differentiate it from *L. gibbus* in the UAM and other collections on the basis of other characters.

Description: Vogt 1973:23–26.
Figures: None available.

Range: Species is known from one specimen, a male, collected in Bradfield Canal, Alaska, at approximately 56°11'N, 131°59'W.

Liparis marmoratus Schmidt, 1950 **festive snailfish**

Northern Bering Sea near St. Lawrence Island; Sea of Okhotsk.

At depths of 100–165 m and probably shallower.

D 41–43; A 35–37; C 14–15; Pec 35–36; PC 25; Vert 47–49.

- **Rosy orange to light brown or yellow, with large, dark reddish to brownish irregularly shaped spots and bars**; peritoneum pale.
- Dorsal body contour not elevated at nape, almost horizontal.
- Head large, 27–29% of standard length; snout blunt at tip; mouth small, maxilla extending to point anterior to eye or to below pupil.
- Dorsal fin not notched; dorsal fin extending along about one-fifth of length of caudal fin, anal fin about one-fourth.
- Disk large, length 43–45% of head length.
- Anus midway between disk and anal fin origin.
- Gill opening extending down in front of 3 or 4 pectoral fin rays.
- Length to 84 mm TL.

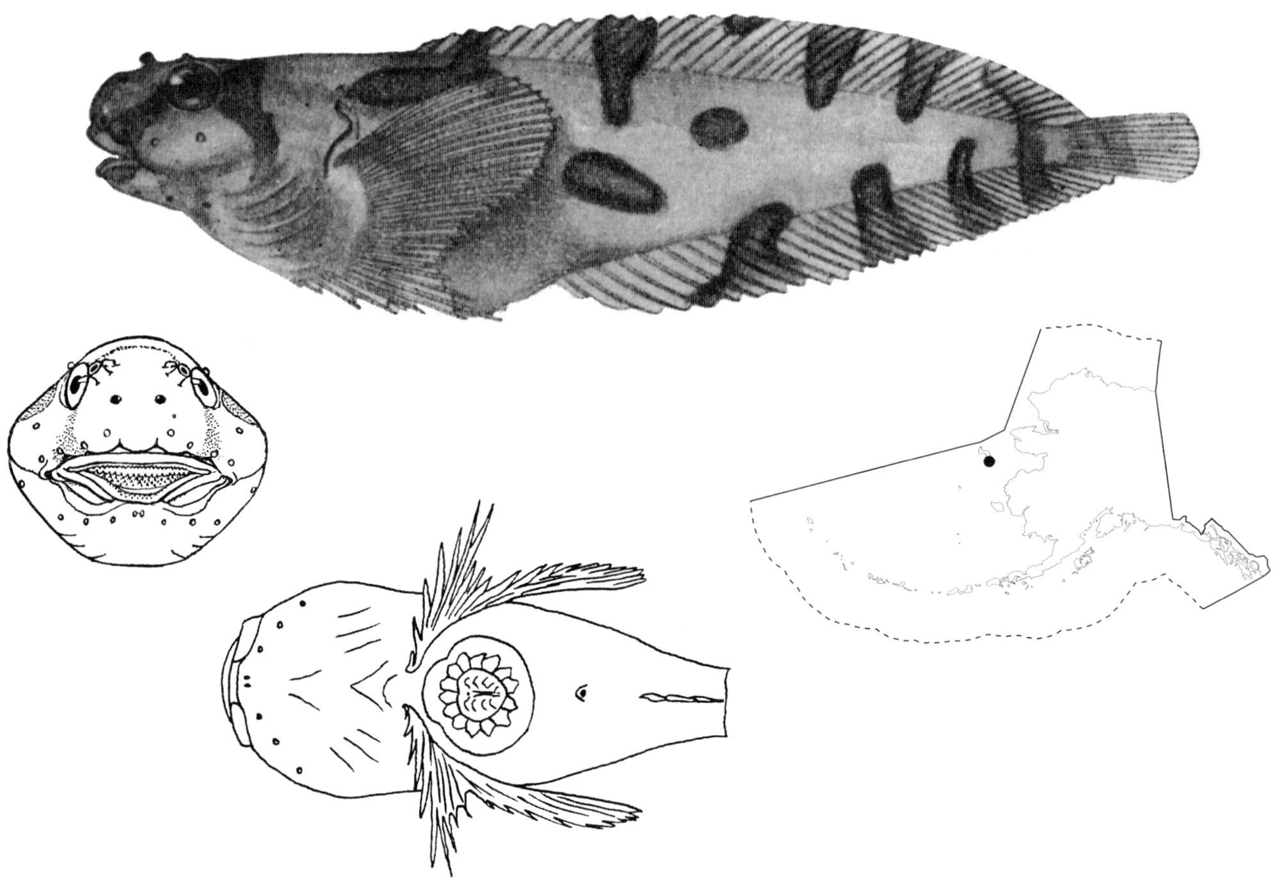

Notes & Sources — *Liparis marmoratus* Schmidt, 1950

Schmidt (1950) considered *L. marmoratus* to be close to *L. tunicatus,* but that its coloration is unique among Sea of Okhotsk and Bering Sea species.

The common name refers to the bright, cheerful-looking coloration.

Description: Schmidt 1950:199–200; Busby and Chernova 2001.

Figures: Lateral and anterior: Schmidt 1950, pl. 16(1) and fig. 15; lectotype. Ventral view: Busby and Chernova 2001, fig. 3 (provided by M. S. Busby).

Range: A juvenile (UW 26332, 50 mm SL, 56 mm TL) collected in 1980 off the northeast coast of St. Lawrence Island at 63°00'N, 169°20'W (depth not known), was identified by Busby and Chernova (2001) as *L. marmoratus.* The other records of occurrence are from the Sea of Okhotsk. The species was described by Schmidt (1950) from two specimens (ZIN 29112, 73 mm SL, 84 mm TL; ZIN 29120, 66 mm SL, 75 mm TL) collected off northeastern Sakhalin Island at depths of 100 and 165 m. The third Sea of Okhotsk specimen (ZIN 37070, juvenile, 49 mm SL, 57 mm TL) was taken in Gizhiginskaya Bay (Chernova 1998). Although the depth of capture was not recorded for the Alaskan specimen (UW 26332), the geographical coordinates place the locality in shallow water, probably less than 50 m.

Liparis tunicatus Reinhardt, 1837 **kelp snailfish**

Arctic Alaska to northern Bering Sea south of St. Lawrence Island and Gulf of Anadyr; circumpolar.

Tidepools and on bottom in coastal waters to depth of 150 m, usually only to 50 m; occurs at shallower depths than *L. gibbus* and *L. fabricii*; commonly associated with kelp.

D 36–45; A 27–38; Pec 32–39; PC 16–49; Vert 42–50.

- Yellowish brown; fin margins generally darker; caudal fin sometimes with dark bars; occasionally boldly banded and blotched with dark brown, and occasionally with distinct creamy white stripes extending from snout to base of caudal fin; **peritoneum pale**.
- **Prickles usually absent**, sometimes present in mature males.
- **Dorsal fin not notched**; dorsal fin extending onto caudal for one-fourth to half its length, anal fin slightly farther; **anal fin rays usually 33–37**; **pectoral rays usually 32–37**.
- Disk length 29–40% of head length.
- **Gill opening** above pectoral or extending down as far as 12th ray, **typically only to rays 4–6**.
- Length to 167 mm TL.

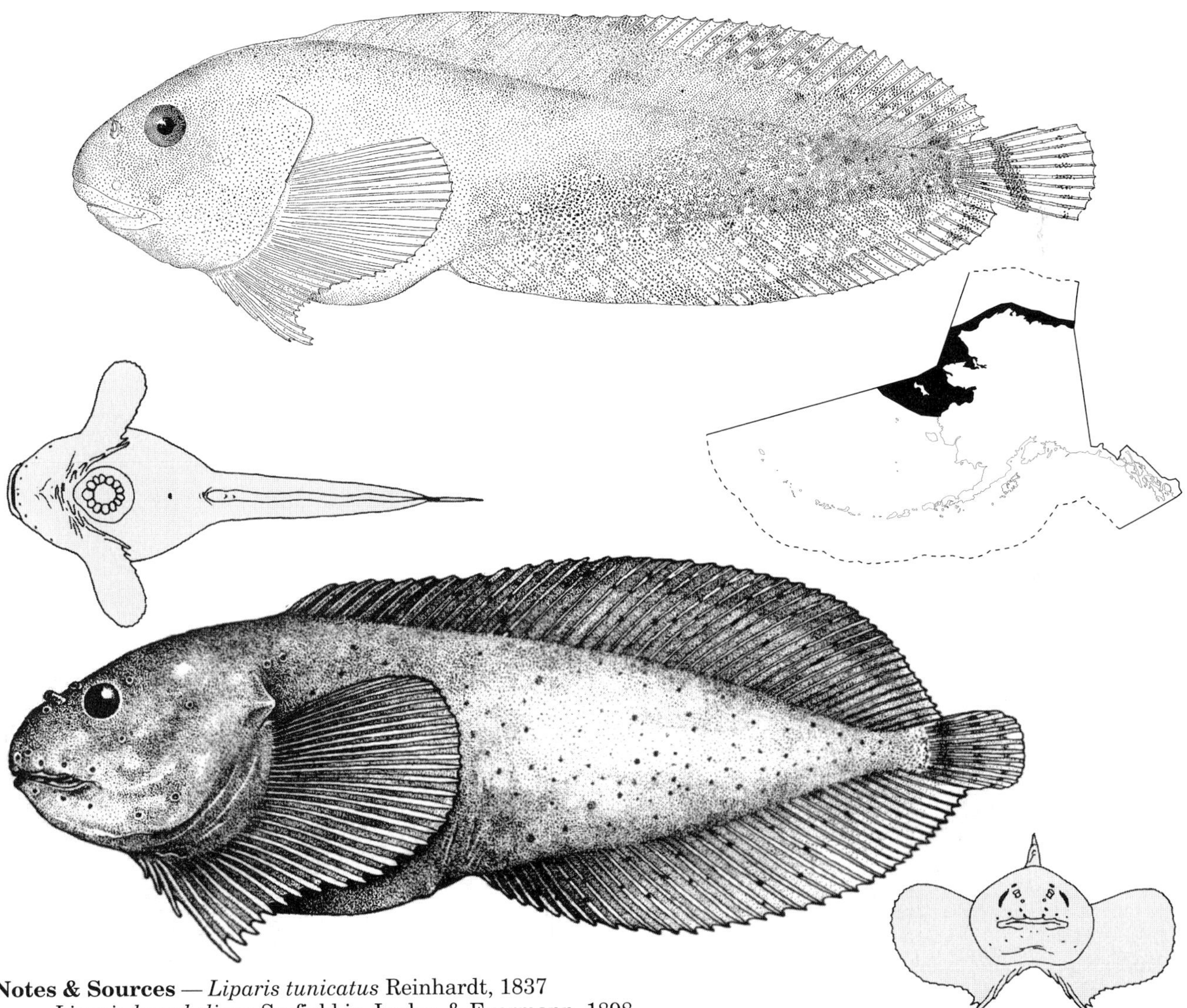

Notes & Sources — *Liparis tunicatus* Reinhardt, 1837
Liparis herschelinus Scofield in Jordan & Evermann, 1898

Description: Burke 1930:73–76; Able and McAllister 1980: 32–40, tables 1–7; Able 1990:484, tables 1–5; Chernova 1991:31–39; Kido and Yabe in Okamura et al. 1995:180.

Figures: Upper: Jordan and Gilbert 1899, pl. 74; Herschel Island, Beaufort Sea. Lower (3 views): Able and McAllister 1980, fig. 8A; 119 mm SL, Cornwallis Island, N.W.T.

Range: Recorded off Alaska as far south as Bering Strait at 65°24'N, 168°43'W (Able and McAllister 1980). The UBC has collections of *L. herschelinus* from as far south as St. Lawrence Island at 63°06'N, 171°42'W (UBC 63-1201). Capture localities depicted on map by Able (1990) indicate distribution to well south of St. Lawrence Island.

Able and McAllister (1980) found the normal habitat of at least small- and medium-sized *L. tunicatus* to be the surface of *Laminaria* fronds, which it resembles in color.

Size: Schmidt 1904a.

Liparis bristolensis (Burke, 1912) **Bristol snailfish**

Known from scattered records from Chukchi Sea to Aleutian Islands and western Gulf of Alaska. Depths of 31–77 m reported for southeastern Bering Sea.

D 38–40; A 30–35; Pec 33–37; PC 16–22.

- Body grayish or brownish; large irregular brown blotches on head and body extending onto dorsal and anal fins; caudal may have brown bar near base; peritoneum pale, with scattered black dots.
- **Thumbtack prickles present**, thick on top of head and sparse along sides of body.
- **Anterior 5 or 6 dorsal fin rays usually set off by shallow notch**; dorsal and anal fins extending along one- to two-fifths the length of the caudal.
- Gill opening extending down in front of 2–5 pectoral fin rays.
- Length of one paratype, 68 mm TL.

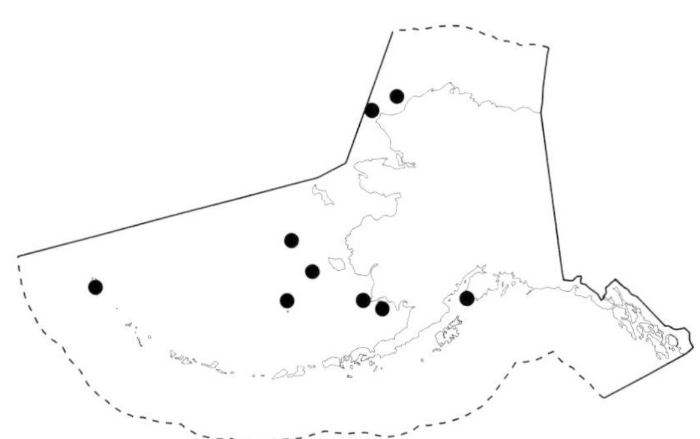

Notes & Sources — *Liparis bristolensis* (Burke, 1912)

Cyclogaster bristolense Burke, 1912

Similar to *Liparis tunicatus,* and probably synonymous. Burke distinguished *L. bristolensis* from *L. tunicatus* on the basis of fewer dorsal fin rays in *L. bristolensis,* presence of prickles only in *L. bristolensis,* and different coloration. With synonymy of *L. herschelinus* in *L. tunicatus* by Able and McAllister (1980), the range of dorsal fin ray counts for *L. bristolensis* is entirely within that for *L. tunicatus*; and Able and McAllister (1980) found prickles on three specimens of *L. tunicatus* (which had previously been identified as *L. bristolensis*; AB 70-244). In both species coloration is variable and can be similar.

Description: Burke 1912b:568–569, 1930:72–73.

Figures: None available of external appearance.

Range: The type specimens (Burke 1912b) were collected by the *Albatross* in the southeastern Bering Sea within Bristol Bay, as reflected in the species name, and west of the bay. Records of this species are as follows. Quast 1972: eastern Chukchi Sea; some of those specimens, from WEBSEC-70 scientific survey, were later referred by Able and McAllister (1980) to *L. tunicatus,* but they did not examine all specimens from that survey that were identified as *L. bristolensis* (AB 70-166, AB 70-179, AB 70-237). Burke 1912b: southeastern Bering Sea, *Albatross* stations 3247, 58°41'N, 162°08'W; 3301, 58°13'N, 160°37'W; 3514, 59°22'N, 168°21'W; and 3518, 60°22'N, 171°42'W. The UBC has collections from Kachemak Bay (UBC 61-516, UBC 61-519); St. Paul Island at Polovina Reef (UBC 62-939); and Nizki Island (52°44'N, 173°59'E; UBC 65-29). Depths: Burke 1912b.

Size: Baxter (1990ms) reported 68.3 mm TL for USNM 64115 (*L. tunicatus* paratype, *Albatross* station 3514). If *L. bristolensis* is, indeed, a species distinct from *L. tunicatus,* specimen AB 70-237 (see Range), if it is correctly identified, could be the largest known, at 104 mm SL.

Liparis megacephalus (Burke, 1912) **bighead snailfish**

Eastern Bering Sea and Aleutian Islands near Amchitka Island; Sea of Japan off South Korea.

Mud and fine sand bottoms at depths of 58–69 m.

D 43–45; A 36–37; Pec 36–42; PC 29–36; Vert 52.

- Body reddish, mottled with dark brown; violet bands radiating from eye; dorsal and anal fins mottled and barred with brown; caudal fin barred with light brown; pectoral fin speckled; peritoneum silvery, with scattered black dots.
- **Head heavy, short, about as wide as deep**; body heavy anteriorly, deep and broad, deepest at dorsal fin origin; **body tapering rapidly to base of caudal**, much compressed posteriorly.
- Thumbtack prickles present or absent.
- **Dorsal fin not notched**; dorsal fin extending onto caudal for two-fifths of caudal; pectoral fin with shallow notch.
- Disk length about half of head length.
- Gill opening extending down in front of 12 pectoral fin rays.
- Length to 267 mm SL, about 280 mm TL.

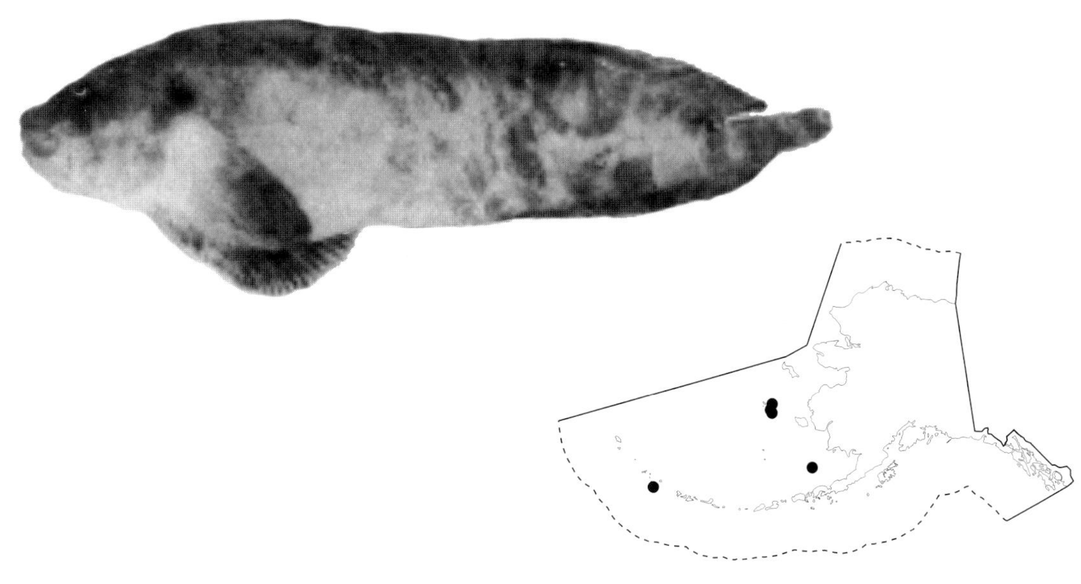

Notes & Sources — *Liparis megacephalus* (Burke, 1912)
Cyclogaster megacephalus Burke, 1912
To Burke (1930) the shape of the body and presence of prickles suggested a close relationship between *L. megacephalus* and *L. bristolensis,* but he considered *L. megacephalus* to be distinct in having a larger number of dorsal fin rays, a larger gill opening, and the dorsal fin notch absent.

Description: Burke 1912b:569–570, Burke 1930:35, 73; Kim et al. 1993:25.

Figure: Kim et al. 1993, pl. 2C; 267.5 mm SL, Sea of Japan.

Range: Previously recorded from the eastern Bering Sea near St. Matthew Island at *Albatross* stations 3518, 60°22'N, 171°42'W; 3519, 60°06'N, 171°25'W; and 3520, 59°28'N, 170°57'W, at depths of 66–69 m (Burke 1912b, 1930); and from Amchitka Island (Isakson et al. 1971), where it was found to be an uncommon species in the "offshore" (depths greater than 37 m) "demersal/rock-sponge" community (Simenstad et al. 1977). Previously unpublished records include UW 28620, a 220-mm-SL specimen collected in 1978 from the eastern Bering Sea at 57°03'N, 163°38'W, at a depth of 62 m; and UW 14760 collected in 1956 from an unknown locality in the Bering Sea at a depth of 58 m. UW 28621, a 250-mm-SL specimen, has no locality data but is probably also from the eastern Bering Sea. Kim et al. (1993) reported a 267.5-mm-SL specimen of *L. megacephalus* from the east coast of South Korea (depth not reported); this is the only record of the species from the western Pacific, and the only record from outside of Alaska.

Size: Kim et al. 1993. Largest recorded by Burke (1930) was 145 mm TL. The 267-mm standard length of the Korean specimen represents about 280 mm in total length.

Liparis fabricii Krøyer, 1847 **gelatinous seasnail**

Arctic Alaska; circumpolar, although not as frequently encountered off Alaska and Siberia as in other regions of the Arctic. *Liparis fabricii* and *L. tunicatus* are the most northerly species of *Liparis.*

Benthic and pelagic at depths of 20–1,880 m, usually taken at 100–300 m.

D 41–49; A 36–42; Pec 32–40; PC 17–35; Vert 48–53.

- Head and body uniformly brownish to dark gray or black; **peritoneum black**.
- Dorsal fin slightly notched or not notched; dorsal and caudal fins extend onto caudal fin for about half of caudal fin length; **anal fin rays usually 37 or more**.
- Disk length 23–28% of head length.
- Anus located midway between disk and anal fin.
- Gill opening extending down in front of 3–16 pectoral fin rays, usually 5–11.
- Length to 194 mm TL.

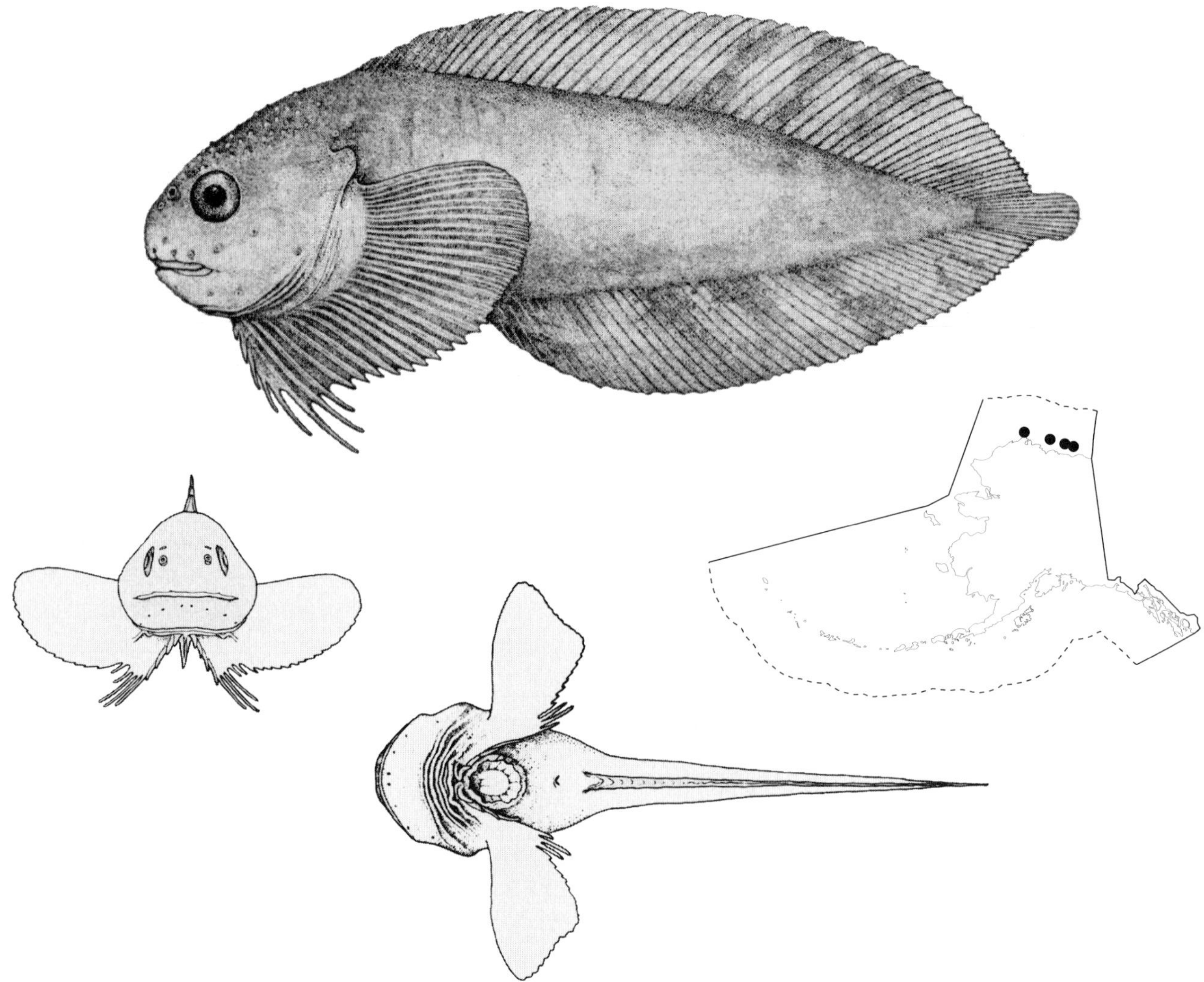

Notes & Sources — *Liparis fabricii* Krøyer, 1847
Liparis koefoedi Parr, 1932

Description: Able and McAllister 1980:18–24, tables 1–7; Able 1990:489–490, tables 1–5; Chernova 1991:46–52; Kido and Yabe in Okamura et al. 1995:178.

Figures: Able and McAllister 1980, fig. 6A; 118 mm SL, Hudson Bay.

Range: Previous Alaskan records: Wilimovsky (1954) and Walters (1955), from Collinson Point (144°54'W) and deep water north of mouth of Colville River (about 151°W); and Able and McAllister (1980), from 44 km north of Maguire Islands (about 146°W). The UBC has a specimen from eastern Chukchi Sea off Point Barrow airport beach (UBC 63-791). Individuals have been found in shallow waters near shore to waters under pack ice over bottom depths of more than 2 km. The exceptional very deep collections reported could result from fish actually being captured in midwater, at any depth, during retrieval of trawl nets from the greater depths (Able 1990).

Size: Baxter (1990ms), from USNM 177626, a specimen taken off Labrador. Andriashev (1954) reported a specimen measuring 182 mm TL from the White Sea.

Liparis fucensis Gilbert, 1896 **slipskin snailfish**

Southeastern Bering Sea and Unimak Pass off Ugamak Island to San Simeon Point, central California.

Shallow to 388 m; frequently encountered around rocky reefs. Juveniles often found in rocky tidepools, adults inhabit deeper water.

D 33–35; A 27–29; C 18–20; Pec 38–43; PC 25–55; Vert 39–41.

- Coloration variable, pale olive brown to dark brown, often tinged with pink; irregular dark bands or blotches on dorsal, anal, caudal, and pectoral fins, sometimes a diagonal light band on caudal fin.
- Dorsal fin unnotched or with shallow notch; dorsal and anal fins extending little, if at all, beyond base of caudal; **tips of dorsal and anal fin rays free**; dorsal fin rays fewer than 36; **more pectoral rays than dorsal rays.**
- Rim of posterior nostril raised anteriorly to form fingerlike projection.
- Disk length 36–40% of head length.
- Anus far back, nearer to anal fin than to disk.
- Gill opening extending down in front of 12–16 pectoral rays.
- Length to 178 mm TL.

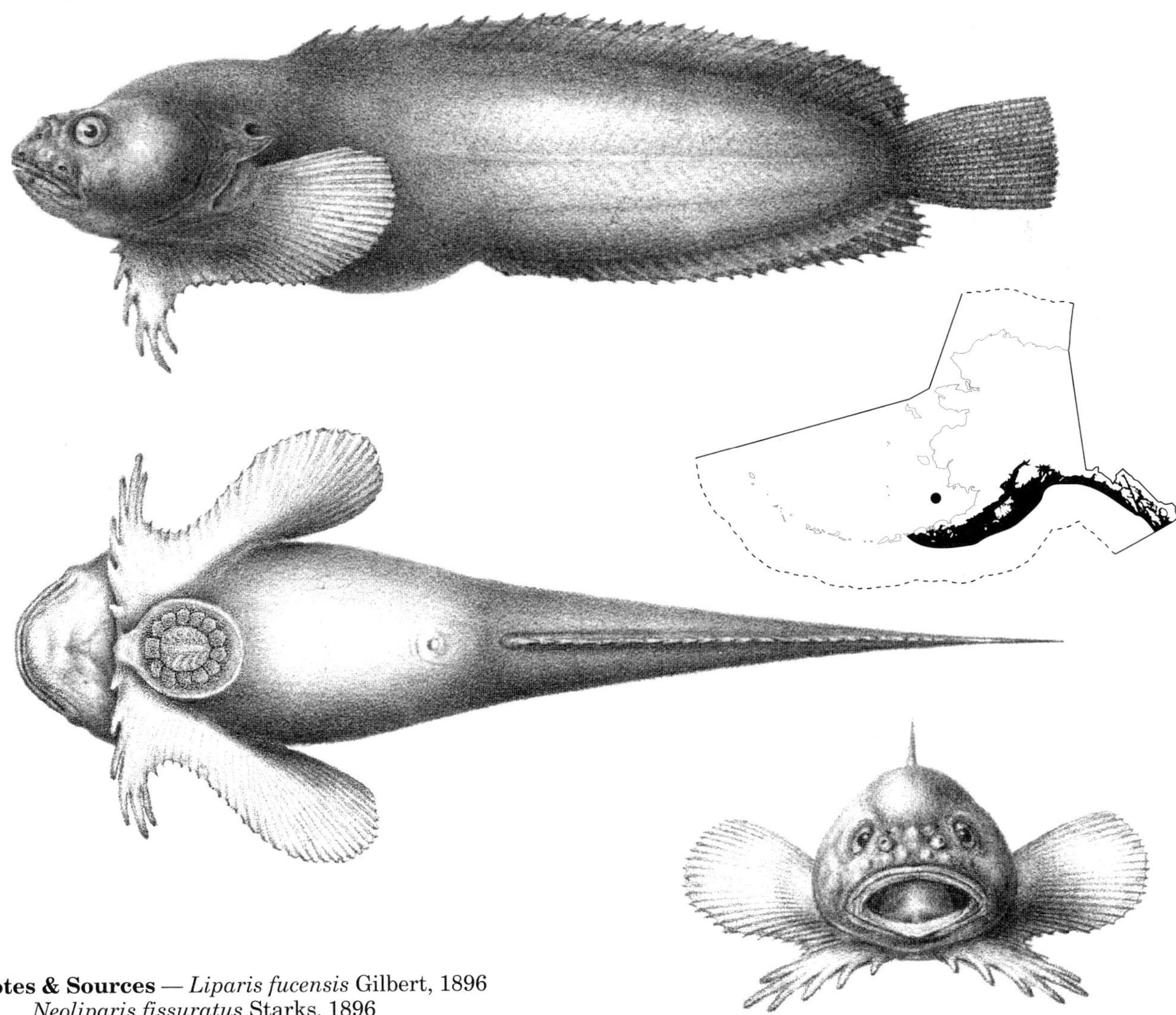

Notes & Sources — *Liparis fucensis* Gilbert, 1896
Neoliparis fissuratus Starks, 1896
Liparis calliodon: Garman 1892.

Description: Gilbert 1896:447; Burke 1930:35, 71–72; Hubbs and Schultz 1934b:6–7; Miller and Lea 1972:138 (vertebral counts).

Figures: Garman 1892, pl. 6, figs. 1, 3, 4.

Range: AB 72-54 is from eastern Bering Sea at 57°20'N, 163°24'W. Schultz and DeLacy (1936) and Quast and Hall (1972) reported it from southeastern Alaska; and Rogers et al. (1986) from Kodiak Island and Cook Inlet. UBC has Gulf of Alaska collections from southeastern Alaska to Kachemak Bay and the Kodiak archipelago and as far west as south Unimak Pass off Ugamak Island (UBC 62-444, UBC 62-663). R. Baxter (unpubl. data) collected *L. fucensis* from Prince William Sound.

Size: Miller and Lea 1972.

Liparis rutteri (Gilbert & Snyder, 1898) **ringtail snailfish**

Aleutian Islands to Duxbury Reef, San Francisco.
Tidepools and shallow water to depth of about 73 m.

D 30–33; A 23–27; C 14; Pec 30–33; PC 23–31.

- Brown to black, sometimes with wavy streaks; usually with **white band on base of caudal fin** and extending onto tips of dorsal and anal fins.
- Anterior dorsal fin rays sometimes separated by shorter rays from rest of fin; anterior rays in males (not shown below) free almost to base and greatly elevated; **dorsal and anal fin margins slightly crenulate**, fins barely extending onto caudal fin; pectoral lobe not always distinct.
- Posterior nostril with low rim, its anterior part elevated into a triangular flap.
- **Disk length distinctly more than half of head length** (59–71%).
- Anus slightly nearer to disk than to anal fin.
- Gill opening entirely above pectoral fin base.
- Length to 168 mm TL.

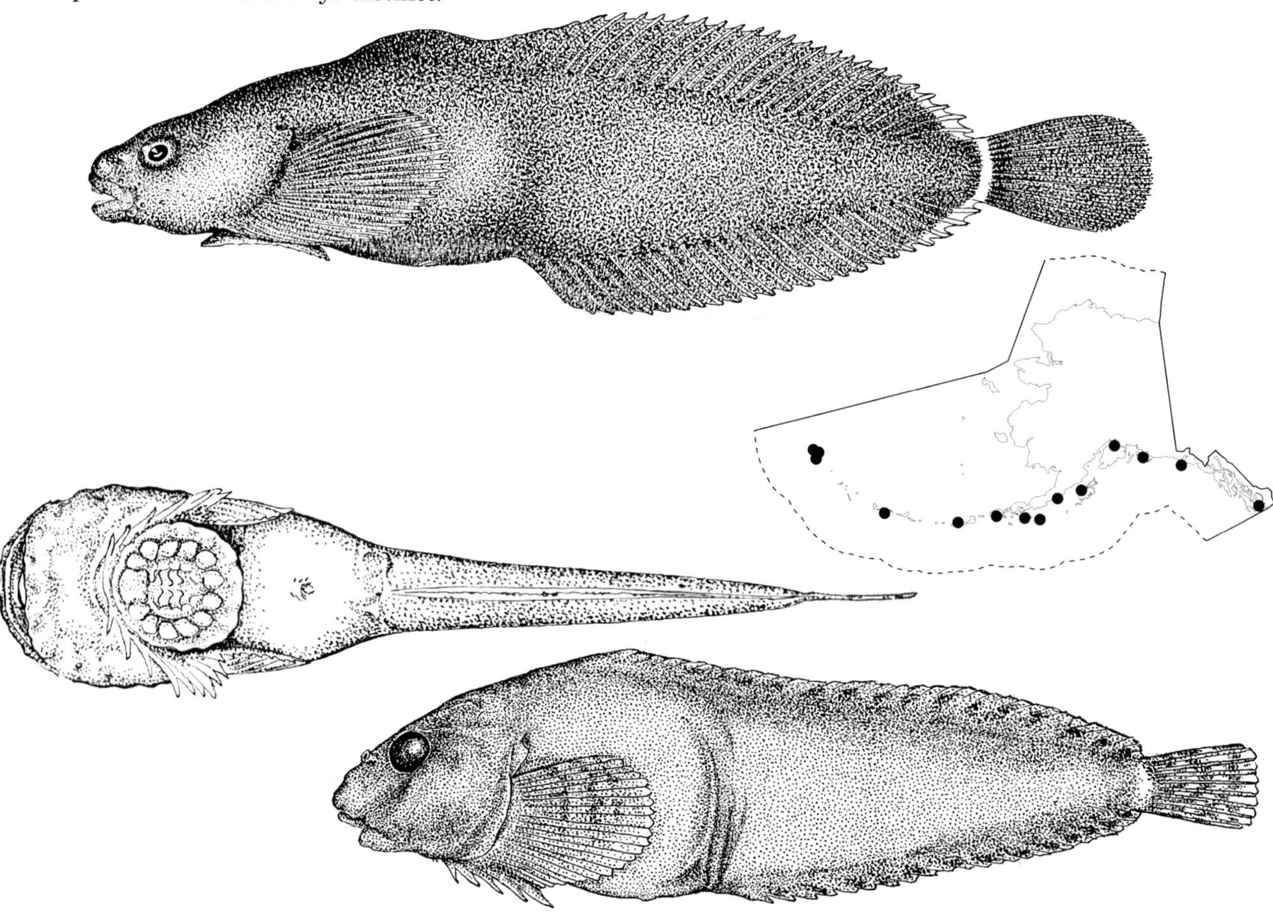

Notes & Sources — *Liparis rutteri* (Gilbert & Snyder in Jordan & Evermann, 1898)
Neoliparis rutteri Gilbert & Snyder in Jordan & Evermann, 1898
Discrepancies in published descriptions and illustrations, as well as among specimens identified as *L. rutteri* in museum collections, suggest that a different, unnamed species has long been confused with *L. rutteri*.

Description: Jordan and Evermann 1898:2108–2110; Rutter 1899:192; Evermann and Goldsborough 1907:331–332; Burke 1930:61–62; Hubbs and Schultz 1934b:4–5.

Figures: Upper: Evermann and Goldsborough 1907, fig. 99; about 61 mm TL, Kodiak Island. Lower, including ventral view: Hart 1973:590; 74 mm TL, Alaska.

Range: Previous Alaskan records include: Rutter (1899) and Evermann and Goldsborough (1907) from Uyak Bay and Karluk, Kodiak Island; Burke (1930) from Naha Bay, Loring; and Wilimovsky (1964) from Agattu, Adak, and Unimak islands. UBC has specimens from Nakalilok Bay, Alaska Peninsula; near Eagle River at 61°19'N, 149°34'W; Chernabura Island; Port Gravina; and Attu, Nizki, Agattu, Adak, Umnak, Unimak, and Shumagin islands. SIO 63-1066 is from Ocean Cape and SIO 69-476 from Womens Bay, Kodiak Island. UBC 63-1174, from Point Barrow and identified as this species, is definitely not (A. E. Peden, pers. comm., 28 Apr. 1999). UW 19663, from south of St. Lawrence Island, is also misidentified as *L. rutteri* (M. S. Busby, pers. comm., 13 Apr. 2000). Specimens from Bering Island described under the name *L. rutteri kussakini* by Pinchuk (1976) represent a different species, not a subspecies of *L. rutteri* (N. V. Chernova via M. S. Busby, 15 Jun. 2000).

Size: Miller and Lea 1972.

Liparis cyclopus Günther, 1861 **ribbon snailfish**

Southeastern Bering Sea and Aleutian Islands to Oregon coast; Commander Islands to Petropavlovsk, Kamchatka.

Rocky tidepools and shallow water to maximum recorded depth of 183 m.

D 34–37; A 29–31; C 12; Pec 29–32; PC 39.

- Color generally uniform; olivaceous; paler ventrally, belly sometimes white; body and pectoral fins finely speckled with olive brown; sometimes with about 4 pale stripes on side.
- **Greatest body depth retained posteriorly to origin of anal fin or beyond**; head broad, low, wider than deep; profile depressed over the eyes.
- **Dorsal fin not notched, or notch faintly indicated**; dorsal and anal fins barely reach caudal fin; fewer pectoral fin rays than dorsal fin rays; pectoral fin notched.
- Disk length 40–50% of head length.
- Anus about midway between disk and anal fin.
- Gill opening extending down in front of 5–10 (usually 6–8) pectoral fin rays.
- Length to 114 mm TL.

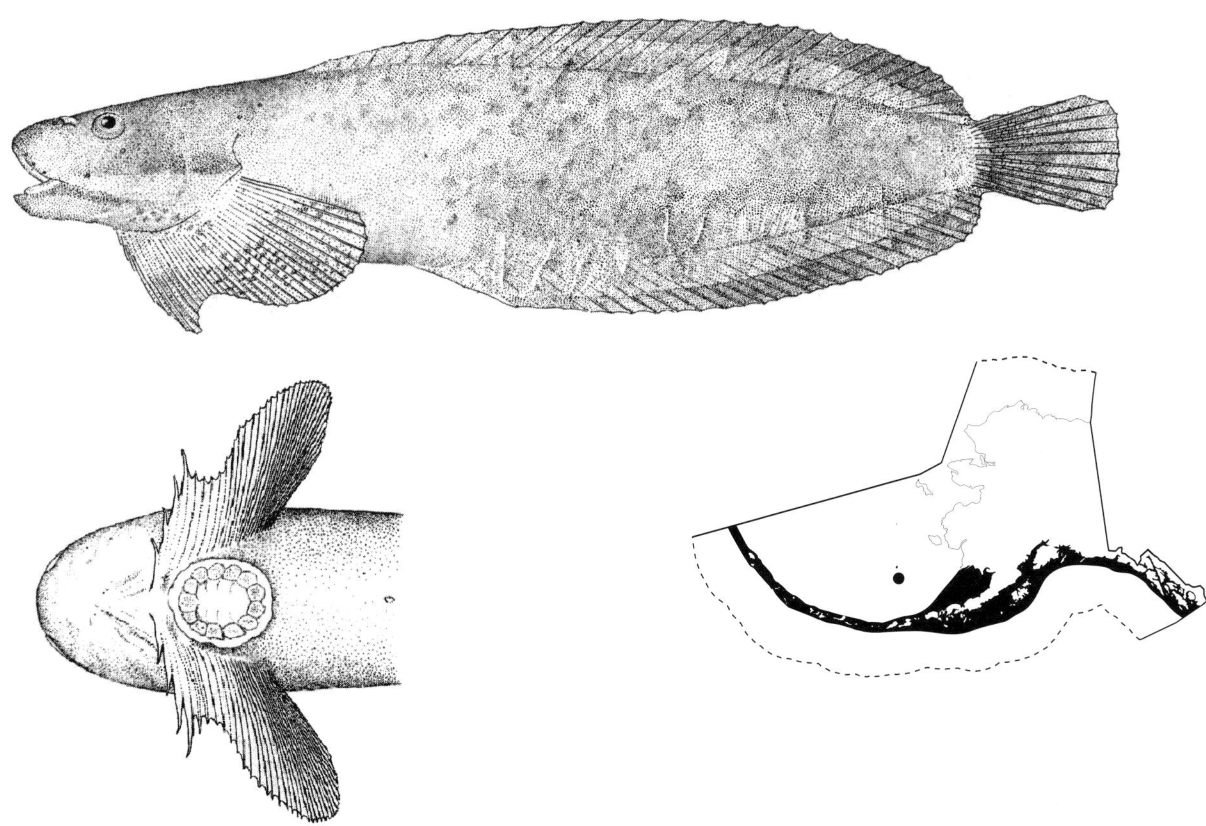

Notes & Sources — *Liparis cyclopus* Günther, 1861

Description: Jordan and Starks 1895:834–835; Burke 1930:69–70; Hart 1973:580–581.

Figures: Jordan and Starks 1895, pl. 97; Elliot Bay, near Seattle.

Range: Previous Alaskan records include the following. Bean 1881b: Unalaska and Port Moller. Turner 1886: Atka Island; he commented that it was not a common fish, as he saw only two during the 4 months of his stay on Atka. Gilbert 1896: Bristol Bay, *Albatross* station 3230. Rogers et al. 1986: Kodiak Island and Cook Inlet. Wilimovsky 1964: Kiska, Adak, Atka, and Unalaska islands, and northwest coast of Alaska Peninsula. Quast and Hall 1972: southeastern Alaska (Little Port Walter, AB 62-7, AB 68-544). AB 75-117 is a specimen from St. George Island. The UBC has collections from Bristol Bay and Izembek Bay; Unalaska Island to Attu Island; Shumagin Islands; Kodiak Island; Kachemak Bay; and Baranof Island. The UW has specimens from Prince William Sound (UW 3939). A. E. Peden (pers. comm., 29 Apr. 1999) examined UBC 63-1118, from Chukchi Sea, and UBC 63-1208, from Bering Strait, and determined they are misidentified as this species.

Size: Jordan and Starks 1895.

Liparis mucosus Ayres, 1855 — slimy snailfish

Kodiak Island, unconfirmed reports; southeastern Alaska at Samsing Cove to Baja California.
Shallow water to depth of about 15 m; usually not in tidepools.

D 30–32; A 24–26; C 10–12; Pec 28–32.

- **Coloration variable**, from plain to reticulate to horizontal stripes, from light yellowish to dark brown, red, and lavender; frequently a blackish bar covers base of caudal fin; lips dark.
- Body deepest below first part of dorsal fin.
- Prickles absent.
- **Dorsal fin lobe low, broadly rounded, hardly evident in some specimens**; dorsal and anal fins extend little if at all onto caudal fin.
- **Disk more than half as long as head.**
- Anus nearer to anal fin than to disk.
- Gill opening above pectoral base or extending down in front of 1–6 rays, usually below 3rd ray.
- Length to about 127 mm TL.

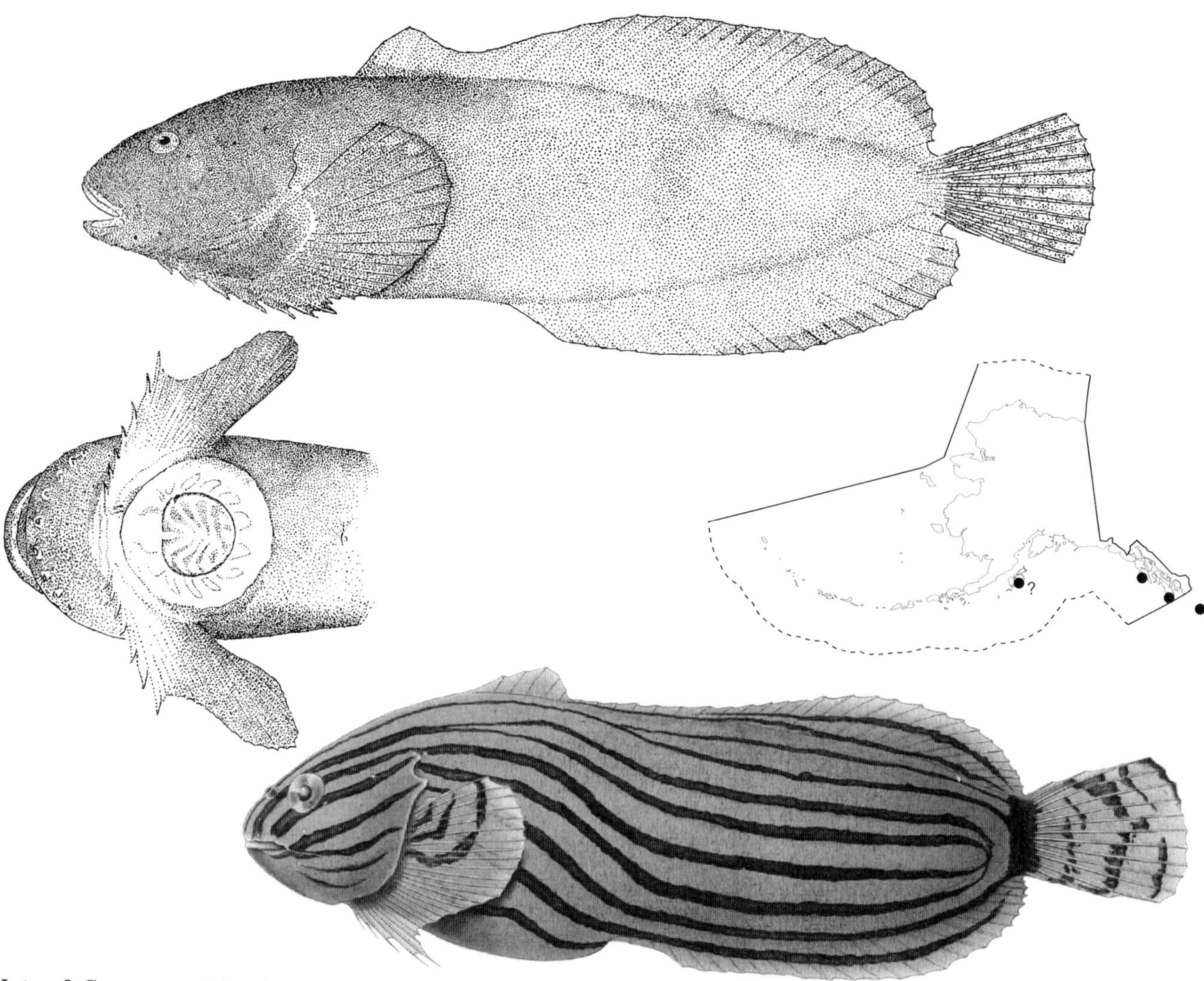

Notes & Sources — *Liparis mucosus* Ayres, 1855
Neoliparis mucosus: Jordan and Evermann 1898.

Description: Jordan and Starks 1895:832–833; Hubbs and Schultz 1934b:3–6. Other descriptions of *L. mucosus* and *L. florae* contain conflicting information.

Figures: Upper: Jordan and Starks 1895, pl. 95; 127 mm TL, off San Francisco. Lower: Royal British Columbia Museum, artist N. Eyolfson, Dec. 1984; BCPM 976-1031, 50 mm SL, British Columbia.

Range: Recorded from southeastern Alaska by Quast and Hall (1972) on basis of AB 64-954 (3 specimens, 37–40 mm SL) from Samsing Cove, about 4 miles south of Sitka. Another southeastern Alaska collection is UBC 65-582, from Baker Island, northeast of Cape Bartolome. Basis for Quast and Hall's (1972) and Rogers et al.'s (1986) listing of *L. mucosus* from Kodiak Island could not be determined; documentation was not given. Peden and Wilson (1976) recorded specimens from as far north in British Columbia as 52°56'N, 129°36'W.

Size: Jordan and Starks 1895. Most records (Hubbs and Schultz 1934b, Peden 1966a, Peden and Wilson 1976) are of specimens less than 55 mm SL.

Liparis florae (Jordan & Starks, 1895) **tidepool snailfish**

Bering Sea and Aleutian Islands reports not verified; Kodiak Island to Point Conception, California. Exposed coast tidepools, where it outnumbers all other species of liparids.

D 31–33; A 21–25; C 10–12; Pec 30.

- **Coloration generally uniform**; yellowish brown to olive brown, red-brown, or purplish; lips white.
- Body deepest below second part of dorsal fin.
- Prickles absent.
- **First dorsal fin distinct, high, often incised behind**; dorsal and anal fins extend onto caudal fin only slightly.
- **Disk less than half of head length** (37.5–45%).
- **Anus slightly closer to disk than to anal fin, sometimes equidistant**, rarely nearer to anal fin (45–51% of distance from disk to anal fin).
- Gill opening extends in front of 2–5 pectoral rays.
- Length to about 183 mm TL.

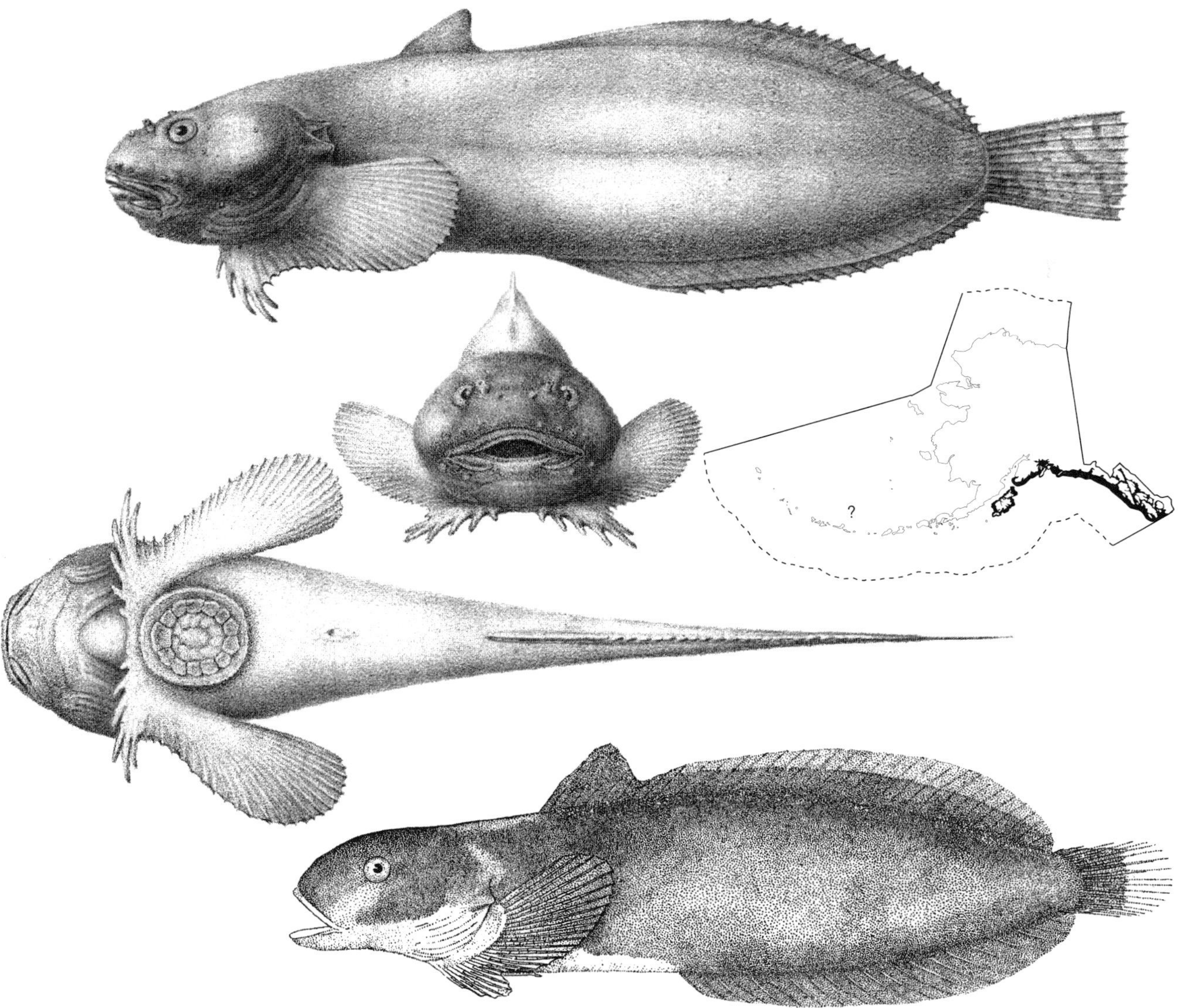

Notes & Sources — *Liparis florae* (Jordan & Starks, 1895)
Neoliparis florae Jordan & Starks, 1895

Description: Jordan and Starks 1895:830–832; Hubbs and Schultz 1934b:3. Descriptions of *L. florae* and *L. mucosus* are confusing. For example, Hubbs and Schultz (1934b) gave the anus in *L. florae* as nearer to the anal fin than to the disk, but the opposite seems to be true (e.g., USNM 103618, 104668, 132499) when not equidistant as in the holotype.

Figures: Garman 1892, pl. 5; identified by Hubbs and Schultz (1934b:5). Bottom: Jordan and Starks 1895, pl. 96; holotype, about 51 mm TL, Waadda Island, Neah Bay, Washington.

Range: Given as north to Bering Sea by Wilimovsky (1954) and Miller and Lea (1972), but to Kodiak Island by Eschmeyer and Herald (1983). Wilimovsky (1964) did *not* list it from the Aleutians as reported by Hart (1973). Some authors may have equated *L. micraspidophorus* with *L. florae.* UBC collections are from Kasitsna Bay to Dall Island.

Size: Miller and Lea 1972.

Liparis micraspidophorus (Gilbert & Burke, 1912) **thumbtack snailfish**

Aleutian Islands to Alaska Peninsula at Cold Bay; Commander Islands.

Tidepools and shallow intertidal area.

D 31; A 25; C 10–12; Pec 31; PC 65.

- **Coloration generally uniform**; reddish brown to olive gray.
- Body depth greatest at first dorsal fin.
- **Body and fins with scattered thumbtack prickles**.
- **Dorsal fin notch deep**; dorsal and anal fins not extending past skin of caudal fin.
- **Disk length more than half of head length** (55–59%).
- **Anus noticeably closer to disk than to anal fin** (30–36% of distance from disk to anal fin).
- Gill opening extending down in front of 4 or 5 pectoral rays.
- Length to less than 100 mm TL.

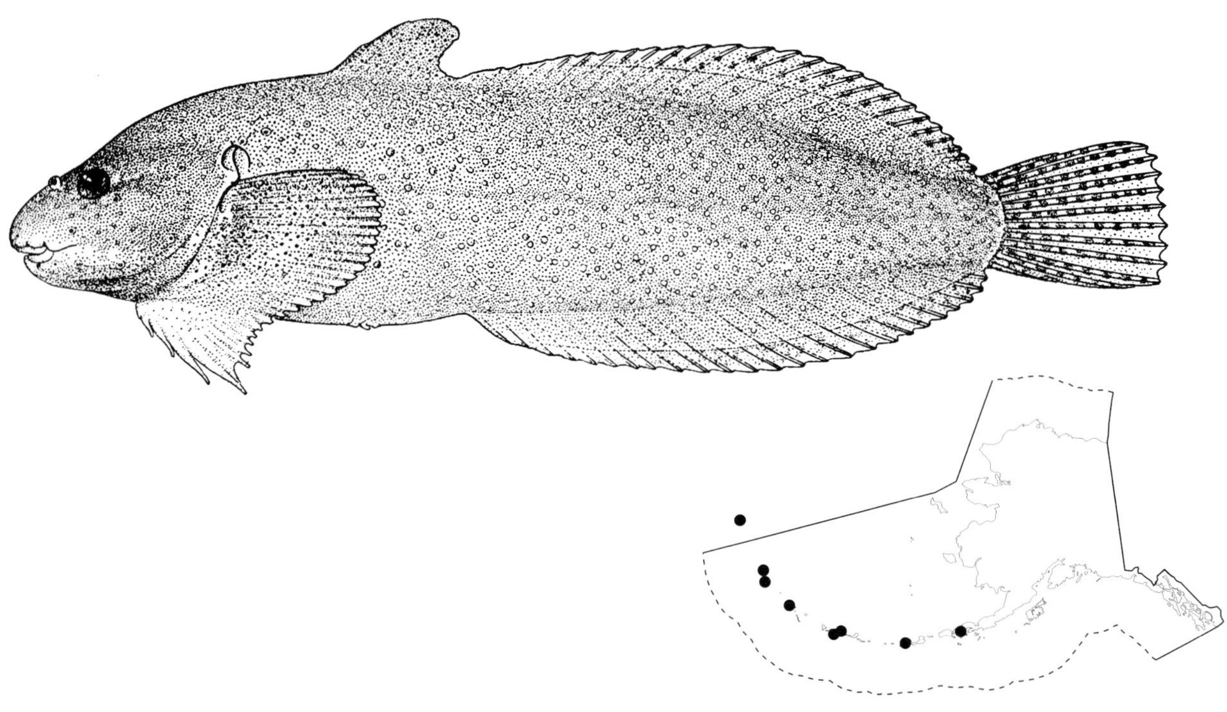

Notes & Sources — *Liparis micraspidophorus* (Gilbert & Burke, 1912)

Cyclogaster (Neoliparis) micraspidophorus Gilbert & Burke, 1912

Gilbert and Burke's (1912a) and Burke's (1930) comments on similarity of *L. micraspidophorus* to *L. mucosus* probably refer not to *L. mucosus* but to *L. florae,* which they mistakenly (Hubbs and Schultz 1934b) synonymized with *L. mucosus.* Hubbs and Schultz (1934b) noted that some specimens of *L. florae* approach *L. micraspidophorus* in one or another of the distinctive features, but did not believe they could be referred to *L. micraspidophorus* or that *L. micraspidophorus* is not a valid species. Later, Dr. Hubbs may have changed his mind. A note in the jar with the holotype of *L. micraspidophorus* (USNM 74379, Bering Island) says "= *Liparis florae.* Ident. by Carl L. Hubbs, 17 May 1952." A note in a jar of two other specimens described by Gilbert and Burke (1912a; USNM 74703, Agattu Island) says "Definitely *Liparis florae.* C. L. Hubbs, 17 May 1952." If so, those specimens comprise the westernmost records of *L. florae.* Examining the specimens, C.W.M. could not differentiate them from *L. micraspidophorus.*

Description: Gilbert and Burke 1912a:71–72; Burke 1930: 35, 67.

Figure: Gilbert and Burke 1912a, fig. 16; type, USNM 74379, 73 mm TL, Nikolski, Bering Island.

Range: Published records are those of Gilbert and Burke (1912a) from Bering Island, Russia and Agattu Island, Alaska; Wilimovsky (1964) from Attu, Agattu, Kiska, Adak, and Great Sitkin-Igitkin islands, and southwest Umnak Island (specimens housed at UBC museum); and Vogt (1973) from the intertidal zone at Cold Bay, Alaska Peninsula. Pinchuk (1976) reported another specimen from Bering Island.

Size: Burke 1930:67: "a small sized species, none of our [4] specimens reaching a length of 100 mm."

Liparis mednius (Soldatov, 1930) — Commander snailfish

Bering and Medny islands, Commander Islands.

Intertidal zone.

D 33–35; A 25–27; C 12; Pec 27–31; PC 77.

- Coloration uniform.
- Body deepest below second part of dorsal fin.
- **Body and fins with scattered prickles**.
- **Dorsal fin notch deep**; dorsal and anal fins not distinctly joined to base of caudal, anal fin extending a little farther than dorsal.
- Disk length 41–44% of head length.
- Anus closer to disk than to anal fin.
- Gill opening extending down in front of 1 or 2 pectoral rays.
- Length to 103.5 mm TL.

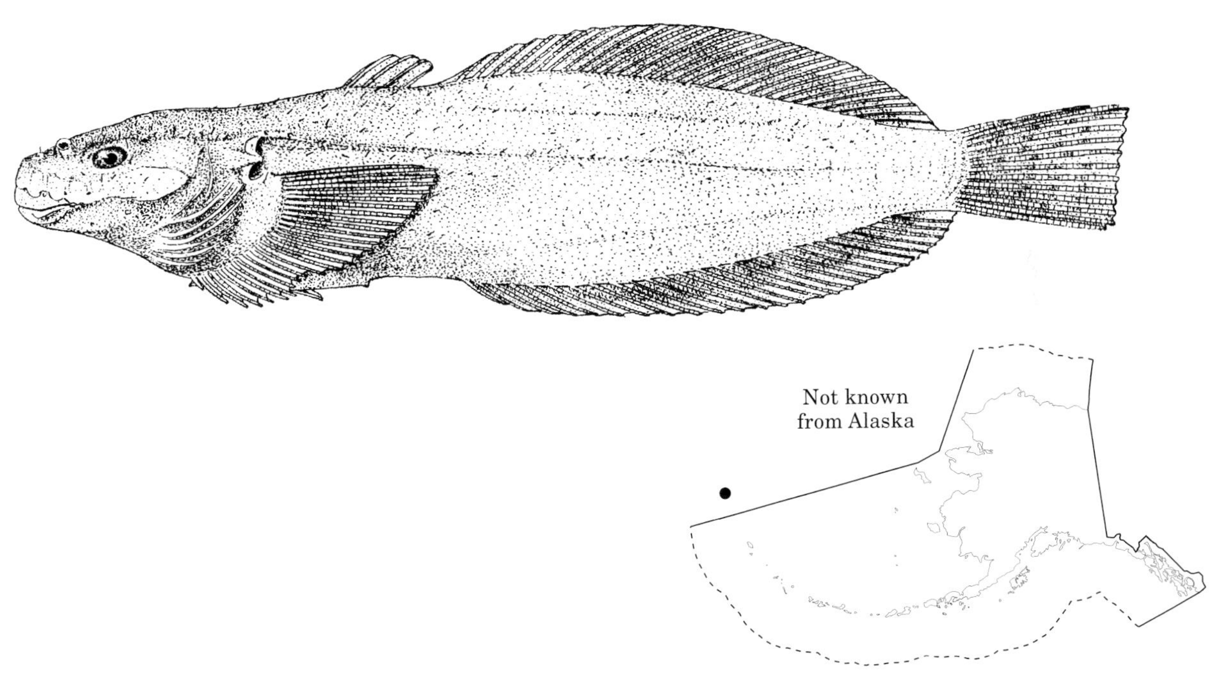

Notes & Sources — *Liparis mednius* (Soldatov in Soldatov & Lindberg, 1930)

Neoliparis mednius Soldatov in Soldatov & Lindberg, 1930

Similar to *L. micraspidophorus,* and possibly not distinct. Features of the neotype designated by Chernova (1998) and other specimens attributed to *L. mednius* should be reported and compared with those of closely related species, including *L. micraspidophorus* and *L. florae.*

Description: Soldatov and Lindberg 1930:339–341; Taranetz 1933:74.

Figures: Soldatov and Lindberg 1930, fig. 55; 92 mm TL, Medny Island. Taranetz (1933) noted that the shape of the head is distorted due to poor fixation and that in his specimens the dorsal fins were connected by a low membrane, not completely separate as in the illustration.

Range: The holotype (unique) was collected from Medny Island on 26 Sep. 1925, and described by Soldatov and Lindberg (1930); it subsequently was lost. Two additional specimens, measuring 103.5 and 89.3 mm TL, 88.7 and 76.3 mm SL, were described by Taranetz (1933), who reported they were collected by E. Kardakova on 19 May 1929 from Bering Island. The labels on the only specimens (ZIN 29007 and 30606) at the Zoological Institute of the Russian Academy of Sciences at St. Petersburg say the specimens were collected by E. Kardakova on 20 May 1931 from Medny Island (B. A. Sheiko, pers. comm., 18 Jan. 1999), and ZIN 30606 measures 66 mm SL, which is different from either of the lengths reported by Taranetz (1933). It is not certain, therefore, that ZIN 29007 and 30606 are the specimens described by Taranetz (1933), and it is important to know this because there are so few specimens. Chernova (1998) designated ZIN 30606 as a neotype of *L. mednius* in the recent catalog of type specimens housed at the Zoological Institute.

Liparis greeni (Jordan & Starks, 1895) **lobefin snailfish**

Pribilof and Aleutian islands to Washington; Commander Islands.

Tidepools to shallow water near shore.

D 37–40; A 29–32; C about 11; Pec 33–37; PC more than 200.

- Light brown, gray, pale pea green, to purplish brown; breast and lower part of head lighter.
- **Profile depressed over eyes, occiput slightly raised**.
- **Eye very small**.
- **Dorsal fin deeply notched anteriorly, forming lobe**; dorsal fin not reaching caudal fin or barely reaching caudal; anal fin extending slightly farther than dorsal.
- Disk length 34–43% of head length.
- Anus midway between disk and anal fin or slightly closer to either one.
- Gill opening extending down in front of 1–4 pectoral rays, sometimes appearing to be above the fin.
- **Pyloric caeca numerous, matted closely together** (more than 200), easily distinguished without counting from most other species of *Liparis*.
- Length to 305 mm TL.

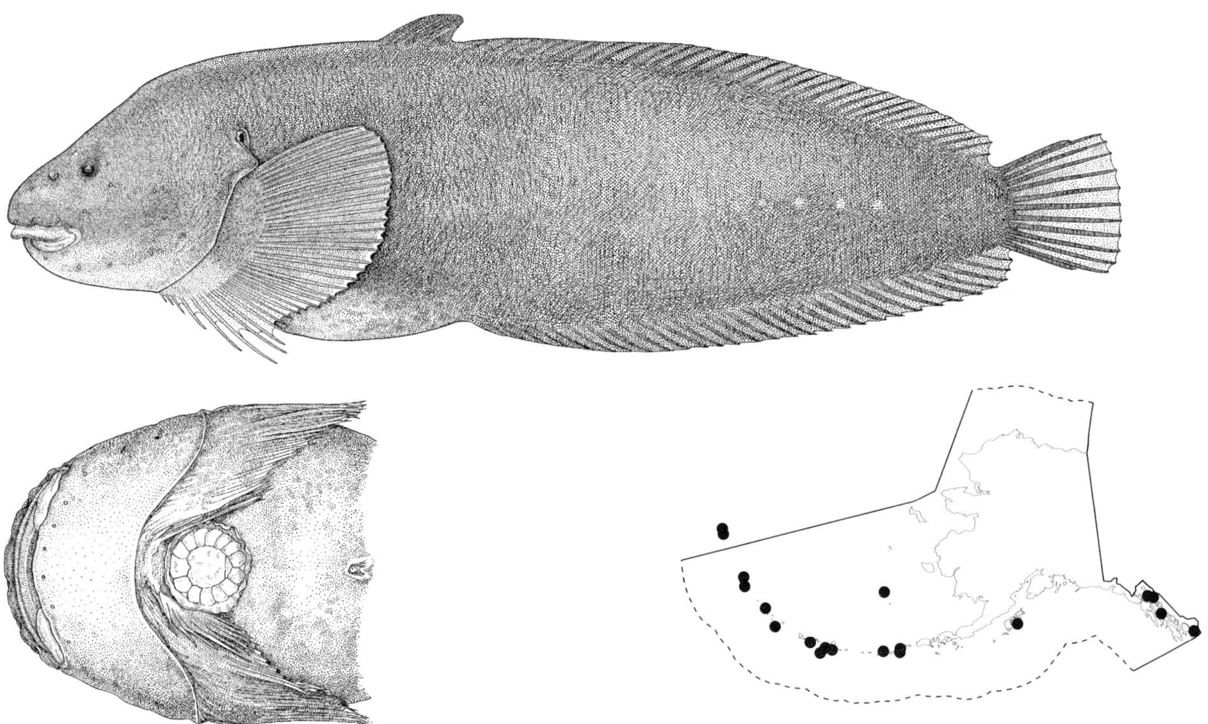

Notes & Sources — *Liparis greeni* (Jordan & Starks, 1895)

Neoliparis greeni Jordan & Starks, 1895

Liparis tunicata Reinhart (?): Bean and Bean 1896:243–244.

Liparis calliodon (Pallas), Günther: Bean and Bean 1896:243 (USNM 47561 only).

Cyclogaster (*Neoliparis*) *beringianus* Gilbert & Burke, 1912

Polypera greeni: Burke 1912b (new genus), 1930.

Polypera beringianus: Burke 1930.

Kido (1988) synonymized *Polypera* with *Liparis*. Some workers maintain the genera are distinct.

Burke (1930) suggested that *L. beringianus* represented immature individuals of *L. greeni*. No Alaskan specimens have been referred to *L. beringianus* since then. Wilimovsky (1958) could find no difference except possibly coloration to distinguish the two forms. After examining specimens attributed to both forms (C.W.M.), we follow N. J. Wilimovsky (pers. comm., 13 Aug. 1996) and A. E. Peden (pers. comm., 5 Sep. 1996) in classifying them as synonymous.

Description: Jordan and Starks 1895:829–830; Gilbert and Burke 1912a:72; Burke 1930:92–94.

Figures: University of British Columbia, artist P. Drukker-Brammall; UBC 65-30, 188 mm SL, Adak Island.

Range: Gilbert and Burke 1912a: Agattu and Unalaska islands. Burke 1930: Kodiak Island. Quast and Hall 1972: southeastern Alaska, based on AB 62-307, south tip Admiralty Island; AB 64-58, Eliza Harbor, Frederick Sound; AB 67-81, Limestone Inlet, Stephens Passage. Isakson et al. 1971: Amchitka Island. UBC collection: St. Paul Island; Attu, Agattu, Nizki, Shemya, Kiska, Amchitka, Adak, Igitkin, Umnak, and Unalaska islands; and Duke Island, southeastern Alaska. Wilimovsky (1964) listed *Polypera* from numerous Aleutian Island localities but did not identify them to species; they are now labeled as *P. greeni* in the UBC fish collection. The UW has specimens from the Rat Islands (UW 28644, 28646) and Lynn Canal (UW 14757).

Size: Clemens and Wilby 1949.

Liparis callyodon (Pallas, 1814) **spotted snailfish**

Bering Sea and Aleutian Islands to Oregon and to Kamchatka.

Tidepools and other intertidal areas, generally on rocky shores.

D 33–35; A 25–27; Pec 29–31; PC 42–66.

- Usually solid olive brown to purplish with slaty cast; dark body and fins, paler ventrally; often spotted with fine black specks on sides and back, and with bars on the fins; skin transparent; peritoneum pale to gray, with light brown spots.
- Skin loose; **prickles absent**.
- **Dorsal fin with deep notch**, forming bluntly pointed lobe; dorsal and anal fins not extending onto caudal fin.
- **Rim of posterior nostril raised anteriorly to form fingerlike projection**.
- Disk length 33–45% of head length.
- Anus slightly nearer to disk than to anal fin, or equidistant.
- Gill opening above pectoral fin or extending down in front of 1st pectoral ray.
- Length to about 127 mm TL.

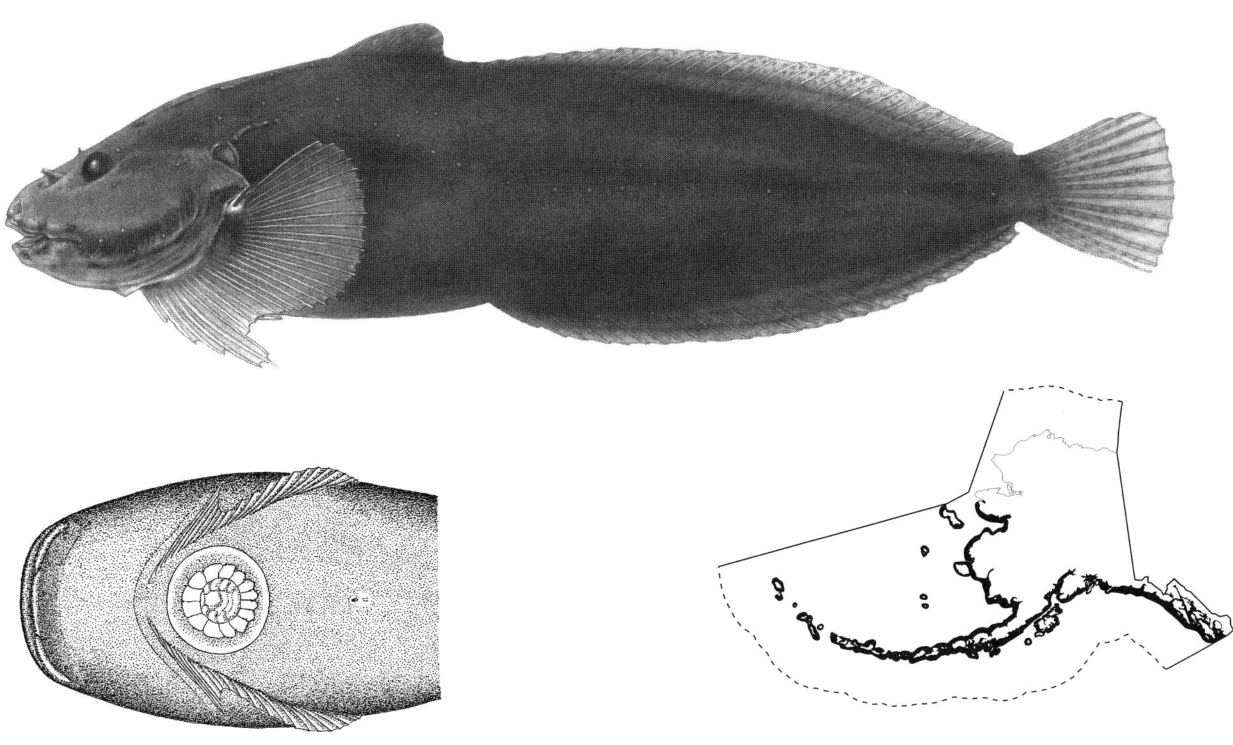

Notes & Sources — *Liparis callyodon* (Pallas, 1814)
Cyclopterus callyodon Pallas, 1814
Neoliparis callyodon: Jordan and Evermann 1898, Evermann and Goldsborough 1907.

Description: Jordan and Evermann 1898:2110; Gilbert and Burke 1912a:71; Burke 1930:62–63; Hart 1973:579–580.

Figures: Full lateral view: University of British Columbia, artist P. Drukker-Brammall, Jan. 1974; UBC 63-1454, 103 mm SL, St. Paul Island, Bering Sea. Ventral: Jordan and Evermann 1898, fig. 760a; 117 mm TL, St. Paul (= Kodiak) harbor, Kodiak Island.

Range: Recorded from Unalaska and Kodiak islands by Jordan and Evermann (1898); north to St. Paul Island by Burke (1930); from Unimak Island to Attu Island by Gilbert and Burke (1912a) and by Wilimovsky (1964); from Kenai Peninsula and southeastern Alaska by Quast and Hall (1972); and from Kodiak Island and Cook Inlet by Rogers et al. (1986). The UBC has numerous collections, including two from a bay at the northeast cape of St. Lawrence Island (UBC 60-384) that could be the northernmost record; although Burke (1930) recorded it "doubtfully" from Plover Bay on the Chukchi Peninsula.

Size: Hart 1973 ("5 inches").

Liparis grebnitzkii (Schmidt, 1904) **Grebnitzki's snailfish**

Commander Islands at Bering Island.

Intertidal zone.

D 32; A 27; C 10; Pec 29; PC about 30.

- Color brown, with darker head and back; fins grayish; pectoral yellowish, without spots.
- Skin loose; **prickles absent**.
- **Dorsal fin with deep notch**; dorsal and anal fins not extending onto caudal fin.
- **Rim of posterior nostril raised anteriorly to form flaplike projection**.
- Disk 45% of head length.
- **Gill opening extending down only to top of pectoral fin base**.
- Length 84 mm TL.

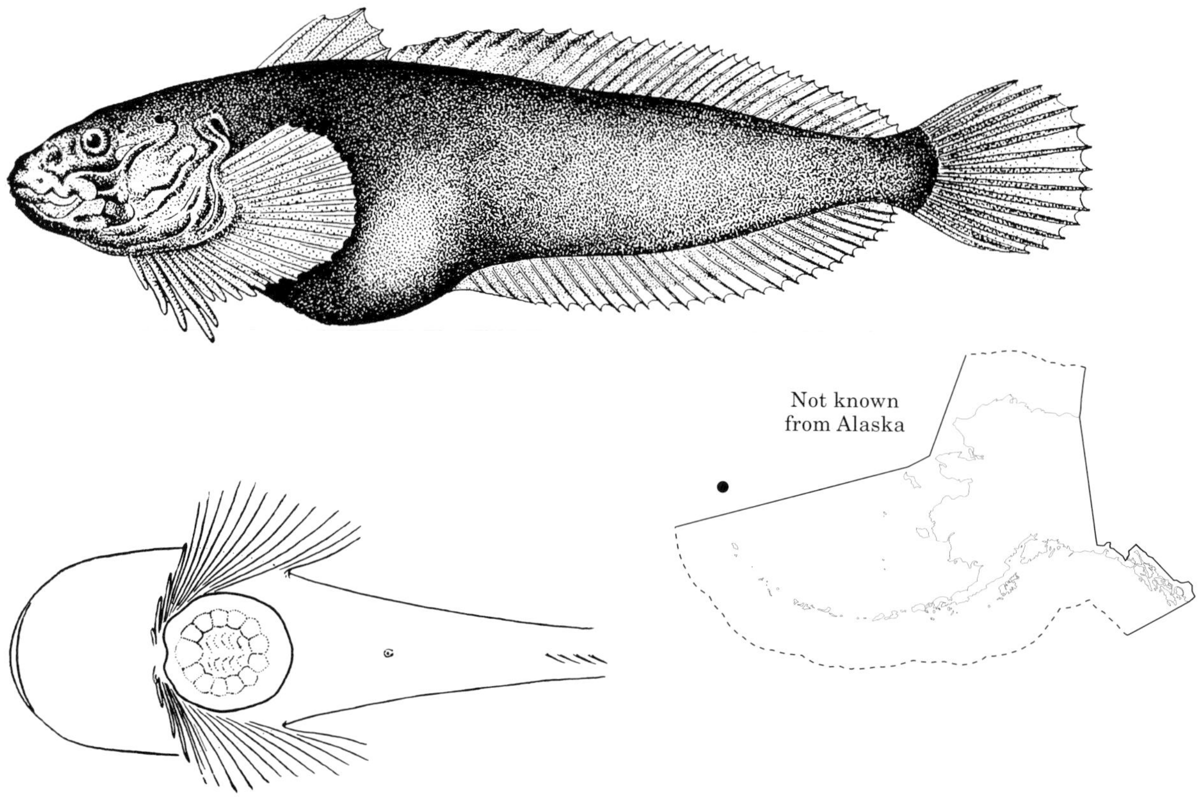

Notes & Sources — *Liparis grebnitzkii* (Schmidt, 1904)

Neoliparis grebnitzkii Schmidt, 1904

From the description (Schmidt 1904) this fish appears to be similar to *L. callyodon* and may not be a distinct species. Schmidt (1904b) believed *L. grebnitzkii* to be close to *L. rutteri,* with, for example, flaps on the posterior nostrils common to both species. However, he overlooked available descriptions of *L. callyodon,* a species which also has a raised projection the posterior nostril rim and has other features similar to *L. grebnitzkii.* Burke (1930:63) believed *L. grebnitzkii* to be a color form of *L. callyodon.* Quast and Hall (1972) listed it as a separate species, and one likely to occur in Alaska. Fedorov and Sheiko (2002) treated it as a synonym of *L. callyodon* in their list of fishes of the Commander Islands. Schmidt's (1904) specimen, which was the only known specimen, was lost, so it cannot be reexamined in light of accumulated knowledge on *Liparis.*

Description: Schmidt 1904b:165–167; Burke 1930:64; Lindberg and Krasyukova 1987:382–383.

Figures: Lindberg and Krasyukova 1987, fig. 223, after Schmidt 1904b, pl. 6; holotype (unique), female full of eggs, 83.7 mm TL, Bering Island. Dorsal fins connected by low membrane according to Schmidt (1904b), not completely separate as they appear to be in the illustration. Chernova (1998) stated that the drawing of the type by Schmidt (1904b) should be recognized as a holotype.

Range: Species is known with certainty only from the holotype. Pinchuk (1976), in a study of intertidal fishes of the Commander Islands, collected four specimens he referred to as "*L. callyodon* = *L. grebnitzkii*" and commented that he could not separate these species. Chernova (1998) considered the report of *L. grebnitzkii* from Peter the Great Bay (Sea of Japan) by Pavlenko (1910) to be dubious.

Prognatholiparis ptychomandibularis Orr & Busby, 2001 **wrinklejaw snailfish**

One specimen from Seguam Pass, Aleutian Islands, Alaska.
Bottom at depth of 455 m.

D 37; A 30; C 12; Pec 30; PC 0; Vert 41.

- Preserved specimen pale brown, with scattered melanophores beneath translucent cutaneous layer; darker on nape and at anterior base of dorsal fin; mouth and gill cavity, stomach, peritoneum pale.
- Subcutaneous gelatinous layer absent.
- Body slender, depth at anal fin origin 19% of standard length; head slightly depressed.
- **Mandible projecting anterior to snout**; maxilla ending well anterior to eye; **snout and jaws with longitudinal folds of skin** bracketing pores of the cephalic seismosensory system.
- Eye small, diameter less than 22% of head length.
- Dorsal and anal fins gradually increasing in height anterior to posterior and extending well onto caudal fin; pectoral fin separated by notch into two lobes, lower rays exserted.
- Teeth trilobed.
- Single pore at mandibular symphysis.
- Disk 37% of head length.
- Anus midway between pelvic disk and anal fin origin.
- Gill opening above first pectoral fin ray.
- Length of holotype 88 mm SL.

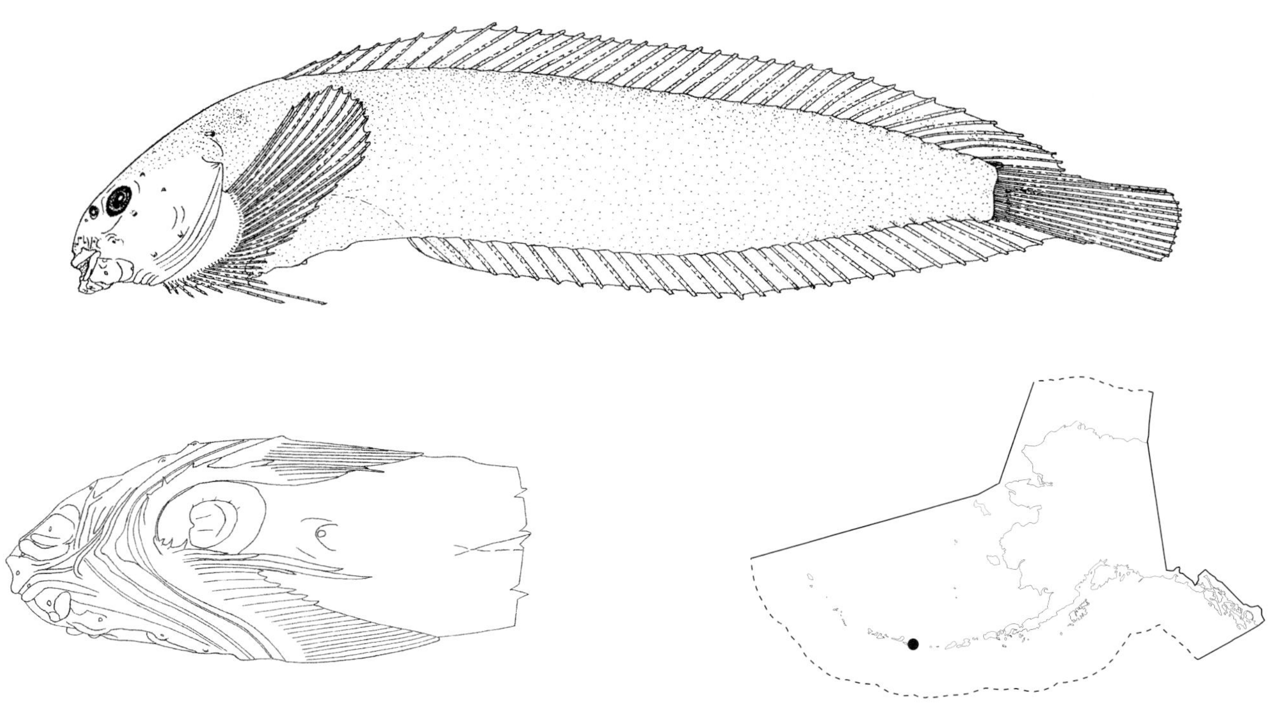

Notes & Sources — *Prognatholiparis ptychomandibularis* Orr & Busby, 2001

Description: Orr and Busby 2001.
Figures: Orr and Busby 2001, figs. 1 and 4; holotype (unique), Aleutian Islands, Alaska (reproduced from copy provided by authors).

Range: Known only from the holotype, taken in Seguam Pass at 52°19'N, 172°45'W, depth 455 m, on 22 Jun. 1997 during triennial groundfish survey of the Aleutian Islands by NMFS, Alaska Fisheries Science Center.

Gyrinichthys minytremus Gilbert, 1896 **minigill snailfish**

One specimen from Bering Sea north of Unalaska Island.

Caught in beam trawl towed at depth of 640 m over mud bottom.

D about 45; C 14; Pec 25.

- Body light brownish gray with minute black spots; peritoneum pale.
- **Head and body strongly depressed**; **head narrow**, a little deeper than wide; **body broad**, wider than depth; tail long, compressed.
- **Head small**, about 15% of total length; snout short, rising abruptly from mouth; eye large, 32% of head length, pupil round.
- Dorsal fin not notched anteriorly; dorsal and anal fins continuous with caudal fin, which is scarcely distinct; anal fin rays extend onto caudal for half its length; **pectoral fin not notched**, lower rays not free.
- Nostril with raised rim in front.
- Disk length almost half (45%) of head length.
- Anus closer to disk than to anal fin (33% of distance from disk to anal fin origin).
- **Gill opening a minute pore** (will not admit a dissecting needle), **high above pectoral fin**.
- Length 72 mm TL.

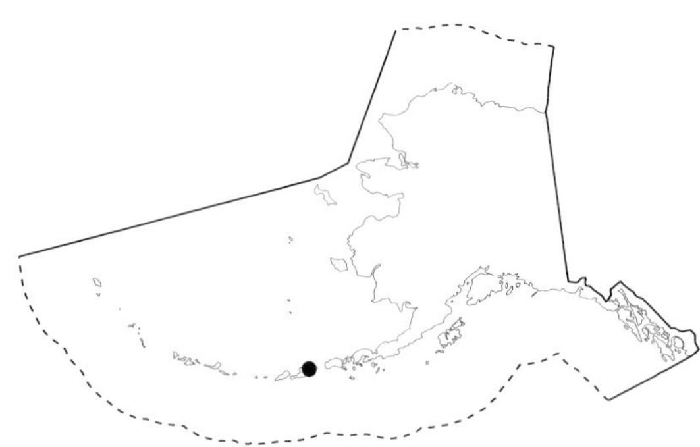

Notes & Sources — *Gyrinichthys minytremus* Gilbert, 1896

Description: Gilbert 1896:444–445; Jordan and Evermann 1898:2137; Burke 1930:152–154. The holotype (USNM 48617), which is the only specimen known, has deteriorated during more than 100 years in alcohol. However, its condition is good enough to allow addition of some information (included above) to the previous descriptions.

Figures: None available of external appearance.

Range: Known from only one specimen, collected from Bering Sea north of Unalaska Island at *Albatross* station 3331, 54°02'N, 166°49'W (Gilbert 1896).

Size: Total length reported by Gilbert (1896) was 67 mm, and by Burke (1930) was 72 mm. Because the specimen is tightly bent, C.W.M. also could not accurately measure its length.

Careproctus candidus Gilbert & Burke, 1912 **bigeye snailfish**

Bering Sea off Attu Island; North Pacific Ocean south of Amukta Pass, Aleutian Islands; Gulf of Alaska at Cook Inlet; western Pacific off southeastern Kamchatka and northern Kuril Islands.

Sand, shell, coarse pebble, and rocky bottoms at depths of 64–400 m.

D 44–48; A 37–39; C 10; Pec 33–37; PC 20.

- Body light reddish dorsally, a little mottled with lighter; whitish ventrally; skin translucent; peritoneum and stomach pale.
- Snout short; profile descends sharply from occiput to front of eye, then more sharply to snout.
- **Eye large, prominent**, 33–36% of head length; **pupil a horizontal slit**.
- **Dorsal fin distinctly but shallowly notched, first 3–5 rays longer than those behind**.
- Nostril in short tube in front of eye.
- Disk flat, well developed, 29–36% of head length.
- Anus close behind disk.
- Gill opening entirely above pectoral fin.
- Length to 106 mm SL.

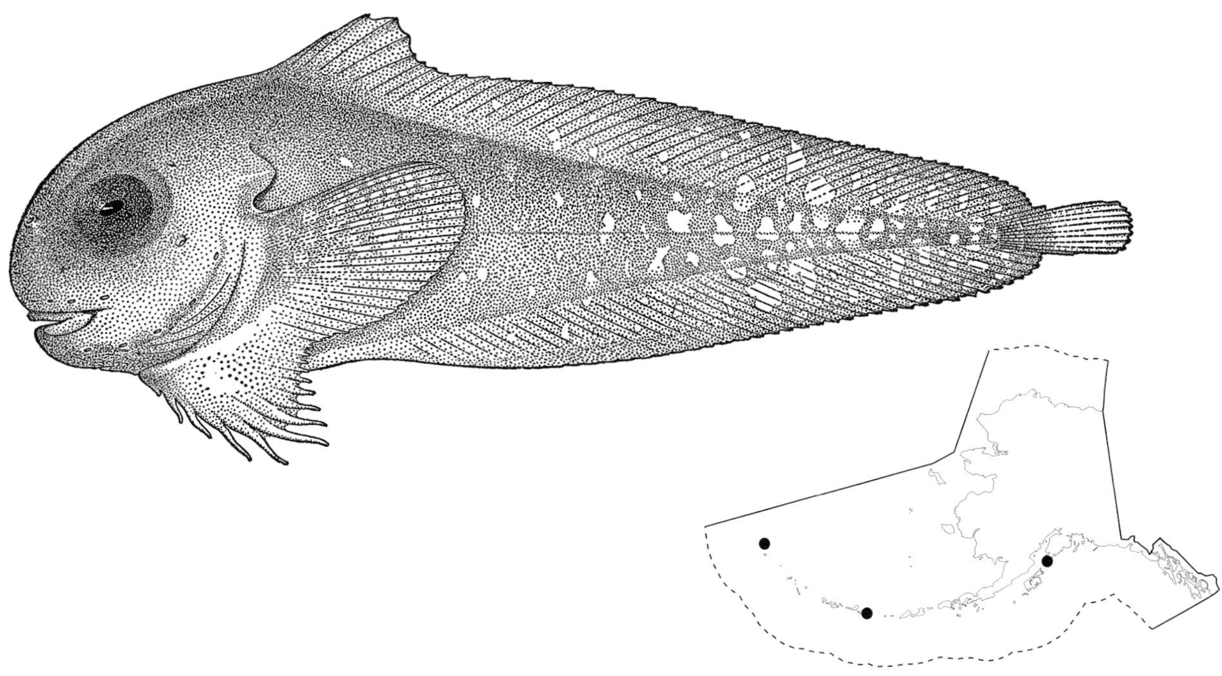

Notes & Sources — *Careproctus candidus* Gilbert & Burke, 1912
Temnocora candida: Burke 1930. Sometimes spelled, incorrectly, *Temnocara*.
Kido (1988:193) returned this species to genus *Careproctus* in his revision of the Liparidae.
Sometimes called crested snailfish (e.g., Sheiko and Fedorov 2000), which is an appropriate name, but bigeye snailfish is the name on the American Fisheries Society–American Society of Ichthyologists and Herpetologists list of names of continental shelf fishes (Robins et al. 1991a).

Description: Gilbert and Burke 1912a:77–78; Burke 1930: 146–147. USNM 74527 (2 paratypes, 66–69 mm TL), USNM 135635 (106 mm SL); AB 64-715 (52 mm TL). The largest specimen (USNM 135635) is more elongate and much less elevated at the nape than in the other, smaller specimens and in the holotype (illustrated above), and may be more typical of adults.

Figure: Gilbert and Burke 1912a, fig. 22; holotype, USNM 74384, 73 mm TL, off Attu Island, Bering Sea.

Range: Species was described by Gilbert and Burke (1912a) from four specimens taken at *Albatross* station 4784, off East Cape, Attu Island, at 52°56'N, 173°26'E, depth 247 m, over a bottom of coarse pebbles. Quast and Hall (1972) reported that a specimen from Cook Inlet was in the ABL collection; this is AB 64-715, taken off south tip of Kenai Peninsula at 58°52'N, 152°31'W, depth 170–197 m, shell bottom. USNM 135635, a specimen labeled "*Liparis* n. sp.," is *C. candidus* (M. S. Busby, pers. comm., 9 Jan. 1998). The specimen is in fair condition, with damaged gill openings and missing most of the epidermis, but character states confirming identification as *C. candidus* can be discerned; e.g., anus close behind disk and absence of pseudobranchs confirm it is a *Careproctus,* and elongate anterior dorsal fin rays, large eye (33% HL), and well-developed disk (35.5% HL) indicate it is *C. candidus* (examined by C.W.M. in 1998 and 1999). It was collected in 1893 from the Pacific Ocean south of Amukta Pass, Aleutian Islands, at *Albatross* station 3480, 52°06'N, 171°45'W, depth 518 m, on a bottom of black sand, coral, and rocks. The extremes of depth given at the top of this page and extension of the known range to Russian coasts are from V. V. Fedorov (unpubl. data via B. A. Sheiko, pers. comm., 12 May 1998).

Size: USNM 135635. Burke (1930) gave 76 mm TL for the largest of the paratypes from Attu Island.

Careproctus zachirus Kido, 1985 **blacktip snailfish**

Amchitka Pass, central Aleutian Islands; Pacific Ocean off southeastern Kamchatka and northern Kuril Islands.

Bottom at depths of 214–850 m.

D 51–53; A 43–45; C 11; Pec 28–31; PC 26–31; Vert 56–58.

- Body pinkish; **posterior part of upper lobe of pectoral fin black; dorsal and anal fins with black submarginal band** joining on caudal fin; mouth and gill cavity, peritoneum, stomach, and pyloric caeca pale.
- Snout slightly projecting.
- Opercular flap projection absent.
- Anterior dorsal and anal fin ray tips buried, posterior tips free; **upper pectoral fin lobe noticeably elongate**.
- Nostril in prominent tube.
- Anterior mandibular pores separate.
- Anus immediately behind disk.
- Gill opening entirely above pectoral fin.
- Length to 252 mm SL.

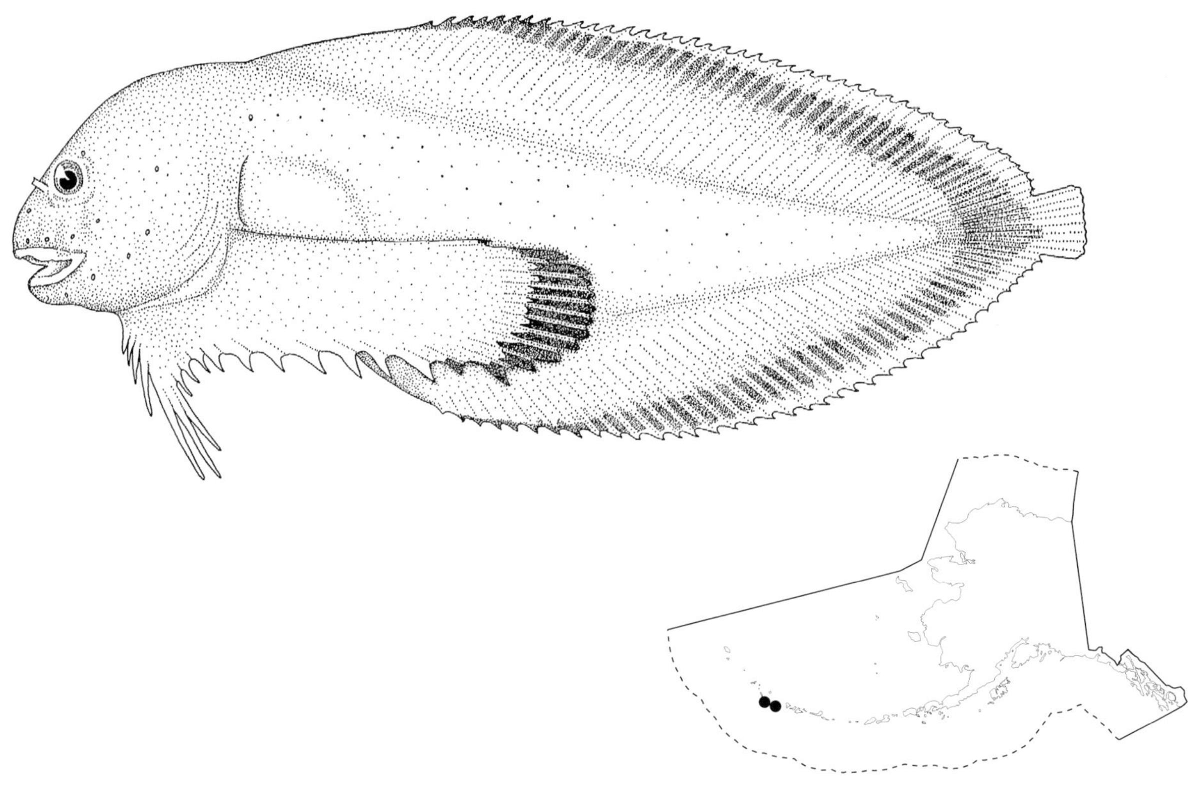

Notes & Sources — *Careproctus zachirus* Kido, 1985

Description: Kido 1985:9–10.

Figure: Kido 1985, fig. 5; holotype, HUMZ 88338, 252 mm SL, near Unalga Island, Aleutian Islands.

Range: Known in Alaska from the four type specimens, which were taken at two localities in Amchitka Pass: 51°35'N, 179°22'W, near Unalga Island; and 51°32'N, 179°45'E, near Amchitka Island. Depths of capture were 300–434 m (Kido 1985). Tokranov (2000a) reported *C. zachirus* at depths of 214–800 m off the northern Kuril Islands in 1995 and 1996. Orlov (1998a) and Sheiko and Fedorov (2000) reported it off southeastern Kamchatka as well, and the latter authors gave a maximum depth of 850 m.

Careproctus canus Kido, 1985 **gray snailfish**

Central and western Aleutian Islands.

Bottom at depths of 244–434 m.

D 51–63; A 43–46; C 11; Pec 33–36; PC 18–24; Vert 55–58.

- **Body uniformly gray**, transparent; **posterior margins of dorsal, anal, and caudal fins dark**; mouth, gill cavity, peritoneum, and stomach pale.
- Snout slightly projecting.
- **Opercular flap projection absent**.
- Anterior rays of dorsal and anal fins buried in gelatinous subcutaneous layer; pectoral fin very shallowly notched.
- Nostril in prominent tube.
- Anterior pair of mandibular pores with a common opening.
- Gill opening entirely above pectoral fin.
- Length to 159 mm SL.

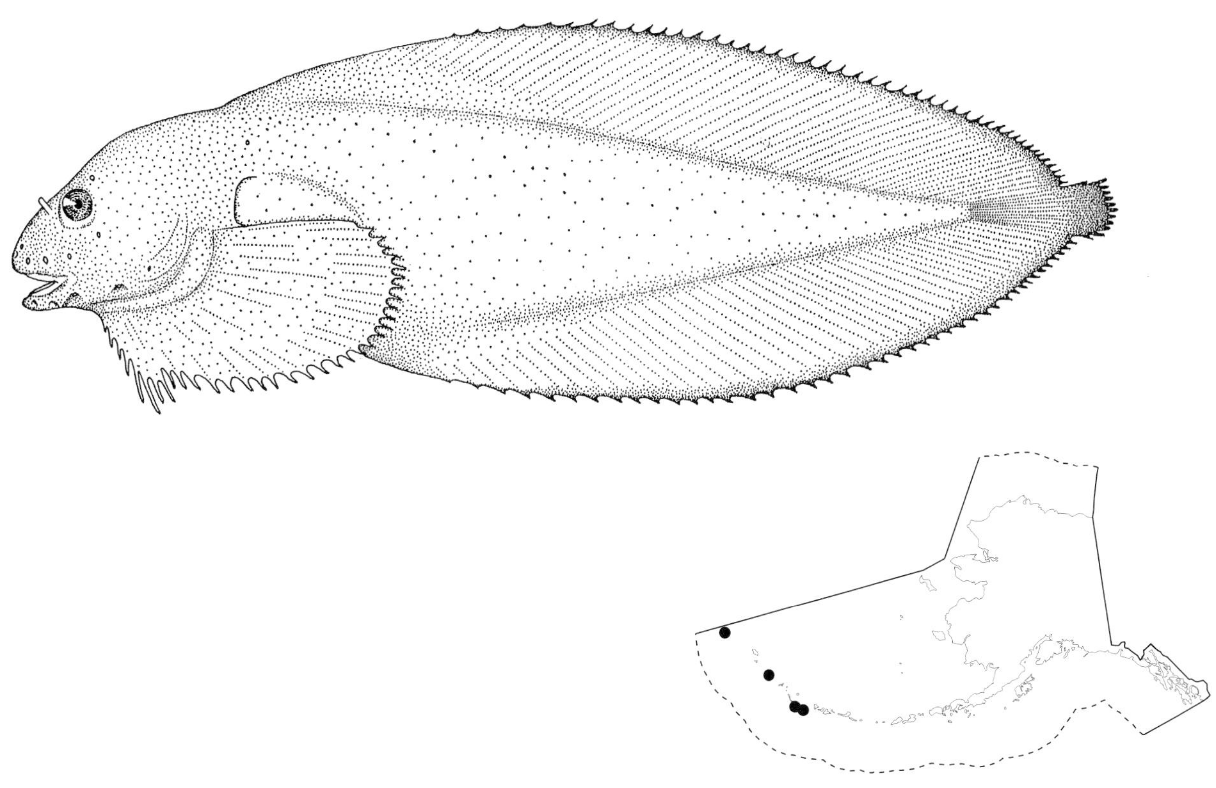

Notes & Sources — *Careproctus canus* Kido, 1985

Description: Kido 1985:6–9.

Figure: Kido 1985, fig. 2; holotype, HUMZ 88339, 154 mm SL, from near Unalga Island, Aleutian Islands.

Range: Known from four specimens taken at four localities in Alaska: 51°35'N, 179°22'W, near Unalga Island; 51°32'N, 179°45'E, near Amchitka Island; 52°16'N, 175°52'E, near Buldir Island; and 52°54'N, 169°50'E, between Medny and Attu islands.

Careproctus pycnosoma Gilbert & Burke, 1912 **stout snailfish**

One confirmed record from Bering Sea northwest of Umnak Island, and one off Simushir Island, Kuril Islands; unconfirmed record from Seguam Pass, Aleutian Islands.

Bottom at depths of 419–610 m.

D 42–45; A 36–39; C 11–12; Pec 37–39; PC 17; Vert 46–49.

- **Body uniformly red** when fresh, pale in alcohol; peritoneum, stomach, and pyloric caeca pale.
- Body short, robust, deepest at anus; **posterior part of body deeper and thicker than that of other *Careproctus*.**
- Snout blunt, broad, not projecting.
- Shallow notch in anterior part of dorsal fin present or absent; **anterior dorsal and anal fin ray tips free, not buried in gelatinous tissue**.
- Nostril in well-developed tube, level with upper half of eye; posterior margin raised into a flap.
- Head pores prominent; **small flap in front of some of the head pores.**
- Anterior pair of mandibular pores separate, not in same pit.
- Anus slightly nearer to disk than to anal fin.
- Gill opening entirely above pectoral fin.
- Length to 79 mm SL.

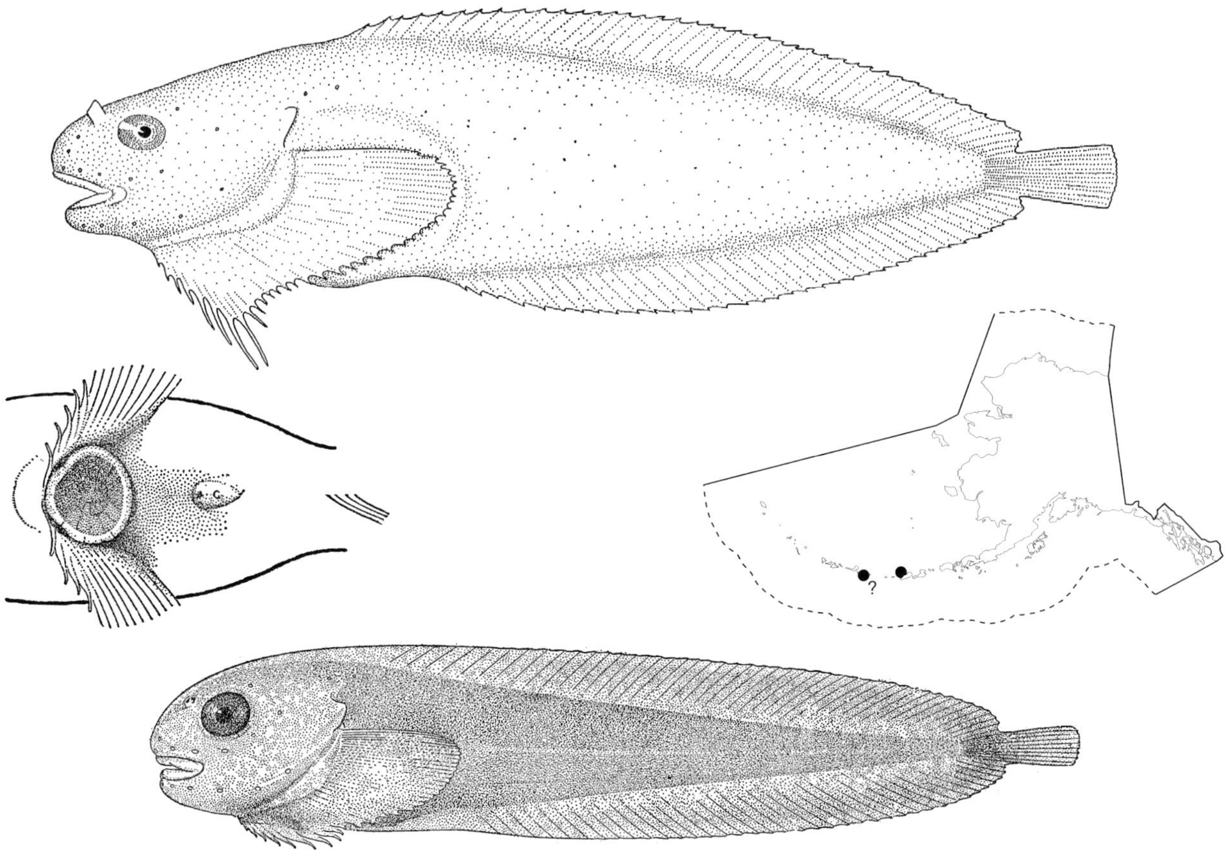

Notes & Sources — *Careproctus pycnosoma* Gilbert & Burke, 1912

Similar to *Allocareproctus jordani* (Burke, 1930) from the Kuril Islands. However, K. Kido (pers. comm., 17 Feb. 1998) maintains they are distinguishable by the color of the peritoneum and, furthermore, that even if they should be the same species the valid name is *C. pycnosoma*. He does not think the genus *Allocareproctus* (Pitruk and Fedorov 1993a) is warranted. The species name, *C. pycnosoma* Gilbert & Burke, 1912 has priority by date of publication over *C. jordani* Burke, 1930 (a new name for *C. gilberti* Jordan & Thompson, 1914), and by page over another possible junior synonym, *C. curilanus* Gilbert & Burke, 1912.

Description: Gilbert and Burke 1912b:372; Burke 1930:108–109; Kido 1985:14–16. Gilbert and Burke's (1912b) and Burke's (1930) descriptions were based on an immature individual (39 mm SL).

Figures: Upper: Kido 1985, fig. 8; HUMZ 88509, 79 mm SL, northwest of Umnak Island. Lower, including ventral view: Gilbert and Burke 1912b, pl. 46-3 and fig. 14; holotype, 46 mm TL, off Simushir Island, Kuril Islands.

Range: Kido (1985) reported the second record for the species and the only confirmed Alaskan specimen, taken northwest of Umnak Island at 53°15'N, 169°03'W, depth 596–610 m. Seventeen specimens taken by bottom trawl farther west in the Aleutian Islands in Seguam Pass at depth of 450 m in 1997 could belong to this species; study is ongoing (M. S. Busby, pers. comm., 19 Jan. 2000).

Careproctus ovigerum (Gilbert, 1896) **abyssal snailfish**

Queen Charlotte Islands, British Columbia, to Oregon.
Bottom at depths of 1,920–2,904 m.

D 43–45; A 34–37; C 10–12; Pec 31–34; PC 16–19; Vert 47–49.

- Light pink, inconspicuously mottled with light brown; fin edges blackish; mouth and gill cavities, stomach, pyloric caeca pale; peritoneum blackish or mottled.
- **Very large mouth** with numerous large, stout, sharp, recurved teeth; snout short, not projecting.
- Dorsal fin unnotched or slightly notched; pectoral and caudal fins large, pectoral rays usually 33, caudal rays usually 11; pectoral deeply notched.
- Wide space between pores nearest mandibular symphysis.
- **Disk large, length 32–38% of head length.**
- Anus in posterior position, distance from disk about same as disk diameter.
- Gill opening extending down in front of about 4 pectoral rays.
- **Pyloric caeca on right side of body**.
- Length to 431 mm SL.

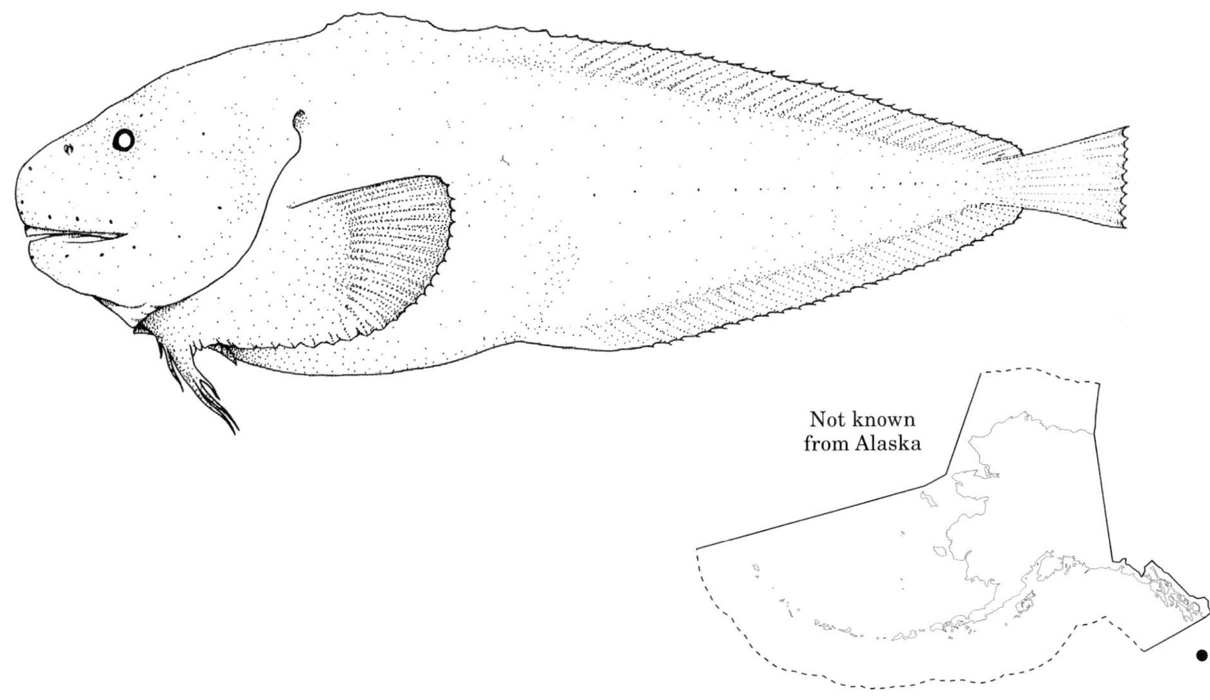

Notes & Sources — *Careproctus ovigerum* (Gilbert, 1896)
Bathyphasma ovigerum Gilbert, 1896
Compared to other liparids from the same depth, *C. ovigerum* is a giant (Stein 1978).

Description: Gilbert 1896:448; Gilbert and Burke 1912a: 131–132; Stein 1978:11–13.

Figure: Stein 1978, fig. 6A; CAS 32345, 431 mm SL, off Tatoosh, Washington.

Range: Hart 1973, Stein 1978. Nearest to Alaska is the holotype, collected off the Queen Charlotte Islands, British Columbia, at *Albatross* station 3342, 52°39'N, 132°38'W, depth 2,904 m. The RBCM has another specimen from British Columbia (A. E. Peden, pers. comm., 5 Sep. 1996), taken father south: BCPM 979-11101-3, collected on 17 May 1979 west of Vancouver Island at 48°37'N, 126°57'W, at depth of 1,920 m (K. Sendall, pers. comm., 25 Mar. 1999). The 1,920-m depth is the shallowest record; others are from 2,510 m or deeper.

Careproctus abbreviatus Burke, 1930 **short snailfish**

One specimen south of Alaska Peninsula; two specimens recorded from northern Sea of Okhotsk.

Mud, sand, and gravel bottoms at depths of 325 m (Sea of Okhotsk) and 1,143 m (south of Alaska Peninsula).

D 39–43; A 32–34; Pec 21–23.

- Body light pinkish; fins brownish toward posterior end; mouth and gill cavity pale; peritoneum and stomach nearly black.
- Snout truncate, deep.
- **Low fin ray counts**; pectoral notch shallow, lower rays about half free.
- Nostril in a short tube directly in front of eye.
- **Disk very deeply cupped** (bell-shaped), central portion hidden in pit formed by the thick, stiff margin.
- Anus a short distance behind disk.
- Gill opening entirely above pectoral fin.
- Length to 100 mm TL.

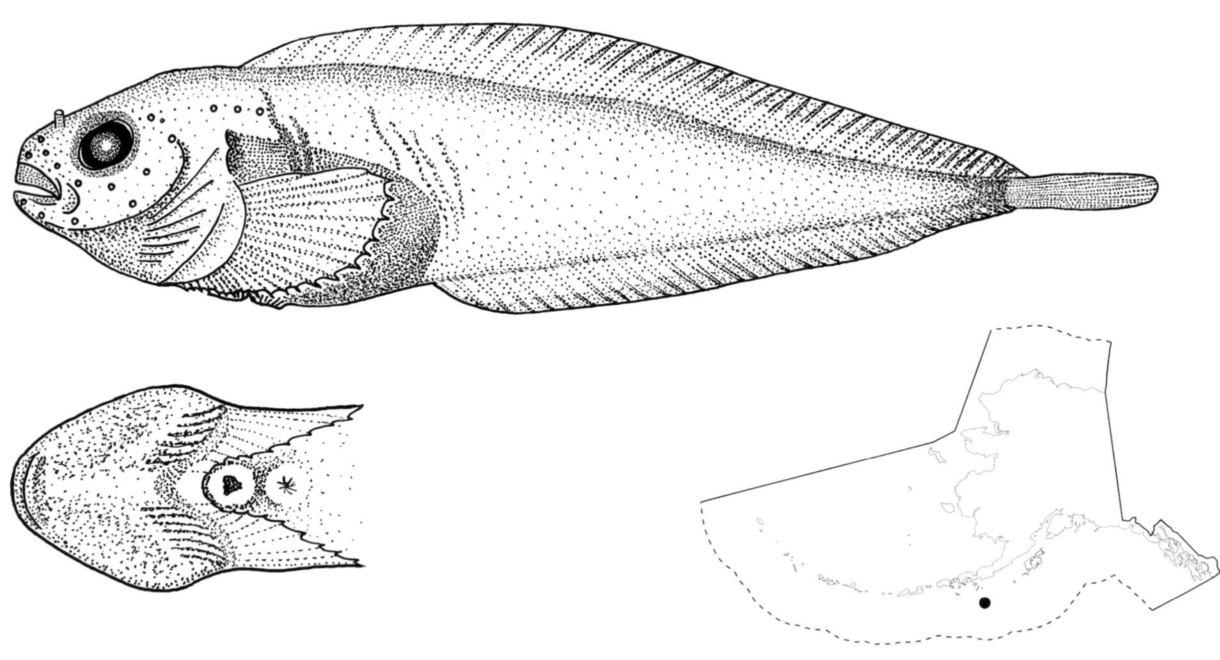

Notes & Sources — *Careproctus abbreviatus* Burke, 1930

Burke (1930) considered *C. abbreviatus* to most closely resemble *C. colletti* in general appearance and shape of disk, but that *C. abbreviatus* was readily distinguishable by its smaller number of fin rays from *C. colletti* and others with which it might be confused.

Description: Burke 1930:128–129; Schmidt 1950:207–208. Schmidt's (1950) specimens, which were larger (female, 100 mm TL; male, 69 mm TL) than Burke's (1930) small specimen (53 mm TL), had small, smooth tubercles covering the body, more densely distributed in the male.

Figures: Russian Academy of Sciences, Zoological Institute, St. Petersburg, artist O. S. Voskoboinikova, Oct. 1999; ZIN 24487, female, 86 mm SL, 100 mm TL, Sea of Okhotsk, one of the specimens described by Schmidt (1950). Free portions of lower pectoral rays missing.

Range: The only Alaskan record is the holotype (unique; Burke 1930), from south of the Alaska Peninsula at *Albatross* station 3338, 54°19'N, 159°40'W, depth 1,143 m, on a bottom of mud and sand. The range to southeastern Alaska given by Wilimovsky (1954, 1958) lacks documentation and we assume it is a mistake, with any voucher specimen subsequently having been identified as some other species. *Careproctus abbreviatus* was recorded by Schmidt (1950) from the northern part of the Sea of Okhotsk at a depth of 325 m over a bottom of gravel and ooze.

Careproctus rastrinus Gilbert & Burke, 1912 **salmon snailfish**

Bering Sea to southeastern Alaska and to Japan and Okhotsk seas.

Soft sand, silt, and mud bottoms at depths of 55–913 m.

D 53–62; A 48–54; C 8–9; Pec 31–38; PC 16–35; Vert 58–67.

- Bright yellowish pink to "salmon"; skin transparent; peritoneum pale; stomach pale to dusky.
- Profile ascends steeply from blunt snout; body deep, about 25–33% or more of standard length.
- Anterior dorsal and anal fin rays buried in gelatinous tissue; pectoral deeply notched, lower rays typically longer than upper and partly free.
- Nostril tube short but prominent.
- Anterior pair of mandibular pores separate.
- Disk 11–20% of head length, triangular.
- Anus close behind disk.
- **Gill opening extending in front of 1–6 pectoral rays, rarely entirely above pectoral fin.**
- Length to 490 mm SL.

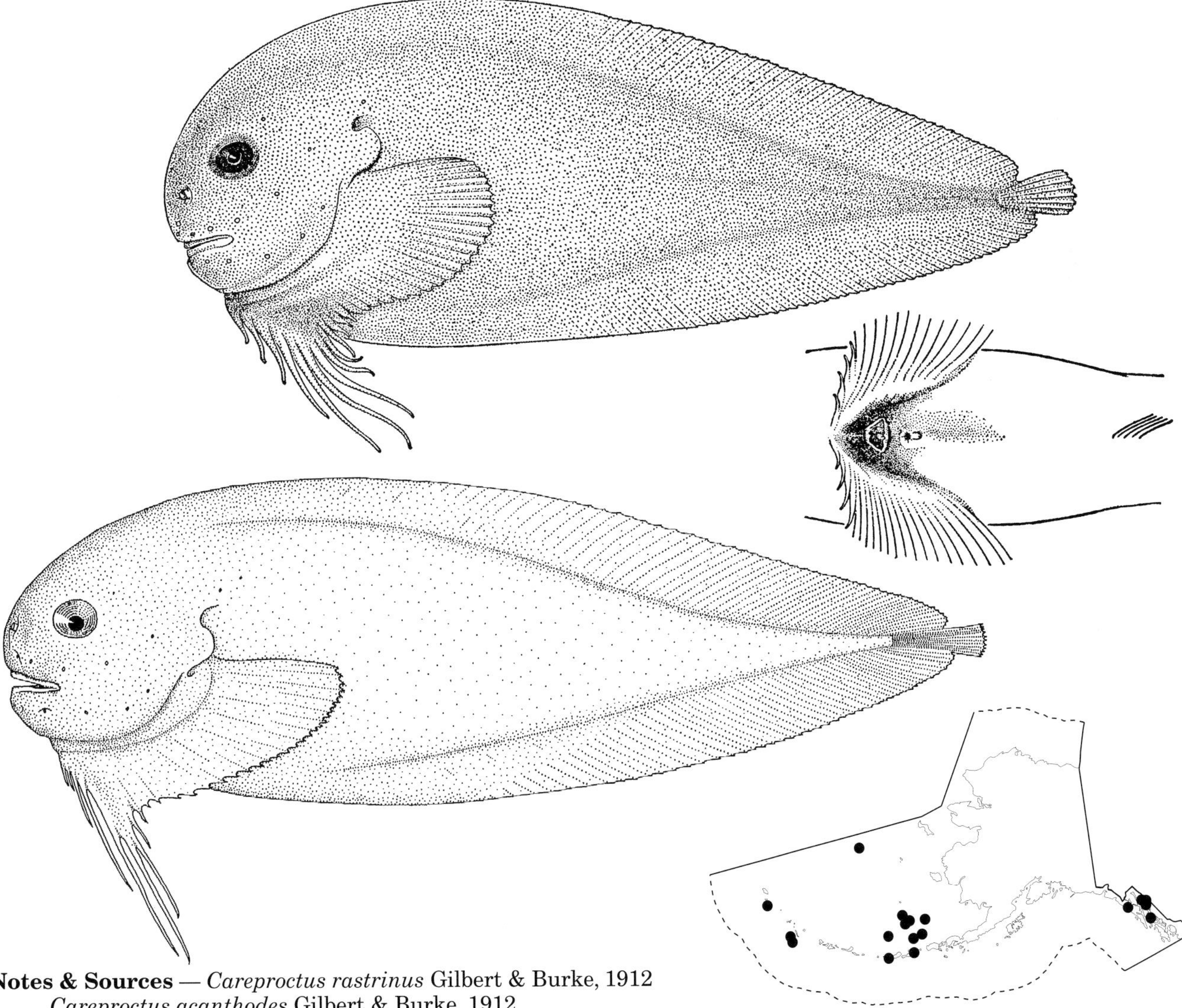

Notes & Sources — *Careproctus rastrinus* Gilbert & Burke, 1912
Careproctus acanthodes Gilbert & Burke, 1912
Careproctus pellucidus Gilbert & Burke, 1912

Description: Burke 1930:136–137; Kido 1988:217–220.

Figures: Upper, with ventral view: Gilbert and Burke 1912b, pl. 43-1, fig. 3; type, USNM 73331, 280 mm TL. Lower: Kido 1988, fig. 48; HUMZ 92882, 303 mm SL. Both Sea of Okhotsk.

Range: The following are identified as *C. rastrinus* but some could be referable to *C. scottae,* if the latter is a valid species (see Notes for *C. scottae*). At ABL: several lots from southeastern Alaska and Bering Sea, on soft bottoms; sometimes on display in ABL aquarium, often taken in crab pots. CAS: south and north of Aleutian Islands (CAS 45100, 45106, 47483, 47690, 47755, 47758). UW 22521: north of Akun Island. SIO: eastern Aleutian Islands (SIO 69-132, 94-171, 94-180). Northernmost is USNM 325590, 59°12'N, 178°26'W. Depth range: 55 m, Auke Bay (AB 68-2); 913 m, Sea of Okhotsk (Dudnik and Dolganov 1992).

Size: Tokranov 2000b: size range in 1,768 specimens collected off southeastern Kamchatka and northern Kuril islands in the 1990s was 11–49 cm SL.

Careproctus scottae Chapman & DeLacy, 1934

peachskin snailfish

Southeastern Alaska.

Bottom at depths of about 8–183 m.

D 52–56; A 47–51; C 8–9; Pec 32–34; PC 15–18.

- Pink to pinkish yellow; body translucent; mouth, gill cavity, peritoneum, and stomach pale.
- Body shorter and deeper than usual in the genus, deepest just in front of dorsal fin origin.
- Snout short, rising abruptly from the mouth.
- Anterior dorsal and anal fin rays buried in gelatinous tissue; pectoral fin deeply notched, rays of lower lobe long and partly free.
- Nostril tube projecting.
- Disk 10–18% of head length, triangular.
- Anus close behind disk.
- **Gill opening entirely above pectoral fin or extending ventrally in front of 1–3 rays.**
- Length to 227 mm SL.

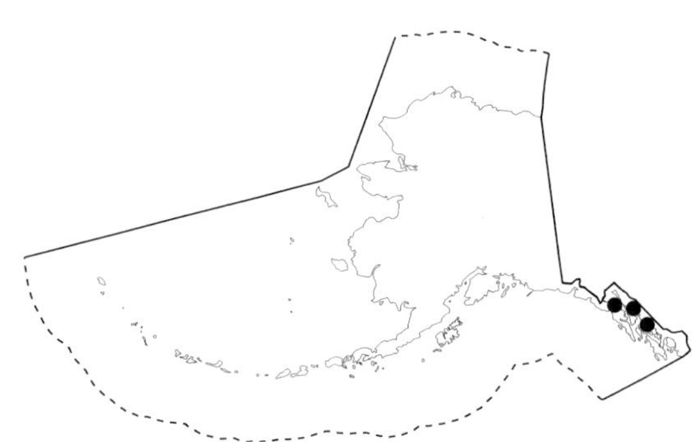

Notes & Sources — *Careproctus scottae* Chapman & DeLacy, 1934

Probably synonymous with *C. rastrinus*. Character states given as diagnostic for *C. scottae* by Chapman and DeLacy (1934) overlap with or are within the range of those for *C. rastrinus*. For example, they gave pectoral ray counts of 32–34 for *C. scottae* versus 34–37 for *C. rastrinus*, but counts subsequently reported (e.g., Kido 1988) have increased the range for *C. rastrinus* to 31–38; the lower rays of the pelvic fins, diagnosed by Chapman and DeLacy (1934) as not extending to the anal fin in *C. scottae*, also fall short of the anal fin in some *C. rastrinus* (e.g., Kido 1988); and the gill opening does not reach the pectoral fin in some *C. rastrinus* (Kido 1988), whereas this condition was believed to be the norm for *C. scottae* but not to occur in *C. rastrinus*. Chapman and DeLacy (1934) believed *C. rastrinus* to be confined to Asian waters, but now there are many specimens in collections identified as *C. rastrinus* from the eastern Bering Sea and southeastern Alaska. C.W.M. could not differentiate Alaskan specimens identified as *C. rastrinus* at the NMFS Auke Bay Laboratory from the types of *C. scottae* (from southeastern Alaska) at the Smithsonian Institution, NMNH. Types of *C. scottae* should be compared to types and other material of *C. rastrinus* from Japan and other localities, to determine if the species are synonymous and, if they are not, to refer specimens correctly and define range of each in Alaska. Vogt (1973) suggested that *C. scottae* is synonymous with *C. pellucidus* from Japan but, since then, Kido (1988) placed *C. pellucidus* in the synonymy of *C. rastrinus*.

Description: Chapman and DeLacy 1934.

Figures: Illustration of adequately documented specimen not available.

Range: Published records comprise the holotype and 10 paratypes collected in 1933 by shrimp trawlers off Petersburg and from Thomas Bay near Petersburg at depths to 183 m (Chapman and DeLacy 1934). Museum catalogs list the following additional lots: NMC 67-100 and 67-101, Glacier Bay, 93–135 m, collected in 1952 by shrimp trawls; NMC 67-98, Tracy Arm, 27 m, 1958, crab pot; NMC 67-99, Thomas Bay, 8–15 m, 1960; UW 3666, Petersburg, 1934; UW 15761, Glacier Bay, 1950. Kessler (1985) reported that *C. scottae* is "uncommon north and south of Alaska Peninsula" but the description provided (e.g., gill opening down to pectoral ray 6) is appropriate for *C. rastrinus*—or the species are synonymous. Allen and Smith (1988) stated in their review of geographic ranges of northeastern North Pacific demersal fish species based on NMFS survey data that good field identification characters to distinguish among *C. rastrinus, C. scottae,* and *C. phasma* were lacking and could not be used to determine range from the NMFS data.

Size: Chapman and DeLacy 1934. Kessler (1985) gave maximum length of 28 cm but this could refer to *C. rastrinus*.

Careproctus colletti Gilbert, 1896 — Alaska snailfish

Bering Sea to northern Gulf of Alaska and to Japan and Okhotsk seas.

Mud and sand bottoms at depths of 64–1,350 m; Alaskan records are from depths greater than 260 m.

D 51–58; A 47–52; C 8–9; Pec 25–31; PC 10–18; Vert 59–65.

- Body reddish black, finely dotted with black; dorsal, anal, and caudal fins black posteriorly; lips, mouth, and gill cavity dusky; **peritoneum black**; stomach pale.
- Snout deep, bluntly rounded, slightly projecting.
- **Teeth long, recurved, lanceolate**.
- **Lower pectoral rays greatly elongate** and mostly free, equal to head length or greater.
- Disk triangular.
- Anus close behind disk.
- Gill opening entirely above pectoral fin.
- Length to 397 mm SL.

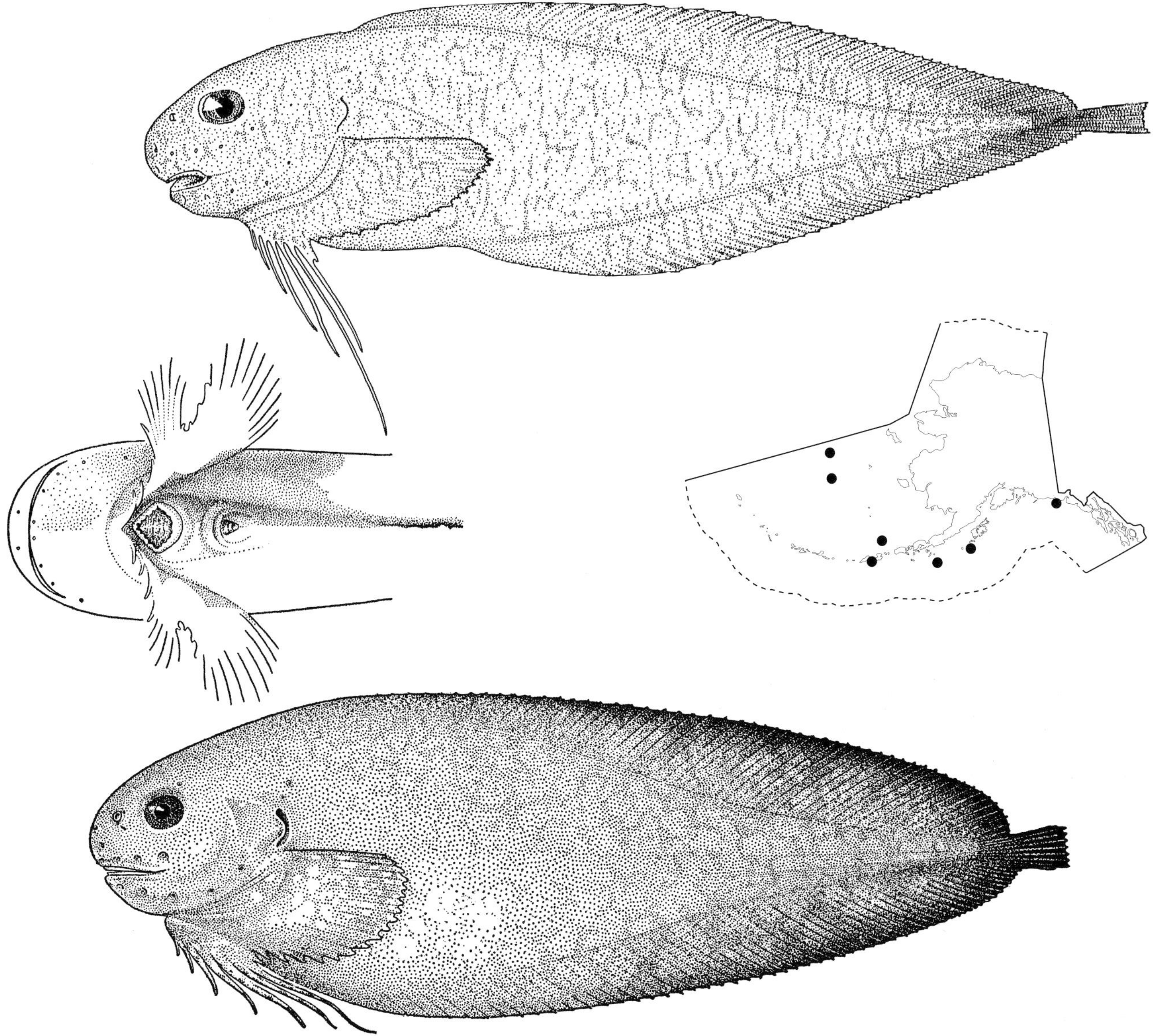

Notes & Sources — *Careproctus colletti* Gilbert, 1896
Careproctus entargyreus Gilbert and Burke, 1912

Description: Burke 1930:142–145; Kido 1988:224–227.

Figures: Upper: Kido 1988, fig. 52; 194 mm SL, Sea of Okhotsk. Lower two: Gilbert and Burke 1912b, pl. 46-1 and fig. 12; approximately 220 mm TL, off Hokkaido.

Range: Gilbert 1896 (syntypes): south of Alaska Peninsula, *Albatross* station 3338, 54°19'N, 159°40'W, bottom of green mud and sand. Burke 1930: station 3325, 53°37'N, 167°50'W, green mud. Kido 1988: 55°10'N, 167°00'W, and several localities within 58°32'N–60°48'N, 176°06'W–179°11'W. NMC 67-89: 80 km southwest of Trinity Islands. A specimen in ABL museum is easternmost Gulf of Alaska record: AB 93-24, 70 mm TL, 59°13'N, 141°25'W, depth 327 m.

Careproctus furcellus Gilbert & Burke, 1912 — emarginate snailfish

Bering Sea and Pacific Ocean off Aleutian Islands to Gulf of Alaska; and to Sea of Okhotsk and Pacific Ocean off Kuril Islands to Hokkaido.

Bottom at depths of 98–1,270 m, usually taken at 175–750 m.

D 61–65; A 54–59; C 10; Pec 32–37; PC 33–49; Vert 67–71.

- **Body pinkish**; caudal fin and posterior portions of body and dorsal, anal, and pectoral fins black; mouth and gill cavity dusky; peritoneum black; stomach and pyloric caeca pale.
- Body tapering gradually to caudal fin but not strongly attenuate.
- **Snout projecting**.
- **Caudal fin slightly emarginate, nearly truncate when spread; pectoral fin notch absent or barely discernible, anterior rays free only at tips**; pectoral base nearly horizontal.
- Pores at mandibular symphysis widely separated.
- Disk triangular, length 12–20% of head length.
- Anus close behind disk.
- Gill opening entirely above pectoral fin.
- Length to 540 mm SL.

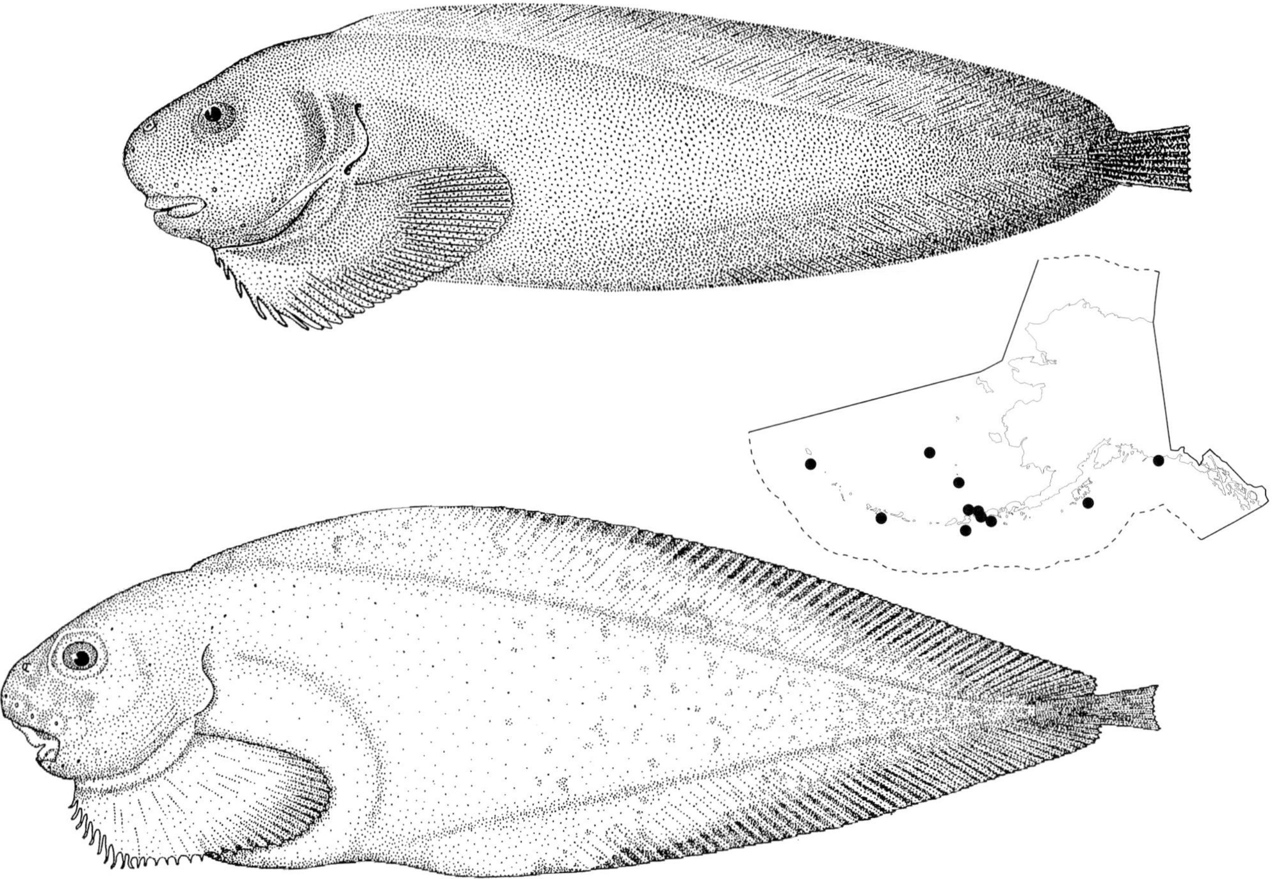

Notes & Sources — *Careproctus furcellus* Gilbert & Burke, 1912

Often confused with *Careproctus cypselurus,* but distinguishable by the characters in bold type above. In occasional specimens the caudal fin is almost falcate, approaching the weakly falcate condition seen in some *C. cypselurus.* The photograph given for *C. cypselurus* in Kessler (1985:99) is probably of *C. furcellus.*

Description: Gilbert and Burke 1912a:80–81; Burke 1930: 126; Kido 1983:378–380, 1988:211–213.

Figures: Upper: Gilbert and Burke 1912a, fig. 25; type, USNM 74387, 130 mm TL, off Agattu Island. Lower: Kido 1983, fig. 6; HUMZ 92716, 394 mm SL, from off Abashiri, Okhotsk coast of Hokkaido.

Range: Alaskan records: Gilbert and Burke (1912a), *Albatross* station 4781, off southwest coast of Agattu Island, 52°14'N, 174°13'E. Kido (1983): southeast of Atka Island, 51°44'N, 175°33'W; north of Unalaska Island, 54°20'N, 167°21'W; central Bering Sea, 57°51'N, 173°58'W. At Auke Bay Laboratory: AB 63-117, off Cape Yakataga; AB 65-53, Albatross Bank; AB 68-132, Davidson Bank; AB 68-90, 53°18'N, 166°20'W; AB 68-566, 54°24'N, 165°47'W; AB 72-61, 54°38'N, 165°42'W. At NMNH: USNM 325459, 58°20'N, 175°02'W; USNM 325518, 56°00'N, 169°14'W; USNM 325581, 54°30'N, 166°39'W; depths 490–740 m. Dudnik and Dolganov (1992) reported maximum depth of 1,270 m; previously recorded to 882 m by Gilbert and Burke (1912a).

Size: Tokranov 2000b: size range in 1,901 specimens taken off southeastern Kamchatka and northern Kuril Islands in the 1990s was 19–54 cm SL.

Careproctus cypselurus (Jordan & Gilbert, 1898) **falcate snailfish**

Eastern Bering Sea; Pacific Ocean off British Columbia and Washington; Oregon, record uncertain; Sea of Okhotsk and Pacific Ocean off Kuril Islands to northern Honshu.

Bottom at depths of 214–1,993 m; most specimens taken at 700–1,600 m.

D 58–64; A 52–58; C 10; Pec 32–40; PC 29–49; Vert 64–70.

- **Purplish indigo when fresh, with red anteriorly; median fins black, especially posteriorly; pectoral fin dusky overall**; mouth and gill cavity dusky; peritoneum black; stomach and caeca pale.
- Body elongate and attenuate, tapering gradually to caudal fin.
- **Snout blunt, not projecting**, or only slightly projecting.
- **Caudal fin falcate**; pectoral slightly notched or not notched, **anterior pectoral rays free for much of length**; pectoral base nearly horizontal.
- Pores at mandibular symphysis widely separated.
- Disk triangular; length 13–17% of head length.
- Anus close behind disk.
- Gill opening above pectoral fin base but large, due to low insertion of pectoral fin.
- Length to 374 mm SL.

Notes & Sources — *Careproctus cypselurus* (Jordan & Gilbert in Jordan & Evermann, 1898)
Prognurus cypselurus Jordan & Gilbert in Jordan & Evermann, 1898
Often confused with *C. melanurus* and *C. furcellus*. *Careproctus cypselurus* is darker, and has more black on the median fins. The strongly falcate caudal fin is a good character but the tail is often damaged.

Description: Jordan and Evermann 1898:2866–2867; Burke 1930:127–128; Stein 1978:16–17; Kido in Masuda et al. 1984:339; Kido 1988:213–215; Peden 1997ms.

Figures: Upper: Jordan and Gilbert 1899, pl. 77; holotype, USNM 48232, 211 mm TL, Bering Sea off Bogoslof Island. Lower: Royal British Columbia Museum, artist P. Drukker-Brammall, May 1971; BCPM 985-476, Pacific off Vancouver Island.

Range: Previous Alaskan records: Jordan and Gilbert (1899), Bering Sea at station 3644 [*not* 3634], off Bogoslof Island; and Kido (1988), central Bering Sea, 58°34'N, 175°05'W. I (C.W.M.) examined USNM 325451 (1; 160 mm SL), from 59°41'N, 178°47'W, depth 900–930 m, and USNM 325453 and 325584 (1 each; 187 and 162 mm SL), from 59°26'N, 178°29'W, depth 700–820 m; collected in 1979. NMC 67-90, a specimen from 60°36'N, 178°56'W, depth 250–400 m, was identified as *C. cypselurus* by A. E. Peden in Aug. 1993. Specimens reported by Quast and Hall (1972) from Gulf of Alaska were later referred by Quast to *C. furcellus* (ABL records). Peden (1997ms) reported the first British Columbia record, a specimen (shown above) captured in a black cod trap west of Vancouver Island. Grinols' (1965:147) Oregon record is unverified (Stein 1978). Depth range: Kido 1988, Dudnik and Dolganov 1992, Tokranov 2000a.

Size: Kido 1988.

Careproctus melanurus Gilbert, 1892 **blacktail snailfish**

Southern Bering Sea and Pacific Ocean south of Aleutian Islands to Baja California; Pacific Ocean off northern Honshu.

Bottom at depths of 89–2,286 m, usually taken at depths greater than about 450 m.

D 52–66; A 47–55; C 10; Pec 27–33; PC 36; Vert 57–68.

- **Pink or rose red**; **caudal fin and posterior portions of dorsal and anal fins black**; **medial side of pectoral fin black**; lips and front of snout and chin often blackish; mouth, gill cavity, and peritoneum black; stomach and pyloric caeca pale.
- Body tapering rapidly, **caudal region stout**.
- **Snout blunt, not projecting**.
- **Dorsal and anal fins gradually extend onto caudal, forming bluntly pointed tail**; pectoral fin slightly notched or not, anterior rays free; pectoral fin base horizontal.
- Anterior mandibular pores close together.
- **Disk oval**, longer than wide; disk length about 14–16% of head length, usually smaller than eye.
- Anus close behind disk.
- Gill opening above pectoral fin base but large, due to low insertion of pectoral fin.
- Length to 350 mm SL.

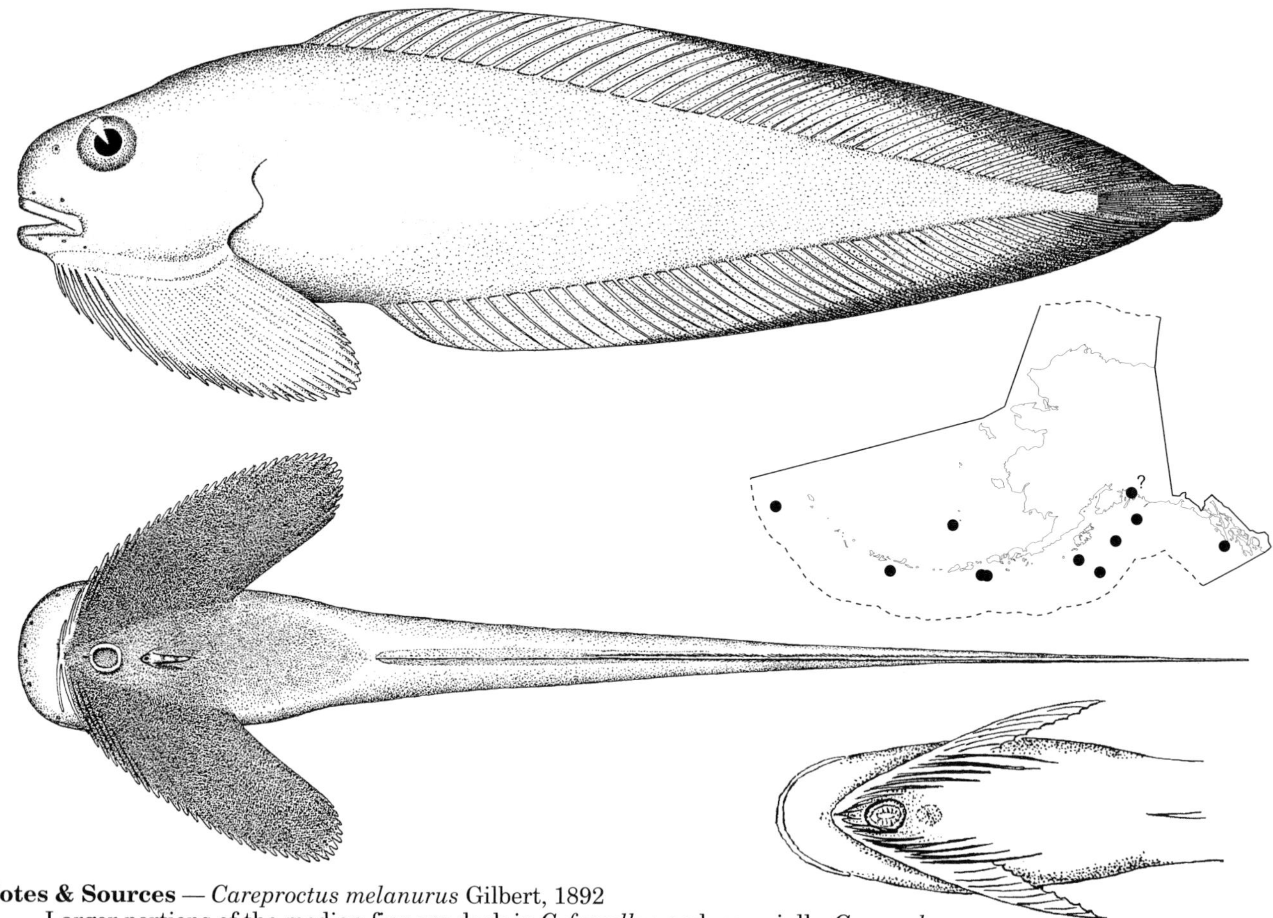

Notes & Sources — *Careproctus melanurus* Gilbert, 1892

Larger portions of the median fins are dark in *C. furcellus* and, especially, *C. cypselurus*.

Description: Gilbert 1892:560–561; Burke 1930:125–126; Forrester and Wilson 1963; Stein 1978:14–16; Kido and Shinohara 1997; Peden 1997ms.

Figures: Smithsonian Institution, NMNH, Division of Fishes, artist A. H. Baldwin, approved 7 Dec. 1891 by C. H. Gilbert; female with ovipositor, 203 mm TL, collected by *Albatross* off coast of Oregon or California. Disk is stylized, but shape (slightly oval) is correct. Ovipositor is used for depositing eggs in gill chambers of crabs, and is also present in ripe females of some other *Careproctus* species. Ventral view at lower right: Hart 1973:574; 300 mm TL.

Range: In describing first record from Honshu, Japan, Kido and Shinohara (1997) used specimens from five Alaskan localities for comparative material: 50°58'N, 171°00'E; 51°44'N, 175°06'W; 56°00'N, 170°19'W; 55°11'N, 156°14'W; and 55°55'N, 135°25'W. The NMC has lots previously identified as *C. spectrum* and *C. attenuatus,* referred to *C. melanurus* by A. E. Peden in Aug. 1993: NMC 67-87, 55°59'N, 154°00'W, depth 184–216 m; NMC 67-88, 53°39'N, 164°45'W, 439–457 m; NMC 67-105, same locality, 420 m; NMC 67-106, 53°38'N, 164°58'W, 430 m. At SIO: SIO 91-59 (2, 265–325 mm SL), 59°15'N, 146°34'W; SIO 63-536 (3, 270–343 mm SL), 58°00'N, 146°00'W. Vogt (1973) reported a possible record (UAM 702) from Port Valdez; C.W.M. could not find the specimen during museum visits in 2000.

Size: Kido and Shinohara 1997.

Careproctus spectrum Bean, 1890 — stippled snailfish

Southeastern Bering Sea and Pacific Ocean south of Unimak Pass to inside waters of southeastern Alaska. Muddy and silty bottoms at depths of 93–201 m.

D 52; A 47; C 10; Pec 32; PC 21.

- **Pale, little or no dark pigment**; abdomen silvery; mouth, gill cavity, stomach, and peritoneum pale.
- **Skin transparent, loose**; body heavy anteriorly, deep, short, tapering rapidly to caudal fin.
- Head broad and flat above; snout blunt.
- Eye about 30% of head length, prominent.
- Dorsal and anal fins gradually extend onto caudal, forming bluntly pointed tail; pectoral fin strongly notched, lower lobe of slender rays free nearly to base.
- **Disk broader than long; length about 25% of head length, smaller than or equal to eye**; margin thick.
- Anus close behind disk.
- Gill opening extending down only to base of 1st pectoral ray; length 30% of head length.
- Length to about 100 mm TL.

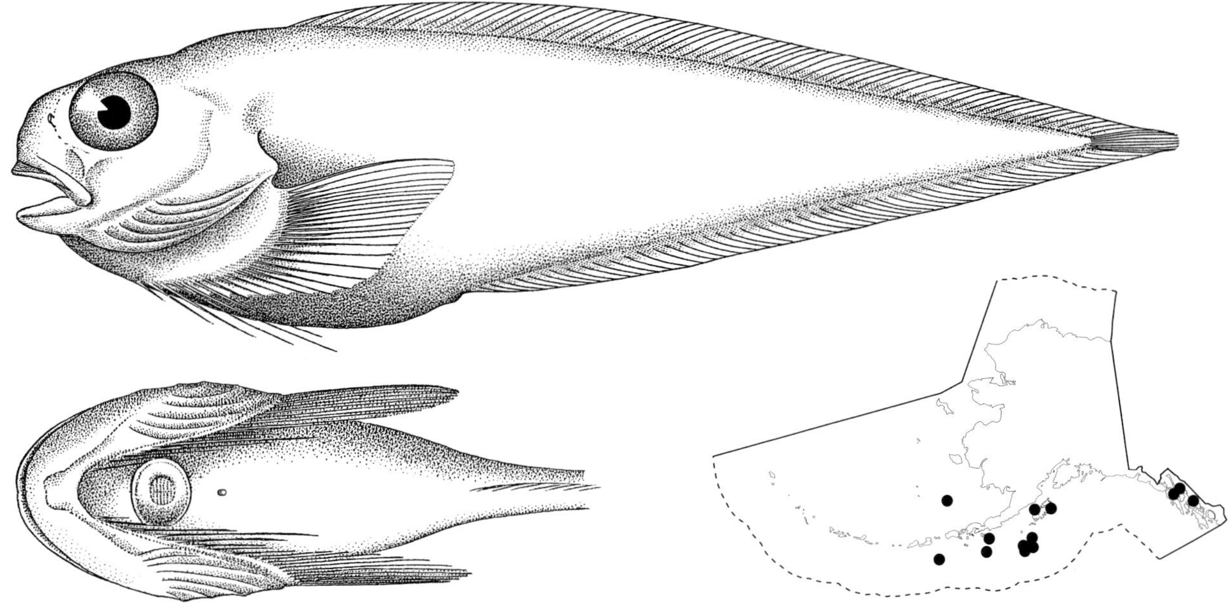

Notes & Sources — *Careproctus spectrum* Bean, 1890

Burke (1912b) referred most of the original 26 specimens in the same jar with the types of *C. spectrum* to *C. gilberti*; he considered *C. spectrum* to be distinguishable by its larger disk, shorter gill slit, and pale stomach. Burke (1930) considered *C. spectrum* to also be closely related to *C. melanurus* but distinguishable from it by having less pigment in the mouth, gill cavity, peritoneum, and posterior part of the body. *Careproctus spectrum* also closely resembles *C. phasma* in general appearance, but Gilbert (1896) and Burke (1930) described *C. phasma* as having a larger disk and thicker, more opaque skin.

Stippled snailfish, the vernacular listed by Robins et al. (1991a), is an odd name for this species, since the fish has little or no pigment. The vernacular could appropriately be exchanged with that of *C. phasma,* the spectral snailfish, which *is* stippled with dark dots. Both specific epithets mean "a spectre."

Description: Bean 1890b:40–41; Gilbert 1896:443 (compared to *C. phasma*); Burke 1930:123–125.

Figures: Smithsonian Institution, NMNH, Division of Fishes, artist S. F. Denton, 31 Jul. 1888; type, 99 mm TL, Shumagin Islands. The drawings partly conflict with Bean's (1890b) description and do not bear a signature of approval (which is found on some other early Division of Fishes illustrations). Since no other illustrations are available we modified these to correct obvious errors, using Bean (1890b) and USNM 60333 and 126711 for guidance.

Range: Bean 1890b (syntypes): *Albatross* station 2848, between Unga and Nagai islands, 55°10'N, 160°18'W, 201 m, green mud bottom. Burke 1930: USNM 60333 (74 mm SL), station 4295, Shelikof Strait off Cape Uyak, 168 m, soft gray mud bottom. USNM 126711 is a specimen (84 mm TL) taken in 1893 at *Albatross* station 3540, 56°27'N, 166°08'W, depth 93 m, green mud and fine sand bottom. AB 64-759 comprises one specimen from Shelikof Strait at 58°38'N, 152°49'W, depth 171–194 m, taken in shrimp trawl on silty bottom. Some others are: NMC 67-89, 55°44'N, 154°55'W; NMC 67-92, 57°47'N, 152°47'W; NMC 67-103, Stephens Passage off southeast tip of Douglas Island; NMC 67-104, Thomas Bay; NMC 67-107, 55°39'N, 155°11'W; UBC 62-715, 55°34'N, 155°30'W; UBC 62-718, 54°15'N, 160°01'W; UBC 62-740, 55°46'N, 155°25'W; UBC 62-744, 53°43'N, 165°01'W; and UW 7348, Tenakee Inlet, Chatham Strait. (USNM 74733, a specimen from *Albatross* station 4781 identified as *C. spectrum*, with gill opening extending down opposite pectoral notch and a dark peritoneum is not this species.)

Careproctus phasma Gilbert, 1896 — spectral snailfish

Eastern Bering Sea; Amchitka Island; Sea of Okhotsk.

Mud, sand, gravel, and shell bottoms at depths of 84–504 m; usually occurring at shallower depths than *C. spectrum,* at least in waters off Alaska.

D 53–54; A 44–45; C 8; Pec 30–34; PC 21.

- **Pale pink in life, white in alcohol**; **body covered with small black dots**; mouth, gill cavity, and peritoneum white or silvery.
- **Skin opaque, thicker than in *C. spectrum***; body heavy anteriorly, short, tapering rapidly to caudal fin.
- Head broad and flat above; snout more blunt than in *C. spectrum.*
- Eye about 25% of head length.
- Anterior rays of dorsal and anal fins buried; rays of lower pectoral lobe equaling the upper lobe in length, lowermost rays free.
- **Disk larger than eye, length 30–38% of head length.**
- Anus close behind disk.
- Gill opening above pectoral fin, not extending down to base of 1st pectoral ray; length less than 25% of head length.
- Length to about 100 mm TL.

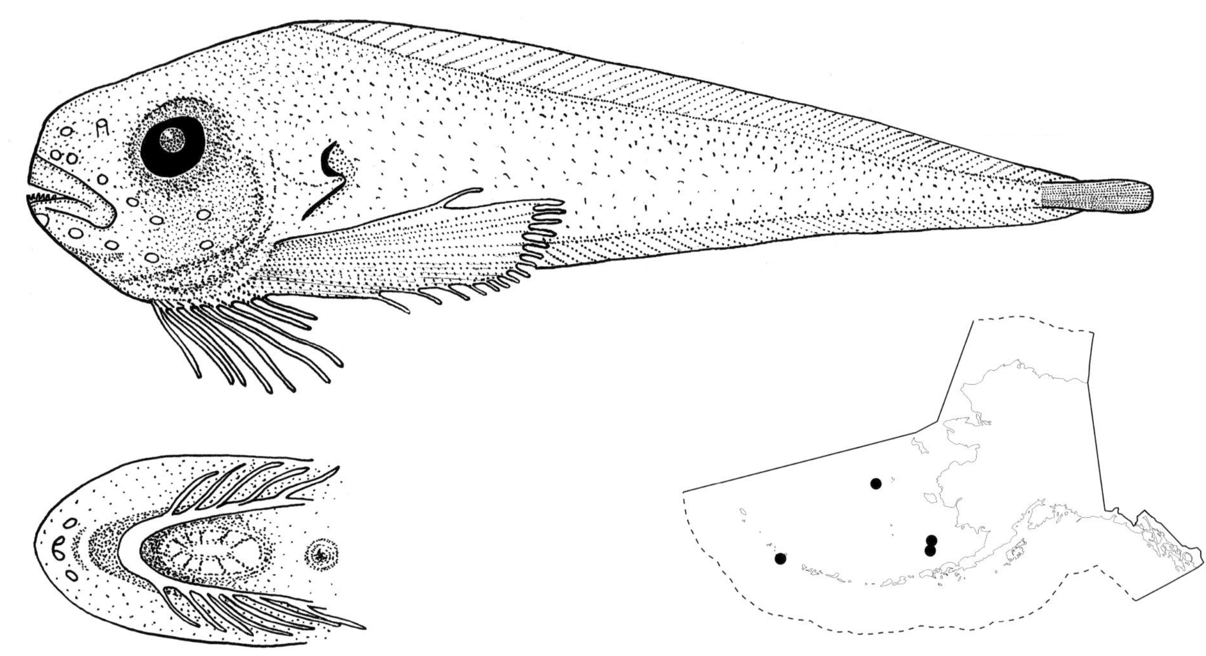

Notes & Sources — *Careproctus phasma* Gilbert, 1896

Possibly confused in surveys and recent popular accounts with, among others, *C. spectrum* and *C. melanurus.* Gilbert (1896) and Burke (1930) considered *C. phasma* to resemble *C. spectrum* in the broad head and in general appearance, but that *C. phasma* is distinguishable by its larger disk and thicker, more opaque skin. Gilbert (1896) emphasized the smaller gill opening in *C. phasma* (length less than 25% of head length versus about 30%, and entirely above the pectoral fin versus reaching the base of the first ray).

Description: Gilbert 1896:443; Burke 1930:123; Schmidt 1950:203–204.

Figures: Russian Academy of Sciences, Zoological Institute, St. Petersburg, artist O. S. Voskoboinikova, Oct. 1999; ZIN 29087, 70 mm SL, 77 mm TL, Sea of Okhotsk, one of the specimens described by Schmidt (1950).

Range: Recorded by Gilbert (1896) from Bristol Bay at *Albatross* station 3254, 56°50'N, 164°27'W, depth 84 m; and station 3256, 56°18'N, 164°34'W, 90 m. The type series comprises one specimen from each of those two stations. Burke (1930) added another record, from station 3530 southwest of St. Matthew Island at 59°39'N, 173°53'W, depth 108 m. Isakson et al. (1971) reported *C. phasma* from Amchitka Island at depths greater than 37 m (their definition of offshore), without giving diagnostic characters or citing voucher specimens. Allen and Smith (1988) noted that NMFS survey records could not be used to determine range because of lack of good field identification characters to distinguish among *C. rastrinus, C. scottae,* and *C. phasma*; other species could have been included as well in the list of species potentially confused with *C. phasma,* such as *C. spectrum* and small *C. melanurus.*

Careproctus simus Gilbert, 1896 **proboscis snailfish**

Central and eastern Bering Sea and Aleutian Islands; southern Sea of Okhotsk off Hokkaido.
Soft bottoms at depths of 410–725 m.

D 54–60; A 47–53; C 10; Pec 31–37; PC 19–28; Vert 59–64.

- Body dark pink or red; caudal fin and posterior portions of dorsal and anal fins black or dusky; mouth, gill cavity, peritoneum, stomach, and pyloric caeca pale.
- **Stout, heavy head, profile ascending gradually from snout; body elongate, tapering gradually to caudal**.
- **Snout thick, rounded, distinctly projecting**.
- Pectoral fin shallowly notched, lower rays partly free.
- Anterior mandibular pores not in same pit.
- Disk smaller than eye, triangular or round, and flat; disk length 17–21 % of head length.
- Anus close behind disk.
- Gill opening entirely above pectoral fin or extending down in front of 1–5 pectoral rays; length 26–38% of head length.
- Length to 186 mm TL.

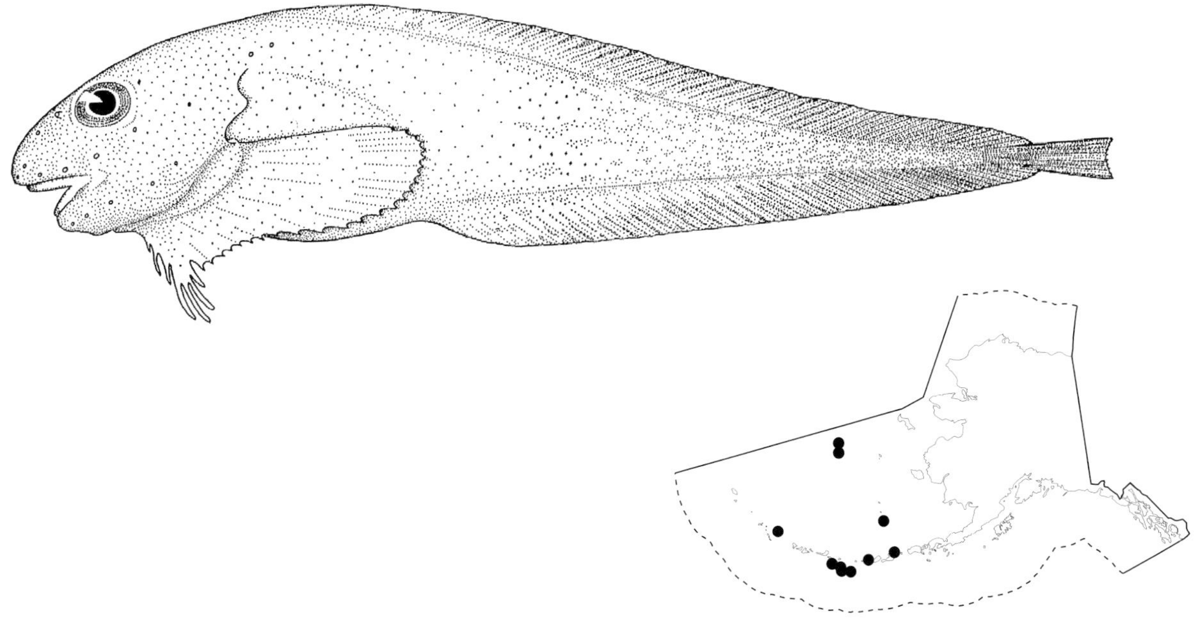

Notes & Sources — *Careproctus simus* Gilbert, 1896

Description: Gilbert 1896:444; Burke 1930:112–113; Kido 1985:11–12; Tsutsui and Amaoka 1997.

Figure: Kido 1985, fig. 6; HUMZ 88447, 123 mm SL, from north of Seguam Island, Aleutian Islands.

Range: Gilbert (1896) described the species from a damaged specimen collected north of Unalaska Island by the *Albatross* (station 3331, mud bottom). The next records were those of Kido (1985:11, fig. 4), who provided a more complete description based on 28 specimens from several localities in the Bering Sea. Tsutsui and Amaoka (1997) recorded the first examples (four specimens) from Japan, which were taken from the Sea of Okhotsk off the north coast of Hokkaido; as well as a new maximum length (186 mm TL).

Careproctus bowersianus Gilbert & Burke, 1912 **Bowers Bank snailfish**

Southeastern and south central Bering Sea and Aleutian Islands.
Soft bottoms at depths of 629–800 m.

D 51–54; A 46–48; C 10–11; Pec 34–38; PC 11–14; Vert 57–59.

- Body uniformly red; in preserved specimens somewhat dusky posteriorly; mouth, gill cavity, and peritoneum pale, **stomach black**.
- Body stout, deep, tapering gradually to caudal; head large, profile tapering fairly steeply from snout to occiput but flat above the eyes.
- Snout blunt, projecting only slightly if at all; **maxilla not extending below front of eye, or just reaching eye** (upper jaw length 33–38% of head length).
- **Eye large, 24–27% of head length, prominent; pupil large**, round.
- Dorsal and anal fins not particularly high, and about same height along length of body; dorsal and anal fins buried in gelatinous tissue anteriorly, tips not showing; pectoral fin shallowly notched, lower rays partly free and exserted.
- Anteriormost pair of mandibular pores separate, but located in same pit (see Notes, below).
- Disk length 18–29% of head length; disk flat and round, margin broad.
- Anus immediately behind disk.
- Gill opening entirely above pectoral fin or extending down in front of 1–3 pectoral fin rays.
- Length to 156 mm SL.

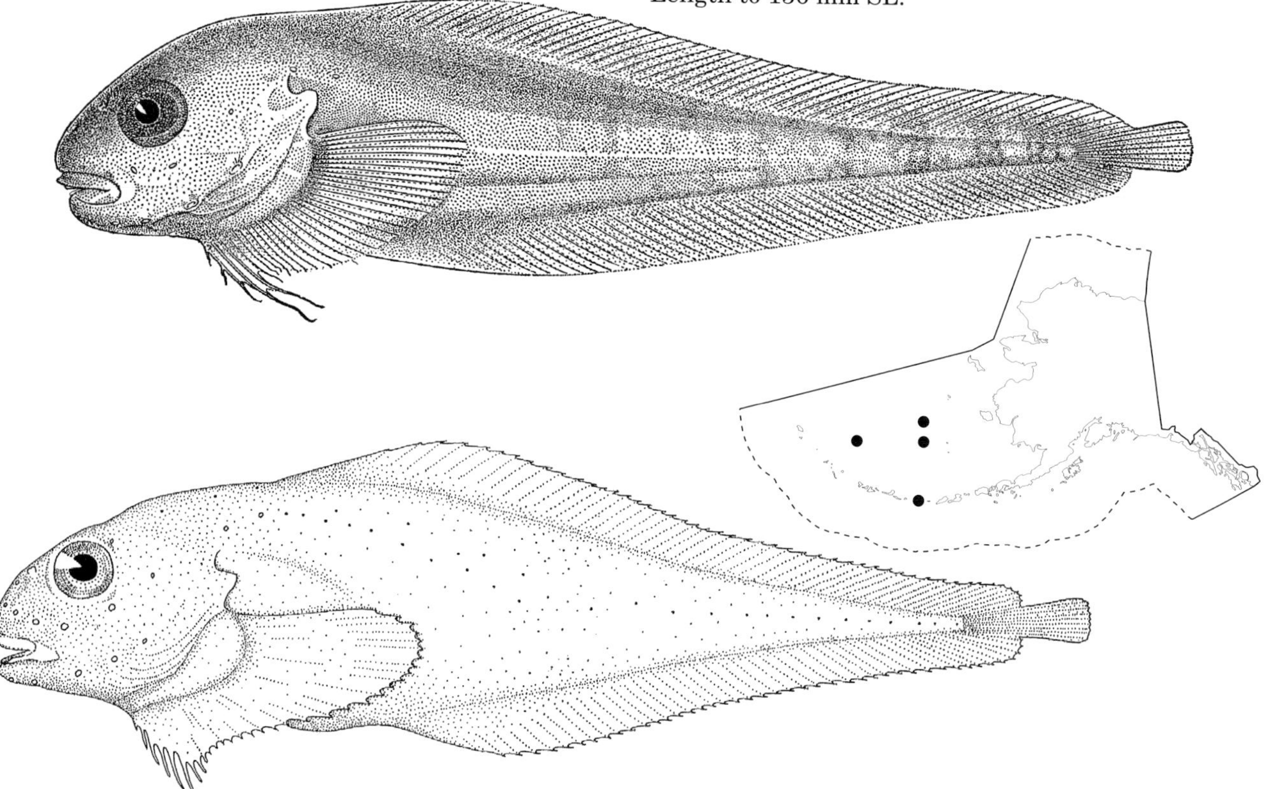

Notes & Sources — *Careproctus bowersianus* Gilbert & Burke, 1912

Burke (1930) considered that *C. bowersianus* differed from *C. mollis* partly in having a smaller disk, but data reported by Kido (1985) indicate the disk length in *C. mollis* falls within the range for *C. bowersianus*. Kido (1985) considered differences in stomach color, eye size, and upper jaw length to be diagnostic; as well as the disposition of the anteriormost pair of mandibular pores, describing them as not being in the same pit in *C. bowersianus* but in the same pit in *C. mollis*. However, examination of types of *C. bowersianus* (USNM 74382) and *C. mollis* (USNM 74383) indicates a different description: *C. bowersianus* has separate pores, with both openings in the same, broad pit, whereas in *C. mollis* the pores are joined, forming one opening in a round pit.

Bigeye snailfish would be an appropriate name for this species, but that name is already in use for *C. candidus*. At a loss for a better vernacular, we use Bowers Bank snailfish after the type locality.

Description: Gilbert and Burke 1912a:76; Burke 1930:115–116; Kido 1985:12–14.

Figures: Upper: Gilbert and Burke 1912a, fig. 20; type, 100 mm TL, Bowers Bank, Bering Sea. Lower: Kido 1985, fig. 7; 126 mm SL, north of Chagulak Island, Aleutian Islands.

Range: Two specimens were recorded by Gilbert and Burke (1912a) from Bowers Bank: one at *Albatross* station 4771, 54°30'N, 179°17'E, depth 779 m; and one at station 4772, 54°30'N, 179°14'E, depth 629–680 m. Kido (1985) recorded six more specimens, from 57°51'N, 173°58'W; 56°33'N, 172°51'W; and 52°46'N, 171°04'W; taken by otter trawl at depths of 710–800 m.

Careproctus mollis Gilbert & Burke, 1912 **everyday snailfish**

Bering Sea off Attu and Agattu islands; Commander Islands; northern Kuril islands.

Soft bottoms at depths of 247–882 m.

D 51; A 47; C 12; Pec 35; PC 8.

- Pink; mouth, gill cavity, peritoneum, and **stomach pale**.
- **Occiput swollen**; **body slightly humped at nape**.
- Snout blunt, not projecting; **maxilla reaching to below anterior part of eye to mideye**, upper jaw length about 42% of head length.
- Eye diameter about 18–21% of head length; **pupil small**, round.
- **Dorsal and anal fins very high, especially posteriorly**; pectoral fin notched, lower rays partly free.
- Anterior pair of mandibular pores with common opening, in circular pit.
- Disk length about 28% of head length; disk flat and round, margin broad.
- Anus close behind disk.
- Gill opening extending down in front of 1–4 pectoral fin rays.
- Length to 85 mm TL.

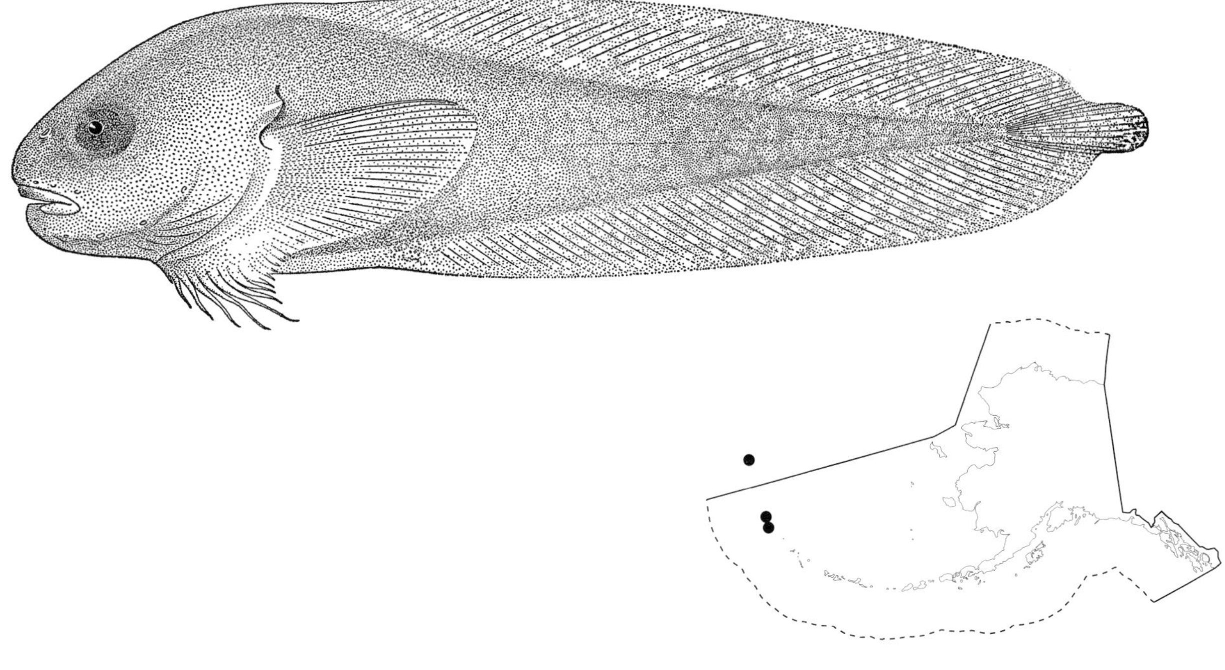

Notes & Sources — *Careproctus mollis* Gilbert & Burke, 1912

Burke (1930) distinguished *C. mollis* from *C. bowersianus* by the smaller eye, humped body, and larger disk of *C. mollis.* Kido (1985) considered the differences in stomach color, eye size, upper jaw length, and anteriormost pair of mandibular pores (see Notes for *C. bowersianus*) to be diagnostic.

"Everyday" in the vernacular alludes to Burke's (1930) characterization of this species as a typical *Careproctus.*

Description: Gilbert and Burke 1912a:77; Burke 1930:113–114.

Figure: Gilbert and Burke 1912a, fig. 21; type, 84 mm TL, Bering Sea off Attu Island.

Range: Recorded by Gilbert and Burke (1912a) from *Albatross* station 4781, 52°14'N, 174°13'E; and 4784, 52°55'N, 173°26'E; at depths of 882 m and 247 m, respectively. V. V. Fedorov collected this species near the Commander Islands and northern Kuril Islands (B. A. Sheiko, pers. comm., 12 May 1998).

Careproctus opisthotremus Gilbert & Burke, 1912 **distalpore snailfish**

One specimen from Aleutian Islands south of Agattu Island (holotype), and one from Bering Sea north of Umnak Island.

Green ooze, mud, sand, and pebble bottoms; holotype taken at depth of 1,913 m, second specimen at 2,562 m.

D 45–46; A 36–42; Pec 32–36; PC 12.

- Color in life not known; pale; mouth slightly dusky at throat; gill cavity, stomach, peritoneum pale.
- Head depressed, broad, width equal to depth; top of head flat from snout to nape; body compressed, slender.
- Snout short, blunt, not projecting.
- Dorsal and anal fins very high, especially posteriorly; pectoral fin notched.
- Disk length 29–33% of head length.
- **Anus far back, nearer anal fin than disk.**
- **Gill opening extending down in front of 5–11 pectoral fin rays.**
- Length to 77 mm SL.

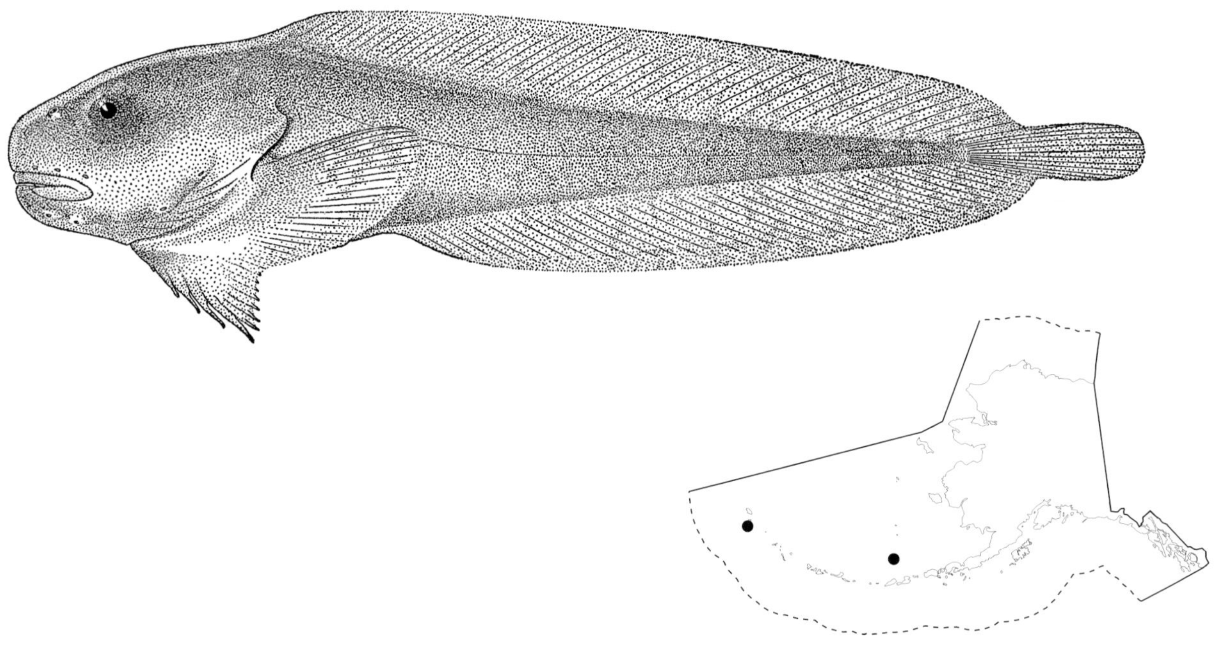

Notes & Sources — *Careproctus opisthotremus* Gilbert & Burke, 1912

The vernacular refers to the position of the anus, away from the disk and closer to the anal fin; the anus is closer to the disk in most other *Careproctus*.

Description: Gilbert and Burke 1912a:78–79; Burke 1930: 133–134. USNM 76497 (1 specimen, 77 mm SL).

Figure: Gilbert and Burke 1912a, fig. 23; holotype, USNM 74385, 50 mm TL, south of Agattu Island.

Range: Described by Gilbert and Burke (1912a) from one specimen obtained at *Albatross* station 4780, south of Agattu Island at 52°01'N, 174°39'E, depth 1,913 m, on bottom of gray mud, sand, and pebbles. Another record is USNM 76497, a specimen from *Albatross* station 3604, north of Umnak Island at 54°54'N, 168°59'W, depth 2,562 m, on bottom of green ooze, collected 12 Aug. 1895. Burke (1930), who studied the Smithsonian Institution's holdings for his review of the family Liparidae, evidently overlooked USNM 76497 (examined by C.W.M.); this specimen has the diagnostic characters of the holotype (USNM 74385), and with its posteriorly located anus and long gill opening it could not be confused with another species. The UW online catalog indicates that a snailfish (UW 15764) collected near St. Lawrence Island in 1949 and identified as *C. opisthotremus* was discarded, so that record cannot be verified. However, the shallow depth (49–53 m) at which it was caught suggests it was not this species.

Size: USNM 76497. The holotype measured 50 mm TL (Burke 1930).

Careproctus attenuatus Gilbert & Burke, 1912 **attenuate snailfish**

South of Agattu Island.

Dredged from bottom at 882 m.

D 48; A 40; Pec about 34; PC about 10.

- Body uniformly pale, tinged with light red; **gill cavity, abdomen, and peritoneum black**.
- Body very slender; head depressed, nearly as wide as deep.
- **Snout abrupt, deep, not projecting**.
- Dorsal and anal fins very high; dorsal fin slightly notched as in *C. ectenes*, with 1st ray longer than next 2 or 3 rays (not evident in drawing); pectoral fin deeply notched, lower rays partly free.
- Disk length about 27% of head length.
- **Anus midway between disk and anal fin**.
- **Gill opening entirely above pectoral fin**.
- Holotype is 37 mm long to base of caudal fin (damaged).

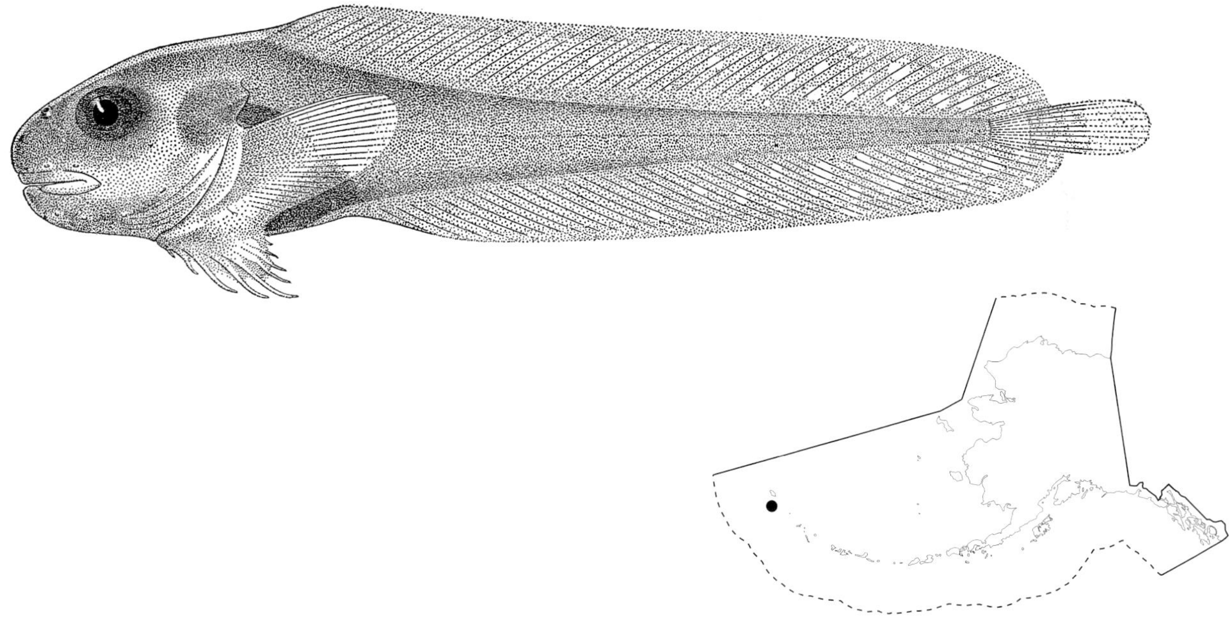

Notes & Sources — *Careproctus attenuatus* Gilbert & Burke, 1912

Description: Gilbert and Burke 1912a:79–80; Burke 1930: 116–117. The holotype is in poor condition, with damaged fins; accurate pectoral fin count not possible.

Figure: Gilbert and Burke 1912a, fig. 24; holotype (unique), USNM 74386, off south side of Agattu Island.

Range: The only unequivocal record is the holotype, obtained off the southwest coast of Agattu Island at *Albatross* station 4781, 52°14'N, 174°13'E. Lindberg and Krasyukova (1987:438) stated that a report of occurrence in the Sea of Okhotsk southeast of Sakhalin Island remains unverified.

Careproctus ectenes Gilbert, 1896 — shovelhead snailfish

Bering Sea north of Rat Islands and Unalaska Island.
Mud, sand, and broken shell bottoms at depths of 494–640 m.

D 48–51; A 44; C about 8; Pec 29–32; PC 0–6.

- Nearly uniform dusky brown to grayish; lighter on snout, belly, and underside of head; **mouth, gill cavity, and peritoneum pale**.
- **Body extremely elongate** and slender; **head depressed, broad**; head length about 17% of standard length.
- **Snout broad, strongly projecting**.
- **Eye large**, 31–33% of head length.
- Dorsal fin notched, 1st ray elongate, next 2 or 3 rays shorter, and the following rays increasing in length, or anterior rays equal in length; pectoral fin deeply notched, **lower pectoral rays long and free**.
- Disk about 21–25% of head length.
- Anus midway between disk and anal fin.
- Gill opening entirely above pectoral fin.
- **Pyloric caeca 0–6**.
- Length to 87 mm TL.

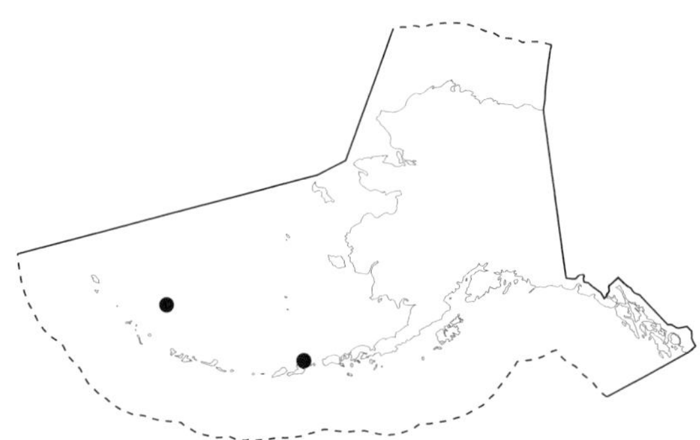

Notes & Sources — *Careproctus ectenes* Gilbert, 1896

Seen from above, and except for the huge eyes, this little fish resembles an extra-long-handled, flat-tipped shovel.

Description: Gilbert 1896:442; Burke 1930:110–112. USNM 53031 (paralectotype, 1 specimen, 51 mm TL) and USNM 64043 (2 specimens, 59–80 mm SL) are in poor condition but permitted addition of some new data, including a few morphometrics, to the description.

Figures: None available of external appearance.

Range: Gilbert (1896) described three specimens (USNM 48618, lectotype; USNM 53031, paralectotype; SU 3091, paralectotype) from *Albatross* station 3331, north of Unalaska Island at 54°01'N, 166°48'W, depth 640 m, muddy bottom. Burke (1930) examined two additional specimens (USNM 64043), from station 3785; locality given by Townsend (1901) as 150 miles north of Rat Islands, depth 494 m, gray sand and broken shell bottom.

Size: Burke 1930.

Careproctus gilberti Burke, 1912 **smalldisk snailfish**

Western Aleutian Islands, Alaska, to Morro Bay, California.

Mud, sand, coral, and rocky bottoms at depths of 172–886 m, possibly as shallow as 80 m.

D 49–55; A 44–48; C 8–9; Pec 30–33; PC 10–12.

- Body pink, slightly darker posteriorly; translucent; fin tips dusky posteriorly; mouth and gill cavity slightly darker than body, but not dusky or blackish; peritoneum pale or silvery with black specks, **stomach black**, pyloric caeca pale.
- Head heavy, body tapering rapidly to caudal fin; large eye.
- Anterior dorsal fin rays buried in thick skin; pectoral fin deeply notched, lower rays partly free.
- **Disk small, length 6–14% of head length**.
- Anus close behind disk.
- **Gill opening extending down in front of about 14 pectoral fin rays**.
- Length to 127 mm SL.

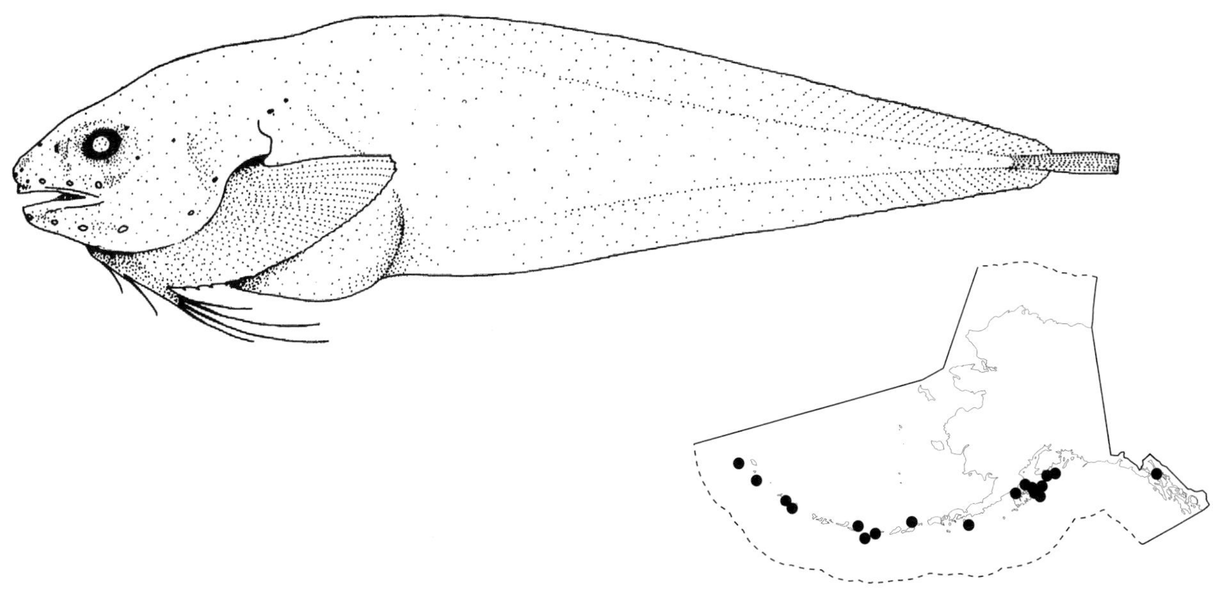

Notes & Sources — *Careproctus gilberti* Burke, 1912
Liparis osborni Townsend & Nichols, 1925

Early records confused *C. gilberti* with other species. Stein (1978:17) gave a detailed synonymy. Recently, M. E. Anderson (pers. comm., 15 Apr. 1999) reported *L. osborni* (known from California) should also be included in the synonymy; he and D. L. Stein independently examined and compared the type to *C. gilberti* and other species, and concur.

Possibly same as *C. ostentum,* but thought to be distinguishable by a larger disk. Disk length in *C. gilberti* was reported by Burke (1930) to be 7.3–9 in the head, or 11–14% HL, by Stein (1978) to be 8–11% HL, and by Kido (1988) to be 6.4–11.2% HL. Kido (1988) also gave a relatively long length of the lower lobe of the pectoral fin (72.4–78.5% HL; N = 4) as a diagnostic character separating it from *C. ostentum.* Also similar in general appearance to *C. spectrum,* but distinguishable by a smaller disk, larger gill opening, and darkly colored stomach.

Description: Burke 1912b:570–571; Burke 1930:138–139; Stein 1978:17–18.

Figure: Stein 1978, fig. 6C; BCPM 72-9-1, 117 mm SL, off British Columbia.

Range: Burke 1912b: *Albatross* station 2848, vicinity of Shumagin Islands, 55°10'N, 160°18'W, depth 201 m, green mud bottom; station 3480, Pacific Ocean south of Amukta Pass, 52°06'N, 171°45'W, 518 m, black sand, coral, and rocky bottom; and stations 4292 and 4293, Shelikof Strait off Cape Uyak, Kodiak Island, 172–205 m, blue mud and fine sand bottom. Isakson et al. 1971: off Amchitka Island. Kido 1988: north of Unalaska Island, 54°34'N, 166°27'W; near Amukta Island, 52°40'N, 172°26'W; near Buldir Island, 52°01'N, 175°09'E; and near Attu Island, 52°08'N, 172°10'E; at depths of 427–600 m. Additional Aleutian Islands records include USNM 333404, 51°57'N, 178°03'E; and USNM 325570, 52°48'N, 170°54'W. Identified as *C. gilberti* at the Auke Bay Laboratory are: AB 62-505, 58°16'N, 135°27'W; 64-675, 59°24'N, 150°31'W; 64-682, 59°27'N, 149°49'W; 64-715, 58°52'N, 152°21'W; 64-754, 58°30'N, 151°48'W; 64-759, Shelikof Strait, northwest of Kodiak Island; 64-850, 57°39'N, 151°57'W; and 66-927, 56°07'N, 156°19'W. CAS 43152 was collected east of Raspberry Island at 58°04'N, 152°16'W, by otter trawl at depth of 80 m. SIO 69-111 includes three specimens from 59°29'N, 150°26'W. Depth range: minimum from Fassett (1905) for *Albatross* station 4292 and maximum from Burke (1912b) for station 4781. With CAS 43152, the minimum recorded depth would be about 80 m.

Size: Largest specimen examined by Stein (1978).

Careproctus ostentum Gilbert, 1896 **microdisk snailfish**

Bering Sea and Aleutian Islands to Gulf of Alaska east of Kodiak Island; Sea of Okhotsk.
Mud to coarse sand, gravel, and rocky bottoms at depths of 165–1,030 m.

D 54; A 47; C 8; Pec 32; PC 10.

- Pale pinkish or reddish; mouth and gill cavity pale; peritoneum silvery, with black dots; **stomach**, base of caeca, and intestines **black**.
- Head heavy; body heavy at the nape, slender posteriorly.
- Snout low, profile retreating gradually from the mouth; upper teeth partly exposed when jaws are closed.
- Cactus-like prickles present on some specimens.
- Anterior dorsal rays short, buried beneath the skin; pectoral fin deeply and broadly notched, with 9 or 10 short, widely spaced rays between upper and lower lobes.
- **Disk minute, 6% or less of head length.**
- Anus close behind disk.
- **Gill opening extending down in front of 8–17 pectoral fin rays.**
- Length to 134 mm TL.

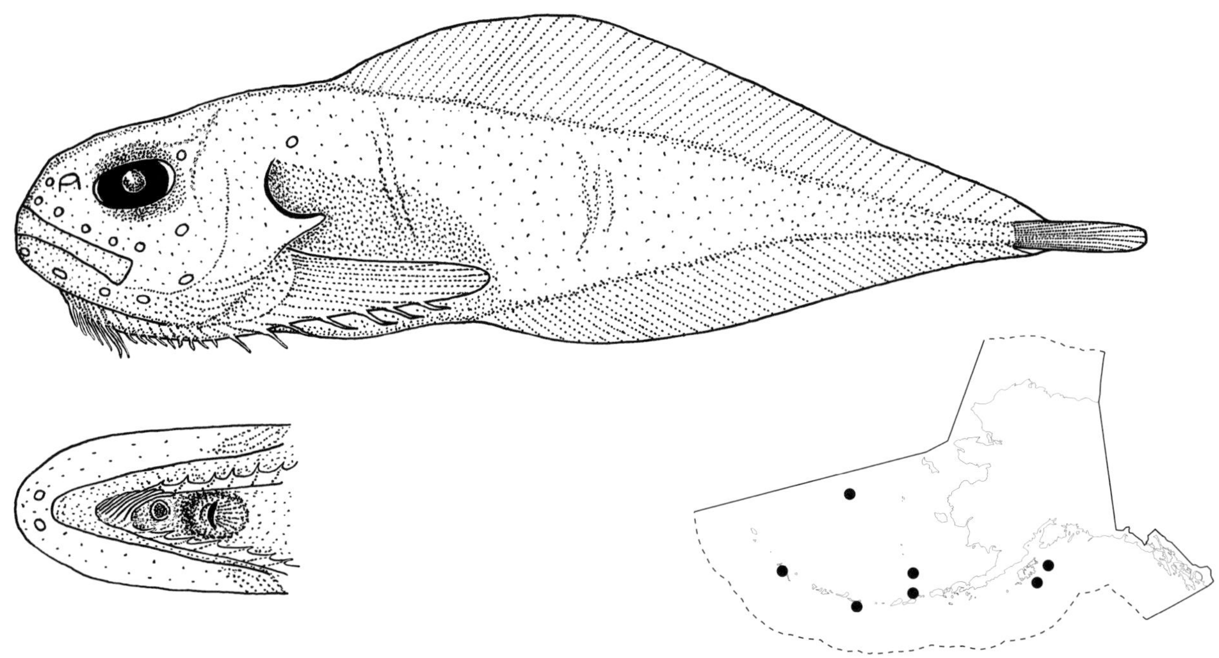

Notes & Sources — *Careproctus ostentum* Gilbert, 1896

The most significant difference from *Careproctus gilberti* is thought to be a smaller disk. Gilbert (1896) described the disk as "a mere rudiment entirely concealed by the anterior (lower) lobes of the pectoral fins"and measuring 1 mm in diameter in a specimen 78 mm long. Burke (1930) reported the disk to be absent in the type and minute, but perfect in structure, in another specimen. He expressed disk length as "more than 9 in the head," or less than 11% HL, and Stein (1978) as 5% HL. Schmidt (1950) gave a disk length of 6.25% HL for the specimen illustrated above. Kido (1988) gave a relatively short length of the lower lobe of the pectoral fin (22.5–42.4% of HL; N = 17) as an additional character distinguishing it from *C. gilberti* and the closely related Sea of Okhotsk species, *C. mederi*. Stein (1978) was not convinced that *C. gilberti* and *C. ostentum* are different species. We could not distinguish the two species in collections at the NMFS Auke Bay Laboratory, other than to sort the specimens by disk length.

Description: Gilbert 1896:444; Burke 1930:140–141; Schmidt 1950:214.

Figures: Russian Academy of Sciences, Zoological Institute, St. Petersburg, artist O. S. Voskoboinikova, Oct. 1999; ZIN 26319, 119 mm SL, 132 mm TL, Sea of Okhotsk, specimen described by Schmidt (1950).

Range: Gilbert 1896: north of Unalaska Island at *Albatross* station 3324, 55°33'N, 167°46'W, depth 199 m; and station 3331, 54°01'N, 166°48'W, depth 640 m. Kido 1988: Bering Sea at 59°20'N, 178°04'W; near Kiska Island, 51°41'N, 177°49'E; and near Amukta Island, 52°40'N, 172°26'W; at depths of 520–610 m. Specimens from Shelikof Strait identified as *C. ostentum* (Quast and Hall 1972) were later reexamined and identified by Quast as *C. gilberti* (ABL records). Currently in the ABL fish collection as *C. ostentum* are lot AB 66-886, from east of Kodiak Island at 57°39'N, 151°59'W; AB 66-1062, off Unalaska Island at 53°50'N, 166°20'W; and AB 68-564, from Makushin Bay, Unalaska Island. The OSUO fish collection includes an uncataloged lot of three specimens taken northeast of Kodiak Island at about 58°N, 151°W, depth 165 m, which R. Baxter (unpubl. data) attributed to this species. Schmidt recorded *C. ostentum* from the Sea of Okhotsk east of Sakhalin at depths of 180–184 m. Dudnik and Dolganov (1992) gave depths of 300–1,030 m for recent Okhotsk Sea catches.

Size: Schmidt 1950.

Crystallichthys cameliae (Nalbant, 1965) **elusive snailfish**

Bering Sea north of Near Islands.

Bottom at depth of about 300 m.

D 50; A 45; C 14; Pec 28; PC 37.

- In alcohol, body pale rose; round or subround, large dusky-bordered gray blotches on head, body, and dorsal and anal fins; all fins pale; mouth and gill cavity whitish rose, peritoneum not pigmented.
- **Head and first part of body high, not strongly compressed; rest of body strongly compressed and tapering gently to caudal fin.**
- Snout projecting; **mouth inferior and oblique**.
- Operculum not produced posteriorly to form projection over gill opening.
- Pectoral fin notched, lower rays thick and partly free.
- Gill opening entirely above pectoral fin.
- Holotype (unique) 84.6 mm SL.

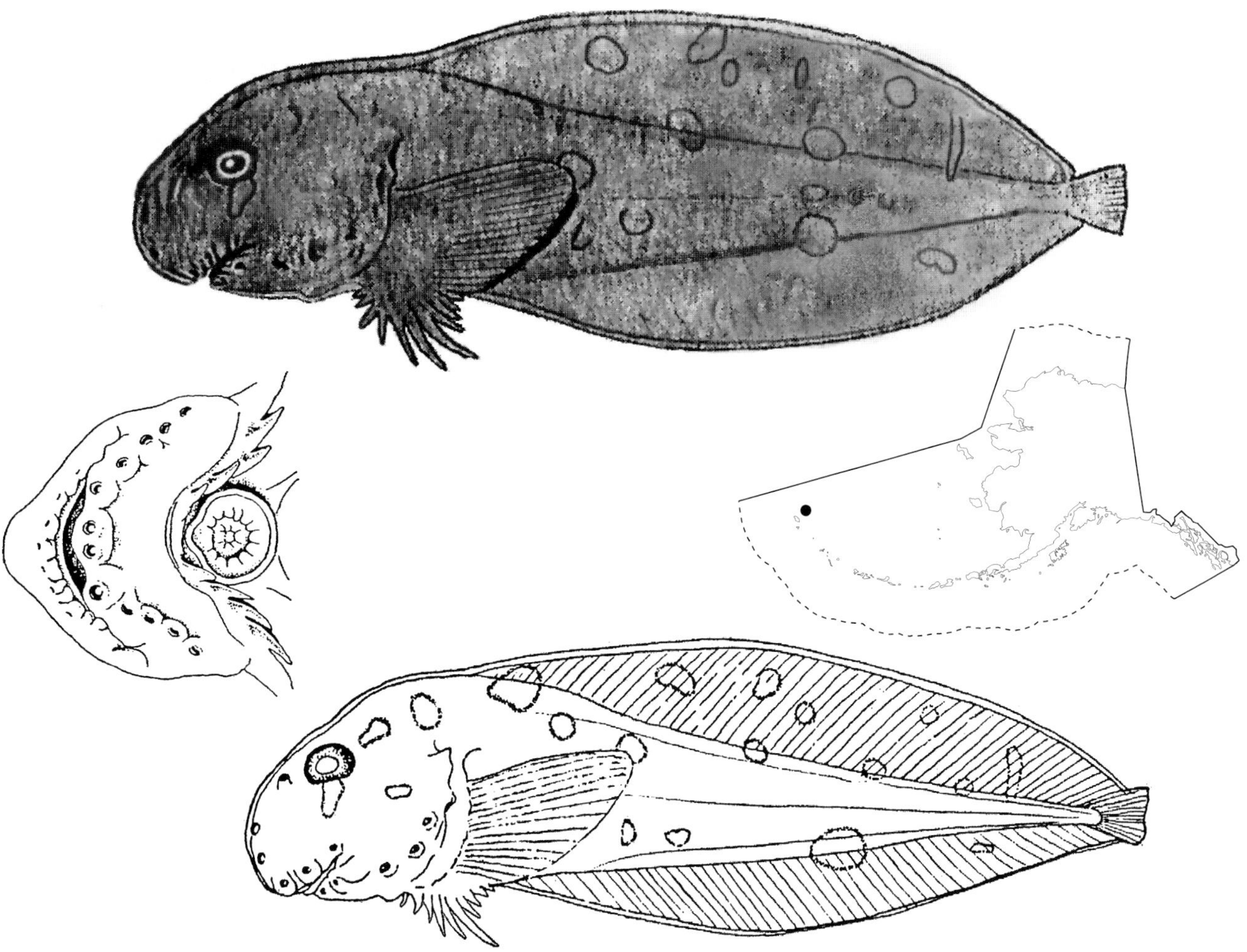

Notes & Sources — *Crystallichthys cameliae* (Nalbant, 1965)
Careproctus cameliae Nalbant, 1965
This species is close to *Crystallichthys mirabilis* and *C. cyclospilus.* Dr. Leonard P. Schultz (formerly NMNH) examined *C. mirabilis* at Dr. Nalbant's request and suggested that *C. cameliae* (in genus *Careproctus* at the time) represented a young stage of *C. mirabilis.* Nalbant (1970), in a report published in the Romanian language, compared his snailfish to photographs of the holotype of *C. mirabilis* and placed it in genus *Crystallichthys* but did not synonymize the species. Dr. Nalbant's (pers. comm., 2 Oct. 1998) opinion is that *C. cameliae* is closer, if not identical, to *C. mirabilis* than to *C. cyclospilus.* However, *C. mirabilis* and *C. cyclospilus* may not be distinct species. At present there is not enough evidence to synonymize *C. cameliae* in either one. A study including specimens of all nominal species of *Crystallichthys* might help to resolve relationships within this group.

Description: Nalbant 1965, 1970.
Figures: Upper: Nalbant 1970, fig. 1. Lower: Nalbant 1965, figs. 1 and 2. (All same specimen.)
Range: The holotype (unique) was taken by the Romanian stern trawler *Galatzi* in 1964 at a depth of 300 m near the shelf of the Near Islands; locality, previously given only as Bering Sea, was specified by Nalbant (1994).
Size: Nalbant 1965.

Crystallichthys mirabilis Jordan & Gilbert, 1898 **wonderful snailfish**

Bering Sea records uncertain; Pacific Ocean off southeastern Kamchatka and northern Kuril Islands. Bottom at depths of 106–318 m.

D 53; A 44; C 12; Pec 30–33; PC 0–40.

- In alcohol grayish or whitish, no blotches; in life pinkish, with reddish pink blotches, some rounded, some barlike, on dorsal region of head, back, and dorsal fin; translucent.
- **Head much compressed, with sides nearly vertical**; body tapering rapidly to caudal fin.
- **Snout conical, strongly projecting** beyond premaxilla; median groove in tip and underside of snout, with or without ridge within the groove; **mouth inferior, oblique**.
- Pupil elliptical, partially divided dorsally by a projection from the iris.
- **Opercular flap small**.
- Anterior dorsal and anal fin rays buried; pectoral fin notched, lower rays thick and partly free.
- Disk normal, 32–38% of head length.
- Gill opening entirely above pectoral fin.
- Pyloric caeca absent from the type, 40 in another specimen.
- Length to 360 mm SL.

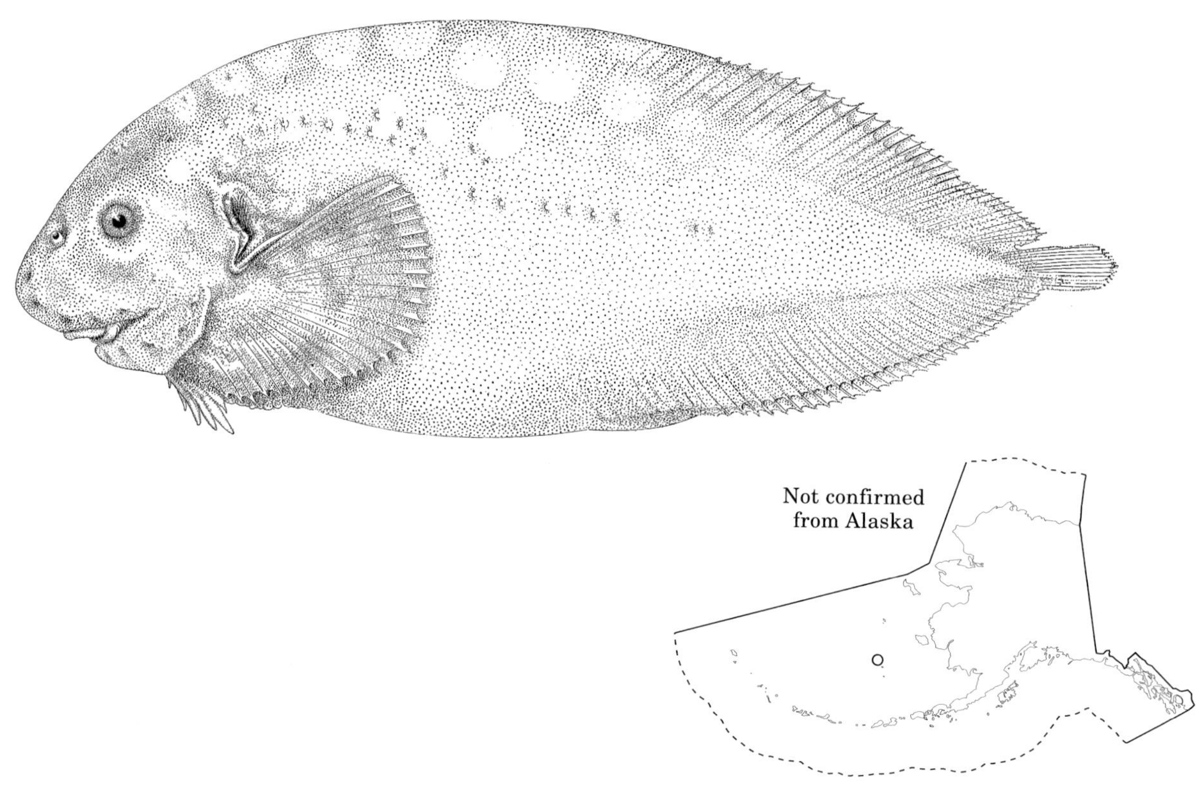

Not confirmed from Alaska

Notes & Sources — *Crystallichthys mirabilis* Jordan & Gilbert in Jordan & Evermann, 1898

Similar to *C. cyclospilus,* but head possibly more compressed, snout longer, and mouth oblique compared to *C. cyclospilus.* Schmidt (1950) believed the two species could be identical.

Description: Gilbert and Burke 1912a:75–76; Burke 1930: 148–150; Schmidt 1950:216. Descriptions by Jordan and Gilbert (in Jordan and Evermann 1898:2864; 1899:476–477) of *C. mirabilis* and an immature individual of *C. cyclospilus* are mixed up (Gilbert and Burke 1912a).

Figure: Jordan and Gilbert 1899, pl. 75; type, USNM 51466, 330 mm TL, off Povorotnaya, Kamchatka. (Their St. Paul Island specimen, pl. 76, is *C. cyclospilus.*)

Range: No firm records from Alaska. Jordan and Gilbert's (1899) and Gilbert and Burke's (1912a) two specimens were from the Pacific Ocean off southeast Kamchatka. Schmidt (1950:216) gave measurements for a specimen reported to be from the Bering Sea, but in that work the Bering Sea was broadly defined to include the Pacific Ocean off southeast Kamchatka, and the specimen may have been collected there. Three fish taken in the vicinity of the Pribilof Islands were identified by R. Baxter (unpubl. data) as *C. mirabilis,* but the data fit descriptions of *C. cyclospilus*; since the specimens were not preserved, the identification cannot be confirmed. Few capture depths have been reported for *C. mirabilis.* Gilbert and Burke (1912a) reported 106 and 183 m for their two specimens. Tokranov (2000a) gave a depth range of 118–318 m for catches in the 1990s in the Pacific off Kamchatka and the Kuril Islands.

Size: Tokranov 2000b: largest of 100 specimens from surveys during the 1990s in the northwestern Pacific was 36 cm SL.

Crystallichthys cyclospilus Gilbert & Burke, 1912 **blotched snailfish**

Bering Sea and Aleutian Islands to Gulf of Alaska south of Shumagin Islands; Sea of Okhotsk.

Mud, sand, and gravel bottoms at depths of 54–265 m.

D 48–50; A 42–43; C 10; Pec 33–35; PC 36.

- Body in alcohol whitish, in life yellowish or pinkish; ovate or round, pink, orange, or red blotches on head, body, and fins; some blotches surrounded by darker border; translucent.
- **Head and body compressed, cheeks vertical.**
- **Snout broadly rounded, moderately projecting; with or without median groove in snout.**
- Pupil elliptical, partially divided dorsally by a projection from the iris.
- Opercle not produced posteriorly to form flap.
- Anterior dorsal and anal fin rays buried; pectoral notched, lower rays thick and tips free.
- Disk 42–45% of head length.
- Gill opening entirely above pectoral fin.
- Length to 287 mm TL.

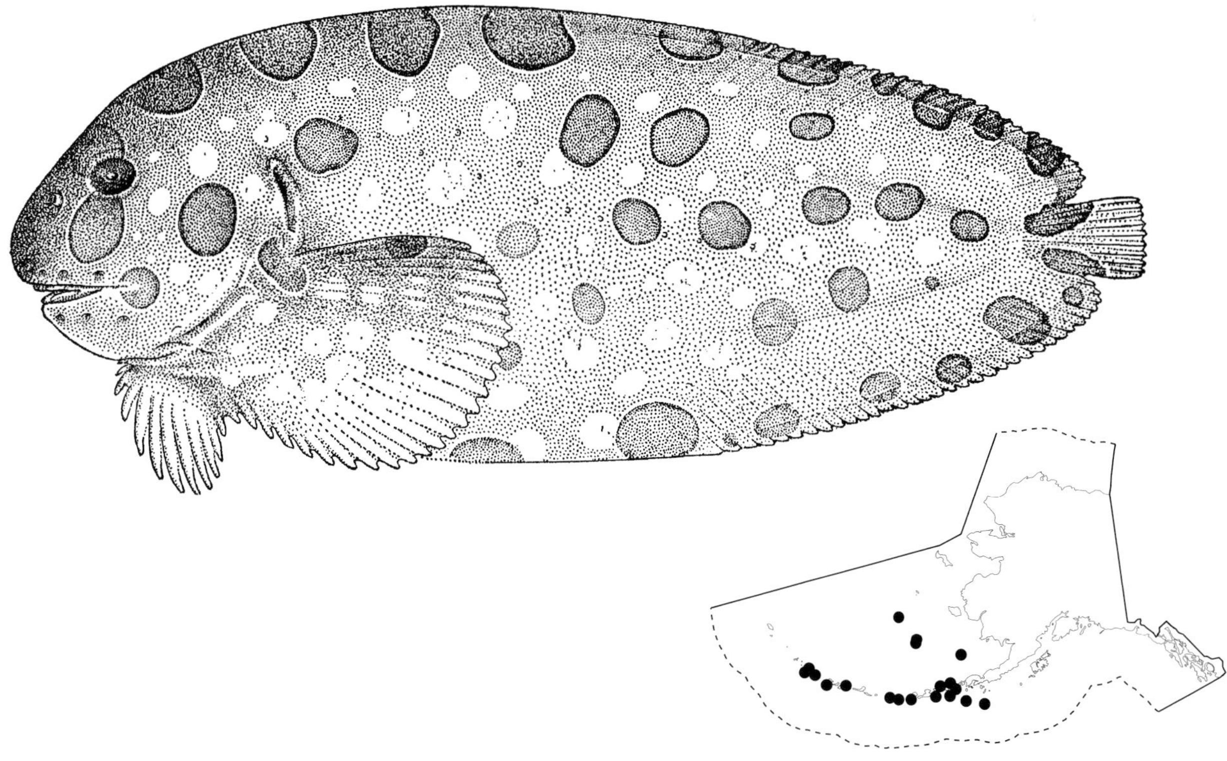

Notes & Sources — *Crystallichthys cyclospilus* Gilbert & Burke, 1912

Liparis cyclostigma Gilbert, 1896 (part, confused with *L. cyclostigma*): Jordan and Evermann 1898; Jordan and Gilbert 1899 (part, pl. 73); Evermann and Goldsborough 1907 (part, pl. 19).

Crystallichthys mirabilis Jordan & Gilbert, 1899 (part, pl. 76)

Gilbert and Burke (1912a:77) explained the confusion with description of *L. cyclostigma* that occurred in earlier works.

Description: Gilbert and Burke 1912a:74–75; Burke 1930: 147; Schmidt 1950:216–217. The significance of the groove along the middle of the snout is not clear. The groove is absent in Bering Sea specimens examined by Burke (1930), and present in Sea of Okhotsk specimens of Schmidt (1950). The latter specimens had longer snouts. C.W.M. found the groove to be absent in AB 66-1034 (2; 126–152 mm SL); AB 66-1056 (1; 174 mm SL); and AB 66-1112 (1; 130 mm SL). M. S. Busby (pers. comm., 29 May 1997) found it to be lacking in a specimen collected in 1997 near the Pribilof Islands.

Figure: Gilbert and Burke 1912a, fig. 19; holotype, USNM 74381, 202 mm TL, Petrel Bank, Bering Sea.

Range: Burke 1930: *Albatross* station 3252, 57°22'N, 164°24'W, black mud bottom; station 3439, 57°06'N, 170°35'W, fine black sand; station 3638, 57°07'N, 170°28'W, gravel; station 4777, 52°11'N, 179°49'E; station 4779, 52°11'N, 179°57'W. Wilimovsky 1964: vicinity of Great Sitkin Island–Igitkin Island. Isakson et al. 1971: Amchitka Island. ABL collections: AB 66-1034, 54°22'N, 165°18'W; AB 66-1056, 54°03'N, 164°47'W; AB 66-1112, 57°06'N, 169°53'W. UBC collections: UBC 63-1012, 51°56'N, 176°02'W; 62-689, 54°80'N, 164°58'W; 62-40, 54°29'N, 164°01'W; 62-692, 54°25'N, 164°15'W; and 62-527, 54°27'N, 160°19'W. Northernmost record in Bering Sea may be SIO 76-392, a 253-mm-SL specimen from 58°24'N, 174°32'W, depth 216 m. Others at SIO are from Aleutian Islands: SIO 76-393, 57°42'N, 169°28'W; 94-184, 52°59'N, 169°59'W; 94-189, 52°43'N, 170°46'W; 94-227, 51°36'N, 177°47'W; 94-233, 52°08'N, 179°53'W. USNM 325569 is from 52°08'N, 175°39'W. Depth record for Alaska is 265 m, from SIO 94-189. Sea of Okhotsk records range down to 250 m.

Size: Schmidt 1950.

Elassodiscus tremebundus Gilbert & Burke, 1912 **dimdisk snailfish**

Eastern Bering Sea over continental and Aleutian Islands slopes; western Bering Sea off Cape Navarin to Pacific Ocean off Kuril Islands and Hokkaido, and Sea of Okhotsk.

Benthic, taken at depths of 130–1,286 m, usually on continental slope.

D 55–69; A 49–63; C 8–9; Pec 25–36; PC 10–20; Vert 62–74.

- Body in life thinly flushed with rose-red, translucent, the red due in part at least to blood vessels; caudal fin and posterior portions of dorsal and anal fins black; mouth, gill cavity, peritoneum, and stomach black.
- Body moderately elongate, deep, strongly compressed; head deep, compressed, occiput high; snout short, deep, rising abruptly from mouth, slightly projecting.
- Anterior dorsal and anal fin rays buried; **rays of lower lobe of pectoral fin relatively short**, not reaching origin of anal fin.
- Teeth trilobed.
- **Disk rudimentary, located in a depression or on the surface of the skin**, sometimes discernible only by preparation with stain.
- Gill opening above pectoral fin, rarely extending down in front of 1–4 rays.
- Length to 390 mm SL.

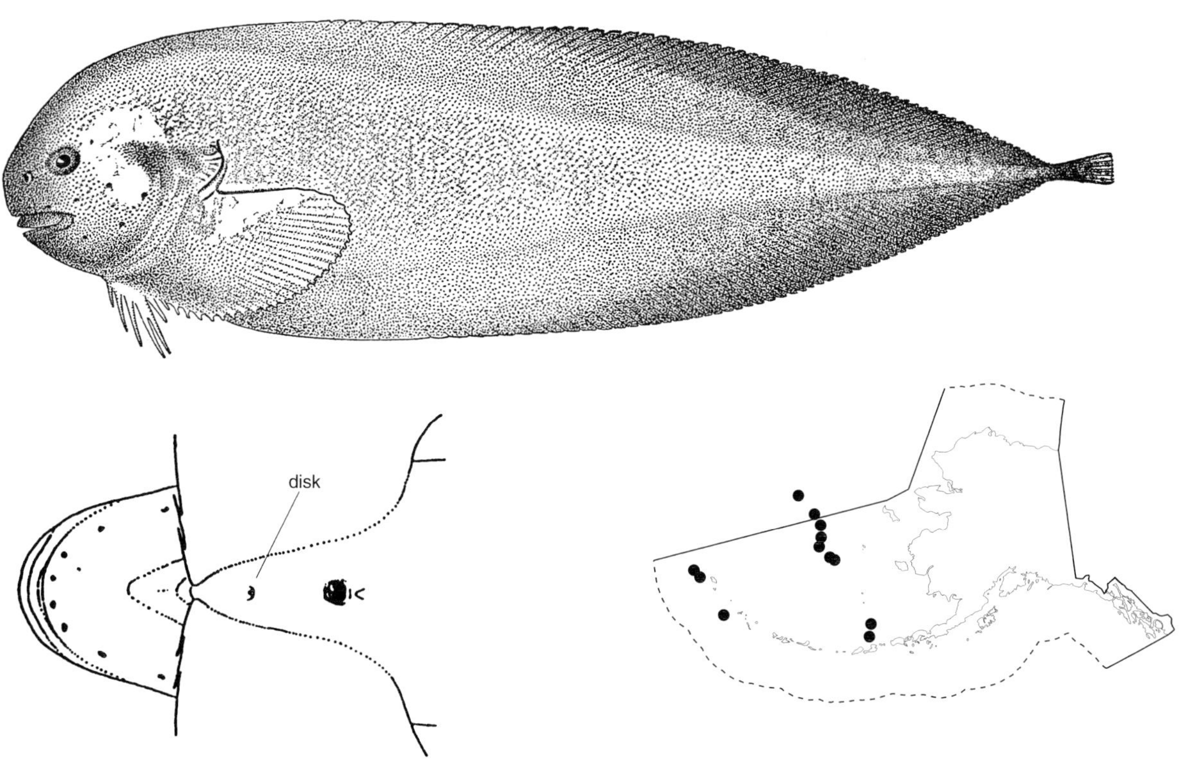

Notes & Sources — *Elassodiscus tremebundus* Gilbert & Burke, 1912

Kido (1988) synonymized *Elassodiscus* with *Paraliparis,* including the absence of a disk as a character in the diagnosis of *Paraliparis.* As recently demonstrated by Pitruk and Fedorov (1993b), however, the original assessment by Gilbert and Burke (1912a) was correct and a rudimentary disk is present (represented by a semicircular fold of skin on the surface or hidden in a pit, and free of the pelvic girdle except for strands of connective tissue).

Description: Gilbert & Burke 1912a:81–82; Burke 1930:154; Schmidt 1950:217; Kido 1992; Pitruk and Fedorov 1993b: 75–79.

Figures: Lateral view: Gilbert and Burke 1912a, fig. 26; holotype, USNM 74388, 214 mm TL, Avacha Bay, Kamchatka. Ventral: Pitruk and Fedorov 1993b, fig. 7.

Range: Kido (1992) listed samples collected from nine eastern Bering Sea localities at depths of 560–915 m. Specimens at NMNH from Alaska include USNM 325576, 58°54'N, 178°57'W; 325578, 58°33'N, 176°22'W; 325591, 58°32'N, 176°06'W; 325460, 58°33'N, 175°05'W; 325585, 58°20'N, 175°02'W; 325588, 54°51'N, 167°42'W; from collected by otter trawl at depths of 497–990 m in 1979. R. Baxter (unpubl. data) examined an uncataloged CAS specimen taken near Attu Island at 52°49'N, 172°14'E, depth 560–600 m. Pitruk and Fedorov (1993b) recorded specimens from northwestern Bering Sea at 60°53'N, 179°18'E, and 61°47'N, 176°38'E. Depth extremes: Dudnik and Dolganov 1992 (300–1,286 m); Pitruk and Fedorov 1993b (130 m).

Size: Tokranov 2000b: maximum size in a sample of 3,034 specimens taken off southeastern Kamchatka and the northern Kuril Islands in the 1990s was 39 cm SL.

Elassodiscus caudatus (Gilbert, 1915) **humpback snailfish**

Eastern Bering Sea, southeastern Alaska, Oregon, and Monterey Bay, California.

Benthic, on continental slope at depths of 335–1,040 m.

D 49–55; A 41–50; C 9–10; Pec 27–29; PC 13–14; Vert 54–62.

- Skin pinkish white, transparent, finely speckled; caudal fin and posterior portions of dorsal and anal fins blackish in most specimens; mouth pale; gill cavity, peritoneum, and stomach black, showing through sides; pyloric caeca pale.
- Head and body compressed; **dorsal profile strongly arched at occiput and nape**; snout short, deep, profile nearly vertical above mouth then rising sharply to occiput.
- **Lower pectoral rays longer than upper and almost completely free**, reaching to or beyond origin of anal fin.
- Teeth trilobed.
- **Disk minute**, not always discernible without staining; almost on symphysis of pectoral fins.
- Gill opening entirely above pectoral fin base or extending down in front of 1–2 rays.
- Length to 183 mm SL, 199 mm TL.

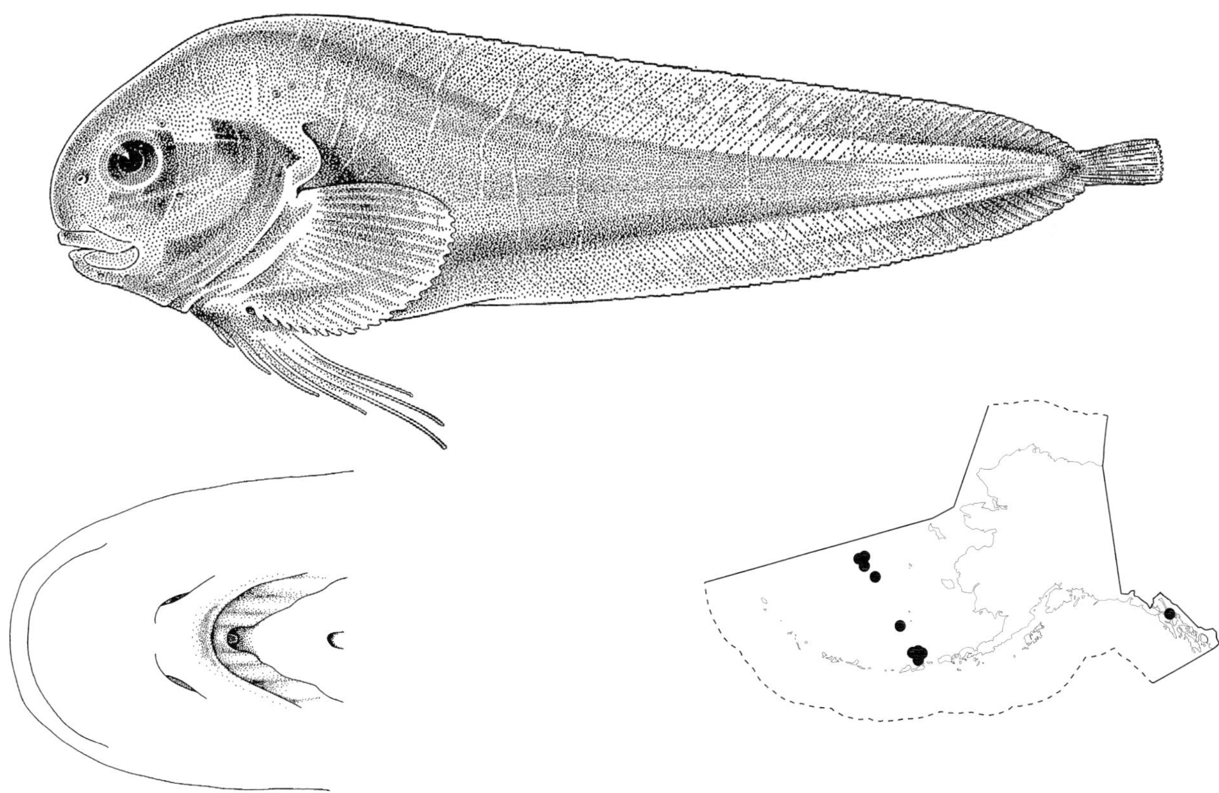

Notes & Sources — *Elassodiscus caudatus* (Gilbert, 1915)

Paraliparis caudatus Gilbert, 1915

Classified in *Elassodiscus* by Stein (1978). Kido (1988) classified *Elassodiscus* as a junior synonym of *Paraliparis.* See note for *E. tremebundus* on preceding page.

With the disk being practically indiscernible, *Elassodiscus caudatus* is easily mistaken for a *Paraliparis.* However, the trilobed teeth distinguish it from all *Paraliparis* except *P. dactylosus,* from which *E. caudatus* may be distinguished by its very long, almost completely free lower pectoral fin rays, more posteriorly inserted pectoral fin, and other characters.

Description: Gilbert 1915:356–357; Stein 1978:26–29; Anderson et al. 1979; Pitruk and Fedorov 1993b:83.

Figures: Lateral view: Gilbert 1915, pl. 18, fig. 14; type, USNM 75815, 86 mm TL, Monterey Bay. Ventral: Stein 1978, fig. 9.

Range: One record from southeastern Alaska, which is that of Quast and Hall (1972) from Stephens Passage, verified by Stein (1978): AB 62-486, from 58°01'N, 134°51'W, depth 618 m. The NMNH collection has 18 fine specimens from the eastern Bering Sea, taken by otter trawl in 1979 at depths of 497–1,040 m: USNM 325452, 58°54'N, 176°06'W; 325454, 59°26'N, 178°29'W; 325455, 59°18'N, 178°18'W; 325456, 58°33'N, 176°22'W; 325517, 54°40'N, 167°49'W; 325521, 54°51'N, 167°41'W; 325522, 56°06'N, 170°51'W; 325524, 54°20'N, 167°20'W; and 325579, 58°32'N, 176°06'W. USNM 325517, taken at 1,030–1,040 m, represents a new depth record.

Size: USNM 325579.

Rhinoliparis barbulifer Gilbert, 1896 **longnose snailfish**

Bering Sea, Umnak Pass, and Pacific Ocean in vicinity of Unalaska Island; southern California; Commander Islands; Sea of Okhotsk and Pacific off Hokkaido to northern Honshu.

Benthopelagic, at depths of 252–1,500 m.

D 63–65; A 57–59; C 3; Pec 18–20; PC 8–9; Vert 68.

- Skin transparent; mouth, gill cavity, and peritoneum black, showing through skin; pyloric caeca pale.
- Body slender, becoming very attentuate posteriorly; head relatively heavy, wider than deep, occiput slightly swollen.
- Snout low, projecting; **2 barbels on tip of snout**; barbels transparent, hence inconspicuous.
- **Dorsal, anal, and pectoral fin ray counts and vertebral count lower than in *R. attenuatus*.**
- **Teeth strongly lobed**.
- Pelvic disk absent.
- Length to 110 mm TL.

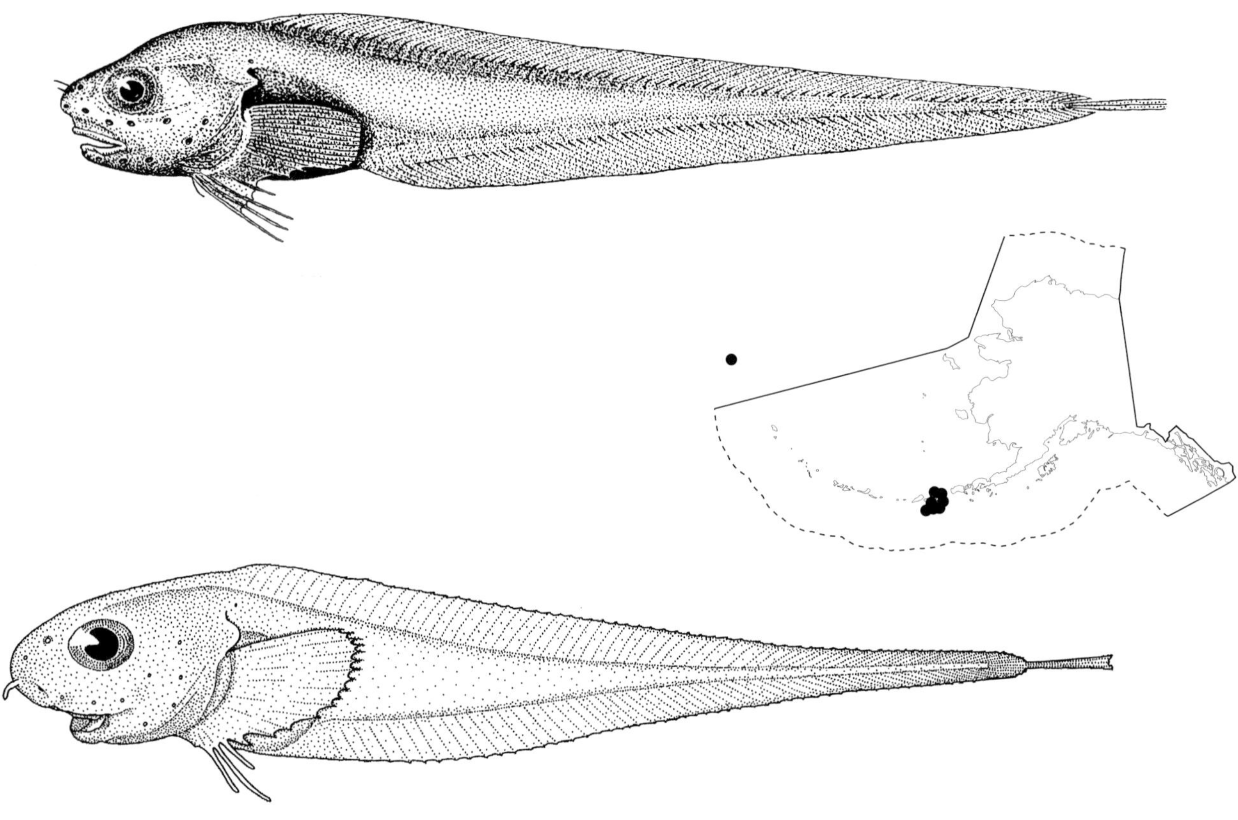

Notes & Sources — *Rhinoliparis barbulifer* Gilbert, 1896

Kido (1988) synonymized *Rhinoliparis* with *Paraliparis,* but not all investigators concur. Considering a related nomenclatural problem (see notes for *R. attenuatus* on next page), Kido (pers. comm., 17 Feb. 1998) suggested the continued use of *Rhinoliparis.*

Description: Gilbert 1896:445; Burke 1930:185–187; Schmidt 1950:223–224; Kido and Kitagawa 1986:table 1; Kido 1988:231.

Figures: Upper: Lindberg and Krasyukova 1987, fig. 282; 69 mm TL, Sea of Okhotsk. Lower: Kido 1988, fig. 55; 53 mm SL, Pacific Ocean off Iwate Prefecture.

Range: Gilbert (1896) described the species from specimens collected at several locations close to each other in the vicinity of the eastern Aleutian Islands: *Albatross* station 3227, 54°36'N, 166°54'W; station 3325, 53°37'N, 167°50'W; station 3326, 53°40'N, 167°42'W; station 3329, 53°57'N, 167°08'W; station 3330, 54°01'N, 166°54'W; station 3331, 54°02'N, 166°59'W; and station 3332, 54°03'N, 166°45'W; at depths of 411–1,053 m. A. E. Peden collected a specimen from the same area in 1980: NMC 81-509, 54°31'N, 165°49'W. Pitruk (1990) reported a maximum depth of capture of 1,500 m in the Sea of Okhotsk.

Size: Burke 1930.

Rhinoliparis attenuatus Burke, 1912 — **slim snailfish**

Eastern Bering Sea; southern British Columbia to Monterey Bay, California.

Pelagic, at depths of 362–2,189 m.

D 74–78; A 70–73; C 2; Pec 21–25; PC 9–10; Vert 80–83.

- Skin transparent, body dusky posteriorly; barbels dark; mouth, gill cavity, and peritoneum black; stomach partially black; pyloric caeca pale.
- Body very slender (attenuated).
- Snout slightly depressed, broad, projecting; **9 snout barbels**, delicate, some usually or always missing due to damage.
- **Dorsal, anal, and pectoral fin ray counts and vertebral counts higher than in *R. barbulifer*.**
- **Teeth simple**, lateral lobes faintly indicated on some teeth.
- Pelvic disk absent.
- Length to 110 mm SL.

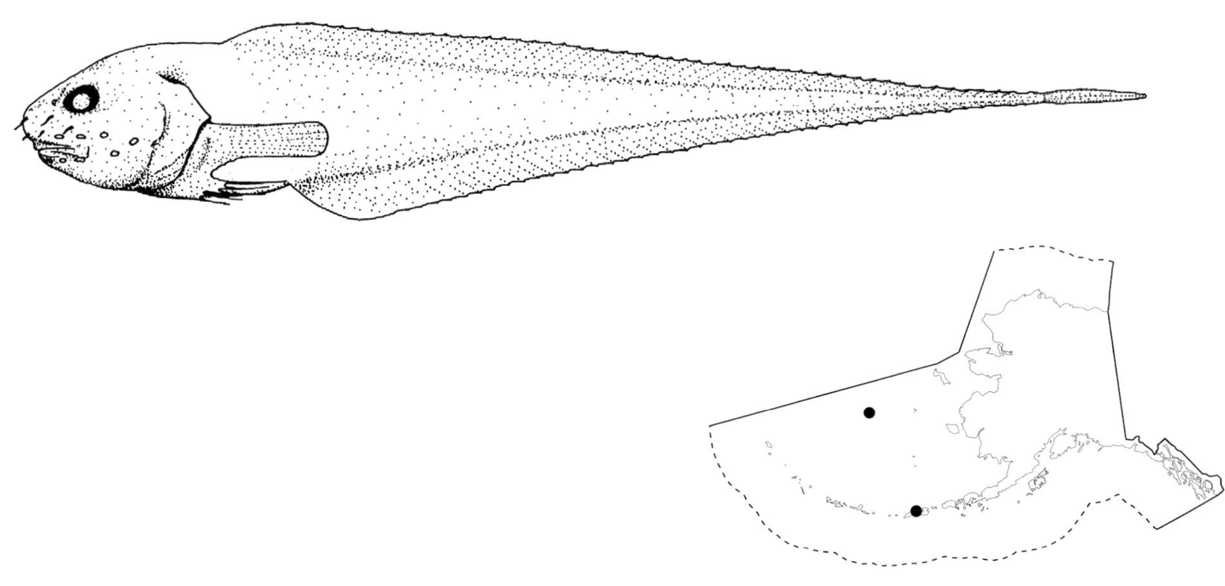

Notes & Sources — *Rhinoliparis attenuatus* Burke, 1912

Kido (1988) synonymized *Rhinoliparis* with *Paraliparis,* but not all workers agree. Moreover, the resulting combination for this species is preoccupied by *Paraliparis attenuatus* Garman, 1899. Consequently, Kido (pers. comm., 17 Feb. 1998) recommended the continued use of *Rhinoliparis,* pending further study.

Description: Burke 1912b:573–574; Burke 1930:187–188; Stein 1978:32–33; Kido and Kitagawa 1986:table 1.

Figure: Stein 1978, fig. 10C; composite of four partially skinned specimens, 62–110 mm SL, from Pacific Ocean off Oregon.

Range: One previous Alaskan record: Burke (1912b), *Albatross* station 3326, 53°40'N, 167°42'W, depth 1,053 m. An additional specimen, USNM 325593, was collected by D. M. Cohen in 1979 at 58°40'N, 177°55'W, depth 735–800 m. The nearest record outside Alaska is a specimen from southern British Columbia at 48°55'N, 126°32'W, depth 400–900 m, reported by Peden (1997ms). Previously, Stein (1978) included two specimens captured a few kilometers to the south (48°38'N, 127°00'W, depth 2,189 m) in his list of material examined.

Size: Stein 1978.

Acantholiparis opercularis Gilbert & Burke, 1912 **spiny snailfish**

North Pacific Ocean near Shumagin Islands, off Oregon, and off southeast Kamchatka; western Bering Sea off northeastern Kamchatka.

Benthic, on lower continental slope and abyssal plain at depths of 1,247–3,609 m.

D 45–52; A 38–47; C 8–10; Pec 20–26; PC 0; Vert 50.

- Dusky reddish; black lips, fin tips, and abdominal region; dusky interior; peritoneum dusky to black, stomach pale.
- Body slender, depressed; head broad, depressed.
- **Operculum with 2 distinct spines directed dorsally and laterally**.
- Pelvic disk absent.
- **Pyloric caeca absent**.
- Length to 83 mm TL.

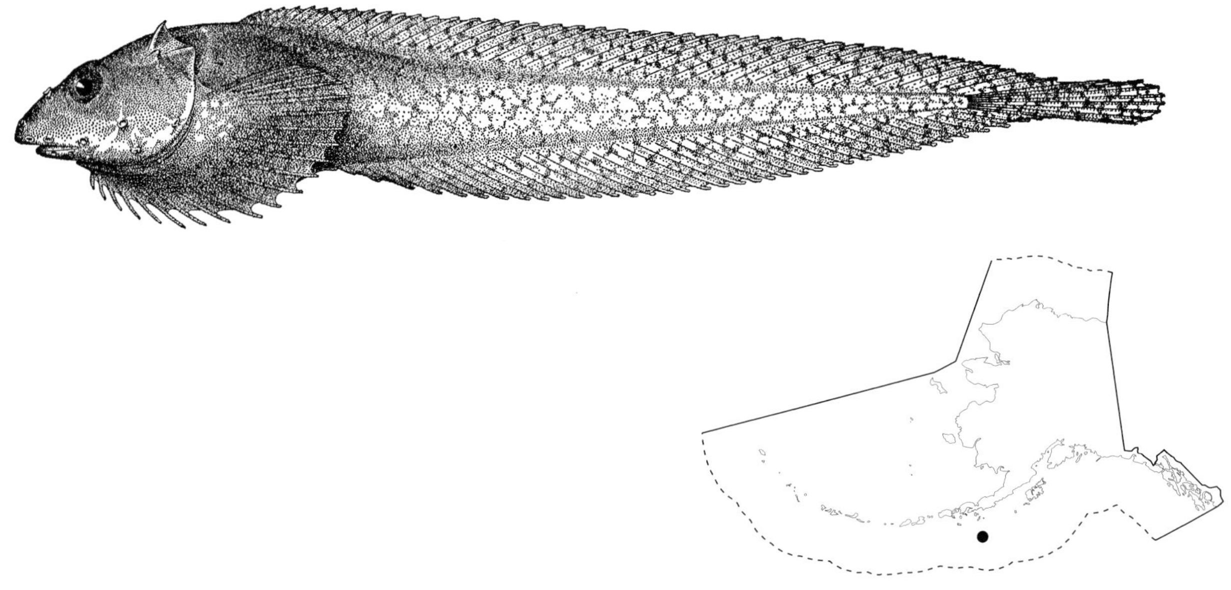

Notes & Sources — *Acantholiparis opercularis* Gilbert & Burke, 1912

Kido (1988) synonymized *Acantholiparis* with *Paraliparis*. However, the spiny armature of *Acantholiparis* seems significant to taxonomists continuing to maintain the distinction (e.g., Nelson 1994).

Description: Gilbert and Burke 1912a:83–84; Burke 1930: 188–189; Grinols 1966d, 1969; Stein 1978:35.

Figure: Gilbert and Burke 1912a, fig. 28; holotype, USNM 74390, 76 mm TL, *Albatross* station 4797, near Staritschkof Island, Avacha Bay, Kamchatka, 1,247 m.

Range: The only Alaskan record is the paratype (USNM 74514) recorded by Gilbert and Burke (1912a) from *Albatross* station 4761, off the Shumagin Islands at 53°57'N, 159°31'W, depth 3,609 m. V. V. Fedorov (unpubl. data provided by B. A. Sheiko, pers. comm., 12 May 1998) has a specimen from northeastern Kamchatka, extending the known range north into the Bering Sea from the holotype collection locality at Avacha Bay, southeastern Kamchatka.

Size: Grinols 1966d.

Paraliparis dactylosus Gilbert, 1896 **polydactyl snailfish**

One record from eastern Bering Sea, one from Pacific Ocean south of Unimak Pass, and others off Oregon, central California, and Commander Islands; doubtful record from vicinity of Agattu Island.

Benthic, on continental slope at depths of 541–960 m.

D 54–61; A 49–55; C 8; Pec 28–30; PC 17–23; Vert 59–67.

- Preserved specimens pale, with scattered speckles; caudal fin and posterior portions of dorsal and anal fins blackish; mouth pale at front, dusky posteriorly; gill cavity and peritoneum black; stomach and pyloric caeca pale.
- Head and abdomen somewhat compressed, cheeks vertical; strongly elevated at occiput; snout deep; body posterior to abdomen strongly compressed.
- **Eye large**, 28–33% of head length.
- Pectoral fin lobed, the intermediate rays widely spaced, lower rays partly free; **more pectoral rays than in most species of *Paraliparis*.**
- **Teeth lobed**, in 12–18 oblique rows (the only *Paraliparis* with trilobed teeth).
- Pelvic disk absent.
- **Gill opening extending down in front of 2–4 pectoral rays.**
- Pyloric caeca relatively numerous.
- Length to 121 mm SL.

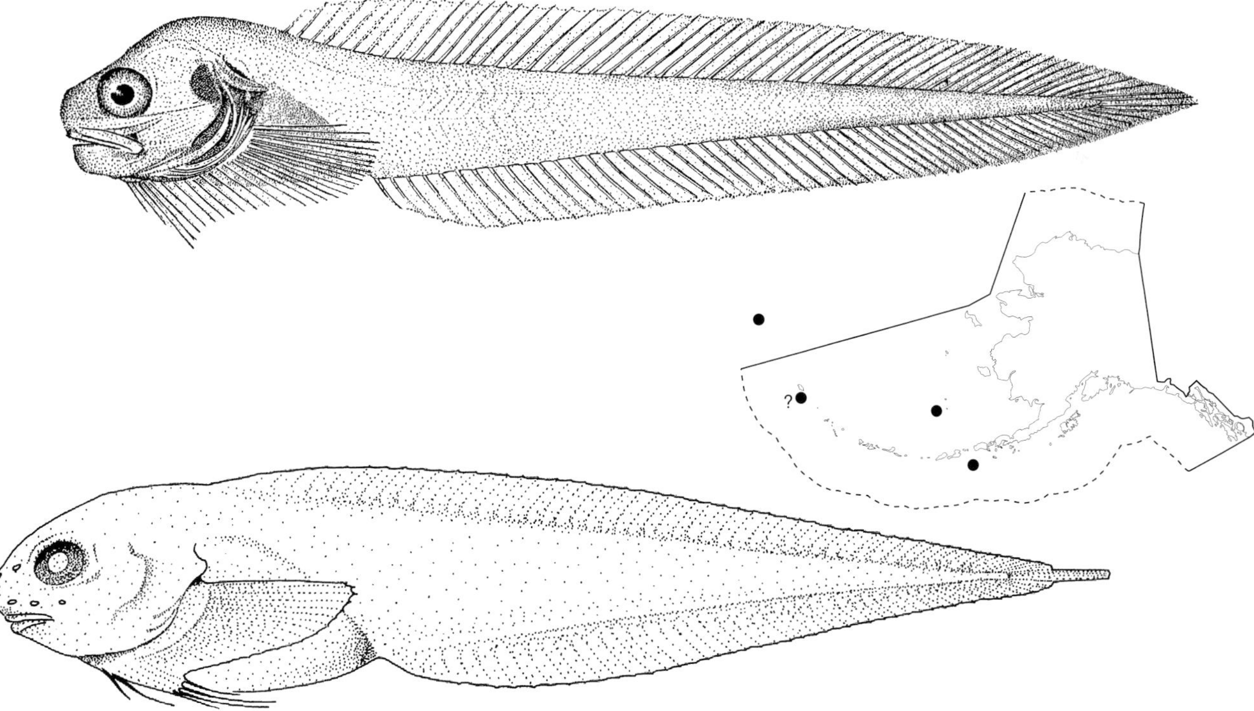

Notes & Sources — *Paraliparis dactylosus* Gilbert, 1896

Burke (1930) believed this to be the most generalized species of the genus, from the trilobed teeth and large numbers of pectoral fin rays and pyloric caeca.

Also called red snailfish (Hubbs et al. 1979), but the only specimen described as red (Gilbert and Burke 1912a) probably belongs to another species. Many snailfishes *are* red, and using this name has led to erroneous reports of this species. "Polydactyl" refers to an important diagnostic feature, the relatively numerous pectoral fin rays.

Description: Gilbert 1896:469–470; Burke 1930:164–166; Stein 1978:47–49. Available descriptions are bewildering in their discrepancies. Data from USNM 74720 (*Albatross* station 4781) are not included in the above description, following Stein (1978). Data from UBC 65-97, including counts from radiographs provided by M. S. Busby (pers. comm., 28 Jan. 1998), are included.

Figures: Upper: Gilbert 1896, pl. 34; type, 78 mm TL, *Albatross* station 3112, off Santa Cruz, California. Lower: Stein 1978, fig. 13B; OSUO 2263, female, 121 mm SL, partially skinned, off Cape Mendocino, California.

Range: Gilbert and Burke (1912a) referred a specimen (USNM 74720) from *Albatross* station 4781, "between Petrel Bank and Agattu Island" (more accurately described as off the south coast of Agattu Island) at 52°14'N, 174°13'E, to this species but Burke (1930) and Stein (1978) doubted the identification. A specimen (USNM 325589) from Bering Sea west of the Pribilof Islands at 56°06'N, 170°51'W, depth 850–890 m, is this species; a note in the jar by D. L. Stein (19 Aug. 1986) provisionally identifies the specimen, and C.W.M. (17 Nov. 1999) found it to have appropriate diagnostic characters, including trilobed teeth. UBC 65-97 comprises two specimens taken southeast of Tigalda Island at 53°38'N, 164°44'W; identification confirmed by M. S. Busby and C.W.M. Fedorov and Sheiko (2002) reported *P. dactylosus* in the vicinity of the Commander Islands. Depth extremes: 541 m (Gilbert 1896) and 960 m (Stein 1978) off California.

Size: Stein 1978.

Paraliparis pectoralis Stein, 1978

pectoral snailfish

Bering Sea, Pacific Ocean off British Columbia and Oregon, and off Okhotsk coast of Hokkaido, Japan. Benthopelagic, over continental slope at depths of 681–1,536 m.

D 55–59; A 49–52; C 7–8; Pec 28–32; PC 6–10; Vert 61–66.

- Dark brown, head darker; speckles scattered over body; mouth, gill cavity, and peritoneum black; stomach and pyloric caeca pale.
- Upper pectoral ray at or little above level of posterior end of maxilla; **more pectoral rays than in most species of *Paraliparis*.**
- Cephalic pores, discernible depending on condition of specimen, include **2 closely spaced suprabranchial pores**; rudimentary pores form lateral line to caudal fin.
- Anteriormost pair of mandibular pores widely separated.
- **Teeth simple**, blunt canines or slightly lanceolate, in narrow bands.
- Pelvic disk absent.
- Gill opening extending down in front of 1–2 pectoral fin rays.
- Length to 218 mm SL.

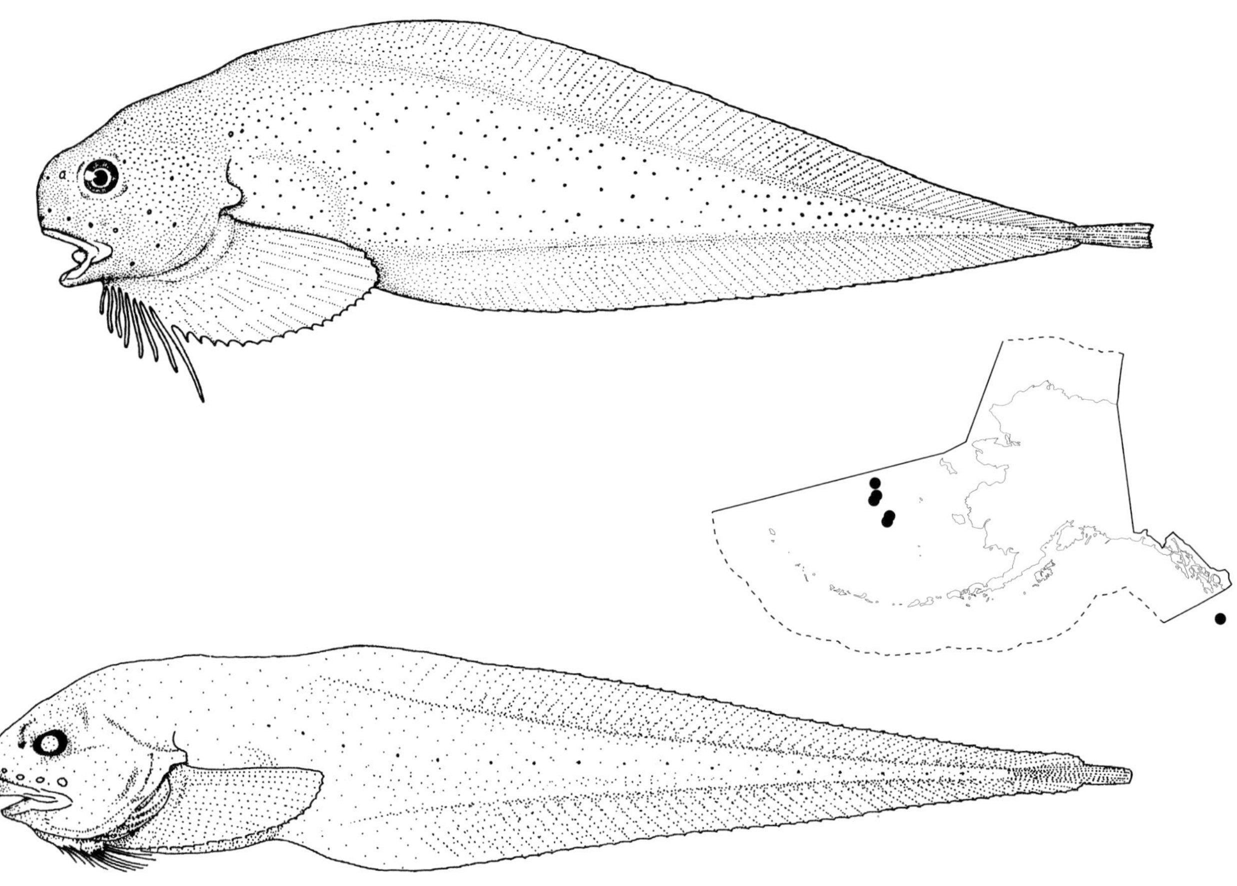

Notes & Sources — *Paraliparis pectoralis* Stein, 1978

Description: Stein 1978:49; Kido 1984b:203–204, 1993:107.

Figures: Upper: Kido 1984b, fig. 1; HUMZ 81964, 140 mm SL, central Bering Sea. Lower: Stein 1978, fig. 13C; holotype, USNM 214606, 135 mm SL, partially skinned, eastern Pacific off Tillamook Head, Oregon.

Range: Kido (1984b) examined 8 specimens from localities in U.S. waters of the Bering Sea: 58°20'N, 175°02'W; 58°15'N, 175°28'W; 59°50'N, 178°47'W; 59°26'N, 178°47'W; 60°24'N, 179°31'W; at depths of 681–990 m. Another Bering Sea specimen is USNM 325587, from 59°26'N, 178°29'W, depth 700–820 m. Peden (1997ms) described the first specimen known from British Columbia, taken at 53°04'N, 132°59'W, depth 1,227 m (BCPM 991-332). Stein (1978) described specimens from the Pacific off Oregon, and Kido (1993) reported the first record from Japan. Depth extremes: Kido 1984b (681 m), Stein 1978 (1,536 m).

Size: Stein 1978.

Paraliparis paucidens Stein, 1978 — toothless snailfish

One specimen from Dixon Entrance, British Columbia, near Alaska border; and two off Oregon.

Benthic, on lower continental slope at depths of 1,536–2,275 m.

D 58–60; A 53–54; C 6–8; Pec 19–24; PC 5–8; Vert 66–67.

- Dark brown, head and snout darker; mouth, gill cavity, and peritoneum dark brown or black; stomach and pyloric caeca pale.
- **Thick, tapered, movable, cartilaginous rod mid-laterally on each side of mandible.**
- Uppermost pectoral fin ray level with lower part of eye, above level of posterior end of maxilla.
- **No teeth on lower jaw; upper jaw teeth absent or few and minute.** (Maxillary papillae can look like teeth, but are soft and flexible.)
- Pelvic disk absent.
- Gill opening entirely above pectoral fin.
- Length to 164 mm SL.

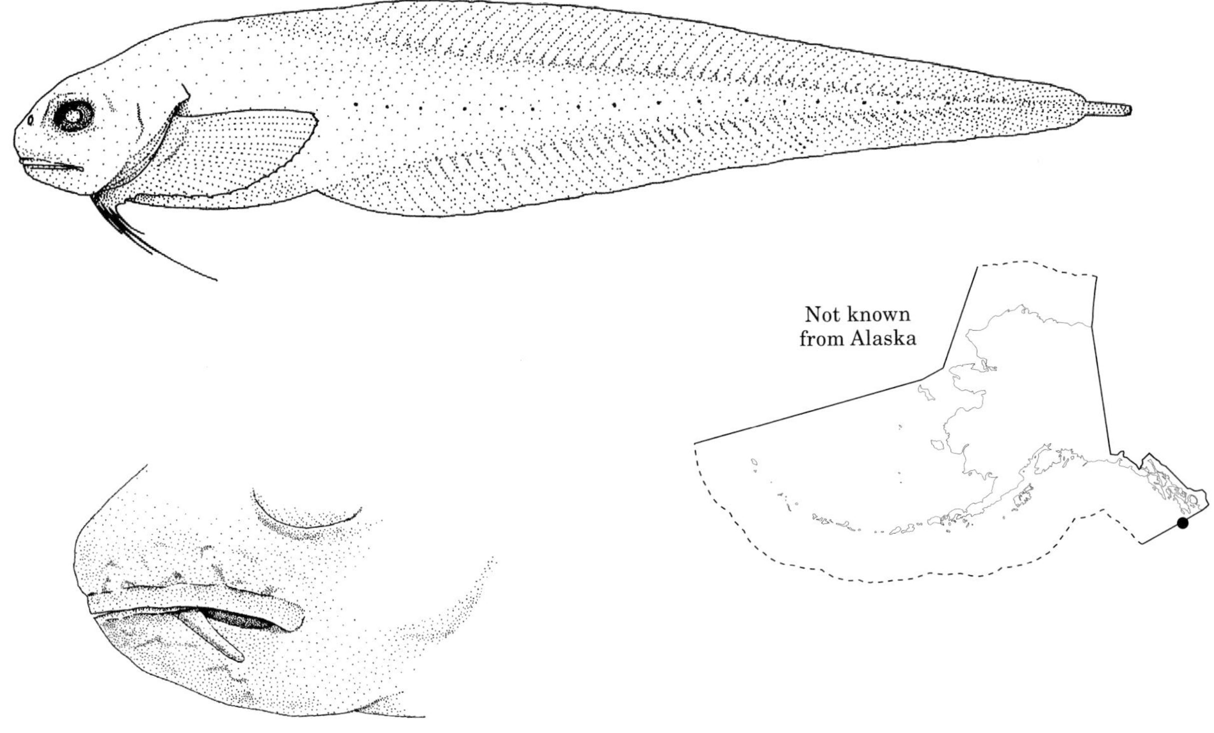

Notes & Sources — *Paraliparis paucidens* Stein, 1978

Description: Stein 1978:43–44; Stein and Peden 1979.

Figures: Stein 1978, figs. 11D and 12; holotype, USNM 214618, 164 mm SL, partially skinned, off Oregon. In detail of mouth, the posterior end of the accessory mandibular rod is pulled down to show more clearly.

Range: British Columbia specimen was taken close to the U.S.–Canada border at 54°32'N, 134°35'W, at a depth of 2,275 m (Stein and Peden 1979).

Size: Stein 1978.

Paraliparis holomelas Gilbert, 1896 **ebony snailfish**

Southeastern Bering Sea to western and central Gulf of Alaska; Pacific Ocean off southeastern Kamchatka and northern Kuril Islands to Sea of Okhotsk.

Benthic, at depths of 617–3,350 m.

D 58–61; A 54; C 5; Pec 23; PC 8.

- Black, including fins, mouth, gill cavity, peritoneum, and stomach; pyloric caeca white.
- Body deepest at nape, sloping rapidly to elongate slender tail; trunk short, not equal to the head; head very large, deep; occiput and nape high, arched; profile not concave over eyes.
- Snout abrupt; mouth horizontal; maxilla extending to a vertical slightly behind posterior margin of eye.
- Pectoral fins with two wholly distinct lobes; **interspace with 2 or 3 rudimentary, buried rays; lower lobe of 5 or 6 almost filamentous rays, all free to base**.
- **Head pores enlarged, oval**; **1 suprabranchial pore**.
- Pelvic disk absent.
- Gill opening large, extending down in front of about 13 pectoral fin rays.
- Length to 100 mm TL.

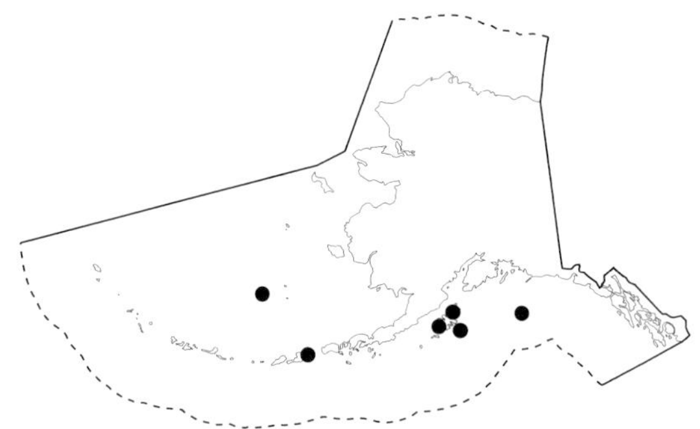

Notes & Sources — *Paraliparis holomelas* Gilbert, 1896

Description: Gilbert 1896:441; Burke 1930:175–176. Caudal fin ray count provided by M. S. Busby (pers. comm., Sep. 1997) from ongoing research on early life history stages of *P. holomelas* based on specimens collected in Shelikof Strait, Alaska.

Figures: None available of external appearance. Busby (pers. comm., 26 Jan. 1999) plans to write an early life history paper with illustrations of juveniles, but the adult specimens are in poor condition and not suitable for drawing.

Range: Recorded from southeastern Bering Sea by Gilbert (1896): *Albatross* station 3308, west of Pribilof Islands, 56°12'N, 172°07'W, 2,972 m; and station 3332, just north of Unalaska Island, 54°03'N, 166°45'W, 743 m. SIO 63-536, a 66-mm-SL specimen, is from north-central Gulf of Alaska at 58°00'N, 146°00'W. UBC has three collections: UBC 62-517, Raspberry Strait off Afognak Island, 58°12'N, 153°12'W; UBC 62-526, off Cape Alitak, southwest Kodiak Island, 56°54'N, 155°00'W; and UBC 62-677, 57°06'N, 152°30'W, off Sitkalidak Island. Dudnik and Dolganov (1992) recorded this species from the Sea of Okhotsk at depths of 617–1,998 m. Maximum known depth of 3,350 m was recorded by Schmidt (1950) from the Sea of Okhotsk. V. V. Fedorov (unpubl. data provided by B. A. Sheiko, pers. comm., 12 May 1998) collected it off the northern Kuril Islands and southeastern Kamchatka.

Size: Gilbert 1896.

Paraliparis deani Burke, 1912 **prickly snailfish**

Western Gulf of Alaska at Shelikof Strait to southern British Columbia; also northern California. Benthic, on continental shelf and slope at depths of 18–1,008 m.

D 56–57; A 44–48; C about 6; Pec 18–22; PC 9.

- Translucent pale brown, silvery with black specks ventrally; lips and fins pinkish; peritoneum dusky, or silvery with dots; stomach black.
- Body deepest at nape, compressed, slender and elongate behind; head short, broad, occiput arched.
- Snout wide, blunt; mouth horizontal; maxilla extending to below posterior part of eye.
- Thumbtack prickles present on epidermis covering base of lower lobe of pectoral fin; prickles not always evident
- **Pectoral fin notched without really being divided into two, lower rays greatly exserted**.
- Pelvic disk absent.
- **Gill opening large, extending down in front of 10–13 pectoral fin rays**.
- Length less than 100 mm TL.

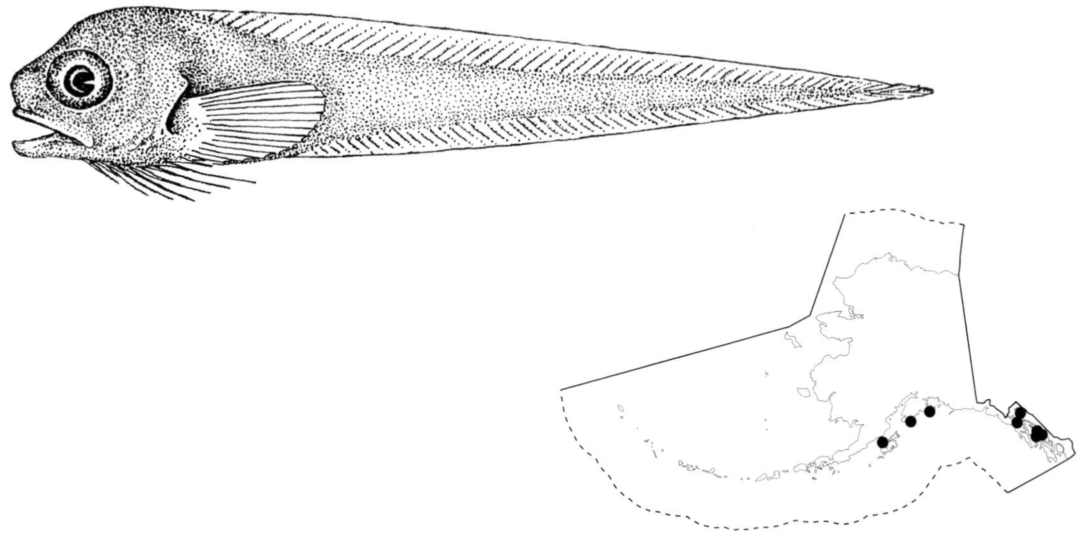

Notes & Sources — *Paraliparis deani* Burke, 1912

Paraliparis holomelas Gilbert: Evermann & Goldsborough, 1907:334 (part, specimens from *Albatross* stations 4194, 4203, 4251, 4253, 4255, 4292, 4293); synonymy from Burke (1912a, 1930).

Called prickly snailfish because of the prickles on the lower lobe of the pectoral fin. Prickles do not appear to be scattered over the entire body, but this cannot be determined with certainty from museum specimens because most of them are lacking the epidermis.

Description: Burke 1912a:571–572, 1930:168–169; Hart 1973:593–594; Stein 1978:47.

Figure: Hart 1973:593; UW 14761, 73 mm TL, Stephens Passage, southeastern Alaska.

Range: The type series (Burke 1912a) comprises specimens from *Albatross* station 4253, Stephens Passage near Thistle Ledge; station 4251, Stephens Passage off Hugh Point; station 4255, Taiya Inlet, Lynn Canal; and stations 4252 and 4293, Shelikof Strait off Cape Uyak; depths 55–501 m. Quast and Hall (1972) recorded collections from the Kenai Peninsula (AB 64-676) at Nuka Bay, 59°36'N, 150°31'W; and Montague Strait (not found). Stein (1978) examined specimens obtained near Karluk (SU 22600, *Albatross*), from Stephens Passage (UW 14761, *Cobb*), and near Petersburg (SU 24974, shrimp trawl, 18–55 m). UBC 65-493 is from Muir Inlet, 58°50'N, 136°05'W. Lower depth limit (1,008 m) is from collections off California (Stein 1978). Species has not been recorded from Oregon or Washington.

Size: Burke 1930.

Paraliparis ulochir Gilbert, 1896 **broadfin snailfish**

Southeastern Bering Sea; Pacific Ocean off Tillamook Head, Oregon; and Gulf of California. Benthic, on continental slope at depths of 720–1,838 m.

D 65–69; A 60–64; C 4; Pec 21–24; Vert 72–74.

- Black; mouth, gill cavity, stomach, and peritoneum black; pyloric caeca pale.
- **Pectoral fin high**, upper edge level with upper part of pupil; upper and lower lobes of closely spaced rays, 4–6 **widely spaced rays in notch; lower lobe of short rays, none of them free.**
- Pelvic disk absent.
- **Gill opening entirely above pectoral fin.**
- Length to 102 mm SL.

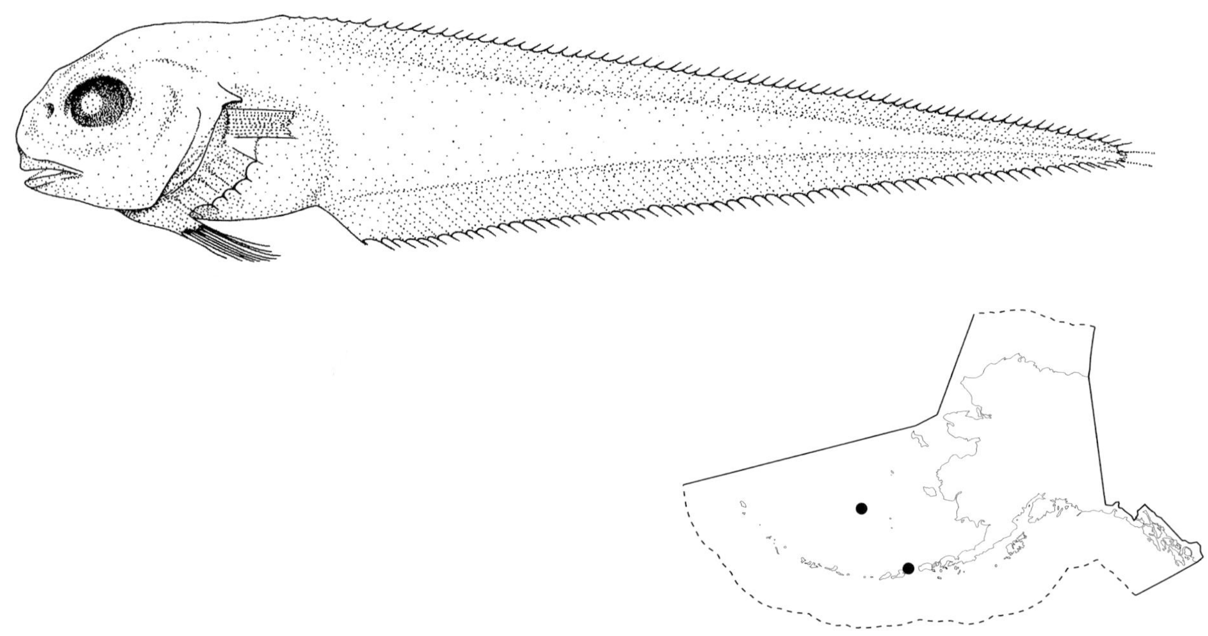

Notes & Sources — *Paraliparis ulochir* Gilbert, 1896

Description: Gilbert 1896:441–442; Burke 1930:171–172; Stein 1978:50. Meristics include additional counts provided by Stein to Matarese et al. (1989).

Figure: Stein 1978, fig. 13D; BCPM 71–194, 102 mm SL, completely skinned, Pacific off Oregon.

Range: Described by Gilbert (1896) from one "young specimen" (USNM 48699) taken in Bering Sea at *Albatross* station 3332, north of Unalaska Island at 54°03'N, 166°45'W, depth 743 m; and a few (3?) specimens from the Gulf of California, depth 1,838 m. USNM 325592 is another specimen from the Bering Sea, taken at 56°58'N, 173°51'W, depth 720 m. Stein (1978) described one specimen taken off Tillamook Head, Oregon, at a depth of 1,554 m.

Size: Stein 1978.

Paraliparis cephalus Gilbert, 1892 **swellhead snailfish**

Bering Sea and Shelikof Strait, western Gulf of Alaska; northern British Columbia to southern California; vicinity of Commander Islands.

Benthic, on continental slope at depths of 294–1,799 m.

D 50–57; A 44–51; C 4; Pec 14–16; PC 6–10; Vert 57–63.

- Light reddish, abdomen blue-black; mouth and gill cavity white to dusky; peritoneum and stomach black; loose, transparent skin.
- **Head, occiput, and anterior part of body greatly swollen; body tapering to very narrow, threadlike, elongate caudal fin**; swollen head and belly particularly evident in young individuals.
- **Mouth oblique; mandibular symphysis with knob that fits into wide notch at juncture of premaxillae**.
- Upper pectoral ray below level of orbit and above level of posterior end of maxilla; middle rays widely spaced, ray tips free, none rudimentary or buried; 2–4 lower lobe rays, free for most of their length; **low total number of pectoral rays**.
- Cephalic pores enlarged.
- Pelvic disk absent.
- Gill opening above pectoral fin; can appear to extend down to 10th pectoral ray due to tearing during capture.
- Length to 82 mm SL or more.

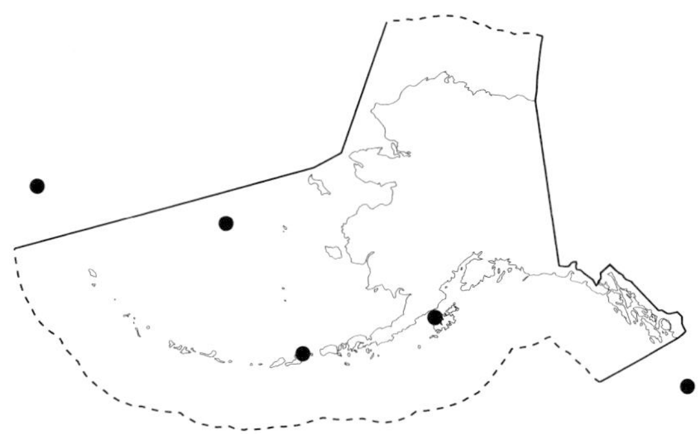

Notes & Sources — *Paraliparis cephalus* Gilbert, 1892

Description: Gilbert 1892:561–562; Burke 1930:177–179; Stein 1978:39–40.

Figures: None available of external appearance.

Range: Previous Alaskan records are those of Gilbert (1896) from *Albatross* station 3330, north of Unalaska Island, 54°01'N, 166°54'W, 642 m; and Burke (1930) from Shelikof Strait off Karluk. USNM 325577 is a specimen from the Bering Sea at 59°19'N, 178°06'W, depth 603–610 m. The nearest record outside Alaska is a specimen (BCPM 71-9) included in a list of materials examined by Stein (1978), from northern British Columbia at 52°07'N, 131°28'W, depth 1,068 m. Fedorov and Sheiko (2002) listed *P. cephalus* from the Commander Islands and gave a depth range of 294–1,799 m. Previously recorded from 519 m off southern California (Gilbert 1892) to 1,384 m off Oregon or California (Stein 1978).

Size: Stein 1978. The species probably reaches greater sizes. Baxter (1990ms) reported a total length of 105 mm for a specimen taken off northern California in a 1990 survey using the Russian vessel *Novokotovsk* (specimen not saved).

Paraliparis rosaceus Gilbert, 1890 — rosy snailfish

Pacific Ocean off northern British Columbia, Oregon, California, and Baja California; Gulf of California; Sea of Okhotsk off Hokkaido.

Benthic, at depths of 1,050–3,358 m.

D 57–69; A 53–60; C 6–8; Pec 18–22; PC 6–9; Vert 67–74.

- **Body rose red, pinkish, or bluish with faint pink when fresh; head and fin margins black**; mouth dusky; gelatinous tissue thick except for caudal fin.
- Mouth horizontal; **head length 17–21% of standard length, depth about equal to head width**.
- **Pectoral fins deeply notched, notch rays often rudimentary in adults**.
- Pelvic disk absent.
- Gill opening small, entirely above pectoral fin.
- Length to 400 mm SL (one of the largest species of *Paraliparis*).

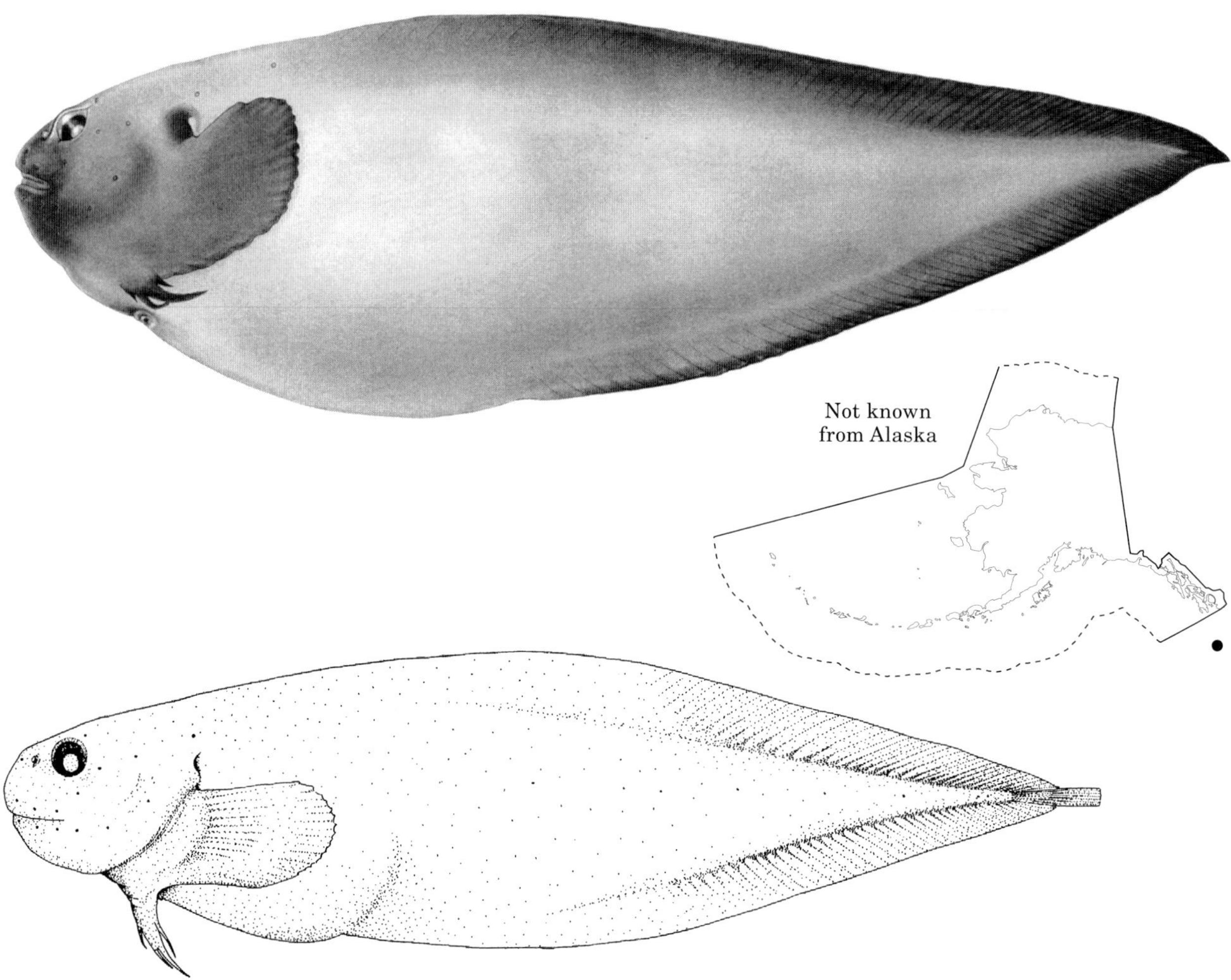

Notes & Sources — *Paraliparis rosaceus* Gilbert, 1890
Paraliparis grandiceps Garman, 1899
Some faunal lists give pink snailfish for the vernacular, but several snailfishes are pink. The name rosy snailfish, after the scientific name, may be less confusing.

Description: Stein 1978:41–43; Peden and Ostermann 1980; Kido 1983:382–384; Kido 1988:235–236.

Figures: Upper: Royal British Columbia Museum, artist P. Drukker-Brammall; BCPM 979-11101, 325 mm SL, off Tasu Sound, British Columbia. Lower: Stein 1978, fig. 11C; OSU 2069, 333 mm SL, off Oregon.

Range: Northernmost record was reported by Peden and Ostermann (1980), a specimen from North Pacific off Tasu Sound, Queen Charlotte Islands, at 52°36'N, 132°19'W, taken in sablefish trap at depth of 2,195 m. Three others were taken in sablefish traps west of Vancouver Island at depth of 1,920 m. Depth range: Kido 1983 (1,050 m, Sea of Okhotsk) and Stein 1978 (3,358 m, Oregon).

Size: Peden and Ostermann 1980: BCPM 979-11101-2, west of Vancouver Island.

Paraliparis melanobranchus Gilbert & Burke, 1912 **phantom snailfish**

One record from British Columbia; two unverified records from Oregon; and holotype, from southern part of Sea of Okhotsk.

British Columbia specimen caught in midwater well off the bottom; Oregon specimens caught at depths of 1,463 m and 1,554 m; holotype at 805 m.

D 52–60; A 48–54; C 4; Pec 17–18; PC 6–7; Vert 64.

- Skin transparent, finely speckled; in life bright orange-red or brick red; chin and isthmus area black; mouth, gill cavity, peritoneum, and stomach black; black coloration of mouth and body cavity generally not evident through orange-red pigment in life but visible through body wall in faded, preserved specimens.
- Skin thin, loose, held away from body by liquid.
- **Pectoral fin rays 17–18** (more than in *Lipariscus nanus*); rays widely spaced, especially in notch area.
- Pelvic disk absent.
- Anus very close to pectoral symphysis.
- **Gill opening entirely above pectoral fin**.
- Larger of the two verified records is 83 mm TL.

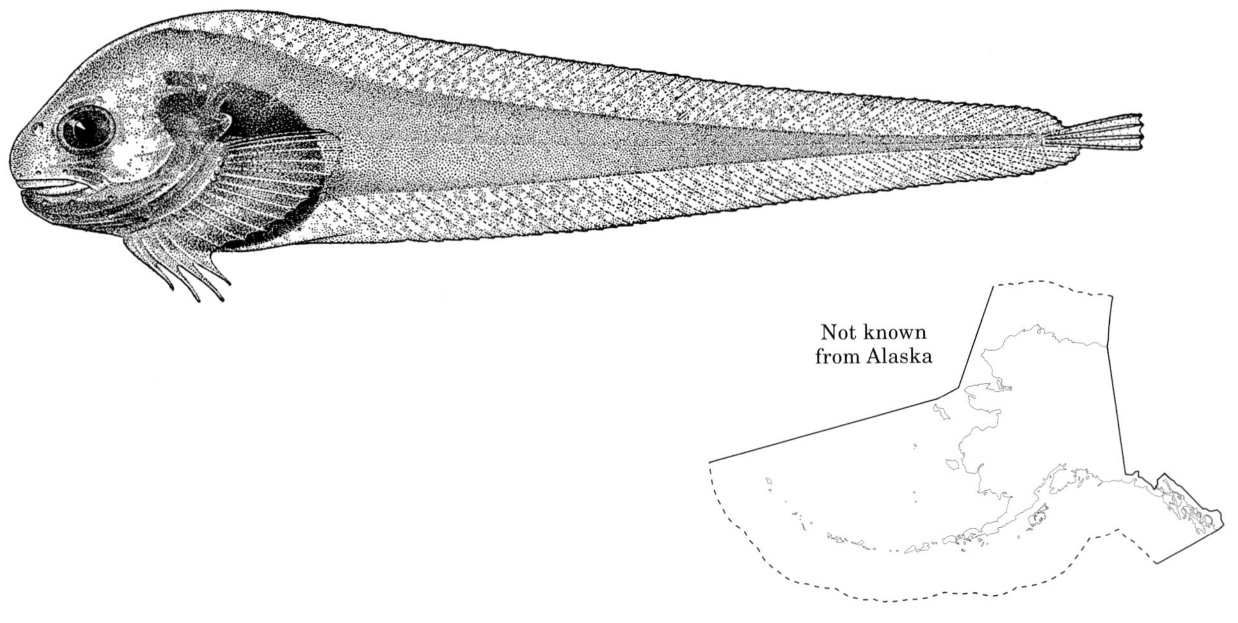

Notes & Sources — *Paraliparis melanobranchus* Gilbert & Burke, 1912

The vernacular, coined by Peden (1997d), refers to the ghostly appearance of the orange-red fish as it lay in the catch bucket in the dim light of a rainy winter day.

Description: Gilbert and Burke 1912b:378; Burke 1930:173–174; Stein 1978:52; Peden 1997ms.

Figure: Gilbert and Burke 1912b, pl. 48, fig. 2; holotype (unique), USNM 73346, 83 mm TL, Sea of Okhotsk.

Range: Record nearest to Alaska is a specimen measuring 67.3 mm SL taken off British Columbia at 48°42'N, 126°26'W (Peden 1997d, 1997ms). Occurrence in both British Columbia and the Sea of Okhotsk suggests a broad distribution in the North Pacific, and possible occurrence in the Gulf of Alaska. In features and possible midwater lifestyle *P. melanobranchus* is similar to *Lipariscus nanus*. Stein (1978) questioned the validity of Oregon records reported by Alton (1972:610) because of the great distance from the Sea of Okhotsk and the limited distribution of many Sea of Okhotsk deepwater species, and the differences in depth of capture (Sea of Okhotsk, 805 m; Oregon, 1,463 and 1,554 m). Stein (1978) could not find the Oregon specimens, which were reported by Alton (1972:610), so they cannot be reexamined in light of the recent (Peden 1997ms) British Columbia record.

Size: Gilbert and Burke 1912b.

Lipariscus nanus Gilbert, 1915

pygmy snailfish

Eastern Bering Sea to Gulf of Alaska near Unimak Pass and southeastern Alaska; British Columbia; Monterey Bay, California; western Bering Sea, Commander Islands, and southern Sea of Okhotsk off Hokkaido, Japan.

Pelagic, usually taken at midwater depths; reported from depths of 58–910 m.

D 40–56; A 37–52; C 4; Pec 12–16; PC 4–8; Vert 60–62.

- Skin transparent, with scattered melanophores; mouth, gill cavity, peritoneum, stomach, and pyloric caeca black.
- Skin thin, loose, held well away from body by liquid.
- **Branchiostegal rays 5**.
- Prickles distributed over entire body, including pectoral fins.
- **Low number of pectoral fin rays**; pectoral fin rays widely spaced.
- Teeth simple, in narrow bands.
- Pelvic disk absent.
- **Anus posterior in position**; in adults, between the lower pectoral lobes anterior to a vertical line through gill opening; in juveniles more posterior, as far distally as end of body cavity.
- **Gill opening entirely above pectoral fin**.
- Length to 71 mm SL.

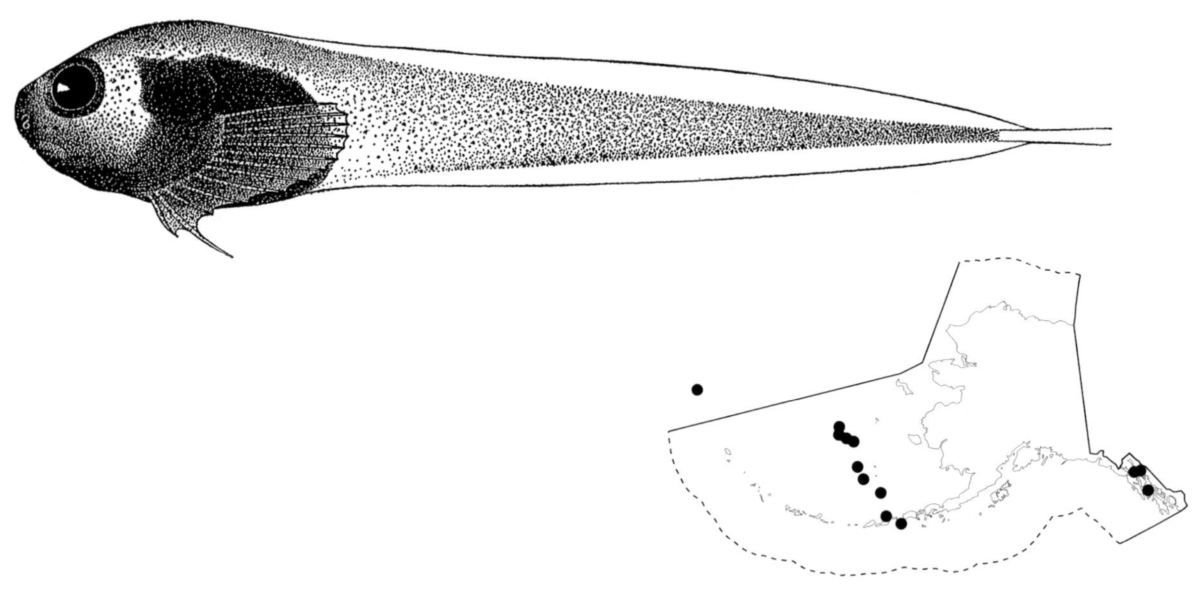

Notes & Sources — *Lipariscus nanus* Gilbert, 1915

Kido (1988) synonymized *Lipariscus* with *Paraliparis,* but other workers (e.g., Balushkin 1996) believed the presence of 5 branchiostegal rays to be a significant character and retained the genus *Lipariscus*.

Description: Stein 1978:29–30; Peden 1981a; Kido 1988:232–234, 1993:107–108; Peden 1997ms. Specimens from the Bering Sea and Japan have higher dorsal and anal fin ray counts than those from the northeastern Pacific, including southeastern Alaska and British Columbia.

Figure: Gilbert 1915, pl. 19, fig. 15; type, USNM 75817, 47 mm TL, California.

Range: Eastern Bering Sea localities given by Kido (1988), for specimens he examined, are: 54°33.5'N, 165°43'E; 58°32'N, 176°10'W; 55°47'N, 168°57'W; 56°29'N, 171°59'W; 54°51'N, 167°03'W; 58°34'N, 175°05'W; 58°22'N, 174°23'W. Additional eastern Bering Sea records are USNM 325574, 58°32'N, 176°06'W; and USNM 325586, 56°29'N, 172°01'W. Southeastern Alaska records include those of Quast (1968) from Lynn Canal at Point Sherman (AB 64-63, AB 64-999) and Point Retreat (AB 64-72). The Auke Bay Laboratory also has a collection from lower Chatham Strait. Also recorded off British Columbia (Stein 1978, Peden 1981a) and from Monterey Bay, California (Gilbert 1915, Stein 1978), and apparently common in both places (Stein 1978). Its small size, which allows it to slip through coarse mesh nets, and deepwater habitat account for its scarceness in collections (Peden 1981a). Kido (1988) considered a southern Sea of Okhotsk record doubtful, but later (Kido 1993) reported the first record off Japan, off the Okhotsk coast of Hokkaido. V. V. Fedorov and B. A. Sheiko (pers. comm., 12 May 1998) collected specimens from the Commander Islands and northwestern Bering Sea. Depth extremes: Gilbert 1915 (58 m), Kido 1988 (910 m).

Size: Kido 1993.

Nectoliparis pelagicus Gilbert & Burke, 1912 **tadpole snailfish**

Bering Sea to Santa Barbara, southern California; and to Sea of Okhotsk.

Pelagic, usually taken at midwater depths; reported to depth of 3,383 m.

D 44–58; A 40–53; C 4–6; Pec 19–25; PC 6–9; Vert 63–66.

- Skin transparent, body tan, head and abdomen very shiny silver; body covered with scattered black chromatophores; mouth and gill cavity brown or black, peritoneum and stomach black, pyloric caeca pale.
- Skin thin, loose, held well away from body by liquid.
- **Pectoral fin divided into two distinct lobes, with 3–5 widely spaced rudimentary rays between the lobes.**
- **Branchiostegal rays 5.**
- Pelvic disk absent.
- Anus in individuals longer than 25 mm SL located anterior to pectoral symphysis on a forward-pointing papilla; in juveniles anus normal, posterior to pectoral symphysis.
- **Gill opening entirely in front of pectoral fin.**
- Length to 65 mm TL.

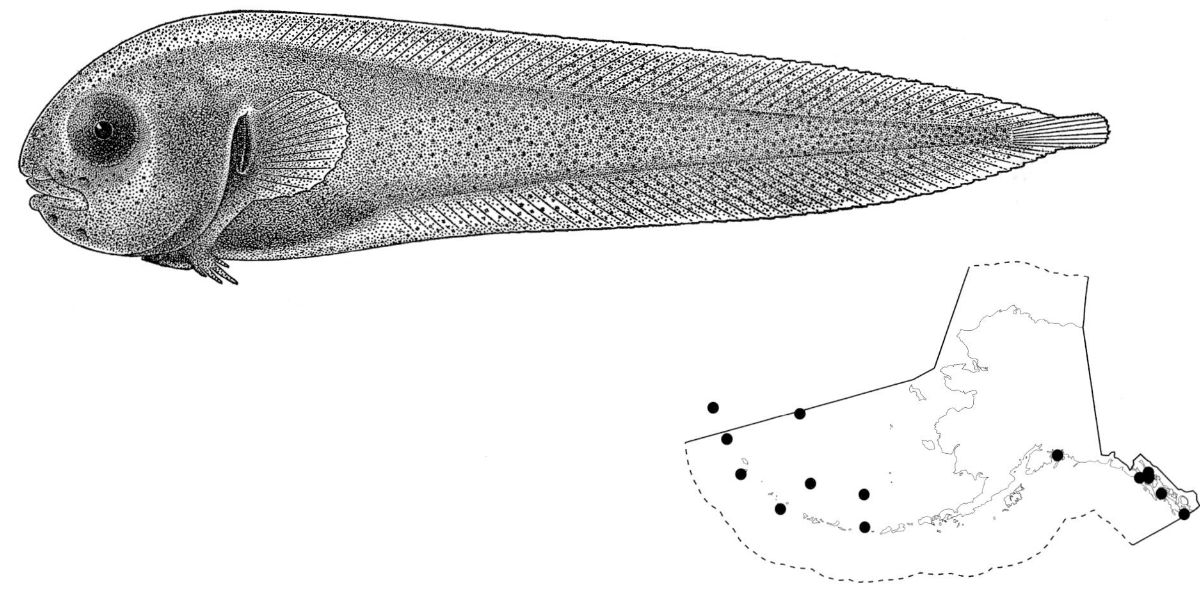

Notes & Sources — *Nectoliparis pelagicus* Gilbert & Burke, 1912

Description: Gilbert and Burke 1912a:82–83; Peden 1981a: fig. 5; Stein 1978:31–32; Kido 1988:246–247.

Figure: Gilbert and Burke 1912a, fig. 27; holotype, USNM 74389, 30 mm TL, Alaska between Attu and Medny islands at *Albatross* station 4785.

Range: Alaskan records are as follows. Gilbert and Burke 1912a: *Albatross* station 4765, 53°12'N, 171°37'W; station 4767, 54°12'N, 179°07'E; station 4781, 52°14'N, 174°13'E; and station 4785, 53°20'N, 170°33'E (the type series). Burke 1930: stations 4252, off Hugh Point, Stephens Passage; and 4257 and 4258, off Clear Point, vicinity of Funter Bay, Lynn Canal. Simenstad et al. 1977: abundant in mesopelagic community off Amchitka Island. Stein 1978: *Albatross* station 4750, off Tolstoi Point, 55°35'N, 132°33'W (southeastern Alaska). Peden 1981a: Prince William Sound. Kido 1988: 58°32'N, 176°10'E. The UBC museum has collections from 55°12'N, 172°38'W, Bering Sea (UBC 63-1198); and 58°12'N, 136°40'W, off Cape Spencer, Cross Sound (UBC 72-32). The ABL has specimens from lower Chatham Strait and several other localities. USNM 207976, 207980, and 207997 are from Lynn Canal and Frederick Sound. Stein (1978) suggested *N. pelagicus* is distributed in neritic and protected waters throughout the North Pacific Ocean north of about 35°N.

Stein's (1978) reported depth of 3,383 m for the type specimens is the deepest record, but it is the maximum depth of the tows and not necessarily the depth at which the fish entered the net. McCosker and Anderson (1976) found the species common at upper mesopelagic depths in Monterey Bay from closing midwater trawl samples. They also kept live specimens in aquaria.

Size: Kido 1988.

Order Perciformes
Perciforms

With about 9,300 species worldwide, including all the typical spiny-rayed fishes and their relatives, the order Perciformes is the largest of all vertebrate orders. This guide provides accounts for 134 perciform species distributed among 27 families, from eel-like, tidepool gunnels to fusiform, pelagic tunas, to large-mouthed, deepsea swallowers. Although about 21% of all the world's perciforms are found in fresh water (Nelson 1994), all of the Alaskan species inhabit marine waters.

Most perciforms have spines in the fins. They have two dorsal fins or, less often, one dorsal fin with a combination of spines and soft rays, but never an adipose fin. Additional characters separating perciforms from lower teleosts, although there are exceptions due to loss of characters, are: scales ctenoid rather than cycloid, or absent; pelvic fins present and thoracic rather than abdominal; upper jaw bordered by the premaxilla, as opposed to both premaxilla and maxilla in other teleosts; and orbitosphenoid, mesocoracoid, and intermuscular bones absent. In contrast to scorpaeniforms, perciforms lack a suborbital stay.

The suborder Zoarcoidei, mainly comprising coldwater fishes, accounts for most of the Alaskan perciforms. All families of the Zoarcoidei are represented in the Alaskan fauna, by at least one species each. By far the greatest number of Alaskan perciform species is included in the Zoarcidae (eelpouts), with 48 or more Alaskan species, followed by the Stichaeidae (pricklebacks), with 23 Alaskan species. Included in this guide but not in previous inventories of Alaskan fishes, are the families Acropomatidae (temperate ocean-basses), Gobiidae (gobies), and Chiasmodontidae (swallowers).

Family Acropomatidae
Temperate ocean-basses

The Acropomatidae is a family of basslike, oceanic perciforms which primarily inhabit temperate seas. Diagnostic characters include two short-based dorsal fins, gill membranes separate from each other and free from the isthmus, 7 branchiostegal rays, and 25 vertebrae. The first dorsal fin has 7–10 spines and the second has no spine or 1 spine and 8–10 soft rays; the anal fin has 2 or 3 spines and 7–9 soft rays (Nelson 1994). The scales are always large and can be cycloid or ctenoid, and deciduous or firmly held. Some members of the family, although not the genus represented in Alaska, have a luminescent organ between the pelvic fins, for which the family is also known as the lanternbellies.

The group is not well defined morphologically and some researchers classify *Howella,* the genus represented in Alaska, in its own family, Howellidae (e.g., Roberts 1993), while others list it in the Percichthyidae (e.g., Eschmeyer 1998). For the present, we take a conservative approach and follow Nelson (1994) in classifying *Howella* in the Acropomatidae.

Occurrence of *Howella* in Alaskan waters was first reported by Busby and Orr (1999), who determined a fish collected south of the Aleutian Islands to be *H. sherborni.* This is not only the first record of *Howella* from Alaska, it is the first record from north of California and Japan. The genus was previously known only from the tropical and temperate regions of the world, and in the North Pacific to about as far north as 40°N.

In *Howella* the bones of the operculum are covered by delicate skin and bear spines along the borders. The configuration of these spines is one of the most important features distinguishing the species of *Howella.* The upper angle of the opercle can have 2 simple spines or a combination of simple and complex spines; the subopercle has 1 long spine to which shorter spines may be joined; the interopercle has 1 spine; and there are short spines along the margin of the preopercle. The number of scale rows between the origin of the second dorsal fin and the lateral line also helps to distinguish *H. sherborni* from *H. brodiei,* a species sympatric with *H. sherborni* in part of its range. *Howella* species have 3 spines in the anal fin and scales on the snout, and the scales on the trunk are tightly adherent. The long pectoral fins, extending past the anal fin origin or past the entire anal fin, are a character shared by closely related members of the family.

Howella measuring more than 102 mm (4 inches) in total length are rarely collected. Most are less than 76 mm (3 inches) long. When caught, they are not taken in great numbers. The typical midwater trawl catch is one or two, and more than five per haul is unusual.

The taxonomy and distribution of *Howella* species were recently analyzed by Fedoryako (1976) and Post and Quéro (1991). It is difficult to distinguish *H. sherborni* from *H. brodiei,* and the two were considered synonymous by Mead and De Falla (1965).

Howella sherborni (Norman, 1930) **shortspine basslet**

North Pacific Ocean south of Krenitzin Islands, Alaska; widely distributed in tropical and temperate seas. Pelagic, taken from surface to depth of about 2,700 m; migrates vertically to upper 800 m at night.

D VII–VIII + I,8–10; A III,7–8; Pec 14–17; Pel I,5; LLs 35–41; GR 7–9 + 19-23 (28–33); Vert 25–26.

- Dark brown, with silvery reflections.
- Snout much shorter than eye.
- **A simple or split upper spine and a complex lower spine, separated by a narrow depression, at upper angle of opercle; upper opercle spine shorter than lower spine**; 1 long spine, sometimes with shorter spines attached, on subopercle; 1 spine, sometimes split, on interopercle; spines on preopercle short, barely extending beyond its margin.
- Dorsal fins well separated; first dorsal fin spine very short; anal fin with 3 spines; pectoral fin long, extending past anal fin origin.
- Body and head with firmly held ctenoid scales; spines only on posterior margin of scales, leaving surface smooth; **4 or 5 scales in row from origin of second dorsal fin to lateral line**.
- Lateral line interrupted near its origin and again just behind first dorsal fin; lateral line not extending onto caudal fin.
- A single row of minute teeth in each jaw; no canines; a few closely set teeth in patch on vomer; palatine teeth in 1 row.
- Gill rakers numerous, longer than the gill filaments, slender, and close-set; **19–23 rakers on lower limb of 1st arch** (including 1 on curve).
- Length to 92 mm SL.

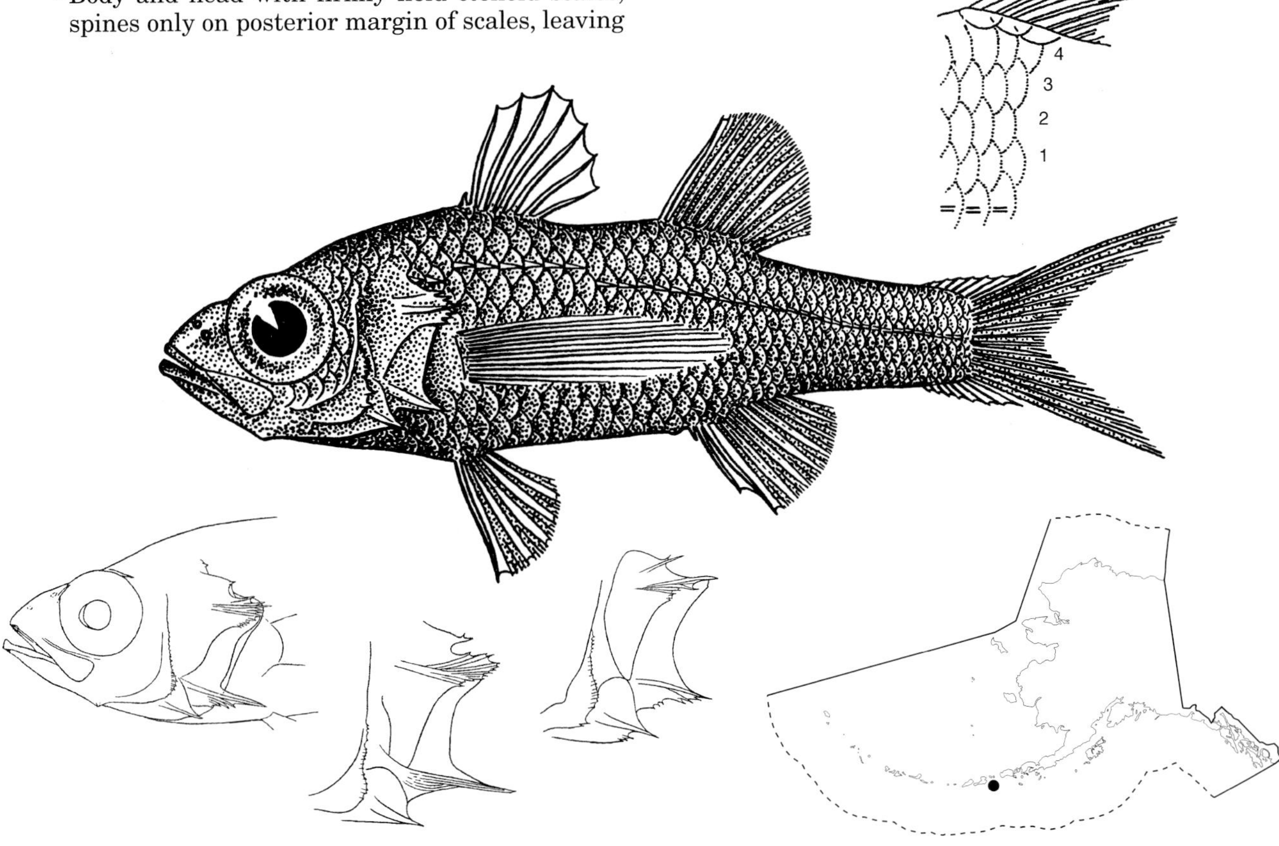

Notes & Sources — *Howella sherborni* (Norman, 1930)
Rhectogramma sherborni Norman, 1930
Shortspine basslet is suggested for the vernacular in reference to the relatively short upper opercular spine; and to distinguish it from the partly sympatric *H. brodiei,* called the pelagic basslet by Eschmeyer and Herald (1983).

Description: Norman 1930:348–349; Fedoryako 1976:168–176; Heemstra in Smith and Heemstra 1986:562; Post and Quéro 1991.

Figures: Norman 1930, fig. 39; holotype, 80 mm SL, off South Africa. (The drawing may not be entirely accurate; e.g., there should be at least 4 scales from 2nd dorsal fin to lateral line.) Opercular spine variations: Fedoryako 1976, fig. 7. Scales below 2nd dorsal: Post and Quéro 1991, fig. 2b.

Range: One record from Alaska: UW 41661, a specimen measuring 78 mm SL collected in June 1993 just south of Krenitzin Islands near Unimak Pass, 53°37'N, 165°06'W, by bottom trawl at a depth of 466 m (Busby and Orr 1999). UW 41662, an 80-mm-SL specimen taken off California at 39°10'N, 124°02'W, by bottom trawl at about 576 m, is one of the most northern known occurrences outside of Alaska. Previously recorded north in Pacific to about 40°N (Fedoryako 1976). Depth: SIO 63-56, taken at the surface; and SIO 63-110, at about 2,700 m.

Family Carangidae
Jacks

The family Carangidae includes about 140 species of jacks, amberjacks, trevallys, and pompanos, collectively called jacks or carangids. Most species are pelagic and inhabit warm seas. Two species have been reported in Alaska. Records of jack mackerel, *Trachurus symmetricus,* in the Gulf of Alaska are well documented but infrequent. Reports of yellowtail jack, *Seriola lalandi,* from the northern and western Gulf of Alaska exist but they are not verifiable due to lack of documentation; a record close to Alaska in northern British Columbia is backed by a voucher specimen. Both species are caught more frequently in the high seas of the North Pacific Ocean south of Alaska and west of British Columbia, but nevertheless are uncommon there compared to the species' abundance farther south, off California. Occurrence at the more northern latitudes is usually noted in warm months or during El Niño events.

Jacks are silvery, streamlined, fast-swimming fishes which range from small schooling planktivorous species to large solitary piscivores. The family is remarkably heterogenous, with species differing greatly in morphology and superficial appearance. However, most species can be identified as carangids by their deeply forked caudal fin, narrow caudal peduncle, and two separate, free spines preceding the anal fin. The separate anal fin spines appear to disappear with age, but are actually covered by skin in large adults.

Jacks have two dorsal fins, the first short-based and composed of spines, and the second long-based and composed mainly of soft rays including "finlet" rays. While jacks do not have finlets of the scombrid type, in some species the last dorsal and anal fin rays can be separate or nearly so. Such rays are included in the second dorsal fin ray and anal fin ray counts because they are not always distinctly separated from those fins.

In contrast to most other percoids, jacks have small, adherent cycloid scales. In *T. symmetricus* and other members of the subfamily Caranginae some of the scales on the lateral line are modified into spiny scutes. The Naucratinae, including *S. lalandi,* do not have scutes on the lateral line. In both subfamilies the number of branchiostegal rays is typically 7 or 8.

Most species of jack reach 30–91 cm (1–3 ft) in total length. With a maximum known length of about 81 cm (32 inches), *T. symmetricus* is typical of the group. Reaching about 152 cm (5 ft), *S. lalandi* is unusually large. These and several other jacks are important in commercial and recreational fisheries.

Key to the Carangidae of Alaska

1 First and second dorsal fins about same height or second slightly higher; scutes present along lateral line . . . . *Trachurus symmetricus,* page 649

1 First dorsal fin much lower than second dorsal fin; no scutes along lateral line . . . . *Seriola lalandi,* page 650 (not confirmed from Alaska)

Trachurus symmetricus (Ayres, 1855) **jack mackerel**

Gulf of Alaska and Pacific Ocean south of Aleutian Islands to southern Baja California at Bahia Magdalena and tropical mid-Pacific; uncommon north of California.

Pelagic, in schools around reefs and offshore; surface to 183 m, rarely to 403 m; young often school near kelp and under piers; large adults often move inshore and north in summer.

D VIII + 0–I,28–40; A II + I,22–34; Pec 22–26; Pel I,5; GR 7–15 + 25–42 (32–61); Vert 23–25.

- Metallic blue to olive green dorsally, silvery ventrally; dark spot at upper rear of operculum; fins mostly clear, caudal fin yellowish to reddish.
- Adipose eyelid present.
- **First dorsal fin slightly higher or about the same height as second dorsal fin**; last rays of dorsal and anal fins sometimes separate, especially in large specimens; forward-directed spine at base of first dorsal fin in small individuals but embedded in larger fish; anal fin origin below front of second dorsal fin; pectoral fin longer than pelvic fin, extending to second dorsal fin.
- **Heavy scutes along main lateral line.**
- Main lateral line slopes sharply downward below origin of second dorsal fin, continues straight to base of caudal fin; accessory lateral line present, extending along base of first dorsal fin to origin of second dorsal fin.
- Length to 81 cm TL; commercial sizes usually 20–38 cm.

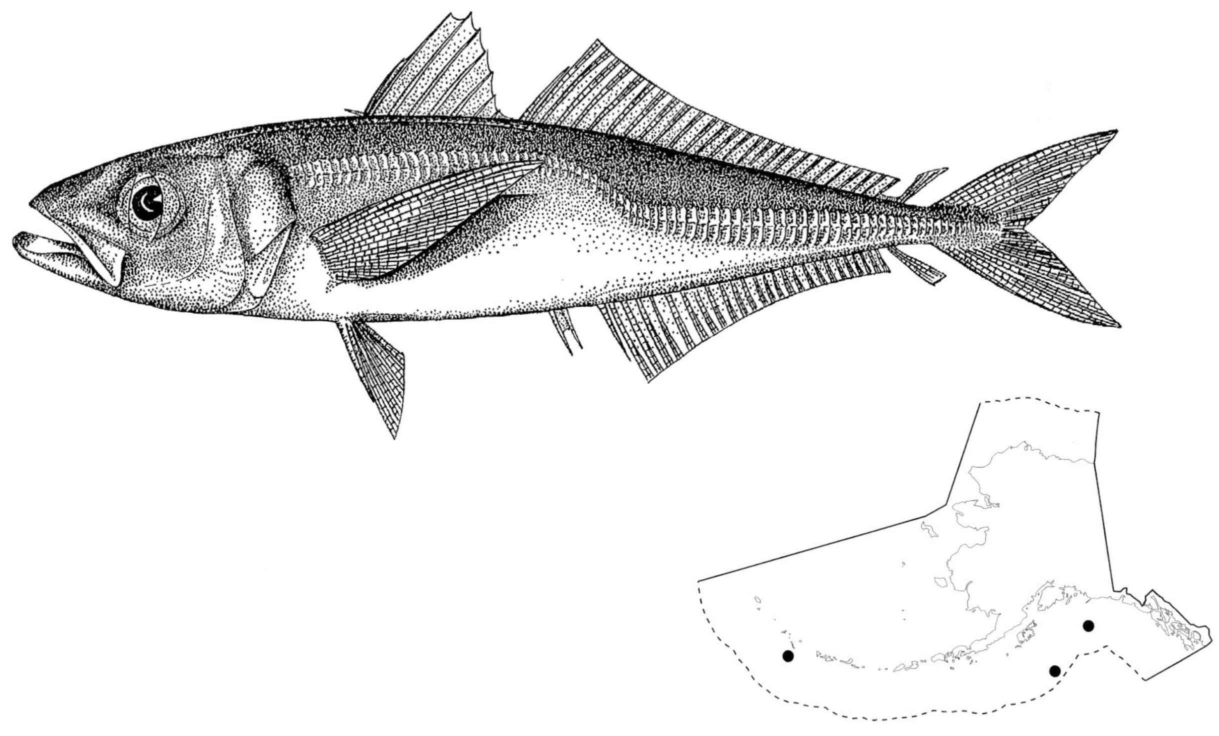

Notes & Sources — *Trachurus symmetricus* (Ayres, 1855)
Caranx symmetricus Ayres, 1855

Description: Roedel 1953:83; Hart 1973:287–288; Eschmeyer and Herald 1983:211.

Figure: Hart 1973:287, modified; 20 cm TL, California.

Range: Neave and Hanavan (1960) showed that distribution of *T. symmetricus* extends farther north as summer progresses, and reported catches in the Gulf of Alaska at about 58°N, 145°W, and about 55°N, 145–155°W (four stations), in August–September of 1956 and 1957. The UW collection includes a specimen taken in July 1958 just south of Amchitka Island at 50°59'N, 178°50'E. No other valid records of occurrence in Alaskan waters, published or in museum collections, were found. The range given by Hart (1973) to northeast Alaska is inaccurate, as is the statement regarding catches in "the whole of the eastern Gulf of Alaska." Other authors have misinterpreted the map by Neave and Hanavan (1960) which shows catches in the region. This species occurs more frequently off southern British Columbia than it does in Alaska, but it has not been taken in British Columbia in commercial quantity and the extent of its occurrence there in recent years is not clear.

Seriola lalandi Valenciennes, 1833

yellowtail jack

Unverifiable reports from Gulf of Alaska off Kodiak Island and Cordova; well documented from Pacific Ocean off northern British Columbia to Chile and Gulf of California; uncommon north of California.

Epipelagic, usually in schools around kelp beds, offshore islands, and other rocky areas; surface to 69 m, usually shallower than 25 m.

D IV–VII + I,31–39; A 0–II + I,19–23; Pel I,5; GR 7–8 + 18–22 (26–30); Vert 25.

- Metallic blue to green dorsally, silvery ventrally; brassy to yellow stripe along side from eye to tail; dorsal and anal fins dusky yellow to nearly black, pectoral and pelvic fins dusky yellow-green, caudal fin dull yellow.
- **First dorsal fin much lower than second**; anal fin origin well behind origin of second dorsal fin; pectoral fin shorter than pelvic fin, not extending beyond first dorsal fin.
- **No scutes on lateral line**; blunt low keel on caudal peduncle.
- Length to 152 cm TL, weight to 36 kg; usually 4.5–9.1 kg.

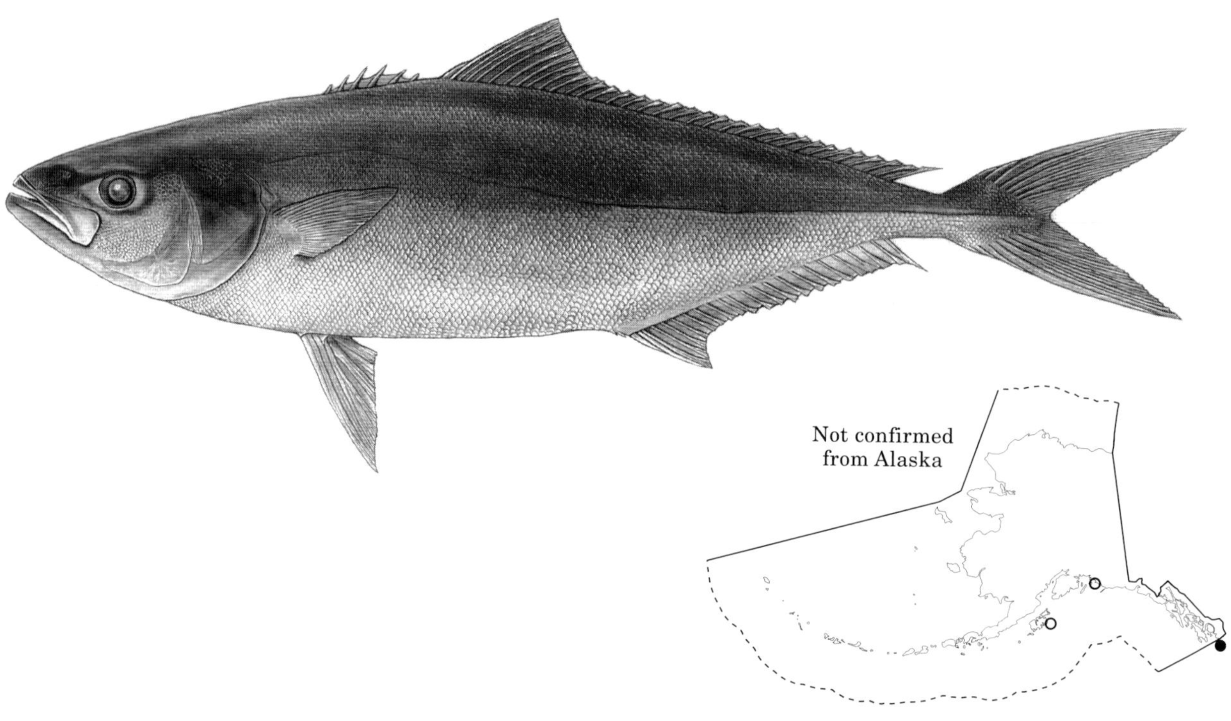

Notes & Sources — *Seriola lalandi* Valenciennes in Cuvier & Valenciennes, 1833
Halatractus dorsalis Gill, 1863
Seriola dorsalis (Gill, 1863): Jordan and Evermann 1896.
Seriola lalandi dorsalis: Peden and Jamieson 1988.

Also called yellowtail kingfish or, simply, yellowtail. As of 22 August 2001, the manuscript for the sixth edition (anticipated for spring 2002) of the American Fisheries Society–American Society of Ichthyologists and Herpetologists list of fish names (J. S. Nelson et al.) calls this fish the yellowtail jack to prevent confusion with other yellowtail species, such as yellowtail rockfish.

Description: Jordan and Evermann 1896:902, 903; Miller and Lea 1972:146; Eschmeyer and Herald 1983:209.

Figure: Royal British Columbia Museum, artist K. Uldall-Ekman, 1983; BCPM 979-11312, 60 cm FL, near Dundas Island, British Columbia.

Range: ADFG biologists reported that two specimens were caught off Cape Chiniak in the sport fishery during the summer of 1997, and that another had previously been taken off Cordova; neither report is documented by a photograph or specimen, but notes on the Cape Chiniak specimens are on file (J. E. Blackburn, pers. comm., 23 Jul. 1998). Nagtegaal and Farlinger (1980) recorded a specimen from northern British Columbia at Caamano Passage between Dundas and Zayas islands, at 54°35'N, 131°00'W (the specimen illustrated on this page). Peden and Jamieson (1988) recorded a specimen from coastal southern British Columbia, and reported that others had been captured in offshore Canadian waters incidental to high seas squid fishing.

Family Bramidae
Pomfrets

The pomfrets, family Bramidae, are a small but widespread group of compressed, deep-bodied, silvery white to metallic blue-black or black oceanic fishes inhabiting tropical and temperate waters, usually near the surface. There are about 20 pomfret species, with 2 of them occurring in Alaska. The Pacific pomfret, *Brama japonica,* is occasionally taken in the Gulf of Alaska and south of the Aleutian Islands in late summer. The rough pomfret, *Taractes asper,* has been reported once from Alaska, off Kodiak Island; throughout its range it is known only from scattered records.

Most pomfrets have a strongly compressed body and blunt snout; a long, single dorsal fin and shorter anal fin; a long pectoral fin; and a forked caudal fin. The dorsal and anal fins typically are high at the front in adults but not in immature fish; and have a few unbranched but unthickened rays, which researchers count with the branched rays. The scales are strongly adherent and bear spines or keels. Scale size, which is reflected in the number of midlateral scales as counted from the gill opening to the end of the scales on the caudal fin, ranges from moderate to large in pomfrets and is useful for identification. The two species occurring in Alaska belong to the subfamily Braminae. In this subfamily the dorsal and anal fins of the adults have scales and are not wholly depressible and the pelvic fins are thoracic.

One species of pomfret, *Taractichthys longipinnis* (not Alaskan), reaches a total length of 85 cm (3.3 ft), but most pomfrets are smaller. *Brama japonica,* the species most likely to be found in Alaska, reaches about 61 cm (2 ft).

Key to the Bramidae of Alaska

1 Forehead strongly convex; scales relatively small, numbering 65–75 from upper end of gill opening to base of midcaudal rays .... *Brama japonica,* page 652

1 Forehead concave to only slightly convex; scales relatively large, numbering 40–50 from upper end of gill opening to base of midcaudal rays .... *Taractes asper,* page 653

Brama japonica Hilgendorf, 1878

Pacific pomfret

Few records from southern Bering Sea; Pacific Ocean from Gulf of Alaska and south of the Aleutian and Commander islands to Peru and to Japan, including midocean.

Epipelagic, oceanic, rarely taken in nearshore waters; in schools; sometimes taken at midwater depths, recorded to 620 m.

D 33–36; A 27–30; Pec 21–23; Pel I,5; Ls 65–75; GR 17–20; Vert 39–41.

- Silvery white in life, rapidly turning black after death.
- **Head blunt**; maxilla extending to mideye; **interorbital space strongly convex, profile of head distinctly arched**.
- Lateral line present in juveniles, indistinct or absent in adults.
- Scales with anchors up and down, arranged in precise longitudinal rows on body, on bases of fins, and all over head except snout; midlateral **scales moderate in size but smaller, and greater in number, than in *Taractes asper***.
- Length to 61 cm TL, perhaps larger.

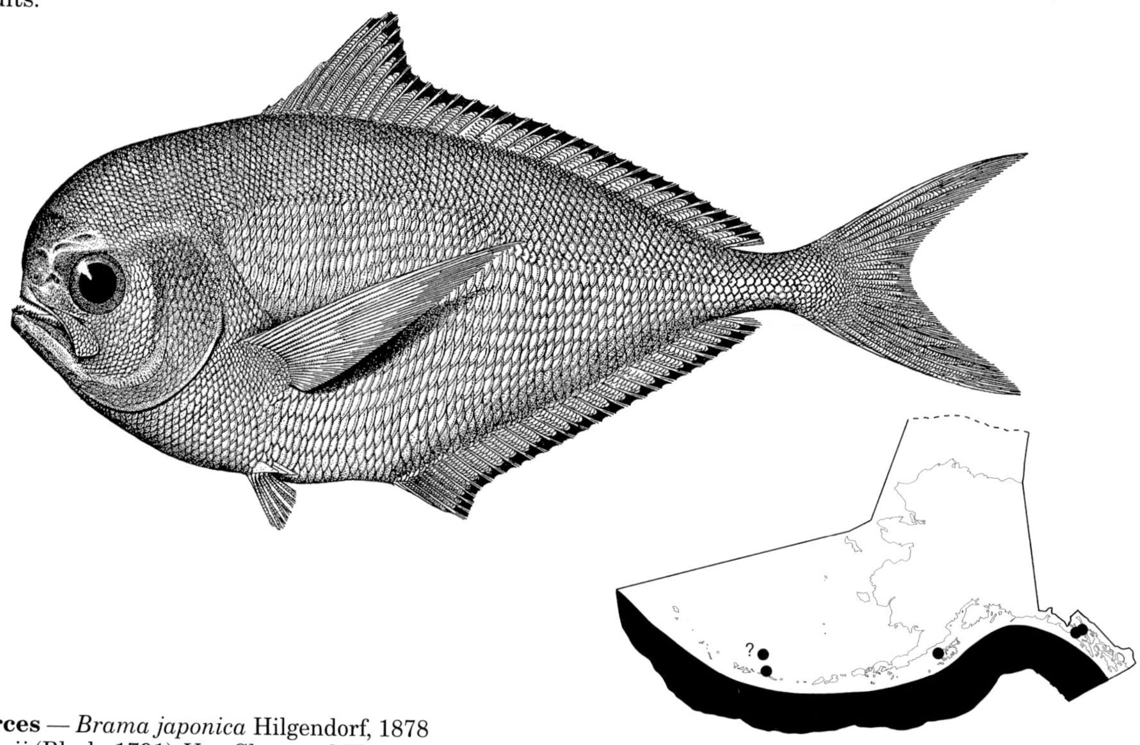

Notes & Sources — *Brama japonica* Hilgendorf, 1878

Brama raii (Bloch, 1791): Van Cleve and Thompson (1938) and others reporting Pacific records.

Brama rayi: Neave and Hanavan 1960; spelling variation.

Brama japonica from the Pacific Ocean and *B. raii* from the Atlantic, the latter now classified as *B. brama* (Bonnaterre, 1788), are currently considered by taxonomists to represent distinct species.

Description: Mead 1972:49–55; Hart 1973:289–290; Eschmeyer and Herald 1983:213; Mochizuki in Masuda et al. 1984:159.

Figure: Lindberg and Krasyukova 1969, fig. 229; 450 mm TL, Japan.

Range: Birman (1958) reported *B. japonica* was caught off the south side of the western Aleutian Islands in 1956. Mead and Haedrich (1965) and Mead (1972) mapped records from the Gulf of Alaska; and Machidori and Nakamura (1971) recorded several more from the Pacific Ocean off the western Aleutian Islands, as far north as 50–51°N. Other records are from northwest Unalaska Island (Wilimovsky 1964; possibly the same as USNM 104471, collected by H. G. Bloom from Unalaska Harbor in September 1933), west coast of Kodiak Island (Van Cleve and Thompson 1938), and Icy Strait and Cross Sound (Karinen et al. 1985). Hanavan and Tanonaka (1959) did not find it in the Bering Sea during surveys to determine distribution in The Gulf of Alaska and Bering Sea in 1956. The only record from the Bering Sea other than USNM 104471 from Unalaska is USNM 103739, taken by a cod fisherman at an unspecified locality in the Bering Sea in summer of 1935; possibly the same as the one specimen reported from the Bering Sea, without specific locality, by Mead (1972:54; not included on Mead's map). Hitz and French (1966) found no Bering Sea records in gill-net and purse-seine data of 1950–1962. Part of the population of Pacific pomfrets moves northward in summer, reaching the northern Gulf of Alaska and Aleutian Islands by August or September (Neave and Hanavan 1960, Machidori and Nakamura 1971, Shimazaki and Nakamura 1981). An analysis of migrations by Savinykh (1994) indicates that foraging 4-year-olds dominate Pacific pomfret aggregations off Alaska in summer. Maximum depth of 620 m was reported by Fedorov and Sheiko (2001).

Size: Reported by Jordan and Evermann (1896:960) to reach 122 cm TL, but the maximum reported by Miller and Lea (1972) is 61 cm and this is the size given by most authors.

Taractes asper Lowe, 1843 **rough pomfret**

Gulf of Alaska off Kodiak Island; Pacific Ocean off British Columbia to southern California and to Japan; widely distributed in all oceans, but not abundant and known only from scattered records.

Oceanic, taken from surface to depths of about 550 m, by gill net, bottom trawl, and other gear.

D 26–34; A 20–30; Pec 16–20; Pel I,5; Ls 40–47; GR 8–15; Vert 41–43.

- Body uniform dark brown, fins darker or lighter.
- **Head not blunt**; maxilla extending past mideye; **interorbital space concave to slightly convex, profile of head not distinctly arched**.
- Caudal peduncle without bony keels.
- Lateral line present in juveniles, indistinct or absent in adults.
- **Body scales large, fewer than in *Brama japonica*, and rough** owing to median ridges which are produced into spines; dorsal, anal, and caudal fins scaled anteriorly; snout, interorbital space, lower jaw scaleless.
- Length to more than 50 cm TL.

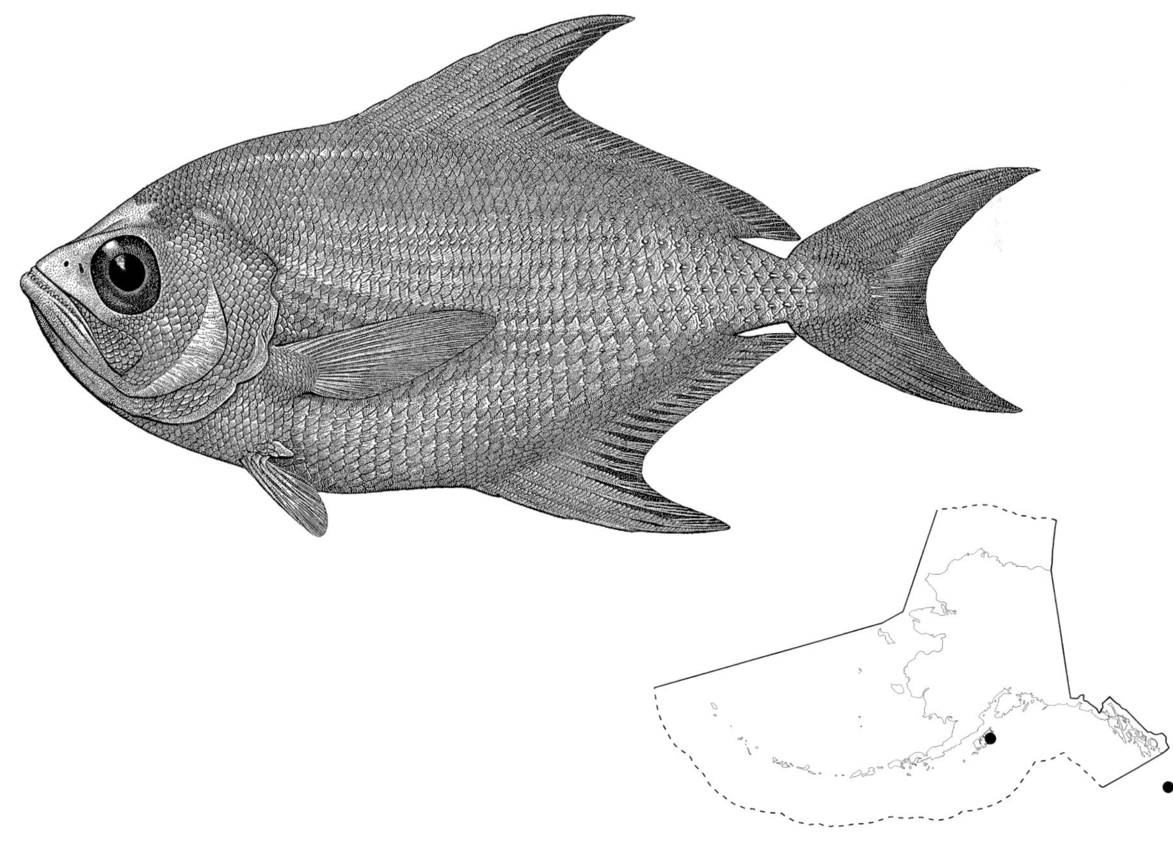

Notes & Sources — *Taractes asper* Lowe, 1843

Description: Mead 1972:21–25; Mochizuki in Masuda et al. 1984:159; Peden and Jamieson 1988:492; Parin and Scherbachev 1998.

Figure: Mead 1972, pl. 2b; 308 mm SL, Norway.

Range: The only published Alaskan record is a single specimen from the vicinity of Kodiak Island, which Mead (1972) reported on the basis of a photograph. At least 10 specimens of *T. asper* have been captured at various localities off the coast of British Columbia; the nearest to Alaska was taken at approximately 52°N, 132°W (Peden and Ostermann 1980, Peden and Jamieson 1988).

Size: Eschmeyer and Herald (1983) gave a maximum length of 50 cm TL. The largest specimen examined by Mead (1972) was 45 cm SL, which likely exceeded 50 cm TL. He reported that larger specimens were caught in the high seas Japanese longline fishery.

Family Caristiidae
Manefishes

Manefishes, also called veilfishes, are meso- to bathypelagic fishes found, albeit rarely, in the Pacific, Indian, and Atlantic oceans. The family is small, comprising four to six species depending on classification followed. At least one species, the bigmouth manefish, *Caristius macropus,* inhabits the eastern North Pacific. This species was listed as a potential addition to the inventory of Alaskan fishes by Quast and Hall (1972) based on its occurrence off British Columbia and pelagic mode of life. Specimens recently collected in the Bering Sea close to the eastern Aleutian Islands confirm the presence of *C. macropus* in Alaskan waters.

Manefishes are easily recognized by their deep, compressed bodies and high, steep foreheads; high, long-based dorsal fin originating on the head; and long pelvic fins. The dorsal, anal, and pelvic fins are depressible into scaly sheaths at the bases of the fins. The bones are weak, and specimens are usually damaged during collection. Family characters also include 1 spine and 5 long rays in the pelvic fins; deciduous, cycloid scales; short, stout gill rakers; and 7 branchiostegal rays. Characters that vary among manefish species include, among others, position of the pelvic fins, in front of or behind the pectoral fins; shape of the caudal fin, either emarginate or round; extension of the maxilla posteriorly relative to the eye; and expression of the lateral line, from distinct to indiscernible.

The habitat and behavior of manefishes are not well known. Although most records are from midwater tows a few adults have been collected demersally by otter trawls at greater depths. This suggests that adults may to some extent be benthopelagic. Observations from a submersible of a small (63 mm SL) *Caristius* individual in its natural habitat indicate that young manefishes feed on siphonophores, steal prey from them, and use them as shelter (Janssen et al. 1989).

Manefishes reach at least 35 cm (13.8 inches) in total length, which is attained in *C. macropus.*

Caristius macropus (Bellotti, 1903) **bigmouth manefish**

Southern Bering Sea and Aleutian Islands to central Baja California near Cedros Island and to Japan.

Pelagic, at depths of 265–1,420 m; typically caught in midwater trawls; adults occasionally taken in bottom trawls.

D 33–35; A 20–23; Pec 14–19; Pel I,5; GR 17–23; Vert 37–40.

- Body gray or brown, fins black; juveniles pale, with distinct bars.
- Body compressed; soft and flabby; bones soft.
- Forehead steeply rising; maxilla extending to or past rear margin of eye.
- Long, high dorsal fin; dorsal and anal fins sheathed at base in soft tissue; pelvic fin placed anterior to pectoral fin; pelvic fin rays drawn out as long filaments; caudal fin emarginate, not forked, rays preceded by short spines.
- Scales small, cycloid, irregular in size and arrangement.
- Lateral line distinct or indistinct.
- Length to 35 cm TL or more.

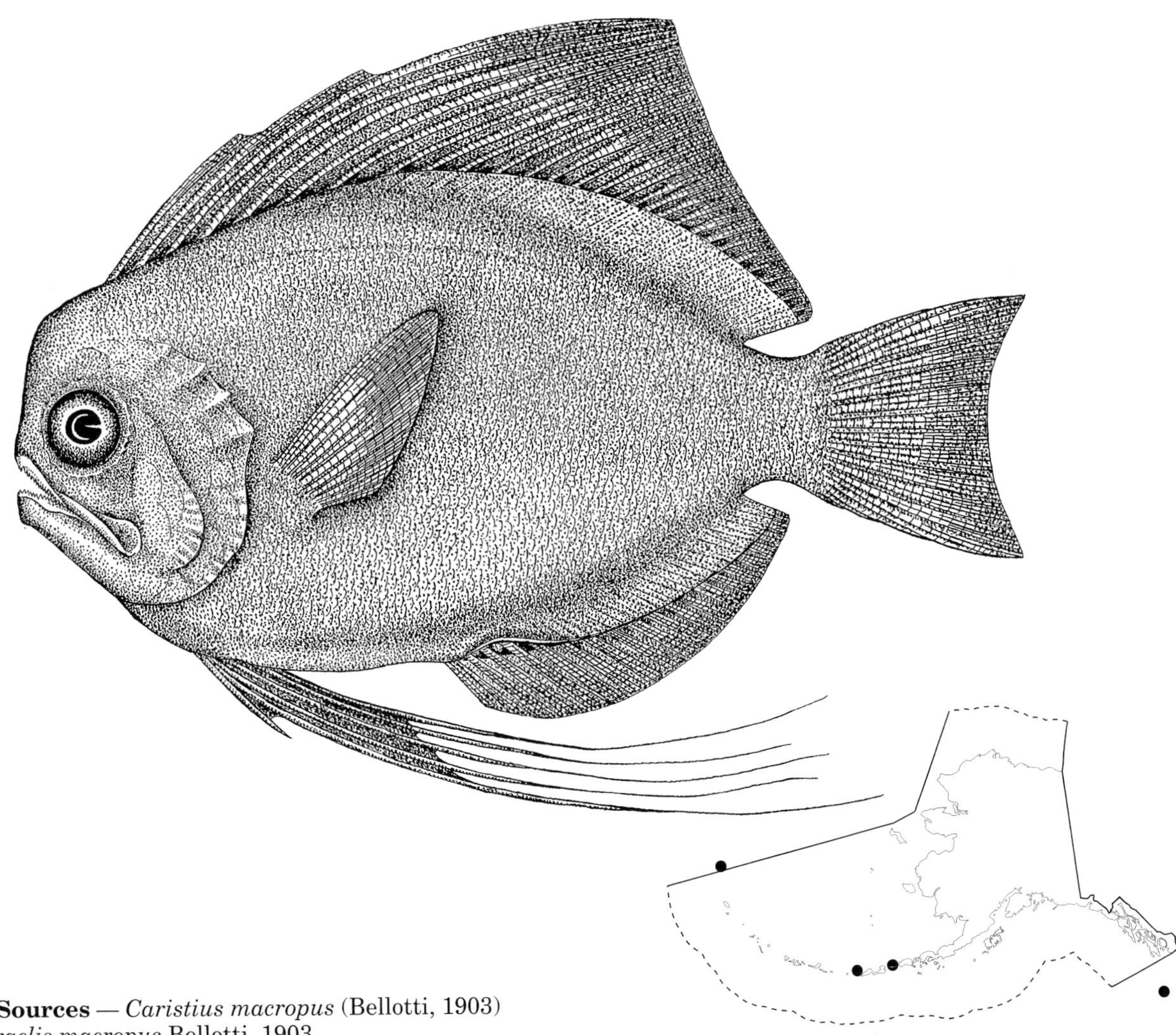

Notes & Sources — *Caristius macropus* (Bellotti, 1903)
Pteraclis macropus Bellotti, 1903

Description: Welander, Alverson, and Bergman 1957:62, 64–66; Hart 1973:291–292; Amaoka in Amaoka et al. 1983:203; Fujii in Masuda et al. 1984:160; Balanov 2000.

Figure: Hart 1973:291; 20 cm TL, off British Columbia.

Range: The first adequately documented records from Alaska are UW 20979, a specimen measuring 307 mm SL obtained at 54°30'N, 165°59'W on 20 Oct. 1982 at a depth of 487 m; UW 22373, 193 mm SL, obtained at 53°16'N, 169°23'W on 10 Jan. 1990, depth 373 m; and UW 22391, 212 mm SL, at 53°08'N, 169°30'W on 22 Jan. 1991, depth 439 m. Balanov (2000) recorded a specimen (171 mm SL) close to U.S. waters in the western Bering Sea at 55°03'N, 170°58'E, collected by trawling at 200–500 m over a bottom depth of 3,880 m. British Columbia records include one individual caught southwest of Tasu Sound, Queen Charlotte Islands, at 52°17'N, 133°10'W, depth 265–280 m (Taylor 1967a,b), and one southwest of Estevan Point, Vancouver Island, depth 384 m (Welander, Alverson, and Bergman 1957). Maximum depth: Amaoka et al. 1983 (500–1,420 m off Japan).

Size: Reported to reach 32 cm TL by Eschmeyer and Herald (1983), but UW 20979, at 307 mm SL, would have a considerably greater total length (not measured by us).

Family Sciaenidae
Drums

The Sciaenidae are a family of noisy fishes which produce loud sounds with their multibranched swim bladders and large otoliths, for which they are called drums or croakers. They are bottom-oriented fishes and inhabit shallow marine waters along continental margins, primarily along sandy shores at warm latitudes. Theirs is one of the largest families of the order Perciformes, with about 270 species (Nelson 1994). In the eastern Pacific alone there are about 100 species, of which 8 inhabit northern latitudes.

One member of the family has been reported from Alaska: the white seabass, *Atractoscion nobilis.* (Its common name is somewhat unfortunate, since this fish is not a seabass at all, but a drum; seabasses, family Serranidae, are not known to occur in Alaska.) White seabass are rarely found north of San Francisco, but there are two reports (Jordan et al. 1930, Radovich 1961) of captures in southeastern Alaska. One reported occurrence was during unusually warm weather in 1958, an El Niño year; further information on the other report was not found.

The combination of a lateral line that extends to the tip of the caudal fin and presence of only one or two spines in the anal fin distinguishes sciaenid fishes from all other perciforms. The anal fin spines typically are weak, but the second spine can be large. Other family characteristics include a long dorsal fin with a deep notch or, less frequently, divided into two by a narrow space; first portion of dorsal fin supported by relatively few (6–13), widely spaced spines and the second by 1 spine and more numerous (20–35) rays, set closer together; a slightly emarginate to rounded caudal fin, never deeply forked; conspicuous pores often present on the snout and lower jaw; a forked upper bony edge to the opercle, with a bony flap above the gill opening; and usually no teeth on the vomer and palatines. Some drum species have one or more barbels on the chin. The mouth is terminal, except subterminal in bottom-feeding species. Sciaenid scales are cycloid or ctenoid.

In addition to a body lateral line extending all the way to the tip of the caudal fin, the sensory canal system of sciaenids includes large cavernous canals in the head. The well-developed sensory system is thought to be an adaptation to murky habitats.

As with many other fishes, in the Sciaenidae the juveniles of some species differ markedly in coloration from the adults. Young white seabass, *A. nobilis,* have several dark vertical bars and used to be called sea trout by fishermen who believed them to be a different species from the adults (Jordan and Gilbert 1881c).

The largest of the eight species occurring in the eastern North Pacific is the white seabass, with a documented maximum length of about 152 cm (5 ft). This species is an excellent food fish, sought commercially as well as by anglers. White seabass have been reported to weigh as much as 41 kg (90 lb). The usual commercial size in the 1950s was 7–9 kg (15–20 lb) and because of fishing pressure is probably less now.

Atractoscion nobilis (Ayres, 1860) **white seabass**

Eastern North Pacific from southeastern Alaska at Juneau to southern Baja California and Gulf of California; uncommon north of San Francisco.

In schools over rocky bottom and in kelp beds, also in surf zone; from surface to about 122 m.

D IX–X + I,19–23; A I–II,8–10; Pec I,14–16; Pel I,5; LLs 88; GR 16–18; Vert 24–25.

- Bluish to gray with dark speckling dorsally, frosted silvery on the sides, and white ventrally; dusky blotch at base of pectoral, extending on whole inner surface of the fin; young less than 30–35 cm with dark vertical bars.
- Maxilla extending beyond rear edge of eye; lower jaw slightly projecting; no chin barbel.
- Raised ridge down midline of belly.
- First and second dorsal fins contiguous; anal fin base much shorter than second dorsal fin; fleshy appendage at base of pelvic fin.
- Scales ctenoid, on body and head to tip of snout.
- Sensory pores on snout and chin minute, barely discernible.
- No enlarged caniniform teeth in upper jaw.
- Length to 152 cm TL, weight to 41 kg.

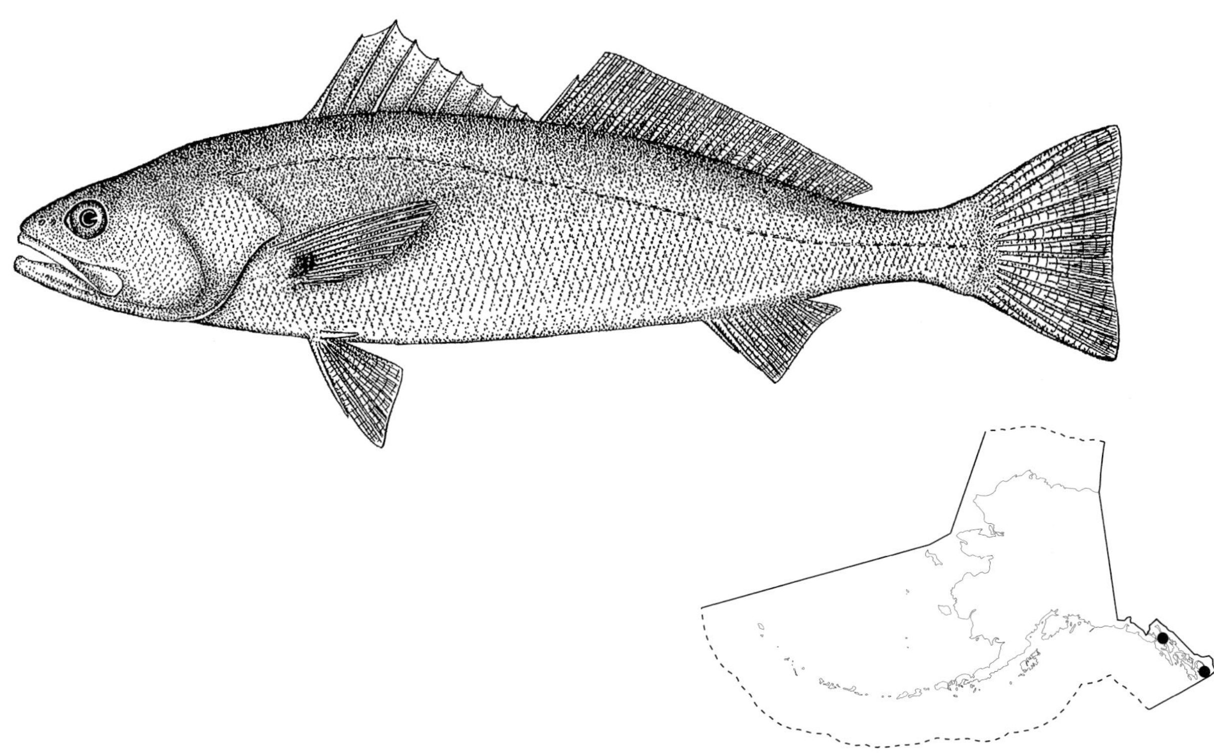

Notes & Sources — *Atractoscion nobilis* (Ayres, 1860)
Johnius nobilis Ayres, 1860
Otolithus californiensis Steindachner, 1876
Cynoscion nobilis: Jordan and Gilbert 1881b.
Atractoscion nobile: Jordan and Gilbert 1881c.

Description: Jordan and Evermann 1898:1413; Walford 1937:130–132; Miller and Lea 1972:154; Hart 1973:295–296; Eschmeyer and Herald 1983:219.

Figure: Hart 1973:295; 122 cm TL, California (after Walford 1937, pl. 19).

Range: Listed from the Boca de Quadra by Jordan et al. (1930), but without providing documentation; this may be the source for reports of range extending northward to southeastern Alaska by Clemens and Wilby (1949) and Wilimovsky (1954). Skogsberg (1939), in a detailed review of the Sciaenidae of California, made no mention of occurrence as far north as Alaska and stated that only one specimen had been recorded north of California; namely, one taken at Victoria, British Columbia, and recorded by Jordan and Evermann (1898). Radovich (1961) reported specimens were caught near Juneau, Alaska, on 2 Sep. 1957; and at Sooke, British Columbia, and off Washington and Oregon in 1957 and 1958. There are no valid records from Alaska since 1957, and no Alaskan specimens in museum collections. The northernmost record for British Columbia is Toba Inlet, off the northern end of the Strait of Georgia at about 50°22'N, 124°42'W, where one white seabass was caught in September 1958 (Clemens and Wilby 1961).

Family Pentacerotidae
Armorheads

Fishes of the family Pentacerotidae are called armorheads because their heads are encased in exposed bones. The family includes shallow- and deepwater forms and has representatives in all oceans, but armorheads mainly inhabit cool, deeper waters and the greatest diversity of species is in the Pacific Ocean. The family comprises seven genera with 11 species (Hardy 1983, Humphreys et al. 1989). One species, the North Pacific pelagic armorhead, *Pseudopentaceros wheeleri,* is found, although rarely, in offshore waters of the Gulf of Alaska and south of the Aleutian Islands. Humphreys et al. (1989) revised the nomenclature of this species from an analysis of morphometrics and life history. However, the nomenclature may not be completely resolved and *Pseudopentaceros* may be a junior synonym of *Pentaceros* (J. S. Nelson and R. N. Lea, pers. comms., 22 Aug. 2001).

The geographic range of the North Pacific pelagic armorhead extends from Japan to the North American coast, with a center of abundance and reproduction at the seamounts of the southern Emperor–northern Hawaiian Ridge. Armorheads have rarely been reported as far north as British Columbia, and only a few times within the 200-mile limit off southern Alaska. During the 2 years between hatching and recruitment armorheads undergo extended migrations through varied pelagic environments, and those that have been found off Alaska are young fish which most likely have strayed from their usual circuit farther south in the Alaska Gyre. The fish may stray during years of unusually high abundance of armorheads. The causes of interannual variations in abundance are poorly understood and are not necessarily related only to increased seawater temperature such as occurs during El Niños. Juveniles and young adults are pelagic, and all of the occurrences reported from Alaska have been pelagic. No benthic occurrences in Alaska have been reported, despite extensive trawling surveys that included seamount areas (Boehlert and Sasaki 1988).

Armorhead characteristics include a strongly compressed body; head encased in exposed, striated bones; single dorsal fin with 4–15 strong spines and 8–29 rays; anal fin with 2–6 strong spines and 6–17 rays; large pelvic fins with 1 spine and 5 rays; and small, ctenoid scales which in some species are united ventrally to form a plastron-like covering. The lateral line is complete, and strongly curved over the pectoral fins. Armorheads lack palatine teeth, but some species have vomerine teeth. The gill membranes are separate, free of the isthmus, and supported by 7 branchiostegal rays. The gill rakers are short to moderate in length and thick. There are numerous pyloric caeca. Armorheads have a large swim bladder.

Pelagic armorheads undergo marked changes in morphology and coloration during the transition from juvenile to adult and in connection with the reproductive cycle. The morphotypes of the North Pacific pelagic armorhead were described by Humphreys et al. (1989). The development of early stages was described by Mundy and Moser (1997). The name boarheads, used by some authors for the Pentacerotidae, reflects the increase in snout length relative to head length that occurs with growth, but that name is used for another family, the Caproidae (not Alaskan). The various armorhead species have maximum recorded sizes of 30–61 cm (1–2 ft) in total length. The North Pacific pelagic armorhead reaches a maximum size of 53 cm (21 inches).

Pseudopentaceros wheeleri Hardy, 1983 **North Pacific pelagic armorhead**

Gulf of Alaska to North Pacific Ocean off central California and south of Japan; center of abundance is seamounts of the southern Emperor–northern Hawaiian Ridge.

Far offshore; juveniles epipelagic, adults benthic; around seamount summits and pelagically in the open ocean from surface to depth of 402 m.

D XIV,8–9; A III–IV,6–8; Pec 16–19; Pel I,5; LLs 70–79; GR 22–28; Vert 24–25.

- Bluish brown, paler ventrally; reddish on head; orange on anal and pelvic fin spines; dark wavy lines or spots dorsolaterally in small individuals.
- Snout long and mouth small, maxilla not extending to below eye; lower jaw slightly projecting in large specimens.
- Spines of dorsal and anal fins originating alternately on either side of the midline, and depressible in a groove; usually 4 anal fin spines; pectoral fin elongate, pointed.
- Small ctenoid scales; more rugose on belly and throat and forming interlocking polygonal plates.
- Teeth very small; present but sparse on vomer.
- Length to 530 mm TL.

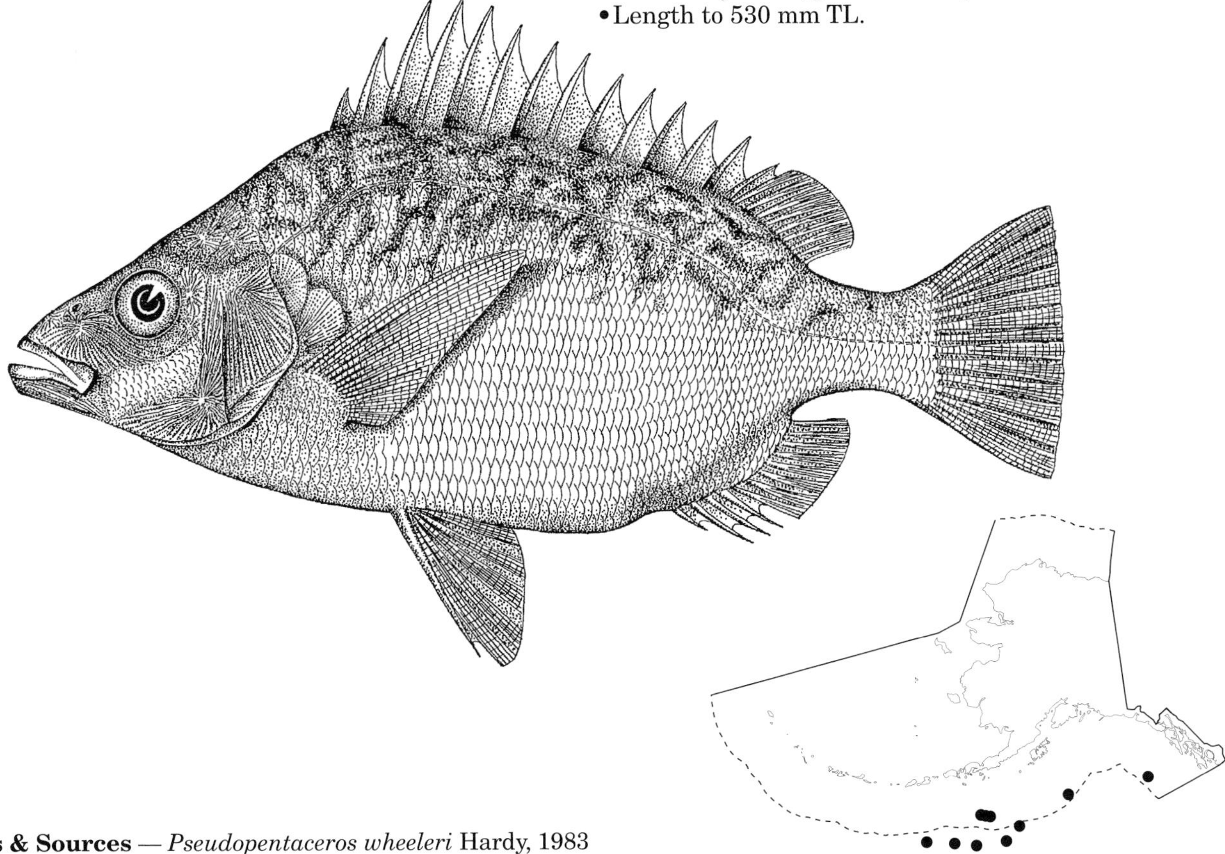

Notes & Sources — *Pseudopentaceros wheeleri* Hardy, 1983
Pseudopentaceros pectoralis Hardy, 1983
North Pacific records of *Pentaceros richardsoni* Smith, 1844 and *Pseudopentaceros richardsoni* (Smith, 1844). Humphreys et al. (1989) compiled a complete synonymy.

Description: Hart 1973:297–298; Eschmeyer and Herald 1983:225–226; Hardy 1983:209–214.

Figure: Hart 1973:297; 29 cm TL, off Vancouver Island.

Range: Erroneously reported to occur north of the Aleutian Islands (Hardy 1983) due to misinterpretation of acquisition data for BPBM 25156. This lot includes two specimens of *P. wheeleri* gillnetted from the *C. H. Gilbert* in 1955 at 45°41'N, 165°05'W. The label also reads "N of Aleutian Is.," and researchers have used this description while overlooking the locality indicated by the coordinates. Latitude 45°41'N is at least 400 statute miles *south* of the Aleutian Islands, in the mid-Pacific Ocean. Dr. A. Suzumoto (pers. comm., 1 Nov. 1994) checked the acquisition data and found missing text, shown in brackets in the following quote: "North [Pacific Ocean; S] of Aleutian Islands . . ."; and verified that the position coordinates were correct. Boehlert and Sasaki (1988) tallied and mapped North Pacific records of *P. wheeleri,* including a few from south of the eastern Aleutian Islands and in the Gulf of Alaska. Exact localities were given for only one of those records, comprising four specimens dipnetted in 1967 at 54°38'N, 150°01'W. Localities for the other dots on our map were estimated from Boehlert and Sasaki's (1988) figure 2A map, and represent sporadic occurrences in the 1950s and 1960s. A specimen caught in the Gulf of Alaska in the summer of 1997 was turned in to the ADFG Kodiak office for identification (*Juneau Empire,* 3 Sep. 1997, "Warm-Water Fish Show Up in Gulf of Alaska off Kodiak"), but there is no further information on capture locality for this specimen (J. E. Blackburn, pers. comm., 12 Aug. 1998).

FAMILY EMBIOTOCIDAE
Surfperches

The silvery, viviparous surfperches occur only along temperate North Pacific coasts, where they may be found in schools in the surf or in shallow water along sandy shores and around floats and pilings. Three or four species occur in southeastern Alaska. The species most commonly reported is the shiner perch, *Cymatogaster aggregata.* A collection of kelp perch, *Brachyistius frenatus,* from Craig and Klawock (Csepp and Wing 2000) recently extended the known range of that species from British Columbia into Alaska. Pile perch, *Rhacochilus vacca,* and striped seaperch, *Embiotoca lateralis,* were reported by Tarp (1952) to occur as far north as Wrangell, but without citing specific documentation. Since then, specimens of *E. lateralis* have been collected at Prince of Wales Island (UBC 61-547, identification confirmed by N. J. Wilimovsky), but they constitute the only adequately documented record of *E. lateralis* in Alaska. The presence of *R. vacca* in Alaska remains unconfirmed; this species has been documented only as far north in southern British Columbia as Vancouver Island, but is abundant there.

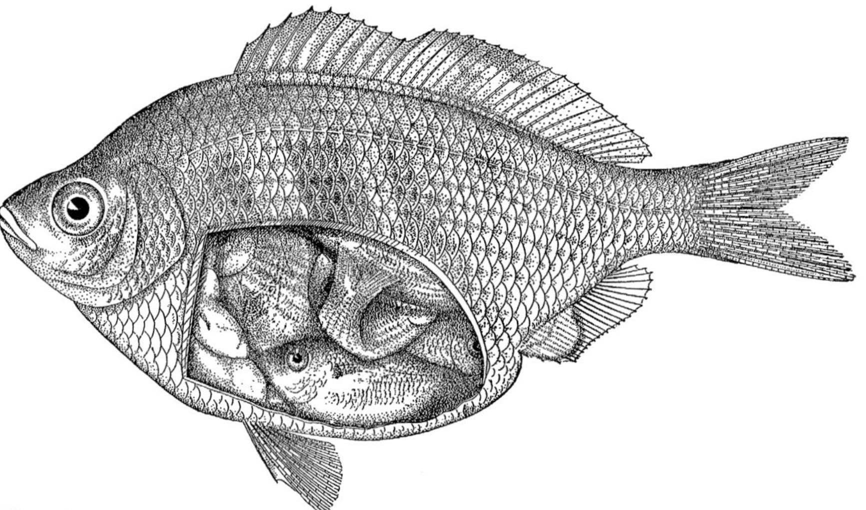

Surfperches are compressed, deep-bodied, and small-mouthed. Their single dorsal fin is composed of spines and soft rays, and has a sheath of scales at its base separated from the body scales by a groove. The anal fin has 3 spines in front of the soft rays, the pelvic fins have 1 spine and 5 rays, and the caudal fin is forked. The lateral line is high on the side and does not extend onto the caudal fin. The scales are cycloid. Surfperches lack vomerine and palatine teeth and pyloric caeca. Their gill openings are wide, with the membranes free from the isthmus or very slightly connected. They have 5 or 6 branchiostegal rays (6 in the Alaskan species) and a large swim bladder.

Brachyistius frenatus is the easiest of the Alaskan surfperches to identify, from its large scales, very small mouth, and concave profile over the eyes. The most useful characters for distinguishing among the other three species in this guide are coloration, numbers of scales, presence or absence of a frenum connecting the lower lip to the jaw, and relative height of the spinous and rayed portions of the dorsal fin. Following the major revision of the family by Tarp (1952), we give lateral line scale counts separately for the scales before and after the end of the hypural. A shortcut scale count can be made from the base of the first dorsal fin spine to the lateral line, where the scales vary from 5 to 10 among the four species treated in this guide.

The viviparity of surfperches has intrigued biologists from as early as 1853, when Louis Agassiz (1807–1873) described and named the family. Surfperch males use the front part of the anal fin, which is thickened, to copulate and achieve internal fertilization. The female nourishes the young in a sac-like enlargement of the oviduct analogous to the uterus. The young are large (2.5–4.1 cm) at birth; most species bear as few as 3–10 per "litter." The illustration above (Jordan and Evermann 1900) shows young near the time of birth in *C. aggregata.*

Individuals of some surfperch species grow to 48 cm (19 inches), but most species are under 25 cm (10 inches). The pile perch, *R. vacca,* reaches 44.2 cm (17.4 inches) and is the largest surfperch treated in this guide.

Three surfperch species listed by Bean (1881b) and Quast and Hall (1972) as probable Alaskan fishes are not included here because they have been recorded no farther north than southern British Columbia and are not commonly found that far north: *Hyperprosopon argenteum, H. ellipticum,* and *Phanerodon furcatus.*

Key to the Embiotocidae of Alaska

1		Lateral line scales total 50 or less	(2)
1		Lateral line scales total more than 60	(3)
2	(1)	Frenum joining lower lip and jaw present	*Brachyistius frenatus,* this page
2		Frenum joining lower lip and jaw absent	*Cymatogaster aggregata,* page 662
3	(1)	Color coppery brown to reddish with blue stripes	*Embiotoca lateralis,* page 663
3		Color silvery gray or brown with 1 or 2 dark bars on the sides and dark spot behind corner of mouth	*Rhacochilus vacca,* page 664 (not confirmed from Alaska)

Brachyistius frenatus Gill, 1862 **kelp perch**

Southeastern Alaska near Sitka at Sandy Cove to central Baja California at Turtle Bay.

In kelp beds, from surface to depth of 30 m.

D VII–X,13–16; A III,20–25; Pec 17–18; Pel I,5; LLs 37–44 + 4–6 caudal; GR 24–29; Vert 31–35.

- Rosy to coppery brown dorsally, lighter ventrally, often with blue spots ventrolaterally; often with whitish areas below lateral line; sometimes rosy overall without distinctive markings.
- Profile slightly concave over eye; **frenum joining lower lip and jaw present**; mouth very small, **maxilla ending well short of eye**.
- Spinous and rayed portions of dorsal fin not markedly different in length.
- **Lateral line scales total 50 or less; scales from first dorsal fin spine to lateral line 5 or 6, usually 6**.
- Length to 220 mm TL.

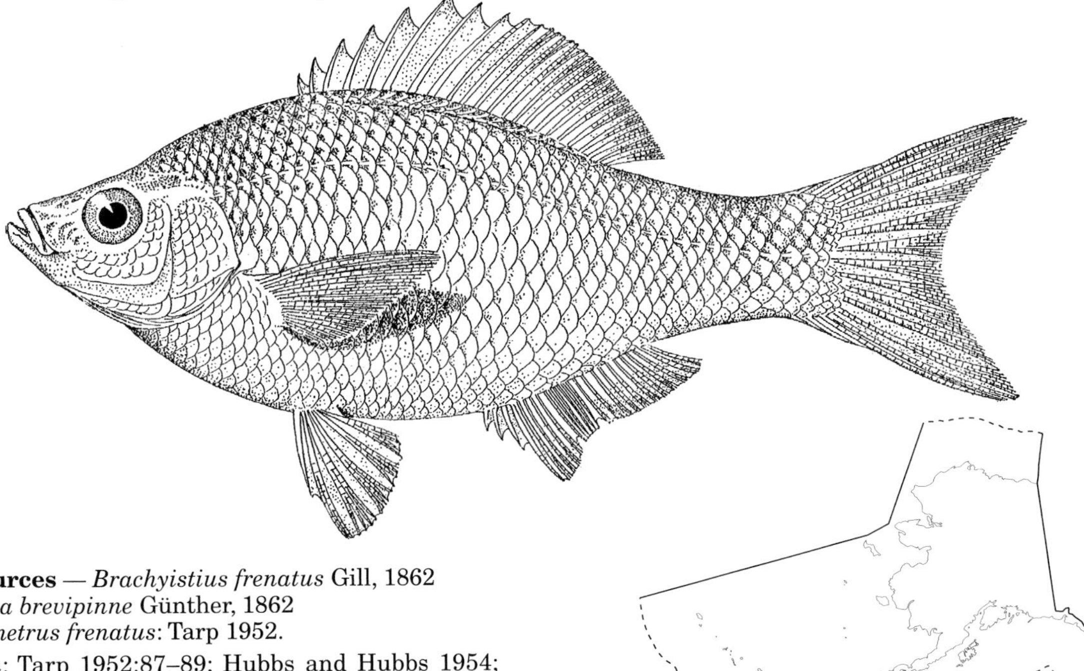

Notes & Sources — *Brachyistius frenatus* Gill, 1862
Ditrema brevipinne Günther, 1862
Micrometrus frenatus: Tarp 1952.

Description: Tarp 1952:87–89; Hubbs and Hubbs 1954; Eschmeyer and Herald 1983:227–228; Humann 1996:178.

Figure: Jordan and Evermann 1900, fig. 580; Monterey Bay.

Range: Thirty-six specimens collected near Klawock and Craig in 1998 (Csepp and Wing 2000) compose the first record from Alaska. Although several localities farther north were sampled in the same study, no additional *B. frenatus* were found. In June 2001, however, Csepp collected several *B. frenatus* at Sandy Cove, just south of Sitka. A voucher specimen from Sandy Cove has been logged into the ABL permanent collection (B. L. Wing, pers. comm., 20 Jun. 2001). The nearest record of occurrence outside Alaska is from northern British Columbia at 54°01'N, 130°36'W, Welcome Harbour, Porcher Island (Peden and Wilson 1976).

Cymatogaster aggregata Gibbons, 1854 **shiner perch**

Southeastern Alaska at Sitka to north central Baja California at Bahia San Quintin.

Shallow waters to depth of about 146 m; along calm areas of exposed coasts and in bays, around eelgrass beds, piers, pilings, and reefs; enters brackish and fresh waters.

D VIII–XI,18–23; A III,22–26; Pec 19–21; Pel I,5; LLs 36–43 + 4–6 caudal; GR 28–33; Vert 34–38.

- Silvery, with dark-spotted scales forming stripes laterally, crossed by 2 or 3 vertical yellow bars which are obscured by black in males in summer; often a black spot above upper lip.
- **Frenum joining lower lip and jaw absent**; maxilla not reaching below eye, in some individuals almost to eye.
- Spinous portion of dorsal fin higher than or about same height as rayed portion.
- **Lateral line scales total 50 or less; scales from first dorsal spine to lateral line 5.**
- Length to 203 mm TL.

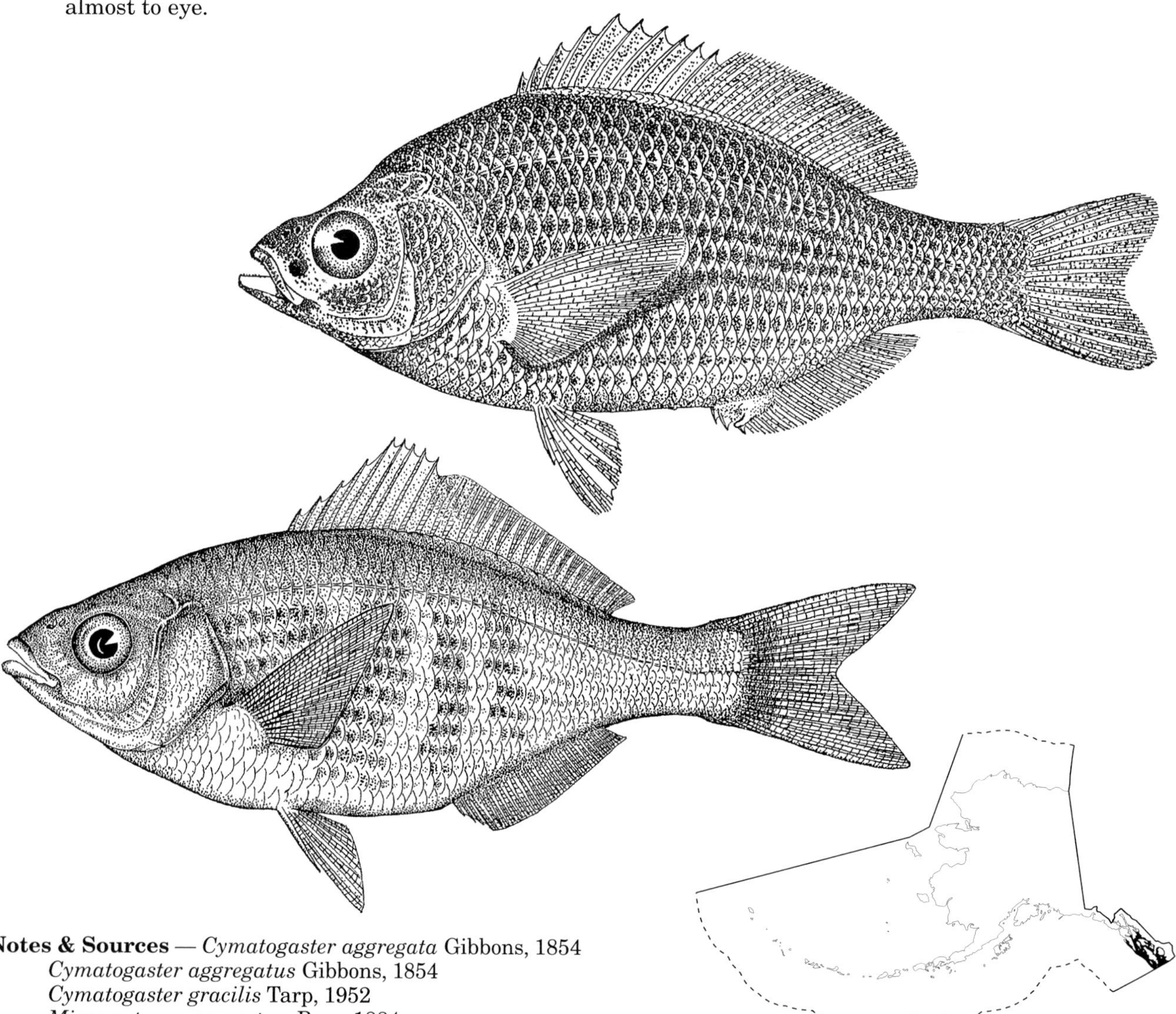

Notes & Sources — *Cymatogaster aggregata* Gibbons, 1854
Cymatogaster aggregatus Gibbons, 1854
Cymatogaster gracilis Tarp, 1952
Micrometrus aggregatus: Bean 1884a.

Description: Tarp 1952:73–76; Hart 1973:304–305; Eschmeyer and Herald 1983:228; Morrow 1980:176–177; Humann 1996:176–177.

Figures: Upper: Jordan and Evermann 1900, fig. 579; male, Wrangell, Alaska. Lower: Hart 1973:304; female, 14 cm TL, Vancouver, British Columbia.

Range: Bean (1884a:361) recorded *C. aggregata* from Port Wrangel (now Wrangell) and noted it was the first embiotocid reported from Alaska. Later recorded from Yes Bay and several localities farther south in southeastern Alaska by Evermann and Goldsborough (1907). Museum collections contain examples from as far north as Petersburg (UBC 65-701, UW 3579). Auke Bay Laboratory biologists collected *C. aggregata* from the Sitka small boat harbor, where it was found to be abundant, in 1998; and the ABL museum has records on file but not specimens from Sitka and localities farther south from salmon trawling and fish habitat studies.

Size: Evermann and Goldsborough (1907) reported maximum of 203 mm TL and mean of 133 mm for 105 females, and maximum of 144 mm and mean of 97 mm for 44 males.

Embiotoca lateralis Agassiz, 1854 **striped seaperch**

Southeastern Alaska at Klakas Inlet, and possibly Wrangell, to northern Baja California at Punta Cabras.

Shallow waters to depth of about 21 m, in rocky areas and kelp beds and around piers; occasionally in sandy surf near rocks.

D X–XII,23–26; A III,29–33; Pec 21–24; Pel I,5; LLs 59–65 + 6–8 caudal; GR 22–27; Vert 33–35.

- Coppery brown to reddish with many narrow, iridescent **blue stripes**; blue spots on head and operculum; fins coppery.
- **Frenum joining lower lip and jaw present**; maxilla extending almost to eye or to anterior edge of eye.
- Spinous portion of dorsal fin lower than rayed portion.
- **Lateral line scales total more than 60; scales from first dorsal spine to lateral line 9 or 10, usually 9**.
- Length to 380 mm TL.

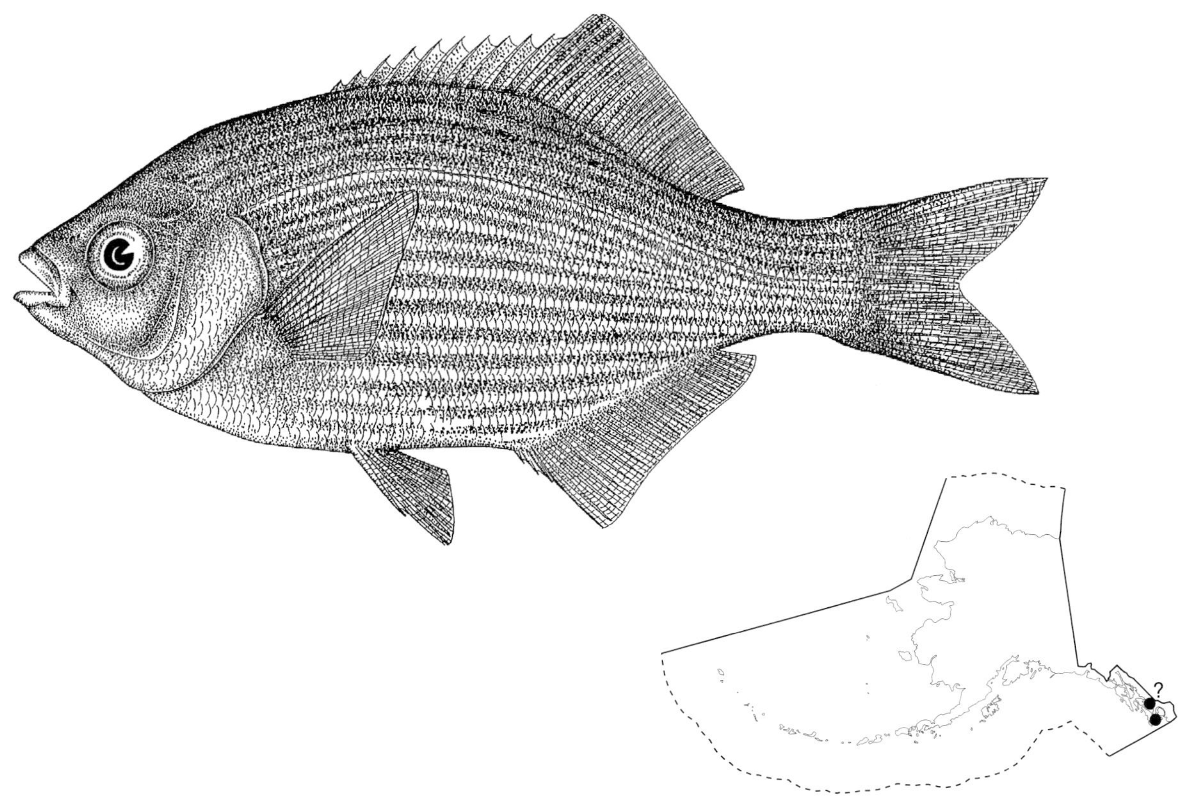

Notes & Sources — *Embiotoca lateralis* Agassiz, 1854
Ditrema laterale: Bean 1881b, 1884a.
Taeniotoca lateralis: Jordan and Evermann 1896a,b.

Description: Tarp 1952:62–64; Hart 1973:206–307; Eschmeyer and Herald 1983:229; Humann 1996:182–183.

Figure: Hart 1973:306; 12 cm TL, Tofino, British Columbia.

Range: Tarp (1952) gave the recorded range of *Embiotoca lateralis, Rhacochilus vacca,* and *Cymatogaster aggregata* as extending north to Port Wrangel (now Wrangell) but without citing documentation. His use of the name Port Wrangel, which was used in the ichthyological literature only in the late 1800s, suggests a misreading of a report by Bean (1884a), who recorded *C. aggregata* from Port Wrangel but *E. lateralis* and *R. vacca* from Departure Bay, in southern British Columbia. However, there is at least one record of *E. lateralis* from farther south in Alaska: UBC 61-547, comprising two specimens from Klakas Inlet, off Cordova Bay on the southwest coast of Prince of Wales Island. The question mark on the above map indicates the Wrangell record is uncertain. Hart (1973) reported it to be "not uncommon" in British Columbia.

Rhacochilus vacca (Girard, 1855) **pile perch**

Unconfirmed record from southeastern Alaska near Wrangell; well documented from southern British Columbia to north central Baja California at Guadalupe Island.

Shallow waters to depth of about 46 m; along rocky and sandy shores, often around pilings, underwater structures, and kelp beds.

D IX–XI,21–25; A III,25–31; Pec 19–22; Pel I,5; LLs 56–59 + 5–8 caudal; GR 18–22; Vert 34–39.

- Silvery gray, occasionally silvery brown, with 1 or 2 sooty vertical bars laterally; **black spot behind corner of mouth**.
- **Frenum joining lower lip and jaw present**; maxilla extending to anterior edge of eye.
- Spinous portion of dorsal fin lower than rayed portion.
- **Lateral line scales total more than 60; scales from first dorsal spine to lateral line 8 or 9, usually 8**.
- Length to 440 mm TL.

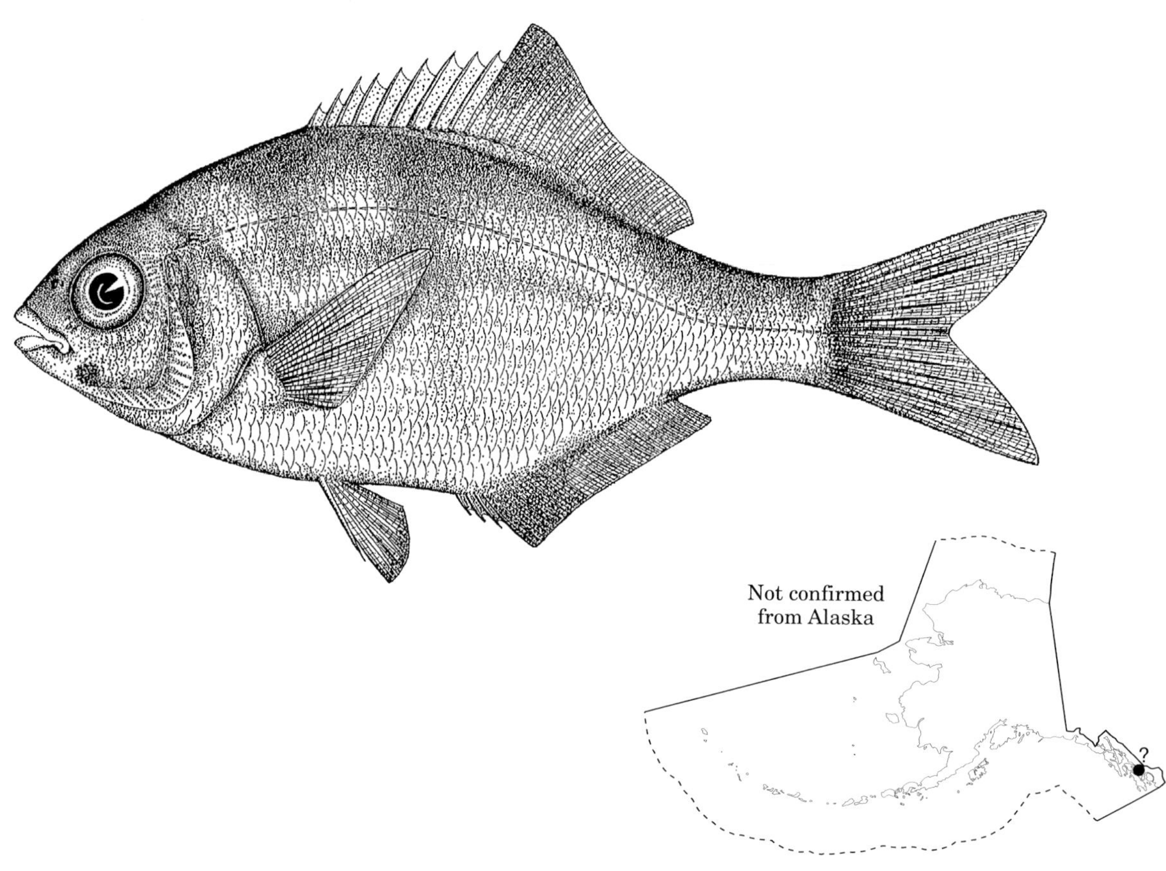

Notes & Sources — *Rhacochilus vacca* (Girard, 1855)
Damalichthys vacca Girard, 1855
Embiotoca argyrosoma Girard, 1856
Damalichthys argyrosomus: Jordan and Gilbert 1881b, Bean 1884a, Jordan and Evermann 1896a,b.

Description: Tarp 1952:56–59; Hart 1973:312–313; Eschmeyer and Herald 1983:228; Humann 1996:182–183.

Figure: Hart 1973:312; 12 cm TL, Vancouver Island.

Range: Reported as far north as Port Wrangel (now Wrangell) by Tarp (1952), without citing documentation. See Notes & Sources for *E. lateralis*. Records to confirm the range given by Tarp (1952) are lacking, and there are no specimens from Alaska in museum collections. Although Evermann and Goldsborough (1907:223) listed *R. vacca* for southeastern Alaska in a summary table, this must have been a mistake. No records from Alaska were mentioned in their text, and the NMNH collection, which formed the basis of their inventory, has no specimens from Alaska. Hart (1973) reported *R. vacca* to be common in southern British Columbia.

Family Bathymasteridae
Ronquils

Ronquils are elongate, cold-water, bottom-dwelling fishes of the North Pacific Ocean. They mainly inhabit rocky shores. The family comprises seven species, with four known from Alaskan waters. The searcher, *Bathymaster signatus,* has the most northern distribution of the ronquils and is frequently encountered in the Bering Sea, where its range extends to Siberia, as well as the Gulf of Alaska. The northern ronquil, *Ronquilus jordani,* despite its common name, has a more southern and eastern distribution and is not found in the western Bering Sea off Siberia or much farther north than the Aleutian Islands. The smallmouth ronquil, *B. leurolepis,* and Alaskan ronquil, *B. caeruleofasciatus,* occur primarily along Gulf of Alaska and Aleutian–Commander island coasts. The range of *B. leurolepis* extends to Japan, but *B. caeruleofasciatus* has been recorded no farther west than the Commander Islands. The bluecheek ronquil, *B. derjugini,* may be restricted to Asian coasts but is included in this guide because *B. caeruleofasciatus* and *B. leurolepis* taken in the vicinity of the western Aleutian Islands are sometimes mistaken for this species. It is not impossible that *B. derjugini* will be found in western Alaska, an eventuality acknowledged by Wilimovsky (1958) when he included it in his provisional keys to the fishes of Alaska.

Ronquils have long dorsal and anal fins that are nearly even in height for their full length. Although some species have one or two spines at the beginning of the dorsal and anal fins, the spines are weak and most researchers count them as soft rays. The pectoral fins are large and round, and the caudal fin round to truncate. The lateral line is distinct and runs high on the body and nearly straight to the end of the dorsal fin. Sensory pores on the top of the head and cheeks are usually distinct. Palatine and vomerine teeth are present. All ronquils have 1 spine and 5 rays in the pelvic fins, and 6 branchiostegal rays. The gill membranes are free of the isthmus, and in the Alaskan species are separate from each other.

Alaskan species of ronquil range in maximum size from about 20 cm (8 inches) in *R. jordani* to more than 38 cm (15 inches) in *B. signatus.*

Key to the Bathymasteridae of Alaska

1		Scales present on cheeks; first 20–30 dorsal fin rays unbranched; lateral line scales enlarged	*Ronquilus jordani,* page 666
1		Head without scales; first 3–5 dorsal fin rays unbranched; lateral line scales not enlarged	(2)
2	(1)	Gill rakers on lower limb of first arch 15–18; black blotch present at anterior end of dorsal fin	*Bathymaster signatus,* page 667
2		Gill rakers on lower limb of first arch 10–14; no black blotch at anterior end of dorsal fin	(3)
3	(2)	Lateral line pores 81–87; pectoral fin rays 18–21; dark blue or black blotch on operculum, almost as large or larger than eye diameter	*Bathymaster derjugini,* page 668 (not known from Alaska)
3		Lateral line pores 87–109; pectoral fin rays 16–19; dark blue or black opercular blotch present or absent	(4)
4	(3)	Maxilla extending to rear margin of eye or beyond; scales rough; caudal fin scaled for more than half its length; scales present on inner rays of pelvic fins	*Bathymaster caeruleofasciatus,* page 669
4		Maxilla extending to about middle of eye; scales smooth; caudal fin scaled for less than half its length; scales absent from pelvic fins	*Bathymaster leurolepis,* page 670

Ronquilus jordani (Gilbert, 1889) **northern ronquil**

Bering Sea north to Pribilof Canyon and west in the Aleutian Islands to Amchitka Island, to central California at Monterey Bay.

On bottom, offshore and nearshore among rocks at depths of 3-275 m, most frequently shallower than 150 m; retreats under boulders or into crevices.

D 41–48; A 31–36; Pec 17–19; Pel I,5; LLp 90–93; LLs about 200; GR 14–15; Vert 49–51.

- Males orange dorsally, olive green ventrally, with vague dark vertical bars; females olive green dorsally, paler ventrally; **dark patch between eyes and before dorsal fin**; yellow or orange stripe or spots curving below eye; fins tipped with yellow or orange; colors fade to brown in preservative.
- Maxilla extending to below mideye.
- **First 20–30 dorsal fin rays (or spines) unbranched**; dorsal fin conspicuously high, more than half of body depth; **pectoral fin extending well past origin of anal fin**; **caudal fin rounded**.
- **Scales weakly ctenoid, almost smooth**, embedded, present on body but not on fins; **fine scales on cheek**; **lateral line scales enlarged**.
- Relatively inconspicuous pores around eyes and on cheeks and top of head.
- Length to 20 cm TL.

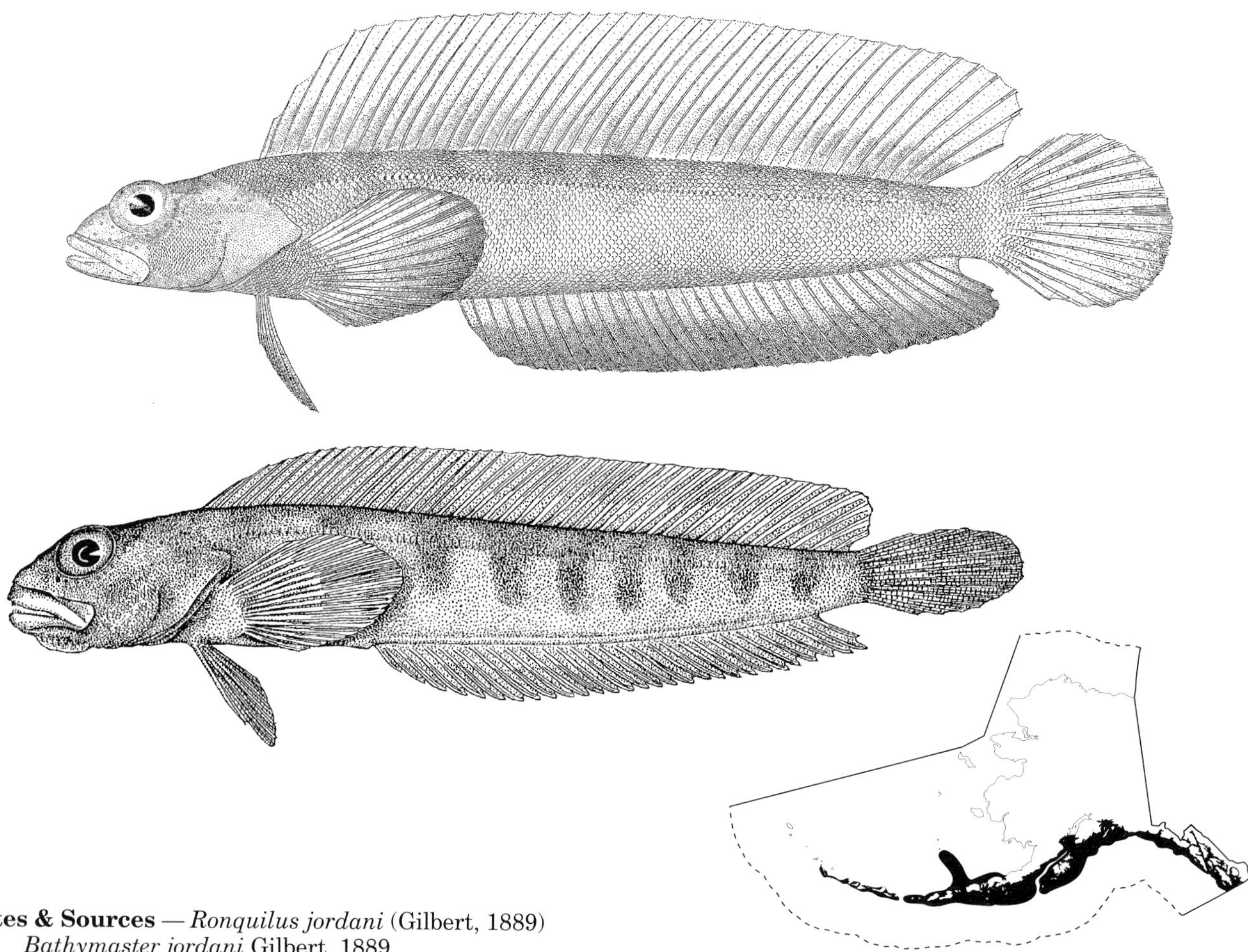

Notes & Sources — *Ronquilus jordani* (Gilbert, 1889)
Bathymaster jordani Gilbert, 1889

Description: Gilbert 1889; Jordan and Evermann 1898:2289; Eschmeyer and Herald 1983:240.

Figures: Upper: Jordan and Starks 1895, pl. 99; Elliot Bay, Washington. Lower: Hart 1973:319; 14 cm TL, Burrard Inlet, British Columbia. Specimens T.A.M. has caught in Lynn Canal, Alaska, have fewer branched rays in the dorsal fin than in Hart's (1973) illustration and, in general, look more like Jordan and Starks' (1895) illustration although the dorsal fin is not quite as high. (In Gilbert's [1889] material the fins were higher in the male, with the longest dorsal ray two-thirds the length of the head.)

Range: Type specimens described by Gilbert (1889) included one from Wrangell, Alaska. NMFS survey data indicate the species' range extends north to the Pribilof Canyon and to Bristol Bay off Port Moller (Allen and Smith 1988) and west to Amchitka Island (Simenstad et al. 1977). *Ronquilus jordani* is represented throughout its known range in Alaska in museum collections, although it is not as common in collections as *Bathymaster signatus*.

Size: Jordan and Starks 1895 (length given as 8 inches).

Bathymaster signatus Cope, 1873 **searcher**

Bering Sea southeast from Navarin Canyon and throughout Aleutian Islands to Washington; East Siberian Sea to eastern Kamchatka and Commander and Kuril islands, Sea of Okhotsk, and Hokkaido.

On bottom, on outer continental shelf on sand and gravel substrate as well as nearshore rock-and-algae habitat; adults at 25–300 m, usually less than 200 m.

D 45–50; A 32–37; Pec 18–22; Pel I,5; LLp 89–127; GR 6–8 + 15–18; Vert 53–55.

- In life light olive brown to dark green dorsally, paler ventrally, with faint vertical bars; **conspicuous black patch at anterior end of dorsal fin** covering first 3–5 rays; **bright orange pores on preopercle** and behind maxilla; anal and pelvic fins black, others dusky; eye bright blue; in preservative colors fade to shades of brown.
- Maxilla extending to below rear margin of eye.
- First 3–5 dorsal fin rays unbranched; **pectoral fin not reaching or barely reaching anal fin**; lower pectoral rays digitate; caudal fin truncate.
- Sensory canals around eye clearly evident; head pores conspicuous.
- **Scales ctenoid, rough**; **head and cheek scaleless**; scales in lateral line not enlarged.
- **Gill rakers 15 or more on lower limb of first arch**.
- Length to 38 cm TL.

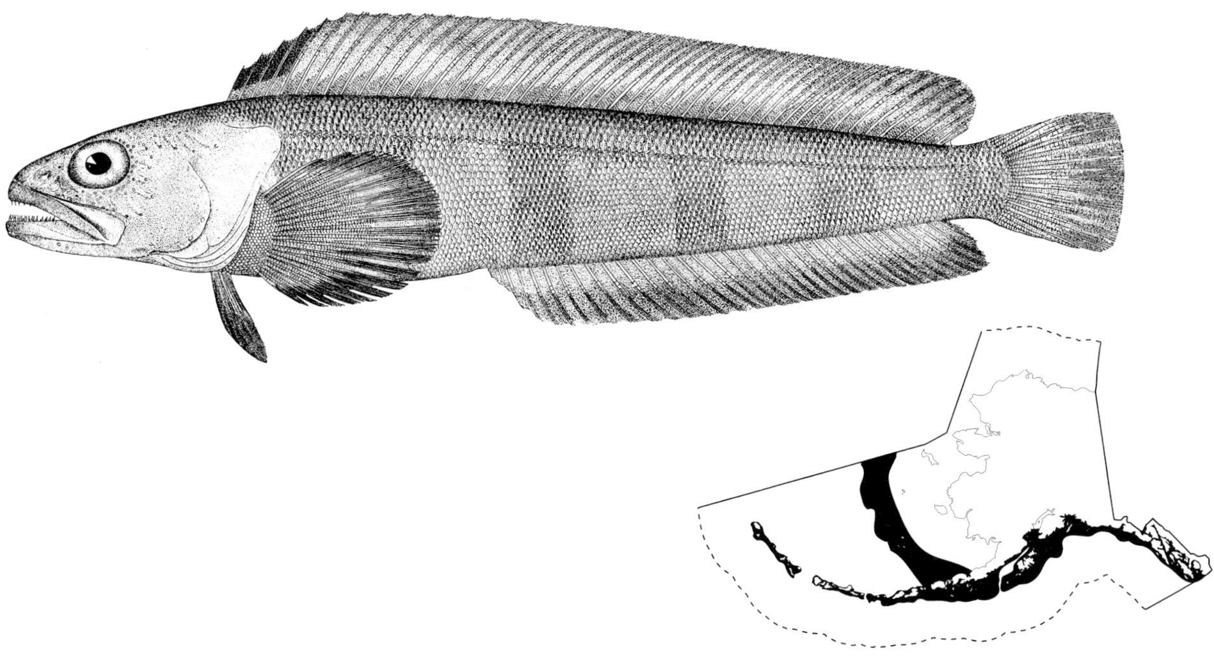

Notes & Sources — *Bathymaster signatus* Cope, 1873

Description: Cope 1873:31–32; Jordan and Evermann 1898: 2288; Taranetz 1933:76–77; Eschmeyer and Herald 1983: 239; Shinohara et al. 1992. Bright blue eyes and sensory canals terminating at bright orange head pores are distinct in freshly caught specimens but soon fade.

Figure: Goode 1884, pl. 118; about 32 cm TL, off Shumagin Islands, Alaska. Jordan and Evermann (1900, fig. 802) reproduced this illustration but modified it by decreasing the size of the dorsal fin blotch. In some of the Alaskan specimens we examined, the blotch is, indeed, as large as shown in Goode's original illustration. However, compared to both Goode's and Jordan and Evermann's depictions, in fresh specimens the anal fin margin is typically more incised between rays, the lower pectoral rays are more digitate, and the opercular flap is lower on the side and does not cover the anterior end of the lateral line.

Range: Described by Cope (1873) from a specimen (ANSP 8982; Böhlke 1984) collected near Sitka, Alaska. By the time of Bean's (1881b) inventory of Alaskan fishes *B. signatus* had been recorded from many Alaskan localities from Sitka to Attu Island and north of the Alaska Peninsula to Port Moller. Allen and Smith (1988) reported distribution in demersal surveys of the Bering Sea and Aleutian Islands. Shinohara et al. (1992) described the first record from Japan, off Kushiro, eastern Hokkaido.

Size: Previously reported to reach 30 cm TL (e.g., Eschmeyer and Herald 1983). A specimen from the Bering Sea examined by Baxter (1990ms) was 383 mm TL (21 Jun. 1984, *Chapman* haul 53). Specimens caught by T.A.M. while recreational fishing using hook and line in 1996 and 1998 off Point Stephens in Lynn Canal, southeastern Alaska, exceeded 310 mm TL and one was 368 mm TL.

Bathymaster derjugini Lindberg, 1930 **bluecheek ronquil**

Kuril Islands and Sea of Okhotsk to Sea of Japan at least as far south as Peter the Great Bay and in Pacific Ocean to southern Hokkaido.

Rocky shore areas.

D 41–44; A 30–33; Pec 18–21; Pel I,5; LLp 81–87; GR 5–6 + 12–14; Vert 14–15 + 33–34.

- Body almost uniform brown; anal and caudal fins blackish, other fins dusky; **conspicuous blue (in life) or black (in preservative) blotch, almost equal to eye diameter, on opercle**.
- **Maxilla extending to below posterior margin of eye or slightly beyond**.
- Pectoral fin reaching to about 5th ray of anal fin; caudal fin truncate.
- Scales ctenoid; no scales on head or dorsal and anal fins; caudal fin scaled for about one-third its length; lateral line scales not enlarged.
- Head pores conspicuous; **lateral line pores fewer than in other *Bathymaster* species**.
- Gill rakers 14 or fewer on lower limb of first arch.
- Length to about 15 cm SL.

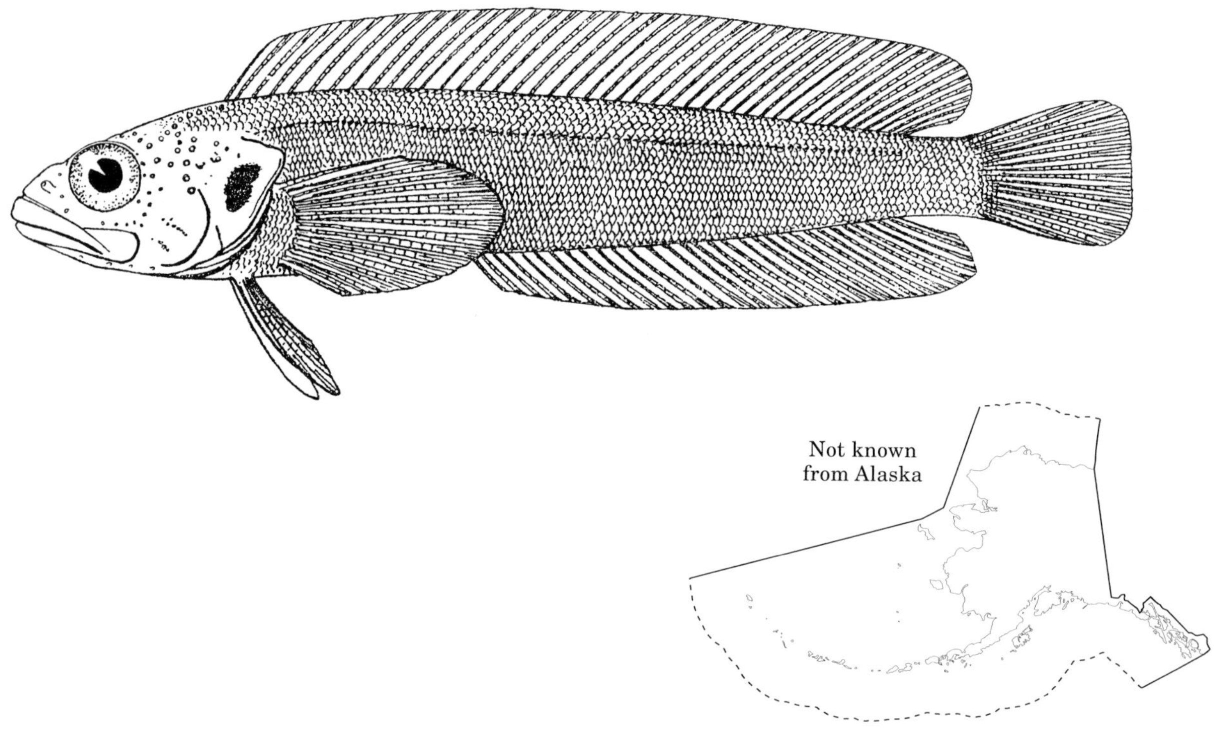

Not known from Alaska

Notes & Sources — *Bathymaster derjugini* Lindberg in Soldatov & Lindberg, 1930

Description: Soldatov and Lindberg 1930:478–481; McPhail 1965:1296; Amaoka in Masuda et al. 1984:289; Kiernan 1990:24.

Figure: Soldatov and Lindberg 1930, fig. 65; 107 mm TL, Peter the Great Bay, Sea of Japan.

Range: Wilimovsky (1958) included *B. derjugini* in his keys to the fishes of Alaska as a species likely to occur in Alaska, although not yet confirmed in the region. Occasionally, fish caught in Alaska are believed to be this species, but they always turn out to be something else. Most recently, fish caught off the western Aleutian Islands in 1998 and tentatively identified as *B. derjugini* were later shown from the fin ray and lateral line pore counts to be *B. caeruleofasciatus* (J. W. Orr, pers. comm., 12 Feb. 1999). Nearest known region of occurrence outside of Alaska is the southern area of the northern Kuril Islands (B. A. Sheiko, pers. comm., 2 Feb. 1999). Wakimoto and Amaoka (1994) described juveniles taken off the coast of Hokkaido and compared them to *B. leurolepis* from the same area.

Size: Amaoka in Masuda et al. 1984.

Bathymaster caeruleofasciatus Gilbert & Burke, 1912 **Alaskan ronquil**

Aleutian Islands to Queen Charlotte Islands, British Columbia, and to Commander Islands.

Subtidal, in rocky habitat, to depth of about 95 m; retreats into holes or crevices if approached.

D 44–50; A 30–37; Pec 16–19; Pel I,5; LLp 87-109; GR 5 + 11–14; Vert 50–53.

- In life reddish brown, with or without blue vertical bars, in alcohol dark brown; head pores blackish; adults occasionally with dark blue or blackish spots on opercle; small specimens paler, often with dark blotch on opercle.
- **Maxilla extending beyond eye**.
- First 4 dorsal rays unbranched; pectoral fin reaching origin of anal fin; caudal fin truncate.
- **Scales ctenoid, rough**; no scales on cheek; **caudal fin scaled for more than half its length; inner rays of pelvic fin scaled**; scales in lateral line not enlarged.
- Head pores conspicuous; **lateral line pores more numerous than in *B. derjugini*.**
- Gill rakers 14 or fewer on lower limb of first arch.
- Length to 30 cm TL.

Notes & Sources — *Bathymaster caeruleofasciatus* Gilbert & Burke, 1912

The description of *B. caeruleofasciatus* by Gilbert and Burke (1912a:84–86) is based on material which contained two forms. McPhail (1965) considered the two to be easily separated on the basis of jaw size and recognized them as distinct species: the long-jawed form, *B. caeruleofasciatus,* and the short-jawed form, *B. leurolepis.*

Description: Taranetz 1933:76–77; McPhail 1965; Peden and Wilson 1976:231; Eschmeyer and Herald 1983:238.

Figures: Upper: University of British Columbia, artist P. Drukker-Brammall, Sep. 1965; UBC 63-905, 208 mm SL, Finger Bay, Adak Island, Alaska. Lower: Royal British Columbia Museum, artist N. Eyolfson, Jul. 1993; BCPM 974-457, 190 mm SL, Parkin Islets, British Columbia.

Range: Recorded west in Aleutian Islands to Agattu Island (holotype; Gilbert and Burke 1912a); and south to Fillmore Island and Cape Fox in southeastern Alaska (Peden and Wilson 1976). Hubbard and Reeder (1965) reported a specimen of *B. caeruleofasciatus* from a Kodiak Island tidepool. The species prefers subtidal habitat. Recorded from Security Inlet, Queen Charlotte Islands, by Peden and Wilson (1976). Paratypes (Gilbert and Burke 1912a) are from Bering, Medny, and Agattu islands, and Petrel Bank.

Bathymaster leurolepis McPhail, 1965 **smallmouth ronquil**

Southeastern Alaska to Pribilof Islands and along Aleutian chain, including Commander Islands, to Pacific coast of Hokkaido.

Tidepools and shallow inshore areas to depth of 9 m, occasionally deeper, to 80 m.

D 43–47; A 30–35; Pec 17–19; Pel I,5; LLp 88–96; GR 4–6 + 12–14; Vert 49–52.

- In life reddish brown, with or without blue vertical bars, in alcohol dark brown; usually a dark blue or blackish blotch at anterior end of dorsal fin in specimens under 125 mm SL; head pores blackish; occasionally with small dark blue or blackish spots on opercle.
- **Maxilla extending to below mideye or rear margin of pupil.**
- First 4 dorsal fin rays unbranched; pectoral fin almost reaching or reaching slightly beyond anal fin origin; caudal fin truncate.
- **Scales weakly ctenoid, nearly smooth**; no scales on head; **caudal fin scaled for less than half its length; no scales on pelvic fin**; scales in lateral line not enlarged.
- Head pores conspicuous; **lateral line pores more numerous than in *B. derjugini*.**
- Gill rakers 14 or fewer on lower limb of first arch.
- Length to 21 cm TL.

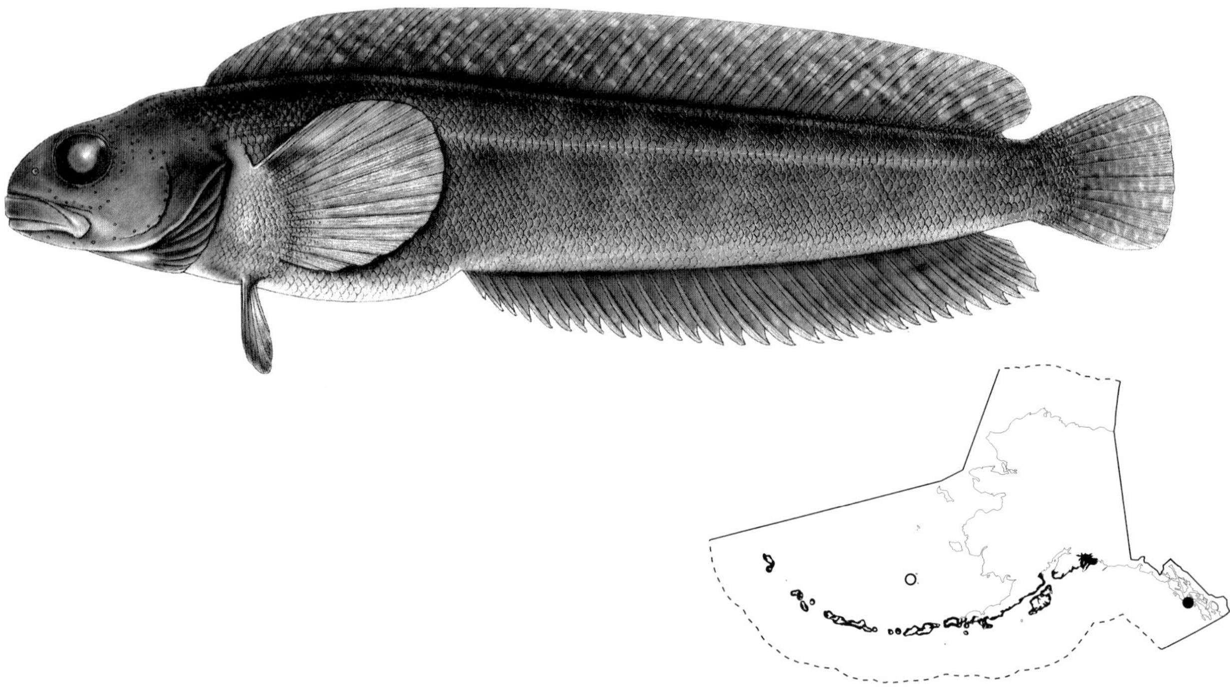

Notes & Sources — *Bathymaster leurolepis* McPhail, 1965

Description: McPhail 1965; Eschmeyer and Herald 1983: 239; Amaoka in Masuda et al. 1984:289.

Figure: University of British Columbia, artist P. Drukker-Brammall, Sep. 1965; holotype, BC 64-214, 186 mm SL, Finger Bay, Adak Island, Alaska.

Range: The species was described by McPhail (1965) using material from numerous Alaskan localities from Kodiak Island and throughout the Aleutian Islands, as well as the Commander Islands of Russia. The type locality is Finger Bay, Adak Island. Rosenthal (1980) claimed an extension of the known range north to Schooner Rock and at least one "other area" of Prince William Sound. NMC 84-152, 84-159, and 84-162 include *B. leurolepis* from Resurrection Bay, off Seward Marine Center dock, collected in 1983 with identification confirmed by A. E. Peden in 1987; caught by hook and line baited with herring. Quast and Hall (1972) gave a general reference to Cook Inlet, confirmed as AB 64-707 (2 specimens, 97–163 mm SL), from southwest tip of Kenai Peninsula. The only confirmed record from southeastern Alaska is AB 68-544 (1 specimen, 105 mm SL), from Little Port Walter (identified by J. C. Quast, confirmed by A. C. Matarese; B. L. Wing, pers. comm., 11 Apr. 1996). R. Baxter (unpubl. data) examined a specimen from the vicinity of the Pribilof Islands, taken by the *Alaska* in haul 22 of cruise 81-4; he indicated the specimen was sent to a museum, but did not say which one. The maximum depth reported by McPhail was 9 m, but Kiernan (1990) examined specimens collected as deep as 80 m. Baxter's (unpubl. data) Pribilof Islands specimen was caught at about 53 m. The ZIN has collections from as deep as 70 m (B. A. Sheiko, pers. comm., 26 Jan. 1999). Wakimoto and Amaoka (1994) described juveniles obtained off the coast of Hokkaido.

Family Zoarcidae
Eelpouts

Eelpouts, family Zoarcidae, are elongate, tapering fishes that inhabit the continental shelves to the abyss in tropical to polar seas and are found mostly on mud bottoms at moderate to great depths. They are primarily species of the North Pacific, North Atlantic, and Arctic oceans, although some are known from the Southern Hemisphere, including the Southern Ocean. Some of the benthic species, including those in the genus *Lycodes,* bury themselves in the mud tail first. A few eelpouts lead a midwater existence. Like deepwater snailfishes (family Liparidae), eelpouts produce their eggs and larvae at the same depths the adults inhabit and larvae are rarely collected in plankton nets. The juveniles of some bottom-dwelling eelpouts inhabit midwater.

The eelpout family belongs to a large group of perciform fishes, the suborder Zoarcoidei, which also includes Bathymasteridae, Stichaeidae, Cryptacanthodidae, Pholidae, Anarhichadidae, Ptilichthyidae, Zaproridae, and Scytalinidae. The only character that consistently separates the Zoarcidae from the other Zoarcoidei is lack of passage of the posterior section of the postorbital canal through the posttemporal and supracleithrum (Anderson 1984, 1994).

Some of the characters that as a group distinguish eelpouts from other fishes are: body and tail elongate, laterally compressed, and tapered posteriorly; head ovoid or dorsoventrally flattened; mouth generally inferior; dorsal and anal fins long, and confluent with caudal fin; dorsal fin with no true spines anteriorly; anal fin with no spines; pectoral fins rudimentary to well developed, with up to 23 rays in Alaskan species; pelvic fin with 2 or 3 rays or absent, and when present, small, located under gill slit or eye; scales cycloid, minute, and not contacting one another, or absent; nostrils single; and vomerine and palatine teeth usually present. The cephalic sensory system is well developed and in many species the pores opening to the outside are conspicuous. The body lateral line can be present in one of several configurations or absent. The gill membranes typically are attached to the isthmus and limit the size of the gill opening, which can extend to the isthmus or be a small pore above the base of the pectoral fin. Pyloric caeca are usually present as 2 small nubs; there are 4 gill arches, with a slit behind the last; pseudobranchia are usually present; and there is no swim bladder. Like other perciforms, eelpouts typically have 6 branchiostegal rays (range 4–7).

Most eelpouts attain lengths of less than 46 cm (18 inches). The largest Alaskan species is the ebony eelpout, *Lycodes concolor,* with a maximum reported length of 760 mm TL (30 inches), while the smallest is the slender eelpout, *Lycodapus leptus,* known to reach a little over 100 mm TL (4 inches).

In the most recent wordwide review of the family Zoarcidae, Anderson (1994) recognized about 200 valid species. Several new eelpout species have been described since that review and others have been collected but not yet named. Many eelpouts are deepsea forms known from only a few specimens and the taxonomy of some others is confused due to inaccurate descriptions and reliance on misunderstood or questionably useful characters. Major works of the past 50 years dealing with the taxonomy of eelpouts in Alaska and adjacent regions include those of Anderson (1982, 1984, 1994, 1995), Anderson and Peden (1988), Andriashev (1954, 1955, 1958), McAllister et al. (1981), Peden and Anderson (1978, 1981), and Toyoshima (1985). Fifty-eight of the species currently recognized as distinct species are treated in this guide. The taxonomy of some of them may change as knowledge of the group increases.

The species accounts are arranged in the informal groups adopted by Anderson (1984): nalbantichthyines (represented in this guide by *Melanostigma, Nalbantichthys, Opaeophacus,* and *Puzanovia*), gymnelines (*Gymnelus*), lycenchelyines (*Derepodichthys, Lycenchelys, Taranetzella*), lycodines (*Lycodes, Pachycara*), and lycodapines (*Bothrocara, Lycodapus*). We do not mean to imply any phylogenetic sequence or relationships of the genera within these groups, but chose them only for convenience; phylogenetic hypotheses are the subject of a later treatment by Anderson (1994). Within the informal groups the species are grouped by overall similarity and presented in the sequence they key out, although sometimes after selecting characters for the key some species ended up farther apart in the accounts than we considered ideal for ease of comparison.

In the **nalbantichthyines** the gill opening is very small, head blunt, pectoral fins very small or rudimentary, and pelvic fins absent. Some species have gelatinous flesh and delicate, loose skin. The body lateral line is present or absent, and when present is mediolateral in position (see lateral line diagrams on next page) but often is indistinct. Scales typically are absent. The three nalbantichthyines known from Alaska have 134–150 vertebrae, far exceeding vertebral counts in other Alaskan eelpouts, and are greatly elongate and slender. Although other characters, such as the

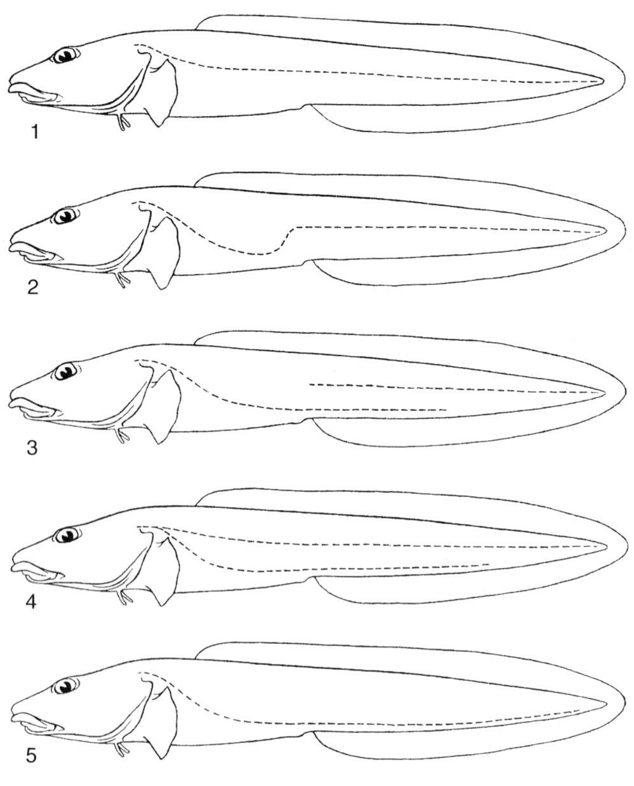

Lateral line configurations in eelpouts
1.—mediolateral; 2.—ventrolateral; 3.—double, incomplete; 4.—double, complete; 5.—ventral. The dorsolateral configuration present anteriorly in some *Bothrocara* is not shown. (After Andriashev 1954.)

unique eye lens of the bulldog eelpout, *Opaeophacus acrogeneius,* are usually sufficient to identify species in the nalbantichthyine group, it could occasionally be necessary to examine the head pores (see diagram of head pores in hypothetical eelpout), which are well developed in some nalbantichthyines.

The Pacific softpout, *Melanostigma pammelas,* is the only one of the four nalbantichthyine species treated in this guide that has not been recorded from Alaska, but its known occurrence off central British Columbia and its pelagic, midwater existence suggests the lack of an Alaskan record may be due to sampling coverage and design. The other three live on the bottom at moderate depths (200–800 m); in Alaska they have been recorded off the Aleutian Islands and in the Bering Sea.

In **gymnelines** the gill slit is broader, in some species extending down as far as the ventral edge of the pectoral fin base, but generally not as large as in lycenchelyines and lycodines; the pectoral fins are larger than in nalbantichthyines, with 9–13 rays; and the pelvic fins are absent. In *Gymnelus* scales are absent, and the body lateral line is present and mediolateral but difficult to discern. Important characters for identifying Alaskan species include presence or absence of the vomerine and palatine teeth and interorbital pore, coloration, position of the dorsal fin origin relative to the base of the pectoral fin, and pectoral fin ray counts and shape.

Gymnelus species inhabit continental shelf bottoms. Species known in Alaska inhabit the shallowest water areas from the intertidal to depths usually no greater than 80 m. In Alaskan waters the Aleutian pout, *G. popovi,* appears to be restricted to the intertidal habitat of the Aleutian Islands to Kodiak Island, whereas the range of the halfbarred pout, *G. hemifasciatus,* and the fish doctor, *G. viridis,* extends into shallow waters of the Arctic Ocean.

Most **lycenchelyines** are strongly elongate, have strongly expressed suborbital and preoperculomandibular pores, and have teeth on the vomer and the palatines. A few species, including the cuskpout, *Derepodichthys alepidotus,* and the ghostly eelpout, *Taranetzella lyoderma,* have loose, delicate skin. The lycenchelyines treated in this guide have 110 or more vertebrae, up to 137, except for *T. lyoderma* and the short

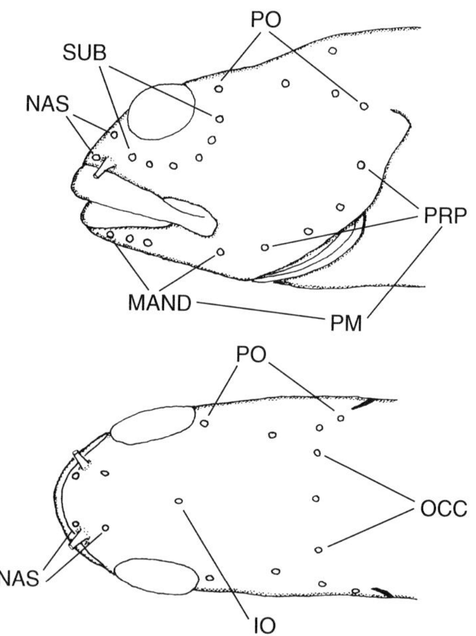

Head pores of hypothetical eelpout
NAS, nasal pores; IO, interorbital pore; SUB, suborbital pores; PO, postorbital pores; OCC, occipital pores; PM, preoperculomandibular pores, including MAND, mandibular, and PRP, preopercular. Nasal and interorbital pores are in the supraorbital canal; other pores are named after like-named canals. (After Anderson 1994.)

eelpout, *Lycenchelys alta,* which have fewer than 100. Some of the most useful characters for distinguishing among species of *Lycenchelys* are scale coverage, lateral line configuration, and head pores. The number of pelvic fin rays, either 2 or 3, is constant by species and useful in identification. The association of the dorsal fin origin with particular vertebrae (Anderson 1995) must, of course, be determined from radiographs or by dissection, but from the vertebral numbers and the position of the dorsal fin origin relative to the pectoral fin, given in the species accounts, one can determine relatively how far back, or retrograde, the dorsal fin is placed. Among the species in this guide, the dorsal fin origin is farthest back in the longnape eelpout, *L. volki,* and keeled eelpout, *L. plicifera.* A special character of some *Lycenchelys* is a raised fold of skin running along the ventral midline from near the base of the pelvic fins to near the anus. This is called a ventral keel, or plica, and is present among the Alaskan species in *L. plicifera.* Occasionally the shape of the opercular lobe is useful for identification, as in *L. volki* and *L. plicifera* in which it is unusually well developed, or the earless eelpout, *L. rassi,* in which the lobe is absent and the operculum is fused to the body leaving only a narrow tube. Coloration is generally not useful for identifying lycenchelyines but a few stand out from the typical brownish to blackish expressions, such as rosy eelpout, *L. rosea*; the rosy red color fades to brown, however, upon preservation.

Lycenchelyines live on the bottom in a wide range of water depths, from the edge of the continental shelf to the abyss, with a depth range of about 200–4,000 m for Alaskan species. Most species seem to prefer water depths greater than 1,000 m. The two most well-known Alaskan lycenchelyines, which are snakehead eelpout, *L. crotalinus,* and Kamchatka eelpout, *L. camchatica,* occur on the continental slope at the shallower end of the depth range. A few lycenchelyines occur in the Arctic Ocean.

Lycodines, including *Lycodes* and *Pachycara,* are generally shorter- and deeper-bodied than most other eelpouts. The species in this guide have 120 or fewer vertebrae (range 87–120), except the black eelpout, *L. diapterus,* which has up to 125. Their pectoral fins have 14–23 rays. The pelvic fins are always present in *Lycodes* and present or absent in *Pachycara,* and when present (in Pacific species) always have 3 rays. Although large in very small juveniles, head pores in *Lycodes* regress and become completely covered with skin with growth of the individual in most species and generally are not useful for identification. Unlike all other eelpouts, *Lycodes* have cartilaginous ridges on the underside of their jaws called chin crests (also called mental crests or submental crests). Presence of the chin crests is an important identifying feature of *Lycodes,* and expression of the crests, whether low or pronounced, and united or not anteriorly, can help identify species. The crests are thought to be a feeding adaptation, used to plow through the mud while "blowing" with the mouth (gill openings closed) to uncover infaunal prey (Anderson 1994).

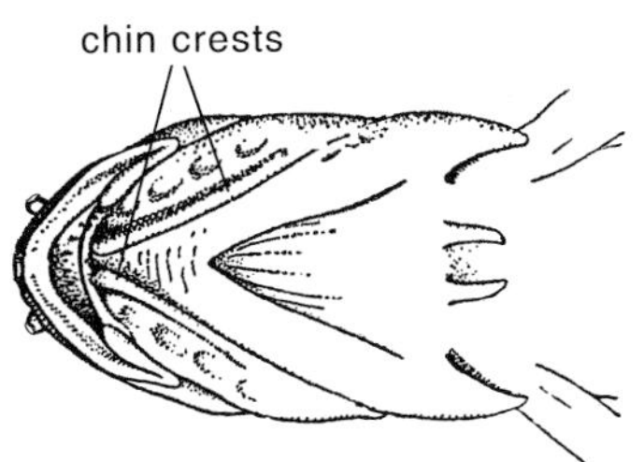

Chin crests, present in *Lycodes*
(After Andriashev 1954.)

The numbers of vertebrae and of rays in the dorsal and anal fins are considered by Toyoshima (1985) to be the most reliable characters for identifying *Lycodes* species, but they are not practical for most people to use since accurate counts are only possible from radiographs or by dissection. The *Lycodes* species in this guide can be identified from coloration; lateral line configuration; scale coverage; pectoral fin shape, length, and ray counts; pelvic fin size, expressed relative to eye diameter; presence and shape of the opercular lobe; and a few morphometric characters, although identifications will be most reliable for adult fishes. Two of the most useful morphometrics for *Lycodes* are size of the head, expressed by head length relative to total length, and the ratio of the anterior part of the body to the posterior part as expressed by preanal length (from tip of snout to anal fin origin) as a percentage of total length. The latter distinguishes between relatively long-tailed and short-tailed species.

Lycodes is the most speciose genus of eelpouts in Alaska and nearby waters, with 23 species included in this guide. In keying out and grouping the species accounts, similar-looking species have been kept together as much as possible. The subject of species groups in *Lycodes* needs further study, but possibilities involving Alaskan species have been suggested by, among other authors, Andriashev (1954), Toyoshima (1985), and Anderson (1994). In the present accounts *L. pacificus* and *L. cortezianus,* each with some palatal tooth loss, represent a possible subgenus *Lycodopsis.* The proposed species of subgenus *Lycodalepis,* with reduced scalation in common, are Arctic in distribution: *L. jugoricus, L. seminudus, L. mucosus, L. turneri,* and *L. polaris. Lycodes raridens, L. reticulatus,* and *L. rossi* seem to be closely related. *Lycodes palearis* and *L. fasciatus* are sometimes treated as subspecies of *L. palearis.* The only representative of subgenus *Furcimanus* (notched pectoral fin) in Alaska is *L. diapterus. Lycodes concolor* and *L. frigidus* are placed together because of their large heads, single, ventral lateral line, very small scales, and solid, dark coloration. Other species are grouped by lateral line configuration although they may not be particularly closely related. For example, *L. pallidus, L. squamiventer,* and *L. eudipleurostictus* have double lateral lines and *L. sagittarius* and *L. soldatovi* have ventrolateral lateral lines.

Treatment of *L. multifasciatus* as banded eelpout, *L. fasciatus,* is the only difference in this guide from the classification presented by Anderson (1994), who followed Toyoshima (1985) in recognizing both forms as distinct species. However, Toyoshima (1985) did not examine specimens of *L. fasciatus.* Boris A. Sheiko (pers. comm., 25 Sep. 1998) examined relevant specimens in the ZIN and KIE collections of the Russian Academy of Sciences, and Sheiko and Fedorov (2000) included *L. multifasciatus* as a synonym of *L. fasciatus* in their catalog of Kamchatka fishes.

Lycodes inhabit soft bottoms, mostly mud, at shallow to moderate depths on the continental shelf and upper slope. None inhabits the intertidal area, and not many frequent depths greater than about 400 m. Although six of the species in this guide have been collected at depths of 1,000 m or more (longear eelpout, *L. seminudus*; dipline eelpout, *L. soldatovi*; scalebelly eelpout, *L. squamiventer*; black eelpout, *L. diapterus*; ebony eelpout, *L. concolor*; glacial eelpout, *L. frigidus*), only *L. frigidus* is typically taken at such depths. *Lycodes* is the only eelpout genus other than *Gymnelus* to occur in the Arctic Ocean off Alaska.

The range statements and maps for several similar-looking species of *Lycodes* may reflect taxonomic confusion and paucity of confirmed records. For example, it is odd that there are no records of shulupaoluk, *L. jugoricus,* from the Beaufort Sea off Alaska, and only one or a few records of threespot eelpout, *L. rossi,* and saddled eelpout, *L. mucosus,* whereas all those species are represented by several records from Canada close to Alaska near Herschel Island and along the Mackenzie Delta. Estuarine eelpout, *L. turneri,* and polar eelpout, *L. polaris,* are often confused and museum collections probably still contain some misidentified records of each species from Alaska.

Pachycara differs from *Lycodes* by the lack of chin crests, presence of an oral valve (palatine membrane), and presence of head pores in adults. Head pores are present in *Pachycara* adults but their numbers are not consistent enough to be useful for identification. Pectoral fin ray numbers (14–19), presence or absence of pelvic fins, scale coverage, and origin of the mediolateral lateral line relative to tip of the pectoral fin are most important for identifying the three species known from nearby waters of British Columbia. These species are known from bathyal and abyssal depths of about 1,700–4,800 m.

Lycodapines, represented in Alaska by *Bothrocara* and *Lycodapus,* lack pelvic fins and oral valve, the flesh is often delicate and gelatinous, and vomerine and palatine teeth are present. In *Bothrocara* scale coverage is extensive, lateral lines are present, and the flesh is relatively firm (compared to *Lycodapus*) except in Alaska eelpout, *B. pusillum.* The lateral line is sometimes doubled in *Bothrocara,* with a mediolateral line and a short dorsolateral line anteriorly. Gill raker shape and pectoral fin length are important in distinguishing twoline eelpout, *B. brunneum,* and soft eelpout, *B. molle.*

Bothrocara are deepwater eelpouts. The three *Bothrocara* species known from Alaska have been collected from a wide range of depths, from 60 to 2,688 m. Although *B. molle* and *B. brunneum* are rarely captured at depths shallower than 400 m, *B. pusillum* is often taken at the shallower depths.

Species of *Lycodapus* have gelatinous flesh and loose, delicate skin; reduced cephalic sensory system (suborbital pores and first mandibular pore absent; see diagram on opposite page); a mediolateral body lateral line, present at least anteriorly; and small pectoral fins (5–9 rays). The gill membranes are free of the isthmus posteriorly, so the gill openings are large. Scales are absent. The mouth is terminal, and adult males have caniniform teeth anteriorly in the jaws. The most important characters for identifying *Lycodapus* species are gill raker ratio (see diagram), dentition, head pore counts, and vertebral counts (75–104 in Alaskan species), as well as a few special characters such as the reduced gill opening (not extending much above the base of the pectoral fin) in smallhead eelpout, *L. parviceps,* and specklemouth eelpout, *L. psarostomatus. Lycodapus* species are difficult to identify since they lack most of the features used in identifying other groups. Closure

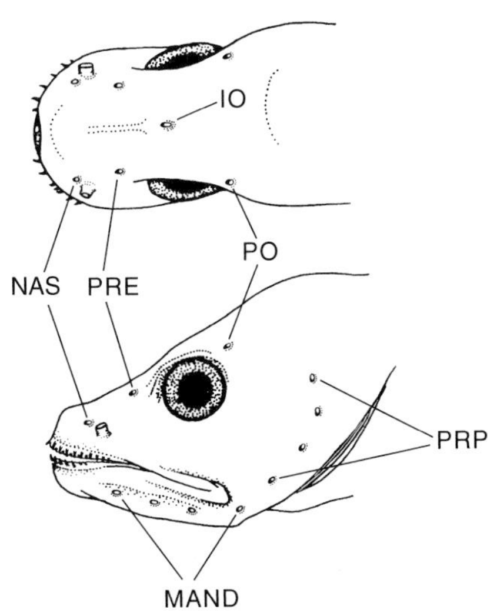

Head pores in *Lycodapus*

NAS, nasal pore; IO, interorbital pore; PRE, preorbital pore; PO, postorbital pore; MAND, mandibular pores; PRP, preopercular pores. (After Peden and Anderson 1978.)

of head pores in adults of some species (pallid eelpout, *L. mandibularis*; slender eelpout, *L. leptus*; variform eelpout, *L. poecilus*) further complicates identification.

Lycodapus is a genus of meso- and bathypelagic eelpouts occurring over the continental shelf and slope. Their loosely attached, gelatinous skin is thought to be an adaptation to aid buoyancy since these fishes lack gas bladders, and is convergent, along with midwater

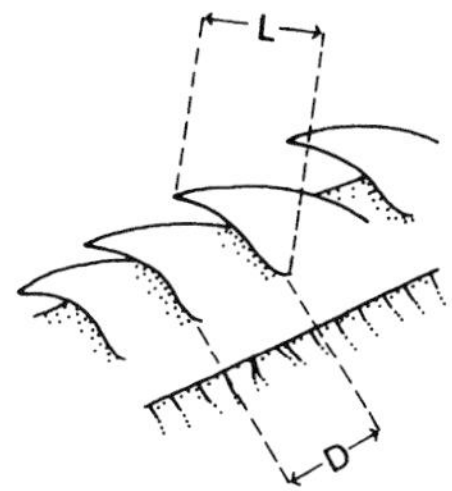

Determining *Lycodapus* gill raker ratio

L, length of fourth gill raker; D, distance between fourth and fifth rakers. (After Peden and Anderson 1978.)

mode of life, with the condition seen in *Melanostigma* in Zoarcidae, *Lipariscus, Nectoliparis,* and *Paraliparis* in Liparidae, and some of the Psychrolutidae (Peden and Anderson 1978). *Lycodapus* have been caught in midwater trawls and nonclosing bottom trawls at a wide range of depths, from near the surface at less than 15 m to near the bottom at about 2,200 m.

The dorsal and anal fin ray counts provided in the line of meristic character values in each species account are not always comparable because some researchers include half the rays of the caudal fin in those counts and, if there was a choice, we reported counts that do not include the caudal fin rays. Gill raker counts are provided if available, but the numbers do not seem to vary much among Alaskan eelpout species. If the number of branchiostegal rays is typically other than 6, which it rarely is in eelpouts, the number is reported in the list of distinguishing (bulleted) characters, not in the line of meristic characters.

Development of the labial lobe (terminology of Toyoshima [1985]) is not provided as a distinguishing character for Lycodinae because it seems to depend largely on age and, possibly, sex. The labial lobe is mentioned only for wattled eelpout, *L. palearis,* because it does seem to be unusually well developed in that species. However, this could be an impression from authors who first described the species and coined the vernacular, and might not apply to all specimens; or, it could be just as strongly developed in other species. In addition, more than one fleshy outgrowth is present on the jaws and authors have not always been clear in referring to these features, making comparisons impossible.

Generally speaking, the characters available for distinguishing eelpout species are limited for some of the same reasons that choice of characters is limited in other poorly known groups, such as the snailfishes (Liparidae). The use of morphometrics is limited by a general lack of adequate sample size for adults and because methods vary among authors and the available data are not comparable. For instance, some authors give total length and some standard length, and for interorbital width some give distance between the pupils and some the distance between the bony orbits. Some features once considered important for identification are now known to vary by age, sex, or locality, including details of coloration and scale coverage, emargination of the pectoral fin rays, and body and fin proportions. Color patterns can be highly variable in detail and, at least in *Lycodes,* partly disappear with growth, whereas scales develop with age. The gelatinous tissues of some species prevent meaningful measurements due to distortion in preservatives.

Several eelpout species have been recorded for the first time from Alaska and closely adjacent waters since Quast and Hall (1972) compiled their inventory. The following newly recognized species were named and described on the basis of specimens from the Bering Sea: *Puzanovia rubra,* described by Fedorov (1975); *Lycodapus endemoscotus* and *L. pachysoma,* by Peden and Anderson (1978); *L. leptus, L. poecilus,* and *L. psarostomatus,* by Peden and Anderson (1981); *Opaeophacus acrogeneius,* by Bond and Stein (1984); and *Lycenchelys alta, L. longirostris,* and *L. rosea,* described by Toyoshima (1985). One new species, *Lycodes sagittarius,* was described from specimens collected in the Beaufort Sea, Alaska, by McAllister (1976).

Recent records that extend the known range of previously recognized species into Alaskan waters include those for *Lycodes eudipleurostictus,* recorded from the Beaufort Sea north of Kaktovik by McAllister et al. (1981); *Lycodapus psarostomatus, L. leptus,* and *L. poecilus,* recorded from the eastern Bering Sea by Peden and Anderson (1981); and *L. endemoscotus,* recorded from the central Aleutian Islands by Anderson (1989). The occurrence of *Lycodes japonicus* just north of the Near Islands, recently reported by Nalbant (1994), is not only the first record of the species for Alaska, but also the first record outside of the Sea of Japan. Finally, adult specimens of *L. pallidus* from the Beaufort Sea off Alaska housed at the National Museum of Natural Sciences, Ottawa, Canada, and identified by M. E. Anderson (NMC records; M. E. Anderson and B. W. Coad, pers. comms., May 1999), extend the known range of that species from nearby Canadian Arctic waters into Alaska.

New eelpout species described from specimens taken in the adjacent waters of British Columbia are the deepwater species *Pachycara gymninium* and *P. lepinium,* described by Anderson and Peden (1988). *Gymnelus pauciporus,* described by Anderson (1982) from specimens taken in shallow waters of the southwestern Bering Sea off Russia, is not included in this guide because it is relatively limited in distribution (M. E. Anderson, pers. comm., 17 Feb. 1998; Chernova 1998b) and is less likely to occur in Alaskan waters.

The known range of several previously recognized species was extended to nearby waters. Three were recorded from the Pacific Ocean off British Columbia: *Lycodapus pachysoma,* by Peden and Anderson (1978, 1979); *Pachycara bulbiceps,* by Anderson and Peden (1988); and *Taranetzella lyoderma,* by Peden and Jamieson (1988). *Lycodes reticulatus* was recorded by Hunter et al. (1984) from western Canada, close to the Alaska border near Herschel Island. *Lycodes frigidus* was recorded from the high Arctic on the Chukchi rise by McAllister et al. (1981).

Several species overlooked in previous inventories are included in this guide. *Lycodes concolor* was described by Gill and Townsend (1897) from specimens collected from the southeastern Bering Sea, Alaska. *Gymnelus popovi* was recorded from Agattu Island, Alaska, by Wilimovsky (1964), and later recorded from other locations in Alaska by Anderson (1982). The holotype of *Lycenchelys micropora,* described by Andriashev (1955a), was captured in U.S. waters in the northern part of the Aleutian Basin. *Lycodes jugoricus, L. pallidus,* and *L. rossi* were all recorded from near Herschel Island, Yukon Territory, by McAllister (1962).

Bothrocara hollandi, Krusensterniella pavlovskii, and *Lyconema barbatum* were incorrectly reported with ranges to the eastern Bering Sea by Matarese et al. (1989). Of those three species, only *K. pavlovskii* has been documented from the Bering Sea, and it appears to have a restricted range off the Kamchatka Peninsula (known only from the vicinity of Cape Afrika) and is not likely to occur in Alaskan waters (M. E. Anderson, pers. comm., 17 Feb. 1998). The documented range of *L. barbatum* is from Oregon to California in the eastern North Pacific, while *B. hollandi* is restricted to the Sea of Japan and the Yellow Sea. The attribution of a Bering Sea range for *L. barbatum* may stem from an incorrect citation by Jordan and Evermann (1896a) of a report by Gilbert (1896), who recorded it from California but not from the Bering Sea; the Gilbert (1896) paper has subsections on fishes from the Bering Sea, California, and Alaska and Washington which have often been confused by subsequent authors.

Three species of *Lycenchelys* which are known only from the unique holotypes described by Andriashev (1955a, 1958) and were collected at abyssal depths of the Kuril–Kamchatka Trench off Paramushir Island could also occur in the Aleutian Basin. They were included on Quast and Hall's (1972) list as potential additions to the Alaskan ichthyofauna: *L. albeola, L. uschakovi,* and *L. vitiazi.* However, to keep this guide within reasonable bounds we do not treat species that are known from only one record and that record is from the Kuril–Kamchatka Trench. *Lycodes bathybius,* known only from the Sea of Okhotsk off the Kamchatka Peninsula yet listed as possibly occurring in Alaska by Quast and Hall (1972), also is not treated in this guide because it is extralimital. Two Asian species of *Lycodapus* that are not treated in this guide are *L. derjugini* and *L. microchir.* Both species are known primarily from the Sea of Okhotsk; there are a few records from the western Bering Sea (Peden and Anderson 1978, 1981; Anderson 1989a), but they are close to Kamchatka and Anderson (pers. comm., 17 Feb. 1998) considers those species unlikely to occur in Alaska. *Lycodapus extensus,* collected in 1890 from the eastern Bering Sea north of Unalaska Island by the *Albatross* (Gilbert 1896) and subsequently counted by authors as an Alaskan species (e.g., Evermann and Goldsborough 1907, Wilimovsky 1954, Quast and Hall 1972), was treated as a nomen dubium by Peden and Anderson (1978) because it was inadequately described and the holotype and only known specimen is in poor condition.

Species in Quast and Hall's (1972) inventory of Alaskan fishes now considered to be junior synonyms of other species are *Gymnelus bilabrus* Andriashev and *Gymnelopsis stigma* (Lay & Bennett), classified in *Gymnelus viridis* (Fabricius) by Anderson (1982); *Lycenchelys birsteini* Andriashev, placed in *L. plicifera* Andriashev by Anderson (1994, 1995); *Lycodes agnostus* Jensen, placed in *L. polaris* (Sabine) by Andriashev (1954); *L. digitatus* Gill & Townsend, placed in *L. palearis* Gilbert by Andriashev (1937); and *L. knipowitschi* Popov, placed in *L. mucosus* Richardson by Anderson (1994). *Lycodapus grossidens* Gilbert was placed in the synonymy of *L. fierasfer* Gilbert by Peden and Anderson (1978), who, in addition, indicated that some specimens from Alaska identified as *L. grossidens* were *L. mandibularis.* Other eelpout species on Quast and Hall's (1972) list have simply undergone name changes due to shifting at the generic level, such as *Lycodes camchaticus* Gilbert & Burke to *Lycenchelys camchatica* (Gilbert & Burke) by Andriashev (1955), Peden (1973), and Anderson et al. (1979).

Recently, Chernova (1998a, 1999a, 1999b, 2000) revised *G. hemifasciatus* and *G. viridis* and described several new *Gymnelus* species. If recognized, the revisions would add several names to the list of species from Alaska and adjacent waters. However, the descriptions suggest, at least partly, forms reflecting ecophenotypic variation rather than distinct species (M. E. Anderson, pers. comms., 1999–2001). Evaluation of the proposed new species is a subject of current research.

Of the 58 eelpout species treated in this guide, 9 are commonly taken in Alaska in research surveys (e.g., Allen and Smith 1988, Barber et al. 1997) and as bycatch in commercial fisheries: *Lycodes turneri, L. polaris, L. raridens, L. brevipes, L. palearis, L. diapterus, L. concolor, Bothrocara brunneum,* and *Lycodapus mandibularis.* Museum vouchers and records in the systematic literature indicate four other species are frequently caught in Alaska, although perhaps they are not as abundant: *Gymnelus hemifasciatus, G. viridis, Lycodes pacificus,* and *B. pusillum.* An additional 8 eelpout species are known from Alaska by occasional records (more than four), and 24 from one to four records. Some of the remaining 13 species, which are not known from Alaska, are commonly taken elsewhere but others are known from very few specimens. The uneven record of information reflects our knowledge of Zoarcidae in general. Few of the 58 eelpout species included in this guide are well known. For many of them our knowledge comes from one to a few specimens, some of which have deteriorated to the point they are useless for confirming characters. Many of the specimens in museum collections, particularly of *Lycodes,* were identified in the 1960s and earlier, and reexamination in conjunction with various ongoing studies will benefit from more recent taxonomic revisions (e.g., McAllister et al. 1981, Toyoshima 1985) and help clarify distribution in Alaska. As well, like other poorly known groups such as the Liparidae, the apparent rarity of some eelpouts could be due to sampling coverage and methods. The paucity of records is most evident for the deepwater species. As pointed out by Anderson and Hubbs (1981), the scarcity of some deepwater eelpouts such as *Derepodichthys* and *Lycodapus* species may be explained by the general use of large-mesh trawls to sample fish populations in deep habitats of the northeastern Pacific. Small, elongate fishes would easily slip through those nets.

The following key to species of eelpouts of Alaska and closely adjacent waters was constructed from numerous sources, notably the key to eelpout genera by Anderson (1994) and keys to *Gymnelus* species by Anderson (1982); *Lycenchelys* species by Andriashev (1954, 1955a) and Anderson (1995); *Lycodes* species by Andriashev (1954), McAllister (1976), McAllister et al. (1981), and Toyoshima (1985); *Pachycara* by Anderson and Peden (1988); and *Lycodapus* by Peden and Anderson (1978, 1981). Anderson (pers. comm., 18 Dec. 1998) provided couplets 16–18. For some species the key will be difficult to use in the field because internal characteristics or others requiring special equipment (e.g., for radiographs) or time-consuming dissections will be needed for proper identification. The reliance on head pores may also be problematic, because they can be obscured by damage to the skin upon collection and by immersion in preservative, and in some species can become overgrown with skin as the individual ages. Careful handling of specimens and saving of vouchers for laboratory verification should accompany field identifications.

The key to eelpouts applies to late juveniles and adults, but not to small juveniles. Gill rakers, tooth counts, scale coverage, and some other characters are not completely developed or are difficult to observe in small juveniles.

Key to the Zoarcidae of Alaska

1 Gill membrane attached to isthmus; pelvic fins present or absent; scales present or absent . . . . . (2)

1 Gill membrane free of isthmus for a few millimeters posteriorly, attached to isthmus by a frenum anteriorly; pelvic fins absent; scales absent . . . . . genus *Lycodapus* (50)

2 (1) Chin crests absent . . . . . (3)

2 Chin crests present . . . . . genus *Lycodes* (23)

3 (2) Pelvic fins absent; or pelvic fins minute, lateral line double, and head pores inconspicuous . . . . . (4)

3 Pelvic fins present; if pelvic fins are minute, lateral line is not double and head pores are conspicuous . . . . . (11)

4 (3) Gill slit a small pore-like opening above pectoral fin base . . . . . (5)

4 Gill slit extending ventrally to opposite second pectoral fin ray or below . . . . . (7)

5 (4) Vomerine and palatine teeth present; lips present . . . . . *Melanostigma pammelas,* page 684 (not known from Alaska)

5 Vomerine and palatine teeth absent; lips absent . . . . . (6)

6 (5) Eye lens with slot-like pit filled with opaque matter; no opening behind last gill arch; branchiostegal rays 6 . . . . . *Opaeophacus acrogeneius,* page 685

6 Eye lens without slot-like pit; small slit behind last gill arch; branchiostegal rays 7 . . . . . *Nalbantichthys elongatus,* page 686

7 (4) Scales present . . . . . (8)

7 Scales absent . . . . . genus *Gymnelus* (9)

8 (7) Scales present only posteriorly on body . . . . . *Puzanovia rubra,* page 687

8 Scale coverage complete or nearly complete . . . . . (45)

9 (7) Vomerine and palatine teeth absent; interorbital pore present; dorsal fin origin close behind head, from vertical at pectoral fin base to vertical at 15–20% of pectoral fin length posterior to pectoral base . . . . . *Gymnelus popovi,* page 688

9 Vomerine and palatine teeth usually present; interorbital pore usually absent; dorsal fin origin behind vertical at 25% of pectoral fin length posterior to pectoral base . . . . . (10)

10 (9) Body and tail with 12–16 dark bars running to lateral line, rarely with heavy, dark, reticulate pigmentation on body (if so tail bars run below lateral line); dorsal and anal fins, particularly anal fin, relatively low; pectoral fin base/length ratio 25–46% (mean = 37.5%); pectoral rays usually 10–11; usually at depths of 40–80 m . . . . . *Gymnelus hemifasciatus,* page 689

10 Body coloration highly variable, when barred, pigmentation always runs below lateral line; dorsal and anal fins relatively high; pectoral fin base/length ratio 39–60% (mean = 50%); pectoral rays usually 11–13; usually intertidal to shallow subtidal . . . . . *Gymnelus viridis,* page 690

11 (3) Pelvic fins appear as a single pair of filaments with a common base placed far forward, under eye . . . . *Derepodichthys alepidotus,* page 691 (not known from Alaska)

11 Pelvic fin rays 3, rarely 2, placed under throat . . . . (12)

12 (11) Flesh gelatinous . . . . *Taranetzella lyoderma,* page 692 (not known from Alaska)

12 Flesh firm, except somewhat gelatinous about head in most deepwater forms . . . . genus *Lycenchelys* (13)

13 (12) Vomerine and palatine teeth absent . . . . *Lycenchelys crotalinus,* page 693

13 Vomerine and palatine teeth present . . . . (14)

14 (13) Scales on nape in front of dorsal fin but not on head . . . . *Lycenchelys jordani,* page 694

14 Scales absent from nape in front of dorsal fin, or if present extend onto head . . . . (15)

15 (14) Abdominal vertebrae more than 27 . . . . (16)

15 Abdominal vertebrae less than 25 . . . . (19)

16 (15) Suborbital pores 7 . . . . *Lycenchelys micropora,* page 695

16 Suborbital pores 8 or 9 . . . . (17)

17 (16) Interorbital pore(s) absent; preoperculomandibular pores 9; lateral line ventral and mediolateral . . . . *Lycenchelys plicifera,* page 696

17 Interorbital pore(s) present; preoperculomandibular pores 8; lateral line ventral only or absent . . . . (18)

18 (17) Body color dark brown or black; postorbital pores 1 or 2, just behind eye; lateral line ventral; pelvic fin rays 2; pyloric caeca absent . . . . *Lycenchelys volki,* page 697 (not known from Alaska)

18 Body color reddish; postorbital pores 4, in line behind eye; lateral line absent; pelvic fin rays 3; pyloric caeca present . . . . *Lycenchelys rosea,* page 698

19 (15) Total vertebrae less than 100 . . . . *Lycenchelys alta,* page 699

19 Total vertebrae more than 100 . . . . (20)

20 (19) Head anterior to line connecting upper ends of gill openings densely scaled; interorbital pore(s) absent . . . . *Lycenchelys camchatica,* page 700

20 Head completely scaleless; interorbital pore(s) present . . . . (21)

21 (20) Snout noticeably broad, with thick, fleshy lobe overhanging mouth; lateral line ventral, running relatively high above anal fin; 2 interorbital pores; vertebrae more than 130 . . . . *Lycenchelys hippopotamus,* page 701 (not known from Alaska)

21 Snout not particularly broad, without fleshy lobe overhanging mouth; lateral line ventral, running at usual height above anal fin; 1 interorbital pore; vertebrae less than 130 . . . . . (22)

22 (21) Lateral line steeply bowed in pectoral axil; occipital pores 3 or 4; pelvic fin rays 3 . . . . . *Lycenchelys ratmanovi,* page 702

22 Lateral line not steeply bowed in pectoral axil; occipital pores 2; pelvic fin rays 2 . . . . . *Lycenchelys rassi,* page 703

23 (2) Teeth absent from vomer; lateral line mediolateral; no vertical bands of color; dark blotch at anterior end of dorsal fin, can be absent in large adults . . . . . subgenus *Lycodopsis* (24)

23 Teeth present on vomer; lateral line mediolateral, ventrolateral, ventral, or double; vertical bands of color present or absent; if dark blotch present at anterior end of dorsal fin, lateral line not mediolateral . . . . . (25)

24 (23) Teeth absent from vomer and palatines . . . . . *Lycodes pacificus,* page 704

24 Teeth absent from vomer, present on palatines . . . . . *Lycodes cortezianus,* page 705

25 (23) Lateral line mediolateral . . . . . (26)

25 Lateral line ventrolateral, ventral, or double . . . . . (33)

26 (25) Scales absent, or present only posteriorly on tail . . . . . subgenus *Lycodalepis* (27)

26 Scales extending anteriorly on sides beyond anal fin origin . . . . . (31)

27 (26) Scales absent; body light, with 7–9 vaguely to sharply defined V-shaped dark bands extending onto dorsal fin; vomerine teeth blunt, round-topped, and numerous (11–14); vertebrae 99–102 . . . . . *Lycodes jugoricus,* page 706 (not known from Alaska)

27 Scales present only posteriorly or absent; body light or dark, with or without dark bands; vertebrae 90–100 . . . . . (28)

28 (27) Opercular lobe (at upper end of gill opening) strongly prominent, rounded, directed dorsally; scales present posteriorly; pectoral fin rays 19–20 . . . . . *Lycodes seminudus,* page 707

28 Opercular lobe not strongly prominent, directed posteriorly; scales absent or only weakly developed posteriorly; pectoral fin rays 15–19 . . . . . (29)

29 (28) Body with large, dark, Y-shaped marks extending onto dorsal and anal fins (on fish under about 200 mm TL), or indistinct light marks on dark background, or solid dark except for light marks on head and anterior part of body; pectoral fin rays 16–19 . . . . . *Lycodes mucosus,* page 708

29 Body and dorsal fin with light or dark bands that are not Y-shaped; pectoral fin rays 15–18 . . . . . (30)

30 (29) Body and dorsal fin with bands outlined by dark edges; pectoral fin rays 18; vertebrae 96–100 . . . . . *Lycodes turneri,* page 709

30 Body and dorsal fin with dark bands not outlined by dark edges; pectoral fin rays 15–17, rarely 18; vertebrae 90–93 . . . . . *Lycodes polaris,* page 710

31 (26) Scales extending anteriorly to well in front of anal fin and including sides below lateral line; scales present on dorsal and anal fins; teeth relatively few and widely spaced; top and upper sides of head blotched or reticulate . . . . *Lycodes raridens,* page 711

31 Scales extending anteriorly in wedge along lateral line, not present on sides below lateral line in front of anal fin; teeth relatively numerous and close-set [uncertain character]; upper sides of head reticulate or not . . . . (32)

32 (31) Dark bands reticulate, particularly the anterior bands; upper sides of head reticulate; pectoral fin rays 19–21; body depth at origin of anal fin 12–14% TL . . . . *Lycodes reticulatus,* page 712
(not known from Alaska)

32 Dark bands never reticulate; head solid-colored or vaguely blotched, not reticulate; pectoral fin rays 17–20, usually 18 or 19; body depth at origin of anal fin 9–11% TL . . . . *Lycodes rossi,* page 713

33 (25) Pectoral fin rays 14 or 15; body and dorsal fin with irregular dark spots and other dark marks . . . . *Lycodes japonicus,* page 714

33 Pectoral fin rays 16 or more; body and dorsal fin without dark marks, except for regular, broad dark bands in one species and dark blotch on anterior portion of dorsal fin in some others . . . . (34)

34 (33) Lateral line ventral or double . . . . (35)

34 Lateral line ventrolateral . . . . (37)

35 (34) Broad dark bands on upper body and dorsal fin . . . . *Lycodes brunneofasciatus,* page 715

35 No dark bands . . . . (36)

36 (35) Lateral line ventral, indistinct; up to 13 very narrow light bands, can be lacking; scales present on dorsal and anal fins; pelvic fins minute, less than half of eye length . . . . *Lycodes brevipes,* page 716

36 Lateral line ventral or double; no very narrow light bars; scales present or absent from dorsal and anal fins; pelvic fin length more than half of eye length, or if this character not clear, scales absent from belly and vertical fins . . . . (40)

37 (34) Lateral line usually distinct; no dark blotch at anterior margin of dorsal fin . . . . (38)

37 Lateral line indistinct, particularly ascending part; dark blotch present at anterior margin of dorsal fin, most distinct in younger specimens . . . . (39)

38 (37) Pectoral fin rays 16–18; lateral line deeply bowed down anteriorly; pelvic fins longer than eye diameter . . . . *Lycodes sagittarius,* page 717

38 Pectoral fin rays 20–23; lateral line bowed down anteriorly, dip relatively shallow; pelvic fins short and knob-like . . . . *Lycodes soldatovi,* page 718
(not known from Alaska)

39 (37) Up to 11 (usually fewer than 9) light bands on body and dorsal fin and 2 light bands in front of dorsal fin, all bars usually absent from adults larger than about 200 mm TL . . . . *Lycodes palearis,* page 719

39 About 12–15 light bands on body and dorsal fin, some cog-shaped with cogs pointing upward, and 2 light bands in front of dorsal fin, some bands persisting on adults over 200 mm TL . . . . *Lycodes fasciatus,* page 720

40 (36) Lateral line double, incomplete . . . . (41)

40 Lateral line double and complete, or ventral . . . . (42)

41 (40) Scales absent from belly and vertical fins . . . . *Lycodes pallidus,* page 721

41 Scales present on belly and vertical fins . . . . *Lycodes squamiventer,* page 722

42 (40) Lateral line double, complete; body and vertical fins with 5–13 light bands; bands simple even in large specimens; pectoral fin slightly emarginate, forming weak lower lobe . . . . . *Lycodes eudipleurostictus,* page 723

42 Lateral line ventral; body and vertical fins with irregular light marks or uniformly colored; pectoral fin lobed or not . . . . (43)

43 (42) Pectoral fin slightly to deeply notched, forming lower lobe; pectoral rays17–19; 6–9 light bars that spread or divide on body, becoming irregular and disappearing in adults; scales not particularly small . . . . *Lycodes diapterus,* page 724

43 Pectoral fin not notched; pectoral fin rays 19–21; uniformly colored; scales very small . . . . (44)

44 (43) Preanal length 43% TL or less; scales extending onto vertical fins; vertebrae more than 110 (114–115) . . . . *Lycodes concolor,* page 725

44 Preanal length more than 43% TL; scales absent from vertical fins, except on base in largest specimens; vertebrae less than 110 (103–107) . . . . *Lycodes frigidus,* page 726 (not known from Alaska)

45 (8) Palatal arch well developed; pseudobranchial filaments 0–6; pelvic fins usually present . . . . genus *Pachycara* (46)

45 Palatal arch weak; pseudobranchial filaments 7–8; pelvic fins absent . . . . genus *Bothrocara* (48)

46 (45) Pelvic fins absent . . . . *Pachycara bulbiceps,* page 727 (not known from Alaska)

46 Pelvic fins present . . . . (47)

47 (46) Pectoral fin rays usually 17 or 18; scales absent from nape or not extending anterior to line connecting gill openings . . . . *Pachycara gymninium,* page 728 (not known from Alaska)

47 Pectoral fin rays usually 15 or 16; scales present on nape, extending to interorbital region . . . . *Pachycara lepinium,* page 729 (not known from Alaska)

48 (45) Body, tail, and belly scaled, nape without scales . . . . *Bothrocara pusillum,* page 730

48 Body, tail, belly, and nape scaled . . . . (49)

49 (48) Gill rakers short and blunt; pectoral fin not reaching a vertical line through anus . . . . *Bothrocara brunneum,* page 731

49 Gill rakers long and pointed; pectoral fin reaching to or beyond vertical through anus . . . . *Bothrocara molle,* page 732

50 (1) Gill rakers on first gill arch very short and blunt; gill raker ratio less than 30% . . . . (51)

50 Gill rakers stout to long; gill raker ratio more than 30% . . . . (52)

51 (50) Preopercular pores 4; vomerine plus inner row of dentary teeth enlarged and not sexually dimorphic in adults; gill slit not extending above pectoral fin base . . . . *Lycodapus parviceps,* page 733

51 Preopercular pores 3; vomerine and dentary teeth small; gill slit sometimes extending slightly above pectoral fin base . . . . . *Lycodapus psarostomatus,* page 734

52 (50) Gill rakers of first gill arch blunt and stout (pointed in young *L. mandibularis*), gill raker ratio 30–150% (rarely 170% in juveniles); when rakers of first arch are pressed downward against the arch, their tips usually lie close to and not beyond base of the adjacent raker down the arch; 1 median interorbital pore, 4 mandibular pores, 4 preopercular pores (except *L. leptus* has less than 4 preopercular pores) . . . . (53)

52 Gill rakers of first gill arch long , slender, and pointed; gill raker ratio usually 150–270%, if less than 150% the gill rakers are pointed and there are 3 preopercular pores; when rakers are pressed downward against the arch, their tips usually lie closer to base of second raker down the arch than base of adjacent raker; a median or paired interorbital pore; 3 or 4 mandibular pores . . . . (56)

53 (52) Total number of vertebrae 75–82 . . . . *Lycodapus pachysoma,* page 735
(not known from Alaska)

53 Total number of vertebrae more than 82 . . . . (54)

54 (53) Preopercular pores 3 (often secondarily closed); total number of vertebrae 94–99; head length 13–15% of standard length. . . . . *Lycodapus leptus,* page 736

54 Preopercular pores 4; total number of vertebrae 79–96; head length 12–23% (usually more than 15%) of standard length. . . . . (55)

55 (54) Vomerine teeth 0–5; palatine teeth 3–13 (usually less than 3 on each side); upper rim of eye reaches level of dorsal profile of head; gill raker ratio 65–165% (lower in adults) (total number of vertebrae 81–96). . . . . *Lycodapus mandibularis,* page 737

55 Vomerine teeth 16–21 (reduced to 4 on some mature males); palatine teeth 8–28 on each side; upper rim of eye of adults below dorsal profile of head; gill raker ratio 57–106% . . . . *Lycodapus endemoscotus,* page 738

56 (52) Usually 2 interorbital pores; 3 preopercular pores; 3 mandibular pores; vertebrae 83 or more . . . . *Lycodapus fierasfer,* page 739

56 One interorbital pore; 3 preopercular pores (frequently 4 in *L. dermatinus*); 4 mandibular pores (frequently 3 in *L. dermatinus*); total number of vertebrae 76–87 . . . . (57)

57 (56) Palatine teeth 2–26 (usually 6–18); vomerine teeth 3–19 (usually 5–12); total number of vertebrae 76–82; precaudal vertebrae 13–15 . . . . *Lycodapus dermatinus,* page 740

57 Palatine teeth 0–4 (usually 0–2); vomerine teeth 1–6 (usually 2–5); total number of vertebrae 80–87; precaudal vertebrae 15–17 . . . . *Lycodapus poecilus,* page 741

Melanostigma pammelas Gilbert, 1896 — **Pacific softpout**

Eastern North Pacific Ocean off Queen Charlotte Islands, British Columbia, to Gulf of Tehuantepec, Mexico. Mesopelagic, in coastal waters; obtained in nets towed as shallow as 97–216 m to as deep as 1,982–2,012 m.

D 84–88; A 69–75; C 6–8; Pec 6–8; Pel 0; GR 11–13; Vert 86–89.

- Brownish black; head and belly intensely black; black internally, including intestines; juveniles silvery blue.
- **Head blunt**, profile rising abruptly from upper jaw, mouth terminal; eye large, round.
- **Flesh gelatinous**, thin, and delicate.
- Pelvic fin absent.
- Scales absent.
- Lateral line absent.
- Branchiostegal rays 6–7.
- **Gill opening a small pore above pectoral fin.**
- Length to about 110 mm TL.

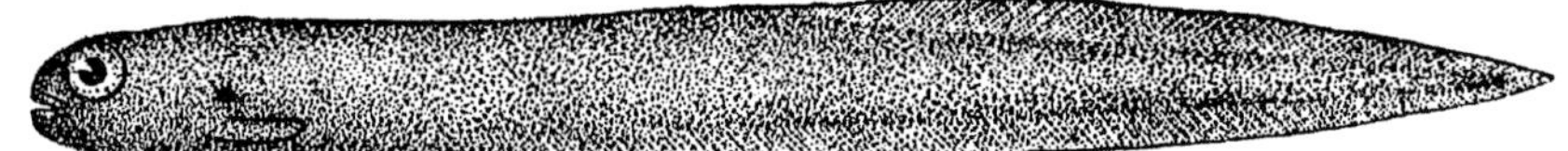

Notes & Sources — *Melanostigma pammelas* Gilbert, 1896

Description: Gilbert 1896:472; McAllister and Rees 1964: 101–102; Hart 1973:247–248; Anderson 1984:84–88, 1994: 36–38. Anderson and Hubbs (1981) corrected Yarberry's (1965) account of the osteology of *M. pammelas* and made comparisons with *Derepodichthys*.

Figure: Gilbert 1896, pl. 35; holotype, 104 mm TL, Monterey Bay, California.

Range: Reports of occurrence in Alaska are based on an incorrect citation by Jordan and Evermann (1896a:481) of Gilbert (1896), who recorded it from California, not from Alaska. The error was soon corrected by Jordan and Evermann (1898:2869) and again by McAllister and Rees (1964), but some authors have overlooked the correction. The nearest record outside Alaska is a specimen captured off the British Columbia coast at 51°53'N, 131°25'W, at a depth range of 700–900 m (Grinols 1966c). *Melanostigma pammelas* is undoubtedly mesopelagic, notwithstanding published accounts that give a benthic existence for the genus (Anderson 1984).

Size: Eschmeyer and Herald 1983. A maximum size of 304 mm was reported by Grey (1956), but such a large size is considered unlikely (McAllister and Rees 1964, Hart 1973). The holotype measured 104 mm TL (Gilbert 1896), the largest of 90 specimens examined by Yarberry (1965) was 98 mm TL, and the largest of 28 specimens measured by Anderson (1984) was 99 mm SL.

Opaeophacus acrogeneius Bond & Stein, 1984 — bulldog eelpout

Bering Sea near Seguam Island and north of Umnak Island.

Bottom at depths of 500–800 m, associated with coral and starfish snagged by longline hooks.

D 141–148; A 121–124; C 8–9; Pec 4–5; Pel 0; GR 14–16; Vert 25–26 + 119–123 (144–149).

- Color bright tangerine orange, fading to light tan in alcohol.
- Lower jaw massive, slightly projecting; head blunt; body very slender and elongate.
- **Slotlike, vertical pit filled with opaque material in lens of eye**.
- **Skin thick and firm**.
- Flesh gelatinous.
- Dorsal and anal fins buried in skin; **pectoral fin greatly reduced**; pelvic fin absent.
- Nostril tubes greatly elongate.
- Scales absent.
- Cephalic sensory pore system complete.
- Lateral line complete, mediolateral.
- Vomerine and palatine teeth absent.
- **Gill opening small, entirely above base of pectoral fin**.
- Length to 154 mm SL.

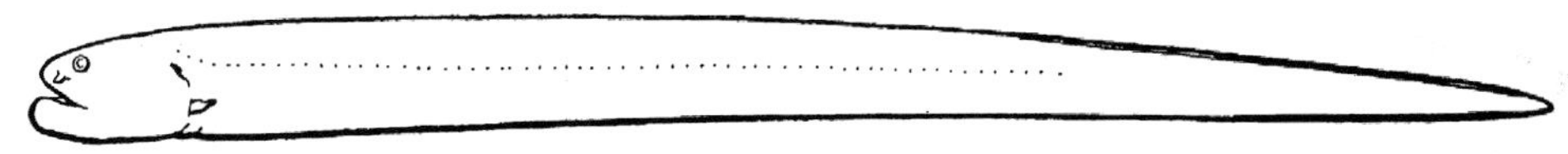

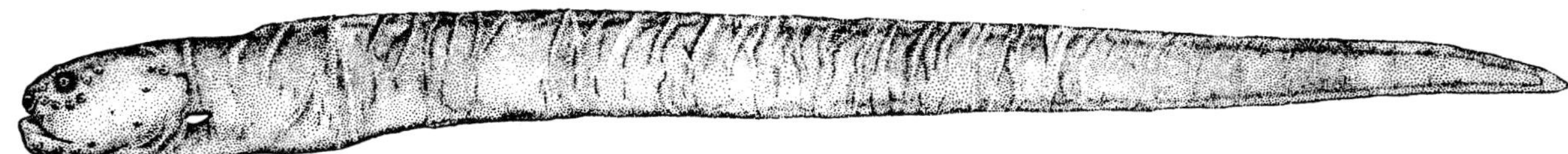

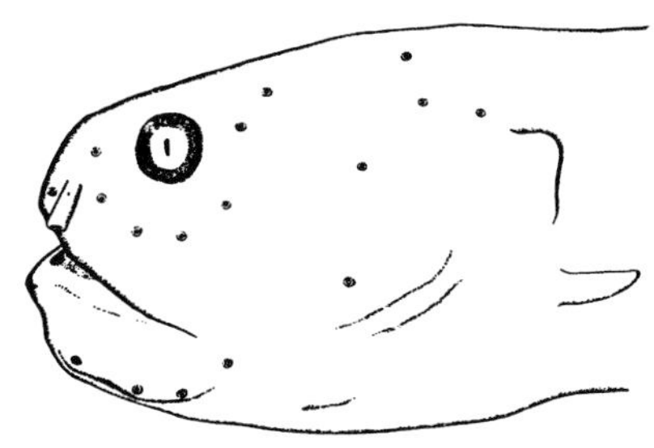

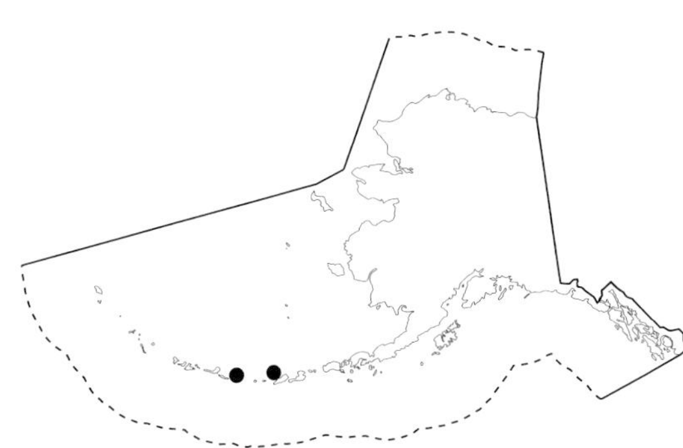

Notes & Sources — *Opaeophacus acrogeneius* Bond & Stein, 1984

Description: Bond and Stein 1984; Anderson 1994:40–42. The unique eye lens may be an adaptation for detecting silhouettes of organisms moving against a dimly lighted background (Bond and Stein 1984).

Figures: Above: Bond and Stein 1984, fig. 1; holotype, USNM 260320, 145 mm SL. Below: Anderson 1994, figs. 58 and 60; paratype, CAS 52802, 153 mm SL.

Range: Known from five specimens obtained at two localities in Alaska: off Seguam Island at 52°42'N, 172°15'W, and north of Umnak Island at 53°33'N, 169°18'W. The four specimens from Seguam Island were associated with an orange coral (order Gorgonacea) close in color to the tangerine hue of the fish. The specimen from north of Umnak Island was associated with black coral (Antipatharia) and basket starfish (Euryalina).

Size: Bond and Stein 1984: largest of the five known specimens.

Nalbantichthys elongatus Schultz, 1967 — **thinskin eelpout**

Bering Sea near western Aleutian Islands.

On or near bottom at depths of 300–520 m.

D 143–152; A 121–127; C 7–10; Pec 6; Pel 0; GR 17; Vert 25 + 119–125 (144–150).

- Lower jaw massive, slightly projecting; head blunt; body very slender and elongate.
- **Skin thin and loose**.
- Flesh gelatinous.
- **Pectoral fin greatly reduced**; pelvic fin absent.
- Nostril tubes greatly elongate.
- Scales absent.
- Cephalic sensory pore system fairly complete; **3 pairs of nasal pores**.
- Lateral line mediolateral, probably complete but not easily discernible.
- Vomerine and palatine teeth absent.
- **Branchiostegal rays 7**.
- **Gill opening small, entirely above base of pectoral fin**.
- Length to 138 mm TL.

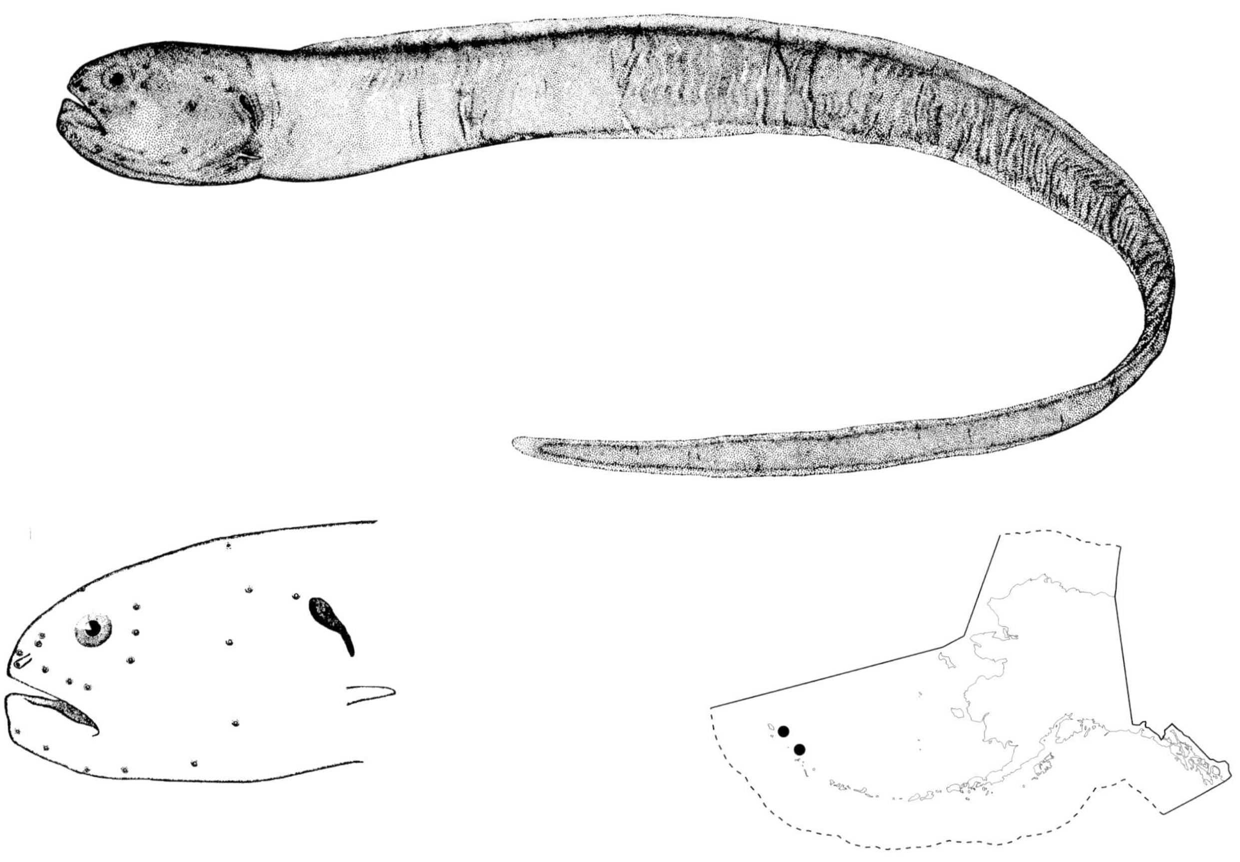

Notes & Sources — *Nalbantichthys elongatus* Schultz, 1967

Description: Schultz 1967; Anderson 1984:88–91; 1994:39–40; Matarese et al. 1989:498; Nalbant 1994:383.

Figures: Anderson 1994, figs. 56 and 57; holotype, USNM 200671, 138 mm TL, Bering Sea, Alaska.

Range: Known from only three specimens. The holotype and paratype were collected together from the Bering Sea off the shelf of the Near Islands by the Romanian trawler *Galatzi* at a depth of about 300 m; latitude and longitude were not reported. Other eelpouts, including *Lycodes raridens* and *L. japonicus*; the poachers *Sarritor frenatus* and *Percis japonica*; rockfishes of the genus *Sebastes*; and a snailfish, *Crystallichthys cameliae,* were also in the haul (Schultz 1967; Nalbant 1970, 1994). Anderson (1984, 1994) listed a third specimen of *N. elongatus* (ZIN 40535), which was collected from the south central Bering Sea at a depth of 520 m by Russian scientists, but did not give details of locality. Positions of the dots on the above map are estimates of the actual collection localities.

Size: Springer and Anderson 1997.

Puzanovia rubra Fedorov, 1975 **tough eelpout**

Bering Sea from Cape Navarin to the Pribilof Islands and north of Unalaska Island, Bowers Bank, and northern Shirshov Ridge; western Pacific off Kuril Islands to Cape Erimo, Hokkaido; Sea of Okhotsk.

Bottom at depths of 200–610 m, usually taken at 250–350 m, always with the dendritic coral *Primnoa resedaeformis*.

D 135–147; A 114–128; C 9–12; Pec 8–12; Pel 0; GR 13–17; Vert 21–24 + 110–125 (134–147).

- Color uniformly pinkish orange or reddish; belly in some specimens dark blue.
- **Head strongly compressed**; lower jaw large, slightly projecting; head blunt; body compressed and very elongate.
- **Body dense, covered with thick skin.**
- Flesh gelatinous.
- **Lips present**, upper lip discontinuous.
- **Pectoral fin not greatly reduced**; pelvic fin absent.
- **Scales present posteriorly**, sparse; difficult to discern (embedded) in some specimens.
- Cephalic sensory pore system well developed; interorbital pore present.
- Lateral line mediolateral, complete; indistinct in some specimens.
- Vomerine teeth absent, palatine teeth present.
- **Gill opening extending down to or almost to level of ventral edge of pectoral fin base.**
- Length to 323 mm TL.

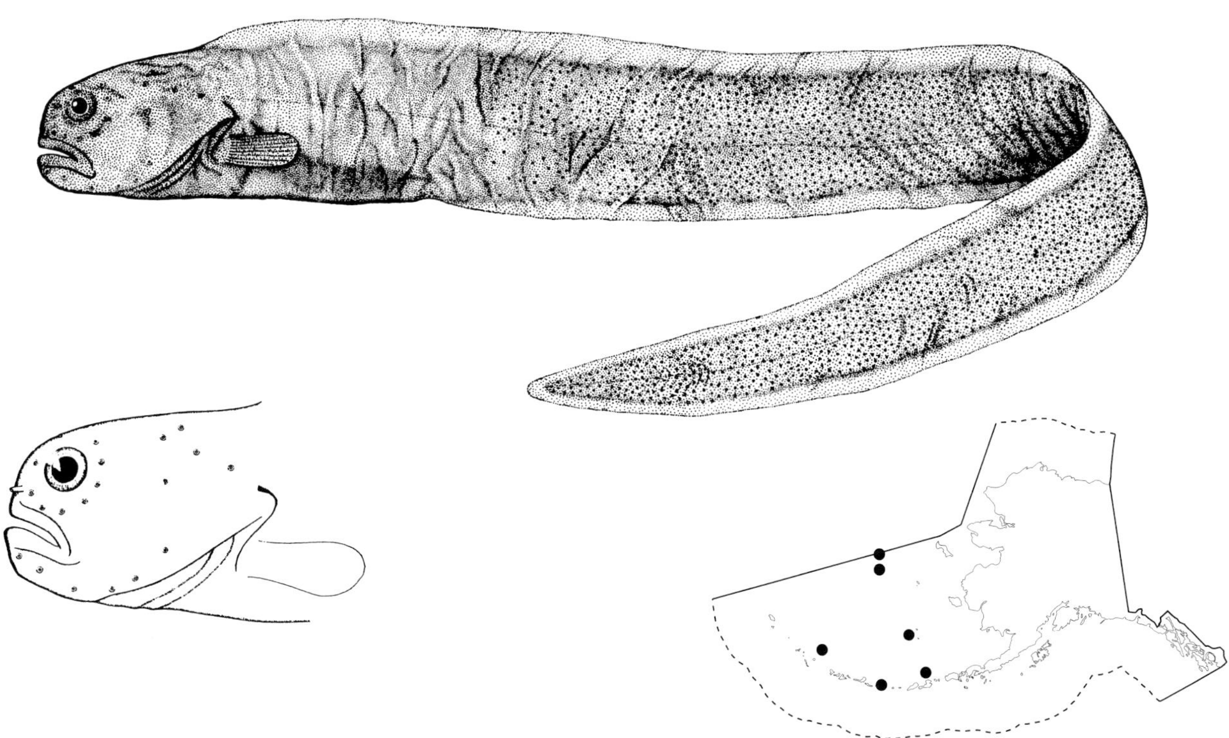

Notes & Sources — *Puzanovia rubra* Fedorov, 1975

Description: Fedorov 1975; Amaoka, Toyoshima, and Inada 1977; Toyoshima in Amaoka et al. 1983:329; Toyoshima in Masuda et al. 1984:306; Matarese et al. 1989:498; Anderson 1994:42–44.

Figures: Anderson 1994, figs. 64 and 66; CAS 47670, 197 mm SL, Aleutian Islands, Alaska.

Range: When he described the new species, Fedorov (1975: 530 in English translation) did not report actual collection localities but gave distribution from trawl catches in the Bering Sea as "on Bauers [= Bowers] Bank to the west of Burevestnik [= Petrel] Bank, in the northern part of the underwater Shirshov range, . . . to the south of Cape Navarin and the Pribilof Islands, as well as to the north of Unalaska." The dots on our map represent estimated positions of those localities. Eschmeyer (1998) reported the capture locality of the holotype (ZIN 39213) to be 61°05'N, 179°20'W, depth 460–475 m. Collection SIO 94-197 includes two specimens taken in 1994 north of Seguam Island at 52°39'N, 172°14'W, with a bottom trawl at a depth of 399 m. Fedorov (1975) reported that the depth range for specimens in his sample was 200–610 m, on or near the bottom, with most specimens taken at 250–350 m. He associated the snakelike shape, tough and relatively thick skin, reddish coloration, and structural peculiarities of the jaw apparatus with habitation among the gorgonian corals.

Size: Toyoshima in Amaoka et al. 1983.

Gymnelus popovi (Taranetz & Andriashev, 1935) **Aleutian pout**

Kodiak Island at Karluk; Aleutian Islands; Commander Islands; Simushir Island.

Intertidal, found from above tidemark in wet seaweed at low tide to water depth of 2 m. Associated with *Laminaria, Fucus, Ulva,* and calcareous red algae or large boulders and gravel where algae is sparse.

D 91–101; A 73–81; C 9–10; Pec 10–13; Pel 0; GR 10–16; Vert 20–26 + 72–80 (92–103).

- Olive brown to cherry red; yellowish ventrally; younger fish with fine dark reticular swathes or spots; older specimens more monotone; anal fin of mature males turns black; black ocelli ringed in white often present on dorsal fin, first appear in juveniles at 45–55 mm SL.
- Dorsal fin origin over pectoral fin base to anterior 15–20% of pectoral length; pectoral fin rays usually 11–12; pectoral fin base/length ratio 42–55% (mean = 49.3%, N = 37) in specimens larger than 80 mm SL.
- Head pores: preoperculomandibular 7–8 (usually 8); suborbital 5–7 (6); **interorbital pore always present**; postorbital 3–5 (4); occipital 3.
- **Vomerine and palatine teeth always absent.**
- Length to 163 mm SL; females mature at about 80–90 mm SL.

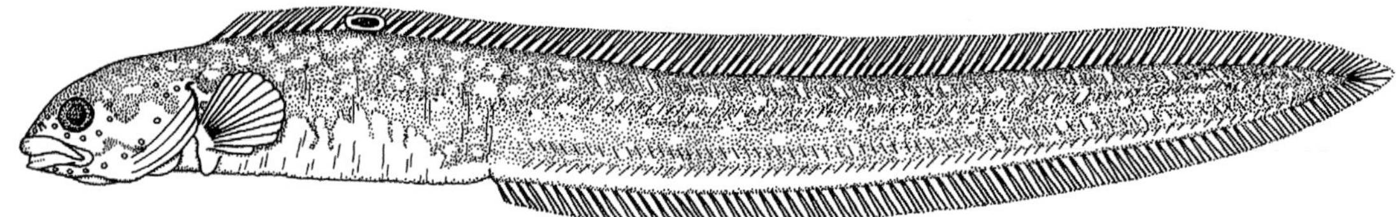

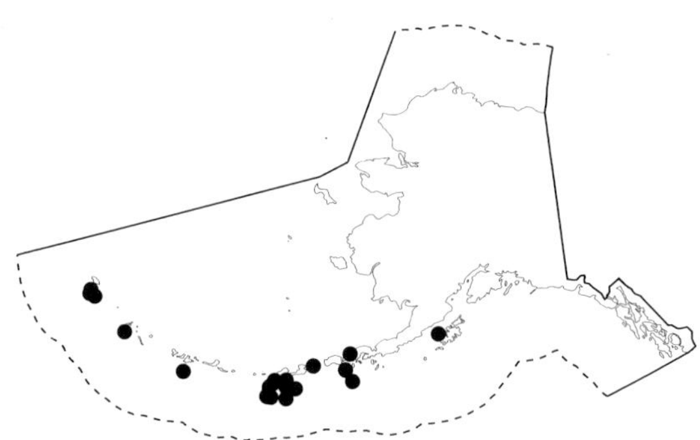

Notes & Sources — *Gymnelus popovi* (Taranetz & Andriashev, 1935)
Commandorella popovi Taranetz & Andriashev, 1935
Commanderella sp.: Wilimovsky 1964:186 (lapsus calami).
Several specimens previously identified as *G. viridis* (non-Fabricius) from various localities in Alaska were referred to *G. popovi* by Anderson (1982:44).

Description: Anderson 1982:44–47, table 2.

Figure: Anderson 1982, fig. 27; UWZ 3558, juvenile female, 88 mm SL, Umnak Island, Alaska.

Range: Reported from as far west in Alaska as Agattu Island at Nikolski Bay by Wilimovsky (1964). The species was first described from specimens collected on the shores of Medny Island of the Commander Islands, Russia, by Taranetz and Andriashev (1935a). Locality data for all recorded specimens, including those from Alaska, were given by Anderson (1982).

Gymnelus hemifasciatus Andriashev, 1937 **halfbarred pout**

Beaufort Sea to northern Gulf of Alaska northeast of Kodiak Island; east in Beaufort Sea to Dease Strait; west to Barents Sea; and to east coast of Kamchatka, Commander Islands, and Sea of Okhotsk.

Most captures are from about 40–80 m, but recorded from intertidal to 200 m; mud and gravel bottoms of inner and outer shelf.

D 81–93; A 69–77; C 9–10; Pec 10–12; Pel 0; GR 9–15; Vert 18–21 + 65–77 (85–95).

- Color in life not reported; body with **12–16 dark vertical bands; bands on tail descend below lateral line only in some large fish, mostly males; females with restricted lateral banding and high, light ventral surface**; anal fin of mature males turns black; juveniles more lightly pigmented than adults; black ocelli ringed in lighter color often occur on dorsal fin, first appearing in juveniles at 50–60 mm SL.
- **Dorsal and anal fins, particularly anal, lower than in other local *Gymnelus***; dorsal fin origin 25–75% of pectoral fin length behind vertical with pectoral base; pectoral fin rays usually 10–11; pectoral fin base/length ratio 25–46% (mean = 37.5%, N = 39) in specimens over 80 mm SL.
- Head pores: preoperculomandibular 7–8 (usually 8); suborbital 6–9 (6); **interorbital pore usually absent**; postorbital 3–5 (4); occipital 2–3 (2).
- **Vomerine and palatine teeth usually present.**
- Length to 140 mm SL; females mature at about 70–80 mm SL.

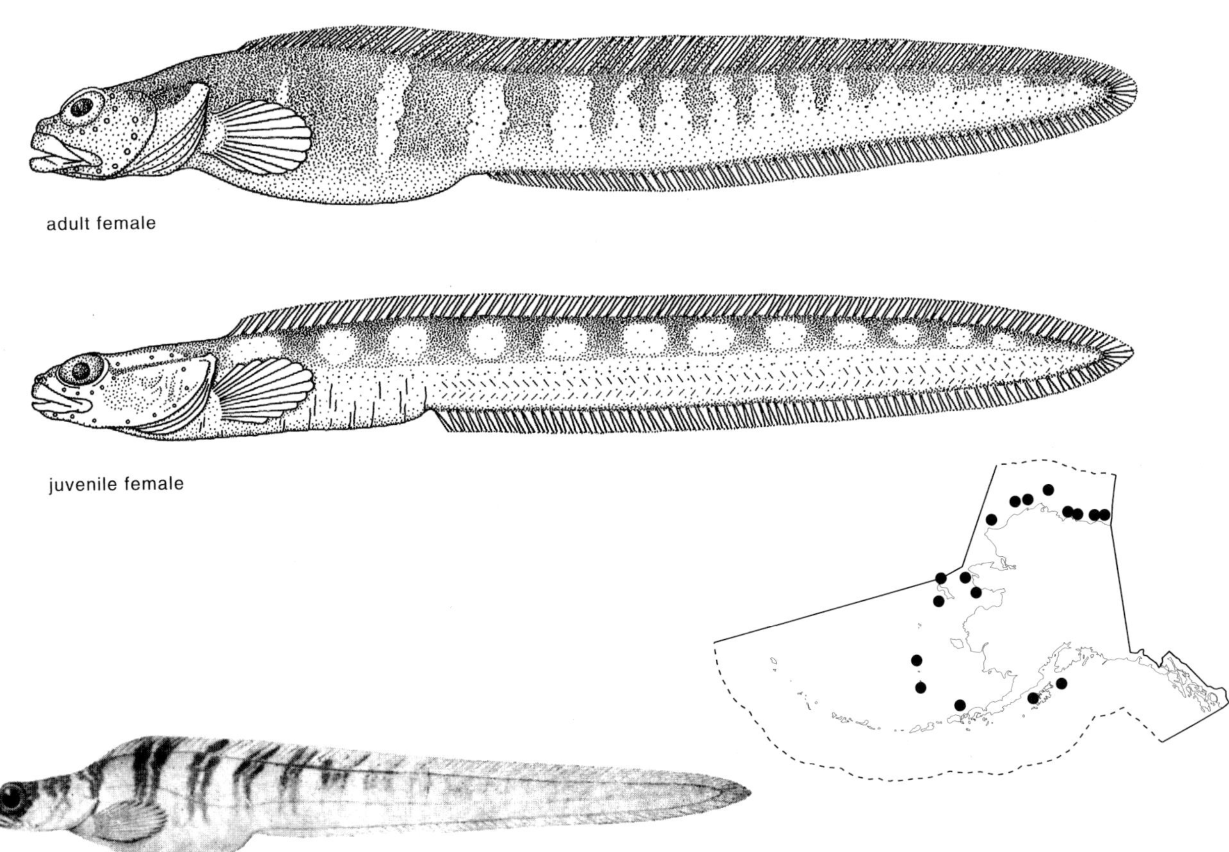
adult female

juvenile female

Notes & Sources — *Gymnelus hemifasciatus* Andriashev, 1937
Gymnelis hemifasciatus Andriashev, 1937
Several specimens previously identified as *G. viridis* (non-Fabricius) from various localities in Alaska were referred to *G. hemifasciatus* by Anderson (1982:38–39).

Description: Anderson 1982:38–44, table 2.

Figures: Upper: Anderson 1982, fig. 24; ZIN 35641, adult female, 115 mm SL, Barents Sea; UA 1225, juvenile female, 65 mm SL, Chukchi Sea. Lower: Andriashev 1937, fig. 23; type, female, 97 mm TL, western Bering Sea near Cape Chukotskiy.

Range: Locality data from museum collections, including several from Alaska, were reported by Anderson (1982). Uncataloged UAM voucher specimens from recent surveys of northeastern Chukchi Sea include adults from 70°13'N, 166°04'W, depth 46 m, collected 13 Sep. 1990; 71°36'N, 163°40'W, depth 46 m, 19 Sep. 1991; and 69°55'N, 168°00'W, depth 47 m, 18 Sep. 1991.

Gymnelus viridis (Fabricius, 1780) **fish doctor**

Beaufort Sea to Islands of Four Mountains in the eastern Bering Sea and to Gulf of Anadyr in the west; circum-Arctic, with most records from Siberia to eastern Canada.

Most captures are from rocky intertidal areas to depth of about 50 m, but known from as deep as 256 m; prefers mud, sand, and gravel bottoms under cover such as rocks, wood debris, and kelp.

D 87–102; A 72–84; C 9–11; Pec 10–14; Pel 0; GR 10–20; Vert 18–23 + 72–84 (92–105).

- Monotone brown to green, banded with bluish bands on yellowish orange background or yellowish bands on greenish brown background, or mottled with white or yellowish reticulations on greenish brown to red background; **when present, bands always extend below lateral line**; anal fin of mature males turns black; youngest fish rarely monotone, usually mottled; ocelli ringed in white or yellow often present on dorsal fin.
- **Dorsal and anal fins relatively high**; dorsal fin origin 50–90% of pectoral fin length posterior to vertical through pectoral base; pectoral fin rays usually 11–13; pectoral fin base/length ratio 39–60% (mean = 50%, N = 37) in fish over 75 mm SL.
- Head pores: preoperculomandibular 7–8 (usually 8); suborbital 5–11 (6–8); **interorbital pore usually absent**; postorbital 2–5 (4); occipital 2–5 (2–3).
- **Vomerine and palatine teeth usually present.**
- Maximum gill raker number expressed by about 120–130 mm SL.
- Length to 256 mm SL; females mature at about 110–120 mm SL.

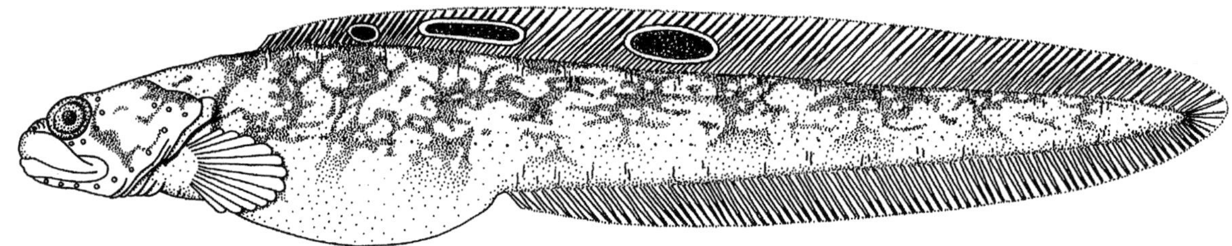

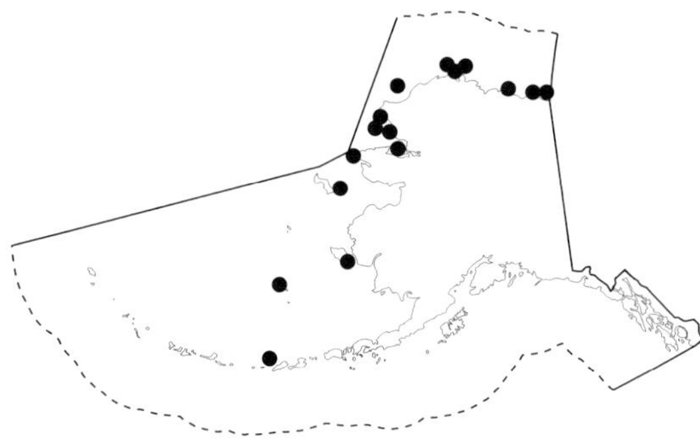

Notes & Sources — *Gymnelus viridis* (Fabricius, 1780)
Ophidium viride Fabricius, 1780
Ophidium stigma Lay & Bennett, 1839
Gymnelis stigma (Lay & Bennett, 1839): Bean 1881b.
Gymnelopsis stigma (Lay & Bennett, 1839): Wilimovsky 1954.
Gymnelus bilabrus Andriashev, 1937
The synonymy is extracted from that of Anderson (1982) and reflects his recent opinion (M. E. Anderson, pers. comm., 30 Apr. 1999). Chernova (1998a) maintained *G. bilabrus* as a distinct species.

Description: Anderson 1982:29–35, table 2; Green and Mitchell 1997. The latter authors found that in specimens (N = 321) from Cornwallis Island, Northwest Territories, more females (73%) than males (48%) were banded, about equal proportions of females (26%) and males (21%) were mottled, and significantly more males (31%) than females (1%) were monotone. Most males, including all of the monotone males, had black anal fins.

Figure: Anderson 1982, fig. 16; NMC 77-1259, adult female, 152 mm SL, Canadian Arctic.

Range: Anderson (1982) reported locality data for most vouchers available at that time. AB 71-134 is an additional Alaskan record, from 71°10'N, 149°19'W, depth 50 m. Uncataloged UAM voucher specimens from recent surveys of the northeastern Chukchi Sea include adults from 69°39'N, 167°38'W, depth 46 m, collected 31 Aug. 1990; 70°45'N, 165°44'W, depth 42 m, 11 Sep. 1990; and 69°49'N, 167°00'W, depth 47 m, 17 Sep. 1991. Chernova (1998a) attributed specimens previously identified as *G. viridis* from the northern Bering Sea and Chukchi Sea to *G. bilabrus*.

Derepodichthys alepidotus Gilbert, 1896 **cuskpout**

Eastern North Pacific off Queen Charlotte Islands, British Columbia; deep basins off southern California; Gulf of California.

Benthopelagic, taken at depths of 1,000–2,904 m; all but two captures have been from below 1,600 m. One record from a rift zone near thermal vents (Gulf of California).

D 110–116; A 94–101; C 8–9; Pec 10–11; Pel 3; GR 11–13; Vert 22–26 + 92–98 (114–122).

- Light to dark brown; body darker posteriorly; median fins gray; pectoral and pelvic fins whitish, with dark margins; abdominal region blue-black in some specimens.
- Head blunt, body long and slender.
- Flesh gelatinous; bones fragile; skin thin, loose, transparent.
- **Pelvic fins each of three joined rays with a common base, placed far forward under the eyes**.
- Scales absent.
- Cephalic sensory pores reduced in number but enlarged.
- Body lateral line absent.
- **Teeth on jaws long, recurved**.
- **Gill opening a narrow vertical slit in front of pectoral fin base**.
- Length to 151 mm SL.

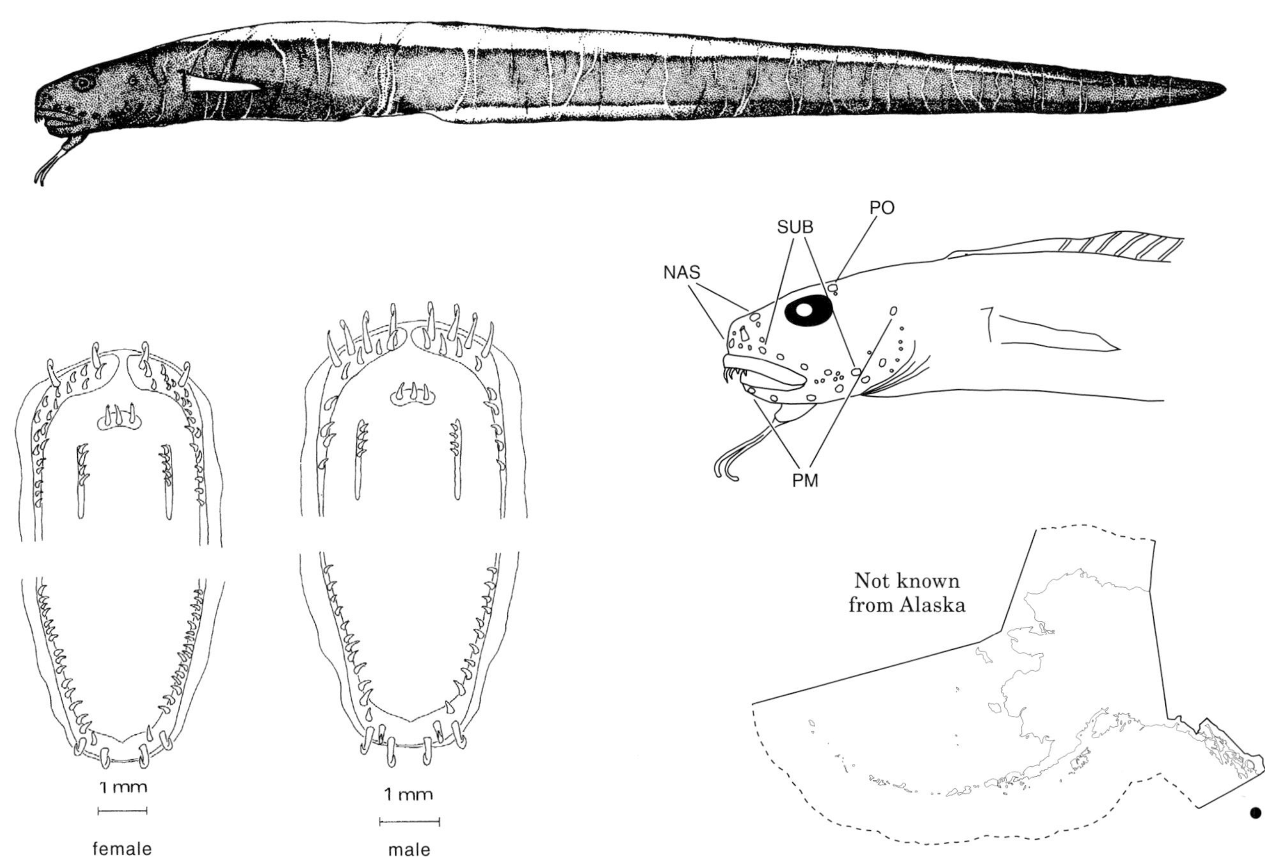

Notes & Sources — *Derepodichthys alepidotus* Gilbert, 1896

Description: Anderson and Hubbs 1981; Anderson 1994:55–57; Fedorov and Parin 1994.

Figures: Full lateral view: Anderson 1994, fig. 99; SIO 65-445, 125 mm SL, off Mexico. Others: Anderson and Hubbs 1981, figs. 2 and 3, modified; southern California.

Range: Nearest known record to Alaska is the holotype, taken off British Columbia at *Albatross* station 3342, 52°39'N, 132°38'W, depth 2,904 m (Gilbert 1896). Twelve specimens taken off California and Mexico were described by Anderson and Hubbs (1981). Since six of those specimens were taken with midwater trawls fished on or close to the bottom and the fragile bones and gelatinous flesh seemed to preclude a burrowing habit, Anderson and Hubbs (1981) concluded that *D. alepidotus* lives slightly above the bottom, continuously roaming in search of invertebrate prey. Fedorov and Parin (1994) described an additional specimen, taken in a rift zone near thermal vents in the Gulf of California.

Size: Anderson and Hubbs 1981: largest of 14 known specimens.

Taranetzella lyoderma Andriashev, 1952 **ghostly eelpout**

Eastern Pacific off southern British Columbia to Oregon, and Guadalupe Island, Mexico; western Bering Sea at Olyutorskiy Bay; Suruga Bay, Japan.

Taken at depths of 986 m in western Bering Sea at Olyutorskiy Bay and 2,225–3,000 m in Pacific Ocean.

D 86–95; A 72–82; C 10; Pec 15–16; Pel 3; GR 14–16; Vert 18–20 + 70–78 (89–97).

- Body low, slender; mouth terminal; snout not projecting.
- Flesh gelatinous; skin thin, loose, transparent.
- Dorsal fin origin associated with vertebrae 3–4.
- Scales present posteriorly.
- **Fleshy lobes between suborbital pores**, look like flaps covering pores.
- Preoperculomandibular pores 9.
- Lateral line absent, or mediolateral and weakly expressed as inconspicuous neuromasts along the midline anteriorly or posteriorly.
- Gill slit extending down to middle of pectoral fin base to near ventral end of pectoral base, but not forward onto throat.
- Length to 160 mm SL, 165 mm TL.

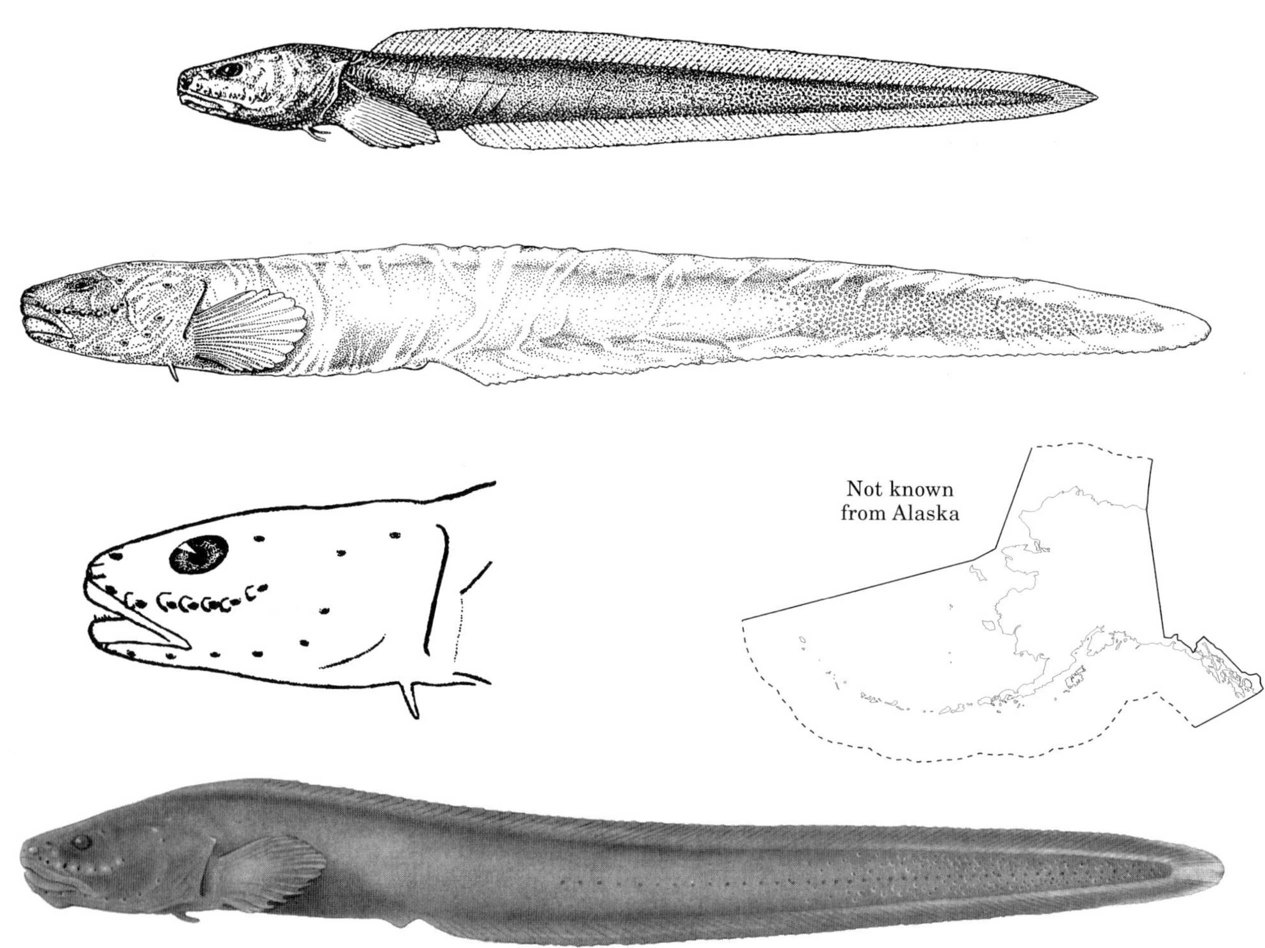

Notes & Sources — *Taranetzella lyoderma* Andriashev, 1952

Description: Andriashev 1952:415–417, 1955a:381–383; Anderson 1984:176–177, 1994:90–92, 1995:107–110; Peden and Jamieson 1988:493. Machida and Ohta 1996: new low-end vertebral count of 89.

Figures: Top: Andriashev 1952; holotype (unique), ZIN 32813, 105 mm TL, Olyutorskiy Bay. Middle, with diagram of head: Anderson 1994, figs. 181 (BMT-186) and 182 (OS 2072), both 158 mm SL, off Oregon. Bottom: Royal British Columbia Museum, artist K. Shuster, Mar. 1986; OSUO 1897, off Oregon. Expression of the body lateral line and ventral extent of the gill slit differ.

Range: Most records are from the Cascadia Abyssal Plain off Washington and Oregon. Nearest records to Alaska are the holotype, described by Andriashev (1952), from Olyutorskiy Bay, Bering Sea, at 59°52'N, 168°17'E, depth 986 m; and two specimens described by Peden and Jamieson (1988), which were collected west of Vancouver Island, British Columbia, at 48°19'N, 127°01'W, depth 2,520 m. Machida and Ohta 1996: Suruga Bay, Japan, at 2,716–2,743 m.

Size: Anderson 1995.

Lycenchelys crotalinus (Gilbert, 1890) **snakehead eelpout**

Eastern Bering Sea along continental slope; eastern Pacific off Sanak Islands and British Columbia to Baja California; western Bering Sea across Shirshov Ridge and Commander Plateau.

Mud bottom at depths of 200–2,816 m, usually taken at 700–1,500 m.

D 118–125; A 103–113; C 10–11; Pec 15–18; Pel 3; GR 15–18; Vert 22–24 + 98–109 (121–131).

- Brownish blue to violet.
- Males with wider, more depressed heads, smaller eyes, and longer upper jaws than females.
- Dorsal fin origin associated with vertebrae 4–6.
- **Scales present on nape and on cheeks.**
- Head pores: suborbital 7–8 + 1–2 (8–10); postorbital usually 2, in positions 1 and 3; occipital and interorbital absent; sensory pores on jaws conspicuous.
- **Lateral line descending to ventral position anteriorly, then rising to mediolateral position at middle of tail.**
- Vomerine and palatine teeth absent.
- Length to 468 mm TL.

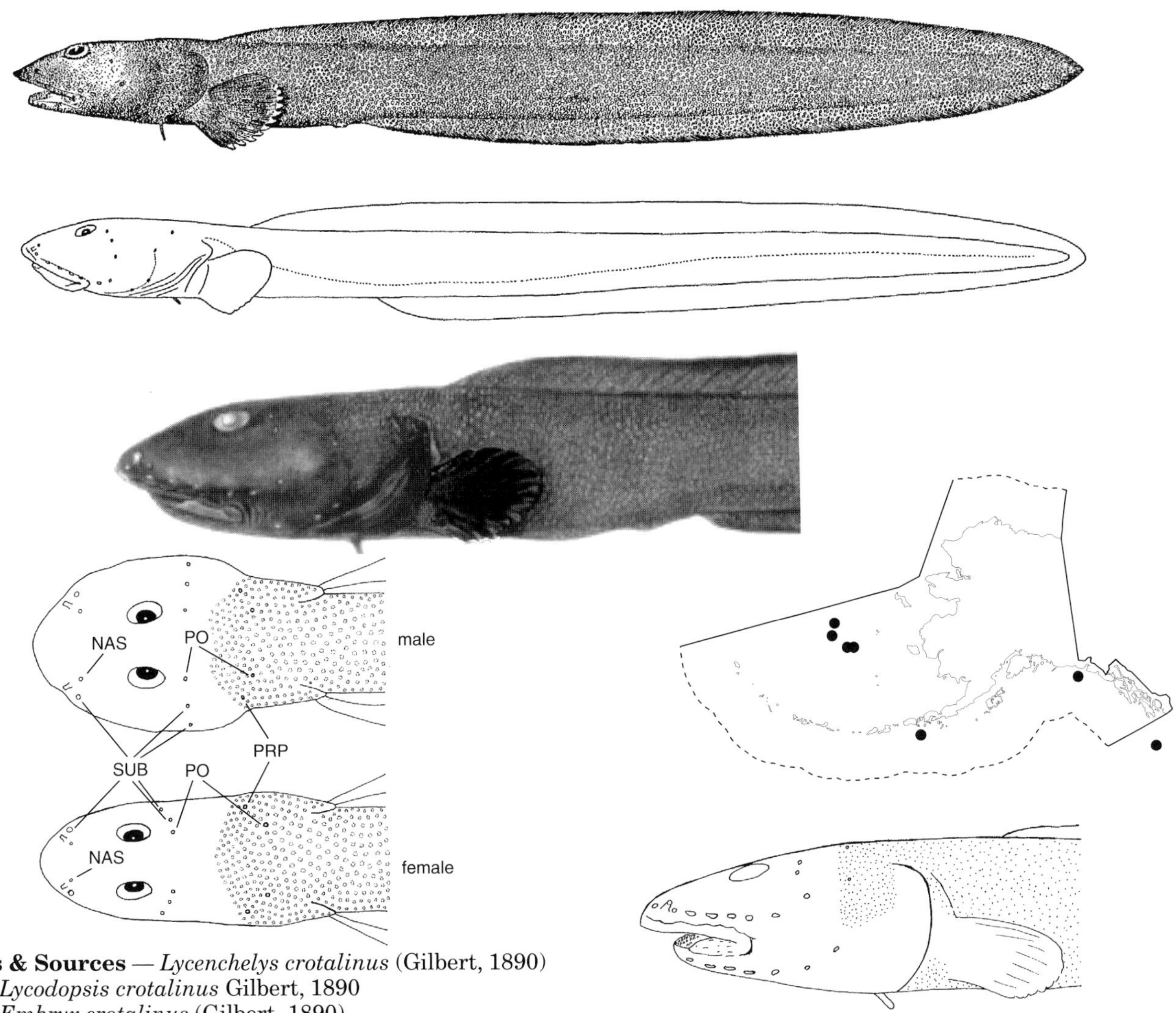

Notes & Sources — *Lycenchelys crotalinus* (Gilbert, 1890)
Lycodopsis crotalinus Gilbert, 1890
Embryx crotalinus (Gilbert, 1890)
Anderson (1984, 1995) synonymized *Embryx* with *Lycenchelys.*

Description: Gilbert 1896:454; Andriashev 1955a:379–380; Peden 1973:119–120; Toyoshima 1985:178–179; Anderson 1995:69–72.

Figures: Top: Jordan and Evermann 1900, fig. 851; USNM 44279, 308 mm TL, Santa Barbara Is. Full diagram: Toyoshima 1985, fig. 32; HUMZ 83403, Bering Sea. Anterior portion: Royal British Columbia Museum, artist P. Drukker-Brammall; BCPM 971-11, British Columbia. Heads, dorsal: Toyoshima, fig. 33, modified; male, HUMZ 83949, 468 mm TL; female, HUMZ 83403, 368 mm TL. Head, lateral: Peden 1973, fig. 1D.

Range: Gilbert (1896): south of Sanak Islands at 54°00'N, 162°40'W. Fedorov (1976) and Toyoshima (1985): Bering Sea and northern Gulf of Alaska localities. USNM 22110 is from 58°14'N, 175°28'W, at 681–818 m. Nearest records outside Alaska in the eastern Pacific are from 53°02'N, 132°52'W (BCPM 71-11) and nearby, reported by Peden (1973) and Anderson (1995).

Lycenchelys jordani (Evermann & Goldsborough, 1907) **shortjaw eelpout**

Eastern Pacific Ocean off Sitka Sound, Alaska; central British Columbia; and Oregon to Cape Colnett, Baja California.

Taken at depths of 1,500–2,570 m.

D 119–124; A 106–114; C 8–10; Pec 16–19; Pel 3; GR 11–15; Vert 24–26 + 102–110 (128–135).

- **Mouth terminal**.
- Dorsal fin origin above middle of pectoral fin, associated with vertebrae 6–8; pectoral fin rays usually 17–18.
- **Scales absent from head, nape in front of dorsal fin, and pectoral fin, base, and axil**.
- Head pores: suborbital 7–8 + 0–1 (7–8); postorbital 3; occipital and interorbital absent.
- Lateral line double (mediolateral and ventral), complete; mediolateral indistinct, observable only in new material.
- Length to 389 mm TL.

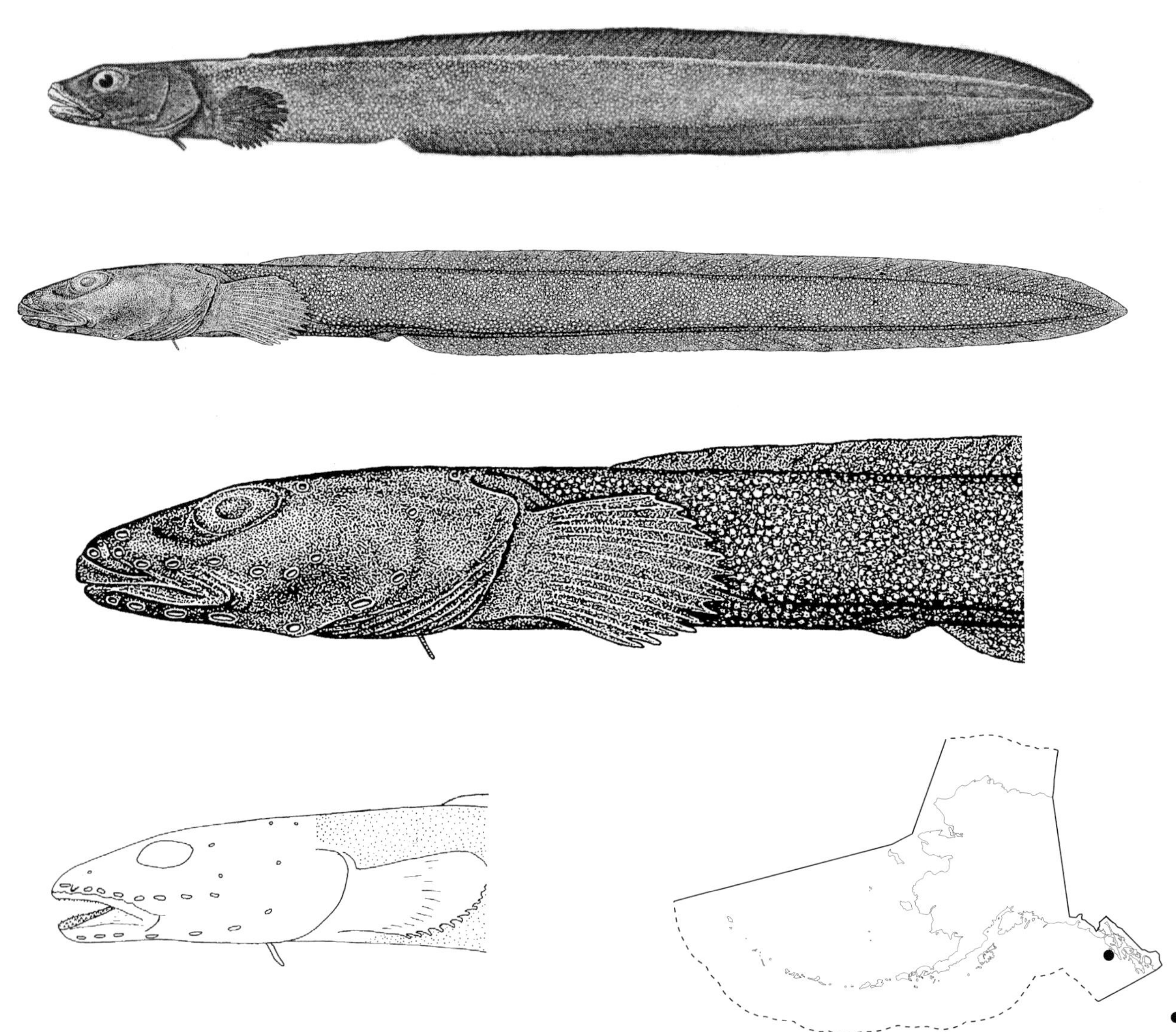

Notes & Sources — *Lycenchelys jordani* (Evermann & Goldsborough, 1907)
Lycodes jordani Evermann & Goldsborough, 1907

Description: Evermann and Goldsborough 1907:343; Peden 1973:118–119; Anderson 1995:80–82.

Figures: Top: Evermann and Goldsborough 1907, fig. 120; holotype, USNM 57828, about 336 mm TL, off Oregon. Lower full lateral and anterior portion: Anderson 1995, fig. 7; CAS 56192, 254 mm SL, off California. Head region diagram: Peden 1973, fig. 1A; British Columbia.

Range: Only one Alaskan record: Evermann and Goldsborough (1907), paratype, *Albatross* station 4267, off Sitka Sound, depth 1,686 m. Nearest record outside Alaska: Peden (1973), 50°54'N, 130°06'W, depth 2,103–2,196 m.

Size: Anderson 1995.

Lycenchelys micropora Andriashev, 1955 **manytoothed eelpout**

Northern Bering Sea; Pacific Ocean off British Columbia and Oregon to Gulf of Tehuantepec, Mexico. Taken at depths of 2,377–3,512 m.

D 115–127; A 99–109; C 8–9; Pec 15–18; Pel 3; GR 10–14; Vert 27–30 + 94–106 (123–135).

- **Nostrils overhang upper lip**.
- Dorsal fin origin above middle of pectoral fin, associated with vertebrae 5–6, rarely 7; pectoral fin rays usually 15–16.
- Scales absent from nape.
- Head pores: suborbital 7 + 0; postorbital 2–3; interorbital and occipital absent; **pores on jaws small and inconspicuous** compared to most *Lycenchelys* species.
- Lateral line double (mediolateral and ventral), complete; mediolateral often indistinct.
- **Head of vomer densely covered with small teeth**; palatine teeth present or absent.
- Branchiostegal rays 6, except 7 in one specimen.
- Length to 349 mm TL.

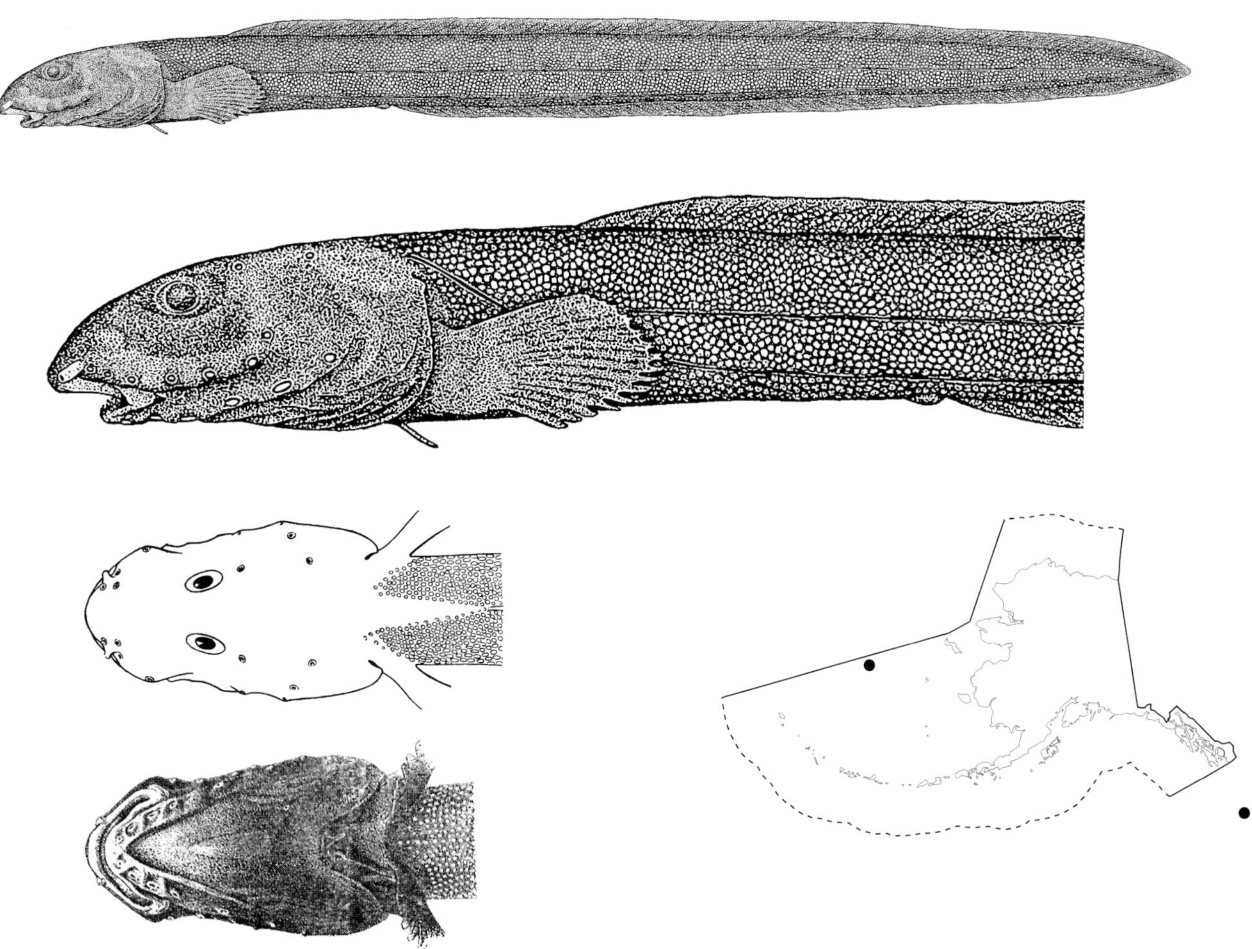

Notes & Sources — *Lycenchelys micropora* Andriashev, 1955
Lycenchelys microporus Andriashev, 1955
Similar to *L. jordani*, but distinguished by its more numerous precaudal vertebrae (27–30 in *L. micropora* vs. 24–26), longer nostril tube (length 7.8–11.6% HL vs. 2.7–3.5% HL), fewer pectoral fin rays (usually 15–16 vs. usually 17–18), and greater depth of occurrence (2,377–3,512 m vs. 1,536–2,570 m) (Anderson 1995).

Description: Andriashev 1955a:367–369; Toyoshima 1985: 152; Anderson 1995:84–86.

Figures: Full lateral view and anterior portion: Anderson 1955, fig. 9; CAS 81708, 259 mm SL, off Farallon Islands, California. Dorsal and ventral views of head: Andriashev 1955a, fig. 12; type, female, 349 mm TL, Bering Sea.

Range: The only Alaskan record is the holotype (Andriashev 1955a), from the Aleutian Basin at 59°43'N, 179°39'E (Eschmeyer 1998). The nearest record outside Alaska is a specimen taken off British Columbia at 48°07'N, 127°04'W, depth 2,510 m; it was deposited in the RBCM collection (A. E. Peden, pers. comm., 5 Sep. 1996; K. Sendall, pers. comm., 5 Nov. 1998).

Size: Largest on record is the holotype.

Lycenchelys plicifera Andriashev, 1955 **keeled eelpout**

Southwestern Bering Sea north of Near Islands (Aleutian Basin); western Pacific Ocean off Paramushir Island (Kuril–Kamchatka Trench).

Collected at depths of 3,820–4,070 m.

D 110–115; A 99–102; C 9–10; Pec 15–16; Pel 2; GR 13–16; Vert 28–30 + 92–98 (122–126).

- Body very elongate, depth at origin of anal fin about 5% of total length.
- **Abdominal skin fold (plica) present, white**, extending back from bases of pelvic fins for a distance equal to about half of head length.
- Opercular lobe well developed.
- Dorsal fin origin above posterior portion of pectoral fin, associated with vertebrae 9–11; rudimentary finfold in front of dorsal fin; **pelvic fin rays 2**.
- Head pores: suborbital 8 + 0–1; postorbital pore 1 present, sometimes doubled; occipital and interorbital absent; pores around mouth nostril-like.
- Lateral line double (mediolateral and ventral); mediolateral distinct in fresh specimens but hardly visible in alcohol.
- Length to 191 mm TL.

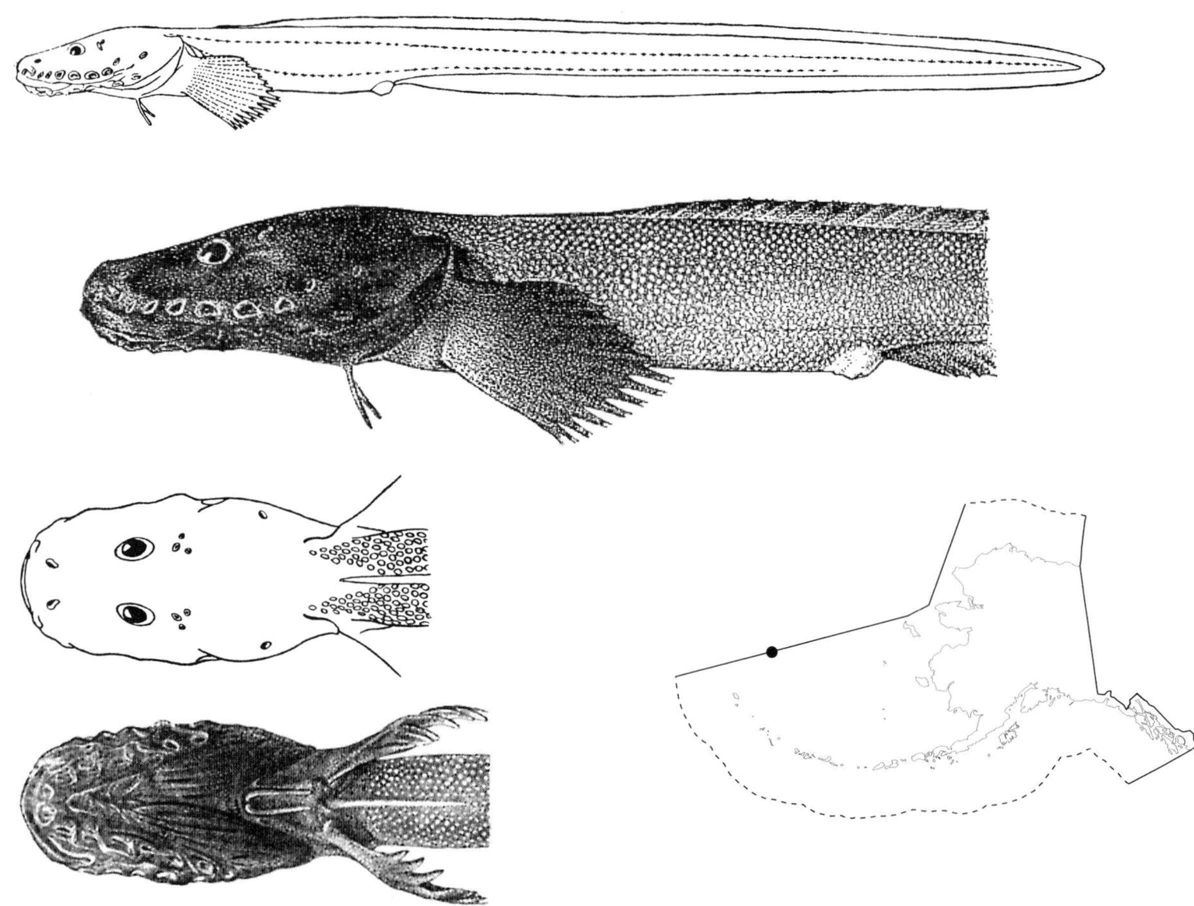

Notes & Sources — *Lycenchelys plicifera* Andriashev, 1955
Lycenchelys pliciferus Andriashev, 1955
Lycenchelys birsteini Andriashev, 1958
Lycenchelys bersteini: Toyoshima 1985 (lapsus calami).

Description: Andriashev 1955a:372–374, 1958:44–46 of transl.; Toyoshima 1985:155; Anderson 1995:94–96.

Figures: Andriashev 1955a, figs. 2-7, 15, 16; holotype, ZIN 32961, 130 mm TL, southwestern Bering Sea.

Range: The only Alaskan record comprises the holotype and one paratype, described by Andriashev (1955a) as taken northeast of Medny Island at 3,820–3,830 m of depth. The coordinates reported by Eschmeyer (1998) for this collection are 56°55'N, 174°20'E, placing it north of Agattu Island and on or close, on the Alaskan side, to the U.S.–Russia border in the Aleutian Basin. The only other specimens which have been reported are the holotype and one paratype of *L. birsteini* (= *L. plicifera*) obtained from the Kuril–Kamchatka Trench at depths of 3,960–4,020 m.

Size: The largest on record is a juvenile (Andriashev 1958).

Lycenchelys volki Andriashev, 1955 **longnape eelpout**

Southwestern Bering Sea northeast of Medny Island (Commander Basin).
Collected at depth of 3,940 m.

D 113; A 101; C 10; Pec 17; Pel 2; GR 16; Vert 30 + 96 (126).

- Opercular lobe well developed, rounded.
- **Dorsal fin origin above pectoral fin tip**, associated with vertebra 11; rudimentary finfold in front of dorsal fin; **pelvic fin rays 2**.
- Lateral line ventral, incomplete, not reaching vertical through anal fin origin.
- Head pores: suborbital 8 + 0; postorbital in position 1, but aberrantly doubled; occipital absent; **interorbital present, anterior to eyes**.
- **Pyloric caeca absent**.
- Length of one specimen: 208 mm TL.

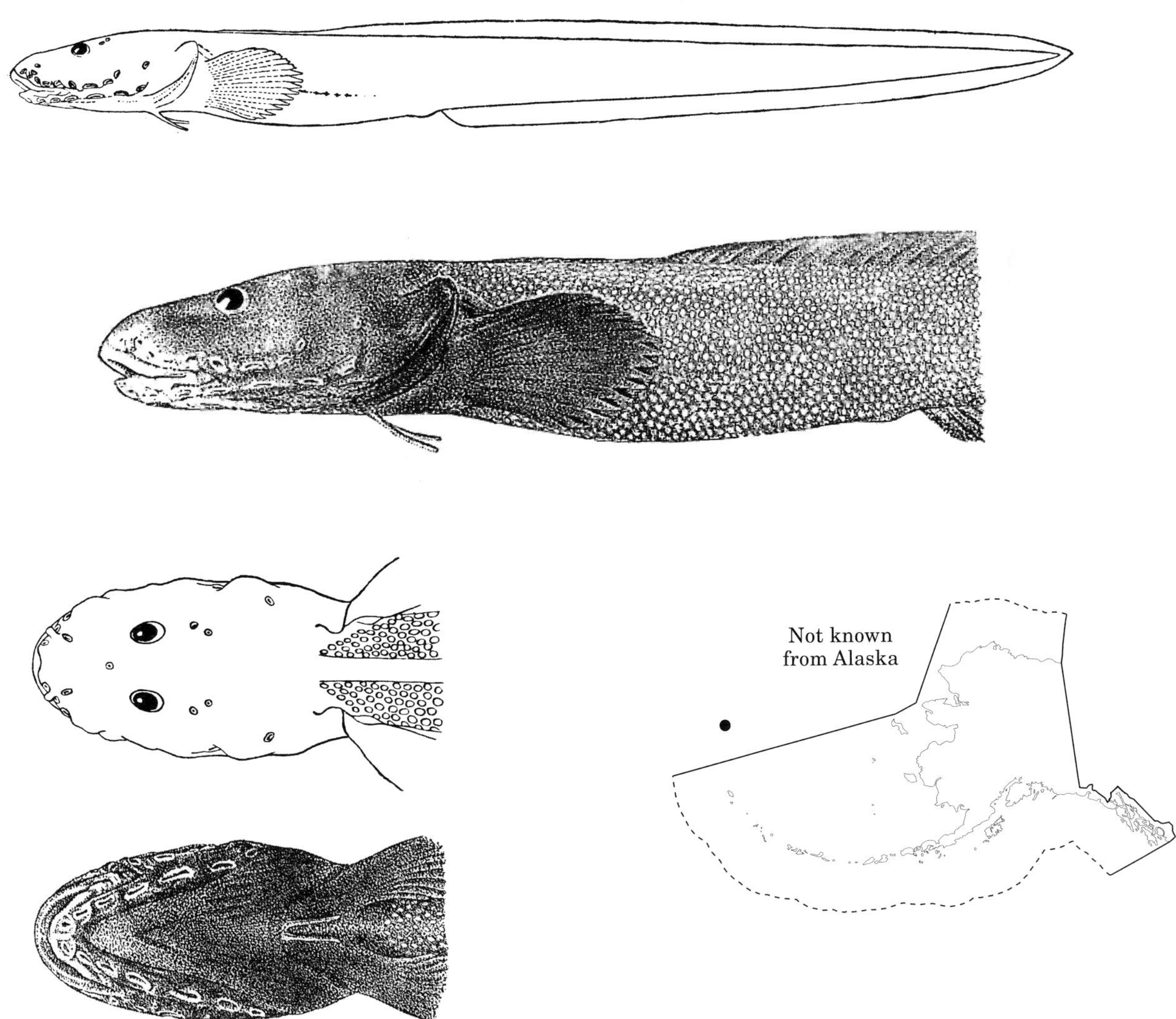

Notes & Sources — *Lycenchelys volki* Andriashev, 1955
The suggested vernacular, longnape eelpout, refers to the retrograde position of the dorsal fin origin.

Description: Andriashev 1955a:369–371; Toyoshima 1985: 152; Anderson 1995:106–107.

Figures: Andriashev 1955a, figs. 2-6, 13, 14; holotype (unique), ZIN 32964, male, 208 mm TL, southwestern Bering Sea.

Range: Known from only one specimen. Coordinates reported by Eschmeyer (1998) for the capture locality are 57°03'N, 168°29'E, placing it northeast of Medny Island and west of the Shirshov Ridge in the Commander Basin.

Lycenchelys rosea Toyoshima, 1985 **rosy eelpout**

Central Aleutian Islands.

Taken at depths of 358 m and 750 m.

D 133; A 117; C 10–11; Pec 14–15; Pel 3; GR 10–11; Vert 28 + 108–109 (136–137).

- Color in life **dull red** without blotches; in alcohol brownish.
- Dorsal fin origin associated with vertebra 2, resulting in predorsal length about equal to or slightly less than head length.
- Head pores: suborbital 7 + 1; **postorbital 4**; **occipital absent**; **interorbital present**.
- **Lateral line absent**.
- Lengths of two specimens, both females: 195 mm and 237 mm TL.

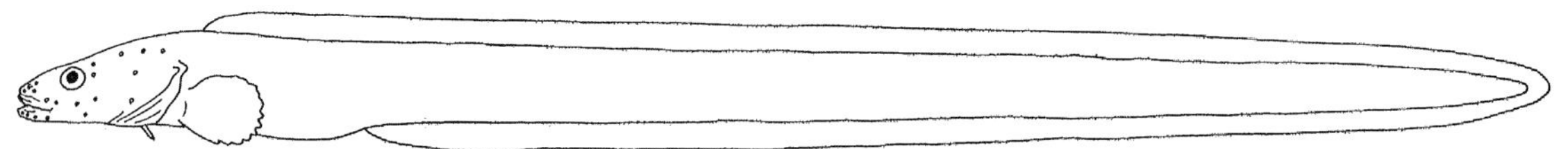

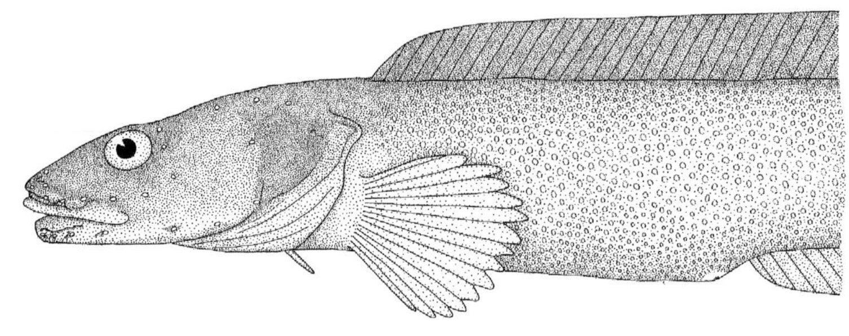

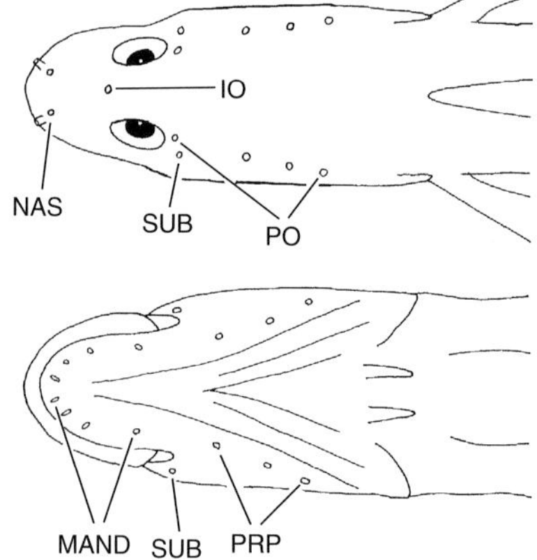

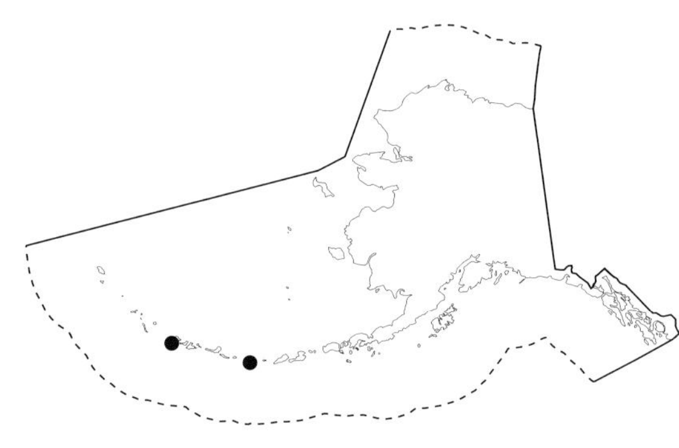

Notes & Sources — *Lycenchelys rosea* Toyoshima, 1985
Lycenchelys roseus Toyoshima, 1985

Description: Toyoshima 1985:152–154; Anderson 1995:103–104.

Figures: Toyoshima 1985, figs. 10, 11 (modified), 31B; HUMZ 88487, female, 237 mm TL, from Aleutian Islands, Alaska.

Range: Only two specimens known: HUMZ 88487, from 52°49'N, 171°02'W, depth 750 m; and HUMZ 89341, at 51°49'N, 178°36'W, depth 358 m (Toyoshima 1985).

Lycenchelys alta Toyoshima, 1985 **short eelpout**

Pacific Ocean southwest of Buldir Island, western Aleutian Islands.

Taken at trawl depth of 336 m.

D 84; A 71; C 9; Pec 18; Pel 3; GR 8–9; Vert 21 + 67 (88).

- **Body deep, depth about 11% of total length; short, head length about 20% of total length;** and number of vertebrae low for a *Lycenchelys*.
- Opercular lobe well developed, angular.
- Dorsal fin origin associated with vertebra 2, resulting in predorsal length about equal to or slightly less than head length; **fewer dorsal and anal fin rays than in other *Lycenchelys* species occurring in Alaska**.
- Head pores: suborbital 5 + 1; postorbital 5; occipital 2; interorbital present.
- Lateral line ventral, complete, traceable as a few groups of neuromasts to tip of tail.
- Length of one specimen: 127 mm TL.

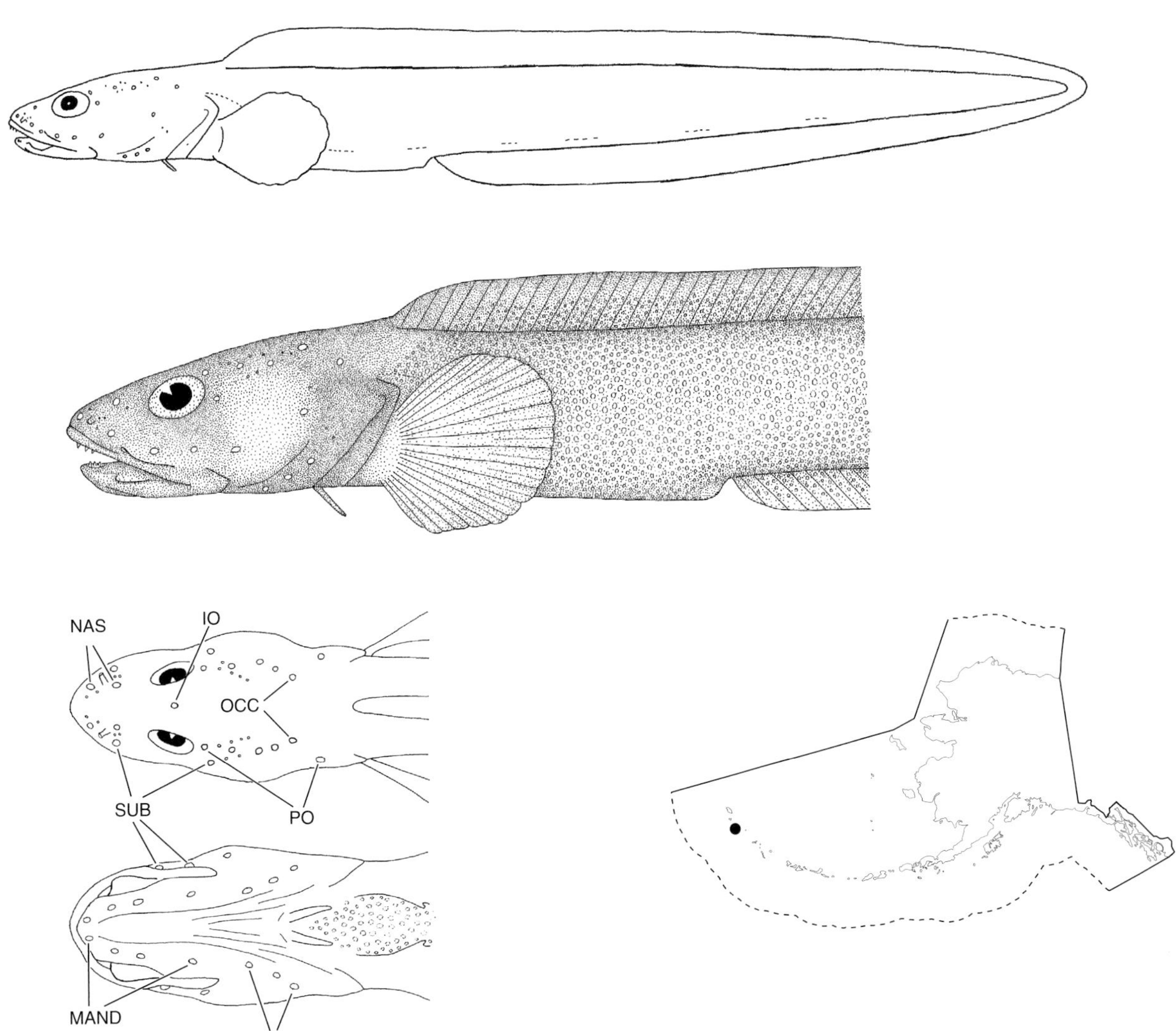

Notes & Sources — *Lycenchelys alta* Toyoshima, 1985
Lycenchelys altus Toyoshima, 1985
The vernacular, short eelpout, refers to the short appearance of this species compared to other *Lycenchelys*.

Description: Toyoshima 1985:158–159; Anderson 1995:59–60.

Figures: Toyoshima 1985, figs. 14, 15, 31D (modified); HUMZ 88704, male, 127 mm TL, south of Buldir Island, Alaska.

Range: Known from one specimen collected southwest of Buldir Island and southeast of Agattu Island at 52°04'N, 175°39'E, depth 336 m.

Lycenchelys camchatica (Gilbert & Burke, 1912) **Kamchatka eelpout**

Bering Sea south of Cape Navarin to near Unalaska Island, over Shirshov Ridge, and off Bering Island; Pacific off Washington to northern Baja California, and Avacha Bay, Kamchatka, to Sea of Okhotsk.

At depths of about 200–2,100 m.

D 112–117; A 100–105; C 9–11; Pec 12–15; Pel 3; GR 14–18; Vert 21–24 + 97–104 (118–125).

- In life bluish purple, or olive brown with greenish gilt on head and pectoral fins; **center of pectoral fin greenish or yellow in life, light in preserved specimens**.
- **Snout greatly produced**, upper teeth visible with mouth closed.
- Dorsal fin origin above middle of pectoral fin, associated with vertebrae 5–6; **pectoral fin rays usually 13–14**.
- Scales present on nape and cheeks.
- Head pores: suborbital 7–8 + 0–1 (7–9); postorbital 2; occipital and interorbital absent.
- Lateral line ventral, steeply sloping on anterior part of body, not traceable to tip of tail.
- Length to 430 mm TL; most specimens are under 250 mm TL.

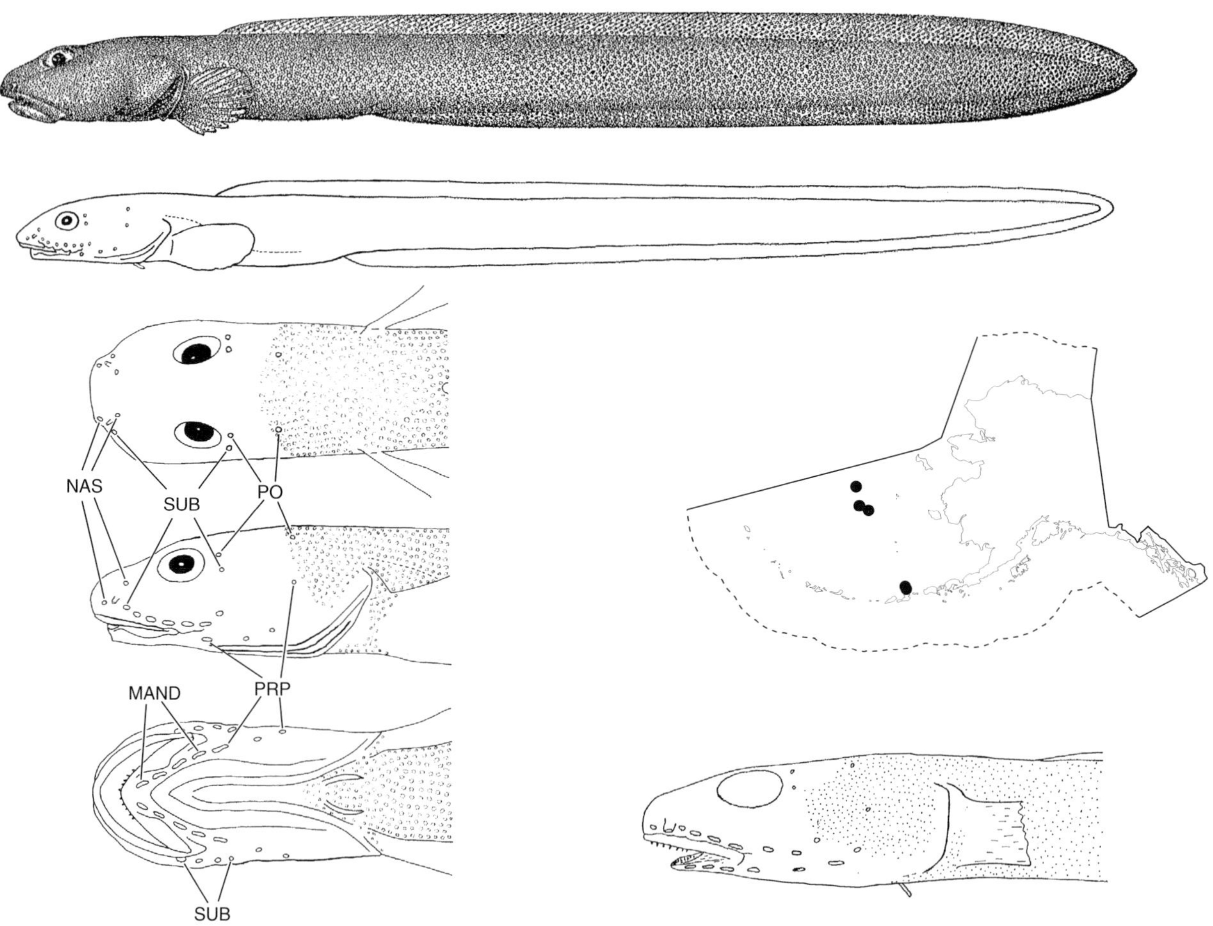

Notes & Sources — *Lycenchelys camchatica* (Gilbert & Burke, 1912)
Lycodes camchaticus Gilbert & Burke, 1912
Easily confused with *L. crotalinus,* but distinguished by having vomerine and palatine teeth, an *incomplete* ventral lateral line, and fewer pectoral fin rays (usually 13–14 in *L. camchatica* and usually 16–17 in *L. crotalinus*).

Description: Gilbert and Burke 1912a:89–90; Andriashev 1955a:364–367, 1958:40–41 of transl.; Peden 1973:117–118; Toyoshima 1985:164–166; Anderson 1995: 63–66.

Figures: At top: Gilbert and Burke 1912a, fig. 34; holotype, USNM 74396, 246 mm TL, off Avacha Bay, southeast Kamchatka; dorsal fin origin modified from examination of specimen by M. E. Anderson. Lateral diagram and heads at left: Toyoshima 1985, figs. 21 and 31F, modified; HUMZ 8223, female, 153 mm TL, eastern Bering Sea, Alaska. Head at lower right: Peden 1973, fig. 1C, Washington.

Range: Fedorov (1976), Toyoshima (1985), and Anderson (1995) reported localities for Bering Sea collections. (The coordinates for HUMZ 83222 and 83223 are correctly 59°49'N, 178°47'W, the same as for duplicate collection USNM 221091.) The minimum reported depth of about 200 m off the west coast of Bering Island (Andriashev 1937) is an estimate, but the record of 256 m off southern California (Anderson et al. 1979) suggests it is not far off (Anderson 1995).

Size: Fedorov 1976.

Lycenchelys hippopotamus Schmidt, 1950 **behemoth eelpout**

Western Bering Sea to southern Sea of Okhotsk.

At depths of 840–1,340 m.

D 125–132; A 113–120; C 9–11; Pec 13–16; Pel 3; GR 12–17; Vert 23–25 + 107–114 (132–137).

- Head somewhat depressed; **snout noticeably broad, bearing thick, fleshy lobe overhanging mouth**; lobe wrinkled and distorted in preserved specimens.
- Dorsal fin origin above anterior quarter of pectoral fin, associated with vertebrae 4–5.
- Scales absent from head, nape, pectoral fin and base, and axil.
- Head pores: suborbital 7–9 + 0–1 (8–10); postorbital 3–4; occipital 1–2; interorbital 1–2; **first suborbital pore at snout tip directly below nostril tube**.
- Lateral line ventral, complete, gently sloping anteriorly on body and running relatively high above anal fin base to tip of tail.
- Length to 223 mm TL.

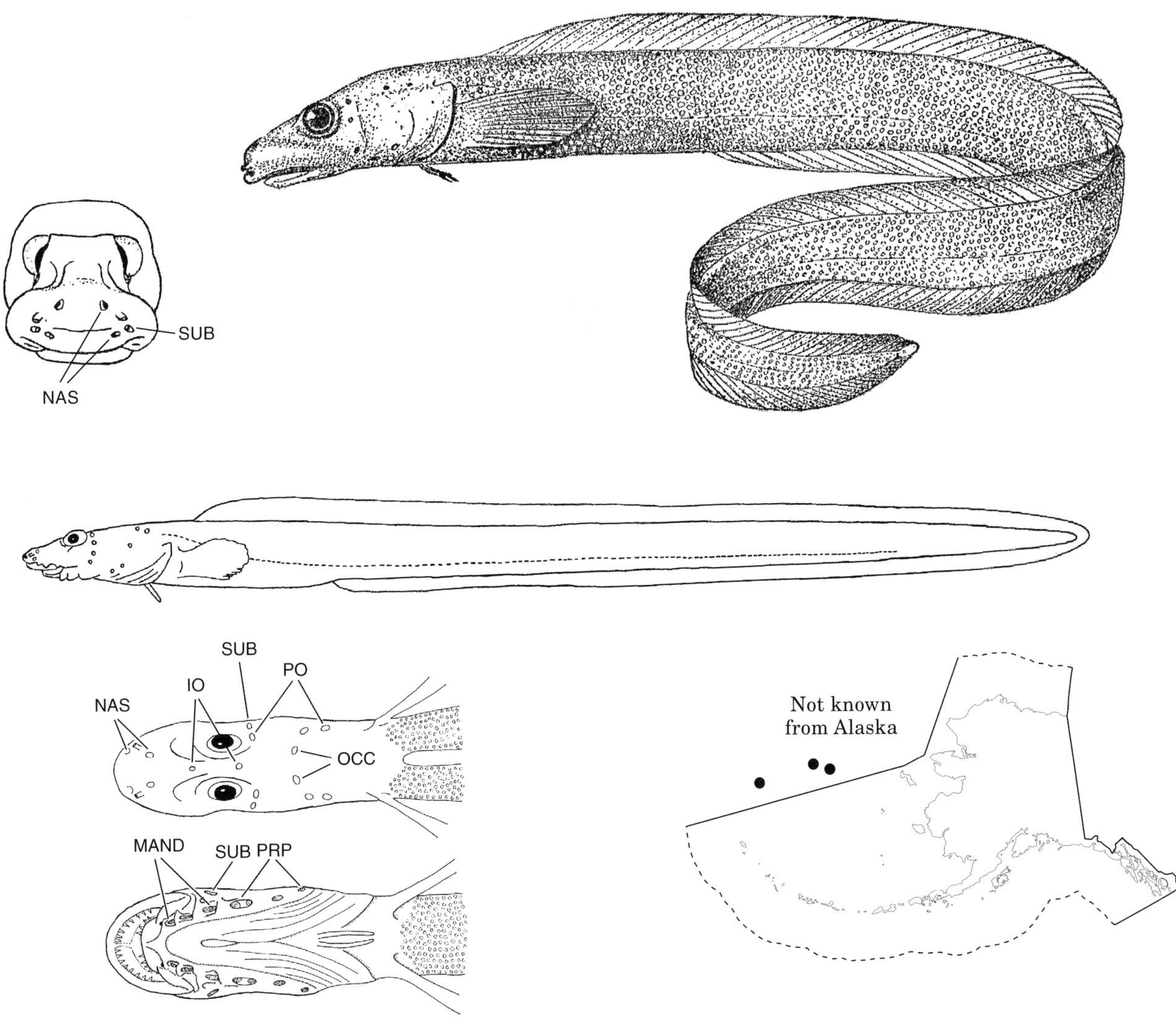

Notes & Sources — *Lycenchelys hippopotamus* Schmidt, 1950

Description: Schmidt 1950:106–107; Andriashev 1955a:361–364; Toyoshima 1985:169–170; Anderson 1995:76–77. Anderson (1995) corrected numerous errors found in the previous works.

Figures: Frontal and flexed lateral views: Schmidt 1950, text fig. 4 (modified) and pl. 9, fig. 1; Sea of Okhotsk. Others: Toyoshima 1985, figs. 25 and 31H, modified; HUMZ 77571, male, 205 mm TL, Sea of Okhotsk.

Range: Recorded from western Bering Sea by Fedorov (1976): ZIN 40536, 57°30'N, 170°25'E; ZIN 42015, 61°03'N, 175°35'E; ZIN 42016, 61°22'N, 177°44'E. Other specimens in ZIN collection are from Sea of Okhotsk.

Size: Largest of 18 known specimens, none of them fully mature (Anderson 1995).

Lycenchelys ratmanovi Andriashev, 1955 **manypore eelpout**

Eastern Bering Sea slope to near Unalaska Island; western Bering Sea southwest of Cape Navarin and off Cape Olyutorskiy; western Pacific off southeast Kamchatka and northern Kuril Islands.

At depths of 620–1,120 m.

D 105–110; A 93–97; C 9–10; Pec 15–18; Pel 3; GR 8–11; Vert 21–23 + 88–93 (110–115).

- Pectoral fin bluish black, in some specimens with greenish blue area in center, this area fading to pale in alcohol.
- Dorsal fin origin above anterior quarter of pectoral fin, associated with vertebrae 3–4.
- **Scales absent from head, nape, pectoral fin and base, and axil.**
- Head pores: suborbital 6–7 + 2–3 (8–10); **postorbital 5**; **occipital 3–4**; interorbital present (more pores than in most other eelpouts).
- **Lateral line ventral, complete, steeply descending in pectoral axil**, not always discernible to end.
- Length to 190 mm TL.

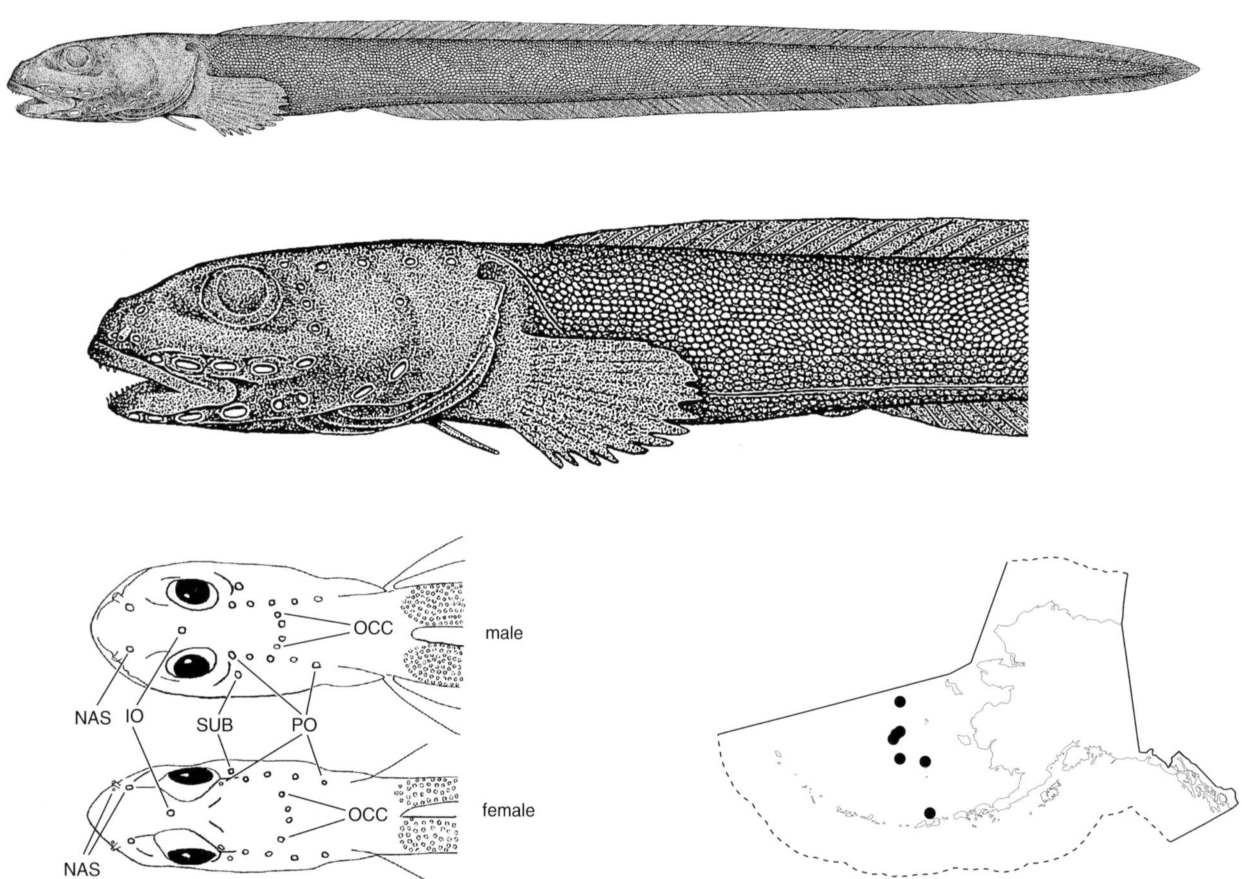

Notes & Sources — *Lycenchelys ratmanovi* Andriashev, 1955
Lycenchelys camchaticus: Andriashev 1937:341–343, figs. 16, 18 (in part, males only, Avacha Bay).
Lycenchelys longirostris Toyoshima, 1985

Description: Andriashev 1955a:355–358; Fedorov 1976:6–7; Toyoshima 1985:166–169, table 3; Anderson 1995:100–103.

Figures: Upper: Anderson 1995, fig. 16; USNM 221249, 135 mm SL, eastern Bering Sea. Head region diagrams: Toyoshima 1985, fig. 23, modified; male, HUMZ 89948, 156 mm TL; female, HUMZ 81914, 144 mm TL.

Range: Fedorov (1976) listed four collections from Alaska: ZIN 40539, off Unalaska Island, 54°19'N, 167°52'W; ZIN 40540, Zhemchug Canyon at 58°13'N, 175°10'W; ZIN 40541, Pribilof Islands, 57°30'N, 170°25'W; and ZIN 40542, west of St. Matthew Island at 61°23'N, 176°18'W. Anderson (1995) reported two other Alaskan collections: USNM 221250, Zhemchug Canyon at 58°20'N, 175°02'W; and USNM 221249, west of the Pribilof Islands at 56°58'N, 173°51'W. The types of *L. longirostris* are from Zhemchug Canyon: HUMZ 81914, at 58°33'N, 175°05'W; and HUMZ 83948, at 58°14'N, 175°28'W.

Size: Andriashev 1955a. Species is known from 14 museum lots, none of the specimens fully mature (Anderson 1995).

Lycenchelys rassi Andriashev, 1955 — earless eelpout

Southeastern Bering Sea north of Unalaska Island; southwestern Bering Sea at Kronotskiy Bay; Sea of Okhotsk.

Soft bottoms at depths of 1,040–1,805 m.

D 117–125; A 105–113; C 9; Pec 14–16; Pel 2; GR 10–13; Vert 23–25 + 98–105 (122–129).

- Head moderately large, 15–16% of total length.
- Dorsal fin origin above anterior quarter of pectoral fin, associated with vertebra 5; **pelvic fin rays 2**.
- **Opercular lobe absent**, since the posterior edge of the opercle is connected with the body and the pectoral fin base by a wide siphon-shaped fold.
- Scales absent from head, nape, pectoral fin and base, and axil.
- Head pores: suborbital 7–8 + 1; postorbital 3–4; occipital 2; interorbital present.
- **Lateral line ventral, complete, without steep decline in pectoral axil**, gently descending to just above anal fin base.
- Lower jaw with elongate, blunt teeth pointing forward.
- Length to 232 mm TL.

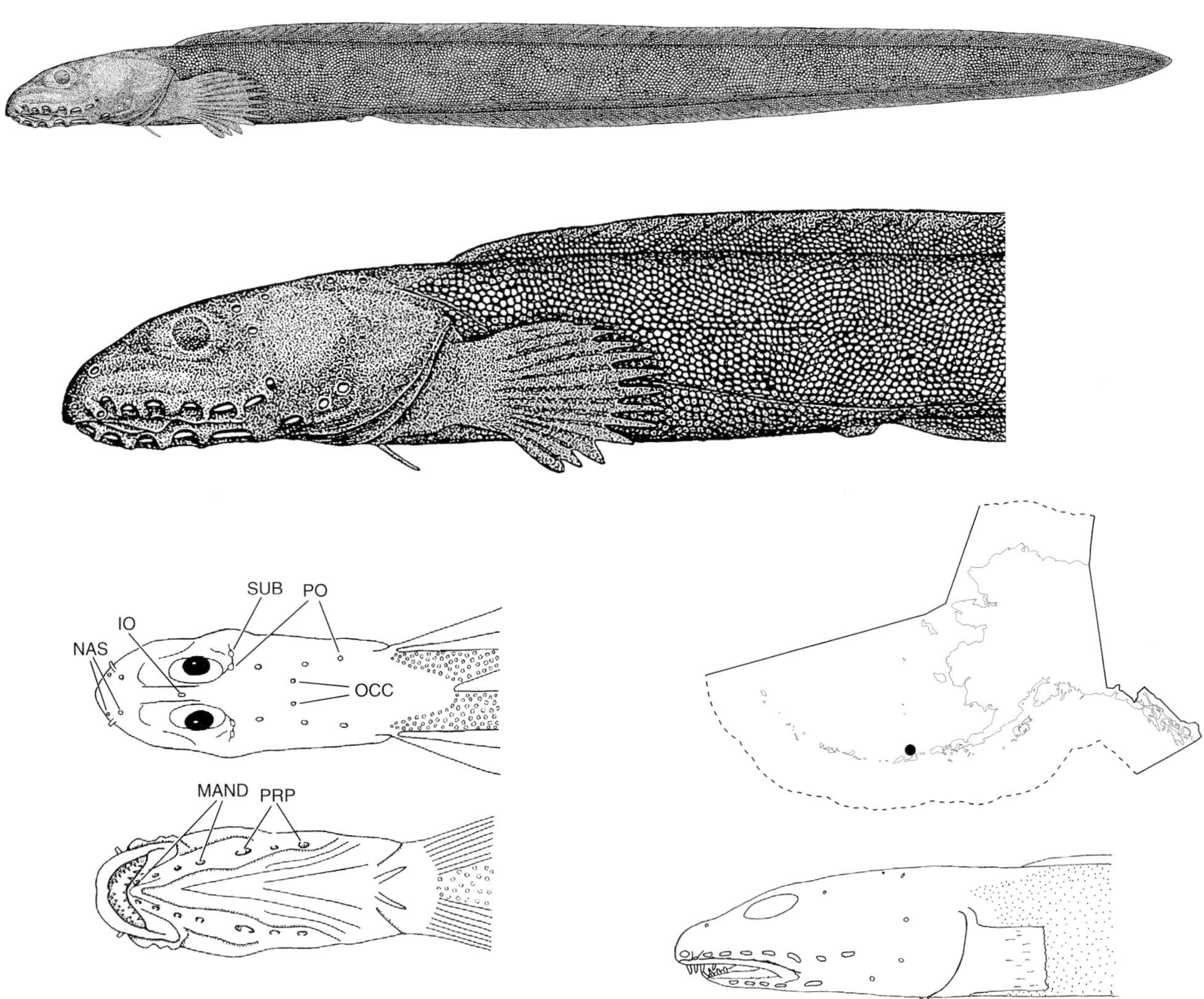

Notes & Sources — *Lycenchelys rassi* Andriashev, 1955

Description: Andriashev 1955a:359–361; Peden 1973:115–117; Toyoshima 1985:173–174; Anderson 1995:98–100.

Figures: Upper views: Anderson 1995, fig. 15; MCZ 34075, 147 mm SL, Sea of Okhotsk. Head region, dorsal and ventral: Toyoshima in Amaoka et al. 1983, fig. 26C,D, modified. Head, lateral: Peden 1973, fig. 1B.

Range: Peden (1973) described the only Alaskan specimens on record, which had been collected by the *Albatross* in 1895 at station 3607, 54°11'N, 167°25'W, on gray mud and black lava sand bottom at a depth 1,805 m.

Size: Toyoshima 1985: largest of the six known specimens (HUMZ 77747).

Lycodes pacificus Collett, 1879 **blackbelly eelpout**

Aleutian Islands and Gulf of Alaska to Pacific Ocean off Baja California.

Muddy bottoms at depths of 9–399 m; frequently taken in shrimp trawls.

D + 1/2C 90–107; A + 1/2C 70–90; Pec 16–19; Pel 3; GR 0–2 + 8–12; Vert 21–23 + 79–85 (102–104).

- Light gray to pale reddish brown; light scale pockets; pale vertical bands edged faintly with black on body, obscure in adults; **black along margin of dorsal fin**, an elongate spot at its anterior end which fades in large adults, and along margin of anal fin posteriorly; **jet black peritoneum, faintly evident through skin of belly**.
- Chin crests inconspicuous, not united anteriorly.
- Scales absent from head and pectoral fin.
- Lateral line mediolateral, fading over anterior portion of anal fin, not discernible in all specimens.
- **Vomerine and palatine teeth absent**.
- Length to 460 mm TL.

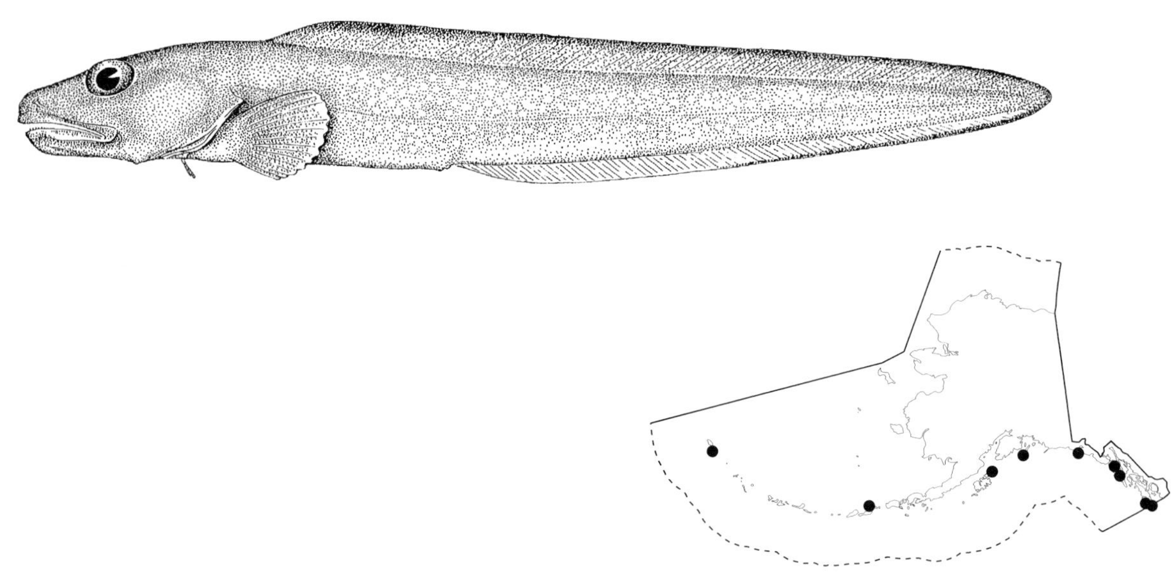

Notes & Sources — *Lycodes pacificus* Collett, 1879
Leurynnis paucidens Lockington, 1880
Lycodopsis pacificus: Gill 1880.

Toyoshima (1985) maintained *Lycodopsis* as a distinct genus by the absence of teeth from both vomer and palatines, whereas Anderson (1984) considered the presence of chin crests more important in linking it with *Lycodes*. Anderson (1994) suggested the presence of a dark blotch on the anterior end of the dorsal fin in *L. pacificus* and *L. cortezianus*, evident particularly in the young, coupled with a degree of palatal tooth loss, may support *Lycodopsis* as a subgenus.

Description: Lockington 1880a:326–328; Jordan and Gilbert 1883:785; Jordan and Evermann 1898:2460; Schultz 1967 (vertebral counts for *Leurynnis* [= *Lycodes*] *paucidens*); Hart 1973:245–246; Matarese et al. 1989:498.

Figure: Hart 1973:245; UBC 59-530, 220 mm TL, Indian Arm, British Columbia.

Range: Alaskan records include those of Bayliff (1959), from Captains Bay on the northeastern side of Unalaska Island, and Afognak Island. ABL holdings comprise two lots from Johnstone Bay (AB 64-663, 59°54'N, 148°52'W, 115 m; AB 64-664, 59°56'N, 148°46'W, 119–133 m); one from Katlian Bay (AB 67-106, 57°10'N, 135°20'W, 128–143 m); and two from Lisianski Inlet (AB 69-30 and AB 69-118, 58°06.5'N, 136°28'W, 37–128 m). The UBC has collections from a lake draining into Armeria Bay, Agattu Island (UBC 65-10, 52°27'N, 173°30'E), and from localities in southeastern Alaska (UBC 61-546, 55°19'N, 133°17'W; UBC 61-547, 54°53'N, 132°23'W). Collection SIO 76-299 includes a specimen from the Kodiak shelf (56°43'N, 153°22'W, 108 m). Fairly common along coasts of southern Alaska but not well documented; not as common there as *L. brevipes* or *L. palearis*. Levings (1969) described reproduction and other aspects of biology in Burrard Inlet, British Columbia, population. Depth: Bayliff 1959.

Size: Jordan and Evermann 1898.

Lycodes cortezianus (Gilbert, 1890) **bigfin eelpout**

Eastern Gulf of Alaska off Prince of Wales Island; Queen Charlotte Sound, British Columbia, to southern California off San Diego.

Mud, sand, and gravel bottoms at depths of 73–800 m, usually taken at 100–450 m. Common in trawl catches south of Alaska, and occasionally taken in sablefish traps.

D 105–109; A 89–92; Pec 18–21; Pel 3; GR 15–17; Vert 23–24 + 89–92 (112–115).

- Light brown to blue-black, lighter ventrally; white scale pockets; black blotch on anterior edge of dorsal fin, fading in large adults; black on posterior portions of dorsal, anal, and caudal fins; pectoral fin with light margin, entirely pale in small specimens.
- **Head broad, depressed, large**; head length more than 20% of total length.
- Chin crests low, not united anteriorly.
- **Pectoral fin large, rounded**.
- Scales absent from head and pectoral fin.
- Lateral line mediolateral.
- **Vomerine teeth absent, palatine teeth present**.
- Length to 493 mm TL.

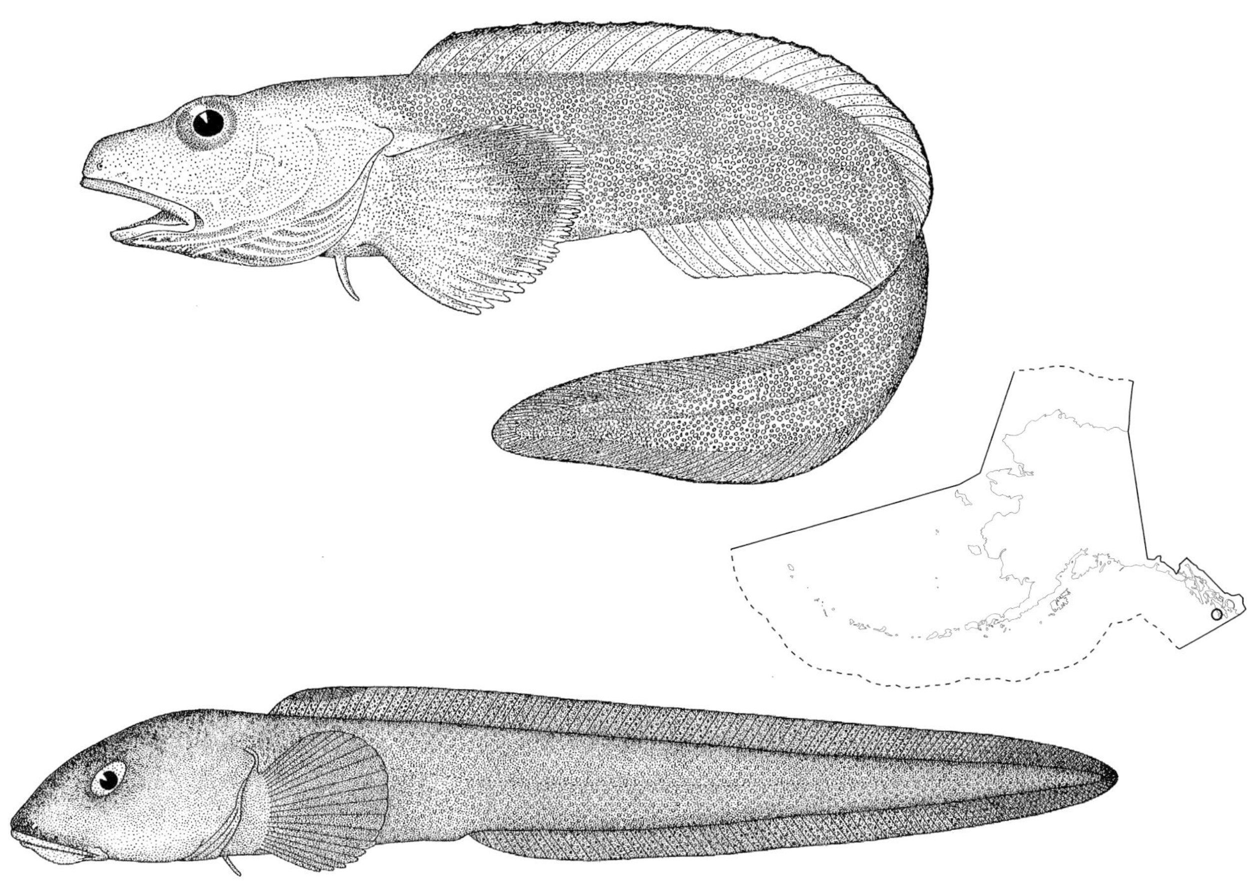

Notes & Sources — *Lycodes cortezianus* (Gilbert, 1890)
Aprodon corteziana Gilbert, 1890
Considered intermediate between *Lycodes* and *Lycodopsis* by Gilbert (1890) due to absence of vomerine teeth and presence of palatine teeth. Toyoshima (1985) maintained distinction of the genus *Aprodon*. Anderson (1994) suggested *Lycodopsis* may be valid as a subgenus, including *Lycodes cortezianus* and *L. pacificus*.

Description: Gilbert 1890:106–107; Bali and Bond 1959; Schultz 1967 (vertebral counts for types); Hart 1973:233–234; Toyoshima 1985:237–238.

Figures: Upper: Jordan and Evermann 1900, fig. 852; type, USNM 46457, Cortes Bank, off San Diego. Lower: Toyoshima 1985, fig. 67; HUMZ 64342, male, 274 mm TL, off San Diego.

Range: Allen and Smith (1988), reviewing NMFS resource assessment data, reported extension of the known range north to Prince of Wales Island; voucher specimens are lacking. They considered survey records west of St. Matthew Island in the Bering Sea and off Stepovak Bay south of the Alaska Peninsula to be highly questionable. Toyoshima (1985) gave a range including the Bering Sea, but without citing records. M. E. Anderson (pers. comm., 17 Feb. 1998) considers Bering Sea reports to be misidentifications, probably confused with *L. palearis*. Consequently, C.W.M. asked B. K. Urbain to examine UW 22039, a Bering Sea specimen identified as *L. cortezianus*, and he reported (pers. comm., 2 Jun. 1998) that it *does* have vomerine teeth; therefore, a misidentification, as suggested by Anderson.

Size: Bali and Bond 1959.

Lycodes jugoricus Knipowitsch, 1906

shulupaoluk

Eastern Beaufort Sea near Herschel Island, Yukon Territory, to Boothia Peninsula, Nunavut; White Sea east to Laptev Sea, New Siberian Islands, near mouth of Kolyma River, and Chukchi Sea.

Soft bottoms in shallow coastal waters; recorded from depths of 9–90 m, usually taken 15 m or shallower.

D + 1/2C 96–111; A + 1/2C 78–88; Pec 16–18; Pel 3; Vert 99–102.

- Adults usually white ventrally, yellowish laterally; top of head dark; narrow, light band straight across occiput; **7–9 vaguely to sharply defined wedge-shaped dark bands with lighter centers, widening dorsally and extending onto dorsal fin**; peritoneum light.
- **Chin crests low, partially fused anteriorly, the tips showing as tubercles.**
- Pectoral fin rays usually 17–18; pectoral fin long, 14–17% of total length.
- **Scales absent.**
- Lateral line mediolateral; widely spaced dorsolateral and predorsal neuromasts.
- **Vomerine teeth blunt, rounded, numerous** (up to 30–37; more than in most northern *Lycodes*).
- Length to 400 mm TL.

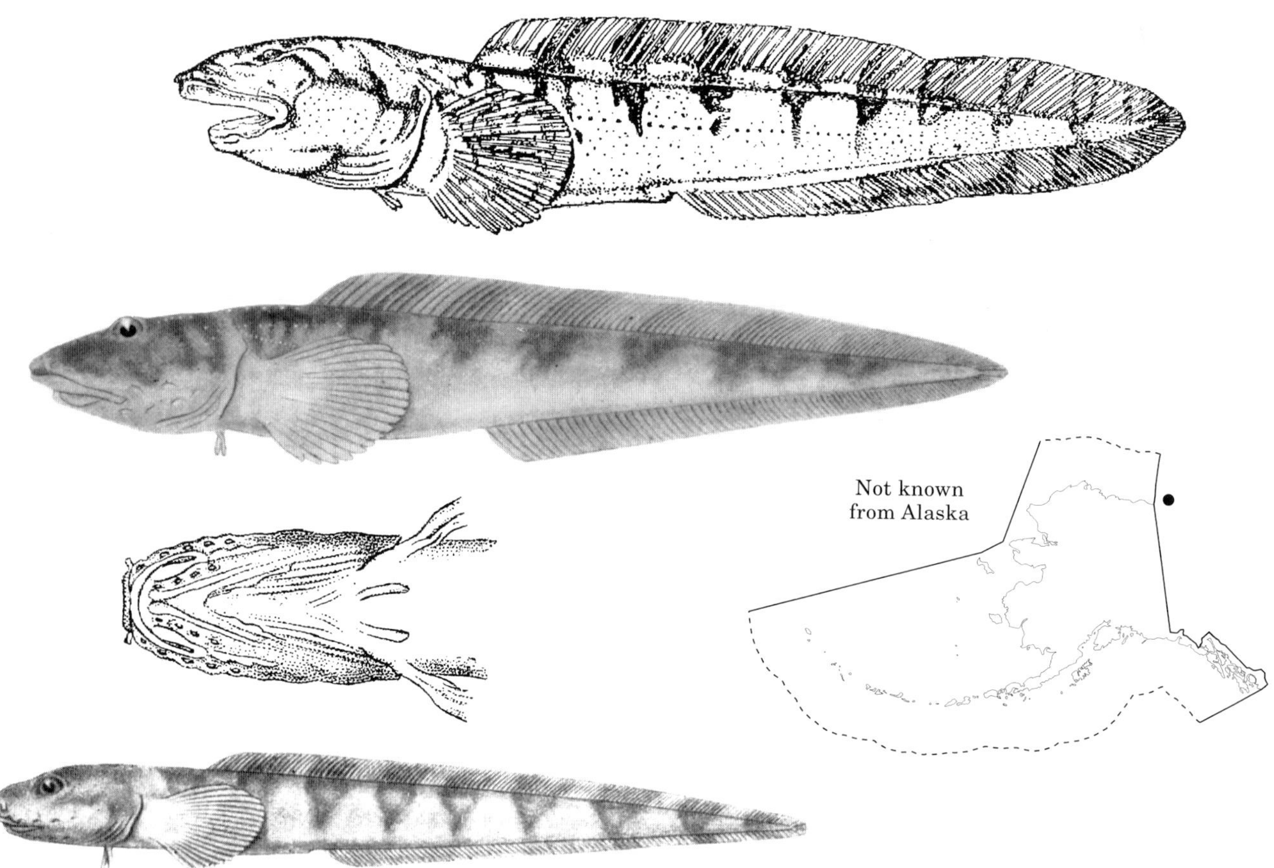

Notes & Sources — *Lycodes jugoricus* Knipowitsch, 1906

Description: Andriashev 1954:275–278, 535; McAllister 1962:27; Andriashev in Whitehead et al. 1986:1139–1140. Andriashev (1954) described white band across the occiput in Russian Arctic specimens; McAllister (1962) described the predorsal region as dark, with no band, in the two Herschel Island, Canada, specimens.

Figures: Andriashev 1954, figs. 145–147. Top: 351 mm TL, White Sea. Middle: 155 mm TL, Laptev Sea. Bottom, including ventral view: juvenile, 61 mm TL, Laptev Sea.

Range: Although Walters (1955) noted that Wilimovsky collected "what appears to be *L. jugoricus*" from the Chukchi Sea, locality or other specimen data were not reported and Wilimovsky (1958) did not include *L. jugoricus* in his keys to Alaskan species. There are no specimens from Alaska in institutional collections. The nearest confirmed record to Alaska is that of McAllister (1962), comprising two specimens taken in the Beaufort Sea near Herschel Island, Yukon Territory. Hunter et al. (1984) confirmed additional records from Canada, including several along Tuktoyaktuk Peninsula, one at Dease Strait, and one at southwest side of Boothia Peninsula in eastern Canada. Andriashev (1954) summarized records from the Russian Arctic; the locality nearest to Alaska was Lyakhovskiy Island in the New Siberian Islands. Andriashev (in Whitehead et al. 1986) listed Chukchi Sea among known records, but did not indicate whether this was on the basis of the indefinite record cited by Walters (1955; see beginning of this note) or if he had a new record.

Lycodes seminudus Reinhardt, 1837 — longear eelpout

Beaufort Sea to Greenland, Norwegian and Kara seas, and north to Franz Josef Land and Spitsbergen. Mud, clay, and stone bottoms in deep water; recorded from depths of 130–1,400 m, usually at 200–600 m.

D + 1/2C 93–97; A + 1/2C 74–78; Pec 19–22; Pel 3; GR 13–15; Vert 96–98.

- Dark gray-brown, some with short, light bands dorsolaterally and extending onto dorsal fin; some with light band, straight, not curved, across occiput.
- **Opercular lobe longer and more dorsally directed than in other *Lycodes*.**
- Chin crests low, bevelled anteriorly, not projecting.
- **Pectoral fin rays relatively numerous**; pectoral fin short, 9–12% of total length.
- **Scales present only posteriorly**.
- Lateral line mediolateral; widely spaced neuromasts dorsolaterally.
- Length to 517 mm TL.

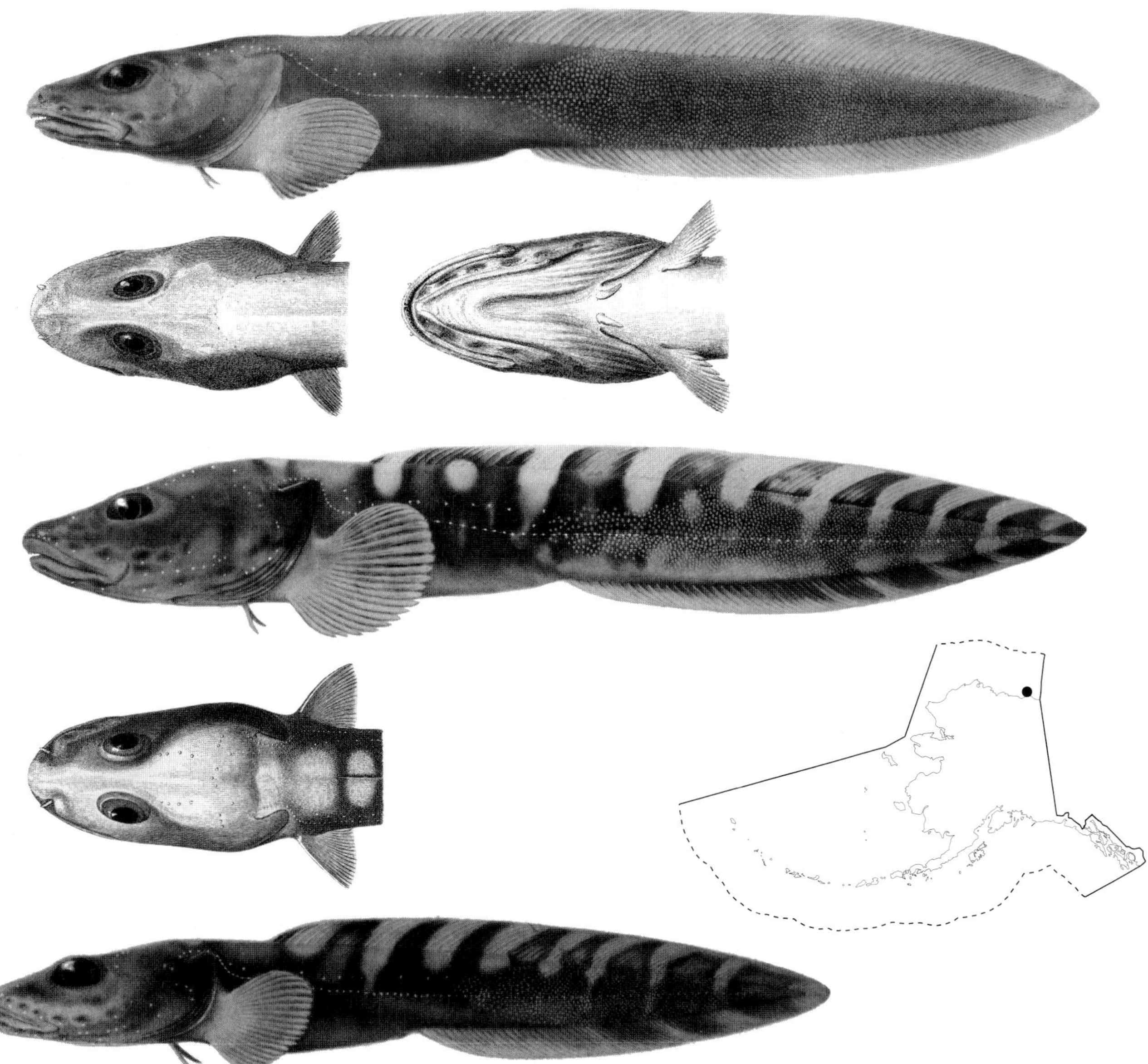

Notes & Sources — *Lycodes seminudus* Reinhardt, 1837

Description: Jensen 1852a:18–22; McAllister et al. 1981: 833–835; Andriashev in Whitehead et al. 1986:1145.

Figures: Jensen 1904, pls. 9 and 10, figs. 11–13. Plain, no stripes: 335 mm TL, west Greenland. Striped: 280 mm and 129 mm TL; east Greenland.

Range: Three specimens taken about 81 km north-northeast of Brownlow Point are the only Alaskan record. They are more than 500 km from the nearest Canadian record, at Franklin Bay, Northwest Territories; and about 3,000 km from the nearest Russian record, in the Kara Sea (McAllister et al. 1981).

Size: Jensen 1952a.

Lycodes mucosus Richardson, 1855 **saddled eelpout**

Alaskan and Canadian Arctic to Bering Sea near Pribilof Islands; Russian Arctic to Gulf of Anadyr. Soft bottoms in shallow water, recorded from depths of 13–80 m.

D 82–85; A 65–67; Pec 16–19; Pel 3; GR 12–15; Vert 24–29 + 65–68 (92–94).

- **Body with dark Y-shaped marks**; light band, variously broken, connecting gill openings; underside of head, lips, and belly light; **light areas decreasing and dark marks becoming indistinct in adults.**
- Opercular lobe not strongly developed.
- Chin crests well developed, not united anteriorly.
- **Scales weakly developed, limited to posterior half of body, absent in smaller specimens.**
- Lateral line mediolateral; row of widely spaced neuromasts dorsally.
- Length to 490 mm TL.

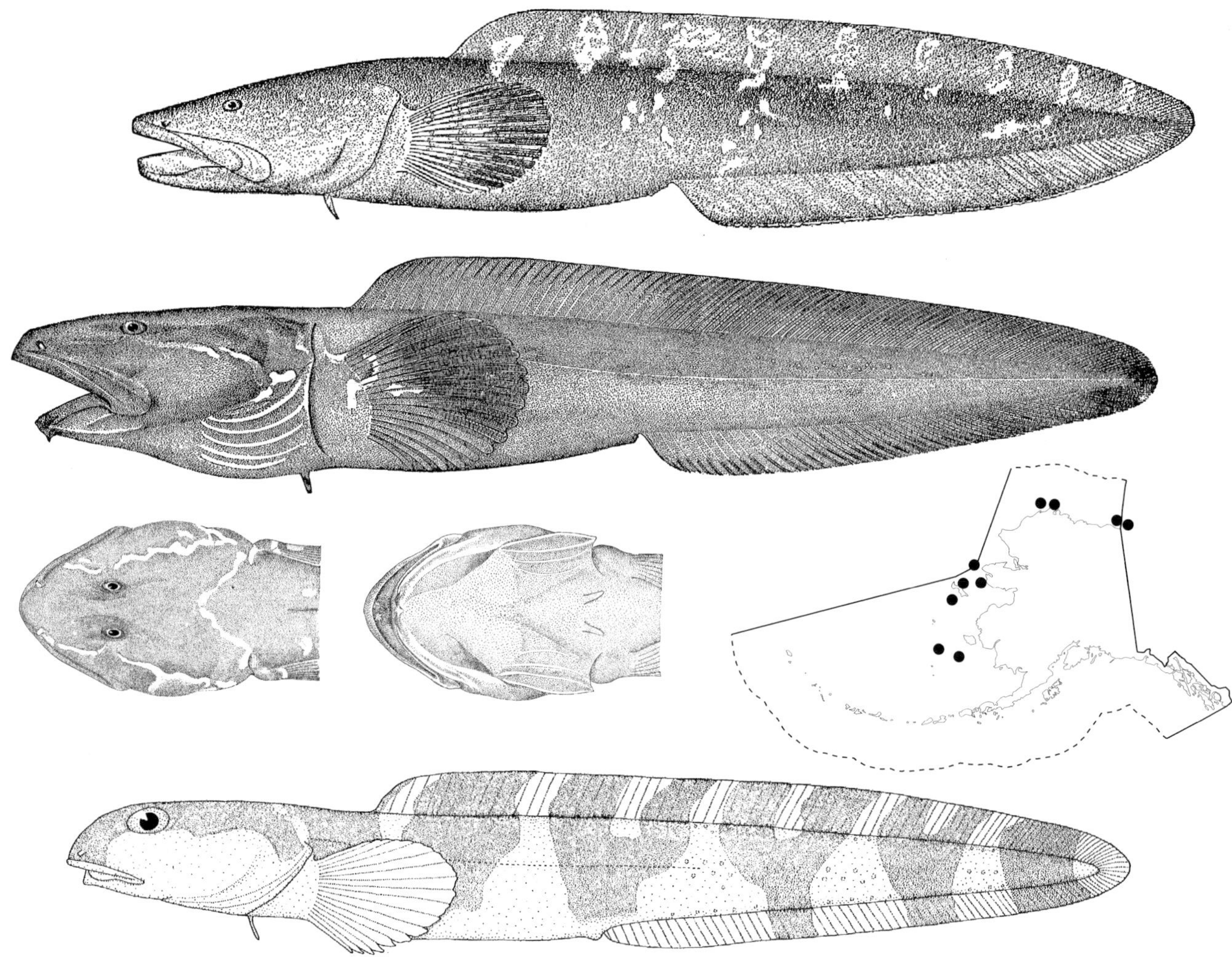

Notes & Sources — *Lycodes mucosus* Richardson, 1855
Lycodes coccineus Bean, 1881
Lycodalepis polaris: Jordan and Evermann 1900, fig. 857 incorrectly labeled (holotype of *Lycodes coccineus* Bean).
Lycodes knipowitschi Popov, 1931
Historically confused in Alaska and adjacent Russian and Canadian Arctic waters with *L. turneri* and *L. polaris.*

Description: Andriashev 1954:278–280; Jensen 1952a:24–26; Toyoshima 1985:195–196, 200–201.

Figures: Top: Jordan and Evermann 1900, fig. 857; USNM 27748, 484 mm TL, off Big Diomede Island, Bering Strait. Middle, with views of head: Goode and Bean 1896, figs. 275, 283a,b; 430 mm TL, Baffin Island. Bottom: Toyoshima 1985, fig. 45; HUMZ 86882, 126.5 mm TL, Bering Strait.

Range: Alaskan records include: Bean (1881a), Big Diomede Island; Andriashev (1954), north of St. Lawrence Island; Quast and Hall (1972), Point Barrow; Toyoshima (1985), Point Barrow and Bering Strait. The UBC has, from north of St. Paul Island: UBC 62-560, 58°21'N, 167°07'W; and UBC 62-562, 58°33'N, 170°12'W. Lot NMC 79-803 is from south of St. Lawrence Island at 62°05'N, 170°17'W, 48 m; and NMC 81-128, Beaufort Sea near Demarcation Bay at 69°40'N, 141°05'W, 13 m. UAM uncataloged: Chukchi Sea at 71°06'N, 158°34'W, depth 52 m, collected 20 Sep. 1991. Closest to Alaska of numerous Canadian Arctic records mapped by Hunter et al. (1984) is Herschel Island.

Size: Andriashev 1954.

Lycodes turneri Bean, 1879 **estuarine eelpout**

Beaufort and Chukchi seas to Bristol Bay in the eastern Bering Sea and to about Cape Olyutorskiy in the western Bering Sea.

Soft bottoms, usually taken shallower than about 50 m, recorded from depths of 10–125 m.

D + 1/2C 85–97; A + 1/2C 67–78; Pec 17–18; Pel 3; Vert 26 + 71 (97–100).

- **Purple, with 10–12 bluish white bands with purplish olive borders, or umber with cream bands and dark umber borders**; underside of head and belly white; anterior bands broken or marbled by intrusion of ground color; first light band curving forward over head, second (variably present) crossing anterior to dorsal fin and joining third band under pectoral fin; **most bands remain distinct in adults**.
- **Head depressed, width about 140% of its depth; interorbital region wide, 10% of head length**.
- **Opercular lobe not prominent**, a weak angle.
- Chin crests well developed, not united anteriorly.
- **Pectoral fin rays 17 or 18, usually 18**.
- Scales absent.
- Lateral line mediolateral.
- Length to 640 mm TL.

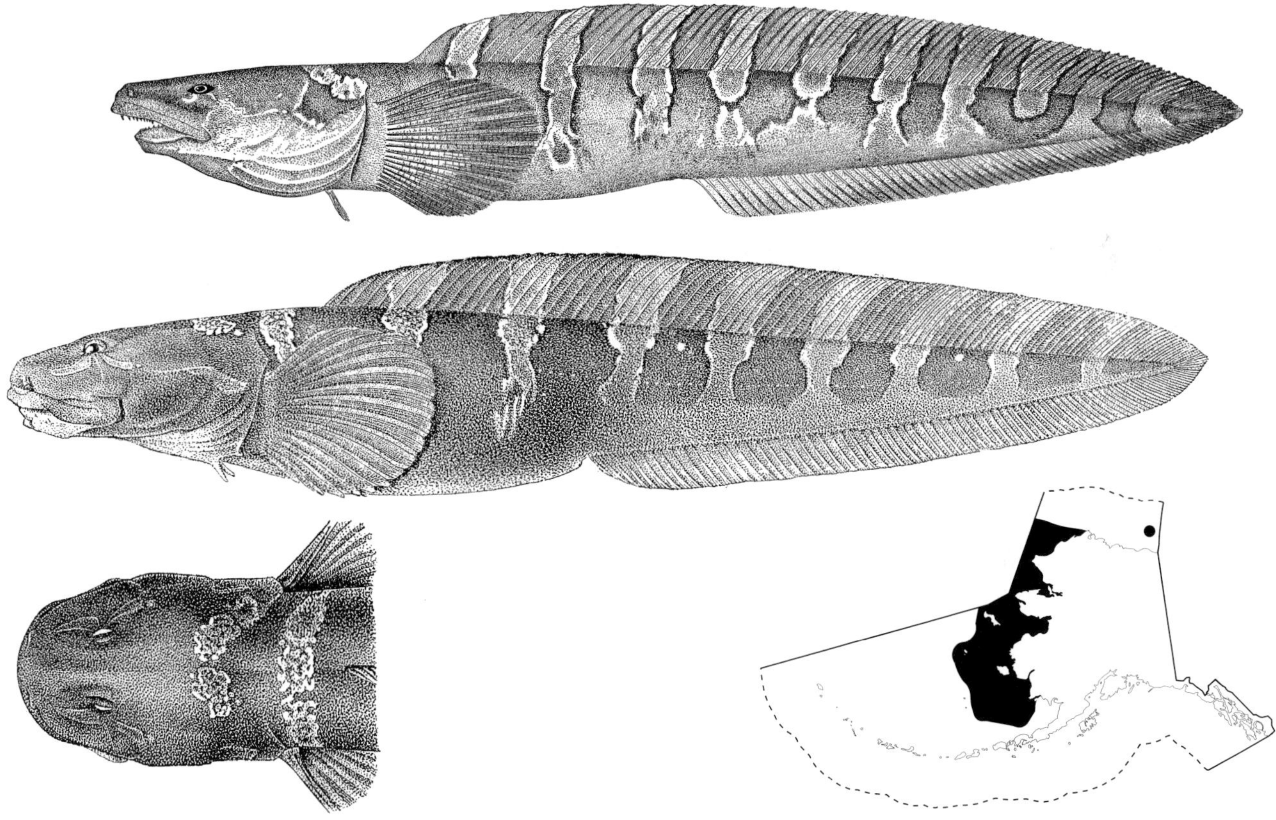

Notes & Sources — *Lycodes turneri* Bean, 1879

Lycodalepis turneri: Jordan and Gilbert 1899, Evermann and Goldsborough 1907.

Frequently confused with *L. mucosus* and *L. polaris*. Andriashev (1973) considered reports of *L. turneri* from the Atlantic Ocean (e.g., Liem and Scott 1966) to represent misidentified *L. polaris*.

The American Fisheries Society (Robins et al. 1991a) calls *L. turneri* the polar eelpout, which we use for *L. polaris*. Estuarine eelpout is the vernacular used for *L. turneri* in Russian literature (B. A. Sheiko, pers. comm., 10 Sep. 1998).

Description: Bean 1879b; Nelson 1887:303; Andriashev 1954:536-537; Schultz 1967 (vertebral counts for type). Frozen, 35-cm specimen from Chukchi Sea near Kivalina (provided by S. C. Jewett and M. Holberg, 17 Nov. 2000) exhibits purple and white coloration originally described by Nelson (1887) from fish collected at Norton Sound.

Figures: Upper: Turner 1886, pl. 4; holotype, USNM 21529, 330 mm TL, St. Michael, Alaska. Lower, including dorsal view of head: Andriashev 1954, figs. 298, 299; 425 mm TL, Gulf of Anadyr, Melkaya Bay, Russia.

Range: Early Alaskan records: Bean (1879b) and Turner (1886), St. Michael; Nelson (1887), Norton Sound; Murdoch (1885) and Scofield (1899), Point Barrow. Allen and Smith (1988) reported it in survey catches from Cape Lisburne to Bristol Bay. The UBC has specimens from Beaufort Sea off Point Franklin at 70°54'N, 141°47'W (UBC 63-1132), and from Chukchi Sea off Barrow and in Kotzebue Sound (UBC 61-74, 61-76, 63-864, 63-1168, 63-1187). Several UAM uncataloged specimens taken in 1989–1991 surveys in eastern Chukchi Sea are *L. turneri* (C.W.M.); northernmost are from 71°06'N, 158°34'W, depth 52 m, to 71°35'N, 163°43'W, depth 42 m; and westernmost was taken at 69°39'N, 167°38'W, depth 46 m. Minimum depth: Sheiko and Fedorov 2000.

Size: Andriashev 1954:537.

Lycodes polaris (Sabine, 1824) **polar eelpout**

Beaufort and Chukchi seas to eastern Bering Sea between Hall Island and St. Lawrence Island and to western Bering Sea off Cape Olyutorskiy; nearly circumpolar along Arctic coasts.

Mud and sandy mud bottoms at depths of 5–236 m, usually taken at 30–150 m.

D + 1/2C 89–94; A + 1/2C 69–76; Pec 15–18; Pel 3; Vert 90–93.

- **Bright orange to light brown**, fading to light tan in preservative; **9–11 dark bands** with light centers across back and dorsal fin, **bands not always well defined**; light band across head uniting gill openings, often separated into 3 spots.
- **Opercular lobe prominent, rounded, projecting posteriorly**.
- Chin crests well developed, not united anteriorly.
- **Pectoral fin rays 15–17, rarely 18**.
- **Scales usually absent**, occasionally present posteriorly on large adults.
- Lateral line mediolateral; widely spaced dorsolateral and predorsal neuromasts.
- Length to about 245 mm TL.

Notes & Sources — *Lycodes polaris* (Sabine, 1824)
Blennius polaris Sabine, 1824
Lycodes agnostus Jensen, 1902
Lycodes turneri atlanticus Vladykov & Tremblay, 1936
Lycodes turneri: Leim and Scott 1966.
Frequently confused with *L. turneri* and *L. mucosus*.
On the American Fisheries Society list (Robins et al. 1991a) *L. polaris* is the Canadian eelpout, but its range is nearly circumpolar and Canadian scientists (e.g., McAllister 1990, Coad 1995) call it the polar eelpout.

Description: Andriashev 1954:272–275; McAllister 1962:27–28; Andriashev in Whitehead et al. 1986:.

Figures: Upper: Andriashev 1954, fig. 143; 180 mm TL, Barents Sea. Lower two: Jensen 1904, pl. 6; 147 mm and 62 mm TL, Kara Sea.

Range: First recorded from Alaska by Andriashev (1954), from Norton Sound. Museum collections contain numerous additional, unreported specimens from Alaska. Many were identified or had their identifications confirmed by eelpout experts M. E. Anderson and D. E. McAllister. The records are numerous enough that we represent range by solid black fill on the above map. Examples, covering the known range off Alaska from southwest to northeast, are: NMC 78-313, 61°49'N, 171°39'W, depth 55 m; NMC 79-811, 61°52'N, 173°29'W, 66 m; UBC 63-1201, 63°06'N, 171°42'W; UBC 61-79, 67°13'N, 167°30'W; UBC 61-103, 68°32'N, 168°52'W; USNM 315543, 69°49'N, 164°10'W, 29 m; UAM uncataloged, collected 19 Sep. 1991, 71°36'N, 163°40'W, 46 m; UBC 63-1206, 71°29'N, 163°09'W; NMC 78-292, 71°45'N, 155°43'W; NMC 74-291, 70°59'N, 149°33'W, 29 m; NMC 78-294, 70°09'N, 141°17'W. Barber et al. (1997) reported *L. polaris* in 1990 survey of northeastern Chukchi Sea, but did not give localities. USNM 315543 (see coordinates above) and several UAM uncataloged specimens are from that survey, and localities are given on the unpublished haul-catch list. Hunter et al. (1984) mapped Canadian Arctic records, some as close to Alaska as the vicinity of Herschel Island.

Size: Andriashev (1954) estimated max. to be 23–24.5 cm TL.

Lycodes raridens Taranetz & Andriashev, 1937 **marbled eelpout**

Chukchi and Bering seas to Bristol Bay; one record from north of Near Islands; off western Bering Sea coasts, including Commander Islands, to Sea of Okhotsk.

Sand and clay bottoms at depths of 8–360 m, rarely deeper than 150 m.

D + 1/2C 83–93; A + 1/2C 72–76; Pec 18–20; Pel 3; GR 13–15; Vert 97.

- Brownish; **body with 7–9 dark bands, reticulate in large specimens; top of head dark, with light spots merging to form mottled or reticulate pattern in adults**; usually with dark oval or triangular spot below eye in pale area; light band, curved forward on top of head, connects gill openings.
- Body depth at origin of anal fin 9–11% TL.
- Chin crests well developed, not united anteriorly.
- **Body covered with scales, except in some Bering and Chukchi sea specimens scales absent from belly and front part of body; scales present on dorsal and anal fins**.
- Lateral line mediolateral.
- **Teeth widely and unequally spaced**.
- Length to 700 mm TL.

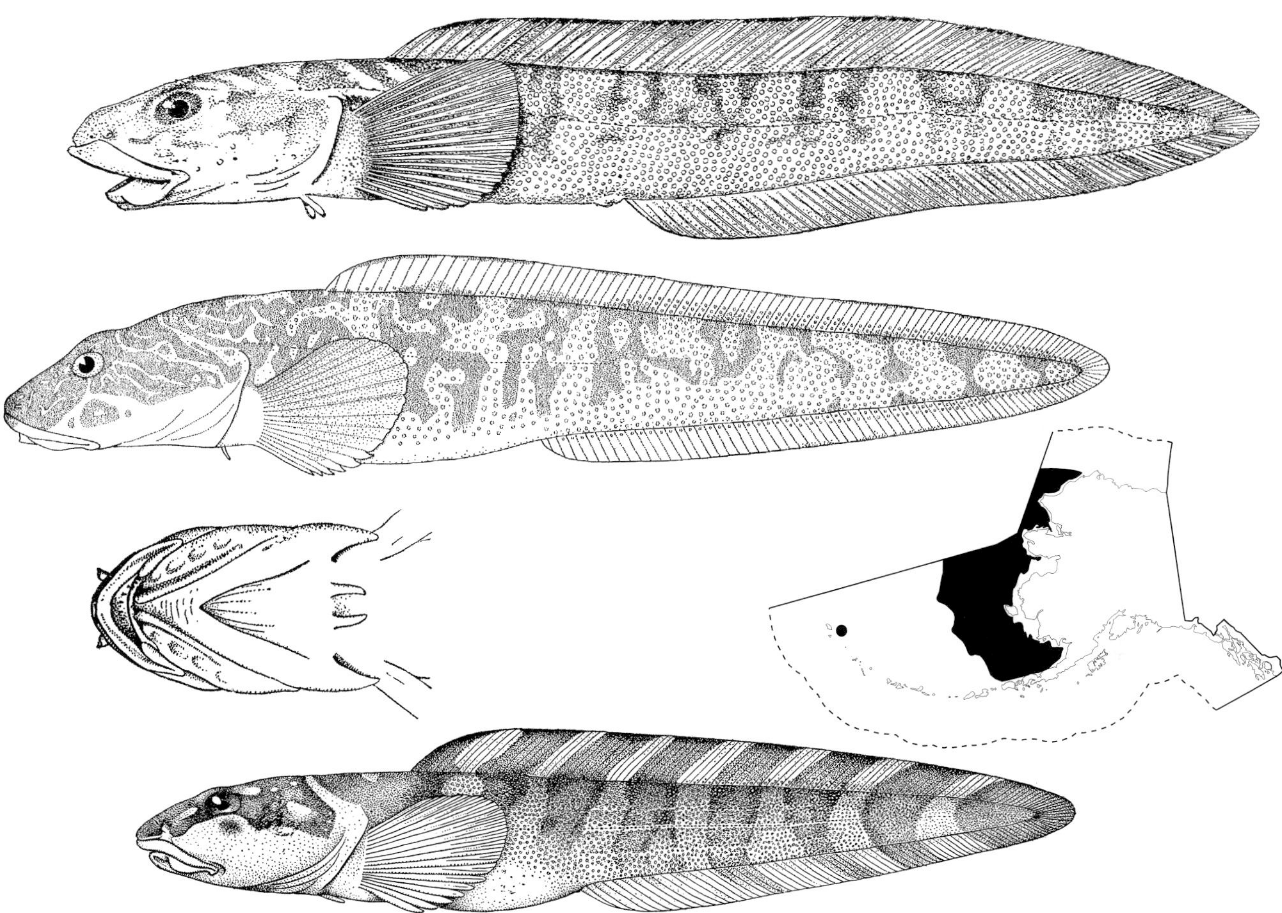

Notes & Sources — *Lycodes raridens* Taranetz & Andriashev in Andriashev, 1937
Lycodes knipowitschi Popov, 1931 (part)

Description: Andriashev 1937:60–63 of transl., 1954:289–291; Lindberg and Krasyukova 1975:162–164; Toyoshima 1985:198–200; Nalbant 1994.

Figures: Top: Schmidt 1950, pl. 5, fig. 2; Sea of Okhotsk. Middle: Toyoshima 1985, fig. 44; female, 200 mm TL, Sea of Okhotsk. Bottom, with ventral view: Andriashev 1937, figs. 14, 15; type, 120 mm TL, Gulf of Anadyr.

Range: Andriashev (1937) recorded specimens from Chukchi Sea southeast of Cape Thompson and Bering Sea southwest of St. Matthew Island. Toyoshima (1985) and Allen and Smith (1988) recorded additional Alaskan localities, including Bristol Bay. Barber et al. (1997) found *L. raridens* to be one of the three most abundant eelpouts (the others were identified as *L. polaris* and *L. palearis*) in surveys of the northeastern Chukchi Sea in 1990 and 1991. Vouchers (UAM uncataloged) from those surveys are from as far north as 70°00'N, 164°56'W, at depth of 38 m (C.W.M.). The unpublished catch list for the 1990 survey gives the northernmost as 71°35'N, 167°47'W, at 48 m. Museum collections contain many examples of *L. raridens* from Alaska. Nalbant (1994) described a specimen taken north of the Near Islands, depth 360 m. Fedorov and Sheiko (2002) reported *L. raridens* to be common at the Commander Islands. Chikilev and Kharitonov (2000) recorded minimum depth: 8–10 m for a 36-cm-TL specimen in brackish water in Anadyr Bay.

Size: Andriashev 1937.

Lycodes reticulatus Reinhardt, 1835 — Arctic eelpout

Arctic Canada to Greenland, south to Gulf of Saint Lawrence and east to Barents, Kara, and Laptev seas. Sandy or muddy bottoms at depths of 20–930 m, usually taken at 380 m or shallower.

D + 1/2C 81–96; A + 1/2C 71–78; Pec 19–21; Pel 3; Vert 93–96.

- Brownish; body with **7–10 dark bands, reticulate in large specimens; light spots on upper side of head form reticulate pattern**; light band across head connecting gill openings.
- Body depth at origin of anal fin 12–14% TL.
- Opercular lobe slightly developed, rounded.
- Chin crests well developed, not united anteriorly.
- Scales cover body behind anal fin origin and extend forward in wedge to about level of dorsal fin origin above lateral line; **scales absent from side anteriorly, belly, and fins**.
- Lateral line mediolateral.
- Length to 760 mm TL.

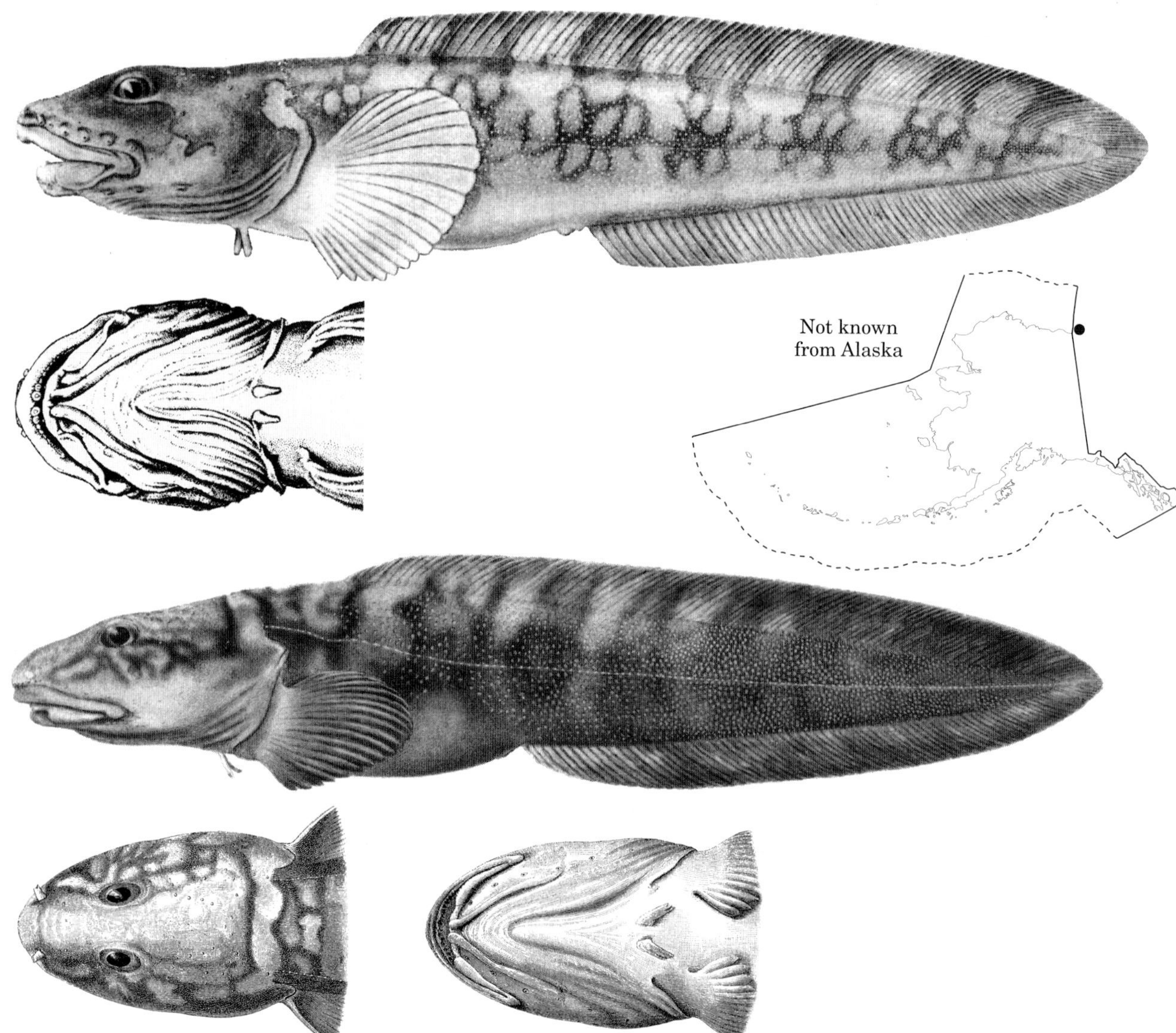

Notes & Sources — *Lycodes reticulatus* Reinhardt, 1835

Most difficult to distinguish from *L. raridens*; also close to *L. rossi*. In *L. reticulatus* and *L. rossi,* scale coverage generally is not as extensive and body is deeper than in *L. raridens*. Teeth are widely spaced in *L. raridens* and close-set in *L. rossi* and *L. reticulatus*.

Description: Jensen 1904:61–70, 1952a:15–18; Andriashev 1954:286–288, 538; Scott and Scott 1988:410–411.

Figures: Upper, with ventral view of head: Andriashev 1954, figs. 158 and 159; male, 365 mm TL, Barents Sea. Lower, with heads: Jensen 1904, pl. 2, fig. 2 and text figs. 9 and 10; male, 255 mm TL, west Greenland.

Range: The nearest records to Alaska are those mapped by Hunter et al. (1984) from east of Herschel Island in Mackenzie Bay and in Franklin Bay, Amundsen Gulf.

Size: Morosova (1982) reported maximum of 76 cm TL, usually 34–60 cm. Andriashev (in Whitehead et al. 1986) gave maximum of 55 cm TL, usually 35–39 cm.

Lycodes rossi Malmgren, 1865 **threespot eelpout**

Chukchi and Beaufort seas off Alaska to Canadian Arctic at Dease Strait; Greenland and Norwegian seas to Kara Sea.

Muddy bottoms; adults taken at depths of 42–365 m, usually deeper than 130 m; juveniles as shallow as 9 m.

D + 1/2C 91–95; A + 1/2C 74–80; Pec 17–20; Pel 3; GR 11–15; Vert 23–25 + 70–75 (95–99).

- Body dark, with 5–9 light bands extending onto dorsal fin, and pale scales; **bands never becoming reticulate** in older fish; light band across top of head, sometimes broken into 2 or 3 spots.
- Body depth at origin of anal fin 9–11% TL.
- **Upper angle of operculum angular, but not elongated**.
- Chin crests well developed, not united anteriorly.
- **Pectoral fin rays usually 18–19**.
- **Scales cover body behind anal fin origin** and extend forward in wedge to about level of dorsal fin origin above lateral line; **scales absent from lower side anteriorly, belly, and fins**.
- Lateral line mediolateral; a few widely spaced dorsolateral and predorsal neuromasts.
- Length to 310 mm TL.

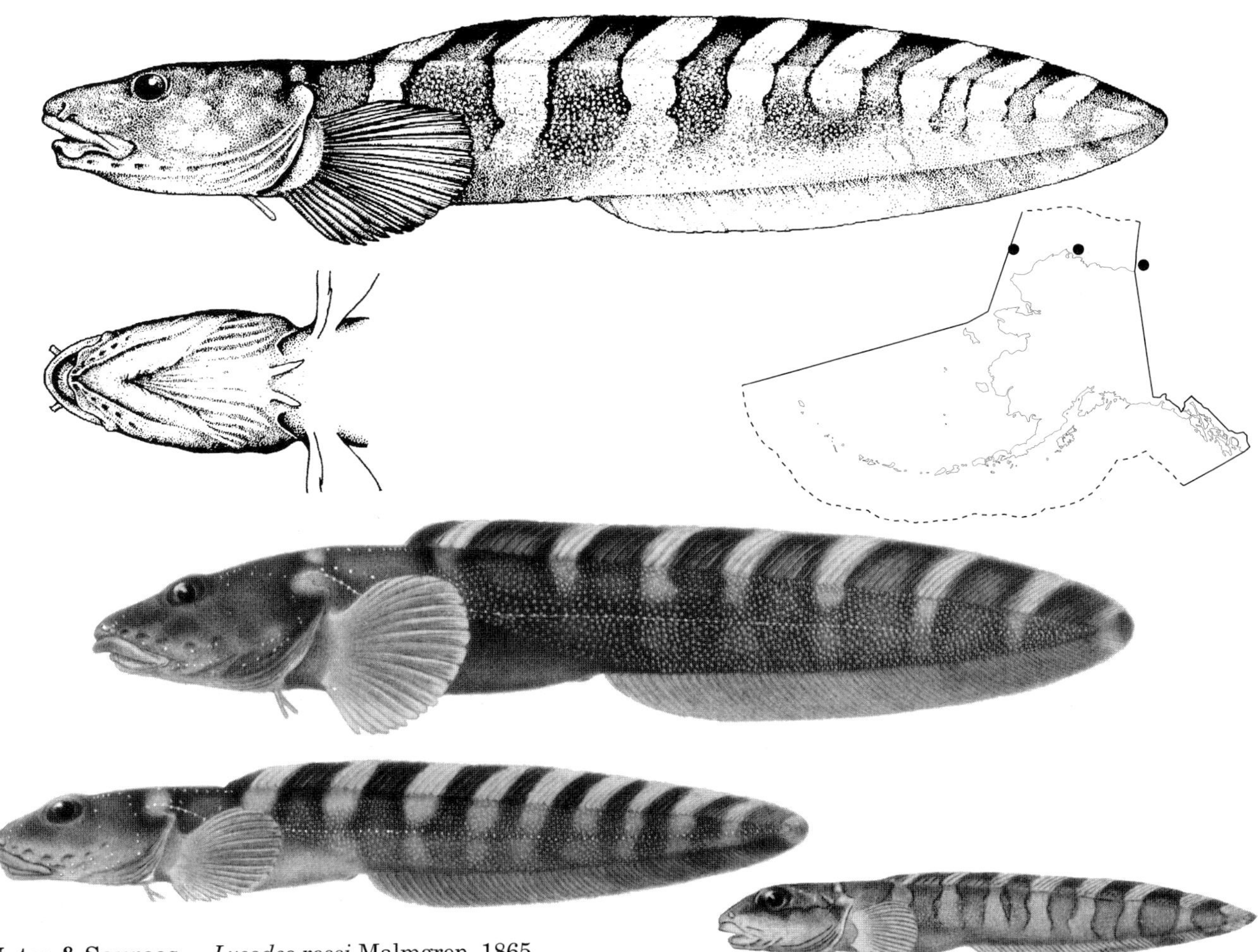

Notes & Sources — *Lycodes rossi* Malmgren, 1865
Most similar to *L. reticulatus* and *L. raridens*. See note for *L. reticulatus*.

Description: Andriashev 1954:284–286; McAllister et al. 1981: 825–827; Andriashev in Whitehead et al. 1986:1143–1144.

Figures: Upper, including ventral view of head: McAllister et al. 1981, fig. 1; NMC 77-976, 223 mm TL, Franklin Bay, Northwest Territories. Lower three: Jensen 1904, pl. 7; 163 mm, 118 mm, and 76 mm TL; Spitsbergen.

Range: Two verifiable records from Alaska: NMC 78-289, a specimen collected by K. J. Frost and L. F. Lowry in Sep. 1978 from the Beaufort Sea about 128 km east of Barrow at 71°19'N, 152°34'W, depth 123 m, and identified by D. E. McAllister; and USNM 315544, collected on 13 Sep. 1990 during a UAF survey of the northeastern Chukchi Sea at 70°29'N, 167°31'W, depth 49 m, and identified by R. Baxter. UAM uncataloged vouchers from the Chukchi Sea surveys of 1990 and 1991 identified as *L. rossi* key out to *L. polaris*; e.g., they have 15 or 16 pectoral fin rays, a prominent opercular lobe, and no scales (C.W.M.). Additional study is needed to sort the records and define range of *L. rossi* in the Alaskan Arctic. The nearest records of occurrence outside Alaska are from just over the Canadian border northeast of Herschel Island, Yukon Territory (McAllister 1962). Several records exist from there to Dease Strait (McAllister et al. 1981, Hunter et al. 1984).

Size: Andriashev 1954.

Lycodes japonicus Matsubara & Iwai, 1951 **Japanese eelpout**

Bering Sea north of Near Islands, Alaska; Sea of Japan off Honshu in Toyama Bay and near Sado Island. Silty bottoms at depths of about 300-303 m.

D 79–84; A 69–73; Pec 14–15; Pel 3; GR 9–13; Vert 19–20 + 68–72 (87–93).

- Light brown; irregular dark brown markings on body, head, and dorsal fin.
- Eye large, 17–23% of head length.
- Chin crests low, united anteriorly.
- Lower pectoral fin rays unbranched, thickened, membranes deeply incised, lower half of fin symmetrical with upper half; **pectoral fin rays 14 or 15**; **pelvic fin long, equal to or greater than eye diameter**, 22–28% of head length, in specimens under about 140 mm TL, becoming relatively shorter in large specimens.
- Scales present on body, including belly, and dorsal and anal fins.
- **Lateral line ventral, incomplete**.
- Length to 340 mm SL.

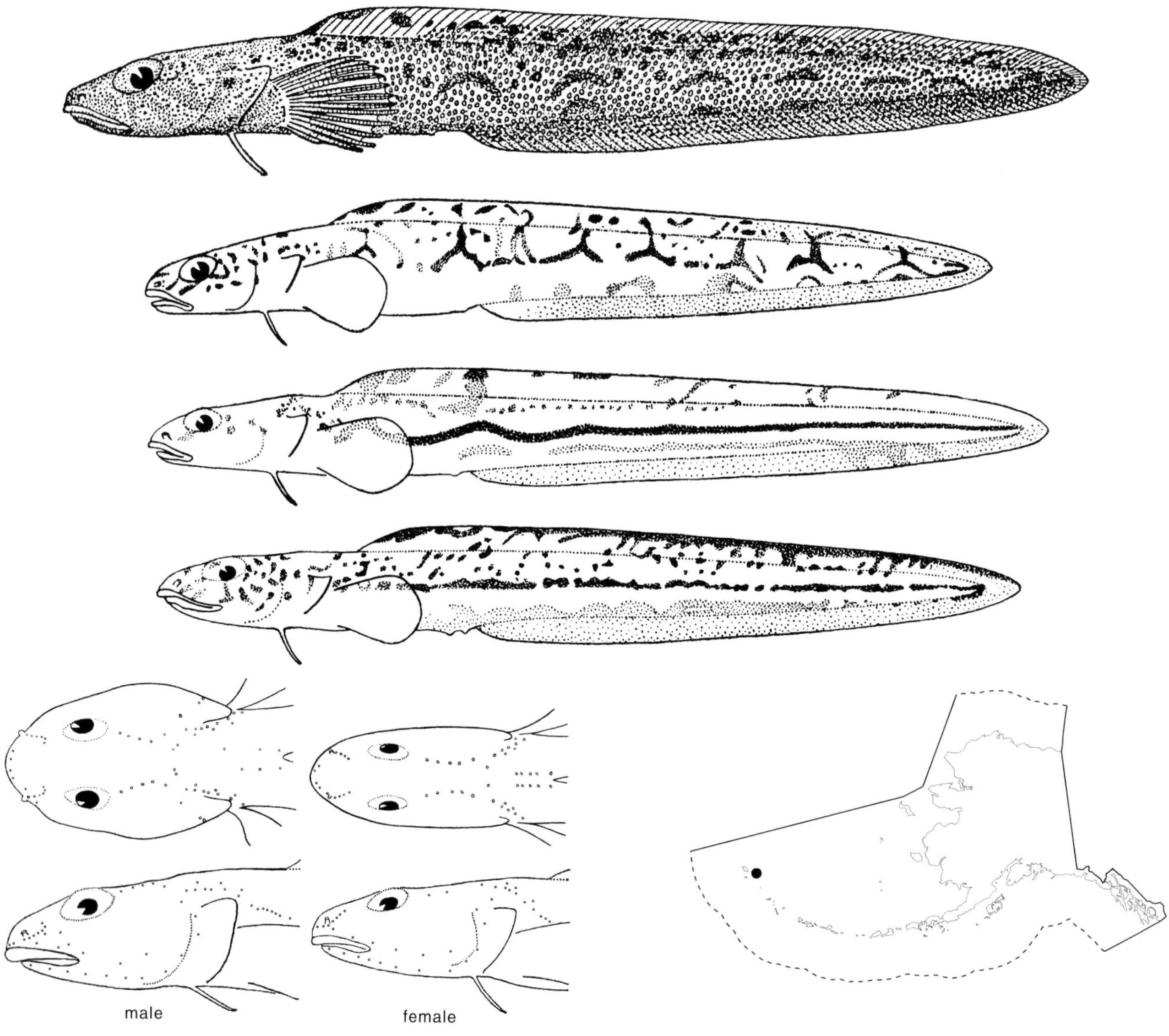

Notes & Sources — *Lycodes japonicus* Matsubara & Iwai, 1951

Description: Matsubara and Iwai 1951; Lindberg and Krasyukova 1975:143–144; Toyoshima 1985:191–192.

Figures: Matsubara and Iwai 1951; Toyama Bay, Sea of Japan. Lateral views, from top: 129, 109, 119, and 116 mm TL. An illustration by Nalbant (1994) of a 360-mm-SL specimen has pelvic fins shorter than eye diameter.

Range: There is one record, comprising one adult female, from Alaska: north of Attu and Agattu islands, taken in 1964 by bottom trawl at depth of about 300 m (Nalbant 1994).

Size: Nalbant 1994. Largest of more than 40 specimens previously recorded was 137 mm TL; considered a "dwarf" species by Matsubara and Iwai (1951).

Lycodes brunneofasciatus Suvorov, 1935 **tawnystripe eelpout**

Eastern Pacific near Unalaska Island; Commander Islands and western Pacific off southeast Kamchatka to south coast of Hokkaido and Sea of Okhotsk.

Bottom at depths of 20–800 m.

D 96–100; A 81–87; Pec 20–22; Pel 3; GR 13–15; Vert 22–23 + 79–86 (101–109).

- Yellowish brown dorsally, mostly gray ventrally; **9 or 10 brown bands on upper part of body, extending onto dorsal fin**; anal fin sometimes with 4 or 5 dark bands; lips, ventral surface of head, margins of lower pectoral fin rays, and base of pectoral fin light; light band over head connecting gill openings; peritoneum brownish.
- **Head gelatinous, large**, 20–25% of total length.
- Chin crests well developed, not united anteriorly.
- Dorsal, anal, and pectoral fins thickened with gelatinous tissue.
- Scales on body and vertical fins; head naked.
- Lateral line ventral, distinct.
- Length to 655 mm TL.

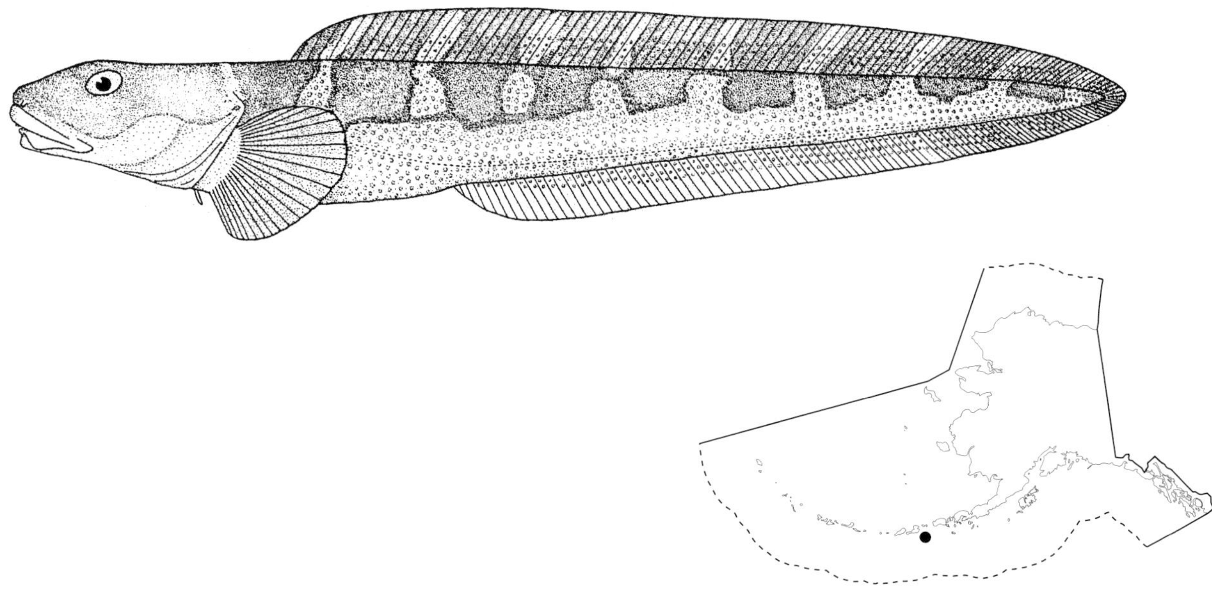

Notes & Sources — *Lycodes brunneofasciatus* Suvorov, 1935

Description: Toyoshima 1985:234–235.

Figure: Toyoshima 1985, fig. 64; HUMZ 56575, male, 353 mm TL, off east coast of Kamchatka.

Range: Only one published Alaskan record, comprising three specimens examined by Anderson (1994): USNM 233629 (345–365 mm SL), from southeast of Unalaska Island at 53°34'N, 165°42'W, depth 348 m. Fedorov and Sheiko (2002) reported new minimum and maximum known depths (20–800 m); previously reported from depths of 88–490 m by Toyoshima (1985). Fedorov and Sheiko (2002) gave first report of occurrence off the Commander Islands. USNM 117931 is from south coast of Hokkaido, taken in 1906 by the *Albatross*; record not previously published.

Size: Toyoshima 1985.

Lycodes brevipes Bean, 1890 — shortfin eelpout

Bering Sea from east of Cape Navarin to Unalaska Island, to eastern Pacific off Fort Bragg, California; and western Bering Sea south to Cape Afrika.

Sandy or muddy bottoms at depths of 27–973 m.

D 93–99; A 78–81; Pec 19–21; Pel 3; GR 11–15; Vert 20–22 + 79–82 (99–103).

- Brown or gray-brown, paler ventrally; lower part of head cream or tan, in some specimens clearly demarcated from dark upper part; up to 13 **narrow light bands** on body and dorsal fin; light band crossing occipital region; light bands sometimes lacking; dorsal and anal fins with dark margins.
- **Chin crests low**, not united anteriorly.
- **Pelvic fin short**, less than half of eye diameter; pectoral fin rounded or slightly indented, with upper rays longest and lower pectoral rays thickened and, in some specimens, slightly exserted.
- Scales cover body and bases of dorsal and anal fins; head naked.
- Lateral line ventral, indistinct.
- Length to 328 mm TL.

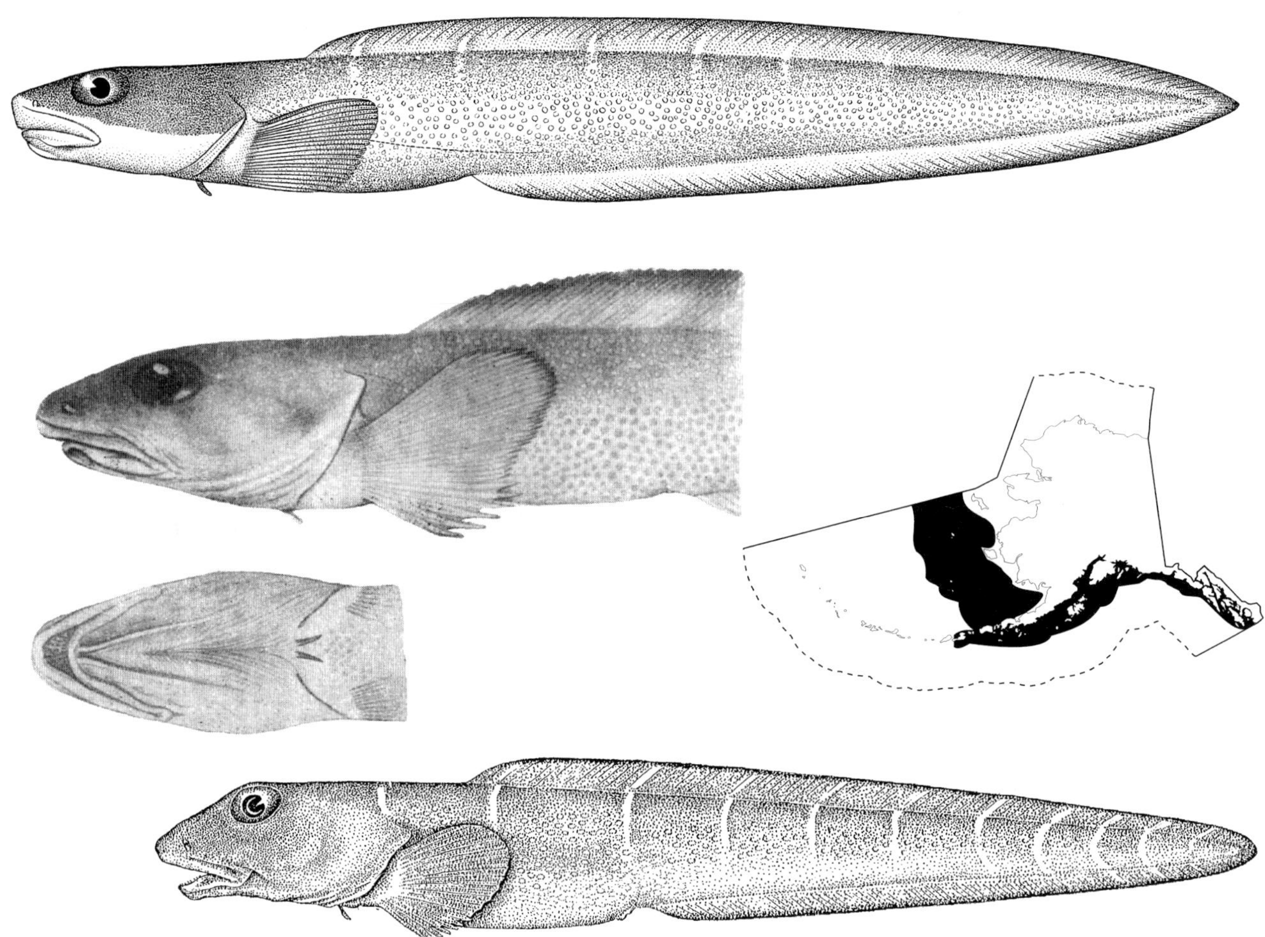

Notes & Sources — *Lycodes brevipes* Bean, 1890
Lycodes brevipes diapteroides Taranetz & Andriashev in Andriashev, 1937
Toyoshima (1985) and Sheiko and Fedorov (2000) treat *L. diapteroides* as a distinct species occurring off Russian coasts from Cape Afrika to Bering Strait, but the published descriptions and treatments by Taranetz and Andriashev (in Andriashev 1937), Schmidt (1950), and Anderson (1994) indicate recognition as a form of *L. brevipes* is more appropriate.

Description: Bean 1890b:38; Andriashev 1937:57–60 of transl.; Hart 1973:242; Toyoshima 1985:233–234.

Figures: Above: Smithsonian Institution, NMNH, Division of Fishes, artist S. F. Denton, 1890; lectotype, 243 mm TL, between Unga and Nagai islands, Alaska. Anterolateral and ventral views: Andriashev 1937, figs. 11 and 12; *L. brevipes diapteroides*, Bering Sea east of Cape Navarin. Below: Hart 1973:242; UBC 62-480, 180 mm TL, Alaska.

Range: Numerous Alaskan records have been documented in the literature since Bean's (1890b) original description, and museum collections include many additional, unpublished records. Allen and Smith (1988) mapped occurrences in NMFS surveys of eastern Bering Sea and North Pacific.

Size: Toyoshima 1985 (HUMZ 76784).

Lycodes sagittarius McAllister, 1976 — archer eelpout

Beaufort Sea, Alaska; Franklin Bay, Northwest Territories; and Kara Sea.

Mud and clay bottoms at depths of 335–600 m.

D + 1/2C 95–107; A + 1/2C 81–92; Pec 16–18; Pel 3; GR 12–15; Vert 19–21 + 77–88 (96–109).

- **Uniformly dark brown or with light bands on back and dorsal fin**; black peritoneum.
- Head length 20–23%, body depth at origin of anal fin 9–11%, and preanal length 37–42% of total length.
- Chin crests well developed, not united anteriorly.
- **Pelvic fin longer than eye diameter**.
- Scales cover body, including belly, and extend onto vertical fins.
- **Lateral line ventrolateral, strongly bowed anteriorly**, usually distinct; widely spaced dorsolateral and predorsal neuromasts.
- Length to 278 mm TL.

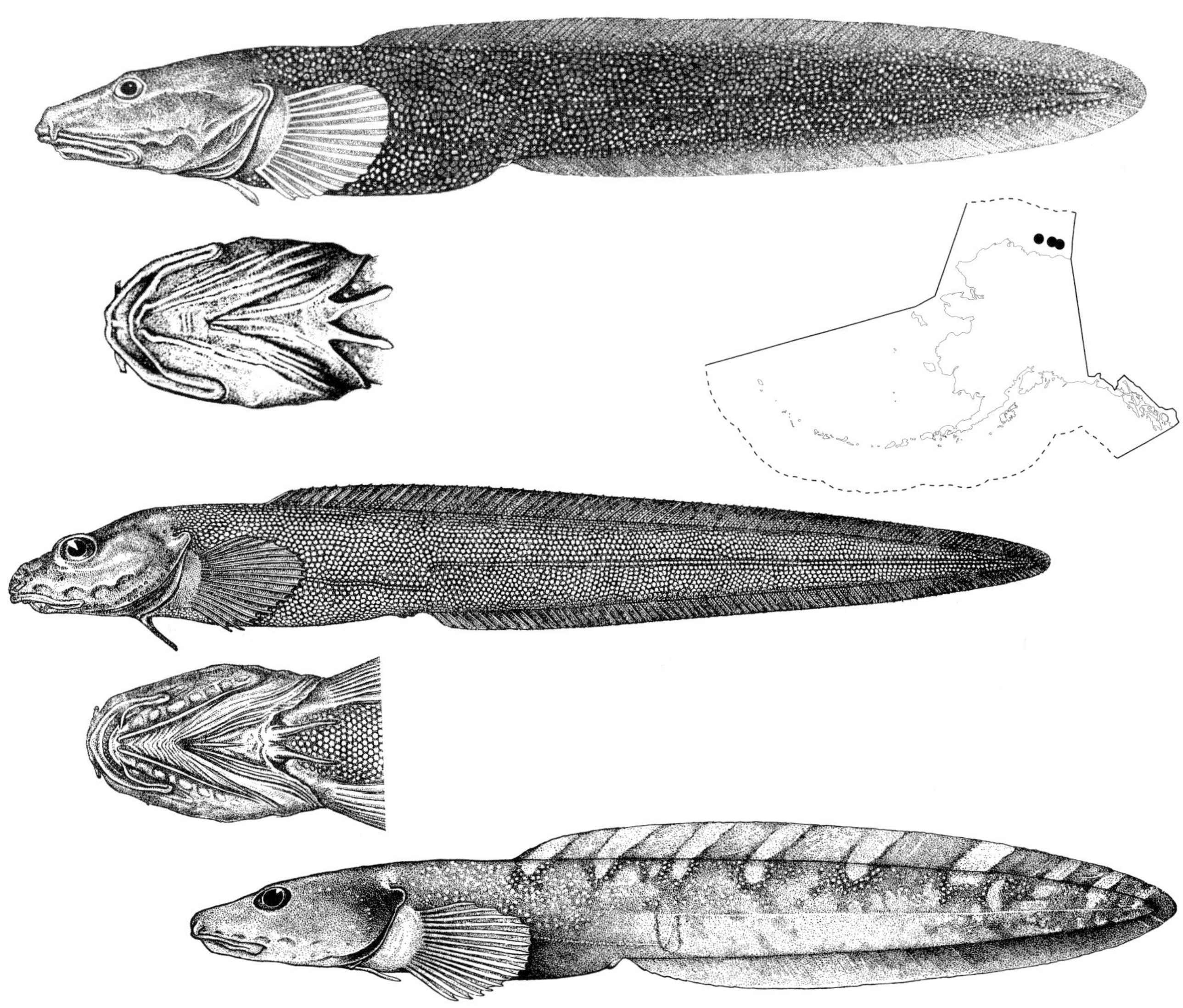

Notes & Sources — *Lycodes sagittarius* McAllister, 1976
Lycodes squamiventer (non-Jensen): Andriashev 1954:297–298 (in part: Kara Sea specimens).

Description: Andriashev 1954:297–298 (Kara Sea specimens); McAllister 1976; McAllister et al. 1981:828–829.

Figures: Top, with ventral view: McAllister 1976, fig. 1; holotype, NMC 74-282, male, 278 mm TL, Beaufort Sea, Alaska. Middle, with ventral view: Andriashev 1954, figs. 167, 169; male, 179 mm TL, Kara Sea. Bottom: McAllister et al. 1981, fig. 3; NMC 77-976, 180 mm TL or less, Franklin Bay, Northwest Territories.

Range: McAllister (1976) described the only specimens known from Alaska, taken by otter trawl in water depths of 357–600 m in Beaufort Sea at 70°43'N, 143°42'W; 70°51'N, 145°17'W; and 71°13'N, 148°34'W. Nearest record outside Alaska is from Franklin Bay, Northwest Territories, over 700 km to the east.

Size: McAllister 1976.

Lycodes soldatovi Taranetz & Andriashev, 1935 **dipline eelpout**

Bering Sea to Okhotsk and Japan seas.
Bottom at depths of 154–1,030 m.

D 91–106; A 76–87; Pec 20–23; Pel 3; GR 15; Vert 20–25 + 76–83 (96–106).

- **Uniformly blackish brown.**
- Head length 23–26%, body depth at origin of anal fin 10–13%, and preanal length 41–49% of total length.
- Chin crests well developed, not united anteriorly.
- **Pelvic fin shorter than eye diameter.**
- Scales cover body, including belly, and extend onto vertical fins.
- **Lateral line ventrolateral**, usually distinct.
- Length to 671 mm TL.

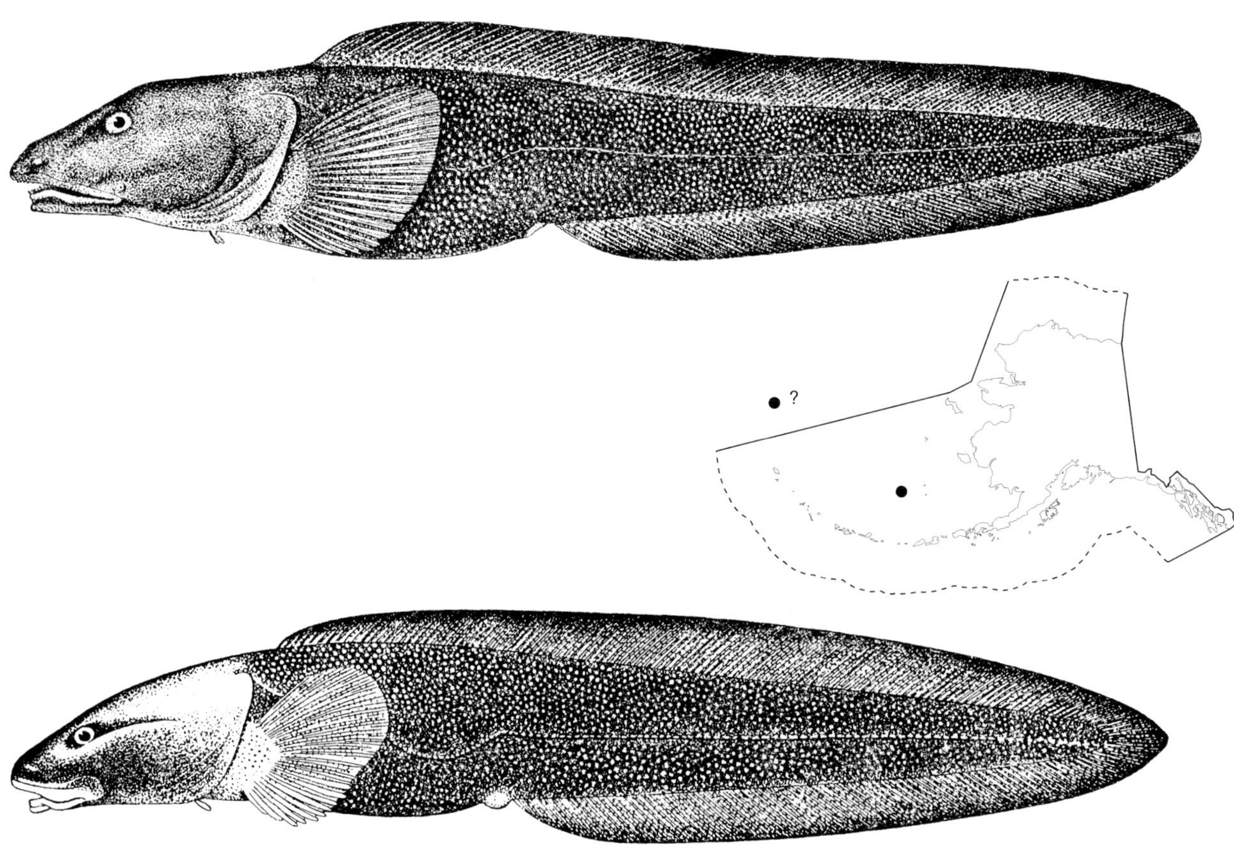

Notes & Sources — *Lycodes soldatovi* Taranetz & Andriashev, 1935

Similar in appearance to *Lycodes concolor* and for a time thought to be the same. However, the two forms are distinguishable, primarily by lateral line configuration (ventrolateral in *L. soldatovi* vs. ventral in *L. concolor*), and taxonomists (e.g., Anderson 1994 and pers. comm., 17 Feb. 1998; Fedorov and Sheiko 2002) currently treat them both as distinct species.

Description: Taranetz and Andriashev 1935b:246–248; Lindberg and Krasyukova 1975:153–155; McAllister 1976: 13; Toyoshima in Amaoka et al. 1983:264, 331; Toyoshima 1985:207–208.

Figures: Upper: Schmidt 1950, pl. 6, fig. 2; Sea of Okhotsk. Lower: Lindberg and Krasyukova 1975, fig. 120, after Taranetz and Andriashev 1935b; 560 mm TL, Sea of Okhotsk.

Range: Previously reported to be common off Alaska (e.g., Allen and Smith 1988), but those reports were due to confusion with *L. concolor.* Andriashev (1937) reported that a specimen from Olyutorskiy Bay at Leningrad State University looked like *L. soldatovi* but that the identification was uncertain. Lindberg and Krasyukova (1975) listed two specimens (ZIN 37978) collected from the Bering Sea in 1963 by V. V. Fedorov, but they did not give a more specific locality. Anderson (1984, 1994) examined one of the specimens (380 mm SL), confirming the identification. The dot on the above map within the Alaska boundary represents that collection (ZIN 37978), for which Anderson's (pers. comm., 1 Dec. 1998) data read "southeastern Bering Sea" and "1963 *Adler* collection." New specimens from the Bering Sea should be preserved for confirmation of identification so that the range can be more precisely defined.

Size: Toyoshima in Amaoka et al. 1983.

Lycodes palearis Gilbert, 1896 **wattled eelpout**

Chukchi Sea, over the continental shelf in the Bering Sea and off the Aleutian Islands to Oregon; and to Sea of Okhotsk.

Muddy or sandy bottoms at depths of 25–925 m; almost always taken in waters shallower than 200 m, and usually less than 150 m.

D 97–106; A 81–88; Pec 17–19; Pel 3; GR 12–18; Vert 23–25 + 83–90 (106–114).

- Brown, lighter ventrally; head and vertical and pectoral fins darker than sides of body; **several light bands on body and dorsal fin; 2 light bars in front of dorsal fin**, with anterior bar joining the gill openings; **bars faint or absent in large specimens; black blotch on anterior margin of dorsal fin**, can disappear with growth.
- **Chin crests well developed, high, projecting anteriorly**, not united; labial lobe unusually well developed.
- Pectoral fin long, rounded, lower rays thickened and often slightly exserted; **pelvic fin shorter than eye diameter but longer than pupil**.
- Scales extending onto head to line connecting gill openings and onto dorsal and anal fins; belly densely scaled.
- Lateral line ventrolateral, the ascending part indistinct or absent.
- Length to 538 mm TL.

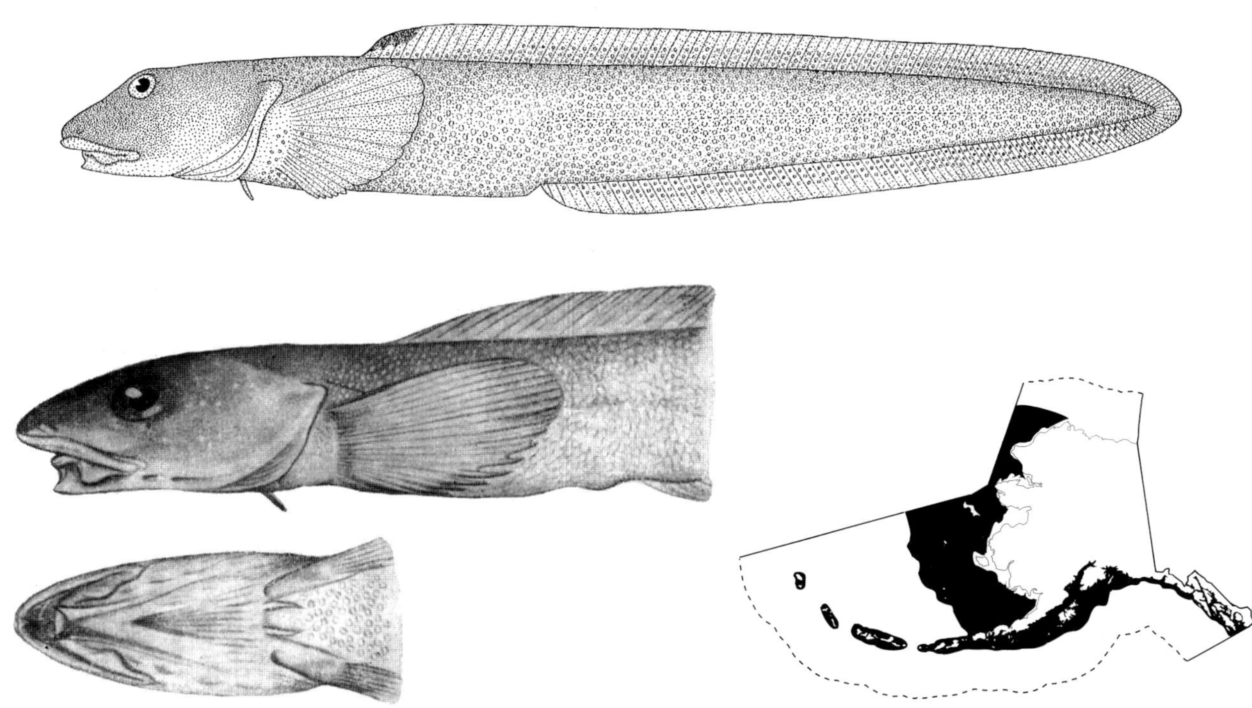

Notes & Sources — *Lycodes palearis* Gilbert, 1896
Lycodes digitatus Gill & Townsend, 1897
Lycodes palearis palearis Gilbert: Andriashev 1937, Taranetz 1937.
Lycodes palearis arcticus Taranetz & Andriashev in Andriashev, 1937

Description: Gilbert 1896:454–455; Gill and Townsend 1897: 232–233; Andriashev 1937:54–57 of transl., 1954:291–293; Toyoshima 1985:212–214.

Figures: Upper: Toyoshima 1985, fig. 50; HUMZ 67489, male, 339 mm TL, Bering Sea. Lower: Andriashev 1954, fig. 162; *L. palearis arcticus,* Bering Sea east of Cape Navarin.

Range: The type locality for *Lycodes palearis* Gilbert, 1896 is Bristol Bay, *Albatross* stations 3253 and 3254. There are numerous published and unpublished records of this species from Alaska, although it is possible that some records pertain to the closely related *L. fasciatus.* Allen and Smith (1988) mapped occurrences from 30 years of NMFS demersal surveys in the eastern Bering Sea and North Pacific but, again, some could have been *L. fasciatus.* Barber et al. (1997) found *L. palearis* to be one of the three most abundant eelpouts (the others were identified as *L. polaris* and *L. raridens*) taken by the UAF in bottom trawl surveys of the northeastern Chukchi Sea in 1990 and 1991. Voucher specimens (UAM uncataloged) from the UAF surveys are from localities as far north as 70°14'N, 166°04'W, at depth of 46 m. The northernmost Alaskan record may be UBC 63-1188, taken off Point Barrow at about 71°23'N, 156°28'W. Depth: Allen and Smith (1988) reported a maximum depth of 925 m, but 96% of the catches (N = 2,477 occurrences) were from no deeper than 200 m.

Size: Baxter 1990ms; Baxter's data include measurements of several large *L. palearis* collected by NMFS and UAF surveys. Hart (1973) reported maximum length of 510 mm TL.

Lycodes fasciatus (Schmidt, 1904) **banded eelpout**

Southern Bering Sea to western Pacific off southeast coast of Kamchatka, Sea of Okhotsk, and northern Sea of Japan.

Bottom at depths of 25–340 m, usually shallower than 200 m.

D 96–105; A 80–89; Pec 17–18; Pel 3; GR 11–15; Vert 23–28 + 78–90 (101–115).

- Color in alcohol dark gray, lighter ventrally; **many light bands on body and dorsal fin, usually with some shaped as cogs pointed upward, especially anteriorly; 2 light bands in front of dorsal fin**; some bands remain in adults; **black blotch on anterior margin of dorsal fin**, disappearing with growth in some individuals.
- Chin crests well developed, not united anteriorly.
- Pelvic fin shorter than eye diameter.
- Scales extending onto head to or a little beyond line connecting upper ends of gill openings; scales present on belly and vertical fins, including the greater parts of the fins posteriorly.
- Lateral line ventrolateral.
- Length to 431 mm TL.

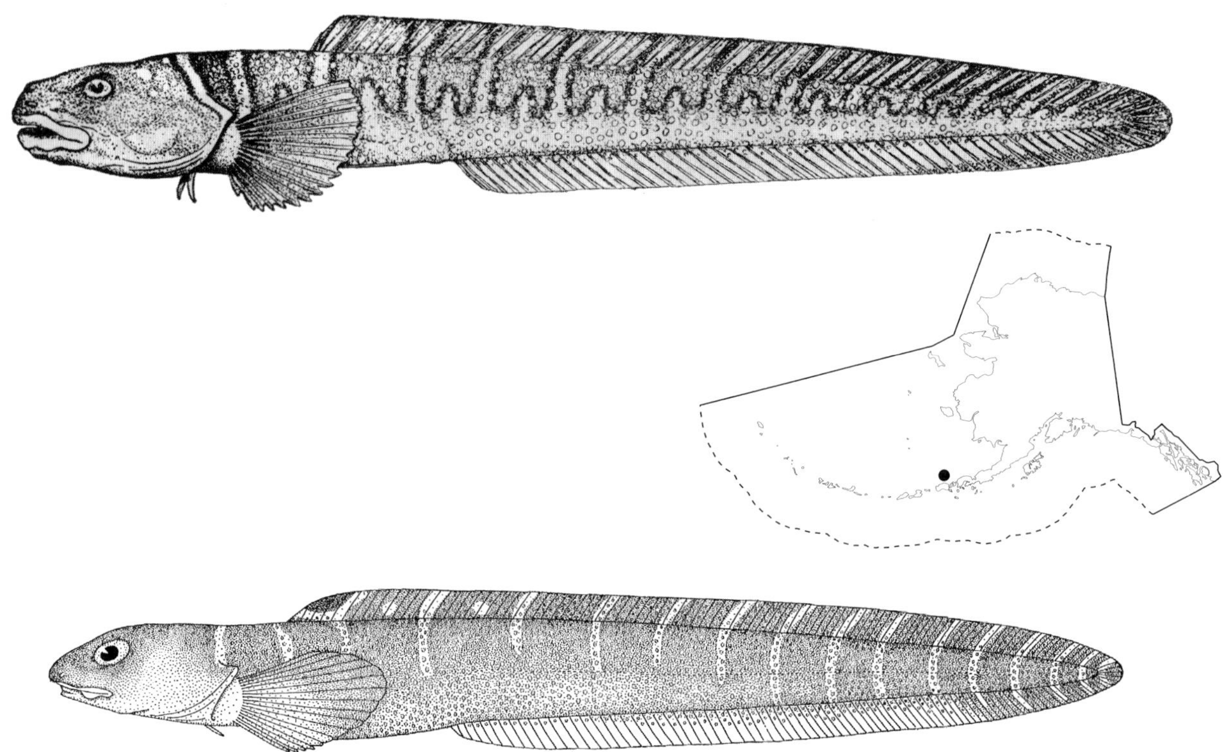

Notes & Sources — *Lycodes fasciatus* (Schmidt, 1904)
Lycenchelys fasciatus Schmidt, 1904
Lycodes palearis fasciatus (Schmidt, 1904)
Lycodes palearis multifasciatus Schmidt, 1950

Toyoshima (1985) treated both *L. multifasciatus* and *L. fasciatus* as species, not as subspecies of *L. palearis* as Schmidt (1950) had done. Anderson (1994) accepted them as species distinct from *L. palearis* but commented (pers. comm., 17 Feb. 1998) on the need for more data on pores, lateral lines, teeth, gill rakers, and other characters, especially in the Sea of Okhotsk types, to better describe the differences. Having studied the types and other specimens (B.A. Sheiko, pers. comm., 25 Sep. 1998), Sheiko and Fedorov (2000) treat *L. multifasciatus* as a synonym of *L. fasciatus,* and *L. fasciatus* as distinct from *L. palearis. Lycodes fasciatus* is highly variable, with, for example, the shape and number of cogs and bands differing by age, geography, and sex; as well, the light marks partly disappear in preservative.

Description: Schmidt 1950:93–96; Lindberg and Krasyukova 1975:158; Toyoshima 1985:214–216.

Figures: Upper: Schmidt 1950, pl. 7, fig. 2; length not reported, between 212 and 298 mm TL; Sea of Okhotsk. Lower: Toyoshima 1985, fig. 51; HUMZ 56526, male, 155 mm TL, Sea of Okhotsk.

Range: Toyoshima (1985) recorded one specimen from southeastern Bering Sea: HUMZ 76612, 55°34'N, 164°45'W, depth 98–100 m; as well as two from western Pacific off Bering Island and southeast Kamchatka, and many from Sea of Okhotsk. Other specimens from the Bering Sea off Alaska and Russia probably exist in museum collections, but attributed to *L. palearis.*

Size: Toyoshima 1985.

Lycodes pallidus Collett, 1879 **pale eelpout**

Beaufort Sea off Alaska, east through Canadian Arctic, and south to Labrador and Gulf of St. Lawrence; Greenland eastward to Laptev Sea; nearly circumpolar in Arctic seas.

Muddy or clay and stone bottoms at depths of 12–1,750 m; often in shallow water, less than 60 m, off Siberia and Alaska, usually at 60–980 m elsewhere.

D + 1/2C 92–104; A + 1/2C 79–91; Pec 17–21; Pel 3; Vert 96–104.

- Pale, yellowish brown; adults more or less uniformly colored; juveniles with 6–12 dark bands, more distinct on dorsal fin than on body and disappearing with age; belly and posterior border of gill cover dark in adults; peritoneum brownish black, visible through body wall in young.
- Preanal length 41–45% of total length.
- Chin crests low, not projecting anteriorly, not fused.
- Pelvic fin shorter than eye length.
- Scales on body extend anteriorly to base of pectoral fin; **scales absent from belly**, head, nape, and fins.
- **Lateral line double, incomplete**; ventral disappearing above anal rays 10–20; mediolateral less distinct, consisting of widely spaced superficial neuromasts extending from above anus to caudal fin.
- Length to 260 mm TL.

Notes & Sources — *Lycodes pallidus* Collett, 1879

Description: Jensen 1904:38–39, 1952a:14–15; Walters 1953b:4–5; Andriashev 1954:293–295 (*L. pallidus pallidus*); McAllister 1962:26. Range of 90–93 for vertebral counts reported by Andriashev (in Whitehead et al. 1986) may be an error; earlier, Andriashev (1954) gave counts of 96–104 from radiographs.

Figures: Jensen 1904, pl. 4; 186 mm, 161 mm, and 102 mm TL; Norwegian Sea.

Range: Specimens from Beaufort Sea in National Museums of Canada collection at Ottawa comprise the first records from Alaska: NMC 74-279, 1 specimen, 89 mm TL, from west of Barter Island at 70°10'N, 144°33'W, depth 27 m; and NMC 74-287, 5 specimens, 59–172 mm TL, from east of Cross Island at 70°30'N, 147°33'W, depth 29 m. Both lots were identified by M. E. Anderson in Aug. 1978. Two other NMC lots from Alaskan Beaufort Sea were tentatively referred by D. E. McAllister and M. E. Anderson to this species, and are not included on above map because of the uncertainty: NMC 78-302, 1 specimen, 119 mm TL, north of Cape Halkett at 71°09'N, 150°17'W, depth 42 m; and NMC 74-285, 8 specimens, 42–192 mm TL, north of Maguire Islands at 70°21'N, 146°32'W, depth 27 m. B. W. Coad (pers. comm., 5 May 1999) provided lengths for the NMC specimens. Nearest literature record outside Alaska is a 114-mm-TL specimen taken southeast of Herschel Island, Yukon Territory (McAllister 1962). Møller and Jørgensen (2000) reported the first specimens taken off western Greenland; previous reports for that region were misidentifications.

Size: Andriashev in Whitehead et al. 1986.

Lycodes squamiventer Jensen, 1904 — scalebelly eelpout

Beaufort Sea off Alaska; Davis Strait off western Greenland; Greenland Sea, Norwegian Sea to north of Faroe–Shetland slope, Barents Sea.

Muddy bottoms at depths of 357–1,808 m.

D + 1/2C 94–99; A + 1/2C 81–87; Pec 17–21; Pel 3; GR 14–15; Vert 19–21 + 77–84 (97–104).

- Light to dark grayish brown with no bands or other marks, except top of head somewhat lighter; peritoneum black.
- Preanal length 38–41% of total length.
- Chin crests low, rectangular or slightly projecting anteriorly and not fused.
- Pelvic fin shorter than eye length, but longer than in *L. pallidus*.
- **Scales cover body, including belly**, extend onto two-thirds of height of dorsal and anal fins.
- **Lateral line double, incomplete**; ventral long, extending almost to end of body; mediolateral frequently indistinct, extending from above anus to caudal fin.
- Length to 260 mm TL.

Notes & Sources — *Lycodes squamiventer* Jensen, 1904
Lycodes pallidus squamiventer Jensen, 1904
Kara Sea records of Andriashev (1954:295, figs. 167 and 169) are not included because they are a different species (McAllister et al. 1981:832).

Description: Jensen 1904:39–40; McAllister 1976:14; McAllister et al. 1981:832–833; Andriashev in Whitehead et al. 1986:1145–1146.

Figures: Jensen 1904, pl. 4, figs. 2a,b; 230 mm and 147 mm TL, Norwegian Sea.

Range: McAllister et al. (1981) described a specimen (NMC 74-282A) that was caught 85 km northeast of Brownlow Point, Alaska, at 70°51'N, 145°17'W, at a depth of 357 m. The nearest record outside Alaska comprises two specimens taken between Baffin Island and Greenland in Davis Strait at 66°32'N, 59°04'W, at a depth of 700 m (Andriashev in Whitehead et al. 1986). Previous to those records the species was known only from the Norwegian Sea at depths of 982–1,750 m (Jensen 1904). Specimens collected during an expedition using a Russian ship in June–August 1998 by M. E. Anderson (pers. comm.,18 Dec. 1998) from the Norwegian Sea at 1,015–1,808 m and the Greenland and Barents seas at 1,250–1,400 m extend the recorded geographic and depth ranges.

Size: Jensen 1904.

Lycodes eudipleurostictus Jensen, 1902 **doubleline eelpout**

Beaufort Sea north of Kaktovik, Alaska; eastern Canada and western Greenland from Smith Sound to Davis Strait; off Iceland; Greenland to Kara seas, north to Svalbard and Severnaya Zemlya.

Muddy bottoms at depths of 25–975 m, rarely found in waters shallower than about 250 m.

D + 1/2C 100–112; A + 1/2C 88–96; Pec 19–23; Pel 3; GR 15–16; Vert 22–23 + 86–91 (105–112).

- Dark brown; **5–13 narrow light bands** (9–10 in the two Alaskan specimens) passing onto dorsal fin and, posteriorly, onto anal fin; sometimes with light band across nape; **bands simple even in large specimens**, not forming complex patterns; black peritoneum makes belly bluish black in young.
- Preanal length less than 44% (37–41%) of total length.
- Chin crests low, not united anteriorly.
- **Pectoral fin emarginate, forming weakly expressed lower lobe**.
- Scales on body, including belly, and extending onto dorsal and anal fins; scales absent from nape, head, and pectoral fin base and axil.
- **Lateral line double, complete**; becomes double almost immediately behind apex of gill opening; not always easily discernible.
- Length to 445 mm TL.

Notes & Sources — *Lycodes eudipleurostictus* Jensen, 1902

Description: Jensen 1902:206, 1904:32–37, 1952a:11–14; Andriashev 1954:298–300; McAllister et al. 1981:830–832; Andriashev in Whitehead et al. 1986:1138–1139; Saito and Okamura in Okamura et al. 1995:195.

Figures: Jensen 1904, pl. 3; 260 mm and 75 mm TL, Norwegian Sea.

Range: Only Alaskan record comprises two specimens taken north of Kaktovik at 70°43'N, 143°43'W, at depth of 464 m. Nearest record outside Alaska is from the eastern Canadian high Arctic off south tip of Ellesmere Island at Jones Sound at 75°54'N, 81°01'W, depth 610 m (Jensen 1952a:13). (Specimens taken off southeastern tip of Baffin Island in Davis Strait at 68°22'N, 59°30'W, 552 m [Møller and Jørgensen 2000], may be second record from Canada, not first as claimed by authors.) Found at numerous localities off western Greenland from Smith Sound (78°14'N, 74°10'W, 672 m) to Davis Strait (e.g., Jensen 1952a). Minimum depth: McAllister et al. (1981), southwest Greenland at 25–260 m; although fish might not have entered net at shallow end of the tow, the 260-m maximum depth of tow is shallower than most other records. Møller and Jørgensen (2000) reported minimum depth of 188 m and maximum of 975 m off western Greenland. Maximum previously reported was 550–914 m in Norwegian Sea, by Collett (1905).

Size: Jensen 1952a. Other authors round to 45 cm.

Lycodes diapterus Gilbert, 1892 — black eelpout

Bering Sea from Navarin Canyon along continental slope and west along Aleutian Islands to Attu Island, to Pacific Ocean off San Diego, California; and to Okhotsk and Japan seas.

Muddy bottoms at depths of 13–1,300 m; usually taken at 100–850 m.

D 105–113; A 92–96; Pec 17–21; Pel 3; GR 14; Vert 19–23 + 92–100 (111–125).

- Pearly, with fine black spots or dusky brown dorsally and blue-black ventrally; **3–9 pale bars extending onto dorsal fin and spreading or dividing on body, faint or lacking in adults**; pectoral, pelvic, and anal fins blue-black; light spots over scales; sometimes with black blotch at anterior end of dorsal fin; mouth, gill cavity, and peritoneum dusky or black.
- **Head small, 17–21% of total length**.
- Preanal length 34–37% of total length.
- Chin crests weakly developed, united anteriorly.
- **Pectoral fin emarginate or notched, forming weak to strong lower lobe**; notch increasing in depth with age.
- Scales cover entire body and vertical fins; scattered scales present on basal half of pectoral fin; no scales on head.
- **Lateral line ventral**.
- Length to 371 mm TL.

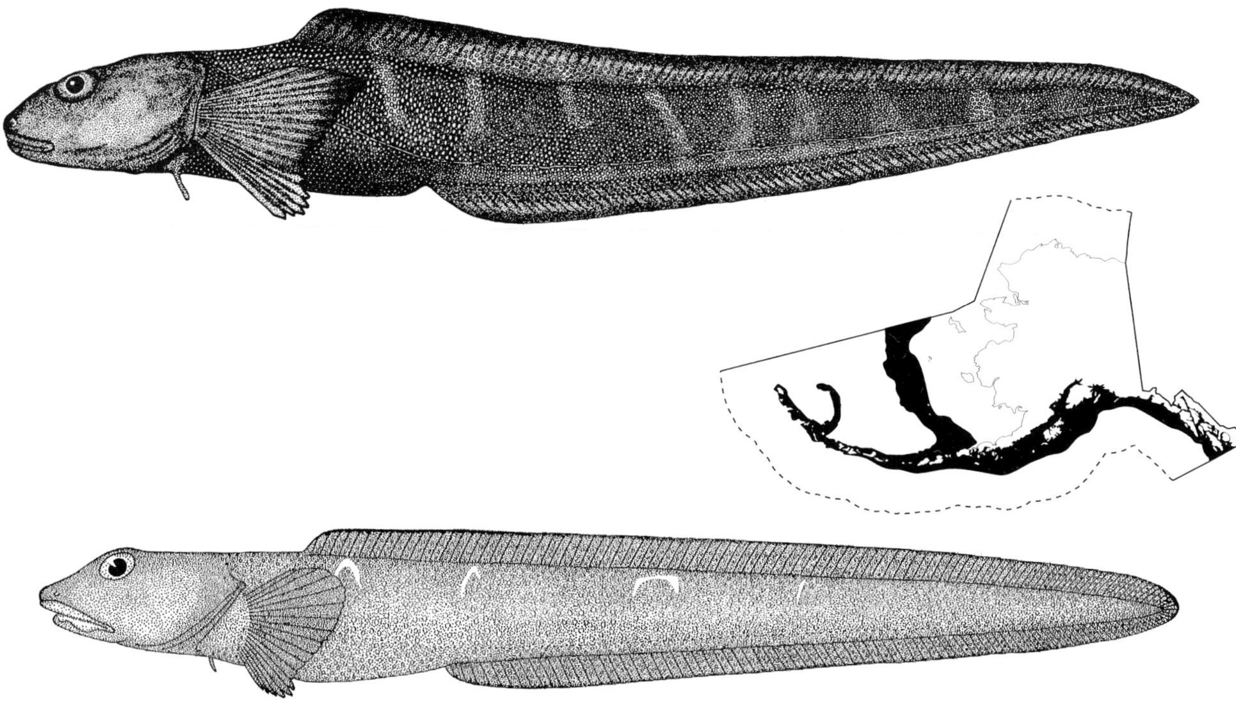

Notes & Sources — *Lycodes diapterus* Gilbert, 1892
Furcimanus diaptera: Jordan and Evermann 1898.
Lycodes (*Furcimanus*) *diapterus beringi* Andriashev, 1935
The genus *Furcimanus,* later used as a subgenus, was erected to reflect the notched pectoral fin of *L. diapterus.* Although other species treated in this guide, including *L. brevipes, L. palearis,* and *L. eudipleurostictus,* sometimes have more or less emarginate pectoral fins they are not closely related; emargination is not as strongly or consistently expressed in them as in other species that seem to form a natural group, including *L. pectoralis* and *L. nakamurae* (Asian species, not known from Alaska).

Description: Gilbert 1892:564–565; Jordan and Evermann 1898:2472–2473; Clemens and Wilby 1961:387–388; Toyoshima 1985:230–231; Matarese et al. 1989:498. The count of 25 pectoral fin rays reported by Miller and Lea (1972) and Matarese et al. (1989) is exceptionally high and is probably an error. The highest count previously reported was 21, by Gilbert (1892). Toyoshima (1985) gave a range of 17–19 from numerous specimens, and M. E. Anderson (pers. comm., 1 Dec. 1998) found the same range in a sample of 30 specimens from Japan and 45 from Oregon and California.

Figures: Upper: Anderson 1994, fig. 127; RUSI 31499, 245 mm SL, Bering Sea. Lower: Toyoshima 1985, fig. 61; HUMZ 56662, male, 317.5 mm TL, Sea of Okhotsk.

Range: Numerous published Alaskan records from Gilbert (1892; syntype, USNM 46716, from Sitka) to Toyoshima (1985; many from Bering Sea) as well as unpublished records in museum collections. Allen and Smith (1988) mapped range from 30 years of NMFS trawl surveys.

Size: Toyoshima 1985.

Lycodes concolor Gill & Townsend, 1897 **ebony eelpout**

One eastern Chukchi Sea record; eastern Bering Sea from Navarin Canyon along continental slope to Aleutian Islands and west to Stalemate Bank, and south of Aleutian Islands to western Gulf of Alaska off Kodiak Island; western Bering Sea to southern Sea of Okhotsk and northern Kuril Islands.

Bottom at depths of 42–1,025 m; usually taken at 250–850 m.

D + 1/2C 117–118; A + 1/2C 98–99; Pec 21; Pel 3; GR 12–14; Vert 22 + 92-93 (114–115).

- Uniformly dark brown to black, **no light bars or blotches**; fin margins darker; scales lighter than ground color.
- **Head large, 20–25% of total length.**
- Preanal length 40–43% of total length.
- Chin crests well developed, not united anteriorly.
- **Pectoral fin rounded, not notched or emarginate, middle rays longest.**
- Body covered with very small scales, entirely separated; scales extending in front of dorsal fin and onto vertical fins; pectoral fin with scattered scales near base; area of smaller scales behind base of pectoral fin and a naked area around upper axil.
- **Lateral line ventral**; in fresh and well-preserved specimens distantly spaced (1–2 cm) superficial neuromasts may be discernible along the mediolateral line of the body.
- Length to about 800 mm TL.

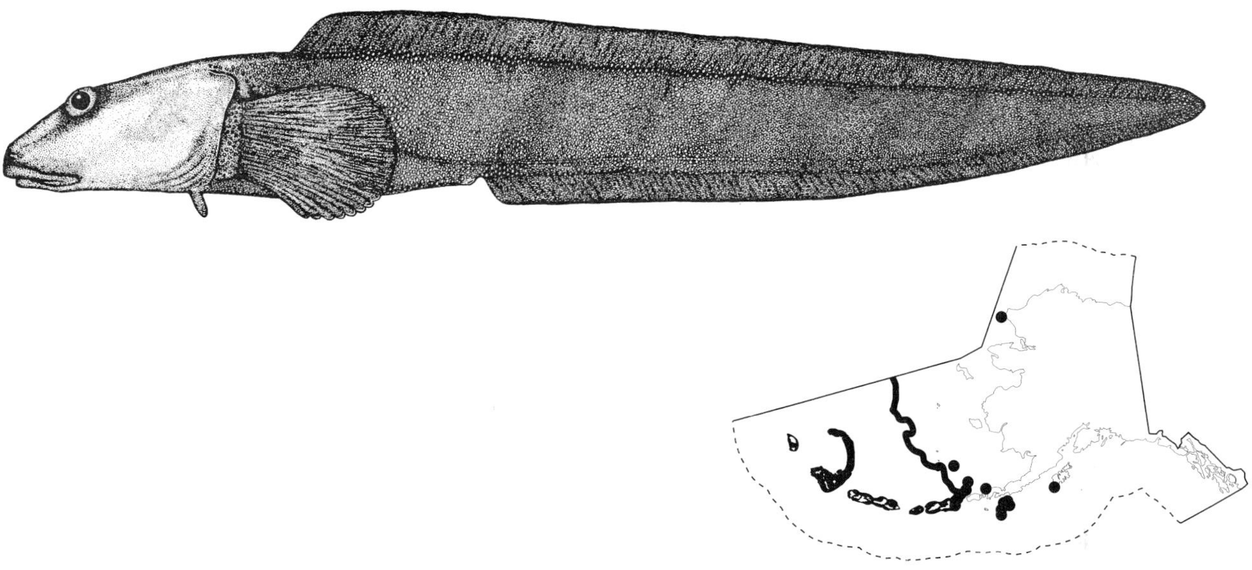

Notes & Sources — *Lycodes concolor* Gill & Townsend, 1897
Lycodes andriashevi Fedorov, 1966

Description: Gill and Townsend 1897:233; Jordan and Evermann 1898:2463–2464; Fedorov 1966; Schultz 1967 (vertebral counts for holotype); Toyoshima 1985:235 (from Fedorov's [1966] description of *L. andriashevi*); Matarese et al. 1989:498 (fin ray and gill raker counts). Not adequately described in the literature. B. A. Sheiko (pers. comm., 17 Oct. 1998) described chin crests as well developed (height about 3 mm), with anterior ends rounded and about 4 mm apart at the bases (KIE 2014, 3 specimens, 640–645 mm TL). See color plate section in this book, which shows specimens from the eastern Bering Sea.

Figure: Anderson 1994, fig. 127; RUSI 31502, 448 mm SL, Bering Sea.

Range: Gill and Townsend 1897: holotype, USNM 48764, Bering Sea, *Albatross* station 3608, 55°19'N, 168°11'W, 505 m. Other USNM specimens are from eastern Bering Sea (USNM 221068, 221077, 221083, 221088, 221094, 221099, 221100, 221104; 420-820 m) and south of the Aleutian Islands (USNM 233919, 52°27'N, 169°33'W, depth 514 m). The UBC has collections from off Point Hope at 68°43'N, 166°23'W (UBC 63-1207); several eastern Bering Sea localities (UBC 62-564, 65-709, 65-713, 65-714, 65-716, 65-717, 65-735); Pacific Ocean south of Unga Island at 55°04'N, 160°47'W (UBC 65-85), and near Nagai Island at 54°33'N, 160°55'W (UBC 65-94); and in vicinity of Kodiak Island off Sitkalidak Island at about 57°07'N, 153°14'W (UBC 65-46), and Alitak Bay, 56°53'N, 154°W (UBC 65-723). The LACM has specimens from the eastern Bering Sea at 54°57'N, 166°02'W, depth 76 m (LACM 35752-4); and 55°15'N, 165°16'W, depth 61 m (LACM 35768-2). Distribution of 189 occurrences in NMFS surveys of eastern Pacific and Bering Sea was reported by Allen and Smith (1988); 96% were between 250 and 800 m. Sheiko and Fedorov (2000) reported a depth range of 125–880 m for catches from Cape Navarin to southeast Kamchatka.

Size: Glubokov and Orlov (2000) reported an average length of 62 cm for 31 specimens collected in 1998 in the western Bering Sea. The largest was a male about 80 cm long (exact length not reported). A specimen measuring 760 mm TL was taken in a 1985 NMFS survey of the eastern Bering Sea at 54°37'N, 165°54'W, depth 391–399 m (Baxter 1990ms and unpubl. data).

Lycodes frigidus Collett, 1879 **glacial eelpout**

Chukchi and East Siberian continental rises, Canadian Basin, Norwegian and Greenland seas north of Faroe–Shetland Ridge, northern part of Laptev Sea, and Eurasian Arctic Basin.

Muddy bottoms at depths of 475–2,750 m, possibly to 3,000 m; mostly taken at depths of 1,000–1,800 m.

D + 1/2C 99–104; A + 1/2C 85–90; Pec 19–21; Pel 3; GR 15; Vert 21–24 + 81–85 (103–107).

- **Uniformly colored at all ages dark brownish gray, brown, or gray-violet**, except darkest on lower part of head, gill membranes, and dorsal and anal fin margins.
- **Head large, 22–28% of total length**.
- Preanal length 43–47% of total length.
- Chin crests barely evident in adults, not united anteriorly.
- **Pectoral fin ovoid, not notched or emarginate, upper rays longest**.
- **Scales very small**, 50 rows or more between anal fin origin and base of dorsal fin; scales cover body forward to pelvic fins and nape; **scales absent from vertical fins**, except present on base of vertical fins in largest specimens; scales first appearing in late juveniles, 10–11 cm TL.
- **Lateral line ventral**.
- Length to 690 mm TL.

Notes & Sources — *Lycodes frigidus* Collett, 1879

Glacial eelpout was suggested by Prouse and McAllister (1986) as a new common name to replace coldwater eelpout, which, they remarked, could apply to almost any eelpout.

Description: Jensen 1904:22–25; Andriashev 1954:302–305; Schultz 1967 (vertebral counts for USNM syntype); McAllister et al. 1981:829–830; Andriashev in Whitehead et al. 1986:1139; Prouse and McAllister 1986.

Figures: Upper: Andriashev 1954, fig. 172; 510 mm TL, Greenland Sea. Lower: Jensen 1904, pl. 5; 232 mm and 50.5 mm TL, Norwegian Sea.

Range: Probably widely distributed in the great depths of the central part of the Arctic Ocean. Currently known patchy distribution is probably due to lack of sampling in deep Arctic waters. Nearest record to Alaska is from Chukchi rise at 77°38'N, 172°43'W, depth 2,215 m. An eelpout in a bottom photograph taken on the Chukchi rise at 78°28'N, 171°01'W, depth 2,653 m, is probably *L. frigidus* also (McAllister et al. 1981).

Size: Nizovtsev et al. 1976.

Pachycara bulbiceps (Garman, 1899) **snubnose eelpout**

Eastern North Pacific Ocean off Queen Charlotte Islands, British Columbia, Oregon, and Guadalupe Island, Mexico, to Gulf of Panama; both sides of North Atlantic Ocean.

Brown and green mud bottoms at depths of 2,400–4,780 m; in North Pacific, at 2,601–4,000 m.

D 104–114; A 86–97; C 8–12; Pec 16–19; Pel 0; GR 11–19; Vert 25–31 + 82–91 (112–119).

- More total vertebrae than in *P. gymninium.*
- Chin crests absent.
- More dorsal and anal fin rays than in *P. gymninium*; **pectoral fin rays usually 17–18; pelvic fin absent**.
- **Scales absent from nape**.
- Head pores small.
- **Lateral line double**; **mediolateral branch originating posterior to pectoral fin margin**.
- Length to 525 mm SL.

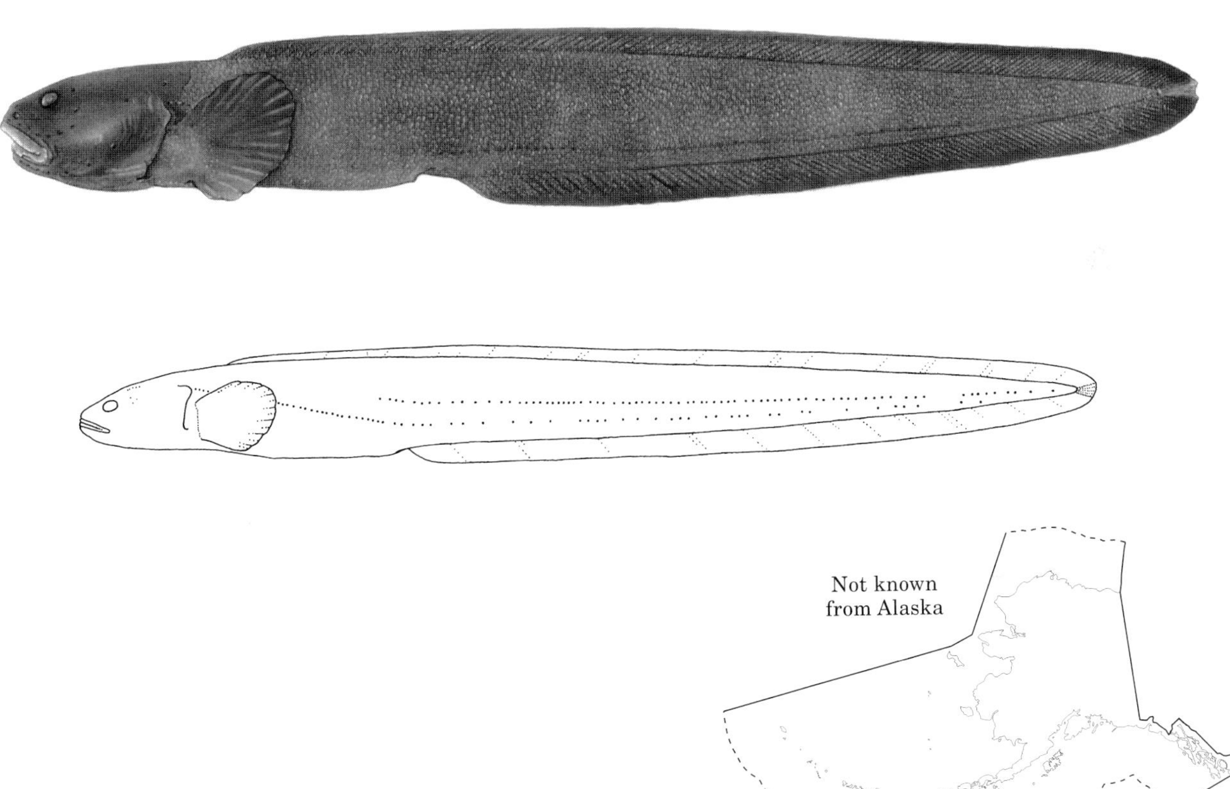

Notes & Sources — *Pachycara bulbiceps* (Garman, 1899)
Maynea bulbiceps Garman, 1899

Description: Garman 1899:140; Anderson and Peden 1988: 84–88.

Figures: Anderson and Peden 1988. Upper: fig. 1; BCPM 980-99, 518 mm SL, off Queen Charlotte Islands (reproduced from original illustration provided by A. E. Peden; artist P. Drukker-Brammall, Dec. 1981). Lower: fig. 2; CAS 55588, 338 mm SL, Gulf of Panama.

Range: Nearest record to Alaska is BCPM 980-99, taken west of Tasu Sound, Queen Charlotte Islands, British Columbia, at 52°38'N, 132°05'W, depth 2,780 m.

Pachycara gymninium Anderson & Peden, 1988 **nakednape eelpout**

Eastern North Pacific Ocean off Queen Charlotte Islands, British Columbia, and Oregon to vicinity of Guadalupe Island, Mexico; Gulf of California.

Brown and green mud bottoms at depths of 1,829–3,219 m. Often taken in traps and trawls with *P. lepinium.*

D 96–103; A 77–84; C 10–12; Pec 14–18; Pel 3; GR 13–19; Vert 28–31 + 73–80 (102–109).

- Fewer caudal and total vertebrae than in *P. bulbiceps,* and usually fewer than in *P. lepinium.*
- Chin crests absent.
- Fewer anal fin rays than in *P. bulbiceps* and *P. lepinium*; **pectoral fin rays usually 17–18**; **pelvic fin present**.
- **Scales absent from nape or not extending anterior to line connecting anterodorsal edges of gill slits**.
- Head pores small.
- **Lateral line double**; **mediolateral branch originating in pectoral axil**.
- Length to 422 mm SL.

Notes & Sources — *Pachycara gymninium* Anderson & Peden, 1988

Description: Anderson and Peden 1988:88–91.

Figure: Anderson and Peden 1988, fig. 5; holotype, USNM 280121, 422 mm SL, off Queen Charlotte Islands (reproduced from original illustration provided by A. E. Peden; artist P. Drukker-Brammall, Nov. 1981).

Range: Nearest record to Alaska is the holotype, taken west of Tasu Sound, Queen Charlotte Islands, British Columbia, at 52°38'N, 132°06'W, in black-cod trap at depth of 2,744 m.

Pachycara lepinium Anderson & Peden, 1988 — **scalynape eelpout**

Eastern North Pacific Ocean off Queen Charlotte Islands, British Columbia, and Oregon to vicinity of Guadalupe Island, Mexico.

Brown and green mud bottoms at depths of 1,728–2,970 m. Often taken in traps and trawls with *P. gymninium*.

D 99–113; A 85–98; C 9–12; Pec 15–18; Pel 3; GR 12–19; Vert 23–26 + 80–94 (105–120).

- Fewer precaudal vertebrae than in *P. bulbiceps* from the Pacific Ocean and in *P. gymninium*.
- Chin crests absent.
- More anal fin rays and usually more dorsal fin rays than in *P. gymninium*; **pectoral fin rays usually 15–16**; **pelvic fin present**.
- **Scales present on nape**, extending to interorbital region.
- Head pores small.
- **Lateral line double**; **mediolateral branch originating at or just posterior to pectoral fin margin**.
- Length to 597 mm SL.

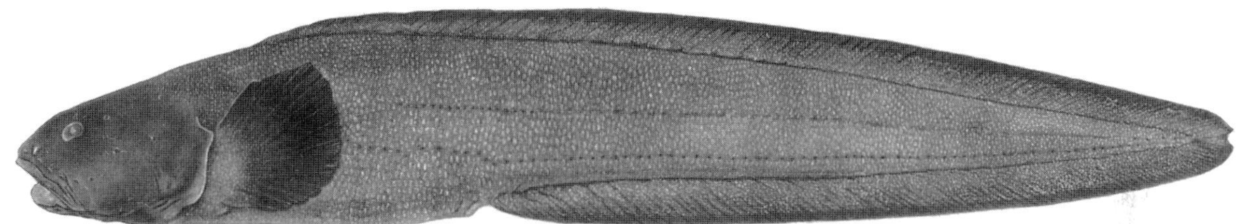

Notes & Sources — *Pachycara lepinium* Anderson & Peden, 1988

Description: Anderson and Peden 1988:91–92.

Figure: Anderson and Peden 1988, fig. 5; holotype, USNM 280120, 465 mm SL, off Queen Charlotte Islands (reproduced from original illustration provided by A. E. Peden; artist P. Drukker-Brammall, Dec. 1981).

Range: Nearest record to Alaska is the holotype, taken west of Tasu Sound, Queen Charlotte Islands, British Columbia, at 52°38'N, 132°06'W, in black-cod trap at depth of 2,744 m.

Bothrocara pusillum (Bean, 1890) **Alaska eelpout**

Eastern Bering Sea to Pacific Ocean off southern British Columbia.
Taken at depths of 91–2,189 m.

D 108–116; A 95–102; C 11; Pec 14–17; Pel 0; Vert 18–20 + 95–101 (114–120).

- **Flesh delicate and transparent, especially in head region.**
- **Eye diameter greater than snout length.**
- Pelvic fin absent.
- Minute scales present on body, tail, and belly; **scales absent from nape.**
- **Lateral line absent.**
- Jaw, vomerine, and palatine teeth nearly uniform.
- Length to 155 mm SL or more (smaller than other Alaskan *Bothrocara* species).

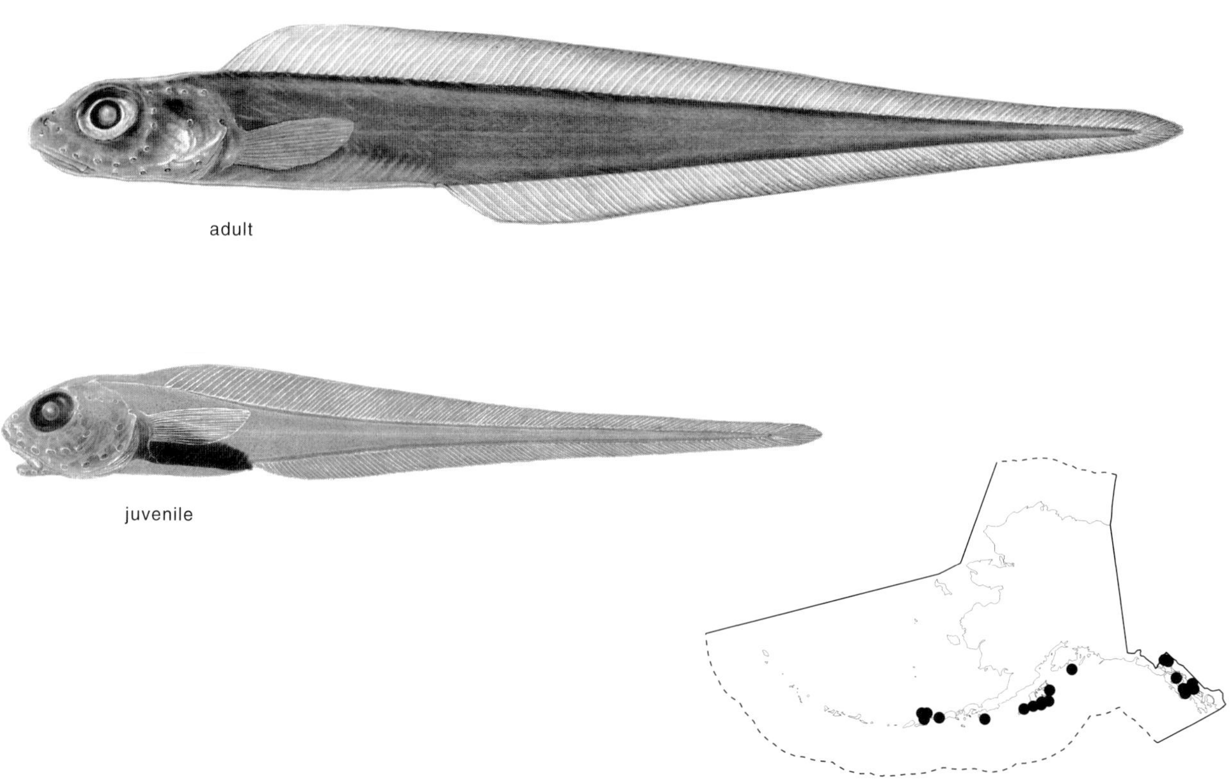

Notes & Sources — *Bothrocara pusillum* (Bean, 1890)
Maynea pusilla Bean, 1890

Description: Bean 1890b:39; Peden 1979b.

Figures: Peden 1979b, figs. 1 and 2. Adult: UBC 73-20, 141 mm SL, near Spruce Island, western Gulf of Alaska. Juvenile: BCPM 976-1293, 57 mm SL, from Gardner Canal, British Columbia.

Range: Alaskan records are as follows. Bean 1890b: off Nagai Island, *Albatross* station 2848, 55°10'N, 160°18'W, depth 201 m (type locality). Gilbert 1896: north of Unalaska Island at stations 3224, 3227, 3330, and 3331; depths 221–642 m. Evermann and Goldsborough 1907: southeastern Alaska at stations 4251, 4252, 4255, 4256 (Stikine River delta and Chilkoot and Taiya inlets); depths 133–474 m. Hubbs and Schultz 1941: Frederick Sound between Frederick Point and Coney Island, and vicinity of Petersburg. The ABL has collections from Pye Island (AB 64-682, 59°27'N, 149°49'W), Alitak Bay (AB 64-825, 56°58'N, 154°00'W; AB 64-826, 57°00'N, 153°59'W; AB 64-827, 57°04'N, 153°56'W), and Marmot Bay (AB 66-893, 57°58'N, 152°04'W) at depths of 91–205 m. The UBC has collections from vicinity of Kodiak Island (UBC 62-703, 56°44'N, 155°27'W; UBC 65-145, 57°20'N, 153°22'W; UBC 73-20, 57°52'N, 152°18'W) and off Douglas Island (UBC 61-542, 58°15'N, 134°16'W). Minimum depth: AB 64-825, taken at 91–132 m. Evermann and Goldsborough (1907) reported that specimens were taken at *Albatross* dredging station 4256; depth given by Fassett (1905) for this station is 133 m. Maximum depth: Peden 1979b.

Size: Peden (1979b) reported a range of 105–155 mm SL in 29 specimens from Alaska. Baxter (1990ms) gave a maximum size of 182 mm TL but did not cite documentation.

Bothrocara brunneum (Bean, 1890) **twoline eelpout**

Bering Sea from Navarin Canyon to Aleutian Islands west to Attu Island, and Pacific Ocean to Coronado Island, Baja California; western Bering Sea and Commander Islands to Sea of Okhotsk.

Continental and island slopes at depths of 199–1,829 m; most occurrences are from about 400 to 950 m.

D 100–112; A 89–100; Pec 14–17; Pel 0; GR 17–20; Vert 22 + 94 (116).

- Large pits on head, due to fossae on bones through which head pores open.
- Eye diameter usually less than snout length.
- Dorsal fin origin posterior to vertical through base of pectoral fin; **pectoral fin not reaching anus**; pelvic fin absent.
- **Lateral line double**: dorsal branch extending to a little posterior to vertical of anus; mediolateral starting from a little anterior to vertical of anus.
- Vomerine and palatine teeth well developed.
- **Gill rakers short and broad**.
- Length to720 mm TL.

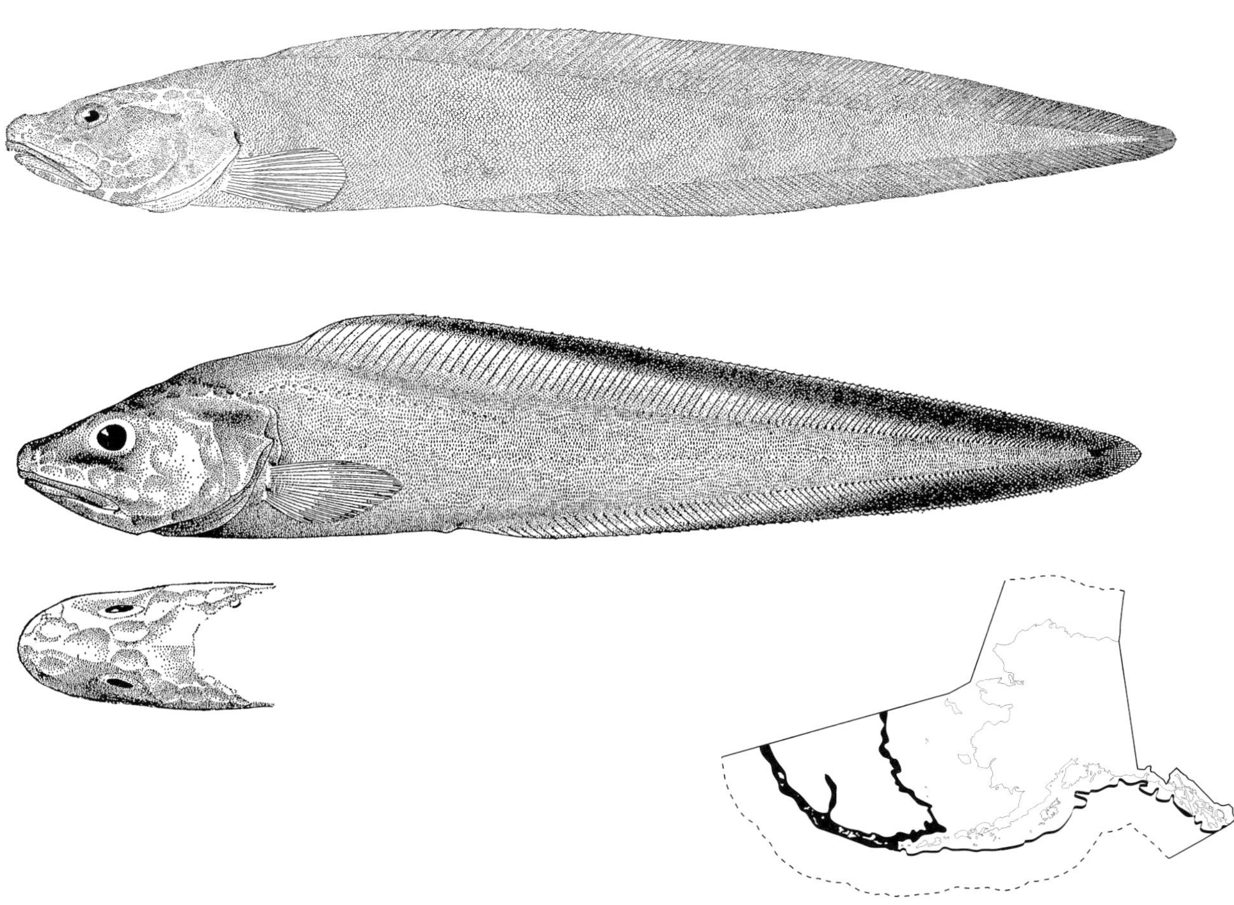

Notes & Sources — *Bothrocara brunneum* (Bean, 1890)
Maynea brunnea Bean, 1890
Lycogramma brunnea (Bean, 1890): Gilbert 1915.
Bayliff (1959) summarized records confused with *B. molle*; the two species were considered to be synonymous from 1898 to 1915.

Description: Bean 1890b:39–40; Gilbert 1915:364–366; Bayliff 1959:79; Westrheim and Pletcher 1966); Hart 1973:235; Matarese et al. 1989:498. Vertebral counts reported by Schultz (1967) for the types of *Maynea brunnea* Bean are not included because, as noted by Springer and Anderson (1997), they actually are counts for types of *Lycodes brunneus* Fowler.

Figures: Upper: Jordan and Gilbert 1899:485 (incorrectly labeled *B. mollis*); USNM 49095, near Bogoslof Island, Aleutian Islands. Lower: Gilbert 1915, pl. 20, fig. 18; California.

Range: Allen and Smith (1988) mapped occurrences in Alaskan waters from NMFS survey records.

Size: Glubokov and Orlov (2000) reported a maximum length of 72 cm (range 44–72 cm) in 208 specimens collected in 1998 from the western Bering Sea. Previously reported to 660 mm TL by Westrheim and Pletcher (1966).

Bothrocara molle Bean, 1890 **soft eelpout**

Southern Bering Sea; Pacific Ocean from northern British Columbia off Queen Charlotte Islands to northern Baja California and Chile, and to northern Honshu; Sea of Japan.

At depths of 60–2,688 m; rarely taken at depths less than about 400 m.

D 110–128; A 93–105; C 14; Pec 13–16; Pel 0; GR 18–24; Vert 18–23 + 93–109 (116–130).

- Large pits on head, due to fossae on bones through which head pores open.
- Eye diameter equal to or slightly less than snout length.
- Dorsal fin origin at or anterior to vertical through base of pectoral fin; **pectoral fin reaching to anus or posterior to anus**; pelvic fin absent.
- **Lateral line double**: dorsal branch extending to a little posterior to vertical of anus; mediolateral starting from a little anterior to vertical of anus; mediolateral branch not always discernible.
- Vomerine and palatine teeth weakly developed or absent.
- **Gill rakers slender and pointed**.
- Length to 587 mm TL.

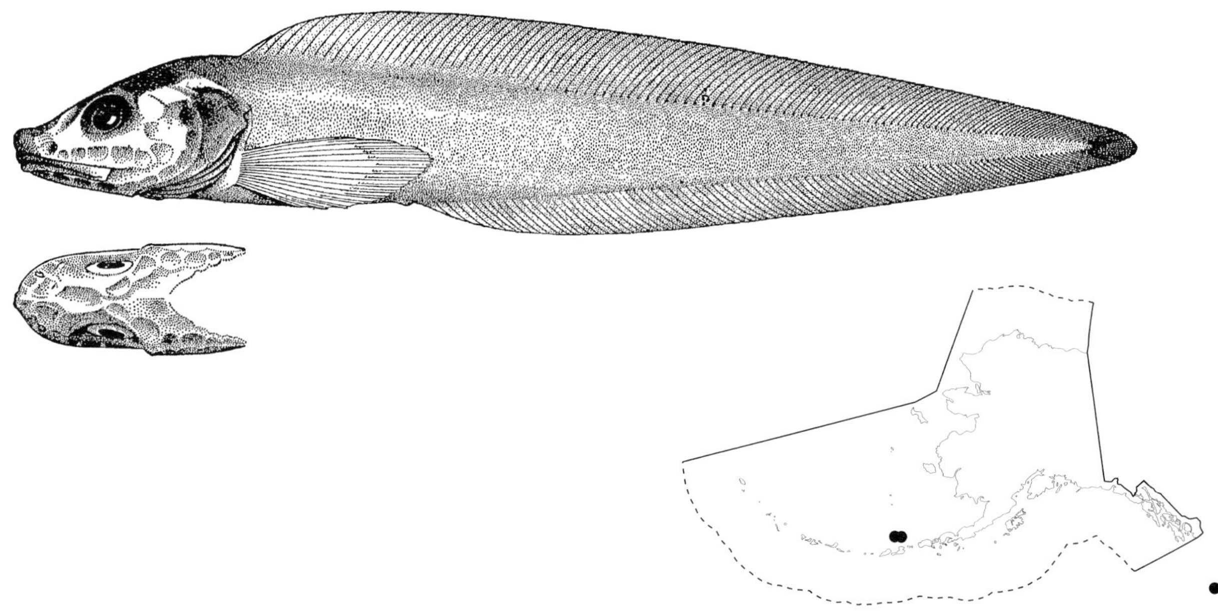

Notes & Sources — *Bothrocara molle* Bean, 1890
Bothrocara mollis Bean: Gilbert and Burke 1912a:90, part, station 4775.
Bothrocara remigera Gilbert, 1915
Anderson (1984, 1994) placed *B. remigerum* in synonymy of *B. molle.*
Since the gender of *Bothrocara* is neuter, the names are correct as *B. molle* and *B. remigerum.*

Description: Bean 1890b:39; Gilbert 1915:366; Schultz 1967 (vertebral counts for the *B. remigerum* holotype); Hart 1973:236–237; Toyoshima in Amaoka et al. 1983:208, 335; Toyoshima in Masuda et al. 1984:309; Matarese et al. 1989:498; Springer and Anderson 1997:22 (fin ray counts for holotype of *B. remigerum,* from note in jar by L. P. Schultz). Bayliff (1959) recounted history of confusion with *B. brunneum.*

Figure: Gilbert 1915, pl. 20, fig. 19; holotype of *B. remigerum,* male, 283 mm TL, from Monterey Bay. The illustration for this species in Hart (1973:236) was probably based on a specimen of *B. pusillum* (UBC 61-542, a 130-mm-TL specimen from southeastern Alaska).

Range: Three specimens from *Albatross* station 3634, off Bogoslof Island, were identified as *B. molle* by Jordan and Gilbert (1899), but their illustration is actually of *B. brunneum,* as noted by Bayliff (1959), and was based on the largest (USNM 49095) of the three specimens; the two smaller specimens (CAS 105653, formerly SU 5653) are *B. molle* (confirmed by M. E. Anderson, pers. comm., 9 Mar. 1998). Bayliff (1959) also referred the specimens from sta. 4775, Bowers Bank, identified by Gilbert and Burke (1912a) as *B. molle,* to *B. brunneum.* Seven specimens (USNM 47588) from sta. 3607, 54°41'N, 168°01'W, collected 13 Apr. 1895, are *B. molle* (confirmed by M. E. Anderson). Some specimens in museum collections identified as *B. brunneum* are probably *B. molle*. Nearest record outside Alaska may be the holotype, described by Bean (1890b), from off Cape St. James, Queen Charlotte Islands (USNM 331716, formerly USNM 45359). Southern extensions of known range were recently reported by M. E. Anderson (pers. comm.), who examined a specimen from Chile (MCZ 45051), and Shinohara et al. (1996), from northern Honshu. Minimum depth: Toyoshima in Amaoka et al. 1983. Maximum: Anderson 1984, 1994.

Size: Baxter 1990ms: from UW 17767, collected off coast of Washington at 46°58'N, 124°49'W. Previously reported to 560 mm TL by Toyoshima (in Amaoka et al. 1983).

Lycodapus parviceps Gilbert, 1896 — smallhead eelpout

Southeastern Bering Sea off Unalaska Island; inlets of southern British Columbia to Washington border in Strait of Juan de Fuca.

Most taken by bottom trawls or nonclosing midwater trawls fishing close to the bottom at depths of 81–457 m.

D 94–98; A 81–86; C 9–10; Pec 8–9; Pel 0; GR 10; Vert 18–20 + 81–85 (100–104).

- **Lining of mouth and gill cavity pale.**
- High vertebral count.
- **Gill slit extending upward not at all or only slightly beyond base of pectoral fin.**
- Pelvic fin absent.
- Head pores: mandibular 4; preopercular 3–4, usually 4; interorbital 1.
- **Inner row of jaw teeth large** in adults; vomerine teeth 2–15, enlarged in adults; palatine teeth 12–20 on each side.
- **Gill rakers mere nubs**, ratio 11–27% (mean = 17%, N = 14).
- Length to 166 mm TL.

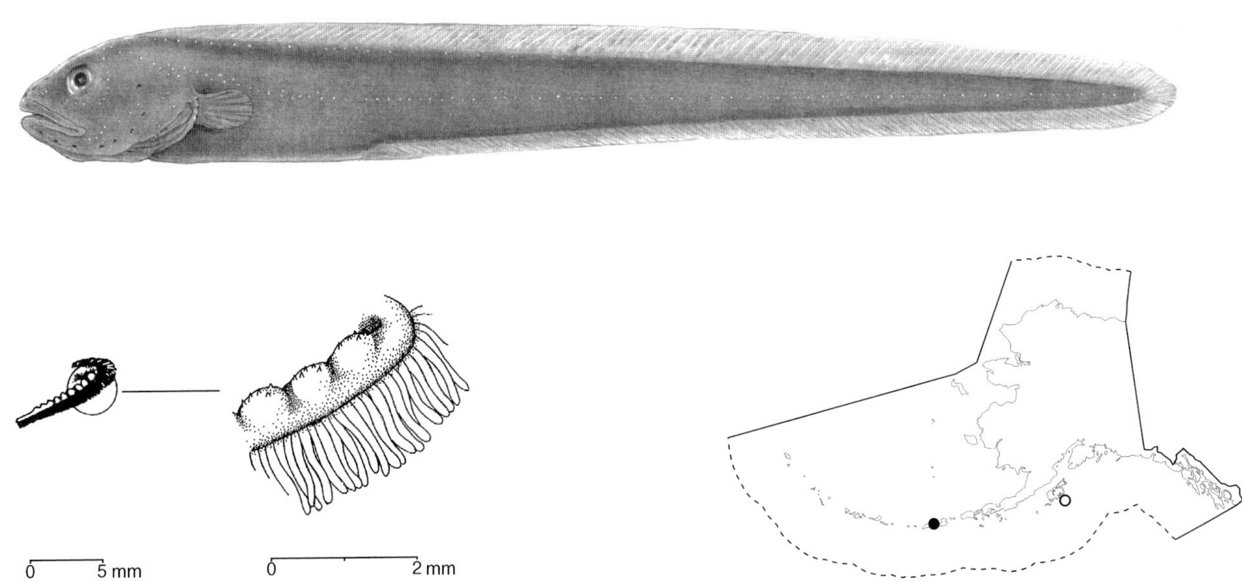

Notes & Sources — *Lycodapus parviceps* Gilbert, 1896

Description: Gilbert 1896:455–456; Peden and Anderson 1978:1929–1935, table 1; 1981: table 2.

Figures: Peden and Anderson 1978, figs. 5 and 13. Adult: BCPM 975-91, 122 mm TL, Alberni Inlet, Vancouver Island.

Range: Gilbert 1896: one specimen, the holotype (unique), collected north of Unalaska Island at *Albatross* station 3324, 53°34'N, 167°47'W, depth 199 m. Baxter (1990ms) identified a specimen taken in 1986 by a NMFS survey of Kodiak Island vicinity as *L. parviceps*; not verifiable, specimen was not saved. Map by Peden and Anderson (1978: fig. 1) shows distribution of other, non-Alaskan records.

Size: Baxter 1990ms: specimen (not saved) from Kodiak area. Largest specimen examined by Peden and Anderson was 116 mm SL, 122 mm TL.

Lycodapus psarostomatus Peden & Anderson, 1981 **specklemouth eelpout**

Eastern Bering Sea; Monterey Bay, California.

Bering Sea specimens were taken in nonclosing bottom trawls towed over the continental slope to depths of 470–590 m; California specimen was taken in a midwater trawl fished near the surface, at 0–15 m.

D 89–98; A 86; C 8–11; Pec 8; Pel 0; GR 10; Vert 17–20 + 77–84 (96–104).

- **Lining of mouth and gill cavity with dark speckles or spots.**
- High vertebral count.
- More pointed snout than in *L. parviceps*.
- **Gill slit extending upward only slightly beyond base of pectoral fin.**
- Pelvic fin absent.
- Head pores: mandibular 4; preopercular 3; interorbital 1.
- Vomerine teeth 7–10; palatine teeth 8–27 on each side.
- **Gill rakers mere nubs**; ratio 8–17% (mean = 12%, N = 5) in Bering Sea specimens, 29% in 1 California specimen.
- Length to 155 mm SL.

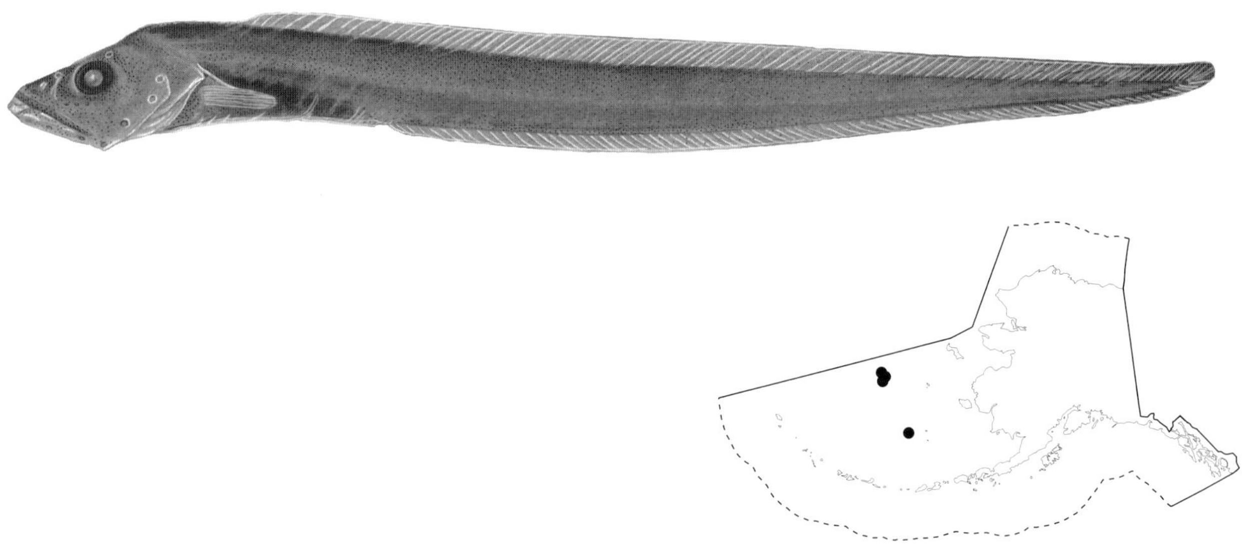

Notes & Sources — *Lycodapus psarostomatus* Peden & Anderson, 1981

Description: Peden and Anderson 1981:668–670, table 2; Anderson 1989a:149–150.

Figure: Peden and Anderson 1981, fig. 4; holotype, USNM 221057, male, 134 mm SL, eastern Bering Sea.

Range: Peden and Anderson (1981) described five specimens taken in eastern Bering Sea in four bottom trawl hauls: USNM 221057, 59°54'N, 178°57'W, depth 564–580 m; USNM 221052, 59°37'N, 178°28'W, depth 470–472 m; USNM 221058, 59°00'N, 178°22'W, depth 568–590 m; USNM 221056, 56°30'N, 172°02'W, depth 530–560 m. The only other record is a specimen taken near the surface in Monterey Bay, California (Anderson 1989).

Lycodapus pachysoma Peden & Anderson, 1978 **stout eelpout**

Eastern Pacific Ocean off central British Columbia to Oregon; Southern Ocean.

Lower continental slopes at depths to 2,000–2,600 m.

D 67–76; A 58–65; C 8; Pec 7–8; Pel 0; Vert 14–18 + 59–65 (75–82).

- **Large head and robust body**; **low vertebral count**.
- Low dorsal and anal fin ray counts; pelvic fin absent.
- Head pores: mandibular 4; preopercular 4; interorbital 1.
- **Teeth usually many and very small**; vomerine teeth 0–19; palatine teeth 10–16 on each side.
- **Gill rakers stout**, ratio 55–88% (mean = 70%, N = 9).
- Length to 200 mm TL.

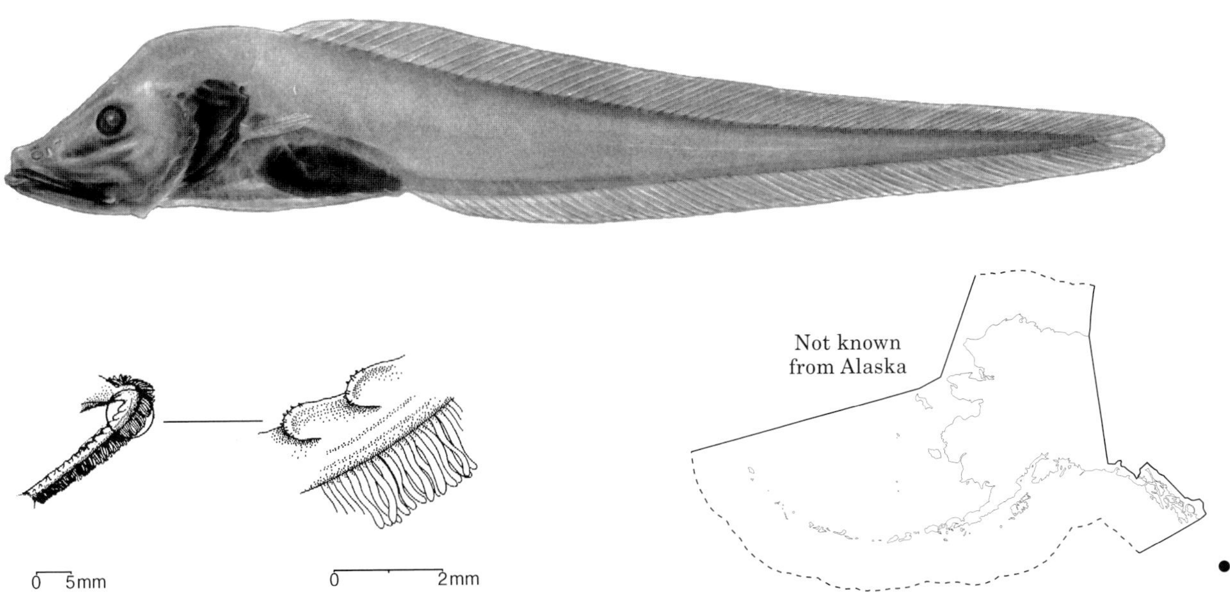

Notes & Sources — *Lycodapus pachysoma* Peden & Anderson, 1978

Description: Peden and Anderson 1978: table 1; 1979a; 1981: table 2; Anderson 1990:266–267.

Figures: Peden and Anderson 1978, figs. 5 and 16; holotype, USNM 216468, female, 138 mm SL, off Oregon.

Range: Nearest record to Alaska is from Pacific Ocean off Triangle Island, British Columbia, at 50°54'N, 130°06'W, depth 2,103–2,196 m (Peden and Anderson 1978, 1979).

Size: Anderson 1990. Maximum known length for northern population is 161 mm SL, and for southern population is 193 mm SL.

Lycodapus leptus Peden & Anderson, 1981 **slender eelpout**

Eastern Bering Sea.

Taken in nonclosing bottom trawls towed to depths of 465–760 m over the continental slope.

D 91–94; C 9–11; Pec 6–8; Pel 0; Vert 16–19 + 78–82 (95–100).

- **Lips speckled; lining of mouth and gill cavity with dark spots or speckles.**
- Slender body, small head; head length 13–15% of standard length; high vertebral count.
- Pelvic fin absent.
- Head pores: mandibular 4; preopercular 3; interorbital 1; some absent or obscured in adults.
- **Vomerine teeth 0–11**, absent in about 17% of individuals; **palatine teeth 0–5** on each side, absent in about 66%.
- **Gill rakers stout**, ratio 38–112% (mean = 87%, N = 35).
- Length to 98 mm SL.

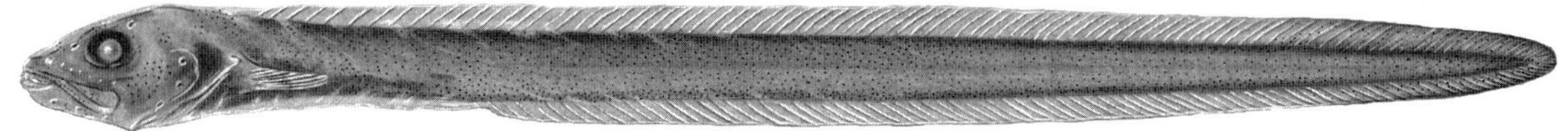

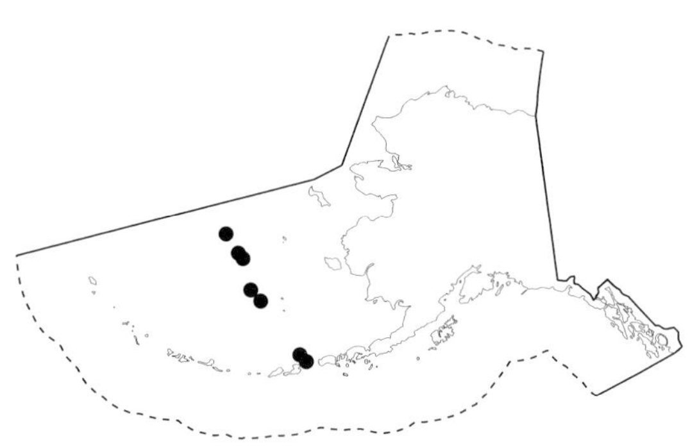

Notes & Sources — *Lycodapus leptus* Peden & Anderson, 1981

Description: Peden and Anderson 1981:671–673, table 2.

Figure: Peden and Anderson 1981, fig. 5; holotype, USNM 222660, female (emaciated, spawned-out), 99 mm SL, eastern Bering Sea.

Range: Peden and Anderson (1981) reported data for specimens taken at six localities, all collected during the *Yakushi Maru* eastern Bering Sea expedition of summer 1979: USNM 222660 and 222661 from 59°00'N, 178°21'W; USNM 221055 from 58°33'N, 175°15'W; CAS 45731, HUMZ 286666, USNM 221054 from 58°32'N, 176°06'W; USNM 222659 from 56°29'N, 172°01'W; USNM 221066 from 54°50'N, 167°19'W; and CAS 45730, HUMZ 83839, USNM 222662 from 54°19'N, 166°40'W. USNM 221059, from 56°58'N, 173°47'W, is another specimen from the same expedition.

Lycodapus mandibularis Gilbert, 1915 **pallid eelpout**

Prince William Sound, Gulf of Alaska, to La Jolla Canyon off southern California.

Typically a midwater species found in depths less than 700 m in submarine canyons or deep northern inlets, recorded to 800 m; sometimes taken in bottom trawls but definitely pelagic.

D 76–90; A 65–79; C 8; Pec 6–9; Pel 0; Vert 14–17 + 67–80 (82–97).

- **Upper orbital rim of adults high, interrupting dorsal profile of head.**
- Pelvic fin absent.
- Head pores: mandibular 4; preopercular 4; interorbital 1; often closed in adults.
- **Vomerine teeth 0–5**, rarely absent; **palatine teeth 2–12** on each side.
- **Gill rakers stout**, ratio 58–161% (mean = 106%, N = 169); more pointed in juveniles.
- Length to 198 mm SL.

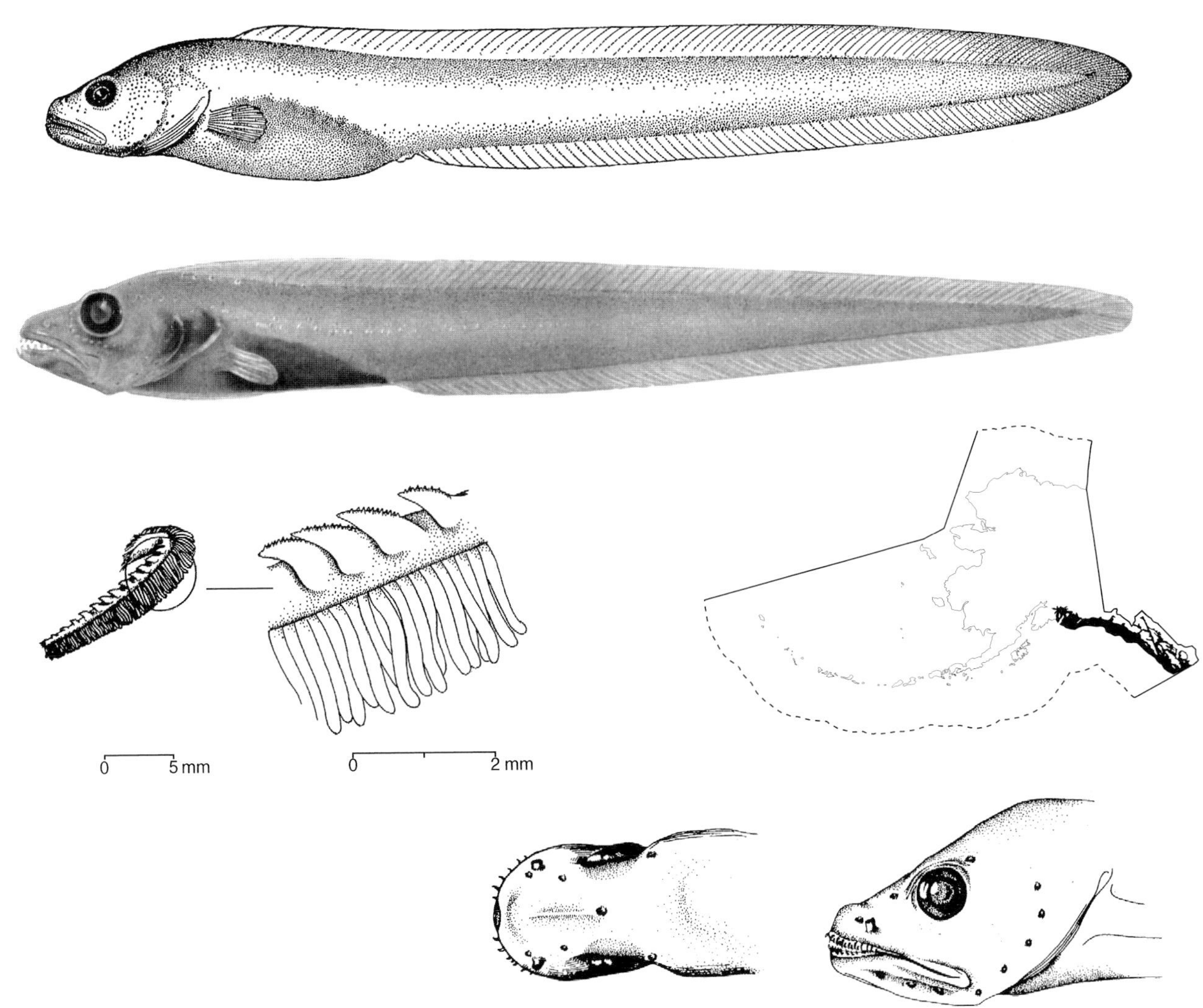

Notes & Sources — *Lycodapus mandibularis* Gilbert, 1915
Lycodapus grossidens Gilbert, 1915 (part)
Detailed synonymy by Peden and Anderson (1978) includes numerous Alaskan specimens.

Description: Gilbert 1915:369–371; Peden and Anderson 1978:1938–1944, table 1; Peden 1979a; Peden and Anderson 1981: table 2.

Figures: Top: Gilbert 1915, pl. 20, fig. 20; holotype, gravid female, Monterey Bay, California. Others: Peden and Anderson 1978, figs. 5, 7, 15; male, BCPM 967-2, 91 mm SL; Georgia Strait, British Columbia.

Range: Known from hundreds of collections from localities extending north to Prince William Sound. The only record for the Bering Sea is an uncertain one: Fedorov's (1973a) *L. lycodon,* which possibly is referable to *L. mandibularis* (Peden and Anderson 1978).

Lycodapus endemoscotus Peden & Anderson, 1978 **deepwater eelpout**

Bering Sea off central Aleutian Islands; eastern Pacific Ocean off southern British Columbia to northern Mexico, Gulf of California, and Peru.

Continental slope at depths of 439–2,225 m.

D 79–91; A 70–81; C 8–10; Pec 6–9; Pel 0; GR 9–11; Vert 14–17 + 69–79 (86–95).

- Pelvic fin absent.
- **Head pores: mandibular 3 or 4; preopercular usually 4; interorbital 1.**
- **Vomerine teeth 4–21, few and large in mature males; palatine teeth 5–28** on each side.
- **Gill rakers stout**; ratio 49–76% (N = 5) in Bering Sea sample; ratio 57–106% (mean = 79%, N = 35) in British Columbia to Gulf of California sample.
- Length to 132 mm SL.

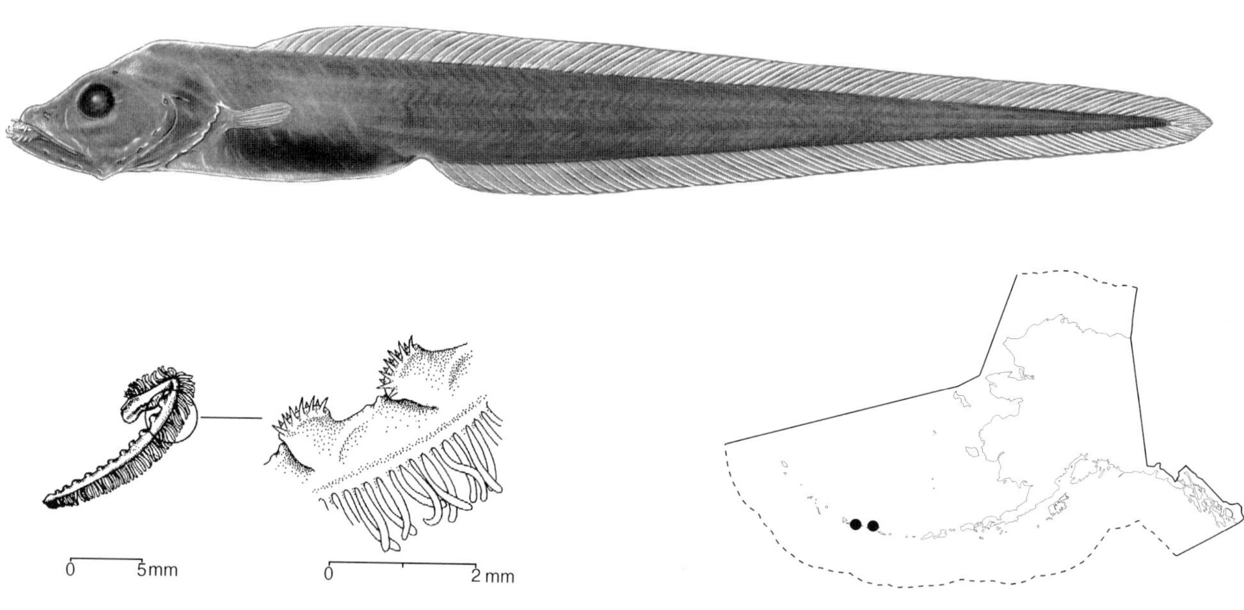

Notes & Sources — *Lycodapus endemoscotus* Peden & Anderson, 1978

Description: Peden and Anderson 1978:1936–1938, table 1; 1981: table 1.

Figures: Peden and Anderson 1978, figs. 5 and 14; holotype, USNM 216471, male, 124 mm SL, off Oregon.

Range: The only Alaskan records are those given by Anderson (1989): CAS 55605, north of Atka Island at 52°16'N, 174°51'W, 468–571 m; and CAS 55606, west of Great Sitkin Island, 52°02'N, 176°23'W, 439–512 m; both collections by otter trawl. The nearest record outside Alaska is from British Columbia at about 50°31'N, 129°00'W (Peden and Anderson 1978).

Lycodapus fierasfer Gilbert, 1890 — blackmouth eelpout

Eastern Bering Sea; eastern Pacific Ocean off central British Columbia to Peru; western Bering Sea on Shirshov Ridge.

Mainly taken in bottom trawls along continental slope but captures in midwater trawls indicate the species is not confined to benthic habitat; taken at depths of 102–2,189 m.

D 78–83; A 68–74; C 6–8; Pec 6–8; Pel 0; Vert 13–15 + 69–77 (83–91).

- **Lips**, mouth, and gill cavity **black** in life.
- Pelvic fin absent.
- Head pores: mandibular 3; preopercular 3; **interorbital 2, rarely 1 or obscure**.
- **Teeth usually many** and small; vomerine teeth 1–13; palatine teeth 0–16 on each side.
- **Gill rakers long and pointed**, ratio 117–256% (mean = 200%, N = 48).
- Length to 141 mm SL.

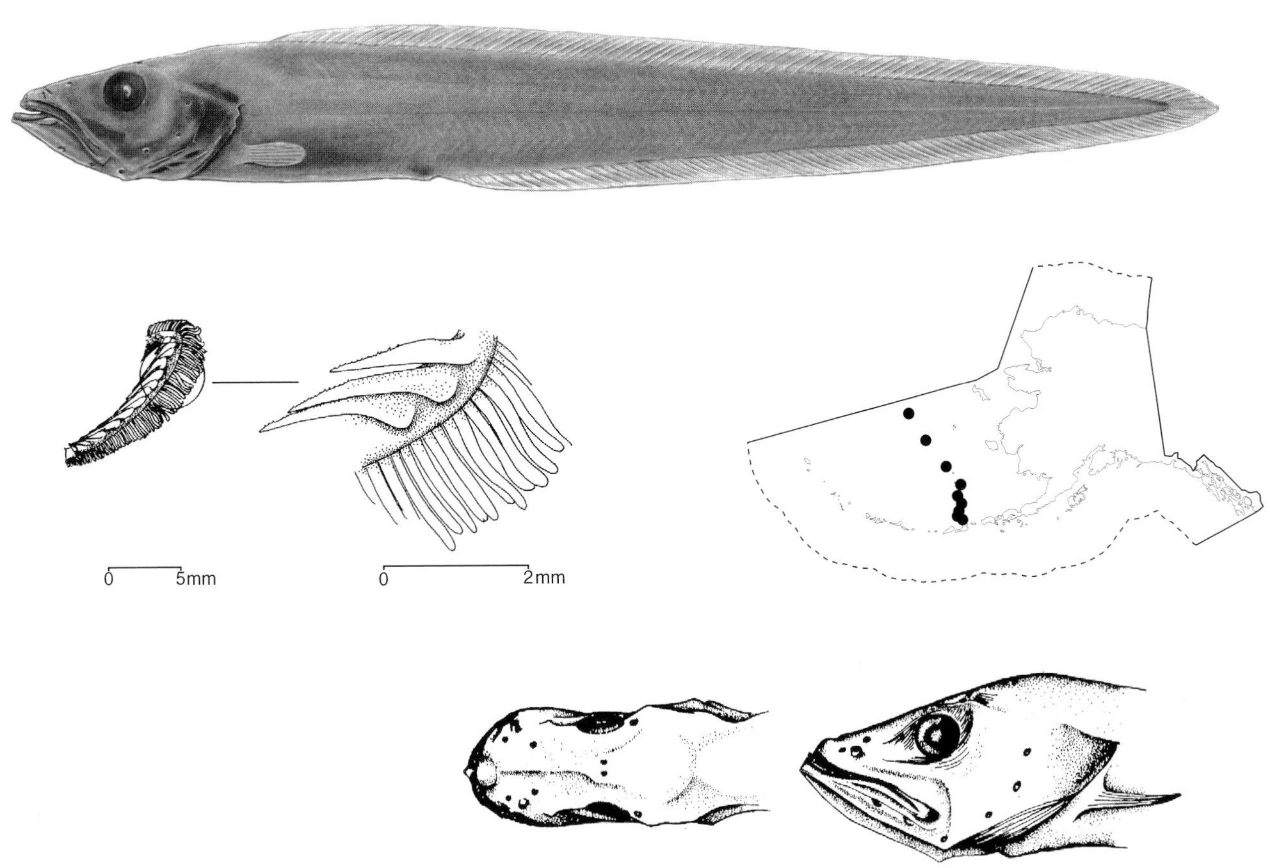

Notes & Sources — *Lycodapus fierasfer* Gilbert, 1890
Lycodapus grossidens Gilbert, 1915 (part, *Albatross* station 3483)
Detailed synonymy of Peden and Anderson (1978) identifies Alaskan specimens that did *not* prove to be *L. fierasfer.*

Description: Peden and Anderson 1978:1952–1956, table 2; 1981: table 2.

Figures: Peden and Anderson 1978, figs. 6, 7, 19; OSU uncataloged, female, 123 mm SL, off Oregon.

Range: Peden and Anderson (1978) noted that most old specimens of *L. fierasfer*, including those collected by the *Albatross* in the 1890s, were too deteriorated to identify, but confirmed two from Alaska: vicinity of Pribilof Islands (catalog number not given, 57°18'N, 171°18'W) and north of Unalaska Island (MCZ 28333, 54°01'N, 166°54'W). Peden and Anderson (1981) examined newer material, including specimens collected by the *Yakushi Maru* in 1979: USNM 221065, 54°51'N, 167°42'W; HUMZ 81830 and 81831, 54°30'N, 167°38'W; HUMZ 81869 and 81870, 55°09'N, 167°58'W; HUMZ 82546, 55°47'N, 168°55'W; HUMZ 83466, 59°54'N, 178°57'W; HUMZ 83817 and 83818, 54°51'N, 167°42'W; and BCPM 980-26, 58°30'N, 176°10'W. Nearest record outside Alaska in Bering Sea is ZIN 49570 (9 specimens), collected in 1989 from Shirshov Ridge at 58°04'N, 170°17'E, determined by A. A. Balanov (B. A. Sheiko, pers. comm., 11 Jan. 1999). Nearest record in eastern Pacific is from off central British Columbia. A specimen described by Anderson (1989) extended the known range south to Peru.

Lycodapus dermatinus Gilbert, 1896 **looseskin eelpout**

Bering Sea and western Gulf of Alaska reports not verifiable; Gulf of Alaska at Welker Seamount; Pacific Ocean off northern Oregon to northern Mexico, Gulf of California, and Peru.

Generally shallower than *L. fierasfer,* at depths of about 450–1,370 m.

D 70–77; A 62–68; C 7–11; Pec 6–8; Pel 0; GR 14; Vert 13–15 + 62–69 (76–82).

- Lips, mouth, and gill cavity black in life.
- **Low vertebral count.**
- Low dorsal and anal fin ray counts; pelvic fin absent.
- Head pores: mandibular 3–4; preopercular 3–4; **interorbital 1.**
- **Vomerine and palatine teeth usually many** and small; vomerine teeth 3–19; palatine teeth 2–26 on each side.
- **Gill rakers long and pointed**, ratio 125–256% (mean = 195%, N = 31).
- Length to 122 mm SL.

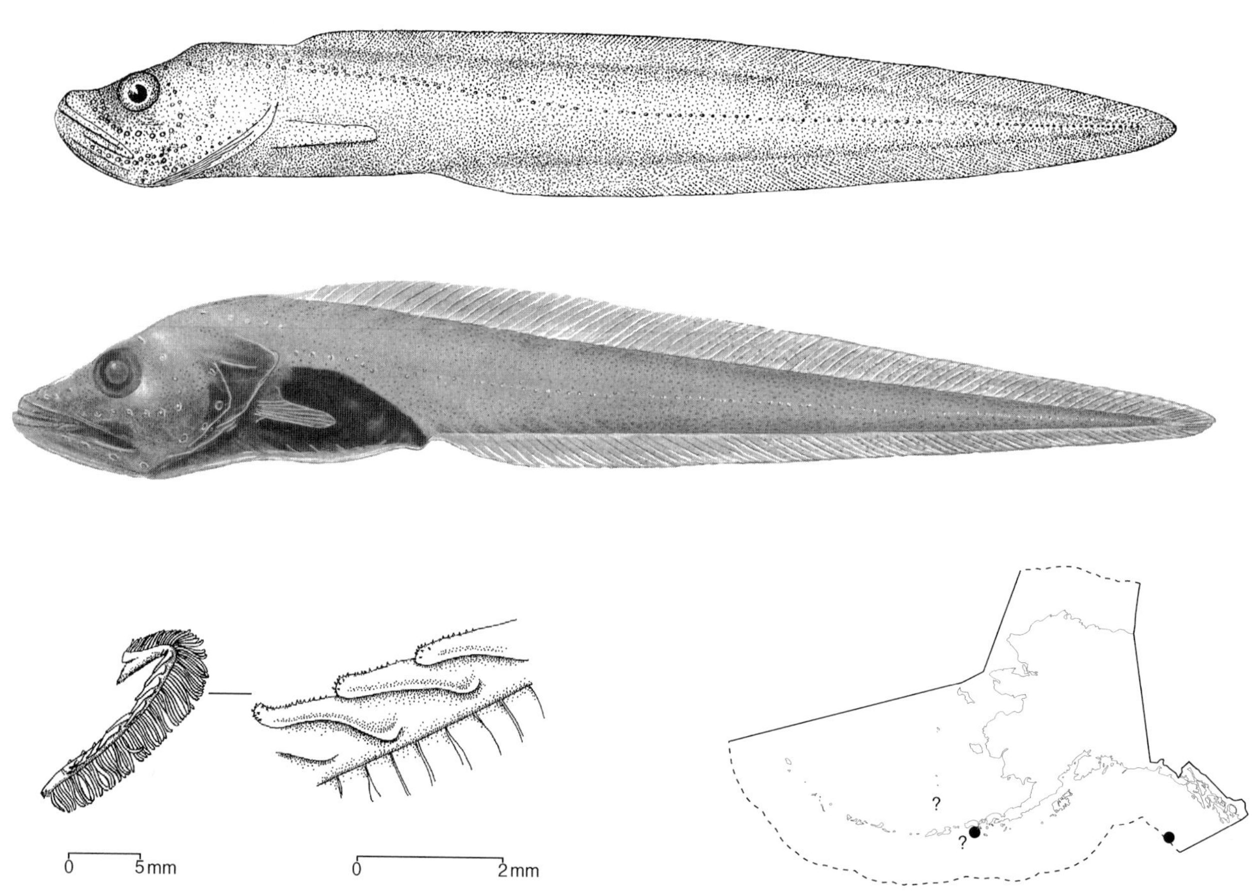

Notes & Sources — *Lycodapus dermatinus* Gilbert, 1896

Description: Gilbert 1896:471–472; Peden and Anderson 1978:1948–1952; 1981: table 2; Anderson, pers. comm., 1 Dec. 1998 (lips and mouth black in freshly caught fish).

Figures: Upper: Gilbert 1896, pl. 35. Others: Peden and Anderson 1978, figs. 6 and 18; LACM uncataloged, female, 82 mm SL, San Pedro Basin.

Range: Peden and Anderson (1978) noted that old specimens which might have been from Alaskan waters could not be verified due to deterioration, but later (1981) reported new specimens from Welker Seamount that, as well as being the only confirmed Alaskan record, are the only *Lycodapus* known to have been taken off the continental shelf in the eastern Pacific. A specimen not verifiable due to cataloging error (SU - Indiana University 6879) could be from Oregon or Alaska; if from Alaska, the coordinates are 54°20'N, 163°37'W (*Albatross* station 3216), south of Unimak Island. A specimen described by Anderson (1989) extended the known range south to Peru.

Lycodapus poecilus Peden & Anderson, 1981 **variform eelpout**

Eastern Bering Sea.

Taken in bottom trawls over the continental slope as deep as 437–900 m.

D 75–83; C 6–8; Pec 5–7; Pel 0; Vert 15–17 + 65–72 (81–88).

- Lips pale or dark; oral and gill cavities black, mouth with or without spots.
- Variable in form: pointed-snout form has straight to concave snout and smaller, delicate pectoral fin; round-snout form is larger, has longer, more robust pectoral fin.
- Pelvic fin absent.
- Head pores: **mandibular 4**, occasionally 3; **preopercular 3**; **interorbital 1**; some pores grown over by skin in some adults.
- **Vomerine teeth 1–6; palatine teeth 0–4, absent in about 35%.**
- **Gill rakers long and pointed**, ratio 108–227%; pointed-snout form, 119–227% (mean = 157%, N = 35); round-snout form, 108–170% (mean = 136%, N = 17).
- Length to 126 mm SL.

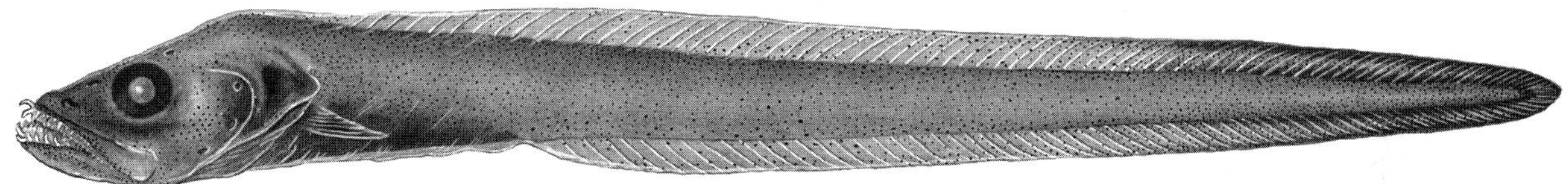

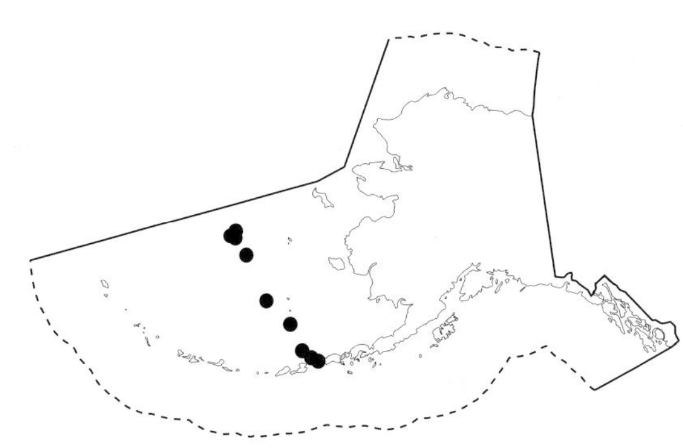

Notes & Sources — *Lycodapus poecilus* Peden & Anderson, 1981

Description: Peden and Anderson 1981:673–675, tables 1 and 2; Anderson, pers. comm., 1 Dec. 1998 (skin grows over pores in some adults).

Figure: Peden and Anderson 1981, fig. 6; holotype, USNM 222663, male, 94 mm SL.

Range: Locality data for all known specimens were reported by Peden and Anderson (1981): USNM 221053, 59°00'N, 178°22'W; USNM 221060, 56°30'N, 172°02'W; USNM 221061, 59°37'N, 178°28'W; USNM 221062 and 222663, 58°32'N, 176°06'W; USNM 221064, 54°20'N, 166°40'W; CAS 46715, 54°19'N, 166°40'W; HUMZ 83800, 56°11'N, 169°22'W; HUMZ 83814 and 83815, 54°51'N, 167°42'W; HUMZ 86650, 58°32'N, 176°06'W; HUMZ 86746 and 86764, 59°37'N, 178°27'W; BCPM 980-24, 59°22'N, 178°03'W; and BCPM 980-595, 54°32'N, 165°49'W.

Size: BCPM 980-595.

Family Stichaeidae
Pricklebacks

Pricklebacks are elongate, compressed, slightly eel-like fishes of the Northern Hemisphere. They occur primarily in the North Pacific Ocean, with a few inhabiting the Arctic and North Atlantic oceans. Pricklebacks live on the bottom in a variety of habitats from shallow subtidal and intertidal areas to rocky reefs or gently sloping sandy or muddy sea floors. Comprising about 54 species, the family is represented by at least 23 species in Alaska. An additional species from nearby waters that may also occur in Alaska makes a total of 24 treated in this guide.

The common name prickleback comes from the stiff spines supporting the dorsal fin, which extends along most of the back. In some species there are a few soft rays at the rear of the fin. The anal fin is also long, as reflected in the preanal distance which usually is equal to or less than the distance from the anal fin origin to the caudal fin; and usually has at least 1 or 2 spines anteriorly. One of the Alaskan species also has spines at the posterior end of the anal fin. In some species the dorsal or the anal fin, or both, extend to and join the caudal fin. The pelvic fins are present or absent, and when present are small and thoracic. The body is usually covered with small overlapping scales, and the head is usually naked. Several species are characterized by the presence of long, fleshy cirri (called tentacles or flaps in the older literature) on their heads and the anterior spines of the dorsal fin. Some pricklebacks are quite colorful, with various markings, and coloration is important in distinguishing those species.

Pricklebacks are similar to gunnels (Pholidae) but have a longer anal fin (shorter preanal distance). Most pricklebacks are smaller than gunnels, typically reaching less than 25 cm (10 inches) in length.

For the Stichaeidae, differences between the current inventory and that of Quast and Hall (1972) are due mainly to differences in nomenclature and coverage of a greater body of literature, not to any new discoveries of species in Alaskan waters. For example, they gave a non-Alaskan range for bearded warbonnet, *Chirolophis snyderi,* but several specimens from Alaska previously identified as other species had been recognized as representing *C. snyderi* by Andriashev (1954) and other investigators. Alaskan records once believed to represent *Chirolophis polyactocephalus* have been referred to decorated warbonnet, *Chirolophis decoratus,* and genus *Bryostemma* is classified as a junior synonym of *Chirolophis.* Stone cockscomb, *Alectrias alectrolophus,* was not on Quast and Hall's (1972) list, but specimens collected in the 1800s from St. Michael, Norton Sound, were confirmed as belonging to this species by Peden (1967). As well, following Makushok (1958, 1961) and most recent authors, we do not include the wrymouths in the family Stichaeidae but classify them in a separate family, Cryptacanthodidae.

Three pricklebacks included as potential additions to the Alaskan ichthyofauna by Quast and Hall (1972) are not treated in this guide because they are extralimital, shallow-water, bottom-dwelling species not likely to occur in Alaska. *Azygopterus corallinus* Andriashev & Makushok has been found no closer to Alaska than the Kuril Islands, and *Allolumpenus hypochromus* Hubbs & Schultz and *Plectobranchus evides* Gilbert have been found no closer than southern British Columbia.

Likewise, *Pholidapus dybowskii* (Steindachner), a prickleback of the subfamily Opisthocentrinae that was included on Quast and Hall's (1972) list, is not treated in this guide. The species has been found no closer to Alaska than the Kuril Islands, and records indicate it is endemic to the western Pacific. On the other hand, a different member of the Opisthocentrinae has been added as a possible component of the Alaskan ichthyofauna: ocellated blenny, *Opisthocentrus ocellatus.* This prickleback is an abundant inhabitant of seaweed beds around the Commander Islands and along southeastern Kamchatka, Russia, to the Sea of Japan as far south as Wonsan, North Korea. Although ocellated blennies are most abundant in shallow water, they have also been found at greater depths than most pricklebacks. Ocellated blennies studied by Shiogaki (1984) were collected from a depth of 335 m off Hokkaido.

The prickleback classification used in this guide follows the revision by Makushok (1958), who apportioned the species among eight subfamilies. Six subfamilies are represented in Alaska. Those subfamilies and the 24 species present in Alaska and nearby waters are fairly easily identified from only a few characters, as shown in the following key and species accounts.

Key to the Stichaeidae of Alaska

1		Lateral line system on body well developed; pelvic fins present	subfamily Stichaeinae (2)
1		Combination not as above: either one or more well-developed lateral lines present and pelvic fins absent; or lateral line absent or weakly developed (sometimes a short canal anteriorly) and pelvic fins present	(3)
2	(1)	Two or more lateral lines present; 2 or 3 spines at posterior end of anal fin	*Eumesogrammus praecisus,* page 746
2		One lateral line; no spines at posterior end of anal fin	*Stichaeus punctatus,* page 747
3	(1)	Head with fleshy cirri	subfamily Chirolophinae (4)
3		Head without fleshy cirri	(10)
4	(3)	Pelvic fins minute; trifid interorbital cirrus present, but few other cirri present on head	*Gymnoclinus cristulatus,* page 748
4		Pelvic fins well developed; numerous cirri on head	(5)
5	(4)	Teeth on jaws incisiform, in 2 alternating rows close together forming continuous cutting edge; vomerine and palatine teeth absent	genus *Chirolophis* (6)
5		Teeth on jaws conical, multiserial, in bands; vomerine and palatine teeth present	genus *Bryozoichthys* (9)
6	(5)	Top and sides of head densely covered with fleshy cirri	*Chirolophis tarsodes,* page 749
6		Cirri most numerous on top of head	(7)
7	(6)	Few or no cirri on cheeks; dorsal fin with several large dark ocelli	*Chirolophis nugator,* page 750
7		Simple or multifid cirri on cheeks; no dark ocelli on dorsal fin	(8)
8	(7)	One pair of long multifid cirri on interorbital space, height more than twice diameter of eye, joined at their bases; a few simple cirri on cheeks, sides of head, and lower jaw	*Chirolophis decoratus,* page 751
8		Two pairs of long multifid cirri on interorbital space, the anterior pair joined at their bases, the posterior pair not joined; multifid cirri on lower jaw in row extending up along edge of preopercle	*Chirolophis snyderi,* page 752
9	(5)	Pair of small cirri on chin near symphysis; scales absent from nape	*Bryozoichthys lysimus,* page 753
9		No cirri on chin near symphysis; short cirrus on posterior end of maxilla and another below it on lower jaw; scales present on nape	*Bryozoichthys marjorius,* page 754

10 (3) Pelvic fins present .... subfamily Lumpeninae (11)

10 Pelvic fins absent .... (17)

11 (10) Maxilla not extending to vertical with eye; scales covering entire head, including cheeks .... *Lumpenella longirostris,* page 755

11 Maxilla extending to vertical with front of eye or beyond; scales not present on entire head .... (12)

12 (11) Lower rays of pectoral fin elongate and with tips free .... *Leptoclinus maculatus,* page 756

12 Lower rays of pectoral fin not elongate and free .... (13)

13 (12) Anal spines 3; vomerine teeth present .... *Poroclinus rothrocki,* page 757

13 Anal spines 1 or 2; vomerine teeth absent .... (14)

14 (13) Dorsal and anal fins connected to caudal fin; gill membranes attached to isthmus under anterior half of eye; vertebrae 70 or fewer .... *Anisarchus medius,* page 758

14 Dorsal and anal fins not connected to anal fin; gill membranes attached to isthmus under posterior edge of eye or farther posteriorly; vertebrae 70 or more .... (15)

15 (14) Irregular brown markings on sides, extending well below midline; scales present on cheeks; dorsal fin spines 61–66; anal fin rays 40–44; vertebrae 70–75 .... *Lumpenus fabricii,* page 759

15 Brown markings mostly on upper sides and back, not extending much below midline; scales present or absent from cheeks; dorsal fin spines 64–76, anal fin rays 41–50, vertebrae 75–80 .... (16)

16 No dark stripe along back below dorsal fin; eye diameter about same as snout length; scales absent from cheeks .... *Lumpenus sagitta,* page 760

16 (15) Dark stripe along entire length of back below dorsal fin; eye diameter less than snout length; on head, scales present only on cheeks .... *Acantholumpenus mackayi,* page 761

17 (10) Pectoral fins large, nearly as long or longer than head length; pectoral fin rays 18–21; 5–7 large dark ocelli on dorsal fin .... *Opisthocentrus ocellatus,* page 762 (not known from Alaska)

17 Pectoral fins minute to moderate in size, obviously shorter than head length; pectoral fin rays 9–15; no large dark ocelli on dorsal fin .... (18)

18 (17) Body with 1 lateral line, not always clearly discernible; median dermal crest present on head .... subfamily Alectriinae (19)

18 Body with 4 lateral lines with vertical branchlets; no median dermal crest on head .... subfamily Xiphisterinae (22)

19 (18) Dermal crest extending from snout only to posterior interorbital region; median interorbital pore present, other interorbital pores paired; scales on body not extending anteriorly past 13th anal fin ray . . . . *Alectridium aurantiacum,* page 763

19 Dermal crest extending from snout to top of head; no median interorbital pore, all interorbital pores paired; scales on body extending anteriorly past 15th anal fin ray . . . . (20)

20 (19) Anal fin joined to caudal fin; gill membranes united, forming broad free fold across isthmus . . . . *Alectrias alectrolophus,* page 764

20 Anal fin not joined to caudal fin; gill membranes united and fused to isthmus, usually not forming free fold posteriorly . . . . genus *Anoplarchus* (21)

21 (20) Dermal crest as high anteriorly as posteriorly; width of isthmus between points of attachment of gill membranes usually more than 75% of eye diameter . . . . *Anoplarchus purpurescens,* page 765

21 Dermal crest lower anteriorly than posteriorly; width of isthmus between points of attachment of gill membranes usually 50% or less of eye diameter . . . . *Anoplarchus insignis,* page 766

22 (18) Pectoral fin small, as large or larger than eye diameter; anal fin with 2 or 3 spines. . . . . *Phytichthys chirus,* page 767

22 Pectoral fin minute, smaller than eye diameter; anal fin with 1 weak spine or spine absent . . . . genus *Xiphister* (23)

23 (22) Dorsal fin origin above pectoral fin; dark bars with darker borders radiate from eye . . . . *Xiphister mucosus,* page 768

23 Dorsal fin origin well behind pectoral fin; dark bars with light borders radiate from eye . . . . *Xiphister atropurpureus,* page 769

Eumesogrammus praecisus (Krøyer, 1837) **fourline snakeblenny**

Beaufort Sea to northeastern Bering Sea and to Sea of Okhotsk; east through Canadian Arctic to Greenland and south to Gulf of St. Lawrence in western North Atlantic.

Sandy or slightly silty bottom with admixture of stones, pebbles, and gravel at depths of 16–400 m; usually at 40–70 m in Bering Sea.

D XLVII–L; A I–II,29–32,II–III; Pec 16–19; Pel I,3; Br 6; Vert 50–52.

- Chocolate brown to gray, with vague, darker bands; fins blackish; **1–3 black spots, often ringed with white, near front of dorsal fin**; base of caudal fin yellowish; margins of anal, caudal, and pectoral fins pale.
- Head large (20–25% SL) and pointed; body deep (16–21% SL).
- **Anal fin with 2 or 3 spines at posterior end**; pelvic fin present.
- **Two lateral lines, each with 2 long branches**; lower branch of upper lateral line longest, extending to or nearly to base of caudal fin; lines variable, some may be missing or partly missing.
- Vomerine and palatine teeth present.
- Gill membranes broadly united, free of isthmus.
- Length to 230 mm TL.

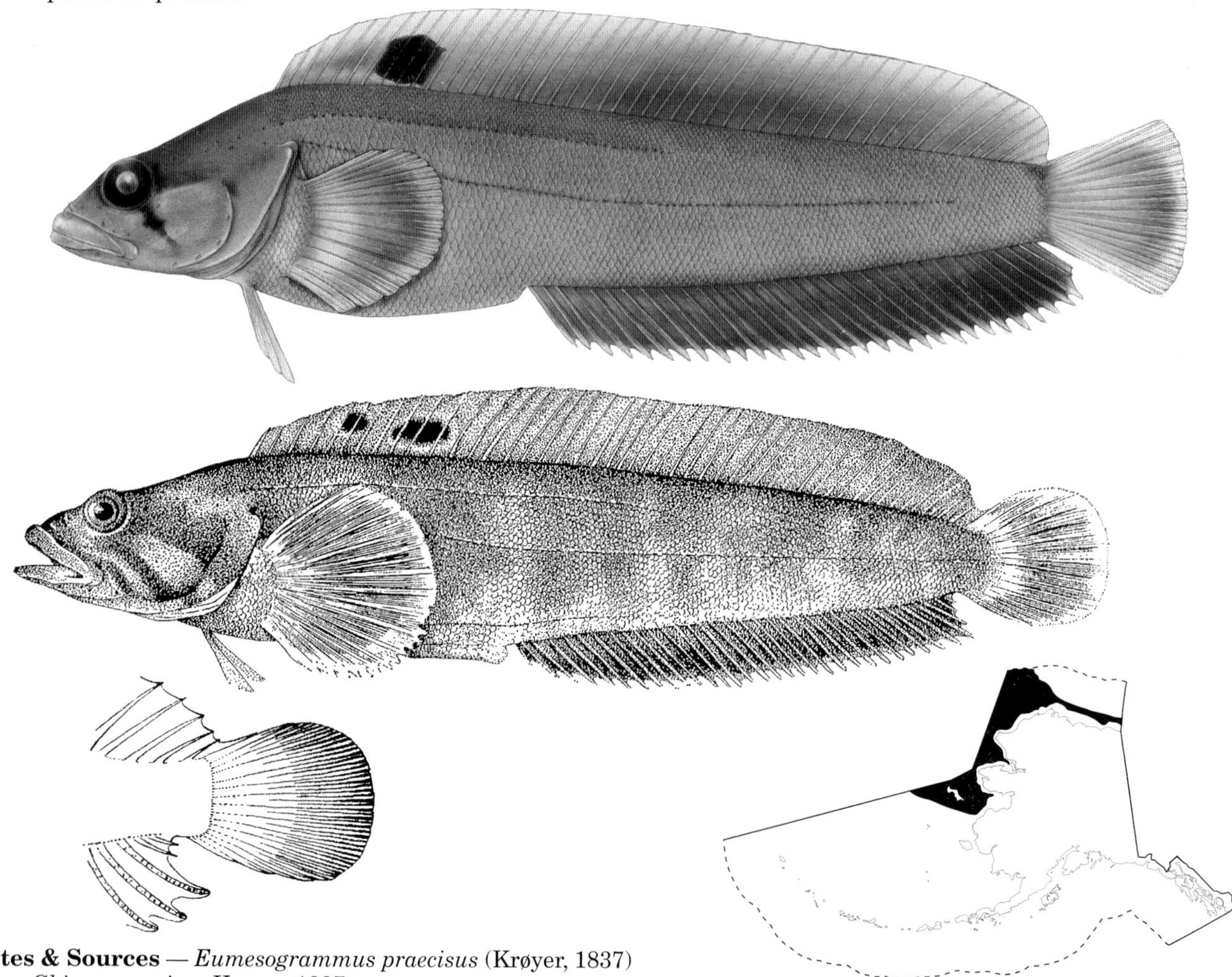

Notes & Sources — *Eumesogrammus praecisus* (Krøyer, 1837)
Chirus praecisus Krøyer, 1837

Description: Jensen 1944:37–39; Andriashev 1954:231–233; Lindberg and Krasyukova 1975:66; Scott and Scott 1988: 416–417.

Figures: Upper: University of British Columbia, artist P. Drukker-Brammall, Aug. 1966; UBC 63-1139, 102 mm SL, from Point Barrow, Alaska. Lower: Leim and Scott 1966:308; eastern Canada. Diagram of tail: Andriashev 1954, fig. 118.

Range: Recorded from the Alaskan Beaufort Sea only as far east as Pitt Point, 71°N, 152°34'W (Frost and Lowry 1983), although occurrence in the Canadian Arctic indicates continuous distribution along the Beaufort coast; and Chukchi Sea (Quast and Hall 1972) to eastern Bering Sea as far south as Norton Sound, 64°18'N, 165°05'W (Sample and Wolotira 1985). There are numerous vouchers from Alaska, including UAM uncataloged specimens from surveys of the northeastern Chukchi Sea in 1989–1991, as well as cataloged lots from Beaufort to Bering seas; NMC 82-26 from western Beaufort Sea; UBC 61-409 and UBC 61-441 from eastern Chukchi Sea; and UBC 63-1139 off Point Barrow.

Stichaeus punctatus (Fabricius, 1780) — Arctic shanny

Beaufort Sea to Aleutian Islands and to northern British Columbia at Skidegate Inlet; to Okhotsk and Japan seas; east across Canadian Arctic to Greenland and Gulf of Maine in western Atlantic; circumpolar.

On bottom in shallow subtidal rocky to sandy areas from shore to depth of 100 m, usually found shallower than 55 m.

D XLVI–LI; A I–II,32–37; Pec 15–16; Pel I,4; Br 6; Vert 51–55.

- Body yellowish brown to bright scarlet with brown streaks and blotches; **dorsal fin with 4–7 dark spots**, each with white or yellow band near posterior margin; anal fin with dark bars.
- Head large (22–25% SL) and pointed; body moderately deep (13–19% SL).
- **No spines at posterior end of anal fin**; caudal rounded to slightly emarginate; pelvic fin present.
- **One lateral line**, ending well before caudal fin.
- Vomerine and palatine teeth present.
- Gill membranes united forward, slightly attached to isthmus.
- Length to 220 mm TL.

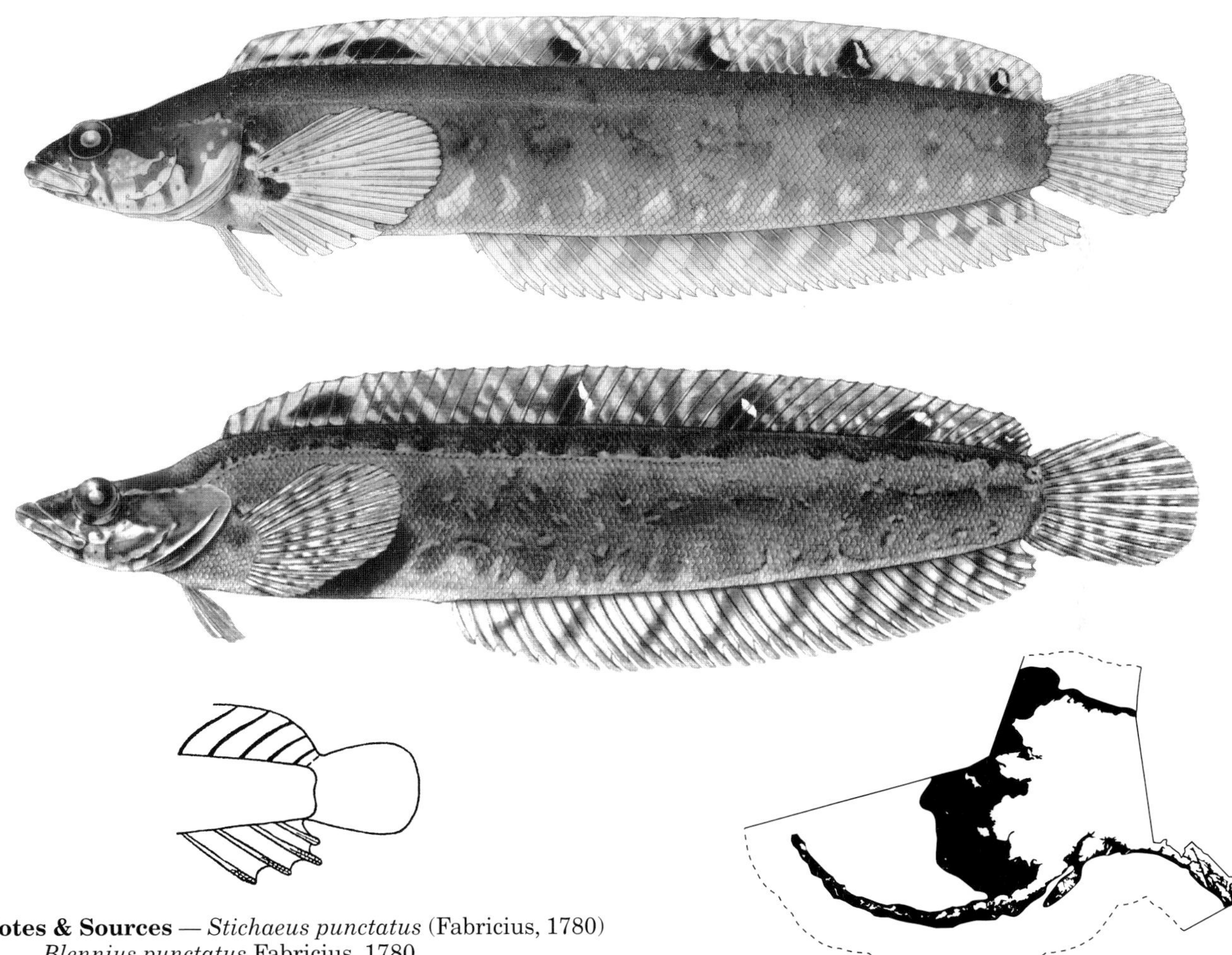

Notes & Sources — *Stichaeus punctatus* (Fabricius, 1780)
Blennius punctatus Fabricius, 1780
Stichaeus rothrocki Bean, 1881

Description: Bean 1879a; Jensen 1944:36–37; Andriashev 1954:230–231; Lindberg and Krasyukova 1975:56–57; Eschmeyer and Herald 1983:253; Scott and Scott 1988:423–424.

Figures: Upper: University of British Columbia, artist P. Drukker-Brammall, Aug. 1966; UBC 63-1034, 110 mm SL, Chiniak Bay, Kodiak Island, Alaska. Lower: Royal British Columbia Museum, artist N. Eyolfson; northern British Columbia. Tail: Makushok 1958, fig. 20.

Range: Previous Alaskan records extend from Beaufort Sea 70 miles east of Point Barrow at Smith Bay (Walters 1955) to three localities in southeastern Alaska just north of British Columbia border (Peden and Wilson 1976). Well represented from areas between those extremes in museum collections, as well as the literature. The only record for the Aleutian Islands west of Unimak Pass seems to be UBC 63-363, from Sweeper Cove, Adak Island. *Stichaeus punctatus* is well known from waters adjacent to Alaska: Hunter et al. (1984) confirmed several western Canadian Arctic records; Peden (1974) recorded it from Skidegate Inlet, British Columbia; and Fedorov and Sheiko (2002) reported it to be abundant in the vicinity of the Commander Islands, Russia.

Gymnoclinus cristulatus Gilbert & Burke, 1912 **trident prickleback**

Amchitka Island, Alaska; eastern Kamchatka, Commander Islands, and Kuril Islands to Hokkaido.

Intertidal to depth of about 40 m; most records are from tidepools and water depths less than 20 m.

D LXI; A 40–43; Pec 14; Pel I,2; Br 6.

- Light olive, with all fins light except the dorsal; **snout and underside of head light, separated from darker upper part by dark line passing through eye**; dorsal fin with or without pale bars; small pale spots along middle of side.
- Snout blunt; eye larger than snout length.
- **Conspicuous trifid interorbital cirrus, each division fringed; similar but smaller cirrus anterior to it**; smaller cirri on snout and upper lip at midline; dermal folds on top of head behind eyes (not all of these structures present or fully developed in the small specimen illustrated).
- **Pelvic fin minute, shorter than eye length**.
- Lateral line present as a mediolateral row of disconnected pores.
- Vomerine and palatine teeth present.
- Gill membranes broadly united, free of isthmus.
- Length to 116 mm SL.

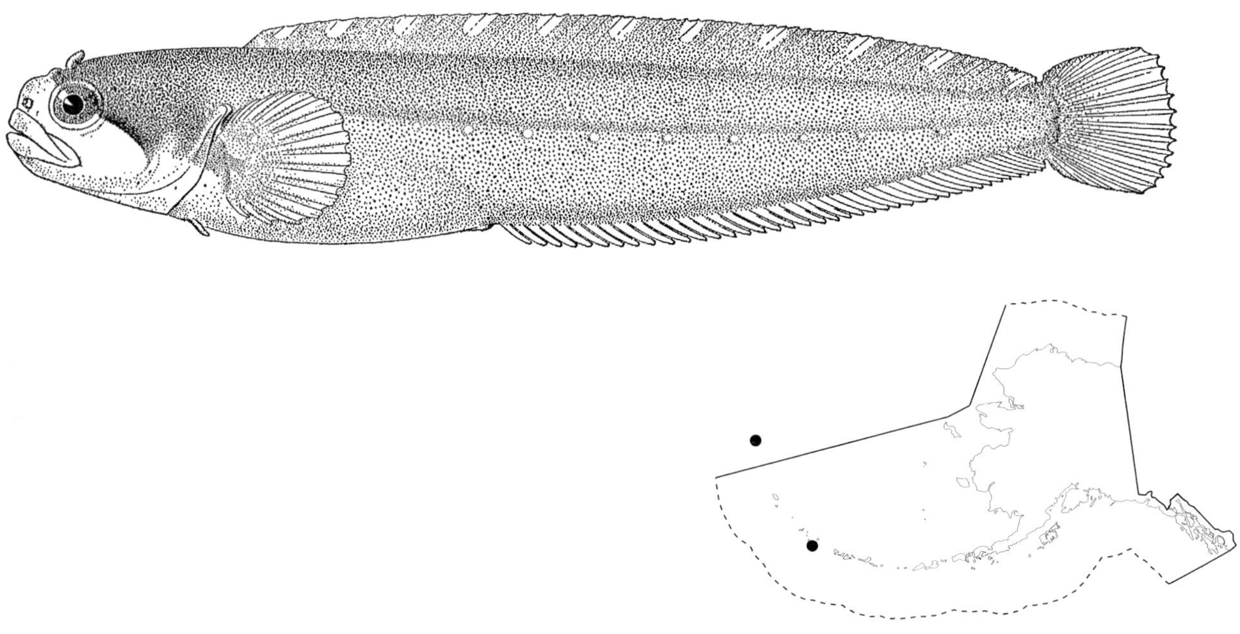

Notes & Sources — *Gymnoclinus cristulatus* Gilbert & Burke, 1912

Hubbs (1927) redefined the genus *Gymnoclinus* on the basis of material overlooked by Gilbert and Burke (1912a). Called wig gunnel by Amaoka et al. (1995:262).

Description: Gilbert and Burke 1912a:86–87; Hubbs 1927: 369–371. Hubbs (1927) described adult material (4 specimens) overlooked by Gilbert and Burke (1912a).

Figure: Gilbert and Burke 1912a, fig. 30; holotype (unique), 37 mm TL, Nikolski, Bering Island, Russia.

Range: Listed for the entire Bering Sea by Andriashev (1939), but we found only one specific Alaskan record: that of Isakson et al. (1971), later repeated (evidently from the same data) by Simenstad et al. (1977), who listed the species among Amchitka Island fishes taken at depths greater than 37 m (their definition of offshore). The species was described from specimens collected at Bering and Medny islands, Russia, where Gilbert and Burke (1912a) found it to be present but rare in the tidepools. The specimens described by Hubbs (1927) were from Simushir Island, in the Kuril Islands, not, as he stated, in Alaska. Sheiko and Fedorov (2000) listed this species for Kamchatka. Sheiko (pers. comm., 2 Feb. 1999) reported that the Kamchatka listing is based on juveniles from Cape Kronotskiy (ZIN 47102) and that, as well, K. Amaoka and A. Balanov collected many juveniles and adults from Shiashkotan Island to Hokkaido, from tidepools to water depths of 20 m.

Chirolophis tarsodes (Jordan & Snyder, 1902) **matcheek warbonnet**

Pacific Ocean south of Sanak Islands and western Gulf of Alaska at Chiniak Bay, Kodiak Island; northern British Columbia at Graham Island.

Sandy bottom in rocky areas near shore at depths of 1–75 m.

D LVIII–LX; A I,43–45; Pec 14–15; Pel I,3–4; Br 6.

- Body and median fins irregularly mottled and blotched; pelvic fin black.
- Snout short; eye large, projecting above profile.
- **Top and sides of head densely covered with cirri**; longer cirri on snout and top of head.
- Pelvic fin well developed.
- Lateral line represented by a few pores anteriorly, concealed by papillae.
- Jaw teeth in 2 close-set rows, their cusps forming a single cutting edge; vomerine and palatine teeth absent.
- Gill membranes united, forming broad fold across isthmus.
- Length to 176 mm SL.

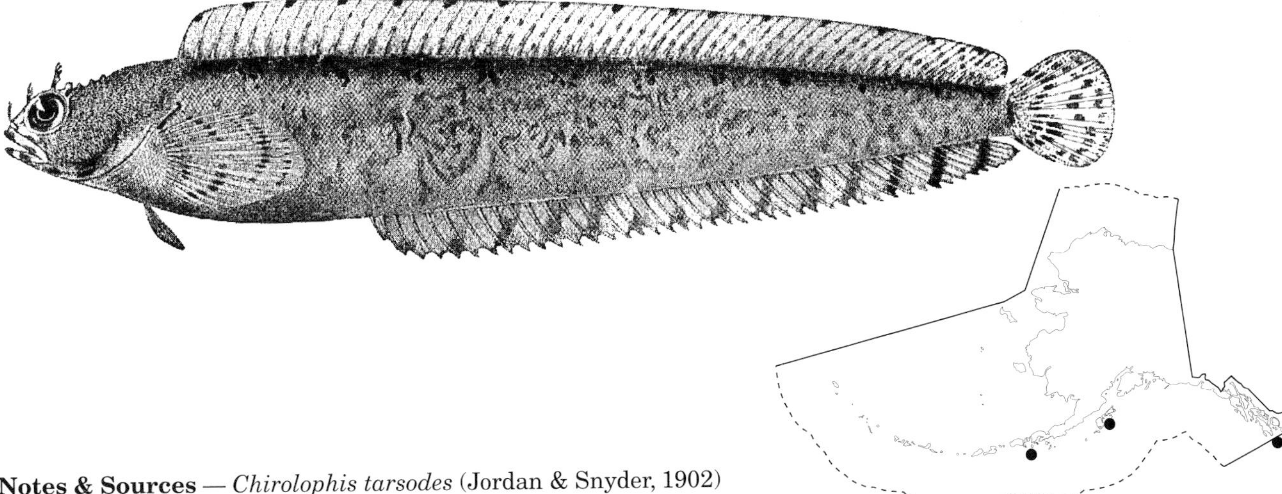

Notes & Sources — *Chirolophis tarsodes* (Jordan & Snyder, 1902)
Bryostemma tarsodes Jordan & Snyder, 1902
Bryostemma polyactocephalum (Pallas): Jordan and Starks 1895:841–843 (in part); Jordan and Evermann 1898:2408–2409 (in part).

Description: Jordan and Snyder 1902d:614–615; Peden 1974:59–60.

Figures: Upper: Royal British Columbia Museum, artist P. Drukker-Brammall; BCPM 72–84, 176 mm SL, Queen Charlotte Islands, B.C. Lower: Jordan and Snyder 1902d, fig. 1; holotype, USNM 50570, 115 mm TL, Alaska; cirri may have been present on the anterior dorsal fin spines but the specimen was damaged in that area.

Range: The holotype (unique) was collected just south of the Sanak Islands, *Albatross* station 3213 (Jordan and Snyder 1902d), at 54°10'N, 162°57'W, depth 75 m (Townsend 1901). Jordan and Snyder (1902d) gave the locality, incorrectly, as "near Unalaska," which may have been the source of later listings from the Bering Sea. Although we did not locate voucher specimens of *C. tarsodes* from the Bering Sea the species evidently does occur there, as Kessler (1985), who participated in NMFS surveys of the Bering Sea and Gulf of Alaska, stated it is rare north and south of the Alaska Peninsula. The only Alaskan record documented by a voucher specimen other than Jordan and Snyder's (1902d) from the Sanak Islands may be UBC 63-1034, from Chiniak Bay on the east coast of Kodiak Island. There is one British Columbia record, comprising four specimens (74–176 mm SL) collected just south of Alaska on the north shore of Graham Island 1 to 2.4 m below low tide (Peden 1974; see upper illustration, this page).

Chirolophis nugator (Jordan & Williams, 1895) **mosshead warbonnet**

Aleutian Islands to southern California at San Miguel Island.

Intertidal to rocky subtidal, often inside empty shells or holes; to depth of 80 m, usually found shallower than 20 m.

D LIII–LV; A I,37–42; Pec 13–14; Pel I,3–4; Br 6.

- Brownish to red-orange and cream; **dorsal fin with 12 or 13 dark brown ocelli** or dark bars, or dark bars anteriorly and ocelli posteriorly; cream-colored bars on body ventrolaterally; pelvic fin pale.
- Snout blunt; eye large, projecting above profile.
- Numerous cirri on top of head and snout; **few cirri on cheeks**.
- Pelvic fin well developed.
- Lateral line not extending beyond pectoral fin.
- Jaw teeth in 2 close-set rows, their cusps forming a single cutting edge; vomerine and palatine teeth absent.
- Gill membranes united, free from isthmus.
- Length to more than 146 mm TL.

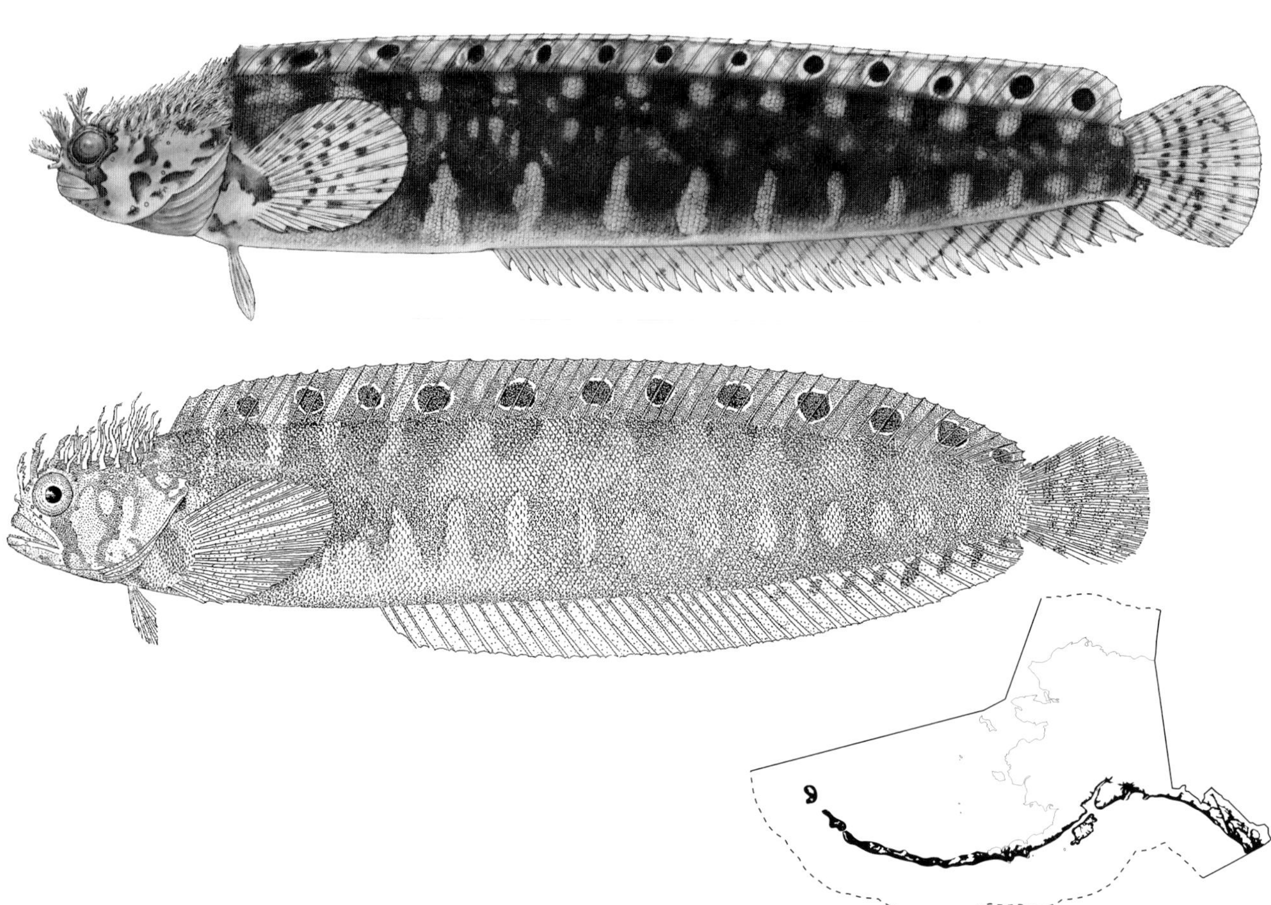

Notes & Sources — *Chirolophis nugator* (Jordan & Williams in Jordan & Starks, 1895)
Bryostemma nugator Jordan & Williams in Jordan & Starks, 1895

Description: Jordan and Starks 1895:843–845; Hart 1973: 333–334; Eschmeyer and Herald 1983:250; Humann 1996:84–85. Presence of ocelli on dorsal fin is not sexually dimorphic as reported by some authors. Jordan and Starks (1895) reported both bars and ocelli on dorsal fin of one specimen, and Peden and Wilson (1976) reported ocelli on dorsal fins of both males and females.

Figures: Upper: University of British Columbia, artist P. Drukker-Brammall; UBC 65-20, 84 mm SL, Agattu Island, Alaska. Lower: Jordan and Starks 1895, pl. 101; syntype, CAS-SU 3134; Elliot Bay, Washington.

Range: Previously recorded as far west in the Aleutian Islands as Amchitka Island (Isakson et al. 1971). Specimens (6) from farther west, at Barnacle Bay, Agattu Island, are in UBC 65-20 (see upper illustration, this page). Occurrence of the species is documented throughout its known range in Alaska by records from, for example, Nikolski Bay, Umnak Island (Hubbard and Reeder 1965); Prince William Sound (Rosenthal 1980); and Sitka (Quast 1968). Peden and Wilson (1976) found it at two localities in southeastern Alaska just north of the British Columbia border, and several south of the border.

Size: The largest specimen examined by Peden and Wilson (1976:240) was 146 mm TL, and they stated they knew of a "considerably larger" specimen.

Chirolophis decoratus (Jordan & Snyder, 1902) **decorated warbonnet**

Eastern Bering Sea and Aleutian Islands to northern California at Humboldt Bay.

Rocky bottom and reef crevices, usually among seaweed, at subtidal depths to 91 m; occasionally found near surface.

D LXI–LXIII; A I,44–47; Pec 14–15; Pel I,4; Br 6; Vert 67–68.

- Shades of brown and orange with pale spots and bands; pelvic fin pale.
- Snout short, about same as eye diameter.
- **One pair of long multifid cirri joined at their bases on anterior part of interorbital space, their height more than twice diameter of eye**; many cirri on top of head; **a few simple cirri on cheeks and sides of head**.
- First 4–9 dorsal fin spines with multifid cirri; pelvic fin well developed.
- Lateral line not extending beyond pectoral fin, each pore below a minute villus.
- Jaw teeth in 2 close-set rows, their cusps forming a single cutting edge; vomerine and palatine teeth absent.
- Gill membranes united, forming broad, V-shaped fold across isthmus.
- Length to 420 mm TL.

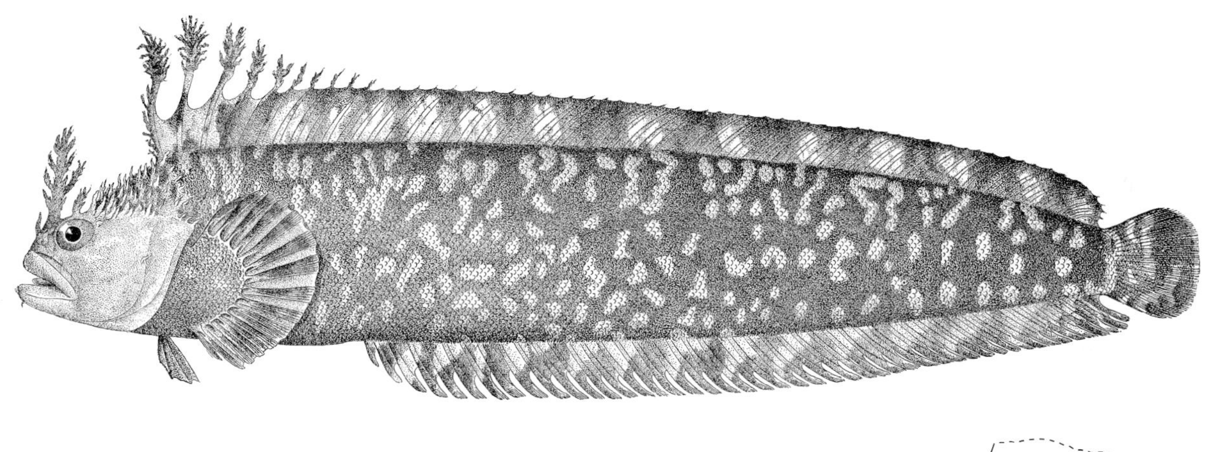

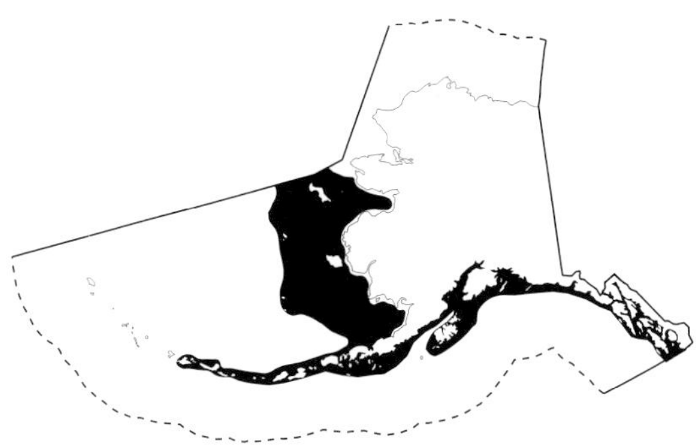

Notes & Sources — *Chirolophis decoratus* (Jordan & Snyder, 1902)

Bryostemma decoratum Jordan & Snyder, 1902

Chirolophus polyactocephalus (Pallas): Bean in Nelson 1887:305 and pl. 15, fig. 2.

Chirolophis polyactocephalus (Pallas): Quast and Hall 1972:34 (in part: specimens from Kodiak Island); and other Alaskan specimens.

Bryostemma polyactocephalum (Pallas): Jordan and Starks 1895:841–843 (in part); Jordan and Evermann 1898:2408–2409 (in part).

Description: Jordan and Snyder 1902d:615–617; Andriashev 1954:237; Peden 1974:60; Eschmeyer and Herald 1983:250; Humann 1996:86–87.

Figure: Nelson 1887, pl. 15-2; St. Michael, Norton Sound.

Range: Alaskan records include: St. Michael, Norton Sound (Nelson 1887); St. Paul Island (Jordan and Gilbert 1899); localities north and south of Alaska Peninsula (Gilbert 1896); Adak Island (Wilimovsky 1964); Kodiak Island (Quast and Hall 1972); Behm Canal and Stephens Passage (Evermann and Goldsborough 1907). Others in permanent collections include: CAS 43946, taken north of Krenitzin Islands; CAS 46314, southwest of Kodiak Island; UBC 65-51 and 65-145, Kodiak Island; and UBC 65-496, northwest Baranof Island. Baxter (1990ms) collected specimens from Kachemak Bay. This species is commonly on display in marine aquaria. Additional records are needed in order to define the extent of the species' range in the northern and western Bering Sea and western Aleutian Islands.

Chirolophis snyderi (Taranetz, 1938) **bearded warbonnet**

Northeastern Chukchi Sea to western Gulf of Alaska; and from at least as far north in western Bering Sea as Cape Olyutorskiy, south to Sea of Okhotsk and west coast of Sakhalin.

Coastal, on soft and rocky bottoms, at depths of 17–68 m.

D LVIII–LXI; A I,43–47; Pec 13–15; Pel I,4; Br 6; Vert 63–65.

- Pinkish orange with lilac-red bands on body and vague spots on dorsal fin; anal fin pink with blurred reddish spots; **two orange or red bars on caudal fin**; pelvic fin dark.
- Snout blunt; eye large, projecting above profile.
- Small median cirrus on snout; **2 pairs of long multifid cirri on interorbital space**, anterior pair close or joined at their bases, posterior widely separated; many simple and multifid cirri on occiput and nape; **widely spaced multifid cirri on lower jaw and preopercle**; sometimes with cirri on opercle and along lateral line anteriorly.
- First 2 or 3 dorsal fin spines with long, flat, multifid cirri, sometimes with additional cirri along length of 1st spine, and smaller, simple or multifid cirri at ends of next several spines; pelvic fin well developed.
- Lateral line short, a few pores above pectoral fin.
- Jaw teeth in 2 close-set rows, cusps forming single cutting edge; vomerine and palatine teeth absent.
- Gill membranes united, forming free fold across isthmus.
- Length to 240 mm TL.

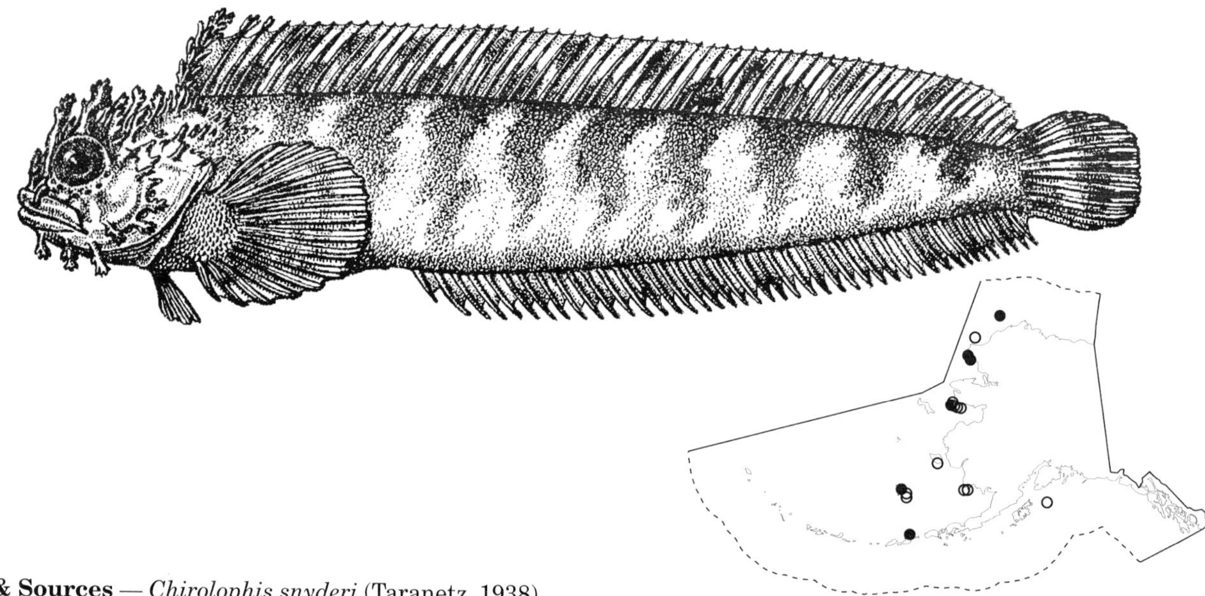

Notes & Sources — *Chirolophis snyderi* (Taranetz, 1938)

Bryostemma polyactocephalum (Pallas): Jordan and Evermann 1898:2408–2409 (in part, specimen from Petropavlovsk; 75-cm size is an error); Jordan and Snyder 1902c:465 (specimen "about 240 mm long" from Petropavlovsk); Andriashev 1937:49 of transl., 136- and 150-mm specimens collected off Cape Olyutorskiy, depth 32 m.

Bryostemma snyderi Taranetz, 1938

Description: Jordan and Snyder 1902c:465; Andriashev 1954:236–237; Lindberg and Krasyukova 1975:81–82; Amaoka and Miki in Masuda et al. 1984:301. Two UAM uncataloged specimens (catch data given under Range).

Figure: Andriashev 1954, fig. 120; 136 mm TL, Bering Sea off Cape Olyutorskiy, Russia.

Range: Reported by Kessler (1985) from NMFS surveys to be uncommon north and rare south of the Alaska Peninsula, and included by Barber et al. (1997) on list of fish caught in UAF surveys of the northeastern Chukchi Sea. Specific localities in Alaska were not previously published. Voucher specimens from the northeastern Chukchi Sea include one (UW 27455) taken at 68°05'N, 166°12'W, depth 24 m, by the *Miller Freeman*, 12 Sep. 1976; one (UAM uncataloged, 174 mm TL) at 71°10'N, 161°55'W, depth 46 m, by the *Ocean Hope III*, 7 Sep. 1990; and one (UAM uncataloged, 113 mm TL) at 68°25'N, 166°40'W, depth 17 m, also by *Ocean Hope III*, 23 Sep. 1991. From farther south, the NMNH has two specimens (USNM 216539, 292585) collected in 1973 by K. Vogt off Nome at depth of 20 m, and off Cape Thompson (depth not given). CAS 46668 and 46669 are from a ridge northwest of St. Paul Island, USNM 53852 was collected by the *Albatross* off Unalaska Island, and RBCM 980-605 by A. E. Peden from Dutch Harbor, Unalaska Island. R. Baxter (unpubl. data) examined specimens (not saved, circles on above map) caught near St. George Island at depths of 47 and 68 m by the *Miller Freeman* in 1984. Other circles on the map, including the one in the Gulf of Alaska, represent additional unvouchered catches from UAF and NMFS surveys (R. Baxter, unpubl. data; D. W. Kessler, pers. comm., 20 Jun. 1994). Possibly the most widely distributed of the Pacific Ocean species of *Chirolophis* (Andriashev 1954), but poorly documented due to its rare occurrence in commercial catches (Grigor'ev 1992) and historical confusion with *C. decoratus*. Few depths of capture were reported for *C. snyderi* before this account.

Bryozoichthys lysimus (Jordan & Snyder, 1902) **nutcracker prickleback**

Eastern Bering Sea in vicinity of St. Matthew Island; Aleutian Islands at Amchitka Pass and Unalaska Bay; western Gulf of Alaska south of Sanak Islands; northern Gulf of Alaska; western Bering Sea off Cape Navarin to Sea of Okhotsk and to northern Sea of Japan and Pacific off Hokkaido.

Soft bottom, usually over outer shelf and upper slope, at depths of 45–490 m.

D LXI–LXVI; A I,47–50; Pec 14–15; Pel I,3; Br 6; Vert 69–75.

- In life and in preservative **brownish**, with indistinct brownish bands; sometimes with dark bar slanting down from eye; dark bands on caudal fin; pectoral fin often orange.
- Long median cirrus on snout; **2 pairs of long multifid cirri on interorbital space**, the anterior ones united at their bases and the posterior pair widely separated; numerous long cirri on occiput and nape; **pair of small cirri on chin**.
- First few dorsal fin spines with cirri at tips; pelvic fin present.
- **Scales not extending anteriorly beyond origin of dorsal fin.**
- Lateral line short, a few pores above pectoral fin base.
- Teeth conical; jaw teeth in bands, not in 2 close-set rows; vomerine and palatine teeth present.
- Gill membranes united, forming broad, V-shaped fold across isthmus.
- Length to 200 mm SL.

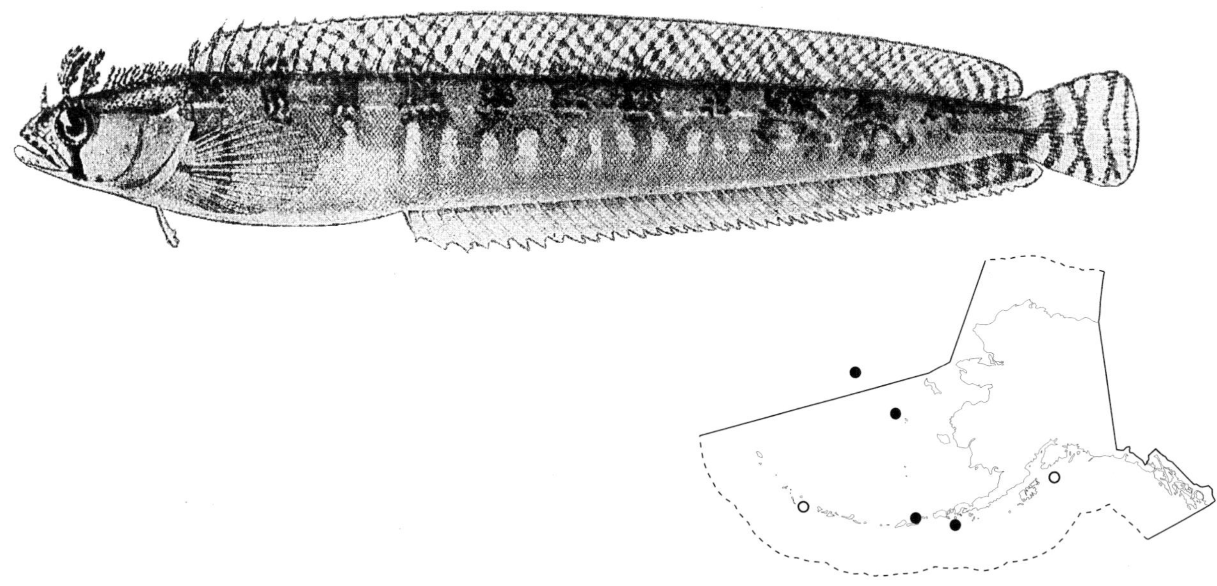

Notes & Sources — *Bryozoichthys lysimus* (Jordan & Snyder, 1902)
Bryolophus lysimus Jordan & Snyder, 1902
So easily confused with *B. marjorius* that a specimen (CAS-SU 3049) described as a paratype of *B. lysimus* by Jordan and Snyder (1902d) was later determined by McPhail (1970) to be *B. marjorius.*
Characters of Japanese specimens of *B. lysimus* and *B. marjorius* described by Amaoka et al. (1977) are inconsistent with the original descriptions of the species and with specimens of *Bryozoichthys* from the Bering Sea examined by C.W.M. A third species may be involved, or *B. lysimus* and *B. marjorius* are not different species, or they may need to be redescribed.

Description: Jordan and Snyder 1902d:617–618; Andriashev 1937:49–50 of transl.; Lindberg and Krasyukova 1975:74–76; Amaoka and Miki in Masuda et al. 1984:301.

Figure: Jordan and Snyder 1902d, fig. 3; holotype, USNM 50571, 100 mm TL, south of Sanak Islands.

Range: Two previous Alaskan records: northwest of St. Matthew Island, in mouth of a Greenland halibut, *Reinhardtius hippoglossoides* (Andriashev 1937); and south of Sanak Islands at *Albatross* station 3213 (Jordan and Snyder 1902d), black sand bottom at depth of 75 m (Townsend 1901). The UW has a specimen (UW 27457) taken from the Bering Sea by NMFS in 1982, but lacking other data. A specimen in NMC 66-8 was collected from north coast of Unalaska Bay, 54°03'N, 166°38'W, depth 77 m, in Nov. 1965. R. Baxter (unpubl. data) examined a specimen taken at Amchitka Pass, 51°58'N, 179°49'E, depth 121 m; and another from the Gulf of Alaska between Seward and Kodiak Island at 58°45'N, 150°00'W, depth 166 m, in 1987 (specimens were not saved). ZIN 46383, a specimen collected in 1982 from the western Bering Sea at 61°50'N, 176°58'E, off Cape Navarin, was determined by V. V. Fedorov to be an example of *B. lysimus* (B. A. Sheiko, pers. comm., 2 Feb. 1999). Few depths of capture have been reported. Lavrova (1990) gave depth range of 45–490 m for Sea of Okhotsk, but the few records from Alaska are from depths shallower than 170 m.

Bryozoichthys marjorius McPhail, 1970 **pearly prickleback**

Aleutian Islands to southern British Columbia at La Perouse Bank.

Bottom, usually on outer shelf and upper slope at depths of 183–310 m.

D LXVII–LXXI; A I,53–55; Pec 15–16; Pel I,3; Br 6; Vert 71–73.

- **Pearly white** in life, tan or brownish in preservative; vague dark saddles; more or less distinct dark bar slanting down from eye; sometimes with dark blotch on dorsal fin anteriorly; caudal fin pale, with 2–5 dark vertical bands; pectoral fin tan or brown, with pale margin.
- Short median cirrus on snout; **1 pair long cirri fused at their bases above anterior margin of orbit**; **3 shorter cirri in row across posterior interorbital space**; 18–20 short cirri on occiput and nape; short **cirrus on posterior end of maxilla and another below it on lower jaw**; **no cirri near symphysis of lower jaw**.
- First 4 dorsal fin spines with cirri at tips; pelvic fin present.
- **Scales present on nape**.
- Lateral line short, a few pores above pectoral fin.
- Teeth conical; jaw teeth in bands, not in 2 close-set rows; vomerine and palatine teeth present.
- Gill membranes united, free of isthmus.
- Length to 305 mm TL.

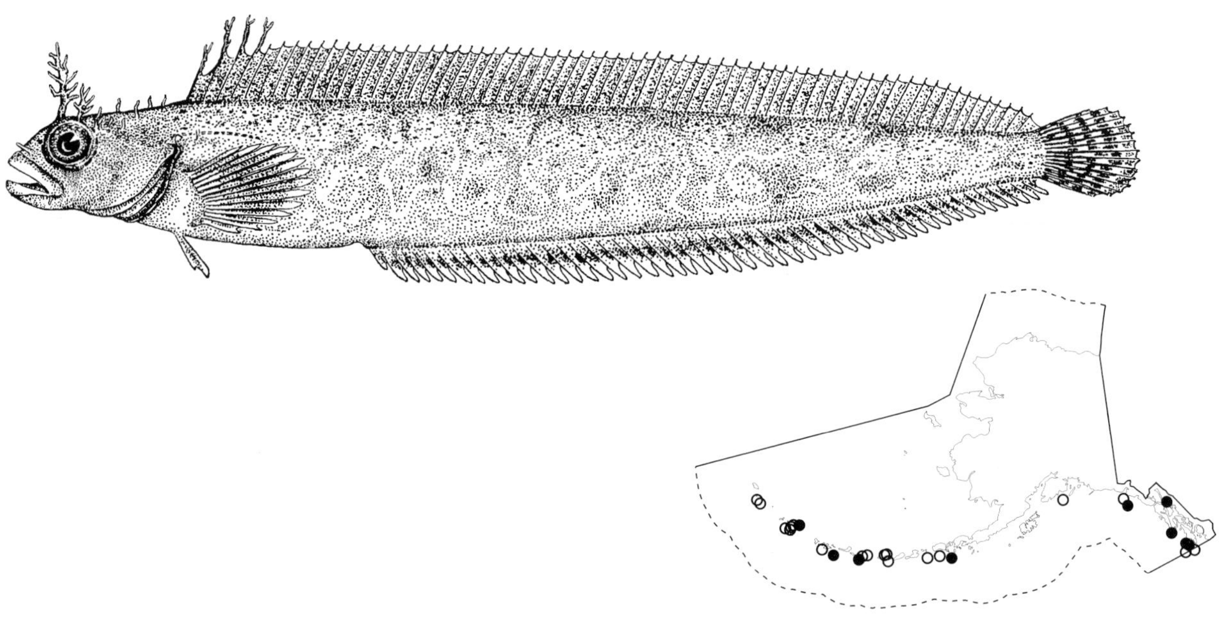

Notes & Sources — *Bryozoichthys marjorius* McPhail, 1970

Species name is sometimes spelled, incorrectly, "*majorius.*" As McPhail (1970) explained it, the specific name *marjorius*, a variant of *margarita* (a pearl), was given for his wife Marjorie and is an allusion to the distinctive pearly white coloration of the species.

This species may not be adequately described. See comment in *B. lysimus* account on preceding page.

Description: McPhail 1970; Eschmeyer and Herald 1983: 249. Hart's (1973:331–332) description was written shortly after McPhail's and reported no new information. Although Matarese et al. (1989:507) gave wider ranges for meristic values, their sources or voucher specimens were not cited. Because of the potential for confusion with *B. lysimus* or the possibility of unresolved problems in the taxonomy of *Bryozoichthys,* we give only the meristics that were provided by McPhail (1970).

Figure: McPhail 1970, fig. 1; holotype, NMC 66-268, 216 mm SL, near Forrester Island, Alaska.

Range: First recorded from Alaska by McPhail (1970) from *Albatross* station 3213 (CAS-SU 3049, 116 mm SL; formerly a paratype of *B. lysimus*), which was located south of the Sanak Islands (not near Unalaska, as some authors reported it), and from off Forrester Island, southeastern Alaska. Recorded by Amaoka et al. (1977) from Petrel Bank off northeast coast of Semisopochnoi Island, south of Adak Island, and eastern Gulf of Alaska at 55°58'N, 135°18'W. The UW has specimens from south of Seguam Island at 52°25'N, 172°40'W, depth 220 m (UW 27456); and northeastern Gulf of Alaska at 58°38'N, 140°33'W (UW 25161). Specimens in lots AB 90-06(4) and AB 93-2(1) were taken off Forrester Island and Snettisham, respectively. Circles on map represent NMFS survey catches provided by D. W. Kessler (pers. comm., 20 Jun. 1994), which are not documented by voucher specimens. Few depths have been reported.

Lumpenella longirostris (Evermann & Goldsborough, 1907) **longsnout prickleback**

Bering Sea and Aleutian Islands to southern British Columbia at Burrard Inlet, and to Sea of Okhotsk and northern Japan; Greenland.

Bottom, usually on outer shelf and upper slope; recorded from depths of 25–1,140 m, typically taken at 100–200 m.

D LXI–LXXI; A II–V,36–42; Pec 13–14; Pel I,2–3; Br 6; Vert 71–75.

- Dark bluish brown to olive brown; fin margins blackish.
- **Snout elongate, projecting beyond and overhanging lower jaw**; maxilla not extending to below eye.
- **Dorsal fin spines unusually stiff and with free tips; typically 3–5 anal fin spines**; spines of anal and pelvic fins rigid and easily discernible from soft rays; pelvic fin present.
- **Scales present on entire head**.
- Lateral line mediolateral, difficult to discern.
- Vomerine and palatine teeth absent.
- Gill membranes narrowly united and attached to isthmus far forward.
- Length to 411 mm TL.

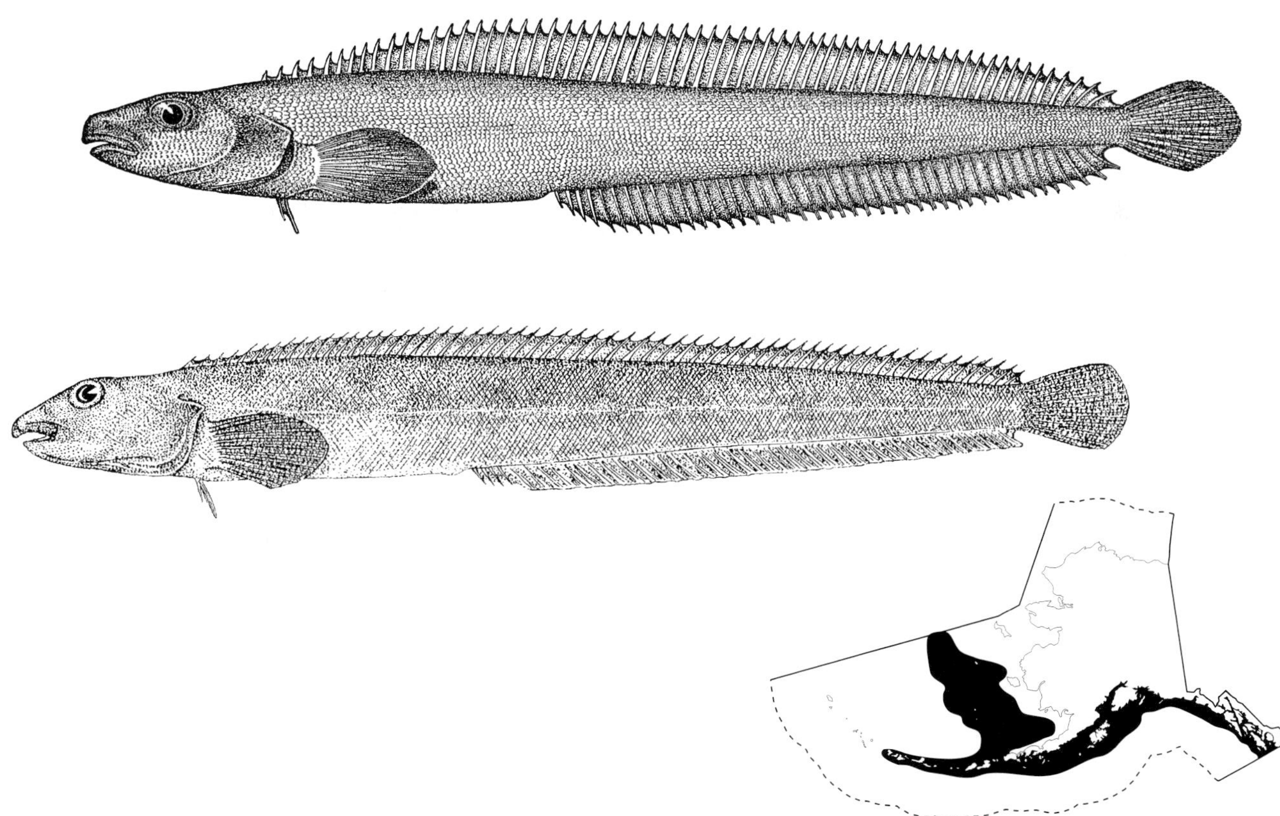

Notes & Sources — *Lumpenella longirostris* (Evermann & Goldsborough, 1907)
Lumpenus longirostris Evermann & Goldsborough, 1907
Lumpenella: New genus defined by Hubbs (1927) on basis of *Lumpenus longirostris.*
Lumpenella nigricans Matsubara & Ochiai, 1952

Description: Evermann and Goldsborough 1907:340–341; Hubbs 1927:378–379; Hart 1973:334–335; Amaoka and Miki in Masuda et al. 1984:301.

Figures: Upper: Evermann and Goldsborough 1907, fig. 115; type, 236 mm TL, Lynn Canal, Alaska. Lower: Hart 1973:334; 27 cm TL, Smith Sound, British Columbia.

Range: NMFS survey data reported by Allen and Smith (1988) extended known range north in the Bering Sea to Navarin Canyon and off the Yukon Delta, and west in Aleutian Islands to Tanaga Island; and indicated a shallower minimum depth of occurrence (25 m) than previous record (Hart 1973) of 91 m. Probably occurs throughout the Aleutian Islands, as Fedorov and Sheiko (2002) reported it to be common at the Commander Islands. Recorded from depths of 300–1,140 m in Sea of Okhotsk by Dudnik and Dolganov (1992); and to 825 m in northeastern Pacific by Allen and Smith (1988). Miki (in Okamura et al. 1995) reported the first record from the Atlantic Ocean: a 70.5-mm-SL prickleback from Greenland at a depth of 734 m.

Size: R. Baxter, unpubl. data: specimen (not saved) from Bering Sea at 54°41'N, 166°15'W, depth 298–302 m, taken by *Argosy* on 26 Aug. 1985, measured 379 mm SL, 411 mm TL; morphological data are on file. Previously recorded to about 35 cm SL (Amaoka and Miki in Masuda et al. 1984).

Leptoclinus maculatus (Fries, 1837) **daubed shanny**

Beaufort Sea through Bering Sea and Aleutian Islands to Unalaska Island and to Puget Sound; Seas of Okhotsk and Japan; North Atlantic Ocean.

Mud, sand, or stone and pebble bottom at depths of 2–475 m, usually shallower than 170 m; as deep as 400 m off Greenland.

D LVII–LXIV; A I–II,34–40; Pec 14–16; Pel I,3–4; Br 6; Vert 66–72.

- Body creamy white to yellowish brown, irregularly marked with dark blotches; dorsal fin with dark spots or oblique bars; caudal fin with 3–5 narrow dark bands; other fins plain yellowish.
- Snout overhangs lower jaw; **maxilla extending to mideye or beyond**.
- Dorsal fin origin far forward, over vertebrae 1–2; first 2–7 dorsal fin spines free or partly free; dorsal and anal fins not connected to caudal fin; caudal fin truncate or slightly emarginate; **lower 5–6 rays of pectoral fin produced and with tips free**; pelvic fin present.
- **Scales present on head, except absent from cheeks**.
- Lateral line mediolateral but indiscernible.
- Jaws each with canine teeth in front; **vomerine** and palatine **teeth present**.
- Gill membranes united forward and narrowly attached to isthmus.
- Length to 200 mm TL.

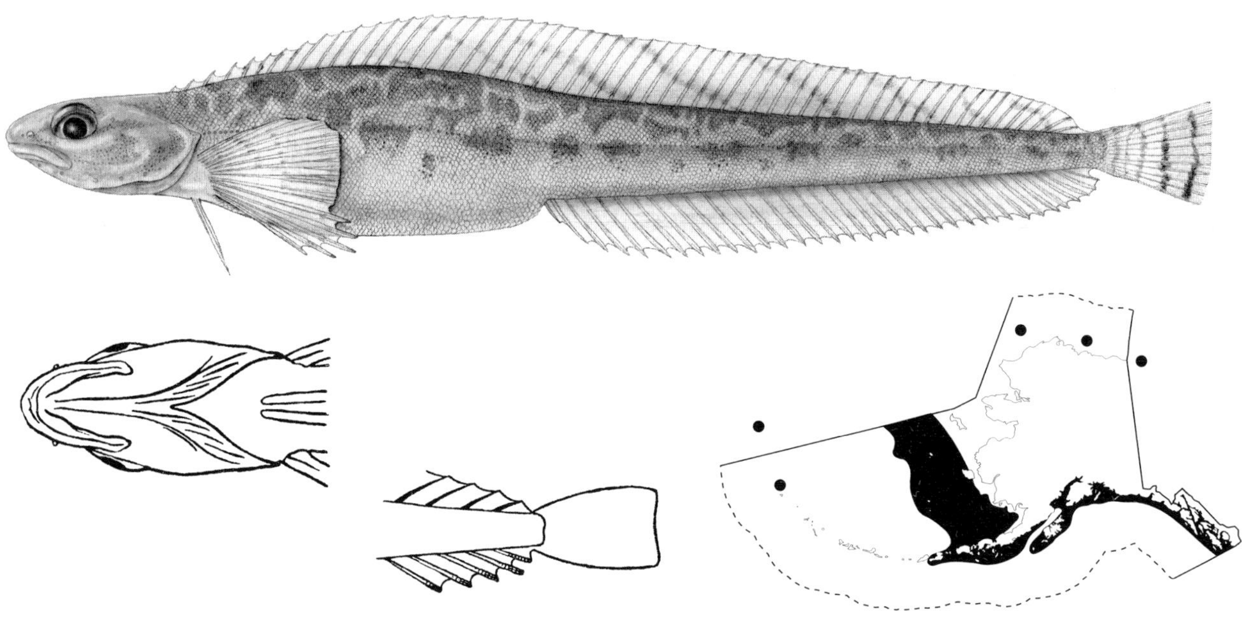

Notes & Sources — *Leptoclinus maculatus* (Fries, 1837)
Clinus maculatus Fries, 1837
Leptoclinus maculatus: Gill 1861a, 1864; Makushok 1958. Detailed synonymies are given in Andriashev (1954:248) and Makushok (in Hureau and Monod 1973:538). Following those authors and Jordan and Evermann (1898), Quast and Hall (1972), Lavrova (1990), McAllister (1990), Coad (1995), Miki (in Okamura et al. 1995), and others, we classify this species in *Leptoclinus* rather than in *Lumpenus* as done by, for example, Eschmeyer and Herald (1983), Scott and Scott (1988), and Robins et al. (1991a).

Some authors (e.g., Andriashev 1937, 1954; Makushok in Hureau and Monod 1973) consider North Pacific specimens to represent a distinct subspecies, *Leptoclinus maculatus diaphanocarus*.

Description: Jordan and Evermann 1898:2433; Jensen 1944:31–32; Andriashev 1954:248–250; Hart 1973:336; Lindberg and Krasyukova 1975:91–93; Eschmeyer and Herald 1983:251; Scott and Scott 1988:420–421.

Figures: University of British Columbia, artist P. Drukker-Brammall, Jan. 1966; UBC 61-494, 145 mm SL, Auke Bay, Alaska. Head, ventral: Andriashev 1954, fig. 125(4). Tail: Makushok 1958, fig. 20.

Range: Recorded northward in Bering Sea to Gulf of Anadyr (Andriashev 1954) and west of St. Lawrence Island (Allen and Smith 1988); west in Aleutians to Unimak Island (Wilimovsky 1964) and Unalaska Island (Allen and Smith 1988); and along Gulf of Alaska coasts, including southeastern Alaska (e.g., Quast and Hall 1972, Blackburn et al. 1980, Blackburn and Johnson 1982). We found only two records from the Arctic Ocean off Alaska and one from the western Aleutian Islands: Beaufort Sea at 71°11'N, 148°32'W, depth 159 m, about 81 km north of the Return Islands (NMC 74-2889); northeastern Chukchi Sea at 71°28'N, 163°47'W (Frost and Lowry 1983); and Attu Island (UBC 65-24). Hunter et al. (1984) recorded specimens from the Canadian Beaufort off Tuktoyaktuk. Fedorov and Sheiko (2002) reported *L. maculatus* to be a common species in the vicinity of the Commander Islands.

Size: To 18 cm in Pacific (Eschmeyer and Herald 1983) and 20 cm off Iceland (Andriashev 1954).

Poroclinus rothrocki Bean, 1890 **whitebarred prickleback**

Southeastern Bering Sea and Aleutian Islands to southern California at San Diego.

Rocky bottom at 46–128 m.

D LVII–LXVII; A III,40–44; Pec 13–15; Pel I,3; Br 6; Vert 65.

- Light brown dorsally, pale ventrally; **10–12 narrow white vertical bars** dorsolaterally on body, fading ventrally; fins without distinct markings; dark smudges variably present on dorsal fin posteriorly and on caudal and pectoral fins.
- Mouth small, maxilla extending to vertical from front of eye to front of pupil.
- **Dorsal and anal fins not connected to caudal fin; anal fin with 3 spines anteriorly**; caudal fin rounded to nearly pointed; pectoral fin rounded, middle rays longest; pelvic fin present.
- **Scales present on cheeks, absent from rest of head.**
- Lateral line mediolateral, indistinct, usually more evident toward head.
- Vomerine and palatine teeth present.
- Gill membranes united forward and firmly attached to isthmus.
- Length to 250 mm TL.

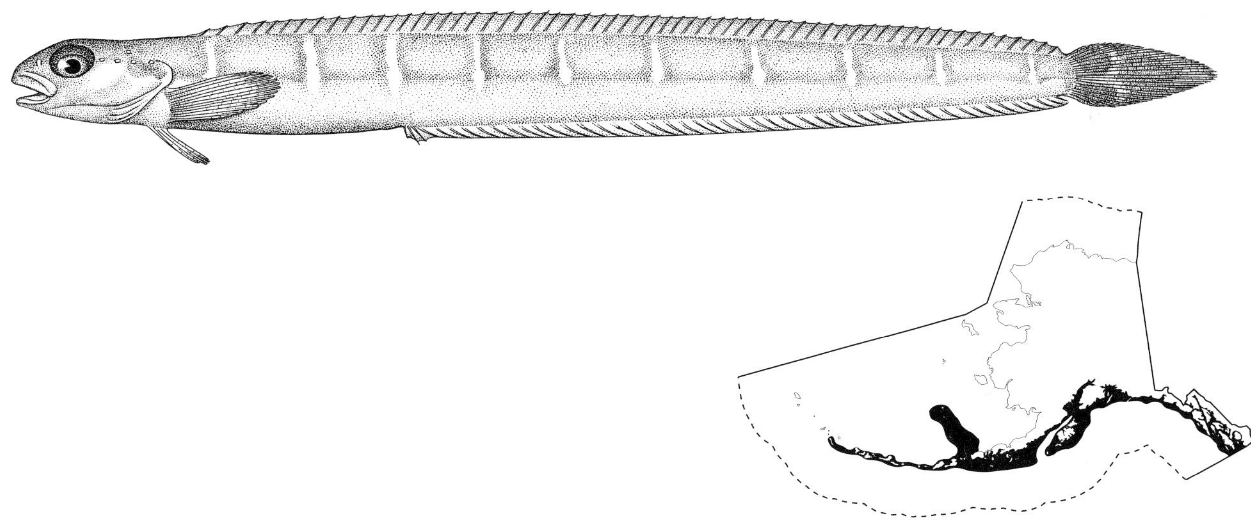

Notes & Sources — _Poroclinus rothrocki_ Bean, 1890

**Description**: Bean 1890b:40; Jordan and Evermann 1898: 2434; Hart 1973:340–341; Eschmeyer and Herald 1983: 252; Springer and Anderson 1997:11 (lengths of holotype).

**Figure**: Smithsonian Institution, NMNH, Division of Fishes, artist S. F. Denton, May 1889; holotype (unique), USNM 45366, 175 mm TL, 155 mm SL, between Nagai and Big Koniuji islands, Alaska.

**Range**: Previous records include: Shumagin Islands between Nagai and Big Koniuji islands, _Albatross_ station 2852, depth 106 m (type locality; Bean 1890b); north of Unalaska Island, _Albatross_ station 3312, depth 82 m (Gilbert 1896); off Amchitka Island (Isakson et al. 1971, Simenstad et al. 1977); off east side Kodiak Island (Blackburn and Jackson 1982); and southeastern Alaska (Quast and Hall 1972). Kessler (1985) reported _P. rothrocki_ to be uncommon north and common south of Alaska Peninsula. The northernmost Bering Sea record found is CAS 124975, off St. Paul Island; UW 22394 is from southwest of St. George Island. Additional museum collections, together with catch localities from the NMFS survey database provided by D. W. Kessler (pers. comm., 20 Jun. 1994), fill out the range outlined by those records.

Anisarchus medius (Reinhardt, 1836) **stout eelblenny**

Beaufort Sea to southeastern Alaska at Auke Bay and to Okhotsk and Japan seas; circumpolar.

Almost exclusively on muddy bottoms from near shore to depth of 150 m, usually shallower than 100 m.

D LVIII–LXIII; A I,37–42; Pec 13–15; Pel I,3; Br 6; Vert 65–70.

- Body creamy white or yellowish to reddish, marked with vague darker spots or monotone; sometimes with oblique red bars on dorsal fin; anal fin without markings; caudal fin banded.
- Body relatively stout, especially toward front.
- Mouth slightly upturned; maxilla extending to anterior margin of eye to pupil.
- **Dorsal and anal fins connected to caudal fin; anal fin increasing gradually in height posteriorly**; caudal fin rounded; pelvic fin present.
- Scales present on cheeks in large specimens.
- Vomerine teeth absent, palatine teeth present.
- **Gill membranes** united far forward, **attached to isthmus under anterior half of eye**.
- Length to 180 mm TL.

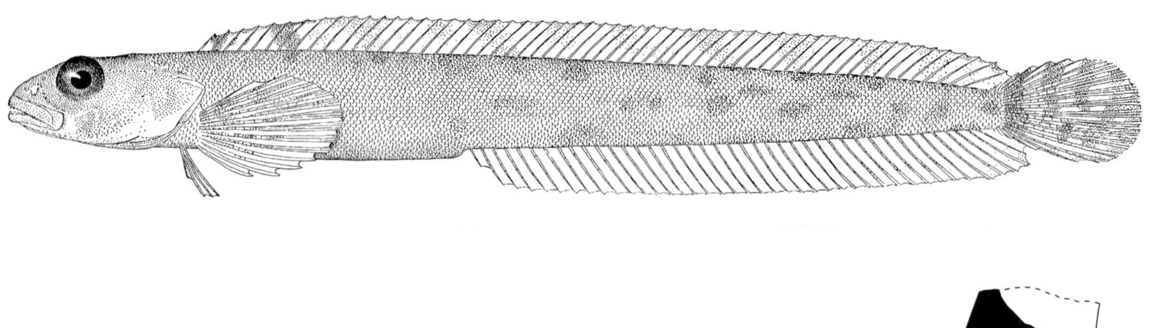

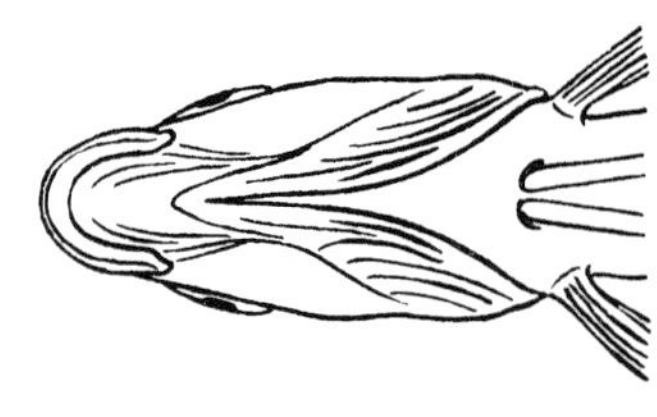

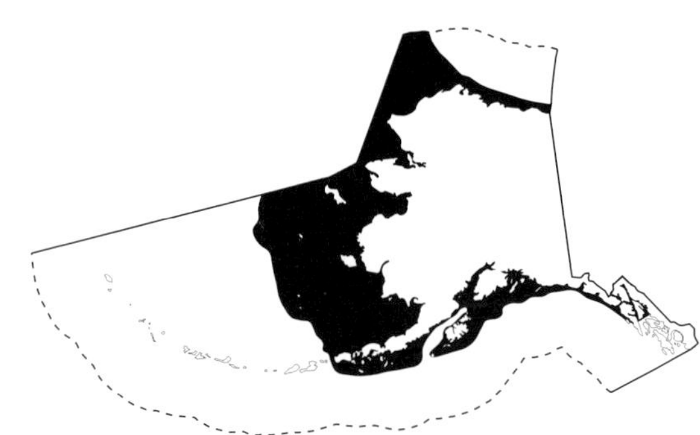

Notes & Sources — *Anisarchus medius* (Reinhardt, 1836)

Lumpenus medius Reinhardt, 1835–1836

Clinus medius Reinhardt, 1837

Anisarchus medius: Gill 1864, Makushok 1958. Detailed synonymies are given in Andriashev (1954:241) and Makushok (in Hureau and Monod 1973:538).

Although valid as *Lumpenus medius* in Wilimovsky (1954), Robins and Ray (1986), and Robins et al. (1991a), the species has most often been classified in *Anisarchus,* as in Gill (1864), Makushok (1958, in Hureau and Monod 1973, in Whitehead et al. 1986), Quast and Hall (1972), Lindberg and Krasyukova (1975), Eschmeyer and Herald (1983), Lavrova (1990), McAllister (1990), Coad (1995), and Miki (in Okamura et al. 1995).

Description: Jensen 1944:34–35; Andriashev 1954:241–243; Lindberg and Krasyukova 1975:89–90; Eschmeyer and Herald 1983: 248; Scott and Scott 1988:422–423.

Figures: Lateral view: Jordan and Gilbert 1899, pl. 81; off Avacha Bay, Kamchatka. Head, ventral: Andriashev 1954, fig. 125(1).

Range: Documented by numerous records from Beaufort Sea at Demarcation Point (Carey 1978) to southeastern Alaska at Auke Bay (Quast 1968), but records are lacking for the Aleutian Islands west of Unimak Pass. Nor has it been recorded from the vicinity of the Commander Islands (B. A. Sheiko, pers. comm., 2 Feb. 1999). Thorsteinson et al. (1991) reported it from the Alaskan Beaufort Sea at Prudhoe and Camden bays at depths as shallow as 2.5 m. Hunter et al. (1984) confirmed records from the Canadian Beaufort Sea off the Mackenzie Delta.

Size: Andriashev (1954) considered 180 mm to be exceptionally large. Lindberg and Krasyukova (1975:90) gave a maximum size of 246 mm, but since that is much larger than previous records and they did not cite documentation for it, it must be a mistake. In the Gulf of Anadyr, where *A. medius* is abundant, it reaches 15 cm TL (Andriashev 1954).

Lumpenus fabricii Reinhardt, 1836 — slender eelblenny

Beaufort Sea to southeastern Alaska at Auke Bay and to Okhotsk and Japan seas; circumpolar.

Sandy to rocky bottom, intertidal to maximum depth of about 175 m, almost always found shallower than 100 m, and usually on inner shelf at depths less than 50 m.

D LXI–LXVI; A I,40–44; Pec 13–16; Pel I,3; Br 6; Vert 70–75.

- Body cream or yellowish with **irregular brown blotches or broken diagonal bars extending onto lower side**; dorsal fin with blotches, caudal fin sometimes with dark markings; other fins pale yellow, unmarked.
- Body more slender than in *Anisarchus medius*.
- Mouth horizontal; maxilla extending nearly to front of pupil to mideye.
- First 1 or 2 dorsal fin spines very short, hardly perceptible, and not united by a common membrane; **dorsal and anal fins not connected to caudal fin; anal fin not increasing in height posteriorly**; caudal fin rounded; pelvic fin present.
- Scales present on cheeks.
- Lateral line mediolateral, indistinct.
- Vomerine teeth absent; a few palatine teeth present in older individuals.
- **Gill membranes** united forward, **attached to isthmus under posterior edge of eye or farther posteriorly**.
- Length to 365 mm TL.

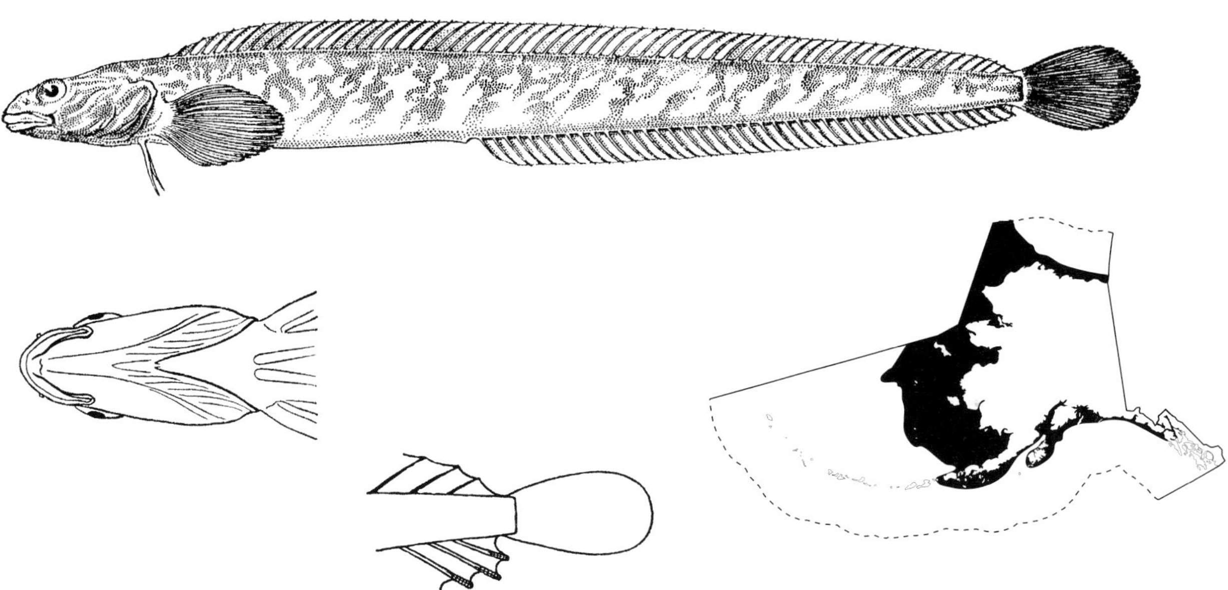

Notes & Sources — *Lumpenus fabricii* Reinhardt, 1836

Description: Jensen 1944:33–34; Andriashev 1954:244–245; Lindberg and Krasyukova 1975:88–89; Scott and Scott 1988:418.

Figures: Andriashev 1954, figs. 125(2) and 126; southern part of Chukchi Sea. Tail: Makushok 1958, fig. 20.

Range: Numerous records exist from the Beaufort, Chukchi, and Bering seas off Alaska. For example, Thorsteinson et al. (1991) collected *L. fabricii* from the Beaufort Sea at Prudhoe and Camden bays; depths were as shallow as 2.5 m. Allen and Smith (1988) mapped catch locations from the NMFS survey database, which were all in the Chukchi and Bering seas. Fechhelm et al. (1984) found *L. fabricii* to rank sixth in total abundance in surveys of the nearshore northeastern Chukchi Sea. Barber et al. (1997) ranked it 13th in abundance in surveys there in 1990 and 1991. Kessler (1985) reported it to be common both north and south of the Alaska Peninsula. Quast (1968) recorded it from Kachemak Bay and Auke Bay. Other Gulf of Alaska records include AB 68-311, Olsen Bay, Prince William Sound; NMC 61-85, Port Etches, Prince William Sound; UBC 63-1301 and 63-1302, Simeonof Island; UBC 65-50, near Kodiak Island; UBC 62-991, Kachemak Bay; and UBC 63-393 and 63-435, Prince William Sound. Could be less common in the southern Bering Sea and Gulf of Alaska than suggested by solid black fill on the above map. Examining specimens in the Russian Academy of Sciences collection at St. Petersburg, B. A. Sheiko (pers. comm., 2 Feb. 1999) found that several specimens from the southern Bering Sea and Sea of Okhotsk identified as *L. fabricii* are *L. sagitta, Anisarchus medius,* or *Leptoclinus maculatus*; and Sheiko and Fedorov (2000) reported *Lumpenus fabricii* off Kamchatka only from Cape Olyutorskiy to Bering Strait. There are no records of *L. fabricii* from the Aleutian Islands west of Unimak Pass or from the Commander Islands.

Lumpenus sagitta Wilimovsky, 1956 — **snake prickleback**

Bering Sea and Aleutian Islands to northern California at Humboldt Bay, and to Seas of Okhotsk and Japan.

Sandy bottom with admixture of silt, pebbles, and stones from shore to depth of 425 m, almost always shallower than 200 m.

D LXIV–LXXII; A I–II,44–50; Pec 13–17; Pel I,3; Br 6; Vert 75–80.

- Light green to tannish or gray dorsally, cream ventrally; **irregular small dark blotches or streaks dorsolaterally**; **line of dark, dash-like or oval marks along midbody**; dorsal fin with dark stripes in some specimens; **4 or 5 irregular narrow bands on caudal fin**; oral cavity pale white.
- Body very elongate and slender.
- **Eye diameter about equal to snout length**; maxilla extending to anterior edge of pupil.
- First few dorsal fin spines very short and free; dorsal and anal fins not connected to caudal fin; **almost always 1 spine in anal fin**; caudal fin slightly rounded; pelvic fin present.
- **Scales present on head, absent from cheeks.**
- Lateral line mediolateral, indistinct.
- Vomerine teeth absent, palatine teeth present.
- Gill membranes attached forward, without free fold across isthmus.
- Length to 51 cm TL, usually less than 25 cm.

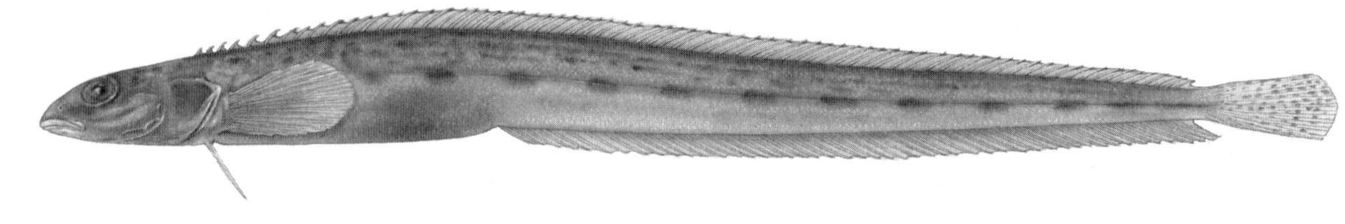

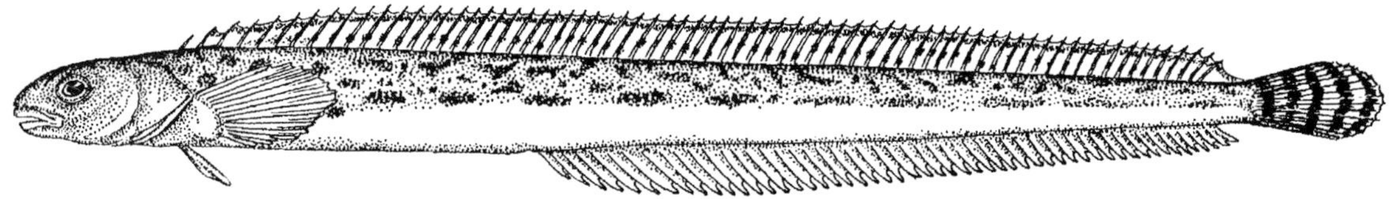

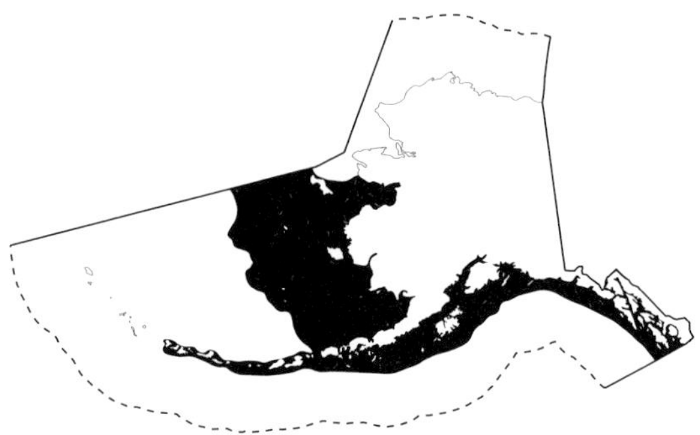

Notes & Sources — *Lumpenus sagitta* Wilimovsky, 1956
Leptogunnellus gracilis Ayres, 1855 (name preoccupied, replaced by *Lumpenus sagitta* Wilimovsky, 1956).
Lumpenus anguillaris: Bean 1881b, 1882, 1883, 1884a; Gilbert 1896; Evermann and Goldsborough 1907.

Description: Hart 1973:337–338; Lindberg and Krasyukova 1975:86–87; Svetovidov 1978:24–25; Eschmeyer and Herald 1983:251; Amaoka and Miki in Masuda et al. 1984:301; Humann 1996:86–87.

Figures: Upper: University of British Columbia, artist P. Drukker-Brammall, Mar. 1974; UBC 65-567, 195 mm SL, lagoon behind Ocean Cape, Alaska. Lower: Hart 1973:337; 23 cm TL, Burrard Inlet, British Columbia.

Range: Recorded north in Bering Sea to St. Lawrence Island by Allen and Smith (1988) from NMFS surveys and west in Aleutian Islands to Adak Island by Wilimovsky (1964). (UBC 63-335 and 63-905 are from Adak Island.) Data from more recent NMFS surveys provided by D. W. Kessler (pers. comm., 20 Jun. 1994) include numerous records for Norton Sound. Records of this species from the Aleutian Islands west of Adak Island are lacking, but Fedorov and Sheiko (2002) reported it to be abundant off the Commander Islands. It is possible, as Sheiko (pers. comm., 2 Feb. 1999) and others have opined, that some species present at the Commander Islands and eastern Aleutian Islands could be absent from the western Aleutian Islands, especially fishes with demersal eggs and short pelagic larval stages.

Acantholumpenus mackayi (Gilbert, 1896) **blackline prickleback**

Southeastern Chukchi Sea, eastern Bering Sea, and Aleutian Islands; northeastern Gulf of Alaska; Canadian Beaufort Sea; Sea of Okhotsk to Sea of Japan and Pacific coast of Hokkaido.

Mud or sand bottoms in shallow water near shore to depth of 56 m; found in brackish waters of lakes and river mouths, as well as more saline waters.

D LXVIII–LXXVI; A II,41–48; Pec 13–16; Pel I,3; Br 6; Vert 76–80.

- Body light yellowish to brownish; **dark line on back at base of dorsal fin, 2 dark broken lines below**; top of head mottled brown; **caudal fin dark, without bands**; roof of mouth dark.
- Body extremely elongate, but usually more robust than *L. sagitta*.
- **Eye diameter less than snout length**; maxilla extending to anterior edge of pupil to mideye.
- Dorsal and anal fins not connected to caudal fin; anterior spines of dorsal fin short but not free; spines of pelvic and anal fins rigid and easily discernible from soft rays; caudal fin rounded in smaller fish, lanceolate in adult males and truncate with rounded corners in adult females; pelvic fin present.
- **Scales present on cheeks and side of head, absent from top and rest of head**.
- Lateral line mediolateral, indistinct.
- Vomerine teeth absent, palatine teeth present.
- Gill membranes united and narrowly attached to isthmus forward of vertical with middle of cheek.
- Length to 70 cm SL.

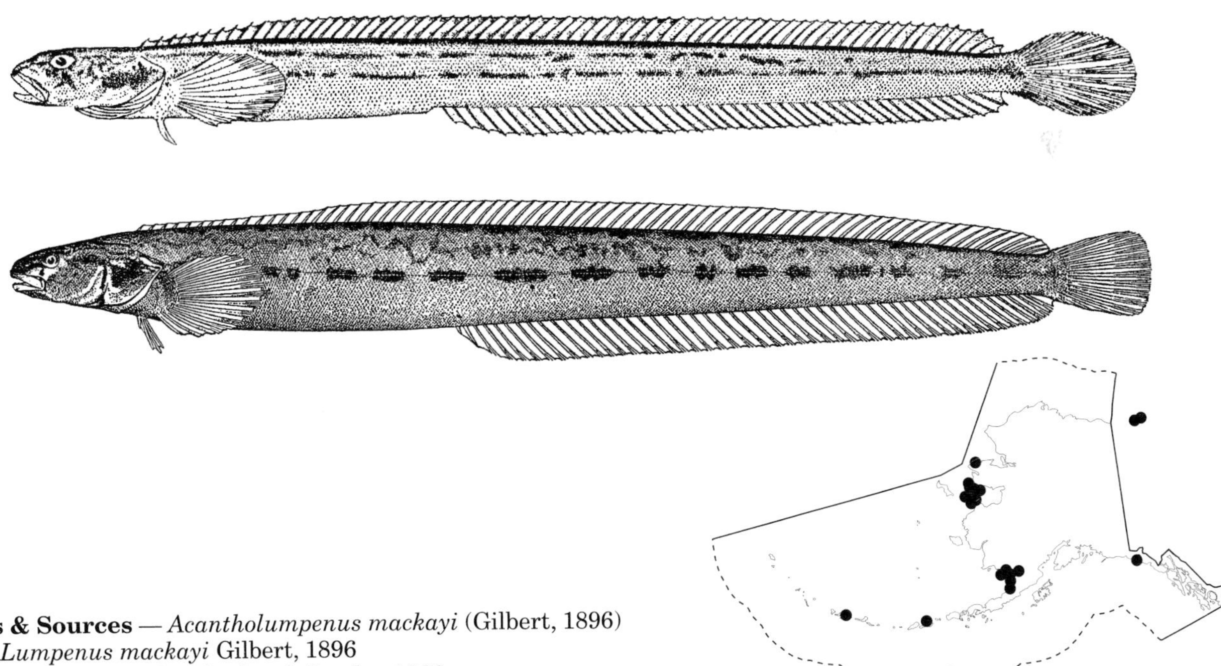

Notes & Sources — *Acantholumpenus mackayi* (Gilbert, 1896)
Lumpenus mackayi Gilbert, 1896
Lumpenus fowleri Jordan & Snyder, 1902

Named for Charles Lesley McKay, of Appleton, Wisconsin, a young ichthyologist who drowned at Nushagak, in Bristol Bay, in 1883 (Jordan and Evermann (1898:2437).

Called pighead prickleback on the American Fisheries Society list, starting with the third edition (Bailey et al. 1970). Blackline prickleback is the name used by Legendre et al. (1975), McAllister (1990), and Coad (1995). The head of this prickleback bears no resemblance to the head of a pig. The black line running along the back below the base of the dorsal fin is an important diagnostic character, as well as the broken black lines running along the side of the body.

Description: Gilbert 1896:450–451; Jordan and Snyder 1902c:500–501; Lindberg and Krasyukova 1975:93–95; Amaoka and Miki in Masuda et al. 1984:301; Houston and McAllister 1990b; Springer and Anderson 1997:10–11.

Figures: Upper: Gilbert 1896, pl. 32; lectotype, about 275 mm TL, near mouth of Nushagak River, Alaska. Lower: Jordan and Snyder 1902c, fig. 28; 315 mm TL, Kushiro, Japan.

Range: Previously recorded from Norton Sound (Sample and Wolotira 1985), Bristol Bay (Gilbert 1896, Quast and Hall 1972), and Unalaska and Adak islands (Wilimovsky 1964; UBC 63-130 and 63-131). Most other Alaskan records are from the same areas: e.g., UW 22303, Bristol Bay at 58°22'N, 159°18'W, depth 11–31 m, May 1988; UBC 56-559, 58-308, and 65-802, Kvichak Bay; and UBC 60-377, between Nome and Safety Sound. Lot UW 27426 may be the only Chukchi Sea record, collected in 1976 at 66°04'N, 167°17'W, depth 18 m. Lot UW 2028, comprising three specimens collected in 1932 in Yakutat Bay, may be the only record from the Gulf of Alaska. Sometimes taken in brackish water, as in river mouths in Alaska (e.g., UW 2586, mouth of Egegik River) and coastal lakes of Hokkaido. Specimens recorded by Hunter et al. (1984) from the vicinity of the Mackenzie Delta to Liverpool Bay on the south side of the Tuktoyaktuk Peninsula are the only Canadian records. Houston and McAllister (1990b) concluded that the Canadian Beaufort Sea records represent the northeastern end of the range.

Opisthocentrus ocellatus (Tilesius, 1811)

ocellated blenny

Commander Islands and southeast coast of Kamchatka to Kuril Islands and Sea of Okhotsk, and Sea of Japan to Wonsan, North Korea.

Shallow coastal areas among seaweed, usually not deeper than about 70 m; collected at depths greater than 300 m off Hokkaido.

D LV–LXII; A II,33–39; Pec 18–21; Pel 0; Br 5; Vert 61–67.

- Greenish to yellowish brown with numerous mottlings and reticulations; **dorsal fin with 5–7 evenly spaced brownish black ocelli**, typically 5; head with vertical dark bar through eye; streaks running obliquely dorsal and posteroventral from eye, can be vague or absent; caudal, anal, and pectoral fins orange yellow; in mature males body turns red, anal fin bluish black, and reticulations darker during breeding season.
- Snouth blunt and short, equal to eye diameter.
- Maxilla extending to front of eye to mideye.
- **Dorsal fin spines slender and flexible except posterior 7–17 spines abruptly stout**; dorsal fin high, especially in mature males; anal fin low; pectoral fin large, rounded; **pelvic fin absent**.
- **Scales present on cheeks and head** anteriorly to interorbital region.
- Interorbital pores 3.
- Dorsal and mediolateral branches of lateral line present, difficult to discern.
- Teeth on upper jaw in 2–3 rows anteriorly; no caniniform teeth in either jaw; vomerine teeth present, palatine teeth absent.
- Gill membranes broadly joined, free of isthmus.
- Length to 200 mm TL.

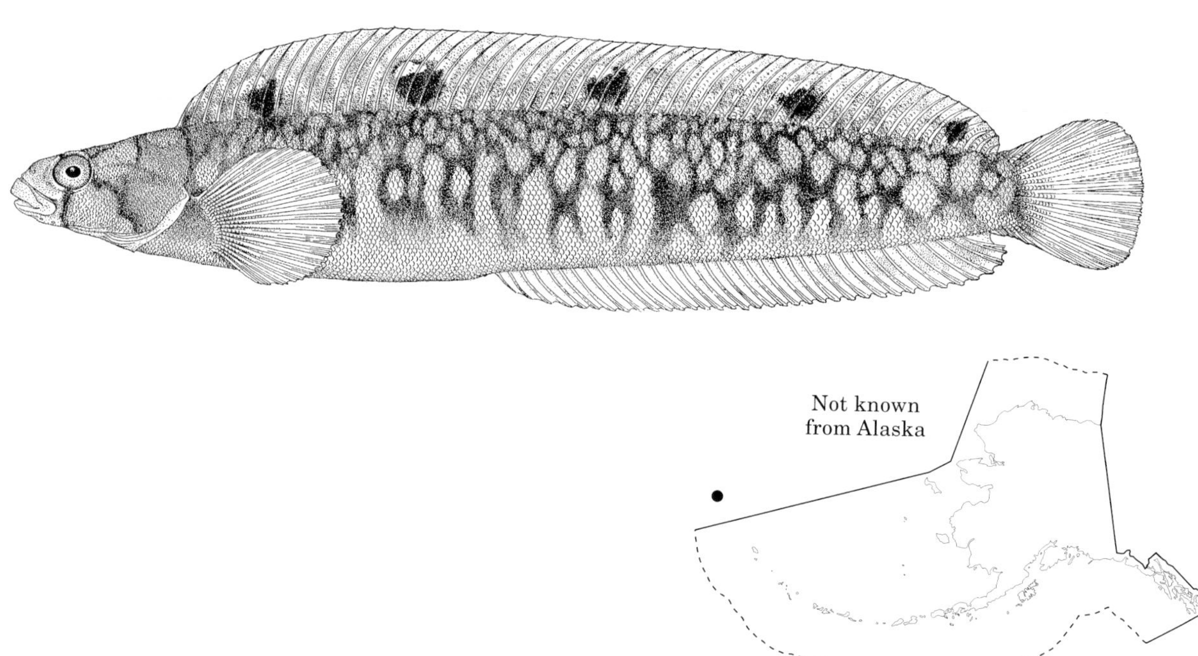

Notes & Sources — *Opisthocentrus ocellatus* (Tilesius, 1811)
Ophidium ocellatum Tilesius, 1811

Description: Lindberg and Krasyukova 1975:104–106; Shiogaki 1982, 1984; Amaoka and Miki in Masuda et al. 1984:302.

Figure: Jordan and Gilbert 1899, pl. 79; Petropavlovsk harbor, Kamchatka, Russia.

Range: Nearest known area of occurrence is Commander Islands, Russia (Shiogaki 1984), where it is reported to be common (Fedorov and Sheiko 2002).

Alectridium aurantiacum Gilbert & Burke, 1912 **lesser prickleback**

Aleutian Islands and north side of Alaska Peninsula to Herendeen Bay, and Gulf of Alaska coasts to Cook Inlet; Commander Islands.

Lower intertidal and subtidal waters to 56 m.

D LII–LXIII; A I,41–44; Pec 11; Pel 0; Br 5; Vert 60–68.

- Body usually dark brown to mottled olive, occasionally bright orange and red; gill membranes with narrow black edge; 2 dark bars below eye with light borders; caudal fin tipped orange; light bar at base of caudal fin.
- Snout steep, round in profile; **narrow dermal crest from snout to posterior interorbital region**, usually ending in front of median interorbital pore.
- **Anal fin barely joined or not joined to base of caudal fin**; pelvic fin absent.
- **Scales present only posteriorly, extending anteriorly as far as 26th to 13th anal fin rays.**
- **Median interorbital pore present, other interorbital pores paired**; median pore sometimes on ridge of dermal crest.
- Two rudimentary lateral lines usually present anteriorly.
- Gill membranes united with each other and fused to isthmus so as to produce a narrow free fold.
- Length to 133 mm TL.

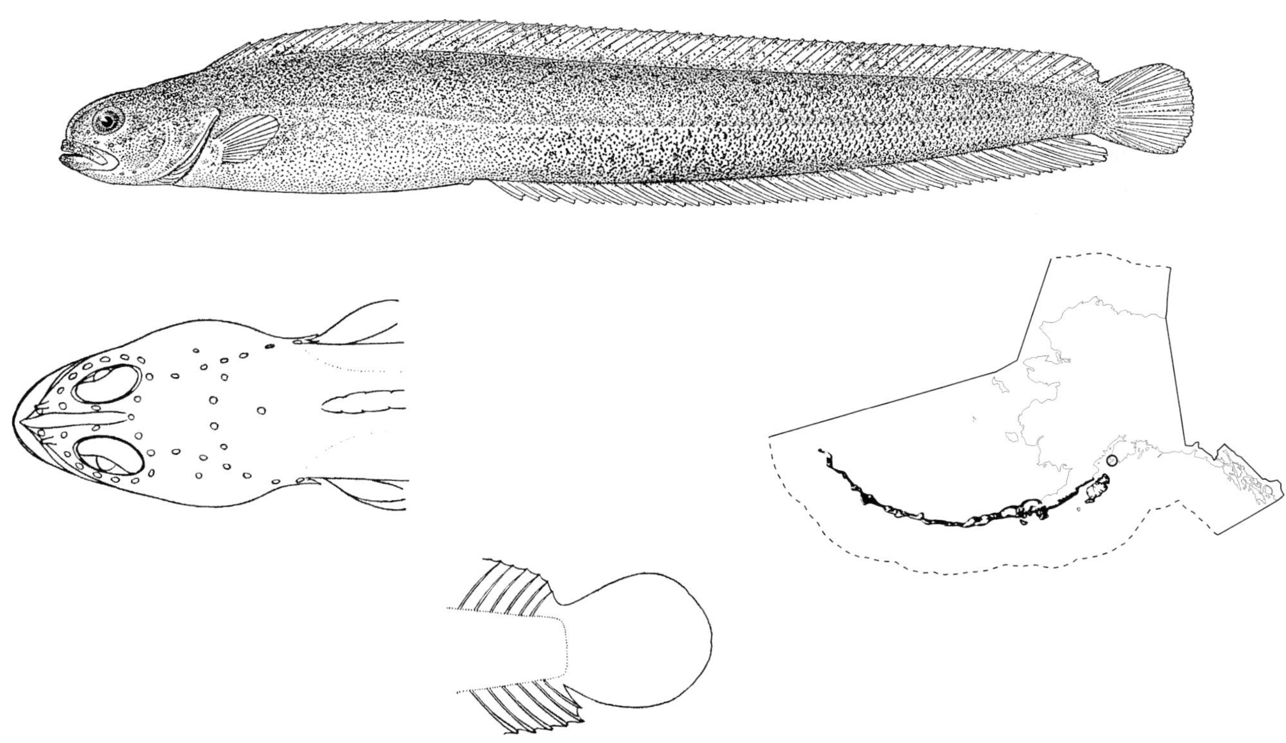

Notes & Sources — *Alectridium aurantiacum* Gilbert & Burke, 1912
Treated as synonymous with *Alectrias alectrolophus* by some authors, but Peden (1967) verified the independent status of the two species and redescribed *Alectridium aurantiacum*.

Description: Gilbert and Burke 1912a:87–88; Peden 1967; Shiogaki 1985.

Figures: Gilbert and Burke 1912a, fig. 31; holotype (unique), 83 mm TL, Nikolski, Bering Island. Head and tail: Shiogaki 1985, figs. 4A and 6A.

Range: Identification of specimens in collections from Attu Island to Kodiak Island was confirmed by Peden (1967) and Shiogaki (1985). Specimens from the Aleutian Islands listed as *Alectrias alectrolophus* by Wilimovsky (1964) are *Alectridium aurantiacum* (Peden 1967). R. Baxter (unpubl. data) collected a specimen (UW 22141, 106 mm TL, 97 mm SL, Aug. 1989) at Herendeen Bay, thereby extending the known range along the north side of the Alaska Peninsula; and one from the intertidal at Cronin Island (not saved, 108 mm TL, 95 mm SL, Jun. 1988), extending the known range to Cook Inlet. Andriashev (1939) and Fedorov and Sheiko (2002) reported it to be common at the Commander Islands, Russia.

Size: R. Baxter, unpubl. data; specimens were 122 mm SL, from intertidal at Dutch Harbor, 27 Jun. 1984; and 106 and 108 mm TL, from Herendeen Bay and Kachemak Bay (other data on file, specimens not saved). Maximum size previously recorded was 89.4 mm SL (Peden 1967).

Alectrias alectrolophus (Pallas, 1814) **stone cockscomb**

Norton Sound at St. Michael; unconfirmed record from Aleutian Islands at Amichitka Island; Commander Islands and southeastern Kamchatka to Sea of Okhotsk and northern Sea of Japan.

Intertidal primarily, but found as deep as 100 m; often in bays with pebble-rock debris bottoms.

D LIX–LXVI; A I,42–45; Pec 9–11; Pel 0; Br 5; Vert 65–69.

- Monotone gray to nearly black to bright spotted with patterns; usually a wavy line extending along back, separating dark portion from lighter spots that continue onto dorsal fin.
- Snout not steep, profile gradually sloping back (excluding crest from profile); **narrow dermal crest from snout to occipital region**, ending in front of median posterior occipital pore.
- **Anal fin joined to caudal fin**; pelvic fin absent.
- **Scales present only posteriorly, but extending anteriorly past 15th anal fin ray.**
- **Pores of interorbital sensory canal paired, no median pore.**
- Two rudimentary lateral lines usually present anteriorly; occasionally, mediolateral line well developed to caudal fin.
- Gill membranes united, forming broad fold across isthmus.
- Length to 128 mm TL.

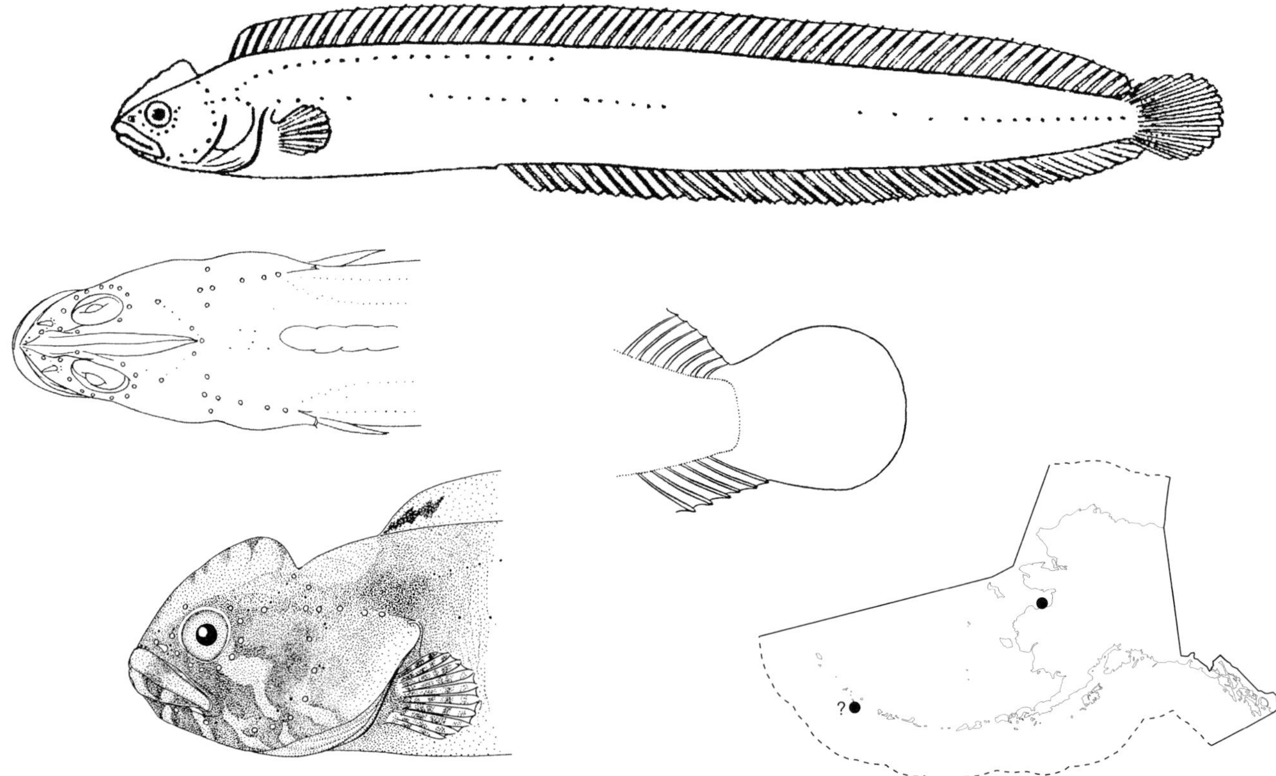

Notes & Sources — *Alectrias alectrolophus* (Pallas, 1814)
Blennius alectrolophus Pallas, 1814
Often confused with *Alectridium aurantiacum.* Peden (1967) described characters distinguishing these species.
Alectrias benjamini Jordan & Snyder, 1904, from the western Pacific is variously treated as a valid species (e.g., Amaoka and Miki in Amaoka et al. 1984, Shiogaki 1985) or as a subspecies of *A. alectrolophus* (e.g., Hubbs 1927, Lindberg and Krasyukova 1975). Hubbs (1927) compared the subspecies.

Description: Andriashev 1954:239–240; Peden 1967; Lindberg and Krasyukova 1975:111–113; Shiogaki 1985. (Meristics given above do not include counts from *A. a. benjamini,* which has fewer dorsal and anal fin elements and vertebrae.)

Figures: Full lateral view: Andriashev 1954, fig. 122; approximately 100 mm TL, Sea of Okhotsk. Others: Shiogaki 1985, figs. 3B, 4C, 6C.

Range: Of several records for Alaska, only those from St. Michael, Norton Sound (USNM 22018, 23979, 32973), were considered valid by Peden (1967). Specimens from the Aleutian Islands reported by Wilimovsky (1964) to be *A. alectrolophus* were determined by Peden (1967) to be *Alectridium aurantiacum.* Listed from Amchitka Island by Isakson et al. (1971) and, in a later treatment of the same data, by Simenstad et al. (1977), but this reference could also be incorrect and based on misidentifications of *A. aurantiacum*; voucher specimens have not been found. However, *Alectrias alectrolophus* was reported to be abundant at the Commander Islands, Russia, by Andriashev (1939) and Fedorov and Sheiko (2002). The statement by Shiogaki (1985:305) that *A. alectrolophus* is widely distributed to "east Alaska" through the Bering Sea is confusing.

Anoplarchus purpurescens Gill, 1861 **high cockscomb**

Pribilof Islands and Aleutian Islands from Attu Island to southern California at Santa Rosa Island. Intertidal and to 30 m, among rocks and algae; found more frequently in the intertidal zone than subtidally.

D LIV–LX; A 36–42; Pec 9–10; Pel 0; Br 5; Vert 58–64.

- Coloration variable, changing to match background, and to some extent sexually dimorphic; body dark brown to blackish or purplish; usually 2 dark bars on cheeks; females sometimes with faint bars on jaws; pale band at base of caudal fin; pectoral and anal fins yellow to orange.
- Numbers of dorsal fin spines, anal fin rays, and vertebrae usually lower than in *A. insignis*.
- Dermal crest from snout to top of head; **crest as high at snout as posteriorly**.
- Anal fin not extending onto caudal fin; pelvic fin absent.
- Scales present only posteriorly, extending forward as far as 12th anal fin ray to anus.
- Gill membranes fused to isthmus, never with free fold posteriorly; **width of isthmus between points of attachment of gill membranes usually more than 75% of eye diameter**.
- Length to 200 mm TL.

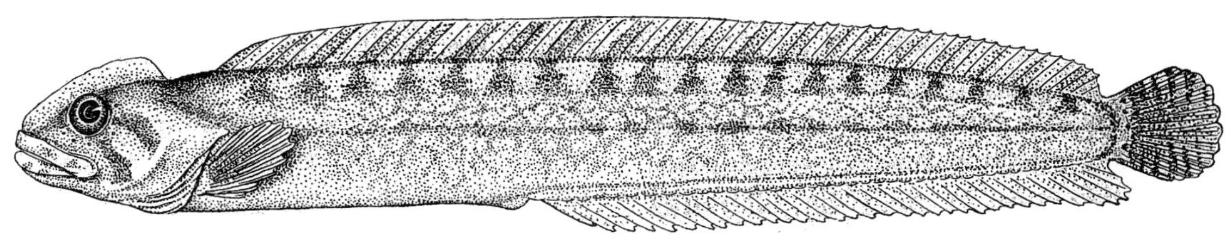

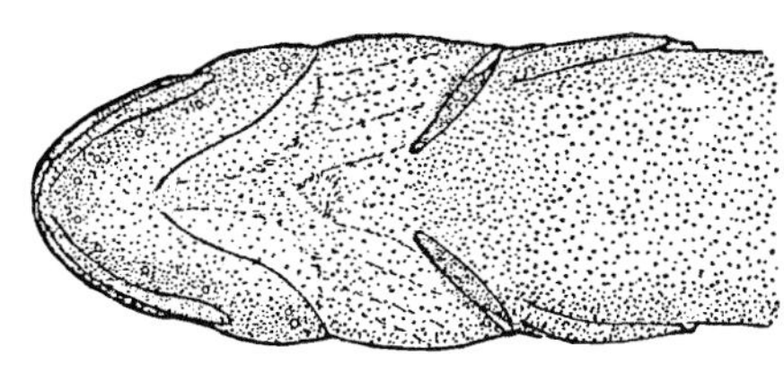

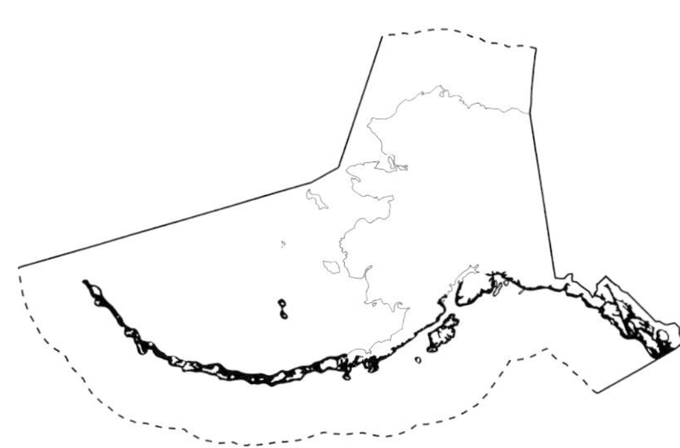

Notes & Sources — *Anoplarchus purpurescens* Gill, 1861

Description: Peden 1966c, 1967; Hubbs 1927:373–377; Hart 1973:329–330; Eschmeyer and Herald 1983:249.

Figures: Full lateral: Hart 1973:329; 10 cm TL, Alaska. Ventral: Peden 1966c, fig. 1.

Range: Well documented from Pribilof Islands and Aleutian Islands through southeastern Alaska (e.g., Gilbert and Burke 1912a, Wilimovsky 1964, Peden 1966c, Quast and Hall 1972). Peden (1966c) found that, among collections from the Aleutian Islands, 91.5% of the specimens found subtidally (0–3 m below lowest tide) were *A. insignis* and 97.5% of specimens found in the higher intertidal zone (*Balanus* and *Fucus* zone) were *A. purpurescens*. In the lower intertidal (*Alaria* zone), 66.2% were *A. purpurescens* and 33.8% were *A. insignis*.

Anoplarchus insignis Gilbert & Burke, 1912 **slender cockscomb**

Southeastern Bering Sea and Aleutian Islands from Attu Island to northern California at Arena Cove.

Intertidal and to 30 m, among rocks and algae; found more frequently in the subtidal zone than the intertidal.

D LVII–LXIV; A 40–46; Pec 9–10; Pel 0; Br 5; Vert 60–69.

- Coloration variable, changing to match background; orange-gray to blackish, rarely bright red; dark bars on jaws, side of head, and over head; pale bars extending from back onto dorsal fin; dorsal fin sometimes with black spots with orange borders; white bar at base of caudal fin.
- Numbers of dorsal fin spines, anal fin rays, and vertebrae usually higher than in *A. purpurescens*.
- Dermal crest from snout to top of head; **crest very low at snout region**.
- Anal fin not extending onto caudal fin; pelic fin absent.
- Scales present only posteriorly, extending forward as far as 15th to 7th anal fin ray.
- Gill membranes fused to isthmus, *usually* not producing free fold posteriorly; **width of isthmus between points of attachment of gill membranes 50% or less of eye diameter**.
- Length to 118 mm TL.

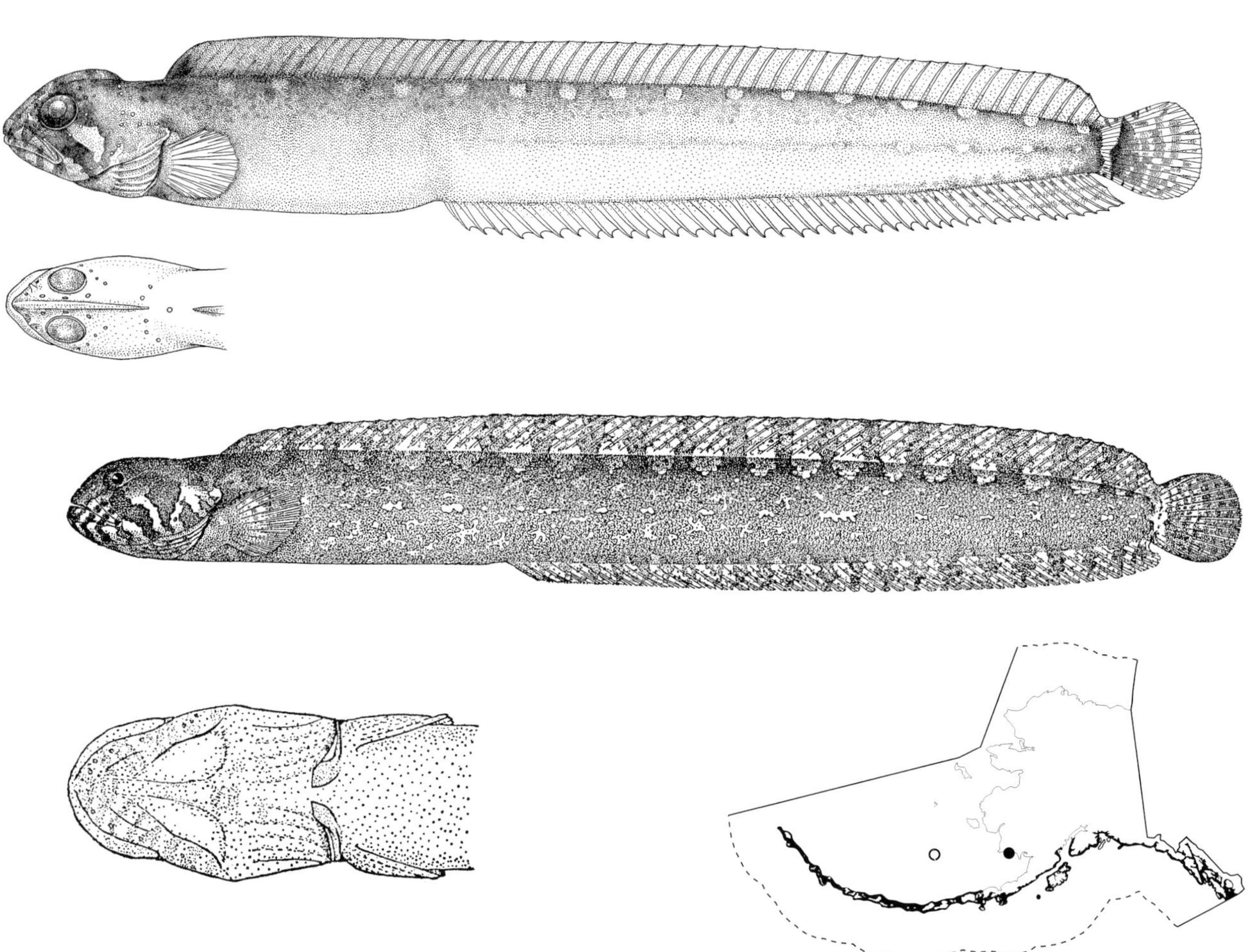

Notes & Sources — *Anoplarchus insignis* Gilbert & Burke, 1912

Considered a subspecies of *A. purpurescens* by Hubbs (1927). Peden (1966c) reexamined and described the species.

Description: Gilbert and Burke 1912a:88; Peden 1966c, 1967; Hart 1973:328–329; Eschmeyer and Herald 1983:248.

Figures: Upper, with dorsal view of head: University of British Columbia, artist P. Drukker-Brammall; UBC 65-8, 87 mm SL, Agattu Island. Lower full lateral: Gilbert and Burke 1912a, fig. 32; type, 102 mm TL, Attu Island. Ventral view of head and isthmus: Peden 1966c, fig. 1.

Range: Well documented from Aleutian Islands through southeastern Alaska (e.g., Gilbert and Burke 1912a, Peden 1966c, Peden and Wilson 1976), although not by nearly as many examples as those of *A. purpurescens*. The ABL has a specimen (AB 82-27) from Metervik Bay, off Bristol Bay. Isthmus and eye measurements by R. Baxter (unpubl. data) from a specimen (not saved) taken in the vicinity of the Pribilof Islands support identification as *A. insignis*.

Size: Peden and Wilson 1976.

Phytichthys chirus (Jordan & Gilbert, 1880) **ribbon prickleback**

Aleutian Islands and Gulf of Alaska coasts to southern California.

Under rocks and in algae in intertidal areas and to depth of about 12 m.

D LXIX–LXXVIII; A II–III,40–50; Pec 14–15; Pel 0; Br 6; Vert 75–76.

- Brownish to olive green or bright green dorsally, yellow to green ventrally; often marbled with red; 4–5 small dark spots laterally that are strongest posteriorly; usually with light and dark streaks radiating down and back from eye; anal fin sometimes with light spots or dark bars.
- Dorsal and anal fins confluent with caudal fin; **dorsal fin origin above pectoral fin**; **anal fin with 2–3 spines; pectoral fin small, but as large as or larger than eye diameter** (larger than in *Xiphister*); pelvic fin absent.
- Four lateral lines, each with short branches extending at right angles dorsally and ventrally; ventral lateral line ending at origin of anal fin.
- Gill membranes united, free of isthmus.
- Length to 211 mm TL.

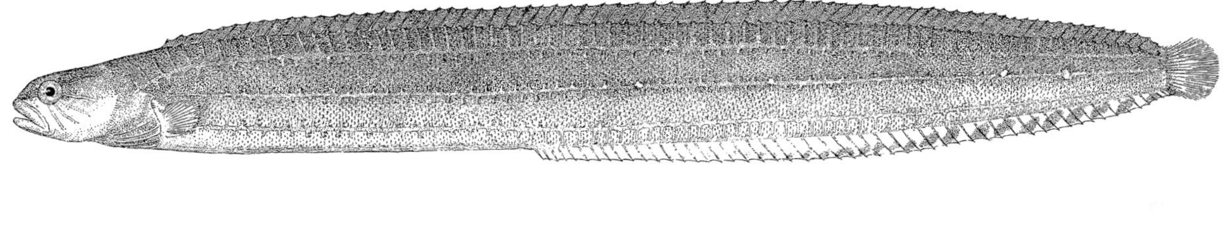

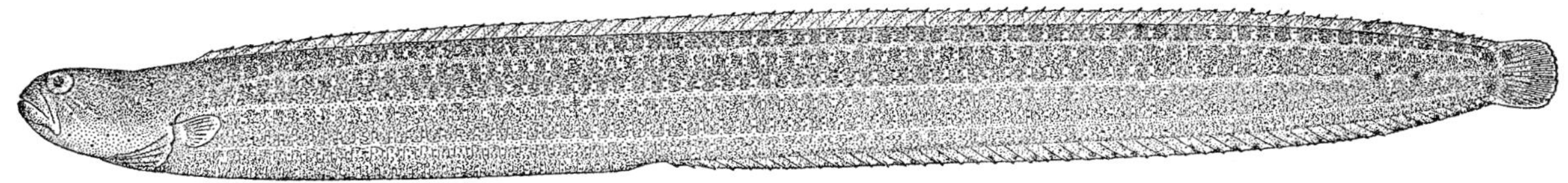

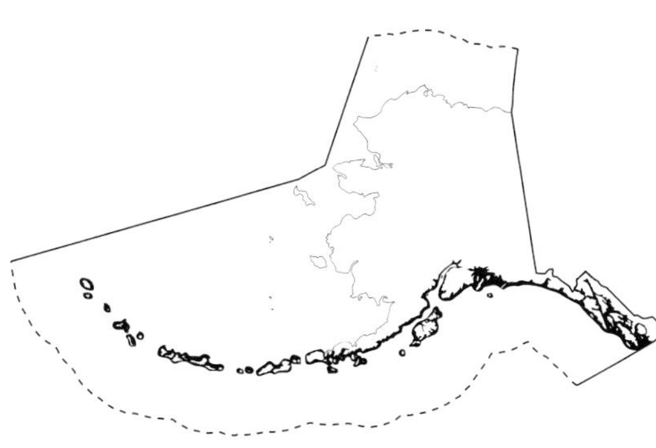

Notes & Sources — *Phytichthys chirus* (Jordan & Gilbert, 1880)
Xiphister chirus Jordan & Gilbert, 1880
Xiphistes ulvae Jordan & Starks, 1895
Xiphistes versicolor Gilbert & Burke, 1912
Hubbs (1927) synonymized the three nominal species and replaced the name *Xiphistes* with *Phytichthys* because the former is preoccupied by a genus of "bugs" (order Hemiptera).

Description: Jordan and Gilbert 1880c:135–136; Jordan and Starks 1895:847–848; Gilbert and Burke 1912a:88–89; Hubbs 1927:380–383; Hart 1973:338; Eschmeyer and Herald 1983:251; Springer and Anderson 1997:9.

Figures: Upper: Jordan and Starks 1895, pl. 102; type of *Xiphistes ulvae*, 127 mm TL, Waadda Island. Lower: Gilbert and Burke 1912a, fig. 33; type of *X. versicolor,* 175 mm TL, Attu Island (head tilted upward from warping due to immersion in preservative).

Range: First recorded from Alaska by Bean (1881b), from specimens collected at Adak and Amchitka islands by W. H. Dall. Gilbert and Burke (1912a) described this species under the name *Xiphistes versicolor* from specimens collected at Attu and Agattu islands. A commonly encountered, well-documented species along the shores of the Gulf of Alaska, including Middleton Island (CAS 149017, 149026, 149033; confirmed by Stoddard [1985]), and throughout the Aleutian Islands. Not recorded from the Commander Islands, Russia.

Size: Peden and Wilson 1976.

Xiphister mucosus (Girard, 1858) **rock prickleback**

Western Gulf of Alaska at Kodiak Island to southern California at Santa Cruz Island.
Under rocks and in algae, particularly along open coast; intertidal to 18 m.

D LXXI–LXXVIII; A 0–I,46–50; Pec 12; Pel 0; Br 6; Vert 73–83.

- Body brown or gray to greenish black; **black bars radiating down and back from eye**.
- Dorsal and anal fins confluent with caudal fin; **dorsal fin origin above pectoral fin; anal fin spine usually absent** or weak; **pectoral fin minute**, less than eye diameter; pelvic fin absent.
- Four lateral lines, each with short branches extending at right angles dorsally and ventrally; ventral lateral line ending at origin of anal fin.
- Gill membranes broadly joined, forming wide free fold.
- Length to 58 cm TL.

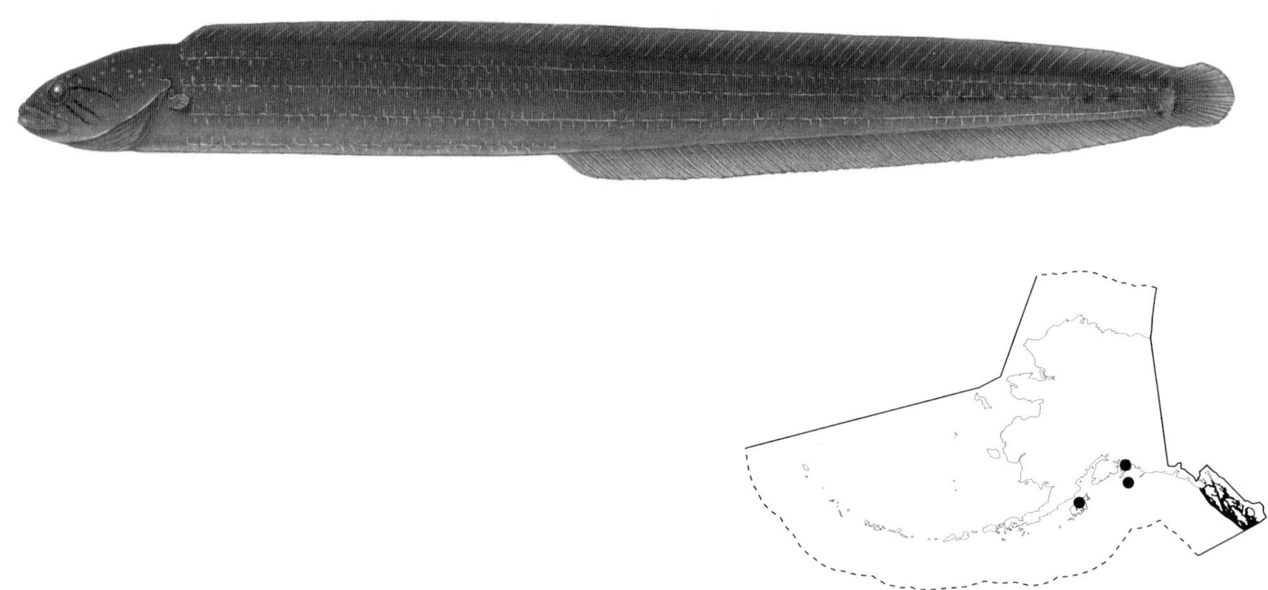

Notes & Sources — *Xiphister mucosus* (Girard, 1858)
Xiphidion mucosum Girard, 1858
Xiphidium cruoreum Cope, 1873
Xiphister was proposed as a new name by Jordan (1880:241) because, he wrote, the name *Xiphidion* or *Xiphidium* is preoccupied by a genus of Orthoptera (grasshoppers). Eschmeyer (1998:2169), however, suggested that *Xiphidium* should probably be used; apparently the name was *not* preoccupied in Orthoptera.
Xiphister cruoreus: Jordan and Gilbert 1880c.
Hubbs (1927:383–384) gave a detailed synonymy.

Description: Hart 1973:343; Eschmeyer and Herald 1983: 253.

Figure: University of British Columbia, artist P. Drukker-Brammall, Aug. 1966; UBC 65-541, 124 mm SL, tidepool at Cape Spencer, Alaska.

Range: Previous Alaskan records include Sitka (Cope 1873), Wrangell (Bean 1882), Mary Island (Bean 1884a), Gabriola Island and Port Ellis (Evermann and Goldsborough 1907), and Forrester Island (Hubbs 1927) in southeastern Alaska; and Port San Juan (Eschmeyer and Herald 1983), Prince William Sound. Westernmost record is Larsen Bay, Kodiak Island (UBC 59-513). Other Alaskan localities on record are: Middleton Island (CAS 148987, 148992, 149004, 149028, 149044); Cape Spencer (UBC 65-540, 65-541, 65-542); Klokachef Island (UBC 65-574); Port Armstrong (UBC 62-591); Coronation Island (UBC 65-521, 65-522); Abbess Island (UBC 61-503); Kuiu Island (AB 60-6); and Waterfall (UW 8291).

Xiphister atropurpureus (Kittlitz, 1858) **black prickleback**

Western Gulf of Alaska at Kodiak Island to northern Baja California at Rio Santo Thomas.

Exposed rocky shorelines under stones and in algae; intertidal zone to 8 m.

D LXV–LXXII; A 0–I,49–55; Pec 11–12; Pel 0; Br 6; Vert 75–80.

- Reddish brown to black; **broad dark bars with white or cream borders radiating down and back from eye**; **white bar across base of caudal fin**, sometimes broken in center.
- Dorsal and anal fins confluent with caudal fin; **dorsal fin origin well behind pectoral fin**; **anal fin spine usually absent** or weak; **pectoral fin minute**, less than eye diameter; pelvic fin absent.
- Four lateral lines, each with short branches extending at right angles dorsally and ventrally; ventral lateral line ending at origin of anal fin.
- Gill membranes broadly joined, forming wide free fold.
- Length to 323 mm TL.

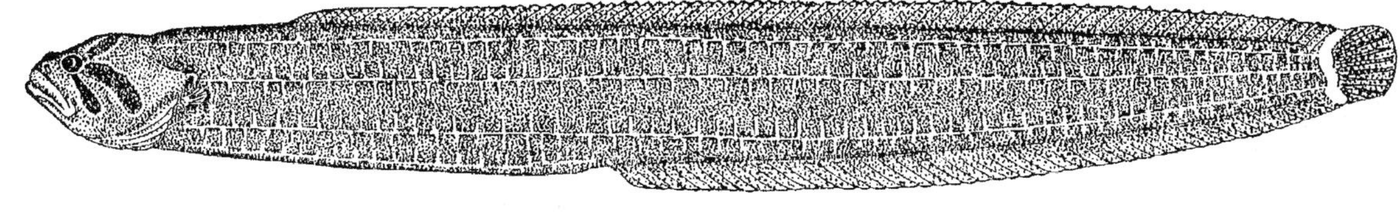

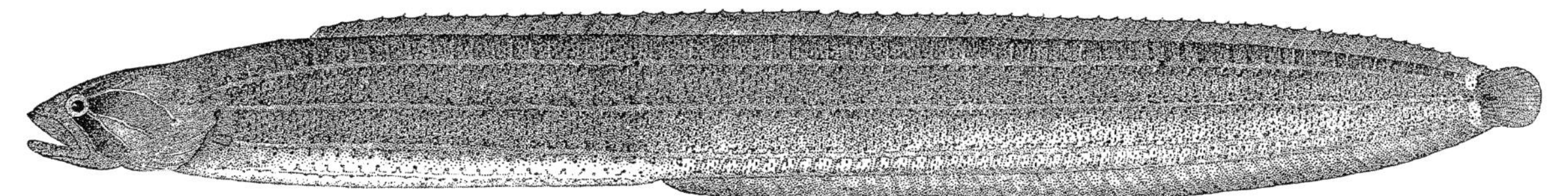

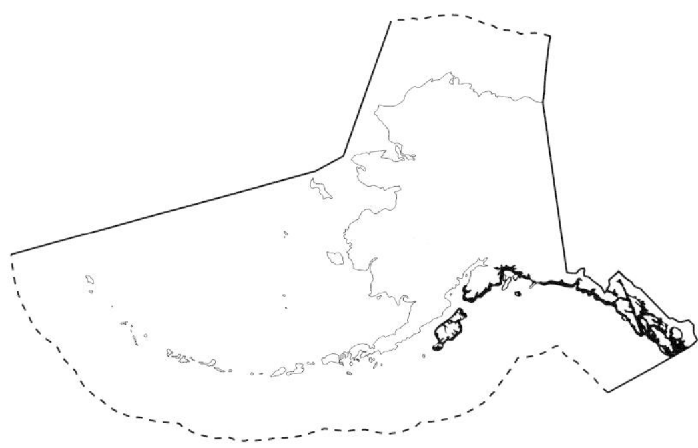

Notes & Sources — *Xiphister atropurpureus* (Kittlitz, 1858)
Ophidium atropurpureum Kittlitz, 1858
Xiphister rupestris Jordan & Gilbert, 1880
Jordan (1880) replaced *Xiphidion* with *Xiphister.*
Xiphidion rupestre: Jordan and Starks 1895.
Epigeichthys: Hubbs 1927:385 (new genus, with *X. rupestris* as the type and also including *X. atropurpureus*).

Description: Jordan and Gilbert 1880c:137–138; Jordan and Evermann 1898:2422–2423; Hubbs 1927:386–388; Hart 1973:341–342; Eschmeyer and Herald 1983:253; Humann 1996:82–83.

Figures: Upper: Hart 1973:341; 17 cm TL, Vancouver Island, British Columbia. Lower: Jordan and Starks 1895, pl. 103; Waadda Island, Washington.

Range: This species was originally described from specimens collected in Alaska, with no definite locality given. Later records extend as far west as Kodiak Island, where *X. atropurpureus* was found in tidepools on the north and south coasts by Hubbard and Reeder (1965). R. Baxter (unpubl. data) collected a 234-mm-TL specimen (not saved) at Tonsina Bay, Kachemak Bay. The CAS has, among others, one specimen from South Bay in Prince William Sound (CAS 42582) and several from Middleton Island (e.g., CAS 149043, with identification confirmed by Stoddard [1985]). During two visits each in 1990 and 1991 to Prince William Sound, a total of 234 specimens were collected (Barber et al. 1995); voucher specimens are at UAM. This is a fairly common species in southeastern Alaska, although not well documented in the literature. Bean (1881b) listed USNM specimens from Sitka, and Evermann and Goldsborough (1907) from Loring. The UBC has numerous lots from Cape Spencer (UBC 65-540) to the southeast tip of Duke Island (UBC 65-508). Lots at ABL include AB 64-954, from Sitka; AB 67-36, Katlian Bay; and AB 69-51, Ketchikan.

Size: R. Baxter, unpubl. data: uncataloged UAM specimen collected in 1989, Prince William Sound. Maximum size previously reported was 30 cm TL (Miller and Lea 1972).

Family Cryptacanthodidae
Wrymouths

The wrymouth family comprises four species of eel-like, burrowing bottom dwellers inhabiting coastal waters of the northern North Pacific and North Atlantic oceans. Wrymouths dig in soft silt, making a system of tunnels with numerous exits, and eat invertebrates, primarily crustaceans. Two species occur only in the eastern North Pacific: giant wrymouth, *Cryptacanthodes giganteus,* and dwarf wrymouth, *C. aleutensis.* Both species are found from the Bering Sea and Aleutian Islands through southeastern Alaska to California.

Wrymouths have considerably elongate bodies which are rounded anteriorly and compressed posteriorly, and broad, depressed heads with eyes set high. The lower jaw projects and the mouth is oblique to nearly vertical. The dorsal fin is composed only of stiff spines. The dorsal and anal fins are long, and join the caudal fin. Pelvic fins are lacking. Scales are absent, except in *C. giganteus* which has small, scattered, cycloid scales. The seismosensory canals of the head do not open to the exterior through pores, and the body lateral line is represented only by widely spaced, superficial neuromasts. All four species have vomerine teeth, and all except *C. aleutensis* have palatine teeth. They have 6 or 7 branchiostegal rays, few pyloric caeca (2–6), and no swim bladder. The gill rakers are not numerous, and are very short. Makushok (1961) noted and corrected errors in previous descriptions of the various forms.

Although wrymouths resemble some pricklebacks (Stichaeidae) which lack pelvic fins, they have flattened rather than compressed heads and different coloration. They lack a head crest and cirri, which are present in many pricklebacks. Reaching lengths of about 30–120 cm (1–4 ft), the two eastern Pacific wrymouths are larger than most pricklebacks and gunnels (Pholidae). Their size, reflected in their common names (giant and dwarf wrymouths), is one of the most useful features for distinguishing between mature specimens of these two species.

The wrymouth classification used in this guide is that of Makushok (1958, 1961). Hence, the Cryptacanthodidae are classified as a separate family from the Stichaeidae, and *Lyconectes* and *Delolepis,* the genera in which the Pacific species of wrymouths were previously placed, are included in *Cryptacanthodes.* Separation by Makushok of the Cryptacanthodidae from the Stichaeidae on the basis of differences in skull and cephalic sensory system structure and proportions of the pectoral radials, as well as differences in external appearance, seems well founded; and all four species of wrymouths differ from each other by such insignificant features that generic separation is not justified. *Delolepis,* for example, was established as a distinct genus by Bean (1882) mainly on the single character of developed scales, which today would not be considered sufficient reason for subdivision in other groups of fishes. Nevertheless, some authors elect not to follow Makushok (1958, 1961) on the taxonomy of this group. Quast and Hall (1972), in their inventory of Alaskan fishes, included the Cryptcanthodidae in the Stichaeidae and used the older generic names. Nelson (1984, 1994), in his systematic treatment of the fishes of the world, followed Makushok (1958) in classifying the Cryptacanthodidae as a separate family but listed the four monotypic genera.

Key to the Cryptacanthodidae of Alaska

1	Scales present on body posteriorly; palatine teeth present; tan to light brown; adult size to 123 cm TL	*Cryptacanthodes giganteus,* page 771
1	Scales absent; palatine teeth absent; red or pink; adult size to 31 cm TL	*Cryptacanthodes aleutensis,* page 772

Cryptacanthodes giganteus (Kittlitz, 1858) **giant wrymouth**

Southeastern Bering Sea and eastern Aleutian Islands from Unalaska Island to northern California at Humboldt Bay.

Level to gently sloping soft bottom, often buried, at depths of 6–128 m, usually shallower than 20 m.

D LXXIII–LXXVII; A II,43–49; Pec 11–14; Pel 0; GR 9–12; Vert 81–85.

- **Light brown** tinged with yellow and violet, lighter ventrally, with a dark brown stripe dorsolaterally and another along lateral line, and an indistinct stripe along anal fin base; dark spots on head and above and below lateral line; lower part of head sometimes white; sometimes tan all over with dark band along lateral line.
- Mouth strongly oblique; maxilla extending beyond eye (with mouth closed).
- Dorsal and anal fins extending to caudal fin base or connected with caudal fin; pelvic fin absent.
- **Scales on body posteriorly and along lateral line anteriorly**; scales small, scattered.
- Lateral line composed of a series of isolated superficial neuromasts.
- Vomerine and **palatine teeth present**.
- Gill membranes connected to isthmus; gill opening 52–56% HL; gill opening interspace 15–26% HL; gill rakers as smooth knobs.
- **Length to 123 cm TL.**

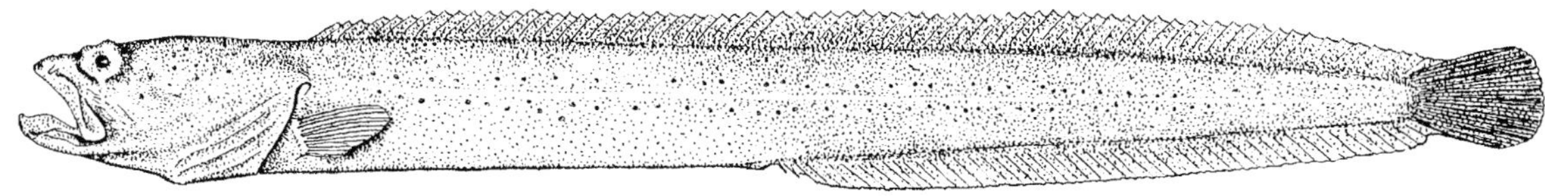

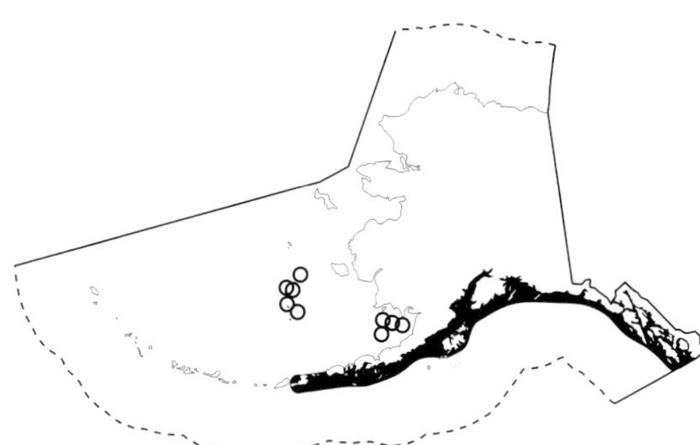

Notes & Sources — *Cryptacanthodes giganteus* (Kittlitz, 1858)
Ophidium giganteum Kittlitz, 1858
Delolepis virgatus Bean, 1882
Delolepis giganteus (Kittlitz): Hubbs 1927:377.

Description: Bean 1882:466–468; Makushok 1961; Hart 1973:355; Eschmeyer and Herald 1983:254; Matarese et al. 1989:520 (vertebral counts); Baxter 1990ms:686 (gill raker counts, gill opening and interspace measurements).

Figure: Hart 1973:355; 65 cm TL, Puget Sound.

Range: Jordan, Evermann, and Clark (1930:472) gave "Siberia" for the type locality of *Ophidium giganteum* Kittlitz. However, an Alaskan or eastern Pacific locality is far more likely. Kittlitz (1858:226) collected the type specimen (which apparently is no longer in existence; Eschmeyer 1998) by angling from the Russian ship *Seniavin,* which he accompanied on the voyage of exploration under Captain Lütke (or Litke) in 1827–1829 from South America to Alaska, stopping at Sitka and Unalaska and continuing to St. Matthew Island before progressing to the Kamchatka Peninsula. Just where along this route he collected the specimen, is not clear from Kittlitz's report. Judging from current knowledge of the species' geographical range, with no records west of the Pribilof Islands, we doubt that the type was from Kamchatka (southern Siberia). Previous, definitely Alaskan records include: Bean (1882) from Wrangel (= Wrangell); Gilbert (1896) and Evermann and Goldsborough (1907) from Unalaska Island; and Wilimovsky (1964) from the Krenitzin Islands. Those records and additional specimens in museum collections document occurrence throughout the area indicated by solid black on the above map. For example, the UBC has one specimen each from Tigalda Island (Krenitzin Islands; UBC 63-1311); Afognak Island (UBC 58-212, UBC 78-133); Sitkalidak Island (UBC 65-46); McLeod Harbor, Prince William Sound (UBC 62-976); Lynn Canal off Shelter Island (UBC 62-615); and other Alaskan localities. The ABL collection has one specimen each from the vicinity of Cape Bingham, northern Chichagof Island (AB 62-1); Little Port Walter (AB 62-105); and Fritz Cove (AB 87-39). Baxter (1990ms) collected specimens (UAM uncataloged) from Kachemak Bay, Cook Inlet. Circles on the above map represent southeastern Bering Sea records from the NMFS survey database (D.W. Kessler, pers. comm., 20 Jun. 1994).

Size: AB 87-39. Previously recorded to 117 cm TL by Clemens and Wilby (1949).

Cryptacanthodes aleutensis (Gilbert, 1896) **dwarf wrymouth**

Southeastern Bering Sea and eastern Aleutian Islands from Unalaska Island to northern California off Eureka.

Soft bottoms, buried, at depths of 28–350 m.

D LX–LXX; A II–III,45–49; Pec 12–13; Pel 0; GR 10–12; Vert 71–77.

- **Bright red or pink** in life, from blood showing through skin; gray in preservative; color mostly uniform.
- Skin loose and transparent.
- Mouth strongly oblique, nearly vertical; maxilla extending to below front edge of eye; nostril tube projects over maxilla.
- Dorsal and anal fins reaching caudal fin base, in some specimens extending onto caudal fin; pelvic fin absent.
- **Scales absent**.
- Lateral line indistinct, a series of distantly spaced superficial neuromasts.
- Vomerine teeth present, **palatine teeth absent**.
- Gill membranes broadly connected to isthmus; gill opening 29–33% HL; gill opening interspace 29–32% HL; gill rakers as spiny plates.
- **Length to 31 cm TL**.

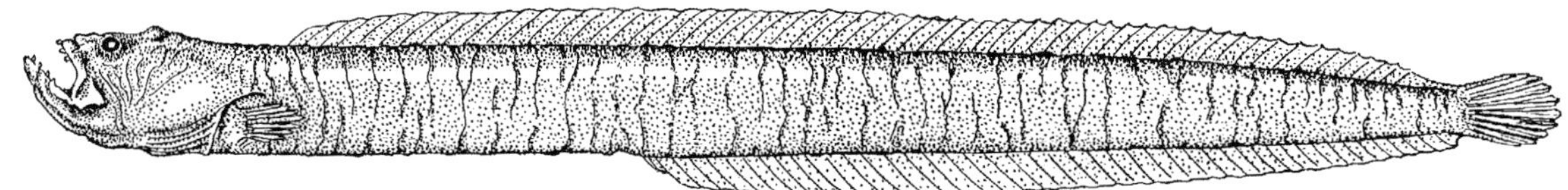

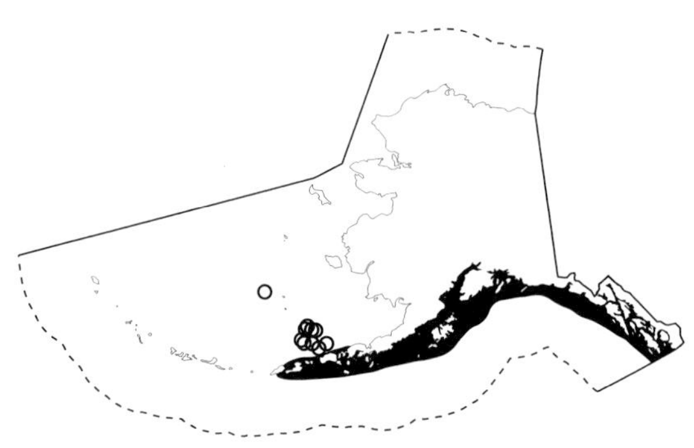

Notes & Sources — *Cryptacanthodes aleutensis* (Gilbert, 1896)
Lyconectes aleutensis Gilbert, 1896
Also called red devil (e.g., Hamada 1981).

Description: Gilbert 1896:452–453; Gilbert and Thompson 1905:986–987; Makushok 1961; Hart 1973:356–357; Hamada 1981; Eschmeyer and Herald 1983:254; Matarese et al. 1989:520 (vertebral counts); Baxter 1990ms:687 (gill raker counts, gill opening and interspace measurements).

Figure: Hart 1973:356; 27 cm TL, Puget Sound.

Range: Gilbert (1896) described the species from one specimen obtained from the Bering Sea north of Unalaska Island at *Albatross* station 3312. Hamada (1981) described a specimen caught near the Shumagin Islands. Blackburn and Jackson (1982) and Baxter (1990ms; UAM uncataloged) collected *C. aleutensis* off the east side of Kodiak Island. Kessler (1985) reported it was common both north and south of the Alaska Peninsula. Specimens from Akutan Bay, Fox Islands (AB 66-1033); Alaska Peninsula at 55°57'N, 159°28'W (AB 65-102); Shelikof Strait (AB 64-774); Day Bay (AB 64-668); Peril Strait (AB 62-517); and Katlian Bay, Baranof Island (AB 67-107) were the basis for a general reference to ABL records by Quast and Hall (1972). Specimen UBC 62-696 was collected near the Alaska Peninsula at 55°30'N, 158°50'W. Circles on the above map represent southeastern Bering Sea records from the NMFS survey database provided by D. W. Kessler (pers. comm., 20 Jun. 1994).

FAMILY PHOLIDAE
Gunnels

Gunnels are elongate, compressed, eel-like fishes of the littoral zone which, like some pricklebacks (family Stichaeidae), are often found under rocks or in tidepools. Although in many characters gunnels are similar to pricklebacks, gunnels typically have shorter anal fins and never have more than one lateral line. Gunnels have no fleshy crest on the head as some pricklebacks do (a wrinkle that could be mistaken for a crest sometimes forms as a result of preservation). About 15 species of gunnels are known, and most of them are found only in the North Pacific. At least five species occur in Alaska, primarily along the southern shores of the state.

Distinguishing characters of gunnels include a single dorsal fin, which is about twice the length of the anal fin and extends from the head to the caudal fin. It is supported by 73–100 spines, while the anal fin has 1–3 spines and 32–53 soft rays; both fins are confluent with the caudal fin, which is rounded. In some species the pectoral fins are absent, although not in the Alaskan species. The pelvic fins are rudimentary, consisting of 1 spine and 1 ray, or are absent. Scales are absent from the head in most species (in all Alaskan species) but the body is covered with tiny cycloid scales which are usually inconspicuous and covered with thick mucus. The basic numbers of head pores are: nasal 2, occipital 3, interorbital 1, postorbital 6, suborbital 6, mandibular 4, and preopercular 5 (see accompanying diagrams). The body lateral line is not evident in preserved specimens, but usually is easily discernible in fresh specimens. The gill membranes are broadly joined to each other and free from the isthmus, and there are 5 branchiostegal rays. Pyloric caeca are absent. Vertebral counts range from 80 to 105. Most gunnels are under 30 cm (1 ft) in length but the penpoint gunnel, *Apodichthys flavidus,* reaches 46 cm (1.5 ft).

The gunnel classification used in this guide follows the revision by Yatsu (1981, 1985), except that we include the species *clemensi, laeta,* and *schultzi* in *Pholis,* whereas Yatsu separated these species from *Pholis* and grouped them in a new nominal genus *Allopholis.* These species are closely similar in appearance, their separation by Yatsu being based on differences in the numbers of suborbital bones and presence or absence of a median interorbital head pore. Peden and Hughes (1984) demonstrated overlap in the number of suborbital bones and considered that presence or absence of a character shared by several genera without other conspicuously distinct features should not by itself be the basis of generic separation. In short, as M. E. Anderson (pers. comm., 18 Nov. 1998) put it, the distinction is too fine. Moreover, as Yatsu (pers. comm., 31 Jul. 1998) pointed out, changing the names of *P. laeta, P. clemensi,* and *P. schultzi,* which are endemic to the eastern Pacific, would be uncomfortable for most North American researchers and naturalists. A few North American workers use the name *Allopholis* (e.g., McAllister 1991), but most (e.g., Robins et al. 1991a) consider the generic distinction insignificant. Yatsu's (1981) shift of the species *dolichogaster* from *Pholis* to the genus *Rhodymenichthys* is well founded, and is a return to the taxonomy of earlier workers (Jordan and Evermann 1896a).

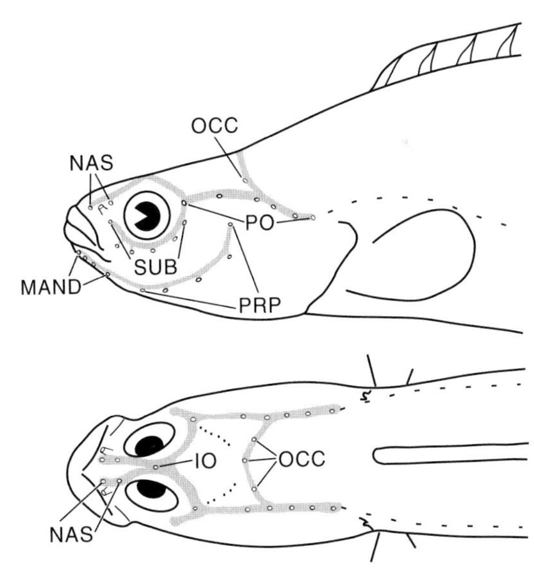

Head pores of hypothetical gunnel
NAS, nasal; IO, interorbital; SUB, suborbital; PO, postorbital; OCC, occipital; MAND, mandibular; PRP, preopercular. (After Makushok 1958, Yatsu 1981.)

The five gunnel species known to exist in Alaska are *Apodichthys flavidus, Rhodymenichthys dolichogaster, P. laeta, P. clemensi,* and *P. fasciata. Pholis clemensi* is relatively new to the list of Alaskan fishes. Its presence in the region was documented for the first time by Peden and Wilson (1976), who collected it from southeastern Alaska at Fillmore Island.

Pholis schultzi, an eastern North Pacific species recorded as far north as Vancouver Island, British Columbia, is also included in this guide, but only as a potential addition to the Alaskan ichthyofauna. The current lack of reports of *P. schultzi* from Alaska may be more an indication of inadequate sampling of open coastal waters (its preferred habitat) than of absence of the species. Peden and Wilson (1976) remarked that lack of sampling coverage might explain its apparent absence from northern British Columbia.

Pholis gilli and *P. ornata,* previously reported to occur in Alaskan waters (Wilimovsky 1954, Quast and Hall 1972), are no longer included in the inventory. Yatsu (1981) suggested that *P. gilli,* named and described on the basis of a specimen collected from the Bering Sea, by Evermann and Goldsborough (1907), is a synonym of *P. fasciata,* known from Greenland, Arctic Canada, and the western Pacific, but the suggested synonymy has generally not been followed in subsequent ichthyological literature. Specimens of both nominal species, including the holotype of *P. gilli,* are essentially identical, confirming the synonymy (C.W.M.). There are numerous reports of *P. ornata* from Alaska, but Peden and Hughes (1984), after examining several thousand specimens of *P. ornata* and closely related species, concluded that previous reports of this species north of Vancouver Island and west to Japan represent either *P. laeta* or an unidentified species, or are mislabeled. Specimens from Alaska collected in the 1990s and identified and curated in museums under the name *P. ornata* also are referable to *P. laeta* (C.W.M., unpubl. data).

Two other species listed by Quast and Hall (1972) are not included among the accounts in this guide. *Pholis picta,* known from the northwest Pacific Ocean from Petropavlovsk to the Sea of Japan, has not been reported from Alaska. Quast and Hall (1972) listed it as a probable Alaskan species, but records in recent years indicate this species is restricted to Asian shores. Lindberg and Krasyukova (1975) incorrectly cited Jordan et al. (1913:388) for suggesting it occurs "possibly also in the Bering Sea"; the latter authors listed only Sea of Okhotsk localities, and Yatsu (1981) indicated those were erroneous. The nearest valid record is that of Popov (1933) from southeastern Kamchatka at Petropavlovsk Harbor. *Pholidapus dybowskii* (Steindachner), which also was listed by Quast and Hall (1972) as a species of gunnel likely to occur in Alaska, is not a gunnel but a prickleback (family Stichaeidae) of the genus *Opisthocentrus* (Makushok 1958), and has a restricted distribution along Asian coasts.

Fin ray counts are used for critical work in distinguishing gunnels, but it is difficult, especially with smaller specimens, to achieve accurate counts without radiographs. Head pore configuration, while important for identification, is also difficult to determine, especially because in some species the pores are not clearly discernible without removing the covering of mucus. However, it is usually possible to distinguish the interorbital pore without such dissection, and this is an important character for identifying some of the Alaskan species. Coloration is an extremely important diagnostic character in gunnels, and patterns, although not the actual colors, can be discernible even after long immersion in preservative. Presence or absence of the pelvic fins, shape and number of the anal fin spines, and length of the anal fin relative to total or standard length are also helpful diagnostic characters.

Key to the Pholidae of Alaska

1		Pelvic fin absent; 1 anal fin spine, which is enlarged	*Apodichthys flavidus,* page 775
1		Pelvic fin present, rarely absent; 2 or 3 anal fin spines, none enlarged	(2)
2	(1)	Body with scattered dark dots; 2 or 3 anal fin spines	*Rhodymenichthys dolichogaster,* page 776
2		Body with light and dark bars or blotches; 2 anal fin spines	(3)
3	(2)	Interorbital pore absent; other head pores conspicuous	*Pholis fasciata,* page 777
3		Interorbital pore present; head pores inconspicuous	(4)
4	(3)	Anal fin length more than 50% SL	*Pholis clemensi,* page 778
4		Anal fin length less than 50% SL	(5)

5 (4) Dorsal fin with 12–16 pale markings bordered by dark crescents . . . . *Pholis laeta,* page 779

5 Dorsal fin with about 16 narrow, pale markings; anal fin with many dark vertical bars; color usually red . . . . *Pholis schultzi,* page 780
(not known from Alaska)

Apodichthys flavidus Girard, 1854 **penpoint gunnel**

Kodiak Island, Gulf of Alaska, to southern California at Santa Barbara.

Intertidal, especially in tidepools, among eelgrass or algae and rocks.

D LXXXVI–XCVI; A I,35–43; Pec 14–15; Pel 0; Vert 49–51 + 47–52 (96–101).

- Color uniformly red to green to brown, except often with row of dark or light spots, or both, laterally; dark streak down from eye, often a second streak from upper rear of eye; with or without silvery bar with orange or black border from mouth through eye to rear of head.
- **Pelvic fin absent**.
- **Anal fin spine large, grooved** (“penpoint”).
- Head pores (inconspicuous): nasal 2, interorbital 1, suborbital 6, postorbital 6, occipital 3, mandibular 4, preopercular 5.
- Length to 460 mm TL.

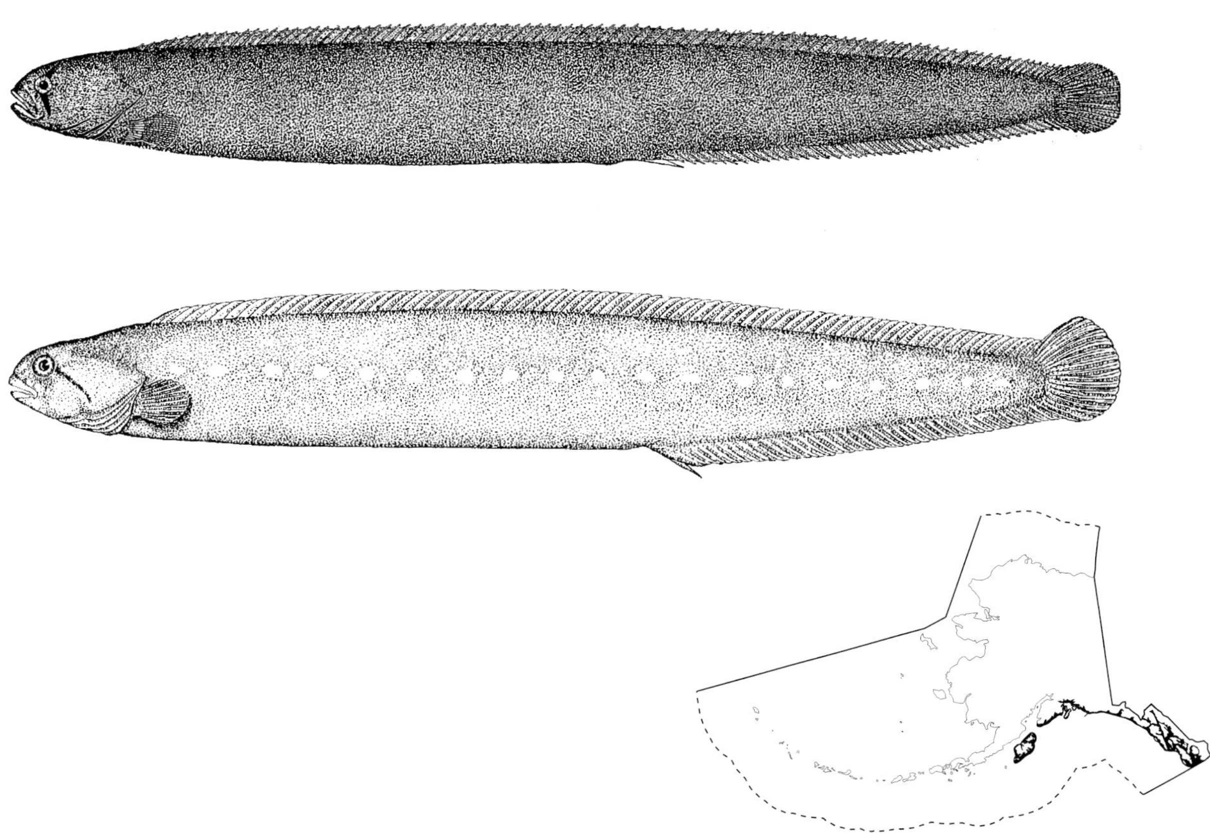

Notes & Sources — *Apodichthys flavidus* Girard, 1854

Description: Jordan and Evermann 1898:2411–2412; Hart 1973:345; Yatsu 1981:183–184; Eschmeyer and Herald 1983:255; Humann 1996:88–89. Some common color variations in Alaska are green with yellow belly and yellow spots along side (e.g., NMC 61-8, Prince of Wales Island); light brown with green streak through eye and light green spots along side (e.g., NMC 61-55, Icy Strait, Scraggy Island); and light brown with silver-blue streak through eye and light blue-green spots along side (e.g., NMC 61-25, Biorka Island, southwest of Sitka).

Figures: Upper: Evermann and Goldsborough 1907, fig. 108; about 20 cm TL, “Sucia Island” (probably Sucia Ledge, southeastern Alaska). Lower: Hart 1973:345, modified to show light-spotted variation; 10 cm TL.

Range: Well represented in institutional collections from eastern Gulf of Alaska coasts to Kodiak Island, where its occurrence was reported by Hubbard and Reeder (1965).

Rhodymenichthys dolichogaster (Pallas, 1814) **stippled gunnel**

Eastern Bering Sea from St. Lawrence Island and Norton Sound to Aleutian Islands; western Bering Sea from Olyutorskiy Bay to Commander Islands, Kuril Islands, and Okhotsk and Japan seas.

Among algae and rocks in intertidal areas and to depth of 148 m; typically found intertidally, frequently in tidepools.

D LXXX–XCVI; A II–III,40–51; Pec 13–15; Pel I,1; Vert 37–45 + 48–57 (87–101).

- **Color highly variable, red to light purple, brown, or olive green, often with scattered minute black dots; silver streak across eye** to pectoral fin base, streak dark in preserved specimens; dorsal and anal fins with light vertical streaks which fade rapidly in preservative.
- Anal fin spines typically 2, rarely 3.
- Head pores (inconspicuous): nasal 2, **interorbital 1, suborbital 5**, postorbital 6, occipital 3, mandibular 4, preopercular 5.
- Length to 250 mm TL.

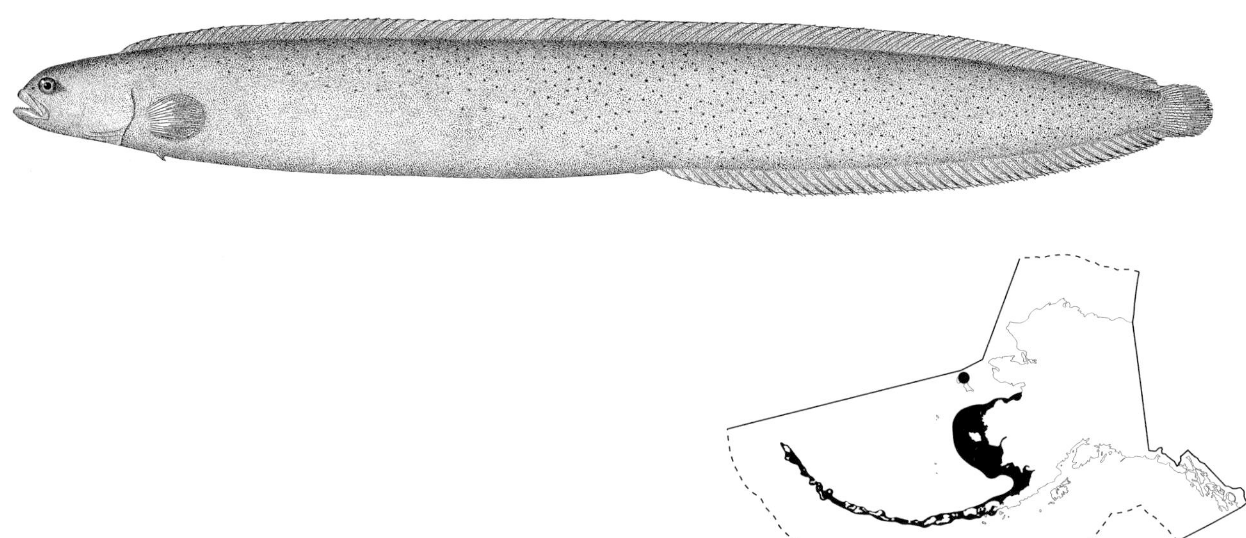

Notes & Sources — *Rhodymenichthys dolichogaster* (Pallas, 1814)
Blennius dolichogaster Pallas, 1814
Gunnellus ruberrimus Cuvier & Valenciennes, 1836
Muraenoides dolichogaster (Pallas): Bean 1881b:245.
Muraenoides ruberrimus (Cuvier & Valenciennes): Nelson 1887:305 and pl. 14.
Rhodymenichthys ruberrimus, R. dolichogaster: Jordan and Evermann 1896a:474 (new genus).
Pholis ruberrimus (Cuvier & Valenciennes): Bean and Bean 1896:247.
Jordan and Evermann (1898:2416–2417) classified *ruberrimus* as a junior synonym of *dolichogaster* in *Pholis,* reducing *Rhodymenichthys* to the level of subgenus.
Pholis dolichogaster (Pallas): Jordan and Gilbert 1899:481.
Placed, again, in *Rhodymenichthys* by Yatsu (1981).

Description: Jordan and Evermann 1898:2416–2417; Lindberg and Krasyukova 1975:41–42; Yatsu 1981:181–182; Amaoka in Masuda et al. 1984:304.

Figure: Nelson 1887, pl. 14, fig. 1; Unalakleet, Alaska.

Range: Collected at Unalakleet (63°52'N, 160°47'W), Norton Sound, by Nelson (1887). A specimen (UAM 42; about 196 mm TL, too curved for accurate measurement) was collected from almost as far north in 1933, from a "stream back of school" at Savoonga (63°42'N, 170°29'W), on the north coast of St. Lawrence Island. Bean (1881b) recorded *R. dolichogaster* from the Aleutian Islands, without exact locality; and Wilimovsky (1964) from Amchitka, Atka, and Unalaska islands. There are no records of *R. dolichogaster* from the Aleutian Islands west of Amchitka, but distribution is probably continuous along Aleutian coasts to the Commander Islands, Russia, where it was recorded by Bean and Bean (1896), Jordan and Gilbert (1899), and Gilbert and Burke (1912a); reported to be abundant there by Fedorov and Sheiko (2002). Recorded from Olyutorskiy Bay, Russia, by Matyushin (1982). Few Alaskan specimens have been reported and few exist in institutional collections. The species could be less commonly distributed in Alaska than indicated by the above map. Maximum depth: Lindberg and Krasyukova 1975.

Pholis fasciata (Bloch & Schneider, 1801) **banded gunnel**

Bering Sea to western Gulf of Alaska at Kodiak Island and in western North Pacific to Okhotsk and Japan seas; and to Arctic Ocean east to Greenland.

Shallow subtidal depths, recorded to 46 m but usually found shallower than 20 m, over rocky substrate and among clumps of red algae; not in tidepools.

D LXXXIII–XCI; A II,41–48; Pec 11–13; Pel I,1 (or absent); Vert 40–44 + 50 (89–98).

- In life bright red, in alcohol yellowish, with **dark sinuous bands reaching belly**; bands highly variable, connections between bands sometimes imparting mottled pattern; **pale blotches containing dark spots extend from back onto dorsal fin; dark band from top of head through eye and down cheek behind mouth, followed by broad white band**.
- Pelvic fin occasionally absent; pectoral fin length 42–49% of head length.
- **Head pores conspicuous**: nasal 2, **interorbital absent**, suborbital 6, postorbital 6, occipital 3, mandibular 4, preopercular 5.
- Length to 300 mm TL.

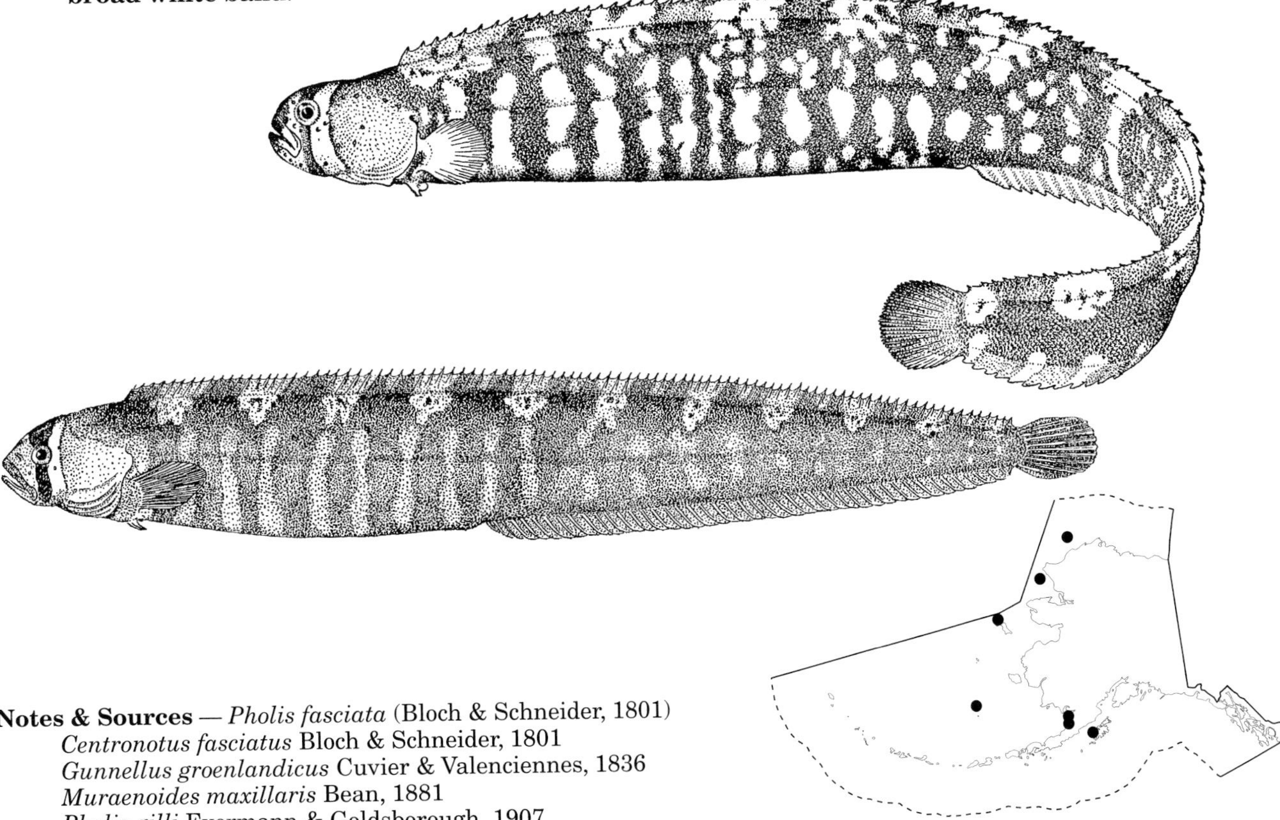

Notes & Sources — *Pholis fasciata* (Bloch & Schneider, 1801)
Centronotus fasciatus Bloch & Schneider, 1801
Gunnellus groenlandicus Cuvier & Valenciennes, 1836
Muraenoides maxillaris Bean, 1881
Pholis gilli Evermann & Goldsborough, 1907

Yatsu (1981) synonymized *P. gilli* in *P. fasciata* but did not have opportunity to examine type specimens (A. Yatsu, pers. comm., 31 Jul. 1998), and the synonymy has not generally been followed (e.g., Robins et al. 1991a). C.W.M. found the holotype and other specimens of *P. gilli* to be identical to specimens cataloged as *P. fasciata* (specimens listed below; 70–220 mm TL), except for minor variations in the banding on the body and fins.

Also called mottled gunnel (e.g., Leim and Scott 1966).

Description: Bean 1881a:147–148; Gilbert 1896:449–450; Jordan and Evermann 1898:2417–2418; Evermann and Goldsborough 1907:337–338; Yatsu 1981:172–173; Scott and Scott 1988:426–427. Cataloged as *P. gilli*: USNM 57826, holotype, Bering Sea; AB 65-116, Kvichak Bay; USNM 338008, UAM 1424 and 1462, Chukchi Sea; USNM 124966, Bering Sea; USNM 60760, St. Paul Island; USNM 38967, Petropavlovsk. As *P. fasciata*: USNM 165411, 177579, 177583, 177586, and 177640, Labrador; USNM 39745, Greenland; USNM 85783 and 126834, St. Paul Island.

Figures: Upper: Evermann and Goldsborough 1907, fig. 110; holotype of *P. gilli,* 178 mm TL, Bering Sea. Lower: Leim and Scott 1966:303; Canadian Arctic.

Range: Previous Alaskan records: St. Paul Island (Bean 1881a, Evermann and Goldsborough 1907); Bristol Bay (Gilbert 1896, *Albatross* stations 3230, 3232–3234; Quast and Hall 1972, based on AB 65-116 from Kvichak Bay); and Karluk (Evermann and Goldsborough 1907). New records: USNM 338008 and UAM 1424, Chukchi Sea near Point Hope at 68°16'N, 166°30'W, 18 m; UAM 1462, west of Point Barrow at 71°12'N, 163°05'W, 46 m; UAM 982 (misidentified as *P. dolichogaster*), Norton Sound, 64°27'N, 165°30'W, 20 m.

Size: Jensen 1942: 30.0 cm off west Greenland. Maximum length of 303 mm TL is attributed by some authors to Green (1970), but he actually gave maximum of 30.3 *mm* for his specimens.

Pholis clemensi Rosenblatt, 1964 **longfin gunnel**

Western Gulf of Alaska at Kodiak Island, record not verifiable; southeastern Alaska off Fillmore Island to northern California at Arena Cove.

Rocky areas at depths of 7–64 m.

D LXXXVII–XCII; A II,48–53; Pec 11–14; Pel I,1; Vert 37–40 + 56–59 (95–98).

- Red to orangish brown or reddish brown, commonly with silvery white or pale spots; 13–16 evenly spaced dark spots each followed by white blotch with dark dots in it extend from upper surface of body onto dorsal fin, or white marks are prominent and dark spots obscure; lower sides with dark mottling, alternating light and dark areas, or mostly red or orange with a series of white spots; coloration highly variable among individuals taken at the same time in the same general habitat.
- **Anal fin long**, usually more than 50% of standard length, with high number (48–53) of soft rays; pectoral fin length 45–49% of head length.
- Head pores (inconspicuous): nasal 2, **interorbital 1**, suborbital 6, postorbital 6, occipital 3, mandibular 4, preopercular 5.
- Length to 134 mm TL.

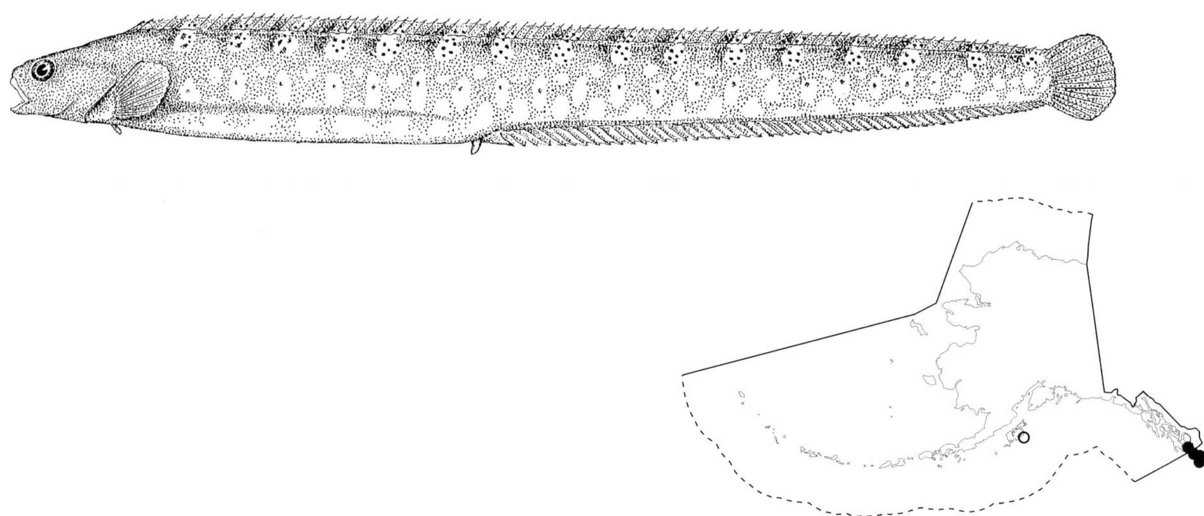

Notes & Sources — *Pholis clemensi* Rosenblatt, 1964
Allopholis clemensi (Rosenblatt): Yatsu 1981, 1985. Separation from *Pholis* is not universally accepted.

Description: Rosenblatt 1964; Hart 1973:346; Yatsu 1981: 179–180; Eschmeyer and Herald 1983:255; Humann 1996: 90–91.

Figure: Hart 1973:346; 11 cm TL, British Columbia.

Range: Recorded from Alaska at two subtidal localities off Fillmore Island: 54°47'N, 130°37'W, and 54°46'N, 130°48'W (Peden and Wilson 1976). A report of this species from near shore off east side of Kodiak Island (Blackburn and Jackson 1982) cannot be verified but does not seem unlikely. J. E. Blackburn (pers. comm., 23 Mar. 1999) wrote that the specimen was "casually identified by people that were getting quite knowledgeable by doing the survey, but not perfect"; the specimen was caught in a beach seine and measured 11 cm to the nearest centimeter. Peden and Wilson (1976) collected specimens from seven subtidal locations in British Columbia just south of the Alaskan border, from 54°45'N, 130°38'W to 53°22'N, 129°15'W.

Size: Peden and Wilson 1976.

Pholis laeta (Cope, 1873) **crescent gunnel**

Aleutian Islands and east along Alaska Peninsula to Port Heiden, and Gulf of Alaska shores to northern California at Crescent City; Commander Islands and southeastern Kamchatka.

Intertidal and shallow subtidal areas among eelgrass, algae, or rocks; to depth of about 73 m.

D LXXIV–LXXXI; A II,32–39; Pec 10–13; Pel I,1; Vert 39–42 + 41–46 (81–89).

- Body yellowish green to orangish brown, paler ventrally; orange or reddish brown anal, caudal, and pectoral fins; pale streaks bordered with black or purple radiate from eye to occiput and to gular region; **brown or blackish, crescent-shaped to nearly circular markings enclosing a yellow or orange area** extend from upper surface of body onto dorsal fin; numerous pale blotches on side.
- Pectoral fin length 31–41% of head length.
- Head pores (inconspicuous): nasal 2, **interorbital 1**, suborbital 6 (rarely 7), postorbital 6 (rarely 7), occipital 3, mandibular 4 (rarely 6), preopercular 5.
- Length to 250 mm TL.

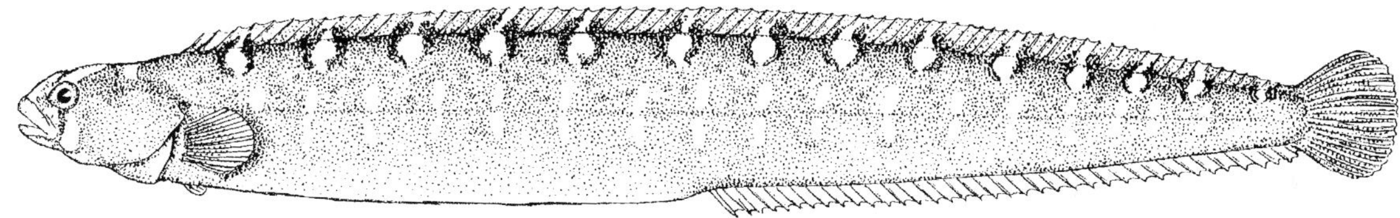

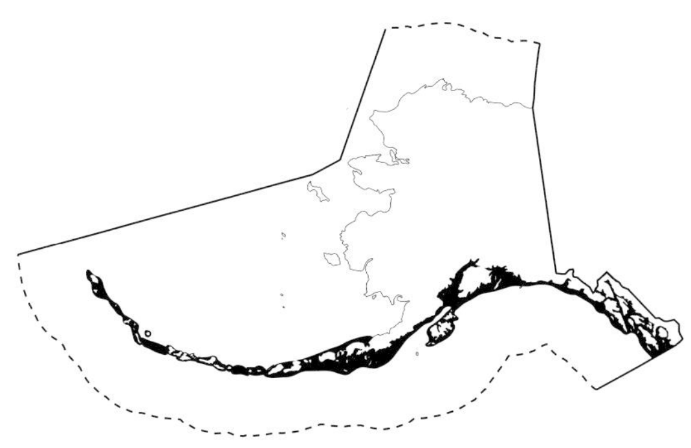

Notes & Sources — *Pholis laeta* (Cope, 1873)
Centronotus laetus Cope, 1873
Pholis laetus (Cope): Hubbs 1928:15.
Allopholis laeta (Cope): Yatsu 1981, 1985. Separation from *Pholis* is not universally accepted.
Peden and Hughes (1984) determined previous records of *P. ornata* from Alaska to be referable to *P. laeta*.

Description: Cope 1873:27–28; Hubbs 1928; Hart 1973:347; Yatsu 1981:178–179; Eschmeyer and Herald 1983:256; Peden and Hughes 1984:293–298; Humann 1996:90–91.

Figure: Hart 1973:347; 12 cm TL, British Columbia.

Range: The type locality is indefinite, but somewhere in Alaska. Cope (1873) described the species from two specimens that, he reported, were collected off Alaska at several points, principally Sitka and Unalaska, by Prof. George Davidson of the U.S. Coast Survey (now U.S. Geological Survey). (The type specimens are missing [Böhlke 1984].) Wilimovsky (1964) recorded the species as far west in the Aleutian Islands as Attu Island. Peden and Hughes (1984) listed 299 collections from throughout the known range in Alaska, and reported the northernmost record in the eastern Bering Sea to be Bristol Bay near Port Heiden, at 57°01'N, 158°38'W.

Pholis schultzi Schultz, 1931 **red gunnel**

British Columbia at Rivers Inlet, north of Vancouver Island, to central California at Diablo Cove.
Open coast in tidal surge channels from intertidal area to depth of about 18 m.

D LXXX–LXXXIX; A II,40–44; Pec 10–13; Pel I,1; Vert 41–43 + 49–52 (89–93).

- **Usually bright, dark red**, sometimes brown to greenish; fairly plain to spotted, blotched, barred, or streaked; sometimes with small black spots along ventral midline; **about 16 light, narrow bars along dorsal fin; anal fin with bars**, which are rarely absent; dark bars below eye.
- Pectoral fin length 38–40% of head length.
- Head pores (inconspicuous): nasal 2, **interorbital 1**, suborbital 6, postorbital 6, occipital 3, **mandibular 3**, preopercular 5.
- Length to 128 mm TL.

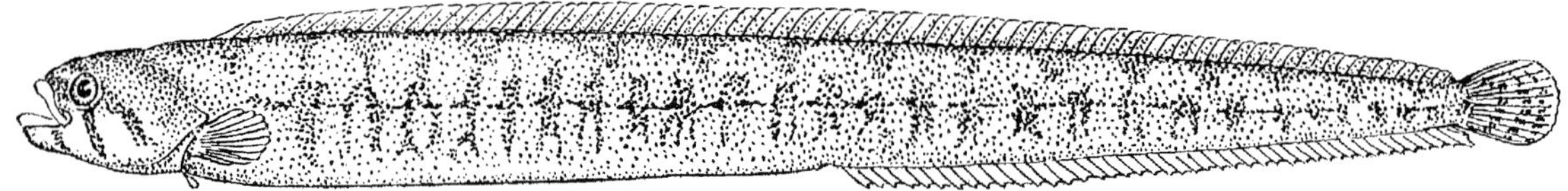

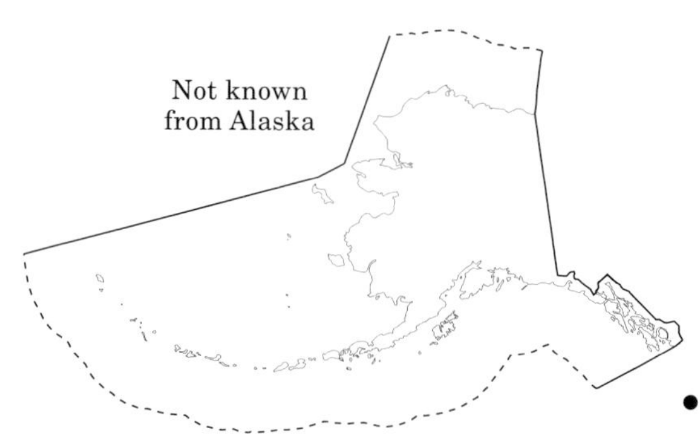

Notes & Sources — *Pholis schultzi* Schultz (ex Hubbs), 1931
Allopholis schultzi (Hubbs): Yatsu 1981, 1985. Separation from *Pholis* is not universally accepted.
Authorship of the scientific name is correctly Schultz. Schultz and Hubbs (1961) and Springer and Anderson (1997) recounted the complex nomenclatural history of this species.

Description: Peden 1966a; Hart 1973:349; Yatsu 1981:180–181; Eschmeyer and Herald 1983:256. Specimens over 80 mm SL collected from British Columbia had numerous dark vertical bars like parr marks along each side of the body (Peden and Wilson 1976).

Figure: Hart 1973:349; 68 mm TL, British Columbia.

Range: Peden and Wilson (1976) reported the nearest known locality: 51°27'N, 127°41'W, at mouth of Rivers Inlet, just north of Vancouver Island, British Columbia. They suggested that *P. schultzi* might have been found farther north if open coastal waters had been more completely sampled. The specimens (44) they collected were found on a subtidal rock face influenced by ocean swell and thickly covered by barnacles and hydroids.

Family Anarhichadidae
Wolffishes

Wolffishes are elongate, carnivorous, demersal inhabitants of shallow to moderately deep waters of the North Pacific and North Atlantic oceans. Most of them feed primarily on hard-shelled benthic prey. Like most other marine carnivorous fishes, wolffishes typically occur as solitary individuals or in small groups, not in large schools.

The wolffish family includes six species, two of them well known in Alaska. The wolf-eel, *Anarrhichthys ocellatus,* frequents caves and crevices. Endemic to the eastern North Pacific, the wolf-eel is found in Alaska primarily along the coasts of the Gulf of Alaska and eastern Aleutian Islands. The Bering wolffish, *Anarhichas orientalis,* inhabits boulder-strewn, sandy and pebbly bottoms along both Asiatic and American shores and in Alaska is known from the northcentral Gulf of Alaska through the Bering Sea and into the Arctic; it is a good food fish and historically was sought by natives of western Alaska. The third species treated this guide, the northern wolffish, *A. denticulatus,* is a benthopelagic inhabitant of deeper waters, primarily of the North Atlantic where it is often taken as bycatch in the halibut fishery. It was listed from Arctic Alaska by Wilimovsky (1958), but this record was questioned by Barsukov (1959) and later by Quast and Hall (1972), who did not include the species in their inventory of Alaskan species. There was a record of *A. denticulatus* from the Canadian high Arctic not far from Alaska at Mould Bay (Walters 1953b) and, since then, a specimen from the Amundsen Gulf area of the Canadian sector of the Beaufort Sea has been tentatively identified as belonging to this species (Smith 1977).

In wolffishes the dorsal fin is long, starting at the head, and composed of flexible spines; the pectoral fins are large; and the pelvic fins are absent. Most species have strong canine teeth at the front of the mouth and molars at the sides, for digging out and crushing clams and other hard-shelled prey. Northern wolffish, *A. denticulatus,* have mostly conical teeth, none of them strongly caniniform or molariform; and a diet which includes fare with relatively weak shells and tough skins such as crabs, sea urchins, and spiny lumpsuckers (family Cyclopteridae). Wolffishes lack scales or have minute cycloid scales. One or two lateral lines are present on the body, although generally indiscernible except in live fish. The gill membranes are attached to the isthmus, and there are 6–8 branchiostegal rays. Wolffishes are the largest of the elongate, compressed fishes of the order Perciformes. The species treated in this guide attain lengths of 1.2–2.4 m (4–8 ft).

The following key emphasizes characters considered diagnostic for the species by Barsukov (1959).

Key to the Anarhichadidae of Alaska

1 — Body extremely elongate and eel-like; dorsal and anal fins confluent with caudal fin, which tapers to a point . . . . *Anarrhichthys ocellatus,* page 782

1 — Body not extremely elongate and eel-like; dorsal and anal fins not connected with caudal fin, which is rounded or truncate . . . . (2)

2 (1) — Vomerine teeth extending posterior to palatine teeth; vertebrae more than 84; anal fin rays usually more than 50; caudal fin rounded . . . . *Anarhichas orientalis,* page 783

2 — Vomerine teeth not extending posterior to palatine teeth; vertebrae less than 84; anal fin rays usually less than 50; caudal fin more or less truncate . . . . *Anarhichas denticulatus,* page 784 (not known from Alaska)

Anarrhichthys ocellatus Ayres, 1855 **wolf-eel**

Southeastern Bering Sea east to Cape Menshikof, west along Aleutian Islands to Krenitzin Islands, and Gulf of Alaska and Pacific Ocean to southern California at Imperial Beach.

Rocky reefs and shorelines, usually in caves or crevices, at depths to 225 m.

D CCXVIII–CCL; A 0–I,180–233; Pec 19–20; Pel 0; GR 15–20; Vert 221–251.

- Dark greenish to gray; **body and dorsal fin covered with ocelli and pale reticulations of various sizes**; head paler than body, especially in males, with finer reticulations; juveniles orangish brown and with more and larger spots than adults.
- **Extremely elongate**.
- **Dorsal and anal fins confluent with caudal fin, which tapers to a point**.
- Vomerine tooth patch longer than palatine tooth patches and extending farther anteriorly; teeth in both jaws caniniform anteriorly, others strongly molariform.
- Length to 240 cm TL.

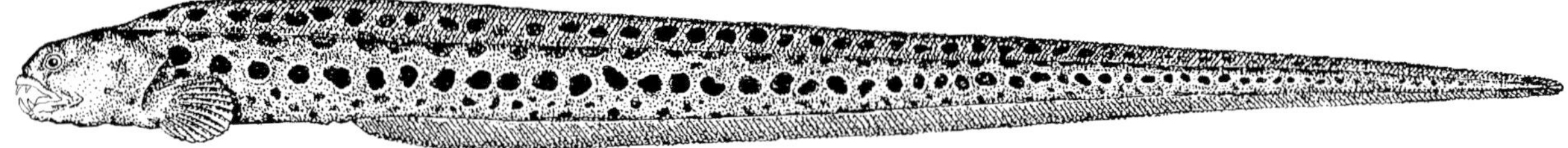

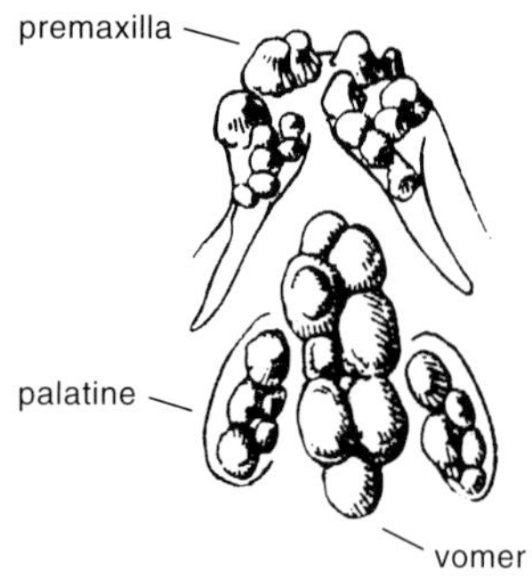

Notes & Sources — *Anarrhichthys ocellatus* Ayres, 1855

The spelling *Anarhichthys* has been used by some authors (e.g., Makushok 1958, Barsukov 1959), but *Anarrhichthys* has priority.

Description: Barsukov 1959:107–108; Hart 1973:351–352; Eschmeyer and Herald 1983:257–258; Humann 1996:80–81.

Figures: Hart 1973:351; 113 cm TL, Alaska. Teeth: Barsukov 1959, pl. I–6.

Range: Recorded from Bering Sea north to 56°04'N, 164°56'W (Larkins 1964) and east along north side of Alaska Peninsula to Cape Menshikof (Isakson et al. 1986); and in Aleutian Islands west to Krenitzin Islands (Wilimovsky 1964). Range in the Gulf of Alaska is well represented in museum collections; e.g., UBC has specimens from Middleton Island, Icy Strait, Cape Ommaney, and McLeod Bay. NMC 61-106 contains a specimen from Wells Passage, northwest Prince William Sound. Quast and Hall (1972) and other authors mistakenly reported its occurrence in the Seas of Japan and Okhotsk and at Petropavlovsk. Grebnitzki (1897) suggested that *A. ocellatus* inhabits the Kamchatka coast but Barsukov (1959), commenting on that suggestion, stated the species was absent from Kamchatka. There are no specimens of *A. ocellatus* in the Russian Academy of Sciences Zoological Institute (A. V. Balushkin, pers. comm., 21 Jun. 1999) or Kamchatka Institute of Ecology (B. A. Sheiko, pers. comm., 17 Aug. 1998) collections. Evidently, the species is endemic to the eastern Pacific.

Anarhichas orientalis Pallas, 1814 **Bering wolffish**

Beaufort and Chukchi seas to northern Gulf of Alaska at Prince William Sound, and to Okhotsk and Japan seas; Canadian Arctic at Bathurst Inlet, Nunavut.

Coastal areas on gravel and sand bottom among stones overgrown with algae; the most shallow-water species of *Anarhichas,* not found deeper than about 100 m and usually taken near shore.

D LXXX–LXXXVIII; A 50–55; Pec 20–22; Pel 0; GR 16–23; Vert 85–89.

- Body brown, reddish brown, or black, mottled and blotched; young with dark stripes on body.
- Head profile gradually sloping to occiput; body not particularly deep, about 17–22% of standard length; elongate; vertebrae more than 84.
- Dorsal and anal fins not confluent with caudal fin; **caudal fin gently rounded**; **anal fin rays usually more than 50**.
- **Vomerine tooth patch longer than and extending behind palatine patches**; **anterior jaw teeth caniniform, others molariform**.
- Length to 124 cm TL, weight to 19.5 kg.

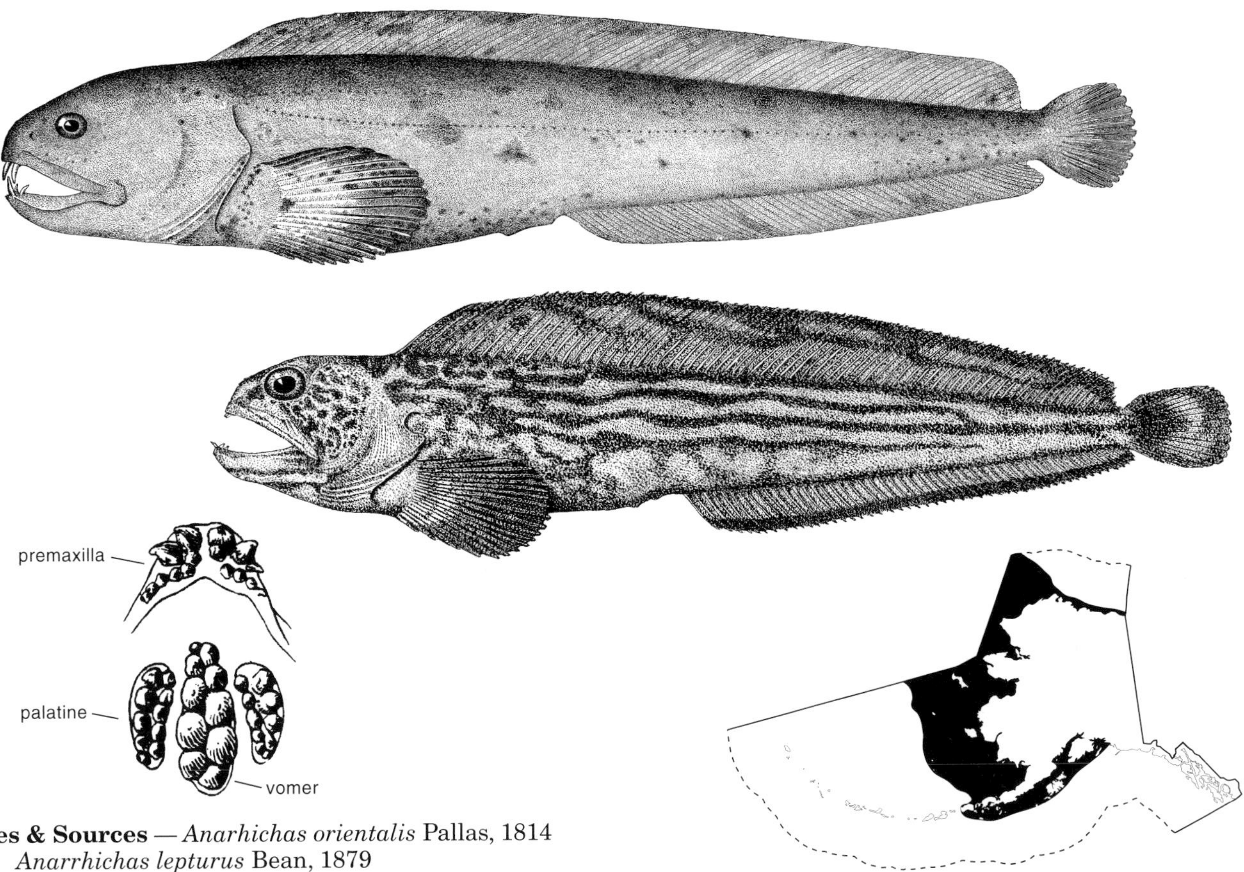

Notes & Sources — *Anarhichas orientalis* Pallas, 1814
Anarrhichas lepturus Bean, 1879
The spelling *Anarhichas* has priority.

Description: Bean 1879d; Andriashev 1954:227; Barsukov 1959:110–115 and throughout; Amaoka in Masuda et al. 1984:304. R. Baxter, unpubl. data: gill raker counts.

Figures: Upper: Turner 1886, pl. 5; 60 cm TL, Saint Michael, Norton Sound. Lower: Nelson 1887, pl. 15, fig. 1; juvenile, Saint Michael. Teeth: Barsukov 1959, pl. I–5.

Range: Early records include Bean (1879d), Turner (1886), and Nelson (1887) from Norton Sound; and Elliott (1882) from the Pribilof Islands. The only records from the Alaskan Beaufort Sea are those of Frugé and Wiswar (1991) from the Camden Bay area at Simpson Cove and off Konganevik Point. UAM uncataloged material includes a juvenile (195 mm TL) collected in 1990 from the Chukchi Sea at 71°10'N, 161°55'W. The easternmost Gulf of Alaska record may be UBC 63-483, from Port Gravina, Prince William Sound. NMC 61-143 is a specimen caught off Rugged Island in Resurrection Bay. The UBC collection also contains specimens from Kachemak Bay and near Nunivak Island and the Pribilof Islands. Quast and Hall (1972) reported *A. orientalis* from Bristol Bay, and Rogers et al. (1986) from Kodiak Island. R. Baxter (unpubl. data) collected specimens from the Chukchi and Bering seas, and Port Dick and Kasitsna Bay in the Gulf of Alaska. Jordan and Evermann (1898) incorrectly reported the range of *A. orientalis* to extend as far south as Vancouver Island (Andriashev 1954, Barsukov 1959). The only Canadian records are from the Arctic at Bathurst Inlet (Hunter et al. 1984, Coad 1995). Sokolovskaya et al. (1998) reported the first record from Peter the Great Bay, Sea of Japan.

Size: R. Baxter, unpubl. data: a specimen caught in Kasitsna Bay, an embayment of Kachemak Bay, Alaska, 17 Jul. 1988. Reported to reach 112 cm TL by Andriashev (1954).

Anarhichas denticulatus Krøyer, 1845 — **northern wolffish**

Canadian high Arctic at Mould Bay, Prince Patrick Island, and possibly Amundsen Gulf; Greenland and western Atlantic south almost to Cape Cod; Iceland to Novaya Zemlya; Arctic seas of the North Atlantic.

Surface to depth of 1,401 m, usually taken over silty bottoms at depths of 150–600 m; diet of bathypelagic and benthic invertebrates reflects demersal lifestyle of adults.

D LXXVI–LXXXI; A 45–50; Pec 19–22; Pel 0; GR 7; Vert 78–82.

- Gray, with bright violet shade or with brown tones of varying intensity; body and dorsal fin covered with dark spots (not shown in illustration below), most distinct dorsally.
- Body and bones soft, flesh watery.
- Head blunt, profile rising sharply to occiput; body deep, about 24–28% of standard length; only moderately elongate; vertebrae fewer than 84.
- Dorsal and anal fins not confluent with caudal; **caudal fin more or less truncate**; **anal fin rays usually fewer than 50**.
- **Vomerine tooth patch shorter than palatine patches, not extending as far posteriorly**; **teeth primarily conical, not molariform**.
- Upper lip noticeably thicker than lower, and covered with papillae (in adults).
- Length to 144 cm TL, weight to more than 20 kg.

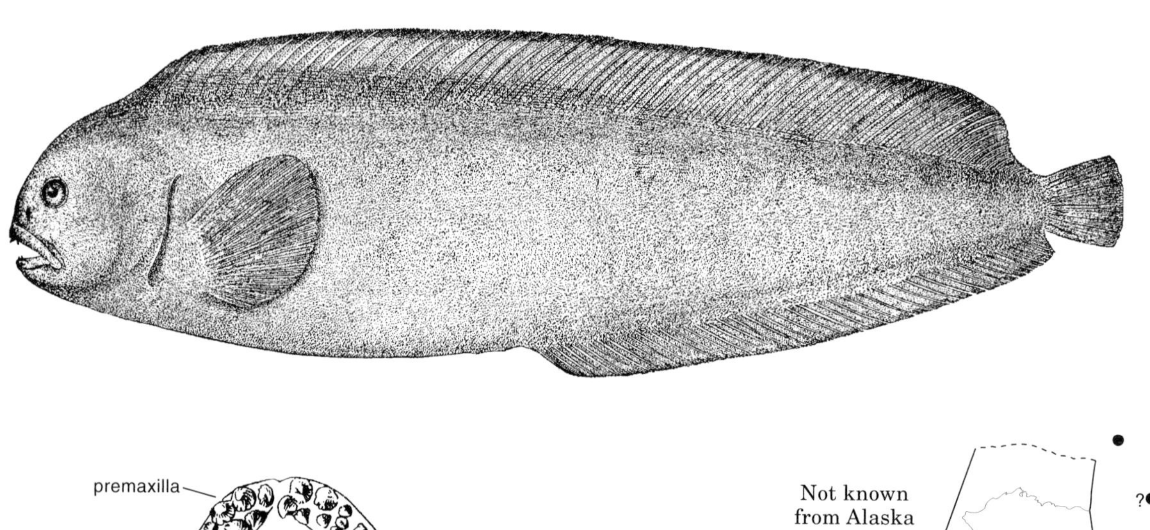

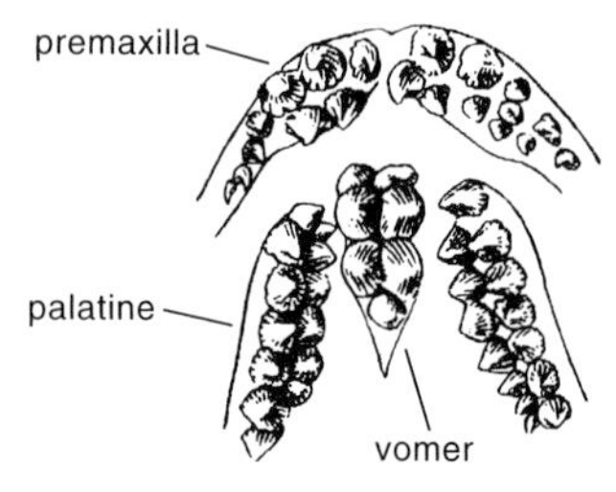

Notes & Sources — *Anarhichas denticulatus* Krøyer, 1845
Anarrhichas latifrons Steenstrup, 1876
Lycichthys denticulatus (Krøyer): Andriashev 1954.
Also called jelly wolffish, for the loose skin and soft, watery flesh.

Description: Andriashev 1954:220–222; Barsukov 1959: 115–127 and throughout; Barsukov in Hureau and Monod 1973:529; Scott and Scott 1988:430–431; Miki in Okamura et al. 1995:212.

Figures: Goode and Bean 1896, fig. 271; western North Atlantic. Teeth: Barsukov 1959, pl. I-1.

Range: Listed from Arctic Alaska by Wilimovsky (1958:85), without documentation. Barsukov (1959) considered the species' inclusion on Wilimovsky's (1958) list of Alaskan fishes "surprising," and Quast and Hall (1972) did not include it in their inventory. Records from Canada suggest probable occurrence off Alaska. Walters (1953b) recorded a specimen of *A. denticulatus* from the western Canadian high Arctic at Mould Bay, Prince Patrick Island. Since then, Smith (1977) reported a possible record from Amundsen Gulf, where a partially eaten wolffish carcass was found on the ice. The carcass was tentatively identified as *A. denticulatus* by D. A. McAllister, from a photograph, but Frugé and Wiswar (1991) thought it possible this fish was *A. orientalis.* Hunter et al. (1984) confirmed the identity of the Prince Patrick Island specimen as *A. denticulatus,* but did not identify the Amundsen Gulf specimen to species. Miki (in Okamura et al. 1995) reported three specimens (41–50 cm) were taken pelagically off the west coast of Greenland at depths of 110 m and 475 m over bottom depths exceeding 2,500 m.

Family Ptilichthyidae
Quillfishes

Ptilichthys goodei, the one extant member of the quillfish family, is occasionally collected from the marine waters off the southern coasts of Alaska. This fish is believed to bury itself in sand and mud during the day, but at night it migrates to the surface in search of prey where it is attracted by lights and can be caught in dip nets from docks and boats. Much of our knowledge of the species comes from specimens found in the stomachs of other fishes, including cods, salmons, and lancetfish.

Quillfish are extremely elongate, have a dorsal fin that extends the length of the body and tapers with the anal fin and reduced caudal fin to a filament, and lack pelvic fins, lateral line, swim bladder, and pyloric caeca. Their gill rakers are low, stout nubs.

Ptilichthys goodei Bean, 1881 **quillfish**

Southern Bering Sea and Pacific Ocean off Pribilof and Aleutian islands to Oregon, and from Litke Strait and Commander Islands to Seas of Okhotsk and Japan.

Surface to depth of about 360 m, possibly buried in the substrate during the day.

D LXXXI–XC + 137–157; A 185–196; Pec 13; Pel 0; Br 3; GR 0 + 8 (8); Vert 227–240.

- Yellow to greenish; throat region orange; longitudinal streak on body; head with dark streaks.
- **Body elongate, eel-like**; head very small, length 4–7% of SL; mouth oblique; **lower jaw projecting, with fleshy appendage at tip**.
- Maxilla barely reaching to below eye.
- **Dorsal fin of isolated spines anteriorly**, soft rays posteriorly; dorsal and anal fins confluent with reduced caudal fin, which tapers to filament.
- Scales very thin and scattered or absent.
- Gill membranes broadly united, free of isthmus.
- Length to 390 mm SL.

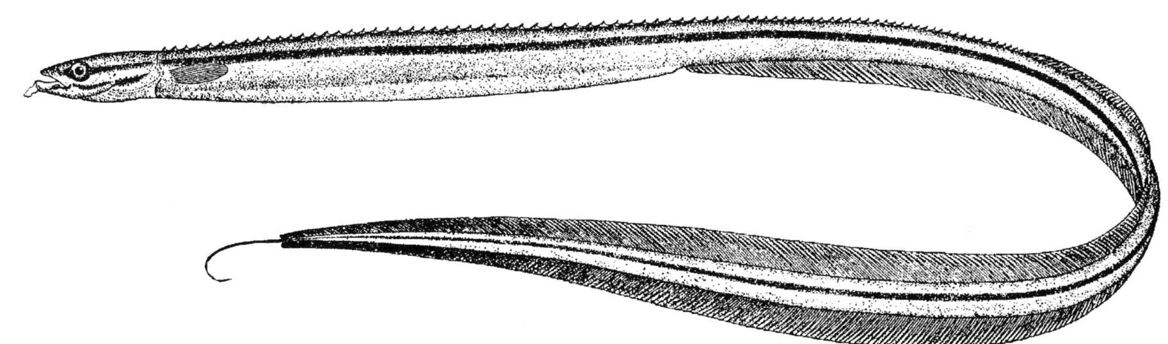

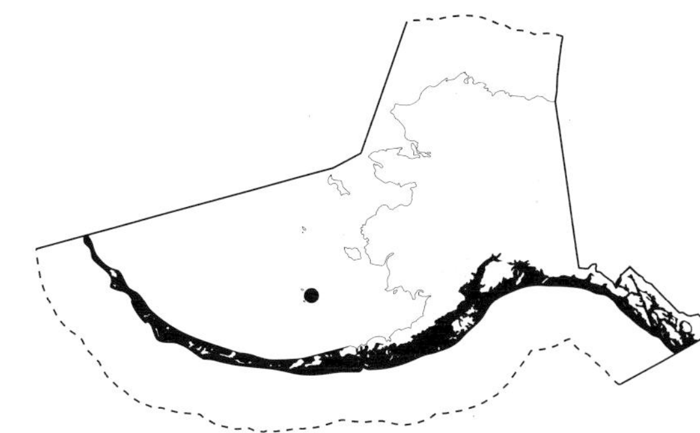

Notes & Sources — *Ptilichthys goodei* Bean, 1881

Description: Bean 1881a:157; Hart 1973:353–354; Richardson and DeHart 1975; Amaoka in Masuda et al. 1984:204; Humann 1996:92–93. Makushok (1958:114–117) presented evidence countering earlier claims that caudal fin and scales are absent.

Figure: Goode and Bean 1896, fig. 304, caudal filament added; holotype, 160 mm with broken filament, Port Levasheff (now Captains Bay), Unalaska Island, depth 18 m.

Range: Only record from north of Aleutian Islands may be a specimen (UW 27011) found in the mouth of a Pacific cod, *Gadus macrocephalus,* taken near the Pribilof Islands at 56°40'N, 168°17'W. Previously documented as far north as Unalaska Island (Bean 1881a, Gilbert 1896) and west to Amchitka Island (Simenstad et al. 1977). USNM 306358 is from vicinity of Attu Island; UBC 62-848, north of Amchitka Island at 52°59'N, 179°00'E; UW 14693, from the stomach of an *Alepisaurus* (lancetfish) taken at Shagak Bay, Adak Island. While occurrence from the Aleutians through southeastern Alaska is well documented by museum collections and the literature (e.g., Evermann and Goldsborough 1907, Quast and Hall 1972), records from Bristol Bay or farther north along the Alaskan mainland are lacking. Known in western Bering Sea from Litke Strait (Andriashev 1937) to the Commander Islands (Fedorov and Sheiko 2002); and to Peter the Great Bay (Sokolovskaya and Sokolovskii 1994). Maximum depth: UW 22359, one specimen, 380 mm TL, taken by trawl at 54°23'N, 165°45'W.

Size: A specimen (UW 27011) found in the mouth of a Pacific cod caught near the Pribilof Islands is the largest on record.

Family Zaproridae
Prowfishes

Zaprora silenus, sole member of its family, is fairly common in commercial fisheries bycatch in the Bering Sea and Gulf of Alaska. Adults are taken near bottom over the continental shelf and upper slope, while juveniles are pelagic and sometimes encountered farther offshore. Young prowfish shelter under jellyfish medusae and are often mistaken for medusafish, *Icichthys lockingtoni.*

Prowfish have large, terminal mouths with razor-sharp uniserial teeth for slicing off pieces of jellyfishes, which are their main prey (Tokranov 1999). *Zaprora silenus* is a stout, compressed fish with a blunt snout; high dorsal and anal fins that are completely separate from the large caudal fin; a deep, short caudal peduncle; large pectoral fins; and no pelvic fins. The dorsal and anal fins are especially high in the young. The dorsal fin is composed of spines, and the anal fin mainly of soft rays; the few spines in the anal fin are weak and most researchers count them as rays.

Zaprora silenus Jordan, 1896 — **prowfish**

Bering Sea to Pacific Ocean off San Miguel Island, California, and Hokkaido, Japan, including Okhotsk Sea. Adults near bottom at depths to 675 m; young fish often taken near surface over deep waters.

D LIV–LVIII; A 24–30; Pec 20–25; Pel 0; Br 6; LLs 200–232; GR 7–9 + 17–20; PC 36–77; Vert 61–64.

- Adults grayish blue to green, with or without darker spots and yellow blotches; head pores with white, yellow, or pale blue margins; young orange brown with dark and light spots and blotches.
- Snout high, blunt; head pores large, numerous.
- Body flaccid, but much less so than in Icosteidae.
- Dorsal and anal fins evenly contoured; caudal fin slightly rounded; pectoral fin longer than head.
- Small ctenoid scales on body and median fins.
- As many as three lateral lines (dorso-, medio-, and ventrolateral), with widely spaced pores.
- Gill membranes united, and free from isthmus.
- Length to 1 m SL or more.

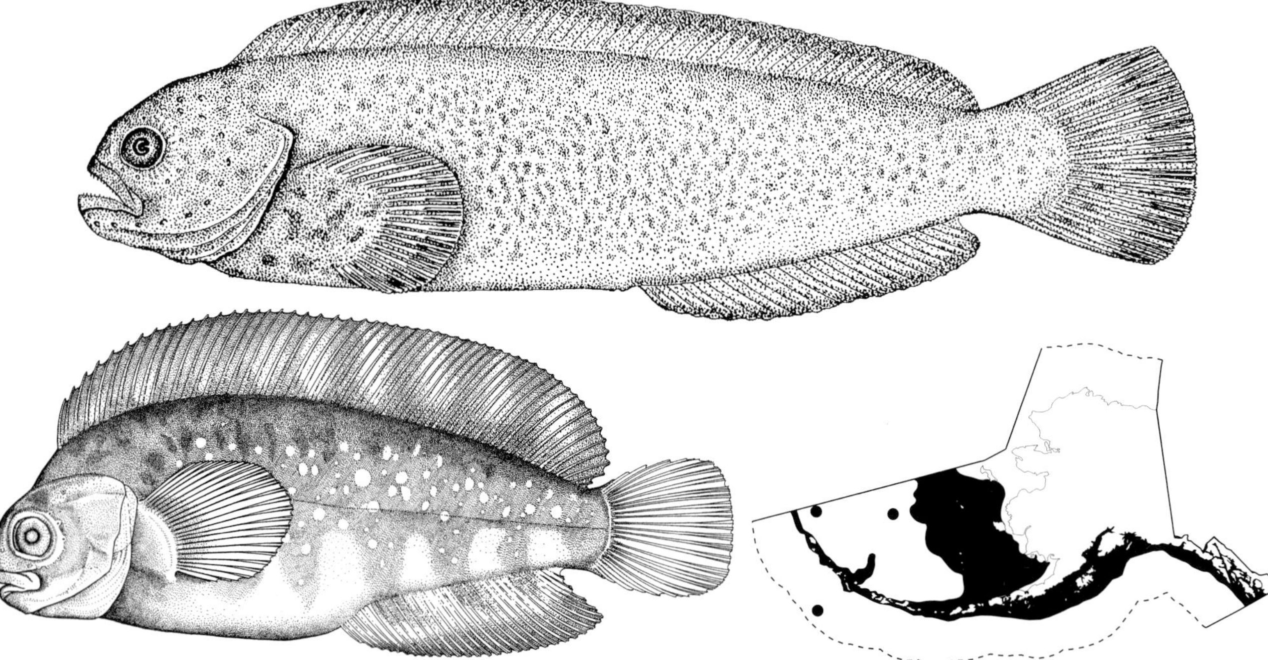

Notes & Sources — *Zaprora silenus* Jordan, 1896

Description: Schultz 1934b; Hart 1973:359–360; Cailliet and Anderson 1975; Amaoka in Masuda et al. 1984:304; Baxter (1990ms, unpubl. data); C.W.M. (AB uncataloged, adult).

Figures: Upper: Hart 1973:359; UBC 63-233, 49 cm TL, Alaska. Lower: University of British Columbia, artist R. Gowby, Sep. 1969; UBC 65-392, 118 mm SL, north of Adak Island.

Range: Nearly all of 468 occurrences in 30 years of NMFS demersal trawl surveys (Allen and Smith 1988) were from Alaska. The solid black fill on the above map also incorporates records of Schultz (1934b), Scheffer (1940), and Wilimovsky (1964), and specimens over 100 mm SL in the ABL, NMNH, UBC, and UW collections. Dots represent a Pacific Ocean locality from Shinohara et al. (1994) for three juveniles, 34–94 mm SL; and Bering Sea localities given by Lindberg and Krasyukova (1975), specimen sizes not reported.

FAMILY SCYTALINIDAE
Graveldivers

Scytalina cerdale, the graveldiver, is the sole member of the family Scytalinidae. This fish inhabits intertidal and shallow subtidal areas from the Aleutian Islands to California, where it burrows in substrates of gravel, sand, and broken shells. Because of their burrowing habit, graveldivers are probably most commonly seen by clam diggers. The genus name is a diminutive of *Scytale,* a genus of serpents, in allusion to the shape of the head and the fanglike canines. The species name *cerdale* means "the wary one" or "the fox," in reference to the graveldiver's escape behavior, as the fish exhibits extraordinary activity in hiding when disturbed.

The eyes of graveldivers are very small and placed high on the head. The dorsal and anal fins begin about halfway back on the body, are confluent with the caudal fin, and composed of soft rays which are weak and are deeply buried in the skin. Pelvic fins, lateral line, scales, pyloric caeca, and swim bladder are lacking. The gill rakers are almost obsolete and there are 6 or 7 delicate branchiostegal rays, which are extremely difficult to discern. Graveldivers have been reported to reach a total length of 15 cm (6 inches), but nearly always much smaller individuals, in the range of 5–10 cm (2–4 inches), are found.

Scytalina cerdale Jordan & Gilbert, 1880 **graveldiver**

Aleutian Islands to central California at Diablo Cove, San Luis Obispo County.

Intertidal and to depth of 7.6 m, along open coast beaches in loose boulders and gravel or tidepools with pebble and broken shell bottoms.

D 41–51; A 36–48; Pec 7–8; Pel 0; Vert 71–72.

- Yellow or light brown to pinkish with purple mottling; caudal fin margin reddish or orange.
- Body elongate, rounded anteriorly, compressed posteriorly; head broader than body, cheeks tumid; prominent pores on jaws.
- Dorsal and anal fins low, rays buried in skin; pectoral fin minute.
- Each jaw with 2 strong canines in front; other teeth close-set and conical.
- Gill membranes united, and free from isthmus.
- Length to 150 mm TL.

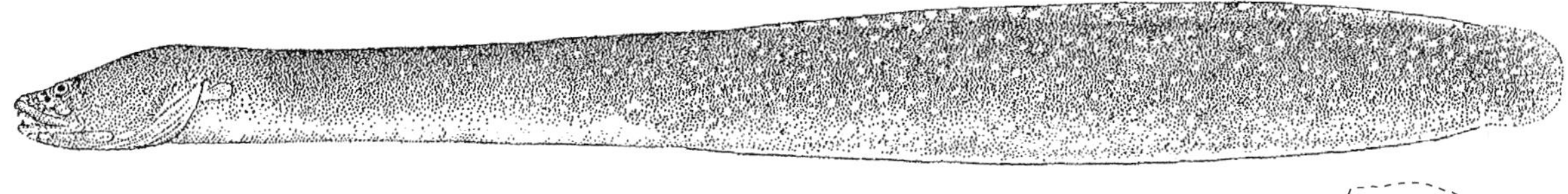

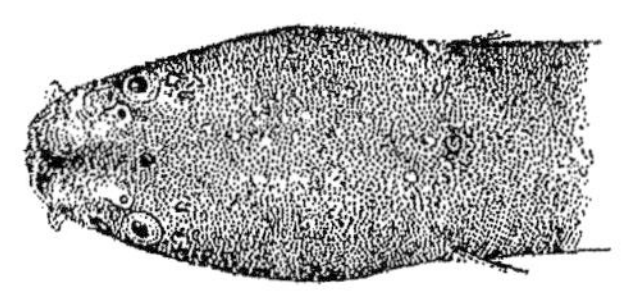

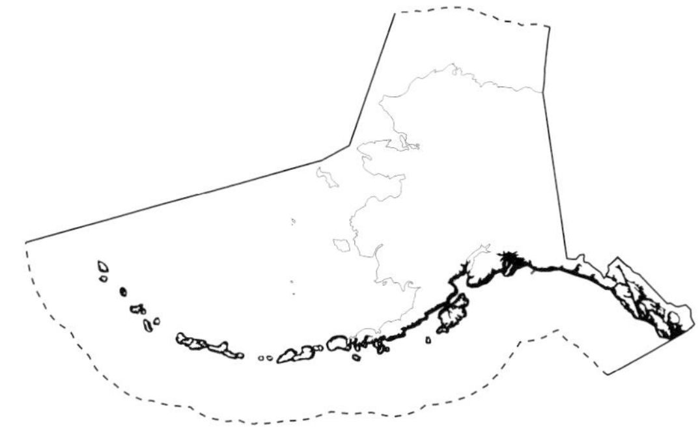

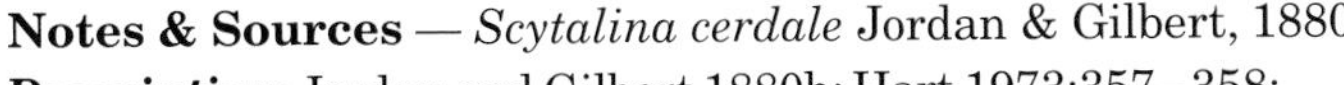

Notes & Sources — *Scytalina cerdale* Jordan & Gilbert, 1880

Description: Jordan and Gilbert 1880h; Hart 1973:357–358; Eschmeyer and Herald 1983:259. AB 63-32 (5 specimens, 49–64 mm SL).

Figures: Jordan and Starks 1895, pl. 104; 86 mm TL, Waadda Island, Neah Bay, Washington.

Range: Documentation for distribution along Bering Sea coasts north of Aleutian Islands is lacking. Recorded from Agattu Island by Gilbert and Burke (1912a); and from Little Port Walter, Baranof Island, by Quast (1968; AB 63-32, the only specimens in ABL museum). NMC 61-11 includes specimens from Prince of Wales Island, and NMC 61-54, from Craggy Island in Icy Strait. UBC has specimens from southeastern Alaska at Big Port Walter (UBC 63-207, 63-238) and Port Conclusion (UBC 65-527, 65-532), Baranof Island; and at Klokachef Island (UBC 65-574). Baxter (1990ms) collected specimens (not saved) from an exposed rocky coast on Hesketh Island, Kachemak Bay. Although not well represented from Alaska in museum collections, as Hart (1973) noted for British Columbia it is probably more abundant than records indicate. Where they have been reported, graveldivers often occur in dense concentrations. Schultz (1930) excavated 32 specimens from a tidepool on San Juan Island, Washington, and Peden and Wilson (1976) observed large numbers in tidepools in northern British Columbia.

Family Chiasmodontidae
Swallowers

Swallowers are oceanic, meso- to bathypelagic carnivorous fishes with adaptations for swallowing large prey. The family contains four genera with about 15 species. Swallowers typically occur widely in tropical and temperate seas but none was known to occur in Alaskan waters until fairly recently. Yabe et al. (1981) recorded a specimen of the shortnose swallower, *Kali indica,* caught by midwater trawl in the eastern Bering Sea over the continental slope. This is the northernmost record of the species and the first from boreal waters, as well as the first record of a swallower from Alaska. The luminous swallower, *Pseudoscopelus scriptus,* has been recorded from areas off the Bering Sea coast of Russia, including the vicinity of the Commander Islands, and probably inhabits deep waters north and south of the Aleutian Islands and in the Gulf of Alaska. Bathypelagic fish species are often proven to be widely distributed, and with *P. scriptus* known to occur in nearby waters it should not be long before its presence in Alaskan waters is confirmed. The black swallower, *Chiasmodon niger,* has been recorded from the eastern North Pacific only as far north as approximately 43°N, but records from cold waters of the North Atlantic are relatively common and include a specimen caught off eastern Greenland.

Swallowers are carnivorous primarily on other fishes and have numerous long, sharp teeth, some of them movable in conjunction with expanding the gape, a highly distensible stomach, and other specializations that allow them to grasp and engulf extremely large prey. Swallowers are often found with large food items, sometimes even larger than they are, in the stomach.

Other swallower family characteristics include an elongate, scaleless body; very large mouth; no vomerine teeth; palatine teeth present or absent; distinct lateral line; and two dorsal fins, the second longer than the first. Pseudobranchs are present in some species. The gill openings are very wide, and the gill membranes only weakly attached anteriorly to the isthmus. Lath-like gill rakers are lacking and are replaced in some species with short gill teeth on nodular bony plates. Swallowers have 6 or 7 branchiostegal rays.

A *K. indica* measuring 26.2 cm SL (10.2 inches) is the largest individual recorded for the family.

The revision by Norman (1929) is the most recent taxonomic treatment of the family Chiasmodontidae as a whole. Johnson (1969) and Johnson and Cohen (1974) revised the genus *Kali.*

Presence or absence of photophores, configuration of pores in the lateral line, jaw shape, and length and position of the anal fin relative to the second dorsal fin should be sufficient for distinguishing the three species treated in this guide. Swallowers are uniformly brown or black, without distinctive markings.

Key to the Chiasmodontidae of Alaska

1		Photophores present	*Pseudoscopelus scriptus,* page 789 (not known from Alaska)
1		Photophores absent	(2)
2	(1)	Jaws curved dorsally and ventrally, not meeting along the middle when mouth is closed; anal fin a little longer than second dorsal fin and commencing before it; lateral line pores in pairs	*Kali indica,* page 790
2		Jaws meet along their length when mouth is closed; anal fin shorter than dorsal fin and commencing behind it; lateral line pores in a single row	*Chiasmodon niger,* page 791 (not known from Alaska)

Pseudoscopelus scriptus Lütken, 1892 **luminous swallower**

Western Bering Sea off northeastern Kamchatka and vicinity of Commander Islands; Kuril Islands; and Suruga and Sagami bays and Ogasawara Islands of Japan; widely distributed in warm waters of Pacific, Atlantic, and Indian oceans.

Oceanic, meso- to bathypelagic; 200–2,100 m.

D VIII + 21–24; A 21–23; Pec 12–14; Pel I,5; Vert 36–37.

- Head without spines; upper and lower jaws meet (not curved away from each other) when mouth is closed; lower jaw not projecting.
- **Anal fin and second dorsal fin about same length and opposite each other**.
- Well-developed sculpturing present on top of head.
- Teeth long, caniniform, numerous; jaw teeth depressible, in 2 or more rows.
- **Small, closely spaced black photophores in a line beginning on isthmus, running along midventral line of body and curving around pelvic fins and along base of anal fin, and rows on each jaw**.
- Lateral line distinct, consisting of large pores in a single row.
- Length to 172 mm SL.

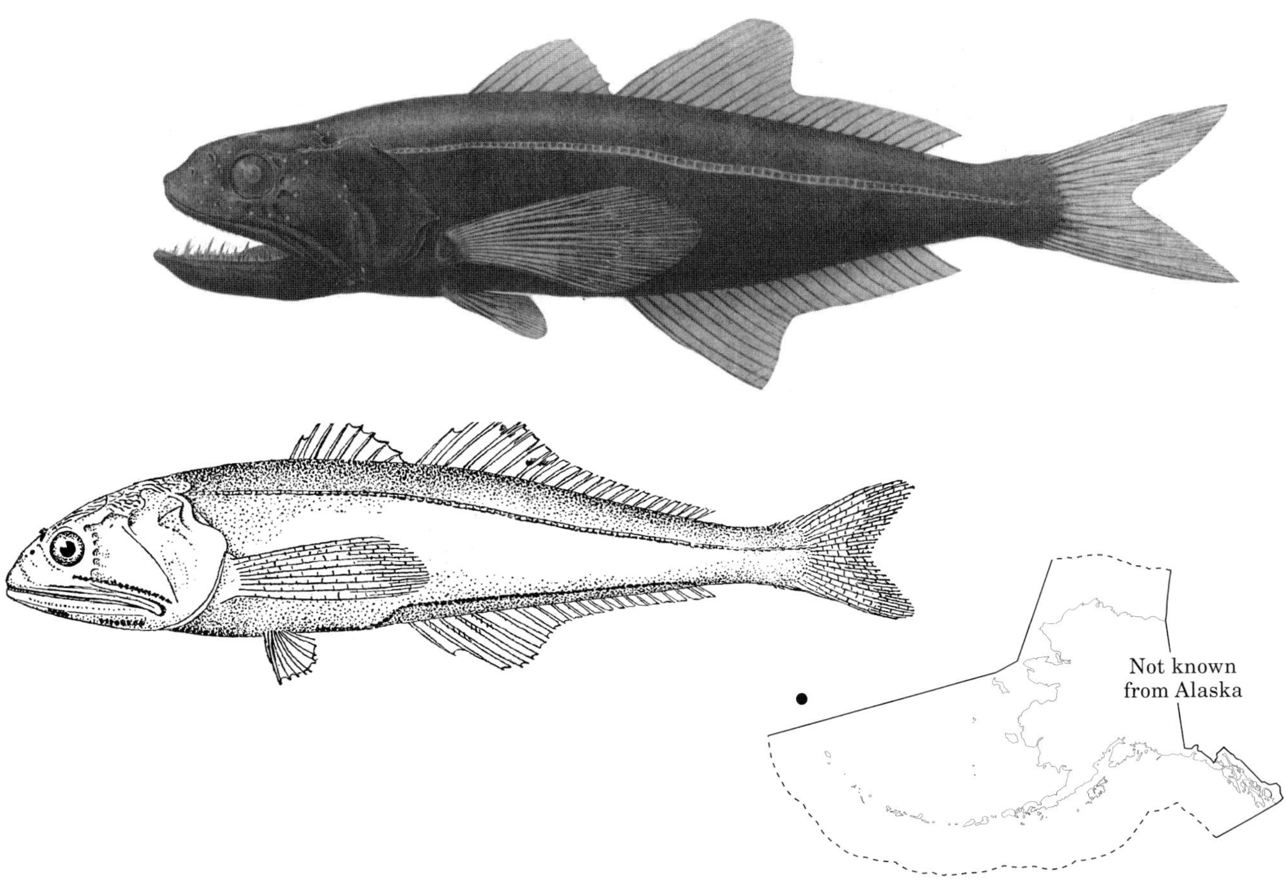

Notes & Sources — *Pseudoscopelus scriptus* Lütken, 1892

Some authors consider North Pacific records of *Pseudoscopelus* to represent a distinct subspecies, *P. scriptus sagamianus* Tanaka, 1908 (e.g., Uyeno in Masuda et al. 1984, Okamura in Okamura et al. 1985), or species, *P. sagamianus* Tanaka (e.g., Nakabo et al. 1992, Shinohara and Matsuura 1997, Sheiko and Fedorov 2000). Tanaka himself first gave the specimen he described subspecies status (Tanaka 1908), only later treating it as a species (Tanaka 1916). Published descriptions do not contain enough information to clearly distinguish the two forms or they indicate only seemingly insignificant differences, so, for convenience and pending future clarification, we classify North Pacific records of *P. sagamianus* in *P. scriptus* Lütken.

Description: Goode and Bean 1896:292–293; Uyeno in Masuda et al. 1984:221; Okamura in Okamura et al. 1985:558, 713; Parin et al. 1995:202.

Figures: Upper: Tanaka 1916, pl. 48, fig. 188; 10.5 cm TL, Sagami Sea, Japan. Lower: Goode and Bean 1896, fig. 266; after Lütken 1892; Old Bahama Channel, Cuba.

Range: Not known from Alaska, but has been taken from Bering Sea off northeastern Kamchatka and vicinity of Commander Islands, Russia (Sheiko and Fedorov 2000). In North Pacific taken in midwater trawls fishing to depths as great as 2,100 m (e.g., SIO 60-243, SIO 60-247).

Size: SIO 63-165, from 29°N, 118°W, depth 0–750 m.

Kali indica Lloyd, 1909 **shortnose swallower**

One record from eastern Bering Sea; circumglobal in tropical and temperate seas, known from widely scattered localities.

Oceanic, bathypelagic; most adults taken at depths greater than 900 m, recorded to about 2,870 m.

D XI–XIII + I,22–24; A I,21–25; Pec 11–13; Pel I,5; Vert 40.

- **Jaws curve concavely away from each other so that they do not meet in the middle when mouth is closed**; lower jaw slightly projecting.
- **Anal fin a little longer than second dorsal fin and commencing before it**.
- Jaw teeth in 2 series; inner teeth very long and strikingly curved; teeth lost in some specimens; none of 3 anteriormost jaw teeth as long as some more posterior teeth in inner row; pharyngeal teeth present.
- Tooth plates present on 1st 3 gill arches.
- Photophores absent.
- **Lateral line** well marked, consisting of **a series of paired pores**, with 5 or more palps between each pair of pores, to fork of caudal fin.
- Pseudobranch present, with 7–10 filaments.
- Length to 262 mm SL.

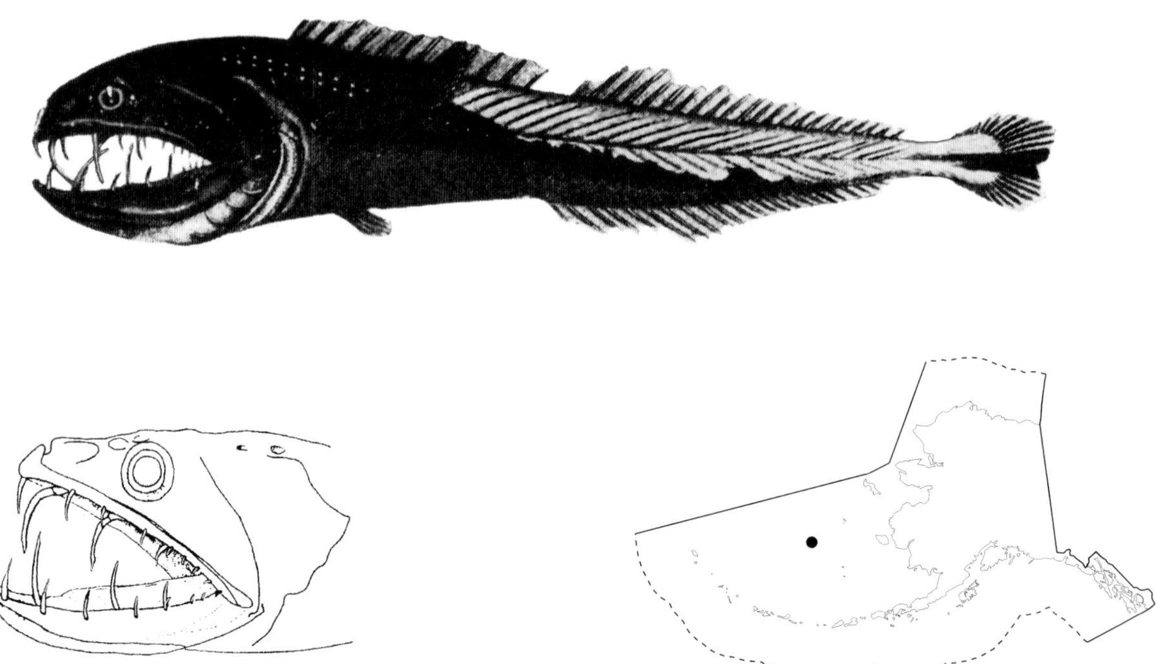

Notes & Sources — *Kali indica* Lloyd, 1909

Description: Lloyd 1909:154–155; Johnson 1969:387–388; Johnson and Cohen 1974:39–41; Johnson and Keene in Smith and Heemstra 1986:733.

Figures: Lloyd 1909, pl. 44, fig. 5; holotype, 17 cm, skin and fins damaged, Bay of Bengal, depth 2,456 m. Diagram of head: Johnson 1969, fig. 1A.

Range: Known in Alaskan waters from one specimen measuring 175 mm SL collected from Bering Sea at 58°22'N, 175°01'W, on 23 Jun. 1979 over a bottom depth of 740 m (Yabe et al. 1981). *Kali indica* has been included on lists of western Bering Sea mesopelagic fish species based on an unpublished record from V. V. Fedorov (e.g., Sinclair et al. 1999), but this record probably refers to *Pseudoscopelus sagamianus* (= *S. scriptus*) (B. A. Sheiko, pers. comm., 4 Oct. 1999). Nearest record from waters south of the Bering Sea comprises specimens measuring 204–211 mm SL from the western Pacific off northern Honshu, Japan, at depths of 930–1,219 m (Shinohara et al. 1996).

Chiasmodon niger Johnson, 1863 **black swallower**

In Pacific Ocean, recorded north to 43°N, in Atlantic north to eastern Greenland; circumglobal in tropical and temperate seas, known from widely scattered localities.

Oceanic, meso- to bathypelagic; recorded from near surface to about 2,740 m, most specimens captured at depths greater than 750 m.

D XI–XIII + 26–29; A I,26–29; Pec 12–15; Pel I,5; Vert 43–46.

- Small but stout spine at lower angle of preopercle; **jaws meet along middle when mouth is closed**; lower jaw projecting.
- **Anal fin not as long as second dorsal fin and commencing behind it**.
- Jaw teeth sharply pointed, in 2 series; 1 or more of 3 anteriormost jaw teeth distinctly longer than any posterior tooth; pharyngeal teeth absent.
- Photophores absent.
- **Lateral line** distinct, in a groove and consisting of **pores in a single row**.
- Pseudobranch absent.
- Length to 194 mm SL.

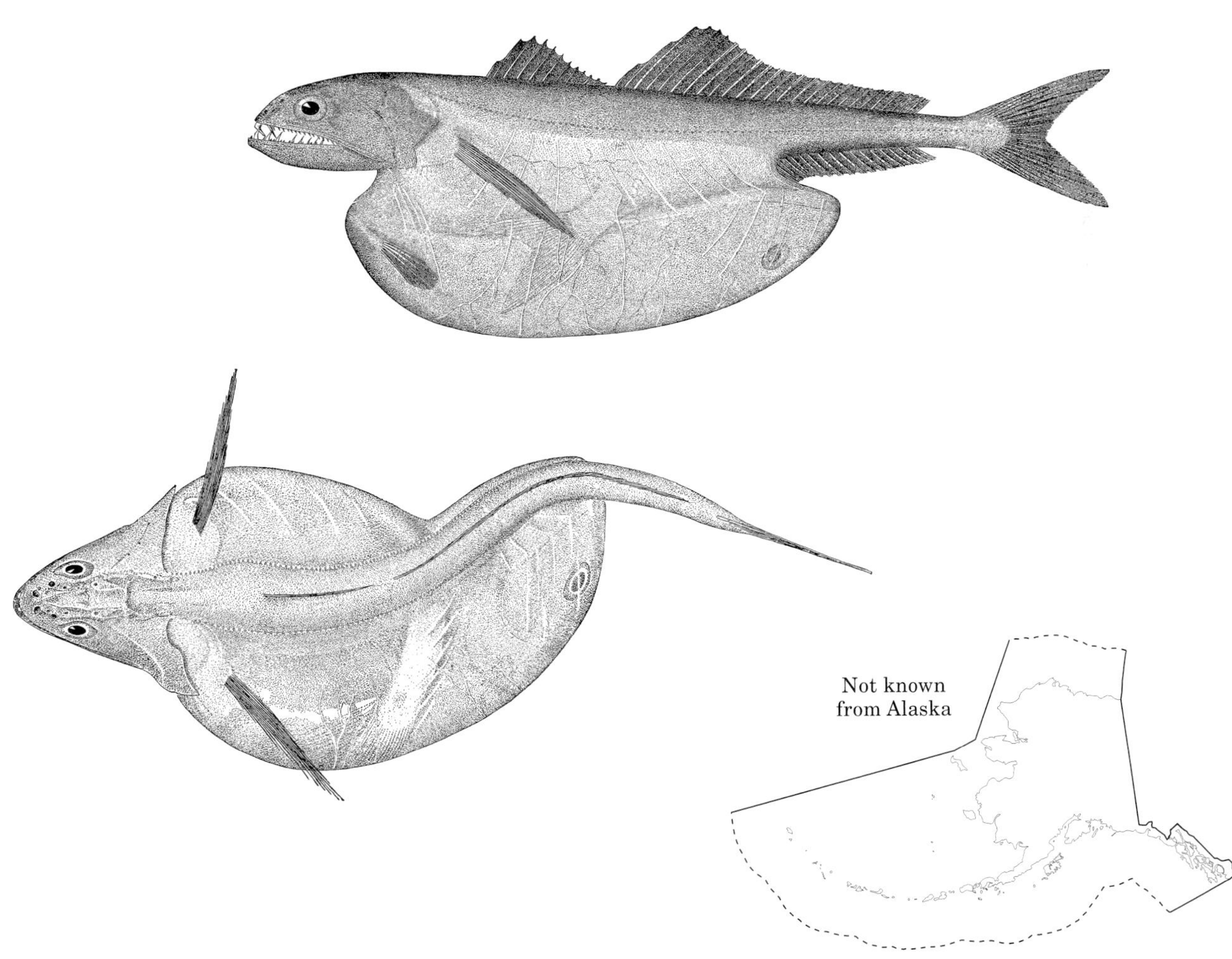

Notes & Sources — *Chiasmodon niger* Johnson, 1863

Description: Goode and Bean 1896:292–293; Johnson and Keene in Smith and Heemstra 1986:731; Parin et al. 1995:202.

Figures: Goode and Bean 1896, fig. 264; northeast Atlantic.

Range: The UW fish collection has specimens from farther north in the Pacific Ocean than previously recorded: UW 21916, 2 specimens, 67–121 mm SL, taken from 42°51'N, 171°01'W, depth 274 m; and UW 21946, 2 specimens, 72–74 mm SL, from 42°47'N, 168°02'W, depth 272 m. They were taken during the same research survey in fall of 1989. Krefft (in Hureau and Monod 1973) reported that a single specimen was found off eastern Greenland. Maximum depth: SIO 60-232, Pacific Ocean a few degrees south of the Equator, midwater trawl.

Size: SIO 72-25, taken from Pacific Ocean at 27°35'N, 155°23'W, with 4,000 m of wire out.

Family Trichodontidae
Sandfishes

Sandfishes, family Trichodontidae, burrow into the sand or mud, where they rest partially buried with only their eyes, lips, and dorsal fins showing. This family comprises two extant species, both inhabiting soft-bottomed coastal areas of the North Pacific Ocean. Pacific sandfish, *Trichodon trichodon,* are commonly found along the shores of the southeastern Bering Sea and Gulf of Alaska. Sailfin sandfish, *Arctoscopus japonicus,* are abundant along the coasts of Japan and are known in Alaska with any certainty from only one record.

Both sandfish species have a strongly compressed, deep body with a nearly straight to slightly concave dorsal head profile; two well-separated dorsal fins, the first supported by spines and the second by soft rays; large, upward-oriented, strongly oblique mouth with fringed lips; preopercle with five sharp spines; a lateral line placed high on the body; and slender, fairly numerous gill rakers. They do not have scales. The gill membranes are joined to each other anteriorly, free of the isthmus, and supported by 5 or 6 branchiostegal rays. The most reliable characters for distinguishing the species are the shape and separation of the dorsal fins, shape of the pectoral and caudal fins, and pigmentation on the nape and back.

The maximum size attained by Pacific sandfish is about 30 cm (12 inches). Sailfin sandfish are smaller, with a maximum recorded length of 16 cm (6.3 inches).

Pacific sandfish are often captured in trawl and set nets, and sea lions, seals, and other fishes feed on them. Waders along beaches may notice sandfish fleeing as the fish are disturbed, or find them buried in the sand in the intertidal area. Juvenile Pacific sandfish occur in mixed schools with fry of pink salmon, *Oncorhynchus gorbuscha,* in the nearshore area in southeastern Alaska (Bailey et al. 1983).

Sailfin sandfish have been reported twice from Alaska: once from the eastern Gulf of Alaska at Sitka (Steindachner 1881) and once from the eastern Aleutian Islands at Akutan Bay (Evermann and Goldsborough 1907). The Sitka locality is probably an error, as pointed out by Jordan and Gilbert (1899). However, the Akutan specimen (USNM 60183), although small (about 2.5 cm), and somewhat deteriorated since it was collected in the late 1800s, exhibits critical diagnostic characters and the museum ledger verifies it was collected in Alaska. Unless evidence to the contrary is discovered, the Akutan record must be treated as valid. There is a discrepancy in the museum records regarding the collection locality, but it is merely a curiosity and does not indicate anything more than that the exact locality is uncertain. The discrepancy involves two similar names for different localities. Three handwritten notes, obviously old, in the jar give Ikatan Bay for the locality, whereas the jar label, which is an original, *Albatross*-era label, and the museum ledger both say Akutan Bay. There is no station number, which suggests the specimen was picked up on the beach or from a tidepool by a shore party. The report on *Albatross* work by Townsend (1901) indicates hydrographic soundings were made during 15–22 July 1894 in the vicinity of Ikatan Bay, and the specimen was collected, according to the museum ledger, on 20 July; so the *Albatross* was in the vicinity of Ikatan Bay at the right time. The discrepancy could have been due to a misspelling or someone may have confused the two localities, but we will probably never know. Akutan Bay, on Akutan Island, is approximately 175 km west of Ikatan Bay, on Unimak Island, so the discrepancy is a minor one. It seems best to follow the early accounts (e.g., Evermann and Goldsborough 1907) and continue to give Akutan Bay for the locality.

Prevailing opinion on trichodontid relationships places the family with the Chiasmodontidae and Ammodytidae in the suborder Trachinoidei. From study of a trichodontid recently discovered in Sakhalin Island Miocene deposits (which is the only known fossil trichodontid) and osteology of the extant species, Nazarkin and Voskoboinikova (2000) proposed classifying the family by itself in a new suborder, Trichodontoidei.

Key to the Trichodontidae of Alaska

1 Dorsal fins low and fairly close together; pectoral fins broadly rounded, with upper middle rays longest; caudal fin forked . . . . *Trichodon trichodon,* page 793

1 Dorsal fins high and triangular, and far apart; pectoral fins truncate, with uppermost rays longest; caudal fin truncate or slightly emarginate . . . . *Arctoscopus japonicus,* page 794

Trichodon trichodon (Tilesius, 1813) **Pacific sandfish**

Bering Sea and Aleutian Islands to central California at San Francisco Bay; Commander Islands and southeastern Kamchatka to Japan; rarely found from Kuril Islands to Japan.

Intertidal to depth of about 375 m, usually shallower than 150 m; buried in sand or mud up to upper part of mouth and back in daytime; active at night, attracted to lights.

D XIII–XVI + I,18–20; A I,28–31; Pec 21–24; Pel I,5; GR 4–5 + 12–14; Vert 44–47.

- Brown dorsally, silvery ventrally; **dark brown on top of head extending back along base of dorsal fin as wide, short bars** and along lateral line as unbroken or broken streak; dark streaks on first dorsal fin and sometimes on second dorsal fin; sometimes dusky areas on pectoral and caudal fins; pelvic and anal fins not marked.
- Mouth strongly oblique to nearly vertical; maxilla extending to mideye.
- **Dorsal fins not triangular**; **both dorsal fins lower, longer-based, and closer together than in *A. japonicus***; **caudal fin forked or strongly indented**; **pectoral fin broadly rounded** when spread, upper middle rays longest and uppermost rays extending to below middle of first dorsal fin.
- Length to 305 mm TL.

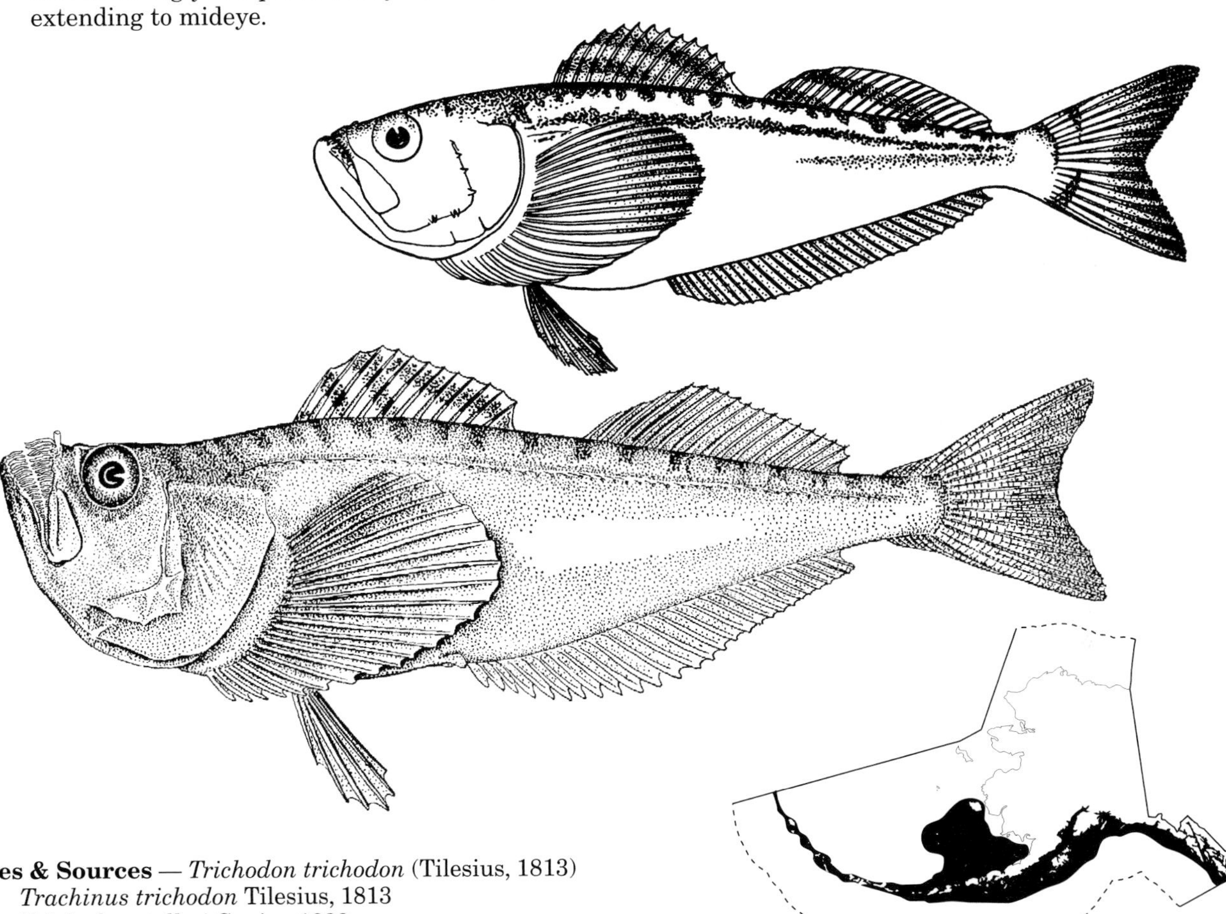

Notes & Sources — *Trichodon trichodon* (Tilesius, 1813)
Trachinus trichodon Tilesius, 1813
Trichodon stelleri Cuvier, 1829

Description: Jordan and Evermann 1898:2295–2296 (same as Jordan and Snyder 1902a:483–484); Lindberg and Krasyukova 1969:422–423; Matarese et al. 1989:532.

Figures: Upper: Lindberg and Krasyukova 1969, fig. 416; Japan. Lower: Hart 1973:316; 20 cm TL, California. Tilting of the head up and back, as shown in the lower illustration, often occurs at death. This exaggerates the vertical orientation of the mouth and gives a false impression of maxillary extension. In unwarped specimens (e.g., UW 26888, 8 specimens, 74–86 mm TL), the mouth is less vertical and the maxilla extends as far as an imaginary vertical line at mideye, like the upper illustration and within the range of expression for *Arctoscopus japonicus*.

Range: The original description was based on specimens from unstated localities at Kamchatka, Russia, and the Aleutian Islands, Alaska (Eschmeyer 1998). Cuvier (1829) described this species from samples collected at Unalaska Island and several localities in Russia, giving it the name *Trichodon stelleri*. Subsequent records document range as far north in western Alaska as Cape Etolin, Nunivak Island (Bean 1881b), and St. Paul Island (Jordan and Gilbert 1899); and as far west as Attu Island (Wilimovsky 1964). Species is well represented throughout its Alaskan range in museum collections. Bean and Bean (1896) recorded *T. trichodon* from the Commander Islands, Russia.

Size: Clemens and Wilby (1949) reported a specimen measuring "about 12 inches in length."

Arctoscopus japonicus (Steindachner, 1881) **sailfin sandfish**

Aleutian Islands at Akutan Bay; Kuril Islands, Sea of Okhotsk, and Sea of Japan to Korea.

Coastal waters on bottom or buried in sandy mud to depths of 200–400 m; spawns among seaweed at depths of 2–10 m.

D VIII–XIV + 12–15; A 29–32; Pec 25–27; Pel I,5; GR 4–5 + 14–16; Vert 45–52.

- Brown dorsally, silvery ventrally; **dark brown mottling on top of head and back to slightly below lateral line**; dark dusky streaks on both dorsal fins; distal half of caudal fin dark dusky; postero-dorsal area of pectoral fin light dusky; pelvic and anal fins not marked.
- Mouth strongly oblique to nearly vertical; maxilla extending to mideye to rear margin of pupil.
- **First dorsal fin triangular**; **both dorsal fins higher, shorter-based, and farther apart than in *T. trichodon***; **caudal fin truncate or slightly emarginate**; **pectoral fin truncate** when spread, with uppermost rays longest and extending to or past insertion of first dorsal fin.
- Length to 168 mm SL.

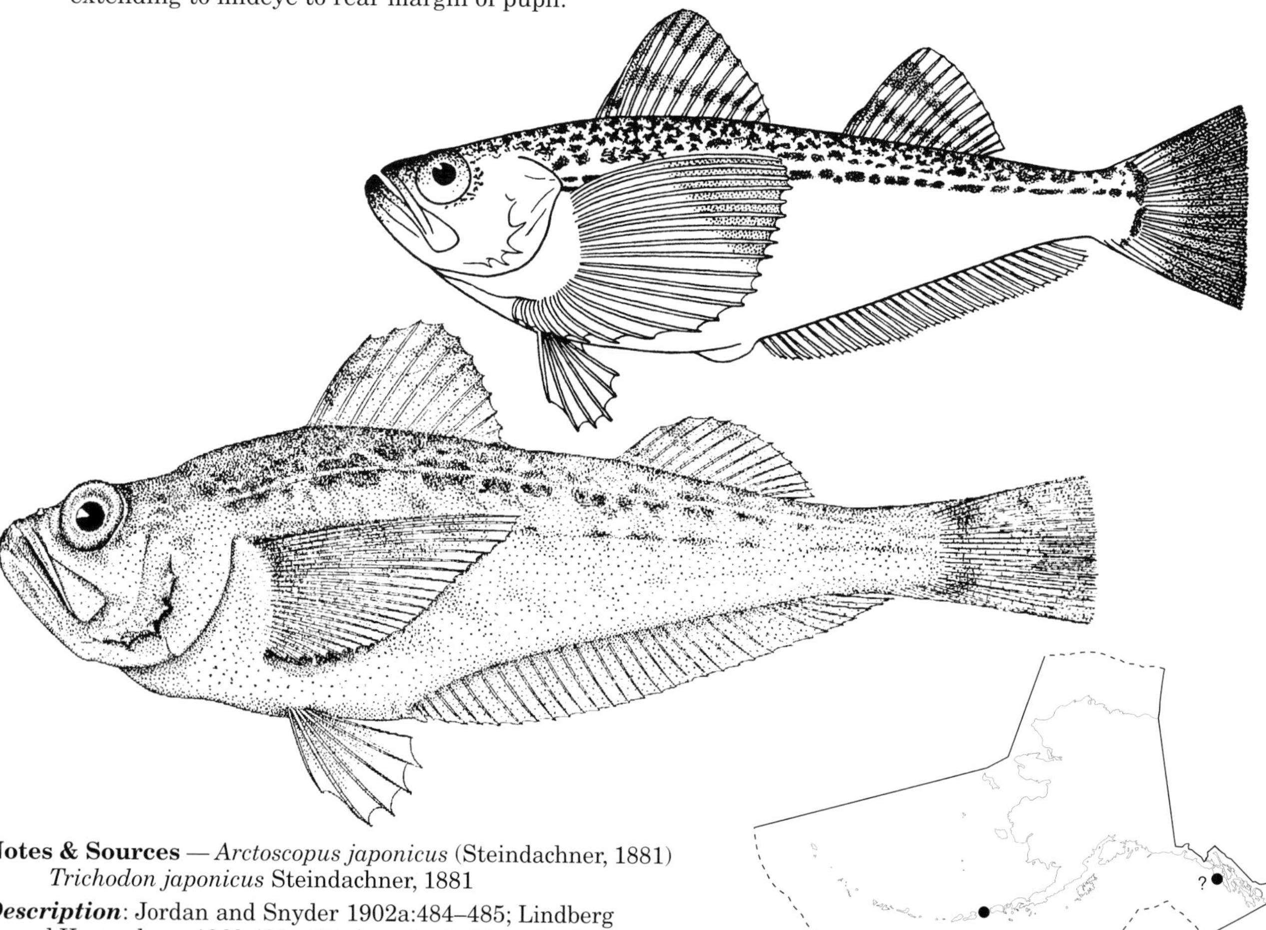

Notes & Sources — *Arctoscopus japonicus* (Steindachner, 1881)
Trichodon japonicus Steindachner, 1881

Description: Jordan and Snyder 1902a:484–485; Lindberg and Krasyukova 1969:421–423; Amaoka in Masuda et al. 1984:221. The description by Jordan and Evermann (1898: 2297) was corrected and expanded by Jordan and Snyder (1902a). Specimens examined by C.W.M. (e.g., UW 26888, 2 specimens, 139–147 mm TL, locality unknown but believed to be Hokkaido) closely match the corrected description.

Figures: Upper: Lindberg and Krasyukova 1969, fig. 415; Japan. Lower: Jordan and Evermann 1900, fig. 807; Iturup Island, Kuril Islands. Shape and ventral extent of the pectoral fin are incorrectly depicted in the lower illustration. Lindberg and Krasyukova's illustration is correct.

Range: Steindachner (1881) listed a specimen from Sitka when he described the species, but other authors, starting with Jordan and Gilbert (1899), considered the locality to be an error. Evermann and Goldsborough (1907) did not mention the possible Sitka record but reported a 1-inch-long specimen (USNM 60183) collected by the *Albatross* at Akutan Bay, Krenitzin Islands. There is no station number, which suggests the specimen was picked up by a shore party. Despite deterioration of the specimen (USNM 60183) since it was collected in 1894, and its small size, characters can be discerned that indicate it is, indeed, an example of *A. japonicus*: dorsal spines 11; dorsal fins separated by large space; pectoral fin truncate; caudal fin probably truncate (most rays broken, but ray in middle is not and is as long as upper and lower rays); dark brown mottling (appearing as small spots with dark centers and darker outlines interspersed with plain, smaller spots) on nape and back, and none of the dorsal bars seen in *Trichodon trichodon*.

Size: Amaoka et al. 1995:270.

Family Ammodytidae
Sand lances

Sand lances, including about 18 species in five or six genera (Ida et al. 1994, Nelson 1994), inhabit the Arctic, Pacific, Atlantic, and Indian oceans. The Pacific sand lance, *Ammodytes hexapterus,* occurs throughout the coastal marine waters of Alaska.

Sand lances occur in enormous schools containing millions of fish and are important as feed for other fishes, birds, and sea mammals. Adult sand lances typically occur in shallow water but can be found far from shore. When not schooling they dive into the sand head first, aided by the pointed lower jaw, and come to rest with only the head protruding. Sometimes they are found buried in sandy beaches after the tide recedes.

Diagnostic features of sand lances include an elongate body with diagonal skin folds (plicae), a fleshy ridge extending the length of the body on either side of the ventral midline, a single dorsal fin which folds back into a groove, a protractile premaxilla, and a projecting lower jaw. The dorsal and anal fins are supported by soft rays only, and most species lack pelvic fins. Teeth and swim bladder are also lacking. The scales are cycloid and minute, the lateral line is high on the body, and gill rakers are long and slender.

Pacific sand lance grow larger, up to 28 cm (11 inches) in total length, in the Bering Sea than they do in most other portions of their range, where they generally grow to 20 cm (8 inches) or less.

In this guide *A. hexapterus* is classified as a species distinct from *A. americanus* of the Atlantic Ocean, following Richards (1982) and Robins et al. (1991a), but the taxonomy of the genus *Ammodytes* is far from settled. Nizinski et al. (1990) discussed alternatives.

Ammodytes hexapterus Pallas, 1814 — **Pacific sand lance**

Western Canadian Arctic to Pacific Ocean off southern California at Balboa Island and to Sea of Japan. Intertidal zone to water depth of about 100 m.

D 54–63; A 24–32; Pec 13–16; Pel 0; Br 6–8; GR 3–6 + 15–23 (20–28); Vert 65–74.

- Metallic blue dorsally, silvery ventrally.
- Body elongate, compressed; symphyseal knob pointed; ventrolateral dermal fold present.
- Caudal fin deeply forked.
- Lateral line high, near base of dorsal fin; numerous close-set, diagonal plicae laterally.
- Gill membranes attached far forward.
- Length to 280 mm TL.

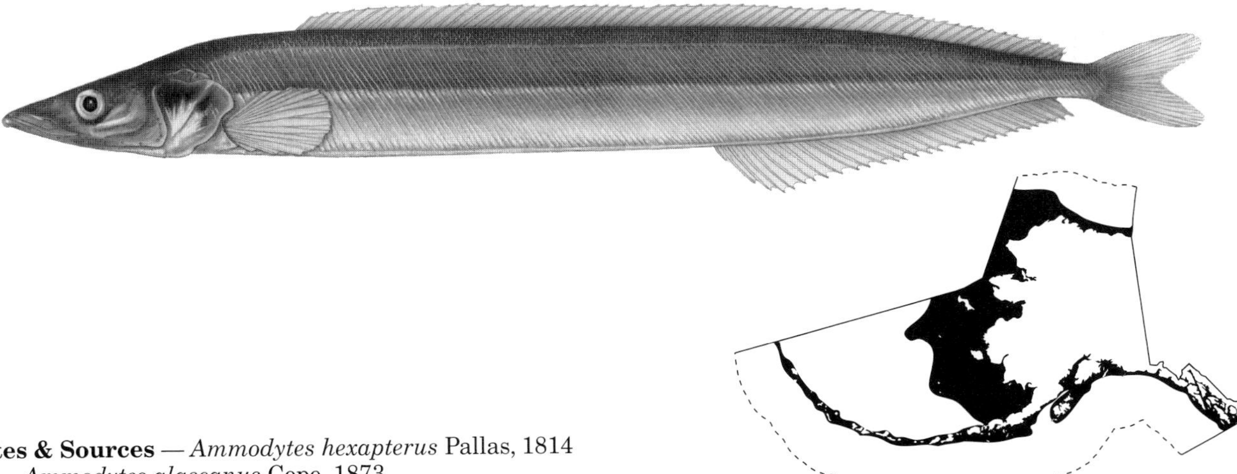

Notes & Sources — *Ammodytes hexapterus* Pallas, 1814
Ammodytes alascanus Cope, 1873
The synonymy by Andriashev (1954) includes other early Alaskan records.
Also called stout sand lance, especially by workers including western Atlantic *A. americanus* in *A. hexapterus* (e.g., Coad 1995). Including Pacific populations only, Chikilev and Datskii (2000) used the name Pacific stout sand lance.

Description: Andriashev 1954:321–322; Hart 1973:361–362; Matarese et al. 1989:540; Ida et al. 1994; Coad 1995:764.

Figure: University of British Columbia, artist P. Drukker-Brammall; UBC 63-146, 146 mm SL, Icy Strait, Alaska.

Range: Allen and Smith (1988) mapped range in Bering Sea and eastern North Pacific from NMFS demersal trawl surveys. Dick and Warner (1982), Blackburn and Anderson (1997), and Robards et al. (1999) studied biology of Alaskan populations. Larvae and juveniles were collected 200 km offshore in the eastern Gulf of Alaska (B. L. Wing, pers. comm., 11 Apr. 1996). Well represented from throughout coastal Alaska, including the Arctic, in museum collections.

Family Icosteidae
Ragfishes

The family Icosteidae includes only one extant species, *Icosteus aenigmaticus,* a meso- to bathypelagic fish with widespread occurrence in the North Pacific Ocean.

Ragfish are limp, like a rag, due to a largely cartilaginous skeleton and an extremely compressed body. The juveniles differ markedly in appearance from the adults and were once thought to represent a separate species. Among other differences, the juveniles have pelvic fins and scales, which are lost in the adults, are spotted and blotched, and have relatively deep bodies. The binomial name itself means a puzzling fish with a flabby body. The flabbiness is especially impressive in the adults, which can reach 213 cm (7 ft) in length. In the first description of an adult ragfish, which was an individual more than 160 cm (5.35 ft) long found on the beach, Willoughby (in Goode and Bean 1896:217) remarked that it could "not bear a weight of 5 pounds pulling on it without severing the head."

Icosteus aenigmaticus Lockington, 1880 **ragfish**

Bering Sea and Pacific Ocean to southern California at Point Loma and to Hokkaido.

Young fish, under about 30 cm TL, in shallow water or offshore near the surface; adults, particularly large individuals, near bottom and deeper, to 1,420 m.

D 50–56; A 33–44; Pec 18–22; Pel 0 (adults); Br 6–7; GR 1–6 + 5–10 (7–17); Vert 66–70.

- Adult dark brown with purplish cast; juvenile light brown blotched with yellow and purple.
- Body compressed, extremely limp; eyes small; body deep in juvenile, elongate in adult.
- One, long dorsal fin; dorsal and anal fins with soft rays only, no spines; caudal fin large, rounded in juvenile, to emarginate in adult.
- Lateral line with slight keel; spiny in juvenile.

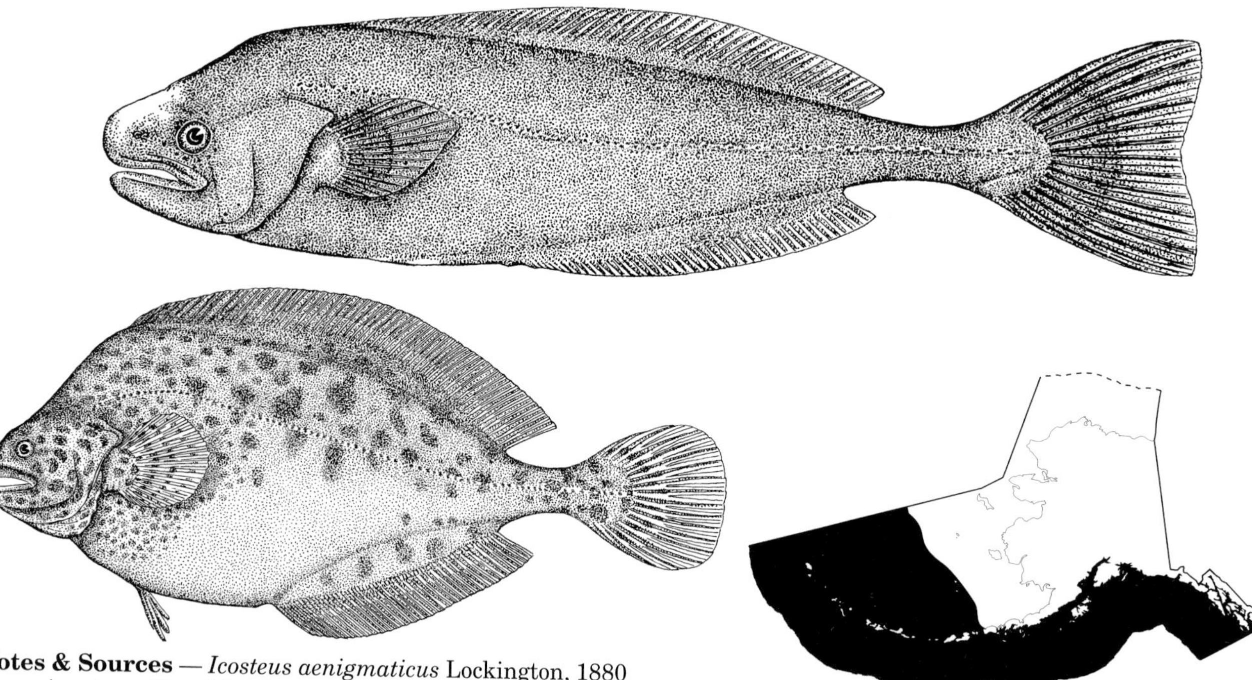

Notes & Sources — *Icosteus aenigmaticus* Lockington, 1880
Acrotus willoughbyi Bean, 1888

Description: Jordan and Evermann 1896:972–973; Fitch 1953:545–546; Kobayashi and Ueno 1956:248; Hart 1973: 386–387; Matarese et al. 1989:538.

Figures: Hart 1973:386. Upper: adult, 53 cm TL, British Columbia. Lower: juvenile, 28 cm TL, Alaska.

Range: Previous records include Petersburg (Schultz et al. 1932) and other southeastern Alaska localities (Quast and Hall 1972). Additional specimens from Gulf of Alaska are in ABL, UBC, and UW collections; CAS 45764 is from north of Unalaska Island. D. W. Kessler (pers. comm., 20 Jun. 1994) provided numerous Bering Sea localities from the NMFS survey database. Not uncommon in Alaska. A couple are taken every year in the Juneau area by NMFS biologists; a ragfish about 183 cm TL was caught there in 1999 (B. L. Wing, pers. comm., 24 Jul. 2000). Kobayashi and Ueno (1956) reported seven specimens (48–74 cm) taken just outside the 200-mile limit southwest of the Near Islands. Fedorov and Sheiko (2002) gave a maximum known depth of 1,420 m. Wing and Kamikawa (1995) reported pelagic eggs to be widely distributed in the eastern Gulf of Alaska.

Family Gobiesocidae
Clingfishes

The Gobiesocidae, or clingfishes, have a ventral adhesive disk composed of the pelvic fins and folds of skin. Theirs is a relatively large family, with 110 species distributed in shallow tropical and temperate waters of the Atlantic, Indian, and Pacific oceans. A few of the tropical species inhabit fast-flowing freshwater streams. Along northeastern Pacific coasts, clingfishes may be found clinging to rocks in the intertidal surge zone, floating kelp, or sea grass, or even settled among the spines of sea urchins. Northern clingfish, *Gobiesox maeandricus,* and kelp clingfish, *Rimicola muscarum,* occur in shallow marine waters of southeastern Alaska. Although *R. muscarum* has been reported only once from Alaska, there is more than one record from adjacent waters of British Columbia. Eschmeyer and Herald (1983) remarked that any clingfish caught north of central California is one of these two species.

Following Nelson (1994), the classification used in this guide places the family Gobiesocidae in the order Perciformes. However, the relationships of clingfishes to other groups are uncertain. Rather than cladistically belonging with the Perciformes, clingfishes may have a closer relationship to paracanthopterygians; there is evidence, for example, of similarity of clingfish spermatozoa to those of batrachoidiforms. No osteological study has been done to demonstrate the cladistic relationships of the family. Nelson (1994) gave a history of clingfish classification and guide to the systematic literature to that time. Parenti and Song (1996) examined innervation patterns of the pectoral and pelvic fin muscles to test hypotheses of teleost phylogeny, and the results suggest alliance of gobiesocids with percomorphs.

Clingfishes have a single dorsal fin, located opposite the anal fin and far back on the body. Their dorsal and anal fins are supported by soft rays only. They lack scales and a swim bladder. In many species, including *G. maeandricus,* the head is depressed and large and the body tapers sharply behind, so that the fish looks like a tadpole from above.

Fishes in three other families have ventral adhesive disks, but those fishes are fairly easily differentiated from the clingfishes. In the gobies (family Gobiidae) the pelvic fins join to form a cone that projects from the body, whereas in the other two families the disk is an integral part of the ventral surface of the body, and is more flat and disklike than conelike. In the snailfishes (Liparidae) and lumpsuckers (Cyclopteridae) the disk is composed of flat "plates" in a ring. Clingfishes have a more complex sucking disk with distinct anterior and posterior portions. For more than a century it was believed that one or the other portion of the gobiesocid disk was supported by pectoral fin bones, but Parenti and Song (1996), from an analysis of nerve patterns, showed that all the elements are pelvic fin bones.

Most clingfish species reach maximum sizes in the range of 6.4–7.6 cm (2.5–3.0 inches). With a maximum recorded length of 16.5 cm (6.5 inches), the northern clingfish, *G. maeandricus,* is large for the group.

Key to the Gobiesocidae of Alaska

1 Head large, depressed, wide; body broad anteriorly, compressed posteriorly; dorsal fin rays 13–16 . . . . *Gobiesox maeandricus,* page 798

1 Head small, narrow; body elongate, gradually tapering; dorsal fin rays 6–8 . . . . *Rimicola muscarum,* page 799

Gobiesox maeandricus (Girard, 1858) northern clingfish

Southeastern Alaska at Noyes Island to southern California; also recorded off northern Baja California, where it was found on drifting kelp between Guadalupe Island and the mainland.

Intertidal zone to water depth of 8 m; clings to underside of rocks, crevice walls, shells, and kelp.

D 13–16; A 12–16; C 11–13; Pec 21–23; Pel disk; Br 6; Vert 32–34.

- Gray-brown to reddish, often with dark, netlike pattern; sometimes with white bar between eyes and extending down onto cheeks.
- **Head large, depressed; body compressed posteriorly**.
- **Adhesive disk large, 40% or more of standard length**.
- **Dorsal and anal fins relatively large, each with 12 or more rays**.
- Gill membranes broadly joined to each other and free of isthmus.
- Length to 165 mm TL (much larger than *Rimicola muscarum*).

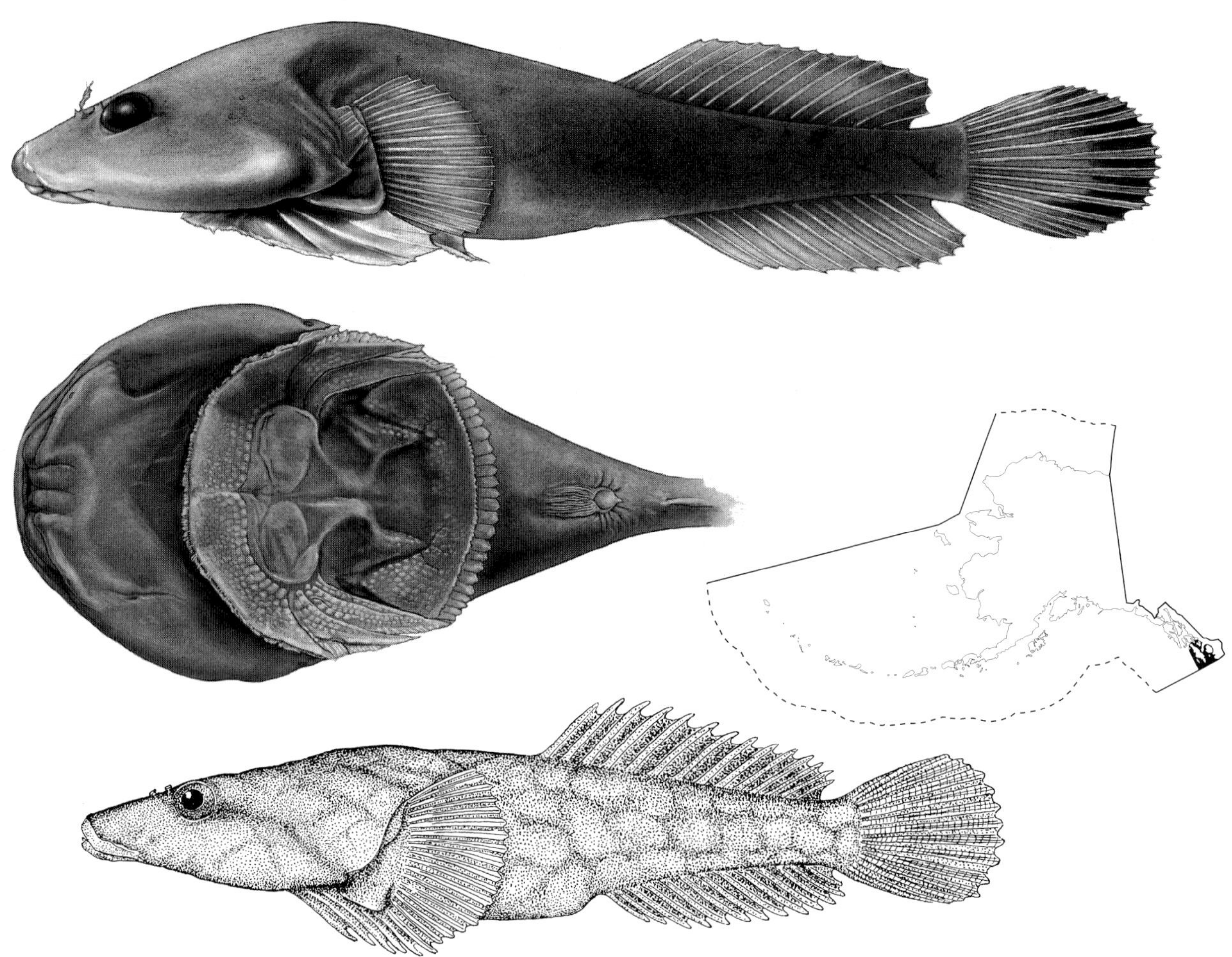

Notes & Sources — *Gobiesox maeandricus* (Girard, 1858)
Lepadogaster maeandricus Girard, 1858
Caularchus maeandricus: Jordan and Evermann 1896, 1898.
Sicyogaster maeandrica: Schultz 1944.
Sicyogaster maeandricus: Parenti and Song 1996.

Description: Briggs 1955:101–102; Hart 1973:210–211; Eschmeyer and Herald 1983:109; Humann 1996:140-141.

Figures: Upper: University of British Columbia, artist P. Drukker-Brammall; UBC 65-512, 82 mm SL, tidepool off Cape Chacon, Prince of Wales Island, Alaska. Lower: Hart 1973:210; 86 mm TL, Alaska–British Columbia boundary; shows dark, netlike pattern.

Range: Previously recorded north to Mud Bay, Revillagigedo Island (55°25'N, 131°46'W), on basis of CAS 13632 by Miller and Lea (1972). UBC 65-512 and 65-513 were taken off Cape Chacon, Prince of Wales Island, UBC 65-508 off Duke Island, and UBC 65-582 from Baker Island. AB 69-51 is from Mountain Point, south of Ketchikan; UAM 334 is from Ketchikan; and UW 4871 is from Noyes Island, about 55°30'N, 133°40'W. Peden and Wilson (1976) found *G. maeandricus* at sites just south of the Alaska–British Columbia boundary. The range of this species extends much farther north than any other species of *Gobiesox*.

Rimicola muscarum (Meek & Pierson, 1895) **kelp clingfish**

Southeastern Alaska at Bartlett Cove, Glacier Bay; northern British Columbia at Tasu Sound to northern Baja California at Todos Santos Bay.

Clings to kelp, often high in canopy, or eelgrass; rarely in tidepools.

D 6–8; A 6–8; C 8; Pec 14–17; Pel disk; Br 5–7; Vert 35–36.

- Emerald green to yellow-brown, changing to match habitat; sometimes with red or orange stripe along side; females sometimes sparsely covered with brownish red, pupil-sized spots.
- **Head small, narrow**; **body elongate, gradually tapering**.
- **Adhesive disk small, about 15% of standard length**.
- **Dorsal and anal fins short-based, each with 8 or fewer rays**.
- Gill membranes connected to each other anteriorly and free of isthmus.
- Length to 70 mm TL (much smaller than *Gobiesox maeandricus*).

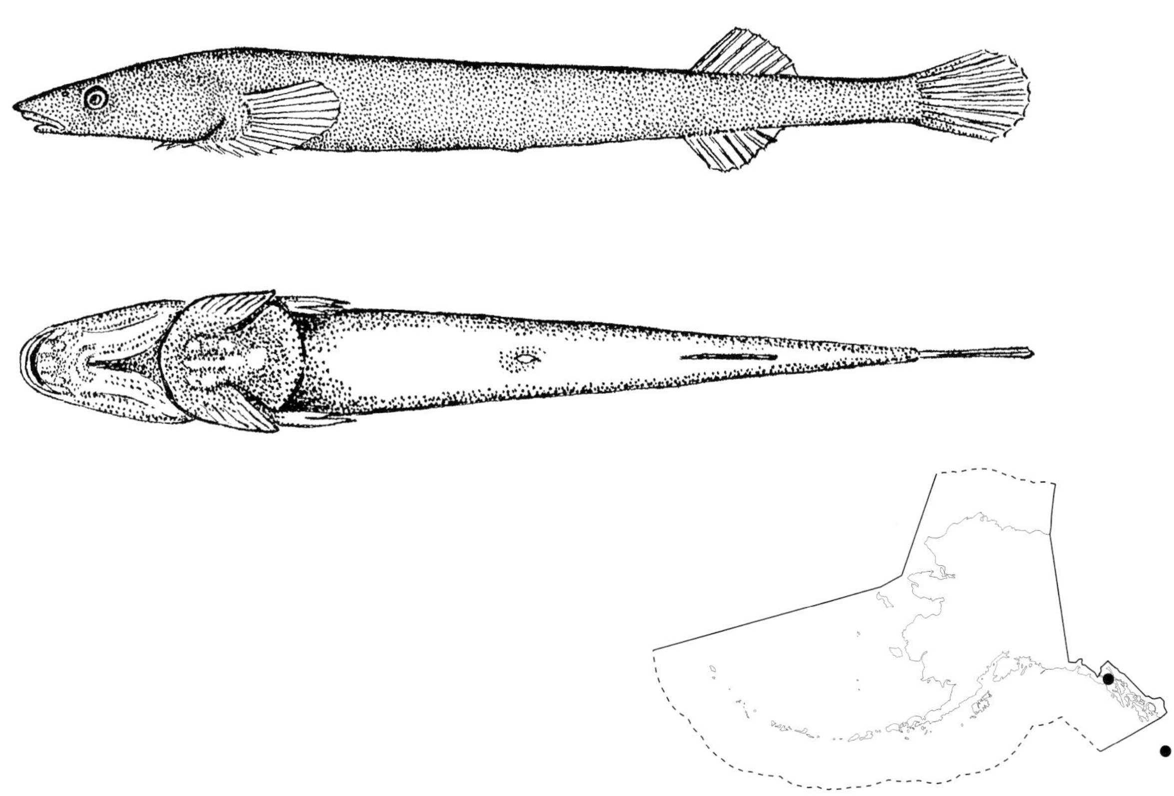

Notes & Sources — *Rimicola muscarum* (Meek & Pierson, 1895)
Gobiesox muscarum Meek & Pierson, 1895
Rimicola eigenmanni (non-Gilbert): Wilby 1936:116; Round Island flats, Clayoquot Sound, British Columbia.

Description: Briggs 1955:80–81; Hart 1973:212–213; Matarese et al. 1989:232 (branchiostegal ray and vertebral counts); Humann 1996:140–141.

Figures: Hart 1973:212; 52 mm TL, British Columbia.

Range: Collected in southeastern Alaska at Bartlett Cove, Glacier Bay, on 4 Jul. 1966 (UAM 1997). Some measurements from the specimen are: TL 26.0 mm, SL 23.1 mm, HL 6.3 mm, BD 2.4 mm (Baxter 1990ms). The Alaskan specimen is in poor condition but keys out to *Rimicola* on the basis of the characters provided above (N. R. Foster, pers. comm., 24 Aug. 1998). It was originally identified as *R. muscarum* partly on the basis of geographic range, by J. E. Morrow. This is the only species of *Rimicola* known to occur north of central California. It was recorded as far north in British Columbia as Goose Island at 51°56'N, 128°28'W by Peden (1966b). A specimen captured slightly farther north at approximately 52°47'N, 132°05'W, was recently reported by Peden (pers. comm., 11 Jan. 1995). The latter specimen is cataloged as RBCM 976-1391, from Lomgon Bay, Tasu Sound, Moresby Island (K. Sendall, pers. comm., 5 Feb. 1999).

Size: Eschmeyer and Herald 1983.

Family Gobiidae
Gobies

The gobies, with, worldwide, about 200 genera and 1,500–2,000 extant species, are the largest family of marine fishes. They occur mostly in tropical marine, brackish, and fresh waters of the world, although some species extend into temperate marine waters. They live on the bottom in shallow to moderately deep muddy or sandy areas, where they rest with their length supported by their pectoral and caudal fins and unique, cone-shaped pelvic fins. They may be encountered in a sedentary state covered with silt up to their eyes, or active, darting about then resting for short periods. Some gobies take refuge in tunnels the fishes burrow in the sand or mud, while others use the burrows of worms, shrimps, and crabs.

Two eastern North Pacific gobiid species have been recorded from Alaska since the inventory by Quast and Hall (1972): blackeye goby, *Rhinogobiops nicholsii,* and bay goby, *Lepidogobius lepidus.* These are the first confirmed records of gobies in Alaska. Blackeye gobies were collected in the summers of 1998 and 1999 from southeastern Alaska at locations near Craig, Klawock, and Sitka by biologists of the National Marine Fisheries Service Auke Bay Laboratory (Csepp and Wing 2000). Previously, blackeye gobies were recorded only as far north as Wales Island, British Columbia (Peden and Wilson 1976), a site that misses being included in Alaska by a technicality. Wales Island was included in the Territory of Alaska until the border was redefined in 1903 (Walbran 1909). The bay goby is known from Alaska by only one specimen (UAM 2852), collected in 1985 in southeastern Alaska at Kegan Cove, Prince of Wales Island, by a University of Alaska Fairbanks biologist (N. R. Foster, pers. comm., 24 Aug. 1998). A third goby species, the arrow goby *Clevelandia ios* Jordan & Gilbert, 1882, occurs in British Columbia but has not been found north of the southern area of the Strait of Georgia (Hart 1973).

The most distinctive diagnostic character of the family Gobiidae is the fusion of well-developed pelvic fins into a cuplike disk which is used for attachment to the substrate, kelp fronds, or other surfaces. Morphological characters uniting the family also include eyes that are positioned near the top of the head, usually close together; the presence of two dorsal fins, the first spinous and the second with one or no spines; and absence of a lateral line.

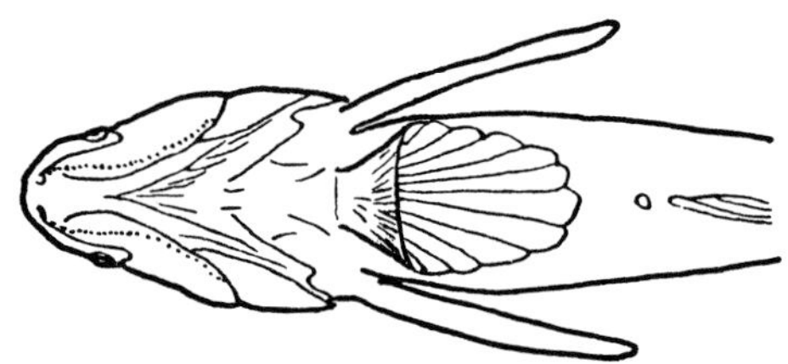

Cuplike ventral disk of gobies
(After Schultz 1936.)

The world's smallest fishes are gobies. A species inhabiting the Indian Ocean measures only 8–10 mm (0.3–0.4 inches) in standard length at maturity. Individuals of some species reach as much as 50 cm (20 inches), but most species are under 10 cm (4 inches). North Pacific species are among the larger gobies, with *L. lepidus* reaching about 10 cm (4 inches), and *R. nicholsii,* 15 cm (6 inches).

Key to the Gobiidae of Alaska

1 Scales obviously large, easy to see; pectoral fin reaches anal fin . . . . *Rhinogobiops nicholsii,* page 801

1 Scales very small, difficult to see; pectoral fin does not reach anal fin . . . . *Lepidogobius lepidus,* page 802

Rhinogobiops nicholsii (Bean, 1882) **blackeye goby**

Southeastern Alaska near Sitka to central Baja California at Punta Rompiente.

Quiet water, on sandy or coarse substrate with vegetation, usually in or near crevices between rocks; typically in shallow waters to depth of about 100 m, occasionally found intertidally; rarely taken at greater depths but adults reported deeper than 640 m and pelagic prejuvenile stages at depths to 2,234 m.

D IV–VIII + I–II,9–16; A 0–I,11–13; Pec 16–23; Pel disk; Ls 24–28; Br 3–5; Vert 26.

- Tan, with brown or greenish speckles; **eye black**; tip of first dorsal fin black; pelvic disk black in breeding males.
- **Fleshy crest on top of head from eyes to dorsal fin**.
- Maxilla extending to anterior part of eye to mideye.
- **Dorsal fins just touching**; **pectoral fin reaching anal fin**; pelvic fins connected, forming hollow cone free of body.
- **Scales conspicuously large**.
- Length to 150 mm TL, usually under 100 mm TL.

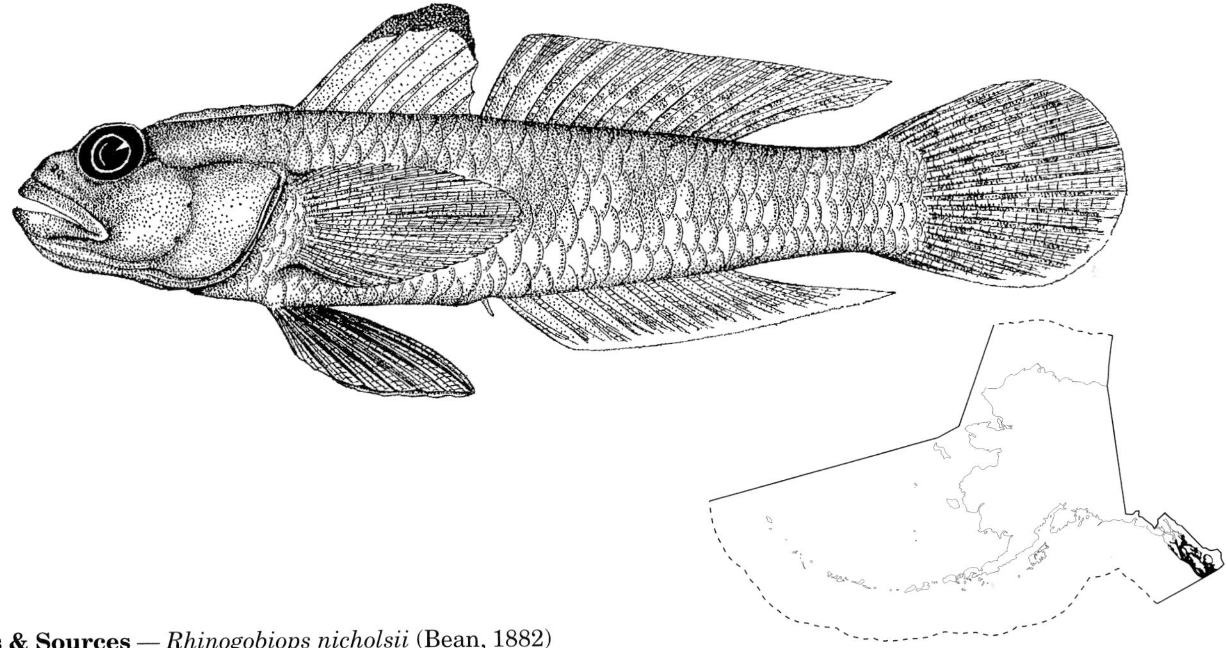

Notes & Sources — *Rhinogobiops nicholsii* (Bean, 1882)

Gobius nicholsii Bean, 1882

Rhinogobiops nicholsii: Hubbs (1926a) created the new genus *Rhinogobiops* for *G. nicholsii*.

Coryphopterus nicholsii: Böhlke and Robins (1960) classified *R. nicholsii* in *Coryphopterus* Gill, 1863, and this has been the usual treatment ever since. Robins (pers. comm., 10 Mar. 2000) was never satisfied that *nicholsii* belonged in *Coryphopterus*. He wrote, "It makes no zoogeographic sense. Its life history, with a long-lived pelagic stage, is totally unlike *Coryphopterus*. I recommend putting it in *Rhinogobiops*. There may well be western North Pacific species that belong with it but *Rhinogobiops* is an early name and is likely to predate any synonyms. I believe that this is a better solution than leaving it with *Coryphopterus* where it clearly seems not to belong." All other temperate eastern Pacific goby genera (those occurring north of San Diego) have affinities with temperate western Pacific genera, and it is likely that the blackeye goby does also (J. S. Birdsong in Randall 1995).

Description: Bean 1882:469–471; Eschmeyer and Herald 1983:261; Follett 1970:478–480; Hart 1973:365–366; Peden and Wilson 1976:230; Matarese et al. 1989:546; Humann 1996:116–117. There is a single pectoral count of 16, from a seemingly aberrant specimen (Peden and Wilson 1976).

Figure: Hart 1973:365, modified to emphasize black eye; 9 cm TL, Sooke, British Columbia.

Range: Reported by Rogers et al. (1986) from southeastern Alaska on list of fishes collected in nearshore waters of Gulf of Alaska between 1976 and 1982, but without giving specific documentation. Specimens were collected by beach seines or observed from a remotely operated vehicle at 15 sites near Craig, Klawock, and Sitka in the summers of 1998 and 1999 (Csepp and Wing 2000). The northernmost capture locality was 57°17'N, 135°35'W, at St. John Baptist Bay north of Sitka. Vouchers are in the ABL permanent collection, and some specimens survived for awhile in ABL display aquaria. Although inside and outside water sites were sampled, blackeye gobies occurred only in outside waters. Csepp and Wing (2000) suggested that those captures may represent the northern range limit for the species in outside waters, as winters are colder north of St. John Baptist Bay. Previously recorded north to Wales Island, British Columbia, by Peden and Wilson (1976), who suggested from the frequency of occurrence at Dundas and Wales islands that blackeye gobies would eventually be found across the Alaskan border.

Size: Eschmeyer and Herald (1983) reported maximum of 150 mm. Largest of 137 specimens from southeastern Alaska measured by Csepp and Wing (2000) was 100 mm TL.

Lepidogobius lepidus (Girard, 1858) **bay goby**

Southeastern Alaska at Kegan Cove, Prince of Wales Island; northern British Columbia at Welcome Harbour to central Baja California at Cedros Island.

Level sand, mud, and silt bottoms; retreats to burrows of echiuroid worms, shrimps, or geoducks when disturbed; intertidal and to water depth of 201 m.

D VI–IX + 0–I,14–18; A 0–I,13–16; Pec 20–23; Pel disk; Ls about 86; Br 3–4; Vert 37–38.

- Tan or reddish brown to pale olive green; often with dark blotches or mottling; tip of first dorsal fin black.
- Maxilla extending about to mideye.
- **Dorsal fins separated by wide gap**; **pectoral fin not reaching anal fin**; pelvic fins connected, forming hollow cone free of body.
- **Scales very small**, barely discernible without magnification.
- Length to 100 mm TL, usually under 75 mm TL.

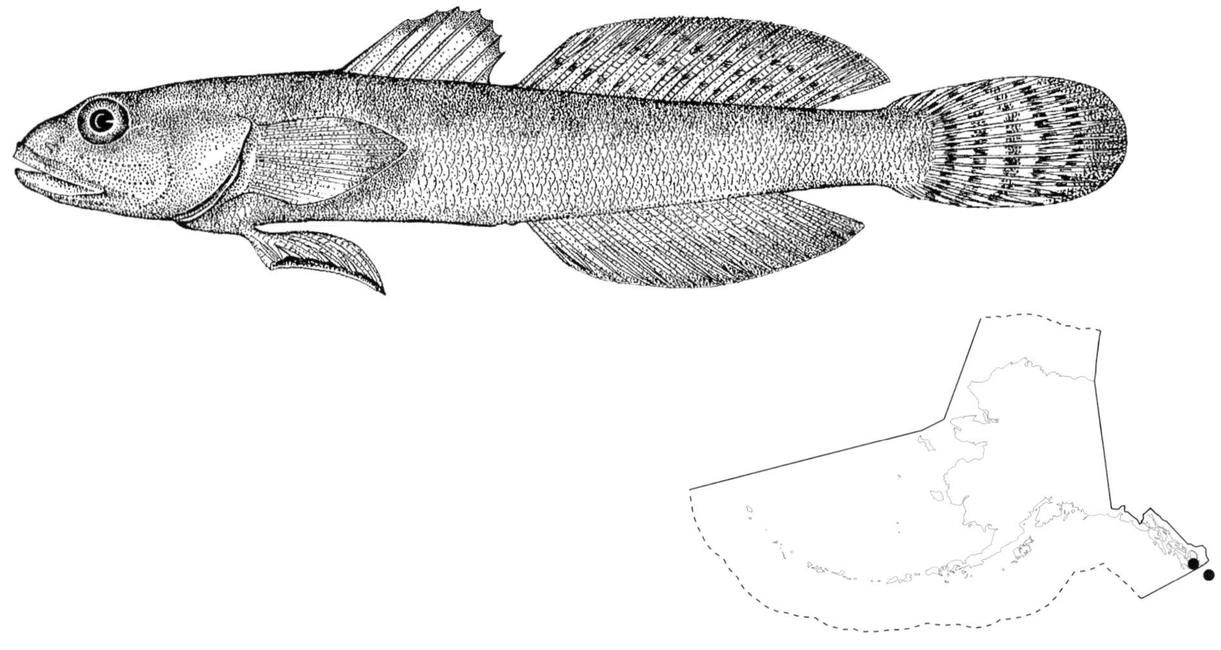

Notes & Sources — *Lepidogobius lepidus* (Girard, 1858)
Gobius lepidus Girard, 1858

The arrow goby, *Clevelandia ios,* which is known to occur as far north in British Columbia as the southern Strait of Georgia, has an overall appearance similar to that of *L. lepidus.* Although *C. ios* is extralimital for purposes of this guide, it might be wise to keep it in mind when identifying gobies found in southern southeastern Alaska. It should be easy to differentiate from the two goby species currently known in Alaska, *L. lepidus* and *Rhinogobiops nicholsii,* from the very large mouth with maxilla extending way past the eye. *Clevelandia ios* is additionally differentiated from *L. lepidus* by having 4 or 5 dorsal fin spines, versus 6–9 in *L. lepidus* (Hart 1973).

Description: Hart 1973:366–367; Eschmeyer and Herald 1983:263; Matarese et al. 1989:548; Humann 1996:118–119.

Figure: Hart 1973:366, modified (margin on first dorsal fin darkened); 10 cm TL, Denman Island, British Columbia.

Range: One record from Alaska, a specimen collected from the intertidal zone at Kegan Cove, Prince of Wales Island, on 2 Jun. 1985: UAM 2852, collected and identified by N. R. Foster; identification confirmed by R. Baxter (unpubl. data). Previously recorded as far north as the north side of Welcome Harbour, British Columbia, about 54°01'N, 130°36'W, by Peden and Wilson (1976).

Family Sphyraenidae
Barracudas

The family Sphyraenidae comprises 20 species of barracuda in one genus, *Sphyraena.* Barracudas inhabit warm waters of the world's oceans, only occasionally straying into colder waters. They are usually seen in small schools near shore or near the surface. Large adults are often solitary. Only one species, the Pacific barracuda, *S. argentea,* occurs in the northeastern Pacific Ocean. Pacific barracudas move north in the summer and south in the autumn, but at any time of the year are rarely encountered north of Point Conception, California. The few known Alaskan records are from the Gulf of Alaska in El Niño years.

Barracudas are predators, and as a group have a reputation for attacking humans. However, it may be only the great barracuda, *S. barracuda,* of the Atlantic Ocean that attacks divers, and such attacks are thought to be rare. The Pacific barracuda may look ferocious, but is not a threat to humans.

Barracudas have an elongate, cylindrical body and a large mouth with protruding lower jaw and large, caniniform teeth. They have two widely spaced dorsal fins; the pelvic fins are abdominal, and located under the first dorsal fin; and the caudal fin is forked. Gill rakers can be absent, or present as vestigial, spiny plates. Barracudas have a single, well-developed lateral line and small, cycloid scales.

Attaining a total length of about 122 cm (4 ft) and weight of 8.2 kg (18 lb), the Pacific barracuda is about the average size for the family. Some species reach at least 183 cm (6 ft).

Sphyraena argentea Girard, 1854 **Pacific barracuda**

Kodiak Island; Prince William Sound; southeastern Alaska to Baja California off Cabo de San Lucas.

Neritic epipelagic, in schools, to depth of about 18 m.

D V + I,8–11; A I,8–11; Pec 14–16; Pel I,5; LLs 139–174; Br 6–7; Vert 24.

- Silvery, tinted blue or brown dorsally; lateral line dark.
- Body elongate, cylindrical; mouth large, snout long, lower jaw protruding.
- Two small, widely spaced dorsal fins; pelvic fin below first dorsal fin; caudal fin forked.
- Teeth daggerlike, prominent.
- Gill rakers as flat, spiny plates.

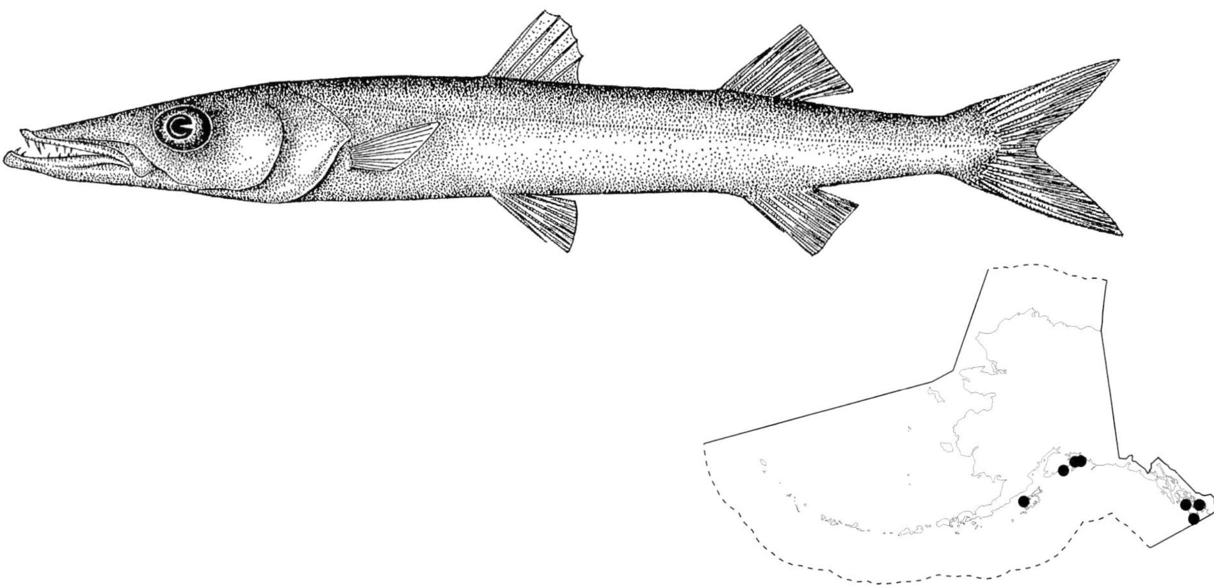

Notes & Sources — *Sphyraena argentea* Girard, 1854

Description: Hart 1973:314–315; Eschmeyer and Herald 1983:234; Humann 1996:172–173. USNM 207056 and LACM uncataloged extend the counts (Baxter 1990ms).

Figure: Hart 1973:314; 13 cm TL, Mexico.

Range: Previous Alaskan records: Cape Uyak, west coast of Kodiak Island (Van Cleve and Thompson 1938); Prince William Sound (Quast 1964b); and Meyers Chuck and Clarence Strait, southeastern Alaska (Karinen et al. 1985). UBC 63-1057 is from Prince William Sound at Culross Passage, UBC 63-1058 near Wrangell, and UBC 63-1059 from Bay of Pillars off Point Ellis. AB 92-8 and AB 92-9 are from Noyes Island and Resurrection Bay.

FAMILY SCOMBRIDAE
Mackerels

The scombrid family includes mackerels, bonitos, and tunas. These are marine, epipelagic, schooling fishes of tropical and temperate seas with streamlined, fusiform shapes. Mackerels and bonitos are primarily coastal fishes, while tunas are oceanic. Several of the tunas migrate extensively and are found worldwide. The family comprises 51 species in 15 genera (Collette 1999). Six species in four genera have been reported from the Gulf of Alaska, but occurrence of one of them in the region has not been confirmed.

Since they are primarily fishes of warm waters, scombrids do not occur consistently off Alaska but appear during periods of unusually high temperatures. The chub mackerel, *Scomber japonicus,* the Pacific bonito, *Sarda chiliensis,* and the albacore, *Thunnus alalunga,* are each known from occasional catches in the Gulf of Alaska. The skipjack tuna, *Katsuwonus pelamis*, and the Pacific bluefin tuna, *T. orientalis*, are known in the region from only one or two records each, although there have been other, unverifiable, reports. The occurrence of yellowfin tuna, *T. albacares,* in Alaska has not been confirmed. A fish that washed up on the beach near Yakutat in 1997 and was initially identified as a yellowfin tuna was later determined to be an albacore, *T. alalunga.*

Distinguishing features of scombrids include two dorsal fins, the first placed well behind the head. The first dorsal fin is supported by spines, and folds down into a groove when the fish is swimming rapidly. Finlets are present posterior to the dorsal and anal fins and a pair of small, obliquely oriented keels is present on each side of the tail at the base of the caudal fin, which is forked. The caudal peduncle is narrow and in the more advanced members of the family, including *Katsuwonus, Sarda,* and *Thunnus,* bears a large median keel anterior to the pair of small keels (Collette and Nauen 1983):

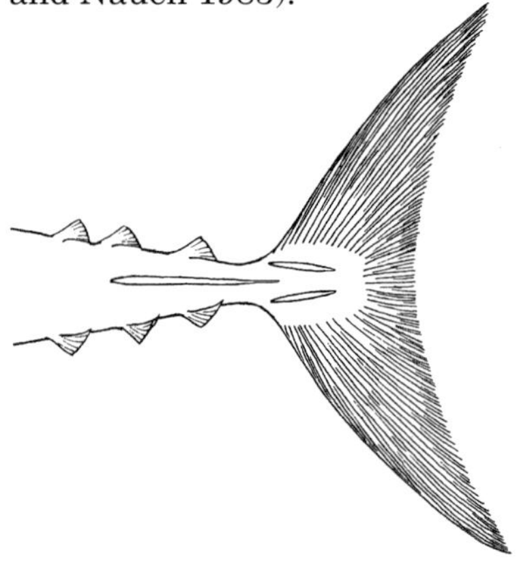

The pectoral fins are high on the body, and the pelvic fins are below the pectorals. An interpelvic process is present and can be single or bifid, small or large (Collette and Nauen 1983). Among the scombrid genera represented in Alaska, it is small and single in *Scomber* and small and bifid in *Katsuwonus, Sarda,* and *Thunnus*:

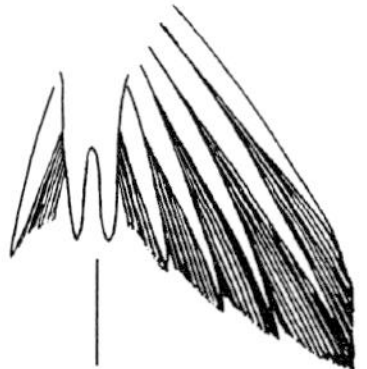

Configuration of the scales is another important feature in identification of scombrids. Some species have small scales all over the body (e.g., *Scomber japonicus*), others have scales only in a "corselet" behind the head and along the anterior part of the lateral line (e.g., *K. pelamis*), and the rest are fully scaly but the scales in the corselet area are enlarged (e.g., *Sarda chiliensis* and *Thunnus* species).

The four genera of the tribe Thunnini, including *Katsuwonus* and *Thunnus* from Alaska, are unique among bony fishes in having countercurrent heat-exchange systems that allow them to retain metabolic heat and stay warmer than the surrounding water. In some species (e.g., *T. alalunga* and *T. orientalis*) the countercurrent heat-exchange system involves the liver (and other viscera), which has a dense vascular network that appears as prominent striations on the ventral surface. The presence or absence of striations can be used to confirm identifications of species.

The vivid, metallic tints and patterns of scombrid coloration are useful for distinguishing among the species, but they quickly fade after death.

Tunas are the largest scombrids. Atlantic bluefin tuna, *T. thynnus,* are reported to reach 4.3 m (14 ft) in length and weigh as much as 910 kg (2,000 lb) (Hart 1973). The California record for *T. orientalis* is 271 cm (8.9 ft) and 458 kg (1,010 lb) (Foreman and Ishizuka 1990). However, adult bluefin tuna are rarely caught anywhere in the eastern Pacific and probably were not taken north of California in the twentieth century (Crockford 1997). Catches in the eastern Pacific rarely exceed 45 kg (99 lb). The smallest scombrids are mackerels of the tribe Scombrini, with the chub mackerel, *Scomber japonicus,* reaching 64 cm (25 inches) and 2.9 kg (6.3 lb).

The first confirmed record of skipjack tuna, *K. pelamis,* in Alaska is from Yakutat Bay; the record is documented by photographs (B. L. Wing, pers. comm., 11 April 1996). The most recent previously published inventory of Alaskan fish species (Quast and Hall 1972) included *K. pelamis* based on an unverified record dating back to 1964. An account for yellowfin tuna, *T. albacares,* is included in this guide because this tuna has occasionally been reported to occur in Alaska, although its presence has not been confirmed. Other differences from the previous inventory (Quast and Hall 1972) are due to changes in the classification of the Scombridae. Consideration of molecular and morphological data led Collette (1999) to raise the Atlantic and Pacific bluefin subspecies to species (*Thunnus thynnus* and *T. orientalis*); and to recognize two subgenera within *Scomber,* classifying the Alaskan species *S. japonicus* in subgenus *Pneumatophorus* Jordan & Gilbert. The name *Pneumatophorus* means swim-bladder bearer, after one of the diagnostic characters of the subgenus. Collette (1999) classified Atlantic and Pacific populations of chub mackerel in separate species: *S. japonicus* in the Indo-Pacific, and *S. colias* in the Atlantic. The latter change does not affect the name of the Pacific Ocean species, but there are morphological differences; e.g., markings are strongly developed on the belly in Atlantic populations but absent or weakly developed in Pacific populations (Collette 1999).

The first few couplets in the following key separate the smaller scombrids from the large tunas.

Key to the Scombridae of Alaska

1 Space between dorsal fins longer than snout length; no median keel on caudal peduncle; body completely covered with scales . . . . *Scomber japonicus,* page 806

1 Space between dorsal fins shorter than snout length; caudal peduncle with median keel; corselet present, may be indistinct . . . . (2)

2 (1) Scales absent posterior of corselet except on lateral line; gill rakers more than 50 on first arch . . . . *Katsuwonus pelamis,* page 807

2 Body fully scaled, with enlarged scales in corselet area and along lateral line . . . . (3)

3 (2) Dark stripes dorsally, slightly oblique; teeth large, usually widely spaced; dorsal spines 17 or more . . . . *Sarda chiliensis,* page 808

3 No dark lines dorsally; teeth small; palatines with or without teeth; gill rakers on lower limb of first arch 25 or less; dorsal spines usually 16 or less . . . . (4)

4 (3) Pectoral fin long, extending beyond insertion of anal fin . . . . *Thunnus alalunga,* page 809

4 Pectoral fin not extending as far as anal fin insertion . . . . (5)

5 (4) Pectoral fin length more than 80% HL, extending beyond origin of second dorsal fin; ventral surface of liver without striations . . . . *Thunnus albacares,* page 810
(not confirmed from Alaska)

5 Pectoral fin less than 80% HL, not reaching beyond origin of second dorsal fin; ventral surface of liver striated . . . . *Thunnus orientalis,* page 811

Scomber japonicus Houttuyn, 1782 **chub mackerel**

Western Gulf of Alaska to Gulf of California and to Pacific Ocean off Chile; in western Pacific south to Philippines; Indo-Pacific in temperate and warm waters.

Coastal pelagic, in large schools; usually over continental slope from surface to depth of about 300 m, reaching greatest depths during the day.

D VIII–XI + I,9–14 + 4–6 finlets; A I,I–II,9–12 + 4–6 finlets; Pec 20–21; Pel I,5;
GR 10–14 + 26–34 (37–47); Vert 29–32.

- Greenish or bluish dorsally grading to silvery ventrally; **dark, oblique, wavy lines dorsally**; sometimes faintly marked with small dark spots ventrolaterally.
- Body rounded.
- Adipose eyelid present.
- **No median keel on caudal peduncle**.
- Maxilla extends to below mideye.
- **Dorsal fins placed far apart**, interspace larger than snout length; 4–6 dorsal and anal finlets, usually 5; first anal fin spine conspicuous, set off from rest of anal fin; **interpelvic process small and single-pointed**.
- Body completely covered with scales; no corselet of larger scales.
- Length to 63.5 cm TL, weight to 2.9 kg; usually less than 41 cm and 0.7 kg.

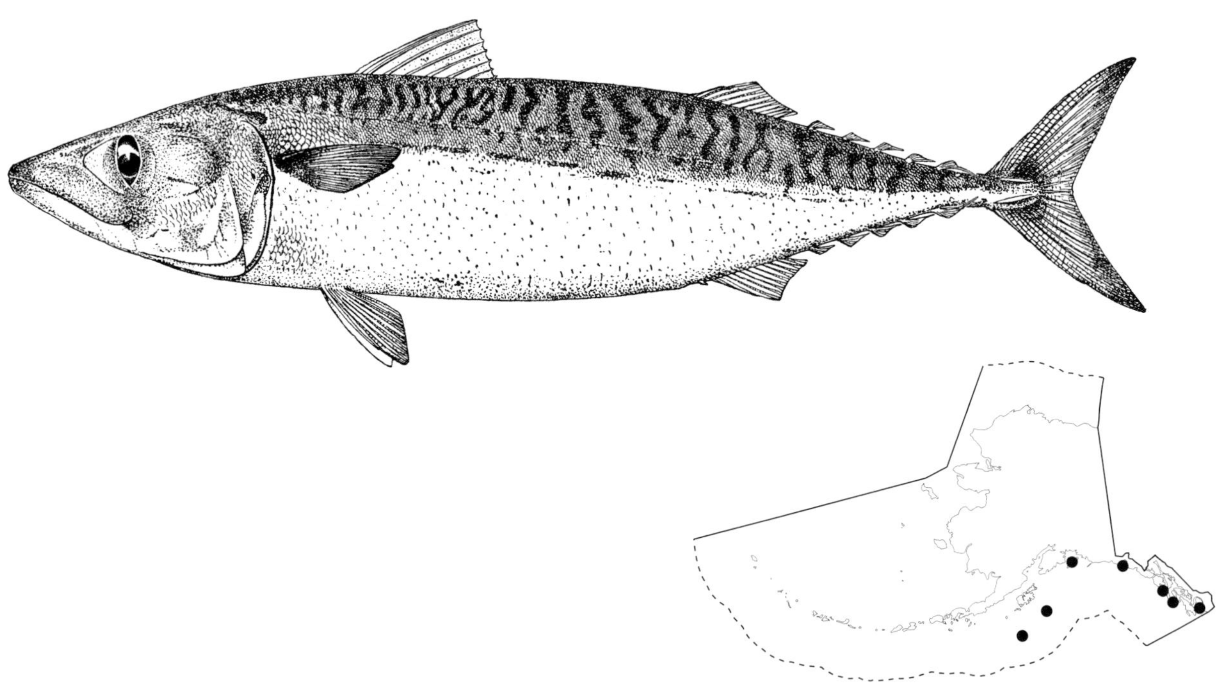

Notes & Sources — *Scomber (Pneumatophorus) japonicus* Houttuyn, 1782
Scomber diego Ayres, 1856
Pneumatophorus diego: Hubbs and Schultz 1929.
Collette (1999) classified *S. japonicus* as a distinct species from Atlantic *S. colias*, and placed both in subgenus *Pneumatophorus* Jordan & Gilbert.
Also called Pacific mackerel.

Description: Miller and Lea 1972:191; Hart 1973:374–376; Collette and Nauen 1983:56–58; Nakamura in Masuda et al. 1984:224; Castro Hernández and Santana Ortega 2000.
Figure: Soldatov and Lindberg 1930, pl. 15.
Range: Reported to be generally distributed in the Gulf of Alaska in late summer (e.g., Brodeur 1988), but documentation is scarce. In 1932 one specimen was found in Prince William Sound herring catches and the *Pacific Fisherman* reported "a lot" were taken at Dall Head, Gravina Island, in southeastern Alaska (Rounsefell and Dahlgren 1934). Macy et al. (1978) reported gill-net and purse-seine catches south of Kodiak Island. J. Koerner (pers. comm., 14 Jan. 1993) has photographs of chub mackerel caught by purse seine and delivered in the summer of 1990 to Ketchikan (photographs also on file at ABL). In July 1993 a specimen was caught in the Kodiak area and taken to the local ADFG office (J. E. Blackburn, pers. comm., 23 Jul. 1998). The ABL permanent collection includes three specimens (AB 93-25) collected on 24 Aug. 1993 near Yakutat by B. L. Wing, who also confirmed a report of a beach seine catch at Sitka in July or August 1993 (B. L. Wing, pers. comm., 17 Aug. 1998). Larkins (1964) reported catches of jack mackerel, *Trachurus symmetricus*, in the Gulf of Alaska that "may" have included some *S. japonicus*.

Katsuwonus pelamis (Linnaeus, 1758) **skipjack tuna**

Yakutat Bay, Alaska; southern British Columbia off Vancouver Island to Chile; worldwide in temperate and tropical seas.

Epipelagic, oceanic, in schools associated with drifting objects, sharks, whales, and other tunas.

D XIV–XVIII + 12–16 + 7–9 finlets; A II,12–16 + 6–8 finlets; Pec 26–28; Pel I,5;
GR 16–22 + 35–44 (53–65); Vert 40–41.

- Bluish to violet dorsally, silvery ventrally; **4–6 dark longitudinal stripes ventrolaterally**, occasionally absent.
- Body fusiform and rounded.
- Strong median keel on caudal peduncle.
- Maxilla extends to below mideye.
- Space between dorsal fins not larger than eye; **first dorsal fin outline concave**; pectoral fin short, triangulate; interpelvic process small and bifid.
- Corselet present; **scales absent posterior to corselet except on lateral line**.
- Gill rakers numerous, more than 50 on first arch.
- Length to 110 cm TL, weight to 25 kg; usually under 65 cm.

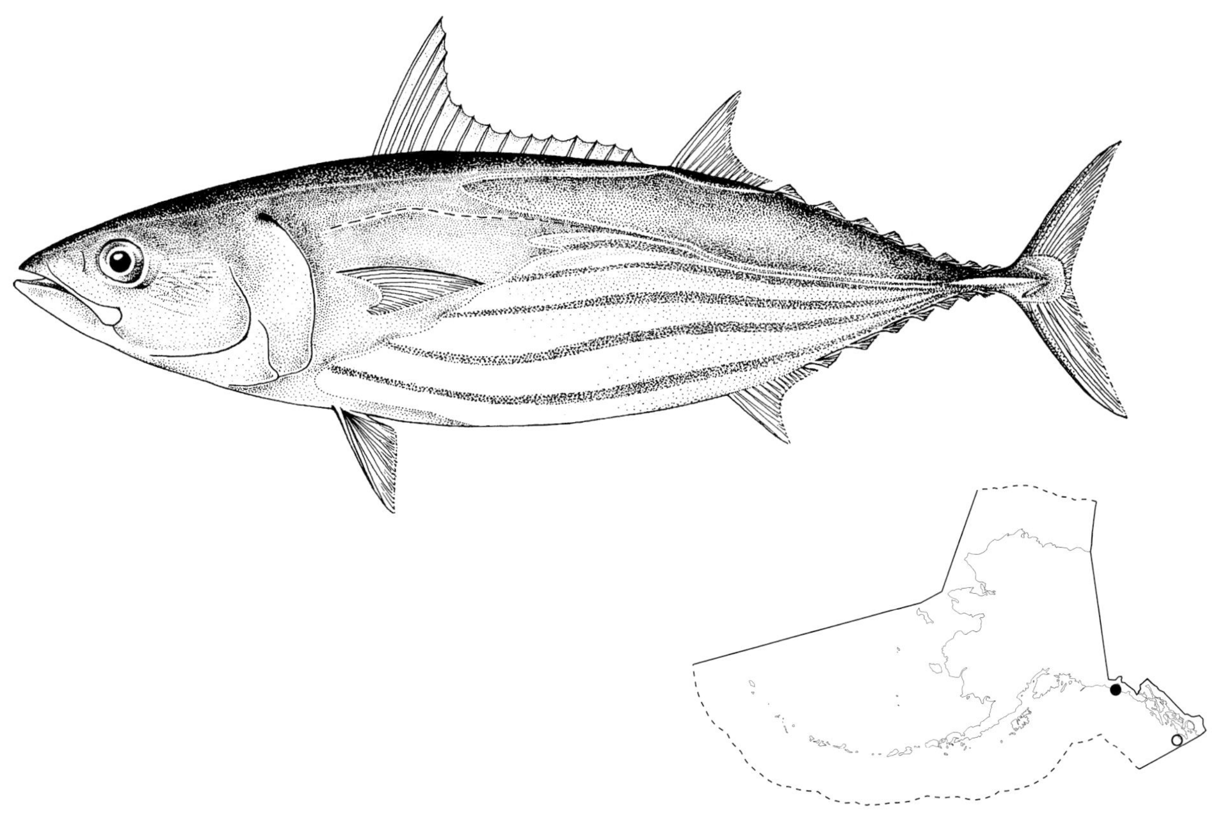

Notes & Sources — *Katsuwonus pelamis* (Linnaeus, 1758)
Scomber pelamis Linnaeus, 1758
Euthynnus pelamis (Linnaeus, 1758): Eschmeyer and Herald 1983, Robins and Ray 1986.
Currently most researchers use the name *Katsuwonus pelamis*; Eschmeyer (1998) listed numerous examples.

Description: Hart 1973:371–372; Collette and Nauen 1983: 42–44; Eschmeyer and Herald 1983:272; Nakamura in Masuda et al. 1984:226.

Figure: Collette and Nauen 1983:42.

Range: The Auke Bay Laboratory has a photograph of a 63-cm-FL specimen caught in a set net at Yakutat Bay on 6 Aug. 1981. J. Koerner (pers. comm., 14 Jan. 1993) recalled seeing specimens collected off southern southeastern Alaska. The nearest occurrences on record from outside of Alaska are Barkley Sound (Hart 1943) and the Strait of Juan de Fuca off Vancouver Island (Neave 1959), British Columbia.

Sarda chiliensis (Cuvier, 1832) **Pacific bonito**

Northeastern Pacific from near mouth of Copper River, Gulf of Alaska, to southern Baja California off Cabo de San Lucas and Revillagigedo Islands; southern population off Peru and Chile.

Epipelagic, neritic, in schools.

D XVII–XIX + I,12–16 + 6–9 finlets; A II,10–13 + 6–7 finlets; Pec 22–26; Pel I,5;
GR 4–10 + 11–18 (20–27); Vert 42–46.

- Greenish blue dorsally, silvery ventrally; **dark stripes dorsally, slightly oblique**.
- Body slightly compressed.
- Well developed median keel on caudal peduncle.
- Maxilla extends to rear of eye or beyond.
- Dorsal fins contiguous or nearly so; **first dorsal fin long, profile straight**; **17 or more dorsal spines**; interpelvic process bifid.
- Body completely covered with scales; corselet of larger scales present.
- Teeth large, usually widely spaced; 18–30 in upper jaw, 14–25 in lower; vomerine teeth absent.
- Length to 102 cm FL, weight to 11.3 kg.

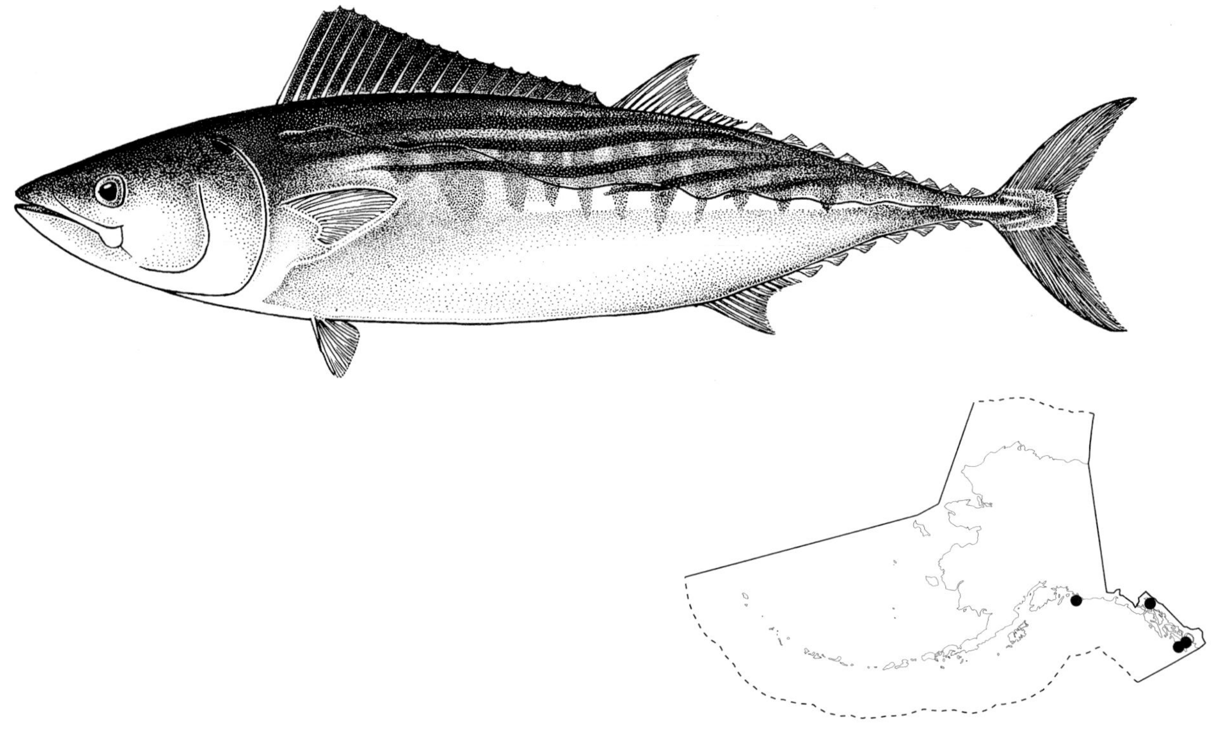

Notes & Sources — *Sarda chiliensis* (Cuvier in Cuvier & Valenciennes, 1832)
Pelamys lineolata Girard, 1858
Pelamys chiliensis Cuvier in Cuvier & Valenciennes, 1832
Some researchers classify the northern population as a separate subspecies, *S. chiliensis lineolata,* from the southern, *S. chiliensis chiliensis.*

Description: Hart 1973:373–374; Collette and Nauen 1983: 51–52; Eschmeyer and Herald 1983:272.

Figure: Collette and Nauen 1983:51.

Range: Taken near the mouth of the Copper River at 60°16'N, 145°32'W (AB 63-141) and in Clarence Strait near Ketchikan (AB 63-107) in 1963 (Quast 1964b). Not reported again in Alaska until the summer of 1983, when bonitos were taken in gill nets in upper Lynn Canal south of Haines (e.g., AB 84-11) and farther south near Klawock, and others were observed at the surface (Karinen et al. 1985). Rarely found north of California.

Thunnus alalunga (Bonnaterre, 1788) **albacore**

Prince William Sound, Gulf of Alaska, to Chile; worldwide in temperate seas.

Epi- and mesopelagic, oceanic, in schools; concentrate where surface temperature is 14.4–16.1°C, along thermal gradients where productive but colder coastal waters meet warmer oceanic waters.

D XII–XVI + 0–III,11–16 + 7–9 finlets; A II,12–15 + 7–8 finlets; Pec 31–34; Pel I,5;
GR 7–10 + 18–22 (25–31); Vert 39.

- Dark blue dorsally, silvery white ventrally; first dorsal fin deep yellow, second dorsal and anal fins light yellow; anal finlets dark; posterior margin of caudal fin white.
- Body fusiform and slightly compressed; **deepest more posteriorly than other tunas, at or only slightly anterior to second dorsal fin**.
- Well developed median keel on caudal peduncle.
- Maxilla extends to below anterior edge of eye.
- Second dorsal fin lower than first dorsal; **pectoral fin remarkably long, extending well beyond front of anal fin**, except in fish smaller than about 50 cm; interpelvic process bifid.
- Body fully scaled, corselet of larger scales present but not very distinct.
- Gill rakers 25–31 on first arch.
- **Liver striated on ventral surface and central lobe largest**.
- Length to 137 cm FL, weight to 43 kg; to 34 kg on Pacific coast.

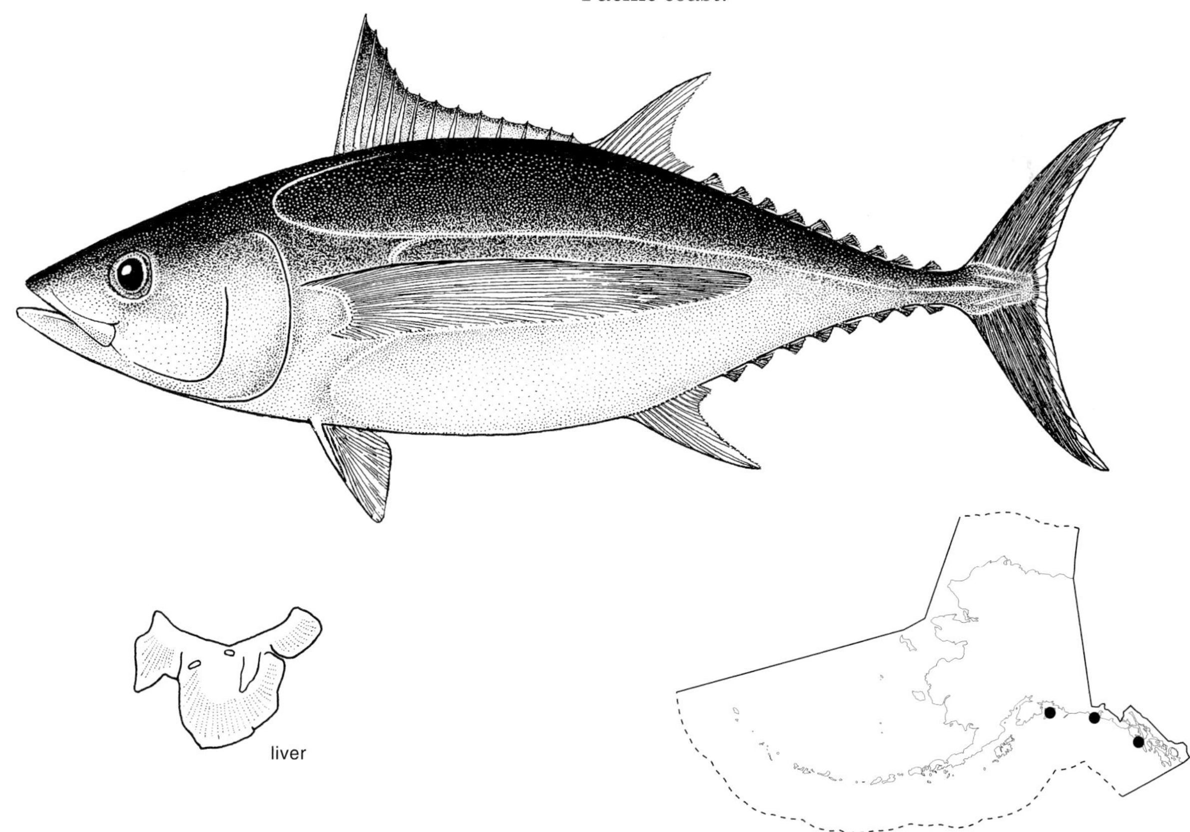

Notes & Sources — *Thunnus alalunga* (Bonnaterre, 1788)
Scomber alalunga Bonnaterre, 1788

Description: Hart 1973:376–378; Collette and Nauen 1983: 81–83; Eschmeyer and Herald 1983:274; Nakamura in Masuda et al. 1984:226.

Figures: Collette and Nauen 1983:81.

Range: Occasionally taken offshore by salmon trollers in the Gulf of Alaska. Taken in several commercial catches off southeastern Alaska and the entrance to Prince William Sound in 1983 (Karinen et al. 1985). A tuna found on the beach near Yakutat in the summer of 1997 was identified as a yellowfin tuna, *T. albacares,* in *Alaska* magazine (May-June 1998:59), but the accompanying photograph is that of an albacore, *T. alalunga.* Although occasionally taken in Alaska, and most frequently in unusually warm years, albacore are not as common in the area as sometimes suggested. For example, commercial catches landed at Kodiak for processing in 1997 were from high seas fishing activity several hundreds of miles to the south. The northern stock of abacore migrates from spawning grounds off Japan to North America in late spring and summer, and northward by late summer and early fall to about 50°N (Neave and Hanavan 1960).

Thunnus albacares (Bonnaterre, 1788) **yellowfin tuna**

Pacific Ocean south of Alaska; southern California to Peru; worldwide in tropical and temperate seas. Epipelagic, oceanic.

D XII–XIV + 14–16 + 8–9 finlets; A 14–16 + 8–9 finlets; Pec 32–35; Pel I,5; GR 8–11 + 19–24 (26–34); Vert 39.

- Dark blue dorsally grading through yellow to silvery gray ventrally; dorsal and anal fins and finlets yellow, finlets edged with black; young with pale, narrow bars and spots ventrally.
- Body fusiform and slightly compressed; **body deepest near middle of first dorsal fin base**.
- Well developed median keel on caudal peduncle.
- Maxilla extends to below anterior portion of eye to mideye.
- Second dorsal fin about same height as first on fish up to about 40 kg, elongate in larger fish, reaching well over 20% FL; **pectoral fin moderately long, but not extending past front of anal fin**; interpelvic process bifid.
- Body fully scaled, corselet of larger scales present but not very distinct.
- Gill rakers 26–34 on first arch.
- **Liver without striations on ventral surface and right lobe largest**.
- Length to over 200 cm FL, weight to 204 kg; rarely more than 57 kg in northeastern Pacific.

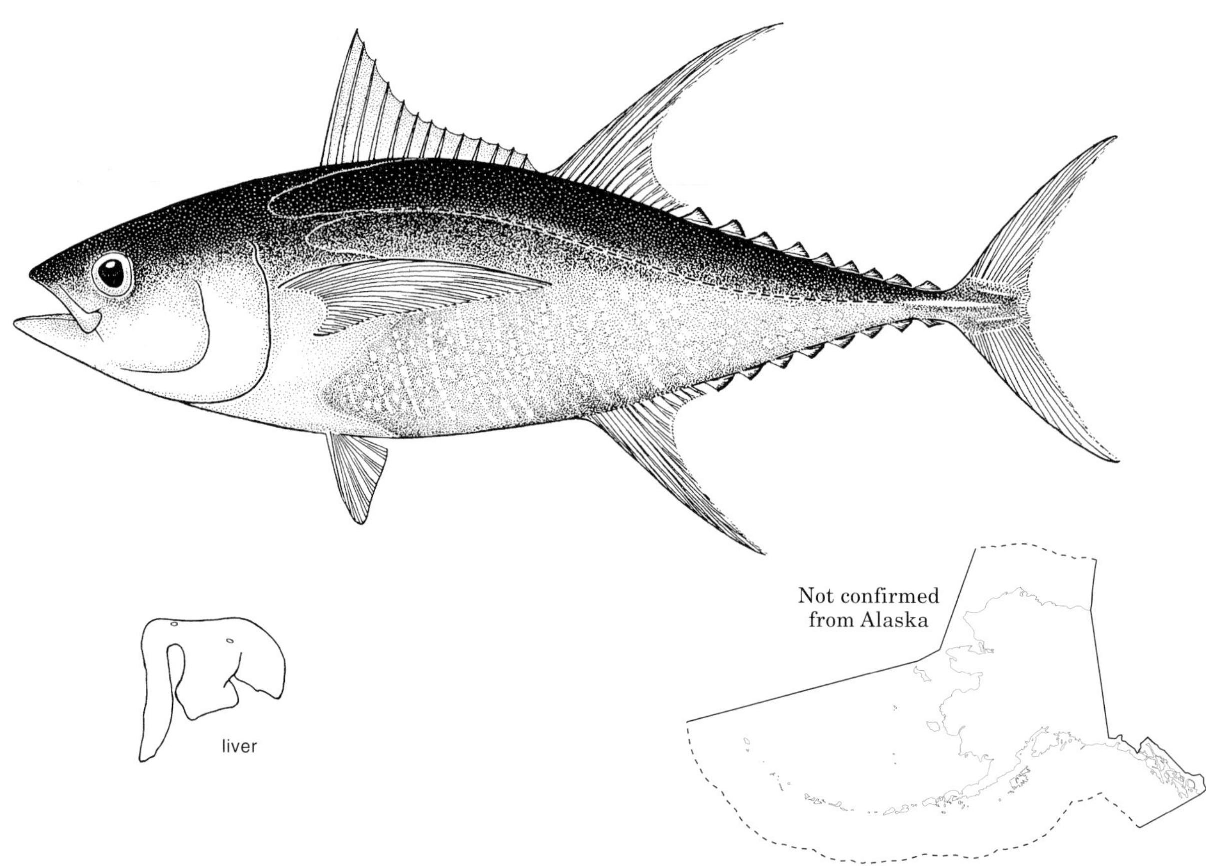

Notes & Sources — *Thunnus albacares* (Bonnaterre, 1788)
Scomber albacares Bonnaterre, 1788

Description: Collette and Nauen 1983:83–85; Eschmeyer and Herald 1983:274; Nakamura in Masuda et al. 1984:226.

Figures: Collette and Nauen 1983:84.

Range: The nearest known occurrence of *T. albacares* to Alaska was recorded by Larkins (1964), from a specimen taken at 50°00'N, 150°02'W (well outside the 200-mile limit), on 24 August 1961 during experimental salmon gillnetting operations. Although a fish found on the beach near Yakutat in the summer of 1997 was reported to be a yellowfin tuna (*Alaska* magazine, May-June 1998:59), the photograph shows an albacore, *T. alalunga*. Rare north of Point Conception, California.

Thunnus orientalis (Temminck & Schlegel, 1844) **Pacific bluefin tuna**

Gulf of Alaska at Shelikof Strait; central British Columbia to southern Baja California; southern Sea of Okhotsk to northern Philippines; endemic to North Pacific.

Epipelagic, usually oceanic but seasonally coming close to shore; in schools.

D XII–XV + 0–I,13–18 + 7–10 finlets; A 0–II,12–15 + 7–9 finlets; Pec 31–38; Pel I,5; GR 9–16 + 21–28 (32–43); Vert 38–39.

- Dark steel-blue to black dorsally; silvery white, usually with white spots and lines, ventrally; first dorsal fin bluish or yellow, second dorsal reddish brown; finlets dusky yellow, edged with black; median caudal keel black in adults.
- Body fusiform and slightly compressed; **body deepest near middle of first dorsal fin base**.
- Well developed median keel on caudal peduncle.
- Maxilla extends to below mideye.
- Second dorsal fin higher than first; **pectoral fin short, not reaching below second dorsal fin**; interpelvic process bifid.
- Body fully scaled, corselet of larger scales present but not very distinct.
- Gill rakers 32–43 on first arch.
- **Liver striated on ventral surface and central lobe largest**.
- Length to more than 300 cm FL, weight to about 680 kg; rarely exceeding 45 kg in eastern North Pacific.

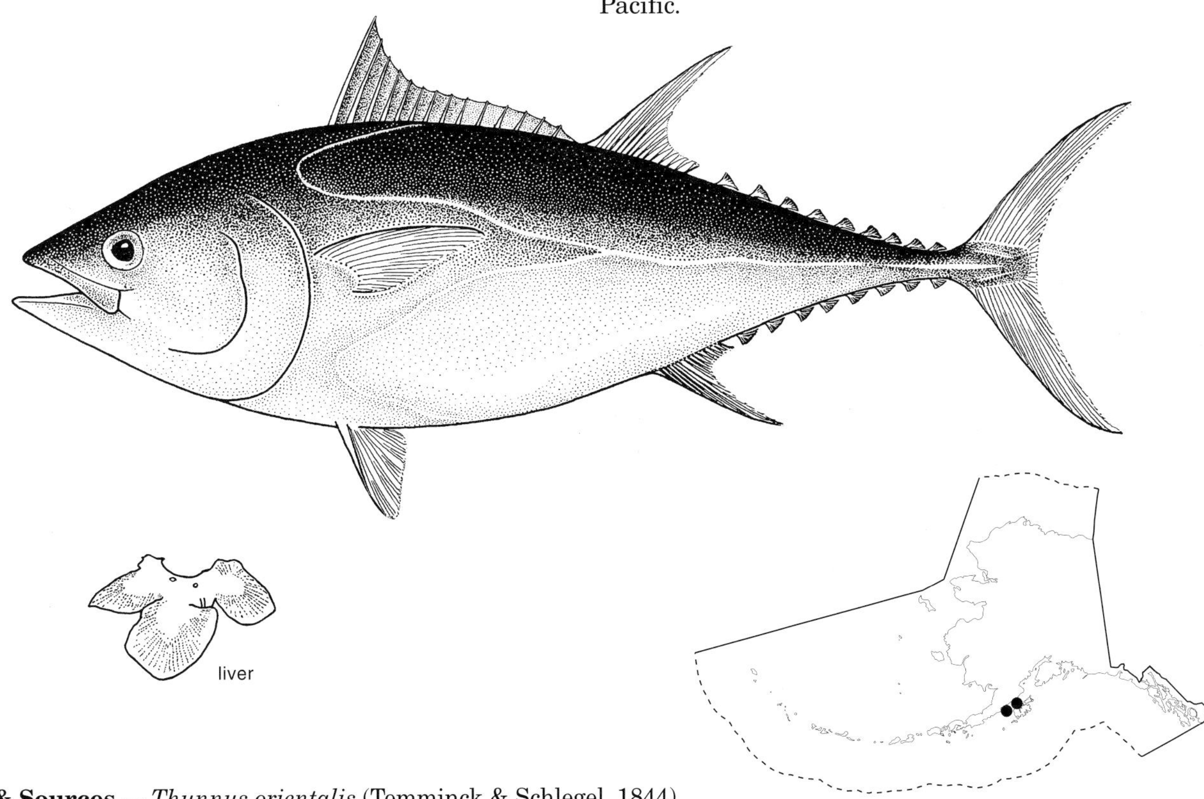

Notes & Sources — *Thunnus orientalis* (Temminck & Schlegel, 1844)
Thynnus orientalis Temminck & Schlegel, 1844
Thunnus saliens Jordan & Evermann, 1926
Thunnus thynnus orientalis: Gibbs and Collette 1967.
Thunnus orientalis: Collette (1999) raised Atlantic and Pacific bluefin tuna subspecies to species.

Description: Hart 1973:379–380; Collette and Nauen 1983: 90–92; Eschmeyer and Herald 1983:275; Nakamura in Masuda et al. 1984:226.

Figures: Collette and Nauen 1983:91.

Range: A 68-cm (27-inch), 6.8-kg (15-lb) specimen taken by a salmon seiner in Shelikof Strait "north of Kodiak Island" on 28 Jul. 1958 was reported as an extension of the known range by Radovich (1961); because of the lack of precise locality data, the position for the dot on the map, above, is estimated. Quast and Hall (1972) also reported a specimen from Shelikof Strait as a range extension. The specimen (AB 63-244), measuring 62 cm SL, was caught on 28 Jul. 1958, the same day as the specimen reported by Radovich (1961), in a purse seine at Wide Bay, Cape Igvak, 57°22'N, 156°17'W, which is west of Kodiak Island. That year, 1958, was a period of intense warming due to El Niño. The nearest record outside Alaska is a specimen taken, also in 1958, west of Queen Charlotte Sound at about 51°N, 130°W. Two others were taken farther south off British Columbia in 1957 (Neave 1959). Sea surface temperatures in the area in 1957, as well as 1958, were warmer than usual (Radovich 1961). The species has not been reported north of California since 1958.

Family Centrolophidae
Medusafishes

One species in each of three families (Centrolophidae, Stromateidae, and Tetragonuridae) of the suborder Stromateoidei has been reported from Alaska or nearby waters of British Columbia. The stromateoids are pelagic fishes of tropical and temperate seas which associate with floating or slowly moving objects and organisms near the surface as young fish, and inhabit greater depths as adults. Some coastal species are abundant and commercially important, but oceanic stromateoids are found only rarely or sporadically. Physical characters of the Stromateoidei include the presence of toothed pouches behind the last gill arch.

Young medusafishes, family Centrolophidae, are often found under jellyfishes, and stomach contents of adults indicate a diet of medusae and ctenophores. One species, *Icichthys lockingtoni,* occurs in Alaskan waters. Although a few dorsal and anal fin spines are present in *I. lockingtoni,* they are weak and most researchers count them with the rays. The body is limp, with soft, flexible bones, and very fragile.

Icichthys lockingtoni Jordan & Gilbert, 1880 **medusafish**

North Pacific south of Aleutian Islands to central Baja California and to Japan.

Pelagic, recorded to depth of 521 m or more; young live near surface among jellyfishes and ctenophores.

D 39–46; A 27–32; Pec 18–21; Pel I,5; LL 100–130; Br 7; GR 18–21; Vert 56–61.

- Adults bluish gray to dark brown with dusky to black fins; fine dark punctulations on head and back; juveniles almost transparent, bluish or pinkish.
- Body limp, compressed; top of head, around eyes and snout spongy; snout bluntly rounded.
- Dorsal fin origin well behind base of pectoral fin; dorsal and anal fins fleshy at base, spines weak.
- Body and head covered with small, cycloid, deciduous scales in adults; scales absent in juveniles.
- Length to about 46 cm TL.

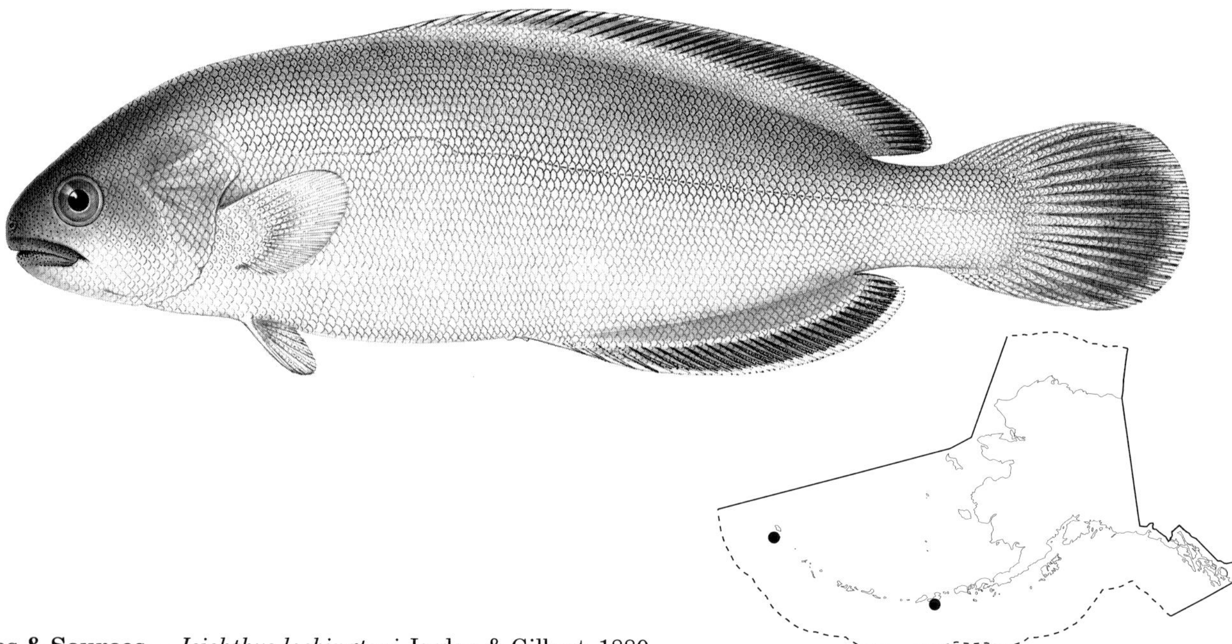

Notes & Sources — *Icichthys lockingtoni* Jordan & Gilbert, 1880

Description: Haedrich 1967:69; Alhstrom et al. 1976:313–316; Lindberg and Krasyukova 1975:324–325.

Figure: Jordan 1923, pl. 1; 181 mm TL, found swimming at the surface under the medusa of a large jellyfish near Monterey, California.

Range: Haedrich (1967) projected the range to include the northern Gulf of Alaska and the Pacific Ocean south of the Aleutian Islands. SIO 63-640 and 63-644, examined by Ahlstrom et al. (1976:316), are from just south of Unalaska and Agattu islands, respectively. We did not find any other records from Alaska in museum collections or databases. The nearest record outside Alaska is from west of Queen Charlotte Sound (BC 65-605; Hart 1973). Sometimes *I. lockingtoni* is confused with juvenile prowfish, *Zaprora silenus,* which also associate with jellyfish medusae. Depth: Specimens were taken at about 521 m off Oregon in 1984 (UW 26461) and 384 m off northern California in 1989 (UW 21887).

Family Tetragonuridae
Squaretails

The Tetragonuridae is a family of oceanic stromateoids of tropical and temperate seas which as young fish occur near the surface with jellyfishes but as adults inhabit meso- or bathypelagic depths. They are the least stromateoid-like members of the suborder and sometimes are placed in their own higher taxon. The bodies of tetragonurids are cylindrical, not compressed; their dorsal fins are in two distinct parts, not single; and the anal fin is much shorter than in other stromateoids.

Tetragonurids are called squaretails because two converging keels on each side of the caudal peduncle make the fish look squarish in cross section. Their adaptations for feeding on coelenterates and ctenophores include sharp, knife-shaped lower teeth used for cutting out pieces and deep, high-sided lower jaws which help to retain them. One of the three known species, the smalleye squaretail, *Tetragonurus cuvieri,* occurs in the offshore waters of southern Alaska.

Tetragonurus cuvieri Risso, 1810 **smalleye squaretail**

North Pacific Ocean south of Aleutian Islands to central Baja California off Cedros Island, and to Japan; off Australia and New Zealand; North Atlantic Ocean.

Pelagic, oceanic; young live near surface among jellyfishes and ctenophores; adults inhabit depths to about 700 m, usually shallower, rise at night to feed.

D XV–XXI + 10–17; A 0–II,9–15; Pec 14–17; Pel I,5; LL 97–114 to keel; Br 5–6; GR 14–20; Vert 51–58.

- Dark brown, with violet and yellow reflections.
- Body elongate, cylindrical; deep, scooplike lower jaw; two keels on each side of caudal peduncle.
- Two dorsal fins, close together; first dorsal of short spines, depressible in a groove; when folded, pelvic fin lies in abdominal groove.
- Body and head covered with multiple-ridged, strongly adherent scales in precise curved rows.
- Numerous close-set, curved-tipped teeth on lower jaw form continuous cutting edge.
- Length to about 38 cm TL in northeastern North Pacific, 62 cm TL off New Zealand.

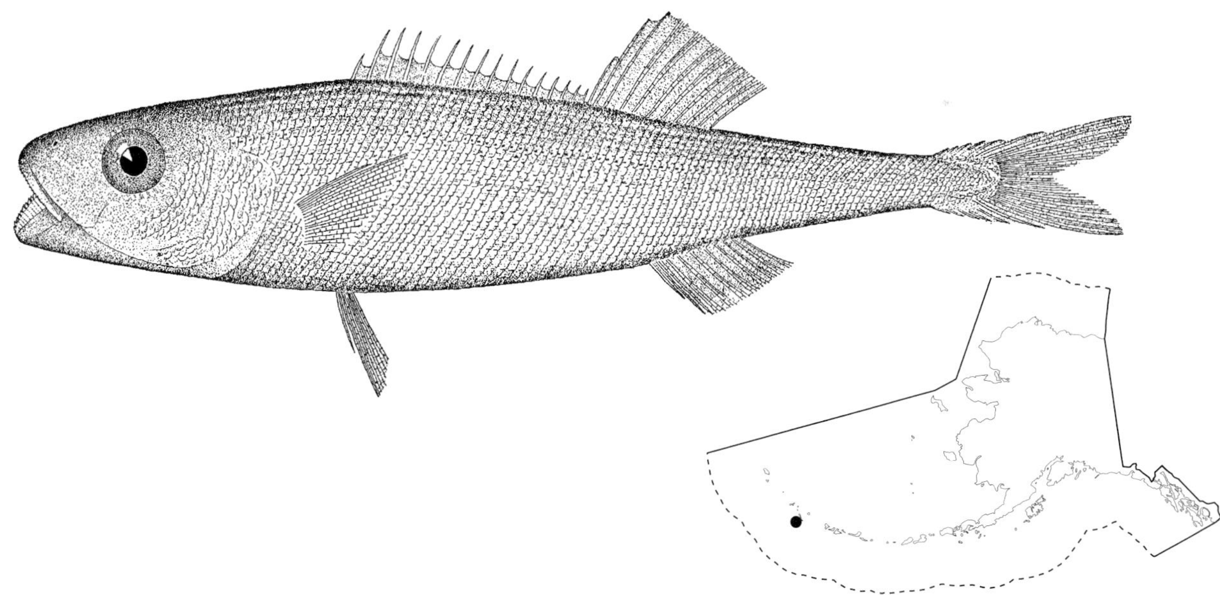

Notes & Sources — *Tetragonurus cuvieri* Risso, 1810

Description: Grey 1955:24–32, 48–56; Haedrich 1967:98; Lindberg and Krasyukova 1975:309–312; Eschmeyer and Herald 1983:282. Pectoral fin rays 19–21 in specimens taken off New Zealand (Grey 1955).

Figure: Goode and Bean 1896, fig. 417; Atlantic Ocean.

Range: Specific records from Alaska were not previously reported. The UW has 3 specimens (UW 15471) collected on 12 Jul. 1958 at 50°59'N, 178°50'E. Considered to be "rather common" (Ahlstrom et al. 1976:329) in the eastern Pacific, but records north of about 40°N are relatively rare. Tanonaka (1957) reported incidental catches of 146 squaretails in 1955 at 45°N, 177°30'E and 167°35'W, at night in gill nets at the surface. Nearest records outside Alaska are two specimens gillnetted at 51°N, 140°W and one at 49°01'N, 134°24'W in 1957 (Neave 1959). Sometimes found in the stomachs of other fishes and whales.

Family Stromateidae
Butterfishes

Butterfishes, family Stromateidae, are brightly iridescent, deep-bodied pelagic fishes of tropical and warm temperate coastal waters. Young butterfishes are found under floating objects and the adults at greater depths, usually near the coast and often in large schools. Only 1 of the 13 or so extant butterfish species occurs anywhere near Alaska. This is the Pacific pompano, *Peprilus simillimus,* which ranges north to British Columbia and is fished commercially, for its excellent flavor, in California. Some authors prefer the popular name Pacific butterfish over Pacific pompano, since the fish is not a true pompano of the family Carangidae.

Distinguishing characters of stromateids typically include a silvery body and rounded head; long, falcate pectoral fins; a forked tail; no pelvic fins in the adults; and, like other stromateoids, a muscular tooth-lined pharynx. The dorsal and anal fins are opposite each other, long, and usually higher anteriorly.

Peprilus simillimus (Ayres, 1860) — **Pacific pompano**

Eastern North Pacific from British Columbia at Queen Charlotte Sound to central Baja California off Cedros Island.

Over sandy bottoms off exposed coasts at shallow depths, from about 9 to 91 m.

D II–IV, 41–48; A II–III, 35–44; Pec 19–23; Pel 0; LL 95–110; Br 6; GR 23–26; Vert 29–31.

- Brilliantly iridescent; green to blue dorsally, silvery ventrally; fins dusky.
- Body deep and strongly compressed; head blunt; mouth small.
- Dorsal and anal fins long and low, higher anteriorly; caudal fin deeply forked; pelvic fin absent.
- Lateral line high, arched, following dorsal profile and ending before base of caudal fin.
- Scales tiny, cycloid, deciduous.
- Length to about 28 cm TL.

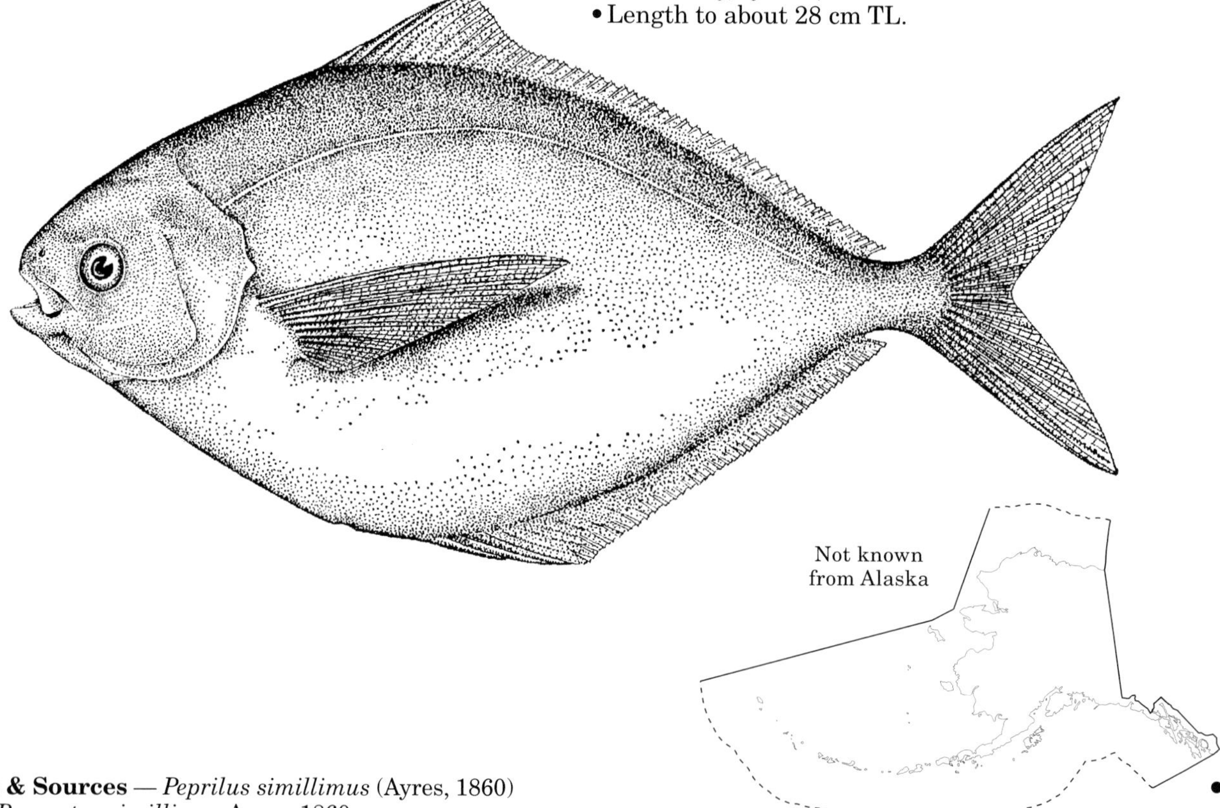

Notes & Sources — *Peprilus simillimus* (Ayres, 1860)
Poronotus simillimus Ayres, 1860
Palometa simillima: Jordan and Evermann 1898:2849.

Description: Horn 1970:185–189; Hart 1973:383–384; Eschmeyer and Herald 1983:280.
Figure: Hart 1973:383; 24 cm TL.

Range: Nearest reported locality is Fitz Hugh Sound off Queen Charlotte Sound, British Columbia, where a specimen was collected in 1951 (Clemens and Wilby 1961).

Order Pleuronectiformes
Flatfishes

Flatfishes live on the bottom, typically in shallow marine waters. Two families are represented in Alaska: the Paralichthyidae, a family of lefteye flounders; and the Pleuronectidae, or righteye flounders.

In adult flatfishes the head is asymmetrical, with both eyes on the same side. The eyes are positioned one on each side in the free-swimming larva, but as the fish grows it is transformed; one eye migrates to the other side and the fish settles to the bottom, blind side down. The body is highly compressed, somewhat rounded on the eyed side but flat on the blind side. Dorsal and anal fins are usually long and the fins are without spines. Flatfishes lack a swim bladder.

The eyed side carries the pigment, while the blind side is usually white or off-white. For identifying specimens the distinction as to whether the blind side is pigmented usually is more helpful than details of coloration on the eyed side, because eyed-side coloration in many species changes to blend with the substrate. The size of the mouth (expressed as extension of the maxilla to some point below the lower eye) varies and is an important distinguishing feature. The lateral line varies from nearly straight to distinctly arching over the pectoral fin. In several species a supratemporal branch extends posteriorly along the base of the dorsal fin, called an accessory dorsal branch, and an anterior branch can extend over the upper eye. Body shape is basically ovate, but can be relatively elongate or deep. The "anal spine" is the tip of a curved bone (first anal pterygiophore) bordering the abdominal cavity posteriorly which in some flatfishes is stiff and enlarged. It may be felt just under the skin in front of the anal fin. In fresh, trawl-caught specimens and in preserved specimens (but not in live fish), the anal spine often projects through the skin. In the following accounts "absent" means the first anal pterygiophore is not stiff and enlarged and its tip cannot be felt externally; "small" or "inconspicuous" means the pterygiophore is enlarged but the point projects only a little or can only be discerned by pressing the area or running a fingernail along the midline; and "pronounced" means the tip is obvious, forming a distinct bulge under the skin or projecting as a large "spine." Although the amount of projection depends partly on the condition of a specimen these general differences are helpful in identification.

Lateral line scale counts reflect scale size, and can help identify some flatfish species. In species of *Citharichthys* and a few other genera the scales are covered by integument and masked by innumerable accessory scales, so counting scales in those species would be impractical. Gill raker counts are crucial for distinguishing *Atheresthes* and *Lepidopsetta* species, and can confirm identifications in some others. Most other counts are less useful for flatfish identification. Flatfishes typically have 6 or 7 branchiostegal rays; a few Alaskan species occasionally have 8. Most Alaskan flatfish species have 6 pelvic fin rays; a few exhibit some variation. Reported counts are for the eyed side.

Family Paralichthyidae
Sand flounders

In sand flounders the eyes and color are typically on the left side of the body, and in *Citharichthys,* the genus represented in Alaska, the pelvic fins are noticeably asymmetrical, with the fin of the eyed side originating on the abdominal ridge. In righteye flounders (Pleuronectidae) the pelvic fins are positioned one on each side of the ridge. Reaching about 30 cm (12 inches), sand flounders are smaller than most righteye flounders.

Called bastard halibuts by Jordan et al. (1930), the family is called the sand flounders by J. S. Nelson et al. in the August 2001 draft of the American Fisheries Society list of fish names (sixth edition). The relationships of the Paralichthyidae are problematical. The group may belong in the family Bothidae (e.g., Hoshino 2001).

Key to the Paralichthyidae of Alaska

1 Lower eye longer than snout; interorbital space concave; high ridge above lower eye . . . . *Citharichthys sordidus,* page 816

1 Diameter of lower eye about equal to snout length; interorbital space flat or convex; no ridge above lower eye . . . . . . *Citharichthys stigmaeus,* page 817

Citharichthys sordidus (Girard, 1854)

Pacific sanddab

Uncertain records from southeastern Bering Sea and Aleutian Islands off Kiska Island; well documented from eastern Gulf of Alaska to southern Baja California off Cabo de San Lucas.

Gravel, sand, or silt bottoms to depth of about 549 m, typically at depths of 50–150 m; the young occur at the shallower depths, and are sometimes found in intertidal or brackish waters.

D 86–102; A 67–81; Pec 12–13; Pel 6; LLs 61–70; GR 6–9 + 12–16; Vert 11–12 + 27–29 (38–40).

- Eyed side light brown with darker mottling, often with yellow or orange spots, occasionally with white spots and blotches; blind side off-white to tan; young fish light olive green with brown, black, and orange speckles, concentrated on fins.
- Dextral individuals are occasionally found.
- **Lower eye longer than snout**; **interorbital space concave**; **high bony ridge above lower eye**; interorbital space relatively broad, with 4–6 rows of scales.
- Maxilla extending to below anterior part of eye.
- Anal spine absent.
- **Pectoral fin projected forward reaches middle of lower eye**; caudal fin slightly rounded.
- Lateral line nearly straight.
- More than 60 lateral line scales; scales ctenoid on eyed side (rough), cycloid on blind side (smooth).
- More gill rakers than in *C. stigmaeus*.
- Length to 41 cm TL.

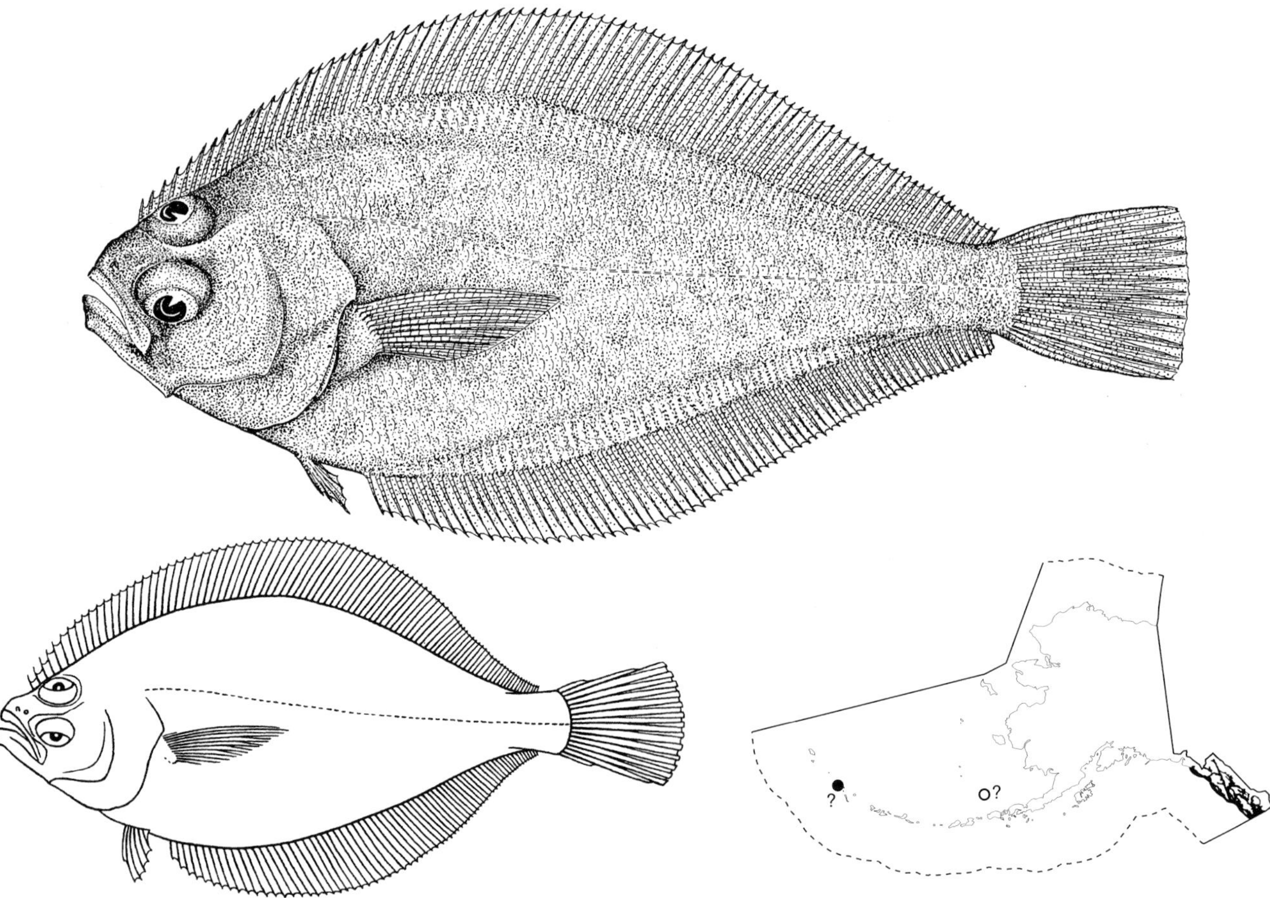

Notes & Sources — *Citharichthys sordidus* (Girard, 1854)
Psettichthys sordidus Girard, 1854

Description: Lockington 1879:83–85; Norman 1934:140–142; Miller and Lea 1972:204–205; Hart 1973:596–597; Matarese et al. 1989:568; Kramer et al. 1995:14–15.

Figures: Upper: Hart 1973:596; 15 cm TL. Lower: Norman 1934, fig. 93.

Range: Reports of *C. sordidus* from the Aleutian Islands (e.g., Wilimovsky 1954, 1964) are based on a specimen from Kiska Island (USNM 54308) recorded by Evermann and Goldsborough (1907); the NMNH online catalog indicates the locality is uncertain. In NMFS survey data reported by Allen and Smith (1988), all of the 701 occurrences of *C. sordidus,* except one "anomalous record" (shown on their map with a question mark) from the eastern Bering Sea, were from Cape Edgecumbe in southeastern Alaska to Los Angeles, California. Three specimens (UW 15458) collected north of Triangle Island, Glacier Bay, at approximately 59°N represent the northernmost record of occurrence in southeastern Alaska. Can occur far offshore; taken at Cobb Seamount, west of Washington, at trawl depths of 200–215 m in surveys in 1976 and 1977 (Snytko 1987).

Citharichthys stigmaeus Jordan & Gilbert, 1882 **speckled sanddab**

Northern Gulf of Alaska at Prince William Sound to southern Baja California at Bahia Magdalena. Sand and mud bottoms near shore to depth of 366 m, usually found shallower than 91 m.

D 75–97; A 58–77; Pec 12; Pel 6; LLs 52–58; GR 3–5 + 7–10; Vert 9–10 + 27–29 (34–39).

- Eyed side brown or tan with fine black speckles and larger spots and blotches; blind side whitish or cream; young fish gray to tan with fine black speckles, almost translucent.
- **Lower eye about same length as snout; interorbital space flat or convex; no bony ridge above lower eye**; interorbital space narrow, with 1 row of scales.
- Maxilla extending to below anterior part of eye.
- Anal spine absent.
- **Pectoral fin projected forward barely reaches or does not reach eye**; caudal fin rounded.
- Lateral line nearly straight.
- Fewer than 60 lateral line scales; scales on both sides of body mostly ctenoid (rough).
- Fewer gill rakers than in *C. sordidus.*
- Length to 17 cm TL, rarely over 13 cm.

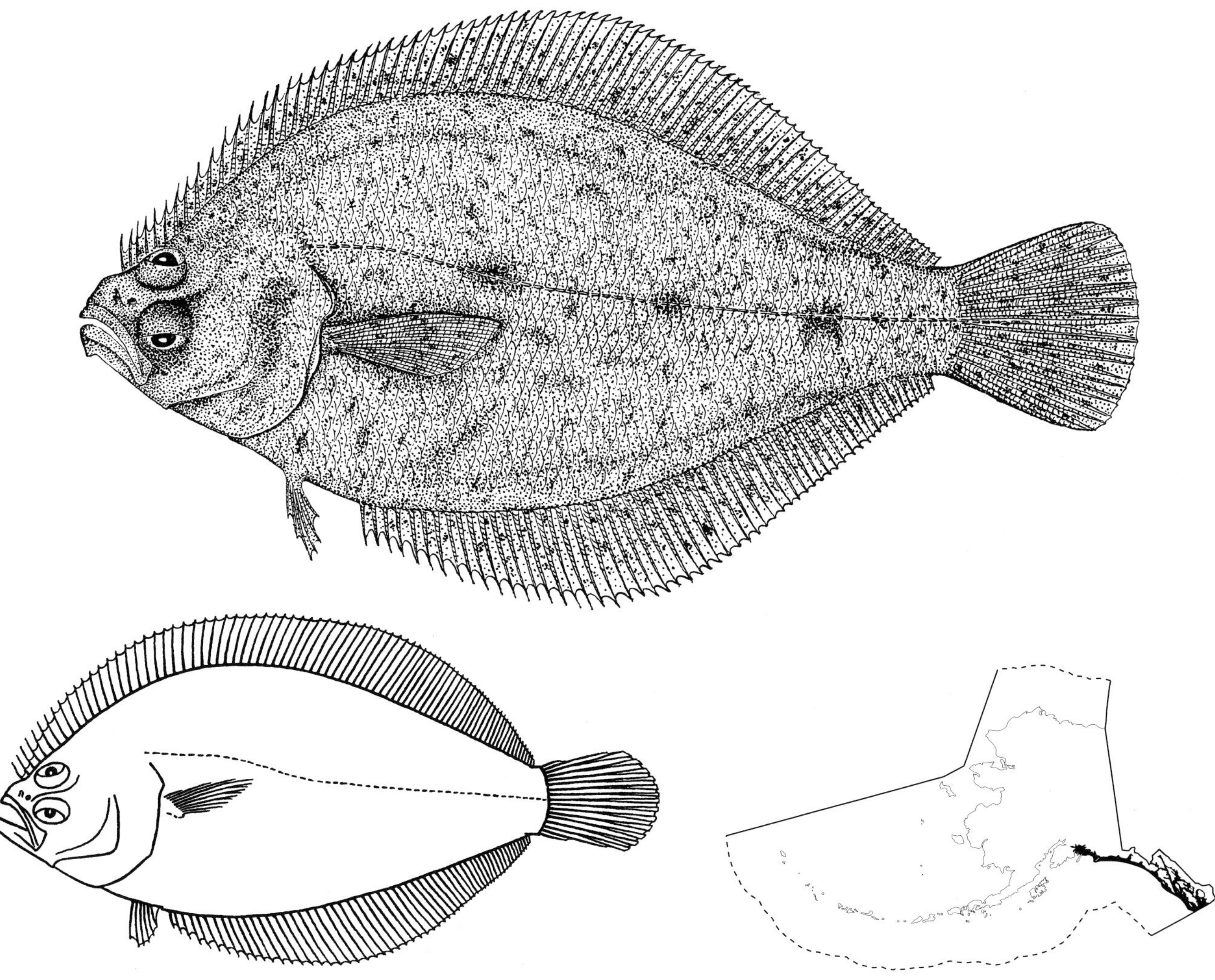

Notes & Sources — *Citharichthys stigmaeus* Jordan & Gilbert, 1882

Description: Norman 1934:143–144; Miller and Lea 1972: 204–205; Hart 1973:598–599; Matarese et al. 1989:570; Kramer et al. 1995:16–17.

Figures: Upper: Hart 1973:598; 15 cm TL. Lower: Norman 1934, fig. 96.

Range: Northern- and westernmost records are from western Prince William Sound at Hanning Bay, Montague Island, 59°58'N, 147°43'W (Townsend 1935); and McClure Bay, 60°30'N, 148°11'W (Orsi et al. 1991). From farther east, records include NMC 61-75 (1 specimen), taken at Monti Bay, northwest of Yakutat at 59°33'N, 139°47'W, depth 37–55 m; and NMC 61-72 (2 specimens), from nearby, at 59°32'N, 139°42'W, depth 0–1 m. A specimen collected from Saint John Baptist Bay (57°17'N, 135°35'W) was displayed in an ABL aquarium in 1988–1989 (B. L. Wing, pers. comm., 26 May 1998). The UW has specimens (UW 15578) from Shelikof Bay, a few kilometers to the south (approximately 57°08'N).

Family Pleuronectidae
Righteye flounders

In the Pleuronectidae the eyes and color are almost always on the right side of the body. The left side is the blind side, which faces or rests on the sea floor. This family includes flounders, soles, turbots, dabs, and plaice. None of these names is restricted to any one taxonomic group, and the names are often used interchangeably for the same species. Most righteye flounders inhabit cold seas. A few occur in the tropics or in brackish and fresh waters. The family is represented in Alaska by 26 species.

In contrast to lefteye flounders, in most righteye flounders the pelvic fins are symmetrically placed, with one on each side of the median ridge; all of the Alaskan righteye flounders have symmetrical pelvic fins. Righteye flounders are typically under 61 cm (2 ft) in length, but several species grow larger. The greatest length recorded, 267 cm (8.75 ft), was attained by a female Pacific halibut, *Hippoglossus stenolepis.*

Twenty-two species of righteye flounders, several of them commercially important, are well known from numerous records in Alaskan waters. Documentation for occurrence in Alaska consists of relatively few records for four other species: C-O sole, *Pleuronichthys coenosus*; curlfin sole, *P. decurrens*; roughscale sole, *Clidoderma asperrimum*; and Korean flounder, *Glyptocephalus stelleri.*

Righteye flounders new to the list of Alaskan species since they were inventoried by Quast and Hall (1972) are *Clidoderma asperrimum, Glyptocephalus stelleri,* and *Lepidopsetta polyxystra.* The roughscale sole, *C. asperrimum,* was first reported from the Aleutian Islands and Bering Sea in a general statement by Lea et al. (1989), and details of documentation for that report and additional records are cited in the species account in this book. The Korean flounder, *G. stelleri,* has been reported from time to time from Alaskan waters although none of the records proved to be unequivocal or verifiable. Lindberg and Fedorov (1993) recently reported a specimen from the vicinity of the Pribilof Islands, which is now permanently archived in the museum of the Pacific Ocean Scientific Research Institute of Fisheries and Oceanography (TINRO) at Vladivostok. Rock sole, *Lepidopsetta bilineata,* was redescribed by Orr and Matarese (2000), who recognized two distinct forms in the eastern Pacific and Bering Sea: southern rock sole, *L. bilineata,* ranging north only to the extreme southeastern Bering Sea; and a new species they call the northern rock sole, *L. polyxystra,* with a range north to St. Lawrence Island and west along the Aleutian Islands.

The existence of dark flounder, *Liopsetta obscura* (= *Pseudopleuronectes obscurus*), in Alaska has been questioned ever since the possibility was introduced by Norman (1934), who examined a specimen from "Alaska?" in the collection of A. M. Popov. All subsequent reports of the species from Alaska are derived from that reference. No other records of dark flounder have been cited for Alaska or adjacent waters, nor are there examples from the region in museum collections or resource databases. J. W. Orr (pers. comm., 6 Aug. 1998) confirmed the lack of dark flounder records in the NMFS survey database. B. A. Sheiko (pers. comm., 17 Aug. 1998) did not find vouchers in Russian Academy of Sciences collections at St. Petersburg or Petropavlovsk-Kamchatsky, or any records of occurrence outside of the Sea of Japan and southern Sea of Okhotsk; rather, he opined, the species is replaced northward in the Pacific Ocean and Bering Sea to the Arctic by *Pleuronectes glacialis.* The species probably does not occur in Alaska.

On the other hand, scalyeye plaice, *Acanthopsetta nadeshnyi,* is added to the inventory as a species to consider when identifying specimens taken in the western Bering Sea in or near U.S. waters. Fadeev (1987) reported *A. nadeshnyi* was taken near Cape Navarin, in close proximity to Alaskan waters.

Platichthys stellatus occasionally hybridizes with other species. The hybrid of *P. stellatus* and *Parophrys vetulus,* sometimes called forkline sole, is the most well known and is included in some faunal accounts. This form was named *Parophrys ischyrus* by Jordan and Gilbert (1880j), and later placed by Jordan and Goss (in Jordan 1885) in *Inopsetta.* Current rules of nomenclature (International Commission on Zoological Nomenclature 1999), however, do not allow binomens for hybrids. If the form ever is shown to be a distinct species, the binomen *Inopsetta ischyra* (Jordan & Gilbert, 1880) might apply. This hybrid is most well known from Puget Sound and is rarely found elsewhere. Jordan et al. (1930:226) indicated its range probably extends northward to Alaska, likely basing their statement on specimens listed as *Parophrys ischyrus* by T. H. Bean in E. W. Nelson's (1887) account of an expedition to Norton Sound. However, the description and illustration in that account seem to represent a different species or hybrid. The records nearest to Alaska that probably represent the hybrid of *Platichthys stellatus* and

Parophrys vetulus are those reported by Clemens and Wilby (1961) from southern British Columbia. Because the hybrid form is extralimital both geographically and biologically it is not included in this guide.

In recent years the revision of the Pleuronectidae by Sakamoto (1984), which was based on a detailed phenetic analysis, has been followed in lists of fishes and guides to eastern North Pacific species (e.g., Robins et al. 1991a, Kramer et al. 1995). However, that revision synonymized several genera with *Pleuronectes,* obscuring the differences among the groups. The monophyly of *Pleuronectes* as defined by Sakamoto (1984) was questioned by researchers (e.g., Chapleau 1993, Nelson 1994, Rass 1996) who noted the need for a cladistic analysis of the Pleuronectidae. Such an analysis was recently completed by Cooper and Chapleau (1998). They resurrected the genera *Isopsetta, Lepidopsetta, Limanda,* and *Parophrys* from synonymy in *Pleuronectes.* However, they classified *Atheresthes* as a junior synonym of *Reinhardtius* and *Embassichthys* as a synonym of *Microstomus,* and we retain *Atheresthes* and *Embassichthys* as separate genera. Other authors have made the same nomenclatural decision (e.g., Orr and Matarese 2000). This course has also been identified by J. S. Nelson and coworkers as the one that will be followed in the sixth edition of the American Fisheries Society list of fish names (draft dated 22 August 2001).

The identification key to the adults of pleuronectids of Alaska and adjacent waters begins with a modification of the couplet from Norman (1934) that separates the species into large- and small-mouthed forms. These are the tribes Hippoglossini and Pleuronectini of Li (1981), and although they are not monophyletic and have been reclassified by Cooper and Chapleau (1998) into a large number of tribes and subfamilies (see classification in the introduction to this guide), the two older groups are still useful for purposes of identification. In the large-mouthed group the mouth is symmetrical or nearly so; the maxilla on the eyed side is at least one-third the length of the head; and the dentition is about equally developed on the eyed and blind sides. Included in the large-mouthed group, in the order they key out and are presented in the following species accounts, are: *Hippoglossus, Psettichthys, Lyopsetta, Eopsetta, Acanthopsetta, Hippoglossoides, Reinhardtius,* and *Atheresthes.* In the small-mouthed group the mouth is asymmetrical, with the jaws on the blind side longer; the maxilla on the eyed side is one-third or less of the length of the head; and the teeth are primarily on the blind side. Alaskan genera in the small-mouthed group are: *Platichthys, Clidoderma, Pleuronectes, Lepidopsetta, Pleuronichthys, Parophrys, Isopsetta, Limanda, Embassichthys, Microstomus,* and *Glyptocephalus.*

Key to the Pleuronectidae of Alaska

1 Mouth large and almost symmetrical, with maxilla on eyed side extending well past mideye and measuring at least one-third of head length, and jaws and dentition nearly equally developed on both sides . . . . (2)

1 Mouth small and asymmetrical, with maxilla on eyed side not extending past mideye, measuring less than one-third of head length, and jaws and dentition better developed on blind side; asymmetry of jaws not always obvious, but mouth always small . . . . (11)

2 (1) Maxilla extending to below mideye or slightly beyond; with or without arch in lateral line . . . . (3)

2 Maxilla extending to posterior edge of eye or beyond; no distinct arch in lateral line . . . . (9)

3 (2) Lateral line strongly arched over pectoral fin; pectoral fin rays 14–19, usually 16 or more . . . . *Hippoglossus stenolepis,* page 823

3 Lateral line without distinct arch over pectoral fin; pectoral fin rays 8–13 . . . . (4)

4 (3) Anterior several dorsal fin rays elongate and mostly free; lateral line with accessory dorsal branch . . . . *Psettichthys melanostictus,* page 824

4 Anterior dorsal fin rays not elongate and mostly free; lateral line without accessory dorsal branch . . . . (5)

5 (4) Teeth in upper jaw in two rows . . . . (6)

5 Teeth in upper jaw in one row . . . . (7)

6 (5) Scales large and deciduous; jaws without distinct caniniform teeth . . . . *Lyopsetta exilis,* page 825

6 Scales small and adherent; jaws with caniniform teeth anteriorly . . . . *Eopsetta jordani,* page 826

7 (5) Eyes and snout densely scaled; scales ctenoid on both sides of body; lateral line distinctly arched above pectoral fin . . . . *Acanthopsetta nadeshnyi,* page 827 (not known from Alaska)

7 Eyes and snout not scaled; scales not ctenoid on both sides of body (scales cycloid on blind side); lateral line slightly curved above pectoral fin or nearly straight . . . . (8)

8 (7) Interorbital space with sharp ridge, nearly naked or with 1 or 2 rows of scales; gill rakers on lower limb of 1st arch usually more than 14, total usually more than 19 . . . . *Hippoglossoides elassodon,* page 828

8 Interorbital space flat, with 2–4 rows of scales; gill rakers on lower limb of 1st arch usually less than 13, total usually less than 17 . . . . *Hippoglossoides robustus,* page 829

9 (2) Blind side dark; posterior margin of preopercle forming right angle . . . . *Reinhardtius hippoglossoides,* page 830

9 Blind side light (gray); posterior margin of preopercle rounded . . . . (10)

10 (9) Portion of upper eye visible from blind side; gill rakers more than 14 on 1st arch, 2 on upper limb of 2nd arch . . . . *Atheresthes stomias,* page 831

10 Upper eye not visible from blind side; gill rakers less than 14 on 1st arch, 1 on upper limb of 2nd arch . . . . *Atheresthes evermanni,* page 832

11 (1) Tubercles on eyed side of body (in adults) . . . . (12)

11 Without tubercles on body, with or without tubercles on head . . . . (13)

12 (11) Tubercles not arranged in rows except along base of dorsal and anal fins; black bands on median fins . . . . *Platichthys stellatus,* page 833

12 Larger tubercles arranged in about 6 irregular rows; without black bands on median fins . . . . *Clidoderma asperrimum,* page 834

13 (11) Postocular ridge with 4–7 bony knobs . . . . *Pleuronectes quadrituberculatus,* page 835

13 Postocular ridge with 2 or without bony tubercles, with or without bony tubercles elsewhere on head . . . . (14)

14 (13) Postocular ridge prominent, rugose, terminating in a larger and a smaller low protuberance .... *Pleuronectes glacialis,* page 836

14 Postocular ridge not as above .... (15)

15 (14) Lateral line with accessory dorsal branch .... (16)

15 Lateral line without accessory dorsal branch .... (21)

16 (15) Lateral line with distinct, high arch; accessory dorsal branch of lateral line not extending beyond operculum .... (17)

16 Lateral line without high arch; accessory dorsal branch of lateral line usually extending beyond operculum .... (18)

17 (16) Total gill raker count on 1st arch 10 or less, on upper limb 3 or less, typically blunt and robust; blind side with muscle bands highlighted with glossy white, especially on anterior portion of body; supraorbital pores more than 4 .... *Lepidopsetta bilineata,* page 837

17 Total gill raker count on 1st arch 10 or more, on upper limb more than 3, typically pointed and slender; blind side uniform creamy white, without glossy white highlights; supraorbital pores less than 4 .... *Lepidopsetta polyxystra,* page 838

18 (16) Anterior 4–12 dorsal fin rays on blind side .... (19)

18 Only anterior 1 or 2 rays on blind side .... (20)

19 (18) Anterior 4–6 dorsal fin rays on blind side; dorsal fin origin above level of angle of jaw, level with upper lip .... *Pleuronichthys coenosus,* page 839

19 Anterior 9–12 dorsal fin rays on blind side; dorsal fin origin below level of angle of mouth .... *Pleuronichthys decurrens,* page 840

20 (18) Head and snout noticeably elongate and pointed; upper eye visible from blind side; scales on eyed side mostly cycloid (smooth) .... *Parophrys vetulus,* page 841

20 Head and snout not noticeably elongate; upper eye not visible from blind side; scales on eyed side strongly ctenoid (rough) .... *Isopsetta isolepis,* page 842

21 (15) Lateral line with distinct, high arch .... (22)

21 Lateral line with low curve or nearly straight .... (24)

22 (21) Profile concave above eyes, snout noticeably produced; maxilla scarcely extending to below anterior edge of eye .... *Limanda proboscidea,* page 843

22 Profile not concave above eyes, snout not noticeably produced; maxilla extending to below anterior part of eye .... (23)

23 (22) Scales on eyed side ctenoid or cycloid, most with 1 spinule, some with 2 or 3; body relatively deep; median fins yellowish; narrow black line at base of dorsal and anal fins (lines fade in preservative) .... *Limanda aspera,* page 844

23 Scales on eyed side mostly ctenoid, with 3–10 spinules; body relatively elongate; median fins brown; without black line at base of dorsal and anal fins .... *Limanda sakhalinensis,* page 845

24 (21) Body deep, about 43–50% TL; upper profile sharply ascending above upper eye, head projecting in front of general profile . . . . *Embassichthys bathybius,* page 846

24 Body elongate, about 28–40% TL; upper profile gradually ascending, head in line with general profile . . . . (25)

25 (24) Teeth primarily on blind side; without large cavities in blind side of head . . . . *Microstomus pacificus,* page 847

25 Teeth well developed on both sides; blind side of head with large cavities . . . . (26)

26 (25) Pectoral fin on eyed side longer than head; snout scaled; anal spine strong; anal fin rays usually more than 80; vertebrae 62–66 . . . . *Glyptocephalus zachirus,* page 848

26 Pectoral fin on eyed side shorter than or equal to head length; snout not scaled; anal fin rays usually less than 80; vertebrae 49–55 . . . . *Glyptocephalus stelleri,* page 849

Hippoglossus stenolepis Schmidt, 1904 **Pacific halibut**

Chukchi Sea to eastern Pacific Ocean off Punta Chamalu, northern Baja California;and to western Pacific Ocean and Japan and Okhotsk seas off Hokkaido.

On a variety of bottom types at depths of 6–1,100 m, usually shallower than 300 m.

D 89–109; A 64–81; Pec 14–19; Pel 6; LLs 145–190; GR 1–2 + 7–10; Vert 16 + 35 (49–51).

- Eyed side grayish to greenish brown or black with dark and light mottling; blind side white.
- Body rather elongate.
- Maxilla extending to below mideye or beyond.
- Anal spine pronounced.
- **Pectoral fin rays usually 16 or more; caudal fin emarginate or double emarginate.**
- **Lateral line strongly arched above pectoral fin.**
- Scales smooth (cycloid), small, adherent.
- Teeth on both jaws large and conical; two rows on upper jaw, one on lower.
- **Gill rakers short and stout.**
- Length to 267 cm TL, weight about 226 kg, but reported to 363 kg; average size in commercial catch about 15 kg.

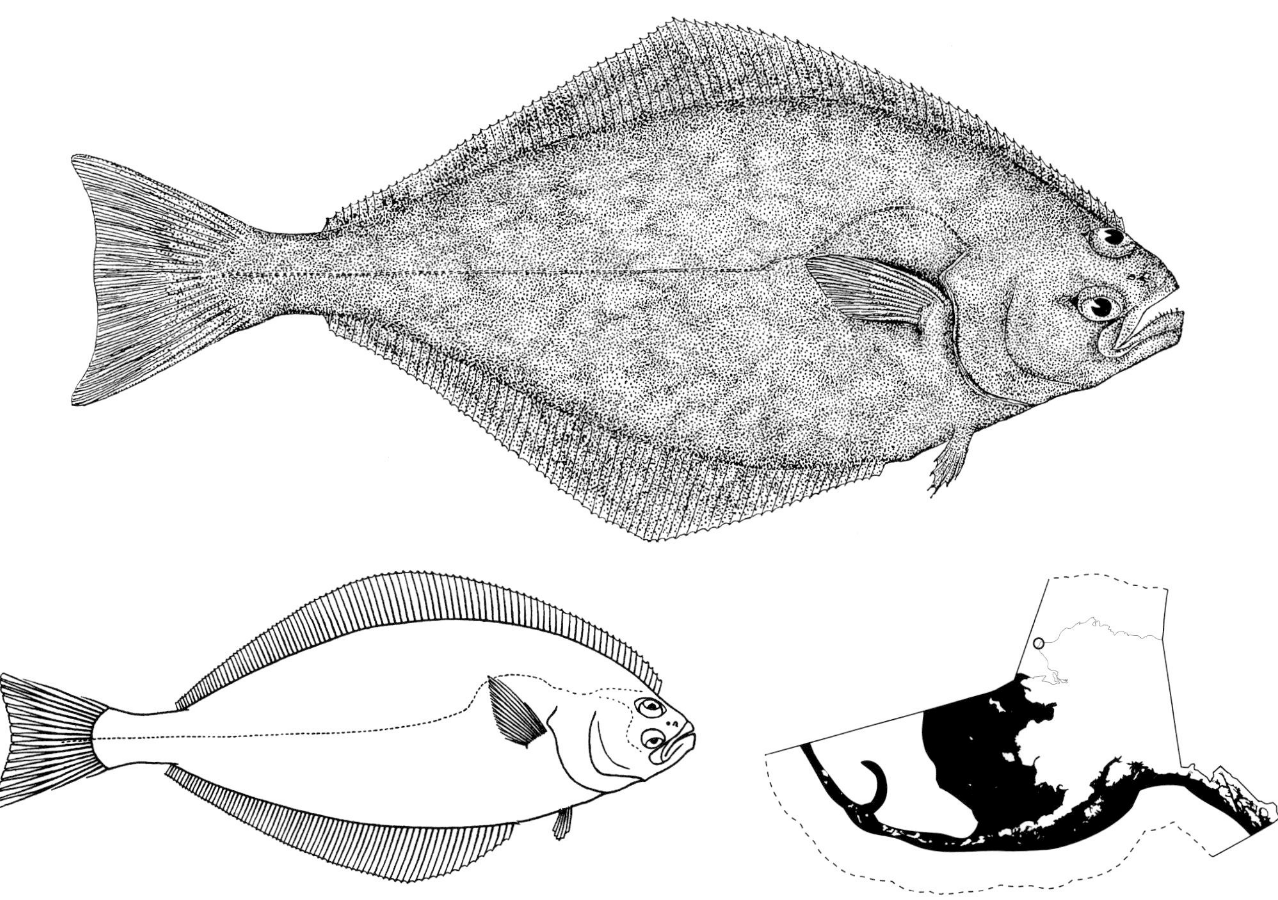

Notes & Sources — *Hippoglossus stenolepis* Schmidt, 1904

Description: Norman 1934:293–294; Hart 1973:614–616; Sakamoto in Masuda et al. 1984:351; Kramer et al. 1995: 54–55.

Figures: Upper: Hart 1973:614, modified; 65 cm TL. Lower: Norman 1934, fig. 218, modified.

Range: Distribution of this well-known species in the Bering Sea and northeastern North Pacific Ocean was mapped by Allen and Smith (1988) from NMFS demersal surveys spanning more than 30 years. Pacific halibut are not often found as far north as the Chukchi Sea. The only record north of the southernmost region of the Chukchi Sea may be that of Barber et al. (1997), who included *H. stenolepis* on a list of fishes taken in 1990 and 1991 UAF bottom trawl surveys of the northeastern Chukchi Sea; *H. stenolepis* was taken at one station in the 1990 survey but was not found in the 1991 survey. Number of specimens and locality were not given by Barber et al. (1997) and voucher specimens of *H. stenolepis* are not among the survey vouchers at the UAF (C.W.M.). However, the unpublished haul-catch listing for the survey (*Ocean Hope III* cruise 90-2) gives one specimen weighing 1.2 kg in haul 30, at 68°58'N, 166°19'W (off Cape Lisburne), depth 27 m.

Size: Eschmeyer and Herald (1983), except average commercial weight of 15 kg is from Kramer et al. (1995).

Psettichthys melanostictus Girard, 1854 **sand sole**

Southeastern Bering Sea from Unalaska Island to Port Heiden, and Gulf of Alaska to Pacific Ocean off southern California at Redondo Beach.

Sandy bottom at depths of 1–325 m, typically shallower than 150 m.

D 72–90; A 53–66; Pec 10–12; Pel 6; LLs 98–118; GR 5–7 + 14–18; Vert 11–12 + 28–30 (37–41).

- Eyed side light green or gray to brown; head and body with fine, dark brown to black speckles; blind side white.
- Body rather elongate.
- Maxilla extending to below mideye or nearly to mideye.
- Anal spine pronounced.
- **First 4–9 dorsal rays elongate and largely free**; caudal fin rounded.
- Lateral line slightly curved above pectoral fin; **accessory dorsal branch extending below first 18–22 dorsal fin rays**.
- Scales on eyed side small, ctenoid, giving skin the texture of fine sandpaper.
- **Teeth large, single series in each jaw with a few caniniform teeth anteriorly**.
- Length to 63 cm TL, weight to more than 2.3 kg.

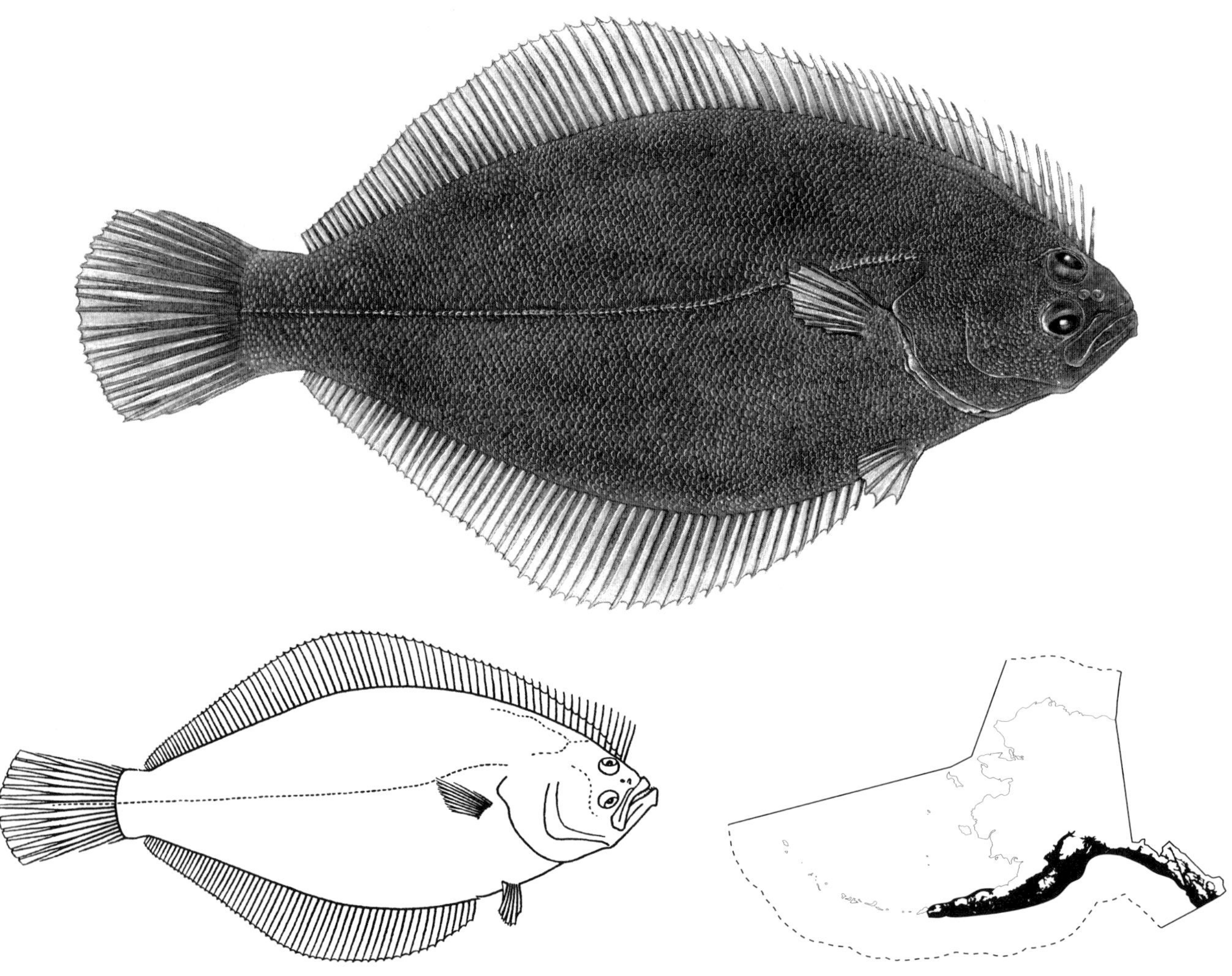

Notes & Sources — *Psettichthys melanostictus* Girard, 1854

Description: Lockington 1879:76–78; Norman 1934:310–311; Hart 1973:636–637; Kramer et al. 1995:92–93.

Figures: Upper: University of British Columbia, artist P. Drukker-Brammall, Jan. 1974; UBC 60-416, 248 mm SL, Queen Charlotte Islands, British Columbia. Lower: Norman 1934, fig. 230, modified.

Range: NMFS resource surveys extended the known range west to Unalaska Island and east in the Bering Sea to northwest of Port Heiden, and provided additional records of occurrence along Gulf of Alaska coasts and south to Eureka, California (Allen and Smith 1988).

Lyopsetta exilis (Jordan & Gilbert, 1880) **slender sole**

Gulf of Alaska east of Kodiak Island at Albatross Bank to Pacific Ocean off southern Baja California west of Punta Pequeña and Punta San Juanico.

Silty or muddy bottoms at depths of 10–800 m, usually 50–350 m.

D 72–88; A 57–66; Pec 10; Pel 6; LLs 65–73; GR 2–3 + 9–11; Vert 11–13 + 32–35 (42–47).

- Eyed side pale olive brown to reddish brown; fins mostly dusky; blind side whitish to pale orange.
- **Body elongate**.
- Upper eye touching edge of head, sometimes partially visible from blind side; **interorbital space with high ridge** extending to lateral line.
- Maxilla extending to or almost to mideye.
- Anal spine pronounced.
- Caudal fin rounded or double truncate.
- Lateral line gently sloping anteriorly.
- **Scales large and deciduous**, often missing from trawl-caught fish; ctenoid on eyed side, mostly ctenoid on blind side.
- **Teeth in two rows on upper jaw, a little enlarged anteriorly but none distinctly caniniform**.
- Length to 35 cm TL, most less than 25 cm.

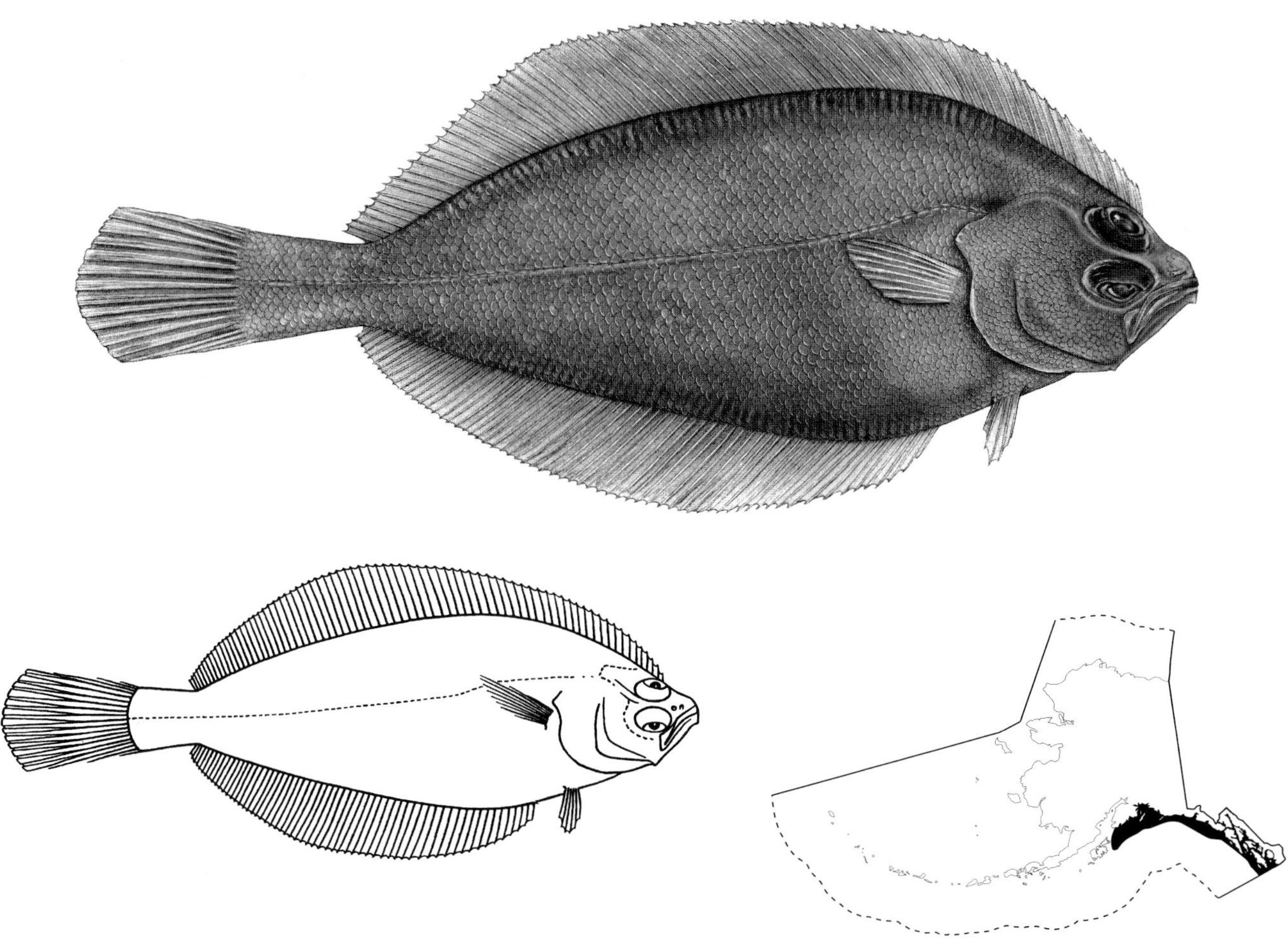

Notes & Sources — *Lyopsetta exilis* (Jordan & Gilbert, 1880)
Hippoglossoides exilis Jordan & Gilbert, 1880
Eopsetta exilis: Sakamoto 1984.

Description: Jordan and Gilbert 1880f; Norman 1934: 306–307; Hart 1973:625–626; Kramer et al. 1995:42–43.

Figures: Upper: University of British Columbia, artist P. Drukker-Brammall, Feb. 1967; UBC 56-91, 201 mm SL, British Columbia. Lower: Norman 1934, fig. 227, modified.

Range: Recorded west in Gulf of Alaska to north Albatross Bank (Allen and Smith 1988). Southernmost known limit of range was extended by catches at 26°04'N, 113°30'W and 26°37'N, 113°55'W at trawl depths of 225–235 m in 1977, documented by Snytko (1987).

Eopsetta jordani (Lockington, 1879) **petrale sole**

Aleutian Islands west at least as far as Unalaska Island, and Gulf of Alaska to northern Baja California off Coronado Islands.

Sandy and muddy bottoms from near shore in shallow water to depth of about 550 m, usually taken at 50–300 m.

D 82–103; A 62–80; Pec 13; Pel 6; LLs 88–100; GR 5 + 14–17; Vert 11 + 30–34 (41–45).

- Eyed side dark to light brown; blind side white; **caudal fin membranes mostly brownish**.
- Body ovate.
- Mandibular articulation rounded.
- Maxilla extending to mideye or slightly beyond; **interorbital space wide and flat, with 4 or 5 rows of scales**.
- Anal spine pronounced.
- Dorsal fin without elongate free rays at origin; caudal fin slightly rounded or double truncate.
- Lateral line gently sloping anteriorly.
- **Scales small and adherent**; mostly ctenoid on eyed side, cycloid on blind side.
- **Two rows of small, arrow-shaped teeth on upper jaw**, one row on lower jaw.
- Length to 70 cm TL, weight to 3.6 kg.

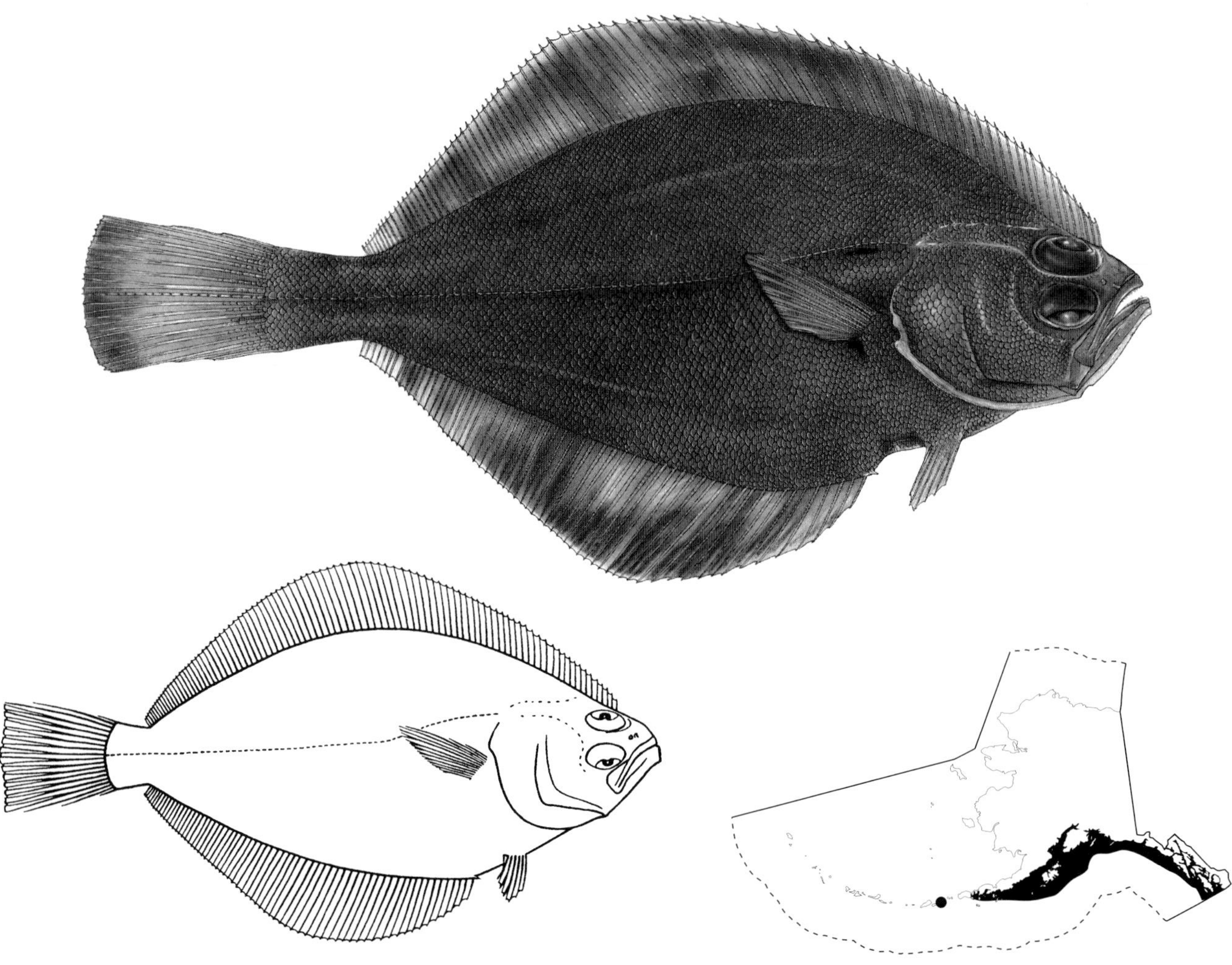

Notes & Sources — *Eopsetta jordani* (Lockington, 1879)
Hippoglossoides jordani Lockington, 1879

Description: Lockington 1879:73–75; Norman 1934:307–308; Hart 1973:607–609; Kramer et al. 1995:44–45.

Figures: Upper: University of British Columbia, artist P. Drukker-Brammall, Mar. 1967; UBC 63-1026, 174 mm SL, Kodiak Island area, Alaska. Lower: Norman 1934, fig. 228.

Range: A specimen collected from Unalaska by Townsend (1887, cited in Evermann and Goldsborough 1907) and identified as *H. jordani* is the only historical record that supports the frequently seen statement that this species is distributed in the Bering Sea and Aleutian Islands. Allen and Smith (1988) reported that in more than 30 years of NMFS demersal surveys, which yielded 1,066 occurrences of *E. jordani,* the species was taken only as far west as the Alaska Peninsula near Kupreanof Point.

Acanthopsetta nadeshnyi Schmidt, 1904 **scalyeye plaice**

Western Bering Sea from Cape Navarin to Pacific Ocean off Hokkaido, southern Sea of Okhotsk, and Sea of Japan to Korea.

Sandy bottom at depths of 29–900 m, and probably deeper; usually taken in deep water.

Pec 9–13; Pel 6; LLs 73–92; GR 3–8 + 7–12; Vert 9–11 + 30–31 (39–42).

- Eyed side uniform dark brown; median fins paler; blind side white.
- Body ovate.
- Maxilla not reaching to below middle of eye.
- Anal spine pronounced.
- Dorsal fin origin above middle to posterior part of eye; caudal fin slightly rounded.
- **Lateral line distinctly arched above pectoral fin**.
- **Scales ctenoid on both sides**; dorsal and anal fin rays more or less scaled on both sides; **snout and upper surface of eyes densely scaled** (except in juveniles).
- **Teeth small, pointed, in single row on both jaws, scarcely enlarged anteriorly**.
- Length to 46 cm TL.

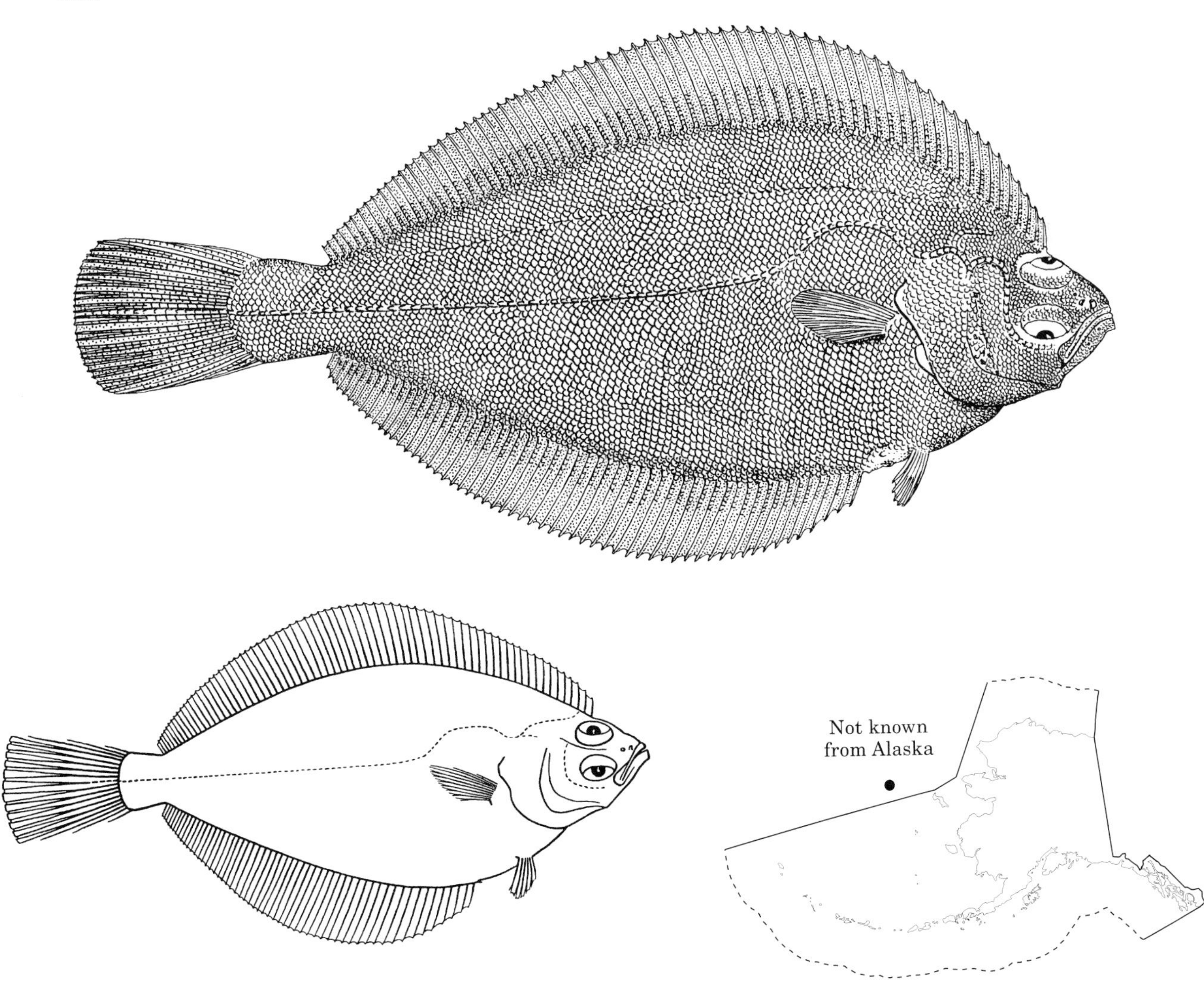

Notes & Sources — *Acanthopsetta nadeshnyi* Schmidt, 1904
Hippoglossoides jordani Lockington, 1879

Description: Hubbs 1915:464–465; Norman 1934:303; Sakamoto in Masuda et al. 1984:351; Lindberg and Fedorov 1993:108–110; Kramer et al. 1995:32–33.

Figures: Upper: Lindberg and Fedorov 1993, fig. 38; 119 mm TL, Sea of Japan. Lower: Norman 1934, fig. 228.

Range: Taranetz (1935a, 1937) reported the known range of *A. nadeshnyi* to extend north in the western Bering Sea to Olyutorskiy Bay. Lindberg and Fedorov (1993) reported it from farther north, off Cape Navarin. Found at great densities as deep as 900 m in winter in northern Sea of Japan, indicating that assemblages probably extend even deeper, probably to 1,000–1,200 m (Kim Sen Tok et al. 1999).

Size: Fadeev 1987.

Hippoglossoides elassodon Jordan & Gilbert, 1880 **flathead sole**

Bering Sea and Aleutian Islands to northern California off Monterey, and to southern Sea of Okhotsk and northern Sea of Japan.

Silty or muddy bottoms from near shore to depth of about 1,050 m, usually less than 366 m.

D 70–94; A 54–73; Pec 9–14; Pel 6; LLs 84–120; GR 2–5 + 14–25; Vert 12–14 + 32–35 (43–47).

- Eyed side brownish; **dorsal and anal fins blotched**; blind side translucent, with white area in center extending above lateral line; **caudal fin membranes mostly clear**.
- Body ovate; **strongly compressed**, especially in small fish.
- Lower jaw projecting, symphyseal knob present; mandibular articulation pointed.
- Maxilla extending to below mideye or beyond.
- **Interorbital space narrow, with sharp ridge, nearly naked or with 1 or 2 rows of scales**.
- Anal spine pronounced.
- Caudal fin rounded or double truncate.
- Lateral line slightly curved above pectoral fin or nearly straight.
- Scales strongly ctenoid on eyed side, mostly cycloid on blind side; dorsal and anal fin rays scaled.
- Teeth conical, in single row in each jaw; anterior teeth enlarged but not distinctly caniniform.
- **Gill rakers on lower limb of 1st arch usually more than 14, total usually more than 19**.
- Length to 56 cm TL.

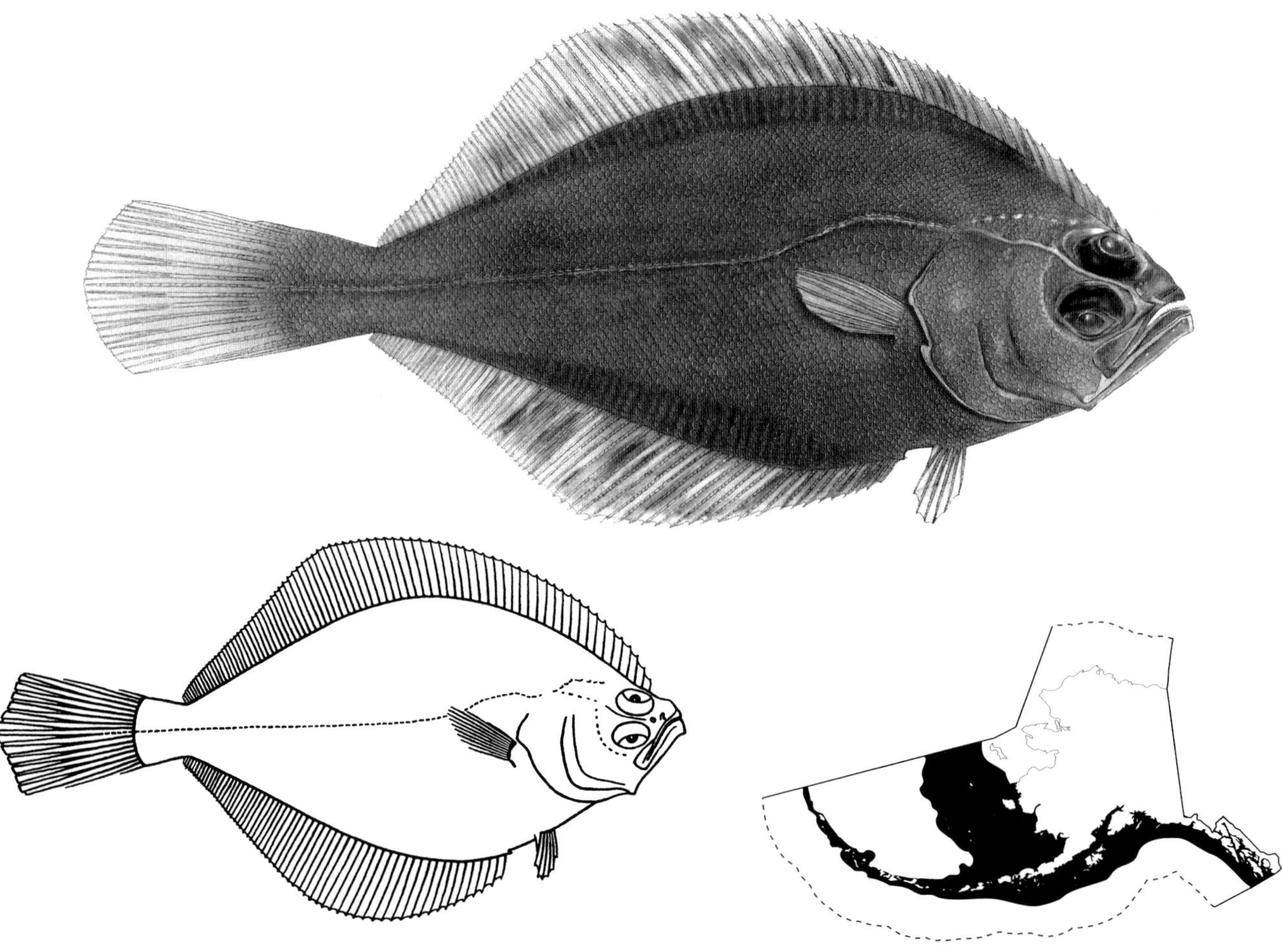

Notes & Sources — *Hippoglossoides elassodon* Jordan & Gilbert, 1880

Also called paper sole and cigarette paper, from the extremely flat (compressed) body and head.

Description: Jordan and Gilbert 1880j:278–279; Norman 1934:299–300; Hart 1973:612–613; Forrester et al. 1977; Sakamoto in Masuda et al. 1984:351; Lindberg and Fedorov 1993:97–101; Kramer et al. 1995:50–51.

Figures: Upper: University of British Columbia, artist P. Drukker-Brammall, Mar. 1967; UBC 65-94, 136 mm SL, near Nagai Island, Alaska. Lower: Norman, fig. 221.

Range: Taken as far west in the Aleutian chain as Stalemate Bank and the Commander Islands and as far north as the Gulf of Anadyr in NMFS surveys (Allen and Smith 1988). Reports of this species from the Chukchi Sea (e.g., Quast and Hall 1972) are probably of *H. robustus* (Allen and Smith 1988). Not reported in surveys of the northeastern Chukchi Sea in 1989–1991 by Barber et al. (1997).

Hippoglossoides robustus Gill & Townsend, 1897 **Bering flounder**

Chukchi Sea, and possibly Beaufort Sea, to Bering Sea off Alaska Peninsula and west to Akutan Island; to western Bering Sea and Pacific Ocean to Sea of Okhotsk and northern Sea of Japan off Hokkaido.

Soft bottom at depths of 18–425 m, usually shallower than 150 m.

D 66–80; A 51–64; Pec 8–12; Pel 6; LLs 85–95; GR 1–4 + 8–17; Vert 12–13 + 32 (44–47).

- Eyed side reddish brown to grayish brown; **dorsal and anal fins not blotched**; blind side white; **caudal fin membranes mostly clear**, sometimes with dark smudges.
- Body ovate.
- Lower jaw projecting, symphyseal knob present; mandibular articulation pointed.
- Maxilla extending to below mideye or a little beyond.
- **Interorbital space narrow, flat, with 2–4 rows of scales**.
- Anal spine pronounced.
- Caudal fin rounded or double truncate.
- Lateral line slightly curved above pectoral fin.
- Scales variable, more or less ctenoid on eyed side, ctenoid or cycloid on blind side; dorsal and anal fin rays scaled.
- Teeth conical, in single row in each jaw; anterior teeth enlarged but not distinctly caniniform.
- **Gill rakers on lower limb of 1st arch usually less than 13, total usually less than 17**.
- Length to 52 cm TL.

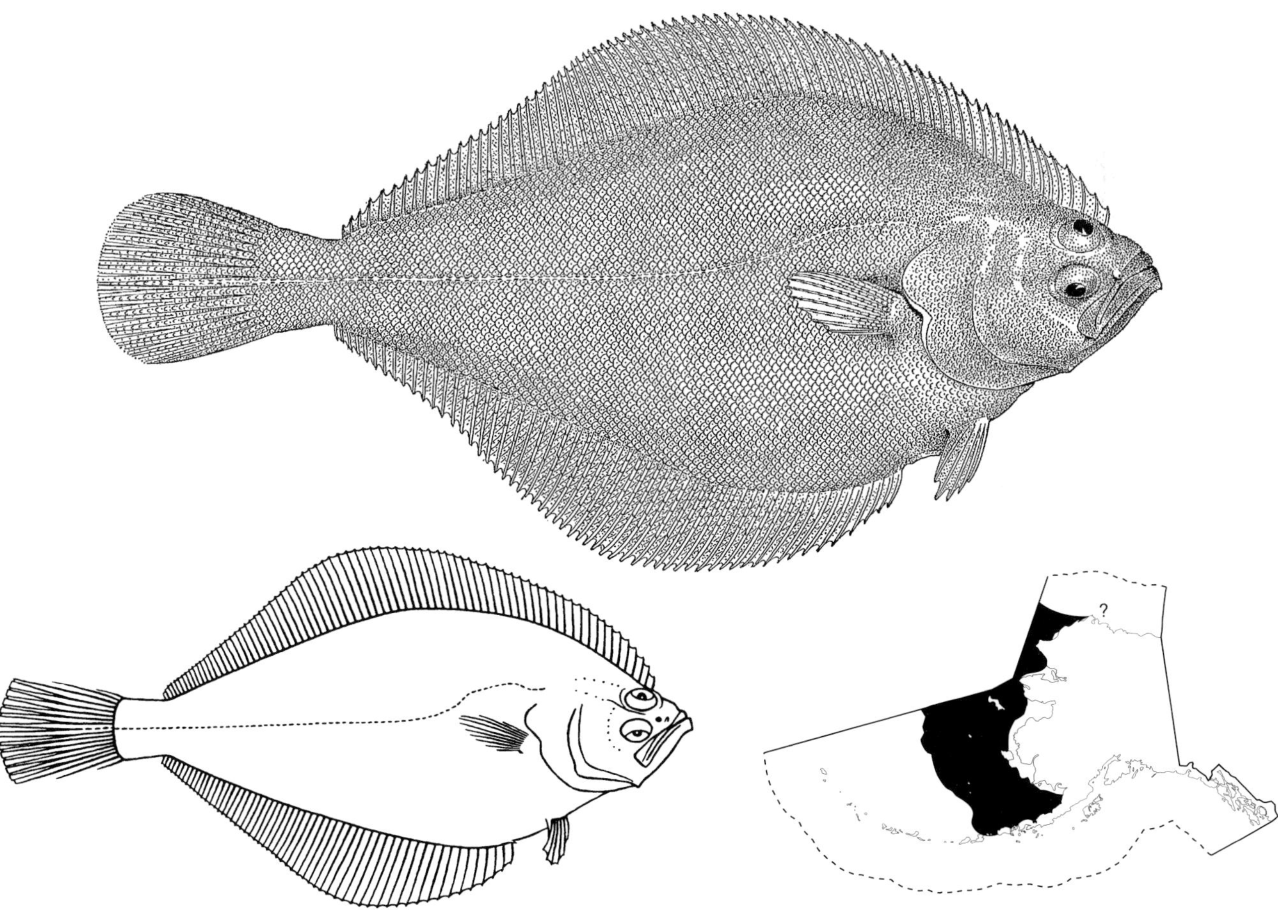

Notes & Sources — *Hippoglossoides robustus* Gill & Townsend, 1897
Hippoglossoides propinquus Hubbs, 1915

Description: Hubbs 1915:469–470; Norman 1934:302; Forrester et al. 1977; Sakamoto in Masuda et al. 1984:351; Kramer et al. 1995:52–53.

Figures: Upper: Hubbs 1915, pl. 26, fig. 5; 383 mm TL, Aniwa Bay, Sakhalin. Lower: Norman 1934, fig. 223, modified.

Range: Described by Gill and Townsend (1897) from *Albatross* station 3541, 56°14'N, 164°08'W. Recorded from the Chukchi Sea near Icy Cape (about 70°N) by Quast (1972), and west off the Aleutian Islands to northwest of Akutan Island by Allen and Smith (1988). In surveys of the northeastern Chukchi Sea this flounder was the most abundant pleuronectid by numbers of fish in 1990 and second most abundant in 1991 (Barber et al. 1997). The haul-catch listing for the 1990 survey (unpublished) lists records of *H. robustus* as far north as 71°49'W, 168°49'W; this suggests the species may occur in the Beaufort Sea as well.

Size: Fadeev 1987.

Reinhardtius hippoglossoides (Walbaum, 1792) **Greenland halibut**

Beaufort and Chukchi seas to eastern Pacific Ocean off northern Baja California near Coronado Islands, and western Pacific to Seas of Okhotsk and Japan; Atlantic Ocean from Greenland to Gulf of Maine.

Soft bottom at depths of 14–2,000 m, usually at 50–650 m; largest specimens at the greater depths.

D 83–109; A 62–84; Pec 11–15; Pel 5–7; LLs 105–119; GR 2–6 + 10–16; Vert 17–19 + 43–46 (60–64).

- **Eyed side dark purplish brown to black; blind side dark.**
- Body elongate.
- **Lower jaw large, projecting.**
- Upper eye visible from blind side; interorbital space flat.
- Maxilla extending to below posterior part of eye or beyond eye; **preopercle with right angle at posterior margin and 4 or 5 pores near edge.**
- Anal spine absent.
- **Dorsal fin origin at rear of or beyond upper eye**; caudal fin slightly emarginate.
- **Lateral line nearly straight**, slightly sloping above pectoral fin.
- Scales small and smooth (cycloid).
- Gill rakers short and blunt.
- Length to 130 cm TL, weight to more than 11.3 kg; average commercial fish about 63.5 cm, 2.3–4.1 kg.

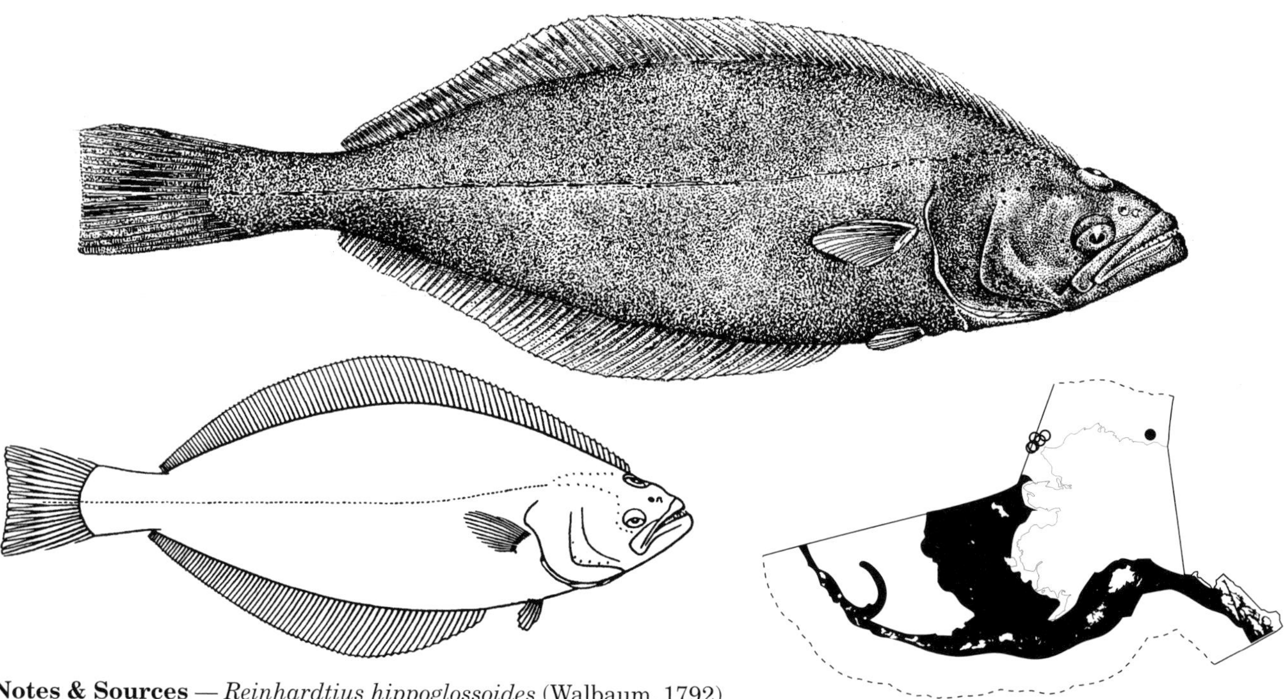

Notes & Sources — *Reinhardtius hippoglossoides* (Walbaum, 1792)
Pleuronectes hippoglossoides Walbaum, 1792
Reinhardtius hippoglossoides matsuurae Jordan & Snyder, 1901, is considered a valid subspecies by some workers (e.g., Lindberg and Fedorov 1993, Sheiko and Fedorov 2000); called Pacific black halibut (Andriashev 1954).

Description: Norman 1934:289–290; Andriashev 1954:474–477; Hubbs and Wilimovsky 1964; Hart 1973:638–639; Sakamoto in Masuda et al. 1984:351; Lindberg and Fedorov 1993:74–77; Kramer et al. 1995: 94–95.

Figures: Upper: Andriashev 1954, fig. 278; 40 cm TL, western Greenland. Lower: Norman 1934, fig. 216.

Range: Reported in NMFS surveys in Alaska as far north as Shishmaref, and most abundantly in Bering Sea (Allen and Smith 1988). UAF surveys of northeastern Chukchi Sea found Greenland halibut in 1990 but not in 1991 (Barber et al. 1997). Voucher specimens of this species from the 1990 survey were not saved, but the unpublished haul-catch listing (*Ocean Hope III,* cruise 90-2) shows one or two individuals weighing less than 45 g each were caught in each of six hauls at depths of 40–51 m (circles on above map); the northernmost was haul 43, at 69°38'N, 167°16'W, depth 46 m. The only record from the Beaufort Sea (NMC 74-282A) is a 26-cm-SL specimen collected in 1972 from about 81 km northeast of Brownlow Point, Alaska, at 70°51'N, 145°17'W at a depth of 357 m, and identified by D. W. McAllister. N. Alfonso (pers. comm., 15 Feb. 2001) confirmed the identification and provided records (NMC 93-0117 and 93-0118; over 40 cm) from southwest of Banks Island, N.W.T. Previously the nearest Canadian Arctic records were from northern Hudson Bay (Hunter et al. 1984, Coad 1995). Greenland halibut are least common in Alaska in the eastern Gulf of Alaska. Four females averaging 95 cm FL were caught in one longline set on 1 Jun. 1988 in Chatham Strait near Funter Bay at depth of 602 m (M. F. Sigler, pers. comm., 23 Mar. 2001). On 15 Aug. 1994 T.A.M. caught a 31-cm specimen while recreational fishing off Aaron Island, Favorite Channel. The species is rare south of Alaska (Eschmeyer and Herald 1983). On 5 Feb. 1994 a specimen (RBCM 994-121-1) was caught at 53°22'N, 133°10'W, in Rennell Sound near Graham Island, depth 585–622 m. Previously known in British Columbia from one record at La Perouse Bank (Westrheim and Pletcher 1966).

Size: Fadeev 1987, Kramer et al. 1995.

Atheresthes stomias (Jordan & Gilbert, 1880) **arrowtooth flounder**

Bering Sea from near Cape Navarin to Aleutian Islands and to Pacific Ocean off central California at San Simeon, and along east coast of Kamchatka to Commander Islands.

Soft bottom at depths of 12–900 m, usually offshore at depths of 50–300 m.

D 92–115; A 72–99; Pec 14–15; Pel 6; LLs about 135; GR 3–5 + 10–16; Vert 12 + 35–38 (47–50).

- Eyed side dark brown; scales darker at edges; blind side off-white to light gray.
- **Upper eye visible from blind side**.
- Body rather elongate.
- Maxilla extending to below posterior edge of eye or beyond; preopercle rounded.
- Anal spine absent.
- Dorsal fin origin over middle of eye; caudal fin emarginate to slightly forked.
- Lateral line slightly curved above pectoral fin.
- Scales large and mostly smooth (only weakly ctenoid).
- Teeth conical, sharp, widely spaced, largest and caniniform in front.
- Gill rakers long and slender; **more than 14 rakers on 1st arch**; **2 on upper limb of 2nd arch**; flat, spiny plates at each end of gill raker row and between some rakers are not counted.
- Length to 86 cm TL, weight to 7.7 kg.

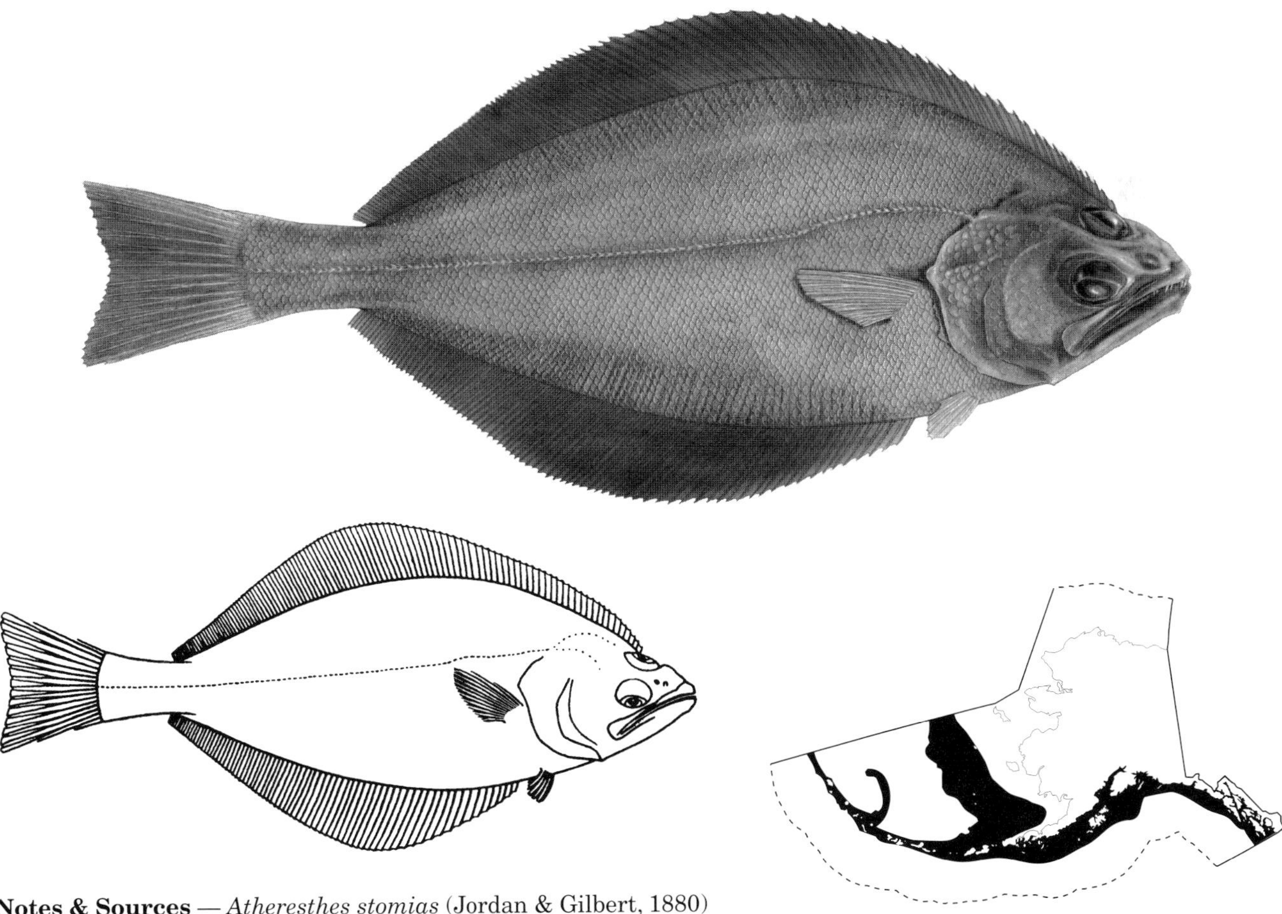

Notes & Sources — *Atheresthes stomias* (Jordan & Gilbert, 1880)
Platysomatichthys stomias Jordan & Gilbert, 1880
Reinhardtius stomias: Cooper and Chapleau 1998.

Description: Jordan and Gilbert 1880m; Norman 1934: 287; Wilimovsky et al. 1967:39–52; Hart 1973:602–603; Yang 1988; Kramer et al. 1995:36–37.

Figures: Upper: University of British Columbia, artist P. Drukker-Brammall, Sep. 1967; UBC 62-565, 170 mm SL, Bering Sea east of St. George Island. Lower: Norman 1934, fig. 214.

Range: *Atheresthes stomias* and *A. evermanni* have both generally been considered to represent *A. stomias* in fisheries surveys (Ranck et al. 1986). Reports of this species from the Chukchi Sea are probably misidentifications (Allen and Smith 1988). Zimmerman and Goddard (1996) mapped distribution of each species of *Atheresthes* in the eastern Bering Sea, Aleutian Islands, and western Gulf of Alaska. In areas where the two occur together, *A. stomias* occupy greater depths than *A. evermanni*. Hart (1973) reported *A. stomias* to be abundant off British Columbia. Allen and Smith (1988) identified the San Pedro record of Miller and Lea (1972) as *Eopsetta exilis*, and gave a range for *A. stomias* to San Simeon.

Atheresthes evermanni Jordan & Starks, 1904 **Kamchatka flounder**

Bering Sea from Gulf of Anadyr to Aleutian Islands and southwestern Gulf of Alaska, and to Sea of Okhotsk and northern Sea of Japan.

Soft bottom at depths of 25–1,200 m, usually taken at 50–500 m.

D 97–117; A 73–95; Pec 11–16; Pel 6; LLs 86–118; GR 2–3 + 9–12; Vert 10–12 + 35–41 (47–53).

- Eyed side dark brown; blind side off-white.
- **Upper eye not visible from blind side**.
- Body rather elongate.
- Maxilla extending to below posterior edge of eye or beyond; preopercle rounded.
- Anal spine absent.
- Dorsal fin origin over middle of eye; caudal fin emarginate.
- Lateral line gradually rising to slightly curved above pectoral fin.
- Scales large and slightly rough (weakly ctenoid).
- Teeth conical, sharp, widely spaced, largest and caniniform in front.
- Gill rakers long and slender; **less than 14 rakers on 1st arch**; **1 on upper limb of 2nd arch**; flat, spiny plates are not included in counts.
- Length to about 110 cm TL.

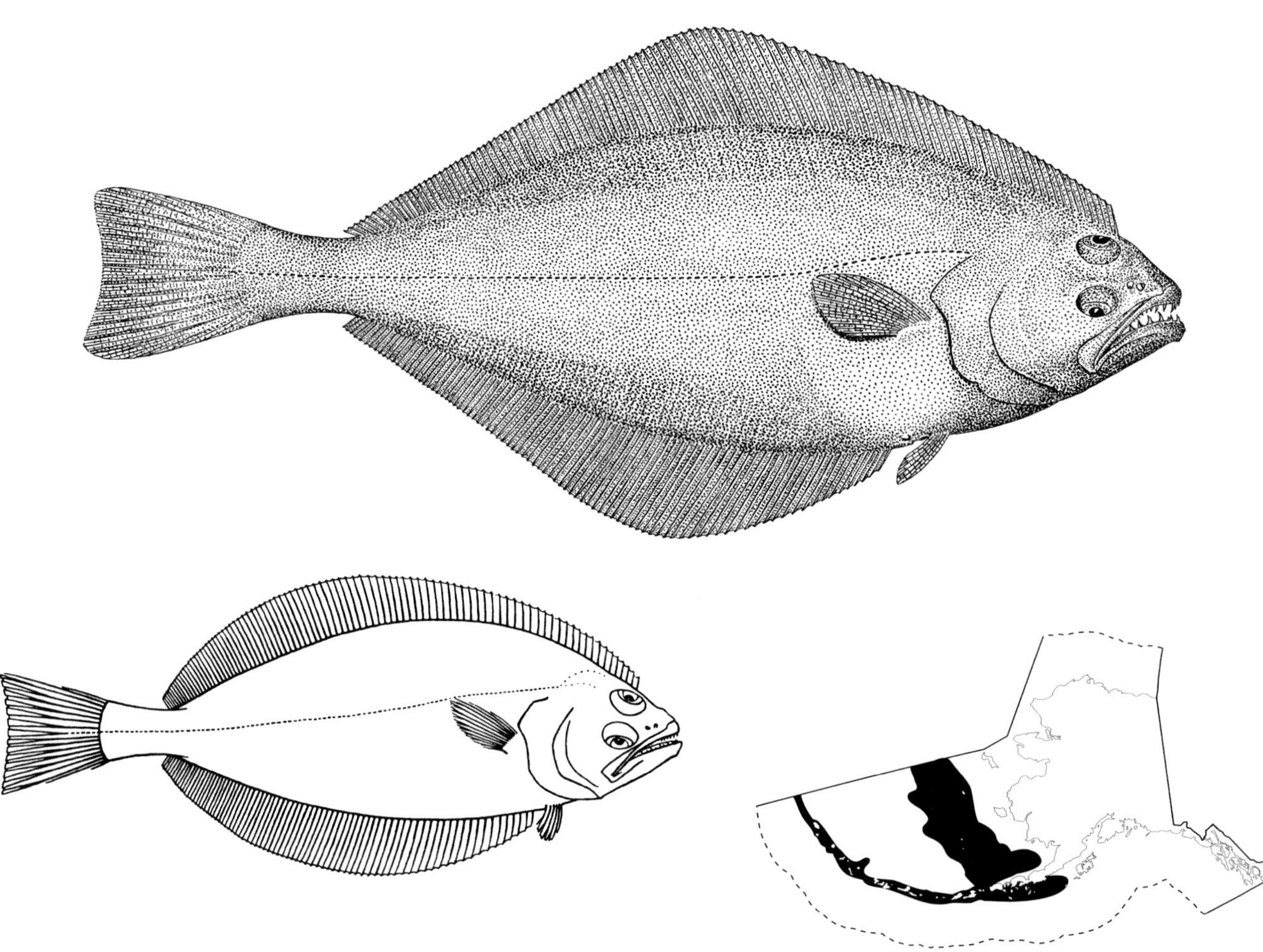

Notes & Sources — *Atheresthes evermanni* Jordan & Starks, 1904
Reinhardtius evermanni: Cooper and Chapleau 1998.

Description: Hubbs 1915:473–474; Norman 1934:288; Wilimovsky et al. 1967:39–52; Sakamoto in Masuda et al. 1984:351; Yang 1988; Lindberg and Fedorov 1993:70–73; Kramer et al. 1995:34–35.

Figures: Upper: Lindberg and Fedorov 1993, fig. 25; 277 mm TL, Kronotskiy Bay, Kamchatka. Lower: Norman 1934, fig. 215.

Range: East to south Shelikof Strait, but occurrence in Gulf of Alaska is relatively rare (Allen and Smith 1988). The similarity between this species and *A. stomias* has resulted in many misidentifications. Zimmerman and Goddard (1996) mapped distribution in the eastern Bering Sea, Aleutian Islands, and western Gulf of Alaska. Coad (1995) reported that a stray was caught in 1965 west of southern Vancouver Island.

Size: Estimated from maximum known length of 1 m SL or more reported by Sakamoto (in Masuda et al. 1984).

Platichthys stellatus (Pallas, 1787) **starry flounder**

Alaskan Beaufort Sea to southern California at Los Angeles Harbor; Canadian Beaufort east to Bathurst Inlet; East Siberian Sea south to Sea of Okhotsk and to Sea of Japan off Korea.

Soft bottoms from intertidal area to depth of 375 m, usually shallower than 100 m; common in estuaries, often found upriver to the limit of tidal influence, as well as in marshes and coastal lakes.

D 51–68; A 35–51; Pec 9–12; Pel 6; LLs 58–83; GR 0–6 + 6–10; Vert 10–12 + 23–26 (34–38).

- Eyed side dark brown; blind side white; **median fins white to orange with black bands**.
- Common either sinistral or dextral.
- Body deep.
- Maxilla extending to below anterior part of eye.
- Anal spine pronounced.
- Caudal fin truncate to slightly rounded.
- Lateral line with slight curve above pectoral fin.
- **Scattered, rough (stellate) tubercles on eyed side**.
- Length to 91 cm TL, weight to 9.1 kg.

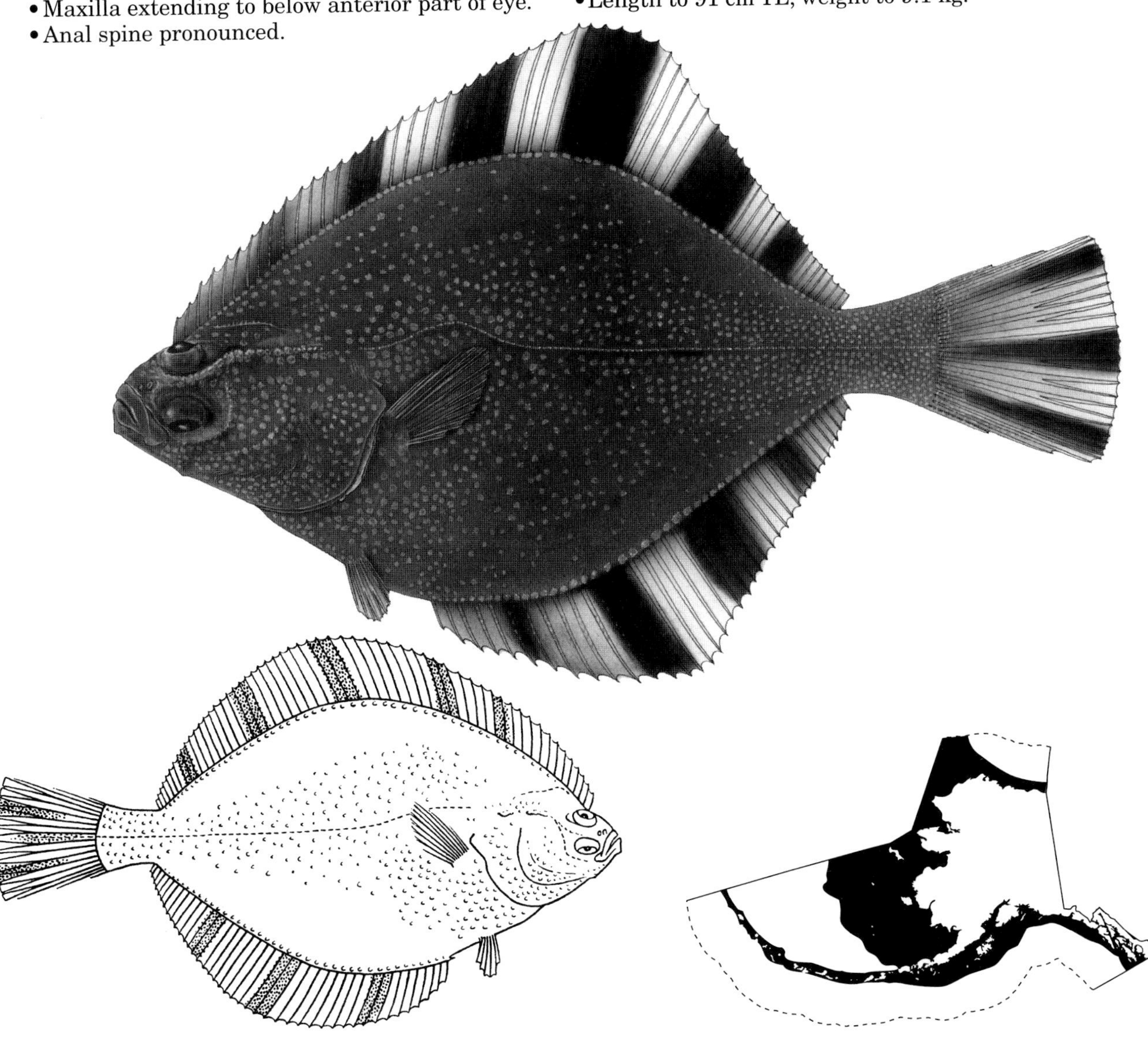

Notes & Sources — *Platichthys stellatus* (Pallas, 1787)

Pleuronectes stellatus Pallas, 1787

From California to eastern Gulf of Alaska 49–66% of specimens are sinistral, in western Gulf of Alaska and eastern Bering Sea 68% are sinistral, and from western Pacific off Kamchatka to Japan and Sea of Okhotsk 100% are sinistral (Forrester 1969, Voronina 1999).

Description: Lockington 1879:91–93; Norman 1934:384–385; Schultz and Smith 1936; Hart 1973:631–633; Morrow 1980: 212–215; Sakamoto in Masuda et al. 1984:353; Lindberg and Fedorov 1993:148–152; Kramer et al. 1995:62–65.

Figures: Upper: University of British Columbia, artist P. Drukker-Brammall, Mar. 1974; UBC 65-371, 236 mm SL, Wingham Island, Alaska. Lower: Norman 1934, fig. 275.

Range: Well documented throughout its range. Morrow (1980) and Allen and Smith (1988) mapped distribution in Alaska.

Size: Miller and Lea 1972.

Clidoderma asperrimum (Temminck & Schlegel, 1846) **roughscale sole**

Bering Sea and Aleutian Islands; southern British Columbia at Estevan Deep to northern California off Punta Gorda; Commander Islands; Okhotsk, Japan, and Yellow seas to Korea.

Muddy bottom at depths of 15–1,900 m off Asian shores, about 150–1,006 m off American shores.

D 75–96; A 61–77; Pec 12–15; Pel 6; GR 3–6 + 8–14; Vert 14 + 31–32 (45–46).

- Eye side brown; blind side grayish brown.
- Body deep.
- Maxilla extending to below anterior part of eye.
- Anal spine inconspicuous.
- Caudal fin slightly rounded or double truncate.
- **Eyed side with rough, bony tubercles, the larger tubercles arranged in irregular rows**; blind side smooth, scales absent.
- Lateral line with low curve above pectoral fin.
- Length to 60 cm TL, weight to 3 kg.

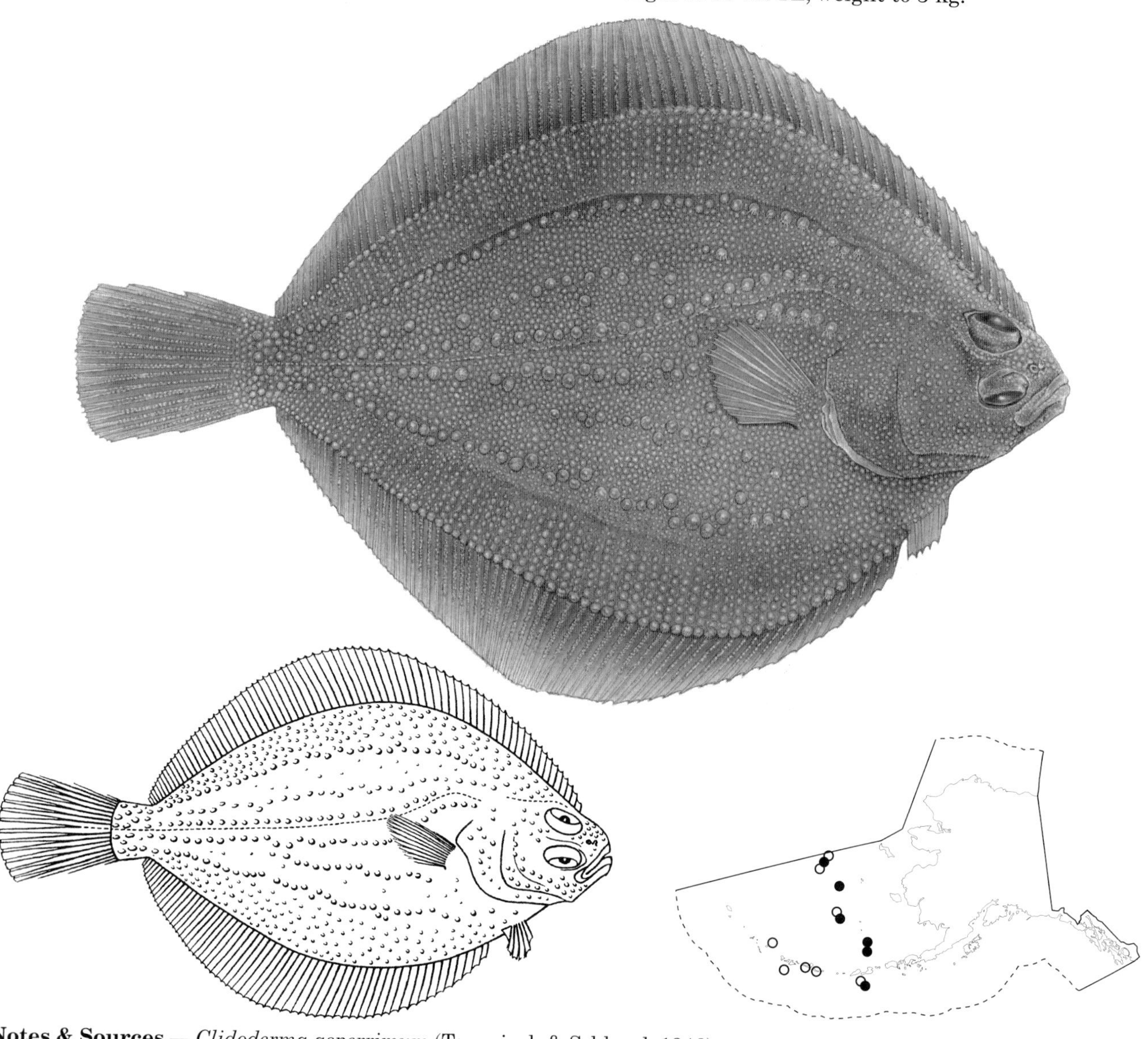

Notes & Sources — *Clidoderma asperrimum* (Temminck & Schlegel, 1846)
Platessa asperrima Temminck & Schlegel, 1846

Description: Jordan and Starks 1906:221–223; Norman 1934:314–315; Hart 1973:604–605; Lindberg and Fedorov 1993:173–176; Kramer et al. 1995:38–39.

Figures: Upper: University of British Columbia, artist P. Drukker-Brammall, Mar. 1974; UBC 56-347, 176 mm SL, Japan. Lower: Norman 1934, fig. 233.

Range: Reported from Aleutian Islands and Bering Sea by Lea et al. (1989). Dots on map represent UW 21210, 55°26'N, 168°20'W; UW 21211, 58°52'N, 175°04'W; UW 21212, 60°26'N, 178°52'W; UW 21214, 55°17'N, 168°22'W; UW 21215, 55°09'N, 167°53'W; and UW 21216, 56°48'N, 173°24'W. Another is RBCM 980-525, 53°07'N, 166°52'W, depth 366 m (A. E. Peden, pers. comm., 11 Jan. 1995). Circles: NMFS resource survey database (D. W. Kessler, pers. comm., 20 Jun. 1994). No depths were given for UW or NMFS records; coordinates place them along the slope in waters 150–400 m deep.

Pleuronectes quadrituberculatus Pallas, 1814 **Alaska plaice**

Chukchi Sea, and possibly Beaufort Sea, through Bering Sea to Unalaska Island and Gulf of Alaska to inside waters of southeastern Alaska; one record off Washington; western Chukchi Sea to Sea of Japan.

Soft bottom at depths of 6–475 m, usually shallower than 150 m.

D 61–74; A 46–56; Pec 8–13; Pel 6–7; LLs 73–88; GR 1–4 + 4–7; Vert 12 + 27–29 (39–42).

- Eyed side greenish gray to almost black; young adults spotted and blotched; blind side yellow.
- Body deep.
- **Postocular ridge with 4–7 bony knobs**.
- Maxilla extending to below anterior edge of eye.
- Anal spine conspicuous.
- Caudal fin rounded.
- Lateral line slightly curved over pectoral fin.
- Length to 62 cm TL; average trawl-caught fish in Bering Sea about 32 cm, weight 0.39 kg.

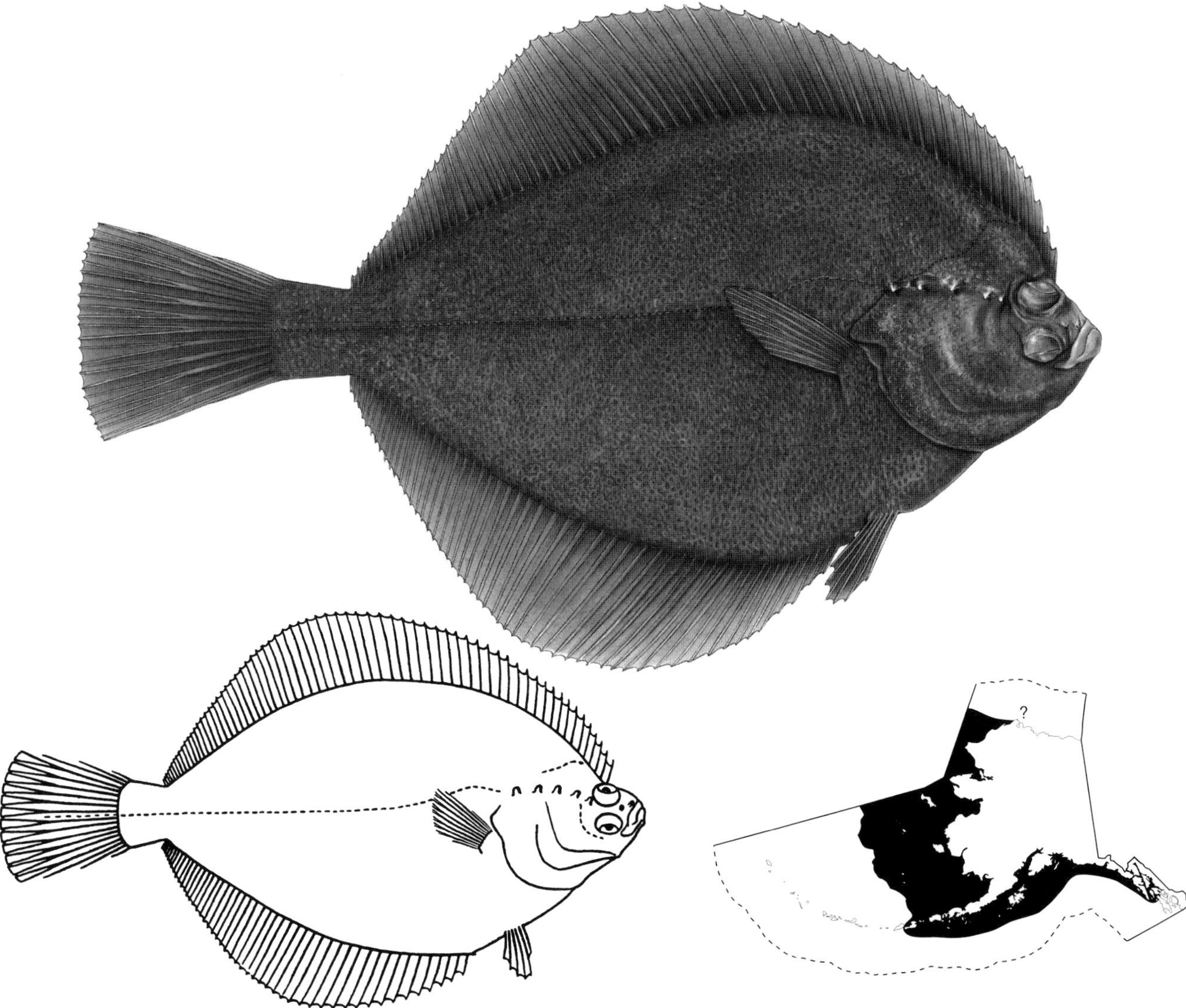

Notes & Sources — *Pleuronectes quadrituberculatus* Pallas, 1814
Pleuronectes pallasii Steindachner, 1880

Description: Norman 1934:349–350; Townsend 1936; Andriashev 1954:494–495; Lindberg and Fedorov 1993: 139–142; Kramer et al. 1995:78–79.

Figures: Upper: University of British Columbia, artist P. Drukker-Brammall, Nov. 1966; UBC 62-432, 282 mm SL, near Ugamik Island, Alaska. Lower: Norman 1934, fig. 256.

Range: This was the third most abundant pleuronectid (by number) in surveys of the northeastern Chukchi Sea in 1990 and 1991 (Barber et al. 1997), which suggests it may also occur in the Beaufort Sea. Recorded west in Aleutian Islands as far as Chernofski Harbor, Unalaska Island (Gilbert 1896). Probably occurs throughout southeastern Alaska, although not abundantly. Carlson et al. (1982) found it in trawl hauls in Fritz Cove, Auke Bay, and along western Chichagof Island, and commented that it was rare in their catches. Reported south to Port Camden by Kramer et al. (1995); D. W. Kessler (pers. comm., 20 Jun. 1994) caught it farther south, near Ketchikan (55°20'N). Townsend (1936) reported four specimens from Bellingham Bay, Washington (as *P. pallasii*).

Size: Maximum: Fadeev 1987. Average: Zhang et al. 1998.

Pleuronectes glacialis Pallas, 1776 **Arctic flounder**

Beaufort Sea to southeastern Bering Sea and Aleutian Islands; Arctic Russia to Sea of Okhotsk and to Labrador.

Shallow, brackish waters of bays and estuaries to depth of about 19 m; rarely, if ever, found in deeper water, but reported to depth of 91 m; sometimes enters fresh waters.

D 48–64; A 33–46; Pec 8–12; Pel 6; LLs 73–100; GR 2–4 + 7–9; Vert 11–13 + 26–27 (37–41).

- Eyed side dark brownish or blackish; fins paler, **dorsal and anal fins usually with dark spots**; blind side chalky white to lime green.
- Body deep.
- **Postocular ridge prominent, terminating in a larger and a smaller low protuberance**.
- Maxilla extending to below anterior edge of eye.
- Anal spine pronounced.
- Caudal fin slightly rounded.
- **Lateral line nearly straight**, rising a little or slightly curved above pectoral fin.
- Scales rougher in males than in females.
- Lower pharyngeals massive, each with more than 2 irregular rows of rounded or molariform teeth.
- Length to 35 cm TL.

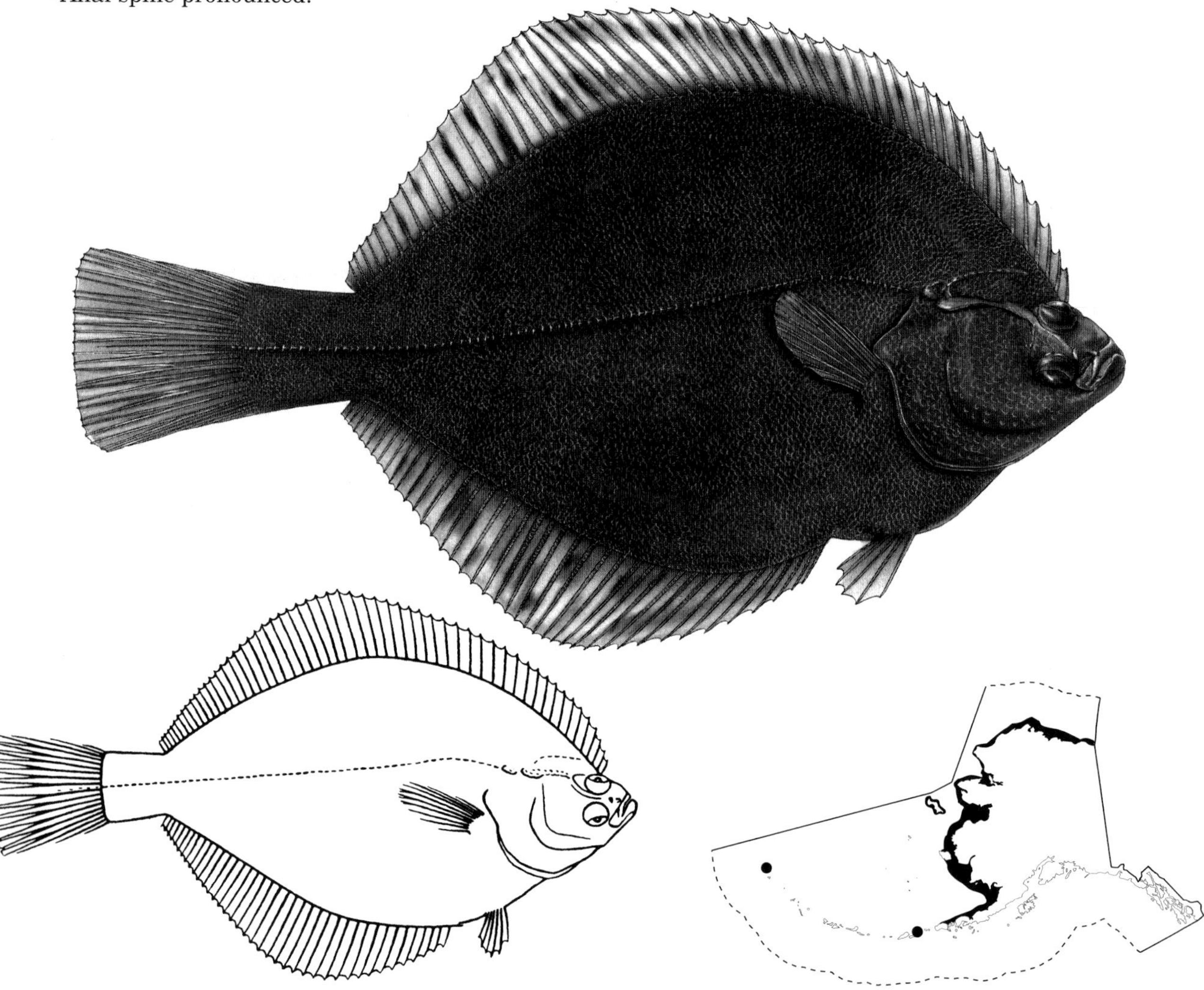

Notes & Sources — *Pleuronectes glacialis* Pallas, 1776

Liopsetta glacialis: Jordan and Evermann 1898, Norman 1934, others. Reestablished in *Pleuronectes* by Sakamoto (1984) and Cooper and Chapleau (1998).

Description: Norman 1934:371–373; Andriashev 1954: 500–503; McAllister 1962:34; Kramer et al. 1995:70–71.

Figures: Upper: University of British Columbia, artist P. Drukker-Brammall, Feb. 1967; UBC 60-384, 150 mm SL, St. Lawrence Island, Alaska. Lower: Norman 1934, fig. 268.

Range: Recorded from Attu and Unalaska islands by Turner (1886) and north side of Alaska Peninsula by Walters (1955) and Isakson et al. (1986). Evermann and Goldsborough (1907) listed early Alaskan records. The UBC has specimens from all along the coasts of Alaska indicated by solid black fill on the above map, including St. Lawrence Island. There are no records of occurrence near the St. Matthew and Pribilof island groups.

Size: Morrow 1980. Rarely exceeds 25 cm (Andriashev 1954).

Lepidopsetta bilineata (Ayres, 1855) **southern rock sole**

Southeastern Bering Sea and Aleutian Islands around Islands of Four Mountains to Baja California. Sand and gravel bottoms to depth of 339 m, usually on continental shelf.

D 67–89; A 54–77; Pec 8–13; Pel 6; LLp 70–91; GR 1–4 + 5–7 (6–11); Vert 11 + 29–30 (40–41).

- Eyed side yellowish brown to greenish brown with scattered dark brown blotches and light spots; brown blotches on median fins; **blind side bright white, with muscle bands, especially anteriorly, highlighted with glossy white**; in preservative blind side uniformly creamy white to yellowish brown.
- Body ovate.
- **Interorbital space narrow**, up to 3 scales at narrowest portion; maxilla extending to below anterior portion of eye.
- Anal spine pronounced.
- Caudal fin rounded or double truncate.
- Lateral line strongly arched above pectoral fin; accessory dorsal branch extending below first 13–18 dorsal fin rays; **supraorbital pores almost always more than 4**, range 3–9.
- Scales on eyed side nearly always rough; always cycloid on blind side anteriorly.
- **Gill rakers broad and robust, total on 1st arch typically 10 or less, on upper limb 3 or less.**
- Length to 58 cm TL.

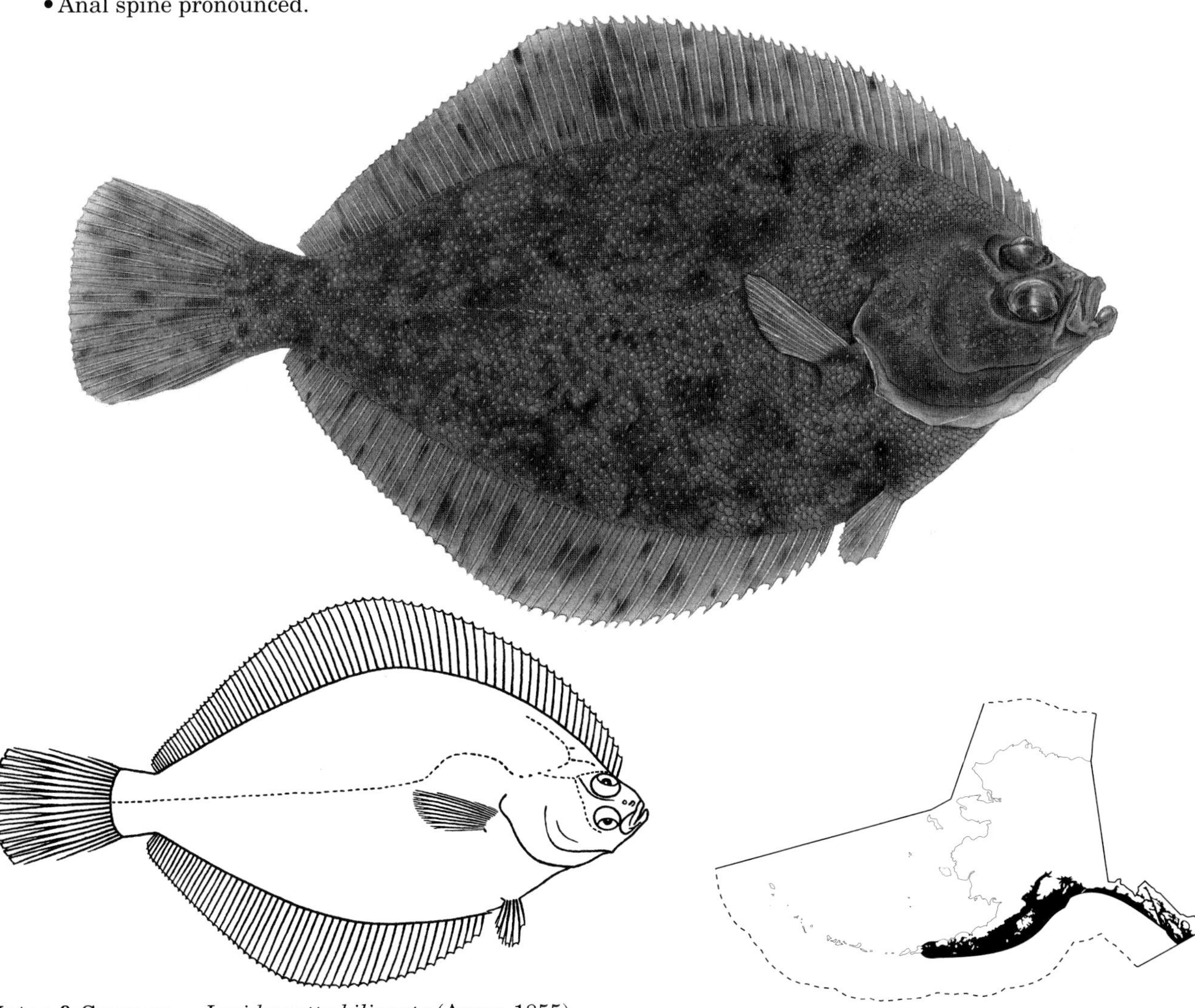

Notes & Sources — *Lepidopsetta bilineata* (Ayres, 1855)
Platessa bilineata Ayres, 1855
Platichthys umbrosus Girard, 1856
Pleuronectes perarcuatus Cope, 1873
Pleuronectes bilineatus: Sakamoto 1984. Complete synonymy was given by Orr and Matarese (2000).

Description: Norman 1934:330–331; Wilimovsky et al. 1967:65–82; Orr and Matarese 2000.

Figures: Upper: University of British Columbia, artist P. Drukker-Brammall, Aug. 1967 ; UBC 65-525, 295 mm SL, Port Conclusion, Baranof Island, Alaska. Lower: Norman 1934, fig. 244, modified from Orr et al. (1997ms).

Range: Orr and Matarese (2000) provided complete documentation of range for this species.

Lepidopsetta polyxystra Orr & Matarese, 2000 **northern rock sole**

Bering Sea from vicinity of St. Lawrence Island south and throughout Aleutian Islands to Puget Sound, Washington; and Gulf of Anadyr to Sea of Okhotsk and northern coast of Hokkaido.

Sandy bottom to depth of 246 m, usually on continental shelf.

D 64–83; A 49–64; Pec 8–13; Pel 6; LLp 76–100; GR 3–6 + 6–9 (9–14); Vert 10–11 + 29–30 (39–41).

- Eyed side yellowish brown to greenish brown with scattered dark brown blotches and light spots; brown blotches on median fins; **blind side uniformly creamy white without glossy white highlights**; in preservative blind side uniformly creamy white to yellowish brown.
- Body ovate.
- **Interorbital space wide**, up to 5 scales at narrowest portion; maxilla extending to below anterior portion of eye.
- Anal spine pronounced.
- Caudal fin rounded or double truncate.
- Lateral line strongly arched above pectoral fin; accessory dorsal branch below first 13–18 dorsal fin rays; **supraorbital pores 1–3**, rarely 4–7.
- Scales on eyed side nearly always rough; always cycloid on blind side anteriorly.
- **Gill rakers usually slender and pointed, total on 1st arch typically 10 or more, on upper limb 3 or more**.
- Length to 69 cm TL.

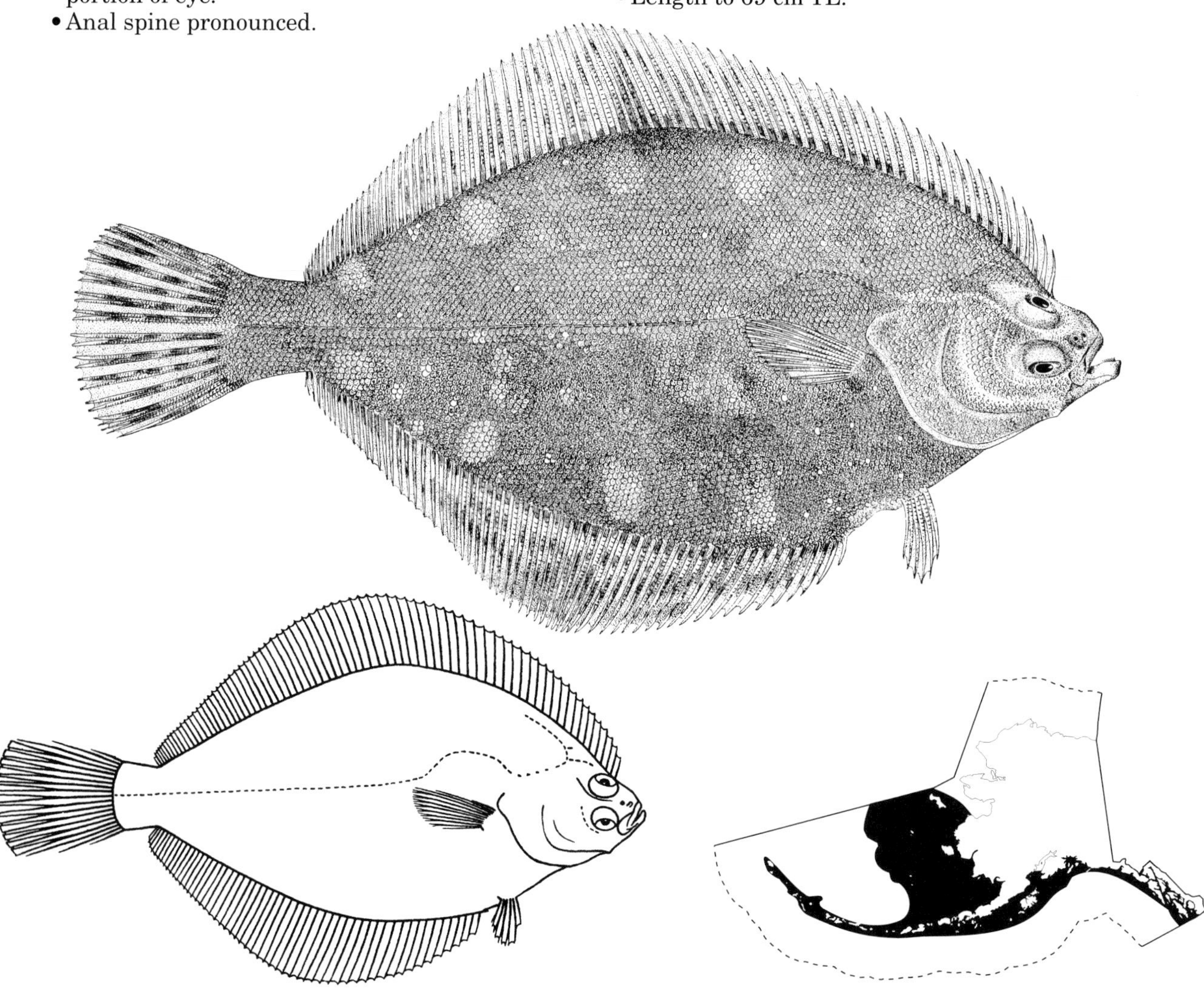

Notes & Sources — *Lepidopsetta polyxystra* Orr & Matarese, 2000

Lepidopsetta bilineata: Goode 1884, pl. 50; Jordan and Evermann 1900, fig. 928. See detailed synonymy in Orr and Matarese 2000.

Coloration of the eyed side is highly variable and exhibits the same patterns seen in *L. bilineata*.

Description: Orr and Matarese 2000.

Figures: Upper: Goode 1884, pl. 50; 35 cm TL, Kodiak Island, Alaska. Lower: Norman 1934, fig. 244.

Range: Orr and Matarese (2000) provided complete documentation of range for this species. Range depicted for *L. bilineata* north of the Aleutian Islands by Allen and Smith (1988) from NMFS survey data represents records of *L. polyxystra*. The specimen chosen as the holotype for this species (UW 14826) was obtained at Constantine Harbor, Amchitka Island, depth 19–42 m.

Pleuronichthys coenosus Girard, 1854 **C-O sole**

Southeastern Alaska, about as far north as Sitka, to northern Baja California at Bahia San Quintin.
Sandy bottom at depths to about 350 m; most common near shore at depths shallower than 15 m.

D 65–79; A 46–56; Pec 9–13; Pel 6; LLs 77–92; GR 3–4 + 8–11; Vert 12–13 + 24–26 (36–39).

- Eyed side dark brown mottled lighter and darker; **usually with dark spot at midbody and dark spot and curved bar (forms inverted C-O) on caudal fin**; blind side creamy white.
- Caudal peduncle deep.
- Interorbital ridge prominent, with blunt, inconspicuous spine at posterior end.
- Maxilla extending as far as anterior part of eye.
- Anal spine small.
- Dorsal and anal fins high; **anterior 4–6 dorsal fin rays on blind side; dorsal fin origin above angle of jaw, on level with upper lip**; caudal fin rounded.
- Lateral line almost straight; **accessory dorsal branch long, extending beyond midbody**.
- Length to 36 cm TL, weight to at least 0.43 kg.

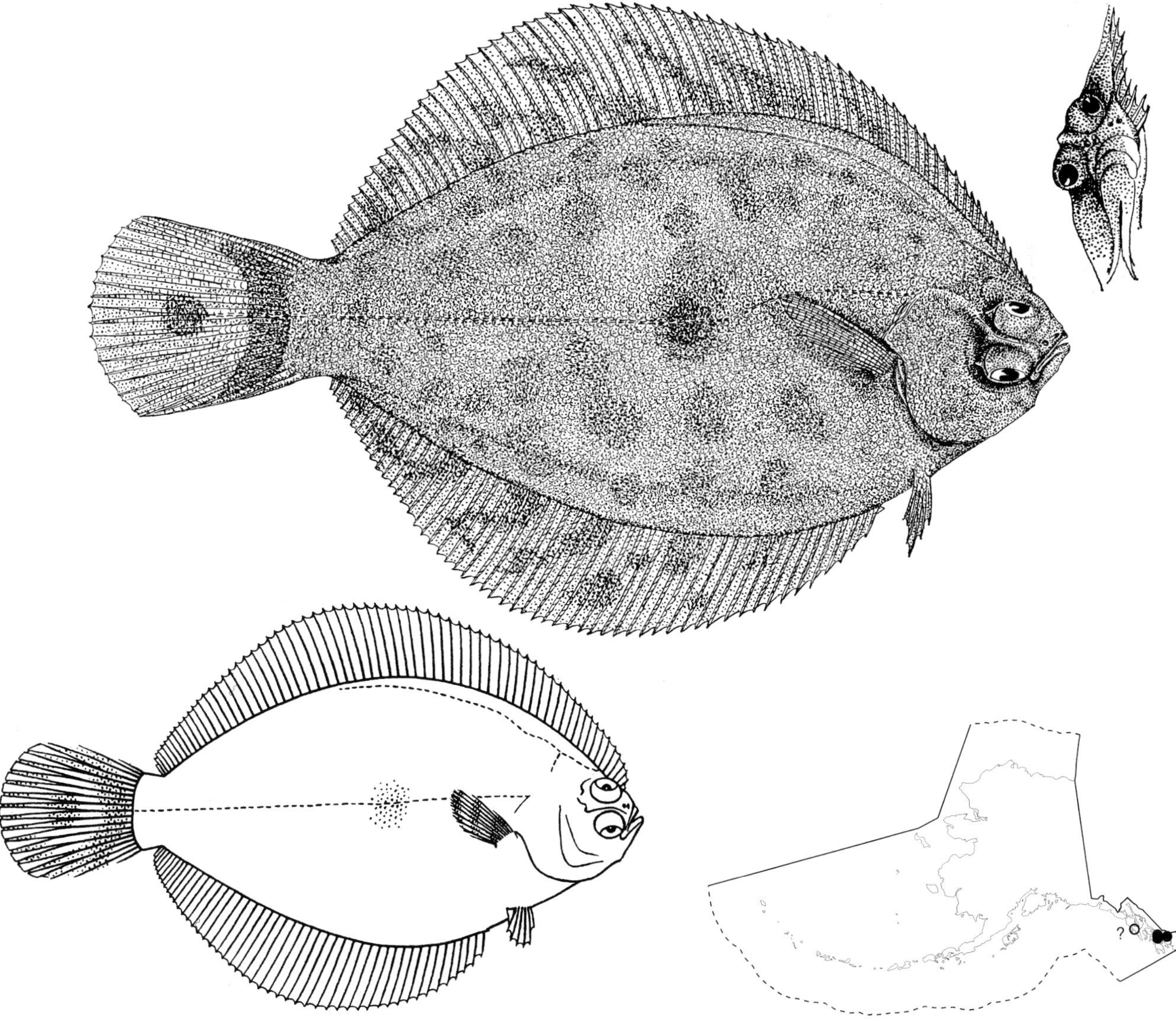

Notes & Sources — *Pleuronichthys coenosus* Girard, 1854

Description: Lockington 1879:97–100; Norman 1934:323–324; Townsend 1936; Fitch 1963:28–31; Hart 1973:633–634; Kramer et al. 1995:84–85.

Figures: Upper: Hart 1973:633; 24 cm TL. Lower: Norman 1934, fig. 239.

Range: Reported as far north as Sitka by Kramer et al. (1995), but probably based on commercial landings at Sitka. The Auke Bay Laboratory museum has specimens taken in NMFS resource surveys farther south in Alaska, from Steamer Bay, Etolin Island (AB 77-119, AB 78-74); and Mountain Point Light, near Ketchikan (AB 69-52).

Size: Length: Miller and Lea 1972. Weight, reported by Fitch (1963), is from a slightly smaller fish, under 33 cm TL.

Pleuronichthys decurrens Jordan & Gilbert, 1881 **curlfin sole**

Southeastern Bering Sea and Gulf of Alaska to southern Baja California off Punta San Juanico.
Level, soft bottom at depths of 8–533 m, usually near shore at depths shallower than 20 m.

D 67–79; A 45–53; Pec 9–14; Pel 4–7; LLs 80–96; GR 3–4 + 6–9; Vert 13–15 + 24–26 (37–41).

- Eyed side dark greenish brown, mottled darker; blind side usually white, sometimes brown.
- Body deep.
- Interorbital ridge prominent, with blunt spine at each end; 2 or 3 bony knobs behind eyes.
- Maxilla extending to below anterior part of eye.
- Anal spine small.
- Dorsal and anal fins high; **anterior 9–12 dorsal fin rays on blind side**; **dorsal fin origin below level of angle of mouth**; caudal fin rounded.
- Lateral line nearly straight; **accessory dorsal branch long, almost to midbody or beyond.**
- Scales depressed, giving dimpled appearance.
- Length to 36 cm TL, weight to 0.77 kg.

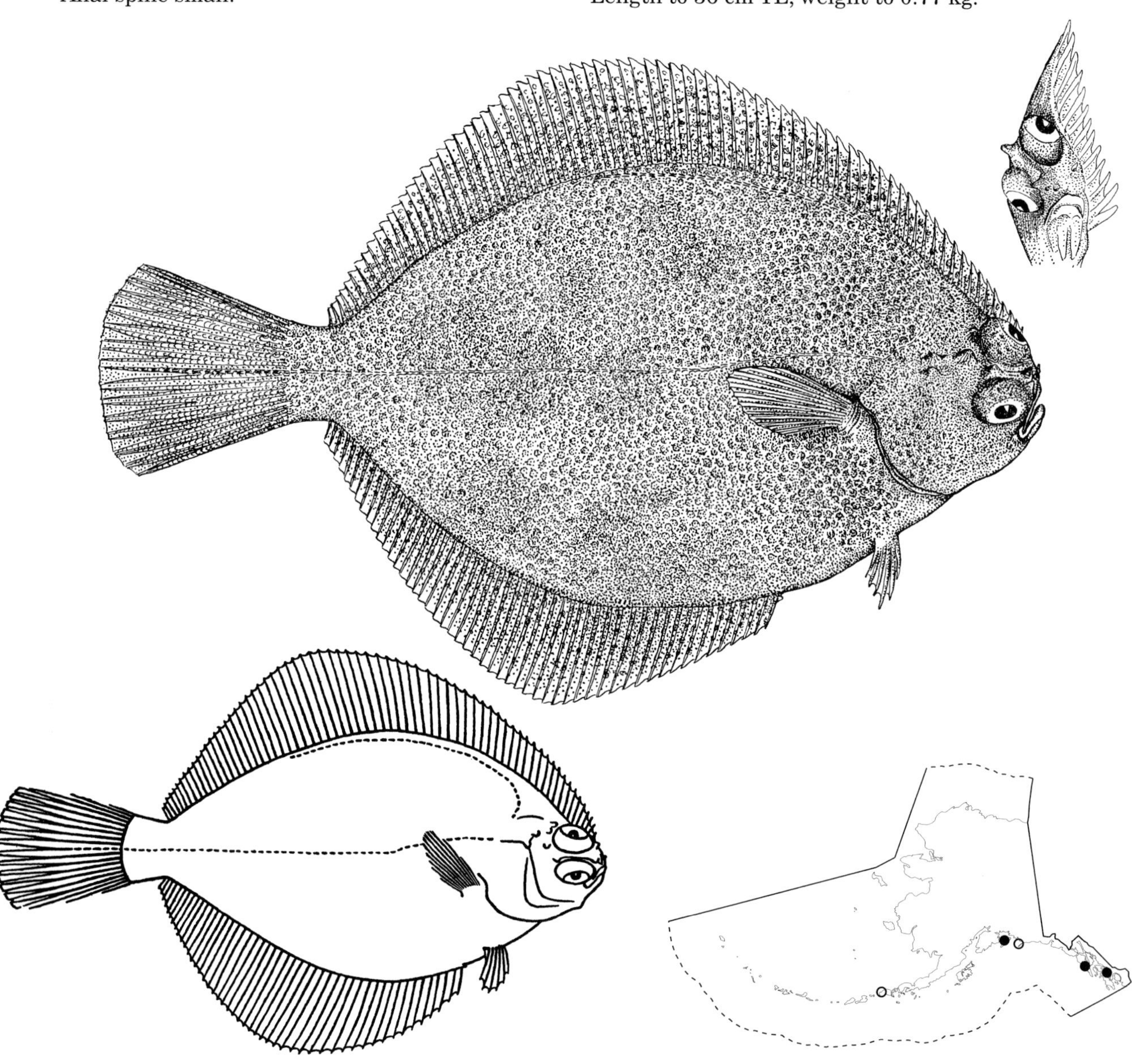

Notes & Sources — *Pleuronichthys decurrens* Jordan & Gilbert, 1881

Description: Norman 1934:318–319; Fitch 1963:20–23; Hart 1973:635–636; Kramer et al. 1995:86–87.

Figures: Upper: Hart 1973:635; 34 cm TL. Lower: Norman 1934, fig. 235.

Range: Schultz et al. (1932): Zaikof Bay, Prince William Sound; and near Wrangell. UW 14464: Sitka Sound. NMFS survey database (D. W. Kessler, pers. comm., 20 Jun. 1994): off northwest coast of Unimak Island, near Kayak Island, and in Sitka Sound. Snytko (1987) extended known range south to 25°59'N, 112°35'W, specimens collected by trawl at depths of 70–75 m.

Size: Fitch 1963: largest of 899 specimens measured.

Parophrys vetulus Girard, 1854 **English sole**

Bering Sea from Nunivak Island to Alaska Peninsula and Aleutian Islands at least as far west as Agattu Island, and Gulf of Alaska to central Baja California at San Cristobal Bay.

Soft bottom from lower intertidal to depth of about 550 m, usually less than 250 m; young flourish in shallow bays and tidal flats.

D 71–93; A 52–70; Pec 10–13; Pel 6; LLs 89–105; GR 4–6 + 10–13; Vert 10–12 + 31–34 (41–47).

- Eyed side uniform reddish brown or olive brown; vague blotching usually disappearing in adults; blind side white to pale yellow.
- Body rather elongate; **head and snout elongate and pointed**.
- **Portion of upper eye visible from blind side**; high, narrow ridge between eyes; **postocular ridge inconspicuous**.
- Maxilla extending to below anterior edge of eye or a little beyond.
- Anal spine pronounced.
- Caudal fin truncate or double truncate.
- Lateral line with low curve above pectoral fin; **accessory dorsal branch long**, extending below first 21–37 dorsal fin rays.
- Scales mostly cycloid; scales not extending onto dorsal and anal fins.
- Length to 61 cm TL; average in commercial fishery about 36 cm.

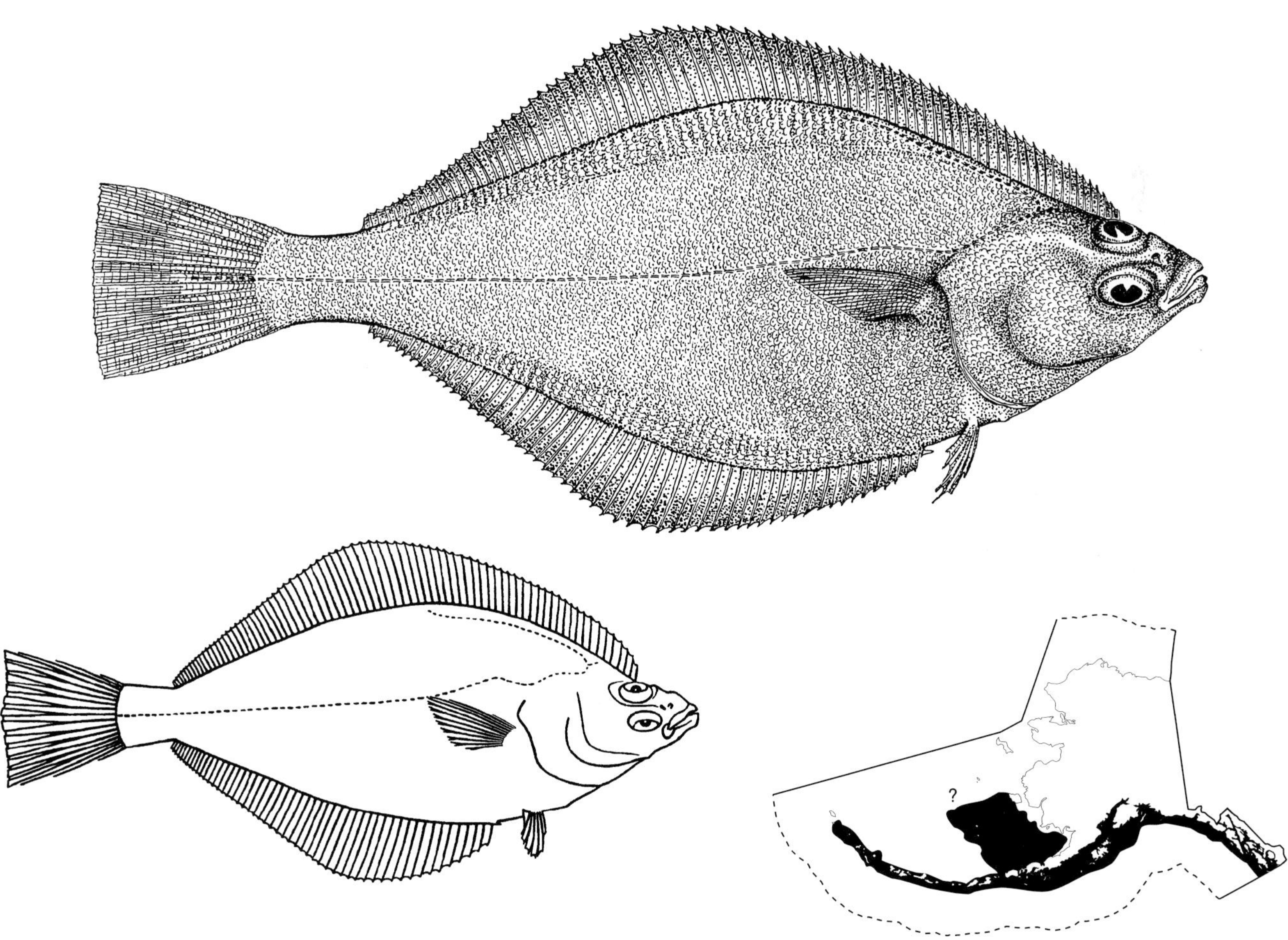

Notes & Sources — *Parophrys vetulus* Girard, 1854

Pleuronectes vetulus: Jordan and Gilbert 1883, Sakamoto 1984.

Norman (1934), Cooper and Chapleau (1998), and other authors changed the spelling of the species name from *vetulus* to *vetula* to agree in gender with *Parophrys* (feminine). However, as Orr and Matarese (2000) pointed out, the original description did not specify the grammatical treatment of *vetulus* and the name may also be treated as a noun in apposition, so changing to *vetula* is incorrect.

Description: Lockington 1879:100–102; Norman 1934:328–329; Schultz and Smith 1936:table 1; Hart 1973:628–630; Kramer et al. 1995:82–83.

Figures: Upper: Hart 1973:628; 30 cm TL. Lower: Norman 1934, fig. 243.

Range: Allen and Smith (1988) mapped records from 30 years of NMFS surveys, extending the known range north to Nunivak Island in the Bering Sea and west to Agattu Island in the Aleutian Islands. Range may extend farther north and west in the Bering Sea, but has not been documented.

Isopsetta isolepis (Lockington, 1880) **butter sole**

Southeastern Bering Sea and Aleutian Islands from Amchitka Island to southern California at Ventura. Muddy bottom at depths of 6–425 m, usually shallower than 150 m.

D 78–92; A 58–69; Pec 10–13; Pel 6; LLs 78–90; GR 4–6 + 7–9; Vert 9–11 + 32 (39–42).

- Eyed side brown, sometimes mottled or blotched; yellow on edges of dorsal and anal fins in freshly caught fish; blind side white.
- Body ovate.
- **Upper eye not visible from blind side**; interorbital space flat; postocular ridge not apparent.
- Maxilla extending to below anterior part of eye.
- Anal spine pronounced.
- Anterior dorsal fin rays partly free but not elongate; caudal fin rounded or double truncate.
- Lateral line with low arch above pectoral fin; **accessory dorsal branch present, extending beyond operculum**, below first 21–28 dorsal fin rays.
- **Scales strongly ctenoid on eyed side**, ctenoid or cycloid on blind side; **scales extend onto dorsal and anal fins**.
- Gill rakers short, few in number.
- Length to 55 cm TL; average in commercial fishery about 20 cm.

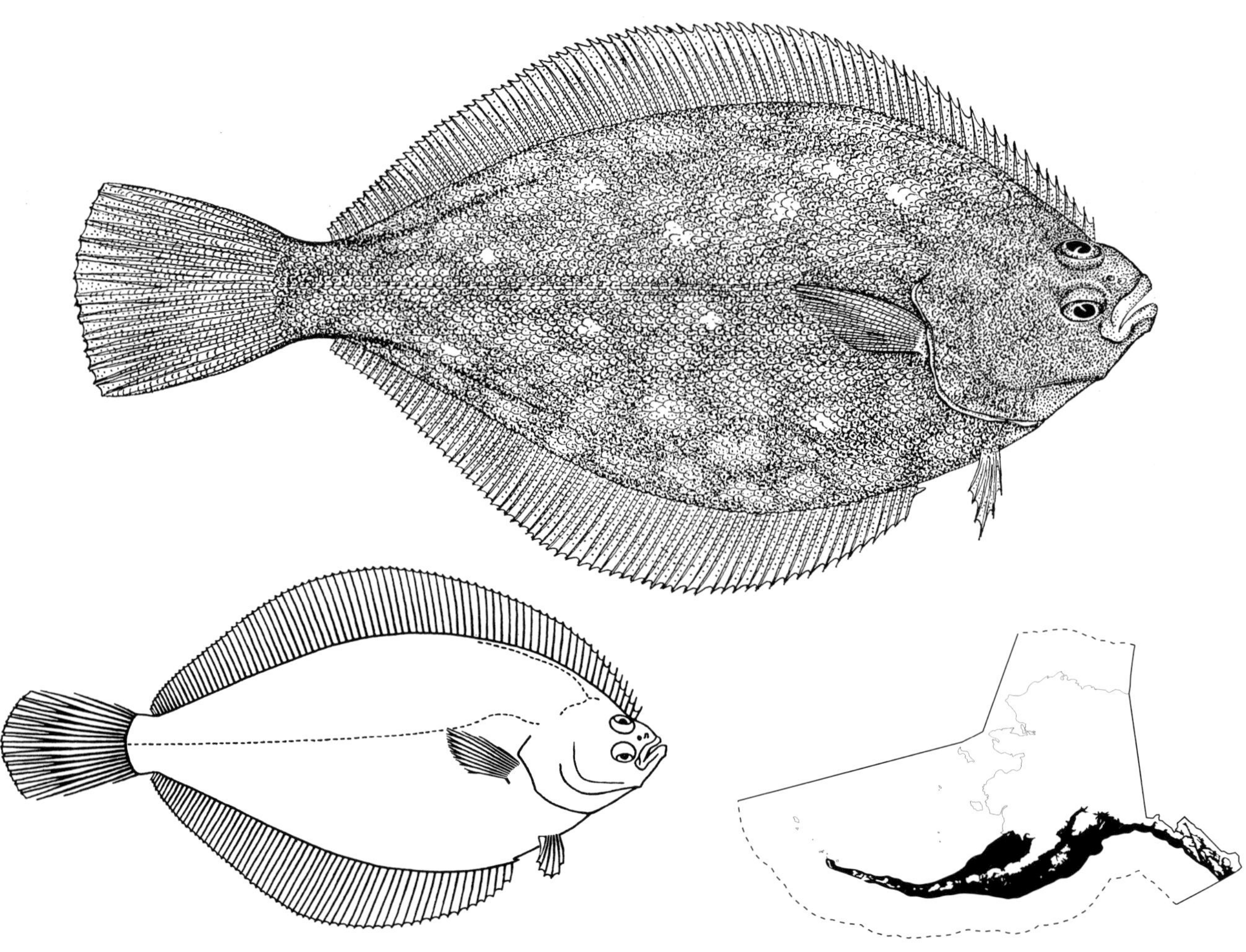

Notes & Sources — *Isopsetta isolepis* (Lockington, 1880)

Lepidopsetta umbrosa (non-Girard): Lockington 1879:106; specimens reidentified and named as new species by Lockington (1880e).

Lepidopsetta isolepis Lockington, 1880

Pleuronectes isolepis: Sakamoto 1984.

Description: Norman 1934:326–327; Townsend 1936; Yesaki and Wolotira 1968; Hart 1973:619–620; Kramer et al. 1995:72–73.

Figures: Upper: Hart 1973:619; 34 cm TL, north of Nagai Island, Alaska. Lower: Norman 1934, fig. 242.

Range: Wilimovsky (1964) reported *I. isolepis* from Amchitka Island, representing the westernmost record in the Aleutian chain. Allen and Smith (1988) reported NMFS survey data that extended the known range to south of Hagemeister Island, Bristol Bay.

Size: Miller and Lea 1972.

Limanda proboscidea Gilbert, 1896 **longhead dab**

Beaufort Sea off Point Barrow, and possibly farther east, to eastern Bering Sea north of Unimak Island, and to Sea of Okhotsk.

Soft bottom at depths of 10–125 m, usually shallower than 100 m.

D 61–77; A 45–58; Pec 9–13; Pel 6; LLs 73–95; GR 4–5 + 8–11; Vert 10–12 + 28–30 (36–40).

- Eyed side grayish brown, covered with small, indistinct whitish spots; **blind side lemon yellow**, brighter at upper and lower edges of body; tips of some rays of median fins bright yellow.
- Body ovate; **head profile concave above eyes; snout produced, longer than eye**.
- Interorbital space flat; **irregular rugose patches on postocular ridge**.
- **Maxilla scarcely extending to below anterior edge of eye**.
- Anal spine pronounced.
- Caudal fin slightly rounded.
- Lateral line with distinct, high arch above pectoral fin.
- Length to 41 cm TL.

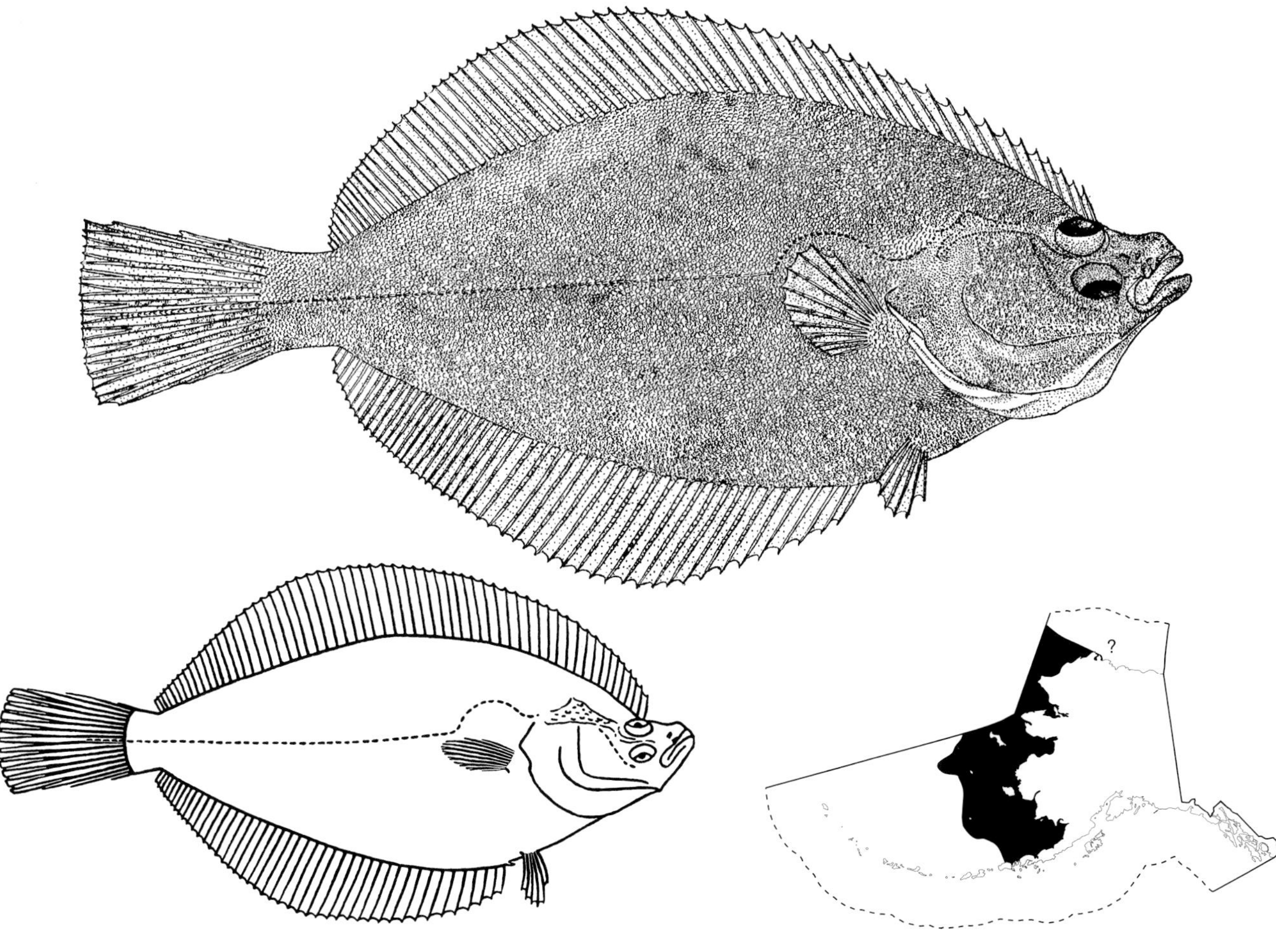

Notes & Sources — *Limanda proboscidea* Gilbert, 1896
Limanda punctatissima proboscidea: Taranetz 1937, Schmidt 1950, Andriashev 1954.
Pleuronectes proboscideus: Sakamoto 1984.

Description: Norman 1934:341; Sakamoto in Masuda et al. 1984:352; Matarese et al. 1989:602; Kramer et al. 1995:76–77.

Figures: Upper: Gilbert 1896, pl. 33; type, about 16 cm TL, Bristol Bay. Lower: Norman 1934, fig. 251.

Range: The type specimens were obtained from Bristol Bay by the *Albatross* (Gilbert 1896). Allen and Smith (1988) reported NMFS survey data indicating range off Alaska from Unimak Island north at least to Cape Krusenstern (about 67°N). Collected in 1990 from northeastern Chukchi Sea in a UAF survey sampling north to Point Barrow, with an estimated abundance of 5 *L. proboscidea* per square kilometer (Barber et al. 1997); none was caught in the 1991 survey of the same area. Voucher specimens of this species from the UAF surveys were not found in searches of the UAM collection in 2000, but the ABL has a 70-mm-TL specimen (AB 70-224) from WEBSEC-70 station 61, off Cape Lisburne at 69°05'N, 166°13'W. The UBC has specimens from both sides of Point Barrow: UBC 63-615, in the Beaufort Sea at 71°22'W, 156°19'N; and UBC 63-1155, in the Chukchi Sea off Browerville at 71°18'N, 156°46'W.

Size: Andriashev 1954.

Limanda aspera (Pallas, 1814) **yellowfin sole**

Beaufort Sea off Point Barrow, and possibly farther east, to Atka Island in the Aleutian Islands and Gulf of Alaska to British Columbia at Barkley Sound, and to Sea of Japan off Korea.

Soft bottom at depths of 10–600 m, usually shallower than 150 m.

D 61–78; A 48–61; Pec 9–13; Pel 6; LLs 72–95; GR 3–9 + 5–10; Vert 10–12 + 28–31 (39–41).

- Eyed side brown; small dark spots on head and body which fade in adults; **median fins yellowish; narrow black line at base of dorsal and anal fins**, fades in preservative; **blind side snowy white**.
- Body ovate, rather deep.
- Interorbital ridge low or of moderate height.
- Maxilla extending to below anterior half of eye.
- Anal spine pronounced.
- Caudal fin rounded.
- Lateral line with distinct, high arch above pectoral fin.
- **Scales on eyed side ctenoid or cycloid, most with single spinule, a few with 2, rarely 3, spinules**.
- Length to 49 cm TL, weight to 1.8 kg.

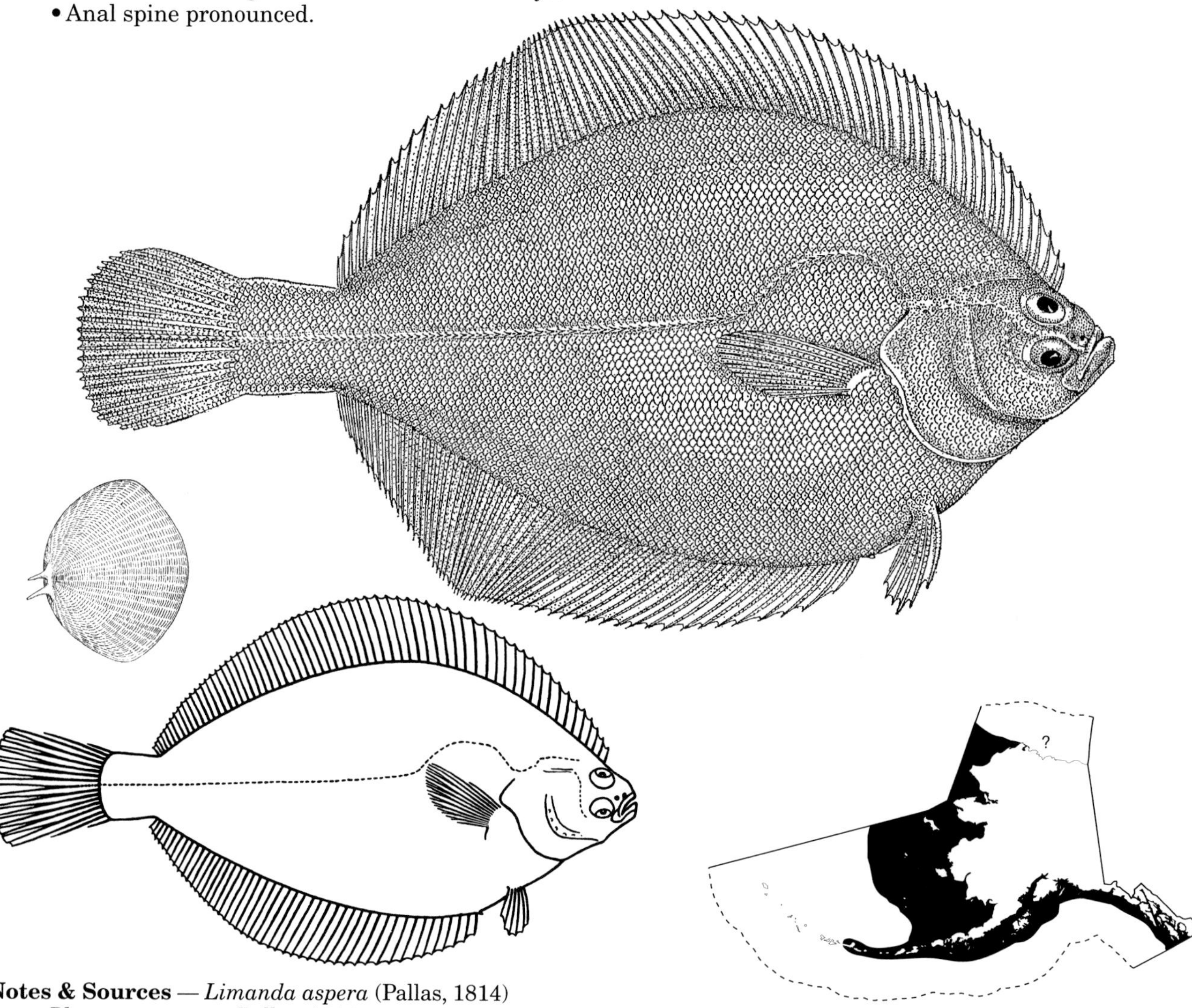

Notes & Sources — *Limanda aspera* (Pallas, 1814)
Pleuronectes asper Pallas, 1814
Limanda asprella Hubbs, 1915
Pleuronectes asper: Sakamoto 1984.

Description: Hubbs 1915:482–483; Norman 1934:336–337; Sakamoto in Masuda et al. 1984:352; Lindberg and Fedorov 1993:120–123; Kramer et al. 1995:66–67.

Figures: Upper: Hubbs 1915, fig. 7 (*L. asprella*). Lower: Norman 1934, fig. 247. Scale: Schmidt 1950, fig. 24a.

Range: Second most abundant flatfish by number of fish caught in UAF survey of northeastern Chukchi Sea in 1990, and most abundant in 1991 (Barber et al. 1997). Range in Bering Sea and Gulf of Alaska was mapped by Allen and Smith (1988). Reported west in Aleutians to Atka Island by Wilimovsky (1964). UBC has examples from Beaufort (UBC 63-789, 63-793, 63-796, 63-823, 63-836) and Chukchi (UBC 63-700, 63-791, 63-1172) seas off Point Barrow.

Size: Fadeev 1987.

Limanda sakhalinensis Hubbs, 1915 — Sakhalin sole

Chukchi Sea to southeastern Bering Sea and to Sea of Okhotsk and Tatar Strait.

Soft bottom at depths of 20–95 m.

D 66–85; A 51–76; Pec 9–12; Pel 6–8; LLs 78–91; GR 4–8 + 5–12; Vert 9–11 + 30–34 (39–45).

- Eyed side uniformly brown or vaguely blotched with darker; **fins brown**; **blind side off-white**.
- Body ovate to slightly elongate (not as deep as in *L. aspera*).
- Interorbital ridge of moderate height.
- Maxilla extending to below anterior edge of eye.
- Anal spine pronounced.
- Caudal fin rounded.
- Lateral line with medium to high arch above pectoral fin.
- **Scales on eyed side mostly ctenoid, with 3–10 spinules**.
- Length to 35 cm TL.

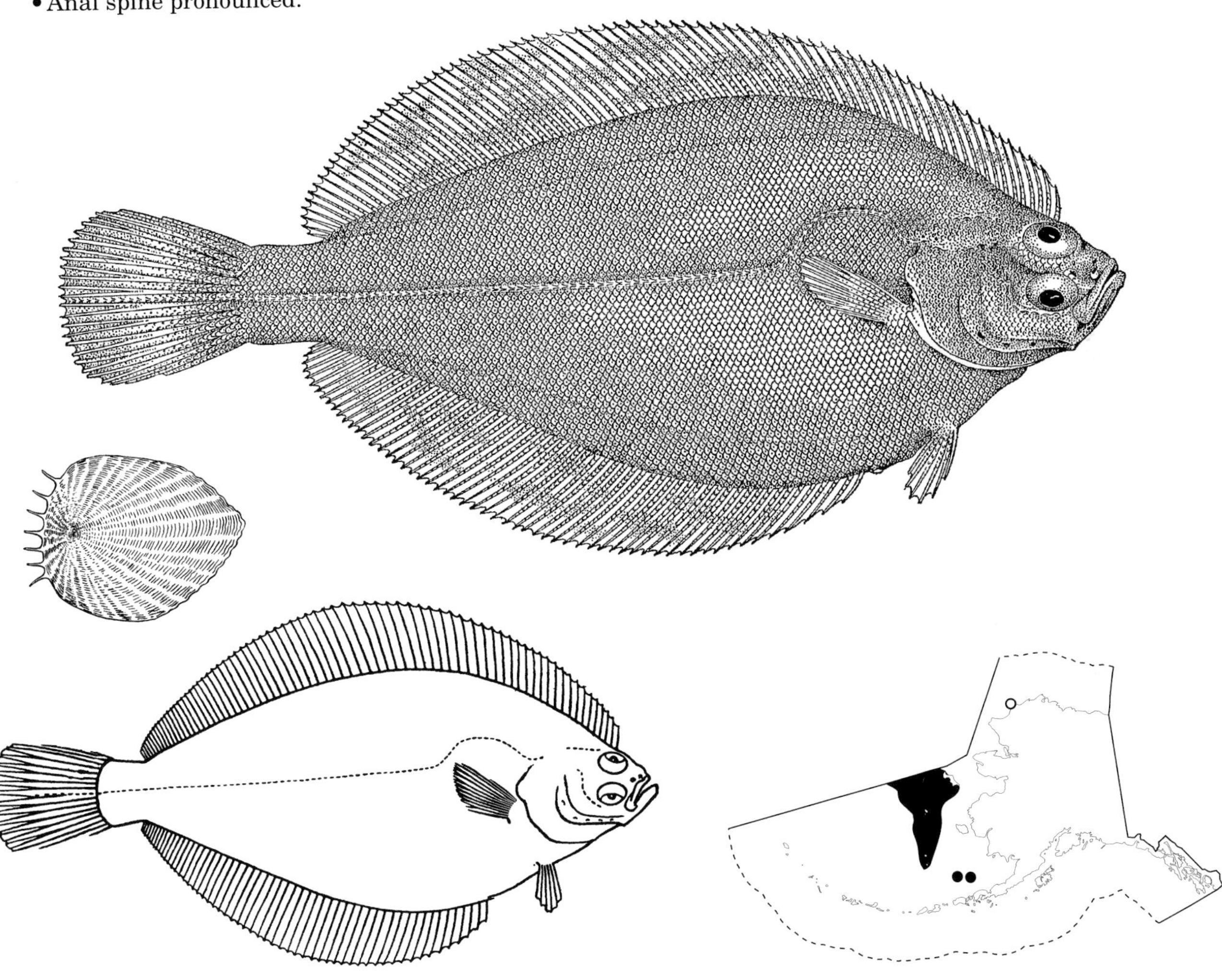

Notes & Sources — *Limanda sakhalinensis* Hubbs, 1915
Pleuronectes sakhalinensis: Sakamoto 1984.

Description: Hubbs 1915:480–482; Norman 1934:337–338; Pitruk 1988; Lindberg and Fedorov 1993:123–126; Kramer et al. 1995:80–81.

Figures: Upper: Hubbs 1915, pl. 26, fig. 6. Lower: Norman 1934, fig. 248. Scale: Schmidt 1950, fig. 24b.

Range: Taken at one station in 1990 in bottom trawl survey of northeastern Chukchi Sea (Barber et al. 1997). Specimens of *L. sakhalinensis* were not found among vouchers for that survey at the UAF (C.W.M.), but the unpublished haul-catch listing gives one specimen in haul 72, at 69°59'N, 163°36'W, depth 26 m; a juvenile weighing less than 45 g. Southernmost records for eastern Bering Sea are from 56°43'N, 165°22'W, depth 95 m (UW 22369); and 56°44'N, 163°34'W, at 73 m (UW 25790). Ivanov and Pitruk collected several specimens (ZIN 47826) in 1985 from the eastern Bering Sea at 60°09'N, 168°47'W (Lindberg and Fedorov 1993). Records provided by D. W. Kessler (pers. comm., 20 June 1994) from NMFS resource surveys include numerous records of *L. sakhalinensis* from St. Lawrence Island southeast to near St. George Island at 56°50'N, 169°52'W, and west to the Gulf of Anadyr and along the Koryak coast and Kamchatka Peninsula. Pitruk (1988) also recorded this species near the Koryak coast.

Embassichthys bathybius (Gilbert, 1890) **deepsea sole**

Bering Sea and Aleutian Islands to California–Mexico border and to Hokkaido, Japan, at Cape Erimo. Muddy bottom at 320–1,433 m, on continental slope and sides of seamounts.

D 108–120; A 93–102; Pec 10–13; Pel 5–6; LLs 165–247; GR 6–9 + 13–16; Vert 13–14 + 44–51 (57–65).

- Eyed side brown to maroon with dark blue and white blotches forming vague, broad bluish bars, fading in preservative; lips and fin margins black; blind side dark gray to brown.
- **Body deep and limp**.
- **Profile sharply angled above upper eye, so that head conspicuously protrudes beyond general outline**.
- Interorbital ridge high and narrow; postocular ridge not apparent.
- Maxilla extending to below anterior edge of eye.
- Anal spine absent.
- Dorsal fin origin above posterior part of eye; caudal fin small and rounded.
- Lateral line with low arch anteriorly.
- Scales small; dorsal and anal fins densely scaled.
- **Teeth nearly equally developed on both sides**; 7–23 on eyed side of upper jaw.
- Length to 52 cm TL.

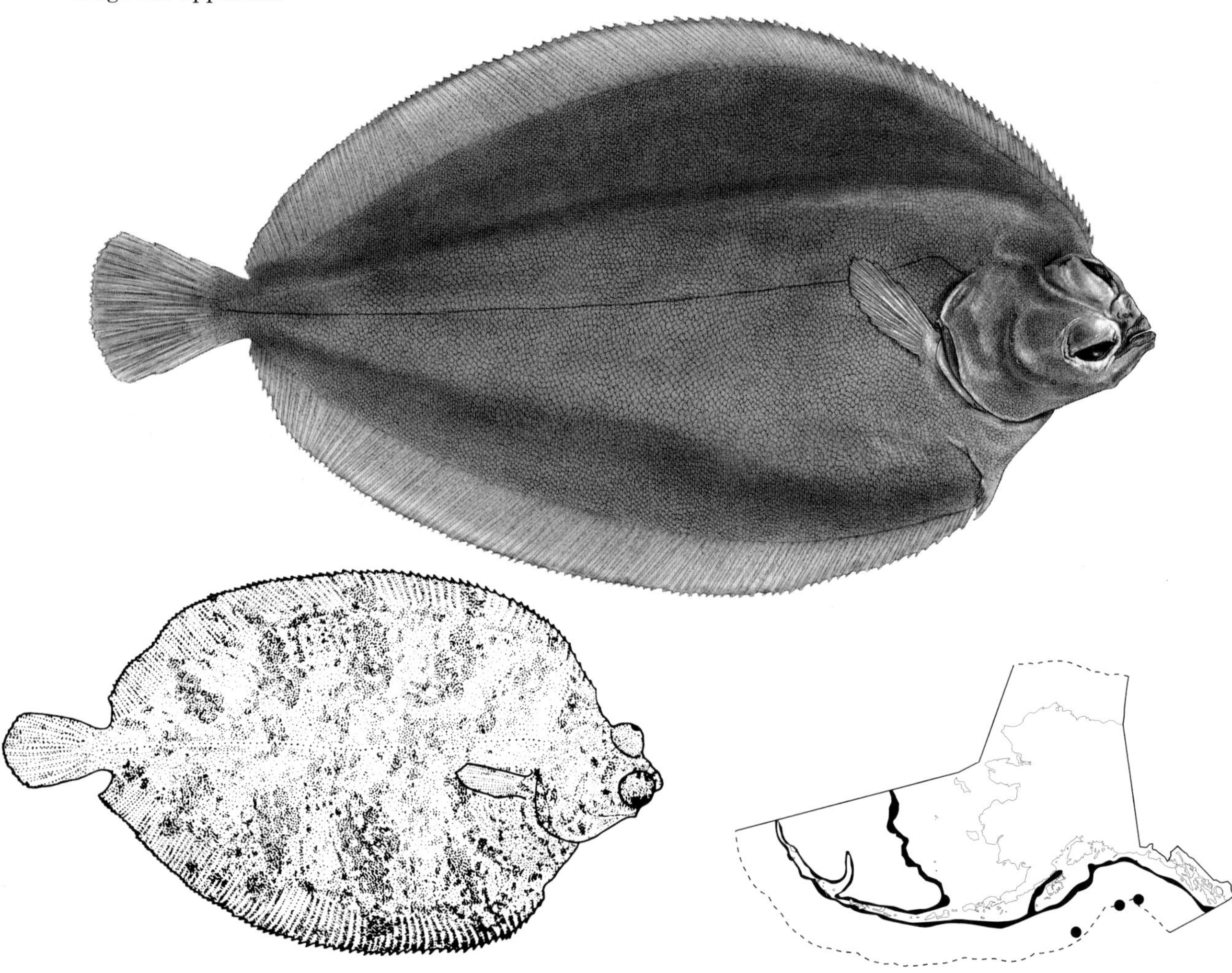

Notes & Sources — *Embassichthys bathybius* (Gilbert, 1890)
Cynicoglossus bathybius Gilbert, 1890
Microstomus bathybius: Cooper and Chapleau 1998.

Description: Norman 1934:361–362; Hart 1973:605–606; Amaoka et al. 1981; Sakamoto in Masuda et al. 1984:353; Kramer et al. 1995:40–41.

Figures: Upper: University of British Columbia, artist P. Drukker-Brammall, Apr. 1974; UBC 62-476, 376 mm SL, east of Sanak I., Alaska. Lower: Miller and Lea 1972:205.

Range: Records include Bering Sea at 60°13'N, 179°06'W; between Bering and Attu islands; north of Unalaska and Islands of Four Mountains; south of Shumagin Is. (Amaoka et al. 1981); Pratt Seamount (Hubbs 1959); Surveyor and Patton seamounts (Hughes 1981). ABL specimens are from south of Unalaska Island (AB 65-46), near Kodiak Island and south of Prince William Sound (AB 66-151, 68-19), and southeastern Alaska off Cape Ommaney (AB 83-5).

Size: B. A. Sheiko, pers. comm., 15 Jan. 1999; *Darwin*, 22 Jul. 1982, 60°37'N, 179°36'E, 620 m, KIE uncataloged.

Microstomus pacificus (Lockington, 1879) **Dover sole**

Southeastern Bering Sea and Aleutian Islands from Stalemate Bank to southern Baja California off Punta San Juanico.

Muddy bottom at depths of 9–1,244 m, usually 50–450 m.

D 88–116; A 75–96; Pec 8–12; Pel 5–6; LLs 137–149; GR 5–8 + 8–11; Vert 11–13 + 38–41 (50–55).

- Eyed side brown, with indistinct darker mottling; **fins blackish at edges**; blind side smudgy off-white to dark brownish gray.
- **Body elongate, soft, and limp**.
- Upper profile of head evenly curved.
- Interorbital ridge present; postocular ridge scarcely apparent.
- Maxilla extending to below anterior part of eye.
- Anal spine absent.
- Dorsal fin origin a little behind middle of eye; caudal fin rounded.
- Lateral line nearly straight, with low curve above pectoral fin; **short anterior branch**.
- Snout, interorbital ridge, and upper surface of eyeballs scaled; median fins densely scaled.
- **Teeth primarily on blind side**; **never more than 3 on eyed side of either jaw**.
- Length to 76 cm TL, weight to 4.6 kg; average trawl-caught fish about 0.45 kg.

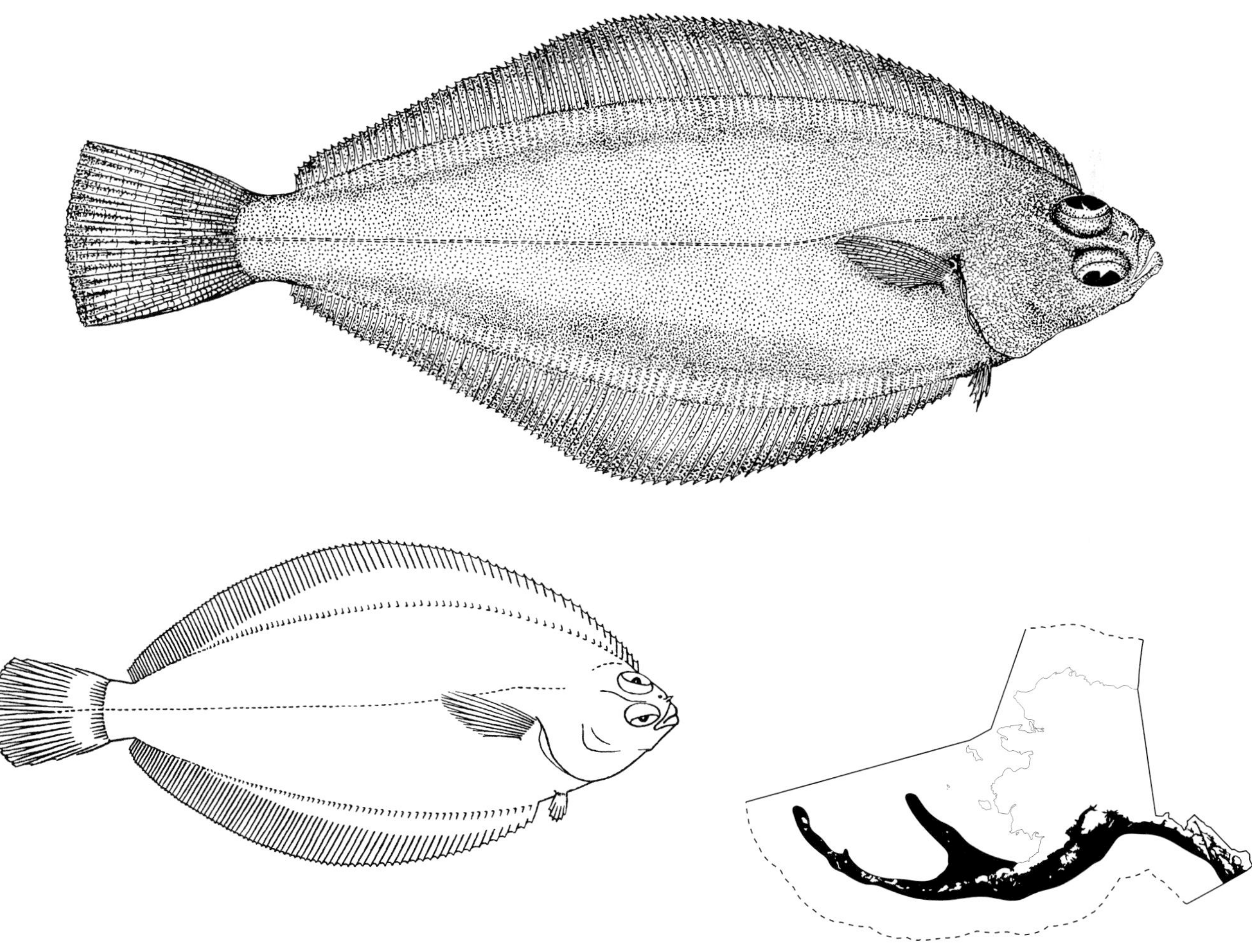

Notes & Sources — *Microstomus pacificus* (Lockington, 1879)
Glyptocephalus pacificus Lockington, 1879

Description: Lockington 1879:86–88; Norman 1934:356, 360–361; Miller and Lea 1972:206; Hart 1973:626–628; Kramer et al. 1995:60–61.

Figures: Upper: Hart 1973:626; 32 cm TL. Lower: Norman 1934, fig. 261.

Range: Allen and Smith (1988) reported NMFS survey data that extended the known range north to Navarin Canyon in the Bering Sea and to west of the Aleutian Islands at Stalemate Bank. Recorded from as far south as 25°59'N, 113°17'W, depth 248–250 m, and from Hodgkins and Cobb seamounts (west of northern British Columbia and Washington) by Snytko (1987).

Glyptocephalus zachirus Lockington, 1879 **rex sole**

Bering Sea from Navarin Canyon and Aleutian Islands from Stalemate Bank to central Baja California off Cedros Island; western Bering Sea to southern tip of Kamchatka.

Sandy or muddy bottom from shallow water near shore to depth of about 850 m, usually 50–450 m.

D 87–110; A 78–93; Pec 11–13; Pel 6; LLs 132–138; GR 0–4 + 5–8; Vert 12–14 + 50–52 (62–66).

- Eyed side light brown to gray; both sides with black speckles; **pectoral fin mostly black**; blind side off-white to dusky.
- Body elongate; limp, slimy; **large mucous cavities in skull, most evident on blind side**; profile of upper margin of head convex; **snout rounded**.
- Interorbital ridge evident in preserved fish; postocular ridge scarcely apparent.
- Maxilla extending to below anterior edge of eye or a little beyond.
- **Anal spine pronounced**.
- Dorsal fin origin above middle or anterior part of eye; **pectoral fin on eyed side longer than head**; caudal fin rounded or double truncate.
- Lateral line nearly straight, with slight rise or low curve anteriorly; **no anterior branch**.
- Snout and interorbital ridge scaled; eyeballs not scaled; caudal fin scaled, other fins not scaled or lightly scaled.
- **Teeth well developed on both sides**; **12–16 on eyed side of upper jaw**.
- Length to 61 cm TL; average trawl-caught fish about 25 cm TL and 0.23 kg.

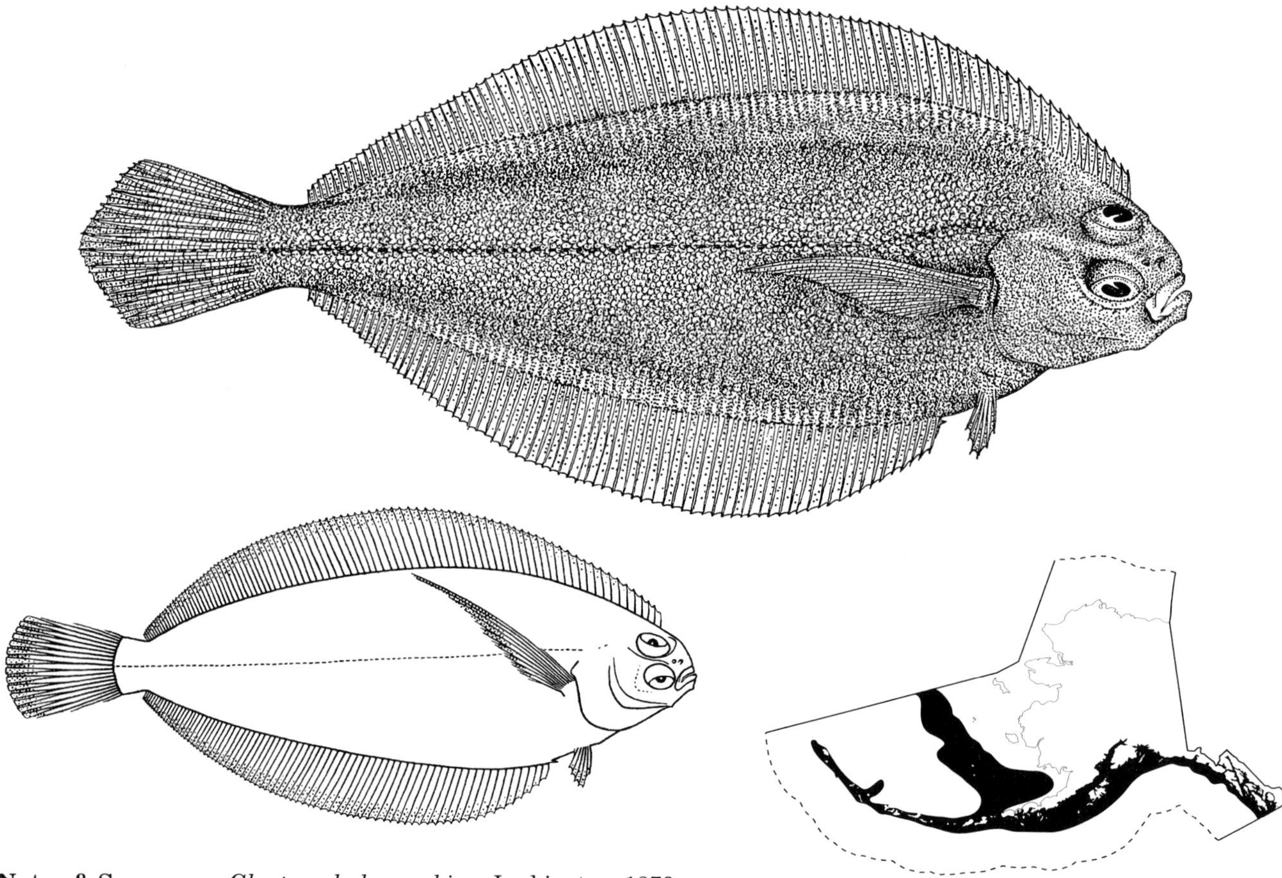

Notes & Sources — *Glyptocephalus zachirus* Lockington, 1879
Errex zachirus: Jordan 1919, Sakamoto 1984.

Description: Lockington 1879:88–91; Norman 1934:367–368; Miller and Lea 1972:204; Hart 1973:610–611; Kramer et al. 1995:46–47.

Figures: Upper: Hart 1973:610; 35 cm TL. Lower: Norman 1934, fig. 266.

Range: Allen and Smith (1988) mapped NMFS survey data indicating extension of the known range northwest in the Bering Sea to Navarin Canyon and off Glubokaya Bay on the Koryak Coast, and to Stalemate Bank west of Attu Island. B. A. Sheiko (pers. comm., 15 Jan. 1999) observed *G. zachirus* in Russian surveys off the Olyutorskiy–Navarin region in 1982, and in the 1990s Tokranov and Vinnikov (2000) observed it in Olyutorskiy Bay and nearby waters over the Shirshov Ridge. A collection off the south tip of Kamchatka in 1998 at 51°04'N, 157°40'E, depth 100–106 m (KIE 2266), is the southernmost record from the western Pacific. Previously recorded off Russia as far south as the Commander Islands (Kulikov 1964). Can occur far offshore; e.g., west of Washington at Cobb Seamount in 1977 at depths of 255–260 m (Snytko 1987).

Glyptocephalus stelleri (Schmidt, 1904) **Korean flounder**

Rare records from Bering Sea and from Pacific Ocean off Kamchatka; most abundant in western Pacific off southern Kuril Islands and in Okhotsk and Japan seas.

Sandy and muddy bottoms at depths of 20–900 m, probably to 1,200 m or more.

D 81–100; A 69–88; Pec 10–13; Pel 6; LLs 85–115; GR 3–6 + 7–10; Vert 11–12 + 41–43 (49–55).

- Eyed side grayish brown; finely speckled; blind side pale gray.
- Body elongate; fewer vertebrae than *G. zachirus*; **large mucous cavities in skull, most evident on blind side**.
- Interorbital ridge high, narrow; postocular ridge scarcely apparent.
- Maxilla extending to a little beyond anterior edge of eye.
- **Anal spine inconspicuous**.
- Dorsal fin origin above middle of eye; **pectoral fin shorter than head**; caudal fin rounded or double truncate.
- Lateral line nearly straight, with slight rise above pectoral fin; **short anterior branch**.
- Snout and interorbital ridge not scaled; eyeballs scaled; median fins scaled; fewer lateral line scales than in *G. zachirus*.
- **Teeth 7 or more on eyed side of upper jaw**.
- Length to 50 cm TL.

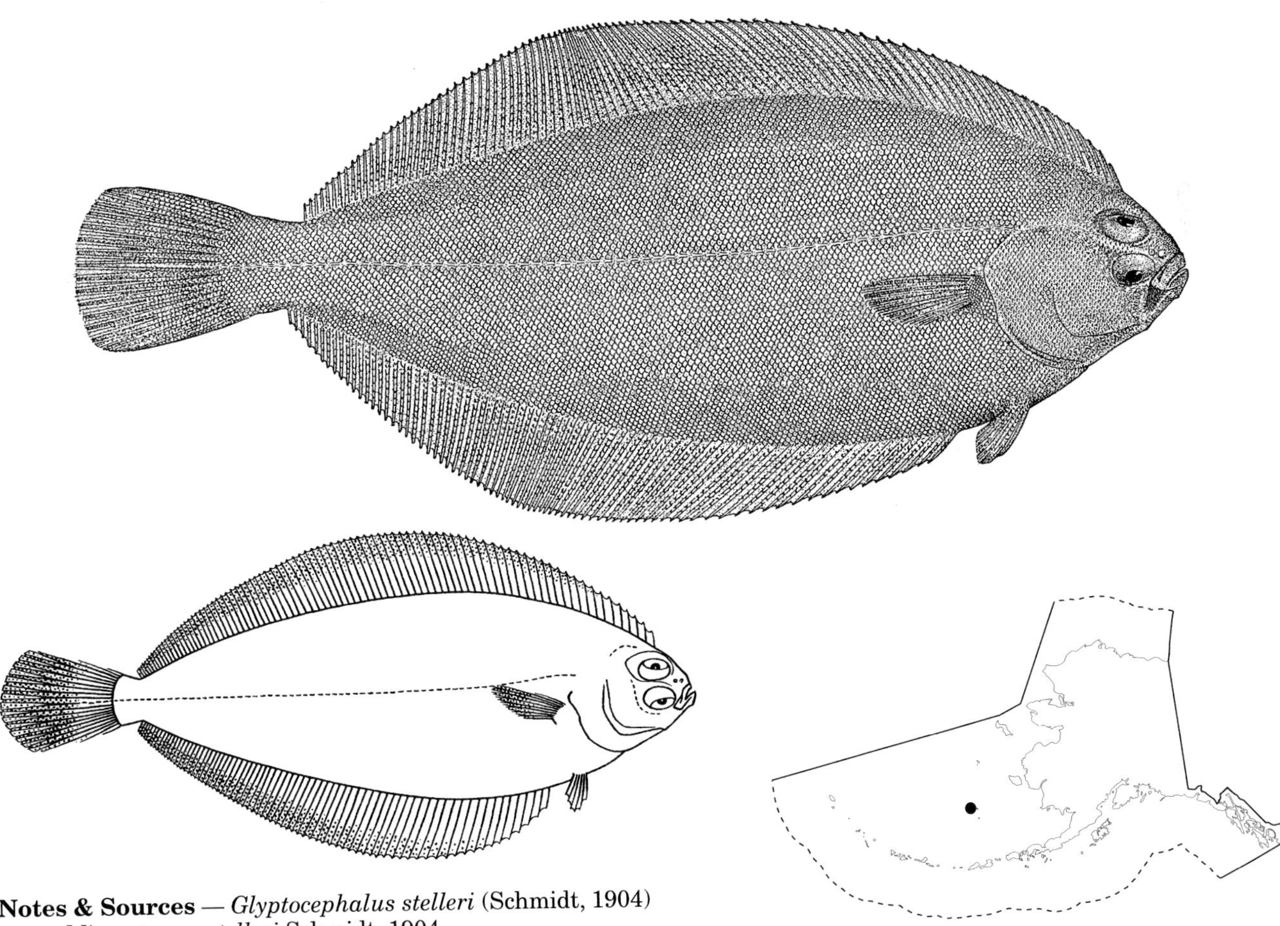

Notes & Sources — *Glyptocephalus stelleri* (Schmidt, 1904)
Microstomus stelleri Schmidt, 1904
Glyptocephalus ostroumowi Pavlenko, 1910
Glyptocephalus sasae Snyder, 1911
Also called small-mouth plaice and Far Eastern long flounder.

Description: Snyder 1911:548–549; Hubbs 1932; Norman 1934:366–367; Schmidt 1950:237–238; Sakamoto in Amaoka et al. 1983:349; Lindberg and Fedorov 1993:157–160; Kramer et al. 1995:48–49.

Figures: Upper: Snyder 1911, pl. 59, fig. 1; type of *G. sasae*, 35 cm TL, Japan. Lower: Norman 1934, fig. 265.

Range: The only record of *G. stelleri* in the eastern Bering Sea is that of Lindberg and Fedorov (1993), who listed a collection (TINRO 3027) from depths of 355–370 m in the vicinity of the Pribilof Islands. A specimen (LACM 35753-1) from north of Cape Sarichef, Unimak Island, labeled "*G. stelleri* (?)" has a long pectoral fin on the eyed side (J. A. Seigel, pers. comm., 5 May 1998) and is more likely to be *G. zachirus*. In the winter fishery trawling to 900 m in Tatar Strait in the 1990s the greatest densities of *G. stelleri* were found below 700 m, indicating that assemblages extend even deeper, to 1,000–1,200 m (Kim Sen Tok et al. 1999).

Order Tetraodontiformes
Tetraodontiforms

The order Tetraodontiformes includes about 330 extant species, most of them inhabitants of tropical or subtropical nearshore waters. One species in the family Balistidae and one in Molidae have been reported from Alaskan waters, but only as rare occurrences during unusually warm conditions.

Tetraodontiforms occur in a great variety of shapes, but with 16–30 vertebrae they generally are ovoid or rounded rather than elongate. Members of some families can enlarge their bodies for protection or territorial display. They are able to inflate their stomachs to an enormous size or, as in the family Balistidae, can slightly enlarge their bodies by expanding a ventral flap supported by a large movable pelvic bone. In most tetraodontiforms the scales are modified to form a bony shield, bony plates, spines, or prickles; a few lack scales. Some species are poisonous.

All members of the Tetraodontiformes have a small gill opening, located in front of the pectoral fin. The mouth is small. In most species the teeth are fused into a beaklike plate, and the maxilla and premaxilla are fused. The spinous dorsal fin is absent or has very few spines, the rayed dorsal fin and anal fin are opposite each other and well back on the body, and pelvic fins are absent. The swim bladder is present except in members of the family Molidae.

Family Balistidae
Triggerfishes

Fishes of the family Balistidae are called triggerfishes in reference to their specialized, upright-locking first dorsal fin spine, or leatherjackets for their thick, scaleless skin. The family comprises 120–135 species. All of them are inhabitants of warm seas. Most triggerfish species are restricted to a narrow strip along the coast, with few frequenting the open ocean.

Diagnostic features of leatherjackets include a greatly compressed body; absence of pelvic fins, or pelvic fins that are reduced and fused to form a small spine or tubercle; a dorsal fin with 2 or 3 spines, the first having a locking mechanism; 12 major rays in the caudal fin; and an upper jaw with two rows of protruding incisorlike teeth. Predators attempting to swallow these fishes can be injured by the rigid first dorsal spine. Most triggerfishes attain lengths under 30 cm (12 inches). The maximum is about 1 m (3.3 ft).

The finescale triggerfish, *Balistes polylepis,* is known in Alaska from one specimen retrieved from a trap in southeastern Alaska at Metlakatla during the 1982–83 El Niño. Unfortunately, the fish was lost before its identity could be confirmed and it was reported to be a black durgon, *Melichthys niger* (Karinen et al. 1985). A black-and-white photograph of the fish shows the third dorsal spine, which is virtually absent in *M. niger* but distinct in *B. polylepis.* The fish in the photograph also appears to be lighter in color than *M. niger* and to lack the pale band at the base of the dorsal and anal fins that is present in *M. niger.* Information on the geographic ranges of these species also substantiates an identification of *B. polylepis* for the Metlakatla specimen. In 1983, the same year it was found in Alaska, *B. polylepis* was found at Willipa Bay, Washington (Schoener and Fluharty 1985), and Yaquina Bay, Oregon (Pearcy et al. 1985). Those discoveries followed a progressive series of range extensions of *B. polylepis* northward from Baja California in previous years (Mearns 1988). *Melichthys niger,* however, has not been confirmed north of Mexico since it was reported off San Diego in the 1800s (Miller and Lea 1972, Eschmeyer and Herald 1983).

Balistes polylepis Steindachner, 1876 **finescale triggerfish**

Southeastern Alaska at Metlakatla; isolated records from Washington to California; most common from Baja California to Chile.

Adults over sandy bottoms and around reefs near shore and to depth of 512 m; juveniles pelagic.

D III + 26–28; A 24–26; Pec 13–15; GR 29–37; Vert 18.

- Light brownish gray, with blue speckles on head.
- Three spines in first dorsal fin, all fully visible.
- Length to about 76 cm TL.

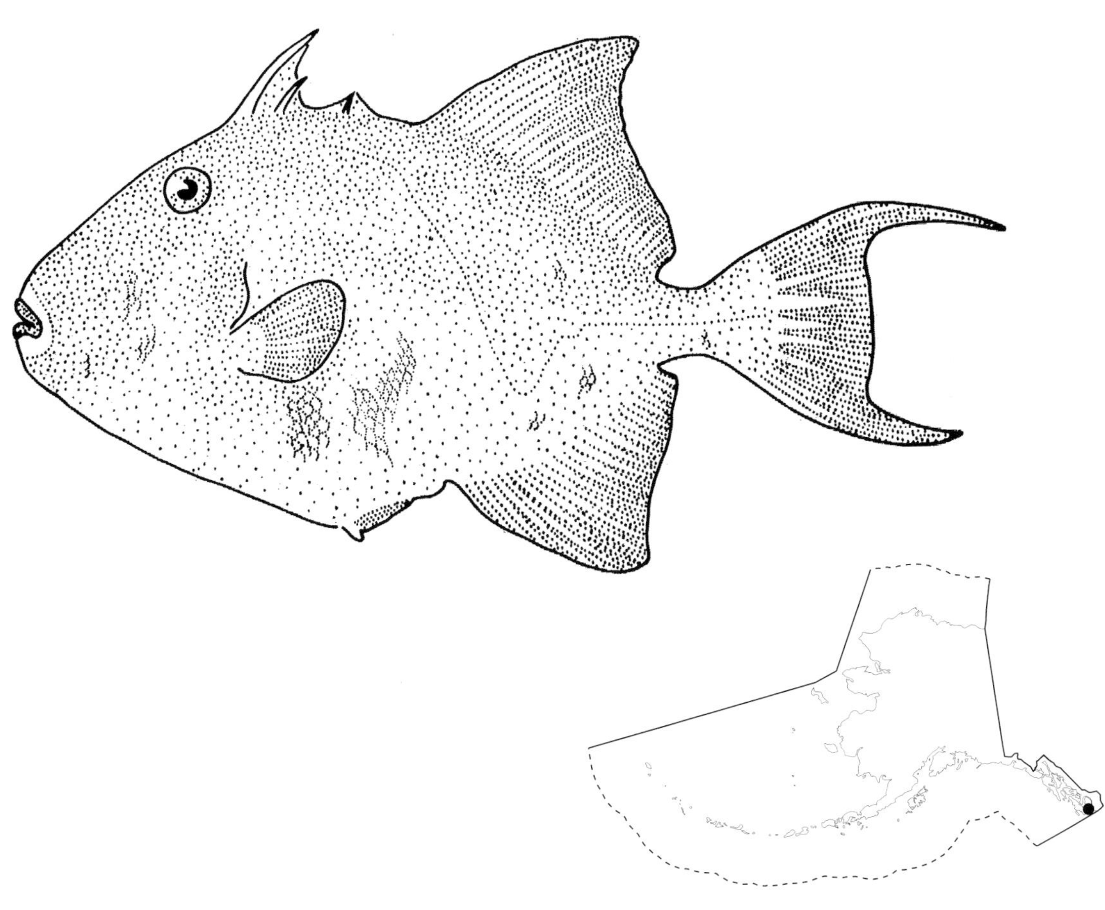

Notes & Sources — *Balistes polylepis* Steindachner, 1876
Melichthys niger: Karinen et al. 1985 (misidentification), Pearcy and Schoener 1987 (range, from same record).

Description: Fitch and Lavenberg 1975:22–24; Eschmeyer and Herald 1983:295; Bussing in Fischer et al. 1995:908.
Figure: Miller and Lea 1972:208.
Range: Known in Alaska from one specimen caught in a trap at Metlakatla in the summer of 1983. In that year a particularly strong El Niño brought several species north, out of their normal range. This particular fish was lost before its identity could be confirmed and it was recorded and referred to black durgon, *Melichthys niger*, by Karinen et al. (1985). The ADFG biologist who retrieved the fish believed it to be an example of *B. polylepis* (J. Koerner, pers. comm., 14 Jan. 1993), but a newspaper article (*Southeastern Log*, October 1983:A–7) called the fish a black triggerfish. The article was accompanied by a black-and-white photograph. The photograph is dark and the fish looks partially dried out, making the fish look blackish, but the third dorsal fin spine characteristic of *B. polylepis* can be seen. The nearest captures of finescale triggerfish outside Alaska occurred during the same exceptionally strong El Niño event that brought the fish to Alaska: two specimens collected at Willipa Bay, Washington (Schoener and Fluharty 1985), and another from Yaquina Bay, Oregon (Pearcy et al. 1985).

FAMILY MOLIDAE
Molas

Molas are markedly compressed, truncate fishes with high dorsal and anal fins, no pelvic fins, and no true caudal fin. They inhabit warm regions of the world's oceans, where they are often seen during calm weather swimming slowly or floating at the surface. Molas primarily feed on jellyfishes and algae. One of the three extant species, the ocean sunfish, *Mola mola,* drifts into Alaskan waters during unusually warm weather.

Molas have a scalloped thickening of the body posteriorly which is used as a rudder, but the clavus, as it is called, is not homologous with the caudal fin of other fishes. Other mola characteristics include two fused teeth, beaklike, in each jaw; a porelike gill opening; two minute nostrils on each side of the head; and 16–18 vertebrae. Molas lack a lateral line and swim bladder. Juvenile and adult molas differ greatly in appearance, although the young already lack a caudal fin.

Ocean sunfish attain a maximum length of about 4 m (13.1 ft) and weight of about 1,500 kg (3,300 lb). The large size of this species, as well as the broad distribution of Molidae in general, is thought to be related to a life of passive drifting as a planktonic fish.

Mola mola (Linnaeus, 1758) **ocean sunfish**

Western Gulf of Alaska to South America; worldwide in tropical and temperate seas.

Epipelagic, both inshore and oceanic.

- Grayish brown dorsally, shading to silvery white to cream ventrally.
- Body compressed, deep, rounded.
- High dorsal and anal fins; posterior margin of body scalloped and thickened.

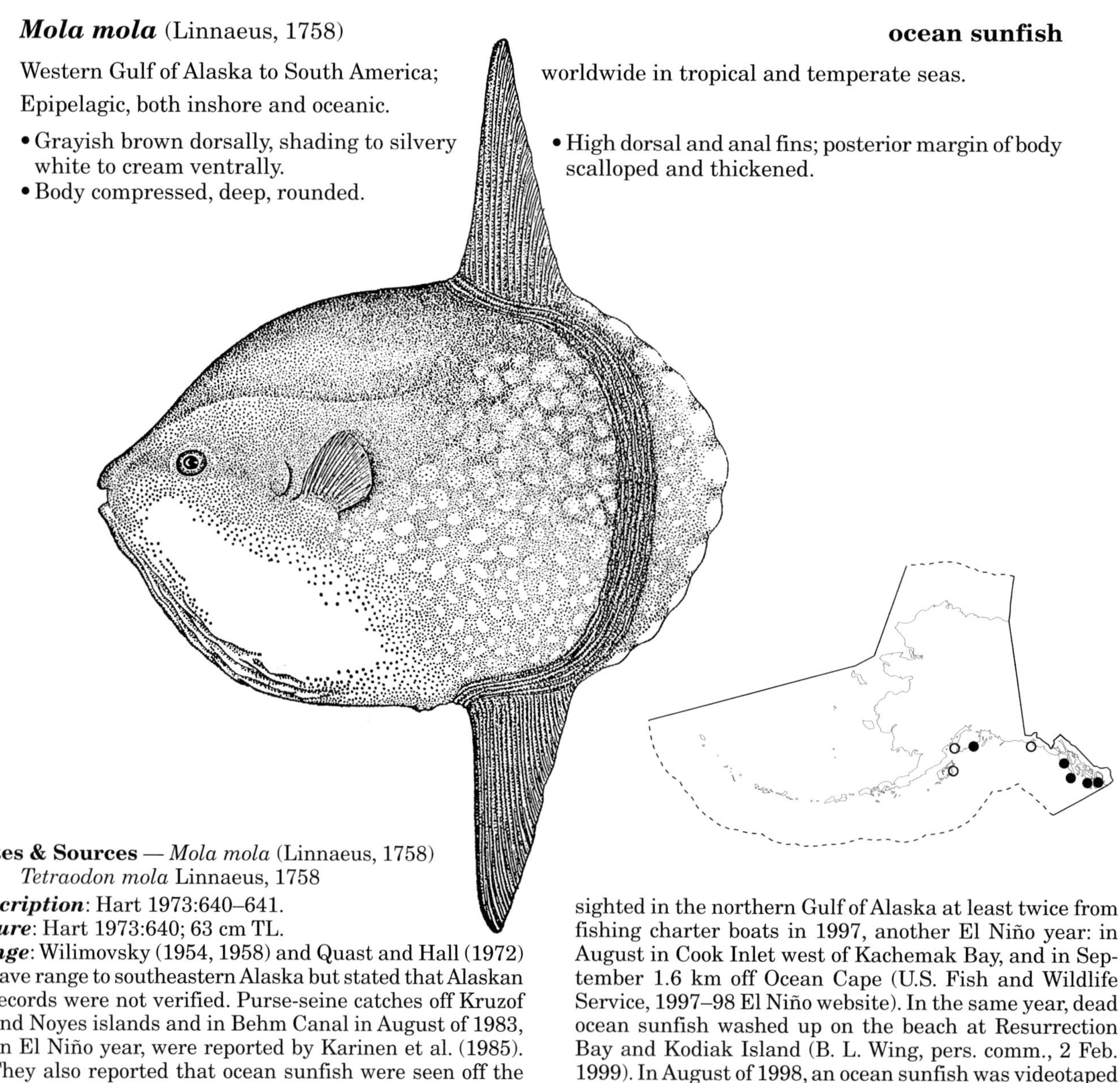

Notes & Sources — *Mola mola* (Linnaeus, 1758)
Tetraodon mola Linnaeus, 1758

Description: Hart 1973:640–641.

Figure: Hart 1973:640; 63 cm TL.

Range: Wilimovsky (1954, 1958) and Quast and Hall (1972) gave range to southeastern Alaska but stated that Alaskan records were not verified. Purse-seine catches off Kruzof and Noyes islands and in Behm Canal in August of 1983, an El Niño year, were reported by Karinen et al. (1985). They also reported that ocean sunfish were seen off the outer coast about 10 years previously. Ocean sunfish were sighted in the northern Gulf of Alaska at least twice from fishing charter boats in 1997, another El Niño year: in August in Cook Inlet west of Kachemak Bay, and in September 1.6 km off Ocean Cape (U.S. Fish and Wildlife Service, 1997–98 El Niño website). In the same year, dead ocean sunfish washed up on the beach at Resurrection Bay and Kodiak Island (B. L. Wing, pers. comm., 2 Feb. 1999). In August of 1998, an ocean sunfish was videotaped in Resurrection Bay (S. C. Meyer, pers. comm., 24 Sep. 1998).

Gazetteer

GAZETTEER

In the following list the term *SE Alaska* is used as a descriptor for place names on the mainland of southeastern Alaska, as opposed to the islands composing the Alexander Archipelago of southeastern Alaska. Use of directional modifiers N, S, E, W, such as in N Russia or W Alaska, is not meant to indicate specific geographic or political entities, only general areas. For British Columbia, N, Central, and S generally refer to the coastal part of the province, not the interior. Obsolete names are generally not listed. Instead, modern equivalents are given in the text; e.g., "Kowuk (= Kobuk) River" or "St. Paul (now city of Kodiak)." Riverbanks are designated right or left from the perspective of a person traveling downstream. Numerous atlases, maps, gazetteers, and collection records were used to create this gazetteer. The major sources are given on page 884.

Aaron Island	Favorite Channel, NW of Point Stephens, N Alexander Archipelago	58°26'N	134°49'W
Abashiri	N Hokkaido, Japan, on Sea of Okhotsk	44°06'N	144°06'E
Abbess Island	W of Wadleigh Island, S Alexander Archipelago, Alaska	55°33'N	133°10'W
Adak Island	Andreanof Islands, Aleutian Islands, Alaska	51°45'N	176°45'W
Admiralty Bay	Head of Dease Inlet, at mouth of Meade River, Beaufort Sea, Alaska	70°53'N	155°43'W
Admiralty Island	Between Chatham Strait and Stephens Passage, N Alexander Arch.	57°40'N	134°20'W
Afognak Island	N of Kodiak Island, W Gulf of Alaska	58°15'N	152°30'W
Agattu Island	Southernmost of Near Islands, Aleutian Islands, Alaska	52°26'N	173°36'E
Ahrnklin River	Flows to Gulf of Alaska SE of Yakutat, Alaska	59°26'N	139°32'W
Aiktak Island	Krenitzin Islands, Aleutian Islands, Alaska	54°11'N	164°50'W
Akun Island	Krenitzin Islands, Aleutian Islands, Alaska	54°11'N	165°32'W
Akutan Bay	E coast Akutan Island, Krenitzin Islands, Alaska	54°11'N	165°43'W
Akutan Island	Krenitzin Islands, Aleutian Islands, Alaska	54°07'N	165°55'W
Akutan Pass	Between Unalaska and Akutan islands, Aleutian Islands, Alaska	54°01'N	166°03'W
Alaska Peninsula	Between Bristol Bay and Gulf of Alaska	56°30'N	159°00'W
Alaska Range	Extends from Iliamna Lake across S Alaska to Canada	59°45'N	156°00'W
Alatna	On N bank Koyakuk River, Alaska	66°34'N	152°40'W
Alatna River	Alaska, flows to Koyakuk River	66°34'N	152°37'W
Alazaya River	Flows to East Siberian Sea, N Russia	71°23'N	154°03'E
Albatross Bank	Shoal SE of Kodiak Island, W Gulf of Alaska	56°30'N	152°30'W
Alberni Inlet	Port Alberni to Barkley Sound, Vancouver Island, British Columbia	48°59'N	124°54'W
Aleutian Basin	Deepwater depression E of Shirshov Ridge, E Bering Sea	55°00'N	177°00'W
Aleutian Islands	Island chain between Bering Sea and Pacific Ocean, Alaska	52°00'N	174°00'W
Aleutian Trench	Pacific Ocean S of Aleutian Islands to S of Kodiak Island, Alaska	51°00'N	171°00'W
Aleutkina Bay	W coast Baranof Island, 4 mi SE of Sitka, Alexander Archipelago	57°00'N	135°17'W
Alexander Archipelago	Islands from Cross Sound and Icy Strait to Dixon Entrance, Alaska	57°00'N	134°00'W
Alice Arm	Head of Observatory Inlet, British Columbia, Canada	55°27'N	129°33'W
Alitak Bay	S coast Kodiak Island, W Gulf of Alaska	56°50'N	154°10'W
Alsek River	Flows S from Canada to NE Gulf of Alaska at Dry Bay	59°03'N	138°34'W

Amak Island	Bristol Bay NW of Izembek Lagoon, NW coast Alaska Peninsula	55°25'N	163°08'W
Amchitka Island	Rat Islands, Aleutian Islands, Alaska	51°30'N	179°00'E
Amchitka Pass	Between Rat Islands and Delarof Islands, Aleutian Islands, Alaska	51°35'N	180°00'E
Amguema River	Flows to Chukchi Sea, N coast Siberia, NE Russia	68°10'N	177°40'W
Amlia Island	Andreanof Islands, Aleutian Islands, Alaska	52°04'N	173°30'W
Amukta Island	Westernmost of Islands of Four Mountains, Aleutian Islands, Alaska	52°30'N	171°16'W
Amukta Pass	Between Andreanof Islands and Fox Islands, Aleutian Islands, Alaska	52°15'N	172°00'W
Amundsen Gulf	Arctic Ocean, W Northwest Territories, Canada	70°33'N	120°47'W
Amur River	On China–Russia border, flows to N Tatar Strait, Russia	50°20'N	137°10'E
Anadyr River	NE Russia, flows to Bering Sea at W end Anadyr Bay	64°41'N	177°32'E
Anadyr Bay	W shore Gulf of Anadyr, W Bering Sea, Russia	64°30'N	177°45'E
Anchorage	S central Alaska on Knik Arm, Cook Inlet	61°13'N	149°53'W
Anderson River	British Columbia, Canada	49°50'N	121°26'W
Anderson River	Northwest Territories, Canada	69°43'N	129°00'W
Andreafsky River	Flows SW to Yukon R. at Pitkas Point, Yukon-Kuskokwim Delta, Alaska	62°02'N	163°15'W
Andreanof Islands	Aleutian Islands between Amchitka Pass and Amukta Pass, Alaska	52°00'N	176°00'W
Aniva Bay, Aniwa Bay	S tip Sakhalin Island, Sea of Okhotsk, Russia	46°15'N	142°45'E
Antilles	West Indies, islands separating Caribbean Sea from Atlantic Ocean	20°00'N	75°00'W
Anton Larsen Bay	N coast Kodiak Island, 10 mi NW of Kodiak, W Gulf of Alaska	57°52'N	152°38'W
Aomori	N coast Honshu, Japan	40°49'N	140°45'E
Apoon Pass	Yukon Delta, W Alaska	63°03'N	163°22'W
Applequist Seamount	Gulf of Alaska about 252 nmi WSW of Cape Edgecumbe, Alaska	55°28'N	142°46'W
Arena Cove	Point Arena, N California	38°54'N	123°42'W
Armeria Bay	NW coast Agattu Island, Aleutian Islands, Alaska	52°27'N	173°30'E
Athabasca River	Alberta, Canada	58°40'N	110°50'W
Atka Island	Largest of Andreanof Islands, Aleutian Islands, Alaska	52°07'N	174°30'W
Atlin Lake	British Columbia and Yukon Territory, Canada	59°35'N	133°47'W
Attu Island	Westernmost of Near Islands, Aleutian Islands, Alaska	52°55'N	172°55'E
Augustine Island	Kamishak Bay, W Cook Inlet, N Gulf of Alaska	59°22'N	153°26'W
Auke Bay	E shore Stephens Passage, 10 mi NW of Juneau, SE Alaska	58°21'N	134°40'W
Aurora Lagoon	E shore Kachemak Bay on Kenai Peninsula, NW Gulf of Alaska	59°42'N	151°06'W
Avacha Bay	NW Pacific Ocean E of Petropavlovsk, SE Kamchatka, Russia	53°00'N	158°45'E
Avatcha Bay	Same as Avacha Bay	53°00'N	158°45'E
Avacha Bight	Off Avacha Bay at Petropavlovk, SE Kamchatka, Russia	53°03'N	158°39'E
Avachinskaya Bay	Same as Avacha Bight	53°03'N	158°39'E
Baffin Bay	Arctic Ocean N of Davis Strait between Greenland and Baffin Island	73°00'N	65°00'W
Baffin Island	E Northwest Territories, Canada	70°06'N	74°15'W
Bahia Magdalena	Pacific coast S Baja California, Mexico	24°38'N	112°00'W

Bahia San Hipolito	Same as Hipolito Bay	27°06'N	114°12'W
Bahia San Quintin	Pacific coast N Baja California, Mexico	30°23'N	115°58'W
Bahia Santa Maria	Pacific coast S Baja California, Mexico	24°40'N	112°11'W
Bahia Sebastian Vizcaino	Pacific coast central Baja California, Mexico	28°00'N	114°30'W
Bahia Tórtolo	SE of Punta Eugenia, Pacific coast central Baja California, Mexico	27°40'N	114°53'W
Baker Island	E shore Gulf of Alaska, W of Prince of Wales Island, Alexander Arch.	55°22'N	133°36'W
Balboa Island	Newport Beach, S California	33°36'N	117°53'W
Baldwin Peninsula	Extends NW from S shore Kotzebue Sound, W coast Alaska	66°45'N	162°20'W
Banks Island	Hecate Strait off mainland, N British Columbia, Canada	53°23'N	130°06'W
Barabara Point	W coast Kenai Peninsula, Kachemak Bay, NW Gulf of Alaska	59°29'N	151°38'W
Baranof Island	Between Gulf of Alaska and S Chatham Strait, Alexander Archipelago	56°45'N	135°10'W
Barents Sea	NW Russia off White Sea, Arctic Ocean	71°00'N	40°00'E
Barkley Canyon	Pacific Ocean W of S Vancouver Island, British Columbia	48°15'N	126°10'W
Barkley Sound	W coast Vancouver Island, S British Columbia, Canada	48°40'N	125°30'W
Barlow Cove	N end Admiralty Island, NW of Juneau, SE Alaska	58°24'N	134°55'W
Barren Islands	NW Gulf of Alaska between Kenai Peninsula and Shuyak Island	67°48'N	152°15'W
Barrier Island	NW coast Prince of Wales Island, Alexander Archipelago	56°13'N	133°40'W
Barrow	Chukchi Sea coast SW of Point Barrow, N Alaska	71°17'N	156°47'W
Barter Island	Beaufort Sea E of Camden Bay, NE coast Alaska	70°07'N	143°40'W
Bartlett Cove	E shore Glacier Bay, SE Alaska	58°27'N	135°55'W
Bashiri	N Hokkaido, Japan, on Sea of Okhotsk	43°57'N	144°31'E
Bathurst Inlet	Coronation Gulf, Arctic Ocean, Northwest Territories, Canada	67°46'N	108°42'W
Bay of Bengal	Indian Ocean	13°00'N	87°00'E
Bay of Pillars	W coast Kuiu Island, Alexander Archipelago	56°35'N	134°15'W
Beacon Hill	Mountain near Victoria, British Columbia, Canada	48°25'N	123°22'W
Bear Creek	Mitkof Island, Alexander Archipelago	56°40'N	132°50'W
Beaufort Sea	S side Arctic Ocean off N coast Alaska and NW coast Canada	71°00'N	141°00'W
Beaver	N Bank Yukon River, interior Alaska	66°21'N	147°23'W
Becharof Lake	Alaska Peninsula, at head of Egegik River	57°56'N	156°23'W
Beechey Point	Beaufort Sea coast E of mouth of Colville River, N Alaska	70°29'N	149°09'W
Behm Canal	Between Revillagigedo Island and mainland, SE Alaska	55°28'N	131°55'W
Bellingham Bay	NW coast Washington on S Strait of Georgia	48°74'N	122°52'W
Bering Island	W island in Commander Islands, Russia	55°00'N	166°15'E
Bering Sea	N part of Pacific Ocean, from Bering Strait to Aleutian Islands	58°00'N	177°00'W
Bering Strait	Connects Chukchi Sea and Bering Sea, between Alaska and Russia	66°00'N	169°00'W
Berners Bay	E shore Lynn Canal, 34 mi NW of Juneau, SE Alaska	58°43'N	135°00'W
Big Diomede Island	Bering Strait, Russia; also called Ratmanov Island	65°46'N	169°06'W
Big Eldorado Creek	Near Fairbanks, interior Alaska	64°55'N	147°49'W

Big Koniuji Island	Shumagin Islands, SW Gulf of Alaska	55°06'N	159°33'W
Big Port Walter	Head of Port Walter, S coast Baranof Island, Alexander Archipelago	56°23'N	134°44'W
Big River	Flows N to Middle Fork Kuskokwim River E of McGrath, W Alaska	61°45'N	154°00'W
Big Sur River	South of Monterey Bay, California	36°16'N	121°51'W
Biorka Island	SW of Sitka off W coast Baranof Island, Alexander Archipelago	56°51'N	135°32'W
Bird Point	N side Turnagain Arm, Alaska	60°56'N	149°22'W
Black River	Flows NW to Porcupine River NE of Fort Yukon, interior Alaska	66°41'N	144°42'W
Blizhni Strait	Opens to NW shore Yakutat Bay, NE Gulf of Alaska	59°50'N	139°46'W
Boca de Quadra	Inlet E of Annette Island, Alexander Archipelago	55°04'N	131°01'W
Bodega Bay	N California between Point Arena and Point Reyes	38°16'N	123°00'W
Bodega Head	Point on N California coast	38°19'N	123°04'W
Bogoslof Island	Bering Sea N of Umnak Island, Fox Islands, Aleutian Islands, Alaska	53°56'N	168°02'W
Bonilla Island	Hecate Strait, N British Columbia	53°30'N	130°40'W
Boothia Peninsula	Between Victoria and Baffin islands, Nunavut, Canada	70°30'N	94°30'W
Bowers Bank	About midway along Bowers Ridge, least depth 11 m, Aleutian Islands	54°18'N	179°30'E
Bowers Basin	Deepwater depression between Rat Islands and Bowers Ridge	53°00'N	177°00'E
Bowers Ridge	Extends in 250-mi curve N and W from Petrel Bank, Aleutian Is., Alaska	54°00'N	179°55'E
Bowie Seamount	E Pacific Ocean west of British Columbia, Canada	53°18'N	135°38'W
Bradfield Canal	Mouth of Bradfield River to Ernest Sound, SE Alaska	56°11'N	131°59'W
Brinnon	Hood Canal, Washington	47°41'N	122°54'W
Bristol Bay	E Bering Sea between Cape Newenham and Alaska Peninsula	57°00'N	162°00'W
Brookings	Oregon coast	42°03'N	124°16'W
Brooks Lake	S of Naknek Lake, Naknek River system, Alaska Peninsula	58°33'N	155°50'W
Brooks Range	Extends from Canada W to Chukchi Sea, N Alaska	68°00'N	156°00'W
Browerville	Chukchi Sea coast NE of Barrow, N Alaska	71°18'N	156°46'W
Brownlow Point	Beaufort Sea coast at W end of Camden Bay, N Alaska	70°10'N	145°51'W
Brundige Inlet	N coast Dundas Island, Dixon Entrance, N British Columbia	54°36'N	130°52'W
Bucareli Bay	Between Baker and Suemez islands, S Alexander Archipelago	55°13'N	133°32'W
Bugomowik Pass	Yukon Delta, W Alaska	62°57'N	164°46'W
Buldir Island	Westernmost of Rat Islands, Aleutian Islands, Alaska	52°21'N	175°56'E
Buldir Pass	Between Near Islands and Buldir Island, Aleutian Islands, Alaska	52°30'N	175°00'E
Burrard Inlet	Strait of Georgia, S British Columbia, Canada	49°18'N	123°00'W
Butedale	N British Columbia, Canada	53°09'N	128°41'W
Caamano Passage	Between Dundas and Zayas islands, N British Columbia, Canada	54°37'N	130°59'W
Cabo Colnett	Pacific coast N Baja California, Mexico	30°56'N	116°19'W
Cabo de San Lucas	S tip Baja California, Mexico	22°51'N	109°57'W
Cambridge Bay	S coast Victoria Island, Dease Strait, Nunavut, N Canada	69°03'N	105°07'W
Camden Bay	Beaufort Sea coast between Barter Island and Point Brownlow, N Alaska	70°09'N	144°45'W

Canning River	North Slope, flows to Camden Bay, Beaufort Sea, N Alaska	70°04'N	145°30'W
Canoe Bay	Head of Pavlof Bay, S coast Alaska Peninsula	55°34'N	161°18'W
Canyon Island	In Taku River, NE of Juneau, SE Alaska	58°43'N	133°40'W
Cape Afrika	Kamchatka Peninsula between Bering Sea and Pacific Ocean, Russia	56°26'N	163°26'E
Cape Alitak	SW coast Kodiak Island, W Gulf of Alaska	56°50'N	154°18'W
Cape Augustine	W coast Dall Island, Alexander Archipelago	54°57'N	133°10'W
Cape Bartolome	S tip Baker Island, S Alexander Archipelago	55°14'N	133°37'W
Cape Belcher	Same as Point Belcher	70°48'N	159°39'W
Cape Bingham	N coast Yakobi Island, Cross Sound, Alexander Archipelago	58°05'N	136°31'W
Cape Breton Island	Between Gulf of St. Lawrence and Atlantic Ocean, Nova Scotia, Canada	46°10'N	60°45'W
Cape Chacon	S tip Prince of Wales Island, Dixon Entrance, Alexander Archipelago	54°41'N	132°01'W
Cape Chaplin(a)	NW shore Bering Sea, SW tip Chukchi Peninsula, Russia	64°23'N	172°35'W
Cape Chiniak	E coast Kodiak Island, 15 mi SE of Kodiak, Alaska	57°37'N	152°10'W
Cape Chukotskiy	NW shore Bering Sea, S tip Chukchi Peninsula, Russia	64°13'N	174°48'W
Cape Cod	Coast of Massachusetts, NW Atlantic	41°50'N	70°00'W
Cape Colnett	Same as Cabo Colnett	30°56'N	116°19'W
Cape Dezhneva	W Bering Strait on NE tip Chukchi Peninsula, Russia (also East Cape)	66°05'N	169°40'W
Cape Edgecumbe	S coast Kruzof Island, 20 mi W of Sitka, Alexander Archipelago	56°59'N	135°51'W
Cape Erimo	SE coast Hokkaido, Japan	41°55'N	143°16'E
Cape Etolin	N coast Nunivak Island, Bering Sea, W Alaska	60°26'N	166°09'W
Cape Falcon	N Oregon, S of Tillamook Head	45°46'N	123°58'W
Cape Fairweather	NE shore Gulf of Alaska between Lituya Bay and Dry Bay	58°48'N	137°57'W
Cape Flattery	NW coast Washington, on Pacific Ocean	48°24'N	124°43'W
Cape Halkett	W point of entrance to Harrison Bay, Beaufort Sea coast, Alaska	70°48'N	152°11'W
Cape Hatteras	Coast of North Carolina, NW Atlantic	35°13'N	75°31'W
Cape Inubo	E tip Honshu Island, Japan	35°37'N	140°53'E
Cape Karluk	W coast Kodiak Island, Shelikof Strait, Alaska	57°35'N	154°30'W
Cape Kozlova	SE Kamchatka, at S end Kamchatka Bay, Russia	54°28'N	161°45'E
Cape Kronotskiy	SE Kamchatka Peninsula, Russia	54°59'N	162°01'E
Cape Kumliun	E of Chignik Bay, S coast Alaska Peninsula, SW Gulf of Alaska	56°30'N	157°54'W
Cape Lisburne	Chukchi Sea coast NE of Point Hope, NW Alaska	68°53'N	166°13'W
Cape Lopatka	S tip Kamchatka Peninsula, Russia	50°52'N	156°38'E
Cape Mendocino	N of Punta Gorda, N California	40°23'N	124°35'W
Cape Menshikof	N coast Alaska Peninsula, SW of Ugashik Bay, Bristol Bay	57°31'N	157°49'W
Cape Muzon	SE tip Dall Island, S Alexander Archipelago	54°39'N	132°41'W
Cape Navarin	NE Kamchatka Peninsula, S of Gulf of Anadyr, Russia	62°16'N	179°10'E
Cape Newenham	Between Bristol and Kuskokwim bays, on Bering Sea, W Alaska	58°38'N	162°10'W
Cape Nizkiy	NE Kamchatka Peninsula between Capes Navarin and Olyutorskiy	61°38'N	173°48'E

Cape Olyutorskiy	NE Kamchatka Peninsula, E shore Olyutorskiy Bay, Russia	59°51'N	170°20'E
Cape Ommaney	S tip Baranof Island, Alexander Archipelago	56°10'N	134°40'W
Cape Peirce	NW Bristol Bay E of Cape Newenham, Bering Sea, SW Alaska	58°33'N	161°46'W
Cape Resurrection	S tip Resurrection Peninsula, SE of Seward, N Gulf of Alaska	59°52'N	149°17'W
Cape Rodney	Bering Sea coast, 30 mi NW of Nome, W Alaska	64°39'N	165°24'W
Cape Sabine	Chukchi Sea coast, E of Cape Lisburne, NW Alaska	68°55'N	164°36'W
Cape St. Elias	SW end Kayak Island, NE Gulf of Alaska	59°54'N	144°36'W
Cape St. James	S tip Moresby Island, Queen Charlotte Islands, N British Columbia	51°56'N	131°02'W
Cape San Lucas	Same as Cabo de San Lucas	22°51'N	109°57'W
Cape Sarichef	W end Unimak Island, Aleutian Islands, Alaska	54°35'N	164°58'W
Cape Serdtse-Kamen'	N coast Chukchi Peninsula, Russia	66°56'N	171°40'W
Cape Shipunskiy	SE Kamchatka between Kronotskiy and Avacha bays, Russia	53°04'N	160°04'E
Cape Sitkinak	E coast Sitkinak Island, W Gulf of Alaska	56°34'N	153°52'W
Cape Spencer	N shore Cross Sound, NE Gulf of Alaska	58°12'N	136°39'W
Cape Suckling	NE shore Gulf of Alaska, E of Okalee Spit and Controller Bay	59°59'N	143°53'W
Cape Terpeniya	E shore Terpeniya Bay, Sakhalin Island, Russia	48°39'N	144°44'E
Cape Thompson	Chukchi Sea coast, SE of Point Hope, NW Alaska	68°08'N	165°58'W
Cape Uyak	W coast Kodiak Island, NE of Karluk, Shelikof Strait, Alaska	57°38'N	154°20'W
Cape Verde Islands	E coast Africa, Indian Ocean	16°00'N	24°00'W
Cape Yakataga	NE shore Gulf of Alaska, W of Icy Bay	60°03'N	142°26'W
Captains Bay	NE coast Unalaska Island, Aleutian Islands, Alaska	53°52'N	166°34'W
Carlisle Island	Islands of Four Mountains, Aleutian Islands, Alaska	52°53'N	170°03'W
Carmel	S of Monterey Bay, central California	36°34'N	121°56'W
Carpenter Bay	SE coast Moresby Island, Queen Charlotte Islands, British Columbia	52°14'N	131°07'W
Carter Bay	Queen Charlotte Strait, S British Columbia, Canada	50°50'N	126°52'W
Cascade Range	Washington State	47°00'N	121°00'W
Cascadia Abyssal Plain	Pacific Ocean west of Washington and Oregon	47°00'N	127°30'W
Casco Cove	SE coast Attu Island, Near Islands, Aleutian Islands, Alaska	52°49'N	173°10'E
Caspian Sea	Inland water body extending from Russia to Iran	42°00'N	50°00'E
Caton Island	Easternmost of Sanak Islands, SW Gulf of Alaska	54°23'N	162°25'W
Cedros Island	Pacific Ocean off central Baja California, Mexico	28°14'N	115°32'W
Celebes Sea	Bounded on N by Philippines and on S by Indonesia	3°00'N	122°00'E
Chagulak Island	Islands of Four Mountains, Aleutian Islands, Alaska	52°34'N	171°08'W
Chakwakamiut Lagoon	Nunivak Island, W Alaska	59°56'N	166°47'W
Chalkyitsik	Village on left bank of Black River NE of Fort Yukon, interior Alaska	66°39'N	143°43'W
Chamalu Bay	N Baja California, Pacific coast	30°50'N	116°11'W
Chamisso Island	Spafarief Bay, Kotzebue Sound, NW Alaska	66°13'N	161°50'W
Chandalar River	Alaska, flows SE to Yukon River	66°36'N	146°00'W

Channel Islands	NE Pacific off S California coast	33°29'N	118°59'W
Chatanika River	Tributary of Tanana River, N of Fairbanks, interior Alaska	65°06'N	147°30'W
Chatham Sound	W coast British Columbia off Dixon Entrance	54°22'N	130°35'W
Chatham Strait	E of Baranof and Chichagof islands, Alexander Archipelago	57°03'N	134°32'W
Chegitun River	NE Chukchi Peninsula, Russia, flows to Chukchi Sea at Arctic Circle	66°30'N	171°05'W
Chena River	Tributary of Tanana River, Fairbanks, interior Alaska	64°48'N	147°55'W
Chenega	S tip Chenega Island, off Kenai Peninsula, SW Prince William Sound	60°19'N	148°05'W
Chernabura Island	Southernmost of Shumagin Islands, S of Alaska Peninsula	54°47'N	159°33'W
Chernofski Harbor	SW coast Unalaska Island, Aleutian Islands, Alaska	53°24'N	167°33'W
Chesapeake Bay	E coast United States, NW North Atlantic	37°00'N	76°00'W
Chichagof Island	Between Gulf of Alaska and N Chatham Strait, Alexander Archipelago	58°00'N	135°30'W
Chignik Bay	SE coast Alaska Peninsula, SW Gulf of Alaska	56°22'N	158°00'W
Chignik Lake	Alaska Peninsula, in course of Chignik River	56°14'N	158°47'W
Chilkoot Inlet	N end Lynn Canal, SE Alaska	59°00'N	135°35'W
Chiniak Bay	NE coast Kodiak Island, W Gulf of Alaska	57°42'N	152°20'W
Chirikof Island	SW Gulf of Alaska SW of Kodiak Island	55°50'N	155°37'W
Chugach Islands	NW Gulf of Alaska off S tip Kenai Peninsula	59°07'N	151°40'W
Chukchi Sea	Between Wrangel Island, Russia, and Point Barrow, Alaska	69°00'N	168°00'W
Chukchi Peninsula	NE Siberia, Russia, on Bering and Chukchi seas	65°40'N	174°28'W
Chukotskiy Peninsula	Same as Chukchi (or Chukchee, Chukot, or Chukotka) Peninsula	65°40'N	174°28'W
Circle	Village on left bank Yukon River 130 mi NE of Fairbanks, Alaska	65°49'N	144°03'W
Clarence Strait	E coast Prince of Wales Island, Alexander Archipelago	54°45'N	131°42'W
Clayoquot Sound	W coast Vancouver Island, British Columbia	49°12'N	126°06'W
Clear Point	W coast Mansfield Peninsula, SW of Juneau, SE Alaska	58°04'N	134°55'W
Cleveland Peninsula	Mainland Alaska between Prince of Wales and Revillagigedo islands	55°45'N	132°00'W
Coast Mountains	Between SE Alaska and British Columbia, Canada	54°00'N	128°00'W
Cobb Seamount	NE North Pacific Ocean, W of Washington	46°45'N	130°45'W
Cold Bay	SW coast Alaska Peninsula, N of Sanak Islands, SW Gulf of Alaska	54°59'N	162°28'W
Collinson Point	Beaufort Sea coast on Camden Bay SW of Barter Island, Alaska	69°59'N	144°54'W
Columbia Glacier	Reaches tidewater at Prince William Sound, SW of Valdez, Alaska	60°59'N	147°02'W
Columbia River	Flows from British Columbia to Oregon and Washington	51°25'N	118°30'W
Colville River	Alaska, North Slope, flows to Harrison Bay, Beaufort Sea	70°27'N	150°07'W
Commander Basin	Deepwater depression W of Shirshov Ridge, W Bering Sea	57°30'N	167°00'E
Commander Islands	Aleutian chain, group between Bering Sea and Pacific Ocean, Russia	54°53'N	167°00'E
Commander Plateau	Shelf surrounding Commander Islands, Russia	55°08'N	166°28'E
Coney Island	S end Frederick Sound SE of Petersburg, Alexander Archipelago	56°41'N	132°38'W
Constantine Harbor	SE coast Amchitka Island, Rat Islands, Alaska	51°24'N	179°19'E
Continental Divide	Line of highest points separating waters flowing W from those flowing N or E; in North America coincides with Rocky Mountains	38°50'N	105°03'W

Controller Bay	NE Gulf of Alaska, SE of Cordova and W of Okalee Spit	60°05'N	144°15'W
Cook Inlet	W of Kenai Peninsula, N Gulf of Alaska	59°05'N	152°30'W
Coos Bay	Oregon coast	43°40'N	124°25'W
Coppermine River	NWT and Nunavut, Canada, flows to Coronation Gulf, Arctic Ocean	67°49'N	115°04'W
Copper River	Flows to N Gulf of Alaska NW of Controller Bay	60°18'N	145°03'W
Cordova	N shore Gulf of Alaska W of Copper River Delta	60°33'N	145°45'W
Cormorant Rock	W shore Uyak Bay, NW coast Kodiak Island, W Gulf of Alaska	57°38'N	153°59'W
Cornwallis Island	Queen Elizabeth Islands, Northwest Territories, Canada	75°25'N	94°32'W
Coronado Bank	Pacific Ocean off N Baja California, Mexico	32°22'N	117°18'W
Coronado Islands	Pacific Ocean off N Baja California, Mexico	32°25'N	117°22'W
Coronation Gulf	Arctic Ocean, South of Victoria Island, Nunavut, Canada	68°06'N	112°25'W
Coronation Island	Between Chatham and Sumner straits, Alexander Archipelago	55°53'N	134°14'W
Cortes Bank	Pacific Ocean S of Tanner Bank, off San Diego, S California	32°30'N	119°10'W
Craggy Island	Icy Strait, N Alexander Archipelago	58°10'N	135°28'W
Craig	Prince of Wales Island, S end Klawak Inlet, Alexander Archipelago	55°28'N	133°09'W
Crescent City	N California	41°46'N	124°12'W
Cronin Island	NE entrance Kasitsna Bay, Kachemak Bay, Alaska	59°29'N	151°31'W
Cross Sound	Icy Strait to Gulf of Alaska, SE Alaska	58°08'N	136°35'W
Crosswind Lake	S Alaska, Copper River system	62°20'N	146°00'W
Culross Passage	E coast Kenai Peninsula, Prince William Sound, N Gulf of Alaska	60°41'N	148°14'W
Cultus Lake	SW British Columbia, Canada, Fraser River system	49°03'N	121°59'W
Cumberland Sound	SE coast Baffin Island, Nunavut, Canada, on NW Atlantic	65°10'N	65°30'W
Dall Head	S tip Gravina Island, S Clarence Strait, Alexander Archipelago	55°08'N	131°45'W
Dall Island	SE Gulf of Alaska N of Dixon Entrance, Alexander Archipelago	54°57'N	133°00'W
Danger Island	W entrance Prince William Sound, SE of Seward, N Gulf of Alaska	59°55'N	148°05'W
Davenport	Central California coast NW of Santa Cruz	37°01'N	122°14'W
Davidson Bank	Extends SW from Sanak Islands into Pacific Ocean, Alaska	54°19'N	163°46'W
Davis Strait	Between Greenland and Baffin Island, E Canada	66°00'N	58°30'W
Day Bay	NW Gulf of Alaska, E of Resurrection Peninsula, SE of Seward	59°57'N	149°10'W
Dease Inlet	Beaufort Sea coast, Alaska, between Point Barrow and Smith Bay	71°12'N	155°24'W
Dease Strait	S of Victoria Island, Northwest Territories, Canada	68°50'N	108°27'W
Delarof Islands	W of Andreanof Islands between Amchitka and Tanaga passes, Alaska	51°30'N	178°45'W
Del Mar	S California	32°57'N	117°15'W
Demarcation Point	Beaufort Sea coast 8 mi W of Alaska–Canada boundary, Alaska	69°41'N	141°19'W
Denman Island	E coast Vancouver Island, Strait of Georgia, S British Columbia	49°33'N	124°48'W
Departure Bay	Strait of Georgia, Vancouver Island, S British Columbia, Canada	49°12'N	123°57'W
Deschutes River	Oregon, Columbia River system	45°40'N	132°25'W
Dezhneva Bay	W Bering Sea between Capes Navarin and Olyutorskiy, Russia	61°42'N	173°35'E

Diablo Canyon	Near San Luis Obispo Bay, California	35°12'N	120°51'W
Diablo Cove	San Luis Obispo Bay, California	35°10'N	120°47'W
Dickins Seamount	Gulf of Alaska 145 nmi W of Cape Muzon, Alaska	54°30'N	137°00'W
Dixon Entrance	Between Queen Charlotte Islands and Alexander Archipelago	54°30'N	132°00'W
Doame River	Flows to Gulf of Alaska at E end Dry Bay, 59 mi SE of Yakutat	59°04'N	138°21'W
Douglas Island	Between Gastineau Channel and Stephens Passage, SE Alaska	58°15'N	134°16'W
Dry Bay	NE shore Gulf of Alaska, SE of Yakutat	59°08'N	138°25'W
Dry Strait	Frederick Sound to mouth of Stikine River, SE Alaska	56°36'N	132°31'W
Duke Island	Clarence Strait S of Annette Island, Alexander Archipelago	54°55'N	131°20'W
Dundas Island	Dixon Entrance, Dundas Islands, N British Columbia, Canada	54°33'N	130°52'W
Durgin Seamount	Gulf of Alaska about 215 nmi WSW of Cape Edgecumbe, Alaska	55°50'N	141°51'W
Dutch Harbor	N coast Unalaska Island, Aleutian Islands, Alaska	53°54'N	166°31'W
Duxbury Reef	Off San Francisco, N California	37°54'N	122°42'W
Eagle River	Flows through Anchorage to Knik Arm, N Gulf of Alaska	61°15'N	149°54'W
East China Sea	S of Yellow Sea, E of China, SW of Japan	29°00'N	125°00'E
East Siberian Sea	W of Chukchi Sea, N Russia	74°06'N	166°15'W
Eel River	N California	40°34'N	124°10'W
Egegik River	Flows to Egegik Bay, N coast Alaska Peninsula, Bristol Bay	58°12'N	157°24'W
Eickelberg Seamount	NE North Pacific Ocean W of Strait of Juan de Fuca	48°30'N	133°10'W
Eleanor Island	N of Knight Island, NE of Chenega, W Prince William Sound, Alaska	60°33'N	147°35'W
Eliza Harbor	SE coast Admiralty Island, Alexander Archipelago	57°09'N	134°17'W
Ellef Ringnes Island	Queen Elizabeth Islands, Arctic Ocean, Nunavut, Canada	78°30'N	102°15'W
Ellesmere Island	Nunavut, Canada, Arctic Ocean W of N Greenland	79°50'N	78°00'W
Elongozhik Pass	Yukon Delta, W Alaska	63°14'N	164°17'W
Emperor Seamounts	Undersea mountain chain, NW North Pacific Ocean	42°00'N	170°00'E
Endicott Causeway	Beaufort Sea coast in Sagavanirktok River delta, N Alaska	70°18'N	147°49'W
Ensenada	N Baja California, Mexico	31°53'N	116°40'W
Eroo River	Same as Yoroo River	47°42'N	96°36'E
Eshamy Bay	E coast Kenai Peninsula, NE of Chenega, Prince William Sound	60°28'N	147°58'W
Estevan Deep	Off SW coast Vancouver Island, S British Columbia, Canada	49°04'N	127°53'W
Estevan Point	SW coast Vancouver Island, S British Columbia, Canada	49°22'N	126°34'W
Etolin Island	Between Prince of Wales and Wrangell islands, Alexander Arch.	56°06'N	132°21'W
Eureka	N California coast	40°48'N	124°10'W
Evans Island	SW Prince William Sound SE of Chenega, N Gulf of Alaska	60°03'N	148°04'W
Fairbanks	Interior Alaska, on Chena River	64°51'N	147°43'W
Fairweather Ground	Bank or bar, NE Gulf of Alaska off Cape Fairweather	58°20'N	138°30'W
False Point Retreat	Lynn Canal, NW coast Mansfield Peninsula, Alexander Archipelago	58°22'N	134°58'W
Farallon Islands	Pacific Ocean off N California, NW of San Francisco	37°44'N	123°02'W

Faroe Islands	E of Iceland in Faroe-Iceland Ridge, Norwegian Sea	62°00'N	7°00'W
Faroe–Shetland Ridge	N North Sea, Faroe Islands, Denmark, to Shetland Islands, Scotland	60°15'N	7°30'W
Favorite Channel	Stephens Passage to Lynn Canal, SE Alaska	58°35'N	135°00'W
Field	S British Columbia, Canada, near Alberta on Kicking Horse River	51°24'N	116°29'W
Fife Point	NE coast Graham Island, Queen Charlotte Is., British Columbia	54°06'N	131°40'W
Fillmore Island	Between Fillmore Inlet and Pearse Canal, Alexander Archipelago	54°50'N	130°33'W
Finger Bay	NE coast Adak Island, Andreanof Islands, Alaska	51°51'N	176°35'W
Fitz Hugh Sound	Queen Charlotte Sound, central British Columbia, Canada	51°37'N	127°56'W
Flannigan Slough	Taku River on and E of Alaska–British Columbia boundary	58°35'N	133°40'W
Flaxman Island	Beaufort Sea NW of Brownlow Point, N Alaska	70°11'N	146°03'W
Forrester Island	SE Gulf of Alaska, W of Dall Island, Alexander Archipelago	54°48'N	133°31'W
Fort Bragg	N California coast	39°26'N	123°49'W
Fort Simpson	Mackenzie River, Northwest Territories, Canada	61°52'N	121°21'W
Fort Tongass	E coast Tongass Island, Alexander Archipelago	54°46'N	130°14'W
Fort Yukon	Right bank Yukon River, Alaska, at junction with Porcupine River	66°34'N	145°16'W
Fox Islands	Aleutian Islands between Samalga Pass and Alaska Peninsula	53°30'N	166°30'W
Franklin Bay	Amundsen Gulf, Northwest Territories, Canada	69°55'N	127°00'W
Franz Josef Land	Arctic N of Barents Sea, Russia	81°00'N	55°00'E
Fraser River	British Columbia, Canada, flows to S Strait of Georgia	49°07'N	123°11'W
Frederick Point	NE coast Mitkof Island, W shore Frederick Sound, Alexander Archipelago	56°48'N	132°49'W
Frederick Sound	Extends E from Chatham Strait to Dry Strait, SE Alaska	56°50'N	134°25'W
Fritz Cove	Stephens Passage, 8 mi N of Juneau, SE Alaska	58°19'N	134°38'W
Funter Bay	W coast Mansfield Peninsula, 19 mi SW of Juneau, SE Alaska	58°14'N	134°55'W
Gabriola Island	Taylor Bay, Cross Sound, SE Alaska	58°16'N	136°30'W
Galapagos Islands	E Pacific W of Ecuador	00°30'S	90°30'W
Galena Bay	SE shore Valdez Arm, N Prince William Sound, N Gulf of Alaska	60°58'N	146°44'W
Gambell	NW tip St. Lawrence Island, Bering Sea, W Alaska	63°47'N	171°45'W
Gardner Canal	Off Hecate Strait, N British Columbia	53°28'N	128°11'W
Garnet Point	S end Kanagunut Island, SE Alaska	54°43'N	130°41'W
Gaviota	N of Santa Barbara, California	34°28'N	120°13'W
Giacomini Seamount	Gulf of Alaska about 198 nmi ESE of Cape Chiniak, Alaska	56°27'N	146°24'W
Gillen Harbour	End of Pemberton Bay, Dewdney Island, British Columbia, Canada	52°58'N	129°36'W
Gizhiginskaya Bay	NE Sea of Okhotsk	60°22'N	155°58'E
Glacier Bay	Off Icy Strait, W of Juneau, SE Alaska	58°22'N	136°00'W
Glass Peninsula	Admiralty Island, along W shore Stephens Passage, Alexander Arch.	57°35'N	133°50'W
Glubokaya Bay	W Bering Sea between Dezhneva Bay and Cape Olyutorskiy, Russia	60°59'N	172°14'E
Golden Gate	Entrance to San Francisco Bay, N California	37°48'N	122°28'W
Golinski Harbor	Unalaska Island, Aleutian Islands, Alaska	53°55'N	166°31'W

Goose Bay	Queen Charlotte Sound, central British Columbia, Canada	51°22'N	127°50'W
Goose Island	Queen Charlotte Sound, central British Columbia, Canada	51°53'N	128°28'W
Gore Point	S coast Kenai Peninsula, Alaska	59°12'N	150°57'W
Graham Island	Queen Charlotte Islands, N British Columbia, Canada	53°30'N	132°30'W
Granite Island	E coast Kenai Peninsula, SW of Seward, NW Gulf of Alaska	59°39'N	149°48'W
Grantley Harbor	Extends SE from Port Clarence, Bering Strait, Alaska	65°17'N	166°15'W
Grass Creek	N side Alaska Peninsula, flows to Herendeen Bay	55°48'N	160°51'W
Gravina Island	Between Revillagigedo and Prince of Wales islands, Alexander Arch.	55°17'N	131°46'W
Great Lakes	United States–Canada	45°00'N	83°00'W
Great Sitkin Island	Andreanof Islands, Aleutian Islands, Alaska	52°03'N	176°06'W
Great Sitkin Pass	S of Great Sitkin Island, Andreanof Islands, Aleutian Islands, Alaska	51°58'N	176°04'W
Great Slave Lake	Northwest Territories, Canada	62°50'N	113°50'W
Greenland	NW Atlantic Ocean	60°00'N	44°00'W
Greenland Sea	E of Greenland	75°00'N	10°00'W
Guadalupe Island	Pacific Ocean W of central Baja California, Mexico	29°00'N	118°15'W
Gulf of Alaska	NE North Pacific Ocean, S coast Alaska	58°00'N	145°00'W
Gulf of Anadyr	S coast Chukchi Peninsula, Russia	64°00'N	178°00'W
Gulf of California	Between Baja California and Mexico mainland	31°00'N	114°00'W
Gulf of Panama	Pacific coast Panama	9°00'N	79°00'W
Gulf of Patience	Same as Terpeniya Bay	49°00'N	143°30'E
Gulf of St. Lawrence	E coast Canada	48°00'N	62°00'W
Gulf of Tatary	Same as Tatar Strait	48°00'N	141°00'E
Gulf of Tehuantepec	S Mexico, on Pacific Ocean	16°00'N	95°20'W
Hagemeister Island	NW Bristol Bay E of Cape Peirce, Bering Sea, SW Alaska	58°39'N	160°54'W
Hakodate	SE coast Hokkaido, Japan	41°52'N	140°52'E
Halfway Point	E coast St. Paul Island, Pribilof Islands, W Alaska	57°09'N	170°10'W
Halibut Cove	E shore Kachemak Bay, Kenai Peninsula, NW Gulf of Alaska	59°37'N	151°14'W
Hall Island	NW of St. Matthew Island, Bering Sea, Alaska	60°40'N	173°06'W
Hanna Shoal	E Chukchi Sea N of Icy Cape, Alaska	72°00'N	162°00'W
Hanning Bay	NW coast Montague Island, Prince William Sound, Alaska	59°58'N	147°43'W
Harrison Bay	Beaufort Sea coast E of Colville River delta, N Alaska	70°40'N	151°30'W
Harrison Lake	Mainland, SW British Columbia, Fraser River system	49°33'N	121°50'W
Hassler Harbor	NE coast Annette Island, Alexander Archipelago	55°13'N	131°26'W
Heceta Head	Oregon coast	44°08'N	124°07'W
Hecate Strait	E of Queen Charlotte Islands, British Columbia, Canada	53°30'N	131°10'W
Herald Island	W Chukchi Sea W of Wrangel Island, Russia (Ostrov Herald or Geralda)	71°23'N	175°40'W
Herald Shoal	W Chukchi Sea N of Chukchi Peninsula, Russia	70°20'N	171°04'W
Herendeen Bay	Port Moller, Bristol Bay, N coast Alaska Peninsula	55°50'N	160°50'W

Herschel Island	NW coast Yukon Territory, Canada	69°35'N	139°37'W
Hesketh Island	S shore Kachemak Bay, Kenai Peninsula, NW Gulf of Alaska	59°30'N	151°31'W
Highpower Creek	Flows NW from Denali Natl. Park to Swift Fork Kuskokwim River, Alaska	63°25'N	153°07'W
Hinchinbrook Entrance	SE entrance to Prince William Sound, N Gulf of Alaska	60°20'N	146°50'W
Hinchinbrook Island	Between N Gulf of Alaska and SE Prince William Sound	60°23'N	146°28'W
Hipolito Bay	Pacific coast central Baja California, Mexico	27°06'N	114°12'W
Hobart Bay	E shore Stephens Passage, SE Alaska	57°24'N	133°28'W
Hodgkins Seamount	NE North Pacific Ocean	53°15'N	135°45'W
Hokkaido (Island)	N Japan	44°00'N	143°00'E
Homer	N shore Kachemak Bay on Kenai Peninsula, Cook Inlet, N Gulf of Alaska	59°39'N	151°33'W
Homer Spit	Extends SE 4 mi from Homer into Kachemak Bay, N Gulf of Alaska	59°37'N	151°27'W
Honshu (Island)	S Japan	36°00'N	138°00'E
Hood Canal	Puget Sound, Washington	47°35'N	123°00'W
Hooper Bay	E shore Bering Sea, Yukon-Kuskokwim Delta, W Alaska	61°27'N	166°00'W
Horton Seamount	Gulf of Alaska	56°00'N	144°30'W
Hotham Inlet	E side Baldwin Peninsula, Kotzebue Sound, NW Alaska	67°00'N	162°00'W
Howe Sound	S Strait of Georgia, British Columbia, Canada	49°25'N	123°30'W
Hudson Bay	E Canada, between Ontario, Manitoba, and Northwest Territories	60°00'N	85°00'W
Hudson Strait	Between Hudson Bay and Davis Strait, E Canada	62°30'N	72°30'W
Hugh Point	S tip Glass Peninsula, Admiralty Island, Alexander Archipelago	57°34'N	133°48'W
Humboldt Bay	N California coast	40°45'N	124°12'W
Hunger Harbour	Tasu Sound, W coast Moresby Island, N. British Columbia, Canada	52°45'N	132°01'W
Huntington Beach	S California coast	33°39'N	117°58'W
Icy Bay	NE Gulf of Alaska, NW of Yakutat, NE Gulf of Alaska	59°55'N	141°33'W
Icy Cape	Chukchi Sea coast, SW of Wainwright, NW Alaska	70°20'N	161°52'W
Icy Point	E shore Gulf of Alaska, NW of Cape Spencer	58°23'N	137°04'W
Icy Point	S coast Douglas Island, 9 mi SW of Juneau, SE Alaska	58°11'N	134°16'W
Icy Strait	NE coast Chichagof Island off Cross Sound, Alexander Archipelago	58°18'N	134°45'W
Igitkin Island	Andreanof Islands, Aleutian Islands, Alaska	51°59'N	175°54'W
Ikatan Bay	SE coast Unimak Island S of tip of Alaska Peninsula, SW Gulf of Alaska	54°47'N	163°15'W
Ilak Island	Delarof Islands, Aleutian Islands, Alaska	51°29'N	178°17'W
Iliamna Lake	N end Alaska Peninsula between Kvichak Bay and Cook Inlet	59°30'N	155°00'W
Imperial Beach	S of San Diego, S California	32°35'N	117°06'W
Indian Arm	Off Burrard Inlet, S British Columbia, Canada	49°20'N	122°50'W
Inuvik	Mackenzie River Delta, Northwest Territories, N Canada	68°21'N	133°43'W
Iony Island	NW Sea of Okhotsk, Russia (Ostrov Iony)	56°26'N	143°25'E
Islands of Four Mountains	Between Fox Islands and Andreanof Islands, Aleutian Is., Alaska	52°45'N	170°00'W
Islas Juan Fernández	Pacific Ocean off Chile	33°00'S	80°00'W

Iturup Island	S Kuril Islands, Russia	45°00'N	148°00'E
Iwate Prefecture	Political district of Honshu, Japan	40°00'N	141°39'E
Izembek Bay	Same as Izembek Lagoon	55°20'N	162°48'W
Izembek Lagoon	S shore Bristol Bay, N coast Alaska Peninsula near W end	55°20'N	162°48'W
Izhut Bay	SE coast Afognak Island, N of Kodiak Island, W Gulf of Alaska	58°11'N	152°15'W
Jakolof Bay	S end Kasitsna Bay, Kachemak Bay, NW Gulf of Alaska	59°28'N	151°32'W
Jakomini Seamount	Gulf of Alaska	56°15'N	145°15'W
Japan Trench	Pacific Ocean east of Honshu	35°00'N	150°00'E
Jens Munk Island	W coast Baffin Island, Nunavut, Canada	69°40'N	79°40'W
Johnstone Bay	SE coast Kenai Peninsula, 30 mi SE of Seward, NW Gulf of Alaska	59°55'N	148°45'W
Johnstone Strait	British Columbia between mainland and NE coast Vancouver Island	50°30'N	126°00'W
Jones Islands	Barrier islands on Beaufort Sea coast, N Alaska	70°32'N	149°36'W
Jones Sound	S tip Ellesmere Island, Nunavut, Canada	76°00'N	85°00'W
Juneau	On Gastineau Channel, SE Alaska (capital of Alaska)	58°18'N	134°25'W
Kachemak Bay	SW coast Kenai Peninsula, SE side Cook Inlet, NW Gulf of Alaska	59°35'N	151°50'W
Kagalaska Island	Andreanof Islands, Aleutian Islands, Alaska	51°48'N	176°21'W
Kaga Point	SW coast Kagalaska Island, Aleutian Islands, Alaska	51°44'N	176°23'W
Kaktovik	Village on N coast Barter Island, Beaufort Sea, N Alaska	70°08'N	143°38'W
Kakul Narrows	E end Salisbury Sound, 25 mi NW of Sitka, Alexander Archipelago	57°22'N	135°42'W
Kamchatka	Same as Kamchatka Peninsula	56°00'N	160°00'E
Kamchatka Bay	NW Pacific, E coast Kamchatka, SW of Commander Islands, Russia	55°35'N	162°20'E
Kamchatka Peninsula	Between Sea of Okhotsk and Pacific Ocean, Russia	56°00'N	160°00'E
Kamchatka Strait	Between Cape Afrika and Commander Islands, Russia	53°00'N	171°00'E
Kamishak Bay	E coast Alaska Peninsula, SW shore Cook Inlet	59°15'N	153°50'W
Kanaga Island	Andreanof Islands, Aleutian Islands, Alaska	51°45'N	177°22'W
Kanagunut Island	Nakat Bay, Alexander Archipelago, at Dixon Entrance	54°45'N	130°42'W
Kantishna Hills	Ridge in Alaska Range extending NE 50 miles from McKinley River	63°40'N	150°35'W
Kanu Island	Andreanof Islands, Aleutian Islands, Alaska	51°56'N	176°02'W
Kara Sea	Arctic Ocean, Russia	75°00'N	65°00'E
Karaginskiy Bay	E coast Kamchatka Peninsula, W Bering Sea, Russia	58°50'N	164°00'E
Karaginskiy Island	E coast Kamchatka Peninsula, W Bering Sea, Russia	58°55'N	164°08'E
Karaginskiy Trench	W Bering Sea off Karaginskiy Island, Russia	58°41'N	164°41'E
Karluk	W coast Kodiak Island, on Shelikof Strait, W Gulf of Alaska	57°34'N	154°27'W
Karluk River	W Kodiak Island, Alaska, flows to Shelikof Strait at Karluk	57°34'N	154°28'W
Kasaan Bay	E coast Prince of Wales Island, Alexander Archipelago	55°24'N	132°06'W
Kasitsna Bay	S shore Kachemak Bay, Cook Inlet, N Gulf of Alaska	59°29'N	151°33'W
Katlian Bay	NW coast Baranof Island, Alexander Archipelago	57°09'N	135°23'W
Katmai River	E coast Alaska Peninsula, flows to Shelikof Strait at Katmai Bay	58°02'N	154°57'W

Katseyedie River	Northwest Territories, Canada	66°30'N	123°05'W
Kauai	W Hawaiian Islands	22°10'N	159°30'W
Kayak Island	N Gulf of Alaska, E of Controller Bay and SE of Cordova	59°56'N	144°23'W
Keats Island	Howe Sound, Strait of Georgia, S British Columbia, Canada	49°23'N	123°28'W
Kegan Cove	SE coast Prince of Wales Island, Alexander Archipelago	55°01'N	132°09'W
Kenai Peninsula	N Gulf of Alaska between Cook Inlet and Prince William Sound	60°00'N	150°00'W
Kenai River	Kenai Peninsula, Alaska, flows to Cook Inlet at Kenai	60°33'N	151°16'W
Kerguelen Islands	Coast of Antarctica, S of Indian Ocean	49°30'S	69°30'E
Ketchikan	SE coast Revillagigedo Island, Alexander Archipelago	55°20'N	131°38'W
Khaz Bay	W coast Chichagof Island, Alexander Archipelago	57°35'N	136°05'W
Khaz Point	W coast Chichagof Island, Alexander Archipelago	57°30'N	136°00'W
Kicking Horse River	S British Columbia W of Yukon Territory boundary	51°18'N	116°59'W
Kiliuda Bay	SE coast Kodiak Island off entrance to Sitkalidak Strait, Alaska	57°16'N	152°54'W
King Cove	SW end Alaska Peninsula E of Cold Bay, SW Gulf of Alaska	55°03'N	162°19'W
Kirilof Point	NW side Constantine Harbor, SE Amchitka Island, Rat Islands, Alaska	51°25'N	179°18'E
Kiska Island	Rat Islands, Aleutian Islands, Alaska	51°58'N	177°30'E
Kiska Pass	Between Buildir Island and Kiska Island, Aleutian Islands, Alaska	52°15'N	176°45'E
Kivalina	Chukchi Sea coast NW of Cape Krusenstern, NW Alaska	67°43'N	164°32'W
Klakas Inlet	SW coast Prince of Wales Island, Alexander Archipelago	54°53'N	132°23'W
Klamath River	Flows into the Pacific Ocean, N California	41°33'N	124°02'W
Klawock	W coast Prince of Wales Island, N of Craig, Alexander Archipelago	55°33'N	133°05'W
Klikitarik	On Klikitarik Bay, S Norton Sound, 17 mi E of Saint Michael, W Alaska	63°28'N	161°28'W
Klokachef Island	SW coast Chichagof Island, N of Salisbury Sound, Alexander Archipelago	57°24'N	135°53'W
Klutina Lake	N of Valdez, Alaska, Copper River system	61°42'N	145°58'W
Knight Island	NW of Montague Island, E of Chenega, W Prince William Sound, Alaska	60°21'N	147°45'W
Knik Arm	Extends NE from Cook Inlet, W of Anchorage, Alaska	61°12'N	150°13'W
Kobuk River	Flows to Chukchi Sea at Hotham Inlet, Kotzebue Sound, NW Alaska	66°54'N	160°38'W
Kodiak Island	W Gulf of Alaska, S of Cook Inlet and E of Alaska Peninsula	57°25'N	153°20'W
Kolyma River	Flows to East Siberian Sea, NE coast Russia	69°30'N	161°00'E
Konganevik Point	Beaufort Sea at Camden Bay, NE coast Alaska	70°01'N	145°10'W
Korea	E Asia, general term including North Korea and South Korea	37°00'N	128°00'E
Korfa Bay	Off Karaginskiy Bay, NE Kamchatka Peninsula, Russia	60°12'N	165°48'E
Koryak Coast	W Bering Sea from Gulf of Anadyr to Karaginskiy Bay, Russia; coastal lowlands of the Koryakskoye Nagor'ye (Koryak Plateau)	62°00'N	175°00'E
Kotel'nyy Island	Laptev Sea, Russia	75°24'N	139°38'E
Kotzebue	NW coast Baldwin Peninsula, Kotzebue Sound, NW Alaska	66°54'N	162°35'W
Kotzebue Sound	Chukchi Sea coast, N of Seward Peninsula, NW Alaska	66°45'N	163°00'W
Koyukuk River	Flows SW to Yukon River NE of Nulato, Alaska	64°55'N	157°32'W

Krenitzin Islands	In Fox Islands group, W of Unimak Pass, Aleutian Islands, Alaska	54°07'N	165°30'W
Krest Bay	NE shore Gulf of Anadyr, W Bering Sea, Russia (Zaliv Kresta)	66°00'N	179°15'W
Kronotskiy Bay	NW Pacific Ocean, SE coast Kamtchatka Peninsula, Russia	53°58'N	160°40'E
Krusenstern Island	Russian name for Little Diomede Island, Alaska	65°43'N	168°55'W
Kruzof Island	W of Baranof Island, 10 mi NW of Sitka, Alexander Archipelago	57°10'N	135°40'W
Kuiu Island	Between Baranof and Prince of Wales islands, Alexander Archipelago	56°35'N	134°00'W
Kukpuk River	NW Alaska, flows to Chukchi Sea NE of Point Hope	68°25'N	166°22'W
Kuk River	Alaska, North Slope, flows to Chukchi Sea SE of Wainwright	70°35'N	159°53'W
Kulukak Bay	N shore Bristol Bay, W of Nushagak Bay, W Alaska	58°49'N	159°44'W
Kupreanof Island	Between mainland and Kuiu Island, Alexander Archipelago	56°45'N	133°30'W
Kupreanof Point	S coast Alaska Peninsula, E of Stepovak Bay, SW Gulf of Alaska	55°34'N	159°36'W
Kuril Islands	Between Sea of Okhotsk and Pacific Ocean, Russia	46°30'N	150°00'E
Kuril–Kamchatka Trench	Pacific Ocean off Kuril Islands and S Kamchatka Peninsula, Russia	47°00'N	155°00'E
Kushiro	SE coast Hokkaido, Japan	42°58'N	144°23'E
Kuskokwim Bay	E Bering Sea at mouth of Kuskokwim River, Alaska	59°00'N	163°00'W
Kuskokwim River	Flows to Bering Sea at Kuskokwim Bay, Yukon Delta, W Alaska	60°05'N	162°25'W
Kvichak Bay	At head of Bristol Bay, W Alaska	58°26'N	157°54'W
Kvichak River	Flows from Iliamna Lake to Kvichak Bay, Alaska Peninsula	58°52'N	157°03'W
Kwatna Inlet	Burke Channel, N British Columbia, Canada	52°05'N	127°32'W
Kyuquot Sound	NW coast Vancouver Island, British Columbia, Canada	50°03'N	127°10'W
Kyushu (Island)	Japan, off S tip Honshu	33°00'N	131°00'E
Labrador	Newfoundland, Canada, on Atlantic Ocean	54°00'N	62°00'W
Labrador Sea	NW Atlantic Ocean off Newfoundland	55°00'N	56°00'W
La Jolla	S California, S of San Diego	32°50'N	117°16'W
La Jolla Canyon	Pacific Ocean off La Jolla, S California	32°53'N	117°17'W
Lake Baikal	Russia, near Mongolia border (deepest lake in the world)	53°00'N	107°40'E
Lake Erie	One of Great Lakes, on U.S.–Canada border	41°40'N	81°40'W
Lake Iliamna	Same as Iliamna Lake	59°30'N	155°00'W
Lake Louise	S Alaska, Susitna River system	62°20'N	146°32'W
Lake Minchumina	Interior Alaska, Tanana River system	63°53'N	152°14'W
Lake Superior	Northern- and westernmost of the Great Lakes, United States-Canada	47°30'N	88°00'W
Lake Union	Seattle, Washington	47°38'N	122°21'W
Lake Washington	Seattle, Washington	47°37'N	122°15'W
Langara Island	NW corner Graham Island, N British Columbia, Canada	54°12'N	133°03'W
La Perouse Bank	Off S Vancouver Island, British Columbia, Canada	48°35'N	125°48'W
La Perouse Glacier	Reaches tidewater NW of Icy Point, Glacier Bay Natl. Park, Alaska	58°27'N	137°17'W
La Pérouse Strait	Between Hokkaido and Sakhalin, Japan–Russia	45°50'N	142°00'E
Lapland	Arctic coast from N Norway to NW Russia, on Barents Sea	70°00'N	25°00'E

Laptev Sea	Arctic Ocean between Kara and East Siberian seas, Russia	75°00'N	125°00'E
Larsen Bay	NW coast Kodiak Island, off Uyak Bay, Shelikof Strait, Alaska	57°32'N	153°58'W
Lavrentiya Bay	Bering Strait, Chukchi Peninsula, Russia	65°40'N	171°05'W
Lawrence Bay	Same as Lavrentiya Bay	65°40'N	171°05'W
Lazy Bay	W shore Alitak Bay, S end Kodiak Island, W Gulf of Alaska	56°53'N	154°14'W
Lena River	N Siberia, flows to Laptev Sea, Arctic Russia	73°20'N	126°20'E
Liard Hot Springs	N British Columbia on Alaska Highway and Liard River	59°26'N	126°06'W
Liard River	Heads in N British Columbia, Canada, flows to Mackenzie River	60°00'N	123°48'W
Limestone Inlet	E shore Stephens Passage, SE Alaska	58°01'N	133°59'W
Lincoln Bight	NW coast St. Paul Island, Pribilof Islands, W Alaska	57°12'N	170°21'W
Lion Rock	Morro Bay, San Luis Obispo County, California	35°20'N	120°51'W
Lisianski Inlet	Cross Sound, NW coast Chichagof Island, Alexander Archipelago	58°07'N	137°27'W
Litke Strait	Between Karagin Island and Kamchatka Peninsula, Russia	59°00'N	163°30'E
Little Diomede Island	Bering Strait, Alaska	65°43'N	168°55'W
Little Port Walter	S coast Baranof Island, N of Port Alexander, Alexander Archipelago	56°23'N	134°38'W
Little Sitkin Island	Rat Islands, Aleutian Islands, Alaska	51°57'N	178°31'E
Lituya Bay	E shore Gulf of Alaska, between Icy Point and Cape Fairweather	58°37'N	137°39'W
Liverpool Bay	S coast Tuktoyaktuk Peninsula, Northwest Territories, Canada	69°54'N	129°30'W
Lomgon Bay	Tasu Sound, W coast Moresby Island, British Columbia, Canada	52°47'N	132°05'W
Long Bay	Prince William Sound, N Gulf of Alaska	60°55'N	147°13'W
Long Beach	S California, facing Channel Islands	33°42'N	118°12'W
Loring	W coast Revillagigedo Island, Alexander Archipelago	55°36'N	131°38W
Los Angeles	S California	33°57'N	118°28'W
Lulu Island	Between Noyes and San Fernando islands, S Alexander Archipelago	55°28'N	133°20'W
Lyakhovskiy Island	East Siberian Sea S of New Siberian Islands, Russia	73°30'N	141°00'E
Lynn Canal	Along mainland coast S to Chatham Strait, N SE Alaska	58°10'N	134°58'W
Mackenzie Delta	Beaufort Sea coast, Northwest Territories, Canada	67°30'N	135°00'W
Mackenzie River	Flows to Beaufort Sea W of Tuktoyaktuk Peninsula, Canada	69°21'N	133°54'W
Madagascar	E coast Africa, Indian Ocean	20°00'S	47°00'E
Magadan	City on N shore Tauyskaya Bay, Sea of Okhotsk, Russia	59°34'N	150°48'E
Maguire Islands	Barrier islands, Beaufort Sea coast W of Flaxman Island, N Alaska	70°14'N	146°30'W
Makushin Bay	W coast Unalaska Island, Fox Islands, Aleutian Islands	53°44'N	167°00'W
Malaspina Glacier	Reaches tidewater 38 mi NW of Yakutat, NE Gulf of Alaska	59°42'N	140°37'W
Malaspina Strait	E side Texada Island, Strait of Georgia, British Columbia	49°40'N	124°15'W
Male Point	SW tip Fillmore Island, Alexander Archipelago	54°48'N	130°37'W
Marmot Bay	E of Whale Island between Afognak and Kodiak islands, Alaska	58°00'N	152°06'W
Martin River	Northwest Territories, Canada, Mackenzie River system	61°55'N	121°35'W
Mary Island	E of Annette Island, SE of Ketchikan, Alexander Archipelago	55°05'N	131°12'W

Masset Inlet	Graham Island off Dixon Entrance, N British Columbia	53°43'N	132°18'W
Mathieson Channel	Central British Columbia, Canada	52°19'N	128°23'W
McClure Bay	E coast Kenai Peninsula, N Gulf of Alaska	60°34'N	148°10'W
McDonald Lake	N of Yes Bay on Cleveland Peninsula, SE Alaska	55°58'N	131°50'W
McGrath	Left bank of Kuskokwim River, SW interior Alaska	62°57'N	155°35'W
McIntyre Bay	NE coast Graham Island, Queen Charlotte Islands, British Columbia	54°01'N	132°05'W
McLeod Bay	SE coast Dall Island, Dixon Entrance, S Alexander Archipelago	54°41'N	132°42'W
McLeod Harbor	NW coast Montague Island, Prince William Sound, N Gulf of Alaska	59°53'N	147°15'W
Meade River	Alaska, North Slope, flows to Beaufort Sea at Admiralty Bay	70°52'N	155°55'W
Mediterranean Sea	Surrounded by Africa, Asia, and Europe	31°20'N	30°00'E
Medny Island	E island in Commander Islands, Russia	54°40'N	167°45'E
Melville Island	Arctic Canada N of Victoria Island	75°30'N	112°00'W
Mendeltna Creek	Flows to Tazlina Lake, Copper River system, S central Alaska	61°58'N	146°25'W
Metervik Bay	N shore Bristol Bay, off Kulukak Bay, W Alaska	58°49'N	159°44'W
Metlakatla	W coast Annette Island, S of Ketchikan, Alexander Archipelago	55°08'N	131°34'W
Meyers Chuck	SW end Cleveland Peninsula, on Clarence Strait, SE Alaska	55°44'N	132°15'W
Middleton Island	N Gulf of Alaska, S of Prince William Sound	59°26'N	146°20'W
Miller Seamount	NE North Pacific	53°35'N	144°15'W
Minto Flats	W of Fairbanks, Alaska, Tanana River lowlands	64°45'N	149°30'W
Missouri River	Montana (headwaters)	47°34'N	111°07'W
Mitkof Island	SE coast Kupreanof Island, NW of Wrangell, Alexander Archipelago	56°40'N	132°50'W
Mitrofania Island	South coast Alaska Peninsula, E of Stepovak Bay, SW Gulf of Alaska	55°53'N	158°50'W
Montague Island	Between N Gulf of Alaska and SW Prince William Sound	60°10'N	147°15'W
Montague Strait	SW Prince William Sound, N side Montague Island, N Gulf of Alaska	60°00'N	147°45'W
Monterey Bay	Central California	36°48'N	121°54'W
Monterey Canyon	Submarine canyon off Monterey Bay, California	36°40'N	122°05'W
Monti Bay	SE shore Yakutat Bay, N Gulf of Alaska	59°34'N	139°50'W
Moresby Island	Queen Charlotte Islands, N British Columbia, Canada	52°50'N	131°55'W
Morro Bay	NE of Point Buchon, S California	35°20'N	120°51'W
Moss Beach	Pacific coast S of Golden Gate, N California	37°31'N	122°30'W
Mould Bay	S coast Prince Patrick Island, Northwest Territories, Canada	76°12'N	119°25'W
Mountain Point	S coast Revillagigedo Island, Alexander Archipelago	55°17'N	131°32'W
Mud Bay	W coast Revillagigedo Island, Alexander Archipelago	55°25'N	131°46'W
Muir Inlet	Off NE side Glacier Bay, N SE Alaska	58°45'N	136°05'W
Murchison River	Nunavut, Canada, N coast mainland, flows to Queen Maud Gulf	68°35'N	93°35'W
Murder Point	SE coast Attu Island, Near Islands, Aleutian Islands, Alaska	52°47'N	173°10'E
Murman coast	N coast Kola Peninsula, Barents Sea, NW Russia	68°00'N	36°00'E
Mussel Point	Monterey Bay, California	36°11'N	119°45'W

Mutsu Bay	N coast Honshu, Japan (also called Mutu Bay)	41°05'N	140°50'E
Nagai Island	Shumagin Islands, S of Alaska Peninsula, SW Gulf of Alaska	55°05'N	160°00'W
Naha Bay	W coast Revillagigedo Island, Alexander Archipelago	55°36'N	131°41'W
Naha River	Flows to Naha Bay, Revillagigedo Island, Alexander Archipelago	55°36'N	131°38'W
Nakalilok Bay	S coast Alaska Peninsula, N of Semidi Islands, W Gulf of Alaska	56°55'N	156°56'W
Nakat Bay	Mainland coast off Dixon Entrance, S SE Alaska	54°46'N	130°47'W
Naknek River	N Alaska Peninsula, flows to Kvichak Bay at head of Bristol Bay	58°43'N	157°04'W
Naktong River	South Korea, flows to Korea Strait	35°07'N	129°03'E
Nass River	British Columbia, Canada, flows to Portland Inlet	54°59'N	129°52'W
Natalii Bay	W Bering Sea, Koryak coast, NE of Cape Olyutorskiy, Russia	61°12'N	172°29'E
Nateekin Bay	In Unalaska Bay, N coast Unalaska Island, Aleutian Islands, Alaska	53°53'N	166°36'W
Navarin Canyon	Bering Sea, N edge Aleutian Basin, S of Cape Navarin	60°45'N	179°45'E
Neah Bay	NW coast Washington	48°22'N	124°37'W
Near Islands	Westernmost group of Aleutian Islands (nearest to Asia)	52°42'N	173°18'E
Near Strait	Between Commander Islands, Russia, and Aleutian Islands, Alaska	54°00'N	170°00'E
Nenana River	Flows N to Tanana River, interior Alaska	64°34'N	149°06'W
Newfoundland	Province of Canada, on NW Atlantic Ocean	53°00'N	60°00'W
New Siberian Islands	Arctic Ocean between Laptev and East Siberian seas, N Russia	75°00'N	142°00'E
New Westminster	Off S Strait of Georgia at Fraser River delta, S British Columbia	49°13'N	122°55'W
Nikolai Cove	SE of Chignik, S coast Alaska Peninsula, SW Gulf of Alaska	56°13'N	158°12'W
Nicola River	British Columbia, Canada, Fraser River system	50°26'N	121°19'W
Nikolski (village)	NW coast Bering Island, Commander Islands, Russia	55°12'N	166°00'E
Nikolski Bay	SW coast Umnak Island, Aleutian Islands, Alaska	52°57'N	168°55'W
Nikol'skoye	Same as Nikolski, Bering Island	55°12'N	166°00'E
Ninilchik	W coast Kenai Peninsula, Cook Inlet, N Gulf of Alaska	60°03'N	151°40'W
Nizki Island	Middle island of Semichi Islands, Near Islands, Aleutian Islands, Alaska	53°10'N	175°43'E
Noatak River	Flows to Chukchi Sea at N shore Kotzebue Sound, NW Alaska	67°25'N	154°53'W
Nome	S coast Seward Peninsula, N shore Norton Sound, W Alaska	64°30'N	165°25'W
Nootka Bay	Same as Nootka Sound	49°35'N	126°35'W
Nootka Sound	W coast Vancouver Island, British Columbia, Canada	49°35'N	126°35'W
North Hawaiian Ridge	Underwater seamounts among Hawaiian Islands	25°54'N	174°15'W
North Slope	Arctic plain and north slope of Brooks Range, Alaska	70°00'N	156°00'W
Northway Junction	On Alaska Highway near Tanana River, Alaska	63°01'N	141°48'W
Northwest Bay	N coast Eleanor Island, W Prince William Sound, Alaska	60°34'N	147°36'W
Northwest Territories	Between Yukon and Nunavut territories, Canada	65°00'N	125°00'W
Norton Sound	Bering Sea between Seward Peninsula and Yukon Delta, Alaska	64°00'N	164°00'W
Norwegian Sea	Arctic Ocean off Norway	70°00'N	10°00'E
Nose Point	Between Brow and Chin points, NW Revillagigedo I., Alexander Arch.	55°48'N	131°42'W

Nova Scotia	E Canada, on Atlantic Ocean	44°59'N	63°29'W
Novaya Zemlya	Arctic Ocean between Barents and Kara seas, N Russia	74°00'N	57°00'E
Nowitna River	Flows NE to Yukon River, interior Alaska	64°56'N	154°16'W
Noyes Island	E Gulf of Alaska, N of Baker Island, Alexander Archipelago	55°30'N	133°40'W
Nuka Bay	SE coast Kenai Peninsula E of Port Dick, NW Gulf of Alaska	59°19'N	150°33'W
Nulato	W Alaska, on right bank Yukon River	64°43'N	158°06'W
Nunavut	Territory E and NE of Northwest Territories, Canada	68°00'N	90°00'W
Nunivak Island	Bering Sea off Yukon-Kuskokwim Delta, W Alaska	60°00'N	166°00'W
Nushagak Bay	N shore Bristol Bay at mouth of Nushagak River, W Alaska	58°30'N	158°30'W
Nushagak River	Flows to N shore Bristol Bay W of Kvichak Bay, W Alaska	60°35'N	156°06'W
Ob River	Flows to Arctic Ocean at Obskaya Gulf, Kara Sea, N Russia	66°42'N	66°18'E
Observatory Inlet	Off Portland Canal, British Columbia, Canada	55°15'N	129°49'W
Ocean Cape	W tip Phipps Peninsula, 4.6 mi W of Yakutat, NE Gulf of Alaska	59°32'N	139°51'W
Ocean Station Papa	Canadian weathership station	50°00'N	145°00'W
Ogasawara Islands	Pacific Ocean SE of S Honshu, Japan	27°00'N	142°10'E
Ogden Passage	W coast Chichagof Island at N end Khaz Bay, Alexander Archipelago	57°38'N	136°10'W
Oglala Pass	Between Rat and Amchitka islands, Aleutian Islands, Alaska	51°42'N	178°30'E
Ogotoruk Creek	NW Alaska, flows to Chukchi Sea SE of Cape Thompson	68°06'N	165°45'W
Okalee Spit	At SE end Controller Bay and NE tip Kayak Island, N Gulf of Alaska	66°02'N	144°15'W
Old Bahama Channel	Off N coast Cuba, Caribbean Sea	22°30'N	78'50'W
Old Harbor	SE coast Kodiak Island on Sitkalidak Strait, W Gulf of Alaska	57°12'N	153°18'W
Oliktok Point	E point Harrison Bay, Beaufort Sea coast, N Alaska	70°31'N	149°51'W
Oliver Inlet	NE end Admiralty Island, SE of Juneau, Alexander Archipelago	58°08'N	134°19'W
Olsen Bay	N edge Port Gravina, E Prince William Sound, N Gulf of Alaska	60°43'N	146°12'W
Olyutorskiy Bay	Koryak coast , NE of Karaginskiy Bay, W Bering Sea, Russia	60°15'N	168°30'E
Ookamok Island	Same as Chirikof Island	55°50'N	155°37'W
Orca Bay	E shore Prince William Sound, 31 mi W of Cordova, N Gulf of Alaska	60°36'N	146°36'W
Oso Flaco Creek	S California	35°02'N	120°35'W
Otter Island	One of Pribilof Islands, S of St. Paul Island, Bering Sea, Alaska	57°03'N	170°24'W
Ozernoy Bay	NE Kamchatka coast, S of Karaginskiy Bay, W Bering Sea, Russia	56°51'N	163°00'E
Paramushir Island	N Kuril Islands, Russia	50°20'N	155°45'E
Parchas Bay	Prince William Sound, N Gulf of Alaska	60°44'N	146°11'W
Parkin Islets	Port Simpson, Chatham Sound, N British Columbia, Canada	54°37'N	130°27'W
Pathfinder Seamount	NE North Pacific Ocean	50°55'N	143°15'W
Patton Seamount	Gulf of Alaska about 166 nmi SE of Cape Sitkinak, Alaska	54°35'N	150°25'W
Paul Bight	E coast Prince of Wales Island, Skowl Arm, Alexander Archipelago	55°24'N	132°23'W
Pavlof Bay	S coast Alaska Peninsula, NW of Shumagin Is., SW Gulf of Alaska	55°20'N	161°38'W
Paxson Lake	S Alaska in course of Gulkana River, Copper River system	62°55'N	145°32'W

Peace River	Heads in British Columbia, flows across Alberta, Canada	56°09'N	120°00'W
Pearse Canal	River, flows from Portland Canal to Dixon Entrance, Alaska	54°56'N	130°20'W
Pechora River	Flows to Barents Sea S of Novaya Zemlya, N Russia	68°13'N	54°15'E
Pedder Bay	Sooke Harbour, S tip Vancouver Island, S British Columbia, Canada	48°20'N	123°33'W
Pendrell Sound	East Rodonda Island, S British Columbia, Canada	50°14'N	124°15'W
Penzhina River	Flows to NE Sea of Okhotsk at Penzhinskaya Gulf, E Russia	62°28'N	165°18'E
Peril Strait	Between Chichagof and Baranof islands, Alexander Archipelago	57°30'N	135°13'W
Pernambuco	Brazil	8°00'S	37°00'W
Perry River	Nunavut, Canada, flows to Queen Maud Gulf	67°43'N	102°14'W
Pervenets Canyon	NE edge Aleutian Basin between Navarin and Zhemchug canyons	59°30'N	178°00'W
Peter the Great Bay	Sea of Japan at Vladivostok, Russia	41°57'N	132°00'E
Petersburg	N end Mitkof Island, Alexander Archipelago	56°48'N	132°58'W
Petrel Bank	Extends 30 mi NE from Semisopochnoi Island, Aleutian Islands, Alaska	52°10'N	179°40'E
Petropaulski	Same as Petropavlovsk or Petropavlovsk-Kamchatskiy	53°01'N	158°39'E
Petropavlovsk-Kamchatskiy	SE Kamchatka Peninsula on Avacha Bight, Russia; also called Petropavlovsk, but there are other cities with that name in Russia	53°01'N	158°39'E
Phipps Peninsula	NE shore Gulf of Alaska on E shore Yakutat Bay	59°32'N	139°48'W
Pillar Bay	W coast Kuiu Island, E of Point Ellis, Alexander Archipelago	56°35'N	134°15'W
Pitkas Point	Between Andreafsky and Yukon rivers, Yukon-Kuskokwim Delta	62°02'N	163°17'W
Pitt Point	Northernmost point on coast of Beaufort Sea, N Alaska	70°55'N	153°10'W
Plover Bay	Gulf of Anadyr, Chukchi Peninsula, Russia	64°22'N	173°00'W
Point Arden	N coast Admiralty I., W shore Stephens Passage, Alexander Archipelago	58°09'N	134°10'W
Point Arena	N California coast	38°57'N	123°44'W
Point Arguello	S California, NE of Point Conception	34°35'N	120°39'W
Point Barrow	Between Beaufort and Chukchi seas, N Alaska	71°23'N	156°28'W
Point Belcher	Chukchi Sea coast NE of Wainwright, NW Alaska	70°48'N	159°39'W
Point Brower	Beaufort Sea coast SE of Beechey Point, N Alaska	70°18'N	147°48'W
Point Buchon	S California, N of Point Arguello	35°15'N	120°53'W
Point Conception	S California, SE of Point Arguello	34°27'N	120°28'W
Point Ellis	W coast Kuiu Island at entrance to Bay of Pillars, Alexander Archipelago	56°34'N	134°19'W
Point Franklin	Between Peard Bay and Chukchi Sea, NE of Point Belcher, Alaska	70°54'N	158°48'W
Point Hope	Chukchi Sea coast SW of Cape Lisburne, NW Alaska	68°20'N	166°51'W
Point Lay	Chukchi Sea coast NE of Cape Lisburne, NW Alaska	69°46'N	163°03'W
Point Loma	Entrance to San Diego Bay, S California	32°42'N	117°15'W
Point Louisa	E shore Stephens Passage, 12 mi NW of Juneau, SE Alaska	58°22'N	134°43'W
Point Marsh	Chukchi Sea coast at entrance to Wainwright Inlet, NW Alaska	70°36'N	160°07'W
Point Montara	South of San Francisco on Pacific Ocean, California	37°32'N	122°31'W
Point Retreat	N tip Admiralty Island on Lynn Canal, Alexander Archipelago	58°24'N	134°57'W

Point Reyes	N California, NW of San Francisco	38°00'N	122°59'W
Point Saint Mary	E shore Lynn Canal, N side of entrance to Berners Bay, SE Alaska	58°44'N	135°01'W
Point Sal	Central California coast, NE of Point Arguello	34°54'N	120°40'W
Point Sherman	E shore Lynn Canal, 46 mi NW of Juneau, SE Alaska	58°51'N	135°09'W
Point Stephens	Favorite Channel at entrance to south arm Tee Harbor, SE Alaska	58°25'N	134°46'W
Point Sur	Central California coast, S of Monterey Bay	36°18'N	121°53'W
Polk Inlet	SE coast Prince of Wales Island S of Kasaan Bay, Alexander Archipelago	55°23'N	132°29'W
Polovina Reef	SE coast St. Paul Island, Pribilof Islands, W Alaska	57°09'N	170°11'W
Porcher Island	N Hecate Strait off mainland coast, N British Columbia, Canada	53°58'N	130°25'W
Porcupine River	Flows from Canada to Yukon River NW of Fort Yukon, Alaska	66°34'N	145°19'W
Port Alexander	SE coast Baranof Island near tip, Alexander Archipelago	56°15'N	133°39'W
Port Althorp	N coast Chichagof Island, Alexander Archipelago	58°08'N	136°20'W
Port Armstrong	SE coast Baranof Island, Alexander Archipelago	56°18'N	134°40'W
Port Bainbridge	E coast Kenai Peninsula, N Gulf of Alaska	59°57'N	148°21'W
Port Camden	E coast Kuiu Island, W of Petersburg, Alexander Archipelago	56°48'N	133°55'W
Port Clarence	SW coast Seward Peninsula, Bering Strait, W Alaska	65°15'N	166°30'W
Port Conclusion	SE coast Baranof Island, Alexander Archipelago	56°17'N	134°38'W
Port Dick	SE coast Kenai Peninsula, NW Gulf of Alaska	59°13'N	151°03'W
Port Etches	SW coast Hinchinbrook Island, Prince William Sound, Alaska	60°20'N	146°37'W
Port Frederick	N end Chichagof Island on Icy Strait, Alexander Archipelago	58°13'N	135°30'W
Port Gravina	N edge Orca Bay, E end Prince William Sound, N Gulf of Alaska	60°38'N	146°23'W
Port Heiden	S shore Bristol Bay, N coast Alaska Peninsula E of Port Moller	56°54'N	158°48'W
Port Houghton	Stephens Passage N of Frederick Sound, Alexander Archipelago	57°19'N	133°30'W
Portillo Channel	Between Lulu and San Fernando islands, S. Alexander Archipelago	55°30'N	133°26'W
Portland Canal	Extends from Pearse Canal between Alaska and British Columbia	55°15'N	130°00'W
Portland Inlet	N British Columbia coast S of Pearse Canal and Portland Canal	54°45'N	130°25'W
Port Lucy	SE coast Baranof Island, Alexander Archipelago	56°20'N	134°39'W
Port McNeill	NE coast Vancouver Island, S British Columbia, Canada	50°35'N	127°06'W
Port Moller	S shore Bristol Bay, N coast Alaska Peninsula E of Izembek Lagoon	55°53'N	160°28'W
Port Orchard	Puget Sound, Washington	47°32'N	122°38'W
Port Orford	S Oregon coast	42°44'N	124°30'W
Port San Antonio	E coast Baker Island off Bucareli Bay, Alexander Archipelago	55°20'N	133°33'W
Port San Juan	Near Valdez, Prince William Sound, Alaska	60°03'N	148°04'W
Port San Juan	SW coast Vancouver Island, Juan de Fuca Strait, British Columbia	48°32'N	124°27'W
Port Townsend	Strait of Juan De Fuca, Washington	48°07'N	122°46'W
Port Valdez	Estuary, head at Valdez, Prince William Sound, N Gulf of Alaska	61°05'N	146°39'W
Port Walter	SE coast Baranof Island, Alexander Archipelago	56°23'N	134°39'W
Port Wells	Prince William Sound, Alaska	60°48'N	148°14'W

Povorotnaya	SE Kamchatka, Russia	52°16'N	158°30'E
Pratt Seamount	Gulf of Alaska about 229 nmi WSW of Cape Edgecumbe, Alaska	56°15'N	142°30'W
Pribilof Canyon	SE edge Aleutian Basin S of Pribilof Islands, Alaska	55°35'N	170°00'W
Pribilof Islands	SE Bering Sea, W Alaska	57°00'N	170°00'W
Prince of Wales Island	Between Gulf of Alaska and Clarence Strait, S Alexander Archipelago	55°00'N	133°00'W
Prince o Wales Island	Arctic Canada, E of Victoria Island	72°30'N	98°30'W
Prince Patrick Island	Queen Elizabeth Islands, M'Clure Strait, Northwest Territories	76°36'N	120°00'W
Prince William Sound	N Gulf of Alaska E of Kenai Peninsula	60°45'N	147°00'W
Provideniya	City on Provideniya Bay, Russia	64°23'N	173°18'W
Providence Bay	Same as Provideniya Bay	64°25'N	173°24'W
Provideniya Bay	SE tip Chukchi Peninsula, Russia, S of Bering Strait	64°25'N	173°24'W
Prudhoe Bay	Beaufort Sea coast, N Alaska	70°22'N	148°22'W
Puale Bay	E coast Alaska Peninsula, Shelikof Strait, W Gulf of Alaska	57°41'N	155°29'W
Puerto Rico Trench	Atlantic Ocean off the Antilles (deepest point of the ocean)	20°00'N	66°00'W
Puffin Bay	S coast Baranof Island, Alexander Archipelago	56°15'N	134°48'W
Puget Sound	NW Washington	47°50'N	122°26'W
Punta Abreojos	Pacific coast S Baja California, Mexico	26°43'N	113°37'W
Punta Baja	Pacific coast N Baja California, Mexico	29°57'N	115°48'W
Punta Banda	Pacific coast N Baja California, Mexico	31°45'N	116°45'W
Punta Blanca	Pacific coast central Baja California, Mexico	29°25'N	115°12'W
Punta Cabras	Pacific coast N Baja California, Mexico	31°20'N	116°30'W
Punta Canoas	Pacific coast N Baja California, Mexico	29°26'N	115°12'W
Punta Chamalu	Pacific coast N Baja California, Mexico	30°50'N	116°11'W
Punta Gorda	N California coast	40°15'N	124°21'W
Punta Pequeña	Pacific coast S Baja California	26°10'N	112°35'W
Punta Rocosa	Pacific coast central Baja California	28°45'N	114°24'W
Punta Rompiente	Pacific coast central Baja California, SE of Cedros Island	27°44'N	115°01'W
Punta San Carlos	Pacific coast N Baja California, Mexico	29°37'N	115°39'W
Punta San Juanico	Pacific coast S Baja California, Mexico	26°00'N	112°15'W
Punta San Pablo	Pacific coast central Baja California, Mexico	27°13'N	114°29'W
Pusan	South Korea on Sea of Japan	35°06'N	128°06'E
Queen Charlotte Islands	N British Columbia, Canada	53°22'N	133°44'W
Queen Charlotte Sound	Between Queen Charlotte Islands and Vancouver Island, B.C.	51°33'N	129°35'W
Queen Elizabeth Islands	Arctic Ocean, Northwest Territories and Nunavut, Canada	76°20'N	114°30'W
Queen Inlet	Off N side Glacier Bay, SE Alaska	58°54'N	136°33'W
Queen Maud Gulf	N coast mainland Canada, Nunavut, E of Dease Strait	68°20'N	102°00'W
Quinn Seamount	Gulf of Alaska about 220 nmi S of Cape St. Elias, Alaska	56°18'N	145°13'W
Rampart	S bank Yukon River, interior Alaska	65°30'N	150°10'W

Ranger Bank	Pacific N of San Benito Islands, W of central Baja California, Mexico	28°34'N	115°30'W
Raspberry Island	Between Kodiak and Afognak islands, W Gulf of Alaska	58°02'N	153°05'W
Raspberry Strait	Between Raspberry and Afognak islands, W Gulf of Alaska	58°02'N	153°00'W
Rat Islands	Between Near Islands and Andreanof Islands, Aleutian Islands, Alaska	52°00'N	178°00'E
Ratmanov Island	Russian name for Big Diomede Island, Russia	65°46'N	169°06'W
Redondo Beach	S of Los Angeles facing Channel Islands, California	33°51'N	118°23'W
Reedsport	Oregon coast	43°42'N	124°06'W
Rennell Sound	W coast Graham Island, Queen Charlotte Islands, British Columbia	53°25'N	132°43'W
Resolute Bay	S coast Cornwallis Island, Nunavut, Canada	74°41'N	94°50'W
Resurrection Bay	SE coast Kenai Peninsula, N Gulf of Alaska	59°48'N	149°30'W
Resurrection Peninsula	SE coast Kenai Peninsula, N Gulf of Alaska	59°52'N	149°17'W
Return Islands	Barrier islands on Beaufort Sea coast, N Alaska	70°27'N	148°47'W
Revillagigedo Island	Between mainland and Prince of Wales Island, Alexander Archipelago	55°35'N	131°20'W
Revillagigedo Islands	N Pacific Ocean W of Mexico	18°05'N	112°00'W
Rio Rosario	Flows to Pacific coast N Baja California, Mexico	30°02'N	115°55'W
Rio Santo Domingo	Flows to Pacific coast S Baja California, Mexico	25°34'N	112°05'W
Rio Santo Thomas	Flows to Pacific coast N Baja California, Mexico	31°33'N	116°41'W
Rivers Inlet	British Columbia, Canada, mainland NE of N tip Vancouver Island	51°28'N	127°35'W
Robben Island	Same as Tyuleniy Island (Ostrov Tyuleniy)	48°30'N	144°38'E
Rose Island	NE coast Prince of Wales Island, Alexander Archipelago	56°05'N	132°51'W
Round Island	Clayoquot Sound, Vancouver Island, British Columbia	49°15'N	126°00'W
Rugged Island	At mouth of Resurrection Bay, S of Seward, N Gulf of Alaska	59°51'N	149°23'W
Sacramento River	California	38°04'N	121°51'W
Sado Island	Sea of Japan off N Honshu, Japan	38°00'N	138°25'E
Safety Sound	N shore Norton Sound E of Nome, W Alaska	64°29'N	164°45'W
Sagami Bay	W Pacific Oean, E coast Honshu, Japan, SW of Tokyo	35°05'N	139°00'E
Sagavanirktok River	Alaska, North Slope, flows to Beaufort Sea at Prudhoe Bay	70°18'N	147°52'W
Saint George Island	Southernmost of Pribilof Islands, SE Bering Sea, W Alaska	56°35'N	169°35'W
Saint John Baptist Bay	NW coast Baranof Island, Alexander Archipelago	57°17'N	135°35'W
Saint Jona Island	Same as Iony Island (Ostrov Iony)	56°26'N	143°25'E
Saint Lawrence Island	N Bering Sea, SW of Nome, W Alaska	63°30'N	170°30'W
Saint Lazaria Islands	Sitka Sound S of Kruzof Island, SW of Sitka, Alexander Archipelago	56°59'N	135°42'W
Saint Matthew Island	E Bering Sea, W of Nunivak Island, Alaska	60°24'N	172°42'W
Saint Michael	E coast St. Michael Island, S shore Norton Sound, W Alaska	63°29'N	162°02'W
Saint Paul Island	Largest of northern Pribilof Islands, SE Bering Sea, W Alaska	57°10'N	170°15'W
Sakhalin Island	Between Tatarskiy Strait and Sea of Okhotsk, Russia	50°21'N	142°49'E
Salisbury Sound	Between Kruzof and Chichagof islands, NW of Sitka, Alexander Arch.	57°22'N	135°50'W
Salmon Fork	Flows SW from Canada to Black River SE of Chalkyitsik	66°33'N	142°32'W

Samsing Cove	W coast Baranof Island, S of Sitka, Alexander Archipelago	56°59'N	135°21'W
Sanak Island	Largest of Sanak Islands, SW Gulf of Alaska	54°25'N	162°40'W
Sanak Islands	SW Gulf of Alaska, SE of Unimak Island	54°23'N	162°35'W
San Benito Island	Pacific Ocean, S Baja California, Mexico	28°15'N	117°25'W
San Benito Islands	Pacific Ocean, S Baja California, Mexico	28°25'N	115°35'W
Sanborn Harbor	W coast Nagai Island, Shumagin Islands, SW Gulf of Alaska	55°10'N	160°04'W
San Carlos Bay	Pacific coast N Baja California, Mexico	29°42'N	115°39'W
San Cristobal Bay	Pacific coast S Baja California, Mexico	27°16'N	114°35'W
San Diego (Bay)	S California coast	32°39'N	117°08'W
Sandman Reefs	NE of Sanak Islands, SW Gulf of Alaska	54°42'N	162°15'W
Sandy Cove	W coast Baranof Island, 4.5 mi S of Sitka, N Alexander Archipelago	56°59'N	135°19'W
San Fernando Island	W of Prince of Wales Island, E of Lulu Island, S Alexander Achipelago	55°30'N	133°20'W
San Francisco Bay	N California	37°42'N	122°16'W
San Joaquin River	California	38°04'N	121°51'W
San Juan Batista Island	W of Prince of Wales Island, E of Baker Island, Alexander Archipelago	55°26'N	133°16'W
San Juan Islands	Washington between Straits of Juan de Fuca and Georgia	48°36'N	122°56'W
San Miguel Island	Westernmost of N Channel Islands, S California	34°02'N	120°22'W
San Nicholas Island	Channel Islands, S California	33°14'N	119°31'W
San Simeon	Central California coast	35°38'N	121°11'W
San Simeon Point	Central California coast	35°38'N	121°12'W
Santa Ana River	Flows to Pacific Ocean at Newport Beach, S California	33°37'N	117°57'W
Santa Barbara	S California, N of San Diego	34°25'N	119°44'W
Santa Barbara Island	Channel Islands, S California	33°28'N	119°02'W
Santa Catalina Island	Channel Islands, S California	33°22'N	118°25'W
Santa Cruz	Central California coast on north shore Monterey Bay	36°58'N	122°02'W
Santa Cruz Island	Channel Islands, S California	34°01'N	119°43'W
Santa Monica Bay	S California coast at Los Angeles	33°56'N	118°27'W
Santa Rosa Island	Channel Islands, S California	33°57'N	120°06'W
Saturna Island	S Strait of Georgia, British Columbia, Canada	48°47'N	123°08'W
Savoonga	N coast St. Lawrence Island, N Bering Sea, Alaska	63°42'N	170°29'W
Schooner Rock	Off NE tip Montague Island in Hinchinbrook Entrance, Alaska	60°18'N	146°54'W
Scraggy Island	In Icy Strait at mouth of Port Frederick, Alexander Archipelago	58°10'N	135°28'W
Sea of Japan	Between Japan and the Koreas and S Russia	40°00'N	135°00'E
Sea of Okhotsk	W of Kamchaka Peninsula and Kuril Islands, Russia and Japan	55°00'N	150°00'E
Seattle	W Washington, at head of Puget Sound	47°35'N	122°20'W
Sebastian Vizcaino Bay	N Baja California, Mexico	28°16'N	114°43'W
Security Inlet	Moresby Island, Queen Charlotte Islands, British Columbia, Canada	53°01'N	132°21'W
Seguam Island	Easternmost of Andreanof Islands, Aleutian Islands	52°19'N	172°30'W

Seguam Pass	Between Seguam and Amlia islands, Andreanof Islands, Alaska	52°10'N	172°45'W
Selawik Lake	NW Alaska, E of Kotzebue Sound	66°30'N	160°45'W
Selawik River	NW Alaska, flows to Selawik Lake	66°37'N	160°18'W
Seldovia	SW coast Kenai Peninsula, E shore Kachemak Bay, N Gulf of Alaska	59°26'N	151°42'W
Semichi Islands	Chain of islands in Near Islands, Aleutian Islands, Alaska	52°44'N	174°00'E
Semidi Islands	SW Gulf of Alaska, SW of Trinity Islands	56°10'N	156°47'W
Semisopochnoi Island	Northeasternmost of Rat Islands, Aleutian Islands, Alaska	51°55'N	179°36'E
Severnaya Zemlya	"North Land"—Islands between Kara and Laptev seas, Russia	80°00'N	100°00'E
Seward	At NW end Resurrection Bay, E coast Kenai Peninsula, Alaska	60°06'N	149°26'W
Seward Peninsula	Between Chukchi Sea and Bering Sea, W Alaska	65°00'N	164°00'W
Seymour Inlet	Queen Charlotte Strait, British Columbia, Canada	51°06'N	127°29'W
Shagak Bay	NW coast Adak Island, Andreanof Islands, Aleutian Islands, Alaska	51°52'N	176°45'W
Shahafka Cove	Opposite Woody Island on NE coast Kodiak Island, W Gulf of Alaska	57°48'N	152°22'W
Shantar Islands	NW Sea of Okhotsk N of Sakhalin Island, Russia	55°00'N	137°36'E
Shearwater Bay	SE coast Kodiak Island off Kiliuda Bay, W Gulf of Alaska	57°20'N	152°55'W
Shelikhov Gulf	NE Sea of Okhotsk, Russia (also Gulf of Shelekhova)	59°45'N	158°00'E
Shelikof Bay	SE Gulf of Alaska, W coast Kruzof Island, Alexander Archipelago	57°08'N	135°49'W
Shelikof Strait	Between Kodiak Island and Alaska Peninsula, W Gulf of Alaska	58°00'N	154°30'W
Shelter Island	W shore Favorite Channel, N of Admiralty Island, Alexander Arch.	58°26'N	134°52'W
Shemya Island	Easternmost of Semichi Islands, Near Islands, Aleutian Islands, Alaska	52°43'N	174°07'E
Ship Creek	Flows to Knik Arm at Anchorage, S Alaska	61°14'N	149°54'W
Shirshov Ridge	Undersea mountains extending S from Cape Olyutorskiy, Russia	58°30'N	170°30'E
Shishmaref	NW coast Seward Peninsula, Alaska	66°15'N	166°04'W
Shumagin Bank	Shoal SE of Shumagin Islands, SW Gulf of Alaska	54°39'N	159°22'W
Shumagin Islands	S of Alaska Peninsula, SW Gulf of Alaska	55°20'N	160°15'W
Siberia	Russian region extending from approximately the Ural Mountains to the Pacific Ocean and from Arctic Ocean to China and Mongolia	65°00'N	135°00'E
Silver Bay	W coast Baranof Island, E of Sitka, Alexander Archipelago	57°02'N	135°12'W
Simeonof Island	Easternmost of Shumagin Islands, SW Gulf of Alaska	54°54'N	159°16'W
Simpson Bay	NE shore Orca Bay, E Prince William Sound, NW of Cordova, Alaska	60°37'N	145°55'W
Simpson Cove	Off Camden Bay, Beaufort Sea, N Alaska	69°57'N	144°54'W
Simpson Lagoon	Beaufort Sea between Jones and Return islands and mainland, N Alaska	70°30'N	149°12'W
Simushir Island	Kuril Islands, Russia	46°54'N	152°00'E
Sinuk	N shore Norton Sound at mouth of Sinuk River, Bering Sea, W Alaska	64°36'N	166°15'W
Sitka	W coast Baranof Island, Alexander Archipelago	57°03'N	135°20'W
Sitkalidak Island	SE coast Kodiak Island, W Gulf of Alaska	57°07'N	153°14'W
Sitka Sound	Between Baranof and Kruzof islands, Alexander Archipelago	57°00'N	135°30'W
Sitkinak Island	Trinity Islands, S of Kodiak Island, SW Gulf of Alaska	56°33'N	154°10'W

Situk River	SE Alaska, flows to NE Gulf of Alaska SE of Yakutat	59°26'N 139°33'W
Skeena River	British Columbia, Canada, flows to Chatham Sound	54°01'N 130°07'W
Skidegate Inlet	S end Graham Island, Queen Charlotte Islands, British Columbia	53°12'N 132°05'W
Skonun River	Flows to McIntyre Bay, Graham Island , British Columbia, Canada	54°59'N 131°55'W
Skowl Arm	Off Kasaan Bay, E coast Prince of Wales Island, Alexander Archipelago	55°26'N 132°16'W
Smith Bay	Beaufort Sea E of Point Barrow, N Alaska	70°54'N 154°19'W
Smith Creek	Cultus Lake, British Columbia, Canada	49°06'N 122°07'W
Smith Sound	Arctic Ocean between Greenland and Ellesmere Island	78°20'N 74°45'W
Smith Sound	British Columbia, Canada, mainland NE of N tip Vancouver Island	51°18'N 127°40'W
Snettisham	E shore Stephens Passage, SE of Juneau, SE Alaska	57°59'N 133°47'W
Snug Harbor	SE coast Knight Island, W Prince William Sound, N Gulf of Alaska	60°15'N 147°43'W
Society Islands	Polynesia, S Pacific Ocean	17°00'S 150°00'W
Somerset Island	Arctic Ocean, Nunavut, Canada	73°30'N 93°00'W
Sooke	S tip Vancouver Island, S British Columbia, Canada	48°19'N 123°38'W
Sooke Harbour	S tip Vancouver Island, S British Columbia, Canada	48°22'N 123°43'W
South China Sea	Between SE China, Indochina, Taiwan, and Philippines	15°00'N 115°00'E
South Emperor Ridge	Mid-North Pacific Ocean chain of seamounts	32°40'N 179°44'W
Spacious Bay	Behm Canal, NE coast Cleveland Peninsula, SE Alaska	55°51'N 131°46'W
Spitsbergen	Largest island in Svalbard archipelago, N of Norway, Arctic Ocean	78°45'N 18°00'E
Spruce Island	NNE of Kodiak Island, N of Kodiak, W Gulf of Alaska	57°55'N 152°25'W
Square Island	Spacious Bay, NE coast Cleveland Peninsula, SE Alaska	55°51'N 131°50'W
Stalemate Bank	Extends about 100 mi W from Attu Island, Aleutian Islands, Alaska	53°00'N 171°00'E
Staritschkof Island	Avacha Bay, NW Pacific Ocean, SE Kamchatka, Russia	52°37'N 158°50'E
Station Papa	Canadian weathership station, NE Pacific Ocean	50°00'N 145°00'W
Steamer Bay	W coast Etolin Island, Alexander Archipelago	56°11'N 132°43'W
Stephens Passage	Portland Island to Frederick Sound, Alexander Archipelago	57°13'N 133°39'W
Stepovak Bay	S coast Alaska Peninsula, N of Shumagin Islands, SW Gulf of Alaska	55°40'N 159°50'W
Stikine River	British Columbia, flows to Frederick Sound N of Wrangell, SE Alaska	56°39'N 131°50'W
Strait of Georgia	Between Vancouver Island and mainland, British Columbia, Canada	49°20'N 124°00'W
Strait of Juan de Fuca	Between Washington State and Vancouver Island, British Columbia	48°15'N 124°00'W
Sucia Ledge	Reef at S end Portillo Channel, S Alexander Archipelago	55°27'N 133°25'W
Suemez Island	E of Bucareli Bay, W coast Prince of Wales Island, Alexander Archipelago	55°16'N 133°21'W
Suruga Bay	W Pacific Ocean, E coast Honshu, Japan, SW of Sagami Bay	35°00'N 138°15°E
Surveyor Seamount	Gulf of Alaska about 235 nmi S of Cape St. Elias, Alaska	56°03'N 144°15'W
Susitna River	S Alaska, flows to Cook Inlet	61°16'N 150°30'W
Svalbard	Archipelago N of Norway in Arctic Ocean	78°00'N 20°00'E
Sweeper Cove	NE coast Adak Island, Andreanof Islands, Alaska	51°52'N 135°08'W
Taiya Inlet	Off Chilkat Inlet, S of Skagway, SE Alaska	59°17'N 135°23'W

Taku Harbor	E shore Stephens Passage, SE of Juneau, SE Alaska	58°03'N	134°02'W
Taku Inlet	E shore Stephens Passage, S of Juneau, SE Alaska	58°12'N	134°06'W
Taku River	Flows from British Columbia to Taku Inlet, SE Alaska	58°59'N	133°09'W
Tanaga Island	Andreanof Islands, Aleutian Islands, Alaska	51°48'N	177°53'W
Tanaga Pass	Between Delarof Islands and Tanaga Island, Aleutian Islands, Alaska	51°38'N	178°20'W
Tanana River	Flows from Northway Junction to Yukon River, interior Alaska	65°09'N	151°57'W
Tanner Bank	Pacific Ocean N of Cortes Bank, off San Diego, S California	32°40'N	119°10'W
Tasman Sea	W South Pacific Ocean between Australia and New Zealand	40°00'S	160°00'E
Tasu Sound	W coast Moresby Island, N British Columbia, Canada	52°50'N	132°05'W
Tatarskiy Strait	Same as Tatar Strait	49°00'N	141°00'E
Tatar Strait	Between W coast Sakhalin Island and mainland Russia	49°00'N	141°00'E
Tauyskaya Bay	N Sea of Okhotsk, Russia	59°30'N	150°00'E
Tava Island	W coast Baranof Island, SW of Sitka, Alexander Archipelago	56°50'N	135°29'W
Taymyr Island	Arctic Ocean N of Taymyr Peninsula, Kara and Laptev seas, Russia	78°07'N	107°06'E
Taymyr Peninsula	On Kara and Laptev seas, Russia	76°00'N	104°00'E
Tazlina Lake	S Alaska, head of Tazlina River, Copper River system	61°53'N	146°30'W
Tazlina River	Tributary of Copper River, S central Alaska	62°02'N	145°23'W
Tee Harbor	E shore Favorite Channel, 15 mi NW of Juneau, SE Alaska	58°25'N	134°45'W
Tenakee Inlet	E central coast Chichagof Island, Alexander Archipelago	57°47'N	134°57'W
Terpeniya Bay	SE coast Sakhalin Island, Sea of Okhotsk, Russia	49°00'N	143°30'E
Teshekpuk Lake	Arctic plain W of Harrison Bay, N Alaska	70°32'N	152°50'W
Teslin Lake	Yukon Territory and British Columbia, Yukon River system	60°15'N	132°58'W
Texada Island	Strait of Georgia, British Columbia	49°40'N	124°25'W
Thetis Island	Beaufort Sea coast, W island of Jones Islands, N Alaska	70°33'N	150°10'W
The Triplets	Island group in Marmot Bay, NE of Kodiak Island, Alaska	57°59'N	152°28'W
Thistle Ledge	E shore Stephens Passage, SE of Juneau, SE Alaska	57°40'N	133°41'W
Thomas Bay	E shore Frederick Sound, N of Petersburg, SE Alaska	57°00'N	132°59'W
Tigalda Island	SW of Unimak Pass in Krenitzin Islands, Aleutian Islands, Alaska	54°06'N	165°05'W
Tillamook Head	Pacific Ocean S of Columbia River, N Oregon	45°57'N	123°59'W
Toba Inlet	Off N Strait of Georgia, British Columbia, Canada	50°22'N	124°42'W
Todos Santos	Pacific coast S Baja California, Mexico	23°27'N	110°13'W
Todos Santos Bay	Pacific coast N Baja California, Mexico, near Ensenada	31°47'N	116°41'W
Tok	At junction of Alaska and Glenn highways, Alaska	63°20'N	142°59'W
Tokyo	SE Honshu, capital of Japan	35°42'N	139°46'E
Toledo Harbor	SE coast Baranof Island, Alexander Archipelago	56°22'N	134°38'W
Tolovana	Interior Alaska, on right bank Tanana River, W of Fairbanks	64°51'N	149°49'W
Tomname Lagoon	N coast St. Lawrence Island, Bering Sea, W Alaska	63°21'N	169°30'W
Tongass Narrows	Between Gravina and Revillagigedo islands, Alexander Archipelago	55°22'N	131°43'W

Tonsina Bay	S shore Kachemak Bay SE of Seldovia, Kenai Peninsula, Alaska	59°18'N	150°54'W
Tonsina Lake	S Alaska, NE of Valdez, Copper River system	61°32'N	145°30'W
Toyama Bay	Sea of Japan off north-central Honshu, Japan	36°50'N	137°10'E
Trail Island	N British Columbia, Canada	54°36'N	130°51'W
Traitors Cove	Behm Canal, W coast Revillagigedo Island, Alexander Archipelago	55°42'N	131°39'W
Trevor Channel	SW coast Vancouver Island, British Columbia	48°52'N	125°08'W
Triangle Island	Queen Inlet at terminus of Carroll Glacier, Glacier Bay, SE Alaska	58°57'N	136°32'W
Triangle Island	Pacific off NW coast Vancouver Island, British Columbia, Canada	50°49'N	129°45'W
Trinity Islands	W Gulf of Alaska off SW coast Kodiak Island	56°33'N	154°20'W
Trois Pistoles	St. Lawrence River estuary, Quebec, Canada	48°06'N	69°02'W
Tsitika River	NE coast Vancouver Island, S British Columbia, Canada	50°28'N	126°35'W
Tufts Abyssal Plain	Pacific Ocean off Oregon	47°00'N	140°00'W
Tuktoyaktuk Peninsula	Mackenzie River Delta, Beaufort Sea, Northwest Territories, Canada	69°45'N	131°20'W
Turnagain Arm	Extends SE from Cook Inlet, S of Anchorage, Alaska	61°06'N	150°12'W
Turtle Bay	Same as Bahia Tórtolo	27°40'N	114°53'W
Tyone Lake	S Alaska, Susitna River system	62°30'N	146°45'W
Tyone River	S Alaska, flows from Tyone Lake to Susitna River	62°42'N	147°13'W
Tyuleniy Island	Sea of Okhotsk off SE coast Sakhalin Island, Russia (Ostrov Tyuleniy)	48°30'N	144°38'E
Ugamak Island	Krenitzin Islands at entrance to Unimak Pass, Aleutian Islands, Alaska	54°12'N	164°50'W
Ugashik River	Flows to Ugashik Bay, NW coast Alaska Peninsula	57°30'N	157°37'W
Ulloa Channel	Between Prince of Wales Island and Suemez Island, Alexander Arch.	53°19'N	133°17'W
Ulm Plateau	NW tip Bowers Ridge, Bering Sea	54°50'N	176°30'E
Umiat	On N bank Colville River S of Harrison Bay, N Alaska	69°22'N	152°08'W
Umnak Island	Fox Islands, Aleutian Islands, Alaska	53°15'N	168°20'W
Umnak Plateau	SE Bering Sea N of E Aleutian Islands, Alaska	54°15'N	170°15'W
Umpqua River	Flows to Pacific Ocean at Reedsport, Oregon	43°40'N	124°12'W
Unalakleet	Norton Sound coastal village near Nome, W Alaska	63°52'N	160°47'W
Unalaska (village)	S shore Unalaska Bay, Unalaska Island	53°52'N	166°32'W
Unalaska Island	Fox Islands, Aleutian Islands, Alaska	53°35'N	166°50'W
Unalga Island	Delarof Islands, Aleutian Islands, Alaska	51°34'N	179°03'W
Unga Island	Largest of Shumagin Islands, SW Gulf of Alaska	55°15'N	160°40'W
Ungava Bay	Hudson Strait, Quebec, Canada	60°00'N	67°30'W
Unimak Pass	Between Unimak Island and Krenitzin Islands, Aleutian Islands, Alaska	54°20'N	165°00'W
Union Seamount	NE North Pacific	49°37'N	132°47'W
Ushishir Island	N Kuril Islands, Russia	47°32'N	152°49'E
Usof Bay	S coast Unalaska Island, Aleutian Islands, Alaska	53°30'N	166°45'W
Uyak Bay	W coast Kodiak Island on Shelikof Strait, W Gulf of Alaska	57°48'N	154°04'W
Valdez	E shore Port Valdez, NE Prince William Sound, N Gulf of Alaska	61°07'N	146°16'W

Valdez Arm	Connects Prince William Sound and Port Valdez, N Gulf of Alaska	60°53'N	146°54'W
Vancouver Island	S British Columbia, Canada	49°30'N	125°30'W
Ventura	S California	34°16'N	119°16'W
Ventura River	S California	34°16'N	119°18'W
Victoria	E shore Vancouver Island near S tip, British Columbia, Canada	48°30'N	123°30'W
Victoria Island	Arctic Canada, E of Amundsen Gulf	71°00'N	110°00'W
Vityaz Ridge	Undersea ridge in Pacific off N Kuril Islands, Russia	48°30'N	154°45'E
Vladivostok	Shore of Peter the Great Bay, Sea of Japan, Russia	43°08'N	131°54'E
Volga Island	Sitka Sound, W coast Baranof Island, Alexander Archipelago	57°02'N	135°21'W
Waadda Island	NW coast Washington	48°23'N	124°35'W
Wadleigh Island	W coast Prince of Wales Island near Craig, S Alexander Archipelago	55°34'N	133°09'W
Wainwright	On Chukchi Sea coast NE of Icy Cape, NW Alaska	70°38'N	160°01'W
Waldron Island	San Juan Islands, Washington	48°42'N	123°01'W
Wales Island	Queen Charlotte Islands, N British Columbia, Canada	54°45'N	130°33'W
Ward Cove	SW coast Revillagigedo Island, Alexander Archipelago	55°23'N	131°44'W
Waterfall	W coast Prince of Wales Island, SW of Craig, Alexander Archipelago	55°16'N	133°14'W
Welcome Harbour	Porcher Island, N British Columbia, Canada	53°53'N	130°31'W
Welker Seamount	Gulf of Alaska about 201 nmi WSW of Cape Ommaney, Alaska	55°06'N	140°20'W
Wells Passage	Extends from Port Wells to Prince William Sound, Alaska	60°46'N	148°04'W
West Cortes Basin	Pacific Ocean off S California	32°23'N	119°25'W
West Creek	Flows to Brooks Lake, N Alaska Peninsula	58°35'N	155°51'W
White Sea	Arctic Ocean off NW Russia, S of Barents Sea	65°30'N	38°00'E
Wiah Point	North Graham Island, British Columbia, Canada	54°07'N	132°19'W
Wide Bay	Shelikof Strait, W of Cape Igvak, Alaska Peninsula	57°22'N	156°11'W
Willapa Bay	Washington	46°22'N	123°57'W
Williams Reef	Off Chiniak Bay NE of Long Island, NE of Kodiak Island, Gulf of Alaska	57°50'N	152°10'W
Wingham Island	Mouth of Controller Bay, E Prince William Sound, Alaska	60°01'N	144°23'W
Wonsan	North Korea on Sea of Japan	40°13'N	127°07'E
Wood River	Flows to Nushagak River, N of Bristol Bay, W Alaska	59°03'N	158°25'W
Woody Island	Chiniak Bay, E coast Kodiak Island, W Gulf of Alaska	57°47'N	152°20'W
Wrangel Island	W Chukchi Sea off NE Siberia, Russia	71°14'N	179°59'W
Wrangell	On N coast Wrangell Island, Alexander Archipelago	56°28'N	132°23'W
Wrangell Harbor	At Wrangell, on N coast Wrangell Island, Alexander Archipelago	56°28'N	132°23'W
Wrangell Island	Between mainland and Etolin Island, Alexander Archipelago	56°16'N	132°12'W
Wright River	Downstream of Canyon Island, flows to Taku River, SE Alaska	58°31'N	133°44'W
Wuluk River	Flows SW to Chukchi Sea at Kivalina Lagoon, NW Alaska	67°44'N	164°31'W
Yakan Point	N Graham Island, Queen Charlotte Islands, British Columbia	53°57'N	131°51'W
Yakobi Island	Off NW coast Chichagof Island, Alexander Archipelago	57°56'N	136°27'W

Yakobi Rock	Off NW coast Yakobi Island, Alexander Archipelago	58°05'N	136°33'W
Yakutat	W end Monti Bay, N Gulf of Alaska	59°33'N	139°44'W
Yakutat Bay	NE shore Gulf of Alaska between Icy Bay and Dry Bay	59°40'N	140°00'W
Yakutat Foreland	Coastal area from Yakutat to Dangerous River, SE Alaska	59°32'N	139°24'W
Yalu River	North Korea–China border, flows to Yellow Sea	39°55'N	124°00'E
Yana River	Flows N to Arctic Ocean at E Laptev Sea, Yakutsk, Russia	71°30'N	136°30'E
Yana River	Flows S to Sea of Okhotsk at Tauyskaya Bay, Magaden, Russia	60°00'N	145°00'E
Yaquina Bay	Oregon coast	44°37'N	124°02'W
Yellow Sea	W North Pacific, off China, North Korea, and South Korea	35°00'N	124°00'E
Yenisei River	Siberia, Russia, flows to Kara Sea, Arctic Ocean	70°08'N	83°13'E
Yes Bay	Off Behm Canal, NE coast Cleveland Peninsula, SE Alaska	55°53'N	131°44'W
Yoroo River	N Mongolia	47°42'N	96°36'E
Yukon Delta	River delta between Norton Sound and Bering Sea, W Alaska	63°00'N	164°00'W
Yukon-Kuskokwim Delta	Delta of Yukon and Kuskokwim rivers, on Bering Sea, W Alaska	61°30'N	164°00'W
Yukon River	Flows from Yukon Territory to Bering Sea at Norton Sound, Alaska	62°32'N	163°54'W
Yukon Territory	Between Alaska and Northwest Territories, Canada	63°00'N	135°00'W
Yunaska Island	Islands of Four Mountains, Aleutian Islands, Alaska	52°38'N	170°40'W
Zaikof Bay	NE coast Montague Island, S Prince William Sound, Alaska	60°19'N	146°58'W
Zaikof Point	NE tip Montague Island, S Prince William Sound, Alaska	60°19'N	146°55'W
Zayas Island	Dixon Entrance, Coastal Islands, British Columbia, Canada	54°38'N	131°02'W
Zhemchug Canyon	E edge Aleutian Basin, Bering Sea, Alaska	57°30'N	175°20'W

The main source for spelling, locations, and history of Alaska place names was Orth's (1967) *Dictionary of Alaska Place Names*. The gazetteer in Hart's (1973) *Pacific Fishes of Canada* and descriptions in Walbran's (1909) *British Columbia Coast Names* provided information on British Columbia names in the early years of work on this book. Various editions of the *United States Coast Pilot,* numbers 7–9, helped find place names in California, Oregon, Washington, and Hawaii, as well as Alaska; bibliographic information for the current editions (National Ocean Service 1997, 1998, 1999) is given in the Bibliography.

In recent years several gazetteers became available on the Internet, and a few proved to be invaluable for completing our gazetteer. Those used most often were the Alexandria Digital Library Gazetteer of the University of California Santa Barbara (for place names worldwide); the Geographic Names Information System of the U.S. Geological Survey (names in United States); the GEOnet Names Server of the National Imagery and Mapping Agency (worldwide excluding United States); and the GeoNames site by Natural Resources Canada. The current (November 2001) Internet addresses for those four sites are, in the same order, as follows:
http://fat-albert.alexandria.ucsb.edu:8827/gazetteer/
http://geonames.usgs.gov/
http://www.nima.mil/gns/html/
http://geonames.nrcan.gc.ca/english/Home.html/

Townsend (1901), Fassett (1905), Gilbert and Burke (1912a), and other collecting records of the U.S. Fish Commission (now National Marine Fisheries Service) were critical for locating stations sampled by the U.S. Fish Commission steamer *Albatross* and referenced in early works on the North Pacific ichthyofauna.

The large collection of maps used to locate names included individual maps published by the National Geographic Society and the *National Geographic Atlas*; *Times Atlas of the World*; *Alaska Atlas and Gazetteer,* containing the U.S. Geological Survey topographic quadrangles; and *British Columbia Recreational Atlas.*

Glossary

GLOSSARY

Definitions for the glossary were adapted from Günther (1880a), Jordan and Evermann (1898), Starks (1921), Schultz (1936), Romer (1962), Pennak (1964), Trautman (1973), Morrow (1980), Cailliet et al. (1986), Smith and Heemstra (1986), Bates and Jackson (1987), Emmett et al. (1991), Coad (1995), Murphy and Willis (1996), Eschmeyer (1998), International Commission on Zoological Nomenclature (1999), and other sources. The objective is not to give a definition of every term used, or all details, but to provide a convenient reference for readers who might not have specialized works such as in ichthyology or comparative anatomy on hand. The glossary supplements the introductions to higher taxa in this book. Some of the most highly specialized terminology is not included in the glossary but is defined, and often illustrated, in the introductions to the taxa having the features; e.g., the posterial teeth of lampreys (Petromyzontidae) or the ventral scutes of herrings (Clupeidae). Likewise, photophores are not defined in the glossary but are shown in diagrams in the family introductions; e.g., bristlemouths (Gonostomatidae) and lanternfishes (Myctophidae). Additional terms and details may be found in the works cited.

Abbreviations used in this book for meristic characters and measurements are listed before the rest of the entries under each letter of the alphabet.

A — abbreviation for anal fin, used to specify anal fin spine and ray counts in the line of meristic values given in the species acounts for ray-finned fishes; roman numerals indicate spines and arabic numerals indicate rays; *see* D.

abdomen — belly; includes the cavity containing the digestive and reproductive organs.

abdominal — pertaining to the belly or abdomen; said of the pelvic fins when the pelvic girdle is not attached to the pectoral girdle, and in this situation the pelvic fins are usually, but not always, located on the abdomen considerably behind the pectoral fins.

abdominal vertebrae — anterior vertebrae that occur dorsal to the body cavity and to which the ribs are attached. They lack the haemal arch and canal, and the haemal spines on their ventral sides.

abyssal — pertaining to or living on the bottom at great depths, below about 4,000 m.

abyssal plain — the more or less flat ocean floor below approximately 4,000 m, excluding trenches.

abyssopelagic — living in the water column at depths of about 4,000 m or more; the abyssopelagic zone.

accessory caudal rays — short, procurrent rays on the upper and lower (rather than posterior) part of the caudal peduncle.

accessory dorsal branch — a branch of the lateral line in certain flatfishes beginning at the head and continuing below the base of the dorsal fin.

actinosts — series of bones at the base of the rays of the paired fins.

acuminate — tapering gradually to a point.

acute — sharply pointed.

adipose eyelid — transparent membrane covering the anterior and posterior parts of the eye of some fishes; e.g., herring (Clupeidae).

adipose fin — fleshy finlike projection behind the rayed dorsal fin present in, e.g., salmons and smelts; lacks typical fin spines or rays; some fishes also have a ventral adipose fin.

adnate — adhering or joined together.

adult — a sexually mature animal.

agape — in a gaping state; jaws open.

air bladder — *see* swim bladder.

alar thorns — specialized prehensile thorns on the upper surface of the disk near the tips of the pectoral fins in male skates.

alevin — the larval stage of trout and salmon that feeds on its yolk sac and lives under gravel.

alisphenoid — a small bone on the anterior lateral wall of the skull.

allopatric — said of distributions that do not overlap geographically.

ammocoete — larval stage of lampreys.

amphiboreal — occurring in both the North Pacific and the North Atlantic but not in the Arctic Ocean (discontinuous distribution).

amphidromous — migrating from fresh to salt water or from salt to fresh water at some stage of the life cycle other than the breeding period; in Alaska, some chars and whitefishes (Salmonidae) exhibit amphidromy.

amphi-North Pacific — a pattern of distribution where a species occurs on the east and west rims of the Pacific Ocean but not on the northern rim (discontinuous distribution).

anadromous — running up; said of marine fishes that migrate from sea and run up rivers to spawn; part of the life cycle is spent in the ocean; e.g., Chinook salmon (Salmonidae) or American shad (Clupeidae).

anaerobic — without oxygen.

anal — pertaining to the anus or vent.

anal fin — fin or fins on the ventral median line behind the anus; composed of rays, sometimes with spines in the front part or, infrequently, back part of the fin.

analogous — said of organs or structures that are similar in function and superficial structure but not in fundamental origin; e.g., the wing of an insect and the wing of a bird.

anal papilla — a fleshy protuberance in front of the genital pore and anal fin through which the end of the intestine passes; *see* genital papilla.

anal spine — a spine at the front of the anal fin, preceding the soft rays; or, in flatfishes, not a fin spine but the free end of the first anal pterygiophore, which may be discernible as a protuberance under the skin in front of the anal fin.

angling — fishing with rod and reel; sportfishing method, but also useful for collecting samples for research.

angular — small bone at the posterior end of each half of the lower jaw.

ankylosed — grown firmly together.

anterior — on or toward the front (head) end of the fish; forward.

antrorse – pointing or turned anteriorly.

anus — the posterior opening of the digestive system; also called the vent.

aphakic space — an extension of the pupil.

arctic region — the ocean north of the 0°C winter isotherm. In the Bering Sea this corresponds to latitude 60°N.

articulate — jointed; sometimes used instead of the equivalent term *segmented* in reference to soft fin rays.

ascidians — tunicate animals, including sea squirts, of the class Ascidiacea.

asymmetrical — not symmetrical; one side not the mirror image of the other; e.g., as in flounders.

atlas — the first vertebra.

attenuate — long and slender, as if drawn out.

available — said of a name that can be used; admissible into zoological nomenclature.

axil — the region under or behind the pectoral fin base.

axillary process — *see* axillary scale.

axillary scale — one or more enlarged, elongate scales lying above the bases of the first rays of the pectoral or pelvic fins in some fishes; e.g., in herrings and anchovies (Clupeiformes); sometimes called an axillary process.

BD — abbreviation for body depth; vertical distance, usually of the body at its deepest part, not including the fins; in eelpouts (Zoarcidae) and some other groups of fish body depth is measured at the origin of the anal fin.

Br — abbreviation for branchiostegal ray used for branchiostegal ray count in the line of meristic values in some species accounts; higher teleosts, such as perciforms, usually have 7; usually provided in the line of meristic characters only if helpful for identification of species; a strong light is helpful in making an accurate count; *see* branchiostegal rays.

band — a vertical mark of color with more or less well-defined edges and generally extending over the greater portion of an area, such as on the side of the body and extending onto the dorsal fin(s).

bar — a vertical or, especially, a diagonal mark of color with more or less well-defined edges, generally shorter than a band.

barbel — elongate, fleshy appendage or projection on the snout, around the mouth, or below the lower jaw.

basal — pertaining to the base; at or toward the base.

base (of a fin) — that part of the fin that is joined to the body; extends from the first ray or spine to the last ray or spine.

basibranchials — three median bones lying end-to-end on the floor of the gill chamber between the paired hypobranchials at the lower ends of the gill arches, and articulating with the basihyal in front.

basihyal — median bone that forms base of tongue; also called glossohyal.

basioccipital — a median posteriorly and ventrally located bone of the skull to which the atlas or first vertebra is attached.

basisphenoid — small, median, Y-shaped bone in rear of orbit.

bathyal — referring to or living on the ocean bottom at depths of about 200 to 4,000 m, primarily on the continental slope and rise.

bathypelagic — inhabiting the water column at depths of about 1,000–4,000 m.

beach seine — nets with or without bags, used in shallow water where net wall can extend from the surface to the bottom; generally set in semicircle and dragged to shore by one or two persons, herding fish into the net; many variations.

beam trawl — bottom-sampling trawl with headline fastened to a heavy beam across the net opening; the groundline scrapes the sea bottom.

benthic — occurring at the bottom of an ocean, lake, or river; or referring to animals that live in or on the bottom.

benthopelagic — occurring near or just above the bottom; demersal; also used to refer to pelagic forms that spend part of their life cycle near the bottom.

Beringia — land mass encompassing northeastern Siberia, Alaska, and the intervening shelves in the Chukchi and Bering seas. Last emerged during the Wisconsinan period of glaciation. The land bridge over the millenia alternately provided a barrier and an access route for dispersal of freshwater fishes between what are now North America and Asia, and for marine fishes between the Arctic and Pacific oceans. See Lindsey and McPhail (1986:641–645) for Pleistocene history of Beringia and, particularly, Alaska.

Bering land bridge — *see* Beringia.

bicuspid — having two points or cusps.

bifid — split or divided into two parts; bifurcate.

bifurcate — divided into two parts.

binomen or **binomial name** — the combination of the two names that constitute the scientific name of a species; the first name is the generic name, and the second is the specific name.

bioluminescence — light produced by an organism.

biserial — arranged in two rows or series.

blind side — used to refer to the side in flatfishes that is opposite the eyed side, and is the same as the side nearest the substrate; also called lower surface, but not ventral surface.

blotch — a poorly defined or irregular mark of color.

boreal region — the oceans of the Northern Hemisphere between the 0 and 13°C winter isotherms. In neritic waters of western North America the boreal region extends from the southern Bering Sea, Alaska, to Point Conception, California.

bottom trawl — a net dragged along the sea bed; variations include beam and otter trawls.

branched ray — a soft or segmented fin ray that is split into two or more parts distally.

branchiae — gills; the respiratory organs of fishes.

branchial — pertaining to the gills.

branchial arch — *see* gill arch.

branchial basket — a network skeleton that in lampreys and chimaeras supports the gill region.

branchiostegal membranes — *see* gill membranes.

branchiostegal rays or **branchiostegals** — bony or cartilaginous supports of the gill membranes, located on the underside of the head, below the opercular bones and behind the lower jaw, and attached to the hyoid arch. In fishes not having the gill membranes joined in the middle, such as herring and other clupeoids, the membranes tend to cling to the gill cover when it is opened up for examination, so the membranes must be pulled inward to expose the branchiostegal rays.

breast — the region on the ventral surface anterior to the pelvic fins and posterior to the isthmus; in front of the belly; chest.

breeding tubercles — small, white, hard protuberances appearing on the scales and skin of some fishes, such as the whitefishes (Coregoninae), at spawning; also called nuptial tubercles or pearl organs.

bristle — a stiff hair or hairlike structure.

buccal — pertaining to the mouth cavity.

bycatch — fishes caught along with the targeted species in a fishery; also called incidental catch.

C — abbreviation for caudal fin used for caudal fin ray counts in the line of meristics in species accounts for ray-finned fishes. Usually only the principal, forked or branched caudal rays are given. A count of III,2 + 11–12 + 3,II indicates that on the dorsal side of the fin there are 3 spines and 2 rays, in the center 11 to 12 major rays, and on the ventral side 3 rays and 2 spines.

caducous — easily shed; deciduous.

caecum, plural **caeca** — an appendage in the form of a blind sac; *see* pyloric caeca.

canine — long, conical, pointed tooth, usually larger than the surrounding teeth.

caniniform — shaped like canine teeth of higher vertebrates; i.e., conical and pointed.

cardiform teeth — small, sharp, slender teeth arranged like the spikes on a wool card.

carinate — keeled; having a ridge along the middle line.

carnivorous — feeding on the flesh of animals.

cartilage — skeletal tissue, usually soft and flexible; in bony fishes, mostly replaced by bone during early growth stages.

catadromous — running down; said of freshwater species that run down rivers to spawn in the sea. There are no strictly catadromous species in Alaska; some populations of prickly sculpin (Cottidae) may migrate downstream to brackish water to spawn.

caudal — pertaining to the tail; e.g., caudal fin.

caudal fin — the fin at the rear end of the fish; tail fin.

caudal peduncle — the part of the body between the dorsal or anal fin and the base of the caudal fin.

caudal peduncle depth — least depth of the peduncle.

caudal peduncle length — measured from the base of the last anal fin ray to the posterior end of the hypural bones or plate.

caudal vertebrae — posterior vertebrae that bear a haemal spine (ventral to the centrum) and lack pleural ribs; the first caudal vertebra is located near the origin of the anal fin.

cavernous — containing cavities, either empty or filled with a mucous secretion.

centrum, plural **centra** — the body of a vertebra.

cephalic — pertaining to the head.

cephalic fin — fin on the head, as on each side of the mouth in mantas; a detached portion of the pectoral fins.

ceratobranchial — bone immediately below the angle in a gill arch.

cf. — when used with a scientific name of an organism, indicates the identification is provisional; confirmation may depend on further study, or might not be possible due to damaged condition of the specimen or other problems; abbreviation for *confer,* meaning "compare."

character — a characteristic or attribute used for identifying or describing taxa.

cheek — area between the eye and the preopercle bone.

chest — the anterior part of the ventral surface of a fish just behind the head.

chin — area between the rami of the lower jaw.

chin crest — outgrowth of the dentary bone of the lower jaw; one on each side of the jaw, converging anteriorly; also called mental or submental crest.

chondrichthyans — cartilaginous fishes, including chimaeras, sharks, and rays.

chondrocranium — cartilaginous cranial skeleton; the primitive skull of cartilaginous fishes.

chromatophore — pigment cell in the skin, responsible for the color of the skin.

ciliated — fringed with projections like eyelashes.

cirrus, plural **cirri** — slender, elongate, fleshy appendage; tendril-like, flexible tuft or tag of skin.

clade — a group defined by a set of shared derived characters inherited from a common ancestor; a monophyletic higher taxon.

cladistics — a method in systematics for determining the evolutionary relationships of organisms, both living and extinct. Developed by a German entomologist, Willi Hennig, in the 1960s, cladistics uses the distribution of shared derived characters (synapomorphies) to test relationships; hence genealogy is the sole criterion for the definition of taxa. Ideally, 20–100 or more characters are used in a cladistic study. Computer programs are used to search for patterns of characters, and sets of relationships suggested by the study are depicted graphically in cladograms. The best cladogram is the one supported by the greatest number of characters and is the basis for revisions in taxonomy. It can never be said to be final, however, as with all scientific hypotheses it is subject to testing and may be only temporarily the best. Extremely sensitive to choice of characters; characters should be as independent of each other as possible. Also called cladism or phylogenetic systematics.

cladogram — a cladistic dendrogram expressing the classificatory relationships among a group of organisms, based on their inferred phylogenetic relationships and in terms of recency of common ancestry. Identities of nodes (ancestors) are not specified, connecting lines usually represent shared derived characters (synapomorphies), and all taxa are terminal in position. Compare with phylogenetic tree.

claspers — extensions of the pelvic fins that function as intromittent (copulatory) organs in male chondrichthyans.

classification — the part of systematics that deals chiefly with the grouping of like things within a system; like things grouped within a system.

clavus — a rudderlike lobe at the end of the body in molas (Molidae).

cleithrum, plural **cleithra** — one on each side, forms the dorsal, and usually anterior, part of the pectoral girdle; extends upward from the pectoral fin base and forms the rear margin of the gill cavity.

cline — a character gradient; continuous variation in expression of a character through contiguous populations; e.g., variation in fin ray or vertebral counts from one part of a species' range to another.

cloaca — pitlike chamber containing the anus and urogenital openings of chondrichthyans.

Code — the 1999 edition, effective 1 January 2000, of *The International Code of Zoological Nomenclature.*

common name — the informal, vernacular name for an organism, which may vary from place to place; *see* vernacular. Many "common" names are contrived and are rarely used, such as those for rare and poorly known fishes. Several new names were coined for this book, in an attempt to establish standard English names for the fishes of Alaska.

complex — term used for convenience for a group of closely related species that have not been adequately differentiated by taxonomists; e.g., Arctic char complex.

compressed — flattened laterally (from side to side); opposite of depressed.

concave — curved inward.

confluent — running or joined together; said of median fins, such as the anal and caudal, when they meet smoothly without forming a notch.

continental rise — gently sloping sea bottom comprising thick layers of sediment between the base of the continental slope and the abyssal plain, at depths of 2,000–5,000 m; width is up to 300 km.

continental shelf — gently sloping sea bottom from the shore out to a depth of approximately 200 m; may extend from a few kilometers off the coastline, as in much of the Gulf of Alaska off southern Alaska, to several hundred kilometers, as in the Bering Sea off western Alaska.

continental slope — steeply sloping sea bottom from approximately 200 to 2,000 m, from the continental shelf to the continental rise; width varies from 20 to 100 km.

continuous — unbroken, usually referring to a dorsal fin in which the spinous part is joined to the soft-rayed part; also refers to an unbroken lateral line series.

convergence — the possession of similar characters or structures by organisms of different groups as a result of similarity in habits or environment; in usage of cladistics, a synonym of parallelism. In oceanography, the meeting of ocean currents or water masses with different densities, temperatures, or salinities, resulting in the sinking of the denser, colder, or more saline water; the line or area in which convergence occurs.

convergent evolution — the development of similar characters or structures in genetically unrelated lineages.

convex — curved outward.

coracoid — the principal posterior bone of the pectoral girdle supporting the pectoral radials.

corselet — a densely scaled area posterior to the base of the pectoral fin of some tunas.

cotype — an obsolete term, once used for either syntype or paratype; not recognized by the Code.

countercurrent heat exchange — heat is exchanged between blood vessels going to the skin and gills and the vessels going to the deep body tissues.

cranial — pertaining to the cranium.

cranium — the part of the skull containing the brain.

crenate — having a margin of small rounded scallops.

crenulate — minutely crenate.

cryptic species — morphologically indistinguishable biological groups that are incapable of interbreeding.

ctenii — toothlike projections, as on the posterior margins of ctenoid scales or forming bony combs along the pelvic fin rays of some fishes.

ctenoid — rough-edged; said of scales with minute toothlike projections or spines (ctenii) on the posterior margin; ctenoid scales give the fish a rough feel when stroked toward the head.

ctenophores — animals, mostly marine, of the phylum Ctenophora, with oval, jellylike bodies bearing rows of comblike plates that aid in swimming; comb jellies.

cusp — a projection or point on a tooth.

cutaneous — pertaining to the skin; dermal.

cycloid — smooth-edged; said of scales when they are smooth posteriorly.

D — abbreviation for dorsal fin, used for dorsal fin spine and ray counts in the line of meristics in accounts for ray-finned fishes. Known range in number of spines is given in roman numerals (e.g., IV–VII) and number of rays in arabic numerals (e.g., 36–40). A comma separates counts in a single fin (e.g., IV–VII,36–40), while a plus sign indicates separate fins (e.g., IV–VII + 36–40).

deciduous — easily falling off; loosely attached; said of scales.

decurved — curved downward.

degenerate — said of a character or structure that has evolved to a less developed state from the ancestral state.

demersal — referring to swimming animals that live near the bottom of an ocean, lake, or river; also referring to eggs that are denser than water and sink to the bottom after being laid.

dendrogram — a treelike diagram depicting the relationships of a group of items sharing a common set of variables.

dentary — bone forming the anterior portion of each half of the lower jaw, usually bearing teeth.
dentate — with toothlike notches; bearing teeth or toothlike projections.
denticle — the toothlike, placoid scale of elasmobranchs; a toothlike, conical projection.
denticular teeth — teeth on the snout and lower jaw of male anglerfishes (Lophiiformes) that are used to attach to the female.
dentigerous — bearing teeth.
dentition — the characteristic arrangement and shape of the teeth.
depressed — flattened from top to bottom, or dorsoventrally.
dermal — pertaining to the skin.
description, original — the first description of a species or other taxon, given when designating the taxon.
desiccated — completely dried out.
diaphanous — translucent.
dichromatic — having two color forms.
dimorphic — having two forms.
diphycercal caudal fin — vertebral column extends straight back to the tip of the body, with the caudal fin symmetrical above and below it; e.g., in chimaeras.
dip net — bag-shaped net on the end of a pole; a circular or square frame holds the mouth open.
disk — in lampreys (Petromyzontidae), the area surrounding the mouth; in skates and rays (Rajiformes), the more or less roundish body, excluding the tail and pelvic fins but incorporating the pectoral fins; in clingfishes (Gobiesocidae), gobies (Gobiidae), and snailfishes (Liparidae), an adhesive disk formed from the pelvic fins.
disk length — in skates, the length from the tip of the snout to the posteriormost margin of the pectoral fin.
disk width — in skates, the greatest distance between the tips of the pectoral fins.
distal — away from the point of attachment.
diurnal — pertaining to daylight activities; most active during daylight.
dorsal — pertaining to the back (dorsum) or, usually, upper part; in flatfishes the dorsum is not the upper surface; *see* eyed side.
dorsal fin — fin or fins on the dorsal median line; composed of spines and rays or either spines or rays.
dorsolateral — refers to the upper area of the side, above the middle.
dorsum — the back, or dorsal surface of the head or body.
double emarginate — refers to a caudal fin that is pointed at the end with the margin dorsal and ventral to the point slightly indented (emarginate).
double truncate — refers to a caudal fin that is pointed at the end with the margin dorsal and ventral to the point straight (truncate).
dredge — heavy-framed bottom sampler; may have teeth, cutting bars, or pressure plates to dig into the substrate or may use hydraulic pumps to remove animals from the substrate.
drift net — unanchored gill net that floats free with prevailing water currents; drift nets must be no longer than 1 nautical mile in U.S. waters, and large-scale nets have been banned on the high seas.
ecophenotype — phenotype exhibiting nongenetic adaptations associated with habitat or environment.
ectopterygoid — paired bone at the roof of the mouth between palatine and quadrate; also called pterygoid.
edentate — without teeth.
eel-shaped — elongate like an eel.
egg case — the keratinous envelope containing the developing embryos of sharks and rays.
elasmobranchs — sharks, rays, and skates.
El Niño — a climatic condition during which northward shifts in distribution of southern species are common in the northeastern Pacific. During an El Niño a warm-water current from the tropics overrides the opposing cold current along the Pacific coasts of North and South America, raising near-surface temperatures, depressing the thermocline, and often suppressing upwelling. These effects are most pronounced along the coast of Peru.
elongate — lengthened; longer than deep.
emarginate — with a slightly concave margin; sometimes used to describe a shallowly forked caudal fin; indented.
embedded — with reference to scales; the scale margin is so enveloped in skin that there is no free edge.
endemic — unique to a particular geographical region.
endoskeleton — the skeleton proper; the inner bony framework of the body.
entire — having a smooth or even margin.
entopterygoid — paired bone articulating with palatine in front.
epibenthic — located on the bottom, as opposed to in the bottom.
epibranchial — bone immediately above the angle in a gill arch.
epifauna — animals living on the surface of the bottom.
epipelagic — living in the upper part of the ocean from the surface to about 200 m, in the sunlit depths.
epural — an elongate bone that supports the upper caudal fin rays.
erectile — susceptible of being raised or erected.
esca — the terminal lure or "bait" on the end of the illicium of anglerfishes (Lophiiformes).
escarpment — a steep slope in topography, such as an undersea cliff.
estuary — a semi-enclosed body of water with an open connection to the sea; here sea and fresh water mix and the influx of nutrients from both sources results in high productivity.
ethmoid — *see* mesethmoid.
eulittoral — marine zone of disturbance by wave action; marine intertidal zone; the shore zone between the highest and lowest seasonal water levels in a lake.
euryhaline — able to live in waters with a wide range of salinity.
exclusive economic zone (EEZ) — waters out to 200 nautical miles from shore; out to the beginning of international waters; also called 200-mile limit.
exoskeleton — hard parts (scales, scutes, plates) on the surface of the body.
exserted — projecting beyond the general level, as fin rays beyond the membrane.
extant — existing or living at the present time; not extinct.

extinct — no longer in existence; no longer living.
extralimital — beyond the limits (of this book or key).
eye diameter — measured lengthwise (horizontal diameter), the shape of the orbit not always being round; most researchers use the greatest diameter of the eye, if the eye is not circular.
eyed side — used to refer to the side in flatfishes that is opposite the blind side, and is the same as the side away from the substrate; also called upper surface, but not dorsal surface.

FL — abbreviation for fork length. Distance from the anteriormost point on the head to the innermost part of the fork of the tail fin.
falcate — sickle-shaped; long, narrow, and curved.
falciform — curved, like a scythe.
fauna — the animals inhabiting a particular region, taken collectively.
filament — threadlike or extremely slender projection running out into a filament.
filiform — in the form of a thread or filament.
fimbriate — having a fringed margin.
finfold — the median body wall folds in hagfishes (Myxinidae); the median fold of tissue in a fish embryo that gives rise to the dorsal, anal, and caudal fins.
fin height — length of the longest ray in the fin.
fin length — measured along the base of the fin.
finlets — a series of small fins consisting of one or two branched rays each, separate from each other and occurring posterior to the dorsal or anal fins.
flora — the plants in a particular region, taken collectively.
foramen — a hole or opening.
foramen magnum — the aperture in the posterior part of the skull for the passage of the spinal cord.
forehead — frontal curve of the head.
forficate — deeply forked; like scissors.
forked — said of the caudal fin when its upper and lower rays diverge or fork from each other.
fork length — *see* FL.
fossa, plural **fossae** — groove or pit.
free — said of fin rays or spines not connected to each other by membrane.
frenum — narrow fold of skin or membrane that joins structures; e.g., the lower lip to the symphysis of the lower jaw, or the upper lip to the snout.
frontal — bone, one on each side, forming most of the top of the cranium.
furcate — forked.
fusiform — spindle-shaped; tapering toward both ends, but more abruptly anteriorly, with sides flattened only slightly or not at all.

GR — abbreviation used in gill raker counts. The gill rakers are counted on the first gill arch, unless otherwise specified. The rakers above and below the angle or bend of the gill arch, on the upper and lower limbs, are counted. The upper number is given first. If a total is given, as well, it is included in parentheses. Rakers in the angle or curve of the arch, if any, are included in the count for the lower limb. Often it is obvious from the curved bases of the gill rakers whether they belong to the upper or the lower limb series. All rudiments are counted.
ganoid scales — thick, nonoverlapping scales or plates of bone covered with enamel-like material, present on some primitive bony fishes.
gape — opening of the mouth.
gas bladder — *see* swim bladder.
genital papilla — fleshy projection in some fishes behind the anus, from which the sperm or eggs are released, as well as urine; in males of some species, including many sculpins (Cottidae), the genital papilla is developed into an intromittent organ equivalent to the penis of higher vertebrates, for internal fertilization of eggs in the female; also called urogenital papilla.
gill — organ for exchanging respiratory gases (oxygen, carbon dioxide) between the blood of the fish and the water; comprises gill arch, gill rakers, and gill filaments.
gill arch — bony support to which the gill filaments and gill rakers are attached; also called branchial arch.
gill chamber — space on each side of the head containing the gills, enclosed by the operculum and the gill or branchiostegal membranes.
gill cover — *see* operculum.
gill filaments — slender, soft, red fringe-like structures along the posterior edge of a gill arch; the gas-exchanging structures of the gill.
gill membranes — membranes, one each side, supported by the branchiostegal rays, which close off the gill chamber, in part; also called branchiostegal membranes. *Gill membranes separate* means the gill membranes are not joined to each other or to the isthmus. *Gill membranes united* means the membrane of one side is united to its fellow of the opposite side across the isthmus. *Gill membranes united, and free from isthmus* means a needle can be moved from side to side over the isthmus under the united gill membranes. *Gill membranes joined to isthmus* means the gill membranes are attached to the isthmus.
gill net — a net hung in the water like a curtain that catches fish by entangling them around the gills; size of fish caught is determined by mesh size.
gill opening — an external opening leading from the gill chamber; also called gill slit; 5–7 gill openings or slits on each side of the head in elasmobranchs, only 1 on each side in bony fishes; the opening of each side is continuous ventrally in some fishes; allows water to exit after passing over the gills.
gill pouch — the internal chambers containing the gills in hagfishes (Myxinidae).
gill rakers — bony protuberances along the anterior edge of the gill arches opposite the gill filaments; prevent food from passing out through the gill slits; counts of the rakers on the upper and lower limbs of the gill arches are useful in identifying some species of fish; *see* GR.
gill slit — *see* gill opening.
glabrous — smooth.
gonad — the reproductive organ: ovary or testis.
graduated — in reference to fin spines, means progressively longer backward; the second longer than the first, the third longer than the second, and so on.

granulated — rough with small prominences.
gravid — full of eggs or embryos; pregnant.
groundfish — fish species that live on or near the bottom; term used most often in reference to commercial fisheries; also called bottomfish.
gular — pertaining to the gula, the region between the chin and isthmus.
guyot — a flat-topped seamount or submarine mountain.
gyre — an ocean current that follows a circular or spiral path around an ocean basin, always clockwise in the Northern Hemisphere and counterclockwise in the Southern Hemisphere.

HL — abbreviation for head length. Measured from the tip of the snout to the extreme posterior margin of the operculum.
habitat — the type of place where a species normally lives; habitat is characterized by its biological components or physical features, such as sandy bottom on the continental shelf, or rocky reefs along exposed outer coast.
hadal — zone included in some ecological systems, referring to the ocean below about 6,000 m; the term is a reference to proximity to hell.
haemal arch — an arch between the haemal spines, for the passage of blood vessels.
haemal canal — the series of haemal arches as a whole.
haemal spine — the lowermost or ventral spine of a caudal vertebra.
halo — circle of color around a spot of another color.
head pores — the external openings of the cephalic sensory system, an extension of the body lateral line system.
height — vertical diameter.
herbivorous — feeding on plants.
heterocercal caudal fin — the tip of the vertebral column turns upward distally, and the greater part of the fin membrane is developed below this axis; the upper lobe is longer than the lower and the vertebrae continue into the upper lobe; e.g., in sharks.
holarctic — in oceanography, the entire arctic region; also a specific biogeographic region, the Holarctic, that includes the arctic and north temperate zones of Europe and Asia (Paleoarctic) and North America (Nearctic).
holotype — a single specimen designated as the name-bearing type of a new species when it was established; or, if no type was specified, the single specimen on which the description of the species was based. If the holotype is the only type it may be referred to as "unique" to emphasize existence of only one type specimen.
homocercal caudal fin — upper and lower lobes are about equal in appearance externally but dissection shows that the tip of the vertebral column turns upward with most of the fin attached below it; the type of caudal fin seen in most teleosts.
homoiothermic — said of animals that regulate their body temperature independent of ambient temperature fluctuations; also called warm-blooded.
homologous — said of organs or other structures, in different taxa, that have a basic similarity due to similar embryonic origin and development (common evolutionary origin); e.g., the pectoral fins of fishes are homologous with the forelimbs of bats, birds, horses, and man.
homology — similarity due to common ancestry; in contrast to homoplasy.
homoplasy — similarity due to convergent, parallel, or reversed evolution; in contrast to homology.
hyaline — transparent.
hybrid — the progeny of two individuals belonging to different species.
hypobranchial — bone of a gill arch below the ceratobranchial.
hyomandibular — a paired bone that articulates with the otic capsule above; part of the articulating mechanism of the lower jaw.
hypurals — bones to which the caudal fin rays are attached; often fused to form a hypural plate in advanced fishes.

ichthyofauna — fish fauna.
ichthyoplankton — fish eggs and larvae in the plankton.
-id (suffix) — indicating membership in a family; e.g., agonid, a member of the Agonidae.
-idae (suffix) — the family name always ends in idae; e.g., Agonidae, Zoarcidae.
-iform (suffix) — indicating membership in an order, e.g., scorpaeniform, perciform; or meaning like or similar in form to something else, e.g., caniniform, like the canine teeth of higher vertebrates.
-iformes (suffix) — the order name always ends in iformes; e.g., Scorpaeniformes, Perciformes.
illicium — a modified, elongate dorsal fin ray on top of the head that serves as a "fishing pole" in anglerfishes (Lophiiformes); illicium is retractable into the head in some species.
imbricate — overlapping like shingles on a roof; refers to scales.
immaculate — unspotted.
imperforate — not pierced through.
-inae (suffix) — the subfamily name always ends in inae; e.g., Brachyopsinae, Lycodinae.
inarticulate — not jointed.
incertae sedis — of uncertain taxonomic position.
-ine (suffix) — indicating membership in a subfamily; e.g., brachyopsine, lycodine.
incised — cut-in; refers to the membranes between the tips of the rays or spines of a fin.
incisiform — said of teeth compressed and wedge-shaped at the tip, forming a cutting edge, like incisors of higher vertebrates.
incisor — tooth compressed at the tip; more often used in reference to incisor teeth at the front of the jaws of land animals than to refer to teeth in fishes.
included — said of a lower jaw that is overlapped by the upper.
indented — in reference to caudal fin, same as emarginate.
infauna — animals living in the substrate of the sea bed.
inferior — below; sometimes used in referring to a mouth located ventrally, on the lower surface of the head, as in sturgeons or some poachers.
inferior pharyngeals — *see* pharyngeals.
infraoral — below the mouth; teeth of the mouth below the oral opening in lampreys.

infra- (prefix) — below.
infraorbital — below the eye; same as suborbital.
infraorbital bones — *see* suborbital bones.
insertion (of a fin) — point where the posterior end of the base of a dorsal or anal fin is connected with the body; or, point where the paired fins arise from the body. For paired fins, origin and insertion are often used interchangeably.
inshore — occurring in shallow nearshore waters and tidepools; landward of the zone of breaking waves.
insular — referring to an island.
interhaemal bones, interhaemals — elements supporting the anal fin rays; *see* pterygiophores.
intermaxillary, plural **intermaxillaries** — *see* premaxilla.
International Code of Zoological Nomenclature — the internationally adopted set of rules governing zoological nomenclature.
interneural bones, interneurals — elements supporting the dorsal fin rays; *see* pterygiophores.
interopercle — bone between the preopercle and the branchiostegal rays; usually anterior to the subopercle when the subopercle is present.
interorbital — between the eyes. The shape of the interorbital space (convex, flat, or concave) refers to the portion of the skull between the eyes and not including cranial ridges or spines. Usually the bony interorbital space is measured, not the distance between the eyeballs.
interpelvic process — fleshy process between the inner edges of the pelvic fins in tunas and other members of the family Scombridae.
interspace — the space between two structures; usually used in reference to dorsal fins.
interspecific — between different species.
intertidal — the shore zone exposed between the high and low tides.
intraspecific — within a species.
invalid — said of a name or nomenclatural act that is not valid under the Code.
isobath — a contour mapping line that indicates a specified constant depth.
isocercal — refers to a tail in which the vertebrae become progressively smaller and end in the median line of the caudal fin; as in cods (Gadidae).
isosmotic — pertaining to solutions that exert the same osmotic pressure.
isotherm — a line connecting points of equal mean temperature for a given sampling period on a chart.
isthmus — narrow triangular portion of the body beneath the head where the gill membranes converge; the fleshy area separating the two gill chambers.

jack — male salmon that spawn after spending a year or two less in the ocean than the majority of individuals; they are noticeably smaller in size than the average size of spawning males of their species.
jugular — pertaining to the throat; said of the pelvic fins when positioned ahead of the attachment of the pectoral fins.
junior synonym — the younger or more recently established name of a taxon.
juvenile — between the larval and adult stages, not sexually mature; in some species a miniature replica of the adult but in others different in appearance. A salmon between about 25 and 110 mm FL that has not entered smolt stage.

keel — a narrow ridge or projection resembling the keel of a boat; e.g., along the ventral midline, on the side, on the caudal peduncle, on the scales, or on the top of the head.
kype — the hooked jaw developed at spawning time by the males of some salmonid fishes.

LLp — pored scales in the lateral line; given instead of lateral line scale count (LLs) for some species in which the lateral line extends only part of the way along the body, or to contrast the count against the total in the lateral series scale count (Ls). For example, in *Ronquilus jordani* LLp = 90–93, while Ls = about 200.
LLs — abbreviation for lateral line scale count, of scales in the lateral line beginning just above the gill opening to the end of the hypurals or hypural plate, omitting any scales on the caudal fin rays.
Ls — abbreviation for lateral series scale count, of the number of scale rows counted similarly to the lateral line scales in fishes without a lateral line or with an interrupted lateral line. In many species scales are very small and difficult to count or may easily be lost, and for them it is more practical to refer to the presence of very small or very large scales in the list of qualitative characters rather than to list the number of scales in the line of meristic characters.
labial — pertaining to the lips.
labial furrow — a fold behind the corner of the mouth that provides slack skin for protruding the jaw in sharks.
lachrymal — the first and largest of the suborbital bones; extends in front of and below the anterior part of the orbit; also spelled lacrimal; also called preorbital bone.
lacustrine — pertaining to, or living in, lakes or ponds.
lagoon — a shallow pond or channel separated from the ocean by a reef or sandbar.
lamella, plural **lamellae** — platelike process or processes.
lamina, plural **laminae** — a small thin plate or plates.
lanceolate — shaped like the blade of a lance; broad at the base and tapering to a point.
La Niña — climatic condition involving cooling in the eastern Pacific, when strong trade winds push warm surface waters westward toward Asia and colder deepsea water upwells to the surface along the Americas. Nutrients become more plentiful.
lapsus calami — slip or slips of the pen; errors made by an author, such as misspelling a name, as opposed to errors made by a printer.
larva, plural **larvae** — early life history stage between the time of hatching and transformation to a juvenile.
lateral — pertaining to the side.
lateralis system — sensory system consisting of a series of pored tubes and canals in the head and body, sometimes extending onto the caudal fin, of a fish; detects movement, low-frequency vibrations, and temperature changes.

lateral line — generally, a line of pores or neuromasts extending along the side of the body; specifically, part of the lateralis system, consisting of pored tubes opening into a canal or superficial neuromasts fed by branches of the lateral line nerve. A body lateral line canal can be single or multiple and have accessory branches (canalicules).
lectotype — a syntype later designated as the one name-bearing type specimen of a taxon.
leptocephalus, plural **leptocephali** — transparent, ribbonlike larva of eels and other elopomorph fishes.
line — in reference to coloration, used for thin mark of any orientation.
lingual — pertaining to the tongue.
littoral — marine environment or depth zone between the lowest low and the highest high tide lines; general habitats in this area include the littoral pelagic zone and the littoral benthic zone; synonymous with intertidal. In older usage, which is obsolete and not recommended, pertained to the depth zone between the shore and a depth of about 200 m.
longline — a fishing line with baited hooks on branch lines at intervals; sometimes several kilometers long; often supported off the bottom by floats.
lower limb — the lower part of a gill arch, below the curve or bend.
lunate — moon-shaped, like a half or crescent moon; having a broadly rounded, rather shallow fork.

malar thorns — spines close to the edge of the disk anterolaterally in male skates.
mandible — lower jaw, composed of paired dentaries, angulars, and retroarticulars.
mandibular pores — pores of the sensory canal system on the lower jaw.
marbled — variegated; clouded.
maxilla, plural **maxillae** — outermost or hindmost, main bone of the upper jaw, one on each side; joined to the premaxilla in front or below, and usually extending farther back than the premaxilla; often lies above the premaxilla; also called maxillary bone.
maxillary, plural **maxillaries** — as noun, maxillary bone(s), but maxilla is used in most current works; *see* maxilla; as adjective, refers to structures on or involving the maxilla, such as a maxillary cirrus.
maxillary extension — an expression of relative mouth size; always judged with mouth closed, because with mouth open the maxilla is displaced farther forward relative to the eye.
medial — toward the center or axial plane running through the middle of the body.
median — situated on the center or axial plane of the body, between the right and left halves; e.g., the dorsal, anal, and caudal fins are median fins.
medusa, plural **medusae** — free-swimming umbrella- or bell-shaped stage in the life history of many hydrozoan coelenterates; common name given to any jellyfish.
melanophore — black dermal pigment cell (chromatophore).
mental crest — *see* chin crest.
meristic character — structure or part that is repeated or divided into segments, hence varying in number and countable; e.g., fin rays, gill rakers, pyloric caeca.
mesethmoid — a median anterior bone of the skull, above the vomer and between the olfactory capsules; also called ethmoid.
mesial — lying in, being in the region of, or directed toward the mesial plane; opposed to distal.
mesial plane — the median vertical longitudinal plane that divides a fish (or other bilaterally symmetrical animal) into right and left halves.
mesocoracoid — a bone of the pectoral girdle, one on each side between the cleithrum (above) and coracoid and scapula (below).
mesopelagic — living in the water column at midwater depths of about 200 to 1,000 m, where the light gradually fades to extinction.
metamorphosis — change in body form; having reference to marked changes occurring in fishes during development from larval to adult stages.
metapterygium — cartilaginous rod supporting the base of each of the pectoral and pelvic girdles in elasmobranchs; modified into claspers in male skates and sharks.
middorsal — along the midline of the back.
midwater — water substantially above the bottom and substantially below the surface; the middle portion vertically of a body of water.
midventral — along the midline of the belly.
midwater trawl — net towed through the water column (as opposed to along the bottom); sometimes used with otter doors or towed by two boats to help keep mouth open, or depressor plates to help the net fish deeper.
molar — blunt tooth used for grinding or crushing.
molariform — shaped like a molar tooth.
monophyletic — said of a group in which all members are descendants of a common ancestor; *see* clade.
monotypic — including only one species.
morphology — the appearance, form, and structure of an organism.
morphometric character — a morphologic measurement or proportion; e.g., total length, or head length as a percentage of total length.
mottled — color spots running together, blotched.
mouth inferior — located much behind and below the tip of the snout, opening more toward front than ventrally.
mouth superior — the lower jaw is somewhat longer than the upper, so that the mouth opens upward.
mouth subterminal — the lower jaw is shorter than the upper, so that the mouth opening is below and behind the tip of the snout.
mouth terminal — the upper and lower jaws are of equal length, so that the mouth opens directly to the front.
mouth oblique — the jaws are at an angle of about 40 degrees or more to the anterior-posterior axis of the body.
mouth ventral — located on underside of the snout, and opening ventrally.
muciferous — producing or containing mucus.
mucous — slimy; adjective form of mucus.
mucus — a slimy secretion from the skin.
multifid — having many branches or forks.
multiserial — arranged in several rows or series.

myomere, plural **myomeres** — muscle segments along the body separated from each other by connective tissue; in most fish species most easily seen in the larval stages; important in identifying larvae since the number of myomeres is the same as the number of vertebrae in the adult.

nape — the portion of the back or dorsum immediately behind the head, from the occiput to the dorsal fin origin; back of the neck in higher vertebrates.
naris, plural **nares** — nostril.
nasal — pertaining to the nostrils; paired bone usually enclosing the nostrils.
nasal capsules — structures enclosing the nostrils.
nasal fossae — grooves in which the nostrils open.
native — organisms historically indigenous to an area.
nekton — organisms that swim in the water column, living above the substrate and moving independently of currents.
neotype — a specimen designated as the name-bearing type of a species or subspecies when no holotype, lectotype, syntype, or prior neotype is known to exist.
neritic — shallow pelagic zone extending from the low tide level to a depth of about 200 m; living in the water column over the sublittoral region; the ocean over the continental shelf.
neural arch — the dorsal arch of a vertebra for the passage of the spinal cord.
neural canal — the cavity formed by the neural arches as a whole.
neural processes — broad plates, one on each side of the centrum of a vertebra, which unite toward their ends and form a spine (the neural spine).
neural spine — the uppermost or dorsal spine of a vertebra.
neuromast — a sensory cell that detects motion or vibration; neuromasts are enclosed in the head and body lateral line canals, freely exposed or sunk in pits on the surface of the skin, or in the inner ear.
neuston — organisms that float or swim in the surface waters.
niche — habitat and role (community relationships, food habits, etc.) of an organism.
nictitating membrane — the movable, membranous fold that partially covers the eye in some sharks.
nocturnal — active at night or pertaining to the night.
nomenclatural — pertaining to nomenclature.
nomenclature — a system of names, and provisions for their formation and use.
nomen dubium — a name of unknown or doubtful application.
notch — in reference to the dorsal and anal fins, an indentation partially dividing the fin into two parts; in reference to the pectoral fin, a broad indentation resulting from the shortening of some of the rays thus dividing the fin into two lobes.
notochord — a cartilaginous rod in the embryo, running from head to tail and supporting the nerve cord; replaced in the larval stage in most fish species by the developing vertebrae, but in some fishes (e.g., hagfishes, chimaeras) persists in the adult and serves as the backbone.
nuchal — pertaining to the nape or nucha.
nuchal thorns — strong spines on the nape in skates.
nuptial tubercles — *see* breeding tubercles.
nyctoepipelagic — migrating from deeper waters to the epipelagic zone at night.

obsolete — faintly marked; scarcely evident.
obtuse — blunt.
occipital — pertaining to the occiput.
occiput — upper back part of the head, in front of the nape.
oceanic — pertaining to the ocean beyond the continental shelf; offshore.
ocellate — with ocelli.
ocellus, plural **ocelli** — an eyelike spot, generally roundish and with a lighter border.
ocular — pertaining to the eye.
olfactory — pertaining to the nasal organs or sense of smell.
ontogeny — development of an individual organism in its various stages of growth through maturity.
opercle — the posterior bone in the operculum or gill cover; largest of the opercular bones.
opercular lobe or **flap** — posterior fleshy part of gill cover supported by prolongation of the upper posterior angle of the opercle.
operculum — cover over the gills on each side of the head; supported by opercle, preopercle, interopercle, and subopercle; also called gill cover.
oral hood — a hoodlike projection leading to the mouth in larval lampreys.
orbit — the bony eye socket.
orbital — pertaining to the orbit.
orbitosphenoid — median bone between the orbits, forming the floor and walls of the anterior end of the cranium.
oreosoma — young fish of the family Oreosomatidae, having scutes or horny protuberances, different in appearance from the adults.
origin — the area of attachment to the body of a median fin at its anterior end; or, point of attachment of paired fins.
osseous — bony.
otolith, plural **otoliths** — bones of the inner ear in bony fishes.
otter trawl — a towed net that strains fish out of the water; "otter boards" on the tow ropes keep the mouth of the net open; commonly used in surveys of demersal species.
oviparous — producing eggs that develop and hatch outside the body of the female.
ovipositor — a specialized organ for depositing eggs.
ovoviviparous — producing eggs that are fertilized and hatch within the body of the mother, but the embryos lack a placental attachment to the oviduct or uterus so do not feed off the mother; young are born as relatively large, free-swimming individuals.
ovum, plural **ova** — egg.

PC — abbreviation for pyloric caeca in the line of meristic values in some species accounts; count includes all pyloric caeca tips; *see* pyloric caeca.
Pec — abbreviation for pectoral fin used for pectoral fin ray count in the line of meristic values in each species account; abbreviated P1 or P by other authors.

Pel — abbreviation for pelvic fin used for pelvic fin spine and ray counts in the line of meristic values in each species account; roman numerals are used for the spines, and arabic for the rays; abbreviated P2 or V (ventral) by other authors.

paired fins — the pectoral and pelvic fins, which correspond to the front and hind legs, respectively, of land animals.

palatal — pertaining to the palate.

palate — roof of the mouth.

palatines — a pair of bones in the roof of the mouth, one on each side, extending outward and backward from the vomer, sometimes bearing teeth; the palatine teeth are often buried in mucus but can be felt by stroking with a needle.

papilla, plural **papillae** — small, fleshy projection.

papillose — covered with papillae.

paralectotype — the type specimens remaining in the type series after a lectotype is designated.

parallel evolution — the development of similar forms by related but distinct phylogenetic lineages.

parallelism — the possession of similar characters by two or more related organisms in separate lineages, often as a result of similar environmental conditions acting upon similar heredities derived from a long-distant common ancestor; the groups, once diverged, evolve in parallel fashion, with similar characters.

paraphyletic — in cladistics, pertaining to a higher taxon that does not contain all the species known to be descended from a given ancestral species.

parasitic males — male anglerfishes that live attached to the females; the body degenerates and draws upon the female for food, while the gonads are well developed.

parasphenoid — long, median bone in the base of the skull below the orbits, between the vomer and basioccipital.

paratype — any specimen, other than the holotype, in a type series.

parietal — bone on each side at the top and back of the head, over the auditory region, behind the frontals and partly or wholly separated by the supraoccipital.

parr — a young, presmolt salmonid before it migrates to the sea.

parr marks — squarish or vertically oblong dark blotches along the sides of presmolt salmons.

pearl organs — *see* breeding tubercles.

pectinate — having toothlike projections as in a comb.

pectoral — pertaining to the breast or the anterior paired fins.

pectoral axil — the region under or behind the pectoral fin base; equivalent of armpit in humans.

pectoral base — that part of the pectoral fin that is joined to the body.

pectoral fin length — measured from the extreme base of the uppermost ray to the farthest tip of the fin.

pectoral fins — the anterior or uppermost of the paired fins, located just behind the head, corresponding to the forelimbs of the higher vertebrates.

pectoral girdle — the bony and cartilaginous skeletal arch posterior to the head, to which the pectoral fins are attached; comprising, on each side, posttemporal, supracleithrum, postcleithrum, cleithrum, scapula, and coracoid; also called shoulder girdle.

pedicel or **pedicle** — a slender stalklike support for a larger part or organ; also called peduncle.

peduncle — a narrow part to which a larger part is attached; *see* caudal peduncle.

pelagic — pertaining to or living in the water column of oceans or lakes.

pelvic fins — paired fins usually located behind and below the pectoral fins, corresponding to the hindlimbs of higher vertebrates; also called ventral fins. Their position is said to be abdominal when they are far behind the pectoral fins on the belly, thoracic when on the chest, or jugular when on the throat in front of the pectoral fins.

pelvic girdle — the skeletal arch supporting the pelvic fins; consists of paired bones, the basipterygia or pelvic bones, to which the fin rays are attached.

perforate — pierced through.

peritoneum — membrane lining the body cavity.

pharyngeal — pertaining to the region of the pharynx.

pharyngeal teeth — lateral teeth present in the wall of the pharynx in many fishes; on the pharyngeal bones.

pharyngobranchials — upper bones of gill arches 1 through 4, which may bear teeth; also called superpharyngeals or superior pharyngeals.

pharynx — region posterior to the mouth into which open the internal gill clefts; first part of the digestive tract.

phenotype — the sum total of observable structural and functional properties of an organism; product of interaction between genotype and environment.

photophore — organ that produces light; small, definite shining spots on body or head.

phylogenetic systematics — the study of systematics with the goal of inferring phylogeny of the organisms investigated. In more restricted usage, the study of systematics using the methods of cladistics.

phylogenetic tree — a dendrogram expressing genealogical relationships among several groups, as inferred from various types of evidence. In cladistics, shows phylogenetic relationships among groups in terms of inferred genealogical history; identities of nodes (ancestors) are specified, connecting lines represent ancestral taxa, and not all the taxa included are terminal in position. Compare with cladogram.

phylogeny — evolutionary relationships and lines of descent in a group of organisms, as opposed to development of an individual organism; or the study of such relationships.

physoclistous — having the swim bladder closed; i.e., no connection with the gut.

physostomous — having the swim bladder connected by a tube with the esophagus.

phytoplankton — plant plankton.

piscivorous — referring to a carnivore that eats fish

placoid scales — thorn-shaped scales of sharks and rays; also called denticles.

plankton — small plants and animals that drift with the ocean currents; includes some fish eggs and larvae.

plesiomorphy — *see* primitive character.

plicate — folded; showing folds or wrinkles, like pleats.

plications — series of small folds or pleats.

plumbeous — lead-colored; dull bluish gray.

polyphyletic — said of a group of organisms that includes two or more groups that are not closely related; sometimes groups are classified together in a polyphyletic group for taxonomic convenience, until their phylogenetic relationships are better understood and the groups can be reclassified in monophyletic groups.

population — a local group of individuals that form a potentially interbreeding community.

pore —tiny opening in the skin; usually involved with sensory perception in fishes.

pored scale — scale that is in the lateral line and has a pore.

postcleithrum, plural **postcleithra** — bone of the pectoral girdle behind the cleithrum; present in salmonids as three pairs of small, scalelike dermal bones.

posterior — at or toward the tail end of a fish; behind.

postorbital or **postocular** — behind the orbit or eye; also a bone in the series around the eye.

posttemporal — bone by which the pectoral girdle is suspended from the skull.

preanal length — in eelpouts (Zoarcidae), the distance from the anteriormost point of the snout to the origin of the anal fin; in other fishes usually measured to the center of the anus (method indicated if used in this book).

precaudal pit — a transverse or longitudinal notch on the caudal peduncle just anterior to the caudal fin in sharks.

precaudal vertebrae — the anterior vertebrae that lack a haemal spine; all but the first few bear pleural ribs.

predator — an animal that captures and eats other animals.

prefrontals — bones forming lateral projections at the anterior margins of the orbits.

premaxilla, plural **premaxillae** — the bones, one on each side, forming the front of the upper jaw; usually larger than the maxillae and commonly bearing most of the upper teeth; in most spiny-rayed fishes higher than Salmonidae the premaxillae form the entire lower border of the upper jaw; also called premaxillary or intermaxillary bone.

premaxillary, plural **premaxillaries** — as noun, premaxillary bone(s), but premaxilla is used in most current works; *see* premaxilla; as adjective, refers to structures on or involving the premaxilla, such as premaxillary suture (point of junction).

preoccupied — said of a genus name predated by use of the same name for another taxon at an earlier date; or, at the species level, a binomen used for another taxon at an earlier date.

preocular — before the eye.

preopercle — the bone in the operculum in front of the opercle and nearly parallel to it; its posterior edge is usually free.

preoperculomandibular canal — sensory canal of the head running along the preopercle and the mandible; preopercular and mandibular segments are sometimes disconnected.

preorbital — the bone or region anterior to and below the eye; first bone of the suborbital series, also called the lachrymal.

presmolt — a juvenile salmon with parr marks; in pink salmon, which lack parr marks, demarcation between a presmolt and smolt is slight, differing chiefly in the latter's more adult shape.

prevomer — *see* vomer.

prey — animals that are the food of predators.

prickle — a scale reduced to a sharp point.

primitive character — a character or character state possessed by an ancestral species; in cladistics, called a plesiomorphy.

principal rays — the longer, obvious fin rays, as opposed to short, anterior rudiments that often are not visible.

priority — seniority of names in taxonomy, fixed by date of publication; the earliest published name has priority.

procumbent — lying down and pointing forward.

procurrent — inclined forward.

procurrent rays — small rays on the upper and lower edges of the caudal fin base.

produced — elongate; projecting; extended.

profile — the contour of the body or head in side view; usually refers to the curve from the front of the dorsal fin to the tip of the snout.

protandrous — sequential hermaphroditism in which the fish functions first as a male and then changes to a female.

protogynous — sequential hermaphroditism in which the fish functions first as a female and then changes to a male.

protractile — capable of being drawn forward; pertaining to the premaxillae and maxillae in some fishes; e.g., sand lances.

protrusible — so made that it can be protruded or thrust out; pertaining to a mouth whose upper lip is not attached to the snout; e.g., the mouth of a sturgeon.

proximal — toward the body or base of attachment; nearest; basal.

pseudobranch — small, gill-like organ on the inner surface of the operculum; the number of pseudobranch filaments or the size of the pseudobranch (expressed relative to some other structure, usually the eye) are useful in distinguishing certain species of fish; also called pseudobranchia or hemibranch.

pseudoceanic — members of a basically oceanic group that are distributed over continental shelf and slope regions and in the vicinity of oceanic islands and that are associated with land-orientated food chains.

pterosphenoids — bones on each side of the skull under the frontal bone; also called alisphenoids.

pterygiophores — bones or cartilages with which the rays of the median fins articulate in teleosts; located between the spines of the vertebrae and the rays of the fins; dorsal fin pterygiophores are also called interneural bones; anal fin pterygiophores are also called interhaemal bones.

pterygoid — *see* ectopterygoid.

punctate or punctulate — dotted with points; either of color or structure.

pungent — sharp like a thorn.

pup — an embryonic or young shark.

pyloric caecum, plural **pyloric caeca** — variously shaped blind sacs on the alimentary canal at the posterior end of the stomach and beginning of the intestine (pylorus); can be long or short, absent to numerous, and simple or branched.

pylorus — passage from stomach to intestine.

quadrate — paired, triangular bone on which the mandible is hinged, connecting the lower jaw to the palatine and hyoid arches.

quincunx — arrangement in sets of five, with one element of a set at each of four corners and the fifth in the center.

range — in this book, refers to the known geographic range; the entire area where a species is known to occur. The range may be continuous or have unoccupied gaps between populations.

ray — one of the cartilaginous rods supporting the membrane of a fin. Rays include flexible, branched or unbranched, segmented soft rays, and stiff, unbranched, unsegmented spines. If neither is specified in this book, soft ray is meant. *See* soft ray and spine.

Recent — the present geological epoch; the Holocene; within the past 10,000 years.

recurved — curved backward or inward.

redd — excavation or nest made by a spawning salmon.

reticulate — marked with a network of lines.

reticulations — markings in the form of a network of lines.

retrograde — said of a structure that is located farther back than is typical of a group.

retrorse — turned backward.

rostral — pertaining to the snout or rostrum.

rostral plate — small plate on the anterior tip of the snout, as in some poachers (Agonidae).

rostral spine — spine on the rostral plate.

rostrum — a projecting snout or beak; produced anterior part of the skull in sharks and rays.

rudimentary — very small and poorly formed; undeveloped.

rugose — rough; wrinkled.

SL — abbreviation for standard length. Distance from the anterior tip of the head to the base of the caudal fin, at the end of the hypural bones or the vertebral column; the posterior point can be found by flexing the caudal fin to the side, which usually produces a crease.

saddle — pigmentation forming a saddle-shaped area over the back and not extending onto the dorsal fin(s), unless so specified.

salmonid — a fish of the family Salmonidae.

salp — a pelagic tunicate (class Thaliacea).

scales — small flattened plates forming an external covering to the body and sometimes to the head and fins; *see* LL and Ls.

scapular thorns — thorns on each side of the anterior midline of the body in skates.

scientific name — the formal name of a taxon; the scientific name of a taxon above species rank consists of one name, that of a species comprises two names (*see* binomen), and that of a subspecies comprises three names (*see* trinomen).

scute — a thickened bony scale bearing a keel or spiny point.

seamount — an undersea mountain.

second dorsal fin — the posterior of two fins, usually comprising soft rays but often including some spines.

seine — net with weights at the bottom and floats along the top that is pulled from the ends through the water.

seismosensory — pertaining to lateral line sense organs and nerves.

senior synonym — the older or earliest established name of a taxon.

septum — thin partition.

serrate, serrated — saw-toothed; notched like a saw.

setaceous — bristly.

setiform — bristlelike; like bristles of a brush.

shared derived character — in cladistics, a character shared by two or more organisms or groups and inherited from an immediately preceding or recent common ancestor; an advanced character held in common by two or more taxa; also called a synapomorphy.

shared primitive character — in cladistics, a character shared by two or more organisms or groups and inherited from a remote or much earlier common ancestor; also called a symplesiomorphy.

shoulder girdle — *see* pectoral girdle.

simple — not divided or branched.

siphonophore — colonial, free-swimming or floating pelagic hydrozoan coelenterate, mostly delicate and transparent, with long filamentous tentacles (order Siphonophora).

smolt — seaward migrating stage of young salmonids; a young salmon that has lost its parr marks. Pink and chum salmon fry usually go to the ocean within a few days of emerging from the streambed and usually do not undergo a visible change in morphology or color in fresh water.

snout — that part of the head in front of the eyes.

snout length — measured from the anteriormost point on the snout or upper lip to the anterior margin of the orbit.

snout rounded — usually referring to the dorsal aspect.

soft dorsal — that part of the dorsal fin that is composed of soft rays.

soft ray — fin ray that is articulated, or segmented, like a stalk of bamboo; can be simple or branched. The segmentation is usually visible in light transmitted through the fin.

soft ray — *see* ray.

spatulate — shaped like a spatula.

sp. — abbreviation for species, used instead of the specific part of a scientific name to indicate a species that has not been formally named and described; also used to mean unknown or unidentifiable due to lack of knowledge or damage to specimens, or in general reference to unspecified species in a genus (in which case plural, spp., may be used in reference to more than one species).

species — a group of actually or potentially interbreeding organisms that are reproductively isolated from all other such groups; a group of organisms formally recognized as distinct from other groups; the fundamental category of classification, intended to designate a single kind.

sphenoid — basal bone of skull.

sphenotic — a lateral, paired bone of the skull behind the orbit.

sphenotic spines — projections of the sphenotic bones in some anglerfishes (order Lophiiformes).
spicule — minute, hard, needlelike or sharp-pointed processes or projections.
spine — a fin ray that is unsegmented (inarticulate), unbranched, and, usually but not always, stiff and sharp-pointed (magnification is usually needed to distinguish a flexible spine from an unbranched ray); fin spines are never branched, as a ray often is; any sharp, projecting point.
spinous — stiff or composed of spines.
spinous dorsal — anterior part of the dorsal fin when that part is composed of spines; dorsal fin composed of spines.
spinule — small, sharp, projecting point (small spine); spinules that occur on the upper preopercular spine in some sculpins (Cottidae) are called thorns or barbs by some authors.
spiracle — an opening behind each eye in sharks, rays, and some other fishes that leads into the mouth cavity and may serve as an opening for water entering the gill chambers. It is not a gill opening.
spot — well-defined circular or subcircular mark of color.
standard length — Usually used as the scientific measurement of body length in fishes because of frequent damage to the tail, which disallows measurement of total length; *see* SL.
state — the particular expression or condition of a character.
stellate — star-like; with ridges or lines radiating from a central point.
stria, plural **striae** — fine lines or grooves, especially parallel grooves in a series, as on the opercula of some fishes.
striate — marked by lines or grooves; striped or streaked.
stripe — a horizontal mark of color with more or less well-defined borders.
strong — easily observed and highly developed.
sub- (prefix) — less than, under, not quite.
subadult — an individual similar in appearance to an adult and approaching adulthood in age and size but still incapable of breeding.
subcylindrical — nearly round in cross-section.
subequal — not quite equal.
sublittoral — marine zone extending from the lower margin of the intertidal (littoral) to the outer edge of the continental shelf at a depth of about 200 m, below which the strongest storms do not stir the water; living on the bottom in this zone; in some schemes divided into inner and outer sublittoral at 50 or 100 m; deeper zone of a lake below the limit of rooted vegetation.
submarine canyon — narrow, deep depression in a continental shelf formed by river or glacial erosion before the shelf was submerged.
subopercle — bone of the operculum immediately below the opercle; the suture connecting the two is often hidden by scales or skin.
suborbital, subocular — below the eye; same as infraorbital.
suborbital bones — a chain of small bones below the eye.
suborbital stay — projection extending from the third (counting the lachrymal as the first) suborbital bone across the cheek to the preopercle in fishes of the order Scorpaeniformes (e.g., rockfishes); easily detected by running a needle downward over the cheek about midway between the eye and the preopercular margin.
subspecies — a taxonomically and geographically distinct subgroup within a species; often isolated geographically from other such groups within the species but, theoretically, interbreeding successfully with these groups where their ranges overlap.
subterminal — not quite at the end and ventral; used to refer to a mouth opening below the anteriormost point of the head..
subtidal — the highly productive shallow zone along a sea coast extending from low tide to a depth of about 100 m, corresponding to the inner area of the continental shelf; often characterized by kelp forests, rich fish fauna, and upwelling bringing nutrients from deeper waters into the nearshore area; the "inner sublittoral" part of the shelf in some ecological schemes.
sucking disk — a disklike part by which a fish may attach itself to rocks or other items.
superior — dorsal to; upward; above.
superior pharyngeals — *see* pharyngobranchials.
suppressed — a name or work that the International Commission on Zoological Nomenclature has ruled is never to be used.
supra- (prefix) — above.
supracleithrum, plural **supracleithra** — bone of the pectoral girdle below the posttemporal bone and connecting it to the cleithrum.
supramaxilla, plural **supramaxillae** — a small bone along the upper rear edge of the maxilla; sometimes there are two, as in anchovies (Engraulidae).
supraoccipital — median bone at the upper rear end of the cranium, often bearing a crest.
supraoral — above the mouth; teeth of the mouth above the oral opening in lampreys.
supraorbital, supraocular — above the eye.
supraorbitals — paired bones along the upper margin of the orbit.
suprapreopercles — small paired dermal tube bones carrying the lateral line canal across the gap between the preopercle and supratemporal; often absent.
supratemporals — paired bones articulating with the posttemporals of the pectoral girdle.
supratemporal canal — sensory canal across the top of the head connecting the lateral lines of each side.
suture — line of union of two bones, as in the skull.
swim bladder — a membranous sac in the body cavity beneath the backbone, usually filled with gases and used to adjust the vertical position of a fish in the water; filled with fat in some fishes, and rudimentary or absent in others; also called air bladder or gas bladder.
symmetrical — having symmetry; each side a mirror image of the other.
sympatric — said of species occupying the same geographic range or overlapping in geographic range.
symphyseal knob — projection or swelling below and in front of the symphysis of the lower jaw.
symphysis — in fishes, the point of junction of the two halves of the lower jaw; tip of chin.

symplesiomorphy — *see* shared primitive character.
synapomorphy — *see* shared derived character.
synonym — a different word having the same or similar meaning. In taxonomy, different names applied to the same taxon are synonyms, and only one can be used; *see* senior synonym, junior synonym, priority.
synonymy — a list of different names that have been applied to a taxon. For example, in a species synonymy if the same species was described independently by two or more scientists, as occasionally happens, the designated names are synonymous and the name that was first applied has priority and the others are said to be junior synonyms.
syntype — any of the specimens on which a species description is based if none of them is designated as a holotype or lectotype.
systematics — the study and classification of organisms with regard to their natural relationships.

TL — abbreviation for total length. The greatest length of a fish from the anteriormost point on the head to the tip of the tail.
tail — the part of the body posterior to the body cavity; in most fishes this is applied to the caudal peduncle and fin inclusive; often used more or less vaguely.
taxon, plural **taxa** — a taxonomic unit; e.g., a family, a genus, a species; a taxon includes its subordinate taxa and individuals.
taxonomy — the study and practice of naming and classifying organisms, as done by taxonomists; part of systematics.
teleost — an advanced or "modern" bony fish; not including elasmobranchs and sturgeons.
temperate region — ocean waters between the 13 and 20°C winter isotherms. The temperate region of the neritic zone along the Pacific coast of North America extends from Point Conception, California, to Bahia Magdalena, Baja California, Mexico.
temporal — pertaining to the region of the temples, the area of the head just behind the eyes.
tentacle — obsolete term for long, fleshy cirrus or papilla, or skin extending from tip of a fin spine or ray.
terete — cylindrical and tapering.
terminal — at the end; refers to a mouth opening at the anteriormost point of the head, the upper and lower jaws being equally far forward.
thermocline — distinct zone of rapid temperature change between warm water above and cold water below.
thoracic — pertaining to the chest or thorax; pelvic fins are said to be thoracic when the pelvic bones are fastened to the pectoral girdle, and in this situation the pelvic fins are located a short distance below or behind the pectoral fins.
thorn — large denticle on the surface of a ray or skate; the thorns are called spines by some authors.
throat — the anterior ventral surface of a fish, under the head.
total length — *see* TL.
toxin — poisonous chemical secreted by an organism.
transverse — extending across; from side to side.
trawl — funnel- or pocket-shaped net that is towed behind a boat through the water and has a weighted footrope at the bottom and buoyed headrope at the top to help keep the net open as it is being towed.
trenchant — compressed to a sharp edge.
tricuspid — having three cusps or points.
trinomen or **trinomial name** — a generic name, a specific name, and a subspecific name that together constitute the scientific name of a subspecies.
tropical region — ocean waters between the 20°C winter isotherms in the Southern and Northern hemispheres. Tropical neritic waters along the Pacific coasts of North and South America extend from the southern tip of Baja California, Mexico, to about 5°S latitude along the coast of Peru.
truncate — ending abruptly or evenly, neither convex nor concave, as if cut squarely off; said of a tail fin with a straight margin.
tubercle — a small knob or rounded prominence; a bump; a modified scale.
tuberculate — covered with tubercles.
Tucker trawl — opening-closing midwater zooplankton trawl.
type, types — one or more specimens upon which the original description of a species is based, or the species upon which the description of a genus is based; the term is used alone, or as part of a compound term to denote a particular kind of type; *see* holotype, lectotype, neotype, paralectotype, paratype, syntype.
type locality — the particular place or locality at which a type was collected.
type series — the original name-bearing specimens used to define a species-group taxon.
type specimen — general term for any specimen in a type series.
typical — said of a structure or character that is the most usual in a given group.

uncinate — hooked at the tip.
ultimate — last or farthest.
uniserial — arranged in a single row or series.
upper limb — the upper part of a gill arch, above the bend.
urogenital papilla — *see* genital papilla.
urohyal — unpaired bone of the hyoid region, arising in a septum between the longitudinal throat muscles.
urostyle — the cartilaginous termination of the vertebral column, formed of fused vertebrae; in salmonids, curves dorsally behind the last three upturned vertebrae; also called ural vertebra.

Vert — abbreviation for vertebrae used for vertebral counts in the line of meristics in species accounts. Usually the total number is given. For some species counts of precaudal and caudal vertebrae are given as well as the total; in this case the total number is given in parentheses. The first precaudal vertebra is the vertebra articulating with the cranium. The first caudal vertebra is the first vertebra bearing a complete haemal spine in most taxa, or bearing a complete haemal arch in some taxa. Some authors include the urostyle or ural vertebra in the caudal vertebra count while others do not, and this is a possible source of discrepancy in vertebral counts.

velar tentacles — tentacles at the junction of the pharynx and esophagus in lampreys.

vent — *see* anus.

ventral — pertaining to the abdominal or, usually, lower surface of the body or head; in flatfishes the ventral surface is not the lower surface; *see* blind side.

ventral fins — *see* pelvic fins.

ventrolateral — refers to the lower area of the side, below the middle.

vermiculations — fine lines more or less wormlike in shape.

vernacular name or **vernacular** — the name of an organism in a language used for general purposes in contrast to a name proposed only for zoological nomenclature; *see* common name.

verrucose — covered with small dermal warts.

vertebra, plural **vertebrae** — bones of the backbone or spinal column; each composed of a centrum with a neural arch and spine above and a haemal arch and spine below.

vertical fins — fins on the median line of the body; the dorsal, anal, and caudal fins; also called median fins.

villiform — said of the teeth when they are small, slender, and crowded into coarse velvety bands or compact patches.

viscous — slimy.

viviparous — giving birth to active, free-swimming young.

vomer — the median, unpaired bone in the roof of the mouth immediately behind the premaxillae and between the palatines, frequently bearing teeth; can bear teeth on the anterior part (the head) or also on the posterior part (the shaft); also called prevomer.

voucher — supporting evidence providing tangible proof of something; in ichthyology, proof of the existence of a species or other taxon, as in a sample from a survey or other collection. Vouchers may include photographs, written records of diagnostic morphological characters, or other evidence. The best kind of voucher may be a voucher specimen.

voucher specimen — a specimen archived in a permanent collection to serve as physical evidence that documents the existence and physical presence of a species. Because the specimen is preserved, it can be examined if confirmation of the identification is necessary. Type specimens are voucher specimens.

warm-blooded — *see* homoiothermic.

water column — the water mass between the surface and the bottom.

weak — scarcely evident.

work — written zoological information, such as a manuscript or publication.

year class — all the individuals of a population of fishes born or hatched in a given year.

zooplankton — animal plankton.

Bibliography

Note: References to original descriptions of species are given in the Bibliography if they were directly consulted for preparation of *Fishes of Alaska*. Complete bibliographic data for works containing all other original descriptions may be found in Eschmeyer (1998, 2001).

BIBLIOGRAPHY

Aagaard, K. A., C. H. Pease, A. T. Roach, and S. A. Salo.

1989. Beaufort Sea mesoscale circulation study: final report. NOAA Tech. Memo. ERL PMEL-90. 114 pp.

Abe, T.

1963. New, rare or uncommon fishes from Japanese waters. VIII. A record of *Rhamphocottus richardsoni.* Jpn. J. Ichthyol. 10(2/6): 51–52.

Abe, T., and M. Funabashi.

1992. A record of an adult female of the deep sea ceratioid angler fish, *Cryptopsaras couesi* Gill, with four parasitic adult males from off Ibaraki Prefecture, Japan. Uo (Jpn. Soc. Ichthyol.) 41: 1–3.

Abe, T., and K. Hiramoto.

1984. Records of *Spectrunculus grandis* (Günther) (Ophidiidae, Teleostei) from off Boso Peninsula, Japan. Uo (Jpn. Soc. Ichthyol.) 34: 1–3. [Cited in Machida et al. 1987.]

Abe, T., and H. Hotta.

1962. An addition to the Japanese piscifauna. Jpn. J. Ichthyol. 8(5/6): 152–156.

Abitia-Cárdenas, L. A., J. Rodríguez-Romero, F. Galván-Magaña, J. de la Cruz-Agüero, and H. Chávez-Ramos.

1994. Systematic list of the ichthyofauna of La Paz Bay, Baja California Sur, Mexico. Cienc. Mar. 20(2): 159–181.

Able, K. W.

1973. A new cyclopterid fish, *Liparis inquilinus,* associated with the sea scallop, *Placopecten magellanicus,* in the western North Atlantic, with notes on the *Liparis liparis* complex. Copeia 1973(4): 787–794.

1990. A revision of Arctic snailfishes of the genus *Liparis* (Scorpaeniformes: Cyclopteridae). Copeia 1990(2): 476–492.

Able, K. W., D. F. Markle, and M. P. Fahay.

1984. Cyclopteridae: development. Pages 428–437 *in* H. G. Moser et al., eds. Ontogeny and systematics of fishes. Am. Soc. Ichthyol. Herpetol., Spec. Publ. 1.

Able, K. W., and D. E. McAllister.

1980. Revision of the snailfish genus *Liparis* from Arctic Canada. Can. Bull. Fish. Aquat. Sci. 208. 52 pp.

Able, K. W., and J. A. Musick.

1976. Life history, ecology, and behavior of *Liparis inquilinus* (Pisces: Cyclopteridae) associated with the sea scallop, *Placopecten magellanicus.* U.S. Natl. Mar. Fish. Serv. Fish. Bull. 74(2): 409–421.

Aizawa, M., and K. Sakamoto.

1993. First record of an arrow eel *Cyema atrum* (Cyematidae: Saccopharyngiformes) from Japan. Jpn. J. Ichthyol. 39(4): 398–400.

Ahlstrom, E. H., J. L. Butler, and B. Y. Sumida.

1976. Pelagic stromateoid fishes (Pisces, Perciformes) of the eastern Pacific: kinds, distributions, and early life histories and observations on five of these from the northwest Atlantic. Bull. Mar. Sci. 26(3): 285–402.

Alcock, A. W.

1890. Natural history notes from H.M. Indian Marine Survey steamer *Investigator,* Commander R. F. Hoskyn, R.N., commanding. No. 18. On the bathybial fishes of the Arabian Sea, obtained during the season 1889–90. Ann. Mag. Nat. Hist., Ser. 6, 6: 295–311.

Alexander, R. McN.

1974. Functional design in fishes. Hutchinson & Co., Ltd., London. 160 pp.

Allen, M. J., and G. B. Smith.

1988. Atlas and zoogeography of common fishes in the Bering Sea and northeastern Pacific. U.S. Dep. Commer., NOAA Tech. Rep. NMFS 66. 151 pp.

Alt, K. T.

1969. Taxonomy and ecology of the inconnu, *Stenodus leucichthys nelma,* in Alaska. Biol. Pap. Univ. Alaska 12. 61 pp.

1971. Occurrence of hybrids between inconnu, *Stenodus leucichthys nelma* (Pallas), and humpback whitefish, *Coregonus pidschian* (Linnaeus) in Chatanika River, Alaska. Trans. Am. Fish. Soc. 100(2): 362-365.

1973. Contributions to the biology of the Bering cisco (*Coregonus laurettae*) in Alaska. J. Fish. Res. Board Can. 30(12): 1885-1888.

1979. Contributions to the life history of the humpback whitefish in Alaska. Trans. Am. Fish. Soc. 108: 156–160.

Alt, K. T., and D. R. Kogl.

1973. Notes on the whitefish of the Colville River, Alaska. J. Fish. Res. Board Can. 30(4): 554–556.

Alton, M. A.

1972. Characteristics of the demersal fish fauna inhabiting the outer continental shelf and slope off the northern Oregon coast. Pages 583–634 *in* A. T. Pruter and D. L. Alverson, eds. The Columbia River estuary and adjacent ocean waters. Bioenvironmental studies. University of Washington Press, Seattle.

Alverson, D. L.

1951. New records for marine fishes from southeastern Alaska. Copeia 1951(1): 86.

1961. Ocean temperatures and their relation to albacore tuna (*Thunnus germo*) distribution in waters off the coast of Oregon, Washington and British Columbia. J. Fish. Res. Board Can. 18(6): 1145–1152.

Alverson, D. L., and W. T. Pereyra.

1969. Demersal fish explorations in the northeastern Pacific Ocean: an evaluation of exploratory fishing methods and analytical approaches to stock size and forecasts. J. Fish. Res. Board Can. 26: 1985–2001.

Alverson, D. L., A. T. Pruter, and L. L. Ronholt.

1964. A study of demersal fishes and fisheries of the northeastern Pacific Ocean. H. R. MacMillan Lectures in Fisheries, Institute of Fisheries, University of British Columbia, Vancouver. 190 pp.

Alverson, D. L., and N. J. Wilimovsky.

1966. Fishery investigations of the southeastern Bering Sea. Pages 843–860 *in* N. J. Wilimovsky and J. N. Wolfe, eds. Environment of the Cape Thompson region, Alaska. U.S. Atomic Energy Commission, Oak Ridge, Tennessee.

Amaoka, K., G. Anma, K. Nakaya, M. Yabe, K. Masuda, and S. Sasaki.

1992. Larval and juvenile fishes collected from the northern Pacific Ocean by T/S *Oshoro-Maru*. Part 1: Salmoniformes, Clupeiformes, Myctophiformes, Cyprinodontiformes, Lophiiformes and Lampriformes. Bull. Fac. Fish. Hokkaido Univ. 43(1): 1–23.

Amaoka, K., K. Matsuura, T. Inada, M. Takeda, H. Hatanaka, and K. Okada, editors.

1990. Fishes collected by the R/V *Shinkai Maru* around New Zealand. Japan Marine Fishery Resource Research Center. 410 pp.

Amaoka, K., K. Nakaya, H. Araya, and T. Yasui, editors.

1983. Fishes from the north-eastern Sea of Japan and the Okhotsk Sea off Hokkaido. Japan Fisheries Resource Conservation Association, Tokyo. 371 pp.

Amaoka, K., K. Nakaya, and M. Yabe.

1995. The fishes of northern Japan. Kita-Nihon Kaiyo Center Co. Ltd., Sapporo, Hokkaido. 391 pp. [In Japanese and English.]

Amaoka, K., K. Sakamoto, and K. Abe.

1981. First record of the deep-sea sole, *Embassichthys bathybius,* from Japan. Jpn. J. Ichthyol. 28(1): 86–90.

Amaoka, K., M. Toyoshima, and T. Inada.

1977. New records of the stichaeid fish *Ascoldia variegata knipowitschi* and the zoarcid fish *Puzanovia rubra* from Japan. Jpn. J. Ichthyol. 24(2): 91–97.

Amaoka, K., M. Toyoshima, and T. Sasaki.

1977. First record of *Bryozoichthys lysimus* from Japan and second record of *B. majorius* [*sic*] from Aleutian Islands and Gulf of Alaska. Bull. Fac. Fish. Hokkaido Univ. 28(4): 175–180.

Anderson, M. E.

1977. Range extension of two marine fishes to the Monterey Bay area. Calif. Fish Game 63(2): 132–133.

1982. Revision of the fish genera *Gymnelus* Reinhardt and *Gymnelopsis* Soldatov (Zoarcidae), with two new species and comparative osteology of *Gymnelus viridis.* Natl. Mus. Nat. Sci. (Ott.) Publ. Zool. 17. 76 pp.

1984. On the anatomy and phylogeny of the Zoarcidae (Teleostei: Perciformes). Ph.D. thesis, College of William and Mary, Williamsburg, Virginia. 253 pp.

1989a. Records of rare eelpouts of the genus *Lycodapus* Gilbert in the north and southeastern Pacific Ocean, with an addition to the California marine fish fauna. Calif. Fish Game 75(3): 148–154.

1989b. Review of the eelpout genus *Pachycara* Zugmayer, 1911 (Teleostei: Zoarcidae), with descriptions of six new species. Proc. Calif. Acad. Sci. 46(10): 221–242.

1990. Zoarcidae. Pages 256–276 *in* O. Gon and P. C. Heemstra, eds. Fishes of the Southern Ocean. J.L.B. Smith Institute of Ichthyology, Grahamstown, South Africa.

1994. Systematics and osteology of the Zoarcidae (Teleostei: Perciformes). J.L.B. Smith Inst. Ichthyol., Ichthyol. Bull. 60. 120 pp.

1995. The eelpout genera *Lycenchelys* Gill and *Taranetzella* Andriashev (Teleostei: Zoarcidae) in the eastern Pacific, with descriptions of nine new species. Proc. Calif. Acad. Sci. 49(2): 55–113.

Anderson, M. E., G. M. Cailliet, and B. S. Antrim.

1979. Notes on some uncommon deep-sea fishes from the Monterey Bay area, California. Calif. Fish Game 65(4): 256–264.

Anderson, M. E., and C. L. Hubbs.

1981. Redescription and osteology of the northeastern Pacific fish *Derepodichthys alepidotus.* Copeia 1981(2): 341–352.

Anderson, M. E., and A. E. Peden.

1988. The eelpout genus *Pachycara* (Teleostei: Zoarcidae) in the northeastern Pacific Ocean, with descriptions of two new species. Proc. Calif. Acad. Sci. 46(3): 83–94.

Andreev, V. L., and Yu. S. Reshetnikov.

1981. Klassifikatsionnye postroeniya s ispol'zovaniyem spiskov vidov presnovodnykh ryb Chukotki i Alyaski [Classificatory constructions using lists of freshwater fishes of Chukotka and Alaska]. Zool. Zh. 60(9): 1285–1296. [In Russian, with English summary.]

Andriashev (Andriyashev, Andriiashev), A. P.

1935. Übersicht der Gattung *Stelgistrum* Jordan und Gilbert (Pisces, Cottidae) nebst Beschreibung einer neuen Art aus dem Beringmeer. Zool. Anz. 111(11/12): 289–297.

1937. K poznaniyu ikhtiofauny Beringova i Chukotskogo morei [A contribution to the knowledge of the fishes from the Bering and Chukchi seas]. Issled. Morei SSSR 25 (Issled. Dal'nevostoch. Morei 5), Leningrad, pp. 292–355, figs. 1–27. [Translation by L. Lanz and N. J. Wilimovsky, 1955, U.S. Fish Wildl. Serv. Spec. Sci. Rep. Fish. 145. 81 pp.]

1939. Ocherk zoogeografii i proiskhozhdeniya fauny ryb Beringova morya i sopredel'nykh vod [An outline of the zoogeography and origin of the fish fauna of the Bering Sea and neighboring waters]. Izdanie Leningradskogo Gosudarstvennogo Universiteta, Leningrad. 187 pp. [Translation by A. Merrivale.]

1949. [On the species composition and distribution of sculpins of the genus *Triglops* Reinh. in the northern seas]. Akad. Nauk SSSR, Tr. Vses. Gibrobiol. Ova. 1: 194–209. [Translation by L. Penny, edited by W. B. Scott, Bureau of Commercial Fisheries, Ichthyological Laboratory, U.S. National Museum, Washington, D.C., Translation No. 30. 21 pp.]

1952. Novaya glubokovodnaya ryba semeistva bel'dyugovykh (Pisces, Zoarcidae) iz Beringova morya [A new deep-sea fish of the eelpout family (Pisces, Zoarcidae) from the Bering Sea]. Tr. Zool. Inst. Akad. Nauk SSSR 12: 415–417. [Translation by Israel Prog. Sci. Transl., 1963, pp. 47–49 *in* A. P. Andriyashev: Selected taxonomic papers on northern marine fishes.]

1954. Ryby severnykh morei SSSR [Fishes of the northern seas of the USSR]. Akad. Nauk SSSR, Zool. Inst., Opredeliteli po Faune SSSR 53. 567 pp. [In Russian; and translation by Israel Prog. Sci. Transl., 1964. 617 pp.]

1955a. Obzor ugrevidnykh likodov [*Lycenchelys* Gill (Pisces, Zoarcidae) i blizkiye formy] morey SSSR i sopredel'nykh vod [A review of the genus *Lycenchelys* Gill (Pisces, Zoarcidae) and related forms in the seas of the U.S.S.R. and adjacent waters]. Tr. Zool. Inst. Akad. Nauk SSSR 18: 349–384. [In Russian; and translation by Israel Prog. Sci. Transl., 1963, pp. 1–36 *in* A. P. Andriyashev: Selected taxonomic papers on northern marine fishes.]

1955b. Novye i redkie vidy ryb semeistva bel'dyugovykh (Pisces, Zoarcidae) s yugo-vostochnogo poberezh'ya Kamchatki [New and rare fish species of the eelpout family (Pisces: Zoarcidae) from the southeast coast of Kamchatka]. Tr. Zool. Inst. Akad. Nauk SSSR 21: 393-400, figs. 1–6. [Translation by M. Grey, edited by B. B. Collette, Ichthyological Laboratory, U.S. National Museum, Washington, D.C., Translation No. 69. 7 pp.]

1955c. O nakhozhdenii na glubine bolee 7 km novoi ryby iz sem. morskikh sliznei (Pisces, Liparidae) [A new fish of the lumpfish family (Pisces, Liparidae) found at a depth of more than 7 kilometers]. Akad. Nauk SSSR, Tr. Inst. Okeanol. 12: 340–344. [Translation by Israel Prog. Sci. Transl., 1963, pages 50–54 *in* A. P. Andriyashev: Selected taxonomic papers on northern marine fishes.]

1955d. A fish new to the fauna of the USSR—*Erilepis* [*Erilepis zonifer* (Lock.), Pisces, Anoplopomatidae] from the Kamchatkan waters of the Pacific Ocean. Vopr. Ikhtiol. (4): 3–9. [Translation by L. Penny, edited by B. B. Collette, Ichthyological Laboratory, U.S. National Museum, Washington, D.C.]

1957. Noviy dlya fauny SSSR vid ryb semeistva treskovykh *Arctogadus glacialis* (Peters) s dreifuyushchei stantsii "Severniy Polyus-6" [*Arctogadus glacialus* (Peters) — A species of cod new to the fauna of the USSR from the drifting research station "North Pole-6." Zool. Zh. 36(11): 1747–1749. [Translation by Israel Prog. Sci. Transl., 1963, pp. 55–58 *in* A. P. Andriyashev: Selected taxonomic papers on northern marine fishes.]

1958. Dobavlenie k obzoru ugrevidnykh likodov (*Lycenchelys* Gill) s opisaniem trekh novykh vidov iz Kurilo-Kamchatskoi vpadiny [An addition to the review of *Lycenchelys* Gill, with a description of three new species from the Kurilo-Kamchatkan Trench. Vopr. Ikhtiol. 11: 171–180. [In Russian; and translation by Israel Prog. Sci. Transl., 1963, pages 37–46 *in* A. P. Andriyashev: Selected taxonomic papers on northern marine fishes.]

1961. Obzor bychkov-kryuchkorogov roda *Artediellus* Jord. (Pisces, Cottidae) Beringova morya [Forms of the hookhorn sculpin genus *Artediellus* Jord. (Pisces: Cottidae) in the Bering Sea]. Vopr. Ikhtiol. 1: 231–242. [In Russian.]

1973. Zoarcidae. Pages 540–547 *in* J. C. Hureau and T. Monod, eds. Check-list of the fishes of the north-eastern Atlantic and of the Mediterranean. Clofnam. Vol. 1. Unesco, Paris.

1986. Review of the snailfish genus *Paraliparis* (Scorpaeniformes: Liparididae) of the Southern Ocean. Theses Zoologicae 7. Koeltz Scientific Books, Koenigstein. 204 pp.

1990. On the probability of the transoceanic (non-Arctic) dispersal of secondary deepwater fish species of Boreal-Pacific origin into the depths of the North Atlantic and Arctic Ocean (Family Liparididae, as example). J. Ichthyol. 30(2): 1–9 [English transl. Zool. Zh. 69(1): 61–67].

Andriashev, A. P., and N. V. Chernova.

1995. Annotated list of fishlike vertebrates and fish of the Arctic seas and adjacent waters. J. Ichthyol. 35(1): 81–123 [English transl. Vopr. Ikhtiol. 34(4): 435–456].

Andriashev, A. P., and V. M. Makushok.

1955. *Azygopterus corallinus* (Pisces, Blennoidei)—novaya ryba bez parnykh plavnikov [*Azygopterus corallinus* (Pisces, Blennioidei)—a new fish without paired fins]. Vopr. Ikhtiol. 3: 50–53. [Translation by L. Penny, Ichthyological Laboratory, U.S. National Museum, Washington, D.C. 5 pp.]

Andriashev, A. P., A. V. Neelov, and V. P. Prirodina.

1977. K metodike izucheniya morfologii i sistematiki ryb semeystva morskikh slizniy (Liparidae) [A method for the study of the morphology and systematics of fishes of the family of sea snails (Liparidae)]. Zool. Zh. 56(1): 141–147. [In Russian, with English summary.]

Andriashev, A. P., and K. I. Panin.

1953. O nakhozhdenii tikhookeanskogo osetra (*Acipenser medirostris* Ayres) v Beringovom more [A find of the Pacific sturgeon (*Acipenser medirostris* Ayres) in the Bering Sea]. Zool. Zh. 32(5): 932–936. [In Russian.]

Andriashev, A. P., and D. L. Stein.

1998. Review of the snailfish genus *Careproctus* (Liparidae, Scorpaeniformes) in Antarctic and adjacent waters. Contrib. Sci. (Los Angel.) 470. 63 pp.

Anonymous.

1996. Fangtooth is B.C.'s "new" species. The Westcoast Fisherman, Vancouver, B.C., December: 26.

Arita, G. S.

1969. Sexual dimorphism in the cyclopterid fish *Eumicrotremus orbis*. J. Fish. Res. Board Can. 26: 3262–3265.

Armstrong, R. H., and J. E. Morrow.

1980. The dolly varden charr, *Salvelinus malma*. Pages 99–140 *in* E. K. Balon, ed. Charrs: salmonid fishes of the genus *Salvelinus*. Dr. W. Junk, The Hague.

Aron, W.

1960. The distribution of animals in the eastern North Pacific and its relationship to physical and chemical conditions. Tech. Rep. Univ. Wash. Dep. Oceanogr. 63. 65 pp.

1962. The distribution of animals in the eastern North Pacific and its relationship to physical and chemical conditions. J. Fish. Res. Board Can. 19(2): 271–314.

Aron, W., and P. McCrery.

1958. A description of a new species of stomiatid from the North Pacific Ocean. Copeia 1958(3): 180–183.

Arora, H. L.

1948. Observations on the habits and early life history of the batrachoid fish, *Porichthys notatus* Girard. Copeia 1948(2): 89–93.

Artyukhin, E. N., and A. E. Andronov.

1990. A morphological study of the green sturgeon, *Acipenser medirostris* (Chondrostei, Acipenseridae), from the Tumnin (Datta) River and some aspects of the ecology and zoogeography of Acipenseridae. J. Ichthyol. 30(7): 11–21 [English transl. Zool. Zh. 69(12): 81–91].

Backus, R. H.

1957. The fishes of Labrador. Bull. Am. Mus. Nat. Hist. 113(4). 337 pp.

Bailey, J. E., B. L. Wing, and J. H. Landingham.

1983. Juvenile Pacific sandfish, *Trichodon trichodon,* associated with pink salmon, *Oncorhynchus gorbuscha,* fry in the nearshore zone, southeastern Alaska. Copeia 1983(2): 549–551.

Bailey, R. G.

1989. Explanatory supplement to ecoregions map of the continents. Environ. Conserv. 16(4). Maps and charts.

Bailey, R. G., P. E. Avers, T. King, and W. H. McNab.

1994. Ecoregions and subregions of the United States. U.S. Department of Agriculture, U.S. Forest Service, Washington, D.C. Maps.

Bailey, R. M.

1980. Comments on the classification and nomenclature of lampreys—an alternative view. Can. J. Fish. Aquat. Sci. 37: 1626–1629.

Bailey, R. M., J. E. Fitch, E. S. Herald, E. A. Lachner, C. C. Lindsey, C. R. Robins, and W. B. Scott.

1970. A list of the common and scientific names of fishes from the United States and Canada, 3rd edition. Am. Fish. Soc. Spec. Publ. 6. 149 pp.

Bailey, R. M., and C. G. Gruchy.

1970. *Occella* to supersede *Occa* for a genus of agonid fishes. J. Fish. Res. Board Can. 27(5): 981–983.

Bailey, R. M., E. A. Lachner, C. C. Lindsey, C. R. Robins, P. M. Roedel, W. B. Scott, and L. P. Woods.
1960. A list of common and scientific names of fishes from the United States and Canada, 2nd edition. Am. Fish. Soc. Spec. Publ. 2. 102 pp.

Bailey, R. M., and C. R. Robins.
1988. Changes in North American fish names, especially as related to the International Code of Zoological Nomenclature, 1985. Bull. Zool. Nomencl. 45(2): 92–103.

Baird, R. C.
1971. The systematics, distribution, and zoogeography of the marine hatchetfishes (family Sternoptychidae). Bull. Mus. Comp. Zool. Harvard Coll. 142(1): 1–128.

Balanov, A. A.
1992. New discoveries of deep-water fishes in pelagic waters of the Bering Sea. J. Ichthyol. [English transl. Vopr. Ikhtiol.] 32(9): 133–137.
2000. Rare mesopelagic fish *Caristius macropus* (Caristiidae) and *Lestidiops ringens* (Paralepididae) in the southern part of the Bering Sea. J. Ichthyol. 40(9): 805–807 [English transl. Vopr. Ikhtiol. 40(6): 850–852].
2001. Feeding and vertical distribution of *Scopelosaurus adleri* and *S. harryi* (Notosudidae) in the northern part of the Pacific Ocean. J. Ichthyol. 41(3): 217–226.

Balanov, A. A., and V. V. Fedorov.
1996. About some deep-sea fishes new to the Bering Sea fauna. J. Ichthyol. [English transl. Vopr. Ikhtiol.] 36(4): 313–316.

Balanov, A. A., and Ye. N. Il'inskiy.
1992. Species composition and biomass of mesopelagic fishes in the Sea of Okhotsk and the Bering Sea. J. Ichthyol. 32(4): 85–93 [English transl. Vopr. Ikhtiol. 32(1): 56–63].

Balanov, A. A., Ye. N. Il'inskiy, and O. A. Ivanov.
1995. Rare mesopelagic fishes, *Scopelosaurus harryi, Arctozenus rissoi, Magnisudis atlantica*, and *Tactostoma macropus* in the northwest Pacific Ocean. Communication 1. Taxonomic descriptions. J. Ichthyol. [English transl. Vopr. Ikhtiol.] 35(4): 88–96.

Balanov, A. A., and V. I. Radchenko.
1995. [Species composition and distribution of fishes in meso- and bathypelagial of the Bering Sea and the Sea of Okhotsk]. Pages 335–343 *in* B. N. Kotenev and V. V. Sapozhnikov, eds. [Integrated researches of the ecosystem of the Bering Sea]. VNIRO, Moscow. [In Russian; selections translated by B. A. Sheiko, 2000, for Point Stephens Research, Auke Bay, Alaska.]
1998. New data on the feeding and consumption behaviors of *Anotopterus pharao*. J. Ichthyol. 38(6): 447–453 [English transl. Vopr. Ikhtiol. 38(4): 492–498].

Balanov, A. A., and V. F. Savinykh.
1999. Redescriptions of *Scopelosaurus harryi* and *S. adleri* (Notosudidae): two valid mesopelagic species inhabiting the northern part of the Pacific Ocean. J. Ichthyol. 39(8): 616–625 [English transl. Vopr. Ikhtiol. 39(5): 642–652].

Baldwin, C. C., and G. D. Johnson.
1996. Interrelationships of Aulopiformes. Pages 355–404 *in* M. L. J. Stiassny, L. R. Parenti, and G. D. Johnson, eds. Interrelationhips of fishes. Academic Press, San Diego.

Bali, J. B., and C. E. Bond.
1959. The bigfin eelpout, *Aprodon cortezianus* Gilbert, common in waters off Oregon. Copeia 1959(1): 74–76.

Balushkin, A. V.
1996. A new genus and species of liparid fish *Palmoliparis beckeri* from the northern Kurile Islands (Scorpaeniformes, Liparidae) with consideration of phylogeny of the family. J. Ichthyol. 36(4): 281–287 [English transl. Vopr. Ikhtiol. 36(3): 293–299]

Balushkin, A. V., and I. A. Chereshnev.
1982. Sistematika roda *Dallia* (Umbridae, Esociformes) [Systematics of the genus *Dallia* (Umbridae, Esociformes)]. Tr. Zool. Inst. Akad. Nauk SSSR 114: 36–56. [In Russian.]

Barber, W. E., R. L. Smith, M. Vallarino, and R. M. Meyer.
1997. Demersal fish assemblages of the northeastern Chukchi Sea, Alaska. U.S. Natl. Mar. Fish. Serv. Fish. Bull. 95: 195–209.

Bardack, D.
1991. First fossil hagfish (Myxinoidea): a record from the Pennsylvanian of Illinois. Science 254: 701–703.

Barnes, P. W., D. M. Schell, and E. Reimnitz, editors.
1984. The Alaskan Beaufort Sea ecosystems and environment. Academic Press, Orlando, Florida. 466 pp.

Barnett, M. A., and R. H. Gibbs.

1968. Validity of the stomiatoid fish species *Bathophilus flemingi* and *B. indicus.* Copeia 1968(1): 197–198.

Barnhart, P. S.

1936. Marine fishes of southern California. University of California Press, Berkeley. 209 pp.

Barraclough, W. E.

1947. A new record of a species of agonid fish, *Occa verrucosa* (Lockington) from the west coast of Vancouver Island, British Columbia. Can. Field-Nat. 61(2): 39.

1950. An inshore record of the bathypelagic fish, *Chauliodus macouni* Bean, from British Columbia. Copeia 1950(3): 241–242.

1952. The agonid fish *Pallasina barbata aix* (Starks), from British Columbia. J. Fish. Res. Board Can. 9(3): 143–147.

1956. The occurrence of the two-pronged hatchetfish, *Argyropelecus sladeni,* in British Columbia. Copeia 1956(2): 109–110.

1967. Number, size, and food of larval and juvenile fish, caught with an Isaacs-Kidd trawl in the surface waters of the Strait of Georgia, April 25–29, 1966. Fish. Res. Board Can. MS Rep. 926: 79 pp.

1971. A sculpin (*Icelus spiniger*) new to the coastal waters of British Columbia. J. Fish. Res. Board Can. 28(12): 1922–1924.

Barraclough, W. E., and T. H. Butler.

1961. Additional records of the argentinid fish, *Leuroglossus stilbius* Gilbert, from British Columbia, with remarks on its taxonomy. J. Fish. Res. Board Can. 18(6): 1167–1169.

1965. First record of the dusky sculpin (*Icelinus burchami*) in British Columbia waters. J. Fish. Res. Board Can. 22(5): 1305–1307.

Barraclough, W. E., and K. S. Ketchen.

1963. First record of the thornback sculpin, *Paricelinus hopliticus,* Eigenmann and Eigenmann, in British Columbia waters. J. Fish. Res. Board Can. 20(3): 851–852.

Barraclough, W. E., and A. E. Peden.

1976. First records of the pricklebreast poacher (*Stellerina xyosterna*), and the cutfin poacher (*Xeneretmus leiops*) from British Columbia, with keys to the poachers (Agonidae) of the Province. Syesis 9: 19–23.

Barrie, L., E. Falck, D. J. Gregor, T. Iversen, H. Loeng, R. MacDonald, S. Pfirman, T. Skotvold, and E. Wartena.

1998. Chapter 3. The influence of physical and chemical processes on contaminant transport into and within the Arctic. Pages 25–166 *in* S. Wilson, J. L. Murray, and H. P. Huntington, eds. AMAP assessment report: Arctic pollution issues. Arctic Monitoring and Assessment Programme (AMAP), Oslo, Norway.

Barsukov, V. V.

1958. Ryby bukhty Provideniya i sopredel'nykh vod Chukotskogo poluostrova [Fishes of Providence Bay and adjacent waters of the Chukotsk Peninsula]. Tr. Zool. Inst. Akad. Nauk SSSR 25: 130–163. [In Russian.]

1959. Sem. zubatok (Anarhichadidae) [The wolffish family (Anarhichadidae)]. Zool. Inst. Akad. Nauk SSSR, Fauna SSSR 5(5): 292 pp. [Translation by Indian National Scientific Documentation Centre, New Delhi, 1972.]

1964. Key to the fishes of the family Scorpaenidae. Tr. Vses. Nauchno-Issled. Inst. Morsk. Rybn. Khoz. Okeanogr. (VNIRO) 53. Izv. Tikhookean. Nauchno-Issled. Inst. Rybn. Khoz. Okeanogr. (TINRO) 52. [Translated by Israel Prog. Sci. Transl., 1968; pages 226–262 *in* P. A. Moiseev, ed. Soviet fisheries investigations in the northeast Pacific, Part III.] [Translation by Edith Roden, U.S. National Museum, Division of Fishes, also available. Page numbers cited in the Scorpaenidae section of this book are from the IPST version.]

1970. Species composition of genus *Sebastes* in the North Pacific and description of a new species. Doklady Akad. Nauk SSSR 195(4): 994–997. [Translated in Doklady Biol. Sci. 195(1–6): 760–763, by Consultants Bureau, Plenum Publ. Corp., 227 West 17th St., New York, NY 10011, in 1971.]

Barsukov, V. V., L. A. Borets, L. S. Kodolov, and V. A. Snytko.

1983. New data on *Adelosebastes latens* Eschmeyer, Abe and Nakano, 1979 (Scorpaenidae). J. Ichthyol. 23(4): 8–13 [English transl. Vopr. Ikhtiol. 23(4): 538–543.]

Barton, M.

1978. First Oregon records for two blennioid fishes. Calif. Fish Game 64(1): 60.

Bates, R. L., and J. A. Jackson, editors.

1987. Glossary of geology, 3rd edition. American Geological Institute, Alexandria, Virginia. 788 pp.

Baxter, R.

1990ms. Annotated keys to the fishes of Alaska. Arctic-Bio, Red Mountain, Alaska. Unpublished manuscript. About 800 pages. Available from Sera Baxter, Red Mountain, Box RDO, Homer, AK 99603.

Bayer, R. D.

1980. Size, seasonality, and sex ratios of the Bay Pipefish (*Syngnathus leptorhynchus*) in Oregon. Northwest Sci. 54(3): 161–167.

Bayliff, W. H.
1959. Notes on the taxonomy and distribution of certain zoarcid fishes in the northeastern Pacific. Copeia 1959(1): 78–80.

Beamish, R. J.
1980. Adult biology of river lamprey (*Lampetra ayresi*) and the Pacific lamprey (*Lampetra tridentata*) from the Pacific coast of Canada. Can. J. Fish. Aquat. Sci. 37: 1906–1923.

Beamish, R. J., and C. D. Levings.
1991. Abundance and freshwater migrations of the anadromous parasitic lamprey, *Lampetra tridentata,* in a tributary of the Fraser River, British Columbia. Can. J. Fish. Aquat. Sci. 48(7): 1250–1263.

Beamish, R. J., and R. E. Withler.
1986. A polymorphic population of lampreys that may produce parasitic and nonparastic varieties. Pages 31–49 *in* T. Uyeno, R. Arai, T. Taniuchi, and K. Matsuura, eds. Indo-Pacific fish biology. Proceedings of the Second International Conference on Indo-Pacific Fishes. Ichthyological Society of Japan, Tokyo.

Beamish, R. J., and J. H. Youson.
1987. Life history and abundance of young adult *Lampetra ayresi* in the Fraser River and their possible impact on salmon and herring stocks in the Strait of Georgia. Can. J. Fish. Aquat. Sci. 44(3): 525–537.

Bean, B. A.
1898. Notes on the capture of rare fishes. Proc. U.S. Natl. Mus. 21(1165): 639–640.

Bean, T. H.
1879a. On the occurrence of *Stichaeus punctatus,* (Fabr.) Kröyer, at St. Michael's, Alaska. Proc. U.S. Natl. Mus. (for 1878) 1: 279–281.
1879b. Description of a species of *Lycodes* (*L. turneri*) from Alaska, believed to be undescribed. Proc. U.S. Natl. Mus. (for 1878) 1: 463–466.
1879c. On the occurrence of *Hippoglossus vulgaris,* Flem., at Unalashka and St. Michael's, Alaska. Proc. U.S. Natl. Mus. (for 1879) 2: 63–66.
1879d. Description of a new fish from Alaska (*Anarrhichas lepturus*), with notes upon other species of the genus *Anarrhichas*. Proc. U.S. Natl. Mus. (for 1879) 2: 212–218.
1880. Descriptions of some genera and species of Alaskan fishes. Proc. U.S. Natl. Mus. (for 1879) 2: 353–359.
1881a. Descriptions of new fishes from Alaska and Siberia. Proc. U.S. Natl. Mus. (for 1881) 4: 144–159.
1881b. A preliminary catalogue of the fishes of Alaskan and adjacent waters. Proc. U.S. Natl. Mus. (for 1881) 4: 239–272.
1882. Notes on a collection of fishes made by Captain Henry E. Nichols, U.S.N., in British Columbia and southern Alaska, with descriptions of new species and a new genus (*Delolepis*). Proc. U.S. Natl. Mus. (for 1881) 4: 463–474.
1883. List of fishes known to occur in the Arctic Ocean north of Bering Strait. Pages 118–120 *in* U.S. Treasury Department, Cruise of the revenue-steamer Corwin in Alaska and the N.W. Arctic Ocean in 1881. Notes and memoranda: medical and anthropological; botanical; ornithological. Washington, D.C., Government Printing Office.
1884a. Notes on a collection of fishes made in 1882 and 1883 by Capt. Henry E. Nichols, U.S.N., in Alaska and British Columbia, with a description of a new genus and species, *Prionistius macellus.* Proc. U.S. Natl. Mus. (for 1883) 6: 353–361.
1884b. Notes on some fishes collected by James G. Swan in Washington Territory, including a new species of *Macrurus*. Proc. U.S. Natl. Mus. (for 1883) 6: 362–364.
1884c. Description of a new species of whitefish (*Coregonus nelsonii*), from Alaska. Proc. U.S. Natl. Mus. (for 1884) 7: 48.
1885. Description of a new species of *Aspidophoroides* (*A. güntherii*) from Alaska. Proc. U.S. Natl. Mus. (for 1885) 8(5): 74–75.
1888. Description of a new genus and species of fish, *Acrotus willoughbyi*, from Washington Territory. Proc. U.S. Natl. Mus. 10(672): 631–632.
1889. Description of *Coregonus pusillus,* a new species of whitefish from Alaska. Proc. U.S. Natl. Mus. 11(748): 526.
1890a. Scientific results of explorations by the U.S. Fish Commission steamer *Albatross.* No. VIII.—Description of a new cottoid fish from British Columbia. Proc. U.S. Natl. Mus. 12(787): 641–642.
1890b. Scientific results of explorations by the U.S. Fish Commission steamer *Albatross.* No. XI.—New fishes collected off the coast of Alaska and the adjacent region southward. Proc. U.S. Natl. Mus. 13(795): 37–45.
1895. Description of a new species of rockfish, *Sebastichthys brevispinis,* from Alaska. Proc. U.S. Natl. Mus. 17(1027): 627–628.

Bean, T. H., and B. A. Bean.
1896. Fishes collected at Bering and Copper islands by Nikolai A. Grebnitski and Leonhard Stejneger. Proc. U.S. Natl. Mus. 19(1106): 237–251.
1897. Notes on fishes collected in Kamchatka and Japan by Leonhard Stejneger and Nicolai A. Grebnitski, with a description of a new blenny. Proc. U.S. Natl. Mus. 19(1112): 381–392, pls. 34–35. [Not 1896 as given by some authors.]

Bean, T. H., and B. A. Bean.

1899. Note on *Oxycottus acuticeps* (Gilbert) from Sitka and Kadiak, Alaska. Proc. U.S. Natl. Mus. 21(1167): 655–656.

Beebe, W., and J. Crane.

1936. Deep-sea fishes of the Bermuda oceanographic expeditions. Family Serrivomeridae. Part I, Genus *Serrivomer.* Zoologica (N.Y.) 20: 53–102.

Begle, D. P.

1989. Phylogenetic analysis of the cottid genus *Artedius* (Teleostei: Scorpaeniformes). Copeia 1989(3): 642–652.

1991. Relationships of the osmeroid fishes and the use of reductive characters in phylogenetic analysis. Syst. Zool. 40(1): 33–53.

1992. Monophyly and relationships of the argentinoid fishes. Copeia 1992(2): 350–366. [See Johnson and Patterson 1996 for corrections.]

Behnke, R. J.

1966. The relationships of the Far Eastern trout, *Salmo mykiss* Walbaum. Copeia 1966(2): 346–348.

1980. A systematic review of the genus *Salvelinus.* Pages 441–480 *in* E. K. Balon, ed. Charrs: salmonid fishes of the genus *Salvelinus.* Dr. W. Junk, The Hague.

1984. Organizing the diversity of the Arctic charr complex. Pages 3–21 *in* L. Johnson and B. L. Burns, eds. Biology of the Arctic charr: Proceedings of the International Symposium on Arctic Charr, Winnipeg, Manitoba, May 1981. University of Manitoba Press, Winnipeg.

1989. Interpreting the phylogeny of *Salvelinus.* Physiol. Ecol. Jpn., Spec. Vol. 1: 35–48.

1992. Native trout of western North America. Am. Fish. Soc. Monogr. 6. American Fisheries Society, Bethesda, Maryland. 275 pp.

Bekker (Becker), V. E.

1964. [Slendertailed luminescent anchovies (genera *Loweina, Tarletonbeania, Gonichthys,* and *Centrobranchus*) of the Pacific and Indian oceans: systematics and distribution]. Tr. Inst. Okeanol. Akad. Nauk SSSR 73: 1–74. [Translation by Israel Prog. Sci. Transl., 1966, pp. 10–78 *in* T. S. Rass, ed. Fishes of the Pacific and Indian oceans: biology and distribution.]

1983. Miktofovye ryby Mirovogo okeana [Myctophid fishes of the World oceans]. Nauka, Moscow. 248 pp. [In Russian.]

1993. Benthopelagic species of *Idiolychnus* and *Diaphus* (Myctophidae) from the southeastern Pacific Ocean with descriptions of two new species. J. Ichthyol. 33(3): 20–29 [English transl. Vopr. Ikhtiol. 32(6): 3–10].

Bekker (Becker), V. E., and Yu. N. Shcherbachev.

1990. Benthopelagic species of the families Neoscopelidae and Myctophidae from the Indian Ocean, with a description of a new species of *Diaphus.* J. Ichthyol. 30(7): 122–134 [English transl. Vopr. Ikhtiol. 30(5): 845–855].

Bell, F. H.

1981. The Pacific halibut: the resource and the fishery. Alaska Northwest Publishing Company, Anchorage. 267 pp.

Bell, F. H., and J. T. Gharrett.

1945. The Pacific Coast blackcod, *Anoplopoma fimbria.* Copeia 1945(2): 94–103.

Bell, F. H., and J. L. Kask.

1936. *Lampris regius* (Bonnaterre), the opah or moonfish from the North Pacific. Copeia 1936(1): 54–56.

Bemis, W. E., E. K. Findeis, and L. Grande.

1997. An overview of Acipenseriformes. Environ. Biol. Fishes 48: 25–71.

Berestovskii, E. G.

1994. Reproductive biology of skates of the family Rajidae in the seas of the far north. J. Ichthyol. [English transl. Vopr. Ikhtiol.] 34(6): 26–37.

Berg, L. S.

1936. Note on *Coregonus (Prosopium) cylindraceus* (Pallas). Copeia 1936(1): 57–58.

1948. Freshwater fishes of the USSR and adjacent countries. Vol. 1, 4th edition. Acad. Sci. USSR Zool. Inst., Fauna USSR 27. 504 pp. [Translation by Israel Prog. Sci. Transl., 1962.]

1949a. Freshwater fishes of the USSR and adjacent countries. Vol. 2, 4th edition. Acad. Sci. USSR Zool. Inst., Fauna USSR 29. 496 pp. [Translation by Israel Prog. Sci. Transl., 1964.]

1949b. Freshwater fishes of the USSR and adjacent countries. Vol. 3, 4th edition. Acad. Sci. USSR Zool. Inst., Fauna USSR 30. 510 pp. Translation by Israel Prog. Sci. Transl., 1965.]

Bernatchez, L., J. A. Vuorinen, R. A. Bodaly, and J. J. Dodson.

1996. Genetic evidence for reproductive isolation and multiple origins of sympatric trophic ecotypes of whitefish (*Coregonus*). Evolution 50(2): 624–635.

Berry, F. H., and H. C. Perkins.

1966. Survey of pelagic fishes of the California Current area. U.S. Fish Wildl. Serv. Fish. Bull. 65(3): 625–682.

Bertelsen, E.

1943. Notes on the deep-sea angler-fish *Ceratias holbölli* Kr. based on specimens in the Zoological Museum of Copenhagen. Vidensk. Medd. fra Dansk Naturh. Foren. 107: 185–206.

1951. The ceratioid fishes: ontogeny, taxonomy, distribution and biology. Dana-Rep. Carlsberg Found. 39: 276 pp.

1984. Ceratioidei: development and relationships. Pages 325–334 *in* H. G. Moser et al., eds. Ontogeny and systematics of fishes. Am. Soc. Ichthyol. Herpetol., Spec. Publ. 1.

Bertelsen, E., G. Krefft, and N. B. Marshall.

1976. The fishes of the family Notosudidae. Dana-Rep. Carlsberg Found. 86. 114 pp.

Bertelsen, E., J. G. Nielsen, and D. G. Smith.

1989. Saccopharyngidae, Eurypharyngidae, and Monognathidae. Pages 636–641 *in* Fishes of the western North Atlantic. Mem. Sears Found. Mar. Res., New Haven, 1(9), Vol. 1.

Bertelsen, E., and T. W. Pietsch.

1983. The ceratioid anglerfishes of Australia. Rec. Aust. Mus. 35: 77–99.

Bertelsen, E., T. W. Pietsch, and R. J. Lavenberg.

1981. Ceratioid anglerfishes of the family Gigantactinidae: morphology, systematics, and distribution. Contrib. Sci. (Los Angel.) 332. 74 pp.

Bertin, L.

1937. Les poissons abyssaux du genre *Cyema* Günther (anatomie, embryology, bionomie). Dana-Rep. Carlsberg Found. 10. 30 pp.

Best, E. A.

1963. Greenland halibut, *Reinhardtius hippoglossoides* (Walbaum), added to California fauna. Calif. Fish Game 49(3): 213–214.

Best, E. A., and P. J. Eldridge.

1969. Range extension of flag rockfish (*Sebastodes rubrivinctus*) to Aleutian Islands. J. Fish. Res. Board Can. 26(7): 1955–1956.

Bickham, J. W., S. M. Carr, B. G. Hanks, D. W. Burton, and B. J. Gallaway.

1989. Genetic analysis of population variation in the Arctic cisco (*Coregonus autumnalis*) using electrophoretic, flow cytometric, and mitochondrial DNA restriction analyses. Biol. Pap. Univ. Alaska 24: 112–122.

Bickham, J. W., J. C. Patton, S. Minzenmayer, L. L. Moulton, and B. J. Gallaway.

1997. Identification of Arctic and Bering ciscoes in the Colville River delta, Beaufort Sea coast, Alaska. Am. Fish. Soc. Symp. 19: 224–228.

Bigelow, H. B., and W. C. Schroeder.

1944. New sharks from the western North Atlantic. Proc. New Engl. Zool. Club. 23: 21–36, pls. 7–10.

1948. Sharks. Pages 59–546 *in* Fishes of the western North Atlantic. Mem. Sears Found. Mar. Res., New Haven, 1(1).

1953. Fishes of the Gulf of Maine. Fish. Bull. Fish Wildl. Serv. 53. 577 pp.

1957. A study of the sharks of the suborder Squaloidea. Bull. Mus. Comp. Zool. 117(1): 1–150, pls. 1–4.

Bird, F. H., and K. Roberson.

1979. Pygmy whitefish, *Prosopium coulteri,* in three lakes of the Copper River system in Alaska. J. Fish. Res. Board Can. 36: 468–470.

Birman, I. B.

1958. O rasprostranenii nekotorykh pelagicheskikh ryb v severnoi chasti Tikhogo okeana [On the distribution of some pelagic fishes in the northern part of the Pacific Ocean]. Zool. Zh. 37(7): 1058–1062. [In Russian.]

Birstein, V. J., R. Hanner, and R. DeSalle.

1997. Phylogeny of the Acipenseriformes: cytogenetic and molecular approaches. Environ. Biol. Fishes 48: 127–155.

Birstein, V. J., A. I. Poletaev, and B. F. Goncharov.

1993. DNA content in Eurasian sturgeon species determined by flow cytometry. Cytometry 14: 377–383.

Black, G. F.

1977. Notes on some fishes collected off the outer coast of Baja California. Calif. Fish Game 63(1): 71–72.

Blackburn, J. E., K. Anderson, C. I. Hamilton, and S. J. Starr.

1980. Pelagic and demersal fish assessment in the lower Cook Inlet estuary system. U.S. Dep. Commer., NOAA, and U.S. Dep. Inter., Minerals Manage. Serv., Environmental Assessment of the Alaskan Continental Shelf, Final Rep., Biol. Stud. 17: 107–450.

Blackburn, J. E., and P. J. Anderson.

1997. Pacific sand lance growth, seasonal availability, movements, catch variability, and food in the Kodiak–Cook Inlet area of Alaska. Pages 409–427 *in* Forage fishes in marine ecosystems. University of Alaska Sea Grant, AK-SG-97-01, Fairbanks.

Blackburn, J. E., and P. B. Jackson.

1982. Seasonal composition and abundance of juvenile and adult marine finfish and crab species in the nearshore zone of Kodiak Island's eastside during April 1978 through March 1979. U.S. Dep Commer., NOAA, and U.S. Dep. Inter., Minerals Manage. Serv., OCSEAP Final Rep. 54: 377–570.

Blaxter, J. H. S.

1985. The herring: a successful species? Can. J. Fish. Aquat. Sci. 42 (Suppl. 1): 21–30.

Bodaly, R. A.

1979. Morphological and ecological divergence within the lake whitefish (*Coregonus clupeaformis*) species complex in Yukon Territory. J. Fish. Res. Board Can. 36(10): 1214–1222.

Bodaly, R. A., and C. C. Lindsey.

1977. Pleistocene watershed exchanges and the fish fauna of the Peel River basin, Yukon Territory. J. Fish. Res. Board Can. 34: 388–395.

Boehlert, G. W., and T. Sasaki.

1988. Pelagic biogeography of the armorhead, *Pseudopentaceros wheeleri,* and recruitment to isolated seamounts in the North Pacific Ocean. U.S. Natl. Mar. Fish. Serv. Fish. Bull. 86(3): 453–465.

Böhlke, E. B.

1984. Catalog of type specimens in the ichthyological collection of the Academy of Natural Sciences of Philadelphia. Acad. Nat. Sci. Phila. Spec. Publ. 14. 246 pp.

Böhlke, J. E.

1953. A catalogue of the type specimens of Recent fishes in the Natural History Museum of Stanford University. Stanford Ichthyol. Bull. 5: 1–168.

Böhlke, J. E., and C. R. Robins.

1960. A revision of the gobioid fish genus *Coryphopterus.* Proc. Acad. Nat. Sci. Phila. 112(5): 103–128.

Bolin, R. L.

1936a. A revision of the genus *Icelinus* Jordan. Copeia 1936(3): 151–159.

1936b. New cottid fishes from Japan and Bering Sea. Proc. U.S. Natl. Mus. 84(3000): 25–38.

1939a. A new stomiatoid fish from California. Copeia 1939(1): 39–41.

1939b. A review of the myctophid fishes of the Pacific coast of the United States and of lower California. Stanford Ichthyol. Bull. 1(4): 89–156.

1944. A review of the marine cottid fishes of California. Stanford Ichthyol. Bull. 3(1): 1–135.

1947. The evolution of the marine Cottidae of California with a discussion of the genus as a systematic category. Stanford Ichthyol. Bull. 3(3): 153–168.

1950. Remarks on cottid fishes occasioned by the capture of two species new to California. Copeia 1950(3): 195–202.

Bond, C. E.

1996. Biology of fishes, 2nd edition. Saunders College Publishing, Fort Worth. 750 pp.

Bond, C. E., and T. T. Kan.

1986. Systematics and evolution of the lampreys of Oregon. Page 919 *in* T. Uyeno, R. Arai, T. Taniuchi, and K. Matsuura, eds. Indo-Pacific fish biology. Proceedings of the Second International Conference on Indo-Pacific Fishes. Ichthyological Society of Japan, Tokyo. [Abstract.]

Bond, C. E., and D. L. Stein.

1984. *Opaeophacus acrogeneius,* a new genus and species of Zoarcidae (Pisces: Osteichthyes) from the Bering Sea. Proc. Biol. Soc. Wash. 97(3): 522–525.

Borkin, I. V., and R. V. Mel'yantsev.

1984. New data on the distribution of polar cod, *Arctogadus glacialis* (Gadidae), in the Arctic region. J. Ichthyol. (English transl. Vopr. Ikhtiol.] 24(2): 101–103.

Borodulina, O. D.

1968. Taxonomy and distribution of the genus *Leuroglossus* (Bathylagidae, Pisces). Probl. Ichthyol. 8(1): 1–10. [English transl. Vopr. Ikhtiol. 8(1): 3–14].

1987. Identification of the remains of mesopelagic fishes from the stomachs of predators. V. Some features of the structure of the jaws of fishes of the superfamily Stomiatoidea. J. Ichthyol. [English transl. Vopr. Ikhtiol.] 27(1): 167–171.

Boulenger, G. A.

1904. A synopsis of the suborders and families of teleostean fishes. Ann. Mag. Nat. Hist. (Ser. 7) 13(75): 161–190.

Boulva, J.

1972. Morphometrics of three sympatric arctic codfishes of the genera *Arctogadus* and *Gadus.* J. Fish. Res. Board Can. 29(3): 243–249.

Bourne, N., and D. E. McAllister.
1969. The black hagfish, *Eptatretus deani,* from British Columbia. J. Fish. Res. Board Can. 26(12): 3246–3248.

Bradbury, M. G.
1967. The genera of batfishes (family Ogcocephalidae). Copeia 1967(2): 399–422.

Bradbury, M. G., and D. M. Cohen.
1958. An illustration and a new record of the North Pacific bathypelagic fish *Macropinna microstoma.* Stanford Ichthyol. Bull. 7(3): 57–59.

Briggs, J. C.
1955. A monograph of the clingfishes (order Xenopterygii). Stanford Ichthyol. Bull. 6. 224 pp.
1960. Fishes of worldwide (circumtropical) distribution. Copeia 1960(3): 171–180.
1974. Marine zoogeography. McGraw-Hill, New York. 475 pp.
1984. Centers of origin in biogeography. Biogeographical Monographs 1, Biogeography Study Group, University of Leeds. Leeds, Yorkshire, U.K. 106 pp.
1986. Introduction to the zoogeography of North American fishes. Pages 1–16 *in* C. H. Hocutt and E. O. Wiley, eds. The zoogeography of North American freshwater fishes. John Wiley & Sons, New York.
1995. Global biogeography. Elsevier, Amsterdam, Netherlands. 553 pp.

Bright, D. B.
1959. The occurrence and food of the sleeper shark, *Somniosus pacificus,* in a central Alaska bay. Copeia 1959(1): 76–77.
1960. A record of the porbeagle, *Lamna nasus,* from Cook Inlet, Alaska. Copeia 1960(2): 145–146.

Brodeur, R. D.
1988. Zoogeography and trophic ecology of the dominant epipelagic fishes in the northern North Pacific. Bull. Ocean Res. Inst. Univ. Tokyo No. 26 (Part II): 1–27.

Brodeur, R. D., and M. S. Busby.
1998. Occurrence of an Atlantic salmon *Salmo salar* in the Bering Sea. Alaska Fish. Res. Bull. 5(1): 64–66.

Brodeur, R. D., and W. G. Pearcy.
1986. Distribution and relative abundance of pelagic non-salmonid nekton off Oregon and Washington, 1979–1984. NOAA Tech. Rep. NMFS 46. 85 pp.

Brodeur, R. D., M. T. Wilson, G. E. Walters, and I. V. Melnikov.
1999. Forage fishes in the Bering Sea: distribution, species associations, and biomass trends. Pages 509–536 *in* T. R. Loughlin and K. Ohtani, eds. Dynamics of the Bering Sea. University of Alaska Sea Grant, AK-SG-99-03, Fairbanks.

Brunner, P. C., M. R. Douglas, and L. Bernatchez.
1998. Microsatellite and mitochondrial DNA assessment of population structure and stocking effects in Arctic charr *Salvelinus alpinus* (Teleostei: Salmonidae) from central Alpine lakes. Mol. Ecol. 7: 209–223.

Buckley, R. M., and I. Erickson.
1977. First record of jack mackerel, *Trachurus symmetricus,* in Puget Sound. Syesis 10: 175.

Burgner, R. L.
1991. Life history of sockeye salmon (*Oncorhynchus nerka*). Pages 1–117 *in* C. Groot and L. Margolis, eds. Pacific salmon life histories. UBC Press, Vancouver.

Burke, C. V.
1912a. Note on the Cyclogasteridae. Ann. Mag. Nat. Hist. (Ser. 8) 9(53): 507–513.
1912b. A new genus and six new species of fishes of the family Cyclogasteridae. Proc. U.S. Natl. Mus. 43: 567–574.
1930. Revision of the fishes of the family Liparidae. U.S. Natl. Mus. Bull. 150. 204 pp.

Busby, M. S.
1998. Guide to the identification of larval and early juvenile poachers (Scorpaeniformes: Agonidae) from the northeastern Pacific Ocean and Bering Sea. NOAA Tech. Rep. NMFS 137. 88 pp.

Busby, M. S., and N. V. Chernova.
2001. Redescription of the festive snailfish, *Liparis marmoratus* (Scorpaeniformes: Liparidae), with a new record from the northern Bering Sea. Ichthyol. Res. 48: 187–191.

Busby, M. S., and J. W. Orr.
2000. A pelagic basslet *Howella sherborni* (family Acropomatidae) off of the Aleutian Islands. Alaska Fish. Res. Bull. 6(1): 49–53. [Dated 1999 on cover and title page, issued in March 2000.]

Butler, J. L., and E. H. Ahlstrom.
1974. Review of the deep-sea fish genus *Scopelengys* (Neoscopelidae) with a description of a new species, *Scopelengys clarkei,* from the central Pacific. U.S. Natl. Mar. Fish. Serv. Fish. Bull. 74(1): 142–150.

Cailliet, G. M., and M. E. Anderson.

1975. Occurrence of the prowfish *Zaprora silenus* Jordan, 1896 in Monterey Bay, California. Calif. Fish Game 61(1): 60–62.

Cailliet, G. M., M. S. Love, and A. W. Ebeling.

1986. Fishes: a field and laboratory manual on their structure, identification, and natural history. Wadsworth Publishing Company, Belmont, California. 194 pp.

Carey, A. G., Jr., editor.

1978. Marine biota (plankton/benthos/fish). Pages 174–237 *in* Environmental assessment of the Alaskan continental shelf, interim synthesis: Beaufort/Chukchi. U.S. Dep. Commer., NOAA, Environ. Res. Lab., Boulder, Colorado.

Carlson, H. R., R. E. Haight, and K. J. Krieger.

1982. Species composition and relative abundance of demersal marine life in waters of southeastern Alaska, 1969–81. NWAFC Processed Report 82-16. 106 pp. Northwest and Alaska Fisheries Center Auke Bay Laboratory, NMFS, NOAA, P.O. Box 155, Auke Bay, AK 99821.

Carr, S. M., D. S. Kivlichan, P. Pepin, and D. C. Crutcher.

1999. Molecular systematics of gadid fishes: implications for the biogeographic origins of Pacific species. Can. J. Zool. 77: 19–26.

Carveth, R. G., and N. J. Wilimovsky.

1983ms. Key to the genus *Myoxocephalus*. Unpublished manuscript. Department of Zoology, University of British Columbia, Vancouver. 17 pp.

Castle, P. H. J., and N. S. Raju.

1975. Some rare leptocephali from the Atlantic and Indo-Pacific oceans. Dana-Rep. 85. 25 pp., 1 pl.

Castro, J. I.

1983. The sharks of North American waters. Texas A&M University Press, College Station. 180 pp.

Castro Hernández, J. J., and A. T. Santana Ortega.

2000. Synopsis of biological data on the chub mackerel (*Scomber japonicus* Houttuyn, 1782). FAO Fisheries Synopsis 157. Food and Agriculture Organization of the United Nations, Rome. 77 pp.

Cavender, T. M.

1978. Taxonomy and distribution of the bull trout, *Salvelinus confluentus* (Suckley), from the American northwest. Calif. Fish Game 64(3): 139–174.

1980. Systematics of *Salvelinus* from the North Pacific Basin. Pages 295–322 *in* E. K. Balon, ed. Charrs: salmonid fishes of the genus *Salvelinus*. Dr. W. Junk, The Hague.

Cavender, T. M., and S. Kimura.

1989. Cytotaxonomy and interrelationships of Pacific basin *Salvelinus*. Physiol. Ecol. Jpn., Spec. Vol. 1: 49–68.

Chapleau, F.

1993. Pleuronectiform relationships: a cladistic reassessment. Bull. Mar. Sci. 52(1): 516–540.

Chapman, W. M.

1939. Eleven new species and three new genera of oceanic fishes collected by the International Fisheries Commission from the northeastern Pacific. Proc. U.S. Natl. Mus. 86(3062): 501–542.

1940. Oceanic fishes from the northeast Pacific Ocean. Occas. Pap. B.C. Prov. Mus. 2. 44 pp.

Chapman, W. M., and A. C. DeLacy.

1934. New species of *Careproctus* from Alaska. J. Pan-Pac. Res. Inst. 9(2): 2–5.

Chapman, W. M., and L. D. Townsend.

1938. The osteology of *Zaprora silenus* Jordan, with notes on its distribution and early life-history. Ann. Mag. Nat. Hist. Ser. 11, 2(8): 89–117.

Chen, L.

1986. Meristic variation in *Sebastes* (Scorpaenidae), with an analysis of character association and bilateral pattern and their significance in species separation. NOAA Tech. Rep. NMFS 45. 17 pp.

Chereshnev, I. A.

1982. The taxonomic status of sympatric diadromous chars of the genus *Salvelinus* (Salmonidae) from eastern Chukotka. J. Ichthyol. [English transl. Vopr. Ikhtiol.] 22(6): 22–38.

1984. The first record of the Bering cisco, *Coregonus laurettae,* from the USSR. J. Ichthyol. 24: 88–95.

1990. Ichthyofauna composition and features of freshwater fish distribution in the northeastern USSR. J. Ichthyol. 30(7): 110–121 [English transl. Vopr. Ikhtiol. 30(5): 836–844].

1996. Annotated list of Cyclostomata and Pisces from the fresh waters of the Arctic and adjacent territories. J. Ichthyol. 36(8): 566–577 [English transl. Vopr. Ikhtiol. 36(5): 597–608].

Chereshnev, I. A., and A. V. Balushkin.

1980. A new species of blackfish, *Dallia asmirabilis* [*sic*] sp. n. (Umbridae, Esociformes) from the Amguema River basin (arctic Chukotka). J. Ichthyol. 20(6): 25–30 [English transl. Vopr. Ikhtiol. 20(6): 800–805].

Chereshnev, I. A., and M. B. Skopets.

1994. The chars (tribe Salvelinini, fam. Salmonidae) of ancient Lake El'gygytgyn (central Chukotka). J. Ichthyol. 34(2): 20–34. [Original manuscript in English.]

Chereshnev, I. A., and S. I. Zharnikov.

1989. On the first record of the American shad, *Alosa sapidissima,* in the Anadyr River. J. Ichthyol. 29(6): 135–138 [English transl. Vopr. Ikhtiol. 29(3): 501–503].

Chernova, N. V.

1991. Liparovye ryby Evroaziatskoy Arktiki [Snailfishes (Liparididae) from the Eurasian Arctic]. Akad. Nauk SSSR, Apatity. 111 pp. [In Russian; English summary.]

1998a. Reestablishment of the validity of species *Gymnelus bilabrus* Andriashev 1937 with characteristics of species *G. viridis* verified (Fabricius, 1780) (Zoarcidae). J. Ichthyol. 38(2): 163–169 [English transl. Vopr. Ikhtiol. 38(2): 182–188].

1998b. A new species *Gymnelus andersoni* sp. nova, from the Arctic seas with refinement of the species status of *G. retrodorsalis* Le Danois and *G. pauciporus* Anderson (Fam. Zoarcidae). J. Ichthyol. 38(9): 708–715 [English transl. Vopr. Ikhtiol. 38(6): 737–744].

1998c. Catalogue of the type specimens of snailfish (Liparidae, Scorpaeniformes) in the Zoological Institute of the Russian Academy of Sciences. J. Ichthyol. 38(9): 730–746 [English transl. Vopr. Ikhtiol. 38(6): 760–775].

1999a. New species *Gymnelus knipowitschi* from the Arctic Ocean and a redescription of *G. hemifasciatus* Andriashev (Zoarcidae). J. Ichthyol. 39(1): 1–9 [English transl. Vopr. Ikhtiol. 39(1): 5–13].

1999b. Four new species of *Gymnelus* (Zoarcidae) from the Arctic regions. J. Ichthyol. 39(5): 343–352 [English transl. Vopr. Ikhtiol. 39(3): 306–315].

2000. Four new species of *Gymnelus* (Zoarcidae) from the Far Eastern seas with genus diagnosis and key to species. J. Ichthyol. 40(1): 1–12 [English transl. Vopr. Ikhtiol. 40(1): 56–16].

Chikilev, V. G., and A. V. Datskii.

2000. Pacific stout sand lance *Ammodytes hexapterus* (Ammodytidae) in the Gulf of Anadyr and adjacent waters. J. Ichthyol. 40(9): 732–739 [English transl. Vopr. Ikhtiol. 40(6): 772–779].

Chikilev, V. G., and A. V. Kharitonov.

2000. Description of eelpout *Lycodes raridens* (Zoarcidae) from the estuary of the Anadyr River. J. Ichthyol. 40(1): 95–97 [English transl. Vopr. Ikhtiol. 40(1): 100–102].

Chikilev, V. G., and O. B. Korotaeva.

2000. Variability in caudal fin coloration of the Pacific halibut *Hippoglossus hippoglossus stenolepis* (Pleuronectidae). J. Ichthyol. 40(3): 273–276 [English transl. Vopr. Ikhtiol. 40(2): 278–281].

Chilton, D. E., and R. J. Beamish.

1982. Age determination methods for fishes studied by the groundfish program at the Pacific Biological Station. Can. Spec. Publ. Fish. Aquat. Sci. 60. 102 pp.

Chute, W. H., R. M. Bailey, W. A. Clemens, J. R. Dymond, S. F. Hildebrand, G. S. Myers, and L. P. Schultz.

1948. A list of common and scientific names of the better known fishes of the United States and Canada. Am. Fish. Soc. Spec. Publ. 1. 45 pp.

Chyung, M. K., and K. H. Kim.

1959. Thirteen unrecorded species of fish from Korean waters. Korean J. Ichthyol. 2(1): 2–10.

Clarke, R.

1950. The bathypelagic angler fish *Ceratias holbölli* Kröyer. Discovery Rep. 26: 1–32, pl. 1.

Claussen, L. G.

1959. A southern range extension of the American shad to Todos Santos Bay, Baja California, Mexico. Calif. Fish Game 45(3): 217–218.

Clemens, H. B.

1961. The migration, age, and growth of Pacific albacore (*Thunnus germo*), 1951–1958. Calif. Dep. Fish Game Fish Bull. 115. 128 pp.

Clemens, W. A., and G. V. Wilby.

1946. Fishes of the Pacific coast of Canada. Fish. Res. Board Can. Bull. 68. 368 pp.

1949. Fishes of the Pacific coast of Canada, revised. Fish. Res. Board Can. Bull. 68. 368 pp.

1961. Fishes of the Pacific coast of Canada, 2nd edition. Fish. Res. Board Can. Bull. 68. 443 pp.

Clothier, C. R.

1950. A key to some southern California fishes based on vertebral characters. Calif. Fish Game Fish. Bull. 79. 83 pp.

Coffie, P. A.

1998. Status of the spinynose sculpin, *Asemicthys* [*sic*] *taylori,* in Canada. Can. Field-Nat. 112(1): 130–132.

Cohen, D. M.

1956. The synonymy and distribution of *Leuroglossus stilbius* Gilbert, a North Pacific bathypelagic fish. Stanford Ichthyol. Bull. 7(2): 19–23.

1958a. *Nansenia candida,* a new species of argentinid fish from the North Pacific, with notes on other species of *Nansenia.* Stanford Ichthyol. Bull. 7(3): 52–57.

1958b. Two new species of *Bathylagus* from the western North Atlantic with notes on other species. Breviora 98: 9 pp.

1963a. The publication dates of Goode and Bean's *Oceanic Ichthyology.* J. Soc. Bibliogr. Nat. Hist. 4(3): 162–166.

1963b. A new genus and species of bathypelagic ophidioid fish from the western North Atlantic. Breviora 196. 8 pp.

1964. Suborder Argentinoidea. Pages 1–70 *in* Fishes of the western North Atlantic. Mem. Sears Found. Mar. Res., New Haven, 1(4).

1966. The North Pacific deepsea fish name *Bathylagus milleri* Gilbert, a senior synonym of *Bathylagus alascanus* Chapman. Copeia 1966(4): 877–878.

1984. Gadiformes: Overview. Pages 259–265 *in* H. G. Moser et al., eds. Ontogeny and systematics of fishes. Am. Soc. Ichthyol. Herpetol., Spec. Publ. 1.

Cohen, D. M., editor.

1989. Papers on the systematics of gadiform fishes. Nat. Hist. Mus. Los Angeles County, Sci. Ser. 32. 262 pp.

Cohen, D. M., T. Inada, T. Iwamoto, and N. Scialabba.

1990. FAO species catalogue. Vol. 10. Gadiform fishes of the world (order Gadiformes). An annotated and illustrated catalogue of cods, hakes, grenadiers, and other gadiform fishes known to date. FAO Fish. Synop. No. 125, Vol. 10. 442 pp.

Cohen, D. M., and J. G. Nielsen.

1978. Guide to the identification of genera of the fish order Ophidiiformes with a tentative classification of the order. U.S. Dep. Commer., NOAA Tech. Rep. NMFS Circ. 417. 72 pp.

Collett, R.

1905. Fiske indsamlede under "Michael sars" Togter i Nordhavet 1900–1902. Rep. Norwegian Fish. Mar. Inv. 2(3): 1–147 + index, pls. 1–2.

Collette, B. B.

1999. Mackerels, molecules, and morphology. Pages 149–164 *in* B. Séret and J.-Y. Sire, eds. Proc. 5th Indo-Pac. Fish Conf., Nouméa, 1997. Soc. Fr. Ichtyol., Paris.

Collette, B. B., and L. N. Chao.

1975. Systematics and morphology of the bonitos (*Sarda*) and their relatives (Scombridae, Sardini). U.S. Fish Wildl. Serv. Fish. Bull. 73(3): 516–625.

Collette, B. B., and C. E. Nauen.

1983. FAO species catalogue. Vol. 2. Scombrids of the world. An annotated and illustrated catalogue of tunas, mackerels, bonitos, and related species known to date. FAO Fish. Synop. No. 125, Vol. 2. 137 pp.

Compagno, L. J. V.

1984. FAO species catalogue. Vol. 4. Sharks of the world. An annotated and illustrated catalogue of shark species known to date. Part 1. Hexanchiformes to Lamniformes. FAO Fish. Synop. No. 125, Vol. 4, Pt. 1, pp. 1–249.

1984. FAO species catalogue. Vol. 4. Sharks of the world. An annotated and illustrated catalogue of shark species known to date. Part 2. Carcharhiniformes. FAO Fish. Synop. No. 125, Vol. 4, Pt. 2, pp. 251–655.

1988. Sharks of the order Carcharhiniformes. Princeton University Press, New Jersey. xxii + 486 pp. followed by numerous figures and 35 plates.

1999a. Systematics and body form. Pages 1–42 *in* W. C. Hamlett, ed. Sharks, skates, and rays. The biology of elasmobranch fishes. Johns Hopkins University Press, Baltimore.

1999b. Checklist of living elasmobranchs. Pages 471–498 *in* W. C. Hamlett, ed. Sharks, skates, and rays. The biology of elasmobranch fishes. Johns Hopkins University Press, Baltimore.

Cook, S. F., and J. Long.

1985. The oxeye oreo, *Allocyttus folletti* Myers, from the Bering Sea. Calif. Fish Game 71(1): 57.

Cooper, J. A., and F. Chapleau.

1998. Monophyly and intrarelationships of the family Pleuronectidae (Pleuronectiformes), with a revised classification. U.S. Natl. Mar. Fish. Serv. Fish. Bull. 96(4): 686–726.

Cope, E. D.

1873. A contribution to the ichthyology of Alaska [Read before the American Philosophical Society, January 17, 1873.]. Proc. Am. Philos. Soc. 13: 24–32.

Cowan, G. I. McT.
1971. Comparative morphology of the cottid genus *Myoxocephalus* based on meristic, morphometric, and other anatomical characters. Can. J. Zool. 49: 1479–1496.
1972a. Relationships within the genus *Myoxocephalus* (Pisces: Cottidae) based on morphological and biochemical data using numerical and conventional methods of analyses. Can. J. Zool. 50: 671–682.
1972b. Comparative morphology of the cottid genus *Myoxocephalus* based on biochemical characters. Can. J. Zool. 50: 683–693.

Cowan, I. McT.
1938. Some fish records from the coast of British Columbia. Copeia 1938(2): 97.

Cox, K. W.
1963. Egg cases of some elasmobranchs and a cyclostome from Californian waters. Calif. Fish Game 49(4): 271–289.

Crabtree, R. E., K. J. Sulak, and J. A. Musick.
1985. Biology and distribution of species of *Polyacanthonotus* (Pisces: Notacanthiformes) in the western North Atlantic. Bull. Mar. Sci. 36(2): 235–248.

Craig, P. C.
1984. Fish use of coastal waters of the Alaskan Beaufort Sea: a review. Trans. Am. Fish. Soc. 113: 265–282.
1989. An introduction to anadromous fishes in the Alaskan Arctic. Biol. Pap. Univ. Alaska 24: 27–54.

Craig, P., and L. Haldorson.
1986. Pacific salmon in the North American Arctic. Arctic 39(1): 2–7.

Craig, P. C., W. B. Griffiths, L. Haldorson, and H. C. McElderry.
1982. Ecological studies of Arctic cod (*Boreogadus saida*) in Beaufort Sea coastal waters, Alaska. Can. J. Fish. Aquat. Sci. 39(3): 395–406.
1985. Distributional patterns of fishes in an Alaskan arctic lagoon. Polar Biol. 4: 9–18.

Cramer, F.
1895. On the cranial characters of the genus *Sebastodes* (rock-fish). Proc. Calif. Acad. Sci., Ser. 2, 5: 573–610, pls. 57–70.

Crockford, S. J.
1997. Archeological evidence of large northern bluefin tuna, *Thunnus thynnus,* in coastal waters of British Columbia and Washington. U.S. Natl. Mar. Fish. Serv. Fish. Bull. 95: 11–24.

Cruz-Aguero, J. de la.
1999. A first Mexican record of the chinook salmon, *Oncorhynchus tshawytscha.* Calif. Fish Game 85(2): 77–78.

Csepp, D. J., and B. L. Wing.
2000. Northern range extensions and habitat observations for blackeye goby *Rhinogopiops nicholsii* and kelp perch *Brachyistius frenatus* in southeastern Alaska. Alaska Fish. Res. Bull. 6(2): 78–84. [Dated 1999 on cover and title page, distributed July 2000.]

Dahlberg, M. L., and D. E. Phinney.
1967. The use of adipose fin pigmentation for distinguishing between juvenile chinook and coho salmon in Alaska. J. Fish. Res. Board Can. 24(1): 209–210.

Dall, W. H.
1870. Alaska and its resources. Lee & Shepard, Boston. 628 pp.
1916. Biographical memoir of Theodore Nicholas Gill, 1837–1914. Biographical Memoirs of the National Academy of Sciences 8: 313–343.

Dames and Moore.
1979. A preliminary assessment of composition and food webs for demersal fish assemblages in several shallow subtidal habitats in lower Cook Inlet, Alaska. Appendix II, pages 383–450 *in* J. E. Blackburn et al., Pelagic and demersal fish assessment in the lower Cook Inlet estuary system. U.S. Dep. Commer., NOAA, and U.S. Dep. Inter., Minerals Manage. Serv., Environmental Assessment of the Alaskan Continental Shelf, Final Rep., Biol. Stud. 17: 107–450.

Darling, J. D., and K. E. Keogh.
1994. Observations of basking sharks, *Cetorhinus maximus,* in Clayoquot Sound, British Columbia. Can. Field-Nat. 108(2): 199–210.

Davenport, D.
1966. Colour variant of bocaccio (*Sebastodes paucispinis*) in British Columbia waters. J. Fish. Res. Board Can. 23(12): 1981.

Dean, T. A., L. Haldorson, D. R. Laur, S. C. Jewett, and A. Blanchard.
2000. The distribution of nearshore fishes in kelp and eelgrass communities in Prince William Sound, Alaska: associations with vegetation and physical habitat characteristics. Environ. Biol. Fishes 57: 271–287.

de Astarloa, J. M. D., D. E. Figueroa, L. Lucifora, R. C. Menni, B. L. Prenski, and G. Chiaramonte.

1999. New records of the Pacific sleeper shark, *Somniosus pacificus* (Chondrichthyes: Squalidae), from the southwest Atlantic. Ichthyol. Res. 46(3): 303–308.

de Carvalho, M. R.

1996. Higher-level elasmobranch phylogeny, basal squaleans, and paraphyly. Pages 35–62 *in* M. L. J. Stiassny, L. R. Parenti, and G. D. Johnson, eds. Interrelationhips of fishes. Academic Press, San Diego.

DeCicco, A. L.

1992. Long-distance movements of anadromous Dolly Varden between Alaska and the U.S.S.R. Arctic 45(2): 120–123.

1997. Movements of postsmolt anadromous Dolly Varden in northwestern Alaska. Am. Fish. Soc. Symp. 19: 175–183.

Dees, L. T.

1961. Sturgeons. U.S. Fish Wildl. Serv. Fishery Leaflet 526. 8 pp.

DeLacy, A. C., and W. M. Chapman.

1935. Notes on some elasmobranchs of Puget Sound, with descriptions of their egg cases. Copeia 1935(2): 63–67.

Dick, M. H., and I. M. Warner.

1982. Pacific sand lance, *Ammodytes hexapterus* Pallas, in the Kodiak Island group, Alaska. Syesis 15: 43–50.

Dobrovol'skii, A. D., A. S. Ionin, and G. B. Udintsev.

1959. History of the exploration of the Bering Sea. *In* P. L. Bezrukov, ed. Geographical description of the Bering Sea. Bottom relief and sediments. Trans. Oceanol. Inst. Acad. Sci. USSR 29: 2–13. [Translation by Israel Prog. Sci. Transl., Jerusalem, 1964.]

Docker, M. F., J. H. Youson, R. J. Beamish, and R. H. Devlin.

1999. Phylogeny of the lamprey genus *Lampetra* inferred from mitochrondrial cytochrome *b* and ND3 gene sequences. Can. J. Fish. Aquat. Sci. 56: 2340–2349.

Dodimead, A. J., F. Favorite, and T. Hirano.

1963. Salmon of the north Pacific Ocean. Part II: Review of oceanography of the Subarctic Pacific Region. Int. North Pac. Fish. Comm. Bull. 13: 195 pp.

Dolganov, V. N.

1982. New records for *Rhinoraja longicauda* (Rajidae, Elasmobranchii) and *Hydrolagus barbouri* (Chimaeridae, Holocephali). J. Ichthyol. [English transl. Vopr. Ikhtiol.] 22(4): 143–145.

1983a. Skaty semeystva Rajidae tikhookeanskogo poberezh'ya Severnoy Ameriki [Skates of the family Rajidae of the Pacific coast of North America]. Izv. Tikhookean. Nauchno-Issled. Inst. Rybn. Khoz. Okeanogr. (TINRO) 107: 56–72. [In Russian.]

1983b. Rukovodstvo po opredeleniyu khryashchevykh ryb dal'nevostochnykh morei SSSR i sopredel'nykh vod [Manual for identification of cartilaginous fishes of Far East seas of USSR and adjacent waters]. TINRO, Vladivostok. 92 pp. [In Russian.]

1985. New species of skates of the family Rajidae from the northwestern Pacific Ocean. J. Ichthyol. [English transl. Vopr. Ikhtiol.] 25(3): 121–132.

1999. Geographical and bathymetric distribution of the skates of the Rajidae family in the Far Eastern seas of Russia and adjacent waters]. J. Ichthyol. 39(4): 340–342 [English transl. Vopr. Ikhtiol. 39(3): 428–430].

2001. Origin and distribution of skates of the suborder Rajoidei of the far east seas of Russia. J. Ichthyol. 41(5): 354–361.

Douglas, M. R., P. C. Brunner, and L. Bernatchez.

1999. Do assemblages of *Coregonus* (Teleostei: Salmoniformes) in the central Alpine region of Europe represent species flocks? Mol. Ecol. 8: 589–603.

Drake, D. E., D. A. Cacchione, R. D. Muench, and C. H. Nelson.

1980. Sediment transport in Norton Sound, Alaska. Mar. Geol. 36: 97–126.

Dryfoos, R. L.

1961. Four range extensions of fishes from the northeastern Pacific. Copeia 1961(4): 476–477.

Dudnik, Yu. I., and V. N. Dolganov.

1992. Distribution and abundance of fish on the continental slopes of the Sea of Okhotsk and of the Kuril Islands during the summer of 1989. J. Ichthyol. [English transl. Vopr. Ikhtiol.] 32(9): 58–76.

Dudnik, Yu. I., L. S. Kodolov, and V. I. Polutov.

1998. On the distribution and reproduction of *Anoplopoma fimbria* off the Kuril Islands and Kamchatka. J. Ichthyol. 38(1): 12–17 [English transl. Vopr. Ikhtiol. 38(1): 16–21].

Dunn, J. R.

1983. Development and distribution of the young of northern smoothtongue, *Leuroglossus schmidti* (Bathylagidae), in the northeast Pacific, with comments on the systematics of the genus *Leuroglossus* Gilbert. U.S. Natl. Mar. Fish. Serv. Fish. Bull. 81(1): 23–40.

Dunn, J. R.

1996a. Charles H. Gilbert, pioneer ichthyologist and fishery biologist. U.S. Natl. Mar. Fish. Serv. Mar. Fish. Rev. 58(1–2): 1–2.

1996b. Charles Henry Gilbert (1859–1928), Naturalist-in-Charge: the 1906 North Pacific expedition of the steamer *Albatross*. U.S. Natl. Mar. Fish. Serv. Mar. Fish. Rev. 58(1–2): 17–28.

1997. Charles Henry Gilbert (1859–1928): pioneer ichthyologist of the American West. Pages 265–278 *in* T. W. Pietsch and W. D. Anderson, eds. Collection building in ichthyology and herpetology. Am. Soc. Ichthyol. Herpetol., Spec. Publ. 3.

Dymond, J. R.

1943. The coregonine fishes of northwestern Canada. Roy. Ontario Mus. Zool. 24: 171–232. [Reprinted from Trans. Roy. Canadian Inst. 24(2): 171–231.]

1964. A history of ichthyology in Canada. Copeia 1964(1): 2–33.

Eagle, R. J.

1969. First records from the northeastern Pacific of the deep-sea ophidioid fish *Parabassogigas grandis*. J. Fish. Res. Board Can. 26(6): 1680–1685.

Ebeling, A. W.

1962. Melamphaidae. I. Systematics and zoogeography of the species of the bathypelagic fish genus *Melamphaes* Günther. Dana-Rep. Carlsberg Found. 58. 164 pp.

1975. A new Indo-Pacific bathypelagic-fish species of *Poromitra* and a key to the genus. Copeia 1975(2): 306–315.

Ebeling, A. W., and G. M. Cailliet.

1990. The vertical distribution and feeding habits of two common midwater fishes (*Leuroglossus stilbius* and *Stenobrachius leucopsarus*) off Santa Barbara, Calif. Coop. Ocean. Fish. Invest. Rep. 31: 106–123.

Ebeling, A. W., and W. H. Weed, III.

1973. Order Xenoberyces (Stephanoberyciformes). Pages 397–478 *in* Fishes of the western North Atlantic. Mem. Sears Found. Mar. Res., New Haven, 1(6).

Ebert, D. A.

1986. Aspects on the biology of hexanchid sharks along the California coast. Pages 437–449 *in* T. Uyeno, R. Arai, T. Taniuchi, and K. Matsuura, eds. Indo-Pacific fish biology. Proceedings of the Second International Conference on Indo-Pacific Fishes. Ichthyological Society of Japan, Tokyo.

1989. Life history of the sevengill shark, *Notorynchus cepedianus* Person, in two northern California bays. Calif. Fish Game 75(2): 102–112.

Ebert, D. A., L. J. V. Compagno, and L. J. Natanson.

1987. Biological notes on the Pacific sleeper shark, *Somniosus pacificus* (Chrondrichthyes: Squalidae). Calif. Fish Game 73(2): 117–123.

Efimkin, A. Ya., and V. I. Radchenko.

1991. State of food resources and distribution of epipelagic fish in the western Bering Sea in fall. Sov. J. Mar. Biol. [English transl. Biol. Morya] 17(1): 18–25.

Ege, V.

1953. Paralepididae I (*Paralepis* and *Lestidium*). Taxonomy, ontogeny, phylogeny and distribution. Dana-Rep. Carlsberg Found. 40. 184 pp.

Eigenmann, C. H., and C. H. Beeson.

1894. A revision of the fishes of the subfamily Sebastinae of the Pacific coast of America. Proc. U.S. Natl. Mus. 17(1009): 375–407.

Eigenmann, C. H., and R. S. Eigenmann.

1892. New fishes from western Canada. Am. Nat. 26(311): 961-964.

Eitner, B. J.

1995. Systematics of the genus *Alopias* (Lamniformes: Alopiidae) with evidence for the existence of an unrecognized species. Copeia 1995(3): 562–571.

Elliott, H. W.

1882. A monograph of the seal-islands of Alaska. U.S. Commission of Fish and Fisheries, Special Bull. 176. Reprinted, with additions, from the report of the fisheries industries of the tenth census. Washington, Government Printing Office. 176 pp., 29 pls.

Ellis, D. V.

1962. Observations on the distribution and ecology of some Arctic fish. Arctic 15(3): 179–189.

Ellis, R., and J. E. McCosker.

1991. Great white shark. Harper-Collins Publ., New York. 270 pp.

Ellson, J. G., D. E. Powell, and H. H. Hildebrand.

1950. Exploratory fishing expedition to the northern Bering Sea in June and July, 1949. U.S. Dep. Inter. Fish Wildl. Serv. Fish. Leafl. 369. 56 pp.

Emmett, R. L., S. A. Hinton, S. L. Stone, and M. E. Monaco.

1991. Distribution and abundance of fishes and invertebrates in West Coast estuaries. Vol. 2. Species life history summaries. ELMR Rep. 8. NOAA/NOS Strategic Environmental Assessments Division, Rockville, Maryland. 329 pp.

Endo, H., and O. Okamura.

1992. New records of the abyssal grenadiers *Coryphaenoides armatus* and *C. yaquinae* from the western North Pacific. Jpn. J. Ichthyol. 38(4): 433–437.

Endo, H., D. Tsutsui, and K. Amaoka.

1994. Range extensions of two deep-sea macrourids *Coryphaenoides filifer* and *Squalogadus modificatus* to the Sea of Okhotsk. Jpn. J. Ichthyol. 41(3): 330–333.

Endo, H., M. Yabe, and K. Amaoka.

1993. Occurrence of the macrourid alevins genera *Albatrossia* and *Coryphaenoides* in the northern North Pacific Ocean. Jpn. J. Ichthyol. 40(2): 219–226.

Eschmeyer, W. N.

1990. Catalog of the genera of Recent fishes. California Academy of Sciences, San Francisco. 697 pp.

Eschmeyer, W. N., T. Abe, and S. Nakano.

1979. *Adelosebastes latens,* a new genus and species of scorpionfish from the North Pacific Ocean (Pisces, Scorpaenidae). Uo (Jpn. Soc. Ichthyol.) 30: 77–84, pl. 1.

Eschmeyer, W. N., editor.

1998. Catalog of fishes. California Academy of Sciences, San Francisco. 2,905 pp., 3 volumes and CD.

2001. Catalog of fishes, online version. Updated 24 April 2001. Address: http://www.calacademy.org/research/ichthyology/catalog/.

Eschmeyer, W. N., and E. S. Herald.

1983. A field guide to Pacific Coast fishes of North America from the Gulf of Alaska to Baja California. Peterson Field Guide 28. Houghton Mifflin, Boston. 336 pp., 48 pls.

Essipov, V. K. (Yessipov, V. K.)

1937. O rybakh polyarnogo basseyna i prilegayushchikh k nemu glubin [On the fishes of the polar basin and adjacent deepwater regions]. Probl. Arktiki 1937(4): 85–97. [In Russian; English summary.]

Everett, R. J., R. L. Wilmot, and C. C. Krueger.

1997. Population genetic structure of Dolly Varden from Beaufort Sea drainages of northern Alaska and Canada. Am. Fish. Soc. Symp. 19: 240–249.

Evermann, B. W., and E. L. Goldsborough.

1907. The fishes of Alaska. Bull. Bur. Fish. (for 1906) 26: 219–360, pls. 14–42.

Evermann, B. W., and H. M. Smith.

1896. The whitefishes of North America. U.S. Fish Commission, Report of the Commissioner of Fish and Fisheries for 1894: 283–324, pls. 11–28.

Fadeev, N. S.

1978. Rasprostranenie i sistematika tikhookeanskikh paltusovidnykh kambal roda *Hippoglossoides* [Distribution and systematics of Pacific flatfishes of the genus *Hippoglossoides*]. Izv. Tikhookean. Nauchno-Issled. Inst. Rybn. Khoz. Okeanogr. (TINRO) 102: 3–18. [Translation by S. Pearson, Natl. Mar. Fish. Serv., 1984.]

1987. Severotikhookeanskie kambaly (rasprostranenie i biologiya) [North Pacific flatfishes (distribution and biology)]. Moscow. 175 pp. [Cited in Lindberg and Fedorov 1993.]

Fassett, H. C.

1905. Records of the dredging and other collecting and hydrographic stations of the fisheries steamer *Albatross* in 1903. Rep. U.S. Fish Comm. (for 1903) 29: 123–138.

Favorite, F., A. J. Dodimead, and K. Nasu.

1976. Oceanography of the Subarctic Pacific Region, 1960–71. Int. North Pac. Fish. Comm. Bull. 33. 187 pp.

Favorite, F., T. Laevastu, and R. R. Straty.

1977. Oceanography of the northeastern Pacific Ocean and eastern Bering Sea, and relations to various living marine resources. U.S. Department of Commerce, NOAA, NMFS, RACE, Seattle, Washington. 280 pp.

Fechhelm, R. G., P. C. Craig, J. S. Baker, and B. J. Gallaway.

1985. Fish distribution and use of nearshore waters in the northeastern Chukchi Sea. U.S. Dep. Commer., NOAA, and U.S. Dep. Inter., Minerals Manage. Serv., OCSEAP Final Rep. 32: 121-298.

Fedorov, V. V.
1966. Novyy vid likoda, *Lycodes andriashevi* Fedorov, sp. n. (Pisces, Zoarcidae) iz Beringova morya [A new species of eelpout, *Lycodes andriashevi* Fedorov n. sp. (Pisces, Zoarcidae), from the Bering Sea]. Vopr. Ikhtiol. vol. 6, part 1(38): 160-164. [In Russian; and transl. by B. A. Sheiko, 1999, for Point Stephens Research, Auke Bay, Alaska.]
1967. Opisaniye *Notosudis adleri* sp. n. (Pisces, Notosudide) novogo vida ryb iz Beringova morya [Description of *Notosudis adleri* sp. n. (Pisces, Notosudidae), a new species from the Bering Sea]. Vopr. Ikhtiol. 7: 967–978. [In Russian; and translation by B. A. Sheiko, 1999, for Point Stephens Research, Auke Bay, Alaska.]
1973a. Ichthyofauna of the continental slope of the Bering Sea and some aspects of its origin and development. Izv. Tikhookean. Nauchno-Issled. Inst. Rybn. Khoz. Okeanogr. (TINRO) 87: 3–41. [Fish. Mar. Serv. Transl. Ser. 3345. Department of the Environment, Fisheries and Marine Service, Pacific Biological Station, Nanaimo, B.C., Canada. 70 pp.]
1973b. A list of Bering Sea fish. Izv. Tikhookean. Nauchno-Issled. Inst. Rybn. Khoz. Okeanogr. (TINRO) 87: 42–71. [Translation by Transl. Bur., Multilingual Services Div., Dep. Secretary of State Canada.]
1975. Description of a new genus and species of a zoarcid fish *Puzanovia rubra,* gen. et sp. n. (Pisces, Zoarcidae) from the northern part of the Pacific Ocean. J. Ichthyol. [English transl. Vopr. Ikhtiol.] 15(4): 527–531.
1976. Novye dannye ob ugrevidnykh likodakh (Pisces, Zoarcidae) severo-zapadnoy chasti Tikhogo okeana i Beringova morya [New data on the eel-like likods (Pisces, Zoarcidae) from the northwestern Pacific Ocean and Bering Sea]. Izv. Tikhookean. Nauchno-Issled. Inst. Rybn. Khoz. Okeanogr. (TINRO) 100: 3–18. [In Russian; and translation by M. Eric Anderson, August 1979.]
1994. *Gigantactis elsmani*, the first report of a species of the family Gigantactinidae (Lophiformes) from the Sea of Okhotsk. J. Ichthyol. 34(8): 132–134 [English transl. Vopr. Ikhtiol. 34(3): 414–415].

Fedorov, V. V., and A. P. Andriyashev.
1993. *Lycenchelys makushok* sp. nova (Perciformes, Zoarcidae) from bathyal depths of the Kuril-Kamchatka Trench. J. Ichthyol. 33(5): 130–135 [English transl. Vopr. Ikhtiol. 33(1): 133–136].

Fedorov, V. V., and N. V. Parin.
1994. *Derepodichthys alepidotus* Gilbert (Zoarcidae), an inhabitant of the hydrothermal zone in the Gulf of California. J. Ichthyol. 34(8): 126–131 [English transl. Vopr. Ikhtiol. 34(3): 411–413].
1998. [Pelagic and benthopelagic fishes of the Pacific waters of Russia]. VNIRO, Moscow. 154 pp. [In Russian. Selections translated by B. A. Sheiko, 2000, for Point Stephens Research, Auke Bay, Alaska.]

Fedorov, V. V., and B. A. Sheiko.
2002. Species composition and structure of the marine ichthyofauna of the Commander Islands. *In* Mammals, birds, and fishes of the Commander Islands. Moscow State University, Russia. [In Russian; translation of manuscript provided by B. A. Sheiko.] In press.

Fedoryako, B. I.
1976. Materialy po sistematike i rasprostraneniyu "okeanicheskikh Cheilodipteridae" [Materials on the systematics and distribution of the "oceanic Cheilodipteridae"]. Tr. Inst. Okeanol. Akad. Nauk SSSR 104: 156–190. [In Russian; and English transl. prepared for Smithsonian Institution, NMNH, by Saad Publications, Karachi, Pakistan, 1987, 65 pp.]

Ferguson, A., and G. Cailliet.
1990. Sharks and rays of the Pacific coast. Monterey Bay Aquarium, Monterey, Calif. 64 pp.

Fernholm, B.
1985. The lateral line system of cyclostomes. Pages 113–122 *in* R. E. Foreman, A. Gorbman, J. M. Dodd, and R. Olsson, eds. Evolutionary biology of primitive fishes. Plenum Press, New York.
1998. Hagfish systematics. Pages 33–44 *in* J. M. Jørgensen, J. P. Lomholt, R. E. Weber, and H. Malte, eds. The biology of hagfishes. Chapman & Hall, London.

Ferraris, C. J., Jr., and W. N. Eschmeyer.
2000. Book review. International Code of Zoological Nomenclature: fourth edition. Copeia 2000(3): 907–908.

Findeis, E. K.
1997. Osteology and phylogenetic interrelationships of sturgeons (Acipenseridae). Environ. Biol. Fishes 48: 73–126.

Fink, W. L.
1985. Phylogenetic interrelationships of the stomiid fishes (Teleostei: Stomiiformes). Misc. Publ. Mus. Zool. Univ. Michigan 171. 127 pp.

Fischer, W., F. Krupp, W. Schneider, C. Sommer, K. E. Carpenter, and V. H. Niem.
1995. Guía FAO para la identificación para los fines de la pesca. Pacifico centro-oriental. Vol. II, Vertebrados, Parte 1, pp. 647–1200. Vol. III, Vertebrados, Parte 2, pp. 1201–1813.

Fitch, J. E.
1951. Studies and notes on some California marine fishes. Calif. Fish Game 37(2): 111–120.
1953. Extensions to known geographical distributions of some marine fishes on the Pacific coast. Calif. Fish Game 39(4): 539–552.

Fitch, J. E.
1963. A review of the fishes of the genus *Pleuronichthys*. Contrib. Sci. (Los Angel.) 76. 33 pp.
1964. The ribbonfishes (family Trachipteridae) of the eastern Pacific Ocean, with a description of a new species. Calif. Fish Game 50(4): 228–240.
1966a. Fishes and other marine organisms taken during deep trawling off Santa Catalina Island, March 3–4, 1962. Calif. Fish Game 52(3): 216–219.
1966b. The poacher *Asterotheca infraspinata* (Gilbert) added to California's marine fauna, and a key to Californian Agonidae (Pisces). Calif. Fish Game 52(2): 121–124.
1973. The taxonomic status of the genus *Asterotheca* and clarification of the distribution of *Bathyagonus pentacanthus* (Pisces: Agonidae). Copeia 1973(4): 815–817.

Fitch, J. E., and R. J. Lavenberg.
1968. Deep-water teleostean fishes of California. California Natural History Guides 25. University of California Press, Berkeley. 155 pp.
1975. Tidepool and nearshore fishes of California. California Natural History Guides 38. University of California Press, Berkeley. 156 pp.

Fitch, J. E., and S. A. Schultz.
1978. Some rare and unusual occurrences of fish off California. Calif. Fish Game 64(2): 74–92.

Fitzinger, L. J. F. J., and J. J. Heckel.
1836. Monographische Darstellung der Gattung *Acipenser*. Ann. Wien. Mus. Naturges. 1(12): 261–326, pls. 25–30.

Follett, W. I.
1970. Benthic fishes cast ashore by giant waves near Point Joe, Monterey County, California. Proc. Calif. Acad. Sci., Ser. 4, 37(15): 473–488.

Follett, W. I., and L. J. Dempster.
1963. Relationships of the percoid fish *Pentaceros richardsoni* Smith, with description of a specimen from the coast of California. Proc. Calif. Acad. Sci., Ser. 4, 32(10): 315–338.

Foreman, R. E., A. Gorbman, J. M. Dodd, and R. Olsson, editors.
1985. Evolutionary biology of primitive fishes. Plenum Press, New York. 463 pp.

Foreman, T. J., and Y. Ishizuka.
1990. Giant bluefin tuna off southern California, with a new California size record. Calif. Fish Game 76(3): 181–186.

Forey, P. L., and P. Janvier.
1993. Agnathans and the origin of jawed vertebrates. Nature 361: 129–134.
1994. Evolution of the early vertebrates. Am. Scientist 82:554–565.

Forey, P. L., D. T. J. Littlewood, P. Ritchie, and A. Meyer.
1996. Interrelationships of elopomorph fishes. Pages 175–191 *in* M. L. J. Stiassny, L. R. Parenti, and G. D. Johnson, eds. Interrelationhips of fishes. Academic Press, San Diego.

Forrester, C. R., A. Peden, and R. M. Wilson.
1972. First records of the striped bass, *Morone saxatilis,* in British Columbia waters. J. Fish. Res. Board Can. 29(3):337–339.

Forrester, C. R., H. Tsuyuki, S. Fuke, J. E. Smith, and J. Schnute.
1977. Flathead sole (*Hippoglossoides*) in the North Pacific. J. Fish. Res. Board Can. 34(4): 455–462.

Forrester, C. R., and R. M. Wilson.
1963. A further record of the blacktail snailfish, *Careproctus melanurus* Gilbert, from British Columbia waters. J. Fish. Res. Board Can. 20(4): 1095–1096.

Francis, M. P., J. D. Stevens, and P. R. Last.
1988. New records of *Somniosus* (Elasmobranchii: Squalidae) from Australasia, with comments on the taxonomy of the genus. N. Z. J. Mar. Freshw. Res. 22: 401–409.

Francis, R. C., A. C. Havens, and M. A. Bell.
1985. Unusual lateral plate variation of threespine sticklebacks (*Gasterosteus aculeatus*) from Knik Lake, Alaska. Copeia 1985(3): 619–624.

Fritzsche, R. A.
1980. Revision of the eastern Pacific Syngnathidae (Pisces: Syngnathiformes), including both recent and fossil forms. Proc. Calif. Acad. Sci. 42(6): 181–227.

Frost, K. J., and L. F. Lowry.
1983. Demersal fishes and invertebrates trawled in the northeastern Chukchi and western Beaufort seas, 1976–77. U.S. Dep. Commer., NOAA Tech. Rep. NMFS SSRF–764. 22 pp.

Fruge, D. J., and D. W. Wiswar.
1991. First records of the Bering wolffish, *Anarhichas orientalis,* for the Alaskan Beaufort Sea. Can. Field-Nat. 105(1): 107–109.

Fujii, E., and T. Uyeno.
1976. On three species of the myctophid genus *Notoscopelus* found in western North Pacific. Jpn. J. Ichthyol. 22(4): 227–233.

Fuller, P. L., L. G. Nico, and J. D. Williams.
1999. Nonindigenous fishes introduced into inland waters of the United States. Am. Fish. Soc., Spec. Publ. 27. 613 pp.

Garman, S.
1892. The Discoboli. Cyclopteridae, Liparopsidae, and Liparididae. Mem. Mus. Comp. Zool. (Harvard) 14(2). 96 pp., 13 pls.
1899. Reports on an exploration off the west coasts of Mexico, Central and South America, and off the Galapagos Islands, in charge of Alexander Agassiz, by the U.S. Fish Commission steamer *Albatross* during 1891, Lieut.-Commander Z. L. Tanner, U.S.N., commanding. XXVI. The fishes. Mem. Mus. Comp. Zool. (Harvard) 24. 431 pp., 97 pls. (2 vols.).

Garrick, J. A. F.
1967. Revision of sharks of genus *Isurus* with description of a new species (Galeoidea, Lamnidae). Proc. U.S. Natl. Mus. 118: 663–694.

Gartner, J. V., Jr., R. E. Crabtree, and K. J. Sulak.
1997. Feeding at depth. Pages 115–193 *in* D. J. Randall and A. P. Farrell, eds. Deep-sea fishes. Academic Press, San Diego.

Gharrett, A. J., A. K. Gray, and J. Heifetz.
2001. Identification of rockfish (*Sebastes* spp.) by restriction site analysis of the mitochondrial ND-3/ND-4 and 12S/16S rRNA gene regions. U.S. Natl. Mar. Fish. Serv. Fish. Bull. 99(1): 49–62.

Gibbs, R. H., Jr.
1960. *Alepisaurus brevirostris,* a new species of lancetfish from the western North Atlantic. Breviora 123. 14 pp.

Gibbs, R. H., Jr., and B. B. Collette.
1967. Comparative anatomy and systematics of the tunas, genus *Thunnus.* U.S. Fish Wildl. Serv. Fish. Bull. 66(1): 65–130.

Gibbs, R. H., Jr., and N. J. Wilimovsky.
1966. Family Alepisauridae. Pages 482–497 *in* Fishes of the western North Atlantic. Mem. Sears Found. Mar. Res., New Haven, 1(5).

Gilbert, C. H.
1889. Description of a new species of *Bathymaster* (*B. jordani*) from Puget's Sound and Alaska. Proc. U.S. Natl. Mus. 11(753): 554.
1890. Scientific results of explorations by the U.S. Fish Commission steamer *Albatross.* No. XII.—A preliminary report on the fishes collected by the steamer *Albatross* on the Pacific coast of North America during the year 1889, with descriptions of twelve new genera and ninety-two new species. Proc. U.S. Natl. Mus. 13(797): 49–126.
1892. Scientific results of explorations by the U.S. Fish Commission steamer *Albatross.* No. XXII.—Descriptions of thirty-four new species of fishes collected in 1888 and 1889, principally among the Santa Barbara Islands and in the Gulf of California. Proc. U.S. Natl. Mus. 14(880): 539–566.
1896. Appendix 6.—The ichthyological collections of the steamer *Albatross* during the years 1890 and 1891. Rep. U.S. Fish Comm. (for 1893) 19: 393–476, pls. 20-35 [3 subtitles: Bering Sea, California, and Alaska and Washington]. [1895 on title page, published in 1896; dates inadvertently switched by Springer and Anderson (1997).]
1897. Descriptions of twenty-two new species of fishes collected by the steamer *Albatross*, of the United States Fish Commission. Proc. U.S. Natl. Mus. 19(1115): 437–457, pls. 49–55.
1904. Notes on fishes from the Pacific coast of North America. Proc. Calif. Acad. Sci., Ser. 3, 3(9): 255–271, pls. 25–29.
1905. Section II. The deep-sea fishes. *In* D. S. Jordan and B. W. Evermann, eds. The aquatic resources of the Hawaiian Islands. Part II. Bull. U.S. Fish Comm. (for 1903) 23: 577–713, pls. 66–101.
1912. A new genus and species of cottoid fish from Departure Bay, Vancouver Island. Contrib. Can. Biol., Mar. Biol. Sta. Can., 1906–1910: 215–216.
1913. Descriptions of two new fishes of the genus *Triglops* from the Atlantic Coast of North America. Proc. U.S. Natl. Mus. 44(1963): 465–468, pl. 64.
1915. Fishes collected by the United States fisheries steamer *Albatross* in southern California in 1904. Proc. U.S. Natl. Mus. 48: 305–380, pls. 14–22.

Gilbert, C. H., and C. V. Burke.
1912a. Fishes from Bering Sea and Kamchatka. Bull. U.S. Bur. Fish. (for 1910) 30: 31–96.
1912b. New cyclogasterid fishes from Japan. Proc. U.S. Natl. Mus. 42(1907): 351–380, pls. 41–48.

Gilbert, C. H., and F. Cramer.

1897. Report on the fishes dredged in deep water near the Hawaiian Islands, with descriptions and figures of twenty-three new species. Proc. U.S. Natl. Mus. 19(1114): 403–435, pls. 36–48.

Gilbert, C. H., and C. L. Hubbs.

1916. Report on the Japanese macruroid fishes collected by the United States Fisheries steamer *Albatross* in 1906, with a synopsis of the genera. Proc. U.S. Natl. Mus. 51(2149): 135–214, pls. 8–11.

Gilbert, C. H., and J. C. Thompson.

1905. Notes on the fishes of Puget Sound. Proc. U.S. Natl. Mus. 28(1414): 973–987.

Gill, T. N.

1859. Description of new generic types of cottoids, from the collection of the North Pacific exploring expedition under Com. John Rodgers. Proc. Acad. Nat. Sci. Phila. 11: 165–166.

1861a. Catalogue of the fishes of the eastern coast of North America, from Greenland to Georgia. Proc. Acad. Nat. Sci. Phila. 13 (Suppl.): 1–63.

1861b. Notes on some genera of fishes of the western coast of North America. Proc. Acad. Nat. Sci. Phila. 13: 164–168.

1864. Note on the family of stichaeoids. Proc. Acad. Nat. Sci. Phila. 16: 208–211.

1872. Arrangement of the families of fishes. Smithson. Misc. Collect. 247: i–xlvi, 1–49.

1880. On the identity of the genus *Leurynnis,* Lockington, with *Lycodopsis,* Collett. Proc. U.S. Natl. Mus. (for 1880) 3: 247–248.

1882. Bibliography of the fishes of the Pacific coast of the United States to the end of 1879. Bull. U.S. Natl. Mus. 11. 73 pp.

1883. Diagnosis of new genera and species of deep-sea fish-like vertebrates. Proc. U.S. Natl. Mus. 6: 253–260.

1891a. On the relations of Cyclopteroidea. Proc. U.S. Natl. Mus. 13(834): 361–376, pls. 28–30.

1891b. The osteological characteristics of the family Hemitripteridae. Proc. U.S. Natl. Mus. 13(835): 377–380, pl. 31.

1903. On the relations of the fishes of the family Lamprididae or opahs. Proc. U.S. Natl. Mus. 26(1340): 915–924.

1909. Angler fishes: their kinds and ways. Smithsonian Report for 1908: 565–615.

Gill, T. N., and C. H. Townsend.

1897. Diagnoses of new species of fishes found in Bering Sea. Proc. Biol. Soc. Wash. 11: 231–234.

Gill, T. N., and J. A. Ryder.

1883. Diagnoses of new genera of nemichthyoid eels. Proc. U.S. Natl. Mus. (for 1883) 6: 260–262.

Gillespie, G. E.

1993. An updated list of the fishes of British Columbia, and those of interest in adjacent waters, with numeric code designations. Can. Tech. Rep. Fish. Sci. 1918. 116 pp.

Gillespie, G. E., and M. W. Saunders.

1994. First verified record of the shortfin mako shark, *Isurus oxyrhinchus* [*sic*], and second records or range extensions for three additional species, from British Columbia waters. Can. Field-Nat. 108(3): 347–350.

Gillespie, G. E., R. D. Stanley, and B. M. Leaman.

1993. Cruise details and biological information from the juvenile rockfish surveys aboard the R/V *Ricker,* May 13–25, 1991, and the F/V *Island Sun,* June 3–11, 1991. Can. Data Rep. Fish. Aquat. Sci. 920.

Gilmore, R. G.

1993. Reproductive biology of lamnoid sharks. Environ. Biol. Fishes 38: 95-114.

Glubokov, A. I., and A. M. Orlov.

2000. Some morphological parameters and feedings characteristics of two species from the family Zoarcidae from the western part of the Bering Sea. J. Ichthyol. 40(8): 651–660 [English transl. Vopr. Ikhtiol. 40(5): 683–692].

Glubokovskiy, M. K., and I. A. Chereshnev.

1981. Unresolved problems concerning the phylogeny of chars (*Salvelinus*) of the Holarctic: I. Migratory chars of the East-Siberian Sea basin. J. Ichthyol. [English transl. Vopr. Ikhtiol.] 21(5): 1–15.

Godsil, H. C.

1945. The Pacific tunas. Calif. Fish Game 31(4): 185–194.

Goldman, K. J.

1997. Regulation of body temperature in the white shark, *Carcharodon carcharias*. J. Comp. Physiol. B 167: 423–429.

Gon, O., and P. C. Heemstra, editors.

1990. Fishes of the Southern Ocean. J.L.B. Smith Institute of Ichthyology, Grahamstown, South Africa. 462 pp.

Goode, G. B.

1884. The fisheries and fishery industries of the United States. Section I. Natural history of useful aquatic animals. Text vol., 895 pp. Plates vol., 277 pls. Government Printing Office, Washington, D.C.

Goode, G. B., and T. H. Bean.
1895a. Scientific results of explorations by the U.S. Fish Commission steamer *Albatross.* No. XXVIII.—On Cetomimidae and Rondeletiidae, two new families of bathybial fishes from the northwestern Atlantic. Proc. U.S. Natl. Mus. 17(1012): 451–454, pl. 17.
1895b. Scientific results of explorations by the U.S. Fish Commission steamer *Albatross.* No. XXIX.—A revision of the order Heteromi, deep-sea fishes, with a description of the new generic types *Macdonaldia* and *Lipogenys.* Proc. U.S. Natl. Mus. 17(1013): 455–470, pl. 18.
1896. Oceanic ichthyology, a treatise on the deep-sea and pelagic fishes of the world, based chiefly upon the collections made by the steamers *Blake, Albatross,* and *Fish Hawk* in the northwestern Atlantic, with an atlas containing 417 figures. Smithsonian Contributions to Knowledge 30 (Contr. 981), 553 pp.; 31 (Contr. 982), 123 pls. [1895 on title pages, 1896 publication date established by Cohen (1963a); dates inadvertently switched by Springer and Anderson (1997).]

Goodrich, E. S.
1909. Vertebrata craniata, first fascicle, cyclostomes and fishes. Part 9 *in* E. R. Lankester, ed. A treatise on zoology. A. & C. Black, London.

Gorbunova, N. N.
1964. Razmnozhenie i razvitie polucheschuinykh bychkov (Cottidae, Pisces). [Reproduction and development of hemilepidotine sculpins (Cottidae, Pisces)]. Tr. Inst. Okeanol., Akad. Nauk SSSR 73: 235–251. [In Russian.]

Gordon, D. J., D. F. Markle, and J. E. Olney.
1984. Ophidiiformes: development and relationships. Pages 308–319 *in* H. G. Moser et al., eds. Ontogeny and systematics of fishes. Am. Soc. Ichthyol. Herpetol., Spec. Publ. 1.

Gorshkov, S. A., Ye. A. Dorofeyeva, V. A. Klyukanov, and N. I. Kulikova.
1979. Osteological features of the Pacific salmon of the genus *Oncorhynchus.* J. Ichthyol. [English transl. Vopr. Ikhtiol.] 19(6): 1–19.

Gosline, W. A.
1971. Functional morphology and classification of teleostean fishes. University Press of Hawaii, Honolulu. 208 pp.

Gotshall, D. W.
1989. Pacific coast inshore fishes, 3rd edition. Sea Challengers, Monterey, Calif. 96 pp.

Gotshall, D. W., and T. Jow.
1965. Sleeper sharks (*Somniosus pacificus*) off Trinidad, California, with life history notes. Calif. Fish Game 51(4): 294–298.

Grande, L., and W. E. Bemis.
1996. Interrelationships of Acipenseriformes, with comments on "Chondrostei." Pages 85–115 *in* M. L. J. Stiassny, L. R. Parenti, and G. D. Johnson, eds. Interrelationhips of fishes. Academic Press, San Diego.

Grebnitskii, N.
1897. Spisok ryb, vodyashchiksya u beregov Komandorskikh ostrovov i p-ova Kamchatka [List of fishes found on the coast of the Commander Islands and Kamchatka peninsula]. Vestn. Ryboprom. 6-7: 323–339.

Green, A. H.
1891. The economic fishes of British Columbia. Pap. Comm. Nat. Hist. Soc. B.C. 1: 6–17.

Green, J. M.
1970. The banded gunnel, *Pholis fasciatus,* in Newfoundland. J. Fish. Res. Board Can. 27: 2120–2121.

Green, J. M., and L. R. Mitchell.
1997. Biology of the fish doctor, an eelpout, from Cornwallis Island, Northwest Territories, Canada. Am. Fish. Soc. Symp. 19: 140–147.

Greene, C. W.
1899. The phosphorescent organs of the toadfish, *Porichthys notatus* Girard. J. Morphol. 15: 667–696.

Greenwood, P. H., D. E. Rosen, S. H. Weitzman, and G. S. Meyers.
1966. Phyletic studies of teleostean fishes, with a provisional classification of living forms. Bull. Am. Mus. Nat. Hist. 131: 339–456.

Gregory, W. K.
1933. Fish skulls: a study of the evolution of natural mechanisms. Trans. Am. Philos. Soc. 23(2): 75–481.

Gregory, W. K., and H. C. Raven.
1934. Notes on the anatomy and relationships of the ocean sunfish (*Mola mola*). Copeia 1934(4): 145–151, 1 pl.

Grewe, P. M., N. Billington, and P. D. N. Hebert.
1990. Phylogenetic relationships among members of *Salvelinus* inferred from mitochondrial DNA divergence. Can. J. Fish. Aquat. Sci. 47: 984–991.

Grey, M.

1955. The fishes of the genus *Tetragonurus* Risso. Dana-Rep. Carlsberg Found. 41: 75 pp.

1956. The distribution of fishes found below a depth of 2000 meters. Fieldiana Zool. 36(2): 75–337.

1964. Family Gonostomatidae. Pages 78–240 *in* Fishes of the western North Atlantic. Mem. Sears Found. Mar. Res., New Haven, 1(4).

Grigor'ev, S. S.

1992. Larvae of Snyder's prickleback, *Chirolophis snyderi* (Stichaeidae). J. Ichthyol. 32(4): 145–149 [English transl. Vopr. Ikhtiol. 31(6): 1025–1028].

Grinols, R. B.

1965. Check-list of the offshore marine fishes occurring in the northeastern Pacific Ocean, principally off the coasts of British Columbia, Washington, and Oregon. M.S. thesis, University of Washington, Seattle. 217 pp.

1966a. Addition of adult anglerfish, *Chaenophryne parviconus* Regan and Trewavas (Pisces: Oneirodidae), to the eastern subarctic Pacific Ocean. Calif. Fish Game 52(3): 161–165.

1966b. Northeastern Pacific records of *Anoplogaster cornuta* Valenciennes (Anoplogasteridae: Pisces) and *Cyema atrum* Günther (Cyemidae: Pisces). J. Fish. Res. Board Can. 23(2): 305–307, 2 pls.

1966c. Northern records of the zoarcid, *Melanostigma pammelas,* in the eastern subarctic Pacific region. Copeia 1966(3): 601–602.

1966d. Southern occurrence of *Acantholiparis opercularis* Gilbert and Burke in the eastern subarctic Pacific region. J. Fish. Res. Board Can. 23(6): 935–937.

1969. A new species of *Acantholiparis* (Pisces: Liparidae) from the eastern subarctic Pacific region, with distribution notes for the genus. J. Fish. Res. Board Can. 26(5): 1237–1242.

Grinols, R. B., and H. Heyamoto.

1965. Description, distribution, and taxonomic status of two species of Alepocephalidae from the northeastern Pacific Ocean. J. Fish. Res. Board Can. 22(5): 1151–1164.

Gross, M. R.

1987. Evolution of diadromy in fishes. Am. Fish. Soc. Symp. 1: 14–25.

Gruchy, C. G.

1969. Canadian records of the warty poacher *Occa verrucosa,* with notes on the standardization of plate terminology in Agonidae. J. Fish. Res. Board Can. 26(6): 1467–1472.

1970. *Occella impi,* a new species of sea poacher from British Columbia with notes on related species (Agonidae, Pisces). J. Fish. Res. Board Can. 27(6): 1109–1114.

Gudkov, P. K.

1994a. Sympatric char of the genus *Salvelinus* from lakes of the Chukotsk Peninsula. J. Ichthyol. 34(2): 48–59 [English transl. Vopr. Ikhtiol. 33(5): 618–625].

1994b. Biology of the Taranets char from Lake Achchen. J. Ichthyol. 34(5): 1–11 [English transl. Vopr. Ikhtiol. 34(1): 58–63].

1998. Bering Sea *Dallia pectoralis* in the Chukchi Peninsula. J. Ichthyol. 38(2): 199–203 [English transl. Vopr. Ikhtiol. 38(2): 252–256].

1999. Relict population of the round whitefish *Prosopium cylindraceum* from the eastern Chukotski Peninsula. J. Ichthyol. 39(4): 294–300 [English transl. Vopr. Ikhtiol. 39(3): 340–346].

Gunter, G.

1942. A list of the fishes of the mainland of North and Middle America recorded from both freshwater and sea water. Am. Midl. Nat. 28(2): 305–326.

Günther, A.

1862. Catalogue of the fishes in the British Museum. Catalogue of the Acanthopterygii, Pharyngognathi and Anacanthini in the collection of the British Museum. Vol. 4. xxi + 534 pp. [Not seen.]

1874. Descriptions of new species of fishes in the British Museum. Ann. Mag. Nat. Hist., Ser. 4, 14(83): 368–371; 14(84): 453–455.

1877. Preliminary notes on new fishes collected in Japan during the expedition of H.M.S. *Challenger.* Ann. Mag. Nat. Hist., Ser. 4, 20(119): 433–446.

1878. Preliminary notices of deep-sea fishes collected during the voyage of H.M.S. *Challenger.* Ann. Mag. Nat. Hist., Ser. 5, 2(7/8/9): 17–28 (July), 179–187 (August), 248–251 (September).

1880a. An introduction to the study of fishes. Adam and Charles Black, Edinburgh. 720 pp.

1880b. Report on the shore fishes procured during the voyage of H.M.S. *Challenger* in the years 1873–1876. *In* Report of the scientific results of the voyage of H.M.S. *Challenger* during the years 1873–76. Part 6: 1–82, pls. 1–32. [Reprinted in 1963 as Historiae Naturalis Classica, Vol. 28, by J. Cramer.]

1887. Report on the deep-sea fishes collected by H.M.S. *Challenger* during the years 1873–76. *In* Report of the scientific results of the voyage of H.M.S. *Challenger* during the years 1873–76. Part 57: 1–335, pls. 1–73. [Reprinted in 1963 as Historiae Naturalis Classica, Vol. 28, by J. Cramer.]

Haas, G. R., and J. D. McPhail.
1991. Systematics and distributions of Dolly Varden (*Salvelinus malma*) and bull trout (*Salvelinus confluentus*) in North America. Can. J. Fish. Aquat. Sci. 48(11): 2191–2211.

Haedrich, R. L.
1967. The stromateoid fishes: systematics and a classification. Bull. Mus. Comp. Zool. (Harvard) 135(2):31–139.
1997. Distribution and population ecology. Pages 79–114 *in* D. J. Randall and A. P. Farrell, eds. Deep-sea fishes. Academic Press, San Diego.

Hagerman, F. B.
1951. An easy method of separating king and silver salmon. Calif. Fish Game 37(1): 53–54.

Haglund, T. R., D. G. Buth, and R. Lawson.
1992a. Allozyme variation and phylogenetic relationships of Asian, North American, and European populations of the threespine stickleback, *Gasterosteus aculeatus*. Copeia 1992(2): 432–443.
1992b. Allozyme variation and phylogenetic relationships of Asian, North American, and European populations of the ninespine stickleback, *Pungitius pungitius*. Pages 438–452 *in* R. L. Mayden, ed. Systematics, historical ecology, and North American freshwater fishes. Stanford University Press, Stanford, California.

Haldorson, L., and P. Craig.
1984. Life history and ecology of a Pacific-Arctic population of rainbow smelt in coastal waters of the Beaufort Sea. Trans. Am. Fish. Soc. 113: 33–38.

Hall, J. V., W. E. Frayer, and B. O. Wilen.
1994. Status of Alaska wetlands. U.S. Fish and Wildlife Service, Anchorage, Alaska. 33 pp.

Hamada, K.
1981. The red devil, *Lyconectes aleutensis* Gilbert, taken in the Gulf of Alaska by a shrimp trawler. Bull. Fac. Fish. Hokkaido Univ. 32(1): 7–9.
1982. A lumpsucker, *Eumicrotremus birulai,* caught in the Gulf of Alaska. Bull. Fac. Fish. Hokkaido Univ. 33(4): 201–205.

Hameedi, M. J., and A. S. Naidu, editors.
1986. The environment and resources of the southeastern Chukchi Sea: a review of scientific literature. U.S. Department of Commerce and U.S. Department of the Interior, Outer Continental Shelf Environmental Assessment Program, Anchorage, Alaska. 103 pp.

Hamlett, W. C., editor.
1999. Sharks, skates, and rays. The biology of elasmobranch fishes. Johns Hopkins University Press, Baltimore. 515 pp.

Hammann, M. G., and M. A. Cisneros-Mata.
1989. Range extension and commercial capture of the northern anchovy, *Engraulis mordax* Girard, in the Gulf of California, Mexico. Calif. Fish Game 75(1): 49–53.

Hampton, M. A., P. R. Carlson, H. J. Lee, and R. A. Feely.
1986. Chapter 5. Geomorphology, sediment and sedimentary processes. Pages 93–143 *in* D. W. Hood and S. T. Zimmerman, eds. The Gulf of Alaska: physical environment and biological resources. U.S. Department of Commerce, NOAA, Ocean Assessments Division, Alaska Office, and U.S. Department of the Interior, Minerals Management Service, Alaska OCS Region. U.S. Government Printing Office, Washington, D.C.

Hanavan, M. G., and G. K. Tanonaka.
1959. Eperimental fishing to determine distribution of salmon in the North Pacific Ocean and Bering Sea, 1956. U.S. Fish Wildl. Serv., Spec. Sci. Rep. Fish. 302. 22 pp.

Hardisty, M. W.
1979. Biology of the cyclostomes. Chapman & Hall, London. 428 pp.

Hardisty, M. W., and I. C. Potter.
1971. The behavior, ecology and growth of larval lampreys, pages 85–125. The general biology of adult lampreys, pages 127–205. Paired species, pages 249–277. *In* M. W. Hardisty and I. C. Potter, eds. The biology of lampreys. Vol. 1. Academic Press, New York.

Hardy, G. S.
1983. A revision of the fishes of the family Pentacerotidae (Perciformes). N. Z. J. Zool. 10: 177–220.

Hare, S. R., N. J. Mantua, and R. C. Francis.
1999. Inverse production regimes: Alaska and West Coast Pacific salmon. Fisheries (Bethesda) 24(1): 6–14.

Hargreaves, N. B., D. M. Ware, and G. A. McFarlane.
1994. Return of Pacific sardine (*Sardinops sagax*) to the British Columbia coast in 1992. Can. J. Fish. Aquat. Sci. 51: 460–463.

Harling, W. R.

1966. Northern range extension record for the pygmy rockfish (*Sebastodes wilsoni*). J. Fish. Res. Board Can. 23(12): 1967–1968.

Harold, A. S.

1993. Phylogenetic relationships of the sternoptychid *Argyropelecus* (Teleostei: Stomiiformes). Copeia(1): 123–133.

1994. A taxonomic revision of the sternoptychid genus *Polyipnus* (Teleostei: Stomiiformes) with an analysis of phylogenetic relationships. Bull. Mar. Sci. 54(2): 428–534.

1998. Phylogenetic relationships of the Gonostomatidae (Teleostei: Stomiiformes). Bull. Mar. Sci. 62(3): 715–741.

Harold, A. S., and S. H. Weitzman.

1996. Interrelationships of stomiiform fishes. Pages 333–353 *in* M. L. J. Stiassny, L. R. Parenti, and G. D. Johnson, eds. Interrelationhips of fishes. Academic Press, San Diego.

Harris, C. K., and A. C. Hartt.

1977. Assessment of pelagic and nearshore fish in three bays on the east and south coasts of Kodiak Island, Alaska, final report. U.S. Dep. Commer. and U.S. Dep. Inter., Environmental Assessment of the Alaskan Continental Shelf, Quarterly Reports, April–June, 1: 483–688.

Harrison, R. C.

1993. Data report: 1991 bottom trawl survey of the Aleutian Islands area. NOAA Tech. Memo. NMFS-AFSC-12. 144 pp.

Harry, R. R.

1952. Deep-sea fishes of the Bermuda Oceanographic Expeditions. Families Cetomimidae and Rondeletiidae. Zoologica (New York) 37(5): 55–72, 1 pl.

Hart, J. L.

1943. News item. *Katsuwonus* and *Trachipterus* in British Columbia. Fish. Res. Board Can. Pac. Progr. Rep. 56: 16.

1973. Pacific fishes of Canada. Fish. Res. Board Can. Bull. 180. 740 pp.

Hays, A. N.

1952. David Starr Jordan, a bibliography of his writings, 1871–1931. Stanford University Press, California. 195 pp.

Healey, M. C.

1991. Life history of chinook salmon (*Oncorhynchus tshawytscha*). Pages 311–393 *in* C. Groot and L. Margolis, eds. Pacific salmon life histories. UBC Press, Vancouver.

Heard, W. R.

1966. Observations on lampreys in the Naknek River system of southwest Alaska. Copeia 1966(2): 332–339.

1991. Life history of pink salmon (*Oncorhynchusgorbuscha*). Pages 119–230 *in* C. Groot and L. Margolis, eds. Pacific salmon life histories. UBC Press, Vancouver.

Heard, W. R., and W. L. Hartman.

1965. Pygmy whitefish *Prosopium coulteri* in the Naknek River system of southwest Alaska. U.S. Fish Wildl. Serv. Fish. Bull. 65(3): 555–579.

Heard, W. R., R. L. Wallace, and W. L. Hartman.

1969. Distributions of fishes in fresh water of Katmai National Monument, Alaska, and their zoogeographical implications. U.S. Fish Wildl. Serv. Spec. Sci. Rep. Fish. 590: 20 pp.

Hedgpeth, J. W.

1945. The United States Fish Commission steamer *Albatross*. The American Neptune 5(1): 5–26.

1947. The steamer *Albatross*. Scientific Monthly 65(1): 17–22.

1957a. Classification of marine environments. Geol. Soc. Am. Mem. 67: 17–27.

1957b. Marine biogeography. Geol. Soc. Am. Mem. 67: 359–382.

Heist, E. J., J. A. Musick, and J. E. Graves.

1996. Genetic population structure of the shortfin mako (*Isurus oxyrinchus*) inferred from restriction fragment length polymorphism analysis of mitochondrial DNA. Can. J. Fish. Aquat. Sci. 53: 583–588.

Hemphill, D. V., and W. I. Follett.

1958. First record of the agonid fish *Pallasina barbata aix* Starks from California. Calif. Fish Game 44(3): 281–283.

Hennig, W.

1966. Phylogenetic systematics. University of Illinois Press, Urbana. 363 pp.

Herring, P. J.

1976. Carotenoid pigmentation of whale fishes. Deep-Sea Res. 23: 235–238.

Herring, P. J., and J. G. Morin.

1978. Bioluminescence in fishes. Pages 273–329 *in* P. J. Herring, ed. Bioluminescence in action. Academic Press, London.

Heyamoto, H., and C. R. Hitz.
1962. Northern range extensions of three species of rockfish (*Sebastodes rubrivinctus, S. aurora,* and *S. helvomaculatus*). Copeia 1962(4): 847–848.

Hildebrand, S. F.
1939. An annotated list of the fishes collected on the several expeditions to Greenland, the Fox Basin region, and the coast of Labrador by Captain R. A. Bartlett, from 1925 to 1935. Medd. Gronl. 125(1): 1–12.
1941. Hugh McCormick Smith and the Bureau of Fisheries. Copeia 1941(4): 216–220.

Hitz, C. R.
1964. Observations on egg cases of the big skate (*Raja binoculata* Girard) found in Oregon coastal waters. J. Fish. Res. Board Can. 21(4): 851–854.
1977. Field identification of the northeastern Pacific rockfish (*Sebastodes*). U.S. Fish Wildl. Serv. Circ. 203, revised in 1977 for Foreign Observer Program. 62 pp.

Hitz, C. R., and R. R. French.
1966. Occurrence of pomfret (*Brama japonica*) in the northeastern Pacific Ocean. U.S. Bur. Commer. Fish., Fishery and Industrial Res. 3(1): 1–7.

Hobbie, J. E.
1984. The ecology of tundra ponds of the Arctic coastal plain: a community profile. U.S. Department of the Interior, U.S. Fish and Wildlife Service, FWS/OBS-83-25. U.S.Government Printing Office, Washington, D.C. 40 pp.

Hocutt, C. H., and E. O. Wiley, editors.
1986. The zoogeography of North American freshwater fishes. John Wiley & Sons, New York. 866 pp.

Hoff, G. R.
2000. Biology and ecology of threaded sculpin, *Gymnocanthus pistilliger,* in the eastern Bering Sea. U.S. Natl. Mar. Fish. Serv. Fish. Bull. 98(4): 711–722.

Holeton, G. F.
1974. Metabolic cold adaptation of polar fish: fact or artefact? Physiol. Zool. 47(3): 137–152.

Hood, D. W., editor.
1986. Processes and resources of the Bering Sea shelf. Continental Shelf Res. 5(1/2). 291 pp.

Hood, D. W., and D. C. Burrell, editors.
1976. Assessment of the Arctic marine environment: selected topics. University of Alaska, Fairbanks, Inst. Mar. Sci., Occas. Publ. 4. 468 pp.

Hood, D. W., and J. A. Calder.
1981. Consideration of environmental risks and research opportunities on the eastern Bering Sea shelf. Pages 1299–1322 *in* D. W. Hood and J. A. Calder, eds. The eastern Bering Sea shelf: oceanography and resources. U.S. Department of Commerce, NOAA, and U.S. Department of the Interior, U.S. Bureau of Land Management. Distributed by University of Washington Press, Seattle, Washington.

Hood, D. W., and J. A. Calder, editors.
1981. The eastern Bering Sea shelf: oceanography and resources. U.S. Department of Commerce, NOAA, and U.S. Department of the Interior, U.S. Bureau of Land Management. Distributed by University of Washington Press, Seattle, Washington. Vol. 1, pp. 1–626. Vol. 2, pp. 627–1339.

Hood, D. W., and E. J. Kelly, editors.
1974. Oceanography of the Bering Sea with emphasis on renewable resources. University of Alaska, Fairbanks, Inst. Mar. Sci., Occas. Publ. 2. 623 pp.

Hood, D. W., and S. T. Zimmerman, editors.
1986. The Gulf of Alaska: physical environment and biological resources. U.S. Department of Commerce, NOAA, Ocean Assessments Division, Alaska Office, and U.S. Department of the Interior, Minerals Management Service, Alaska OCS Region. U.S. Government Printing Office, Washington, D.C. 655 pp.

Hopkins, D.
1994. Beringia revisited. Pages 21–23 *in* R. H. Meehan, V. Sergienko, and G. Weller, eds. Bridges of science between North America and the Russian Far East. Proceedings of the 45th Arctic Science Conference, 25–26 August 1994, Anchorage, Alaska. Arctic Division, AAAS, Fairbanks, Alaska.

Horn, M. H.
1970. Systematics and biology of the stromateoid fishes of the genus *Peprilus.* Bull. Mus. Comp. Zool. (Harvard) 140(5): 165–262.
1977. Observations on feeding, growth, locomotor behavior, and buoyancy of a pelagic stromateoid fish, *Icichthys lockingtoni.* U.S. Natl. Mar. Fish. Serv. Fish. Bull. 75(2): 453–456.
1984. Stromateoidei: development and relationships. Pages 620–628 *in* H. G. Moser et al., eds. Ontogeny and systematics of fishes. Am. Soc. Ichthyol. Herpetol., Spec. Publ. 1.

Hoshino, K.

2001. New hypothesis of intrarelationships of the Pleuronectiformes (Teleostei) based on myological and osteological characters. Page 80 *in* Program book and abstracts. Joint Meeting of Ichthyologists and Herpetologists, State College, Pennsylvania, 5–10 July 2001.

Houston, J.

1988. Status of the green sturgeon, *Acipenser medirostris,* in Canada. Can. Field-Nat. 102(2):286-290.

Houston, J., and D. E. McAllister.

1990a. Status of the Bering wolffish, *Anarhichas orientalis,* in Canada. Can. Field-Nat. 104(1): 20–23.

1990b. Status of the blackline prickleback, *Acantholumpenus mackayi,* in Canada. Can. Field-Nat. 104(1): 24–28.

Howe, K. M., and S. L. Richardson.

1978. Taxonomic review and meristic variation in marine sculpins (Osteichthyes: Cottidae) of the northeast Pacific Ocean. Final report, NOAA-NMFS Contract 03-78-MO2-120, 1 January 1978 to 30 September 1978. Northwest and Alaska Fisheries Center, 2725 Montlake Blvd. E., Seattle, WA 98112. 142 pp.

Howes, G. J.

1991a. Anatomy, phylogeny and taxonomy of the gadoid fish genus *Macruronus* Günther, 1873, with a revised hypothesis of gadoid phylogeny. Bull. Br. Mus. (Nat. Hist.) Zool. 51(1): 77–110.

1991b. Biogeography of gadoid fishes. J. Biogeogr. 18: 595–622.

Hubbard, J. D., and W. G. Reeder.

1965. New locality records for Alaskan fishes. Copeia 1965(4): 506–508.

Hubbs, C. L.

1915. Flounders and soles from Japan collected by the United States Bureau of Fisheries steamer *Albatross* in 1906. Proc. U.S. Natl. Mus. 48: 449–496, pls. 25–27.

1925. A revision of the osmerid fishes of the North Pacific. Proc. Biol. Soc. Wash. 38: 49–55.

1926a. Notes on the gobioid fishes of California, with descriptions of two new genera. Occas. Pap. Mus. Zool. Univ. Mich. 169. 6 pp., 1 pl.

1926b. Descriptions of new genera of cottoid fishes related to *Artedius*. Occas. Pap. Mus. Zool. Univ. Mich. 170. 16 pp.

1926c. A revision of the fishes of the subfamily Oligocottinae. Occas. Pap. Mus. Zool. Univ. Mich. 171. 18 pp.

1927. Notes on the blennioid fishes of western North America. Pap. Mich. Acad. Sci. Arts Lett. 7(1926): 351–394.

1928. A checklist of the marine fishes of Oregon and Washington. J. Pan-Pac. Res. Inst. 3(3): 9–16.

1932. The Japanese flounders of the genera *Tanakius, Microstomus* and *Glyptocephalus.* Occas. Pap. Mus. Zool. Univ. Mich. 249. 8 pp.

1942. Peculiar variants of the agonid fish *Odontopyxis trispinosus.* J. Fish. Res. Board Can. 6(1): 30–36.

1943. John O. Snyder. Copeia 1943(4): 265–266.

1958. *Dikellorhynchus* and *Kanazawaichthys*: nominal fish genera interpreted as based on prejuveniles of *Malacanthus* and *Antennarius,* respectively. Copeia 1958(4): 282–285.

1959. Initial discoveries of fish faunas on seamounts and offshore banks in the eastern Pacific. Pac. Sci. 13(4): 311–316.

1964a. History of ichthyology in the United States after 1950. Copeia 1964(1): 42–60.

1964b. David Starr Jordan. Syst. Zool. 13(4): 195–200.

1967. Occurrence of the Pacific lamprey, *Entosphenus tridentatus,* off Baja California and in streams of southern California, with remarks on its nomenclature. Trans. San Diego Society Nat. Hist. 14: 301–312.

Hubbs, C. L., and W. I. Follett.

1947. *Lamna ditropis,* new species, the salmon shark of the North Pacific. Copeia 1947(3): 194.

1978. Anatomical notes on an adult male of the deep-sea ophidiid fish *Parabassogigas grandis* from off California. Proc. Calif. Acad. Sci. 41(17): 389–399.

Hubbs, C. L., W. I. Follett, and L. J. Dempster.

1979. List of the fishes of California. Occas. Pap. Calif. Acad. Sci. 133. 51 pp.

Hubbs, C. L., and L. C. Hubbs.

1954. Data on the life history, variation, ecology, and relationships of the kelp perch, *Brachyistius frenatus,* an embiotocid fish of the Californias. Calif. Fish Game 40(2): 183–198.

Hubbs, C. L., and R. Ishiyama.

1968. Methods for the taxonomic study and description of skates (Rajidae). Copeia 1968(3): 483–491.

Hubbs, C. L., and K. F. Lagler.

1958. Fishes of the Great Lakes region, revised edition. Cranbrook Inst. Sci. Bull. 26. 213 pp.

Hubbs, C. L., G. W. Mead, and N. J. Wilimovsky.
1953. The widespread, probably antitropical distribution and the relationship of the bathypelagic iniomous fish *Anotopterus pharao.* Bull. Scripps Inst. Oceanogr. 6(5): 173–189.

Hubbs, C. L., and I. C. Potter.
1971. Distribution, phylogeny, and taxonomy. Pages 1–65 *in* M. W. Hardisty and I. C. Potter, eds. The biology of lampreys. Vol. 1. Academic Press, New York.

Hubbs, C. L., and L. P. Schultz.
1929. The northward occurrence of southern forms of marine life along the Pacific coast in 1926. Calif. Fish Game 15(3): 234–241.
1932. A new blenny from British Columbia with records of two other fishes new to the region. Contrib. Can. Biol. Fish. 7(22): 319–324.
1934a. *Elephantichthys copeianus,* a new cyclopterid fish from Alaska. Copeia 1934(1): 21–26, 1 pl.
1934b. The reef liparid fishes inhabiting the west coast of the United States. J. Pan-Pac. Res. Inst. 9(4): 2–7.
1939. A revision of the toadfishes referred to *Porichthys* and related genera. Proc. U.S. Natl. Mus. 86(3060): 473–496.
1941. Contribution to the ichthyology of Alaska, with descriptions of two new fishes. Occas. Pap. Mus. Zool. Univ. Mich. 431. 31 pp.

Hubbs, C. L., and N. J. Wilimovsky.
1964. Distribution and synonymy in the Pacific Ocean, and variation, of the Greenland halibut, *Reinhardtius hippoglossoides* (Walbaum). J. Fish. Res. Board Can. 21(5): 1129–1154.

Hubbs, C. L., and R. L. Wisner.
1980. Revision of the sauries (Pisces, Scomberesocidae) with descriptions of two new genera and one new species. U.S. Natl. Mar. Fish. Serv. Fish. Bull. 77(3): 521–566.

Hughes, G. W., and R. K. Kashino.
1984. First records of the agonid fish *Sarritor frenatus* from British Columbia. Syesis 17: 101.

Hughes, S. E.
1981. Initial U.S. exploration of nine Gulf of Alaska seamounts and their associated fish and shellfish resources. U.S. Natl. Mar. Fish. Serv. Mar. Fish. Rev. (January): 26–33.

Hulet, W. H., and C. R. Robins.
1989. The evolutionary significance of the leptocephalus larva. Pages 669–677 *in* Fishes of the western North Atlantic. Mem. Sears Found. Mar. Res., New Haven, 1(9), Vol. 2.

Humann, P.
1996. Coastal fish identification: California to Alaska. New World Publications, Inc., Jacksonville, Florida. 205 pp.

Humphreys, R. L., Jr., G. A. Winans, and D. T. Tagmi.
1989. Synonymy and life history of the North Pacific pelagic armorhead, *Pseudopentaceros wheeleri* Hardy (Pisces: Pentacerotidae). Copeia 1989(1):142–153.

Hunter, J. G., S. T. Leach, D. E. McAllister, and M. B. Steigerwald.
1984. A distributional atlas of records of the marine fishes of Arctic Canada in the National Museums of Canada and Arctic Biological Station. Syllogeus (Ottawa) 52. 35 pp.

Hureau, J. C., and T. Monod, editors.
1973. Check-list of the fishes of the north-eastern Atlantic and of the Mediterranean. Vol. 1: 683 pp. Vol. 2: 331 pp. Unesco, Paris.

Ida, H., P. Sirimontaporn, and S. Monkolprasit.
1994. Comparative morphology of the fishes of the family Ammodytidae, with a description of two new genera and two new species. Zool. Stud. 33(4): 251–277.

Il'inskii, E. N., and V. I. Radchenko.
1992. Distribution and migration of smooth lumpsucker in the Bering Sea. Sov. J. Mar. Biol. (Engl. Transl. Biol. Morya) 18(3/4): 75–79.

Il'inskiy, Ye. N.
1991. Long-term changes in the composition of bottom fish catches on the continental slope in the western part of the Bering Sea, along the Pacific seaboard of Kamchatka and the Kurils. J. Ichthyol. [English transl. Vopr. Ikhtiol.] 31(3): 117–127.

Il'inskiy, Ye. N., A. A. Balanov, and O. A. Ivanov.
1995. Rare mesopelagic fishes—*Scopelosaurus harryi, Arctozenus rissoi, Magnisudis atlantica,* and *Tactostoma macropus* from the northwest Pacfic. 2. Spatial distribution and biology. J. Ichthyol. [English transl. Vopr. Ikhtiol.] 35(6): 1–19.

Inada, T.

1989. Current status of the systematics of Merlucciidae. Pages 197–207 *in* D. M. Cohen, ed. Papers on the systematics of gadiform fishes. Nat. Hist. Mus. Los Angeles County Sci. Ser. 32.

International Commission on Zoological Nomenclature.

1985. International Code of Zoological Nomenclature, 3rd edition. University of California Press, Berkeley. 338 pp.

1992. Opinion 1673. LIPARIDAE Gill, 1861 (Osteichthyes, Scorpaeniformes: spelling confirmed. Bull. Zool. Nomencl. 49(1): 95–96.

1993. Corrigenda. Bull. Zool. Nomencl. 50(4): 311.

1999. International Code of Zoological Nomenclature, 4th edition. The International Trust for Zoological Nomenclature 1999, c/o The Natural History Museum, Cromwell Road, London SW7 5BD, UK. 306 pp.

Isaacson, P. A.

1965. Southern range extension of the tomcod, *Microgadus proximus.* Calif. Fish Game 51(1): 58.

Isakson, J. S., C. A. Simenstad, and R. L. Burgner.

1971. Fish communities and food chains in the Amchitka area. BioScience 21(12): 666–670.

Isakson, J. S., J. P. Houghton, D. E. Rogers, and S. S. Parker.

1986. Fish use of inshore habitats north of the Alaska Peninsula: June–September 1984 and June–July 1985. U.S. Dep. Commer., NOAA, and U.S. Dep. Inter., Minerals Manage. Serv., OCSEAP Final Rep. 55: 1–380.

Ishida, M.

1994. Phylogeny of the suborder Scorpaenoidei (Pisces: Scorpaeniformes). Bull. Nansei Natl. Fish. Res. Inst. 27: 1–112.

Ishihara, H.

1987. Revision of the western North Pacific species of the genus *Raja.* Jpn. J. Ichthyol. 34(3): 241–285.

1990. The skates and rays of the western North Pacific: an overview of their fisheries, utilization, and classification. Pages 485–497 *in* H. L. Pratt, Jr., S. H. Gruber, and T. Taniuchi, eds. Elasmobranchs as living resources: advances in the biology, ecology, systematics, and the status of the fisheries. NOAA Tech. Rep. NMFS 90.

Ishihara, H., and R. Ishiyama.

1985. Two new North Pacific skates (Rajidae) and a revised key to *Bathyraja* in the area. Jpn. J. Ichthyol. 32(2): 143–179.

1986. Systematics and distribution of the skates of the North Pacific (Chondrichthyes, Rajoidei). Pages 269–280 *in* T. Uyeno, R. Arai, T. Taniuchi, and K. Matsuura, eds. Indo-Pacific fish biology. Proceedings of the Second International Conference on Indo-Pacific Fishes. Ichthyological Society of Japan, Tokyo.

Ishiyama, R.

1952. Studies on the rays and skates belonging to the family Rajidae, found in Japan and adjacent regions. 4. A revision of three genera of Japanese rajids, with descriptions of one new genus and four new species mostly occurring in northern Japan. J. Shimonoseki Coll. Fish. 2(1): 1–34, pls. 1–4.

Ishiyama, R.

1967. Fauna Japonica. Rajidae (Pisces). Biogeographical Society of Japan, Tokyo. 84 pp., 32 pls.

Ishiyama, R., and C. L. Hubbs.

1968. *Bathyraja,* a genus of Pacific skates (Rajidae) regarded as phyletically distinct from the Atlantic genus *Breviraja.* Copeia 1968(2): 407–410.

Ishiyama, R., and H. Ishihara.

1977. Five new species of skates in the genus *Bathyraja* from the western North Pacific, with reference to their interspecific relationships. Jpn. J. Ichthyol. 24(2): 71–90.

Issacs, J. D., and R. A. Schwartzlose.

1975. Active animals of the deep sea floor. Sci. Am. 233(4): 85–91.

Ivanov, O. A.

1997. Composition and biomass of the fishes and cephalopods of the upper mesopelagial of the Kuril and Kamchatka waters of the Pacific Ocean. J. Ichthyol. 37(2): 147–168 [English transl. Vopr. Ikhtiol. 37(2): 167–178].

Iwamoto, T.

1979. Eastern Pacific macrourine grenadiers with seven branchiostegal rays (Pisces: Macrouridae). Proc. Calif. Acad. Sci. 42(5): 135–179.

Iwamoto, T., and D. L. Stein.

1974. A systematic review of the rattail fishes (Macrouridae: Gadiformes) from Oregon and adjacent waters. Occas. Pap. Calif. Acad. Sci. 111. 79 pp.

Iwamoto, T., and Yu. I. Sazonov.

1988. A review of the southeastern Pacific *Coryphaenoides* (sensu lato) (Pisces, Gadiformes, Macrouridae). Proc. Calif. Acad. Sci. 45(3): 35–82.

Izmyatinskii, D. V., P. V. Kalchugin, and N. L. Aseeva.

1999. First occurrence of *Brama japonica* (Bramidae) in waters off Primorye. J. Ichthyol. 39(7): 547 [English transl. Vopr. Ikhtiol. 39(4): 557].

Jackson, K. L., and J. S. Nelson.

1998. *Ambophthalmos*, a new genus for "*Neophrynichthys*" *angustus* and "*Neophrynichthys*" *magnicirrus*, and the systematic interrelationships of the fathead sculpins (Cottoidei, Psychrolutidae). Can. J. Zool. 76: 1344–1357.

James, G. D., T. Inada, and I. Nakamura.

1988. Revision of the oreosomatid fishes (Family Oreosomatidae) from the southern oceans, with a description of a new species. N. Z. J. Zool. 15: 291–326.

Jamieson, I. G., D. M. Blouw, and P. W. Colgan.

1992. Parental care as a constraint on male mating success in fishes: a comparative study of threespine and white sticklebacks. Can. J. Zool. 70: 956–962.

Janssen, J., R. H. Gibbs, Jr., and P. R. Pugh.

1989. Association of *Caristius* sp. (Pisces: Caristiidae) with a siphonophore, *Bathyphysa conifera*. Copeia 1989(1): 198–201.

Janssen, J., N. W. Pankhurst, and G. R. Harbison.

1992. Swimming and body orientation of *Notolepis rissoi* in relation to lateral line and visual function. J. Mar. Biol. Assoc. U.K. 72(4): 877–886.

Jarvela, L. E., and L. K. Thorsteinson.

1999. The epipelagic fish community of Beaufort Sea coastal waters, Alaska. Arctic 52(1): 80–94.

Jean, Y., A. E. Peden, and D. E. McAllister.

1981. English, French and scientific names of Pacific fish of Canada. British Columbia Provincial Museum, Heritage Record 13. 51 pp.

Jensen, A. S.

1902. Ichthyologiske studier. III. Om en ny art af slaegten *Lycodes*. Vidensk. Medd. Dansk Naturhist. Foren. Khobenhavn 1901: 191–215.

1904. The North-European and Greenland Lycodinae. Dan. Ingolf-Exped. 2(4): 1–99, 10 pls.

1942. Contributions to the ichthyofauna of Greenland 1–3. Spolia Zool. Mus. Haun. 2. 44 pp.

1944. Contributions to the ichthyofauna of Greenland 4–7. Spolia Zool. Mus. Haun. 4. 60 pp., 8 pls.

1948. Contributions to the ichthyofauna of Greenland 8–24. Spolia Zool. Mus. Haun. 9. 182 pp., 4 pls.

1952a. Recent finds of Lycodinae in Greenland waters. Medd. Grønl. 142(7): 1–28, pls. 1–2.

1952b. On the Greenland species of the genera *Artediellus, Cottunculus,* and *Gymnocanthus* (Teleosti, Scleroparei, Cottidae). Medd. Grønl. 142(7): 1–21, pl. 1.

Johnson, C. R.

1969. Contributions to the biology of the showy snailfish, *Liparis pulchellus* (Liparidae). Copeia 1969(4): 830–835.

Johnson, G. D.

1986. Scombroid phylogeny: an alternative hypothesis. Bull. Mar. Sci. 39(1): 1–41.

1993. Percomorph phylogeny: progress and problems. Bull. Mar. Sci. 52(1): 3–28.

Johnson, G. D., and C. Patterson.

1993. Percomorph phylogeny: a survey of acanthomorphs and a new proposal. Bull. Mar. Sci. 52(1): 554–626.

1996. Relationships of lower euteleostean fishes. Pages 251–332 *in* M. L. J. Stiassny, L. R. Parenti, and G. D. Johnson, eds. Interrelationhips of fishes. Academic Press, San Diego.

Johnson, R.

1980. The arctic charr, *Salvelinus alpinus*. Pages 15-98 *in* E. K. Balon, ed. Charrs: salmonid fishes of the genus *Salvelinus*. Dr. W. Junk, The Hague.

Johnson, R. K.

1969. A review of the fish genus *Kali* (Perciformes: Chiasmodontidae). Copeia 1969(2): 386–391.

1974. A revision of the alepisauroid family Scopelarchidae (Pisces: Myctophiformes). Fieldiana Zool. 66. 249 pp.

1982. Fishes of the families Evermannellidae and Scopelarchidae: systematics, morphology, interrelationships, and zoogeography. Fieldiana Zool., new series 12. 252 pp.

Johnson, R. K., and D. M. Cohen.

1974. Results of the research cruises of FRV Walther Herwig to South America. XXX. Revision of the chiasmodontid fish genera *Dysalotus* and *Kali*, with descriptions of two new species. Arch. Fischereiwiss. 25(1/2): 13–46.

Johnson, S. E.

1918. Osteology of the gruntfish, *Rhamphocottus richardsoni*. J. Morphol. 31(3): 461–477, 4 pls.

Johnson, W. R.

1988. Physical oceanography. Pages 29–38 *in* M. J. Hameedi and A. S. Naidu, eds. The environment and resources of the southeastern Chukchi Sea: a review of scientific literature. U.S. Department of Commerce and U.S. Department of the Interior, Outer Continental Shelf Environmental Assessment Program, Anchorage, Alaska.

Jones, A. C.

1962. The biology of the euryhaline fish *Leptocottus armatus* Girard (Cottidae). Univ. Calif. Publ. Zool. 67(4): 321–367.

Jones, B. C., and G. H. Geen.

1976. Taxonomic reevaluation of the spiny dogfish (*Squalus acanthias* L.) in the northeastern Pacific Ocean. J. Fish. Res. Board Can. 33: 2500–2506.

1977. Observations on the brown cat shark, *Apristurus brunneus* (Gilbert), in British Columbia coastal waters. Syesis 10: 169–170.

Jordan, D. S.

1878. Manual of the vertebrates of the northern United States, including the district east of the Mississippi River and north of North Carolina and Tennessee, exclusive of marine species; 2nd edition, revised and enlarged. Chicago. 407 pp.

1880. Description of new species of North American fishes. Proc. U.S. Natl. Mus. (for 1879) 2: 235–241.

1885. A catalogue of the fishes known to inhabit the waters of North America, north of the Tropic of Cancer, with notes on the species discovered in 1883 and 1884. Rep. U.S. Fish Comm. 13:789–973. [Report published in 1887. Separate in 1885: 185 pp.]

1891. Relations of temperature to vertebrae among fishes. Proc. U.S. Natl. Mus. 14(845): 107–120.

1896. Notes on fishes, little known or new to science. Proc. Cal. Acad. Sci., 2nd Ser., 6: 201–244, pls. 20–43.

1900. Notes on recent fish literature. Am. Nat. 34 (407, Nov.): 897–899.

1903. [Generic names of fishes.] Am. Nat. 37(437, May): 360.

1905. Guide to the study of fishes. Henry Holt & Co., New York. Vol. 1: 624 pp. Vol. 2: 599 pp.

1906. A review of the sand lances or Ammodytidae of the waters of Japan. Proc. U.S. Natl. Mus. 30(1464): 715–719.

1919. New genera of fishes. Proc. Acad. Nat. Sci. Phila. (for 1918) 70: 341–344.

1922. The days of a man: being memories of a naturalist, teacher and minor prophet of democracy. World Book Co., Yonkers-on-Hudson, New York. Vol. 1: 710 pp. Vol. 2: 906 pp.

1923. Note on *Icichthys lockingtoni* Jordan and Gilbert, a pelagic fish from California. Proc. U.S. Natl. Mus. 63(2472): 1–3, pl. 1.

1931. History of zoological explorations of the Pacific coast. Calif. Fish Game 17(2): 156–158.

Jordan, D. S., and B. M. Davis.

1891. A preliminary review of the apodal fishes or eels inhabiting the waters of America and Europe. Rep. U.S. Fish Comm. (for 1888) 16: 581–677.

Jordan, D. S., and B. W. Evermann.

1896a. A check-list of the fishes and fish-like vertebrates of North and Middle America. Rep. U.S. Fish Comm.(for 1895) 21, Append. 5: 207–584.

1896b. The fishes of North and Middle America: a descriptive catalogue of the species of fish-like vertebrates found in the waters of North America, north of the Isthmus of Panama. Part I. U.S. Natl. Mus. Bull. 47. i–lx, 1–1240.

1898. The fishes of North and Middle America: a descriptive catalogue of the species of fish-like vertebrates found in the waters of North America, north of the Isthmus of Panama. Part II. U.S. Natl. Mus. Bull. 47. i–xxx, 1241–2183.

1898. The fishes of North and Middle America: a descriptive catalogue of the species of fish-like vertebrates found in the waters of North America, north of the Isthmus of Panama. Part III. U.S. Natl. Mus. Bull. 47. i–xxiv, 2183a–3136.

1900. The fishes of North and Middle America: a descriptive catalogue of the species of fish-like vertebrates found in the waters of North America, north of the Isthmus of Panama. Part IV. U.S. Natl. Mus. Bull. 47. i–ci, 3137–3313, 392 pls.

Jordan, D. S., B. W. Evermann, and H. W. Clark.

1930. Check list of the fishes and fishlike invertebrates of North and Middle America north of the northern boundary of Venezuela and Columbia. Rep. U.S. Comm. Fish. for 1928, Appendix X. 670 pp. Reprinted by Government Printing Office, Washington, D.C., 1955.

Jordan, D. S., and H. W. Fowler.

1902. A review of the ophidioid fishes of Japan. Proc. U.S. Natl. Mus. 25(1303): 743–766.

Jordan, D. S., and C. H. Gilbert.

1877. On the genera of North American freshwater fishes. Proc. Acad. Nat. Sci. Phila. 26(1338): 897–911.

1880. Description of a new flounder (*Pleuronichthys verticalis*), from the coast of California, with notes on other species. Proc. U.S. Natl. Mus. (for 1880) 3: 49–51.

Jordan, D. S., and C. H. Gilbert.

1880a. Description of a new species of *Sebastichthys* (*Sebastes miniatus*), from Monterey Bay, California. Proc. U.S. Natl. Mus. (for 1880) 3: 70–73.

1880b. Description of a new species of ray (*Raia stellulata*) from Monterey, California. Proc. U.S. Natl. Mus. (for 1880) 3: 133–135.

1880c. Descriptions of new species of *Xiphister* and *Apodichthys,* from Monterey, California. Proc. U.S. Natl. Mus. (for 1880) 3: 135–140.

1880d. Description of two new species of *Sebastichthys* (*Sebastes entomelas* and *Sebastichthys rhodochloris*), from Monterey Bay, California. Proc. U.S. Natl. Mus. (for 1880) 3: 142–146.

1880e. Description of a new agonoid fish (*Brachyopsis xyosternus*), from Monterey Bay, California. Proc. U.S. Natl. Mus. (for 1880) 3: 152–154.

1880f. Description of a new flounder (*Hippoglossoides exilis*) from the coast of California. Proc. U.S. Natl. Mus. (for 1880) 3: 154–156.

1880g. Description of a new species of ray, *Raia rhina,* from the coast of California. Proc. U.S. Natl. Mus. (for 1880) 3: 251–253.

1880h. Description of two new species of fishes, *Ascelichthys rhodorus* and *Scytalina cerdale,* from Neah Bay, Washington Territory. Proc. U.S. Natl. Mus. (for 1880) 3: 264–268.

1880i. Description of two new species of scopeloid fishes, *Sudis ringens* and *Myctophum crenulare,* from Santa Barbara Channel, California. Proc. U.S. Natl. Mus. (for 1880) 3: 273–276.

1880j. Description of two new species of flounders (*Parophrys ischyrus* and *Hippoglossoides elassodon*) from Puget's Sound. Proc. U.S. Natl. Mus. (for 1880) 3: 276–279.

1880k. Description of seven new species of sebastoid fishes, from the coast of California. Proc. U.S. Natl. Mus. (for 1880) 3: 287–298.

1880l. Description of a new embiotocid (*Abeona aurora*), from Monterey, Caliufornia, with notes on a related species. Proc. U.S. Natl. Mus. (for 1880) 3: 299–301.

1880m. Description of a new flounder (*Platysomatichthys stomias*), from the coast of California. Proc. U.S. Natl. Mus. (for 1880) 3: 301–303.

1880n. Description of a new species of deep-water fish (*Icichthys lockingtoni*), from the coast of California. Proc. U.S. Natl. Mus. (for 1880) 3: 305–308.

1880o. Description of a new scorpaenoid fish (*Sebastichthys maliger*), from the coast of California. Proc. U.S. Natl. Mus. (for 1880) 3: 322–324.

1880p. Description of a new scorpaenoid fish (*Sebastichthys proriger*), from Monterey Bay, California. Proc. U.S. Natl. Mus. (for 1880) 3: 327–329.

1880q. Description of a new agonid (*Agonus vulsus*), from the coast of California. Proc. U.S. Natl. Mus. (for 1880) 3: 330–332.

1880r. Description of a new species of notidanoid shark (*Hexanchus corinus*), from the Pacific coast of the United States. Proc. U.S. Natl. Mus. (for 1880) 3: 352–355.

1881a. Description of a new species of *Nemichthys* (*Nemichthys avocetta*), from Puget Sound. Proc. U.S. Natl. Mus. (for 1880) 3: 409–410.

1881b. List of the fishes of the Pacific coast of the United States, with a table showing the distribution of the species. Proc. U.S. Natl. Mus. (for 1880) 3: 452–458.

1881c. Notes on the fishes of the Pacific coast of the United States. Proc. U.S. Natl. Mus. (for 1881) 4: 29–70.

1881d. Description of *Sebastichthys mystinus.* Proc. U.S. Natl. Mus. (for 1881) 4: 70–72.

1881e. Note on *Raia inornata*. Proc. U.S. Natl. Mus. (for 1881) 4: 73–74.

1883. Synopsis of the fishes of North America. Bull. U.S. Natl. Mus. 16. 1,018 pp. [1882 on title page.]

1899. The fishes of Bering Sea. Pages 433–492 *in* D. S. Jordan, ed. The fur seals and fur-seal islands of the North Pacific Ocean, Part 3. Government Printing Office, Washington, D.C.

Jordan, D. S., and D. K. Goss.

1889. A review of the flounders and soles (Pleuronectidae) of America and Europe. Rep. U.S. Fish. Comm. (for1886) 14: 225–342, pls. 1–9.

Jordan, D. S., and A. C. Herre.

1907. A review of the lizard-fishes or Synodontidae of the waters of Japan. Proc. U.S. Natl. Mus. 32(1544): 513–524.

Jordan, D. S., and J. O. Snyder.

1902a. A review of the trachinoid fishes and their supposed allies found in the waters of Japan. Proc. U.S. Natl. Mus. 24(1263): 461–497.

1902b. A review of the salmonoid fishes of Japan. Proc. U.S. Natl. Mus. 24(1265): 567–593.

1902c. A review of the blennioid fishes of Japan. Proc. U.S. Natl. Mus. 25(1293): 441–504.

1902d. On certain species of fishes confused with *Bryostemma polyactocephalum.* Proc. U.S. Natl. Mus. 25(1300): 613–618.

Jordan, D. S., and E. C. Starks.

1895. The fishes of Puget Sound. Proc. Calif. Acad. Sci., Ser. 2, 5: 785–855, pls. 76–104.

1903a. A review of the fishes of Japan belonging to the family of Hexagrammidae. Proc. U.S. Natl. Mus. 26(1348): 1003–1013.

1903b. A review of the synentognathous fishes of Japan. Proc. U.S. Natl. Mus. 26(1319): 525–540.

1904a. A review of the scorpaenoid fishes of Japan. Proc. U.S. Natl. Mus. 27(1351): 91–175, 2 pls.

1904b. A review of the Cottidae or sculpins found in the waters of Japan. Proc. U.S. Natl. Mus. 27(1358): 231–335.

1904c. A review of the Japanese fishes of the family of Agonidae. Proc. U.S. Natl. Mus. 27(1365): 575–599.

1904d. List of fishes dredged by the steamer *Albatross* off the coast of Japan in the summer of 1900, with description of new species and a review of the Japanese Macrouridae. Bull. U.S. Fish Comm. 22: 577–630, pls. 1–8.

1906. A review of the flounders and soles of Japan. Proc. U.S. Natl. Mus. 31(1484): 161–246.

Jordan, D. S., S. Tanaka, and J. O. Snyder.

1913. A catalogue of the fishes of Japan. J. Coll. Sci. Imp. Univ. Tokyo 33(1): 1–497.

Jordan, D. S., and W. F. Thompson.

1914. Record of the fishes obtained in Japan in 1911. Mem. Carnegie Mus. 6(4): 205–313, pls. 24–42.

Jow, T.

1963. A record-size daggertooth taken off northern California. Calif. Fish Game 49(3): 215–216.

Kanayama, T.

1980. Intraspecific variation in the agonid fish, *Sarritor frenatus.* Jpn. J. Ichthyol. 26(4): 364–366.

1981. Scorpaenid fishes from the Emperor Seamount chain. Research Institute of North Pacific Fisheries, Hokkaido University, Special Volume: 119–129.

1991. Taxonomy and phylogeny of the family Agonidae (Pisces: Scorpaeniformes). Mem. Fac. Fish. Hokkaido Univ. 38(1.2). 199 pp.

Kanayama, T., and S. Maruyama.

1979. Agonid fishes, *Anoplagonus occidentalis* and *Bothragonus occidentalis,* from Japanese waters. Jpn. J. Ichthyol. 25(4): 278-282.

Karinen, J. F., B. L. Wing, and R. R. Straty.

1985. Records and sightings of fish and invertebrates in the eastern Gulf of Alaska and oceanic phenomena related to the 1983 El Niño event. Pages 253-267 *in* W. S. Wooster and D. L. Fluharty, eds. El Niño north: Niño effects in the eastern subarctic Pacific Ocean. Washington Sea Grant Program, University of Washington, Seattle.

Karmovskaya (Karmowskaya), E. S.

1977. Izucheniye taksonomii i rasprostraneniya roda *Borodinula* (Nemichthyidae, Osteichthyes) s opisaniem novogo vida [Studies on taxonomy and distribution of the genus *Borodinula* (Nemichthyidae, Osteichthyes) with description of a new species]. Tr. Inst. Okeanol. Akad. Nauk SSSR 109: 186–210. [In Russian; English summary.]

1982. Sistematika i nekotorye ovobennosti ekologii nitekhvostykh ugrei semeistva Nemichthyidae (Pisces, Anguilliformes) [Systematics and some aspects of ecology of the family Nemichthyidae (Pisces, Anguilliformes)]. Tr. Inst. Okeanol. Akad. Nauk SSSR 118: 151–161. [In Russian; English summary.]

1990. Leptocephali of eels of the genus *Nemichthys* (Nemichthyidae, Osteichthyes). J. Ichthyol. 30(5): 28–42 [English transl. Vopr. Ikhtiol. 30(4): 551–563].

1996. Occurrence of mesopelagic sawtooth snipe eel, *Serrivomer lanceolatoides* (Serrivomeridae) in the northwestern Pacific. J. Ichthyol. 36(2): 200–202 [English transl. Vopr. Ikhtiol. 36(2): 276–278].

Karrer, C.

1976. Über fischarten aus der Davisstrasse und Labradorsee. Mitt. Zool. Mus. Berlin 52: 371–376.

Kashkin, N. I.

1995. Vertical distribution of *Cyclothone* (Gonostomatidae) in the Pacific Ocean (brief review). J. Ichthyol. 35(8): 53–60 [English transl. Vopr. Ikhtiol. 35(4): 440–444].

Kato, F.

1991. Life history of masu and amago salmon (*Oncorhynchus masou* and *Oncorhynchus rhodurus*). Pages 447–520 *in* C. Groot and L. Margolis, eds. Pacific salmon life histories. UBC Press, Vancouver.

Kawaguchi, K.

1971. Gonostomatid fishes of the western North Pacific. Jpn. J. Ichthyol. 18(1): 411–429.

Kawaguchi, K., and J. L. Butler.

1984. Fishes of the genus *Nansenia* (Microstomatidae) with descriptions of seven new species. Contrib. Sci. (Los Angel.) 352. 22 pp.

Keivany, Y., and J. S. Nelson.

2000. Taxonomic review of the genus *Pungitius,* ninespine sticklebacks (Teleostei, Gasterosteidae). Cybium 24(2): 107–122.

Keleher, J. J.

1961. Comparison of largest Great Slave Lake fish with North American records. J. Fish. Res. Board Can. 18(3): 417–421.

Kendall, A. W., Jr.

1991. Systematics and identification of larvae and juveniles of the genus *Sebastes*. Environ. Biol. Fishes 30: 173–190.

2001. An historical review of *Sebastes* taxonomy and systematics. Mar. Fish. Rev. 62(2): 1–23.

Kendall, A. W., Jr., and B. Vinter.

1984. Development of hexagrammids (Pisces, Scorpaeniformes) in the northeastern Pacific Ocean. NOAA Tech. Rep. NMFS 2. 44 pp.

Kenya, V. S.

1982. New data on the migration and distribution of Pacific sardines in the northwest Pacific. Sov. J. Mar. Biol. [English transl. Biol. Morya] 8(1): 41–48.

Kessler, D. W.

1985. Alaska's saltwater fishes and other sea life. Alaska Northwest Publishing Company, Anchorage. 358 pp.

Kharin, V. E.

1984. Two new species of deep water anglerfish (Ceratioidei: Himantolophidae, Gigantactinae [*sic*] from the North Pacific. J. Ichthyol. [English transl. Vopr. Ikhtiol.] 24(3): 112–117.

Kido, K.

1983. New and rare liparidid species from the Okhotsk and Bering seas and their adjacent waters. Jpn. J. Ichthyol. 29(4): 374-384.

1984a. The third specimen of cyclopterid fish, *Eumicrotremus barbatus,* from Japan. Jpn. J. Ichthyol. 31(1): 83–85.

1984b. Occurrence of the liparidid fish, *Paraliparis pectoralis,* in the Bering Sea. Jpn. J. Ichthyol. 31(2): 203–204.

1985. New and rare species of the genus *Careproctus* (Liparididae) from the Bering Sea. Jpn. J. Ichthyol. 32(1): 6–17.

1988. Phylogeny of the family Liparididae, with the taxonomy of the species found around Japan. Mem. Fac. Fish. Hokkaido Univ. 35(2): 125–256.

1992. Redescription of *Paraliparis tremebundus* (Liparididae). Jpn. J. Ichthyol. 39(3): 251–254.

1993. New records of *Paraliparis pectoralis* and *P. nanus* (Liparidae) from Japan. Jpn. J. Ichthyol. 40(1): 107–109.

Kido, K., and D. Kitagawa.

1986. Development of larvae and juveniles of *Rhinoliparis barbulifer* (Liparididae). Pages 697–702 *in* T. Uyeno, R. Arai, T. Taniuchi, and K. Matsuura, eds. Indo-Pacific fish biology: Proceedings of the Second International Conference on Indo-Pacific Fishes. Ichthyological Society of Japan, Tokyo.

Kido, K., and G. Shinohara.

1996. *Pelagocyclus vitiazi* Lindberg & Legeza, 1955, a junior synonym of *Aptocyclus ventricosus* (Pallas, 1769) (Scorpaeniformes: Cyclopteridae). Ichthyol. Res. 43(2): 175–177.

1997. First record of a liparid fish, *Careproctus melanurus* (Teleostei, Scorpaeniformes), from Japan. Bull. Natl. Sci. Mus. (Tokyo) Ser. A, 23(2): 127–130.

Kiernan, A. M.

1990. Systematics and zoogeography of the ronquils, family Bathymasteridae (Teleostei: Perciformes). Ph.D. thesis, University of Washington, Seattle. 190 pp.

Kim, I.-S., E.-J. Kang, and C.-H. Youn.

1993. New records of eight species of the suborder Cottoidei (Pisces: Scorpaeniformes) from Korea. Korean J. Zool. 36: 21–27. [In Korean.]

Kim, I.-S., and C.-H. Youn.

1992. Synopsis of the family Cottidae (Pisces: Scorpaeniformes) from Korea. Korean J. Ichthyol. 4(1): 54–78.

Kim Sen Tok, I. A. Biryukov, and E. V. Pometeev.

1999. Species composition, distribution, and structural changes in the flatfish community of the Tatarskii Strait during the fishery period 1994–1997. J. Ichthyol. 39(6): 433–440 [English transl. Vopr. Ikhtiol. 39(4): 469–477].

Kitagawa, D., J. Hashimoto, Y. Ueno, K. Ishida, and J. Iwakiri.

1985. Distributional property of the kichiji rockfish (Scorpaenidae) in the deep sea region off Sanriku. Pages 107–117 *in* Deepsea research using the submergible "Shinkai 2000" system. Tech. Rep. JAMSTEC (Japan Marine Science and Technology Center) 1985.

Kittlitz, F. H. von.

1858. Denkwürdigkeiten einer Reise nach dem russischen Amerika, nach Mikronesien und durch Kamtschatka. Gotha, Perthes. Vol. 1: 383 pp. Vol. 2: 462 pp. [Original not seen. Excerpt reproduced by Hubbs (1927).]

Klein, D. R., D. E. Murray, R. H. Armstrong, and B. A. Anderson.

1998. Alaska. Pages 707–745 *in* M. P. Mac, P. A. Opler, C. E. Puckett Haecker, and P. D. Doran, eds. Status and trends of the nation's biological resources. Vol. 2. U.S. Geological Survey, Reston, Virginia.

Klyukanov, V. A.

1969. Morfologicheskie osnovy sistematiki koryushek roda *Osmerus* (Osmeridae) [Morphological basis of classification of smelts of the genus *Osmerus*]. Zool. Zh. 48(1): 99–109. [In Russian; English summary.]

Knaggs, E. H., J. S. Sunada, and R. N. Lea.

1975. Notes on some fishes collected off the outer coast of Baja California. Calif. Fish Game 61(1): 56–59.

Knipowitsch, N. M.

1907. Zur Ichthyologie des Eismeeres. Die von der Russischen Polar-Expedition im Eismeer gesammelten Fische. Zap. Akad. Nauk 8(5). 53 pp., 2 pls.

Kobayashi, B. N.

1973. Systematics, zoogeography, and aspects of the biology of the bathypelagic fish genus *Cyclothone* in the Pacific Ocean. Ph.D. thesis, University of California, San Diego. [Pages 1, 11–13, 83–94, fig. 1 only.]

Kobayashi, K., M. Mikawa, and J. Ito.

1968. Descriptions of the young and one immature adult specimens of coster dory, *Allocyttus verrucosus* (Gilchrist) from the northern part of the Pacific. Bull. Fac. Fish. Hokkaido Univ. 19(1): 1–5, 1 pl., 1 table.

Kobayashi, K., and T. Ueno.

1956. Fishes from the northern Pacific and from Bristol Bay. Bull. Fac. Fish. Hokkaido Univ. 6(4): 239–265.

1966. Record of a bathypelagic melamphid fish, *Promitra* [*sic*] (*Melamphaes*) *cristiceps* (Gilbert) obtained from the stomach of salmon taken in the North Pacific Ocean. Jpn. J. Ichthyol. 13(4/6): 213–219.

Kobayashi, K., T. Ueno, H. Omi, and K. Abe.

1968. Records of some rare deep-sea anglerfishes obtained from the waters of Hokkaido. Bull. Fac. Fish. Hokkaido Univ. 19(1): 7–18, 2 pls.

Kobayashi, T., M. Wake,and M. Naito.

1968. Studies on the life history of the Pacific saury, *Cololabis saira* (Brevoort). I. Aggregative characteristics of adults of the spawning population. Sci. Rep. Hokkaido Fish. Exp. Sta. 9: 1–45.

Kobylianskiy, S. G. (Kobylyansky, S. H.)

1985. Material for the revision of the genus *Bathylagus* Günther (Bathylagidae): the group of "light" deepsea smelts. J. Ichthyol. 25(2): 1–17 [English transl. Vopr. Ikhtiol. 25(1): 51–67].

1986. Materialy k revizii semeystva Bathylagidae (Teleosti, Salmoniformes) [Materials for a revision of the family Bathylagidae (Teleostei, Salmoniformes)]. Tr. Inst. Okeanol. Akad. Nauk SSSR [Trans. P. P. Shirshov Inst. Oceanol.] 121: 6–50. [In Russian; English summary.]

1990. Taksonomicheskiy status mikrostomovykh ryb i nekotorye voprosy klassifikatsii podotryada Argentinoidei (Salmoniformes, Teleostei) [Taxonomic status of microstomatid fishes and problems of classification of suborder Argentinoidei (Salmoniformes, Teleostei)]. Tr. Inst. Okeanol. Akad. Nauk SSSR 125: 147–177. [In Russian.]

Kobylianskiy (Kobylianskii), S. G., and V. V. Fedorov.

2001. A new species of the genus *Dolichopteryx* — *D. parini* (Opistoproctidae [sic], Salmoniformes) from the mesopelagial zone of the Sea of Okhotsk and the Bering Sea. J. Ichthyol. 41(1): 115–118 [English transl. Vopr. Ikhtiol. 41(1): 125–128].

Kondrat'ev, M. A.

1996. K biologii golubogo okunya *Sebastes glaucus* v Tauyskoy gube Okhotskogo morya[On the biology of the blue rockfish in Tauyskaya Bay, Sea of Okhotsk]. Biol. Morya 22(4): 252–254. [In Russian.]

Konstantinov, K. G., and G. P. Nizovtsev.

1979. The basking shark, *Cetorhinus maximus,* in Kandalaksha Bay of the White Sea. J. Ichthyol. [English transl. Vopr. Ikhtiol.] 19(1): 155.

Kotlyar, A. N.

1984. Slovar' nazvaniy morskikh ryb na shesti yazykakh [Dictionary of names of marine fishes in six languages]. Vses. Nauchno-Issled. Inst. Morsk. Rybn. Khoz. Okeanogr. [All Union Research Institute of Marine Fisheries and Oceanography]. Moscow, Russkiy Yazyk. 288 pp.

1986. Classification and distribution of fishes of the family Anoplogasteridae (Beryciformes). J. Ichthyol. [English transl. Vopr. Ikhtiol.] 26(4): 133–152.

1995. Osteology and distribution of *Barbourisia rufa* (Barbourisiidae). J. Ichthyol. [English transl. Vopr. Ikhtiol.] 35(6): 140–150.

Kottelat, M.

1997. European freshwater fishes. Biologia, Bratislava 52 (suppl. 5): 1–271.

Kramer, D. E., W. H. Barss, B. C. Paust, and B. E. Bracken.

1995. Guide to northeast Pacific flatfishes: families Bothidae, Cynoglossidae, and Pleuronectidae. University of Alaska Sea Grant, Fairbanks, Marine Advisory Bull. 47. 104 pp.

Kramer, D. E., and V. M. O'Connell.
1988. Guide to northeast Pacific rockfishes genera *Sebastes* and *Sebastolobus*. University of Alaska Sea Grant, Fairbanks, Marine Advisory Bull. 25. 78 pp.

Krejsa, R. J.
1964. Reproductive behavior and sexual dimorphism in the manacled sculpin, *Synchirus gilli* Bean. Copeia 1964(2): 448–450.

Krieger, K. J.
1992. Shortraker rockfish, *Sebastes borealis,* observed from a manned submersible. U.S. Natl. Mar. Fish. Serv. Mar. Fish. Rev. 54(4): 34–37.
1993. Distribution and abundance of rockfish determined from a submersible and by bottom trawling. U.S. Natl. Mar. Fish. Serv. Fish. Bull. 91: 87–96.

Krieger, K. J., and D. H. Ito.
1999. Distribution and abundance of shortraker rockfish, *Sebstes borealis,* and rougheye rockfish, *S. aleutianus,* determined from a manned submersible. U.S. Natl. Mar. Fish. Serv. Fish. Bull. 97: 264–272.

Kriksunov, Ye. A., and M. I. Shatunovskiy.
1979. Some questions of population structure variability in the smelt, *Osmerus eperlanus.* J. Ichthyol. [English transl. Vopr. Ikhtiol.] 19(1): 48–55.

Kukuev, E. I.
1998. Systematics and distribution in the world ocean of daggertooth fishes of the genus *Anotopterus* (Anotopteridae, Aulopiformes). J. Ichthyol. 38(9): 716–729 [English transl. Vopr. Ikhtiol. 38(6): 745–759].

Kulikov, M. Yu.
1964. Noviyye dannyye ob ikhtiofaune Komandorskikh ostrovov [New data on ichthyofauna of Commander Islands]. Izv. Tikhook. Nauchno-Issled. Inst. Rybn. Khoz. Okeanogr. [Proc. Pacific Res. Inst. Fish. Oceanogr.] (TINRO) 55: 249–250. [In Russian; and selections translated by B. A. Sheiko, 1999, for Point Stephens Research, Auke Bay, Alaska.]

Kynard, B., and K. Curry.
1976. Meristic variation in the threespine stickleback, *Gasterosteus aculeatus,* from Auke Lake, Alaska. Copeia 1976(4): 811–813.

Laidig, T. E., P. B. Adams, K. R. Silberberg, and H. E. Fish.
1997. Conversions between total, fork, and standard lengths for lingcod, *Ophiodon elongatus.* Calif. Fish Game 83(3): 128–129.

Lamb, A., and P. Edgell.
1986. Coastal fishes of the Pacific Northwest. Harbour Publishing, Madeira Park, British Columbia. 224 pp.

Lapko, V. V., and O. A. Ivanov.
1993. Composition and distribution of the fauna in the sound-scattering layer in the Pacific waters near Kuril Islands. Oceanology 33(4): 574–578. [In Russian.]

Larkins, H. A.
1964. Some epipelagic fishes of the North Pacific Ocean, Bering Sea, and Gulf of Alaska. Trans. Am. Fish. Soc. 93(3): 286–290.

Laur, D., and L. Haldorson.
1996. Coastal habitat studies: the effect of the *Exxon Valdez* oil spill on shallow subtidal fishes in Prince William Sound. Am. Fish. Soc. Symp. 18: 659–570.

Laurs, R. M., and R. J. Lynn.
1977. Seasonal migration of North Pacific albacore, *Thunnus alalunga,* into North America coastal waters: distribution, relative abundance, and association with Transition Zone waters. U.S. Natl. Mar. Fish. Serv. Fish. Bull. 75(4): 795–822.

Lavenberg, R. J., and J. E. Fitch.
1966. Annotated list of fishes collected by midwater trawl in the Gulf of California, March–April 1964. Calif. Fish Game 52(2): 92–110.

Lavin, P. A., and J. D. McPhail.
1987. Morphological divergence and the organization of trophic characters among lacustrine populations of the threespine stickleback (*Gasterosteus aculeatus*). Can. J. Fish. Aquat. Sci. 44: 1820–1829.

Lavrova, T. V.
1990. Predvaritel'nyy spisok i rasprostraneniye vidov ryb semeistva Stichaeidae v Okhotskom more [A preliminary list and distribution of species of the family Stichaeidae in the Okhotsk Sea]. Tr. Zool. Inst. Akad. Nauk SSSR 213: 46–54. [In Russian.]

Lay, G. T., and E. T. Bennett.

1839. Fishes. Pages 41–75, plates 15–23 *in* The zoology of Captain Beechey's voyage to the Pacific and Behring's Straits in His Majesty's ship *Blossom,* in the years 1825, 26, 28, and 28. H. G. Bohn, London.

Lea, R. N.

1974. First record of Puget Sound sculpin, *Artedius meanyi,* from California. J. Fish. Res. Board Can. 31(7): 1242–1243.

1987. On the second record of *Barbourisia rufa,* the velvet whalefish, from California. Calif. Fish Game 73(2): 124.

Lea, R. N., and L. J. Dempster.

1982. Status and nomenclatural history of *Agonus vulsus* Jordan and Gilbert, 1880 (Pisces—family Agonidae). Calif. Fish Game 68(4): 249–252.

Lea, R. N., K. A. Karpov, and L. F. Quirollo.

1989. Record of the roughscale sole, *Clidoderma asperrimum,* from northern California with a note on the Pacific lined sole, *Achirus mazatlanus.* Calif. Fish Game 75(4): 239–241.

Lea, R. N., R. D. McAllister, and D. A. VenTresca.

1999. Biological aspects of nearshore rockfishes of the genus *Sebastes* from central California, with notes on ecologically related sportfishes. Calif. Dep. Fish Game Fish. Bull. 177. 109 pp.

Lea, R. N., and L. F. Quirollo.

1986. First record of *Hemitripterus bolini,* the bigmouth sculpin, from Californian waters. Calif. Fish Game 72(2): 117–119.

Lea, R. N., and R. H. Rosenblatt.

1987. Occurrence of the family Notacanthidae (Pisces) from marine waters of California. Calif. Fish Game 73: 51–53.

LeBrasseur, R. J.

1964. Data record, collections of fish taken in Isaacs–Kidd midwater trawl from northeastern Pacific Ocean 1958–59. Fish. Res. Board Can., Manuscr. Rep. Ser. (Oceanogr.–Limnol.) 175. 25 pp.

1967. Line fishing at Ocean Station P, 50°00'N, 145°00'W. J. Fish. Res. Board Can. 24(10): 2201–2203.

Lecointre, G., and G. Nelson.

1996. Clupeomorpha, sister-group of Ostariophysi. Pages 193–207 *in* M. L. J. Stiassny, L. R. Parenti, and G. D. Johnson, eds. Interrelationhips of fishes. Academic Press, San Diego.

Lee, D. S., C. R. Gilbert, C. H. Hocutt, R. E. Jenkins, D. E. McAllister, and J. R. Stauffer, Jr.

1980 et seq. Atlas of North American freshwater fishes. North Carolina State Museum of Natural History, Raleigh. 854 pp.

Lee, R. S.

1974. *Thalassobathia nelsoni,* a new species of bathypelagic ophidioid fish from Chilean waters. Copeia 1974(3): 629–632.

Legendre, V., J. G. Hunter, and D. E. McAllister.

1975. French, English, and scientific names of marine fishes of Arctic Canada. Syllogeus 7: 1–15.

Leim, A. H., and W. B. Scott.

1966. Fishes of the Atlantic coast of Canada. Bull. Fish. Res. Board Can. 155. 485 pp.

Leipertz, S. L.

1985. A review of the fishes of the agonid genus *Xeneretmus* Gilbert. Proc. Calif. Acad. Sci. 44(3): 17–40.

1988. The rockhead poacher, *Bothragonus swani* (Teleostei: Agonidae): selected osteology, with comments on phylogeny. Copeia 1988(1): 64–71.

Levings, C. D.

1969. The zoarcid *Lycodopsis pacifica* in outer Burrard Inlet, British Columbia. J. Fish. Res. Board Can. 26: 2403–2412.

Leviton, A. E., and R. H. Gibbs, Jr.

1988. Standards in herpetology and ichthyology standard symbolic codes for institution resource collections in herpetology and ichthyology. Supplement No. 1: additions and corrections. Copeia 1988(1): 280–282.

Leviton, A. E., R. H. Gibbs, Jr., E. Heal, and C. E. Dawson.

1985. Standards in herpetology and ichthyology: Part I. Standard symbolic codes for institutional resource collections in herpetology and ichthyology. Copeia 1985(3): 802–832.

Li, S. Z.

1981. On the origin, phylogeny and geographical distribution of the flatfishes (Pleuronectiformes). Trans. Chin. Ichthyol. Soc. 1981(1): 11–20.

Liem, K. F.

1986. The pharyngeal jaw apparatus of the Embiotocidae (Teleostei): a functional and evolutionary perspective. Copeia 1986(2): 311–323.

Lien, J., and L. Fawcett.

1986. Distribution of Basking Sharks, *Cetorhinus maximus,* incidentally caught in inshore fishing gear in Newfoundland. Can. Field-Nat. 100: 246–252.

Lincoln, R., G. Boxshall, and P. Clark.

1998. A dictionary of ecology, evolution and systematics, 2nd edition. Cambridge University Press. 361 pp.

Lindberg, G. U.

1935. O nakhozhdenii ivasi i anchousa na Kamchatke [A find of ivasi and anchovy on Kamchatka]. Priroda 5: 47–48. [In Russian.]

1950. Description of a new species in the genus *Anoplagonus* Gill (Pisces, Agonidae) from the Sea of Japan. Issled. Dal'nevost. Morei SSSR 2: 303–304. [In Russian.] [Cited in Kanayama and Maruyama 1979.]

1973. Fishes of the world: a key to families and a checklist. Translated from Russian by Hilary Hardin. Halsted Press, John Wiley & Sons, New York. 545 pp. [Translation of Opredelitel' i kharakteristika semeistv ryb mirovoi fauny. Izdatel'stvo "Nauka," Leningrad, 1971.]

Lindberg, G. U., and V. V. Fedorov.

1993. Fishes of the Sea of Japan and the adjacent areas of the Sea of Okhotsk and the Yellow Sea. Part 6. Teleostomi, Osteichthyes, Actinopterygii. XXXI. Pleuronectiformes (CXCV. Family Psettodidae–CCI. Family Cynoglossidae). Zool. Inst. Ross. Akad. Nauk, Faune 166: 272 pp. [In Russian.]

Lindberg, G. U., and Z. V. Krasyukova.

1969. Fishes of the Sea of Japan and the adjacent areas of the Sea of Okhotsk and the Yellow Sea. Part 3. Teleostomi. XXIX. Perciformes: Percoidei (XC. Serranidae—CXLIV. Champsodontidae). Acad. Sci. USSR Zool. Inst., Fauna USSR 99. 498 pp. [Translation by Israel Prog. Sci. Transl., 1971.]

1975. Fishes of the Sea of Japan and the adjacent areas of the Sea of Okhotsk and the Yellow Sea. Part 4. Teleostomi. XXIX. Perciformes: 2. Blennioidei—13. Gobioidei (CXLV. Anarhichadidae—CLXXV. Periophthalmidae). Nauka Publishers, Leningrad. [Translation by Smithsonian Institution Libraries and National Science Foundation, Washington, D.C., B. B. Collette, editor, 1989. 602 pp.]

1987. Fishes of the Sea of Japan and the adjacent areas of the Sea of Okhotsk and the Yellow Sea. Part 5. Teleostomi, Osteichthyes, Actinopterygii. XXX. Scorpaeniformes (CLXXVI. Scorpaenidae—CXCIV. Liparididae). Zool. Inst. Akad. Nauk SSSR, Faune 150. 526 pp. [In Russian.]

Lindberg, G. U., and M. I. Legeza.

1955. Obzor rodov i vidov ryb podsemeistva Cyclopterinae (Pisces) [Review of genera and species of fishes of the subfamily Cyclopterinae (Pisces)]. Tr. Zool. Inst. Akad. Nauk SSSR 18: 389–458. [In Russian; and translation by Israel Prog. Sci. Transl., 1964.]

1959. Fishes of the Sea of Japan and the adjacent areas of the Sea of Okhotsk and the Yellow Sea. Part 1. Amphioxi, Petromyzones, Myxini, Elasmobranchii, Holocephali. Acad. Sci. USSR, Zool. Inst., Fauna USSR 68. 198 pp. [Translation by Israel Prog. Sci. Transl., 1967.]

1965. Fishes of the Sea of Japan and the adjacent areas of the Sea of Okhotsk and the Yellow Sea. Part 2. Teleostomi. XII. Acipenseriformes—XXVIII. Polynemiformes. Acad. Sci. USSR, Zool. Inst., Fauna USSR 84. 389 pp. [Translation by Israel Prog. Sci. Transl., 1969.]

Lindsey, C. C.

1962. Distinctions between the broad whitefish, *Coregonus nasus,* and other North American whitefishes. J. Fish. Res. Board Can. 19(4): 687–714.

Lindsey, C. C., and J. D. McPhail.

1986. Zoogeography of fishes of the Yukon and Mackenzie basins. Pages 639–674 *in* C. H. Hocutt and E. O. Wiley, eds. The zoogeography of North American freshwater fishes. John Wiley & Sons, New York.

Lisitsyn, A. P.

1959. Bottom sediments of the Bering Sea. *In* P. L. Bezrukov, ed. Geographical description of the Bering Sea. Bottom relief and sediments. Trans. Oceanol. Inst. Acad. Sci. USSR 29: 65–178. [Translation by Israel Prog. Sci. Transl., Jerusalem, 1964.]

Lissner, A. L., and J. H. Dorsey.

1986. Deep-water biological assemblages of a hard-bottom bank-ridge complex of the southern California continental borderland. Bull. S. Calif. Acad. Sci. 85(2): 87–101.

Lloyd, R. E.

1909a. A description of the deep-sea fish caught by the R.I.M.S. ship *Investigator* since the year 1900, with supposed evidence of mutation in *Malthopsis.* Mem. Indian Mus. 2(3): 139–180.

1909b. Illustrations of the zoology of the Royal Indian marine survey ship *Investigator*, . . . Fishes. Calcutta. Part 10, pls. 44–50. [Accompanied Lloyd 1909a.]

Lockington, W. N.

1878. Walks around San Francisco. No. 3. Lake Honda and Seal Rock. Am. Nat. 12(12): 786–793.

1879. Review of the Pleuronectidae of San Francisco. Proc. U.S. Natl. Mus. (for 1879) 2: 69–108.

1880a. Descriptions of new genera and species of fishes from the coast of California. Proc. U.S. Natl. Mus. (for 1879) 2: 326–332.

1880b. Description of a new fish from Alaska (*Uranidea microstoma*). Proc. U.S. Natl. Mus. 3: 58–59.

1880c. Description of a new species of Agonidae (*Brachyopsis verrucosus*), from the coast of California. Proc. U.S. Natl. Mus. 3: 60–63.

1880d. Description of a new genus and some new species of California fishes (*Icosteus aenigmaticus* and *Osmerus attenuatus*). Proc. U.S. Natl. Mus. 3: 63–68.

1880e. Description of a new chiroid fish, *Myriolepis zonifer,* from Monterey Bay, California. Proc. U.S. Natl. Mus. 3: 248–251.

1880f. Note on a new flatfish (*Lepidopsetta isolepis*) found in the markets of San Francisco. Proc. U.S. Natl. Mus. 3: 325.

1880g. Description of a new species of *Hemitripterus* from Alaska. Proc. Acad. Nat. Sci. Phila. 32(7 Sep.): 233–236. [Presentation date on volume is 7 Sep.]

1881. Description of a new genus and species of Cottidae. Proc. U.S. Natl. Mus. 4: 141–144.

Logan, J. E., K. L. Day, M. Marks, and O. Assemien.

1993. Occurrence of the codling (*Halargyreus johnsonii,* Moridae), in the eastern North Pacific. Calif. Fish Game 79(1): 39–41.

López, J. A., P. Bentzen, and T. W. Pietsch.

2000. Phylogenetic relationships of esocoid fishes (Teleostei) based on partial cytochrome *b* and 16S mitochondrial DNA sequencing. Copeia 2000(2): 420–431.

Loughlin, T. R., and K. Ohtani, editors.

1999. Dynamics of the Bering Sea. University of Alaska Sea Grant, AK-SG-99-03, Fairbanks. 838 pp.

Love, M. S.

1974. New geographic and bathymetric records for fishes from southern California. Calif. Fish Game 60(4): 212–216.

Love, M. S., and R. N. Lea.

1997. Range extension of the quillback rockfish, *Sebastes maliger,* to the Southern California Bight. Calif. Fish Game 83(2): 78–83.

Low, Loh-Lee, H. W. Braham, J. C. Olsen, P. J. Gould, and A. M. Shimada.

1998. Marine resources. Pages 806–814 *in* M. P. Mac, P. A. Opler, C. E. Puckett Haecker, and P. D. Doran, eds. Status and trends of the nation's biological resources. Vol. 2. U.S. Department of the Interior, U.S. Geological Survey, Reston, Virginia.

Lowe, C. G., and K. J. Goldman.

2001. Thermal and bioenergenetics of elasmobranchs: bridging the gap. Environ. Biol. Fishes 60: 251–266.

Lowry, L. F.

1993. Chapter 6. Foods and feeding ecology. Pages 201–238 *in* J. J. Burns, J. J. Montague, and C. J. Cowles, eds. The bowhead whale. Society for Marine Mammalogy, Spec. Publ. 2. Allen Press, Lawrence, Kansas.

Lowry, L. F., and K. J. Frost.

1981. Distribution, growth, and foods of Arctic cod (*Boreogadus saida*) in the Bering, Chukchi, and Beaufort seas. Can. Field-Nat. 95: 186–191.

MacCrimmon, H. R.

1971. World distribution of rainbow trout (*Salmo gairdneri*). J. Fish. Res. Board Can. 28: 663–704.

MacCrimmon, H. R., and J. S. Campbell.

1969. World distribution of brook trout, *Salvelinus fontinalis.* J. Fish. Res. Board Can. 26: 1699–1725.

MacCrimmon, H. R., B. L. Gots, and J. S. Campbell.

1971. World distribution of brook trout, *Salvelinus fontinalis*: further observations. J. Fish. Res. Board Can. 28: 452–456.

Macdonald, J. S., and K. Brewer.

1980. Range extensions of the whitebait smelt (*Allosmerus elongatus*) (Ayres) in British Columbia. Syesis 13: 209.

Machida, Y., and S. Ohta.

1996. First finding of the deep-sea eelpout, *Taranetzella lyoderma,* from Japan (Zoarcidae, Lycodinae). Ichthyol. Res. 43(1): 90–92.

Machida, Y., S. Ohta, and O. Okamura.

1987. Newly obtained specimens and information on a deep-sea fish *Spectrunculus grandis* (Günther) (Ophidiidae, Ophidiiformes) from Japan. Rep. Usa Mar. Biol. Inst. Kochi Univ. 9: 189–200.

Machidori, S., and S. Nakamura.

1971. Distribution and some biological informations of pomfret (*Brama raii*) in the northwestern North Pacific Ocean. Bull. Far Seas Fish. Res. Lab. (Shimizu) 5: 131–145.

Macy, P. T., J. M. Wall, N. D. Lampsakis, and J. E. Mason.

1978. Resources of non-salmonid pelagic fishes of the Gulf of Alaska and eastern Bering Sea. Parts 1 and 2. Final report to OCSEAP, Bureau of Land Management, U.S. Department of the Interior. 714 pp.

Madison, R. J., T. J. McElhone, and C. Zenone.

1987. National water summary 1986: Alaska groundwater quality. U.S. Geological Survey Water Supply Paper 2325: 149–156.

Magnin, E.

1959. Répartition actuelle des acipenserides. Rev. Trav. Inst. Pêches Marit. 23(3): 277–285.

Maisey, J. G.

1985. Relationships of the megamouth shark, *Megachasma*. Copeia 1985(1): 228–231.

Makhrov, A. A., K. V. Kuzishchin, and G. G. Novikov.

1998. Natural hybrids of *Salmo salar* with *Salmo trutta* in the rivers of the White Sea basin. J. Ichthyol. 38(1): 61–66 [English transl. Vopr. Ikhtiol. 38(1): 67–72].

Makushok, V. M.

1958. Morfologicheskie osnovy sistemy stikheevykh i blizkikh k nim semeistv ryb (Stichaeoidae, Blennioidei, Pisces) [The morphology and classification of the northern blennioid fishes (Stichaeoidae, Blennioidei, Pisces)]. Tr. Zool. Inst. Akad. Nauk SSSR 25: 3–129. [In Russian; and translation by A. R. and W. A. Gosline, Ichthyological Laboratory, U.S. Fish Wildl. Serv., U.S. Natl. Mus., Washington, D.C., 1959. 105 pp.]

1961. Dopolnitel'nye dannye po morfologii i sistematike krivorotov (Cryptacanthodidae, Blennioidei, Pisces) [Additional information on the morphology and systematics of wrymouths (Cryptacanthodidae, Blennioidei, Pisces)]. Tr. Inst. Okeanol. Akad. Nauk SSSR 43: 184–197. [In Russian; and translation by B. A. Sheiko, 1999, for Point Stephens Research, Auke Bay, Alaska.]

1964. The specific identity of *Nematonurus longifilis* (Günther, 1877) and *N. clarki* (Jordan and Gilbert, 1898) and some remarks on age-dependent variations in Macruridae (Pisces). Tr. Inst. Okeanol. Akad. Nauk SSSR 73: 139–162. [Translation by Israel Prog. Sci. Transl., 1966, pp. 147–172 *in* T. S. Rass, ed. Fishes of the Pacific and Indian oceans: biology and distribution.]

1970. Data on fishes collected during the 39th voyage of the R/V *Vityaz* in the Kurile–Kamchatka Trench area during the summer of 1966. Pages 541–565 *in* V. G. Bogorov, ed. Fauna of the Kurile–Kamchatka Trench and its environment. Proc. Shirov Inst. Oceanol. Acad. Sci. USSR 86. [Translation by Israel Prog. Sci. Transl., 1972.]

Malkin, E. M., and A. A. Churikov.

1972. Spawning of capelin off the eastern coast of Sakhalin. Rybn. Khoz. 8: 19–21. [Translation by Israel Prog. Sci. Transl., IPST 651590.]

Mandritsa, A. S. (Mandrytza, S. A.)

1991. A new species of the genus *Eumicrotremus* (Pisces, Cyclopteridae) from the Sea of Okhotsk. J. Ichthyol. 31(9): 120–124. [First published in Russian in Zool. Zh. 70(7): 148–151 (1991), with author name spelled S. A. Mandrytza.]

Manzer, J. I.

1965. *Sarda lineolata* (Girard), a Pacific bonito, in the Strait of Georgia, British Columbia. J. Fish. Res. Board Can. 22(3): 853–855.

Markle, D. R.

1978. Taxonomy and distribution of *Rouleina attrita* and *Rouleina maderensis* (Pisces: Alepocephaloidea). U.S. Natl. Mar. Fish. Serv. Fish. Bull. U.S. 76(1): 79–87.

Marliave, J. B.

1976. A theory of storm-induced drift dispersal of the gasterosteid fish *Aulorhynchus flavidus*. Copeia 1976(4): 794–796.

Marshall, N. B.

1955. Studies of alepisauroid fishes. Discovery Rep. 27: 303–336.

1966. Family Scopelosauridae. Pages 194–204 *in* Fishes of the western North Atlantic. Mem. Sears Found. Mar. Res., New Haven, 1(5).

Martin, M. H.

1997. Data report: 1996 Gulf of Alaska bottom trawl survey. NOAA Tech. Memo. NMFS-AFSC-82. 235 pp.

Martin, M. H., and D. M. Clausen.

1995. Data report: 1993 Gulf of Alaska bottom trawl survey. NOAA Tech. Memo. NMFS-AFSC-59. 217 pp.

Martin, N. V., and C. H. Olver.

1980. The lake charr, *Salvelinus namaycush*. Pages 205–277 *in* E. K. Balon, ed. Charrs: salmonid fishes of the genus *Salvelinus*. Dr. W. Junk, The Hague.

Martini, F. H.

1998. The ecology of hagfishes. *In* J. M. Jørgensen, J. P. Lomholt, R. E. Weber, and H. Malte, eds. The biology of hagfishes. Chapman & Hall, London.

Mason, J. C., and A. C. Phillips.

1985. Biology of the bathylagid fish, *Leuroglossus schmidti,* in the Strait of Georgia, British Columbia, Canada. Can. J. Fish. Aquat. Sci. 42: 1144–1153.

Masuda, H., K. Amaoka, C. Araga, T. Uyeno, and T. Yoshino, editors.

1984. The fishes of the Japanese archipelago. English edition. Tokai University Press, Tokyo. Text vol.: 437 pp. Plates vol.: 370 pls.

1992. The fishes of the Japanese archipelago. 3rd English edition. Tokai University Press, Tokyo. Text vol.: 437 pp. + appendix, pp. 441–456. Plates vol.: 370 pls. + appendix, pls. 371–378.

Matallanas, J.

1986. Notes ostéologiques sur *Nansenia problematica* Lloris et Rucabado, 1985, avec discussion de son statut générique. Cybium 10(4): 389–394.

Matarese, A. C., A. W. Kendall, Jr., D. M. Blood, and B. M. Vinter.

1989. Laboratory guide to early life history stages of northeast Pacific fishes. U.S. Dep. Commer., NOAA Tech. Rep. NMFS 80. 652 pp.

Matarese, A. C., and D. L. Stein.

1980. Additional records of the sculpin *Psychrolutes phrictus* in the eastern Bering Sea and off Oregon. U.S. Natl. Mar. Fish. Serv. Fish. Bull. 78(1): 169–171.

Mathisen, O. A., and K. O. Coyle, editors.

1996. Ecology of the Bering Sea: a review of Russian literature. University of Alaska Sea Grant, AK-SG-96-01, Fairbanks. 306 pp.

Matsubara, K., and T. Iwai.

1951. *Lycodes japonicus,* a new ophidioid fish from Toyama Bay. Jpn. J. Ichthyol. 1(6): 368–375.

Matsui, T.

1991. Description of young of the mesopelagic platytroctids *Holtbyrnia latifrons* and *Sagamichthys abei* (Pisces, Alepocephaloidea) from the northeastern Pacific Ocean. U.S. Natl. Mar. Fish. Serv. Fish. Bull. 89: 209—219.

Matsui, T., and R. H. Rosenblatt.

1971. Ontogentic changes in patterns of light organs in searsids and the taxonomy of *Sagamichthys* and *Persparsia.* Copeia 1971(3): 440–448.

1979. Two new searsid fishes of the genera *Maulisia* and *Searsia* (Pisces: Salmoniformes). Bull. Mar. Sci. 29(1): 62–78.

1987. Review of the deep-sea fish family Platytroctidae (Pisces: Salmoniformes). Bull. Scripps Inst. Oceanogr. 26: 1–159.

Matyushin, V. M.

1982. On the intertidal fish fauna of eastern Kamchatka. Biol. Morya (Vladivost.) 4: 60–62. [Translation from Russian by B. A. Sheiko, 1999, for Point Stephens Research, Auke Bay, Alaska.]

1990. *Porocottus quadrifilis* Gill, 1859 (Cottidae) in the littoral zone of the Chukotka Peninsula. J. Ichthyol. 30(8): 119–121 [English transl. Vopr. Ikhtiol. 30(5): 860–861].

Mayden, R. L.

1991. Cyprinids of the New World. Pages 240–263 *in* I. J. Winfield and J. S. Nelson, eds. Cyprinid fishes: systematics, biology and exploitation. Chapman & Hall, London.

Mayden, R. L., editor.

1992. Systematics, historical ecology, and North American freshwater fishes. Stanford University Press, Stanford, California. 970 pp.

McAllister, D. E.

1959. A collection of oceanic fishes from off British Columbia with a discussion of the evolution of black peritoneum. Natl. Mus. Can. Bull. 172: 39–43.

1960. List of the marine fishes of Canada. Natl. Mus. Can. Bull. 168. 76 pp.

1961. Northward range extension of the flathead chub and trout-perch to Aklavik, N.W.T. J. Fish. Res. Board Can. 18(1): 141.

1962. Fishes of the 1960 "Salvelinus" program from western Arctic Canada. Natl. Mus. Can. Bull. 185: 17–39.

1963a. A revision of the smelt family, Osmeridae. Natl. Mus. Can. Bull. 191. 53 pp.

1963b. Systematic notes on the sculpin genera *Artediellus, Icelus,* and *Triglops* on Arctic and Atlantic coasts of Canada. Natl. Mus. Can. Bull. 185: 50–59.

1964. Distinguishing characters for the sculpins *Cottus bairdii* and *C. cognatus* in eastern Canada. J. Fish. Res. Board Can. 21(5): 1339–1342.

McAllister, D. E.

1968. Mandibular pore pattern in the sculpin family Cottidae. Natl. Mus. Can. Bull. 223: 58–69.

1976. A new species of Arctic eelpout, *Lycodes sagittarius,* from the Beaufort Sea, Alaska, and the Kara Sea, USSR (Pisces: Zoarcidae). Natl. Mus. Nat. Sci. (Ott.) Publ. Biol. Oceanogr. 9: 16 pp. [1975 on title page, distributed in 1976.]

1990. A list of the fishes of Canada. Syllogeus (Ottawa) 64. 310 pp.

McAllister, D. E., M. E. Anderson, and J. G. Hunter.

1981. Deep-water eelpouts, *Zoarcidae,* from Arctic Canada and Alaska. Can. J. Fish. Aquat. Sci. 38: 821–839.

McAllister, D. E., and J. Aniskowicz.

1976. Vertebral number in North American sculpins of the *Myoxocephalus quadricornis*-complex. J. Fish. Res. Board Can. 33: 2792–2799.

McAllister, D. E., and C. C. Lindsey.

1961. Systematics of the freshwater sculpins (*Cottus*) of British Columbia. Natl. Mus. Can. Bull. 172: 66–89.

McAllister, D. E., and E. I. S. Rees.

1964. A revision of the eelpout genus *Melanostigma* with a new genus and with comments on *Maynea*. Natl. Mus. Can. Bull. 199: 85–110.

McAllister, D. E., and S. J. Westrheim.

1965. Widow rockfish, *Sebastodes entomelas,* new to British Columbia waters. J. Fish. Res. Board Can. 22: 1559–1561.

McCart, P.

1970. Evidence for the existence of sibling species of pygmy whitefish (*Prosopium coulteri*) in three Alaskan lakes. Pages 81-98 *in* C. C. Lindsey and C. S. Woods, eds. Biology of coregonid fishes. University of Manitoba Press, Winnipeg, Canada.

1980. A review of the systematics and ecology of Arctic char, *Salvelinus alpinus,* in the western Arctic. Can. Tech. Rep. Fish. Aquat. Sci. 935. 89 pp.

McCart, P., and P. Craig.

1971. Meristic differences between anadromous and freshwater-resident Arctic char (*Salvelinus alpinus*) in the Sagavanirktok River Drainage, Alaska. J. Fish. Res. Board Can. 28(1): 115–118.

McCart, P., and V. A. Pepper.

1971. Geographic variation in the lateral line scale counts of the Arctic grayling, *Thymallus arcticus.* J. Fish. Res. Board Can. 28(5): 749–754.

McConnell, R. J., and G. R. Snyder.

1972. Key to field identification of anadromous juvenile salmonids in the Pacific Northwest. U.S. Dep. Commer., NOAA Tech. Rep. NMFS Circ. 366. 6 pp.

McCormick, J. H., B. R. Jones, and R. F. Syrett.

1971. Temperature requirements for growth and survival of larval ciscos (*Coregonus artedii*). J. Fish. Res. Board Can. 28(6): 924–927.

McCosker, J. E., and M. E. Anderson.

1976. Aquarium maintenance of mesopelagic animals: a progress report. Bull. S. Calif. Acad. Sci. 75(2): 211–219.

McDowall, R. M.

1987. The occurrence and distribution of diadromy among fishes. Am. Fish. Soc. Symp. 1: 1–13.

McDowell, S. B.

1973. Order Heteromi (Notacanthiformes). Pages 1–31 *in* Fishes of the western North Atlantic. Mem. Sears Found. Mar. Res., New Haven, 1(6).

1973. Family Notacanthidae. Pages 124–207 *in* Fishes of the western North Atlantic. Mem. Sears Found. Mar. Res., New Haven, 1(6).

McEachran, J. D., and K. A. Dunn.

1998. Phylogenetic analysis of skates, a morphologically conservative clade of elasmobranchs (Chondrichthyes: Rajidae). Copeia 1998(2): 271–290.

McEachran, J. D., K. A. Dunn, and T. Miyake.

1996. Interrelationships of the batoid fishes (Chondrichthyes: Batoidea). Pages 63–84 *in* M. L. J. Stiassny, L. R. Parenti, and G. D. Johnson, eds. Interrelationhips of fishes. Academic Press, San Diego.

McEachran, J. D., and H. Konstantinou.

1996. Survey of the variation in alar and malar thorns in skates: phylogenetic implications (Chondrichthyes: Rajoidei). J. Morphol. 228: 165–178.

McEachran, J. D., and T. Miyake.

1990a. Phylogenetic interrelationships of skates: a working hypothesis (Chondrichthyes, Rajoidei). Pages 285–304 *in* H. L. Pratt, Jr., S. H. Gruber, and T. Taniuchi, eds. Elasmobranchs as living resources: advances in the biology, ecology, systematics, and the status of the fisheries. NOAA Tech. Rep. NMFS 90.

1990b. Zoogeography and bathymetry of skates (Chondrichthyes, Rajoidei). Pages 305–326 *in* H. L. Pratt, Jr., S. H. Gruber, and T. Taniuchi, eds. Elasmobranchs as living resources: advances in the biology, ecology, systematics, and the status of the fisheries. NOAA Tech. Rep. NMFS 90.

McGinnis, S. M.

1984. Freshwater fishes of California. California Natural History Guides 49. University of California Press, Berkeley. 316 pp.

McGowan, M. F., and F. H. Berry.

1984. Clupeiformes: development and relationships. Pages 108–126 *in* H. G. Moser et al., eds. Ontogeny and systematics of fishes. Am. Soc. Ichthyol. Herpetol., Spec. Publ. 1.

McKinnell, S., and A. J. Thomson.

1997. Recent events concerning Atlantic salmon escapees in the Pacific. ICES J. Mar. Sci. 53: 1221–1225.

McKinnell, S., A. J. Thomson, E. A. Black, B. L. Wing, C. M. Guthrie III, J. F. Koerner, and J. H. Helle.

1997. Atlantic salmon in the North Pacific. Aquac. Res. 28: 145–157.

McPhail, J. D.

1960. Annotated bibliography on Arctic North American freshwater fishes. Museum Contribution 6. Inst. Fish., Univ. British Columbia, Vancouver. 24 pp.

1961. A systematic study of the *Salvelinus alpinus* complex in North America. J. Fish. Res. Board Can. 18(5): 793–816.

1963. Geographic variation in North American ninespine sticklebacks, *Pungitius pungitius.* J. Fish. Res. Board Can. 20(1): 27–44.

1965. A new ronquil, *Bathymaster leurolepis,* from the Aleutian Islands. J. Fish. Res. Board Can. 22(5): 1293–1297.

1966. The *Coregonus autumnalis* complex in Alaska and northwestern Canada. J. Fish. Res. Board Can. 23(1): 141–148.

1969. Two rare sculpins (Cottidae) new to the marine fauna of British Columbia. Can. Field-Nat. 83(4): 1 p.

1970. A new species of prickleback, *Bryozoichthys marjorius* (Chirolophinae), from the eastern North Pacific. J. Fish. Res. Board Can. 27(12): 2362–2365.

McPhail, J. D., and C. C. Lindsey.

1970. Freshwater fishes of northwestern Canada and Alaska. Fish. Res. Board Can. Bull. 173: 381 pp.

1986. Zoogeography of the freshwater fishes of Cascadia (the Columbia system and rivers north to the Stikine). Pages 615–637 *in* C. H. Hocutt and E. O. Wiley, eds. The zoogeography of North American freshwater fishes. John Wiley & Sons, New York.

McPhail, J. D., and E. B. Taylor.

1999. Morphological and genetic variation in northwestern longnose suckers, *Catostomus catostomus*: the Salish sucker problem. Copeia 1999(4): 884–893.

Mead, G. W.

1972. Bramidae. Dana-Rep. Carlsberg Found. 81. 166 pp., 9 pls.

Mead, G. W., E. Bertelsen, and D. M. Cohen.

1964. Reproduction among deep-sea fishes. Deep-Sea Res. 11: 569–596.

Mead, G. W., and J. E. De Falla.

1965. New oceanic cheilodipterid fishes from the Indian Ocean. Bull. Mus. Comp. Zool. 134(7): 261–274.

Mead, G. W., and R. L. Haedrich.

1965. The distribution of the oceanic fish *Brama brama.* Bull. Mus. Comp. Zool. 134(2): 29–68.

Mead, G. W., and F. H. C. Taylor.

1953. A collection of oceanic fishes from off northeastern Japan. J. Fish. Res. Board Can. 10(8): 560–582.

Mearns, A. J.

1988. The "odd fish": unusual occurrences of marine life as indicators of changing ocean conditions. Pages 137–176 *in* D. F. Soule and G. S. Kleppel, eds. Marine organisms as indicators. Springer-Verlag, New York.

Mecklenburg, C. W.

2001. Notes on taxonomy of fishes of Alaska. Paper presented at annual meeting of the American Society of Ichthyologists and Herpetologists, State College, Pennsylvania, 5-10 July 2001. 22 pp.

Mecklenburg, C. W., K. L. Jackson, J. S. Nelson, and B. A. Sheiko.

2001. Lost *Thecopterus aleuticus* (Psychrolutidae) of Alaska found? Paper presented at annual meeting of the American Society of Ichthyologists and Herpetologists, State College, Pennsylvania, 5-10 July 2001. 15 pp.

Mednikov, B. M., and V. G. Prokhorov.
1956. Novyy vid *Cyclopteropsis* (Pisces, Cyclopterinae) v Beringovom more [A new species of *Cyclopteropsis* (Pisces, Cyclopterinae) from the Bering Sea]. Doklady Akad. Nauk SSSR 111(3): 717–719. [In Russian.]

Mednikov, B. M., E. A. Shubina, M. H. Melnikova, and K. A. Savvaitova.
1999. The genus status problem in Pacific salmons and trouts: a genetic systematics investigation. J. Ichthyol. 39(1): 10–17 [English transl. Vopr. Ikhtiol. 39(1): 14–21].

Medvedeva, K. D., and K. A. Savvaitova.
1980. Intrapopulation and geographic variability of the skull in charrs. Pages 435-440 *in* E. K. Balon, ed. Charrs: salmonid fishes of the genus *Salvelinus*. Dr. W. Junk, The Hague.

Meléndez, R., and D. F. Markle.
1997. Phylogeny and zoogeography of *Laemonema* and *Guttigadus* (Pisces; Gadiformes; Moridae). Bull. Mar. Sci. 61(3): 593–670.

Messersmith, J. D.
1965. Southern range extensions for chum and silver salmon. Calif. Fish Game 51(3): 220.

Migdalski, E. C.
1962. Angler's guide to the fresh water sport fishes. Ronald Press, New York. 431 pp.

Miller, D. J., and R. N. Lea.
1972. Guide to the coastal marine fishes of California. Calif. Dep. Fish Game Fish Bull. 157. 235 pp.
1976. Addendum, pages 237–249 *in* Guide to the coastal marine fishes of California. Calif. Dep. Fish Game Fish Bull. 157. 249 pp. [Reprint with addendum.]

Miller, R. G.
1993. History and atlas of the fishes of the Antarctic Ocean. Foresta Institute for Ocean and Mountain Studies, Carson City, Nevada. 792 pp.

Miller, R. R.
1947. A new genus and species of deep-sea fish of the family Myctophidae from the Philippine Islands. Proc. U.S. Natl. Mus. 97(3211): 81–90.

Miller, R. R., and D. S. Erdman.
1948. The range and characters of *Synchirus gilli,* a remarkable cottid fish of the northeastern Pacific. Copeia 1948(2): 85–89.

Milliman, J. D., and R. H. Meade.
1983. World-wide delivery of river sediment to the oceans. J. Geology 91(1): 1–21.

Milner, A. M.
1997. Glacial recession and ecosystems of coastal Alaska. Pages 303–330 *in* A. M. Milner and M. W. Oswood, eds. Freshwaters of Alaska: ecological syntheses. Springer-Verlag, New York.

Milner, A. M., and G. S. York.
2001. Factors influencing fish productivity in a newly formed watershed in Kenai Fjords National Park. Arch. Hydrobiol. 151(4): 627–647.

Miya, M.
1994. *Cyclothone kobayashii,* a new species of gonostomatid fish (Teleostei: Stomiiformes) from the Southern Ocean, with notes on its ecology. Copeia 1994(1): 191—204.
1995. Some aspects of the biology of *Bathylagus ochotensis* (Pisces: Bathylagidae) in Sagami Bay, central Japan. Bull. Mar. Sci. 56(1): 173–184.

Miya, M., and M. Nishida.
1996. Molecular phylogenetic perspective on the evolution on the deep-sea fish genus *Cyclothone* (Stomiiformes: Gonostomatidae). Ichthyol. Res. 43(4): 375–398.
2000. Molecular systematics of the deep-sea fish genus *Gonostoma* (Stomiiformes: Gonostomatidae): two paraphyletic clades and resurrection of *Sigmops.* Copeia 2000(2): 378–389.

Møller, P. R.
1997. Identity of the Atlantic eelpouts *Lycodes terraenovae* Collett, 1896, *L. atlanticus* Jensen, 1902 and *L. agulhensis* Andriashev, 1959 (Pisces: Zoarcidae). Steenstrupia 22: 45–58.

Møller, P. R., and O. A. Jørgensen.
2000. Distribution and abundance of eelpouts (Pisces, Zoarcidae) off West Greenland. Sarsia 85: 23–48.

Møller, P. R., and Æ. Petersen
1997. New data on the rare eelpout *Lycodes luetkeni* (Zoarcidae) from Greenlandic and Icelandic waters. Cybium 21(3): 289–296.

Mollet, H. F., G. Cliff, H. L. Pratt, Jr,., and J. D. Stevens.

2000. Reproductive biology of the female shortfin mako, *Isurus oxyrinchus* Rafinesque, 1810, with comments on the embryonic development of lamnoids. U.S. Natl. Mar. Fish. Serv. Fish. Bull. 98: 299–318.

Molnia, B. F., and K. B. Taylor, editors.

1994. Proceedings of the Interagency Arctic Research Policy Committee Workshop on Arctic Contamination, May 2–7, 1993, Anchorage, Alaska. Arctic Research of the United States 8: 1–313.

Moore, J., and R. Boardman.

1991. List of type specimens in the fish collection at the Yale Peabody Museum, with a brief history of ichthyology at Yale University. Postilla 206. 36 pp.

Mori, T.

1952. Checklist of the fishes of Korea. Zoology Department, Hyogo University of Agriculture, Sasayama, Japan. 228 pp. [Not seen.]

Morosova, G. N.

1982. Distribution, relative abundance and size composition of three species of eelpouts in the Labrador and Newfoundland areas. J. Northwest Atl. Fish. Sci. 3: 159–164.

Morrow, J. E.

1964. Family Malacosteidae. Pages 523–549 *in* Fishes of the western North Atlantic. Mem. Sears Found. Mar. Res., New Haven, 1(4).

1965. First record of the trout-perch, *Percopsis omiscomaycus,* from Alaska. Copeia 1965(2): 232.

1973. A new species of *Salvelinus* from the Brooks Range, northern Alaska. Biol. Pap. Univ. Alaska 13: 1–8.

1974. Illustrated keys to the fresh-water fishes of Alaska. Alaska Northwest Publishing Company, Anchorage. 78 pp.

1980a. Analysis of the dolly varden charr, *Salvelinus malma,* of northwestern North America and northeastern Siberia. Pages 323–338 *in* E. K. Balon, ed. Charrs: salmonid fishes of the genus *Salvelinus.* Dr. W. Junk, The Hague.

1980b. The freshwater fishes of Alaska. Alaska Northwest Publishing Company, Anchorage. 248 pp.

Morrow, J. E., and R. H. Gibbs, Jr.

1964. Family Melanostomiatidae. Pages 351–511 *in* Fishes of the western North Atlantic. Mem. Sears Found. Mar. Res., New Haven, 1(4).

Morton, W. M.

1970. On the validity of all subspecific descriptions of North American *Salvelinus malma* (Walbaum). Copeia 1970(4): 581–587.

1980. Charr or char: a history of the English name for members of the salmonid genus *Salvelinus.* Pages 4–6 *in* E. K. Balon, ed. Charrs: salmonid fishes of the genus *Salvelinus.* Dr. W. Junk, The Hague.

Moser, H. G.

1996. Opisthoproctidae: spookfishes. Pages 216–223 *in* H. G. Moser, ed. The early stages of fishes in the California Current region. CALCOFI (California Cooperative Oceanic Fisheries Investigations) Atlas No. 33. U.S. Department of Commerce, NOAA, NMFS, Southwest Fisheries Science Center, La Jolla, California.

Moser, H. G., W. J. Richards, D. M. Cohen, M. P. Fahay, A. W. Kendall, Jr., and S. L. Richardson, editors.

1984. Ontogeny and systematics of fishes. Am. Soc. Ichthyol. Herpetol., Spec. Publ. 1. 760 pp.

Moyle, P. B., and J. J. Cech, Jr.

1988. Fishes: an introduction to ichthyology, 2nd edition. Prentice Hall, Englewood Cliffs, New Jersey. 559 pp.

Mukhacheva, V. A.

1964. O vidovom sostave roda *Cyclothone* (Pisces, Gonostomatidae) v Tikhom okeane [The composition of species of the genus *Cyclothone* (Pisces, Gonostomidae) in the Pacific Ocean]. Tr. Inst. Okeanol. Akad. Nauk SSSR 73: 93–138. [In Russian, with English summary; and English translation by Israel Prog. Sci. Transl., 1966, pages 98–146 *in* T. S. Rass, ed. Fishes of the Pacific and Indian oceans, biology and distribution.]

1969. Bristlemouth (genus *Cyclothone,* fam. Gonostomatidae). Pages 182–199 *in* The Pacific Ocean. Biology of the Pacific Ocean. Book 3, Fishes of the open waters, part 2, chapter 3. [In Russian.] [Cited in Kawaguchi 1971.]

1972. Materialy po sistematika, rasprostraneniye i biologiya vidov roda *Gonostoma* (Pisces, Gonostomatidae) [Materials on the systematics, distribution, and biology of the species of *Gonostoma* (Pisces, Gonostomatidae)]. Tr. Inst. Okeanol. Akad. Nauk SSSR 93: 205–249. [In Russian, with English summary; and English translation prepared for Smithsonian Institution by Saad Publications, Karachi, Pakistan, 1987.]

1974. Tsiklotony (rod *Cyclothone,* sem. Gonostomatidae) Mirovogo okeana i ikh rasprostraneniye [Cyclothones (genus *Cyclothone,* fam. Gonostomatidae) of the World ocean and their distribution]. Tr. Inst. Okeanol. Akad. Nauk SSSR 96: 189–254. [In Russian.]

Mukhametov, I. N., and A. V. Volodin.

1999. Capture of two rare fish species and one fish species new to the fauna of the northern Kurils. J. Ichthyol. 39(4): 338–339 [English transl. Vopr. Ikhtiol. 39(3): 426–427].

Mulligan, H. L., A. W. Kendall, Jr., and A. C. Matarese.
1995. The significance of morphological variation in adults and larvae of the rock sole, *Pleuronectes bilineatus,* from the Bering Sea and northeastern Pacific Ocean. Pages 133–150 *in* Proceedings of the International Symposium on North Pacific Flatfish. University of Alaska Sea Grant, AK-SG-95-04, Fairbanks.

Mundy, B. C., and H. G. Moser.
1997. Development of early stages of pelagic armorhead *Pseudopentaceros wheeleri* with notes on juvenile *Ps. richardsoni* and larval *Histiopterus typus* (Pisces, Percoidei, Pentacerotidae). Bull. Mar. Sci. 61(2): 241–269.

Murdoch, J.
1884. Fish and fishing at Point Barrow, Arctic Alaska. Trans. Am. Fish-Cultural Association (1884): 111–115.
1885. Fishes. Pages 129–132 *in* P. H. Ray. Report of the International Polar Expedition to Point Barrow, Alaska, in response to the resolution of the House of Representatives of December 11, 1884. U.S. Signal Office, Arctic Series of Publications, No. 1. Government Printing Office, Washington, D.C.

Murphy, B. R., and D. W. Willis, editors.
1996. Fisheries techniques, 2nd edition. American Fisheries Society, Bethesda, Maryland. 732 pp.

Murphy, M. L., S. W. Johnson, and D. J. Csepp.
2000. A comparison of fish assemblages in eelgrass and adjacent subtidal habitats near Craig, Alaska. Alaska Fish. Res. Bull. 7:11–21.

Murray, J. L.
1998. Chapter 2. Physical/geographical characteristics of the Arctic. Pages 9–24 *in* S. Wilson, J. L. Murray, and H. P. Huntington, eds. AMAP assessment report: Arctic pollution issues. Arctic Monitoring and Assessment Programme (AMAP), Oslo, Norway.

Murray, J. L., G. E. Brigette de March, and B. T. Hargrave.
1998. Chapter 4. Ecological characteristics of the Arctic. Pages 117–139 *in* S. Wilson, J. L. Murray, and H. P. Huntington, eds. AMAP assessment report: Arctic pollution issues. Arctic Monitoring and Assessment Programme (AMAP), Oslo, Norway.

Muto, F., M. Yabe, and K. Amaoka.
1994. A new cottid species, *Artediellus neyelovi,* from the southeastern coast of the Oshima Peninsula, Hokkaido, Japan. Jpn. J. Ichthyol. 41(3): 275–280.

Myers, G. S.
1934. A new name for the Alaskan cottoid fish *Ulca marmorata* (Bean). Copeia 1934(1): 44.
1946. On a recently proposed new family of deep-sea fishes (Barbourisiidae, Parr, 1945). Copeia 1946(1): 41-42.
1951. David Starr Jordan, ichthyologist. Stanford Ichthyol. Bull. 4(1): 2–6.
1960. A new zeomorph fish of the family Oreosomatidae from the coast of California, with notes on the family. Stanford Ichthyol. Bull. 7(4): 89–98.
1964. A brief sketch of the history of ichthyology in America to the year 1950. Copeia 1964(1): 33–41.

Nafpaktitus, B. G.
1977. Family Neoscopelidae. Pages 1–12 *in* Fishes of the western North Atlantic. Mem. Sears Found. Mar. Res., New Haven, 1(7).

Nagasawa, K.
1993. Distribution of daggertooth (*Anotopterus pharao*) in the North Pacific Ocean. Nat. Res. Inst. Sea Fish.: 107–109. [Cited in Balanov and Radchenko 1998.]

Nagasawa, K., A. Nishimura, T. Asanuma, and T. Marubayashi.
1997. Myctophids in the Bering Sea: distribution, abundance, and significance as food for salmonids. Pages 337–350 *in* Forage fishes in marine ecosystems. University of Alaska Sea Grant, AK-SG-97-01, Fairbanks.

Nagtegaal, D. A.
1983. First record of an adult oreo, *Allocyttus folletti* Myers, from British Columbian waters. Syesis 16: 89–90.

Nagtegaal, D. A., and S. P. Farlinger.
1980. First record of two fishes, *Seriolis dorsalis* (Gill) and *Medialuna californiensis* (Steindachner), from waters off British Columbia. Syesis 13: 207–208.

Nakabo, T.
2000. Fishes of Japan with pictorial keys to the species, 2nd edition. Tokai University Press. Vol. 1, pp. i–lvi + 1–866. Vol. 2, pp. i–vii + 867–1748. [In Japanese.]

Nakabo, T., U. Yamada, and M. Aizawa.
1992. New record of *Pseudoscopelus scutatus* (Chiasmodontidae) from Japan. Uo (Jpn. Soc. Ichthyol.) 41: 19–23.

Nakano, H., and K. Nagasawa.
1996. Distribution of pelagic elasmobranchs caught by salmon research gillnets in the North Pacific. Fish. Sci. (Tokyo) 62(5): 860–865.

Nakamura, R.

1976. Temperature and the vertical distribution of two tidepool fishes (*Oligocottus maculosus, O. snyderi*). Copeia 1976(1): 143–152.

Nakamura, I., and N. V. Parin.

1993. FAO species catalogue. Vol. 15. Snake mackerels and cutlassfishes of the world (families Gempylidae and Trichiuridae). FAO Fish. Synop. No. 125, Vol. 15. 136 pp.

Nakaya, K.

1971. Descriptive notes on a porbeagle, *Lamna nasus,* from Argentine waters, compared with the North Pacific salmon shark, *Lamna ditropis.* Bull. Fac. Fish. Hokkaido Univ. 21: 269–279.

Nakaya, K., K. Amaoka, and K. Abe.

1980. A review of the genus *Lepidion* (Gadiformes, Moridae) from the northwestern Pacific. Jpn. J. Ichthyol. 27(1): 41–47.

Nalbant, T. T.

1965. *Careproctus cameliae,* a new species of sea-snail from the Bering Sea (Pisces, Liparidae). Senckenb. Biol. 46(4): 271–273.

1970. Noi contributii la studiul ihtiofaunei din oceanul Pacific de nord. Bul. Inst. Cercet. Proiect. Piscic. 29 (1-2): 57–61, 1 pl. [In Romanian, with English and Russian summary.]

1994. Fishes obtained during the first cruise (1964) of M/S *Galati* in the Bering Sea. I. Family Zoarcidae (Pisces: Perciformes). Travaux de Muséum d'Histoire naturelle "Grigore Antipa" 34: 381–390.

Narver, D. W.

1969. Phenotypic variation in threespine sticklebacks (*Gasterosteus aculeatus*) of the Chignik River system, Alaska. J. Fish. Res. Board Can. 26(2): 405–412.

National Ocean Service.

1997. United States Coast Pilot 7. Pacific coast: California, Oregon, Washington, and Hawaii, 31st edition. U.S. Department of Commerce, NOAA, National Ocean Service, Washington, D.C. 453 pp. + indexes.

1998. United States Coast Pilot 9. Pacific and Arctic coasts Alaska: Cape Spencer to Beaufort Sea, 19th edtion. U.S. Department of Commerce, NOAA, National Ocean Service, Washington, D.C. 341 pp. + indexes.

1999. United States Coast Pilot 8. Pacific coast Alaska: Dixon Entrance to Cape Spencer, 23rd edtion. U.S. Department of Commerce, NOAA, National Ocean Service, Washington, D.C. 266 pp. + indexes.

National Research Council.

1996. The Bering Sea ecosystem. National Academy of Science Press, Washington, D.C. 307 pp.

Nazarkin, M. V., and O. S. Voskoboinikova.

2000. New fossil genus and species o Trichodontidae and the position of this family in the order Perciformes. J. Ichthyol. 40(9): 687–703 [English transl. Vopr. Ikhtiol. 40(6): 725–742].

Neave, F.

1959. Records of fishes from waters off the British Columbia coast. J. Fish. Res. Board Can. 16(3): 383–384.

Neave, F., and M. G. Hanavan.

1960. Seasonal distribution of some epipelagic fishes in the Gulf of Alaska region. J. Fish. Res. Board Can. 17(2): 221–233.

Neyelov (Neelov), A. V.

1976. Obzor bakhromchatykh bychkov roda *Porocottus* Gill i blizkikh k nemu rodov (Cottidae, Myoxocephalinae) [Survey of the fringed sculpins of the genus *Porocottus* Gill and closely related genera (Cottidae, Myoxocephalinae)]. Pages 78–112 *in* V. M. Korovina, ed. Zoogeografiya i sistematika ryb [Zoogeography and systematics of fishes]. Zool. Inst., Akad. Nauk SSSR. [In Russian.]

1979. Seismosensornaya sistema i klassifikatsiya kerchakovykh ryb (Cottidae: Myoxocephalinae, Artediellinae) [Seismosensory system and classification of sculpins (Cottidae: Myoxocephalinae, Artediellinae)]. Leningrad, Nauka. 208 pp. [In Russian.]

Nelson, D. W.

1984. Systematics and distribution of cottid fishes of the genera *Rastrinus* and *Icelus.* Occas. Pap. Calif. Acad. Sci. 138. 58 pp.

1986. Two new species of the cottid genus *Artediellus* from the western North Pacific Ocean and the Sea of Japan. Proc. Acad. Nat. Sci. Phila. 138(1): 33–45.

Nelson, E. W.

1887. Field notes on Alaskan fishes, by Edward W. Nelson, with additional notes by Tarleton H. Bean. Pages 295–322, plates 13–21 *in* Report upon natural history collections made in Alaska between the years 1877 and 1881 by Edward W. Nelson, edited by Henry W. Henshaw. Arctic Series of Publications Issued in Connection with the Signal Service, U.S. Army, No. 3. Government Printing Office, Washington, D.C.

Nelson, J. S.
1968. Distribution and nomenclature of North American kokanee, *Oncorhynchus nerka*. J. Fish. Res. Board Can. 25(2): 409–414.
1982. Two new South Pacific fishes of the genus *Ebinania* and contributions to the systematics of Psychrolutidae (Scorpaeniformes). Can. J. Zool. 60: 1470–1504.
1984. Fishes of the world, 2nd edition. John Wiley & Sons, New York. 523 pp.
1989. *Cottunculus nudus,* a new psychrolutid fish from New Zealand (Scorpaeniformes: Cottoidei). Copeia 1989(2): 401–408.
1994. Fishes of the world, 3rd edition. John Wiley & Sons, New York. 600 pp.
2000. Editorial and introduction: the species concept in fish biology. Rev. Fish Biol. Fish. 9: 277–280.

Niebauer, H. J., and D. M. Schell.
1993. Chapter 2. Physical environment of the Bering Sea population. Pages 23–43 *in* J. J. Burns, J. J. Montague, and C. J. Cowles, eds. The bowhead whale. Society for Marine Mammalogy, Spec. Publ. 2. Allen Press, Lawrence, Kansas.

Nielsen, J. G., D. M. Cohen, D. F. Markle, and C. R. Robins.
1999. FAO species catalogue. Vol. 18. Ophidiiform fishes of the world (order Ophidiiformes). An annotated and illustrated catalogue of pearlfishes, cusk-eels, brotulas and other ophidiiform fishes known to date. FAO Fish. Synop. No. 125, Vol. 18. 178 pp.

Nielsen, J. G., and J.-C. Hureau.
1980. Revision of the ophidiid genus *Spectrunculus* Jordan & Thompson, 1914, a senior synonym of *Parabassogigas* Nybelin, 1957 (Pisces, Ophidiiformes). Steenstrupia 6(11): 149–169.

Nielsen, J. G., and J. M. Jensen.
1967. Revision of the Arctic cod genus, *Arctogadus* (Pisces, Gadidae). Medd. Grønl. 184(2):1–26.

Nielsen, J. G., and D. G. Smith.
1978. The eel family Nemichthyidae (Pisces, Anguilliformes). Dana-Rep. Carlsberg Found. 88. 71 pp., 2 pls.

Nikiforov, S. N., S. N. Safronov, and N. S. Fadeev.
1983. Distinguishing characters of rock sole, *Lepidopsetta bilineata,* and mochigar sole, *L. mochigarei* (Pleuronectidae). J. Ichthyol. [English transl. Vopr. Ikhtiol.] 23: 36–44.

Nikol'skii, G. V.
1961. Special ichthyology (Chastnaya ikhtiologiya), 2nd edition. Israel Program for Scientific Translations, Jerusalem. 538 pp.

Nishimoto, J.
1970. Western range extension of the rosethorn rockfish, *Sebastes helvomaculatus* (Ayres). Calif. Fish Game 56(3): 204–205.

Nizinski, M.S., B. B. Collette, and B. B. Washington.
1990. Separation of two species of sand lances, *Ammodytes americanus* and *A. dubius,* in the western North Atlantic. U.S. Natl. Mar. Fish. Serv. Fish. Bull. 88: 241–255.

Nizovtsev, G. P., V. P. Ponomarenko, and M. S. Shevelev.
1976. Deepsea fishes of the Norwegian Sea. Vopr. Ikhtiol. 16: 1013–1014. [Translation by American Fisheries Society, 1977.]

Norman, J. R.
1929. The teleostean fishes of the family Chiasmodontidae. Ann. Mag. Nat. Hist. (Ser. 10) 3: 529–544.
1930. Oceanic fishes and flatfishes collected in 1925–1927. Discovery Rep. 2: 261–370, pls. 2.
1934. A systematic monograph of the flatfishes (Heterosomata). Vol. 1. Psettodidae, Bothidae, Pleuronectidae. British Museum (Natural History), London. 459 pp.

Norris, K. S.
1957. Second record of the green sturgeon in southern California. Calif. Fish Game 43(4): 317.

Novikov, N. P.
1970. Biology of *Chalinura pectoralis* in the North Pacific. Pages 304–331 *in* P. A. Moiseev, ed. Soviet fisheries investigations in the northeastern Pacific. Part V. All-Union Scientific Research Institute of Marine Fisheries and Oceanography (VNIRO) Proceedings Vol. 70, Pacific Scientific Research Institute of Fisheries and Oceanography (TINRO) Proceedings Vol. 72. [Translation by Israel Prog. Sci. Transl., 1972.]

O'Connell, C. P.
1953. The life history of the cabezon, *Scorpaenichthys marmoratus* (Ayres). Calif. Dep. Fish Game Fish Bull. 93: 76 pp.

O'Connell, V. M.
1993. Submersible observations on lingcod, *Ophiodon elongatus,* nesting below 30 m off Sitka, Alaska. U.S. Natl. Mar. Fish. Serv. Mar. Fish. Rev. 55(1): 19–24.

O'Connell, V. M., D. A. Gordon, A. Hoffmann, and K. Hepler.
1992. Northern range extension of the vermilion rockfish (*Sebastes miniatus*). Calif. Fish Game 78(4): 173.

Odemar, M. W.
1964. Southern range extension of the eulachon, *Thaleichthys pacificus*. Calif. Fish Game 50(4): 305–307.

Ogilby, J. D.
1899. Additions to the fauna of Lord Howe Island. Proc. Linn. Soc. N.S.W. 23(4): 730–745.

Okada, S., and K. Kobayashi.
1968. Hokuyo-gyorui-zusetsu [Illustrations and descriptions of the fishes of the northern seas]. Sanseido, Tokyo. 179 pp. [In Japanese.]

Okada, Y.
1955. Fishes of Japan. Maruzen Co., Ltd., Tokyo. 434 pp.

Okamura, O.
1970. Fauna Japonica. Macrourina (Pisces). Academic Press of Japan, Tokyo. 216 pp., 44 pls.

Okamura, O., K. Amaoka, M. Takeda, K. Yano, K. Okada, and S. Chikuni, editors.
1995. Fishes collected by the R/V Shinkai Maru around Greenland. Japan Marine Fishery Resources Research Center, Tokyo. 304 pp.

Okamura, O., and T. Kitajima, editors.
1984. Fishes of the Okinawa Trough and the adjacent waters. Vol. 1. The intensive research of unexploited fishery resources on continental slopes. Japan Fisheries Conservation Association, Tokyo. Pages 1–414.

Okamura, O., and Y. Machida.
1986. Additional records of fishes from Kochi Prefecture, Japan. Mem. Fac. Sci. Kochi Univ. Ser. D Biol. 7: 17–41.
1987. Additional records of fishes from Kochi Prefecture, Japan (II). Mem. Fac. Sci. Kochi Univ. Ser. D Biol. 8: 101–112.

Okamura, O., Y. Machida, T. Yamakawa, K. Matsuura, and T. Yatou, editors.
1985. Fishes of the Okinawa Trough and the adjacent waters. Vol. 2. The intensive research of unexploited fishery resources on continental slopes. Japan Fisheries Conservation Association, Tokyo. Pages 417–781.

Okazaki, T.
1984. Genetic divergence and its zoogeographic implications in closely related species *Salmo gairdneri* and *Salmo mykiss*. Jpn. J. Ichthyol. 31(3): 297–310.

Olney, J. E., G. D. Johnson, and C. C. Baldwin.
1993. Phylogeny of lampridiform fishes. Bull. Mar. Sci. 52(1): 147–169.

Orlov, A. M.
1994. Some characteristics of distribution and biological status of *Eumicrotremus soldatovi* (Cyclopteridae) in the northeastern part of the Sea of Okhotsk during the spring. J. Ichthyol. 34(2): 122–127 [English transl. Vopr. Ikhtiol. 33(5): 720–723].
1998a. Demersal ichthyofauna of Pacific waters around the Kuril Islands and southeastern Kamchatka. Russ. J. Mar. Biol. [English transl. Biol. Morya] 24(3): 144–160.
1998b. On feeding of mass species of deep-sea skates (*Bathyraja* spp., Rajidae) from the Pacific waters of the northern Kurils and southeastern Kamchatka. J. Ichthyol. 38(8): 635–644 [English transl. Vopr. Ikhtiol. 38(5): 659–668].
1998b. The diets and feeding habits of some deep-water benthic skates (Rajidae) in the Pacific waters off the northern Kuril Islands and southeastern Kamchatka. Alaska Fish. Res. Bull. 5(1): 1–17. [Contains the same information as published earlier in the same year in the J. Ichthyol.; see preceding entry.]
1999. Capture of especially large sleeper shark *Somniosus pacificus* (Squalidae) with some notes on its ecology in northwestern Pacific. J. Ichthyol. 39(7): 548–553 [English transl. Vopr. Ikhtiol. 39(4): 558–563].

Orlov, A. M., and P. N. Kochkin.
1995. Distinctive features of the spatial distribution and size composition of the large-fin thornyhead, *Sebastolobus macrochir* (Scorpaenidae), on the slope of southeastern Sakhalin, summer 1993. J. Ichthyol. [English transl. Vopr. Ikhtiol.] 38: 219–225.

Orr, J. W.
1991. A new species of the ceratioid anglerfish genus *Oneirodes* (Oneirodidae) from the western North Atlantic, with a revised key to the genus. Copeia 1991(4): 1024–1031.

Orr, J. W., and D. C. Baker.
1996a. New North American records of the northeast Pacific scorpaenids *Adelosebastes latens* and *Sebastes glaucus*. Alaska Fish. Res. Bull. 3(2): 94–102.
1996b. Southern range extension of the harlequin rockfish, *Sebastes variegatus* (Scorpaenidae). Calif. Fish Game 82(3): 133–136.

Orr, J. W., D. C. Baker, and M. A. Brown.
1997ms. Field key to the flatfishes from Point Conception to the Arctic (draft). [Available from J. W. Orr, National Marine Fisheries Service, Alaska Fisheries Science Center, 7600 Sand Point Way NE, Seattle, WA 98115-0070.]

Orr, J. W., J. Blackburn, J. A. Lopez, and P. Bentzen.
1997. Systematics of *Sebastes ciliatus*: a case of mistaken identity? American Society of Ichthyologists and Herpetologists Annual Meeting. [Abstract.] [Available from J. W. Orr, National Marine Fisheries Service, Alaska Fisheries Science Center, 7600 Sand Point Way NE, Seattle, WA 98115-0070.]

Orr, J. W., M. A. Brown, and D. C. Baker.
1998. Guide to rockfishes (Scorpaenidae) of the genera *Sebastes, Sebastolobus,* and *Adelosebastes* of the northeast Pacific Ocean. U.S. Dep. Commer., NOAA Tech. Memo. NMFS-AFSC-95. 46 pp.
2000. Guide to rockfishes (Scorpaenidae) of the genera *Sebastes, Sebastolobus,* and *Adelosebastes* of the northeast Pacific Ocean, 2nd edition. U.S. Dep. Commer., NOAA Tech. Memo. NMFS-AFSC-117. 47 pp.

Orr, J. W., and M. S. Busby.
2001. *Prognatholiparis ptychomandibularis,* a new genus and species of the fish family Liparidae (Teleostei: Scorpaeniformes) from the Aleutian Islands, Alaska. Proc. Biol. Soc. Wash. 114(1): 51–57.

Orr, J. W., and A. C. Matarese.
2000. Revision of the genus *Lepidopsetta* Gill, 1862 (Teleostei: Pleuronectidae) based on larval and adult morphology, with a description of a new species from the North Pacific Ocean and Bering Sea. Fish. Bull. 98(3): 539–582.

Orsi, J. A., R. K. Gish, and B. L. Wing.
1991. Northern range extensions of four nearshore marine fishes in Alaska. Can. Field-Nat. 105(1): 82–86.

Orsi, J. A., and J. H. Landingham.
1985. Numbers, species, and maturity stages of fish captured with beach seines during spring 1981 and 1982 in some nearshore marine waters of southeastern Alaska. U.S. Dep. Commer., NOAA Tech. Memo. NMFS F/NWC-86. 34 pp.

Orth, D. J.
1967. Dictionary of Alaska place names. Reprinted 1971 with minor revisions. U.S. Geological Survey Professional Paper 567. U.S. Government Printing Office, Washington, D.C. 1,084 pp., 12 maps.

Osburn, R. C., and J. T. Nichols.
1916. Shore fishes collected by the *Albatross* expedition in Lower California, with descriptions of new species. Bull. Am. Mus. Nat. Hist. 35(16): 139–181.

Osinov, A. G.
1999. Salmonid fish of the genera *Salmo, Parasalmo,* and *Oncorhynchus*: genetic divergence, phylogeny, and classification. J. Ichthyol. 39(8): 571–587 [English transl. Vopr. Ikhtiol. 39(5): 595–611].
2001. Evolutionary relationships between the main taxa of the *Salvelinus alpinus–Salvelinus malma* complex: results of a comparative analysis of allozyme data from different authors. J. Ichthyol. 41(3): 192–208.

Osinov, A. G., and S. D. Pavlov.
1994. Genetic similarity between Kamchatkan and North American rainbow trout. J. Ichthyol. 34(2): 60–68 [English transl. Vopr. Ikhtiol. 33(5): 626–630].
1998. Allozyme variation and genetic divergence between populations of Arctic char and Dolly Varden (*Salvelinus alpinus–Salvelinus malma* complex). J. Ichthyol. 38(1): 42–55 [English transl. Vopr. Ikhtiol. 38(1): 47–61].

Oswood, M. W.
1989. Community structure of benthic invertebrates in interior Alaskan (USA) streams and rivers. Hydrobiologia 172: 97–110.

Oswood, M. W., K. R. Everett, and D. M. Schell.
1989. Some physical and chemical conditions of an arctic beaded stream. Holarct. Ecol. 12: 290–295.

Oswood, M. W., J. B. Reynolds, G. G. Irons III, and A. M. Milner.
2000. Distributions of freshwater fishes in ecoregions and hydroregions of Alaska. J. N. Am. Benthol. Soc. 19(3): 405–418.

Page, L. M., and B. M. Burr.
1991. A field guide to freshwater fishes of North America north of Mexico. Peterson Field Guide 42. Houghton Mifflin, Boston. 432 pp.

Pallas, P. S.
1814. Zoographia Rosso-Asiatica. Petropoli. Vol 3. [Cited by Jordan and Evermann (1896b), giving year as 1811. Date of publication fixed as 1814 by International Commission of Zoological Nomenclature, Opinion 212.]

Palmen, A. T.
1954. Occurrence of the eel-pout, *Aprodon cortezianus,* in Queen Charlotte Sound, B.C. Wash. Dep. Fish. Fish. Res. Pap. 1(2). 45.

Palmer, G., and H. A. Oelschläger.

1976. Use of the name *Lampris guttatus* (Brünnich, 1788) in preference to *Lampris regius* (Bonnaterre, 1788) for the opah. Copeia 1976 (2): 366–367.

Panchenko, V. V.

1996. Data on the biology of the blue rockfish *Sebastes glaucus* (Scorpaenidae) in the southern Sea of Okhotsk. J. Ichthyol. 36(1): 124–125 [English transl. Vopr. Ikhtiol. 36(1): 130–131].

Panin, K. I.

1936. O nakhozhdenii dal'nevostochnoi sardiny-ivasi (*Sardinops melanosticta*) v vodakh vostochnoi Kamchatki [A find of the Pacific sardine-ivasi (*Sardinops melanosticta*) in the waters of eastern Kamchatka]. Dokl. Akad. Nauk SSSR 3(12), 1(96): 41–44.

Parenti, L. R.

1993. Relationships of atherinomorph fishes. Bull. Mar. Sci. 52(1): 170–196.

Parenti, L. R., and J. Song.

1996. Phylogenetic significance of the pectoral–pelvic fin association in acanthomorph fishes: a reassessment using comparative anatomy. Pages 427–444 *in* M. L. J. Stiassny, L. R. Parenti, and G. D. Johnson, eds. Interrelationships of fishes. Academic Press, San Diego.

Parin, N. V.

1961. Raspredelenie glubokovodnykh ryb verkhnego sloya batipelagiali v subarkticheskikh vodakh severnoi chasti Tikhogo okeana [Distribution of deepwater fishes in the upper layer of the bathyal zone in subarctic waters of the North Pacific]. Tr. Inst. Okeanol. Akad. Nauk SSSR 45. [In Russian.]

1968. Ichthyofauna of the epipelagic zone. Acad. Sci. USSR, Inst. Oceanology. 205 pp. [Translation by Israel Prog. Sci. Transl., 1970, IPST No. 5528.]

1984. Oceanic ichthyologeography: an attempt to review the distribution and origin of pelagic and bottom fishes outside continental shelves and neritic zones. Arch. Fischerei Wiss. 35(1): 5–41.

Parin, N. V., and A. W. Ebeling.

1980. A new western Pacific *Poromitra* (Pisces: Melamphaidae). Copeia 1980(1): 87–93.

Parin, N. V., V. V. Fedorov, O. D. Borodulina, and V. E. Bekker.

1995. New records of mesopelagic and epipelagic fishes in Pacific waters off the southern Kuril Islands. J. Ichthyol. 35(9): 193–204 [English transl. Vopr. Ikhtiol. 35(6): 732–739].

Parin, N. V., and A. N. Kotlyar.

1998. *Melamphaes suborbitalis* and *Scopeloberyx robustus* (Melamphaidae) from the Russian part of the Sea of Okhotsk. J. Ichthyol. [English transl. Vopr. Ikhtiol.] 38(6): 481–482.

Parin, N. V., and Y. I. Kukuyev.

1983. Reestablishment of the validity of *Lampris immaculata* Gilchrist and the geographical distribution of Lampridae. J. Ichthyol. [English transl. Vopr. Ikhtiol.] 23(1): 1–12.

Parin, N. V., and N. S. Novikova.

1974. Sistematika khauliodov (Chauliodontidae, Osteichthyes) i ikh rasprostranenie v mirovom okeane [Taxonomy of viperfishes (Chauliodontidae, Osteichthyes) and their distribution in the world ocean]. Tr. Inst. Okeanol. Akad. Nauk SSSR 96: 255–315. [In Russian; English summary.]

Parin, N. V., and Yu. N. Scherbachev.

1998. *Taractes asper* (Bramidae) in the waters of California. J. Ichthyol. 38(4): 338–339 [English transl. Vopr. Ikhtiol. 38(4): 420–421].

Parks, N. B., and H. Zenger.

1979. Trawl survey of demersal fish and shellfish resources in Prince William Sound, Alaska: spring 1978. NWAFC Processed Report 79–2. 49 pp. Northwest and Alaska Fisheries Center, NMFS, NOAA, 2725 Montlake Blvd. E., Seattle, WA 98112.

Parr, A. E.

1926. Investigations on the Cyclopterini. Bergens Mus. Aarbok 1924–25, Naturvidensk. raekke 7. 31 pp., 1 pl.

1930. On the probable identity, life-history and anatomy of the free-living and attached males of the ceratioid fishes. Copeia 1930(4): 129–135.

1931. Scientific results of the second oceanographic expedition of the *Pawnee,* 1926. Deepsea fishes from off the western coast of North and Central America. Bull. Bingham Oceanogr. Collect. Yale Univ. 2(4). 53 pp.

1933. Scientific results of the third oceanographic expedition of the *Pawnee,* 1927. Deepsea Berycomorphi and Percomorphi from the waters around the Bahama and Bermuda islands. Bull. Bingham Oceanogr. Collect. Yale Univ. 3(6): 1–51.

1934. Report on experimental use of a triangular trawl for bathypelagic collecting with an account of the fishes obtained and a revision of the family Cetomimidae. Bull. Bingham Oceanogr. Collect. Yale Univ. 4 (art. 6): 1–59.

Parr, A. E.
1945. Barbourisidae, a new family of deep sea fishes. Copeia 1945(3): 127–129, 1 pl.
1946a. A new species of *Gyrinomimus* from the Gulf of Mexico. Copeia 1946(3): 116–117, 1 pl.
1946b. On taxonomic questions related to the classification of *Barbourisia,* the Cetomimidae and the Iniomi. Copeia 1946(4): 260–262.
1960. The fishes of the family Searsidae. Dana-Rep. Carlsberg Found. 51. 108 pp.

Parrish, R. H., R. Serra, and W. S. Grant.
1989. The monotypic sardines, *Sardina* and *Sardinops*: their taxonomy, distribution, stock structure, and zoogeography. Can. J. Fish. Aquat. Sci. 46(11): 2019–2036.

Patterson, C.
1993. Lampriformes or lampriform, Lamprididae or Lampridae? Bull. Mar. Sci. 52(1): 168–169.

Patterson, C., and D. E. Rosen.
1989. The Paracanthopterygii revisited: order and disorder. Pages 5–36 *in* D. M. Cohen, ed. Papers on the systematics of gadiform fishes. Nat. Hist. Mus. Los Angeles County, Sci. Ser. 32.

Paulin, C. D.
1989. Moridae: overview. Pages 243–250 *in* D. M. Cohen, ed. Papers on the systematics of gadiform fishes. Nat. Hist. Mus. Los Angeles County, Sci. Ser. 32.

Paulson, A. C., and R. L. Smith.
1974. Occurrence of Pacific staghorn sculpin (*Leptocottus armatus*) in the southern Bering Sea. J. Fish. Res. Board Can. 31(7): 1262.

Pavlov, Yu. P.
1989. Some data on the morphometrics and distribution of species of the genus *Taractes* (Bramidae) in the Pacific Ocean. J. Ichthyol. 29(6): 164–165 [English transl. Vopr. Ikhtiol. 29(4): 660–662].

Paxton, J. R.
1972. Osteology and relationships of the lanternfishes (family Myctophidae). Nat. Hist. Mus. Los Angel. County Sci. Bull. 13. 81 pp.
1979. Nominal genera and species of lanternfishes (family Myctophidae). Contrib. Sci. (Los Angel.) 322: 28 pp.
1989. Synopsis of the whalefishes (family Cetomimidae) with descriptions of four new genera. Rec. Aust. Mus. 41: 135–206.
1990. Whalefishes: little fishes with big mouths. Aust. Nat. Hist. 23(5): 378–385.

Paxton, J. R., E. H. Ahlstrom, and H. G. Moser.
1984. Myctophidae: relationships. Pages 239–244 *in* H. G. Moser et al., eds. Ontogeny and systematics of fishes. Am. Soc. Ichthyol. Herpetol., Spec. Publ. 1.

Pearcy, W. G., J. Fisher, R. Brodeur, and S. Johnson.
1985. Effects of the 1983 El Niño on coastal nekton of Oregon and Washington. Pages 188–204 *in* W. S. Wooster and D. L. Fluharty, eds. El Niño north: Niño effects in the eastern subarctic Pacific Ocean. Washington Sea Grant Program, University of Washington, Seattle.

Pearcy, W. G., T. Nemoto, and M. Okiyama.
1979. Mesopelagic fishes of the Bering Sea and adjacent northern North Pacific Ocean. J. Oceanogr. Soc. Jpn. 35:127–135.

Pearcy, W. G., and A. Schoener.
1987. Changes in the marine biota coincident with the 1982–1983 El Niño in the northeastern subarctic Pacific Ocean. J. Geophys. Res. 92(C13): 14,417–14,428.

Pearcy, W. G., D. L. Stein, and R. S. Carney.
1982. The deep-sea benthic fish fauna of the northeastern Pacific Ocean on Cascadia and Tufts abyssal plains and adjoining continental slopes. Biol. Oceanogr. 1(4): 375–428.

Pearson, D. E., D. A. Douglas, and B. Barss.
1993. Biological observations from the Cobb Seamount. U.S. Natl. Mar. Fish. Serv. Fish. Bull. 91: 573–576.

Peden, A. E.
1966a. Occurrences of the fishes *Pholis schultzi* and *Liparis mucosus* in British Columbia. J. Fish. Res. Board Can. 23(2): 313–316.
1966b. Rare marine fishes from British Columbia with first records of silver perch, *Hyperprosopon ellipticum,* and shanny, *Leptoclinus maculatus.* J. Fish. Res. Board Can. 23(8): 1277–1280.
1966c. Reexamination of two species in the stichaeid genus, *Anoplarchus.* Copeia 1966(2): 340–345.
1967. Redescription of a North Pacific prickleback, *Alectridium auranticum* [*sic*]. J. Fish. Res. Board Can. 24(1): 1–8.
1967. Erratum: correct spelling of *Alectridium aurantiacum.* J. Fish. Res. Board Can. 24(12): 2641.

Peden, A. E.

1968. Two new specimens of the notacanthid fish *Macdonaldia challengeri* in the eastern North Pacific Ocean. J. Fish. Res. Board Can. 25(1): 181–188.

1970. A new cottid fish, *Nautichthys robustus,* from Alaska and British Columbia. Natl. Mus. Nat. Sci. (Ottawa) Publ. Biol. Oceanogr. 2: 1–10.

1971. Extension of the known range of the masked greenling, *Hexagrammos octogrammus,* to British Columbia. J. Fish. Res. Board Can. 28(6): 927–928.

1972. New records of sculpins (Cottidae) from the coasts of British Columbia and Washington. Can. Field-Nat. 86(2): 168–169.

1973. Records of eelpouts of the genus *Lycenchelys* and *Embryx* from the northeastern Pacific Ocean. Syesis 6: 115–120.

1974. Rare fishes including first records of thirteen species from British Columbia. Syesis 7: 47–62.

1976. First records of the notacanth fish, *Notacanthus chemnitzi* Bloch, from the northeastern Pacific. Calif. Fish Game 62(4): 304–305.

1977. First record of Atka mackerel, *Pleurogrammus monopterygius* (Hexagrammidae), in British Columbia. Can. Field-Nat. 91(2): 175–176.

1978. A systematic revision of the hemilepidotine fishes (Cottidae). Syesis 11: 11–49.

1979a. Meristic variation of *Lycodapus mandibularis* (Pisces: Zoarcidae) and oceanic upwelling on the west coast of North America. J. Fish. Res. Board Can. 36(1): 69–76.

1979b. Occurrence of the eelpout, *Bothrocara pusillum* (Zoarcidae), off British Columbia. Syesis 12: 183–184.

1979c. Rare captures of two fishes, *Benthodesmus* and *Paralepis,* off British Columbia. Syesis 12: 179–180.

1981a. Meristic variation of four fish species exhibiting lowest median counts in Georgia Strait, British Columbia. Can. J. Zool. 59(4): 679–683.

1981b. On the identity of two cottid subspecies, *Icelinus burchami burchami* and *I. b. fuscescens.* Copeia 1981(2): 482–484.

1981c. Recognition of *Leuroglossus schmidti* and *L. stilbius* (Bathylagidae, Pisces) as distinct species in the North Pacific Ocean. Can. J. Zool. 59(12): 2396–2398.

1984. Redefinition of *Icelinus fimbriatus* and *I. oculatus* (Cottidae, Pisces), and their corrected geographic distributions, with a new key to the genus. Syesis 17: 67–80.

1997a. Dreamers and sea devils. The Westcoast Fisherman, Vancouver, B.C., February: 35–36.

1997b. The California slickhead, B.C.'s "missing fish." The Westcoast Fisherman, Vancouver, B.C., March: 39.

1997c. One species or two? The Westcoast fisherman, Vancouver, B.C., April: 41.

1997d. Phantoms and other snailfish. The Westcoast Fisherman, Vancouver, B.C., May: 50.

1997e. "Blob" says it all: how the blob sculpin got its name. The Westcoast Fisherman, Vancouver, B.C., June: 40.

1997ms. Confirmatory records of snailfishes (Liparidae) of British Columbia: including notes on life history of *Careproctus melanurus, Lipariscus nanus,* and *Paraliparis melanobranchus*; and first records of *C. cypselurus, Liparis gibbus,* and *P. pectoralis.*

1998. Marine fishes. Pages 5–23 *in* The vertebrates of British Columbia: scientific and English names. Standards for Components of British Columbia's Biodiversity No. 2. Resources Inventory Committee, Province of British Columbia. [Available on the Internet or printed on demand through: www.publications.gov.bc.ca.]

Peden, A. E., and M. E. Anderson.

1978. A systematic review of the fish genus *Lycodapus* (Zoarcidae) with descriptions of two new species. Can. J. Zool. 56(9): 1925–1961.

1979. Erratum: A systematic review of the fish genus *Lycodapus* (Zoarcidae) with descriptions of two new species. Can. J. Zool. 57(2): 472–473.

1981. *Lycodapus* (Pisces: Zoarcidae) of eastern Bering Sea and nearby Pacific Ocean, with three new species and a revised key to the species. Can. J. Zool. 59(4): 667–678.

Peden, A. E., and C. A. Corbett.

1973. Commensalism between a liparid fish, *Careproctus* sp., and the lithodid box crab, *Lopholithodes foraminatus.* Can. J. Zool. 51: 555–556.

Peden, A. E., and C. G. Gruchy.

1971. First record of the bluespotted poacher, *Xeneretmus triacanthus,* in British Columbia. J. Fish. Res. Board Can. 28(9): 1347–1348.

Peden, A. E., and G. W. Hughes.

1984. Distribution, morphological variation, and systematic relationship of *Pholis laeta* and *P. ornata* (Pisces: Pholididae) with a description of the related form *P. nea* n. sp. Can. J. Zool. 62(2): 291–305.

1986. First records, confirmatory records, and range extensions of marine fishes off Canada's west coast. Can. Field-Nat. 100(1): 1–9.

Peden, A. E., and G. S. Jamieson.
1988. New distributional records of marine fishes off Washington, British Columbia and Alaska. Can. Field-Nat. 102(3): 491–494.

Peden, A. E., and W. Ostermann.
1980. Three fish species previously unknown from marine waters off British Columbia. Syesis 13: 215–217.

Peden, A. E., W. Ostermann, and L. J. Pozar.
1985. Fishes observed at Canadian weathership ocean station Papa (50°N, 145'W) with notes on the trans-Pacific cruise of the CSS *Endeavor.* British Columbia Provincial Museum, Heritage Record 18. 50 pp.

Peden, A. E., and K. Sendall.
1997ms. *Careproctus* sp. nov. Peden and Sendall.

Peden, A. E., and D. E. Wilson.
1976. Distribution of intertidal and subtidal fishes of northern British Columbia and southeastern Alaska. Syesis 9: 221–248.

Pennak, R. W.
1964. Collegiate dictionary of zoology. The Ronald Press Company, New York. 583 pp.

Percy, R., W. Eddy, and D. Munro.
1974. Anadromous and freshwater fish of the outer Mackenzie Delta. Interim report, Beaufort Sea Project Study B2. Beaufort Sea Project, 512 Federal Building, 1230 Government St., Victoria, B.C. V8W 1Y4. 51 pp.

Pereyra, W. T., J. E. Reeves, and R. G. Bakkala.
1976. Demersal fish and shellfish resources of the eastern Bering Sea in the baseline year 1975. Data appendices. Processed Report. 534 pp. Northwest Fisheries Center, NMFS, NOAA, 2725 Montlake Blvd. East, Seattle, WA 98112.

Perminov, G. N.
1936. Obzor vidov roda *Eumicrotremus* Gill [Review of species of the genus *Eumicrotremus* Gill]. Vestnik Dal'nevostochnogo Filiala Akademii Nauk SSSR [Bull. Far-East. Branch Acad. Sci. USSR] 19: 115–129. [In Russian.]

Phillips, R. B., and K. A. Pleyte.
1991. Nuclear DNA and salmonid phylogenetics. J. Fish. Biol. 39 (Suppl. A): 259–275.

Phillips, J. B.
1953. Sleeper shark, *Somniosus pacificus,* caught off Fort Bragg, California. Calif. Fish Game 39(1): 147–149.
1953. Additional Pacific cod taken off central California. Calif. Fish Game 39(4): 559.
1957. A review of the rockfishes of California (family Scorpaenidae). Calif. Dep. Fish Game Fish Bull. 104. 158 pp.
1958. Southerly occurrences of three northern species of fish during 1957, a warmwater year on the California coast. Calif. Fish Game 44(4): 349–350.
1959. A review of the lingcod, *Ophiodon elongatus.* Calif. Fish Game 45(1): 19–27.
1964. Life history studies on ten species of rockfish (genus *Sebastodes*). Calif. Dep. Fish Game Fish Bull. 126. 70 pp.
1966. Skilfish, *Erilepis zonifer* (Lockington), in Californian and Pacific Northwest waters. Calif. Fish Game 52(3): 151–156.
1967. A longfin sanddab, *Citharichthys xanthostigma,* and a skilfish, *Erilepis zonifer,* taken in Monterey Bay. Calif. Fish Game 53(4): 297–298.

Phinney, D. E.
1972. Occurrence of the Bering poacher (*Occella dodacaedron*) [*sic*] and the Pacific staghorn sculpin (*Leptocottus armatus*) near Chignik, Alaska. J. Fish. Res. Board Can. 29(1): 107–108.

Phinney, D. E., and M. L. Dahlberg.
1968. Western range extension of the surf smelt, *Hypomesus pretiosus pretiosus.* J. Fish. Res. Board Can. 25(1): 203–204.

Pietsch, T. W.
1972. A review of the monotypic deep-sea anglerfish family Centrophrynidae: taxonomy, distribution and osteology. Copeia 1972(1): 17–47.
1973. A new genus and species of deep-sea anglerfish (Pisces: Oneirodidae) from the northern Pacific Ocean. Copeia 1973(2): 193–199.
1974. Osteology and relationships of ceratioid anglerfishes of the family Oneirodidae, with a review of the genus *Oneirodes* Lütken. Nat. Hist. Mus. Los Angel. County Sci. Bull. 18. 113 pp.
1975. Systematics and distribution of ceratioid anglerfishes of the genus *Chaenophryne* (family Oneirodidae). Bull. Mus. Comp. Zool. 147(2): 75–100.

Pietsch, T. W.

1976. Dimorphism, parasitism and sex: reproductive strategies among deepsea ceratioid anglerfishes. Copeia 1976(4): 781–793.

1984. Lophiiformes: development and relationships. Pages 320–325 *in* H. G. Moser et al., eds. Ontogeny and systematics of fishes. Am. Soc. Ichthyol. Herpetol., Spec. Publ. 1.

1986. Systematics and distribution of bathypelagic anglerfishes of the family Ceratiidae (order: Lophiiformes). Copeia 1986(2): 479–493.

1994. Systematics and distribution of cottid fishes of the genus *Triglops* Reinhardt (Teleosti: Scorpaeniformes). Zool. J. Linn. Soc. 109(4) for 1993: 335–393.

Pietsch, T. W., and C. P. Zabetian.

1990. Osteology and interrelationships of the sand lances (Teleostei: Ammodytidae). Copeia 1990(1): 78–100.

Pinchuk, V. I.

1976. Ikhtiofauna litorali Komandorskikh Ostrovov [Ichthyofauna of the intertidal zone of the Commander Islands]. Biol. Morya (Vladivost.) 1976(5): 28–37. [In Russian; English summary.]

Pinkas, L.

1967. First record of a Pacific cod in southern California waters. Calif. Fish Game 53(2): 127–128.

Pitruk, D. L.

1988. New data on the Sakhalin flounder, *Limanda sakhalinensis*. J. Ichthyol. [English transl. Vopr. Ikhtiol.] 27(6): 116–119.

1990. A preliminary list and distribution of species of fishes of the family Liparididae in the Okhotsk Sea. Tr. Zool. Inst. Akad. Nauk SSSR 213: 35–45. [In Russian.]

Pitruk, D. L., and V. V. Fedorov.

1990. A new species of the genus *Osteodiscus* Stein (Liparididae) from the Sea of Okhotsk. J. Ichthyol. 30(8): 112–118 [English transl. Vopr. Ikhtiol. 30(5): 856–860].

1993a. *Allocareproctus* gen. novum (Scorpaeniformes, Liparidae)—a new genus of snailfishes from the northwest Pacific Ocean. J. Ichthyol. 33(5): 99–107 [English transl. Vopr. Ikhtiol. 33(1): 16–20].

1993b. The validity of the genus *Elassodiscus* Gilbert and Burke, 1912 (Scorpaeniformes, Liparidae) with a description of a new species from the Sea of Okhotsk. J. Ichthyol. 33(6): 68–84 [English transl. Vopr. Ikhtiol. 33(2): 165–175].

1994. *Squaloliparis* (Scorpaeniformes, Liparidae)—a new genus of snailfishes from the Sea of Okhotsk. J. Ichthyol. 34(2): 8–19 [English transl. Vopr. Ikhtiol. 33(5): 602–608].

Poltev, Yu. N., and I. N. Mukhametov.

1999. Captures of big-mouth sculpin *Ulca bolini* in Pacific waters of the northern Kurils and the southeastern extremity of Kamchatka. J. Ichthyol. 39(8): 679–681 [English transl. Vopr. Ikhtiol. 39(5): 708–710].

Poltorykhina, A. N.

1974. Morphological characteristics and variability of the Siberian lamprey (*Lampetra japonica kessleri*) from the upper Irtysh Basin. J. Ichthyol. 14(2): 192–202.

Polutov, I. A.

1966. [Pharaoh's fishes from the northern part of the Pacific Ocean]. Vopr. Geografii Kamchatki 4: 136–139. [In Russian. Selections translated by B. A. Sheiko, 1999, for Point Stephens Research, Auke Bay, Alaska.]

Ponomarenko, V. P.

1979. An interesting find of the blue wolffish *Anarhichas denticulatus*. J. Ichthyol. [English transl. Vopr. Ikhtiol.] 19(16): 151–152.

Popov, A. M.

1928. K sistematike roda *Eumicrotremus* Gill [On the systematics of the genus *Eumicrotremus* Gill]. Izv. Tikhookean. Nauchno-Issled. Inst. Rybn. Khoz. Okeanogr. [Bull. Pac. Sci. Inst. Fish. Oceanogr.] 1(2): 47–63, 2 pls. [In Russian; English summary.].

1930. A short review of the fishes of the family Cyclopteridae. Ann. Mag. Nat. Hist., Ser. 10, 6(31): 69–76.

1933. Fishes of Avatcha Bay on the southern coast of Kamtchatka. Copeia 1933(2): 59–67.

Post, A.

1968. Ergebnisse der Forschungsreisen des FFS *Walter Herwig* nach Südamerika. V. *Notolepis rissoi* (Bonaparte, 1841) (Osteichthyes, Iniomi, Paralepididae). Arch. Fischereiwiss. 19(2/3): 103–113.

1987. Results of the research cruises of FRV *Walter Herwig* to South America. LXVII. Revision of the subfamily Paralepidinae (Pisces, Aulopiformes, Alepisauroidei, Paralepididae). I. Taxonomy, morphology and geographical distribution. Arch. Fischereiwiss. 38(1/2): 75–131.

Post, A., and J.-C. Quéro.

1991. Distribution et taxinomie des *Howella* (Perciformes, Percichthyidae) de l'Atlantique. Cybium 15(2): 111–128.

Potter, I. C.
1980. The Petromyzoniformes with particular reference to paired species. Can. J. Fish. Aquat. Sci. 37: 1595–1615.

Potter, I. C., and R. W. Hilliard.
1987. A proposal for the functional and phylogenetic significance of differences in the dentition of lampreys (Agnatha: Petromyzontiformes). J. Zool. (Lond.) 212(4): 713–737.

Power, G.
1980. The brook charr, *Salvelinus fontinalis.* Pages 141–203 *in* E. K. Balon, ed. Charrs: salmonid fishes of the genus *Salvelinus.* Dr. W. Junk, The Hague.

Proshutninsky, A. J., and M. A. Johnson.
1997. Two circulation rregimes of the wind-driven Arctic Ocean. J. Geophys. Res. 102(C6): 12493–12514.

Prouse, N. J., and D. E. McAllister.
1986. The glacial eelpout, *Lycodes frigidus,* from the Arctic Canadian Basin, new to the Canadian ichthyofauna. Can. Field-Nat. 100(3): 325–329.

Pruter, A. T., and D. L. Alverson.
1962. Abundance, distribution, and growth of flounders in the south-eastern Chukchi Sea. J. Cons. Cons. Int. Explor. Mer 27(1): 81–99.

Pshenichnov, L. K.
1997. A dogfish species new for ichthyofauna of subantarctic regions: *Squalus acanthias* (Squalidae). J. Ichthyol. 37(8): 678–679 [English transl. Vopr. Ikhtiol. 37(5): 713–714].

Quast, J. C.
1964a. Meristic variation in the hexagrammid fishes. U.S. Fish Wildl. Serv. Fish. Bull. 63(3): 589–609.
1964b. Occurrence of the Pacific bonito in coastal Alaskan waters. Copeia 1964(2): 448.
1965. Osteological characteristics and affinities of the hexagrammid fishes, with a synopsis. Proc. Calif. Acad. Sci., Ser. 4, 31(21): 563–600.
1968. New records of thirteen cottoid and blennioid fishes for southeastern Alaska. Pac. Sci. 22(4): 482–487.
1971. *Sebastes variegatus,* sp. n. from the northeastern Pacific Ocean (Pisces, Scorpaenidae). U.S. Fish Wildl. Serv. Fish. Bull. 69(2): 387–398.
1972. Preliminary report on the fish collected on WEBSEC-70. Pages 203–206 *in* WEBSEC-70, an ecological survey in the eastern Chukchi Sea, September–October 1970. U.S. Coast Guard Oceanogr. Rep. 50.
1987. Morphometric variation of Pacific ocean perch, *Sebastes alutus,* off western North America. U.S. Natl. Mar. Fish. Serv. Fish. Bull. 85(4): 663–680.

Quast, J. C., and E. L. Hall.
1972. List of fishes of Alaska and adjacent waters with a guide to some of their literature. U.S. Dep. Commer., NOAA Tech. Rep. NMFS SSRF–658. 47 pp. [With errata sheet dated 20 Dec. 1972.]

Radchenko, V. I., and I. I. Glebov.
1998. On vertical distribution of Pacific salmon in the Bering Sea, collected by trawling data. J. Ichthyol. 38(8): 603–608 [English transl. Vopr. Ikhtiol. 38(5): 627–632].

Radovich, J.
1961. Relationships of some marine organisms of the northeast Pacific to water temperatures particularly during 1957 through 1959. Calif. Dep. Fish Game Fish Bull. 112. 62 pp.

Ranck, C. L., F. M. Utter, G. B. Milner, and G. B. Smith.
1986. Genetic confirmation of specific distinction of arrowtooth flounder, *Atheresthes stomias*, and Kamchatka flounder, *A. evermanni.* U.S. Natl. Mar. Fish. Serv. Fish. Bull. 84(1): 222–226.

Randall, J. E.
1987. Refutation of lengths of 11.3, 9.0, and 6.4 m attributed to the white shark, *Carcharodon carcharias.* Calif. Fish Game 73(3): 163–168.
1992. Review of the biology of the tiger shark (*Galeocerdo cuvier*). Aust. J. Mar. Freshwater Res.43: 21–31.
1995. *Fusigobius* Whitley, a junior synonym of the gobiid fish genus *Coryphopterus* Gill. Bull. Mar. Sci. 56(3):795–798.
1998. Zoogeography of shore fishes of the Indo-Pacific region. Zool. Stud. 37(4): 227–267.

Raschi, W., and J. D. McEachran.
1991. *Rhinoraja longi*, a new species of skate from the outer Aleutian Islands, with comments on the status of *Rhinoraja* (Chondrichthyes, Rajoidei). Can. J. Zool. 69: 1889–1903

Rass, T. S.
1954. Deep-sea fish of far eastern seas of the USSR. Zool. Zh. 33(6): 1312–1324. [Translation by Israel Prog. Sci. Transl., 1960, 22 pp.]

Rass, T. S.

1955. Glovokovodnye ryby Kurilo–Kamchatskoi vradin. [Deep-sea fishes of the Kurile–Kamchatka Trench]. Tr. Inst. Okeanol. Akad. Nauk SSSR 12: 328–339. [Translation by Natural History Museum, Stanford University,.]

1996. On taxonomy of Pleuronectini (Pleuronectidae). J. Ichthyol. 36(7): 546–548 [English transl. Vopr. Ikhtiol. 36(4): 569–571].

Rathbun, R.

1884. The North Pacific Exploring Expedition. Bull. U.S. Natl. Mus. 27: 532–534.

Reed, P. H.

1964. Recent occurrences of intergeneric hybrid flounders, *Inopsetta ischyra* (Jordan and Gilbert), from California and Oregon. Calif. Fish Game 50(2): 118–121.

Reed, R. K., and J. D. Schumacher.

1986. Physical oceanography. Pages 57–75 *in* D. W. Hood and S. T. Zimmerman, eds. The Gulf of Alaska: physical environment and biological resources. U.S. Department of Commerce, NOAA, Ocean Assessments Division, Alaska Office, and U.S. Department of the Interior, Minerals Management Service, Alaska OCS Region. U.S. Government Printing Office, Washington, D.C.

Reed, R. K., and P. J. Stabeno.

1994. Flow along and across the Aleutian Ridge. J. Mar. Res. 52: 639–648.

1999. The Aleutian North Slope Current. Pages 177–193 *in* T. R. Loughlin and K. Ohtani, eds. Dynamics of the Bering Sea. University of Alaska Sea Grant, AK-SG-99-03, Fairbanks.

Regan, C. T., and E. Trewavas.

1929. The fishes of the families Astronesthidae and Chauliodontidae. Danish Dana Exped. 1920–22, No. 5. 39 pp., 7 pls.

1930. The fishes of the families Stomiatidae and Malacosteidae. Danish Dana Exped. 1920–22, No. 6. 143 pp., 14 pls.

1932. Deep-sea angler-fishes (Ceratioidea). Dana-Rep. Carlsberg Found. 2. 113 pp., 10 pls.

Reinhardt, J. C.

1834. [Om *Gymnelus*]. Page 4 *in* H. C. Örsted, ed. Overs. Danske Vidensk. Selsk. Forhandl Kjobenhavn 1831–32: 1–30. [Not seen.]

Reist, J. D.

1987. Comparative morphometry and phenetics of the genera of esocoid fishes (Salmoniformes). Zool. J. Linn. Soc. 89: 275–294.

Reist, J. D., J. D. Johnson, and T. J. Carmichael.

1997. Variation and specific identity of char from northwestern Arctic Canada and Alaska. Am. Fish. Soc. Symp. 19: 250–261.

Reist, J. D., J. Vuorinen, and R. A. Bodaly.

1992. Genetic and morphological identification of coregonid hybrid fishes from Arctic Canada.

Renaud, C. B.

1989. Systematics of *Gadus*: a preliminary view. Pages 237–242 *in* D. M. Cohen, ed. Papers on the systematics of gadiform fishes. Nat. Hist. Mus. Los Angeles County, Sci. Ser. 32.

Rendall, H.

1931. Fische aud dem östlichen Sibirischen Eismeer und dem Nordpazifik. Arkiv f. Zool. 22A(10): 1–81.

Reshetnikov, Yu. S., N. G. Bogutskaya, E. D. Vasil'eva, E. A. Dorofeeva, A. M. Naseka, O. A. Popova, K. A. Savvaitova, V. G. Sideleva, and L. I. Sokolov.

1997. An annotated check-list of the freshwater fishes of Russia. J. Ichthyol. 37(9): 687–736 [English transl. Vopr. Ikhtiol. 37(60): 723–771].

Reshetnikov, Yu. S., A. N. Kotlyar, T. S. Rass, and M. I. Shatunovskiy.

1989. Pyatiyazychny slovar' nazvaniy zhivotnykh. Ryby [Dictionary of animal names in five languages. Fishes]. Moscow, Russkiy Yazyk. 735 pp.

Reynolds, J., editor.

1997. Fish ecology in Arctic North America. Am. Fish. Soc. Symp 19.

Richards, J. E., R. J. Beamish, and F. W. H. Beamish.

1982. Descriptions and keys for ammocoetes of lamprey from British Columbia, Canada. Can. J. Fish. Aquat. Sci. 39: 1484–1495.

Richards, L. J., and S. J. Westrheim.

1988. Southern range extension of the dusky rockfish, *Sebastes ciliatus,* in British Columbia. Can. Field-Nat. 102(2): 251–253.

Richardson, J.

1836. Fauna Boreali-Americana or the zoology of the northern parts of British America. Part 3: The fish. Richard Bentley, London. 327 pp., 23 pls. [Reprinted by Arno Press, New York, 1978.]

Richardson, S. L.

1981. Current knowledge of larvae of sculpins (Pisces: Cottidae and allies) in northeast Pacific genera with notes on intergeneric relationships. U.S. Natl. Mar. Fish. Serv. Fish. Bull. 79(1): 103–121.

Richardson, S. L., and C. Bond.

1978. Two unusual cottoid fishes from the northeast Pacific. Paper presented at Annual Meeting of American Society of Ichthyologists and Herpetologists, Tempe, Arizona. 33 pp.

Richardson, S. L., and D. A. DeHart.

1975. Records of larval, transforming, and adult specimens of the quillfish, *Ptilichthys goodei,* from waters off Oregon. U.S. Natl. Mar. Fish. Serv. Fish. Bull. 73(3): 681–685.

Robards, M. D., J. F. Piatt, A. B. Kettle, and A. A. Abookire.

1999. Temporal and geographic variation in fish communities of lower Cook Inlet, Alaska. U.S. Natl. Mar. Fish. Serv. Fish. Bull. 97(4): 962–977.

Robards, M. D., J. F. Piatt, and G. A. Rose.

1999. Maturation, fecundity, and intertidal spawning of Pacific sand lance in the northern Gulf of Alaska. J. Fish Biol. 54: 1050–1068.

Roberts, C. D.

1993. Comparative morphology of spined scales and their phylogenetic significance in the Teleostei. Bull. Mar. Sci. 52(1): 60–113.

Robins, C. H., and C. R. Robins.

1989. Family Synaphobranchidae. Pages 207–253 *in* Fishes of the western North Atlantic. Mem. Sears Found. Mar. Res., New Haven, 1(9), Vol. 1.

Robins, C. R.

1989. The phylogenetic relationships of the anguilliform fishes. Pages 9–23 *in* Fishes of the western North Atlantic. Mem. Sears Found. Mar. Res., New Haven, 1(9), Vol. 1.

Robins, C. R., R. M. Bailey, C. E. Bond, J. R. Brooker, E. A. Lachner, R. N. Lea, and W. B. Scott.

1980. A list of common and scientific names of fishes from the United States and Canada, 4th edition. Am. Fish. Soc., Spec. Publ. 12. 174 pp.

1991a. Common and scientific names of fishes from the United States and Canada, 5th edition. Am. Fish. Soc., Spec. Publ. 20. 183 pp.

1991b. World fishes important to North Americans exclusive of species from the continental waters of the United States and Canada. Am. Fish. Soc., Spec. Publ. 21. 243 pp.

Robins, C. R., and R. R. Miller.

1957. Classification, variation, and distribution of the sculpins, genus *Cottus,* inhabiting Pacific slope waters in California and southern Oregon, with a key to the species. Calif. Fish Game 43(3): 213–233.

Rodríguez-Romero, J., L. A. Abitia-Cárdenas, J. de la Cruz-Agüero, and F. Galván-Magaña.

1992. Systematic list of marine fishes of Bahia Concepcion, Baja California Sur, Mexico. Cienc. Mar. 18(4): 85-95.

Roedel, P. M.

1953. Common ocean fishes of the California coast. Calif. Dep. Fish Game Fish Bull. 91. 184 pp.

Rofen, R. R.

1959. The whale-fishes: families Cetomimidae, Barbourisiidae and Rondeletiidae (order Cetunculi). Galathea Rep. 1: 255–260, 2 pls.

1966a. Family Paralepididae. Pages 205–461 *in* Fishes of the western North Atlantic. Mem. Sears Found. Mar. Res., New Haven, 1(5).

1966b. Family Anotopteridae. Pages 498–510 *in* Fishes of the western North Atlantic. Mem. Sears Found. Mar. Res., New Haven, 1(5).

Rogers, B. J., and M. E. Wangerin.

1980. Seasonal composition and food web relationships of marine organisms in the nearshore zone of Kodiak Island—including ichthyoplankton, zooplankton, and fish. U.S. Dep. Commer., NOAA, and U.S. Dep. Inter., Minerals Manage. Serv., Environ. Assess. Alaskan Continental Shelf, Final Rep., Biol. Stud. 17: 541–658.

Rogers, D. E., B. J. Rogers, and R. J. Rosenthal.

1986. The nearshore fishes. Pages 399–415 *in* D. W. Hood and S. T. Zimmerman, eds. The Gulf of Alaska: physical environment and biological resources. U.S. Department of Commerce, NOAA, Ocean Assessments Division, Alaska Office, and U.S. Department of the Interior, Minerals Management Service, Alaska OCS Region. U.S. Government Printing Office, Washington, D.C.

Roguski, E. A., and E. Komarek, Jr.

1971. Monitoring and evaluation of Arctic waters with emphasis on North Slope drainages: Arctic Wildlife Range study. Alaska Dep. Fish Game, Fed. Aid Fish Restor., Ann. Rep. Progress, Proj. F-9-3, Job G-III-A. 12: 1–22.

Romanov, N. S.

1999. Morphological variability of some fish of the genera *Sebastes* and *Sebastolobus* (Scorpaenidae). J. Ichthyol. 39(6): 471–474 (English transl. Vopr. Ikhtiol. 39(4): 569–572].

Romer, A. S.

1962. The vertebrate body, 3rd edition. W. B. Saunders Company, Philadelphia. 627 pp.

Rosen, D. E.

1973. Interrelationships of higher euteleosteans. Pages 397–513 *in* P. H. Greenwood, R. S. Miles, and C. Patterson, eds. Interrelationships of fishes. Academic Press, London. J. Linn. Soc. Lond. Zool. 53, Suppl. 1.

Rosenblatt, R. H.

1964. A new gunnel, *Pholis clemensi,* from the coast of western North America. J. Fish. Res. Board Can. 21(5): 933–939.

Rosenblatt, R. H., and W. J. Baldwin.

1958. A review of the eastern Pacific sharks of the genus *Carcharhinus*, with a redescription of *C. malpeloensis* (Fowler) and California records of *C. remotus* (Duméril). Calif. Fish Game 44(2): 137–159.

Rosenblatt, R. H., and L.-C. Chen.

1972. The identity of *Sebastes babcocki* and *Sebastes rubrivinctus.* Calif. Fish Game 58(1): 32–36.

Rosenblatt, R. H., and G. D. Johnson.

1976. Anatomical considerations of pectoral swimming in the opah, *Lampris guttatus.* Copeia 1976(2): 367–370.

Rosenblatt, R. H., and D. Wilkie.

1963. A redescription of the rare cottid fish, *Artedius meanyi,* new to the fauna of British Columbia. J. Fish. Res. Board Can. 20(6): 1505–1511.

Rosenthal, R. J.

1980. Shallow water fish assemblages in the northeastern Gulf of Alaska: habitat evaluation, species composition, abundance, spatial distribution, and trophic interaction. U.S. Dep. Commer., NOAA, and U.S. Dep. Inter., Minerals Manage. Serv., Environmental Assessment of the Alaskan Continental Shelf, Final Rep., Biol. Stud. 17: 451–540.

Rosenthal, R. J., V. Moran-O'Connell, and M. C. Murphy.

1988. Feeding ecology of ten species of rockfishes (Scorpaenidae) from the Gulf of Alaska. Calif. Fish Game 74(1): 16–37.

Rounsefell, G. A., and E. H. Dahlgren.

1934. Occurrence of mackerel in Alaska. Copeia 1934(1): 42.

Royce, W. F.

1963. First record of white shark (*Carcharodon carcharias*) from southeastern Alaska. Copeia 1963(1): 179.

Ruban, G. I.

1997. Species structure, contemporary distribution and status of the Siberian sturgeon, *Acpenser baerii* Environ. Biol. Fishes 48:221–230.

Ruiz-Campos, G., and S. Gonzalez-Guzman.

1996. First freshwater record of Pacific lamprey, *Lampetra tridentata,* from Baja California, Mexico. Calif. Fish Game 82(3): 144–146.

Russell, R.

1980. A fisheries inventory of waters in the Lake Clark National Monument area. Alaska Dep. Fish Game, Sport Fish Div., Juneau. 197 pp., appendixes.

Rutecki, T. L., and D. M. Clausen.

1988. Fishing log: 1987 triennial bottom trawl survey of the eastern Gulf of Alaska, July–September 1987. U.S. Dep. Commer., NWAFC Processed Report 88–20. 60 pp. NOAA, NMFS, AFSC, Auke Bay Laboratory, P.O. Box 155, Auke Bay, AK 99821.

Rutecki, T. L., M. F. Sigler, and H. H. Zenger, Jr.

1997. Data report: National Marine Fisheries Service longline surveys, 1991–96. U.S. Dep. Commer., NOAA Tech. Memo. NMFS AFSC-83. 64 pp.

Rutter, C.

1899. Notes on a collection of tide-pool fishes from Kadiak Island in Alaska. Bull. U.S. Fish Comm. 18: 189–192.

Sakamoto, K.

1930. Two new species of fishes from the Japan Sea. J. Imp. Fish. Inst. 26: 15–19.

1984. Interrelationships of the family Pleuronectidae (Pisces: Pleuronectiformes). Mem. Fac. Fish. Hokkaido Univ. 31(1/2): 95–215.

Sakurai, Y., and K. Kido.

1992. Feeding behavior of *Careproctus rastrinus* (Liparididae) in captivity. Jpn. J. Ichthyol. 39(1): 110–113.

Salo, E. O.

1991. Life history of chum salmon (*Oncorhynchus keta*). Pages 231–309 *in* C. Groot and L. Margolis, eds. Pacific salmon life histories. UBC Press, Vancouver.

Sample, T. M., and R. J. Wolotira, Jr.

1985. Demersal fish and shellfish resources of Norton Sound and adjacent waters during 1979. U.S. Dep. Commer., NOAA Tech. Memo. NMFS F/NWC–89. 208 pp.

Sandercock, F. K.

1991. Life history of coho salmon (*Oncorhynchus kisutch*). Pages 395–445 *in* C. Groot and L. Margolis, eds. Pacific salmon life histories. UBC Press, Vancouver.

Sandercock, F. K., and N. J. Wilimovsky.

1968. Revision of the cottid genus *Enophrys.* Copeia 1968(4): 832–853.

Sanford, C. P. J.

1990. The phylogenetic relationships of salmonoid fishes. Bull. Brit. Mus. (Nat. Hist.), Zool. 56(2): 145–153.

Saruwatari, T., J. A. López, and T. W. Pietsch.

1997. A revision of the osmerid genus *Hypomesus* Gill (Teleostei: Salmoniformes), with the description of a new species from the southern Kuril Islands. Species Diversity 2(1): 59–82.

Sasaki, T.

1981. Ecological studies on the pomfret (*Brama japonica* Hilgendorf). II. A north-south distribution of the pomfret along longitude 175°30'E in late July. Bull. Fac. Fish. Hokkaido Univ. 32(3): 225–233.

1972. Demersal fishes collected in the southeastern shelf waters of Alaska. Bull. Fac. Fish. Hokkaido Univ. 22(4): 281–289.

Saunders, M. W., and G. A. McFarlane.

1993. Age and length at maturity of the female spiny dogfish, *Squalus acanthias,* in the Strait of Georgia, British Columbia, Canada. Environ. Biol. Fishes 38: 49–57.

Savin, A. B.

1993. Distribution and migration of *Laemonema longipes* (Moridae) in the northwestern Pacific. J. Ichthyol. 33(6): 107–117 [English transl. Vopr. Ikhtiol. 33(2): 190–197].

Savinykh, V. F.

1993. The epipelagic ichthyocene of subtropical and mixed waters in the northwestern Pacific Ocean during winter. J. Ichthyol. 33(5): 1–11 [English transl. Vopr. Ikhtiol. 33(1): 46–52].

1994. Migrations of the Pacific pomfret *Brama japonica.* Russ. J. Mar. Biol. [English transl. Biol. Morya] 20(4): 205–210.

1998. Nekton composition of near-surface waters of the subarctic front zone in the northwest part of the Pacific Ocean according to the data of drift-net catches. J. Ichthyol. 38(1): 18–27 [English transl. Vopr. Ikhtiol. 38(1): 22–32].

Savinykh, V. F., and A. A. Balanov.

2000. Distribution, migrations, and some biological traits of *Scopelosaurus adleri* and *S. harryi* (Notosudidae)]. J. Ichthyol. 40(2): 155–164 [English transl. Vopr. Ikhtiol. 40(2): 193–202].

Savvaitova, K. A.

1980. Taxonomy and biogeography of charrs in th Palearctic. Pages 281-294 *in* E. K. Balon, ed. Charrs: salmonid fishes of the genus *Salvelinus.* Dr. W. Junk, The Hague.

Sazonov, Yu. I.

1976a. Novye vidy ryb semeystva Searsiidae (Salmoniformes, Alepocephaloidei) iz Tikhogo Okeana [New species of fishes of the family Searsiidae (Salmoniformes, Alepocephaloidei) from the Pacific Ocean]. P. P. Shirshov Inst. Okeanol., Akad. Nauk SSSR., Tr. 104: 13–25. [In Russian; English summary.]

1976b. Materialy po sistematike i rasprostraneniy ryb semeystva Searsiidae (Salmoniformes, Alepocephaloidei) [Materials on the systematics and distribution of fishes of the family Searsiidae (Salmoniformes, Alepocephaloidei)]. P. P. Shirshov Inst. Okeanol., Akad. Nauk SSSR., Tr. 104: 26–72. [In Russian; English summary.]

1980. Replacement of the family name Searsiidae Parr, 1951 by the senior subjective synonym Platytroctidae Roule, 1919. J. Ichthyol. [English transl. Vopr. Ikhtiol.] 20(6): 142–143.

1992. *Matsuichthys* gen. novum, a new genus of the fish family Platytroctidae (Salmoniformes) with notes on the classification of the subfamily Platytroctinae. J. Ichthyol. 32(4): 26–37 [English transl. Vopr. Ikhtiol. 32(1):3–12].

Sazonov, Yu. I., A. A. Balanov, and V. V. Fedorov.

1993. Gladkogolovovidnye ryby (Alepocephaloidei) severo-zapadnoy chasti Tikhogo okeana [Slickheads (Alepocephaloidei) from the western North Pacific Ocean]. Tr. Inst. Okeanol. Ross. Akad. Nauk 128: 40–68. [In Russian; short English summary.]

Sazonov, Yu. I., and A. N. Ivanov.

1980. Gladkogolovy (Alepocephalidae i Leptochilichthyidae) talassobatiali Indiy-skogo okeana [Slickheads (Alepocephalidae and Leptochilichthyidae) from the thallasobathyal zone of the Indian Ocean]. Tr. Inst. Okeanol. Akad. Nauk SSSR 110: 7–104. [In Russian; English summary.]

Scanlon, B. P.

2000. The ecology of the Arctic char and Dolly Varden in the Becharof Lake drainage, Alaska. M. S. thesis, University of Alaska Fairbanks. 126 pp.

Scheffer, V. B.

1940. Two recent records of *Zaprora silenus* Jordan from the Aleutian Islands. Copeia 1940(3): 203.

1959. Invertebrates and fishes collected in the Aleutians, 1936–38. N. Am. Fauna 61: 365–406.

Schmidt, P. J. (Shmidt, P. Yu.)

1904. Ryby vostochnykh morey Rossiyskoi Imperii [Fishes of the eastern seas of the Russian Empire]. St. Petersburg, Izdanie Russkogo geograficheskogo Obshchestva. 466 pp., 6 pls. [In Russian; and selections translated by B. A. Sheiko, 1999, for Point Stephens Research, Auke Bay, Alaska.]

1916. Ichthyological notes. I. On some new and little known Cottidae of North Pacific. Ann. Mus. Zool. Acad. Imp. Sci. Petrograd 20(1915): 611–627, figs. 1–6. [In Russian.]

1927. A revision of the cottoid fishes of the genus *Artediellus.* Proc. U.S. Natl. Mus. 71(2685): 1–10.

1929. A revision of the genus *Triglops* Reinhardt (Pisces, Cottidae). Ann. Mus. Zool. Acad. Sci. URSS 30: 513–523.

1933. Description of a new myctophid fish from off Bering Island. Copeia 1933(3): 131–132.

1936. On the systematics and distribution of the genus *Agonus* Bloch and Schneider. Copeia 1936(1): 58–59.

1937a. On the Pacific genera *Eurymen* Gilbert and Burke and *Gilbertidia* C. Berg (Pisces, Cottidae). C. R. (Dokl.) Acad. Sci. URSS 15(5): 279–281.

1937b. Two new species of *Artediellus* Jordan from the Sea of Okhotsk. C. R. (Dokl.) Acad. Sci. URSS 15(9): 571–572.

1950. Ryby Okhotskogo Morya [Fishes of the Sea of Okhotsk]. Akad. Nauk SSSR, Tr. Tikhookeanskogo Komiteta [Acad. Sci. USSR, Trans. Pac. Committee] 6. 370 pp., 20 pls. [In Russian; and translation by Israel Prog. Sci. Transl., 1965. 392 pp.]

Schoener, A., and D. L. Fluharty.

1985. Biological anomalies off Washington in 1982–83 and other major Niño periods. Pages 211–225 *in* W. S. Wooster and D. L. Fluharty, eds. El Niño north: Niño effects in the eastern subarctic Pacific Ocean. Washington Sea Grant Program, University of Washington, Seattle.

Scholander, P. F., W. Flagg, R. J. Hock, and L. Irving.

1953. Studies on the physiology of frozen plants and animals in the Arctic. J. Cell. Comp. Physiol. 42, Suppl. 1: 1–56.

Schott, J. W.

1966. A Greenland halibut, *Reinhardtius hippoglossoides* (Walbaum) recorded in southern California. Calif. Fish Game 52(1): 55–56.

Schroeder, W. C.

1940. Some deep sea fishes from the North Atlantic. Copeia 1940(4): 231–238.

Schultz, L. P.

1930. Miscellaneous observations on fishes of Washington. Copeia 1930(4): 137–140.

1934a. A new ceratiid [ceratioid] fish from the Gulf of Alaska. Copeia 1934(2): 66–68.

1934b. *Zaprora silenus* Jordan from Alaska. Copeia 1934(2): 98.

1936. Keys to the fishes of Washington, Oregon and closely adjoining regions. Univ. Wash. Publ. Biol. 2(4): 103–228.

1937. Redescription of the capelin *Mallotus catervarius* (Pennant) of the North Pacific. Proc. U.S. Natl. Mus. 85(3029): 13–20.

1938a. A new genus and two new species of cottoid fishes from the Aleutian Islands. Proc. U.S. Natl. Mus. 85(3038): 187–191.

1938b. Review of the fishes of the genera *Polyipnus* and *Argyropelecus* (family Sternoptichidae), with descriptions of three new species. Proc. U.S. Natl. Mus. 96(3047): 135–155.

1940. Two new genera and three new species of cheilodipterid fishes, with notes on the other genera of the family. Proc. U.S. Natl. Mus. 88(3085): 403–423.

1941. Hugh McCormick Smith. Copeia 1941(4): 194–209.

1961a. A short history of the Division of Fishes, United States National Museum, December 17, 1856 to December 15, 1956. Copeia 1961(1): 120–123.

1961b. Revision of the marine silver hatchetfishes (family Sternoptychidae). Proc. U.S. Natl. Mus. 112 (3449): 587–649.

Schultz, L. P.

1964. Family Sternoptychidae. Pages 241–273 *in* Fishes of the western North Atlantic. Mem. Sears Found. Mar. Res., New Haven, 1(4).

1967. A new genus and new species of zoarcid fish from the North Pacific Ocean. Proc. U.S. Natl. Mus. 122(3598): 1–5.

Schultz, L. P., and A. C. DeLacy.

1935–36. Fishes of the American Northwest. A catalogue of the fishes of Washington and Oregon, with distributional records and a bibliography. J. Pan-Pacific Res. Inst. *in* Mid-Pacific Mag. 10: 365–380; 11: 63–78, 127–142, 211–226, 275–290.

Schultz, L. P., J. L. Hart, and F. J. Gunderson.

1932. New records of marine West Coast fishes. Copeia 1932(2): 65–68.

Schultz, L. P., and C. L. Hubbs.

1961. Early nomenclatural history of the nominal cyprinid genus *Oregonichthys* and of the blennioid *Pholis schultzi,* fishes of western North America. Copeia 1961(4): 477–478.

Schultz, L. P., and R. T. Smith.

1936. Is *Inopsetta ischyra* (Jordan and Gilbert), from Puget Sound, Washington, a hybrid flatfish? Copeia 1936(4): 199–203.

Schultz, L. P., and A. D. Welander.

1935. A review of the cods of the northeastern Pacific with comparative notes on related species. Copeia 1935(3): 127–139.

Schweigert, J. F.

1988. Status of the Pacific sardine, *Sardinops sagax,* in Canada. Can. Field-Nat. 102(2): 296–303.

Scofield, N. B.

1899. List of fishes obtained in the waters of Arctic Alaska. Pages 493–509 *in* D. S. Jordan, ed. The fur seals and fur-seal islands of the North Pacific Ocean. Part 3. Government Printing Office, Washington, D.C.

Scofield, W. L.

1941. Occurrence of the tiger shark in California. Calif. Fish Game 27: 271–272.

Scott, W. B., and E. J. Crossman.

1973. Freshwater fishes of Canada. Fish. Res. Board Can. Bull. 184. 966 pp.

Scott, W. B., and M. G. Scott.

1988. Atlantic fishes of Canada. Can. Bull. Fish. Aquat. Sci. 219. 731 pp.

Seeb, L. W.

1986. Biochemical systematics and evolution of the scorpaenid genus *Sebastes.* Ph.D. thesis, University of Washington, Seattle. 176 pp.

Seigel, J. A., D. J. Long, J. M. Rounds, and J. Hernandez.

1995. The tiger shark, *Galeocerdo cuvier,* in coastal southern California waters. Calif. Fish Game 81(4): 163–166.

Selkregg, L. L.

1974–1976. Alaska regional profiles. Six vols. Southcentral Alaska, 255 pp. Arctic, 218 pp. Southwest, 313 pp. Southeast, 233 pp. Northwest, 265 pp. Yukon, 346 pp. Arctic Environmental Information and Data Center, Anchorage.

Shaboneyev, I. Ye.

1980. Systematics, morpho-ecological characteristics and origin of carangids of the genus *Trachurus.* J. Ichthyol. [English transl. Vopr. Ikhtiol.] 20(6): 15–24.

Shaposhnikova, G. Kh.

1970. On the taxonomy of whitefishes from the USSR. Pages 195-207 *in* C. C. Lindsey and C. S. Woods, eds. Biology of coregonid fishes. University of Manitoba Press, Winnipeg, Canada.

Shapovalov, L., A. J. Cordone, and W. A. Dill.

1981. A list of the freshwater and anadromous fishes of California. Calif. Fish Game 67(1): 4–38.

Shapovalov, L., W. A. Dill, and A. J. Cordone.

1959. A revised check list of the freshwater and anadromous fishes of California. Calif. Fish Game 45(3): 159–180.

Shaw, F. R.

1999. Life history traits of four species of rockfish (genus *Sebastes*). M.S. thesis, University of Washington, Seattle. 178 pp.

Sheiko, B. A.

1993. Katalog ryb semeystva Agonidae s. l. (Scorpaeniformes: Cottoidei) [A catalogue of fishes of the family Agonidae sensu lato (Scorpaeniformes: Cottoidei)]. Tr. Zool. Inst. Akad. Nauk SSSR [Proc. Zool. Inst. Acad. Sci. USSR] (for 1991) 235: 65–95. [In Russian; English summary.]

Sheiko, B. A., and V. V. Fedorov.

2000. Chapter 1. Class Cephalaspidomorphi — Lampreys. Class Chondrichthyes — Cartilaginous fishes. Class Holocephali — Chimaeras. Class Osteichthyes — Bony fishes. Pages 7–69 *in* Katalog pozvonochnykh Kamchatki i sopredel'nykh morskikh akvatoriy [Catalog of vertebrates of Kamchatka and adjacent waters]. Kamchatsky Pechatny Dvor, Petropavlovsk-Kamchatsky, Russia. 166 pp. [In Russian.]

Sheiko, B. A., and A. G. Tranbenkova.

1998. New for the Russian fauna and rare marine fishes from Kamchatka and the Kuril and Commander islands. Pages 62-63 *in* Abstracts, All-Russian conference on problems in fish taxonomy, 17–19 November 1998, St. Petersburg, Russia. [Translation by B. A. Sheiko, 1998, for Point Stephens Research, Auke Bay, Alaska.]

Shelekhov, V. A., and D. V. Baginskii.

2000. Finding of toothless specimens of daggertooth *Anotopterus nikparini* (Anotopteridae) during winter off the southern Kuril Islands. J. Ichthyol. 40(6): 485 [English transl. Vopr. Ikhtiol. 40(4): 571–572].

Sherman, K., and A. M. Duda.

1999. Large marine ecosystems: an emerging paradigm for fishery sustainability. Fisheries (Bethesda) 24(12): 15–26.

Shimazaki, K., and S. Nakamura.

1981. Ecological studies of the pomfret (*Brama japonica* Hilgendorf). I. The seasonal distributional pattern and ecological considerations. Pages 91–103 *in* S. Mishima, ed. Pelagic animals and environments around the Subarctic boundary in North Pacific. Res. Inst. North Pacific Fish., Fac. Fish. Hokkaido Univ. Spec. Vol.

Shimizu, T.

1978. Record of the beryciform fish, *Anoplogaster cornuta,* from the western North Pacific. Jpn. J. Ichthyol. 25(1): 65.

Shimokawa, T., K. Amaoka, Y. Kajiwara, and S. Suyama.

1995. Occurrence of *Thalassenchelys coheni* (Anguilliformes; Chlopsidae) in the west Pacific Ocean. Jpn. J. Ichthyol. 42(1): 89–92.

Shinohara, G.

1994. Comparative morphology and phylogeny of the suborder Hexagrammoidei and related taxa (Pisces: Scorpaeniformes). Mem. Fac. Fish. Hokkaido Univ. 41(1): 1–97.

Shinohara, G., and K. Amaoka.

1993. Albino specimen of *Sebastolobus macrochir* collected from off the Shimokita Peninsula, northern Japan. Jpn. J. Ichthyol. 39(4): 395–397.

1994. *Stellistius katsukii* Jordan et Tanaka, 1927, a junior synonym of *Pleurogrammus azonus* Jordan et Metz, 1913 (Scorpaeniformes: Hexagrammidae). Jpn. J. Ichthyol. 40(4): 487–490.

Shinohara, G., H. Endo, and K. Matsuura.

1996. Deep-water fishes collected from the Pacific coast of northern Honshu, Japan. Mem. Natl. Sci. Mus. (Tokyo) 29: 153–185.

Shinohara, G., and K. Matsuura.

1997. Annotated checklist of deep-water fishes from Suruga Bay, Japan. Natl. Sci. Mus. (Tokyo) Monogr. 12: 269–318, pls. 1–2.

Shinohara, G., M. Yabe, K. Amaoka, and T. Meguro.

1992. A psychrolutid, *Malacocottus gibber,* collected from the mesopelagic zone of the Sea of Japan, with comments on its intraspecific variation. Jpn. J. Ichthyol. 38(4): 419–424.

Shinohara, G., M. Yabe, and T. Honma.

1994. Occurrence of the scorpaenid fish, *Sebastes ciliatus,* from the Pacific coast of Hokkaido, Japan. Bull. Biogeogr. Soc. Jpn. 49(1): 61–64.

Shinohara, G., M. Yabe, K. Nakaya, G. Anma, S. Yamaguchi, and K. Amaoka.

1994. Deep-sea fishes collected from the North Pacific by the T/S *Oshoru-Maru.* Bull. Fac. Fish. Hokkaido Univ. 45(2): 48–80.

Shinohara, G., H. Yoshida, and M. Yabe.

1992. First record of *Bathymaster signatus* (Perciformes: Bathymasteridae) from Japan. Jpn. J. Ichthyol. 39(2): 163–166.

Shirai, S.

1992. Squalean phylogeny, a new framework of "squaloid" sharks and related taxa. Hokkaido University Press, Sapporo. 151 pp., 58 pls.

1996. Phylogenetic interrelationships of neoselachians (Chondrichthyes: Euselachii). Pages 9–34 *in* M. L. J. Stiassny, L. R. Parenti, and G. D. Johnson, eds. Interrelationhips of fishes. Academic Press, San Diego.

Shiogaki, M.

1982. Life history of the stichaeid fish *Opisthocentrus ocellatus.* Jpn. J. Ichthyol. 29: 77–85.

Shiogaki, M.

1984. A review of the genera *Pholidapus* and *Opisthocentrus* (Stichaeidae). Jpn. J. Ichthyol. 31(3): 213–224.

1985. A new stichaeid fish of the genus *Alectrias* from Mutsu Bay, northern Japan. Jpn. J. Ichthyol. 32(3): 305–314.

Shuntov, V. P.

1963. Osobennosti raspredeleniya ikhtiofauny v yugo-vostochnoy chasti Beringova morya [Peculiarities of the distribution of ichthyofauna in the southeastern Bering Sea]. Zool. Zh. 42(5): 704–714. [In Russian.]

Shuntov, V. P., A. F. Volkov, and A. I. Abakumov.

1990. Composition and present status of the fish community in epipelagic waters of the Sea of Okhotsk. J. Ichthyol. 30(4): 116–129 [English transl. Vopr. Ikhtiol. 30(4): 587–608].

Simenstad, C. A., J. S. Isakson, and R. E. Nakatani.

1977. Marine fish communities. Pages 451–492 *in* M. L. Merritt and R. G. Fuller, eds. The environment of Amchitka Island, Alaska. Technical Information Center, Energy Research and Development Administration, Oak Ridge, Tennessee.

Sinclair, E. H., A. A. Balanov, T. Kubodera, V. I. Radchenko, and Y. A. Fedorets.

1999. Distribution and ecology of mesopelagic fishes and cephalopods. Pages 485–508 *in* T. R. Loughlin and K. Ohtani, eds. Dynamics of the Bering Sea. University of Alaska Sea Grant, AK-SG-99-03, Fairbanks.

Skogsberg, T.

1939. The fishes of the family Sciaenidae (croakers) of California. Calif. Fish Game, Fish Bull. 54. 62 pp.

Small, G. J.

1981. A review of the bathyal fish genus *Antimora* (Moridae: Gadiformes). Proc. Calif. Acad. Sci. 42(13): 341–348.

Smith, D. G.

1979. Guide to the leptocephali (Elopiformes, Anguilliformes, and Notacanthiformes). NOAA Tech. Rep. NMFS Circ. 424. 39 pp.

1989a. Order Saccopharyngiformes. Family Cyematidae. Pages 629–635 *in* Fishes of the western North Atlantic. Mem. Sears Found. Mar. Res., New Haven, 1(9), Vol. 1.

1989b. Introduction to leptocephali. Pages 657–668 *in* Fishes of the western North Atlantic. Mem. Sears Found. Mar. Res., New Haven, 1(9), Vol. 2.

1994. Catalog of type specimens of Recent fishes in the National Museum of Natural History, Smithsonian Institution, 6: Anguilliformes, Saccopharyngiformes, and Notacanthiformes (Teleostei: Elopomorpha). Smithson. Contrib. Zool. 566. 50 pp.

Smith, D. G., and J. G. Nielsen.

1989. Family Nemichthyidae. Pages 441–459 *in* Fishes of the western North Atlantic. Mem. Sears Found. Mar. Res., New Haven, 1(9), Vol. 1.

Smith, G. R., and R. F. Stearley.

1989. The classification and scientific names of rainbow and cutthroat trouts. Fisheries (Bethesda) 14(1): 4–10.

Smith, H. M.

1904. A new cottoid fish from Bering Sea. Proc. Biol. Soc. Wash. 17 (December 27, 1904): 163–164.

Smith, J. G.

1965. A second record of the pelagic armorhead, *Pentaceros richardsoni* Smith 1849, in California waters. Calif. Fish Game 51(3): 213–214.

Smith, M. M., and P. C. Heemstra, editors.

1986. Smiths' sea fishes. Springer-Verlag, Berlin. 1,047 pp.

Smith, R. L., W. E. Barber, M. Vallarino, J. Gillespie, and A. Ritchie.

1997a. Population biology of the Arctic staghorn sculpin in the northeastern Chukchi Sea. Am. Soc. Symposium 19: 133–139.

Smith, R. L., M. Vallarino, E. Barbour, E. Fitzpatrick, and W. E. Barber.

1997b. Population biology of the Bering flounder in the northeastern Chukchi Sea. Am. Fish. Soc. Symp. 19: 127–132.

Smith, T. G.

1977. The wolffish, cf. *Anarhichas denticulatus,* new to the Amundsen Gulf area, Northwest Territories, and a probable prey of the ringed seal. Can. Field-Nat. 91(3): 288.

Smith-Vaniz, W. F.

1984. Carangidae: relationships. Pages 522–530 *in* H. G. Moser et al., eds. Ontogeny and systematics of fishes. Am. Soc. Ichthyol. Herpetol., Spec. Publ. 1.

Smitt, F. A., editor.

1893. A history of Scandinavian fishes, 2nd edition. Norstedt and Sönern, Stockholm.

Snyder, J. O.
1911. Descriptions of new genera and species of fishes from Japan and the Riu Kiu Islands. Proc. U.S. Natl. Mus. 40(1836): 525–549.
1912. Japanese shore fishes collected by the United States Bureau of Fisheries steamer *Albatross* expedition of 1906. Proc. U.S. Natl. Mus. 42(1909): 399–450, pls. 51–61.
1913. Notes on *Ranzania makua* Jenkins and other species of fishes of rare occurrence on the California coast. Proc. U.S. Natl. Mus. 44(1961): 455–460, pls. 63.

Snytko, V. A.
1986. New distribution records of rockfishes of the subfamily Sebastinae in the northern Pacific Ocean. J. Ichthyol. [English transl. Vopr. Ikhtiol.] 26(3): 124–130.
1987. New data on the distributions of some species of fish in the North Pacific. J. Ichthyol. [English transl. Vopr. Ikhtiol.] 27(1): 142–146.

Snytko, V. A., and V. V. Fedorov.
1974. New data on the distribution of scorpaenid fishes of the subfamily Sebastinae and notes on their biology. J. Ichthyol. 14: 811–818 [English transl. Vopr. Ikhtiol. 14(6): 939–947].
1975. The southern and northern borders of the areas of distribution of some fishes near the Pacific coast of North America. Izv. Tikhookean. Nauchno-Issled. Inst. Rybn. Khoz. Okeanogr. 96: 175-180.

Sobolevsky, Ye. I., T. G. Sokolovskaya, A. A. Balanov, and I. A. Senchenko.
1996. Distribution and trophic relationships of abundant mesopelagic fishes of the Bering Sea. Pages 159–168 *in* O. A. Mathisen and K. O. Coyle, eds. Ecology of the Bering Sea: a review of Russian literature. Alaska Sea Grant College Program Report 96-01, University of Alaska Fairbanks.

Sokolovskaya, T. G., and A. S. Sokolovskii.
1994. *Ptilichthys goodei,* a fish species new for the waters of Primor'e. Vopr. Ikhtiol. 34(6): 841–842. [Cited in Sokolovskaya et al. 1998.]

Sokolovskaya, T. G., A. S. Sokolovskii, and E. I. Sobolevskii.
1998. A list of fishes of Peter the Great Bay (Sea of Japan). J. Ichthyol. 38(1): 1–11 [English transl. Vopr. Ikhtiol. 38(1): 5–15].

Soldatov, V. K., and G. U. Lindberg.
1930. Obzor ryb dal'nevostochnykh morey [A review of the fishes of the seas of the Far East]. Izv. Tikhookean. Nauchn. Inst. Rybn. Khoz. [Bull. Pac. Sci. Fish. Inst.] 5: 576 pp., 15 pls. [In Russian and English.]

Soldatov, V. K., and M. N. Pavlenko.
1915. Two new genera of Cottidae from Tatar Strait and Okhotsk Sea. Ezh. Zool. Muz. Imp. Akad. Nauk 20: 638–640.

Somerton, D. A., and W. Donaldson.
1998. Parasitism of the golden king crab, *Lithodes aequispinus,* by two species of snailfish, genus *Careproctus*. U.S. Natl. Mar. Fish. Serv. Fish. Bull. 96(4): 871–884.

Springer, S.
1979. A revision of the catsharks, family Scyliorhinidae. U.S. Dep. Commer., NOAA Tech. Rep. NMFS Circ. 422: 152 pp.

Springer, S., and P. W. Gilbert.
1976. The basking shark, *Cetorhinus maximus,* from Florida and California, with comments on its biology and systematics. Copeia 1976(1): 47–54.

Springer, V. G.
1982. Pacific plate biogeography, with special reference to shorefishes. Smithson. Contrib. Zool. 367: 182 pp.
1993. Definition of the suborder Blennioidei and its included families (Pisces: Perciformes). Bull. Mar. Sci. 52(1): 472–495.

Springer, V. G., and M. E. Anderson.
1997. Catalog of type specimens of Recent fishes in the National Museum of Natural History, Smithsonian Institution, 8: Suborder Zoarcoidei (Anarhichadidae, Bathymasteridae, Pholidae, Ptilichthyidae, Scytalinidae, Stichaeidae, Zoarcidae). Smithson. Contrib. Zool. 589: 27 pp.

Squire, J. L., Jr.
1990. Distribution and apparent abundance of the basking shark, *Cetorhinus maximus,* off the central and southern California coast, 1962–85. U.S. Natl. Mar. Fish. Serv. Mar. Fish. Rev. 52(2): 8–11.

Stabeno, P. J., J. D. Schumacher, and K. Ohtani.
1999. The physical oceanography of the Bering Sea. Pages 1–28 *in* T. R. Loughlin and K. Ohtani, eds. Dynamics of the Bering Sea. University of Alaska Sea Grant, AK-SG-99-03, Fairbanks.

Starks, E. C.

1895. Description of a new genus and species of cottoid fishes from Puget Sound. Proc. Acad. Nat. Sci. Phila. 47: 410–412.

1911. Results of an ichthyological survey about the San Juan Islands, Washington. Ann. Carnegie Mus. 7(2): 162–212, pls. 29–31.

1921. A key to the families of marine fishes of the West Coast. Calif. Fish Game Comm., Fish Bull. 5. 16 pp.

Stearley, R. F., and G. R. Smith.

1993. Phylogeny of the Pacific trouts and salmons (*Oncorhynchus*) and genera of the family Salmonidae. Trans. Am. Fish. Soc. 122(1): 1–33.

Stehmann, M.

1986. Notes on the systematics of the rajid genus *Bathyraja* and its distribution in the world oceans. Pages 261–268 *in* T. Uyeno, R. Arai, T. Taniuchi, and K. Matsuura, eds. Indo-Pacific fish biology: Proceedings of the Second International Conference on Indo-Pacific Fishes. Ichthyological Society of Japan, Tokyo.

Stein, D. L.

1978. A review of the deepwater Liparidae (Pisces) from the coast of Oregon and adjacent waters. Occas. Pap. Calif. Acad. Sci. 127. 55 pp.

Stein, D. L., and A. P. Andriashev.

1990. Liparididae. Pages 231–255 *in* O. Gon and P. C. Heemstra, eds. Fishes of the Southern Ocean. J.L.B. Smith Institute of Ichthyology, Grahamstown, South Africa.

Stein, D. L., and C. E. Bond.

1978. A new deep-sea fish from the eastern North Pacific, *Psychrolutes phrictus* (Pisces: Cottidae [Psychrolutinae]). Contrib. Sci. (Los Angel.) 296. 9 pp.

Stein, D., and J. Butler.

1971. A notacanthid *Macdonaldia challengeri* collected off the Oregon coast. J. Fish. Res. Board Can. 28(9): 1349–1350.

Stein, D. L., and A. E. Peden.

1979. First record of *Paraliparis paucidens* Stein (Pisces: Liparidae) from British Columbia waters. Syesis 12: 181.

Steindachner, F.

1880. Über zwei neue *Agonus*-Arten aus Californien. Ichthyologische beiträge (IX). Sitzungsber. Akad. Wiss. Wien, Math.-Naturwiss. Kl., Abt 1, 82: 253–255 (pls. 6, figs. 1, 1a, 1b).

Stepanov, Yu. N.

1986. Morphological characteristics of Pacific saury, *Cololabis saira* (Scombresocidae), from two regions of the northwestern Pacific Ocean. J. Ichthyol. [English transl. Vopr. Ikhtiol.] 27(2): 124–127.

Steyskal, G. C.

1980. The grammar of family-group names as exemplified by those of fishes. Proc. Biol. Soc. Wash. 93(1): 168–177.

Stiassny, M. L. J.

1996. Basal ctenosquamate relationships and the interrelationships of the myctophiform (scopelomorph) fishes. Pages 405–426 *in* M. L. J. Stiassny, L. R. Parenti, and G. D. Johnson, eds. Interrelationhips of fishes. Academic Press, San Diego.

Stiassny, M. L. J., and J. Moore.

1992. A review of the pelvic girdle of acanthomorph fishes, with a provisional hypothesis of acanthomorph intrarelationships. J. Zool. Lond. 104: 209–242.

Stoddard, K. M.

1985. A phylogenetic analysis of some prickleback fishes (Teleostei, Stichaeidae, Xiphisterinae) from the North Pacific Ocean, with a discussion of their biogeography. M.A. thesis, California State University, Fullerton. 88 pp.

Strauss, R. E.

1993. Relationships among the cottid genera *Artedius, Clinocottus,* and *Oligocottus* (Teleostei: Scorpaeniformes). Copeia 1993(2): 518–522.

Sulak, K. J., and Y. N. Shcherbachev.

1997. Zoogeography and systematics of six deep-living genera of synaphobranchid eels, with a key to taxa and description of two new species of *Ilyophis.* Bull. Mar. Sci. 60(3): 1158–1191.

Sulak, K. J., R. E. Crabtree, and J.-C. Hureau.

1984. Provisional review of the genus *Polyacanthonotus* (Pisces, Notacanthidae) with description of a new Atlantic species, *Polyacanthonotus merretti*. Cybium 8(4): 57–68.

Sund, O.

1943. Et brugebarsel [A basking shark giving birth]. Naturen 67(9): 285–286. [In Norwegian; translation by Markus Leppä, University of Joensuu, Karelian Institute Department of Ecology, FIN-80101 Joensuu, Finland.]

Suzuki, K., and S. Kimura.

1980. First record of the deep-sea cottid fish *Psychrolutes inermis* from Japan. Jpn. J. Ichthyol. 27(1): 77–81.

Svetovidov, A. N.

1936. *Lepidion schmidti*, eine neue Fischart. Zool. Anz. 113: 266–269.

1948. Gadiformes. Acad. Sci. USSR, Zool. Inst., Fauna USSR 9(4) New Ser. 34: 221 pp. [Translation by Israel Prog. Sci. Transl., 1962. 304 pp.]

1952. Clupeidae. Acad. Sci. USSR, Zool. Inst., Fauna USSR 11(1) New Ser. 48: 331 pp. [Translation by Israel Prog. Sci. Transl., 1963. 428 pp.]

1965. O vidovykh otlichiyakh mezhdu evropeyskoy i tikhookeanskoy navagami i o sistematicheskom polozhenii navagi arkticheskoy Alyaski i Kanady [On the specific differences between the European and the North Pacific *Eleginus* species and the systematic position of the form of Arctic Alaska and Canada]. Zool. Zh. 44(2): 220–227. [In Russian; brief English summary.]

1978. Tipy vidov ryb, opisannykh P. S. Pallasom v "Zoographia rosso-asiatica" (s ocherkom istorii opublikovaniya etogo truda) [The types of the fish species described by P. S. Pallas in "Zoographia rosso-asiatica" (with a historical account of publication of this book)]. Nauka, Leningrad. 34 pp. + 27 pls. [In Russian.]

Swan, J. G.

1880a. The surf-smelt of the Northwest Coast, and the method of taking them by the Quillehute Indians, west coast of Washington Territory. Proc. U.S. Natl. Mus. (for 1880) 3: 43–46.

1880b. The eulachon or candle-fish of the Northwest Coast. Proc. U.S. Natl. Mus. (for 1880) 3: 257–264.

Swift, C. C., T. R. Haglund, M. Ruiz, and R. N. Fisher.

1993. The status and distribution of the freshwater fishes of southern California. Bull. So. Calif. Acad. Sci. 92(3): 101–167.

Tanaka, S.

1911. *Paraceratias mitsukurii* (Tanaka). (Ceratiidae.) Figures and descriptions of the fishes of Japan, including Riukiu Islands, Bonin Islands, Formosa, Kurile Islands, Korea and southern Sakhalin 2: 30–32, pls. 8 (fig. 25). [In Japanese and English.]

1912. *Cyclolumpus asperrimus* Tanaka. (Cyclopteridae.) Figures and descriptions of the fishes of Japan, including Riukiu Islands, Bonin Islands, Formosa, Kurile Islands, Korea and southern Sakhalin 5: 86, pl. 21 (figs. 80–83); 6: 87. [In Japanese and English.]

1912. *Acipenser mikadoi* Hilgendorf. (Acipenseridae.) Figures and descriptions of the fishes of Japan, including Riukiu Islands, Bonin Islands, Formosa, Kurile Islands, Korea and southern Sakhalin 7: 125–127, pl. 33 (figs. 127–129). [In Japanese and English.]

1912. *Eumicrotremus spinosus* (Müller). (Cyclopteridae.) Figures and descriptions of the fishes of Japan, including Riukiu Islands, Bonin Islands, Formosa, Kurile Islands, Korea and southern Sakhalin 7: 127–128, pl. 34 (figs. 130–133); 8: 129–130. [In Japanese and English.]

1916. *Pseudoscopelus sagamianus* (Tanaka). (Chiasmodontidae.) Figures and descriptions of the fishes of Japan, including Riukiu Islands, Bonin Islands, Formosa, Kurile Islands, Korea and southern Sakhalin 10: 180–183, pl. 48 (fig. 188); 8: 129–130. [In Japanese and English.]

Tanner, Z. L.

1885. Report of the construction and outfit of the United States Fish Commission steamer *Albatross.* Appendix A *in* Rep. U.S. Fish Comm. (for 1883) 11: 1–111.

1889. Explorations of the fishing grounds of Alaska, Washington Territory, and Oregon during 1888, by the U.S. Fish Commission steamer *Albatross.* Bull. U.S. Fish Comm. (for 1888) 8. 95 pp.

1893. Report upon the investigations of the U.S. Fish Commission steamer *Albatross* from July 1, 1889, to June 30, 1891. Rep. U.S. Fish Comm. (for 1889 to 1891) 17: 207–342.

1894. Report upon the investigations of the U.S. Fish Commission steamer *Albatross* for the year ending June 30, 1892. Rep. U.S. Fish Comm. (for 1892) 18: 1–64.

1896. Report on the work of the Fish Commission steamer *Albatross,* for the year ending June 30, 1893. Rep. U.S. Fish Comm. (for 1893) 19: 305–341.

1897. Deep-sea exploration: a general description of the steamer *Albatross,* her appliances and methods. Bull. U.S. Fish Comm. (for 1896) 16: 257–428.

Tanonaka, G. K.

1957. The occurrence of the squaretail, *Tetragonurus cuvieri,* on the high-seas south of the Aleutian Islands. Copeia 1957(1): 53–54.

Taranetz, A. Ya.

1933. Novye dannye po ikhtiofaune Beringova morya [New data on the ichthyofauna of the Bering Sea]. Vestnik Dv. Filiala Akademii Nauk SSSR [Bull. Far Eastern Branch Acad. Sci. USSR] 1933(1-2-3): 67–78. [In Russian; new species and summary in English; and selections translated by B. A. Sheiko, 1999, for Point Stephens Research, Auke Bay, Alaska.]

Taranetz, A. Ya.

1935a. Nekotorye izmeneniya v sistematike ryb sovetskogo Dal'nego Vostoka s zametkami ob ikh rasprostranenii [Some changes in the classification of fishes of the Soviet Far East with notes on their distribution]. Vestnik Dv. Filiala Akademii Nauk SSSR [Bull. Far Eastern Branch Acad. Sci. USSR] 13: 89–101. [In Russian; English summary.]

1935b. Kratkiy obzor vidov roda *Porocottus* [A short review of the species of the genus *Porocottus* with a note on *Myoxocephalus sellaris*]. Vestnik Dv. Filiala Akademii Nauk SSSR [Bull. Far Eastern Branch Acad. Sci. USSR] 14: 177–180. [In Russian; English summary; and translation by B. A. Sheiko, 1999, for Point Stephens Research, Auke Bay, Alaska.]

1936. Description of three new species of the genus *Icelus* Kröyer (Pisces, Cottidae) from the Sea of Japan and from Okhotsk Sea. Comptes Rendus (Doklady) de l'Académie des Sciences de l'URSS (N. S.) vol. 4 (13), no. 3 (107): 149–152.

1937. Kratkiy opredelitel' ryb sovetskogo Dal'nego Vostoka i prilezhashchikh vod [Handbook for identification of fishes of the Soviet Far East and adjacent waters. Izv. Tikhookean. Nauchno-Issled. Inst. Rybn. Khoz. Okeanogr. [Bull. Pac. Sci. Inst. Fish. Oceanogr.] 11. 200 pp. [In Russian.]

1938. O novykh nakhodkakh yuzhnykh elementov v ikhtiofaune severo-zapandnoi chasti Yaponskogo morya [New finds of southern elements in the ichthyofauna of the northwestern part of the Sea of Japan]. Vestnik Dv. Filiala Akademii Nauk SSSR [Bull. Far Eastern Branch Acad. Sci. USSR] 28(1): 113–129. [In Russian; English summary.]

1941. On the classification and origin of the family Cottidae. Bull. Acad. Sci. USSR, Biol. Ser. 1941(3): 427–447. [Translated from the Russian by N. J. Wilimovsky and E. Lanz, 1959. Mus. Contrib. 5, Inst. Fish., University of British Columbia, Vancouver. 28 pp.]

Taranetz, A., and A. Andriashev.

1935a. On a new fish of the family Zoarcidae from the littoral zone of the Komandorskiye Islands. Comptes Rendus (Doklady) de l'Académie des Sciences de l'URSS (N. S.) 1(4): 269–270.

1935b. Vier neue Fischarten der Gattung *Lycodes* Reinh. aus dem Ochotskischen Meer. Zool. Anz. 112(9-10): 242–253.

Tarp, F. H.

1952. A revision of the family Embiotocidae (the surfperches). Calif. Dep. Fish Game Fish Bull. 88. 99 pp.

Taylor, F. H. C.

1967a. Midwater trawl catches from Queen Charlotte Sound and the open ocean adjacent to the Queen Charlotte Islands. Fish. Res. Board Can. Tech. Rep. 11. 44 pp.

1967b. Unusual fishes taken by midwater trawl off the Queen Charlotte Islands, British Columbia. J. Fish. Res. Board Can. 24(10): 2101–2115.

1968. The relationship of midwater trawl catches to sound scattering layers off the coast of northern British Columbia. J. Fish. Res. Board Can. 25(3): 457–472.

Taylor, G. T.

1959. The occurrence of lesser lancetfish (*Anotopterus pharao* Zugmayer) in the northeast Pacific Ocean. Fish. Res. Board Can. Prog. Rep. Pac. Coast Stn. 113: 10–12.

Templeman, W.

1968. A review of the morid fish Genus *Halargyreus* with first records from the western North Atlantic. J. Fish. Res. Board Can. 25(5): 877–901.

1970. Distribution of *Anotopterus pharao* in the North Atlantic and comparison of specimens of *A. pharao* from the western North Atlantic with those from other areas. J. Fish. Res. Board Can. 27(3): 499–512.

Teshima, K., and S. Tomonaga.

1986. Reproduction of Aleutian skate, *Bathyraja aleutica* with comments on embryonic development. Pages 303–309 *in* T. Uyeno, R. Arai, T. Taniuchi, and K. Matsuura, eds. Indo-Pacific fish biology. Proceedings of the Second International Conference on Indo-Pacific Fishes. Ichthyological Society of Japan, Tokyo.

Teshima, K., and T. K. Wilderbuer.

1990. Distribution and abundance of skates in the eastern Bering Sea, Aleutian Islands region, and the Gulf of Alaska. Pages 257–267 *in* H. L. Pratt, Jr., S. H. Gruber, and T. Taniuchi, eds. Elasmobranchs as living resources: advances in the biology, ecology, systematics, and the status of the fisheries. NOAA Tech. Rep. NMFS 90.

Thompson, G. R., and J. Turk.

1997. Modern physical geology. Saunders College Publishing. 1 vol., various pagination.

Thompson, W. F.

1915. A new fish of the genus *Sebastodes* from British Columbia with notes on others. Province of British Columbia, Report of the Commissioner of Fisheries for 1914: 120–122, 1 pl.

1917. Further notes on *Erilepis,* the giant bass-like fish of the North Pacific. B.C. Prov. Mus. Rep. 1916: 20–22.

Thompson, W. F., and R. Van Cleve.

1936. Life history of the Pacific halibut. 2. Distribution and early life history. Rep. Int. Fish. Comm. 9. 184 pp.

Thorsteinson, L. K., P. R. Becker, and D. A. Hale.

1989. The Yukon Delta: a synthesis of information. U.S. Department of Commerce, OCS Study, MMS 89-081. 89 pp.

Thorsteinson, L. K., L. E. Jarvela, and D. A. Hale.

1991. Arctic fish habitat use investigations: nearshore studies in the Alaskan Beaufort Sea, summer 1990. Annual report, National Oceanic and Atmospheric Administration, National Ocean Service, Office of Ocean Resources Conservation and Assessment, Grace Hall, Suite 300, 4230 University Drive, Anchorage, AK 99508-4626. 134 pp. + appendixes.

Thys, T.

1994. Swimming heads: an underwater encounter with the giant ocean sunfish. Nat. Hist. 103(8): 36–39.

Tighe, K. A.

1989. Family Serrivomeridae. Pages 613–628 *in* Fishes of the western North Atlantic. Mem. Sears Found. Mar. Res., New Haven, 1(9), Vol. 1.

Tilesius, W. G. von.

1811. Piscium Camtschaticorum descriptiones et icones. Mem. Acad. Imp. Sci. St. Petersburg 3: 225–285, pls. 8–13.

Tkachenko, V. A., and L. N. Domanevskiy.

1970. A find of the smalleye squaretail [*Tetragonurus cuvieri* (Risso)] (Tetragonuridae Pisces) off the northwest African coast. J. Ichthyol. [English transl. Vopr. Ikhtiol.] 10(6): 841–843.

Tokranov, A. M.

1984. Reproduction of great sculpin, *Myoxocephalus polyacanthocephalus* (Cottidae), in Kamchatka waters. J. Ichthyol. [English transl. Vopr. Ikhtiol.] 24(4): 119–127.

1993. Sexual dimorphism in sea poachers (Agonidae) off Kamchatka. J. Ichthyol. 33(3): 113–122 [English transl. Vopr. Ikhtiol. 32(6): 81–89].

1994. Distribution and population of the northern Far East belligerent sculpin, *Megalocottus platycephalus platycephalus* (Cottidae), in the Bol'shaya River estuary (western Kamchatka). J. Ichthyol. 34(5): 149–153 [English transl. Vopr. Ikhtiol. 34(1): 127–129].

1998a. Some traits of biology of *Bathymaster signatus* (Bathymasteridae) in the Pacific waters of southeastern Kamchatka and the northern Kurils. J. Ichthyol. 38(6): 488–490 [English transl. Vopr. Ikhtiol. 38(4): 571–573].

1998b. Some features of the biology of *Thyriscus anoplus* (Cottidae) in the Pacific waters of northern Kuril Islands. J. Ichthyol. 38(8): 677–679 [English transl. Vopr. Ikhtiol. 38(5): 701–703].

1998c. Distribution and size–age composition of *Sebastes aleutianus* (Scorpaenidae) in Pacific waters of the northern Kurils, eastern Kamchatka, and the western Bering Sea. J. Ichthyol. 38(9): 758–765 [English transl. Vopr. Ikhtiol. 38(6): 787–793].

1999. Some features of biology of the prowfish *Zaprora silenus* (Zaproridae) in the Pacific waters of the northern Kuril Islands and southeastern Kamchatka. J. Ichthyol. 39(6): 475–478 [English transl. Vopr. Ikhtiol. 39(4): 573–576].

2000a. Specific composition and spatially-bathymetrical distribution of snailfish (Liparidae) in the Pacific waters of southeastern Kamchatka and the northern Kuril Islands. J. Ichthyol. 40(2): 139–149 [English transl. Vopr. Ikhtiol. 40(2): 176–186].

2000b. Size-age composition of liparids (Liparidae) in the Pacific Ocean of southeastern Kamchatka and north Kuril Islands. J. Ichthyol. 40(5): 364–369 [English transl. Vopr. Ikhtiol. 40(3): 347–352].

2000c. Feeding of Liparidae in the Pacific waters off southeastern Kamchtaka and the northern Kuril Islands. J. Ichthyol. 40(7): 536–542 [English transl. Vopr. Ikhtiol. 40(4): 530–536].

2000d. Distribution and some features of the biology of *Bathyagonus nigrippinis* (Agonidae) in Pacific waters of southeast Kamchatka and the northern Kurils. J. Ichthyol. 40(8): 585–591 [English transl. Vopr. Ikhtiol. 40(5): 614–620].

2001. Some biological characteristics of the hook-eared sculpin *Artediellichthys nigripinnis* (Cottidae) in the Pacific waters of the northern Kuril Islands and southeastern Kamchatka. J. Ichthyol. 41(8): 584–588.

Tokranov, A. M., and I. I. Davydov.

1997. Some aspects of biology of the shortraker rockfish *Sebastes borealis* (Scorpaenidae) in the Pacific waters of Kamchatka and western part of the Bering Sea: 1. Spatial and bathymetric distribution. J. Ichthyol. 37(9): 761–768 [English transl. Vopr. Ikhtiol. 37(6): 798–805].

1998. Some aspects of biology of the shortraker rockfish *Sebastes borealis* (Scorpaenidae) in the Pacific waters of Kamchatka and western part of the Bering Sea: 2. Size and age composition. J. Ichthyol. 38(1): 37–41 [English transl. Vopr. Ikhtiol. 387(1): 42–46].

Tokranov, A. M., and Yu. P. D'yakov.

1996. A new record of the skillfish [*sic*] *Eripelis zonifer* (Anoplopomatidae) from the coastal waters of Russia. J. Ichthyol. 36(8): 674–675 [English transl. Vopr. Ikhtiol. 36(5): 708–709].

Tokranov, A. M., and A. M. Orlov.

2001a. Some specific biological features of Psychrolutidae in the Pacific waters of southeastern Kamchatka and the northern Kuril Islands. Communication 1. Spatial-bathymetric distribution. J. Ichthyol.41(7): 515–523.

2001b. Some biological features of Psychrolutidae in the Pacific waters of southeastern Kamchatka and the northern Kuril Islands. Communication 2. Size-age and sex composition and feeding. J. Ichthyol. 41(8): 575–583.

Townsend, C. H.

1887. Notes on the natural history and ethnology of northern Alaska. Pages 81–102 with 4 plates *in* M.A. Healy, Report of the cruise of the Revenue Marine steamer *Corwin* in the Arctic Ocean in the year 1885. House of Representatives, 49th Congress, 1st Session, Ex. Doc. 153. Washington, Government Printing Office.

1901. Dredging and other records of the United States Fish Commission steamer *Albatross,* with bibliography relative to the work of the vessel. Rep. U.S. Fish Comm. (for 1900) 26: 387–562.

1924. The passing of the *Albatross.* Natural History 24: 619–620.

Townsend, C. H., and J. T. Nichols.

1925. Deep sea fishes of the *Albatross* Lower California expedition. Bull. Am. Mus. Nat. Hist. 52(1): 1–21, pls. 1–4, and 1 map.

Townsend, L. D.

1935. Notes on *Citharichthys sordidus* and *C. stigmaeus* with an extension of range. Copeia 1935(4): 193.

1936. Variations in the meristic characters of flounders from the northeastern Pacific. Rep. Int. Fish. Comm. 11. 24 pp.

Toyoshima, M.

1985. Taxonomy of the subfamily Lycodinae (family Zoarcidae) in Japan and adjacent waters. Mem. Fac. Fish. Hokkaido Univ. 32(2): 131–243.

Trautman, M. B.

1973. A guide to the collection and identification of presmolt Pacific salmon in Alaska with an illustrated key. U.S. Dep. Commer., NOAA Tech. Memo. NMFS ABFL-2. 20 pp.

Trewavas, E.

1933. On the structure of two oceanic fishes, *Cyema atrum* Günther and *Opisthoproctus soleatus* Vaillant. Proc. Zool. Soc. Lond. 1933 (2): 601–614, pls. 1–2.

Trunov, I. A.

1998. A chiasmodontid species from genus *Kali* (Chiasmodontidae) new for the Antarctic. J. Ichthyol. 38(1): 138–139 [English transl. Vopr. Ikhtiol. 38(1): 146–147].

Tsutsui, D., and K. Amaoka.

1997. First record of the snail fish, *Careproctus simus* (Scorpaeniformes: Liparidae), from Japan. Ichthyol. Res. 44(1): 89–91.

Tsuyuki, H., and S. J. Westrheim.

1970. Analysis of the *Sebastes aleutianus – S. melanostomus* complex, and description of a new scorpaenid species, *Sebastes caenaematicus,* in the northeast Pacific Ocean. J. Fish. Res. Board Can. 27(12): 2233–2254.

Tucker, D. W., and J. W. Jones.

1951. On a rare deep-sea fish *Notacanthus phasganorus* Goode (Heteromi-Notacanthidae) from the Arctic Bear Isle fishing-grounds. Bull. Brit. Mus. (Nat. Hist.) Zool. 1(5): 69–79.

Tully, J. P.

1964. Oceanographic regions and assessment of the temperature structure in the seasonal zone of the North Pacific Ocean. J. Fish. Res. Board. Can. 21(5): 941–969.

Turner, L. M.

1886. Fishes. Pages 87–113, plates 1–15 *in* Contributions to the natural history of Alaska. Results of the investigations made chiefly in the Yukon District and the Aleutian Islands; conducted under the auspices of the Signal Service, United States Army, extending from May, 1874, to August, 1881. Arctic Series of Publications Issued in Connection with the Signal Service, U.S. Army, No. 2. Government Printing Office, Washington, D.C.

Tyler, J. C.

1980. Osteology, phylogeny, and higher classification of the fishes of the Order Plectognathi (Tetraodontiformes). National Oceanic and Atmospheric Administration, Tech. Rep. NMFS Circular 434. 422 pp.

Udintsev, G. B., I. G. Boichenko, and V. F. Kanaev.

1959. Rel'ef dna Beringova morya [The bottom relief of the Bering Sea]. *In* Geographicheskaya kharakteristika Beringova morya. Rel'ef dna i donnye otlozheniya [Geographical description of the Bering Sea: bottom relief and sediments]. Tr. Inst. Okeanol. Akad. Nauk SSSR 29: 17–64 [Trans. Oceanol. Inst. Acad. Sci. USSR 29: 14–64]. [Translation by Israel Prog. Sci. Transl., Jerusalem, 1964.]

Ueber, E.

1989. Xanthic, gigantic, China rockfish. Calif. Fish Game 75(1): 47–48.

Ueno, Tatsuji.

1954. Studies on the cyclopterid fishes from northern Japan and adjacent regions. I. Remarks on two genera, *Cyclolumpus* and *Eumicrotremus.* Bull. Fac. Fish. Hokkaido Univ. 4(4): 273–295.

1970. Fauna Japonica. Cyclopteridae (Pisces). Academic Press of Japan, Tokyo. 233 pp., 13 pls.

1971. List of the marine fishes from the waters of Hokkaido and its adjacent regions. Sci. Rep. Hokkaido Fish. Exp. Stn. 13: 61–102.

United States Department of State.

1977. Public Notice 526, Fishery Conservation Zone: notice of limits. Federal Register 42(44)(7 March): 12937–12938.

United States Department of the Interior.

1952. Alaska: a reconnaissance report of the potential development of water resources in the Territory of Alaska for irrigation, power production, and other beneficial uses. House Document 197, 82D Congress, First Session. Washington, D.C. 287 pp.

United States National Museum.

1947. A list and index of the publications of the United States National Museum (1875–1946). U.S. Natl. Mus. Bull. 193: 306 pp.

Uyeno, T., K. Matsuura, and E. Fujii, editors.

1983. Fishes trawled off Surinam and French Guiana. Japan Marine Fishery Resource Research Center. 519 pp.

Uyeno, T., and S. Kishida.

1977. First record of the neoscopelid fish, *Scopelengys tristis* from Japan. Jpn. J. Ichthyol. 23(4): 239–241.

Van Cleve, R., and W. F. Thompson.

1938. A record of the pomfret and barracuda from Alaska. Copeia 1938(1): 45–46.

Van Guelpen, L.

1986. Hookear sculpins (genus *Artediellus*) of the North American Atlantic: taxonomy, morphological variability, distribution, and aspects of life history. Can. J. Zool. 64: 677–690.

Vasil'eva, E. D.

1997. Morphological divergence of two species of gadid fishes *Eleginus navaga* and *E. gracilis* (Gadidae) with disjunctive area. J. Ichthyol. 37(9): 754–760 [English transl. Vopr. Ikhtiol. 37(6): 791–797].

Vermeij, G. J.

1991. Anatomy of an invasion: the trans-Arctic interchange. Paleobiology 17(3): 281–307.

Vladykov, V. D.

1973. *Lampetra pacifica*, a new nonparasitic species of lamprey (Petromyzontidae) from Oregon and California. J. Fish. Res. Board Can. 30(2): 205–213.

Vladykov, V. D., and W. I. Follett.

1958. Redescription of *Lampetra ayresii* (Günther) of western North America, a species of lamprey (Petromyzontidae) distinct from *Lampetra fluviatilus* (Linnaeus) of Europe. J. Fish. Res. Board Can. 15(1): 47–77.

1965. *Lampetra richardsoni,* a new nonparasitic species of lamprey (Petromyzonidae) from western North America. J. Fish. Res. Board Can. 22(1): 139–158.

1967. The teeth of lampreys (Petromyzonidae): their terminology and use in a key to the holarctic genera. J. Fish. Res. Board Can. 24(5): 1067–1075.

Vladykov, V. D., and E. Kott.

1978. A new nonparasitic species of the holoarctic lamprey genus *Lethenteron* Creaser and Hubbs, 1922, (Petromyzonidae) from northwestern North America with notes on other species of the same genus. Biol. Pap. Univ. Alaska 19: 74 pp.

1979a. List of Northern Hemisphere lampreys (Petromyzonidae) and their distribution. Can. Dep. Fish. Oceans, Ottawa, Misc. Spec. Publ. 42. 30 pp.

1979b. Satellite species among the holarctic lampreys (Petromyzonidae). Can. J. Zool. 57(4): 860–867.

Vladykov, V. D., and J. L. Tremblay.

1936. Nouvelles espèces de *Lycodes* (Pisces, Zoarcidae) du St.-Laurent et revision de toutes les espèces du même genre de d'Atlantique occidental. Fauna et Flora Laurentianae 1: 1–45. [Cited in Andriashev 1973.]

Vogt, K. D.

1973. New distributional records and description of a new species of liparid from Alaska. Biol. Pap. Univ. Alaska 13: 22–27.

Vogt, K. D.

1987a. On two unique reports of species of *Liparis* in Alaska and adjacent waters. Jpn. J. Ichthyol. 34(1): 116.

1987b. *Malacocottus kincaidi* Gilbert et Thompson: a south central Alaskan species? Jpn. J. Ichthyol. 34(2): 239–240.

1988a. Liparidae Gill, [30 September] 1861 (Osteichthys, Scorpaeniformes): proposed confirmation of spelling. Bull. Zool. Nomencl. 45(2): 130–131.

1988b. The occurrence of *Lampetra tridentatus* in the northern Bering Sea. Jpn. J. Ichthyol. 35(4): 403.

Volpe, J. P., E. B. Taylor, D. W. Rimmer, and B. W. Glickman.

2000. Evidence of natural reproduction of aquaculture-escaped Atlantic salmon in a coastal British Columbia river. Conserv. Biol. 14(3): 899–903.

Voronina, E. P.

1999. Morphology and systematics of river flounders of the genus *Platichthys*. J. Ichthyol. 39(8): 588–599 [English transl. Vopr. Ikhtiol. 39(5): 612–624].

Voronina, E. P., and S. A. Evseenko.

2001. Morphology and systematics of Arctic flounders of the genus *Liopsetta* (sensu Norman, 1934) (Pleuronectidae, sensu Chapleau and Keast, 1988). J. Ichthyol. 41(7): 486–498.

Wagner, T. A.

1988. Survey of fishery resources in the Port Moller–Balboa Bay pipeline corridor. U.S. Fish and Wildlife Service, King Salmon Fishery Assistance Office, P.O. Box 277, King Salmon, AK 99613. 37 pp.

Wahle, R. J., and R. E. Pearson.

1987. A listing of Pacific coast spawning streams and hatcheries producing chinook and coho salmon (with estimates on number of spawners and data on hatchery releases). U.S. Dep. Commerce, NOAA Tech. Memo., NMFS F/NWC-122. 109 pp.

Wakimoto, H., and K. Amaoka.

1994. Occurrence of juveniles of two bathymasterid species from Hokkaido, Japan. Jpn. J. Ichthyol. 41(2): 222–226.

Walbran, J. T.

1909. British Columbia coast names, 1592–1906. Government Printing Bureau, Ottawa. [Reprint, 1971, Douglas & McIntyre, Vancouver, and University of Washington Press, Seattle. 546 pp.]

Walford, L. A.

1931. Handbook of common commercial and game fishes of California. Calif. Fish Game Fish Bull. 28. 181 pp.

1935. The sharks and rays of California. Calif. Fish Game Fish Bull. 45. 66 pp.

1974. Marine game fishes of the Pacific coast from Alaska to the Equator. Reprint of the 1937 edition, with new introduction. Reprinted by T.F.H. Publications, Inc., for Smithsonian Institution Press, Washington, D.C. 205 pp., 69 pls.

Walker, H. J., Jr., and R. H. Rosenblatt.

1988. Pacific toadfishes of the genus *Porichthys* (Batrachoididae) with descriptions of three new species. Copeia 1988(4): 887–904.

Walters, V.

1953a. The fishes collected by the Canadian Arctic Expedition, 1913–18, with additional notes on the ichthyofauna of western Arctic Canada. Natl. Mus. Can. Bull. 128: 257–274.

1953b. Notes on fishes from Prince Patrick and Ellesmere islands, Canada. Am. Mus. Novit. 1643. 17 pp.

1955. Fishes of western arctic America and eastern arctic Siberia: taxonomy and zoogeography. Bull. Am. Mus. Nat. Hist. 106, Article 5: 255–368.

Washington, B. B.

1986. Systematic relationships and ontogeny of the sculpins *Artedius, Clinocottus,* and *Oligocottus* (Cottidae: Scorpaeniformes). Proc. Calif. Acad. Sci. 44(9): 157–224.

Washington, B. B., W. N. Eschmeyer, and K. M. Howe.

1984. Scorpaeniformes: relationships. Pages 438–447 *in* H. G. Moser et al., eds. Ontogeny and systematics of fishes. Am. Soc. Ichthyol. Herpetol., Spec. Publ. 1.

Watanabe, M.

1960. Fauna Japonica. Cottidae (Pisces). Biogeographical Society of Japan, Tokyo. 218 pp., 40 pls.

Weinberg, K. L.

1994. Rockfish assemblages of the middle shelf and upper slope off Oregon and Washington. U.S. Natl. Mar. Fish. Serv. Fish. Bull. 92(3): 620–632.

Weingartner, T. J.

1997. A review of the physical oceanography of the northeastern Chukchi Sea. Am. Fish. Soc. Symp. 19: 40–59.

Weingartner, T., and J. C. "Craig" George.

2001. Chukchi Sea oceanography: regional and global issues. Pages 297–302 *in* D. W. Norton, ed. Fifty more years below zero: tributes and meditations for the Naval Arctic Research Laboratory's first half century at Barrow, Alaska. University of Alaska Press, Fairbanks.

Weitzman, S. H.

1974. Osteology and evolutionary relationships of the Sternoptychidae, with a new classification of stomiatoid families. Bull. Am. Mus. Nat. Hist. 53: 327–478.

1997. Systematics of deep-sea fishes. Pages 43–77 *in* D. J. Randall and A. P. Farrell, eds. Deep-sea fishes. Academic Press, San Diego.

Welander, A. D.

1940. Notes on the dissemination of shad, *Alosa sapidissima* (Wilson), along the Pacific coast of North America. Copeia 1940(4): 221–223.

Welander, A. D., and D. L. Alverson.

1954. New and little known fishes of the eastern Pacific. Wash. Dep. Fish. Fish. Res. Pap. 1(2): 37–44.

Welander, A. D., D. L. Alverson, and P. Bergman.

1957. Rare fishes from the eastern North Pacific Ocean. Wash. Dep. Fish. Fish. Res. Pap. 2(1): 60–66.

Welander, A. D., R. C. Johnson, and R. A. Hajny.

1957. Occurrence of the boar fish, *Pseudopentaceros richardsoni,* and the zeid, *Allocyttus verrucosus,* in the North Pacific. Copeia 1957(3): 244–246.

Welch, D. W., L. Margolis, M. A. Henderson, and S. McKinnell.

1991. Evidence for attacks by the bathypelagic fish *Anotopterus pharao* (Myctophiformes) on Pacific salmon (*Oncorhynchus* spp.). Can. J. Fish. Aquat. Sci. 48: 2403–2407.

Westrheim, S. J.

1964. Rockfish (*Sebastodes brevispinis*) in British Columbia waters. J. Fish. Res. Board Can. 21(4): 855–856.

1965. Northern range extensions for four species of rockfish (*Sebastodes goodei, S. helvomaculatus, S. rubrivinctus,* and *S. zacentrus*) in the North Pacific Ocean. J. Fish. Res. Board Can. 22(1): 231–235.

1966a. Northern range extension records for two rockfish species (*Sebastodes caurinus* and *S. elongatus*). J. Fish. Res. Board Can. 23(9): 1455–1456.

1966b. Northern range extensions for three species of rockfish (*Sebastodes flavidus, S. paucispinis,* and *S. pinniger*) in the North Pacific Ocean. J. Fish. Res. Board Can. 23(9): 1469–1471.

1968. First records of three rockfish species (*Sebastodes aurora, S. ciliatus,* and *Sebastolobus altivelis*) from waters off British Columbia. J. Fish. Res. Board Can. 25(11): 2509–2513.

1970. Survey of rockfishes, especially Pacific ocean perch, in the northeast Pacific Ocean, 1963–66. J. Fish. Res. Board Can. 27(10: 1781–1809.

1973. Preliminary information on the systematics, distribution, and abundance of the dusky rockfish, *Sebastes ciliatus.* J. Fish. Res. Board Can. 30(8): 1230–1234.

Westrheim, S. J., and B. M. Leaman.

1976. A selected bibliography of northeastern Pacific rockfishes (*Sebastes* and *Sebastolobus*) other than *Sebastes alutus*. Environment Canada, Fish. Mar. Serv. Tech. Rep. 659. 20 pp.

Westrheim, S. J., and F. T. Pletcher.

1966. First records of the twoline eelpout, *Bothrocara brunneum,* Greenland halibut, *Reinhardtius hippoglossoides,* and shortbelly rockfish, *Sebastodes jordani,* in British Columbia waters. J. Fish. Res. Board Can. 23(2): 309–312, 3 pls.

Westrheim, S. J., and H. Tsuyuki.

1967. *Sebastodes reedi,* a new scorpaenid fish in the northeast Pacific Ocean. J. Fish. Res. Board Can. 24(9): 1945–1954.

1971. Taxonomy, distribution, and biology of the northern rockfish, *Sebastes polyspinis.* J. Fish. Res. Board Can. 28(10): 1621–1627.

1972. Synonymy of *Sebastes caenaematicus* with *Sebastes borealis,* and range extension record. J. Fish. Res. Board Can. 29(5): 606–607.

Whitehead, P. J. P.

1985a. FAO species catalogue. Vol. 7. Clupeoid fishes of the world (suborder Clupeoidei). Part 1. Chirocentridae, Clupeidae and Pristigasteridae. FAO Fisheries Synopsis No. 125, Vol. 7, part 1, pp. 1–303.

1985b. King herring: his place amongst the clupeoids. Can. J. Fish. Aquat. Sci. 42 (Suppl. 1): 3–20.

Whitehead, P. J. P., M.-L. Bauchot, J.-C. Hureau, J. Nielsen, and E. Tortonese, editors.

1984. Fishes of the north-eastern Atlantic and the Mediterranean. Vol. I, pp. 1–510. Paris, Unesco. [Reprint with corrections, 1989.]

Whitehead, P. J. P., M.-L. Bauchot, J.-C. Hureau, J. Nielsen, and E. Tortonese, editors.

1986. Fishes of the north-eastern Atlantic and the Mediterranean. Vol. II, pp. 511–1008. Vol. III, pp. 1009–1473. Paris, Unesco.

Whitehead, P. J. P., G. J. Nelson, and T. Wongratana.

1988. FAO species catalogue. Vol. 7. Clupeoid fishes of the world (suborder Clupeoidei). Part 2. Engraulididae. FAO Fisheries Synopsis No. 125, Vol. 7, part 2, pp. 305–579.

Wilby, G. V.

1934. Ichthyological treasures from the *Albatross* expeditions in Canadian waters. Can. Field-Nat. 48(8): 121–126.

1936. On the gobiesocid genus *Rimicola*. Copeia 1936(2): 116.

1936. A second record of the cottoid fish *Asemichthys taylori* Gilbert. Copeia 1936(2): 117; photograph on p. 116.

1937. The lingcod, *Ophiodon elongatus* Girard. Biol. Board Can., Bull. 54. 24 pp.

Wild, P. W.

1967. An occurrence of a chum salmon, *Oncorhynchus keta* (Walbaum), in the California troll fishery. Calif. Fish Game 53(4): 299–300.

Wiley, E. O.

1981. Phylogenetics, the theory and practice of phylogenetic systematics. Wiley, New York. 439 pp.

Wilimovsky, N. J.

1954. List of the fishes of Alaska. Stanford Ichthyol. Bull. 4(5): 279–294.

1956. A new name, *Lumpenus sagitta*, to replace *Lumpenus gracilis* (Ayres), for a northern blennioid fish (family Stichaeidae). Stanford Ichthyol. Bull. 7(2): 23–24.

1958. Provisional keys to the fishes of Alaska. U.S. Fish and Wildlife Service, Fisheries Research Laboratory, Juneau, Alaska. 113 pp.

1964. Inshore fish fauna of the Aleutian archipelago. Proc. Alaska Sci. Conf. 14: 172–190.

1966. Synopsis of previous scientific explorations. Pages 1–5 *in* N. J. Wilimovsky and J. N. Wolfe, eds. Environment of the Cape Thompson region, Alaska. U.S. Atomic Energy Commission, Division of Technical Information, Oak Ridge, Tennessee.

1974. Fishes of the Bering Sea: the state of existing knowledge and requirements for future effective effort. Pages 243–256 *in* D. W. Hood and E. J. Kelley, eds. Oceanography of the Bering Sea with emphasis on renewable resources. University of Alaska, Fairbanks, Inst. Mar. Sci., Occas. Publ. 2.

1979ms. Provisional key to known genera of living cottoid fishes with a nomenclator of nominal marine forms. Unpublished manuscript. University of British Columbia, Institute of Resource Ecology, Vancouver. 64 pp.

Wilimovsky, N. J., L. S. Incze, and S. J. Westrheim, editors.

1988. Species synopses: life histories of selected fish and shellfish of the northeast Pacfic and Bering Sea. University of Washington, Washington Sea Grant Program and Fisheries Research Institute, Seattle. 111 pp.

Wilimovsky, N. J., A. Peden, and J. Peppar.

1967. Systematics of six demersal fishes of the North Pacific Ocean. Fish. Res. Board Can. Tech. Rep. 34. 95 pp.

Wilimovsky, N. J., and D. E. Wilson.

1978. A new species of Agonidae, *Agonomalus mozinoi,* from the west coast of North America. Syesis 11: 73–79.

Wilimovsky, N. J., and J. N. Wolfe, editors.

1966. Environment of the Cape Thompson region, Alaska. U.S. Atomic Energy Commission, Division of Technical Information, Oak Ridge, Tennessee. 1,250 pp., 6 pls.

Williams, H.

1958. Landscapes of Alaska: their geologic evolution. Cambridge University Press, London. 148 pp.

Willis, J. M.

1984. Mesopelagic fish faunal regions of the northeast Pacific. Biol. Oceanogr. 3(2): 167–185.

Willis, J. M., and W. G. Pearcy.

1982. Vertical distribution and migration of fishes of the lower mesopelagic zone off Oregon. Mar. Biol. 70(1): 87–98.

Willis, J. M., W. G. Pearcy, and N. V. Parin.

1988. Zoogeography of midwater fishes in the Subarctic Pacific. Bull. Ocean Res. Inst. Univ. Tokyo No. 26 (part II): 79–142.

Wilson, D. E.

1973. Revision of the cottid genus *Gymnocanthus*, with a description of their osteology. M.S. thesis, University of British Columbia, Vancouver. 223 pp.

Wilson, D. E., and G. W. Hughes.

1978. The first record of the brown cat shark, *Apristurus brunneus* (Gilbert, 1891) from Alaskan waters. Syesis 11:283.

Wilson, P. C., and J. S. Beckett.
1970. Atlantic Ocean distribution of the pelagic stingray, *Dasyatis violacea.* Copeia 1970(4): 696–707.

Wilson, R. R., Jr.
1984. Taxonomic and biological studies on the abyssal grenadiers *Coryphaenoides armatus* and *C. yaquinae* in the eastern and central North Pacific, with special reference to otoliths. Ph.D. thesis, Univ. California, San Diego. 194 pp.
1994. Interrelationships of the subgenera of *Coryphaenoides* (Gadiformes: Macrouridae): comparison of protein electrophoresis and peptide mapping. Copeia 1994(1): 42–50.

Wilson, R. R., Jr., and R. S. Waples.
1983. Distribution, morphology, and biochemical genetics of *Coryphaenoides armatus* and *C. yaquinae* (Pisces, Macrouridae) in the central and eastern North Pacific. Deep-Sea Res. 30: 1127–1145.
1984. Electrophoretic and biometric variability in the abyssal grenadier *Coryphaenoides armatus* of the western North Atlantic, eastern South Pacific and eastern North Pacific oceans. Mar. Biol. 80: 227–237.

Wing, B. L., C. M. Guthrie III, and A. J. Gharrett.
1992. Atlantic salmon in marine waters of southeastern Alaska. Trans. Am. Fish. Soc. 121: 814–818.

Wing, B. L., and D. J. Kamikawa.
1995. Distribution of neustonic sablefish larvae and associated ichthyoplankton in the eastern Gulf of Alaska, May 1990. NOAA Tech. Memo. NMFS-AFSC-53. 54 pp.

Wing, B. L., J. M. Murphy, and T. L. Rutecki.
2000. Occurrence of Pacific sardine, *Sardinops sagax,* off southeastern Alaska. U.S. Natl. Mar. Fish. Serv. Fish. Bull. 87:881–883.

Winkler, G. R., E. M. MacKevett, Jr., G. Plafker, D. H. Richter, D. S. Rosenkrans, and H. R. Schmoll.
2000. A geologic guide to Wrangell-Saint Elias National Park and Preserve, Alaska: a tectonic collage of northbound terranes. U.S. Geological Survey Professional Paper 1616. U.S. Government Printing Office, Washington, D.C. 166 pp.

Winkler, P.
1988. Environmentally induced color polymorphism in the penpoint gunnel, *Apodichthys flavidus* (Pisces: Pholididae). Copeia 1988(1): 240–242.

Winters, G. H.
1970. Record size and age of Atlantic capelin, *Mallotus villosus.* J. Fish. Res. Board Can. 27(2): 393–394.

Wisner, R. L.
1959. Distribution and differentiation of the North Pacific myctophid fish, *Tarletonbeania taylori.* Copeia 1959(1): 1–7.
1970. Distribution and characters of the North Pacific myctophid fish *Lampanyctus jordani* Gilbert. Copeia 1970(3): 420–429.
1974a. Descriptions of five new species of myctophid fishes from the Pacific, Indian, and Atlantic oceans. Occas. Pap. Calif. Acad. Sci. 110. 37 pp.
1974b. The taxonomy and distribution of lanternfishes (family Myctophidae) of the eastern Pacific Ocean. NORDA Rep. 3, Navy Ocean Research and Development Activity, Bay St. Louis, Mississippi. 229 pp.

Wisner, R. L., and C. B. McMillan.
1990. Three new species of hagfishes, genus *Eptatretus* (Cyclostomata, Myxinidae), from the Pacific coast of North America, with new data on *E. deani* and *E. stoutii*. U.S. Natl. Mar. Fish. Serv. Fish. Bull. 88: 787–804.

Wolotira, R. J., Jr., T. M. Sample, S. F. Noel, and C. R. Iten.
1993. Geographic and bathymetric distributions for many commercially important fishes and shellfishes off the west coast of North America, based on research survey and commercial catch data, 1912–84. U.S. Dep. Commer., NOAA Tech. Memo. NMFS-AFSC-6. 184 pp.

Woods, L. P., and P. M. Sonoda.
1973. Order Berycomorphi (Beryciformes). Pages 263–396 *in* Fishes of the western North Atlantic. Mem. Sears Found. Mar. Res., New Haven, 1(6).

Wooton, R. J.
1976. The biology of the sticklebacks. Academic Press, New York. 387 pp.
1984. A functional biology of sticklebacks. University of California Press, Berkeley. 265 pp.

Workman, G. D., N. Olsen, and A. R. Kronlund.
1998. Results from a bottom trawl survey of rockfish stocks off the west coast of the Queen Charlotte Islands, September 5 to 23, 1997. Can. MS Rep. Fish. Aquat. Sci. 2457. 86 pp.

Yabe, M.

1981. Osteological review of the family Icelidae Berg, 1940, (Pisces; Scorpaeniformes), with comment on the validity of this family. Bull. Fac. Fish. Hokkaido Univ. 32(4): 293–315.

1985. Comparative osteology and myology of the superfamily Cottoidea (Pisces: Scorpaeniformes), and its phylogenetic classification. Mem. Fac. Fish. Hokkaido Univ. 32(1). 130 pp.

1991. *Bolinia euryptera,* a new genus and species of sculpin (Scorpaeniformes: Cottidae) from the Bering Sea. Copeia 1991(2): 329–339.

1995. A new species of sculpin, *Zesticelus ochotensis* (Scorpaeniformes: Cottidae), from the southwestern Okhotsk Sea. Jpn. J. Ichthyol. 42(1): 17–20.

Yabe, M., D. M. Cohen, K. Wakabayashi, and T. Iwamoto.

1981. Fishes new to the eastern Bering Sea. U.S. Natl. Mar. Fish. Serv. Fish. Bull. 79(2): 353–356.

Yabe, M., S. Maruyama, and K. Amaoka.

1983. First records of five cottid fishes and a psychrolutid fish from Japan. Jpn. J. Ichthyol. 29(4): 456–464.

Yabe, M., A. Soma, and K. Amaoka.

2001. *Icelinus pietschi* sp. nov. and a rare species, *Sigmistes smithi,* from the southern Kuril Archipelago (Scorpaeniformes: Cottidae). Ichthyol. Res. 48(1): 65–70.

Yabe, M., D. Tsutsui, T. Shimokawa, and T. Kinoshita.

1995. A psychrolutid fish, *Psychrolutes pustulosus,* collected from the southwestern Okhotsk Sea off Hokkaido, Japan. Jpn. J. Ichthyol. 42(2): 200–202.

Yang, M.-S.

1988. Morphological differences between two congeneric species of pleuronectid flatfishes: arrowtooth flounder, *Atheresthes stomias,* and Kamchatka flounder, *A. evermanni.* U.S. Natl. Mar. Fish. Serv. Fish. Bull. 86(3): 608–611.

Yang, M.-S., and B. N. Page.

1999. Diet of Pacific sleeper shark, *Somniosus pacificus,* in the Gulf of Alaska. U.S. Natl. Mar. Fish. Serv. Fish. Bull. 97: 406–409.

Yarberry, E. I.

1965. Osteology of the zoarcid fish *Melanostigma pammelas.* Copeia 1965(4): 442–462.

Yatsu, A.

1981. A revision of the gunnel family Pholididae (Pisces, Blennioidei). Bull. Natl. Sci. Mus. (Tokyo) Ser. A (Zool.) 7(4): 165–190.

1985. Phylogeny of the family Pholididae (Blennioidei) with a redescription of *Pholis* Scopoli. Jpn. J. Ichthyol. 32(3): 273–282.

1986. Phylogeny and zoogeography of the subfamilies Xiphisterinae and Cebidichthyinae (Blennioidei, Stichaeidae). Pages 663–678 *in* T. Uyeno, R. Arai, T. Taniuchi, and K. Matsuura, eds. Indo-Pacific fish biology: Proceedings of the Second International Conference on Indo-Pacific Fishes. Ichthyological Society of Japan, Tokyo.

Yesaki, M., and R. J. Wolotira, Jr.

1968. Extension of recorded range of butter sole, *Isopsetta isolepis,* into the Bering Sea. J. Fish. Res. Board Can. 25(5): 1077–1078.

Yoshida, H., and H. Yamaguchi.

1985. Distribution and feeding habits of the pelagic smooth lumpsucker, *Aptocyclus ventricosus* (Pallas), in the Aleutian Basin. Bull. Fac. Fish. Hokkaido Univ. 36(4): 200–209.

Youson, J. H., and R. J. Beamish.

1991. Comparison of the internal morphology of adults of a population of lampreys that contains a nonparasitic life-history type, *Lampetra richardsoni,* and a potentially parasitic form, *L. richardsoni* var. *marifuga.* Can. J. Zool. 69: 628–637.

Zahuranec, B. J.

2000. Zoogeography and systematics of the lanternfishes of the genus *Nannobrachium* (Myctophidae: Lampanyctini). Smithson. Contrib. Zool. 607. 69 pp.

Zhang, C. I., T. K. Wilderbuer, and G. E. Walters.

1998. Biological characteristics and fishery assessment of Alaska plaice, *Pleuronectes quadrituberculatus,* in the eastern Bering Sea. U.S. Natl. Mar. Fish. Serv. Mar. Fish. Rev. 60(4): 16–27.

Zimmermann, M., and P. Goddard.

1996. Biology and distribution of arrowtooth, *Atheresthes stomias,* and Kamchatka, *A. evermanni,* flounders in Alaskan waters. U.S. Natl. Mar. Fish. Serv. Fish. Bull. 94: 358–370.

Zolatov, S. F.

1997. Occurrence of chinook salmon, *Oncorhynchus tschawytscha,* in the Sea of Japan. J. Ichthyol. 37(2): 200–201 [English transl. Vopr. Ikhtiol. 37(2): 270–271].

Zorzi, G. D., and M. E. Anderson.

1988. Records of the deep-sea skates, *Raja (Amblyraja) badia* Garman, 1899 and *Bathyraja abyssicola* (Gilbert, 1896), in the eastern North Pacific, with a new key to California skates. Calif. Fish Game 74(2): 87–105.

1990. Summary of records of the deep-water skates, *Raja (Amblyraja) badia* Garman, 1899 and *Bathyraja abyssicola* (Gilbert, 1896), in the eastern North Pacific. Pages 389–390 *in* H. K. Pratt, Jr., S. H. Gruber, and T. Taniuchi, eds. Elasmobranchs as living resources: advances in the biology, ecology, systematics, and the status of the fisheries. NOAA Tech. Rep. NMFS 90.

Zugmayer, E.

1911. Diagnoses de poissons nouveaux provenant des campagnes du yacht *Princesse Alice* 1901 à 1910. Bull. Inst. Oceanogr. Monaco 193: 1–14.

Note: After this book went to press the following paper came to our attention:

Møller, P. R.

2001. Redescription of the *Lycodes pallidus* species complex (Pisces, Zoarcidae), with a new species from the Arctic/North Atlantic Ocean. Copeia 2001(4): 972–996. [Issue received 11 Jan. 2002.]

Møller includes the Alaskan species *Lycodes concolor, L. pallidus,* and *L. squamiventer* with other species in a complex of species having a complete ventral lateral line and an incomplete, mediolateral row of neuromasts from above the anal fin origin toward the caudal fin. In this book we include *L. concolor* among species with a single, ventral lateral line, following Anderson (1994). We note the presence of widely spaced superficial neuromasts along the mediolateral line of the body in some fresh and well-preserved specimens of *L. concolor,* but this row fades more rapidly in alcohol than the ventral lateral line of closely spaced superficial neuromasts and we do not attach any significance to it for identification of species. Møller provides more complete descriptions of these species than previously available, and presents evidence (number and size of pharyngobranchial teeth) that supports the separation of *L. squamiventer* from *L. pallidus.*

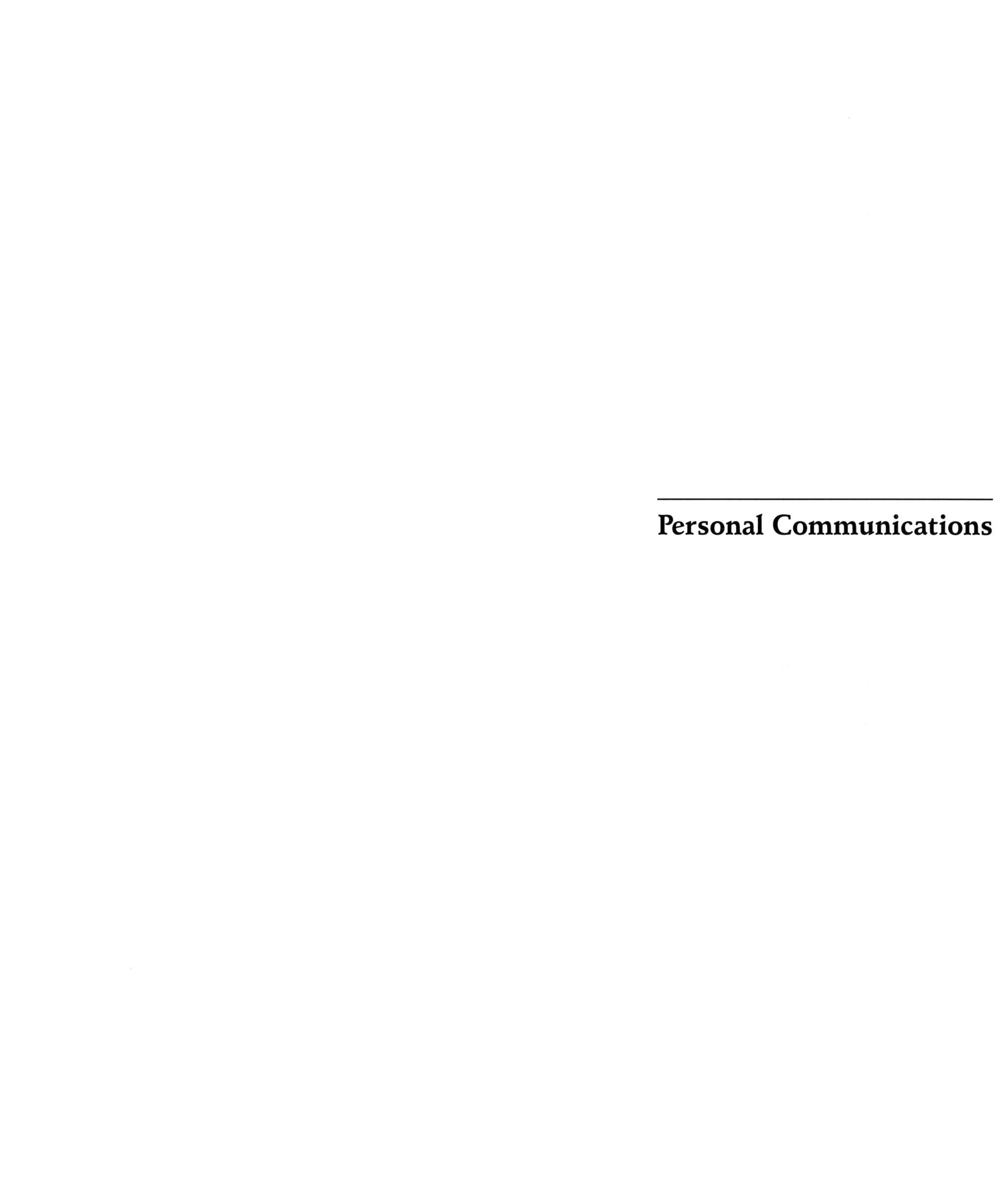

Personal Communications

PERSONAL COMMUNICATIONS

Noel A. Alfonso. Canadian Museum of Nature, Research Services Division, Ottawa, Ontario.

Kenneth T. Alt. Alaska Department of Fish and Game, Sport Fish Division, Fairbanks (retired).

M. Eric Anderson. J. L. B. Smith Institute of Ichthyology, Grahamstown, South Africa.

David C. Baker. National Marine Fisheries Service, Domestic Observer Program, Seattle, Washington.

Andrey A. Balanov. Russian Academy of Sciences, Far East Division, Institute of Marine Biology, Vladivostok.

Arcady V. Balushkin. Russian Academy of Sciences, Zoological Institute, Ichthyology Laboratory, St. Petersburg.

Robert J. Behnke. Colorado State University, Department of Fishery and Wildlife Biology, Fort Collins.

James E. Blackburn. Alaska Department of Fish and Game, Kodiak.

Morgan S. Busby. National Marine Fisheries Service, Alaska Fisheries Science Center, Resource Assessment and Conservation Engineering Division, Seattle, Washington.

Natalia V. Chernova. Russian Academy of Sciences, Zoological Institute, Ichthyology Laboratory, St. Petersburg.

Brian W. Coad. Canadian Museum of Nature, Ottawa, Ontario.

David J. Csepp. National Marine Fisheries Service, Alaska Fisheries Science Center, Auke Bay Laboratory, Juneau, Alaska.

Joel Curtis. National Weather Service, Anchorage Forecast Office, Alaska.

Jack L. Dean. U.S. Fish and Wildlife Service, Anchorage, Alaska (retired).

Alfred L. DeCicco. Alaska Department of Fish and Game, Sport Fish Division, Fairbanks.

Margaret F. Docker. University of Windsor, Ontario, Canada.

Vladimir N. Dolganov. Russian Academy of Sciences, Far East Division, Institute of Marine Biology, Vladivostok.

Steve Ebbert. U.S. Fish and Wildlife Service, Alaska National Maritime Wildlife Refuge, Homer.

David A. Ebert. Ocean Resource Consulting Associates, Moss Landing, California.

William N. Eschmeyer. California Academy of Sciences, Department of Ichthyology, San Francisco.

Vladimir V. Fedorov. Russian Academy of Sciences, Zoological Institute, Ichthyology Laboratory, St. Petersburg.

Nora R. Foster. University of Alaska Museum, Fairbanks.

Graham Gillespie. Department of Fisheries and Oceans, Pacific Biological Station, Nanaimo, British Columbia, Canada.

Gerald R. Hoff. National Marine Fisheries Service, Alaska Fisheries Science Center, Resource Assessment and Conservation Engineering Division, Seattle, Washington.

Philip N. Hooge. U.S. Geological Survey, Alaska Biological Science Center, Glacier Bay Field Station, Gustavus, Alaska.

Lee B. Hulbert. National Marine Fisheries Service, Alaska Fisheries Science Center, Auke Bay Laboratory, Juneau, Alaska.

Tomio Iwamoto. California Academy of Sciences, Department of Ichthyology, San Francisco.

Keith L. Jackson. University of Alberta, Department of Biological Sciences, Edmonton, Alberta, Canada.

John F. Karinen. National Marine Fisheries Service, Alaska Fisheries Science Center, Auke Bay Laboratory, Juneau, Alaska.

Kaoru Kido. Shimokita, Aomori, Japan.

Jerrold Koerner. Alaska Department of Fish and Game, Ketchikan.

Robert N. Lea. California Department of Fish and Game, Monterey.

Milton Love. University of California, Santa Barbara, Marine Science Institute.

Douglas F. Markle. Oregon State University, Department of Fisheries and Wildlife, Corvallis.

Don E. McAllister. National Museums of Canada, National Museum of Natural Sciences, Ichthyology Section, Ottawa, Ontario (deceased).

John D. McEachran. Texas A&M University, Department of Wildlife and Fisheries Sciences, College Station.

J. Donald McPhail. Professor Emeritus, University of British Columbia, Department of Zoology, Vancouver.

James E. Morrow. Professor Emeritus, University of Alaska, Department of Biological Sciences, Fairbanks.

Scott C. Meyer. Alaska Department of Fish and Game, Homer.

Kristen M. Munk. Alaska Department of Fish and Game, Age Determination Unit, Juneau.

Fumihito Muto. Hokkaido University, Faculty of Fisheries, Laboratory of Marine Zoology, Hakodate, Japan.

Teodor T. Nalbant. Institute of Biology, Department of Taxonomy and Evolution, Bucuresti, Romania.

Joseph S. Nelson. University of Alberta, Department of Biological Sciences, Edmonton, Alberta, Canada.

James W. Orr. National Marine Fisheries Service, Alaska Fisheries Science Center, Resource Assessment and Conservation Engineering Division, Seattle, Washington.

Wayne A. Palsson. Washington Department of Fish and Wildlife, Mill Creek.

John R. Paxton. Australian Museum, Sydney.

Alex E. Peden. Curator Emeritus, Royal British Columbia Museum, Victoria, British Columbia, Canada.

Claude B. Renaud. Canadian Museum of Nature, Ottawa, Ontario.

C. Richard Robins. University of Kansas, Natural History Museum, Lawrence.

David G. Roseneau. U.S. Fish and Wildlife Service, Anchorage, Alaska.

Jeffrey A. Seigel. Natural History Museum of Los Angeles County, Los Angeles, California.

Kelly Sendall. Royal British Columbia Museum, Victoria, British Columbia, Canada.

Boris A. Sheiko. Russian Academy of Sciences, Zoological Institute, Ichthyology Laboratory, St. Petersburg.

Gento Shinohara. National Science Museum, Department of Zoology, Tokyo, Japan.

Michael F. Sigler. National Marine Fisheries Service, Alaska Fisheries Science Center, Auke Bay Laboratory, Juneau.

Elizabeth H. Sinclair. National Marine Fisheries Service, Alaska Fisheries Science Center, National Marine Mammal Laboratory, Seattle, Washington.

David G. Smith. Smithsonian Institution, National Museum of Natural History, Division of Fishes, Washington, D.C.

Arnold Suzumoto. Bernice P. Bishop Museum, Department of Ichthyology, Honolulu, Hawaii.

Brian Urbain. University of Washington, School of Aquatic and Fishery Sciences, Fish Collection, Seattle.

Kenneth D. Vogt. University of Alaska, Department of Biology, Anchorage.

Norman J. Wilimovsky. University of British Columbia, Institute of Fisheries, Vancouver (deceased).

Jeffrey C. Williams. U.S. Fish and Wildlife Service, Alaska Maritime National Wildlife Refuge, Adak.

Bruce L. Wing. National Marine Fisheries Service, Alaska Fisheries Science Center, Auke Bay Laboratory, Juneau, Alaska.

Mamoru Yabe. Hokkaido University, Faculty of Fisheries, Laboratory of Marine Zoology, Hakodate, Japan.

Akihito Yatsu. National Research Institute of Far Seas Fisheries, Shizuoka, Japan.

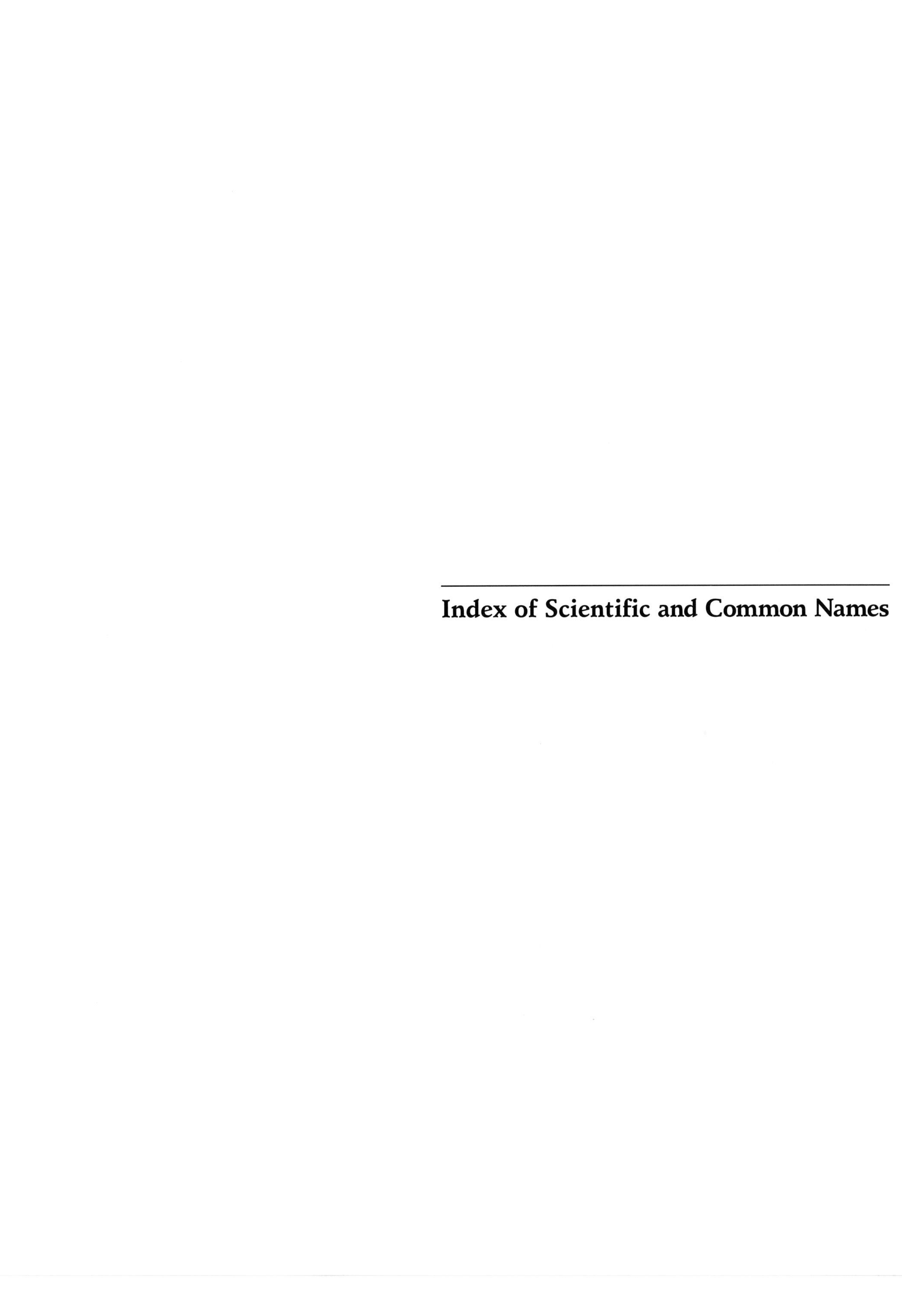

Index of Scientific and Common Names

INDEX OF SCIENTIFIC AND COMMON NAMES

Names in capital letters and bold type are families with accounts in this book. Page numbers in bold type indicate species accounts and the first page of introductions to families, orders, and other higher taxa. Where alternate spellings or names are given for species the page number in bold type indicates the version currently recognized as correct. Page numbers in italic type indicate reference in keys to the families or species. Roman numerals indicate color plates. The Systematic Section (pages 1–852) is indexed, not the beginning and end materials.

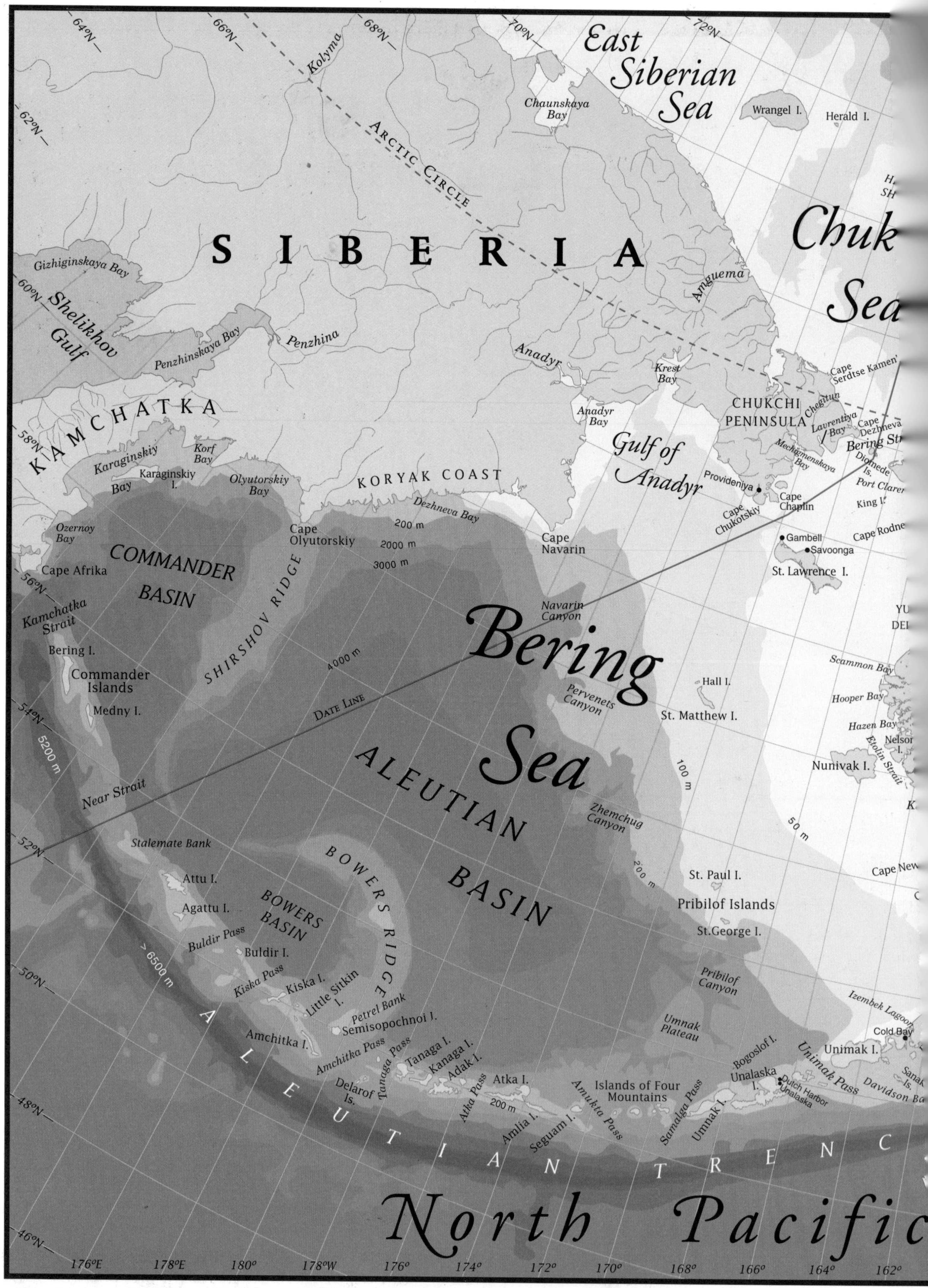
East Siberian Sea
Chaunskaya Bay
Wrangel I.
Herald I.
Kolyma
Arctic Circle
SIBERIA
Chuk
Sea
Gizhiginskaya Bay
Shelikhov Gulf
Penzhinskaya Bay
Penzhina
Amguema
Anadyr
Krest Bay
Cape Serdtse Kamen'
KAMCHATKA
Anadyr Bay
CHUKCHI PENINSULA
Chegitun
Lavrentiya Bay
Cape Dezhneva
Bering St
Gulf of Anadyr
Mechigmenskaya Bay
Diomede Is.
Karaginskiy Bay
Korf Bay
Karaginskiy I.
Olyutorskiy Bay
KORYAK COAST
Provideniya
Cape Chaplin
Port Clarer
King I.
Dezhneva Bay
Cape Chukotskiy
Ozernoy Bay
200 m
Cape Olyutorskiy
2000 m
3000 m
Cape Navarin
Gambell
Savoonga
Cape Rodne
COMMANDER BASIN
Cape Afrika
St. Lawrence I.
Kamchatka Strait
SHIRSHOV RIDGE
Navarin Canyon
Bering Sea
Bering I.
Commander Islands
4000 m
Scammon Bay
Hall I.
Medny I.
Date Line
Pervenets Canyon
Hooper Bay
St. Matthew I.
Hazen Bay
5200 m
Nelson I.
Etolin Strait
Nunivak I.
ALEUTIAN BASIN
100 m
Near Strait
Zhemchug Canyon
50 m
Stalemate Bank
BOWERS RIDGE
Cape New
Attu I.
200 m
St. Paul I.
Agattu I.
BOWERS BASIN
Pribilof Islands
St.George I.
Buldir Pass
Buldir I.
> 6500 m
Pribilof Canyon
Kiska Pass
Kiska I.
Little Sitkin I.
Izembek Lagoon
Petrel Bank
Semisopochnoi I.
Umnak Plateau
Cold Bay
Amchitka I.
Amchitka Pass
Tanaga Pass
Tanaga I.
Kanaga I.
Adak I.
Bogoslof I.
Unimak I.
Unimak Pass
Unalaska I.
Dutch Harbor
Unalaska
Delarof Is.
Atka Pass
Atka I.
Amukta Pass
Islands of Four Mountains
Samalga Pass
Umnak I.
Davidson Ba
Sanak Is.
200 m
Amlia I.
Seguam I.
ALEUTIAN TRENC
North Pacific
64°N
66°N
68°N
70°N
72°N
62°N
60°N
58°N
56°N
54°N
52°N
50°N
48°N
46°N
176°E
178°E
180°
178°W
176°
174°
172°
170°
168°
166°
164°
162°